FOURTEENTH EDITION

SCHROEDER'S

ANTIQUES

PRICE GUIDE

Edited by Sharon & Bob Huxford

COLLECTOR BOOKS

A Division of Schroeder Publishing Co., Inc.

The current values in this book should be used only as a guide. They are not intended to set prices, which vary from one section of the country to another. Auction prices as well as dealer prices vary greatly and are affected by condition as well as demand. Neither the Editors nor the Publisher assumes responsibility for any losses that might be incurred as a result of consulting this guide.

Searching For A Publisher?

We are always looking for knowledgable people considered experts within their fields. If you feel that there is a real need for a book on your collectible subject and have a large comprehensive collection, please contact Collector Books.

Additional copies of this book may be ordered from:

COLLECTOR BOOKS
P.O. Box 3009
Paducah, Kentucky 42002-3009

@$14.95. Add $2.00 for postage and handling.

Copyright: Schroeder Publishing Co., Inc. 1996

Introduction

As the editors and staff of *Schroeder's*, our goal is to compile the most useful, comprehensive, and accurate background and pricing information possible. Our guide encompasses nearly seven hundred categories, many of which you will not find in other price guides. Our sources are varied; we use auction results, dealer lists, trade paper ads, and we consult with national collectors' clubs, recognized authorities, researchers, and appraisers. We have by far the largest Advisory Board of any similar publication on the market. Each year we add several new advisors and now have over 425 who cover over 500 categories. They go over our computer print-outs line by line, deleting listings that are misleading or too vague to be of merit; they often send background information and photos. We appreciate their assistance very much. Only through their expertise and experience in their special fields are we able to offer with confidence what we feel are useful, accurate evaluations that provide a sound understanding of the dealings in the market place today. Correspondence with so large an advisory panel adds months of extra work to an already monumental task, but we feel that to a very large extent this is the foundation that makes *Schroeder's* the success that it has become.

Our Directory, which you will find in the back of the book, lists each contributor by state. These are people who have allowed us to photograph various examples of merchandise from their show booths, sent us pricing information, or in any way have contributed to this year's book. If you happen to be traveling, consult the Directory for shops along your way. We also list clubs who have worked with us and auction houses who have agreed to permit us the use of photographs from their catalogs.

Our Advisory Board lists only names and home states, so check the Directory for addresses and telephone numbers should you want to correspond with one of our experts. Remember, when you do, **always** enclose a self-addressed, stamped envelope (SASE). Thousands of people buy our guide, and hundreds contact our advisors. The only agreement we have with our advisors is that they edit their categories. They are in no way obligated to answer mail. Some are dealers who do many shows a month. The time they spend at home may be very limited, and they may not be open to contacts. There's no doubt that the reason behind the success of our book is their assistance. We regret seeing them becoming more and more burdened by phone and mail inquiries. We have lost some of our good advisors for this reason, and when we do, the book suffers and consequently, so do our readers. Many of our listed reference sources report that they constantly receive long distance calls (at all hours) that are really valuation requests. If they are registered appraisers, they make their living at providing such information and expect a fee for their service and expertise.

If you find you need more information than *Schroeder's* provides, there are other sources available to you. Go to your local library; check their section on reference books. Museums are public facilities that are willing and able help you establish the origin and possibly even the value of your particular treasure. Check the yellow pages of your phone book. Other cities' phone books are available from either your library or from the telephone company office. Look under the heading *Antique Dealers*. Those who are qualified appraisers will mention this credit in their advertisement. But remember that if you sell to a dealer, he will expect to buy your merchandise at a price low enough that he will be able to make an appreciable profit when he sells it. Once you decide to contact one of these appraisers, unless you intend to see them directly, you'll need to get photographs. Don't send photos that are under or over exposed, out of focus, or shot against a background that detracts from important details you want to emphasize. It is almost impossible for them to give you a value judgement on items they've not seen when your photos are of poor quality. Shoot the front, top, and the bottom; describe any marks and numbers (or send a pencil rubbing), explain how and when you acquired the article, and give accurate measurements and any further background information that may be helpful.

The auction houses listed in the Directory nearly all have a staff of appraisal experts. If the item you're attempting to research is of the caliber of material they deal with, they can offer extremely accurate evaluations. Of course, most have a fee. Be sure to send them only professional-quality photographs. Tell them if you expect to consign your item to their auction. If you disagree with the value they suggest, you are under no obligation to do so.

Nearly seven hundred categories are included in our book. We have organized our topics alphabetically, following the most simple logic, usually either by manufacturer or by type of product. If you have difficulty in locating your subject, consult the index. Our guide is unique in that much more space has been allotted to background information than any other publication of this type, and it is easier to read due to the larger-than-average print. Our readers tell us that these are features they enjoy. To be able to do this, we have adopted a format of one-line listings wherein we describe the items to the fullest extent possible by using several common-sense abbreviations; they will be easy to read and understand if you will first take the time to quickly scan through them.

The Editors

Editorial Staff

Editors
Sharon and Bob Huxford

Research and Editorial Assistants
Michael Drollinger, Nancy Drollinger, Steven Drollinger, Linda Holycross, Donna Newnum, Loretta Woodrow

Layout
Beth Ray, Gail Ashburn, and Michelle Dowling

Cover Design
Beth Summers

On the cover, clockwise from right:
Hull Vase, Wildflower, $30.00–45.00. Courtesy of Beth Summers.
1961 Ponytail Barbie, $200.00. Courtesy of Beth Summers. Barbie is wearing the outfit called Friday Night Date, $100.00.
Rhinestone pin, gold leaves with yellow topaz colored dome cut marquise stones marked Kramer, $25.00. Courtesy of Cherri Simonds.
Bowl, Wild Strawberry, 9", amethyst, $250.00.
Bambi Bookends marked Made in Japan, $25.00. Courtesy of Beth Summers.
Gulf one-piece glass globe, $500.00–750.00, as shown in *Value Guide to Gas Station Memorabilia* by B. J. Summers and Wayne Priddy.

Listing of Standard Abbreviations

The following is a list of abbreviations that have been used throughout this book in order to provide you with the most detailed descriptions possible in the limited space available. No periods are used after initials or abbreviations. When two dimensions are given, height is noted first. If only one dimension is listed, it will be height, except in the case of bowls, dishes, plates, or platters, when it will be diameter. The standard two-letter state abbreviations apply.

For glassware, if no color is noted, the glass is clear. Hyphenated colors, for example blue-green, olive-amber, etc., describe a single color tone; colors divided by a slash mark indicate two or more colors, i.e. blue/white. Teapots, sugar bowls, and butter dishes are assumed to be 'with cover.' Condition is extremely important in determining market value. Common sense suggests that art pottery, china, and glassware values would be given for examples in pristine, mint condition, while suggested prices for utility wares such as Redware, Mocha, and Blue and White Stoneware, for example, reflect the probability that since such items were subjected to everyday use in the home they may show minor wear (which is acceptable) but no notable damage. Values for other categories reflect the best average condition in which the particular collectible is apt to be offered for sale without the dealer feeling it necessary to mention wear or damage. For instance, advertising items are assumed to be in excellent condition since mint items are scarce enough that when one is offered for sale the dealer will most likely make mention of that fact. The same holds true for Toys, Banks, Coin-Operated Machines, and the like. A basic rule of thumb is that an item listed as VG (very good) will bring 40% to 60% of its mint price — a first-hand, personal evaluation will enable you to make the final judgement; EX (excellent) is a condition midway between mint and very good, and values would correspond.

Am . . . American	drw . . . drawer	ldgl . . . leaded glass	rnd . . . round
appl . . . applied	dtd . . . dated	litho . . . lithograph	rpl . . . replaced
att . . . attributed to	dvtl . . . dovetail	lt . . . light	rpr . . . repaired
bbl . . . barrel	emb . . . embossed, embossing	M . . . mint	rpt . . . repainted
bk . . . back	embr . . . embroidered	mahog . . . mahogany	rstr . . . restored
bl . . . bl	eng . . . engraved, engraving	mc . . . multicolor	rtcl . . . reticulated
blk . . . black	EPNS . electroplated nickel silver	MIB . . . mint in box	rvpt . . . reverse painted
brd . . . board	etch . . . etched, etching	MIG . . . Made in Germany	s&p . . . salt and pepper
brn . . . brown	EX . . . excellent	mk . . . mark	sgn . . . signed
bulb . . . bulbous	fr . . . frame, framed	MOP . . . mother-of-pearl	SP . . . silverplated
bsk . . . bisque	Fr . . . French	mt, mtd . . . mount, mounted	sq . . . square
b3m . . . blown 3-mold	ft, ftd . . . foot, feet, footed	NE . . . New England	std . . . standard
C . . . century	G . . . good	NM . . . near mint	str . . . straight
c . . . copyright	gr . . . green	NP . . . nickel plated	sz . . . size
ca . . . circa	grad . . . graduated	opal . . . opalescent	trn . . . turned, turning
can . . . canister	grpt . . . grain painted	orig . . . original	turq . . . turquoise
cb . . . cardboard	H . . . high, height	o/l . . . overlay	uphl . . . upholstered
CI . . . cast iron	hdl, hdld . . . handle, handled	o/w . . . otherwise	VG . . . very good
compo . . . composition	HP . . . hand painted	Pat . . . patented	Vict . . . Victorian
cr/sug . . . creamer and sugar	illus . . . illustration, illustrated by	pc . . . piece	W . . . width
c/s . . . cup and saucer	imp . . . impressed	ped . . . pedestal	wht . . . white
cvd . . . carved	ind . . . individual	pk . . . pink	w/ . . . with
cvg . . . carving	int . . . interior	pnt . . . paint	w/o . . . without
dbl . . . double	Invt T'print . . Inverted Thumbprint	porc . . . porcelain	X, Xd . . . cross, crossed
decor . . . decoration	irid . . . iridescent	prof . . . professional	yel . . . yellow
dk . . . dark	L . . . length, long	re . . . regarding	(+) . . . has been reproduced
Dmn Quilt . . . Diamond Quilted	lav . . . lavender	rfn . . . refinished	

A B C Plates

Children's plates featuring the alphabet as part of the design were popular from as early as 1820 until after the turn of the century. The earliest English creamware plates were decorated with embossed letters and prim moralistic verses, but the later Staffordshire products were conducive to a more relaxed mealtime atmosphere, often depicting playful animals and riddles or scenes of pleasant leisure-time activities. They were made around the turn of the century by American potters as well. All featured transfer prints, but color was sometimes brushed on by hand to add interest to the design. Braille plates were made for the blind, but these are rather scarce and usually more valuable. You may also find an occasional bowl or mug.

Ceramic

American Sports — Baseball, Out on
Third Base, black transfer, RM mark,
6¼", $220.00.

A Stands for Anemones, blk transfer w/mc, Staffordshire, 8" 200.00
Alpine shepherd, blk w/mc, red rim stripe, Staffordshire, 5" 65.00
Badger, brn transfer, Staffordshire, 8", NM 120.00
Bear w/cubs, 7½" 90.00
Blind Girl, Victorian children, mc transfer, 5¾" 150.00
Bull charging couple by stream, purple transfer, 7", EX 95.00
Cat & fan, flow bl, W Adams & Sons Tunstall England, 7" 165.00
Catch It Carlo When I Throw, blk transfer w/mc, 5½", NM 110.00
Chairs To Mend, blk transfer w/bl edge, ironstone, 7", EX 165.00
Christ resurrected, blk transfer w/mc enamel, Meakin, 6⅛" 75.00
Clock center, blk transfer w/gr, ironstone, Pat 1882, 8½" 90.00
Drill, blk transfer w/mc enamel, Staffordshire, 5⅞" 90.00
Dwarfs ride lg insects, ABC rim, Germany 65.00
Floral transfer w/mc decor, Staffordshire, 7" 60.00
Football, blk transfer w/mc enamel, Meakin, 6¼" 85.00
Franklin's Proverb, Silks & Satins..., 5" 150.00
He That by the Plough..., blk transfer, Meakin, 5¼" 85.00
Lone Fisherman, gr transfer, Staffordshire, 7" 110.00
Mug, A&B, brn transfer w/red enameling, Staffordshire, 2½" 165.00
My Face Is My Fortune, bl-gr transfer, Staffordshire, 7½" 65.00
Nations of the World, Japanese 85.00
Organ grinder & children, gr transfer, Staffordshire, 6¾" 105.00
Pet of Village, blk transfer w/mc enamel, Staffordshire, 7" 75.00
Poor Richard's Way to Wealth, red transfer, Staffordshire, 7" 50.00
Ready for Ride, blk transfer w/mc enamel, Staffordshire, 6" 85.00
Robinson Crusoe at Work, Staffordshire 125.00
Robinson Crusoe Finding Footprints, Staffordshire 110.00
Soldiers, 2 children & dog, Staffordshire, 7" 50.00

Squirrel & flowers, brn transfer, Staffordshire, 6⅜" 40.00
Stilt Walking, blk transfer w/mc enamel, Meakin, 5¼" 95.00
That Girl Wants Pup Away, blk transfer, Staffordshire, 6" 90.00
Their First Day, chicks in basket, gold ABCs, 6¼" 65.00
Village Blksmith, mc transfer, 7" 135.00
Youthful man w/basket, mc transfer, Meakin, 7" 110.00
Zouaves, blk w/mc enamel, Staffordshire, 6" 135.00

Glass

Clock, Thousand Eye, amber, ABC rim 125.00
Ducks, ABC rim, 6" 60.00
Elephant w/howdah on bk, ABC rim, Ripley & Co, 6" 90.00
Garfield, ABC rim 100.00
Independence Hall, scalloped, 6¾" 110.00
Proud Dog, ABC rim 65.00
Rooster, hen & chicks, ABC rim 65.00

Tin

Bust of Washington, dents, 6⅛" 170.00
Cow, mini, 1½" 85.00
Girl's portrait in oval medallion, Lava soap premium, 6¼" 85.00
Grinding Old Into Young, mini 165.00
Hi Diddle Diddle, 8¾" 85.00
Jumbo, dk gray, 6½", EX 100.00
Mary Had a Little Lamb, 8" 135.00
Who Killed Cock Robin?, 8" 100.00

Abingdon

From 1934 until 1950, the Abingdon Pottery Co. of Abingdon, Illinois, made a line of art pottery with a white vitrified body decorated with various types of glazes in many lovely colors. Novelties, cookie jars, utility ware, and lamps were made in addition to several lines of simple yet striking art ware. Fern Leaf, introduced in 1937, featured molded vertical feathering. La Fleur, in 1939, consisted of flowerpots and flower-arranger bowls with rows of vertical ribbing. Classic, 1939-40, was a line of vases, many with evidence of Chinese influence. Several marks were used, most of which employed the company name. In 1950 the company reverted to the manufacture of sanitary ware that had been their mainstay before the Art Ware Division was formed.

Highly decorated examples and those with black, bronze, or red glaze usually command at least 25% higher prices.

Bookend, Black Russian,
9", $150.00.

#102, vase, Beta, maroon, 10" **58.00**
#104, vase, Delta Classic, 10" **28.00**
#109, vase, Alpha, wht, 6" **20.00**
#116, vase, Classic, 10", from $18 to **22.50**
#118, vase, Classic, 10" **25.00**
#126, candle holders, Classic, wht, 2", pr **38.00**
#142, vase, Classic, bl, mini, 5½" **25.00**
#266D, vase, scalloped, pk w/decor, 8" **40.00**
#301, jar, Ming, turq, 7¼" **80.00**
#305, bookends, sea gull, 6½", pr **60.00**
#306, ashtray, 8x3" **18.00**
#310, jar, Chang, wht matt, 1934-36, 10½" **245.00**
#315, vase, Athena Classic, wht, 1934-36, 9" **38.00**
#322, goblet, Swedish, gr **50.00**
#339, plate, salad; dk bl, sq, 7½" **32.00**
#363, bookends, colt, 5¾", pr **65.00**
#375, wall pocket, dbl morning-glory, wht, 7¾" **45.00**
#390, vase, morning-glory, turq, 1934-50, 10" **60.00**
#3903, seated nude, 7", minimum value **300.00**
#3905b, chessman, bishop, bronze/blk, 1937, rare **250.00**
#3906, shepherdess & fawn, yel w/gold traces, 11½" **200.00**
#400, tea tile, geisha, sq, 5" **50.00**
#402, vase, Box, 5½" **45.00**
#404, candle holder, triple, Chain, beige, 3x8½" **35.00**
#408, bowl, leaf, beige, 1937, 6½" **50.00**
#412, vase, Volute, wht, 1937-40, 15½" **125.00**
#416, peacock, wht, 1937-38 & 1942, 7" **40.00**
#420, vase, Fern Leaf, no decor, 7¼" **20.00**
#429, vase/candle holder, Fern Leaf, 8" **25.00**
#430, pitcher, Fern Leaf, wht, 1937-38, 8" **150.00**
#434, candle holder, Fern Leaf, 5½x3" **27.50**
#437, bowl (window box), Han Pansy, 10½" L **20.00**
#441, bookend, horse head, wht, pr **55.00**
#442, vase, Laurel, turq matt, 1938-39, 5½" **33.00**
#460, bowl, Panel, 8" **40.00**
#464, vase, medallion, 8" **25.00**
#466, vase, wheel hdl, wht matt, 8" **30.00**
#486, vase, acanthus, gray, 11" **40.00**
#493, wall pocket, dbl, turq, 1940, 8½" **50.00**
#504, vase/planter, shell, wht, 7¼" **17.50**
#513, vase, swirl, 9", from $15 to **25.00**
#516, vase, Acadia, 7" **22.00**
#522, vase, Barre, 9" **23.00**
#527, bowl, hibiscus, pk, 1941-48, 10" dia **35.00**
#540, bowl, flare, 11½x8" **30.00**
#544, bowl, Streamliner, 9" L **15.00**

#563, vase, urn form, bl w/decor, 9" **20.00**
#565, cornucopia, blk, 1942-47, 7" **25.00**
#568, mint compote, pk, ftd, 1942-47, 6" dia **28.00**
#569D, cornucopia, bl w/decor **27.50**
#574, heron, 5¼" **30.00**
#581, cornucopia, dbl, pk, 8¼" **22.00**
#593, vase, bow knot, bl, 9" **25.00**
#615, ashtray, blk gloss, Ohio, 4" **17.50**
#616, vase, cactus, 6½" **40.00**
#649, wall bracket, acanthus, wht, rare, 8¾" **72.00**
#660, ashtray, leaf, blk & yel, 5½" dia **38.00**
#661, swan, chartreuse, 3¾" **35.00**
#681/#682, sugar bowl & creamer, daisy **27.50**
#700, bowl, pineapple, 14¼" H **125.00**
#705, vase, Modern, bl gloss, 8" **28.00**
#709, bowl, irregular, 13½" H **15.00**
#712, string holder, mouse, 8½" **72.50**
#716, candlesticks, bamboo, decor, 3½" sq, pr **28.00**
Cookie jar, #471, Old Lady, plain or decor, 1942 ....**210.00**
Cookie jar, #471, Old Lady, rare gr **195.00**
Cookie jar, #495, Fat Boy **240.00**
Cookie jar, #549, Hippo, decor, 1942 ....**225.00**
Cookie jar, #561, Baby, Blk decor **300.00**
Cookie jar, #588, Money Bag, 1947 ....**70.00**

Cookie jar, #602-D, Hobby Horse, marked Abingdon USA, $185.00.

Cookie jar, #611, Jack-in-Box **255.00**
Cookie jar, #622, Miss Muffet **205.00**
Cookie jar, #651, Choo Choo (Locomotive) **150.00**
Cookie jar, #653, Clock, 1949 ....**85.00**
Cookie jar, #663, Humpty Dumpty **250.00**
Cookie jar, #664, Pineapple **60.00**
Cookie jar, #665, Wigwam, minimum value **300.00**
Cookie jar, #674, Pumpkin, 1949 ....**310.00**
Cookie jar, #677, Daisy, 1949 ....**45.00**
Cookie jar, #678, Windmill **185.00**
Cookie jar, #692, Witch, minimum value **350.00**
Cookie jar, #693, Little Girl **60.00**
Cookie jar, #694, Bo Peep **240.00**
Cookie jar, #695, Mother Goose **295.00**
Cookie jar, #696, Three Bears **90.00**
G-1, oil jar, tall **200.00**
G-2, Palm vase, squat **200.00**
G-3, Rope vase, lg **180.00**
P-7, jardiniere, 6" **24.00**

Draped Vase, courting couple decal with gold, #557, 10½", $75.00.

Adams

Wm. Adams, whose potting skills were developed under the tutelage of Josiah Wedgwood, founded the Greengates Pottery at Tunstall, England, in 1769. Many types of wares including basalt, ironstone, parian, and jasper were produced; and various impressed or printed marks were employed. Until 1800 'Adams Co.' or 'Adams' impressed in block letters identified the company's earthenwares and a fine type of jasper similar in color and decoration to Wedgwood's. The latter mark was used again from 1845 to 1864 on parian figures. Most examples of their product found on today's market are transfer-printed dinnerwares with ornate backstamps which often include the pattern name and the initials 'W.A. & S.' This type of product was made from 1820 until about 1920. After 1890 the word 'England' was included in the mark; 'Tunstall' was added after 1896. From 1914 through 1940, a printed crown with 'Adams, Estbd 1657, England' identified their products. From 1900 to 1965, they produced souvenir plates with transfers of American scenes, many of which were marketed in this country by Roth Importers of Peoria, Illinois. In 1965 the company affiliated with Wedgwood. Although there were other Adams potteries in Staffordshire, their marks incorporate either the first name initial or a partner's name and so are easily distinguished from those of this company. See also Spatter; Staffordshire; Adams Rose.

Bowl, Dr Syntax Stopt by Highwaymen, 10¼" 70.00
Creamer, bl jasper, wht classical figures, 3¼" 45.00
Cup & saucer, handleless; stick spatter w/gaudy floral, EX 55.00
Plate, Columbia, red transfer, mk, 10¾" 40.00
Plate, cut sponge, 4-color, floral, blk sponged rim, 8" 75.00
Plate, Dr Syntax Bound to a Tree, 9" 50.00
Plate, Mt Washington Steamer, bl transfer, 8" 37.50
Plate, Seasons (Winter), pk transfer, 9½" 65.00
Plate, soup; Caledonia, red transfer, 11", EX 40.00
Platter, 2 stags, 3 does, bl transfer, 1850s, 16" 300.00

Adams Rose, Early and Late

In the second quarter of the 19th century, the Adams and Son Pottery produced a line of hand-painted dinnerware decorated in large, red brush-stroke roses with green leaves on whiteware, which collectors call Adams Rose. Later, G. Jones and Son (and possibly others) made a similar ware with less brilliant colors on a gray-white surface.

Bowl, early, rare sz, 9", M 750.00
Bowl, late, England, 5½" 65.00
Bowl, late, mk Imperiale Royale, Belgium, 3x5½" 35.00
Bowl, vegetable; late, Staffordshire, England, oval, 8½" 80.00
Coffeepot, early, scroll hdl, dome lid, Adams, rpr,12", EX 575.00
Coffeepot, early, red/gr/bl, tall, rare, NM 850.00
Creamer, early, 3", EX 150.00
Creamer, early, 5¾", M 295.00
Creamer, late, scalloped rim, England/#d, 5½", EX 110.00
Cup plate, early, scalloped, Adams, 4", EX 95.00
Pitcher, early, scalloped rim w/emb scrolls, mk Adams, 8", EX ...450.00
Pitcher, late, 8½", VG 235.00
Pitcher, late, 6¾", M 325.00
Plate, early, plain rim, mk Adams, 7½" 70.00
Plate, early, 9", M 195.00
Plate, late, Staffordshire England, imp mk, 8¾", EX, 6 for 150.00
Plate, toddy; early, plain rim, mk Adams, 5", EX 120.00
Platter, early, scalloped rim, Adams, 20x16½", NM 2,075.00
Platter, late, 12", EX 135.00

Soup plate, early, plain rim, mk Adams, 9½", NM 90.00
Soup plate, early, scalloped rim, Adams, 10¾" 200.00
Soup plate, early, wear/minor stains/glaze flakes, 9" 80.00
Sugar bowl, late, England, rpr, 6", EX 200.00
Sugar bowl, w/lid, early, M 350.00
Tea bowl & saucer, late, M 125.00
Teapot, late, M 325.00
Wash bowl, late, emb floral vine at rim, 14½" 160.00
Wash pitcher & bowl, 14¾", 13½" dia, EX 350.00

Advertising

The advertising world has always been a fiercely competitive field. In an effort to present their product to the customer, every imaginable gimmick was put into play. Colorful and artfully decorated signs and posters, thermometers, tape measures, fans, hand mirrors, and attractive tin containers (all with catchy slogans, familiar logos, and often-bogus claims) are only a few of the many examples of early advertising memorabilia that are of interest to today's collectors.

Porcelain signs were made as early as 1890 and are highly prized for their artistic portrayal of life as it was then . . . often allowing amusing insights into the tastes, humor, and way of life of a bygone era. As a general rule, older signs are made from a heavier gauge metal. Those with three or more fired-on colors are especially desirable.

Tin containers were used to package consumer goods ranging from crackers and coffee to tobacco and talcum. After 1880 can companies began to decorate their containers by the method of lithography. Though colors were still subdued, intricate designs were used to attract the eye of the consumer. False labeling and unfounded claims were curtailed by the Pure Food and Drug Administration in 1906, and the name of the manufacturer as well as the brand name of the product had to be printed on the label. By 1910 color was rampant with more than a dozen hues printed on the tin or on paper labels. The tins themselves were often designed with a second use in mind, such as canisters, lunch boxes, even toy trains. As a general rule, tobacco-related tins are the most desirable, though personal preference may direct the interest of the collector to peanut butter pails with illustrations of children, or talcum tins with irresistible babies or beautiful ladies. Coffee tins are popular, as are those made to contain a particularly successful or well-known product.

Perhaps the most visual of the early advertising gimmicks were the character logos, the Fairbank Company's Gold Dust Twins, the goose trademark of the Red Goose Shoe Company, Nabisco's ZuZu Clown and Uneeda Kid, the Campbell Kids, the RCA dog Nipper, and Mr. Peanut, to name only a few. Any example of these brings a high price on the market today.

Our listings are alphabetized by company name or, in lieu of that information, by word content or other pertinent description. When no condition is indicated, the items listed below are assumed to be in excellent condition, except glass and ceramic items, which are assumed mint. Remember that condition greatly affects value (especially true for tin items). For instance, a sign in excellent or mint condition may bring twice as much as the same one in only very good condition, sometimes even more. On today's market, items in good to very good condition are slow to sell, unless they are extremely rare. Mint (or near-mint) examples are high.

As a general rule, beer tip trays in near-mint condition are worth $150.00 to $250.00 Spool cabinets (depending on condition) may be evaluated at $100.00 to $150.00 per drawer.

We have several advertising advisors; See specific subheadings. For further information we recommend *Zany Characters of the Ad World* by Mary Jane Lamphier, *Advertising Character Collectibles* by Warren Dotz, *Value Guide to Advertising Memorabilia* by B.J. Summers, and *Huxford's Collectible Advertising* by Sharon and Bob Huxford. All of these books are available at your local bookstore or from Collector Books. See also Advertising Dolls; Advertising Cards; Automobilia; Coca-Cola; Banks; Calendars; Cookbooks; Paperweights; Posters; Sewing Items.

Key:
cb — cardboard
cl — celluloid
lcs — litho on canvas sign
pp — pre-prohibition
ps — porcelain sign
sf — self-framed
tc — tin container
ts — tin sign

Blanke's Coffee, tin litho store bin, large, EX, $600.00.

Abbey Pipe Tobacco, pocket tin, vertical, VG	100.00
AC Spark Plugs, display, metal, revolves, '30s, 9x11" dia, NM	475.00
AC Spark Plugs, display, metal, yel cage, 14½x7" dia, EX	200.00
Admiration Coffee, tc, Blk lady & couple, keywind, 1-lb, VG	65.00
Air Float Borated Baby Powder, tc, baby in reserve, NM	105.00
Airway Castor Motor Oil, curb sign, metal, w/fr, 47x20x32", G	275.00
Albert Talc, tc, baby in tub on bk, EX	190.00
Alemite Motor Oil, pump plate, porc diecut, 5¾" dia, NM	500.00
Amalie Motor Oil, ts, red/wht/blk, 11½x35½", EX	70.00
American Bosch Sales & Service, sign, porc, 3-color, 24x16", G	210.00
American Wringer Co, display rack, wood, mc pnt, 54x14x5", VG	35.00
Amoco, sign, porc, 3-color, chips, 15x24", VG	45.00
Amrico Talcum Powder, tc, slant sided, EX	70.00
Angelus Marshmallows, tc, sample sz, EX	60.00
Anheuser-Busch, plate, tin, Victorian lady, 1905, NM	275.00
Arm & Hammer Soda, sign, cb, Snipe, 1908, 11½x14¼", EX	70.00
Artex Motor Oil, tc, Am Oil Co, 5-gal, 14x9½", VG	75.00
AT&T, flange sign, porc, 2-sided, 1950s, 18x18½", NM	310.00
Atlantic, pump sign, porc, minor stains, 9x13", EX	50.00
Atlantic Imperial, sign, metal, In a Class..., 5x17¾", EX	35.00
Aunt Dina Molasses, tc, Aunt Dina litho, lt wear, 5¼x5"	70.00
Auto Lite, clock, rvpt glass, red/wht/bl, 18" dia, VG	175.00
Auto Lite, flange sign, metal, 4-color, 12x18", VG	50.00
Automotive Maintenance Assoc, sign, porc, 24x24", VG	50.00
Baby's Own Talcum, tc, reserve on yel, sq sides, EX	62.00
Ballantine Beer, clock, wht/bl/brn letters, 15x15", VG	60.00
Banner Glass, sign, cb, lady's portrait, orig fr, 16x23", EX	85.00
Barking Dog Cigarettes, carton, empty, EX	30.00
Beach Motor Hair Nets, display tin, car litho, '18, 5½", EX	250.00
Beech-Nut Coffee, tc, Trial Tin Not For Sale, 4-oz, EX	50.00
Bell System, flange sign, porc, bl & wht, 11x11¾", EX	250.00
Berina Malted Milk Food, sign, porc, pre-1920, 24x60", EX	410.00
Bernard & Algers Crop Manure, sign, porc, turnip, 20x12", VG	275.00

Betsy Ross 5¢ Cigars, sf ts, Betsy w/flag, 24x20", EX	450.00
Big Ben Tobacco, pocket tin, EX	35.00
Big Buster Popcorn, tc, full, 10-oz, EX	75.00
Biltrite Rubber Heels & Soles, push bar, porc, 3x30", EX	65.00
Bireley's, door push, tin litho, dents/wear, 3¾x10", VG	35.00
Bireley's Beverage, sign, metal, yel w/red letters, 10x28", EX	40.00
Black & White Scotch Whisky, ts, Morning Nip, fr, 25x23", EX	150.00
Blatz Brewing, watch chain spinner, EX	145.00
Blue Ribbon Bourbon, oleograph, farm, rprs, fr, 38x48", EX	525.00
Borax-O, soap dispenser, metal, mc pnt, 1950s, MIB	35.00

Borden's, Elsie display figure, painted composition, repaired horn, 1950s, 10½", $395.00.

Borden's Ice Cream, light-up clock, Elsie's head, EX	225.00
Boston Daily & Sunday Globe, ts, globe man, 17½x11", EX	650.00
Bowl of Roses, pocket tin, vertical, short, EX	100.00
Bridgestone Motorcycles, sign, metal, 3-color, 57x33½", EX	200.00
Brooke Bond Tea, sign, porc, blk & wht on red, 30x20", EX	120.00
Buckeye Gasoline, pump nozzle, brass, 14", EX	30.00
Buckhorn Tobacco, pocket tin, vertical, EX	80.00
Buckingham Tobacco, pocket tin, vertical, EX+	110.00
Budd's Baby Shoes, sf ts, children, 1900-10, 19½x14½", EX	350.00
Bull Durham Tobacco, box, cb, 9 full packs & papers, EX	60.00
Bull Durham Tobacco, sign, compo, 3-D, 18x22x7½"	1,600.00
Bull Durham Tobacco, ts in wooden fr, 38x36", EX	2,200.00
Bulldog Tobacco, pocket tin, vertical, short, EX+	500.00
Buss Auto Fuses, box, metal, blk & yel, 8½x7¼", EX	80.00

Buster Brown

Buster Brown was the creation of cartoonist Richard Felton; his comic strip first appeared in the *New York Herald* on May 4, 1902. Since then Buster and his dog Tige (short for Tiger) have adorned sundry commercial products but are probably best known as the trademark for the Brown Shoe Company established early in this century. Today hundreds of Buster Brown premiums, store articles, and advertising items bring substantial prices from many serious collectors.

Advertising, Ponds Extract, BB & Tige, 1904, 7x5", NM	235.00
Bandana, Smilin' Ed, Froggy, BB & Tige, 22x24", 1940s, M	150.00
Bank, BB & Tige w/horse & horseshoe, EX pnt	200.00
Bill hook, BB figural, tin, EX	36.00
Blotter, BB & Tige, ca 1910, EX	25.00

Bowl, cereal; red w/BB & Tige transfer, porc, EX 42.50
Cigar, w/BB band, 1920s, EX 8.00
Clicker, 1930s, EX 25.00
Clock, BB Shoes, store type, M 675.00
Comic book, Fun Maker, 1912, 10x16", EX 300.00
Comic book, Latest Frolics, 1906, 11x16", EX 125.00
Cup & saucer, BB pouring tea, ceramic 120.00
Dealer sign, 1950s, 15x15", MIB 150.00
Figurine, BB & Tige, bsk, Germany, 5", NM 65.00
Frame, 1950s decal, 5x7" 30.00
Kite, paper, 1940s, M 28.00
Magic Pad 25.00
Mask, BB Shoes, heavy paper diecut, 1905, NM 75.00
Mechanical card, BB & Tige, mc, Hearst Am, 1906, 5½x6¾" ...100.00
Paint box, BB Stocking, BB & Tige, 1902, 5½x3½", VG 95.00
Pencil, mechanical 45.00
Periscope, EX 25.00
Pin-bk button, BB Hose Supporters, BB & Tige, 1900s, ⅞", EX ...40.00
Pitcher, cream; BB & girl, china, 1900s, 3", NM 90.00
Plate, dessert; china, gold trim, +c/s, EX 125.00
Ring, BB Club, gold finish 40.00
Shoehorn 42.50
Sign, BB & Tige, Authorized BB Dealer, hardboard, 14x14", EX .120.00

Sign, tin litho diecut of Buster Brown &
Tige, H.D. Beach Co., 10", $1,000.00.

Sign, BB & Tige emb, pressed board/compo, 17" dia, EX 600.00
Slippers, red felt, 1930s, pr, EX 95.00
Stand-up, BB & Tige, on plastic stand, 7½x6" 35.00
Valentine, BB & Tige, Tuck, 1904, 5½x3½", unused, EX 37.50
Waffle iron, BB & Tige on bk, sm 80.00
Watch fob 200.00
Whistle, wooden, paper label w/BB & Tige 45.00
Wristwatch, BB Shoes, Ingersoll, 1930s, EX orig 315.00

C.D. Kenny

C.D. Kenny was determined to be a successful man, and he was.
Between 1890 and 1934, he owned seventy-five groceries in fifteen
states. He realized his success in two ways: fair business dealings and

premium giveaways. These ranged from trade cards and advertising mirrors to tin commemorative plates and kitchen items. There were banks
and toys, clocks and tins. Today's collectors are finding scores of these
items, all carrying Kenny's name.

Tray, girl with doll, holly band at rim, ca
1910, 10⅛" diameter, EX, $30.00.

Doll, pnt bsk, premium, printed mk, 4", NM 90.00
Figurine, Indian in canoe, EX 22.50
Pin-bk button, flags, Welcome United Singers, 1900s, 1½", VG ..12.00
Plate, tin, child in snow scene 90.00
Salt shaker, Geisha Girl 15.00
Stamp holder, cl, Dutch waitresses 16.50
Tape measure, retractable 48.00
Tip tray, lady in woods, flower border, M 120.00

Camel Tobacco, tc, RJ Reynolds, 1950s, 3¼x3½", EX 30.00
Campbell's Coffee, pail, tin, men & camels, 4-lb, EX 65.00
Canada Dry, clock, plastic face, metal fr, 16x16", EX 35.00
Canada Dry, door push, tin litho, 3½x12", EX 70.00
Capudine, door push, cl over metal, 3½x10", VG 60.00
Caravan Condoms, tc, unopened, M 45.00
Case Equipment, eagle on globe, CI, 2-pc, pnt chips, 57½" 2,350.00
Champion Spark Plugs, sign, metal, 4-color, 27½x10½", EX 145.00
Chemists Powder, tc, flowers on creme, EX 60.00
Chesterfield, banner, linen, mc, 1930s-40s, 30x56", EX 150.00
Chevrolet, clock, metal, neon, 3-color, 20½" dia, EX 575.00
Chevrolet, clock, plastic & metal, 24x13", VG 65.00
Chevrolet, sign, plastic, 4-color, lights up, 27" dia, EX 200.00
Chrysler, promo card, Hopalong Cassidy, 1942, 3¼x5", M 35.00
Clabber Girl Baking Powder, tc, sample sz, EX 65.00
Cleanzum Hand Cleaner, tc, 5½x13" dia, EX 70.00
Co-Re-Ga Tooth Powder, sample tin, NMIB 38.00
Cockshutt Plows, sign, cb, factory, orig fr, 13x23", NM 160.00
Coleman Mustard, box, wood, paper label, 4x21x12", EX 20.00
Colgan's Violet Chips, tc, 1½" dia, EX 20.00
Colgate's Baby Talc, tc, baby in oval on gr, EX 165.00
Colgate's Borated Baby Powder, tc, blond baby on wht, VG+ 95.00
Collins Hand Axe, sign, porc, 2-sided, blk & gray, 18x11", EX 95.00
Confy Talc, tc, baby crawling on creme bkground, NM 135.00
Conoco Aviation Gasoline, crate, paper label, 15¼x21", VG 55.00
Continental Coffee, tc, keywind, 1-lb, EX 50.00
Continental Cubes Tobacco, tc, sample sz, EX 250.00
Corbett's Extra Old Stock Ale, radio, bottle form, 24", EX 300.00

Crystal Club Ginger Ale, thermometer, metal, 27x7", EX **90.00**
Cunningham Radio Tubes, sign, tin, mc, 5x5", NM **120.00**
Dad's Old Fashioned Root Beer, ts, blk/red/yel, 19x27", NM **190.00**
Daisy Fly Killer, tc, daisies, unused, 6x3½", NM **50.00**

Dan Patch Roasted Coffee, tin container, trotter reserve, 10½", G, $800.00.

Daniel's Gall Cure, flange sign, metal, blk & yel, 6¼x13¾", G ..**185.00**
DeKalb Hybrid Corn, ts, red/creme/yel, St Thomas, 13x19", EX ..**175.00**
Delco Batteries, sign, metal, 3-color, 20x28", EX **125.00**
Delco Batteries, sign, porc, 3-color, 17¾x24", EX **200.00**
Diamond Dyes, book, hard bound, 16-pg, 5x9", EX **12.00**
Diamond Dyes, cabinet, court jester, much rstr to pnt **400.00**
Diamond Dyes, cabinet, governess, tin, orig pnt, NM **1,900.00**
Diamond Dyes, cabinet, maypole, tin, orig pnt, VG **475.00**
Diamond Dyes, cabinet, washer lady, tin, faded pnt **600.00**
Diamond F Mixture, tc, sq corners, 4", VG **65.00**
Dill's Best Tobacco, sign, cb, lady & tin, 26x20", EX **140.00**
Dodger Beverage, sign, pressed steel, mc diecut, 65x16", EX **450.00**
Double Cola, flange sign, metal, mc, c 1947, 15x18", EX **295.00**
Double Cola, thermometer, red & wht, 12" dia, NM **80.00**
Dr Caldwell's, door push, porc, 4x6½", VG **105.00**
Dr Hess Heave Powder, package, man w/horse, unopened, 7x4", EX ..**30.00**
Dr Hess Instant Louse Killer, package, unopened, NM **30.00**

Dr. Pepper

A young pharmacist, Charles C. Alderton, was hired by W.B. Morrison, owner of Morrison's Old Corner Drug Store in Waco, Texas, around 1884. Alderton, an observant sort, noticed that the drugstore's patrons could never quite make up their minds as to which flavor of extract to order. He concocted a formula that combined many flavors, and Dr. Pepper was born. The name was chosen by Morrison in honor of a beautiful young girl with whom he had once been in love. The girl's father, a Virginia doctor by the name of Pepper, had discouraged the relationship due to their youth, but Morrison had never forgotten her. On December 1, 1885, a U.S. patent was issued to the creators of Dr. Pepper. Our advisors for Dr. Pepper listings are Craig and Donna Stifter; they are listed in the Directory under Illinois.

Bottle, seltzer; Cherrio-Memphis **165.00**
Bottle, 1937, 6½ -oz **35.00**

Bottle topper, 4½x8½", NM **35.00**
Calendar, shows Miss East, West, North, South, 1941, NM **150.00**
Calendar, 1951, 3-pg, 20x12", EX **40.00**
Clock, milk glass face, lights up, 1950s, EX orig **295.00**
Clock, Pam, 15" sq, EX **175.00**
Clock, plastic, bottle cap shape, 14" dia, EX **110.00**
Dispenser, syrup; china w/metal legs, cylindrical, 18", EX **1,350.00**
Door pull, metal, bottle form, EX **75.00**
Door push, tin, red/gold/wht, NM **60.00**
Marker, store; brass **60.00**
Postcard, 10¢ coupon, M **5.00**
Sign, cb, girl at car, orig wood fr, 1940s, NM **225.00**
Sign, cb, lady at stadium being handed bottle, 15x25", NM **185.00**
Sign, rvpt glass, 4-color, 1930s, rare, 14x11", NM **1,800.00**

Tin litho thermometers, 5-color, 1939, 17¼", EX, $500.00; Drink a Bite To Eat, 1936, NM, $750.00; 3-color, 17¼", EX, $300.00.

Tray, roses, King of Beverages, Vienna **265.00**
Watch fob, Billiken, brass, EX **110.00**

Drink Lift, ts, plane on bottle, 24x12", VG **185.00**
Drummond's Horse Shoes, sign, cb diecut, girl/shoe, 21x17", EX ...**170.00**
Dryden Oil, sign, metal, 3-color, 23⅝x27⅝", EX **35.00**
Duke's Mixture, door push, porc, some fading, 4x6½", VG **130.00**
Dunlap's Seeds, sign, paper, Ottman litho, 23x17"+fr, EX **550.00**
Dunlop Tires, sign, metal, creme & bl, oval, 17x21½", EX **275.00**
Dunlop Tires, ts, emb letters, 3-color, 20x27½", NM **110.00**
Duplex Marine Engine Oil, sign, metal, 3-color, 10x20", VG **80.00**
Duplex Marine Engine Oil, sign, metal, 3-color, 24x48", G- **50.00**
Dupont Paint, clock, metal w/glass face, electric, 15" dia, VG **80.00**
Dutch Masters Cigars, ts, 6 men at table, oval, 9x11", VG **70.00**
Dyer's Indian Herb Cough Drops, tc, Indians/forest, VG **130.00**
Eagle Musical Strings, display, tin & glass, 12x9½x6½" **175.00**
Eame's Good Breads, door push, aluminum, mc, 3x6", VG **25.00**
Early Morn Coffee, pin, cl, 1-lb for 19¢, 2¾", EX **70.00**
Edison Mazda Lamps for Automobiles, sign, metal, 22x11", VG ...**160.00**
Edward Pure Rye..., ts, bartender/maid, 1890-1915, 33x23", VG ..**425.00**
Effecto Auto Red Enamel, tc, paper label, 3x6" dia, VG **35.00**
Egyptian Prettiest Cigarettes, sign, cb, lady, 14x10½", VG **150.00**
Egyptian Straights, sign, paper, orig fr, 16x14", EX **185.00**
El Moriso Cigars, sign, cb, 5-color, 10¼x13½", EX **40.00**
English Bird's Eye Tobacco, box, red on yel, horizontal, EX **40.00**
Epicure Tobacco, pocket tin, vertical, full, EX **210.00**

Esso Credit Cards Honored, sign, porc, 2-sided, 33½x26", NM ..**165.00**
Esso Oil, tc, red/wht/bl, 1950s, unopened, M **5.00**
Eveready Batteries, sign, cb, boy & skunks, 26x14", VG **45.00**
Ex-Lax, door push, plastic, 3½x7½", EX **28.00**
Ex-Lax, thermometer, porc, red/wht/bl/blk, 36x8", EX **130.00**
Exide Batteries, sign, metal, 3-color, 15½x47", NM **120.00**
Export Cigarettes, change mat, rubber, 7x6", NM **10.00**
Farmer's Pride, spice tin, farmer & girl, 1½ -oz, EX **24.00**
Fatima Cigarettes, thermometer/barometer, porc, 27½", EX **150.00**
Fehr's Ambrosia, tray, tin, 3 Romans, 1917-20, 13" dia, EX **220.00**
Ferguson System, sign, porc, tractor, rust/scratches, 35x60" **185.00**
Fire Chief Gasoline, sign, porc, helmet on wht, 18x12", EX **80.00**
Firestone Tires, curb sign, porc w/iron base, 60" H, VG **375.00**

Fleischmann's Yeast, tin sign, bright colors, Sentenne & Green, 13¾x19¾", EX, $1,700.00.

Fleishmann's Yeast, door push, coated porc, 3x4", NM **115.00**
Ford, symbol, compo, shield shape, 5-color, 20¼x17", G **85.00**
Four Roses Tobacco, pocket tin, vertical, flat top, 4x3", NM **350.00**
French Market Coffee, pail, tin, 4-lb, VG **45.00**
Friskies Dog Food, ts, mc dog's face, comic, 9½x30", EX **85.00**
Frostie Root Beer, sf cb sign, For Goodness..., 15x29½", EX **25.00**
Frostie Root Beer, sign, cb diecut, mc, 12x21", EX **25.00**
Frostie Root Beer, sign, metal, bottle cap form, 36", VG **300.00**
Full Dress Tobacco, canister, slip lid, 6x5", EX **330.00**
Full Dress Tobacco, pocket tin, vertical, EX **260.00**
Gargoyle Mobiloil, flange sign, porc, 3-color, 15½x24", EX **375.00**
Glass Mirrors Agency, flange sign, metal, Indian, mc, 14x19" **200.00**
Glenwood Motor Oil, tc, racing car, 2-gal, 11x8½x5¾", VG **100.00**
Gold Bond Tobacco, pocket tin, VG **125.00**
Gold Seal Champagne, tip tray, creme/blk/gold, 6½x4½", EX **40.00**
Golden Leaf Coffee, tc, paper label, pry top, 1-lb, EX **55.00**
Golden Rule Coffee, tc, 1-lb, EX **60.00**
Golden Rule Spices, tc, mc, 5", EX **15.00**
Goodrich Sport Shoes, sign, Indian cb diecut, fr, 41x26", EX **260.00**
Goodyear Tires, sign, porc w/wrought fr, 25⅝x47½", EX **230.00**
Grant Batteries, sign, metal, 3-color, 38½x12½", EX **80.00**
Grapette, sign, porc, red/wht/bl, oval, 1940s, 10x7", EX **165.00**
Graphinoil, flange sign, metal, blk & orange, 9x18½", EX **65.00**
Green River Tobacco, cb container, Blk man w/horse, 6x5", EX ..**175.00**
Gulf, sign, metal, 3-color, 28" dia, NM **115.00**
Gulf, sign, porc, 2-sided, 3-color, 66" dia, VG **210.00**
Gurd's Ginger Beer, display bottle, stoneware, 30", EX **875.00**
Hall's Distemper, sign, porc, figures & house, 18x48", EX **750.00**
Hamilton's Funeral Home, thermometer, metal, 36x9", EX **110.00**
Happy Foot Health Socks, sign, cb, Santa, mc, 14x29", EX **26.00**
Happy Foot Health Socks, sign, plastic, easel bk, 5x12", EX **26.00**
Harley-Davidson, sales envelope, 4x9½", EX **15.00**

Harley-Davidson, vest, leather, emblem on bk, EX **110.00**
Harry Horne Marshmallows, tc, comic figure, lid hat, NM **210.00**
Hartford Fire Insurance, flange sign, metal, 28x18", EX **325.00**
Hartford Insurance, clock, rvpt, lights up, 15x15", EX **165.00**
Harvester Cigars, sf ts, girl on yel, blk border, 13x9", EX **140.00**
Hastings Piston Rings, sign, metal, 3-color, 27x20", VG **100.00**
Heinz Vinegar, dispenser, glass, bbl shape, early, 10" **250.00**
Helmar Cigarettes, sign, porc, 27½x10", VG **110.00**
Helmar Turkish Cigarettes, sign, paper, mc, fr, 30x20", VG **200.00**
Herbert Tareyton Cigarettes, sign, cb stand-up diecut, 20", NM ..**80.00**
Hercules Overalls, door push, porc, 4x6", EX **200.00**
Hi-Plane Tobacco, pocket tin, 2-engine, vertical, NM **150.00**
Highlander Pilsner Brew, ts, mc, 14x19", EX **275.00**

Hires

Charles E. Hires, a drugstore owner in Philadelphia, became interested in natural teas. He began experimenting with roots and herbs and soon developed his own special formula. Hires introduced his product to his own patrons and began selling concentrated syrup to other soda fountains and grocery stores. Samples of his 'root beer' were offered for the public's approval at the 1876 Philadelphia Centennial. Today's collectors are often able to date their advertising items by observing the Hires boy on the logo. From 1891 to 1906, he wore a dress. From 1906 until 1914, he was shown in a bathrobe; and from 1915 until 1926, he was depicted in a dinner jacket. The apostrophe may or may not appear in the Hires name; this seems to have no bearing on dating an item. Our advisors for Hires listings are Craig and Donna Stifter; they are listed in the Directory under Illinois.

Hires Root Beer, sign, reverse painting on glass, with frame and chain hanger, 8¼x7¼", NM, $1,500.00.

Bottle stopper, metal & rubber **10.00**
Coaster, ceramic, Mettlach, rare, 4¼", EX **665.00**
Door push, tin, bottle on wht, 14x4", EX **70.00**
Mug, ceramic, boy lifts mug, Mettlach, EX **175.00**
Mug, ceramic, England, 4", NM **250.00**
Mug, stoneware, Drink...It Is Pure, 6" **110.00**
Note pad, blk, w/1890 calendar **50.00**
Pocket mirror, cl, lady w/roses, rare, NM **350.00**
Sign, cb, Haskell Coffin artwork, 1910s, 15x21", EX **350.00**
Sign, cb, Hires boy, 1880-90, 24x20", EX **1,100.00**
Sign, die-cut tin bottle, 1960s, 28", NM **125.00**
Sign, emb tin, Josh Slinger, ca 1915, 18x9", VG **375.00**
Sign, menu board, tin, 1950s, 20x28", EX **150.00**
Sign, rvpt child w/mug, chain fr, 8¼x7¼", NM **1,500.00**

Sign, tin, dbl-sided flange, 1940s, EX 150.00
Sign, tin, emb oval w/bottle diecut, 40x55", VG 600.00
Sign, tin, girl & top of bottle, mc, 28x10", EX 450.00
Thermometer, tin, mc, 17x5", EX+ 30.00
Trade card, boy on ladder adjusting clock, 1893, EX 32.00
Tray, baby points finger, oval, c 1907, VG 175.00
Tray, girl on wood-grained bkground, 10½x13", EX 95.00

Holland Dairy Foods, clock, windmill on face, lights up, EX 150.00
Home Investment Savings Assoc, sign, porc, bl/wht, 12x18", EX .150.00
Honeymoon Tobacco, pocket tin, vertical, EX 100.00
Hood's Sarsaparilla, puzzle calendar, 1903, M in envelope 30.00
Hood Tires, sign, metal, bl & wht, 77½x18", EX 350.00
Hugh Campbell's Shag, pocket tin, 10¢, vertical, 2-oz, EX 350.00
Hulman's Coffee, bin, slant front, 18x18x16", EX 125.00
Humphrey's Remedies, case, wood & metal, 21x18x7", EX 250.00
Hushpuppies, lighter, MIB 12.00
Imperial Club Cigars, ts, cigar box, mc, 10x13½", EX 60.00
Imperial Roll Films, sign, porc, gr & wht, 2-sided, 14x10", EX ...220.00
Incandescent Light & Stove, change tray, EX 75.00
Ingersoll Watches, case, metal, mc, 15x10x6", EX 100.00
Invador Motor Oil, sign, metal, emb letters, mc, 12x15", VG 160.00
Jergens Oriental, tc, Oriental lady in reserve, VG 96.00
Jergens Talcum Powder, tc, roses on yel, EX 97.00
JHP 5¢ Cigar, door push w/match striker, porc, 4x16", VG 140.00
Joe Grein's Sauerkraut Juice, pocket mirror, Chicago, EX 35.00
Johnson's Belladonna Plaster, cabinet, tin, 5-drw, 15x13x9" 250.00
Johnson's Peacemaker Coffee, tc, log cabin, no chimney, VG 750.00
Juicy Orange, door push, porc, chips, 3½x8", VG 125.00
Junge's Bread, door push, porc, 4x9", EX 50.00
Kelly Tires, porc sign, Lotta Miles, 3-color, 33x34", VG 900.00
Kern's Root Beer, door push, tin litho, wear, 3x9¾", G 75.00
Kik Cola, door push, tin, red & wht, 3x10", EX 37.00
Kik Cola, door push, tin, 3-color, French, 3½x10", EX 33.00
King Aerator, sign, tin, barn, 4-color, 19x13", VG 125.00
King Cole Tea, door push, porc, 3-color, 11x3", NM 170.00
King Cole Tea, door push, tin, blk on yel, 3x30", EX 38.00
Kirk's Flake Soap, sign, porc, red/blk/wht, 15x40", NM 650.00
Kis-Me Gum, fold-out fan, 10", VG 85.00
Kist, door push, aluminum, red & gold, 3x30", EX 50.00
Kleinert's Dress Shields, pocket mirror, cl, EX 35.00
Kodak, sign, metal w/wrought hanger, Verichrome, 17x17" 280.00
Kodak Film, sign, tin, 2-sided, 14x18", NM in shipping box 125.00
Kool Cigarettes, fan, cb, on stick, EX 45.00
L&M Cigarettes, lighter, pack form, MIB 12.00
La Flor de Erb, sign, tin on cb, man in bl on gray, 6x14", EX 70.00
La Palina Cigars, jar & lid, glass w/wood base, 8x6½", EX 120.00
Labatt's Union Made, tray, porc, creme & red, 12x16", EX 60.00
Lash's Kidney & Liver Bitters..., sign, wood, 20x14", VG 350.00

Leak Proof Piston Rings, clock, metal & glass, 14" dia, VG 130.00
Lions Internat'l, sign, porc, lions' heads, 30" dia, G 100.00
Lions Internat'l, sign, porc w/steel fr, 2-sided, 30" dia, NM 375.00
Listerine Shaving Cream, bank, frog figural, EX 20.00

Log Cabin Syrup

Bank, glass cabin figural, EX 35.00
Can opener, Towle's, metal 14.00
Container, plastic wigwam, yel letters, 1950, 2x2" dia 7.50
Syrup tin, bear in door, cartoon ends, Towle's, 5-lb 145.00
Syrup tin, blacksmith, 33-oz 140.00
Syrup tin, boy w/lasso, 1-lb 115.00
Syrup tin, cartoon all sides, sm 115.00
Syrup tin, child in door, 4¾" 115.00
Syrup tin, children, man by pump, Towle's, 33-oz 155.00
Syrup tin, children playing, Towle's, 33-oz, NM 145.00
Syrup tin, Dr RU Well, cartoon style, rare 255.00
Syrup tin, Express Office, coach, Towle's, 33-oz 155.00
Syrup tin, Frontier Inn, cowboys & horse, 5-lb 225.00
Syrup tin, Frontier Jail, 12-oz 155.00
Syrup tin, hand w/finger pointing on top, Towle's, med 165.00
Syrup tin, Home Sweet Home, 12-oz 155.00
Syrup tin, pancakes, VG 15.00
Syrup tin, paper label, sample sz, rare, 2x1½" 310.00
Syrup tin, red, 5-lb 55.00
Syrup tin, Stockade School, Towle's, 33-oz 155.00
Syrup tin, wigwam, 1-lb, very rare, 4x3¼x3½" 515.00
Teaspoon 20.00

Lowe Brothers Paints, sign, porc, yel/bl/wht, 20x28", EX 45.00
Lowney's, spoon, brass, emb, 4" 15.00
Lowney's Chocolates, ts, blk on yel, 12½x16", EX 52.00
Lowney's Oh Henry, ts, red & wht, 23x35", NM 110.00
LTS Rubber Heels, sign, paper, sgn Frise, 21x19", NM 180.00
Lucky Strike Cigarettes, carton, flat, unformed, EX 55.00
Lucky Strike Tobacco, pocket tin, vertical, sample sz, EX 150.00
Lucky Strike Tobacco, pocket tin, vertical, sample sz, VG 80.00
Lunch Ice Cream Soda, sign, porc, bl & wht, early, 10x52", EX .280.00
Lyons' Tea, door push, metal, mc, 3x5½", EX 25.00
Lyons' Tea, sign, tin, blk & wht, 10x17", NM 60.00
Marathon Gasoline, sign, porc, 3-color, 35x72", G 230.00
Marathon Motor Oil, tc, runner, 2-gal, 11x8½x5¾", VG 210.00
Marathon Motor Oil, ts, 3-color, 9⅝x13⅝", VG 185.00
Marvels Cigarettes, thermometer, tin, 12x3¾", EX 95.00
Mason & Rich Pianos, letter opener, tin & paper, 6x1½", EX 90.00
Master Feeds, sign, porc, yel w/red banner, 15x26½", EX 75.00
Maven's Biscuits, push bar, porc, 3x30", EX 55.00
May Day Coffee, tc, bl, keywind, 1-lb 55.00
McCormick-Deering, sign, paper, early tractor, 23x33", VG 185.00
McCormick-Deering Machines, ts, bl & yel, 12x16", EX 80.00
Medaglia D'oro, tc, keywind, full, unopened, NM 25.00
Mi Lola Cigars, humidor, emb glass, NM 30.00
Michelin Tires, ashtray, Bakelite, Michelin Man on rim 75.00
Michelin Tires, tire man, reinforced plaster, 32", VG 1,125.00
Miller High Life, sign, porc, red/wht/blk, 34x45½", EX 320.00
Miss Wonderful Cutters, display, wood & glass, 22x16x2½", EX ..55.00
Mission Orange, blotter, bright colors, EX 8.00
Mission Orange, sign, cb, life-sz lady figural, 60", EX 275.00
Mitchell Car, ts, bl & wht litho, 19⅝x13½", EX 1,200.00
Mobil Travel Information Center, flanged sign, metal, 8x34", EX ..80.00
Mobilgas, pump plate, porc, wht/bl/red, 12x11", EX 80.00
Mobiloil, crate, wood, paper label, 11x28x11½", VG 90.00

Leisey's Light Beer, electric sign, yellow & blue with eagle logo, 15" diameter, NM, $950.00 at auction.

Mobiloil, plaque, compo, mc, chips, 9½x7½", VG 85.00
Mobiloil Aero, tc, w/contents, 1-qt, 5x4½", NM 160.00
Molson's Ales, match striker, tin, 9x4", EX 55.00
Monarch Coffee, tc, sample sz, EX 35.00
Moore Push Pins, display, metal, revolves, '30s, 15", EX 140.00
MoPar Mufflers, ts, 3-color, 46½x35", EX 85.00
Morris' Supreme Peanut Butter, pail, 12-oz, EX 180.00

Moxie

The Moxie Company was organized in 1884 by George Archer of Boston, Massachusetts. It was at first touted as a 'nerve food' to improve the appetite, promote restful sleep, and in general to make one 'feel better!' Emphasis was soon shifted, however, to the good taste of the brew, and extensive advertising campaigns rivaling those of such giant competitors as Hires and Coca-Cola resulted in successful marketing through the 1930s. Today the term Moxie has become synonymous with courage and audacity, traits displayed by the company who dared compete with such well-established rivals. Our advisors for Moxie are Craig and Donna Stifter; they are listed in the Directory under Illinois.

Tray, glass over metal, lady with glass, 1910, 10", EX, $475.00.

Bottle, Moxie Nerve Food, Hutchinson type, aqua, 26-oz 17.50
Candy tin, Moxiemobile, scarce 165.00
Case, wooden, Crystal Lake Bottling, holds 24 7-oz bottles 18.00
Clicker, Moxie boy, rnd, NM 48.00
Display, wooden diecut, butler, 35x10x10", VG 400.00
Fan, cb, lady w/full glass, 1920s, 9x8", NM 60.00
Folder, President Roosevelt & Moxie, 4½x7", EX 80.00
Label, Mad About...1884, 28-oz, late 1960s, NM 12.00
Mug, china, girl transfer, flared ft, 4¼x3" dia, EX 150.00
Pin, Moxie girl, 1910, scarce 400.00
Sheet music, Moxie boy pointing on cover, 1921, EX 30.00
Sign, tin, bottle pouring, 19x54", EX 235.00
Sign, tin flange, Drink Moxie, oval, 9x18", VG 125.00
Thermometer, girl w/glass & bottle, F Archer, 1910s-20s, rstr 900.00
Thermometer, tin, orange & gr, 25x10", EX 425.00
Tip tray, I Just Love..., girl w/glass, 6" dia, G 120.00
Token, bottle wagon, NM 45.00
Wooden nickel, M 3.00

Murad, sign, paper, Vanderbilt Cup Race, '09, 13½x9½", EX 155.00
Murad Turkish Cigarettes, ts, lady w/tray, 1900-25, 39x29", EX ..900.00
Nabisco Nat'l Biscuit Co, bin cover, Pat 1923, 11x10" 25.00
Nadruco Royal Rose Talc Powder, tc, red rose, EX+ 105.00

New & True Coffee, clicker, EX 8.00
New York Coach Oil, tc, coach, 1-pt, 6½x2⅞", EX 120.00
Niagara Shoes, ts, Falls, mc, Am Art Works, 8½x10", NM 160.00
Nigger Hair Tobacco, pail, tin litho, mc, VG 325.00
North Star Oil, pail, tin litho, mc, 10-lb, EX 20.00
NuGrape, tray, hand holding bottle, 13x10", VG+ 52.00
NuGrape, ts, red & blk on yel, 1950s, 19x27", EX 40.00

Novia Candies, tin pail, Uncle Wiggily at the Seashore, VG, $250.00.

O-Cedar, rack, metal, mc, ca 1925, 41x14x12", EX 120.00
Oh Boy Gum, ts, bl w/creme & yel, wood fr, 12½x16½", VG 175.00
Oilzum Motor Oil, sign, metal, 3-color, 1949, 10x15½", EX 600.00
Oilzum Tar Remover, tc, man's face, 1-pt, 6¼x2¾", EX 160.00
Old Gold Cigarettes, door pull, tin litho, 4x12", EX 70.00
Old Judge Million Dollar Coffee, tc, keywind, 1-lb, EX 30.00
Olympian Coffee, tc, discus thrower, EX 250.00
Omar Cigarettes, sign, cb, Joy of Life, orig fr, 25x18", EX 250.00
Omar Cigarettes, ts, lettering on blk, 14x8", EX 115.00
Orange-Crush, bottle, 7-oz 6.00
Orange-Crush, decal, premium, 1940s, M in envelope 16.00
Orange-Crush, door push, porc, gr/blk/orange, 9x3½", EX 280.00
Orange-Crush, door push, tin litho, 1920s, 12x3¼", NM 300.00
Orange-Crush, hat, paper, mc, 11x14", NM 6.00
Orange-Crush, letter head, Crushie & bottle, 1950s, 11x8½" 5.00
Orange-Crush, sign, cb, 1920 bottle, 11x14", NM 75.00
Orange-Crush, thermometer, tin, bottle diecut, 28x7", EX 110.00
Orange-Crush, thermometer, tin, bottle on wht, 19x6", EX 80.00
Orange-Crush, ts, Ask For a..., 4-color, 3½x26", EX 78.00
Osh Kosh B'Gosh Overalls, sign, porc, neon, Uncle Sam, EX+ ..750.00
Pabst Blue Ribbon Beer, bottle opener, bottle form, '30s, EX 20.00
Pabst Blue Ribbon Beer, sign, cb, red & wht, 36x27", EX 650.00
Pabst's Okay Special, mirror, wood fr, 9x12", EX 75.00
Palmer's Root Beer, sign, porc, bbl form, 14x19", EX 350.00
Parke-Davis Products, sign, glass, 3-color, 25x13", EX 60.00
Parker Pens, display, wood & glass, lights up, 9x21x9", NM 85.00
Patterson Sargent Paint, sign, 2-sided porc diecut, 24x33", EX 75.00
Peg Top Cigar, door push, porc, mc, 12½x4", NM 130.00
Penn Drake Lubricants, flange sign, metal, mc, 20x14", VG 200.00
Penn's Spells Quality Tobacco, box, tin, hinged, 2½x6½", EX 30.00
Penn Soo Oil, tc, minor soiling, ½-gal, 8x4¾", EX 20.00
Pennzoil, chalk board, lt rust at edges, 23½x17½", NM 45.00
Pennzoil, flange sign, porc, 2-sided, NM 135.00
Pennzoil, sign, metal, 2-sided, Sound Your Z, 12x16½", NM 100.00
Pennzoil, sign, porc, 2-sided, oval, NM 110.00

Pepsi-Cola

Pepsi-Cola was first served in the early 1890s to customers of Caleb D. Bradham, a young pharmacist who touted his concoction to be medicinal as well as delicious. It was first called 'Brad's Drink' but was renamed Pepsi-Cola in 1898. Our advisors for Pepsi are Craig and Donna Stifter; they are listed in the Directory under Illinois.

Blotter, Hayden artwork, 1945, NM **95.00**
Bottle, clear glass emb w/appl color label, 1950s, NM **12.00**
Bottle, fountain syrup **20.00**
Bottle, seltzer; glass, Delicious Healthful, EX **600.00**
Bottle opener, heavy SP metal, flat w/emb ad, 1950s-60s, NM **50.00**
Bottler's coin, bronze, emb ad, 1950s-60s, NM **50.00**
Calendar, Rolf Armstrong artwork, 1920, 5x7", VG **2,300.00**
Can, pull tab, 1950s, 7-oz, NM **12.00**
Cigarette lighter, bottle form, ca 1930s-40s, NMIB **80.00**

Clock, plastic front with metal back, 1963, 16x15⅝", NM, $85.00.

Clock, can form, General Electric, 1950s, NMIB **55.00**
Clock, dbl bubble glass, Think Young, lights up, 1950s, NM **375.00**
Clothes brush, Great in Bottles, VG **140.00**
Cooler, metal table top, creme/red/bl, 1940, 13x27x15", EX **500.00**
Deposit ticket, for empty bottle return, VG **15.00**
Door push, porc, 5-color, 3x30", EX **60.00**
Door push, porc, 5-color, 3x30", NM **85.00**
Fan, cb, boy w/glass, 1938, 12", VG **15.00**
Fan, girl at fountain sipping from bottle, 1912, 8x9", G **700.00**
Hanger, 1940s, war Victory Paper on bk, 16x16", NM **450.00**
Ice pick, yel hdl, ca 1960s, VG **30.00**
Letter opener, Lucite hdl, 1970s **20.00**
Money clip, plastic, 1950s, EX **15.00**
Napkin holder, bottle motif, 1970s, M **45.00**
Pencil, gold w/enameled cap logo on clip, 1950s, NM **25.00**
Pocketknife, bone-colored plastic hdl, 1950s, NM **30.00**
Postcard, shows outdoor ad sign on brick building, NM **15.00**
Radio, bottle form, Bakelite, rpt label, working, VG **300.00**
Radio, bottle-shape transistor, 1970s, 8½", NM **35.00**
Radio, machine-type transistor, 1940s, EX, +leather case **175.00**
Sewing kit, cl cover, 1930s-40s, VG **25.00**
Sign, cb, picnic scene, Light Refreshment, 1950s, 20x18", G **85.00**
Sign, cb, promotes bottle sales for 5¢, sepia, 16x11", G **20.00**
Sign, cb, red & creme on bl, 21" dia, EX **210.00**
Sign, cb diecut, Pepsi & Pete w/6-pack, 1930s, EX **275.00**
Sign, cb diecut, Santa, Rockwell, easel bk, 1950s, 48", NM **60.00**
Sign, cb w/metal fr, 2-sided, lady in fur hat, 13x27", EX **40.00**
Sign, cl, Refresh..., Blk lady & phone, 1950s, 12x8", EX **30.00**

Sign, emb tin, Enjoy...Bigger-Better, 1940, 40x22", VG **125.00**
Sign, gloss-coated cb, Pepsi w/Rum drinks, easel bk, 12x6", M ..**200.00**
Sign, plastic, Say Pepsi & Taste the Difference, 1970s, NM **15.00**
Sign, porc, Enjoy a Pepsi, w/cap on yel, 12x30", EX **125.00**
Sign, sf cb, Erbit artwork, 1940, EX **400.00**
Sign, tin, die-cut bottle w/5¢ on it, 1940, 12x45", EX **400.00**
Sign, tin, Peps You Up..., Canadian, 18x28", VG **170.00**
Sign, tin, Pepsi & Pete, late 1930s, 3½x21", G **100.00**
Skirt, mini; Feeling Free, 1960s, NM **25.00**
Syrup drum, red & wht, 1930s-40s, EX **75.00**
Telephone, can shape, M in orig packaging **36.00**
Thermometer, Bigger & Better, 1942, 6¼x16", EX **275.00**
Thermometer, later repro w/1909 girl, wood, dtd 1973, NM **35.00**
Thermometer, Say Pepsi Please, yel, 1960s, NM **85.00**
Tie bar, cap logo, enameled, 1940s, EX **40.00**
Tip tray, flowers on blk, 1950s, VG **30.00**
Toy truck, Hong Kong, 1960s, 2", NM **35.00**
Toy truck, metal, red w/bl top, Nylint, 16½", EX **200.00**
Toy truck, metal, Tonka, 1978, 8", NM **80.00**
Toy truck, Nylint, 1950s, 16", NMIB **225.00**
Toy truck, wht plastic w/decal on rear, 1½", NM **75.00**
Tray, tin, Hits the Spot, musical notes, 3-color, 10x14", NM **90.00**
Tray, tin, red, wht & bl bottle cap, 12" dia, EX **150.00**
Watch fob, emb eagle & 2 bottles, ca 1900-05, EX **55.00**
Whistle, plastic, dual bottles, partial decal, 1940s, G **15.00**

Philip Morris, sign, heavy cb diecut, fr, 15x5½", EX **125.00**
Philip Morris Cigarettes, carton, cb, Johnny, EX **40.00**
Pickwick Ale, sign, tin on cb, horses w/wagon, 6½x23", VG **75.00**
Pickwick Ale & Beer, tray, horses pull wagon, 12" dia, EX **95.00**
Picobac Tobacco, pocket tin, hand/leaf, vertical, short, NM **75.00**
Pittston Gazette, sign, porc, bl & wht, 8x16", NM **100.00**

Planters Peanuts

Mr. Peanut, the dashing peanut man with the top hat, spats, monocle, and cane, has represented the Planters Peanut Company since 1916, although he took on a decidedly more modern appearance after the company was purchased by Standard Brands in 1961. He remains, however, perhaps the most highly recognized logo of any company in the world.

Mr. Peanut has promoted the company's products by appearing on premium giveaways, store displays, jars, and all company products, as well as in a special peanut costume at promotional events. Among the favored treasures of collectors today are the glass display jars which were sent to retailers nationwide to stimulate 'point-of-sale' trade. They come in a variety of shapes and styles — some are square, some hexagonal, some barrel shaped, and others round. The earliest, issued in the early 1920s, was a tall pedestal or apothecary jar, and it is unmarked except for a narrow paper label at the neck. In 1926 an octagonal jar was issued, and this is often called the 'pennant jar' or the 'eight-sided jar.' This jar has been widely reproduced (sometimes marked Made in Italy on the bottom; sometimes identified by the unusually wide space between the 'E' and 'R' in 'PLANTERS' on the jar neck), but most original jars of any shape are marked 'MADE IN USA' on the bottom. In a second octagonal style, a paper label adorned one of the sides.

In 1930 a 'fishbowl' jar was introduced, and in 1932 a 'four-corner peanut' jar (arguably the most beautiful) with a blown-out peanut on each of the four corners was issued. Perhaps the rarest jar, the 'football' shape, was also introduced in the 1930s, as were the large 'barrel' jar, 'six-sided' jar with yellow decals, and 'square' jar. All of these early jars had glass lids, some with a peanut finial. In the 1940s, jars with tin lithographed lids were introduced, including the 'leap year,' 'clipper,' and 'streamline' models. Due to rusting, good tin lids are harder to find than the jars they covered. All told, at least fifteen different styles were developed, and several of these (octagon, barrel, four-corner, and clipper) have been recently reproduced in Asia.

In the late 1920s, the first premiums were introduced in the form of coloring/painting books, and in the 1930s, the wooden jointed doll and tin nut dishes (which were still made into the 1970s) were distributed. Post-WWII items were made of plastic: salt and pepper shakers, light switch pulls, drinking mugs, banks, mechanical pens and pencils, walking Mr. Peanut, small cars and trucks, cookie cutters, and almost any other form and shape imaginable. In recent years, the company (now owned by RJR-Lifesavers) has continued to make and distribute a wide variety of premiums. Today's collectors are able to find a treasure trove of advertising memorabilia depicting that debonair gentleman, Mr. Peanut. Our advisor for Planters Peanuts is Neil Williams; he is listed in the Directory under Massachusetts.

Bag, glassine, Planters Salted Peanuts, 1920s 5.00
Bag, mesh, filled w/marbles (+) 3.00
Bag, plastic, filled w/marbles, 1950s 18.00
Bank, plastic, Mr peanut, blk & gold, 1990, M in pkg 25.00
Bank, plastic, Mr peanut, red/lt bl/tan/gr, 8½" 10.00
Bear, plush, Honey Bear, 8", M 25.00
Bookmark, cb, Mr Peanut, 1930s-50s 15.00
Business card, cb, peanut shape, 1940s 20.00
Can, tin, Cocktail Peanuts, 1930s, 8-oz, EX 10.00
Can, tin, Salted Peanuts, blk/red graphics, 1910s, 10-lb, EX 50.00
Cap, golf; Mr Peanut, M 10.00
Cap, ski; knit, Mr Peanut, 18" 15.00
Coloring/painting book, Famous Men, 1930s 35.00
Coloring/painting book, Presidents, 1950s 10.00
Coloring/painting book, Presidents, 1977 ....5.00
Coloring/painting book, 12 Months, 1980s 5.00
Coloring/painting book, 50 States, 1960s 5.00
Costume, plastic, Mr Peanut, gold emb letters, 1960s 500.00
Dishes, tin, Mr peanut, 1930s-70s, 1 lg+4 sm pcs 10.00
Doll, Mr Peanut, jtd wood, bl/blk/wht, 1930s, 8½" 200.00
Glass, champagne style, plastic, Mr Peanut, red/wht/bl, 1950s 25.00
Jar, Barrel, running Mr Peanut, EX paper label, orig lid 275.00
Jar, Barrel, running Mr Peanut, no label, orig lid 200.00
Jar, Clipper, orig tin lid, NM 150.00

Jar, Octagon, 7 sides emb, orig lid 150.00
Jar, Octagon, 8 sides emb, orig lid 250.00
Jar, rnd, frosted label, orig knob-finial lid, 1950s 50.00
Jar, Streamline, G orig tin lid 50.00
Jar, supermarket; Chocolate...Cashews, label, tin lid, 1940s 25.00
Jar, supermarket; Mixed Nuts, label, orig tin lid, 1940s 25.00
Jar, supermarket; Peanut Butter, label, orig tin lid, 1950s 25.00
Jar, 4-corner, w/orig lid 225.00
Jar, 6-sided, yel decals, PLANTERS emb on orig lid 100.00
Knife, plastic, Mr Peanut, 1940s 20.00
Knife, plastic, Mr Peanut, 1950s 5.00
Knife/fork/spoon set, SP, Mr Peanut, 1950s 50.00
Light pull, plastic, Mr Peanut, 1950s 5.00
Lunch box, vinyl, Mr Peanut, NM 25.00
Measuring cup, clear plastic, Mr Peanut, 1950s 10.00
Mug, pewter, beer stein, 1980s 35.00
Mug, plastic, Lifesaver, hard-to-find logo 20.00
Mug, plastic, Mr Peanut, red/lt bl/tan/gr, 1950s 5.00
Mug, plastic, Mr Peanut, yel & pk, 1950s 10.00
Mug, SP, 1950s, baby sz 100.00
Nut grinder, tin litho, peanuts & Mr Peanut, 1930s-60s, EX 5.00
Peanut butter maker, plastic, Mr Peanut figural, 1970s, MIB 25.00
Pencil, mechanical; plastic, Mr Peanut, red/tan/bl/yel, 1950s 5.00
Pin, tin, Mr Peanut, tab bk, 1½" dia, NM 10.00
Plate, metal, Planters Snacks Super Bowl XIII, M 50.00
Puzzle, cb, Just Nuts About Mr Peanut, 1970s, MIB 25.00
Radio, plastic, Mr Peanut figural, 10", MIB 75.00
Snow globe, plastic, 1988, M 25.00
Spooky picture card, cb, Mr Peanut, bl & wht, 1940s 5.00
Spoon, nut server, gold wash, Mr Peanut, NM 10.00
Spoon, nut server, SP, Mr Peanut, NM 10.00
Tape measure/key chain, Mr Peanut, M 20.00
Trade card, Big Game Series, 1930s, 2¼x2", ea 7.50
Tray, tin, oval, 1980s, M 20.00
Whistle, plastic, police style 3.00

Jar, Fish Bowl with rectangular label, peanut finial lid, 13", $150.00.

Jar, Football, PLANTERS emb on orig lid 275.00
Jar, Leap Year, G orig tin lid, 1940 ....50.00
Jar, Octagon, VG paper label, orig lid 200.00
Jar, Octagon, 6 sides emb, orig lid 125.00

Peter Hand Brewery Co., tray, detailed graphics, Chas. Shonk litho, 15x18½", NM, $1,500.00.

Plow Boy Tobacco, container, cb, slip lid, 6x5", EX 150.00
Plow Boy Tobacco, tc, boy on plow, Liggett & Myers, 6x5", VG .50.00
Polarine Motor Oil, sign, porc, 3-color, 29½", VG 250.00
Poll Parrot, sign, porc, neon, mc parrot, chips, 41x21", EX 950.00
Pratt & Lambert Paint, sign, porc, 2-sided, mc, 24x36", EX 75.00
Prest O'Lite, door push, porc, 3x10", NM 225.00
Prestone, clock, metal, bl & silver, 10" dia, EX 40.00
Prestone Antifreeze, rack, metal, 3-color, 20x21x17", EX 35.00
Pro-phy-lac-tic Toothbrush, display cabinet, 1935, 8x20x12" 250.00
Pure Spring, clock, plastic face, 4-color, 12" dia, EX 35.00
Pure Spring Ginger Ale, door push, porc, 4-color, NM 46.00
Pursuit Gasoline, decal on glass, prof fr, 13½x17", EX 70.00

Quaker State Motor Oil, clock, neon, metal band, 21" dia, EX ..**500.00**
Quaker State Motor Oil, sign, metal, Buy Quality, 35x95", EX **70.00**
Quaker State Motor Oil, sign, metal, gr & wht, 24" dia, EX **90.00**
Quaker State Motor Oil, sign, metal, gr & wht, 29x26½", NM ..**100.00**

RCA Victor

Nipper, the RCA Victor trademark, was the creation of Francis Barraud, an English artist. His pet's intent fascination with the music of the phonograph seemed to him a worthy subject for his canvas. Although he failed to find a publishing house who would buy his work, the Gramophone Co. in England saw its potential and adopted Nipper to advertise their product. Nipper and the painting were later acquired by the Victor Talking Machine Co. and were purchased by RCA in 1929. The trademark is owned today by EMI in England and by General Electric in the U.S. Nipper's image appeared on packages (for use in the United States), accessories, in ads and brochures. If you are very lucky you may find a life-size statue of him; but all are not old, they have been manufactured for the owner throughout RCA history and are marketed currently by licensees BMG Inc. and Themson Consumer Electronics (DBA RCA). Except for the years between 1968 and 1976, Nipper has seen active duty, and with his image spruced up only a bit for the present day, the ageless symbol for RCA still listens intently to 'His Master's Voice.' Our advisor for RCA Victor is Roger R. Scott; he is listed in the Directory under Oklahoma.

Bank, Nipper figural, metal, 1940s **125.00**
Buckle, His Master's Voice, brass, Nash Tiffany London **25.00**
Catalog, record; performers' photos, leatherette cover, 1917 ....**45.00**
Clock, RCA Victor Records, w/Nipper **350.00**
Doll, RCA majorette, jtd wood, 1930s, EX **700.00**
Figure, Nipper, crystal, Fenton, 4" **40.00**
Figure, Nipper, molded plastic, 36", EX **235.00**
Figure, Nipper, papier-mache, fitted for sound, 40" **1,650.00**
Figure, Nipper, papier-mache, 14", EX **350.00**
Figure, Nipper, papier-mache, 36", EX **1,000.00**
Necktie, Nipper, M **35.00**
Oleograph, Nipper w/early phonograph, 24x30", EX **550.00**
Pin-bk button, Little Nipper Club Member, 1930s, 1½", EX **70.00**
Record display, dog & phonograph, chalk **150.00**
Shakers, ceramic, Nipper figural, Lenox, 1930s, pr **50.00**
Shakers, ceramic, S&P, 1940s, pr **40.00**
Shakers, dog & RCA phonograph, plastic, pr **45.00**
Sign, paper, His Master's Voice, textured, fr, 25x29", EX **675.00**
Sign, plastic/metal, lights up, 1940s, 15x37", EX **200.00**
Watch fob, EX **30.00**

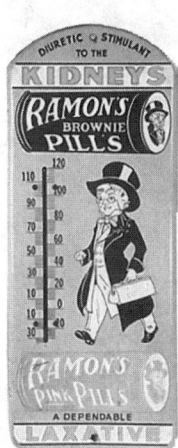

Ramon's Brownie and Pink Pills, metal thermometer, yellow, green and creme, light fading and rust, 21x8½", **$325.00.**

Radiola, dealer's sign, porc, 3-color, bent, 19x14½" **100.00**
Rajah Motor Oil, ts, die-cut man's head, 2-color, 28x20", EX ...**1,400.00**
Raleigh Tobacco, door push, tin litho, 3x8¼", EX **75.00**
Rameses Cigarettes, sign, cl on cb, 11x8", EX **85.00**
Red Bell Motor Oil, tc, bell in circle, 2-gal, 11x8½x5¾", G **75.00**
Red Belt Tobacco, pocket tin, EX **75.00**
Red Cross Mills Coffee, container, cb, paper label, 6x4¾", EX **75.00**
Red Crown Deodorized Gasoline, crate, wood, label, 15x21", VG .**255.00**
Red Devil Tools, display, pnt metal, devil, 13x20x5", EX **40.00**

Red Goose Shoes

Realizing that his last name was difficult to pronounce, Herman Giesceke, a shoe company owner resolved to give the public a modified, shortened version that would be better suited to the business world. The results suggested the use of the goose trademark with the last two letters, 'ke,' represented by the key that this early goose held in his mouth. Upon observing an employee casually coloring in the goose trademark with a red pencil, Giesceke saw new advertising potential and renamed the company Red Goose Shoes. Although the company has changed hands down through the years, the Red Goose emblem has remained. Collectors of this desirable fowl increase in number yearly, as do prices. Beware of reproductions; new chalkware figures are prevalent.

Address book, EX **7.50**
Bank, cb w/tin top, EX **78.00**
Bell, Ring For Red Goose Shoes **30.00**
Bill hook, tin goose figural **35.00**
Calendar, 1938, 10x17", EX **40.00**
Counter display, cb diecut, boy running, easel bk, 1940s **265.00**
Counter display, cb diecut, girl, easel bk, ca 1905 ....**545.00**
Counter display, paper on wood, boy on goose, 1920s **275.00**
Decal, 1930s, 2", M **6.00**
Dictionary, giveway, w/Red Goose ads, 1927 ....**30.00**
Display figure, goose, plaster, 11", NM **100.00**
Eraser **25.00**
Mirror, floor type, 21x14½" **135.00**
Pencil box, ca 1920, EX **65.00**
Shoe bench, seats 3 ....**875.00**
Thermometer, porc, For Boys & Girls, 27x7", EX **260.00**
Whistle, EX **22.00**

Red Indian Aviation Motor Oil, sign, porc, mc, 11x14", EX **700.00**
Red Jacket Coal, ts, Indian on blk & yel, 11½x23½", NM **230.00**
Red Ribbon Beer, change tray, EX **125.00**
Red Rose Coffee, ts, red & creme, 19x27", EX **60.00**
Red Rose Tea, door push, tin, red/wht/bl, 3x30", EX **30.00**
Red Rose Tea, ts, red & wht, 18x22", EX **80.00**
Red Rose Tea, ts, 3-color, 1930s, 12x16", EX **65.00**
Remington Game Loads, display, hunter/game, folds, 18x48", NM ..**230.00**
Retonga Medicine, sign, cb stand-up, man & lady, 41x27½" **175.00**
Revelation Tobacco, pocket tin, vertical, trial sz, EX **100.00**
Rexall Violet Talcum Powder, tc, violets, EX **58.00**
Ridenour-Johnson Hdw, sign, cb, Indian & lady, 1922, 27x16", VG .**70.00**
Roe Feeds, sign, metal, edge wear, 12x7", VG **85.00**

Roly Poly

The Roly Poly tobacco tins were patented on November 5, 1912, by Washington Tuttle and produced by Tindeco of Baltimore, Maryland. There were six characters in all: Satisfied Customer, Storekeeper, Mammy, Dutchman, Singing Waiter, and Inspector. Four brands of tobacco were packaged in selected characters; some tins carry a printed tobacco box on the back to identify their contents. Mayo and Dixie Queen Tobacco were packed in all six; Red Indian and U.S. Marine Tobacco in only Mammy, Singing Waiter, and Storekeeper. Of the set, the Inspector is considered the rarest and in excellent condition may fetch more than $1,100.00 on today's market.

Dutchman, Mayo, EX 500.00
Dutchman, Mayo, NM 675.00

Mammy, 6½", EX, $600.00.

Inspector from Scotland Yard, Mayo, EX 1,100.00
Satisfied Customer, Mayo, VG 425.00
Singing Waiter, Mayo, EX 600.00
Singing Waiter, US Marine, VG 450.00
Storekeeper, Mayo, NM 695.00
Storekeeper, VG 365.00

Royal Crown Cola, sf ts, emb bottle, chips, 36x16", EX 185.00
Royal Crown Cola, sf ts, 2 bottles, 17⅝x53½", EX 185.00
RPM Motor Oil, clock, cb, metal fr, 15½x15½", VG 100.00
RPM Motor Oil, sign, porc, red/wht/bl, 28" dia, NM 275.00
Salada Tea, door push, porc, yel & dk bl, 9½x2½", EX 180.00
Salada Tea, sign, porc, bl on yel, 3x15", NM 100.00
Salada Tea Bags, door push, porc, red & creme, 3x30", EX 55.00
Sanka Coffee, tc, key wind, full, 1-lb, EX 20.00
Savoy Beer, sf ts, US Brewing, 19½x15½", EX 2,500.00
Schmidt's Beer & Ale, figure, bronze, bartender, 7¾", EX 150.00
Schoenling Lager Beer, clock, neon, 8-sided, EX 275.00
Schweppes Ginger Ale, door push, tin, 3x30", VG 40.00
Sea-L-Tite Oysters, pail, tin, mermaid, no lid, 8x7", EX 215.00
Sears Roebuck, coffee pail, gr & blk, bail hdl, 4-lb, EX 45.00
Sentinal Dental Floss, cb stand-up, 12 boxes, 8x10" 90.00
Shell Aviation Gasoline, crate, wood, paper label, 15x21", EX 75.00
Shell Aviation Motor Spirit, flange sign, porc, 15x24", EX 2,800.00
Shell X-100 Motor Oil, bottle, glass w/pnt label, 11¼", NM 135.00
Sherwin-Williams Paints, sign, porc, 2-sided, mc, 10x24", EX ...120.00
Shot Crushed Plug, pocket tin, vertical, full sz, VG 110.00
Sinclair H-C Gasoline, sign, porc, 2-sided, fr, 48" dia, EX 275.00
Sinclair Motor Oils, sign, metal, 3-color, 1936, 12x16", EX 140.00
Sir Walter Raleigh Tobacco, pocket tin, cut-down sample sz, NM ..65.00
Sky Ranger, pump plate, 10" dia, NM 950.00
Smith Bros Cough Drops, display, metal, lt rust, 11x4x4" 165.00

Socony Aircraft Oils, sign, porc, 20x30", NM 2,100.00
Solitaire Coffee, tc, cowboy, red & yel, keywind, 1-lb, EX 40.00
Solo Drink, ts, plane & pilot litho, Gen Steel, 30x15", NM 400.00
Speedboat Mixture Tobacco, tc, '30s-style boat, 3¼x5¾", EX 230.00
Spicy Steamro Red Hots, sign, porc, 3-color, 2¼x17", VG 180.00
Stag Tobacco, pocket tin, vertical, flat, tall, EX 88.00
Standard Ale, sign, cb, truck w/oxen, fr, 12½x16", EX 80.00
Standard Brewing, tray, factory, Mankato MN, 12" dia, EX 550.00
Standard Motor Oil, sign, porc, 3-color, 18x36", VG 125.00
Star Tobacco, door push, porc, chip, 3½x6¼", EX 180.00
Star Tobacco, pocket tin, vertical, EX+ 195.00
Star Tobacco, sign, porc, mc, 24x12", VG 135.00
Star Weekly, door push, porc, red & wht, 3x30", NM 50.00
Sterling Cards Honored, sign, porc, 10x18", G 140.00
Stewart's Coffee, tc, creme & brn, keywind, 1-lb, EX 40.00
Stewart Warner, menu board, counter; neon, 2-sided, 22x18" ...395.00
Sun Light Oil, tip tray, tin, 3-color, 4" dia, EX 75.00
Sun Oil, sign, porc, Charge Accounts Honored Here, 18x24", VG ..70.00
Sun Oil, sign, porc, yel & bl, 24x12", EX 75.00
Sunoco Motor Oil, case, porc, 23x29x19¼", VG 425.00
Sunoco Motor Oil, flange sign, metal, sunset, 19½x25", G 120.00
Sunoils Sunoco, flange sign, porc, chips, 19½x26", VG 325.00
Sunset Soap Dye, cabinet, tin, w/79 boxes, 1915, 16x23x4" 225.00
Super Aeroline Motor Oil, tc, NY Motor Oil Co, 9x6¼", VG ...125.00
Supreme Auto Oil, tc, Gulf Refining, 1-gal, 5½x8½", VG 75.00
Sweet Cuba Fine Cut, canister, tin litho, 8x8x10", EX 95.00
Sweet Heart Products, door push, porc, 5x5", EX 55.00
Swift Hazard of Oz Peanut Butter, pail, tin litho, 34-oz, EX 50.00
Target Tobacco, pocket tin, vertical, EX 50.00
Tech Beer, sf ts, hunt scene, 18½x26½", EX 140.00
Texaco, banner, blk, red & wht, 29x42½", EX 45.00
Texaco, paperweight, glass, 3" dia 125.00
Texaco, thermometer, metal, 3-color, 23½x7", EX 120.00
Texaco, ts, Buy the Best Buy, 4-color, 24x40", G 200.00
Texaco Aviation Products, sign, porc, 2-sided, rstr, 24" dia 4,750.00
Texaco Motor Oil, sign, porc, 2-sided, 3-color, 30x30", EX 300.00
Texaco Spica Oil, tc, w/contents, 1-pt, 5⅜x3⅜", EX 130.00
Thermo Anti-Freeze, tc, snowman, 1-qt, 5x4½", NM 45.00
Tiger Oil, tc, Will Not Scratch White, 8x4¼", EX 65.00
Tiger Tobacco, pocket tin, flat, EX 95.00
Tubular Cream Separators, match holder, tin litho, 7x2", EX 375.00

Tucketts Marguerite Cigar, tin sign, A. Asti, 28x22", NM, $2,900.00.

Tucketts Marguerite Cigar, sf ts, prof rpr, 28x22", EX 2,100.00
Turnbull's Scotch Whisky, ts, bottle, 5-color, 18x12¼", EX 70.00

Tuxedo Tobacco, canister, slip top, 5½x4", EX **75.00**
Tuxedo Tobacco, pocket tin, vertical, sample sz, EX **72.50**
Tydol Motor Oil, tc, w/contents, lt dents, 1-qt, 5x4½", EX **40.00**
Uncle Sam War Savings Stamps, window display, 30", EX **105.00**
Uneeda Biscuits, letter opener, boy in raincoat **65.00**
Union Leader, pocket tin, Trial Package, vertical, EX **55.00**
Union Leader Tobacco, pocket tin, Uncle Sam, vertical, VG **75.00**
United Service Motors, mercury vacameter, CI/glass, 75x18", EX .**160.00**
United Service Motors, sign, porc, neon, 20½x35x8", NM **1,500.00**
United States Tires, sign, chalkboard & metal, 29½x21⅝", G **45.00**
United States Tires, sign, porc, 3-color, 17⅝x72", NM **110.00**
US Royal Tires, sign, porc, 2-sided, mc, 33½x26", NM **150.00**
US Savings Bonds, cb stand-up, Lady Liberty, 60x40", MIB **600.00**
Utica Supreme...Knives, case, wood & glass, 13x18x6", EX **35.00**
Utica Tools, case, wood & glass, 33x22x3", EX **80.00**
Valora Oil, ts, emb letters, bl & wht, 9¾x13¾", VG **180.00**
Veedol Motor Oil, sign, metal, 3-color, 10½x17½", VG **110.00**
Velvet Pipe Tobacco Sold Here, sign, porc, 12x39", VG **155.00**
Velvet Tobacco, pocket tin, vertical, sample sz, EX **165.00**
Vernor's Ginger Ale, tray, gr w/yel lettering, 10½x13", EX **35.00**
Vicks, door push, porc, 159 Million, 4x6½", VG **50.00**
Vicks, door push, porc, 17 Million, 4x6½", VG **100.00**
Violet Talc, tc, violets, EX **90.00**
W Harold Weiss Michelin Tires, sign, porc, mc, 30x60", VG **600.00**
Wagner Lockhead Brake Service, sign, lights up, 13x26", VG **50.00**
Watkins Talc, tc, blk/wht/bl, EX **48.00**
Weatherbird Shoes, sign, porc, neon, chicken, 26x17", EX **1,700.00**
West Virginia Pilsner Beer, sign, cb, lady, 22x14", EX **85.00**
Western Assurance, ledger ruler, tin, VG **110.00**
Western Employment Counselors, pocket mirror, Kansas City **30.00**
Western Union Telegraph, sign, porc, side mt, 17x25", G **135.00**
Western Union Telegraph & Cable, sign, porc, 2-sided, 24x48" ..**250.00**
Westinghouse Refrigerators, sign, lights up, 9¼x25x6", EX **100.00**
Whale Smoking Tobacco, pack, cloth, tax stamp, 7½x4½", NM ..**230.00**
Whistle, sign, cb, 3-D elves, easel-bk, 14x19", EX **85.00**
Whistle, ts, bottle pushed in dolly, mc, 26x30", NM **310.00**
White Rose Imperial Oil, tc, wht rose, 1-qt, 6½x4", EX **30.00**
Whitman's Chocolates, sign, cb diecut, Whitman Man, 34x48" ..**125.00**
Wild Wood Talc, tc, flowers on wht, slim, sq sides, tall, EX **135.00**
Winner Cut Plug Tobacco, lunch pail, race car, 4x8x5¼", VG ..**160.00**
Winter Richlube Motor Oil, banner, bl/wht/yel, 36x69", VG **15.00**
Winterton's Satsuma Wafers, tc, 1½" dia, EX **40.00**
Wishing Well Orange, door push, porc, blk & yel, 3x30", EX **100.00**
Wolf's head, flange metal sign, blk/wht/red, 22x17", NM **125.00**
Wonder-Mist Cleanser & Polisher, tc, 1-qt, 5½x4¼", VG **50.00**
Wrigley's Gum, sample card w/3 sticks of gum, 3¼x6", NM **35.00**
Wynola, door push, tin, red & gr on wht, 14x4", EX **70.00**
Yacht Club Tobacco, pocket tin, vertical, full, EX+ **600.00**
Yeast Foam, door push, porc, mc, 2x7", EX **140.00**
Yeast Foam, wall dispenser, tin, yel & red, 18x3", EX **66.00**
7-Up, calendar, pinup artwork, full pad, 1942, 7x12", EX **125.00**
7-Up, door push, Come In, 7-Up Likes You, emb tin, 1940s, G **60.00**
7-Up, door push, tin, 4-color on wht, 3x30", EX **40.00**
7-Up, menu, full color, never printed, early 1960s, 12x10", EX **8.00**
7-Up, menu, masonite, 12x21", EX **70.00**
7-Up, poster, cb, Beef Sandwich &..., post-1960, 10x17", NM **10.00**
7-Up, sf ts, Fresh Up, orange & blk, 39½x30", EX **700.00**
7-Up, sign, cb, man w/case, easel bk, 1948, 12x10", EX **40.00**
7-Up, sign, porc, Fresh Up w/7-Up, 1951, 40x15½", EX **185.00**
7-Up, sign, tin, shows 6-pack, Canadian, 1950s, 36x60", NM **400.00**
7-Up, sign, tin over cb, 7-Up Some Mixer, 6x6¼", NM **90.00**
7-Up, thermometer, porc, 4-color, 15x6", EX **100.00**
7-Up, ts, Fresh Up w/7-Up, 2-sided, 12x19", EX **90.00**
7-Up, ts, hand w/bottle on creme & gr, ca 1951, 12x30¼", EX **95.00**

7-Up, paperboard hanging display, flowers in basket, 3-D effect, minor damage, 20", G, $150.00.

Advertising Cards

Advertising trade cards enjoyed great popularity during the last quarter of the 19th century when the chromolithography printing process was refined and put into common use. The purpose of the trade card was to aquaint the public with a business, product, service, or event. Most trade cards range in size from 2" x 3" to 4" x 6"; however, many are found in both smaller and larger sizes.

There are two classifications of trade cards: 'private design' and 'stock.' Private design cards were used by a single company or individual; the images on the cards were designed for only that company. Stock cards were generics that any individual or company could purchase from a printer's inventory. These cards usually had a blank space on the front for the company to overprint their own name and product information. In these listings a stock card is indicated by 'stk.' If there is no such reference, it is assumed the card is a private design. Values are given for cards in near-mint condition.

Four categories of particular interest to collectors are:

Mechanical — a card which achieves movement through the use of a pull tab, fold-out side, or movable part.

Hold-to-light — a card that reveals its design only when viewed before a strong light.

Diecut — a card in the form of something like a box, a piece of clothing, etc.

Metamorphic — a card that by folding down a flap shows a transformed image, such as a white beard turning black after use of a product.

For a more thorough study of the subject, we recommend *Reflections 1* and *Reflections 2* by Kit Barry; his address can be found in the Directory under Vermont.

Am Eagle Tobacco, pitcher in center, baseball game beyond **300.00**
Am Puzzle Cards, Where Is the Herdsman?, stk **5.00**
Arbuckle Coffee, Esquimau, caribou, sled dogs, killing seals **4.00**
Arbuckle Coffee, North Dakota Bad Lands, Sioux chief, farm **5.00**
Aromatic Pino-Palmine Mattress, palms, baby vignette **12.00**
AST Co, girl at easel w/boy pointing at drawing **5.50**
AST Co, The Old Woman Who Lived in a Shoe **12.00**
Austen's Forest Flower Cologne, girl sprays cologne at cat **5.00**
Ayer's Ague Cure, swamp scene, frog & alligators vignette **6.00**
Ayer's Hair Vigor, mermaids combing hair, ships sinking **4.00**
Bear-ly an Escape, man w/2 dogs run from bear, stk **6.50**
Bensdor's Cocoa, Dutch scene, 2 men talk to sm girl **6.50**
Boy w/jack-in-the box & girl w/cat, 4 cats on floor, stk **3.00**
Buckingham's Dye for Whiskers, metamorphic, wht-to-blk beard ...**12.00**

Castoria, Jumbo Feeds Baby Castoria 8.00
Clipper ship Mary, Glidden & Williams Line, red & gold on wht .175.00
Columbia Bicycles & Tricycles, 2 riders w/in front wheel fr 15.00
Diamond Dyes, Class in Economy, teacher/students dye clothes 7.50
Diamond Dyes, lady advises friend to use Diamond Dyes 8.00
Donkey serenading bird standing on porch, stk 10.00
Dr Kilmer's Indian...Cure, children read book w/Indian cover 25.00
Dr Thomas Electric Oil, cat in product box, paw on bottle 7.50
Espey's Fragrant Cream, girl in yel holds fan, fr w/flowers 16.00
Fishing in Earnest, man pulls friend out of water, stk 4.00
Florence Machine Co, lady baking, children play croquet 12.00
Florence Oil Stoves, before & after picnicking w/ & w/o stove 8.00
Girl pnts at easel on beach, boy watches over shoulder 4.00
Girl swings stick at tree, pug dog at ft, stk 6.00
Girl talks to parrot on bird stand, stk 6.00
Globe Shirt Collar & Cuff, metamorphic, clothes, happy lady 28.00
Going to Plantation, Blks w/mule & buggy in accident, stk 10.00
Gold Soap, Tally Ho coach, throwing soap in streets 20.00
Harness Racing, Mattie Hunter, 2.14, stk 18.00
Hood's Pills, cure liver ills, girl diecut in gold fr 5.50

J&P Coats Thread, girl on hay bale holding puppy 4.00
J&P Coats Thread, 3 children & dog have picnic 4.00
J&P Coats Thread, 4 cats sit on ottomans & sew 6.00
Jack the Giant Killer, Little Giant School Shoes, No 1 ....5.00
Jackson's Best, 4 smiling men w/tobacco, 1 frowning w/none 20.00
Kendall Mfg, French laundry soap, boy climbs rope on star 4.00
Keystone Watch Case, keystone diecut, man/telescope/comet 12.00
Lautz Bros & Co, Acme Soap, grinning man holds bar 12.00
League Favorites, Find the Referee, puzzle card 6.50
Lutten's Cough Drops, 3 people ride toboggan down hill, stk 6.50
Maison Demorest Reliable Patterns, Raphael's angel, stk 4.00
Margaret Mather, actress portrait, gold border, stk 2.50
Merchants Gargling Oil, mule kicking, man w/club 12.00
Mme Demorest's Reliable Patterns, roses & open book on blk 3.00
Page Fence, lady & child at fence as bull charges 16.00
Parker Gun, men shoot clay pigeons, cocked bbl in corner 100.00
Pearline, girl w/finger to mouth stands on chair 3.50
Pearline, Highway Robbery, goose stole cookie from girl 4.00
Pearline, sailor boy on deck, boat tied in bkground 6.50
Polar bear attacking seal, snowy mtns beyond, stk 6.50
Putnam Nail, Whoa Aunty!, Blks picking cotton 5.00
Quakeress Cigar, Quaker lady stands by brick house 10.00
Ray Hubbell's Oil Cloths, 2 adults before stove w/2 angels 12.00
Reids Seeds, boys on bikes, girl w/bouquets, man w/seeds 12.00
Scourene, big-headed women scrubbing coffeepot 12.00
Singer Mfg, American Singer Series, cardinal, No 7 ....8.00
Smith & Anthony Stoves, Hub range, tobogganing, stove vignette .12.00
Soapine, box layout, scrubbing whale wht 15.00
Soapine, man atop telephone pole, birds spell Soapine 5.00
Soapine, parrot & 2 crows watch crow clean itself wht 15.00
Solar Tip Shoes, boys playing ball as girls watch 3.00
Spalding's, baseball player diecut, holds bat, bats on ground 75.00
Target Plug, boy & 2 girls shoot arrows at target & pigs 26.00
Tippecanoe Medicine, 8 Indians riding in lg canoe 16.00
Union Web Hammock, lady in hammock reading, horseshoe fr ...18.00
Warner's Safe Cure, girl riding St Bernard dog 6.00
Waterbury, My Waterbury Says Supper's Ready, lady serving 15.00
Weir Stove Co, Glenwood, girl looking at poster of stove 15.00
White Sewing Machine, girl picks daisies, morning-glory border 4.00
Williams Clark & Co Fertilizers, jester, April 1885 calendar 8.50
Winter scene w/2 girls, pks & bls surrounded by roses, stk 6.50
Woman in bl w/tambourine walking down steps, stk 8.50

Hood's Sarsaparilla, First Lesson, 3x5", $6.00.

Hood's Sarsaparilla, lily pad & flower diecut w/scene 8.00
Hood's Sarsaparilla, Who Said Hood's Sarsaparilla? 5.50
Horseshoe Cross Bar, boy & dog jump horseshoe w/tobacco plug .20.00
Household Sewing Machine, girl & boy carry girl in basket 8.00

Humpty Dumpty and Punch & Judy mechanical banks, bright colors, ca 1880s, NM, $750.00 each.

Ivorine, I Couldn't Keep House w/o..., girl doing dishes 6.50
J&P Coats Thread, girl lying in field w/flowers 4.00

Advertising Dolls

    Whether your interest in ad dolls is fueled by nostalgia or strictly because of their amusing, often clever advertising impact, there are several points that should be considered before making your purchases. Condition is of utmost importance; never pay book price for dolls in poor condition, whether they are cloth or of another material. Restoring fabric dolls is usually unsatisfactory and involves a good deal of work. Seams must be opened, stuffing removed, the doll washed and dried, and then reassembled. Washing old fabrics may prove to be disastrous. Colors may fade or run, and most stains are totally resistant to washing. It's usually best to leave the fabric doll as it is.

    Watch for new dolls as they become available. Save related advertising literature, extra coupons, etc., and keep these along with the doll to further enhance your collection. Old dolls with no marks are sometimes challenging to identify. While some products may use the same familiar trademark figures for a number of years (the Jolly Green Giant, Pillsbury's Poppin' Fresh, and the Keebler Elf, for example) others appear on the market for a short time only and may be difficult to trace. Most libraries have reference books with trademarks and logos that might provide a clue in tracking down your doll's identity. Children see advertising figures on Saturday morning cartoons that are often unfamiliar to adults, or other ad doll collectors may have the information you seek.

Some advertising dolls are still easy to find and relatively inexpensive, ranging in cost from $1.00 to $100.00. The hard plastic and early composition dolls are bringing the higher prices. Advertising dolls are popular with children as well as adults. For a more thorough study of the subject, we recommend *Advertising Dolls* by Joleen Robison and Kay Sellers. Our advisor for this category is Jim Rash; he is listed in the Directory under New Jersey.

Kernal Renk, vinyl figure for midwestern seed company, 1970, M, $400.00.

Adams Gum, rabbit, cloth, 11", NM 150.00
Air-India, East Indian man in turban, on base, 4½" 15.00
Alka Seltzer, Speedy, vinyl store display figure, 1970s, 8" 500.00
Am Rice Food, Cook's Teddy Bear, uncut cloth, 1907 ....135.00
APW Paper Co, litho cloth girl, check skirt, 1925, 12", EX 135.00
Aunt Jemima Pancake Flour, Uncle Mose, cloth, 1905, 15" 175.00
Babbitt Cleanser, boy, compo & cloth, 1916, 15", NM 600.00
Beaver Enterprises, beaver, brn plush, 1972, 12" 15.00
Big Boy Restaurant, Big Boy, cloth pillow style, 1978, MIP 15.00
Big Boy Restaurant, Dolly, litho cloth, 1978, 14" 15.00
Borden, Elsie cow, plush, 1987, M 70.00
Borden, Elsie cow, vinyl & plush, 1950, 12", VG 70.00
Brunswick Corp, Itylyti, litho cloth, 1968, 16" 20.00
Buster Brown Shoes, Buster Brown, litho cloth, 1902, 13" 150.00
Campbell Soup Co, Campbell Kid vinyl squeaker, 1974, 7", NM .20.00
Campbell Soup Co, Cheerleader, Ideal, all orig, 1957-61, 9½" 20.00
Ceresota Flour boy, stuffed cloth, EX 200.00
Chesty Potato Chips, Chesty Boy, squeaks, 1950s, 8", NM 300.00
Chiquita Banana, cloth, 1940, EX 45.00
Clark Candy, bar boy, squeeze toy, 1960s, 9" 200.00
Coronet Brandy, waiter w/tray, compo, on base, 19", NM 50.00
Dash Dog Food, basset dog, plush, 11x19", NM 12.00
Dean's Curly Locks, cloth, EX 95.00
Downey's Honey-Butter, bee, plush, w/ribbon & tag, 10", NM 8.00
Drewry Beer, pointing man, hard plastic, 1960s 45.00
Dutch Maid Egg Noodles, Dutch Maid, cloth, 1976, 12", M 6.00
Exxon, tiger, cloth litho, 1960, 17", NM 12.00
Fletcher's Castoria, Mammy Castoria, cloth litho, 1930s, 11" 165.00
Freddie Fastgas, jtd vinyl, Dakin, 1976, 7" 75.00
Fresca, dog, plush, 1970, 28", M 15.00
General Foods, Trix Playmate rabbit, vinyl squeaker, 1977, 9" 12.00
Gerber Products, baby, orig clothes, Sun Rubber, 1954, 12" 45.00
Gold Medal Flour, girl, cloth litho, ca 1920s, 7½", EX 75.00
Green Giant, vinyl figure, Product People, 1974, 8" 75.00
Hamburger Helper, Helping Hand, plush, 1976, 14" 10.00

Hires Root Beer, Blk Cow, inflatable, 1976, 40" L, M 20.00
Ice Capades, Icee Bear, vinyl bank, 1974 ....10.00
Ideal Flour, Simple Sam, cloth litho, 14", M 30.00
Jack's Restaurant, man, cloth litho, 16", M 15.00
Just Rite Restaurant, Li'l Miss Just Rite, Dakin, 1965, 8", M 60.00
Keebler, Ernie Elf, 23", MIB 35.00
Kellogg's, Tony the Tiger, cloth/plush, 1970, 13", NM 20.00
Kellogg's, Toucan Sam, cloth litho, 1964, 9x12", M 25.00
Kellogg's, Toucan Sam, movable plastic, Talbot, 4" 15.00
Kentucky Fried Chicken, Colonel Sanders bank, 1965, 12½" 30.00
Libby, Libby, cloth, yarn hair, orig clothes, 14", M 45.00
Little Debbie, Little Debbie Cakes, porc head, 30th Anniv, MIB ...35.00
Long John Silver's, parrot, cloth litho, unmk, M 15.00
Malted Cereal, Gretchen, cloth litho, 1905, 8", EX 145.00
McDonald Corp, Grimace, purple plush & vinyl, Remco, M 10.00
McDonald Corp, Ronald, cloth litho, 1971, M 8.00
Morton Salt, girl, yarn hair, Mattel, 15", MIB 30.00
Mr Bubble, Mr Bubble soap container, plastic, 10", M 40.00
Mr Wiggle, hand puppet, rubber & vinyl, 1966 ....225.00
Nabisco, kangaroo, bl plush, 17", M 10.00
Nestle, Little Hans, cloth litho, 1970, M 20.00
Old Crow Whiskey, Old Crow, cloth, ca 1970, 28", NM 30.00
Oxol, boy, cloth litho, 1931, uncut, M 100.00
Pappy Parker's Chicken House, man, molded vinyl, 6½", M 20.00
Pepto Bismol, 24-Hour Bug bank, 1973 ....75.00
Philip Morris, Johnny Bellhop, compo & cloth, 1940s, 11", EX .275.00
Pillsbury, Poppie Fresh, knit velour, 1972, M 25.00
Pizza King, chef, cloth, all orig, w/label, 15", NM 15.00
Post Cereals, Sugar Bear, plush & cloth, 1972, 12½", NM 12.00
Quaker Oats, Cap'n Crunch, cloth, 1978, 15½", M 15.00
Quaker Oats, Puffy soldier, cloth litho, 1930, 16", M 150.00
Rodkey's Flour, Rag Darling, cloth litho, uncut, M 130.00
Seven-Up, Freshen Up Freddie, vinyl, 1959, 8" 250.00
Shaklee Products, Small Wonder rabbit, vinyl, 6½", NM 15.00
Snoboy Apples, Snuggly Snoboy, plush, Princess Mfg, 12" 15.00
Stoney's Beer, Stoney bartender, molded plastic, on base, 8" 50.00
Texas Dairy Queen Assoc, Sweet Nell, cloth, 1975, 15", M 7.50
Tillie From Tillamook, squeeze toy, Rempel, 1958 ....40.00
Travelodge Internat'l, Sleepy Bear, plush, 1967, 12", M 10.00
Vanta Baby Garments, baby, Amburg Toy, all orig, 1927, 21½" ...225.00
Whitman's, delivery man, jigsaw wooden display, 18" 1,800.00
Yukon Flour Mills, Peter Rabbit, cloth litho, 7", EX 65.00

Agata

Agata is New England peachblow (the factory called it 'Wild Rose') with an applied metallic stain which produces gold tracery and dark blue mottling. The stain is subject to wear, and the amount of remaining stain greatly affects the value. It is especially valuable (and rare) when found on peachblow of intense color. Caution! Be sure to use only gentle cleaning methods.

Currently rare types of art glass have been realizing erratic prices at auction; until they stablize, we can only suggest an average range of values. In the listings that follow, examples are glossy unless noted otherwise. Our advisors for this category are Betty and Clarence Maier; they are listed in the Directory under Pennsylvania. See also Green Opaque.

Bowl, pie-crust ruffles, 2½x5" 770.00
Creamer, sq rim, mottled reed hdl, M mottle 1,800.00
Pitcher, water; reeded hdl, outstanding color, 7½" 3,000.00
Plate, fluted, 6½" 850.00
Punch cup, 2½" 350.00
Spooner, allover mottling, crimped top, 5" 1,500.00

Spooner, worn staining, sqd top, 4½" **350.00**
Sugar bowl, VG mottling, reeded hdls **750.00**
Toothpick holder, sqd rim, 2" **750.00**
Toothpick holder, tricorner, NE Glass, 2¼" **725.00**
Tumbler, gold spiderweb tracery, outstanding color, 3¾" **1,000.00**
Tumbler, good color, 3⅞" **695.00**
Tumbler, lemonade; M mottling, 5" **1,200.00**
Vase, lily; good color, 8" **900.00**
Vase, lily; outstanding color, 7¾" **1,265.00**

Akro Agate

The Akro Agate Co., founded in 1914 primarily as a marble maker, operated in Clarksburg, West Virginia, until 1951. Their popular wares included children's dishes, powder jars, flowerpots, and novelty items along with the famous 'Akro Aggies.' Much of their glass was produced in the distinctive marbleized colors they called Red Onyx, Blue Onyx, etc.; solid opaque and transparent colors were also produced. Most of the wares are marked with their trademark, a crow flying through the letter 'A' holding an Aggie in its beak and one in each claw. Other marks include 'J.P.' on children's pieces, 'J.V. Co., Inc.,' 'Braun & Corwin,' 'N.Y.C. Vogue Merc Co. U.S.A.,' 'Hamilton Match Co.,' and 'Mexicali Pickwick Cosmetic Corp.' on novelty items. In 1936 Akro obtained the molds from the Balmer-Westite Co. of Weston, West Virginia. Westite produced a similar line of products for several years. Their ware is drab in color when compared to Akro and is generally unmarked. The embossed Westite logo does appear occasionally on the bottoms of some pieces. Westite is commonly accepted as a companion collectible of Akro.

For more information we recommend *The Collector's Encyclopedia of Children's Dishes* by Margaret and Kenn Whitmyer, available at your local bookstore. Our advisor for miscellaneous Akro Agate is Albert Morin; he is listed in the Directory under Massachusetts.

Chiquita

Creamer, cobalt, 1½" **14.00**
Creamer, crystal **21.00**
Cup, gr opaque, 1½" **4.00**
Plate, cobalt, 3¾" **7.00**
Saucer, baked-on colors, 3⅛" **3.00**
Set, baked-on colors, 16-pc, MIB **75.00**
Set, gr opaque, 22-pc, MIB **78.00**
Sugar bowl, opaque colors other than gr, 1½" **16.00**
Teapot, gr opaque, w/lid, 3" **14.00**

Concentric Rib

Concentric Rib, opaque green and white, Teapot, 3⅜", $12.00; Plate, 3¼", $3.00; Cup and saucer, $7.00.

Plate, opaque colors other than gr or wht, 3¼" **7.00**
Set, gr or wht opaque, 8-pc, MIB **33.00**
Sugar bowl, gr or wht opaque, 1¼" **10.00**
Teapot, wht opaque, w/lid, 3⅜" **12.00**

Concentric Ring

Cereal, lg, any opaque color, 3⅜" **22.00**
Creamer, lg, bl marbleized, 1⅜" **45.00**
Cup, lg, any opaque color, 1¼" **30.00**
Cup, lg, bl marbleized, 1⅜" **40.00**
Cup, sm, cobalt transparent, 1¼" **30.00**
Plate, sm, bl marbleized, 3¼" **22.00**
Saucer, sm, any opaque color, 2¾" **3.50**
Set, lg, bl marbleized, 21-pc, MIB **750.00**
Sugar bowl, lg, any opaque color, w/lid, 1⅜" **27.00**
Sugar bowl, lg, cobalt transparent, 1⅜" **45.00**
Sugar bowl, sm, any opaque color, 1¼" **18.00**
Teapot, lg, cobalt transparent, w/lid, 3¾" **65.00**

Interior Panel, Stippled Interior Panel

Cereal, lg, azure bl, 3⅜" **30.00**
Cereal, lg, red & wht, 3⅜" **32.00**
Creamer, lg, bl & wht, 1⅜" **32.00**
Creamer, lg, topaz transparent, 1⅜" **22.00**
Creamer, lg, yel opaque, 1⅜" **35.00**
Creamer, sm, azure bl, 1¼" **32.00**
Creamer, sm, pk lustre, 1¼" **27.00**
Cup, lg, lemonade & oxblood, 1⅜" **25.00**
Cup, sm, bl & wht, 1¼" **22.00**
Cup, sm, gr & wht, 1¼" **15.00**
Cup, sm, gr lustre, 1¼" **10.00**
Cup, sm, pumpkin, 1¼" **20.00**
Pitcher, sm, topaz transparent, 2⅞" **15.00**
Plate, lg, pk lustre, 4¼" **8.00**
Plate, lg, red & wht, 4¼" **16.00**
Plate, lg, yel opaque, 4¼" **10.00**
Plate, sm, gr lustre, 3¼" **5.00**
Plate, sm, gr transparent, 3¼" **6.00**
Plate, sm, red & wht, 3¼" **12.00**
Plate, sm, yel, 3¼" **10.00**
Set, lg, bl & wht, 21-pc, MIB **400.00**
Set, lg, topaz transparent, 21-pc, MIB **200.00**
Set, lg, yel opaque, 21-pc, MIB **450.00**
Set, sm, azure bl, 16-pc, MIB **265.00**
Set, sm, red & wht, 16-pc, MIB **275.00**
Sugar bowl, lg, gr transparent, w/lid, 1⅜" **27.00**
Sugar bowl, lg, red & wht, w/lid, 1⅜" **40.00**
Sugar bowl, lg, yel opaque, w/lid, 1⅜" **45.00**
Sugar bowl, sm, azure bl, 1¼" **35.00**
Sugar bowl, sm, bl & wht, 1¼" **27.00**
Sugar bowl, sm, pk lustre, 1¼" **27.00**
Sugar bowl, sm, topaz, 1¼" **20.00**
Teapot, lg, lemonade & oxblood, w/lid, 3¾" **65.00**
Teapot, lg, red & wht, w/lid, 3¾" **65.00**
Teapot, lg, topaz transparent, w/lid, 3¾" **35.00**
Teapot, sm, azure bl or yel, w/lid, 3⅜", ea **45.00**
Teapot, sm, gr & wht, 3⅜" **35.00**
Teapot, sm, red & wht, 3⅜" **40.00**
Teapot, sm, topaz transparent, w/lid, 3⅜" **22.00**
Tumbler, sm, gr lustre, 2" **45.00**
Tumbler, sm, gr transparent, 2" **8.50**

J.P. (Made for J. Pressman Company)

Cereal, lg, baked-on color, 3¾" 10.00
Creamer, lg, gr transparent, 1½" 40.00
Cup, lg, cobalt w/ribs, 1½" 6.00
Plate, lg, cobalt w/ribs, 4¼" 6.00
Plate, lg, lt bl or crystal, 4¼", ea 10.00
Set, lg, baked-on color, 17-pc, MIB 96.00
Sugar bowl, lg, lt bl or crystal, 1½", ea 30.00
Teapot, lg, lt bl or crystal, w/lid, 2¾", ea 40.00

Miss America

Creamer, orange & wht 55.00
Creamer, wht w/decal 55.00
Cup, forest gr 45.00
Cup, wht 40.00
Plate, wht 25.00
Plate, wht w/decal 45.00
Saucer, forest gr 15.00
Saucer, wht 15.00
Set, wht, 17-pc, MIB 495.00
Set, wht w/decal, 17-pc, MIB 600.00
Sugar bowl, forest gr, w/lid 65.00
Sugar bowl, wht, w/lid 55.00
Teapot, orange & wht, w/lid 125.00
Teapot, wht, w/lid 75.00

Octagonal

Cereal, lg, gr or wht, 5⅜", ea. 10.00
Cereal, lg, lt bl, 3⅜" 20.00
Creamer, lg, dk bl, closed hdls, 1½" 10.00
Creamer, sm, bl or wht, 1¼", ea 14.00
Cup, lg, pumpkin, closed hdl, 1½" 15.00
Pitcher, sm, dk gr, 2⅞" 18.00
Plate, sm, yel, 3⅜" 6.00
Set, lg, gr or wht, 21-pc, MIB, ea 140.00
Sugar bowl, lg, dk bl w/decal, w/lid, 1½" 21.00
Sugar bowl, lg, lt bl, closed hdl, w/lid, 1½" 18.00
Tumbler, sm, wht, 2" 10.00

Raised Daisy

Creamer, sm, yel, 1¼" 45.00
Cup, sm, gr, 1¾" 18.00
Plate, sm, bl, 3" 14.00
Saucer, sm, yel, 2½" 9.00
Sugar bowl, sm, yel, 1¼" 45.00
Teapot, sm, gr, no lid, 2⅜" 30.00
Teapot, sm, yel, w/lid, 2⅜" 45.00
Tumbler, sm, beige, 2" 30.00
Tumbler, sm, bl, 2" 55.00

Stacked Disc

Creamer, sm, any opaque color other than gr or wht, 1¼" 14.00
Cup, sm, any opaque color other than gr or wht, 1¼" 12.00
Cup, sm, wht, 1¼" 6.00
Pitcher, sm, any opaque color other than gr or wht, 2⅞" 14.00
Plate, sm, gr or wht, 3¼", ea 3.00
Saucer, sm, any opaque color other than gr or wht, 2¾" 4.00
Set, sm, gr opaque, 21-pc, MIB 120.00

Sugar bowl, sm, gr opaque, 1¼" 10.00
Teapot, sm, opaque gr, w/lid, 2" 12.50
Tumbler, sm, gr opaque, 2" 7.50
Tumbler, sm, pumpkin, 2" 21.00

Stacked Disc and Interior Panel

Cereal, lg, any solid opaque color, 3⅜" 25.00
Cereal, lg, gr transparent, 3⅜" 22.00
Creamer, lg, bl marbleized, 1⅜" 45.00
Creamer, sm, any solid opaque color, 1¼" 18.00
Creamer, sm, cobalt transparent, 1¼" 35.00
Cup, lg, bl marbleized, 1⅜" 40.00
Cup, sm, cobalt transparent, 1¼" 35.00
Cup, sm, gr transparent, 1¼" 18.00
Pitcher, sm, cobalt transparent, 2⅞" 27.00
Plate, lg, any solid opaque color, 4¼" 12.00
Plate, lg, bl marbleized, 4¼" 20.00
Plate, sm, any solid opaque color, 3¼" 8.00

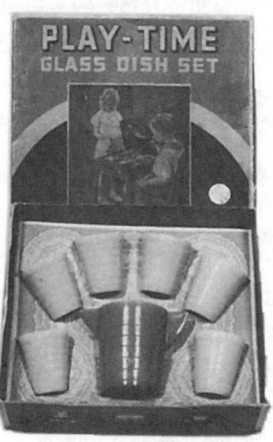

Stacked Disc, Play-Time Set, small green pitcher with 6 white tumblers, M in EX box, $65.00.

Set, lg, bl marbleized, 21-pc, MIB 685.00
Set, sm, bl marbleized, 16-pc, MIB 450.00
Set, sm, cobalt transparent, 8-pc, MIB 125.00
Set, water; sm, gr transparent, 7-pc, MIB 90.00
Sugar bowl, lg, cobalt transparent, w/lid, 1⅞" 50.00
Sugar bowl, sm, bl marbleized, 1¼" 40.00
Teapot, lg, cobalt transparent, w/lid, 3¾" 70.00
Teapot, lg, gr transparent, w/lid, 3¾" 55.00
Teapot, sm, cobalt transparent, w/lid, 3⅜" 45.00
Tumbler, sm, gr transparent, 2" 12.00

Stippled Band

Creamer, lg, gr transparent, 1½" 20.00
Creamer, sm, gr transparent, 1¼" 30.00
Cup, sm, amber transparent, 1¼" 8.00
Plate, lg, amber transparent, 4¼" 8.50
Plate, sm, gr transparent, 3¼" 6.00
Saucer, sm, amber transparent, 2¾" 2.50
Set, lg, gr transparent, 17-pc, MIB 150.00
Sugar bowl, lg, gr transparent, w/lid, 1½" 22.00

Sugar bowl, sm, gr transparent, 1¼" 30.00
Teapot, lg, amber transparent, w/lid, 3¾" 40.00

Miscellaneous

Goodrich tire ashtray, gray/black marbleized, $38.00; Goodrich tire pen holder, ivory/orange marbleized, $95.00.

Ashtray, gr/wht, Atlantic Foundry, rare 675.00
Ashtray, marbleized, leaf shape 9.00
Ashtray, marbleized, 5" heavy sq 65.00
Ashtray, red/wht marbleized, Akro Agate Ware 125.00
Ashtray, transparent amber, Camel Cigarette, rare 750.00
Bell, crystal, #725 ....28.00
Bell, crystal, fine ribbed 48.00
Bell, orange, #725 ....225.00
Bowl, marbleized, ftd, unmk, lg 275.00
Bowl, Royal Bl, Fiesta type, rare 700.00
Bowl, Royal Bl, Graduated Dart, #320 ....24.00
Candlesticks, blk/wht marbleized, pr 400.00
Cornucopia, bl/wht marbleized, hand held, #766 ....18.00
Cornucopia, HP Niagara Falls, #765 ....35.00
Flowerpot, bl, ribbed top, #291 ....12.00
Flowerpot, bl/wht marbleized, Stacked Disc, 3" 12.00
Flowerpot, gr/wht marbleized, Stacked Disc, 4" 18.00
Flowerpot, ivory, #1311 ....165.00
Flowerpot, marbleized, Banded Dart, #302 ....75.00
Flowerpot, marbleized, Grandaddy, #308 ....175.00
Flowerpot, orange, factory decor, #1309 ....195.00
Flowerpot, orange, Graduated Dart, fully sgn, 3" 35.00
Flowerpot, orange/wht marbleized, Ribs & Flutes, #297 ...8.00
Flowerpot, Royal Bl, Banded Dart, #301 ....45.00
Flowerpot, Royal Bl, Graduated Dart, #307 ....28.00
Flowerpot, yel, Ribs & Flutes, #305 ....20.00
J Vivaudou, mortar & pestle jar, wht, #331 ....12.00
J Vivaudou, puff box, pk, #334 ....125.00
J Vivaudou, shaving mug, blk, #335 ....45.00
Knife, amber, grid style, #739 ....200.00
Knife, crystal, grid style, #739 ....38.00
Lamp, bl/wht marbleized, sawtooth base 125.00
Lamp, ivory, 5-pc 48.00
Marble box, tin, #200 ....500.00
Marble box, 100 #0 assorted Royals 350.00
Marble box, 25 #2 Carnelians 550.00
Marble box, 50 #4 Opals 400.00
Milk bottle cover, yel, mk w/Crow trademk 650.00
Planter, blk, rnded rectangle, #652 ....95.00
Planter, marbleized, rectangular, #656 ....10.00
Planter, orange, Graduated Dart, #651 ....28.00
Powder jar, bl, Scotty dog form 85.00
Powder jar, crystal, apple form 65.00
Powder jar, marbleized gr/wht, treasure trunk form 95.00

Powder jar, marbleized or wht, Ivy design, #323 ....45.00
Powder jar, orange, apple form 250.00
Tire ashtray, crystal, Atlas Tires 75.00
Tire ashtray, crystal, US Rubber 70.00
Tire ashtray, gray/blk marbleized, US Rubber 85.00
Tire pen holder, gray/blk marbleized, Goodrich 145.00
Vase, blk, tab hdls, #317 ....150.00
Vase, bud; Royal Bl, #315, rare, 7¾" 350.00
Vase, yel, Ribs & Flutes, #311 ....125.00
Westite ashtray, transparent gr, hexagonal 25.00
Westite ashtray, triangle, Lion Match Co 35.00
Westite bowl, Graduated Dart, sgn 45.00
Westite flowerpot, brn/wht marbleized, #303 ....50.00
Westite planter, scalloped top, #651 ....28.00
Westite vase, brn/wht marbleized, plain, #310 ....95.00
Westite vase, bud; orange/wht, #315 ....200.00

Alexandrite

Alexandrite is a type of art glass introduced around the turn of the century by Thomas Webb and Sons of England. It is recognized by its characteristic shading, pale yellow to rose and blue. Although it was also produced by other companies, only examples made by Webb command premium prices. Amount and intensity of blue determines value. Our advisors for this category are Betty and Clarence Maier; they are listed in the Directory under Pennsylvania.

Finger bowl, honeycomb, crimped/ruffled, 3¾", +underplate ..2,000.00
Goblet, honeycomb, amber stem, 4½" 745.00
Punch cup, 2¾x2¼" 550.00
Toothpick holder, honeycomb, bulbous w/hexagonal rim, 2½" .2,000.00
Vase, ribbed, ruffled morning-glory form, scalloped ft, 5" 2,000.00
Vase, ribbed, star-cut base, flared U-form, Moser, 7" 275.00
Vase, ruffled, 2¾" 450.00

Alhambra China

A line of dinnerware made in Vienna during this century, the Alhambra pattern is strongly geometric with bold colors and gold trim. It is marked with the line name and the country of origin.

Teapot, 3", $80.00.

Compote, sm 85.00
Cup & saucer 55.00
Jam jar, w/lid & underplate 110.00
Nappy, gold loop hdl 22.00

Plate, 7½" **15.00**
Plate, 8¼" **17.50**

Almanacs

The earliest evidence indicates that almanacs were used as long ago as Ancient Egypt. Throughout the Dark Ages they were circulated in great volume and were referred to by more people than any other book except the Bible. *The Old Farmer's Almanac* first appeared in 1793 and has been issued annually since that time. Usually more of a pamphlet than a book (only a few have hard covers), the almanac provided planting and harvesting information to farmers, weather forecasts for seamen, medical advice, household hints, mathematical tutoring, postal rates, railroad schedules, weights and measures, 'receipts,' and jokes. Before 1800 the information was unscientific and based entirely on astrology and folklore. The first almanac in America was printed in 1639 by William Pierce Mariner; it contained data of this nature. One of the best-known editions, Ben Franklin's *Poor Richard's Almanac,* was introduced in 1732 and continued to be printed for twenty-five years.

By the 19th century, merchants saw the advertising potential in a publication so widely distributed, and the advertising almanac evolved. These were distributed free of charge by drug stores and mercantiles and were usually somewhat lacking in information, containing simply a calendar, a few jokes, and a variety of ads for quick remedies and quack cures.

Today their concept and informative, often amusing, text make almanacs popular collectibles that may usually be had at reasonable prices. Because they were printed in such large numbers and often saved from year to year, their prices are still low. Most fall within a range of $4.00 to $15.00. Very common examples may be virtually worthless; those printed before 1860 are especially collectible. Quite rare and highly prized are the Kate Greenaway 'Almanacks,' printed in London from 1883 to 1897. These are illustrated with her drawings of children, one for each calendar month.

1904, Studebaker Farmer's Almanac, Studebaker Wagons, 48-page, 8½x5¼", EX, $15.00.

1757, Colonial American, by Nathaniel Ames, Boston, EX **85.00**
1781, NE or Lady's & Gentleman's Diary, Bickerstaff, EX **65.00**
1806, MS, NH, CT, RI, VT; I Thomas Jr, Father Time/cherubs, EX ..**21.50**
1813, Houghton's Genuine, Isaiah Thomas, Am shield/tools, EX ..**12.50**
1817, MS Register & US Calendar, 286 pgs, index, EX **18.50**
1817, Town & Co, Worcester, MS, Father Time/cherubs, EX **9.50**
1818, Lady's & Gentleman's Diary, Asa Houghton, VT, EX **9.50**
1825, Old Farmer's, RB Thomas, Boston, EX **5.00**
1840, Boston, RR map, 130+ pgs, EX **12.50**
1849, Illus Christian, charts slave population, 60+ pgs **12.50**
1850, New England Farmer's, EX **20.00**
1862, Robert B Thos Civil War, gr illus wraps **6.50**
1882-83, Green's Diary, GG Green, Woodbury NJ, 36-pg, VG **12.00**

1883, Simmon's Liver Regulator, red & blk, 28-pg, 5x7½" **15.00**
1886, Routledge's Japanese, Beatty & Co, 24-pg, G **22.00**
1887, Barker's, Blk comics, 6x8", G **12.50**
1888, NY Almanac, colorful, EX **12.50**
1893, Hostetter's Illustrated CA Almanac, 7¾x5¼", EX **35.00**
1897, Western Farmer's, 4½x2", EX **27.00**
1931, Dr Pierce's Treasure Chest, NM **5.50**
1947, Indiana Botanic Gardens, The Herbalist, VG **10.00**

Aluminum

Aluminum, though being the most abundant metal in the earth's crust, always occurs in combination with other elements. Before a practical method for its refinement was developed in the late 19th century, articles made of aluminum were very expensive. After the process for commercial smelting was perfected in 1916, it became profitable to adapt the ductile, non-tarnishing material to many uses.

By the late thirties, novelties, trays, pitchers, and many other tableware items were being produced. They were often handcrafted with elaborate decoration. Russel Wright designed a line of lovely pieces such as lamps, vases, and desk accessories that are becoming very collectible. Many who crafted the ware marked it with their company logo, and these signed pieces are attracting the most interest. Wendell August Forge (Grove City, PA) is a mark to watch for; this firm produced some particularly nice examples and upwardly mobile market values reflect their popularity with today's collectors. In general, 'spun' aluminum is from the thirties or early forties, and 'hammered' aluminum is from the fifties.

For further information, refer to *Hammered Aluminum, Hand Wrought Collectibles,* by Danny Woodard, and *Collectible Aluminum, An Identification and Value Guide* by Everett Grist. Our advisor for this category is Ted Haun; he is listed in the Directory under Indiana. See also Russel Wright.

Pitcher, Chrysanthemum, Continental Silver Co., $30.00; Matching tumbler, $7.50.

Ashtray, emb dog/ducks & shotgun, 3-rest, Everlast **45.00**
Basket, china insert w/Indian Tree pattern, unmk, 6x7" **30.00**
Basket, emb chrysanthemums, strap hdl, Hand Forged, 7x9" **10.00**
Basket, hammered & serrated rim, appl leaf ft, unmk, 4x4" **18.00**
Bookends, bass leap over water sprays, 7x5x3", pr **185.00**
Bowl, stylized waves, anodized copper, fluted, Kraftware, 11" **10.00**
Bowl, tulips, scalloped, Rodney Kent, 8x12½" **12.00**
Bowl, vintage pattern, scalloped & serrated edge, 1x6" **15.00**
Butter dish, scroll pattern, leaf finial, unmk, 2x7x4" **8.00**
Candelabra, 3-arm, Buenilum, 12", pr **175.00**

Candy bowl, w/lid, Farber 15.00
Candy dish, emb roses, 2 joined bowls w/center hdl, 16" L 10.00
Candy dish, orchid pattern, 3-compartment, ¾x9½x7¼" 10.00
Casserole, emb bamboo pattern w/bamboo finial, Everlast, 4x7" ..15.00
Casserole, emb tomatoes, flower finial, Everlast, 5x9" 20.00
Chocolate pot, Chrysanthemum pattern, continental, 10x5" 85.00
Coaster, emb roses, Everlast, common 2.00
Coaster, hammered cap over glass sunburst design bottom, 4½" 5.00
Compote, wild rose pattern, ftd, continental, 5x5" 20.00
Crumber & tray, Greek Key pattern, unmk 15.00
Double boiler, polished, wood finial & hdl, Buenilum, 7" dia 25.00
Ice bucket, medieval helmet form, Hong Kong, 16x10" 20.00
Lazy susan, emb fruit & flowers, serrated rim, 16" dia 10.00
Matchbox cover, emb shotgun & ducks, Wendell August Forge ..50.00
Meat server, tulip & scroll pattern, 'tree' drain, unmk, 18" L 15.00
Percolator, Universal No 79, Landers, Frary & Clark, 1905 ....37.50
Pitcher, bamboo pattern, ice lip, rolled edge, Everlast, 8x5" 45.00
Pitcher, hammered, ice lip appl inside, unmk, 7x6" 20.00
Pitcher & 4 tumblers, hammered, Italy 35.00
Plaque, water lily medallion, Wendell August Forge, 18" 45.00
Plate, 1904 IL Athletic Club, 8½" 15.00
Silent butler, emb berries, Everlast, 6" 20.00
Tray, bar; emb anchor/rope/gulls, hdls, Everlast, 15x9" 60.00
Tray, bar; water lily pattern, self-hdls, A Armour, 17x8" 45.00
Tray, bread; apple blossom pattern, fluted, unmk, 13x9" 10.00
Tray, bread; rose pattern, self-hdls, Farber & Shlevin, 12x5" 10.00
Tray, sandwich; dogwood pattern, fluted edge, 10" dia 10.00
Tray, serving, allover emb flowers & vines, loop hdls, 18x11" 25.00
Tray, serving; emb goldfish, walnut hdls, unmk, 14x10" 45.00
Tray, serving; emb grapes, wire loop hdls, unmk, 17" dia 15.00
Tray, tidbit; rose pattern, T-hdl, Made in Canada, 8" dia 10.00
Tumbler, anodized color, various hallmks, ea 5.00

AMACO, American Art Clay Co.

AMACO is the logo of the American Art Clay Co. Inc., founded in Indianapolis, Indiana, in 1919, by Ted O. Philpot. They produced a line of art pottery from 1931 through 1938 that is today beginning to interest collectors. The company is still in business but now produces only supplies, implements, and tools for the ceramic trade.

Values for AMACO have risen sharply, especially those for figurals, items with Art Deco styling, and pieces with uncommon shapes. Our advisor for this category is Virginia Heiss; she is listed in the Directory under Indiana.

Figure, #141, Madonna, bl gloss, 10" 225.00
Figure, #155, head, bl gloss, 6" 125.00
Figure, #159, head, wht gloss, 7" 150.00
Vase, #S-10, bl gloss, w/lid, 3" 45.00

Vase, #25, green to yellow, decorated handles, 8x9", $175.00.

Vase, #S-10, yel matt, 3" 30.00
Vase, #27, blk matt w/buttress, 6" 110.00
Vase, #35, Deco gourd, orange, 5½" 115.00
Vase, #4, bl, hdls, 4" 40.00
Vase, #42, maroon, bulbous bottom, 7" 75.00
Vase, #43, yel to plum, w/hdls, 7½" 115.00
Vase, #44, gr matt, melon shape, 7½" 95.00
Vase, #8, mauve, 8¼" 95.00

Amberina

Amberina, one of the earliest types of art glass, was developed in 1883 by Joseph Locke of the New England Glass Company. The trademark was registered by W.L. Libbey, who often signed his name in script within the pontil.

Amberina was made by adding gold powder to the batch, which produced glass in the basic amber hue. Part of the item, usually the top, was simply reheated to develop the characteristic deep red or fuchsia shading. Early amberina was mold-blown, but cut and pressed amberina was also produced. The rarest type is plated amberina, made by New England for a short time after 1886. It has been estimated that less than 2,000 pieces were ever produced. Other companies, among them Hobbs and Brockunier, Mt. Washington Glass Company, and Sowerby's Ellison Glassworks of England, made their own versions, being careful to change the name of their product to avoid infringing on Libbey's patent. Prices have been erratic at auction for several months; values given below are in the average range.

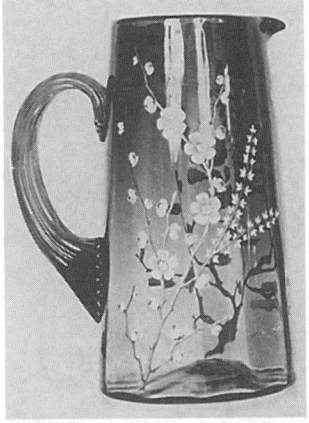

Pitcher, paneled tankard, floral decoration, 10", $400.00.

Bowl, heavy gold floral, 6-crimp top, ftd, 3¾x5¾" 325.00
Bowl, int florals, swirl ribs, 4-fold Hobnail rim, 4½x9" 200.00
Bowl, Invt T'print, 6¾x7½" 225.00
Bowl, ribbed, waisted, slightly scalloped, 2¾x5½" 825.00
Canoe, Daisy & Button, pierced for hanging, lg 275.00
Celery vase, Dmn Quilt, scalloped sq top, NE Glass 485.00
Celery vase, 10 low scallops, Mt WA; ornate Pairpoint fr 795.00
Compote, flared wide rim, 3x7½" 440.00
Condiment set, Invt T'print, 3½" s&p, bbl mustard, SP holder ..750.00
Cordial, tapered, 4½" 300.00
Creamer, Invt Panels, 4¾" 275.00
Creamer, swirl, amber hdl, 4½x3⅜" 135.00
Cruet, Invt T'print, invt goblet mold, amber hdl & stopper 375.00
Cruet, 8 optic panels, NE Glass, 6½" 400.00
Cup, eggnog; HP florals allover 230.00
Cup, punch; Dmn Quilt 125.00
Cup, punch; HP dragonflies & flowers, amber hdl 125.00

Cup, punch; Optic Rib 95.00
Decanter, reverse Dmn Quilt, matching stopper, 11" 650.00
Decanter, swirl, swirl/bubble stopper, 8¾x4¾" 245.00
Finger bowl, Dmn Quilt, 2" H 210.00
Finger bowl, Dmn Quilt w/tricorner rim, 3¼x4½" 275.00
Finger bowl, vertical ribbing w/paneled dmns, ruffled, 6" 135.00
Pitcher, Coin Spot & Honeycomb, amber hdl, 9x9½" 300.00
Pitcher, Daisy & Button, Hobbs Brockunier, 5x3", EX 400.00
Pitcher, Dmn Quilt, reeded amber hdl, 6x6" 215.00
Pitcher, Invt T'print, bulbous w/sq rim, amber hdl, 7¾" 300.00
Pitcher, Invt T'print, rope hdl, NE Glass, 4x4½" 920.00
Pitcher, Invt T'print, scrolled amber hdl, NE Glass, 2½" 450.00
Pitcher, Invt T'print, str neck, 5½" 250.00
Pitcher, tankard, ribbed, amber hdl, 8" 250.00
Plate, Daisy & Button, sq, 5¾" 180.00
Rose bowl, Invt T'print, triangular top, 6" H 250.00
Salad servers, Dmn Quilt hdls, 11", pr 450.00
Shakers, Blossom Time; SP Wilcox fr, pr 600.00
Shot glass, dbl; Optic Dmn, polished pontil, 2½x2" 150.00
Spooner, Dmn Quilt, squatty, scalloped, 4¾" 300.00
Toothpick holder, Daisy & Button, ftd, 2¾" 250.00
Toothpick holder, Dmn Quilt, corset shape 225.00
Toothpick holder, Dmn Quilt, sq top, Libbey 250.00
Toothpick holder, lattice on hexagonal form, 2" 175.00
Toothpick holder, Venetian Dmn, 2½" 300.00
Tumbler, Dmn Quilt, 3¾" 105.00
Tumbler, Invt T'print, ftd, 4x2⅝" 70.00
Tumbler, Invt T'print, 3½x2½" 45.00
Vase, amber trim at collar, amber ft, cylindrical, 12", pr 525.00
Vase, clear spiral trim, 8x2¼" 195.00
Vase, emb ribs, appl ft on cylindrical shape, 12" 250.00
Vase, Invt T'print, amber rigaree collar, scalloped rim, 3" 600.00
Vase, Invt T'print, sq top, reeded hdls, 2¾" 550.00
Vase, Invt T'print, 5⅜" 250.00
Vase, lily; ribbed, 7" 285.00
Vase, lily; swirl w/pinched amber trim, 20" 495.00
Vase, ribbed, squatty, flanged rim, 2x3½" 325.00
Vase, 4-sided, appl amber edge, 8½x3½" 325.00

Plated Amberina

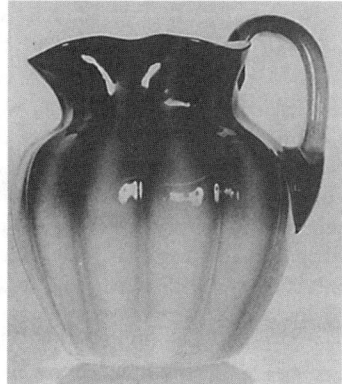

Pitcher, ribbed, amber handle,
6¾", $7,200.00.

Bowl, squatty, 2½x5¼" 3,000.00
Mug, amber hdl 2,200.00
Pitcher, ribbed, tricorn rim, 4½" 5,000.00
Pitcher, water; amber hdl, 7½" 7,200.00

Plate, ruffled, 6⅜" 1,250.00
Punch cup, EX color 1,850.00
Tumbler, 4" 2,400.00

American Bisque

The American Bisque Pottery operated in Williamstown, West Virginia, from 1919 to 1982. The company was begun by Mr. B.E. Allen and remained an Allen-family business until its sale in 1982. Figural pottery was produced from approximately 1937 until about the time the pottery sold in 1982.

American Bisque pottery is often identified by the 'wedges' or dry-footed cleats on the bottom of the ware. Many cookie jar designs are unique to the American Bisque Company, such as cookie jars with blackboards and magnets, cookie jars with lids that doubled as serving trays, and cookie jars with 'action pieces' which show movement. American Bisque pieces are very collectible and are available in a broad variety of color schemes; some items are decorated with 22-24k gold. Many items are modeled after highly popular copyrighted characters.

For further information, we recommend *American Bisque, Collector's Guide With Prices,* by our advisor Mary Jane Giacomini; she is listed in the Directory under California.

Bank, Casper the Ghost 475.00
Bank, Diaper Pin Pig, gold trim 175.00
Bank, Dino Flintstone 525.00
Bank, girl pig, dimples in knees 32.00
Bank, Little Audrey 775.00
Bank, pig w/purse, For Your Rainy Day 75.00
Bank, Popeye 450.00
Bank, snowman w/top hat 32.00
Bank, Sweet Pea 850.00
Bank, yarn doll, boy or girl, ea 20.00
Cookie jar, Baby Elephant, w/baseball cap 150.00
Cookie jar, Baby Elephant, w/sailor hat 115.00
Cookie jar, Chef, w/tray lid 425.00
Cookie jar, Chick, w/tam & jacket 75.00

Cookie jar, Clown with
Blackboard, $300.00.

Cookie jar, Cowboy Boots 200.00
Cookie jar, Feed Bag 100.00

Cookie jar, Fred Flintstone 1,200.00
Cookie jar, Gift Box 125.00
Cookie jar, Jack-in-the-Box 140.00
Cookie jar, Kittens on Beehive, pastel gr 65.00
Cookie jar, Magic Bunny 95.00
Cookie jar, Olive Oyl 3,000.00
Cookie jar, Pig in a Poke 85.00
Cookie jar, Poodle 135.00
Cookie jar, Ring for Cookies Bell 50.00
Cookie jar, Rudolph the Red-Nosed Reindeer 750.00
Cookie jar, Santa Claus 400.00
Cookie jar, Sitting Horse 950.00
Cookie jar, Stern Wheeler (Tugboat) 225.00
Cookie jar, Sweethearts (Umbrella Kids) 350.00
Cookie jar, Treasure Chest, w/open lid 150.00
Cookie jar, Yogi Bear, mk Hanna Barbera 500.00
Lamp, chick, underglaze, no shade 55.00
Lamp, chick, wht w/cold pnt, no shade 35.00
Mug, Santa Claus 25.00
Night light, Davy Crockett 45.00
Pitcher, Santa Claus 350.00
Planter, bear, rag doll, baseball 24.00
Planter, bear, rag doll, baseball, w/24k gold 36.00
Planter, blk panther w/bloom through bk 24.00
Planter, boy yarn doll w/block 20.00
Planter, Davy Crockett canoe 60.00

Planters: Davy Crockett moccasins, pouch, canoe, and powder horn, $60.00 each.

Planter, elf reclining on mushroom 30.00
Planter, gazelle 22.00
Planter, gazelle w/flower bloom through bk 26.00
Planter, girl yarn doll w/house 20.00
Planter, gypsy w/cart 12.00
Planter, hen w/chicks 20.00
Planter, lamb w/cart 10.00
Planter, lamb w/cart, 24k gold trim 20.00
Planter, mare w/foal 30.00
Planter, paddle boat 24.00
Planter, puppy w/slipper 18.00
Planter, sailfish 50.00
Planter, sleeping kitten w/slipper 8.00
Planter, Southern Belle, dbl sided 38.00
Planter, stork w/bassinette 10.00
Planter, stork w/bassinette, w/24k gold 20.00
Planter, wailing kitten w/bunny 22.00
Sprinkler bottle, Siamese cat, mk Cardinal 85.00
Wall pocket, birdhouse 24.00
Wall pocket, birdhouse, w/24k gold 36.00

American Encaustic Tiling Co.

A.E. Tile was organized in 1879 in Zanesville, Ohio. Until its closing in 1935, they produced beautiful ornamental and architectural tile equal to the best European imports. They also made vases, figurines, and novelty items with exceptionally fine modeling and glazes.

Ashtray, frog form, matt gr, mk 95.00
Frieze, cattail & florals, 5 6" sq tiles, vertical, EX 500.00
Tile, Alexander G Bell portrait, bl, mk, dtd 1897, 3" 65.00
Tile, classical figure, 1892 plant opening commemorative, 4" 175.00
Tile, cockatoo on branch, brn hi-glaze, 6x12", NM 170.00
Tile, Deco deer, silver on blk, silver decor corners, 6" 125.00
Tile, fish on waves, 4-color, 2x4" 65.00
Tile, lady in classical headdress, amber majolica, 8x8" 125.00
Tile, maid on bench, 2 children w/grain, mauve gloss, 12x18" ...325.00
Tile, purple flowers & gr foliage on pk, AF506, 6"+fr 225.00
Tile, stylized Indian in headdress holds shield, mc, 12x8" 385.00

American Indian Art

That time when the American Indian was free to practice the crafts and culture that was his heritage has always held a fascination for many. They were a people who appreciated beauty of design and colorful decoration in their furnishings and clothing; and because instruction in their crafts was a routine part of their rearing, they were well accomplished. Several tribes developed areas in which they excelled. The Navajo were weavers and silversmiths, the Zuni, lapidaries. Examples of their craftsmanship are very valuable. Today even the work of contemporary Indian artists — weavers, silversmiths, carvers, and others — is highly collectible. For a more thorough study we recommend *Arrowheads and Projectile Points*, *Indian Axes*, and *Indian Artifacts of the Midwest*. All three have been written by our advisor, Lar Hothem; you will find his address in the Directory under Ohio.

Key:
bw — beadwork   p-h — prehistoric
dmn — diamond   S — Southern
E — Eastern   W — Western
NE — Northeastern   x — cross

Apparel and Accessories

Before the white traders brought the Indian women cloth from which to sew their garments and beads to use for decorating them, clothing was made from skins sewn together with sinew, usually made of animal tendon. Porcupine quills were dyed bright colors and woven into bags and armbands and used to decorate clothing and moccasins. Examples of early quillwork are scarce today and highly collectible.

Early in the 19th century, beads were being transported via pony pack trains. These 'pony' beads were irregular shapes of opaque glass imported from Venice. Nearly always blue or white, they were twice as large as the later 'seed' beads. By 1870 translucent beads in many sizes and colors had been made available, and Indian beadwork had become commercialized. Each tribe developed its own distinctive methods and preferred decorations, making it possible for collectors today to determine the origin of many items. Soon after the turn of the century, the craft of beadworking began to diminish.

Belt, Cree, beaded, mk Hudson Bay Co in beaded letters, 24" 135.00
Bonnet, Plains child's, deer hide, quillwork/ribbon, 1920s 400.00
Breech cloth, Woodlands, mc floral bw, 61x16", VG 130.00

Cap, Nez Perce lady's, twined corn husk, geometrics/Vs, 1935 ...**440.00**
Clout, Winnebago, trade cloth w/ribbonwork, bw floral, 1900 ...**325.00**
Cuffs, Plains, full bw, 1930s, 9" **145.00**
Dress, Crow, lady's, trade cloth/felt/ribbon/shells, 1925 ....**500.00**
Dress, Nez Perce, full bw yoke on buckskin, fringe, 1920 ....**1,400.00**
Dress skirt, Navajo, blk wool, red/bl panels, 1870s, 50x30" **6,600.00**
Dress skirt, Sioux, hide w/bw fringe/ties, 1890, 40x30" **875.00**
Gauntlets, Santee Sioux, flag/birds/etc bw, fringe, 1910, 12" **220.00**
Gloves, Tlingit, bw floral on moose hide/fur trim, 1920, 14" **135.00**
Hat, Hupa lady's, twined basketry w/blk & red designs, 1900 .....**440.00**
Hat, Iroquois, trade coth w/floral bead decor, 1880, 11x5" **350.00**
Hat, Nez Perce lady's, corn husk/wool fez w/blk motif, 1930 ....**550.00**
Jacket, Chippewa, moosehide w/floral bw, 1910, rpr, 32" **850.00**
Jacket, Chippewa child's, moose hide, bw florals/fringe, 1900 ....**545.00**
Jacket, lady's, wht buckskin w/floral bw pockets, 1940 ....**135.00**
Leggings, Cheyenne, hide w/geometric bw bottom/sides, 1930 ...**220.00**
Leggings, Crow lady's, full bw geometrics, 1900, 14x9" **935.00**
Leggings, Flathead, panel on new cloth, floral bw, 1890 ....**330.00**
Mittens, Athabascan, hide/fur w/appl leather floral, 1920 ....**245.00**
Moccasins, Arapaho, sinew sewn on buffalo hide, 1800s **2,600.00**
Moccasins, Assiniboine, bw on buffalo hide, 1800s, EX quality .**2,500.00**
Moccasins, Cheyenne, full bw, parfleche soles, 1800, M **1,000.00**
Moccasins, N Plains, star design, 4-color bw, 4½", EX **275.00**
Moccasins, Ojibwa, mc bw, center seam toe, 10¼" **245.00**
Moccasins, Sioux, full bw geometrics, hard sole, 1940 ....**165.00**
Moccasins, Sioux, full bw geometrics, split bw tongue, 1920 ......**825.00**
Moccasins, Sioux, man's, 5-color bw, 1910s, 9¾" **550.00**
Moccasins & leggings, Cheyenne child's, full bw, 1875 ....**1,800.00**
Sash, Hopi, cotton w/wool embr, fringe, 1940s, 48" **300.00**
Skirt, Kiowa girl's, cloth w/mc ribbonwork, 1930s, 24" **70.00**
Turban, Prairie-style, otter w/tail, bw, wool lining **450.00**

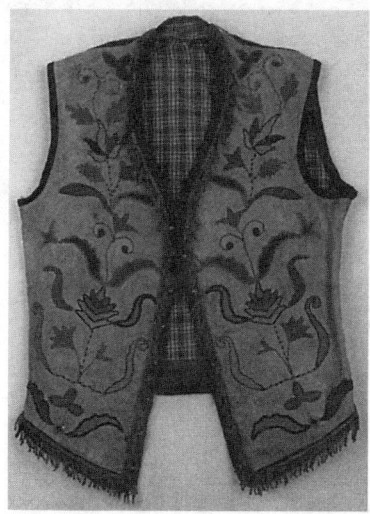

Vest, Northern Plains, beaded hide, linen lined, silver 'bullion' fringe, brass ball buttons, minor fabric losses, $1,500.00.

Vest, Kootenai, hide, mc floral bw front & bk, 1925 ....**220.00**
Vest, Piegan, full bw, muslin lined, stroud bk, 1800s, choice ...**8,800.00**
Vest, Sioux, full bw w/2 equestrians & 2 flags on wht, 1890s ..**5,100.00**

Arrowheads and Points

Relics of this type usually display characteristics of a general area, time period, or a particular location. With study, those made by the

Plains Indians are easily discerned from those of the West Coast. Because modern man has imitated the art of the Indian by reproducing these artifacts through modern means, use caution before investing your money in 'too good to be authentic' specimens.

Andice, 3¼x2⅜" **150.00**
Bonham, TX, tan, 1⅛", EX **9.00**
Cache River, TN, gray, side notch, 1¼", EX **9.00**
Covington, TX, tan, 1⅞" **12.00**
Darl, TN, tan, 2¼" **12.00**
Elora, TN, gray, 2", EX **12.00**
Frazier, TN, off-wht w/gray spots, 1⅜", VG **9.00**
Godar, AK, pk/gray, 1½", EX **12.00**
Halifax, VA, gray, 2", VG **9.00**
Hamilton, TN, blk, 1¼", EX **12.00**
Hidden Valley, AK, gray/wht, 1⅞", EX **16.00**
Jeff, AL, pk, 1½", VG **18.00**
Kalapuyan, Columbia River, red jasper, serrated, 1", EX **12.00**
Kinney, TX, gray, 1⅜", VG **9.00**
Opalescent Agate, EX color, shape, workmanship, 2¾" **190.00**
Perdiz, TX, lt grn, ⅞", EX **6.00**
Perdiz type, CO, translucent wht agate, thin, 1¼" **18.00**
Scallorn, AR, tan, 1⅛", NM **12.00**
Scottsbluff, AK, tan, minor chips, 1⅜" **18.00**
Washita, TX, tan, ⅝", EX **9.00**

Arts and Crafts

Basket, quilled birchbark, squirrel on lid, 2x6" **250.00**
Blanket, Tlingit, 1000 shell buttons form whale, 61x64" **600.00**
Box, Sioux, pnt parfleche, 20th C, 9½x17½" **495.00**
Crucifix, catlinite, made for church, 1880, 7x2" **275.00**
Cvg, Zuni, antler, 10 Mud Heads on serpent, 1940, 7x18" **495.00**
Oil on canvas, Navajo Girls, Yellowknife, 1965, 40x30" **300.00**
Pillowcase, Prairie, blk felt w/floral bw, 1900, 20" dia **575.00**
Print, Apache Women at the Fiesta, Gene Kloss, 1945, 11x14" .**690.00**
Salad set, Navajo, hand-hammered silver w/turq, 1935 ....**275.00**
Tapestry, Chimayo, blk w/geometrics, dmn center, 1950, 84x49" ..**300.00**
Totem, Tlingit, cvd cedar, 3-animal, open legs, 1800s, 21" **875.00**
Wall pocket, Sioux, cloth w/pictorial bw, 1900, 13x10" **200.00**
Watercolor, rooster/skunk/corn/rainbow, John Martinez, 13x10" ..**220.00**

Bags and Cases

The Indians used bags for many purposes, and most display excellent form and workmanship. Of the types listed below, many collectors consider the pipe bag to be the most desirable form. Pipe bags were long, narrow, leather and bead or quillwork creations made to hold tobacco in a compartment at the bottom and the pipe, with the bowl removed from the stem, in the top. Long buckskin fringe was used as trim and complemented the quilled and beaded design to make the bag a masterpiece of Indian Art.

Apache, medicine bag, bw ea side/beaded fringe, 1800s, 6x13" ..**400.00**
Arapaho, geometric bw on hide, fringe, 1910, 13x6" **715.00**
Arapaho, pipe bag, bw on antelope, quilled slats, 1870, 37" **3,900.00**
Cheyenne, medicine bag, unborn cow head, beads/quills, 1880, 9" ..**500.00**
Chippewa, bandolier, full bw floral/bead fringe, 1880, 44x18" ...**1,750.00**
Crow, knife case, full geometric bw, rawhide/leather, 1975 ....**110.00**
Crow, medicine bag, gr pnt/fringe/bw geometrics, 1870, 7x2" **495.00**
Huron, floral bw w/mc bead fringe, 6-sided, 1880, 11x9" **770.00**
Kiowa, medicine pouch, bw/bead drops/twist fringe, 4x11" **650.00**
Nez Perce, belt pouch, contour bw, 1900, 2½x2½" **190.00**
Nez Perce, pipe, full bw pony on elk hide, fringe, 1890, 34" **5,200.00**

Nez Perce, twined corn husk, geometrics ea side, 1910, 18x13" ..**770.00**
Nez Perce, twined corn husk w/mc geometrics ea side, 1890, 10" ...**440.00**
Nez Perce, twined corn husk/yarn, mc motif, 1910, 10½x12" **300.00**
Northern Plains, parfleche, mc geometrics, 1900s, 27x14" **495.00**
Ojibway, pipe bag, velvet w/floral bw ea side, fringe, 1880 ....**245.00**
Plains, tab pouch, 4-color bw, 1900s, 14" **360.00**
Plateau, bw florals/foliage, 1910, 10x11" **275.00**
Plateau, contour bw floral, 1890, 12x11" **825.00**
Sioux, scissors case, bw buckskin, 1890, 6½x2" **110.00**
Wasco, medicine pouch, bw humans/elk, 20th C, 3½x9" **1,000.00**
Woodlands, mc floral w/edge bw on blk velvet, 1890s, 6½" **250.00**
Yakima, contour bw chief's portrait, EX work, 1920, 13x15" **700.00**
Yakima, dmn bw, 3-color on bl-wht, 6⅛x7¼" **195.00**

Baskets

In the following listings, examples are basket form and coiled unless noted otherwise.

Apache, bowl, geometrics in martynia & willow, 1890s, 11¾" ...**580.00**
Apache, bowl w/dk arrowheads, 1930, 1½x6" **165.00**
Apache, burden, twined, worn dye, leather rpr, 1900, 16x15" **220.00**
Apache, burden, twined design, fringe, tin cones, 1910, 9x4" **235.00**
Apache, olla, many Xs, men, dogs, dmns, 1920, 14x12" **1,925.00**
Apache, tray, willow & martynia, 18 figures, 1920s, 5x21" **990.00**
Apache, twined, allover pitch, horsehair hdls, 1940, 6x11" **220.00**
Apache, water jar, int/ext pitched, ca 1901, 6¾x10⅝" **195.00**
Klickitat, berry basket, imbricated, EX work, 1800s, 12x13" **600.00**
Klickitat, burden, imbricated, compound rim finish, 1930, 2" **185.00**
Macha, mc boats & ducks, finial damage, 5" dia **30.00**
Macha, mc geometrics, 3¾" dia **40.00**
Macha, oval, mc boats & whale, 3¼" **85.00**
Maidu, fine weave 3-rod willow & redbud w/flowers, 1930, 4x3" ..**440.00**
Mission, bowl w/mc rattlesnake, 1910, 7x18" **880.00**

Mohawk, ash splint with wicker design of colorful ash splints and ribbon motifs, 12⅜x11", $190.00.

Navajo, wedding basket, braided rim & 18 points, 1960, 12" **110.00**
NW Coast, cedar & twined beargrass, 4x5⅜" **220.00**
Ojibway, bark w/allover mc quillwork, 1920, 3x7½" **195.00**
Papago, olla, lt geometrics, 1920, 15x13" **400.00**
Papago, 4 geometric dmns, 1960, 17½x12" **275.00**
Pima, bowl, whirling fret in martynia & willow, 10¼" **360.00**
Pima, tray, Pima fret design, 1910, 4x18½" **220.00**

Pima, whirlwind in blk, shallow, 1920, 13" **600.00**
Pima, willow, 5 male figures in dk martynia, soiled, 11" **825.00**
Pima, 3 stylized horses, 1920s, 2x10½" **375.00**
Pima, 8 Gila monsters, 1920, 1½x10" **1,200.00**
Pitt River, 6 radiating elements, dk brn on tan, 1910, 9x14" **750.00**
Seri, tray, mc 4-petal star, 1960, 19x5", M **220.00**
Tulare, Friendship, continuous line of men & women, 1920 ......**880.00**
Western Apache, bowl, willow & martynia, men & horses, 3x12" .**1,045.00**
Yavapai, tray, 10 humans/10 dogs, 1890s, 17" **3,700.00**

Blankets, Navajo

Pueblo Indians first made blankets centuries ago, but today most are made by Navajo Indians. Pendleton and Hudson's Bay blankets became widely available in the 1800s; around the turn of the century, rugs were developed because tourists were more likely to buy them as floor coverings and wall-hangings. Rugs or blankets are made in various regional styles; an expert can usually identify the area where one was made, sometimes even the individual who made it. The colors of wool are natural (gray-white, brown-black), vegetal (from plant dyes), or artificial (aniline, from synthetic chemicals). Value factors include size, tightness of weave, artistry of design, and condition. Examples by artists whose names are well known command the higher prices.

Woman's wearing blanket, tightly woven stepped crosses on orange-red with ivory and dark brown linear field, ca 1890, 46x48", EX, $2,200.00.

Child's wearing, handspun w/indigo, 1880, 44x28" **880.00**
Child's wearing, orig condition, museum quality, 1880s, 54x32" .**4,675.00**
Saddle, dmn twill design, 1960, dbl sz, 60x35" **165.00**
3rd Phase Chief's, stepped dmns/fine stripes, 1910, 67x57" ..**2,875.00**
3rd Phase Chief's, transitional, 1910, 59x54" **1,000.00**

Ceremonial Items

Bowl, beaver effigy, wood/abalone & bone inlay, 1920s, 14" ...**3,200.00**
Dance wand, Plains, buffalo horn sceptre, cloth wraps, 1900 ......**230.00**
Drum, Cochiti, pnt wood, 4 rattlesnake tails, 1920, 5½" H **1,000.00**
Drum, Cochiti, pnt wood w/hide-wrap hdls, 1920, 21", +beater .**1,725.00**
Drum, Taos, cottonwood & rawhide, traditional, 1960, 10" **80.00**
Effigy, Mound Builder, cvd stone turtle, p-h, 7x4" **135.00**
Fetish, turtle, full bw, umbilical cord, 20th C, 8x5" **165.00**
Flask, Apache, pnt rawhide w/beads, 1850, 3x1" **275.00**
Mask, Cherokee 'Booger,' 1890, 12x9" **220.00**

Mask, Iroquois, corn husk around entire circumference, 1890 ...**495.00**
Mask, Iroquois, False Face, cvd wood, long hair, 20th C, 13x8" .**375.00**
Mask, Iroquois, False Face, tin insets/long hair, 1900 ....**245.00**
Necklace, personal medicine; Crow, full bw, 1880 ....**385.00**
Rattle, Hopi, gourd pnt w/rain clouds, wood hdl, 1890s, 7½" **575.00**
Rattle, Hopi, gourd w/3-color traditional designs, 1950, 11" **50.00**
Rattle, Iroquois False Face Society, turtle shell, 15½" **250.00**
Rattle, turtle shell w/bead hdl, fringe, 20th C, 16x8" **400.00**
Shield, dance; Pueblo, pnt muslin, snakes/animals, 1890, 19" **660.00**
Shield, Pueblo, rawhide dome shape, pnt motif, 1900, 19" **1,750.00**
Spoon, effigy, horn w/tack eyes, bw hdl/cones/horsehair, 9½" **230.00**

Dolls

Blackfoot, buckskin male, bw moccasins/war bonnet, 1920, 19" ...**495.00**
Kachina, Apache, cvd/pnt, Gan dancer, 11" **330.00**
Kachina, Clown, w/watermelon & cowboy boots, Cleveland, 12" .**275.00**
Kachina, Crow Dancer, full attire, 1920, 30x10" **770.00**
Kachina, Hopi, Navuk-China dancer, pnt/cvd costume, 9¼" **100.00**
Kachina, Mouse, sgn Bob Tubbs/dtd 1981, 24x9" **135.00**
Kachina, Mudhead, cvd/pnt cottonwood, Alvin James Sr, 16" ...**690.00**
Kachina, Ogre Woman, cvd w/little pnt, Loren Phillips, 12" **900.00**
Kachina, Shalako, sgn Royel Jackson, 1981, 18" **165.00**
Navajo, decorated velvet dress, w/jewelry, 1950, 24x8" **110.00**
Plains, cloth/hide, pnt face/wool braids, bw, 1890s, 11", pr **2,700.00**

Jewelry and Adornments

As early as 500 A.D., Indians in the Southwest drilled turquoise nuggets and strung them on cords made of sinew or braided hair. The Spanish introduced them to coral, and it became a popular item of jewelry; abalone and clam shells were favored by the Coastal Indians. Not until the last half of the 19th century did the Indians learn to work with silver. Each tribe developed its own distinctive style and preferred design, which until about 1920 made it possible to determine tribal origin with some degree of accuracy. Since that time, because of modern means of communication and travel, motifs have become less distinct.

Quality Indian silver jewelry may be antique or contemporary. Age, though certainly to be considered, is not as important a factor as fine workmanship and good stones. Pre-1910 silver will show evidence of hammer marks, and designs are usually simple. Beads have sometimes been shaped from coins. Stones tend to be small; when silver wire was used, it is usually square. To insure your investment, choose a reputable dealer.

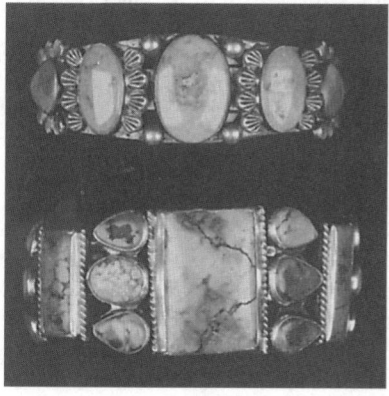

Cuff bracelets, Navajo, silver and turquoise, Top: 5 stones, 2½", $400.00; Bottom: 3-wire with 15 Blue Gem stones, 2¾", $825.00.

Belt, Navajo, Old Pawn, 11 conchos/buckle, 1940 ....**275.00**
Belt, Navajo, stamped/emb silver, 6 conchos+spacers, 1950 ....**385.00**
Belt, Navajo, 6 conchos+7 butterflies, stamped/emb, 1950 ....**385.00**
Belt, Zuni, 13 lg inlaid butterflies+buckle, Rosetta Wallace **1,200.00**
Bolo, Zuni sunface, coral/jet/pearl/turq, Leahtz, 1940, 3" **165.00**
Bracelet, Navajo, coin silver, 3 natural turq, 1935, 1½" W **135.00**
Bracelet, Zuni, EX shell/stone inlay, +ring & earrings, 1935 ......**975.00**
Bracelet, Zuni, kachina form, mixed inlay, 1940s **230.00**
Breast plate, Crow, hairpipe w/brass beads, moon shell, 22x8" ...**440.00**
Breast plate, Souix, old bone hairpipe w/brass beads, restrung **145.00**
Choker, Crow, hairpipe w/bl & brass bead spacers, 1930, 31x1" ..**165.00**
Collar, 11-strand grad turq heishi on felt, 1900, 17½x9" **600.00**
Necklace, lg amber beads w/handmade silver & wood beads, 24" .**195.00**
Necklace, made from Liberty dimes/quarters/1881 dollar, 1945 ..**200.00**
Necklace, Navajo, all silver, 12 squash blossoms/naja, 1920 ....**245.00**
Necklace, Navajo, silver beads w/rnd cluster pendant, 1950 ....**200.00**
Necklace, Pueblo, 2-strand turq slabs on heishi, 1940, 29" **165.00**
Necklace, Pueblo, 3-strand nugget/tube coral/cones, 1940 ....**300.00**
Necklace, silver dollar squash blossom w/Liberty dimes, 1945 ....**400.00**
Necklace, silver/turq squash blossom w/8 bear claws, 1975 ....**245.00**
Necklace, turq/silver squash blossom w/12 bear claws, 1975 ......**300.00**
Necklace, turq/silver squash blossoms, sandcast naja, 1930 ....**195.00**
Necklace, 2-row w/mc inlay squash blossoms, 1985, +earrings ...**330.00**
Ring, Zuni, snake, inlaid coral/turq, by Calabasa, 1935 ....**85.00**
Roach, Crow, deer hair, w/shaping stick, 1890 15x4" **220.00**
Trade beads, blk w/wht & red dots, w/squash beads **65.00**
Trade beads, Lewis & Clark beads w/1 rare red chevron, 23" **385.00**
Trade beads, lg grad chevrons, museum quality, 30" **525.00**
Trade beads, lg oval cobalt Peking glass beads, 27" **110.00**

Knives and Chipped Blades

The knife was an indispensable tool to the Indian whether he was in battle, hunting game, or doing chores at the campsite. Before the white man's metal blades, all were made of copper, obsidian, flint, or chert. Knife cases, fashioned of leather with intricate decorations of quilling or beadwork, were sometimes suspended from the neck, or they were attached to the belt.

Agate Basin, MO, 4¼" **100.00**
Clovis, WI, 4¼" **285.00**
Crooked, blade made from file, hide wrapped, 1800s, 9½" **400.00**
Crooked, Great Lakes, cvd hdl, leather blade cover, 1910, 9" ...**135.00**
Crooked, hdl cvd w/3 stacked hearts, copper wire wrap, 8" **800.00**
Crooked, hdl: chip-cvd rolled-up belt, blade: Keen razor **500.00**
Dalton, MO, 4¼" **200.00**
Dovetail, IL, 4½" **90.00**
Etley, MO, 6" **275.00**
Flint, MO, off-wht, sq bk, 4½" **65.00**
Hardin, MO, 5¼" **575.00**
Kinney, TX, off-wht, sq bk, thin, well made, 3", NM **65.00**
Sedalia, TX, 7" **345.00**
Spear, AR, Bulverde, off-wht & tan, 3¼", VG **35.00**
Sq bk, AR, cave find, p-h, EX **35.00**
Steel, NW Coast, handmade, eagle cvd on hdl, 1900, 21x2" **200.00**

Pipes

Pipe bowls were usually carved from soft stone, such as catlinite or pipestone, an argilaceous sedimentary rock composed mainly of clay. Granite was also used. Some ceremonial pipes were simply styled, while others were intricately designed naturalistic figurals, sometimes in bird or frog forms called effigies. Their stems, made of wood and often covered with leather, were sometimes nearly a yard in length.

Pipe tomahawk, notched and incised lead trade pipe bowl, hardwood stem decorated with copper wire and brass tacks, beaded and fringed hide suspension, 19½x8⅜", $2,200.00 at auction.

Bird, gr-brn steatite, drilled/incised decor, KY, p-h, 8¼" **400.00**
Bowl only, catlinite, eagle claw form, 2½x7", +stand **690.00**
Bowl only, catlinite, T-form w/telescopic cvg, 1890s, 8" **140.00**
Bowl only, Omaha, catlinite disk shape, 1850, 1½" **165.00**
Iroquois, vulture, gray-gr steatite, drilled/cvd, 3¼x2¼" **300.00**
N Plains, catlinite, bowl held in cvd claw, 1880, 8", +stand **440.00**
Plains, catlinite T-bowl w/pewter inlay, bear-paw pnt stem **270.00**
Plains, catlinite/pewter inlay, cvd/burned stem, 1800s, 26x5" **440.00**
Sioux, catlinite, incised scallops, quill braid wrap, 34" **550.00**
Sioux, catlinite T bowl, quill-wrap stem w/duck breast, 1870 .**1,265.00**
Sioux, cvd/inlaid, quillwork wrap, horsehair drops, 31" **3,700.00**

Pottery

Indian pottery is nearly always decorated in such a manner as to indicate the tribe that produced it or the pueblo in which it was made. For instance, the designs of Cochiti potters were usually scattered forms from nature or sacred symbols. The Zuni preferred an ornate repetitive decoration of a closer configuration. They often used stylized deer and bird forms, sometimes in dimensional applications.

Acoma, jar, white slip with black checkered and stepped geometric and bat devices, red base and inner lip, 11¼", $6,000.00 at auction.

Acoma, water jar, mc on wht slip, 1890s, 11x10⅛" **8,580.00**
Cochiti, bowl, full-decor int, ½" red slip band, mc, 1950, 7" **135.00**
Cochiti, jar, stylized birds etc, 1920, 11x9½" **990.00**
Gila, shoulder olla, blk on buff geometrics, p-h, 4x6" **330.00**
Hawikuh, Kiva dish, stepped wall construction, p-h, 4x6" **495.00**
Hohokam, bowl, red on buff, flared, Z lines inside, p-h, 9" **550.00**
Hohokam, shoulder jar, red curvilinears on buff, p-h, 3x4" **190.00**
Hopi, jar, bird/butterfly, Rena Leslie hallmk, 1950, 7x7" **165.00**

Hopi, jar, classic Nampeyo design, EX quality, 1910, 9x6" **550.00**
Hopi, jar, redware w/cvd butterfly, sgn Thos Nampeyo, 2¾" **300.00**
Hopi, plaque, mc stylized bird, Frieda Poleahla, 1958, 8x6" **150.00**
Hopi, seed jar, sgn Adele Nampeyo, 1975, 3x5" **135.00**
Hopi, storage vessel, plainware, fire clouds, 1880, 9" **110.00**
Hopi, vase, umber avian design w/red ochre on cream slip, 9" **195.00**
Hopi, wedding vase, stylized mc birds/etc, Frog Woman, 11x9" .**495.00**
Jeddito, bowl, buff; w/brn geometrics in & out, p-h, 3x8" **220.00**
Jemez, bowl, blk geometrics on cream slip on red-brn base, 6" **75.00**
Jemez, jar, EX decor, sgn M Tosa, 1985, 10x9" **220.00**
Laguna, olla, pnt designs, early 20th C, 12x12" **440.00**
Laguna, wedding jar, traditional, 20th C, 9x11" **275.00**
Maricopa, bowl, snake encircles rim, mc, M Sunn, 1950, 2½x7" ..**110.00**
Moundbuilder, pot, turtle form, cvd detail, sm rpr, p-h, 7x6" **250.00**
Pueblo, olla, birds, museum quality, 1850, 7x5½" **440.00**
Roosevelt, jar, blk on wht w/geometrics, p-h, 4½x5" **275.00**
Santa Clara, bowl, blkware, highly polished, Cookie Tafoya, 4" ...**100.00**
Santa Clara, bowl, blkware w/cvd snake, Chavarria, 3½" **230.00**
Santa Clara, bowl, blkware w/cvd snake, M Tafoya, 1930s, 8" ...**575.00**
Santa Clara, jar, blk on blk Avanyu, Nicolaso & Roberto, 8x6" ...**220.00**
Santa Clara, olla, blkware w/bear print, Clara Sisneros, 10" **900.00**
Santa Clara, owl effigy, mc, Margaret & Luther, 1965, 3x2" **190.00**
Santa Clara, seed bowl, life forms etched on red, S Romero **175.00**
Santa Clara, seed jar, mc Avenu, Margaret & Luther, 5½" **550.00**
Santa Clara, sugar/creamer on tray, plain blkware, M Tofoya **450.00**
Santa Clara, vase, cvd blkware, Helen Shupla, 1960, 7x5" **250.00**
Santa Clara, vase, mc serpent, Lela & Luther, 1950s, 3" **200.00**
Santa Clara, vase, mc serpent, Margaret & Luther, 1980, 6" **700.00**
Santo Domingo, jar, blk floral on creamy slip, 1900, 5¼" **250.00**
Snowflake, bowl, blk on wht w/geometrics/lines, p-h, 5x11" **550.00**
Tonto, olla, intricate mc geometrics, p-h, 13x9" **1,000.00**
Zia, jar w/3 mc naturalistic deer, 1930, 7½x6" **220.00**
Zuni, Kiva pot, raised frogs/owls/birds, 1920, 8x5" **600.00**
Zuni, Kiva pot w/spotted bas relief frogs, 1880, 6x4" **275.00**
Zuni, olla, curvilinear/foliate motif, 1900, 10x9½" **365.00**
Zuni, olla, polychrome deer etc, 1900, sm **385.00**

Pottery, San Ildefonso

The pottery of the San Ildefonso pueblo is especially sought after by collectors today. Under the leadership of Maria Martinez and her husband Julian, experiments began about 1918 which led to the development of the 'black-on-black' design achieved through exacting methods of firing the ware. They discovered that by smothering the fire at a specified temperature, the carbon in the smoke that ensued caused the pottery to blacken. Maria signed her work (often 'Marie') from the late teens to the 1960s; she died in 1980. Today a piece with her signature may bring prices in the $500.00 to $4,500.00 range.

Bowl, blk on red, serpent, Tonita, ca 1920s, 3x8" **300.00**
Bowl, blkware, feathers, Bl Corn, 1930s, minor rstr, 10" **2,300.00**
Bowl, blkware, geometrics, Bl Corn, 2½x5" **250.00**
Bowl, blkware, plain, Marie & Santana, int rstr, 1950s, 10" **1,300.00**
Bowl, blkware w/design, Anna, 1930, 2½x5" **135.00**
Bowl, mc geometric bands, 1910, 3½x9" **300.00**
Bowl, mc geometrics, Rose, 1960, 2½x8" **80.00**
Jar, blkware, cvd rain cloud design, sgn Rose, 1940, 6x7" **495.00**
Jar, blkware, cvd steps, sgn Bl Corn, 1970, 6x5¾" **465.00**
Jar, blkware, feathers, Marie & Santana, 3⅝x4½" **525.00**
Jar, blkware, geometrics, Maria Popovi, 4½x6¼", NM **1,950.00**
Jar, blkware, geometrics/feathers, Bl Corn, 1950s, 4½" **430.00**
Jar, blkware, highly polished, Lupeto Martinez, 3¼x5¼" **70.00**
Jar, blkware, plain, finely polished, sgn Marie, 1923, 7" **440.00**
Jar, blkware, polished, Lupita Martinez, 3x4½" **60.00**

Jar, blkware, wide neck band, EX work, sgn Desederia, 7x7" 550.00
Olla, blkware, finely polished, Maria Poveka, 1930s, 7" 2,300.00
Plate, blkware, arrowheads etc, sgn Ramona, 1930, 9" 220.00
Plate, blkware, polished, Marie & Julian, 1930s, 7" 450.00
Plate, blkware w/geometrics, unsgn, 1930, 2x11" 95.00
Platter, blkware, polished, Marie & Julian, 1930, 11½" 900.00
Pot, blkware, cvd serpent, sgn Rose, 1940, 7x4½" 385.00

Rugs, Navajo

Coal Mine Mesa, vegetal dye, raised outline, 1985, 42x28" 220.00
Crystal, natural wool, 4-barbell center motif, 1930, 60x28" 385.00
Crystal, serrated dmns/stripes, vegetal, 1940s, 61x45", EX 375.00
Dmn design (early), 4-color, wool, ca 1910, 83x58" 495.00
Early West Reservation, central dmns, 4-color, 74x64" 935.00
Ganado, dmns/rectangles, natural/aniline, 1920, 50x35", EX 550.00
Ganado, serrated dmns/geometrics, 1930s, 81x41" 575.00
Ganado, tight weave, 5-color, 1940, 90x70" 950.00
Key designs w/serrate border, 5-color, 70x39" 385.00
Klagetoh, geometrics/feathers/zigzags, 1950s, 63x43" 750.00
Klagetoh, gray field, red/wht/blk border, 1930, 81x51" 495.00
Klagetoh, storm pattern, stylized corn stalks, 1930, 64x44" 990.00
Klagetoh, stylized storm pattern, 6-color, 1950, 64x41" 550.00
Pictorial, lg Yeibichi figure in center, 1925, 82x56" 2,300.00
Pictorial, mtn/stream w/animals & birds, contemporary, 45x35" .1,000.00
Pictorial, Xs/arrows, 1930, 27x27" 220.00
Red Mesa, mc geometrics, 1935, 66x42" 650.00
Serrated dmn, heavy yarn/med weave, natural, 1930, 83x43" 465.00
Serrated dmn, tight/fine weave, EX colors, 1940, 60x33" 1,100.00
Storm, feather design border, 1930, 75x45" 700.00
Storm, fine weave/intricate, vegetal, 20th C, 84x58", M 2,700.00
Storm, water bugs/2 valero stars, natural wool, 1940, 54x30" 385.00
Teec Nos Pos outline, EX example, 1930s, 93x49" 5,500.00
Teec Nos Pos outline, EX/mc triangles, 1930, 65x39" 1,650.00
Transitional, central lozenge, 1910, 65x49" 275.00
Transitional, soft weave, striped, 1890, 78x54" 550.00
Two Gray Hills, Chief's Blanket design, 1930, 45x43" 275.00
Two Gray Hills, Valero stars/hooked border, 1964, 96x140" ...5,300.00

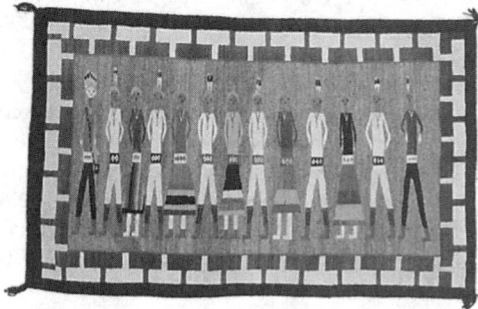

Yei, pictorial weaving in natural and analine-dyed home-spun, multicolor on gray ground, 46x79", $1,600.00.

Yei, mc figures on red, 42x35" 415.00
Yei, 13-figure, Greek Key border, 1930s, 132x66" 6,325.00
Yei, 4-figure tapestry corn stalk, Lukachukai, 1970, 35x25" 190.00
Yei Fox Dancer, 8-figure, EX color, 1975, 69x32" 330.00
2 vertical zigzags ea side block track design, 1940, 61x31" 660.00

Stone Artifacts

Banner stone, butterfly, brn, IL, 3¼x5¼" 135.00

Birdstone, blkish gray-gr, OH, 2x5¾" 125.00
Bowl, Mound Builder, cvd gr turkey effigy, TN, p-h, 4" 300.00
Discoidal, brn-cream, IL, 2¼x4¼" 125.00
Pestle, blk steatite, pecked/polished, shows use, 13½" 150.00
Pestle, gray granite, pecked/polished, Columbia River, 12¾" 125.00
Pestle, NW Coast, blk, 6¾x4" 175.00

Tools

Axe, blk granite, full-grooved, shape rough, polished, 4½" 60.00
Axe, blk/gray granite, full-groved, OH, 2½x6¼x2¾" 115.00
Axe, granite, full-groved, edge w/some damage, p-h, 7", +hdl 200.00
Fish hook, NW Cost, cvd cedar w/stylized loon, 1800s, 10" 550.00
Hide scraper, Blackfeet, elk horn, 1860s, 14½" 400.00
Hoe, flint, 1 side flat, hump on other, lg flakes, MO, 8" 120.00
Maul, greystone, ¾-grooved, pecked/polished, 4x3½" 30.00
Scraper, Conerly, gray/brn, TN, 2⅞", VG 9.00
Scraper, N Plains, elk antler w/iron blade, 14" 135.00
Trade axe, lady's, hand forged, rusty/pitted, 1960, 6" 75.00

Weapons

Arrow, Plains, sinew-wrap stone head, tipped/fletched, 23" 175.00

Bow, quiver, and bow case, Apache, sinew-sewn hide quiver with fringed cuffs, paint decoration, inscribed 'Geronimo' on fringed case, painted and incised wood 46" bow, EX, $2,300.00.

Club, blk egg-shape head, full bw hdl, 20th C, 26x6" 190.00
Club, fish killing; Kwakiult, wood w/head of creature, 23" 2,000.00
Club, Plains, stone w/lead inlay, horsehair braid-wrap hdl 170.00
Club, Sioux, pnt-filled grooves, bw strip/hdl, losses, 6x20" 425.00
Club, Sioux, tomahawk shape, bw/cones/fluffs, 1890, 5x20" 200.00
Club, Sioux, wht bauxite, dbl pointed, 5¾", bw strap/hdl 175.00
Club, stone, hide-wrapped hdl/oval head w/some bw, 21" 575.00
Club, wood, ball top, effigy on bk of hdl, 22" 920.00
Club head, wht/gray bauxite, 6-sided, drilled, 6¼" 175.00
Tomahawk, Plains, trade head, wood stem w/tack decor, 1890s .400.00

Miscellaneous

Back rest, Plains, willow rods w/mc pnt decor & beads, 55" 1,000.00
Blanket, saddle; Nez Perce, bw on bl stroud, 19th C, 26x64" 600.00
Blanket, trade; Oregon City label, 1910, 72x51" 190.00
Book, N Am Indian Vol XII Hopi, ES Curtis, Plimpton Press ...6,325.00
Cradle, Paiute, woven, sun shade/decor/shell drops, 1940, 29" ...495.00
Cradle, wood w/bw sun shade, cvd stars/tacks, 20th C, 30" 165.00
Fiddle, Apache, cactus wood w/images & fire brands, 1900, 11" ...750.00
Gold tone, Nez Perce in full regalia, ES Curtis, 1925, 10x10" 220.00
Ladle, Plains, horn w/sm cvd circles, 1800s, 7½" 60.00
Map, Hudson Bay Trading Post & territory, +trade token, 1950 ..130.00

Peace medal, Andrew Johnson, silver, 1865, 3" dia 235.00
Peace medal, Franklin Pierce, silver, 1853, 3" dia 225.00
Peace medal, Geo Washington, 1795, 2½x3½" 300.00
Photograph, Plains encampment, 1900, 10x8" 85.00
Photograph, Plains Indian Chief, Schnitzmyer, 1900, 11x14" 220.00
Photograph, Pottery Maker - Hopi, RR Reed, tinted sky 250.00
Photogravure, John Abbott - Osage, ES Curtis, lg folio 250.00
Photogravure, Lower Columbia, ES Curtis, Van Gelder, 17x12" ..460.00
Photogravure, On the Beach - Nokoaktok, Curtis, #339, 11x16" ..550.00
Photogravure, Woista - Cheyenne Woman, ES Curtis, lg folio ..225.00
Saddle, Chas Shipley, orig tool bag, restrung, 1900 ....440.00
Staff, Plains, cvd stone ram head/horsehair-wrap hdl, 1800s 230.00
Toy cradle, wood w/bw sun shade & bib, tacks, 1900s, 15" 135.00
Wampum, Plateau, pump-drilled shells w/trade beads, 1800s, 34" ..500.00

Amethyst Glass

The term amethyst simply describes the rich color of this glassware, made by many companies both here and abroad since the 19th century.

Bottle, scent; HP stork, ped ft, orig lily stopper, 7" 110.00
Box, HP florals, ormolu ft, brass rings on sides, 4¾" dia 245.00
Box, patch; HP florals, 1¼x2" dia 110.00
Ring tree, mc florals, gold leaves, 3¾x3¾" 110.00
Salt cellar, hexagonal, flint glass, chip, 2" 85.00
Tumbler, HP florals & wht dots w/gold, 3¾x2½" 25.00
Vase, appl flowers, thorn hdls, 14⅜x5⅜" 275.00
Vase, mc flowers & gold leaves, 4¼x3¼" 85.00

Amphora

The Amphora Porcelain Works in the Teplitz-Turn area of Bohemia produced Art Nouveau-styled vases and figurines during the latter part of the 1800s through the first few decades of the 20th century. They marked their wares with various stamps, some incorporating the name and location of the pottery with a crown or a shield. Because Bohemia was part of the Austro-Hungarian empire prior to WWI, some examples are marked Austria; items marked with the Czechoslovakia designation were made after the war. Our advisor for this category is Jack Gunsaulus; he is listed in the Directory under Michigan.

Vase, Art Nouveau nymph applied to side of stoneware gourd shape with jeweled blossoms, marked, #6168, 10½", $1,250.00.

Basket, child sitting on edge feeding chicks, ca 1900, rpr 295.00
Basket, roses, oval, 5½x9½" 225.00
Bust, lady in 18th-C garb, brn/rust/pk, mk Austria, 12", EX 350.00
Bust, maid in off-shoulder gown above scenic reserve, 18" ...3,100.00
Candlestick, irid, swirl ribs, organic mold, #3538, 8" 850.00

Compote, poppies/whiplash stems in high relief, gold/mc, 12" ...950.00
Ewer, HP florals w/gilt, rtcl rim, mk, 15¾x6¼" 495.00
Pitcher, laughing cat w/red bow tie form, mk, 10x4¼" 145.00
Pitcher, lg leaf ea side, hdl is stem, mc irid, 9½" 900.00
Tray, Nouveau ladies' heads ea end, Wahliss, 11" 375.00
Vase, appl vintage on bl irid, 8¾" 275.00
Vase, appl vintage on gr to pk irid, ped ft, hdls, 8¾" 295.00
Vase, appl vintage on pale gr & cobalt, hdls, 10½" 395.00
Vase, Arts & Crafts emb tree scene, bk: peasants, 18", EX 1,300.00
Vase, bluebird emb on tan, 6" 125.00
Vase, cup over 4 appl lily pads on rnd base, bl/wht, 9" 250.00
Vase, Deco floral emb, strap hdls, 11" 550.00
Vase, Deco mc flower bands, blk rim, mk, 14½" 700.00
Vase, HP flowers & bird on slender form, 8" 110.00
Vase, HP geometric decor, cobalt trim, hdls, 13½" 850.00
Vase, icicles descend from rim, 4 form hdls, tan/gr/pk, 7" 300.00
Vase, jeweled flowers, salamander hdls, crown mk, 9¾" 395.00
Vase, mc metallic on irregular gourd form w/long hdls, 11" 1,200.00
Vase, Nouveau lady's face, gold leaves & lilies, 18" 1,100.00
Vase, parrots atop rim-to-width hdls, ftd, mc, 8" 280.00
Vase, portrait of lady/jewels/sun, much gold, 7x5" 1,800.00
Vase, scenic, bottle form w/gold cobra hdls, RS&K, 9" 175.00
Vase, stylized upright bud, rtcl rim, beaded hdls, 7" 300.00

Animal Dishes with Covers

Covered animal dishes have been produced for nearly two centuries and are as varied as their manufacturers. They were made in many types of glass (slag, colored, clear, and milk glass) as well as china and pottery. On bases of nests and baskets, you will find animals and birds of every sort. The most common was the hen.

Some of the smaller versions made by McKee, Indiana Tumbler and Goblet Company, and Westmoreland Specialty Glass of Pittsburgh, Pennsylvania, were sold to food-processing companies who filled them with prepared mustard, baking powder, etc. Occasionally one will be found with the paper label identifying the product and processing company still intact.

Many of the glass versions produced during the latter part of the 19th century have been recently reproduced. As early as the 1960s, the Kemple Glass Company made the rooster, fox, lion, cat, lamb, hen, horse, turkey, duck, dove, and rabbit on split-ribbed or basketweave bases. They were made in amethyst, blue, amber, and milk glass, as well as a variegated slag. It is sometimes necessary to compare items in question to verified examples of older glass in order to recognize reproductions. Reproduction is continued today.

For more information, we recommend *Covered Animal Dishes* by our advisor, Everett Grist, whose address is in the Directory under Illinois. In the listings below, when only one dimension is given, it is the greater one, usually length.

Boar's head, milk glass, Atterbury Pat May 29, 1888, 9½" 1,500.00
Bull's head, milk glass, spoon tongue (missing), mk 175.00
Cat on lacy base, milk glass, mk WG (Westmoreland) 130.00
Chick in egg on sleigh, any color, Westmoreland repro, 5½" 95.00
Conestoga wagon, clear, LE Smith 35.00
Dolphin on sauce dish, milk glass, att Westmoreland, 7¼" 100.00
Dolphin w/sawtooth edge, milk glass, Kemple repro 75.00
Duck, Atterbury; milk glass, Pat Applied For on base, 11" 375.00
Duck, Pintail; on split-rib base, bl opaque, 5½" 110.00
Duck, Swimming; amber, Vallerysthal, 5" 120.00
Duck on cattail base, milk glass, unmk, 5½" 85.00
Eagle mother, milk glass, Westmoreland reissue w/WG mk 100.00
Elephant standing, blk, Co-operative Flint Glass, 9" 130.00

Elephant w/rider, milk glass, Vallerysthal, 7" 350.00
Fish, Entwined; milk glass, lacy base, dtd lid, 6" dia 200.00
Fish, Flat; bl opaque 165.00
Fish on collared base, clear frosted, Central Glass 150.00
Hand & dove, milk glass, lacy rectangular base, Atterbury, dtd ..125.00
Hen, milk glass, Challinor, Taylor & Co, 8" 110.00
Hen, str-headed, clear w/red pnt details, Imperial, sm 25.00
Hen & chicks on basketweave, milk glass, att Smith, med sz 35.00
Hen w/chicks on split-rib base, milk glass, unmk McKee, 5½" ...165.00
Horse on split-rib base, milk glass, repro, 5½" 75.00
Jack rabbit on oval ribbed base, clear, att Flaccus 150.00
Lamb on split-rib base, amber, recent, 5½" 45.00
Lion on scroll base, milk glass, unmk, 5½" 75.00
Mule-eared rabbit on picket base, milk glass, pk ears & eyes 50.00
Quail on scroll base, milk glass, 5½" 65.00
Rabbit emerging from horizontal egg, milk glass, worn pnt 85.00
Rabbit on wheat base, milk glass, Flaccus 350.00
Ribbed fox on ribbed base, milk glass, dtd 175.00
Robin on nest w/ped ft, bl opaque, Vallerysthal 90.00
Rooster, goofus on milk glass base, att Westmoreland, 5½" 65.00
Rooster on basketweave base, bl opaque, Westmoreland, lg 125.00
Rooster on wide-rib base, bl w/wht head, 5½" 70.00
Snail on strawberry, milk glass, Vallerysthal, 5¼" 120.00
Swan, clear frosted, Vallerysthal, 5½" 65.00
Swan, Closed-Neck; on basketweave base, milk glass, WG mk 75.00
Swan, Raised-Wing; milk glass, glass eyes, att Atterbury 185.00
Swan on knobby basketweave base, amber, Pat Applied For, 7" .165.00
Swan on split-rib base, milk glass, mk Mckee, 5½" 250.00
Turkey, Standing; clear, US Glass, lg 250.00
Turtle, milk glass, knobby bk, unmk, lg 100.00

Antiquities

The ancient Egyptians, Romans, and the early craftsmen of Indian and China have left us with exquisite treasures bearing mute witness of their esthetic convictions that even a water carrier, a knife, or a rug should be created a thing of beauty. Though time and the elements have taken their toll on the more fragile works of these ancient artisans, it is incredible that many remain intact to this day. The thin-walled tear and scent bottles blown by Roman artisans from the last century A.D., and examples of the red or black predynastic potteries of Egypt, though understandably quite rare, can yet occasionally be found on the market today. Jewelry, often interred with the dead, has survived the centuries well; figurines of marble and terra cotta, ceremonial masks, earthenware vessels, and other relics such as these offer us of the 20th century the only tangible link possible to the ancient world. Our advisor for this category is Alex G. Malloy; he is listed in the Directory under New York.

Bronze

Figure, Egpyt, 1070-712 BC, Nefertum striding w/scepter, 10⅝" .10,000.00
Figure, Egypt, Anubis seated & wearing kilt, 6⅞" 7,500.00
Figure, Egypt, 644-30 BC, Bastet w/sistrum & basket, 5⅝" 4,000.00
Figure, Egypt, 945-525 BC, cat's head & shoulders, 3¾" 10,000.00
Figure, Rome, 100-200 AD, Apollo, hands & ft missing, 3¾" .1,150.00
Figure, Rome, 100-200 AD, Lar dancing w/rhyton in hand, 4⅛" .4,000.00
Group, Egypt, 644-30 BC, Isis & Harpocrates on base, 6⅛" 3,000.00
Handle, Rome, 200 AD, boy on dolphin form, 5½" 3,500.00
Helmet, Corinth; Greek, 600 BC, hammered sheet, 9⅛" 20,000.00

Hardstones

Bowl, 2700-2200 BC, cycladic marble, rolled rim, 2¼x8" 3,500.00

Caponic jar, Egypt, 1550-1070 BC, limestone, Hapy lid, 12½" 3,500.00
Caponic jar lid, Egypt, 1550-1070 BC, pnt head form, 4¾" 1,500.00
Cosmetic palette, Egypt, 3500-3000 BC, schist, fish form, 10" ..7,500.00
Fragment, Cypriote, 500-400 BC, nude dwarf, 21¾" 6,000.00
Fragment, Rome, 100-200 AD, foot & sandal, marble, 7¼" ...3,500.00
Head, S Arabia, 2nd half 1st Millenniun BC, alabaster, 5¾"..10,000.00
Heart-scarab, Egypt, 1070-664 BC, olivine basalt, 2¼" 4,000.00
Scarab, Graeco-Phoenicia, 500 BC, Poseidon relief, jasper, ⅝" ..2,500.00

Jewelry and Adornments

Cross, Byzantine, 500-600 AD, cut sheet gold w/decor & loop ..5,000.00
Ring, Byzantine, 500-600 AD, solid cast gold w/eng bezel 5,000.00
Ring, Rome, 100-200 AD, gold w/carnelian intaglio eng head ..1,500.00

Pottery

Amphora, Cypriot, 1000-700 BC, painted in brown with horizontal bands, circles and plants, 27", $850.00.

Baby feeder, Apulia, 320-200 BC, Gnathia Ware, canteen shape .1,500.00
Epichysis, Apulia, 400 BC, blk glass, appl face hdls, 10⅛" 2,300.00
Lekanis, Etruria, 400 BC, Gnathia Ware, pnt vines, 6¾" 1,380.00
Lekanis, Sicily, 350-325 BC, Gnathia Ware, w/lid, 5⅛" dia 2,500.00
Mug, Apulia, 400 BC, Red Figure, hdl, 3⅛", pr 1,495.00
Oinochoe, 600-500 BC, bl core, yel spirals & zigzags, 3¼" 1,725.00
Pectoral, Egypt, 300-100 BC, shrine form, faience, 3½" 1,000.00
Plate, Apulia, 325 BC, Gnathia Ware, birds & flowers, 7⅜" ...2,185.00

Terra Cotta

Dove, Apulian, 400-200 BC, wht w/red details, 6½" 1,000.00
Figure, Asia Minor, 200-300 AD, Aphrodite on base, 16½" 3,000.00
Figure, Boeotia, 625-550 BC, bird-face woman, pnt details, 6¾" .2,500.00
Figure, Canosa, 300-200 BC, Eros seated, pnt traces, 4" 800.00

Miscellaneous

Beaker, Rome, 400-500 AD, gr translucent glass, conical, 7½" ...2,000.00
Mask, Egypt, late period, mummy, wooden, pigment traces, 18" 600.00
Shabti, Egypt, 1070-712 BC, Priest of Ptah, bl faience, 4¼" 1,000.00

Appliances, Electric

Today all vintage appliances are being collected. Toasters, irons and percolators top the list. Electric fans have become very much sought after in the last few years, the earliest ones being the most desirable.

Prices listed below are for examples in very good to excellent condition and in good working order. Be sure to check any old appliance for safety before plugging it in. If you have questions regarding antique appliances, please contact our advisor, Jim Barker; he is listed in the Directory under Pennsylvania.

Beater, Chicago, electric, jadite bowl 45.00
Blender, Waring, chrome base, heavy glass, EX 45.00
Fan, Electric Edison, 1890s 500.00
Fan, Emerson, brass cage, 6-blade, 1908 ....150.00
Fan, Fitzgerald, oscillating, Art Deco style w/enameling 45.00
Fan, Fresh-N-Air, chrome w/blk Bakelite blades, table model 175.00
Fan, Mesco DC Fan #3695 ....85.00
Fan, Ohio Electric Works, 9" blade 350.00
Fan, Star Rite, #431 ....75.00
Fan, Westinghouse, 10" brass blade & cage 145.00
Fan, White Cross, 8" 65.00
Heater, Sunbeam, early, 5" dia, EX 40.00
Iron, Silver Streak, glass w/int red color, 9", EX 550.00
Percolator, Coffee Maid, Deco style, chrome, 1950s 45.00
Percolator, Hotpoint #114P20 ....50.00
Percolator, Hotpoint #114517 ....85.00
Percolator, Manning Bowman K336 ....50.00
Percolator, Manning Bowman set, K4591 ....85.00
Percolator, Porcelier Perc 85.00
Percolator, Royal Rochester, ceramic & metal, EX 150.00
Percolator, Star Rite set, #8039 ....75.00
Percolator, Westinghouse #283881 ....65.00
Refrigerator, General Electric, coil top 300.00
Toaster, Armstrong, table/toaster/stove, wht enamel 65.00
Toaster, Bersted #74, EX 65.00
Toaster, Bersted #80, EX 65.00
Toaster, Estate #77, EX 165.00
Toaster, Hotpoint #125-T-18 ....55.00
Toaster, Manning Bowman #1410, table/toaster/stove 95.00
Toaster, Strite Automatic, cast aluminum, 4-slice, 1930s 195.00
Toaster, Sun Chief #680 ....25.00
Toaster, Sunbeam T-9, EX 95.00

Toaster, Sunbeam, chrome with black trim, $85.00.

Toaster, Toastermaster #1-A-1, 1-slice, chrome design, 1929 ....75.00
Toaster, Toastmaster #1-A-4 ....45.00
Toaster, Torrid Swing Around, EX 85.00
Toaster, Universal E7722, EX 75.00
Toaster, Universal E9912, EX 75.00
Toaster, Westinghouse #196158, table/toaster/stove 75.00

Waffle iron, Lady Hibbard on ceramic insert, Bakelite hdls 135.00
Whipper/beater, Challenger, 1930s, MIB 35.00

Arc-En-Ciel

The Arc-En-Ciel Pottery Company operated in Zanesville, Ohio, from 1903 until 1907. Artware was produced only until 1905, typically finished in a high lustre gold glaze. Though not always marked, those pieces that are carry the half-circle rainbow logo containing the company name.

Vase, gold lustre, Radford mold, 7½", $225.00.

Vase, gold lustre, mk, 12" 200.00
Vase, oak leaves at rim, stems form swirls, lt gr-bl, 6½" 300.00
Vase, rose & gold irid, flared base & neck, #549, 6" 75.00

Arequipa

The Arequipa Pottery operated from 1911 until 1918 at a sanitorium near Fairfax, California. Its purpose was two-fold: therapy for the patients and financial support for the institution. Frederick H. Rhead was the originator and director. The ware, made from local clays, was often hand thrown, simply styled and decorated. Marks were varied but always incorporated the name of the pottery and the state. A circular arrangement encompassing the negative image of a vase beside a tree is most common.

Examples are evaluated according to quality of artwork; size and shape are less important. Those done by Rhead himself are most desirable.

Bowl, turq matt, #752, 3x9" 175.00
Jar, lt bl matt, cvd geometric band, hdls, w/lid, 5x6" 300.00
Vase, brn matt, imp mk, #1524, 3½" 170.00
Vase, cvd flowering branch on tan bsk, bulb w/long neck, 8" 690.00
Vase, cvd stylized flowers on blk gloss, 3x3" 200.00
Vase, dbl ribbing on plum matt, inv't baluster, 1914, 6" 285.00
Vase, emb flowers on gray/pk matt, hand thrown, 3x4" 250.00
Vase, floral branch at everted mouth, natural tan, ovoid, 8" 700.00
Vase, HP floral, gun metal on dk bl, 4" 500.00
Vase, spades/lines, squeezebag decor, wht/brn/purple, 3½" 1,500.00
Vase, stylized berry band, yel on gr mottle, rpr, 9x3" 1,900.00

Argy-Rousseau, G.

Gabriel Argy-Rousseau produced both fine art glass and quality commercial ware in Paris, France, in 1918. He favored Art Nouveau as well as Art Deco and in the twenties produced a line of vases in the Egyptian manner, made popular by the discovery of King Tut's tomb. One of the most important types of glass he made was pate-de-verre. Most of his work is signed. Items listed below are pate-de-verre unless noted otherwise.

Bowl, Etoiles, stephanotis clusters, violet on wht/gr, 4" H 3,680.00
Bowl, lg stylized flower front/bk, lg scroll leaf hdls, 8½" 2,900.00
Bowl vase, gray/bl, 16-facet sides on 8-sided ft, 6½" H 2,500.00
Box, allover floral, violet/wht w/blk centers, dome lid, 4" 5,700.00
Tray, emb fruit border, clear/mc mottle w/orange & blk, 12" ..1,400.00

Vase, molded bowl form with amethyst and purple flowers, black stamen centers, white accents, impressed mark, 3x4¾", $6,900.00.

Vase, continuous line of dancing maids/horizontal bands, 10" ..40,250.00
Vase, lg flower front/bk, lg scroll leaf hdls, 8" L 5,175.00
Vase, purple flowers w/wht accents, blk centers, 3x4¾" 6,900.00
Vase, rows of lozenges/geometrics, lav/red/blk, U-form, 3½" ...4,300.00
Vase, thistles (4 repeats), amber/gr/red on mottle, 6" 5,100.00
Vase, 3 beetle shoulder band, EX color contrast, 6x5" 5,500.00
Vase, 3 pr feathers, wine/gr on gray mottle, 6x4½" 4,300.00
Veilleuse, conical shade w/3 pk roses & bands, 7" 5,100.00

Art Deco

To the uninformed observer, 'Art Deco' evokes images of chrome and glass, streamlined curves and aerodynamic shapes, mirrored prints of pink flamingos, and statues of slender nudes and greyhound dogs. Though the Deco movement began in 1925 at the Paris International Exposition and lasted to some extent into the 1950s, within that period of time the evolution of fashion and taste continued as it always has, resulting in subtle variations.

The French Deco look was one of opulence — exotic inlaid woods, rich material, lush fur and leather. Lines tended toward symmetrical curves. American designers adapted the concept to cover every aspect of fashion and home furnishings from small inexpensive picture frames, cigarette lighters, and costume jewelry to high-fashion designer clothing and exquisite massive furniture with squared or circular lines. Vinyl was a popular covering, and chrome-plated brass was used for chairs, cocktail shakers, lamps, and tables. Dinnerware, glassware, theaters, and train stations were designed to reflect the new 'Modernism.'

The Deco movement made itself apparent into the fifties in wrought iron lamps with stepped pink plastic shades and Venetian blinds. The sheer volume of production during those twenty-five years provides collectors today with fine examples of the period that can be bought for as little as $10.00 or $20.00 up to the thousands. Chrome items signed

'Chase' are prized by collectors, and blue glass radios and tables with blue glass tops are high on the list of desirability in many areas.

Those interested in learning more about this subject will want to read *Collector's Guide to Art Deco* by our advisor, Mary Frank Gaston. She is listed in the Directory under Texas. See also Bronzes; Chase; Frankart; Furniture; Jewelry; Lalique; Radios; etc.

Andirons, silver-bronze cobra form, in Brandt's style, 12", pr ..3,200.00
Ashtray stand, tall nude std, NuArt, 26" 215.00
Bookends, nude, arched bk, flowing hair, bronze wash, 7", pr 90.00
Bookends, sailboats, Bronze Art, 7", pr 225.00
Box, powder; dancing nude atop rnd form, ceramic, Germany ...100.00
Candle holders, bronze, opposing Cs, Carl Sorensen, 5", pr 400.00
Candle holders, chrome, stylized fish-form hdls, 4", pr 45.00
Candle holders, sailboat form, frosted bl glass, 5½", pr 65.00
Cigarette case, Bakelite & pigskin, A Rolinx, MIE 100.00
Clock, mantel; cast figures at sides on marble base, 14x18" 200.00
Clock, metal & compo reclining musician at side, marble base ..950.00
Clock, shelf; ceramic & chrome, gilt dog atop, unmk, 11½x10" .150.00
Clock, walnut, ceramic nudes, floral-emb pewter dial, 12" 500.00
Cocktail shaker, Zeppelin, chrome-plated, gold int, 9x3", G 325.00
Coffee set, chrome w/Catalin hdls, Manning Bowman, 4-pc 550.00
Console, 4 leaf straps under marble demilune, Bergue 30" W ..8,000.00
Figurine, draped nude, ceramic, Kent Art Ware, 11" 175.00
Figurine, nude running w/torch, porc, Germany, 9" 375.00
Figurine, seated nude, ceramic, Guiraud Riviere, 14" 1,725.00
Figurine, Spanish lady, pot metal & ivorene, marble base, 10" ...300.00
Flower frog, dancing nude, ceramic, Germany, 7" 60.00
Hors d'oeuvres server, chrome w/Bakelite hdl, 11½" 80.00
Ice bucket, chrome, cobalt glass insert, Hazel Atlas, 11x8" 85.00
Incense burner, Egyptian lady figural, ceramic, Lisne, 6½" 400.00
Incense burner, girl w/flowers by basket, bronzed metal, 5½" 45.00
Inkwell, hammered copper & cast brass, wide rnd base 150.00
Lamp, chrome gazelles on blk glass base, conical shade, 9" 75.00
Lamp, draped nude supports globe in hands, wht metal, 20" 425.00
Lamp, table; Easy Edges, stacked laminated cb, Frank Gehry 550.00
Lamp, vanity; stylized nudes, wht metal w/bronze finish, pr 400.00
Luminaire, cvd glass semicircle w/peacock feathers, onyx base ..2,600.00
Luminaire, fan form w/wrought iron cobra base, Fr, 22½" 1,100.00
Mirror, hammered wrought iron, scrolls/foliage, fr, 39x46" 800.00
Mirror, pnt scene: nude w/bird, leaping deer, Toran, 60x40" 485.00
Necklace, orange & clear plastic cubes & blk beads 18.00
Picture frame, beveled glass w/etched roses, '40s, 17x14" 100.00
Pin, gr stone set in blk & turq enamel, silver trim 40.00
Pitcher & bowl, Rose Marie, HP geometrics, Fr, 9¼", 12½" 300.00
Rug, wool, repeating clamshells in shades of gr, 143x109" 1,100.00
Sconce, bronze, stork w/scrolling wings, Cheuret, 36x27" 7,500.00
Sconce, gold irid shade w/molded geometrics in 9" holder, pr 95.00
Stem, cocktail; nude supports pk glass bowl, unmk, 5" 65.00
Tea set, copper w/simple brass detail, 2 pots+cr/sug 90.00
Tumbler, sterling, flared mouth, lg rnd base, Cartier 125.00
Urn, bronze, sea creature panel ea side, hdls, Brandt, 10" 11,500.00
Vase, acid-cut geometrics, ftd cone form, mk Kaza, 10" 265.00
Vase, dk gr glass, Zeppelin shape, unmk, 9" 35.00
Vase, sterling floral decor on bronze, Heintz, 12" 300.00
Wall brackets, bronze w/oval glass bk & tray, 29x12", pr 500.00
Wall pocket, lady's head w/hat, pottery, wht glaze 70.00

Art Glass Baskets

A popular novelty and gift item during the Victorian era, these one-of-a-kind works of art were produced in just about any type of art glass in use at that time. They were never marked, since these were not true production pieces but 'whimsies' made by glassworkers to relieve the tedium of the long work day. Some were made as special gifts. The more decorative and imaginative the design, the more valuable the basket.

Amber w/spatter & gold mica over cranberry, amber hdl, 6½" ...350.00
Amberina irid ribbed swirl, shaped rim, clear hdl/ft, 9" 295.00
Basketweave w/emb florals, bl, 5½x6½x4" 100.00
Bl, wht & crystal int w/mica, ruffled rim, thorn hdl, 8½" 275.00
Bl w/vaseline band, wht rim, orange enamel, thorn hdl, 7½" 415.00
Bluerina, clear twist thorn hdl, 7½" 525.00
Coinspot, wht opal, rainbow spatter int, crystal rim, 7½" 415.00
Cranberry, appl medallions to hdl, clear base, 14x9x8½" 350.00
Cranberry threading on crystal, appl flowers, 11½" 650.00
Dmn Quilt, frosted chartreuse to clear, frosted hdl, 4¼x5" 85.00
Dmn Quilt, mc spatter, sq thorn hdl, 7½x5½" 175.00
Dmn Quilt, pk opal, appl vaseline leaves & hdl, 6½x5" 145.00
Dmn Quilt, yel opaque, ruffled, clear hdl, 5¾x4¾" 88.00
Dmn Quilt MOP, pk cased, clear thorn hdl, 8½x7½" 795.00
Gold & pk spatter w/clear thorn hdl, 7¾x5" 155.00
Hobnail, peachblow w/appl amber hdls, Sandwich, 6½x6" 250.00
Lime gr, clear ft, ruffle & hdl, thorny nubs allover, 8x4" 135.00
Lime gr opal, clear ruffled rim & hdl, 6½x5¾" 145.00
Mc spatter, emb rosette & swirl pattern, clear hdl, 6x5" 100.00
Mc spatter, int melon ribs, clear hdl, 5¾x4⅞" 135.00
Mc spatter cased, clear thorn hdl, 7⅛x4¾" 165.00
Mc spatter cased, star-shaped top, clear twist hdl, 6¼x5⅜" 100.00
Oxblood red & opaline swirls w/gold mica, clear hdl, 7½" 285.00
Peachblow color, appl flowers/branch/leaves/ft/rim, 13x13" ...1,000.00
Pk o/l, clear braided hdl, 5½x5½" 85.00
Pk o/l w/mica, clear thorn hdl, 8-crimp, 7¼x4⅛" 185.00
Pk over wht, amber thorn hdl, crimped rim, 6x7" 100.00
Ruby iris form w/crystal petals, petals form hdl, 7x3⅝" 118.00
Tomato w/yel ext, 15-rib, 4-lobe rim, twist hdl, 9x6" 225.00

Yellow and pink stripes, white interior, ruffled rim, clear thorn handle, 8", $125.00.

Yel cased, ruffled, clear twisted hdl, 6½x4x4¾" 85.00
Yel opaque, emb swirls & beads, clear thorn hdl, 6x4¾" 95.00

Art Nouveau

From the famous 'L'Art Nouveau' shop in the Rue de Provence in Paris, 'New Art' spread across the continent and belatedly arrived in America in time to add its curvilineal elements and asymmetrical ornamentations to the ostentatious remains of the Rococo revival of the 1800s. Nouveau manifested itself in every facet of decorative art. In glassware Tiffany turned the concept into a commercial success that lasted well into the second decade of this century and created a style that inspired other American glassmakers for decades. Furniture, lamps, bronzes, jewelry, and automobiles were designed within the realm of its dictates. Today's market abounds with lovely examples of Art Nouveau, allowing the collector to choose one or several areas that hold a special interest. Our advisor for this category is Steven Whysel; he is listed in the Directory under Arkansas. See also Bronzes; Galle; Jewelry; Loetz; Tiffany; Silver; specific manufacturers.

Table lamp, bronze, winged maiden supports openwork domical shade with fringe, signed R. Elias, 30", $3,200.00.

Box, jewel; brass w/florals/leaves, lid w/portrait, 6x8" 525.00
Bust of maid, marble, 3 irises at bust, titled Ireos, 25" 575.00
Candelabrum, SP, 3 branches w/leaves & flower cups, 16" 100.00
Centerpc, pewter, veined leaf, leaf hdl, mk Hanny, 14", EX 230.00
Curio, inlaid copper/brass/wood lilies, 2 ldgl doors, mahog 3,500.00
Ewer, pewter, emb vintage, very slim w/vine hdl, Osiris, 14" 150.00
Ewer, porc, woman draped around hdl, mk Wahlis, rpr, 10" 600.00
Plant stand, brass, cast w/dolphins/dragonflies, 38" 300.00
Vase, ceramic, bronze frwork of leaves/berries, 1897, 17" 2,500.00
Vase, ceramic, pewter framework of vines & flower, mk CN, 14" .1,750.00
Vase, ceramic bottle in bronze fr w/2 lg dragonflies, 7" 2,800.00

Arts and Crafts

The Arts and Crafts movement began in England during the last quarter of the 19th century, and its influence was soon felt in this country. Among its proponents in America were Elbert Hubbard (see Roycroft) and Gustav Stickley (see Stickley). They rebelled against the mechanized mass production of the Industrial Revolution and against the cumulative influence of hundreds of years of man's changing taste. They subscribed to a theory of purification of the styles: that designs be geared strictly to necessity. At the same time they sought to elevate these basic ideals to the level of accepted 'art.' Simplicity was their virtue; to their critics it was a fault.

The type of furniture they promoted was squarely built, usually of heavy oak, and so simple was its appearance that as a result many began to copy the style which became known as 'Mission.' Soon factories had geared production toward making cheap copies of their designs. In 1915 Stickley's own operation failed, a victim of changing styles and tastes. Hubbard lost his life that same year on the ill-fated *Lusitania*. Within the decade the style had lost its popularity.

Metalware was produced by numerous crafts people, from experts such as Dirk van Erp and Albert Berry to unknown novices. Prices for Arts and Crafts accessories rose dramatically in 1988, but by the beginning of 1991 leveled off and (in some cases) dropped. Metal items or hardware should not be scrubbed or scoured; to do so could remove or damage the rich, dark patina typical of this period. Our advisor for this category is Bruce Austin; he is listed in the Directory under New York. See also Furniture; Roycroft; Silver; Stickley; specific manufacturers.

Andirons, brass, sq shaft w/appl design, no mk, 20", pr 1,600.00
Ashstand, ET Hurley, sea horse shaft, starfish ft, dtd, 30" 1,800.00
Blotter, Burton, MOP inlay on hammered copper, 3x6" 45.00
Bookends, Berry Shop, hammered copper triangle w/mtn scene, pr ..150.00
Bowl, hanging; Kalo, hammered copper, appl monogram, 7" 150.00
Bowl, JF Hewes, hammered copper, scalloped, 2½x8½", VG 200.00
Bowl, van Erp, hammered copper, incurvate, rfn, 6x13" 1,500.00
Box, copper lid w/enameling, att Boston School, 5 " dia 400.00
Box, hammered copper, strap hinge, riveted flared legs, 3x8" 250.00
Box, hammered copper w/arrowheads wrapped in silver, 7" L .1,000.00
Box, Liberty & Co, Tudric SP w/turq enamel, #085, 5x4½" 550.00
Box, oak, cylindrical, lid cvd/pnt w/village scene, 3x5" 90.00
Candlestick, Jarvie, brass, 1-pc, no mk, 6" 375.00
Candlesticks, Benedict, hammered copper, strap hdl, 6½", pr 450.00
Candlesticks, Chas Rohlfs, oak 'h' form w/brass mts, 21", pr 650.00
Candlesticks, Jarvie, Alpha, brass, pencil std, 11", VG, pr 600.00
Candlesticks, Jarvie, brass, lathe-trn pencil std, 9x4½", pr 475.00
Candlesticks, Jarvie, Delta, sgn, 14", VG, pr 700.00
Candlesticks, Kipp, sq base, 2-strap std, EX orig, 7½", pr 1,300.00
Chafing dish, hammered copper/silver w/oak hdls & base, VG ..240.00
Chafing dish, Shreve & Co, copper/silver, oak hdls/base, VG 240.00
Chandelier, Prairie School, 4 sm ldgl tulip shades, 24x19" 1,600.00
Clock, van Erp, copper, shaped triangle w/appl 'AOS,' 4½" 900.00
Compote, Heintz, appl silver flowers, lg sqd hdls, ftd, 6x12" 300.00
Costumer, Limbert #229, 4-leg base w/dbl X stretcher, 72" 850.00
Desk pc, silvered copper, pentray/blotter+4 boxes, appl 'R' 300.00
Desk set, Heintz, silver on bronze, 9-pc, lt cleaning, VG 900.00
Fr, Revere, rtcl floral over slag glass, 12x9" 400.00
Humidor, Heintz, appl fox hunt on gr/brn patina, 6x5½" 400.00
Jardiniere, hammered copper w/swirling floral, London, 9x10" ..350.00
Lamp, boudoir; Heintz, bronze w/silver geometrics, 11x8" 950.00
Lamp, table; Heintz, silver-inlay copper, cut-out shade 1,000.00
Lamp, table; Limbert #376, rtcl mica (rpl)-lined 16" shade 3,500.00
Lamp, table; 4-sided slag glass 15" shade; sqd oak base 600.00
Lamp, van Erp, 4 mica panels in 17" shade; hammered base ...6,250.00
Lantern, copper top & fr w/4 slag glass panels, 18x12" 600.00
Letter holder & opener, Carence Crafters, geometrics, NP, VG .325.00
Letter opener, van Erp, hammered copper w/appl monogram, 10" .200.00
Linen centerpc, embr 4-color geometrics, fringed, 40" dia, EX ...400.00
Magazine stand, 5 sq cutouts over 3 magazine slots, no mk, VG .550.00
Mat, leather, w/lg lotus flowers & leaves, some wear, 14" 150.00
Pillow, 3 lg poinsettias, red/gr on cream, 19x19", EX 290.00
Pitcher, hammered copper, riveted bands, str flared sides, 12" 300.00
Purse, leather, red/gr pnt flowers on blk, silver clasp, 8" 70.00
Table linen, embr pastel geometrics & blk, lace ends, 21x51" 250.00
Tablecloth, embr linen w/tulips, 38x38", +6 napkins 90.00
Tray, van Erp, concave scallops at rim, mk, rfn, 17½" dia 1,100.00
Umbrella stand, hammered brass, waisted form, 25", VG 600.00
Umbrella stand, 4 posts w/beveled caps, orig pan, 30" 300.00
Vase, Avon, hammered copper, scalloped/flared, rfn, 8¾", pr 425.00
Vase, Benedict, hammered copper, 2 ear hdls, 8x12", EX 550.00
Vase, Dixon, hammered copper, bowl base, long neck, 5½x5" ...400.00
Vase, Dixon, hammered copper, bulb bottom, 6x4", EX 250.00
Vase, hammered brass, upright shoulder hdls, orig, 20" 150.00
Vase, hammered copper, bulb w/can neck, ring hdls, 13", VG ...240.00

Vase, Tudric, pewter, 3-hdld, #0226, 7½", pr 325.00
Vase, van Erp, copper, closed-in top, cleaned, 3½x4½" 475.00
Vase, van Erp, hammered copper, bulbous w/rolled rim, 7½" ..1,400.00
Vase, van Erp, hammered copper, orig patina, 11x6" 3,500.00
Vase, van Erp, hammered copper, scalloped/flared, 2½", pr 275.00
Vase, van Erp, hammered copper, squat w/rolled rim, rfn, 6½" ...475.00

Attwell, Mabel Lucie

Born in London in 1879, Mabel Lucie Atwell put her talent in illustration and design toward many outlets. Merchandise ranging from children's books and dinnerware, postcards, advertising, dolls, calendars, and greeting cards were marketed under her direction. She also designed a line of china called Nursery Ware for the Shelley China Company (See also Shelley). Our advisor for this category is David Ehrhard; he is listed in the Directory under California.

Ad, Just Lovely, Erasmic Vanishing Cream, Punch, 1919 ....40.00
Book, Alice in Wonderland, L Carroll, Tuck & Sons, 12 plates .135.00
Book, Lucie Attwell's Pop-Up Book of Rhymes, 1973 ....75.00
Calendar, Never Froget If the World Goes Wry...Standing By ...125.00
Candy dish, Fairies Love Motoring, sq 85.00
Figurine, BooBoo w/mushroom 450.00
Figurine, Bride 600.00
Figurine, Diddums, Shelley 500.00
Figurine, Little Mermaid 450.00
Game, Valentine's Party Games, Age-Endings, Valentine 35.00
Hanky set, Lucie Attwell Hanky Book 200.00
Magazine cover, Pictorial Review, Who's Afraid, Nov 1913 ....70.00
Nursery Ware, bowl, Look at This Wee Jolly..., Shelley 185.00
Nursery Ware, plate, Don't Forget The Fairies..., Shelley 125.00
Nursery Ware, plate, We've Just Come From..., Shelley, oval 225.00
Nursery Ware, saucer, Oh! Mr Rabbit..., Shelley 75.00
Plaque, This Is Home Not an Ashtray, Valentine/Sons of Dundee ..95.00
Print, Evacuation of School Children..., Aug 1939, from book 75.00
Print, False Perjured Clarence, Tatler, Jan 1921 ....60.00
Print, Muvver's Pretty Pet 60.00

Tea set, mushroom house pot, BooBoo creamer and toadstool sugar bowl, $600.00; Sarah figurine by Wade, $95.00; Crawford biscuit tin, $450.00; Chamber pot, $400.00.

Tray, Mischief, I'm Nuts About You, Wright's Biscuits 150.00

Austrian Glass

Many examples of fine art glass were produced in Austria during the time of Loetz and Moser that cannot be attributed to any glasshouse in particular, though much of it bears striking similarities to the products of both artists.

Finger bowl, red floral w/gold, w/underplate, 6 for 285.00
Vase, appl purple plums & leafy branch on webbed irid, 13" 250.00
Vase, Nouveau floral, gold on irid, att F Heckert, 4½" 150.00
Vase, pulled chain band, gr-blk irid w/gold specks, 6" 465.00
Vase, silver o/l floral on cased burnt orange, 6" 175.00
Vase, silver o/l floral on orange irid, bulbous, 2¾" 465.00

Austrian Ware

From the late 1800s until the beginning of WWI, several companies were located in the area known at the turn of the century as Bohemia. They produced hard-paste porcelain dinnerware and decorative items primarily for the American trade. Today examples bearing the marks of these firms are usually referred to by collectors as Austrian ware, indicating simply the country of their origin. Of those various companies, these marks are best known: M.Z. Austria; Victoria, Carlsbad, Austria (Schmidt and Company); and O. & E.G. (Royal) Austria.

Though most of the decorations were transfer designs which were sometimes signed by the original artist, pieces marked Royal Austria were often hand painted and so indicated alongside the backstamp.

Of these three companies, Victoria, Carlsbad, Austria, is the most highly valued. Collectors should note that in our listings transfer decorations showing 'signatures' (sgn), such as 'Wagner,' 'Kauffmann,' 'LeBrun,' etc., were not actually painted by those artists but were merely based on their original paintings.

Bust, Victorian lady in bonnet & jacket, Depose, EW Turn, 9" .150.00
Cake plate, floral w/gold, scalloped rim w/hdls, mk, 9½" 25.00

Cake plate, roses on green with gold border, R.S. Prussia mold, Wheelock, 11" diameter, $125.00.

Ewer, floral, w/gold, circle hdl, RH crown mk, 6" 45.00
Ewer, wild roses w/gold, scroll hdl, 4-ftd, 11¾x6" 155.00
Figurine, German shepherd, Keramos, 18" L 110.00
Plate, lady's portrait, sgn Carlsen, mk Carlsbad, 10" 55.00
Vase, HP carnations w/gold, emb leaves, hdls, mk, 13½x5" 210.00
Vase, maid w/wreath in hair in woods, gold hdls, Tenner, 9" 325.00

Autographs

Autograph collecting, also known as 'philography' or 'love of writing,' used to be a hobby shared by a few thousand dedicated collectors.

But in recent years, autograph collecting has become a serious pursuit for more than 2,000,000 collectors worldwide. And in the past decade, more investors are adding rare and valuable autograph portfolios to their traditional investments. One reason for this sudden interest in autograph investing relates to the simple economic law of supply and demand. Rare autographs have a 'fixed' supply, meaning that unlike diamonds, gold, silver, stock certificates, etc., no more are being produced. There are only so many Abraham Lincoln, Marilyn Monroe, and Charles Lindbergh autographs available. In the meantime, it's estimated that more than 20,000 new collectors enter the market each year, thus creating an ever-increasing demand. Hence, the rare autographs generally rise steadily in value each year. Because of this scarcity, a serious collector will pay over $10,000 for a photograph signed by both Wilbur and Orville Wright, or as much as $25,000 for a handwritten letter of George Washington.

But by far, the majority of autograph collectors in the country do it for the love of the hobby. A polite letter and self-addressed, stamped envelope sent to a famous person will often bring the desired result. And occasionally one receives not only an autograph but a nice handwritten letter thanking the fan as well!

In terms of value, there are five general types of autographs: 1) mere signatures on an album page or card; 2) signed photographs; 3) signed documents; 4) typed letters signed; and 5) handwritten letters. The signatures are the least valuable, and handwritten letters the most valuable. The reasoning here is simple: with a handwritten letter, not only do you get an autograph but the handwritten message of the person as well. And this content can sometimes increase the value many times over. A handwritten letter of Babe Ruth thanking a fan for a gift might fetch a few thousand dollars. But if the letter were to mention Ruth's feelings on the day he retired, it could easily sell for $10,000 or more.

There are several major autograph collector organizations where members can exchange celebrity addresses or buy, sell, and trade their autographed wares. Philography can be a fun and rewarding hobby. And who knows! In ten or twenty years, those autographs you got for free could be worth a small fortune!

In the listings below, photos are assumed black and white unless noted color. Our advisor for autographs is Tim Anderson; he is listed in the Directory under Utah.

Key:
ADS — handwritten document signed
ALS — handwritten letter signed
ANS — handwritten note signed
AQS — autograph quotation signed
CS — counter signed
DS — document signed
ins — inscription
ISP — inscribed signed photo
LH — letterhead
LS — signed letter, typed or written by someone else
PLH — personal letterhead
sig — signature
SP — signed photo

Adams, John; DS, 4-language ship's paper, 1797, EX 1,300.00
Autry, Gene; sig on colored postcard 15.00
Baer, Max Sr; sig on 3x5" card 75.00
Banks, Ernie; SP, 8x10" 25.00
Barton, Clara; ALS, financial worry/etc, 4-pg, 1906, EX 400.00
Bendix, William; sig on theatre bill 20.00
Bernhardt, Sarah; ALS, monogrammed stationery, 2-pg, EX 130.00
Bronson, Charles; SP, blk & wht, 8x10" 15.00
Byrd, Richard E; sig in book: Little America, 1930, EX 35.00
Carnegie, Andrew; sign on PA RR pass, 1860, EX 110.00
Carpentier, George; SP, sitting ringside, 7½x4¾" 60.00
Carter, Jimmy; SP, 8x10" 75.00
Caruso, Enrico; sig on self-caricature on postcard, 1906, EX 650.00
Castalini, Rocky; sig on 3x5" card 40.00

Clay, Henry; ALS, asking favor, 1-pg, 1834, EX **400.00**
Cody, William; SP, photo from magazine, laid down, EX **280.00**
Coolidge, Calvin; LS, thank-you, 1-pg, 1932, EX **130.00**
Coolidge, Calvin; sig on White House card, matted/fr, EX **220.00**
Cooper, J Fenimore; sgn check, pew rent, matted & fr, 1844, EX .**130.00**
Crawford, Joan; LS **50.00**

Bette Davis, signed photograph, inscribed in lower right-hand corner, ca 1930s, 11x9" (excluding frame), $575.00.

Davis, Jefferson; ALS, as Governor of NH, 1-pg, 1855, EX **1,400.00**
Dickens, Charles; DS, to bankers, 1-pg, 1867, EX **450.00**
Doyle, Sir Arthur Conan; sig on card, EX **200.00**
Edison, Thomas A; SP, silverprint, semiprofile, 9½x7½" **1,100.00**
Eisenhower, Dwight D; LS, as President, 1-pg, 1955, EX **160.00**
Eisenhower, Dwight D; SP, close-up portrait, 1953, 10x8", EX ..**250.00**
Faye, Alice; SP, 8x10", blk & wht **30.00**
Garner, James; SP, 8x10" glossy **15.00**
Garrett, Pat T; ALS, to wife on hotel stationery, 1-pg, 1892 ...**1,500.00**
Godfrey, Arthur; SP, 7x9" **30.00**
Hancock, John; DS, as President of Congress, 13½x8½", EX ..**2,500.00**
Harding, Warren G; sgn/inscr engraving, pencil, 13¼x9½", EX .**400.00**
Harris, Julie; SP, 8x10" glossy **15.00**
Harrison, Benjamin; ALS, to sister, 1½-pg, 1834, EX **750.00**
Harrison, Benjamin; LS, travel plans, 1900, 1-pg, EX **900.00**
Harrison, William Henry; DS, as Aide-de-Camp, 1794, 4x8¼" ..**750.00**
Hayes, Rutherford B; request note sgn 3 times on bk, 1885 ....**250.00**
Hemingway, Ernest; LS, 1-pg **550.00**
Hoover, Herbet; SP, Harris & Ewing cabinet card **200.00**
Howard, Leslie; SP, by Elmer Fryer, 8x10", EX **250.00**
Huxley, Aldous; ALS, on request for autograph, 1-pg, 1931 ....**80.00**
Irving, Washington; ALS, acknowledgement, 1-pg, 1855, EX **350.00**
Jabbar, Kareem Abdul; SP, color, 5x7" **35.00**
Jefferson, Thomas; DS, ship's passport, 1-pg, EX **1,600.00**
Joplin, Janice; sig on sm paper w/album Cheap Thrills, EX **300.00**
Lahr, Bert; sig on theatre bill **160.00**
Landon, Michael; sig on horse show program **35.00**
Lee, Bruce; SP, 8x10" glossy **400.00**
Lee, Robert E; DS, as Captain of US Engineers, 1839, 3x8" **2,800.00**
Leno, Jay; SP, 8x10" glossy **15.00**
MacArthur, Douglas; SP, sepia toned, 13¾x10¾", EX **350.00**
Madison, James; DS, ship's passport w/seal, 1-pg **950.00**
Martin, Dean; SP, 8x10" **20.00**
McCormick, Cyrus H; sig on bank draft, 1878, EX **280.00**

McKinley, William; DS, military appointment, 1900, 1-pg, EX .**500.00**
Mitchum, Robert; SP, color, 8x10" **20.00**
Monroe, James; DS, ship's passport, countersigned JQ Adams ...**1,100.00**
Murphy, George; SP, blk & wht, 8x10" **65.00**
Musial, Stan; SP, 8x10" **25.00**
Nixon, Richard; LS **120.00**
Parrish, Maxfield; bold sig on 3x5" card, 1940s **125.00**
Peck, Gregory; SP, blk & wht, 8x10" **20.00**
Pershing, John J; LS, to President of France, 1919, EX **100.00**
Polk, James K; DS, military appointment, as President, 1848 .....**950.00**
Power, Tyrone; ISP, in Marine uniform, 8x10" **175.00**
Raye, Martha; SP, 8x10" **24.00**
Reagan, Ronald; LS, tax reform mentioned, 1-pg, 1967, EX **200.00**
Reynolds, Burt; sig on script of Evening Shade **25.00**
Robinson, Jackie; sig in book: Wait Till Next Year, 1960, EX **550.00**
Roosevelt, Franklin D; LS, Navy Department, 1915, 1-pg **150.00**
Roosevelt, Theodore; SP postcard, portrait, 1908, EX **500.00**
Rose, Axl; sig on cover of Rolling Stone magazine **50.00**
Russell, Jane; SP, hayloft scene, 8x10" **40.00**
Schumann-Heink, Ernestine; ISP, portrait, 1930, 12¾x8½", VG .**50.00**
Shaw, Geo Bernard; note on postcard, 1904, EX **500.00**
Sinclair, Upton; SP, blk & wht, 8x10", EX **40.00**
Stewart, Jimmy; SP, 8x10" glossy **25.00**
Taft, William; LS, re becoming Supreme Court Justice, 1-pg **160.00**
Thompson, Lea; SP, 8x10" glossy **18.00**
Tierney, Gene; SP, pinup, 8x10" **50.00**
Tolstoy, Leo; sgn portrait postcard, 1904, EX **900.00**
Truman, Harry; LS, White House stationery, 1-pg, 1948, EX **300.00**
Twain, Mark; sig on postcard, EX **400.00**
Verne, Jules; inscription & sig on portrait postcard, 1903 ....**1,000.00**
Wallace, Lew; SP, cabinet card, Jno F Burrow NY, EX **220.00**
Welch, Racquel; SP, blk & wht, 8x10" **15.00**
Whittier, John Greenleaf; ALS, sympathy, 2-pg, EX **140.00**
Wilson, Woodrow; LS, as President of Princeton, 1903, EX **180.00**
Wright, Orville; sgn photogravure, First Man Flight, 1903 ......**2,800.00**
Young, Brigham; LS, to Governor of NH, 1-pg, 1856, EX **1,300.00**

Automobilia

While some automobilia buffs are primarily concerned with restoring vintage cars, others concentrate on only one area of collecting. For instance, hood ornaments were often quite spectacular. Made of chrome or nickel plate on brass or bronze, they were designed to represent the 'winged maiden' Victory, flying bats, sleek greyhounds, soaring eagles, and a host of other creatures. Today they often bring prices in the $75.00 to $200.00 range. R. Lalique glass ornaments go much higher!

Horns, radios, clocks, gear shift knobs, and key chains with company emblems are other areas of interest. Generally, items pertaining to the classics of the thirties are most in demand. Paper advertising material, manuals, and catalogs in excellent condition are also collectible.

License plate collectors search for the early porcelain-on-cast-iron examples. First year plates (e.g., Massachusetts, 1903; Wisconsin, 1905; Indiana, 1913) are especially valuable. The last of the states to issue regulation plates were South Carolina and Texas in 1917, and Florida in 1918. While many northeastern states had registered hundreds of thousands of vehicles by the 1920s making these plates relatively common, those from the southern and western states of that period are considered rare. Naturally, condition is important. While a pair in mint condition might sell for as much as $100.00 to $125.00, a pair with chipped or otherwise damaged porcelain may sometimes be had for as little as $25.00 to $30.00.

For more information we recommend *American Automobilia: An Illustrated History and Price Guide* by our advisors for this category, Jim and Nancy Schaut. They are listed in the Directory under Arizona. See also Gas Globes and Panels.

Ashtray, Firestone Deluxe Champion, tire form w/glass insert **25.00**
Ashtray, Seiberling Safe-Air, tire form w/glass insert **20.00**
Badge, chauffer's, CO, 1953 ....**15.00**
Badge, chauffer's, NY, 1925 ....**27.50**
Book, Modern Motorcycle Mechanics, c 1945, 9x5", EX **30.00**
Book, 1894-1963 World's Motorcycles, 8¾x6", NM **30.00**
Booklet, Auburn, full color, no date, ca 1930 ....**32.50**
Booklet, Packard, full color, touring cars, 1937 ....**23.50**
Brochure, Buick, 1965, 44-pg **15.00**
Brochure, Harley-Davidson Sales, 1928, 12x9", VG **65.00**
Buckle, AMA Gypsy Tour, lt tarnish, 1932, 1¾x2¼" **150.00**
Catalog, showroom, Buick, 1925, EX **45.00**
Coin, GM Motorama, 1954 ....**10.00**
Diecut, Plymouth countertop promo, 1932, 5x7" **30.00**
Folder, Oldsmobile Holiday Sedans, mc, ca 1955 ....**25.00**
Horn, copper & brass w/rubber bulb, ca 1910, 24" L **65.00**
Key chain, Chrysler, pictorial, 1942, NM **30.00**
Key chain, General Motors Powerama, 1955 ....**10.00**
Kit, tube repair, Cornell, 7¾x2¼" dia, EX **15.00**
License plate, porc, early 1900s, EX, ea, minimum value **50.00**
License plate, porc, early 1900s, M, ea, minimum value **100.00**
License plate attachment, FL, lady in swimsuit & palm, M **100.00**
License plate attachment, Pegasus, pnt metal, 2⅝x5", EX **25.00**
License plate attachment, Phillips 66 Safety Pays, EX **65.00**
Lithograph, Ferrari, red & wht, sgn, 36x45", EX **25.00**
Manual, owner's, Chevrolet, 1936 ....**45.00**
Manual, owner's, Oakland Auto, 1926 ....**65.00**
Manual, owner's, Studebaker, 1940 ....**30.00**
Manual, salesman's, Chevrolet, 1959, M **125.00**
Manual, shop; Chevrolet, 1940 ....**60.00**
Mug, Chevy Truck Sales Award, ceramic w/gold, 1961 ....**25.00**
Mug, 1954 B Vukovich, 1930.840 mph, frosted glass, Indy 500 ....**50.00**
Nodder, St Bernard fuzzy pup, Japan, 6", EX **15.00**
Paperweight, GM Golden Milestones...1908-58, Lucite cube **45.00**
Pencil, mechanical; Indian Motorcycles, silver, 4¾", VG **90.00**
Photo, 1931 ½-ton open cab pickup truck, fr, 13¼x16" **20.00**
Pin, AAA Patrol Service, sm shield, 1950s **10.00**
Pin, AMA Gypsy Tour, 1962, M on card **25.00**
Pin, NDRA Rivertown Reunion Drags, 1988 ....**8.00**

Poster, Austin Healy/MK III Sports Convertible, England, 1960s, 25x35", $110.00.

Promotional car, 1954-55 Corvette, plastic/metal, 6½", EX **130.00**
Promotional car, 1955 Thunderbird, plastic, friction, 7¼", EX **65.00**

Promotional car, 1957 Pontiac, plastic, 8¼", G **35.00**
Promotional car, 1957, Thunderbird, MIB **125.00**
Promotional car, 1959 Corvette, missing 2 hubcaps **150.00**
Promotional car, 1959 Edsel **50.00**
Promotional car, 1959 Ford **50.00**
Promotional car, 1959 Thunderbird, plastic & metal, 8", NM **70.00**
Promotional car, 1962 Thunderbird plastic, friction, 8¼", EX **85.00**
Promotional car, 1965 Mustang Pace Car, wht, 7¼", VG **110.00**
Promotional car, 1966 Mustang, red plastic, 7¼", EX **70.00**
Promotional car, 1977 Corvet, plastic, 7½", NMIB **75.00**
Promotional radio, 1964 Thunderbird form, battery op, 8", EX **95.00**
Radiator flag holder set, 1940s, MIB **18.00**
Radio, for Tucker auto, M in orig factory box **475.00**
Service pin, Sarcony, 25 Years, w/diamond **100.00**
Tag attachment, Studebaker **35.00**
Tin container, Standard Oil of NJ, WWII era, 2-oz, EX **10.00**

Autumn Leaf

In 1933 the Hall China Company designed a line of dinnerware for the Jewel Tea Company, who offered it to their customers as premiums. Although you may hear the ware referred to as 'Jewel Tea,' it was officially named 'Autumn Leaf' in the 1940s. In addition to the dinnerware, frosted Libbey glass tumblers, stemware, and a melmac service with the orange and gold bittersweet pod were available over the years, as were tablecloths, plastic covers for bowls and mixers, and metal items such as cake safes, hot pads, coasters, wastebaskets, and canisters. Even shelf paper and playing cards were made to coordinate. In 1958 the International Silver Company designed silverplated flatware in a pattern called 'Autumn' which was to be used with dishes in the Autumn Leaf pattern. A year later, a line of stainless flatware was introduced. These accessory lines are prized by collectors today.

One of the most fascinating aspects of collecting the Autumn Leaf pattern has been the wonderful discoveries of previously unlisted pieces. Among these items are two different bud-ray lid one-pound butter dishes; most recently a one-pound butter dish in the 'Zephyr' or 'Bingo' style; a miniature set of the 'Casper' salt and pepper shakers; coffee, tea, and sugar canisters; a pair of candlesticks; an experimental condiment jar; and a covered candy dish. All of these china pieces are attributed to the Hall China Company. Other unusual items have turned up in the accessory lines as well and include a Libbey frosted tumbler in a pilsner shape, a wooden serving bowl, and an apron made from the oilcloth (plastic) material that was used in the 1950s tablecloth. These latter items appear to be professionally done, and we can only speculate as to their origin. Collectors believe that the Hall items were sample pieces that were never meant to be distributed.

Hall discontinued the Autumn Leaf line in 1978. At that time the date was added to the backstamp to mark ware still in stock in the Hall warehouse. A special promotion by Jewel saw the reintroduction of basic dinnerware and serving pieces with the 1978 backstamp. These pieces have made their way into many collections. Additionally, in 1979 Jewel released a line of enamel-clad cookware and a Vellux blanket made by Martex which were decorated with the Autumn Leaf pattern. They continued to offer these items for a few years only, then all distribution of Autumn Leaf items was discontinued.

It should be noted that the Hall China Company has produced several limited edition items for the National Autumn Leaf Collectors Club (NALCC): a New York-style teapot (1984); an Edgewater vase (1987, different than the original shape); candlesticks (1988); a Philadelphia-style teapot, creamer and sugar set (1990); a tea-for-two set and a Solo tea set (1991), a donut jug, and a large oval casserole. New items for the NALCC: small ball jug, 1-cup French teapot, and a set of four chocolate mugs. The NALCC has also given their club members special items over the past few years made for them by Hall China: a sugar packet holder, a chamberstick, and an oyster cocktail. Other items are scheduled for production. All of these are plainly marked as having been made for the NALCC and are appropriately dated. A few other pieces have been made by Hall as limited editions for an Ohio company, but these are easily identified: the Airflow teapot and the Norris refrigerator pitcher (neither of which was previously decorated with the Autumn Leaf decal), a square-handled beverage mug, and the new-style Irish mug. A production problem with the square-handled mugs halted their production. The company then issued a regular conic-style mug with a round handle. Additional items available now are a covered onion soup, tall bud vase, china kitchen memo board, and egg drop-style salt and pepper shakers with a mustard pot. They have also issued a deck of playing cards and Libbey tumblers.

Our advisor for this category is Gwynne Harrison; she is listed in the Directory under California.

Baker, oval, Fort Pitt 90.00
Batter bowl, Saf-Hdl 2,500.00
Bean pot, 1-hdl 800.00
Bean pot, 2-hdl, 2¼ -qt 135.00
Bowl, cereal; 6" 10.00
Bowl, coupe soup 12.00
Bowl, cream soup; 2-hdl 30.00
Bowl, fruit; 5½" 6.00
Bowl, metal, enamelware, set of 3 ....450.00
Bowl, mixing; set of 3: 6¼", 7½", 9" 250.00
Bowl, Royal Glas-Bake, set of 4 ....60.00
Bowl, salad 20.00
Bowl, stackette; set of 3: 18-oz, 24-oz, 34-oz, w/lid 75.00
Bowl, vegetable; divided, 10½" 90.00
Bowl, vegetable; oval, w/lid, 10" 50.00
Bowl, vegetable; oval, 10½" 15.00
Bowl, vegetable; rnd, 9" 90.00
Bowl cover set, plastic, 8-pc: 7 assorted covers in pouch 50.00
Bread box, metal 350.00
Butter dish, 1-lb 325.00
Butter dish, ¼ -lb 150.00
Butter dish, ¼ -lb, Square Top 500.00

Butter dish, ¼ -lb, Wings, $1,400.00.

Cake plate, 9½" 12.00
Cake safe, metal, motif on top & sides, 5" 35.00
Cake safe, metal, side decor only, 4½x10½" 30.00
Cake stand, metal base, orig box 175.00
Candy dish 400.00
Canister, metal, rnd, w/coppertone lid, set of 4 ....200.00
Canister, metal, rnd, w/ivory plastic lid 10.00
Canister, metal, rnd, w/matching lid, 6" 15.00
Canister, metal, rnd, w/matching lid, 7" 25.00
Canister, metal, rnd, w/matching lid, 8¼" 35.00
Canister, metal, sq, set of 4: 8½" & 4½" 175.00

Casserole, Royal Glas-Bake, deep, w/clear glass lid 25.00
Casserole, Royal Glas-Bake, shallow, w/clear glass lid 20.00
Casserole, Tootsie-hdl, w/lid 22.00
Casserole/souffle, swirl, 3-pt 15.00
Casserole/souffle, 10-oz 10.00
Casserole/souffle, 2-pt 60.00
Cleanser can, metal, sq, 6", M 700.00
Clock, orig works 400.00
Coaster, metal, 3⅛" 4.00
Coffee dispenser/canister, metal, wall type, 10½x19" dia 175.00
Coffee maker, 5-cup, all china, w/china insert 250.00
Coffee maker, 9-cup, w/metal dripper, 8" 35.00
Coffee percolator, electric, all china 225.00
Coffee percolator/carafe, Douglas, w/warmer base, MIB 250.00
Cookie jar, Tootsie 200.00
Creamer, New Style 8.00
Creamer, Old Style, 4¼" 15.00
Cup & saucer 8.00
Cup & saucer, St Denis 22.00
Custard cup 4.00
Flatware, silverplate, ea 30.00
Flatware, stainless, ea 25.00
Fruit cake tin, metal 10.00
Golden Ray base, to use w/candy dish or cake plate, pr 50.00
Gravy boat 18.00
Hot pad, metal, red or gr felt-like bking, rnd 15.00
Hot pad, oval 12.00
Hurricane lamp, Douglas, w/metal base, pr 400.00
Kitchen utility chair, metal 450.00
Marmalade jar, 3-pc 55.00
Mixer cover, Mary Dunbar, plastic 50.00
Mug, beverage 55.00
Mug, Irish coffee 95.00
Mustard jar, 3½" 55.00
Napkin, ecru muslin 35.00
Pickle dish or gravy liner, oval, 9" 18.00
Picnic thermos, metal 325.00
Pie baker, 9½" 18.00
Pitcher, utility; 2½ -pt, 6" 15.00
Place mat, paper, scalloped 25.00
Place mat, set of 8, M in orig package 325.00
Plate, 10" 12.00
Plate, 6" or 7", ea 4.00
Plate, 8" 8.00
Plate, 9" 10.00
Platter, 11½" 15.00
Platter, 13½" 18.00
Playing cards, regular or Pinochle, dbl deck 160.00
Range set, shakers & covered drippings jar 35.00
Sauce dish, serving; Douglas, Bakelite hdl 150.00
Shakers, Casper, pr 18.00
Shakers, range, hdl, pr 18.00
Sugar bowl, New Style 12.00
Sugar bowl, Old Style, 3½" 18.00
Tablecloth, cotton sailcloth w/gold stripe, 54x54" 100.00
Tablecloth, cotton sailcloth w/gold stripe, 54x72" 110.00
Tablecloth, ecru muslin, 56x81" 300.00
Tablecloth, plastic 150.00
Teakettle, metal enamelware 200.00
Teapot, Aladdin 38.00
Teapot, long spout, 7" 45.00
Teapot, Newport 175.00
Teapot, Newport, dtd 1978 ....150.00
Toaster cover, plastic, fits 2-slice toaster 25.00

Towel, dish; pattern & clock motif **45.00**
Towel, tea; cotton, 16x33" **35.00**
Trash can, metal, red **250.00**
Tray, glass, wood hdl, 19½x11¼" **95.00**
Tray, metal, oval **55.00**
Tray, red w/allover red & yel design, red border **65.00**
Tray, tidbit; 2-tier **75.00**
Tray, tidbit; 3-tier **100.00**
Tumbler, Brockway, 13-oz **30.00**
Tumbler, Brockway, 16-oz **35.00**
Tumbler, Brockway, 9-oz **35.00**
Tumbler, frosted, 14-oz, 5½" **12.00**
Tumbler, frosted, 9-oz, 3¾" **30.00**
Tumbler, gold frost etched, flat, 10-oz **40.00**
Tumbler, gold frost etched, flat, 15-oz **50.00**
Tumbler, gold frost etched, ftd, 10-oz **60.00**
Tumbler, gold frost etched, ftd, 6½ -oz **45.00**
Vase, bud; 6" **175.00**
Warmer base, oval **150.00**
Warmer base, rnd **110.00**
Warmer base, rnd, w/4 orig candles, orig mk box **125.00**

Aviation

Aviation buffs are interested in any phase of flying, from early developments with gliders, balloons, airships and flying machines to more modern innovations. Books, catalogs, photos, patents, lithographs, ad cards, and posters are among the paper ephemera they treasure alongside models of unlikely flying contraptions, propellers and rudders, insignia and equipment from WWI and WWII, and memorabilia from the flights of the Wright Brothers, Lindbergh, Earhart, and the Zeppelins. See also Militaria. Our advisor for this category is John R. Joiner; he is listed in the Directory under Georgia.

Binder, Bureau of Aeronautics Publications, 1946 ....**85.00**
Blanket, Southern Airlines, lt gray, lap sz **40.00**
Blanket, United Air Lines, pre-war logo in gray, lap sz **85.00**
Book, Airplane & Its Engine, Chaffield & Taylor, 1928 ....**30.00**
Book, Boys Book of Famous Fliers, Grayson, 1951, EX **5.00**
Book, Story of Lindbergh Lone Eagle, 1st ed, 1927, EX **40.00**
Bookends, Charles Lindbergh, 1929, EX, pr **175.00**
Bookmark, Wright Bros, brass metal, early 1900s **65.00**
Brochure, Pan-American, mc, 1945, lg **20.00**
Butter pat, American Airlines, china, rare **78.00**
Certificate, Ambassador's Club, TWA, 1951 ....**22.00**
Coffee mug, Northrup B-2 ....**22.00**
Cuff links, Western Airlines, The Only Way To Fly **30.00**
Cup, Air Atlanta, china, platinum trim **7.00**
Cup, demitasse; Eastern Airlines, platinum trim **4.50**
Cup & saucer, Northwest Royal Imperial **36.00**
Flight bag, Pan-American **9.00**
Folio, TWA picture series, 1944, set of 12 prints **48.00**
Key chain, British Airways **8.00**
Magazine, Flying Aces, Von Hindenburg Zeppelin cover, 1936 ...**75.00**
Model, Am Airlines SST by Boeing, cast resin, 37", EX **660.00**
Model, BOAC Clipper Flying Boat, cast metal, 20½", EX **3,200.00**
Model, Boeing C-97 Strato Freighter, cast metal, 24½", EX **635.00**
Model, Braniff Internat'l Ariways DC-7, aluminum, 30", NM **880.00**
Model, Eastern Airlines Prop-Jet Electra, aluminum, 29", EX **935.00**
Model, Ozark Airlines DC-9, aluminum, 25", EX **635.00**
Model, Pan-American Airways Sikorski S38, cast metal, 12", NM .**300.00**
Model, T29 Navigation Trainer, cast medal, tray base, 6½", EX ...**145.00**
Napkin, Air Atlanta, lt bl, 21x16" **4.50**

Paperweight, United Airlines, sgn WA Patterson, bronze **40.00**
Pennant, Welcome Home Captain Charles A Lindbergh...1927 ..**95.00**
Photo, Am single-engine scout planes on field, 1940s, 4½x3" **15.00**
Pin, lapel; TWA **10.00**
Place mat, Pan-American, paper, M **5.00**
Plate, Debonair, United Airlines, 6¼", pr **28.00**
Plate, Delta, china, platinum trim, 8" **9.00**
Service pin, Capital Airlines **50.00**
Service pin, Pan-American **50.00**
Shakers, Eastern Airlines, glass w/metal top, pr **7.00**
Shakers, United Airlines, pr, +cr/sug **45.00**
Swizzle stick, Pan-American **1.00**
Swizzle stick, TWA 50th Anniversary, 1976 ....**3.00**
Token, Apollo 11, bronze, Metallic Art Co, 2½", MIB **25.00**
Watch fob, Eddie Rickenbacker, hat in ring, WWI **35.00**
Watch fob, Spirit of St Louis & airship, early 1900s **65.00**
Wings, Delta, plastic pin-bk, child's **1.00**
Wings, Eastern Airlines, gold plastic, child's **1.25**

Avon

The California Perfume Company, the parent of the Avon Co., was founded in 1886. Although an 'Avon' line was introduced by the company in the mid-twenties, not until 1939 did it become known as Avon Products, Inc. Collectible Avon items include not only figural bottles and jars but jewelry, awards, product samples, magazine ads, and catalogs as well. For more information concerning the Avon Collectors Club, see the Clubs, Newsletters, and Catalogs section of the Directory. See also California Perfume Company.

For more information, we recommend *Hastin's Avon Collector's Price Guide, 14th Edition,* by Bud Hastins.

Decanter, Calling for Men, gold paint on clear glass with black plastic parts, 1969, 8½", M, $12.00.

ALBEE 1961 Woman of Achievement Award, W Germany **300.00**
Cape Cod wine goblet, 1975 ....**5.00**
Country Cupboard Talc, peach or strawberry **2.00**
Fostoria Salt Cellar, w/silver spoon, 1969 ....**10.00**
George & Martha Washington Candle Holders, 1975, pr **10.00**
Little Folks Gift Box, 4 perfumes, 1931 ....**250.00**
Moonwind pin/scarf holder, 1973 ....**10.00**
Perfume Jewelry a la Glace, Baby Grand/etc, 6 scents, 1971, MIB ..**10.00**
Tenderness Plate, Spain, 1974, 9" dia **10.00**
Victoriana pitcher & bowl, gr, 1971 ....**15.00**

Avon Works

In 1902 a firm based in Wheeling, West Virginia, absorbed several small local potteries; the Vance Avon Faience Co. of Tiltonville, Ohio, was one of them. They continued in operation at Tiltonville until 1905, when Avon moved to the Wheeling location. The production of artware was discontinued in an effort to produce a more commercially profitable semiporcelain ware; but by 1907 even that proved to be unsuccessful, and the Wheeling department closed in 1907. For more information on the earlier pottery, see Vance Avon.

Pitcher, piped-on leaves on turq irid, dtd 1906, 6", EX 260.00
Tankard, decal portrait on brn, mk, +6 portrait mugs 500.00
Vase, incised stylized floral, bl/gr on dk bl gloss, mk, 5" 500.00
Vase, landscape, glossy, 6" 400.00
Vase, 3-branch floral, squeezebag decor, Rhead, #126, 5x7" 1,200.00

Baccarat

The Baccarat Glass company was founded in 1765 near Luneville, France, and continues to this day to produce quality crystal tableware, vases, perfume bottles, and figurines. The firm became famous for the high-quality millefiori and caned paperweights produced there from 1845 until about 1860. Examples of these range from $300.00 to as much as several thousand. Since 1953 they have resumed the production of paperweights on a limited edition basis. Our advisors for this category are Randall Monsen and Rod Baer; their address is listed in the Directory under Virginia. See also Paperweights.

Wash bowl and pitcher, Rose Tiente Swirl, 13", 5½x15", $1,100.00.

Bottle, Guerlain Coque d'Or, bl crystal 250.00
Bottle, scent; Ybry, gr w/enameled metal cap 600.00
Box, cameo floral/scrolls, pk on clear, 5¼" dia 400.00
Fairy lamp, bl, Pinwheel, 5x5¾", pr 300.00
Fairy lamp, Rose Tiente Pinwheel, shouldered top, plate base 265.00
Fairy lamp, Rose Tiente Sunburst, mk, 4½x5½" 245.00
Flower holder, sapphire bl, Swirl, bridge shape, 5x12x2" 195.00
Humidor, gr texture w/gilt & red floral & scrolls, 5" 400.00
Punch bowl, pk to yel w/swirled floral, undulating rim, 15" 850.00
Tumbler, Rose Tiente Sunburst, mk, 4x2⅞" 55.00
Vase, cameo cyclamen, pk on acid-etch clear, ruffled, 5" 325.00
Vase, cameo opal leaves, gold coiled snake on stick neck, 8" .. 1,500.00
Vase, cameo roses/gilt, wine on opal, bulbous mouth, 12" 575.00

Badges

The breast badge came into general usage in this country about 1840. Since most are not marked and styles have changed very little to the present day, they are often difficult to date. The most reliable clue is the pin and catch. One of the earliest types, used primarily before the turn of the century, involved a 't-pin' and a 'shell' catch. In a second style, the pin was hinged with a small square of sheet metal, and the clasp was cylindrical. From the late 1800s until about 1940, the pin and clasp were made from one continuous piece of thin metal wire. The same type, with the addition of a flat back plate, was used a little later. There are exceptions to these findings, and other types of clasps were also used. Hallmarks and inscriptions may also help pinpoint an approximate age.

Badges have been made from a variety of materials, usually brass or nickel silver; but even solid silver and gold were used for special orders. They are found in many basic shapes and variations — stars with five to seven points, shields, disks, ovals, and octagonals being most often encountered. Of prime importance to collectors, however, is that the title and/or location appear on the badge. Those with designations of positions no longer existing (City Constable, for example) and names of early western states and towns are most valuable.

Badges are among the most commonly-reproduced (and faked) types of antiques on the market. At any flea market, ten fakes can be found for every authentic example. Genuine law badges start at $30.00 to $40.00 for recent examples (1950-1970); earlier pieces (1910-1930) usually bring $50.00 to $90.00. Pre-1900 badges often sell for more than $100.00. Authentic gold badges are usually priced at a minimum of scrap value (karat, weight, spot price for gold); fine gold badges from before 1900 can sell for $400.00 to $800.00, and a few will bring even more. A fire badge is usually valued at about half the price of a law badge from the same circa and material. Our advisor for this category is Gene Matzke; he is listed in the Directory under Wisconsin.

Board of Public Safety, 14k yellow gold and enamel, dates 1902 and 1903, EX, $250.00; AS1ST. Engineer F.F.D., 14k yellow gold shield form with enameled pumper, marked Cg BC, EX, $300.00.

ACL RR Police Patrolman, NP shield, 1⅜x2" 100.00
Bristol CT Police, cut-out star, hallmk Noble & Westbrook 100.00
Chauffer, KS, 1943 .... 22.50
Chauffer, MO, 1924, no pin 32.50
Newsboy, Bridgeport CT, 1914 .... 40.00
Old Orchard Police, hallmk Iver Johnson 75.00
Portland City Police, SP, rare 150.00
SAL Ry Police, nickel w/emb blk enamel 75.00
Special Deputy Sheriff Rennselear NY, brass shield 35.00
Special KCC Constable, brass shield, ca 1940s, EX 40.00
Special Police, Monsanto IL 27.50
Sun Oil Co Guard, brass 40.00
US Inspector, Steam Vessels #132, SP, 1¾" 75.00

WWI shipbuilding, bronze 45.00

Banks

This year the continuing impact of auctions shows in the listings. Again, condition, condition, condition is what is driving the market. In addition, some banks with outstanding provenances were available, and they brought prices that reflect their individual value to a specific collector but distort the real market value of similar banks. The spread between a bank in good condition and an excellent or original condition example continues to widen. It is imperative that you realize the importance of paint and the completeness of a bank. Also some banks have a wide margin of value based on color variations. It becomes more and more important that you attend as many shows and auctions as possible. Direct contact with collectors and knowledgeable dealers is the only way you can get a feel for prices and the desirability of banks, both mechanical and still. Banks continue to hold their value. However, it is becoming extremely important for collectors to understand the market.

Let's take a look at the price variations possible on an Uncle Sam mechanical bank. If you find one with considerable paint missing but with some good color showing, the price would be around $1,000.00. If it has repairs or restoration, the value would drop to something like $800.00 or less. If you had another example, and it had two thirds of its original paint and no repairs, it would be priced around $1,800.00. One with minor nicks and 90% of the original paint could go as high as $3,500.00. Or if you find one that is in near-original paint and has no repairs, $5,000.00 would not be out of line. This should help you see what causes price variations. After considering all of these factors, remember the final price is always determined by what a willing buyer and seller agree on for a specific bank.

The category of mechanical banks is unique. Along with cast-iron bell toys, they are among the most outstanding products of the Industrial Revolution and are recognized as some of the most successful of the mass-produced products of the 19th century. The earliest mechanicals were made of wood or lead; but when John Hall introduced Hall's Excelsior, a cast-iron mechanical bank, it was an immediate success. J. & E. Stevens produced the bank for Hall and soon began to make their own designs. Several companies followed suit, most of which were already in the hardware business. They used newly developed iron-molding techniques to produce these novelty savings devices for the emerging toy market. Mechanical banks reflect the social and political attitudes of the times, racial prejudices, the excitement of the circus, and humorous everyday events. Their designers made the most of simple mechanics to produce banks with captivating actions that served not only to amuse but to promote the concept of thrift to the children. The quality of detail in the castings are truly remarkable. The most collectible examples were made during the period of 1870 to 1900; however, they continued to be made until the early days of World War II. J. & E. Stevens, Shepard Hardware, and Kyser and Rex are some of the more well-known manufacturers; most made still banks as well.

Still banks are widely collected, and you can literally choose from thousands of banks. No one knows exactly how many different banks were made, but at least three thousand have been identified in the various books published on the subject. Cast-iron examples still dominate the market, but the lead banks from Europe are growing in value. Tin and early pottery banks are drawing more interest as well. American pottery banks which were primarily collected by Americana collectors are becoming more important in the still bank field. This market has not been as volatile as the mechanical banks, but the number of collectors is growing. The auction market on still banks is not as extensive as with the mechanicals, but some nice examples do turn up. Collectors and dealers are still the best source.

The popularity of old mechanicals has created a market for reproductions and fakes. Reproductions may have minor value as such, but not as true collectibles. A few of the fakes have attained collectible status but are still not regarded as true mechanical banks.

As both value and interest continue on the increase, it becomes even more important to educate one's self to the fullest extent possible. We recommend these books for your library: *The Dictionary of Still Banks* by Long and Pitman, *The Penny Bank Book* by Moore, and *The Bank Book* by Norman. If you are primarily interested in mechanicals, *Penny Lane*, a book by Davidson, is considered the most complete reference available. It contains a cross-reference listing of numbers from all other publications on mechanical banks.

In the listings that follow, banks are identified by L for Long, G for Griffith, M for Moore, N for Norman, D for Davidson, and W for Whiting. Our advisor is Diane Patalano; she is listed in the Directory under New Jersey.

Key:
CI — cast iron   NPCI — nickel-plated cast iron
EPCI — electroplated cast iron

Advertising

Acey Chicken, Arctic Circle Drive-In, compo, 6", NM 85.00
Admiral Appliance, Admiral figure 20.00
Alka Seltzer, Speedy, molded vinyl, 1960s, 5½", NM 250.00
Alpo, Garfield figural 25.00
Atlantic Premium Gas, gas pump, tin, 5", NM 45.00
Boker Coffee, can shape, tin, 1970s, NM.....................................15.00
Boscul Coffee, tin, 2¼ x 2½" dia, EX 20.00
Calumet Baking Powder, tin, child atop, pat 1924, EX 300.00
Campbell's Soups, can shape, tin, 4½", EX 9.50
Cap'n Crunch Cereal, plastic 25.00
Count Chocula, vinyl 40.00
Esso Tiger, gr plastic, bust form, M 22.50

Esso, Watch Your Savings Grow, block form, 1920s, 5x5", $125.00.

Eveready Batteries, blk cat, hard plastic, 1981, NM 22.00
Frisch's Big Boy, Big Boy figural, vinyl, 1973 ....15.00
General Electric refrigerator, CI, EX 42.50
Hush Puppy, dog figural, plastic 20.00
Icee Bear, M in package 45.00
Little Sprout, vinyl 6.00
Old Black Joe Speckled Butter Beans, can form, M 6.00
Orange Bird, FL, M 35.00
Oscar Mayer Weinermobile, 9½" 45.00
Patton's Paint, tin litho pail, oval, 2" 85.00
Pepto Bismol, bug form 65.00
Richmond Ice Cream, freezer, M-12370, pnt CI, 4¼", EX 250.00

Rival Dog Food, tin can form, EX **45.00**
Shell, bl & creme w/orange shell, pnt scuffs, 3½", VG **160.00**
Sunoco, metal w/bl & yel pnt, 4x2", NM **120.00**
Taco Bell, bus figural, M **15.00**

Mechanical

Always Did 'Spise a Mule, boy on bench, pnt CI, yel base, EX ..**1,725.00**
Artillery Bank, Stevens, CI, mc pnt, Union variation, 6", VG/EX ..**3,200.00**
Baby Elephant, N-1140A, pnt CI, unlocks at 10 o'clock, NM ..**8,000.00**
Bear Beating Drum, pnt lead & tin, 3¾", EX **650.00**
Bear w/Honey Pot, M-717, CI, grainy pnt traces, 6½" **60.00**
Billy Bounce, M-15, pnt CI, 4¾", EX **825.00**
Billy Goat Bank, N-1240B, pnt CI, missing trap, EX **500.00**
Boy & Bulldog, N-1340A, CI, purple japanning traces, 5¼" **250.00**
Boy on Trapeze, N-1350A, mc pnt, rpr leg, 9½", G **2,000.00**
Bulldog, N-1430A, glass eyes, J&E Stevens, 7¾", G **880.00**
Butting Goat, N-1580C, pnt CI, wht goat, NM **2,700.00**
Butting Ram, N-1590, pnt CI, NM **11,000.00**
Cabin, N-1610A, CI, mc pnt, lt wear, 3¾", VG **600.00**
Cabin, N-1610B, CI, mc pnt, lt wear, 4¼", VG **635.00**
Cat & Mouse, N-1700A, cat balancing, CI, worn pnt, 11½", VG ..**1,425.00**
Chief Big Moon, N-1740B, CI, worn mc pnt, 10⅛", VG ......:....**1,925.00**
Confectionery, N-1970A, CI, EX mc pnt, rpl trap, 7¾" **1,550.00**
Creedmore, N-2000B, pnt CI, 10¼", EX **750.00**
Crescent Cash Register, N-2010, pnt CI, EX **475.00**
Darktown Battery, N-2080A, pnt CI, EX **3,000.00**

Dentist, D-152, painted cast iron, J.&E. Stevens, 1880-90, 9½", EX+, $8,500.00.

Dome Bank, M-1182, CI, gold & silver pnt, 4¾", VG **60.00**
Eagle & Eaglets, N-2230B, CI, worn mc pnt, rpl eyes, 6" **275.00**
Eagle & Eaglets, N-2230B, pnt CI, EX **1,300.00**
Elephant, N-2280A, man pops out, pnt CI, EX **475.00**
Elephant & 3 Clowns, N-2250B, pnt CI, NM **5,000.00**
Elephant Pull Tail, N-2300A, pnt CI, EX **1,025.00**
Frog on Rnd Base, N-2530, pnt CI, hairline crack **550.00**
Frog on Rock, N-2520, pnt CI, NM **1,000.00**
Hall's Excelsior, N-2710A, CI, mc pnt, minor wear, rprs, 5¼" ...**275.00**
Hall's Liliput, N-2740C, CI, mc pnt, 4¼", EX **675.00**
Hoop-La Bank, N-2870, pnt CI, NM **6,100.00**
Indian & Bear, N-2980A, old mc pnt, wht bear, 10½" L, VG .**1,320.00**
Joe Socko, N-3050, pnt tin, NMIB **650.00**
Jolly 'N,' N-3270, pnt aluminum, NM **150.00**
Jolly 'N,' N-3370C, CI, bl coat, yel tie, worn, VG **1,000.00**
Jolly 'N,' N-3370, pnt CI, NM **2,900.00**
Jonah & the Whale, N-3490, CI, worn mc pnt, 10¼", G **1,000.00**
Kitty, M-349, CI, mc pnt, lt wear, 4⅞" L **55.00**

Lion Hunter, N-3660, pnt CI, hairline crack, EX **4,100.00**
Magic Bank, N-2730A, CI, worn mc pnt, 5¼", G **578.00**
Mule Entering Barn, N-4030B, pnt CI, VG **1,000.00**
Musical Bank, M-797, pnt CI, 5¾", EX **5,000.00**
Organ Bank, cat & dog, N-4320, pnt CI, NM **2,250.00**
Owl, N-4380B, turns head, pnt CI, NM **4,000.00**
Owl, N-4380D, CI, orig gray & wht pnt, glass eyes, 7¼", VG **500.00**
Pig in Highchair, N-4570, pnt CI, EX **950.00**
Popeye Knockout, N-4620, tin, pitting, 4½" **115.00**
Presto Bank, N-4650, pnt CI, EX **325.00**
Punch & Judy, N-4740A, CI, worn mc pnt, rpl screw, 7⅜", G- ..**440.00**
Rabbit, Standing; N-4810A, CI, japanning traces, 5¾" **470.00**
Rabbit in Cabbage, N-4790, CI, worn mc pnt, 4¼", VG **700.00**
Sharecropper, M-173, CI, worn mc pnt, 5½" **77.50**
Stump Speaker, N-5370B, CI, orig mc pnt, 10", EX- **1,980.00**
Tammany, N-5420A, CI, mc pnt, 5¾", VG **425.00**
Teddy & Bear, N-5460A, CI, orig mc pnt, 9¼", G **1,200.00**
Trick Dog, N-5630, pnt CI, gr base, EX **1,400.00**
Trick Dog, N-5630A, pnt CI, EX **1,650.00**
Uncle Sam, N-5740, CI, rpr, 11¼", VG **500.00**
Uncle Sam, N-5740, CI, orig mc pnt, lt wear, 11½", EX **1,760.00**
Uncle Tom, N-5760b, pnt CI, EX **675.00**
William Tell, N-5940, CI, worn orig pnt, 10½", VG+ **935.00**
Zoo, N-6070, CI, mc pnt, lt wear, loose shutters, 4¼" **635.00**

Registering

Capitol, 10¢ registering, orig pnt **60.00**
Circus, 10¢ registering, M **20.00**
Imperial 3-coin registering, CI & steel, worn pnt, 4½" **380.00**
Little Orphan Annie, 10¢ registering, 1936, EX **90.00**
NY World's Fair Daily, 10¢ registering, M **30.00**
Pail, M-912, 1¢ registering, pnt CI, 2¾", EX **130.00**
Pail, M-912 variant, 1¢ registering, pnt CI, 2¾", EX **110.00**
Popeye, Daily Dime w/Savings Tally, litho tin, 2½", VG/EX **50.00**
Popeye, Daily Quarter, USA Kalon, 5x3½", NM+ **850.00**
Prince Valiant, 10¢ registering, c KFS, 1959, M **110.00**
Prudential, CI, 10¢ registering, orig label, 7⅜", NM **400.00**
Prudential, pnt CI, 25¢ registering, orig label, 7⅜", NM **425.00**
Prudential, pnt CI, 5¢/10¢ registering, 7⅜", EX **275.00**
Save for Victory, 10¢ registering, pnt tin & wood, 4¾", EX **200.00**
Snow White & 7 Dwarfs, 10¢ registering, WDE, 1938, EX **160.00**
Stafford, CI & steel, 5½", EX **80.00**
Trunk, M-947 variant, pnt CI, 10¢ registering, 3¾", EX **90.00**
1964 World's Fair, 10¢ registering, orig pnt **80.00**

Still

Alphabet Block, M-1604, pnt CI, 3⅞", EX **2,200.00**
Arabian Safe, M-882, CI, worn gold pnt, casting hole, 4½" **75.00**
Armoured Car, M-1424, pnt CI, turret rpr, 3¾", EX **1,400.00**
Aunt Jemima, M-169, CI, worn mc pnt, 6" **150.00**
Bailey's Centennial Money Bank, M-807, pnt CI, 4½", EX **110.00**
Baseball on 3 Bats, M-1608 variant, pnt CI, 5⅜", EX+ **1,200.00**
Battleship Oregon, M-1450, CI w/brn japanning & gold, 5", EX ..**275.00**
Bear, M-694, CI, worn blk pnt, 4" L, G **100.00**
Bear w/Honey Pot, M-717, pnt CI, 6½", EX **120.00**
Beauty Horse, M-542, CI, worn blk & gold pnt, 5", VG **85.00**
Begging Bear, M-715, CI, gold & silver traces, 5⅜" **60.00**
Black Boy, M-84, 2-faced, CI, worn gold & blk pnt, 3", G **100.00**
Boxer Dog, M-357, CI, EX gold pnt, 4⅜" **75.00**
Buffalo, M-560, CI, worn brn rpt, 4⅜" L **75.00**
Bulldog, N-1450, standing, pnt CI, EX **675.00**
Bullet Head, M-1400, pnt steel, 4½", NM **70.00**

Bungalow, M-999, pnt CI & steel, 3¾", EX-	325.00
Buster Brown & Tige, M-241, CI, dull gold rpt, 5¼"	78.00
Buster Brown & Tige, M-241, pnt CI, 5½", EX	200.00
Camel, Kneeling; M-2270, pnt CI, 2½", EX-	625.00
Camel, M-767, CI, worn mc pnt, rpr leg, 7¼"	45.00
Camel, Oriental; M-769, pnt CI, 3¾", EX	550.00
Cash Register, M-925, CI, worn red & gold pnt, 3¾"	72.50
Castle, M-954, pnt CI, 3", EX	525.00
Cat on Tub, M-358, CI, pnt traces, 4⅛"	120.00
Cat w/Bow, M-364, pnt CI, 4⅜", EX	275.00
Chandler's Bank, N-1720, pnt CI & steel, EX	975.00
Christmas Roast, M-613, pnt CI, 3¼", EX	175.00
Church Towers, M-956 variant, pnt CI, 6¾"	650.00
Clown, M-211, CI, worn pnt, minor rust, 6¼"	75.00
Clown, M-211, pnt CI, 6¼", EX	150.00
Cockatoo, M-656, pnt wht metal, 5", EX	500.00
Colonial House, M-993, pnt CI, 3", EX	155.00
Columbia, M-1703, pnt CI, 8¾", EX	1,250.00
Columbian Magic Savings, N-1960B, pnt CI, EX	300.00
Crosley Radio, M-820, CI & tin, gr pnt, 4¼", VG	300.00
Crown, M-1227, CI, worn yel & red pnt, rpl screw, 3"	105.00
Crown, M-1316, worn brn japanning, 3½"	77.50
Cupola Bank, M-1146, pnt CI, 4⅛", EX	160.00
Cupola Bank, M-1147, CI, worn pnt, rpl screw, 3⅜"	105.00
Daffy Duck at Tree Trunk, M-280, pnt wht metal, 4¼", NM	110.00
Domed Bank, M-1182, CI, silver & gold pnt, lt wear, 4¾"	75.00
Domed Bank, M-1183, CI, old silver rpt w/gold & blk, 5"	30.00
Donkey, M-499, CI, worn gold pnt, 4⅝"	95.00
Doughboy, M-48, pnt CI, 7", EX	875.00
Duck, M-624 variant, pnt wht metal, 5⅛", EX	110.00
Dutch Girl, M-16, pnt CI, 6½", EX	750.00
Elephant, M-455, swivel trunk, pnt CI, wear & rust, 3⅝"	60.00
Elephant, M-459, CI, worn gold pnt, 4" L	75.00
Elephant on Tub, M-484, pnt CI, 5⅜", EX	215.00
Elephant on Wheels, M-446, CI, worn gold & red pnt, 4¼"	120.00
Elephant w/Blanket, M-487, pnt CI, 3⅛", EX	650.00
Elephant w/Blanket, N-2340, 3 stars, pnt CI, NM	600.00
Elephant w/Howdah, M-457, pnt CI, 2½", EX	100.00
Elephant w/Howdah, M-474, CI, gold pnt, 4⅞", G	40.00
Elephant w/Howdah, M-476, CI, EX gold & red pnt, 4⅞"	150.00
Elmer Fudd at Tree Trunk, M-308, pnt wht metal, 5½", NM	125.00
Fido, M-417, CI, EX mc pnt, 5"	65.00
Fido on Pillow, M-443, CI, mc pnt, minor wear, 5¼"	235.00
General Butler, M-14, CI, worn pnt, 6½"	2,700.00
General Sheridan, M-50, pnt CI, 6", EX	425.00
Give Me a Penny, M-167, pnt CI, 5⅝", EX	275.00
Goose, M-615, CI, gold pnt w/touch up, rpl screw, 5"	110.00
Goose, M-615, CI, very worn gold over silver traces, 5"	150.00
Gorilla, M-744, pnt wht metal, 4¼", NM	390.00
Graf Zeppelin, M-1428, CI, EX silver pnt, 6¾"	250.00
Hansel & Gretel, M-1016, pnt tin, 2¼", EX	80.00
Hen on Nest, M-546, pnt CI, slot on underside, 3", VG+	1,100.00
High Rise, M-1220, pnt CI, 3¼", EX	155.00
Home Savings, M-1201, pnt CI, 10½", EX	1,100.00
Home Savings, M-1237, pnt CI, 5¾", EX	475.00
Honey Bear, M-696, pnt CI, 2½", VG+	850.00
Horse, M-533, CI, worn blk pnt, 4⅛"	60.00
Horse, Prancing; M-517, CI, very worn gold, 4¼"	72.50
Horse, Prancing; M-520, NPCI, 7¼", EX	110.00
Horse, Saddle; M-523, pnt CI, 2¾", EX	170.00
Horse on Tub, M-409, CI, worn mc pnt, rpl screw, 5½"	130.00
Horse on Tub, M-510, pnt CI, 4¼", EX	200.00
Horse on Wheels, M-512, CI, worn gold & silver pnt, 5"	150.00
House w/Bay Window, M-1213, pnt CI, 4⅞", EX	2,000.00
Independence Hall, M-1242, CI, worn pnt, 10", VG	525.00
Independence Hall Tower, M-1202, CI, bronze pnt, 9½", EX	580.00
Iron Master's House, M-1027, pnt CI, 4¼", NM	1,700.00
Japanese Safe, M-883, CI, old polished surface, 5⅜"	85.00
Junior Safe Deposit, M-897, CI, blk w/yel traces, 4⅝"	50.00
King Midas, M-13, CI, no pnt, 4½"	350.00
King Midas, M-13, pnt CI, 4½", EX	2,400.00
Liberty Bell, M-809, CI, worn bronze pnt, 3⅜"	30.00
Lion, M-742, CI, gold pnt, 3½"	60.00
Lion, M-754, CI, worn gold pnt w/varnish, 6½"	75.00
Lion, M-755, tail right, pnt CI, 4", VG	40.00
Lion, M-759, CI, worn gold pnt, 4½"	160.00
Lion on Tub, M-746, CI, worn mc pnt, sm casting hole, 5½"	125.00
Lion on Tub, M-747, CI, worn gold pnt, 4¼"	127.50
Main Street, M-1469, CI, worn gold pnt, rpl wheels, 6⅝"	130.00
Mammy w/Hands on Hips, M-176, pnt CI, 5¼", EX	210.00
Mammy w/Spoon, M-168, pnt CI, 5⅞", EX	275.00
Man in Fez, M-273 variant, pnt tin, 2¼", NM	200.00
Man w/Cane at Ball, pnt lead & tin, 3⅛", NM	140.00
Marietta Silo, M-1246, pnt CI, 5½", EX	750.00
Middy Bank, M-36, CI, worn blk pnt, clapper missing, 5⅛"	105.00
Moody & Sankey, M-1288, pnt CI, 5", EX	2,100.00
Mutt & Jeff, M-157, pnt CI, 4¼", EX	130.00
Newfoundland Dog, M-440, CI, pnt traces, 5¼"	85.00
North Pole Freezer, M-1373, CI, worn pnt, 4¼", VG	375.00
Old South Church, pnt lead, 9", VG/EX	700.00
Owl, M-598, Be Wise Save Money, CI, no pnt, 5"	60.00
Owl, N-4360A, slot in book, pnt CI, EX	1,100.00
Owl, N-4370, slot in head, pnt CI, EX	550.00
Parlor Stove, M-1357, CI, old pnt traces, 7"	165.00
Parlor Stove, M-1357, pnt CI, 6⅞", NM	325.00
Penny Trust Co, M-877, milk glass & tin, 2⅞", NM	125.00
Polar Bear, M-716, CI, worn gr rpt, 5¼", G	66.00
Policeman, M-182, pnt CI, 5½", NM	600.00
Pup, M-414, CI, worn red & blk pnt, lt rust, 3⅞"	45.00
Rabbit, M-574, CI, EX gold & red pnt, rpl screw, 6½"	188.00
Rabbit Begging, M-455, CI, worn gold pnt, 5"	200.00
Rabbit Begging, M-566, CI, worn gold pnt, 5½", G	66.00
Rabbit in Cabbage, N-4790A, pnt CI, EX	975.00
Radio Bank, M-829, CI & tin, gr pnt, 3", NM	260.00
Retriever, M-440, CI, gold traces, 5¼"	50.00
Roly Poly Monkey, M-1277, pnt tin, 6", NM	750.00
Roof Bank, M-1122, CI, worn pnt, 5¼"	275.00
Rooster, M-547, CI, worn blk pnt w/red & silver, rpr, 4¾"	100.00
Rooster, M-548, CI, gold pnt w/red trim, 4⅞", EX	300.00
Rooster, M-548, CI, red & gold pnt, lt wear, 5¾"	45.00
Round Duck, M-619, CI, EX mc pnt, 4"	226.00
Royal Safe Deposit, CI, blk & gold rpt, orig decoupage, 6"	75.00
Santa, M-45, NPCI, removable tree, 7¼"	850.00
Santa at Chimney, M-104, pnt lead, 3¾", EX	425.00
Santa w/Tree, M-61, pnt CI, 5⅞", EX	850.00
Security Safe Deposit, CI, worn pnt, brass dial, 4½"	100.00
Sharecropper, M-173, pnt CI, 5½", EX	150.00
Six-Sided Building, M-1007, pnt CI, 2⅜", EX	675.00
Spitz, M-409, pnt CI, 4¼", EX	350.00
St Bernard w/Pack, M-439, CI, pnt traces, lt rust, 5½" L	60.00
Stag, M-737, CI, 9¼", EX	125.00
State Bank, M-1078, pnt CI, 8", EX	550.00
State Bank, M-1080, old gold rpt, 5¾"	200.00
Statue of Liberty, M-1165, pnt CI, 6⅜", EX	170.00
Stop Sign, M-1479, pnt CI, 4½", EX	300.00
Stop Sign, M-1481, pnt CI, 5⅝", EX	625.00
Street Car, M-1468, CI, worn red & gold pnt, rpl pin, 4½"	175.00
Tank Bank, M-1435, CI, worn gold pnt, sm casting hole, 5¾"	95.00

Teddy Bear, M-698, CI, worn gold pnt, 3⅞" L 105.00
Time Is Money, M-1555, pnt CI & tin, 4⅞", NM 1,200.00
Trolley, M-1472, pnt CI, rpl turnpin, 3¾", VG 200.00
Trolley Car, M-1474, pnt CI, 2¾", EX 450.00
Two Kids, M-594, pnt CI, 4½", EX 1,275.00
Uncle Sam Bank, M-1383, pnt tin, 3¼", NM 45.00
United Bank, M-1100, pnt CI, 2¾", EX 300.00
US Mail, M-842, CI, gr & gold pnt, rpl nut, 3¾", G 65.00
US Tank Bank, M-1438, CI, worn gold pnt, 4" L 70.00
US Tank Bank 1918, M-1437, pnt CI, 2⅜", EX 175.00
US Treasury, M-1053, NPCI & steel, 3¼", EX 325.00
Whale, N-4930D, wht metal, red pnt, NM 550.00
Wise Pig, M-609, CI, pk & wht, lt wear, 6⅝" 75.00
World Time Bank, M-1539, CI & paper, 4⅛", EX 275.00

Barber Shop Collectibles

Even for the stranger in town, the local barber shop was easy to find, its location vividly marked with the traditional red and white striped barber pole that for centuries identified such establishments. As far back as the 12th century, the barber has had a place in recorded history. At one time he not only groomed the beards and cut the hair of his gentlemen clients but was known as the 'blood-letter' as well, hence the red stripe for blood and the white for the bandages. Many early barbers even pulled teeth! Later, laws were enacted that divided the practices of barbering and surgery.

The Victorian barber shop reflected the charm of that era with fancy barber chairs upholstered in rich wine-colored velvet; rows of bottles made from colored art glass held hair tonics and shaving lotion. Backbars of richly carved oak with beveled mirrors lined the wall behind the barber's station. During the late 19th century, the barber pole with a blue stripe added to the standard red and white as a patriotic gesture came into vogue.

Today the barber shop has all but disappeared from the American scene, replaced by modern unisex salons. Collectors search for the barber poles, the fancy chairs, and the tonic bottles of an era gone but not forgotten. See also Bottles; Razors; Shaving Mugs.

Blade bank, pole form, blk & red stripes, mk Blades, EX 32.00
Catalog, Guarantee Barbers' Supply, Phila, 1916, 184-pg, EX 350.00
Catalog, Maher & Grosh, razors, strops, etc, 1899, 4x6½" 85.00
Chair, child's, car shape, rstr 2,000.00
Chair, child's, fire engine w/ladders, rstr 2,000.00

Chair, Koken, carved oak, restored red leather, chrome trim, EX, $1,200.00.

Chair, tufted leather, rnd, Koken, full rstr, M 1,500.00
Chair, walnut, cvd lion's head, 1880, rstr 1,000.00
Jar, Burma Shave, bl glass, unused contents 8.00
Jar, Santek Cellucotton neck strips, aluminum lid, EX 165.00
Mug rack, oak, holds 10, 7x28x8½" 200.00
Mug rack, oak, 20-drw, holds 108 mugs, 103x60x10", EX 650.00
Paperweight, glass, Koken Barbers' Supply..., rectangular 100.00
Photo, 1920s shop interior scene, 5x7", EX 25.00
Pole, cvd wood, orig pnt, early, 72" 650.00
Pole, ldgl/illuminated, wall mt, porc-on-iron brackets, 32" 350.00
Pole, leaded glass, Victorian, Koken, 48" 1,200.00
Pole, porc & ldgl, Koken, 48", NM 1,200.00
Pole, trn wood, ball ea end, worn/weathered pnt, 72" 935.00
Pole, wood, red & wht strips w/finials ea end, 24", EX 85.00
Pole, yel & gr porc, revolves, Koch, NM 475.00
Sharpener, razor; glass, Glix Blades, Glix Always Clicks 8.00
Showcase, Remington/Dupont Cutlery, wood/glass, 20x14x9" ...155.00
Sign, porc over steel, Ask for Wildroot, 12½x39½" 65.00
Sign, Tom the Barber, Shave 10¢, pnt wood, 1930s, 42x25" 650.00
Stand, shaving; wire w/attached soap dish, mirror & bars, 59" ...125.00
Stand, shoeshine; bent wire highchair w/shelf & shoe rest 250.00
Stationery & envelope, Philip Eisemann...Supply letterhead 50.00
Steamer, NP copper, Ideal Metal Wks, 61" 415.00
Sterilizer, Dewit Steri-Tool, E Liverpool OH, 5x9½x5½" 32.00
Strop, leather, wood hdl w/sheath, 4-sided, Lamont, 14", EX 55.00

Barometers

Barometers are instruments designed to measure the weight or pressure of the atmosphere in order to anticipate approaching weather changes. Those made prior to the turn of the century (earlier in England and on the continent) were beautifully housed in period cases of mahogany, rosewood, walnut, or cherry, often with brass trim. Pocket barometers/altimeters were produced for surveying and personal use.

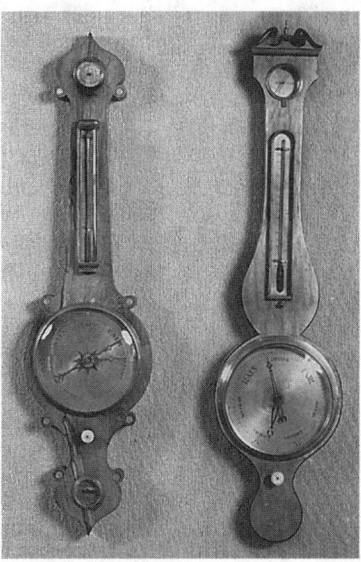

Banjo types: English, rosewood case with thermometer, ivory knobs, 1800s, 38", $350.00; Gallione Galli & Co., New York, satinwood with ebony edge, 39½", $400.00.

Abatte Oakham, mahog inlay, early 1800s, 40½x9½" 660.00
English oak, aneroid, C/F scales, working, 1920, 24" 80.00
Gardner & Lyle, aneroid, silvered scales, cvd oak case, 31" 275.00
Holosteric, cvd walnut case, 11½" dia, EX 150.00
Keuffel & Esser NY, aneroid, brass, 1900s, 2⅝" dial, EX 125.00
Peter Oltt Frankfurt, mercury stick, mahog, 1800s, 37" 600.00
R Fuest Berlin-Steglitz, WWII German U-boat, brass, 6½" 325.00

Barware

Back in the thirties when social soirees were very elegant affairs thanks to the influence of Hollywood in all its glamour and mistique, cocktails were often served up in shakers styled as miniature airplanes, zeppelins, skyscrapers, lady's legs, penguins, roosters, bowling pins, etc. Some were by top designers such as Norman Bel Geddes and Russel Wright. They were made of silverplate, glass, and chrome, often trimmed with colorful Bakelite handles. Today these are hot collectibles, and even the more common Deco-styled chrome cylinders are often priced at $25.00 and up. Ice buckets, trays, and other bar accessories are also included in this area of collecting. Our advisor for this category is Stephen Visakay, who is listed in the Directory under New Jersey.

Ice bucket, aluminum, emb penguins, West Bend Alum Co, 1944 ...35.00
Picks, bottle forms in red Bakelite 'bar,' 4½x5" 95.00
Picks, bottle forms in wood 'bar' w/chrome, 4½x5" 45.00
Rack, tumbler; gyroscopic, chrome, 20x8½" dia, +4 tumblers 200.00
Shaker, aluminum, Chicago Century of Progress, 1933 ....45.00
Shaker, aluminum, Precision Cooler, 11¼x4¼" 75.00
Shaker, chrome & plastic w/glass insert, mk Ritz, 1930s 75.00
Shaker, chrome bell form w/wood hdl, side spout, 11x5¾" 35.00
Shaker, chrome bell form w/wood hdl that unscrews, 11x6" 65.00
Shaker, chrome w/Catalin lid, Revere, 1937, 12⅛" 350.00
Shaker, chrome zeppelin form, complete w/case, Germany 2,000.00
Shaker, clear glass, w/strainer, rooster's head lid, Heisey 75.00
Shaker, clear glass w/emb dmns, plastic lid, 1928, 12½" 40.00
Shaker, cobalt glass, Tally Ho, horse & rider, 10" 48.00
Shaker, cobalt glass w/silver o/l, 1920s, 11", +8 tumblers 350.00
Shaker, cobalt glass w/SP trim, chrome lid, 1935, +6 tumblers ...450.00
Shaker, cobalt w/wht angel fish, chrome top, Hazel Atlas, 10" 28.00
Shaker, cranberry flashed & cut, SP lid, 10½" 150.00
Shaker, frosted glass dumbbell w/SP trim, Nat'l, +12 martinis 500.00
Shaker, onyx glass w/silk-screened recipes, chrome lid, 11½" 175.00
Shaker, ruby glass w/silver hunt scene, chrome lid, 1-qt 175.00
Shaker, ruby glass w/silver roosters, SP lid, 1-qt 175.00
Travel bar, SP plane breaks apart for shaker, etc, '28, 17½" 5,000.00
Travel bar, SP plane breaks apart for 12" decanter/etc, '28 ......2,200.00
Tray, gyroscopic, glass/chrome, 24" dia, +shaker & 8 tumblers ...750.00

Basalt

Basalt is a type of unglazed black pottery developed by Josiah Wedgwood and copied by many other companies during the late 18th and early 19th centuries. It is also called 'Egyptian Black.' See also Wedgwood.

Creamer, emb floral/acanthus bands, leaf hdl, oval, 6" L 185.00
Creamer, Wellington, lion spout, snake hdl, teapot form, 6" 350.00
Spill vase, emb cherubs, copper lustre int, 4¾" 200.00
Teapot, Wellington, lion spout, snake hdl, 9" L, EX 600.00

Baskets

Basket weaving is a craft as old as ancient history. Baskets have been used to harvest crops, for domestic chores, and to contain the catch of fishermen. Materials at hand were utilized, and baskets from a specific region are often distinguishable simply by analyzing the natural fibers used in their construction. Early Indian baskets were made of corn husks or woven grasses. Willow splint, straw, rope, and paper were also used. Until the invention of the veneering machine in the late 1800s, splint was made by water-soaking a split log until the fibers were soft-ened and flexible. Long strips were pulled out by hand and, while still wet and pliable, woven into baskets in either a cross-hatch or hexagonal weave.

Most handcrafted baskets on the market today were made between 1860 and the early 1900s. Factory baskets with a thick, wide splint cut by machine are of little interest to collectors. The more popular baskets are those designed for a specific purpose, rather than the more commonly found utility baskets that had multiple uses. Among the most costly forms are the Nantucket Lighthouse baskets, which were basically copied from those made there for centuries by aboriginal Indians. They were designed in the style of whale-oil barrels and named for the South Shoal Nantucket Lightship where many were made during the last half of the 19th century. Cheese baskets (used to separate curds from whey), herb-gathering baskets, and finely woven Shaker miniatures are other highly-prized examples of the basket weaver's art.

In the listings that follow, assume that each has a center bentwood handle (unless handles of another type are noted) that is not included in the height. Unless another type of material is indicated, assume that each is made of splint.

For further information we recommend *Collector's Guide to Country Baskets* by Don and Carol Raycraft, available from Collector Books. See also American Indian; Eskimo; Sewing; Shaker.

Market or utility basket, white oak splint, woven handle, New England, late 1800s, 13" to top of handle, 15½" long, $200.00.

Buttocks, dbl lids, weathered, 10½x22x15" 85.00
Buttocks, Eye-of-God hdls, old worn brn pnt, 7½x12x12" 110.00
Buttocks, Eye-of-God hdls, worn patina, 9x16x14" 225.00
Buttocks, faded gr & natural, well made, 9x18x13" 135.00
Buttocks, finely woven, natural patina, 3¾x7x6½" 160.00
Buttocks, finely woven, 7x11x10" 220.00
Buttocks, natural & bl-gr, 3¼x5½x5" 295.00
Buttocks, natural patina, minor damage, 6x10x10" 85.00
Buttocks, old finish, minor damage, 9x18x16" 95.00
Buttocks, old varnish, minor damage, 10x21x17" 220.00
Buttocks, pnt traces, good age, 3½x6x5½" 175.00
Buttocks, some age & wear, 7x15x14" 85.00
Buttocks, weathered patina, 7x17½x13" 130.00
Buttocks, well made, natural patina, minor damage, 6x11x12" ..150.00
Buttocks, well shaped, EX age & color, 4x8½x7¼" 200.00
Buttocks, 1-egg, mini, 2x3⅝x3" 120.00
Cheese, woven splint, wht rpt, 16" dia 30.00
Gathering, old worn varnish, 5x15½x12" 75.00
Gathering, rectangular, worn, 20x31x21" 75.00
Goose feather, dome lid, hdls, 25" 225.00
Goose feather, minor rpr, 21½" 165.00
Herb drying, openweave bottom, 6¾x16", EX 240.00
Laundry, lg weave, rim hdls, dk finish, damage, 16x26" 50.00
Laundry, minor damage, 12x40x22" 60.00
Laundry, oblong w/ribs, open rim hdls, damage, 11x24x20" 95.00
Laundry, old dk bl pnt, minor damage, 14x29x18" 385.00
Loom, dk patina w/blk & faded red, hanging, 8½x11½" 75.00

Nantucket, swing hdl, old paper label, 5¼x10" 600.00
Nantucket, swing hdl, some damage, 5x9", VG 375.00
Nantucket, swing hdl, 4x8" 400.00
Rye straw, rim hdls, partially rstr, 9x18" dia 100.00
Rye straw, 5x20" 85.00
Splint, concave bottom, 15x14" dia 65.00
Splint, dmn at hdls, ftd, EX detail, 3¾x6¾" 60.00
Splint, dmn at hdls, ftd, 3¾x6¾", EX 50.00
Splint, faded brn & bl, some damage, 5x11x11" 130.00
Splint, finely woven, EX detail & patina, 6x9" dia 385.00
Splint, gr pnt w/mc fruit, 9¼x4¾" 105.00
Splint, natural & bl, rim hand holds, minor damage, 13x16", EX .45.00
Splint, natural & blk, 4¾x9" 115.00
Splint, natural & dk brn w/pnt designs, 3½x11½" 95.00
Splint, natural & faded bl, sq, 4½x12x12" 200.00
Splint, natural w/printed mc designs, 3½x14½" 140.00
Splint, old bl rpt, old rpr, 6x11" 110.00
Splint, old patina, 9x22" 180.00
Splint, rectangular, well made, lt patina, 7¼x9½x11½" 130.00
Splint, swivel hdls, oblong, OH, old finish, 7x18½x12" 150.00
Splint, swivel hdls, worn, 7x14½x10" 135.00
Splint, well made, dk patina, 8x15x12" 250.00
Splint, yel & red pnt, oblong, sgn MT 1867, 5½x14x11" 135.00
Splint & sweet grass, 4x3" 30.00
Wedding, bamboo, red & blk, 21" H 25.00

Batchelder

Ernest A. Batchelder was a leading exponent of the Arts and Crafts movement in the United States. His influential book, *Design in Theory and Practice,* was originally published in 1910. He is best known, however, for his artistic tiles which he first produced in Pasedena, California, from 1909 to 1916. In 1906 the business was relocated to Los Angeles where it continued until 1932, closing because of the Depression.

In 1938 Batchelder resumed production in Pasedena under the name of 'Kinneola Kiln.' Output of the new pottery consisted of delicately cast bowls and vases in an Oriental style. This business closed in 1951. Tiles carry a die-stamped mark; vases and bowls are hand incised. Our advisor for this category is Jack Chipman, author of *Collector's Encyclopedia of California Pottery*; he is listed in the Directory under California.

Vase, oblong, 6¼x8", $100.00; Bowl, low, incised marks, 1½x7", $125.00.

Bowl, bl w/ivory int, flared, 3¼x7½" 100.00
Bowl, gray, 3" 75.00
Tile, bud w/leaves, engobe, 3" sq 65.00
Tile, grapevine, patina glaze, 3" sq 60.00
Tile, Hispanic geometrics, mc, satin matt, 1928, 6" 75.00
Tile, lion, buff clay on bl matt, 3¾" sq 225.00

Tile, medieval landscape, engobe, 4" 150.00
Tile, peacock, engobe, 6" 175.00
Tile, 2 doves in star, bl & brn slip, unglazed, 3¾" 85.00
Vase, gray, cylindrical, 9½" 200.00
Vase, lt gr glossy drip, bulbous, 3½" 250.00
Vase, yel, flared rim, 6" 125.00
Vase, yel, pillow form, 4¾x5½" 100.00
Vase, yel, sq shape, 7" 150.00

Battersea

Battersea is a term that refers to enameling on copper or other metal. Though originally produced at Battersea, England, in the mid-18th century, the craft was later practiced throughout the Staffordshire district. Boxes are the most common examples. Some are figurals, and many bear an inscription. Values are given for examples with only minimal damage, which is normal. Our advisor for this category is John Harrigan; he is listed in the Directory under Minnesota.

Box, bluebird on foliage, hinged lid, 1½" 285.00
Box, Esteem the Giver, scenic lid w/mirror, ¾x1½x1" 275.00
Box, Present From..., scenic reserve, gold bands, 2" 180.00
Box, Trifle From London, floral garland, 1½" L, EX 350.00
Candlesticks, floral, scalloped drip pans, baluster, 9", pr 1,485.00
Needle case, floral & insects on yel, rstr, 4¾" L 550.00
Opera glasses, children hunting & fishing, 4" W, in case 425.00

Bauer

Originally founded in Paducah, Kentucky, in 1885, the J.A. Bauer Company moved to Los Angeles where it was re-established in 1909. Until the 1920s, their major products were terra cotta gardenware, flowerpots, and stoneware and yellowware bowls. During prohibition they produced crocks for home use. A more artful form of product began to develop with the addition of designer Louis Ipsen to the staff in 1915. Some of his work, a line of molded vases, flowerpots, bowls, etc., was awarded a bronze medal at the Pacific International Exposition the following year.

In 1930 the first of many dinnerware lines was tested on the market. Their initial pattern, Plain Ware, was well accepted and led the way to the introduction of the most popular dinnerware in their history and with today's collectors, Ring Ware. It was produced from 1932 into the early 1960s in solid colors of jade green, royal blue, Chinese yellow, light blue, orange-red, and (in very limited quantities) black or white. Its simple pattern was a design of closely-spaced concentric ribs, either convex or concave. Over the years, more than one hundred shapes were available. Some were made in limited quantities, resulting in rare items to whet the appetites of Bauer buffs today. Other patterns were La Linda, produced during the 1940s and 1950s, and Monterey Moderne, introduced in 1948 and remaining popular into the 1950s (made in pink, black, gray, brown, and green).

After WWII a flood of foreign imports drastically curtailed their sales, and the pottery began a steady decline that ended in failure in 1962. Prices listed below reflect the California market. For more information, we recommend *The Collector's Encyclopedia of California Pottery* by Jack Chipman, our advisor for this category. Mr. Chipman's address may be found in the Directory under California.

Ashtray, Monterey, wht, rare 150.00
Ashtray, plain, sq, all colors but blk, 4" 45.00
Bean pot, plain, all colors but blk, no hdl, 1-pt 45.00
Bean pot, plain, blk, hdls, 4-qt 200.00

Bowl, batter; Ring, blk, 1-qt 175.00
Bowl, beater; Ring, orange-red, dk bl or ivory, 1-qt 75.00
Bowl, fruit; Monterey, wht, 6" 22.00
Bowl, fruit/dessert; Al Fresco, speckled, gr, or gray, 5" 10.00
Bowl, fruit/dessert; Contempo, all colors, 5" 10.00
Bowl, mixing; plain, all colors but blk, 1½-gal 145.00
Bowl, mixing; Ring, blk, #9, 1-gal 250.00
Bowl, ramekin; La Linda, burgundy or dk brn 10.00
Bowl, ramekin; Ring, blk, 4" 40.00
Bowl, serving; Monterey, all colors, 9½" 37.50
Bowl, soup; Al Fresco, coffee brn or Dubonnet, w/lid, 5½" 20.00
Bowl, vegetable; Al Fresco, coffee brn or Dubonnet, 9½" 25.00
Bowl, vegetable; La Linda, burgundy or dk brn, 10" 35.00
Bowl, vegetable; Monterey Moderne, blk, oval, 9" 60.00
Candlestick, Monterey, all colors but wht 50.00
Candlestick, Ring, orange-red, spool shape, 2½" 65.00
Casserole, Al Fresco, speckled, gr or gray, w/lid, 1½-qt 35.00
Casserole, French; Contempo, all colors, w/lid, ind 30.00
Chop plate, all colors but wht, 13" 50.00
Coffee server, Monterey, wht, 8-cup 45.00

Coffee server, Ring, jade green, 6-cup, $45.00; Black lid, $30.00.

Cookie jar, Ring, yel, jade gr, or lt bl 200.00
Creamer, La Linda, burgundy or dk brn, new shape 20.00
Cup, jumbo coffee; La Linda, lt brn, pk, or ivory 30.00
Cup & saucer, Al Fresco, coffee brn or Dubonnet 18.00
Cup & saucer, Monterey, wht 40.00
Cup & saucer, Ring, orange-red, dk bl or ivory, tea sz 45.00
Flowerpot, Ring Gardenware, jade gr or lt bl, ruffled, 5" 22.00
Gravy boat, Al Fresco, coffee brn or Dubonnet 18.00
Gravy bowl, Ring, blk 175.00
Honey jar, Ring, all colors but blk 350.00
Jardiniere, Ring, orange-red, dk bl or wht, 10" 100.00
Marmalade, plain, blk 200.00
Oil jar, all colors but blk, #129, 20" 800.00
Pitcher, beer; Ring, orange-red, dk bl, or wht, cylindrical 300.00
Pitcher, La Linda, gr, yel, or turq, ice lip, 2-qt 65.00
Plate, Al Fresco, speckled, gr, or gray, 8" 8.00
Plate, Contempo, all colors, 10" 10.00
Plate, grill; Monterey Moderne, all colors but blk, rnd 20.00
Plate, grill; Monterey Moderne, blk, sq, rare 60.00
Plate, Monterey, wht, 9" 22.00
Plate, Monterey Moderne, all colors but blk, 10½" 20.00
Plate, salad; Ring, blk, 7½" 45.00
Platter, La Linda, lt brn, pk, or gray, 12" 22.00
Platter, Monterey Moderne, blk, oval, 12" 45.00
Platter, rnd, plain, all colors but blk, oval, 12" 25.00
Rack, holds Ring coffee server & 6 6-oz tumblers 65.00
Relish plate, Monterey, all colors but wht, oval, 10½" 55.00
Sherbet, Ring, orange-red, dk bl, or burgundy 50.00

Souffle dish, Ring, jade gr or dk bl 200.00
Spice jar, plain, blk, 4½x3½" 200.00
Stein, Ring, blk, cylindrical, 5" 200.00
Sugar bowl, plain, blk, w/lid 85.00
Teapot, Contempo, all colors, 6-cup 35.00
Teapot, Monterey Moderne, all colors but blk, 6-cup 60.00
Teapot, plain, all colors but blk, 6-cup 100.00
Tumbler, La Linda, gr, yel, or turq, 8-oz 15.00
Tumbler, Ring, blk, cylinder, no hdl, 6-oz 45.00
Vase, Ring Gardenware, blk, cylinder, 10" 150.00
Vase, Ring Gardenware, dk bl or ivory, 12" 125.00
Vase, Ring Gardenware, yel, jade gr, or lt bl, cylinder, 8" 75.00

Bavaria

Bavaria, Germany, was long the center of that country's pottery industry; in the 1800s, many firms operated in and around the area. Chinaware vases, novelties, and table accessories were decorated with transfer prints as well as by hand by artists who sometimes signed their work. The examples here are marked with 'Bavaria' and the logos of some of the various companies which were located there.

Ashtray, rose medallions w/gold tracery, Schumann, 4¼x3¼" 10.00
Bowl, souvenir; Niagara Falls, rtcl rim w/gold, 5¼" 5.00
Coffee set, mc florals w/gold, Creidlitz, 9¼" pot+cr/sug 125.00
Creamer & sugar bowl, roses, lustre trim 32.00
Cup & saucer, Wigsburg Schloss (castle) w/gold, ftd, mini 45.00
Leaf dish, pk & wht blossoms on oak leaf w/gold, 11x4½" 20.00
Mug, bl flowers w/gold 30.00
Pitcher, mc florals w/gold, Carlsbad, 10" 75.00
Plate, roses & cat, 8½" 35.00
Plate, roses w/gold lattice & leafy swags, 6", 5 for 20.00
Urn, floral spray w/gold, w/dome lid, Waldershof, 12x7" 55.00

Beer Cans

When the flat-top can was first introduced in 1934, it came with printed instructions on how to use the triangular punch opener. Cone-top cans, which are rare today, were patented in 1935 by the Continental Can Company. By the 1960s, aluminum cans with pull tabs had made both types obsolete.

The hobby of collecting beer cans has been rapidly gaining momentum over the past ten years. Series types, such as South African Brewery, Lion, and the Cities Series by Schmit and Tucker, are especially popular.

Condition is an important consideration when evaluating market price. Grade 1 must be in like-new condition with no rust. However, the triangular punch hole is acceptable. Grade 2 cans may have slight scratches or dimples but must be free of rust. For Grade 3, light rust, minor scratching, and some fading may be acceptable. When these defects are more pronounced, a can is defaulted to Grade 4. Those in less-than-excellent condition devaluate sharply. In the listings that follow, cans are arranged alphabetically by brand name, not by brewery. Unless noted otherwise, values are for 11- to 12-oz. cans in Grade 1 condition.

ABC, ABC Brewery, flat top, red/wht/bl 50.00
Acme Bock, Acme Brewery, flat top, wht w/lamb's head 200.00
Adler Brau, Walter Brewery, pull top, red w/gold bird 10.00
All American, flat top, wht over bl 45.00
Alpine, Fox Deluxe Brewery, flat top, wht w/gold trim 200.00
Alpine, pull top, wht w/bl & gold 10.00
Ambassador, Kreuger Brewery, flat top, w/people dancing 55.00

American Dry, Eastern Brewery, flat top, gold w/red/wht/bl 25.00
Arrow, Globe Brewery, pull top, gold w/2 red arrows on bottom ..200.00
Ballantine, Falstaff Brewery, pull top, Liberty Bell on flag 1.00
Bantam Ale, flat top, wht & gr w/rooster, 8-oz 40.00
Beverwyck Cream Ale, flat top, gr 4-leaf clover 105.00
Big Mac, flat top, Golden Gate bridge pictured 95.00
Blk Forest Light, cone top, red & wht 175.00
Brut's, Lone Star Brewery, pull top, bl/gold/red 30.00
Buffalo, pull top, buffalo pictured on tan can 1.00
Bull Dog Malt Lager, flat top, gold w/wht & bl, 8-oz 25.00
Bullfrog, Monarch Brewery, flat top, wht w/gold 45.00
Busch Bavarian, pull top, no 'Half Quart' at top, 15- to 16-oz 10.00
Coors, flat top, gold ring at base, 7-oz 15.00
Country Club Lager, cone top, gr over wht 50.00
Country Club Malt Lager, no Xs in crown, 8-oz 20.00
Custom Club, Grace Brewery, flat top, red w/wht letters 85.00
Denver, Tivoli Brewery, flat top, picture of city 45.00
Dutch Lunch, flat top, stein & bread pictured 175.00
El Ray, Grace Brewery, flat top, bl crown w/glass on gold 225.00
Encore, pull top, gold over wht, 10-oz 15.00
F&G, Drewrys Brewery, flat top, red & wht 65.00
Fitzgerald's Ale, cone top, red & cream, 1940s, EX 175.00
French 76 Malt Lager, pull top, picture of Eiffel Tower, 8-oz 55.00
GBX Malt Lager, Grain Belt Brewery, pull top, bl w/silver letters ..6.00
Gibbons, cone top, red w/wht letters 55.00
Gibbons, pull top, Christmas 100.00
Golden Crown Draft, Maier, pull top, bl w/gold & wht letters 16.00
Grace Bros Bavarian Beer, flat top, shield in middle, 8-oz 75.00
Haa's Pilsner, cone top, blk/red/gold 125.00
Hampden Mild Ale (1947), flat top, gr w/tan center 250.00
Hop Gold, Star Brewery, flat top, gold w/bl star 350.00
Jax, pull top, wht over gold w/red letters, 10-oz 10.00
Knickerbocker Dark, flat top, gold/brn/wht 50.00
Lebanon Valley, flat top, wht & gold w/bl border trim 85.00
Metbrew Near Beer, pull top, picture of stein on front 1.00
Miller Malt Liqueur, pull top, red w/gold eagle, 15- to 16-oz 3.00
National Bohemian, flat top, wht w/brn & bl, 7-oz 17.00
NY Special, flat top, bl & wht city, red ribbon w/name 1,000.00
Paul Bunyan, Wisconson Brewery, flat top, PB pictured 90.00
Pearl, pull top, country scene w/running brook, 8-oz 2.00
Pikes Peak Malt Lager, flat top, wht w/name in ribbon, 8-oz 40.00
Rahr's All Star, flat top, wht w/red star, gold border 22.00
Shaefer Irish Cream Ale, flat top, wht w/gr 3-leaf clover 30.00
Soul Mellow Yellow, pull top, wht over red, 15- to 16-oz 225.00
State Fair, pull top, silver w/bl letters & picture 75.00
Turborg, pull top, gold w/red circle, 10-oz 8.00
Winchester, Walter Brewery, 15- to 16-oz 10.00
Yankee, flat top, wht & red w/clipper ship, 16-oz 95.00
76 Ale, Terre Haute Brewery, cone top, gr/wht/red 75.00

Bellaire, Marc

Marc Bellaire was born in Toledo, Ohio. He studied at the Toledo Museum of Art while employed as a designer for the Libbey Glass Company. During World War II, while serving in the Navy, he travelled extensively throughout the Pacific resulting in his enriched sense of design and color.

Marc settled in California in the 1950s where his work attracted the attention of national buyers and agencies who persuaded him to create ceramic lines of his own, employing hand-decorated techniques throughout. This resulted in the building of a studio in Culver City. He produced high-quality ceramics, often decorated with ultra-modern figures or geometric patterns. His work was executed with a distinctive

flair. His most famous line was Mardi Gras, decorated with slim dancers of spattered and striped colors of black, blue, pink and white.

During the period of 1951-1956, Mark was named one of the top ten artware designers by Giftwares Magazine. After 1956 he taught and lectured on art, design, and ceramic decorating techniques from coast to coast. Many pieces were one of a kind, commissioned throughout the United States.

During the 1970s he set up a studio in Marin County, California, and eventually moved to Palm Springs where he set up his final studio/gallery. There he produced large pieces with a Southwestern style. Mr Bellaire died in 1994. Our advisor for this category is Marty Webster; he is listed in the Directory under Michigan.

Ashtray, Bird Isle, blk on cream, 8" 85.00
Ashtray, Clown, mc on cream, 7" 45.00
Ashtray, Geometric Designs, blk/brn on cream, 8x15" 85.00
Ashtray, Mardi Gras, figures on blk, 14x14" 225.00
Ashtray, Still Life, matt fruits & leaves, 10x15" 100.00
Bottle, Flowers, gr top & bottom, 16" 150.00
Compote, Cave Painting, 4-ftd, 6x12" 125.00
Compote, Woman w/Blue Bird, 4-ftd, 8x17" 125.00

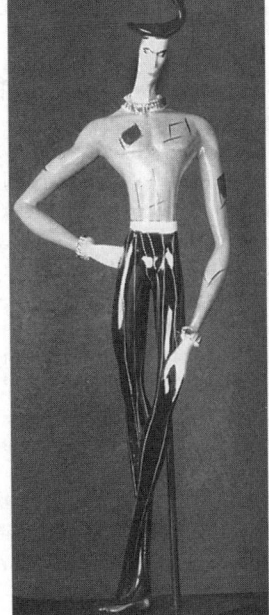

Figurine, Mardi Gras, man standing, very slim, 24", $1,000.00.

Figurine, Mardi Gras, reclining man, very slim, 18" 1,000.00
Figurine, Polynesian, standing man 400.00
Platter, Mardi Gras, figures on blk, 12x18" 250.00
Tile, Flower w/Butterfly, 6" sq 125.00
Tray, Polynesian man, blk & gr, 12" dia 200.00
Vase, Balinese women, hourglass shape, 8" 125.00

Belleek, American

From 1883 until 1930, several American potteries located in New Jersey and Ohio manufactured a type of china similar to the famous Irish Belleek soft-paste porcelain. The American manufacturers identified their porcelain by using 'Belleek' or 'Beleek' in their marks. American Belleek is considered the highest achievement of the American porcelain industry. Production centered around artistic cabinet pieces and luxury tablewares. Many examples emulated Irish shapes and decor with marine themes and other naturalistic styles. While all are highly collectible, some companies' products are rarer than others. The best-known manufacturers are Ott and Brewer, Willets, The Ceramic Art Company (CAC), and Lenox. You will find more detailed information in those specific categories. Our advisor for this category is Mary Frank Gaston; you will find her address in the Directory under Texas.

Key:
AAC — American Art China Company
ABC — American Beleek Works
CAP — Columbian Art Pottery Works

Bowl, tiny flowers w/in & w/o, gold rim, AAC, 2½x5" 350.00
Creamer & sugar bowl, HP flowers, pk int, gold trim, AAC 650.00
Hatpin holder, silver Art Deco decor, obelisk shape, mk, 7" 165.00
Pitcher, grape pods & spider in web, A Cannon, 1900, 5½" 250.00
Shell dish, wht w/pk lustre int, ABC mk, 4x5" 150.00
Stein, currants & leaves, red & gr on brn, 5" 200.00
Tankard, 3 cherubs along shore, gold scrolls, 14" 450.00
Teapot, gold paste decor on dragon shape, red CAP mk, 9" L ..1,500.00
Vase, chrysanthemums, mc, sgn, gr mk, 13" 450.00
Vase, poppies on shoulder, sgn MP, 8" 150.00

Belleek, Irish

Belleek is a very thin translucent porcelain that takes its name from the village in Ireland where it originated in 1859. The glaze is a creamy ivory color with a pearl-like lustre. The tablewares, baskets, figurines, and vases that have always been made there are being crafted yet today. Shamrock, Tridacna, Echinus, and Thorn are but a few of the many patterns of tableware which have been made during some periods(s) of the pottery's history. Throughout the years, their most popular pattern has been Shamrock.

It is possible to date an example to within twenty to thirty years of crafting by the mark. Pieces with an early stamp often bring prices nearly triple that of a similar but current item. With some variation, the marks have always incorporated the Irish wolfhound, Celtic round tower, harp, and shamrocks. The first three marks (usually in black) were used from 1863 to 1946. A series of green marks identified the pottery's offerings from 1946 until the seventh mark (in gold/brown) was introduced in 1980 (it was discontinued in 1992). The most current mark, the eighth, is blue. Belleek Collector's International Society limited edition pieces are designated with a special mark in red. In the listings below, numbers designated with the prefix 'D' relate to the book Belleek, The Complete Collector's Guide and Illustrated Reference, Second Edition published by Wallace-Homestead Book Company, One Chilton Way, Radnor, PA 19098-0230. The author, Richard K. Degenhardt, is our advisor for Belleek; he is listed in the Directory under North Carolina.

Key:
A — plain (glazed only)
B — cob lustre
C — hand tinted
D — hand painted
E — hand-painted shamrocks
F — hand gilted
G — hand tinted and gilted
H — hand-painted shamrocks and gilted
J — mother-of-pearl
K — hand painted and gilted
L — bisque and plain
M — decalcomania
N — special hand-painted decoration
T — transfer design

I — 1863-1890
II — 1891-1926
III — 1926-1946
IV — 1946-1955
V — 1955-1965
VI — 1965-3/31/1980
VII — 4/1/1980-12/22/1992
VIII — 1/4/1993-current

Further information concerning Periods of Crafting (Baskets):
1 — 1865-1890, BELLEEK (three-strand)
2 — 1865-1890, BELLEEK CO. FERMANAGH (three-strand)
3 — 1891-1920, BELLEEK CO. FERMANAGH IRELAND (three-strand)
4 — 1921-1954, BELLEEK CO. FERMANAGH IRELAND (four-strand)
5 — 1955-1979, BELLEEK® CO. FERMANAGH IRELAND (four-strand)
6 — 1980-1985, BELLEEK® IRELAND (four-strand)
7 — 1985-1989, BELLEEK® IRELAND 'ID NUMBER' (four-strand)
8-12 — 1990 to present (Refer to Belleek, The Complete Collector's Guide and Illustrated Reference, 2nd Edition, Chapter 5)

Bamboo Teapot, D515-I, A, lg 625.00
Belleek Flowerpot, ftd, D51-II, J, 10½" 2,400.00
Bonbonniere, flowered, D1812-VII, K, 1980, ltd ed 160.00
Calawite Candle Extinguisher & Stand, D1507-I, A, 3½" 850.00
Celtic Tea Ware Tea & Saucer, D1437-III/D1438-III, K&B 200.00
Chinese Tea Ware Tea Urn, D482-I, K, lg 12,000.00
Cone Tea Ware Tea & Saucer, D432-II, A 195.00
Dolphin Spill, D189-II, C, 6½" 375.00
Echinus Tea Ware Mustache Cup, D664-I (C), F, 2½" 375.00
Erne Tea Ware Creamer, D448-II, B, 2¾" 190.00
Figure of Erin, D1-I, L 8,000.00
Figurine, Boy & Girl Basket Bearers, D19-I/D17-I, A, pr 3,600.00
Florence Jug, D813-VII, K 95.00
Grass Tea Ware Milk Jug, D753-I, K, 6" dia 450.00
Henshall Basket, D121-10, 4-strand, A, 8" 1,100.00
Hexagon Tea Ware Coffee & Saucer, D397-II, G 190.00
Hexagon Tea Ware Teapot, D392-II, C 550.00
Irish Pot & Cream, D232-III, A, sz 2 ....145.00
Ivy Trunk Stump Spill, D153-I, D, 5" 275.00
Limpet Tea Ware Plate, D1372-III, B, 8" 75.00
Limpet Tea Ware Tea, D549(C)-II, B, 3¾" 85.00
Lithophane, Farm Girl w/Goat, D1537-III, A, 8½x6¾" 3,000.00
Neptune Tea Ware Plate, D422-II, A, 6" 85.00
Nile Vase, D84-II, A, lg, 12" 500.00
Pierced Shamrock Vase, D1217-II, H, 8½" 225.00
Rathmore Oval Basket, D117-7, 4-strand, D 7,200.00
Ribbon Cream & Sugar, D243-IV, B 78.00
Round Tower Vase, D1777-VI, D&E, 8¼" 485.00
Shamrock Tea Ware, Kettle, D386-II, E, lg 500.00
Shamrock Tea Ware Bread Plate, D379-V, E, 10¼" 90.00
Shamrock Tea Ware Cream & Sugar, D369-II/D368-II, E, sm ...255.00
Shamrock Tea Ware Slop, D380-III, E, 2½x4½" 75.00
Shamrock Ware, Teapot, D367-III, E, med sz 325.00
Shell Comport, D27-I, A, 3¾x9¾" 475.00
Spaniel on Cushion Paperweight, D1555-VI, L, 3" 100.00
Summer Briar Covered Sugar, D2050-VII, D 65.00
Sydenham Twig Basket, D108-2, 3-strand, J, 11¼" 3,500.00
Thorn Napkin Ring, D2067-VII, D 25.00
Toy Shell Cream, D250-II (CR), D, 3¾" 90.00
Tridacna Tea Ware Plate, D464-II, B, 5" 75.00
Tridacna Tea Ware Tea & Saucer, D454-II, B 130.00
Tulip Vase, D93-I, K, lg, 12" 3,200.00
Violet Holder, D1185-I, C, 4½" 875.00

Bells

Some areas of interest represented in the study of bells are history, religion, and geography. Since Biblical times, bells have announced morning church services, vespers, deaths, christenings, school hours, fires, and community events. Countries have used them en masse to peal out the good news of Christmas, New Year's, and the endings of World Wars I and II. They've been rung in times of great sorrow, such as the death of Abraham Lincoln.

Dorothy Malone Anthony is the author of a series of nine books entitled *World of Bells*. Her address is in the Directory under Kansas. All have over two hundred colored pictures covering many bell categories. See also Schoolhouse Collectibles.

China bell, Colonial lady figural, yellow gown with blue ruffle, Germany, 3", $45.00.

Brass, trn wood hdl, 10x5"	75.00
Bronze, Dutch girl w/jug figural, 4½"	125.00
China, floral emb on wht, cherub hdl, Italy, no mk	35.00
Collar bells, 5 bell-shape bells on leather strap, 21", pr	330.00
Saddle chimes, Russian type, 6-arm outside clappers	135.00
School, brass w/trn wooden hdl, old red pnt, 7¾"	50.00
Silver, lady w/shawl over face figural, A Mano, Peru, 4"	85.00
Sleigh, brass, 17 grad bells on 78" leather strap	225.00
Sleigh, brass, 23 grad bells on 94" leather strap	295.00
Sleigh, brass, 29 #d grad bells on new leather strap	260.00
Sleigh, brass, 3 2½" bells on metal strap	28.00

Bennett, John

Bringing with him the knowledge and experience he had gained at the Doulton (Lambeth) Pottery in England, John Bennett opened a studio in New York City around 1877, where he continued his methods of decorating faience under the glaze. Early wares utilized imported English biscuit, though subsequently local clays (both white and cream-colored) were also used. His first kiln was on Lexington Avenue; he built another on East Twenty-Fourth Street. Pieces are usually signed 'J. Bennett, N.Y.,' often with the street address and date. Later examples may be marked 'West Orange, N.J.,' where he retired. The pottery was in operation approximately six years in New York. Pieces signed with other initials are usually worth less. Our advisor for this category is Robert Tuggle; he is listed in the Directory under New York.

Charger, insects & flowers on honeycomb, sgn/1878, 14½"	4,620.00
Jardiniere, apple blossoms on blk mottle, sgn, 6½x8"	2,090.00
Vase, bird & vintage on gr mottle, sgn, 8⅝"	925.00
Vase, cattleya orchids on gr mottle, sgn, 9½"	2,250.00
Vase, wht/rose blossoms on yel, sgn/1883, 9"	2,420.00

Bennington

Although the term has become a generic one for the mottled brown ware produced there, Bennington is not a type of pottery, but rather a town in Vermont where two important potteries were located. The Norton Company, founded in 1793, produced mainly redware and salt-glazed stoneware; only during a brief partnership with Fenton (1845-47) was any Rockingham attempted. The Norton Company endured until 1894, operated by succeeding generations of the Norton family. Fenton organized his own pottery in 1847. There he manufactured not only redware and stoneware, but more artistic types as well — graniteware, scroddled ware, flint enamel, a fine parian, and vast amounts of their famous Rockingham. Though from an esthetic standpoint his work rated highly among the country's finest ceramic achievements, he was economically unsuccessful. His pottery closed in 1858.

It is estimated that only one in five Fenton pieces were marked; and although it has become a common practice to link any fine piece of Rockingham to this area, careful study is vital in order to be able to distinguish Bennington's from the similar wares of many other American and Staffordshire potteries. Although the practice was without the permission of the proprietor, it was nevertheless a common occurrence for a potter to take his molds with him when moving from one pottery to the next, so particularly well-received designs were often reproduced at several locations. Of eight known Fenton marks, four are variations of the '1849' impressed stamp: 'Lyman Fenton Co., Fenton's Enamel Patented 1849, Bennington, Vermont.' These are generally found on examples of Rockingham and flint enamel. A raised, rectangular scroll with 'Fenton's Works, Bennington, Vermont,' was used on early examples of porcelain. From 1852 to 1858, the company operated under the title of the United States Pottery Company. Three marks — the ribbon mark with the initials USP, the oval with a scrollwork border and the name in full, and the plain oval with the name in full — were used during that period.

Among the more sought-after examples are the bird and animal figurines, novelty pitchers, figural bottles, and all of the more finely-modeled items. Recumbent deer, cows, standing lions with one forepaw on a ball, and opposing pairs of poodles with baskets in their mouths and 'coleslaw' fur were made in Rockingham, flint enamel, and occasionally in parian. Numbers in the listings below refer to the book *Bennington Pottery and Porcelain* by Barret. Our advisors for Bennington (except for parian and stoneware) are Barbara and Charles Adams; they are listed in the Directory under Massachusetts.

Key: c/s — cobalt on salt glaze

Coffeepot, flint enamel with fluted finial, olive and mottled amber, marked, ca 1849-58, 12¾", NM, $13,000.00; Slop jar, flint enamel with scalloped ribs, brown with green and yellow, professional repair, 14¼", $550.00.

Bottle, Departed Spirits G, flint enamel, book form, 5½"	595.00
Bottle, flint enamel, book form, Kossuth, sticker, 7¾"	1,100.00
Candlesticks, Rockingham, 2 appl rings, rnd base, att, 8", pr	900.00

Chamber set, flint enamel, Alternate Rib, pitcher/bowl/soap	1,975.00
Creamer, Rockingham, cow form, mk F under base, 7" L	450.00
Cuspidor, flint enamel, faint 1849 mk, 9½"	440.00
Cuspidor, flint enamel, side vents, no mk	110.00
Cuspidor, Rockingham, 1849 mk, 9¾"	275.00
Dog w/fruit basket in mouth, coleslaw & Rockingham, 9½"	4,500.00
Frame, flint enamel, plain scalloped edge, crack, 11"	985.00
Frame, flint enamel, 1 w/rpr, 5x4½", pr	425.00
Frame, plain scalloped edge, 6½x6"	825.00
Lamp base, flint enamel, olive w/brn stepped base, 9"	1,750.00
Lion, flint enamel, coleslaw mane, rpr, 10"	3,000.00
Lion, flint enamel, facing left/tongue up, no base, rstr, 11"	4,400.00
Pie plate, flint enamel, mk, 11"	450.00
Pipkin, Rockingham, att, 5½"	425.00
Pitcher, brn lead glaze, hound hdl, 9"	465.00
Pitcher, flint enamel, Alternate Rib, mk, 10½"	1,100.00
Pitcher, flint enamel, paneled, 1849 mk, flaw, 11¾"	750.00
Pitcher, graniteware, presentation, gold/bl grapevines, 7½"	875.00
Pitcher, Rockingham, emb grapes, Lyman R Fenton..., 1840s, 7"	400.00
Pitcher, Rockingham, grape relief, mk, 1845, rpr, 7"	400.00
Poodle, olive flint, w/basket in mouth, no base, 8½"	4,500.00
Poodle, Rockingham, basket in mouth, no base, att, 8", NM, pr	11,000.00
Snuff jar, flint enamel, olive gr, mk, rstr lid/jar, 4½"	850.00
Spaniel, Rockingham, seated, base chips, 10½"	4,000.00
Swiss lady bar counter coin cover, Rockingham, 6½"	3,000.00
Tiebk, Rockingham, att, 1850s, 4¼" dia, pr	250.00
Toby bottle, flint enamel, holding mug, 10½", NM	935.00
Toby bottle, Rockingham, w/mustache/tassles/bottle, mk, 11"	1,100.00
Toby pitcher, Rockingham, Ben Franklin w/pipe & goblet, 6½"	550.00
Toby pitcher, Rockingham, 6"	300.00
Toby snuff jar, Rockingham, mk, 4¼", NM	825.00
Vase, tulip; flint enamel, 10", NM, pr	2,100.00
Wash basin, flint enamel, emb floral/scroll rim, mk, 13½"	900.00
Whiskey barrel, flint enamel, Rockingham Whiskey, 6"	275.00

Stoneware

Key: c/s — cobalt on salt glaze

Churn, #5/floral spray, c/s, E&LP Norton, rpr, 18"	350.00
Cooler, water; #5/floral spray, c/s, J&E Norton, 15", EX	1,900.00
Jug, #1/bird on branch, c/s, J&E Norton, ca 1855, rpr, 12"	500.00
Jug, #4/birds (2), c/s, J Norton & Co, ca 1860, 17", EX	1,050.00
Jug, #4/floral, c/s, J&E Norton, ca 1855, 17", EX	575.00
Jug, peacock on stump, c/s, J&E Norton, ca 1855, 13", EX	575.00
Jug, peacock on stump, c/s, J&E Norton, 3-gal, 15½", NM	3,100.00
Jug, rooster on branch, c/s, Norton & Co, 2-gal, 14", EX	1,250.00

Beswick

In the early 1890s, James Wright Beswick operated a pottery in Longston, England, where he produced fine dinnerware as well as ornamental ceramics. Today's collectors are most interested in the figurines made since 1936 by a later generation Beswick firm, John Beswick, Ltd. They specialize in reproducing accurately detailed bone-china models of authentic breeds of animals. Their Fireside Series includes dogs, cats, elephants, horses, the Huntsman, and an Indian figure, which measure up to 14" in height. The Connoisseur line is modeled after the likenesses of famous racing horses. Beatrix Potter's characters and some of Walt Disney's are charmingly recreated and appeal to children and adults alike. Other items, such as character Tobys, have also been produced. The Beswick name is stamped on each piece. The firm was absorbed by the Doulton group in 1973.

Figurine, Airdale	50.00
Figurine, Aunt Petitoes	60.00
Figurine, cat, blk w/gr eyes	50.00
Figurine, Cocker Spaniel, wht & blk	50.00
Figurine, Corgi	50.00
Figurine, Dachshund, sitting up	55.00
Figurine, Dalmation	50.00
Figurine, fox, seated, matt	55.00
Figurine, fox hound	55.00
Figurine, Foxy Whiskered Gentleman	90.00
Figurine, Golden Retriever	50.00
Figurine, J Townmouse	60.00
Figurine, Labrador, blk	55.00
Figurine, owl	55.00
Figurine, Persian cat, recumbent, 4½x7"	75.00
Figurine, Peter Rabbit	49.00
Figurine, Sally Heney Penny	60.00
Figurine, Samuel Whiskers	49.00
Figurine, Spaniel, Staffordshire type	90.00
Figurine, Spaniel puppies, 5 seated before tray	30.00
Figurine, Tabitha Twitch & Miss Moppet	90.00
Figurine, Yorkie	55.00

Big Little Books

The first Big Little Book was published in 1933 and copyrighted in 1932 by the Whitman Publishing Company of Racine, Wisconsin. Its hero was Dick Tracy. The concept was so well accepted that others soon followed Whitman's example; and though the 'Big Little Book' phrase became a trademark of the Whitman Company, the formats of his competitors (Saalfield, Goldsmith, Van Wiseman, Lynn, and World Syndicate) were exact copies. Today's Big Little Book buffs collect them all.

These hand-sized sagas of adventure were illustrated with full-page cartoons on the right-hand page and the story narration on the left. Colorful cardboard covers contained hundreds of pages, usually totaling over an inch in thickness. Big Little Books originally sold for 10¢ at the dime store; as late as the mid-1950s when the popularity of comic books caused sales to decline signaling an end to production, their price had risen to a mere 20¢. Their appeal was directed toward the pre-teens who bought, traded, and hoarded Big Little Books. Because so many were stored in attics and closets, many have survived. Among the super heroes are G-Men, Flash Gordon, Tarzan, the Lone Ranger, and Red Ryder; in a lighter vein, you'll find such lovable characters as Blondie and Dagwood, Mickey Mouse, Little Orphan Annie, and Felix the Cat.

In the early to mid-'30s, Whitman published several Big Little Books as advertising premiums for the Coco Malt Company, who packed them in boxes of their cereal. These are highly prized by today's collectors, as are Disney stories and super-hero adventures. Our advisor for this category is Ron Donnelly; he is listed in the Directory under Florida.

Lone Ranger and the Red Renegades, Better Little Book, 1939, VG, $32.50.

Adventures of Pete the Tramp, hard bk, Saalfield, 1935, VG **32.00**
Adventures of Tim Tyler, Saalfield, hard bk, 1934, EX **50.00**
Air Fighters of America, Whitman, 1941, NM **42.00**
Alley Oop & Dinny on Jungle of Moo, Whitman, 1938, VG **22.00**
Andy Panda & Mad Dog Mystery, Whitman, 1947, NM **38.00**
Apple Mary & Dennie's Lucky Apples, Whitman, 1939, EX **32.00**
Arizona Kid on Bandit Trail, Whitman, 1936, EX **25.00**
Bambi's Children, Whitman, Disney, 1943, G **15.00**
Barny Baxter in Air w/Eagle Squadron, Whitman, 1938, VG **15.00**
Big Chief Wahoo & the Lost Pioneers, Whitman, 1938, VG **30.00**
Blaze Brandon w/Foreign Legion, Whitman, 1938, VG **22.50**
Blondie, Count Cookie in Too!; Whitman, 1947, VG **25.00**
Blondie & Bouncing Baby Dumpling Whitman, 1940, VG **27.50**
Blondie or Life Among Bumsteads, Whitman, 1944, VG **22.50**
Brick Bradford w/Brocco Modern Buccaneer, Whitman, 1938, VG ..**25.00**
Bronc Peeler Lone Cowboy, Whitman, 1937, EX **32.50**
Buck Jones & 2-Gun Kid, Whitman, 1937, VG **40.00**
Buck Rogers & Doom Comet, Whitman, 1935, NM **125.00**
Buck Rogers in War w/Planet Venus, Whitman, 1938, VG **65.00**
Bugs Bunny, Whitman, All Picture Comics series, 1943, VG **35.00**
Bullet Benton, Saalfield, 1939, NM **38.00**
Buz Sawyer & Bomber 3, Whitman, 1946, EX **50.00**
Captain Frank Hawks, Air Ace & League of 12, 1938, EX **45.00**
Captain Midnight & Sheik Jomak Khan, Whitman, 1946, NM ...**75.00**
Chuck Malloy RR Detective on Streamliner, Whitman, 1938, EX ..**37.50**
Clyde Beatty Daredevil Lion & Tiger Tamer, Whitman, 1939, EX ..**60.00**
Convoy Patrol Thrilling US Navy Story, Whitman, 1942, EX **35.00**
Cowboy Millionaire, movie version, Saalfield, 1935, VG **32.00**
Dan Dunn Operative 48 & Crime Master, Whitman, 1937, VG ..**30.00**
Daniel Boone, World Syndicate, 1934, VG **22.50**
Detective Dick Tracy & Spider Gang, Whitman, 1937, EX **100.00**
Dick Tracy & Yogee Yamma, Whitman, 1946, EX **60.00**
Dickie Moore in Little Red Schoolhouse, 1936, EX **50.00**
Don O'Dare Finds War, Whitman, 1940, VG **35.00**
Donald Duck, Ghost Morgan's Treasure; 1946, EX **90.00**
Donald Duck, Hunting for Trouble; 1938, VG **45.00**
Down Cartridge Creek, Saalfield, 1938, VG **17.50**
Dumbo of the Circus, Only His Ears Grew; 1941, NM **100.00**
Flame Boy & Indians' Secret, Whitman, 1938, VG **27.50**
Flash Gordon in Red Sword Invaders, 1945, EX **60.00**
Flint Roper & 6-Gun Showdown, Whitman, 1941, VG **24.00**
Freckles & Lost Dmn Mine, Whitman, 1937, EX **17.50**
George O'Brien in Gun Law, movie edition, Whitman, 1935, EX ..**55.00**
In Name of Law, Whitman, 1937, EX **35.00**
Jack Pearl as Detective Baron Munchausen, Goldsmith, 1934, VG ..**25.00**
Just Kids, Whitman, 1937, EX **45.00**
Kazan in Revenge of North, Whitman, 1937, VG **22.50**
Ken Maynard & Gun Wolves of Gila, Whitman, 1939, EX **40.00**
Li'l Abner in New York, Al Capp, Whitman, 1936, EX **75.00**
Little Orphan Annie & Chizzler, 1933, VG **45.00**
Mandrake the Magician, Whitman, 1935, EX **60.00**
Masked Man of the Mesa, Saalfield, 1939, VG **22.50**
Mickey Mouse & Pluto the Racer, 1936, VG **65.00**
Mickey Mouse in Blaggard Castle, 1934, VG **65.00**
Mickey Rooney & Judy Garland, Whitman, 1941, VG+ **35.00**
Myra North Special Nurse & Foreign Spies, Whitman, '38, EX ...**32.00**
Pat Nelson Ace of Test Pilots, Whitman, 1937, G **15.00**
Phantom, Whitman, 1936, VG **55.00**
Phantom in Desert Justice, 1941, EX **55.00**
Prairie Bill & Covered Wagon, premium, Whitman, 1934, VG ...**37.50**
Red Barry Ace Detective Hero of Hour, Whitman, 1935, EX **45.00**
Red Ryder, Hoofs of Thunder; 1939, EX **45.00**
Red Ryder the Fighting Westerner, 1940, NM **50.00**
Red-Hot Holsters, Saalfield, 1938, VG **20.00**

Riders of Lone Trails, Whitman, 1937, EX **35.00**
Roy Rogers Range Detective, 1950, EX **30.00**
Shadow & Living Death, Whitman, 1940, EX **185.00**
Smilin' Jack & Coral Princess, Whitman, 1938, EX **45.00**
Smitty in Going Native, Whitman, 1938, VG **20.00**
Speed Douglas & Mole Gang, 1941, NM **35.00**
Story of Shirley Temple, Saalfield, 1934, EX **65.00**
Tailspin Tommy & Hooded Flyer, Whitman, 1937, EX **55.00**
Tailspin Tommy & Sky Bandits, Whitman, 1938, EX **50.00**
Tarzan Escapes, Burroughs, Whitman, 1936, VG **65.00**
Tarzan of the Apes, Burroughs, Whitman, 1933, VG **78.00**
Texas Kid, Whitman, 1937, VG **18.00**
Tom Beatty Ace of Service & Big Brain, Whitman, 1939, EX **50.00**
Tom Mix Circus on the Barbary Coast, 1940, VG **30.00**
Tom Mix in Range War, Whitman, 1937, EX **45.00**
Up Dead Horse Canyon, Saalfield, 1940, VG **12.50**
Vic Sands of US Flying Fortress, Whitman, 1943, VG **24.00**
Wells Fargo, Whitman, 1938, VG **37.50**
Will Rogers, photo cover, Saalfield, 1935, VG **25.00**
Windy Wayne & His Flying Wing, Whitman, 1942, VG **24.00**
Zane Grey's King of Royal Mounted, premium, Whitman, 1935, NM ..**80.00**
Zip Saunders King of Speedway, Whitman, 1939, NM **35.00**

Bing and Grondahl

In 1853 brothers M.H. and J.H. Bing formed a partnership with Frederick Vilhelm Grondahl in Copenhagen, Denmark. Their early wares were porcelain plaques and figurines designed by the noted sculptor Thorvaldsen of Denmark. Dinnerware production began in 1863, and by 1889 their underglaze color 'Copenhagen Blue' had earned them worldwide acclaim. They are perhaps most famous today for their Christmas plates, the first of which was made in 1895. See also Limited Edition Plates.

Figurine, accordion player **175.00**
Figurine, ballerina, #2344, 9½" **170.00**
Figurine, ballerina sitting on floor, #4642, 6¼x6¾" **250.00**
Figurine, blacksmith at anvil, #2225, 12" **500.00**
Figurine, boy kissing girl, #2162 ....**100.00**
Figurine, boy sits w/cup, #1713 ....**185.00**
Figurine, boy w/bear, wht, #2231 ....**70.00**
Figurine, boy w/trumpet, #1792, 6½" **175.00**
Figurine, foundry worker pouring hot metal, #2335, 11¾" **250.00**
Figurine, girl feeding cat, #1745 ....**120.00**
Figurine, girl tennis player, #1745, 5½" **170.00**
Figurine, girl w/cat in apron, #1779 ....**90.00**
Figurine, Little Mother, #1779 ....**150.00**
Figurine, parrot, bl & tan, #2019, 5¾" **160.00**
Figurine, polar bear, #1785, 12½" L **160.00**
Figurine, seal, brn overtones, #1733, 6¾x8" **150.00**
Figurine, starling, #1880, 7½" **190.00**
Figurine, Toothache **45.00**
Figurine, Vagabond, hands in pockets, #2473, 8½" **345.00**
Figurine, 2 boys, #1648 ....**115.00**
Figurine, 2 children w/coat, #2312 ....**95.00**
Vase, stork's nest, #1302/6250, 8½" **190.00**
Vase, windmill scene, 11" **240.00**

Binoculars

There are several types of binoculars, and the terminology used to refer to them is not consistent or precise. Generally, 'field glasses' refer to simple Galilean optics, where the lens next to the eye (the ocular) is concave and dished away from the eye. By looking through the large lens (the objective), it is easy to see that the light goes straight through the two lenses. These are lower power, have a very small field of view, and do not work nearly as well as prism binoculars. In a smaller size, they are opera glasses, and their price increases if they are covered with mother-of-pearl (fairly common but very attractive), abalone shell (more colorful), ivory (quite scarce), or other exotic materials. Field glasses are not valuable unless very unusual or by the best makers, such as Zeiss or Leitz. Prism binoculars have the objective lens offset from the eyepiece and give a much better view. This is the standard binocular form, called Porro prisms, and dates from around 1900. Another type of prism binocular is the roof prism, which at first resembles the straight-through field glasses, with two simple cylinders or cones, here containing very small prisms. These can be distinguished by the high quality views they give and by a thin diagonal line that can be seen when looking backwards through the objective. In general, German binoculars are the most desirable, followed by American, English, and finally French, which can be of good quality but are very common unless of unusual configuration. Japanese optics of WWII or before are often of very high quality. 'Made in Occupied Japan' binoculars are very common, but collectors prize those by Nippon Kogaku (Nikon). Some binoculars are center focus (CF), with one central wheel that focuses both sides at once. These are much easier to use but more difficult to seal against dirt and moisture. Individual focus (IF) binoculars are adjusted by rotating each eyepiece and tend to be cleaner inside in older optics. Each type is preferred by different collectors. Very large binoculars are always of great interest. All binoculars are numbered according to their magnifying power and the diameter of the objective in millimeters. 6 x 30 optics magnify six times and have 30 millimeter objectives.

Prisms are easily knocked out of alignment, requiring an expensive and difficult repair. If severe, this misalignment is immediately noticeable on use by the double-image scene. Minor damage can be seen by focusing on a small object and slowly moving the binoculars away from the eye, which will cause the images to appear to separate. Overall cleanliness should be checked by looking backwards (through the objective) at a light or the sky, when any film or dirt on the lenses or prisms can easily be seen. Pristine binoculars are worth far more than when dirty or misaligned, and broken or cracked optics lower the value far more. Cases help keep binoculars clean but do not add materially to the value. The following listings assume a very good overall condition, with generally clean and alligned optics.

Our advisor for this category is Peter Abrahams, who studies and collects binoculars and other optics. Please contact, especially to exchange reference material. Mr. Abrahams is listed in the Directory under Oregon.

Field Glasses

Folding, modern, hinged flat case, oculars outside 10.00
Folding or telescoping, no bbls, old 125.00
Goerz 5x40, military drab gr, WWI, IF, many other makers 40.00
Ivory covered, various sm szs & makers 180.00
LeMaire, bl leather/brass, various szs, other Fr makers same 25.00
Metal, emb hunting scene, various sm szs & makers 35.00
Pearl covered, various sm szs & makers 90.00
Porc covered, delicate painting, various sm szs & makers 175.00
US Naval Gun Factory Optical Shop 6x30 ....75.00
Zeiss 'Galan' 2x5x34, modern design look, early 1920s 80.00

Prism Binoculars (Porro)

Barr & Stroud, 7x50, Porro II prisms, IF, WWII 110.00
Bausch & Lomb, 6x30, IF, WWI, Signal Corps 40.00
Bausch & Lomb, 7x50, IF, WWII, other makers same 45.00

Bausch & Lomb Zephyr, 7x35 & other, CF 100.00
Bausch & Lomb/Zeiss, Pat 1897, 8x17, CF 140.00
Crown Optical, 6x30, IF, WWI, filters 45.00
France, various makers & szs, if not unusual 30.00
Goertz Trieder Binocle, various szs, unusual adjustment 65.00
Leitz 6x30 Dienstglas, IF, good optics 65.00
Leitz 8x30 Binuxit, CF, outstanding optics 150.00
Nikon 9x35, 7x35, CF, 1950s 65.00
Nippon Kogaku 7x50, IF, Made in Occupied Japan 85.00
Ross Stephada, 7x30, CF, wide angle, 1930s 90.00
Sard 6x42, IF, very wide angle, WWII 750.00
Toko (Tokyo Opt Co) 7x50, IF, Made in Occupied Japan 45.00
Universal Camera 6x30, IF, WWII, other makers same 40.00
US Naval Gun Factory Optical Shop 6x30, IF, filters, WWI 70.00
US Naval Gun Factory Optical 10x45, IF, WWI 140.00
US Navy, 20x120, various makers, WWII & later 2,000.00
Warner & Swasey (important maker) 8x20, CF, 1902 ....250.00
Zeiss, Starmobi 12/24/42x60, turret eyepcs, 1920s 2,000.00
Zeiss Deltrintem 8x30, CF, 1930s 95.00
Zeiss Teleater 3x13, CF, bl, leather 85.00
Zeiss 15x60, CF or IF, various models 600.00
Zeiss 8x40 Delactis, CF or IF, 1930s 150.00

Roof Prism Binoculars

Hensoldt, Dialyt, various szs, long tapered bbl, 1930s-80s 110.00
Hensoldt Universal Dialyt, 6x26, 3.5x26, cylindrical, 1920s 80.00
Leitz Trinovid, 7x42 & other, CF, 1960s-80s, EX 375.00
Zeiss Dialyt, 8x30, CF, 1960s 400.00

Birdcages

Birdcages can be found in various architectural styles and in a range of materials such as wood, wicker, brass, and gilt metal with ormolu mounts. Those that once belonged to the wealthy are sometimes inlaid with silver or jewels. In the 1800s, it became fashionable to keep birds, and some of the most beautiful examples found today date back to that era. Musical cages that contained automated bird figures became popular; today these command prices of several thousand dollars. In the latter 1800s, wicker styles came into vogue. Collectors still appreciate their graceful lines and find they adapt easily to modern homes.

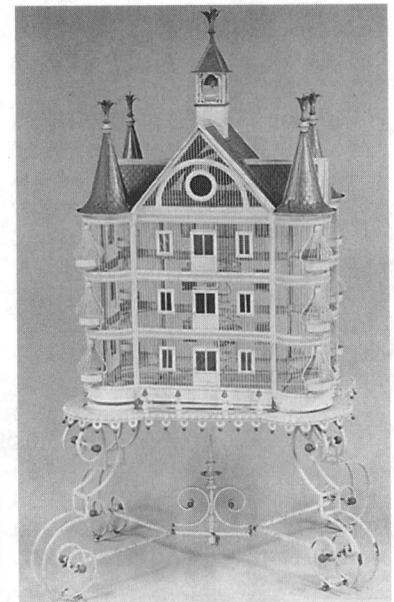

Metal and wood mansion form with four turrets and pitched roof with tower, spiral staircase inside, 57¾x26", on wrought-iron stand, $5,250.00 at auction.

Brass, Hendryx, Pat 1906, 9x13" 110.00
Pine/wire, Fr Provincial, arched bonnet, 18x24x11" 465.00
Poplar w/pnt traces, wire bars, house style, weathered, 26", EX ..250.00
Tin, minor pitting & rust, 19¼" H 220.00
Tole, tin/wire/trn wood finial, worn orig 5-color pnt, 17" 125.00
Wicker, hand-cvd fr of fruits/leaves, 1880s, 15x12x9", EX 240.00
Wire ware on wood fr, copper tray, blk pnt, 22x15x24" 165.00

Bisque

Bisque is a term referring to unglazed earthenware or porcelain that has been fired only once. During the Victorian era, bisque figurines became very popular. Most were highly decorated in pastels and gilt and demonstrated a fine degree of workmanship in the quality of their modeling. Few were marked. See also Heubach; Nodders; Dolls; Piano Babies.

Am Indian (& African chief), EX quality, 11", pr 1,200.00
Boy w/basket, lav, bl & pk, good detail, 13¾" 225.00
Boy w/plumed hat by side, much gold, 11½x3¼" 195.00
German Shepherd, tan w/blk details, 5x6" 175.00
Girl in nightie w/kittens, dog & cat, Germany, 8½" 145.00
Girl in pk dress & tam holding shell to breast, 12" 100.00
Girl in short dress & lg hat holding sheaf of wheat, 14" 150.00
Grandmother & 2 children, Ernst Bohne, bl anchor mk, 5¾" 225.00
Lady holds mask, much gold, Maruyama, 12¼" 62.00
Lady in long floral gown, lg feathered hat, 9" 38.00
Lamp, man (& lady), brass rtcl base, 1930s, Germany, 11", pr ...385.00
Man & lady under pk umbrella, pastels, 5⅜x3" 195.00
Man on bench w/musical instrument, mk Gardner, Russia, 7" ...495.00
Pastille burner, cottage figural, mc, 3½x7¼" 75.00
Pastille burner, dog wearing hat w/feather, mc, 5" 200.00
Toothpick holder, figure of a boy in long jacket, Germany, 6" 30.00
Vase, lady in purple by tree before sq receptacle, 7½x5" 75.00
Vase, Nouveau maid stands before lg lily, Germany, 18" 440.00

Black Americana

Black memorabilia is without a doubt a field that encompasses the most widely exploited ethnic group in our history. But within this field there are many levels of interest: arts and achievements such as folk music and literature, caricatures in advertising, souvenirs, toys, fine art, and legitimate research into the days of their enslavement and enduring struggle for equality. The list is endless.

In the listings below are some with a derogatory connotation. Thankfully, these are from a bygone era and represent the mores of a culture that existed nearly a century ago. They are included only to convey the fact that they are a part of this growing area of collecting interest. Black Americana catalogs featuring a wide variety of items for sale are available; see the Directory under Clubs, Newsletters, and Catalogs for more information. See also Cookie Jars; Postcards; Posters; Sheet Music.

Ashtray, boy rolling dice, pnt bsk, Japan, 3" 40.00
Ashtray, Coon Chicken Inn, purple & red print on glass, 4¼" 30.00
Ashtray, Go Away...Dis Ain't Yo Hive, ceramic, Japan, 3¼" 65.00
Ashtray, Mammy figural, rpt CI, 4" 100.00
Ashtray, man playing banjo, pnt CI, 3⅞", NM 170.00
Ashtray, 2 boys pushing dice cart, bsk, 4¾" 30.00
Bell, Mammy figural, lacquered brass, lt wear, 3⅞" 55.00
Bell, Mammy figural, porc, mc, Japan, 3¼", EX 70.00
Book, Am Slave Code, Wm Goodell, 1853, EX 310.00
Book, Budget Negro Songs, Harris & Carroll, 1880, EX 50.00

Book, Little Blk Sambo, Bannerman, jtd moving pictures, G 40.00
Book, Little Blk Sambo, Donahue, ca 1919, G 25.00
Book, Wonderful Tar Baby, JC Harris, Disney, 1945, VG 40.00
Bottle, banjo player, mc ceramic, J Baulmi, 12", EX 90.00
Bottle, man's head form, amber glass w/mc pnt, 6¼" 75.00
Bowl, Coon Chicken Inn, Shenango, 5½", G 145.00
Brush holder, Red Cap, molded/pnt compo, 8", EX 60.00
Cigarette caddy, Who Left This Behind, bsk, mc, 3½", EX 15.00
Cigarette/match holder, figure by baskets, bone china, 6" 75.00
Cigarette/match holder, shoeshine boy by box, ceramic, 6½" 40.00
Clothespin bag, Mammy washing clothes print on linen, 26x18"..35.00
Cookie jar, Aunt Jemima, F&F 325.00
Creamer, Mammy figural, pnt ceramic, Japan, 2¾", EX 90.00
Creamer & sugar bowl, Aunt Jemima & Uncle Mose, F&F 150.00

Figurine, boy and girl seated, each holding melon slice, molded and painted bisque, Germany, ca 1900-20s, 7x4", $250.00.

Figurine, boy on potty w/watermelon, pnt bsk, 4¼" 125.00
Figurine, man smoking cigar, pnt CI, sm chips, 3⅛" 200.00
Figurine, 2 children on potty, pnt bsk, 3¼", EX 70.00
Hitching post, stable boy, pnt CI, 48", G 325.00
Humidor, bald man w/pipe, pnt bsk, Germany, 4½" 250.00
Humidor, dapper man, rpt plaster, 13" 475.00
Humidor, girl in pigtails, pnt bsk, minor chips, 4⅜" 250.00
Humidor, head of sailor, glazed ceramic, 7½", EX 350.00
Humidor, Mammy w/open mouth, pnt bsk, hairline, 5½" 425.00
Humidor, man smiling, pnt ceramic, hairline, 5" 300.00
Incense burner, head of smiling man, pnt plaster, 3½", EX 40.00
Incense urn, crying baby on potty, pnt lead & metal, 6" 70.00
Lamp, Mammy, pnt ceramic, metal bracket, hangs, 7½" 195.00
Lawn ornament, boy in red pants & yel shirt, CI, 40x12", EX 400.00
Lure, boy in bbl, bbl lifts, 3½", NMIB mk Sam-bo 150.00
Match holder, boys & cotton bale, bronze, 2⅝" 65.00
Match holder, scrub woman, ceramic, mc, 4", EX 95.00
Memo holder, Mammy, pnt wood, Hampden Novelty, 10½", EX .65.00
Mug, Chef, ceramic, mk Japan 135.00
Opener, Blk face, pnt CI, DJ Crowley, 4¼" 350.00
Opener, smiling man, brass, 4¼", EX 60.00
Pad & pencil holder, Mammy, pnt chalk, Miller, 1954, 9½" 75.00
Planter, Mammy, pnt bsk, Japan, 4", EX 120.00
Planter, Mammy, pnt ceramic, Pfaltzgraff, 7" 180.00
Plaque, lady's head, pnt plaster, red bow tie, 6", VG 25.00
Plate, dinner; Coon Chicken Inn, tan, oval, Inca Ware 325.00
Plate, Famous & Dandy, transfer print on china, 6½" 125.00
Plate, Sambo Meets Molly, 3-compartment, porc, Germany, 8"..165.00
Pot holder plaque, Mammy, pnt wood, 9", VG 50.00
Print, Cake Walk, dancing couples, fr, 5x4", EX 225.00
Print, Colored Man Is No Slacker, Renesch, 1918, 20x16", VG ...55.00
Print, Diana & Wade cut-out dolls, paper litho, 19x49", EX 200.00

Print, Sambo Was a Gentleman, color litho, Rees, 15x7", EX 120.00
Recipe box, Aunt Jemima, unmk F&F 125.00
Saucer, Coon Chicken Inn, 6" 100.00
Scouring pad holder, lady holds out apron, ceramic, Germany ...135.00
Shaker, Mammy, ceramic, wht/bl/brn/gr, 6" 65.00
Shakers, Aunt Jemima & Uncle Mose, F&F, 3½", pr 60.00
Shakers, Blk & Wht Chefs, CA Pottery, 4¼", EX, pr 75.00
Shakers, boy w/watermelon slice, ceramic, Japan, 3½", pr 100.00
Shakers, children in basket, pnt ceramic, 5½", pr 85.00
Shakers, lady w/watermelon, nodder, pnt bsk, 3¼", pr 80.00
Shakers, Mammy & Chef, ceramic, mc, Japan, 8½", EX, pr 40.00
Shakers, Mammy & Chef, ceramic, red & wht, 4", 4¼", pr 75.00
Shakers, Mammy & Chef, unmk, pr 60.00
Shakers, native children, pnt bsk, Germany, 3", EX 50.00
Shakers, native riding whale, pnt ceramic, Japan, 2¾", pr 85.00
Sheet music, Amos 'N Andy, Kalmar & Ruby, VG 25.00
Smoking stand, Butler, pnt wood, holds metal tray, 38", VG 250.00
Spice containers, Aunt Jemima, F&F, 4", VG, set of 9 ....350.00
Spoon holder nodders, Mammy & Chef, ceramic, 3½", EX, pr ...200.00
Spoon rest, Mammy, pnt ceramic, Japan, discoloration, 9" 45.00
String holder, Bell Hop, pnt clay, Fredericksburg, 6" 150.00
String holder, Mammy's face, pnt ceramic, Japan, 6" 200.00
Sugar bowl, Chef figural, pnt ceramic, CC Co, 6½" 220.00
Syrup, Aunt Jemima, pnt plastic, F&F, 5¼", EX 40.00
Tambourine, boy w/watermelon on paper, wood & metal fr, 3" dia ..400.00
Teapot, Mandy, ceramic, Japan 175.00
Teapot, Native on elephant, porc, Japan, rpr, 10" 55.00
Timer, Chef holding sand timer, ceramic, Germany, 3½" 55.00

Black Cats

Made in Japan during the fifties, these novelty cats may be found bearing the labels of several different importers, all with their own particular characteristics. The best known and most collectible of these cats are from the Shafford line. Even when unmarked, they are easily identified by their red bows, green eyes, and white whiskers, eyeliners, and eyebrows. Relco/Royal Sealy cats are tall and slender, and their bow ties are gold with red dots. Wales is a wonderful line with yellow eyes and gold detailing; Enesco cats have blue eyes, and there are other lines as well. When evaluating your black cats, be sure to inspect their paint and judge them accordingly. 50% paint should relate to 50% of our suggested values, which are given for cats in mint (or nearly mint) paint.

Milk pitchers, Shafford, 6½" and 6", $85.00 each.

Ashtray, head shape w/open mouth, Shafford, 3" 18.00
Cigarette lighter, Shafford, 5½" 150.00
Condiment set, 2 heads, J&M bows w/spoons, Shafford, 4" 65.00

Cookie jar, lg cat head, Shafford 85.00
Creamer & sugar bowl, cat-head lids are shakers, 5⅜" 45.00
Cruet, oil & vinegar; co-joined cats, 1-pc, Royal Sealy 40.00
Cruets, he w/O eyes, she w/V eyes & hair bow, Shafford, pr 50.00
Decanter, upright cat holds bottle w/cork stopper, Shafford 50.00
Demitasse pot, tail hdl, bow finial, Shafford, 7½" 95.00
Desk caddy, pen forms tail, spring body holds letters, 6½" 8.00
Egg cup, cat face on bowl, ped ft, Shafford 25.00
Grease jar, sm cat head, Shafford 60.00
Measuring set, 4 cups on wood rack w/cat's face, Shafford 150.00
Pincushion, cushion on bk, tongue measure 22.50
Pot holder caddy, 'teapot' cat, 3-hook, Shafford 85.00
Shaker, long cat, salt in 1 end, pepper in other, Shafford 75.00
Shakers, rnd-bodied teapot cat, Shafford, pr 35.00
Shakers, seated, bl eyes, Enesco label, 5¾", pr 15.00
Spice set, yel eyes, 9 sq shakers w/appl red bows, wood rack 125.00
Spice set, 6 sq shakers in wood rack, Shafford 125.00
Strainer, w/cat face, long wood hdl, Shafford 60.00
Teapot, bulbous body, head lid, gr eyes, Shafford, 6½" 45.00
Teapot, dbl-chamber, Shafford 95.00
Teapot, panther-like, gold eyes, sm 20.00
Teapot, upright cat, paw spout, yel eyes, red bow, Wales, 8¼" 60.00
Toothpick holder, cat by vase atop book, Occupied Japan 12.00
Wall rack, long flat cat w/hooks for utensils, Shafford 85.00
Wine, emb cat's face, gr eyes, Shafford, sm 20.00

Black Glass

Black glass is a type of colored glass that when held to strong light usually appears deep purple, though since each glasshouse had its own formula, tones may vary. It was sometimes etched or given a satin finish; and occasionally it was decorated with silver, gold, enamel, coralene, or any of these in combination. The decoration was done either by the glasshouse or by firms that specialized in decorating glassware. Crystal, jade, colored glass, or milk glass was sometimes used with the black as an accent. Black glass has been made by many companies since the 17th century. Contemporary glasshouses produced black glass during the Depression, seldom signing their product. It is still being made today.

To learn more about the subject, we recommend *A Collector's Guide to Black Glass*, written by our advisor, Marlena Toohey; she is listed in the Directory under Colorado. Look for her newly updated value guide. See also Tiffin, L.E. Smith, and other specific manufacturers.

Ashtray, hat shape, emb Dobbs on brim, 2½" H 25.00
Atomizer, gold decor on satin, ca 1930s 7" 55.00
Bonbon, clear swan neck & head hdl, Viking, #974-1S, 5¼" 30.00
Bottle, beer; Anchor Hocking, metal closure, 8½" 25.00
Bottoms Up cocktail tumbler, legs together, 1932 ....25.00
Bowl, mayonnaise; silver decor, LE Smith, #635, 1930s 15.00
Bowl, rolled edge, 1920s-30s, 11" 45.00
Bowl, shallow, cupped, ca 1920s, 10¼" 30.00
Candle holders, dbl; Dbl Shield, LE Smith, pr 40.00
Candlesticks, 3-light, 4x7½", pr 70.00
Comport, HP florals, scalloped edge, McKee, #157, 1930s 35.00
Creamer & sugar bowl, Ovide, Hazel Atlas 22.00
Flowerpot & saucer, LE Smith, 4" 25.00
Ivy ball, Hobnail, ftd, LE Smith, #85, 5" 15.00
Jug, emb tavern scene, European, ca 1900, 5" 50.00
Pin tray, heart shape, 5" 18.00
Plate, 2 sides rolled up, hdls, LE Smith, 7" 18.00
Salver, US Glass, ca 1926, 11½" 45.00
Tumbler, 10-scallop ft, 8-oz 15.00
Vase, bud; gold decor, att HC Fry 25.00

Vase, fan form w/8-sided ft, LE Smith, #1000, 1920s 40.00
Vase, urn form, LE Smith, 7¾" 22.00
Window box, Snake Dance, LE Smith, #404 ....30.00

Blown Glass

Blown glass is rather difficult to date; 18th and 19th century examples vary little as to technique or style. It ranges from the primitive to the sophisticated, but the metallic content of very early glass caused tiny imperfections that are obvious upon examination, and these are often indicative of age.

In America, Stiegel introduced the English technique of using a patterned, part-size mold, a practice which was generally followed by many glasshouses after the Revolution. From 1820 to about 1850, glass was blown into full-size three-part molds. In the listings below, glass is assumed clear unless color is mentioned. Numbers refer to a standard reference book, *American Glass* by Helen McKearin. See also Bottles and specific manufacturers. Our advisor for this category is Mark Vuono; he is listed in the Directory under Connecticut.

Bottle, pinch; lt gr, appl ft & rigaree, stain, 6¼" 50.00
Bottle, whimsey, cobalt, dog form, chip on ft, 6¼" 55.00
Bowl, amethyst, folded rim, faint ribs, 2¾x4" 165.00
Bowl, bl opal, broken blister, 3x6" 70.00
Bowl, Pillar mold, flared rim, 6½" 55.00

Bowl, olive-amber with lily pad decorations, footed, attributed Lancaster, 1830-50, 4½x7⅜", $9,900.00; Pitcher, aqua with threaded decoration, Redford Glass Works, NY, ca 1840, 8½", $1,045.00.

Cake stand, hollow stem w/wafers, gallery rim, 7¼x10¾" 370.00
Candlestick, flint, hollow cut stem & socket, 11" 60.00
Canister, 2 appl rings, pressed lid, 10" 75.00
Compote, flint, cut dmn point band, appl ft, 7x8" 77.50
Compote, Petal & Loop, hexagonal baluster stem, 9¼x12¼" 400.00
Creamer, deep violet, appl hdl, 3" 55.00
Creamer, ribbed mold, appl ribbed hdl, 3¾" 15.00
Cruet, 14 ribs, appl hollow hdl, no stopper, 6½" 50.00
Decanter, elongated t'print, bulbous lip, flint, 10¾" 125.00
Decanter, frosted bands & SP vintage o/l, 8⅞" 150.00
Decanter, pinched sides, 8 pcs of appl rigaree, 9⅜" 110.00
Decanter, 2 appl rings, 3¾"+stopper 220.00
Funnel, wine; appl rim, 21" 155.00
Goblet, wheel-eng vintage, 6", 4 for 44.00
Hat whimsey, 15 ribs, appl cobalt rim, 2¾" 115.00
Jar, blk amethyst, pontil scar, tooled rim, 5⅜" 190.00
Jar, deep olive-amber, flared mouth, 11½" 75.00
Mug, eng hops, figures, dtd 10-11-87, pewter lid, 7¾" 200.00

Mug, fiery opal w/mc floral & Forget-Me-Not, 4⅛" 85.00
Pan, aqua, folded rim, 1½x3¾" 60.00
Pan, clear w/cobalt band at rim, pontil scar, 1860s, 2x6⅛" 100.00
Pan, sapphire bl, 16 broken swirl ribs, folded rim, 6" 1,450.00
Pitcher, appl threading at neck, flake, 3⅞" 130.00
Pitcher, cobalt, 19 ribs, appl cobalt ft & hdl, 4¾" 300.00
Pitcher, etched foliage, appl hdl, 8" 135.00
Pitcher, lt gr, 17 swirled ribs, appl hdl, 2⅞" 20.00
Pitcher, orange-red, Loop, appl clear hdl, 9½" 220.00
Pitcher, red-amber, pontil scar, hollow hdl, 1830-50, 5½" 525.00
Pitcher, 15 broken swirl ribs, appl hollow hdl, 4⅞" 110.00
Pokal, cut decor, amber flashed, 13¼" 90.00
Sugar bowl, electric bl w/wht looping, opal cased, 7" 1,925.00
Sugar bowl, molded panels & 10 ribs, appl ft, w/lid, 7" ..1,100.00
Taster, canary yel, 9 panels, pontil scar, 1½", NM 85.00
Taster, cobalt, 12 panels, smooth base, tooled rim, 1½" 70.00
Tumbler, amethyst, 8 panels, pontil scar, sm chip, 3¼" 130.00
Tumbler, bright gr, 8 panels, polished pontil, 1880s, 3½" 250.00
Tumbler, cobalt, 6 panels, pontil scar, ca 1870s, 3¾" 120.00
Tumbler, dk sapphire bl, 8 panels, pontil scar, 1870s, 3⅛" 90.00
Tumbler, emerald gr, 8 panels, polished pontil, 1880s, 3¼" 210.00
Tumbler, eng floral wreath, 3½" 85.00
Tumbler, fiery opal w/mc bird & floral, 4" 225.00
Tumbler, lt ice bl, 6 panels, pontil scar, 1870s, 3⅛" 160.00
Tumbler, lt pk-amethyst, 9 panels, pontil scar, 1870s, 3½" 220.00
Tumbler, yel-amber, 6 panels, pontil scar, ca 1870s, 3¼" 210.00
Vase, cobalt, cut decor w/ormolu fittings, chip, 7¼" 55.00
Vase, gr, appl ring, 11" 65.00
Wine, eng floral band, wafer stem, 3¾" 50.00
Wine, peacock gr, 4¾" 17.50

Blown Three-Mold Glass

A popular collectible in the 1920s, '30s, and '40s, blown three-mold glass has again gained the attention of many. Produced from approximately 1815 to 1840 in various New York, New England, and Midwestern glasshouses, it was a cheaper alternative to the expensive imported Irish cut glass.

Distinguishing features of blown three-mold glass are the three distinct mold marks and the concave-convex appearance of the glass. For every indentation on the inner surface of the ware, there will be a corresponding protuberance on the outside. Blown three-mold glass is most often clear with the exception of inkwells and a few known decanters. Any colored three-mold glass commands a premium price.

The numbers in the listings that follow refer to the book *American Glass* by George and Helen McKearin. Our advisor for this category is Mark Vuono; he is listed in the Directory under Connecticut.

Creamer, GII-7, bbl form, Keene, w/stopper, 1-pt 200.00
Decanter, GII-18, 3 appl rigaree rings, rpl stopper, 8¼" 40.00
Decanter, GII-18, 3 appl rings, open blister, w/stopper, 8" 150.00
Decanter, GII-21, 3 appl rings, stain, 6¾" 165.00
Decanter, GII-7, pouring spout, rpl stopper, 6⅞" 120.00
Decanter, GIII-6, rpl stopper, 5⅛" 175.00
Decanter, GIV-7, rpl stopper, 8⅞" 85.00
Decanter, GV-16, minor stain, w/stopper, 8¼" 415.00
Decanter, GV-8, Baroque pattern, 8¼" 50.00
Hat whimsey, GII-21, 2½" 12.50
Inkwell, GII-2, deep olive-amber, sm chip, 2⅜" 30.00
Pan, GI-5, pontil scar, tooled & folded rim, 1820s, 5⅞" 110.00
Pan, GII-28, pontil scar, tooled & folded rim, 1⅝x4⅛" 170.00
Pitcher, GI-25, milk glass, smooth base, appl hdl, 8⅛" 2,000.00
Pitcher, GII-18, appl hdl, 5½" 578.00

Tumbler, GII-22, 5¾" 20.00
Tumbler, GIII-26, 5⅞" 45.00

Blue and White Stoneware

Blue and white stoneware, much of which was decorated with such in-mold designs as grazing cows and Dutch children, was made by practically every American pottery from the turn of the century until the mid-1930s. Crocks, pitchers, wash sets, rolling pins, and canisters are only a few of the items that may be found in this type of 'country' pottery that has become one of today's popular collectibles.

Roseville, Brush-McCoy, Uhl Co., and Burley Winter were among those who produced it; but very few pieces were ever signed. Naturally, condition must be a prime consideration, especially if one is buying for resale; pieces with good, strong color and fully molded patterns bring premium prices. Normal wear and signs of age are to be expected since this was utility ware and received heavy use in busy households. In the listings that follow, crocks and jars are assumed without lids unless noted otherwise. For further information we recommend *Blue and White Stoneware* by Kathryn McNerny. See also specific manufacturers.

Batter jar, Wildflower, thick appl hdl, 8x7" 275.00
Bean pot, Boston Baked Beans, Swirl, heavy diffused pattern 300.00
Beer cooler, Elves, brass spigot, 18x14" 850.00
Bowl, Apricot, 9½" 85.00
Bowl, batter; Wildflower, w/hdl 400.00
Bowl, Daisy on Waffle, 10¾" 95.00
Bowl, Gadroon Arches (Feather Panels), 4½x9½" 150.00
Bowl, mixing; Flying Bird, 4x7½" 225.00
Bowl, Reverse Pyramids w/Reverse Picket Fence, 2½x4½" 150.00
Bowl, Wildflower, 4½x7" 100.00
Butter crock, Butterfly, orig lid & bail, 6½" 225.00
Butter crock, Daisy & Trellis, orig lid & bail, 4½" 200.00
Butter crock, Eagle, orig lid & bail, M 450.00
Butter crock, Grapes & Leaves, dbl ring around rim, 3x6½" 175.00
Canister, Basketweave, Cereal, orig lid, 7½" 350.00
Canister, Basketweave, Cloves, orig lid, 5" 250.00
Canister, Basketweave, Coffee, orig lid, 7½" 250.00
Canister, Basketweave, Pepper, orig lid, 5" 250.00
Canister, Basketweave, Put Your Fist In, orig lid, 7½" 700.00
Canister, Basketweave, Sugar, orig lid, 7½" 250.00
Canister, Basketweave, Tobacco, orig lid, 7½" 500.00
Canister, Snowflake, rpl lid, 6½x5¾" 150.00
Chamberpot, Wildflower, stenciled pattern, 6x11" 135.00
Coffeepot, Oval, Diffused Bl, bl-tipped knob, str sides, 11x4" 250.00
Coffeepot, Swirl, 'spurs' on hdl, acorn finial, 11½x6" 450.00
Cookie jar, Brickers, flat button finial, 8x8" 325.00
Cookie jar, Turkey Eye color drip, Diffused Bl bands, 9x8" 250.00
Cookie/biscuit jar, Flying Bird, orig lid, 9x6¾" 650.00
Cup, Bow tie, bird transfer, 3¾x3½" 95.00
Cup, Wildflower w/emb Ribbon & Bow, 4½x2½" 85.00
Custard cup, Fishscale, 5x2½" 75.00
Egg storage crock, Barrel Staves, bail hdl, 5½x6" 185.00
Foot warmer, Diffused Bl, A Warm Friend, 12½x6½" 275.00
Grease jar, Flying Bird, orig lid 650.00
Ice crock, Barrel Staves, rope/tongs/ice block emb, 4½x6" 225.00
Iced tea cooler, Blue Band, flat lid, complete, 13x11" 295.00
Measuring cup, Spearpoint & Flower Panels, 6x6¾" 150.00
Milk crock, Daisy & Lattice, 4x8", NM 125.00
Milk crock, Lovebird, rstr bail & handgrip, 5½x9" 145.00
Mug, beer; advertising, Diffused Bl, sqd hdl 150.00
Mug, Cattails 150.00

Mug, Basketweave and Flower, roped square-top handle, 5x3", $125.00.

Mug, Flying Bird, 5x3" 225.00
Mug, plain 65.00
Mug, Windy City (Fannie Flagg), Robinson Clay Products 200.00
Pickle crock, Blue Band, advertising, recessed lid, 12x9" 225.00
Pickle crock, Heart Band, advertising, rolled rim, w/lid, 8x8" 225.00
Pie plate, Blue Walled Brick-Edge star emb base, 10½" 100.00
Pitcher, Acorns, stenciled, 8x6½" 135.00
Pitcher, American Beauty Rose, 10" 350.00
Pitcher, Apricot, 8" 250.00
Pitcher, Avenue of Trees, allover bl, 9x7" 200.00
Pitcher, Barrel, +6 mugs 395.00
Pitcher, Basketweave & Flower, 9" 225.00
Pitcher, Bl Band, plain 100.00
Pitcher, Bl Band Scroll 160.00
Pitcher, Bl Sawtooth, Wht Hall 150.00
Pitcher, Bluebird, 9x7" 250.00
Pitcher, Butterfly, 9x7" 250.00
Pitcher, Castle & Fishscale, 8" 195.00
Pitcher, Cattails, 7½" 150.00
Pitcher, Cattails, 9" 185.00
Pitcher, Cherries & Leaves, w/printing, 9½" 350.00
Pitcher, Cherry Cluster, 7½" 195.00
Pitcher, Cherry Cluster & Basketweave, 10" 175.00
Pitcher, Cosmos 195.00
Pitcher, Cow, 8½" 250.00
Pitcher, Doe & Fawn, EX color 250.00
Pitcher, Doe & Fawn, sparce bl, 8½" 185.00
Pitcher, Dutch Boy & Girl by Windmill, 9" 225.00
Pitcher, Dutch Landscape, stenciled, tall 200.00
Pitcher, Eagle 450.00
Pitcher, Eagle w/Shield & Arrows, rare 500.00
Pitcher, Edelweiss, metal thumb rest, 9x5" 300.00
Pitcher, Fishscale & Wild Rose, 10" 160.00
Pitcher, Flying Bird, 9" 700.00
Pitcher, Grape Cluster on Trellis, allover bl, 7x7" 200.00
Pitcher, Hunting Scene, rare, 7x8" 400.00
Pitcher, Indian Boy & Girl, 6" 350.00
Pitcher, Indian Good Luck, stenciled 250.00
Pitcher, Indian Head in War Bonnet, dl bl, waffled body, 9" 435.00
Pitcher, Iris, 9" 225.00
Pitcher, Lady w/Harp, deep cobalt 200.00
Pitcher, Leaping Deer, 8½" 175.00
Pitcher, Lincoln, allover deep bl, 10x7" 600.00
Pitcher, Lincoln, allover deep bl, 4¾x4¾" 175.00
Pitcher, Lincoln, allover deep bl, 6x4" 250.00
Pitcher, Lincoln, allover deep bl, 7x5" 300.00
Pitcher, Lincoln, allover deep bl, 8x6" 350.00
Pitcher, Lincoln w/Log Cabin 525.00
Pitcher, Lovebird, arc bands, deep color, 8½" 450.00
Pitcher, Lovebird, pale color, 8½", EX 300.00
Pitcher, Peacock, 7¾x6½" 450.00

Pitcher, Pine Cone, 9½" 200.00
Pitcher, Poinsettia, 6½" 275.00
Pitcher, Rose & Fishscale, 6" 165.00
Pitcher, Rose on Trellis 165.00
Pitcher, Scroll & Leaf, advertising, 8" 250.00
Pitcher, Stag & Pine Trees, 9" 295.00
Pitcher, Swan, long beak, arched neck, deep color, 8½" 275.00
Pitcher, Swan, lt bl, 8½" 295.00
Pitcher, tavern scene, Flemish Jugs...Kinney & Levan, 9" 165.00
Pitcher, Tulip, 8x4" 275.00
Pitcher, Wild Rose, sponged bands, 9" 295.00
Pitcher, Wild Rose, 9x6" 185.00
Pitcher, Wildflower, stenciled 250.00
Pitcher, Windmill & Bush, 9" 225.00
Pitcher, Windy City (Fannie Flagg), Robinson Clay, 8½" 450.00
Pitcher, 2 old men w/canes, dog's-head spout, Germany, 11" 200.00
Roaster, Diffused Bl, appl hdls, flat lid finial, 9x19" 225.00
Roaster, Wildflower, domed lid, 8½x12" 195.00
Rolling pin, Bl Band, advertising, 14x4" 350.00
Rolling pin, Swirl, orig wooden hdls, 13" 475.00
Rolling pin, Wildflower, w/advertising, 15x4½" 450.00
Salt crock, Apricot, orig lid 200.00
Salt crock, Butterfly, orig lid 185.00
Salt crock, Daisy on Snowflakes, orig lid, 6½x6" 220.00
Salt crock, Flying Bird, orig lid, 9" 350.00
Salt crock, Grapevine on Fence, pale bl, orig lid, 6½x6¾" 225.00
Soap dish, Beaded Rose 125.00
Soap dish, cat's head 150.00
Soap dish, Indian in War Bonnet 150.00
Syrup dispenser, Pep-So, rpl lid, 12x9" 325.00
Teapot, Swirl, dbl wire bail hdl, ball shape, 9x6½" 450.00
Toothbrush holder, Bow Tie, stenciled flower 50.00
Vase, Swirl, cone shape 300.00
Wash set, Rose on Trellis, 2-pc 300.00
Water cooler, Apple Blossom, brass spigot, 17x15" 700.00
Water cooler, Bl Band, orig lid 175.00
Water cooler, Cupid, brass spigot, patterned lid, 15x12" 700.00
Water cooler, Polar Bear, brass NP spigot, rare, 17x15" 700.00
Water jug, Diffused Bl, cork affixed to stopper, 7x7" 195.00

Blue Ridge

Blue Ridge dinnerware was produced by Southern Potteries of Erwin, Tennessee, from the late 1930s until 1956 in twelve basic styles and two thousand different patterns, all of which were hand decorated under the glaze. Vivid colors lit up floral arrangements of seemingly endless variation, fruit of every sort from simple clusters to lush assortments, barnyard fowl, peasant figures, and unpretentious textured patterns. Although it is these dinnerware lines for which they are best known, collectors prize the artist-signed plates from the forties and the limited line of character jugs made during the fifties most highly. Examples of the French Peasant pattern are valued at double the prices listed below; very simple patterns will bring 25% to 50% less.

Our advisors, Betty and Bill Newbound, have compiled two lovely books, *Blue Ridge Dinnerware, Revised Third Edition*, and *The Collector's Encyclopedia of Blue Ridge*, both with beautiful color illustrations and current market values. They are listed in the Directory under Michigan. For information concerning the National Blue Ridge Newsletter, see the Clubs, Newsletters, and Catalogs section of the Directory.

Ashtray, advertising, rnd 50.00
Ashtray, advertising, w/rest 65.00
Bonbon, divided, center hdl 85.00

Bowl, cereal/soup; Premium, 6" 15.00
Bowl, divided, 8" 20.00
Bowl, fruit; 5" 4.00
Bowl, hot cereal 10.00
Bowl, mixing; sm 15.00
Bowl, salad; 10½" 45.00
Bowl, vegetable; divided, oval, 9" 25.00
Bowl, vegetable; oval, 9" 20.00
Box, candy; rnd w/lid, rare 95.00
Box, cigarette 65.00
Box, Dancing Nudes, rare 300.00
Box, Mallard, rare 450.00
Box, powder; rnd 125.00
Box, Rose Step 100.00
Butter dish, Woodcrest 60.00
Butter pat/coaster 1,500.00
Cake tray, Maple Leaf 55.00
Carafe, w/lid 60.00
Casserole, w/lid 40.00
Celery, Skyline shape 30.00
Child's cereal bowl 30.00
Child's feeding dish 30.00
Child's mug 25.00
Child's plate 35.00
Chocolate pot, pedestal, china 175.00
Coffeepot 100.00
Creamer, Fifties shape 12.00
Creamer, Pedestal 55.00
Creamer, regular 8.00
Cup, dessert; glass 12.00
Cup & saucer, demitasse; china 30.00
Cup & saucer, Premium 45.00
Cup & saucer, regular 10.00
Custard cup 12.00
Deviled egg dish 32.50
Dish, baking; 13x8", w/metal stand 35.00
Egg cup, Premium 30.00
Gravy boat 20.00
Jug, batter; w/lid 70.00
Jug, character; china, rare 600.00
Jug, syrup; w/lid 80.00
Lazy susan, center bowl w/lid 160.00
Leftover, w/lid, lg 30.00
Pitcher, fancy, china 95.00

Pitcher, Tralee Rose, Spiral, 7", $65.00.

Plate, artist sgn, china 650.00
Plate, Christmas Tree 65.00

Plate, dinner; 9½" 12.00
Plate, divided 20.00
Plate, Language of Flowers 75.00
Plate, party; w/cup well & cup 22.50
Plate, sq, novelty pattern, 6" 45.00
Plate, Square Dance, 14" 85.00
Plate, 11½" 28.00
Plate, 8" sq 9.00
Platter, regular pattern, 15" 30.00
Platter, Thanksgiving Turkey 195.00
Platter, Turkey w/Acorns 195.00
Platter, 11" 11.00
Platter, 12½" 15.00
Ramekin, w/lid, 5" 28.00
Ramekin, w/lid, 7½" 32.00
Relish, Charm House 125.00
Relish, crescent shape, ind 15.00
Relish, heart shape, sm 45.00
Relish, Maple Leaf, china 55.00
Salad fork 32.00
Salad spoon 30.00
Server, center hdl 25.00
Shakers, Apple, pr 12.00
Shakers, Bud Top, pr 32.50
Shakers, Charm House 95.00
Shakers, ftd, china, tall, pr 50.00
Shakers, Good Housekeeping 75.00
Shakers, Palisades, pr 30.00
Shakers, regular, short, pr 12.00
Shakers, Skyline, pr 20.00
Sugar bowl, demitasse; china 35.00
Sugar bowl, regular, w/lid 13.00
Sugar bowl, Rope hdl, w/lid 20.00
Sugar bowl, Waffle, w/lid 20.00
Teapot, Ball shape 60.00
Teapot, Chevron hdl 90.00
Teapot, Colonial 90.00
Teapot, demitasse; china 125.00
Teapot, Mini Ball, china 95.00
Tidbit, 2-tier 25.00
Toast, covered 100.00
Tray, cake; Maple Leaf 45.00
Tray, chocolate pot; china 400.00
Tray, flat shell, china 80.00
Tray, snack; Martha 95.00
Tumbler, juice; glass 12.00
Vase, boot, 8" 80.00
Vase, rnd, china, 5½" 70.00
Vase, ruffled top, 9¼" 90.00
Vase, tapered, china 90.00
Wall sconce 65.00

Bluebird China

Made from 1910 to 1934, Bluebird china is lovely ware decorated with bluebirds flying among pink flowering branches. It was inexpensive dinnerware and reached the height of its popularity in the second decade of this century. Several potteries produced it; shapes differ from one manufacturer to another, but the decal remains basically the same. Among the backstamps you'll find W.S. George, Cleveland, Carrolton, Homer Laughlin, Limoges China of Sebring, Ohio; and there are others.

Because examples of this line are relatively scarce, we seldom find new listings. If you have some to add, let us hear from you.

Bowl, deep, 5" 25.00
Bowl, fruit; Deerwood, 5½" 12.50
Bowl, fruit; Hopewell China, 5" 10.00
Bowl, gravy; w/saucer, Hopewell China 50.00
Bowl, sauce; SP Co, 4½" 12.50
Bowl, soup; PMC Co, 8" 30.00
Butter dish, 4½" holder w/in 7" dia dish, Steubenville 85.00
Casserole, Royal China Internat'l, 7x11½" 125.00
Casserole, w/lid, Ostro China, 10½" dia 95.00
Creamer & sugar bowl, w/lid, Homer Laughlin 45.00

Cup, footed, 3½", $35.00; Creamer, 4¼", $20.00.

Cup, coffee; unmk, 3½" 25.00
Cup, tea; unmk 15.00
Ladle, sauce; gold scrolling 40.00
Plate, dessert; Limoges, 6" 8.00
Plate, Homer Laughlin, 8½" 15.00
Plate, rtcl, sq, unmk, 9" 35.00
Plate, Steubenville China, 9" 15.00
Platter, Hopewell China, 13x10" 65.00
Platter, Hopewell China, 17½x13" 95.00
Platter, unmk, 9x7" 35.00
Syrup, unmk, 4" 35.00
Teapot, ELP Co, 8½x8½" 125.00

Boch Freres

Founded in the early 1840s in La Louviere, Boch Freres Keramis became the foremost producer of art pottery in Belgium. Though primarily they served a localized market, in 1844 they earned worldwide recognition for some of their sculptural works on display at the International Exposition in Paris.

In 1907 Charles Catteau of France was appointed head of the art department. Before that time, the firm had concentrated on developing glazes and perfecting elegant forms. The style they pursued was traditional, favoring the re-creation of established 18th-century ceramics. Catteau brought with him to Boch Freres the New Wave (or Art Nouveau) influence in form and decoration. His designs won him international acclaim at the Exhibition d'Art Decoratif in Paris in 1925, and it is for his work that Boch Freres is so highly regarded today. He occasionally signed his work as well as that of others who under his direct supervision carried out his preconceived designs. He was associated with the company until 1950 and lived the remainder of his life in Nice, France, where he died in 1966. The Boch Freres Keramis factory continues to operate today, producing bathroom fixtures and other utilitarian wares. A variety of marks have been used, most incorporating some combination of 'Boch Freres,' 'Keramis,' 'BFK,' or 'Ch Catteau.' A shield topped by a crown and flanked by a 'B' and an 'F' was used as well.

Box, jewel; mc Deco gr abstracts, brass trim, 5½x4½" **325.00**
Jardiniere, stylized floral band/zigzags, 1890, 10x11" **825.00**
Vase, checkerbrd panels are wht fluted, brn sun rays, 13" **865.00**
Vase, Deco floral on volcanic glaze, stoneware, 10" **650.00**
Vase, deer between bands of geometric circles, Catteau, 20" ...**2,185.00**
Vase, lg vibrant floral on wht w/yel dots, blk top/base, 14" **690.00**
Vase, lush flowers/leaves, mc/orange on blk, Keramis, 12" **950.00**
Vase, multifloral, mc/blk on aubergine, gilt rim/hdls, 9" **175.00**
Vase, 3 lg deer/leaves, blk/bl/gr on wht crackle, bulbous, 9" **1,100.00**

Boehm

Boehm sculptures were the creation of Edward Marshall Boehm, a ceramic artist who coupled his love of the art with his love of nature to produce figurines of birds, animals, and flowers in lovely background settings accurate to the smallest detail. Sculptures of historical figures and those representing the fine arts were also made and along with many of the bird figurines, have established secondary-market values many times their original prices. His first pieces were made in the very early 1950s in Trenton, New Jersey, under the name of Osso Ceramics. Mr. Boehm died in 1969, and the firm has since been managed by his wife. Today known as Edward Marshall Boehm, Inc., the private family-held corporation produces not only porcelain sculptures but collector plates as well. Both limited and non-limited editions of their works have been issued. Examples are marked with various backstamps, all of which have incorporated the Boehm name since 1951. 'Osso Ceramics' in upper case lettering was used in 1950 and 1951.

In our descriptions, those ending in (A) are auction values. All others are dealer's asking prices. As you can see, there is a wide variance.

Birds

Ruffled Grouse pair, #456, issued 1960, $1,400.00 (A).

Baby Bald Eagle, perched on rocks, 10" (A) **450.00**
Baby Buntings, 3½" (A) **160.00**
Baby Cedar Waxwing, #432 ....**250.00**
Baby Chickadee, #461 ....**250.00**
Baby Chickadee, 3" (A) **60.00**
Baby Crested Flycatcher, #458E **229.00**
Baby Crested Flycatcher, 5" (A) **100.00**
Baby Robin, 3½" (A) **75.00**
Baby Wood Thrush, #444 ....**250.00**
Black-Capped Chickadee on Holly, 8" **220.00**
Bluejays on Strawberries w/Chameleon **3,500.00**
Canadian Geese, #408RR **625.00**
Cardinal, wht bsk, rnd porc base, 8½" (A) **175.00**
Cardinals **465.00**
Common Tern, 1968 ....**935.00**

Crested Flycatcher on Sweet Gum **550.00**
Cygnet, 6⅝" (A) **195.00**
Cygnet on lily pad, 4¼" (A) **385.00**
Fledgling Blackburnian Warbler, #478RR **250.00**
Fledgling Great Horned Owl, #479D **240.00**
Fledgling Kingfisher, #4499 ....**325.00**
Fledgling Red Poll, #495 ....**250.00**
Green Jays w/Blk Persimmons **1,650.00**
Hummingbird, by pk cactus flower (A) **400.00**
Killdeer Pr w/Bluebells **440.00**
Prothonotary Warbler, #445 ....**325.00**
Rearing Arabian Stallion, #RPC 309-03, 9½" **875.00**
Road Runner w/Horned Toad, 1968 ....**585.00**
Seal Pup, wht w/blk eyes, 2½" (A) **105.00**
Snowy Owl, #10177 ....**1,945.00**
Snowy Owl, Boehm Porc Expo, Moscow 1987, 18x14" (A) **1,200.00**
Tree Sparrow, 8" (A) **125.00**
Tufted Titmouse, on snowy branch, 13" **945.00**
Western Bluebirds, #494 ....**475.00**
White Mouse, pk features, gr leaf, 3½" (A) **90.00**
Wood Thrushes w/Azaleas **525.00**
Young American Bald Eagle, #4998B **795.00**

Bohemian Glass

The term 'Bohemian glass' has come to refer to a type of glass developed in Bohemia in the late 16th century at the Imperial Court of Rudolf II, the Hapsburg Emperor. The popular artistic pursuit of the day was stone carving, and it naturally followed to transfer familiar procedures to the glassmaking industry. During the next century, a formula was discovered that produced a glass with a fine crystal appearance which lent itself well to deep, intricate engraving, and the art was further advanced.

Although many other kinds of art glass were made there, collectors today use the term 'Bohemian glass' to most often indicate clear glass overlaid or stained with color through which a design is cut or etched. (Unless otherwise described, the items in the listing that follows are of this type.) Red or yellow on clear glass is common, but other colors may also be found. Another type of Bohemian glass involves cutting through and exposing two layers of color in patterns that are often very intricate. Items such as these are sometimes further decorated with enamel and/or gilt work. Our advisor for this category is Thomas P. Bradshaw; he is listed in the Directory under California.

Beaker, gr, daffodils, mc enamel & gold, 19th C, 5¼" **750.00**
Beaker, red, deer & trees, 5⅜" **70.00**
Bowl, red, naturalistic scenes, 5x6" **110.00**
Box, powder, red, girl feeding chickens, 3½" **145.00**
Compote, red, stag in wooded landscape, 1930s, 11½" **350.00**
Decanter, cobalt, leaves & berries, 7" **90.00**
Goblet, red, view of Battle Monument Baltimore, 7" **465.00**
Jar, red, scrolling vintage, w/lid, 7" **90.00**
Pitcher, amber, HP 24k gold leaf, 1950s, 15½", +4 tumblers **245.00**
Pokal, amber, paneled, faceted knob, acorn finial, 19th C, 14" ..**350.00**
Powder dish, red, bird in branches w/gold **72.50**
Stein, red, dog in forest, pewter mts, 5½x3¼" **325.00**
Urn, amber, nature scene, tall knob std w/eng base, 20" **1,250.00**
Vase, amber, florals, 1920s, 11" **210.00**
Vase, red, triple dmn, scalloped, 10" **82.50**

Bookends

Though a few were produced before 1880, bookends became a necessary library accessory and a popular commodity after the printing industry was revolutionized by Mergenthaler's invention, the linotype. Books became abundantly available at such affordable prices that almost every home suddenly had need for bookends. They were carved from wood, cast in iron, bronze, or brass, or cut from stone. Today's collectors may find such designs as ships, animals, flowers, and children. Patriotic themes, art reproductions, and those with Art Nouveau and Art Deco styling provide a basis for a diverse and interesting collection.

Abraham Lincoln bust on plinth, bronzed metal	45.00
Am Congress on Surveying & Mapping logo, brass, 1941, 6"	125.00
Amish couple, CI, mc pnt, 4¾"	200.00

Boy and dog, bronze finish, Frankart, 1920s, 6¾x5½", $190.00.

Cactus, copper, Craftsman	30.00
Cowboy, ceramic, cubist style, wht crackle, Fabre France	430.00
Dayton OH etched landscape band, brass, Frost, 4½x6"	90.00
Eagle, CI, EX detail, 7"	300.00
Flower silhouette, bronze, sgn G Matthew, 1928	100.00
German Shepherd, brass, old	65.00
Great Dane, bronze finish	40.00
Horse head w/flowing mane, bronze-look ceramic	12.00
Indian's head w/headdress, CI, orig mc pnt, 6½"	188.00
Lady in pk dress, Doulton style, 6x3¾"	145.00
Maid w/book, 2nd on knee, metal, after Gerdago, 7½"; 6¾"	485.00
Monk reading from crouched position, CI, B&H	135.00
Nude, seated w/book in lap, bronze w/gr patina, Verrier, 7"	345.00
Paneled door, dome window above, pillars, bronze, Handel	450.00
Peek-A-Boo, gr, Frankart	190.00
Satyr boy (& girl), silvered bronze, sgn Silvestre, 4x10"	200.00
Scottie dog, Frankart	145.00
Ship's wheel, metal, Jennings Brothers	60.00
Sitting Bull, pot metal, mc pnt, 1920s, 7x5x3"	70.00
Teddy Roosevelt	75.00
Terriers, porc, blk & wht	150.00
Wire-Haired Terrier, bronze, EB Parsons, 6x8"	250.00

Bootjacks and Bootscrapers

Bootjacks were made from metal or wood. Some were fancy figural shapes, others strictly business! Their purpose was to facilitate the otherwise awkward process of removing one's boots. Bootscrapers were handy gadgets that provided an effective way to clean the soles of mud and such. Our advisor for this category is Louis Picek; he is listed in the Directory under Iowa.

Bootjacks

Am Bull Dog, pistol shaped, CI, blk pnt, 8"	75.00
Beetle, CI, orig worn pnt, Reading PA, 4x11x3", EX	120.00
Beetle, openwork bk, CI, 11¾x5x2", EX	110.00
Cricket, CI, no paint, Webster Bros, Reading PA, 11"	55.00
Dachshund, CI, worn blk pnt, early 1900s, 24x8x5½"	185.00
Heart figural, scalloped sides, CI, 13" L	135.00
Hickory, bentwood hdl, hinged/folds, use w/out bending over	85.00
Naughty Nellie, CI, EX pnt, no rust, 9¾"	200.00
Naughty Nellie, CI, pnt traces & rust, 9¾"	105.00
V-shape, ornate CI, VG	48.00

Bootscrapers

Dachshund, full body, blk pnt w/red trim, 20"	80.00
Duck, full bodied, scraper on bk, CI, 14½" L	350.00
Griffins jtd at wings & tails, CI, marble base, 18"	880.00
Lyre on oval scalloped base, CI, 9x11"	110.00
Pig silhouette, cut-out eye, CI, 8½x12"	200.00
Pointer on 'bridge,' brushes in base missing, CI, rpt, 6"	335.00
Scottie silhouette w/edge tooling, cast steel, pnt, 9"	110.00
Wrought iron w/scrolled finials, 11½"	75.00

Boru, Sorcha

Sorcha Boru was the professional name used by California ceramist Claire Stewart. She was a founding member of the Allied Arts Guild of Menlo Park (California) where she maintained a studio from 1932 to 1938. From 1938 until 1955, she operated Sorcha Boru Ceramics, a production studio in San Carlos. Her highly acclaimed output consisted of colorful, slip-decorated figurines, salt and pepper shakers, vases, wall pockets, and flower bowls. Most production work was incised 'S.B.C.' by hand.

Bowl, maroon, appl peony on lid, 6"	75.00
Figurine, bluebird, 5x10"	100.00
Figurine, Penelope, fawn, 6"	85.00
Pitcher, pk lustre florals w/gold centers, beading, 6½"	65.00
Planter, appl flowers	75.00
Shakers, mouse w/jacket, pr	50.00
Shakers, sailor boy & girl, pr	85.00
Sugar shaker, lady figural, 6"	85.00
Vase, appl florals & leaves, 8"	60.00

Bossons Artware

Bossons artware has been on the international market since 1948 when the first high-relief wall plaques were made to depict English scenes and floral subjects. Though floral plaques are still produced with many new releases becoming popular, it is Bossons character wall masks (life-like sculptures) and figurines that have been so popular as gift-store items since they were introduced in 1958/59. Today's collectors appreciate their extremely fine modeling and artistry, and interest is on the increase on an international basis. Masks most often found are usually subjects of men from all nations and walks of life (women are rare, two of the three 'Children Studies,' 1968, are extremely rare), and some of the larger wall figurines include an animal. Nearly all are made of a strong plaster medium that is easily chipped or scuffed. Mint or mint-in-box discontinued examples are few.

In most every case, Bossons have the sculpture name incised under the collar, or at the base of the figurine, with a date indicating when the mold was created. Also, on the reverse side of these sculptures will appear the following incision: 'Bossons Copyright Reserved,' and often 'Congleton, England,' with date. **Those dates will not change though** that model may be issued for years, but collectors seek out the variations in color and particularly sculptural changes that often occur during the mask's span of production. Collectors and dealers must be aware of many directly molded illegal copies, e.g., 'Pancho and Rawhide,' or 'fakes' and 'look-alikes' cast in everything from plaster, rubber, and even metal. They are some **English** character masks of good quality produced by the Legend Company. They can have a striking resemblance to Bossons in that Fred Wright, principal sculptor for Bossons from 1957 to 1972, left Bossons to work at the Legend factory. The Bossons resident sculptor/artist several years before Wright and since 1972 is Mrs. Alice Brindley. Mr. W. Ray Bossons, son of the founder, W.H. Bossons, is Chairman and Managing Director of the company.

Being molded in plaster, Bossons are frequently found in deplorable condition, and avid collectors pay the premium prices mentioned here for only the most perfect examples, either in factory 'mint' states or perfectly returned to their original structural and coloring beauty by a restoration artist recommended by Bossons.

Bossons also made a series of both domestic animals and wildlife in plaster as well as a hard plastic called 'Stonite.' Full-length plaster Oriental figures were made in a limited number as were clocks, mirrors and other decorative items. Bossons also produces their 'Ivorex' plaques, formerly Osborne Editions. All Bossons products are hand painted by individual artists and highly collectible. The discontinued editions and some of the rarer examples in perfect condition command prices in excess of $1,000.00.

Our advisor for this category is Dr. Don Hardisty; he is recommended by Bossons to restore their products and is listed in the Directory under New Mexico.

Key:
DC — Dickens Character Series   DS — Dog of Distinction

Arug Barbarossa, 5", current retail	68.00
Bill Sikes, DC, current retail	42.00
Black Labrador, DS, 4½", current retail	27.00
Boxer, DS, 4½", current retail	27.00
Desert Hunters, 2nd edition (dog's mouth open), 7"	175.00
Dog, Series II, Alsatian, 4¾"	125.00
Dog, Series II, Corgi, 4"	75.00
Dog, Series II, Double Terriers	100.00
Dog, Series II, Pekingese, 3¼"	75.00
Dogs & Cats, Series I & II, 1959-61, 3" to 4", $125 to	300.00
Eagle, Bossons Ceramic	150.00
Full-length wall figure, Peon, 15", $150 to	275.00
Full-length wall figure, Sherpa, 15", $175 to	350.00
Koalas, orig model, 10½"	300.00
Lords of the Desert, 10"	125.00
Series A, Abdhul, 8", $75 to	125.00
Series A, Coolie, 8"	175.00
Series A, Deccan Hunters, brn-eyed cat, 8½", $175 to	250.00
Series A, Deccan Hunters, gr-eyed cat, 8½", $150 to	200.00
Series A, Eskimo, 8½"	125.00
Series A, Romany, orig model, 8½"	150.00
Series A, Saracen, wht hat, 8"	185.00
Series A, Saracen, yel hat, 8"	165.00
Series B, Albanian, pk hat, 5½"	145.00
Series B, Corsican, 5½", $85 up to	125.00
Series B, Jock, orig model w/tooth, 5½", $85 to	150.00
Series B, Lichensteiner, 5½", $150 to	175.00
Series B, Paddy, 5½", current retail	38.00
Series B, Smuggler, 5½", current retail	37.00
Series B, Tibetan, 5½", $75 to	125.00
Shelf ornament, Himalayan, 1 of 4	215.00
Yorkshire Terrier, bl hair bow, DS, 5", current retail	27.00

Bottle Openers

Around the turn of the century, manufacturers began to seal bottles with a metal cap that required a new type of bottle opener. Now the screw cap and the flip top have made bottle openers nearly obsolete. There are many variations, some in combination with other tools. Many openers were used as means of advertising a product. Various materials were used including silver and brass.

A figural bottle opener is defined as a figure designed for the sole purpose of lifting a bottle cap. The actual opener must be an integral part of the figure itself. A base-plate opener is one where the lifter is a separate metal piece attached to the underside of the figure. The major producers of iron figurals were Wilton Products, John Wright Inc., Gadzik Sales, and L & L Favors. Openers may be free-standing and three-dimensional, wall hung or flat. They can be made of cast iron (often painted), brass, bronze or aluminum.

Numbers within the listings refer to a new reference book printed by the FBOC (Figural Bottle Opener Collectors) organization. Those seeking additional information are encouraged to contact FBOC, whose address can be found in the Directory under Clubs, Newsletters, and Catalogs.

Alligator, F-136, CI, mc pnt, EX	90.00
Bear's head, F-426, CI, worn mc pnt, 3¾"	120.00
Bulldog, F-425A, brass, Wilton Products, 4"	40.00
Clown, F-417, brass	30.00
Cowboy, F-27, CI, NM pnt, 1950, 4¾"	135.00
Donkey, F-60, CI, mc pnt	32.00
Donkey, F-61, CI, mc pnt, EX	42.00
Double Eye, F-414, bald man, EX pnt	48.00

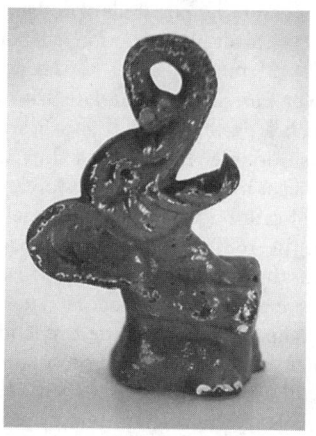

Elephant with trunk up, F-48, cast iron with gray paint, light wear, 3¾", $30.00.

Goat, F-71, pnt CI, tall, EX	65.00
High Hat Sign Post Drunk, F-12, CI, mc pnt, EX	25.00
Lamp Post Drunk, F-2A, bronze w/blk highlights, 4"	22.00
Leg, F-206, brass	35.00
Lobster, F-168, CI, red & blk pnt	32.00
Miss 4-Eyes, F-408, EX pnt	55.00
Monkey, F-89A, brass, 2½"	40.00
Mr Dry, F-416, VG mc pnt	80.00
Negro w/wide mouth, F-402C, smooth eyes, brass	30.00
Nude, F-171, brass, Russwood, 1946	50.00
Nude, F-177, brass	40.00
Nude w/wreath, F-173, pot metal, copper finish, 5¾"	15.00
Parrot, F-108, CI, mc pnt, plain stand	55.00
Parrot on perch, F-114, ornate base, CI, EX mc pnt, 5½"	300.00
Pelican, F-129, CI, mc pnt, EX	55.00
Pretzel, F-232, EX pnt	40.00
Sea Gull, F-123, CI, 3-color pnt	60.00

Shoe, F-209, aluminum, no pnt, 3¾" 100.00
Sign Post Drunk, F-11, CI, worn pnt 22.50
Squirrel, F-91, CI, worn mc pnt, 3" 90.00
Straw Hat Sign Post Drunk, F-13, CI, mc pnt, EX 40.00
Streetwalker, F-5, aluminum, 4½", NM 65.00
Tennis Racquet, brass 6.00
Trout, F-159, CI, mc pnt 120.00

Bottles and Flasks

As far back as the 1st century B.C., the Romans preferred blown glass containers for their pills and potions. Though you're not apt to find many of those, you will find bottles of every size, shape, and color made to hold perfume, ink, medicine, soda, spirits, vinegar, and many other liquids. American business firms preferred glass bottles in which to package their commercial products and used them extensively from the late 18th century on. Bitters bottles contained 'medicine' (actually herb-flavored alcohol), and judging from the number of these found today, their contents found favor with many! Because of a heavy tax imposed on the sale of liquor in 17th-century England by King George, who hoped to curtail alcohol abuse among his subjects, bottlers simply added 'curative' herbs to their brew and thus avoided taxation. Since gin was taxed in America as well, the practice continued in this country. Scores of brands were sold; among the most popular were Dr. H.S. Flint & Co. Quaker Bitters, Dr. Kaufman's Anti-Cholera Bitters, and Dr. J. Hostetter's Stomach Bitters. Most bitters bottles were made in shades of amber, brown, and aquamarine. Clear glass was used to a lesser extent, as were green tones. Blue, amethyst, red-brown, and milk glass examples are rare. (Please note that color is a strong factor when pricing bottles. For example, an amber Hostetter's bitters sells for $25.00 or less, but a green variant can bring hundreds of dollars. An aqua scroll flask may bring $50.00, but a cobalt blue variation will command over $1,000.00.)

Perfume or scent bottles were produced abroad by companies all over Europe from the late 16th century on. Perfume making became such a prolific trade that as a result beautifully decorated bottles were fashionable. In America they were produced in great quantities by Stiegel in 1770 and by Boston and Sandwich in the early 19th century. Cologne bottles were first made in about 1830 and toilet-water bottles in the 1880s. Rene Lalique produced fine scent bottles from as early as the turn of the century. The first were one-of-a-kind creations done in the cire perdue method. He later designed bottles for the Coty Perfume Company with a different style for each Coty fragrance. Prices for commercial perfumes hinge on condition. Their values appreciate according to these factors: are they still sealed or full; do they retain all factory labels; is the original box or packing included? Deluxe versions bring premium prices. Example: blue flat Dans La Nuit cologne by Rene Lalique, value for 6" size, $250.00. Dans La Nuit, enameled with stars by Rene Lalique, 3" round ball, $900.00.

Spirit flasks from the 19th century were blown in specially designed molds with varied motifs including political subjects, railroad trains, and symbolic devices. The most commonly used colors were amber, dark brown, and green.

From the 20th century, early pop and beer bottles are very collectible as is nearly every extinct commercial container. Dairy bottles are a relatively new area of interest; look for round bottles in good condition with both city and state as well as a nice graphic relating to the farm or the dairy.

Bottles may be dated by the methods used in their production. For instance, a rough pontil indicates a date before 1845. After the bottle was blown, a pontil rod was attached to the bottom, a glob of molten glass acting as the 'glue.' This allowed the glassblower to continue to manipulate the extremely hot bottle until it was finished. From about 1845 until approximately 1860, the molten glass 'glue' was omitted.

The rod was simply heated to a temperature high enough to cause it to afix itself to the bottle. When the rod was snapped off, a metallic residue was left on the base of the bottle; this is called an 'iron pontil.' A seam that reaches from base to lip marks a machine-made bottle from after 1903, while an applied or hand-finished lip points to an early mold-blown bottle. The Industrial Revolution saw keen competition between manufacturers, and as a result, scores of patents were issued. Many concentrated on various types of closures; the crown bottle cap, for instance, was patented in 1892. If a manufacturer's name is present, consulting a book on marks may help you date your bottle.

Among our advisors for this category are Madeleine France (see the Directory under Florida), Mark Vuono (Connecticut), Steve Ketcham (Minnesota), Monsen and Baer (Virginia), and John Tutton (Virginia). In the listings that follow (most of which have been taken from auction catalogs), glass is assumed to be clear unless color is indicated. Numbers refer to a standard reference book, *American Glass*, by George and Helen McKearin. See also Advertising, various companies; Avon; Barber Shop Collectibles; Blown Glass; Blown Three-Mold Glass; California Perfume Company; Czechoslovakia; De Vilbiss; Fire Fighting; Lalique; Medical Collectibles; Steuben.

Key:
am — applied mouth
bbl — barrel
bt — blob top
b3m — blown 3-mold
cm — collared mouth
fm — flared mouth
gm — ground mouth
gp — graphite pontil
grd — ground pontil
GW — Glass Works
ip — iron pontil
ps — pontil scar
rm — rolled mouth
sb — smooth base
sl — sloping
sm — sheared mouth
tm — tooled mouth

Barber Bottles

Amethyst, HP daisies 150.00
Arabian Nights, cranberry opal, Beaumont Glass Co, 1899 ....495.00
Bl opal, Daisy & Fern, rm 185.00
Cobalt, floral/enamel dot decor 175.00
Cobalt w/yel & gold Nouveau decor, ps, rm, 1890-1920, 7½" 325.00
Cologne & butterfly pnt on fiery opal milk glass, 8⅝" 150.00
Cranberry opal, melon stripes 200.00
Cranberry swirl opal, sq base, rm 250.00
Lime gr, Persian design 160.00
Stars & Stripes, turq opal, polished pontil, rm, 7⅛" 180.00
Turq w/emb ribs, orange & wht enamel, open pontil, sm, 7⅞" ...160.00

Bitters Bottles

A Hoffeld's Liver...KY, med amber, semi-cabin, 9¾" 575.00
Baker's Orange Grove, med amber, sb, am, spots, 9⅜" 150.00
Baker's Orange Grove, med yel-amber, sb, am, 9⅝" 275.00
Bell's Cocktail..., amber, sb, am, lady's leg, 10½" 185.00
Big Bill Best, amber, sm, tm, faded labels, 12⅛" 90.00
Bismark..., med amber, sb, tm, 1890s, 6⅛" 85.00
Bourbon Whiskey, med salmon-puce, stained labels, 9¼" 400.00
Bourbon Whiskey, smoky plum-puce, flake, 9¼" 275.00
Brown's Celebrated Indian..., dk chocolate, Indian queen, 12" ..925.00
Brown's Celebrated Indian..., med amber, Indian queen, 12" 375.00
Canton (star), med yel-amber, lady's leg, 12" 185.00
Clarke's Vegetable Sherry Wine, aqua, sb, am, 11¾" 180.00
Congress, aqua, sb, am, semi-cabin, 10⅜" 275.00
Constitution...Seware & Bentley, med amber, am, potstone, 9" .425.00
Dandelion Trade Mark, med amber, sb, tm, chips, 7⅜" 300.00
Dr Ball's Vegetable Stomachic..., aqua, am, 1840s, 6⅞" 200.00

Dr Bishop's Wahoo..., med yel-amber, semi-cabin, 10⅛" **475.00**
Dr Blake's Aromatic..., aqua, am, cleaned, 1850s, 7" **90.00**
Dr CW Roback's Stomach Cincinnati O, med amber, bbl, 9⅜" .**145.00**
Dr CW Roback's Stomach Cincinnati O, med yel-amber, bbl, 10".**450.00**
Dr CW Roback's Stomach Cincinnati O, orange-amber, bbl, 9⅜" ..**155.00**
Dr Fisch's WH Ware Pat 1866, med amber, fish, 11½" **160.00**
Dr Fleshhut's Celebrated Stomach, aqua, sb, am, 8⅝" **300.00**
Dr HA Jackson's, aqua, ps, am, 7½" **375.00**
Dr J Hostetter's Stomach, deep olive-amber, sb, am, 8⅜" **130.00**
Dr J Hostetter's Stomach, dk olive-amber, sb, am, 9⅝" **110.00**
Dr J Hostetter's Stomach, yel w/olive tone, sb, am, 8¾" **110.00**
Dr Loew's Celebrated Stomach & Nerve, med yel-apple gr, 9½" ..**150.00**
Dr Lyford's Bitters CP Herrick Tilton NH, aqua, sb, 8½" **100.00**
Dr Manly Hardy's Genuine Jaundice, aqua, sm, ps, 6¾" **180.00**
Dr Marcus' Universal Philada, aqua, ps, am, lt haze, 7⅞" **250.00**
Dr Owen's European Life..Detroit, dk aqua, ps, am, 7" **150.00**
Dr Skinner Celebrated 25 Cent, aqua, ps, am, stain, 8½" **80.00**
Dr Skinner Sherry Wine, aqua, ps, am, 8⅝" **110.00**
Dr Soule's Hop 1872, dk root beer-amber, semi-cabin, 9" **90.00**
Dr Soule's Hop 1872, lt gold-amber, sb, semi-cabin, 7¾" **135.00**
Dr Stephen Hewett's Celebrated..., potstone, bl-aqua, 7½" **90.00**
Dr Wood's Sarsaparilla & Wild Cherry, aqua, ps, am, 9" **240.00**
Drake's Plant'n Pat 1869, amber, sb, am, 9⅞" **75.00**
Drake's Plant'n Pat 1869, root beer-amber, 5-log, 9⅞" **180.00**

E.J. Rose's Magador Bitters For Stomach, Kidney & Liver..., amber, tooled lip, smooth base, 8¾", NM, $80.00.

E Baker's Premium..., aqua, am, cleaned, 6½" **170.00**
Edw Wilder's Stomach Patented..., clear, semi-cabin, 10½" **170.00**
EE Hall New Haven...Est 1842, yel-amber, bbl, 9¾", EX **120.00**
Established 1845 Schroeder's..., amber, lady's leg, 5¼" **300.00**
F Brown Boston Sarsaparilla & Tomato, aqua, ps, am, 9½" **95.00**
Garnett's Compound Vegetable, amber, sb, tm, 6⅜" **425.00**
GC Segur's Golden Seal, aqua, ps, am, 8¼", NM **160.00**
General Bolivar, apple gr, sb, tm, 6¾" **550.00**
Gilbert's Sarsaparilla, med yel-amber, sb, am, 8⅞" **400.00**
Globe Mfg Only by Byrne Bros NY, amber, cannon, 10¾" **285.00**
Golden Geo C Hubbel & Co, aqua, semi-cabin, 10¼" **275.00**
Great Tonic Dr Caldwell's Herb, med amber, ip, am, 12½" **185.00**
Greeley's Bourbon, deep plum-puce, bbl, 9¼" **235.00**
Greeley's Bourbon, med strawberry-puce, bbl, 9¼" **350.00**
Greeley's Bourbon, smoky puce, bbl, 9¼" **275.00**
Greeley's Bourbon, smoky topaz w/olive tone, bbl, 9⅛" **575.00**
Hart's Star OBLPC 1868, aqua, sb, tm, scratches, 9⅛" **250.00**

Hartwig Kantorowicz Pozen Germany, milk glass, sb, 3¾" **110.00**
Highland & Scotch Tonic, amber, am, bbl, 9½" **550.00**
Holtzermann's Pat Stomach, amber, faded label, 4-roof, 9¾" **325.00**
Holtzermann's Pat Stomach, med amber, 2-roof, 9⅜" **1,300.00**
Holtzermann's Pat Stomach, med amber, 4-roof, 9⅝" **140.00**
Holtzermann's Pat Stomach, red-amber, tm, sb, 4-roof, 9¾" **190.00**
Hops & Malt Trade Mark, med amber, semi-cabin, chip, 10" **140.00**
HP Herb Wild Cherry, amber, sb, tm, cabin form, 10" **220.00**
Hutching's Dyspepsia NY, aqua, ps, am, stain, 8¼" **125.00**
Indian Vegetable & Sarsaparilla Geo C Goodwin, aqua, 8¼" **210.00**
Jacob Pinkerton Wahoo..., puce-amber, semi-cabin, 9⅞" **275.00**
Jacob Pinkerton Wahoo..., yel-amber to amber, sb, am, 10⅜" **450.00**
JNO Moffat NY Phoenix Price $1, yel-olive gr, ps, am, 5½" **450.00**
John W Steele's Niagara..., amber, sb, am, semi-cabin, 10" **575.00**
Johnson's Calisaya, dk reddish copper-puce, am, 10" **350.00**
Johnson's Indian Dispeptic, aqua, ps, am, 6⅝" **350.00**
Kelly's Old Cabin Pat 1863, med amber, sb, am, cabin, 9" **1,650.00**
Keystone, amber, sb, am, bbl, 9¾" **525.00**
Kimball's Jaundice, yel olive-amber, am, 7" **375.00**
Lash's Natural Tonic Laxative, amber, sb, tm **20.00**
Lediard's Celebrated Stomach, bl-gr, sb, am, 10" **750.00**
Lediard's Celebrated Stomach, med to dk emerald gr, 10" **1,900.00**
Loftus Peach, gr w/yel tone, sb, am, scratches, 11½" **160.00**
Loveridges Wahoo Buffalo NY, med yel-olive, sb, 7" **300.00**
Lowell's Invigorating, aqua, sb, am, open bubble, 7⅞" **70.00**
Morning (star) Inceptum 48699 Pat 4869, yel-amber, 12⅝" **200.00**
Moulton's Oloroso Trade Mark, bl-aqua, sb, am, 11⅜" **350.00**
Mrs E Emma Cobb's Dr Cobb's Compound, amber, sb, tm, 8¼" .**275.00**
National Pat 1867, amber, sb, am, ear of corn, 12½" **275.00**
National Pat 1867, med amber, sb, am, ear of corn, 12⅜" **300.00**
Old Continental, lt to med yel-amber sb, am, semi-cabin, 9⅞" ..**230.00**
Old Homestead Wild Cherry, med yel-amber, cabin, 9¾" **120.00**
Old Sachem & Wigwam Tonic, med yel-amber, bbl, 9⅜" **325.00**
Old Sachem & Wigwam Tonic, reddish puce, bbl, 9⅜" **220.00**
Oswego 25¢, med amber, sb, tm, 1880s, 7" **75.00**
Patd Oct 1st 1870 by AL Lacraix, aqua, pineapple, 8⅞" **1,700.00**
Peruvian Tonic, med yel-amber, sb, am, 10¼" **210.00**
Reed's, amber, sb, am, lady's leg, 12¾" **170.00**
Rocky Mountain Tonic 1840 Try Me 1870, yel-amber, 9¾" **150.00**
Romaine's Crimean Pat 1863..., yel-amber, semi-cabin, 10" **325.00**
Royal Italian Registered...Genova, pk-amethyst, sb, am, 13⅜" ...**550.00**
Sazerac Aromatic PHD & Co, milk glass, lady's leg, 10" **275.00**
Schroeder's Bitters Louisville Ky, yel-amber, lady's leg, 12" **325.00**
Simon's Centennial Trade Mark, aqua, Washington bust, 10" ...**500.00**
Solomon's Strengthening & Invigorating, cobalt, 9½" **625.00**
ST Drakes 1860 Plant'n X Pat 1862, peach-puce, 6-log, 9¾" **180.00**
Suffolk Philbrook & Tucker Boston, yel-amber, am, 10" **650.00**
Sunny Castle Stomach Jos Dudenhoefer..., amber, sb, tm, 9¼" **65.00**
Swains Bourbon, med yel-olive, sb, am, 1880s, 9" **250.00**
W&Co NY, bright yel-gr, ip, am, pineapple, 8½" **4,100.00**
W&Co NY, med bl-gr, ps, am, pineapple, 8¼" **4,100.00**
WA Graham & Co Tonic, amber, sb, am, flake, 9", NM **110.00**
Walker's Tonic, med yel-amber, lady's leg, 11½", NM **425.00**
Warner 1880 German Hop...Mich, med amber, sb, tm, 8" **230.00**
Whitewell's Temperance, aqua, ps, am, ca 1850s, 7¾" **130.00**
WR Tryee's Chamomile, med amber, sb, tm, semi-cabin, 8¾" ...**525.00**
Zingari F Rather, amber, sb, am, lady's leg, 11¾" **150.00**

Blown Glass Bottles and Flasks

Chestnut flask, cobalt, ps, sm, shallow chip, 1800s, 3½" **240.00**
Chestnut flask, golden yel-amber, 24 swirled ribs, 8¼" **600.00**
Chestnut flask, gr-aqua, rm, sm pontil bruise, 1800s, 5½" **65.00**
Chestnut flask, med olive gr, ps, rm, crude, 1800s, 5⅛" **145.00**

Chestnut flask, yel w/amber tone, ps, rm, 1800s, 6½" 145.00
Flask nurser, cobalt, ps, ca 1840, 7¼" 210.00
Flask nurser, gr-aqua, 20 vertical ribs, fm, ps, 6¼" 75.00
Gemel, gr-aqua w/wht loopings, ps, 1870-1900, 9" 80.00
Gemel, med emerald gr, ps, rm, 1850-60, 4¾" 160.00
Nurser, gr-aqua, 16 vertical ribs, ps, sm, 6½" 80.00
Nurser, lt gr-aqua, 19 dmn pattern, sm, ps, 5¾" 90.00
Pitkin flask, med yel olive gr, 36-rib swirled to right, 5" 210.00
Pitkin flask, yel olive-amber, 36 broken rib swirl, 6½" 275.00

Cologne, Perfume, and Toilet Water Bottles

Blown, dk sapphire bl, 19 ribs swirl to left, ps, 5¾" 350.00
Blown, med sapphire bl, 16 vertical ribs, ps, tm, 6⅛" 475.00
B3m, GI-3 type 2, cobalt, ribs swirl to left, ps, 5½" 250.00
B3m, GI-3 type 2, dk sapphire bl, ribs swirl to left, 5½" 180.00
B3m, GI-7 type 4, sapphire bl, vertical ribs, ps, 6" 190.00
Cylindrical, powder bl opal, ps, Am, ca 1850, 14⅜" 250.00
Herringbone corners, dk purple amethyst, sb, rm, 7¾" 375.00
Label under glass, EN Lightner & Co, sb, w/stopper, 6¼" 250.00
Label under glass, tm, ps, Eau de Cologne label, 6" 135.00
Polygonal, teal gr, rm, sb, Am, 1860-75, 4¾" 180.00
Sunburst, cobalt, tm, Am, ca 1860, 3" 400.00
12-sided, cobalt, ps, rm, sm chips, 1860-70, 10" 625.00
12-sided, deep sapphire bl, rm, sb, Am, 1870s, 7½" 160.00
12-sided, dk amethyst, t&fm, ps, long neck, Am, 1870s, 9¼" 180.00
12-sided, sapphire bl, rm, sb, Am, 1860s, 8¾" 160.00
8-sided w/corset waist, cobalt, rm, sb, Am, 1865-80, 5⅞" 525.00
8-sided w/corset waist, med amethyst, sb, rm, 4½" 625.00

Commercial Perfume Bottles

Asuma, Coty, frosted ball w/emb flowers, 2⅜", +box 200.00
Attente, Verlayne, clear fan shape, Baccarat, 3¼" 120.00
Bal a Versailles, J Despres, court ladies label, 4¼", +box 80.00
Ben Hur, Jergens, frosted gr flower stopper, 5½" 140.00
Blue Grass, E Arden, turq mare & colt overcap, 2¾", +box 385.00
Candide Effuve, Guerlain, hat shape, Baccarat, 5" 200.00
Casanova, Grenoville, clear w/silver stopper, 3½", +box 50.00
Chantilly, Houbigant, attached to parasol, 2", +box 150.00
Charm, Molyneux, apothecary shape, disk stopper, 6" 115.00
Chu Chin Chow, Bryenne, bl glass figure, wht opal cap, 2¼" 415.00
Coeur Joie, Nina Ricci, heart shape, pk ribbon, 1¼", +box 275.00
Dark Brilliance, Lentheric, gold enamel & cap, 1½", +box 145.00
Divine, D'Orsay, clear urn form, gold label, 7", +box 385.00
Divine, D'Orsay, clear w/gold cap, 2⅜", +gold bag & box 132.00
Escaramouche, J Desprez, sword w/blk label, mc tassel, 4¾" 85.00
Essence Rare, Houbigant, clear 'ice,' silver label, 6½" 175.00
Evening in Paris, Bourjois, 7-pc gift set, M in worn box 95.00
Farouche, Nina Ricci, clear & frosted, gold band, 4", +box 330.00
Fath's Love, Fath, clear w/gold label, 4", +gr flocked box 72.50
Fille d'Eve, Nina, apple form, sgn Lalique, +basket 360.00
Flambeau, Faberje, whistle form, w/label, near full, 3", +box 60.00
Gamine, Fragonard, gold urn shape, no label, 4½" 275.00
Gitanjali, Gueldy, clear flask, frosted stopper, 3½", +box 60.00
Glycine, Gabilla, blossom label on clear, Baccarat, 3" 110.00
Guerillas, Guerlain, oval w/horizontal bands, Baccarat, 3" 200.00
Hypnotic, Hattie Carnegie, lady's head & shoulders, 4" 220.00
Impromptu, L Lelong, clear & frosted futuristic shape, 4½" 200.00
It's You, E Arden, hand w/vase, rose stopper, Baccarat, 6¼" 935.00
Jabot, L Lelong, ornate bow shape, w/label, 2¼" 415.00
Kai Sang, Corday, blk glass w/gold/red/wht Oriental decor, 3" ...825.00
L'Or, Coty, slim teardrop shape, Baccarat emblem, 6¼" 60.00
Le Debut Noir, R Hudnut, blk glass octagon, no label, 2" 200.00

Le Gui, Duvelle, gr opaque cylinder, metallic label, 6½" 100.00
Le Vertige, Coty, clear w/gold label, 3", +box 165.00
Madrigal, Molinard, frosted urn shape w/emb dancers, 6" 330.00
Magie, Lancome, baton w/emb stars, gold cap, 5", +box 85.00
Massatta, Lazell, clear w/blk glass flower stopper, 3", +box 120.00
Muse, Coty, clear w/frosted overcap, gold label, 3¼", +box 115.00
My Own Jasmin, Safuran, Japanese doll in kimono, 2¾" 85.00
Narcissus, AJ Co, molded beads, gold label, 3¾", +box 130.00
New Horizons, Ciro, stylized eagle form, 3½", +box 175.00
Nuit de Noel, Caron, blk glass flask shape, 3", +box 165.00
Ode, Guerlain, frosted & clear, bud stopper, Baccarat, 5¾" 360.00
Oeillet, Worth, emb flowers, gold label, Lalique, 3⅜", +box 300.00
Oeillet Fane, Grenoville, clear w/rooster stopper, 3¼" 255.00
Oh La La, Ciro, clear w/frosted stopper, 3¾", +box 300.00
On Dit, E Arden, 2 whispering ladies, frosted, 3¾" 550.00
Parfum des Champs Elysees, Guerlain, turtle, Baccarat, 4¾" 525.00
Parfum Ideal, Houbigant, Nouveau label on clear, Baccarat, 5" ..200.00
Presence, Houbigant, logo enamel name, 3½", +box 110.00
Princess Marie, Matchabelli, orange marbleized slag, 3½" 715.00
Prophesy, Matchabelli, gold & enamel crown, 2½" 230.00
Quand?, Corday, blk glass, gold enamel, 2½", MIB 275.00
Quelques Fleurs, Houbigant, clear w/brass cap, 1½", +basket 90.00
Radical, Caron, clear w/frosted 'ice,' worn label, 8" 200.00
Rose Lilliput, Lubin, clear, sterling cap, Baccarat, 2½", +box 550.00
Ruffles, Oscar de la Renta, boat shape, 10¼" 175.00
Safari, R Lauren, clear cut look, plastic 'silver' cap, 10" 185.00
Sirocco, L Lelong, emb logo on clear, gold cap, 1½", +box 72.00
Souvenir d'un Soir, Mary Chess, clear/frosted fountain, 3½" 550.00
Succes Fou, Shiaparelli, wht glass w/fig leaf overcap, 3" 525.00
Sweet Pea, Renaud, clear w/bl stripes, brass cap, 2⅜", +box 40.00
Toujours Fidele, D'Orsay, pillow form, dog stopper, 3½" 286.00
Une Rose, Guerlain, clear w/floriform stopper, 7¾", +box 415.00
White Diamonds, E Taylor, clear, gold metal stopper, 11" 990.00
Wild Musk, Max Factor, acorn form on chain, 1¾", +box 50.00
Windsong, Matchabelli, crown shape, gold cap, 1½", +box 100.00
With Pleasure, Caron, keg w/gold bands, Baccarat, 3½" 340.00
Zut, Schiaparelli, lady's torso, gr ribbon, gold label, 2¼" 715.00

Dairy

AG Smalley Boston New York, tin top & hdl, 1898, qt 85.00
Alamito Omaha's Pioneer Dairy, pyro covered wagon/mtns, qt 75.00
Borden's Dairy Delivery Co, modern cream top, pyro, 1940, qt 75.00
Carrigan's Niagara Dairy Co, gr, 1930, qt 550.00
Dairy Maid Milk Depot Holland, Mich, ½-pt 10.00

Cloverleaf Blue Ribbon Farms, Stockton, California, Store Bottle, red pyro, 1-qt, $28.50.

Dellinger Dairy Jeffersonville Ind Gold Medal Herd, pyro, qt **75.00**
Empire State Tairy, tin top w/o cap seat, 1890, pt **60.00**
Fauquier Farms Goat Milk Warrenton VA, ½-pt **50.00**
Freeman's Buttermilk Dairy, amber, 1920-30, qt **130.00**
Highland Farms Baltimore MD, pyro barn & trees, qt **25.00**
J Kelso Boscawen NH, pyro Ayrshire milk cow, qt **35.00**
Liberty Dairy Utica NY, pyro Statue of Liberty, ½-pt **15.00**
Maid of California Milk Co Villejo Cal, milkmaid, qt **75.00**
Purity Maid Products, bl, rnd ¾-oz creamer **25.00**
Registered...Empire State Dairy, tm w/o cap seat, 9" **60.00**
Saco Dairy, emb baby face, 1940, qt **90.00**

Figural Bottles

Bear, X Bazin Philada, clambroth, 1840-55, 3¾" **300.00**
Cherub holding medallion, emerald gr, tm, 11" **175.00**
Cherub holding medallion, med purple amethyst, tm, 11" **180.00**
Cucumber, med sapphire bl, 10-rib, ps, Am, ca 1890, 7¾" **70.00**
Fish, EX orig wht & bl-gray pnt on clear, metal cap, 8¾" **80.00**
Lady acrobat on ball, Depose, pontil scar, sm stain, 16" **75.00**
Lady standing, bl opaque, Alsace DD Depose, crown top, 13⅜" .**350.00**

German porcelain figural crown-top bottle: lady in long gown, Coronet mark, 5¾", $100.00.

Man smoking pipe, amber, tm, sb, Germany, ca 1900, 11½" **750.00**
Pineapple, med yel-amber, sb, am, bruise, 1870s, 8⅞" **110.00**
2 children climbing tree, clear/frosted, Depose, 12" **150.00**

Flasks

Benjamin Franklin/Dyott, GI-94, aqua, ps, sm, 1-pt **230.00**
Bust of Columbia/Eagle, GI-122, clear, ps, sm, 1-pt **3,500.00**
Byron/Scott, GI-114, med yel-amber, ps, sm, ½-pt **250.00**
Clasped Hands/Eagle, GXII-21, amber, sb, am, stain, 1-pt **100.00**
Cornucopia/Urn, GIII-17, med to deep bl-gr, 1-pt **450.00**
Cornucopia/Urn, GIII-6, med emerald gr, am, 1-pt **235.00**
Cornucopia/Urn, GIII-7, deep yellowish olive-amber, ½-pt **90.00**
Cornucopia/Urn, GIII-7, dk olive-amber, s&rm, ps, ½-pt **100.00**
Cornucopia/Urn, GIII-7, med emerald gr, sm, ½-pt **185.00**
E Pluribus Unum.../Eagle, GII-43, clear, ps, sm, ½-pt **800.00**
Eagle/Cornucopia, GII-43, aqua, sm, milky stain, ½-pt **275.00**
Eagle/Cornucopia, GII-45, aqua, ps, sm, ½-pt, 5⅝" **150.00**
Eagle/Cornucopia, GII-72, yel-amber, ps, sm, stain, 1-pt **85.00**
Eagle/Cornucopia, GII-73, med olive gr, sm, 1-pt **120.00**
Eagle/Eagle, GII-40, bl-gr, ps, sm, ca 1825-35, 1-pt **775.00**
Eagle/Eagle, GII-40, emerald gr, ps, sm, 1-pt **900.00**

Eagle/Eagle, GII-40, med yel-amber, ip, sm, ca 1830-40, 1-pt .**2,100.00**
Eagle/Morning-Glory, GII-19, aqua, ps, sm, stain, 1-pt **300.00**
Eagle/Sunburst, GII-7, clear w/faint vaseline tint, 1-pt **2,200.00**
Eagle/Tree, GII-41, aqua, sm, scarce, 1-pt **130.00**
Eagle/Willington Glass Co, GII-52, deep olive-amber, 1-pt, EX ...**70.00**
For Pike's Peak/Prospector-Hunter, GXI-45, olive gr, 1-pt **360.00**
Franklin/Franklin, GI-97, emerald gr, ps, sm, 1825-35, 1-qt ..**2,300.00**
Hunter/Fisherman, GXIII-4, orange-amber, am, calabash **220.00**
Lafayette/Liberty Cap, GI-85, yel-amber, ps, sm, 1-pt **300.00**
Liberty/Willington Glass Co, GII-63, deep olive gr, ½-pt **160.00**
Masonic Arch/Eagle, GIV-1, deep aqua, ps, sm, 1-pt **150.00**
Masonic Arch/Eagle, GIV-1, med aqua, ps, sm, 1-pt **130.00**
Masonic Arch/Eagle, GIV-18, med yel-olive, sm, 1-pt **140.00**
Masonic Arch/Eagle, GIV-32, red-amber, ps, sm, 1-pt, 5½" **350.00**
Masonic Arch/Masonic Arch, GIV-28a, emerald gr, ½-pt, NM .**550.00**
Monument/Capt Brag, GVI-1, strawberry puce, 1830-35, ½-pt .**6,200.00**
Ringgold/Rough & Ready, GI-71, aqua, ps, sm, 1-pt **120.00**
Scroll, GIX-8, med yel-olive, ps, sm, haze, 7" **210.00**
Sheaf of Grain/Star, GXIII-38, med bl-gr, ps, am, 1-qt **250.00**
Sheaf of Grain/Star, GXIV-1, dk yel olive-amber, haze, 1-qt **150.00**
Sheaf of Grain/Westford, GXIII-35, olive-amber, sb, am, 1-pt ...**120.00**
Sheaf of Grain/Westford, GXIII-37, dk root beer-amber, ½-pt **90.00**
Soldier/Hound, GXIII-16, yel w/olive tone, ps, am, 1-qt **280.00**
Star/Ravenna Glass Works, GXIII-83, deep aqua, sm, 1-pt **220.00**
Success to RR/Horse Pulling Cart, GV-5, dk olive gr, 1-pt **130.00**
Success to RR/Locomotive, GV-I, aqua, sm, 1-pt **225.00**
Sunburst, GVIII-10, yel olive-amber, sm, ½-pt **475.00**
Sunburst, GVIII-14, lt emerald gr, ps, sm, ½-pt **675.00**
Sunburst, GVIII-16, med yel-olive gr, crude, 1815-25, ½-pt **600.00**
Sunburst, GVIII-18, yel-amber, ps, sm, ½-pt, 6⅜" **375.00**
Sunburst, GVIII-25, med pinkish-puce, ps, sm, ½-pt, NM **2,400.00**
Tree/Tree, GX-17, med gr, ps, sm, 1855-65, 1-pt **825.00**
Urn & Cornucopia, GIII-4, amber, broken blister, 6⅞" **75.00**
Washington/Eagle, GI-2, lt gr, sm, 1-pt **190.00**
Washington/Jackson, GI-32, med yel-olive, sm, 1830-40, 1-pt ...**140.00**
Washington/Taylor, GI-25, aqua, ps, sm, haze, 1-qt **110.00**
Washington/Taylor, GI-40a, yel olive-gr, ps, sm, 1-pt **275.00**
Washington/Taylor, GI-40c, yellowish olive gr, ps, sm, 1-pt **375.00**
Zanesville/Eagle, GIV-32, yel-amber, ps, sm, 1830-35, 1-pt **425.00**

Food Bottles and Jars

Aker's Select Tea Finley Acker & Co..., bright yel-gr, 11⅛" **275.00**
Mustard, HJ Neuhauser, clear, ps, rm, 5" **85.00**
Peppersauce, Cleveland, aqua, cathedral, sb, am, 1870s, 8½" **275.00**
Peppersauce, lt to med bl-gr, cathedral, lt stain, 10¼" **235.00**

Cathedral-style pickle jars: Light green with yellow tint, iron pontil, American, 1850-60, 11½", $525.00; Deep aqua, iron pontil, rolled lip, American, 1850-60, 11¼", $185.00.

Peppersauce, med bl-gr, cathedral, open pontil, am, 8¾" 110.00
Pickle, aqua, cathedral, rm, sb, open bubble, ca 1870, 13¾" 185.00
Pickle, aqua, cathedral, 6-sided, sb, rm, 12¾" 120.00
Pickle, bl-aqua, cylindrical w/fluted shoulder, ip, 11½" 150.00
Pickle, bright yel-gr, unemb bbl, tm, ps, 1860s, 9½" 135.00
Pickle, cobalt goofus, sb, gm, sm chips, 1900-15, 15" 500.00
Pickle, dk aqua, cathedral, rm, sb, ca 1870, 13¾" 250.00
Pickle, gr-aqua, cathedral, rm, sb, 8¾" 130.00

Ink Bottles

B3m, dk yel-olive gr, ps, tm, Am, ca 1800-20, 1½" 90.00
B3m, yel-amber, ps, tm, Am, ca 1810-30, 1⅜" 100.00
Domed, med amber, sb, sm, Am, ca 1880, 1⅞" 120.00

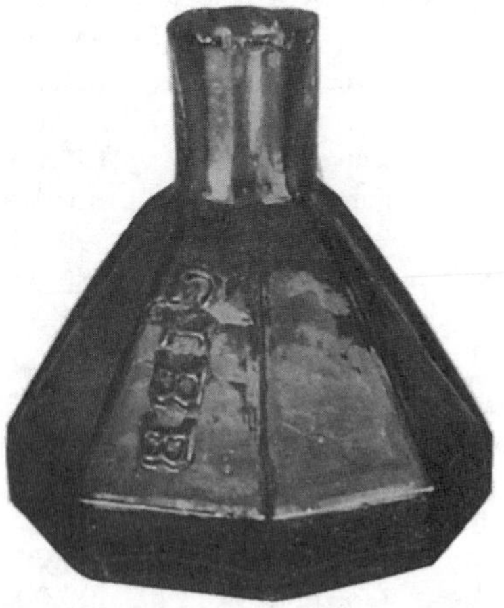

Gibb, dark blue aqua, umbrella form, burst top, smooth base, American, 1860-70, very rare, 2⅝", $275.00.

Harrison's Columbian Ink, aqua, igloo shape, sb, stain, 1½" 160.00
Harrison's Columbian Ink, aqua, 8-sided, stain, 3⅛" 60.00
Hover Phila, lt to med bl-gr, ps, fm, 1835-55, 6" 160.00
Pitkin, med olive gr, 36 swirls to right, 1800s, 1⅝" 650.00
Teakettle, dk amethyst, sb, chips, 1880s, 2" 375.00
Teakettle, lime-gr opaque, sb, Am, ca 1880s, 2" 650.00
Teakettle, med yel-gr, gm w/neck ring, sb, 1880s, 2¾" 850.00
Teakettle, turq, cut & polished dmns in panels, 1880s, 2⅜" 650.00
Tinta American, clear flint, ps, tooled & rm, ca 1850, 1¾" 230.00
Umbrella, amber, 8-sided, open pontil, sm, 1840s, 2½" 150.00
Umbrella, lt gr, 12-sided, ps, rm, haze, 1850s, 2⅝" 240.00
Umbrella, med amber, 8-sided, open pontil, rm, 1840s, 2⅜" 120.00
Umbrella, yel w/amber tone, 8-sided, ps, open bubble, 2⅜" 750.00
Umbrella, yel-olive, 8-sided, open pontil, rm, 1840s, 2⅜" 325.00
18 vertical ribs, aqua, ps, tm, crude, 1850s, 1⅞" 240.00

Medicine Bottles

A H Bull's Ext of Sarsaparilla..., aqua, am, ps, haze, 7" 100.00
American Compound Phila, aqua, ps, am, 5⅞" 85.00
Brunet's Universal Remedy Philada, aqua, ps, lt stain, 8" 240.00
C Heimstreet & Co Troy NY, sapphire bl, 8-sided, stain, 7" 160.00
Doct Robt B Folger's Olosaonian NY, aqua, am, 7⅛" 50.00
Dr Blendigo's Celery Tonic..., amber, sb, tm, 9½" 205.00
Dr Brunet's Worm Syrup, aqua, am, ps, 1850s, lt haze, 6¾" 250.00
Dr Hough's Anti Scrofula Syrup, aqua, am, ps, stain, 9½" 160.00
Dr Kilmer's Swamp Root...Cure, aqua, sb, am, 8½" 10.00
Dr Myers Bilious King Smith Myers & Co, amber, sb, am, 9" 85.00
Dr N Angell's Rheumatic Gin, dk aqua, ps, am, 7⅜" 275.00
Dr Pierce's Gold Med Disc, aqua, sb, am, 8" 10.00
DR W Burton's Syrup Philada, lt gr, ps, am, haze, 6¼" 400.00
ES Reed's Apothecary..., milk glass, sb, heart stopper, 4½" 65.00
H Lake's Indian Specific, aqua, ps, am, 8⅜" 425.00
HH Warner & Co Tippecanoe, amber, am, 9⅛" 85.00
Kickapoo Indian Cough Cure, aqua, sb, am, 6⅛" 10.00
Kikapoo Indian Sagwa, aqua, sb, am, 8¾" 15.00
Kr Kilmer's Swamp Root...Remedy, aqua, sb, am, 7½" 5.00
Laughlin Bushfield Druggists Wheeling Va, bl-aqua, ip, 7⅝" 135.00
LQC Wishart's Pine Tree Tar Cordial, emerald gr, sb, am, 8" 220.00
LQC Wishart's Pine Tree Tar Cordial, med bl-gr, sb, am, 8⅛" ...130.00
LQC Wishart's Pine Tree Tar Cordial, sapphire, sb, 9¾" 725.00
LQC Wishart's Pine Tree Tar Cordial, yel-gr, sb, am, 8" 110.00
Lydia Pinkham's Veg Comp, aqua, sb, am, 8½" 10.00
One Minute Cough Cure, aqua, sb, am, 5¾" 10.00
Paine's Celery Compound, amber, sb, am, 9¾" 10.00
Radam's Microbe Killer, amber, sb, tm, 10¼" 100.00
Rheumatic Trade Mark Syrup 1882..., med amber, sb, am, 9¾" .160.00
Squire Eckstein...Cincinnati Ohio, sapphire bl, ps, am, 6½" 475.00
Swaim's Vermifuge Fever Dysentery Cholera..., aqua, ps, 4¼" 125.00
Thomson's Compound Syrup of Tar..., aqua, ps, am, 1840s, 5¾" ..55.00
Warner's Safe Nervine, amber, sb, am, 9¼" 125.00
Zollickoffer's Anti Rheumatic Cordial, yel olive-amber, 6⅜" ..1,450.00

Mineral Water and Soda Bottles

AB Schellentrager Cleveland Ohio, dk root beer-amber, 9⅛" 160.00
Buffum Sarsaparilla & Lemon, cobalt, 10-sided, ip, 7½" 300.00
Buffum Sarsaparilla & Lemon, dk aqua, 10-sided, ip, 7⅞" 210.00
Caladonia Spring Wheelock VT, yel-amber, sb, am, 9½" 600.00
Congress & Empire Spring Co..., emerald gr, sb, am, 1-pt, 8" 155.00
DA Knowlton Saratoga NY, dk olive-amber, sb, am, 1-qt 100.00
DL Ormsby New York Philadelphia XX..., dk teal gr, 6⅝" 170.00
Eagle Bottling...Goldfield Nev, sun-colored amethyst, 8¼" 1,050.00
El Dorado, med emerald gr, sb, am, stain, 7¼" 45.00
EM Gatchell & Co...Soda Water, med emerald gr, ip, am, 7½" ..300.00
Empire Soda Works Vallejo, med bl-gr, emb eagle, sb, 7½" 90.00
G Morris & Co City Bottling..., sapphire bl, Hutchinson, 6¾" ..140.00
Genuine Belfast Ginger Ale John Ryan..., gr-aqua, 9⅜" 110.00
Geyser Spring Saratoga Springs..., bl-aqua, sb, stain, 7⅝" 90.00
GW Weston & Co, olive gr, ps, am, 9⅝" 170.00
Hamakua Soda Works, Hutchinson, sb, tm, flakes, 7⅝" 160.00
Highrock Congress Spring..., teal bl, sb, am, 1860s, 7⅝" 230.00
Hutchinson & Co Celebrated..., med cobalt, ip, am, 7¼" 230.00
JA Dearborne NY Union Glass Works..., cobalt, ip, am, 7½" 135.00
JN Gerdes SF Mineral Water, gr-aqua, 8-sided, sb, 7¼" 50.00
John Ryan Excelsior...1859 Union Glass Works..., cobalt, 7⅛" ..110.00
John Ryan 1866 Augusta GA, sapphire bl, sb, am, 7¼" 90.00
JW Harris Soda Water..., lt sapphire bl, 8-sided, ip, 7⅜" 375.00
LD Williams Woodbury NJ W, emerald gr, sb, am, 1860s, 6⅞" ..240.00
Meinchke & Ebberwein 1882..., electric cobalt, stains, 7⅞" 60.00
MS Johns Pittsburgh J, bl-aqua, ip, am, 7⅝" 150.00
Norwich Bottling Works..., orange-amber, Hutchinson, 6⅜" 140.00
Owen Casey Eagle Soda Works, cobalt, sb, am, 7⅛" 100.00
Seitz & Bro...Premium Soda Waters, cobalt, 8-sided, ip, 7⅛" 155.00
Union Soda Works, bl-aqua, sb, am, crude, 7" 200.00

Poison Bottles

HK Mulford Co Chemists, cobalt, sb, ca 1900, 3¼" 110.00
Jno Wyeth & Bro Philadelphia, cobalt, w/labels, 2⅝" 90.00
Lattice & Dmn pattern, cobalt, orig Poison stopper, 7" 80.00
Morph Hydrochl Poison, cobalt w/orange & wht enamel, 4¼" ..275.00
Poison & gridwork emb on amber, UDCo/WGW on sb, 3¼" 650.00
Poison emb on amber, S&D on sb, tm, flakes, 4¾" 300.00
Poison Pat Appl'd For emb on skull form, cobalt, 4⅛" 1,000.00
Poison Poison, amber, Antiseptic Tablets label, 4½" 70.00

Phoenix - Old - (phoenix rising from flames) Trade Mark - Bourbon - Naber, Alfs and Brune - S.F. - Sole Agts., light amber, tooled lip, smooth base, ca 1879-1888, 1-pt, $300.00.

Sarsaparilla Bottles

Ayer's Comp Ext, aqua, sb, am, 8½" 10.00
Dr Belding's Wild Cherry, aqua, sb, am, 9½" 75.00
Dr Townsend NY, bright emerald gr, ps, am, 9¾", NM 150.00
Dr Townsend NY, bright med bl-gr, ps, am, flake, 9¾" 210.00
Dr Townsend's Albany NY, dk gr w/yel tones, ip, am, 9⅜" 215.00
Dr Townsend's Albany NY, dk olive-amber, ps, am, 9½" 150.00
Dr Townsend's Albany NY, emerald gr, metallic pontil, 9½" 230.00
Dr Townsend's Albany NY, med emerald gr, sb, am, 9¼" 140.00
Dr Townsend's Albany NY, olive-amber, crude, 9½" 170.00
Dr Townsend's Albany NY, yel-olive gr, ps, am, 9½" 135.00
Itood's, aqua, sb, am, 8¾" 10.00
Old Dr J Townsend NY, dk bl-gr, ps, am, dull, 9¾" 275.00
Old Dr J Townsend NY, med emerald gr, ps, am, haze, 9¾" 150.00
Old Dr Townsend NY, med emerald gr, ps, am, variant, 9¾" 275.00
Wynkoop's Katharismic NY, med sapphire bl, am, 10" 6,500.00

Spirits Bottles

AM Bininger & Co...Gin, yel w/olive tone, sb, am, stain, 10" 140.00
Binninger's Old KY Bourbon 1849 Reserve..., yel-olive, 9¾" 170.00
CI Lewis 3 So 5th St Phila, med amber, ip, am, pocket flask 220.00
Dougherty's Old Rye Whiskey label under glass, 8¾", EX 200.00
Duffy's Malt Whiskey, Baltimore, sb, am, 10⅜" 35.00
EG Booz's...Whiskey, yel-amber, sb, am, cabin, 7¾" 1,050.00
EP Middleton Bro Phila Wheat 1825...on appl seal, amber, 12" .190.00
Henry Chapman & Co Sole Agents..., amber, teardrop, 5¾" 100.00
IW Harper Rye, label only, amber, sb, am, 11¾" 25.00
Nathans Bros 1863 Phila on appl seal, amber, sb, 9½" 110.00
PF Hering on appl banner seal, olive-amber, am, ps, 9½" 140.00
Star emb on appl seal, dk olive-amber, b3m, ps, am, 9¼" 350.00
Sunny Brook Whiskey, bar decanter, gold letters, gp, tm, 8¼" 35.00
Tom Moore Bourbon, jug-style bar bottle, gp, tm, 6⅜" 40.00
Udolpho Wolfe's Schiedam...Schnapps, med pk-amethyst, 8¼" .350.00
Udolpho Wolfe's Schiedam...Schnapps, root beer-amber, 7¾" ...150.00
Wine, olive-amber to blk, long neck, ps, am, 1770s, 8⅜" 85.00
Wine or champagne, med olive-amber, long neck, ps, 1790s, 11" .160.00

Miscellaneous

Lavender Salts, Goetting & Co, see California Perfume Co
Nurser, Best Feeding...Japan, tm, 1920s, 7¼", MIB 90.00

Nurser, Feed the Baby, frosted emb baby's face, sb, tm, 4" 200.00
Nurser, Standard WM McCully & Co, sb, tm, ca 1900, 6¼" 95.00
Nurser, The Empire Nursing Bottle, monogram, 5½" 35.00
Nurser, Universal Feeder, monogram, tm, 6¼" 35.00
Pearson & Co Circassian Hair Rejuvenator..., med amber, 7" 550.00
Renovo For The Hair D Skidmore & Co..., dk amethyst, 7¾" ..1,500.00
Storage, aqua, globular, rm, ps, Am, ca 1800-30, 9" 45.00
Storage, med olive gr, globular, ps, rm, 1820s, 10¼" 350.00
Storage, yel-amber, ps, am, Am, ca 1800-30, 11" 150.00
Sweet 16, Goetting & Co, see California Perfume Co
Utility, olive gr, ps, rm, Am, ca 1800, 10½" 75.00
Wheeler's Teaberry Tooth Wash Philada, aqua, rm, 3⅞" 110.00

Boxes

Boxes have been used by civilized man since ancient Egypt and Rome. Down through the centuries, specifically designed containers have been made from every conceivable material. Precious metals, papier-mache, Battersea, Oriental lacquer, and wood have held riches from the treasuries of kings, snuff for the fashionable set of the last century, China tea, and countless other commodities. See also Toleware; specific manufacturers.

Apple, pine, sq nails, 9½" 88.00
Band, bentwood, orig wallpaper covering, 15½" L 85.00
Band, bentwood pine w/laced seams, old patina, 16¾" 135.00
Bentwood, Harvard Shaker type w/fingers, varnish, 5½" 50.00
Bentwood, nailed lapping seam, old red rpt, 9¾" 195.00
Bentwood, old bl rpt, 7¾" 185.00
Bentwood pine, laced seams, gr rpt, 15¼" 225.00
Bentwood pine, orange pnt w/mc floral, laced seams, 13" dia 195.00
Bentwood poplar, orig pnt w/bl & wht decor, PA, 4½" 300.00
Bird's-eye veneer on poplar, age cracks, 13" 75.00
Bride's, bentwood, orig mc floral, rpl bottom brd, 17½" 465.00
Bride's, bentwood, orig mc pnt, chicken on lid, 1870s, 15" 220.00
Bride's, bentwood pine w/orig mc floral & decoupage, 20" 990.00
Bride's, bentwood pine w/orig mc pnt w/floral decor, 18¾" 770.00
Bride's, pine, orig mc floral pnt w/deer & hare, 19" 770.00
Candle, dvtl butternut, shaped crest, pnt traces, 18" 1,100.00
Candle, dvtl curly maple, slide lid w/cvd rooster, 13½" 415.00
Candle, dvtl pine, minor rpr, 13¼" 95.00
Candle, dvtl pine, slide lid w/2 cvd finger notches, 12", VG 170.00
Candle, grpt in mustard & red, slide top, dtd 1869, 18x10x8" 225.00
Candle, pine, slant lid, red pnt traces, 6½x13x5¾" 115.00
Cardboard, wallpaper covered, lined w/1839 newspaper, 7¾" 275.00
Cardboard, wallpaper covered, lt wear, 3x4½" 195.00
Cherry, dvtl, slide lid (rstr), soft patina, 9" 75.00
Document, brn sponged, hinged lid/dvtl, brass hinges, 7x7x10" ..170.00
Dome top, burl veneer, brass fittings w/abalone inlay, 5½" 95.00
Dome top, dvtl pine, orig grpt, German inscription, 1800, 15" ...470.00
Dome top, dvtl pine & poplar, yel grpt, 24", EX 700.00
Dome top, leather covered, brass studs, NY, rprs, 12" 45.00
Dome top, mc swags & flowers on brn japanning, 10" 415.00
Dome top, orig mc floral pnt, staple hinges, 7½" 300.00
Dome top, pine & poplar, orig grpt, EX age & color, 13¼" 495.00
Dome top, poplar, orig vinegar grpt, wrought lock, 20" 195.00
Hanging, dvtl walnut, high cut-out crest, 13x12½" 935.00
Hat, wallpaper covered, Am, 1800s, 26", G 300.00
Horn w/cvd geometric decor, iron lid finial, oval, 2⅞x3½" 220.00
Knife, curly maple w/inlaid hearts/stars/etc, rfn, 14x10" 335.00
Knife, dvtl walnut, cutout in hdl, dk finish, 16x12" 195.00
Knife, pine, worn blk rpt, 14x10¼" 115.00
Lehnware, poplar w/orig floral pnt on saffron, rpr, 5" 470.00

Pine, dvtl, brass hinges & lock, 1850s, 5¾x11⅞x7⅝" **75.00**
Pine, dvtl, hinged lid, bottom drw, brass hinges, 12x7x7" **295.00**
Pine, dvtl, wrought strap hinges, brass hdls, 17½" **385.00**
Pine, hasp closure, old orig dk gr pnt, 9x16½x10¼", VG **75.00**
Pipe, tiger maple, shell-cvd drw, 16½" H **250.00**
Poplar, dk pnt w/roses on lid, dvtl, 5¼x15x10" **300.00**
Poplar, dvtl, plk pnt w/gold striping traces, 14" **72.50**
Poplar w/orig free-hand & stencil decor, wire hinges, 10" **525.00**
Spice, pine, arched bkbrd, 9 drws w/wire pulls, nailed, 20x12" ...**290.00**
Spice, wood/tin, holds 8 stencil-label canisters, 3½x10" **180.00**
Trinket, pine w/dome lid, appl molded rim/base, rfn, 8" **140.00**
Walnut w/marquetry inlay, book shape w/drw, 6¼" **120.00**
Work, rosewood w/brass inlay medallion, fitted int, 9⅝" **100.00**
Writing, mahog veneer w/brass mts, ca 1860s, 20" **440.00**
Writing, mahog w/inlay, brass mts, Bussing, NY, 7½x29x11" **495.00**
Writing, rosewood veneer w/silver inlay, 16" **80.00**

Boyd Crystal Art Glass

Boyd Crystal Art Glass is a small but productive glass factory located in Cambridge, Ohio. It was established in 1978 when the Boyd family bought out the Degenhart factory. Over the years Boyd has produced more than 200 molds; while many were their own design, they acquired others from glasshouses no longer in business. All the Boyd pieces are marked with a distinct logo of a 'B' in diamond. Further dating is possible because a line was added under the diamond in 1983, and an additional line was added above the diamond in 1988. In September 1993 another line was added, this one on the right of the diamond. Boyd's glass is prized because of the colors they formulated and the fact that once a piece is produced in a particular color it will not be produced in that color again, even if that color is brought back years later. All pieces are hand pressed from glass that is from a single-day tank. Colors are made for about six weeks or less, thus limiting the number of pieces that can be produced in that color. More than three hundred different colors have been used and developed by the Boyds. Much like Degenhart glass, the colors can be confusing and difficult to identify. Exceptional slags and hand-painted pieces can command up to 50% higher prices. Satin glass variations are priced 10% to 30% higher when they can be found.

In the following listings, (N) indicates a mold that was new in 1993-94. (R) indicates a yearly special edition of a retired piece. Our advisor for this category is Joyce Pringle; she is listed in the Directory under Texas.

Airplane, Classic Black Satin **17.00**
Airplane, Heather Gray **16.75**
Airplane, Vaseline **25.00**
Artie Penguin, Nile Green **8.00**
Artie Penguin, Primrose **8.00**
Aunt Sheila's Pin Dish, Daffodil **5.00**
Bingo the Deer, Caramel **8.00**
Bingo the Deer, Milk White **8.00**
Bingo the Fawn, Cobalt (R) **10.00**
Bingo the Fawn, Lilac (R) **12.00**
Bird Salt, Forest Green **14.00**
Bird Salt, Tomato Cream Slag **14.00**
Bird Shakers, Forest Green, pr **22.50**
Bird Shakers, Tomato Cream Slag, pr **20.00**
Bow Slipper, Aqua Diamond **8.00**
Bow Slipper, Crown Tuscan **20.00**
Bow Slipper, Maverick Blue **8.75**
Boyd Special, Cobalt, 6-pc train **72.50**
Brian the Bunny, Cornsilk **10.00**
Brian the Bunny, Vaseline **16.00**

Brian the Bunny, Winter Swirl **15.00**
Bunny on a Nest, Bamboo **10.00**
Bunny on a Nest, Platinum **14.00**
Buzz Saw Wine, Apricot **7.00**
Cat Slipper, Bermuda Slag **32.50**
Cat Slipper, Enchantment **20.00**
Cat Slipper, Waterloo **9.00**
Chick Salt, Banana Cream, 1" **6.75**
Chick Salt, Lavender, 1" **12.00**
Chick Salt, Sunglo Carnival, 1" **16.00**
Chicken, Caramel, 3" **14.00**
Chicken, Heatherbloom, 3" **16.00**
Colonial Doll #2, Caramel **12.00**
Colonial Doll #2, Milk White **12.00**
Debbie Duckling, Bermuda, 1¼" **5.00**
Debbie Duckling, Mint Green, 1¼" **4.00**
Duck Salt, Copper Brown, w/lid **7.75**
Duck Salt, Lime Carnival, w/lid **7.00**
Fuzzy Bear, Banana Cream (R) **15.00**
Heart Jewel Box, Spinnaker Blue **16.00**
Hen, Ice Blue, 5" **30.00**
Hen, Ruby Gold, 5" **50.00**
Hen, Vanilla Coral, 5" **14.00**
Hen, Vaseline, 5" **35.00**
JB Scotty, Cobalt **35.00**
JB Scotty, Cobalt Carnival (R) **10.00**
JB Scotty, Cornsilk **10.00**
Joey Horse, Bermuda **20.00**
Joey Horse, December Swirl **20.00**
Joey Horse, Flame **25.00**
Joey Horse, Light Rose **12.00**
Joey Horse, Lilac **16.00**
Joey Horse, Ruby **22.50**
Joey Horse, Sandpiper **14.00**
Lil Joe, Cobalt, 2½x1½" **6.00**
Lil Joe, Plum, 2½x1½" **5.00**
Lil Lucky Unicorn, Cobalt Blue **7.00**
Lil Lucky Unicorn, Jadite **6.00**
Louise Doll, Apricot **20.00**
Louise Doll, Cobalt, HP **30.00**
Louise Doll, Furr Green **14.00**
Louise Doll, Ice Green **25.00**
Louise Doll, Olympic White Carnival **18.00**
Louise Doll, Snow **18.00**
Louise Doll, Sunburst **12.00**
Louise Doll, Willow Blue **14.00**
Louise Doll Bell, Mistletoe Satin, 1980 ....**16.00**
Louise Doll Bell, Misty Green, 1st, 1979 ....**25.00**
Lucky Unicorn, Caramel **10.00**
Lucky Unicorn, Lemonade **10.00**
Lucky Unicorn, Ruby **20.00**
Marguerite Doll, Enchantment Pink **15.00**
Marguerite Doll, Lime Carnival **20.00**
Mini Vase, Daffodil, HP **22.50**
Mini Vase, December Swirl **14.00**
Owl, Bernard Slag **18.00**
Owl, Classic Black **9.00**
Owl, Ebony **14.00**
Owl, Lemon Ice **20.00**
Owl, Olympic White Carnival **25.00**
Owl, Sandpiper **14.00**
Owl Bell, Golden Delight, 4" **9.00**
Rex the Dinosaur, Aqua Diamond (N) **15.00**
Rooster Holder, Milk Wht **10.00**

Sonny the Gorilla, Vaseline (N) 8.50
Teddy Tug Boat, Cobalt 20.00
Teddy Tug Boat, Mint Green 15.00
Turkey Salt, Banana Cream Carnival, 1" (N) 7.75
Turkey Salt, Cobalt, 1" (N) 8.75
Virgil Clown, Nile Green 9.00
Virgil Clown, Vaseline 12.00
Woodsie the Owlet, Azure Blue 6.00
Woodsie the Owlet, Custard 5.00
Zak the Elephant, Alice Blue (R) 20.00
Zak the Elephant, Crown Tuscan 20.00
Zak the Elephant, Flame (R) 37.50
Zak the Elephant, White Opal (R) 22.50

Bradley and Hubbard

The Bradley and Hubbard Mfg. Company was a firm which produced metal accessories for the home. They operated from about 1860 until the early part of this century, and their products reflected both the Arts and Crafts and Art Nouveau influence. Their logo was a device with a triangular arrangement of the company name containing a smaller triangle and an Aladdin lamp. Our advisor for this category is Daniel Batchelor; he is listed in the Directory under New York.

Lamps

Banquet, wireware shade/std/base, rpl glass insert, 24" 400.00
Bent 6-panel 20" shade w/etched urns; 4 lions on mk std 345.00
Delft scene pnt on 8" ball shade; fancy metal base 300.00

Fluid lamp, ornate cast gilt metal, 8" opal glass ball shade with hand-painted blue and white Delft-style windmill scene, 18", $400.00.

Metal filigree 16½" 6-panel slag-lined shade; mk std 975.00
Paneled 17" mica shade w/appl metal; bronzed std 1,500.00
Piano, brass/wrought iron, frosted Beaded Drape 10" shade 550.00
Slag glass 16" 8-sided shade w/foliate fr; simple mk std 865.00

Miscellaneous

Andirons, #390, brass w/faceted rivets, mk, 21x11x22" 400.00
Andirons, CI winged griffin form, #9537, 20½" 2,500.00
Bookends, monk reading, wall of books behind him, CI, mk, pr .135.00
Candlesticks, brass, sq w/pyramidal base, cleaned, 11", pr 110.00
Plaque, lady gazes at butterfly on shoulder, bronzed, 8" 150.00

Smoking set, brass, Greek Key motif, mk, humidor/box+2 pcs ...200.00

Brass

Brass is an alloy consisting essentially of copper and zinc in variable proportions. It is a medium that has been used for both utilitarian items and objects of artistic merit. Today, with the inflated price of copper and the popular use of plastics, almost anything made of brass is collectible. Our advisor, Mary Frank Gaston, has compiled a lovely book, *Antique Brass and Copper*, with full-color photos; you will find her address in the Directory under Texas. See also Candlesticks.

Architectural pc, star w/beveled edges, 1900s, 8" dia 40.00
Basket, iron bail hdl, Hayden's Pat, 7¾x12" 60.00
Bucket, Hayden's Pat, 9½" dia 50.00
Bucket, spun, wire bail hdl, dk patina, 10½" dia 55.00
Dipper, wrought iron hdl, 2¾" dia, 17¼" L 95.00
Kettle, Am Brass Kettle label, bail hdl, 10x17" 95.00
Kettle, iron hdl, 7x12" 50.00
Kettle, spun, heavy, iron bail hdl, 6¾x13½" 85.00
Ladle, tasting; dmn shape in wrought iron hook hdl, 8x2" 85.00
Lamp filler, polished, 4⅞" 75.00
Memo clip, emb florals, Merry Phipson Parker's..., 6" 50.00
Mold, spoon, 8" 175.00
Pan, sauce; iron hdl w/copper rivets, 5½" dia 50.00
Pan, sauce; pour spout, 7½" hollow riveted hdl, 7" dia 85.00
Shelf, kettle; grillwork top, 5x10x6" 105.00
Skimmer, wrought iron hdl, Canton O '86, 20" 85.00
Teapot, footed, amber glass hdl, England, 1850s 300.00
Teapot, goose spout, ftd, Scotland, mid-1800s, 4¾x7½" 195.00
Tray, roses on swirl surface, mk Depose, 11x7½" 75.00
Wick trimmer, scissors style, w/tray 72.50

Brastoff, Sascha

The son of immigrant parents, Sascha Brastoff was encouraged to develop his artistic talents to the fullest, encouragement that was well taken, as his achievements aptly attest. Though at various times he was a dancer, sculptor, Hollywood costume designer, jeweler, and painter, it is his ceramics that are today becoming highly regarded collectibles.

Sascha began his career in the United States in the late 1940s. In a beautiful studio built for him by his friend and mentor, Winthrop Rockefeller, he designed innovative wares that even then were among the most expensive on the market. All designing was done personally by Brastoff; he also supervised the staff which at the height of production numbered approximately 150. Wares signed with his full signature (not merely backstamped 'Sascha Brastoff') were personally crafted by him and are valued much more highly than those signed 'Sascha B.,' indicating work done under his supervision. Until his death in 1993, he continued his work in Los Angeles, in his latter years producing 'Sascha Holograms,' which were distributed by the Hummelwerk Company.

Another medium he used in his work was resin, and such pieces are also very collectible, though extremely scarce. In the listings below, all items are ceramic and signed 'Sascha B.' unless 'full signature' is indicated.

Our advisor for this category is Jack Chipman, author of *Collector's Encyclopedia of California Pottery*; Mr. Chipman is listed in the Directory under California. See also *Collector's Encyclopedia of Sascha Brastoff* by Steve Conti, A. DeWayne Bethany, and Bill Seay.

Ashtray, abstract florals, enamel on metal, 6½" 30.00
Ashtray, Eskimo face, Alaska line, turq & wht, 7x5" 75.00
Ashtray, floral, 5x8½" 35.00

Ashtray, gold & blk clam-shell shape 30.00
Ashtray, gold bird decor, chimneyed, 6" 40.00
Ashtray, houses, gray, 7" dia 40.00
Ashtray, seal, Alaska line, gray on brn & wht triangle 70.00
Bowl, geometric decor, beige & brn, oval, 3x9x5" 50.00
Bowl, horse on gr, sq, mk, 5½" 55.00
Bowl, walrus, Alaska line, gray, ftd, 3½" 45.00
Box, horse on shaded gray, mk, 7¼x4½" 75.00
Box, leaves, mc on kelly gr, 2x7x4" 85.00
Cigarette box, flowers, gold & silver on wht, 1½x6x3" 85.00
Cigarette lighter, gold HP florals, +holder 40.00
Mug, fruit design, 5" 45.00
Mug, gold & wht bird, 5" 45.00
Planter, floral on lt bl, 4x5" 50.00

Figure of rooster, heavy gold, 16½", $295.00.

Shakers, Alaska, pr 38.00
Vase, Alaska, 8" 95.00
Vase, enamel & copper, 5" 65.00
Vase, floral on turq, 8x3" 80.00
Vase, houses & trees, rooftops line, 5½" 65.00
Vase, lion inscr on bl, #H13, 6x5½" 100.00
Vase, 2-faced, bl molded resin, 10" 195.00

Brayton, Laguna

Durlin E. Brayton made handcrafted vases, lamps, and dinnerware in a small kiln at his Laguna Beach, California, home in 1927. He soon married, and with his wife, Ellen Webster Grieve, as his partner, the small business became a successful commercial venture. They are most famous for their amusing, well-detailed figurines, some of which were commissioned by Walt Disney Studios. Though very successful even through the Depression years, with the influx of imported novelties that deluged the country after WWII, business began to decline. By 1968 the pottery was closed. For more information on this as well as many other potteries in the state, we recommend *The Collector's Encyclopedia of California Pottery* by Jack Chipman; he is listed in the Directory under California.

Candle holder, Blackamoor 75.00
Candy dish, Fr peasant design, rnd 60.00
Cookie jar, Gingham Dog 575.00
Cookie jar, Granny, mk 500.00
Cookie jar, Matilda 695.00

Cookie jar, Swedish maiden 700.00
Creamer & sugar bowl, duck head 65.00
Creamer & sugar bowl, Gingham Dog & Calico Cat 175.00
Figurine, baby on pillow 60.00
Figurine, Blk Sultan, Blackamoor line 100.00
Figurine, calf, brn & cream spots, rough texture, unmk, RR-81 ....65.00
Figurine, cat, Fifi & Zizi, rare, pr 225.00
Figurine, cat, stylized, 11" 85.00
Figurine, cowboy boot, sgn Kaye Kinney 75.00
Figurine, duck, lg 35.00
Figurine, Gay Nineties, bartender w/2 men at bar, 9x9" 100.00
Figurine, Gay Nineties, Bedtime, couple in nightclothes, 8½" ...100.00
Figurine, Gay Nineties, Honeymoon, couple in bathing suits 100.00
Figurine, Gay Nineties, 1 Year Later, couple w/baby 100.00
Figurine, gazelles, aqua & gold, pr 225.00
Figurine, organ grinder w/monkey 85.00
Figurine, penguin, brn & wht crackle, 7" 80.00
Figurine, Pluto, recumbent, HH-81 ....155.00
Figurine, purple cow family, 3-pc 275.00
Figurine, roosters, lg, pr 175.00
Figurine, Southern lady in yel dress 85.00
Figurine, toucan, 11x12" 75.00
Figurine, vendor pushing cart 100.00
Figurine, Zulu w/shield 95.00
Flower holder, peasant lady 75.00
Flower holder, Sally, apron holds flowers 25.00
Flower holder, Swedish Maid 75.00
Pitcher, old woman w/blueberries figural 495.00
Planter, Provincial wheelbarrow 20.00
Plate, dinner; eggplant color, hand thrown, 10" 60.00
Shakers, Dutch couple, pr 125.00
Shakers, Mammy & Chef, pr 150.00
Teapot, brn stain w/wht crackle decor, CX-35 ....50.00
Teapot, peasant lady, mc, 1930s, NM 250.00
Wall pc, Blackamoor holds wall planter, gold trim, 16", 2-pc 250.00

Bread Plates and Trays

Bread plates and trays have been produced not only in many types of glass but in metal and pottery as well. Those considered most collectible were made during the last quarter of the 19th century from pressed glass with well-detailed embossed designs, many of them portraying a particularly significant historical event. A great number of these plates were sold at the 1876 Philadelphia Centennial Exposition by various glass manufacturers who exhibited their wares on the grounds. Among the themes depicted are the Declaration of Independence, the Constitution, McKinley's memorial 'It Is God's Way,' Remembrance of Three Presidents, the Purchase of Alaska, and various presidential campaigns, to mention only a few.

'L' numbers correspond with a reference book by Lindsey; 'S' refers to a book by Stuart. Our advisor for this category is Darlene Yohe; she is listed in the Directory under Arkansas.

American Flag, 38 stars, L-51, 11x8" 235.00
Angel Head, milk glass, B-7f 30.00
Bates, L-375 ....65.00
Be Industrious, beehive center, ornate border, 11½x8" 125.00
Black Builders of Bicentennial, 1776-1976 ....35.00
Bunker Hill, Prescott/1775/Stark, L-44, 13¼x9" 120.00
California Bear, 1894 Expo, L-104 ....140.00
Cleveland/Thurman busts, clear/frosted, L-325, 9½x8½" 215.00
Columbia, shield shape, bl, L-54, 11½x9½" 165.00
Continental Hall, hand hdls, 12¾" L 75.00

Cupid & Venus, 10½" dia **55.00**
Do Unto Others **55.00**
Egyptian, Cleopatra center, 13" L **55.00**
Eureka, motto, L-103 ....**32.00**
Frosted Lion, Give Us This Day, 12½x9" **175.00**
Garden of Eden, Give Us This Day, 12½x9" **35.00**
Garfield Memorial, L-302, 10" L **40.00**
Give Us This Day, Sheaf of Wheat, 13" L **75.00**
Grand Army of the Republic **90.00**
Heroes of Bunker Hill **70.00**
Jewel Band, Bread Is Staff of Life **45.00**
Kansas, motto **50.00**
Knights of Labor, amber, oval, L-512, 12" **145.00**
Liberty Bell, John Hancock, oval, 13" **65.00**
Lotus & Serpent **55.00**
McKinley, Gothic border, milk glass, F-549 ....**85.00**
Memorial Hall **65.00**
Mormon Temple, w/eye & beehive **315.00**
Nelly Bly, L-136, 12" L **185.00**
Niagara Falls, clear/frosted, L-489, 16" L **135.00**
Old State House, for water set **50.00**
Polar Bear, ship, L-486, 16" **165.00**
Rock of Ages, dtd, milk glass center, F-569 ....**175.00**
Ruth the Gleaner, Gillinder **145.00**
Teddy Roosevelt, dancing bears, L-357, 10¾" L **145.00**
Three Presidents, In Remembrance, 12½x10" **95.00**
Union Pacific Railroad **85.00**
US Grant, Let Us Have Peace, amber, 10½" dia **90.00**
Warrior **80.00**
Washington, First in War/First in Peace, L-27, 12x8½" **100.00**
Washington & 13 stars, milk glass, B-1 ....**50.00**
Wildflower, sq **28.00**

Bretby

The Bretby Art Pottery was an English firm whose roots can be traced to the 1880s, an offspring of the earlier Tooth & Company Ltd. The Bretby mark was first used circa 1885. 'England' was added in later years of the 19th century, and by the 1920s, 'Made in England, Bretby,' was the standard mark.

Figurine, cat w/yarn, blk faience, gr glass eyes, 10¼" L **325.00**
Vase, red, yel & gr flambe, 5½" **145.00**

Bride's Baskets and Bowls

Victorian brides were showered with gifts, as brides have always been; one of the most popular gift items was the bride's basket. Art glass inserts from both European and American glasshouses, some in lovely transparent hues with dainty enameled florals, others of Peachblow, Vasa Murrhina, satin or cased glass, were cradled in complementary silverplated holders. While many of these holders were simply engraved or delicately embossed, others such as those from Pairpoint and Wilcox were wonderfully ornate, often with figurals of cherubs or animals. The bride's basket was no longer in fashion after the turn of the century.

Watch for 'marriages' of bowls and frames. To warrant the best price, the two pieces should be the original pairing. If you can't be certain of this, at least check to see that the bowl fits snugly into the frame. Beware of later-made bowls (such as Fenton's) in Victorian holders.

In the listings that follow, if no frame is described, the price is for a bowl only.

Multicolor tortoise-shell spatter, white interior, crimped rim; original footed silverplate frame with fretwork and embossed florals, **$395.00.**

Aqua o/l w/mica flecks, ruffled, 2½x8" **65.00**
Beaded Drape, gr opal; worn SP fr **150.00**
Bl Herringbone MOP, pk int, mini, 4¼" **125.00**
Bl o/l w/floral, ruffled w/frosted edge, 5x10½" **245.00**
Cameo beasts/flowers, turq on wht, Mt WA, 4x10"; SP basket ...**1,400.00**
Coralene, coral on wht to bl shaded; ftd Meriden fr **550.00**
Cranberry Hobnail; ornate SP fr **395.00**
Cranberry o/l, ruffled; orig Acme SP fr, mini **150.00**
Cranberry opal Spanish Lace, ruffled, 10"; orig SP fr **300.00**
Cranberry w/HP decor; Rogers triple gold-plate fr w/cherubs **900.00**
Gold satin w/birds & floral, clear ruffle, 13"; mk fr, 13" **495.00**
Gr satin w/pk satin int, 4½x10½x5" **250.00**
Hobnail, wht to pk w/appl bl rim, Mt WA; ftd Barbour fr, 14" ...**650.00**
Lemon satin w/pk int & much gold; SP fr w/3 6" winged cherubs ...**2,800.00**
Lemon w/HP florals & dots, Mt WA; rstr SP fr, 12x10½" **425.00**
Peachblow w/daffodils, gold & gr leaves, 5x10½" **450.00**
Peachblow w/emb fleur-de-lis, NE Glass **175.00**
Peachblow w/florals & scrolls sqd/ruffled; fr w/rtcl hdl **350.00**
Peachblow-cased wht, sq, 11" **125.00**
Pk o/l, ruffled, Webb; rstr SP fr, 12½x10" **400.00**
Pk o/l w/dimples & Hobnails, clear rim; floral SP fr, 14x10" **295.00**
Pk o/l w/floral/dots/lacy foliage, scalloped, 4x11" **175.00**
Pk o/l w/wht opaque & vaseline ruffle, 3⅜x11¼" **195.00**
Pk ruffled w/mica; ornate ftd orig Tufts fr **450.00**
Pk satin o/l w/appl ribbon & HP florals; SP fr, 11½x9x6" **335.00**
Pk satin w/Hobnail edge, gold scrolls/mc roses, ruffled, 15" **725.00**
Pk satin w/HP decor, ruffled, NE Glass, 10½" **100.00**
Pk shaded w/floral & gold, wht ext; 4 rtcl ft, ornate hdl **240.00**
Purple to wht o/l, ruffled; rstr SP fr **225.00**
Rose o/l, ruffled, Mt WA; orig SP fr, 12¼x12" **400.00**
Rose to pink o/l, scalloped; orig Toronto SP fr w/berries **395.00**
Tomato, 4-sided fluted rim, 4x9" **295.00**
Wht w/florals/scrolls/birds, pleated; ornate SP fr, 13x11" **350.00**
Wht w/pk floral, bl ribbed int w/gold; Meriden fr w/bird, 15" **750.00**
Yel o/l w/floral, ruffled, 6½"; brass ormolu fr, 9½" **235.00**

Bristol Glass

Bristol is a type of semi-opaque opaline glass whose name was derived from the area in England where it was first produced. Similar glass was made in France, Germany, and Italy. In this country, it was made by the New England Glass Company and to a lesser extent by its contemporaries. During the 18th and 19th centuries, Bristol glass was imported in large amounts and sold cheaply, thereby contributing to the demise of the earlier glasshouses here in America. It is very difficult to distinguish the English Bristol from other opaline types. Style, design, and decoration serve as clues to its origin; but often only those well versed in the field can spot these subtle variations.

Biscuit jar, tan, HP herons, rstr SP rim/lid/hdl, 7¼" 235.00
Biscuit jar, turq, HP daisies & leaves, rstr SP trim, 6½" 225.00
Biscuit jar, turq, HP herons & trees, SP top/lid/hdl, 7½" 235.00
Bottle, scent; apple gr w/gold decor, ball stopper, 4x2⅜" 85.00
Bottle, scent; gr w/gold, appl hdls, 9½x3¼" 100.00
Bottle, scent; turq, HP florals, w/stopper, 5¼x2¼" 100.00
Bottle, scent; turq w/gold florals & blk trim, 8¾x3¼" 110.00
Box, jewel; pk w/cupids & flowers in gold, ftd, 5¼x7" dia 375.00
Box, patch; pk, HP bird, 1x1¼" dia 95.00
Candlestick, turq, HP florals w/gold, 6½x3⅜" 88.00
Creamer, wht, HP floral swag, appl hdl, 4⅜" 45.00
Lamp, miniature; bl to wht, HP florals & bird, 10x4¾" 850.00
Mug, wht, enamel traces, appl hdl, 3⅝" 10.00
Ring tree, turq, HP yel & gold leaves, 3x3¼" 75.00
Rose bowl, turq, gold ropes & tassels, HP dots, 4⅛x3¼" 75.00
Rose bowl, turq w/gold florals, 6-crimp, 4¾x4⅝" 125.00
Tumbler, gray, HP florals, 3¾x2¾" 60.00

Vase, blue flowers and bird with gold highlights and trim on cream, footed, 12", $100.00.

Vase, turq, HP bird & flowers, bk: bee, w/gold, sq base, 10½" 195.00
Vase, turq, HP florals, gold bands, 6½x3½" 145.00
Vase, turq, HP florals & dots, ftd, 5x2½", pr 145.00
Vase, turq, HP florals w/gold, ewer form, 4½", pr 135.00

British Royalty Commemoratives

Royalty commemoratives have been issued for royal events since Edward VI's 1547 coronation through modern-day events, so it's possible to start collecting at any period of history. Many collectors begin with Queen Victoria's reign, collecting examples for each succeeding monarch and continuing through modern events.

Some collectors identify with a particular royal personage and limit their collecting to that era, ie., Queen Elizabeth's life and reign. Other collectors look to the future, expanding their collection to include the heir apparents Prince Charles/Princess Diana and their first-born son, Prince William.

Royalty commemorative collecting is often further refined around a particular type of collectible. Nearly any item with room for a portrait and a description has been manufactured as a souvenir. Thus royalty commemoratives are available in glass, ceramic, metal, fabric, plastic and paper. This wide variety of material lends itself to any pocketbook.

The range covers expensive limited edition ceramics to inexpensive souvenir key chains, puzzles, matchbooks, etc.

Many recent royalty headline events have been commemorated in a variety of souvenirs. Buying some of these modern commemoratives at the moderate issue prices could be a good investment. After all, today's events are tomorrow's history.

For further study we recommend *British Royal Commemoratives* by our advisor for this category, Audrey Zeder; she is listed in the Directory under California.

Key:
anniv — anniversary
chr — christening
com — commemorative
cor — coronation
EPNS — electroplated nickel silver
ILN — Illustrated London News
inscr — inscribed
jub — jubilee
LE — limited edition
mem — memorial
wed — wedding

Album, Geo V 1935 jub, 50 mc cigarette cards, Wills 40.00
Album, Geo VI 1937 cor, 50 mc cigarette cards, Player 35.00
Bank, Geo VI cor, oval shape, bl w/bl & wht portrait, tin 45.00
Bank, Henry 1984 birth, Bunnykins design by Royal Doulton 60.00
Beaker, Edward VII cor, King's Dinner, Royal Doulton 130.00
Beaker, Geo V cor, gift to school children, Royal Doulton 90.00
Beaker, Geo V cor, gr portrait, ships of war, Whitley 150.00
Beaker, Geo VI cor, mc portraits, Official Design 55.00
Beaker, Victoria 1897 jub, pnt decor, 3¾" 175.00
Bottle, Charles/Diana 1981 wed, amber glass, Millville 75.00
Bottle, Geo V cor, emb decor, clear glass, flat sided 125.00
Bottle, Victoria cor, emb decor on sceptre, stoneware, Greene ..700.00
Bowl, Geo V 1935 jub, baby's, mc portrait, Shelley, 7½" 175.00
Bowl, Princess Royal 1858 wed, pnt decor, pk lustre 250.00
Bowl, Victoria 1851, pnt decor, pk lustre, 6¼x3½" 250.00
Bust, Geo V/Mary, parian, G details, 5½", pr 250.00
Bust, Geo V/Mary, pnt, G detail, 7½", pr 225.00
Bust, Victoria 1871, amber celluloid on blk ped, 4¼" 195.00
Bust, Victoria 1887, milk glass, 3x3¾x3¾" 165.00
Chalice, William 1982 birth, gray w/mc cradle, 5½" 60.00
Coin, Geo III 1797 copper cartwheel penny 45.00
Coin, Henry III 1200's half penny, Canterbury 75.00
Coin, William & Mary 1689 Maudy Money, 2 pence 100.00
Coin, William IV 1831 penny 50.00
Compact, Princess Elizabeth 1937, mc portrait, 1⅞" 75.00
Covered dish, Geo V cor, cut glass w/EPNS emb portrait lid 85.00
Covered dish, Prince William 1982 birth, bsk, relief, Worcester ...165.00
Cup & saucer, Geo V cor w/mc portrait, fluted shape 155.00
Cup & saucer, Geo VI 1939 Canada Visit, Wedgwood & Co 150.00
Cup & saucer, Princess Margaret birth, Paragon 125.00
Cup & saucer, Victoria/Albert 1951, pk lustre w/portraits 250.00
Ephemera, Charles/Diana 1981 wed place mat, luncheon sz 5.00
Ephemera, Charles/Diana 1981 wed matchbooks, unused set of 6 ..10.00
Ephemera, Elizabeth II 1953 cor ILN Record Number 50.00
Ephemera, Elizabeth II 1953 cor paper napkin 55.00
Ephemera, Geo V 1935 jub ILN Record Number 65.00
Ephemera, Geo VI 1937 cor ILN Record Number 60.00
Ephemera, Geo VI 1937 cor Royal Beverage label, pr 20.00
Figure, Elizabeth II riding horse & 2 guards, lead on wood 85.00
Figure, Sarah 1986 wed, china, LE, Royal Doulton, 8½" 500.00
Fork, pickle; Geo VI 1937 cor, brass w/pnt portrait/decor, 6" 30.00
Fork, toasting; Geo V 1935 jub, brass, 20" 75.00
Glass, Charles/Diana wed plate, heather, pressed, 3½" 30.00
Glass, Edward VII 1902 cor pitcher, etched portrait, 4½" 150.00
Glass, Elizabeth II beaker, powder bl w/mc decor, gold rim 25.00
Glass, Elizabeth II plate, gr, 3½" 25.00

Glass, Geo VI 1939 Canada visit beaker, clear w/bl design 30.00
Glass, Queen Mother 85th birthday plate, bl, 3½" 25.00
Glass, Victoria 1827 cor plate, clear, pressed, 3½" 190.00
Glass, Victoria/Albert 1840 wed plate, clear, pressed, 3½" 190.00
Jewelry, Edward VIII pin, mc portrait/MOP, silver-tone bezel 60.00
Jewelry, Elizabeth cor bracelet, bl pnt & sterling silver 50.00
Jewelry, Geo V 1935 pin, mc photo in rnd brass fr 45.00
Jewelry, Victoria 1890 pin, emb portrait on brass 50.00
Jewelry, Victoria 1900 pendant, emb portrait, w/generals 95.00
Loving cup, Elizabeth II, emb portrait, maroon/tan, 3½x6" 75.00
Loving cup, Victoria 1897 jub, bl w/bl transfer, 9x6" 425.00
Magazine, Charles/Diana ILN Royal Wedding Number 1981 ....35.00
Magazine, Princess Alexandra wed, ILN, May 4, 1963 ....25.00
Magnet, Elizabeth II, 40th yr of cor, 1953 mc portrait 5.00
Magnet, Princess Diana 1993 visits, mc portrait, set of 3 ....15.00
Matches, Edward VII cor, brass vespa, portrait on book form 125.00
Matches, Geo V/Queen Mary, matchbox labels, unused, pr 25.00
Matches, Geo VI cor matchbox holder, metal, Bryant & Mays 75.00
Matches, Geo VI matchbook holder, pnt on chrome 45.00
Matches, Victoria matchbox label, 6½x5¾", unused 75.00
Medal, Edward VII cor, emb portrait on brass, ¾" 35.00
Medal, Elizabeth I 1602, high relief on bronze, 1½" 300.00
Medal, Geo V 1919 victory, brass, 1½" 35.00
Medal, Geo VI cor, Cadbury Chocolates giveaway, 1¼" 40.00
Miniature, crowns, 1959 investiture & 1981 wed 60.00
Miniature, Geo V cor pitcher, mc portrait, 2½x1½" 60.00
Mug, Charles 1969 investiture, red Welch dragon & castle 30.00
Mug, Charles 1969 investiture, sepia portrait 60.00
Mug, Charles/Diana 1981 wed, mc portraits, china 35.00
Mug, Charles/Diana 1992 separation, mc portraits 30.00
Mug, Duke of York 1928 visit to Pudsey, mc decor 155.00
Mug, Elizabeth 1992 Annus Horribulus, w/events, mc portrait 25.00
Mug, Geo V cor, mc portrait, child's sz, 2½" 50.00
Mug, Geo VI cor, circus theme, lion hdl, Myott 125.00
Mug, William 1993 1st birthday, mc portrait, St George 45.00
Newspaper, Caroline trial 1820, Columbian Sentinal of Boston ..35.00
Newspaper, Elizabeth 1947 wed, Mason City Globe Gazette 45.00
Novelty, Diana letter opener w/mc portrait, gold-tone 10.00
Novelty, Geo V jug brass safety-pin holder, relief design 60.00
Novelty, Henry 1984 birth nail clipper, mc family group 10.00
Pin-bk, Geo VI cor, mc portrait, w/orig card 60.00
Pitcher, Edward VIII cor, gold portrait, sq Deco shape 60.00
Pitcher, Geo IV 1920 anniv 1689 Battle Boyne, lustre, 4¾" 725.00
Pitcher, Prince of Wales Edward 1863 wed, emb decor, 4½" 225.00
Pitcher, Princess Royal 1858 wed, pk lustre, 5" 295.00
Pitcher, Victoria 1897 jub, royal bl, stoneware, Doulton, 9" 875.00
Pitcher, William IV 1831 cor, blk/wht portrait & decor, 6" 725.00
Plaque, Elizabeth II cor, emb portrait on brass, 6" dia 25.00
Plaque, Geo VI 1937 cor, celluloid, 5x7" 60.00
Plaque, Geo VI 1939 visit, emb portrait, Winton, 6½" dia 60.00
Plaque, Victoria 1889, emb portrait on bronze, 7x10" 375.00
Plate, Andrew/Sarah wed, mc portrait, bl rim, 7" 30.00
Plate, Charles 1969 investiture, Spode, 10½" 175.00
Plate, Charles/Diana 1981 wed, portrait/filigree, Minton, 10½" ..195.00
Plate, Diana, mc portrait, leaning on pillar, Danbury, 8" 75.00
Plate, Edward VII cor, portrait, rectangle, Doulton, 3½x2½" 90.00
Plate, Edward VII 1900s, portrait/commonwealth coat of arms ..125.00
Plate, Elizabeth 1959 opens St Lawrence Seaway, Tuscan, 4¼" 30.00
Plate, Geo V 1911 cor, mc portrait, Royal Doulton, 4¼" 75.00
Plate, Princess Anne 1973 wed, bl jasper, Wedgwood, 4½" 65.00
Plate, Princess Eliz 1926 birth, hexagon, Paragon, 5½" 150.00
Plate, Victoria mem, Edward VII accession, mc portrait, 9" 225.00
Plate, Victoria 1837 in garden, blk decor w/enamel/lustre, 7" .1,150.00
Plate, Victoria 1840 at opera, bl portrait, hexagon, 5½" 1,000.00

Plate, Victoria 1847 on throne, enamel & blk, hexagon, 7½" 695.00
Plate, Victoria 1890s, mc decor, heart shape, Foley, 3½" 50.00
Plate, Victoria 1897 jub, sepia/mc neamel, Allerton, 6¾" 160.00
Platter, 200th anniv Wm III Battle of Boyne, lustre, 1890s 175.00
Pocketknife, Elizabeth II cor, mc portrait, corkscrew, 2¾" 40.00
Pocketknife, Geo V cor, ivory w/gold portrait & trim, 3½" 65.00
Postcard, Charles 25th anniv Prince of Wales, LE 500 ....5.00
Postcard, Elizabeth II state visit Canada 1994, LE 500 ....5.00
Pot lid, Albert 1861, mc portrait, Pratt, 4" 175.00
Pot lid, Victoria portrait, Cherry Toothpaste 110.00
Print, Geo V/Mary, pr tipped in w/mc views, 11x16" 40.00
Print, Victoria 1880s, ind ovals of relatives, 10x16" 35.00
Print, Victoria 1901 mem, Tuck, fr, 11½x9½" 150.00
Puzzle, Charles/Diana wed w/mc engagement picture, in box 35.00
Puzzle, Diana 30th birthday, 4x6", 16-pc 6.00
Puzzle, Elizabeth II collage of 1953 cor tins, 11x14" 25.00
Spoon, Diana, emb portrait & decor, SP 15.00
Spoon, Elizabeth II cor, emb portrait, SP 25.00
Spoon, Elizabeth II cor, mc portrait, pnt bowl, SP 60.00
Spoon, Elizabeth II jub, SP, set of 6 in orig box 75.00
Spoon, Geo VI 1939 Canada visit, SP by Internat'l 45.00
Spoon, Princess Elizabeth, emb portrait, EPNS 45.00
Spoon, Victoria 1897 jub, emb portrait, sterling 150.00
Stamps, Elizabeth 40th wed, M stamps on souvenir pg 15.00
Tankard, Charles 1969 investiture, Caernarvon Castle, Wedgwood ..100.00
Teapot, Elizabeth II 1953 cor, crown shape, chrome, 2-cup 75.00
Teapot, Geo V 1911 cor, mc portrait in Naval uniform, 1-cup ...145.00
Teapot, Queen Mother/Margaret/Anne 1990 royal birthdays 75.00
Textile, Elizabeth II 1953 cor tablecloth, 36" sq 85.00
Textile, Geo V cor handkerchief, mc portrait, 12x12" 60.00
Textile, Geo VI cor handkerchief, bl portrait, 18x18" 65.00
Textile, Victoira 1897 jub, 4 generations, 28x28" 200.00
Tin, Geo VI cor, family portrait, octagonal, 5½x4x2" 45.00
Tin, Prince of Wales 1930s, mc portrait, counter, 9x7½x3" 165.00
Tin, Princess Mary w/WWI troups, brass, 5x3¼" 95.00
Tin, Victoria, flat hinged, Parkinsons, 3x3½x1½" 165.00
Toby mug, Diana, HP, Kevin Francis, LE 295.00
Toby mug, Geo V & Queen Mary, pr 495.00
Toy, Princess Elizabeth/Margaret, cup & saucer from set 35.00
Trading cards, packs in unopened counter display, Press Pass 80.00
Trading cards, 13 in deluxe pkg, Press Pass 2.00
Vehicle, Elizabeth II 40 yrs on throne, Thornycroft van 40.00
Vehicle, Elizabeth II 40th wed anniv dbl-decker bus, LLEDO 50.00

Broadmoor

In the October of 1933, the Broadmoor Art Pottery was formed and space rented at 217 East Pikes Peak Avenue, Colorado Springs, Colorado. Most of the pottery produced would not be considered elaborate and only a handful was decorated. Many pieces were signed by P.H. Genter, J.B. Hunt, Eric Hellman, and Cecil Jones. It is reported that this plant closed in 1936, and Genter moved his operations to Denver.

Broadmoor pottery is marked in several ways: a Greek or Egyptian-type label depicting two potters (one at the wheel and one at a tile-pressing machine) and the word Broadmoor; an ink-stamped 'Broadmoor Pottery, Colorado Springs (or Denver), Colorado'; and an incised version of the latter.

The bottoms of all pieces are always white and can be either glazed or unglazed. Glaze colors are turquoise, green, yellow, cobalt blue, light blue, white, pink, pink with blue, maroon red, black, and a copper lustre. Both matt and high gloss finishes were used.

The company produced many advertising tiles, novelty items, coasters, ashtrays, and vases for local establishments around Denver and as far away as Wyoming. An Indian head was incised into many of the advertising items, which also often bear a company or a product name. A series of small animals (horses, dogs, elephants, lamb, squirrels, a toucan bird, and a hippo), each about 2" high, are easily recognized by the style of their modeling and glaze treatments, though all are unmarked. Our advisors for this category are Carol and Jim Carlton, authors of *Collector's Encyclopedia of Colorado Pottery*; they are listed in the Directory under Colorado.

Ashtray, dog finial center 45.00

Bookends, head forms, 6", $150.00 each.

Coaster, cobalt, baker advertising, 3" 30.00
Cornucopia, bl & mauve, 6" 45.00
Figurine, squirrel 45.00
Lamp base, cream wht swirl, C Jones, 15", minimum value 200.00
Pitcher, gr w/gold floral, E Hellman, 15", minimum value 200.00
Relish tray, 3-petal flower form, sm center hdl, 10" 45.00
Vase, emb floral on wht ball form, 6" 45.00
Vase, honeycomb glaze, ftd, 12" 140.00
Vase, Mongol red, w/sticker, 4" 65.00
Vase, pk spongeware, incurvate rim 65.00
Vase, red swirl, bulbous, 17", minimum value 175.00

Broadsides

Webster defines a broadside as simply a large sheet of paper printed on one side. During the 1880s, they were the most practical means of mass-communication. By the middle of the century, they had become elaborate and lengthy with information, illustrations, portraits, and fancy border designs. Those printed on coated stock are usually worth more.

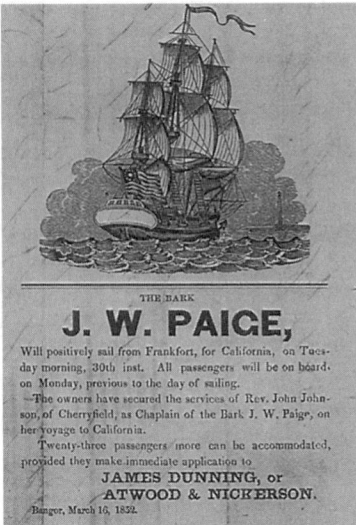

The Bark, J.W. Paige, sailing ship leaving for California, March 16, 1852, 9", $550.00.

Bank Against People!, Jackson campaign, 1832, 15x14" 750.00
Cleveland, Medina & Seville Stage Line...1866, 16½x12½" 300.00
Congratulatory Order from General Custer, April 1865, EX ...1,300.00
Execution of Powars for Murder of T Kennedy, 1820, 10½x8" ...925.00
Fourth Party in Field!, women's political action, 1850, 13x9" .1,500.00
Girl's suicide report, prose explanation, MS, 1845, 16½ x7" 600.00
Insurance Agency, ship woodcuts, Balch, Boston, 1824, 10x6" ..150.00
Jones' Chemical Washing Fluid, NY, 1859, 8x13½", VG 20.00
Last Night's Performance...Richard the 3rd...1805, 11x9" 375.00
Masonic, re: new church, balloon ascension, NH, 1825, 15x11" ..275.00
Nat'l Theatre Complimentary Benefit... 1839, on silk, 7x15" 450.00
New Goods! Union Must & Shall Be Preserved, PA, 1861, EX ...1,700.00
New Steamboat Henry Clay, illustration, 1833, 11x20", EX ...3,800.00
New Year's Address...Carriers...Providence Daily, 1866, 18x12" ...150.00
News of Lee's surrender, April 1865, 1-pg, EX 750.00
Nonsense of It, TW Hissinson, women's suffrage, 1867, 9¼x6" ..150.00
Pottstown Track Horse Races/4th of July Fireworks, 1870s 80.00
PT Barnum...1835 Joice Heth Exhibition, 8 vo, VG 3,000.00
Public Sale...Marshallville, O, 1873, fr, 37½x23¼" 185.00
Removal on restrictions of trade west, sgn A Johnson, 1865 ......150.00
Slave & land sale, NC, 1-pg, sm folio 950.00
State of RI...in General Assembly..., forming militia, 1-pg 1,300.00
Theatre, Shakespeare performed by Cooper, Boston, 1805, 11x9" ..375.00
Unrecorded Revolutionary War period verse, Bounce, 12x6½" ..2,750.00
Verse, 20 verses made up as party invitation, 1844, 11x8" 150.00
Webster's Academy of Penmanship..., swan vignette, 1842, 16x10" ..425.00
Women's politics, 4th Party in Field, Cambridge, 1850, 13x9" ...1,500.00
Women's suffrage, Nonsense of It, Boston, Thos Wentworth, 10" .150.00
Young Republic Rally..., Jas A Garfield, woodcut, 38¾x20¾" 550.00

Bronzes

Thomas Ball, George Bessell, and Leonard Volk were some of the earliest American sculptors who produced figures in bronze for home decor during the 1840s. Pieces of historical significance were the most popular, but by the 1880s a more fanciful type of artwork took hold. Some of the fine sculptors of the day were Daniel Chester French, Augustus St. Gaudens, and John Quincy Adams Ward. Bronzes reached the height of their popularity at the turn of the century. The American West was portrayed to its fullest by Remington, Russell, James Frazier, Hermon MacNeil, and Solon Borglum. Animals of every species were modeled by A.P. Proctor, Paul Bartlett, and Albert Laellele, to name but a few.

Art Nouveau and Art Deco influenced the medium during the twenties, evidenced by the works of Allen Clark, Harriet Frismuth, E.F. Sanford, and Bessie P. Vonnoh.

Be aware that recasts abound. While often esthetically satisfactory, they are not original and should be priced accordingly. In much the same manner as prints are evaluated, the original castings made under the direction of the artist are the most valuable. Later castings from the original mold are worth less. A recast is not made from the original mold. Instead, a rubber-like substance is applied to the bronze, peeled away, and filled with wax. Then, using the same 'lost wax' procedure as the artist uses on completion of his original wax model, a clay-like substance is formed around the wax figure and the whole fired to vitrify the clay. The wax, of course, melts away, hence the term 'lost wax.' Recast bronzes lose detail and are somewhat smaller than the original due to the shrinkage of the clay mold.

A Bofill, boy seated on anchor post w/coil of rope, 17" 935.00
A Falguiere, Diana, poised on left toes, marble base, 18" 1,725.00
A Laessel, bust of a boy, red marble base, 15" 575.00
Austrian, Arab man in tent selling artifacts, mc, 12" 3,450.00
Austrian, Arab on prayer rug, staff & shoes beside, mc, 5" 935.00
Austrian, lamp, dancers & boy under cloth stall, Gesch, 20" ..2,750.00

After Adrien-Etienne Gaudez, Orientalist Maiden, Possibly Judith, cold-painted patina of browns and red, rouge marble base, $3,500.00.

Austrian, praying man, cold pnt, 1800s, 4½" L 300.00
Bayre, seated lion, 1900, 10" 3,500.00
Beach, standing nude, marble base, Kunst Foundry NY, 9¾" 460.00
Bergman, Arab maid under canopy is fanned by boy, mc, 16" .2,900.00
Bergman, Namgreb, 2 Arabs under lg palm, mechanical, 13" ..2,900.00
Biegas, nude male emerging from billowing robe, 15" 3,700.00
Bitter, nymph sits w/doe, holds fawn, marble base, 11x30" 1,600.00
Bitter, sleeping faun, curious deer, marble base, 33" L 1,840.00
Bitter, 2 children/2 fauns, gr patina, marble base, 11x23" 345.00
Bouraine, 2 nude dancers, marble base, 21" 1,000.00
Carlier, sitting Boston Bull, dk brn patina, LAMY mk, 5½" 225.00
Chiparus, boy w/accordion, cold-pnt bronze & ivory, 9½" 1,000.00
Chiparus, dancer in loin wrap/scarf on head, marble std, 27" .4,600.00
Clodion, satyr groups, male & female w/infants, 18", pr 3,450.00
Collas, Diana the Huntress w/prancing stag, 20" 1,300.00
Cormier, kneeling nude, right arm to top of head, 16" 1,265.00
De la Grange, bust of woman, long hair/hood, 13" 1,300.00
De Matteis, girl w/water jugs, dk patina, dtd 1883, 21" 225.00
Descomps Cormier, couple kissing, on tall base w/skulls, 31" ..2,450.00
Drivier, archer, resting on knee, bow aloft, Rudier mk, 20" 6,325.00
Drouot, female sprinter, marble base, late 1800s, 21" 1,375.00
Erte, Woman & Satyr, 18" 2,500.00
Erte, 3 Graces, 16" 2,500.00
Fiala, nude reclining on cornucopia, faces in base, 18" 2,300.00
Gallo, young woman in short dress, greyhound aside, 26x16" 575.00
Gemignani, satyrs, 1 crashing cymbals to annoy 2nd, 24" 5,700.00
Gerome, Julius Caesar Crossing Rubicon, marble base, 15" 5,750.00
Grasegger, Siegfried, in loincloth, raising sword, 24" 1,150.00
Guillamin, standing Napoleon, rnd marble base, 9" 635.00
Guiraud-Riviere, 2 horses/charioteer, silvered, 1928, 14x34" ..4,100.00
H Mueller, Richard Wagner bust, red marble ped, 1900s, 11½" .450.00
Hatvany, figure of a doe, brn patina, mk Susse Frs, 5¾" 865.00
Hatvany, figure of a dog, brn patina, mk Susse Frs, 15" 1,800.00
Hoyt, standing cocker spaniel, gr/brn patina, mk OFGY, 5" L 125.00
J D'aste, reclining nude w/lamb, dk brn patina, 8x23" 1,650.00
Johnson (GMJ), stalking cat, dk brn patina, 1909, 4x8" 200.00
JW Learned, buffalo, ltd edition, 6½" 300.00
Kalish, reclining nude, face down, on mound, 7x15" 1,000.00
Kelety, Charioteer, 2 horses/chariot, gr-brn patina, 15x32" 3,000.00
Kemeys, cat observing terrapin, dk brn, mk KFI 1972, 3x6½" 175.00
Korschann, maid holds flowers to breast, floral base, 13" 920.00
Larche, lamp, Pan sits under flowering branch, gilt, 13½" 2,900.00
LeCoinay, little girl w/broken jug, 12" 250.00
Maindron, Velleda, standing by tree trunk, harp on bk, 18" ..1,265.00
Marceaux, Harlequin, arms Xd, standing on platform, 27" 1,000.00
Mengin, nude w/billowing cape on crescent moon, 30" 4,000.00
Muller, bust of maid in garland of flowers, 5" 230.00

Muller, inkwell, nude male in sea, 8½x15" 900.00
Nachtmann, kneeling nude Amazon archer in headdress, 12" ...1,000.00
Nikki, Winged Victory, gilt patina/marble columnar base, 14" ..495.00
O Opitz, Maiden Standing w/Lute, sq marble base, 10" 350.00
Ofner, Nouveau-style lady, brn patina, marble base, 14½" 475.00
Picciole, Ne Me Touchez Pas, tough boy, 11" 250.00
PJ Mene, stallion by fence, after Barre, 1876, 16" L 1,300.00
PJ Mene, 2 hounds, chained, hare in corner, recast, 15" 2,000.00
PJ Mene, 2 playful whippets, oval base, 6" 850.00
Pompon, owl, brn patina, mk Valsuani, 7" 2,000.00
Pompon, swan, silvered/gilded, mk Valsuani, 4" 1,300.00
Rancoulet, Pluto & Persephone w/3-headed dog on rocks, 34" ..4,400.00
Sauvage, female bust, long hair swept bk, marble base, 21" 1,200.00
Seifert, maid leans forward to drink from bowl, 15" 920.00
Silvestre, nude on hands & knees before charging ram, 14x33" ..1,300.00
Silvestre, prancing lamb, gr-brn patina, 5x5½" 125.00
Talconnet, standing nude female, sq base, 23" 600.00
Unmk, bust of maid, hair draped in cloth, gilt/marble, 9½" 250.00
Villanis, Dalila, bust of woman, ped base, now lamp, 17" 1,265.00
Villanis, Diane, bust of woman, 1900, 24" 690.00
Wiegand, kneeling nude, marble base, 6½x16" 1,000.00
Zach, dancer en pointe, breast exposed, marble base, 21" 1,150.00

Brownies by Palmer Cox

Created by Palmer Cox in 1883, the Brownies charmed children through the pages of books and magazines, as dolls, on their dinnerware, in advertising material, and on souvenirs. Each had his own personality, among them The Bellhop, The London Bobby, The Chairman, and Uncle Sam. But the oversized, triangular face with the startled expression, the protruding tummy, and the spindlelegs were characteristics of them all. They were inspired by the Scottish legends related to Cox as a child by his parents, who were of English descent. His introduction of the Brownies to the world was accomplished by a poem called *The Brownies Ride*. Books followed in rapid succession, thirteen in the series, all written as well as illustrated by Palmer Cox.

By the late 1890s, the Brownies were active in advertising. They promoted such products as games, coffee, toys, patent medicines, and rubber boots. 'Greenies' were the Brownies' first cousins, created by Cox to charm and to woo through the pages of the advertising almanacs of the G.G. Green Company of New Jersey. Perhaps the best-known endorsement in the Brownies' career was for the Kodak Brownie, which became so popular and sold in such volume that their name became synonymous with this type of camera.

Ashtray, RS Germany, 1913 ....50.00
Basket, SP, Brownies w/chocolate advertising, Tufts 165.00
Book, Brownies Their Book, Cox illus, 1887, EX 50.00
Book, Queer People, Palmer Cox illus, 1894, EX 45.00
Box, Log Cabin Brownies, cabin form, Nat'l Biscuit Co, '20s 135.00
Brownie Blocks, McLoughlin, litho decor, wood box, 13½x11" .250.00
Candlestick, Uncle Sam, 7½" 325.00
Cloth, 6 printed dolls to stuff, uncut, NM 450.00
Comic sheet, 1907, lg, EX 30.00
Creamer, Little Boy Blue verse & 4 Brownies, gold trim, china 85.00
Cup & saucer, Brownie golfers, ca 1900 ....195.00
Dish, child's, SP, 19 Brownies, 8½" 125.00
Game, Brownie Artillery, wood people/cannon/balls, 10x12", EX ...800.00
Game, 9 Brownies on wooden bases, bowling, c 1892, EX 425.00
Humidor, Brownie w/stocking cap, 6" 185.00
Ice cream bag, Cox illus, 5¢ orig value, 1930s, M 20.00
Ice cream mold, pewter, full figure, hinged, E&Co, 4¾" 195.00

Inkwell, majolica 135.00
Label, fruit crate; 1920s, 10x12", M (+) 20.00
Needle book, Brownies, 1892 World's Fair, rare 35.00
Paperweight, 3 intaglio-cut Brownies in glass base, gold pnt, 3" ..135.00
Picture frame, paper on wood, 8x10" 40.00
Plate, SP, Brownies on rim, 8½" 50.00
Plate, 5 Brownies wrapped in Am flag, china, 7½" 50.00
Table set, brass, emb Brownies, 3-pc (knife/fork/spoon) 80.00
Tray, 2 fencing Brownies, self hdls, china, 6¼x4½" 75.00

Brush

George Brush began his career in the pottery industry in 1901 working for the J.B. Owens Pottery Co. in Zanesville, Ohio. He left the company in 1907 to go into business for himself, only to have fire completely destroy his pottery less than one year after it was founded. Brush became associated with J.W. McCoy in 1909 and for many years served in capacities ranging from General Manager to President. (From 1911 until 1925, the firm was known as The Brush-McCoy Pottery Co.; see that section for information.) After McCoy died, the family withdrew their interests, and in 1925 the name of the firm was changed to The Brush Pottery. The era of hand-decorated art pottery had passed for the most part and would soon be completely replaced by the production of commercial lines. Of all the wares bearing the later Brush script mark, their figural cookie jars are the most collectible, and several have been reproduced.

For additional information on Brush cookie jars, we recommend *The Collector's Encyclopedia of Cookie Jars* by Joyce and Fred Roerig; they are listed in the Directory under South Carolina. See also Brush-McCoy for information on a second reference book.

Cookie Jars

Antique Touring Car, minimum value 650.00
Bear, #46 ....450.00
Boy w/Balloons, minimum value 600.00
Chick in Nest 450.00
Cinderella Pumpkin, #32 ....200.00
Circus Horse, gr, minimum value 900.00
Circus Horse, pk, minimum value 950.00
Clown, yel pants 185.00
Clown Bust 225.00
Cookie House, #31 ....75.00
Covered Wagon, dog finial, #30, minimum value 695.00
Cow w/Cat on Bk, brn 110.00
Cow w/Cat on Bk, purple, minimum value 1,000.00

Davy Crockett, no gold, marked USA, $300.00; Puppy Police, marked W 39 Brush USA, $585.00.

Davy Crockett, gold trim, minimum value 800.00
Dog & Basket, #33 ....300.00
Donkey w/Cart, ears down, #33, gray 650.00
Donkey w/Cart, ears up, #33, brn 600.00
Elephant w/Baby Bonnet & Ice Cream Cone, wht 500.00
Elephant w/Monkey on Bk, minimum value 1,000.00
Fish 500.00
Formal Pig, gr hat & coat, minimum value (+) 350.00
Gas Lamp, K1 ....75.00
Granny, pk apron, bl dots on skirt 325.00
Granny, plain skirt, minimum value 400.00
Happy Bunny, wht, #25 ....225.00
Happy Hippo 425.00
Hillbilly Frog, minimum value (+) 4,500.00
Hobby Horse, #55, minimum value 500.00
Humpty Dumpty, w/beany & bow tie 265.00
Humpty Dumpty, w/peaked brn hat & shoes 200.00
Laughing Hippo 500.00
Little Angel, minimum value 850.00
Little Boy Blue, gold trim, K25 USA, sm, minimum value 700.00
Little Boy Blue, K24 Brush USA, lg 800.00
Little Girl, #017 ....375.00
Little Red Riding Hood, gold trim, mk, lg, minimum value 750.00
Little Red Riding Hood, no gold, K24 USA, sm 465.00
Nite Owl 120.00
Old Clock 165.00
Panda, #21 ....240.00
Peter Pan, gold trim, lg 800.00
Peter Pan, sm 600.00
Pumpkin w/Lock on Door, W24 ....325.00
Raggedy Ann, #16 ....465.00
Sitting Pig 465.00
Squirrel on Log, #26 ....85.00
Squirrel w/Top Hat, blk coat & hat 250.00
Squirrel w/Top Hat, gr coat 235.00
Stylized Owl 425.00
Stylized Siamese, #41 ....460.00
Teasure Chest, #28 ....150.00
Teddy Bear, feet apart 250.00
Teddy Bear, feet together 150.00
3 Bears 100.00

Miscellaneous

Baby shoe, wht, #22, 2", ea 15.00
Candle holder, Christmas tree form 45.00
Custard cup, Rainbow Ovenware, yel, 1935, 5-oz 15.00
Figurine, boxer dog, #352, 1952 ....30.00
Figurine, rabbit w/removable carrot, 1950s, 9" 60.00
Figurine, squirrel standing, #482, 1949, 8½" 125.00
Flower arranger, Fleur-de-Lis, ftd, #FL4, 1964, 4x8" 25.00
Planter, bear on log, #205, 1954, 5¼x6" 25.00
Planter, Mary & Lamb, creme, #291, 1958, 6" 20.00
Planter, police hat, early 1950s 35.00
Planter, Red Riding Hood, #619, 1941, 5x6" 50.00
Vase, Glo Art, #750, 1930s 30.00
Vase, gr, ftd, #303, 1972, 3½x4½" 10.00
Vase, Ring & Leaf, brn, #806, 1931, 8" 35.00

Brush-McCoy

The Brush-McCoy Pottery was formed in 1911 in Zanesville, Ohio, an alliance between George Brush and J.W. McCoy. Brush's original pottery had been destroyed by fire in 1907; McCoy had operated his own business in Roseville, Ohio, since 1899. After the merger, the company expanded and produced not only their staple commercial wares but also fine artware. Lines such as Navarre, Venetian, Oriental, and Sylvan were of fine quality equal to that of their larger competitors. Because very little of the ware was marked, it is often mistaken for Weller, Roseville, or Peters and Reed.

In 1918 after a fire in Zanesville had destroyed the manufacturing portion of that plant, all production was contained in their Roseville (Ohio) plant #2. A stoneware type of clay was used there; and as a result, the artware lines of Jewel, Zuniart, King Tut, Florastone, Jetwood, Krakle-Kraft, and Panelart are so distinctive that they are more easily recognizable. Examples of these lines are unique and very beautiful, also quite rare and highly prized!

The Brush-McCoy Pottery operated under that name until after 1925 when it became the Brush Pottery. The Brush-Barnett family retained their interest in the pottery until 1981 when it was purchased by the Dearborn Company. For more information we recommend *The Guide to Brush-McCoy Pottery,* written by Martha and Steve Sanford and edited by David P. Sanford, our advisors for this category. They are listed in the Directory under California. See also Brush.

Bowl, gr matt, #195, 6" 65.00
Candlestick, Bl Onyx, #032, 10½", pr 225.00
Candlestick, Jetwood, #030, 7", ea 500.00
Casserole, Grape Ware, w/lid, #178, 1913 ....200.00
Cuspidor, Frog, #02, 1912 ....150.00
Fern dish, Zuniart, #055, 5" 450.00
Flower block, Florastone, #05, 3½" 200.00
Jardiniere, Bluebird, #229, 1915, 9" 400.00
Jardiniere, Bon-Ton, #214, 1916, 6¼" 65.00

Jardiniere and pedestal, Blended, #2360, 26", $950.00.

Mug, Flemish Bl, bluebird, sm 100.00
Mug, KolorKraft, keg form, #397, 15-oz 20.00
Pitcher, Nurock, #351, 5-pt, 8½" 135.00
Spill vase, Vogue, #046, 1916, 12" 150.00
Stein, Corn Line, #49, 1910, 16-oz 100.00
Vase, Brn Onyx, #063, 12" 125.00
Vase, bud; Jewel, bsk, #047, 10" 450.00
Vase, Cleo, #044, 1915, 11" 450.00
Vase, Jetwood, type 1, #041, 12" 1,000.00
Vase, King Tut, #051, 4" 750.00

Vase, Krackle-Kraft, #053, 3" 400.00
Vase, Panelart, #071, 9" 1,500.00

Buffalo Pottery

The founding of the Buffalo Pottery in Buffalo, New York, in 1901, was a direct result of the success achieved by John Larkin through his innovative methods of marketing 'Sweet Home Soap.' Choosing to omit 'middle-man' profits, Larkin preferred to deal directly with the consumer and offered premiums as an enticement for sales. The pottery soon proved a success in its own right and began producing advertising and commemorative items for other companies, as well as commercial tableware. In 1905 they introduced their Blue Willow line after extensive experimentation resulted in the development of the first successful underglaze cobalt achieved by an American company. Between 1905 and 1909, a line of pitchers and jugs were hand decorated in historical, literary, floral, and outdoor themes. Twenty-nine styles are known to have been made. These have been found in a wide array of color variations.

Their most famous line was Deldare Ware, the bulk of which was made from 1908 to 1909. It was hand decorated after illustrations by Cecil Aldin. Views of English life were portrayed in detail through unusual use of color against the natural olive green cast of the body. Today the 'Fallowfield Hunt' scenes are more difficult to locate than 'Scenes of Village Life in Ye Olden Days.' A Deldare calendar plate was made in 1910. These are very rare and are highly valued by collectors. The line was revived in 1923 and dropped again in 1925. Every piece was marked 'Made at Ye Buffalo Pottery, Deldare Ware Underglaze.' Most are dated, though date has no bearing on the value. Emerald Deldare, made with the same olive body and on standard Deldare Ware shapes, featured historical scenes and Art Nouveau decorations. Most pieces are found with a 1911 date stamp. Production was very limited due to the intricate, time-consuming detail. Needless to say, it is very rare and extremely desirable.

Abino Ware, most of which was made in 1912, also used standard Deldare shapes, but its colors were earthy and the decorations more delicately applied. Sailboats, windmills, and country scenes were favored motifs. These designs were achieved by overpainting transfer prints and were often signed by the artist. The ware is marked 'Abino' in handprinted block letters. Production was limited; and as a result, examples of this line are scarce today. Prices only slightly trail those of Emerald Deldare Ware.

The many uncataloged items that have been found over the years indicate that Buffalo Pottery decorators were free to use their own ideas and talents to create many beautiful one-of-a-kind pieces.

Our advisors for this category are Fred and Lila Shrader; they are listed in the Directory under California.

Abino

Bowl, sailing scene, 9" 850.00
Bowl, windmill on pond scene, 5" 450.00
Chamberstick, w/finger ring 850.00
Plate, windmill on pond scene, 10" 675.00
Vase, sailing scene, 13" 1,250.00
Vase, windmill scene, cylindrical, 6½" 875.00

Deldare

Bowl, cereal; Ye Olden Days, 6½" 150.00
Bowl, fern; Emerald Art Nouveau, w/insert, 3½x8" 1,150.00
Bowl, fruit; Dr Syntax Reading His Tour..., 9" 995.00
Bowl, fruit; Fallowfield Hunt, 9" 640.00
Bowl, rimmed soup; Ye Village Scenes, 9" 250.00

Bowl, vegetable; Ye Olden Times, 8½x6½" 395.00
Candle holder, Ye Olden Times, shield bk, 7" 950.00

Candle holder, Colonial couple before Tudor-style house, shield back with handle, dated 1909, 5", $975.00.

Candlestick, Emerald Art Nouveau, 9" 950.00
Candlesticks, City Scenes, 9", pr 795.00
Chamberstick, City Scenes, w/finger ring 495.00
Chocolate pot, Ye Village Street, 6-sided, 9" 2,000.00
Creamer, Fallowfield Hunt scene (uncaptioned) 195.00
Creamer, Ye Village Scenes 195.00
Cup & saucer, chocolate; Fallowfield Hunt Scene (uncaptioned) ..550.00
Cup & saucer, chocolate; Ye Village Street 425.00
Cup & saucer, Fallowfield Hunt 275.00
Cup & saucer, Ye Olden Days 225.00
Humidor, Emerald, Dr Syntax Returned Home 900.00
Humidor, Emerald, There Was an Old Sailor 900.00
Humidor, Ye Lion Inn 600.00
Mug, Emerald, Dr Syntax, I Give the Law..., 2¼" 545.00
Mug, Fallowfield Hunt, The Death, 4½" 365.00
Mug, Ye Lion Inn, 4½" 310.00
Pin tray, Ye Olden Days, 6¼x3½" 325.00
Pitcher, Emerald, Dr Syntax...the Lake, 8½" 1,170.00
Pitcher, Fallowfield Hunt, Breaking Cover, 10" 795.00
Pitcher, Robin Hood (on Deldare Body), 8¼" 1,250.00
Pitcher, Their Manner of Telling Stories, 6" 500.00
Pitcher, To Spare an Old Broken Soldier, 7" 535.00
Plaque, Emerald, Dr Syntax Stretching..., 12" 1,150.00
Plate, At Ye Lion Inn, 6¼" 95.00
Plate, calendar; 1910, 9¾" 1,650.00
Plate, chop; Emerald, Dr Syntax Sells Grizzle, 13½" 1,250.00
Plate, Deldare Ware, salesman's sample, 7" 1,050.00
Plate, Emerald, Dr Syntax Soliloquising, 7¼" 495.00
Plate, Fallowfield, The Hunt, 6½" 145.00
Plate, Fallowfield, The Start, 9¼" 235.00
Plate, Ye Town Crier, 8½" 145.00
Plate, Ye Village Scenes, 10" 210.00
Platter, Fallowfield, The Start, 8½x6½" 675.00
Powder jar, Ye Village Street, w/lid 375.00
Relish dish, Fallowfield, The Dash, 12x6" 495.00
Sugar bowl, Fallowfield (untitled), 6-sided, 3½" 300.00
Sugar bowl, Village Life 225.00
Tankard, Emerald, Art Nouveau decor, 12" 1,400.00
Tankard, Emerald, Dr Syntax Entertained, 10" 1,385.00
Tea tile, Emerald, Dr Syntax Taking Possession 550.00
Teapot, Emerald, Dr Syntax Disputing..., 5½" 1,175.00
Teapot, Scenes of Village Life, 5¾" 425.00
Tray, calling card; Ye Lion Inn, 7½" 350.00
Tray, dresser; Dancing Ye Minuet, 12x9" 625.00

Tray, tea; heirlooms, 12x10¼" 725.00
Vase, kingfisher & irises, 7¾x6½" 2,645.00
Vase, Village Scenes, hourglass shape, 9" 375.00
Vase, Ye Village Parson, 8½" 950.00

Miscellaneous

Ashtray/matchbox holder, Tahoe Tavern 50.00
Bowl, cereal; Blue Willow, 7½" 35.00
Bowl, fruit; natural wood design, 5½" 45.00
Bowl, vegetable; Blue Willow, 9" 145.00
Bowl, wash; Chyrsanthemum, 14½" 290.00
Butter pat, American Mail, side stamped 65.00
Butter pat, Blue Willow 22.00
Butter pat, Diary Lunch 25.00
Butter pat, Eastern Steamship 45.00
Butter pat, Indian Tree 10.00
Butter pat, Park Lane 18.00
Butter pat, Vienna 20.00
Butter pat, YPH (Yellowstone Park Hotel) 45.00
Creamer, Ahwahnee Hotel, rust & blk geometrics, 3" 25.00
Creamer, Blue Willow, no hdl, ind, 2½" 25.00
Creamer, Standard Oil, 3" 125.00
Cup, bouillon; Brown Derby 18.00
Cup & saucer, Blue Willow, farmer sz, cup 6½" across 75.00
Cup & saucer, Globe Dairy Lunch, Los Angeles 25.00
Dish, child's feeding; Campbell Kids, w/alphabet 85.00
Dish, child's feeding; nursery rhyme 65.00
Egg cup, Blue Lune, Colorido, or Cafe au Lait 12.00
Game set, 15x11" platter+6 9" plates w/deer decor 485.00
Mug, Remember the Maine, 4½" 85.00
Mug, Sea Cave, Multifleure, 4½" 45.00
Pitcher, Argyle, 7½" 425.00
Pitcher, Bluebird, 7" 175.00
Pitcher, Holland jug, 6" 475.00
Pitcher, Landing of Roger Williams, mc 750.00
Pitcher, Robin Hood, 8¼" 540.00
Pitcher, The Genesee, wht w/gold, str sides, 7½" 135.00
Pitcher, Whirl of the Town, mc, 7" 725.00
Plate, advertising; Advance, 7½" 78.00
Plate, Ahwahnee, rust & blk geometrics, 9½" 55.00
Plate, Gaudy Willow, 8" 125.00
Plate, Mt Vernon, historical series, 10½" 75.00
Plate, Pat's Cafe, 6" 15.00
Plate, Pink's Pittsburgh Inn, Multifleure ware, 8" 35.00
Plate, Roosevelt Bears, 8" 265.00
Platter, Dr Syntax Theme, bl & wht w/floral border, 14x11" ..365.00
Teapot, Argyle, bl & wht tea roses, w/metal tea ball 200.00
Teapot, Blue Willow, sq, 4-cup, 5½" 165.00
Vase, Geranium, mc, rose-bowl style, 4" 95.00
Wash bowl & pitcher, tea roses on wht 375.00
Wash set, Chrysanthemum, pitcher+bowl+chamber pot+vase ...475.00

Buggy Steps

The recent increase in horse-drawn vehicle refurbishing and restoration has increased the requirement for original antique iron buggy steps. The purpose of these steps is to allow the passenger to enter or exit the vehicle without the driver releasing his hold. Steps are exceedingly convenient and may be hinged, pivoted, adjustable, or folding. Some doubled as foot scrapers with multiple patterns of raised projections designed to remove soil and mud from the feet of passengers before they entered the buggy.

The carts, wagons, buggies, and surries utilized iron steps which were cast, malleable, and steel. The elaborate handwork of blacksmiths in creating iron steps was equal to the wheelwrights, carpenters, and leather workers performing the state of the art labors in the manufacture of early wheeled vehicles (ca 1865-1910). Prices are shown for steps in mint to good condition. Rust, breaks and pitting reduce value. Our advisor for this category is John Waddell; he is listed in the Directory under Texas.

Henny Buggy Co., oval, trifork mount, 5x3½", $40.00; **Dean & Co.**, oval, tee mount, 5¼x3½", $45.00; **Studebaker**, rectangle, trifork mount, 5x3¼", $40.00.

Beebe Cart, 3x3" sq, bolt on 18.00
Cole, 3½x2¼" eared oval, slot mt 25.00
CW Co, 3½x3½" sq shield, bolt on 18.00
Emerson, 5x3½" oval, tee mt 40.00
Folding step, spring offset, open mt 18.00
Grate step, open, 4½x4", trifork mt 40.00
Moon Bros, 4½x3½" oval, trifork mt 40.00
Ornamental step, w/scraper & scroll, trifork mt 55.00
Peru, 4½" dia, tee mt 45.00
Staver, 4½x3½" oval, trifork mt 40.00
Surry step, 8½x6½" oval, branch arm mt 110.00
Thompson Wagon Co, rectangle w/shield & branch 45.00
WG Hesse & Son, 4" dia, tee mt 45.00

Burmese

Burmese glass was patented in 1885 by the Mount Washington Glass Co. It is typically shaded from canary yellow to a rosy salmon color. The yellow is produced by the addition of uranium oxide to the mix. The salmon color comes from the addition of gold salts and is achieved by reheating the object (partially) in the furnace. It is thus called 'heat sensitive' glass. Thomas Webb of England was licensed to produce Burmese and often added more gold, giving an almost fuchsia tinge to the salmon in some cases. They called their glass 'Queen's Burmese,' and this is sometimes etched on the base of the object. This is not to be confused with Mount Washington's 'Queen's Design,' which refers to the design painted on the object. Both companies added decoration to many pieces. Mount Washington-Pairpoint produced some Burmese in the late 1920s and Gunderson and Bryden in the '50s and '70s, but the color and shapes are different. Our advisors for this category are Dolli and Wilfred Cohen; they are listed in the Directory under California. In the listings that follow, examples are assumed to have the satin finish unless noted 'shiny.' See also Lamps, Fairy.

Biscuit jar, grapes & leaves, SP rim, hdl & lid, 6" 650.00
Bottle scent; floral & butterfly, sterling lid, 3½" 600.00
Bowl, crimped rim, Mt WA, 1½x4¾" 200.00
Bowl, Dmn Quilt, tapered, 4-fold rim, 4 stick ft, Webb, 5½" 750.00
Bowl, ivy & berries, waisted/ruffled, Webb, 3½"; SP fr 500.00
Bowl, pine cones & leaves, 8-crimped flared top, 2¾x4" 350.00
Bowl, shiny, rigaree, ruffled, 2½x5"; SP hdld/ftd fr 475.00
Bowl, shiny, ruffled, 3¼x10" 200.00
Bowl, wide ruffled rim, att Mt WA, 4x8" 220.00
Candlestick, vines & floral, ruffled, Webb Queen's, 6½" 800.00
Creamer, burmese hdl, 4" 275.00
Creamer, shiny, Pairpoint, 2½x2¾" 75.00
Cruet, shiny, ribbed, matching stopper, 5" 1,195.00
Cup, chocolate; mallards in flight w/gilt rim, 3" 650.00
Epergne, 1 lily+2 cups & 2 lg leaves on mirror, Webb, 12" 700.00
Ewer, peonies & dragons, gilt, petticoat body, 10" 2,500.00
Finger bowl, 9-crimp, Mt WA, 2¼x4⅜" 225.00
Pin dish, berries & leaves, collared top, 2x3½" dia 325.00
Pitcher, Hobnail, 'blossom' base, flaring sides, Mt WA, 5½" 600.00
Pitcher, leaf & vine rigaree, reeded hdl, Mt WA, 9" 1,100.00
Pitcher, milk; tea roses & Thos Hood verse, 7½" 3,000.00
Plate, boat & mtns in brn tones, 11" 325.00
Plate, coupe; 10" 175.00
Plate, rimmed, 10" 125.00
Rose bowl, 8-crimp, Webb, 2¼x2¼" 175.00
Shakers, butterfly in bl/red, red/gold floral, Webb, 3½", pr 850.00
Sugar bowl, Mt WA, 2x3¾" 100.00
Sugar bowl, wishbone ft, berry pontil, Mt WA, 3" 650.00
Sugar shaker, dainty floral, Mt WA, 4" 1,000.00
Toothpick holder, florals on melon ribs, star-form rim, ...400.00
Toothpick holder, pnt decor, ribbed, fluted, Mt WA, 2¼" 525.00
Toothpick holder, shiny, Dmn Quilt, sq top, Mt WA 525.00
Toothpick holder, sq top, 2¼" 250.00
Tumbler, Mt WA, 3¾" 200.00
Tumbler, shiny, Mt WA, 3¾" 250.00
Vase, acorns, fluted rim, 4" 325.00
Vase, asters, wht/gold, scroll hdls, stick neck, Mt WA, 13" 1,200.00
Vase, autumn leaves, stick neck, mk Webb Queen's, 10" 650.00
Vase, ball shape w/star-shaped top, Webb, 3x2⅝" 200.00
Vase, bud; SP hdld fr, Webb, 8¼" 515.00
Vase, crimped top, petal base, 4" 250.00
Vase, floral, mc w/blk bands, unmk Webb, 3½x3" 275.00
Vase, floral, mc/lav, ruffled trumpet top, 3¾" 275.00
Vase, floral branches, collared 6-sided top, 2½x2" 295.00
Vase, jack-in-pulpit; Mt WA, 7¼x3½" 345.00
Vase, jack-in-pulpit; shiny, 9" 440.00
Vase, mc floral, Webb, 8⅛x3⅞" 750.00
Vase, owl/branch/poem by Gray, bk: birds, stick neck, 12" 2,700.00
Vase, prunus on long leafy stem, 8¾" 700.00
Vase, ruffled rim, crimped ped base, 4¼x1½" 210.00
Vase, ruffled rim, Webb, 3⅞x2⅞" 225.00
Vase, slim form w/fluted top, ped ft, 6" 200.00
Vase, striped look, unsgn Webb, 4x2⅞" 225.00
Whiskey taster, Dmn Quilt, Mt WA, 3" 195.00

Butter Molds and Stamps

The art of decorating butter began in Europe during the reign of Charles II. This practice was continued in America by the farmer's wife who sold her homemade butter at the weekly market to earn extra money during hard times. A mold or stamp with a special design, hand carved either by her husband or a local craftsman, not only made her product more attractive but also helped identify it as hers. The pattern became the trademark of Mrs. Smith, and all who saw it knew that this was her butter. It was usually the rule that no two farms used the same mold within a certain area, thus the many variations and patterns available to the collector today. The most valuable are those which have animals, birds, or odd shapes. The most sought-after motifs are the eagle, cow, fish, and rooster. These works of early folk art are quickly disappearing from the market.

Molds

Cornflower, EX cvg, rnd case w/plunger, 4¾" dia	95.00
Cow, clear glass, wooden hdl, 4½" dia	85.00
Cow, rectangular w/hinged box, continental, 11"	160.00
Flower & leaves, 4x3¾", EX	110.00
Pear w/geometric border, rnd case, worn varnish, 5"	165.00
Pineapple & leaves, dtd Pat April 17, 1867, ½-lb, EX	130.00
Pineapple on sq, Shaker	185.00
Pomegranate, rnd case, 4¾"	40.00
Sheaf of wheat, brass fittings & plunger, dbl, 5¾x3½"	145.00
Sheaf of wheat, dbl, 2½x3¾" L	80.00
Star (dbl), rectangular case, 4½x5¼"	150.00
Strawberries & leaves, appl hdl, 3½" dia, EX	115.00
Swan, old finish, 5" dia	110.00

Wheat pattern, small crack, EX patina, 4¾" diameter, $65.00.

Stamps

Basket of fruit, elongated trn hdl, scrubbed, 4"	330.00
Cow, EX patina, trn threaded hdl	220.00
Cow, trn screw hdl, worn patina, 2⅝"	165.00
Eagle, star flower on reverse, lollipop style, 9"	990.00
Eagle, well cvd, trn hdl, 3¾"	385.00
Eagle, 1-pc trn hdl, scrubbed, 4⅜"	220.00
Fish, hardwood w/some curl in hdl, 2¾" dia	195.00
Floral, 2-pc trn hdl, dk patina, 3¾"	105.00
Floral (stylized), in X-hatched crescent-shaped bowl, 4"	50.00
Floral (stylized), trn hdl, 5⅛"	140.00
Floral (stylized), 1-pc trn hdl, dk patina, 4¾"	110.00
Floral (stylized), 1-pc trn hdl, old patina, 3½"	85.00
Floral (stylized), 1-pc trn hdl, scrubbed, 4⅝"	95.00
Floral ea side, minor damage, 5¼"	300.00
Floral w/incised leaves, notched rim, 3⅞" dia	55.00
Leaf, wear & age crack, 3¾"	60.00
Leaf, 1-pc trn hdl, worn patina, 2¾"	215.00
Leaf (stylized), missing hdl, scrubbed, 4⅞"	85.00
Pineapple, semicircular, trn inserted hdl, scrubbed, 7"	215.00
Pineapple, trn hdl, old scrubbed gray patina, 4¼"	110.00
Pineapple (stylized), 1-pc trn hdl, scrubbed, 4½"	165.00

Pinwheel, inserted hdl, primitive, 5¼"	415.00
Pomegranate & foliage, concave surface, 1-pc trn hdl, 5⅛"	250.00
Pomegranate & foliage, 1-pc trn hdl, scrubbed, 4¼"	75.00
Sheaf of wheat, deeply cvd, 1-pc trn hdl, 4¼"	330.00
Sheaf of wheat, EX detail & patina, 1-pc trn hdl, 4⅝"	450.00
Sheaf of wheat, 1-pc trn hdl, soft patina, crack, 4¾"	60.00
Star flower, lollipop style, G worn patina, 7⅜"	300.00
Star flower, lollipop style, primitive, 9"	110.00
Star flower, well cvd, trn hdl, 5"	165.00
Star flower, 1-pc trn hdl, dk brn patina, 2⅞"	165.00
Strawberry & leaf, inserted trn hdl, soft patina, 3½"	165.00
Sunburst, dk patina, 4¾"	195.00
Swan, appl stick hdl, 6x3½" dia	115.00
Swan, trn screw-in hdl, worn patina, 2⅞"	85.00
Thistle, concentric circle border, knob hdl, 1-pc, 4" dia	65.00
Tulip, 1-pc w/whittled hdl, worn patina, 3½x3⅝"	220.00
Tulip (stylized), EX detail & patina, missing hdl, 4½"	55.00
Tulip (stylized), well cvd, trn hdl, 4¼"	300.00
Tulip & floral, dbl sided, scrubbed, 3½"	77.00
Tulip & floral, sgn NH/dtd 1820, rpl hdl, 3x5½"	120.00
Tulip & thistle (stylized), dbl sided, scrubbed, 4"	55.00
2 hearts w/initials, trn hdl, EX patina, 4"	270.00
4-Leaf design, trn inserted hdl, 3¾"	95.00
6-Petal rosette, sm stars between petals, cvd leaves, 4" dia	175.00
6-Pointed star, notched rim, 4½" dia	75.00
6-Pointed star w/cvd petals, lollipop type, 4" dia	190.00
6-Pointed star w/petals & cvd border, bk: plume, 5" dia	350.00
8-Pointed star, bk: rosette w/star points, lollipop type, 3½"	330.00

Buttonhooks

The earliest known written reference to buttonhooks (shoe hooks, glove hooks, or collar buttoners) is dated 1611. They became a necessary implement in the 1850s when tight-fitting high-button shoes became fashionable. Later in the 19th century, ladies' button gloves and men's button-on collars and cuffs dictated specific types of buttoners, some with a closed wire loop instead of a hook end. Both shoes and gloves used as many as twenty-four buttons each. Usage began to wane in the late 1920s following a fashion change to low-cut laced shoes and the invention of the zipper. There was a brief resurgence of use following the 1948 movie 'High Button Shoes.' For a simple, needed utilitarian device, buttonhook handles were made from a surprising variety of materials: natural wood, bone, ivory, agate and mother of pearl to plain steel, celluloid, aluminum, iron, lead and pewter, artistic copper, brass, silver, gold, and many other materials, in lengths that varied from under 2" to over 20". Many designs folded or retracted, and buttonhooks were often combined with shoehorns and other useful implements. Stamped steel buttonhooks often came free with the purchase of shoes, gloves or collars. Material, design, workmanship, condition and relative scarcity are the primary market value factors. Prices range from $1.00 to over $100.00. Buttonhooks are fairly easy to find, and they are interesting to display. Our advisor for this category is Richard Mathes; he is listed in the Directory under Ohio.

Buttonhook/penknife, ivory side plates, man's	40.00
Glove hook, gold plated, retractable, 3"	75.00
Glove hook, loop end, agate hdl, 2½"	35.00
Shoe hook, colored celluloid hdl, 8"	10.00
Shoe hook, faux ivory celluloid hdl, 8"	5.00
Shoe hook, stamped steel, advertising, 5"	3.00
Shoe hook, wooden hdl, 8"	8.00
Shoe hook/shoehorn combination, steel & celluloid, 9"	20.00

Calendar Plates

Calendar plates were advertising giveaways most popular from about 1906 until the late twenties. They were decorated with colorful underglaze decals of lovely ladies, flowers, animals, birds and, of course, the twelve months of the year of their issue. During the 1950s they came into vogue again, but never to the extent they were originally. Those with exceptional detailing, or those with scenes of a particular activity are most desirable, so are any from before 1906 or after 1930.

Our advisor for this category is Elizabeth M. Stout; she is listed in the Directory under Missouri.

1907, ladies **45.00**
1908, pk rose border **30.00**
1909, Gibson Girl **38.00**
1909, Santa in sled, holly, 9½" **48.00**
1910, lighthouse & sailboats **35.00**
1910, Lighthouse from Anaheim Store **35.00**
1910, poppies, NY City **36.00**
1910, sailboats on water **35.00**
1910, St Bernard dog **38.00**
1911, Delft windmill/boat scene **32.00**
1911, 4-leaf clover **35.00**
1911-12, months form border **40.00**
1912, owl **35.00**
1913, farm boy **39.00**
1914, automobile **42.00**
1915, Dutch children, 9" **48.50**
1915, Panama Canal completion **30.00**
1923, fish in center **45.00**
1930, parrot, Schulz Produce, Spencer NE **65.00**
1966, eagle, USA in center, gold on wht, unmk **2.50**

Calendars

Calendars are collected for their colorful prints, often attributed to a well-recognized artist of the period. Advertising calendars from the turn of the century often have a double appeal when representing a company whose tins, signs, store displays, etc., are also collectible. See also Parrish, Maxfield.

1886, Hood's Sarsaparilla, blond child, partial pad, 5x7", EX **40.00**
1887, Blk man bitten by dog falls on melon, ad, 5x7", G **65.00**
1894, Hood's Sarsaparilla, girl diecut, 8¾x5½", G **50.00**
1894, Youth's Companion Dainty Calendar, mc scenes, 2x3", G .**25.00**
1903, Hanan Shoe Co, elves, Indians, etc, EX **190.00**
1904, St Mary's Academy, Notre Dame IN, 5½x6½", G **30.00**
1905, Tongaline Liquid Tablets, Indian portrait, EX **95.00**

1906-07, Wales Goodyear Rubbers, stylish ladies in winter scene, framed, $200.00.

1906, Domestic Sewing Maching, mother & daughter w/doll, EX ...**375.00**
1907, Bristol Steel Rods, fisherman/guide in canoe, 20x15", EX ...**1,100.00**
1907, SM Hess & Bro, child w/flowers, Hayes c 1901, 22x15", EX ..**140.00**
1908, Antikammia Tablets..., boy w/missing tooth, EX **110.00**
1909, Columbus Brewing, emb diecut, boy & girl, EX **750.00**
1909, Harrington & Richardson Arms, grandpa w/shotgun, 26x14", EX .**500.00**
1910, Katherine Pyle Calendar, children w/animals, 14x18", G .**125.00**
1910, Osborn Harvesting Machines, implements/woman/horse, NM ..**475.00**
1911, Detroit Journal Carriers, Dutch people, 3-part, 13½", G **25.00**
1911, Orange Candy, boy w/violin diecut, 18½x14½", EX **60.00**
1912, Haberle Congress Beer, men toasting girl, 23x17", EX **285.00**
1912, Harrison Fisher lady's portrait, full pad, NM **95.00**
1912, Youth's Companion, lady, Am Litho, 2-part, 5x8½", G **22.50**
1913, Bristol...Fishing Rod, Catch of Season, 23x16", EX **800.00**
1913, Peters Cartridge, Getting Ready, 27x14", EX **400.00**
1914, Brinker Horse Supplies, girl w/horse, full pad, NM **450.00**
1916, Bell Plaine Candy, couple in gazebo, emb diecut, EX **110.00**
1919, Cream City Sash & Door, Santa's elves/factory, 16", EX ..**350.00**
1920, Western Cartridge, Respectors of Limits, 30x15", EX **275.00**
1924, Doe-Wah Jack Peaceful Counsel emb, EX **65.00**
1924, Western Ammunition, Saving the Day, A Russell, 31x15", EX .**350.00**
1926, US Shot Cartridges, man painting decoy, 28x15", G **450.00**
1931, Maas & Steffen, Winged Invader, 27x14", G **175.00**
1931, Western World...Ammunition, Bird Scents, 28x15", EX ..**250.00**
1932, Am Stores, children & flag, full pad, 25x12", VG **65.00**
1932, Champion Mars Guy-Llewelyn Setter, on point, 16x12", EX ..**350.00**
1933, Maas & Steffen, Terror in Tops, RC Prathe, 28x14", VG ...**265.00**
1936, Jewel Tea, Flying High, children & kites, 13x7½", G **15.00**
1937, Gibson Bros Oil Co, traffic cop, full pad, 46x21", EX **35.00**
1937, Hercules Powder, Autumn Fields, 30x13", VG **150.00**
1940, Good Year Rubber Goods, Boy Scout, full pad, 37x20", NM ..**45.00**
1941, Hercules Powder, boy w/dog, Rockwell, 29½x13", EX **125.00**
1941, Protect Wild Life, Obey the Law, men & moose, 22x16", G ..**75.00**
1944, Earl Moran pinup girls, desk type, M **50.00**
1944, Varga pinup girls, 12 poses, orig 25¢ envelope, M **165.00**
1945, Earl Moran pinup girl, pocket type, G **25.00**
1946, Rockwell cover, full pad, 14½x8", M in mailer **30.00**
1947, Munson pinup girls, M in illus envelope **95.00**
1948, Perdew Handmade Game Calls & Decoys, sepiatone, 16x9", VG .**100.00**
1949, Hock Paint & Chemicals, Thoroughbred, 33x16", NM **55.00**
1951, Lee Johnson Furniture, man fishing near bridge, 44x30", EX ..**75.00**
1952, Rockwell cover, full pad, 14½x8", M **30.00**
1954, Kik Cola, child at beach, full pad, 1954, 33x16", NM **40.00**
1954, nude Marilyn Monroe w/lace o/l, 15x9", NM **350.00**
1956, Kik Cola, full pad, 26x13", NM **40.00**
1960, Winnick's Auto Parts, Elvgren girl, 33x16", VG **45.00**
1962, Playboy, Stella Stevens w/dog, etc, M **85.00**
1966, Fritz Willis pinup portraits, M **75.00**

California Faience

California Faience was the trade name used by William V. Bragdon and Chauncy R. Thomas on vases, bowls, and other artware produced at their pottery known as 'The Tile Shop' in Berkeley, California, from 1920 to 1930. Faience tile was the principal product of the business during these years and is the favorite with today's collectors. Items in a glossy glaze are rare and therefore more valuable. Tiles were marked 'California Faience' with a die stamp.

Bowl, bl on turq, turq int, fluted, 2½x6" **150.00**
Bowl, lt bl gloss, vertical ribs, 3x7" **90.00**
Bowl, lt bl matt, 2x10½" **175.00**
Flower frog, 2 ducks, aqua glossy, mk, 5½" **100.00**

Tile, desert scene, mc, 5½" dia	450.00
Tile, stylized tulips, gr on ochre, 4½" dia	295.00
Vase, dk rose gloss, vertical lines, incurvate can form, 5½"	150.00
Vase, emb leaves, lt brn matt, ovoid, 5x3"	450.00
Vase, lovebirds & trees, frieze on red, 6¼"	300.00
Vase, ochre/gray, cylinder w/cvd vertical lines, 5½x3¾"	600.00
Vase, turq glossy, bulbous, 5½"	165.00

California Perfume Company

D.H. McConnell, Sr., founded the California Perfume Company (C.P. Company; C.P.C.) in 1886 in New York City. He had previously been a salesman for a book company, which he later purchased. His door-to-door sales usually involved the lady of the house, to whom he presented a complimentary bottle of inexpensive perfume. Upon determining his perfume to be more popular than his books, he decided that the manufacture of perfume might be more lucrative. He bottled toiletries under the name 'California Perfume Company' and a line of household products called 'Perfection.' In 1928 the name 'Avon' appeared on the label, and in 1939 the C.P.C. name was entirely removed from the product. The success of the company is attributed to the door-to-door sales approach and 'money back' guarantee offered by his first 'Depot Agent,' Mrs. P.F.E. Albee, known today as the 'Avon Lady.'

The company's containers are quite collectible today, especially the older, hard-to-find items. Advanced collectors seek bottles and other items labeled Goetting & Co., New York; Goetting's; or Savoi Et Cie, Paris. Such examples date from 1871 to 1896. The Goetting Company was purchased by D.H. McConnell; Savoi Et Cie was a line which they imported to sell through department stores. Also of special interest are packaging and advertising with the Ambrosia or Hinze Ambrosia Company label. This was a subsidiary company whose objective seems to have been to produce a line of face creams, etc., for sale through drugstores and other such commercial outlets. They operated in New York from about 1875 until 1954. Because very little is known about these companies and since only a few examples of their product containers and advertising material have been found, market values for such items have not yet been established. Other items sought by the collector include products marked Gertrude Recordon, Marvel Electric Silver Cleaner, Easy Day Automatic Clothes Washer, pre-1930 catalogs, and California Perfume Company 1909 and 1910 calendars.

There are hundreds of local Avon Collector Clubs throughout the world that also have C.P.C. collectors in their membership. If you are interested in joining, locating, or starting a new club, contact the National Association of Avon Collectors, Inc., listed in the Directory under Clubs, Newsletters, and Catalogs. Those wanting a National Newsletter Club or price guides may contact Avon Times, listed in the same section. Inquiries concerning California Perfume Company items and the companies or items mentioned in the previous paragraph should be directed toward our advisor, Dick Pardini, whose address is given under California. (Please send a large SASE; not interested in Avons, 'Perfection' marked C.P.C.'s, or Anniversary Keepsakes.)

American Ideal Dbl Compact, brass, powder & rouge, 1921, M	50.00
American Ideal Toilet Soap, gr box, 2 bars, 1925, M	65.00
Baby Set, toilet water, soap & powder, 1923, M	225.00
Bandoline, cork stopper, 1915, M	50.00
Bay Rum, metal cap, 1929, 16-oz	65.00
Benzoin, metal stopper, 1915, 2-oz or 4-oz, M, ea	70.00
California Baby Soap in box, 1902, M	60.00
Daphne Eyebrow Pencil, metal tube, 1925, M	20.00
Daphne Glycerin Soap, gr box, 2 bars, 1925, M	65.00
Daphne Threesome Set, toilet water/talc/sachet, 1923, M	220.00
Eau De Quinine, shaker cap, 1900, 6-oz, M	65.00

French Perfumes, glass stopper, 1910s, ¼-oz to 4-oz, M, ea	85.00
Gertrude Recordon's Peach Lotion, 1925, MIB	80.00

**Little Folks Set, 4 perfume bottles
with corks, 1904, M, $250.00.**

Perfume, glass stopper, ca 1896, 1-oz, M	75.00
Shaving Soap, 1 bar in wrapper, 1905, M	55.00
Toilet Water, glass stopper, 1910, 8-oz, M	75.00
Tooth Powder, metal coned cap, 1908, M	75.00
Trailing Arbutus Brillantine, frosted glass stopper, 1923, M	90.00
Trailing Artubus...Perfume, metal cap/glass stopper, 1-oz, '23, M	110.00
Vernafleur Quintette Set, holds 5 items, 1929, M	200.00
Vernafleur Toilet Soap Set, 3 bars, 1928, M	75.00
Violet Almond Meal, glass, metal shaker lid, 1912, M	90.00
Witch Hazel, 1896, 8-oz	110.00
Witch Hazel, 1908, 4-oz, 8-oz, or 16-oz, M, ea	80.00

Calling Cards, Cases, and Receivers

The practice of announcing one's arrival with a calling card borne by the maid to the mistress of the house was a social grace of the Victorian era. Different messages (condolences, a personal visit, or a good-by) were related by turning down one corner or another. The custom was forgotten by WWI. Fashionable ladies and gents carried their personally engraved cards in elaborate cases made of such materials as embossed silver, mother-of-pearl with intricate inlay, tortoise shell, and ivory. Card receivers held cards left by visitors who called while the mistress was out or 'not receiving.' Calling cards with fringe, die-cut flaps that cover the name, or an unusual decoration are worth about $3.00 to $4.00, while plain cards usually sell for around $1.00.

Cases

Abalone, pearl & tortoise shell w/ornate eng, minor damage, 4"	120.00
Abalone & pearl harlequin design w/tortoise & ivory edge, 4"	50.00
Abalone & pearl w/cameo, minor damage, 4"	40.00
Coin silver w/presentation eng, 3½", w/chain	75.00
MOP, dmn-shaped panels, SP center & corners	80.00
MOP, dmn-shaped panels, 4"	60.00
Silver filigree, lobed/scalloped sides	100.00
Silver w/eng & cast cherubs, w/chain, 4"	100.00
Sterling, rtcl foliage, emb Windsor Castle etc, 1837, 4"	325.00
Sterling w/floral eng, jade at clasp, w/chain, 4"	95.00
Tortoise shell w/detailed emb florals, 4"	85.00
Tortoise shell w/eng ivory inlay, loose hinge, 4"	85.00

Receivers

Bl Dmn Quilt MOP w/camphor edge, SP base, 6½x8"	250.00
Gilt bronze, putti emb on rnd tray, std: 3 putti/dolphins, 14"	1,500.00
Sapphire bl glass teardrop shape in SP fr, 6x4x3½"	325.00
SP, boy & girl atop shell shape, #49	250.00
SP, cherub playing violin on hdl, Derby #3522	475.00
SP, cherub w/harp at side, floral hdl, Reed & Barton #1830	350.00

SP, fancy apron, floral hdl, ftd base, Tufts #115 ....140.00
SP, ped base w/leaf decor, Reed & Barton 70.00

Camark

The Camden Art and Tile Company (commonly known as Camark) of Camden, Arkansas, was organized in the Fall of 1926 by Samuel J. 'Jack' Carnes. Using clays from Arkansas, John Lessell, who had been hired as Art Director by Carnes, produced the initial lustre and iridescent Lessell wares for Camark ('CAM'den, 'ARK'ansas) before his death in December 1926. Before the plant opened in the Spring of 1927, Carnes brought John's wife, Jeanne, and step-daughter Billie to oversee the art department's manufacture of Le-Camark. Production by the Lessell family included variations of J.B. Owens' Soudanese and Opalesce and Weller's Marengo and Lamar. Camark's version of Marengo was called Old English. They also made wares identical to Weller's LaSa. Pieces made by John Lessell back in Ohio were signed 'Lessell,' while those made by Jeanne and Billie in Arkansas during 1927 were signed 'Le-Camark.' By 1928 Camark's production centered on traditional glazes. Drip glazes similar to Muncie Pottery were produced, in particular the green drip over pink. In the 1930s commercial castware with simple glossy and matt finishes became the primary focus and would continue so until Camark closed in the early 1960s. Between the 1960s and 1980s the company operated mainly as a retail store selling existing inventory, but some limited production occurred. In 1986 the company was purchased by the Ashcraft family of Camden, but no pottery has yet been made at the factory.

Our advisor for this category is David Edwin Gifford. He is listed in the Directory under Arkansas. Mr. Gifford is starting an Arkansas Pottery Collector's Society (Camark, Niloak, and others) and seeks those who are interested in joining to write him.

Vase, Iris, 8½", $48.50.

Bowl, Nor-so grape leaf, w/pelican flower frog 50.00
Bowl, orchid flower, #624 ....36.00
Cup & saucer, flower form, Arkansas sticker 20.00
Pitcher, emb iris, scalloped lip 125.00
Shakers, S&P shapes, pr 15.00
Tray, bl & wht matt, ruffled rim, sm mk, 13½" 75.00
Vase, iris ea side, basket hdl 60.00

Cambridge Glass

The Cambridge Glass Company began operations in 1901 in Cambridge, Ohio. Primarily they made crystal dinnerware and well-designed accessory pieces until the 1920s when they introduced the concept of color that was to become so popular on the American dinnerware mar-

ket. Always maintaining high standards of quality and elegance, they produced many lines that became best-sellers; through the twenties and thirties they were recognized as the largest manufacturer of this type of glassware in the world.

Of the various marks the company used, the 'C in triangle' is the most familiar. Production stopped in 1958. For a more thorough study of the subject, we recommend *Colors in Cambridge Glass* by the National Cambridge Collectors, Inc.; their address may be found in the Directory under Clubs. *Glass Animals and Figural Flower Frogs of the Depression Era* by Lee Garmon and Dick Spencer is a wonderful source for an in-depth view of their particular aspect of glass collecting. They are both listed in the Directory under Illinois. See also Carnival Glass; Glass Animals.

Apple Blossom, crystal; ashtray, heavy, 6" **50.00**
Apple Blossom, crystal; bowl, 4-part, 12" **40.00**
Apple Blossom, crystal; comport, tall, 7" **35.00**
Apple Blossom, crystal; plate, tea; 7½" **9.00**
Apple Blossom, crystal; saucer **4.00**
Apple Blossom, crystal; tumbler, #3400, ftd, 12-oz **17.50**
Apple Blossom, pk or gr; bowl, baker; 10" **85.00**
Apple Blossom, pk or gr; butter dish, w/lid, 5½" **350.00**
Apple Blossom, pk or gr; pitcher, #3025, 64-oz **295.00**
Apple Blossom, pk or gr; shakers, pr **90.00**
Apple Blossom, pk or gr; tumbler, #3025, 4-oz **19.00**
Apple Blossom, pk or gr; vase, 5" **45.00**
Apple Blossom, yel or amber; bowl, cereal; 6" **25.00**
Apple Blossom, yel or amber; bowl, 13" **60.00**
Apple Blossom, yel or amber; cup **22.00**
Apple Blossom, yel or amber; plate, dinner; 9½" **65.00**
Apple Blossom, yel or amber; platter, 11½" **60.00**
Apple Blossom, yel or amber; stem, water; #3130, 8-oz **22.00**
Candlelight, candle holder, #3900/67, 5", ea **37.50**
Candlelight, creamer, #3900/41 ....**20.00**
Candlelight, cup, #3900/17 ....**27.50**
Candlelight, icer, cocktail; #968, 2-pc **65.00**
Candlelight, plate, #3900/20, 6½" **12.50**
Candlelight, plate, salad; #3900/22, 8" **15.00**
Candlelight, saucer, #3900/17 ....**5.00**
Candlelight, stem, wine; #3111, 2½-oz **35.00**
Candlelight, sugar bowl, #3900/41 ....**17.50**
Candlelight, vase, #6004, ftd, 6" **35.00**
Caprice, crystal; ashtray, #215, 4" **7.00**
Caprice, crystal; bowl, fruit; #18, 5" **30.00**
Caprice, crystal; bowl, salad; #80, cupped, 13" **75.00**
Caprice, crystal; butter dish, #52, ¼-lb **225.00**
Caprice, crystal; candy dish, #165, w/lid, 3-ftd, 6" **42.50**
Caprice, crystal; celery or relish dish, #124, 3-part, 8½" **20.00**
Caprice, crystal; coaster, #13, 3½" **15.00**
Caprice, crystal; creamer, #38, med **11.00**
Caprice, crystal; cruet, oil; #101, w/stopper, 3-oz **30.00**
Caprice, crystal; ice bucket, #201 ....**60.00**
Caprice, crystal; nut dish, #94, divided, 2½" **25.00**
Caprice, crystal; plate, cake; #36, ftd, 13" **150.00**
Caprice, crystal; plate, salad; #23, 7½" **15.00**
Caprice, crystal; saucer, #17 ....**2.50**
Caprice, crystal; shakers, #96, flat, pr **28.00**
Caprice, crystal; stem, cocktail; #301, blown, 3-oz **20.00**
Caprice, crystal; stem, water; #300, blown, 9-oz **18.00**
Caprice, crystal; tray, #42, oval, 9" **22.00**
Caprice, crystal; tumbler, #9, ftd, 12-oz **22.50**
Caprice, crystal; vase, #240, ball shape, 9¼" **140.00**
Caprice, crystal; vase, #252, blown, 4½" **40.00**
Caprice, pk or bl; bottle, bitters; #186, 7-oz **350.00**

Caprice, pk or bl; bowl, #81, shallow, 4-ftd, 11½" 100.00
Caprice, pk or bl; bowl, pickle; #102, 9" 60.00
Caprice, pk or bl; candlestick, #74, 3-light, ea 115.00
Caprice, pk or bl; cigarette holder, #205, triangular, 2x2¼" 65.00
Caprice, pk or bl; cracker jar, #202, w/lid 900.00
Caprice, pk or bl; cup, #17 ....35.00
Caprice, pk or bl; mustard jar, #87, w/lid, 2-oz 165.00
Caprice, pk or bl; pitcher, #178, tall, Doulton style, 90-oz 4,250.00
Caprice, pk or bl; plate, #28, 4-ftd, 14" 100.00
Caprice, pk or bl; salver, #31, 2-pc, 13" 450.00
Caprice, pk or bl; stem, wine; #6, 3-oz 125.00
Caprice, pk or bl; sugar bowl, #41, lg 22.00
Caprice, pk or bl; tumbler, tea; #300, ftd, 12-oz 40.00
Caprice, pk or bl; vase, ivy bowl; #232, 5" 180.00
Chantilly, bowl, oval, 4-ftd, 12" 37.50
Chantilly, bowl, relish/pickle; 7" 20.00
Chantilly, bowl, tab hdls, 11" 35.00
Chantilly, butter dish, ¼-lb 210.00
Chantilly, candlestick, 3-light, 6", ea 37.50
Chantilly, candy box, w/lid, rnd 60.00
Chantilly, comport, 5½" 30.00
Chantilly, creamer 14.50
Chantilly, cup 3.00
Chantilly, decanter, ftd 150.00
Chantilly, hat, sm 150.00
Chantilly, ice bucket, w/chrome hdl 65.00
Chantilly, marmalade, w/lid 55.00
Chantilly, mustard, w/lid 50.00
Chantilly, pitcher, Doulton style 265.00
Chantilly, plate, dinner; 10½" 57.50
Chantilly, plate, salad; 8" 12.50
Chantilly, salad dressing bottle 85.00
Chantilly, stem, cordial; #3779, 1-oz 60.00
Chantilly, stem, oyster cocktail; #3775, 4½-oz 15.00
Chantilly, stem, water; #3600, 10-oz 20.00
Chantilly, stem, wine; #3775, 2½-oz 30.00
Chantilly, sugar bowl 13.50
Chantilly, tumbler, juice; #3775, ftd, 5-oz 14.00
Chantilly, tumbler, water; #3625, ftd, 10-oz 17.50
Chantilly, tumbler, 13-oz 22.00
Chantilly, vase, bud; 10" 30.00
Cleo, all colors but bl; #3115, 9-oz 30.00
Cleo, all colors but bl; almond, ind; 2½" 70.00
Cleo, all colors but bl; bowl, comport, 4-ftd, 6" 35.00
Cleo, all colors but bl; bowl, cranberry; 6½" 27.50
Cleo, all colors but bl; bowl, pickle; Decagon, 9" 30.00
Cleo, all colors but bl; bowl, relish; 2-part 22.00
Cleo, all colors but bl; bowl, 8½" 40.00
Cleo, all colors but bl; candy box, w/lid 125.00
Cleo, all colors but bl; cup, Decagon 15.00
Cleo, all colors but bl; decanter, w/stopper 225.00
Cleo, all colors but bl; ice pail 60.00
Cleo, all colors but bl; mayonnaise, ftd 35.00
Cleo, all colors but bl; pitcher, w/lid, 22-oz 175.00
Cleo, all colors but bl; platter, 12" 100.00
Cleo, all colors but bl; server, center hdl, 12" 35.00
Cleo, all colors but bl; stem, fruit; #3115, 6-oz 15.00
Cleo, all colors but bl; sugar cube tray 175.00
Cleo, all colors but bl; toast, w/lid, rnd 350.00
Cleo, all colors but bl; tobacco humidor 350.00
Cleo, all colors but bl; vase, 11" 130.00
Cleo, all colors but bl; wafer tray 225.00
Cleo, bl; basket, 2-hdld, Decagon, 11" 50.00
Cleo, bl; bowl, cream soup; w/saucer, 2-hdld, Decagon 50.00

Cleo, bl; bowl, oval, 11" 40.00
Cleo, bl; plate, 7" 15.00
Cleo, bl; salt cellar, 1½" 100.00
Cleo, bl; stem, wine; #3077, 3½" 95.00
Cleo, bl; sugar bowl, ftd 30.00
Cleo, bl; tumbler, #3077, ftd, 5-oz 50.00
Crown Tuscan, basket, 10" 475.00
Crown Tuscan, cake plate, ftd, #3500/39, 12" 125.00
Crown Tuscan, candy dish, 3-part, #3500/57 ....55.00
Crown Tuscan, cornucopia, sm 27.50
Crown Tuscan, Nautilus shakers, pr 375.00
Crown Tuscan, vase, bud; #274, 10" 45.00

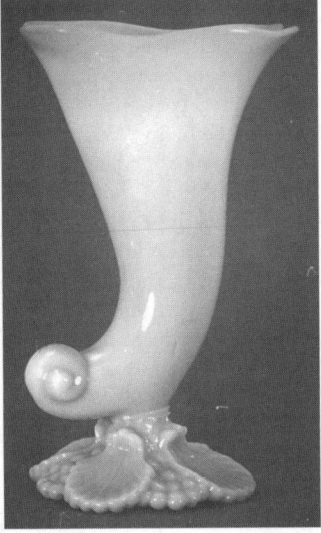

Crown Tuscan, vase, cornucopia;
10", $80.00.

Decagon, pastels; bowl, bouillon; w/liner 7.50
Decagon, pastels; bowl, cereal; flat rim, 6" 10.00
Decagon, pastels; bowl, cranberry; belled, 3½" 15.00
Decagon, pastels; bowl, relish; 2-part, 11" 10.00
Decagon, pastels; bowl, vegetable; rnd, 9" 14.00
Decagon, pastels; celery tray, 11" 10.00
Decagon, pastels; creamer, ftd 9.00
Decagon, pastels; ice bucket 35.00
Decagon, pastels; plate, bread & butter; 6¼" 3.00
Decagon, pastels; plate, grill; 10" 8.00
Decagon, pastels; relish tray, 6 inserts 75.00
Decagon, pastels; saucer 1.00
Decagon, pastels; stem, water; 9-oz 15.00
Decagon, pastels; sugar bowl, scalloped edge 9.00
Decagon, pastels; tumbler, ftd, 8-oz 12.00
Decagon, red or bl; bowl, almond; ind, 2½" 35.00
Decagon, red or bl; bowl, berry; 10" 20.00
Decagon, red or bl; bowl, bonbon; 2-hdld, 6¼" 17.00
Decagon, red or bl; bowl, fruit; belled, 5½" 10.00
Decagon, red or bl; comport, tall, 7" 35.00
Decagon, red or bl; cup 10.00
Decagon, red or bl; mayonnaise, w/liner & ladle 80.00
Decagon, red or bl; pickle tray, 9" 17.50
Decagon, red or bl; plate, salad; 8½" 10.00
Decagon, red or bl; plate, service; 12½" 17.50
Decagon, red or bl; sauce boat & plate 75.00
Decagon, red or bl; server, center hdld 20.00
Decagon, red or bl; service tray, oval, 15" 40.00
Decagon, red or bl; stem, cocktail; 3½-oz 20.00
Diane, bottle, bitters 125.00

Diane, bowl, baker; 10" 40.00
Diane, bowl, berry; 5" 20.00
Diane, bowl, celery or relish; 3-part, 9" 30.00
Diane, bowl, cereal; 6" 25.00
Diane, bowl, flared, 4-ftd, 12" 40.00
Diane, bowl, relish; 2-part, 7" 20.00
Diane, bowl, 4-ftd, 11" 40.00
Diane, butter dish, rnd 120.00
Diane, candlestick, 5", ea 17.50
Diane, cigarette urn 42.50
Diane, cocktail icer, 2-pc 60.00
Diane, comport, blown, 5⅜" 35.00
Diane, creamer 14.00
Diane, cruet, oil; w/stopper, 6-oz 115.00
Diane, cup 20.00
Diane, decanter, ftd, lg 165.00
Diane, ice bucket, w/chrome hdl 65.00
Diane, martini pitcher 600.00
Diane, mayonnaise, divided, w/liner & ladle 40.00
Diane, plate, bonbon; ftd, 2-hdld, 8" 11.00
Diane, plate, bread & butter; sq, 6" 5.00
Diane, plate, salad; 8" 10.00
Diane, plate, service; 4-ftd, 12" 35.00
Diane, plate, torte; 14" 40.00
Diane, platter, 13½" 70.00
Diane, saucer 5.00
Diane, stem, wine; #1066, 3-oz 25.00
Diane, tumbler, ftd, 8-oz 22.00
Diane, tumbler, juice; ftd, 5-oz 27.00
Diane, tumbler, water; #3122, 9-oz 15.00
Diane, tumbler, 13-oz 30.00
Diane, tumbler tea; #1066, 12-oz 20.00
Diane, vase, bud; 10" 45.00
Diane, vase, flower; 13" 95.00
Elaine, bowl, finger; #3104, w/liner 27.50
Elaine, bowl, pickle/relish; 7" 20.00
Elaine, candlestick, 5", ea 17.50
Elaine, cocktail icer, 2-pc 55.00
Elaine, creamer, ind 12.00
Elaine, decanter, ftd, lg 175.00
Elaine, ice bucket, w/chrome hdl 60.00
Elaine, pitcher, upright 185.00
Elaine, plate, salad; 8" 15.00
Elaine, plate, torte; 4-ftd, 13" 30.00
Elaine, saucer 3.00
Elaine, shakers, ftd, pr 30.00
Elaine, stem, cocktail; #1402, 3½" 20.00
Elaine, stem, cordial; #3104, 1-oz 135.00
Elaine, stem, cordial; #3500, 1-oz 57.50
Elaine, stem, goblet; #1402 ....20.00
Elaine, stem, sherbet, #3121, low, 6-oz 15.00
Elaine, stem, water; #3500, 10-oz 20.00
Elaine, tumbler, tea; #1402, 12-oz 27.50
Elaine, vase, ftd, 6" 35.00
Elaine, vase, keyhole; ftd, 9" 55.00
Flower frog, see Glass Animals and Figurines
Gloria, crystal; bowl, cereal; rnd, 6" 12.00
Gloria, crystal; bowl, finger; ftd 15.00
Gloria, crystal; bowl, flared rim, 13" 25.00
Gloria, crystal; bowl, fruit; 2-hdld, 11" 30.00
Gloria, crystal; bowl, salad; tab hdls, 9" 20.00
Gloria, crystal; candlestick, 6", ea 17.50
Gloria, crystal; comport, tall, 7" 35.00
Gloria, crystal; icer, w/insert 60.00

Gloria, crystal; pitcher, ball shaped, 80-oz 160.00
Gloria, crystal; plate, bread & butter; 6" 6.00
Gloria, crystal; plate, cake; sq, ftd, 11" 60.00
Gloria, crystal; platter, 11½" 55.00
Gloria, crystal; relish tray, center hdl, 2-part 25.00
Gloria, crystal; saucer, sq 2.00
Gloria, crystal; stem, wine; #3130, 2½-oz 20.00
Gloria, crystal; sugar bowl, ftd 11.00
Gloria, crystal; tumbler, #3115, ftd, 8-oz 12.00
Gloria, crystal; tumbler, juice; #3115, 5-oz 12.00
Gloria, crystal; vase, 11" 45.00
Gloria, gr, pk or yel; bowl, cranberry; 4-ftd, 3" 50.00
Gloria, gr, pk or yel; comport, fruit cocktail; 4" ...20.00
Gloria, gr, pk or yel; creamer, ftd 17.50
Gloria, gr, pk or yel; cup, sq, 4-ftd 65.00
Gloria, gr, pk or yel; plate, dinner; sq 75.00
Gloria, gr, pk or yel; plate, dinner; 9½" 75.00
Gloria, gr, pk or yel; stem, goblet; #3115, 9-oz ...30.00
Imperial Hunt Scene, colors; comport, #3085, 5½" ...35.00
Imperial Hunt Scene, colors; decanter 235.00
Imperial Hunt Scene, colors; tobacco humidor 365.00
Imperial Hunt Scene, colors; tumbler, #3085, ftd, 2½-oz ...35.00
Imperial Hunt Scene, crystal; bowl, cereal; 6" 15.00
Imperial Hunt Scene, crystal; ice bucket 40.00
Imperial Hunt Scene, crystal; plate, 8" 12.00
Imperial Hunt Scene, crystal; saucer 10.00
Imperial Hunt Scene, crystal; stem, #1402, 18-oz ...60.00
Imperial Hunt Scene, crystal; stem, sherbet; #1402, 6½-oz ...35.00
Imperial Hunt Scene, crystal; stem parfait; #3085, 5½-oz ...60.00
Imperial Hunt Scene, crystal; sugar bowl, ftd 15.00
Mt Vernon, amber or crystal; ashtray, #63, 3½" 8.00
Mt Vernon, amber or crystal; bowl, #43, deep, 10½" ...30.00
Mt Vernon, amber or crystal; bowl, #44, flared, 12½" ...35.00
Mt Vernon, amber or crystal; bowl, finger; #23 ...10.00
Mt Vernon, amber or crystal; bowl, fruit; #6, 5¼" ...10.00
Mt Vernon, amber or crystal; box, #17, w/lid, sq, 4" ...30.00
Mt Vernon, amber or crystal; candelabrum, #38, 13½" ...50.00
Mt Vernon, amber or crystal; celery tray, #79, 10½" ...17.50
Mt Vernon, amber or crystal; coaster, #60, plain, 3" ...5.00
Mt Vernon, amber or crystal; comport, #397, 6½" ...17.50
Mt Vernon, amber or crystal; creamer, #4, ind 10.00
Mt Vernon, amber or crystal; honey jar, #74, w/lid ...30.00
Mt Vernon, amber or crystal; ice bucket, #92, w/tongs ...35.00
Mt Vernon, amber or crystal; lamp, hurricane; #1607, 9" ...70.00
Mt Vernon, amber or crystal; mug, #84, stein shaped, 14-oz ...27.50
Mt Vernon, amber or crystal; pitcher, #13, 66-oz ...85.00
Mt Vernon, amber or crystal; plate, salad; #5, 8½" ...7.00
Mt Vernon, amber or crystal; plate (finger bowl liner), #23 ...4.00
Mt Vernon, amber or crystal; relish tray, #101, 2-part, hdld, 8" ...17.50
Mt Vernon, amber or crystal; rose bowl, #106, 6½" ...18.00
Mt Vernon, amber or crystal; salt cellar, #24, ind ...7.00
Mt Vernon, amber or crystal; saucer, #7 ....7.50
Mt Vernon, amber or crystal; sugar bowl, #86 .....10.00
Mt Vernon, amber or crystal; tumbler, #56, 5-oz ...12.00
Mt Vernon, amber or crystal; tumbler, #59, tall, 14-oz ...22.00
Mt Vernon, amber or crystal; tumbler, old fashioned; #57, 7-oz ...15.00
Nude stem, amber; vase, bud 750.00
Nude stem, amethyst; ashtray 295.00
Nude stem, amethyst; brandy, 6¼" 125.00
Nude stem, amethyst; champagne 145.00
Nude stem, amethyst; claret 160.00
Nude stem, amethyst; ivy bowl, frosted stem, 9¾" ...200.00
Nude stem, amethyst; wine 250.00
Nude stem, carmen; brandy 145.00

Nude stem, carmen; claret 165.00
Nude stem, cobalt; ashtray 250.00
Nude stem, cobalt; claret 140.00
Nude stem, Crown Tuscan; compote, 6x5½" 125.00
Nude stem, Crown Tuscan/topaz; cocktail, 6½" 245.00
Nude stem, crystal; goblet, water; 9" 115.00
Nude stem, crystal; shell compote 350.00
Nude stem, crystal; vase, bud 225.00
Nude stem, forest gr; shell compote 400.00
Nude stem, gr frost; comport, tall 150.00
Nude stem, gr; ivy ball, 9¾" 175.00
Nude stem, moonlight; ashtray 400.00
Nude stem, pistachio; brandy 195.00
Nude stem, pistachio; cocktail 165.00
Nude stem, pk; ashtray 475.00
Nude stem, pk; cocktail 125.00
Nude stem, red; compote, cupped, 7" 220.00
Portia, bowl, bonbon; tab hdls, ftd, 7" 22.00
Portia, bowl, cranberry; 3½" 22.50
Portia, bowl, flared, 4-ftd, 10" 40.00
Portia, bowl, flared, 4-ftd, 12" 45.00
Portia, bowl, grapefruit or oyster; 6" 17.00
Portia, bowl, relish; 2-part, 6" 16.00
Portia, candlestick, 5", ea 20.00
Portia, candy box, w/lid, rnd 67.50
Portia, celery tray, 11" 27.50
Portia, comport, 5½" 27.50
Portia, creamer, ind 12.50
Portia, decanter, sherry; w/stopper, ftd, 29-oz 175.00
Portia, mayonnaise, w/liner & ladle 40.00
Portia, pitcher, ball shape 130.00
Portia, plate, dinner; 10½" 65.00
Portia, plate, salad; 8" 12.50
Portia, shakers, flat, pr 25.00
Portia, stem, brandy; #3126, low ftd, 1-oz 45.00
Portia, stem, cocktail; #3121, 3-oz 20.00
Portia, stem, cordial; #3121, 1-oz 55.00
Portia, stem, goblet; #3121, 10-oz 22.50
Portia, stem, goblet; #3124, 10-oz 18.00
Portia, stem, goblet; #3126, 9-oz 20.00
Portia, stem, oyster cocktail; #3121, 4½" 15.00
Portia, stem, wine; #3124, 3-oz 25.00
Portia, stem, wine; #3130, 2½-oz 25.00
Portia, sugar bowl, ind 11.50
Portia, tumbler, #3124, 3-oz 13.00
Portia, tumbler, juice; #3124, 5-oz 12.50
Portia, tumbler, tea; #3126, 12-oz 22.00
Portia, tumbler, water; #3126, 10-oz 15.00
Portia, vase, bud; 10" 40.00
Portia, vase, flower; 13" 95.00
Portia, vase, ftd, 6" 45.00
Rosalie, amber; bottle, French dressing 85.00
Rosalie, amber; bowl, cranberry; 3½" 22.00
Rosalie, amber; bowl, soup; 8½" 30.00
Rosalie, amber; candlestick, 2 styles, 4", ea 20.00
Rosalie, amber; gravy boat, dbl; w/platter 85.00
Rosalie, amber; nut dish, ftd, 2½" 45.00
Rosalie, amber; plate, cheese & cracker; 11" 40.00
Rosalie, amber; plate, dinner; 9½" 35.00
Rosalie, amber; salt cellar; ftd, 1½" 40.00
Rosalie, amber; sugar shaker 195.00
Rosalie, amber; tumbler, #3077, ftd, 10-oz 20.00
Rosalie, bl, pk or gr; bowl, console; 13" 50.00
Rosalie, bl, pk or gr; bowl, cream soup 25.00

Rosalie, bl, pk or gr; bowl, fruit; 5½" 15.00
Rosalie, bl, pk or gr; celery tray, 11" 35.00
Rosalie, bl, pk or gr; comport, 5¾" 30.00
Rosalie, bl, pk or gr; creamer, ftd 12.00
Rosalie, bl, pk or gr; cup 35.00
Rosalie, bl, pk or gr; ice tub 70.00
Rosalie, bl, pk or gr; plate, 2-hdld, 7" 15.00
Rosalie, bl, pk or gr; platter, 12" 65.00
Rosalie, bl, pk or gr; stem, goblet, #801, 10-oz 30.00
Rosalie, bl, pk or gr; vase, ftd, 6" 75.00
Rose Point, ashtray, #721, sq, 2½" 32.50
Rose Point, basket, favor; #3500/79, 3" 275.00
Rose Point, bell, dinner; #3121 ....145.00
Rose Point, bowl, #1398, 13" 110.00
Rose Point, bowl, #221, 3-part, 8½" 150.00
Rose Point, bowl, #222, 3-part, 10½" 195.00
Rose Point, bowl, #3500/17, ftd, 12" 110.00
Rose Point, bowl, bonbon; #3400/1180, 2-hdld, 5½" 30.00
Rose Point, bowl, cereal; #3400/10, 6" 77.50
Rose Point, bowl, cranberry; #3400/70, 3½" 85.00
Rose Point, bowl, finger; #3106, w/liner 85.00
Rose Point, bowl, fruit; #1534, blown, 5" 75.00
Rose Point, bowl, fruit; #3400/1188, 11" 90.00
Rose Point, bowl, salad; Pristine #427, 10" 135.00
Rose Point, butter dish, #3400/52, w/lid, 5" 170.00
Rose Point, candlestick, #3121, 7", ea 70.00
Rose Point, candlestick, #3500/108, 2½", ea 30.00
Rose Point, candlestick, #3500/31, 6", ea 87.50
Rose Point, candy box, #300, w/rose finial, 3-ftd, 6" 265.00
Rose Point, candy box, #3500/103, w/lid, blown, 5⅜" 155.00
Rose Point, celery & relish tray, #3900/126, 3-part, 12" 60.00
Rose Point, celery tray, #3400/652, 12" 45.00
Rose Point, cheese dish, #980, w/lid, 5" 425.00
Rose Point, cigarette box, #615, w/lid 120.00
Rose Point, comport, #3900/135, 5" 42.50
Rose Point, cup, punch; #488, 5-oz 37.50
Rose Point, decanter, #1380, sq, 26-oz 415.00
Rose Point, hat, #1703, 6" 425.00
Rose Point, honey dish, #3500/139, w/lid 275.00
Rose Point, ice bucket, #1402/52 ....195.00
Rose Point, ice pail, #3400/851 ....120.00
Rose Point, mustard jar, #151, 3-oz 135.00
Rose Point, pitcher, #3400/38, ball shaped, 80-oz 195.00
Rose Point, pitcher, #70, w/ice lip, 20-oz 235.00
Rose Point, plate, #3400/1186, 2-hdld, 12½" 65.00
Rose Point, plate, bread & butter; #3400/60, 6" 13.50
Rose Point, plate, breakfast; #3400/62, 8½" 20.00
Rose Point, plate, cake; Martha #170, ftd, 13" 235.00
Rose Point, plate, canape; #693, 6⅛" 155.00
Rose Point, plate, dinner; #3900/24, 10½" 125.00
Rose Point, plate, luncheon; #3400/63, 9½" 40.00
Rose Point, plate, salad; #3400/176, 7½" 15.00
Rose Point, plate, torte; #3400/65, 14" 125.00
Rose Point, punch set, Martha, 15-pc 4,125.00
Rose Point, saucer, after dinner; #3400/69 ....55.00
Rose Point, shakers, #1468, egg shaped, pr 85.00
Rose Point, stem, brandy; #3106, ¾-oz 110.00
Rose Point, stem, claret; #3500, 4½-oz 80.00
Rose Point, stem, cocktail; #3106, 3-oz 35.00
Rose Point, stem, sherbet; #3121, tall, 6-oz 22.00
Rose Point, stem, sherry; #3106, 2-oz 45.00
Rose Point, stem, water goblet; #3106, 10-oz 35.00
Rose Point, stem, wine; #3121, 3½" 60.00
Rose Point, sugar bowl, #3500/14 ....20.00

Rose Point, relish tray, 3-part, $65.00.

Rose Point, tray, #3500/67, rnd, 12" 150.00
Rose Point, tumbler, #3106, ftd, 3-oz 25.00
Rose Point, tumbler, #3121, ftd, 2½-oz 65.00
Rose Point, tumbler, #3400/115, 13-oz 45.00
Rose Point, urn, #500/42, w/lid, 12" 625.00
Rose Point, vase, #1301, ftd, 10" 75.00
Rose Point, vase, #572, 6" 130.00
Rose Point, vase, #6004, ftd, 12" 85.00
Rose Point, vase, keyhole; #1237, ftd, 9" 85.00
Rose Point, vase, sweet pea; #629 ....250.00
Valencia, ashtray, #3500/124, rnd, 3¼" 10.00
Valencia, bowl, #1402/88, 11" 35.00
Valencia, bowl, cereal; #3500/37, 6" 20.00
Valencia, celery tray, #1402/94, 12" 30.00
Valencia, creamer, #3500/14 ....15.00
Valencia, ice pail, #1402/52 ....65.00
Valencia, nut dish, #3400/71, 4-ftd, 3" 55.00
Valencia, plate, torte; #3500/38, 13" 25.00
Valencia, saucer, #3500/1 ....3.00
Valencia, shakers, #3400/18, pr 50.00
Valencia, stem, cocktail; #3500, 3-oz 18.00
Valencia, stem, goblet; #1402 ....20.00
Valencia, stem, oyster cocktail; #1402 ....16.00
Valencia, stem, wine; #1402 ....30.00
Valencia, sugar bowl, #3500/14 ....15.00
Valencia, tumbler, #3400/92, 2½-oz 17.50
Valencia, tumbler, #3500, ftd, 16-oz 20.00
Valencia, tumbler, #3500, ftd, 5-oz 14.00
Wildflower, bowl, #3900/34, 2-hdld, 11" 45.00
Wildflower, bowl, celery/relish; 5-part, 12" 35.00
Wildflower, bowl, relish; 3-part, 6½" 17.50
Wildflower, butter dish, #3400/52, 5" 115.00
Wildflower, candlestick, #3400/646, 5", ea 25.00
Wildflower, cocktail icer, #968, 2-pc 65.00
Wildflower, creamer, #3900/41 ....12.50
Wildflower, cruet, oil; #3900/100, w/stopper, 6-oz 80.00
Wildflower, hat, #1703, 6" 200.00
Wildflower, plate, #3400/62, 8½" 15.00
Wildflower, plate, torte; #3900/167, 14" 37.50
Wildflower, shakers, #3900/1177, pr 32.50
Wildflower, stem, water; #3121, 10-oz 25.00
Wildflower, stem, wine; #3121, 3½-oz 30.00
Wildflower, tumbler, juice; #3121, 5-oz 17.50
Wildflower, vase, bud; #1528, 10" 35.00

Cambridge Pottery

The Cambridge Art Pottery operated in Cambridge, Ohio, from 1900 until 1909. During that time, several lines of artware were developed under the direction of C.B. Upjohn, an established ceramic artist of the period. Their standard brown-glazed line was Terrhea, examples of which are often found bearing the signature of the artist responsible for the underglaze decoration. Oakwood was a second brown-glazed line, without the slip painting. Other lines were Acorn (introduced in 1904) and Otoe, a matt green ware (introduced in 1907) that utilized already existing shapes from earlier lines. However, their most successful product was a line of cookware called Gurnsey, made from a red-brown clay with a white-glazed interior. Sales proved to be so profitable that by 1908 all artware was discontinued in favor of its exclusive production. By the following year, the firm had elected to change the name of their pottery to the Gurnsey Earthenware Company. Marks varied, but all incorporated a device comprised of the letters 'CAP'; with the cojoined 'AP' usually contained within a larger-scale 'C.'

Note: Cambridge's brown-glazed artware is compatible in value to Roseville's Rozane line or Weller's Louwelsa.

Bowl, gr matt crystalline, 4-ftd, 5x9" 190.00
Pitcher, emb leaves/berries, gr crystalline matt, no mk, 6" 100.00
Vase, gr crystalline, flared cylinder, 10", NM 140.00

Cameo

The technique of glass carving was perfected 2,000 years ago in ancient Rome and Greece. The most famous ancient example of cameo glass is the Portland Vase, made in Rome around 100 A.D. After glass blowing was developed, glassmakers devised a method of casing several layers of colored glass together, often with a light color over a darker base, to enhance the design. Skilled carvers meticulously worked the fragile glass to produce incredibly detailed classic scenes. In the 18th and 19th centuries Oriental and Near-Eastern artisans used the technique more extensively. European glassmakers revived the art during the last quarter of the 19th century. In France, Galle and Daum produced some of the finest examples of modern times, using as many as five layers of glass to develop their designs, usually scenics or subjects from nature. Hand carving was supplemented by the use of a copper engraving wheel, and acid was used to cut away the layers more quickly.

In England, Thomas Webb and Sons used modern machinery and technology to eliminate many of the problems that plagued early glass carvers. One of Webb's best-known carvers, George Woodall, is credited with producing over four hundred pieces. Woodall was trained in the art by John Northwood, famous for reproducing the Portland Vase in 1876. Cameo glass became very popular during the late 1800s, resulting in a market that demanded more than could be produced, due to the tedious procedures involved. In an effort to produce greater volume, less elaborate pieces with simple floral or geometric designs were made, often entirely acid etched with little or no hand carving. While very little cameo glass was made in this country, a few pieces were produced by James Gillinder, Tiffany, and the Libbey Glass Company. Though some continued to be made on a limited scale into the 1900s (and until about 1920 in France), for the most part, inferior products caused a marked reduction in its manufacture by the turn of the century. Beware of new 'French' cameo glass from Romania and Taiwan. Some of it is very good and may be signed with 'old' signatures. Watch for stencil-cut designs that are 'disconnected' and segmented. Know your dealer! Our advisor for this category is Don Williams; he is listed in the Directory under Missouri. See also specific manufactures.

Key: fp — fire polished

English

Biscuit jar, apple blossoms, wht on citron, SP trim, 5x6" 3,000.00
Biscuit jar, dogwood flowers, wht on bl, SP trim, 5½x5" 3,000.00
Rose bowl, allover floral, wht on red, miniature, 1½" dia 800.00
Rose bowl, lg flowers/leaves, wht on red, 2¼" 1,500.00
Sweetmeat, daisies, wht on red, silver rim/bail/lid, 5" 1,600.00
Sweetmeat, Dolce Relievo, floral vine, rose on wht, 4½x5" 750.00
Toothpick holder, leaves, wht on raisin, 2" 550.00

Vase, detailed floral, white on pink shaded to apricot, 4¼", $1,300.00.

Vase, anemones/leaves, bk: butterflies, wht on red, 8x6" 2,500.00
Vase, floral, 2-color on bl, stick neck, 4" 750.00
Vase, floral/butterfly, wht/red on citron, bulbous, 2¼" 1,000.00
Vase, gooseberries/pomegranates, wht on red, 3" 2,600.00
Vase, leaves/berries, wht on red, stick neck, 7½" 1,800.00
Vase, morning-glories, wht on citron, stick neck, 9¼" 1,800.00
Vase, morning-glories, wht on red, leaf-banded rim, 5x3½" 1,225.00
Vase, palms/fruit/leaves, wht on gr texture, 2½x3" 400.00
Vase, rose & buds on leafy stem, wht on lime, 5" 600.00
Vase, rose & 3 buds, bk: palm frond, red on wht, 10" 3,500.00

French

Lamp base, windmill/sailboat on brn to yel, Peynaud, 10" 350.00
Rose bowl, carnations, orange/lav on texture, St Louis, 5" 225.00
Vase, abstracts/Xs at shoulder on frost, Pantin/Brevete, 6" 150.00
Vase, clover buds, purple on shaded purple, C Vessier, 8x6" 600.00
Vase, floral, brn/orange mottle on clear, Degue, 7x7" 400.00
Vase, grapes, cranberry on irid, Pantin, 6" 300.00
Vase, hydrangeas, gr/bl on wht fr, Arsall, 15" 1,500.00
Vase, leaves, pk on clear, Vallerysthal, 6" 1,000.00
Vase, lg flowers, brn/gr, Desire Christian, 12" 2,500.00
Vase, lg tulips, maroon on frost, ovoid, Cristiro, 8" 210.00
Vase, overall leafy stems/flowers, red on yel, Arsall, 12" 935.00
Vase, pine grove/mtns/castle titled Spesbourg-Sites, 10" 650.00
Vase, stylized floral/leaves, orange/brn on yel, Degue, 17" 1,400.00

Canary Ware

Canary ware was produced from the late 1700s until about the mid-19th century in the Staffordshire district of England. It was potted of yellow clay and the overglaze was yellow as well. More often than not, copper or silver lustre trim was added. Decorations were usually black-printed transfers, though occasionally hand-painted polychrome designs were also used.

Creamer, milkmaid reserve, blk transfer, 4½" 85.00
Creamer, red & gr floral, fluted, 4", EX 75.00
Cup & saucer, fisherman, red transfer, Sewell, rpr 110.00
Lamp, T'print & arch hex font, baluster stem, 9¼" 665.00
Mug, children & beehive, red transfer, pk lustre band, 2½" 170.00
Pitcher, basketweave, vintage, mask spout, mc enamel, rpr, 6" ...115.00
Pitcher, mc floral w/brn striping, leaf hdl, prof rpr, 4½" 195.00
Saucer, tea party, blk transfer, Adams 215.00
Sugar bowl, silver lustre floral, Leeds, 4½", EX 600.00
Waste bowl, classical lady & child, red transfer, 3x6" 300.00

Candle Holders

The earliest type of candlestick, called a pricket, was constructed with a sharp point on which the candle was impaled. The socket type, first used in the 16th century, consisted of the socket and a short stem with a wide drip pan and base. These were made from sheets of silver or other metal; not until late in the 17th century were candlesticks made by casting. By the 1700s, styles began to vary from the traditional fluted column or baluster form and became more elaborate. A Rococo style with scrolls, shellwork, and naturalistic leaves and flowers came into vogue that afforded the individual silversmith the opportunity to exhibit his skill and artistry. The last half of the 18th century brought a return to fluted columns with neoclassic motifs. Because they were made of thin sheet silver, weighted bases were used to add stability. The Rococo styles of the Regency period were heavily encrusted with applied figures and flowers. Candelabra with six to nine branches became popular. By the Victorian era when lamps came into general use, there was less innovation and more adaptation of the earlier styles. See also Silver; specific manufacturers.

Key: QA — Queen Anne

Brass, hex base w/cast cherubs, 11¼", pr 330.00
Brass, mid-drip, soldered rprs, 8½", pr 385.00
Brass, Neoclassical, side pushup, 7⅝", pr 385.00
Brass, octagonal base, resoldered stem, early, 6" 195.00
Brass, push-up tab, saucer base, 5¾x4" dia 98.00
Brass, QA, cut-corner base, minor rpr, 6½" 165.00
Brass, QA, octagonal base, soldered stem, polished, 7¼" 195.00
Brass, QA, petal base, soldered rpr, polished, 7" 165.00
Brass, QA, scalloped base, 7⅜" 220.00
Brass, QA style, old but not period, 8", pr 225.00
Brass, scalloped base, ejector mechanism, early, 8x4½", pr 500.00
Brass, slush molded, polished, 4x2" base dia, pr 130.00
Brass, sq base, early, 5½" 130.00
Brass, sq base, short ft, no seam in stem, early, 8¼" 260.00
Brass, sq base w/paw ft, 6¾" 250.00
Brass, sq base w/paw ft, 8" 300.00
Brass, twist stem, soldered rprs, 18¾", pr 80.00
Bronze, Neoclassical w/fire gilding & gr patina, 11½", pr 625.00
Bronze, Regency, owl std w/prisms, petal-edge glass cup, pr 700.00
Chamberstick, tin, wide saucer base, brass pushup, 8½" dia 85.00
Hogscraper, brass, Am or England, early 1800s, 6¼", pr 575.00
Hogscraper, sheet iron w/brass band, fan-shape ejector, 7½" 290.00
Hogscraper, steel, w/pushup, no lip hanger, 7¼" 90.00
Hogscraper, steel w/worn tin wash, w/pushup & hanger, 5¼" 120.00
Hogscraper, steel w/worn tin wash, w/pushup & hanger, 6¼" 120.00
Hogscraper, worn tin plate, w/pushup & lip hanger, 5⅜" 100.00
Hogscraper, worn tin plate, w/pushup & lip hanger, 7" 115.00
Rush light holder, wrought, mushroom-head counterweight, 10" .275.00
Sconce, brass, pierced arm w/stylized deer, 3-branch, 9½" 100.00
Sconce, cast brass, beveled mirror w/worn silvering, 18", pr 77.50

Sconce, punched tin, primitive, 11¼"	**75.00**
Sconce, tin, crown & heart design, Continental, 1800s, 6"	**430.00**
Sconce, tin, mirrored, Am, 1800s, 6½" dia	**315.00**
Silverplate, hexagonal, repousse figures/flowers, '20s, 13", pr	**125.00**
Sterling, Georgian, oval serpentine std/base, 9", pr	**350.00**
Sticking tommy, wrought iron, pitted, 14"	**140.00**
Tin, saucer base, CI finger hdl, ejector, 4x5½"	**60.00**
Wrought iron, 4-socket, twist details, late 1800s, 12½"	**420.00**

Candlewick

Candlewick crystal was made by the Imperial Glass Corporation, a division of Lenox Inc., Bellaire, Ohio. It was introduced in 1936, and though never marked except for paper labels, it is easily recognized by the beaded crystal rims, stems, and handles inspired by the tufted needlework called candlewicking, practiced by our pioneer women. During its production, more than 741 items were designed and produced. In September 1982 when Imperial closed its doors, thirty-four pieces were still being made.

Identification numbers and mold numbers used by the company help collectors recognize the various styles and shapes. Most of the pieces are from the #400 series, though other series numbers were also used. Stemware was made in eight styles — five from the #400 series made from 1941 to 1962, one from #3400 series made in 1937, another from #3800 series made in 1941, and the eighth style from the #4000 series made in 1947. In the listings that follow, some #400 items lack the mold number because that information was not found in the company files.

A few pieces have been made in color or with a gold wash. At least two lines, Valley Lily and Floral, utilized Candlewick with floral patterns cut into the crystal. These are scarce today. Other rare items include gifts such as the desk calendar made by the company for its employees and customers; the dresser set comprised of a mirror, clock, puff jar, and cologne; and the chip and dip set.

Ashtray, #1776/1, heart shape, 4½"	**9.00**
Ashtray, #400/64, ind	**6.00**
Ashtray, #400/653, sq, 5¾"	**37.50**
Basket, #400/73/0, hdld, 11"	**225.00**
Bell, #400/108, 5"	**85.00**

Bottles, 6-oz, $55.00; 4-oz, $45.00; on tray, $42.50.

Bowl, #400/124A, oval, 11"	**240.00**
Bowl, #400/17F, shallow, 12"	**47.50**
Bowl, #400/182, 3-ftd, 8½"	**110.00**
Bowl, #400/183, 3-ftd, 6"	**60.00**
Bowl, #400/232, sq, 6"	**110.00**
Bowl, #400/49H, heart shape, 9"	**90.00**
Bowl, #400/7F, rnd, 8"	**37.50**
Bowl, centerpiece; #400/13B, flared, 11"	**45.00**

Bowl, cottage cheese; #400/85, 6"	**25.00**
Bowl, cream soup; #400/50, 5"	**40.00**
Bowl, finger; #3800	**27.50**
Bowl, float; #400/92F, 12"	**40.00**
Bowl, jelly; #400/59, w/lid, 5½"	**60.00**
Bowl, pickle/cereal; #400/57, 7½"	**25.00**
Bowl, relish; #400/208, 3-part, 3-ftd, 10"	**85.00**
Bowl, salad; #400/75B, 10½"	**40.00**
Butter & jam set, #400/204, 5-pc	**245.00**
Cake stand, #400/103D, high ftd, 11"	**67.50**
Candle holder, #400/207, 3-toed, 4½"	**40.00**
Candle holder, #400/81, w/finger hold, 3½"	**42.50**
Candle holder, #400/86, mushroom shape	**22.00**
Candy box, #400/259, w/lid, 7"	**135.00**
Candy box, #400/59, rnd, 5½"	**45.00**
Cigarette box, #400/134, w/lid	**30.00**
Cigarette holder, #400/44, bead ft, 3"	**40.00**
Clock, rnd, 4"	**265.00**
Coaster, #400/226, w/spoon rest	**13.00**
Coaster, #400/78, 4"	**6.00**
Compote, #400/63B, 4½"	**25.00**
Compote, cheese & cracker; #400/88, hdld, 2-pc	**37.50**
Creamer, #400/126, flat, bead hdl	**32.50**
Creamer, bridge; 400/122, ind	**7.50**
Cruet, oil; #400/275, bulbous bottom, 6-oz	**55.00**
Cup, after dinner; #400/77	**17.50**
Cup, punch; #400/211	**7.50**
Decanter, #400/18, w/stopper, 18-oz	**365.00**
Deviled egg server, #400/154, center hdl, 12"	**100.00**
Fork & spoon, #400/75, set	**35.00**
Ice tub, #400/168, hdls, 7"	**195.00**
Jar tower, #400/655, 3-section	**300.00**
Knife, butter; #4000	**250.00**
Ladle, mayonnaise; #400/135, 6¼"	**10.00**
Mustard jar, #400/156, w/spoon	**30.00**
Pitcher, #400/19, low ft, 16-oz	**210.00**
Pitcher, #400/424, plain, 80-oz	**55.00**
Pitcher, Manhattan; #400/18, 40-oz	**225.00**
Plate, #400/124, oval, 12½"	**75.00**
Plate, #400/266, triangular, 7½"	**85.00**
Plate, #400/34, 4½"	**6.00**
Plate, #400/62D, hdls, 8½"	**12.00**
Plate, #400/72D, hdls, 10"	**17.50**
Plate, bread & butter; #400/1D, 6"	**8.00**
Plate, luncheon; #400/7D, 9"	**13.50**
Plate, salad; #400/5D, 8"	**9.00**
Plate, service; #400/13D, 12"	**30.00**
Plate, torte; #40017D, 14"	**42.50**
Platter, #400/131D, 16"	**175.00**
Salt spoon, #400/616	**9.00**
Sauce boat, #400/169	**100.00**
Sauce boat liner, #400/169	**35.00**
Saucer, tea or coffee; #400/35 or #400/37, ea	**2.50**
Shakers, #400/109, ind, pr	**10.00**
Snack jar, #400/139/1, w/lid, bead ft	**425.00**
Stem, #400/18, domed ft	**115.00**
Stem, claret; #3800	**30.00**
Stem, cocktail; #3800, 4-oz	**25.00**
Stem, parfait; #3400, 6-oz	**50.00**
Stem, tea; #4000, 12-oz	**20.00**
Stem, wine; #400/190, 5-oz	**22.50**
Stem, wine; #4000, 5-oz	**25.00**
Toast, #400/123, w/lid, 7¾"	**245.00**
Tray, #400/29, 6½"	**15.00**

Tray, relish; #400/102, 5-section	65.00
Tumbler, #3400, ftd, 12-oz	16.00
Tumbler, #3800, 12-oz	25.00
Tumbler, #400/19, 10-oz	12.00
Tumbler, cocktail; #400/19, ftd, 3-oz	15.00
Tumbler, juice; #3400, ftd, 5-oz	15.00
Tumbler, old-fashioned; #400/18, 7-oz	32.50
Tumbler, sherbet; #400/18, 6-oz	40.00
Tumbler, water; #400/18, 9-oz	40.00
Tumbler, wine; #400/19, ftd, 3-oz	16.00
Vase, #400/193, ftd, 10"	165.00
Vase, bud; #400/186, ftd, 7"	225.00
Vase, bud; #400/28C, bead ft, 8½"	75.00

Candy Containers

Figural glass candy containers were first created in 1876 when ingenious candy manufacturers began to use them to package their products. Two of the first containers, the Liberty Bell and Independence Hall, were distributed for our country's centennial celebration. Children found these toys appealing, and an industry was launched that lasted into the mid-1960s.

Figural candy containers include animals, comic characters, guns, telephones, transportation vehicles, household appliances, and many other intriguing designs. The oldest (those made prior to 1920) were usually hand painted and often contained extra metal parts in addition to the metal strip or screw closures. During the 1950s these metal parts were replaced with plastic, a practice that continued until candy containers met their demise in the 1960s. While predominately clear, they are found in nearly all colors of glass including milk glass, green, amber, pink, emerald, cobalt, ruby flashed, and light blue. Usually the color was intentional, but leftover glass was used as well and resulted in unplanned colors. Various examples are found in light or ice blue, and new finds are always being discovered. Production of the glass portion of candy containers was centered around the western Pennsylvania city of Jeannette. Major producers include Westmoreland Glass, West Bros., Victory Glass, J.H. Millstein, J.C. Crosetti, L.E. Smith, Jack Stough, and T.H. Stough. While 90% of all glass candies were made in the Jeannette area, other companies such as Eagle Glass, Play Toy, and Geo. Borgfeldt Co. have a few to their credit as well.

Buyer beware! Many candy containers have been reproduced. Some, including the Camera and the Rabbit Pushing Wheelbarrow, come already painted from distributors. Others may have a slick or oily feel to the touch. The following list may also alert you to possible reproductions:

E&A #149/L #12 Chicken on Nest
E&A #180/L #24 Dog (clear and cobalt)
E&A #539/L #38 Mule and Waterwagon (original marked Jeannette, PA)
E&A #601/L #47 Rabbit Pushing Wheelbarrow (eggs are speckled on the repro; solid on the original)
E&A #618/L #55 Peter Rabbit
E&A #651/L #58 Rocking Horse (original in clear only)
E&A #342/L #76 Independence Hall (original is rectangular; repro has offset base with red felt-lined closure)
E&A #208/L #89 Happifats on Drum (no notches on repro for closure to hook into)
E&A #345/L #90 Jackie Coogan (marked inside 'B')
E&A #349/L #91 Kewpie (must have Geo. Borgfeldt on base to be original)
E&A #546/L #94 Naked Child
E&A #674/L #103 Santa (original has plastic head; repro is all glass and opens at bottom)
E&A #162/L #114 Mantel Clock (originally in ruby flashed, milk

glass, clear and frosted only)
#144 Amber Pistol (first sold full in the 1970s, not listed in E&A)
E&A #303/L #168 Uncle Sam's Hat
E&A #111/L #233 Santa's Boot
E&A #132/L #242 Carpet Sweeper (currently being sold with no metal parts)
E&A #133/L #243 Carpet Sweeper (currently being sold with no metal parts)
E&A #177/L #246 Display Case
E&A #521/L #254 Mailbox
E&A #543/L #255 Drum Mug
E&A #661/L #268 Safe (original in clear, ruby flashed, and milk glass only)
E&A #577/L #289 Piano (original in only clear and milk glass, both painted)
E&A #60/L #356 Auto
E&A #33/L #377 Auto
E&A #121/L 238 Camera (original says 'Pat Apld For' on bottom, (reproduction says 'B. Shakman' or is ground off)
E&A #56/L #378 Station Wagon
E&A #213/L #386 Fire Engine
E&A #137/L #83 Charlie Chaplin (original has 'Geo. Borgfeldt' on base; reproduction comes in pink and blue)
Others are possible.

Our advisor for this category is Jeff Bradfield; he is listed in the Directory under Virginia. You may contact him with questions, if you will include an SASE. See Clubs, Newsletters, and Catalogs for the address of the Candy Container Collectors of America. A bimonthly newsletter offers insight into new finds, reproductions, updates, and articles from over four hundred collectors and members, including all authors of books on candy containers.

'L' numbers used in this guide refer to a standard reference series, *An Album of Candy Containers*, Vols 1 and 2, by Jennie Long. 'E&A' numbers correlate with *The Compleat American Glass Candy Containers Handbook* by Eikelberner and Agadjanian, revised by Adele Bowden. Values are given for undamaged examples with original paint and metal parts when applicable or unless noted otherwise. Repaired pieces (often repainted) are worth only a small fraction of one that is perfect. The symbol (+) at the end of some of the following lines was used to indicate items that have been reproduced. See also Christmas; Halloween.

Turkey, L #61, (E&A #790) 1924-29, 3½", $175.00.

Airplane, P-51; L #327 (E&A #5)	45.00
Airplane, Passenger; L#323 (E&A #7)	275.00
Airplane, Spirit of Goodwill; L #320 (E&A #8)	160.00
Amos 'N Andy, G pnt, L #77 (E&A #21)	450.00
Angeline Coach, L #398 (E&A #166)	450.00
Auto, rear trunk, L #367 (E&A #38), G pnt	140.00
Baby Dear Bottle, L #64 (E&A #555)	20.00
Basket, grape design, L #223 (E&A #81)	35.00

Basket, ruby flashed, L #225 ....35.00
Battleship on Waves, L #335 (E&A #96) 175.00
Bell, Hand; wood hdl, L #494 ....200.00
Billiken, L #82 (E&A #90) 125.00
Black Cat for Luck, L #4 (E&A #136-1) 800.00
Bucket, Kid Kandy; L #508 ....450.00
Bulldog #2, cb closure, L #16 (E&A #186) 40.00
Bureau, G pnt, L #125 (E&A #112) 200.00
Bus, Jitney; closure, L #340 (E&A #114) 365.00
Candy Pay Station, L #239 (E&A #120) 150.00
Cannon, cobalt bbl, rpl carriage, L #534 (E&A #122) 300.00
Cannon, Quick Firer; orig carriage, L #537 ......1,000.00
Cannon #3, 4-wheel carriage, all orig, L #139 (E&A #125) 800.00
Car, Electric Coupe #2; closure, L #356 (E&A #47)(+) 60.00
Car, Ribbed-Top Sedan; closure, L #376 (E&A #32) 25.00
Charlie Chaplin by Bbl, Borgfeldt, G pnt/closure, (E&A #137) .150.00
Chick in Eggshell Auto, G pnt, L #7 (E&A #144) 350.00
Chicken on Oblong Basket, closure, gr, L #10 (E&A #147) 50.00
Chicken on Rnd Base, L #11 (E&A #146) 250.00
Circus Dog w/Hat, L #478 ....30.00
Coupe, Long Hood; #1, L #357 (E&A #50) 150.00
Defense Field Gun, orig gun, L #142 (E&A #128) 300.00
Dog, Mutt, L #20 (E&A #194) 55.00
Dog w/Glass Hat, L #22 (E&A #181), lg 25.00
Duck, rectangular basket, L #27 (E&A #198) 80.00
Esther Coach, all orig, L #397 (E&A #165) 400.00
Fairy Pups, L #23 (E&A #193) 35.00
Fancy Boot, L #232 ....20.00
Fannie Farmer, cowboy, L #528 ....150.00
Felix by Barrel, G pnt, L #85 (E&A #211) 600.00
Fire Engine, bl glass, L #381 (E&A #218-1) 110.00
Flatiron, orig pnt & closure, L #249 (E&A #344) 385.00
Flossie Fisher Bed, L #127 (E&A #234) 900.00
Foxy Doctor, L #657 ....100.00
Frog, milk glass, L #36 (E&A #238) 825.00
Genteel Elephant, L #33 (E&A #207) 250.00
Grocery Truck, L #458 (E&A #783) 775.00
Gun, cork closure, L #540 ....25.00
Gun, Kolt #1; screw cap, L #151 (E&A #285) 75.00
Horn, Millsteins, L #282 (E&A #311) 20.00
Horn, 3-valve, w/mouthpiece, L #281 (E&A #312) 175.00
Irish Hat, L #167 (E&A #302) 800.00
Jack-O'-Lantern, blk cat, L #158 (E&A #349-1) 450.00
Jeep Scout Car, L #390 (E&A #350) 35.00
Kaleidoscope, L #250 (E&A #353) 3,000.00
Kangaroo, L #453 (E&A #354) 1,200.00
Kewpie by Bbl, L #91 (E&A #359) (+) 125.00
Kewpie on Radio, L #533 ....500.00
Lantern, barn type #2, L #178 (E&A #427-B) 75.00
Lantern, beveled glass w/gilt & ruby stain, L #175 (E&A #396) ...85.00
Lantern, brass cap, #184, (E&A #403) 20.00
Lantern, Crossette-Little One; L #200 (E&A #386) 20.00
Lantern, domed closure, L #576 ....45.00
Lantern, fancy trim, L #190 (E&A #403) 30.00
Lantern, Japanese paper type, L #572 (E&A #389) 300.00
Lantern, magnifying lens, L #176 (E&A #438) 115.00
Lantern, Victory Glass #1, L #191 (E&A #443)(+ by Avon) 20.00
Liberty Bell, L #495 (E&A #86) 125.00
Library Lamp, orig fringe, L #207 (E&A #372) 500.00
Limousine, Yel Taxi; L #596 (E&A #43) 700.00
Locomotive, dbl sq windows, orig closure, L #414 (E&A #497) .110.00
Lucky Lindy Candy Air Mail, L #666 ....300.00
Lynne Clock Bank, L #119 (E&A #159) 350.00
Mailbox, silver pnt, orig closure, L #254 (E&A #521) (+) 115.00

Mantel Clock #1, L #115 (E&A #164) 150.00
Maud Muller Milk Carrier, L #69 ....175.00
Military Hat, L #170 (E&A #131) 30.00
Model Cruiser, orig closure, L #339 (E&A #98) 22.00
Mounted Policeman, G pnt, L #551 ....2,600.00
Mr Rabbit w/Hat, no pnt, L #39 (E&A #610) 1,100.00
Naked Child, Victory Glass, L #94 (E&A #546) 40.00
Nurser Bottle, Waisted; L #71 (E&A #548) 25.00
Opera Glasses, celluloid fr, L #625 ....225.00
Pencil, paper label, L #263 (E&A #567) 65.00
Peter Rabbit, L #55 (E&A #618) (+) 30.00
Phonograph, glass horn, L #286 (E&A #576) 300.00
Pocket Watch, 'Jeannette' on paper face, L #457 (E&A #825) ..450.00
Poodle Dog, glass head, L #471 ....20.00
Pumpkin Head Witch, L #165 (E&A #594) 565.00
Puss in Boots, L #468 ....125.00
Rabbit, aluminum ears, L #487 (same, no ears $125) 425.00
Rabbit Crouching, L #41 (E&A #615), EX pnt 105.00
Rabbit in Eggshell, gold pnt, L #48 (E&A #608) 75.00
Rabbit Pushing Cart, G pnt, L #44 (E&A #602) 285.00
Rabbit Running on Log, G pnt, L #42 (E&A #603) 250.00
Rabbit w/Layed-Bk Ears, EX pnt, L #40 (E&A #616) 100.00
Rocking Horse #1, L #58 (E&A #651)(+) 350.00
Rocking Settee, L #134 (E&A #653) 450.00
Santa Claus, banded coat, L #97 (E&A #669) 215.00
Santa Claus, plastic head, L #103 (E&A #674)(+) 65.00
Sedan, 4-door, orig tin wheels, no pnt, L #370 (E&A #57) 80.00
Seltzer Bottle, L #505 ....350.00
Soldier on Monument, L #107 (E&A #682) 825.00
Stutz Bearcat, L #429 (E&A #639) 2,000.00
Telephone, Redlich's #5; L #296 (E&A #749) 75.00
Telephone, Stough's #3; L #308 (E&A #751) 40.00
Telephone, Victory Glass #6, L #303 (E&A #738) 45.00
Trophy, 3-hdl, L #631 ....50.00
Valise, L #220 (E&A #599) 265.00
Wagon, tin, L #442 (E&A #820) 150.00
Wheelbarrow, lg wheel, L #610 (E&A #832) 100.00
Whip, glass hdl, L #274 (E&A #836) 900.00
Windmill, pewter top, all orig, L #443 (E&A #840) 415.00
Windmill, shaker top, orig blades, L #445 (E&A #842) 250.00
World Globe, L #506 ....45.00

Papier-Mache, Composition

Peter the Pumpkin Bellhop, Germany, 7", $375.00.

Brownie cop on rabbit, glass eyes, 6", EX 350.00

Chick, cloth clothes, 6½", VG 135.00
Chick baby rolly polly on wheels, 5", EX 200.00
Chick in fez, yel w/red & brn, glass eyes, 6" 215.00
Clown rabbit, opens at neck, 6", EX 425.00
Clown rabbit on egg, w/mica, 4", EX 250.00
Duck, compo w/wire legs, on base, mc, Germany, 5½" 100.00
Duck emerging from egg, glass eyes, 4", EX 275.00
Duck w/jtd neck, papier-mache & wood, lead ft, 6", VG 195.00
Football, Germany, ca 1910, 2½x3½", EX 80.00
Foxy Grandpa nodder on rabbit, glass eyes, 6", VG 285.00
Girl rabbit, glass eyes, crepe paper clothes, 7" 385.00
Golf Bunny, wood base, Germany, 6½", EX 200.00
Humpty Dumpty, mc, 5" 265.00
Irish boy, gr, 4" 95.00
Rabbit couple, glass eyes, 7", EX, pr 450.00
Rabbit emerging from egg, 5", EX 250.00
Rabbit in carrot zeppelin, Japan, 5" 175.00
Rabbit in coveralls, glossy pnt, 16", EX 250.00
Rabbit in egg, pk, Germany, 4" 195.00
Rabbit in tin car, 6½", VG 300.00
Rabbit lady, glass eyes, 8", EX 330.00
Rabbit nodder, glass eyes, 7", VG 110.00
Rabbit on log, mc, 4" 250.00
Rabbit pulling wooden cart, glass eyes, 10½", EX 240.00
Rabbit seated, Reutter label, 14", EX 300.00
Rabbit w/carrot, glass eyes, 7", EX 125.00
Turkey, mc, Germany, ca 1900, 4x2½x2½", EX 125.00
Turkey, papier-mache, HP, wht metal ft, glass eyes, rpr, 14" 525.00
Turkey, unmk West Germany, 5½" 95.00
Turkey hen, compo, Germany, early, 6", EX 150.00
2 chickens, wood/cb/papier-mache, orig pnt, Germany, 3½" 135.00
2 rabbits carrying litter w/lg egg, 13x16" 250.00

Canes

Fancy canes and walking sticks were once the mark of a gentle-man. Hand-carved examples are collected and admired as folk art from the past. The glass canes that never could have been practical are unique whimseys of the glass-blower's profession. Gadget and container sticks, which were produced in a wide variety, are highly desirable. Character, political, and novelty types are also sought after as are those with handles made of precious metals.

For more information we recommend *American Folk Art Canes, Personal Sculpture,* by George H. Meyer, Sandringham Press, 100 West Long Lake Rd., Suite 100, Bloomfield Hills, MI 48304. Our advisor for this category is Bruce Thalberg.

One-piece carved ebony, silver-overlay ears, eye brows and nose, ivory teeth, glass eyes, 34", $950.00.

Bamboo, cvd mongoose relief, EX 120.00
Bamboo, metal tip unscrews for telescoping fly rod, root hdl 200.00
Bamboo, sterling plate on hdl, sterling scrolls on shaft 90.00
Bamboo w/silver-gilded wht-metal knob of smiling head, 35" 50.00
Blown glass, aqua spatter w/spiral twist at hdl & end, 31" 200.00
Blown glass, red & bl spirals, 49" 195.00
Curly maple w/stag horn hdl, 35" 65.00
Cvd, monkey automata, ivory ears/glass eyes, snakewood shaft .. 825.00
Eagle cvd hdl, Union shields/etc cvd along shaft, 36" 300.00
Ebonized, gold-plated head, name/1891 .... 140.00
Ebony wood, hammered silver hdl, 3 copper bugs, 34" 200.00
Ebony wood, horse's head bone hdl, silver ferrule, 35" 325.00
Ebony wood, Oriental man's head ivory hdl, gold ferrule 525.00
Gambler's, faux bamboo, w/trn walnut screw-off end holds dice .. 335.00
Hardwood, brass tip w/mechanical pencil in hdl, 35" 95.00
Hardwood, screw-off brass ice chipper tip & screw end, 37" 85.00
Hardwood w/X-hatched cvg, NP brass trim, horn tip 75.00
Horn w/amber inserts, steel core, 36" 70.00
Ivory shaft w/ebony spacers, ivory monkey's fist knob, 1800s .. 1,200.00
Leather encased, braided hdl w/1" cut stone, 36" 300.00
Malacca, cvd lady's leg hdl, 35" 150.00
Malacca shaft, ivory hdl w/terrier finial, gold ferrule 500.00
Music box in fan-shaped hdl, pierced/stained horn tip, 35" 250.00
Riding crop, leather-covered w/stag horn hdl, silver inlay 100.00
Root head, cvd mouse's head hdl, natural, 36" 95.00
Root head, gnarled shaft w/2-faced head hdl, red stain 75.00
Rosewood, gr jadeite hdl w/faceted crystal bands 400.00
Shark vertebrae, baleen cap, dividers & tip, 34½" 175.00
Steel, horse hdl opens to 7½" steel knife, 4-section, 36" 310.00
Sterling, lg eagle's head cane & collar, rosewood shaft 660.00
Sterling L hdl w/hunting scene in high relief, ebony shaft 525.00
Thornwood, repousse floral on silver hdl, metal tip, 35" 250.00
Tiger maple & oak joined by wide brass band, 1800s, 35½" 85.00
Tin w/wht cast-metal knob w/bust of McKinley & 1896, 33" 140.00
Tortoise veneer w/eng sterling knob, 34" 600.00
Walnut, Spanish neillo silver hdl w/eng vines, 35" 250.00
Whale ivory, clenched fist on bar, ivory shaft 1,800.00
Whale ivory, lady's leg, high-button shoe, mahog shaft 475.00
Whale ivory, nude woman's figure, silver collar, ebony shaft .. 1,100.00
Whalebone, cvd decor, ivory hdl inset w/metal disk, 1800s 550.00
Whalebone, hammerhead knob, 1800s, 35¾" 400.00
Whalebone, trn & incised knob, 1800s, 38" 365.00
Whalebone shaft, ivory serpent hdl w/inlaid eyes, 34" 990.00
Whalebone 8-sided shaft, cvd ivory hdl w/2 separators, 31", VG .. 200.00
Wood, alligator hdl, brass tip 90.00
Wood, antler whistle hdl, repousse sterling ferrule, 34" 150.00
Wood, dog's head hdl w/glass eyes, 1890 .... 125.00

Canton

Canton is a blue and white porcelain that was first exported in the 1790s by clipper ships from China to the United States, a practice that continued into the 1920s. Canton became very popular along the East coast where the major ports were located. Its popularity was due to several factors: it was readily available, inexpensive, and (due to the fact that it came in many different forms) appealing to the housewife.

The porcelain's blue and white color and simple motif (teahouse, trees, bridge, and a rain-cloud border) have made it a favorite of people who collect early American furniture and accessories. Buyers of Canton should shop at large outdoor shows and up-scale antique shows. Collec-tions are regularly sold at auction. Collectors usually prefer a rich, deep tone rather than a lighter blue. Cracks, large chips, and major repairs will substantially affect values. Prices of Canton have escalated sharply over the last twenty years, and rare forms are highly sought after by advanced collectors. Our advisor for this category is Hobart D. Van Deusen; he is listed in the Directory under Connecticut.

Bowl, fruit; low, 1850s, 9¾", pr 600.00
Bowl, fruit; sq w/canted corners, 1850s, 10" 1,100.00
Bowl, fruit; w/undertray, 1800s, 10¾" 1,035.00
Bowl, octagonal, deep, 11¼" 315.00
Bowl, octagonal, deep, 1850s, 13¾" L 465.00
Bowl, petal edge, 10" 520.00
Bowl, vegetable; 10¼" L 275.00
Brush box, rectangular, divided int, 1800s, 7¼x3⅜x3" 635.00
Butter dish, w/lid & strainer, 1800s, 7½" dia 550.00
Hot water dish, oblong, 1800s, 14" L 385.00
Hot water dish, 1800s, 9" dia 235.00
Pitcher, cream; 3¼" 130.00
Pitcher, milk; 7½" 975.00
Plate, 8¾" 100.00
Platter, ftd, oval, 14⅞" 1,150.00
Platter, octagonal, 16½x13½" 475.00
Platter, octagonal, 18½x15¼" 600.00
Platter, oval, 13½" 260.00
Platter, oval, 1840s, 15" 400.00
Platter, oval, 1840s, 19½" 700.00
Platter, well & tree; 19th C, minor chip, 17" 900.00
Tureen, soup; w/lid, 12" 935.00

Capo-Di-Monte

Established in 1743 near Naples and sponsored by Charles II, who was King of Naples at that time, Capo-Di-Monte produced soft-paste porcelain figurines and dinnerware usually marked with a 'crown over N' device, though a fleur-de-lis was used on occasion. The factory was closed throughout the 1760s but reopened in 1771 in the city of Naples. There both hard- and soft-paste porcelains were made, sometimes decorated with applied florals in high relief. Their technique as well as their marks were blatantly copied. As a result, this type of encrusted decoration is often referred to today as Capo-Di-Monte. The original factory closed in 1821. Some of their molds were purchased by the Docceia Porcelain factory in Florence which continues to operate to the present time. Most examples on the market today are of fairly recent manufacture. Capo-Di-Monte type wares have been made in Hungary and Germany as well as France and Italy. Many of these pieces continue to bear the 'crown over N' gold stamp. As more collectors recognize and appreciate the quality of the older ware, buyer demand drives prices higher.

Urns, cherubs and 4 applied mask figures, reticulated lid with cherub finials, repairs, 31", $1,600.00 for the pair.

Box, Bacchanalian scenes, hinged, 3¼x5" 340.00
Box, classical figures, relief swirls, hinged lid, 5½x8" 535.00
Box, classical scenes w/cherubs, mc w/gold, late, 11" 600.00
Box, cupids, gold scrolls/stripes, hinged lid, 3x5x2½" 210.00
Box, mythological scenes, ormolu mts, 5x6½x5" 575.00
Candelabra, figural parrots, floral arms, metal mt, 13", pr 850.00
Figurine, romantic couple, cat w/pheasant, 9½x9" 395.00
Plaque, Adam & Eve w/angel, octagonal ebonized/brass fr, 20" ..550.00
Stein, classical figures, rampant lion finial, 1920s, 11" 365.00
Stein, figures in deep relief, ca 1850, 2-liter, 16½", NM 1,250.00
Teapot, nudes bathing, bird-head spout, twig hdl, late, 5" 180.00
Vase, cylindrical w/rim flange, hdls, ftd, sq base, 8", pr 1,100.00
Vase, mythological scenes, oval columnar shape, 5½", pr 200.00

Carlton Ware

Carlton Ware was the product of Wiltshaw and Robinson, who operated in the Staffordshire district of England from about 1890. During the 1920s, they produced ornamental ware with enameled and gilded decorations such as flowers and birds, often on a black background. In 1958 the firm was renamed Carlton Ware Ltd. Their trademark was a crown over a circular stamp with 'W & R, Stoke on Trent,' surrounding a swallow. 'Carlton Ware' was sometimes added by hand.

Bowl, iris on cream, oval, Australian pattern 25.00
Bowl, kingfisher, Lustered Bleu Royale, hdls, oval 195.00
Box, kingfisher & willow, mc w/gold, ball ft 200.00
Butter dish, yel daisy shape, w/daisy knife, 4" dia, MIB 110.00
Jam dish, raspberries, red on pk, 4½" dia, MIB 120.00
Leaf dish, Rouge Royale 95.00
Pitcher, classic ladies emb, Stoke on Trent 125.00
Pitcher, Rouge Royale, 6" 37.50
Vase, kingfisher, gold hdls, ovoid w/everted rim, 4¼" 185.00
Vase, kingfisher & willow, mc w/gold, baluster, ftd, 6" 200.00

Carnival Collectibles

Carnival items from the early part of this century represent the lighter side of an America that was alternately prospering and sophisticated or devastated by war and domestic conflict. But whatever the country's condition, the carnival's thrilling rides and shooting galleries were a sure way of letting it all go by — at least for an evening.

For further information on chalkware figures, we recommend *The Carnival Chalk Prize* by Thomas G. Morris, who is listed in the Directory under Oregon. Our advisors for shooting gallery targets are Richard and Valerie Tucker; their address is listed in the Directory under Texas.

Chalkware figure, Abe Lincoln bust, 1940-50, 12" 55.00
Chalkware figure, Blk boy w/melon, mk Buelah, 1930-40, 7½" 80.00
Chalkware figure, boy & dog, mk Pals, 1935-45, 10x9" 55.00
Chalkware figure, boy angel, bookend, 1920-30, 8" 45.00
Chalkware figure, Charlie McCarthy, seated, 1930-40, 9½" 55.00
Chalkware figure, Chinaman, mk Chinky, 1920-30, 9½" 85.00
Chalkware figure, cowboy, ashtray, 1930-40, 8¼" 35.00
Chalkware figure, dancing girl, HP, airbrushed, 1930-40, 14" 95.00
Chalkware figure, Dead End Kid, 1930-40, 15" 95.00
Chalkware figure, Frenchie, Jenkins, 1924, rare, 15" 185.00
Chalkware figure, girl sitting in flower, HP, 1920, 11" 120.00
Chalkware figure, Jackie Coogan, mk My Boy, 1930s, 17" 165.00
Chalkware figure, Kewpie vamp, HP, jtd arms, veil, 1920s, 11" ..125.00
Chalkware figure, Little Sheba, orig feathers, HP, 1920s, 13" 155.00
Chalkware figure, Mae West, mk Rainwater, ca 1936, 14" 95.00

Chalkware figure, Maggie and Jiggs, titled Armistice on base, KFS, 1925-40, 11½", $250.00.

Chalkware figure, Pluto, 1930-40, 6" 30.00
Chalkware figure, Popeye, saluting, 1930-40, 11½" 115.00
Chalkware figure, Sailor, saluting, flat bk, 1930s, 13½" 30.00
Chalkware figure, Shirley Temple, ca 1935-45, 14½" 190.00
Chalkware figure, St Nicholas by chimney w/bag, 1930-40, 12½" ...50.00
Chalkware figure, Uncle Scrooge, w/money bag, 1940-50, 8" 35.00
Chalkware figure, US Capitol, lamp, 1930-40, 11x11x17" 120.00
Chalkware figure, Wimpy, 1930-40, 8" 45.00
Shooting gallery target, bird, brass, worn pnt, 5x5x1½" 88.00
Shooting gallery target, bird, CI, old gold rpt, 3¼" 105.00
Shooting gallery target, buffalo, CI, worn wht pnt, 6½" 90.00
Shooting gallery target, convict, pnt wood & tin, 1930s, 12" 325.00
Shooting gallery target, cow, pine w/leather ears, 46x47" 365.00
Shooting gallery target, eagle, CI, worn pnt, 1900s, 20x15" 850.00
Shooting gallery target, eagle, worn pnt, 1900s, 11½x10½" 750.00
Shooting gallery target, hen w/chick, CI, worn pnt, 15x12¾" .1,200.00
Shooting gallery target, lion, jumping, CI, 1900s, 11x7" 195.00
Shooting gallery target, owl, old mc pnt, 1900s, 11" 275.00
Shooting gallery target, rabbit, jumping, no pnt, 8½x6½" 225.00
Shooting gallery target, squirrel, CI, worn pnt, early, 5" 85.00
Shooting gallery target, star on stand, pnt CI, 6x3", EX 65.00
Shooting gallery target, Tom turkey, mk Evans, 7" 175.00
Shooting gallery target, WWI soldier w/rifle, old pnt, 7½" 125.00

Carnival Glass

Carnival glass is pressed glass that has been coated with a sodium solution and fired to give it an exterior lustre. First made in America in 1905, it was produced until the late 1920s and had great popularity in the average American household; for unlike the costly art glass produced by Tiffany, carnival glass could be mass-produced at a small cost. Colors most found are marigold, green, blue, and purple; but others exist in lesser quantities and include white, clear, red, aqua opalescent, peach opalescent, ice blue, ice green, amber, lavender, and smoke.

Companies mainly responsible for its production in America include the Fenton Art Glass Company, Williamstown, West Virginia; the Northwood Glass Company, Wheeling, West Virginia; the Imperial Glass Company, Bellaire, Ohio; the Millersburg Glass Company, Millersburg, Ohio; and the Dugan Glass Company (Diamond Glass), Indiana, Pennsylvania. In addition to these major manufacturers, lesser producers included the U.S. Glass Company, the Cambridge Glass Company, the Westmoreland Glass Company, and the McKee Glass Company.

Carnival glass has been highly collectible since the 1950s and has been reproduced for the last twenty-five years. Several national and state collectors' organizations exist, and many fine books are available on old carnival glass, including *The Standard Encyclopedia of Carnival Glass* by Bill Edwards.

A Dozen Roses (Imperial), bowl, marigold, rare, 10" 650.00
Acanthus (Imperial), plate, marigold, 10" 200.00
Acorn (Fenton), bowl, gr, 8½" 85.00
Acorn Burrs (Northwood), bowl, amethyst, flat, 5" 40.00
Acorn Burrs (Northwood), cup, punch; aqua opal 575.00
Apple Blossom Twigs (Dugan), plate, gr 300.00
Apple Panels (English), creamer, marigold 35.00
Apple Tree (Fenton), tumbler, bl 65.00
April Showers (Fenton), vase, gr 150.00
Arched Panels, tumbler, marigold 85.00
Arcs (Imperial), bowl, amethyst, 8½" 60.00
Asters, bowl, marigold 60.00
August Flowers, shade, marigold 42.00
Autumn Acorns (Fenton), bowl, gr, 8¼" 80.00
Aztec (McKee), tumbler, marigold, rare 650.00
Baby's Bouquet, plate, marigold, scarce, child sz 115.00
Baker's Rosette, ornament, marigold 75.00
Ballard-Merced, CA (Northwood), bowl, amethyst 950.00
Balloons (Imperial), compote, smoke 90.00
Band (Dugan), hat, peach opal 75.00
Banded Diamonds (Crystal), tumbler, amethyst, rare 40.00
Banded Diamonds & Bars, decanter, marigold, complete 175.00
Banded Grape (Fenton), tumbler, wht 95.00
Banded Grape & Leaf (English), pitcher, water; marigold, rare ..650.00
Banded Panels (Crystal), sugar bowl, amethyst 45.00
Banded Rose, vase, marigold, sm 175.00
Beaded Bull's Eyes (Imperial), vase, amethyst, 14" 125.00
Beaded Hearts (Northwood), bowl, marigold 50.00
Beaded Panels (Westmoreland), compote, amethyst 55.00
Beaded Shell (Dugan), creamer or spooner, amethyst, ea 90.00
Beaded Shell (Dugan), tumbler, bl 180.00
Beaded Spears (Crystal), pitcher, marigold, rare 490.00
Beaded Stars (Fenton), bowl, rose; marigold 60.00
Beads (Northwood), bowl, gr, 8½" 70.00
Bells & Beads (Dugan), bowl, bl, 7½" 120.00
Bells & Beads (Dugan), hat, amethyst 60.00
Birds & Cherries (Fenton), bonbon, marigold 45.00
Birds & Cherries (Fenton), compote, pastel colors 95.00
Blackberry (Fenton), hat, marigold, open edge 40.00
Blackberry (Fenton), plate, bl, rare 400.00
Blackberry (Northwood), compote, bl 75.00
Blackberry Banded (Fenton), hat, gr 55.00
Blackberry Block (Fenton), tumbler, gr 85.00
Blackberry Bramble (Fenton), compote, bl 55.00
Blackberry Miniature (Fenton), compote, bl, sm 265.00
Blackberry Spray (Fenton), compote, gr 55.00
Blackberry Wreath (Millersburg), plate, amethyst, rare, 6" 2,700.00
Blackberry Wreath (Millersburg), spittoon whimsey, gr, rare 250.00
Blocks & Arches (Crystal), tumbler, amethyst, rare 90.00
Blossomtime (Northwood), compote, gr 350.00
Blueberry (Fenton), pitcher, bl, scarce 700.00
Border Plants (Dugan), bowl, peach opal, flat, 8½" 180.00
Boutonniere (Millersburg), compote, marigold 195.00
Bow & English Hob (English), bowl, nut; marigold 50.00
Briar Patch, hat, amethyst 50.00
Brocaded Summer Gardens, bowl, centerpc; pastel color, ftd 120.00
Brocaded Summer Gardens, tray, cake; pastel colors 110.00
Broken Arches (Imperial), bowl, gr, 10" 75.00
Brooklyn, bottle, amethyst, w/stopper 95.00
Bubbles, lamp chimney, pastel colors 50.00
Butterfly (Fenton), ornament, bl 200.00
Butterfly (Fenton), tray, card; bl 60.00
Butterfly (US Glass), tumbler, marigold, rare 5,800.00
Butterfly & Berry (Fenton), bowl, marigold, ftd, 10" 100.00

Butterfly & Berry (Fenton), butter dish, marigold, w/lid 150.00
Butterfly & Berry (Fenton), spooner, gr 190.00
Butterfly & Berry (Fenton), vase, gr, rare 200.00
Butterfly & Fern (Fenton), tumbler, bl 65.00
Butterfly Bush (Crystal), compote, amethyst, lg 175.00
Buttermilk (Fenton), goblet, amethyst 70.00
Buttress (US Glass), pitcher, marigold, rare 400.00
Buzz Saw (Cambridge), cruet, gr, rare, 4" 400.00
Buzz Saw (Cambridge), shade, marigold 45.00
Cane (Imperial), bowl, pastel colors, 10" 50.00
Cane & Scroll (Sea Thistle) (English), rose bowl, bl 75.00
Captive Rose (Fenton), bowl, marigold, 10" 75.00
Captive Rose (Fenton), plate, amethyst, 7" 190.00
Carnation (New Martinsville), punch cup, marigold 57.00
Carnival Honeycomb (Imperial), bonbon, amethyst 55.00
Carolina Dogwood (Westmoreland), bowl, aqua opal, 8½" 500.00
Cathedral (Sweden), chalice, bl, 7" 190.00
Cathedral (Sweden), compote, bl, 2 szs, ea 80.00
Cathedral Arches (English), bowl, punch; marigold, 1-pc 350.00
Central Shoe Store (Northwood), bowl, amethyst, 7" 1,200.00
Chatelaine (Imperial), tumbler, amethyst, rare 510.00
Chatham (US Glass), candlesticks, marigold, pr 90.00
Checkerboard (Westmoreland), goblet, marigold, rare 350.00
Checkerboard (Westmoreland), vase, amethyst 2,700.00
Cherry (Dugan), bowl, amethyst, flat, 5" 50.00
Cherry (Millersburg), bowl, amethyst, 4" 85.00
Cherry (Millersburg), bowl, ice cream; marigold, 10" 250.00
Cherry (Millersburg), butter dish, gr, w/lid 450.00
Cherry (Millersburg), creamer or spooner, amethyst, ea 275.00
Cherry (Millersburg), plate, gr, rare, 7½" 1,150.00
Cherry (Millersburg), tumbler, amethyst, 2 variations, ea 190.00
Cherry & Cable (Northwood), tumbler, marigold, rare 425.00
Cherry & Daisies (Fenton), banana boat, bl 1,050.00
Cherry Chain (Fenton), bonbon, amethyst 60.00
Cherry Circles (Fenton), bowl, amethyst, 8" 65.00
Cherub, lamp, pastel colors, rare 150.00
Chrysanthemum (Fenton), bowl, gr, flat, 9" 95.00
Circle Scroll (Dugan), bowl, amethyst, 10" 80.00
Circle Scroll (Dugan), tumbler, amethyst, rare 600.00
Cobblestones (Dugan), plate, amethyst, rare 1,300.00
Cobblestones (Imperial), bowl, marigold, 8½" 75.00
Coin Dot (Fenton), bowl, gr, 10" 40.00
Coin Dot VT (Westmoreland), compote, aqua opal 270.00
Coin Spot (Dugan), compote, peach opal 200.00
Colonial (Imperial), goblet, lemonade; marigold 110.00
Columbia (Imperial), compote, gr 65.00
Concave Diamonds (Dugan), pitcher, vaseline, w/lid 550.00
Concord (Fenton), bowl, marigold, scarce, 9" 175.00
Constellation (Dugan), compote, marigold 150.00
Coral (Fenton), plate, bl, rare, 9½" 1,200.00
Corinth (Westmoreland), vase, gr 75.00
Cornucopia (Fenton), candlesticks, marigold, 5", pr 80.00
Cosmos & Cane, bowl, marigold, 10" 75.00
Cosmos & Cane, plate, chop; marigold, rare 1,450.00
Cosmos & Cane, rose bowl, marigold, lg 1,275.00
Cosmos VT (Fenton), bowl, amethyst, 10" 65.00
Cosmos VT (Fenton), plate, peach opal, rare, 10" 400.00
Country Kitchen (Millersburg), butter dish, amethyst, w/lid 750.00
Country Kitchen (Millersburg), vase whimsey, marigold, rare 600.00
CR (Argentina), ashtray, bl 135.00
Crab Claw (Imperial), bowl, gr, 10" 65.00
Crab Claw (Millersburg), pitcher, scarce 650.00
Crackle (Imperial), bowl, amethyst, 5" 18.00
Crackle (Imperial), pitcher, gr, domed base 160.00

Crackle (Imperial), plate, gr 60.00
Crackle (Imperial), vase, auto; gr 35.00
Cut Arcs (Fenton), compote, bl 55.00
Dahlia (Dugan), bowl, wht, 10" 290.00
Dahlia (Dugan), butter dish, wht 350.00
Dahlia (Dugan), creamer or spooner, wht, ea 220.00
Dahlia (Dugan), tumbler, marigold, rare 170.00
Dahlia & Drape (Fenton), tumble-up, marigold, complete 150.00
Daisy (Fenton), bonbon, bl, scarce 300.00
Daisy & Cane (English), spittoon, bl, rare 250.00
Daisy & Drape (Northwood), vase, aqua opal 700.00
Daisy & Plum (Northwood), rose bowl, peach opal 175.00
Daisy Squares, compote, marigold, rare 500.00
Daisy Squares, rose bowl, gr 675.00
Daisy Web (Dugan), hat, amethyst, rare 500.00
Dandelion (Northwood), mug, bl 500.00
Dandelion (Northwood), pitcher, marigold 395.00
Deep Grape (Millersburg), compote, bl, rare 3,000.00
Diamond & Daisy Cut (US Glass), pitcher, bl 450.00
Diamond & Rib (Fenton), vase, marigold, 7" 45.00
Diamond & Sunburst (Imperial), bowl, amethyst, 8" 55.00
Diamond & Sunburst (Imperial), wine, marigold 55.00
Diamond Band (Crystal), float set, marigold 400.00
Diamond Checkerboard, cracker jar, marigold 85.00
Diamond Checkerboard, tumbler, marigold 100.00
Diamond Fountain (Higbee), cruet, marigold, rare 750.00
Diamond Lace (Imperial), bowl, amethyst, 11" 110.00
Diamond Lace (Imperial), tumbler, marigold 190.00
Diamond Point, rose bowl, amethyst, rare 1,400.00
Diamond Point Columns (Imperial), butter dish, marigold 70.00
Diamond Point Columns (Imperial), vase, pastel colors 55.00
Diamond Points (Northwood), vase, peach opal, 14" 300.00
Diamond Ring (Imperial), bowl, amethyst, 5" 30.00
Diamonds (Millersburg), tumbler, marigold 70.00
Diving Dolphins (English), bowl, gr, ftd, 7" 280.00
Dogwood Sprays (Dugan), compote, marigold 270.00
Dolphins (Millersburg), compote, bl, rare 6,000.00
Double Dolphins (Fenton), plate, cake; pastel colors, center hdl .85.00
Double Loop (Northwood), creamer, bl 190.00
Double Scroll (Imperial), bowl, amethyst 55.00
Double Star (Cambridge), pitcher, marigold, scarce 750.00
Double Stem Rose (Dugan), bowl, marigold, dome base, 8½" 100.00
Dragon & Lotus (Fenton), bowl, bl, flat, 9" 115.00
Dragon & Strawberry (Fenton), bowl, gr, flat, scarce, 9" 900.00
Dragon's Tongue (Fenton), bowl, marigold, scarce, 11" 950.00
Drapery (Northwood), vase, gr 110.00
Drapery VT (Fenton), pitcher, marigold, rare 510.00
Duckie, powder jar, marigold, w/lid 40.00
Dugan Fan (Dugan), sauce boat, peach opal, 5" 145.00
Dugan's Many Ribs, vase, bl 75.00
Dutch Mill, plate, marigold, 8" 50.00
Dutch Twins, ashtray, marigold 50.00
EA Hudson Furniture (Northwood), plate, amethyst 1,000.00
Elegance, bowl, marigold, rare, 8¼" 2,800.00
Elks (Fenton), bell, bl, 1914 Parkersburg 2,300.00
Elks (Fenton), bowl, Detroit; amethyst, scarce 900.00
Embroidered Mums (Northwood), plate, gr 695.00
Enameled Grape (Northwood), pitcher, bl 400.00
English Hob & Button (English), bowl, marigold, 7" 60.00
English Hob & Button (English), epergne, marigold, metal mts .145.00
Engraved Grapes (Fenton), tumbler, marigold 30.00
Estate (Westmoreland), mug, marigold, rare 75.00
Estate Stippled (Westmoreland), vase, pastel colors, 3" 200.00
Fancy Flowers (Imperial), compote, gr 175.00

Fans (English), tumbler, marigold 150.00
Fantail (Fenton), bowl, bl, ftd, 5" 220.00
Farmyard (Dugan), bowl, gr, rare, 10" 8,500.00
Fashion (Imperial), bowl, fruit; marigold, w/base 70.00
Fashion (Imperial), bowl, rose; marigold, rare 450.00
Fashion (Imperial), bowl, gr, 9" 90.00
Feather Stitch (Fenton), bowl, bl, 10" 80.00
Feather Swirl (US Glass), vase, marigold 65.00
Feathered Serpent (Fenton), bowl, bl, 5" 42.00
Feathered Serpent (Fenton), bowl, gr, 10" 70.00
Fentonia, bowl, gr, ftd, 9½" 75.00
Fentonia, tumbler, bl 75.00
Fentonia Fruit (Fenton), vase whimsey, bl, rare 160.00
Fern (Northwood), compote, bl 100.00
Fern Panels (Fenton), hat, bl 50.00
Field Flower (Imperial), pitcher, gr, scarce 365.00
Field Flower (Imperial), pitcher, milk; amethyst, rare 200.00
Field Thistle (US Glass), plate, marigold, rare, 6" 350.00
Field Thistle (US Glass), spooner, marigold, rare 80.00
Field Thistle (US Glass), tumbler, marigold, scarce 45.00
File (Imperial & English), pitcher, amethyst, rare 445.00
Fine Block (Imperial), shade, gr 45.00
Fine Cut & Roses, (Northwood), rose bowl, gr, ftd 200.00
Fine Cut Flowers & VT (Fenton), compote, gr 75.00
Fine Rib (Northwood, Fenton & Dugan), bowl, gr, 9" 75.00
Fine Rib (Northwood, Fenton & Dugan), plate, amethyst, 9" 90.00
Fishscale & Beads (Dugan), bowl, amethyst, 6" 45.00
Fishscale & Beads (Dugan), plate, amethyst, 7" 200.00
Five-Lily Epergne, amethyst, metal mts, complete 250.00
Fleur-De-Lis (Czechoslovakia), bowl, gr, flat, 8½" 300.00
Fleur-De-Lis (Czechoslovakia), bowl, marigold, ftd, 8" 260.00
Floral & Grape (Dugan), pitcher, marigold 145.00
Floral & Grape (Fenton), pitcher, amethyst, 2 variations, ea ...285.00
Floral & Scroll, shade, various shapes, ea 45.00
Floral & Wheat (Dugan), compote, bl 45.00
Floral Oval (Higbee), bowl, marigold, 8" 50.00
Flower & Beads, plate, amethyst, 6-sided, 7½" 115.00
Flowering Dill (Fenton), hat, bl 40.00
Flowers & Frames (Dugan), bowl, marigold, 10" 70.00
Flowers & Spades (Dugan), bowl, peach opal, 5" 80.00
Flute (Millersburg), bowl, marigold, 10" 65.00
Flute (Millersburg), vase, gr, rare 425.00
Flute (Northwood), creamer or sugar bowl, gr, ea 95.00
Flute (Northwood), tumbler, marigold, 3 variations, ea 50.00
Flute #3 (Imperial), cruet, marigold 90.00
Flute #3 (Imperial), spooner, marigold 90.00
Flying Bat, hatpin, scarce 195.00
Folding Fan (Dugan), compote, aqua opal 295.00
Footed Prism Panels (English), vase, bl 100.00
Footed Shell (Westmoreland), marigold, 5" 40.00
Forget-Me-Not (Fenton), tumbler, marigold 30.00
Formal #600 (Dugan), vase, jack-in-pulpit; pastel colors, rare ...150.00
Fountain, lamp, marigold, complete, scarce 290.00
Four Flowers, bowl, gr, 6¼" 50.00
Four Flowers VT, bowl, gr, 9" 70.00
Four Flowers VT, bowl, peach opal, metal base, rare 300.00
Four Pillars (Northwood & Dugan), vase, aqua opal 175.00
French Knots (Fenton), hat, amethyst 50.00
Frosted Block (Imperial), bowl, marigold, 7½" 30.00
Frosted Block (Imperial), pickle dish, marigold, hdld, rare 60.00
Frosty, bottle, marigold 30.00
Fruit & Berries (English), bean pot, bl, w/lid, rare 425.00
Fruit & Flowers (Northwood), bonbon, bl, stemmed 275.00
Fruit Lustre, tumbler, marigold 40.00

Fruit and Flowers (Northwood), plate, amethyst, 9½", $225.00.

Fruit Salad (Westmoreland), cup, amethyst, rare 40.00
Garden Mums (Northwood), bowl, bl, 10" 85.00
Garden Path (Dugan), bowl, fruit; amethyst, 10" 115.00
Garden Path VT (Dugan), bowl, fruit; amethyst, 9" 375.00
Garland (Fenton), rose bowl, marigold, ftd 55.00
Georgia Bell (Dugan), compote, amethyst, ftd 75.00
Gervutz Brothers, (Northwood), bowl, amethyst 750.00
God & Home (Dugan), pitcher, bl, rare 2,000.00
Golden Cupids (Crystal), bowl, pastel colors, rare, 5" 225.00
Golden Grapes (Dugan), bowl, amethyst, 7" 45.00
Golden Harvest (US Glass), wine, marigold 25.00
Golden Honeycomb (Imperial), plate, 7" 55.00
Good Luck (Northwood), bowl, gr, 8¼" 475.00
Good Luck VT (Northwood), bowl, marigold, rare, 8¼" 300.00
Gooseberry Spray, bowl, gr, 5" 125.00
Graceful (Northwood), vase, gr 120.00
Grape, Heavy (Dugan), bowl, amethyst, rare, 5" 185.00
Grape, Heavy (Imperial); cup, custard; gr 35.00
Grape (Fenton's Grape & Cable), orange bowl, marigold, ftd ...110.00
Grape (Imperial), bowl, amethyst, 10" 80.00
Grape (Imperial), nappy, gr 40.00
Grape (Imperial), pitcher, milk; gr 300.00
Grape (Imperial), plate, marigold, 12" 90.00
Grape (Imperial), tumbler, gr 30.00
Grape (Imperial), wine, amethyst 40.00
Grape (Northwood's Grape & Cable), bonbon, marigold 65.00
Grape (Northwood's Grape & Cable), bottle, scent; gr, w/top ...220.00
Grape (Northwood's Grape & Cable), bowl, punch; bl w/base, sm .850.00
Grape (Northwood's Grape & Cable), candle lamp, gr, complete ..500.00
Grape (Northwood's Grape & Cable), cup, amethyst 27.00
Grape (Northwood's Grape & Cable), orange bowl, amethyst, ftd ..250.00
Grape (Northwood's Grape & Cable), pitcher, gr, standard 300.00
Grape (Northwood's Grape & Cable), plate, bl, ftd 135.00
Grape (Northwood's Grape & Cable), sherbet, ice cream; gr 60.00
Grape & Cherry (English), bowl, bl, rare, 8½" 180.00
Grape & Gothic Arches (Northwood), bowl, amethyst, 5" 40.00
Grape & Gothic Arches (Northwood), butter dish, bl 125.00
Grape & Gothic Arches (Northwood), tumbler, gr 70.00
Grape Arbor (Northwood), pitcher, amethyst 650.00
Grape Delight (Dugan), rose bowl, amethyst, ftd, 6" 80.00
Grape Leaves (Northwood), bowl, gr, 8¼" 85.00
Grape Wreath (Millersburg), bowl, ice cream; marigold, 10" ...120.00
Grapevine Lattice (Dugan), plate, marigold, 9" 75.00
Grapevine Lattice (Fenton), tumbler, marigold, rare 55.00
Greek Key (Northwood), bowl, gr, 7" 150.00
Greek Key (Northwood), tumbler, gr, rare 210.00
Handled Vase (Imperial), tumbler, marigold 105.00
Hattie (Imperial), bowl, marigold 47.00
Hattie (Imperial), plate, gr, rare 500.00
Headdress, bowl, bl, 2 variations, 9", ea 52.00

Heart & Horseshoe (Fenton), bowl, marigold, 8½" 900.00
Heart & Vine (Fenton), bowl, marigold, 8½" 80.00
Heart & Vine (Fenton), plate, amethyst, rare, 9" 475.00
Heart Band Souvenir (McKee), mug, gr, sm 100.00
Heavy Diamond (Imperial), vase, gr 65.00
Heavy Hobnail (Fenton), vase, amethyst, rare 550.00
Heavy Prisms (English), vase, celery; bl, 6" 95.00
Heavy Shell (Fenton), candle holder, pastel colors, ea 100.00
Heavy Web (Dugan), bowl, peach opal, 10" 1,300.00
Heisey #357, tumbler, marigold 65.00
Heisey Flute, cup, punch; marigold 35.00
Hex Base, candlesticks, amethyst, pr 125.00
Hickman, caster set, marigold, 4-pc 250.00
Hobnail (Millersburg), creamer or spooner, gr, rare, ea 450.00
Hobnail (Millersburg), tumbler, amethyst, rare 500.00
Hobnail VT (Millersburg), jardiniere, amethyst, rare 950.00
Hobstar (Imperial), bowl, berry; pastel colors, 10" 50.00
Hobstar (Imperial), bowl, fruit; amethyst, w/base 85.00
Hobstar (Imperial), creamer or spooner, gr, ea 75.00
Hobstar & Arches (Imperial), bowl, fruit; gr, w/base 75.00
Hobstar & Cut Triangles (English), bowl, gr 60.00
Hobstar & Feather (Millersburg), bowl, amethyst, rnd, 5" 450.00
Hobstar & Feather (Millersburg), butter dish, rare 1,800.00
Hobstar & Feather (Millersburg), creamer, gr, rare 800.00
Hobstar & Feather (Millersburg), cup, punch; marigold, scarce 30.00
Hobstar & Waffle Block (Imperial), basket, marigold 150.00
Hobstar Band (Imperial), bowl, marigold, rare 90.00
Hobstar Flower (Northwood), compote, bl, scarce 80.00
Hobstar Panels (English), creamer, marigold 45.00
Hobstar Reversed (English), butter dish, bl 70.00
Hobstar Whirl (Whirligig), compote, bl, 4½" 60.00
Holly (Fenton), bowl, marigold, 10" 75.00
Holly (Fenton), bowl, rose; bl 500.00
Holly Berry (Dugan), gravy boat, bl, hdl 140.00
Holly Panelled (Northwood), bonbon, gr, ftd 75.00

Holly Sprig (Whirl), bowl, amethyst, ruffled, 10", $58.00.

Holly Sprig (Whirl), bowl, gr, ruffled, 10" 60.00
Holly Sprig (Whirl), bowl, sauce; amethyst, deep, rare 275.00
Holm Spray, atomizer, marigold, 3" 65.00
Honeycomb & Clover (Fenton), bonbon, marigold 40.00
Horseshoe, shot glass, marigold 50.00
Hot Springs Souvenir, vase, marigold, 9⅞" 115.00
Hourglass, vase, bud; marigold 50.00
Idyll (Fenton), vase, amethyst, rare 750.00
Illusion (Fenton), bonbon, marigold 55.00
Illusion (Fenton), bowl, bl 90.00
Imperial Daisy (Imperial), shade, marigold 45.00
Imperial Grape (Imperial), shade, marigold 85.00
Inca, vase, marigold, rare, 7" 900.00

Intaglio Feathers, cup, marigold 25.00
Intaglio Stars, tumbler, marigold 600.00
Interior Poinsettia (Northwood), tumbler, marigold, rare 485.00
Interior Rays (Westmoreland), butter dish, marigold, w/lid 65.00
Interior Swirl, spittoon, peach opal 95.00
Inverted Coin Drop (Northwood-Fenton), pitcher, marigold 325.00
Inverted Coin Drop (Northwood-Fenton), rose bowl, gr 60.00
Inverted Feather (Cambridge), cracker jar, amethyst, w/lid 1,000.00
Inverted Feather (Cambridge), tumbler, marigold, rare 500.00
Inverted Strawberry, bowl, marigold, 10½" 100.00
Inverted Strawberry, butter dish, amethyst, w/lid 750.00
Inverted Strawberry, compote, bl, sm, rare 350.00
Inverted Strawberry, tumbler, amethyst, rare 250.00
Inverted Thistle (Cambridge), bowl, gr, rare, 9" 350.00
Inverted Thistle (Cambridge), pitcher, amethyst, rare 3,500.00
Iris, Heavy (Dugan); tumbler, amethyst 80.00
Iris (Fenton), compote, marigold 50.00
Isaac Benesch, bowl, amethyst, advertising, 6½" 350.00
Jack-in-the-Pulpit (Dugan), vase, bl 80.00
Jester's Cap (Westmoreland), vase, gr 55.00
Jewel Box, inkwell, marigold 150.00
Jeweled Heart (Dugan), bowl, amethyst, 10" 95.00
Jeweled Heart (Dugan), tumbler, marigold, rare 100.00
Jewels (Imperial- Dugan), bowl, amethyst, various szs, ea 50.00
Jockey Club (Northwood), bowl, amethyst, 7" 600.00
Kangaroo (Australian), bowl, marigold, 9" 175.00
Kingfisher & Vt (Australian), bowl, marigold, 5" 50.00
Kittens (Fenton), cup & saucer, bl, scarce 650.00
Kittens (Fenton), spooner, bl, rare, 2½" 275.00
Knotted Beads (Fenton), vase, bl, 4" 40.00
Kookaburra & VTS (Australian), bowl, marigold, 5" 75.00
Lacy Dewdrop (Westmoreland), compote, pastel colors, w/lid ...350.00
Lacy Dewdrop (Westmoreland), creamer, pastel colors 160.00
Large Kangaroo (Australian), bowl, marigold, 5" 60.00
Late Enameled Strawberry, tumbler, marigold, tall 175.00
Lattice & Daisy (Dugan), bowl, marigold, 9" 60.00
Lattice & Daisy (Dugan), tumbler, pastel colors 60.00
Lattice & Points (Dugan), vase, marigold 40.00
Lattice Heart (English), bowl, amethyst, 10" 75.00
Laurel, shade, pastel colors 50.00
Laurel Leaves (Imperial), plate, amethyst 55.00
Leaf & Beads (Northwood-Dugan), bowl, gr, 9" 700.00
Leaf & Beads (Northwood-Dugan), bowl, rose; marigold, ftd 90.00
Leaf & Little Flowers (Millersburg), compote, marigold, mini 450.00
Leaf Chain (Fenton), plate, gr, 9¼" 175.00
Leaf Swirl & Flower (Fenton), vase, marigold 55.00
Leaf Tiers (Fenton), bowl, marigold, ftd, 5" 30.00
Leaf Tiers (Fenton), tumbler, gr, ftd, rare 90.00
Lined Lattice (Dugan), vase, peach opal, 14" 160.00
Little Beads (Imperial), bowl, peach opal, 8" 45.00
Little Fishes (Fenton), bowl, bl, flat or ftd, 5½", ea 185.00
Little Flowers (Fenton), bowl, amethyst, rare, 5½" 80.00
Little Owl, hatpin, marigold 450.00
Little Stars (Millersburg), bowl, marigold, 7" 100.00
Loganberry (Imperial), vase, gr 395.00
Long Hobstar, bowl, marigold, 10½" 60.00
Long Leaf (Dugan), bowl, peach opal, ftd 165.00
Long Thumbprint (Dugan), compote, marigold 35.00
Long Thumbprint (Dugan), creamer or sugar bowl, smoke, ea 50.00
Lotus & Grape (Fenton), bonbon, gr 70.00
Louisa (Westmoreland), candy dish, gr, ftd 65.00
Louisa (Westmoreland), rose bowl, marigold 55.00
Lucille, tumbler, bl, rare 800.00
Lucky Bell, bowl, marigold, 8¾" 80.00

Lustre & Clear (Fenton), vase, fan; marigold 40.00
Lustre & Clear (Imperial), bowl, pastel colors, 10" 50.00
Lustre & Clear (Imperial), creamer or sugar bowl, amethyst, ea ...65.00
Lustre & Clear (Lightolier), shade, marigold 45.00
Lustre Flute (Northwood), bowl, gr, 8" 54.00
Lustre Rose (Imperial), bowl, amethyst, flat, 11" 45.00
Lustre Rose (Imperial), bowl, berry; gr, 9" 48.00
Lustre Rose (Imperial), bowl, sugar; marigold 40.00
Lustre Rose (Imperial), fernery, bl 45.00
Lustre Rose (Imperial), tumbler, gr 40.00
Magnolia Drape (McKee), pitcher, marigold 275.00
Malaga (Dugan), bowl, marigold, 9" 60.00
Many Fruits (Dugan), cup, bl 45.00
Many Stars (Millersburg), bowl, vaseline, ruffled, 9" 1,850.00
Maple Leaf (Dugan), bowl, gr, stemmed, 4½" 50.00
Maple Leaf (Dugan), creamer or spooner, marigold, ea 50.00
Maple Leaf (Dugan), tumbler, marigold 30.00

Marilyn (Millersburg), pitcher, amethyst, rare, $975.00.

Marilyn (Millersburg), tumbler, marigold 150.00
Mary Ann (Dugan), vase, amethyst, 2 variations, 7", ea 135.00
Mayan (Millersburg), bowl, gr, 10" 200.00
Mayflower, bowl, marigold, 7½" 30.00
Mayflower, hat, amethyst 50.00
Maypole, vase, gr, 6¼" 60.00
Memphis (Northwood), bowl, amethyst, 5" 45.00
Memphis (Northwood), cup, marigold 30.00
Mikado (Fenton), compote, bl, lg 700.00
Milady (Fenton), tumbler, gr 150.00
Miniature Intaglio (Westmoreland), cup, nut; wht, stemmed 700.00
Mirrored Lotus (Fenton), bonbon, bl 95.00
Mirrored Lotus (Fenton), plate, marigold, 7½" 400.00
Mirrored Peacocks, tumbler, marigold 400.00
Mittered Diamonds & Pleats (English), bowl, bl, shallow, 8½" 45.00
Moonprint (English), butter dish, marigold 100.00
Moonprint (English), candlestick, marigold 50.00
Moonprint (English), jar, bl, w/lid 85.00
Morning Glory (Imperial), vase, gr, 8" 80.00
Moxie, bottle, pastel colors 90.00
Multi-Fruits & Flowers (Millersburg), cup, marigold 50.00
My Lady, powder jar, marigold, w/lid 90.00
Napoleon, bottle, pastel colors 85.00
Nautilus (Dugan-Northwood), compote, marigold, giant sz 3,000.00
Nell (Higbee), mug, marigold 75.00
Nesting Swan (Millersburg), bowl, marigold, tricornered 500.00
Nesting Swan (Millersburg), ruffled, 10" 500.00
Night Stars (Millersburg), bonbon, gr 400.00
Nippon (Northwood), bowl, amethyst, 8½" 220.00
Northern Star (Fenton), tray, card; marigold, 6" 40.00
Northwood Jack-in-the-Pulpit, vase, amethyst, various szs, ea 50.00
Northwood's Poppy, pickle dish, gr, oval 235.00

Nu-Art (Imperial), plate, marigold 3,800.00
Number 2351 (Cambridge), cup, punch; amethyst 65.00
Number 270 (Westmoreland), compote, amethyst 90.00
Number 600 (Fostoria), toothpick holder, marigold 45.00
Octagon (Imperial), bowl, pastel colors, 8½" 80.00
Octagon (Imperial), butter dish, marigold 90.00
Octagon (Imperial), creamer or spooner, gr, ea 65.00
Octagon (Imperial), vase, gr 125.00
Octet (Northwood), bowl, marigold, 8½" 60.00
Oklahoma (Mexican), tumbler, marigold 500.00
Open Rose (Imperial), bowl, fruit; pastel colors, 7" 70.00
Optic & Buttons (Imperial), bowl, marigold, 5" 30.00
Optic & Buttons (Imperial), goblet, marigold 60.00
Optic Flute (Imperial), bowl, amethyst, 5" 45.00
Orange Peel (Westmoreland), cup, marigold 20.00
Orange Tree (Fenton), bowl, ice cream; bl, w/stem, sm 35.00
Orange Tree (Fenton), butter dish, marigold 250.00
Orange Tree (Fenton), cup, gr 36.00
Orange Tree (Fenton), mug, marigold, 2 szs, ea 70.00
Orange Tree (Fenton), rose bowl, amethyst 65.00
Orange Tree (Fenton), sugar bowl, bl 75.00
Orange Tree & Scroll (Fenton), pitcher, marigold 495.00
Orange Tree Orchid (Fenton), pitcher, gr 550.00
Ostrich (Australian), compote, marigold, lg 200.00
Oval & Round (Imperial), bowl, amethyst, 9" 45.00
Oval & Round (Imperial), plate, marigold, 10" 65.00
Oval Star & Fan (Jenkins), rose bowl, amethyst 60.00
Pacifica (US Glass), tumbler, marigold 400.00
Palm Beach (US Glass), bowl, pastel colors, 5" 50.00
Palm Beach (US Glass), plate, pastel colors, 9" 225.00
Palm Beach (US Glass), rose bowl whimsey, marigold 90.00
Palm Beach (US Glass), vase whimsey, amethyst 125.00
Panelled Dandelion (Fenton), tumbler, marigold 50.00
Panelled Diamond & Bows (Fenton), vase, gr, 14" 40.00
Panelled Hobnail (Dugan), vase, marigold, 10" 40.00
Panelled Tree Trunk (Dugan), vase, peach opal, 12" 150.00
Pansy (Imperial), bowl, amethyst, 8¾" 95.00
Pansy (Imperial), plate, gr, ruffled 120.00
Panther (Fenton), bowl, marigold, ftd, 5" 55.00
Parlor Panels, vase, amethyst, 11" 190.00
Pastel Panels (Imperial), tumbler, pastel colors 75.00
Peach (Imperial), tumbler, wht 100.00
Peach (Northwood), creamer, sugar bowl or spooner, marigold, ea .275.00
Peacock, Fluffy (Fenton); pitcher, amethyst 600.00
Peacock, lamp, gr carnival base 495.00
Peacock (Millersburg), bowl, gr, 5" 240.00
Peacock (Millersburg), bowl, ice cream; bl, 5" 390.00
Peacock & Dahlia (Fenton), bowl, marigold, 7½" 50.00
Peacock & Grape (Fenton), bowl, marigold, 7¾" 50.00
Peacock & Urn (Fenton), compote, marigold 55.00
Peacock & Urn (Fenton), goblet, marigold, rare 70.00
Peacock & Urns VTS (Millersburg), bowl, gr, ruffled, 6" 210.00
Peacock at the Fountain (Dugan), tumbler, amethyst 90.00
Peacock at the Fountain (Northwood), bowl, marigold, 5" 45.00
Peacock at the Fountain (Northwood), sugar bowl, bl 250.00
Peacock at the Fountain (Northwood), tumbler, bl 80.00
Peacock Tail (Fenton), bonbon, amethyst 75.00
Peacock Tail (Fenton), plate, marigold, 6" 70.00
Peacock Tail VT (Millersburg), compote, amethyst 120.00
Pearl & Jewels (Fenton), basket, wht, 4" 200.00
Pebble & Fan (English), vase, bl, 11¼" 750.00
Perfection (Millersburg), tumbler, marigold 600.00
Persian Garden (Dugan), bowl, berry; amethyst, 5" 60.00
Persian Garden (Dugan), bowl, ice cream; marigold, 6" 140.00

Persian Garden (Dugan), bowl fruit; amethyst, w/base 420.00
Persian Medallion (Fenton), bowl, bl, 10" 550.00
Persian Medallion (Fenton), bowl, punch; gr, w/base 500.00
Persian Medallion (Fenton), plate, amethyst, 9½" 450.00
Petal & Fan (Dugan), bowl, gr, 5" 50.00
Petals (Dugan), compote, marigold 50.00
Pigeon, paperweight, marigold 120.00
Pillar & Flute (Imperial), celery vase, amethyst 90.00
Pillar & Sunburst (Westmoreland), bowl, peach opal, 9" 70.00
Pin-Ups (Australian), bowl, marigold, 8¾" 110.00
Pine Cone (Fenton), bowl, amethyst, 6" 250.00
Pineapple (English), bowl, bl, 7" 70.00
Pineapple (English), compote, bl 60.00
Pineapple (English), creamer, marigold 70.00
Pinwheel (Dugan), bowl, peach opal, 6" 85.00
Pinwheel (English), vase, marigold, 6½" 100.00
Plaid (Fenton), bowl, bl, 8¾" 200.00
Plain Jane (Imperial), basket, smoke 60.00
Plain Petals (Northwood), nappy, gr 90.00
Pleats & Hearts, shade, pastel colors 90.00
Plume Panels, vase, marigold, 7" 50.00
Poinsettia (Imperial), pitcher, milk; gr 275.00
Poinsettia (Northwood), bowl, marigold, flat ot ftd, 8½" 400.00
Pond Lily (Fenton), bonbon, gr 65.00
Poodle, powder jar, marigold, w/lid 30.00
Poppy (Millersburg), compote, gr 500.00
Poppy Show (Imperial), vase, gr, 12" 950.00
Poppy Show (Northwood), bowl, marigold, 8½" 750.00
Portland (US Glass), bowl, pastel colors, 9½" 170.00
Premium (Imperial), candlesticks, amethyst, pr 90.00
Pretty Panels (Northwood), tumbler, marigold 60.00
Primrose (Millersburg), bowl, amethyst, ruffled, 8¾" 185.00
Primrose & Fishnet (Imperial), vase, red, 6" 750.00
Primrose Ribbon, light shade, marigold 90.00
Prism, tray, marigold, 3" 50.00
Prism & Cane (English), bowl, amethyst, 5" 65.00
Prism & Daisy Band (English), bowl, marigold, 8" 32.00
Prism & Daisy Band (Imperial), vase, marigold 30.00
Prism Band (Fenton), pitcher, amethyst w/decor 350.00
Prisms (Westmoreland), compote, gr, 5" 100.00
Pulled Loop (Dugan), vase, gr 50.00
Puzzle (Dugan), compote, amethyst 50.00
Question Marks (Dugan), bonbon, amethyst 55.00
Question Marks (Dugan), compote, peach opal 75.00
Ragged Robin (Fenton), bowl, marigold, 8¾" 75.00
Rambler Rose (Dugan), pitcher, gr 275.00
Ranger (Mexican), pitcher, milk; marigold 175.00
Raspberry (Northwood), bowl, amethyst, 9" 70.00
Raspberry (Northwood), sauce boat, gr, ftd 275.00
Raspberry (Northwood), tumbler, amethyst 45.00
Rays & Ribbons (Millersburg), bowl, amethyst, 8½" 90.00
Rays & Ribbons (Millersburg), bowl, marigold, sq 115.00
Regal Swirl, candlestick, marigold 75.00
Rib & Panel (Fenton), vase, amethyst 60.00
Ribbed Holly (Fenton), compote, bl 60.00
Ribbed Swirl, tumbler, gr 80.00
Ribbon Tie (Fenton), bowl, gr, 8¼" or 8¾", ea 75.00
Ribs (Czechoslovakia), dresser tray, marigold 110.00
Ribs (Czechoslovakia), ring tree, marigold 60.00
Ripple (Imperial), vase, amethyst, various szs, ea 150.00
Robin (Imperial), mug, pastel colors, old only 55.00
Rococo (Imperial), bowl, gr, 5" 150.00
Roll, tumbler, marigold 40.00
Rosalind (Millersburg), bowl, amethyst, 10" 260.00

Rose Bouquet, creamer, marigold 60.00
Rose Column (Millersburg), vase, gr 1,200.00
Rose Garden, bowl, amethyst, 6" 90.00
Rose Garden (Sweden), bowl, marigold, 8¾" 80.00
Rose Show VT (Northwood), bowl, marigold, 8¾" 500.00
Rose Spray (Fenton), compote, marigold 175.00
Rosetime, vase, marigold 100.00
Rosettes (Northwood), bowl, amethyst, ftd, 7" 80.00
Round-Up (Dugan), bowl, wht, 8¾" 180.00
Royalty (Imperial), cup, marigold 30.00
Ruffled Rib (Northwood), vase, marigold, 14" 75.00
Rustic (Fenton), vase, funeral; amethyst, 20" 150.00
S-Band (Australian), compote, marigold 70.00
S-Repeat (Dugan), cup, amethyst 120.00
Sailboats (Fenton), compote, marigold 150.00
Sailboats (Fenton), goblet, bl 70.00
Saint (English), candlestick, marigold, ea 300.00
Salamanders, hatpin, amethyst 75.00
Sawtooth Prisms, jelly jar, marigold 60.00
Scale Band (Fenton), bowl, peach opal, 6" 80.00
Scales (Westmoreland), bonbon, aqua opal 300.00
Scales (Westmoreland), plate, peach opal, 9" 110.00
Scotch Thistle (Fenton), compote, gr 75.00
Scroll (Westmoreland), pin tray, marigold 50.00
Scroll & Feather Panels (Imperial), vase, amethyst, 10" 250.00
Scroll Embossed (Imperial), bowl, amethyst, 8½" 65.00
Scroll Embossed (Imperial), compote, gr, sm 60.00
Scroll Embossed VT (English), ashtray, marigold, hdld, 5" 45.00
Sea Gulls (Dugan), bowl, marigold, 6½" 80.00
Seacoast (Millersburg), pin tray, marigold 425.00
Seaweed (Millersburg), bowl, marigold, 6½" 80.00
Seaweed (Millersburg), bowl, marigold, 9" 275.00
Shell (Imperial), bowl, amethyst, 9" 250.00
Shell & Jewel (Westmoreland), creamer, marigold, w/lid 55.00
Shell & Jewel (Westmoreland), sugar bowl, gr, w/lid 60.00
Sheraton (US Glass), creamer or spooner, pastel colors 75.00
Shrine (US Glass), toothpick holder, amethyst 650.00
Singing Birds (Northwood), bowl, amethyst, 10" 75.00
Singing Birds (Northwood), sugar bowl, gr 150.00
Single Flower (Dugan), bowl, gr, 8" 45.00
Single Flower Framed (Dugan), bowl, amethyst, 8¾" 70.00
Six-Sided (Imperial), candlestick, gr, ea 250.00
Ski-Star (Dugan), bowl, banana; peach opal 290.00
Ski-Star (Dugan), bowl, bl, 10" 175.00
Small Blackberry (Northwood), compote, gr 60.00
Small Rib (Dugan), compote, amethyst 45.00
Smooth Panels (Imperial), bowl, marigold, 6½" 30.00
Smooth Panels (Imperial), pitcher, gr 175.00
Smooth Rays (Northwood-Dugan), bowl, amethyst, 9" 80.00
Smooth Rays (Northwood-Dugan), compote, amethyst 50.00
Soda Gold (Imperial), candlestick, marigold, 3½", ea 55.00
Soda Gold Spears (Dugan), bowl, marigold, 4½" 30.00
Soutache (Dugan), bowl, peach opal, 10" 200.00
Souvenir (US Glass), vase, peach opal, 6½" 150.00
Souvenir Banded, mug, marigold 85.00
Sowerby Wide Panel (Sowerby), bowl, marigold 45.00
Spiderweb (Northwood), candy dish, smoke, w/lid 40.00
Spiral (Imperial), candlesticks, amethyst, pr 185.00
Spiralled Diamond Point, vase, marigold, 6" 90.00
Spokes (Fostoria), bowl, pastel colors, 10" 100.00
Spring Basket (Imperial), basket, marigold, hdld, 5" 50.00
Springtime (Northwood), bowl, amethyst, 5" 55.00
Springtime (Northwood), tumbler, gr 200.00
Sq Daisy & Button (Imperial), toothpick holder, pastel colors 125.00

Stag & Holly (Fenton), bowl, gr, ftd, 13"	400.00
Stag & Holly (Fenton), plate, marigold, ftd, 9"	700.00
Star & Fan, vase, marigold, 9½"	250.00
Star & File (Imperial), bonbon, marigold	35.00
Star & File (Imperial), bowl, marigold, 9½"	35.00
Star & File (Imperial), bowl, rose; gr	115.00
Star Center (Imperial), bowl, amethyst, 8½"	40.00
Star Medallion (Imperial), bowl, marigold, 9"	30.00
Star Medallion (Imperial), cup, custard; pastel colors	45.00
Star Medallion (Imperial), pitcher, milk; marigold	80.00
Star Medallion (Imperial), plate, marigold, 5"	60.00
Star Medallion (Imperial), tumbler, gr	50.00
Star of David & Bows (Northwood), bowl, gr, 8½"	75.00
Star Spray (Imperial), bowl, marigold, 7"	35.00
Starbright, vase, amethyst, 6½"	45.00
Starfish (Dugan), compote, gr	75.00
Stark & Rushes (Dugan), cup, bl	35.00
Stars & Stripes (Old Glory), plate, marigold, 7½"	150.00
Stippled Diamond Swag (English), compote, gr	65.00
Stippled Petals (Dugan), basket, amethyst, hdld	150.00
Stippled Petals (Dugan), bowl, peach opal, 9"	90.00
Stippled Rays (Fenton), plate, marigold, 7"	50.00
Stippled Rays (Imperial), creamer, gr, stemmed	50.00
Stippled Rays (Northwood), bowl, marigold, 10"	45.00
Stippled Strawberry (Jenkins), butter dish	85.00
Stork & Rushes (Dugan), creamer or spooner, amethyst	90.00
Strawberry (Fenton), bonbon, bl	60.00
Strawberry (Millersburg), bowl, gr, 6½"	140.00
Strawberry (Millersburg), bowl, marigold, tricornered, 9½"	390.00
Strawberry (Northwood), plate, amethyst, 9"	450.00
Strawberry Scroll (Fenton), tumbler, bl	250.00
Stream of Hearts (Fenton), compote, marigold	95.00
Stretched Diamond (Northwood), tumbler, marigold	175.00
Studs (Imperial), tumbler, juice; marigold	40.00
Style, bowl, amethyst, 8"	95.00
Sunflower (Millersburg), pin tray, gr	350.00
Sunflower (Northwood), bowl, amethyst, 8½"	70.00
Sunflower & Diamond, vase, bl, 2 szs, ea	110.00
Sunk Diamond Band (US Glass), pitcher, marigold	150.00
Sunken Daisy (English), sugar bowl, bl	40.00
Sweetheart (Cambridge), tumbler, marigold	650.00
Swirl (Imperial), mug, marigold	90.00
Swirl (Northwood), pitcher, gr	800.00
Swirl Hobnail (Millersburg), spittoon, amethyst	750.00
Swirl VT (Imperial), pitcher, marigold, 7½"	100.00
Swirl VT (Imperial), vase, gr, 6½"	45.00
Swirled Flute (Imperial), vase, marigold, 12"	50.00
Swirled Ribs (Northwood), tumbler, amethyst	75.00
Swirled Threads, goblet, marigold	95.00
Taffeta Lustre, perfume bottle, marigold, w/stopper	90.00
Taffeta Lustre (Fostoria), bowl, console; gr, 11"	150.00
Target (Fenton), vase, gr, 11"	60.00
Ten Mums (Fenton), bowl, marigold, 11"	95.00
Thin Rib & Drape (Fenton), vase, amethyst, 14"	50.00
Thin Rib & VTS (Northwood), vase, gr, 11"	50.00
Thistle (Fenton), compote, bl	70.00
Thistle & Thorn (English), bowl, marigold, ftd, 6"	50.00
Thistle & Thorn (English), bowl, nut; marigold	75.00
Three Diamonds (Dugan), vase, amethyst, 10"	50.00
Three Fruits (Northwood), bonbon, gr, stemmed	80.00
Three Fruits (Northwood), bowl, marigold, 9"	45.00
Three Fruits Medallion (Northwood), bowl, gr, ftd, 10½"	240.00
Three-In-One (Imperial), bowl, marigold, 8¾"	30.00
Three-In-One (Imperial), rose bowl, marigold	200.00

Thumbprint & Spears, creamer, gr	60.00
Tiered Thumbprint, candlesticks, marigold, pr	120.00
Tiger Lily (Imperial), tumbler, amethyst	60.00
Tiny Hobnail, lamp, marigold	110.00
Top Hat, vase, pastel colors	50.00
Tornado (Northwood), vase, gr, plain	500.00
Toy Punch Set (Cambridge), bowl, marigold, ftd	60.00
Tracery (Millersburg), bonbon, gr	650.00
Tree Bark (Imperial), bowl, marigold, 7½"	20.00
Tree Bark VT, pitcher, marigold	60.00
Tree of Life (Imperial), basket, marigold, hdld	30.00
Tree Trunk (Northwood), vase, gr, 12"	95.00
Triad, hatpin, amethyst	55.00
Triands (English), celery vase, marigold	55.00
Triplets (Dugan), bowl, marigold, 8"	35.00
Tulip (Millersburg), compote, gr, 9"	800.00
Tulip & Cane (Imperial), goblet, marigold, 8-oz	45.00
Tulip & Cane (Imperial), wine, marigold, 2 szs, ea	85.00
Tulip Scroll (Millersburg), vase, gr, 12"	300.00
Twins (Imperial), bowl, gr, 9"	50.00
Twitch (Bartlett-Collins), cup, marigold	30.00
Two Flowers (Fenton), bowl, bl, ftd, 8"	50.00
Two Flowers (Fenton), plate, gr, ftd, 9"	675.00
Two Row (Imperial), vase, amethyst	1,100.00
Victorian, bowl, amethyst, 12"	500.00
Vineyard (Dugan), tumbler, marigold	25.00
Vining Leaf & VT (English), spittoon, marigold	350.00
Vining Twigs (Dugan), bowl, gr, 7½"	50.00
Vintage (Dugan), powder jar, marigold, w/lid	70.00
Vintage (Fenton), bowl, bl, 6½"	45.00
Vintage (Fenton), cup, bl	40.00
Vintage (Fenton), fernery, marigold, 2 variations, ea	55.00
Vintage (Millersburg), bowl, amethyst, 9"	900.00
Vintage Banded (Dugan), mug, smoke	45.00
Vintage Leaf (Fenton), bowl, amethyst, 5½"	35.00
Virginia Blackberry (US Glass), pitcher, bl, sm	250.00
Waffle Block (Imperial), bowl, punch; marigold	175.00
Waffle Block (Imperial), vase, marigold, 11"	40.00
Waffle Weave, inkwell, marigold	95.00
Water Lily (Fenton), bonbon, amethyst	50.00
Water Lily (Fenton), bowl, amethyst, 5"	50.00
Water Lily (Fenton), bowl, bl, ftd, 10"	250.00
Water Lily & Cattails (Fenton), bonbon, bl	90.00
Water Lily & Cattails (Northwood), tumbler, marigold	110.00
Water Lily & Dragonfly (Australian), bowl, amethyst, 10½"	185.00
Weeping Cherry (Dugan), bowl, amethyst, dome base	130.00
Whirling Leaves (Millersburg), bowl, gr, rnd or ruffled, 9", ea	450.00
Whirling Star (Imperial), bowl, punch; marigold, w/base	135.00
Wide Bouquet, basket, marigold, 3½"	75.00
Wide Panel (Northwood-Fenton-Imperial), bowl, amethyst, 9"	90.00
Wide Rib (Dugan), vase, marigold	55.00
Wild Blackberry (Fenton), bowl, gr, 8½"	110.00

Wild Strawberry (Dugan), bowl, marigold, 9", $85.00.

Wild Rose, syrup, marigold 700.00
Wild Rose (Northwood), bowl, marigold, flat, 8" 40.00
Wildflower (Northwood), compote, amethyst, plain interior 350.00
Windflower (Dugan), nappy, bl, hdls 185.00
Windmill (Imperial), bowl, fruit; gr, 10½" 40.00
474 (Imperial), bowl, gr, 9" 85.00
474 (Imperial), goblet, gr 65.00
474 (Imperial), spooner, marigold 65.00
474 VT (Sweden), compote, gr, 7" 90.00

Carousel Figures

For generations of Americans, visions of carousel horses revolving majestically around lively band organs rekindle wonderful childhood experiences. These nostalgic memories are the legacy of the creative talent from a dozen carving shops that created America's carousel art. Skilled craftsmen brought their trade from Europe where American carvers took the carousel animal from a folk art creation to a true art form. The 'Golden Age of Carousel Art' lasted from 1880 to 1929.

There are two basic types of American carousels. The largest and most impressive is the 'park style' carousel built for permanent installation in major amusement centers. These were created in Philadelphia by Gustav and William Dentzel, Muller Brothers, and E. Joy Morris who became the Philadelphia Toboggan Company in 1902. A more flamboyant group of carousel animals was carved in Coney Island, New York, by Charles Looff, Marcus Illions, Charles Carmel and Stein & Goldstein's Artistic Carousel Company. These park-style carousels were typically three, four and even five rows with forty-five to sixty-eight animals on a platform. Collectors often pay a premium for the carvings by these men. The outside row animals are larger and more ornate and command higher prices. The horses on the inside rows are smaller, less decorated and of lesser value.

The most popular style of carousel art is the 'country fair style.' These carousels were portable affairs created for mobility. The horses are smaller and less ornate with leg and head positions that allow for stacking and easy loading. These were built primarily for North Tonawanda, New York, near Niagara Falls, by Armitage Herschell Company, Herschell Spillman Company, Spillman Engineering Company and Allen Herschell. Charles W. Parker was also well known for his portable merry-go-rounds. He was based in Leavenworth, Kansas. Parker and Herschell Spillman both created a few large park-style carousels as well, but they are better known for their portable models.

Horses are by far the most common figure found, but there are two dozen other animals that were created for the carousel platform. Carousel animals, unlike most other antiques, are oftentimes worth more in a restored condition. Figures found with original factory paint are extraordinarily rare and bring premium amounts. Typically, carousel horses are found in garish, poorly applied 'park paint' and oftentimes are missing legs or ears. Carousel horses are hollow. They were glued up from several blocks for greater strength and lighter weight. Bass and poplar woods were used extensively.

If you have an antique carousel animal you would like to have identified, send a clear photograph and description along with a LSASE to our advisor, William Manns, who is listed in the Directory under New Mexico. Mr. Manns is the author of *Painted Ponies*, containing many full-color photographs, guides, charts, and directories for the collector. (Note: market values remain virtually unchanged since the last edition.)

Key:
IR — inside row   OR — outside row
MR — middle row   PTC — Philadelphia Toboggan
                                        Company

Coney Island Style

Carmel, IR jumper, unrstr 7,000.00
Carmel, MR jumper, unrstr 12,500.00
Carmel, OR jumper w/cherub, rstr 48,000.00

Illions inside row jumper, ca 1910, restored, $5,000.00 to $6,500.00.

Illions, MR stander, rstr 20,000.00
Illions, OR stander, eagle saddle, rstr 44,000.00
Looff, IR jumper, unrstr 6,000.00
Looff, OR jumper, unrstr 21,500.00
Stein & Goldstein, IR jumper, unrstr 4,500.00
Stein & Goldstein, MR jumper, rstr 17,000.00
Stein & Goldstein, OR stander w/bells, unrstr 35,000.00

European Horses

Anderson, English, unrstr 4,000.00
Bayol, French, unrstr 3,000.00
Heyn, German, unrstr 5,000.00
Hubner, Belgian, unrstr 3,800.00
Savage, English, unrstr 3,500.00

Menagerie Animals (Non-Horses)

Dentzel, bear, unrstr 28,000.00
Dentzel, cat, unrstr 35,000.00
Dentzel, lion, unrstr 55,000.00
Dentzel, pig, unrstr 9,000.00
Dentzel, rabbit, unrstr 40,000.00
E Joy Morris, deer, unrstr 14,500.00
Herschell Spillman, cat, unrstr 17,000.00
Herschell Spillman, chicken, portable, unrstr 7,500.00
Herschell Spillman, dog, portable, unrstr 9,000.00
Herschell Spillman, frog, unrstr 25,000.00
Looff, camel, unrstr 9,000.00
Looff, goat, rstr 18,500.00
Muller, tiger, rstr 30,000.00

Philadelphia Style

Dentzel, IR 'topknot' jumper, unrstr 6,000.00
Dentzel, MR jumper, unrstr 18,000.00
Dentzel, OR stander, rstr 45,000.00
Dentzel, prancer, rstr 9,500.00
Morris, IR prancer, rstr 8,000.00
Morris, MR stander, unrstr 9,500.00
Morris, OR stander, rstr 29,000.00
Muller, IR jumper, rstr 8,900.00
Muller, MR jumper, unrstr 12,500.00

Muller, OR stander, rstr	46,000.00
Muller, OR stander w/military trappings	85,000.00
PTC, chariot (bench-like seat), rstr	8,900.00
PTC, IR jumper, rstr	5,500.00
PTC, MR jumper, rstr	15,500.00
PTC, OR stander, armored, rstr	46,000.00
PTC, OR stander, unrstr	29,500.00

Portable

Allan Herschell, all aluminum, ca 1950	700.00
Allan Herschell, half & half, wood & aluminum head	1,500.00
Allan Herschell, IR Indian pony, unrstr	2,600.00
Allan Herschell, OR, rstr	3,200.00
Allan Herschell, OR Trojan-style jumper	4,700.00
Armitage Herschell, track machine jumper	3,500.00
Dare, jumper, unrstr	3,900.00
Herschell Spillman, chariot (bench-like seat)	3,500.00
Herschell Spillman, IR jumper, unrstr	3,000.00
Herschell Spillman, MR jumper, unrstr	3,200.00
Herschell Spillman, OR, eagle decor	6,000.00
Herschell Spillman, OR, park machine	12,000.00
Parker, MR jumper, unrstr	4,500.00
Parker, OR jumper, park machine, unrstr	14,000.00
Parker, OR jumper, rstr	9,500.00

Carpet Balls

Carpet balls are glazed china spheres decorated with intersecting lines or other simple designs that were used for indoor games in the British Isles during the early 1800s. Mint condition examples are rare. Our examples are for those that are in excellent to near-mint condition.

Bl stick spatter floral, 3⅛"	188.00
Blk & wht stick spatter, 3"	226.00
Blk & wht stripes, 3⅛"	165.00
Gr stick spatter, 3¼"	195.00
Red & wht plaid, 3⅜"	165.00
Red & wht stripes, 3⅜"	195.00

Cartoon Art

Collectors of cartoon art are interested in many forms of original art — animation cels, sports, political or editorial cartoons, syndicated comic strip panels, and caricature. To produce even a short animated cartoon strip, hundreds of original drawings are required, each showing the characters in slightly advancing positions. Called 'cels' because those made prior to the 1950s were made from a celluloid material, collectors often pay hundreds of dollars for a frame from a favorite movie. Prices of Disney cels with backgrounds vary widely. Background paintings, model sheets, storyboards, and preliminary sketches are also collectible — so are comic book drawings executed in India ink and signed by the artist. Daily 'funnies' originals, especially the earlier ones portraying super heroes, and Sunday comic strips, the early as well as the later ones, are collected. Cartoon art has become recognized and valued as a novel yet valid form of contemporary art.

Key:
ab — airbrushed	cel — celluloid
C — Courvosier	wc — watercolor

Animation Cel, Full Color

Snow White and the Seven Dwarfs, Dopey, gouache on partial celluloid applied to Courvosier ground, 5½" square, $1,980.00.

Adventures in Magic Kingdom, Disney, Tinker Bell, '70s, 4x4"	825.00
Alice in Wonderland, Disney, Dodo, gouache on cel, '51, 7x7"	900.00
Aristocats, Disney, 2 dancing, gouache on cel, '70, 4x13"	825.00
Blk Cauldron, Disney, Gorgi & Taran, gouache on cel, 7x9"	280.00
Jungle Book, Disney, King Louie, gouache on cel, '67, 6x4"	675.00
Jungle Book, Disney, Shere Kahn, gouache on cel, '67, 4x5"	330.00
Lady & Tramp, Disney, gouache on cel, Tramp, 1955, 4x3½"	935.00
Melody Time, Disney, J Appleseed, gouache on cel, 1948, 9x9"	330.00
Mickey Mouse, Disney, in space suit, gouache on cel, '85, 5x2"	725.00
Peter Pan, Disney, Father Darling, gouache on cel, '53, 9x7"	880.00
Peter Pan, Disney, mermaid, gouache on cel, 1953, 4x2½"	365.00
Peter Pan, Disney, Tinker Bell, gouache on cel, '53, 2x3"	900.00
Pluto, Disney, Pluto, gouache on cel, 1950s, 4½x3½"	715.00
Rescuers, Disney, Madame Medusa, gouache on cel, '77, 7x7"	440.00
Rescuers, Disney, Orville, gouache on cel, 1977, 5x8"	330.00
Robin Hood, Disney, Robin Hood, gouache on cell, '73, 11x14"	660.00
Sleeping Beauty, Disney, the kiss, gouache on cel, 8½x12"	1,980.00
Yel Submarine, McCartney & clown, gouache on cel, '68, 8x8"	600.00

Animation Drawing

Dumbo, Disney, Timothy Mouse, mc pencils, 1941, 4½x5"	550.00
Grasshopper & Ants, Disney, busy ant, pencil, 1934, 5x7"	525.00
Gulliver Mickey, Disney, Mickey/children, pencil, '34, 4x6"	360.00
Jungle Jitters, Iwerks, Willie Whopper/girl, pencil, '34, 6x7"	415.00
Mickey's Amateurs, Disney, smiling Mickey, pencil, '37, 4x4"	715.00
Mickey's Garden, Disney, Mickey, red & blk pencil, '35, 6x6"	715.00
Puppy Love, Disney, Pluto & Fifi, pencils, '33, 9x6"	400.00
Sleeping Beauty, Disney, Maleficent, pencil, '59, 9x6"	1,550.00
Steamboat Willie, Disney, piloting paddle wheeler, '28, 5x4"	1,900.00

Daily Newspaper Comic Strip

Barney Google, DeBeck, India ink on brd, 1935, 4x16½"	550.00
Blondie, Young, India ink & shading on brd, 1948, 6x18"	250.00
Brick Bradford, Norris, India ink on brd, 1966, 5x18"	77.00
Flash Gordon, Barry, India ink on paper, 1962, 4½x15"	200.00
Flintstones, Hazelton, India ink on brd, 1965, 6½x20½"	165.00
Harold Teen, Ed, India ink on brd, sgn twice, 1931	115.00
Henry, Anderson, pencil/India ink on brd, 1957, 5½x20"	165.00
Little Lulu, Armstrong, India ink on brd, 1964, 6x20"	88.00
Mandrake the Magician, Davis, ink on paper, 1945, 5x17"	275.00
Mickey Mouse, Disney Studio, India ink on paper, 1976, 5x18"	330.00
Mickey Mouse, Gottfredson/Disney, India ink, 1965, 6x18"	495.00
Mutt & Jeff, Fisher, India ink on brd, 1914, 8x25"	360.00
Nancy, Bushmiller, India ink on brd, 1962, 5x20"	175.00
Pogo, Kelly, pencil/ink on paper, 1963, 5x18"	480.00

Popeye, Sagendorf, India ink on brd, 1976, 6x16½" **95.00**
Terry & Pirates, Wunder, India ink on brd, 1951, 6½x22" **60.00**
Twin Earths, McWilliams, India ink on brd, 1954, 5½x21" **90.00**

Storyboard

Bambi, Disney, 2 mice in shelter, pastels, '42, 15x17" **650.00**
Fantasia, Disney, fairies, pastel on blk paper, '40, 5x6" **675.00**
Peter Pan, Disney, Hook/Mr Smee/children, pastels, '53, 6x8" ...**300.00**
You Can't Win, Disney, Goofy & gambling, '49, 3-pg, 14x17" ...**350.00**

Miscellaneous

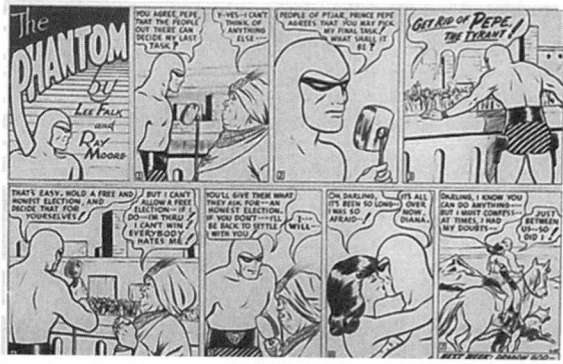

Original art for Sunday 'funnies,' The Phantom, Lee Falk and Ray Moore, June 29, 1947, 19x28", $1,035.00.

Book cover, Donald Duck, wc on brd, 1985, 14x18" **450.00**
Color book illustration, Robin Hood, Hubbard, 1973, 11x11" ...**350.00**
Daily orig, Terry & Pirates, Caniff, ink on brd, '46, 7x22" **330.00**
Panel, Out Our Way, Williams, India ink on brd, 1929, 12x12" ..**120.00**
Portrait, Deadman, sgn N Adams, pencil on paper, 1970s, 10x7" ...**275.00**
Portrait, Jungle Girl, Frazetta, pencil on paper, '70s, 9x7" **1,430.00**
Story sheet, Bambi, Disney, w/bunnies, pencil/crayon, '42, 4x6" ...**600.00**
Sunday page, Katzenjammer Kids, India ink on brd, '53, 14x19" ..**175.00**

Cartoon Books

'Books of cartoons' were printed during the first decade of the 20th century and remained popular until the advent of the modern comic book in the late thirties. Cartoon books, printed in both color and black and white, were merely reprints of current newspaper comic strips. The books, ranging from thirty to seventy pages and in sizes from 3½" x 8" up to 11" x 17", were usually bound with cardboard covers and were often distributed as premiums in exchange for coupons saved from the daily paper. One of the largest of the companies who printed these books was Cupples and Leon, producer of nearly half of the two hundred titles on record. Among the most popular sellers were *Mutt and Jeff, Bringing Up Father,* and *Little Orphan Annie.*

Bringing Up Father, #1, King Features, Star, EX **125.00**
Bringing Up Father, #18, Cupples & Leon, scarce, EX **65.00**
Bringing Up Father, #4, Cupples & Leon, EX **75.00**
Charlie Chaplin in the Army, Donahue, EX **100.00**
Exploits of Dick Tracy, Resdon, 1946, NM **100.00**
Famous Comics, Captain & Kids, Whitman, 1934, EX **50.00**
Famous Comics, Ella Cinder, Whitman, NM **65.00**
Felix the Cat, McLoughlin, 1931, EX **200.00**

Happy Hooligan, 50-pg, 1903, EX **120.00**
How Dick Tracy...Caught Rocketeers, Cupples & Leon, '33, EX ..**150.00**
Komical Katzenjammer Kids, 1910, EX **75.00**
Krazy Kat, Holt, 1946, VG **65.00**
Little Annie Rooney, McKay, 48-pg, 1935, NM **60.00**
Little Orphan Annie Never Say Die, Cupples & Leon, VG **45.00**
Little Orphan Annie Shipwrecked, Cupples & Leon, NM **85.00**
Mutt & Jeff, 1930, NM **40.00**
Mutt & Jeff Big Book, Cupples & Leon, hardcover, 1929, NM ..**165.00**
Nebbs, Cupples & Leon, 1928, EX **40.00**
Skeezix & Uncle Walt, Reilly & Lee, 1924, NM **65.00**
Skeezix at the Circus, Reilly & Lee, 1926, EX **45.00**
Smitty, Cupples & Leon, 1928, VG **35.00**
Tillie the Toiler, #1, Cupples & Leon, 1925, EX **36.00**
Tillie the Toiler, #4, Cupples & Leon, EX **30.00**
Tricks of Katzenjammer Kids, 1905, NM **150.00**
Trouble of Bringing Up Father, color, Embee, 1921, EX **165.00**
Winnie Winkle, #3, Cupples & Leon, EX **28.00**

Cash Registers

By 1970 antique cash registers had risen to become blue chip collectibles, joining the ranks of fine paintings, bronzes, firearms, clocks, and other categories having permanent, established worth. Some extremely scarce and elegant cash registers will command up to $25,000.00 on today's market.

Register prices are determined by make, model, size, desirability of pattern and accessories such as add-on clocks, topsigns and personalized nameplates (which may be cast as topsigns or 'lid ovals' and on occasion cast into the register's front or back plates). Of immense consideration is the register's condition.

This column uses 'mint' condition (M) to indicate registers which have been cleaned, oiled, polished and lacquered by a professional and have perfect glass, keytops, and indicators. Some restorers will replace the velvet underneath the lid (where applicable), which is an added touch of elegance. 'Very good' condition (VG) describes unrestored, unpolished registers which are complete and operating. Their values are usually about half of the restored model's value. All prices may vary as much as 20%, depending on geography and demand.

For further information we recommend the highly informative books *Antique Cash Registers, 1880-1920,* by Bartsch and Sanchez (Mr. Bartsch's address may be found in our Directory under Oregon); and *The Incorruptible Cashier,* Vols. I & II, currently available from our other advisor, John Apple, listed in our Directory under Wisconsin.

NCR #1, American detail adder, VG **2,650.00**
NCR #1000, glass atugoraphic box attachment, 1910-16, M ..**1,200.00**
NCR #1000, glass autographic box attachment, 1920-16, VG ...**650.00**
NCR #129-130, bronze, VG **850.00**
NCR #13 or #14, Ionic CI, 1899, G **750.00**
NCR #130, Art Nouveau cabinet, M **1,600.00**
NCR #135, Art Nouveau pattern, CI, 31-key, 1905, VG **600.00**
NCR #2 or #3, detail adder, scroll pattern, VG **900.00**
NCR #2 or #3, inlaid oak or mahog, scarce **2,250.00**
NCR #215 or #216, bronze fleur-de-lis, VG **850.00**
NCR #226, w/rare bilingual topsign, EX orig **900.00**
NCR #250 or #251, bronze, VG **900.00**
NCR #3, inlay mahog, deep wood drw, ca 1886 ....**4,500.00**
NCR #30, bronze, total adder, VG **1,400.00**
NCR #312, #313, or #317, dolphin pattern, M **1,400.00**
NCR #312, #313, or #317, dolphin pattern, VG **800.00**
NCR #313, dolphin design, M rstr **1,400.00**
NCR #313, EX orig **775.00**

NCR #322, #323, or #327, marble 3 sides, extended base, M ..1,800.00
NCR #322, #323, or #327, marble 3 sides, extended base, VG..1,050.00
NCR #324, Woolworth sz, M 1,050.00
NCR #33, $5 maximum, CA, 1903, VG 900.00
NCR #332, #333, #349 or #356, orig topsign, M 1,150.00
NCR #332, #333, #349 or #356, orig topsign, VG 550.00
NCR #337, dolphin design, M 1,150.00
NCR #338, dogwood pattern, English numerals, CA, 1910-16, VG .475.00
NCR #441-#452, Empire pattern, M 1,750.00
NCR #441-#452, Empire pattern, VG 700.00
NCR #441-2, Empire design w/quartered oak base, M 1,750.00
NCR #441E-#452E, electric, M 2,250.00
NCR #441E-#452E, electric, VG 950.00
NCR #442E-L, EX orig 950.00
NCR #452, 22x25x16", EX 750.00
NCR #47, oak or mahog inlay, up to $6, VG 2,250.00
NCR #5, narrow scroll, glass topsign, EX orig 2,750.00
NCR #50, Renaissance design, orig clock, EX orig 2,500.00
NCR #50 or #51, Renaissance pattern, VG 1,350.00
NCR #52, Renaissance design, orig clock, extended base, M ..3,800.00
NCR #52 or #52¼, Renaissance pattern, extended base, VG ..2,900.00
NCR #52¼, dolphin design, extended base, M 2,200.00
NCR #522, 2-drw, electric bar model, 1910-16, M 2,500.00
NCR #522, 2-drw, electric bar model, 1910-16, VG 1,800.00
NCR #64, Bohemian pattern, iron, 25-key, 1901, VG 600.00
NCR #7 or #8, detail adder, fleur-de-lis, VG 850.00
NCR #711-#717, mahog grain finish on steel, M 275.00

Cast Iron

In the mid-1800s, the cast-iron industry was raging in the United States. It was recognized as a medium extremely adaptable for uses ranging from ornamental architectural filigree to actual building construction. It could be cast from a mold into any conceivable design that could be reproduced over and over at a relatively small cost. It could be painted to give an entirely versatile appearance. Furniture with openwork designs of grapevines and leaves and intricate lacy scrollwork was cast for gardens as well as inside use. Figural doorstops of every sort, bootjacks, trivets, and a host of other useful and decorative items were made before the 'ferromania' had run its course. Our advisor for this category is J.M. Ellwood; he is listed in the Directory under Arizona. See also Kitchen, Cast-Iron Bakers and Kettles; and other specific categories.

Architectural pc, Bacchus head, old brn pnt, 8½x8x3" 165.00
Armchair, fern design, rust/pitting, 35½" 550.00
Armchair, rustic limbs w/oak leaves & acorns, rpr, rust, 31" 715.00
Ashtray, eagle, ca 1860, 3¼x6" 95.00
Bench, fern details, Kramer, rebolted, rprs, 35x58" 880.00
Bench, floral details, bird-head arms, rprs, 34x42" 1,100.00
Bench, rococo details w/fishscale-grate bk, Carr, 36x46" 1,100.00
Bench, rococo florals w/Minerva-head bk, 42x45", EX 1,760.00
Bench, rustic limbs w/oak leaves & acorns, rprs, rust, 32x38" 660.00
Bench, rustic limbs w/oak leaves & acorns, rprs, 33x51" 990.00
Bench, rustic limbs w/oak leaves & acorns, 32x48", EX 1,155.00
Bench, vintage details, wht rpt, 37", EX 100.00
Bracket supports, lacy curvilinear designs, 1880s, 17x11", pr 85.00
Bust, McKinley, old mc pnt w/minor touch up, 11¼" 85.00
Cannon, EX detail, old blk pnt, 17¾" L 385.00
Chair, floral scrolls & lyre bk, old wht rpt, 32", pr 440.00
Chair, swivel base, floral scroll details, pitting, 32½" 550.00
Cookie mold, cornucopia w/fruit, 5⅝" 50.00
Fence post, fluted column, no finial, pitted, 42" 195.00
Finial, eagle, old rusted finish, 23½" wingspan 275.00

Fountain, egrets support 3 bowls, crown finial, 80x70" 7,975.00
Frog, I Croak for Webtser Wagon, pnt traces, 5" 100.00
Grate, lacy openwork floral design, 14" dia 36.00
Hitching post, Blk boy on sq base, EX detail, old pnt, 46" 3,300.00
Hitching post, horse-head finial, tapered column, 67½" 1,100.00
Hitching post, horse-head finial w/ring, pitted, 45" 770.00
Hitching post, jockey, old mc rpt, wear/rust, 48" 415.00
Hitching post, jockey on sq base, Champion...OH, rpt, 50" 715.00
Humidor, relief molded, emb OMSB 1823, 10" 350.00
Lamp post, tapered w/fluted & flanged detail, 105" 275.00
Lawn ornament, deer on metal base, pnt, 63x52" 1,600.00
Lawn ornament, rabbit, seated, old wht, pnt, 12½x12x5¼" 225.00
Lawn ornament, rabbit, 11" 195.00
Lawn sprinkler, Enterprise, dtd 1890 ....235.00
Ornament, birds, fruit compote & scrolls, rpt, 32" L 225.00
Paperweight, lion figural, old gold pnt, 4⅜" L 60.00
Road sign, tombstone shape, Cincinnati/Cleveland, 29x15" 880.00
Rosette maker, serrated edge, wood grip, 17½" L 60.00
Slave plate, 1x9" dia 120.00
Stove plate, arch floral panels/twist columns, pitted, 24x20" 150.00
Street post, fluted, paw ft, from New Orleans 950.00
Table, dbl-ped base w/floral details, marble top, 28x36x24" 185.00
Table, 4 foliage/scroll legs, rnd rtcl top, 27x39" dia 105.00
Tie rod, fleur-de-lis form, old blk pnt, late 1800s, 9½x9" 55.00
Trough, rectangular, JL Mott, Iron Works NY, 20x46x24" 1,430.00

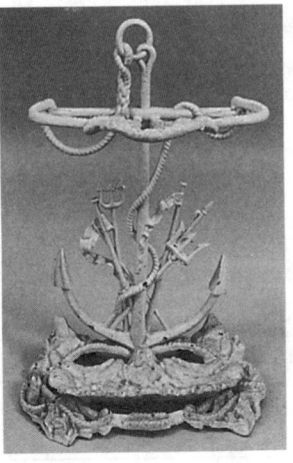

Umbrella stand, nautical motif, white paint, 29", $825.00.

Umbrella rack, leaf details, old pnt, Wilson...NY, 39½" 415.00
Urn, arches on sides, uptrn hdls, ped base w/leaves, 45" 775.00
Urn, classic design, short hdls, rprs, 24x20" 250.00
Urn, emb florals & buffalo heads, Kramer, pnt traces, 56", pr .7,925.00
Urn, foliage/scroll ear hdls, wht rpt, Kramer Bros, 35", pr 550.00
Urn, on plinth, scrolled ear hdls, pnt traces, 49", pr 2,200.00
Urn, 3-part griffin stem w/dolphins, rebolted, 40x35" dia 1,265.00
Waffle iron, Am eagle, 5½" dia, 31" hdl w/shaped finial 130.00
Waffle iron, heart shape w/dmn, 34" hdl w/ball finials 225.00
Window guard, radiating scrolls in sq fr, 1850, pr 400.00

Castor Sets

Castor sets became popular during the early years of the 18th century and continued to be used through the late Victorian era. Their purpose was to hold various condiments for table use. The most common type was a circular arrangement with a center handle on a revolving pedestal base that held three, four, five, or six bottles. Some had extras; a few were equipped with a bell for calling the servant. Frames were made of silverplate, glass, or pewter. Though most bottles were of pressed glass, some of the designs were cut, and on rare occasion, colored glass with enameled decorations was used as well. To maintain authenticity and value, castor sets should have matching bottles. Prices listed below are for those with matching bottles and in frames with plating that is in excellent condition (unless noted otherwise).

Watch for new frames and bottles in both clear and colored glass; these have recently been appearing on the market.

Key: D&B — Daisy and Button

3-bottle, D&B, clear/blown; pressed glass fr	135.00
3-bottle, Invt T'print, ruby stain; orig fr	195.00
3-bottle, rubena, cut panels; orig SP fr, 5x4¼"	165.00
4-bottle, cranberry; glass fr	250.00
5-bottle, amberina w/eng leaf; Aurora fr w/eng presentation	1,500.00
5-bottle, Bellflower, rpl period stoppers; pewter fr, 11"	150.00
5-bottle, D&B, vaseline, rstr fr w/bell revolves, 17"	450.00
5-bottle, Honeycomb; ornate Wilcox fr, EX	275.00
6-bottle, cut, panelled; Meriden fr revolves, EX	295.00
6-bottle, cut; Paul Storr armorial fr, 1810, 12"	5,000.00
6-bottle, D&B; ornate emb 19" fr w/winged cherub	395.00
6-bottle, etched; Rogers rstr SP fr revolves, 19"	325.00
7-bottle, wreath cutting; 22" ornate openwork fr revolves, rstr	625.00

Catalina Island

Catalina Island pottery was made on the island of the same name, which is about twenty-six miles off the coast of Los Angeles. The pottery was started in 1927 at Pebbly Beach, by Wm. Wrigley, Jr., who was instrumental in developing and using the native clays. Its principal products were brick and tile to be used for construction on the island. Garden pieces were first produced, then vases, bookends, lamps, ashtrays, novelty items, and finally dinnerware. The ware became very popular and was soon being shipped to the mainland as well.

Some of the pottery was hand thrown; some was made in molds. Most pieces are marked Catalina Island or Catalina with a printed incised stamp or handwritten with a pointed tool. Cast items were sometimes marked in the mold; a few have an ink stamp, and a paper label was also used.

The color of the clay can help to identify approximately when a piece was made: 1927 to 1932, brown to red clay; 1931 to 1932, an experimental period with various colors; 1932 to 1937, mainly white clay, but tan to brown were also used on occasion.

Items marked Catalina Pottery are listed in Gladding McBean. For further information we recommend *The Collector's Encyclopedia of California Pottery* by our advisor, Jack Chipman; he is listed in the Directory under California.

Dinnerware

Catalina Island, bowl, cereal	45.00
Catalina Island, bowl, vegetable; rnd, 8½"	65.00
Catalina Island, cup, coffee/tea	45.00
Catalina Island, custard cup	25.00
Catalina Island, pitcher, squat base	100.00
Catalina Island, plate, dinner; wide rim, 10½"	30.00
Catalina Island, sugar bowl, w/lid	45.00
Catalina Island, teapot, traditional English style	250.00
Catalina Island, tumbler, 4"	25.00
Rope Edge, casserole, w/lid	50.00
Rope Edge, chop plate, 13½"	60.00
Rope Edge, creamer	35.00
Rope Edge, cup & saucer	35.00

Rope Edge, plate, dinner; 10½"	25.00
Rope Edge, plate, salad; 8½"	20.00
Rope Edge, sugar bowl	45.00
Rope Edge, teapot	150.00

Miscellaneous

Bookends, monk design, gr matt, pr	750.00
Bowl, gr matt, str rim, 3x9"	175.00
Candelabrum, turq, 3-holed, str	200.00
Candle holder, yel, 5½", ea	125.00
Charger, HP Mexican scene, mk, ca 1932, 11½"	600.00
Shakers, tulip, pr	65.00
Tile, Spanish, mc, 6x6"	165.00
Tray, turq, rolled edge, 14½", w/forged iron hdl	175.00
Vase, bl matt, sq hdls, 5x6"	195.00
Vase, Monterey Brn, flowerpot form, old mk, 5½"	125.00
Vase, red-orange, squat base, conical neck, 8"	235.00
Vase, Toyon red, bulbous base, 6"	175.00
Vase, wht, #611, 10"	225.00
Vase, wht, #619, 7½"	195.00
Vinegar bottle, bl matt, gourd shape	100.00
Wall pocket, gr matt, basketweave, 9"	200.00

Catalogs

Catalogs are not only intriguing to collect on their own merit, but for the collector with a specific interest, they are often the only remaining source of background information available, and as such they offer a wealth of otherwise unrecorded data. The mail-order industry can be traced as far back as the mid-1800s. Even before Aaron Montgomery Ward began his career in 1872, Laacke and Joys of Wisconsin and the Orvis Company of Vermont, both dealers in sporting goods, had been well established for many years. The E.C. Allen Company sold household necessities and novelties by mail on a broad scale in the 1870s. By the end of the Civil War, sewing machines, garden seed, musical instruments, even medicine, were available from catalogs. In the 1880s Macy's of New York issued a 127-page catalog; Sears and Spiegel followed suit in about 1890. Craft and art supply catalogs were first available about 1880 and covered such varied fields as china painting, stenciling, wood burning, brass embossing, hair weaving, and shellcraft. Today some collectors confine their interests not only to craft catalogs in general but often to just one subject. There are several factors besides rarity which make a catalog valuable: age, condition, profuse illustrations, how collectible the field is that it deals with, the amount of color used in its printing, its size (format and number of pages), and whether it is a manufacturer's catalog verses a jobber's catalog (the former being the most desirable).

A Shuman & Co, clothiers, color cover, 1890, NM	35.00
Beck Motorcycle Accessories, 1945	38.00
Bloomingdale's Holiday, detailed illus, 1892, EX	90.00
Butler Bros Christmas, toys, 662-pg, 1927, EX	90.00
Chas B Shipley Saddlery & Westernware, 1950, 54-pg	45.00
Chicago Skates, roller skates, blk & wht & color, 1935, EX	20.00
F Wenter Cabinetware, Chicago, 1885, 32-pg	35.00
Fenton Co, labels & ad stickers, ca 1910	30.00
Friske Tires, circus cutouts, giveaway, 1929, EX	38.00
Geo H Bowman, mini cooking sets, blk & wht illus, 1929, EX	20.00
Gowing Detrich Syracuse, creamery machinery, 1918, 322-pg	35.00
Hohner Accordions, detailed mc illus, 1926, 72-pg	60.00
Hohner Harmonicas, many illus, 1926, 4-pg, 9¼x12", EX	25.00
Hub Cycle Co, cycles & velocipedes, blk & wht illus, 1919, EX	40.00

Huther Saws, 1929, 107-pg, EX **20.00**
Ives Trains, mc cover, blk & wht illus, 1930s, EX **50.00**
JB Clow & Sons Modern Plumbing for schools, 1916, 88-pg **45.00**
Jenny Semple Hill, furniture, ca 1925, 300-pg, EX **35.00**
Keystone, toys, blk & wht illus, 1942-43, G- **30.00**
Kilgore, CI toys, color, 1929, M in envelope **300.00**
L&C Mayers Co, jewelry, flatware, etc, 1935, 386-pg, EX **45.00**
Lionel Electric Trains, color & blk & wht illus, 1926, EX **45.00**
Lionel Electric Trains, 1933, 51-pg, 11½x8¼", EX **35.00**
M Gordon Boston MA, toys, 1904 ....**55.00**
Marshall Field, toys, 1969 reprint, 35-pg, M **20.00**
Monarch Bicycles, 1898, 36-pg, 4¾x9", EX **40.00**
Motorola Radios, radios & record players, 1946, 32-pg, EX **23.00**
MW Savage, 1933-34, 153-pg, EX **20.00**
Nash Sporting Goods, 1961, EX **25.00**
NY Sporting Goods Camp Outfits & Firearms, 1920s, #95, EX **50.00**
P&O Vehicles, buggies/wagons/etc, 1915, 92-pg **76.00**
Paramount Electrical Supply, lighting fixtures, '20s, 88-pg **32.00**
Pathex Motion Pictures for Home, lists silent films, 1925 ....**27.50**
Ranger Bicycles, blk & wht & color illus, 1921, EX **55.00**
Ranger Bicycles, 1922, 48-pg, 8½x11", VG **40.00**
Remington Bicycles, 1893, EX **195.00**
Remington Bicycles, 1893, 24-pg, 6x9", VG **70.00**
Rexall Drugs, 1926, 340-pg, EX **60.00**
Rochester Can Co, metal ware, ca 1920, 50-pg, 8x10½" **45.00**
Schoenhut Toys, Humpty Dumpty Circus shown, ca 1912, EX **95.00**
Schoenhut Toys, wood dolls, 1912, EX **35.00**
Sears, Fall & Winter 1931-32, EX **45.00**
Sears, hardcover, 1902 ....**220.00**
Sears, Roebuck & Co, bicycles, 1918, 18-pg, 8½x11", VG **22.50**
Sears Roebuck, Spring & Summer, 1920, EX **65.00**
Sears Sporting Goods, Fall & Winter 1924-25, EX **50.00**
Shriber Co Charlton IA, carriages, ca 1910, 20-pg, 8x9½" **65.00**
Simplex Movie Projectors, 1916, 70-pg, 6x9" **35.00**
Singer Sewing Machines, mc, ca 1903, EX **30.00**
Spencer Fireworks, many illus, 1936 ....**90.00**

Spiegel, Home Coming Bargain Book,
1917, unpaged, 15x11", EX, $25.00.

Spiegel, Christmas 1956 ....**45.00**
Spiegel, Christmas 1971 ....**12.00**
Spiegel, Fall & Winter 1947 ....**35.00**
Star Bicycles & Tricycles, 1887, 35-pg, 6½x9½", EX **180.00**
Structo Toys, blk & wht & color illus, 1922, VG **230.00**
Thomas Mills & Bros, confectioners' machinery, 1924, 219-pg ..**140.00**
Tinker Toys & Games, mc illus, 1920, EX **25.00**
United Indurated Fibre Co, Chicago, 1891, 18-pg **25.00**
US Buggy & Cart Co, 1880, 50-pg **65.00**
Wards, Christmas 1942, EX **50.00**
Wards, Midsummer 1947 ....**25.00**
WM Radford Guaranteed Building Plans, Chicago, 1915, 256-pg ..**45.00**

WS Darley, fire trucks & equipment, 1944, 99-pg, EX **60.00**
WS Darley Municipal Supplies, fire engines etc, '40, 84-pg, VG ..**45.00**

Caughley Ware

The Caughley Coalport Porcelain Manufactory operated from about 1775 until 1799 in Caughley, near Salop, Shropshire, in England. The owner was Thomas Turner, who gained his potting experience from his association with the Worcester Pottery Company. The wares he manufactured in Caughley are referred to as 'Salopian.' He is most famous for his blue-printed earthenwares, particularly the Blue Willow pattern, designed for him by Thomas Minton. For a more detailed history, see Coalport.

Bowl, junket; bl foral fruit transfers, emb shells, 10" **675.00**
Cup & saucer, chinoiserie, 1750s mk, M **185.00**
Cup & saucer, girl w/bundle of sticks on head, mini **375.00**
Cup & saucer, mc HP stylized florals, vine band, mk **100.00**
Cup & saucer, roses, mc/brn transfer, mk **145.00**
Jug, fruit/flowers, bl transfer, ovoid, 1785, 4½" W **325.00**
Plate, Horse Chestnut, imp CPUS clover, 8¾" **300.00**
Sauce dish, house & people, mc/brn transfer, mk, 4½" **65.00**
Saucer, fallow deer, mc **115.00**
Teapot, fruit clusters, bl transfer, bulbous, 1790, 4½" **495.00**

Ceramic Art Company

Jonathan Coxon, Sr., and Walter Scott Lenox established the Ceramic Art Company in 1889 in Trenton, New Jersey, where they produced fine belleek porcelain. Both were experienced in its production, having previously worked for Ott and Brewer. They hired artists to hand paint their wares with portraits, scenes, and lovely florals. Today artist-signed examples bring the highest prices. Several marks were used, three of which contain the 'CAC' monogram. A green wreath surrounding the company name in full was used on special-order wares, but these are not often encountered. Coxon eventually left the company, and it was later reorganized under the Lenox name. See also Lenox. Our advisor for this category is Mary Frank Gaston; she is listed in the Directory under Texas.

Bell, tulip shape, wht w/silver decor, unmk **160.00**
Chocolate pot, emb fish, mermaid spout & hdl, gold trim, 12" .**1,400.00**
Clock, HP florals & gold, bl beading, Ansonia works, mk, 9" ...**1,000.00**
Cup, demitasse; gold paste florals on wht, ring hdl, mk, 2" **120.00**
Ewer, gold paste florals on creamy matt, mk, 7½" **475.00**
Jug, pharmacy; Rx silver o/l on brn glossy, 4½" **375.00**
Mug, HP apples on orange, gr mk, 6" **150.00**
Salt cellar, mixed florals w/gold, mk **40.00**
Stein, HP monk, mk CAC/Lenox, copper & silver lid, ½-litre ...**470.00**
Table lamp, plain wht w/scalloped base, unmk, 20½" **275.00**
Vase, gold paste florals on dk gr & brn, cabbage shape, 6½" **650.00**
Vase, HP lav & wht flowers, ewer form, gold hdls, mk, 18" **800.00**
Vase, lg HP roses, gilt hdls, flared neck, mk, 10" **600.00**
Vase, violets & gold scrolls on cream, classic form, mk, 22½" **800.00**
Vase, wht neck w/purple lustre body, gr mk, 3¾" **125.00**

Ceramic Arts Studio, Madison

The Ceramic Arts Studio Company began operations sometime prior to the 1940s, but it was about then that Betty Harrington started marketing her goods through this company. Betty Harrington is the designer primarily responsible for creating the line of figurines and knick-knacks that has become so popular with collectors. There were two others — Ulli Rebus, who not only designed several of the animals and various other pieces but taught Betty the art of mold-making as well; and Ruth Planter, who's work may have been very limited. About 65% of these items are marked, but even unmarked items become easily recognizable after only a brief study of their distinctive styling and glaze colors. At least eight different marks were used, among them the black ink stamp and the incised mark: 'Ceramic Arts Studio, Madison, Wisc.' A paper sticker was used in the early years.

After the 1955 demise of the company in Madison, the owner (Ruben Sand) went to Japan where he continued production under the same name using many of the same molds. After a short time, the old molds were retired, and new and quite different items were produced. Most of the Japan pieces can be found with a Ceramic Arts Studio backstamp. The Japan identification was on a paper label and is often missing. Japan pieces are never marked Madison, Wisc., but not all Madison pieces are either. Red or blue backstamps are exclusively Japanese.

Another company that also produced figurines operated at about the same time as the Madison studio. It was called Ceramic Art (no 's') Studio; do not confuse the two.

A second and larger building in the C.A.S. complex in Madison was for the exclusive production of metal accessories. The creator and designer of this related line was Zona Liberace, Liberace's stepmother, who was Art Director for the line of figurines as well. These pieces are rising fast in value and because they weren't marked can sometimes be found at bargain prices. They were so popular that other ceramic companies bought them to complement their own lines, so they may also be found with ceramic figures other than C.A.S.'s.

For those seeking additional information, videotapes (Series 1 and 2) are available from the author, BA Wellman, whose address can be found under Massachusetts. 1996-1997 price guides are also available. Mr. Wellman encourages collectors to write him with any new information concerning company history and/or production. He sends Vera a 'thank you' for helping us with this year's updates.

Figurine, Comedy and Tragedy, $150.00 for the pair.

Bank, Skunky, 4"	85.00
Bell, Winter Belle, 5¼" (+)	68.00
Bowl, Bonita Stripe, 3¾"	40.00
Candle holder, Hear No Evil, angel, 5"	50.00
Figurine, accordion lady, standing, 8½"	145.00
Figurine, Adam & Eve, 1-pc, 12"	565.00
Figurine, Alice & wht rabbit, 4½", 6", pr	185.00
Figurine, angel w/candle, 5"	35.00
Figurine, Annie & Benny (elephants), 3¼", 3½", pr	45.00
Figurine, Archibald the Dragon, 8"	175.00

Figurine, Bali-Hai, topless, 8"	115.00
Figurine, bass viol boy, 4¾"	60.00
Figurine, birch bark canoe, 8" L	65.00
Figurine, Bright Eyes (cat), 3"	32.00
Figurine, Burmese Clinthe, 5¾"	75.00
Figurine, child w/towel, 5"	55.00
Figurine, Cinderella & Prince Charming, pr	135.00
Figurine, collie pup playing, 2½"	18.00
Figurine, colonial boy & girl, 5", 5¼", pr	65.00
Figurine, Daisy ballerina, standing, 5¼"	50.00
Figurine, drum girl, 4¼"	45.00
Figurine, Dutch Love boy & girl, 5", pr	45.00
Figurine, Encore man & woman, 8¼", 8¾", pr	195.00
Figurine, french horn man, sitting, 6½"	145.00
Figurine, Gay '90s man & lady, #2, pr	100.00
Figurine, gremlin boy & girl, early, rare, 4", 2½", pr	185.00
Figurine, Hans & Katinka, chubby, 6½", 6¼", pr	90.00
Figurine, harem girl, sitting, 4½"	35.00
Figurine, Harlequin boy & girl, 7¾", pr	275.00
Figurine, Harry & Lillibeth, 6¼", pr	85.00
Figurine, Hiawatha, 3½"	95.00
Figurine, kitten scratching, wht, 2"	18.00
Figurine, kitten sleeping, w/bow, wht, 1"	18.00
Figurine, Lady Rowena on charger, 8½"	185.00
Figurine, leopards, fighting, 3½", 6¼", pr	135.00
Figurine, Little Bo Peep & Little Boy Blue, pr	55.00
Figurine, Little Jack Horner, #2	50.00
Figurine, Little Miss Muffet, #1	55.00
Figurine, lovebirds, 1-pc, 2¾"	30.00
Figurine, Lu Tang & Wing Sang, 6¼", pr	45.00
Figurine, Lucinda & Col Jackson, pr	85.00
Figurine, Madonna w/Bible, 9½"	125.00
Figurine, Madonna w/Child, 1-pc, 6½"	85.00
Figurine, mermaid baby on tummy, 2½"	45.00
Figurine, Minnehaha, 6½"	95.00
Figurine, mouse, 3" L	35.00
Figurine, Mr Monk, 4"	45.00
Figurine, Mr Skunky, 3" to tail (+)	35.00
Figurine, Palomino colt, 5¾"	75.00
Figurine, Peek-a-Boo pixie boy, 2½" (+)	32.00
Figurine, Pioneer Sam & Susie, pr	75.00
Figurine, Piper girl running, 3¼"	38.00
Figurine, Polish boy & girl, 6¾", 6", pr	75.00
Figurine, Poncho & Pepita, 4½", pr	68.00
Figurine, Praise & Blessing (angels), 6", 5¾", pr (+)	75.00
Figurine, Ralph the goat, w/flower, 4"	35.00
Figurine, shepherd & shepherdess, 8½", 8", pr	185.00
Figurine, squirrel w/jacket, 2¼"	30.00
Figurine, St Francis of Assisi, 7"	65.00
Figurine, Sultan, 4½"	55.00
Figurine, Summer Sally, 3½"	50.00
Figurine, Swish & Swirl (fish), 2½", 3", pr	48.00
Figurine, toadstool, 3"	20.00
Figurine, Toby horse, 2¾"	32.00
Figurine, violin lady, standing, 8½"	145.00
Figurine, Willing, 4¾"	50.00
Figurine, zebra, 5"	40.00
Flowerpot, rnd, 1"	18.00
Jug, Adam & Eve, twig hdl, 3"	45.00
Jug, George Washington, 2¾"	48.00
Jug, toby, 3½" (+)	45.00
Planter, Barbie head, 7"	75.00
Planter, Lorelei on seashell, 6"	95.00
Planter, Svea & Sven, 6", 6½", pr	135.00

Plaque, Attitude & Arabesque, gr, 9½", pr 85.00
Plaque, Harlequin & Columbine, 8", pr 140.00
Plaque, Neptune, 6" 135.00
Plaque, Shadow Dancers, left & right, 7", pr 80.00
Plaque, Zor & Zorina, pr 95.00
Shakers, Blk Sambo & Tiger, 3½", 5" L, pr 325.00
Shakers, Chirp & Chip, 4", pr 68.00
Shakers, cocks, fighting, 3¾", pr 45.00
Shakers, FiFi & FuFu (dogs), 3", 2½", pr 85.00
Shakers, fish, swimming, 3½", pr 45.00
Shakers, frog & toadstool, 2", 3", pr 38.00
Shakers, lion & lioness, 5¼" L, pr 165.00
Shakers, Paul Bunyan & evergreen, 4½", 2½", pr 95.00
Shakers, ram & ewe, modern, 2", 1¾", pr 35.00
Shakers, snuggle bear mom & baby, brn, 4¼", pr 65.00
Shakers, snuggle boy in chair, 2¼", pr 62.00
Shakers, snuggle cow & calf, 5¼", pr 75.00
Shakers, snuggle doe & fawn, stylized, 3¾", 2", pr 75.00
Shakers, snuggle elephant & native boy, 5", 2¾", pr 165.00
Shakers, snuggle mother monkey & baby, pr 75.00
Shakers, snuggle mouse in cheese, 2½", pr 38.00
Shakers, snuggle Willing & Lover Boy, 4¾", pr (+) 125.00
Shakers, Sootie & Taffie (Scotties), 3", pr 48.00
Shakers, spaniel mom & pup, sitting, 2¼", 1¾", pr 65.00
Shakers, Spaniel mom & pup, 2¼", 1¾", pr 65.00
Shakers, Waldo & Sassy, 3¼", 2¼", pr 75.00
Shakers, Wee Chinese boy & girl, 3", pr 20.00
Shakers, Wee French girl & boy, pr 50.00
Shakers, Wee Indian boy & girl, 3", pr 48.00
Shakers, Wee Piggies boy & girl, 3¼", 3½", pr 45.00
Shelf sitter, baby w/ball up, wht, 4½" 95.00
Shelf sitter, Bali boy & girl, 5½", pr 125.00
Shelf sitter, boy w/dog, 4¼" 55.00
Shelf sitter, canary, left & right, 5", pr 56.00
Shelf sitter, Chinese boy & girl, 4", pr 45.00
Shelf sitter, Dutch boy & girl, 4½", pr 45.00
Shelf sitter, harmonica boy, 4" 45.00
Shelf sitter, Jack & Jill, 4¾", 5", pr 48.00
Shelf sitter, Maurice & Michele, 7", pr 85.00
Shelf sitter, Pudgie & Budgie (birds), 5", pr 65.00
Shelf sitter, Sun-Li & Sun-Lin, chubby, 5½", pr 48.00
Shelf sitter, Tuffy (cat), wht, 5¼" 45.00
Shelf sitters, girl w/cat & boy w/dog, pr 100.00
Shelf sitters, Jack & Jill, pr 48.00
Vase, bird motif, rnd, 2" 20.00
Vase, duck for Encore, 4¼" 55.00
Vase, Lotus & Manchu, head form, pr 180.00
Vase, textured, sq, 2½" 22.00

Metal Accessories

Arched window, for Madonna w/child 45.00
Artist palette, left & right, 12", pr 65.00
Artist palette w/shelves, left & right, 12", pr 75.00
Beanstalk for Jack, rare 125.00
Birdcage w/perch, 14" 65.00
Diamond shadow box, for Attitude & Arabesque 55.00
Free-form, left & right, pr 75.00
Free-form w/shelf, left & right, pr 65.00
Pyramid shelves, ea 35.00
Shadow box, w/wood, sq, 13" 30.00
Sofa, for Maurice & Michele 32.00
Star, holds any 1 of angel trio, 9" 35.00
Triple ring shelves, ea 65.00

Chalkware

Chalkware figures were a popular commodity from approximately 1860 until 1890. They were made from gypsum or plaster of Paris formed in a mold and then hand painted in oils or watercolors. Items such as animals and birds, figures, banks, toys, and religious ornaments modeled after more expensive Staffordshire wares were often sold door to door. Their origin is attributed to Italian immigrants. Today regarded as a form of folk art, 19th century American pieces bring prices in the hundreds of dollars. Carnival chalkware from this century is also collectible, especially figures that are personality related. For those, see Carnival Collectibles.

Bulldog's head, mc pnt, hanging, hollow, 7x6½x6½" 110.00
Cat, blk & wht w/red & bl ribbon, wear, 12", EX 165.00
Cat, orig yel & blk pnt w/faded red, minor wear, 10" 165.00
Cat sleeping, orig yel & blk w/mc trim, wear, 12¼" L 110.00
Deer, detailed pnt, removable antlers, early 1900s, 18x15x9" 160.00
Deer, orig red, brn & blk pnt, pnt wear, rprs, early, 5½" 280.00
Dog, wht w/blk, red & gr pnt, lt wear, 8¾" 220.00

Girl reading, light paint wear, 1800s, 18½", $1,200.00.

Lamb, reclining, brn tones, rectangular base, 14" 250.00
Lion, worn mc pnt w/gr base, 10" L, VG 95.00
Pig, standing, blk/yel features, rpr, 17" L 550.00
Rooster, EX mc pnt, minor damage, early, 7¼" 800.00
Sheep w/lamb, pnt faded, 1800s, 7", VG 85.00

Champleve

Champleve, enameling on brass, differs from cloisonne in that the design is depressed or incised into the metal, rather than being built up with wire dividers as in the cloisonne procedure. The cells, or depressions, are filled in with color, and the piece is then fired.

Candlestick, onyx body & base w/metal neck/tripod ft, 8", pr 225.00
Chamberstick, cream bobeche, bl stem 200.00
Chamberstick, porc plaque w/cherubs & flowers, 6½", pr 275.00
Floor lamp, Chinese, no fixture, 61" 650.00
Inkwell, mc scrolls, 4" oval scalloped tray, hinged lid 140.00
Inkwell, onyx pots/hexagonal base, metal lids/base border 1,800.00
Inkwell, urn form w/sea horse hdls, on ftd/shaped tray 325.00

Lamp, floral, mc on bl w/yel panels & gold, marble base, pr **1,300.00**
Tray, plaque w/romantic scene, serpentine, 7½" **225.00**
Urn, gilt bronze, scroll hdls, champleve base/lid, 9" **250.00**
Urn, porc body w/portrait, metal neck/lid/base, 21", pr **3,800.00**

Chase Brass & Copper Company

Americans were shocked in 1923 when an invitation to stage an exhibit at the first major postwar fair, *The 1925 Exposition des Arts Decoratifs et Industriels*, was declined by the American government because the U.S. could not comply with the exposition's requirement that only original work would be exhibited. Even though American industry produced a vast quantity of varied goods, there was very little 'original American' to show, since most design ideas were being brought in from Europe.

This blow to American prestige and the uproar that resulted prompted a dispatch of designers (among them Donald Deskey, Walter Dorwin Teague, and Russel Wright) to the Paris exhibition. They were to determine what steps would be necessary in order for U.S. designs to compete with European standards. They returned championing the new modernist style. By the mid-1930s, products were being designed and marketed that were attractive to the reluctant consumer insistent upon buying a streamline style that was uniquely American. During the decade of the thirties, the Chase Brass & Copper Company offered lamps, smoking acessories, and housewares similar to those Americans were seeing on the Hollywood screen at prices the average buyer could afford. These products are highly valued today not only because of their superior quality but also because of those who created them. Walter von Nessen, Gerth & Gerth, Rockwell Kent, Russel Wright, Laurelle Guild, and Dr. A. Reimann were some of Chases' well-known designers. Emily Post, who served as spokesperson for Chase, promoted a trend away from expensive silver and toward chromium serving pieces.

Besides chromium, Chase manufactured many products in brass, copper, nickel plate, or a combination of these metals; all are equally collectible. Some items had glass inserts which collectors also seek.

Nearly all Chase products were marked, either on the item itself or on a screw or rivet. On sets containing several pieces, the trademark may appear on only one. Be cautious. Check unmarked items to make sure they measure up to Chase's standard of quality, and lighting fixtures that are unmarked may be compared with pictures of verified examples. For safety's sake, replace both cords and internal wiring before attempting to use any electrical product. Not only will you be protected against possible loss from fire, but you will enhance the value of your collectible as well.

For more thorough study we recommend *Art Deco Chrome, The Chase Era*, and *Art Deco Chrome, Book 2, A Collector's Guide, Industrial Design in the Chase Era*. Both are authored by Richard J. Kilbride; Mrs. Kilbride is listed in the Directory under Connecticut. In the listings that follow, examples are polished unless noted satin. Prices are an average of values reported by members of the Chase Collector's Society. See Directory, Clubs and Newsletters.

Ash receiver, Pentad, chrome, #840 ....**10.00**
Ashtray, Aristocrat, copper/brass, 4" #835 ....**35.00**
Ashtray, Golfer's, copper, 4¼" #890 ....**50.00**
Bell, Ming, chrome w/blk ball hdl, #13007, 3" **65.00**
Bookends, Cat, satin nickel w/blk, #17042, 7⅜", pr **550.00**
Bookends, Davy Jones, brass, #90142, pr..**85.00**
Bookends, Gothic, brass/copper, #17021, 5", pr **350.00**
Bookends, Spiral, satin nickel/blk, #17018, 4½", pr **275.00**
Bowl, Diana Flower, chrome & walnut, #15005, 6¾x10" **50.00**
Bowl, ice; chrome w/curved hdl, #28002, 7", w/tongs **70.00**
Bowl, sauce; Lotus, chrome w/lk hdl, #17045, +ladle & tray..........**55.00**
Box, Dolphin, copper w/wht base, #856, 3¾x3" **45.00**

Box, occasional; chrome w/blk heart trim, #90144, 5¼" **50.00**
Box, Tournament, chrome w/blk, #888, 3¾x3" **60.00**
Breakfast set, chrome w/blk, #26003, tray +cr/sug **70.00**
Bud holder, 4-tube, chrome, #11230, 9" **35.00**
Candle holder, Sunday Supper, copper, #24002, 3⅜", 4 for **40.00**
Candlestick, Taurex, chrome, U-shpae, #24003, 7⅛", ea..............**75.00**
Candlestick, Bubble, chrome/bl glass, #17063, 2½", pr **75.00**
Candlestick, Diana, chrome/walnut, #24009, 1⅞x3½", pr **45.00**
Candy dish, brass w/fruit finial, glass insert, #90011, 7" **30.00**
Cigarette box, Band Box, chrome w/red, #852, 7⅛" **90.00**
Cigarette box, Rockwell Kent, bronze, #847, 6½"...................**1,200.00**
Cigarette server, Ball, copper & wht, #853, 3⅜" **60.00**
Cocktail Ball, chrome w/red rubber base, #90071, 3⅜" **30.00**
Cocktail shaker, Blue Moon, chrome w/bl top, #90066....................**90.00**
Cocktail shaker, Gaiety, chrome w/blk rings, #90034 ....**45.00**
Coffee service, Comet, chrome, #90120, 4 pcs+tray **325.00**
Coffee service, Continental, chrome, #17054, 3 pcs **200.00**
Coffee service, Coronet, chrome, #17029, 4 pcs+tray **350.00**
Cup, cocktail; Blue Moon, chrome w/bl glass, #90067, 3½" **30.00**
Cup, cocktail; chrome hemisphere, #26002, 2¾"............................**5.00**
Cup, iced drink; chrome w/leaf-hdl stirrer, #90085, 5¼" **30.00**
Cup, old-fashioned cocktail; chrome, #90063, 2⅞", w/muddler.....**30.00**
Dinner gong, chrome, #11251, 8¼", w/hammer **175.00**
Goblet, Bacchus, chrome, #90032, 6" **40.00**
Jelly dish, Duplex, chrome basket w/glass insert, #90062, 5½" **35.00**
Jigger, High Hat, chrome, #28014, 1¾" **30.00**
Lamp, Binnacle, brass, wired/battery, #25001/#15002, 5½", ea......**40.00**
Lamp, Circle, chrome, w/rpl shade, #1004, 14" **75.00**
Lamp, desk; chrome, rpl shade, #1003, 14" **75.00**
Lighter, automatic table; chrome/blk, #851, 2⅜ **75.00**
Lighter, Fire Ball, chrome, #851, 2⅜...**75.00**
Mint & nut dish, chrome, twin bowls, loop hdl, #29003................**35.00**
Napkin holder, chrome w/wht hdl, #90148, 6x4⅛" **45.00**
Pancake & corn set, chrome w/cobalt glass, #28003, 4 pcs **220.00**
Pitcher, water; Sparta, chrome, wht plastic hdl, #90055, 8"...........**70.00**
Plant pot, Tom Thumb, copper, #4010 ....**5.00**
Relish dish, Fairfax, chrome w/glass & wht hdl, #90128 ....**45.00**
Salt & Pepper Spheres, chrome, #28004, 1¾", 1⅛", pr **60.00**
Sauce, Olympia, chrome, #90072, 6⅜" **15.00**
Serving fork & spoon, chrome w/wht plastic hdls, #90076, pr.......**35.00**
Silent Butler, chrome w/wht plastic hdl, #17111 ....**40.00**
Sugar Sphere, chrome shaker, #90078, 2⅝" **40.00**
Tidy Crumber, chrome w/wht, lg/sm scrapers, #90092 ....**45.00**
Tray cocktail; chrome, #09013, 15⅞x5⅜" **30.00**
Tray, Ring, chrome, etched circular design, #90058, 12" **45.00**
Tray, Triple, chrome, folding, all metal, #09001 ....**30.00**
Vase, Calyx, copper, #3008, 7½" **45.00**
Vase, Minerva, chrome w/wht plastic, #03012, 6⅜" **45.00**
Vase, Ring, chrome w/blk, #17039, 9½" **55.00**
Vase, Trophy, chrome, #3005, 9" **70.00**

Chelsea

The Chelsea Porcelain Works operated in London from the middle of the 18th century, making porcelain of the finest quality. In 1770 it was purchased by the owner of the Derby Pottery and for about twenty years operated as a decorating shop. Production periods are indicated by trademarks: 1745-1750 — incised triangle, sometimes with 'Chelsea' and the year added; early 1750s — raised anchor mark on oval pad; 1752-1756 — small painted red anchor, only rarely found in blue underglaze; 1756-1769 — gold anchor; 1769-84 — Chelsea Derby mark with the script 'D' containing a horizontal anchor. Many reproductions have been made; be suspicious of any anchor mark larger than ¼".

Scent bottles: boy with bagpipes figural, bright colors, flame finial, 2¾", EX, $1,100.00; Vase with mixed flowers form, rose and butterfly stopper, ca 1760, 3¼", EX, $1,700.00.

Figurine, gentleman (& lady), red anchor mk, 4¼", pr 325.00
Figurine, lady hunter w/greyhound, gold anchor mk, 7½" 475.00
Figurine, lady w/lamb (male musician), boscage, 11", VG, pr 385.00
Figurine, man (& lady), 18th-C attire, w/baskets, 11", pr 500.00
Figurine, seated gent (& lady), gold anchor mk, 7", pr 435.00

Chelsea Dinnerware

Made from about 1830 to 1880 in the Staffordshire district of England, this white dinnerware is decorated with lustre embossings in the grape, thistle, sprig, or fruit and cornucopia patterns. The relief designs vary from lavender to blue, and the body of the ware may be porcelain, ironstone, or earthenware. Because it was not produced in Chelsea as the name would suggest, dealers often prefer to call it 'Grandmother's Ware.'

Grape, bowl, 8" 30.00
Grape, coffeepot, stick hdl, 2-cup, 7" 65.00
Grape, creamer 35.00
Grape, cup & saucer 25.00
Grape, egg cup 25.00
Grape, pitcher, milk; 40-oz 50.00
Grape, plate, 6" 12.00
Grape, plate, 7" 18.00
Grape, plate, 8" 20.00
Grape, sauce boat 30.00
Grape, sugar bowl, w/lid 50.00
Grape, teacup 25.00
Grape, teapot, 2-cup 65.00
Grape, waste bowl 40.00
Sprig, cup & saucer 40.00
Sprig, pitcher, milk 45.00
Sprig, plate, cake; 9" 40.00
Sprig, plate, dinner 25.00
Sprig, plate, 7" 18.00
Thistle, butter pat 15.00
Thistle, cup & saucer 35.00
Thistle, plate, 7" 15.00

Chelsea Keramic Art Works

Established in 1872 in Chelsea, Massachusetts, by several members of the Robertson family who later formed the Dedham Pottery, this firm is most noted for its experiments in attempting to re-create the ancient Oriental oxblood-red glaze. They succeeded in this in 1885 and also developed several other outstanding glazes as a result of their perseverance. One was their Oriental crackle glaze which they ultimately used in the manufacture of the very successful Dedham dinnerware. Though

their very early artware utilized a redware body, by the late 1870s it was replaced with yellow- or buff-burning clay. A line called Bourgla-Reine (underglaze slip-decorated ware with primarily blue and green backgrounds) was produced, though not to any great extent. Other pieces were designed in imitation of metalware, even to the extent that surfaces were 'hammered' to further enhance the effect. Occasionally live flora was pressed into the damp vessel walls to leave a decorative impression. The pottery closed in 1889. Early wares were not marked; those made from 1875 to 1880 were marked with either two or three lines containing 'Chelsea Keramic Art Works, Robertson and Son,' the 'C-KA-W' cipher, or 'CPUS' in a 4-leaf clover. These were used up to 1889. A paper label was used for a short time on the crackleware. See also Dedham.

Plaque, landscape, bl on ivory, RCR, 11" dia 1,650.00
Plaque, Muse Calliope/merman cvd on bl gloss, sgn, 11", NM ...440.00
Plate, pineapple, impressed CPUS clover, 8½" 500.00
Plate, Rabbit, imp clover, 10" 350.00
Plate, Rabbit, imp clover, 8¾" 250.00
Vase, butterfly, cobalt/bl/lav on craquel, CKAW, 1888, 5½" ..1,100.00
Vase, cream crackle w/red flashing, hdld flask form, rpr, 10" 230.00
Vase, dragon's blood irid, beige outer rim, HCR, 1888, 8" 2,750.00
Vase, floral relief on yel, Josephine Day, 1880, 4¾", EX 440.00
Vase, gr w/brn streaks & spatters, cut/folded rim, 3¾" 2,400.00

Chicago Crucible

For only a few years during the 1920s, the Chicago (IL) Crucible Company made a limited amount of decorative pottery in addition to their regular line of architectural wares. Examples are very scarce today; they carry a variety of marks, all with the company name and location.

Flower frog, frog form, gr matt, 5x6" 275.00
Vase, gr/caramel matt, 8" 110.00
Vase, mottled bl/gr, bottle form w/swirled base, 8", NM 400.00
Vase, 2-tone gr, cvd swirls, bulbous, 4½" 750.00
Vase, 6 vertical leaves, olive gr over brn & aqua, 6½" 450.00

Children's Books

Children's books, especially those from the Victorian era, are charming collectibles. Colorful lithographic illustrations that once delighted little boys in long curls and tiny girls in long stockings and lots of ribbons and lace have lost none of their appeal. Some collectors limit themselves to a specific subject, while others may be far more interested in the illustrations. First editions are more valuable than later issues, and condition and rarity are very important factors to consider before making your purchase.

Arabian Nights, Milo Winter illus, 1912, EX 35.00
Beauty & Beast, Perrault, McLoughlin, ca 1880, 16-pg, EX 135.00
Bedtime Story Calendar, Burgess, 1st edition, 1915, NMIB 150.00
Bertie's Escapade, Grahame, Lippincott, 1949, EX 65.00
Bobbsey Twins at School, Hope, gr cloth cover, 1941, NM 15.00
Bobbsey Twins in Washington, Hope, 1919, VG 12.00
Book of Cowboys, Holling, Platt & Munk, 1936, EX 65.00
Brave Mr Buckingham, Kunhardt, 1st edition, 1935, EX 125.00
Cat in the Hat, Seuss, 1st edition, NY, 1956, VG+ 95.00
Christmas on Stage, pop-up, Byj, spiral bound, 1940, EX 45.00
Cinderella, Perrault, 1st edition, inscr, NY, 1985, M 55.00
Country Noisy Book, MW Brown, illus, Harper, 1940, VG+ 30.00
Dr Seuss's Sleep Book, Seuss, 1st edition, 1962, EX 170.00

Ed Emberley's ABC, Emberly, London, picture cover, 1979, NM .**35.00**
Flower Children, Gordon, 1st edition, 1910, 5½x8", VG **60.00**

Freckles, Gene Stratton-Porter, Grosset and Dunlap, 1916, EX, $15.00.

Friendly Fairies, Gruelle, MA Donohue, 1919, VG+ **85.00**
Gingham Dog & Calico Cat, Field, 1926, VG **225.00**
Grimm's Household Tales, 1st edition, London, 1946, VG **130.00**
Hosie's Zoo, Baskin, Viking Press, 1981, EX, w/dust jacket **40.00**
Jemima Remembers, Dragonwagon, Macmillan, 1984, EX+ **22.50**
Kid From Mars, Friend, Flack illus, NY, 1949, EX **35.00**
King Arthur, Howard Pyle illus, 1927, EX **35.00**
Last of Plainsmen, Z Gray, Grosset & Dunlap, 1908, EX **22.50**
Little Brown Bear, Winter, Merrill, 1937, 16-pg, VG **20.00**
Little Child's Home ABC, McLoughlin, 1899, VG w/wraps **60.00**
Little Lulu at Grandma's Farm, Marge Henderson, 1946, VG **25.00**
Little Red Riding Hood, Brundage, 1929, 12-pg, EX **40.00**
Little Red Riding Hood, McLoughlin, ca 1890s, VG w/wraps **30.00**
Lord of Rushie River, Barker, illus, 1976 ed, VG **10.00**
Mother Goose, James Marshall, 1st edition, 1979, NM **30.00**
Mysterious Island, Verne, Wyeth, Scribner, 1940, NM w/jacket ..**50.00**
Night Before Christmas, pop-up, Moore, 1944, VG **45.00**
Nights w/Uncle Remus, Harris, Winter, Houghton Mifflin, 1917, EX ..**65.00**
Noddy Has an Adventure, Blyton, London, 1st edition, VG **25.00**
Pandy, Bouthton, 1st edition, Volland, 1930, VG **22.00**
Peter's Wagon, Biesterveld, picture cover, Whitman, 1968 ....**20.00**
Pets & Toys, muslin, Saalfield, 6-pg, wraps, VG **45.00**
Philomena, Seredy, 1st edition, 1955, VG w/dust jacket **85.00**
Pooh Get-Well Book, Milne, Shepard, NY, 1973, NM **25.00**
Princess & Apple Tree, Milne, 1st edition, 1937, 40-pg, VG **70.00**
Raggedy Ann Stories, Gruell, mc illus, 1918, 6x9", VG **50.00**
Reaches of Heaven, Singer, 1st edition, 1980, NM w/dust jacket .**32.00**
Red Riding Hood, pop-up, Kubasta illus, London, 1961, VG **30.00**
Rule of Three, Nister, mc illus, ca 1890s, VG **37.50**
Scarcrow of Oz, Baum, Reilly & Lee, 10 color plates, VG **35.00**
Shari Lewis Puppet Book, Lewis, Leipzig, NY, 1958, VG+ **35.00**
Tale of Tom Kitten, Potter, ca 1910-18, VG **98.00**
Uncle Wiggly & Fling Rug, Whitman, 1st edition, 1940, VG **50.00**
Violet Fairy Book, Land, Simont illus, NY, 1948, VG **20.00**
Wait Till Moon Is Full, MW Brown, illus, Harper, 1948, VG **25.00**
What Color Is Love? cloth, Anglund, 1st edition, 1966 EX **25.00**
Whiskers, Frees, Rand McNally, 1941 reprint, VG **17.50**
Wild Swan, HC Anderson, Dial Press NY, 1981, 40-pg, EX **40.00**
Wizard of Oz, Baum, Weekly Reader Club, 1983, EX **18.00**
Wizard of Oz, Baum, 8 color illus, Golden Book, 1986, VG **15.00**

Children's Things

Nearly every item devised for adult furnishings has been reduced to

child size — furniture, dishes, sporting goods, even some tools. All are very collectible. During the late 17th and early 18th centuries, miniature china dinnerware sets were made both in China and in England. They were not intended primarily as children's playthings, however, but instead were made to furnish miniature rooms and cabinets that provided a popular diversion for the adults of that period. By the 19th century, the emphasis had shifted, and most of the small-scaled dinnerware and tea sets were made for children's play.

Late in the 19th century and well into the 20th, toy pressed glass dishes were made, many in the same pattern as full-scale glassware. Today these toy dishes often fetch prices in the same range as those for the 'grown-ups'!

Authorities Margaret and Kenn Whitmyer have compiled a lovely book, *The Collector's Encyclopedia of Children's Dishes,* with full-color photos and current market values; you will find their address in the Directory under Ohio. We also recommend *Children's Glass Dishes, China, and Furniture,* by Doris Anderson Lechler, available at your local bookstore or public library. See also A B C Plates; Canary Lustre; Clothing; Stickley; Willow Ware; etc.

Key:
ds — doll size　　　　　　　Fr — French
Emp — Empire

China

Bowl, Children Fishing, Noritake, 5⅞" **18.00**
Bowl, Tommy Tucker, Shenango **22.50**
Mug, A Present for My Dear Boy, Staffordshire, 2" **330.00**
Mug, cat in bonnet w/glasses, 2⅜" **75.00**
Mug, children playing, purple transfer w/mc, Staffordshire **80.00**
Mug, Fishing Party, 2¾" **68.00**
Mug, girl w/sheep & boy w/donkey, blk transfer, English **95.00**
Mug, Goddess of War, purple transfer, Staffordshire, 2½" **98.00**
Mug, gr stripes w/gold lustre, 2⅜" **80.00**
Mug, Present for My Dear Girl, canary yel, England, 1800s, 2" ..**385.00**
Plate, Franklin Maxim: It Is Hard for an Empty Bag, 6½" **70.00**
Plate, Little Bo Peep, Royal Doulton, 8" **48.00**
Tea set, Birthday Party, pastels w/gold trim, Japan, 15-pc **195.00**
Tea set, Circus Tricks, lustre on porc, Germany, serves 4 ....**165.00**
Tea set, Donald Duck, porc, 13-pc, MIB **395.00**
Tea set, ironstone, child w/cat & dog transfer, 15-pc **165.00**
Tea set, ironstone, Mother Hubbard, brn transfer, 11-pc **120.00**
Tea set, Mickey Mouse, tan lustre, 23-pc, NM in orig box **475.00**
Tea set, scenic view in pk lustre, Czech, 5-pc, rare **165.00**
Tea set, Sprig, pearlware, 1800s, 11-pc **165.00**
Tea set, Wind Flower, England, ca 1830, serves 4 ....**925.00**
Teapot, Nursery Scenes, Germany, 4½" **40.00**
Tumbler, Hey Diddle Diddle, Royal Doulton, 3¾" **65.00**

Furniture

Examples with no dimensions given are child size unless noted doll size.

Armchair, ladderbk, new splint seat, rfn, 25" **140.00**
Armchair, ladderbk, woven cane seat, 25½", VG **40.00**
Armchair, 2-slat ladderbk, EX trn detail, fiber seat, 25" **400.00**
Armchair rocker, Adirondack style, bl pnt w/mc daubs, 20" **95.00**
Bed, soft wood, old blk pnt, 15x21x12" **330.00**
Bed, walnut, rondel crests, spindle sides, SP Hovely, 32" **225.00**
Cabinet, pine w/stencil decor, glass doors, spindles, 43" **150.00**
Chair, blk lacquer, corner style, 18¼" **360.00**
Chair, captain's style, 1850s, rstr **195.00**
Chair, ladderbk, rpl tape seat, 22" **220.00**

Chair, side, caned seat & bk, old rprs, European, 31" **90.00**
Chair, side, curly maple, saber leg, rpl cane seat, 27" **425.00**
Chair, Windsor, gr w/mc eagle & flowers w/gold, 1830s, 30" **175.00**
Chest, cigar box wood, tramp art, appl drw molding, 18x9" **100.00**
Chest, cigar box wood, tramp-art cvg, 11x10" **65.00**
Chest, factory made, veneer/mirror, Depression era, 17" **110.00**
Chest, feather grpt pine, handmade, nailed, dtd 1887, 11x10" ...**450.00**
Chest, mahog English Hplwht bow front, lid folds bk, 26x22x21" .**400.00**
Chest, oak, handmade, swivel mirror, nailed, 14" **65.00**
Cradle, bird's-eye maple, handmade repro, some age, 30x40x20" .**1,100.00**
Cradle, dvtl cherry, hooded style, minor damage, 17" **660.00**
Cradle, dvtl pine, twin sz, old rpr, rpl rockers, 59" **165.00**
Cradle, dvtl poplar, scrolled sides, cut-out rockers, 42" **385.00**
Cradle, dvtl poplar w/cherry finish, heart cutouts, 37" **300.00**
Cradle, dvtl walnut, cut-out edge detail, rprs, 39½" **330.00**
Cradle, dvtl walnut, ds, 22½" **275.00**
Cradle, pine, hooded, wire nails, old red flame grpt, 25" **250.00**
Cradle, poplar, hooded style, 25" **440.00**
Cradle, poplar, worn lt gr pnt, 20½" **50.00**
Cradle, walnut, trn posts & finials, spindle rails, 27x40x22" **265.00**
Cupboard, from crate wood, 2-door top/base, step-bk, 24" **95.00**
Cupboard, poplar, 2 glass doors over step-bk base, 29" **300.00**
Dresser w/mirror, cherry, factory made, early 20th C, 25" **240.00**
Dresser w/mirror, cigar box wood, tramp art, ornate, 46x22" **450.00**
Dresser w/mirror, Eastlake style, handmade, 1880s, rfn, 39" **250.00**
Dresser w/mirror, pine, early 20th C, 11x9" **60.00**
Footstool, cigar box wood, shaped ends, nailed, 4x6x4" **35.00**
Highchair, hardwood, spindle-bk, string seat, gr pnt, 36" **1,295.00**
Highchair, primitive, gr pnt, trn posts/ft/finials, 35" **215.00**
Highchair, wood, Strombecker, ds, 8" **15.00**
Magazine rack, walnut, handmade, latticework/brass tacks, 14" **35.00**

Rocker, oak with clear finish, pressed Yellow Kid on back, turned features, caned seat, restored, 30", $275.00.

Secretary, Victorian style, cvd walnut, 46x30x17", EX **1,550.00**
Settee, Classical mahog veneer, upholstered, 1850s, 27x45x19" ...**470.00**
Sideboard, crate wood, tramp art, superstructure, 36x20", EX **225.00**
Sideboard w/mirror, handmade, very ornate, 1890s, 18x11" **160.00**
Stand, library; oak, 2-shelf, 1920s, 19x11x11" **175.00**
Table, pine, handmade, trn drop ea corner, shaped legs, 10" **55.00**
Trunk, wood & cb, paper litho int, Little Traveler, 7" L, EX **85.00**
Wash bench, w/wringer, wooden tub & washboard, EX **210.00**
Washstand, crate wood, tramp art, towel bar, allover cvg, 26" **275.00**
Washstand w/swivel oval mirror, oak, factory made, 25" **100.00**

Glass

Bowl, master berry; Lacy Daisy **15.00**

Butter dish, Pennsylvania, gr **185.00**
Butter dish, Whirligig **30.00**
Cake stand, Baby Thumbprint **150.00**
Cake stand, Beautiful Lady **30.00**
Cake stand, Daisy & Star **35.00**
Creamer, Doyle #500 ....**30.00**
Creamer, Grapevine w/Ovals **60.00**
Creamer, Grapevine w/Ovals, bl **50.00**
Creamer, Hobnail w/T'print, bl **45.00**
Creamer, Lamb **50.00**
Creamer, Liberty Bell **95.00**
Creamer, Michigan w/Carnation **50.00**
Creamer, Rex **25.00**
Cup, Lion **35.00**
Cup, Nursery Rhymes, milk glass **22.00**
Cup, Prism & Pinwheel **27.50**
Cup & saucer, Grape Stippled Leaf **30.00**
Mug, Baby Animals, milk glass **34.00**
Mug, Bird in Nest, milk glass **50.00**
Mug, Birds & Owl, amber **30.00**
Mug, Butterfly, milk glass **22.00**
Mug, Cupid & Venus **27.00**
Mug, Good Girl, milk glass **40.00**
Mug, Gooseberry **25.00**
Mug, Monkey & Vines, milk glass **55.00**
Mug, Robin, bl opaque **42.00**
Pitcher, water; Galloway **30.00**
Pitcher, water; Michigan, gold trim **35.00**
Pitcher, water; Portland, gold trim **28.00**
Pitcher, water; Rex **55.00**
Plate, Wee Branches **50.00**
Punch bowl, Invt Strawberry **45.00**
Punch bowl, Oval Star **48.00**
Punch bowl, Tulip & Honeycomb **25.00**
Punch bowl, Wheat Sheaf, +4 cups **60.00**
Punch bowl, Whirligig **30.00**
Punch bowl, Wild Rose, opal **85.00**
Spooner, Colonial, Cambridge, gr **35.00**
Spooner, Hawaiian Lei, w/bee **25.00**
Spooner, Menagerie, amber, fish **145.00**
Spooner, Nursery Rhymes **45.00**
Spooner, Stippled Vine & Beads, sapphire bl **100.00**
Spooner, Whirligig **15.00**
Sugar bowl, Drum **115.00**
Sugar bowl, Duncan #42 ....**80.00**
Sugar bowl, Lion, w/lid **110.00**
Sugar bowl, Oval Star **25.00**
Sugar bowl, Rex **35.00**
Sugar bowl, Sawtooth Band, Heisey **115.00**
Tray, Doyle #500, bl **70.00**
Tumble up, gr pitcher w/blk hdl & matching tumbler, 5" **275.00**
Tumbler, Oval Star **8.00**
Tumbler, Pattee Cross **15.00**

Miscellaneous

Bean pot, brn stoneware, 2¾" **45.00**
Book, prayer; celluloid covers, 1936 ....**20.00**
Carpet sweeper, Little Queen, Bissell **50.00**
Clothes brush, china girl as hdl, pk bristles, mk Germany **35.00**
Cup & saucer, bl graniteware **25.00**
Kiddykook Bake Set, aluminum, 10-pc **45.00**
Ladle, lt bl speckled graniteware, 4½", EX **40.00**
Noisemaker, all wood, worn finish, 10" L **200.00**

Pans, copper, 3-pc set	**90.00**
Pie plate, stoneware, cobalt int, 1¼" dia	**35.00**
Plate, enamel on tin	**14.00**
Plate, 2 children w/hoops, ABC rim, CI, mini, 2⅞"	**150.00**
Pot, hammered aluminum, hdls, w/lid, 2"	**14.00**
Rattle, tin, ABCs, For...Child & Eagle, whistle hdl, 5½"	**175.00**
Rocking horse, cvd 1-pc body, orig pnt, leather saddle, 32"	**375.00**
Rocking horse, wood, old brn rpt, metal patches, 64" L	**660.00**
Sled, pnt wood w/stencil, metal-tipped runners, 1909, 33"	**385.00**
Spelling board, heavy cb, Richmond School Fun, '40, 9½x13"	**125.00**
Tableware, pewter, 6-place set	**110.00**
Tea set, boy & girl in garden, tin litho, 15-pc	**150.00**
Tea set, Frolicking Children, graniteware, Germany, 6-place	**450.00**
Tea set, Geisha Women, tin litho, Ohio Art, 8-pc	**250.00**
Tea set, Kittens, tin litho, Ohio Art, 1930s, 6-pc	**250.00**
Tea set, She Loves Me...Loves Me Not, tin litho, 9-pc	**125.00**
Teething ring, sterling & MOP, bl enameling, 1880s	**125.00**
Teething ring/rattle, sterling, cat figural	**95.00**
Wagon, Daisy & PM Co, blk striping/red stencil on wood, 33"	**600.00**

Chocolate Glass

Jacob Rosenthal developed chocolate glass, a rich shaded opaque brown sometimes referred to as caramel slag, in 1900 at the Indiana Tumbler and Goblet Company of Greentown, Indiana. Later, other companies produced similar ware. Only the latter is listed here. See also Greentown. Our advisors for this category are Jerry and Sandi Garrett; they are listed in the Directory under Indiana.

Bowl, Aldine, oval, w/lid	**1,650.00**
Bowl, Beaded Triangle, 4½"	**400.00**
Bowl, Cattail & Water Lily, 8¼"	**550.00**
Bowl, Geneva, oval, 10½"	**450.00**
Bowl, Shield w/Daisy & Button, 8⅜"	**1,350.00**
Butter dish, Chrysanthemum Leaf	**1,400.00**
Butter dish, Wild Rose & Bow Knot, McKee & Bros, 5"	**500.00**
Creamer, Chrysanthemum Leaf	**650.00**
Creamer, Strigal, tankard form	**165.00**
Hatpin holder, Orange Tree	**700.00**
Mug, Serenade, 5"	**250.00**
Mug, Swirl	**600.00**
Nappy, Masonic, hdls	**175.00**
Pitcher, milk; Feather	**1,350.00**
Pitcher, Rose Garland	**2,850.00**
Salt cellar, Honeycomb, 1¾" dia	**475.00**
Spooner, Wild Rose w/Bowknot	**225.00**
Syrup, Chrysanthemum Leaf, metal lid	**1,000.00**
Toothpick holder, Chrysanthemum Leaf	**850.00**
Tray, Venetian, 10x8"	**450.00**

Christmas Collectibles

Christmas past . . . lovely mementos from long ago attest to the ostentatious Victorian celebrations of the season.

St. Nicholas, better known as Santa, has changed much since 300 A.D. when the good Bishop Nicholas showered needy children with gifts and kindnesses. During the early 18th century, Santa was portrayed as the kind gift-giver to well-behaved children and the stern switch-bearing disciplinarian to those who were bad. In 1822 Clement Clark Moore, a New York poet, wrote his famous *Night Before Christmas*, and the Santa he described was jolly and jovial — a lovable old elf who was stern with no one. Early Santas wore robes of yellow, brown, blue, green, red, white, or even purple. But Thomas Nast, who worked as an illustrator for Harper's Weekly, was the first to depict Santa in a red suit instead of the traditional robe and to locate him here the entire year at the North Pole headquarters.

Today's collectors prize early Santa figures, especially those in robes of fur or mohair or those dressed in an unusual color. Some early examples of Christmas memorabilia are the pre-1870 ornaments from Dresden, Germany. These cardboard figures — angels, gondolas, umbrellas, dirigibles, and countless others — sparkled with gold and silver trim. Late in the 1870s, blown glass ornaments were imported from Germany. There were over 6,000 recorded designs, all painted inside with silvery colors. From 1890 through 1910, blown glass spheres were often decorated with beads, tassels, and tinsel rope.

Christmas lights, made by Sandwich and some of their contemporaries, were either pressed or mold-blown glass shaped into a form similar to a water tumbler. They were filled with water and then hung from the tree by a wire handle; oil floating on the surface of the water served as fuel for the lighted wick.

Kugels are glass ornaments that were made as early as 1820 and as late as 1890. Ball-shaped examples are more common than the fruit and vegetable forms and have been found in sizes ranging from 1" to 14" in diameter. They were made of thick glass with heavy brass caps, in cobalt, green, gold, silver, red, and occasionally in amethyst.

Although experiments involving the use of electric light bulbs for the Christmas tree occured before 1900, it was 1903 before the first manufactured socket set was marketed. These were very expensive and often proved a safety hazard. In 1921 safety regulations were established, and products were guaranteed safety approved. The early bulbs were smaller replicas of Edison's household bulb. By 1910 G.E. bulbs were rounded with a pointed end, and until 1919 all bulbs were hand blown. The first figural bulbs were made around 1910 in Austria. Japan soon followed, but their product was never of the high quality of the Austrian wares. American manufacturers produced their first machine-made figurals after 1919. Today figural bulbs (especially character-related examples) are very popular collectibles. Bubble lights were popular from about 1945 to 1960 when miniature lights were introduced. These tiny lamps dampened the public's enthusiasm for the bubblers, and manufacturers stopped providing replacement bulbs.

Feather trees were made from 1850 to 1950. All are collectible. Watch for newly manufactured feather trees that have lately been reintroduced.

For further information concerning Christmas collectibles, we recommend these highly informative books, *Christmas Collectibles, Vols. 1* and *2*, by Margaret and Kenn Whitmyer and *Christmas Ornaments, Lights, and Decorations, A Collector's Identification and Value Guide*, by George Johnson. All books are available from Collector Books or your local bookstore.

Bulbs

Early clear glass German bulbs: Jester head, NM paint, 3", $85.00; Indian, worn paint, 3¾", $145.00; Clown head, EX paint, 3", $75.00.

Aviator, purple coat, pk hat, gold trim, milk glass, 3", EX 55.00
Ball w/stars, red 12.00
Bell w/Santa face on ea side, milk glass 12.00
Betty Boop, mc pnt 85.00
Boy in hip boots, worn pnt, milk glass 55.00
Chick, mc pnt, milk glass, NM 55.00
Clown on ball, bl suit w/yel ruffle, milk glass, 3" 85.00
Cross, pk pnt, milk glass, 3" 25.00
Darla, girl in pk dress, orange hair, milk glass, NM 65.00
Dick Tracy, EX pnt, milk glass, 3" 145.00
Donald Duck, mc pnt, clear glass 65.00
Drama face, happy/sad, mc pnt, Germany, EX 195.00
Ducklings, mc pnt, milk glass, sm, NM 48.00
Dunce head, EX pnt, milk glass 65.00
Elephant w/trunk up, no pnt, milk glass 95.00
Grapes, mc w/gr leaves, milk glass, 3¼" 15.00
Hayseed Farmer, EX pnt, milk glass 95.00
Indian head, pk & orange, 2" 175.00
Jack-o'-lantern, EX pnt, milk glass 65.00
Kayo, squatting, milk glass, 1935, EX 110.00
Lantern, VG pnt, milk glass, Japan, sm 12.00
Lion w/tennis racket, mc pnt, milk glass, NM 110.00
Little Orphan Annie, mc pnt, milk glass, c 1935, 3⅛" 165.00
Mickey Mouse, mc pnt, milk glass, EX 80.00
Owl, mc pnt, clear glass, Germany 75.00
Paramount shooting star, EX pnt, 4" 40.00
Pig, bl tie, gr jacket, yel pants, milk glass, 3" 150.00
President bust, worn pnt 110.00
Rabbit, sitting, yel & red pnt, milk glass, NM 120.00
Santa, bright colors, 9" 175.00
Santa, full figure w/pack, mc pnt, milk glass, EX 45.00
Santa atop chimney, mc pnt, milk glass, EX 75.00
Santa in oval, mc pnt, milk glass, 3¾", NM 65.00
Smitty, milk glass, VG 85.00
Snowman, red hat, bl bag, milk glass, 3" 20.00
Star w/face, EX pnt, milk glass 15.00
Teddy bear, red pnt, milk glass, EX 110.00
Woman in shoe, mc pnt, milk glass, NM 125.00
Zeppelin, EX pnt, milk glass 110.00
3 Men in a Tub, mc pnt, EX 135.00

Candy Containers

Cornucopia, crepe paper, die-cut decor 65.00
Deer w/antlers, papier-mache & lead, glass eyes, 11", EX 850.00
Dwarf, cb, glitter, pnt face, 5" 45.00
House w/cotton Santa on cotton roof, mk, Japan 95.00
Jockey cap, Dresden, blk brim, mk MIG, 1¾x4x2⅜" 150.00
Santa, cb, cloth trim, gr cloth sack, 12", VG 300.00
Santa, cb, cotton clothes, Fr, 8½", EX 135.00
Santa, cb w/clay face, cloth dressed, 10½", VG 220.00
Santa, cb w/gold flecks, mk Germany on base, 15", EX 230.00
Santa, chenille type, papier-mache face, fur beard, 7", EX 255.00
Santa, papier-mache, red coat, bl pants, 4" 130.00
Santa, papier-mache, red w/gold flecks, rstr, 6", EX 245.00
Santa, papier-mache & cb, basket on bk, wood base, 10", EX ..3,500.00
Santa, papier-mache & cb, bl & red clothes, 10", VG 285.00
Santa, papier-mache & cb, bl pants, 8½", VG 350.00
Santa, papier-mache & cb, cloth dressed, bl pants, 10", NM 500.00
Santa, papier-mache & cb, cotton clothes, 11½", EX 150.00
Santa, papier-mache & cb, cotton clothes, 14", EX 300.00
Santa, papier-mache & cb, snow on coat, 10", EX 600.00
Santa, papier-mache & cb, wire arms, bl pants, 17", EX 635.00
Santa, papier-mache & cb, wire arms, rstr base, 13", VG 300.00

Santa, papier-mache/wire/cb w/mica, on wood pile, 5", VG 230.00
Santa on deer, compo, metal horns, Dresden trim, Germany, 10"...625.00
Santa on sleigh, papier-mache & wire, cloth dressed, 14" 1,200.00
Santa on wicker tricycle w/feather tree, Germany, 10", EX 775.00
Santa w/bird on sleeve, papier-mache & cb, 10", EX 635.00
Snowman, papier-mache/egg carton w/Blk features, 9" 98.00
Star medallion, Dresden, cb w/glitter, 3" 120.00
Wreath, Dresden, 4¼" 150.00

Ornaments

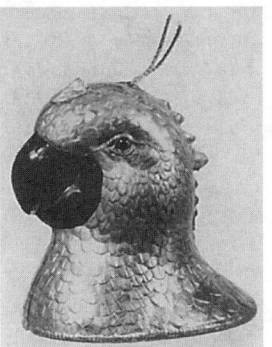

Parrot's head of pressed paper with color highlights, Dresden, EX, 2", $425.00.

Angel, diecut w/spun glass wings, 2-sided, 3½x4" 85.00
Angel, Tuck diecut, in spun glass circle, 4¼" 85.00
Angel's head, diecut, in spun glass circle, 2½", VG 65.00
Angel w/lg wings, blown, flesh w/mc details, 1940s, 3" 60.00
Apple w/leaf, mold blown, red & yel-gr, ca 1900, 2¾x2¼" 25.00
Baboon, blown, pearly gold/blk/red, 1920s, 2¼" 110.00
Baby face ea side, blown, glass eyes, ca 1920 ....185.00
Balloon, wire-wrapped, w/Father Xmas diecut, 6" w/tinsel tail ...165.00
Banjo, Dresden, orange & tan stripes, 3" 165.00
Bear w/hump holding beach ball, mold blown, mc, 1910s, 3" 165.00
Beetle, blown, pk w/gr wings, 3" 165.00
Bell, blown, gold w/wht & gr flower, 3" 22.00
Berry w/leaf, blown, pk, unsilvered, 1900, 2½", EX 25.00
Bird, blown, bl & silver w/spun glass tail, Germany, 5½" 15.00
Bird w/trn head, blown, mc w/spun glass tail, 4¼" 15.00
Birdcage, blown, bird w/spun glass tail inside, 3" 90.00
Boat, wire-wrapped, unsilvered, w/Father Christmas diecut, 9" ..145.00
Boy, blown, pearly wht, pk hat/scarf/belt, 3" 110.00
Brownie head, blown, pearly wht/blk/gold, 1900s, 2½" 265.00
Butterfly, blown, red 65.00
Carousel, blown, silver w/red & gr, early, 3" 85.00
Cat in slipper, blown, pearly wht/pk/yel, 3½" 155.00
Cello, blown, gold w/red & bl, 1920s, 3¼" 22.00
Cherries on ovoid, blown, pearly wht/red/gr, 4" 32.00
Clown, blown, brn w/pnt details, silver hair, '30, 2½" 60.00
Clown, blown, fat, mc, silvered, 3¼" 50.00
Cockatoo, blown, pk/gr/red, on clip, 3" 65.00
Cross on heart, blown, gold on wht, 2" 27.50
Cuckoo clock, blown, red & dk gold, paper face 65.00
Dinner bell, blown, bl, 4¼" 22.50
Dog begging, blown, pearly wht w/blk spots, 4" 95.00
Doll's head, blown, glass eyes, silver hair, 1910s, 2¾" 115.00
Eagle flying, Dresden, tan & brn, 5½" wingspan, NM 295.00
Egg shape w/emb rabbit ea side, blown, mc, Germany, 2½" 200.00
Father Christmas, cotton, gold Dresden belt, die-cut face, 5" 235.00
Fish, blown, pearly silver w/mc, 1920, 2½" 55.00
Fish, blown w/cb tail, silver/wht/blk/red, 1910, 4½" 125.00
Flower, blown, orange, 3" 20.00
Flower girl, blown, flesh face, gold hair, mc flowers, 4" 150.00

Flower w/lg petal, blown, red, 1920s, 1½" 35.00
Fruit basket, blown, mc fruits, 3" 65.00
Girl in bag, blown, yel hair, pk bag, 3" 80.00
Good Luck horseshoe, blown, pearly wht/blk/gold, 2½" 110.00
Hag, blown, 2-faced, pearly pk, 2" 130.00
Horn, blown, silver/gold/bl/red, 1920x, 4" 14.00
House w/turkey, blown, wht/bl-gr/red, 1910s, 3" 65.00
Humpty-Dumpty, blown, wht/blk/red/gold, 1920s, 3¼" 235.00
Icicle, blown, pearly bl, 1930, 6" 12.50
Indian head, blown, copper, red & gray feathers, 3" 325.00
Jockey, Dresden, flesh face, pk shirt, silver horse, 3" 395.00
Kittens in basket, blown, pearly wht, pk basket, 3" 95.00
Lady on urn, blown, silver matt w/gold, 3½" 30.00
Lamb, blown, pk & gr, 4½" 95.00
Lobster, Dresden, orange & beige, 4" 325.00
Madonna w/Child in arms, blown, mc, 3", VG 150.00
Mandolin, blown, pk w/long blk stem, 6" 42.00
Moonface, diecut w/in spun glass circle, on clip, 5" 90.00
Mountain climber, blown, flesh face, mc clothes, 6" 85.00
Old lady in glasses, blown, mc, 1920s, 3½" 200.00
Owl head, blown, pearly silver/blk/red, ca 1920, 3x3" 150.00
Peach w/leaf, yel to pk, flocked, 1910s, 2½" 35.00
Pear, blown, orange to yel, fabric leaf, 3" 14.00
Pig, Dresden, fat/sitting, flesh color, rare, 3¼" 275.00
Pipe, blown, red/wht/bl, ca 1930s, 5¾" 38.00
Rail car, blown, silver matt w/orange & gr, 3" 65.00
Red Riding Hood, blown, pk & red, rpl glass eyes 110.00
Rose, blown, pearly wht w/bl-gr at top, 1910, 1¾x2" 12.50
Santa, scrap, red robe, in oval, 5" 22.50
Santa in basket, blown, red w/gold, 3" 135.00
Skeezix, blown, pearly wht, pk clothes, gr tie, 4" 150.00
Snake, blown, pearly bl-gr, 1920s, 5½" 135.00
Spaniel, blown, silver w/gr ears & legs, red bow, 3" 110.00
Storks w/open bills, mold blown, 4" spun glass tails, on clip ...110.00
Strawberry, blown, gold 12.50
Street lamp, blown, pk, gr & red panels, 4" 30.00
Tree, blown, gr & wht, EX molding, 1920s, 2" 18.00
Turkey, blown, silver/blk/red, 1920s, 2½x2¼x1½" 150.00
Turtle, Dresden, gray, 3½" 250.00
Uncle Sam, blown, wht/blk/red/bl, ca 1930, 3¾", M 220.00
Vase, wire-wrapped, w/paper flower, 1940s, 6¼" 65.00
Walnut, blown, gold, 1920s, 1½" 12.00
Web, wire-wrapped, w/glass spider, 4¼" rods form web 130.00
Witch, blown, 4-colored pnt, unsilvered, 5" 265.00
6-pointed star w/indents, blown, silver/red/gold, 4½" 35.00

Miscellaneous

Angel, wax on compo, spun glass wings, 6", VG 135.00
Bells, St Nicholas Electric Bells, late 1940s, MIB 95.00
Candle, light-up, CI base w/cb tubes, 1930s, EX, pr 70.00
Candle holder, Deco-style Santa, chalkware, 1940s, 14", EX 65.00
Candle holder, Santa, red glass, Fenton 35.00
Candle holder, tin w/clay counterbalances, mc pnt, 1890s 45.00
Candles, outdoor, Bakelite base, electric, Paramount, 42", pr ...120.00
Church, coated cb building, Japan, 5" 45.00
Cube puzzle, Santa, paper on wood, McLoughlin, 1897, 13x11", EX..1,500.00
Diecut, Santa in plane, cb w/mica, 11", EX 85.00
Doll, Santa, compo & cloth, rpt, redressed, 21", G 200.00
Doll, Santa, compo & cloth, w/bell, redressed, Germany, 17", EX..500.00
Doll, Santa, pressed cloth face, cloth body, redressed, 21" 200.00
Fence, CI, gr & gold pnt, 10 pcs 11½" L/4 8" posts/2 gates 225.00
Fence, dowel posts, wht w/gold, ca 1900, 84" 135.00
Fence, pnt tin wire, 20" sq w/2-part 6" gate 110.00

Fence, pnt wicker w/12 wooden posts, AW Drake...PA, 38" sq ..265.00
Fence, pnt wood, flat rails, Valley Novelty...PA, 4½x18" 85.00
Figurine, Santa at child's bed, bsk, Japan, 3", EX 110.00
Figurine, Santa driving train, bsk, unmk, 3", EX 120.00
Figurine, Santa w/gr pack, bsk, Japan, 4½", EX 50.00
Figurine, Santa w/horse, bsk, Germany, 3", EX 200.00
Figurine, Santa w/reindeer, bsk, Germany, 3" 110.00
Head vase, girl in red w/holly on muff, Napco, 1959 ....50.00
Kugel, acorn, yel, orig metal cap, 1⅝" 160.00
Kugel, ball, pk-red, orig metal cap, 4¾" 200.00
Kugel, ball, ruby, orig metal cap, 1½" 135.00
Kugel, ball w/ribs, emerald gr, orig metal cap, 5" 250.00
Kugel, grapes, bl, rpl period metal cap, 5¼" 325.00
Kugel, grapes, cobalt, orig metal cap, 2¾" 250.00
Kugel, grapes, cranberry, orig metal cap, 4" 250.00
Kugel, grapes, gold to blk in tip, orig metal cap, 2¾" 170.00
Kugel, grapes, purple to dk amethyst, orig metal cap, 2¾" 400.00
Kugel, grapes, yel-gr, orig metal cap, 2¾" 295.00
Kugel, pear, gr, orig metal cap, spotting, 5¾" 250.00
Kugel, pear, ribbed pattern, silver, metal cap, 2⅞" 125.00
Lamp, Santa figural, molded fibre, Ungers Fibre..., 18", EX 300.00
Lamp, signal; Santa figural, EX pnt, ca 1950s 40.00
Lamp, signal; Santa's head form, battery operated, Japan 95.00
Light, bust of King Edward, Eclipse Lamp..., amethyst, 4⅛" 650.00
Light, bust of Queen Victoria, lt aqua, Hearn Wright, 4" 180.00
Light, Expanded Dmn, bright yel-amber, folded rim, 2⅞" 125.00
Light, Expanded Dmn, dk gr w/yel tone, folded rim, 3" 125.00
Light, Expanded Dmn, emerald gr, Brock's Illumination, 3⅝" 80.00
Light, Expanded Dmn, purple amethyst, pontil scar, 3⅝" 90.00
Light, grapes, lt aqua, Hearn Wright, 3⅞" 110.00
Light, Harlequin Dmns, dk emerald gr, smooth base, 3½" 195.00
Light, Harlequin pattern, dk purple amethyst, 3⅜" 250.00
Light, ribs, lt smoky amethyst, pontil scar, 2⅝" 165.00
Light, swirl ribs, pk-amethyst, flared/folded rim, 3⅜" 140.00
Lights, Betty Boop, string of 10, NM 300.00
Lights, Noma Bubble Lights, string of 12, EX working 85.00
Mask, Santa, papier-mache & cotton, Germany, 20", EX 850.00
Nativity set, cb litho, 9-pc+manger, Concordia, 1950s, EX 65.00
Nodder, Santa, papier-mache & cb w/wire arms, 26", EX 1,200.00
Nutcracker, Santa, cvd wood, mc pnt, contemporary, 9½", M 45.00
Party set, Holly & Spruce, Taylor-Smith-Taylor, 1960s, 12-pc ..195.00
Pin, angel, gold plated w/rhinestones, from $15 to 45.00
Plaque, Santa face in holly oval, plastic, lights up, 1950s 60.00
Plaque, Santa head, molded fiber, pnt & cotton decor, 18", EX ...85.00
Print, baby on chair beside tree, Maude Humphrey, 8x10" 75.00
Rolly polly, Santa, papier-mache, gray hat, 8½", EX 470.00
Rolly polly, Santa, papier-mache, Schoenhut, rpt, 8" 415.00
Rolly polly, Santa, papier-mache, Schoenhut, 14", VG 2,000.00
Santa, bsk, flannel coat, US War Zone Germany, 7" 175.00
Santa, celluloid w/cb bk, lights up, 24", NMIB 65.00
Santa, chalkware, purple-brn coat w/gold, 1800s, 18" 950.00
Santa, compo, basket on bk, yel plush coat, Germany, 11", EX ..250.00
Santa, compo & cb, clay face, star on belt, 10", EX 125.00
Santa, compo & cb, w/squeaker (silent), Germany, 7" 125.00
Santa, papier-mache, Belsnickle, cloth trim, 11", G 300.00
Santa, papier-mache, Belsnickle, mica on coat, 6½", EX 450.00
Santa, papier-mache, Belsnickle, much gold & mica, 14", EX ..1,200.00
Santa, papier-mache, Belsnickle, pk-wht coat w/mica, 10½" 440.00
Santa, papier-mache, Belsnickle, red w/gold, 9½", EX 1,200.00
Santa, papier-mache, Belsnickle, wht coat w/mica, 11½", VG ...900.00
Santa papier-mache, Belsnickle, w/feather tree, mc, 8", VG 275.00
Santa, papier-mache, felt clothes, in moss car, Germany, 7", EX ..1,265.00
Santa, papier-mache, glass eyes, mechanical, 12", EX 560.00
Santa, papier-mache & cb, paper belt, Japan, 13", EX 85.00

Santa face, celluloid & cb, lights up, 1950s, 14" 55.00
Santa in sleigh, compo & wire, felt clothes, Germany, 7", EX 225.00
Santa in sleigh, tin & plastic, battery op, Japan, 17", EX 200.00
Santa in sleigh w/2 reindeer, celluloid, Japan, 18", VG 45.00
Santa in sleigh w/3 reindeer, papier-mache/wood, Germany, 25" ...300.00
Santa on reindeer, plastic, lights up, 1950s, MIB 45.00
Santa w/pack, compo & wood squeaker, 7½", EX 110.00
Sheep, wood w/flocked coats, Germany, ca 1900, 5" 85.00
Teapot, Lucky Santa Claus, ceramic, Made in England, 7" 110.00
Tree, feather; dk gr w/red berries, 1900s, 22", EX 225.00
Tree stand, emb metal, musical key wind-up, 1870s, 15" dia 695.00
Tree stand, metal pot in center, 8 series lamps, Noma, 1940s 85.00
Wreath, chenille, Reliance, early, MIB 37.50

Chrysanthemum Sprig, Blue

This is the blue opaque version of Northwood's popular pattern, Chrysanthemum Sprig. It was made at the turn of the century and is today very rare, as its values indicate. Prices are influenced by the amount of gold remaining on the raised designs. Our advisors for this category are Betty and Clarence Maier; they're listed in the Directory under Pennsylvania.

Bowl, berry; sm 325.00
Bowl, master fruit; 10½" W 600.00
Butter dish 850.00
Compote, jelly 475.00
Condiment tray, rare, VG gold 750.00

Creamer, $385.00; Sugar bowl with lid, $450.00.

Cruet, 6½" 1,000.00
Pitcher, water 1,100.00
Shakers, pr 450.00
Spooner 265.00
Toothpick holder 450.00
Tumbler 250.00

Circus Collectibles

The 1890s — the Golden Age of the circus. Barnum and Bailey's parades transformed mundane city streets into an exotic never-never land inhabited by trumpeting elephants with jeweled gold headgear strutting by to the strains of the calliope that issued from a fine red- and gilt-painted wagon extravagantly decorated with carved wooden animals of every description. It was an exciting experience. Is it any wonder that collectors today treasure the mementos of that golden era? See also Posters.

Key:
B&B — Barnum & Bailey   RB — Ringling Bros.

Banner, Bearded Lady, Snapp Wyatt 1,000.00
Banner, Eeka Geek Show, Hiner 600.00
Button, pin-bk; Clyde Beatty & cub, Coles Bros, blk/wht, EX 12.50
Date sheet, Beatty-Cole Bros, color litho, 1967, 36x42" 50.00
Invitation, opening performance; B&B, 1911 ....30.00
Magazine, RB B&B, Coles Bros, 1947, EX 25.00
Pass, work; Beaty, 1976 ....5.00
Photograph, Earle's Midgets, inscr, 1934 ....35.00
Postcard, photo of B&B giants, 1930s 20.00
Program, B&B, color cover, 1911, EX+ 85.00
Program, Polack, Shrine, 1950, EX 20.00
Program, RB B&B, 1954, EX 30.00
Rope ladder 150.00
Sheet, official route; B&B, mc graphics, 1942 ....15.00
Ticket, Clowns Vs Braves, baseball, Blk player shown, unused 75.00

Clambroth

Clambroth is a term that refers to a type of glass popular in the Victorian period. It was semi-opaque and gray-white in color, said to resemble the broth of the clam. See also Sandwich.

Candlestick, sq base, fluted std, petal socket, 8¾" 100.00
Ladle, 9½" 52.00
Spill holder, ltly sanded, Dmn Quilt, 3 bull's-eye dmns, 4½" 185.00
Toothpick holder, floral at rim, Sandwich, 2" 100.00

Clarice Cliff

Between 1928 and 1935 in Burslem, England, as the director and part owner of Wilkinson and Newport Pottery Companies, Clarice Cliff and her 'paintresses' created a body of hand-painted pottery whose influence is felt to the present time.

The name for the oevre was Bizarre Ware, and the predominant sensibility, style, and appearance was Deco. Almost all pieces are signed and include the pattern names. There were over 160 patterns and more than 400 shapes, all of which are illustrated in A *Bizarre Affair — the Life and Work of Clarice Cliff*, published by Harry N. Abrams, Inc., written by Len Griffen and our advisors, Susan and Louis Meisel, whose address is listed in the Directory under New York.

Clarice Cliff died in 1972, shortly after the Victoria and Albert Museum showed her work in retrospect, and collectors (primarily in England) began seeking and admiring her work. In September of 1982, the Metropolitan Museum of Art in New York acquired and placed on view a selection of six pieces.

Note: Non-hand-painted work (transfer printed) was produced after World War II and into the 1950s. Some of the most common names are 'Tonquin' and 'Charlotte.' These items, while attractive and enjoyable to own, have no value in the collector market.

Beaker, Sunray, orange bands, 3" 230.00
Bowl, Alpine, orange band, flared, 9" 200.00
Bowl, orange-roofed cottages/stylized trees, ftd, 9" 325.00
Bowl, Woodland, octagonal rim, 6" 250.00
Candle holders, My Garden, kneeling female w/basket, 7", pr 400.00
Charger, Bizarre in Clouvre pattern, 17½" dia 6,400.00
Charger, Bizarre in Oranges pattern, 18" dia 5,225.00
Coffee service, Crocus, 7½" pot, cr/sug, pitcher, 6 c/s 485.00
Coffee service, Ravel, 6" pot, cr/sug, 6 c/s, 6 cake plates 800.00

Isis jug, Abstract, mc bands, 1-hdl, 10" 920.00
Jug, Conical, Fantasque Bizarre in Broth pattern, 7" 1,000.00
Jug, Poppy Delecia, pear shape w/angle hdl, 7" 325.00
Lemonade set, Abstract, 8" pitcher, 4 cylindrical cups 690.00
Lotus jug, Autumn, orange/gr bands, 1-hdl, 11½" 1,265.00
Lotus jug, Bizarre, Lightning pattern, 1-hdl, 11½" 3,600.00
Lotus jug, Fantasque Bizarre, Autumn pattern, 1-hdl, 11½" 2,200.00
Lotus jug, Fantasque Bizarre, Bl W pattern, 1-hdl, 11¾" 8,000.00
Lotus jug, Garland, mc florals, hdls, 12" 800.00
Lotus jug, Nasturtium, yel/orange rim band, 12" 460.00

Lotus jug, Sunrise, orange and yellow bands, marked, 12", $950.00.

Pitcher, stork body as spout, neck as hdl, 7½" 525.00
Plaque, Fantasque Bizarre in Pastel Autumn pattern, 10¼" 575.00
Plate, Autumn, yel/gr banding, scalloped, 11" 365.00
Plate, Bizarre, orange medallion, bl triangles, 8-sided, 8¾" 525.00
Plate, Bizarre in Latona Tree pattern, mc on cream, 9" 400.00
Plate, Devon, yel/gr bands, 10½" 435.00
Plate, Fantasque Bizarre in Melon pattern, mc w/blk bands, 9" ..575.00
Plate, Forest Glen, 10" 90.00
Plate, Sunrise, orange/gr bands, scalloped, 10¾" 250.00
Preserve pot, Bl Firs, flat-sided, cylindrical ft, 4" 250.00
Preserve pot, Trees & House, cherry finial, 3½" 175.00
Sugar sifter, Autumn, conical, 5½" 365.00
Sugar Sifter, Bonjour in Rhodanthe pattern, 5¼" 375.00
Sugar sifter, Conical, Fantasque Bizarre, Gibralter, 5½" 2,400.00
Sugar sifter, Conical, Fantasque Bizarre, House & Bridge, 5½" ...975.00
Vase, Bizarre, Clouvre Butterfly, arch motif, #363, 6¼" 2,200.00
Vase, Bizarre in Bl Ribbon pattern, baluster, 9" 975.00
Vase, emb crocus, purple/gr on ivory, 6" 300.00
Vase, Inspiration, abstracts, baluster, 9" 435.00
Vase, landscape on stippled cafe-au-lait yel, cylinder, 8" 365.00
Vase, Patina Tree, lg tree on bl spattered ground, ftd, 6½" 600.00

Cleminson

A hobby turned to enterprise, Cleminson is one of several California potteries whose clever hand-decorated wares are attracting the attention of today's collectors. The Cleminsons started their business at their El Monte home in 1941 and were so successful that eventually they expanded to a modern plant that employed more than 150 workers. They produced not only dinnerware and kitchen items such as cookie jars, canisters, and accessories, but novelty wall vases, small trays, plaques, etc., as well. Though nearly always marked, Cleminson wares are easy to spot as you become familiar with their distinctive glaze colors. Their grayed-down blue and green, berry red, and dusty pink say 'Cleminson' as clearly as their trademark. Unable to compete with for-

eign imports, the pottery closed in 1963. Our advisor for this category is Jack Chipman, author of *The Collector's Encyclopedia of California Pottery*; he is listed in the Directory under California.

Ashtray, stylized fruit, 10" L 36.00
Ashtray, stylized fruit, 7" 22.00
Butter dish, Distlefink 30.00
Cigarette holder 30.00
Cleanser shaker, girl figure, 5 holes 25.00
Cookie jar, Carrot Head 65.00
Cookie jar, Cottage House 210.00
Cookie jar, Gingerbread house 200.00
Cookie jar, pig, pnt flakes on lid rim 175.00
Creamer & sugar bowl, Distlefink 24.00
Cup & saucer, Gramma's 25.00
Cup & saucer, His, man on front 32.00
Cup & saucer, My Old Man, lg 32.00
Darner 22.00
Dish, clown w/pointed hat lid 60.00
Drip jar, Cherry, w/lid 36.00
Egg cup, lady w/apron & spoon 35.00
Egg cup, man w/blk coat & striped pants 35.00
Gravy boat, Distlefink, w/ladle 36.00
Hairpin holder, soldier 25.00
Match safe, Cherry 26.00
Mug, Morning After; ice-pack lid 25.00
Mustard & ketchup pumps, pr 22.00
Pitcher, Cherry, oil-can shape 22.00
Plaque, heart shape, orig ribbon 15.00
Plaque, teapot, A Kitchen Bright... ....35.00
Plaques, whistling farm boy & farm girl, pr 35.00
Ring holder, bulldog 22.00
Ring holder, Chef 45.00
Salt box, Cherry 45.00
Shakers, Cherry, sm, pr 22.00
Shakers, Distlefink, lg, pr 16.00
Shakers, Katrina, pr 40.00
Shakers, range; Cherry, pr 45.00
Spoon rest, Cherry 18.00
Spoon rest, fruit 15.00
Sprinkler bottle, Chinaman 35.00
String holder, heart form 35.00
Tray, Distlefink, leaf shape, 3-compartment 35.00
Tray, Distlefink, 12" 25.00
Tray, Gala Gray, sectional 21.00
Wall pocket, coffee grinder 30.00
Wall pocket, coffeepot, Let's Have Another Cup..., metal hdl 30.00
Wall pocket, frying pan 25.00
Wall pocket, kettle 25.00
Wall pocket, teapot, Penny Saved Is a Penny... ....35.00

Clewell

Charles Walter Clewell was a metal worker who perfected the technique of plating an entire ceramic vessel with a thin layer of copper or bronze treated with an oxidizing agent to produce a natural deterioration of the surface. Through trial and error, he was able to control the degree of patina achieved. In the early stages, the metal darkened and, if allowed to develop further, formed a natural turquoise-blue or green corrosion. He worked alone in his small Akron, Ohio, studio from about 1906, buying undecorated pottery from several Ohio firms, among them Weller, Owens, and Cambridge. His work is usually marked. Clewell died in 1965, having never revealed his secret process to others.

Prices for Clewell have advanced rapidly during the past few years along with the Arts and Crafts market in general. Right now, good examples are bringing whatever the traffic will bear.

Bowl, copper panels w/rivets, brass advertising plate, 4" 150.00
Bowl, geometric design at lip, 4 buttresses, 3x7" 450.00
Cider set, riveted copper, 11" pitcher+4 mugs 700.00
Humidor, riveted, cleaned patina, bbl shape, 6x6" 250.00
Jardiniere, simple form, orig patina, 10x14" 1,600.00
Vase, brn to gr, cylindrical, #328-2-6, 9½" 800.00
Vase, bronze to gr patina, #321-1, 6" 425.00
Vase, bud; 7½" 460.00

Vase, copper clad with outstanding red and green patina, incised mark, #256, 13", $2,200.00.

Vase, copper over Roseville Rozane vase w/slip floral, 4¾" 125.00
Vase, copper patina, bulbous w/flaring rim on long thin neck, 7" ..325.00
Vase, copper patina, cylindrical, no mk, 9½" 250.00
Vase, copper/gr patina, inverted trumpet form, #4333-25, 4" 475.00
Vase, cvd flowers/emb stylized flowers at base, 6½x6" 475.00
Vase, dk orange/gr, EX patina, shouldered cylinder, 7¼" 520.00
Vase, gr/bl patina, classic form, #378-25, 14½" 2,100.00
Vase, gr/bl/copper patina, tiny rim, 6" 475.00
Vase, gr/bl/orange patina, swollen cylinder, #313-2-7, 13" 1,800.00
Vase, gr/brn patina, waisted neck, #418-2-9, 5½x6½" 600.00
Vase, gr/copper patina, incurvate, #443-25, 4½" 475.00
Vase, orange to mint gr, ovoid w/short neck, #308, 7x3¼" 550.00
Vase, red & gr, EX patina, #256, ovoid, 13" 2,200.00
Vase, red to bl-gr, EX patina, can neck, bulbous, #100-2-8, 7" ...500.00
Vase, rust to gr, trumpet neck, ftd, #4133-6, 8x3¼" 400.00
Vase, 3 winged pharaohs w/cut-bk ground, orig patina, 9" 700.00

Clews

Brothers Ralph and James Clews were potters who operated in Cobridge in the Staffordshire district from 1817 to 1835. They are best known for their blue and white transfer-printed earthenwares, which included American Views, Moral Maxims, Picturesque Views, and English Views. A series called *Three Tours of Dr. Syntax* contained thirty-one different scenes with each piece bearing a descriptive title. Another popular series was *Pictures of Sir David Wilkie* with seven prints. (Though we once thought that the Don Quixote series was made by Clews, new information seems to indicate that it was made instead by Davenport.) Both printed and impressed marks were used, often incorporating the pattern name as well as the pottery. See also Staffordshire, Historical.

Bowl, vegetable; Dr Syntax, dk bl transfer, w/lid, 12" L 500.00
Coffeepot, Water Girl, dome lid, dk bl transfer, rpr, 12", EX 425.00

Creamer, Christmas, Wilkie's Designs, dk bl transfer, 5½" 250.00
Cup & saucer, Christmas Eve, Wilkie, dk bl transfer 225.00
Pitcher, Water Girl, dk bl transfer, mk, rpr hdl/spout, 7" 400.00
Plate, Beehive, dk bl transfer, 6" 65.00
Plate, Dr Syntax Mistakes Gentleman's Home..., 1830s, 10¼" ...175.00
Plate, Dr Syntax Reading His Tour, dk bl transfer, 10¼" 140.00
Plate, Dr Syntax Returned From His Tour, dk bl transfer, 9" 300.00
Plate, Dr Syntax Taking Possession..., dk bl transfer, 10" 245.00
Plate, Playing at Draughts, dk bl transfer, 10" 245.00
Plate, Valentine, Wilkie's Designs, dk bl transfer, 8⅞" 99.00
Platter, Advertisement for a Wife, dk bl transfer, 15¼" 1,450.00
Platter, Letter of Introduction, dk bl transfer, 12⅜" 580.00
Saucer, Christmas Eve, dk bl transfer 30.00
Wash pitcher & bowl, Select Views, dk bl transfer 1,850.00

Clifton

Clifton Art Pottery of Clifton, New Jersey, was organized ca 1903. Until 1911 when they turned to the production of wall and floor tile, they made artware of several varieties. The founders were Fred Tschirner and William A. Long. Long had developed the method for underglaze slip painting that had been used at the Lonhuda Pottery in Steubenville, Ohio, in the 1890s. Crystal Patina, the first artware made by the small company, utilized a fine white body and flowing, blended colors, the earliest a green crystalline. Indian Ware, copied from the pottery of the American Indians, was usually decorated in black geometric designs on red clay. (On the occasions when white was used in addition to the black, the ware was often not as well executed; so even though two-color decoration is very rare, it is normally not as desirable to the collector.) Robin's Egg Blue, pale blue on the white body, and Tirrube, a slip-decorated matt ware, were also produced.

Bowl vase, Indian Ware, 3-color, 5½x7" 180.00
Humidor, Indian Ware, abstract bird, blk/flesh on red, 4x6" 225.00
Pitcher, Indian Ware, Chevlon #247 ....185.00
Teapot, Crystal Patina, yel to golden brn, 3¼x9½" 100.00
Teapot, Indian Ware, geometrics, blk on red, 6½" 225.00
Vase, buff to celadon semi-matt, barrel shape, 1905, 3¼" 125.00
Vase, Crystal Patina, buff to celadon, egg shape, 4½" 175.00
Vase, Crystal Patina, yel/buff mottle, 4-side flared neck, 7" 275.00
Vase, gr crystal patina, 1905, 9" 200.00
Vase, gr crystalline over lt gr matt, 1906, 5½x3½" 175.00
Vase, gr crystalline over tan matt, shouldered, mk/#d, 4½" 250.00
Vase, gr/cream runs over brn/tan, spherical, 5x7" 400.00
Vase, Indian Ware, blk/tan geometric on red, #208, 3x4" 175.00
Vase, Indian Ware, geometric band, blk on red, no mk, 3½x4½" .150.00
Vase, Indian Ware, outstanding geometrics, 3-color, 9x15" 1,500.00
Vase, lg crane/flowers on burgundy matt, Haubrich, 12x6" 1,800.00
Vase, Tirrube, jonquils, yel/wht/gr on brick red, 8x4" 300.00

Clocks

In the early days of our country's history, clock makers were influenced by styles imported from Europe. They copied the European's cabinets and reconstructed their movements. But needed materials were in short supply; modifications had to be made. Of necessity was born mainspring motive power and spring clocks. Wooden movements were made on a mass-production basis as early as 1808. Before the middle of the century, metal movements had been developed.

Today's collectors prefer clocks from the 18th and 19th centuries with pendulum-regulated movements. Bracket clocks made during this period utilized the shorter pendulum improvised in 1658 by Fromentiel, a prominent English clock maker. These smaller square-face clocks usually were made with a dome top fitted with a handle or a decorative finial. The case was usually walnut or ebony and was sometimes decorated with pierced brass mountings. Brackets were often mounted on the wall to accommodate the clock, hence the name. The banjo clock was patented in 1802 by Simon Willard. It derived its descriptive name from its banjo-like shape. A similar but more elaborate style was called the lyre clock.

Prices have been stable for several years. Unless noted otherwise, values are given for clocks in excellent condition. Clocks that have been altered, damaged, or have had parts replaced are worth considerably less.

Our advisor is Bruce A. Austin; he is listed in the Directory under New York. Our novelty clock advisors are DLK Nostalgia and Collectibles; their address is given under Pennsylvania.

Key:
br — brass
dl — dial
esc — escapement
mcr — mercury
mvt — movement
og — ogee
pnd — pendulum
reg — regulator
rswd — rosewood
T — time only
wt — weight
vnr — veneer
2nds — seconds

Novelty Clocks

Ballerina, not animated, Lux, 1920s, scarce, NM 185.00
Black boy shining lady's shoes, Lux 375.00
Bluebird, animated, w/oak leaves & acorns, Keebler 30.00
Bluebirds, #8720, Lux 50.00
Bulldog in house, animated cat pnd, Keebler 175.00
Christopher Columbus on boat, brass 90.00
Cottage, cuckoo style, Lux, sm 60.00
Cottage, cuckoo style, 8-day, Lux, lg 140.00
Cottage, Keebler 50.00
Cottage scene w/horse & wagon on oval bl tin front, Lux 425.00
Dog, pug-faced, cvd wood, Osuhr, 9" 350.00
Doll, bsk, swings from tree branch, tin can works, Ansonia 1,300.00
Fire Chief Petunia, pendulette, Peek-A-Bee pnd w/50% pnt 100.00
Happy Days (Beer Drinkers), Lux 345.00
Horseshoe, horse hoofs, jockey's cap, brass, Junghans, 7", VG 180.00
Hunting scene, rabbit & fowl, cuckoo type, Lux, 5¾x9½" 100.00
Jack & Jill, VG pnt, M label, Lux 550.00
Joe Lewis, United, 1939 ....395.00
Man on trapeze, oak case, Junghans, dl mk Germany, 15" 900.00
Octagonal pendulette w/bl checkered border, Keebler 70.00
Organ grinder, animated monkey, alarm, Lux, EX 185.00
Owl on book clock, dl eyes, cvd wood, Osuhr, 5½" 300.00
Owl w/moving eyes, cvd wood wall type, Mi-ken Japan 55.00
Racing car, animated litho, Jaz, NM 30.00
Rooster standing by basket, wht metal, Maroue Fabrique, 10", EX .350.00
Rudolph the Red-Nosed Reindeer, #21574, Lux 135.00
Scotty dog, pressed wood, #8722, Lux 200.00
Scotty in doghouse, cuckoo style, #333, Lux 300.00
Seaman on anchor smoking pipe, iron, Gustav Becker 245.00
Ship's wheel, pendulette, plastic, red/wht sailboat, Westclox 95.00
Showboat, wheel revolves, Lux, NM 190.00
Skull w/moving eye dl, cvd wood, German, 4½" 525.00
Totem pole pnd, eyes move, Japan 85.00
Uncle Sam's Little Wonder, tin front w/wood-mtd pendulette ...200.00

Shelf Clocks

Ansonia, pnt iron, architectural, open esc porc dl, 1890 ....150.00
Atkins, Empire-style rswd, orig dl/tablet/hands, 1860, 17" 280.00

Atkins, octagon-top walnut, orig finish/tablet, 1860, 14" 135.00
Chauncey Jerome, 30-hr cottage w/alarm, mahog, orig table, 1850 .110.00
CW Feishtinger, Victorian Kitchen Calendar, walnut, 1890 ......700.00

Mantel clock, Deniere y Mate-lyn, Empire gilt-bronze, Cupid's wings support clock with white enamel dial and black Roman numerals, France, 1820s, 16¾", $4,600.00.

E Hotchkiss Jr, Empire, mahog vnr, pnd, 34" 110.00
Fr, blk marble mantel, T/strike on bell, open esc, porc dl 250.00
Fr, blk slate/marble, mcr pnd, open esc, striker, 1915, 19" 475.00
Fr, carriage, brass/glass, repeating mvt, 4½" 650.00
Fr, carriage, brass/glass, 4¾", +case 275.00
Fr, mahog bracket, lancet top, slate dl, open esc, gong, 1890 ......350.00
Fr, marble/bronze architectural, gilt dl sgn Stowell, 1890 ....225.00
Fr crystal reg, made for Tiffany, mcr pnd, 1880, 11" 500.00
Geo Mitchell label, wood works, groaner mvt, 1840 ....175.00
German, balloon style, mahog, mvt mk Kienzle, 1890 ....185.00
Gilbert, ebonized walnut w/cherubs ea side, all orig, 1890 ....275.00
Gilbert, 30-hr steeple, 1870, full sz, all orig 160.00
Ingraham, Adrian, blk, orig dl/finish/label, 1920 ....65.00
Ingraham, pressed oak gingerbread, rfn/rstr/rpl dl, 1890 ....120.00
Iron front, Bristol style, onion-shaped case, rpr dl, 1850s 95.00
Jerome, Rocket, octagon top, poplar case, label, 1850, 13" 80.00
Kroeber, walnut gingerbread, Kroeber mvt/pnd, 1880 ....150.00
New Haven, beehive, orig dl/rvpt flaking, vnr good, 1860, 19" ..230.00
New Haven, Gothic walnut case, 30-hr T/alarm, 1890, 13" 160.00
New Haven, oak architectural gingerbread, rnd columns, 1890 .125.00
New Haven, rfn oak, cast ft & side decor, 1900, 12" 75.00
New Haven, walnut gingerbread w/leaf cutouts, 1900 ....220.00
Seth Thos, Adamantine Hollis, rpl ft, 1920 ....75.00
Seth Thos, Chime Clock #14, Westminster chimes, 1920 ....240.00
Seth Thos, Cottage (label), lg 8-day mvt, 1920, 13" 95.00
Seth Thos, 8-day tambour, 1920 ....55.00
Smith Patterson, Fr carriage w/cloisonne pillars, 1900 ....300.00
Statue of female on park bench, Fr, marble, 1920, 16" 300.00
Statue of girl w/wheat, Fr spelter, 8-day T/strike, 12" 130.00
Statue of Napoleon's marshal seated by lion-mtd mvt, bronze ..2,200.00
Statue of nymph, Viox de la Lyre by Causse, bronze/marble, 21" ..875.00
Statue of seated maid w/lyre, HP inset, Japy Freres mvt, 13" 935.00
Statue: Rosee de Printemps, Moreau, spelter/onxy, 28" 550.00
Terry & Andrews, rswd 8-day cottage, orig dl/tablet, 1850 ....220.00
Terwilliger reissue, Jubilee, 400-day disk pnd, 1981, M 275.00
Waterbury, Parlor #10, rose porc w/emb scrolls, 1890, 11", VG .185.00

Tall Case Clocks

Chpndl, walnut, dvtl bonnet, English works, 92" 8,800.00

Colonial Co, Arts & Crafts, overhang top w/arch corbels, 85" ...3,000.00
Curly birch, Country style, brass works, rstr, 84"+finials 770.00
Geo IV, mahog w/inlay, moon phase, 3 dl, broken arch pediment ..1,400.00
Houghton, Geo III, figured mahog, moon phase, broken arch .2,100.00
Ithaca, mahog w/brass trim, 11" rstr dl, 8-day spring, 1920 ....425.00
L Watson, cherry w/mahog veneer, 92½", EX 2,300.00
Mission oak, ldgl on 3 sides, 2-wt, 75" 270.00
Otelli, Georgian Provincial, broken arch pediment, 1780 ....800.00
Pembroke label, pine w/bl rpt, rstr, 84" 660.00
Rswd, lg scrolls under rnd top, raised panels, English 3,000.00
S Hoadley Plymouth, cherry, orig finish, 88" 4,600.00
Walnut, cvd, music box in center, Lenzkirch mvt, 86" 7,400.00

Wall Clocks

Anglo American, Superior 8-day, standard American movement, some rippling to veneer, repainted pendulum, 1860s, 34", 17" diameter, $350.00.

Atkins, rnd-top short drop, 11" worn dl, T, rpl tablet, 1855 ....275.00
Austrian picture-fr, 30-hr silk thread mvt, 1850, 12x12" 100.00
Dutch, mahog, arched crest w/pnt face: moon phases, pnd, 52" .825.00
EN Welch, Gentry, short-drop school, pressed oak, 1900 ....275.00
EN Welch, rswd short-drop octagon, 11" rpl dial, T, 11" 250.00
English, gallery, rpt dl, 1900, 11" dl 160.00
English, single fusee postal, oak, 24-hr dl sgn Ball & Sons 300.00
German, cvd walnut, rpt 11" silvered dl, 1890, 35x17" 325.00
German, HP 2-wt cartel, chain-drive mvt, 1950 ....30.00
German, picture-fr, brass dl surround w/2 maids, 1860, 9x11" 200.00
Gilbert, reg #302, mahog (no bottom), nickel wt+pulley, rpl pnd .1,600.00
Gilbert, store reg, flat top/shaped apron, 1910 ....225.00
Ingraham, Boston long drop, oak, orig dl/finish, T, 1900 ....200.00
Ingraham, Landau, oak (orig), 8-day T/strike/calendar, 1900 .....250.00
Ingraham, Nayanza banjo, orig rvpt, 38" 275.00
Ingraham, pressed oak long drop, T, rfn, 1900 ....300.00
Ingraham, Treasure Island banjo, eagle w/rpr, 1910 ....400.00
Ithaca, hanging office #4, dbl dl, calendar, rpl dl, 1880 ....800.00
Junghans, Vienna-style reg, porc dl, 1880, 26" 165.00
New Haven, banjo, VG rvpt, 1920, 31" 175.00
New Haven, short-drop octagon school, oak, Hebrew #d dl, 1920 .250.00
New Haven, store reg, pressed oak (rfn), rpl tablet/dl, 1900 ....225.00
New Haven, Waring banjo, rpl rvpt, rpl trim, orig finish 225.00
New Haven, Whitney banjo, all orig, w/label, rod strike, 30" 125.00
New Haven, 8" reg, rnd-drop school, mahog, 1880, 22" 270.00
Riggs & Bro, 9¾" rnd iron dl w/8" chapter ring, 1850 ....500.00
Schatz & Sons, 4-glass case, platform esc, chimes, 1950, 9" 100.00
Sempire, Elechrometer, oak, 45" 725.00
Sessions, gallery, rnd, 11" dl w/new paper, 1920 ....100.00

Sessions, Kitchenklok, w/label, 1920, 14" 85.00
Sessions, Narragansett banjo, 1930, 27" 95.00
Sessions, short-drop school, 12" dl, rfn oak, 1920, 27" 210.00
Sessions, store reg, golden oak, rpl dl, 1900 ....250.00
Seth Thos, #2 mvt in cherry case, Riggs pnt dl, 1910, 50" 650.00
Seth Thos, Derby, City Series, walnut, no pnd, 1909 ....190.00
Seth Thos, Globe, sharp bottom version, rpl dl, rfn oak 410.00
Seth Thos, lobby, oak (losses), 1900, 18" 750.00
Seth Thos, school, oak w/8" drop, repapered dl, T, 1910, 17" 175.00
Seth Thos, ship's bell #66, striking, brass, 5½" dl, 1890 ....300.00
Seth Thos, ship's outside bell, rpl bell shimmed out, 1890 ....250.00
Seth Thos, store reg, T/calendar, new paper dl, 1890 ....235.00
Seth Thos, Sunburst, composition, dbl wind, T, 1920, 24" 80.00
Seth Thos, World, long-drop school, rfn mahog, rpt dl, 1900 .....350.00
Tledhill-Brooke, factory time punch, 240v motor, 1930 ....125.00
Waterbury, Cane, store reg, pressed oak, rpl dl, T, 1890, 37" 310.00
Waterbury, school, gilt banding, 8-day T/strike, 1900 ....350.00
Waterbury, 10"-drop school, mahog, orig dl/label, T, 22" 380.00
Waterbury, 12-sided, mahog vnr, rpt 11" dl, rfn, 1880, 15" 200.00
Waterbury, 8" drop, rswd w/gilt banding, 1900 ....425.00

Cloisonne

Cloisonne is a method of decorating metal with enameling. Fine metal wires are soldered onto the metal body following the lines of a predetermined design. The resulting channels are filled in with enamels of various colors, and the item is fired. The final step is a smoothing process that assures even exposure of the wire pattern. The art is predominately Oriental and has been practiced continuously, except during war years, since the 16th century. The most excellent examples date from 1865 until the turn of the century. The early 20th-century export variety is usually lightweight and the workmanship inferior. Modern wares are of good quality and are produced in Taiwan as well as China.

Several variations of the basic art include plique-a-jour, achieved by removing the metal body after firing, leaving only the transparent enamel work; foil cloisonne, using transparent or semitranslucent enameling over a layer of embossed silver covering the metal body of the vessel; wireless cloisonne, made by removing the wire dividers prior to firing; and cloisonne executed on ceramic, wood, or lacquer rather than metal.

Bowl, bird center, 16 floral panels, ext: butterflies, 6" 350.00
Bowl, bird/floral center, floral border, low, 19/20th C, 12" 350.00
Bowl, floral, mc on blk, 4x4½" 100.00
Candle holder, writhing winged dragon std, 17" 550.00
Cane hdl, ball end w/dragon on pk, 7" 250.00
Charger, 5 cranes/mass of flowers on bl, 19th C, 18", EX 550.00
Jar, genre reserves on blk, w/lid, 1930s, 16½" 185.00
Jar, ginger; peonies, mc on gr, teakwood base, 10", pr 300.00
Jar, 2 floral reserves on lt bl, w/lid, 1800s, 6" 650.00
Jardiniere, dragons, 12x15" 850.00
Lamp base, cvd/emb floral band, 2 petal bands, Ming, 12" 550.00
Plaque, 3 lg blk/wht birds & floral on pk, 12" dia 395.00
Teapot, floral on red, sq, late, 6x4" 200.00
Vase, dragon on midnight bl, hexagonal, slender, 7" 150.00
Vase, dragon panel, cobalt on lt bl, lion/ring hdls, 15x9" 400.00
Vase, dragons in waves, bl floral neck/base bands, 15" 300.00
Vase, floral on yel, dog finial, sq, w/lid, now lamp, 17", pr 850.00
Vase, floral sakura/fence on cobalt, Kichisaro Ota, 6" 550.00
Vase, lotus on wht, ornate hdls w/loose rings, 14" 600.00
Vase, mums & mixed flowers, mc on bl, 8", pr 595.00
Vase, mums/sm floral on bl, classic form, facing pr, 9" 650.00
Vase, scenes w/lg cranes, 6-sided, hdls, 18" 600.00

Vase, wisteria on dk bl, sgn Nanuko Inaba, 6", orig box **2,200.00**
Vase, wisteria on midnight bl, hexagonal, Japan, 6" **200.00**
Vase, 6 floral reserves on dk bl, silver wire, 6-sided, 10" **875.00**

Clothing and Accessories

'Second-hand' or 'vintage?' It's all a matter of opinion. But these days it's considered good taste (downright fashionable) to wear clothing from Victorian to styles from the sixties. Jackets with padded shoulders from the thirties are 'trendy.' Jewelry from the Art Deco era is just as beautiful and often less expensive than current copies. But why settle for new when the genuine article can be bought for the same price with exquisite lace that no reproduction can rival! When once the 'style' of the day was so strictly obeyed, today, in New York and the larger cities of California and Texas, in particular, nothing well-designed and constructed is 'out of style.' And though costumes by such designers as Chanel, Fortuny, and Lanvin may bring four-figure prices at fine auction houses, as a general rule, prices are very modest considering the wonderful fabrics one may find in vintage clothing, many of which are no longer available. Cashmere coats, elegant furs, and sequined or beaded gowns can be bought for only a small fraction of today's retail. Though some are strictly collectors, many do buy their clothes to wear. Care must be given to alterations, and gentle cleaning methods employed to avoid damage that would detract from their value.

Key:
cap/s — cap sleeves   n/s — no sleeves
embr — embroidery   plt — pleated
hs — hand sewn   s/p — shoulder pads
lgth — length   s/s — short sleeves
l/s — long sleeves   /s — sleeves
ms — machine sewn

Child's dress, lace inserts, short sleeves, EX, $50.00.

Apron, tea; dimity w/embr flowers & crochet trim, M **7.50**
Bathing suit, bl cotton jersey, ca 1920, VG **25.00**
Bathing suit, navy & wht sailor style w/skirt & bloomers **60.00**
Bathing suit, wool, Bradley, 1930s, EX **32.00**
Blouse, blk silk brocade, jet trim, l/s, pre-1900, EX **78.00**
Blouse, cotton w/lace, s/s, 1950s, EX **20.00**
Blouse, lav cotton, n/s, 1940s, EX **20.00**
Blouse, peasant; wht, silk embr, l/s, drawstrings, EX **30.00**
Blouse, wht dotted net & lace, l/s, pre-1900, VG **50.00**
Blouse, wht lawn, lace inserts, ¾/s, jewel neck, 1900s, VG **40.00**
Blouse, wht sheer nylon, lace yoke/glass buttons, l/s, 1940s **12.50**
Bonnet, blk silk, plaid lining, 1850s, EX **48.00**
Bonnet, child's; velvet w/ribbon trim, late 1800s, EX **65.00**
Bonnet, mourning; w/veil, 1860s, EX **55.00**
Bonnet, nester's, bl wool crochet, lined, 1860s, VG **42.00**
Camisole, wht cotton, wide straps w/lace, EX **27.50**

Camisole, yel crepe w/lace trim, ca 1920, EX **20.00**
Cape, child's; blk velvet, w/hood, lined, 1920s, NM **50.00**
Cape, dk plush, ca 1920s, EX **50.00**
Cape, opera; blk mohair, ankle lgth, 1930s, EX **85.00**
Coat, blk velvet, jet trim, ¾-lgth, pre-1900, EX **115.00**
Coat, boy's, cream linen w/belt, 20", EX **22.00**
Coat, child's, ecru silk, puffy, much embr, lined **60.00**
Coat, velvet, scalloped cuffs & collar, full lgth, '20s, EX **100.00**
Collar, stand-up neck, Irish lace, EX **32.00**
Corset cover jacket, wht cotton, l/s, ca 1810, EX **40.00**
Dress, blk velvet, l/s, jewel neck/covered buttons, '30s, EX **40.00**
Dress, calico, prairie style, 1900s, NM **85.00**
Dress, calico, Victorian **100.00**
Dress, child's, calico, mutton/s, high waist, 1860s **120.00**
Dress, child's, coat style, ecru silk w/embr, cape collar **65.00**
Dress, child's, plique-a-line, eyelet, ruffles, 1860s **60.00**
Dress, child's, wht cotton, s/s, shirred embr yoke, 1930s **20.00**
Dress, child's, wht lawn & lace, drop waist, l/s, 1910s, EX **80.00**
Dress, cotton print, s/s, 1950s, EX **22.50**
Dress, Edwardian wht lace w/lily embr, EX **90.00**
Dress, evening; blk lace, deep V, full skirt, 1930s, EX **90.00**
Dress, evening; blk silk, l/s, 1930s, EX **100.00**
Dress, evening; nylon net/satin, n/s, sq drop neck, '50s, M **32.00**
Dress, evening; pk satin, puffed/s, full skirt, '30s, EX **55.00**
Dress, linen, wisteria embr inserts, Irish lace trim, l/s, NM **165.00**
Dress, purple taffeta, jet buttons, l/s, 1920s, EX **75.00**
Dress, purple wool flannel, shirtwaist, 1950s, EX **45.00**
Dress, red polka-dot voile, cap/s, walnut buckle, 1930s, EX **25.00**
Dress, toddler's, Edwardian lace w/much embr, EX **80.00**
Dress, wht batiste w/embr, l/s, 1900s, EX **155.00**
Dress, wht dimity lawn, l/s, shirtwaist, ca 1910, EX **85.00**
Dress, wht organdy, mini lgth, 1970s, EX **40.00**
Fur boa, full silver fox w/head, glass eyes, pom-pom tail **55.00**
Fur coat, gray mink, full lgth, 1930s, EX **125.00**
Fur coat, mouton, padded shoulders, ¾-lgth, 1940s, EX **65.00**
Fur coat, Persian lamb, full lgth, EX **60.00**
Fur muff, child's, wht, neck strap, 5" dia, EX **14.00**
Gloves, ball; gold satin, 1890s, EX **215.00**
Gloves, crochet lace, 1940s, pr **8.00**
Gloves, wht kidskin, pearl button, 22", M **42.00**
Gown, christening; much lace & shirring, 43" **85.00**
Gown, christening; puffed/s, embr yoke & lace, 34", EX **45.00**
Hat, baby's, Edwardian lace, corded, wide brim **65.00**
Hat, child's, midnight bl velvet, ca 1880s **65.00**
Hat, lady's, bl velvet beret, 1940s, EX **15.00**
Hat, lady's, brn velvet w/berries trim, 1870s **70.00**
Hat, lady's, jet blk, Victorian, 1880s **68.00**
Hat, lady's, lilac plush, knit band, rhinestone buckle, EX **18.00**
Hat, lady's, plush beaver w/leather trim, Edwardian **65.00**
Hat, lady's, plush beaver w/plumed bird **100.00**
Hat, lady's, purple plush velvet, 1950s, EX **10.00**
Hat, lady's, straw w/Edwardian wide brim, flower trim **110.00**
Hat, lady's, straw w/ostrich feathers, ca 1880 ....**70.00**
Hat, lady's, sunbonnet w/ruffled/tatted brim, neck protector **20.00**
Hat, lady's, wht eyelet, 1890s **65.00**
Hat, man's, blk beaver, western style, ca 1930, EX **65.00**
Hat, man's, brn felt, 1930s, EX **20.00**
Hat, man's, Derby type, blk straw, narrow band, lined, '20s **25.00**
Hat, man's, straw, wide red & wht cloth band, early 1900s, EX **45.00**
Hoop, for full Victorian skirt, wire & tape, EX **85.00**
Jacket, bolero style, wht ostrich feathers, 1950s **50.00**
Jacket, jet beads allover, beaded fringe, Victorian, EX **165.00**
Jacket, lined Battenburg lace, ca 1910, EX **215.00**
Jacket, pk wool flannel, Eisenhower style, s/s, 1950s, EX **40.00**

Nightgown, peach rayon, ecru lace bodice, ties, M **24.00**
Pajamas, pk flannel, baby-doll style, 1970s, EX **25.00**
Pantaloons, tucked, drawstring waist, eyelet trim, long, M **35.00**
Pantaloons, wht, split style, VG **10.00**
Parasol, child's; pongee silk **80.00**
Petticoat, bl stripes, 1920s **30.00**
Petticoat, blk silk, ca 1900, VG **35.00**
Petticoat, velvet w/embr mc top stitching, 1880s **85.00**
Shawl, Chantilly lace, ca 1860 ....**45.00**
Shawl, gold embr, ball trim **65.00**
Shawl, mourning; blk wool, Victorian, 96", NM **75.00**
Shawl, paisley pattern, woven wool, 1870s, 72x72", NM **325.00**
Shawl, paisley pattern cotton & wool, 65x67" **95.00**
Shawl, paisley pattern woven wool, 68x67", VG **115.00**
Shift, blk & wht check polyester, l/s, 1960s, EX **25.00**
Shift, polka-dot cotton, s/s, 1960s, EX **35.00**
Shirt, man's, cotton silkscreen pullover, 1950s, EX **35.00**
Shirt, man's, homespun linen, partial button front, early **45.00**
Shoes, lady's, high tops, wht, M, pr **125.00**
Shoes, lady's, pumps, lav satin, ca 1920s, EX, pr **25.00**
Shoes, lady's, wht, 1830s, pr **55.00**
Skirt, blk crepe, ca 1930s, VG **45.00**
Skirt, blk faille, ca 1920, G **25.00**
Skirt, tennis; bl cotton w/embr, ca 1920, VG **45.00**
Skirt, turq cotton, circle cut, 1950s, VG **25.00**
Skirt, wht batiste w/crochet panels, ca 1920, EX **75.00**
Skirt, wht cotton, ca 1900, EX **95.00**
Skirt, wht linen w/embr, ca 1910, EX **85.00**
Slacks, bl wool, lined, Evan Picone, 1970s, EX **25.00**
Slip, navy satin, 2-tier ruffled hem, long, 1940s, M **18.00**
Stockings, blk lisle, ca 1900, VG **12.00**
Suit, boy's sailor, wool, Victorian, EX **60.00**
Suit, lady's walking; navy gabardine, ca 1910, EX **165.00**
Sweater, wht rabbit fur trim w/beading, EX **42.00**
Uniform, pk nylon seersucker, 1940s, EX **30.00**
Vest, navy cotton/wool blend, scalloped w/embr, Victorian **35.00**
Waist, blk silk, boned, l/s, 1890s, EX **65.00**
Waist, wht, Victorian, EX **55.00**
Wrapper, brn calico, leg-of-mutton/s, EX **125.00**

Cluthra

The name Cluthra is derived from the Scottish word 'clutha,' meaning cloudy. Glassware by this name was first produced by J. Couper and Sons, England. Frederick Carder developed Cluthra while at the Steuben Glass Works, and similar types of glassware were also made by Durand and Kimball. It is found in both solid and shaded colors and is characterized by a spotty appearance resulting from small air pockets trapped between its two layers. See also Steuben.

Chalice, gr/wht, sgn Stanhope, 10½" **165.00**
Vase, gr, #1812, Kimball, 12" **200.00**
Vase, mauve/wht, classic form, #K-1710-4-Dec-100, 4½" **300.00**
Vase, orange/gray, polished pontil, Kimball, #1910-6, 7x5" **625.00**
Vase, wht, #1968-6, Kimball, 6" **200.00**
Vase, wht, 1968, Kimball, 6" **225.00**
Vase, yel/opal mottle, ftd cylinder, Kimball, 12½" **250.00**
Vase, yel/orange/yel mottle, trumpet neck, Kimball, 11" **350.00**

Coalport

In 1745 in Caughley, England, Squire Brown began a modest busi-

ness fashioning crude pots and jugs from clay mined in his own fields. Tom Turner, a young potter who had apprenticed his trade at Worcester, was hired in 1772 to plan and oversee the construction of a 'proper' factory. Three years later he bought the business, which he named Caughley Coalport Porcelain Manufactory. Though the dinnerware he produced was meant to be only everyday china, the hand-painted florals, birds, and landscapes used to decorate the ware were done in exquisite detail and in a wide range of colors. In 1780 Turner introduced the Willow pattern which he produced using a newly perfected method of transfer printing. (Wares from the period between 1775 and 1799 are termed 'Caughley' or 'Salopian'; see section on Caughley.) John Rose purchased the Caughley factory from Thomas Turner in 1799, adding that holding to his own pottery which he had built two years before in Coalport. (It is from this point in the pottery's history that the wares are termed 'Coalport.') The porcelain produced there before 1814 was unmarked with very few exceptions. After 1820 some examples were marked with a '2' with an oversize top loop. The term 'Coalbrookdale' refers to a fine type of porcelain decorated in floral bas relief, similar to the work of Dresden.

After 1835 highly decorated ware with rich ground colors imitated the work of Sevres and Chelsea, even going so far as to copy their marks. From about 1895 until the 1920s, the mark in use was 'Coalport' over a crown with 'England A.D. 1750' indicating the date claimed as the founding, not the date of manufacture. From the 1920s until 1945, 'Made in England' over a crown and 'Coalport' below was used. Later, the mark was 'Coalport' over a smaller crown with 'Made in England' in a curve below.

Each of the major English porcelain companies excelled in certain areas of manufacture. Coalport produced the finest 'jeweled' porcelain, made by picking up a heavy mixture of slip and color and dropping it onto the surface of the ware. These 'jewels' are perfectly spaced and are often graduated in size with the smaller 'jewels' at the neck or the base of the vase. Some ware was decorated with very large 'jewels' resembling black opals or other polished stones. Such pieces are in demand by the advanced collector.

It is common to find considerable crazing on old Coalport, since the glaze was thinly applied to increase the brilliance of the colors. Many early vases had covers; look for a flat surface that would have supported a lid (just because it is gilted does not mean the vase never had one). Pieces whose lids are missing are worth about 40% less. Most lids have a finial which may have been broken and restored. You should deduct about 10% for a professional restoration on a finial.

In 1926 the Coalport Company moved to Shelton in Staffordshire and today belongs to a group headed by the Wedgwood Company. Our advisors for this category are Henry and Geneva Tyler; they are listed in the Directory under Florida. See also Indian Tree.

Ewer, large jewels with gold, shape #2446C, 1893, 11¾x4¼", $6,500.00.

Box, high-heel shoe shape, bl w/floral/gold, 1900, 5" 1,250.00
Cup & saucer, jeweled clover shape, 1½" H.............................$750.00
Urn, lake on cobalt w/gold scrolls & jewel dots, ftd, 10" 1,100.00
Vase, encrusted floral/estate scene, hdld, w/lid, 18" 3,500.00

Coca-Cola

    J.S. Pemberton, creator of Coca-Cola, originated his world-famous drink in 1886. From its inception the Coca-Cola Company began an incredible advertising campaign which has proven to be one of the most successful promotions in history. The quantity and diversity of advertising material put out by Coca-Cola in the last one hundred years is literally mind-boggling. From the beginning, the company has projected an image of wholesomeness and Americana. Beautiful women in Victorian costumes, teenagers and schoolchildren, blue- and white-collar workers, the men and women of the Armed Forces (even Santa Claus) have appeared in advertisements with a Coke in their hands. Some of the earliest collectibles include trays, syrup dispensers, gum jars, pocket mirrors, and calendars. Many of these items fetch prices in the thousands of dollars. Later examples include radios, signs, lighters, thermometers, playing cards, clocks, and toys — particularly toy trucks.

    In 1970 the Coca-Cola Company initialed a multimillion-dollar 'image-refurbishing campaign,' which introduced the new 'Dynamic Contour' logo, a twisting white ribbon under the Coca-Cola and Coke trademarks. The new logo often serves as a cut-off point to the purist collector. Newer and very ardent collectors, however, relish the myriad of items marketed since that date, as they often cannot afford the high prices that the vintage pieces command. For more information we recommend *Petretti's Coca-Cola Collectibles Price Guide*, 1994 edition (available from Nostalgia Publications whose address you will find under Auctions in the Directory); *Huxford's Collectible Advertising, Second Edition*, and *Collectible Coca-Cola Toy Trucks* by our advisor Gael deCourtivron, who is listed in the Directory under Florida. For further information call the Cocaholics Hotline: 813-355-COLA.

Key:
b/o — battery operated   tm — trademark

Reproductions and Fantasies

    Beware of reproductions! Prices are given for the genuine original articles, but the symbol (+) at the end of some of the following lines indicate items that have been reproduced. Warning! The 1935 calendar has been reproduced. It is identical in almost every way; only a professional can tell them apart. It is *very* deceiving! Watch for frauds: genuinely old celluloid items ranging from combs, mirrors, knives and forks to doorknobs that have been recently etched with a new double-lined trademark. Still another area of concern deals with reproduction and fantasy items. A fantasy item is a novelty made to appear authentic with inscriptions such as 'Tiffany Studios,' 'Trans Pan Expo,' 'World's Fair,' etc. In reality, these items never existed as originals. For instance, don't be fooled by a Coca-Cola cash register; no originals are known to exist! Large mirrors for bars are being reproduced and are often selling for $10.00 to $50.00.

    Of the hundreds of reproductions (designated 'R' in the following examples) and fantasies (designated 'F') on the market today, these are the most deceiving.

Belt buckle, no originals thought to exist (F), up to 10.00
Bottle, dk amber, w/arrows, heavy, narrow spout (R) 10.00
Bottle carrier, wood, yel w/red logo, holds 6 bottles (R) 10.00
Cooler, Glascock Jr, made by Coca-Cola USA (R) 250.00
Doorknob, glass etched w/tm (F) 3.00
Knife, bottle shape, 1970s, many variations (F), ea 5.00

Knife, fork or spoon w/celluloid hdl, newly etched tm (F) 5.00
Letter opener, stamped metal, Coca-Cola for 5¢ (F) 3.00
Pocketknife, yel & red, 1933 World's Fair (F) 2.00
Sign, cb, lady w/fur, dtd 1911, 9x11" (F) 3.00
Soda fountain glass holder, word 'Drink' not on orig (R) 5.00
Thermometer, bottle form, DONASCO, 17" (R) 10.00
Trade card, copy of 1905 'Bathtub' foldout, emb 1978 (R) 25.00
Watch, pocket; often old watch w/new face (R) 10.00

    The following items have been reproduced and are among the most deceptive of all:
    Pocket mirrors from 1905, 1906, 1908, 1909, 1910, 1911, 1916, and 1920.
    Trays from 1899, 1910, 1913, 1914, 1917, 1920, 1923, 1925, 1926, 1934, and 1937.
    Tip trays from 1907, 1909, 1910, 1913, 1914, 1917, and 1920.
    Knives: many versions of the German brass model.
    Cartons: wood versions, yellow with logo.
    Calendars: 1924, 1925, and 1935.
    These items are currently being marketed:
    Brass button, Taiwan, 18", (R)
    Brass thermometer, bottle shape, Taiwan, 24"
    Cast-iron toys (none ever made)
    Cast-iron door pull, bottle shape, made to look old
    Poster, Yes Girl (R)
    Button sign, has 1 round hole while original has 4 slots, most have bottle logo, 12", 16", 20" (R)
    Bullet trash receptacles (old cans with decals)
    Paperweight, rectangular, with Pepsin Gum insert
    1949 cooler radio (reproduced with tape deck)
    Straw holders (no originals exist)
    Countless trays — most unauthorized (must read 'American Art works; Coshocton, OH.')

Centennial Items

    1986 was the year for the Coca-Cola Company to celebrate its 100th birthday, and amidst all the fanfare came many new collectible items, all sporting the 100th anniversary logo. These items are destined to become an important part of the total Coca-Cola Collectible spectrum. The following pieces are among the most popular centennial items.

Bottle, gold dipped, in velvet sleeve, 6½-oz 60.00
Bottle, Hutchinson, amber, Root Co, ½-oz, 3 in case 275.00
Bottle, International, set of 9 in plexiglas case 350.00
Bottle, leaded crystal, 100th logo, 6½-oz, MIB 150.00
Medallion, bronze, 3" dia, w/box 80.00
Pin set, wood fr, 101 pins 450.00
Scarf, silk, 30x30" 40.00
Thermometer, glass cover, 14" dia, M 22.00

Coca-Cola Originals

Bank, 1960s, dispenser form, missing insert lever, VG in box 60.00
Blotter, 1904, Drink CC..., Deutch & Heitmann, horizontal, NM ..100.00
Blotter, 1906, Restores Energy, red/wht, EX 125.00
Blotter, 1909, Delicious, Refreshing, Invigorating, red/wht, NM .100.00
Blotter, 1926, Refresh Yourself, red/bl on wht, NM 25.00
Blotter, 1942, girl in boat, NM 15.00
Blotter, 1942, I Think It's Swell, 3½x7½", NM 5.00
Blotter, 1947, Coke Knows No Season, snow scene, NM 10.00
Blotter, 1950, Be Prepared..., 6x2¾", NM 15.00
Blotter, 1960, Over 60 Million a Day, 3½x7½", M 5.00
Bottle, display; 1923, no cap, NM 300.00
Bottle, Portsmouth OH, amber 100.00

Blotter, 1926, Restores Energy, Strengthens the Nerves, red on white, EX, $125.00.

Bottle, Rochester NY, gr, 30-oz, NM 150.00
Bottle, Rochester NY, script lettering, pale bl, 30-oz 160.00
Bottle opener, 1950s, flat, EX 10.00
Calendar, 1925, lady in bl turban w/glass, w/o full pad, EX (+) ..325.00
Calendar, 1957, Skater Girl, Canada, 6 pgs, 14x14", NM 60.00
Calendar, 1958, couple w/skis, Fr Canadian, 22x13", VG 40.00
Calendar, 1963, Santa & train, NM 60.00
Calendar, 1976, Olympics, 4 pgs, 12x9", NM 8.00
Calendar top, 1927, girl w/glass, matted & fr, EX 250.00
Can, 1990, Summer Pop Art, M 3.00
Chalkboard, 1940, red button on gr, Make Good Food, 18x26", EX ..135.00
Chinese checkerboard, wood & cb, no marbles, 16½", EX 40.00
Cooler, 1940s, emb metal, red/wht, 32½x29x22" 575.00
Cup, paper, 1 side English, other side Fr, 3½" 3.00
Dominoes, ea pc w/bottle, complete set, NMIB 65.00
Door push, late 1930s, porc, red/yel/wht, Fr, 6½x4", NM 200.00
Door push, porc, Enjoy CC Here, red/yel/wht, 3x30", EX 150.00
Door push, 1940s, porc, red/yel/wht, Fr, 12x4", NM 125.00
Game, 1938, Steps to Health, orig pcs & envelope, 11x26", NM ..125.00
Inkwell, plastic, holds fountain pen, drw front, 3", EX 275.00
Match book, 1929-35, bottle tilted, w/matches, NM 15.00
Match striker, 1938-39, porc, 4-color, Fr, 4x4", NM 250.00
Mirror, 1920s, rvpt, Please Pay Cashier..., 11" dia, EX 350.00
Music box, 1950s, cooler form, missing doll on top, 7x12x9½" ..800.00
Note pad, 1931, Rockwell boy w/dog, 10x7", EX 50.00
Playing cards, 1943, girl in reserve on red, EX in box 80.00
Playing cards, 1943, nurse bks, airplane spotters, EX in box 90.00
Playing cards, 1951, cowgirl w/bottle, NMIB 60.00
Playing cards, 1951, girl w/bottle at party, NMIB 60.00
Playing cards, 1963, girl in red w/tray on wht, EX in box 35.00
Playing cards, 1976, CC Adds Life to Everything Nice, sealed 17.50
Puzzle, 1950s, party w/bottles in tub, 12x18", EX 80.00
Radio, 1949, cooler form, minor pnt chips, working 800.00
Sign, 1939, paper, bottle & button on iceberg, 19x57", EX 300.00
Sign, 1939, porc, Drink CC Sold Here Ice Cold, 12x29", EX 200.00
Sign, 1939, porc, 4-color, 28x12", VG 150.00
Sign, 1941, tin, red Coke button on gr, 27½x19½", EX 200.00
Sign, 1943, cb, B-26 bomber, crease, 13x15", EX 50.00
Sign, 1945, cb, Got Enough Coke on Ice, Canada, 30x56½", EX ...350.00
Sign, 1950, cb, Hospitality, lady w/flower in hair, 27x56", EX 350.00
Sign, 1975, Olympics symbols, wood fr, 6x15", EX 15.00
Straw box, late 1940s, 11", NM 115.00
String dispenser, tin, carton in yel circle on red, 16x12", EX 450.00
Telephone, bottle form, exact sz of 10-oz bottle, MIB 40.00
Thermometer, late 1930s, porc, silhouette girl, 18x16", VG 300.00
Thermometer, 1950s, tin, bottle, 16", NM 150.00
Tip tray, 1909, Hilda Clark, St Louis World's Fair, 4½x6", NM ..425.00
Toy dispenser, plastic, Drink CC, red/wht, 10x11x6", NM 40.00
Toy dispenser, 1950s, b/o, Linemar, 9x5x7", EX 445.00

Toy picnic cooler, plastic, 6" L, EX 90.00
Toy truck, Big Wheel, 1980s, plastic/metal b/o, Atlanta, 10", EX ..80.00
Toy truck, Big Wheel, 1980s, plastic/metal b/o, Atlanta, 10", MIB .125.00
Toy truck, Buddy-L, yel GMC, w/8 cases, 15", EX 325.00
Toy truck, Buddy-L, 1960s, yel, 15", EX 250.00
Toy truck, Buddy-L, 1970s, Can Racer, plastic, 4½", EX 35.00
Toy truck, Buddy-L, 1980s, CC Trailer, metal/plastic, 14", EX 25.00
Toy truck, Dinky Toy #402, 1965, EX 275.00
Toy truck, Lesney-Matchbox #37, 1950s, staggered load, EX+ 75.00
Toy truck, Lesney-Matchbox #37, 1960, blk wheels, MIB 80.00
Toy truck, Marx, 1950, stake truck, steel, red/yel, 20¼", EX 275.00
Toy truck, Marx, 1950s, delivery truck, tin, 12½", EX 275.00
Toy truck, Marx, 1950s, plastic, Ford style, no cracks, 11", EX ...250.00
Toy truck, Marx #1090, 1950s, w/litho cases, 17½", EX 750.00
Toy truck, Matchbox K31 Superking, 1970s, 12¼", MIB 45.00
Toy truck, Matchbox-Yesteryears Y12, 1978, 3½", MIB 65.00
Toy truck, Metalcraft, 1930s, pressed steel, 10 bottles, 11", EX ..475.00
Toy truck, Pyro, 1950s, yel plastic, smooth wheel, 5½", NM 50.00
Toy truck, Rosko, 1950s, Beverage Delivery, friction, 8", EX 450.00
Toy truck, Sanyo, 1960s, yel/wht, b/o, 12½", NM in EX box 350.00
Toy truck, Smith-Miller, 1949, red GMC, metal & wood, 14" ...850.00
Toy truck, Smith-Miller, 1978, metal, yel, 6 cases, 14", EX 650.00
Toy truck, 1980s, Siku-Oldtimer, metal, 5¾" 45.00
Tumbler, tulip shape, dbl syrup lines, NM 12.50

Trays

Values are given for trays in excellent condition (C8). Those that have been reproduced are marked with a (+). The 1934 Weismuller and O'Sullivan tray has been reproduced at least three times. To be original, it must have a black back and must say 'American Artworks, Coshocton, Ohio.' It was not reproduced by Coca-Cola in the 1950s.

Tray, 1928, Soda Jerk, 13¼x10½", EX, $625.00.

1897, Victorian lady, 9¼" dia, EX+ 10,000.00
1901, Hilda Clark, 9¾" dia, EX+ 3,750.00
1903, Hilda Clark, oval, 18½x15", EX+ 5,000.00
1906, Juanita, glass or bottle version, 10½x13¼" 2,500.00
1907, Relieves Fatigue, 10½x13¼", EX+ 2,000.00
1909, St Louis Fair, 10½x13¼" 1,500.00
1909, St Louis Fair, 13½x16½" 2,000.00
1910, Girl in Lg Hat, Hamilton King, 10½x13¼" (+) 750.00
1913, Girl in Lg Hat, Hamilton King, oval, 12¼x15¼" (+) ..650.00
1914, Betty, oval, 12¼x15¼" (+) 600.00

1914, Betty, 10½x13¼" (+) 575.00
1916, Elaine, 8½x19" (+) 325.00
1920, Garden Girl, oval, 12¼x15¼" 800.00
1921, Autumn Girl, 10½x13¼" 750.00
1922, Summer Girl, 10½x13¼" 750.00
1923, Flapper, 10½x13¼" 400.00
1924, Smiling Girl, 10½x13¼" 625.00
1925, Party, 10½x13¼" (+) 400.00
1926, Golfers, 10½x13¼" (+) 600.00
1927, Curbside Service, 10½x13¼" 650.00
1928, Bobbed Hair, 10½x13¼" 600.00
1929, Girl in Swimsuit w/Glass, 10½x13¼" 400.00
1930, Swimmer, 10½x13¼" 400.00
1930, Telephone, 10½x13¼" 350.00
1931, Boy w/Sandwich & Dog, 10½x13¼" 675.00
1932, Girl in Swimsuit on Bench, Hayden, 10½x13¼" 575.00
1933, Francis Dee, 10½x13¼" 425.00
1934, Weismuller & O'Sullivan, 10½x13¼" (+), from $650 to ..750.00
1935, Madge Evans, 10½x13¼" 325.00
1936, Hostess, 10½x13¼" 300.00
1937, Running Girl, 10½x13¼" (+) 275.00
1938, Girl in Afternoon, 10½x13¼" 225.00
1939, Springboard Girl, 10½x13¼" 250.00
1940, Sailor Girl, 10½x13¼" 275.00
1941, Ice Skater, 10½x13¼" 250.00
1942, Roadster, 10½x13¼" 250.00
1950, Girl w/Wind in Hair, screened bkground, 10½x13¼" (+) ...60.00
1950, Girl w/Wind in hair, solid bkground, 10½x13¼" (+) 150.00
1955, Menu, 10½x13¼" 50.00
1957, Birdhouse, 10½x13¼" 80.00
1957, Rooster, 10½x13¼" 125.00
1957, Umbrella Girl, 10½x13¼" 225.00
1961, Pansy Garden, 10½x13¼" 25.00

Vendors

Though interest in Coca-Cola machines of the 1949–1959 era rose dramatically over the last few years, values currently seem to have leveled off and actually dropped 15% to 20%. The major manufacturers of these curved-top, 5¢ and 10¢ machines were Vendo (V), Vendorlator (VMC), Cavalier (C or CS), and Jacobs.

Cavalier, model #CS72, EX orig 900.00
Cavalier, model #CS72, M rstr 2,500.00
Cavalier, model #C27, EX orig 1,400.00
Cavalier, model #C27, M rstr 3,000.00
Cavalier, model #C51, EX orig 650.00
Cavalier, model #C51, M rstr 2,000.00
Jacobs, model #26, EX orig 1,500.00
Jacobs, model #26, M rstr 3,000.00
Vendo, model #23, EX orig 650.00
Vendo, model #23, M rstr 1,500.00
Vendo, model #39, EX orig 850.00
Vendo, model #39, M rstr 2,250.00
Vendo, model #44, EX orig 2,000.00
Vendo, model #44, M rstr 3,500.00
Vendo, model #56, EX orig 1,200.00
Vendo, model #56, M rstr 3,000.00
Vendo, model #80, EX orig 650.00
Vendo, model #80, M rstr 1,500.00
Vendo, model #81, EX orig 1,250.00
Vendo, model #81, M rstr 3,000.00
Vendorlator, model #27, EX orig 1,500.00
Vendorlator, model #27, M rstr (on stand) 2,500.00

Vendorlator, model #27A, EX orig 800.00
Vendorlator, model #27A, M rstr 2,000.00
Vendorlator, model #33, EX orig 800.00
Vendorlator, model #33, M rstr 2,000.00
Vendorlator, model #44, EX orig 1,800.00
Vendorlator, model #44, M rstr 3,200.00
Vendorlator, model #72, EX orig 750.00
Vendorlator, model #72, M rstr 2,500.00

Coffee Grinders

The serious collector of kitchenwares and country store items rank coffee mills high on the list of desirable examples. A trend is developing toward preferring items whose manufacturers are easily identifiable. Names to look for include Adams, Arcade, Baldwin Bros., Daisy, Elgin National, Elma, Enterprise, Lane Bros., Parker, Regal, and Sun Mfg. Co.; there are many others. Any of these marks found on coffee mills represent companies who were in business at or before the turn of the century.

Side mills usually have a brass tag located on the tin hopper. If the hopper was made of cast iron, the name was usually cast into the metal. Some of the less expensive versions had no identification. Decals were often used on the front of lap mills and table styles, though sometimes you will find these decals on the inside of the drawer. Because decals are prone to flake off and fade, and since they are often destroyed when the mill is being refinished, lap and table mills are the most difficult types to attribute to a specific manufacturer. Canister mills had names and patent dates molded into the cast-iron housing or on the canister itself. Commercial mills used in country and general stores were made of cast iron. Important information such as manufacture and patent dates was usually cast into the wheels, housing, or base of the mill. Such identification contributes considerably toward value.

Good examples of early coffee mills are rapidly becoming difficult to find. Beware of the many imported imposters that are on the market today.

A Kendrick & Sons No 1, lap, CI w/brass hopper, CI drw 140.00
Adams Pat, lap, pewter hopper, wood box, porc knob 135.00
AK & Sons #237707, CI, octagon base, rnd hopper, heavy 185.00
American Beauty, canister, CI & tin, orig cup & papers 65.00
Arcade, Crystal No 44, CI w/glass hopper, Arcade lid & cup 95.00
Arcade, Favorite No 27, side, CI w/orig lid 75.00
Arcade, Favorite No 47, wood box, CI hopper 155.00
Arcade, Favorite No 7, side, CI, orig lid, grind adjustment front ..75.00
Arcade, Imperial, lap, CI closed hopper, wood box, EX 110.00
Arcade, Imperial, table, closed CI hopper, wood box 95.00
Arcade, Imperial No 200, lap, CI hopper w/eagle, Pat 88, 89 .....135.00
Arcade, IXL, table, ornate CI hopper, hdl on side, 1-lb, EX 175.00
Arcade, Jewel, canister, rectangular glass hopper, w/lid, EX 155.00
Arcade, lap, fancy CI top & hopper, wood box, EX 110.00
Arcade, Royal, canister, CI cup, tin hopper 95.00
Arcade, Sunbeam, CI w/glass hopper, orig lid & cup, EX 95.00
Arcade, table, w/decal, Pat 6-5-1884, 1-lb 95.00
Arcade, Telephone, canister, CI front, Pat Sept 25 '88 ....355.00
Arcade No 147, lap, fancy CI closed hopper, wood box, EX 95.00
Arcade No 3, canister, CI w/glass hopper, orig lid 95.00
Arcade No 4, canister, CI w/glass hopper, orig Arcade lid 95.00
Arcade No 40, canister, CI/glass 95.00
Arcade No 5, side, CI, Pat June '94 ....75.00
Arcade No 700, lap, w/dust cover, Sears 1908 catalog, EX 105.00
Blksmith-made, funnel shape, 1-hdl, open hopper, wall mt 225.00
Blksmith-made, funnel shape, 2-hdl, wall mt to 2x4" 225.00
Bronson-Walton Ever Ready No 2, canister, Pat 1905 ....95.00
Bronson-Walton Monitor, coffee, tin 55.00
Bronson-Walton Monitor, table, tin, ca 1909 ....55.00

Bronson-Walton Monitor, tin w/tin cup underneath, Pat 1909 ....80.00

C Ibach stamp on hdl, dvtl walnut, CI hopper 145.00

Caravan, canister, CI works, tin hopper, ca 1910, VG 85.00

Cavanaugh Bros, table, front fill, 1-lb 135.00

Cavanaugh's, table, CI, ornate legs, front fill, wood box 285.00

Clark & Clawson No 1, CI, dbl grind, Pat 1886, 6" wheel 195.00

Coffee Bean Roaster, tin hopper, CI trivet, wood hdl 155.00

Coles Mfg No 7, counter, CI, Pat 1887, 16" wheels, 27", EX 695.00

Common unmk, lap, open CI hopper, orig drw, wood box, VG 70.00

Common unmk, table, orig drw, screw cap on top, VG 75.00

Crescent, table, wood, top fill, cylinder, 13" 235.00

Daisy No 667, miniature, CI top, wood box & drw, orig decal 80.00

DeVe, Holland made, lap, copper-plated hopper, decals 65.00

Elgin Nat'l, floor, silver hopper, 24" wheels 1,100.00

Elgin Nat'l No 40, counter, CI, red pnt, 2 wheels, orig, VG 575.00

Elgin Nat'l No 44, CI/red pnt, w/eagle & pan, 5" wheels, 24" 525.00

Elgin Nat'l No 48, CI w/eagle, orig lily decal, 2-wheel 575.00

Elma, counter, CI, closed hopper, 10" single wheel, 17" 165.00

Enterprise, counter, CI, brass hopper, Pat 1873, 6" wheels, EX ..575.00

Enterprise, counter, CI, CI drw, closed hopper, Pat 1873, VG ...225.00

Enterprise, counter, CI, eagle on hopper, 2-wheel, Pat 1873 ......575.00

Enterprise, floor, CI, CI hopper, Pat 1898, 39" wheels, VG 2,500.00

Enterprise, table clamp-on, CI w/CI cup, blk w/gold decal 80.00

Enterprise No 1, CI w/CI drw, hdl, covered hopper 225.00

Enterprise No 1, counter, open hopper, hdl, Pat 1873, 11", VG .225.00

Enterprise No 116½, floor, Pat 1873, 39" wheels, 72", EX 3,675.00

Enterprise No 12, counter, w/eagle, 2-wheel, Pat 1898 ....695.00

Enterprise No 3, counter, CI w/wood drw, orig decals/pnt 575.00

Enterprise No 7, counter, CI, w/eagle, orig pnt, 17" wheel 675.00

Enterprise No 9, CI, brass eagle, Pat 1898, 19" wheels, 28", VG ..750.00

Enterprise Pioneer, floor, CI, Pat 1873, 34" wheels, 65", VG ..2,795.00

Euclid No 4, counter, aluminum hopper, 10" wheels, VG 395.00

Fairbanks Morse, floor, CI, brass hopper, 2-wheel, 72", EX 2,600.00

Golden Rule, canister, w/orig glass, CI front, wood box, EX 375.00

Grand Union Tea, canister, red pnt, orig writing, Pat 1910 ....95.00

Grand Union Tea, table, CI sq base, rnd hopper, mfg Griswold .235.00

Griswold, coffee bean roaster, rnd, CI, wood hdl, 3-pc 595.00

Griswold, counter, CI, 2 wheels, Pat 1897 ....675.00

Hobart Electric Model No 265, covered hopper 375.00

J Fisher, dvtl mahog, pewter hopper, handmade 195.00

J Fisher Warranted, lap, dvtl walnut, pewter hopper, unique 195.00

Japy Freres, ornate woodwork, brass hopper, ftd 135.00

Juvenile, lap, CI, top, wood box, orig drw & decal, sm, EX 85.00

K&M, lap, maple, aluminum closed hopper, clips on drw side 55.00

L'il Tot, miniature, CI hopper & drw front, wood box 80.00

L&S, side, CI, on orig brd 75.00

Landers, Frary & Clark, canister, CI & tin, Pat 1905, VG 95.00

Landers, Frary & Clark, CI, rnd, sq base, ornate, Pat 1875 ....265.00

Landers, Frary & Clark, Crown No 10, counter, 8" wheels 695.00

Landers, Frary & Clark, lap, fancy, CI top, wood box 95.00

Landers, Frary & Clark, Regal No 44, canister, CI/tin, orig 95.00

Landers, Frary & Clark, Standard, lap, 1878 ....145.00

Landers, Frary & Clark, table, CI, Pat Feb 14, 1905, VG 95.00

Landers, Frary & Clark, Universal No 10, table, tin 85.00

Landers, Frary & Clark Crown No 01, table, CI 75.00

Landers, Frary & Clark No 20, blk, 10" wheels 595.00

Landers, Frary & Clark No 50, counter, CI, 12" wheels, EX+ 550.00

Lap, CI, brn pnt, octagon base & hopper, cup in base, 4x4x4" ...135.00

Lees, canister, CI works, rnd glass hopper, EX 70.00

Lightning, canister, CI works, tin hopper, 1-lb, EX 95.00

Logan & Strobridge, Franco-American, lap, ornate CI hopper ...125.00

Logan & Strobridge, Queen, canister, glass hopper, tin lid 155.00

Luther, side, CI, tin hopper, brass plate, Pat 1843 ....175.00

Mimosa, table mt, CI, open hopper, heavy 85.00

Miniature, canister, boy & girl, 5½x1½" 85.00

Nat'l, coffee & spice counter, CI, 12" wheels, 25", VG 475.00

Nat'l, coffee & spice counter, CI, 17" wheels, 28", VG 525.00

Nat'l, counter, CI works, covered hopper, wood drw, 1-wheel 95.00

Nat'l No 5, CI body & drw, 12" wheels, VG 525.00

Nat'l Specialty No 0, table clamp-on, CI, covered hopper 95.00

Nat'l Specialty...Philadelphia, CI, 25" wheels, VG 595.00

New Home, table, CI top, enclosed hopper, wood box, 1-lb, EX+ ..80.00

New Model, lap, CI w/CI drw, bottom opens all 4 sides 85.00

None Such, Bronson Co Cleveland OH, table, tin, pnt 75.00

Parker, Charles; table, tall/thin, CI & tin top, hdl on top 125.00

Parker, side, Pat 1876, CI, on orig brd, grind adjustment front 75.00

Parker Eagle No 50, side, CI, Pat 1860 ....95.00

Parker No 2, counter, CI w/orig decals, 9" wheels, EX 575.00

Parker No 260, table, CI top & hdl, side grind 225.00

Parker No 260 Columbia, table, side grind, 1-lb 195.00

Parker No 350, side, CI, orig lid, Pat 4/1876 ....75.00

Parker No 400 Series, lap, split covered top, ornate 135.00

Parker No 449, canister, CI works, rnd glass hopper, VG 85.00

Parker No 49, side, tin hopper w/brass eagle, tin lid 95.00

Parker No 5000, counter, CI, Pat 1897, 12" wheels, 17", VG 575.00

Parker No 5005, counter, CI, 12½" wheels, 17", EX 575.00

Parker No 555, Challenge Fast Grind, table, 1-lb, orig, EX 95.00

Parker No 560, table, side crank, wood drw 375.00

Parker No 60, tin hopper on side, brass eagle, Parker lid 75.00

Parker No 700, counter, CI, wood drw, 17" wheels 675.00

Parker Union, side, CI, gear drive, Pat 1855 ....125.00

Parker Victor No 535, table, wood/tin hopper, hdl 135.00

Peck, Stow & Wilcox, lap, ornate CI top, Pat 1877 ....155.00

Peck, Stow & Wilcox International #360, lap, unusual 155.00

Persepolis, table, CI & brass, unique 275.00

Peugot Freres, lap, wood box, tin-covered hopper, Fr 45.00

Primitive, lap, cherry, brass hopper, handmade/unique, 4x4" 195.00

Primitive, lap, dvtl, red buttermilk pnt, orig drw, pewter 195.00

Primitive, lap, dvtl walnut, wrought iron, brass hopper 175.00

Primitive, pyramid shape, wooden box, brass hopper, cast-iron top, $165.00.

PS&W No 3500, side, CI, orig lid, britannia hopper 85.00

PS&W Standard No 31, lap, CI open hopper, wood box 125.00

PS&W Vortex No 40, lap, CI hopper, wood box 145.00

PSW&Co No 6, side, orig CI lid, EX 75.00

Queen, miniature, CI hopper & drw front, wood box, decal 80.00

Rock Hard, Garant-Sewaarborge, lap, imported 55.00

Royal, side, CI w/CI cup, open hopper, Pat Apr 15, 1890, VG 65.00

RR Kreiterr, Lewisberry, York Co PA, dvtl, pewter hopper 165.00

Russell & Erwin Mfg Co, lap, top adjustment, CI hopper, wood box ..95.00

Russell & Erwin Mfg Co No 1008, CI hopper, wood box 90.00

Russell & Erwin Mfg Co No 60, britannia hopper, wood box 90.00
S&H, counter, CI, w/drw, 19" wheels, 21", VG 525.00
School Bell, canister, similar to Golden Rule, CI & wood 375.00
Selsor, Cook & Co, lap, name on hdl, Pat 1859 ....165.00
Simmons Hardware Co, Delmar Coffee, table, CI cover 295.00
Star, canister, tin w/CI works, Pat 1910, VG 75.00
Star, counter, tin drw, blk, 1-wheel, sm, VG 325.00
Star, floor, brass hopper, 2 CI wheels 975.00
Star No 7, counter, CI, w/pan, 2-wheel, VG 475.00
Sun No 1080, Challenge Fast Grind, Columbus OH, table 80.00
Sun No 1050 Improved, lap, wood, tin hopper 85.00
Swift, drug mill, CI, open hopper, Pat June 30, 1874 ....525.00
Swift, side, CI, Pat 1845, Pat Aug 16, 1859, top missing 95.00
Swift No 13, counter, orig tin drw, red pnt, 12" wheels, 19" 475.00
Swift No 15, counter, orig decals/pnt, Pat 1875, 19" wheels 875.00
Turkish, brass cylinder, seal of sultan, folding hdl, old 75.00
Turkish, primitive, table, lg sq box on 28" brd, ornate, old 195.00
Universal No 109, blk tin w/gr decal, Pat 1905, EX 95.00
W Cross & Sons, lap, CI w/orig CI drw, brass hopper & pull 85.00
Waddel Improved No 40, lap, CI hopper 115.00
Walton, Bronson, canister, tin & CI, Pat 1911 ....85.00
Walton, Clevis, canister, orig cup, Pat 7/0/1901, orig, EX 95.00
Wilson, Increase, side, CI & tin 60.00
Wrights Hdwe Co, Brighton, table, 1-lb, 8" 85.00
WW Weaver Warranted, dvtl walnut, pewter hopper, ca 1830 ..225.00
Xray, canister, CI works, tin hopper w/glass, EX 95.00

Coin-Operated Machines

Coin-operated machines may be the fastest-growing area of collector interest in today's market. Many machines are bought, restored, and used for home entertainment. Older examples from the turn of the century and those with especially elaborate decoration and innovative accessories are most desirable.

Vending machines sold a product or a service. They were already in common usage by 1900 selling gum, cigars, matches, and a host of other commodities. Peanut and gumball machines are especially popular today. The most valuable are those with their original finish and decals. Older machines made of cast iron are especially desirable, while those with plastic globes have little collector value. When buying unrestored peanut machines, beware of salt damage.

The coin-operated phonograph of the early 1900s paved the way for the jukeboxes of the twenties. Seeburg was first on the market with an automatic 8-tune phonograph. By the 1930s Wurlitzer was the top name in the industry with dealerships all over the country. As a result of the growing ranks of competitors, the forties produced the most beautiful machines made. Wurlitzers from this era are probably the most popularly sought-after models on the market today. The model #1015 of 1946 is considered the all-time classic and often brings prices in excess of $7,000.00.

Last year Sotheby's auctioned a coin-operated strength machine for $107,000.00.

Coin-Op Newsletter; Jukebox Collectors' Newsletter; Antique Amusements, Slot Machine, and Jukebox Gazette; and *Classic Amusements Magazine* are all excellent publications for those interested in coin-operated machines; see the Clubs, Newsletters, and Catalogs section of the Directory for publishing information.

Jackie and Ken Durham are our advisors (for all but jukeboxes); they are listed in the Directory under the District of Columbia. Our advisor for jukeboxes is Norman Nelson; he is listed in the Directory under Ohio.

Arcade Machines

Atlas 5¢ Tilt Test, formica case, flat-top game, EX 425.00

Brunswick, pool table, ca 1890, EX orig 4,600.00
Caille Mickey Finn Strength Tester, rstr 4,600.00
Exhibit Cupid's Post Office, ca 1920, EX orig 3,000.00
Exhibit Egyptian Mummy, EX orig 1,550.00
Exhibit Grandfather's Clock, ca 1925, VG orig 2,500.00
Exhibit Kiss-O-Meter, EX orig 715.00
Exhibit 1¢ Five Ball shooter, rstr 825.00
Gottleib Gold Star, 1954, EX orig 550.00
Little Whirl Wind 1¢, flip ball game, counter-top, sm, VG 450.00
Mercury Grip Tester, EX orig 300.00
Mexican 1¢ Baseball, 2-player, metal case, EX orig 425.00
Mills Punching Bag, ca 1900, EX orig 1,800.00
Mutoscope Indian Front, ca 1900, NM 7,000.00
Mutoscope Love Analyst, fancy cabinet, EX orig 775.00
Rockola World Series, pinball, EX 1,200.00
Seeburg Chicken Sam, ca 1931, EX orig 775.00
What Kind of Person Are You?, counter-top, 11x9x18", EX 550.00
Whiting Sculptoscope, EX orig 700.00

Jukeboxes

AMI #1200, EX orig 1,750.00
AMI A, EX orig 3,100.00
AMI F-80, pk, EX orig 1,200.00
Cremona #3, rstr 3,600.00
Mills Empress, ca 1939, EX orig 2,000.00
Mills Throne of Music, ca 1939, EX orig 1,575.00
Packard Manhattan, 1946, EX orig 4,200.00
Rockola, #1468, EX orig 1,600.00
Rockola #1422, Magic Glo series, EX rstr 3,500.00
Rockola #1484, wall mt, EX orig 900.00
Rockola #1555, EX orig 125.00
Rockola #39, counter-top, EX orig 2,500.00
Rockola Dialatune, wall type 325.00
Rockola Monarch, ca 1938, NM 1,575.00
Rockola Princess, EX orig 1,000.00

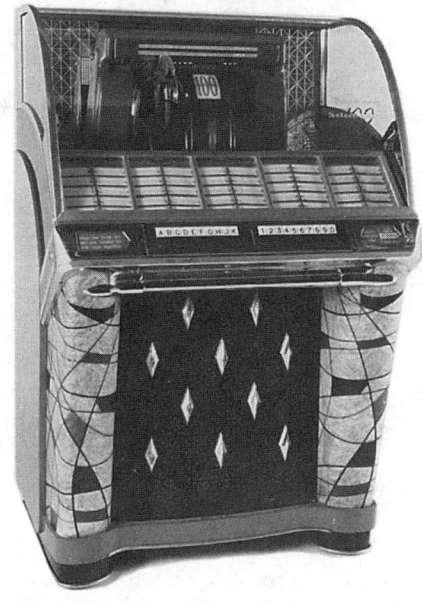

Seeburg W, EX original, $3,900.00.

Seeburg #100C, ca 1940, EX rstr 3,500.00
Seeburg A, rstr 2,500.00
Seeburg E, oak, w/xylophone, rstr 8,650.00
Seeburg G, EX orig 1,650.00

Seeburg LSI, EX orig	300.00
Seeburg V, ca 1955, EX	3,750.00
Seeburg WS1Z, wall type, EX orig	170.00
Williams Music Mite, w/stand	900.00
Wurlitzer #1015, M rstr	8,500.00
Wurlitzer #1100, EX orig	7,000.00
Wurlitzer #1100, M rstr	8,500.00
Wurlitzer #1800, ca 1955, EX orig	2,000.00
Wurlitzer #2000, EX orig	2,500.00
Wurlitzer #2200, ca 1958, NM	2,200.00
Wurlitzer #3010, EX orig	175.00
Wurlitzer #412, EX orig	2,800.00
Wurlitzer #500, ca 1938, EX orig	2,200.00
Wurlitzer #5207, EX orig	140.00
Wurlitzer #5250, EX orig	150.00
Wurlitzer #570E, 2 rpl plastics, G orig	350.00
Wurlitzer #700, orig plastics, EX	3,500.00
Wurlitzer #750, rstr	8,500.00
Wurlitzer #780, 1940, EX orig	5,000.00
Wurlitzer #81, counter-top, NM	9,000.00
Wurlitzer Peacock, M rstr	18,000.00

Slot Machines

Bally 5¢ Spark Plug Horse Race, metal front, 14x16x11", EX	2,750.00
Bonus Horse head, EX orig	2,500.00
Caille Blk Cat, musical cabinet, 1902, 66", EX rstr	18,000.00
Caille Superior Bell, nude on hdl, ca 1926, EX	2,800.00
Caille 5¢ New Century Detroit, upright w/music, EX	13,000.00
Caille 5¢ Silent Sphinx, EX orig	2,600.00
Dutch boy & girl 5¢, rstr	2,000.00
Jennings 1¢ Little Duke, EX orig	2,000.00
Jennings 1¢ Little Duke, w/side vendor, rstr	2,400.00

Jennings $1 Sun Chief, nickel-plated front with brass Indian head, 27", VG, $3000.00; Mills 25¢ Golden Gate, cast iron with wooden base, some restoration, 25½", G, $2,000.00.

Jennings 10¢ Golf Ball, rstr	4,700.00
Jennings 10¢ Indian front, EX orig	1,800.00
Jennings 25¢ Standard Chief, EX orig	2,000.00
Jennings 25¢ Sun Chief, EX orig	1,250.00
Jennings 5¢ Dixie Bell, ca 1937, EX	1,275.00
Jennings 5¢ Duchess, rstr	1,400.00
Jennings 5¢ Operator Bell	1,500.00

Jennings 5¢ Peacock, rstr	2,300.00
Jennings 5¢ Silver Moon, console, ca 1940, EX orig	1,150.00
Jennings 5¢ 4-Star Scene Chief, 1936, NM	18,000.00
Lincoln 10¢ De Lux, old rstr, repro bk door	1,600.00
Mills 1¢ Cricket, upright, ca 1904, EX orig	10,000.00
Mills 1¢ QT Dmn Front, 19x12½x13½", VG	1,100.00
Mills 10¢ Bonus Hi Top, EX orig	1,600.00
Mills 10¢ Golden Falls, rstr	1,400.00
Mills 25¢ Bursting Cherry, 1941, VG orig	2,000.00
Mills 25¢ Extra Bell, ca 1946, EX orig	1,600.00
Mills 25¢ Poinsettia, EX orig	1,300.00
Mills 25¢ War Eagle, ca 1932, NM	2,800.00
Mills 5¢ Bonus Horse Head, ca 1939, EX orig	2,500.00
Mills 5¢ Bursting Cherry, rstr	1,900.00
Mills 5¢ Castle Front, rstr	2,500.00
Mills 5¢ Dewey Jackpot, upright, oak case, decals, EX	8,500.00
Mills 5¢ Futurity, rpt, EX	3,200.00
MIlls 5¢ Lion Front, EX orig	2,500.00
Mills 5¢ Owl, upright, EX orig	7,000.00
Mills 5¢ Poinsettia w/jackpot, rstr	2,500.00
Mills 5¢ Skyscraper, rstr	1,900.00
Pace Chrome Deluxe, EX orig	1,800.00
Pace 5¢ Comet	1,800.00
Schall 5¢ Sun, 1-wheel, counter-top, rstr	5,800.00
Watling 1¢ Rol-A-Top w/Gold Coin Award, rstr	3,900.00
Watling 10¢ Rol-A-Top, bird & coin cast front, 1935, EX	4,000.00
Watling 10¢ Rol-A-Top, w/mint vendor, rstr	4,300.00
Watling 25¢ Bird of Paradise, rstr	4,000.00
Watling 25¢ Blue Seal, gooseneck jackpot, 1929, rstr	2,400.00
Watling 5¢ Rol-A-Top Checkerboard, EX orig	2,700.00
Watling 5¢ Treasury, eagle & coins on front, rare, VG	4,750.00

Trade Stimulators

Ad Lee 1¢ Try It, dice game, decals, rstr	400.00
Bally Reserve, EX orig	250.00
Bar Boy 5¢, EX orig	500.00
Caille Junior Bell, EX orig	900.00
Caille Puritan Bell, CI, EX orig	850.00
Caille 1¢ Baseball, 1-reel, ca 1911, EX orig	6,000.00
Columbus Bi-Mor, EX orig	500.00
Daval 1¢ Penny Pack, 3-reel, ca 1939, 9x11x9", EX	415.00
Daval 5¢ Derby Horse Race, ca 1937, NM	700.00
Gee Whiz Horse Race, EX orig	375.00
Groetchen 1¢ Gold Rush, rstr	465.00
Groetchen 5¢ Klix 21, 5-reel, w/gum vendor, EX orig	425.00
Jennings Grandstand, EX orig	395.00
Jennings 1¢ Target Indian Front, coin drop, EX orig	625.00
Mercury 1¢ Pay Out, EX orig	300.00
Mills Bell Boy, EX orig	1,600.00
Mills Perfection, upright, rpl marque, ca 1901, EX	1,750.00
National Target, cast aluminum, penny flip, EX orig	300.00
Punt Return 5¢ Game of Skill, decal on front, 1950s, EX	400.00
Puritan 1¢ Confection, Chicago Mint Co, EX orig	575.00
Rockola 1¢ Official Sweepstakes Horse Race, rstr	1,300.00
Skill Cards 5¢ Poker, EX orig	375.00
Stephens Magic Beer Barrel, pretzels, 3-reel, EX orig	850.00
Stephens 1¢ Draw Poker, reels spin, rpt, EX	465.00

Vendors

Abby 3-Way, nuts, EX orig	200.00
Advance, 1¢ Hershey, chocolate bars, EX orig	250.00
Advance #11 Big Mouth, peanuts, 1923, rstr	200.00

Advance D, gumball, 1923, EX orig 150.00
Atlas Master, gumball, NM orig 65.00
Atlas 1¢ Matchbox, ca 1915, 17", EX orig 800.00
Atlas 1¢/5¢ Masters Hi Top, EX orig 300.00
Butter Kist 1¢, peanuts, Holcomb & Hoke, 1923, EX, on roaster..1,900.00
Challenger, hot nuts, ca 1947, EX, on stand 375.00
Columbus, peanuts, CI, 1910, rstr 225.00
Columbus #21, EX orig 400.00
Columbus A, gumball, flat coin entry, 1946, EX orig 325.00
Columbus M, EX pnt & decals, working 225.00
Columbus Triple, gumball, M orig 885.00
E-Z, gumball, aluminum base, 18", EX 750.00
Exhibit Exco 2¢, cards, EX orig 250.00
Ford, gumball, chrome, w/orig base, marque top, rstr 90.00

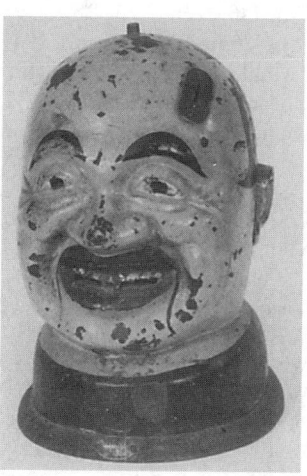

Happy Jap 1¢ gum machine, cast iron, clockwork mechanism, 1902, 15", VG, $3,000.00.

Jennings in the Bag, ca 1934, EX orig 750.00
Kandy King, 2-sided, EX 75.00
Manikin Baker Boy, gum, animated, EX 4,500.00
National Hunter, gumball, EX orig 375.00
Northwestern #22, peanuts, frosted globe, orig locks, rstr 400.00
Perfection 1¢, gum, Appleton Novelty, orig marque, '27, EX 650.00
Price Collar Button, glass & pnt CI, 11", EX orig 900.00
Pulver Gum, Clown, porc, 1899, NM 1,500.00
Pulver Gum, Foxy Grandpa, 4-panel, EX orig 1,200.00
Pulver Gum, Yel Kid, animated, 2-panel, 24", EX orig 750.00
Scoopy Gum, clockwork, man drops gum from scoop, 20", EX .1,650.00
Shipman Mfg 10¢, postage cards, 3 for 10¢, EX orig 150.00
Silver Comet 1¢, stick gum, EX orig 200.00
Silver King 1¢, peanuts, CI, 1930s, EX 100.00
Star, popcorn, floor model, EX orig 785.00
Toy 'N Joy, gumball, late 1950s, EX 25.00
Victor Baby Grand, gumball, EX orig 55.00
Victor K, gumball, sidewinder, rstr 275.00
Victor Vendorama, full glove, EX orig 75.00
Victor 1¢ Halfback, gumball, 1950s, EX orig 60.00
Victor 1¢ Topper, gumball, metal w/glass, 16x6¼x6¼", EX 95.00
Zeno 1¢, gum, wood/CI, clockworks, 17x10x9", EX orig 850.00

Miscellaneous

Columbus Tri More, w/stand 1,075.00
Master Fantail 1¢/5¢, EX orig 1,500.00
Masters 1¢, wht porc, EX orig 195.00
Mills Quarterscope, drop card machine 1,600.00
Triple Scoopy 1,300.00
Watling 1¢ Lollipop Fortune Teller Scale, bl porc w/witch, EX ..4,000.00

Watling 1¢ Scale, Philadelphia, 1918, 73", EX orig 775.00

Comic Books

For almost sixty years, the American public has been thrilled by the monthly adventures of everyone's favorite comic book heroes such as Superman, Captain Marvel, and Spiderman. Each 10¢ comic book issue, featuring a new saga of adventure and mystery, was met with excitement and anticipation by the youngsters who eagerly purchased them from their neighborhood candy store or newsstand. Unfortunately, the vast majority of these comic books were eventually discarded in favor of other worldly pursuits. Due to this fact, most comic books from the '30s and '40s did not survive, making them a very scarce and desirable collectible in today's world.

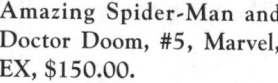

Amazing Spider-Man and Doctor Doom, #5, Marvel, EX, $150.00.

X-Men, Guest Starring the Mighty Avengers, #12, Marvel, NM, $100.00.

Action Comics, #147, Superman cover, DC Comics, 1950, NM ..300.00
Action Comics #96, Superman cover, DC Comics, 1946, NM ...468.00
Alley Oop, #1, Argo, 1955, EX 28.00
Amazing Fantasy, #15, Spider-Man, Marvel, 1962, EX 3,200.00
Amazing Spider-Man, #1, Marvel Comics, 1963, EX 5,390.00
Amazing Spider-Man, #2, Marvel, Ditko art, 1963, EX 1,045.00
Andy Panda, #25, Four Color, 1943, EX 165.00
Apache, #1, Fiction House, 1951, NM 62.00
Aquaman, #2, DC, 1962, EX 34.00
Archie Comics, #20, Archie Pub, 1946, EX 32.00
Archies Girls, Betty & Veronica; #4, 1951, NM 130.00
Batman, #64, scarce, 1951, EX 330.00
Batman Annual, #1, 1st Batman collection, 1961, EX 220.00
Blondie Comics, #16, Harvey, 1950, NM 16.00
Bulletman, #3, Fawcett, 1941, EX 160.00
Captain America, #76, scarce, 1954, EX 825.00
Cimarron Strip, #1, Dell, EX 7.00
Cisco Kid, #41, Dell, 1958, EX 18.00
Columbia Comics, #1, WH Wise, 1943, EX 43.00
Cosmo Cat, #3, Fox, 1946, EX 13.00
Daffydils, Cupples & Leon, 1911, EX 30.00
Dandy Comics, #1, EC Comics, 1947, EX 54.00
Death Valley, #1, Comic Media, 1953, EX 14.00
Detective Comics, #113, Batman cover, 1946, NM 255.00
Detective Comics, #115, Batman & Robin, Air Wave, 1946, NM ..415.00
Detective Comics, #22, DC, VG 200.00
Dick Tracy, #24, Dell, 1949, EX 40.00
Don Winslow of the Navy, #2, Fawcett, EX 75.00

Donald Duck Adventures, #1, Gladstone, 1987, NM	3.30	Stumbo Tinytown, #1, Harvey, 1963, EX	33.00
Eagle, #1, Fox, 1941, EX	220.00	Super Cat, #56, Star, 1953, EX	20.00
Famous Funnies, #210, Frazetta cover, 1954, EX	187.00	Super Heroes, #1, Dell, 1967, NM	12.00
Flash Comix V1, #1, blk & wht, Fawcett, Jan 1940, 8-pg, EX	3,100.00	Super Rabbit, #1, Timely, 1944, EX	115.00
Flash Gordon, #2, Harvey, 1950, EX	40.00	Superman, #10, National, 1940, EX	400.00
Flintstones, #1, Charlton, 1970, NM	15.00	Swamp Thing, #1, National, 1972, NM	27.00
Flipper, #1, Gold Key, 1966, EX	9.00	Swift Arrow, #1, Ajax/Farrell, 1954, EX	20.00
Foodini, #5, Continental, 1950, EX	8.00	Tales of Horror, #1, Toby Press, 1952, EX	95.00
Forbidden Worlds, #2, 1951, EX	85.00	Tales of the Unexpected, #2, National, 1956, EX	60.00
Gene Autry Comics, #2, Fawcett, EX	156.00	Tales to Astonish, #1, Atlas, 1959, EX	170.00
Girl From UNCLE, #1, Gold Key, EX	14.00	Terrifying Tales, #11, Star, 1953, EX	60.00
Gunsmoke Trail, #4, Ajax-Farrell/4 Star, EX	8.00	Texan, #1, St John, 1948, EX	26.00
Hawkman, #1, National Periodical, 1964, EX	80.00	Three Mouseketeers, #1, National, 1956, EX	33.00
Heckle & Jeckle, #2, St Johns, 1951, EX	27.00	Tormented, #1, Sterling, 1954, EX	20.00
Hillbilly Comics, #4, Charlton, 1956, NM	15.00	Trail Blazers, #1, Street & Smith, 1941, EX	50.00
Howdy Doody, #2, Dell, 1950, EX	32.00	True Life Secrets, #1, Romantic Love Stories, 1951, NM	42.00
HR Puf 'n Stuf, #1, Gold Key, 1970, NM	6.00	True Western, #1, Marvel, 1949, EX	28.00
It Really Happened, #11, Standard, 1947, EX	15.00	Twinkle Comics, #1, Spotlight, 1945, EX	28.00
Jesse James, Avon, #1, 1950, EX	35.00	Uncanny Tales, #1, Atlas, 1952, EX	78.00
Jetsons, #2, Gold Key, 1963, EX	42.00	Uncle Milty, #1, Victoria, 1950, EX	73.00
Joe Palooka, #2, Columbia, 1942, EX	35.00	Unseen, #5, Standard, 1952, EX	33.00
Johnny Quest, #1, Gold Key, 1964, EX	40.00	US Marines in Action, #1, Avon, 1952, EX	12.00
Kid Colt Outlaw, #1, Marvel, 1948, EX	125.00	USA Comics, #3, Timely, 1941, EX	400.00
King Classics, #3, David McKay, 1936, EX	300.00	Vampirella, #1, Warren, 1969, EX	43.00
Krazy Kat Comics, #1, Dell, 1951, NM	33.00	Vic Flint, #1, Argo, 1956, NM	25.00
Land of the Lost, #1, DC Comics, 1946, EX	65.00	Visions, #1, Visions Pub, 1979, NM	125.00
Legends of Daniel Boone, #2, National Periodical, 1955, EX	65.00	Wagon Train, #1, Gold Key, 1964, EX	11.00
Little Archie, #1, 1956, EX	175.00	War Action, #1, Atlas, 1952, EX	21.00
Little Dot, #2, Harvey, 1953, EX	80.00	War Birds, #1, Fiction House, 1952, EX	21.00
Lone Ranger, #1, Dell, 1948, EX	150.00	Warlord, #1, National, 1976, NM	17.00
Looney Tunes & Merrie Melodies, #13, Dell, 1942, NM	140.00	Washable Jones & Shmoo, #1, Harvey, 1953, NM	85.00
Magic Comics, #3, David McKay, 1939, EX	110.00	Wedding Bells, #1, Quality, 1954, EX	21.00
Marines in Battle, #1, Atlas, 1954, EX	17.50	Weird Comics, #1, Fox, 1940, EX	370.00
McHale's Navy, #1, Dell, 1963, NM	20.00	Weird Terror, #1, Allen Hardy, 1952, EX	45.00
Mighty Mouse, #1, Timely-Marvel, 1946, EX	175.00	Western Bandit Trails, #1, St John, 1949, EX	35.00
Miss Liberty, #1, Burten, 1945, EX	48.00	Wilbur Comics, #1, MLJ, 1944, EX	85.00
Mister Mystery, #1, Media, 1951, EX	75.00	Wild Frontier, #1, Charlton, 1955, EX	12.00
Moon Mullins, #2, Michel, 1947, EX	17.00		
My Girl Pearl, #1, Atlas, 1955, EX	16.00		
Mystery Tales, #1, Atlas, 1952, EX	70.00		
PJ Warlock, #1, Eclipse, 1986, NM	2.50		
Popeye, #25, Four Color, 1943, NM	330.00		
Public Enemy, #1, DS, 1948, EX	28.00		
Quick-Draw McGraw, #1, Charlton, 1970, EX	6.00		
Ralph Kiner, Home Run King; Fawcett, 1950, EX	85.00		
Rat Patrol, #1, Dell, 1967, NM	31.00		
Rawhide Kid, #2, Atlas/Marvel, 1955, EX	42.00		
Richie Rich, #2, Harvey, 1960, EX	110.00		
Rifleman, #2, Dell, 1960, EX	24.00		
Saint, #2, Avon, 1947, EX	55.00		
Scooby Doo, #1, Gold Key, 1970, EX	10.00		
Sea Devils, #1, National, 1961, EX	82.00		
Secret Romance, #1, Superior, 1951, EX	21.00		
Select Detective, #1, DS, 1948, EX	30.00		
Sheena, Queen of the Jungle, #1, Fiction House, 1942, EX	360.00		
Shorty Shiner, #1, Dandy, 1956, EX	9.00		
Showcase, #43, Dr No, DC Comics, 1963, EX	330.00		
Soldier Comics, #1, Fawcett, 1952, EX	31.00		
Space Action, #1, Ace, 1952, EX	94.00		
Space Mouse, #1, Avon, 1953, EX	14.00		
Sparky Watts, #1, Columbia, 1942, EX	57.00		
Strange As It Seems, #1, United Feature, 1939, EX	52.00		
Strange Journey, #1, America's Best, 1957, EX	23.00		
Strange Tales, #1, Atlas, 1951, EX	280.00		

Compacts

The use of cosmetics before WWI was looked upon with disdain. After the war women became liberated, entered the work force, and started to use cosmetics. The compact, a portable container for cosmetics, became a necessity. The basic compact contains a mirror and a powder puff.

The vintage compacts were fashioned in a myriad of shapes, styles, materials, and motifs. They were made of precious metals, fabrics, plastics, and in almost any other conceivable medium imaginable. Commemorative, premium, patriotic, figural, Art Deco, plastic and gadgetry compacts are just a few of the most sought-after types available today. Those that are combined with other accessories (music/compact, watch/compact, cane/compact) are also very much in demand. Vintage compacts are an especially desirable collectible since the workmanship, design, techniques, and materials used in their execution would be very expensive and virtually impossible to duplicate today.

Our advisor, Roselyn Gerson, has written two highly informative books, *Ladies' Compacts of the 19th and 20th Centuries* and *Vintage Vanity Bags and Purses*, the first book devoted solely to bags and purses that incorporate compacts. She is listed in the Directory under the state of New York. See Clubs and Newsletters for information concerning the compact collectors' club and their periodical publication, *The Powder Puff*.

Bracelet type, hinged to fit on wrist, gold-tone, w/mirror 215.00

Carryall, wht plastic, metal disk on front lid, 3¼x6¼" 125.00
Christian Dior, gold-tone, fine ribs, 3x3½", EX 45.00
Copper, hammered finish, unmk, 3½" dia, VG 55.00
Coty, gold-tone wallet type w/fold-over lid, 2½x3½" 40.00
Coty, silver w/bird logo, 2x2", EX 30.00
Elgin, gold-tone w/blk enamel & etched floral, 3" sq, VG 25.00
Elgin, gray & wht MOP check pattern, sq, MIB 45.00
Elgin, rnd w/MOP lid, gold medallion in center, blk cord, M 42.50
Elgin Am, gold-tone w/eng hearts, mirror & puff, VG 35.00
Elgin Am, satin silver carryall w/bronze fawns, 4½x3", NM 150.00
Elizabeth Arden, rhinestones on gold-tone, 4" dia, EX 55.00
Estee Lauder, gold-tone, eng ea side, w/chain, M 50.00
Estee Lauder, lady's cameo profile on gold-tone lid w/eng, rnd 45.00
Evans, gold-tone, watch-case type, 2½" sq 75.00
Evans, mc stones on gold-tone, compartmental, 3x5½", NM 175.00
Evans, pk, yel & wht basketweave metal carryall, 3x5½", NM ... 150.00
Evans, rhinestones on gold floral pattern on lid, sq 85.00
Evening in Paris, Bourgois, SP, eng/pnt decor, 2¼x3¼" 60.00
Floral petit point, tortoise plastic, France, 2½" dia 60.00
Girey, 1939 World's Fair, turq speckled camera type, 1¾x3¼" ... 100.00
Gold-tone & copper, woven design, 5" dia, EX 60.00
Gold-tone w/bl & wht floral, 3¼" sq, EX 30.00
Heart shape, MOP lid, M 48.00
Lentheric, gold-tone, plain, 2½x3½" 12.50
Lucretia Vanderbuilt, bl enamel w/butterfly, 1½x2¼" 50.00
Max Factor, Deco-look dmns on rectangular shape, 2½x3½", NM ... 25.00
Pen Art, silver-tone w/wht enamel florals, 4½" dia 100.00
Plastic w/gold rhinestones, no cord or puff, early 185.00
Revlon, fancy gold-dotted surface, 3½x2½", M 22.50
Rex, 24k gold-plated w/eng floral, flapjack type, 4" 50.00
Rex Fifth Avenue, celluloid flapjack type w/flowers 60.00
Rhinestonnes allover lid, gold fr, sq, M 55.00
Schildkraut, AM Airlines, gold-tone w/faux MOP, 2½" dia 50.00
Silver gilt, lid w/miniature painting on ivory, rectangle 185.00
Silver gilt w/enamel lady & cupids, serpentine oval 220.00
Silver gilt w/enamel portrait of a maid, red shawl, bl borders 165.00
Silver-tone w/blk enamel Deco lady & children, 2x2½" 60.00
Statue of Liberty, lt bl, 2¾" dia 45.00
Sterling w/emb floral decor, mirror, 3" dia, VG 65.00
Stratton, silver metal w/scalloped edge & stars allover, 3" dia 30.00
Stratton, Wedgwood gr jasper ware, 3½" dia 100.00
Vogel, ladies w/parasol petit point, gold-tone, 2¼" sq 75.00
Volupte, sterling box type w/ribbon decor, 3" sq 70.00
Woolworth Bldg, NY, gold-tone pnt on plastic w/rhinestones 45.00
14k yel gold, fluted/rectangular, +lipstick case, 126.7dwt 1,035.00

Computing Devices

Computing, calculating and adding devices come in many shapes, sizes and weights. Some are complex machines with many moving parts while others, such as slide rules, are quite simple in construction. These devices were used by scientists, accountants, engineers and many other professionals when mathematical computations and exactness were required. Examples of devices and machines with early patent dates are usually of greatest interest to collectors. Our advisor for this category is Dale Beeks; he is listed in the Directory under Idaho.

Adder, addometer, 7 numbered wheels, in case, EX 20.00
Adder, Gem, chain drive, pocket sz 45.00
Adder, Webb, Pat 1867, wooden base, EX 300.00
Adder, Webb, Pat 1889, all metal, EX 165.00
Adder, Webb type, unsgn, all metal, EX 110.00
Curta, pepper-grinder type, w/case, EX 200.00

Machine, Burroughs, push button glass sides, lg 95.00
Machine, Comptometer, copper case, push button 45.00
Machine, Comptometer, wooden case, G 200.00
Machine, Millionaire, metal case, heavy, lg, VG 750.00
Machine, Monroe, push button, suitcase sz 75.00
Slide rule, beginner's, w/case, EX 12.00
Slide rule, circular, Gilson, w/case, EX 35.00
Slide rule, demonstration, Pickett, 7-ft long, EX 120.00
Slide rule, Keuffel & Esser NY, typical, EX 22.00
Slide rule, Thachers, cylindrical, Pat 1882, w/case, EX 800.00

Consolidated Lamp and Glass

The Consolidated Lamp and Glass Company of Coraopolis, Pennsylvania, was incorporated in 1894. For many years their primary business was the manufacture of lighting glass such as oil lamps and shades for both gas and electric lighting. The popular 'Cosmos' line of lamps and tableware was produced from 1894 to 1915. (See also Cosmos.) In 1926 Consolidated introduced their Martele line, a type of 'sculptured' ware closely resembling Lalique glassware of France. (Compare Consolidated's 'Lovebirds' vase with the Lalique 'Perruches' vase.) It is this line of vases, lamps, and tableware which is often mistaken for a very similar type of glassware produced by the Phoenix Glass Company, located nearby in Monaca, Pennsylvania. For example, the so-called Phoenix 'Grasshopper' vases are actually Consolidated's 'Katydid' vases.

Items in the Martele line were produced in blue, pink, green, crystal, white, or custard glass decorated with various fired-on color treatments or a satin finish. For the most part, their colors were distinctively different from those used by Phoenix. Although not foolproof, one of the ways of distinguishing Consolidated's wares from those of Phoenix is that most of the time Consolidated applied color to the raised portion of the design, leaving the background plain, while Phoenix usually applied color to the background, leaving the raised surfaces undecorated. This is particularly true of those pieces in white or custard glass.

In 1928 Consolidated introduced their Ruba Rombic line, which was their Art Deco or Art Moderne line of glassware. It was only produced from 1928-1932 and is quite scarce. Today it is highly sought after by both Consolidated and Art Deco collectors.

Consolidated closed its doors for good in 1964. Subsequently a few of the molds passed into the hands of other glass companies that later reproduced certain patterns; one such reissue is the 'Chickadee' vase, found in avocado green, satin-finish custard, or milk glass. Our advisor for this category is Jack D. Wilson, author of *Phoenix and Consolidated Art Glass, 1926 - 1980*; he is listed in the Directory under Illinois.

Key: mg — milk glass

Bird of Paradise, fan vase, pk wash, 6" 85.00
Bittersweet, vase, purple cased, 9½" 295.00
Blackberry, umbrella vase, gold highlighting on glossy mg, 18" .. 500.00
Catalonian, bowl, salad; amethyst, str sides, #1114 .... 40.00
Catalonian, cigarette box, honey, #1107 .... 45.00
Catalonian, plate, russet, rare color, 6" 100.00
Catalonian, vase, red, triangular, #1101, 10" 100.00
Catalonian, vase, yel, ftd, flared, #1148 .... 40.00
Chrysanthemum, vase, 2-color highlighting on satin mg, 12" 150.00
Cockatoo, vase, straw opal, ormolu mts, 8½" 450.00
Con-Cora, cookie jar, roses decor, mg, 6½" 95.00
Dancing Nymph, bowl, bl wash, rare, 8" 275.00
Dancing Nymph, cup & saucer, frosted 100.00
Dancing Nymph, fan vase, crysal, rare 75.00
Dancing Nymph, goblet, pk crystal 100.00
Dancing Nymph, platter, gr wash, bowl shape, palace sz 525.00

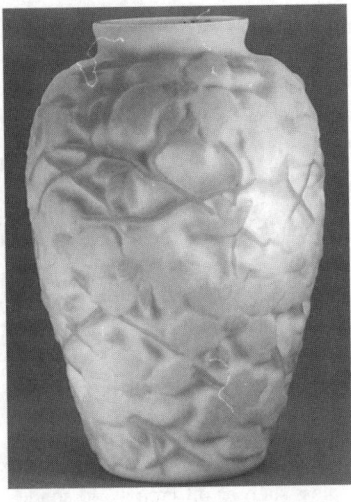

Dogwood, vase, tricolor highlighting on satin custard, 11", $150.00.

Dogwood, lamp, 3-color highlights on satin mg, 11" 125.00
Five Fruits, jug, yel wash, ftd, ½-gal 250.00
Five Fruits, plate, purple wash, 14" 150.00
Florentine, vase, gr, #2200, 7" 195.00
Hummingbird, powder jar, purple wash, 5" 75.00
Iris, candlestick, gr wash, tall 75.00
Iris, jug, gr transparent over wht casing, ½-gal, rare 300.00
Katydid, vase, ovoid, bl on satin mg, 7" 165.00
Katydid, vase, ovoid, reverse gr highlighting on mg, 7" 150.00
Line 700, candlesticks, bl crystal, pr 55.00
Line 700, compote, French crystal 25.00
Line 700, lamp, red·slag on satin, 7" 325.00
Line 700, plate, wht, 8" 55.00
Line 700, vase, dk bl on crystal, 6½" 110.00
Love Bird, vase, 3-color on satin custard, 10½" 375.00
Orchids, candlestick, yel wash 95.00
Ruba Rombic, bottle, toilet; lav 250.00
Ruba Rombic, bowl, jade, flared, 9" 175.00
Ruba Rombic, creamer, lav 75.00
Ruba Rombic, sugar bowl, Jungle Gr, 3" 150.00
Ruba Rombic, tumbler, juice; smoky topaz 65.00
Ruba Rombic, tumbler, Sunshine, 9-oz 75.00
Ruba Rombic, vase, Jade Gr, 2¾" 250.00
Ruba Rombic, vase, Jungle Gr, 9½" 275.00
Screech Owls, vase, sepia cased, 5¾" 250.00
Sea Gulls, vase, gr cased, 11" 375.00
Spanish Knobs, goblet, yel, ftd 35.00
Spanish Knobs, tumbler, amethyst 25.00
Tropical Fish, tray, French crystal, rare 185.00
Tropical Fish, vase, orange on gr satin, 9" 185.00

Cookbooks

Cookbooks from the 19th century, though often hard to find, are a delight to today's collectors both for their quaint formats and printing methods as well as for their outmoded, often humorous views on nutrition. Recipes required a 'pinch' of salt, butter 'the size. of an egg' or a 'walnut,' or a 'handful' of flour. Collectors sometimes specialize in cookbooks issued as advertising premiums. Especially desirable are the figurals that were shaped like a jar, a slice of bread, or some other form relative to the product. Others with unique features such as illustrations by well-known artists or references to famous people or places are priced in accordance. Cookbooks written earlier than 1874 are the most valuable and when found command prices as high as $200.00; figurals usually sell in the $10.00 to $15.00 range.

As is true with all other books, if the original dust jacket is present and in nice condition, a cookbook's value goes up by at least $5.00. Right now, books on Italian cooking from before circa 1940 are in demand, and bread-baking is important this year. For further information we recommend A *Guide to Collecting Cookbooks* by Col. Bob Allen and *Price Guide to Cookbooks and Recipe Leaflets* by Linda Dickinson. Our advisor for this category is Charlotte Safir; she is listed in the Directory under New York.

Key:
CB — Cookbook   dj — dust jacket

Adventures in French Cooking, J Childs, 1970, 374-pg, NM 20.00
American Woman's CB, Berolzheimer, 1947, 824-pg, EX 25.00
Art of Bread Making, Northwestern Yeast, 1935, 28-pg, NM 6.00
Aunt Jane's CB, McConnon Products, 1939, 48-pg, EX 12.00
Avon Active Woman's CB, soft cover, 1980, 80-pg, M 5.00
Batter Breads, Fleischmann...Yeast Baking; 1962, 50-pg, NM 2.00
Better Homes & Gardens Junior CB, 1963, 77-pg, M 24.00
Betty Crocker Barbecue Lovers #22, 1987, 94-pg, M 2.50
Betty Crocker Cake Mix Magic, 1951, 26-pg, EX 3.50
Betty Crocker Pie Parade, 1957, 38-pg, M 6.50
Borden's Eagle Brand 70 Magic Recipes, 1952, 24-pg, M 7.50
Borden's Quick 'N Easy Dietary Dishes, 31-pg, NM 7.50
California Dried Fig Recipes, 1939, 23-pg, M 8.00
Calumet Baking Secrets, 1942, 34-pg, EX 7.50
Campbell's Cooking w/Soup, hardbk, 1959, 199-pg, M 6.00
Campfire Marshmallow Cookery, 1934, 19-pg, EX 12.00
Cape Cod's Famous Cranberry Recipes, Ocean Spray, '41, 30-pg ...7.00
Ceresota CB, Ceresota Flour, 42-pg, VG 12.50
Chamberlain Sampler of Amrican Cooking, 1961, 232-pg, NM 5.00
Chiquita Banana's Recipe Book, 1950, 24-pg, NM 7.50

Corn Products Cook Book, 1916, EX, $14.00.

Country Inn Cookware, West Bend, 1938, 38-pg, NM 2.50
Cranberries & How To Cook Them, 1938, 20-pg, EX 20.00
Dining Delights, RT French Co, 1951, 30-pg, EX 7.50
Dishes Children Love, Culinary Arts Institute, 1972, 68-pg 3.50
Dr Morse's Indian Root Pills CB, VG 12.50
Everyday French Cooking, HP Pellaprat, hardbk, 1959, 562-pg, M ..20.00
Family Circle Fast Meals, hardbk, 1979, 96-pg, M 2.50
Family Fare, US Dept of Agriculture, 1950, NM 4.00
Farm Journal's Country CB, hardbk, 1959, 420-pg, EX 15.00
Festive Christmas Foods From Many Lands, 1958, 16-pg, NM 6.00

Glamour Magazine After 5 CB, hardbk, 1952, 258-pg, EX **8.00**
Glorious Eating for Weight Watchers, 1961, 95-pg, NM **6.00**
Good Housekeeping CB, hardbk, 1935, 254-pg, EX **14.50**
Good Housekeeping CB, hardbk, 1958, 760-pg, EX **12.00**
Good Housekeeping's Dreamy Desserts, 1967, 64-pg, NM **3.50**
Hershey's Cocoa CB, paperbk, 1979, 96-pg, M **2.50**
I Hate To Cook CB, Peg Bracken, 1950, 144-pg, M **8.00**
Jean Anderson's Processor Cooking, hardbk, 1979, 446-pg, NM **8.00**
Jell-O Recipes for Delicious Ice Cream, 1936, 15-pg, EX **25.00**
Jeremiah Towers New American Classics, 1986, 233-pg, M **20.00**
Jewish Cookery, Leah Leonard, hardbk, 1949, 495-pg, VG **25.00**
Kelvinator Book of Recipes, 1928, 32-pg, EX **12.50**
Kerr Home Canning Book, 1952, 56-pg, EX **7.00**
Kerr Modern Homemaker, 1943, 23-pg, M **12.00**
Kraft Good Ideas Keep Popping Up, Vol II, 1981, 15-pg, NM **2.50**
Libby Hillman's Gourmet CB, 1972, 356-pg, NM **20.00**
Lily Wallace New American CB, hardbk, 1948, 930-pg, EX **6.00**
Mazola, New Dressings Galore; 24-pg, M **7.50**
Meat Recipes for the Family Chef, 1952, 40-pg, M **2.00**
Modern Approach to Everyday Cooking, hardbk, 1966, 223-pg, M .**5.00**
New Delineator Recipes, hardbk, 1930, 222-pg, EX **32.00**
New Fashioned Old Fashioned Recipes, Arm & Hammer, 1948, NM .**3.00**
New Perfection Oil Stove, 1923, worn cover, 63-pg, VG **12.50**
Pierre Franey's Kitchen, soft cover, 1984, 262-pg, NM **15.00**
Pillsbury Nice 'N Easy CB, 1968, 96-pg, M **10.00**
Pillsbury 100 Grand National Recipes, 1953, 96-pg, NM **50.00**
Playboy's Gourmet CB, paperbk, 1971, 264-pg, M **2.00**
Playboy's Host & Bar Book, hardbk, 1971, 339-pg, M **12.00**
Rawleigh's Good Health Guide, 1953, 32-pg, NM **5.00**
Rodale's Naturally Great Foods CB, hardbk, 1977, 408-pg, NM ..**12.00**
Royal Baker & Pastry CB, 1911, 45-pg, EX **22.00**
Royal CB, 1928, 49-pg, EX **17.50**
Shefford 100 Recipes w/Cheese, 1935, 32-pg, EX **10.00**
Sunbeam Controlled Heat Frypan Recipe Booklet, 1953, 19-pg, VG .**2.00**
Sunkist Recipes for Every Day, 1934, 40-pg, NM **15.00**
Swanson Best Loved Chicken & Turkey Recipes, 23-pg, M **4.00**
Tante Marie's French Kitchen, hardbk, 1949, 323-pg, NM **12.00**
Teen Time Cooking w/Carnation, 1959, 16-pg, M **7.50**
Waldorf Astoria CB, hardbk, 1969, 266-pg, M **12.50**
Weight Watchers 365 Day Menu CB, soft cover, 1983, 371-pg, M ..**2.50**
What Shall I Cook Today?, Spry, 1930s, 48-pg, NM **8.00**
Woman's Day Book of New Mexican Cooking, 1984, 253-pg, NM .**6.00**
Woman's Day Collector's CB, hardbk, 1973, 519-pg, NM **12.00**
World Famous Chef's CB Rare Old Recipes, 1st ed, 1941, 637-pg ..**55.00**
10 Cakes Husbands Like Best, Spry, 1940s, 17-pg, NM **6.00**
253 Food Ideas By Hormel, 1948, 47-pg, NM **5.00**
500 Tasty Sandwiches #14, Culinary Arts, 1941, 48-pg **10.00**

Cookie Cutters

Early hand-fashioned cookie cutters have recently been commanding stiff prices at country auctions, and the ranks of interested collectors
are growing steadily. Especially valuable are the figural cutters; and the
more complicated the design, the higher the price. A follow-up of the
carved wooden cookie boards, the first cutters were probably made by
itinerant tinkers from leftover or recycled pieces of tin. Though most of
the 18th-century examples are now in museums or collections, it is still
possible to find some good cutters from the late 1800s when changes in
the manufacture of tin resulted in a thinner, less expensive material.
The width of the cutting strip is often a good indicator of age; the wider
the strip, the older the cutter. While the very early cutters were 1" to
1½" deep, by the twenties and thirties, many were less than ½" deep.
Crude, spotty soldering indicates an older cutter, while a thin line of

solder usually tends to suggest a much later manufacture. The shape of
the backplate is another clue. Later cutters will have oval, round, or
rectangular backs, while on the earlier type the back was cut to follow
the lines of the design. Cookie cutters usually vary from 2" to 4" in size,
but gingerbread men were often made as tall as 12". Birds, fish, hearts,
and tulips are common; simple versions can be purchased for as little as
$12.00 to $15.00. The larger figurals, especially those with more imaginative details, often bring $75.00 and up. The cookie cutters listed here
are tin and handmade unless noted otherwise.

Rabbit, tin with flat back, 4¼x5½", $37.00.

Bird, standing, strap hdl, 3½x2½" **20.00**
Bird, strap hdl, 6" **65.00**
Bird flying, strap hdl, 4x3" **20.00**
Bird w/long tail (stylized), loose seams, 6½" **30.00**
Boot, strap hdl, 5¼" **30.00**
Cat, sitting, strap hdl, 3¾x2½" **30.00**
Chicken, strap hdl, 5⅜" **25.00**
Christmas tree, rectangular bk, strap hdl, 5½x4x1" **35.00**
Cow (stylized), strap hdl, 5¼" **77.50**
Crimped leaf w/tulip, strap hdl, 4¾" **25.00**
Dbl tulip & leaf in crimped oval, strap hdl, 3¾x2¾" **25.00**
Dog, strap hdl, 4x3" **16.00**
Duck, strap hdl, 4x3" **16.00**
Dutchman dancing, strap hdl, dk patina, 7" **225.00**
Dutchman w/lg head, strap hdl, 7¼" **170.00**
Eagle, simple cvg, no hdl, 4x5" **30.00**
Elephant, good detail, strap hdl, 4¾" **65.00**
Fish, no hdl, 2½x5½" **15.00**
Fish, strap hdl, 4" **20.00**
Fish, strap hdl, 6¾" **25.00**
Goose, simple, strap hdl, 6½" **35.00**
Hatchet, strap hdl, 7" **55.00**
Heart, flat bk, 3½x3¾" **25.00**
Heart, strap hdl, 3x3" **20.00**
Heart, strap hdl, 6½" **30.00**
Heart in hand, hdl missing, soldered rprs, 4¼" **260.00**
Heart in heart, strap hdl, some resoldering, 3½" **100.00**
Hen, strap hdl, 3⅝x3⅞" **18.00**
Horse, no hdl, 6½x6¼" **65.00**
Horse, standing, strap hdl, 3⅝x3¼" **35.00**
Horse, standing, strap hdl, 4x5" **40.00**
Horse, standing, strap hdl, 6½" **55.00**
Horse, trotting, no hdl, 2¾x1⅝" **75.00**
Lady in long skirt, strap hdl, 4½" **30.00**
Lion, strap hdl, 3x4" **25.00**
Man & lady, strap hdls, 4", pr **55.00**
Man in bowler hat, strap hdl, ca 1900, 9½x5½x3" **60.00**
Man in top hat & frock coat, folded rim, no hdl, 7x3½" **180.00**
Man w/boots, strap hdl, resoldered, 8" **85.00**
Man w/coat tails, strap hdl, 6¼" **66.00**
Man w/hat, strap hdl, 4½x2¼" **40.00**

Man w/outstretched hand, flat bk, 9¾"	385.00
Man wearing hat on horsebk, galvanized, no hdl, 9½x8½"	180.00
Pea hen, strap hdl, 4x2⅞"	20.00
Penguin, standing, strap hdl, 3⅝x2½"	20.00
Rabbit, no hdl, 5x8¾"	40.00
Rabbit, running, strap hdl, 3¾x2½"	18.00
Rabbit, running, strap hdl, 7¾"	38.00
Rabbit jumping, strap hdl, 6½x4¾"	36.00
Razorbk hog, strap hdl, 4¼"	42.50
Reindeer, detailed antlers, no hdl, 4¾x5"	175.00
Reindeer, leaf-shaped inset, no hdl, 4¼x6½"	50.00
Rocking horse, strap hdl, 4¾x4¾"	45.00
Rooster, hdl missing, 4½"	35.00
Santa Claus, no hdl, bl partly open, mk Joseph Germany, 4x9"	55.00
Santa w/tree, strap hdl, 10¼"	66.00
Santa w/tree, strap hdl, 5"	35.00
Sheep, inset division in legs, no hdl, 3¼x5¼"	30.00

Cookie Jars

The appeal of the cookie jar is universal; folks of all ages, both male and female, love to collect 'em! The early thirties' heavy stoneware jars of a rather nondescript nature quickly gave way to figurals of every type imaginable. Those from the mid to late thirties were often decorated over the glaze with 'cold paint,' but by the early forties underglaze decorating resulted in cheerful, bright, permanent colors and cookie jars that still have a new look fifty years later.

With few exceptions, unmarked jars, unless properly identified and rare, bring the lowest prices, while cookie jars trimmed in gold are usually highly valued. For further information we recommend *The Collector's Encyclopedia of Cookie Jars* by Fred and Joyce Roerig; they are listed in the Directory under South Carolina. Another good source is *An Illustrated Guide to Cookie Jars* by Ermagene Westfall. Our advisors for this category are Charlie and Rose Snyder; they are listed in the Directory under Kansas.

The examples listed below were made by companies other than those found elsewhere in this book; see also specific manufacturers.

Chef and Mammy, Pearl China, both with 22k gold trim, $600.00 and $925.00.

Alice's Adventures in Wonderland, Japan	125.00
Avon Cookie Jar, Avon lady at door	70.00
Baby Bear, Treasure Craft, EX	45.00
Bambi, Twin Winton	225.00
Barney Rubble, Made in Taiwan	60.00
Basket Handle Mammy, Maruhon Ware	1,250.00
Basket of Tomatoes, Doranne of California, EX	37.50
Betsy Ross, Imports, Enesco, Japan	175.00
Betty Boop, Vandor, Made in Japan, 1983, sm	80.00

Big Bird Chef, California Originals	125.00
Birdhouse, Treasure Craft, EX	45.00
Butler w/Herringbone Trousers, Japan	1,500.00
C-3PO, Star Wars TM, c 1977	225.00
Caterpiller, David Kirschner, 1980, rare	1,200.00
Chipmunk, w/acorn, blk & wht stripes, DeForest of California	155.00
Christmas Tree, California Originals	400.00
Circus Wagon, mk Circus Parade, Enesco, 1980, EX	40.00
Coffee Grinder, #861, California Originals	50.00
Cookie Catcher, brn, Twin Winton	95.00
Cookie Coach, brn, unmk Twin Winton	85.00
Cookie Time Clock, California Originals, EX	65.00
Cookieville, Treasure Craft	35.00
Cookstove Mammy, Wisecarver, 1988	225.00
Cowmen Mooranda, Vandor, 1988	350.00
Cream of Wheat Chef, Japan, 10", minimum value	1,500.00
Crook-Neck Squash, Doranne	95.00
Dachshund, DeForest of California	75.00
Dog on Stump, California Originals	32.00
Donald Duck, standing, EX	450.00
Donald Duck Cylinder, California Originals	75.00
Dopey, Treasure Craft	80.00
Duck w/Mixing Bowl, brn, Twin Winton	230.00
Dutch Boy, brn pnts, wht top, Pottery Guild	125.00
Dutch Boy, solid color, Pottery Guild	78.00
Elephant, gr, Doranne of California	35.00
Elf Bakery, yel & wht, Twin Winton	120.00
Ernie & Bert Fine Cookies, California Originals	525.00
Famous Amos, Fitz & Floyd	70.00
Famous Amos Bag of Cookies, Treasure Craft, MIB	65.00
Ferdinand, #870, California Originals	75.00
Fire Engine, brn, Twin Winton	125.00
Fire Engine, red, Twin Winton	175.00
Garbage Can, Doranne of California, EX	28.00
Garfield, c 1978, 1981 United Features Syndicate, Inc	85.00
Gigantic Clown, all under glaze, Maurice of California	225.00
Gigantic Clown, cold pnt, Maurice of California	175.00
Gingerbread House, snowy roof, Treasure Craft	125.00
Grandma's Cookies, Monmouth, Ill USA	50.00
Green Pepper, Doranne of California, 1984	35.00
Gumball Machine, orig red pnt, California Originals, EX	65.00
Gun Fighter Rabbit, brn, Twin Winton	125.00
Happy Bull, brn, Twin Winton	115.00
Happy Bull, Collector Series	175.00
Harley-Davidson Gas Tank, Taiwan	95.00
Hey Diddle Diddle, no gold, Robinson Ransbottom	225.00
Hobo, Treasure Craft	40.00
Holstein Cow, Japan	60.00
Horse, unmk Sierra Vista	385.00
Horse Mechanic, Japan	45.00
Howdy Doody, Puritan, EX	565.00
Jeep, Doranne	95.00
Juggling Clown, #876, California Originals	85.00
Katrina, Treasure Craft, minimum value	700.00
Keystone Cop, Marcia of California	85.00
Lamb, For Good Little Lambs Only, brn, unmk	50.00
Liberty Bell, #884, California Originals	85.00
Man in Barrel, #873 on lid, California Originals	85.00
Marsh Pig w/Apple, unmk Marsh Ceramics, 1967	145.00
Mexican Bandito, Treasure Craft	65.00
Mickey & Minnie in Big Black Car, Schmid	90.00
Mickey Mouse, wht, Treasure Craft, EX	100.00
Milk Bone Dog Biscuits, Made in Thailand label	60.00
Minnie Jumping Rope, plastic, musical, Schmid	32.00

Miss Piggy, purple dress, unmk 60.00
Mixing Bowl Mammy, Wisecarver 225.00
Monk, Thou Shalt Not Steal Cookies, Treasure Craft 45.00
Monkey in Barrel, Doranne of California 70.00
Mother Goose, Twin Winton, 1962 ....125.00
Mrs Santa, Houston Foods, 1987 ....35.00
Noah's Ark, brn tone, Twin Winton 95.00
Old-Fashioned Phonograph, #891, California Originals 155.00
Old-Fashioned Telephone, Cardinal, EX 65.00
Ole King Cole, Twin Winton 225.00
Panda, Fitz & Floyd, c 1984 ....125.00
Pappy Bust, Wisecarver 225.00
Peter Pumpkin Eater, Robinson Ransbottom 250.00
Petting Zoo, Fitz & Floyd 125.00
Pickup Truck, red, orig issue, Treasure Craft 550.00
Pig, Twin Winton 125.00
Pillsbury Dough Boy, 1988 ....65.00
Plaid Apron Mammy, Japan 650.00
Police Chief Bear, Twin Winton, EX 95.00
Quaker Oats, Regal 130.00
Rabbit, Maurice of California 50.00
Raggedy Ann, Bobbs Merrill, 1972 ....400.00
Ranger Bear, brn, Twin Winton 65.00
Rooster, G-22, Gilner 50.00
Rooster, Hand Painted Pottery Guild of America 75.00
Sailor Monkey, yel hat, DeForest of California 165.00
Santa (head), c Carolina Enterprises...1973 ....35.00
Scarecrow, Royal Sealy, Japan 28.00
Shedd's Spread Butter Tub, unmk 35.00
Snoopy & Woodstock, Willets Design Snoopy, c 1958-66 ....120.00
Space Ship, brn tone, Sierra Vista California 375.00
Space Ship, glazed yel, Sierra Vista California 425.00
Stan Laurel, California Originals 675.00
Strawberry Shortcake, American Greetings Corp 125.00
Superman, #846, California Originals 350.00
Teddy Bear, brn, Twin Winton 120.00
Tigger, California Originals 150.00
Tony the Tiger, plastic, 1968, EX 75.00
Train, Smile Face; mk California, EX 55.00
Upside Down Turtle, #2627, California Originals 175.00
Victorian House, Treasure Craft, EX 35.00
Wilber the Blue Ribbon Pig, unmk 125.00
Ye Old Cookie Bucket, brn, Twin Winton 35.00
Ziggy, on top of stack of Oreos, Designer's Collection 425.00

Cooper, Susie

A 20th-century ceramic designer whose works are now attracting the attention of collectors, Susie Cooper was first affiliated with the A.E. Gray Pottery in Henley, England, in 1922 where she designed in lustres and painted items with her own ideas as well. (Examples of Gray's lustreware is rare and costly.) By 1930 she and her brother-in-law, Jack Beeson, had established a family business. Her pottery soon became a success and she was subsequently offered space at Crown Works, Burslem. In 1940 she received the honorary title of Royal Designer for Industry, the only such distinction ever awarded by the Royal Society of Arts solely for pottery design. Miss Cooper received the Order of the British Empire in the New Year's Honors List of 1979. She was the chief designer for the Wedgwood group from 1966 until she resigned in 1972. Since 1980 she has worked on a free-lance basis.

Bowl, Cubist, Gray's Period, 8" 380.00
Bowl, sgraffito squirrels, 4½" 450.00

Chocolate pot, Patricia Rose, pk rose, 7½" 95.00
Coffeepot, yel wash w/blk lines, Kestrel shape, 7¾" 200.00
Cup & saucer, dk gr w/sgraffito leaves, 2½" 45.00
Egg gup, Gray Leaves w/gr wash 35.00
Jug, Crocus, turq, 6" 185.00
Meat dish, Dresden Spray, gr wash border, 14" L 80.00
Plate, circus clown & lady, gr & blk border, Gray's Period, 10" ..225.00
Plate, fruit in center, wide yel band, 8½" 80.00
Plate, Swansea Spray, br wash band, 7" 30.00
Sauce boat, Gray Leaf w/gr wash 45.00
Teapot, Nosegay, 5" 70.00

Coors

The firm that became known as Coors Porcelain Company in 1920 was founded in 1908 by John J. Herold, originally of the Roseville Pottery in Zanesville, Ohio. Though still in business today, they are best known for their artware vases and Rosebud dinnerware produced before 1939.

Coors vases produced before the late thirties were made in a matt finish; by the latter years of the decade, high-gloss glazes were also being used. Nearly fifty shapes were in production, and some of the more common forms were made in three sizes. Typical colors in matt are white, orange, blue, green, yellow, and tan. Yellow, blue, maroon, pink, and green are found in high gloss. All vases are marked with a triangular arrangement of the words 'Coors Colorado Pottery' enclosing the word 'Golden.' You may find vases (usually 6" to 6½") marked with the Colorado State Fair stamp and dated 1939. For such a vase, add $10.00 to the suggested values given below.

For further information we recommend *Collector's Encyclopedia of Colorado Pottery, Identification and Values,* by Carol and Jim Carlton, who provide miscellaneous listings. Our Rosebud advisor is Jo Ellen Winther. All are listed in the Directory under Colorado.

Rosebud

Apple baker, 4¾" dia 30.00
Baking pan, rectangular, 2x12x8" 40.00
Bowl, cereal; 6" 15.00
Bowl, pudding; 2-pt, sm 30.00
Cake knife, 10" 60.00
Casserole, Dutch; 3½-cup 40.00
Casserole, service; w/lid & underplate, 3½-pt 45.00
Casserole, w/lid, 14-cup 45.00
Creamer, 3" 15.00
Honey pot, w/lid & ladle 175.00
Jar, utility; 2½-pt 45.00
Muffin set, 8" plate w/5½" dome lid 125.00
Pitcher, open, 4-pt 85.00
Plate, soup; 4" 25.00
Plate, 7¼" 8.00
Plate, 9" 15.00
Platter, 12x9" 20.00
Saucer, 5½" 6.50
Shakers, str sides, 4½", pr 18.00
Shakers, 2½", pr 25.00
Teapot, 2-cup 85.00
Tumbler, either style, 8½-oz or 12-oz, ea 75.00
Water server, commemorative, corked stopper, 3-pt 150.00
Water server, corked stopper, 6-cup 90.00

Miscellaneous

Cake knife, Hawthorne, decalcomania 75.00

Clown bank, $150.00.

Cookie jar, HP decor, lg	38.00
Creamer & sugar bowl, Mello-Tone	25.00
Mortar & pestle, cobalt, porc	55.00
Pie plate, Coorado	55.00
Pitcher, Coorado Dinnerware, lg	95.00
Plate, dinner; bl sponging on wht	100.00
Plate, dinner; Floree, decalcomania	75.00
Platter, Mello-Tone, 15"	45.00
Shakers, Rockmount, pr	15.00
Statue, buffalo, stamped inside, 5x8½", minimum value	500.00
Teapot, Tulip, decalcomania	110.00
Vase, Aspen, tan matt, flared rim, ftd, 12"	125.00
Vase, bud; yel gloss, 8"	30.00
Vase, Empire, burgundy gloss, stepped form, 10"	100.00
Vase, Golden, gr matt, Deco shape w/integral circular hdls, 8"	70.00
Vase, Matchless, gr matt, ribbed body, 8"	70.00
Vase, Trinidad, orange matt, classic urn form w/hdls, 6"	45.00
Water server, Open Window, decalcomania	150.00

Copper

Handcrafted copper was made in America from early in the 18th century until about 1850, with the center of its production in Pennsylvania. Examples have been found signed by such notable coppersmiths as Kidd, Buchanan, Babb, Bently, and Harbeson. Of the many utilitarian items made, teakettles are the most desirable. Early examples from the 18th century were made with a dovetailed joint which was hammered and smoothed to a uniform thickness. Pots from the 19th century were seamed. Coffeepots were made in many shapes and sizes and along with mugs, kettles, warming pans, and measures are easiest to find. Stills ranging in sizes of up to fifty-gallon are popular with collectors today. Our advisor, Mary Frank Gaston, has compiled a lovely book, *Antique Brass and Copper*, with many full-color photos and current market values; you will find her address in the Directory under Texas.

Silent butler, Kregarian Copper mark, $50.00.

Bowl, candy-making; dvtl w/wrought-iron hdls, 17½"	110.00

Coffeepot, str spout, hinged lid, brass finial, 8½x5¼"	145.00
Dipper, deep conical bowl, Camp CW, 4" bowl, 10½" hdl	50.00
Fat pot, hinged lid, ribbon hdl, arched spout, 6"	100.00
Kettle, apple butter; dvtl, hinged iron hdl, rpr, 15x23"	245.00
Kettle, dvtl, iron bail hdl, battered, rpr, 12½x19"	60.00
Kettle, preserving; riveted brass hdls, 5x16" dia	285.00
Pan, lg bent iron hdls, mk Chas Dennery, 20½"	260.00
Pitcher, Chas C Schenck...Pat 1898 on brass label, 8½"	85.00
Pot, cooking; strap hdl, domed lid, 12x10"	210.00
Saucepan, dvtl, CI hdl, 4x6½"	50.00
Saucepan, dvtl, wrought copper hdl, 5¼x9½"	75.00
Scoop, riveted base plate extends for wooden hdl insert	95.00
Teakettle, dvtl, brass trim, minor dents, 12"	65.00
Teakettle, dvtl, oval, brass trim, minor dents, 12"	100.00
Teakettle, dvtl, well made, polished, 8¼"+hdl	220.00
Teakettle, dvtl w/rnd bottom, iron hdl, 15½"	140.00
Teakettle, gooseneck, brass finial, sgn Getz, rpr, 10" dia	490.00
Teakettle, gooseneck, brass finial, sgn Kidd, rpr lid, 9" dia	200.00
Teakettle, gooseneck, brass knob, sgn Schlosser, 11" dia	1,150.00
Teakettle, gooseneck, dvtl, acorn finial, 10x12"	290.00

Copper Lustre

Copper lustre is a term referring to a type of pottery made in Staffordshire after the turn of the 19th century. It is finished in a metallic rusty-brown glaze resembling true copper. Pitchers are found in abundance, ranging from simple styles with dull bands of color to those with fancy handles and bands of embossed, polychromed flowers. Bowls are common; goblets, mugs, teapots, and sugar bowls much less so. It's easy to find, but not in good condition. Pieces with hand-painted decoration and those with historical transfers are the most valuable.

Bowl, mc emb lady & dog on wide dk bl band, 5"	40.00
Creamer, canary band, women & children brn transfer w/mc, 4¾"	165.00
Figurine, dog, seated, hairlines, 8", G	55.00
Figurine, hounds, allover lustre, facing pr, 1850s, 6", NM	465.00
Loving cup, mc floral, ped ft, scroll hdls, 4½"	45.00
Mug, mc floral emb in wide bl band, scroll hdl, 3½", NM	60.00
Pitcher, clock face, 11½"	200.00
Pitcher, clock face magenta transfer & Charity, 6¾"	60.00
Pitcher, emb deer, bl arch & dot design below rim, ftd, 6"	45.00
Pitcher, mc emb flower basket on bl band, mask spout, 5", EX	50.00
Shaker, bl band, 4½"	75.00
Tumbler, wide bl band w/lustre floral, 3¼"	35.00

Coralene Glass

Coralene is a unique type of art glass easily recognized by the tiny grains of glass that form its decoration. Lacy allover patterns of seaweed, geometrics, and florals were used, as well as solid forms such as fish, plants, and single blossoms. (Seaweed is most commonly found and not as valuable as the other types of decoration.) It was made by several glasshouses both here and abroad. Values are based to a considerable extent on the amount of beading that remains. Our advisors for this category are Betty and Clarence Maier; they are listed in the Directory under Pennsylvania.

Bowl, bl, Dmn Quilt, fleur-de-lis motif, 6¼"	225.00
Ewer, lav satin, seaweed motif, 8½"	275.00
Pitcher, bl/wht striped satin, seaweed motif, amber hdl, 5"	425.00
Pitcher, rose Dmn Quilt MOP, yel seaweed motif, reed hdl, 5"	450.00
Toothpick holder, shiny peachblow, seaweed motif, sq	700.00

Tumbler, pk glossy Dmn Quilt w/seaweed motif, 3¾" 250.00
Vase, aqua w/yel seaweed motif, stick neck, 6" 300.00
Vase, bl, seaweed motif, long can neck, bulb bottom, 9" 250.00
Vase, brn satin, bl seaweed motif, hdld/ruffled, Webb, 4½" 400.00
Vase, peachblow w/seaweed motif & gold, Mt WA 1870s, 7½" ..675.00

Vase, pink with allover gold seaweed motif, numbered on base, 5¼", $450.00.

Vase, pk, Dmn Quilt, fern motif, ruffled, 9½" 275.00
Vase, pk striped MOP, seaweed motif, 3½" 225.00
Vase, sapphire bl, mc floral/butterfly/birds motif, ftd, 19" 895.00
Vase, yel satin, seaweed motif, 6", EX 120.00
Vase, yel satin w/mc top, seaweed motif, amber ft, 5½", NM 400.00

Cordey

The Cordey China Company was founded in 1942 in Trenton, New Jersey, by Boleslaw Cybis. The operation was small with less than a dozen workers. They produced figurines, vases, lamps, and similar wares, much of which was marketed through gift shops both nationwide and abroad. Though the earlier wares were made of plaster, Cybis soon developed his own formula for a porcelain composition which he called 'Papka.' Cordey figurines and busts were characterized by old-world charm, Rococo scrolls, delicate floral appliques, ruffles, and real lace which was dipped in liquified clay to add dimension to the work.

Although on rare occasions some items were not numbered or signed, the 'basic' figure was cast both with numbers and the Cordey signature. The molded pieces were then individually decorated and each marked with its own impressed identification number as well as a mark to indicate the artist-decorator. Their numbering system began with 200 and in later years progressed into the 8000s. As can best be established, Cordey continued production until sometime in the mid-1950s. Boleslaw Cybis died in 1957, his wife in 1958. Our advisor for this category is Sharon A. Payne; she is listed in the Directory under Washington.

Key: ff — full figure

#302, lady, ff, flowing dress, 16" 195.00
#32-5001, bust of lady 65.00
#5026, bust of lady w/mantilla, Jr Miss Group 65.00
#5034, bust of Raleigh, Raleigh Group 75.00
#5039, lady, Josephine, Raleigh Group 75.00
#5042, man, ff, red hair, lacy jacket, scroll base, 10½" 175.00
#5043, man, ff, Colonial attire 175.00
#5045, Neopolitan boy w/breadsticks 145.00
#5088, lady, ff, HP roses on dress, 11" 175.00
#6004, bluebird on stump 150.00
#6029, box, roses on lid, 5x7x5½" 65.00
#627, ginger jar, w/lid, 7½x6" dia 150.00
#7004, tray (or shallow bowl), 13x9" 100.00

#8002, pin/ashtray, 4" sq 30.00
#852, wall decoration, nosegay, experimental 110.00
Lamp, lady in dk bl w/much lace (12"), 17 ....150.00
Lamp, pk roses w/gold on wht 85.00
Lamp, 18th-C lady w/much lace, 12" 150.00
Wall pocket, lady's face, ringlets, #902, 10¾" 200.00

Corkscrews

The history of the corkscrew dates back to the mid-1600s, when wine makers concluded that the best-aged wine was that stored in smaller containers, either stoneware or glass. Since plugs left unsealed were often damaged by rodents, corks were cut off flush with the bottle top and sealed with wax or a metal cover. Removing the cork cleanly with none left to grasp became a problem. The task was found to be relatively simple using the worm on the end of a flintlock gun rod. So the corkscrew evolved. Endless patents have been issued for mechanized models. Handles range from carved wood, ivory, and bone to porcelain and repousse silver. Exotic materials such as agate, mother-of-pearl, and gold plate were also used on occasion. Celluloid lady's legs are popular.

In the following descriptions, values are for examples in excellent condition, unless noted otherwise. Our advisor for this category is Roger Baker; he is listed in the Directory under California.

Black bulldog, Syroco wood, 1920-30s **45.00**
English, champagne tap, screw in cork, hdl makes faucets, ca 1890s ..**60.00**
English, mk Lund Patentee London, rack & pinion, 1855 ....**275.00**
English, 4-finger pull, w/button, ca 1895 ....**23.00**
French, made of horn, octagonal shape, dbl wooden hdl, rnd fr **65.00**
German, all NP, swivel cap, 2¼" worm **30.00**
German, Hercules, wood hdl **40.00**
German, lady's leg w/gr stripes, ca 1910 ....**350.00**
German, lady's legs, gr & wht stripes w/shiny boots, 1890s **290.00**
German, swivel over collar, rubber ring on lower fr, mid-1900s **25.00**
Italy, dbl lever, bar man shape, 10½" **45.00**
Lady's leg, tooled brass w/striped celluloid inlay, 2⅝" **150.00**
London, John Dewar & Son Distillery, bottle type **35.00**
Monkey (or dog), gold jeweled, corkscrew tail **20.00**
R-11 Parrot, corkscrew tail **20.00**
Sommerlier, dbl lever, chrome **30.00**
US, Alaskan ivory tusk **30.00**
US, crocodile tail hdl, copper-plated end caps, 1900s **75.00**
US, H&B Mfg Co, rosewood hdl w/brush & ivory plug on end **49.00**
US, Haff Mfg Co, New York, wooden hdl, mk Pat 4/14/86 ....**135.00**
US, Hollwig, advertising Pabst Milwaukee, 1891 ....**125.00**
US, James E Wolcott & Co, Cornhill Rye, bottle type, 1821 ....**40.00**
US, Pepper Distillery, handmade sour mash, bottle type, 1780 .....**40.00**
US, rnd steel shaft w/2" worm, wooden hdl **35.00**
US, Roundlet, bullet shape **50.00**
US, staghorn hdl, sterling silver cap, late 1800s, 8½" **75.00**
US, staghorn hdl, sterling silver cap ea end, 1900s **115.00**
US, walrus tusk w/sterling silver end, SP worm cap, mk Pat 1906 .**150.00**
Walker, 1900 mechanism, wooden hdl **30.00**

Cosmos

Cosmos, sometimes called Stemless Daisy, is a patterned glass tableware produced from 1894 through 1915 by Consolidated Lamp and Glass Company. Relief-molded flowers on a finely crosscut background were painted in soft colors of pink, blue, and yellow. Though nearly all were made of milk glass, a few items may be found in clear glass with the designs painted on. In addition to the tableware, lamps were also made.

Bottle, cologne; orig stopper, rare 150.00
Butter dish, 6x8" 235.00
Creamer 150.00
Lamp, banquet; kerosene, 24" 475.00
Lamp, banquet; slender base, rnd globe, all orig, 16" 525.00

Lamp, miniature, 7", $365.00.

Lamp, 10" 400.00
Pickle castor, mk SP fr 500.00
Pitcher, milk; 5" 170.00
Pitcher, syrup; 6" 200.00
Pitcher, water 250.00
Shakers, tall, orig lids, pr 100.00
Spooner 125.00
Sugar bowl, open 150.00
Sugar bowl, w/lid 185.00
Sugar shaker 230.00
Tumbler, 3¾" 65.00

Cottageware

You'll find a varied assortment of novelty dinnerware items, all styled as cozy little English cottages or huts with cone-shaped roofs; some may have a waterwheel or a windmill. Marks will vary. English-made Price Brothers or Beswick pieces are valued in the same range as those marked Occupied Japan, while items marked simply Japan are considered slightly less pricey. Our advisor for this category is Grace Klender; she is listed in the Directory under Ohio.

Biscuit jar, Maruhon Ware, Occupied Japan, 6½" 65.00
Bowl, salad; English 65.00
Butter dish, English 45.00
Butter pat, emb cottage, rectangular, Occupied Japan 18.00
Chocolate pot, English 135.00
Condiment set, 2 shakers & mustard on tray, Occupied Japan 45.00
Cookie jar, pk/brn/gr, sq, Japan, 8½x5½" 65.00
Cookie jar/canister, cylindrical, English 85.00
Cookie or biscuit jar, Occupied Japan 85.00
Creamer & sugar bowl, English, 2½", 4½" 45.00
Creamer & sugar bowl, w/lid, on tray, Occupied Japan 50.00
Cup & saucer, English, 2½", 4½" 45.00
Demitasse pot, English 100.00
Dish w/cover, Occupied Japan, sm 35.00
Grease jar, Occupied Japan 18.00
Marmalade, English 40.00
Marmalade & jelly, 2 houses cojoined, Price Brothers 85.00
Mug, Price Bros 50.00
Pin tray, English, 4" dia 20.00

Pitcher, water; English 150.00
Platter, oval, 11¾x7½" 45.00
Sugar box, for cubes, English, 5¾" L 45.00
Tea set, Japan, child's, serves 4 ....150.00
Teapot, English or Occupied Japan, 6½" 50.00
Toast rack, English 60.00
Tumblers, Occupied Japan, 3½", set of 6 ....60.00

Coverlets

The Jacquard attachment for hand looms represented a culmination of weaving developments made in France. Introduced to America by the early 1820s, it gave professional weavers the ability to easily create complex patterns with curved lines. Those who could afford the new loom adaptation could now use hole-punched pasteboard cards to weave floral patterns that before could only be achieved with intense labor on a draw-loom.

Before the Jacquard mechanism, most weavers made their coverlets in geometric patterns. Use of indigo-blue and brightly colored wools often livened the twills and overshot patterns available to the small-loom home weaver. Those who had larger multiple-harness looms could produce warm double-woven, twill-block, or summer-and-winter designs.

While the new floral and pictorial patterns' popularity had displaced the geometrics in urban areas, the mid-Atlantic, and the Midwest by the 1840s, even factory production of the Jacquard coverlets was disrupted by cotton and wool shortages during the Civil War. A revived production in the 1870s saw a style change to a center-medallion motif, but a new fad for white 'Marseilles' spreads soon halted sales of Jacquard-woven coverlets. Production of Jacquard carpets continued to the turn of the century.

Rural and frontier weavers continued to make geometric-design coverlets through the 19th century, and local craft revivals have continued the tradition through this century. All-cotton overshots were factory produced in Kentucky from the 1940s, and factories and professional weavers made cotton-and-wool overshots during the past decade. Many Jacquard-woven coverlets have dates and names of places and people (often the intended owner — not the weaver) woven into corners or borders. In the listings that follow, examples are blue and white unless noted otherwise.

Jacquard

Birds & flowers, Bird of Paradise mk corners, 2-pc, 82x81" 395.00
Christian & Heathen/flowers/peacocks, 2-pc, wear, 100x74" 330.00
Floral, buildings border, 4-color, 1-pc, worn, 97x75" 195.00
Floral, eagle corners, OH/1847, 4-color, 2-pc, 79x66" 415.00
Floral, floral/bird border, 4-color, sgn Schnell/1858, VG 400.00
Floral, fruit border, eagle corners, 3-color, 2-pc, 92x86" 1,700.00
Floral, Greek key border, 1848 in corners, 2-pc, 84x70" 495.00
Floral, turkey in tree corners, red/wht, 2-pc, 90x78" 600.00
Floral, United We Stand...1841 border, 2-pc, wear, 88x76" 500.00
Floral medallion, bird & floral border, maroon/natural, 90x84" .395.00
Floral medallion, capitol bldgs border, 3-color, 1-pc, 81x77" 495.00
Floral medallion w/eagles & banners, 3-color, 1-pc, 84x72" 468.00
Floral medallions, eagle/bldg border, 4-color, 1-pc, 86x74" 550.00
Floral medallions, rose border, 2-pc, 1840, 90x67" 600.00
Floral medallions/dmns/rose/etc, red/bl/wht, 2-pc, 86x69" 550.00
Geometric floral, 1848 in corners, red/natural, 2-pc, 89x80" 525.00
Geometric floral w/house & bird border, 1859, 2-pc, 88x72" 685.00
Hempfield Railroad, floral center, wear, 77x85" 2,860.00
Hempfield Railroad, navy/tomato red, 2-pc, dbl weave, 88x75" ..3,520.00
Oak leaf/acorn wreath, angels in corners, 4-color, sgn, NM 500.00
Roses & stars, 2-pc, single weave, 90x68" 220.00

Snowflake & pine tree, 2-pc, dbl weave, 82x74" 195.00
Star flower w/wreath center, 4-color, 2-pc, 88x73" 660.00
Stars, dbl tree border, 2-pc, lt stain, 98x76" 475.00

Overshot

Bow ties & dmns, 4-color, 2-pc, lt wear, 93x66" 220.00
Optical pattern, navy/tomato red/natural, 86x72" 330.00
Optical pattern, 3-color, 2-pc, minor wear, 96x80" 195.00
Optical pattern, 4-color, 3-pc, minor wear, 81x81" 250.00
Twill weave, 3-color, 2-pc, minor wear, 88x81" 140.00

Cowan

Guy Cowan opened a small pottery near Cleveland, Ohio, ca 1909, where he made tile and artware on a small scale from the natural red clay available there. He developed distinctive glazes — necessary, he felt, to cover the dark red body. After the war and a temporary halt in production, Cowan moved his pottery to Rocky River, where he made a commercial line of artware utilizing a highly-fired white porcelain. Although he acquiesced to the necessity of mass-production, every effort was made to insure a product of highest quality. Fine artists, among them Waylande Gregory, Margaret Postgate, and Viktor Schreckengost, designed pieces which were often produced in limited editions, some of which sell today for prices in the thousands. Most of the ware was marked 'Cowan' or 'Lakewood Ware,' not to be confused with the name of the 1930 mass-produced line called 'Lakeware.' Falling under the crunch of the Great Depression, the pottery closed in 1931.

The use of an asterick (*) in the listing below indicates a nonfactory name that is being provided as a suggested name for the convenience of present-day collectors. One example is the glaze Original Ivory*, which is a high-gloss white that resembles undecorated porcelain. It was used on many of Cowan's lady 'flower figures' (Cowan's more graceful term for what some people call frogs). Our advisor for this category is Mark Bassett; he is listed in the Directory under Ohio.

Jazz bowl, earthenware, molded black on blue decoration, inverted bell form, Viktor Schreckengost, ca 1931, 8¼" high, $15,000.00; Danse Moderne plate, earthenware, black on blue dry-point decoration, Viktor Schreckengost, 11¼", $4,000.00.

Bookends, boy/girl, Special Ivory, Wilcox, #519, 6½", pr 250.00
Bookends, elephant, Egyptian bl, Postgate, #E-2, 7½", pr 850.00
Bookends, Sunbonnet Girl, Antique Gr, #521, 7½", pr 450.00
Bookends, unicorn, Foliage, W Gregory, #961, 7", pr 600.00
Bowl, console; emb leaves, 3 lobed ft, Parchment Gr, 16" 250.00
Bowl, console; pterodactyl hdls, April, #739, 15" 130.00
Bowl, console; rnd scalloped, Amalfi, #733-A, 11¾" 75.00
Bowl, console; sq, scalloped, April, #732, 11½" 75.00
Bowl, console; Verbena, sea horse hdls, #727, 16" 200.00

Bowl, mantel; fluted, floral hdls, Marigold, #538 ....80.00
Candelabra, nude, Special Ivory, R Guy Cowan, #745, pr 850.00
Charger, thunderbird, Egyptian Bl, A Blazys, #750, 15" 750.00
Cigarette holder, sea horse, Special Ivory, #726, 3½" 35.00
Comport, shell form, Apple Blossom Pk, #C-12, 8" 45.00
Figure, Bird & Wave, Melon Gr, Blazys, #749-A 750.00
Figure, Introspection, blk, AD Jacobson, #D-1, 8" 1,000.00
Figure, Radio Girl, hand decor, att T Frazier, #853, 9" 2,500.00
Figure, Russian Peasants, Parchment, ltd ed, 8¼", 4 for 4,000.00
Figure, Spanish Dancers, Primrose, Anderson, #793/#794, 9", pr .1,250.00
Figurine, Introspection, Deco owl, gray semigloss, #D-1, 8" 1,100.00
Flower figure, Duet*, Special Ivory, RG Cowan, #685, 8" 275.00
Flower figure, Heavenward*, Special Ivory, RG Cowan, #680, 8" ..275.00
Flower figure, Pavlova*, Orig Ivory*, Cowan/Sinz, #698, 6½" 200.00
Flower figure, Repose*, Special Ivory, RG Cowan, #712, 6" 300.00
Flower figure, Scarf Dancer*, Special Ivory, RG Cowan, #686, 6" .275.00
Flower figure, Swan, Special Ivory, Gregory, #F-7, 11½" 650.00
Flower figure, Swirl Dancer*, Orig Ivory*, att Cowan, #720, 10" .275.00
Flower figure, Tambourine Dancer*, Special Ivory, 10" 750.00
Lamp, Aztec man*, Antique Gr, 13" 650.00
Lamp, Deco fountain form, October, 10" 450.00
Lamp, Deco sunburst, April Gr, 6" 300.00
Paperweight, elephant, Oriental Red, #D-3, 4½" 350.00
Pitcher, Larkspur, #621-A, ½-pt, 3½" 75.00
Pitcher, orange lustre, 3½" 50.00
Vase, Azure, #V-15, 12", +custom wrought-iron stand, 30" 750.00
Vase, bud; Oriental Red w/mottled brn crystals, #V-86, 6½" 150.00
Vase, bulbous, Larkspur, #585, 9½" 250.00
Vase, Chinese Dragon, Melon Gr, RG Cowan, #V-747, 11½" ...750.00
Vase, classical, Delphinium, 3569, 11" 250.00
Vase, fan; October, #801, 5" 125.00
Vase, fish dry-point decor, Melon Gr & blk, #V-91, 6" 450.00
Vase, Jet-Yel Lustre flambe, 13" 750.00
Vase, paneled, Marigold, #691-B, 9½" 175.00
Vase, pillow; October, #V-853, 6" 125.00
Vase, ribbed, bulbous, Azure, #V-38, 6½x8" 250.00
Vase, ribbed, Plum, #V-30, 4½" 95.00
Vase, ribbed, wheel-thrown look, MOP, #V-847, 12" 275.00
Vase, sea horse fan (lg), Melon Gr, #715-B, 8" 200.00
Vase, Squirrel, MOP, Gregory, #V-19, 8½" 750.00

Cracker Jack

Kids have been buying Cracker Jack since it was first introduced in the 1890s. By 1912 it was packaged with a free toy inside. Before the first kernel was crunched, eager fingers had retrieved the surprise from the depth of the box — actually no easy task, considering the care required to keep the contents so swiftly displaced from spilling over the side! Though a little older, perhaps, many of those same kids still are looking — just as eagerly — for the Cracker Jack prizes. Point of sale, company collectibles, and the prizes as well have over the years reflected America's changing culture. Grocer sales and incentives from around the turn of the century — paper dolls, postcards and song books — were often marked Rueckheim Brothers (the inventors of Cracker Jack) or Reliable Confections. Over the years the company made some changes, leaving a trail of clues that often help collectors date their items. The company's name changed in 1922 from Rueckheim Brothers & Eckstein to The Cracker Jack Company. Their Brooklyn office was open from 1914 until it closed in 1923, and the first time the sailor Jack logo was used on their packaging was 1919. For packages and 'point of sale' dating, note that the word 'prize' was used from 1912 to 1925, 'novelty' from 1925 to 1932, and 'toy' from 1933 on.

The first loose-packed prizes were toys made of wood, clay, tin, metal, and lithographed paper. Plastic toys were introduced in 1946. Paper wrapped for safety purposes in 1948, subjects echo the 'hype' of the day — Yo-Yos, tops, whistles, and sports cards in the simple, peaceful days of our country, propaganda and war toys in the forties, games in the fifties, and space toys in the sixties. Few of the estimated 15 billion prizes were marked. Advertising items from Angelus Marshmallow and Checkers Confections (cousins of the Cracker Jack family) are also collectible. When no condition is indicated, the items listed below are assumed to be in excellent condition. 'CJ' indicates that the item is marked. Note: An often-asked question concerns the tin Toonerville Trolley marked 'CJ.' No data has been found in the factory archives to authenticate this item; it is assumed that the 'CJ' merely refers to its small size. Our advisor for this category is Wes Johnson; he is listed in the Directory under Kentucky.

Cast-Metal Prizes

Badge, shield, CJ Jr Detective, silver, 1931, 1¼" 40.00
Badge, 6-point star, mk CJ Police, silver, 1931, 1¼" 40.00
Button, stud bk, Me for Cracker Jack, boy & dog, oval 33.00
Button, stud bk, Xd bats & ball, CJ pitcher/etc series, 1928 ....88.00
Chair, T (Tootsie), 3 different sectional pcs, pnt, mini, ea 12.00
Coins, Presidents, 31 series, CJ, 1933, ea 8.00
Dollhouse items: lantern, mug, candlestick, etc; no mk, ea 6.50
Horse & wagon, CJ, 3-D, silver or gold, early, 2½", ea 250.00
Pistol, soft lead, inked, CJ on barrel, early, rare, 2⅛" 180.00
Ring, alphabet letter setting (series), unmk, ea 3.00
Rocking horse, no rider, 3-D, inked, early, 1⅛" 9.00
Rocking horse w/boy, 3-D, inked, early, 1½" 29.00
Spinner, early pkg in center, 'More You Eat...,' CJ, rare 295.00
Tootsietoy series: boats, cars, animals; '31, ¾"-1½", ea 7.00

Dealer Incentives and Premiums

Badge, pin-bk, celluloid, pretty lady, CJ label, 1905, 1¼" 65.00
Bat, baseball; wood, Hillerich & Bradsby, CJ, full sz 125.00
Blotter, CJ question mk box, yel, 7¾x3¾" 225.00
Book, pocket; jester on cover, CJ 73.00
Book, pocket; riddle/sailor boy/dog on cover, RWB, CJ, 1919 ....60.00
Book, recipe; Angelus, 1930s 22.00
Book, Uncle Sam Song Book, CJ, 1911, ea 60.00
Cart w/2 movable wheels, wood dowel tongue, CJ 75.00
Corkscrew/opener, metal plated, CJ/Angelus, 3" 79.00
Corkscrew/opener, metal plated, CJ/Angelus, 3¾" tube case 79.00
Golf tee set, CJ, 1920s, EX 725.00
Harmonica, full scale, emb CJ, early, 5⅛" 385.00
Jigsaw puzzle, CJ or Checkers, 1 of 4, 7x10", in envelope 35.00
Marbles, Akro set of 12 in box, CJ, 1929 ....950.00
Mask, Halloween; paper, CJ, 10" or 12", ea 22.00
Match holder, hinged, eng gold-tone case, CJ, 2½x1⅞" 650.00
Mirror, oval, Angelus (redhead or blond) on box 89.00
Palm puzzle, mirror bk, CJ, mk Germany/RWB, 1910-14, 1½" 110.00
Pen, ink; w/nib, tin litho bbl, CJ 650.00
Pencil top clip, metal/celluloid, oval boy & dog logo 210.00
Pencil top clip, metal/celluloid, tube shape w/package 190.00
Postcard, bear, 1 of 16, CJ, 1907, ea 30.00
Riddle card, 2 series of 20, w/package/from factory, CJ, '07, ea 7.00
Tablet, school; CJ, 1929, 8x10" 195.00
Thimble, aluminum, CJ Co/Angelus, red pnt, rare, ea 165.00
Wings, air corps type, silver or blk, stud-bk, CJ, '30s, 3", ea 80.00

Packaging

Box, popcorn; Question Mark box end for CJ 'Toy,' 1923-27 ....85.00

Box, popcorn; red scroll border, CJ 'Prize,' 1912-25, ea 95.00
Box, popcorn; store display, CJ 'Novelty,' 1925-32, ea 90.00
Canister, tin, CJ Candy Corn Crisp, 10-oz 75.00
Canister, tin, CJ Coconut Corn Crisp, 1-lb 55.00
Canister, tin, CJ Coconut Corn Crisp, 10-oz 65.00
CJ Commemorative canister, mc scene, 1990s, ea 9.00
CJ Commemorative canisters, wht w/red scroll, 1980s, ea 6.50
Crate, shipping; wood, CJ, Rueckheim Bros Eck, 1902-22, lg 175.00

Paper Prizes

Baseball CJ score counter, 3⅜" L 145.00
Book, Animals (or Birds), to color, Makatoy, 1949, mini 35.00
Book, Bess & Bill on CJ Hill, series of 12, 1937, mini 95.00
Book, Birds We Know, CJ, 1928, mini 75.00
Book, Chaplin flip book, CJ, 1920s, ea 115.00
Book, drawing w/tracing paper, CJ, 1920s, mini 110.00
Book, Twigg & Sprigg, CJ, 1930, mini 95.00
Booklet, stickers/wise cracks/riddles, Borden, CJ, 1965 on 2.50
Decal, cartoon or nursery rhyme figure, 1947-49, CJ 12.00
Disguise, ears, red (punch out from carrier), 1950, pr 40.00
Disguise, glasses, hinged, cellophane lenses, CJ, 1933 ....145.00
Disguise, glasses, hinged, w/eyeballs, 1933 ....6.00
Disguise, mustache, blk/brn, in carrier, CJ, 1949 ....60.00
Fortune Teller, boy/dog on film in envelope, CJ, '20s, 1¾x2½" 75.00
Fortune wheel, 2-pc litho, turn for fortune, CJ, 1¾" 70.00
Game, Midget Auto Race, wheel spins, CJ, 1949, 3⅜" H 45.00
Game spinner, ...baseball at home, rectangle, CJ, 2¾" W 125.00
Game spinner, ...baseball at home, unmk, 1946, 1½" dia 40.00
Hat, fold out, More You Eat/More You Want, CJ, early 75.00
Hat, Indian headdress, CJ, 1931, 2½" H 110.00
Hat, Indian headdress, CJ, 1950s, 5⅜" H 275.00
Hat visor, baseball, CJ, 1931 ....120.00
Magic game book, erasable slate, series of 13, 1946, ea 27.00
Movie, boy at blkboard, turn wheel: draws/erases, CJ, '31, 2" 185.00
Movie, Goofy Zoo, turn wheel(s): change animals, 1939 ....12.00
Movie, pull tab for 2nd picture, series, CJ, 1943, 1¼", ea 82.00
Movie, pull tab for 2nd picture, yel, early, 3", in envelope 125.00
Top, golf game, wood stick center, CJ, 1933 ....57.00
Transfer, iron on, sport figure or patriotic, CJ, 1939, ea 18.00
Whistle, Blow for More, CJ box/boy/dog, yel, 1931, ea 55.00
Whistle, Blow for More, CJ/Angelus packages, 1928, '31 or '33, ea ..45.00
Whistle, pressed paper, series of 10, 1948-49, CJ, 1¼x2", ea 34.00
Whistle, Razz Zooka, C Carey Cloud design, CJ, 1949 ....32.00

Plastic Prizes

Animals, standup, letter on bk, series of 26, Nosco, 1953, ea 3.50
Animals, standup on base, assorted, Nosco or CJ, 1947 on, ea 1.50
Baseball players, 3-D, bl or gray team, 1958, 1½", ea 7.00
Disc, emb comic character, series of 12, 1954, 1½" dia 9.00
Disc, emb fish plaque, oval, series of 10, 1956, ea 7.00
Dog, 3-D, hollow base, series of 10, CJCO, 1954, ea 4.50
Figure, circus; stands on base, 1 of 12, Nosco, 1951-54 ....1.75
Figure on rocking base, semi-flat, 1 of 9, cloud design, '56 ......3.00
Fob, alphabet letter w/loop on top, 1 of 26, 1954, 1½" 2.25
Magnifying glass, many designs/shapes, from 1961, ea 1.00
Palm puzzle, ball(s) roll into holes, plastic dome, from 1966 .....2.50
Pinball game, lever shoots ball/score in holes, 1964 to recent 5.00
Sand picture, sand pours for action, series of 14, 1967, ea 9.00
Ships in a bottle, 6 different, 1960, ea 5.00
Signs, road; Stop, Caution, etc, yel, series of 10, 1954-60, ea ...3.00
Spinner, varied colors, 10 designs, from 1948, ea 1.50
Toys, take apart/assemble, variety, from '62, assembled, ea 1.00

Toys, take apart/assemble, variety, from '62, unassembled, ea **2.25**
Whistle, tube w/animals on top, CJ, 1 of 6, 1950-53, 1⅜" **6.50**

Tin Prizes

Badge, emb/plated CJ officer, 2⅜" or 1⅝", early, ea **110.00**
Badge, litho, red/wht/bl, boy/dog, CJ, 1920s, 1¼" dia **150.00**
Bank, 3-D book form, red/gr/or blk, CJ Bank, early, 2" **95.00**
Bookmark, dogs, 4 different, 1941, 3", ea **22.00**
Boy & dog, diecut, complete w/bend-over tab, CJ **150.00**
Boy & dog, diecut, w/o tab at top **85.00**
Boy & dog, stand-up litho rectangle, est 1916, lg or sm, ea **145.00**
Brooch or pin, various designs on card, CJ/logo, early, ea **125.00**
Cash register, litho, More You Eat, CJ, early, 1⅞" **275.00**
Clicker, 'Noisy CJ Snapper,' pear shape, aluminum, 1949 ....**32.00**
Doll dishes, tin plated, CJ, '31, 1¾", 1⅞", & 2⅛" dia, ea **35.00**
Fortune Wheel, 2-pc litho, CJ, 1939-41, 1¾" **55.00**
Helicopter, yel propeller, wood stick, unmk, 1937, 2⅝" **24.00**
Horse & wagon, litho diecut, CJ & Angelus, 2⅛" **65.00**
Horse & wagon, litho diecut, gray/red mks, CJ, 1914-23, 3⅛" **395.00**
Model T Ford, License: NY 1915 #999, blk/wht, CJ, rare, 2" **410.00**
Oval standup, Am flag, 1 of 4, unmk, 1936-46 ....**35.00**
Oval standup, comic character, 1 of 10, CJ, 1936-46, ea **125.00**
Pocket watch, silver or gold, CJ as numerals, 1931, 1½" **65.00**
Sled, tin plated, CJ, 1931, 2" L **39.00**
Small box shape: electric stove litho, unmk, 1⅛" **90.00**
Small box shape: garage litho, unmk, 1⅛" **85.00**
Small box shape: radio litho, bl, unmk, 1⅛" **80.00**
Soldier, litho, die-cut standup, officer/private/etc, unmk, ea **17.00**
Tall box shape: Frozen Foods locker freezer, '47, unmk, 1¾" **65.00**
Tall box shape: grandfather clock, unmk, 1947, 1¾" **55.00**
Tall box shape: radio, Tune in w/CJ, brn/yel, 1939, 1¾" **115.00**
Tall box shape: Refrigerator Car, CJ 2006, 1947, 1¾" L **155.00**
Train, engine & tender, litho, CJ Line/512 ....**125.00**
Train, litho coach only, red, unmk, 1941 ....**24.00**
Train, litho engine only, red, 1941, unmk **20.00**
Tray, emb, litho w/early package, smaller version **115.00**
Tray, emb, litho w/early package, 2¼x1¾" **95.00**

Truck, tin litho, red, white and black, CJ/Angelus, 1931, $65.00.

Wagon shape: caterpillar tractor, unmk, 1931, 1¾" L **29.00**
Wagon shape: CJ Shows, yel circus wagon, series of 5, ea **135.00**
Wagon shape: Playtime Trailer (auto trailer), unmk, 1947 ....**40.00**
Wagon shape: tank, orange/red/gr camouflage, unmk **65.00**
Wagon shape: Tank Corps No 57, gr & blk, 1941 ....**30.00**
Wheelbarrow, tin plated, bk leg in place, CJ, 1931, 2½" L **40.00**

Miscellaneous

Ad, comic book, CJ, ea **9.00**
Ad, Saturday Evening Post, mc, CJ, 1919, 11x14" **18.00**
Hat, ball park vendor cap, CJ, 1930s **30.00**

Lunch box, tin, 2 hdls, CJ, 1980s, 4½x5x6" **25.00**
Lunch box, tin emb, CJ, 1970s, 4x7x9" **30.00**
Medal, CJ salesman award, brass, 1939, scarce **125.00**
Sign, bathing beauty, 5-color cb, CJ, early, 17x22" **300.00**
Sign, boy or girl w/box of CJ, 5-color cb, early, 17x22", ea **300.00**
Sign, Jack & Bingo, die-cut litho, easel standup, CJ, early **285.00**
Sign, Jack & Bingo, standing on early CJ pkg, mc cb, rare **345.00**
Sign, Santa & prizes, mc cb, Angelus, early, lg **200.00**
Sign, Santa & prizes, mc cb, Checkers, early, lg **1,000.00**
Sign, Santa & prizes, mc cb, CJ, early, lg **250.00**

Cranberry

Cranberry glass is named for its resemblance to the color of cranberry juice. It was made by many companies both here and abroad, becoming popular in America soon after the Civil War. It was made in free-blown ware as well as mold-blown. Today cranberry glass is being reproduced, and it is sometimes difficult to distinguish the old from the new. Ask a reputable dealer if you are unsure.

For further information we recommend *American Art Glass* by John A. Shuman III, available from Collector Books or your local bookstore. See also Cruets; Salts; Sugar Shakers; Syrups.

Basket, ribbed optic w/clear rigaree ft, snake hdl, 7½" **265.00**
Biscuit jar, gold floral/leaves, 4-sided, SP mts, 7x4½" **295.00**
Biscuit jar, Invt T'print, HP flowers/etc w/gold, SP trim, 8" **450.00**
Bottle, scent; floral/dots/gilt, bulbous shoulder, 3½x2" **185.00**
Bottle, scent; HP florals, cranberry bottle stopper, 5¾" **195.00**
Bowl, appl crystal berry prunts/fans/ft, Webb, 5½x6" **245.00**
Bowl, swirl ribs, crystal collar, 5"; SP bird-ftd fr, 8x12" **400.00**
Box, patch; encased in gold-tone filigree **220.00**
Creamer & sugar bowl, appl shell ft, 4¼", 3½" **145.00**
Cruet, gold flowers & scrolls, clear bubble stopper, 10½" **195.00**
Cruet, HP thistles w/gold, 8¼x3⅜" **195.00**
Decanter, clear blown stopper/hdl, 12½x5", pr **325.00**
Decanter, eng flower/wheat, clear disk ft/faceted stopper, 12" **195.00**
Decanter, fans/dots/scrolls in wht, clear bubble stopper, 9" **265.00**
Decanter, flattened sides, appl clear rope hdl, 10x4½" **145.00**
Decanter, gold flower baskets & scrolls, bubble stopper, 12" **165.00**
Decanter, wht/gold flowers, 7¾", +13" tray & 6 2" mugs **500.00**
Muffineer, ribbed, metal top **95.00**
Pitcher, clear hdl, 4¾x4" **88.00**
Pitcher, Invt T'print, fluted top, 6¼x3⅞" **120.00**
Pitcher, Optic, bulbous, clear reeded hdl, 6¼x3½" **85.00**
Pitcher, Optic, fluted top, clear hdl, 4⅞x3⅛" **65.00**
Pitcher, tankard, clear reeded hdl, 8½x4⅜" **135.00**
Sugar bowl, in SP spoon-holder fr w/rabbit hdls, lid, +spoons **375.00**
Tray, tiny flowers in bl/wht, oval, 10¾" **160.00**
Tumbler, juice; HP florals w/gold, 4x2½" **75.00**
Tumbler, 3½" **42.00**
Tumbler, 4¼" **50.00**
Vase, bud; pk opal ruffled rim, sterling silver base, 6" **175.00**
Vase, clear rigaree on collared top, 4¼x4½" **60.00**
Vase, Fleurette, 4-lobed top, spherical, 4¾", pr **165.00**
Vase, HP florals w/gold, flared top, 4⅝x3⅜" **69.00**
Vase, Invt T'print, HP daisies, trefoil, 6½" **170.00**
Vase, wht sanded Greek Key band/scallops, ormolu claw ft, 6" ...**135.00**
Wine, clear stem & base, 5" **52.00**

Creamware

Creamware was a type of earthenware developed by Wedgwood in the 1760s and produced by many other Staffordshire potteries, including Leeds. Since it could be potted cheaply and was light in weight, it became popular abroad as well as in England, due to the lower freight charges involved in its export. It was revived at Leeds in the late 19th century, and the type most often reproduced was heavily reticulated or molded in high relief. These later wares are easily distinguished from the originals since they are thicker and tend to craze heavily. See also Leeds.

Bowl, rtcl floral, ftd, 3x8½" 85.00
Bowl, triangular, rtcl rim, 8½" 140.00
Bust, Alexander AET .35 Moscow Burnt Europe Preserved., 10" .275.00
Creamer, floral, pear shape, English, 1800s 300.00
Fruit basket, rtcl, molded feather hdls, 9¾", +tray, NM 385.00
Mug, mc floral w/bl transfer band inside rim, 2¼" 40.00
Pitcher, band of hearts & swags, 1800s, 7¾" 175.00
Pitcher, Werter...Shoot Himself/Charlotte Weeping..., 6½" 460.00
Plate, basketweave w/rtcl rim, 8¼", EX 110.00
Puzzle jug, 2 rtcl bands, ftd pear shape, 1880, 8", EX 500.00
Sauce boat, duck, brn spatter w/bl & gr wings & head, 8" 550.00

Crown Milano

Crown Milano was introduced in 1894 by the Mt. Washington Glass Company of New Bedford, Massachusetts. Along with Burmese, it was their best-selling line. The glass is very pale, almost ivory. It was blown, free-form or in molds, highly decorated with flowers and colored enamels, and fired. Made to compete with the English Porcelain Companies, Crown Milano required only about half as many steps to produce as the porcelain (for which it is often mistaken, especially when viewed from a distance). This enabled Mt. Washington to make very attractive pieces at competitive prices. Some of the very early pieces are referred to as 'Albertine'; these had a glossy finish. Satin pieces were marked 'CM,' and some were shipped with paper labels. One of the most outstanding Crown Milano decorators was Frank Guba, who preferred subjects such as flying ducks or other birds. Pieces decorated by him command very high prices. Our advisors for this category are Henry and Geneva Tyler; they are listed in the Directory under Florida. In the descriptions that follow, the glassware is assumed to be satin unless noted glossy.

Biscuit jars: Art Deco floral decoration, 6x5¼", $925.00; Seaweed starfish with jewels, 5½x7¼", $1,725.00.

Biscuit jar, berries, mc on pk, ribbed, SP mts, #d, 7x7" 1,800.00
Biscuit jar, floral/gold on dk/lt bl swirl, lid w/turtle, 7" 1,350.00
Biscuit jar, pansies/roses/gold on pnt Burmese, SP lid/bail 1,100.00
Biscuit jar, violets/gold scrolls, emb lid w/appl butterfly 900.00

Bowl, pansies/multiflora on wht & yel-gr, gold, 3x9½" 460.00
Box, jewel; wild roses/traceries, gold/pk/wht, mk/#d, 2x4" 400.00
Box, stylized herons on spiral twist lid, 4x7" L 2,400.00
Creamer & sugar bowl, emb floral w/gold, w/lid 385.00
Creamer & sugar bowl, violets w/gold, 3½", 4½" dia 915.00
Cup & saucer, demi; mc floral/tan shadow leaves & scrolls 2,500.00
Ewer, lotus/pods, gold/gr on lt gr, aqua hdl, 8x8" 2,400.00
Pickle castor, floral by Candy on shaded bl; orig fr w/tongs 900.00
Pitcher, birds/reeds, much gold, dimpled, cut-out rim, 9" 2,800.00
Pitcher, gold lilies, silver/gr trim, snake hdl, #d, 8" 2,450.00
Pitcher, holly leaves/berries, gold dividers, bulbous, 8" 2,750.00
Sweetmeat, pk & bl flowers, SP lid & hdl 875.00
Syrup, floral w/mc dots, SP trim 1,245.00
Vase, boy & girl fr by garland in lav tones w/gold, 8" 850.00
Vase, dancing children in scroll reserve, bulbous, hdls, 7" 1,380.00
Vase, floral bouquets, swirled, bulbous, ruffled, 6" 725.00
Vase, floral on swirled bulb w/sm ruffled mouth, 6" 965.00
Vase, gold leaves over satin scrolls, hdld long neck, 10" 1,600.00
Vase, ivy, gr & brn w/gold, unmk, 10½" 2,295.00
Vase, lg ferns/gold/shadow leaves on wht, 4-lobe rim, 5" 1,000.00
Vase, pansies in gold/blk/bl, pk shadows, stick neck, 9½" 2,750.00
Vase, roses/buds, gold on shaded pk, petal rim, 4½" 650.00
Vase, sea creatures, gilt/jewels on bl, spherical, 6½x7" 2,000.00
Vase, spider mums w/gold, shadow medallions, mk, 11½" 1,000.00

Cruets

Cruets, containers made to hold oil or vinegar, are usually bulbous with tall, narrow throats and a stopper. During the 19th century and for several years after, they were produced in abundance in virtually every type of glassware available. Those listed below are assumed to be with stopper and mint unless noted otherwise. Our advisor for this category is Elaine Ezell; she is listed in the Directory under Maryland.

Alaska, vaseline opal 225.00
Amazon 85.00
Argus Swirl, wht opaque w/decor 195.00
Atlanta, ruby stain 375.00
Azalea, Noritake 225.00
Baroque, Azure, Fostoria 400.00
Barred Ovals 65.00
Barred Ovals, ruby stain 195.00
Bead Swag, emerald gr 195.00
Beaded Swirl & Lens, ruby stain 195.00
Bl w/wht crackle, bulbous, Stevens & Wms, 8" 145.00
Bulging Loops, yel cased 375.00
Bull's Eye & Buttons, EX gold 55.00
Button Arches, ruby stain 195.00
Buzz Saw, gr 450.00
Cape Cod, yel, Imperial 40.00
Caprice, bl 95.00
Cathedral, amber 135.00
Challinor's Forget Me Not, clear frosted, sm 125.00
Chrysanthemum Base Swirl, bl opal 380.00
Chrysanthemum Base Swirl, wht opal 210.00
Circle Scroll, gr opal 595.00
Coinspot, amberina 495.00
Coinspot, cranberry opal, tall cut stopper 365.00
Cord Drapery, chocolate 450.00
Cranberry w/floral, clear stopper/hdl, 7¾" 195.00
Crown Milano, Mt WA 9,000.00
Daisy & Button, vaseline 150.00
Daisy & Fern, Apple Blossom mold, bl opal 225.00

Daisy & Fern, swirl mold, bl opal 165.00
Esther, gr w/HP decor, lg 300.00
Fandango, Heisey 145.00
Feather, amber stain 235.00
Florette, pk satin, 4-oz 350.00
Fluted Scrolls w/flowers, bl opal 225.00
Galle, cameo 700.00
Georgia Gem, custard 200.00
Gonterman Swirl, bl 300.00
Hero 40.00
Hobbs Swirl, bl opal 275.00
Hobnail, vaseline opal, Hobbs 395.00

Import peachblow with amber handle and stopper, $425.00.

Indiana mold, peachblow, Wheeling 1,100.00
Invt T'print, cranberry, Hobbs tapered mold 200.00
Iris w/Meander, vaseline 375.00
Jacob's Ladder, orig Maltese Cross stopper 85.00
Janice, lt bl 70.00
Jeweled Heart, gr 185.00
Kings 500, cobalt w/EX gold 650.00
Nestor, amethyst w/HP decor 170.00
Nestor, gr 100.00
Pansy & Butterfly, Pomona 700.00
Queen Anne's Lace on sapphire bl, teardrop stopper, 7½" 375.00
Ranson, vaseline w/gold 175.00
Rosby, milk wht, Imperial 55.00
Sapphire bl w/wht flowers, paneled, clear stopper/hdl, 8½" 145.00
Scroll /wAcanthus, purple slag 225.00
Seaweed, bl opal 425.00
Shoshone, gr 125.00
Stars & Bars, amber 95.00
Swirl, cranberry opal, Hobbs 365.00
Thousand Eye, amber, 3-knob 170.00
Tokyo, bl opal 225.00
Wild Bouquet, bl opal 300.00
Wild Bouquet, custard, 7" 825.00
1000 Eye, vaseline 295.00

Cup Plates, Glass

Before the middle 1850s, it was socially acceptable to pour hot tea into a deep saucer to cool. The tea was sipped from the saucer rather than the cup, which frequently was handleless and too hot to hold. The cup plate served as a coaster for the cup. It is generally agreed that the first examples of pressed glass cup plates were made about 1826 at the Boston and Sandwich Glass Co. in Sandwich, Cape Cod, Massachusetts. Other glassworks in three major areas (New England, Philadelphia, and the Midwest, especially Pittsburgh) quickly followed suit.

Antique glass cup plates range in size from 2⅝" up to 4¼" in diameter. The earliest plates had simple designs inspired by cut glass patterns, but by 1829 they had become more complex. The span from then until about 1845 is known as the 'Lacy Period,' when cup plate designs and pressing techniques were at their peak. To cover pressing imperfections, the backgrounds of the plates were often covered with fine stippling which endowed them with a glittering brilliance called 'laciness.' They were made in a multitude of designs — some purely decorative, others commemorative. Subjects include the American eagle, hearts, sunbursts, log cabins, ships, George Washington, the political candidates Clay and Harrison, plows, beehives, etc. Of all the patterns, the round George Washington plate is the rarest and most valuable — only three are known to exist today.

Authenticity is most important. Collectors must be aware that contemporary plates which have no antique counterparts and fakes modeled after antique patterns have had wide distribution. Condition is also important, though it is the exceptional plate that does not have some rim roughness. More important considerations are scarcity of design and color.

Our advisor for this category is John Bilane; he is listed in the Directory under New Jersey. The book *American Glass* by George and Helen McKearin has a section on glass cup plates. The definitive book is *American Glass Cup Plates* by Ruth Webb Lee and James H. Rose. Numbers in the listings that follow (computer sorted) refer to the latter. When no condition is indicated, the examples listed below are assumed to have only minor rim roughness as is normal. See also Staffordshire; Pairpoint.

R-100, rare, VG- 65.00
R-101, scarce, G 42.00
R-103, rare, G- 45.00
R-107B, scarce, VG- 50.00
R-129, EX- 45.00
R-134A, scarce, G 49.00
R-151A, G 30.00
R-154A, EX 40.00
R-159A, scarce, G+ 41.00
R-160A, G 28.00
R-162, scarce, G+ 41.00
R-164A, EX 40.00
R-164B, VG 35.00
R-166B, rare, VG- 72.00
R-169A, EX 40.00
R-169B, EX 40.00
R-173, EX 42.00
R-175, scarce, VG+ 52.00
R-176, very rare, G- 61.00
R-176A, VG 34.00
R-180, G 28.00
R-180A, scarce, G+ 45.00
R-184, very rare, G 95.00
R-20, VG+ 32.00
R-226, G+ 26.00
R-228A, rare, VG- 70.00
R-229B, scarce, VG- 44.00
R-230, rare, G 105.00
R-230B, scarce, VG 50.00
R-232, rare, G+ 64.00
R-247, rare, VG 77.00
R-260, scarce, VG 75.00
R-284, very rare, G- 275.00
R-310B, G+ 23.00
R-310B, scarce, G+ 23.00
R-324, honey amber, G 65.00
R-342, opaque wht, rare, G 70.00

R-371, VG- 14.00
R-396, bl, rare, G+ 75.00
R-410, G 11.00
R-411, VG- 12.00
R-412, VG- 12.00
R-444A, G 28.00
R-45, scarce, VG+ 65.00
R-465J, VG 19.00
R-465L, bl opal, scarce, VG 85.00
R-467, VG 19.00
R-467A, G 15.00
R-499, G 14.00
R-501, bl, rare, G+ 90.00
R-505, scarce, VG 30.00
R-508, G- 11.00
R-522, bl opal, VG+ 65.00
R-522, dk amethyst, rare, G+ 75.00
R-525, scarce, G+ 26.00
R-526A, G- 14.00
R-532, VG 19.00
R-547, G 14.00
R-565A, VG+ 33.00
R-566, rare, VG- 60.00
R-566A, scarce, G- 33.00
R-568X2, scarce, VG+ 100.00
R-571, rare, VG- 100.00
R-575, scarce, VG+ 70.00
R-576, scarce, VG 68.00
R-610, EX 50.00
R-610B, VG 34.00
R-624A, scarce, G 53.00
R-643B, G+ 18.00
R-654A, very rare, VG+ 305.00
R-655, rare, G 170.00
R-656, very rare, G- 165.00
R-666B, scarce, VG 48.00
R-670, scarce, VG 64.00
R-670C, rare, G- 55.00
R-671, very rare, G 105.00
R-675, G+ 34.00
R-676C, scarce, G- 37.00
R-677, G+ 34.00
R-677A, G- 27.00
R-680C, very rare, G+ 101.00
R-680D, VG- 32.00
R-693, scarce, G 70.00
R-694, rare, VG- 124.00
R-699, rare, G- 83.00
R-80, rare, VG 96.00
R-82, bl opal, very rare, G+ 300.00
R0672, scarce, G+ 56.00

Currier & Ives by Royal

During the 1950s dinnerware decorated with transfer-printed scenes taken from prints by Currier and Ives was manufactured by Royal China and given as premiums through A&P stores. Though it was also made in pink, green and brown as well; the blue is by far the most popular. In addition to the dinnerware, a line of Fire-King baking pans and accessories was also available, as were vinyl place mats and various sizes of glass tumblers. Today it is readily available at reasonable prices, and it has become a very popular collectible at malls and flea markets around the country. Included this year in our listings are pieces from

Hostess sets, which should be of great interest to collectors. These pieces are noted in the lines with an asterisk (*). Our advisors for this category are Treva and Jack Hamlin; they are listed in the Directory under Ohio.

Ashtray 12.00
Bowl, cereal; rimmed 10.00
Bowl, cereal; tab hdl, mk, rare, 6⅜" 25.00
Bowl, fruit; 5½" 3.00
Bowl, lug soup; deep, tab hdl, 2¾x4¾" 20.00

Bowl, Maple Sugaring, 9", $18.00.

Bowl, soup; flat, mk, 8½" 8.00
Bowl, vegetable; 10" 20.00
Bowl, 9" 18.00
Butter dish, ¼-lb 25.00
Cake plate, ftd, 10" (*) 30.00
Cake plate, 10" (*) 20.00
Calendar plate, ca 1970s-85, ea 12.00
Candle lamp & globe, rare, tall, 3¾" base 40.00
Candy bowl, 7¾" (*) 20.00
Casserole, angle hdls, w/lid 75.00
Casserole, tab hdls, w/lid, old 100.00
Chop plate, mk, 11" dia 20.00
Chop plate, mk, 12" dia 25.00
Chop plate, mk, 13" dia 40.00
Creamer 7.50
Cup & saucer 5.00
Deviled egg plate, 11" (*) 40.00
Dip bowl, 4⅜" (*) 15.00
Gravy boat 13.00
Gravy ladle 20.00
Mug, soup or coffee; mk, 2¾x3¾" (*) 18.00
Pie baker, 11" 25.00
Pie plate (6 decals made), mk 20.00
Pie server, scarce 20.00
Plate, bread & butter; 6" 7.50
Plate, dinner; mk, 10½" 6.00
Plate, luncheon; mk, 9" 10.00
Plate, mk, 6" 2.50
Plate, salad; mk, 7⅜" 7.00
Plate, serving; 7" (*) 7.00
Platter, oval, 13" 25.00
Shakers, pr 20.00
Sugar bowl, w/lid 12.00
Teapot 100.00
Tidbit server, 3-tier 28.00
Tumbler, juice 13.00
Tumbler, milk glass 7.00
Tumbler, old-fashioned, 3¼" 10.00

Tumbler, 9-oz, 4¾" 13.00
Underplate, tab hdls, sm (for gravy boat) 12.00

Custard

As early as the 1880s, custard glass was produced in England. Migrating glassmakers brought the formula for the creamy ivory ware to America. One of them was Harry Northwood, who in 1898 founded his company in Indiana, Pennsylvania, and introduced the glassware to the American market. Soon other companies were producing custard, among them Heisey, Tarentum, Fenton, and McKee. Not only dinnerware patterns but souvenir items were made. Today custard is the most expensive of the colored pressed glassware patterns. The formula for producing the luminous glass contains uranium salts which imparts the cream color to the batch and causes it to glow when it is examined under a black light.

Argonaut Shell, bowl, master berry; gold & decor, 10½" L 265.00
Argonaut Shell, bowl, sauce; ftd, gold & decor 65.00
Argonaut Shell, butter dish, gold & decor 350.00
Argonaut Shell, butter dish, no gold 275.00
Argonaut Shell, compote, jelly; gold & decor, scarce 145.00
Argonaut Shell, creamer, gold & decor 135.00
Argonaut Shell, creamer, no gold 110.00
Argonaut Shell, cruet, gold & decor 700.00
Argonaut Shell, pitcher, water; gold & decor 435.00
Argonaut Shell, shakers, gold & decor, pr 345.00
Argonaut Shell, spooner, gold & decor 135.00
Argonaut Shell, sugar bowl, w/lid, gold & decor 200.00
Argonaut Shell, tumbler, gold & decor 110.00
Bead Swag, bowl, sauce; floral & gold 50.00
Bead Swag, goblet, floral & gold 65.00
Bead Swag, tray, pickle; floral & gold, rare 260.00
Bead Swag, wine, floral & gold 60.00
Beaded Circle, bowl, master berry; floral & gold 245.00
Beaded Circle, butter dish, floral & gold 450.00
Beaded Circle, creamer, floral & gold 180.00
Beaded Circle, cruet, floral & gold, rare 1,175.00
Beaded Circle, pitcher, water; floral & gold 675.00
Beaded Circle, shakers, floral & gold, pr 800.00
Beaded Circle, spooner, floral & gold 175.00
Beaded Circle, sugar bowl, w/lid, floral & gold 275.00
Beaded Circle, tumbler, floral & gold, very rare 100.00
Cane Insert, berry set, 7-pc 450.00
Cane Insert, table set, 4-pc 450.00
Cherry & Scales, bowl, master berry; nutmeg stain 130.00
Cherry & Scales, butter dish, nutmeg stain 225.00
Cherry & Scales, creamer, nutmeg stain 115.00
Cherry & Scales, pitcher, water; nutmeg stain, scarce 325.00
Cherry & Scales, spooner, nutmeg stain, scarce 110.00
Cherry & Scales, sugar bowl, w/lid, nutmeg stain, scarce 125.00
Cherry & Scales, tumbler, nutmeg stain, scarce 50.00
Chrysanthemum Sprig, bowl, master berry; gold & decor 275.00
Chrysanthemum Sprig, bowl, master berry; no gold 175.00
Chrysanthemum Sprig, bowl, sauce; ftd, gold & decor 50.00
Chrysanthemum Sprig, butter dish, gold & decor 300.00
Chrysanthemum Sprig, celery vase, gold & decor, rare 375.00
Chrysanthemum Sprig, compote, jelly; gold & decor 135.00
Chrysanthemum Sprig, compote, jelly; no decor 95.00
Chrysanthemum Sprig, creamer, gold & decor 125.00
Chrysanthemum Sprig, cruet, gold & decor, 6¾" 350.00
Chrysanthemum Sprig, pitcher, water; gold & decor 470.00
Chrysanthemum Sprig, shakers, gold & decor, pr 300.00

Chrysanthemum Sprig, cruet,
no gold, clear faceted stopper,
6¾", $275.00.

Chrysanthemum Sprig, spooner, gold & decor 130.00
Chrysanthemum Sprig, spooner, no gold 75.00
Chrysanthemum Sprig, toothpick holder, gold & decor 300.00
Chrysanthemum Sprig, toothpick holder, no decor 165.00
Chrysanthemum Sprig, tray, condiment; gold & decor, rare 595.00
Chrysanthemum Sprig, tumbler, gold & decor 55.00
Dandelion, mug, nutmeg stain 165.00
Delaware, bowl, sauce; pk stain 65.00
Delaware, creamer, breakfast; pk stain 70.00
Delaware, tray, pin; gr stain 75.00
Delaware, tumbler, pk stain 55.00
Diamond w/Peg, bowl, master berry; roses & gold 215.00
Diamond w/Peg, bowl, sauce; roses & gold 40.00
Diamond w/Peg, butter dish, roses & gold 235.00
Diamond w/Peg, creamer, ind; no decor 30.00
Diamond w/Peg, creamer, ind; souvenir 45.00
Diamond w/Peg, creamer, roses & gold 75.00
Diamond w/Peg, mug, souvenir 50.00
Diamond w/Peg, napkin ring, roses & gold, rare 150.00
Diamond w/Peg, pitcher, roses & gold, 5½" 260.00
Diamond w/Peg, shakers, souvenir, pr 175.00
Diamond w/Peg, sugar bowl, w/lid, roses & gold 160.00
Diamond w/Peg, toothpick holder, roses & gold 150.00
Diamond w/Peg, tumbler, roses & gold 60.00
Diamond w/Peg, water set, souvenir, 7-pc 650.00
Diamond w/Peg, wine, roses & gold 55.00
Diamond w/Peg, wine, souvenir 40.00
Everglades, bowl, master berry; gold & decor 215.00
Everglades, bowl, sauce; gold & decor 60.00
Everglades, butter dish, gold & decor 395.00
Everglades, creamer, gold & decor 155.00
Everglades, shakers, gold & decor, pr 375.00
Everglades, spooner, gold & decor 160.00
Everglades, sugar bowl, w/lid, gold & decor 235.00
Everglades, tumbler, gold & decor 100.00
Fan, bowl, master berry; good gold 135.00
Fan, bowl, sauce; good gold 55.00
Fan, butter dish, good gold 225.00
Fan, creamer, good gold 110.00
Fan, ice cream set, good gold, 7-pc 500.00
Fan, pitcher, water; good gold 275.00
Fan, spooner, good gold 100.00
Fan, sugar bowl, w/lid, good gold 150.00
Fan, tumbler, good gold 75.00
Fan, water set, good gold, 7-pc 700.00
Fine Cut & Roses, rose bowl, fancy int, nutmeg stain 100.00
Fine Cut & Roses, rose bowl, plain int 85.00

Geneva, bowl, master berry; floral decor, ftd, oval, 9" L 90.00
Geneva, bowl, master berry; floral decor, rnd, 9" 120.00
Geneva, bowl, sauce; floral decor, oval 45.00
Geneva, bowl, sauce; floral decor, rnd 45.00
Geneva, butter dish, floral decor 225.00
Geneva, butter dish, no decor 135.00
Geneva, compote, jelly; floral decor 95.00
Geneva, creamer, floral decor 100.00
Geneva, cruet, floral decor 465.00
Geneva, pitcher, water; floral decor 250.00
Geneva, shakers, floral decor, pr 280.00
Geneva, spooner, floral decor 100.00
Geneva, sugar bowl, open, floral decor 85.00
Geneva, sugar bowl, w/lid, floral decor 150.00
Geneva, syrup, floral decor 475.00
Geneva, toothpick holder, floral w/M gold 375.00
Geneva, tumbler, floral decor 50.00
Georgia Gem, bowl, master berry; good gold 135.00
Georgia Gem, bowl, master berry; gr opaque 115.00
Georgia Gem, butter dish, good gold 190.00
Georgia Gem, celery vase, good gold 145.00
Georgia Gem, creamer, good gold 100.00
Georgia Gem, creamer, no gold 60.00
Georgia Gem, mug, good gold 45.00
Georgia Gem, powder jar, w/lid, good gold 80.00
Georgia Gem, shakers, good gold, pr 160.00
Georgia Gem, spooner, souvenir 55.00
Georgia Gem, sugar bowl, w/lid, no gold 95.00
Grape (& Cable), bottle, scent; orig stopper, nutmeg stain 600.00
Grape (& Cable), bowl, master berry; nutmeg stain, ftd, 11" 375.00
Grape (& Cable), bowl, nutmeg stain, 7½" 60.00
Grape (& Cable), bowl, sauce; nutmeg stain, ftd 50.00
Grape (& Cable), butter dish, nutmeg stain 275.00
Grape (& Cable), compote, jelly; open, nutmeg stain 145.00
Grape (& Cable), compote, nutmeg stain, 4½x8" 300.00
Grape (& Cable), cracker jar, nutmeg stain 800.00
Grape (& Cable), creamer, breakfast; nutmeg stain 80.00
Grape (& Cable), humidor, bl stain, rare 950.00
Grape (& Cable), humidor, nutmeg stain, rare 900.00
Grape (& Cable), nappy, nutmeg stain, rare 60.00
Grape (& Cable), pitcher, water; nutmeg stain 400.00
Grape (& Cable), plate, nutmeg stain, 7" 50.00
Grape (& Cable), plate, nutmeg stain, 8" 65.00
Grape (& Cable), powder jar, nutmeg stain 350.00
Grape (& Cable), punch bowl, w/base, nutmeg stain 1,750.00
Grape (& Cable), spooner, nutmeg stain 145.00
Grape (& Cable), sugar bowl, breakfast; open, nutmeg stain 75.00
Grape (& Cable), sugar bowl, w/lid, nutmeg stain 195.00
Grape (& Cable), tray, dresser; nutmeg stain, scarce, lg 350.00
Grape (& Cable), tray, pin; nutmeg stain 135.00
Grape (& Cable), tumbler, nutmeg stain 75.00
Grape & Gothic Arches, bowl, master berry; pearl w/gold 200.00
Grape & Gothic Arches, bowl, sauce; pearl w/gold, rare 80.00
Grape & Gothic Arches, butter dish, pearl w/gold 235.00
Grape & Gothic Arches, creamer, pearl w/gold, rare 100.00
Grape & Gothic Arches, favor vase, nutmeg stain 80.00
Grape & Gothic Arches, goblet, pearl w/gold 75.00
Grape & Gothic Arches, pitcher, water; pearl w/gold 300.00
Grape & Gothic Arches, spooner, pearl w/gold 85.00
Grape & Gothic Arches, sugar bowl, w/lid, pearl w/gold 135.00
Grape & Gothic Arches, tumbler, pearl w/gold 65.00
Grape Arbor, vase, hat form 90.00
Heart w/T'print, creamer 85.00
Heart w/T'print, lamp, good pnt, scarce, 8" 435.00

Heart w/T'print, sugar bowl, ind 80.00
Honeycomb, wine 65.00
Horse Medallion, bowl, gr stain, 7" 80.00
Intaglio, bowl, master berry; gold & decor, ftd, 9" 250.00
Intaglio, bowl, sauce; gold & decor 50.00
Intaglio, butter dish, gold & decor, scarce 300.00
Intaglio, compote, jelly; gold & decor 125.00
Intaglio, creamer, gold & decor 125.00
Intaglio, cruet, gold & decor 475.00
Intaglio, pitcher, water; gold & decor 395.00
Intaglio, shakers, gold & decor, pr 235.00
Intaglio, spooner, gold & decor 125.00
Intaglio, sugar bowl, w/lid, gold & decor 165.00
Intaglio, tumbler, gold & decor 75.00
Inverted Fan & Feather, bowl, master berry; gold & decor 250.00
Inverted Fan & Feather, bowl, sauce; gold & decor 65.00
Inverted Fan & Feather, butter dish, gold & decor 350.00
Inverted Fan & Feather, compote, jelly; gold & decor, rare 500.00
Inverted Fan & Feather, creamer, gold & decor 150.00
Inverted Fan & Feather, cruet, gold & decor, scarce, 6½" 1,100.00

Inverted Fan and Feather,
pitcher, gold and decoration,
7¼", $600.00.

Inverted Fan & Feather, punch cup, gold & decor 250.00
Inverted Fan & Feather, shakers, gold & decor, pr 600.00
Inverted Fan & Feather, spooner, gold & decor 145.00
Inverted Fan & Feather, sugar bowl, w/lid, gold & decor 225.00
Inverted Fan & Feather, tumbler, gold & decor 95.00
Jackson, bowl, master berry; good gold, ftd 135.00
Jackson, bowl, sauce; good gold 45.00
Jackson, creamer, good gold 85.00
Jackson, pitcher, water; good gold 250.00
Jackson, pitcher, water; no decor 175.00
Jackson, shakers, good gold, pr 195.00
Jackson, tumbler, good gold 50.00
Louis XV, berry set, w/nutmeg, 7-pc 375.00
Louis XV, bowl, master berry; good gold 165.00
Louis XV, bowl, sauce; good gold, ftd 47.00
Louis XV, butter dish, good gold 200.00
Louis XV, creamer, good gold 80.00
Louis XV, cruet, good gold 365.00
Louis XV, pitcher, water; good gold 225.00
Louis XV, spooner, good gold 80.00
Louis XV, sugar bowl, w/lid, good gold 150.00
Louis XV, tumbler, good gold 65.00
Maple Leaf, bowl, master berry; gold & decor, scarce 335.00
Maple Leaf, bowl, sauce; gold & decor, scarce 95.00
Maple Leaf, butter dish, gold & decor 350.00
Maple Leaf, compote, jelly; gold & decor, rare 455.00
Maple Leaf, creamer, gold & decor 150.00
Maple Leaf, cruet, gold & decor, rare 3,000.00

Maple Leaf, pitcher, water; gold & decor 400.00
Maple Leaf, shakers, gold & decor, very rare, pr 800.00
Maple Leaf, spooner, gold & decor 155.00
Maple Leaf, sugar bowl, w/lid, gold & decor 230.00
Maple Leaf, tumbler, gold & decor 95.00
Panelled Poppy, lamp shade, nutmeg stain, scarce 800.00
Peacock & Urn, bowl, ice cream; nutmeg stain, sm 80.00
Peacock & Urn, bowl, ice cream; nutmeg stain, 10" 350.00
Punty Band, shakers, pr 175.00
Punty Band, spooner, floral decor 100.00
Punty Band, tumbler, floral decor, souvenir 65.00
Ribbed Drape, bowl, sauce; roses & gold 40.00
Ribbed Drape, butter dish, scalloped, roses & gold 375.00
Ribbed Drape, compote, jelly; roses & gold, rare 200.00
Ribbed Drape, creamer, roses & gold, scarce 180.00
Ribbed Drape, cruet, roses & gold, rare 650.00
Ribbed Drape, pitcher, water; roses & gold, rare 365.00
Ribbed Drape, shakers, roses & gold, rare, pr 360.00
Ribbed Drape, spooner, roses & gold 180.00
Ribbed Drape, toothpick holder, roses & gold 475.00
Ribbed Drape, tumbler, roses & gold 65.00
Ribbed Thumbprint, wine, floral decor 80.00
Ring Band, bowl, master berry; roses & gold 150.00
Ring Band, bowl, sauce; roses & gold 45.00
Ring Band, butter dish, roses & gold 250.00
Ring Band, compote, jelly; roses & gold, scarce 195.00
Ring Band, creamer, roses & gold 115.00
Ring Band, cruet, roses & gold 450.00
Ring Band, pitcher, roses & gold, 7½" 335.00
Ring Band, shakers, roses & gold, pr 155.00
Ring Band, spooner, roses & gold 110.00
Ring Band, syrup, roses & gold 465.00
Ring Band, toothpick holder, roses & gold 135.00
Ring Band, tray, condiment; roses & gold 200.00
Singing Birds, mug, nutmeg stain 75.00
Tarentum's Victoria, bowl, master berry; gold & decor 200.00
Tarentum's Victoria, butter dish, gold & decor, rare 300.00
Tarentum's Victoria, celery vase, gold & decor, rare 275.00
Tarentum's Victoria, creamer, gold & decor, scarce 135.00
Tarentum's Victoria, pitcher, water; gold & decor, rare 375.00
Tarentum's Victoria, spooner, gold & decor 135.00
Tarentum's Victoria, sugar bowl, w/lid, gold & decor 160.00
Tarentum's Victoria, tumbler, gold & decor 70.00
Vermont, butter dish, bl decor 195.00
Vermont, toothpick holder, bl decor 155.00
Vermont, vase, floral decor, jeweled 95.00
Wide Band, bell, roses 195.00
Wild Bouquet, butter dish, gold & decor, rare 700.00
Wild Bouquet, creamer, no gold 145.00
Wild Bouquet, cruet, no decor, w/clear stopper 995.00
Wild Bouquet, sauce, gold & decor 60.00
Wild Bouquet, spooner, gold & decor 160.00
Wild Bouquet, tumbler, no decor 95.00
Winged Scroll, bowl, master berry; gold & decor, 11" L 175.00
Winged Scroll, bowl, sauce; good gold 45.00
Winged Scroll, butter dish, good gold 200.00
Winged Scroll, butter dish, no decor 150.00
Winged Scroll, celery vase, good gold, rare 400.00
Winged Scroll, cigarette jar, scarce 195.00
Winged Scroll, compote, ruffled, rare, 6¾x10¾" 495.00
Winged Scroll, cruet, good gold, clear stopper 375.00
Winged Scroll, hair receiver, good gold 135.00
Winged Scroll, pitcher, water; bulbous, good gold 350.00
Winged Scroll, shakers, bulbous, good gold, rare, pr 400.00

Winged Scroll, shakers, str sides, good gold, pr 195.00
Winged Scroll, sugar bowl, w/lid, good gold 150.00
Winged Scroll, syrup, good gold 395.00
Winged Scroll, tumbler, good gold 75.00

Cut Glass

The earliest documented evidence of commercial glass cutting in the United States was in 1810; the producers were Bakewell and Page of Pittsburgh. These first efforts resulted in simple patterns with only a moderate amount of cutting. By the middle of the century, glass cutters began experimenting with a thicker glass which enabled them to use deeper cuttings, though patterns remained much the same. This period is usually referred to as Rich Cut. Using three types of wheels — a flat edge, a mitered edge, and a convex edge — facets, miters, and depressions were combined to produce various designs. In the late 1870s, a curved miter was developed which greatly expanded design potential. Patterns became more elaborate, often covering the entire surface. The Brilliant Period of cut glass covered a span from about 1880 until 1915. Because of the pressure necessary to achieve the deeply cut patterns, only glass containing a high grade of metal could withstand the process. For this reason and the amount of handwork involved, cut glass has always been expensive. Bowls cut with pinwheels may be either foreign or of a newer vintage, beware! Identifiable patterns and signed pieces that are well cut and in excellent condition bring the higher prices on today's market. See also Dorflinger; Hawkes; Libbey; Tuthill; Val St. Lambert; other specific manufacturers.

Key:
dmn — diamonds   X-cut — crosscut
strw — strawberry   X-hatch — crosshatch

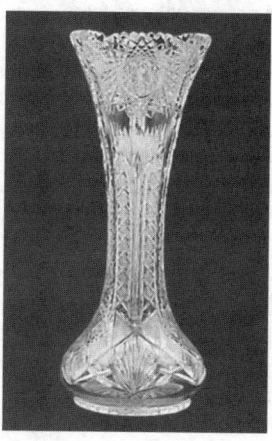

Vase, Camelia, Clark shape and pattern (unsigned), flared rim, 18", $625.00.

Ashtray, hobstar in base, triangular, lg 40.00
Basket, cut/eng butterflies/flowers, ornate silver hdl, 17" 1,100.00
Berry set, buzz stars/hobstars, Clark, 7-pc 1,000.00
Bottle, scent; heart pattern, bulbous, faceted stopper, 5" 135.00
Bowl, Alhambra, 4¼x9" 1,400.00
Bowl, Belmont, hobstars/buzz stars, shallow, 8" 110.00
Bowl, central hobstar fr w/hobstars, shallow, Clark, 5¼" 35.00
Bowl, cluster of hobstars, shallow, Corning, 7" 150.00
Bowl, cobwebs, floral garlands, cobalt hdls, 10" 265.00
Bowl, Comet, 3½x8" 235.00
Bowl, fruit; buttons on oval helmet form, 4x12" 250.00
Bowl, Harvard variant w/buttons, 8" 120.00
Bowl, Heart pattern, att Strauss, 9" dia 300.00
Bowl, hobstars/fans/X-hatching/hobnails, Blackmere, 9½" 275.00
Bowl, hobstars/notched vesicas, triple-notched hdls, 6x7" 325.00

Bowl, hobstars/X-hatching/hobnails/mitres, Strauss, 9" 300.00
Bowl, radiant star, sq, 8" 175.00
Bowl, Royal, Hunt, 8" 110.00
Bowl, salad; hobstars w/silver florals, 4¾x12½", +plate 1,650.00
Bowl, stars/dmns, Clark, 8" 110.00
Bowl, stars/X-hatching, Hoare, 8" 150.00
Bowl, X-Ray, allover cut, rtcl silver rim, Hoare, 2x11" 200.00
Butter dish, chain of hobstars/buttons, faceted knob, 6x8" 200.00
Candlesticks, oval notches, 8½", pr 100.00
Candlesticks, rayed bottom, teardrop in stem, Meriden, 6", pr ...500.00
Canoe, Harvard, 11½" L 200.00
Carafe, Carolyn, Hoare, 8", EX 200.00
Carafe, hobstars, stars & X w/miters, bowling pin shape, 9" 150.00
Carafe, water; Peerless, Empire, 8" 110.00
Champagne, flute cut, dbl teardrop stem, hobstar base 100.00
Cheese & cracker, geometrics, florals, 12" 85.00
Cheese dish, Harvard, daisies, scalloped plate, 6¾x8" 235.00
Compote, hobstar/dmn point, scalloped rim, rayed base, 7x8" 250.00
Compote, hobstars, teardrop stem w/notched swirl knob, 11" 375.00
Compote, hobstars/X-hatching, 24-point hobstar base, 13½" 700.00
Compote, Memphis, shallow, 2 hdls, short std, 10" dia 160.00
Creamer & sugar bowl, Aberdeen, Jewel Cut Glass Co, 2½" 250.00
Creamer & sugar bowl, florals, ped ft, 2¾" 155.00
Creamer & sugar bowl, hobstars, dmns & fans, dbl-cut hdls 225.00
Creamer & sugar bowl, Pluto, Hoare 395.00
Creamer & sugar bowl, Ruby, Blackmere, 4" dia 130.00
Creamer & sugar bowl, thistles, Clark, 3½" dia 125.00
Cruet, Harvard & band, flaring base, 8½" 75.00
Decanter, alternating hobstars & fans, notched hdl, 13" 400.00
Decanter, bird/nest/flowers, EX quality, 12", pr 450.00
Decanter, Buzz, Enterprise Cut Glass Co 250.00
Decanter, Harvard band frames florals, step-cut neck, 15" 500.00
Decanter, Manila, Higgins & Seiter, 7" 325.00
Dish, ice cream; palm & fan, 6", set of 4 ....250.00
Ewer, hobstars/X-hatching w/in dmn-field band, ped ft, 10" 350.00
Ferner, hobstars/fans, 3-ftd, Hoare, 7½" dia 130.00
Ferner, Plymouth, short stem, hobstar/fan-cut ft, liner, 6" 200.00
Flower center, lg pinwheels, stepped neck, Strauss, 9x10" 800.00
Fork, hobstar hdl, SP tines, 12", G 100.00
Frame, tulips & leaves, notching around edge, 9x7" 275.00
Goblet, florals, stepped std, rnd ft, 7", set of 4 ....85.00
Ice bucket, expanding stars, 6x6" 125.00
Ice tub, band of hobstars/dmns, upright hdls, 5½", EX 175.00
Jardiniere, Xd Ovals, 4 lg 32-point hobstars, 9x10½" 700.00
Jug, whiskey; fluted, silver o/l stopper, faceted neck, 9" 150.00
Ladle, egg nog; fans, X-hatching, SP bowl, 11" 200.00
Lamp, intaglio roses & spear prisms, 19", EX 1,050.00
Mayonnaise, chain of hobstars, X-hatching, +underplate 275.00
Mayonnaise, Propeller, 2¾x6", +underplate 575.00
Mug, coffee; Arcadia, 16-point hobstar on base 250.00
Nappy, #1 Spray, w/hdl, Illig, 6" dia 350.00
Nappy, Elfin, Hoare, 7" 110.00
Nappy, Harvard, step-cut tall ped ft, hdls, 9x11" 400.00
Paperweight, hobstars/buttons/X-hatching, heart shape, 3½" 195.00
Pitcher, buzz stars/X-hatching, low/bulbous, Maple City, 7½" 270.00
Pitcher, cosmos, flowers & leaves, appl hdl, 10½" 225.00
Pitcher, geometric, notched hdl, bulbous, 7" 175.00
Pitcher, Harvard, 10", +6 tumblers 625.00
Pitcher, hobstars, eng poinsettias, cut hdl & rim, water sz 225.00
Pitcher, hobstars w/V bands of cane, notched hdl, 11½" 350.00
Pitcher, tankard; brilliant cut, sterling repousse rim, 10" 650.00
Pitcher, tankard; Harvard, notched hdl, 14" 625.00
Pitcher, tankard; hobstars/band of cane, fans, 12" 275.00
Pitcher, tankard; pinwheels, hobstars & fans, slim, 10¼" 125.00

Pitcher, tankard; sunflowers, notched hdl, 12½" 500.00
Planter, window; hobstars & fans, rayed base, 2x9x2½" 225.00
Plate, hobnail, rayed center, cranberry to clear, 7" 225.00
Plate, hobstars/nailhead/cane/strw dmn, 8" 215.00
Plate, Mortenson's Butterfly, 7" 150.00
Plate, sandwich; hobstars & prisms, 10" 195.00
Plate, Star of David, 6", set of 6 ....570.00
Punch bowl, hobstars/vesicas, 13x13", EX 550.00
Punch bowl, lg hobstars/X-hatching, 2-pc, 17x13" 2,250.00
Punch bowl, pinwheel variant, 12x12" 550.00
Punch bowl, Strw Dmn & Star, 1-pc, Clark, 5x12" 400.00
Relish, eng ivy vines/leaves, 2-part oval, 14" 120.00
Relish, expanding star, 4-section, dbl-notched hdls, 8" dia 200.00
Relish, prism cut, prism & hobstar ends, 4½x8" 75.00
Relish, strw variant, 3-part boat shape, 12" L 525.00
Ring tree, red/yel cut bk to clear w/stars & ovals, 3" 210.00
Roll dish, Regal, stars/eng flowers, 12¾" 110.00
Sachet jar, engr florals, mushroom lid 45.00
Sandwich server, intaglio & brilliant cuttings, sgn Hunt 325.00
Server, cut florals, sawtooth rim, center hdl 50.00
Shade, Russian pattern, mushroom shape, 5x7" 85.00
Sherbet, Russian, lapidary knob stem, pattern-cut base, 4" 50.00
Shot glass, hobstars/fan/elongated punty, set of 6 ....100.00
Spoon rest, hobstars/vesicas, 5½" 150.00
Spooner, stars/hobnails/mitres, Egginton, 8" 80.00
Syrup, dmn fields of nailhead/shooting stars, saucer base 250.00
Tazza, expanding star, fan, strw dmn, teardrop stem, 8x6" 150.00
Tazza, hobstars base, file stem, Star of David on top, 12" 550.00
Tray, bread; caning/hobstars/fans, eng leaves, Clark, 13" 275.00
Tray, hobstars/fans/X-hatching, sawtooth rim, Hoare, 13" 325.00
Tray, hobstars/shooting stars, cloverleaf shape, 10", NM 195.00
Tray, ice cream; carnation panels, 10" dia 850.00
Tray, ice cream; Festoon variant, 11x18" 1,200.00
Tray, ice cream; hobstars/punch cutting, 8x11½" 300.00
Tray, lg star centering miters/stars, scalloped, Hoare, 15" 1,600.00
Tray, Russian, oval, 10" 140.00
Vase, allover hobstar/sunbursts, heavy, 18" 1,000.00
Vase, cane/hobstars/prisms/bull's eye, cylindrical, 14" 450.00
Vase, canes/notched prisms, silver repousse rim, 11" 800.00
Vase, checkerboard-style hobstars, fine X-hatching, 12" 125.00
Vase, Harvard w/hobstars & canes, 24-hobstar ft, heavy, 10x9" ..650.00
Vase, sweet pea; Lily of the Valley, flared/ftd, 5¼" 175.00
Vase, Victoria, cylindrical, Egginton, 12" 190.00
Vase, X-hatching/miters/stars, waisted, Hoare, 6" 80.00
Wine, Russian, cranberry cut to clear 250.00
Wine, Split Square, 4½", pr 85.00
Wine, strw dmn, teal cut to clear, 4½" 225.00

Cut Overlay Glass

Glassware with one or more overlying colors through which a design has been cut is called 'Cut Overlay.' It was made both here and abroad.

Bottle, scent; wht cut to clear w/cloverleaves, gilt, 5½" 200.00
Decanter, red cut to clear w/fans & dmns, bulbous, 8" 170.00
Shaker, cobalt cut to clear w/gilt panels, brass cap, 4½" 175.00
Vase, fruit reserves/ornate borders, bl cut to vaseline, 15" 440.00

Cut Velvet

Cut Velvet glassware was made during the late 1800s. It is characterized by the effect achieved through the execution of relief-molded patterns, often ribbing or diamond quilting, which allows its white inner casing to show through the outer layer.

Ewer, Dmn Quilt, pk, appl hdl, 8"	150.00
Rose bowl, Dmn Quilt, Am Beauty Rose Red, 3½x3½"	225.00
Rose bowl, Dmn Quilt, gr, 4-crimp top, 4x3"	175.00
Rose bowl, Dmn Quilt, lav-pk, egg shape, 4x3"	165.00
Rose bowl, Dmn Quilt, pk, 4-crimp top, 4x3"	165.00
Rose bowl, Dmn Quilt, red, 6-crimp top, 3½x3½"	225.00
Rose bowl, Dmn Quilt, sky bl, 4-crimp top, 3½x3¼"	145.00

Vase, Diamond Quilted in deep rose, white lining, ruffled rim, 7", $375.00.

Vase, Dmn Quilt, bl, appl frosted bellflower & leaf, 5½"	165.00
Vase, Dmn Quilt, bl, bottle form, 7¼x3½"	135.00
Vase, Dmn Quilt, bl, bulbous, 8¾"	325.00
Vase, Dmn Quilt, bl, sq top, 6x3⅛"	175.00
Vase, Dmn Quilt, pk w/3 camphor branch ft, ruffled, 5¾"	135.00
Vase, Dmn Quilt, tan, bulbous, 5x5⅝"	175.00
Vase, Ribbed, pk, 6⅞x3⅜"	95.00

Cybis

Boleslaw Cybis was a graduate of the Academy of Fine Arts in Warsaw, Poland, and was well recognized as a fine artist by the time he was commissioned by his government to paint murals in the Polish Pavillion's Hall of Honor at the 1939 World's Fair. Finding themselves stranded in America at the outbreak of WWII, the Cybises founded an artists' studio, first in Astoria, New York, and later in Trenton, New Jersey, where they made fine figurines and plaques with exacting artistry and craftsmanship entailing extensive handwork. The studio still operates today producing exquisite porcelains on a limited edition basis.

Allegra	295.00
American Bullfrog	200.00
Ballerina, On Cue, wht, on wood stand, 12½"	450.00
Ballerinas, Aurora & Florimund	1,500.00
Bathsheba, #452, 14"	2,350.00
Burro, Benjamin	150.00
Calla Lily, #427, 16"	750.00
Chipmunk w/Bloodroot	395.00
Cupid, 6½"	325.00
Duckling, 4" L	125.00
Eagle Bowl	195.00
Eskimo Mother	2,250.00

Folk Singer	495.00
Funny Face, clown, 8¾"	425.00
Girl's Head, wht w/wood ped, 9½"	500.00
Grouse, on raspberry bush, wooden base, 7"	125.00
Harp Seal	95.00
Holiday Child, w/panda bear, 6¼"	195.00
Jennifer Bust	250.00
Jester, wht/orange costume, holding mask in hand, #74, 15"	500.00
Juliet	1,800.00
Kangaroo Mouse, by leafy stump, 6"	150.00
Little Boy Blue, 9"	450.00
Little Indian Princess, 9½"	375.00
Little Miss Muffet, 7"	300.00
Little Red Riding Hood, 6¾"	200.00
Lucy Locket	295.00
Madame Butterfly, #321, 13½"	2,000.00
Madonna, bl veil	225.00
Magnolias, #391, 8"	350.00
Male Jogger, 14½"	350.00
Moses the Great Lawgiver	1,995.00
Narcissus	295.00
Owl, wht on mc branch, 4½"	95.00
Penguins, Steppin' Out	200.00
Performing Dog, 8¼"	250.00
Pollyanna, 7½"	350.00
Psyche	300.00
Queen Esther, #98, 13"	1,100.00
St Francis, w/2 lambs & 3 birds, wht bsk, 12"	250.00
Turtle, w/frog on bk, 5" L	100.00
Woman in medieval gown, w/falcon on wrist, #317, 15"	625.00
Wood Duck	650.00
Wood Wren, w/dogwood, 5½"	350.00

Czechoslovakian Collectibles

Czechoslovakia came into being as a country in 1918. Located in the heart of Europe, it was a land with the natural resources necessary to support a glass industry that dates back to the mid-14th century. This ware has recently captured the attention of today's collectors, and for good reason. There are beautiful vases — cased, ruffled, applied with rigaree or silver overlay — fine enough to rival those of the best glasshouses. Czechoslovakian art glass baskets are quite as attractive as Victorian America's, and the elegant cut glass perfumes made in colors as well as crystal are unrivaled. There are also pressed glass perfumes, molded in lovely Deco shapes, of various types of art glass. Some are overlaid with gold filigree set with 'jewels.' Jewelry, lamps, porcelains, and fine art pottery are also included in the field.

More than seventy marks have been recorded, including those in the mold, ink stamped, acid etched, or on a small metal nameplate. The newer marks are incised, stamped 'Royal Dux Made in Czechoslovakia' (see Royal Dux), or printed on a paper label which reads 'Bohemian Glass Made in Czechoslovakia.' (Communist controlled from 1948, Czechoslovakia once again was made a free country in December 1989. Today it no longer exists; since 1993 it has been divided to form the world's two newest countries, the Czech Republic and the Slovak Republic.) For a more thorough study of the subject, we recommend you refer to the books *Made in Czechoslovakia* And *Made in Czechoslovakia, Book 2,* by Ruth A. Forsythe; she is listed in the Directory under Ohio. Another fine book is *Czechoslovakian Glass & Collectibles* by Dale and Diane Barta. In the listings that follow, when one dimension is given, it refers to height; decoration is enamel unless noted otherwise. See also Erphila.

Perfume bottles: Crystal cut base with etched floral on fan-shaped stopper, 5", $98.00; Pressed crystal, faceted brass cap with brass decoration and 2 white elephants dangling from chain, 2½", $60.00.

Candy Baskets

Bl mottle, yel top, jet hdl, 8"	130.00
Blk w/silver mica, bl int, blk hdl, 8"	115.00
Cased mc mottle, blk rim & hdl, 7"	175.00
Gr varicolored w/red o/l at base, flared rim, 8½"	125.00
Mc mottle, crystal flat-top hdl, slender, incurvate, 8½"	100.00
Mc streaks, clear hdl, 9½"	100.00
Pk varicolored, pk hdl, 8"	90.00
Red & yel mottle, twisted crystal thorn hdl, 7"	135.00
Red w/dk streaks, clear twisted thorn hdl, 5½"	155.00
Solid color w/blk petal rim, crystal hdl, 6½"	125.00

Cased Art Glass

Bowl, cameo-cut vine, dk gr on lt orange, ftd, 5½"	425.00
Candlesticks, blk w/red flared rim, 3", pr	60.00
Candy jar, yel, appl florals, w/lid, 3¾"	110.00
Mayonnaise, varicolored, ball finial, 5½"	90.00
Pitcher, exotic bird on orange, blk hdl, 11½"	125.00
Vase, bl pull-ups on bl, flared cylinder, 7"	75.00
Vase, blk & yel mottle w/wht serpentine decor, ruffled, 9⅝"	100.00
Vase, bud; dk orange w/silver splotches, 11"	50.00
Vase, bud; orange, silver-deposit florals, 6¼"	32.50
Vase, enamel medallions, blk on orange, blk-lined rim & ft, 8½"	65.00
Vase, gr trumpet form w/clear gr hdls, 5½"	70.00
Vase, jack-in-pulpit; yel w/mc mottle at base, 7½"	60.00
Vase, mc mottle, stick form, wide base, 8½"	45.00
Vase, mottled, metal flower arranger, 5½"	55.00
Vase, orange w/silver & blk Roman figure, 12"	150.00
Vase, pk, canes, red o/l veins, hdls, 7"	365.00
Vase, varicolored, ball form, 6"	115.00
Vase, wht, clear ruffled rim, 5½"	50.00
Vase, wht, rose int, ruffled sphere, 5½"	78.00
Vase, yel, slim w/ruffled blk rim, 8½"	65.00
Vase, yel gourd shape w/enamel landscape, 9½"	190.00
Vase, yel satin, mc pastoral scene, flared cylinder, 9½"	195.00
Vase, yel w/pnt Niagara Falls scene, blk at rim & ft, 6¼"	50.00
Wine, yel, tall blk stem & base, 7½"	27.50

Cut Glass Perfume Bottles

Amber, shouldered form w/faceted amber stopper, 6⅛"	155.00
Amber, 4 scrolling ft, frosted floral teardrop stopper, 7⅞"	465.00
Amber cut to clear on lamp-like form, atomizer, 8½"	200.00
Amethyst, flared base, frosted nude stopper, 6⅝"	425.00
Amethyst, shouldered form, frosted floral stopper, 4¾"	155.00
Amethyst arched form w/jewels, frosted floral stopper, 5⅜"	500.00
Blk opaque, stepped Deco form, crystal stopper, 4⅝"	120.00
Crystal, stepped sides, bl shield-form stopper, 6½"	125.00
Crystal, wide base, frosted lady stopper, 5⅝"	265.00
Crystal & frosted, waffled cuts, butterfly stopper, 5½"	120.00
Gr, wide shoulders, frosted florals in stopper, 6½"	135.00
Gr low shape w/4 ft, frosted spear-shape stopper, 7¼"	155.00
Gr w/gold jewels, gr frosted stopper, 4¾"	400.00
Red, shouldered form, crystal cut stopper, 5⅞"	425.00

Lamps

Base, variegated mottle, cased, brass top, 4½"	80.00
Basket, crystal beads, glass fruit, metal trim, 10"	600.00
Desk, acid-cut counterbalance shade, slim trn std, 10"	175.00
Desk, acid-cut shade, floral decor on ft, 10"	175.00
Mottled satin base & shade, 12½"	190.00
Student, acid-cut shade w/floral design, 21"	365.00
Table, dk bl lustre, classic form, rpl shade, 13"	95.00
Table, pnt milk glass, kerosene burner, 12¾"	125.00
Table, pottery w/brass base, pnt leaves decor, 30½"	150.00
Vanity, clear base w/HP flowers & leaves, brass top, 12"	75.00

Mold-Blown and Pressed Bottles

Amethyst & crystal w/enamel daisies, 7"	115.00
Bl, sloped shoulders, atomizer, 3"	65.00
Clear w/emb decor & chain dangles w/jewels, 2½"	60.00
Clear w/mc daisies, fat cylinder form, 3⅜"	50.00
Gold & jewels encase clear shouldered form, 2"	125.00
Gr frosted w/blk & wht Deco enameling, 6"	60.00
Gr w/appl blk serpentine decor, atomizer, 8"	110.00
Gr w/wht veins, low-shouldered base, orange stopper, 7"	45.00
Mc mottle satin, cased, atomizer, Mar Franc Paris, 6½"	135.00
Orange cased, blk base & stopper, 6¼"	65.00
Purple lustre, flattened bulb form w/flower finial, 4½"	95.00
Topaz tinted, pillow form, jet stopper, 5"	35.00

Opaque, Crystal, Colored Transparent Glass

Candy jar, gr, appl apricot ped base, knob finial, 6"	160.00
Decanter, amber, floral cuttings, cylindrical, 8"	65.00
Figurine, Henry VIII, gr & red coat, foil label, 9¼"	350.00
Pitcher, amber, yel o/l pull-ups, quilted, 11½"	175.00
Pitcher, orange & gr, stacked cone form, clear hdl, 12½"	95.00
Shakers, pk, cut decor, 4¾", pr	155.00
Tumbler, bl, enameled exotic bird, 5½"	40.00
Vase, clear cylinder w/red spiral threading, 8¼"	70.00
Vase, coralene florals on bl to wht, classic form, 7½"	50.00
Vase, crystal, red spiral threading, ftd cylinder, 8¼"	75.00
Vase, golden topaz, orange pull-ups, fan form, 8"	200.00
Vase, jet w/orange spiral decor, slim cylinder, 6½"	70.00
Vase, mauve, acid etched, flared ruffled rim w/blk trim, 5⅝"	115.00
Vase, mc mottle, fan form, 9¼"	150.00
Vase, orange w/yel o/l, fan form, 8"	150.00
Vase, pk lustre w/threading at top, ftd cylinder, 9⅜"	275.00
Wine, gr bubbly glass, enameled riding scene, 4¼"	42.50

Pottery, Porcelain, Semiporcelain

Clock, faux marble w/flower basket, German works, 7"	120.00
Creamer, chicken figural, 4"	45.00
Creamer, cow, sitting, marigold irid, 6"	45.00

Creamer, Dutchman w/pipe figural, 4½" 30.00
Creamer, elk head 45.00
Creamer, mini mc florals on wht w/gold trim, 5¼" 20.00
Creamer, tomato form, 3½" 30.00
Creamer, wht w/blk trim, cat figural hdl, 4⅜" 35.00
Cup & saucer, rooster, brn on tan w/gr, child's sz 35.00
Dinnerware, Sylvia pattern, 8-place set w/serving pcs 375.00
Dresser box, enameled couple on lid w/mirror, 3¼" dia..............50.00
Figurine, elephant w/howdah, mc pnt, EX details, 4½" 50.00
Flower holder, bird on stump form, 5⅜" 40.00
Flower holder, bird perched on stump, mc pnt, 3½" 40.00
Plate, fruit & flowers, Peasant Art, sgn Mrazek, scarlet, 10" 150.00
Potato server, potato form w/butter pat finial, 5" 17.50
Teapot, Art Deco fruit & flower, Peasant art, sgn Mrazek, 7" 350.00
Teapot, pk lustre, bulbous, 6⅛" 35.00
Wall pocket, bird atop apple cluster, mc pnt, 4¾" 45.00
Wall pocket, bird perched at side of wishing well, mc pnt, 6" 45.00

D'Argental

D'Argental cameo glass was produced in France from the 1870s until about 1920 in the Art Nouveau style. Browns and tans were favored colors used to complement florals and scenic designs developed through acid cuttings. Our advisor for this category is Don Williams; he is listed in the Directory under Missouri.

Lamp, wooded lake scene on 12" shade and base, red on yellow frost, 24", $15,000.00.

Cameo

Bowl, honeysuckle, purple-brn on citron, 3¾x3½" 350.00
Box, leafy boughs, red/purple on gray opal, domical, 4" H 1,250.00
Vase, bud; floral, brn on gray/amber mottle, 7½" 650.00
Vase, mulberry branches, wine on lt bl, ovoid, 8" 725.00
Vase, palm trees/mtns/man in boat, gr/dk gr on opal, 8" 850.00
Vase, pine cones/needles, bl/citron on dk bl, 9" 1,000.00
Vase, poppies/leaves, rust on citron, trumpet top, 8" 900.00
Vase, tall trees/river/house/castle, lt/dk brn on yel, 14" 900.00
Vase, thistles, bl on yel frost, ovoid, 5" 545.00
Vase, 5-petal floral, brn on yel, 9½x6" 650.00

Daum Nancy

Daum was an important producer of French cameo glass, operating from the late 1800s until after the turn of the century. They used vari-

ous techniques — acid cutting, wheel engraving, and handwork — to create beautiful scenic designs and nature subjects in the Art Nouveau manner. Virtually all examples are signed. Our advisor for this category is Don Williams; he is listed in the Directory under Missouri.

Key: fp — fire polished

Cameo

Bottle, scent; desert, cut/pnt on wht mottle, 1½" 1,700.00
Bottle, scent; sm floral on yel/orange body & stopper, 5" 2,000.00
Bowl, autumn leaves/raspberries on mc mottle, 2¼x6¼" 1,250.00
Bowl, bleeding hearts, red on gr/yel/red, ridged/ftd, 4" 1,000.00
Bowl, fuchsia, gr/brn/red on purple to wht, 2½x5½" 1,750.00
Box, bird/fox in winter, cut/pnt on opal, flat lid, 5" dia 4,400.00
Box, clovers/blossoms, cut/pnt on opal, dome lid, 3" dia 2,500.00
Box, irises/gilt on yel opal, 5½" dia 2,000.00
Box, roses/honey bee/5 cabachons, cut/pnt/gilt, 6" dia 4,800.00
Ewer, tulips/flower frieze, cut/pnt on gr/orange mottle, 4½" 2,500.00
Lamp, perfume; gold daisies on orange texture, wavy base, 7" .1,500.00
Salt bucket, windmill/harbor, blk on opal texture, hdls, 1¼" 500.00
Toothpick holder, winter scene, 2½" 950.00
Vase, bare trees/road, cut/pnt on yel/rust, bottle form, 7½" 1,800.00
Vase, birch trees cut/pnt on bl shaded, 12" 3,000.00
Vase, bleeding hearts, cut/pnt on mc mottle, ftd, 8" 1,400.00
Vase, bleeding hearts, red on amber/frost mottle, 3½" 800.00
Vase, blkberries, dk bl/gr on bl & frost mottle, ftd, 15" 3,400.00
Vase, bud; poppies, orange on yel/brn w/gold, 7x2" 1,500.00
Vase, butterfly/berries, wine/gilt on stripes, stick neck, 6" 1,500.00
Vase, carnations, gr on pk/opal martele w/fp, 5x5" 3,200.00
Vase, cornflowers, cut/pnt/gilt on gray/pk mottle, 8" 3,300.00
Vase, cornflowers, cut/pnt/gilt on yel/amethyst, 3½" 1,400.00
Vase, currants & leaves, cut/pnt on yel & purple mottle, 3½" 750.00
Vase, lake/trees, gr on yel & wht, cross mk, slender, 25" 3,600.00
Vase, leafy branches, brn on purple mottle & gold, 9x10" 1,200.00
Vase, leaves/seed pods, brn on yel/orange mottle, 3" 210.00
Vase, morning-glories, red/gr-blk on yel, trumpet form, 23" 2,400.00
Vase, orchids/buds, maroon on citron to blk, trumpet neck, 4" ...1,300.00
Vase, rampant lion, gold on emerald texture, slim, 12" 3,000.00
Vase, roses w/gold bee etc on textured pk, cylindrical, 6" 900.00
Vase, snow scene, yel & red w/mottling, 8" 1,600.00
Vase, trees fr village silhouette, gr on orange/yel, 11" 4,000.00
Vase, trees/grass, gr/red on lt bl, bbl form, 2" 850.00
Vase, trees/mtns, orange/gr on yel, ftd/shouldered, 16", EX 2,750.00
Vase, violets, cut/pnt on purple shaded, 4-sided, 4½x2" 1,800.00
Vase, 1 gilt iris/butterly on amethyst texture, sqd, 7½" 425.00

Miscellaneous

Bottle, scent; thistles, etch/pnt on amethyst, bulbous, 4" 220.00
Bowl, ice-gr w/sm bubbles, flat notched edge, thick, 10" 275.00
Bowl, 4-color mottle, pinched to form sq rim, 3½x9" 690.00
Box, smoky amber w/etched concentric rings, 3x5" dia 375.00
Candlestick, brn stripe on rope-twist std, 21" 575.00
Decanter, windmill/lake/man in boat HP on opal, 9½x4½" 2,200.00
Tray, pate-de-verre frog on rim of lily pad, 2¼x6½" 1,600.00
Tumbler, orange-amber mottle, swollen cylinder, 5" 230.00
Vase, etched angle panels on rings, clear on smoke, 16" 485.00
Vase, etched chevrons/geometrics on amber w/gold foil, 10" ..4,000.00
Vase, etched geometrics/stepped designs on amber, 15x11" 3,000.00
Vase, etched overlapping sqs, clear on frost, U-form, 10" 865.00
Vase, etched scroll & dot panels, frost/fp amber, 12½" 575.00
Vase, etched zigzag berry branches, amber, flared neck, 17" 575.00
Vase, int dk bl over bl-gr flecks, ribbed clear ext, 15" 575.00

Vase, lt gr, tapered cylinder w/incurvate rim, 9" 230.00
Vase, smoke, banded, flared rim, 10" 690.00
Vase, streaky amber blown into iron scrollwork fr, 14½" 1,150.00
Vase, topaz, Deco ribs/facets, polished, U-form, 11½" 440.00
Vase, winter scene w/houses HP on gold frost, 16" 525.00
Vase, yel/bl mottle, flat-sided oval w/sqd rim, 5x7" 210.00

De Vez

De Vez was a type of acid-cut French cameo glass produced by Cristallerie de Pantin in Paris around the turn of the century. Our advisor for this category is Don Williams; he is listed in the Directory under Missouri.

Cameo

Atomizer, sailboats/rowboat on lake, dk gr/orange, mk, 12" 1,500.00
Rose bowl, trees/water, blk on gold w/pk satin, 3" H 650.00
Vase, berried branch, gr on red/yel mottle, slim baluster, 7" 400.00
Vase, floral, bl on yel, ovoid, 6" 250.00
Vase, mtn scene, bl on yel, 7" 750.00
Vase, palms/river/bldg/mtns/birds, EX colors, 8" 1,150.00
Vase, river/house/girl w/geese, tapered, 7½" 1,000.00
Vase, trees, tan on lime/bl, tapered, 8" 500.00
Vase, water/village/mtns, red shades w/gr trees, 9½" 850.00

De Vilbiss

Perfume bottles, atomizers, and dresser accessories marketed by the De Vilbiss Company are appreciated by collectors today for the various types of lovely glassware used in their manufacture as well as for their pleasing shapes. Various companies provided the glass, while De Vilbiss made only the metal tops. They marketed their merchandise not only here but in Paris, England, Canada, and Havana as well. Their marks were acid stamped, ink stamped, in gold script, molded in, or on paper labels. One is no more significant than another. For more information we recommend *Bedroom and Bathroom Glassware of the Depression Years* by Margaret and Kenn Whitmyer; their address is listed in the Directory under Ohio. Our advisor for this category is Randy Monsen; he is listed in the Directory under Virginia.

Atomizer, dk bl enamel w/blk decor, orig bulb & cord, 5¼" 65.00
Atomizer, ebony, long cord, tasseled bulb, 6¼" 110.00
Atomizer, gold crackle, beaded flower on top, 4¾" 85.00
Atomizer, Imperial line, cased glass w/jewels, complete, 7¼" ..3,575.00

Atomizer, smoke with gold duck decoration, paper stickers, 6", $75.00.

Atomizer, lt gr, Opalescent Windows, 5" 95.00
Bottle, scent; allover gold, 8" 200.00
Bottle, scent; cut, gold-encrusted, sgn Hawkes, 10" 450.00
Bottle, scent; orange o/l w/Deco decor, 6¾", +7" atomizer 525.00
Bottle, scent; smoke gray, hand blown, sm 300.00
Dresser set, atomizer+2 jars+tray, gold enamel w/mc florals 415.00
Lamp, perfume; Fairies at My Garden Gate, brass base, 7¼" 360.00
Lamp, perfume, Deco nude trio, blk on wht, brass trim, 10¾" 715.00
Lamp, perfume, nude figure on glass insert, 7" 245.00
Pin tray, blk matt w/gold trim 40.00

Decanters

Ceramic whiskey decanters were brought into prominence in 1955 by the James Beam Distilling Company. Few other companies besides Beam produced these decanters during the next ten years or so; however, other companies did eventually follow suit. At its peak in 1975, at least twenty prominent companies and several on a lesser scale made these decanters. Beam stopped making decanters in mid-1992. Now only a couple of companies are still producing these collectibles.

Liquor dealers have told collectors for years that ceramic decanters are not as valuable, and in some cases worthless, if emptied or if the federal tax stamp has been broken. Nothing is further from the truth. Following are but a few of many reasons you should consider emptying ceramic decanters:

1) If the thin glaze on the inside ever cracks (and it does in a small percentage of decanters), the contents will push through to the outside. It is then referred to as a 'leaker' and worth a fraction of its original value.

2) A large number of decanters left full in one area of your house poses a fire hazard.

3) A burglar, after stealing jewelry and electronics, may make off with some of your decanters just to enjoy the contents. If they are empty, chances are they will not be bothered.

4) It is illegal in most states for collectors to sell a full decanter without a liquor license.

Unlike years ago, few collectors now collect all types of decanters. Most now specialize. For example, they may collect trains, cars, owls, Indians, clowns, or any number of different things that have been depicted on or as a decanter. They are finding exceptional quality available at reasonable prices, especially when compared with many other types of collectibles.

We have tried to list those brands that are the most popular with collectors. Likewise, individual decanters listed are the ones (or representative of the ones) most commonly found. The following listing is but a small fraction of the thousands of decanters that have been produced.

These decanters come from all over the world. While Jim Beam owned its own china factory in the U.S., some of the others have been imported from Mexico, Taiwan, Japan and elsewhere. They vary in size from miniatures (approximately 2-oz.) to gallons. Values range from a few dollars to more than $3,000.00 per decanter.

Most collectors and dealers define a 'mint' decanter as one with no chips, no cracks, and label intact. A missing federal tax stamp or lack of contents have no bearing on value. All values are given for 'mint' decanters. A 'mini' behind a listing indicates a miniature. All others are fifth or 750 ml unless noted otherwise. Our advisor for this category is Roy Willis; he is listed in the Directory under Kentucky.

Aesthetic Specialties (ASI)

Golf, Bing Crosby 40th 38.00

Stanley Steamer, 1909, gr or blk, ea 50.00
World's Greatest Golfer 40.00

Beam

Casino Series, Barney's Slot, 1.75 L 30.00
Casino Series, Slot Machine, bl 18.00
Casino Series, Slot Machine, gray 10.00
Customer Series, ABC Liquors 6.00
Customer Series, Bohemian Girl 20.00
Customer Series, Delco Battery 30.00
Customer Series, Harry Hoffman 5.00
Customer Series, Ponderosa House 8.00
Customer Series, Travelodge 10.00
Executive Series, 1967 Prestige 15.00
Executive Series, 1968 Presidential 12.00
Executive Series, 1969 Sovereign 10.00
Executive Series, 1970 Charisma 12.00
Executive Series, 1971 Fantasia 12.00
Executive Series, 1972 Regency 12.00
Organization Series, Bowling Proprietors 10.00
Organization Series, Chili Society 10.00
Organization Series, Ducks Unlimited #13, 1987 ....45.00
Organization Series, Ducks Unlimited #14, 1988 ....40.00
Organization Series, Ducks Unlimited #15, 1989 ....100.00
Organization Series, Ducks Unlimited #16, 1990 ....45.00
Organization Series, Ducks Unlimited #17, 1991 ....30.00

Beam, Wheel Series, Fire Chief's Car, 1928, MIB, $110.00.

Wheel Series, Ambulance 75.00
Wheel Series, Cable Car, 1983 ....55.00
Wheel Series, Chevy, 1953 Corvette, wht 175.00
Wheel Series, Chevy, 1957 Bellair Convertible, red 90.00
Wheel Series, Chevy, 1957 Corvette, blk 70.00
Wheel Series, Chevy, 1969 Camaro, bl 55.00
Wheel Series, Chevy, 1978 Corvette, red or yel, ea 70.00
Wheel Series, Circus Wagon 25.00
Wheel Series, Duesenberg, 1934 Convertible, dk bl 130.00
Wheel Series, Duesenberg, 1934 Convertible, lt bl 110.00
Wheel Series, Fire Engine, 1930 Ford 175.00
Wheel Series, Ford, Police Paddy Wagon 175.00
Wheel Series, Ford, 1934 Roadster, cream 80.00
Wheel Series, Ford, 1956 Thunderbird, gr or gray, ea 85.00
Wheel Series, Ford, 1964 Mustang, red 80.00
Wheel Series, Race Car, Olsonite Eagle 75.00
Wheel Series, Tractor Trailer, Jim Beam, wht 70.00
Wheel Series, Train, Boxcar, brn or yel, ea 65.00
Wheel Series, Train, Caboose, red, yel or gray, ea 70.00

Wheel Series, Train, Coal Tender for Grant 75.00
Wheel Series, Train, Dining Car 100.00
Wheel Series, Train, Locomotive, General 110.00
Wheel Series, Train, Locomotive, JB Turner 150.00
Wheel Series, Train, Locomotive, Grant 85.00
Wheel Series, Train, Passenger Car 50.00
Wheel Series, Train, Track, per section 20.00
Wheel Series, Train, Wood Tender for General 85.00
Wheel Series, Volkswagen, bl or red, ea 75.00
Wheel Series, Wood Tender for JB Turner 75.00

Brooks

American Legion, Denver, 1972 ....18.00
Amvets, Polish Legion 10.00
Bareknuckle Fighter 10.00
Cannon 8.00
Cards, Jack, Queen or King, ea 12.00
CB Convoy 7.00
Clown w/Accordion or Balloons 25.00
Clydesdale 18.00
Deadwagon 10.00
Delta Belle 12.00
Elephant, Asian 18.00
Foremost Astronaut 10.00
Grandfather Clock 10.00
Greensboro Open, 1972 ....25.00
Groucho Marx 50.00
Harold's Club Dice 10.00
Indy Racer #21 ....45.00
Jayhawk, Kansas 10.00
Kitten on Pillow 12.00
Liquor Square 8.00
Maine Potato 10.00
Owl #1, Ol' Ez 30.00
Owl #2, Eagle 60.00
Owl #3, Snowy 35.00
Owl #4, Scops 25.00
Owl #5, Great Gray 35.00
Pontiac Race Car 40.00
Sailfish 10.00
Ski Boot 10.00
Spirit of St Louis 12.00
Stove, Potbelly 10.00
Ticker Tape 8.00

Cyrus Noble

Assayer 110.00
Bartender 125.00
Bartender, mini 18.00
Gambler's Lady 45.00
Mine Shaft 40.00
Music Man 30.00
Snowshoe Thompson 150.00
Snowshoe Thompson, mini 20.00

Double Springs

Bentley, 1927 ....30.00
Cadillac, 1913 ....22.00
Matador 12.00
Mercer, 1911 ....30.00
Owl, brn or red, ea 12.00

Eagle, Rare

#1, 1979	25.00
#2, 1980	30.00
#3, 1981	35.00
#4, 1982	35.00
Nature Series, #1, 1983	75.00
Nature Series, #2, 1984	75.00

Famous Firsts

Dewitt Clinton Locomotive	25.00
Lockheed C-130	85.00
P-51 Mustang	125.00
Riverboat, Robert E Lee	80.00
Sewing Machine	50.00
Sewing Machine, mini	22.00
Telephone, French	65.00
Telephone, Johnny Reb	25.00

Grenadier

Frosty the Snowman	35.00
Horse, Saddlebred	30.00
Horse, Tennessee Walking	25.00
Lafayette	30.00
Napoleon	35.00

Hoffman

Betsy Ross	50.00
Cats, 6 different, mini, ea	14.00
Children of the World, 6 different, ea	25.00
Eagle, Bicentennial	45.00
Horses, 6 different, mini, ea	18.00
Mr Lucky Series, Bartender	35.00
Mr Lucky Series, Bartender, mini	15.00
Mr Lucky Series, Railroad Engineer	35.00
Mr Lucky Series, Railroad Engineer, mini	16.00
Mr Lucky Series, Stockbroker	40.00
Mr Lucky Series, Stockbroker, mini	15.00

Lionstone

Annie Oakley	20.00
Bath, Saturday Nite	75.00
Bath, Saturday Nite, mini	22.00
Bluebirds, Eastern	25.00
Bluebirds, Western	20.00
Clowns, 6 different, ea	40.00
Clowns, 6 different, mini, ea	22.00
Cowboy	20.00
Engineer, Railroad	25.00
Fireman, #1 Holding Hose, red hat	100.00
Fireman, #1 Holding Hose, yel hat	125.00
Fireman, #2 Carrying Child	95.00
Fireman, #3 Sliding Down Pole	85.00
Frontiersman	20.00
Indian, Proud	18.00
Laundryman, Chinese	18.00
Lonely Luke	28.00
Lonely Luke, mini	15.00
Molly Brown	20.00
Sheriff	18.00

Swallow, Capistrano	30.00
Swallow, Capsitrano, mini	10.00
Telegrapher	25.00
Woodhawk	20.00

McCormick

Austin, Stephen	20.00
Clark, Captain William	25.00
Durante, Jimmy	45.00
Elvis, Gold Tribute	190.00
Elvis, Gold Tribute, mini	125.00
Elvis, Karate	250.00
Elvis, Karate, mini	80.00
Elvis, Sergeant	275.00
Elvis, Sergeant, mini	80.00
Elvis, Silver Anniversary	125.00
Elvis, Silver Anniversary, mini	70.00
Iwo Jima	130.00
Iwo Jima, mini	75.00
JR Ewing	40.00

McCormick, Gunfighter Series, Black Bart, 14", $35.00.

Marilyn Monroe	375.00
Marilyn Monroe, mini	95.00
Telephone, Strowger	30.00
Train, Jupiter Locomotive	20.00
Train, Mail Car or Passenger Car, ea	30.00
Train, set of 4, mini	40.00
Train, Wood Tender	20.00

Michter

Goddess Selket	35.00
Goddess Selket, mini	25.00
Goddess Selket, 1.75 L	45.00
Queen Nefertiti	38.00
Queen Nefertiti, mini	25.00
Queen Nefertiti, 1.75 L	75.00

Mike Wayne

Barrel, Elijah Wayne 25.00
Mercedes, 450 SL 25.00
Pope John Paul II 22.00
Rockwell Portraits, 4 different, ea 25.00

Old Bardstown

Iron Worker 35.00
Kentucky Colonel 25.00
Trucker 30.00
Wildcat #1 ....65.00
Wildcat #2 ....35.00
Wildcat #3 ....225.00

Old Commonwealth

Auburn Tigers 35.00
Boot, Western 25.00
Boot, Western, mini 12.00
Fisherman, Keeper 45.00
Irish, Idyll 15.00
Irish & the Sea 28.00
Leprechaun #1, 1980 ....35.00
Lumberjack 30.00
Virginia, University of 8.00
Waterfowler #1, 1978 ....50.00

Old Fitzgerald

Four Seasons, ea 5.00
Leprechaun, 1968 Praise God 30.00
Leprechaun, 1983 Praise Be 250.00
Old Ironsides 5.00

Pacesetter

Fire Truck, Pirsch Pumper 65.00
Shell Gas Pump 50.00
Tractor, Green Machine, 4-wheel drive 150.00
Tractor, Steiger, 4-wheel drive 150.00

Ski Country

Barrel Racer 65.00
Barrel Racer, mini 25.00
Caveman 25.00
Caveman, mini 15.00
Duck, Mallard, 1980 ....60.00
Duck, Mallard, 1980, mini 40.00
Duck, Merganzer, Male 75.00
Duck, Merganzer, Male, mini 20.00
Eagle, Majestic 300.00
Eagle, Majestic, mini 110.00
Eagle, Mountain 110.00
Eagle, Mountain, mini 80.00
Owl, Barred Wall Plaque 100.00
Owl, Barred Wall Plaque, mini 35.00
Pelican 50.00
Pelican, mini 30.00
Ruffed Grouse 60.00
Ruffed Grouse, mini 25.00
Wild Turkey 110.00

Wild Turkey, mini 95.00

Wild Turkey

Series I, #1, #2, #3, or #4, mini, ea 15.00
Series I, #1, 1971 ....260.00
Series I, #2 ....160.00
Series I, #3 or #4, ea 70.00
Series I, #5 ....35.00
Series I, #6 or #7, ea 25.00
Series I, #8 ....45.00
Series I, set of #5, #6, #7 & #8, mini 130.00
Series II, Lore #1 ....25.00
Series II, Lore #2 ....35.00
Series II, Lore #3 ....45.00
Series II, Lore #4 ....50.00
Series III, #1, In Flight 110.00
Series III, #1, In Flight, mini 45.00
Series III, #10, Turkey & Coyote 90.00
Series III, #10, Turkey & Coyote, mini 45.00
Series III, #11, Turkey & Falcon 90.00
Series III, #11, Turkey & Falcon, mini 45.00
Series III, #12, Turkey & Skunks 90.00
Series III, #12, Turkey & Skunks, mini 45.00
Series III, #2, Turkey & Bobcat 140.00
Series III, #2, Turkey & Bobcat, mini 45.00
Series III, #3, Fighting Turkeys 160.00
Series III, #3, Fighting Turkeys, mini 45.00
Series III, #4, Turkey & Eagle 90.00
Series III, #4, Turkey & Eagle, mini 80.00
Series III, #5, Turkey & Raccoon 90.00
Series III, #5, Turkey & Raccoon, mini 45.00
Series III, #6, Turkey & Poults 90.00
Series III, #6, Turkey & Poults, mini 45.00
Series III, #7, Turkey & Red Fox 90.00
Series III, #7, Turkey & Red Fox, mini 45.00
Series III, #8, Turkey & Owl 90.00
Series III, #8, Turkey & Owl, mini 45.00
Series III, #9, Turkey & Bear Cubs 90.00
Series III, #9, Turkey & Bear Cubs, mini 45.00

Decoys

American colonists learned the craft of decoy making from the Indians who used them to lure birds out of the sky as an important food source. Early models were carved from wood such as pine, cedar, balsa, etc., and a few were made of canvas or papier-mache. There are two basic types of decoys: water floaters and shorebirds (also called 'stick-ups'). Within each type are many different species, ducks being the most plentiful since they migrated along all four of America's great waterways. Market hunting became big business around 1880, resulting in large-scale commercial production of decoys which continued until about 1910 when such hunting was outlawed by the Migratory Bird Treaty.

Today decoys are one of the most collectible types of American folk art. The most valuable are those carved by such artists as Laing, Crowell, Ward, and Wheeler, to name only a few. Each area, such as Massachusetts, Connecticut, Maine, the Illinois River, and the Delaware River, produces decoys with distinctive regional characteristics. Examples of commercial decoys produced by well-known factories — among them Mason, Stevens, and Dodge — are also prized by collectors. Though mass-produced, these nevertheless required a certain amount of hand carving and decorating. Well-carved examples, especially those of rare species, are appreciating rapidly, and those with original paint are more desirable. Writer Carl F. Luckey has compiled a fully illustrated identification and value guide, *Collecting Antique Bird Decoys*; you will find his address in the Directory under Alabama. In the listings that follow, all decoys are solid-bodied unless noted hollow.

Key:
OP — original paint   RP — repaint
ORP — old repaint   WOP — worn original paint
OWP — original working paint   WRP — working repaint

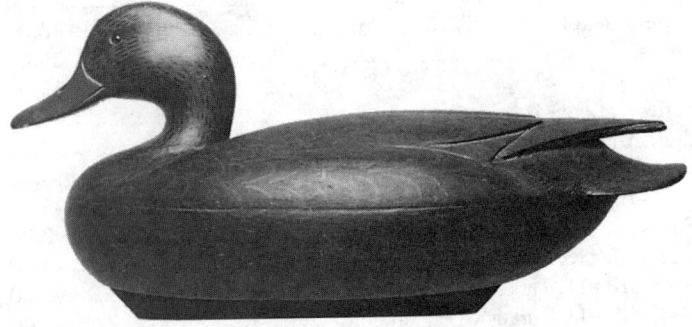

Black Duck, John McLoughlin, hollow carved with crossed wing tips, EX details on NM paint, structurally EX, oversized, 20½", $1,900.00.

Blk Duck, Al McCormick, cork body, NM OP, pr 125.00
Blk Duck, Dude Crane, hollow, WOP hairline 125.00
Blk Duck, John Blair, preening, ORP worn to OP, roughness ..1,500.00
Blk Duck, Ira Hudson, football body, EX OP, sm crack, '20s ...1,000.00
Blk Duck, Ira Hudson, football type, WOP, some RP, EX 500.00
Blk Duck, Jester Family, M OP 100.00
Blk Duck, Keyes Chadwick, NM OP, sm split & dents 300.00
Blk Duck, Premier Grade, Mason Factory, NM OP, hairline ...2,300.00
Blk Duck, sleeping, E Crowell, rstr pnt, pre-stamp style 1,050.00
Blk Duck, Wildfowler Factory, EX OP, magnum sz 50.00
Blk-Bellied Plover, Chief Cuffee, 3-pc body, M 400.00
Blk-Bellied Plover, Mason Factory, tack eyes, EX OP 900.00
Bluebill hen, Premier Grade, Mason Factory, EX OP w/some RP ..550.00
Bluebill hen, WH Wilkens, NM OP, tiny dents 175.00
Bluebill pr, James Currier, EX OP, ca 1930 ....950.00
Bluebill pr, Premier Grade, Mason Factory, EX OP, dents 1,500.00
Bluebill pr, Ward Bros, slightly trn heads, 1972, M 1,750.00
Bluewing Teal drake, Standard Grade, Mason Factory, EX OP ..850.00
Brandt, R Madison Mitchell, preening, M OP, sgn, dtd 1976 .2,500.00
Canada Goose, Joseph Lincoln, detailed NM OP, nail in neck ..3,000.00
Canada Goose, R Madison Mitchel, NM OP, sgn, dtd 1974 ......475.00
Canada Goose, swimming, Charles Wilbur, NM OP, sm crack ..250.00
Canvasbk drake, Challenge Grade, Mason Factory, EX OP 1,200.00
Canvasbk drake, Jim Currier, high head, EX OP, ca 1918 ....500.00
Canvasbk drake, John Graham, high head, EX OP, ca 1900, rprs ..225.00
Canvasbk drake, Ward Bros, trn head, EX OP, 1930s, rstr 800.00
Canvasbk pr, Premier Grade, Mason Factory, NM OP, chip/shot .2,250.00
Canvasbk pr, Virgil Lashbrook, trn heads, NM OP 400.00
Coot, preening, Ben Schmidt, orig keel & weight, NM OP 800.00
Dove, Herters Factory, molded, NM OP, structurally EX 125.00
Dowicher, Mason Factory, glass eyes, EX OP, shot, EX 500.00
Golden Plover, Joseph Lincoln, tack eyes, NM OP, lightly shot ..1,500.00
Goldeneye drake, Premier Grade, Mason Factory, EX OP, rstr ..1,400.00
Goldeneye hen, Augustus Wilson, WOP, glass eyes, 1920s 300.00
Goldeneye hen, Challenge Grade, Mason Factory, EX OP, rprs .900.00
Greenwing Teal drake, Charles Hart, EX cvg, NM OP 5,000.00
Mallard drake, Billy Shaw, EX OP, sm crack, ca 1925, EX 500.00
Mallard drake, Challenge Grade, Mason Factory, EX OP, rprs ...550.00

Mallard drake, Charles Perdew, RP in Perdew style, sm rpr 450.00
Mallard drake, R Madison, M OP, sgn, dtd 1958 ....175.00
Mallard hen, Challenge Grade, Mason Factory, EX OP, lt shot .300.00
Mallard hen, Lem & Steve Ward, EX OP, 1960, NM 1,200.00
Pintail drake, Miles Hancock, EX OP, sm hairline in bill 325.00
Pintail drake, Robert F McGraw, WOP, ca 1925-30 ....750.00
Pintail drake, Ward Bros, balsa body, trn head, old RP 475.00
Pintail hen, Ward Bros, slightly trn head, EX OP, ca 1936 .....2,750.00
Redbreasted Robin Snipe, Elmer Crowell, NM OP, sm flake 550.00
Redhead drake, att Walter Bailey, EX old RP, rpr cracks 125.00
Redhead drake, Captain Ben Dye, old RP, teardrop form, EX ...650.00
Redhead drake, Harry V Shourds, full bodied, NM OP, EX 7,000.00
Redhead drake, Premier Grade, Mason Factory, WOP, ca 1900 .300.00
Redhead hen, Paul Gibson, EX OP, minor crack, ca 1945 ....170.00
Redhead pr, Ward Bros, trn heads, NM OP, ca 1969 ....1,700.00
Robin, Elmer Crowell, NM OP w/EX patina, hairline crack 850.00
Ruddy drake, Elmer Crowell, NM OP, tiny flake 600.00
Ruddy Turnstone, Strater & Sohier, folding, tin, Pat 1874, EX ..200.00
Scaup drake, Tom Gaskill, NM OP, ca 1900-10 ....850.00
Scaup hen, Premier Grade, Mason Factory, rpt, ca 1900, EX 180.00
Surf Scoter, Joseph Lincoln, canvas covered, old RP, EX 425.00
Widgeon drake, Ben Schmidt, trn head, NM OP, 1940s 1,700.00
Widgeon drake, Miles Hancock, NM OP, structurally EX 900.00
Wood Duck drake, Ben Schmidt, OP & detailed cvg, M 2,400.00
Yellowlegs, Marc McNair, Cape Cod style, NM OP, raised wings ..800.00

Dedham Pottery

Originally founded in Chelsea, Massachusetts, as the Chelsea Keramic Works, the name was changed to Dedham Pottery in 1895 after the firm relocated in Dedham, near Boston, Massachusetts. The ware utilized a gray stoneware body with a crackle glaze and simple cobalt border designs of flowers, birds, and animals. Decorations were brushed on by hand using an ancient Chinese method which suspended the cobalt within the overall glaze. There were thirteen standard patterns, among them Magnolia, Iris, Butterfly, Duck, Polar Bear, and Rabbit, the latter of which was chosen to represent the company on their logo. On the very early pieces, the rabbits face left; decorators soon found the reverse position easier to paint, and the rabbits were turned to the right. In addition to the standard patterns, other designs were produced for special orders. These and artist-signed pieces are highly valued by collectors today.

Though their primary product was the blue-printed, crackle-glazed dinnerware, two types of artware were also produced: crackle glaze and flambe. Their notable volcanic ware was a type of the latter. The mark is incised and often accompanies the cipher of Hugh Robertson. The firm was operated by succeeding generations of the Robertson family until it closed in 1943. Our advisor for this category is Dale MacLean; he is listed in the Directory under Massachusetts. See also Chelsea Keramic Art Works.

Dinnerware

Ashtray, Rabbit, stamped registered, 3¾" 220.00
Bacon rasher, Rabbit, stamped/imp, 9¾x6¼" 375.00
Bonbon, Rabbit, stamped registered, 3½x5½" 400.00
Bowl, Chick, oblong, #6, rstr, 2x7½" 800.00
Bowl, Crab, #7, flakes, 2x3½" 400.00
Bowl, Rabbit, sq, stamped registered, 2½x8" 500.00
Bowl, Rabbit, stamped, 2¾x6" 225.00
Bowl, Rabbit, stamped, 3½x7¾" 450.00
Bowl, soup; Rabbit, deep, lg rim, stamped/imp, 1½x9¼" 210.00
Bowl, soup; Single-Ear Rabbit, shallow, stamped, 1¼x8¼" 300.00

Bowl, whipped cream; Elephant & Baby, stamped registered, 7½" .700.00
Bowl, whipped cream; Rabbit, stamped, 2½x7¼" 250.00
Butter pat, Wild Rose, stamped registered, 3½" 275.00
Candlesticks, Rabbits, stamped registered, 1½x3½", pr 450.00
Casserole, Rabbit, Robertson rebus, stamped/imp, 2x8¼" 350.00
Charger, Rabbit, stamped, 12" 475.00
Cheese tray, Rabbit, stamped registered, 5½x5½" 750.00
Creamer, Horse Chestnut, stamped, 3½x5½" 250.00
Creamer, Rabbit, stamped registered, 3½x3¾" 350.00
Cup & saucer, bouillon; Rabbit, stamped, 2x5¼", 6" 170.00
Cup & saucer, coffee; Elephant & Baby, stamped registered 400.00
Cup & saucer, coffee; Rabbit, stamped, 2x4½", 6" 230.00
Cup & saucer, demitasse; Rabbit, stamped, 2⅛x3", 4½" 250.00
Egg cup, Rabbit, 2½x2¼" 170.00
Goblet, Rabbit, ovoid, ped ft, stamped, 4¾x3" 450.00
Knife rest, Rabbit form, EX details, stamped, rstr, 3½" L 425.00
Marmalade, Azalea, stamped, 4¾x4¼" 400.00
Nappy, Double Turtle, stamped registered, 1½x5¾" 500.00
Nappy, Grape, flared rim, stamped, 2⅛x9¾" 240.00
Nappy, Rabbit, flared rim, stamped registered, 2x7¼" 210.00
Nappy, Rabbit, flared rim, stamped registered, 2x9¼" 250.00
Pitcher, Night & Morning scenes, stamped, 5" 600.00
Pitcher, Rabbit, early, #3, 8½" 450.00
Pitcher, Rabbit, long neck, stamped registered, 5¼" 425.00
Pitcher, Rabbit, stamped registered, exhibition sticker, 4½" 400.00
Pitcher, Rabbit, 2 bl/1 floral band, early, #7, 8¾x6" 500.00
Pitcher, Standing Rabbit, stamped, 4½" 800.00
Plate, Bird in Potted Orange Tree, imp, 10⅛" 750.00
Plate, Butterfly, stamped/imp, 8¼" 500.00
Plate, Day Lily, Davenport rebus, stamped/imp, 8½" 1,000.00
Plate, Dolphin, stamped, 8¾", NM 600.00
Plate, Double Turtle, stamped registered, 6" 750.00
Plate, Duck, stamped/imp, 8½" 275.00
Plate, Elephant, stamped, child's, 1x7½" 800.00
Plate, Elephant & Baby, stamped/imp, 6" 500.00
Plate, Grape, stamped registered/imp, 7½" 145.00
Plate, Grape, stamped/imp, 8½" 160.00
Plate, Horse Chestnut, stamped/imp, 6" 165.00
Plate, Horse Chestnut, stamped/imp, 8½" 250.00
Plate, Iris, stamped registered/imp rabbits, 6" 180.00
Plate, Lion Tapestry, stamped/imp, 8½", EX 925.00
Plate, Lobster, stamped registered/imp, 6" 425.00
Plate, Magnolia, Davenport rebus, stamped/imp, 10", NM 300.00
Plate, Magnolia, Davenport rebus, stamped/imp, 6" 280.00
Plate, Magnolia, stamped, 8½" 195.00
Plate, Owl, stamped/imp, 6¼", NM 2,300.00
Plate, Polar Bear, stamped registered/imp, 8½" 700.00
Plate, Polar Bear, stamped Tercentenary, 6" 650.00
Plate, Pond Lily, Davenport rebus, stamped/imp, 6" 290.00
Plate, Pond Lily, Davenport rebus, stamped/imp, 9¾" 340.00
Plate, Pond Lily, stamped/imp, 8¼" 235.00
Plate, Rabbit, Davenport rebus, stamped/imp, 6" 210.00
Plate, Rabbit, stamped, 10" 240.00
Plate, Rabbit, stamped registered/imp, 7½" 180.00
Plate, Snow Tree, Davenport rebus, stamped/imp, 6" 250.00
Plate, Swan, stamped registered/imp, 8½" 350.00
Plate, Tufted Duck, imp, 6¼" 300.00
Plate, Turkey, Davenport rebus, stamped, 10", NM 325.00
Plate, Turkey, stamped, 6" 275.00
Plate, White Lobster, sgn HR, stamped/imp, rstr, 8½" 800.00
Platter, roast; Rabbit, stamped, 17½x10½", NM 900.00
Platter, steak; Wolf Chasing Owl, stamped/imp, 14x8½" 16,000.00
Shaker, Azalea, stamped, 2⅛x2¼" 110.00
Shakers, Rabbit, floral bands at shoulders, pnt mk, 2¾", pr 400.00

Stein, Rabbit, Davenport rebus, inscribed/stamped, 4¾" 600.00
Sugar bowl, Rabbit, w/lid, stamped, 4½x5" 475.00
Teapot, Rabbit, sticker ca 1948, 6½" 800.00
Toothpick holder, White Tulip, stamped registered, 2½" 900.00

Miscellaneous

Vase, brn/wht/bl drip glaze, trial, sgn HCR, 8" 525.00
Vase, buff-colored gloss, can neck, bulbous base, HCR, 3½x3¾" ..175.00
Vase, irid oxblood drip, trial, HCR, 7½" 880.00
Vase, oxblood/bl volcanic glaze, trial, sgn WA, 6", NM 385.00
Vase, sang-de-boeuf w/gold lustred finish, provenance, 5½" 2,000.00
Vase, thick sang-de-boeuf metallic irid, can neck, mk, 5", NM ..550.00

Degenhart

The Crystal Art Glass factory in Cambridge, Ohio, opened in 1947 under the private ownership of John and Elizabeth Degenhart. John had previously worked for the Cambridge Glass Company and was well known for his superior paperweights. After his death in 1964, Elizabeth took over management of the factory, hiring several workers from the defunct Cambridge Company, including Zack Boyd. Boyd was responsible for many unique colors, some of which were named for him. From 1964 to 1974, more than twenty-seven different moulds were created, most of them resulting from Elizabeth Degenhart's work and creativity, and over 145 official colors were developed. Elizabeth died in 1978, requesting that the ten moulds she had built while operating the factory were to be turned over to the Degenhart Museum. The remaining moulds were to be held by the Island Mould and Machine Company, who (complying with her request) removed the familiar 'D in heart' trademark. The factory was eventually bought by Zack's son, Bernard Boyd. He also acquired the remaining Degenhart moulds, to which he added his own logo.

In general, slags and opaques should be valued 15% to 20% higher than crystals in color.

Toothpick holders: Forget-Me-Not, Baby Pink Slag, $30.00; Beaded Oval, Amber, $25.00; Daisy and Button, Sapphire, $15.00.

Beaded Oval Toothpick, Amberina 25.00
Beaded Oval Toothpick, Cobalt 20.00
Beaded Oval Toothpick, Maverick 45.00
Beaded Oval Toothpick, Opal 20.00
Beaded Oval Toothpick, Rubina 60.00
Beaded Oval Toothpick, Teal 15.00
Bell, Butterscotch 25.00
Bell, Misty Green 12.00
Bell, Pearl Gray 20.00
Bird Salt & Pepper, Apple Green 50.00
Bird Salt & Pepper, Emerald Green 30.00
Bird Salt & Pepper, Ivory 45.00

Bird Salt & Pepper, Mint Green	50.00
Bird Salt & Pepper, Pink	40.00
Bird Salt & Pepper, Smoky Heather	35.00
Bird Salt w/Cherry, Angel Blue	15.00
Bird Salt w/Cherry, Burnt Amber	20.00
Bird Salt w/Cherry, Fog	15.00
Bird Salt w/Cherry, Lavender Marble	45.00
Bird Salt w/Cherry, Tomato	45.00
Bow Slipper, Olive	25.00
Bow Slipper, Willow Green	25.00
Chick Covered Dish, Aqua, 2"	30.00
Chick Covered Dish, Cobalt, 2"	20.00
Chick Covered Dish, Lemon Custard, 2"	60.00
Chick Covered Dish, Red, 2"	35.00
Coaster, Amberina	15.00
Coaster, Peach Blo	10.00
Coaster, Vaseline	8.00
Daisy & Button Creamer & Sugar, Bluebell	75.00
Daisy & Button Creamer & Sugar, Cobalt	90.00
Daisy & Button Salt, Amberina	15.00
Daisy & Button Salt, Cambridge Pink	15.00
Hand, Bittersweet	20.00
Hand, Desert Sun	12.00
Hand, Honey	6.00
Hand, Pine Green	15.00
Heart & Lyle Cup Plate, Brown	8.00
Heart & Lyle Cup Plate, Emerald Green	8.00
Heart & Lyle Cup Plate, Milk Blue	15.00
Heart Jewel Box, Chocolate Creme Slag	35.00
Heart Jewel Box, Cobalt Carnival	60.00
Heart Jewel Box, Fawn	20.00
Hen Covered Dish, 3", April Green	30.00
Hen Covered Dish, 3", Bittersweet	60.00
Hen Covered Dish, 3", Canary	25.00
Hen Covered Dish, 3", Gold	20.00
Hen Covered Dish, 3", Ivory	25.00
Hen Covered Dish, 3", Milk White	20.00
Hen Covered Dish, 3", Pigeon Blood	50.00
Hen Covered Dish, 3", Ruby	45.00
Hen Covered Dish, 5", Amber	40.00
Hen Covered Dish, 5", Caramel	100.00
Hen Covered Dish, 5", Crystal	35.00
Hen Covered Dish, 5", Mint Green	65.00
Kat Slipper, Blue Green	35.00
Kat Slipper, Concord Grape	20.00
Kat Slipper, Green Slag	35.00
Kat Slipper, Jade	40.00
Lamb Covered Dish, Amethyst	50.00
Lamb Covered Dish, Canary	35.00
Lamb Covered Dish, Cobalt	40.00
Lamb Covered Dish, Forest Green	50.00
Lamb Covered Dish, Ruby	75.00
Mini Pitcher, Cobalt Carnival	20.00
Mini Pitcher, Jade	25.00
Owl, Amberina	50.00
Owl, Bluebird #1 w/Custard	125.00
Owl, Buttercup	50.00
Owl, Chartruese	50.00
Owl, Crown Tuscan	36.00
Owl, Crystal	15.00
Owl, Dickie Bird	150.00
Owl, Elizabeth's Delight	300.00
Owl, Green Slag	45.00
Owl, Indigo	100.00

Owl, Lemonade	65.00
Owl, Orchid	35.00
Owl, Sea Foam	50.00
Owl, Tiger	40.00
Owl, Wondor Blue	45.00
Pooch, Brownie	15.00
Pooch, Caramel Custard Slag	35.00
Pooch, Cobalt Carnival	35.00
Pooch, Gray Blue Marble	22.50
Pooch, Green	20.00
Pooch, Old Lavender	25.00
Pooch, Sapphire	15.00
Pooch, Toffee	25.00
Portrait Plate, Amber	35.00
Portrait Plate, Blue & White Slag	200.00
Pottie, Amber	6.00
Pottie, Cobalt Carnival	20.00
Pottie, Fog	15.00
Pottie, Nile Green	15.00
Priscilla, Blue Lady	125.00
Priscilla, Daffodil	125.00
Priscilla, Periwinkle	95.00
Robin Covered Dish, Amber	35.00
Robin Covered Dish, Aqua	65.00
Robin Covered Dish, Custard Slag	125.00
Robin Covered Dish, Lavender Blue	90.00
Robin Covered Dish, Tangerine	175.00
Roller Skate, Apple Green	50.00
Roller Skate, Milk Blue	35.00
Seal of Ohio Cup Plate, Cobalt	15.00
Seal of Ohio Cup Plate, Heliotrope	25.00
Seal of Ohio Cup Plate, Sapphire	10.00
Star & Dewdrop Salt, Cobalt	15.00
Star & Dewdrop Salt, Heatherbloom	40.00
Star & Dewdrop Salt, Snow White	15.00
Stork & Peacock Child's Mug, Baby Green	25.00
Stork & Peacock Child's Mug, Sunset	20.00
Texas Boot, Chocolate Slag	25.00
Texas Boot, Sapphire	15.00
Texas Creamer & Sugar, Aqua	50.00
Texas Creamer & Sugar, Custard	100.00
Texas Creamer & Sugar, Ruby	120.00
Tomahawk, Blue & White Slag	75.00
Tomahawk, Milk Blue (NS)	50.00
Tomahawk, Sapphire	25.00
Turkey Covered Dish, Bluina	125.00
Turkey Covered Dish, Green Marble	85.00
Turkey Covered Dish, Tomato	125.00
Wildflower Candle Holder, Amber	25.00
Wildflower Candle Holder, Ruby	60.00
Wildflower Candy Dish, Bloody Mary	70.00
Wildflower Candy Dish, Crystal	20.00

Delatte

Delatte was a manufacturer of French cameo glass. Founded in 1921, their style reflected the influence of the Art Deco era with strong color contrasts and bold design. Our advisor for this category is Don Williams; he is listed in the Directory under Missouri.

Cameo

Lamp, floral, red on butterscotch, bullet form, 15"	2,785.00

Lamp, sea gulls, bl on olive frost shade & base, 17" **3,500.00**
Vase, fuchsia vines, rose on wht/raspberry mottle, 11" **1,000.00**
Vase, landscape along river, maroon/rose on wht, hdls, 9" **1,300.00**
Vase, rhododendron, wine on mc mottle, metal base, 16" **1,800.00**

Miscellaneous

Vase, abstract Deco motif, mc on cased red, bottle form, 11" **475.00**

Delft

Old Delftware, made as early as the 16th century, was originally a low-fired earthenware coated in a thin opaque tin glaze with painted-on blue or polychrome designs. It was not until the last half of the 19th century, however, that the ware became commonly referred to as Delft, acquiring the name from the Dutch village that had become the major center of its production. English, German, and French potters also produced Delft, though with noticeable differences both in shape and decorative theme.

In the early part of the 18th century, the German potter, Bottger, developed a formula for porcelain; in England, Wedgwood began producing creamware — both of which were much more durable. Unable to compete, one by one the Delft potteries failed. Soon only one remained. In 1876 De Porcelyne Fles reintroduced Delftware on a hard white body with blue and white decorative themes reflecting the Dutch countryside, windmills by the sea, and Dutch children. This manufacturer is the most well known of several operating today. Their products are now produced under the Royal Delft label. Examples listed here are blue on white unless noted otherwise. See also specific manufacturers.

Ashtray, floral, 3 rests, De Porcelyne mk, 1⅞x6½" **12.00**
Ashtray, windmill scene, appl shoes, 3 rests, 4x4⅝" **15.00**
Ashtray, windmill scene, shoe form, Delfts Holland, 2⅝" **8.00**
Bear jar, Dutch, mc on bl & mangagese, sgn JG/R, 10", VG ...**1,500.00**
Bottle, English, floral, 1770, rim chips, 9½" **450.00**
Bowl, barber's; Dutch, foliate scrolls & flowers, 18th C **215.00**
Bowl, Bristol, Oriental floral landscape, 1750s, 12", VG **1,300.00**
Bowl, fruit; English, florals/house, 1700s, 10½" **250.00**
Bowl, vegetable; Bl Parsley, w/lid, De Porcelyne mk, 9½" **42.00**
Butter tureen, Dutch, chinoiserie, w/lid, 18th C, 13" dia **185.00**
Butterdish, windmill scene, ¼-lb **16.50**
Charger, Dutch, boy/dolphin, floral/leaf border, 1700s, 14" **1,000.00**
Charger, English, Chinaman seated by fence, mc, 1750, rstr, 12" ...**385.00**
Charger, English, floral center/rim, mc, rpr, 13½" **300.00**
Creamer & sugar bowl, Bl Parsley, De Porcelyne mk **45.00**
Cup, English, floral landscape, int: I:S 1712, 2", VG **495.00**
Figurine, Dutch, recumbent cow, florals, 1780s, rstr, 9" **985.00**
Humidor, Dutch, floral cartouch titled St Vincent, 9", VG **220.00**
Pitcher & underplate, stylized flowers, Royal Delft, 3x2½" **22.00**
Plaque, Dutch, sea view/mother & child, earthenware, 1900s, pr .**925.00**
Plaque, harbor & windmills, Saxony, early **195.00**
Plate, canal scene, Bonneville, Royal Sphinx, 15" dia **75.00**
Plate, Dutch, Oriental landscape amid 8 panels, 1750s, 19" **185.00**
Plate, English, floral wheel, sm sqs in border, rstr, 14" **235.00**
Platter, Bl Parsley, De Porcelyne mk, 11½" dia **30.00**
Posset pot, Dutch, fence/flowers/birds, lid, 1750, 8" L, EX **975.00**
Relish, Bl Parsley, De Porcelyne mk, oval, 9½x5½" **20.00**
Shoes, English, scrolled band w/lace, 1720s, 3", EX, pr **3,500.00**
Tankard, Dutch, mc floral, pewter mts/lid, 1780s, 7", VG **275.00**
Vase, Dutch, floral landscape, w/lid, 1780s, rpr/chips, 17" **600.00**
Vase, Dutch, floral panels/scroll, dome lid, 1780s, 16", EX **1,000.00**
Vase, men of war (ships) in reserves, w/lid, 10" **225.00**

Denver

The Denver China and Pottery Company began production in 1901 in Denver, Colorado. The founder, William A. Long, used materials native to Colorado and produced underglaze-decorated brownware as well as other artware lines. Several marks were used: an impressed 'Denver' (often with the Lonhuda Faience cipher inside a shield), an imprinted 'Denaura,' and an arrow mark.

Bowl vase, gr, ftd form w/inverted rim, Denaura, 6x7" **250.00**
Vase, burro on brn, ovoid, 9½x5½" **275.00**
Vase, cvd lines at shoulder, bl satin w/dk bl int, 4½x3" **150.00**
Vase, floral on bl, sgn WL, bsk, ovoid, 9½x5½" **1,000.00**
Vase, floral on brn, integral hdls, 6x9", EX **500.00**

Denver White

In 1894 Frederick and Frank White settled in Denver, Colorado, and formed the F.J. White & Son pottery company. They located at 1434 Logan Street. After the death of Frederick in 1919, Frank moved the pottery to 1560 South Logan, where he remained until the company closed. He had a kiln set up at home and worked each day on the pottery, often selling his products in his front yard. On many occasions he was commissioned to produce specialty items for customers.

Each piece is hand thrown and many are dated. They are usually incised with the name Denver and the letter 'W' inside the capital 'D.' Many items are decorated with Colorado scenery. Though most pieces are matt glazed with a glossy interior, some later examples were completely glossy. The Whites would also add a small band to some of the ware, similar to what you see on Wedgwood pottery today. They created a line with swirled colors as well. On March 6, 1960, Frank White died at the age of 91.

Our advisors for this category are Jim and Carol Carlton, authors of *Collector's Encyclopedia of Colorado Pottery*; they are listed in the Directory under Colorado.

Bowl, gnarled trees, red on red, 6x10", minimum value **200.00**
Bowl, gray, incurvate rim, 6x8" **150.00**
Pitcher, dk gr, cylindrical, 7" **75.00**

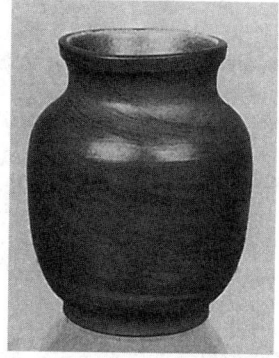

Vase, swirl, 6", $125.00.

Vase, brn & bl swirl, classic form, 6" **150.00**
Vase, cobalt, shouldered form w/hdls, 10" **125.00**
Vase, pine cones, sgn Stabler, glossy int, 6", minimum value **125.00**

Depression Glass

Depression Glass is defined by Gene Florence, author of several best-selling books on the subject, as 'the inexpensive glassware made primarily during the Depression era in the colors of amber, green, pink, blue, red, yellow, white, and crystal.' This glass was mass produced, sold through five-and-dime stores and mail-order catalogs, and given away as premiums with gas and food products.

The listings in this book are far from being complete. If you want a more thorough presentation of this fascinating glassware, we recommend *The Collector's Encyclopedia of Depression Glass*, *The Pocket Guide to Depression Glass*, *Elegant Glassware of the Depression Era*, and *Very Rare Glassware of the Depression Years* by Gene Florence, whose address is listed in the Directory under Kentucky.

Key:
AOP — allover pattern   PAT — pattern at top

Adam, ashtray, pk, ¾" 27.00
Adam, bowl, gr, 7¾" 22.00
Adam, bowl, pk, oval, 10" 27.50
Adam, candy jar, gr, w/lid, 2½" 90.00
Adam, cup, gr 20.00
Adam, pitcher, pk, 32-oz, 8" 37.50
Adam, plate, grill; gr, 9" 16.00
Adam, saucer, pk, sq, 6" 7.00
Adam, sugar bowl, gr 18.00
Adam, tumbler, pk, 4½" 27.50
American Pioneer, bowl, console; gr, 10¾" 60.00
American Pioneer, bowl, pk or crystal, hdld, 5", ea 15.00
American Pioneer, coaster, pk or crystal, 3½", ea 26.00
American Pioneer, creamer, gr, 2¾" 21.00
American Pioneer, goblet, cocktail; gr, 3¾", 3-oz 36.00
American Pioneer, ice bucket, pk, 6" 45.00
American Pioneer, mayonnaise, gr, 4¼" 90.00
American Pioneer, plate, pk or crystal, 6", ea 12.50
American Pioneer, saucer, gr 6.50
American Sweetheart, bowl, cereal; cremax, 6" 8.00
American Sweetheart, bowl, cereal; monax, 6" 12.00
American Sweetheart, bowl, cream soup; pk, 4½" 70.00
American Sweetheart, bowl, soup; pk, flat, 9½" 55.00
American Sweetheart, creamer, pk, ftd 12.00
American Sweetheart, creamer, red, ftd 80.00
American Sweetheart, cup, bl 95.00
American Sweetheart, pitcher, pk, 60-oz, 7½" 625.00
American Sweetheart, plate, bread & butter; pk, 6" 4.00
American Sweetheart, plate, chop; monax, 11" 15.00
American Sweetheart, plate, dinner; monax, 9¾" 20.00
American Sweetheart, plate, salad; smoke trim, 8" 25.00
American Sweetheart, plate, salver; smoke trim, 12" 85.00
American Sweetheart, saucer, bl 22.50
American Sweetheart, saucer, pk 3.00
American Sweetheart, sugar bowl, red, open, ftd 80.00
American Sweetheart, tumbler, pk, 5-oz, 3½" 70.00
Aunt Polly, bowl, berry; bl, lg, 7⅞" 40.00
Aunt Polly, bowl, berry; gr, 4¾" 8.00
Aunt Polly, bowl, bl, hdld, 5½" 20.00
Aunt Polly, butter dish, gr 210.00
Aunt Polly, candy dish, gr, hdls, w/lid 60.00
Aunt Polly, creamer, bl 42.00
Aunt Polly, plate, sherbet; gr, 6" 6.00
Aunt Polly, sherbet, bl 12.00
Aunt Polly, vase, bl, ftd, 6½" 40.00
Aurora, bowl, cereal; pk, 5⅜" 15.00
Aurora, bowl, cobalt or pk, deep, 4½", ea 35.00
Aurora, creamer, cobalt, 4½" 20.00
Aurora, cup, cobalt 15.00

Aurora, plate, pk, 6½" 11.00
Aurora, saucer, pk 6.00
Aurora, tumbler, cobalt, 10-oz, 4¾" 19.00
Avocado, bowl, pk, hdls, 5¼" 25.00
Avocado, bowl, relish; pk, ftd, 6" 23.00
Avocado, bowl, salad; gr, 7½" 50.00
Avocado, creamer, ftd 12.00

Avocado, pitcher, milk glass, $395.00.

Avocado, pitcher, pk, 64-oz 750.00
Avocado, plate, luncheon; gr, 8¼" 19.00
Avocado, saucer, pk, 6⅜" 25.00
Avocado, tumbler, gr 250.00
Beaded Block, bowl, bl, rnd, flared, 7¼" 20.00
Beaded Block, bowl, gr, rnd, 6¼" 8.00
Beaded Block, bowl, lily; gr, rnd, 4½" 9.50
Beaded Block, bowl, pickle; amber, hdls, 6½" 13.00
Beaded Block, bowl, pk, hdld, 5½" 7.50
Beaded Block, bowl, vaseline, rnd, plain edges, 7½" 25.00
Beaded Block, jelly jar, crystal, stemmed, 4½" 9.50
Beaded Block, plate, milk glass, sq, 7¾" 7.00
Beaded Block, sugar bowl, pk 15.00
Beaded Block, vase, bouquet; gr, 6" 12.00
Block Optic, bowl, berry; gr, lg, 8½" 25.00
Block Optic, bowl, cereal; pk, 5¼" 22.50
Block Optic, bowl, gr, 4¼" 7.50
Block Optic, butter dish, gr 45.00
Block Optic, candy dish, yel, w/lid, 2¼" 55.00
Block Optic, goblet, cocktail; gr, 4½" 32.00
Block Optic, goblet, yel, 9-oz, 7¼" 32.00
Block Optic, mug, gr 32.00
Block Optic, pitcher, pk, 80-oz, 8" 75.00
Block Optic, plate, grill; yel, 9" 38.00
Block Optic, plate, luncheon; pk, 8" 5.00
Block Optic, saucer, pk, w/cup ring, 6⅛" 6.00
Block Optic, shakers, gr, ftd, pr 35.00
Block Optic, sherbet, yel, 6-oz, 4¾" 15.00
Block Optic, tumbler, gr, flat, 5-oz, 3½" 19.00
Block Optic, tumbler, gr, 3" 45.00
Block Optic, tumbler, pk, ftd, 3-oz, 3¼" 19.00
Block Optic, vase, gr, blown, 5¾" 265.00
Block Optic, whiskey, 2-oz, 2¼" 25.00
Bowknot, bowl, berry; gr, 4½" 15.00
Bowknot, bowl, cereal; gr, 5½" 18.00
Bowknot, cup, gr 8.00
Bowknot, plate, salad; gr, 7" 12.00
Bowknot, sherbet, gr, low ftd 15.00

Bowknot, tumbler, ftd, 10-oz, 5" 18.00
Cameo, bowl, cream soup; gr, 4¾" 110.00
Cameo, bowl, salad; gr, 7¼" 50.00
Cameo, bowl, vegetable; gr, oval, 10" 22.00
Cameo, butter dish, yel, w/lid 1,300.00
Cameo, candy dish, yel, w/lid, 4" 65.00
Cameo, cookie jar, gr, w/lid 47.50
Cameo, cup, crystal w/platinum ring, 2 styles, ea 5.50
Cameo, goblet, water; pk, 6" 160.00
Cameo, pitcher, juice; gr, 36-oz, 6" 55.00
Cameo, plate, cake; gr, 3-legged, 10" 19.00
Cameo, plate, cake; pk, flat, 10½" 130.00
Cameo, plate, dinner; yel, 9½" 9.00
Cameo, plate, grill; pk, 10½" 45.00
Cameo, plate, sherbet; gr, 6" 3.00
Cameo, sherbet, gr, blown, 3⅛" 12.50
Cameo, sugar bowl, pk, 4¼" 98.00
Cameo, tray, domino; gr, 7", w/3" indentation 125.00
Cameo, tray, relish; crystal w/platinum ring, 3-part, 7½" ...130.00
Cameo, tumbler, gr, 15-oz, 5¼" 65.00
Cameo, tumbler, juice; gr, 5-oz, 3¾" 26.00
Cameo, vase, gr, 8" 35.00
Cherry Blossom, bowl, berry; pk, 4¾" 14.00
Cherry Blossom, bowl, fruit; pk, 3-legged, 10½" 75.00
Cherry Blossom, bowl, soup; gr, flat, 7¾" 50.00
Cherry Blossom, bowl, vegetable; delphite, oval, 9" ...45.00
Cherry Blossom, butter dish, gr, w/lid 80.00
Cherry Blossom, creamer, delphite 18.00
Cherry Blossom, mug, pk, 7-oz 185.00
Cherry Blossom, pitcher, gr, PAT, flat, 42-oz, 8" 50.00
Cherry Blossom, plate, cake; gr, 3-legged, 10¼" 25.00
Cherry Blossom, plate, gr, oval, 11" 38.00
Cherry Blossom, plate, grill; pk, 9" 24.00
Cherry Blossom, plate, sherbet; gr, 6" 7.00
Cherry Blossom, saucer, pk 6.00
Cherry Blossom, tray, sandwich; delphite, 10½" 18.00
Cherry Blossom, tumbler, gr, PAT, flat, 12-oz, 5" ...67.50
Cherry Blossom, tumbler, pk, AOP, scalloped ft, 8-oz, 4½" ...30.00
Cherryberry, bowl, pk, 4" 8.50
Cherryberry, bowl, salad; irid, deep, 6½" 16.00
Cherryberry, butter dish, gr or pk, w/lid, ea 155.00
Cherryberry, creamer, gr or pk, sm, ea 17.00
Cherryberry, plate, sherbet; irid, 6" 6.00
Cherryberry, sugar bowl, gr or pk, open, sm, ea 17.00
Cherryberry, tray, pickle; crystal, oval, 8¼" 9.00
Cherryberry, tumbler, gr or pk, 9-oz, 3⅝", ea 32.50
Chinex Classic, bowl, cereal; brownstone, 5¾" 5.50
Chinex Classic, bowl, vegetable; decor, 9" 22.00
Chinex Classic, butter dish, castle decal, w/lid 115.00
Chinex Classic, plate, sandwich; castle decal, 11½" ...22.50
Chinex Classic, plate, sherbet; decor, 6¼" 3.50
Chinex Classic, sugar bowl, brownstone, open 5.50
Circle, bowl, gr, 4½" 8.00
Circle, bowl, pk or gr, 8", ea 15.00
Circle, decanter, pk or gr, hdld, ea 37.50
Circle, pitcher, pk or gr, 80-oz, ea 30.00
Circle, plate, sandwich; pk or gr, 10", ea 12.50
Circle, sugar bowl, pk or gr, ea 7.00
Circle, tumbler, tea; pk or gr, 10-oz, 5", ea 16.00
Cloverleaf, ashtray, blk, match holder in center, 4" ...67.50
Cloverleaf, bowl, dessert; gr, 4" 18.00
Cloverleaf, bowl, salad; yel, deep, 7" 47.50
Cloverleaf, creamer, gr, ftd, 3⅝" 10.00
Cloverleaf, plate, luncheon; pk, 8" 7.00

Cloverleaf, plate, sherbet; blk, 6" 35.00
Cloverleaf, shakers, yel, pr 100.00
Cloverleaf, sugar bowl, gr, ftd, 3⅝" 10.00
Cloverleaf, tumbler, pk, flat, flared, 10-oz, 5¾" 19.00
Colonial, bowl, berry; pk, 4½" 14.00
Colonial, bowl, cream soup; pk or gr, 4½", ea 60.00
Colonial, bowl, vegetable; gr, oval, 10" 33.00
Colonial, butter dish, pk, w/lid 600.00
Colonial, goblet, cocktail; crystal, 3-oz, 4" 15.00
Colonial, goblet, water; gr, 8½-oz, 5¾" 28.00
Colonial, pitcher, pk, 68-oz, 7¾" 65.00
Colonial, plate, luncheon; pk or gr, 8½", ea 9.00
Colonial, platter, pk, oval, 12" 30.00
Colonial, tumbler, iced tea; pk, 12-oz 42.00
Colonial, tumbler, juice; gr, 5-oz, 3" 24.00
Colonial, whiskey, gr, 1½-oz, 2½" 14.00
Colonial Block, bowl, pk or gr, 4", ea 6.50
Colonial Block, butter dish, pk or gr, ea 45.00
Colonial Block, candy jar, pk or gr, w/lid, ea 35.00
Colonial Block, creamer, wht 7.00
Colonial Block, pitcher, pk or gr, ea 38.00
Colonial Block, sherbet, pk or gr, ea 8.00
Colonial Fluted, bowl, berry; gr, 4" 5.50
Colonial Fluted, bowl, salad; gr, 2½x7½" 16.00
Colonial Fluted, cup, gr 5.00
Colonial Fluted, plate, luncheon; gr, 8" 5.00
Colonial Fluted, sugar bowl, gr 5.00
Columbia, bowl, cereal; crystal, 5" 15.00
Columbia, butter dish, crystal, w/lid 20.00
Columbia, cup, pk 20.00
Columbia, plate, snack; crystal 37.50
Columbia, saucer, pk 8.00
Columbia, tumbler, water; crystal, 9-oz 25.00
Coronation, bowl, berry; pk, 4¼" 4.50
Coronation, bowl, nappy; Royal Ruby, 6½" 12.00
Coronation, pitcher, pk, 68-oz, 7¾" 400.00
Coronation, plate, sherbet; pk, 6" 2.00
Coronation, tumbler, ftd, 10-oz, 5" 20.00
Cremax, bowl, vegetable; ivory, 9" 6.50
Cremax, plate, bread & butter; decor, 6¼" 4.00
Cremax, plate, sandwich; decor, 11½" 11.00
Cube, bowl, dessert; pk, 4½" 6.50
Cube, butter dish, pk or gr, w/lid, ea 60.00
Cube, cup, gr 9.00
Cube, shakers, pk or gr, pr 35.00
Cube, tumbler, pk, 9-oz, 4" 60.00
Diamond Quilted, bowl, bl or blk, crimped edges, 7", ea ...16.00
Diamond Quilted, bowl, cream soup; pk or gr, 4¾", ea ...8.00
Diamond Quilted, candy jar, pk or gr, ftd, w/lid, ea ...60.00
Diamond Quilted, goblet, cordial; pk or gr, 1-oz, ea ...11.00
Diamond Quilted, ice bucket, bl or blk, ea 85.00
Diamond Quilted, plate, salad; pk or gr, 7", ea 6.00
Diamond Quilted, saucer, bl or blk, ea 5.00
Diamond Quilted, tumbler, water; pk or gr, 9-oz, ea ...12.00
Diamond Quilted, whiskey, pk or gr, 1½-oz, ea 8.00
Diana, ashtray, crystal, 3½" 2.50
Diana, bowl, amber, scalloped edges, 12" 16.00
Diana, bowl, cream soup; pk, 5½" 22.00
Diana, cup, crystal 3.00
Diana, plate, bread & butter; pk, 6" 4.00
Diana, saucer, amber 2.00
Diana, tumbler, pk, 9-oz, 4⅛" 42.00
Dogwood, bowl, berry; pk, 8½" 55.00
Dogwood, bowl, cereal; pk or gr, 5½" 25.00

Dogwood, creamer, gr, flat, thin, 2½" 42.00
Dogwood, plate, bread & butter; monax or cremax, 6", ea 21.00
Dogwood, plate, salver; pk, 12" 25.00
Dogwood, saucer, gr 6.50
Dogwood, tumbler, pk, molded band 20.00
Doric, bowl, berry; pk, 4½" 7.00
Doric, bowl, cereal; gr, 5½" 60.00
Doric, butter dish, gr, w/lid 80.00
Doric, creamer, gr, 4" 13.00
Doric, pitcher, pk, ftd, 48-oz, 7½" 425.00
Doric, plate, cake; pk, 3-legged, 10" 22.00
Doric, plate, sherbet; gr, 6" 5.00
Doric, platter, gr, oval, 12" 22.00
Doric, shakers, gr, pr 35.00
Doric, tray, serving; pk, 8" sq 18.00
Doric & Pansy, bowl, berry; gr or teal, 4½", ea 16.50
Doric & Pansy, bowl, pk or crystal, hdls, 9", ea 15.00
Doric & Pansy, butter dish, gr or teal, w/lid, ea 495.00
Doric & Pansy, plate, sherbet; gr or teal, 6", ea 10.00
Doric & Pansy, saucer, pk or crystal, ea 6.00
Doric & Pansy, shakers, gr or teal, pr 425.00
Doric & Pansy, tumbler, gr or teal, 9-oz, 4½", ea 70.00
English Hobnail, ashtray, pk or gr, 3", ea 20.00
English Hobnail, bowl, celery; pk or gr, 12", ea 26.00
English Hobnail, bowl, grapefruit; pk or gr, 6½", ea 16.00
English Hobnail, bowl, nappy; ice bl, rnd, 4½" 27.50
English Hobnail, bowl, nappy; pk or gr, sq, 6", ea 12.00
English Hobnail, bowl, pk or gr, ftd, 8", ea 50.00
English Hobnail, bowl, rose; pk or gr, 4", ea 45.00
English Hobnail, candy dish, pk or gr, 3-ftd, ea 45.00
English Hobnail, cigarette box, ice bl, w/lid, 4½x2½" 45.00
English Hobnail, compote, honey; pk or gr, rnd, ftd, 6", ea ...30.00
English Hobnail, cup, ice bl 20.00
English Hobnail, ice tub, ice bl, 5½" 100.00
English Hobnail, mayonnaise, pk or gr, w/lid, 6", ea 36.00
English Hobnail, pitcher, pk or gr, rnd, 60-oz, ea 265.00
English Hobnail, plate, pk or gr, 6½", ea 5.00
English Hobnail, saucer, pk or gr, ea 4.00
English Hobnail, stem, cocktail; ice bl, ftd, 3-oz 35.00
English Hobnail, sugar bowl, ice bl, ftd, hexagonal 45.00
English Hobnail, tumbler, ginger ale; pk or gr, 5-oz, ea 14.00
English Hobnail, vase, flip; pk or gr, 7½", ea 65.00
English Hobnail, vase (straw jar), pk or gr, 10", ea 85.00
Fire-King Philbe, bowl, cereal; crystal, 5½" 18.00
Fire-King Philbe, bowl, vegetable; bl, oval, 10" 150.00
Fire-King Philbe, creamer, pk or gr, ftd, 3½", ea 110.00
Fire-King Philbe, pitcher, crystal, 56-oz, 8½" 365.00
Fire-King Philbe, plate, grill; bl, 10½" 60.00
Fire-King Philbe, plate, luncheon; pk or gr, 8", ea 40.00
Fire-King Philbe, sugar bowl, pk or gr, ftd, 3¼", ea 110.00
Fire-King Philbe, tumbler, juice; crystal, ftd, 3½" 35.00
Floral, bowl, berry; pk, 4" 15.00
Floral, bowl, vegetable; gr, w/lid, 8" 45.00
Floral, butter dish, pk, w/lid 80.00
Floral, candlesticks, pk, 4", pr 70.00
Floral, coaster, gr, 3¼" 10.00
Floral, pitcher, lemonade; pk, 48-oz, 10¼" 225.00
Floral, platter, gr, oval, 10¾" 17.00
Floral, shakers, pk, ftd, 4", pr 45.00
Floral, sherbet, gr 18.00
Floral, tumbler, juice; gr, ftd, 5-oz, 4" 20.00
Floral, tumbler, water; delphite, ftd, 7-oz, 4¾" 175.00
Floral & Diamond Band, bowl, nappy; pk or gr, hdld, 5¾", ea ...11.00
Floral & Diamond Band, butter dish, pk, w/lid 130.00

Floral & Diamond Band, compote, gr, tall, 5½" 16.00
Floral & Diamond Band, pitcher, pk, 42-oz, 8" 85.00
Floral & Diamond Band, sherbet, gr 8.00
Floral & Diamond Band, tumbler, water; pk, 4" 18.00
Florentine No 1, ashtray, crystal or gr, 5½", ea 22.00
Florentine No 1, bowl, cereal; yel, 6" 22.00
Florentine No 1, butter dish, pk, w/lid 155.00
Florentine No 1, creamer, gr 10.00
Florentine No 1, cup, cobalt bl 75.00
Florentine No 1, plate, grill; yel, 10" 13.00
Florentine No 1, plate, sherbet; crystal or gr, 6", ea 6.00
Florentine No 1, saucer, pk or yel, ea 4.00
Florentine No 1, tumbler, iced tea; cobalt, 9-oz, 5¼" 100.00
Florentine No 2, bowl, berry; crystal or gr, 4½", ea 11.00
Florentine No 2, bowl, cereal; yel, 6" 35.00
Florentine No 2, bowl, vegetable; yel, oval, w/lid, 9" 60.00
Florentine No 2, candy dish, crystal or gr, w/lid, ea 100.00
Florentine No 2, compote, pk, ruffled, 3½" 12.00
Florentine No 2, custard cup, yel 80.00
Florentine No 2, pitcher, pk, 48-oz, 7½" 110.00
Florentine No 2, plate, grill; yel, 10¼" 11.00
Florentine No 2, plate, salad; pk, 8½" 9.00
Florentine No 2, platter, pk, oval, 11" 15.00
Florentine No 2, saucer, amber 15.00
Florentine No 2, tumbler, crystal or gr, ftd, 5-oz, 4", ea 14.00
Florentine No 2, tumbler, juice; yel, 5-oz, 3⅜" 20.00
Flower Garden w/Butterflies, bowl, orange; blk, ftd, 11" 225.00
Flower Garden w/Butterflies, candlesticks, amber, 4", pr 42.50

Flower Garden with Butterflies, candy dish, blue, heart shape, $1,250.00.

Flower Garden w/Butterflies, candy dish, pk, flat, 6" 155.00
Flower Garden w/Butterflies, compote, canary, 2⅞", ea 28.00
Flower Garden w/Butterflies, cup, pk 60.00
Flower Garden w/Butterflies, plate, blk, indented, 10" 175.00
Flower Garden w/Butterflies, plate, crystal, 7" 16.00
Flower Garden w/Butterflies, saucer, gr or bl-gr, ea 22.50
Flower Garden w/Butterflies, vase, pk or gr, 10½", ea 125.00
Fortune, bowl, berry; pk or crystal, 4", ea 3.50
Fortune, candy dish, pk or crystal, flat, w/lid, ea 22.50
Fortune, cup, pk or crystal, ea 4.00
Fortune, tumbler, water; pk or crystal, 9-oz, 4", ea 9.00
Fruits, bowl, berry; gr, 5" 22.50
Fruits, plate, luncheon; pk or gr, 8", ea 6.50
Fruits, sherbet, gr 8.00
Fruits, tumbler, gr, 12-oz, 5" 95.00
Georgian, bowl, berry; gr, 4½" 8.00
Georgian, bowl, vegetable; gr, oval, 9" 60.00
Georgian, creamer, gr, ftd, 3" 11.00

Georgian, plate, dinner; gr, 9¼" 25.00
Georgian, saucer, gr 3.00
Georgian, tumbler, gr, flat, 12-oz, 5¼" 100.00
Hex Optic, bowl, berry; pk or gr, lg, 7½", ea 9.00
Hex Optic, bowl, mixing; pk or gr, 10", ea 22.00
Hex Optic, bowl, mixing; pk or gr, 7¼", ea 12.00
Hex Optic, bucket reamer, pk or gr, ea 55.00
Hex Optic, ice bucket, pk or gr, metal hdl, ea 18.00
Hex Optic, pitcher, pk or gr, ftd, 48-oz, 9", ea 40.00
Hex Optic, plate, sherbet; pk or gr, 6", ea 2.50
Hex Optic, platter, pk or gr, 11" dia, ea 14.00
Hex Optic, shakers, pk or gr, pr 26.00
Hex Optic, sugar shaker, pk or gr, ea 135.00
Hex Optic, tumbler, pk or gr, 12-oz, 5", ea 7.00
Hex Optic, whiskey, pk or gr, 1-oz, 2", ea 8.00
Homespun, ashtray/coaster, pk or crystal, ea 10.00
Homespun, bowl, cereal; pk or crystal, 5", ea 18.00
Homespun, bowl, pk or crystal, closed hdls, 4½", ea 10.00
Homespun, butter dish, pk or crystal, w/lid, ea 55.00
Homespun, cup, pk or crystal, ea 10.00
Homespun, plate, dinner; pk or crystal, 9¼", ea 15.00
Homespun, saucer, pk or crystal, ea 4.00
Homespun, sugar bowl, pk or crystal, ftd, ea 9.50
Homespun, tumbler, iced tea; pk or crystal, 13-oz, 5¼", ea 27.50
Homespun, tumbler, pk or crystal, ftd, 15-oz, 6¼", ea 24.00
Indiana Custard, bowl, cereal; French ivory, 6½" 20.00
Indiana Custard, bowl, vegetable; French ivory, oval, 9½" 26.00
Indiana Custard, creamer, French ivory 17.50
Indiana Custard, cup, French ivory 37.50
Indiana Custard, plate, dinner; French ivory, 9¾" 25.00
Indiana Custard, plate, salad; French ivory, 7½" 15.00
Indiana Custard, sugar bowl, French ivory, w/lid 30.00

Iris, all pieces in clear:
Goblet, 5½", $24.00;
Wine, 4½", $16.00;
Pitcher, 9½", $37.50.

Iris, bowl, salad; gr or pk, ruffled, 9½", ea 95.00
Iris, bowl, sauce; irid, ruffled, 5" 24.00
Iris, bowl, soup; crystal, 7½" 150.00
Iris, butter dish, irid, w/lid 40.00
Iris, candlesticks, crystal, pr 40.00
Iris, coaster, crystal 92.50
Iris, cup, irid 14.00
Iris, goblet, wine; irid, 4" 30.00
Iris, plate, luncheon; crystal, 8" 100.00
Iris, saucer, irid 11.00
Iris, sugar bowl, crystal, w/lid 23.00
Iris, tumbler, crystal, ftd, 6" 18.00
Iris, vase, pk or gr, 9", ea 125.00
Jubilee, bowl, fruit; yel, hdld, 9" 110.00
Jubilee, bowl, pk, 3-ftd, 13" 250.00

Jubilee, cheese & cracker set, yel 250.00
Jubilee, cup, pk 40.00
Jubilee, plate, salad; yel, 7" 12.00
Jubilee, saucer, pk, 2 styles 12.00
Jubilee, stem, yel, 3-oz, 4⅞" 135.00
Jubilee, sugar bowl, pk 35.00
Jubilee, tumbler, water; pk, 10-oz, 6" 75.00
Jubilee, vase, yel, 12" 350.00
Lace Edge, bowl, cereal; pk, 6⅜" 17.50
Lace Edge, bowl, crystal, 8¼" 11.00
Lace Edge, bowl, pk, plain or ribbed, 9½", ea 20.00
Lace Edge, butter dish, pk, w/bonbon lid 60.00
Lace Edge, candy jar, pk, ribbed, w/lid 45.00
Lace Edge, compote, pk, 7" 22.50
Lace Edge, cookie jar, pk, w/lid 55.00
Lace Edge, creamer, pk 21.00
Lace Edge, plate, dinner; pk, 10½" 25.00
Lace Edge, plate, relish; pk, 3-part, 10½" 22.50
Lace Edge, plate, salad; pk, 8¼" 20.00
Lace Edge, platter, pk, 12¾" 27.50
Lace Edge, saucer, pk 10.00
Lace Edge, tumbler, pk, flat, 5-oz, 3½" 30.00
Laced Edge, bowl, bl or gr opal, 5", ea 35.00
Laced Edge, bowl, fruit; bl or gr opal, 4⅜" to 4¾", ea 27.00
Laced Edge, bowl, vegetable; bl or gr opal, 9", ea 95.00
Laced Edge, creamer, bl or gr opal, ea 38.00
Laced Edge, cup, bl or gr opal, ea 33.00
Laced Edge, plate, bread & butter; bl or gr opal, 6½", ea 18.00
Laced Edge, plate, dinner; bl or gr opal, 10", ea 85.00
Laced Edge, platter, bl or gr opal, 13", ea 145.00
Laced Edge, tumbler, bl or gr opal, 9-oz, ea 58.00
Lake Como, bowl, cereal; wht, 6" 22.00
Lake Como, bowl, soup; wht, flat 90.00
Lake Como, plate, dinner; wht, 9¼" 27.50
Lake Como, plate, salad; wht, 7¼" 17.50
Lake Como, platter, wht, 11" 57.50
Lake Como, saucer, wht 11.00
Laurel, bowl, berry; wht opal or jade gr, 5", ea 6.50
Laurel, bowl, Poudre bl, 11" 55.00
Laurel, bowl, soup; French ivory, 7⅞" 30.00
Laurel, cup, wht opal or jade gr 8.00
Laurel, plate, salad; French ivory, 7½" 10.00
Laurel, saucer, Poudre bl 7.50
Laurel, tumbler, French ivory, flat, 12-oz, 5" 45.00
Loraine, bowl, berry; yel, deep, 8" 135.00
Loraine, bowl, cereal; crystal or gr, 6", ea 35.00
Loraine, cup, crystal or gr, ea 11.00
Loraine, plate, luncheon; crystal or gr, 8⅜", ea 16.00
Loraine, plate, salad; yel, 7¾" 15.00
Loraine, platter, yel, 11½" 40.00
Loraine, saucer, yel 6.00
Loraine, sugar bowl, crystal or gr, ftd, ea 15.00
Loraine, tumbler, yel, ftd, 9-oz, 4¾" 27.00
Madrid, ashtray, gr, 6" sq 150.00
Madrid, bowl, berry; pk, lg, 9⅜" 20.00
Madrid, bowl, sauce; amber, 5" 6.00
Madrid, bowl, soup; bl, 7" 30.00
Madrid, bowl, vegetable; amber, oval, 10" 15.00
Madrid, butter dish, gr, w/lid 75.00
Madrid, cookie jar, amber, w/lid 45.00
Madrid, cup, pk 7.50
Madrid, hot dish coaster, amber 40.00
Madrid, jam dish, gr, 7" 18.50
Madrid, pitcher, pk, 60-oz, sq, 8" 35.00

Madrid, plate, luncheon; gr, 8⅞" 9.00
Madrid, plate, relish; pk, 10¼" 12.50
Madrid, plate, sherbet; bl, 6" 8.00
Madrid, platter, amber, oval, 11½" 15.00
Madrid, saucer, pk 5.00
Madrid, shakers, gr, ftd, 3½", pr 80.00
Madrid, tumbler, amber, 9-oz, 4¼" 15.00
Manhattan, ashtray, crystal, 4" dia 11.00
Manhattan, bowl, berry; crystal or pk, hdls, 5⅜", ea 17.50
Manhattan, bowl, berry; pk or crystal, lg, 7½", ea 14.00
Manhattan, bowl, salad; crystal, 9" 20.00
Manhattan, coaster, crystal, 3½" 15.00
Manhattan, creamer, pk or crystal, oval, ea 10.00
Manhattan, pitcher, crystal, 24-oz 30.00
Manhattan, plate, salad; crystal, 8½" 14.00
Manhattan, sherbet, crystal 6.50
Manhattan, vase, crystal, 8" 17.50
Mayfair Federal, bowl, cereal; crystal, 6" 9.50
Mayfair Federal, bowl, sauce; amber, 5" 8.50
Mayfair Federal, creamer, gr, ftd 18.00
Mayfair Federal, cup, amber 9.00
Mayfair Federal, plate, grill; amber or gr, 9½", ea 14.00
Mayfair Federal, plate, salad; crystal, 6¾" 4.00
Mayfair Federal, saucer, amber or gr, ea 4.00
Mayfair Federal, tumbler, crystal, 9-oz, 4½" 13.00

Mayfair/Open Rose, pitchers, both in blue, 8½", $180.00; 8", $160.00.

Mayfair/Open Rose, bowl, cereal; bl, 5½" 45.00
Mayfair/Open Rose, bowl, cream soup; pk, 5" 40.00
Mayfair/Open Rose, bowl, gr, low, flat, 11¾" 35.00
Mayfair/Open Rose, bowl, vegetable; yel, 10" 115.00
Mayfair/Open Rose, celery dish, gr or yel, 10", ea ...105.00
Mayfair/Open Rose, creamer, bl, ftd 75.00
Mayfair/Open Rose, goblet, water; gr, 9-oz, 5¾" 55.00
Mayfair/Open Rose, goblet, water; pk, 9-oz, 5¾" ...200.00
Mayfair/Open Rose, goblet, wine; gr, 3-oz, 4½" 400.00
Mayfair/Open Rose, pitcher, gr or yel, 80-oz, 8½", ea ...500.00
Mayfair/Open Rose, plate, grill; pk, 9½" 40.00
Mayfair/Open Rose, plate, luncheon; bl, 8½" 50.00
Mayfair/Open Rose, saucer, pk, w/cup ring 30.00
Mayfair/Open Rose, shakers, gr, flat, pr 1,000.00
Mayfair/Open Rose, sherbet, pk, ftd, 3" 16.00
Mayfair/Open Rose, tumbler, juice; bl, 5-oz, 3½" ...110.00
Mayfair/Open Rose, vase, sweet pea; gr 275.00
Miss America, bowl, berry; gr, 4½" 11.00
Miss America, bowl, vegetable; crystal, oval, 10" ...15.00
Miss America, butter dish, pk, w/lid 550.00
Miss America, coaster, pk, 5¾" 15.00

Miss America, cup, Royal Ruby 200.00
Miss America, goblet, wine; pk, 3-oz, 3¾" 67.50
Miss America, pitcher, crystal, 65-oz, 8" 46.00
Miss America, plate, dinner; pk, 10¼" 25.00
Miss America, plate, gr, 6¾" 7.50
Miss America, saucer, crystal 4.00
Miss America, shakers, pk, pr 55.00
Miss America, tumbler, water; pk, 10-oz, 4½" 28.00
Moderntone, bowl, berry; amethyst, 5" 22.50
Moderntone, bowl, cream soup; cobalt, 4¾" 20.00
Moderntone, bowl, soup; cobalt, 7½" 110.00
Moderntone, butter dish, cobalt, w/metal lid 100.00
Moderntone, creamer, amethyst 10.00
Moderntone, plate, dinner; amethyst, 8⅞" 12.00
Moderntone, plate, sherbet; cobalt, 5⅞" 6.50
Moderntone, saucer, cobalt 5.00
Moderntone, tumbler, cobalt, 5-oz 40.00
Moondrops, bowl, amber, concave top, ftd, 8⅜" 22.00
Moondrops, bowl, amber, hdld, oval, 9¾" 23.00
Moondrops, bowl, soup; bl or red, 6¾", ea 75.00
Moondrops, bowl, vegetable; bl or red, oval, 9¾", ea ...33.00
Moondrops, butter dish, gr, w/lid 250.00
Moondrops, candlesticks, bl or red, ruffled, 2", pr ...40.00
Moondrops, candy dish, cobalt, ruffled, 8" 20.00
Moondrops, compote, bl or red, 4", ea 23.00
Moondrops, creamer, amethyst, mini, 2¾" 11.00
Moondrops, decanter, crystal, med, 8½" 42.00
Moondrops, goblet, amber, 8-oz, 5¾" 19.00
Moondrops, goblet, wine; bl or red, 4-oz, 4", ea 22.00
Moondrops, gravy boat, bl or red, ea 120.00
Moondrops, mayonnaise, pk, 5¼" 32.00
Moondrops, plate, bl or red, 5⅞", ea 11.00
Moondrops, plate, salad; gr, 7⅛" 10.00
Moondrops, platter, bl or red, oval, 12", ea 35.00
Moondrops, saucer, amethyst 5.00
Moondrops, tumbler, bl or red, 8-oz, 4⅜", ea 16.00
New Century, ashtray/coaster, gr or crystal, 5⅜", ea ...28.00
New Century, bowl, casserole; gr or crystal, w/lid, 9", ea ...55.00
New Century, bowl, cream soup; gr or crystal, 4¾", ea ...17.50
New Century, cup, pk, cobalt or amethyst, ea 19.00
New Century, decanter, gr or crystal, w/stopper, ea ...50.00
New Century, goblet, wine; gr or crystal, 2½-oz, ea ...23.00
New Century, plate, grill; gr or crystal, 10", ea 10.00
New Century, plate, salad; gr or crystal, 8½", ea 9.00
New Century, plate, sherbet; gr or crystal, 6", ea 3.00
New Century, saucer, gr or crystal, ea 2.00
New Century, tumbler, gr or crystal, 5-oz, 3½", ea ...12.00
New Century, tumbler, pk, cobalt or amethyst, 10-oz, 5", ea ...14.00
New Century, whiskey, gr or crystal, 1½-oz, 2½", ea ...15.00
Newport, bowl, berry; cobalt, 4¾" 16.00
Newport, bowl, cereal; cobalt, 5¼" 35.00
Newport, bowl, cream soup; amethyst, 4¾" 17.50
Newport, creamer, cobalt 16.00
Newport, cup, amethyst 10.00
Newport, plate, dinner; cobalt, 8¾" 27.50
Newport, plate, luncheon; amethyst, 8½" 11.00
Newport, platter, cobalt, oval, 11¾" 40.00
Newport, saucer, amethyst or cobalt, ea 5.00
Newport, sherbet, amethyst 14.00
Newport, tumbler, cobalt, 9-oz, 4½" 35.00
No 610 Pyramid, bowl, berry; crystal, 4¾" 11.00
No 610 Pyramid, bowl, pk, oval, 9½" 30.00
No 610 Pyramid, creamer, gr 23.00
No 610 Pyramid, pitcher, yel 450.00

No 610 Pyramid, tray, pk (for creamer & sugar bowl) 22.00
No 610 Pyramid, tumbler, gr, ftd, 11-oz 52.50
No 612 Horseshoe, bowl, berry; gr, 4½" 20.00
No 612 Horseshoe, bowl, salad; yel, 7½" 22.50
No 612 Horseshoe, bowl, vegetable; gr, oval, 10½" 20.00
No 612 Horseshoe, butter dish, gr, w/lid 700.00
No 612 Horseshoe, creamer, yel, ftd 16.00
No 612 Horseshoe, pitcher, gr, 64-oz, 8½" 225.00
No 612 Horseshoe, plate, salad; yel, 8⅜" 10.00
No 612 Horseshoe, plate, sandwich; gr, 11½" 16.00
No 612 Horseshoe, saucer, gr or yel, ea 5.00
No 612 Horseshoe, tumbler, gr, flat, 9-oz, 4¼" 160.00
No 612 Horseshoe, tumbler, gr or yel, ftd, 12-oz, ea 135.00
No 616 Vernon, creamer, gr or yel, ftd, ea 24.00
No 616 Vernon, cup, crystal 8.00
No 616 Vernon, plate, luncheon; gr or yel, 8", ea 25.00
No 616 Vernon, saucer, gr or yel, ea 4.00
No 616 Vernon, tumbler, crystal, ftd, 5" 14.00
No 618 Pineapple & Floral, ashtray, crystal, 4½" 17.50
No 618 Pineapple & Floral, bowl, cereal; amber or red, 7", ea 20.00
No 618 Pineapple & Floral, cup, crystal 10.00
No 618 Pineapple & Floral, plate, dinner; red, 9⅜" 15.00
No 618 Pineapple & Floral, plate, sandwich; crystal, 11½" 15.00
No 618 Pineapple & Floral, saucer, amber or red, ea 5.00
No 618 Pineapple & Floral, tumbler, crystal, 8-oz, 4¼" 35.00
Normandie, bowl, berry; amber, 5" 6.00
Normandie, bowl, cereal; pk, 6½" 20.00
Normandie, bowl, vegetable; irid, oval, 10" 15.00
Normandie, creamer, amber, ftd 8.50
Old Cafe, bowl, berry; pk, 3¾" 4.00
Old Cafe, bowl, cereal; Royal Ruby, 5½" 10.00
Old Cafe, lamp, Royal Ruby 25.00
Old Cafe, pitcher, crystal or pk, 80-oz, ea 90.00
Old Cafe, tumbler, water; Royal Ruby, 4" 16.00
Old English, bowl, pk, gr or amber, flat, 4", ea 17.50
Old English, bowl, pk, gr or amber, flat, 9½", ea 35.00
Old English, candy jar, pk, gr or amber, w/lid, ea 50.00
Old English, creamer, pk, gr or amber, ea 17.50
Old English, pitcher, pk, gr or amber, ea 65.00
Old English, sherbet, pk, gr or amber, 2 styles, ea 20.00
Old English, tumbler, pk, gr or amber, ftd, 5½", ea 32.00
Old English, vase, pk, gr or amber, ftd, 12", ea 55.00
Ovide, bowl, berry; wht w/decor, 4¾" 7.00
Ovide, creamer, blk 6.50
Ovide, cup, gr 3.50
Ovide, plate, luncheon; Art Deco, 8" 45.00
Ovide, plate, sherbet; gr, 6" 2.50
Ovide, platter, wht w/decor, 11" 22.50
Ovide, saucer, blk 3.50
Ovide, tumbler, Art Deco 80.00
Oyster & Pearl, bowl, crystal or pk, 1-hdl, 5½", ea 7.00
Oyster & Pearl, bowl, fruit; Royal Ruby, deep, 10½" 45.00
Oyster & Pearl, plate, sandwich; crystal or pk, 13½", ea 16.00
Oyster & Pearl, relish, crystal or pk, oblong, 10¼", ea 10.00
Parrot, bowl, berry; gr, 5" 22.00
Parrot, bowl, soup; amber, 7" 30.00
Parrot, bowl, vegetable; gr, oval, 10" 52.50
Parrot, creamer, amber, ftd 50.00
Parrot, jam dish, amber, 7" 30.00
Parrot, plate, dinner; gr, 9" 50.00
Parrot, plate, salad; gr, 7½" 35.00
Parrot, platter, amber, oblong, 11¼" 65.00
Parrot, saucer, gr or amber, ea 15.00
Parrot, tumbler, gr, 12-oz, 5½" 150.00

Patrician, bowl, cereal; pk, 6" 22.00
Patrician, bowl, cream soup; amber or crystal, 4¾", ea 15.00
Patrician, butter dish, gr, w/lid 100.00
Patrician, creamer, pk, ftd 10.00
Patrician, jam dish, amber, crystal or pk, ea 26.00
Patrician, plate, grill; amber or crystal, 10½", ea 13.50
Patrician, plate, luncheon; gr, 9" 11.00
Patrician, plate, sherbet; pk, 6" 8.00
Patrician, saucer, amber, crystal, pk or gr, ea 9.50
Patrician, tumbler, pk, 14-oz, 5¼" 28.00
Patrick, bowl, console; yel, 11" 125.00
Patrick, bowl, fruit; pk, hdld, 9" 165.00
Patrick, candlesticks, yel, pr 77.50
Patrick, creamer, pk 75.00
Patrick, cup, yel 37.50
Patrick, goblet, juice; pk, 6-oz, 4¾" 90.00
Patrick, mayonnaise, pk, 3-pc 195.00
Patrick, saucer, pk 20.00
Patrick, tray, yel, center hdl, 11" 60.00
Petalware, bowl, cereal; pk, 5¾" 10.00
Petalware, bowl, cream soup; crystal, 4½" 4.50
Petalware, creamer, pk, ftd 7.50
Petalware, cup, monax plain 5.00
Petalware, plate, salad; monax plain, 8" 4.00
Petalware, plate, salver; pk, 12" 9.00
Petalware, platter, pk, oval, 13" 15.00
Petalware, saucer, crystal 1.50
Petalware, tumbler, crystal, 6-oz, 3⅝" 32.50
Primo, bowl, yel or gr, 4½", ea 10.00
Primo, coaster/ashtray, yel or gr, ea 8.00
Primo, cup, yel or gr, ea 9.00
Primo, plate, dinner; yel or gr, 10", ea 16.00
Primo, saucer, yel or gr, ea 3.00
Primo, sherbet, yel or gr, ea 9.00
Primo, tumbler, yel or gr, 9-oz, 5¾", ea 16.00
Princess, ashtray, gr, 4½" 67.50
Princess, bowl, cereal; pk, 5" 22.00
Princess, bowl, vegetable; topaz or apricot, oval, 10", ea 55.00
Princess, cake stand, pk, 10" 26.00
Princess, coaster, gr 32.50
Princess, cup, gr or pk, ea 12.00
Princess, pitcher, gr or pk, 60-oz, 8", ea 50.00
Princess, plate, dinner; topaz or apricot, 9½", ea 14.50
Princess, plate, grill; gr or pk, 9½", ea 12.00
Princess, shakers, gr or pk, 4½", pr 50.00
Princess, tumbler, juice; gr, 5-oz, 3" 25.00
Princess, tumbler, water; pk, 9-oz, 4" 24.00
Queen Mary, ashtray, pk, oval, 2x3¾" 5.00
Queen Mary, bowl, berry; crystal, 4½" 4.00
Queen Mary, bowl, berry; pk, 5" 10.00
Queen Mary, bowl, cereal; crystal, 6" 8.00
Queen Mary, bowl, pk, sm, 7" 12.00
Queen Mary, butter dish, pk, w/lid 100.00
Queen Mary, candy dish, crystal, w/lid 20.00
Queen Mary, coaster, pk, 3½" 4.00
Queen Mary, compote, pk, 5¾" 12.50
Queen Mary, creamer, pk, oval 8.00
Queen Mary, plate, salad; crystal, 8¾" 5.00
Queen Mary, plate, sandwich; pk, 12" 14.00
Queen Mary, saucer, pk 2.00
Queen Mary, tumbler, water; pk, 9-oz, 4" 12.00
Raindrops, bowl, berry; gr, 7½" 37.50
Raindrops, bowl, fruit; gr, 4½" 5.00
Raindrops, creamer, gr 8.00

Raindrops, plate, luncheon; gr, 8" 6.00
Raindrops, saucer, gr 1.50
Raindrops, sugar bowl, gr 7.00
Raindrops, tumbler, gr, 10-oz, 5" 9.00
Raindrops, tumbler, gr, 4-oz, 3" 5.00
Raindrops, whiskey, gr, 1-oz, 1⅞" 7.00
Ribbon, bowl, berry; blk, lg, 8" 30.00
Ribbon, bowl, berry; gr, 4" 10.00
Ribbon, creamer, gr, ftd 14.00
Ribbon, cup, gr 5.00
Ribbon, plate, luncheon; blk, 8" 12.50
Ribbon, saucer, gr 2.00
Ribbon, sherbet, gr, ftd 5.00
Ribbon, tumbler, gr, 10-oz, 6" 25.00
Ring, bowl, berry; crystal, 5" 3.50
Ring, bowl, crystal, divided, 5¼" 9.50
Ring, cocktail shaker, w/decor or gr, ea 25.00
Ring, cup, crystal 4.50
Ring, decanter, crystal, w/stopper 22.00
Ring, goblet, wine; w/decor or gr, 3½-oz, 4½", ea 15.00
Ring, pitcher, crystal, 80-oz, 8½" 18.00
Ring, plate, luncheon; w/decor or gr, 8", ea 4.50
Ring, saucer, crystal 1.50
Ring, sugar bowl, w/decor or gr, ftd, ea 5.50
Ring, tumbler, juice; crystal, ftd, 3½" 5.50
Ring, vase, crystal, 8" 16.00
Rock Crystal, bonbon, crystal, scalloped, 7½" 18.00
Rock Crystal, bowl, pickle; cobalt, 7" 30.00
Rock Crystal, bowl, red, scalloped, 4½" 30.00
Rock Crystal, bowl, salad; red, scalloped, 7" 68.00
Rock Crystal, butter dish, crystal, w/lid 310.00
Rock Crystal, candelabra, cobalt, 2-light, pr 77.50
Rock Crystal, candy dish, crystal, rnd, w/lid 42.50
Rock Crystal, compote, red, 7" 65.00
Rock Crystal, cup, crystal, 7-oz 16.00
Rock Crystal, lamp, electric; red 650.00
Rock Crystal, pitcher, gr, scalloped, 1-qt 210.00
Rock Crystal, plate, bread & butter; crystal, scalloped edge, 6" 6.00
Rock Crystal, plate, red, scalloped, 10½" 165.00
Rock Crystal, salt cellar, crystal 35.00
Rock Crystal, saucer, red 22.00
Rock Crystal, spooner, crystal 37.50
Rock Crystal, stemware, yel, 7-oz 24.00
Rock Crystal, tumbler, juice; red, 5-oz 55.00
Rock Crystal, vase, red, ftd, 11" 155.00
Rose Cameo, bowl, berry; gr, 4½" 8.50
Rose Cameo, bowl, cereal; gr, 5" 14.00
Rose Cameo, plate, salad; gr, 7" 11.00
Rose Cameo, sherbet, gr 11.00
Rose Cameo, tumbler, gr, ftd, 2 styles, 5", ea 17.50
Rosemary, bowl, berry; amber, 5" 5.50
Rosemary, bowl, cereal; pk, 6" 33.00
Rosemary, bowl, cream soup; gr, 5" 20.00
Rosemary, creamer, amber, ftd 8.50
Rosemary, plate, dinner; gr 12.50
Rosemary, plate, grill; pk 18.00
Rosemary, platter, pk, oval, 12" 28.00
Rosemary, saucer, gr 5.00
Rosemary, tumbler, amber or gr, 9-oz, 4¼", ea 28.00
Roulette, bowl, fruit; gr, 9" 13.00
Roulette, pitcher, pk or gr, 65-oz, 8", ea 35.00
Roulette, plate, luncheon; gr, 8½" 6.00
Roulette, saucer, pk or gr, ea 3.00
Roulette, tumbler, juice; pk or gr, 5-oz, 3¼", ea 20.00

Roulette, tumbler, water; gr, 9-oz, 4⅛" 22.00
Roulette, whiskey, pk or gr, 1½-oz, 2½", ea 14.00
Round Robin, bowl, berry; gr, 4" 5.00
Round Robin, creamer, irid, ftd 6.50
Round Robin, domino tray, gr 32.00
Round Robin, plate, luncheon; gr or irid, 8", ea 4.00
Round Robin, saucer, gr or irid, ea 2.00
Round Robin, sherbet, gr 5.00
Round Robin, sugar bowl, irid 6.00
Roxana, bowl, berry; yel, 5" 8.50
Roxana, bowl, cereal; yel, 6" 13.00
Roxana, bowl, wht, 4½x2⅜" 13.00
Roxana, plate, sherbet; yel, 6" 6.50
Roxana, plate, yel, 5½" 7.50
Roxana, tumbler, yel, 9-oz, 4¼" 17.50
Royal Lace, bowl, berry; gr, rnd, 10" 28.00
Royal Lace, bowl, berry; pk, 5" 25.00
Royal Lace, bowl, cream soup; crystal, 4¾" 11.00
Royal Lace, bowl, nut; pk or gr, ea 350.00
Royal Lace, bowl, vegetable; bl, oval, 11" 55.00

Royal Lace, butter dish, clear, $65.00.

Royal Lace, butter dish, bl, w/lid 550.00
Royal Lace, cookie jar, pk, w/lid 48.00
Royal Lace, creamer, crystal, ftd 12.00
Royal Lace, plate, dinner; pk, 9⅞" 18.00
Royal Lace, plate, sherbet; crystal, 6" 5.00
Royal Lace, platter, gr, oval, 13" 38.00
Royal Lace, saucer, gr 9.00
Royal Lace, tumbler, gr, 10-oz, 4⅞" 58.00
Royal Lace, tumbler, pk, 5-oz, 3½" 23.00
Royal Ruby, bonbon, 6½" 8.50
Royal Ruby, cigarette box/card holder, w/ruby top, 6⅛x4" 55.00
Royal Ruby, creamer, ftd 9.00
Royal Ruby, cup, rnd 5.50
Royal Ruby, goblet, ball stem 10.00
Royal Ruby, pitcher, 42-oz 30.00
Royal Ruby, plate, salad; 7" 5.00
Royal Ruby, saucer, rnd 2.50
Royal Ruby, tray, 6x4½" 12.50
Royal Ruby, tumbler, water; 9-oz 6.50
Royal Ruby, vase, 2 styles, 9", ea 16.00
S Pattern, bowl, cereal; crystal, 5½" 4.00
S Pattern, creamer, yel or crystal w/trim, ea 7.00
S Pattern, cup, crystal, thick or thin, ea 5.00
S Pattern, plate, dinner; amber or crystal w/trim, 9¼", ea 8.00
S Pattern, plate, grill; yel, amber or crystal w/trim, ea 9.00
S Pattern, saucer, crystal 2.00
S Pattern, tumbler, crystal, 10-oz, 4¾" 7.00

S Pattern, tumbler, crystal, 5-oz, 3½" 5.00
Sandwich (Indiana), basket, amber or crystal, high, 10", ea 35.00
Sandwich (Indiana), bowl, amber or crystal, 6", ea 4.00
Sandwich (Indiana), bowl, teal bl, hexagonal, 6" 14.00
Sandwich (Indiana), candlesticks, pk or gr, 3½", pr 42.00
Sandwich (Indiana), creamer, crystal 9.00
Sandwich (Indiana), cup, teal bl 8.50
Sandwich (Indiana), decanter, red, w/stopper 80.00
Sandwich (Indiana), goblet, amber or crystal, 9-oz, ea 13.00
Sandwich (Indiana), pitcher, red, 68-oz 130.00
Sandwich (Indiana), plate, sandwich; amber or crystal, 13", ea 13.00
Sandwich (Indiana), plate, sherbet; teal bl, 6" 7.00
Sandwich (Indiana), saucer, red 7.00
Sandwich (Indiana), tumbler, cocktail; amber, ftd, 3-oz 7.50
Sandwich (Indiana), wine, red, 4-oz, 3" 12.50
Sharon, bowl, berry; amber, 5" 8.50
Sharon, bowl, berry; gr, lg, 8½" 30.00
Sharon, bowl, cereal; pk, 6" 22.50
Sharon, butter dish, amber, w/lid 47.50
Sharon, cheese dish, pk, w/lid 850.00
Sharon, cup, pk 14.00
Sharon, plate, bread & butter; gr, 6" 8.00
Sharon, plate, cake; pk, ftd, 11½" 40.00
Sharon, plate, dinner; amber, 9½" 12.00
Sharon, shakers, pk, pr 47.50
Sharon, sherbet, gr, ftd 32.00
Sharon, tumbler, amber, thick, 9-oz, 4⅛" 25.00
Sharon, tumbler, pk, ftd, 15-oz, 6½" 45.00
Ships, bowl, ice; bl & wht 30.00
Ships, cocktail mixer, bl & wht, w/stirrer 25.00
Ships, plate, bread & butter; bl & wht, 5⅞" 20.00
Ships, plate, salad; bl & wht, 8" 21.00
Ships, saucer, bl & wht 16.00
Ships, tumbler, iced tea; bl & wht, 12-oz 20.00
Ships, tumbler, juice; bl & wht, 5-oz, 3¾" 11.00
Ships, tumbler, old fashioned; bl & wht, 8-oz, 3⅜" 15.00
Ships, tumbler, whiskey; bl & wht, 3½" 25.00
Sierra, bowl, cereal; pk, 5½" 11.00
Sierra, bowl, mixing; gr, 7" 8.50
Sierra, creamer, pk 18.00
Sierra, plate, dinner; gr, 9" 20.00
Sierra, platter, pk, oval, 11" 40.00
Sierra, saucer, gr 7.00
Sierra, tray, serving; pk, hdls, 10¼" 15.00
Sierra, tumbler, gr, ftd, 9-oz, 4½" 67.50
Spiral, bowl, berry; gr, 4¾" 5.00
Spiral, bowl, vegetable; gr, oval, 9¼" 88.00
Spiral, creamer, gr, flat or ftd 7.50
Spiral, pitcher, gr, 58-oz, 7⅝" 30.00
Spiral, platter, gr, 12" 25.00
Spiral, saucer, gr 2.00
Spiral, shakers, gr, pr 32.50
Spiral, sherbet, gr 4.00
Spiral, tumbler, gr, ftd, 5⅞" 14.00
Spiral, tumbler, juice; gr, 5-oz, 3" 4.50
Starlight, bowl, crystal or wht, closed hdls, 8½", ea 9.00
Starlight, bowl, pk, 2¾x12" 24.00
Starlight, cup, pk 5.00
Starlight, plate, luncheon; crystal or wht, 8½", ea 5.00
Starlight, plate, sandwich; pk, 13" 17.50
Starlight, saucer, crystal or wht, ea 2.00
Starlight, shakers, crystal or wht, pr 22.50
Strawberry, bowl, berry; crystal or irid, 4", ea 6.50
Strawberry, bowl, salad; pk or gr, deep, 7½", ea 22.00

Strawberry, butter dish, crystal or irid, w/lid, ea 135.00
Strawberry, compote, pk or gr, 5¾", ea 19.00
Strawberry, pickle dish, pk or gr, oval, 8¼", ea 13.00
Strawberry, plate, sherbet; crystal or irid, 6", ea 5.00
Strawberry, sugar bowl, pk or gr, w/lid, lg, ea 80.00
Strawberry, tumbler, pk or gr, 8-oz, 3⅝", ea 30.00
Sunflower, ashtray, pk, center design only, 5" 9.00
Sunflower, creamer, pk 16.00
Sunflower, plate, cake; pk or gr, 3-legged, 10", ea 15.00
Sunflower, plate, dinner; gr, 9" 18.00
Sunflower, saucer, pk 7.00
Sunflower, trivet, gr, turned-up edges, 3-legged, 7" 300.00
Sunflower, tumbler, gr, ftd, 8-oz, 4¾" 30.00
Swirl, bowl, cereal; pk, 5¼" 10.00
Swirl, bowl, salad; ultramarine, 9" 25.00
Swirl, butter dish, pk, w/lid 190.00
Swirl, candy dish, ultramarine, w/lid 145.00
Swirl, creamer, delphite, ftd 12.00
Swirl, cup, pk 7.00
Swirl, plate, pk, 7¼" 6.50
Swirl, plate, ultramarine, 10½" 28.00
Swirl, platter, delphite, oval, 12" 35.00
Swirl, saucer, pk 3.00
Swirl, sugar bowl, pk, ftd 10.00
Swirl, tumbler, pk, 9-oz, 4⅝" 17.50
Swirl, vase, pk, ruffled, ftd, 6½" 16.00
Tea Room, bowl, banana split; pk, ftd, 7½" 77.50
Tea Room, bowl, finger; gr 50.00
Tea Room, bowl, salad; gr, deep, 8¾" 80.00
Tea Room, creamer, pk, rectangular 17.00
Tea Room, creamer, pk or gr, 3¼", ea 26.00
Tea Room, ice bucket, gr 57.50
Tea Room, mustard jar, gr, w/lid 135.00
Tea Room, pitcher, gr, 64-oz 140.00
Tea Room, relish tray, gr, divided 22.50
Tea Room, saucer, pk or gr, ea 25.00
Tea Room, sugar bowl, gr, rectangular 20.00
Tea Room, tumbler, pk, ftd, 11-oz 40.00
Tea Room, vase, gr, ruffled edge, 6½" 98.00
Tea Room, vase, gr, str, 11" 90.00
Thistle, bowl, cereal; pk, 5½" 20.00
Thistle, bowl, fruit; gr, lg, 10¼" 175.00
Thistle, cup, pk, thin 20.00
Thistle, plate, grill; pk, 10¼" 20.00
Thistle, plate, luncheon; gr, 8" 14.00
Thistle, saucer, pk 9.50
Tulip, bowl, amethyst or bl, 6", ea 10.00
Tulip, creamer, amber, crystal or gr, ea 10.00
Tulip, cup, amethyst or bl, ea 10.00
Tulip, plate, amber, crystal or gr, 9", ea 4.00
Tulip, saucer, amethyst or bl, ea 2.50
Tulip, tumbler, whiskey; amber, crystal or gr, ea 10.00
Twisted Optic, bowl, amber, 9" 15.00
Twisted Optic, bowl, cereal; gr, 5" 5.50
Twisted Optic, bowl, pk, tall, 10" 40.00
Twisted Optic, candlesticks, pk or gr, 3", pr 18.00
Twisted Optic, candy jar, canary yel, ftd, w/lid, tall 35.00
Twisted Optic, cologne bottle, pk, w/stopper 35.00
Twisted Optic, creamer, pk or gr, ea 7.50
Twisted Optic, mayonnaise, amber 20.00
Twisted Optic, pitcher, bl, 64-oz 30.00
Twisted Optic, plate, salad; canary yel, 7" 3.00
Twisted Optic, powder jar, pk, w/lid 30.00
Twisted Optic, saucer, gr 2.00

Twisted Optic, vase, gr, 2-hdld, str edge, 8" 25.00
US Swirl, bowl, gr, hdl, 5½" 10.00
US Swirl, bowl, pk or gr, oval, 8¼", ea 25.00
US Swirl, creamer, gr 14.00
US Swirl, pitcher, pk or gr, 48-oz, 8", ea 50.00
US Swirl, shakers, pk or gr, pr 45.00
US Swirl, tumbler, pk or gr, 8-oz, 3⅝", ea 10.00
US Swirl, vase, gr, 6½" 16.00
Victory, bonbon, amber, pk or gr, 7", ea 12.00
Victory, bowl, console; amber, pk or gr, 12", ea 35.00
Victory, bowl, soup; blk or bl, flat, 8½", ea 40.00
Victory, creamer, blk or bl, ea 45.00
Victory, plate, salad; amber, pk or gr, 7", ea 7.00
Victory, platter, blk or bl, 12", ea 70.00
Victory, sugar bowl, amber, pk or gr, ea 15.00
Vitrock, bowl, berry; wht, 4" 4.50
Vitrock, bowl, fruit; wht, 6" 5.50
Vitrock, bowl, vegetable; wht, 9½" 12.00
Vitrock, creamer, wht, oval 4.50
Vitrock, plate, soup; wht, 9" 14.00
Vitrock, saucer, wht 2.00
Waterford, ashtray, crystal, 4" 7.50
Waterford, bowl, berry; crystal, lg, 8¼" 10.00
Waterford, bowl, cereal; pk, 5½" 27.50
Waterford, coaster, crystal, 4" 3.50
Waterford, cup, pk 14.00
Waterford, pitcher, pk, 52-oz, 6¾" 27.50
Waterford, plate, dinner; crystal, 9⅝" 11.00
Waterford, saucer, pk 6.00
Windsor, bowl, cream soup; crystal, 5" 6.00
Windsor, bowl, salad; crystal, 10½" 9.00
Windsor, coaster, gr, 3¼" 16.00
Windsor, plate, chop; pk or gr, 13⅝", ea 45.00
Windsor, plate, salad; pk, 7" 16.00
Windsor, tumbler, pk, 9-oz, 4" 18.00

Derby

William Duesbury operated in Derby, England, from about 1755, purchasing a second establishment, The Chelsea Works, in 1769. During this period fine porcelains were produced which so impressed the King that in 1773 he issued the company the Crown Derby patent. In 1810, several years after Duesbury's death, the factory was bought by Robert Bloor. The quality of the ware suffered under the new management, and the main Derby pottery closed in 1848. Within a short time, the work was revived by a dedicated number of former employees who established their own works on King Street in Derby.

The earliest known Derby mark was the crown over a script 'D'; however this mark is rarely found today. Soon after 1782, that mark was augmented with a device of crossed batons and six dots, usually applied in underglaze blue. During the Bloor period, the crown was centered within a ring containing the words 'Bloor' above and 'Derby' below the crown, or with a red printed stamp — the crowned Gothic 'D.' The King Street plant produced figurines that may be distinguished from their earlier counterparts by the presence of an 'S' and 'H' on either side of the crown and crossed batons.

In 1876 a new pottery was constructed in Derby, and the owners revived the earlier company's former standard of excellence. The Queen bestowed the firm the title Royal Crown Derby in 1890; it still operates under that name today. See also Royal Crown Derby.

Cup & saucer, exotic bird, Kakiemon palette, 1815 ....225.00

Figurine, pointer by stump, natural colors, 1795, 6" L 825.00
Figurine, Venus/Cupid on dolphin, 1765, rpr, 10", VG 1,100.00
Potpourri, flower-filled comport form, masks, 7", VG 1,100.00
Vase, floral, gold trim, bulbous w/slim neck, 11½x4½" 900.00
Waste bowl, stylized roots, leaf rim, bl w/gold, 1820, 6" 450.00

Desert Sands

As early as the 1850s, the Evans family living in the Ozark Mountains of Missouri produced domestic clay products. Their small pot shop was passed on from one generation to the next. In the 1920s it was moved to North Las Vegas, Nevada, where the name Desert Sands was adopted. Succeeding generations of the family continued to relocate, taking the business with them. From 1937 to 1962 it operated in Boulder City, Nevada; then it was moved to Barstow where it remained until it closed in the late 1970s.

Desert Sands pottery is similar to Mission Ware by Niloak. Various mineral oxides were blended to mimic the naturally occuring sand formations of the American West. A high-gloss glaze was applied to add intensity to the colorful striations that characterize the ware. Not all examples are marked, making it sometimes difficult to attribute. Marked items carry an ink stamp with the Desert Sands designation. Paper labels were also used.

Bowl, 3", $15.00; Vase, 5", $25.00; Vase, 3½", $35.00.

Ashtray, 6½" 20.00
Bowl, console; hand thrown, 9½" 45.00
Butter dish 45.00
Candle holder, swirled colors, 3" 15.00
Shakers, swirled colors, pr 25.00
Tumbler, swirled colors 15.00
Vase, swirled colors, slim form, 3½" 15.00

Devon, Crown Devon

Devon and Crown Devon were trade names of S. Fielding and Company, Ltd., an English firm founded after 1879. They produced majolica, earthenware mugs, vases and kitchenware. In the 1930s they manufactured an exceptional line of Art Deco vases that have recently been much in demand.

Box, cigarette; musical, I Love a Lassie, H Lauder, 4x5½" 175.00
Jug, Irish Junting Cart, Killarny, verse, musical, 7x4⅜" 165.00
Jug, John Peel, fox hdl, musical, 8¼x6" 195.00

Mug, John Peel, riding crop hdl, musical, 6½" 175.00
Mug, toasting figures, Auld Lang Syne, musical, 4¾x4½" 165.00
Vase, String of Pearls, gold hdls, ftd, 10¼" 45.00

Documents

Although the word 'document' is defined in the general sense as 'anything printed or written, etc., relied upon to record or prove something. . .,' in the collectibles market, the term is more diversified with broadsides, billheads, checks, invoices, letters and letterheads, land grants, receipts, and waybills some of the most sought after. Some documents in demand are those related to a specific subject such as advertising, mining, railroads, military, politics, banking, slavery, nautical, or legal (deeds, mortgages, etc.). Other collectors look for examples representing a specific period of time such as colonial documents, Revolutionary, or Civil War documents, early western documents or those from a specific region, state, or city.

Aside from supply and demand, there are five major factors which determine the collector-value of a document. These are:

1) Age — Documents from the eastern half of the country can be found that date back to the 1700s or earlier. Most documents sought by collectors usually date from 1700 to 1900. Those with 20th-century dates are still abundant and not in demand unless of special significance or beauty.

2) Region of origin — Depending on age, documents from rural and less-populated areas are harder to find than those from major cities and heavily populated states. The colonization of the West and Mid-West did not begin until after 1850, so while an 1870s billhead from New York or Chicago is common, one from Albuquerque or Phoenix is not, since most of the Southwest was still unsettled.

3) Attractiveness — Some documents are plain and unadorned, but collectors prefer colorful, profusely illustrated pieces. Additional artwork and engravings add to the value.

4) Historical content — Unusual or interesting content, such as a letter written by a Civil War soldier giving an eye-witness account of the Battle of Gettysburg or a western territorial billhead listing numerous animal hides purchased from a trapper, will sell for more than one with mundane information.

5) Condition — Through neglect or environmental conditions, over many decades paper articles can become stained, torn, or deteriorated. Heavily damaged or stained documents are generally avoided altogether. Those with minor problems are more acceptable, although their value will decrease anywhere from 20% to 50%, depending upon the extent of damage. Avoid attempting to repair tears with scotch tape — sell 'as is' so that the collector can take proper steps toward restoration.

Foreign documents are plentiful; and though some are very attractive, resale may be difficult. The listings that follow are generalized; prices are variable depending entirely upon the five points noted above. Values here are based upon examples with no major damage. Common grade documents without significant content are found in abundance and generally have little collector value. These usually date from the late 1800s and early 1900s. It should be noted that the items listed below are examples of those that meet the criteria for having collector value. There is little demand for documents worth less than $5.00. For more information we recommend *Owning Western History* by our advisor Warren Anderson. His address and ordering information may be found in the Directory under Utah.

Key:
illus — illustrated   vgn — vignette

Bank draft, Dakota Territory, vgns, 1885, 4x9", EX 20.00

Bank note, Confederate, for $20, cherub & lady vgn, 1861 ....30.00
Book, account; Civil War Union clothing, unbound, EX 125.00
Certificate, baptismal; parchment, England, 1585, EX 400.00
Contract, AT&SF RR, land purchase, 1873, 11x20" 45.00
Currency, Confederate, Blks hoeing cotton, $100 ....75.00
Deed, tract of land in CT, 1798, EX 16.00
Directory, US Army Retired Officers, 6 states, 1961, 51-pg 6.50
Discharge, Revolutionary War, sgn twice, 1790, EX 100.00

Engraved parchment commission, signed by Andrew Johnson and Edwin M. Stanton, dated 1866, 15x18", framed, $600.00.

Envelope, illus of Steamer Bell of Shreveport, M 85.00
Examination, school teacher's, VT, 1876, 4-pg, 2¾x5⅜" 15.00
Indenture papers, vellum, PA, 2 wax seals, 1779, 15x26" 28.00
Inventory of estate, GA, assets/slaves, 1848, 8x12", VG 125.00
Invoice, Corning & Co Distillery, illus of plant, 1914, 6x8" 7.50
Land grant, sgn James Monroe 700.00
Leaflet, WWII propaganda, as dropped on Germans, EX 15.00
Ledger, OH River, Steamer JC Kerr wharf charges, 1884-87 ....55.00
Letter, Kansas City Athletic club fund-raising, 1919, 1-pg 12.50
Letter, much business, Boston, 1784, 1-pg, EX 24.00
Letter, re title to land, Omaha, 1870 ....30.00
Letter, soldier to mother, Aug 1917, 4-pg, EX 25.00
Letterhead, JM Curley campaign office in Boston, 1940s, EX 6.50
Marriage certificate, PA, Dec 29, 1900, silver fr, 16x20" 50.00
Note, Navy related, sgn Louis Warrington, 1832 ....185.00
Orders, delivery of textiles, 1773, EX 20.00
Passenger list, US Mail Coach, coach vgns, 1841, 9x14" 20.00
Patent papers, Magician bank, WC Bull, 2-pg, EX 240.00
Pay order, amount due for military services, bl paper, 1854 ....5.00
Pay order, pre-printed, service in army, 1780 ....50.00
Pension request, Confederate soldier's widow, 1900, EX 6.00
Promissory note, CA mining camp, handwritten, 1863, 4x6" 30.00
Receipt, Am Express, list of goods, St Louis, 1884, 4x5", pr 20.00
Receipt, bail; handwritten, NY, 1763, 4x5", VG 98.00
Receipt, Lake Keuka Navigation Co, bbl of wine, 1909, EX 10.00
Receipt, NYNH&H RR, transportation of merchandise, 1878, EX ...7.50
Receipt, purchase of steer for $19, 1776, EX 25.00
Receipt, shares in AK bank, printed, 1830s, 7⅛x9⅜" 15.00
Receipt, tax payments, AR Territory, 1883, 4x6", EX 25.00
Recital program, VA College for Young Ladies, 1899, 3-pg 6.50
Report, health inspection of ship, for entering port, 1808, EX 10.00
Report, re income from slaves, dtd 1834, EX 32.00
Scrip, PA mining co, Kewenaw County MI, sgn Sam Hill, 1864 ..50.00
Slave sale, GA, list of 7 w/amounts for ea, 1833, 7x8" 150.00
Sworn statement, witness of slave sale, 1805, 5x9" pg 85.00
Ticket, commencement, Harvard University, 1928, EX 5.00
Voucher, military 'pay,' unissued, 1850s, 10x16", EX 15.00
Warrant, treasury; Texas, $3, 1864, EX 25.00

Writ, order to appear to testify, Cornwall, 1798, 6x8", EX **27.50**

Dollhouses and Furnishings

Dollhouses were introduced commercially in this country late in the 1700s by Dutch craftsmen who settled in the East. By the mid-1800s, they had become meticulously detailed, divided into separate rooms, and lavishly furnished to reflect the opulence of the day. Originally intended for the amusement of adults of the household, by the latter 1800s their status had changed to that of a child's toy. Though many early dollhouses were lovingly hand-fashioned for a special little girl, those made commercially by such companies as Bliss and Schoenhut are highly valued.

Furniture and furnishings in the Biedermeier style featuring stenciled Victorian decorations often sell for several hundred dollars each. Other early pieces made of pewter, porcelain, or papier-mache are also quite valuable. Certainly less expensive but very collectible, nonetheless, is the quality, hallmarked plastic furniture produced during the forties by Renwal and Acme, and the 1960s Petite Princess line produced by Ideal. In the listings that follow, dollhouses are litho paper on wood, unless otherwise noted. When no manufacturer or country of origin is noted, examples are German, turn of the century. For more information, see *Schroeder's Collectible Toys, Antique to Modern*. Our advisor for this category is Barbara Rosen; she is listed in the Directory under New Jersey. See also Miniatures.

Furniture

Bathinette, Renwal, #122 ....**12.00**
Bathtub, Plasco **12.00**

6-piece bedroom set, Bliss, lithographed paper on wood, ca 1895, some damage, $350.00.

Bench, Renwal, #L-75 ....**3.00**
Chaise lounge, Plasco **16.00**
Chest, Renwal, #B-85 ....**6.00**
Clock, red, Renwal, #10 ....**8.00**
Coal bucket & shovel, CI **10.00**
Cookstove, CI **30.00**
Crib, rocking type w/baby, Renwal, #120 ....**20.00**
Desk, office; w/swivel chair, Renwal, #35/#36 ....**40.00**
Dining set, Arcade, pnt CI, table+6 chairs+hutch+sideboard, VG ..**300.00**
Dining set, walnut wood, Strombecker, 7-pc **165.00**
Easy chair, Renwal, #L-76 ....**14.00**
Hamper, Plasco **3.00**
Ironing board, Renwal, #32 ....**10.00**
Lamp, floor type, Renwal **10.00**
Patio fountain, Plasco **12.00**
Playpen, Renwal, #118 ....**12.00**

Radio/record player, Renwal, #18 ....**20.00**
Range, Modern Maid decal, 1950s **20.00**
Rocker, Renwal, #65 ....**10.00**
Rocking horse, Acme **12.00**
Sink, bathroom; Plasco **6.00**
Sink, Renwal, ivory w/red stencil **5.00**
Slide (playground), #20 ....**9.00**
Stove, Renwal, #K-69 ....**13.00**
Table, dressing; Plasco, #B-1, +stool **10.00**
Table, dressing; Renwal, #B-82 ....**10.00**
Table, kitchen; Renwal, #K-67 & 4 chairs, #K-53 ....**16.00**
Table, kitchen; Tootsietoy, +2 chairs **26.00**
Table, patio; rnd, w/4 chairs, Plasco **20.00**
Table, Renwal, #L-73 ....**5.00**
Teeter totter, Acme **9.00**
Telephone, cradle style, Tootsietoy **15.00**
Tub & shower, pnt tin, Germany, 7", VG **275.00**
Wringer washer, Renwal, #31 ....**22.00**

Houses, Shops, and Single Rooms

Victorian cottage, printed paper on wood, double veranda, 18x9½x9", EX, $420.00.

Bliss, mc trim w/metal porch lattice, hinged door, 17", G **600.00**
Bliss, trn porch balusters, hinged door, rpt, 16", G **800.00**
Dunham Cocoanut, 4-story, wood litho, 12x29", G **275.00**
Germany, bake shop, papered wood/glass, 10x26", +80 pcs **650.00**
Germany, coffee shop, pnt/papered wood, 9x21+, +18 pcs **300.00**
Germany, grocery store, pnt wood, counters+accessories, 8x10" ...**500.00**
Germany, tea shop, litho on wood, 12 containers, 15x6", VG **210.00**
Germany, Victorian room, papered cb, 10 furniture pcs, 12x22" ..**150.00**
Germany, wrapping counter, desk/cabinet/papers, 21x18", EX ...**575.00**
Germany, 2-story/2-room, paper on wood, 17", G **415.00**
Kitchen, pnt wood diorama, 2 celluloid dolls+50 pcs, 17x34" **525.00**
Marx, house w/breezeway, tin litho, complete, unassembled, NM ...**100.00**
Marx, Modern Kitchen Set, tin diorama, complete, 5x26", NM ..**190.00**
Parker Bros, Toy Town Grocery, paper litho, 8x17", +36 pcs **350.00**
Schoenhut, bungalo, yel/red w/red roof, trn posts, 11x15x13", EX .**360.00**
Tudor stable, pnt & stucco wood, 4 animals, 15x14" **160.00**
Wolverine, Corner Grocery, tin litho, 16x12", G **110.00**

Dolls

Collecting dolls of any sort is one of the most rewarding hobbies in the United States. The rewards are in the fun, the search, and the finds — plus there is a built-in factor of investment. No hobby, be it dolls, glass, or anything else, should be based completely on investment; but any collector should ask: 'Can I get my money back out of this item if I should ever have to sell it?' Many times we buy on impulse rather than with logic, which is understandable; but by asking this question we can save ourselves a lot of 'buyer's remorse' which we have all experienced at one time or another.

Since we want to learn to invest our money wisely while we are having fun, we must become aware of defects which may devaluate a doll. In bisque, watch for eye chips, hairline cracks and chips, or breaks on any part of the head. Composition should be clean, not crazed or cracked. Vinyl and plastic should be clean with no pen or crayon marks. Though a quality replacement wig is acceptable for bisque dolls, composition and hard plastics should have their originals in uncut condition. Original clothing is a must except in bisque dolls, since it is unusual to find one in its original costume.

A price guide is only that — a guide. It suggests the average price for each doll. Bargains can be found for less-than-suggested values, and 'unplayed-with' dolls in their original boxes may cost more. Dealers must become aware of condition so that they do not overpay and therefore overprice their dolls — a common occurrence across the country. Quantity does not replace quality, as most find out in time. A faster turnover of sales with a smaller margin of profit is far better than being stuck with an item that does not sell because it is overpriced. It is important to remember that prices are based on condition and rarity. When no condition is noted, dolls are assumed to be in excellent condition with the exceptions of Armand Marseille, Madame Alexander, and Effanbee dolls, which are priced in mint condition. In relation to bisque dolls, excellent means having no cracks, chips, or hairlines, being nicely dressed, shoed, wigged, and ready to to be placed into a collection. For a more thorough study of the subject, we recommend you refer to the many lovely doll books written by authority Pat Smith, available at your favorite bookstore or public library.

Key:
bjtd — ball-jointed	o/c/m — open closed mouth
blb — bent limb body	o/m — open mouth
bsk — bisque	p/e — pierced ears
c/m — closed mouth	pnt — painted
hh — human hair	pwt — paperweight eyes
hp — hard plastic	RpC — replaced clothes
jtd — jointed	ShHd — shoulder head
MIG — Made In Germany	ShPl — shoulder plate
NC — no clothes	SkHd — socket head
o/c — open closed eyes	str — straight
OC — original clothes	trn — turned

American Character

Baby, compo/cloth, mk AC, 1930s-40s, 14" 85.00
Baby Lou, plastic (1-pc mold), molded hair, RpC, 1950, 8" 20.00
Butterball, plastic/vinyl, lg rnd o/c, 1961, OC, 19" 140.00
Child, compo, mk AC, OC, 14" 165.00
Groom, hp, OC, 20" 450.00
Puggy, compo, pnt eyes, frowning mouth, OC, mk Petite, 13" ...500.00
Ricky Jr, vinyl (1-pc mold), o/c, pnt hair, '55, RpC, 13" 85.00
Sally Says, hp/vinyl, talker, o/c, 1964, OC, 19" 95.00
Sally Says, plastic/vinyl, talker, 1965, OC, 19" 85.00
Sweet Sue, hp, OC (red ball gown), 14" 285.00
Sweet Sue, hp, orig ball gown, 1958, 10½" 175.00
Sweet Sue, hp, walker, OC, 18", minimum value 365.00
Sweet Sue, vinyl, curly brn hair, 1955, OC, 17" 325.00
Talking Marie, plastic/vinyl, battery-op record player, 18" 95.00
Teeny Weeny Tiny Tears, vinyl, o/c, o/m nurser, '64, OC, 8½" ...25.00
Toodles, vinyl, brn flirty eyes, curly hair, 1956, RpC, 22" 200.00
Tressie, heavy makeup, hair 'grows,' OC, 12½" 55.00
Whimette, hp/vinyl, pnt eyes, red hair, 1963, RpC, 18" 35.00

Annalee

Baby Angel, felt w/pnt features, 1960s, 7"-8", ea 325.00
Baby Angel, felt w/pnt features, diaper, 1956, 10", minimum 600.00
Ballerina Pig, felt w/pnt features, tutu & parasol, 1981 ....145.00
Baseball Kid, felt w/pnt features, 1984, 7" 200.00
Bear w/bee on nose, felt, 1938, OC, 18", minimum value 200.00
Child, felt w/pnt features, 1950s, rare, 10", minimum value 2,000.00
Clown, felt w/pnt features, orange hair, 1984, 10" 150.00
Elf, felt w/pnt features, 1970s, 7" 200.00
Go Go Girl, felt w/pnt features, 10", NM, minimum value 115.00
Indian, felt w/pnt features, 1970s, 7" 200.00
Indian, felt w/pnt features, 1980s, 18", minimum value 250.00
Monk w/ski, felt w/pnt features, 1970, 9" 175.00
Monkey w/banana & trapeze, felt w/pnt features, 1981, 12" 250.00
Mrs Santa Claus, felt w/pnt features, 1970s, 26" 200.00
Naughty Angel, felt w/pnt features, 1985, 12" 130.00
Rabbit in Easter crate, felt w/pnt features, 1978, 8" 115.00
Rooster, felt w/cloth features, 1976, 15" 1,000.00
Santa, felt w/pnt features, 1970s, 7" 75.00
Santa Fox, felt w/pnt features, 1981, 18", minimum value 295.00
Santa Frog, felt w/pnt features, 1980, 18" 235.00
Skiing Kid, felt w/pnt features, 1986, 7" 70.00
Snowman, felt w/pnt features, 1971, 7" 275.00
Valentine Bunny, felt w/pnt features, 1984, 7" 130.00

Armand Marseille

Alma, ShHd, 12" 150.00
Alma, ShHd, 26" 485.00
AM, Darling Baby, 1906, 12" 350.00
AM, Floradora, ShHd, 23" 425.00
AM, Floradora, SkHd, 15" 250.00
AM, Floradora, SkHd, 17" 325.00
AM, Floradora 1374, ShHd, fur eyebrows, 21" 425.00
AM, Indian, SkHd, o/c, 1890s, 8" 450.00
AM, Kiddiejoy, ShHd, 9" 225.00
AM, My Playmate (body), closed dome & c/m, 18" 1,800.00
AM, Roseland, 1910, 18" 485.00
AM, SkHd, c/m, 14" 950.00
AM, SkHd, o/m, blk, 12" 475.00
AM, SkHd, 17" 250.00
AM, SkHd, 8" 165.00
AM, trn ShHd, talks, 16" 500.00
AM 1894, SkHd, blk, 12" 375.00
AM 1894, SkHd, wht, 16½" 325.00
AM 1894, SkHd, 14" 250.00
AM 200, SkHd, googly eyes, 11½" 2,500.00
AM 231, Fany, baby, c/m, 1913, 25" 8,400.00
AM 250, mk GB (Geo Borgfeldt), SkHd, c/m, molded hair, 10½" ..500.00
AM 252, SkHd, googly eyes, 1915, 9½" 1,100.00
AM 253, SkHd, googly eyes, 6½" 750.00
AM 254, SkHd, googly eyes, molded hair, 8" 750.00
AM 257, baby, SkHd, 1914, 22" 550.00
AM 315, Queen Louise, SkHd, 27" 850.00
AM 3200, ShHd, some trn, 15" 275.00
AM 3200, ShHd, some trn, 1898, 16" 265.00
AM 3200, ShHd, some trn, 26" 600.00
AM 323, SkHd, googly eyes, 7½" 900.00
AM 327, SkHd, baby, fur hair, 1914, 12" 350.00
AM 327, SkHd, 1914, 20" 450.00
AM 329, girl, SkHd, 9" 275.00
AM 341, My Dream Baby, flange, c/m, 15" 450.00
AM 341, My Dream Baby, flange, c/m, 1924, 7" 245.00

AM 341, My Dream Baby, SkHd, c/m, 16" 650.00
AM 3500, ShHd, 17" 400.00
AM 351, My Dream Baby, flange, o/m, 26" 900.00
AM 351, Wee One, rubber body, 1922, 7" 165.00
AM 3524, Baby Gloria, flange neck, 18" 1,000.00
AM 370, fur eyebrows (rare), 22½" 350.00
AM 370, 15" 225.00
AM 370, 19½" 350.00
AM 372, Kiddiejoy, ShHd, molded hair, 1926, 9" 350.00
AM 390, My Dearie, SkHd, 1908-22, 18" 400.00
AM 390, o/m, 7½" 175.00
AM 390, SkHd, 22" 385.00
AM 390, SkHd, 9½" 225.00
AM 390n, Patrice, 18" 500.00
AM 450, SkHd, c/m, provincial attire, 19" 2,000.00
AM 500, Infant Berry, molded hair, 1908, 5" 185.00
AM 550, SkHd, c/m, 16" 2,200.00
AM 590, Hoopla Girl, o/c & mouth, 16" 1,800.00
AM 800, Baby Sunshine, 'Mama' talker in head, 1925, 16" 2,200.00
AM 95, trn ShHd, 20" 325.00
AM 970, Lady Marie, Otto Gans, 1916, 20" 700.00
AM 975, Sadie, baby, SkHd, 1914, 24" 800.00
AM 980, baby, SkHd, 14" 325.00
AM 990, Happy Tot, baby, SkHd, 13" 400.00
AM 990, Happy Tot, baby, SkHd, 1910, 21" 625.00
AM 991, Kiddiejoy, baby, SkHd, 14" 425.00
AM 995, baby, SkHd, 12" 300.00
AM 997, Kiddiejoy, baby, SkHd, 14" 425.00
Lily, ShHd, 1913, 17" 350.00
Mabel, ShHd, 1898, 17" 375.00
Queen Louise, 100, Germany, SkHd, 1910, 12" 250.00
Wonderful Alice, SkHd, fur eyebrows, 26" 650.00

Barbie Dolls and Related Dolls

Though the face has changed three times since 1959, Barbie is still as popular today as she was when she was first introduced. Named after the young daughter of the first owner of the Mattel Company, the original Barbie had a white iris but no eye color. These dolls are nearly impossible to find, but there is a myriad of her successors and related collectibles just waiting to be found. When no condition is indicated, the dolls listed below are assumed to be in mint condition (without original box) unless otherwise specified. For further information we recommend *The World of Barbie Dolls* and *The Wonder of Barbie, 1976 – 1986*, by Paris, Susan, and Carol Manos; *The Collector's Encyclopedia of Barbie Dolls and Collectibles* by Sibyl DeWein and Joan Ashabraner, and *Barbie Exclusives* by Margo Rana. *Barbie Fashion, Vol I, 1959 – 1967*, by Sarah Sink Eames, gives a complete history of the wardrobes of Barbie, her friends, and her family. Many of Patricia Smith's books contain chapters on Barbies as well as other dolls by Mattel. Our advisor for Barbie Dolls is Karen Martin; she is listed in the Directory under Michigan.

Allen, 1964, 12" 95.00
Barbie, 1958-59, #1, doll only, 11½", M 2,500.00
Barbie, 1958-59, #1, holes in ft, metal cylinders, 11½", MIB ...3,000.00
Barbie, 1960, #3, curved brows, mk, as nurse, 11½" 500.00
Barbie, 1961, #4, bubble cut, 11½", minimum value 140.00
Barbie, 1961, #4, mk Pat Pend, 11½" 275.00
Barbie, 1961, Friday Nite Date, 11½" 250.00
Barbie, 1963, Career Girl, 11½" 200.00
Barbie, 1963, Fashion Queen, 2 wigs, 11½", minimum value 200.00
Barbie, 1963, Movie Date, 11½" 225.00
Barbie, 1963, Ski Queen, 11½" 260.00
Barbie, 1963, Swinging Easy, 11½" 300.00

Barbie, 1964, Drum Major, 11½" 225.00
Barbie, 1964, Guinevere, 11½" 400.00
Barbie, 1964, ponytail, swirl bands, 11½", minimum value 200.00

Barbie doll with Lifelike Bendable Legs, 1965, M in EX box, $3,000.00.

Barbie, 1967-68, Twist 'N Turn, 11½" 175.00
Barbie, 1968, Spanish Talking, 11½", minimum value 225.00
Barbie, 1969-70, Twist 'N Turn, 11½" 150.00
Barbie, 1970, Standard, gr & gr striped swimsuit, 11½" 200.00
Barbie, 1972, Growing Pretty Hair, 11½" 175.00
Barbie, 1972, Miss America, 11½" 200.00
Barbie, 1972, Ward's Anniversary, 11½" 550.00
Barbie, 1975, Free Moving, 11½" 65.00
Barbie, 1975, Gold Medal Skater, 11½" 60.00
Barbie, 1977, Super Star, 11½" 50.00
Barbie, 1979, Kissing, 11½" 50.00
Barbie, 1982, Magic Curl, 11½" 35.00
Barbie, 1982, Oriental, 11½" 110.00
Barbie, 1983, Horse Lovin', 11½" 35.00
Barbie, 1985, Peaches & Cream, 11½" 35.00
Brad, 1971, bend knees, 11½" 90.00
Christie, 1968, Blk, 11½", minimum value 75.00
Debbie Boone, 1979, 11½" 22.00
Francie, 1966, 11½", minimum value 100.00
Kelly, 1973, Quick Curl, 11½" 60.00
Ken, bend knees, minimum value 325.00
Ken, flocked hair, minimum value 125.00
Ken, Malibu, minimum value 25.00
Ken, mod hair, minimum value 50.00
Midge, 1963, freckles, 11½", minimum value 130.00
PJ, 1971, Live Action, 11½" 65.00
PJ, 1976, Quick Curl, 11½" 40.00
Ricky, 1965, red hair & freckles, minimum value 75.00
Skipper, 1963, minimum value 85.00
Skipper, 1967, Funtime, bend knees 80.00
Tutty, 1965, 6", minimum value 75.00

Barbie Gifts Sets and Related Accessories

When no condition is indicated, the items listed below are assumed to be mint and in the original box or package. Items in only excellent condition may be worth 40% to 60% less.

Airplane, minimum value 1,000.00
Autograph book, 1962 ....30.00

Case, Barbie & Francie, bl, rnd, 1965, rare, EX 40.00
Clothes, Barbie Color Coordinates, #1832 ....750.00
Clothes, Campus Corduroys (Ken), #1410 ....75.00
Clothes, Country Clubbin' (Ken), #1400 ....135.00
Clothes, Drum Majorette, 1963 ....150.00
Clothes, Easter Parade, #900 series, 1958 ....900.00
Clothes, Enchanted Evening, pk gown, 1958 ....250.00
Clothes, Golden Glory, 1965 ....70.00
Clothes, Hollywood Premier, 1992 ....30.00
Clothes, Long 'N Short of It (Skipper), 1970 ....55.00
Clothes, Patio Party, 1966 ....100.00
Clothes, Pretty as a Picture, #1652 ....225.00
Clothes, Snow 'N Ride, 1988 ....55.00
Clothes, Sophisticated Lady, pk gown, red cape, 1963 ....300.00
Clothes, Travel Togethers, #1688 ....275.00
Cycle 30.00
Dune buggy, minimum value 90.00
Family House, minimum value 75.00
Game, Barbie Miss Lively Livin', Mattel, 1971, EX in box 25.00
Gift set, Barbie Foaming Beauty Bath, 1960s 110.00
Gift set, Ice Breaker, MIB, minimum value 600.00
Gift set, Living Barbie Action Accents, 1970 ....430.00
Gift set, Olympic Gymnast, minimum value 85.00
Gift set, Round the Clock Wedding Party, 1965, minimum value .850.00
Gift set, Tutti Nighty Night Sleep Tight, 1965 ....175.00
Mercedes, gr, 1963, NMIB 150.00
Photo album 40.00
Record tote 25.00
Starcycle, #2149, 1978 ....12.00
Wristwatch, from $20 to 45.00

Belton

Concave head, 2 or 3 hole, EX bsk, o/c or c/m w/wig, 10" 1,100.00
Concave head, 2 or 3 hole, EX bsk, o/c or c/m w/wig, 13" 1,600.00
Concave head, 2 or 3 hole, EX bsk, o/c or c/m w/wig, 15" 2,300.00
Concave head, 2 or 3 hole, EX bsk, o/c or c/m w/wig, 16" 2,400.00
Concave head, 2 or 3 hole, EX bsk, o/c or c/m w/wig, 17" 2,600.00
Concave head, 2 or 3 hole, EX bsk, o/c or c/m w/wig, 20" 3,200.00
Concave head, 2 or 3 hole, EX bsk, o/c or c/m w/wig, 22" 3,300.00
Concave head, 2 or 3 hole, EX bsk, o/c or c/m w/wig, 23" 3,400.00
Concave head, 2 or 3 hole, EX bsk, o/c or c/m w/wig, 26" 4,000.00
Concave head, 2 or 3 hole, EX bsk, o/c or c/m w/wig, 8" 1,000.00

Bru

Bru Jne, bisque socket head with closed
mouth, paperweight eyes, kid and wood
body, bisque lower arms, 21", $26,000.00.

Closed mouth, all kid body, bsk lower arms, Bru, 13" 8,500.00
Closed mouth, all kid body, bsk lower arms; Bru, 18" 13,000.00
Closed mouth, all kid body, bsk lower arms; Bru, 26" 26,000.00
Closed mouth, kid/wood body, bsk lower arms; Bru Jne, 14" .18,500.00
Closed mouth, kid/wood body, bsk lower arms; Bru Jne, 20" .24,000.00
Closed mouth, kid/wood body, bsk lower arms; Bru Jne, 28" .36,500.00
Closed mouth, mk Bru, circle dot, 16" 20,000.00
Closed mouth, mk Bru, circle dot, 19" 24,000.00
Closed mouth, mk Bru, circle dot, 26" 28,000.00
Open mouth, compo walker's body, throws kisses, 22" 8,300.00
Open mouth, nursing (Bebe), high color, late SFBJ, 12" 2,600.00
Open mouth, nursing (Bebe), high color, late SFBJ, 18" 3,500.00
Open mouth, nursing Bru (Bebe), early, EX bsk, 15" 8,200.00
Open mouth, socket head, compo body; Bru, R, 14", EX bsk ..6,500.00
Open mouth, socket head, compo body; Bru, R, 22", EX bsk ..8,300.00
Open mouth, socket head, compo body; Bru, R, 28", EX bsk ..11,500.00

Cabbage Patch

Black boy or girl w/pacifier, 1984, MIB, minimum value 175.00
Black boy, shaggy hair, freckles, 1983, MIB, minimum value 600.00
Boy or girl w/no dimples, 1983, MIB, ea from $50 to 75.00
Boy w/red shaggy hair & pacifier, 1983, MIB, from $400 to 500.00
Boy w/tan shaggy hair & freckles, 1983, MIB 150.00
Girl w/brunette ponytail, 1 tooth, 1985, MIB, minimum value ..200.00
Girl w/gray eyes, 1985, MIB, from $50 to 75.00
Girl w/2 blond ponytails & freckles, 1983, MIB, from $175 to 300.00

Celebrity

Barry Goldwater, Remco, 1964, NM 30.00
Betty Grable, compo, 1940s, OC, 21", NM 150.00
Boy George, vinyl, 1980s, 11½", MIB 150.00
Cheryl Tiegs, Matchbox, 1989, MIB 35.00
Diahann Carol (Julia), Mattel, OC, 11½", MIB 140.00
Dolly Parton, hp/vinyl, Eegee, 1987, 18", MIB 65.00
Elizabeth Taylor, World Dolls, 1988, 11½", M 50.00
Elvis Presley, Graceland, plastic/vinyl, 1984, MIB 70.00
Farrah Fawcett, jtd vinyl, Mego, 1977, 12¼", NM 40.00
Flying Nun, Hasbro, 12", MIB 200.00
Jackie Kennedy, plastic/vinyl, Horsman, 1961, OC, 25" 175.00
Laurel & Hardy, Goldberger, 1986, 12", MIB, ea 45.00
Linda Evans (Crystal), jtd vinyl, World Doll, 1988, MIB 150.00
Mae West, Effanbee, Great Legends series, MIB 120.00
Marilyn Monroe, Tri-Star, 1983, 12", MIB, ea from $50 to 100.00
Marilyn Monroe, vinyl, 19802, 11½", MIB, from $50 to 100.00
Mary Poppins, plastic/vinyl, Horsman, 1964, OC, 12" 35.00
Michael Jackson, LJN, Thriller outfit, 1984, 11½", MIB 40.00
Michael Jackson, vinyl, 1980s, OC, 11½", MIB 40.00
Michael of Mary Poppins, plastic/vinyl, Horsman, 1965, OC, 8" ..30.00
Patty Duke, Horsman, 1965, rare, MIB 450.00
Richard Chamberlain (Dr Kildare), rare, 11½", MIB 350.00
Susan Dey (Laurie Partridge), Remco, 1973, OC, 19", MIB 100.00
Twiggy, Mattel, 1967, rare, 11½", MIB 250.00

China, Unmarked

Adelina Patti, center part, curls at temples, 1860s, 14" 275.00
Adelina Patti, center part, curls at temples, 1860s, 18" 450.00
Adelina Patti, center part, curls at temples, 1860s, 22" 485.00
Biedermeier or Bald Head, takes wig, RpC, 14" 625.00
Biedermeier or Bald Head, takes wig, RpC, 20" 875.00
Brown Eyes (pnt), any hairstyle or date, 16" 575.00
Brown Eyes (pnt), any hairstyle or date, 20" 950.00

Common Hairdo, blond or blk hair, RpC, after 1905, 12" 145.00
Common Hairdo, blond or blk hair, RpC, after 1905, 23" 285.00
Common Hairdo, blond or blk hair, RpC, after 1905, 8" 80.00
Covered Wagon Style, sausage curls, RpC, 1840s-70s, 12" 285.00
Covered Wagon Style, sausage curls, RpC, 1840s-70s, 24" 900.00

Curly Top, loose ringlet curls, redressed, 1845-60, 20", $725.00; Flat Top, black hair with mid-part and short curls, redressed, ca 1860, 23", $475.00.

Curly Top, loose ringlet curls, RpC, 1845-60s, 16" 500.00
Dolly Madison, modeled ribbon & bow, RpC, 1870-80s, 14" 250.00
Dolly Madison, modeled ribbon & bow, RpC, 1870-80s, 18" 475.00
Dolly Madison, modeled ribbon & bow, RpC, 1870-80s, 21" 550.00
Flat Top, blk hair, mid-part/short curls, RpC, ca 1860, 17" 300.00
Flat Top, blk hair, mid-part/short curls, RpC, ca 1860, 20" 350.00
Glass Eyes, various hairstyles, RpC, 1840s-70s, 14" 1,400.00
Japanese, blk or blond hair, mk or unmk, RpC, 1910-20s, 14" 185.00
Japanese, blk or blond hair, mk or unmk, RpC, 1910-20s, 17" 250.00
Man or Boy, glass eyes, side part, RpC, 14" 2,200.00
Man or Boy, pnt eyes, side part, RpC, 14", EX 1,200.00
Man or Boy, pnt eyes, side part, RpC, 16" 1,400.00
Man or Boy, pnt eyes, side part, RpC, 21½" 2,400.00
Peg Wood Body, early hairdo, 1840s, 16", EX 2,200.00
Pet Name, molded shirtwaist w/name on front, RpC, 1905, 19" .265.00
Pet Name, molded shirtwaist w/name on front, RpC, 1905, 8" ...125.00
Pierced Ears, various hairstyles, RpC, 14" 475.00
Pierced Ears, various hairstyles, RpC, 18" 675.00
Snood/Combs, any appl hair decor, RpC, 14" 650.00
Snood/Combs, any appl hair decor, RpC, 17" 800.00
Spill Curls, w/or w/out head band, RpC, 14" 400.00
Spill Curls, w/or w/out head band, RpC, 22" 850.00
Wood Body, articulated/slim hips, RpC, 1840s-50s, 12" 1,500.00
Wood Body, articulated/slim hips, RpC, 1840s-50s, 17" 3,200.00
Wood Body, jtd hips, covered-wagon hairdo, 1840s-50s, 12" 985.00
Wood Body, jtd hips, covered-wagon hairdo, 1840s-50s, 15" ..1,800.00

Cloth

Chase, Blk lady, pnt arms & legs, OC, 25" 7,450.00
Cotton cloth stuffed w/cotton, pencil face, 1880s, OC, 18" 225.00
Litho on muslin girl, cotton stuffed, EX color, OC, 26" 285.00
Little Bo Peep, 1920s, EX 150.00
Mary Had a Little Lamb, 1920s 150.00
Mask face, swivel head, yarn hair, 1940s, RpC, 24" 125.00
Merrie Marie, litho on cotton, jtd knees, 30", EX 250.00
Oil-pnt muslin, mitt hands, pnt shoes/socks, OC, 1850s, 17" 800.00
Oil-pnt rag, cotton stuffed, jtd, ca 1900, OC, RpC, 18", EX 600.00
Pitti Sing, 4 on uncut litho cloth sheet 150.00

Raggedy Ann, unbleached cotton, Gruelle type, early, 15" 950.00
Raggedy Ann & Andy, Mollye Goldman, 1920s, OC, 18", pr .1,200.00

Eegee

Andy, hp/vinyl, pnt eyes to side, 1961, OC, 12" 35.00
Ballerina, plastic/vinyl, 1958, RpC, 20" 45.00
Chubby Schoolgirl, hp/vinyl, bl o/c, walker, RpC, 10½" 15.00
Georgette, vinyl/cloth, gr o/c, orange hair, 1971, OC, 22" 45.00
Janie, vinyl, bl o/c, rooted hair, 1956, OC, 8½" 20.00
Kid Sister, plastic/vinyl, pnt features, blond hair, OC, 9¼" 15.00
Miss Debby, vinyl, bl o/c, 1958, OC (bride), 14" 30.00
Robert, latex/vinyl, bl o/c, molded/pnt hair, 1956, OC, 21" 60.00

Effanbee

Bernard Fleischaker and Hugo Baum became business partners in 1910, and after two difficult years of finding toys to buy and a retail market to sell them in, they decided to manufacture dolls of their own. Their lovely dolls were a decided success largely because of their dedication to their work and the mutual trust and respect they held for each other. This is reflected in the Effanbee trademark — Eff stands for Fleischaker and bee for Baum. The company still exists today.

Alyssia, hp walker, vinyl head, 1958, OC, 20" 250.00
Ann Shirley, compo, 1936-40, OC, 17" 350.00
Babyette, compo & cloth, sleeping, OC, 16" 350.00
Compo head & limbs, cloth body, o/c/m, 1920s, OC, 18" 165.00
Currier & Ives, plastic/vinyl, OC, 12" 40.00
Fluffy, vinyl, 1954, OC, 10" 45.00
Honey, compo, flirty eyes, 1947-48, 21" 450.00
Howdy Doody, compo/cloth, string-op mouth, 1947, OC, 17" ...185.00
Laurel (girl) by Jan Hagara, 1984, OC, 15" 50.00
Little Lady, compo, 1939-47, OC, 15" 350.00
Mae Starr, compo/cloth, record player inside, OC, 30" 465.00
Mary Jane, plastic/vinyl, walker, 1960, OC, 31" 265.00
Patsy, compo, 1927-30s, OC, 14" 365.00
Patsy Ann, vinyl, 1959, OC, 15" 200.00
Patsy Mae, 1932, OC, 20", minimum value 785.00
Santa Claus, compo, molded beard & hat, OC, 19", minimum .1,200.00
WC Fields, compo/cloth, 1938, OC, 22" 500.00

Half Dolls

Half dolls, lovely porcelain figures awaiting attachment to secure bases, were never meant to be objects of play. Most of these lovely ladies were firmly sewn into pincushion bases that were beautifully decorated and served as the skirt of their gown. Other skirts were actually covers for items on milady's dressing table. Some were used for parasol or brush handles or for tops to candy containers or perfume bottles. Most popular from 1900 to about 1930, they will most often be found marked with the country of their origin — Bavaria, Germany, France, and Japan. You may also find some fine quality pieces marked Goebel, Dressel and Kester, and Heubach.

Germany, arms & hands attached, common type, 3" 25.00
Germany, arms & hands attached, common type, 5" 35.00
Germany, arms & hands attached, common type, 8" 55.00
Germany, arms & hands completely away, 12" 950.00
Germany, arms & hands completely away, 3" 145.00
Germany, arms & hands completely away, 5" 285.00
Germany, arms & hands completely away, 8" 650.00
Germany, arms extended, hands attached, 3" 75.00

Germany, arms extended, hands attached, 5" 115.00
Germany, arms extended, hands attached, 8" 160.00
Japan mk, 3" 20.00
Japan mk, 5" 30.00
Japan mk, 8" 50.00

Handwerck

#189, o/m, RpC, 14" 325.00
#421 21 Handwerk Germany, bsk head, o/m, jtd, RpC, 42" 3,200.00
#79 or #89, c/m, RpC, 21", minimum value 2,300.00
Bsk ShHd, o/m, kid body, RpC, 16" 350.00
Bsk SkHd, bjtd, brn o/c, o/m, p/e, hh wig, RpC, 28" 950.00
Child, bsk head, bjtd, o/c or set eyes, after 1885, RpC, 25" 750.00
Child, bsk head, bjtd, o/c or set eyes, after 1885, RpC, 36" 1,450.00
Child, bsk head, bjtd, o/c or set eyes, mold mks, RpC, 12" 450.00

Hertel, Schwab and Company

#119, bsk head, pnt eyes, c/m, jtd compo, RpC, 16" 4,900.00
#126, Skippy, bsk head, molded hair, o/c/m & eyes, 12" 1,000.00
#154, bsk head, c/m, RpC, 16" 2,400.00
#163, googly eyes, c/m, RpC, 12" 3,000.00
#217, googly eyes, c/m, wig, RpC, 7½" 875.00
#222, Our Fairy, molded hair, pnt eyes, RpC, 9" 1,500.00
#254, Patsy, bsk head, o/c eyes, bent limb body, RpC, 14" 1,000.00
Prize Baby, bsk 1-pc body & head, glass eyes, 6" 300.00

Heubach

#1017, baby-faced toddler, bsk head, o/m, RpC, 18" 1,600.00
#2850, bsk head, o/c/m w/teeth, molded braids, RpC, 16" 9,400.00
#5636, laughing child, intaglio pnt eyes, 2 teeth, RpC, 9" 850.00
#6692, ShHd, smiling, intaglio eyes, RpC, 15", minimum value ...900.00
#7129, laughing character, ShHd, cloth body, RpC, 11" 675.00
#7602, long face pouty, pnt eyes & hair, c/m, RpC, 16" 2,200.00
#7603, pouty ShHd, intaglio eyes, cloth body, RpC, 18" 995.00
#7644, ShHd, chubby cheeks, kid body, bsk arms, RpC, 16" 800.00
#7701, pouty, intaglio eyes, RpC, 16" 1,500.00
#7781, baby, squinted eyes, yawning, RpC, 15" 1,800.00
#7959, intaglio eyes, molded-on bonnet & hair, RpC, 17" 3,500.00
#8197, ShHd, c/m, molded curls, kid body, RpC, 17", minimum .8,700.00
#9141, winking glass eyes, RpC, 9" 1,500.00

Heubach-Koppelsdorf

Heubach, Ernst; Both #312 children with bisque socket heads, blue sleep eyes, open mouths with upper teeth, jointed wood and composition bodies, original dresses and undies, replaced shoes and socks, marked Heubach-Kopplesdorf, 15", $350.00 each.

#250-12/0 Germany, compo, o/c, o/m w/teeth, RpC, 11", EX 125.00
#267, baby, o/m, flirty eyes, metal eyelids, RpC, 17" 600.00
#300, baby, 5-pc bent-limb body, o/m, o/c, 1910s, 10" 285.00
#300 3/0, SkHd, bl o/c, 2 teeth, saran wig, RpC, 14" 250.00
#338, c/m, o/c, pnt hair, cloth body, 1925, RpC, 13" 675.00
#339, o/c, pnt hair, celluloid hands, cloth body, 9½" 425.00
Child, bsk ShHd w/bsk arms, o/m, kid body, RpC, 14" 225.00

Horsman

Ballerina, vinyl, 1-pc body & legs, jtd elbows, 1957, OC, 18" 75.00
Betty Jane, compo, OC, 25" 350.00
Bootsie, hp/vinyl, brn o/c, rooted blk hair, 1969, OC, 12" 10.00
Brother, compo/cloth, OC, 22", G, minimum value 300.00
Child, compo, 1930-40s, OC, 14" 145.00
Compo, mk EIH, 1910s-20s, RpC, 12" 185.00
Dimples, compo/cloth, 1928-33, RpC, 16" 225.00
Ella Cinders, compo/cloth, 1925, RpC, 14" 425.00
Mimi Thirsty Baby, jtd, glassine eyes, OC, 6" 25.00
Peek-a-Boo, compo/cloth, G Drayton, OC, 7½", minimum 145.00
Pippi Longstocking, vinyl/cloth, 1972, OC, 18" 35.00
Pudgie Baby, plastic/vinyl, 1979, 12" 40.00
Renee Ballerina, stuffed vinyl, bl o/c, rooted hair, OC, 18" 45.00
Sleepy Baby, vinyl/cloth, molded closed eyes, 1965, 24" 50.00
Tuffie, vinyl, molded upper lip over lower, 1966, OC, 16" 50.00

Ideal

April Showers, battery-op, splashes w/hands, '69, 14", M 25.00
April Showers, hp/vinyl, battery-op, 1968, 14" 32.00
Baby Coos, cloth/plastic/vinyl, o/c, molded hair, 1948, 20" 85.00
Baby Giggles, vinyl, eyes to side, mechanical giggler, 18" 120.00
Baby Herman, hp/vinyl, pnt features, molded hair, 1965, OC, 9" .35.00
Baby Snooks Flexie, wire & compo, OC, 12", minimum value ...285.00
Betty Big Girl, plastic & vinyl, 1968, OC, 30" 245.00
Bizzie Lizzie, vinyl, o/c, battery-op, OC, 18" 40.00
Bonnie Braids, hp & vinyl, 1951, OC, 13" 95.00
Brandi, hp/vinyl, pnt eyes, swivel waist, OC, 18" 80.00
Brother/Baby Coos, compo/hp/cloth, 1951, OC, 25" 100.00
Cinnamon, hp/vinyl, pnt eyes, hair 'grows,' 1971, OC, 12" 70.00
Compo baby, cloth body, c/m, o/c, 1930s-40s, OC, 16" 200.00
Compo child, o/c, o/m, OC, 14" 165.00
Deanna Durbin, compo, 1939, OC, 14" 575.00
Dina, hp/vinyl, pnt eyes, hair 'grows,' 1971, OC, 15" 90.00
Flossie Flirt, compo & cloth, flirty eyes, 1938-45, OC, 20" 265.00
Happi Returns, cloth/vinyl, walks & laughs, 1983-84, OC 20.00
Harmony, battery-op, 1971, OC, 21" 50.00
Judy Garland, compo, 1939, OC, 14" 1,000.00
Little Miss Revlon, hp/vinyl, bl o/c, jtd waist, OC, 10½" 95.00
Magic Lips, vinyl-coated cloth & vinyl, teeth, 1955, OC, 24" 95.00
Mia of Crissy Family, 1970, OC, 15½" 45.00
Patty Petite, vinyl, bl o/c, posable head, brn hair, OC, 19" 75.00
Pebbles, plastic & vinyl, 1963, OC, 8" 18.00
Peter Playpal, 1961, OC, 36" 500.00
Pinocchio, compo & wood, 1938-41, OC, 10" 300.00
Queen of Ice, jtd compo, mohair curls, OC & skates, 16" 150.00
Samantha the Witch, hp/vinyl, pnt eyes, 1965, OC, 12" 85.00
Sara Ann, hp, saran wig, 1952 on, OC, 14", minimum value 185.00
Snoozie, compo & cloth, molded hair, o/c, 1933, OC, 13" 175.00
Tabitha, vinyl & cloth, pnt eyes, 1966, OC, 15" 65.00
Tippy Tumbles, hp/plastic, does flips, battery-op, OC, 16½" 40.00
Tony, hp, red nylon wig, OC, 14", minimum value 250.00
Tubbsy, hp/vinyl, pnt eyes, battery-op, RpC, 18" 40.00
Uneeda Kid, compo & cloth, pnt eyes & hair, OC, 1914-19, 16" ..450.00

Jumeau

Emile Jumeau took over his father's doll company sometime in the 1870s. He brought many new innovations and ideas to the business. One fascination Jumeau had concerned dolls' eyes and led to the patents for eyelids that dropped over the eye itself; a second type allowed the doll to 'sleep.' Jumeau's distaste for German dolls is apparent in the booklets that were packaged with his dolls. These booklets referred to the German dolls as cheap and ugly and and as having 'stupid' faces. In reality, these less-expensive dolls were the downfall of the French doll manufacturers, and in 1899 the Jumeau company had to combine with several others in an effort to save the French doll industry from German competition.

Closed mouth, blue paperweight eyes, pierced ears, blond human hair wig, wood and composition body with straight wrists, marked EJ (incised) Jumeau, 16", $6,600.00.

Closed mouth, mk EJ (incised) Jumeau, rpr ft, 24" 8,700.00
Closed mouth, mk EJ (incised) Jumeau, 14" 5,800.00
Closed mouth, mk EJ (incised) Jumeau, 19" 6,800.00
Closed mouth, mk Tete Jumeau, 10" 3,000.00
Closed mouth, mk Tete Jumeau, 16" 4,100.00
Closed mouth, mk Tete Jumeau, 21" 4,800.00
Closed mouth, mk Tete Jumeau, 25" 5,600.00
Closed mouth, mk Tete Jumeau, 30" 6,800.00
Depose/Tete Jumeau, swivel head, p/e, long curls, adult, 22" ..7,400.00
Jumeau 1907, SkHd, appl ears, o/m, 18" 2,400.00
Jumeau 1907, swivel head, o/m, o/c, p/e, 23" 2,800.00
Long face, c/m, 21" 23,000.00
Long face, c/m, 30" 30,000.00
Open mouth, mk Tete Jumeau, 10" 995.00
Open mouth, mk Tete Jumeau, 16" 2,300.00
Open mouth, mk Tete Jumeau, 21" 3,100.00
Open mouth, mk Tete Jumeau, 25" 3,500.00
Open mouth, mk Tete Jumeau, 30" 4,600.00
Open mouth, mk 1907 Jumeau, 17" 2,500.00
Open mouth, mk 1907 Jumeau, 25" 3,300.00
Open mouth, mk 1907 Jumeau, 32" 4,000.00
Phonograph in body, o/m, 25" 12,000.00
Portrait Jumeau, c/m, 20" 7,800.00

Kammer and Reinhardt

#100, baby, pnt hair & eyes, o/c/m, 15" 650.00
#101, boy or girl w/glass eyes, 12" 4,100.00
#101, boy or girl w/glass eyes, 20" 8,000.00
#101, boy or girl w/pnt eyes, 12" 2,000.00
#101, boy or girl w/pnt eyes, 20" 5,000.00

#107, Carl, pnt eyes, pouty mouth, orig mohair wig, 12½" 13,000.00
#109, rare, w/glass eyes, 18" 26,000.00
#109, rare, w/pnt eyes, 18" 22,000.00
#112, rare, w/glass eyes, 18" 19,000.00
#112, rare, w/pnt eyes, 18" 17,000.00
#114, rare, w/glass eyes, 15" 5,900.00
#114, rare, w/pnt eyes, 11" 2,950.00
#114, rare, w/pnt eyes, 18" 5,500.00
#115 or #115a, c/m, 18" 4,900.00
#115 or #115a, o/m, 15" 1,400.00
#115 or #115a, o/m, 22" 2,600.00
#116 or #116a, c/m, 18" 3,500.00
#116 or #116a, o/m, 15" 1,400.00
#116 or #116a, o/m, 22" 2,600.00
#117, c/m, 24" 6,900.00
#117a, c/m, 18" 5,400.00
#117a, c/m, 30" 8,200.00
#126, sleeping/flirty glass eyes, o/m, silent, 28" 1,550.00
Dolly face, o/m, mold #400-403-109, etc, 16" 600.00
Dolly face, o/m, mold #400-403-109, etc, 24" 850.00
Dolly face, o/m, mold #400-403-109, etc, 38" 2,800.00

Kestner

Johannes D. Kestner made buttons at a lathe in a Waltershausen factory in the early 1800s. When this line of work failed, he used the same lathe to turn doll bodies. Thus the Kestner company began. It was one of the few German manufacturers to make the complete doll. By 1860, with the purchase of a porcelain factory, Kestner made doll heads of china and bisque as well as wax, worked-in-leather, celluloid, and cardboard. In 1895 the Kestner trademark of a crown with streamers was registered in the U.S. and a year later in Germany. Kestner felt the mark was appropriate since he referred to himself as the 'king of German dollmakers.'

A, ShHd, o/m, MIG/Kestner, 19" 685.00
B/6, ShHd, kid w/bsk ½-arms, o/m w/teeth, o/c, 19" 685.00
Century Doll Co, flanged closed dome, c/m, 15" 685.00
D/8, SkHd & ShHd, kid w/bsk ½-arms, c/m, 15" 800.00
E/9, SkHd, o/m, 1892, 26" 1,200.00
G/11, Hilda, SkHd, o/c, o/m w/2 teeth, 1920s, 15" 3,600.00
G/8, trn ShHd, o/m, MI/JDK, 19" 800.00
G11, SkHd, jtd, bl eyes, o/m, mohair wig, 19" 800.00
H/12, SkHd, o/c/m, JDK, 1892, 23" 3,000.00
Hilda, toddler, jtd body, o/m, o/c, 1914, rstr, 15" 4,800.00
I/13, SkHd, o/m, JDK, 1892, 26" 985.00
JDK, bsk head, glass eyes, c/m, appl ears, OC, 20", EX 4,800.00
JDK, bsk head on celluloid, R Gummi Co, turtle mk, 18" 500.00
JDK 12, SkHd, pwt, o/m, bent limbs, RpC, 15", VG 475.00
K/12, ShHd, made for Century, o/c/m, molded hair, 21" 3,600.00
L/15, SkHd, bsk ShPl, c/m, 21" 3,000.00
N/17, SkHd, o/m, 1892, 17" 725.00
SkHd, Oriental, o/m, JDK/Kestner, 14" 4,800.00
Trn ShHd, brn eyes, o/m, orig wig, kid body, 22", EX 750.00
10, SkHd, bsk ShPl, c/m, 21" 2,900.00
10/G, SkHd, c/m, JDK, 1912, 12" 600.00
11, SkHd, pnt eyes to side, o/c/m, JDK/MIG, 11" 550.00
13, SkHd, o/m, JDK/MIG, 18" 700.00
143, ShHd, jtd compo, o/c, o/m, mohair wig, 14", EX 850.00
143, ShHd, kid w/bsk ½-arms, o/m, 17" 1,100.00
145, ShHd, kid w/bsk ½-arms, o/c mouth, 15" 1,500.00
145, SkHd, c/m, 143/4/0/JDK, 11" 325.00
147, trn ShHd, o/m, JDK, 25" 900.00
148, ShHd, kid w/bsk ½-arms, o/m, 7½, 21" 700.00

150.1, bsk, Kestner seal on body, 8" 500.00
154, SkHd/ShHd, kid w/bsk ½-arms, o/m/teeth, DEP, 17" 725.00
154, SkHd/ShHd, kid w/bsk ½-arms, o/m/teeth, DEP, 21½" 750.00
16, SkHd, o/m, JDK/MIG, 21" 650.00
167, SkHd, jtd compo, o/m, p/e, F 1/2/MI6 1/2/G, 16" 675.00
168, SkHd, o/m, MID/G7, 26" 1,000.00
169, SkHd, jtd compo, o/c, c/m, B 1/2/BI6 1/2G, 18" 2,700.00
171, SkHd, jtd compo, o/c, o/m, 'Daisy,' F/M110, 18" 700.00
171, SkHd, jtd compo, o/c, o/m, 'Daisy,' F/M110, 32" 1,300.00
201, ShHd, celluloid on kid, o/m, set eyes/lashes, JDK, 19" 685.00
215, SkHd, jtd compo, fur eyebrows, o/m, MI9/GJDK, 21" 850.00
221, jtd compo, googly eyes, c/m smile, wig, JDK, 15" 5,200.00
235, toddler, kid body, 16" 750.00
245, SkHd, 5-pc baby, G/MIG/11/JDK Jr/1914 Hilda, 14" 3,300.00
257, SkHd, 5-pc baby, o/m, G/JDK, 10" 425.00
257, SkHd, 5-pc baby, o/m, G/JDK, 20" 850.00
260, flirty-eyed toddler, OC, 16" 1,900.00

Lenci

Eleanora Scavani, separated from her husband who was in the service of Italy during WWI, found herself painfully alone after the death of her baby. With her brother as her partner, this talented artist began designing lovely felt-covered dolls with beautiful hand-painted features. These dolls became her children, and she regarded them as a tribute to her lost daughter.

Following the war, her husband returned and joined the firm as a partner. The Lenci firm (a name he used as a term of endearment for his wife) soon became well-known in the doll-making industry. Great care was taken in every detail. Characteristics of Lenci dolls include seamless, steam-molded felt heads, quality clothing, childishly plump bodies, and painted eyes that glance to the side. Fine mohair wigs were used, and the middle and fourth fingers were sewn together. Look for the factory stamp on the foot, though paper labels were also used. Dolls under 10" are known as mascots and usually sell for $125.00 to $150.00. The Lenci factory continues today, producing dolls of the same high quality.

African man w/sword & shield, 17" 1,850.00
Baby, 16", minimum value 1,800.00
Bali Dancer, 18" 1,800.00
Boy, side part, 18", minimum value 2,200.00
Boy, winking, o/c/m, pnt teeth, 1920s, 11" 2,800.00
Child, 14", minimum value 800.00
Child, 18", minimum value 1,200.00
Clown, 18" 1,600.00
Golfer, 16" 2,400.00
Lady w/adult face, flapper style, 14" 1,200.00
Mascot, 5", minimum value 250.00
Pan, hooved ft, 9½" 2,100.00
Surprise eyes, rnd pnt eyes, O-shaped mouth, 15" 1,900.00

Madame Alexander

Beatrice Alexander founded the Alexander Doll company in 1923 using a lovely doll that was designed after her daughter Mildred. With the help of her three sisters, the company prospered; and by the late 1950s there were three factories with over six hundred employees making Madame Alexander dolls. The company still produces these lovely dolls today.

Abigail Fillmore, 1st Ladies Series, Louisa, 1982-84 ....90.00
Active Miss, hp, Violet/Cissy, 1954, 18" 550.00
Alexander-Kin, bend-knee nonwalker, cotton dress, 1965 ....125.00
Alexander-Kin, bend-knee walker, coat & hat, 1956-64, 8" 200.00

Alexander-Kin, str-leg nonwalker, nightgown, 1953, 7½" 250.00
Alexander-Kin, str-leg walker, school dress, 1955 ....250.00
Alice in Wonderland, compo, Little Betty, 1930s, 9" 325.00
All Star, wht or Blk hp, Americana series, 8" 60.00
Anna Kerenina, Jacqueline, 1991, 21" 340.00
Anna McGuffey, compo, Tiny Betty, 1935-39, 7" 290.00
Antoinette, compo, Wendy Ann, 1946, 21" 2,200.00
Army WAAC, compo, Wendy Ann, 1943-44, 14", minimum value .650.00
Artie, plastic/vinyl, 1962, 12" 300.00
Babs, hp, Maggie, 1949, 20" 650.00
Ballerina, compo, Wendy Ann, 1936-38, 11" 275.00
Barbara Jane, cloth & vinyl, 1952 only, 29" 500.00
Best Man, hp, Wendy Ann, 1955 only, 8" 750.00
Bitsy, hp head, 1949-51, 11" 70.00
Bride, hp, Maggie or Margaret, 1949-55, 18" 600.00
Bride, porc, Jacqueline, full lace, 1965, 21", minimum value 900.00
Bridesmaid, hp, Elice, 1957-59, 16½" 425.00
Butch McGuffey, compo & cloth, 1940-41, 22" 200.00
Carmen, compo, Wendy Ann, 1937-40, 14" 365.00
Christening Baby, cloth & vinyl, 1951-54, 11" 80.00
Cinderella, compo, Betty, 1935-37, 15" 450.00
Cissy, hp, street dress, 1955-59, 20", minimum value 300.00
Coco, plastic & vinyl, 1966, 21", minimum value 2,000.00
Curly Locks, hp, Wendy Ann, 1955 only, 8" 900.00
David Copperfield, compo, Tiny Betty, 1936-38, 7" 300.00
Dionne Quint, compo, toddler, 1938-39, 10" 750.00

Dionne Quintuplets, composition heads with molded and painted hair, all original clothes, 7½", M unplayed-with condition, $3,200.00.

Dolly, Storybook Series, Wendy Ann, 1988-89, 8" 80.00
Edith w/Golden Hair, cloth, 1940s, 18" 625.00
Emily, cloth & felt, 1930s 625.00
Fairy Princess, compo, Tiny Betty, 1940-43, 8" 285.00
France, compo, Tiny Betty, 1936-43, 7" 235.00
Germany, hp, str leg, mk Alex, 1973-75, 8" 60.00
Godey Bride, hp, Margaret, 1950, 14", minimum value 825.00
Grandma Jane, plastic & vinyl, Mary Ann, 1970-72, 14" 285.00
Groom, bend knee, 1958, 8" 425.00
Happy, cloth & vinyl, 1970 only, 20" 260.00
Honeyette Baby, compo & cloth, 1941-42, 16" 125.00
Huckleberry, hp, Storybook Series, Wendy Ann, 1989-91, 8" 58.00
Ireland, hp, bend-knee walker, Wendy Ann, 1965 only, 8" 175.00
Jamaica, str legs, Wendy Ann, 1986-88, 8" 75.00
Jane Withers, compo, c/m, 1937, 12", minimum value 975.00
Jeannie Walker, compo, 1940s, 13" 550.00
Juliet, compo, Wendy Ann, 1937-40, 18", minimum value 1,200.00
Kate Greenaway, compo, Little Betty, 1936-39, 9" 300.00

Kathryn Grayson, hp, Margaret, 1949 only, 20", minimum value .2,400.00
Kathy Baby, rooted or molded hair, 1954-56, 18" 100.00
Kelly, hp, Lissy, 1959 only, 12" 450.00
Klondike Kate, hp, Cissette, 1963, 10", minimum value 1,200.00
Lady Hamilton, hp & vinyl, Cissy, 1957 only, 20" 850.00
Lila Bridesmaid, compo, Tiny Betty, 1938-40, 8" 275.00
Little Angel, latex & vinyl, 1950-57, 9" 100.00
Little Bo Peep, hp, str legs, Wendy Ann, mk Alex, 1973-75, 8" ...60.00
Little Genius, compo & cloth, 1935-40 & 1942-46, 12" 120.00
Little Godey, hp, Wendy Ann, 1953-55, 8", minimum value ..1,200.00
Little Shaver, cloth, 1940-44, 10", minimum value 465.00
Little Woman, plastic & vinyl, Nancy Drew, 1969-82, 12" 50.00
Lord Nelson, vinyl, Nancy Drew, 1984-86, 12" 60.00
Louisa of Sound of Music, Cissette, 1971-73, 10" 265.00
Lucy Bride, compo, Wendy Ann, 1937-40, 17" 425.00
Madeline, hp, jtd elbows & knees, 1950-53, 17", minimum value ...950.00
Maggie Mixup, hp, as angel, 1961, 8" 1,000.00
Marine, compo, Wendy Ann, 1943-44, 14" 750.00
Mary Louise, compo, Wendy Ann, 1938, 1946-47, 21" 2,300.00
Melanie, hp & vinyl, Cissy, 1961, 21", minimum value 800.00
Melinda, plastic & vinyl, party dress, 1963, 22" 500.00
Mistress Mary, compo, Tiny Betty, 1937-41, 7" 275.00
Molly Cottontail, cloth & felt, 1930s 650.00
Muffin, vinyl, Janie, 1989-90, 12" 75.00
Nina Ballerina, compo, Little Betty, 1939-41, 9" 325.00
Nurse, compo, Tiny Betty, 1938-39, 7" 300.00
Opening Night, Cissette, gold sheath & overskirt, 1989, 10" 80.00
Parlour Maid, hp, Wendy Ann, 1956 only, 8", minimum value ..1,500.00
Pinky, cloth, 1940s, 16" 550.00
Pocahontas, hp, bend knees, Wendy Ann, 1967-70, 8" 475.00
Pollyana, rigid vinyl, Marybell, 1960-61 (mk 1958), 16" 425.00
Prince Charles, hp, Wendy Ann, 1957 only, 8", minimum value ..575.00
Princess Elizabeth, compo, o/m, 15", minimum value 525.00
Pussy Cat, cloth & vinyl, 1965-85, 14" 75.00
Queen, hp & vinyl, Cissy, brocade gown, 1955, 20" 875.00
Queen Alexandrine, compo, Wendy Ann, 1939-41, 21" 2,200.00
Rapunzel, Cissette, gold velvet dress, 1989-92, 10" 105.00
Red Riding Hood, hp, str legs, mk Alex, 1973-75, 8" 60.00
Renoir Child, plastic & vinyl, Nancy Drew, 1967 only, 12" 200.00
Romeo, compo, Wendy Ann, 1949, 18", minimum value 1,400.00
Russia, str legs, mk Alex, 1973-75, 8" 60.00
Scarlett O'Hara, compo, Tiny Betty, 1937-42, 7" 400.00
Scarlett O'Hara, plastic/vinyl, Mary Ann, 1968, 14" 500.00
Scarlett O'Hara, str legs, flowered gown, 1988-89, 8" 65.00
Smarty, plastic & vinyl, 1962-63, 12" 365.00
Spanish Boy, hp, bend-knee walker, Wendy Ann, 1964-68, 8" ..365.00
Special Girl, cloth & compo, 1942-46, 23", minimum value 500.00
Sugar Darlin', cloth & vinyl, 1964 only, 14" 100.00
Swiss, compo, Tiny Betty, 1936, 7" 245.00
Timmy Toddler, plastic & vinyl, 1960-61, 23" 165.00
Tommy, hp, Lissy, 1962 only, 12" 1,100.00
Topsy-Turvy, compo, Tiny Betty, 1935 only 200.00
Treena Ballerina, hp, Margaret, 1952 only, 15", minimum value ..750.00
Union Officer, Scarlett Series, Nancy Drew, 1990-91, 12" 80.00
Victoria, compo, Wendy Ann, 1939, 1941, 21", minimum value ...2,200.00
Vietnam, hp, Wendy Ann, 1968-69, 8" 360.00
Wendy Ann, hp, 1948-50, 16" 775.00
Wendy from Peter Pan, plastic & vinyl, Mary Ann, 1969, 14" ...325.00
Yolanda, Brenda Star, 1965 only, 12" 325.00

Mattel

Baby Beans, vinyl w/beanbag body, pnt eyes, 1971, OC, 11" 18.00
Baby First Step, hp/vinyl, o/c, battery-op, 1968, RpC, 10" 35.00

Baby Fun, vinyl, pnt eyes, rooted hair, 1968, OC, 8" 20.00
Big Jack, hp/vinyl, pnt eyes & hair, fully jtd, OC, 9½" 75.00
Bucky Love Notes, press for tunes, 1974, OC, 12" 30.00
Chatty Cathy, bl o/c, blond curls, RpC, 1960 ....35.00
Dr Doolittle, vinyl, molded & pnt features, OC, 6" 25.00
Randy Reader, hp/vinyl, bl eyes, wht hair, battery-op, RpC, 19" ..40.00
Sister Belle, plastic/cloth, yarn hair, talker, OC, 17" 25.00
Sweet 16, hp/vinyl, pnt eyes, blond hair, 1975, OC, 11½" 85.00
Talking Baby Tenderlove, working, OC 20.00
Wet Noodles, vinyl, pnt eyes, orange hair, 1969, OC, 3½" 15.00

Papier-Mache

Clown, o/c/m, molded hair or wig, 5-pc body, RpC, 10" 265.00
Coiled braids over ears, RpC, 20", minimum 2,200.00
Early type w/cloth body, wooden limbs, braids, RpC, 12" 600.00
French/French type, o/m w/bamboo teeth, glass eyes, RpC, 15" .1,400.00
German, molded hair, glass eyes, c/m, RpC, 14" 525.00
German, molded hair, pnt eyes, c/m, RpC, 1870-1900, 23" 475.00
German character head, glass eyes, cm, fully jtd, RpC, 15" 1,100.00
Greiner, molded hair, pnt eyes, cloth body, 19" 1,400.00
M&S Superior, ShHd, molded hair, pnt eyes, RpC, 16" 400.00
Milliner's model, braided bun, side curls, 1820-60, RpC, 10" 785.00
Molded bonnet, kid body, wooden limbs, RpC, 15", minimum ..2,000.00
Motschmann type, glass eyes, c/m, solid dome, RpC, 15" 725.00
ShHd, cloth body, blond wig, OC, 14" 250.00
Trn ShHd, solid dome, glass eyes, c/m, compo arms, RpC, 17" ...750.00
1920s & later, cloth body, bright coloring, wig, RpC, 8" 80.00

Parian

Bald solid dome head, ear details, takes wigs, 1850s, RpC, 14" ...775.00
Man or boy, parted hair, cloth body, shirt & tie, 16" 900.00
Molded comb, glass eyes, cloth body, RpC, 16" 1,700.00
Molded hat, blond or blk hair, pnt eyes, 15" 2,200.00
Molded hat, glass eyes, RpC, 16" 3,100.00
Molded head band, Alice, RpC, 14" 400.00
Molded head band, pnt eyes, unpierced ears, RpC, 18" 1,200.00
Molded necklace, glass eyes, p/e, RpC, 21", minimum value ...2,500.00
Molded scarf, pnt features, cloth body, RpC, 14", minimum ...1,000.00
Plain, no decor in hair or on shoulders, RpC, 10" 175.00
Swivel neck, glass eyes, RpC, 21" 3,700.00

Remco

Baby Grow-a-Tooth, 1969, OC, 14" 30.00
Gingersnap, brn hp/vinyl, brn pnt eyes, curly hair, OC, 18" 50.00
Hug-a-Bug, gr vinyl, pnt clothes/features, clip on bk, 3½" 6.00
Jan, fully jtd, blk rooted hair, 1965, OC, 5½" 12.50
Mimi, hp/vinyl, pnt eyes, blond hair, OC, 19" 65.00
Sweet April, vinyl, stationary eyes, arms move, RpC, 5½" 6.00
Tumbling Tomboy, hp/vinyl, 1969, Oc, 16" 25.00

Schoenhut

Albert Schoenhut left Germany in 1866 to go to Pennsylvania to work as a repairman for toy pianos. He eventually applied his skills to wooden toys and later designed an all-wood doll which he patented on January 17, 1911. These uniquely jointed dolls were painted with enamels and came with a metal stand. Some of the later dolls had stuffed bodies, voice boxes, and hollow heads; some were made with heads of imitation bisque. These innovations influenced the development of the popular Bye-Lo Baby which was introduced in 1924. Due to the changing economy and fierce competition, the company closed in the mid-1930s.

Baby, bent-limb body, pnt hair, decal eyes, OC, 12" 525.00
Boy, cvd & pnt hair, bl pnt eyes, c/m, scuffed, RpC, 17" 2,600.00
Boy, cvd hair, pnt eyes, walker, nude, 16½", VG 2,800.00
Boy, pnt bl intaglio eyes, cvd hair, c/m, RpC, 15", EX 2,000.00
Character child, intaglio eyes, o/c/m w/teeth, OC, 14" 1,600.00
Child, cvd hair, molded ribbon, c/m, OC, 14" 2,500.00
Compo, molded curls, Patsy-style body, label, OC, 13" 1,600.00
Dolly face, decal eyes, o/c/m w/teeth, OC, 14" 625.00
Girl, bl pnt eyes, c/m, brn hh wig, RpC, 11" 250.00
Girl, brn decal eyes, o/c/m w/4 teeth, RpC, 17", EX 625.00
Girl, brn decal eyes, 4 pnt teeth, orig wig, 1911, RpC, 21½" 785.00
Girl, brn decal eyes, 4 teeth, hh wig, RpC, 21½", EX 785.00
Girl, brn pnt eyes, brn hh wig, orig dress, 15", EX 500.00
Girl, intaglio eyes, cvd hair w/braids, c/m, RpC, 16", EX 600.00
Girl, intaglio eyes, pouty mouth, rpl wig, rpt, RpC, 21½" 785.00
Girl, pnt eyes, c/m, rpl wig, rpt, RpC, 15" 675.00
Girl, pnt eyes, 4 pnt teeth, cvd hair, rpt, RpC, 16" 700.00
Man, cvd hair, OC, 19", minimum value 3,000.00
O/c, o/m w/cvd teeth, OC, 17" 1,350.00
Toddler, OC, 12" 850.00
Tootsie Wootsie, pnt hair, o/c/m w/tongue/teeth, OC, 14" 2,100.00
Walker, pnt eyes, o/c or c/m, OC, 18" 1,100.00
Wood & compo, intaglio eyes, fully jtd, OC, 19", EX 1,400.00

SFBJ

By 1895 Germany was producing dolls of good quality at much lower prices than the French dollmakers because of lower wages in German factories. This was a serious threat to the French companies, and in a supreme effort to save the doll industry, several leading French manufacturers united to form one large company in the hope they could combine their strengths to save the French market. Bru, Raberry and Delphieu, Pintel and Godshaux, Fleischman and Bodel, and Jumeau united to form the company today known as SFBJ. Their dolls did well while Germany was otherwise occupied with WWII, but after the war German doll production proved to be too strongly competitive, and SFBJ closed in 1958.

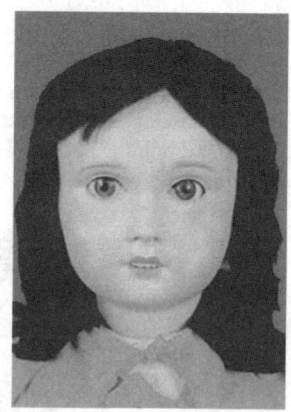

Child, bisque socket head with blue set eyes, open mouth with six upper teeth, human hair wig, jointed wood and composition body, nicely dressed, 33", $2,000.00.

Celestine, bsk SkHd on papier-mache, o/m, inset eyes, 18" 900.00
Tete Jumeau, p/e, o/m, o/c/lashes, 18" 1,600.00
15, o/c, o/m w/teeth, wood/compo body, RpC, 15", EX 1,500.00
203, 1900 bsk head on compo, o/c/m, inset eyes, 20" 3,000.00
223, bsk, closed dome, o/m w/8 teeth, molded hair, 17" 2,000.00
227, brn swivel closed dome head, animal skin wig, 18" 2,500.00
228, toddler, papier-mache body, c/m, inset eyes, 16" 2,200.00
229, wood walker, o/c/m, inset eyes, 18" 4,000.00
230, SkHd, p/e, o/m, o/c, 23" 2,400.00
235, closed dome, molded hair, o/c/m & eyes, 8" 500.00

236, laughing Jumeau, o/m, o/c, dbl chin, 17" 1,800.00
236, laughing Jumeau, o/m, o/c, dbl chin, 22" 2,300.00
239, Poulbot, c/m, street urchin, red wig, 14" 8,500.00
245, boy, o/c/m, lg glass eyes, googly, pnt shoes, 12" 2,600.00
247, toddler, o/c/m/2 inset teeth, 16" 2,400.00
247, toddler, o/c/m/2 inset teeth, 24" 3,200.00
251, toddler, 25" 2,600.00
252, pouty, c/m, inset eyes, papier-mache body, 18" 6,200.00
257, 1900 toddler, o/c/m, inset eyes, 16" 2,500.00
301, bsk SkHd on compo, o/m, inset eyes, 16" 725.00
301, bsk SkHd on compo, o/m, inset eyes, 24" 1,400.00
301, bsk SkHd on compo, o/m, inset eyes, 30" 1,900.00
60, kiss-blower, cryer/walker, 22" 2,300.00
60, o/m w/teeth, o/c, jtd body & wrists, 25½" 950.00
60, SkHd, papier-mache/compo, plunger cryer, o/m, 1-pc, 11" ...575.00

Shirley Temple

Compo, 13", Captain January, pk organdy dress & hat 750.00
Compo, 13", Curly Top, MIB 700.00
Compo, 15", flirty eyes, plaid dress, all orig 700.00
Compo, 15", Stand Up & Cheer 650.00
Compo, 16", Now & Forever, cotton pique dress, 1934 ....650.00
Compo, 17", Baby Take a Bow, MIB 750.00
Compo, 17", trenchcoat 750.00
Compo, 18", Bright Eyes, cotton dress, 1934, all orig 750.00
Compo, 20", Poor Little Rich Girl 865.00
Compo, 22", swivel head, cloth body, RpC 925.00
Compo, 27", Captain January, sailor suit 1,000.00
Compo/cloth, 20", baby, all orig 1,100.00
Vinyl, 12", Captain January, sailor suit, 1958, M 200.00
Vinyl, 12", Ideal, 1961, MIB 200.00
Vinyl, 15", Cinderella, 1961 ....325.00
Vinyl, 15", Heidi, 1960, M 325.00
Vinyl, 15", Little Bo Peep 325.00
Vinyl, 15", Montgomery Ward, 1972, MIB 325.00
Vinyl, 15", Wee Willie Winkie, 1959, M 325.00
Vinyl, 15", 1950s, all orig 325.00
Vinyl, 16", red polka dot dress, 1973, M 125.00
Vinyl, 35", RpC, 1960 ....1,800.00

Simon and Halbig

Simon and Halbig was a large German doll firm that operated from ca 1870 until the 1930s. They were a popular supplier of bisque heads to French dollmakers of the 1870s and '80s. This company made dolls for such famous companies as Gimbel Bros., Jumeau, Kammer and Reinhardt, as well as many others. Halbig became the sole owner of the company in 1895 but did not register 'S&H' as his trademark until ten years later.

AW, SkHd, o/m, SH/13, 21" 850.00
Baby Blanche, SkHd, o/m baby, S&H, 21" 950.00
CM Bergmann, SkHd, o/m, 1895, Halbig/S&H5, 30" 1,300.00
Elenore, SkHd, o/m, CMB/Simon & Halbig, 18" 650.00
Handwerck, SkHd, o/m, G/Halbig, 4, 26" 850.00
Handwerck, SkHd, o/m, S&H, 30" 1,100.00
Handwerck, SkHd, o/m, 1895, G/S&H/1, 16" 450.00
Handwerck, SkHd, o/m w/teeth, Simon & Halbig, rpl wig, 32" ..1,300.00
10, SkHd, o/m, G/Halbig/S&H, 16" 600.00
10, SkHd, o/m, G/Halbig/S&H, 22" 900.00
100, SkHd, o/m, Simon & Halbig/S&C/G, 15" 500.00
1039, SkHd, flirty bl eyes, jtd walking body, p/e, wig, 22" 995.00
1078, SkHd, o/m, pwt, p/e, S&H, RpC, 18½" 725.00

1159, SkHd, adult, 1905, G/Simon & Halbig/S&H7, 18" **1,900.00**
1159, SkHd, swivel on ShPl, wood w/kid fashion, o/m, 19" **2,000.00**
1160, Louisa May Alcott, bsk head, cloth body, 7", EX **400.00**
1296, SkHd, 1911, FS&Co/Simon & Halbig, 14" **525.00**
156, SkHd, 1925, S&H, 18" **625.00**
156, SkHd, 1925, S&H, 22" **725.00**
179, SkHd, o/m, Simon & Halbig S11H DEP, 20" **700.00**
282, SkHd, o/m, SH, 18" **650.00**
383, SkHd, flapper body, SH, 14" **1,200.00**
409, SkHd, o/m, S&H, 26" **850.00**
50, SkHd, c/m, Simon & Halbig, 16" **1,800.00**
540, SkHd, o/m, G/Halbig/S&H, 16" **600.00**
570, SkHd, o/m, walking, head turns, G/Halbig S&H, 18" **750.00**
670, SkHd, o/m, Simon & Halbig, 16" **600.00**
719, SkHd, c/m, S&H DEP, 16" **2,300.00**
739, SkHd, c/m, brn, S 5 H DEP, 14" **1,600.00**
739, SkHd, o/m/4 teeth, brn stationary eyes, p/e, DEP, OC, 17" .**1,300.00**
769, SkHd, c/m, S&H DEP, 17" **2,600.00**
908, SkHd, swivel on ShPl, c/m, SH, 16" **2,700.00**
929, SkHd, c/m, S&H, DEP, 25" **4,900.00**
939, SkHd, c/m, S 11H DEP, 23" **3,500.00**
940, SkHd, closed dome, o/c/m, S 2 H, 26" **3,600.00**
945, SkHd, c/m, S 2 H DEP, 16" **2,200.00**

Steiner

Jules Nicholas Steiner established one of the earliest French doll manufactories in 1855. Having been a clockmaker, he began with mechanical dolls and his patents grew to include walking and talking dolls. In 1880 he registered a patent for a doll with moving eyes. This doll could be put to sleep by turning a rod that operated a wire attached to its eyes. Though these new innovations brought much acclaim to the Steiner company, it closed around 1910 because it could not compete with the less-expensive German dolls that were flooding the market at that time.

A Series, c/m, wire eyes, jtd body, RpC, 21" **6,500.00**
A Series Child, cb pate, c/m, pwt, jtd, RpC, 15" **4,400.00**
A Series Child, cb pate, c/m, pwt, jtd, RpC, 25" **7,500.00**
A Series Child, cb pate, o/m, pwt, jtd, RpC, 22" **6,500.00**
A Series Le Parisien, c/m, RpC, 21" **6,400.00**
A Series Le Parisien, c/m, RpC, 9" **2,800.00**
A Series Le Parisien, o/m, RpC, 16" **2,400.00**
B Series, c/m, pwt, jtd body, RpC, 24" **5,400.00**
Bourgoin, c/m, pwt, jtd body, RpC, 20" **6,700.00**
Bsk head & hip, Motschmann-style body, RpC, 18", minimum .**7,000.00**
C Series, c/m, wire eyes, jtd, RpC, 17" **5,200.00**
C Series Child, c/m, rnd face, pwt, ca 1880, RpC, 18" **5,400.00**
Wht bsk, rnd face, o/m w/teeth, unmk, early, Rpc, 16" **4,200.00**

Uneeda

Baby Dana, hp/vinyl, nurser, 1975, OC, 20" **25.00**
Betsy McCall, hp/vinyl, brn o/c, posable head, OC, 11½" **100.00**
Bride Sue, vinyl, bl o/c, high-heel ft, OC, 10½" **35.00**
Donna Fashion Doll, hp/vinyl, pnt eyes, 1970, OC, 5½" **10.00**
Magic Meg, hp/vinyl, bl o/c, hair 'grows,' 1971, OC, 16" **35.00**
Moonmaid, hp/vinyl, brn pnt eyes, blond hair, 1966, OC, 11½" ..**45.00**
Patti-Cake, hp/vinyl, bl o/c, wht hair, music box, OC, 20" **8.00**
Serenade, vinyl, battery-op talker, 1962, OC, 21" **50.00**
Toddles, hp/vinyl, bl o/c, hinged legs, RpC, 1952 ....**20.00**

Vogue

Angela, Debutant series, hp, 1953, OC, 8" **450.00**

Angela, hp, Debutante Series, 1953, OC, 8" **450.00**
Baby Dear, 1960-61, OC, 12" **60.00**
Baby Wide Eyes, vinyl, lg brn o/c, 1976, OC, 16" **40.00**
Black Ginny Baby, vinyl/cloth, o/c, c/m, 1964, OC, 12" **25.00**
Character baby, vinyl, o/c, molded/pnt hair, 1966, OC, 16" **65.00**
Fairy Godmother, 1986, OC **165.00**
Ginny, hp, molded lashes, walker, 1954-57, OC, minimum value ..**300.00**
Ginny, hp, pnt lashes, strung, OC, 8", minimum value **450.00**
Ginny Hawaiian, brn/blk, OC, 8", minimum value **725.00**
Ginny International, vinyl, 1977, OC, minimum value **1,400.00**
Jeff, plastic/vinyl, OC (Phantom Skater), minimum value **200.00**
Jeff, 1957, OC, 10" **165.00**
Lil Imp, vinyl, OC, 11" **45.00**
Littlest Angel, brn hp/vinyl, brn o/c, 1963, OC, 13" **30.00**
Wee Imp, red wig, OC, 8" **500.00**

Wax, Poured Wax

Alice headband hairdo, RpC, 14" **475.00**
Common type, worn wax, RpC, 12" **150.00**
Lady, poured head & limbs, glass eyes, cloth body, RpC, 24" ..**3,600.00**
Lever-operated eyes, 1850s, RpC, 17" **950.00**
Molded hat, RpC, 16" **3,200.00**
Over compo, sleep eyes, cloth body, wood limbs, 1860s, RpC, 16" ..**850.00**
Poured head & limbs, glass eyes, cloth body, RpC, 16" **1,400.00**
Poured head & limbs, glass eyes, cloth body, RpC, 22" **1,900.00**
2-faced, laughing & crying, Bartenstein, 1890s, RpC, 16" **950.00**

Door Knockers

Door knockers, those charming precursors of the door bell, come in an intriguing array of shapes and styles. The very rare ones come from England. Cast iron examples made in this country were often produced in forms similar to the more familiar doorstop figures.

Butterfly, gold pnt **60.00**
Butterfly, orig factory pnt **225.00**
Cherries, CI, orig pnt, 3¼" **145.00**
Couple kissing, bronze, 10½" **45.00**
Cow's head, brass **165.00**
Flower basket w/bow, CI, orig pnt, 3⅝" **125.00**
Gargoyle, cherubs & shield on bronze, no striker, 12" **235.00**
Lady's hand holding apple, CI, EX **65.00**
Lion's head, CI, worn gold pnt, 6½x4" **80.00**

Lion's head with ring through nose, copper, 6", $85.00.

Little girl knocking at door, CI, orig pnt, Hubley, 3½" 185.00
Oval w/eng name & 1805, brass, 7¾" 85.00
Owl, brass, old 40.00
Parrot in flight, pnt CI, EX 185.00
Pistol, brass 165.00
Poinsettia, CI, orig pnt, 3" 195.00
Urn form, cast brass 35.00
Woodpecker, CI, Hubley 135.00

Doorstops

Although introduced in England in the mid-1800s, cast iron doorstops were not made to any great extent in this country until after the Civil War. Once called 'door porters,' their function was to keep doors open to provide better ventilation. They have been produced in many shapes and sizes, both dimensional and flat backed, and in the past few years have become a popular, yet affordable collectible. While cast iron examples are the most common, brass, wood, and chalk were also used. An average price is in the $100.00 to $200.00 range, though some are valued at more than $400.00. Doorstops retained their usefulness and appeal well into the thirties.

The prices below reflect market values in the East where doorstops are at a premium. For other areas of the country, it may be necessary to adjust prices down about 25%. In the listings below, when no condition code is present, items are assumed to be in excellent original condition, flat backed unless noted full figured, and cast iron unless another material is mentioned. For further information we recommend *Doorstops, Identification and Values*, by Jeanne Bertoia.

Key:
B&H — Bradley & Hubbard   ff — full figured

Aunt Jemima, arms akimbo, ff, 13¼x8" 165.00
Basket of Flowers, orig mc pnt w/blk & silver basket, 8" 100.00
Beagle, sits facing right, w/collar, 8x6½" 175.00
Bear w/Honey, stands & holds honey w/both arms, 15x6½" 500.00
Bellhop, carries bag in arm, suitcase beside, 7½x5⅛" 375.00
Bobby Blake, holds teddy bear at waist, 9½x5¼" 410.00
Boy w/Fruit Basket, top hat, basket at waist, 9¼x3⅞" 375.00
Campbell Kid, standing girl, 9½" 320.00
Castle, on mountain w/winding road, 8x5¼" 275.00
Clown, sits w/arms & legs crossed, w/rubber knobs, 8x3½" 475.00
Comical Dog, Greenblatt #17, 1927, 10x4¾" 90.00
Comical Man, w/umbrella & dog, worn mc rpt, 11¼" 165.00
Covered Wagon, Hubley, w/paper label, 6½" L 110.00
Crocodile, walking w/mouth open, wedge, 5¼x11½" 100.00
Dolly, bow in hair, holds doll at waist, 9½x5½" 410.00

Donald Duck, holding stop sign, smiling, 8⅜x5¼" 200.00
Dutch Girl, Littco #33, yoke w/buckets, label, 13x10" 360.00
Elephant, Hubley, trunk over head, 8¼x10" 125.00
Elephant by Palm, trunk in top of tree, wedge, 13¾x10¼" 250.00
Elk, standing on rocks, looking back, 11x10" 150.00
Fireplace, woman w/spinning wheel in front, 6¼x8" 265.00
Frog, Lg; standing erect, ff, 14x7" 500.00
Frog on Mushroom, ff, 4½x3⅝" 165.00
Geisha, Hubley, on knees playing instrument, ff, 7x6" 200.00
Giraffe, Hubley, 12½x9" 500.00
Girl w/Full Dress, wedge, 8½x6" 240.00
Gnome Smoking Pipe, ff, 6½x10" 360.00
Halloween Girl, pointed hood, w/pumpkin, 14x10" 500.00
Horse on Base, rearing in front of a dog, 7¼x8½" 150.00
Huckleberry Finn, big hat, w/pole & bucket, 12½x9⅝" 475.00
Humpty Dumpty, w/bow tie, sitting on wall, ff, 4½x3½" 275.00
Knight, in full armor, 13¼x6" 225.00
Koala, Taylor Cook, #5, on log, 7¼x5½" 385.00
Lafayette, left hand at side, sword in right, 11⅝x6⅜" 460.00
Lion & serpent, cast brass, 10½" 165.00
Little Blk Lady, hands in apron pockets, ff, 4x2⅜" 165.00
Little Colonial Lady, tiered skirt, hands at waist, ff, 4⅝" 80.00
Little Girl by Wall, hand at mouth, ff, 5¼x3¼" 165.00
Lobster, 12½x6½" 410.00
Maid of Honor, Hubley, holds flowers/skirt held up, 8x5" 240.00
Mary Quite Contrary, watering flowers, 11⅜x9⅝" 500.00
Olive Picker, man w/mule & baskets, 7¾x8¾" 500.00
Outhouse, 8x6½" 350.00
Owl, on stump facing left, 10x6" 225.00
Owl, on 2 books, 9¼x6½" 435.00
Pansy Bowl, Hubley #256, 7x6½" 180.00
Parrot, mk 1289, w/rubber knobs, 8x3⅞" 320.00
Parrot, on perch, 8x3⅞" 175.00
Parrot in Ring, unmk B&H, 8x7" 85.00
Peacock, in full bloom, 6¼x6¼" 165.00
Peasant Girl, Hubley, fruit basket on head, 8¾x5" 175.00
Pekingese, Hubley, stands, faces left, ff, 14½x9" 425.00
Pheasant, Hubley, facing backwards, 8½x7½" 250.00
Pied Piper, sits on mushroom, plays flute, 7¼x5" 300.00
Police Boy, in diaper & hat, w/whistle & dog, 10⅝x7¼" 375.00
Puppies in Basket, 3 looking out, 7x7⅜" 325.00
Rabbit w/Top Hat, Albany, in tuxedo, 9⅞x4¾" 375.00
Reading Girls, 2 girls in bonnets sit bk to bk, 5x8⅝" 450.00
Setter, Hubley, in point stance, ff, 8¾x15⅞" 165.00
Skier, holds skis in right arm, ff, 12½x5" 425.00
Southern Belle, holding hat & flowers in 1 hand, 11¼x6" 125.00
Spaniel, sits facing left, collar w/chain across bk, 9x7" 300.00
Squirrel, on stump eating nut, 9x6⅜" 165.00
St Bernard, w/sm barrel around neck, 8x10½" 175.00
Stork, Hubley, ff, 12¼x7" 465.00
Swallows, 2 in berry tree, Hubley, #480, 8½x7½" 300.00
Twin Penguins, standing side by side, facing away, 7¼x7½" 175.00
Uncle Sam, dressed in red, wht & bl, 12x5½" 500.00
Wht Caddie, w/golf bag, 8x6" 500.00
Woman w/Muff, hands in muff, looking right, ff, 9¼x5" 200.00
Woodsman, English, w/axe, pipe & dog, 13¼x9" 250.00

Dorchester Pottery

Taking its name from the town in Massachusetts where it was organized in 1895, the Dorchester Pottery Company made primarily utilitarian wares, though other types of items were made as well. By 1940 a line of decorative pottery was introduced, some of which was

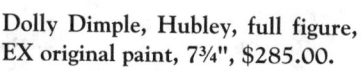

Dolly Dimple, Hubley, full figure, EX original paint, 7¾", $285.00.

painted by hand with scrollwork or themes from nature. The buildings were destroyed by fire in the late 1970s, and the pottery was never rebuilt. In the listings that follow, the decorations described are all in cobalt unless otherwise noted.

Basket, high-glaze wht, flared rim, paper label, 11¾x9¼" 120.00
Bottle, scent; Colonial Lace, striped hdl, sgn, stamped, 4½" 120.00
Bottle, scent; Full Scroll, spherical, mk, 5½x4½" 130.00
Bowl, breakfast; Blueberry, swirled int, stamped, 2⅛x5¾" 60.00
Bowl, breakfast; Flower Blossom, sgn RB, stamped, 2¼x5½" 210.00
Bowl, breakfast; Good Morning..., clown face, stamped, 2x5¾" .180.00
Bowl, Clematis, spongeware ext, sgn, stamped, 3⅛x8½" 400.00
Candy dish, Butterfly & Flower, sgn, stamped, 1½x6¼" 240.00
Candy dish, Pussy Willow, sgn, stamped, 1½x6½" 130.00
Casserole, Colonial Lace, hdls, sgn, stamped, 4½x7¾" 275.00
Casserole, Pine Cone, hdls, sgn, stamped, 4½x7¼" 200.00
Casserole, Pine Cone, sgn CAH, stamped, 2¾x5¼" 150.00
Chamberstick, Pine Cone, sgn CAH, stamped, 1¼x5¾" 125.00
Cookie jar, Apple, sgn, stamped, sealed crack, 9x8¾" 425.00
Creamer & sugar bowl, Blueberry, sgn, stamped, 3", 3½" 150.00

Creamer and sugar bowl, Pussy Willow, incised and stamped, 4¼" diameter, $200.00 for the pair.

Cup, demitasse; Half Scroll, sgn CAH, stamped, 2x3¾" 55.00
Cup, Good Morning, clown's face, sgn, stamped, 7¼" 180.00
Cup, Happy Day, clown's face, All Gone in bottom, mk, 2¾" 90.00
Cup & saucer, demitasse; Blueberry, sgn, stamped, 2" 55.00
Cups, Double Band, striped hdl, sgn, stamped, 2¾" 50.00
Decanter, Pine Cone, sperical cap w/bl florals, mk, 9x7" 140.00
Jell-O mold, Fluted Blueberry & Stripe, stamped, 2½x5¼" 100.00
Mug, Anchor, striped hdl, sgn CAH, stamped, 4½" 60.00
Mug, Anchor, stylized anchor & rope on ivory, stamped, 4½" 65.00
Mug, Half Scroll, striped hdl, sgn CAH, stamped, 4½" 50.00
Mug, Pine Cone, sgn CAH, stamped, 4½" 40.00
Mug, Pine Cone & Blizzard, ...Blizzard of 1978, stamped, 4⅛" 175.00
Mug, Sea Horse, dbl bl bands, striped hdl, sgn, stamped, 4½" 60.00
Mug, Whale, sgn CAH, stamped, 4½" 60.00
Pitcher, water; Pine Cone, sgn RB, stamped, 7½" 150.00
Plate, bamboo-type decor, swirled int, sgn, stamped, 10¼" 210.00
Plate, flower blossoms, sgn CAH, stamped, 10½" 160.00
Plate, Strawberry, sgn RT, stamped, 9¾" 180.00
Sugar bowl, Pine Cone, sgn CAH, stamped, 3¼" 120.00
Sugar jar, Lace, bulbous, sgn JM, stamped, 3¼x3" 210.00
Syrup, Blueberry, bulbous, w/lid, sgn, stamped, 5" 125.00
Syrup, Full Scroll, striped hdl, w/lid, sgn, stamped, 4½", EX 125.00
Syrup, Half Scroll, striped hdl, w/lid, sgn, stamped, 4¾" 125.00
Syrup, Pine Cone, w/lid, sgn, stamped, 5⅛" 140.00
Vase, 2-tone bl, 4-sided, crimped mouth, bulbous, mk, 4½x5" 40.00

Dorflinger

C. Dorflinger was born in Alsace, France, and came to this country

when he was ten years old. When still very young, he obtained a job in a glass factory in New Jersey. As a young man, he started his own glassworks in Brooklyn, New York, opening new factories as profits permitted. During that time he made cut glass articles for many famous people including President and Mrs. Lincoln, for whom he produced a complete service of tableware with the United States Coat of Arms. In 1863 he sold the New York factories because of ill health and moved to his farm near White Mills, Pennsylvania. His health returned, and he started a plant near his home. It was there that he did much of his best work, making use of only the very finest materials. Christian died in 1915, and the plant was closed in 1921 by consent of the family.

Dorflinger glass is rare and often hard to identify. Very few pieces were marked — many only carried a small paper label which was quickly discarded.

Bottle, 'Cologne' eng, cut honeycomb & floral, sterling top, 12" 900.00
Bowl, Old Irish, 9" 500.00
Decanter, gr to clear, Dmn Point & oval cuttings, w/stopper 295.00
Jug, whiskey; Renaissance, faceted hdl/stopper, 9½" 450.00
Pitcher, Crosscut Dmn & Fan w/stars, triple-cut hdl, 2-pt 500.00
Plate, cranberry to clear, strawberry dmns, star center, 7" 295.00
Relish, Dmn & Fan cutting w/stars, triple-cut hdl, 2-part 500.00
Shot glass, cut, Old Colony 42.00
Wine, Strawberry Dmn, cranberry to clear 175.00

Dragon Ware

Dragon ware is fairly accessible and is still being made today. The 'new' Dragon ware is distinguishable by the lack of detail in the dragon. In the older pieces, much care is given to the slipwork dragon's eyes, scales, and wings. In the new ware, the dragon is 'flat' and lacks detail.

Colors are 'primary,' referring to background color, not the color of the dragon. The primary color of a 'new' piece has more shine than the older ware. Old colors are vibrant but for the most part not shiny (except for the lustre colors). 'New' colors include green, lavender, yellow, pink, blue, pearlized, and orange as well as the classic blue/black. Old colors include orange, green, yellow, blue, pearlized, and blue/black. In addition to lustre finishes, you will find some background colors that are applied unevenly (and without shine), producing a 'cloud' effect behind the dragon.

Many Dragon ware cups have lithophanes in the bottoms, often the face of a geisha girl. Nude lithophanes are more scarce but can sometimes be found in cups and saki cups. New pieces may also have lithophanes, but they are lacking in detail and tend to be flat.

Items listed below are unmarked unless noted otherwise. Our advisor for this category is Suzi Hibbard; she is listed in the Directory under California.

Ashtray, tricorner, Nippon mk, 5½" 135.00
Box, cigarette; gray w/bl, pk & gold highlights 15.00
Condiment set, 2 cruets+shakers+mustard w/lid on 10x6" tray 65.00
Creamer & sugar bowl, slip on gray-gr lustre w/gold, souvenir 28.00
Cup & saucer, coffee; orange lustre int, Japan 10.00
Cup & saucer, demitasse; jewels & gold, scalloped rim, ftd 15.00
Cup & saucer, demitasse; orange lustre int w/bl irid, Japan 12.50
Cup & saucer, demitasse; pearlized int, bl highlights 8.50
Ferner, ftd, scalloped rim, Nippon mk, 7½" 325.00
Lemon dish, gray & wht w/bl, loop hdl, 5½" sq 15.00
Lemon dish, red w/gray & wht dragons, loop hdl, 5½" sq 20.00
Plate, brn edge, 7½" 12.00
Plate, brn on beige w/pk & bl, brn rim, Japan, 7" 12.00
Plate, gold dragon, gold rim, HP Japan, 7½" 10.00
Shakers, sm, pr 12.50

Sugar bowl, wht w/gold dragon, gold rim 15.00
Tea set, figures on brn w/gold, lithophane cups, Nippon, 15-pc .350.00
Tea set, pastel moriage, brn trim, 3-pc 55.00
Teapot, orange, MIJ, pot+cr/sug 55.00

Teapot, 7¼", with creamer and sugar bowl, classic style, ca 1940s, Made in Japan, $55.00 for the set.

Vase, orange lustre int, fancy hdls, Hinode, 9x6x3½" 80.00
Vase, wht dragon w/turq, orange lustre int, hdls, Japan, 8¾" 160.00

Dresden

The term Dresden is used today to indicate the porcelains that were produced in Meissen and Dresden, Germany, from the very early 18th century well into the next. John Bottger, a young alchemist, discovered the formula for the first true porcelain in 1708 while being held a virtual prisoner at the palace in Dresden because of the King's determination to produce a superior ware. Two years later a factory was erected in nearby Meissen with Bottger as director. There fine tableware, elaborate centerpieces, and exquisite figurines with applied details were produced. In 1731, to distinguish their product from the wares of such potters as Sevres, Worcester, Chelsea, and Derby, the Meissen company adopted their famous crossed swords trademark. During the next century, several potteries were producing porcelain in the 'Meissen style' in Dresden itself. Their wares were often marked with imitations of Meissen's crossed swords.

The Carl Theime factory produced dinnerware as well as decorative pieces in the Meissen style from 1872 until 1972. Openwork pieces were their specialty. Their mark was an intertwined 'SP' with the word Dresden below. Other companies followed suit, and in 1883 began using the crown mark along with the Dresden indication. There were several variations of this mark employed over the years. Many of these companies produced Meissen-type wares well into the 20th century. See also Meissen.

Bowl, floral reserves, appl fruit/floral, scroll ends, 14" L 700.00
Bowl, mc floral w/gold, deep, mk Dresden, late, 4⅝" 45.00
Boy (& girl), baskets on bk, scythe in hand, 12", pr 350.00
Candelabra, 3-arm, appl florals, 3-D couple base, 17", pr 465.00
Celery dish, HP florals w/gold, scalloped, ca 1881, 5x13" 195.00
Compote, mc floral w/gold, rtcl edge, mk Dresden, lg 145.00
Compote, parrot & owl perched on ea side floral ped, 15" 725.00
Compote, rtcl bands on bowl & knop ft, HP florals, 7x9" 225.00
Compote, rtcl/HP floral, 3 figures stand on base, 1800s, 12" 600.00
Compote, rtcl/oval, 2 cupids on flower-appl stump base, 12" 440.00
Ewer, garden scene (continuous), wine top/bottom, 1890s, 12" ..750.00
Figurine, ballerina, silver gray hair, mk Dresden, 6" 135.00
Figurine, chess players, couple at table, much gold 345.00
Figurine, dancing pr, 18th-C attire, 1900s, #11349, 7" 220.00
Figurine, gentleman in lav coat, 1800s, 8¾" 200.00

Figurine, romantic pr on rock base w/basket of flowers, 12" 350.00
Figurine, Spanish dancer, lacy dress, 9", NM 350.00
Figurine, 2 ladies by Rococo mirror & console table, 15" 700.00
Inkwell, dbl; pastel flowers w/gold, ca 1905 ....300.00
Lamp, 3 appl cupids w/birds & flowers, ca 1920, 16"+fittings 450.00
Plaque, Madonna & Child w/donors & children, 6x4½" 700.00
Porringer, floral, mc on wht, mk Dresden 65.00
Tete-a-tete, battle scenes on cobalt w/gilt, 8-pc 1,000.00
Tray, dresser; mc floral w/gold, 10¼x7" 100.00
Tray, fruit; romantic couple, garland/rtcl border, 12" 285.00
Tray, garden chess match, scalloped/gilt border, 4-lobe, 11" 435.00
Vase, floral/gold on wht, soft paste, no mk/#d, 1890s, 6" 50.00

Dresser Accessories

Dresser sets, ring trees, figural or satin pincushions, manicure sets — all those lovely items that graced milady's dressing table — were at the same time decorative as well as functional. Today they appeal to collectors for many reasons. The Victorian era is well represented by repousse silver-backed mirrors and brushes and pincushions that were used to display ornamental pins for the hair, hats, and scarves. The hair receiver — similar to a powder jar but with an opening in the lid — was used to hold long strands of hair retrieved from the comb or brush. These were wound around the finger and tucked in the opening to be used later for hair jewelry and pictures, many of which survive to the present day. (See Hair Weaving.)

Celluloid dresser sets were popular during the late 1800s and early 1900s. Some included manicure tools, pill boxes, and buttonhooks, as well as the basic items. Because celluloid tends to break rather easily, a whole set may be hard to find today. (See also Plastics.) With the current interest in anything Art Deco, sets from the thirties and forties are especially collectible. These may be made of crystal, Bakelite, or silver, and the original boxes just as lavishly appointed as their contents.

Box, gr frosted glass coach form, blk lid w/crown final 110.00

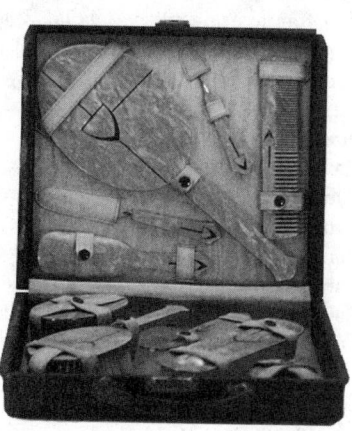

Dresser set, green marbleized celluloid, 10-piece set, M in case, $125.00.

Hairbrush, brass w/HP medallion & colored stones, +mirror 195.00
Hairbrush, gilt metal w/portrait on bk, +hand mirror 230.00
Hand mirror, bl hard rubber & celluloid, Indian portrait, 7" 100.00
Hand mirror, tortoise, cvd stylized floral medallion, lg 140.00
Nail buffer, tortoise, silver mt w/Birmingham mk 80.00
Nail file, Nouveau lady w/flowing hair, mk Sterling, 7½" 65.00
Set, china, yel roses, unmk Germany, 5-pc+8x11" tray 265.00
Set, glass, cut & frosted, chrome tops, Germany, 7-pc 475.00
Set, gold-tone metal wHP floral medallion, 1930s, 9-pc, MIB 225.00
Set, pk blown glass w/gold, 2 7" bottles+powder box 88.00
Set, sterling, Old Colony repousse, Gorham, 3-pc, +case 200.00

Set, tortoise, 8-pc, in fitted case 300.00
Set, vaseline glass, mk Shari, 4-pc on 2x7" tray 165.00
Shoe horn, ivory w/silver mts 45.00

Dryden

James Dryden founded Dryden Pottery in July, 1946, in Ellsworth, Kansas. For ten years Dryden produced pottery from clay dug from the hills of Ellsworth County. Pieces were cast in molds and then glazed using processes Dryden learned while studying ceramics at the University of Kansas. Glazes were produced from volcanic ash, and recipes for them were a guarded secret. James Dryden is still numbered among the few potters who possessed the secret of decorative glazing with just one firing. Ellsworth Dryden was shipped to over six hundred retail outlets in forty different states. In the 1950s Dryden sold some pottery to Van Briggle to offset losses in counter sales. When I-70 opened, taking tourist traffic away from Dryden's plant, James Dryden moved to Hot Springs, Arkansas, in 1956. Since the late 1960s, most of the pottery has been wheel thrown.

It is easy to recognize those pieces produced in Kansas because they were made with a dark tan clay. Arkansas pottery pieces are pure white. Almost all of the pottery is marked with the Dryden signature. Kansas pieces may also show a mold number and a paper label. Of special interest to collectors are those pieces in animal shapes (elephants, panthers, and donkeys, for instance) and those sold as souvenirs (i.e., the K.U. jug). Our advisor for this category is Ralph Winslow; he is listed in the Directory under Kansas.

Ashtray, #7B, 2" 12.00
Bookends, Scotty, #80, 4" 35.00
Boot, souvenir, aqua, #47, 4½" 20.00
Bowl, oblong, #44 ....25.00
Figurine, elephant, blk, #10, 11" 60.00
Figurine, panther, brn 60.00
Figurine, stork, mauve, #720, 9" 25.00
Jug, souvenir, #102, 5" 16.00
Mug, Kansas State, blk, #7, 5" 20.00
Mug, souvenir, blk, #1, 3½" 15.00
Pitcher, bl, #39, 6" 30.00
Pitcher, bl, #98, 5½" 17.50
Pitcher, gr, #50, 6½" 15.00
Pitcher, souvenir, maroon, 5½" 24.00
Planter, cow, blk, #80, 5¾" 17.50
Planter, flowerpot, maroon, #86 ....30.00
Planter, Madonna, brn, #87, 4" 30.00
Planter, pony, blk, #5, 6½" 25.00
Planter, rooster, avocado, #Y 28.00
Shakers, gr, 6", pr 20.00
Shakers, souvenir, #73, 4", pr 20.00
Teapot, bl, #108B 20.00
Vase, aqua, #41, 6½" 25.00
Vase, Bull Shoals Dam, sq, #A3 ....55.00
Vase, cactus, gr, #B1 ....25.00
Vase, donkey, #21, 4½" 22.00
Vase, elephant, #313, 3" 18.00
Vase, fish, gr, #88, 8" 35.00
Vase, leaf, souvenir, 37K, 4½" 17.50
Vase, mustard, #800, 10" 50.00

Duncan and Miller

The firm that became known as the Duncan and Miller Glass

Company in 1900 was organized in 1874 in Pittsburgh, Pennsylvania, a partnership between George Duncan, his sons Harry and James, and his son-in-law Augustus Heisey. John Ernest Miller was hired as their designer. He is credited with creating the most famous of all Duncan's glassware lines, Three Face. (See Pattern Glass.) The George Duncan and Sons Glass Company, as it was titled, was only one of eighteen companies that merged in 1891 with U.S. Glass. Soon after the Pittsburgh factory burned in 1892, the association was dissolved, and Heisey left the firm to set up his own factory in Newark, Ohio. Duncan built his new plant in Washington, Pennsylvania, where he continued to make pressed glassware in such notable patterns as Bagware, Amberette, Duncan Flute, Button Arches, and Zippered Slash. The firm was eventually sold to U.S. Glass in Tiffin, Ohio, and unofficially closed in August 1955.

In addition to the early pressed dinnerware patterns, today's Duncan and Miller collectors enjoy searching for opalescent vases in many patterns and colors, frosted 'Satin Tone' glassware, acid-etched designs, and lovely stemware such as the Rock Crystal cuttings. Milk glass was made in limited quantity and is considered a good investment. Ruby glass, Ebony (a lovely opaque black glass popular during the twenties and thirties), and, of course, the glass animal and bird figurines are all highly valued examples of the art of Duncan and Miller.

Expect to pay at least 25% more than values listed for other colors for ruby and cobalt, as much as 50% more in the Georgian, Pall Mall and Sandwich lines. Pink, green, and amber Sandwich is worth approximately 30% more than the same items in crystal. Milk glass examples of American Way are valued up to 30% higher than color, 50% higher in Pall Mall. Add approximately 40% to listed prices for opalescent items. Etchings, cuttings, and other decorations will increase values by about 50%. For further study we recommend *The Encyclopedia of Duncan Glass*, by Gail Krause; she is listed in the Directory under Pennsylvania. Also refer to *Glass Animals and Figural Flower Frogs of the Depression Era* by Lee Garmon and Dick Spencer; they are both listed under Illinois. See also Glass Animals.

Astaire, crystal; top hat vase, 3¾" 45.00
Canterbury, crystal; goblet, water 12.50
Canterbury, crystal; tray, cloverleaf 12.50
Canterbury, crystal; vase, crimped, 3" 8.00
Canterbury, pk opal; candy dish, 3-part, w/lid 65.00

Canterbury, blue opalescent; three-part candy dish with lid, $95.00.

Caribbean, bl; bowl, flared, 9½" 95.00
Caribbean, bl; bowl, soup; 7" 50.00
Caribbean, bl; bowl, 5" 35.00
Caribbean, bl; champagne 45.00
Caribbean, bl; cocktail, 3¾-oz, 4⅛" 45.00
Caribbean, bl; creamer & sugar bowl 75.00
Caribbean, bl; goblet, water 40.00

Caribbean, bl; oyster cocktail 95.00
Caribbean, bl; pitcher, milk 350.00
Caribbean, bl; pitcher, water 950.00
Caribbean, bl; plate, hdld, 6" 18.00
Caribbean, bl; plate, 13½" 55.00
Caribbean, bl; relish, 2-part, 6" 30.00
Caribbean, bl; relish, 5-part, 12½" 110.00
Caribbean, bl; sherbet, low 30.00
Caribbean, bl; vase, oval, 10½x5½" 75.00
Caribbean, crystal; tray (for creamer & sugar bowl) 30.00
Chanticleer, amber; cocktail shaker 65.00
Chanticleer, crystal; tumbler, 3" 30.00
Festive, bl; comport, 7¾" 75.00
Festive, bl; creamer & sugar bowl 45.00
Festive, bl; relish, divided 65.00
Festive, honey; creamer & sugar bowl 45.00
Festive, honey; mayonnaise bowl 25.00
First Love, crystal; bowl, flared, ftd, 12" 60.00
First Love, crystal; bowl, fluted, flared, 10" 55.00
First Love, crystal; candle holders, 2-light, #30, pr 90.00
First Love, crystal; champagne 15.00
First Love, crystal; cordial 45.00
First Love, crystal; goblet, champagne 25.00
First Love, crystal; goblet, water; 6¾" 37.00
First Love, crystal; pitcher, water 150.00
First Love, crystal; relish, 2-part, #115, 8" 30.00
First Love, crystal; saucer champagne 25.00
First Love, crystal; shaker 25.00
First Love, crystal; tumbler, ftd, 5-oz 24.00
First Love, crystal; vase, urn form, 5½" 55.00
Georgian, gr; bowl, 4½" 8.00
Georgian, gr; creamer, 3" 11.00
Georgian, gr; cup & saucer 13.00
Georgian, gr; plate, 8½" 9.00
Georgian, gr; server, center hdl 30.00
Georgian, gr; sherbet 13.50
Georgian, gr; sugar bowl, w/lid, 3" 45.00
Hobnail, bl opal; candy dish, w/lid 125.00
Hobnail, bl opal; pitcher, water 325.00
Hobnail, bl opal; plate, 13¼" 85.00
Hobnail, bl opal; tumbler, iced tea; flat 30.00
Hobnail, bl opal; tumbler, juice; flat 22.50
Hobnail, bl opal; tumbler, water; flat 25.00
Hobnail, crystal; candy dish, w/lid 35.00
Hobnail, crystal; champagne 8.00
Hobnail, crystal; coaster 4.00
Hobnail, crystal; cup & saucer 12.50
Hobnail, crystal; goblet, water 14.50
Hobnail, crystal; tray, 8" 10.00
Hobnail, crystal; vase, crimped, 5½" 22.50
Hobnail, pk opal; basket, 5" 95.00
Hobnail, pk opal; champagne 22.50
Hobnail, pk opal; cocktail 30.00
Hobnail, pk opal; goblet, water 35.00
Hobnail, pk opal; tumbler, juice; flat 22.50
Hobnail, pk opal; tumbler, water; flat 30.00
Indian Tree, crystal; comport, low, #115, 6" 45.00
Indian Tree, crystal; mayonnaise bowl 22.50
Indian Tree, crystal; plate, 8½" 16.00
Indian Tree, crystal; relish, 3-part, 9" 27.50
Indian Tree, crystal; tumbler, iced tea 22.50
Indian Tree, crystal; vase, crimped, 4½" 55.00
Pall Mall, Biscayne gr; swan, 10½" 50.00
Pall Mall, bl opal; swan, swag bk 175.00

Pall Mall, chartreuse; swan, 10½" 50.00
Pall Mall, crystal; ashtray, duck etch, rectangular, 8" 65.00
Pall Mall, crystal; swan, w/cutting, 10½" 225.00
Pall Mall, crystal; swan, 4¼" 35.00
Pall Mall, wisteria; swan, 7" 125.00
Plaza, pk; bowl, deep, 8" 150.00
Radiance, lt bl; cheese comport 45.00
Radiance, lt bl; cup & saucer 25.00
Radiance, lt bl; mint dish, ftd, 5" 47.50
Radiance, lt bl; plate, 8⅝" 20.00
Radiance, lt bl; relish, 3-part, 7½" 55.00
Radiance, lt bl; sugar bowl 20.00
Radiance, red; punch cup 15.00
Radiance, red; relish, 2-part, #4224, 7" 45.00
Radiance, red; sugar bowl 22.50
Sandwich, crystal; basket, 11½" 175.00
Sandwich, crystal; celery tray, 10" 22.50
Sandwich, crystal; cheese dish 125.00
Sandwich, crystal; goblet, water 25.00
Sandwich, crystal; sherbet 8.00
Sandwich, crystal; syrup, 13-oz 95.00
Sandwich, crystal; tumbler, iced tea; ftd 15.00
Sandwich, crystal; vase, 10" 65.00
Sandwich, dk bl; goblet, wine 35.00
Seahorse etch, red/crystal; cocktail, ftd, 3-oz 35.00
Seahorse etch, red/crystal; tumbler, ftd, 13-oz 37.50
Seahorse etch, red/crystal; tumbler, ftd, 9-oz 30.00
Seahorse etch, red/crystal; whiskey, ftd, 2-oz 45.00
Spiral Flutes, amber; ashtray 30.00
Spiral Flutes, amber; cigarette box, w/silver o/l 30.00
Spiral Flutes, amber; cup, bouillon 14.50
Spiral Flutes, amber; cup, seafood 12.50
Spiral Flutes, amber; grapefruit, ftd 17.50
Spiral Flutes, amber; plate, 6" 4.50
Spiral Flutes, amber; saucer 4.50
Spiral Flutes, crystal; comport, low, 4½" 10.00
Spiral Flutes, crystal; sweetmeat, 4½" 10.00
Spiral Flutes, crystal; vase, 10½" 60.00
Spiral Flutes, crystal; whiskey, ftd 4.00
Spiral Flutes, gr; cigarette box, w/silver o/l 35.00
Spiral Flutes, gr; cup & saucer 13.00
Spiral Flutes, gr; goblet, wine 14.50
Spiral Flutes, gr; pickle dish, 8½" 15.00
Spiral Flutes, gr; sweetmeat 25.00
Spiral Flutes, gr; tumbler, 5¼" 10.00
Spiral Flutes, gr; vase, 10½" 40.00
Spiral Flutes, gr; vase, 8½" 30.00
Spiral Flutes, pk; tumbler, iced tea; flat, 5½" 40.00
Sylvan, crystal; swan, 12" 125.00
Teardrop, crystal; ashtray, 4½" 12.00
Teardrop, crystal; goblet, water; 7" 14.50
Teardrop, crystal; plate, hdls, 6" 6.00
Teardrop, crystal; relish, divided, 5½" 10.00
Teardrop, crystal; relish, 3-part, 10½" 22.50
Teardrop, crystal; relish, 5-part, 11¾" 30.00
Teardrop, crystal; sugar bowl, lg 9.00
Terrace, cobalt; plate, hdls, 5" 35.00
Terrace, crystal; bowl, 5" 12.50
Terrace, crystal; cordial 45.00
Terrace, crystal; cup & saucer, demitasse 35.00
Terrace, crystal; plate, dinner 45.00
Terrace, crystal; plate, luncheon 20.00
Terrace, crystal; plate, 7½" 8.50
Terrace, red; ashtray, sq 35.00

Terrace, red; creamer 42.50
Three Feathers, pk opal; vase, lg 85.00

Durand

Durand Art Glass was a division of Vineland Flint Glass Works in Vineland, New Jersey. This division was geared toward the manufacture of fine hand blown art glass in the style of Tiffany and Steuben. Lustered glass and opal glass were used as a basis to create such patterns as King Tut, Heart and Vine, Peacock Feather and Egyptian Crackle. Crystal, cased and overlay glass were used to produce cut designs. Production began in 1924 and continued until 1931. Early art glass was unmarked. Later pieces were generally signed Durand, often written across a large 'V,' all in script. The numbers that sometimes appear along with the signature indicate shape and height of the object. Owner Victor Durand employed several employees as well as the owner of the failed Quezal Art Glass and Decorating Company, which explains why early Durand is often mistaken for Quezal. Our advisor for this category is Edward J. Meschi; he is listed in the Directory under New Jersey.

Bowl, centerpc; Egyptian, red crackle, 11" dia 350.00
Bowl, centerpc; red crackle, stretched & ruffled, 11" 385.00
Bowl, cranberry, ftd, 2½x4¾" 75.00
Candlesticks, bl flanged rim w/wht pulled feather, 3x5" 575.00
Candlesticks, King Tut, opal on bl irid, baluster stem, 10", pr .1,100.00
Cordial, feathers on bl cup, lt yel stem 300.00
Lamp base, feathers, bl on wht w/gold threading, 7", pr 750.00
Rose bowl, leaves/vines, opal on bl irid, sgn/#1995, 4" 700.00
Rose bowl, yel-amber irid, floral/wreath etch, ftd, 4¾" 375.00

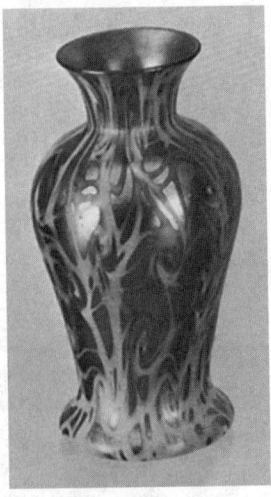

Vase, blue iridescent with opaque coil decoration, 7", $800.00.

Vase, allover threading on bl irid, classic form, 8" 550.00
Vase, allover threading on orange-gold, classic form, 8" 400.00
Vase, ambergris w/allover fissured gold, ribbed, 12" 1,000.00
Vase, bl irid, tapered w/open top, sgn/#1972, 8" 550.00
Vase, cut band at neck, bl/wht feathers, ftd, 6½" 500.00
Vase, dk amber w/optic ribs, #1987-8, 8x6" 400.00
Vase, feathers, gr on pale yel, 10½x6" 500.00
Vase, feathers, opal/gr on gold, much threading, #1970, 8" 700.00
Vase, feathers & threading, opal on orange-gold, #20102, 14" ...575.00
Vase, gold irid, beehive shoulder, sgn/#1978, 9" 850.00
Vase, heart vine, gold on cobalt, ovoid, 9" 1,265.00
Vase, hearts/vines, bl irid, #1812-7, 7" 1,200.00
Vase, King Tut, dk bl w/silver & gold irid, 9¾x5½" 1,100.00
Vase, King Tut, gr on amber to opal, gold int, bulbous, 8" 1,200.00

Vase, orange-gold, classic form, #1812-8, 8" 575.00
Vase, swirled/crackled gr & wht, lid w/berry finial, 10" 990.00

Durant Kilns

The Durant Pottery Company operated in Bedford Village, New York, in the early 1900s. Its founder was Mrs. Clarence Rice; she was aided by L. Volkmar to whom she assigned the task of technical direction. (See also Volkmar.) The artware and tableware they produced was simple in form and decoration. The creative aspects of the were carried on almost entirely by Volkmar himself, with only a minimal crew to help with production. After Mrs. Rice's death in 1919, the property was purchased by Volkmar, who chose to drop the Durant name by 1930. Prior to 1919 the ware was marked simply 'Durant' and dated. After that time a stylized 'V' was added.

Vases, Oriental blue glossy ribbed form with brown matt base, marked and dated 1920, 11½", $350.00 for the pair.

Bowl, aubergine semigloss, flaring petal sides, 1936, 11" 300.00
Candlestick, petals top & base, stems up column, wht, 12" 265.00
Planter, crackled Persian bl, ftd (3 rstr), 1913, 7x20x8" 500.00
Vase, blk satin, spherical/ftd, mfg flaw, 5½x5¾" 175.00

Elfinware

Made in Germany from about 1920 until the 1940s, these miniature vases, boxes, salt cellars, and miscellaneous novelty items are characterized by the tiny applied flowers that often cover their entire surface. Pieces with animals and birds are the most valuable, followed by the more interesting examples such as diminutive grand pianos, candle holders, etc. Items covered in 'spinach' (applied green moss) can be valued at 75% to 100% higher than pieces that are not decorated in this manner. See also Salts, Open.

Baby shoe, rose appl on lt bl, 4" 45.00
Box, w/lid 25.00
Card holder 25.00
Cradle, mini 20.00
Piano, mini 20.00
Slipper 25.00

Epergnes

Popular during the Victorian era, epergnes were fancy centerpieces often consisting of several tiers of vases (called lilies), candle holders, or dishes, or a combination of components. They were made in all types of art glass, and some were set in ornate plated frames.

Amethyst w/gold flowers, 1-lily, ruffled, 12½" 500.00
Bl o/l w/HP florals, 1-lily, matching base, 15½ x10½" 495.00
Cranberry & gr, 3-lily, 20" 850.00
Cranberry bud vase w/cast deer support on rnd SP base 225.00
Cranberry w/ribs & twists, crystal rigaree, 3-lily, 16" 900.00
Cranberry w/rigaree, 2 ea: sm & lg vases/canes/baskets, 22" 600.00
Cranberry w/wht opaque threading, 1-lily, 15¼ x11½" 295.00
Gr & wht, 4-lily, 19½" 1,250.00
Purple opal to clear w/emb decor, 1-lily, NP fr, 14x9½" 295.00
Turq, 4-lily, 3 baskets, fancy, 20½" 1,300.00
Vaseline, 4-lily, 17½" 550.00
Venetian latticinio, twisted mc ribbons, 3-lily, 16½x11½" 725.00

Erphila

Ebeling and Ruess, an importing company in Philadelphia, began operations in 1886. The acronym 'Erphila' was frequently substituted for the manufacturer's mark on the imported items. It appears that the Erphila mark was used through the late 1930s and then again after WW II on products from U.S. Zone Germany as well as from other areas. The company imported from factories such as Fustenberg, W. Goebel, Villeroy and Boch, Heinrich, Keramos, and Schumann, to name a few. Figurines, art pottery, and some utilitarian items can be found bearing the Erphila mark. Examples are hard to find. Early German marks (those prior to 1900) often contain the word 'Fayence.' After the turn of the century, a rectangular mark in green ink was used. Following WW I, porcelain items were imported from Czechoslovakia. These sometimes carried gold and silver labels. A small variety of marks were used in the 1920s and '30s, but they all contained the name Erphila. Sticker labels were also used. 'Bavaria,' 'Black Forest,' and 'Italy' are sometimes found in combination with 'Erphila.'

Ebeling and Ruess continue the importing business, but it appears that since the 1940s they are also using an 'E' and 'R' on a bell-shaped mark. Because this mark does not contain the name 'Erphila,' we do not consider it to be such. We assume that they stopped using this name sometime in the 1950s.

Figurines, four-piece dog family, largest: 4¾", green stamped mark, $100.00.

Ashtray, bird & 2 chicks on rim, oval 20.00
Ashtray/cigarette/match holder, alligator shape, bl/mc, MIG 65.00
Basket, porc, desert scene w/sphinx, Czech 56.00
Bookends, Colonial girl & boy, wht & pk, Czech 60.00
Bowl, leaf shape, gr w/gold veins, Czech, sm 32.00
Cake plate, wht flowers, MIG 16.00
Candlesticks, bl & wht, ea dbl, Czech, pr 45.00
Celery dish, leaf shape, wht, MIG 27.00

Cookie jar, coach scene, egg shape, 8¼" 300.00
Creamer, dog form, wht & blk, MIG, 8" 33.50
Creamer, gr & wht, dog hdl, MIG 75.00
Creamer, pig form, pk & blk, MIG, 8" 98.00
Dinnerware, Colonial scenes, sepia on beige, service for 8 ....425.00
Dresser doll, lady w/pk dress, MIG 115.00
Figurine, Airedale dog, wht/blk/brn, MIG 25.00
Figurine, bird, gr, MIG, 5", pr 30.00
Figurine, bull terrier dog, MIG, 5" L 40.00
Figurine, cat, sitting, blk & wht, MIG, 4½" 35.00
Figurine, cat, wht w/gold ball, MIG, 12" L 150.00
Figurine, Colonial couple, sitting, MIG 60.00
Figurine, fox, wht & tan, MIG, pr 55.00
Figurine, goat on hind legs, mc, MIG, 8" 65.00
Figurine, goose, wings spread, wht & gray, MIG 35.00
Figurine, Mrs Gamp, wht & orange, MIG, 3" 35.00
Figurine, Pekingese dog, blk & wht, MIG, 3" 33.50
Figurine, pirate w/parrot on shoulder, MIG 35.00
Figurine, rooster, wht, Czech, lg 45.00
Figurine, setter, dog in hunting pose, blk & wht, MIG, 10" L 60.00
Pitcher, chicken figural, red/yel/blk, Czech, chip, 9" 90.00
Pitcher, fruit, bl on wht, Czech, ½-liter, 6" 28.00
Planter, Art Deco, rings, mc, Czech 50.00
Planter, red flowers, ring hdls, Czech, 4" 30.00
Plate, cake; carnations, MIG, 11" 30.00
Plate, cake; wht flowers, MIG, w/server 22.00
Teapot, cat form, gray & blk, MIG, 8" 100.00
Teapot, dog form, gray & blk, MIG, 8" 110.00
Teapot, duck form, gr/bl/brn, MIG, 8¼" 130.00
Teapot, rabbit form, brn & blk, MIG, 7¾" 140.00
Vase, bl iris, narrow neck, Czech, 6" 68.00

Eskimo Artifacts

While ivory carvings made from walrus tusks or whale teeth have been the most emphasized articles of Eskimo art, basketry and woodworking are other areas in which these Alaskan Indians excell. Their designs are effected through the application of simple yet dramatic lines and almost stark decorative devices. Though not pursued to the extent of American Indian art, the unique work of this northern tribe is beginning to attract the serious attention of today's collectors.

Adze, antler w/jade blade, highest quality, 1800, 12x8" 385.00
Basket, coiled, geometric design, w/lid, 5x5¾" 100.00
Basket, 3-color sealskin embrication, w/lid, 1900, 7" 200.00
Cribbage brd, cvd ivory, seals/fish, bk: walrus/kayak, 21" 290.00
Cribbage brd, detailed genre scenes, walrus ivory, 1920, 21" 690.00
Cribbage brd, etch fish etc, bear w/turq eyes at end, 1890, 8" 460.00
Cribbage brd, tusk cvg of seal heads/sleds/people/etc, 26" 250.00
Cvg, whale bone, man in hooded jacket, 1920, 13½" 600.00
Fetish, walrus ivory seal, stylized cvg, 400-800 AD, 4¾" 1,150.00
Fish hook, bone, drilled hole, 7" 60.00
Harpoon head, ivory w/steel blade, 1800s, 6" 500.00
Knife, fighting; copper, split scroll-tip hdl, 1800, 20" 550.00
Knife, ivory w/steel blade, used to prepare fish & game, 5" 350.00
Knife hdl, fossilized ivory, cvd fox w/blk eyes, 2¾" 230.00
Lance tip, copper w/ivory foreshaft, for whale hunting, 13" 575.00
Necklace, cvd bone, early, needs restrung 300.00
Necklace, hunter's; trade beads/fossilized walrus ivory, 1800s ...135.00
Ornament, fossilized ivory, bi-lateral w/metal inlay, 5" 145.00
Pictograph, excavated ivory w/hunting scene, 20th C, 3½ x2" ...110.00
Pipe, blk stone, wood stem, 1850, EX quality, 7x1" 440.00
Reel, harpoon-line; hand forged, 1890, 20x10" 275.00

Fairings

Fairings, small chinaware figural groups that portray amusing (if not risque) scenes of courting couples, marital woes, and family feuds, were popular purchases and prizes at 19th-century English fairs. From 1840 through the 1850s, their bases were embossed with marks that identified the manufacturer as well as the artist who applied the polychrome enameling. From 1860 until 1870, they were no longer marked and became smaller in size. During the 1870s they retained their smaller size but once again were marked in relief, indicating manufacturer and artisan. Through the 1880s all marks were omitted; but the bases were much more shallow than those from the 1860s. About 1890 the Staffordshire potters sold the molds to German manufacturers who marked their product with the name of their country until about 1900. Examples from this period are most commonly encountered. Fairings made in Germany in the early 20th century often have two holes in their bases.

Generally, the more complex groups and those that are marked bring the higher prices. Earlier examples from the sixties and seventies are of better quality. Similar items such as small boxes and match holders with much the same type of theme and figural decoration are also listed here.

Will We Sleep First or How?, 5¼x4", $195.00.

Bank, pk cottage w/Present From Scarborough in gold, 4" W 150.00
Box, baby asleep on pillow, ruffled edge, 2½" 250.00
Box, baby holding gold rattle, unmk German bsk, 4½" 195.10
Box, boy w/chicken on fireplace mantel w/mirror, 4¾" 165.00
Box, cat w/frog, English, 3" 90.00
Box, child in bed w/kitten, 4¼" 120.00
Box, child on bed pulls on pajama bottoms, Elbogen mk, 4" 120.00
Box, child w/trumpet, doll in basket, Staffordshire, 3¾" 175.00
Box, lion on gr matt, emb leaves on wht base w/gold, 3½" 195.00
Box, pigeon w/letter on lid, 2½ x2½" 95.00
Christ child w/lamb, EX colors, NM 75.00
For Heaven's Sake Maria..., lady by man in bed, German mk 210.00
Happy Father, What 2?..., couple & twins, 1880s, 3½" 110.00
I Am Off w/Him, lady w/dog & basket 175.00
Last in Bed To Put Out the Light 145.00
Looking Down Upon His Luck, couple w/twins, Germany, 3½" .100.00
O Do Leave Me a Drop, 2 cats at box 175.00
Returning at One O'clock in the Morning, rare 150.00
Tug of War, girl & dog by fence tugging at doll, 2¾x5¼" 185.00
Wedding Night, man on knee to lady, gold trim, Germany 180.00
Who Said Rats?, cat in draped bed, mice on table 165.00

Fans

The Japanese are said to have invented the fan. From there it went to China, and Portuguese traders took the idea to Europe. Though usually considered milady's accessory, even the gentlemen in 17th-century England carried fans! More fashionable than practical, some were of feathers and lovely hand-painted silks with carved ivory or tortoise sticks. Some French fans had peepholes. There are mourning fans, calendar fans, and those with advertising.

Fine antique fans (pre-1900) of ivory or mother-of-pearl have recently escalated in value. Those from before 1800 often sell for upwards of $1,000.00. Examples with mother-of-pearl sticks are most desirable; least desirable are those with sticks of celluloid. Our advisor for this category is Vicki Flanigan; she is listed in the Directory under Virginia.

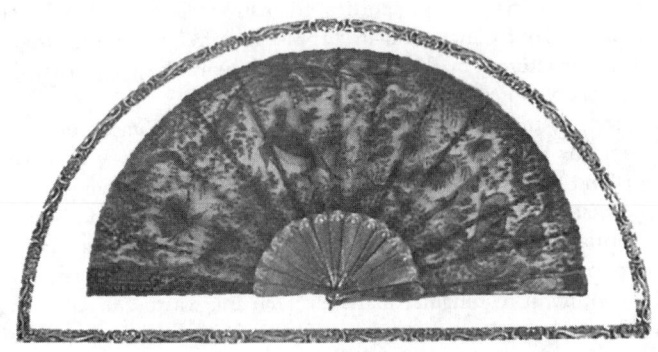

French black lace and gilt-pique mother-of-pearl with lady and cherubs among flowering shrubs, ca 1860s, 24", in wooden shadow box frame, $350.00.

Abalone shell w/printed & hand-colored cloth, Fr, 17x24" 85.00
Blk Chantilly lace, ornate cvd/gilt MOP sticks, 1870s, 10½" 565.00
Chinese figures cvd in continuous scene on ivory, 1830s, 7½" ...250.00
Courting couples HP on vellum, bone sticks, French, 1890s 525.00
Lace sprays on net, pierced/cvd MOP sticks, 1870s, 11" 565.00
Oriental boating scene on silk, tortoise shell sticks, 1890s 215.00
Orientals HP on paper, ivory sticks, Canton, 1850s, 11" 675.00
Rosepoint lace, cvd/gilt MOP sticks, Continental, 1900, 12" 725.00
Scrolling florals on wht metal filigree, China, 1850s, 7½" 675.00
Silk w/HP flowers, ivory sticks, French, in 30" W fr 375.00

Farm Collectibles

Country living in the 19th century entailed plowing, planting, and harvesting; gathering eggs and milking; making soap from lard rendered on butchering day; and numerous other tasks performed with primitive tools of which we in the 20th century have had little firsthand knowledge. Our advisor for this category is Lar Hothem; his address is listed in the Directory under Ohio. See also Cast Iron; Woodenware; Wrought Iron.

Booklet, hog raising, 1917, EX 15.00
Corn dryer, 10 iron prongs 17.50
Corn sheller, hand; CI, Decker, Keokuk IA 50.00
Cranberry picker, steel tines, long wooden hdl 100.00
Cranberry scoop, wood, tin & galvanized hardware cloth, 18" ...140.00
Cream separator, McCormick-Deering, electric or crank, 1940s ...175.00
Egg crate, wood, wire tabs, old brn-red pnt, 15x13x12", EX 70.00
Hog catcher, CI, Dr Rinehart Handy Hog Holder, Pat 1931, EX .36.00

Husking peg, hand-cvd wood, w/leather strap 15.00
Implement seat, Buckeye 145.00
Implement seat, Moline 145.00
Implement seat, Nash & Bro 145.00
Implement seat, Oliver Chilled Plow Works 145.00
Leather-marking tool, iron shank w/serrated wheel, wood hdl 17.50
Manual, Deerborn plow, 1951 ....15.00
Manual, John Deere side rake, 1951 ....20.00
Rope maker, CI, New Era..., 4-strand, Pat 1911, EX 225.00
Shovel, grain; all wood, gold pnt traces, 36" 140.00
Spinner, Minneapolis Moline, dtd 1915, NM 45.00
Stool, milking; maple, 3 wedged stick legs, 1820s, 11x13" 140.00
Token, McCormick Reaper International Harvester 7.50
Yoke, cow; bentwood U-shape, 13x26" 55.00
Yoke, goat; bentwood U-shape, 14x9½" 45.00
Yoke, oxen; wooden, dbl, 38" W 45.00

Fenton

Frank and John Fenton were brothers who founded the Fenton Art Glass Company in 1906 in Martin's Ferry, Ohio. The venture, at first only a decorating shop, began operations in July of 1905 using blanks purchased from other companies. This operation soon proved unsatisfactory, and by 1907 they had constructed their own glass factory in Williamstown, West Virginia. John left the company in 1909 and organized his own firm in Millersburg, Ohio.

The Fenton Company produced over 130 patterns of carnival glass. They also made custard, chocolate, opalescent, and stretch glass. This company has always been noted for its various colors of glass and has continually changed its production to stay attune with current tastes in decorating. In 1925 they produced a line of 'handmade' items that incorporated the techniques of threading and mosaic work. Because the process proved to be unprofitable, the line was discontinued by 1927. Even their glassware made in the past twenty-five years is already regarded as collectible. Various paper labels have been used since the 1920s; only since 1970 has the logo been stamped into the glass. For information concerning Fenton Art Glass Collectors of America, Inc., see the Clubs, Newsletters, and Catalogs section of the Directory. See also Carnival Glass; Custard Glass; Stretch Glass.

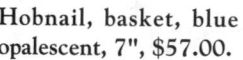

Hobnail, basket, blue opalescent, 7", $57.00.

Apple Blossom Crest, candlestick, #7271 ....40.00
Apple Blossom Crest, compote, dbl-crimped, ftd, #7228, 7" 45.00
Apple Blossom Crest, vase, dbl-crimped, #7254, 4" 40.00
Apple Tree, vase, milk glass, #1561, 10" 125.00
Aqua Crest, candle holders, cornucopia form, 6", pr 48.00

Aqua Crest, pitcher, 7" 67.50
Aqua Crest, plate, 8½" 20.00
Aqua Crest, tidbit tray, 2-tier 65.00
Aqua Crest, vase, dbl-crimped, 4" 22.50
Aqua Crest, vase, 4½" 40.00
Baroque, candy dish, lav satin, w/lid, 7½" 95.00
Beaded Melon, creamer, milk glass, 4" 24.00
Beaded Melon, rose bowl, gr o/l, 3½" 25.00
Beaded Melon, vase, gr o/l, 4" 35.00
Bicentennial, bell, Patriot, red 52.50
Bicentennial, comport, Patriot, chocolate, w/lid 195.00
Bicentennial, paperweight, Eagle, wht satin 27.50
Bicentennial, plate, Lafayette, chocolate 16.50
Bicentennial, plate, Patriot, milk glass 15.00
Big Cookies, basket, Mandarin Red, wicker hdl, 10½" 170.00
Big Cookies, basket, red 110.00
Black Rose, vase, tulip form, 8" 150.00
Block & Star, candlesticks, milk glass, #5670, pr 18.00
Block & Star, shakers, milk glass, pr 28.00
Blossoms & Berries, vase, burmese, tulip form 50.00
Blue Overlay, basket, 6" 38.00
Blue Ridge, vase, French opal spiral, 7" 57.50
Bubble Optic, vase, honey-amber, 11½" 135.00
Burmese, basket, pk roses, sgn M Walrath, 5" 47.50
Burmese, pitcher, no decor, 4½" 50.00
Burmese, tumbler, bbl shape, no decor, 4" 47.50
Cherry, pitcher, rosalene, 4" 50.00
Chinese Yellow, candlestick, #315, 3½", ea 55.00
Coin Dot, basket, French opal, #1522, 10" 98.00
Coin Dot, bowl, bl opal, 10" 90.00
Coin Dot, bowl, cranberry opal, crimped 47.50
Coin Dot, bowl, lime opal, 7" 78.00
Coin Dot, creamer, cranberry opal, 4" 55.00
Coin Dot, creamer, French opal, 4" 32.00
Coin Dot, tumbler, cranberry opal, flat, 4¼" 35.00
Coin Dot, vase, cranberry opal, #3005, 7½" 65.00
Coin Dot, vase, cranberry opal, tricorner, 7" 65.00
Coin Dot, vase, cranberry opal, 8¾" 130.00
Crystal Crest, basket 7" 125.00
Daisy & Button, bell, Lime Sherbet 22.00
Daisy & Button, candlesticks, milk glass, 2-light, pr 40.00
Daisy & Button, vanity set, rose, #957, 3-pc on fan tray 175.00
Dancing Ladies, lamp base/vase, Mongolian Gr, ftd, 9" 225.00
Dancing Ladies, vase, Moonstone, #901 ....200.00
Diamond Lace, candle holders, French opal, pr 40.00
Diamond Optic, basket, ruby o/l, 7" 65.00
Diamond Optic, ivy ball & base, gr opal, #1722 ....125.00
Diamond Optic, pitcher, rosalene, 7½" 72.50
Diamond Optic, vase, bl opal, flared, 8½" 50.00
Diamond Optic/Beaded Melon, vase, cranberry opal, 8" 62.50
Dogwood, vase, dusty rose o/l, 8" 65.00
Dolphin, bowl, royal bl, etched, sq, #1621-E, 9½" 75.00
Dolphin, candy box, Velva Rose, w/lid 37.50
Dolphin, compote, red, ftd, 7½" 58.00
Dolphin, fan vase, rosalene, pk roses, hdls, 5½" 135.00
Dot Optic, cruet, cranberry opal w/pearlized finish, lg 120.00
Dot Optic, jug, cranberry opal, #192, 6" 90.00
Dot Optic, pitcher, gr opal, 9" 155.00
Dot Optic, sugar shaker, cranberry opal, 4⅞" 110.00
Dot Optic, tumbler, cranberry opal, flat, #1353, 4" 27.50
Ebony, candlesticks, #449, 8½", pr 90.00
Emerald Crest, bowl, #662, 9½" 42.00
Emerald Crest, cake plate, high std, #7213, 13" 75.00
Emerald Crest, compote, low std, #7329 ....32.50

Emerald Crest, plate, 8½"	28.00
Fern Optic, vase, cranberry opal, dbl-crimped, 11"	140.00
Fruits & Flowers, bonbon, bl satin	16.00
Georgian, claret, ruby, #1611, 4½ -oz	20.00
Georgian, cup & saucer, red, ftd, #1611	12.00
Georgian, sherbet, red, 8"	7.50
Georgian, tumbler, red, ftd, 9-oz, 5½"	18.00
Gold Crest, compote, low ftd	36.00
Gold Crest, sugar bowl	35.00
Grape & Cable, humidor, rosalene	145.00
Hobnail, banana boat, milk glass	45.00
Hobnail, basket, bl opal, 4"	50.00
Hobnail, basket, French opal, #389, 6¼"	65.00
Hobnail, basket, peachblow, shallow, 5½"	45.00
Hobnail, basket, topaz opal, 7"	125.00
Hobnail, bell, aqua opal	23.00
Hobnail, bonbon, bl opal, 6"	36.00
Hobnail, bonbon, French opal, hdl, 5"	27.50
Hobnail, bottle, cologne; cranberry opal, 4"	55.00
Hobnail, bowl, cranberry opal, dbl-crimped, #3927, 6"	40.00
Hobnail, bowl, cranberry opal, dbl-crimped, 7"	67.50
Hobnail, bowl, French opal, dbl-crimped, ftd, 11"	90.00
Hobnail, bowl, plum opal, 6-sided, crimped, ftd, 8½"	100.00
Hobnail, bowl, topaz opal, dbl-crimped, ftd, 11"	125.00
Hobnail, butter dish, French opal, rnd lid	100.00
Hobnail, candle bowl, milk glass	24.00
Hobnail, candle holders, bl opal, cornucopia shape, 3½", pr	42.00
Hobnail, candle holders, cranberry opal, hdl, pr	120.00
Hobnail, candle holders, milk glass, fingered, pr	27.50
Hobnail, candle holders, plum opal, #3974, pr	98.00
Hobnail, candle holders, topaz opal, squat, pr	48.00
Hobnail, candy dish, orange, #3784, w/lid	45.00
Hobnail, candy jar, milk glass, ftd, 9"	37.50
Hobnail, champagne/sherbet, French opal, 4⅛"	18.00
Hobnail, creamer & sugar bowl, bl opal, star-shaped top	40.00
Hobnail, creamer & sugar bowl, French opal, star-shaped top	35.00
Hobnail, creamer & sugar bowl, French opal, 3½"	22.00
Hobnail, creamer & sugar bowl, pastel gr	45.00
Hobnail, creamer & sugar bowl, topaz opal, 2"	40.00
Hobnail, cruet, bl opal, 4"	32.00
Hobnail, cruet, cranberry opal, lg, 5"	100.00
Hobnail, decanter, plum opal, hdld, 10"	300.00
Hobnail, epergne, bl opal, 3-lily, apartment sz	100.00
Hobnail, epergne, plum opal, #3801, apartment sz, 4-pc	225.00
Hobnail, fan vase, bl opal, ftd, 6"	32.00
Hobnail, fan vase, topaz opal, 4"	45.00
Hobnail, goblet, French opal, plain ft	16.50
Hobnail, hat vase, bl opal, 4"	37.50
Hobnail, jam set, cranberry opal, w/lid & spoon	45.00
Hobnail, mustard, French opal, w/lid	24.00
Hobnail, mustard set, bl opal, 3-pc	60.00
Hobnail, pitcher, cranberry opal, squat, 4¾"	60.00
Hobnail, pitcher, juice; yel opal, +6 tumblers	195.00
Hobnail, shakers, bl opal, flat, pr	45.00
Hobnail, shakers, French opal, flat, pr	45.00
Hobnail, toothpick holder, French opal, top hat shape, 1¾"	37.00
Hobnail, top hat, bl opal, 2¾"	27.00
Hobnail, top hat, bl opal, 3½"	37.50
Hobnail, top hat, French opal, #2	35.00
Hobnail, tumbler, bl opal, flat bbl form, 4¾"	24.00
Hobnail, tumbler, gr, 4¼"	27.50
Hobnail, tumbler, juice; bl opal, flat, 3¼"	13.00
Hobnail, tumbler, water; French opal, flat, 4"	14.00
Hobnail, tumbler, water; yel opal, flat, 4"	20.00

Hobnail, tumbler, yel opal, flat bbl form, 4¾"	25.00
Hobnail, vase, bl o/l, 8"	82.50
Hobnail, vase, bud; topaz opal, ftd, 8"	32.50
Hobnail, vase, cameo opal, 4½"	42.50
Hobnail, vase, Colonial Amber, 4½"	24.00
Hobnail, vase, cranberry opal, dbl-crimped, 8"	75.00
Hobnail, vase, cranberry opal, 4"	27.50
Hobnail, vase, French opal, dbl-crimped, 6"	30.00
Hobnail, vase, French opal, dbl-crimped, 8"	37.00
Hobnail, vase, French opal, tricorner	20.00
Hobnail, vase, gr opal, 4"	20.00
Hobnail, vase, lime gr, fluted, 6"	47.00
Hobnail, vase, peachblow, 6"	72.50
Hobnail, vase, plum opal, #3755, 9"	150.00
Hobnail, vase, swung; plum opal, 11"	145.00
Hobnail, vase, topaz opal, dbl-crimped, 8"	70.00
Hobnail, vase, topaz opal, tricorner, 3¾"	35.00
Hobnail, vase, topaz opal, tricorner, 8½"	155.00
Hobnail/Spiral Optic, vase, cranberry opal, 7"	75.00
Inverted Strawberry, bell, crystal velvet	16.00
Ivory Crest, bowl, cone shape, 7"	50.00
Ivory Crest, bowl, 10"	45.00
Ivory Crest, vase, #186, 8"	50.00
Jacqueline, creamer & sugar bowl, gr	90.00
Jade, vase, hand decor, w/ebony 5-ftd base, #612, 6¼"	350.00
Jamestown, vase, silver, #7262, 12"	95.00
Lilac, biscuit jar, w/lid, rare	350.00
Lilac, shell bowl, cased, #9020, 10"	100.00
Lily of the Valley, candy jar, cameo opal, 7"	50.00
Lincoln Inn, cup & saucer, pk	24.00
Lincoln Inn, shakers, blk, pr	47.50
Lincoln Inn, sherbet, ruby, 4¾"	27.50
Mandarin Red, console set, 10" bowl+2 6¾" candlesticks	185.00
Mandarin Red, flip vase, 7"	85.00
Mandarin Red, vase, ftd, 5½"	85.00
Maple Leaf, pitcher, burmese	50.00
Melon Rib, bottle, scent; mulberry, low, w/stopper, 9"	105.00
Melon Rib, vase, mulberry w/blk stand, 11"	88.00
Melon Rib, vase, rosalene, pk roses, 7"	98.00
Melon Rib/Silver Crest, bottle, scent; w/stopper, 7"	35.00
Ming Rose, vase, #621, 6½"	40.00
Orange Tree, jelly compote, crystal	20.00
Owl, ring tree, Crystal Velvet	10.00
Paisley, bell, Copper Rose, 7"	35.00

'Pancake' lamp, light pink with cut decoration, #G70, $250.00.

Peach Crest, basket, milk glass hdl, #203, 7" 75.00
Peach Crest, pitcher, #192 ....78.00
Peach Crest, shell bowl, #9020 ....70.00
Peach Crest, vase, pk roses, dbl-crimped, 8" 88.00
Peach Crest, vase, triangular, narrow neck, 8" 42.50
Peach Crest, vase, tulip form, #7250, 8½" 65.00
Peacock, vase, burmese, 8" 85.00
Pekin Blue, candle holders, 3", pr 65.00
Pekin Blue, candlesticks, 8½", pr 132.00
Pekin Blue, temple jar 48.00
Persian Medallion, compote, custard satin, 6½" 25.00
Persian Medallion, compote, Velva Bl 47.50
Pineapple, fairy lamp, rosalene 88.00
Plymouth, champagne, ruby, 4" 22.00
Plymouth, goblet, red, 6" 20.00
Plymouth, tumbler, juice; red 17.50
Polka Dot, rose bowl, cranberry opal, 5" 115.00
Polka Dot, top hat, French opal, 4" 95.00
Polka Dot, vase, cranberry opal, #3160, 6" 100.00
Poppy, rose bowl, custard satin 32.00
Poppy, rose bowl, Lime Sherbet 26.00
Rib Optic, shakers, cranberry opal, pr 95.00
Rosalene, paperweight, fish, 5" 65.00
Rosalene, paperweight, lovebird, glossy 50.00
Rosalene, vase, bud; plain top 24.50
Rosalene, vase, tulip; glossy, 10" 135.00
Rose, bowl, console; Velva Bl 36.00
Rose, comport, custard satin, 7½" 32.00
Rose, vase, bud; pearlized Shell Pink, 9½" 26.00
Rose, vase, Provincial Bl opal, ped ft, 9" 42.50
Rose Crest, pitcher, #192A, 9" 50.00
Rose Crest, vase, dbl-crimped, 4½" 20.00
Rose Overlay, basket, #1924, 5" 55.00
Rose Overlay, bowl, 10" 35.00
Rose Overlay, bowl, 7" 25.00
Ruby Overlay, vase, tricorner, 6" 40.00
Scroll, vase, Lime Sherbet, 8" 67.50
Scroll, vase, rose satin, 8" 77.50
Scroll & Eye, nut dish, cameo opal, 5" 38.00
Sea Mist opal, rose candy box, butterfly lid 45.00
Sheffield, bowl, bl, ruffled, 12½" 28.00
Sheffield, bowl, Velva Bl, ftd 22.50
Sheffield, creamer & sugar bowl, ruby 80.00
Silver Crest, banana bowl, high std 45.00
Silver Crest, banana bowl, low std 40.00
Silver Crest, basket, #7233, 13" 90.00
Silver Crest, basket, 7½" 36.00
Silver Crest, bell 35.00
Silver Crest, bowl, dbl-crimped, #7224 ....45.00
Silver Crest, bowl, melon ribs, ftd, 11" 30.00
Silver Crest, bowl, salad; 9½" 45.00
Silver Crest, bowl, sq, tall, ftd, #7330 ....60.00
Silver Crest, cake plate, low std, #5813, 13" 45.00
Silver Crest, cake stand, high std 50.00
Silver Crest, candle holders, low, pr 37.50
Silver Crest, candlesticks, #7474, 6", pr 55.00
Silver Crest, candlesticks, cornucopia form, pr 55.00
Silver Crest, compote, ftd, 4" 25.00
Silver Crest, epergne, 12" 145.00
Silver Crest, fan vase, 12" 80.00
Silver Crest, plate, 10¾" 30.00
Silver Crest, plate, 6½" 14.00
Silver Crest, plate, 8½" 27.50
Silver Crest, shakers, pr 42.50

Silver Crest, vase, 8" 28.00
Silver Crest/Melon Rib, vase, beaded, 5x3" 10.00
Silver Crest/Spanish Lace, cake plate, ftd, 11" 52.50
Snow Crest, bowl, ruby, heart shape 35.00
Snow Crest, vase, cranberry opal, #1458, 8½" 150.00
Spanish Lace, basket, cranberry opal, crimped, 8" 67.50
Spiral Optic, vase, bl opal, 4" 47.50
Stars & Stripes, tumbler, cranberry opal, 5¼" 50.00
Strawberry, basket, rosalene, ftd, 4½" 50.00
Strawberry, toothpick holder, burmese, 3" 35.00
Stretch, candy dish, aquamarine, #531 ....38.00
Swirled Feather, fairy lamp, cranberry opal satin, #2092 ....88.00
Turquoise Crest, creamer, #1924 ....50.00
Vasa Murrhina, basket, gr/bl aventurine, 11¼" 110.00
Venetian Red, candlesticks, #449, 8¾", pr 165.00
Violets in Snow, bell 25.00
Waffle, rose bowl, gr opal 37.00
Waffle, vase, gr opal, cupped, 4¼" 40.00
Waffle, vase, swung; gr opal, 11" 45.00
Water Lily, basket, Crystal Velvet 35.00
Water Lily, basket, custard satin 36.00
Water Lily, basket, Twilight Bl opal, 7" 32.50
Water Lily, candlesticks, bl satin, pr 36.00
Water Lily, candlesticks, rosalene, pr 47.50
Water Lily, compote, Velva Rose, lg 47.50
Water Lily, compote, Velva Rose, sm 35.00
Water Lily, jardiniere, custard satin 36.00
Water Lily, pitcher, bl satin, #8464, 30-oz 57.50
Water Lily, pitcher, wht satin, #8464, 30-oz 55.00
Water Lily, vase, bud; Lime Sherbet 22.00
Water Lily & Cattails, bowl, amethyst opal, crimped, 9" 75.00
Wistaria, basket, wht satin, #1684 ....65.00
Wistaria, pitcher, crystal satin, #1355, lg 130.00

Fiesta

Fiesta is a line of dinnerware produced by the Homer Laughlin China Company of Newell, West Virginia, from 1936 until 1973. It was made in eleven different solid colors with over fifty pieces in the assortment. The pattern was developed by Frederick Rhead, an English Stoke-on-Trent potter who was an important contributor to the art-pottery movement in this country during the early part of the century. The design was carried out through the use of a simple band-of-rings device near the rim. Fiesta Red, a strong red-orange glaze color, was made with depleted uranium oxide. It was more expensive to produce than the other colors and sold at higher prices. Today's collectors still pay premium prices for Fiesta Red pieces. During the fifties the color assortment was gray, rose, chartreuse, and dark green. These colors are relatively harder to find and along with Fiesta Red and medium green (new in 1959) command the higher prices.

Fiesta Kitchen Kraft was introduced in 1939; it consisted of seventeen pieces of kitchenware such as pie plates, refrigerator sets, mixing bowls, and covered jars in four popular Fiesta colors.

As a final attempt to adapt production to modern-day techniques and methods, Fiesta was restyled in 1969. Of the original colors, only Fiesta Red remained. This line, called Fiesta Ironstone, was discontinued in 1973.

Two types of marks were used: an ink stamp on machine-jiggered pieces and an indented mark molded into the hollowware pieces.

In 1986 HLC reintroduced a line of Fiesta dinnerware in five colors: black, white, pink, apricot, and cobalt (darker and denser than the original shade). Since then yellow, turquoise, seafoam green, 'country' blue, lilac, and persimmon have been added. Collectors have found that the new line poses no theat to their investments.

In the listings below, 'original colors' indicates only three of the original six — light green, turquoise, and yellow (or those remaining after specific original colors have been priced). Red, ivory and cobalt values are listed separately. For more information we recommend *The Collector's Encyclopedia of Fiesta, Harlequin, and Riviera* (values updated in 1994) by Sharon and Bob Huxford, available at your local bookstore or from Collector Books.

Dinnerware

Ashtray, '50s colors	70.00
Ashtray, orig colors	37.50
Ashtray, red, cobalt or ivory	45.00
Bowl, covered onion soup; cobalt or ivory	450.00
Bowl, covered onion soup; red	500.00
Bowl, covered onion soup; turq, minimum value	2,000.00
Bowl, covered onion soup; yel or lt gr	325.00
Bowl, cream soup; '50s colors	60.00
Bowl, cream soup; med gr, minimum value	2,800.00
Bowl, cream soup; orig colors	32.50
Bowl, cream soup; red, cobalt or ivory	48.00
Bowl, dessert; '50s colors, 6"	42.00
Bowl, dessert; med gr, 6"	265.00
Bowl, dessert; orig colors, 6"	32.00
Bowl, dessert; red, cobalt or ivory, 6"	42.00
Bowl, fruit; '50s colors, 4¾"	28.00
Bowl, fruit; '50s colors, 5½"	30.00
Bowl, fruit; med gr, 4¾"	285.00
Bowl, fruit; med gr, 5½"	60.00
Bowl, fruit; orig colors, 11¾"	140.00
Bowl, fruit; orig colors, 4¾"	22.00
Bowl, fruit; orig colors, 5½"	24.00
Bowl, fruit; red, cobalt or ivory, 11¾"	180.00
Bowl, fruit; red, cobalt or ivory, 4¾"	25.00
Bowl, fruit; red, cobalt or ivory, 5½"	27.00
Bowl, ftd salad; orig colors	190.00
Bowl, ftd salad; red, cobalt or ivory	230.00
Bowl, ind salad; med gr, 7½"	80.00
Bowl, ind salad; red, turq or yel, 7½"	60.00
Bowl, nappy; '50s colors, 8½"	40.00
Bowl, nappy; med gr, 8½"	90.00
Bowl, nappy; orig colors, 8½"	30.00
Bowl, nappy; orig colors, 9½"	40.00
Bowl, nappy; red, cobalt or ivory, 8½"	38.00
Bowl, nappy; red, cobalt or ivory, 9½"	50.00
Bowl, Tom & Jerry; ivory w/gold letters	225.00
Bowl, unlisted; red, cobalt, or ivory	265.00
Bowl, unlisted; yel	75.00
Candle holders, bulb; orig colors, pr	70.00
Candle holders, bulb; red, cobalt or ivory, pr	90.00
Candle holders, tripod; orig colors, pr	325.00
Candle holders, tripod; red, cobalt or ivory, pr	375.00
Carafe, orig colors	145.00
Carafe, red, cobalt or ivory	185.00
Casserole, '50s colors	235.00
Casserole, French; standard colors other than yel	450.00
Casserole, French; yel	210.00
Casserole, med gr	400.00
Casserole, orig colors	110.00
Casserole, red, cobalt or ivory	160.00
Coffeepot, '50s colors	220.00
Coffeepot, demi; orig colors	185.00
Coffeepot, demi; red, cobalt or ivory	235.00
Coffeepot, orig colors	135.00

Coffeepot, red, cobalt or ivory	175.00
Compote, orig colors, 12"	115.00
Compote, red, cobalt or ivory, 12"	140.00
Compote, sweets; orig colors	48.00
Compote, sweets; red, cobalt or ivory	65.00

Creamer, individual, red, $145.00; Sugar bowl, yellow, with lid, $75.00; Tray, figure-8 shape, turquoise, $190.00.

Creamer, '50s colors	26.00
Creamer, ind; turq	235.00
Creamer, ind; yel	48.00
Creamer, med gr	48.00
Creamer, orig colors	18.00
Creamer, red, cobalt or ivory	24.00
Creamer, stick hdld, orig colors	30.00
Creamer, stick hdld, red, cobalt or ivory	40.00
Cup, demi; '50s colors	225.00
Cup, demi; orig colors	50.00
Cup, demi; red, cobalt or ivory	55.00
Egg cup, '50s colors	125.00
Egg cup, orig colors	40.00
Egg cup, red, cobalt, or ivory	55.00
Lid, for mixing bowl #1-#3, any color, minimum value	550.00
Lid, for mixing bowl #4, any color, minimum value	600.00
Marmalade, orig colors	150.00
Marmalade, red, cobalt or ivory	190.00
Mixing bowl, #1, orig colors	90.00
Mixing bowl, #1, red, cobalt, or ivory	120.00
Mixing bowl, #2, orig colors	70.00
Mixing bowl, #2, red, cobalt or ivory	80.00
Mixing bowl, #3, orig colors	80.00
Mixing bowl, #3, red, cobalt or ivory	85.00
Mixing bowl, #4, orig colors	90.00
Mixing bowl, #4, red, cobalt or ivory	95.00
Mixing bowl, #5, orig colors	100.00
Mixing bowl, #5, red, cobalt or ivory	110.00
Mixing bowl, #6, orig colors	125.00
Mixing bowl, #6, red, cobalt or ivory	140.00
Mixing bowl, #7, orig colors	160.00
Mixing bowl, #7, red, cobalt or ivory	185.00
Mug, Tom & Jerry; '50s colors	85.00
Mug, Tom & Jerry; ivory w/gold letters	60.00
Mug, Tom & Jerry; orig colors	50.00
Mug, Tom & Jerry; red, cobalt or ivory	65.00
Mustard, orig colors	125.00
Mustard, red, cobalt or ivory	170.00
Pitcher, disk juice; gray	1,200.00

Pitcher, disk juice; red 250.00
Pitcher, disk juice; yel 40.00
Pitcher, disk water; '50s colors 200.00
Pitcher, disk water; med gr, minimum value 600.00
Pitcher, disk water; orig colors 80.00
Pitcher, disk water; red, cobalt or ivory 115.00
Pitcher, ice; orig colors 80.00
Pitcher, ice; red, cobalt or ivory 110.00
Pitcher, jug, 2-pt; '50s colors 95.00
Pitcher, jug, 2-pt; orig colors 47.50
Pitcher, jug, 2-pt; red, cobalt or ivory 70.00
Plate, '50s colors, 10" 38.50
Plate, '50s colors, 6" 7.00
Plate, '50s colors, 7" 10.00
Plate, '50s colors, 9" 16.00
Plate, cake; lt gr or yel 550.00
Plate, cake; red, cobalt or ivory 600.00
Plate, calendar; 1954 or 1955, 10" 32.00
Plate, calendar; 1955, 9" 37.50
Plate, chop; '50s colors, 13" 60.00
Plate, chop; '50s colors, 15" 80.00
Plate, chop; med gr, 13" 110.00
Plate, chop; orig colors, 13" 26.00
Plate, chop; orig colors, 15" 35.00
Plate, chop; red, cobalt or ivory, 13" 38.00
Plate, chop; red, cobalt or ivory, 15" 50.00
Plate, compartment; '50s colors, 10½" 42.00
Plate, compartment; orig colors, 10½" 25.00
Plate, compartment; orig colors, 12" 50.00
Plate, compartment; red, cobalt or ivory, 10½" 28.50
Plate, compartment; red, cobalt or ivory, 12" 45.00
Plate, deep; '50s colors 42.00
Plate, deep; med gr 90.00
Plate, deep; orig colors 32.00
Plate, deep; red, cobalt or ivory 40.00
Plate, med gr, 10" 80.00
Plate, med gr, 6" 15.00
Plate, med gr, 7" 22.50
Plate, med gr, 9" 35.00
Plate, orig colors, 10" 25.00
Plate, orig colors, 6" 4.00
Plate, orig colors, 7" 7.00
Plate, orig colors, 9" 8.50
Plate, red, cobalt or ivory, 10" 32.00
Plate, red, cobalt or ivory, 6" 6.00
Plate, red, cobalt or ivory, 7" 8.50
Plate, red, cobalt or ivory, 9" 15.00
Platter, '50s colors 45.00
Platter, med gr 90.00
Platter, orig colors 22.50
Platter, red, cobalt or ivory 35.00
Sauce boat, '50s colors 52.50
Sauce boat, med gr 95.00
Sauce boat, orig colors 32.00
Sauce boat, red, cobalt or ivory 48.00
Saucer, '50s colors 5.00
Saucer, demi; '50s colors 62.50
Saucer, demi; orig colors 12.00
Saucer, demi; red, cobalt or ivory 12.50
Saucer, med gr 8.00
Saucer, orig colors 3.00
Saucer, red, cobalt or ivory 4.00
Shakers, '50s colors, pr 34.00
Shakers, med gr, pr 70.00

Shakers, orig colors, pr 16.50
Shakers, red, cobalt or ivory, pr 23.00
Sugar bowl, ind; turq 275.00
Sugar bowl, ind; yel 75.00
Sugar bowl, w/lid, '50s colors, 3¼x3½" 50.00
Sugar bowl, w/lid, med gr, 3¼x3½" 100.00
Sugar bowl, w/lid, orig colors, 3¼x3½" 35.00
Sugar bowl, w/lid, red, cobalt or ivory, 3¼x3½" 45.00
Syrup, orig colors 200.00
Syrup, red, cobalt or ivory 235.00
Teacup, '50s colors 35.00
Teacup, med gr 50.00
Teacup, orig colors 22.00
Teacup, red, cobalt or ivory 26.00
Teapot, lg; orig colors 120.00
Teapot, lg; red, cobalt or ivory 150.00
Teapot, med; '50s colors 210.00
Teapot, med; med gr 425.00
Teapot, med; orig colors 120.00
Teapot, med; red, cobalt or ivory 140.00
Tray, figure-8; cobalt 60.00
Tray, figure-8; yel 195.00
Tray, relish; mixed colors, no red 175.00
Tray, utility; orig colors 28.00
Tray, utility; red, cobalt or ivory 32.00
Tumbler, juice; chartreuse, Harlequin yel or dk gr 275.00
Tumbler, juice; orig colors 27.50
Tumbler, juice; red, cobalt or ivory 32.00
Tumbler, juice; rose 38.00
Tumbler, water; orig colors 45.00
Tumbler, water; red, cobalt or ivory 55.00
Vase, bud; orig colors 50.00
Vase, bud; red, cobalt or ivory 65.00
Vase, orig colors, 10" 450.00
Vase, orig colors, 12" 540.00
Vase, orig colors, 8" 365.00
Vase, red, cobalt or ivory, 10" 500.00
Vase, red, cobalt or ivory, 12" 635.00
Vase, red, cobalt or ivory, 8" 425.00

Kitchen Kraft

Bowl, mixing; lt gr or yel, 10" 80.00
Bowl, mixing; lt gr or yel, 6" 55.00
Bowl, mixing; lt gr or yel, 8" 70.00
Bowl, mixing; red or cobalt, 10" 90.00
Bowl, mixing; red or cobalt, 6" 60.00
Bowl, mixing; red or cobalt, 8" 80.00
Cake plate, lt gr or yel 42.00
Cake plate, red or cobalt 48.00
Cake server, lt gr or yel 80.00
Cake server, red or cobalt 90.00
Casserole, ind; lt gr or yel 115.00
Casserole, ind; red or cobalt 130.00
Casserole, lt gr or yel, 7½" 70.00
Casserole, lt gr or yel, 8½" 85.00
Casserole, red or cobalt, 7½" 80.00
Casserole, red or cobalt, 8½" 95.00
Covered jar, lg; lt gr or yel 210.00
Covered jar, lg; red or cobalt 230.00
Covered jar, med; lt gr or yel 190.00
Covered jar, med; red or cobalt 210.00
Covered jar, sm; lt gr or yel 200.00
Covered jar, sm; red or cobalt 225.00

Covered jug, lt gr or yel 170.00
Covered jug, red or cobalt 180.00
Fork, lt gr or yel 70.00
Fork, red or cobalt 78.00
Metal frame for platter 22.00
Pie plate, lt gr or yel, 10" 38.00
Pie plate, lt gr or yel, 9" 35.00
Pie plate, red or cobalt, 10" 42.00
Pie plate, red or cobalt, 9" 40.00
Platter, lt gr or yel 65.00
Platter, red or cobalt 72.00
Platter, spruce gr 225.00
Shakers, lt gr or yel, pr 75.00
Shakers, red or cobalt, pr 85.00
Spoon, lt gr or yel 75.00
Spoon, red or cobalt 85.00
Stacking refrigerator lid, ivory 150.00
Stacking refrigerator lid, lt gr or yel 45.00
Stacking refrigerator lid, red or cobalt 52.00
Stacking refrigerator unit, ivory 150.00
Stacking refrigerator unit, lt gr or yel 32.00
Stacking refrigerator unit, red or cobalt 36.00

Fifties Modern

Postwar furniture design is marked by organic shapes and lighter woods and forms. New materials from war research such as molded plywood and fiberglass were used extensively. For the first time, design was extended to the mass, and the baby-boomer generation grew up surrounded by modern shape and color, the perfect expression of postwar optimism. The top designers in America worked for Herman Miller and Knoll Furniture Company. These include Charles Eames, George Nelson and Eero Saarinen.

Italian glass from the fifties represents some of the most beautiful designs of the period. The color and expressive forms that came from the island of Murano during this time were the perfect expression of Italian style and flair.

This information was provided to us by Richard Wright. See also Italian Glass.

Key: uph — upholstered

Hanging lamp, Poul Henningsen, artichoke shape, segmented metal fixture with copper exterior and white enameled interior, 21x24", $1,300.00.

Airchair, Chas Eames, fiberglass shell, wire base, VG 400.00
Armchair, Platner, uphl circular bk/sides, steel rod fr 350.00
Armchair, Risom, birch fr w/wht webbing, shaped seat, 30" 225.00
Armchair, shell w/blk vinyl uphl, blk wire cradle base, VG 400.00
Armchair, 6-band rattan, Frankl style, vinyl uphl, 34x37" 375.00
Bench, Geo Nelson, slats w/6 metal legs, 15x18x98", EX 2,500.00
Bench, vanity; Geo Nelson, concave seat cushion, birch fr 40.00
Bench, vanity; Geo Nelson, red wool seat, walnut fr, G 210.00
Cabinet, Geo Nelson, w/drop-front desk, rosewood, 56" W, VG .2,500.00
Cabinet, Geo Nelson, walnut color, 2 4-drw banks, 30x57", VG ...450.00
Cabinet, Geo Nelson, 5-drw, door, primavera finish, 34x40" 750.00
Candlesticks, Palmer Smith, aluminum, 4 grad stems, 11x9x6" ..230.00
Chair, lounge; Eames, blk wire shell, armless, VG 375.00
Chair, lounge; Eames, rosewood shell w/blk leather, +ottoman ..1,400.00
Chair, lounge; Mathsson, woven birch, uphl headrest, +ottoman .1,200.00
Chair, side; Heywood Wakefield, Streamline, solid bk, 4 for 230.00
Chair, side; McCobb, blk iron 10-dowel bk, 'tray' seat 250.00
Chaise lounge, Thonet, bentwood/caning, scroll arms/supports ..2,500.00
Chest, Frankl, birch, 2 5-drw banks, 'X' pulls, 32x73", VG 220.00
Chest, Heywood Wakefield, Niagara, 5-drw, bow-tie hdls, EX ...450.00
Chest, Heywood Wakefield, 5-drw, birch (blond), 44x38", EX ..300.00
Clock, Geo Nelson, blk perforated metal dish w/wood markers ..375.00
Clock, Geo Nelson, radiating chrome rods, 24" dia, EX 325.00
Clock, Geo Nelson, Sunflower, woven walnut plywood, 28" dia ..425.00
Clock, Howard Miller, ceramic disk, sq markers, 14", VG 375.00
Credenza, Knoll, 4 wht lacquered doors, walnut case, 75" L 1,100.00
Desk, Sarrinen, bird, 4-drw, open shelf under shaped top 325.00
Dresser, Geo Nelson, 5-drw, orig primavera finish, 34x40" 800.00
Figurine, Gambone, ceramic donkey, 6x4" 550.00
Floor lamp, Geo Nelson, elongated bubble on tripod, 36", G 230.00
Floor lamp, Italian, 4 chrome tubes ea w/'windmill' arm 900.00
Jewelry chest, Geo Nelson, teak w/rosewood fronts, 20" W 3,500.00
Lamp, desk; dumbbell-shaped chrome arm on Lucite ring, EX ...180.00
Lamp, desk; Kennedy-Baratelli, Bakelite, for Polaroid, G 350.00
Lamp, desk; Weinberg, abstract brass horse, 4-leg base, VG 400.00
Lamp base, iron skyscraper form w/bronze patina, 31", EX 975.00
Mobile, Calder style, red pnt metal forms on blk wire, 20x30" ...650.00
Ottoman, multi-banded rattan, vinyl cushion, 12x23x23" 200.00
Rocker, Chas Eames, shaped fiberglass, birch rockers, G 240.00
Rug, Matisse, Mimosa, #d edition, 58x36", EX 4,250.00
Stool, Chas & Ray Eames, trn walnut, Time-Life, 15x13" dia 350.00
Stool, Gilbert Rohde, 'Z,' chromed steel, vinyl seat, VG 100.00
Table, cocktail; Heywood Wakefield, birch, sq w/rnd corners 160.00
Table, cocktail; J Keil, sculptural free-form mahog, 68", VG 110.00
Table, cocktail; Paul Frankl, lacquered cork 36" dia top, VG 170.00
Table, cocktail; 48" dia glass top on bent aluminum base 250.00
Table, coffee; Eames, 37" dia aluminum top w/geometrics, VG ..325.00
Table, coffee; Frankl style, multi-banded rattan, oak top 60.00
Table, coffee; Noguchi, 3-side glass on 2-part ebonized fr 850.00
Table, coffee; Wormley, free-form glass top on brass/wood fr 700.00
Table, console; Ponti, blond w/inset enamel by de Poli, G 750.00
Table, dinette; Noguchi, formica w/spiral chrome dowel base 900.00
Table, dining; Eames, wht laminate top/birch legs, 54", G 425.00
Table, dining; Heywood Wakefield, drop leaf, 3 arched legs 750.00
Table, end; Paul Frankl, cork top, magazine storage, rfn 300.00
Table, Heywood Wakefield, Streamline, oval extension, VG 220.00
Tray, Machine Age, chromed metal w/rvpt Deco graphic, 18" ...425.00
Vanity, Geo Nelson, flip-top between 4-drw banks, 3-unit, VG .425.00
Vanity, Heywood Wakefield, lg rnd rpl mirror, 2 3-drw banks ...325.00
Vase, Cabat, blk/brn/yel crystalline, 4" 450.00
Vase, Cabat, lt gr crystalline on dk apple gr, 3" 400.00
Vase, CAC Habana, ceramic, geometrics, #592/A, 12x6" 115.00
Vase, CAS Vetri, ceramic, gondolier on bl, 12" 105.00
Vase, ceramic, yel/gun-metal brn drip, 4" 600.00

Vase, Fantoni/Raymor, cvd abstracts, sqd, 17x4" 220.00

Finch, Kay

Kay Finch and her husband, Braden, operated a small pottery in Corona Del Mar, California, from 1939 to 1963. The company remained small, employing from twenty to sixty local residents who Kay trained in all but the most requiring tasks, which she herself performed. The company produced animal and bird figurines, most notably dogs, Kay's favorites. Figures of 'Godey' type couples were also made, as were tableware (consisting of breakfast sets) and other artware. Most pieces were marked. Kay Finch died on June 21, 1993. Prices for her work have been climbing.

Our advisor for this category is Jack Chipman, author of *The Collector's Encyclopedia of California Pottery*; he is listed in the Directory under California. Original model numbers are included in the following descriptions — three-digit numbers indicate pre-1946 models. After 1946 they were assigned four-digit numbers, the first two digits representing the year of initial production. *Kay Finch Ceramics Identification Guide* (published in 1992), containing many reprints of original catalog pages, is available from Frances Finch Webb; she is also listed in the Directory under California.

Christmas bell 75.00
Creamer, Briar Rose 25.00
Figurine, angel, pk, standing, #114B or #114C, ea 45.00
Figurine, angel boy (bust), #212 ....55.00
Figurine, angel in wht, bl wings, blond hair, 5" 35.00
Figurine, bear, standing, #5004, sm 75.00
Figurine, cat, #4834, sm 55.00
Figurine, cat, Ambrosia, #155, 10¾" 350.00
Figurine, choir boy, kneeling, #211, 5½" 75.00
Figurine, circus monkey, #4841 ....85.00
Figurine, cockatoo, for Freeman McFarlin, lg 125.00
Figurine, cocker spaniel, #5260, 4½" 150.00
Figurine, duck, Peep, #178, 4" 45.00
Figurine, elephant, #191, 9" 175.00
Figurine, elephant, #4626, 5" 125.00
Figurine, Godey lady w/muff & shawl, pk & bl, #160, 7½" 75.00
Figurine, hen, Biddy, yel-tan, #177, 8" 50.00
Figurine, hippo, #5019 ....100.00
Figurine, kittens, Muff & Puff, #182 & #183, 3¼", pr 90.00
Figurine, lamb, kneeling, #136, sm 40.00
Figurine, lamb, w/bow, wht & pk, #167, rare, 20" 1,100.00
Figurine, Madonna & Child, wht, 2-pc 100.00
Figurine, owl, Hoot, #187, 8¾" 175.00
Figurine, owl, Toot, #188, 5¾" 65.00
Figurine, owl, Tootsie, #189, 3¾" 40.00
Figurine, peasant boy, pk & gr, #113, 6¾" 55.00
Figurine, pig, Smiley, #164, 6¾" 125.00
Figurine, pig, Winkie, #185, 3¾" 65.00
Figurine, Scandie boy & girl, #127/#126, 5¼", pr 100.00
Figurine, squirrel, upright, #108 ....30.00
Figurine, swan, #4958, sm 45.00
Figurine, terrier, #156 ....65.00
Figurine, turkey, #5360, 10" 275.00
Figurine, turkey, brn, #4853, 5" 75.00
Figurine, Yorkie pup, #170, 5½" 200.00
Figurine, Yorkie pup, #171, 6" 225.00
Flowerpot, daisies, 3508 ....25.00
Mug, Santa, arm hdl 95.00
Stein, marlin fish hdl, 7" 65.00
Tile, Yorkie, 5¾" 55.00

Tureen, turkey, #5361, w/lid, 8" 150.00

Findlay Onyx and Floradine

Findlay, Ohio, was the location of the Dalzell, Gilmore, and Leighton Glass Company, one of at least sixteen companies that flourished there between 1886 and 1901. Their most famous ware, Onyx, is very rare. It was produced for only a short time beginning in 1889 due to the heavy losses incurred in the manufacturing process.

Onyx is layered glass, usually found in creamy white with a dainty floral pattern accented with metallic lustre that has been trapped between the two layers. Other colors found on rare occasions include a light amber (with either no lustre or with gilt flowers), light amethyst (or lavender), and rose. Although old tradepaper articles indicate the company originally intended to produce the line in three distinct colors, long-time Onyx collectors report that aside from the white, production was very limited. Other colors of Onyx are very rare, and the few examples that are found tend to support the theory that production of colored Onyx ware remained for the most part in the experimental stage. Even three-layered items have been found (they are extremely rare) decorated with three-color flowers. As a rule of thumb, using white Onyx prices as a basis for evaluation, expect to pay two to five times more for colored examples.

Floradine is a separate line that was made with the Onyx molds. A single-layer rose satin glassware with white opal flowers, it is usually priced in the general range of colored Onyx.

Chipping around the rims is very common, and price is determined to a great extent by condition. Our advisors for this category are Betty and Clarence Maier; they are listed in the Directory under Pennsylvania.

Floradine

Bowl, fluted, squat bulbous base, 4" 775.00
Box, dresser; 5½" 800.00
Celery vase, fluted cylinder neck, bulbous body, 6½", EX 750.00
Celery vase, NM 1,800.00
Creamer, bulbous, flared neck, 4⅝" 750.00
Mustard pot, NM 1,550.00
Mustard pot, 3¾", EX 600.00
Spooner 535.00
Sugar bowl, bulbous, w/lid, 5½" 850.00
Sugar shaker 600.00
Syrup pitcher 1,250.00
Toothpick holder, 2½" 800.00
Tumbler, slightly bulbous, 3⅝" 700.00

Onyx

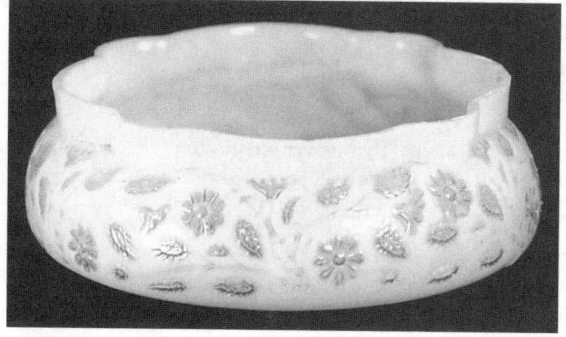

Onyx bowl, white with silver decoration, 8", $400.00.

Bowl, wht w/silver decor, flattened ovoid, 4" 300.00
Butter dish, wht w/silver decor, 5¾" dia 800.00
Celery vase, wht w/silver decor, 6½" 250.00
Creamer, wht w/silver decor, 4½" 275.00
Jam jar, wht w/silver decor 500.00
Mustard pot, wht w/silver decor, hinged metal top, 3" 650.00
Pitcher, wht w/silver decor, rim chips, flakes, 4½" 275.00
Pitcher, wht w/silver decor, 8" 1,200.00
Spooner, wht w/silver decor, 4¼" 250.00
Sugar bowl, wht w/silver decor, w/lid, EX 325.00
Sugar shaker, raspberry 4,100.00
Sugar shaker, wht w/silver decor, 5½" 485.00
Syrup, wht w/silver decor, metal thumb-lift cover, 7" 875.00
Tumbler, apricot 2,400.00
Tumbler, wht w/silver decor, 3¾x2⅞" 325.00

Fire Marks

During the early 18th century, insurance companies used fire marks — signs of insurance — to indicate to the volunteer firefighters which homes were covered by their company. Handsome rewards were promised to the brigade that successfully extinguished the blaze, so competition was fierce between rivals and sometimes resulted in an altercation at the scene to settle the matter of which brigade would be the one to fight the fire! Fire marks were originally made of cast iron or lead; later examples were sometimes tin or zinc. They were used abroad as well as in this country, and those from England tended to be much more elaborate. When municipal fire departments were organized in the mid- to late 1860s, volunteer departments and fire marks became obsolete.

FA (Fire Association), CI, gr pnt, EX 180.00
FA (Fire Association), CI, oval, pitting, 11¼ x7¼" 110.00
Fire Assurance of Philadelphia, CI, oval, 11x7½" 85.00
Fire Department Insurance, mc pnt on CI, oval, 11½" 375.00
Hose & FA, CI, oval, old dk gr rpt, 11½x7¼" 75.00

Invicta and famous white horse of Kent, lead, 8¾x6½", $350.00.

Mutual Insurance, angel flying over Charleston, 9½x7½" 65.00
Protector Fire Ins Co London, copper, 1835, VG 50.00
United Firemen's Ins Co Phila PA, CI, 11⅜x8¾", VG 100.00

Firefighting Collectibles

Firefighting collectibles have always been a good investment in terms of value appreciation. Many times the market will be temporarily affected by wild price swings caused by the 'supply and demand principle' as related to a small group of aggressive collectors. These collectors will pay well over market value for a particular item they need or want. Once their desires are satisfied, prices seem to return to their normal range. It has been noticed that during these periods of high prices, many items enter the marketplace that otherwise would remain in collections. This may (it has in the past) cause a price depression (due again to the 'supply and demand principle' of market behavior). But when all is said and done, the careful purchase of quality, well-documented firefighting items has been an enjoyable hobby and an excellent investment opportunity.

Today there is a large, active group of collectors for fire department antiques (items over 100 years old) and an even larger group seeking related collectibles (those less than 100 years old). Our advisors for this category (except grenades) are H. Thomas and Patricia Laun; they are listed in the directory under New York.

Fire grenades preceded the pressurized metal fire extinguishers used today. They were filled with a mixture of chemicals and water and made of glass thin enough to shatter easily when thrown into the flames. Many varieties of colors and shapes were used. Our fire grenades advisor is Lawrence Meyer; he is listed in the Directory under Illinois.

Key:
S&A — soda & acid

Alarm box, Autocall Co, break-glass type, VG 20.00
Alarm box, auxiliary; Gamewell, pull ring, fancy door, 1888 ......100.00
Alarm box, Chicago Fire Alarm, CI, brass mechanism, 1911, EX ..275.00
Alarm box, Gamewell, CI, rnd top, slanted fist style, EX 325.00
Alarm box, Oakland Electrical Dept, CI, 18", EX 175.00
Albumen print, early ladder truck w/members, 11x13" 35.00
Ambrotype, man w/helmet & red tinted shirt, EX in case 50.00
Axe, parade; Rescue 4 on hdl, tole-pnt blade, 36", pr 350.00
Axe, parade; Viking style, orig handle, 24½" L head, EX 225.00
Axe, parade; Viking style, sm, EX 400.00
Badge, A Ulrich, Retired...1924-50, gilt silver, pin-bk 50.00
Badge, Deputy Chief Milton FD, NP, worn 20.00
Badge, Fire Police 10 Greenwich, steel, VG 40.00
Badge, Keystone Fire Chief's Ass'n, enamel w/gold & red, EX 25.00
Badge, Liberty 5 Reading PA, w/steamer, 2-pc, EX 60.00
Badge, Middleton Fire Dept 1, steel, motorized truck, EX 25.00
Badge, Monmouth IL 1897, gilt on brass die-cut star, 2-part 85.00
Badge, Reading Fire Dept #932, steel, EX 35.00
Badge, Watertown FD E Carney 54, steel, EX 40.00
Badge, Worcester FD, stainless, 2¾", EX 65.00
Ballot box, wooden, plain/unlettered, w/blk & wht marbles, EX ..65.00
Banner, Welcome Fireman, Loyal To Our Duty, muslin, 54x34", EX .130.00
Bed key, wrought iron, unmk, lg, EX 100.00
Bed key, wrought iron, 4-sided, R Timmins & Sons, EX 100.00
Bell, Am LaFrance, eagle finial, 12", w/bracket 550.00
Bell, apparatus; Franklin Sq HC...1923, acorn finial, 12" 275.00
Bell, apparatus; missing clapper, 10" 50.00
Bell, brass muffin style w/wooden hdl, CI ring, 5" dia, EX 300.00
Bell, engine; brass, orig swing mt, 9½" dia, EX 450.00
Bell, engine; brass w/NP traces, acorn finial, 10" dia 325.00
Bell, engine; gun-metal gray, w/bracket & clapper, 9¾" dia 350.00
Bell, hand tub; acorn finial, w/bracket, 9" dia, 34" overall 650.00
Belt, parade; blk leather, Barnicoat, dtd 1852, EX 110.00
Belt, parade; blk leather w/Nashua Vet, dtd 1891, EX 60.00
Belt, parade; leather, worn orig pnt, Hampden, 42", EX 75.00
Belt, parade; red & wht leather, VG 45.00
Belt, parade; wht leather, Foreman Randolph Mass, VG 95.00
Boots, ALF, rubber, pr, EX 55.00

Box, alarm; Gamewell, CI cottage style, complete, 11" 130.00
Box, Gamewell Telegraph Station, red oval, complete, 13" 180.00
Box, Gamewell Terminal, CI, red cottage style 120.00
Bucket, leather, Fire Commissioner, dtd 1899-1903, VG 350.00
Bucket, leather, Gen Taylor portrait, lt pnt loss, EX 300.00
Bucket, leather, old gr rpt w/blk & gold, 12¼", EX 600.00
Bucket, leather, pnt unicorn & lion, European, VG 110.00
Bucket, leather, red & gr pnt, Malden Fire Club 1822, EX 800.00
Bucket, leather, vines & leaves w/name, dtd 1846, EX 400.00
Buggy whip, presentation; silver ferrules, ivory hdl, 1861 ......1,200.00
Extinguisher, Accurate Junior, copper & brass, S&A, pony sz 190.00
Extinguisher, apparatus; Babcock, copper/brass, 5-gal, 30" 350.00
Extinguisher, apparatus; Elkhart, foam, 2½-gal, EX 125.00
Extinguisher, apparatus; Elkhart, NP, 2½-gal, VG 125.00
Extinguisher, apparatus; LaFrance, copper/brass, 2½ -gal 160.00
Extinguisher, Autofyrstop, glass carbon-tet, mushroom shape 25.00
Extinguisher, Automatic by Firetox, ceiling mt, VG 40.00
Extinguisher, Babcock, red-pnt copper w/brass plaque, 5-gal 275.00
Extinguisher, Badger's, copper/brass, pony sz, 11" 120.00
Extinguisher, Badger's Pony, copper, S&A, 2½-gal, 20", EX 35.00
Extinguisher, Keystone, J Boyd & Bro, S&A, 2½-gal, G 40.00
Extinguisher, LaFrance, nickel/copper, 1926, EX 45.00
Extinguisher, Rameses, tin tube, powder, EX 45.00
Extinguisher, Russ Bro, Handi Warr Dry Chemical..., NM 35.00
Extinguisher, Universal, brass/copper, S&A, pony sz 110.00
Extinguisher, unmk, NP, S&A, pony sz, 19", EX 40.00
Extinguisher, Utica Pat Applied For, nickel, 21", EX 40.00
Frontispc, Engine 4 LFD, leather, 8", EX 80.00
Frontispc, Franklin R FS, red w/gold letters, 7½", EX 190.00
Frontispc, leather, Driver-3-Truck-LFD, red, 8", G 100.00
Frontispc, leather, Engineer-3-HMH, blk, 8", EX 100.00
Frontispc, leather, Hose-12-LFD, blk, 6¼", EX 75.00
Frontispc, leather, Super Pumper, 5¼", EX 45.00
Frontispc, Ringgold Hose Co, admiral portrait, 7½", EX 350.00
Gauge, pressure; Lonergan Phila, brass bezel, 11½" 40.00
Gauge, Seagrave, brass, 0-400psi, 3¼", EX 65.00
Gong, Fight style, 10" bell w/wooden hdl, CI base, 1 stroke, EX ...185.00
Gong, Fire Gong Rope Fire Escape Co Phila, 8" bell, EX 85.00
Gong, Gamewell, brass, turtle style, wind indicator, 10", EX 190.00
Gong, Gamewell, chrome, turtle style, center wind, 6" 70.00
Gong, Gamewell, NP, Excelsior style, center wind, 10" bell 125.00
Gong, Gamewell, Pat 1880 & 1881, 6", in wood case, EX 775.00
Gong, Utica, brass, 8", in 21" oak case 700.00
Gong indicator, Gamewell, 15", wood case w/3 dials, EX 5,500.00
Grenade, Deutsche...Eberhardt, med gold-amber, 1890s, 8⅜" 875.00
Grenade, Harden's, no Star in circle, turq, 6⅝" 135.00
Grenade, Harden's Hand...Pat, med cobalt, ftd base, 4¾" 80.00
Grenade, Harden's Star, cobalt, ca 1890, 1-pt, 6⅝" 160.00
Grenade, Harden's Star, lt 'electric' bl, ca 1890, 6½" 180.00
Grenade, Harden's Star Hand London, turq, ca 1890, 6½" 325.00
Grenade, Harden's Star...May 27 84, clear, partial label, 8" 300.00
Grenade, Harden's Star...May 27 84, yel-gr, 1-qt, 7⅞" 185.00
Grenade, Hayward Hand...NY, cobalt, 1880s, 6" 210.00
Grenade, Hayward's...Pat 1871-SF Hayward...NY, apple gr, 6⅜" ..190.00
Grenade, Hayward's...Pat 1871-SF Hayward...NY, clear, 6⅛" 120.00
Grenade, Hayward's...Pat 1871-SF Hayward...NY, yel-amber, 6⅛" .120.00
Grenade, Hayward's...407 Broadway...Pat...1871, cobalt, 6" 230.00
Grenade, Hayward's..407 Broadway NY, clear, 1880s, 5⅞" 70.00
Grenade, Healey's Hand Fire Extinguisher, yel, 10¾" 875.00
Grenade, Purrett's Pat Magic Fire Extinguisher label, 9⅛" 375.00
Grenade, unmk Am, horizontal ribs, dk sapphire bl, 1880s, 6" ...100.00
Helmet, aluminum, low front, Lower 1 Allen, complete, EX 110.00
Helmet, leather, Anderson & James, w/frontispc, rprs, EX 375.00
Helmet, leather, English, brass frontispc/rosettes/band 150.00

Helmet, leather, high eagle, Cairns, Boston FD frontispc, EX 280.00
Helmet, leather, high eagle, Cairns, Boston FD Honorary Chief, EX ...400.00
Helmet, leather, high eagle, Cairns, NAFD frontispc, EX 250.00
Helmet, leather, high eagle, Cairns, no frontispc, VG 245.00
Helmet, leather, high eagle, District 3 Chief frontispc, EX 400.00
Helmet, leather, high eagle, Neptune 8 Newburyport RNP, VG ..325.00
Helmet, leather, high eagle, Oak Hall Boston, w/frontispc, EX ..425.00
Helmet, leather, low eagle, Engine 2 BFD frontispc, EX 150.00
Helmet, leather, low front, Cairns, HCFD frontispc, EX 200.00
Helmet, leather, Roulstone, 4-comb, no frontispc, early 450.00
Helmet, leather, war baby, Cairns, no frontispc, VG 110.00
Helmet, leather, war baby, Cairns, 4-comb, w/frontispc, VG 125.00
Hose, leather, ca 1850, 30-ft, EX 675.00
Key, alarm mechanism, brass, 3½" 45.00
Lamp, brass, 19" trumpet, 29", EX 125.00

Lantern, marked Wm. Porter & Sons - Pat'd Apr. 23, 67 - Aug. 3, 69, solid brass, etched H. Drapper - Engineer on globe, 16", NM, $700.00.

Lantern, chief's, Peter Gray, brass, gr/clear globe, EX 575.00
Lantern, Dietz, Chief model, brass, orig globe, VG 330.00
Lantern, Dietz Fire King, brass, slide-off cage, 1889, EX 250.00
Lantern, Dietz Fire King, tin w/copper bottom, EX 140.00
Lantern, Dietz King, ALF, VG 260.00
Lantern, Dietz King, Seagrave...Columbus OH, brass, VG 450.00
Lantern, Dietz Mill, red pnt, G 45.00
Lantern, Hamm's for Boston Woven Hose...Co, nickel/brass, EX ..425.00
Lantern, Kingsford Fire Co, whale oil burner, EX 325.00
Lantern, wrist; John B Chase 4, fixed gr globe, VG 850.00
Lantern, wrist; Porter, brass, clear globe, complete, EX 300.00
Medal, Valor FDNY, gold-tone metal, scarce, EX 280.00
Nameplate, apparatus; Ahrens-Fox, EX 120.00
Nozzle, brass, AJ Morse, shut-off, 2 hdls, 61", EX 300.00
Nozzle, brass, Cole, w/open/close control, 10", EX 75.00
Nozzle, brass, from hand tub, early, 73½" 1,500.00
Nozzle, brass, Henry Barnes Boston, 19" 70.00
Nozzle, brass, Larkin, w/flow control, 15½", EX 140.00
Nozzle, brass, leather cover, Larkin, flow control, 26" 210.00
Nozzle, brass, SF Hayward, flow control, 10", EX 90.00
Nozzle, brass, steamer type, 36½"w/1½" tip, EX 100.00
Nozzle, chrome, ALF Foamite Corp July 1919, 10", EX 125.00
Nozzle, chrome, Fabric Fire Hose Co NY, w/Pat date, 7", EX 200.00
Nozzle, copper & brass, from hand tub, early, 64", VG 675.00
Nozzle, fog; brass, Fire Appliance Co, 8½", EX 45.00
Nozzle, leather covered, Callahan Boston, 22", EX 200.00
Oil can, NP brass, from steamer, EX 175.00
Photo, horse-drawn ladder wagon, E Weymouth MA, EX 40.00
Pin, presentation; sterling, 5-pc, mk Tiffany & Co 320.00
Playing cards, Play the Game-Well, complete deck, EX in box ..300.00
Pump, Merryweather & Sons, brass, 19½" 25.00
Rack, wire, to hold 3 Hayward grenades, EX 130.00

Rattle, oak, single reed, early, 11", working, EX 100.00
Rattle, oak, swing type to use when walking, 11x15", EX 200.00
Register, ADT System, brass, paper tape, take-up reel, EX 325.00
Register, alarm; JH Bunnell & Co NY, brass, ½" tape, EX 80.00
Register, Horni, polished brass, 1" tape, EX 140.00
Shield, H on red leather, 5", G 25.00
Shirt, red w/ST FD buttons, VG 230.00
Siren, Sterling Siren Fire Alarm, hand-crank, EX 475.00
Spotlight, apparatus; Dietz, brass, 10" dia, w/mt base 130.00
Staff, warden's, wooden w/solid brass head, 50", EX 325.00
Tintype, man in bibbed shirt, parade belt & cap, EX 90.00
Torch, parade; brass, mtd on trn wooden hdl, 26" 100.00
Torch, parade; brass, ornate, gimballed 4 ways, wood hdl, 30" 150.00
Torch, parade; brass w/acorn finial, trn walnut hdl, 32", pr 275.00
Torch, parade; brass w/iron spike end, 36", EX 375.00
Torch, parade; brass w/trn wood hdl, 27", EX 200.00
Torch, parade; brass w/trn wooden hdl, 1800s, 43", EX 850.00
Trumpet, parade; eng SP, Warren PA, 17", VG 650.00
Trumpet, presentation; SP, dtd 1863, eagle sash mts, 22½" 900.00
Trumpet, presentation; SP, winged eagle eng on bell, EX 900.00
Trumpet, presentation; sterling, ornate eng, dtd 1874, EX 2,200.00
Trumpet, working; NP, missing tassel mt, 16", VG 315.00
Trumpet, working; NP brass, 15½", EX 235.00

Fireglow

Fireglow is a type of art glass that first appears to be an opaque cafe au lait, but glows with rich red 'fire' when held to a strong source of light.

Ewer, bird on branch, brn monotone satin, 7" 75.00
Lamp, brn leaves/wht flowers on 5½" globe & base, mini 250.00
Vase, birds on floral branches, 11¾x5" 225.00
Vase, pk & purple flowers, gold metal ftd fr, 10" 175.00
Vase, stylized flowers in bl & red, 3 crystal thorn ft, 7" 120.00

Fireplace Implements

In the colonial days of our country, fireplaces provided heat in the winter and were used year round to cook food in the kitchen. The implements that were a necessary part of these functions were varied and have become treasured collectibles, many put to new use in modern homes as decorative accessories. Gypsy pots may hold magazines; copper and brass kettles, newly polished and gleaming, contain dried flowers or green plants. Firebacks, highly ornamental iron panels that once reflected heat and protected masonry walls, are now sometimes used as wall decorations. By Victorian times the cookstove had replaced the kitchen fireplace, and many of these early utensils were already obsolete; but as a source of heat and comfort, the fireplace continued to be used for several more decades. See also Wrought Iron.

Andirons, bell metal, lemon top, rnd plinth, 14", pr 220.00
Andirons, brass, Arts & Crafts, tapered posts w/balls, 24", pr 270.00
Andirons, brass, ball finials, matching fire dogs, 17", pr 445.00
Andirons, brass, ball finials, 17", pr 225.00
Andirons, brass, dbl lemon top, ca 1800s, 20", +tongs/shovel 715.00
Andirons, brass, lemon-shaped finials, early, 13¼", pr 300.00
Andirons, brass, steeple top, ca 1800s, 22", +shovel/tongs 1,250.00
Andirons, CI, Blk sailor, 20", pr 900.00
Andirons, CI, dolphins, bk ends of rods incomplete, 14", pr 165.00
Andirons, CI, eagle finials, OH, 12", pr 725.00
Andirons, CI, Hessian soldier, worn mc pnt, 10¼", pr 300.00
Andirons, CI, owl w/glass eyes, worn blk pnt, 14½", pr 350.00

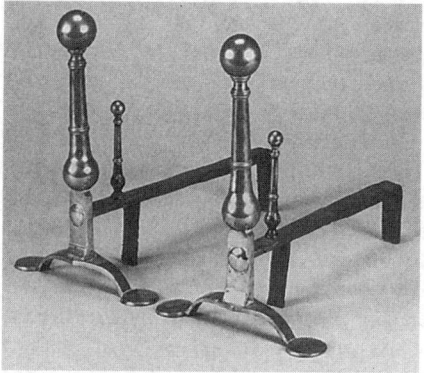

Andirons, Queen Anne, brass, Rhode Island, ca 1740, 14", $1,760.00 for the pair.

Andirons, CI, spaniel dog form, 13", pr 400.00
Andirons, wrought, Arts & Crafts, ca 1900, 23x13", pr 110.00
Andirons, wrought iron, gooseneck finial, penny ft, 14", pr 135.00
Andirons, wrought iron, gooseneck finial, 17½", pr 110.00
Bellows, orig grpt w/striping, brass nozzle, 17¾", EX 250.00
Bellows, orig yel pnt w/fruit stencil, worn leather, 14" 175.00
Bellows, turtle bk, gold floral rpt on red, rstr, 16½" 115.00
Bellows, wood/leather w/simple punched decor, iron spout, 20" .100.00
Fender, brass, rtcl grill & top rail 360.00
Fender, brass & wire, early 1800s, 12x52", EX 978.00
Fender, brass wire work, England, 1800s, 60" 750.00
Fender, wire w/iron fr & brass rail w/2 finials, 9x43" 600.00
Fender, wire w/iron fr & brass rail w/3 finials, 10x45" 775.00
Fireback, CI, caricatured figure, 18th C, 24", EX 575.00
Fireback, CI, heraldic lion, 18th C, 33", EX 575.00
Fireback, CI, horse & rider, 18th C, 24", EX 800.00
Fireback, CI, hunt scene, Pat 1890, 32x26", EX 300.00
Fireback, CI, mask, dtd 1763, 15½", EX 200.00
Grate, CI & brass, classic style, urn finials, 19x24x12" 700.00
Mantel, gr/blk marble, cvd rosettes, fluted columns, 48x72" 525.00
Mantel, pine Country Classical Revival, tan rpt, 45x62" 195.00
Mantel, soft wood, fluted pilasters, oval sunbursts, 62x62" 1,650.00
Spit-jack, brass, complete w/key, iron wheel, hangers, 14" 225.00
Toaster, heavy wire, wooden hdl, 1890s, 18½" 45.00
Toaster, wrought iron, rotary style, 26" 300.00
Toaster, wrought w/dbl jaws, scrolled ends, trn hdl, 26" 140.00
Tongs, ember; iron w/looped hdls, ca 1865, 16½" 55.00
Trivet, wrought iron, scrolled platform ft, trn hdl, 9x20x9" 230.00

Fisher, Harrison

Harrison Fisher (1875-1934), noted illustrator and creator of the Fisher Girl, was the son of landscape artist, Hugh Antoine Fisher. His career began in his teens in San Francisco where he did artwork for the Hearst papers. Later in New York his drawings of beautiful American women attracted much attention and graced the covers of the most popular magazines of the day such as *Puck, Ladies' Home Journal, Saturday Evening Post,* and *Cosmopolitan.* He also illustrated novels, and his art books are treasured. His drawings appeared on thousands of postcards and posters. His creation of the Fisher Girl and his panel of six scenes of the *Greatest Moments in a Woman's Life* made him the most sought-after and well-paid illustrator of his day.

Banner, Red Cross, nurse, w/Foringer's Madonna, 41½x8½", EX ..110.00
Book, American Beauties, Bobbs Merrill, 1st ed, 1909, EX 200.00
Book, Bachelor Bells, Fisher illus, 1908, EX 75.00
Book, Dream Fair Women, Fisher color illus, 1909, 20-pg, VG ..100.00
Book, Fair Americans, 1911, EX 195.00
Book, Harrison Fisher Book, 1907, EX 200.00

Bookplate, American Beauties, 1909, 11x8½" **75.00**
Candy tin, Snowbird, Tindeco, 1⅜x4" **42.50**
Postcard, Greatest Moments, set of 6 in orig matting & fr **110.00**
Print, American Belles, 1911 ....**295.00**
Print, Bachelor Bells, 1908, EX **175.00**
Print, Danger, ca 1908, old fr **90.00**
Print, Dream of Fair Women, 1907 ....**210.00**
Print, King of Hearts, orig fr, 11x13" **85.00**

Fishing Collectibles

Collecting old fishing tackle is becoming more popular every year. Though at first most interest was geared toward old lures and some reels, rods, advertising, and miscellaneous items are quickly gaining ground. Values are given for examples in excellent or better condition and should be used only as a guide. For more information contact our advisor Randy Hilst, an appraiser and collector whose address and phone number are listed in the Directory under Illinois.

Box, Hopper Coop-Live for Insects, Pat Appl For, tin, VG **95.00**
Creel, half-moon; wood & tin, orig blk pnt, early 1800s, 10" **200.00**
Creel, whole willow, orig sliding peg latch & hangers, EX **75.00**
Gaff, brass, telescopic, wood hdl, knurled butt cap, VG **130.00**
Landing net, Ed Cummings, laminated wood, old, NM **65.00**
Landing net, Peek & Sons, brass, telescopic, wood hdl, VG **230.00**

Lure, Crazy Leg, green with yellow eyes, treble hooks, 3¼", EX, $17.00.

Lure, Creek Chub Giant Pikie, glass eyes, MIB **75.00**
Lure, Heddon Model 'O' Dowagiac Minnow, glass eyes, 3¼" **375.00**
Lure, Joseph Pepper New Century Minnow, 3 trebles, ca 1900, 2½" .**375.00**
Lure, K&K Animated Minnow, glass eyes, pnt chips, 4¼", VG ..**375.00**
Lure, Martin wht redhead, glass eyes, lg, MIB **50.00**
Lure, Martin yel redhead, glass eyes, lg, MIB **50.00**
Lure, Pflueger Neverfail Minnow, glass eyes, 3-hook, 2¾", EX ...**190.00**
Lure, Pflueger Surprise, red & wht, glass eyes, VG **95.00**
Minnow trap, CF Orvis Manchester VT, all orig, EX **85.00**
Reel, Bill Ballan, classic S hdl, 3", NM **200.00**
Reel, Fowler Gem, Pat June 1872, rare, NM **4,000.00**
Reel, Hardy Perfect w/duplicated Mark II stamping, 3⅛", VG **200.00**
Reel, Julius Vom Hofe Size 1, NP, 2⅞" dia, G **125.00**
Reel, Leonard Atwood Boston, Pat 1918, 3⅝" dia, VG **400.00**
Reel, Neversink, German silver & hard rubber, 2¾", VG **45.00**
Reel, Pflueger Hawkeye, German silver, 80-yd sz, VG **175.00**
Reel, Pflueger Supreme #1573, cub hdl, MIB **85.00**
Reel, Talbot, Star, Kansas City MO **650.00**
Reel, 4 Brothers Delite, NP & hard rubber, 2¼", G **95.00**
Rod, fly; GH Howells Custom Made, 1963, 8'9", VG **300.00**
Rod, fly; Orvis Western Series , 2-pc, 8'9", EX in bag & tube **175.00**
Rod, salmon; LL Bean Atlantic, 3-pc, 2-tip, 9½', NM in case **125.00**

Rod, trout; FE Thomas Dirigo, 3-pc, 8', VG in bag & case **575.00**
Rod, trout; Leonard Catskill, wraps, 3-pc, 8', VG in bag **500.00**
Rod, trout; Sam Carlson, 2-pc, rfn, 7½', EX **300.00**
Rod, WG Soeffker, dk flaming, 3-pc, 8', M in bag & tube **1,250.00**
Tackle box, Knickerbocker, oil-skin covered wood, 13x17x9", EX ..**100.00**

Flags of the United States

The brevity and imprecise language of the first Flag Act of 1777 allowed great artistic license for America's early flag makers. This resulted in a rich variety of imaginative star formations which coexisted with more conventional union patterns. In 1912 inviolate design standards were established for the new 48-star flag, but the banners of our past history continue to survive:

The 'Great Star' pattern — configured from the combined stars of the union, appeared in various star denominations for about 50 years, then gradually disappeared in the post-Civil War years.

The utilitarian 'scatter' pattern — created through the random placement of stars, is traceable to the formative years of our nation and remained a design influence through most of the 19th century.

The 'wreath' pattern — first appearing in the form of simple single-wreath formations, eventually evolved into the elegant double- and triple-wreath medallion patterns of the Centennial period.

Acquisition of specific star denominations is also a primary consideration in the collecting process. Pre-Civil War flags of 33 stars or less are very scarce and are typically treated as 'blue chip' items. Civil War-era flags of 34 and 35 stars also stand among the most sought-after denominations. Market demand for 36-, 37- and 38-star flags is strong but less broad-based, while interest in the unofficial 39-, 40-, 41- and 42-star examples is largely confined to flag aficionados. The very rare 43 remains in a class by itself and is guaranteed to attract the attention of the serious collector.

Row-patterned flags of 44, 45 and 46 stars still turn up with some frequency and serve as a source of more modestly priced vintage flags. Ordinary 48-star flags flood the flea markets and are priced accordingly, while the short-lived 49 is regarded as a legitimate collectible. 13-star flags, produced over a period of more than 200 years, surface in many forms and must be assessed on a case-by-case basis.

Many flag buffs favor sizes that are manageable for wall display. Extra-large flags may or may not be regarded as desirable, depending upon the beholder. Allowances are typically made for the normal wear and tear found on original period flags. Conversely, there is little or no collector demand for modern-day flag repros, regardless of condition.

The dollar value of a flag is by no means based upon age alone. The wide price swings in the listing below have been influenced by a variety of determining factors related to age, scarcity and aesthetic merit. In fact, almost any special feature that stands out as unusual or distinctive is a potential asset. Imprinted flags and inscribed flags; 8-point stars, gold stars, and added stars; extra stripes, missing stripes, tri-color stripes and war stripes are all part of the pricing equation. And while political and military flags may rank above all others in terms of prestige and price, any flag with a significant and well-documented historical connection has 'star' potential (pardon the pun). Our advisor for this category is Robert Banks; he is listed in the Directory under Maryland.

13 stars, (4-5-4), sea captain's, ca 1860s, 74x140" **280.00**
13 stars, Betsy Ross flag, by grandaughter, 1903, 8x12" **550.00**
13 stars, in semi-wreath, hand sewn, 1870s, 54x102" **180.00**
13 stars, printed, w/advertisement, 1880s, 4x7" **40.00**
13 stars, US Navy boat ensign, dtd Sept 1904, 44x78" **75.00**
13 stars, 3rd MD pattern, hand sewn, 1840s, 32x45" **575.00**
16 stars, naval ensign, hand sewn, CW era, 44x60" **600.00**
19 stars, 16 orig+3, sewn scrap fabric, 39x66" **960.00**

20 stars, handembr into Great Star, rare, 24x32" 1,050.00
23 stars, Civil War related, home-sewn muslin, 48x96" 200.00
24 stars, folk art, hand-tatted construction, 12x18" 225.00
25 stars, stenciled burlap on 24" wood tripod pole, 5x7" 220.00
26 stars, Great Star, embr on sewn silk, 30x43" 630.00
29 stars, entirely hand sewn, poor condition, 43x68" 410.00
30 stars, gold stars/fringe, silk, delicate, 52x68" 425.00
31 stars, Great Star, Lincoln related, printed, 11x14" 185.00
31 stars, Great Star, 14 stripes, hand sewn, 39x69" 600.00
31 stars, row pattern, hand-stitched bunting, 104x247" 580.00
32 stars, dbl wreath of inset stars, hand sewn, 36x48" 535.00

33-Star, double wreath pattern, hand sewn, undersized canton, ten stripes, pre-Civil War, 77x127", $450.00.

33 stars, hand-/machine-sewn wool bunting, 66x92" 475.00
34 stars, dbl-wreath pattern, printed silk, 18x28" 225.00
34 stars, Great Star, mixed fabrics, sewn, 91x154" 670.00
34 stars, row pattern, pieced printed silk, 64x104" 390.00
34 stars form shield, all hand sewn, worn, 51x66" 600.00
34 stars in pentagonal clusters, hand sewn, 63x95" 620.00
35 stars, recruiting flag, sewn bunting, 50x116" 585.00
35 stars, row pattern, hand/machine sewn, 96x180" 510.00
36 stars, Civil War, 8-pointed, in sewn wreath, 78x90" 720.00
36 stars, in 6 rows, hand-sewn wool bunting, 71x114" 210.00
36 stars, sailing ship's, inscr & dtd, 75x142" 235.00
37 stars, printed silk, 32x40" 55.00
37 stars, row pattern, stitched bunting, 30x48" 180.00
37 stars, wreath pattern, hand-sewn cotton, 72x106" 290.00
37 stars, 6-pointed, hand-/machine-stitched cotton, 60x84" 375.00
38 stars, Blaine campaign, printed cotton, 17x27" 340.00
38 stars, Centennial 1876, printed cotton, 15x24" 70.00
38 stars, dbl-wreath pattern, sewn muslin, 87x128" 220.00
38 stars, from SS America, hand sewn, 68x108" 420.00
38 stars, Great Star, printed silk, gold fringe, 12x17" 65.00
38 stars, in rows, hand/machine-stitched bunting, 71x116" 145.00
38 stars, medallion-wreath pattern, printed cotton, 12x17" 55.00
38 stars, 1776-1876 pattern, printed linen, 27½x46" 330.00
39 stars, in rows, all machine-stitched bunting, 40x84" 150.00
39 stars, originally 34 Great Star, sewn, 69x129" 400.00
39 stars, row pattern variation, printed silk, 12x24" 45.00
39 stars, scatter pattern, hand sewn, 78x120" 185.00
39 stars, triple wreath, hand-sewn bunting, 60x108" 250.00
39 stars (6-5 pattern), printed gauze bunting, 19x34" 32.00
40 stars, unofficial, hand/machine sewn, 61x115" 110.00
40 stars, wreath-in-box pattern, hand sewn, 43x82" 160.00
41 star printed flags (17), uncut muslin, rare, 24x263" 300.00
42 stars, printed cotton, unhemmed, 18x24" 22.00

42 stars, sewn cotton, from Ft Hamilton NY, 120x177" 135.00
42 stars, Union scatter pattern, hand sewn, 48x72" 134.00
43 stars, machine-sewn bunting, extremely rare, 29x70" 425.00
43 stars (1 side only), 98989 pattern, homemade, 38x48" 175.00
44 stars, hand-sewn bunting, 70x144", EX 110.00
44 stars, machine-sewn cotton bunting, 53x82" 65.00
45 stars, hand-sewn wool bunting, 92x135" 55.00
45 stars, HP w/sewn muslin stripes, 38x70" 42.00
45 stars, machine-sewn cotton bunting, 80x108" 40.00
45 stars, printed silk w/red ribbon ties, 32x46" 38.00
45 stars, triple-wreath GAR flag, printed muslin, 11x16" 40.00
46 stars, machine-sewn wool bunting, 72x138" 40.00
46 stars, printed silk, in baton-type carrying tube, 12x17" 17.00
46 stars, random pattern, machine sewn, 40x100" 55.00
47 stars, unofficial, sewn bunting, 108x137" 170.00
48 stars, machine-sewn cotton bunting, 60x96" 25.00
48 stars, naturalization, sewn names, 1914, 14x24" 75.00
48 stars, sewn to form 'USA,' unauthorized WWI, 45x69" 175.00
48 stars, staggered rows (early), printed muslin, 13x23" 10.00
48 stars, Whipple Peace Flag, printed silk, 14x24" 220.00
48 stars, WWII liberation, from Liege, homemade, 68x93" 95.00
48 stars, 10-9 pattern, printed bunting, rare, 39x61" 55.00
49 stars, embr w/sewn stripes, gold fringe, 48x72" 60.00
49 stars, machine-sewn cotton, 36x60" 25.00
49 stars, 3 uncut flags, printed cottonsheet, 37x36" 18.00
50 stars, Carter campaign, printed plastic, 12x18" 15.00
50 stars, oddity, printed/sewn in gr & wht, 36x60" 65.00
52 stars, Spanish Am war era, home sewn, rare, 44x84" 215.00
56 stars, printed crepe paper, Oriental, 1920s, 9x9" 18.00

Florence Ceramics

Figurines marked 'Florence Ceramics' were produced in the forties and fifties in Pasadena, California. The quality of the ware and the attention given to detail are prompting a growing interest among today's collectors. The names of these lovely ladies, gents, and figural groups are nearly always incised into their bases. The company name is ink-stamped. Because this is a relatively new area of collecting and the rarity of many items has yet to be determined, examples are evaluated by size and intricacy of design. Our advisor for this category is Jack Chipman, author of *The Collector's Encyclopedia of California Pottery*; he is listed in the Directory under California.

Abigail, bl or gr, 8½", ea 95.00
Bea, w/gold, 6" 85.00
California Quail, wht matt bird, rare, 7½" 325.00
Camille, bl, 8½" 150.00
Camille, pk, net shawl, 8½" 175.00
Cardinal, mc bird, rare, 4½" 325.00
Catherine, seated on settee, 8x7" 275.00
Charles, wht w/gold, 8½" 95.00
Chinese Blossom Birl, wht w/gold, 8½" 75.00
Chinese couple, flower holders, blk & wht, 8", pr 125.00
Chinese couple, She-Ti & Kiu, wht, 10¼", pr 325.00
Chinese Lantern Boy, wht w/gold, 8½" 75.00
Choir Boy, 6" 45.00
Clarissa, gold trim, 8" 100.00
David, holds top hat, wht & gold, 8" 75.00
David & Betsy, lamps, pr 350.00
Delia, gold trim, 7½" 95.00
Edward, seated, 7" 150.00
Elaine, 6" 75.00
Eugenie, teal w/gold, 9" 200.00

Eve, wht w/gold, 8½" 100.00
Her Majesty, violet w/gold, 7½" 125.00
Irene, wht, 6" 60.00
Jennifer, pk, 8" 150.00
Jim, 6¼" 70.00
Josephine, bl, 9" 100.00
Kay, planter, 6" 55.00
Lillian, pk, 8" 65.00

Lillian Russell, bow at waist of pink dress, gold trim, 13", $350.00.

Linda Lou, 8" 95.00
Louis XV, red w/gold, 12½" 300.00
Marie Antoinette & Louis XVI, wht w/gold, pr 650.00
Marilyn, pk, 8½" 150.00
Matilda, bl, 8½" 100.00
Melanie, teal, 7½" 75.00
Mocking bird family, damage to flower, rare, 8½" 325.00
Musette, red, 9" 200.00
Pat & Mike, children, 6", 6¼", pr 125.00
Pinky & Blue Boy, 12", pr 650.00
Roberta, moss, 8½" 110.00
Rose Marie, rose w/gold, 9½" 225.00
Sarah, gray, 7½" 75.00
Scarlett, articulated fingers, ornate, red /wgold, 9" 150.00
Scarlett, gray & maroon, simple, 9" 100.00
Victor, bl 200.00
Victoria, burgundy dress, gray sofa, 8¼x7" 325.00
Vivian, holds parasol, purple, 9½" 225.00
Wendy, planter, 6" 50.00

Florentine Cameo

Although the appearance may look much like English cameo, the decoration on this type of glass is not wheel cut or acid etched. Instead a type of heavy paste — usually a frosty white — is applied to the face to create a look very similar to true cameo. It was produced in France as well as England; it is sometimes marked 'Florentine.'

Vase, bird & leaf, brn & wht, 8" 495.00
Vase, flowers & leaves, wht on bl, ruffled/bulbous, 8" 265.00
Vase, lady, doves & flowers on citron, 11¼" 265.00
Vase, trumpet flowers, wht on red, 6" 175.00

Flow Blue

Flow Blue ware was produced by many Staffordshire potters;
among the most familiar were Meigh, Podmore and Walker, Samuel Alcock, Ridgway, John Wedge Wood (who often signed his work Wedgewood), and Davenport. It was popular from about 1825 through 1860 and again from 1880 until the turn of the century. The name describes the blurred or flowing affect of the cobalt decoration, achieved through the introduction of a chemical vapor into the kiln. The body of the ware is ironstone, and Oriental motifs were favored. Later issues were on a lighter body and often decorated with gilt.

Our advisor, Mary Frank Gaston, has compiled a lovely book, *The Collector's Encyclopedia of Flow Blue China*, with full-color illustrations and current market values; you will find her address in the Directory under Texas.

Abbey, creamer, G Jones 115.00
Acme, sauce tureen ladle, Hancock 275.00
Aldine, bone dish, Grindley 35.00
Aldine, sugar bowl, w/lid, Grindley 135.00
Alexandria, plate, Hancock & Sons, 9½" 67.50
Amoy, cup & saucer, handleless; Davenport 115.00
Amoy, cup plate, Davenport 125.00
Amoy, plate, Davenport, 10½" 175.00
Amoy, plate, Davenport, 8¼" 120.00
Amoy, plate, 9" 130.00
Amoy, platter, Davenport, 15½" 500.00
Amoy, soup, flanged, Davenport, 10⅜" 185.00
Amoy, teapot, Davenport, prof rpr 895.00
Arabesque, creamer, Dmn Cut, rare 350.00
Arabesque, platter, 13" 295.00
Arabesque, teapot, +cr/sug 1,300.00
Arcadia, bowl, vegetable; w/lid, Wilkinson 325.00
Argyle, bowl, vegetable; Grindley, w/lid 345.00
Argyle, cup & saucer, Grindley 90.00
Argyle, plate, Grindley, 10" 95.00
Argyle, plate, Grindley, 7" 40.00
Argyle, plate, Grindley, 8¾" 90.00
Argyle, platter, Grindley, 10¼x7" 175.00
Argyle, platter, Grindley, 17" 365.00
Argyle, platter, Grindley, 19⅝x13½" 425.00
Ashburton, bowl, vegetable; Grindley, w/lid 275.00
Ashburton, pitcher, milk; Grindley, 2-qt 450.00
Ashburton, platter, 16" 275.00
Ashburton, soup bowl, Grindley 88.00
Astoria, bone dish, New Wharf Pottery 55.00
Astral, gravy boat, Grindley, w/undertray 230.00
Astral, plate, Grindley, 9⅜" 82.50
Astral, platter, Grindley, 11" 150.00
Beaufort, butter pat, Grindley, 10 for 285.00
Belmont, butter pat, Meakin 45.00
Blue Danube, pitcher, Johnson Bros, 7¼" 250.00
Blue Rose, bowl, Grindley, 6¼" 45.00
Burleigh, bowl, vegetable; w/lid, Burgess & Leigh 82.50
Burleigh, soup bowl, Burgess & Leigh 88.00
California, platter, Wedgwood, ca 1884, 14" 425.00
Candia, cup & saucer, Cauldon 95.00
Candia, soup bowl, Cauldon, 10⅛" 98.00
Candia, soup tureen, w/lid, unmk, lg 945.00
Cashmere, cup, Ridgway & Morley 135.00
Cashmere, plate, Morley, 8½" 150.00
Chain of States, cup & saucer 95.00
Chapoo, plate, Wedge Wood, 6½" 95.00
Chapoo, plate, Wedge Wood, 8⅜" 115.00
Chapoo, platter, Wedge Wood, 18¼" 875.00
Chapoo, teapot, Wedge Wood 850.00
Chatsworth, teapot, Myott 600.00

Chen-Si, cup & saucer, handleless; Meir 155.00
Chen-Si, plate, Meir, 9½" 125.00
Chinese, bowl, vegetable; Dimmock, 8½x6" 275.00
Chinese, plate, Dimmock, 6¾" 85.00
Chinese, plate, mc, Dimmock, 9¼" 125.00
Chinese, teapot, Dimmock 775.00
Chusan, plate, Ashworth, 9¼" 145.00
Chusan, platter, Clementson, 18" 650.00
Chusan, platter, Fell, 16¾" 510.00
Claremont, bowl, vegetable; w/lid, 11" 110.00
Clarence, bowl, vegetable; 10" dia 125.00
Clayton, bacon dish, Johnson Bros 67.50
Clayton, butter pat, Johnson Bros 35.00
Clayton, creamer, Johnson Bros 175.00
Coburg, cup & saucer, handleless; Edwards 145.00
Coburg, platter, Edwards, 16" 390.00
Coburg, relish, Edwards 275.00
Constance, soup bowl, ca 1902, 8½" 55.00
Conway, bowl, vegetable; New Wharf Pottery, 8⅞" ...65.00
Conway, plate, New Wharf Pottery, 10⅛" 75.00
Conway, plate, New Wharf Pottery, 9⅛" 65.00
Conway, platter, oval, New Wharf Pottery, 10¾" 150.00
Corea, platter, Wedgwood, 12¼" 235.00
Country Scenes, bowl, rimmed soup; Wood & Sons, 9" ...60.00
Cows, plate, Wedgwood, 10" 145.00
Crumlin, bone dish, Myott 65.00
Crumlin, sauce tureen, w/lid, Myott 275.00
Dainty, plate, Maddock, 8" 62.50
Dainty, plate, Maddock, 9" 75.00
Daisy, plate, Maastrich, 9½" 98.00
Del Monte, sauce bowl, Johnson Bros, 5" 27.50
Devon, bowl, soup; Meakin 85.00
Devon, plate, luncheon; Meakin 65.00
Devon, platter, Meakin, 19" 195.00
Dundee, cup & saucer, Ridgway 75.00
Dundee, plate, Ridgway, 9" 50.00
Florence, bowl, vegetable; w/lid, Wood & Son 200.00
Florida, cup & saucer, Johnson Bros 88.00
Florida, plate, Johnson Bros, 8" 55.00
Florida, plate, Johnson Bros, 9" 68.00
Formosa, plate, Mayer, 10½" 185.00
Formosa, plate, Ridgway, 6¼" 88.00
Formosa, platter, 17½ x14" 715.00
Geneva, bowl, vegetable; w/lid, New Wharf Pottery, rpr ...185.00
Georgia, cup & saucer, Johnson Bros 85.00
Gironde, gravy boat, w/underplate, Grindley 225.00
Gothic, bowl, vegetable; w/lid 675.00
Grace, bone dish, Grindley 60.00
Grace, butter pat, Grindley 40.00
Grace, sauce tureen & underplate, Grindley 350.00
Grande, bowl, vegetable; gold accents, w/lid 215.00
Haddon, bowl, vegetable; w/lid, Grindley, 12x7½" ...335.00
Haddon, butter pat, Grindley 25.00
Haddon, creamer, Grindley, 5" 175.00
Haddon, cup & saucer, Grindley 60.00
Haddon, pitcher, Grindley, 8" 298.00
Haddon, platter, Grindley, 16x11" 285.00
Haddon, soup tureen, w/lid, Grindley 550.00
Hamilton, plate, Maddock, 7" 36.00
Hindustan, platter, Maddock, 18" 825.00
Honc, plate, Regout, 8¾" 92.50
Hong Kong, bowl, vegetable; w/lid, Meigh 495.00
Hong Kong, cup & saucer, Meigh 135.00
Hong Kong, gravy boat, Meigh 375.00

Hong Kong, plate, Meigh, 8¾" 120.00
Hong Kong, plate, Meigh, 9¼" 130.00
Hong Kong, sauce tureen & underplate, w/lid, Meigh ...775.00
Idris, plate, 10" 30.00
Idris, plate, 7¾" 20.00
Idris, saucer 10.00
Indian, mitten relish 125.00
Indian, plate, F&R Pratt, 9" 120.00
Indian, plate, Meigh, 7¼" 77.50
Indian, plate, Meigh, 9" 120.00
Indian, platter, F&R Pratt, 17" 575.00
Indian, platter, Meigh, 13¼" 330.00
Indian, teapot, lg 1,095.00
Indian Jar, cup & saucer 125.00
Indian Jar, teapot, Furnival, rpr 745.00
Jenny Lind, bowl, vegetable; Wilkinson, 1895, 7½" ...225.00
Kaolin, creamer, Podmore Walker 325.00
Kaolin, cup & saucer, Podmore Walker 110.00
Kaolin, teapot, Podmore Walker 825.00
Kaolin, teapot, Podmore Walker, prof rpr 700.00
Kaolin, waste bowl, Podmore Walker 325.00
Kelvin, plate, 7" 35.00
Kensington, cracker jar, Doulton, w/lid & underplate ...335.00
Kin Shan, cup, Challinor 80.00
Kin Shan, plate, Challinor, 7¾" 98.00
Kin Shan, plate, Challinor, 8¾" 100.00
Kin Shan, soup bowl, Challinor 145.00
Kyber, plate, Adams, 10" 110.00
Kyber, plate, Adams, 7¼" 55.00
Kyber, platter, Adams, 10x7⅜" 100.00
Kyber, platter, Adams, 18x14" 445.00
La Belle, bowl, oval, Wheeling 300.00
La Belle, bowl, scalloped, Wheeling, 9" 225.00
La Belle, celery tray, Wheeling 265.00
La Belle, charger, Wheeling, 12¾" 265.00
La Belle, soup bowl, Wheeling 88.00
La Francaise, bowl, serving; scalloped, French China, 9½" ...75.00
La Francaise, creamer & sugar bowl, French China 35.00
La Francaise, cup & saucer, French China 40.00
La Francaise, plate, French China, 7¼" 20.00
La Francaise, plate, French China, 9¼" 30.00
La Francaise, platter, mc, French China, 15", +6 9¼" plates ...650.00
La Francaise, sauce bowl, French China 25.00
Ladras, soup bowl, Ridgway, 9" 77.50
Lahore, coffee cup, Phillips 120.00
Lahore, plate, Phillips, 8½" 100.00
Lahore, plate, Phillips, 9" 115.00
Lahore, platter, Phillips, 18" 575.00
Lancaster, gravy boat, New Wharf Pottery 75.00
Lancaster, soup bowl, flanged, New Wharf Pottery, 9" ...88.00
Le Pavot, bowl, vegetable; oval, w/lid, 7x9" 275.00
Le Pavot, bowl, vegetable; w/lid, 8" 275.00
Lobelia, sugar bowl 385.00
Lonsdale, cup & saucer, Ford 80.00
Lorne, bowl, vegetable; w/lid, Grindley 220.00
Lorne, platter, Grindley, 14" 235.00
Luzurne, plate, Mercer, 7⅞" 70.00
Madras, plate, Doulton, 9½" 105.00
Madras, plate, Upper Hanley Pottery, 9" 110.00
Madras, sauce ladle, Doulton 235.00
Madras, saucer, Doulton, 6⅜" 65.00
Maltese, cup & saucer 60.00
Mandarin, plate, Pountney, 7¼" 60.00
Mandarin, plate, Pountney, 9¼" 70.00

Manhattan, butter pat, Alcock 45.00
Manilla, gravy boat, Podmore Walker 310.00
Manilla, plate, Podmore Walker, 7⅜" 90.00
Manilla, plate, Podmore Walker, 8⅝" 130.00
Manilla, plate, Podmore Walker, 9⅞" 145.00
Manilla, platter, Podmore Walker 425.00
Manilla, teapot, Podmore Walker, prof rpr 785.00
Marechal Neil, bone dish 60.00
Marguerite, cup & saucer, Grindley 70.00
Marguerite, plate, Grindley, 6" 32.00
Marguerite, platter, Grindley, 18" 350.00
Marquis, plate, Grindley, 10" 80.00
Melbourne, plate, Grindley, 10" 67.50
Melbourne, platter, Grindley, 16¼" 220.00
Melbourne, saucer, Grindley 15.00

Melrose, gravy boat, Doulton, 4", $120.00.

Melrose, sauce tureen ladle 275.00
Melton, pitcher, 7" 315.00
Mikoda, cup & saucer, Wilkinson 85.00
Mongolia, bowl, Johnson Bros, 7⅛" 55.00
Mongolia, platter, oval, Johnson Bros, 11" 200.00
Morning-Glory, cup & saucer 125.00
Nankin, bowl, vegetable; w/lid 495.00
Non Pareil, bowl, berry; Burgess & Leigh 65.00
Non Pareil, bowl, vegetable; Burgess & Leigh 160.00
Non Pareil, bowl, vegetable; w/lid, Burgess & Leigh 475.00
Non Pareil, butter pat, Burgess & Leigh 30.00
Non Pareil, cake plate, Burgess & Leigh, 11" 225.00
Non Pareil, cup & saucer, Burgess & Leigh 85.00
Non Pareil, pitcher, Burgess & Leigh, 7¾" 665.00
Non Pareil, plate, Burgess & Leigh, 6" 42.50
Non Pareil, plate, Burgess & Leigh, 8½" 88.00
Non Pareil, plate, Burgess & Leigh, 9¾" 110.00
Non Pareil, platter, Burgess & Leigh, 12" 275.00
Non Pareil, platter, Burgess & Leigh, 13¼" 295.00
Non Pareil, platter, Burgess & Leigh, 15½" 325.00
Non Pareil, sauce dish, Burgess & Leigh 32.00
Non Pareil, soup bowl, Burgess & Leigh, 8⅝" 85.00
Non Pareil, soup tureen, w/lid, Burgess & Leigh, 10" 600.00
Non Pareil, teapot, Burgess & Leigh, prof rpr 775.00
Norfolk, plate, Royal Doulton, 1891, 10" 98.00
Normandy, bowl, vegetable; Johnson Bros 165.00
Normandy, plate, Johnson Bros, 6⅜" 45.00
Normandy, plate, Johnson Bros, 9¼" 77.50
Normandy, waste bowl, Johnson Bros, 5⅞x3¼" 150.00
Orchid, plate, Maddock, 10⅜" 55.00

Orchid, plate, Maddock, 7⅞" 36.00
Orchid, plate, Maddock, 9" 50.00
Orchid, soup bowl, flanged, Maddock, 10⅜" 68.00
Oregon, bowl, berry; Mayer 95.00
Oregon, plate, Mayer, 9½" 125.00
Oregon, platter, Mayer, 10¾x8⅛" 235.00
Oregon, platter, Mayer, 13⅜" 385.00
Oregon, relish, Mayer 285.00
Oriental, bowl, Ridgway, 6½" 65.00
Oriental, bowl, rimmed soup; Ridgway 75.00
Oriental, creamer, Alcock 425.00
Oriental, plate, L&Co, 9½" 68.00
Oriental, platter, Ridgway, 17¼" 450.00
Osborne, bowl, vegetable; oval, hdls, Grindley, 12" 140.00
Osborne, creamer, Ridgway 145.00
Osborne, cup & saucer, Grindley 65.00
Osborne, plate, Ridgway 30.00
Osborne, platter, Rathbone, 13⅜" 150.00
Oxford, plate, Johnson Bros, 7" 30.00
Paisley, cup & saucer, Mercer 88.00
Pekin, gravy boat w/tray, mc, Whieldon 110.00
Pelew, cup & saucer, Challinor 175.00
Portman, cream soup 85.00
Raleigh, compote, Grindley, 5x9" dia 295.00
Raleigh, cup & saucer, Burgess & Leigh, mini 40.00
Rhone, cup, ped ft, hdl, Furnival, rare, early 175.00
Rhone, teapot, Furnival 775.00
Rock, platter, 12½" 365.00
Rose, bowl, vegetable; Ridgway, 10" 135.00
Rosette, plate, Burgess & Leigh, 9" 25.00
Roseville, butter pat, Maddock 40.00
Roseville, cup & saucer, Maddock 88.00
Roxbury, sauce tureen ladle, Ford 275.00
Royal Blue, cup & saucer, Burgess Campbell 65.00
Ruins, platter, Copeland, ca 1848, 9⅛x6⅝" 230.00

Salem, plate, Warranted, 9", $70.00.

Scinde, cup & saucer, handleless; Alcock 185.00
Scinde, plate, Alcock, 10½" 110.00
Scinde, plate, Alcock, 9½" 100.00
Scinde, platter, Alcock, rpr, 16" 600.00
Scinde, platter, Alcock, 13x10" 365.00
Scinde, teapot, Alcock 775.00
Seville, plate, Wood & Sons, 6⅞" 55.00
Sevres, creamer, New Wharf Pottery, 5" 190.00
Shanghai, coffeepot, Grindley, rare 450.00
Shell, cup & saucer, handleless; Challinor 135.00
Shell, cup & saucer, handleless; Challinor 170.00
Shell, plate, Challinor, 10¼" 125.00

Shell, plate, Challinor, 9⅝" 100.00
Shusan, teacup, Pratt 80.00
Sicily, plate, 10¼" 42.50
Temple, cup & saucer, handleless; Podmore Walker 150.00
Temple, plate, Podmore Walker, 8¾" 120.00
Temple, plate, 8¾" 115.00
Temple, sugar bowl, lion hdls, Podmore Walker, rare 415.00
Togo, bowl, vegetable; oval, Colonial Pottery, 10⅜" 115.00
Togo, creamer, Colonial Pottery 100.00
Togo, plate, Colonial Pottery, 8" 65.00
Togo, plate, Colonial Pottery, 9¾" 80.00
Togo, sauce bowl, Colonial Pottery, 5" 32.00
Tokio, platter, Adams, 12x9", NM 125.00
Tonquin, cup, ped ft, hdl, 12-panel, Adams, rare 175.00
Tonquin, cup & saucer, Adams 135.00
Tonquin, plate, Heath, 7⅞" 80.00
Tonquin, platter, Adams, 15½" 625.00
Tonquin, platter, Heath, 10¾" 300.00
Tonquin, sugar bowl, Heath 265.00
Touraine, bone dish, Stanley 65.00
Touraine, bowl, berry; Stanley 47.50
Touraine, bowl, vegetable; Alcock 200.00
Touraine, butter pat, Stanley 55.00
Touraine, cream soup, Stanley 85.00
Touraine, cup & saucer, Stanley 95.00
Touraine, plate, Alcock, 6½" 40.00
Touraine, plate, Stanley, 7⅝" 42.50
Touraine, platter, Stanley, 12½" 170.00
Touraine, saucer, Stanley 17.50
Touraine, soup bowl, flangeless, Stanley 98.00
Troy, platter, Meigh, 19½" 1,275.00
Troy, waste bowl, Meigh 365.00
Turin, sauce bowl, Johnson Bros, 5⅛" 24.00
Venice, bowl, berry; Johnson Bros 47.50
Venice, butter pat, Johnson Bros 40.00
Vermont, butter pat, Burgess & Leigh 32.00
Virginia, butter pat, Maddock 28.00
Virginia, cup & saucer, Maddock 55.00
Virginia, plate, Maddock, 7" 42.00
Virginia, plate, Maddock, 8" 55.00
Virginia, plate, Maddock, 9" 66.00
Virginia, platter, oval, Maddock, 10½" 235.00
Virginia, sauce bowl, Maddock 32.50
Virginia, soup bowl, Maddock, 8" 67.50
Waldorf, bowl, vegetable; New Wharf Pottery, 9" 160.00
Waldorf, cup & saucer, New Wharf Pottery 90.00
Waldorf, plate, New Wharf Pottery, 10" 80.00
Waldorf, plate, New Wharf Pottery, 8⅞" 77.50
Waldorf, waste bowl, New Wharf Pottery 180.00
Warwick, saucer, Johnson Bros 25.00
Watteau, plate, Doulton, 10½" 90.00
Watteau, plate, Doulton, 7" 55.00
Watteau, soup, Doulton, 7½" 65.00
Waverly, butter pat, Maddock 45.00
Waverly, plate, Maddock, 6¼" 42.50
Waverly, plate, Maddock, 9" 60.00
Waverly, platter, Maddock, 17" 340.00
Waverly, soup tureen, w/lid, Maddock 500.00
Willow, plate, Allerton, 10" 65.00
Windflower, cup & saucer 55.00
Windsor Royal, butter pat 42.50
Windsor Royal, cup & saucer, Edwards 100.00
Yeddo, platter, Ashworth, 15¼" 240.00
Yeddo, tureen stand, Ashworth, 15" 300.00

Flue Covers

When spring housecleaning started and the heating stove was taken down for the warm weather season, the unsightly hole where the stovepipe joined the chimney was hidden with an attractive flue cover. They were made with a colorful litho print behind glass with a chain for hanging. Although scarce today, some scenes were actually reverse painted on the glass itself. The most popular motifs were florals, children, animals, and lovely ladies. Occasionally flue covers were made in sets of three — one served a functional purpose, while the others were added to provide a more attractive wall arrangement. They range in size from 7" to 14", but 9" is the average. Our advisor for this category is Cara J. Washburn; her address is in the Directory under Wisconsin.

Blue jay on branch HP on brass, 10" dia 36.00
Brunette (in red dress), wht wicker fr, 14" 75.00
Brunette in jeweled dress & helmet, 8½", EX 70.00
Giving Thanks, crimped pewter edge, orig chain, 12", EX 35.00
Greek scenic, couple in foreground, 8½" 25.00
Oriental boy w/bouquet, tin border, orig chain, 8½x7½" 50.00
Steamship, rvpt, brn & gold border, G 30.00

Folk Art

That the creative energies of the mind ever spark innovations in functional utilitarian channels as well as toward playful frivolity is well documented in the study of American folk art. While the average early settler rarely had free time to pursue art for its own sake, his creative energy exemplified itself in fashioning useful objects carved or otherwise ornamented beyond the scope of pure practicality. After the advent of the Industrial Revolution, the pace of everyday living became more leisurely, and country folk found they had extra time. Not accustomed to sitting idle, many turned to carving, painting, or weaving. Whirligigs, imaginative toys for the children, and whimsies of all types resulted. Though often rather crude, this type of early art represents a segment of our heritage and as such has become valued by collectors.

Values given for drawings, paintings, and theorems are 'in frame' unless noted otherwise. See also Baskets; Decoys; Frakturs; Samplers; Trade Signs; Weathervanes; Wood Carvings.

Birdhouse, inverted pyramid shape, pnt wood, 1930s, 18x8x8" 85.00
Birdhouse, made from firkin, tin roof, 12¾x8½" 55.00
Calligraphy, bird & flourishes, pen/ink, 9½x12" 245.00
Calligraphy, horse & snake, blk ink on paper, fr, 22x26" 300.00
Calligraphy, lion roaring, brn ink on paper, fr, 19x25" 50.00
Calligraphy, swans/eagle/ABCs, sgn/1800s, 19x23" 375.00
Charcoal drawing, children w/cows, titled, fr, 19x24" 105.00
Charcoal drawing, Cupid w/quiver & flowers, grpt fr, 13x11" 40.00
Cyclist, pnt wood w/tin propellers, mc pnt, 17x29" 550.00
Dancing man, articulated figure, sheet metal, mc pnt, 16" 360.00
Dancing man, pnt tin, attached to iron rod w/wooden hdl, 11" 175.00
Drawing, pencil & watercolor, fruit & foliage, fr, 17x22" 110.00
Figure, dachshund, welded pipes w/worn brn pnt, 1930s, 16" 145.00
Horse, wood & papier-mache, orig palomino pnt, 5" 30.00
Mirror, pine cones & branches on wooden base, 1900s, 25x9" 135.00
Oil on panel, primitive landscape, sgn/1897, fr, 11x16" 250.00
Painting on velvet, hen on nest, sgn/1900s, fr, 14x16" 200.00
Paper cutout, birds/flowers/men on horsebk, OH, 14x12" 300.00
Parrot, wood w/mc pnt, 2 tin paddle wings, 1930s, 22x16x4" 95.00
Pencil drawing on paper, colonial buildings, sgn/1840, 18x21" 525.00
Theorem on cotton, pear in yel/red/gr, stain, fr, 8x5¾" 175.00
Theorem on paper, bird, brn/yel/gr watercolor, fr, 5½x8" 75.00

Theorem on velvet, bowl w/fruit, soft colors, fr, 25x29" 660.00
Theorem on velvet, fruit in flower wreath, fr, 20x20" 500.00
Valentine, watercolor/ink on paper, Am, 1800s, 20x17", EX 500.00
Watercolor on paper, roses & mixed flowers, fr, 12x9½" 85.00
Whirligig, bearded farmer sawing wood, pnt wood, 27x15x9" 135.00
Whirligig, Blk banjo player & jigger, pnt wood & metal, 20" 260.00
Whirligig, Blk man sawing wood, pnt masonite/wood/metal, 20" ...65.00
Whirligig, boy w/cap, pnt wood, tack buttons, 1900s, 19" 1,100.00
Whirligig, flying Canadian goose, pnt wood, tack eyes, 30x22" ..160.00
Whirligig, Mammy churning butter, pnt wood & metal, 15½" 55.00
Whirligig, Mammy hitting man on head, pnt wood, 14½" 170.00
Whirligig, Mammy hitting man over head, crayon on wood, 18" 80.00
Whirligig, man sawing wood, wood & sheet zinc, 1930s, 15x32" ..115.00
Whirligig, man w/oversz waving arms, pnt wood, 1900s, 20", EX ..185.00
Whirligig, soldier, pnt wood, tin belt & sword, 1900s, 16" 1,155.00
Whirligig, woodpecker pecking board, pnt wood, 1930s, 24x15" ..125.00
Yard ornament, couple cutting wood, pnt wood, 1930s, 19x16" .145.00
Yard ornament, crane, wood w/wire legs, 1930s, 36x32x1" 65.00

Fostoria

The Fostoria Glass Company was built in 1887 at Fostoria, Ohio, but by 1891 it had moved to Moundsville, West Virginia. During the next two decades, they produced many lines of pressed patterned tableware and lamps. Their most famous pattern, American, was introduced in 1915 and was produced continuously until 1986 in well over two hundred different pieces. From 1920 to 1925, top artists designed tablewares in colored glass — canary (vaseline), amber, blue, orchid, green, and ebony — in pressed patterns as well as etched designs. By the late thirties, Fostoria was recognized as the largest producer of handmade glassware in the world. The company ceased operations in Moundsville in 1986.

Many items from both the American and Coin Glass lines are currently being reproduced by Lancaster Colony. In some cases the new glass is superior in quality to the old. Since the 1950s, Indiana Glass has produced a pattern called 'Whitehall' that looks very much like Fostoria's American, though with slight variations. Because Indiana's is not handmade glass, the lines of the 'cube' pattern and the edges of the items are sharp and untapered in comparison to the fire-polished originals. Three-footed pieces lack the 'toe' and instead have a peg-like foot, and the rays on the bottoms of the American examples are narrower than on the Whitehall counterparts. The Home Interiors Company currently offer several pieces of American look-alikes which were not even produced in the United States. Be sure of your dealer and study the books suggested below to become more familiar with the original line.

Coin Glass reproductions are flooding the market. Among items you may encounter are an 8" round bowl, 9" oval bowl, 8¼" wedding bowl, 4½" candlesticks, urn with lid, 6¼" candy jar with lid, footed comport, sugar and creamer; there could possibly be others. Colors in production are crystal, green, blue, and red. The red color is very good, but the blue is not the original color, nor is the emerald green. Buyer beware!

For further information see *Elegant Glassware of the Depression Era* by Gene Florence; *Fostoria, the Popular Years, Third Edition Price Guide*, by Jo Ann Schliesman; and *Fostoria, an Identification and Value Guide of Pressed, Blown & Hand Molded Shapes* by Ann Kerr. *Glass Animals and Figural Flower Frogs of the Depression Era* by Lee Garmon and Dick Spencer offers an in-depth look at that particular aspect of Fostoria's production. (See also Glass Animals.) Their addresses are listed in the Directory under Illinois. Items with (+) at the end of the lines are currently being reproduced; prices are for original issues.

Alexis, crystal; butter dish, w/lid 55.00
Alexis, crystal; nappy, 8" 13.00
Alexis, crystal; toothpick holder 18.00

Allegro, crystal w/gold band; goblet, #2, 11-oz, 8¼" 14.00
Ambassador, crystal w/gold band; goblet, #2, 11-oz, 6⅛" 15.00
Ambassador, crystal w/gold band; tumbler, wine; #21, 4-oz, 4⅝" ..14.00
American, crystal; almond, oval, 2¾" 15.00
American, crystal; appetizer tray, sq 27.50
American, crystal; ashtray, oval, 5½" 27.50
American, crystal; boat, 12" 30.00
American, crystal; bottle, water 375.00
American, crystal; bowl, banana split 350.00
American, crystal; bowl, ftd, sq, 7" 100.00
American, crystal; bowl, punch; low ft, 18" 300.00
American, crystal; bowl, watercress 33.00
American, crystal; box, cigarette; w/lid 35.00
American, crystal; butter dish, oblong, w/lid 35.00
American, crystal; candlesticks, 6", pr 60.00
American, crystal; comport, 8½" 45.00
American, crystal; cup, ftd 7.00
American, crystal; finger bowl, w/underplate 70.00
American, crystal; ladle 16.00
American, crystal; napkin ring, 2" 7.00
American, crystal; olive dish, 6" 15.00
American, crystal; plate, dinner; 9⅓" 20.00
American, crystal; pretzel jar 250.00
American, crystal; relish, 3-part 50.00
American, crystal; rose bowl, 5" 33.00
American, crystal; spoon 35.00
American, crystal; sundae, 6-oz 13.00
American, crystal; toothpick holder 25.00
American, crystal; tumbler, wine; 2½-oz 15.00
American, crystal; vase, str, 12" 125.00

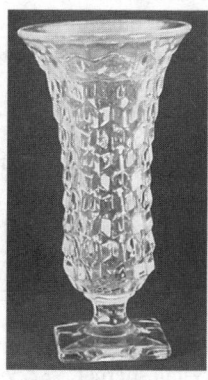

American, crystal, vase, flared, 10", $85.00.

American Lady, crystal; finger bowl, #495 ....8.00
American Lady, crystal; plate, #549, 7" 8.00
Andover, crystal; goblet, #2, 10-oz, 6⅝" 15.00
Andover, crystal; tumbler, juice; #88, 5-oz, 4⅝" 15.00
Anniversary, crystal; goblet, #2, 10-oz, 6⅛" 15.00
Anniversary, crystal; plate, #549, 7" 8.00
Announcement, crystal; creamer, #681, ftd 10.00
Announcement, crystal; tumbler, brandy; #31, 3½-oz, 3⅞" 15.00
Argus, crystal; creamer, 6" 15.00
Argus, crystal; plate, dessert; #330, 8" 8.00
Astrid, crystal; cordial, #29, 1-oz, 1⅞" 18.50
Astrid, crystal; plate, #549, 7" 8.00
Aurora, crystal; plate, #550, 8" 8.00
Aurora, crystal; wine/cocktail, #27, 4-oz, 5¼" 15.00
Baroque, bl; bonbon, #137, 3-toed, 7⅜" 30.00
Baroque, bl; candlesticks, #315, 4", pr 60.00
Baroque, bl; floating garden, 10" 90.00
Baroque, bl; plate, #552, 9" 66.00

Baroque, crystal; celery, 11" 20.00
Baroque, crystal; comport, 6½" 24.00
Baroque, crystal; jelly jar, w/lid 33.00
Baroque, crystal; mint dish, hdld 25.00
Baroque, crystal; punch cup 10.00
Baroque, topaz; bowl, hdld, 10" 42.00
Baroque, topaz; cocktail, ftd 25.00
Baroque, topaz; sweetmeat 41.00
Bedford, crystal; bonbon, 6" 10.00
Bedford, crystal; bottle, water 65.00
Bedford, crystal; bowl, Royal Berry, 8" 20.00
Bedford, crystal; claret 18.00
Bedford, crystal; creamer 22.00
Bedford, crystal; goblet 15.00
Bedford, crystal; mug 20.00
Bedford, crystal; salt cellar, oval 10.00
Bedford, crystal; syrup 35.00
Bedford, crystal; whiskey jug & stopper 70.00
Beloved, crystal; goblet, #2, 11½-oz, 6⅜" 14.00
Beloved, crystal; plate, #549, 7" 8.00
Beloved, crystal; relish, #643, 4-part 17.00
Berkshire, crystal; bowl, dessert; #495 ....8.00
Berkshire, crystal; sherbet, #11, 9-oz, 5¾" 10.00
Berkshire, crystal; wine, #26, 6-oz, 5¾" 12.00
Betrothal, crystal; goblet, #2, 11-oz, 8¼" 15.00
Betrothal, crystal; liqueur, 2-oz, 4¼" 12.00
Biscayne, crystal; goblet, #2, 11-oz, 6⅜" 12.00
Biscayne, crystal; highball, #64, 14-oz, 4¾" 10.00
Bracelet, crystal; cordial, #29, 2-oz, 3⅜" 15.00
Brazilian, crystal; bottle, water 70.00
Brazilian, crystal; bowl, oblong, 9" 18.00
Brazilian, crystal; creamer 25.00
Brazilian, crystal; olive dish, hdld 15.00
Brazilian, crystal; spooner 27.50
Brazilian, crystal; tankard 100.00
Brazilian, crystal; vase, 11" 50.00
Brilliant, crystal; bowl, berry; 7" 18.00
Brilliant, crystal; butter dish, w/lid 50.00
Brilliant, crystal; creamer 22.00
Brilliant, crystal; pickle dish 15.00
Brilliant, crystal; pitcher 75.00
Brilliant, crystal; spoon 15.00
Brilliant, crystal; tumbler 15.00
Brocade, crystal; claret, #25, 8-oz, 5¾" 13.00
Brocade, crystal; sherbet, #22, 9-oz, 5⅝" 8.00
Camelot, crystal; champagne/dessert, #11, 9-oz, 6⅜" 10.00
Camelot, crystal; magnum, #35, 16-oz, 7¾" 20.00
Candlelight, crystal; cordial, #29, 1-oz, 3½" 18.00
Candlelight, crystal; plate, #549, 7" 8.00
Capri, crystal; cordial, #29, 1½-oz, 2⅝" 12.00
Capri, crystal; plate, #549, 7" 8.00
Capri, crystal; tumbler, juice; #88, ftd, 7¼-oz, 4⅝" 8.00
Caribbean, crystal; candle holder, #318, 5½" 13.00
Caribbean, crystal; sherbet, #12, 8-oz, 5⅛" 9.00
Cascade, crystal; goblet, #2, 9¾-oz, 7" 18.00
Cascade, crystal; tumbler, juice; ftd, 5½-oz, 4⅞" 16.00
Celebrity, crystal; goblet, #2, 12-oz, 7" 10.00
Celebrity, crystal; plate, #550, 8" 8.00
Celebrity, crystal; sherbet, #11, 9-oz, 5¾" 6.00
Celebrity, crystal; tumbler, juice; #88, ftd, 5-oz, 4⅝" ...12.00
Cellini, crystal; cordial, #29, 1-oz, 3¾" 20.00
Century, crystal; basket, w/reed hdl, 10½" 90.00
Century, crystal; bowl, #249, flared, 12" 43.00
Century, crystal; bowl, fruit; #421, 5" 15.00

Century, crystal; candy jar, #351, 4¾" 35.00
Century, crystal; cocktail, #20, 3½-oz, 4⅛" 18.00
Century, crystal; condiment set, #686 ....130.00
Century, crystal; creamer, #688, ind, 3½" 8.00
Century, crystal; cruet, #528, 5-oz, 6" 45.00
Century, crystal; cup, #396, ftd 12.50
Century, crystal; lily pond, #237, 11¼" 60.00
Century, crystal; plate, #548, 6" 10.00
Century, crystal; plate, cake; #306, 9½" 45.00
Century, crystal; plate, party; 8" 25.00
Century, crystal; plate, torte; #573, 16" 35.00
Century, crystal; platter, #560, oval, 12" 44.00
Century, crystal; saucer, #397 ....3.00
Century, crystal; shakers, #654, 3¼", pr 20.00
Century, crystal; tray, snack; #729, 10½" 25.00
Century, crystal; tumbler, ftd, 5-oz, 4¾" 18.00
Century, crystal; vase, hdl, 7½" 100.00
Chalice, crystal; tumbler, juice; ftd, 5½-oz, 4½" 9.00
Chalice, crystal; wine/cocktail, 4½-oz, 3¾" 8.00
Chateau, crystal; plate, #549, 7" 8.00
Chateau, crystal; tumbler, juice; ftd, 5-oz, 5" 9.00
Cherish, crystal; brandy, #31, 4½-oz 15.00
Cherish, crystal; tulip wine, #26, 7-oz, 6⅜" 13.00
Classic Gold, crystal; plate, #549, 7" 8.00
Coin, crystal; ashtray, #114, rnd, 7½" 22.00
Coin, crystal; ashtray, #123, 1-coin, 5" 12.00
Coin, crystal; bowl, #189, oval, 9" 36.00
Coin, crystal; bowl, nappy; #499, hdld, 5⅜" 35.00
Coin, crystal; bowl, wedding; #162, w/lid, 8¼" 50.00
Coin, crystal; candle holders, #316, 4½", pr 42.00
Coin, crystal; candlestick, #326, 8" 25.00
Coin, crystal; candy box, #354, w/lid, 6⅜" 35.00
Coin, crystal; cigarette holder & ashtray, w/lid 25.00
Coin, crystal; compote, #199, ftd, 8½" 43.00
Coin, crystal; creamer, #680, 3½" 16.00
Coin, crystal; cruet, #531, w/stopper, 7-oz 35.00
Coin, crystal; decanter, #400, w/stopper 90.00
Coin, crystal; goblet, #2, 10½" 27.00
Coin, crystal; iced tea, #58, 14-oz 28.00
Coin, crystal; jelly jar, #448, ftd, 3¾" 16.00
Coin, crystal; lamp, oil; #310, 9¾" 90.00
Coin, crystal; plate, #550, 8" 18.00
Coin, crystal; punch bowl, #600, 1½-gal, 14" 250.00
Coin, crystal; punch bowl, #602, ftd, 14" 75.00
Coin, crystal; salver, #630, 10" 80.00
Coin, crystal; shaker, #652, chrome top, 3¼", ea 25.00
Coin, crystal; sherbet, #7, 9-oz, 5⅝" 17.50
Coin, crystal; sugar bowl, #673, w/lid, 5⅜" 25.00
Coin, crystal; tumbler, juice; #81, 9-oz, 3⅝" 27.00
Coin, crystal; tumbler, water; #73, 9-oz, 4¼" 30.00
Coin, crystal; urn, #829, ftd, w/lid, 12¾" 68.00
Coin, crystal; wine, #26, 5-oz, 5¼" 35.00
Coin, emerald gr, red or bl; ashtray, #119, center coin, 7½" 66.00
Coin, emerald gr, red or bl; bowl, 8" 135.00
Coin, emerald gr, red or bl; cigarette urn, #374, w/lid, 5¾" 90.00
Coin, emerald gr, red or bl; dbl old-fashioned, #23 ....20.00
Coin, emerald gr, red or bl; punch cup, #615, 3½" 40.00
Coin, emerald gr, red or bl; vase, bud; #799, 8" 45.00
Coin, olive gr or amber; ashtray, #115, oblong, 3x4" 16.00
Coin, olive gr or amber; ashtray, 10" 33.00
Coin, olive gr or amber; bowl, nappy; 4½" 40.00
Coin, olive gr or amber; candy jar, #347, w/lid, 6⅜" 40.00
Coin, olive gr or amber; condiment tray, #738, 9" 35.00
Coin, olive gr or amber; pitcher, #453, 1-qt, 6⅝" 88.00

Coin, olive gr or amber; tumbler, iced tea; #64, 12-oz, 5⅛" 50.00
Colfax, crystal; bowl, dessert/finger; #495 ....8.00
Colfax, crystal; champagne, 6-oz, 4⅞" 14.00
Colonial Dame, crystal; cordial, #29, 1-oz, 3¼" 15.00
Colonial Dame, crystal; oyster cocktail, #33, 4½-oz, 3⅞" 8.00
Colonial Dame, crystal; plate, #550, 8" 8.00
Colonial Prism, crystal; boat, 11" 14.00
Colonial Prism, crystal; bowl, fruit salad 30.00
Colonial Prism, crystal; butter dish, w/lid 40.00
Colonial Prism, crystal; celery tray, 12" 15.00
Colonial Prism, crystal; creamer, hotel sz 14.00
Colonial Prism, crystal; dish, oval, 10½" 14.00
Colonial Prism, crystal; jar, ftd, w/lid 28.00
Colonial Prism, crystal; nappy, 6" 7.50
Colonial Prism, crystal; pickle jar, w/lid 28.00
Colonial Prism, crystal; toothpick holder 17.50
Colonial Prism, crystal; vase, 12" 14.00
Colony, crystal; ashtray, rnd, 3" 11.00
Colony, crystal; bonbon, #135, 5" 13.00
Colony, crystal; bowl, flared, 11" 43.00
Colony, crystal; bowl, vegetable; #836, oval, 10½" 48.00
Colony, crystal; cake salver, #630, 12" 45.00
Colony, crystal; celery, 10½" 25.00
Colony, crystal; cracker plate, 12½" 20.00
Colony, crystal; finger bowl 12.00
Colony, crystal; lemon dish, 6½" 35.00
Colony, crystal; pitcher, ice; 2-qt, 7¾" 85.00
Colony, crystal; plate, torte; #563, 13" 33.00
Colony, crystal; rose bowl, 6" 48.00
Colony, crystal; sweetmeat, hdld, 5" 13.00
Colony, crystal; urn, ftd, w/lid 50.00
Continental, crystal; cordial, #29, 1¼-oz, 3⅛" 15.00
Continental, crystal; plate, #550, 8" 8.00
Continental, crystal; tumbler, iced tea; #60, 13-oz, 9⅛" 9.00
Contour #2638, crystal; ashtray, #116, 1-lip, 3" 6.00
Contour #2638, crystal; bowl, #152, 5½" 8.00
Contour #2638, crystal; tray, #720, 7" 10.00
Contour #2666, crystal; bonbon, #136, 6⅞" 12.00
Contour #2666, crystal; celery, #360, 9" 14.00
Contour #2666, crystal; mayonnaise ladle 12.00
Contour #2666, crystal; plate, #549, 7" 7.00
Contour #2666, crystal; plate, canape; #309, 7⅜" 10.00
Contour #2666, crystal; saucer, #397 ....4.00
Coventry, crystal; bonbon, #135 ....11.00
Coventry, crystal; creamer, #680, 3⅞" 10.00
Coventry, crystal; pickle dish, #540 ....10.00
Daisy & Button, crystal; butter dish, #300, w/lid, 9½" 25.00
Daisy & Button, crystal; nappy, hdld, sq, 4¾" 10.00
Dawn, crystal; bowl, dessert; #495, 6-oz, 1⅞" 5.00
Dawn, crystal; tumbler, juice; #89, 5-oz, 3½" 4.00
Decorator, crystal; ashtray, ind, 2⅝" 3.00
Decorator, crystal; creamer, 3¼" 10.00
Decorator, crystal; saucer, regular 4.00
Decorator, crystal; sugar bowl, w/lid, 3¼" 12.00
Diana, crystal; bowl, berry; 4½" 7.00
Diana, crystal; celery 18.50
Diana, crystal; salver, 9" 32.50
Diana, crystal; syrup 27.50
Drape, crystal; bonbon, hdld 10.00
Drape, crystal; butter dish, w/lid 56.00
Drape, crystal; comport, 10" 24.00
Drape, crystal; creamer 22.00
Drape, crystal; plate, 9" 8.00
Drape, crystal; tumbler 16.00

Edgewood, crystal; bowl, berry; 4½" 12.50
Edgewood, crystal; custard 8.00
Edgewood, crystal; pickle jar, w/lid 33.00
Edgewood, crystal; tankard 95.00
Embassy, crystal; goblet, #2, 11½-oz, 6¼" 7.50
Enchantment, crystal; plate, #549, 7" 8.00
Envoy, crystal; sherbet, 5½-oz, 3¼" 7.00
Essex, crystal; cabaret, 10" 10.00
Essex, crystal; cordial 12.00
Essex, crystal; pickle dish 15.00
Essex, crystal; sugar shaker 15.00
Fairfax, crystal; bouillon 10.00
Fairfax, crystal; candlesticks, 3", pr 20.00
Fairfax, crystal; cracker plate 8.00
Fairfax, crystal; ice bucket 35.00
Fairfax, crystal; platter, oval, 15" 40.00
Fairmont, crystal; pickle dish, #540, 7¾" 7.00
Fairmont, crystal; sherbet, #7, 6-oz, 4⅜" 6.00
Flame, crystal; bowl, oval, 12½" 30.00
Flame, crystal; candlesticks, 4½", pr 30.00
Flame, crystal; sauce boat tray 12.00
Flemish, crystal; basket, 11" 50.00
Flemish, crystal; bowl, jelly; w/lid 30.00
Flemish, crystal; molasses can 30.00
Flemish, crystal; sherbet, med 7.00
Flemish, crystal; vase, 10" 15.00
Frisco, crystal; bowl, 7" 16.50
Frisco, crystal; comport, 6" 8.00
Frisco, crystal; spooner 28.00
Glacier, crystal; bonbon, hdld 10.00
Glacier, crystal; bowl, cream soup; w/underliner 20.00
Glacier, crystal; mustard jar, w/lid & spoon 22.00
Glacier, crystal; plate, flat, 16" 35.00
Glacier, crystal; shakers, pr 16.00
Glacier, crystal; tray, sq, 10" 22.00
Golden Belle, crystal; relish, #620, 2-part 8.00
Grape Leaf, crystal; almond, ind 5.00
Grape Leaf, crystal; mint dish, hdld, 4" 10.00
Halo, crystal; goblet, #2, 11-oz 14.00
Hartford, crystal; bowl, oblong, 8" 19.00
Hartford, crystal; comport, 8" 35.00
Hartford, crystal; spooner 29.00
Heritage, crystal; coaster, utility; #380 ....4.00
Heritage, crystal; pastry server, #733 ....16.00
Hermitage, crystal; beer mug, ftd, 9-oz 30.00
Hermitage, crystal; bowl, cereal; 6" 12.00
Hermitage, crystal; decanter, w/stopper 60.00
Hermitage, crystal; plate, luncheon; 8" 15.00
Horizon, crystal; coaster 5.00
Horizon, crystal; mayonnaise, w/plate & ladle 25.00
Illusion, crystal; bowl, dessert; #495 ....8.00

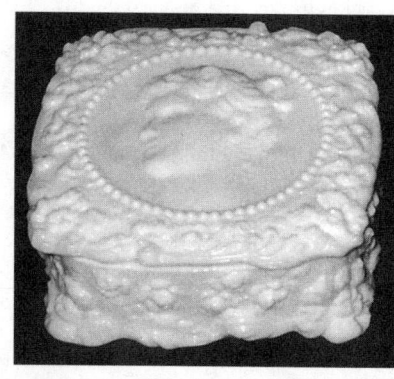

Jenny Lind, milk glass, handkerchief box, 5¼" square, $68.00.

Jamestown, crystal; bowl, serving; #648 ....30.00
Jamestown, crystal; creamer, #681, ftd, 4" 12.00
Jamestown, crystal; muffin tray, hdld, 9⅜" 30.00
Jamestown, crystal; salver, #630, rnd, 10" 35.00
Jamestown, crystal; tumbler, water; #73, 9-oz, 4¼" 12.00
Kent, crystal; ashtray 6.00
Kent, crystal; plate, 12" 18.00
Kent, crystal; urn, ftd, 7½" 23.00
Lafayette, crystal; baker, oval, 10" 12.00
Lafayette, crystal; bowl, cereal; 6" 8.00
Lafayette, crystal; olive dish, 6½" 11.00
Lafayette, crystal; platter, 12" 22.00
Lafayette, crystal; vase, 7" 14.00
Lincoln, crystal; catsup, w/ground stopper 38.00
Lincoln, crystal; comport, w/lid, deep, 8" 40.00
Lincoln, crystal; custard 7.50
Lincoln, crystal; nut bowl 8.00
Lincoln, crystal; salver, 10" 40.00
Lincoln, crystal; sugar sifter 23.00
Louise, crystal; butter dish, w/lid 65.00
Louise, crystal; celery 30.00
Louise, crystal; nappy, 8" 10.00
Louise, crystal; pitcher, ½-gal 65.00
Louise, crystal; spoon 25.00
Lucere, crystal; berry saucer, 4½" 3.00
Lucere, crystal; bowl, fruit 14.00
Lucere, crystal; celery tray 15.00
Lucere, crystal; cordial 10.00
Lucere, crystal; creamer 20.00
Lucere, crystal; plate, 8½" 8.00
Lucere, crystal; sundae 6.00
Lucere, crystal; vase, 12" 35.00
Mademoiselle, crystal; cordial, #29, 1-oz, 3⅝" 15.00
Mantilla, crystal; plate, #550, 8" 8.00
Mayfair, crystal; bonbon, hdls 12.50
Mayfair, crystal; condiment tray 28.00
Mayfair, crystal; creamer, ftd 13.00
Mayfair, crystal; plate, bread & butter; 6" 7.00
Maypole, crystal; bowl, #195, 9" 30.00
Mesa, crystal; coaster, #380, 3⅝" 3.00
Mesa, crystal; creamer, #680, 4½" 7.00
Mesa, crystal; tumbler, juice; #84, 7-oz, 4¼" 6.00
Moonstone, crystal; tumbler, #64 ....6.00
Myriad, crystal; ashtray, oblong, 4" 10.00
Myriad, crystal; bowl, fruit; 11" 25.00
Myriad, crystal; lily pond, 10½" 18.00
Niagara, crystal; bowl, berry; 8" 19.00
Niagara, crystal; jug/tankard 100.00
Niagara, crystal; spooner 25.00
Old English, crystal; bouquet holder, 9" 30.00
Old English, crystal; comport, 4½" 6.00
Old English, crystal; custard 8.00
Old English, crystal; molasses can 35.00
Old English, crystal; pickle dish 15.00
Old English, crystal; sundae 6.00
Orleans, crystal; brandy, #31, 1½-oz, 4⅛" 12.50
Orleans, crystal; plate, #549, 7" 5.00
Pebble Beach, crystal; bowl, dessert; #421, 4¾" 6.00
Pebble Beach, crystal; creamer, #680, 3¼" 4.00
Pebble Beach, crystal; cup, punch; #615, 6½" 35.00
Pebble Beach, crystal; plate, cake; 11" 6.50
Pebble Beach, crystal; tumbler, iced tea; #58, 14-oz, 5¾" 4.50
Pioneer, crystal; ashtray, sm 5.00
Pioneer, crystal; bowl, cereal; 6" 9.00

Pioneer, crystal; cup 5.00
Pioneer, crystal; plate, chop; 13" 25.00
President's House, crystal; cordial, 1½" 16.00
President's House, crystal; wine, #28, 8-oz, 5¾" 12.00
Pressed Glass, crystal; bowl, berry; 8" 22.50
Pressed Glass, crystal; creamer 10.00
Pressed Glass, crystal; tankard 105.00
Princess, crystal; plate, #549, 7" 5.00
Priscilla, crystal; plate, #549, 8" 5.00
Promise, crystal; goblet, #2, 11-oz, 7¾" 12.50
Promise, crystal; wine, #26, 7-oz, 6⅜" 11.00
Puritan, crystal; creamer, hotel style 14.00
Puritan, crystal; finger bowl 6.00
Puritan, crystal; tumbler 7.00
Queen Anne, crystal; bowl, centerpiece; 9" 50.00
Queen Anne, crystal; bowl, oblong, 13" 85.00
Queen Anne, crystal; mint dish 20.00
Radiance, crystal; bowl, salad; 12" 14.00
Radiance, crystal; creamer, 3¼" 5.00
Radiance, crystal; platter, 15" 16.00
Radiance, crystal; sugar bowl, 2¾" 6.00
Raleigh, crystal; bonbon 13.00
Raleigh, crystal; bowl, fruit; 13" 19.00
Raleigh, crystal; bowl, serving; hdls, 8½" 15.00
Raleigh, crystal; comport, 5" 9.00
Raleigh, crystal; lemon dish 12.00
Raleigh, crystal; plate, cake; #306, 10" 14.00
Raleigh, crystal; sweetmeat 7.00
Rambler, crystal; bowl, berry; 4½" 9.00
Rambler, crystal; custard 9.00
Rambler, crystal; nappy, 10" 20.00
Rambler, crystal; vase, 13" 30.00
Reception, crystal; creamer, #581, ftd 7.00
Reception, crystal; relish tray, #620, 2-part 8.00
Reception, crystal; sherbet, #11, 7-oz 10.00
Reflection, crystal; candlesticks, #315, 4", pr 18.00
Reflection, crystal; creamer, #680 ....7.00
Reflection, crystal; saucer, #397 ....3.00
Reflection, crystal; tumbler, juice; #88, ftd, 5-oz 10.00
Regal, crystal; celery tray 13.00
Regal, crystal; custard 7.00
Regal, crystal; mint dish, ftd 10.00
Regal, crystal; sweetmeat 8.00
Regal, crystal; water bottle 25.00
Rehearsal, crystal; bowl, #224, ftd, 10" 10.00
Rehearsal, crystal; creamer, #681, ftd 7.00
Rhapsody, crystal; bowl, dessert; #495 ....6.00
Rhapsody, crystal; tumbler, juice; #88, 5½-oz, 4⅞" 8.00
Ringlet, crystal; cocktail, #20, 3¼-oz, 3⅞" 7.50
Ringlet, crystal; plate, #550, 8" 6.00
Robin Hood Ware, crystal; bowl, berry; 6" 21.00
Robin Hood Ware, crystal; creamer 20.00
Robin Hood Ware, crystal; cruet, oil 30.00
Rosby, crystal; bowl, 7½" 10.00
Rosby, crystal; creamer 17.50
Rosby, crystal; pickle dish, 8" 10.00
Rosby, crystal; plate, serving; 10" 26.00
Rosby, crystal; punch bowl, ftd, 16" 395.00
Rutledge, crystal; cordial, #29, 1-oz, 3¼" 13.00
Rutledge, crystal; parfait, #18, 5½-oz, 5⅞" 10.00
Seascape, crystal; bowl, salad; 10" 45.00
Seascape, crystal; bowl, 11½" 42.00
Seascape, crystal; bowl, 8" 28.00
Seascape, crystal; plate, buffet; 14" 55.00

Seascape, crystal; salver, 12" 45.00

Seascape, crystal; tray, mint; 7½" 25.00

Sheffield, crystal; bowl, #224, 10" 17.00

Sheffield, crystal; creamer, #680 ....7.00

Sheffield, crystal; cup, #396 ....6.00

Sheffield, crystal; saucer, #397 ....3.00

Sheffield, crystal; tumbler, juice; ftd, 5-oz 14.00

Shell Pearl, crystal; bowl, #189, oval 8.00

Shell Pearl, crystal; creamer, #680 ....8.00

Shell Pearl, crystal; goblet, #2, 10-oz 20.00

Shell Pearl, crystal; plate, serving; #568, 14" 18.00

Sheraton, crystal; cordial, #29, 1-oz, 3⅝" 25.00

Sheraton, crystal; plate, #549, 7" 5.00

Silhouette, crystal; goblet, #24, lg, 11-oz, 8" 18.00

Silver Flutes, crystal; cocktail, #21, 4-oz, 5" 10.00

Silver Flutes, crystal; goblet, #3, 9-oz, 6⅜" 12.00

Silver Flutes, crystal; parfait, #18, 6-oz, 6⅛" 13.00

Simplicity, crystal; bowl, salad; #221, 10½" 12.00

Simplicity, crystal; candlesticks, #315, 4", pr 18.00

Simplicity, crystal; creamer, #679, ftd 5.00

Simplicity, crystal; tumbler, iced tea; #63, ftd, 12-oz 14.00

Sonata, crystal; bowl, #249, flared, 12" 15.00

Sonata, crystal; celery tray, 11" 12.00

Sonata, crystal; pickle dish, 8" 8.00

Sonata, crystal; plate, cracker 14.00

Sonata, crystal; plate, sandwich; #557, 11" 17.00

Sorrento, crystal; goblet, #2, 9-oz, 6" 11.00

Sorrento, crystal; plate, #550, 8" 6.00

Sorrento, crystal; sherbet, #7, 6½-oz, 3⅝" 7.00

Splendor, crystal; goblet, #2, 10½-oz, 5⅞" 15.00

Splendor, crystal; plate, #550, 8" 6.00

Spool, crystal; ashtray, ind, 3⅛" 4.50

Spool, crystal; bowl, centerpiece 15.00

Spool, crystal; bowl, oval, 11" 30.00

Sun-Ray, crystal; ashtray, sq 5.00

Sun-Ray, crystal; bonbon, 3-toed 11.00

Sun-Ray, crystal; bowl, fruit; 5" 6.00

Sun-Ray, crystal; candlesticks, 3", pr 25.00

Sun-Ray, crystal; coaster 5.00

Sun-Ray, crystal; decanter, w/stopper, 18-oz 30.00

Sun-Ray, crystal; mustard jar, w/lid & spoon 28.00

Sun-Ray, crystal; pitcher, 1-pt 32.00

Sun-Ray, crystal; plate, torte; 11" 25.00

Sun-Ray, crystal; salt cellar 6.00

Sun-Ray, crystal; tray, hdld, oval 16.00

Sun-Ray, crystal; vase, 7" 15.00

Sydney, crystal; bowl, ice cream 8.00

Sydney, crystal; butter dish, w/lid 35.00

Sydney, crystal; comport, 4½" 8.00

Sydney, crystal; creamer 16.00

Sydney, crystal; pickle dish, 7" 14.00

Sydney, crystal; shaker, blown, ea 12.00

Sylvan, crystal; butter dish, w/lid 57.50

Sylvan, crystal; celery tray 20.00

Sylvan, crystal; finger bowl 13.00

Sylvan, crystal; olive tray, sq or tricornered, ea 8.00

Sylvan, crystal; punch bowl 40.00

Tea Room, crystal; coaster 5.00

Tea Room, crystal; creamer, ind 9.00

Tea Room, crystal; cruet, oil; 6-oz 43.00

Tea Room, crystal; goblet 15.00

Tea Room, crystal; parfait, 5-oz 15.00

Tea Room, crystal; tumbler, 8-oz 11.00

Trousseau, crystal; creamer, #679, ftd 8.00

Tuxedo, crystal; banana jar 20.00

Tuxedo, crystal; bonbon, ftd 10.00

Tuxedo, crystal; bowl, crushed fruit; w/lid 35.00

Tuxedo, crystal; bowl, nut; ftd 15.00

Tuxedo, crystal; comport, 8" 20.00

Tuxedo, crystal; olive dish 12.00

Tuxedo, crystal; spoon, crushed fruit 20.00

Tuxedo, crystal; straw jar 85.00

Tuxedo, crystal; tankard, ½-gal 110.00

Valencia, crystal; bowl, nut 15.00

Valencia, crystal; bowl, 8" 17.00

Valencia, crystal; cruet set 75.00

Valencia, crystal; molasses can 65.00

Valencia, crystal; tumbler 15.00

Vermeil, crystal; creamer, #681, ftd 10.00

Verona, crystal; bowl, w/lid, 8" 30.00

Verona, crystal; bowl, 6" 12.00

Verona, crystal; butter dish, w/lid 35.00

Verona, crystal; comport, open, 8" 16.00

Verona, crystal; custard, hdld 6.00

Verona, crystal; goblet 14.00

Verona, crystal; molasses can 40.00

Verona, crystal; salver, 8" 25.00

Verona, crystal; tumbler 15.00

Versailles, crystal; goblet, #2, 14-oz, 6⅞" 16.00

Vesper, crystal; tumbler, iced tea; #63, ftd, 13-oz, 6¼" 12.00

Victoria, crystal; bowl, 8" 30.00

Victoria, crystal; butter dish, w/lid 100.00

Victoria, crystal; celery tray 27.00

Victoria, crystal; cocktail, 4-oz 10.00

Victoria, crystal; creamer 35.00

Victoria, crystal; custard plate 6.00

Victoria, crystal; nappy, 10" 30.00

Victoria, crystal; pickle castor 130.00

Victoria, crystal; saucer, ice cream 12.50

Victoria, crystal; shot glass 100.00

Virginia, crystal; bonbon, sq 8.00

Virginia, crystal; bottle, water 65.00

Virginia, crystal; bowl, jelly 10.00

Virginia, crystal; butter dish, w/lid 50.00

Virginia, crystal; candlesticks, #319, 6", pr 20.00

Virginia, crystal; comport, #171, ftd 15.00

Virginia, crystal; comport, 9" 18.00

Virginia, crystal; finger bowl 10.00

Virginia, crystal; nappy, 9" 16.00

Virginia, crystal; pitcher, ½-gal 65.00

Virginia, crystal; plate, 10" 8.00

Virginia, crystal; salver, 11" 30.00

Vogue, crystal; ashtray 8.00

Vogue, crystal; banana split dish, ftd 10.00

Vogue, crystal; bowl, nut; sq, 4½" 8.00

Vogue, crystal; bowl, oval 8" 12.00

Vogue, crystal; bowl, sauce 8.00

Vogue, crystal; box, cigarette; w/lid, lg 25.00

Vogue, crystal; celery tray 10.00

Vogue, crystal; creamer 10.00

Vogue, crystal; honey jar 15.00

Vogue, crystal; lemon dish, w/lid 18.00

Vogue, crystal; mug 8.00

Vogue, crystal; nappy, 8¾" 10.00

Vogue, crystal; pickle dish, 8" 12.00

Vogue, crystal; pitcher, qt 20.00

Vogue, crystal; sauce ladle 15.00

Vogue, crystal; spoon 15.00

Vogue, crystal; tray, buffet 10.00
Vogue, crystal; tub, sm 8.00
Vogue, crystal; vase, 9" 13.00
Wedding Bells, crystal; bottle, water 70.00
Wedding Bells, crystal; bowl, berry; 7" 25.00
Wedding Bells, crystal; butter dish, w/lid 88.00
Wedding Bells, crystal; custard 12.50
Wedding Bells, crystal; decanter, 1-qt 120.00
Wedding Bells, crystal; punch bowl 200.00
Wedding Bells, crystal; spooner 30.00
Wedding Bells, crystal; tankard 105.00
Wedding Ring, crystal; bowl, salad; #2364/195, 9" 20.00
Wedding Ring, crystal; candlesticks, #2324/315, 4", pr 22.00
Wedding Ring, crystal; cup, #2666/396 ....7.50
Westchester, crystal; goblet, #2, 10-oz, 6⅞" 15.00
Westchester, crystal; plate, #550, 8" 6.00
Wilma, crystal; claret, #27, 6½-oz, 6½" 14.00
Wilma, crystal; tumbler, juice; #88, ftd, 5-oz, 4⅝" 12.00

Windsor Crown, gold, scarce, $125.00; crystal, perfume with stopper, 4¾", $75.00.

Windsor, crystal; bowl, dessert; #485 ....6.00
Windsor, crystal; cocktail, #21, 4-oz, 4⅞" 7.00
Windsor, crystal; parfait, #18, 6¾-oz, 6" 8.50
Windsor, crystal; tumbler, iced tea; ftd, 15½-oz, 6¼" 10.00
Wistar, crystal; bonbon, 3-toed 12.50
Wistar, crystal; bowl, fruit; 13" 19.00
Wistar, crystal; bowl, nut; 3-toed 16.00
Wistar, crystal; bowl, salad; 10" 21.00
Wistar, crystal; creamer, ftd 12.00
Wistar, crystal; mayonnaise, w/plate & ladle 27.00
Wistar, crystal; plate, torte; 14" 17.50
Woodland, crystal; bowl, #517, 7" 12.00
Woodland, crystal; jelly jar, #448, ftd 10.00
Woodland, crystal; plate, serving; 10" 10.00
Woodland, crystal; vase, bud 10.00
York, crystal; bowl, berry; 4½" 5.00
York, crystal; butter dish, w/lid 55.00
York, crystal; creamer 22.50
York, crystal; custard 8.00
York, crystal; spoon 25.00

Frakturs

Fraktur is a German style of black letter text type. To collectors the fraktur is a type of hand-lettered document used by the people of German descent who settled in the areas of Pennsylvania, New Jersey, Maryland, Virginia, North and South Carolina, Ohio, Kentucky, and Ontario. These documents recorded births and baptisms and were used as bookplates and as certificates of honor. They were elaborately deco-

rated with colorful folk-art borders of hearts, birds, angels, and flowers. Examples by recognized artists and those with an unusual decorative motif bring prices well into the thousands of dollars, in fact, some have sold at major auction houses in excess of $5,000.00. Frakturs made in the late 1700s after the invention of the printing press provided the writer with a prepared text that he needed only to fill in at his own discretion. The next step in the evolution of machine-printed frakturs combined woodblock-printed decorations along with the text which the 'artist' sometimes enhanced with color. By the mid-1800s, even the coloring was done by machine. The vorschrift was a handwritten example prepared by a fraktur teacher to demonstrate his skill in lettering and decorating. These are often considered to be the finest of frakturs. Those dated before 1820 are most valuable.

The practice of fraktur art began to diminish after 1830 but hung on even to the early years of this century among the Pennsylvania Germans ingrained with such customs. Our advisor for this category is Frederick S. Weiser; he is listed in the Directory under Pennsylvania.

Key:
lp — laid paper   wc — watercolored
p/i — pen and ink   wp — wove paper
pr — printed

Taufschein, watercolor and printed, tulips decoration, signed Martin Brechall, Pennsylvania, 1797, 13x8", EX, $528.00.

Birth Records

Gerburts und Taufschein, Ebner, PA, 1823, fr, 19x16" 120.00
Geburts und Taufschein, OH, 1865, 12½ x9½" 120.00
P/i/wc/lp, birds/trees/data, 4-color, 1808, 12x10" 1,150.00
P/i/wc/lp, hearts/parrots/etc, 5-color, sgn/1805, 20" W, EX 1,800.00
P/i/wc/lp, sgn/dtd 1776, fr, 18½x15" 220.00
P/i/wc/wp, angel/dots/rose, PA, 1840, 16x14" 440.00
P/i/wc/wp, birds from 1777 to 1806, 4-color, 19x15", EX 800.00
P/i/wc/wp, stylized flowers, OH, 1815, stains, 10x15" 2,100.00
P/i/wc/wp, 3-color florals, 1786-1819 data, 17x12", VG 1,350.00
Pr, angels/hearts/etc, 1805, Peters, PA, fr, 20x17", VG 105.00
Pr, block letters, Peters, OH, 1833, 17x14" 105.00
Pr/hc, angels/birds, Ritter, 1842, stains, fr, 17x14" 95.00
Pr/p/i/wc, flowers, birds, 5-color, 1805, 16x18", EX 385.00
Pr/wc, angels/eagle/etc, Blummer & Busch, PA, 1832, 18x15", G ...85.00
Pr/wc, flowers, couple, OH, 1830, rprs, fr, 13x11" 825.00
Pr/wc, flowers & heart, Baumann, 1812, fr, 15x18", EX 300.00

Miscellaneous

Bookplate, p/i/wc, lg mc floral cutout, sgn, lt soil, 6¼x4" **160.00**

Bookplate, p/i/wc on lp, flowers, 5-color, 2-pg, 1788, 17x22" **500.00**
Bookplate, p/i/wc on paper, mc roses, 1854, fr, 11x8" **110.00**
Bookplate, p/i/wc on wp, sgn/1810, much damage/stain, 11x9" ..**385.00**
Bookplate, p/i/wc/lp, birds/vines/name/1843, 2-pg, book intact ..**400.00**
Bookplate, p/i/wc/lp, 3-color, 1804, fr, 6x8" **260.00**
Bookplate, p/i/wp, blk ink, 1843, 8½x6" **150.00**
Motto, p/i/wc/lp, intricate floral, 13¾x9", EX **120.00**
P/i/wc, inscription/heart/flowers, 1828, fr, 11x16" **165.00**
P/i/wc/lp, vorschrift, 4-color, 11x9", EX **300.00**
Wc/wp, basket of flowers, 4-color, sgn/1838, 11x9" **700.00**

Frames

Styles in picture frames have changed with the fashion of the day, but those that especially interest today's collectors are the deep shadow boxes made of fine woods such as walnut or cherry, those with Art Nouveau influence, and the oak frames decorated with molded gesso and gilt from the Victorian era. Our advisor for this category is Michael Hinton; he is listed in the Directory under Pennsylvania.

Gutta percha, dated 1855, contains photo of small boy, 5¼x4¾", EX, $60.00.

Architectural, wood, Florentine Gothic w/angel Gabriel, 29" **500.00**
Cast brass, Cupid design, 20x12" **225.00**
Cast iron, floral design, 14x8" **75.00**
Cherry w/pearl heart at ea cross corner, folky style, 15x11" **50.00**
Copper w/emb floral, easel bk, 8½x6½" **55.00**
Cut brass, filigree, Italian, 1700s, 9x6" **575.00**
Pine & grpt, beveled edge, 1¼" molding, 15x12" **75.00**
Pine & walnut, 2¾" molding, old finish, 10¾x14½" **75.00**
Poplar, blk pnt, 1⅝" molding, 18x14" **30.00**
Shaving, CI, EX detail, old blk pnt, 20¾" **200.00**
SP, crown/cupid crest, scroll ft, easel bk, 8½" **275.00**
Walnut, beveled, 2" molding, 17x14" **90.00**
Walnut, narrow gold inner border, 17x15" **90.00**

Frances Ware

Frances Ware, produced in the 1880s by Hobbs, Brockunier and Company of Wheeling, West Virginia, is either clear or frosted with amber-stained rim bands. The most often found pattern is Hobnail, but Swirl was also made.

Hobnail, clear; bowl, 7½" **65.00**
Hobnail, clear; butter dish **95.00**
Hobnail, clear; creamer **60.00**
Hobnail, clear; finger bowl, 4" **35.00**
Hobnail, clear; pitcher, 8½" **125.00**
Hobnail, clear; spooner **40.00**

Hobnail, frosted; bowl, ftd, berry pontil, 6x10" **150.00**
Hobnail, frosted; bowl, oblong, 8" **75.00**
Hobnail, frosted; bowl, sq, 7½" **70.00**
Hobnail, frosted; bowl, 2½x5½" **40.00**
Hobnail, frosted; bowl, 4½" **30.00**
Hobnail, frosted; bowl, 8" **75.00**
Hobnail, frosted; bowl, 9" **85.00**
Hobnail, frosted; butter dish **120.00**

Hobnail, frosted; candy dish, $185.00.

Hobnail, frosted; celery vase **75.00**
Hobnail, frosted; chandelier, amber font, brass fr, 14" dia **950.00**
Hobnail, frosted; creamer **75.00**
Hobnail, frosted; cruet **550.00**
Hobnail, frosted; finger bowl, 4" **35.00**
Hobnail, frosted; marmalade **125.00**
Hobnail, frosted; pitcher, milk **150.00**
Hobnail, frosted; pitcher, water; sq top, 8½" **175.00**
Hobnail, frosted; plate, sq, 5¾" **25.00**
Hobnail, frosted; sauce dish, sq, 4" **28.00**
Hobnail, frosted; shakers, very rare, pr **180.00**
Hobnail, frosted; spooner **70.00**
Hobnail, frosted; sugar bowl, w/lid **80.00**
Hobnail, frosted; syrup, pewter lid **165.00**
Hobnail, frosted; toothpick holder **60.00**
Hobnail, frosted; tray, cloverleaf, 12" **125.00**
Hobnail, frosted; tray, oblong, 14" **150.00**
Hobnail, frosted; tumbler, water **45.00**
Swirl, clear; shakers, pr **55.00**
Swirl, clear; syrup **90.00**
Swirl, frosted; bowl, 3¾" H **40.00**
Swirl, frosted; cruet **175.00**
Swirl, frosted; cruet, orig stopper, mini **260.00**
Swirl, frosted; mustard jar **140.00**
Swirl, frosted; shakers, pr **105.00**
Swirl, frosted; sugar shaker, orig lid **125.00**
Swirl, frosted; syrup, Pat dtd **145.00**
Swirl, frosted; tumbler **35.00**

Franciscan

Franciscan is a trade name used by Gladding McBean and Co., founded in northern California in 1875. In 1923 they purchased the Tropico plant in Glendale where they produced sewer pipe, gardenware, and tile. By 1934 the first of their dinnerware lines, El Patio, was produced. It was a plain design made in bright, attractive colors. El Patio Nouveau followed in 1935, glazed in two colors — one tone on the inside, a contrasting hue on the outside. Coronado, a favorite of today's collectors, was introduced in 1936. It was styled with a wide, swirled border and was made in pastels, both satin and glossy. Before 1940 fifteen patterns had been produced. The first hand-decorated lines were introduced in 1937, the ever-popular Apple pattern in 1940, Desert Rose in 1941, and Ivy in 1948. Many other hand-decorated and decaled patterns were produced there from 1934 to 1984.

Dinnerware marks before 1940 include 'GMcB' in an oval, 'F' within a square, or 'Franciscan' with 'Pottery' underneath (which was later changed to 'Ware.') A circular arrangement of 'Franciscan' with 'Made in California USA' in the center was used from 1940 until 1949. At least forty marks were used before 1975; several more were introduced after that. At one time, paper labels were used.

The company merged with Lock Joint Pipe Company in 1963, becoming part of the Interpace Corporation. In July of 1979 Franciscan was purchased by Wedgwood Limited of England, and the Glendale plant closed in October, 1984.

Our advisors for this category are Mick and Lorna Chase (Fiesta Plus); they are listed in the Directory under Tennessee. Authority Delleen Enge has compiled an informative book, *Franciscan Ware.* You will find her address in the Directory under California. See also Gladding McBean.

Coronado

Bowl, cereal	12.00
Bowl, cream soup	23.00
Bowl, vegetable; serving, oval	20.00
Bowl, vegetable; serving, rnd	15.00
Butter dish	45.00
Candlesticks, pr	28.00
Casserole, w/lid	35.00
Cigarette box	40.00
Coffeepot, demitasse	95.00
Creamer & sugar bowl, w/lid	30.00
Cup & saucer	12.00
Cup & saucer, demitasse	22.00

Coronado, gravy boat with attached plate, $28.00.

Nut cup, ftd	16.00
Plate, chop; 12"	25.00
Plate, chop; 14"	35.00
Plate, 6½"	8.00
Plate, 7½"	10.00
Plate, 8½"	12.00
Platter, 11½"	25.00
Platter, 15½"	35.00
Saucer, cream soup	12.00
Shakers, pr	15.00

Sherbet	10.00
Teapot	65.00

El Patio

Bowl, cereal	12.00
Bowl, fruit	12.00
Bowl, salad; 3-qt	25.00
Bowl, vegetable; oval	30.00
Butter dish	40.00
Creamer	10.00
Cup	10.00
Cup, jumbo	18.00
Cup & saucer, demitasse	28.00
Gravy boat, w/attached underplate	35.00
Plate, bread & butter	7.00
Plate, 10½"	15.00
Plate, 8½"	12.00
Platter, 13"	45.00
Saucer	4.00
Saucer, jumbo	8.00
Sherbet	10.00
Sugar bowl, w/lid	18.00
Teapot, w/lid, 6-cup	45.00

Franciscan Fine China

The main line of fine china was called Masterpiece. There were at least four marks used during its production from 1941 to 1977. Almost every piece is clearly marked. This china is true porcelain, the body having been fired at a very high temperature. Many years of research and experimentation went into this china before it was marketed. Production was temporarily suspended during the war years. More than 170 patterns and many varying shapes were produced. All are valued about the same with the exception of the Renaissance group, which is 25% higher.

Bowl, vegetable; serving, oval	50.00
Cup	20.00
Plate, bread & butter	18.00
Plate, dinner	30.00
Plate, salad	25.00
Saucer	12.00

Hand-Painted Embossed Earthenware

Values listed here apply to the following: Apple, Desert Rose, Ivy, Meadow Rose, Forget-Me-Not, October, Strawberry Time, Strawberry Fair, Fresh Fruit, and other hand-painted patterns. Daisy and Cafe Royal are both worth approximately 30% less, Poppy about 50% more. For Wildflower, double the listed values. Not all of the pieces described below were made in every pattern.

Ashtray, ind; from $18 to	25.00
Bowl, batter	125.00
Bowl, bouillon; lug hdl, w/lid, sm, from $75 to	95.00
Bowl, cereal	16.50
Bowl, cereal; ftd, from $28 to	32.00
Bowl, fruit; sm	12.00
Bowl, mixing; lg	150.00
Bowl, mixing; sm	100.00
Bowl, rim soup; from $28 to	38.00
Bowl, vegetable; sm	32.00
Boxl, mixing; med	125.00
Butter dish, ¼-lb, stick type	40.00

Casserole, ind	45.00
Coaster, 3¾", from $15 to	20.00
Coffeepot, from $95 to	125.00
Compote, lg	85.00
Creamer, ind	42.00
Creamer, reg	32.00
Cup & saucer, demitasse; from $45 to	65.00
Cup & saucer, jumbo	65.00
Egg cup, from $25 to	35.00
Goblet, ceramic, minimum value	75.00
Mug, 10- or 12-oz, ea	45.00
Mug, 7-oz	25.00
Napkin ring, from $25 to	35.00
Pickle dish, 10¼"	35.00
Pitcher, milk; from $75 to	95.00
Pitcher, water; from $85 to	125.00
Plate, chop; 14"	75.00
Plate, grill/divided; 10¾", from $95 to	125.00
Plate, 10½", from $15 to	20.00
Plate, 6½", from $9 to	12.00
Plate, 8½", from $18 to	22.00
Plate, 9½", from $12 to	18.00
Platter, 12½"	45.00
Platter, 14½"	65.00
Platter, 19½", from $250 to	350.00
Relish, 3-part, 11"	65.00
Shaker & pepper mill, 6", pr, from $195 to	225.00
Shakers, sm, pr	24.00
Shakers, tall, pr, from $45 to	60.00
Sugar bowl, ind; open, sm	75.00
Sugar bowl, w/lid, lg, from $32 to	45.00
Syrup pitcher, from $65 to	80.00
Tray, 3-tier	75.00
Tumbler, juice; from $25 to	35.00
Tumbler, water; from $25 to	32.00

Miscellaneous

Trio, Duet, Oasis, and similar patterns are comparable in value to Starburst, having Art Deco shapes and styling, but '50s colors.

Starburst, bowl, oval, 8"	15.00
Starburst, bowl, salad; 12"	80.00
Starburst, bowl, 2-part, 8"	18.00
Starburst, butter dish	40.00
Starburst, coffeepot	90.00
Starburst, cup & saucer	6.50
Starburst, plate, bread & butter	4.00
Starburst, plate, dinner	9.00
Starburst, relish, 3-part	27.00
Starburst, shakers, pr	16.00

Frankart

During the 1920s Frankart, Inc., of New York City, produced a line of accessories that included figural nude lamps, bookends, ashtrays, etc. These white metal composition items were offered in several finishes including verde green, jap black, and gun-metal gray. The company also produced a line of caricatured animals, but the stylized nude figurals have proven to be the most collectible today. With few exceptions, all pieces were marked 'Frankart, Inc.' with a patent number or 'pat. appl. for.' All pieces listed are in very good original condition unless otherwise indicated. Our advisor for

this category is Walter Glenn; he is listed in the Directory under Georgia.

Aquarium, 3 kneeling nudes encircle 10" aqua bowl, 10½"	750.00
Ashtray, ballerina in center of 8" dia tray, 10"	450.00
Ashtray, bk-to-bk nudes hold rack of 4 rnd inserts, 8"	395.00
Ashtray, gr opaque, held out by upright nude, #230	450.00
Ashtray, nude on horseshoe base holds tray aloft, 23"	550.00
Ashtray, nude on tiptoe bends bkward, holds tray, 10½"	425.00
Ashtray, nudes holds overhead 6" pottery ashbowl, 13"	375.00
Ashtray, seated honey bear holds honey-pot ashtray, 5½"	195.00
Ashtray, stylized giraffe bends to drink from ashtray, 7"	225.00
Bookends, boy w/sailboat playing w/dog, pr	190.00
Bookends, fan dancing nudes hold books, 10", pr	395.00
Bookends, futuristic long-necked female heads, 7", pr	250.00
Bookends, metal nudes sits atop metal book, 10", pr	325.00
Bookends, nudes on tapered base w/sm frog, #215	485.00
Bookends, Peek-A-Boo, gr, pr	190.00
Bookends, Romanesque masks, 7½", pr	375.00
Box, bk-to-bk nudes support etched gr box w/lid, #218	775.00
Clock, 2 nudes kneel & hold 10" dia glass clock, 12½"	1,550.00
Lamp, ladies in sailor attire walking, 16", pr	1,150.00
Lamp, modernistic prancing horse, parchment shade, 7"	250.00
Lamp, nude kneels before 4" bubble ball, 8"	625.00
Lamp, nude on bk, legs up to support globe, #201, pr	1,550.00
Lamp, nude stands ea side of 8" glass globe, 9", pr	1,600.00
Lamp, sm globe ea side of seated nude, #207	1,100.00
Lamp, standing nude silhouettes against glass panel, 10"	395.00

Lamp, 2 nudes kneel facing 8" crackle glass globe, 10", $750.00.

Lamp, 2 nudes stand, support lg globe, #202	1,500.00
Lamp, 2 nudes stand bk to bk, hold skyscraper globe, 21"	695.00
Lamp, 2 nudes stand either side carved rectangular glass, 10½"	975.00
Lamp, 3 nudes w/rnd pottery bowl nested between heads, #211	1,850.00
Lamp, 4 standing nudes surround sq glass cylinder, 13"	895.00
Tray, nude w/10" dia tray at ft	450.00
Wall plaques, Diana the Huntress, 8" sq, pr	550.00

Frankoma

The Frank Pottery, founded in Oklahoma in 1933 by John Frank, became known as Frankoma in 1934. The company produced decorative figurals, vases, and such, marking their ware from 1936-38 with a pacing leopard 'Frankoma' mark. These pieces are highly sought. The entire operation was destroyed by fire in 1938, and new molds were cast — some from surviving pieces — and a similar line of production was pursued. The body of the ware was changed in 1955 from a honey tan (called 'Ada clay,' referring to the name of the town near the area where it was dug) to a red brick clay (known as Sapulpa), and this, along with the color of the glazes (over forty have been used), helps determine the period of production. A Southwestern theme has always been favored in design as well as in color selection.

In 1965 they began to produce a limited-edition series of Christmas plates, followed by a bottle vase series in 1969. Considered very collectible are their political mugs, bicentennial plates, Teenagers of the Bible plates, and the Wildfire series. Their ceramic Christmas cards are also very popular items with today's collectors.

Frankoma celebrated their 50th Anniversary in 1983. On September 26 of that same year, Frankoma was again destroyed by fire. Because of a fire-proof wall, master molds of all 1983 production items were saved, allowing plans for rebuilding to begin immediately.

Frankoma filed for Chapter 11 in April, 1990, and eventually sold to a Maryland investor in February of 1991, thereby ending the family-ownership era. For a more thorough study of the subject, we recommend that you refer to *Frankoma Treasures* and *Frankoma and Other Oklahoma Potteries* by Phyllis and Tom Bess, our advisors; you will find their address in the Directory under Oklahoma.

Ashtray, Okla, natural gas, 1956 ....25.00
Ashtray, red clay, free-form, #30 ....35.00
Baker, Aztec gr, w/lid, #7U, 10-oz 35.00
Bookends, boot w/horseshoe, pr 35.00
Bookends, Mountain Girl, Ada clay, pr 350.00
Bowl, Golda Corn; Desert Gold 25.00
Bowl, mint; Red Bud, Ada clay, #35 ....45.00
Bowl, Royal Bl, oval, Ada clay, #205 ....30.00
Bowl, swan, open tail, #230, 12" 150.00
Bowl, Terra Cotta Rose, #45 ....40.00
Candle holders, Oral Roberts, Christ Light of World, pr 17.50
Canteen, Thunderbird, Prairie Gr, leather thong, 6¼" 20.00
Christmas card, 1950-56, ea 75.00
Christmas card, 1952 ....85.00
Christmas card, 1958-65, ea 60.00
Christmas card, 1973-74, ea 30.00
Christmas card, 1975, bird in hand, Grace Lee, rare 115.00
Christmas card, 1979 ....30.00
Cornucopia, gr, Ada clay, #57 ....40.00
Cup & saucer, Wagon Wheel, Prairie Gr 10.00
Donkey mug, 1976, Centennial Red 35.00
Donkey mug, 1978, Woodland Moss 30.00
Donkey mug, 1983, wisteria 30.00
Elephant mug, 1976, Centennial Red 35.00
Elephant mug, 1981, Reagan-Bush 20.00
Gravy boat, Plainsman, Desert Gold 8.00
Jug, Prairie Gr, w/stopper, 3-cup 65.00
Jug, Terra Cotta Rose, #86, w/stopper, 2-qt 65.00
Mug, Plainsman, Desert Gold, 5⅜" 7.50
Pipe rest 100.00
Pitcher, Aztec, Terra Cotta Rose, #551 ....20.00
Pitcher, honey, #831, 16-oz 10.00
Planter, swan, gr, red clay, #229 ....45.00
Plate, Bicentennial, 'staits' error, 1972 ....125.00
Plate, Christmas, 1987 ....25.00
Plate, Christmas Annunciation, 1973, 8½" 40.00
Plate, Conestoga Wagon, 1971 ....85.00
Plate, David, Teenager of the Bible, 1974 ....40.00
Plate, Easter, Jesus the Carpenter, 1972 ....40.00
Plate, Easter, Oral Roberts, 1972 ....15.00
Plate, Helen Keller 40.00

Plate, Oklahoma, 'Jubilee' error, 1982 ....65.00
Plate, Rural Letter Carrier, Ada clay 75.00
Plate, Wildlife, Prairie Chicken, 1974 ....75.00
Platter, Red Bud, 13" 35.00
Sculpture, camel 450.00
Sculpture, Cocker Spaniel, 8½" 250.00
Sculpture, English Setter 65.00
Sculpture, Fan Dancer, Dove Gray, #113 ....350.00
Sculpture, Fan Dancer, gr, red clay, #113, 1955, 8½x13½" 200.00
Sculpture, Flower Girl, #700 ....80.00
Sculpture, Indian Chief, Flame, 8" 100.00
Sculpture, Ponytail Girl 35.00
Sculpture, Prancing Percheron, blk, Ada clay 350.00
Sculpture, puma, seated, blk, Ada clay, #114, 7½" 100.00
Sign, Indian on tee-pee, rare 400.00
Sugar bowl, Wagon Wheel, Terra Cotta Rose, #510 ....25.00
Teapot, Wagon Wheel, Prairie Gr, 2-cup 30.00
Tray, Dogwood, Robin Bl, #204A, 6" 5.00
Tray, leaf form, Terra Cotta Rose, #225 ....25.00
Trivet, Gov & Mrs David Boren, 1975 ....15.00
Trivet, stylized eagle, Woodland Moss, sq, #117 ....35.00
Trivet, 5 Tribes 10.00
Vase, Cactus, Red Bud, #4 ....45.00
Vase, fan-form shell, Red Bud, #54 ....45.00
Vase, pillow; Red Bud, #63, 7" 35.00
Vase, ram's head, gr, Ada clay, #38 ....40.00
Vase, reed, gr, Ada clay, #61 ....45.00
Vase, stepped hdl, gr, Ada clay, #41 ....75.00
Vase, Wagon Wheel, Ada clay, #94 ....35.00
Wall mask, African man & woman, Flame, #124/#125, pr 150.00
Wall mask, Phoebe, gr, Ada clay, #730 ....100.00
Wall pocket, acorn, Red Bud, #190 ....35.00
Wall pocket, Billiken, gr 75.00
Wall pocket, Jester, 1954 ....75.00
Wall pocket, Wagon Wheel, Prairie Gr, Ada clay 37.50
Wall pocket, Wagon Wheel, Red Bud, #510 ....40.00

Fraternal Organizations

Fraternal memorabilia is a vast and varied field. Emblems representing the various organizations have been used to decorate cups, shaving mugs, plates, and glassware. Medals, swords, documents, and other ceremonial paraphernalia from the 1800s and early 1900s are especially prized. Our advisor for Odd Fellows is Greg Spiess; he is listed in the Directory under Illinois. Information on Masonic memorabilia has been provided by David Smies, who is listed under Kansas.

Elks

Flask, ceramic, emb symbols, wht w/brn, dtd 1912, 4½x2½" 125.00
Gaming chip, Tucson 10.00
Note pad & pencil, Ladies Night, 1916, EX 37.50
Plate, metal, 1907 reunion 34.00
Ribbon, Syracuse Lodge...1885, w/2½" bronze pin 8.00
Watch button, celluloid, w/2 1933 ribbons 22.50
Watch fob, clothing ad, 1912 ....30.00

Masons

Decoration, CI, compass, T-sq & C emblems, 1800s, 7x6x1¼" 60.00
Emblem, bl & wht enamel on copper, post & bolt, 3" 15.00
Sign, gilt wood, compass, sq & G, 1800s, 33" 725.00

Tie clip, 12k gold-filled, emblem hangs from chain, early 8.00

Odd Fellows

Banner, symbols on bl, gold braid, 30x18", EX 88.00
Book, Code of General Laws, 1916, EX 8.50
Medal, Grand Lodge...San Francisco, 1904, w/purple ribbon 20.00
Pin-bk button, clasped hands, celluloid, Whitehead-Hoag 70.00
Sash, red & wht stripes, stars on bl at top, 1890s, 39x5" 48.00
Shaving mug, symbols, Dresden china, EX 35.00
Wristwatch, symbols on dial, silver case, Waltham, NM 225.00

Shrine

Cup, Indian head in relief, mc pnt on glass, 1903 ....40.00
Emblem, sword/moon/Egyptian, metal, orig pnt, 1920, 12x12" 90.00
Measure, dbl liquor; cranberry & clear glass, St Louis, 1909 ....65.00
Mug, glass, Atlantic City, 1904 ....75.00
Tumbler, officers & donkey on milk glass, sq, 1917 ....110.00

Fruit Jars

As early as 1829, canning jars were being manufactured for use in the home preservation of foodstuffs. For the past twenty-five years, they have been sought as popular collectibles. At the last estimate, over four thousand fruit jars and variations were known to exist. Some are very rare, perhaps one-of-a-kind examples known to have survived to the present day. Among the most valuable are the black glass jars, the amber Van Vliet, and the cobalt Millville. These often bring prices in excess of $3,000.00 when they can be found. Aside from condition, values are based on age, rarity, color, and special features. Our advisor for this category is John Hathaway; he is listed in the Directory under Maine.

Millville Atmospheric Fruit Jar, aqua, 1-quart, $35.00.

ABC aqua, clear, qt 298.00
ABGMCo, wax sealer, aqua, qt 35.00
Acme Seal (script), regular mouth, clear, pt 145.00
Agee Special, amber, qt 30.00
Almy, aqua, qt 128.00
Am (eagle & flag) Fruit Jar, lt gr, ½-gal 148.00

Anchor (block letters) below slanting anchor, qt 48.00
Atlas Clover Good Luck, clear, ½-gal 20.00
Atlas E-Z Seal, aqua, 48-oz 15.00
Atlas E-Z Seal, bl, qt 22.00
Atlas E-Z Seal, gr, qt 20.00
Atlas Mason Improved Pat'd, aqua, pt 8.00
Atlas Mason Improved Pat'd, gr, pt 40.00
Ball, olive gr, qt 98.00
Ball (script) Mason's Patent 1858 Ghost Pat Apld For, qt 33.00
Ball (3 L loops), aqua, crude, qt 5.00
Ball (3 loops) Mason, gr, qt 30.00
Ball Ideal Pat'd July 14th 1908, clear, ½-gal 12.00
Ball Jar Mason Patent Nov 30th 1858, aqua, ½-gal 10.00
Ball Mason, bk: Mason's Patent Nov 30th 1858, aqua, ½-gal 38.00
Ball Perfect Mason, amber, ½-gal 38.00
Ball Perfect Mason, olive-amber, qt 85.00
Ball Perfect Mason (Ball offset to right), med gr, qt 25.00
Ball Perfect Mason (dbl-lined letters), clear, qt, NM 73.00
Baltimore Glass Works, aqua, no closure, qt 325.00
Bamberger's Mason Jar, bl, pt 18.00
Banner circled by Pat dates, aqua, qt 148.00
BBGMCo, aqua, qt 75.00
Beaver (beaver chewing log over word), clear, qt 30.00
Best, aqua, ½-gal 30.00
Best, lt gr, qt 25.00
Bosco Double Seal, clear, qt 40.00
Calcutt's Patent Apr 11th Nov 7th 1893 (on lid), clear, qt 38.00
Canton Domestic Fruit Jar, clear, qt 83.00
Champion Pat Aug 31 1869, aqua, orig clamp, qt 205.00
Cohansey Glass Mfg Co Philada (base), amber, pt 35.00
Columbia (base), clear, ½-gal 15.00
Crown Imperial, aqua, qt 12.00
Crystal, aqua, qt 88.00
Curtis & Moore TM Mono (Boston Mass), clear, ½-gal 20.00
Dexter (encircled by fruits & vegetables), aqua, qt 63.00
Dictator D, bk: Pat DI Holcomb...1869, wax sealer, aqua, qt 68.00
Dominion Mason, clear, qt 2.00
Doolittle, aqua, no closures, qt 38.00
Drey Sq Mason, clear, pt 6.00
Eagle, aqua, qt 125.00
ECGCo, wax sealer, aqua, qt 20.00
Eclipse Jar, aqua, qt 445.00
Edwardsburg Corn Syrup, clear, qt 28.00
Empire, aqua, repro clamps, ½-gal 98.00
Empire (in stippled cross), clear, pt 6.00
Eureka Pat'd Dec 27th 1864, aqua, ½-gal 78.00
Excelsior Improved, aqua, ½ -gal 48.00
Flaccus Bros Steers Head Fruit Jar, milk glass, repro lid, pt 148.00
Franklin Fruit Jar, aqua, qt 50.00
Garden Queen, clear, qt 8.00
Gem, aqua, qt 8.00
Gilberts Improved (star) Jar, aqua, orig wire, qt 200.00
Gimbel Brothers Pure Food Store Phil, clear, qt 50.00
GJCo, aqua, qt 28.00
Golden Crown Maple Syrup, clear, pt 20.00
Hahne & Co Newark NJ (around star) Mason's Pat 1858, aqua, pt .40.00
Haines Pat'd Mar 1st 1870, aqua, ½-gal 118.00
Hansee's Palace Home Jar, clear, qt 88.00
Haserot Company Cleveland Mason Patent, aqua, qt 12.00
Hero Improved, aqua, qt 22.00
Heroine, aqua, tin lid, pt 140.00
Home Jar Scranton PA, aqua, qt 58.00
Ideal, aqua, ½-gal 18.00
John Agnew & Son Pittsburgh around star, aqua, qt, chip 15.00

Johnson & Johnson New Brunswick NJ USA, amber, qt	28.00
Kerr Self Sealing Mason, amber, qt	18.00
Keystone (Improved), aqua, qt	8.00
Kline's Pat'd Oct 27 63 (on blown stopper), aqua, qt	123.00
Knowlton Vacuum (star) fruit jar, bl, qt	28.00
Knox (K in Keystone) Mason, clear, zinc lid, qt	5.00
Kohrs Davenport IA (vertical), pt	15.00
KYGW (base), wax sealer, aqua, qt	23.00
L&W, aqua, no closure, qt	48.00
Lafayette (script), aqua, pt	200.00
Lamb Mason, qt	2.00
Lindell Glass Co (base), wax sealer, amber, qt, NM	20.00
Lockport Mason, clear, ½-gal	10.00
Maltese Cross on base, wax sealer, aqua, ½-gal	98.00
Mason (shepherd's crook), aqua, pt	14.00
Mason Improved ABGA, gr, ½-gal	45.00
Mason Jar of 1872, aqua, qt	35.00
Mason's (cross) Patent Nov 30th 1858, amber, qt	148.00
Mason's (Keystone) Keystone, aqua, qt	130.00
Mason's Crystal Jar, clear, ½-gal	40.00
Mason Straight Line, amber, pt	73.00
Moore's Patent Dec 30 1861, aqua, qt	90.00
New Paragon, aqua, qt	125.00
Patent Applied For, wax sealer, aqua, qt	73.00
Peerless, aqua, qt	123.00
Perfection, clear, ½-gal	58.00
Princess (on shield in fr), clear, pt	25.00
Protector (recessed panels), aqua, qt	48.00
Puritan, bk: L&Co, aqua, qt	163.00
Putnam Glass Works Zanesville O, wax sealer, aqua, qt	33.00
Queen, aqua, qt	23.00
Rau's Improved Pat'd Applied For Groove Ring Jar, qt	40.00
Registered U S Pat Office (on heel), aqua, 1½-pt	38.00
Royal, aqua, orig insert & band, qt	148.00
S McKee & Co on shoulder, wax sealer, aqua, ½-gal	28.00
Safety, amber, pt	323.00
Safety Valve Triangles Base, emerald gr, repro closure, pt	98.00
Sierra Mason Jar Made in Calif, clear, pt	60.00
Standard (arched), wax sealer, aqua, qt	25.00
Star Glass Co New Albany Ind, wax sealer, aqua, ½-gal	48.00
Stevens Tin Top Patented July 27 1875, wax sealer, aqua, ½-gal	75.00
Swazee's Improved Mason, dk gr, qt	50.00
TM Lightning, amber, qt	40.00
TM Lightning (base) Putnam, aqua, 1½-pt	45.00
Trade Mark the Dandy, clear, pt	58.00
Trademark Banner Registered (in banner), clear, qt	10.00
Trademark Keystone Registered, clear, pt	7.00
Union, wax sealer, aqua, qt	45.00
Valve Jar Co Philadelphia, aqua, repro wire, ½-gal	235.00

Fry

Henry Fry established his glassworks in 1901 in Rochester, Pennsylvania. There, until 1933 when it was sold to the Libbey Company, he produced glassware of the finest quality. In the early years they produced beautiful cut glass; and when it began to wane in popularity, Fry turned to the manufacture of occasional pieces and oven glassware. He is perhaps most famous for the opalescent pearl glass called 'Foval.' It was sometimes made with blue or jade green trim in combination. Because it was in production for only a short time in 1926 and 1927, it is hard to find. Our advisor for this category is Ron Damaska; he is listed in the Directory under Pennsylvania. See also Kitchen Collectibles, Glassware.

Baker, pearl ovenware, oval, 13"	35.00
Baker, pearl ovenware, 9" sq	35.00
Bean pot, pearl ovenware, w/lid, 1924, 1-qt	120.00
Bowl, cut, Basket of Flowers, str sides, heavy, 4x10"	265.00
Cake pan, pearl ovenware, 9" dia	25.00
Candle holder, Royal Blue, wide saucer base, ea	15.00
Candlesticks, Foval, bl spiral threaded stems/wafers, 11", pr	250.00
Candy dish, etched, floral spray, center hdl	45.00
Casserole, pearl ovenware, oval, w/lid, 10"	45.00
Casserole, pearl ovenware, w/lid, child sz, 4½"	75.00
Casserole, pearl ovenware, w/lid, 7" dia	35.00
Casserole, pearl ovenware, w/lid, 8½" dia	40.00
Champagne, etched, Rose, hollow stem	45.00

Chicken roaster, ovenware, #1946, 14", $60.00.

Coquette, pearl ovenware, 6"	30.00
Creamer & sugar bowl, cut, Monaca, pr	185.00
Cup & saucer, Foval, gr hdl	60.00
Cup & saucer, Fuchsia	50.00
Finger bowl, etched, Grape	20.00
Loaf pan, pearl ovenware, rectangular, 10½"	45.00
Loaf pan, pearl ovenware, rectangular, 9"	30.00
Measuring cup, pearl ovenware, 3-spout, 8-oz	120.00
Mug, lemonade; Foval, jade gr hdl	75.00
Pie pan, pearl ovenware, 10" dia	25.00
Pitcher, cut, Orient	265.00
Plate, cut, Flower Basket, 9"	175.00
Plate, grill; amber, 3-part	25.00
Refrigerator dish, pearl ovenware, w/lid, 8" sq	85.00
Relish, cut, Asteroid, oblong, 13"	150.00
Teacup & saucer, Azure bl	20.00
Tray, sandwich; emerald gr, center hdl	35.00
Tumbler, iced tea; etched, Japanese Maid, hdld	60.00
Vase, cut, Ivy, slim form, 14"	275.00
Vase, cut, Orient w/Buzz Star & Zipper neck, sgn, 12"	195.00
Vase, cut, Vardin, trumpet form, 9"	120.00
Vase, etched, Honeysuckle, slim form, #811 line, 12"	45.00
Vase, reeded crystal w/emerald threading	90.00

Fulper

The Fulper Pottery was founded in 1899, after nearly a century of producing utilitarian stoneware under various titles and managements. Not until 1909 did Fulper venture into the art pottery field. Vasekraft, their first art line, utilized the same heavy clay body used for their utility ware. Although shapes were unadorned and simple, the glazes they developed were used with such flair and imagination (alone and in unexpected combined harmony) that each piece was truly a work of art. Graceful Oriental shapes were produced to complement the important 'famille rose' glaze developed by W.H. Fulper, Jr. Other shapes and glazes were developed in line with the Arts and Crafts movement of the same period.

During WWI, doll's heads and Kewpies were made to meet the demand for hard-to-find imports. Figural perfume lamps and powder boxes were made both in bisque and glazed ware. Examples prized most highly by collectors today are those made before a devastating fire destroyed the plant in 1929, resulting in an operations takeover by Martin Stangl later that same year.

Several marks were used: a vertical 'Fulper' in a line reserve, a horizontal mark, a Vasekraft paper label, 'Rafco,' 'Prang,' and 'Flemington.' Fulper values are to a major degree determined by the desirability of the glazes and forms. And, of course, larger examples command higher prices. Lamps with colored glass inserts are rare and highly prized. Our advisor for this category is Douglass White; he is listed in the Directory under Florida.

Bookends, Rameses II, cucumber gr, pr 575.00
Bowl, bl crystalline/gr, 3 rim extensions hold center ring 325.00
Bowl, centerpc; moss-to-rose flambe matt, rtcl ft, 4¾x17" 500.00
Bowl, dk rose w/cream highlights, 10-sided, #455, 9" 160.00
Bowl, mirror blk over caramel w/cat's-eye flambe, 16" 235.00
Effigy bowl, gr/blk crystalline, 3 figure supports, 7⅛" H, NM 300.00
Flower frog, Pan, #383, 6" 150.00
Jar, powder; Art Deco lady, aqua, 6¾" 225.00
Jug, musical; ivory gloss over mustard matt, 9½x5" 225.00
Lamp, gr w/gun metal, shallow 14" dome shade w/inset glass ..5,000.00
Lantern, gr gloss, 12 glass panels, riveted cone top, 12" 1,100.00
Night light, ballerina figure, peach, 6" 210.00
Vase, bl flambe w/cream & gr, wide gourd form, drilled, 11½" ...270.00
Vase, brn crystalline drip over bl matt, gourd form, 7½" 250.00
Vase, cat's-eye flambe, hdls, #T25, 6½x10" 275.00
Vase, copper dust, bulbous, 5½x4¾", pr 425.00
Vase, copper dust crystalline, downward-sloping hdls, 9" 375.00
Vase, Flemington gr, hdls, 7x7" 175.00
Vase, Flemington gr over cucumber, 17" 2,000.00
Vase, gr w/charcoal, hammered, bulbous w/hdls, 13x12" 650.00
Vase, ivory drip gloss on mustard matt, 12x5¾" 850.00
Vase, leopard skin, #577, 5¼" 225.00
Vase, lt bl flambe w/matt crystals, hdls, 9" 250.00
Vase, lt to dk bl gloss w/heavy matt crystals, bulb body, 8" 275.00

Vases: Mirrored black drip over green crystalline, ovoid, rectangular mark, 13x6", $700.00; Green leopard skin on urn shape with handles, #490, vertical oval ink stamp mark, 12x11x9", $1,350.00.

Vase, mirror blk, 4 integral hdls at incurvate neck, 9x9", EX 500.00
Vase, mirror blk streaks on copper dust, mk, #608, 15" 1,500.00

Vase, mirror blk/cafe au lait, Arts & Crafts type, hdls, 11" 475.00
Vase, Mission brn, #23, 8x7" 650.00
Vase, moss-to-Chinese bl flambe, 4 shoulder hdls, rpr, 13x10" ...600.00
Vase, pea gr to robin's-egg bl gloss, hdls, #643, 8x5½" 200.00
Vase, periwinkle crystalline, squat, 6x10" 300.00
Vase, purple matt, classic form, 9" 350.00
Vase, red matt w/gray & gr crystalline, 3-hdld, 7" 225.00
Vase, wisteria, bl highlights at top, #646, 8" 325.00
Wall pocket, royal bl matt, imp Greek Key border, 8½" 275.00

Furniture

From the cabinetmaker's shop of the early 1800s with apprentices and journeymen who learned every phase of the craft at the side of the master carpenter, the trade had evolved by the mid-century to one with steam-powered saws and turning lathes and workers who specialized in only one operation. By 1870 the Industrial Revolution was in progress, and large factories in the East and Midwest turned out increasingly elaborate styles, ornately machine carved and heavily inlaid. Rococo, Egyptian, and Renaissance Revival furniture adapted well to factory production. Eastlake offered a welcome respite from Victorian frumpery and a return to quality handcrafting. All of these styles remained popular until the turn of the century.

As early as 1880, factories began using oak; early mail-order catalogs offered oak furniture, simply styled and lighter in weight, since long-distance shipping was often a factor. Mission, or Craftsman, a style introduced around 1890, was simple to the extreme. Stickley and Hubbard were two of its leading designers. Other popular Victorian styles were Colonial Revival, Cottage, Bentwood, and Windsor. Prices are as variable as the styles.

Though the market is showing a recovery, some items are still selling below market value. Because of this, items that have sold at auction for at least 25% lower than their normal market values will be designated with (*). Items listed in the lines that are designated with (**) are pieces in the best of form and of museum quality. Mahogany furniture, machine made, from the 1900s to the 1930s in traditional styling (Hepplewhite, Sheraton and Duncan Phyfe) is very popular right now, as is furniture decorated in the Chinoiserie and English Regency styles. These are all escallating in value at this time. On the down side, ordinary oak furniture is still selling well below its highs of a few years ago.

Learn to tell the difference between handmade and machine-made furniture. Condition is the most important factor to consider in determining value, and it's important to remember that *where* a piece sells, has a definite bearing on the price it will realize, due simply to regional preference. Our advisor for this category is Suzy McLennan Anderson, ISA, of Heritage Antiques, whose address is listed in the Directory under New Jersey. To learn more about furniture, we recommend *The Collector's Encyclopedia of American Furniture* by Robert and Harriet Swedberg.

Note: When only one dimension is given for blanket chests, dry sinks, tables, settees, and sofas, it is length.

Key:
Am — American	Fr — French
brd — board	ftbd — footboard
Chpndl — Chippendale	G — good
Co — Country	Geo — Georgian
cvd — carved	grpt — grainpainted
cvg — carving	hdbd — headboard
c&b — claw and ball	hdw — hardware
do — door	Hplwht — Hepplewhite
drw — drawer	mar — marriage
Emp — Empire	NE — New England
Fed — Federal	QA — Queen Anne

trn — turning
uphl — upholstered/upholstery
Vict — Victorian

W/M — William and Mary
: — over (example: 1 do:2 drw =
1 door over 2 drawers)

Beds

Canopy, maple Co Sheraton, trn & reeded ft posts, 61x75x56" ..1,540.00
Canopy, walnut Sheraton, tall trn posts, 88" w/flat-top fr 1,450.00
Day, cherry & walnut Co Emp, fold-down bk, 1-cushion, 80" 660.00
Day, rope; cherry Co Emp, trn posts & rails, 28x76x27", EX 500.00
Day, trn maple, mid-1800s, old surface, 31" H 350.00
Day, walnut Co Emp, adjustable headrest, 3-cushion, 80" 450.00
Half tester, rosewood Rococo Revival, elaborate hd/ftbd ** 6,000.00
Mahog Fed style, trn posts, twin sz, pr 500.00
Oak, w/appl decor crest, ca 1890, 82" 1,200.00
Pencil-post style, birch w/pine hdbd, rfn, 83x74x38" 250.00
Pencil-post style, maple w/pine hdbd, repro, 83x79x55" 1,045.00
Rope, birch & pine, cannonball finials, 48x74x53" 250.00
Rope, curly maple, high ft, scrolled hdbd, 50x69x53" 1,760.00
Rope, curly maple, spool posts w/trn finials, 56x71x45" 330.00
Rope, maple Co Emp, tall posts w/acorn finials, 80x70x53" 1,485.00
Rope, maple w/some curl, trn posts, rpl ftbd, 52x74x56" 990.00
Rope, old red & blk grpt w/gold stencil, trn posts, 48x76x49" 425.00
Rope, poplar, cannonball finials on posts, rpt, 43x69x39" 440.00
Rope trundle, short trn posts w/wooden wheels, old red 90.00
Tall post, cvd Fed, old dk finish, 1800s, 73x44½", EX 1,760.00
Walnut Victorian w/burl decor, ornate, 89" H 1,500.00

Benches

Kneeling, pine Co w/splayed chestnut legs, reuphl, 42" 95.00
Limbert #243 ½ , flaring sides ea w/4 sq cutouts, 24x18" 2,500.00
Mammy's, poplar Co, high bk at 1 end, trn legs & posts, 57" ..1,045.00
Pine Co, cut-out legs & trestle, old brn grpt, 18x56x15" 135.00
Settle, bamboo Windsor, blk rpt, rpr seat, 96" 660.00
Settle, Co Emp, plank seat, 2 wide vase splats, rfn, 80" 415.00
Settle, gray-gr rpt w/stencil & freehand floral, 82" 685.00
Settle, oak English Co, 2-drw, cvd arms, worn grpt, 72" 1,100.00
Water, Co pine w/ivory rpt over gray, 1-brd ends, 59x36" ** ..1,650.00
Water, dbl-do base, mortised shelves, rpl brace, 64x32x11" ** ..1,700.00
Water, poplar Co, bootjack legs, gallery, old pnt, 24x32x16" 330.00

Blanket Chests, Coffers, and Mule Chests

Cherry Co, dvtl, trn ft, till w/lid, 35x44x20" 550.00
Cherry Co Chpndl, 2 dvtl drw, 6-brd, lift lid, rprs, 42x44" 2,200.00
Mule, pine, 2 dvtl drw, lift lid, 6-brd, orig grpt, 45x42" 1,100.00
Pine, dvtl 6-brd, truncated front panel w/cvg, 42" 660.00
Pine, yel & brn comb grpt over bl, dvtl, 23x43x19" 435.00
Pine Co, dvtl case & till w/lid, bracket ft, rfn, 44" 440.00
Pine Co, 2-drw/2 false drw, 6-brd, rprs/rfn, 44x39x17" 500.00
Pine Co, 6-brd, staple hinges, old red pnt, 24x36x17" 360.00
Pine Co Chpndl, 3 dvtl drw, rpl brasses/rprs, 40x39x17" 1,265.00
Pine Co Chpndl, 3-drw, 6-brd, worn grpt (rpt), rprs, 41x38" ..1,300.00
Pine European, orig pnt w/rose mulled decor, 24x51" 600.00
Pine w/old bl sponged pnt, dvtl drw, 32x39x20" 2,200.00
Pine w/PA German decor, bl w/blk/wht/pk, 2-drw, 24x50" ** ..11,000.00
Pine w/red-brn grpt on yel, gr ft, dvtl, 22x36x19" 2,200.00
Pine w/red-brn grpt on yel w/blk trim, w/till, 44" 1,045.00
Poplar, red/blk grpt, trn ft, dtd 1837, 28x44x20" 495.00
Poplar, worn brn flame grpt, dvtl, 22x38x18", EX 385.00
Poplar w/old grpt w/yel trim, dvtl case, w/till, 29x49x23" 1,650.00
Poplar w/orig combed grpt, dvtl case, till, 48" 685.00
Sea, pine, iron bound w/end hdls, strap hinges, rpt, 29" 165.00

Sea, pine/poplar, pnt scenes/wild animals, 38" 1,000.00
Sea, poplar, 5-brd w/till, becket hdls, blk pnt, 43" 195.00
Walnut & poplar, dvtl, trn ft, till, 23x37x17" 330.00
Walnut Chpndl, dvtl drws, orig brasses, 32x55x23" 3,200.00
Walnut Co, corner posts, paneled sides/ends, 42" 385.00
Walnut Co, dvtl bracket ft, single brd, 25x44x22" 1,100.00
Walnut Co, dvtl ft, till w/lid, iron hinges, 22x41x18" 715.00
Walnut transitional Chpndl to Hplwht, PA, 50" 2,425.00

Bookcases

Cherry Chpndl glass do on fr, ca 1800, 86½ x72x19", EX 6,000.00
Limbert #359, 2 do ea w/2 horizontal panes, mk, rfn, 57x47" ..2,500.00
Limbert #377, 1 6-pane do (3 sm:3 lg), no mk, varnished, 60" 1,500.00
Walnut Am Gothic, fretwork frieze, tracery cvgs on glass do ..1,300.00
Walnut veneer English QA secretary, 3-drw, 2-pc, 88x38x19" ...4,000.00

Bureaus, See Chests

Cabinets

Cellarette, Limbert #751, slide-out glass shelf, brand, M 5,250.00
China, Lifetime, bksplash, rnded sides, orig finish, 61x45" 1,000.00
China, oak, curved glass front, mirror, many press-cvgs, lg 1,250.00
China, plain/quarter-sawn cvd oak, 3 convex glass panels, 65" ..2,800.00
China, quarter-sawn oak, swell-front shelves, c&b ft, 68x40x16" ..1,300.00
Curio, oak, lg glass do, 3-shelf, gallery, 48x23x11½" 150.00
Hoosier kitchen, oak, flat panel do, enamel work top, 90x40" ...1,500.00
Majorelle, glazed do, sm birch tree-inlay do, 68x28" 7,700.00

Candlestands

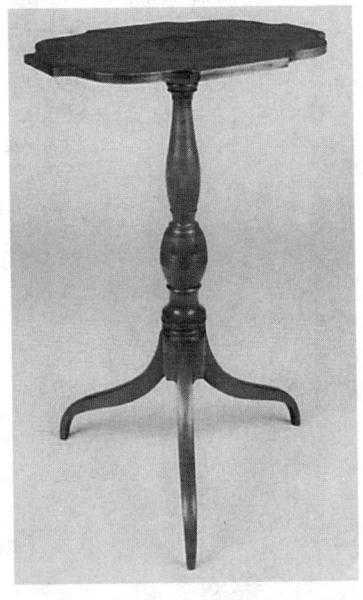

Candlestand, cherry inlaid and carved Federal, flame birch veneer, tilt top, early 1800s, 30½x18x13⅜", $4,400.00.

Cherry Co, tripod base, 1-brd top, rfn, 29x18x18" 525.00
Cherry Co, tripod base w/spider legs, 29x20x17" 360.00
Cherry Co Chpndl, tripod base, snake ft, sq top, 27x16x16" 435.00
Cherry Co Chpndl, tripod base, 1-brd top, 18" dia 770.00
Co Hplwht, tilt top, tripod base, dk stain, rprs, 22x18" 330.00
Curly maple, trn column & base, scroll ft, OH, 21x13x10" 5,170.00
Mahog Chpndl, tilt top, tripod base w/snake ft, 28x22x22" 400.00
Mahog Chpndl style, snake ft, trn column, rprs, 29x23" dia 125.00
Maple Co, tripod base, trn column, 1-brd top, 28x18x16" 360.00
Walnut Chpndl, tripod w/snake ft, 1-brd top, 20" dia ** 14,500.00

Walnut Co, tripod base, turtle-bk top, rpt, 15x15" 500.00

Chairs

Arm, bamboo Windsor, cut-down spindle bk, splayed base, 34" .120.00
Arm, bamboo Windsor, rfn/rprs/rpl, 33" 300.00
Arm, bamboo Windsor, 7-spindle bow bk, rpt, 38" 470.00
Arm, cherry Co Chpndl, pierced splat/shaped crest, rprs, 39" 440.00
Arm, Co ladderbk, 4-slat, old rpt, poor splint seat, 41" 80.00
Arm, Fr style, cvd mahog fr, worn tapestry uphl, 1900s, 33" 400.00
Arm, Fr style, cvd wood w/wht pnt, brocade uphl, 48" 175.00
Arm, Harden, Mission style, 5-slat bk, 4 ea side, orig, VG 600.00
Arm, J&J Meeks, Stanton Hall, gentleman's armchair ** 4,000.00
Arm, ladderbk, 5 grad arched slats, rfn hardwood, 45" 770.00
Arm, Lifetime #706½ , 4-slat arms, leather bk/seat (torn), VG ..350.00

Armchair by Louis Majorelle, mahogany, carved continuous wing arms, damask upholstery, 42½", $4,000.00.

Arm, Louis XVI style, tapestry, giltwood fr, 1880s, pr 1,000.00
Arm, Louis XVI style, worn uphl, old rpt, 1800s, 40", pr 650.00
Arm, mahog Fed fr w/cvd swans in crest rail, uphl seat 275.00
Arm, Michigan Chair Co, Flemish scroll, cane seat & bk, 51" ...125.00
Arm, Morris, Handcraft, oak Mission, leather cushions, 40" ...1,400.00
Arm, oak, leather uphl w/brass-head pins, animal ft, 1890s 175.00
Arm, oak Mission, even-arm cube, 3-slat sides, 33", VG 650.00
Arm, oak Mission style, rstr uphl, ca 1920, rstr, 38" 185.00
Arm, walnut Chpndl, cabriole legs, trifid ft, slip seat, 40" ** ..8,250.00
Arm, walnut Co Chpndl, wingbk, old uphl remains, 46½" 1,300.00
Arm, Windsor, bow bk, brn grpt (rpt), saddle seat, 33½" 220.00
Arm, Windsor, bow bk, bulbous trn, saddle seat, rfn 1,450.00
Arm, Windsor, bowbk, old red & blk pnt, rprs, 37½" 965.00
Arm, Windsor, spindle bow bk, saddle seat, 37x18½" 675.00
Arm/writing, oak, velvet uphl on swivel seat, ca 1890, 40" 170.00
Arm/writing, Windsor, drw under shaped seat, rpt/rpl 2,000.00
Bishop's, chestnut & pine, 1-brd ends, hooded, drw, 61" 1,980.00
Corner, Cherry Co Chpndl, deep apron, reuphl seat, rpr, 33" .1,550.00
Corner, oak European, relief-cvd bk, wood seat, 30" 275.00
Corner, walnut Chpndl style, rush seat, rfn, 32½" 330.00
Parlor, laminated rosewood, C-scroll/floral crest cvg, pr 2,000.00
Rocker, PA sewing; orig brn pnt w/wht striping, floral crest ** 95.00
Rocker, sewing; mahog Emp, worn rush seat, old finish, 29" 50.00
Rocker/arm, bamboo Windsor, comb bk, worn pnt w/gold, 42" ..495.00
Rocker/arm, bamboo Windsor scroll, shaped seat, 40½" 220.00
Rocker/arm, Co Windsor, blk rpt w/mc decor, 30" 100.00
Rocker/arm, comb bk, arrow spindles, old rpt, 43¾" 550.00

Rocker/arm, high bk, fruit stencil on gr pnt w/gold, 41" 550.00
Rocker/arm, JM Young, Mission style, orig finish, 34" 400.00
Rocker/arm, Limbert #1654, 5-slat bk, 3 ea side, rstr, 35", VG ...550.00
Rocker/arm, maple, 4-slat bk, trn finial, rpt, 44" 105.00
Rocker/arm, 3-slat bk, scrolled arms, splint seat, 39" 125.00
Rosewood Am Rococo, floral-cvd fr, tufted uphl, 1850s 1,100.00
Side, bamboo Windsor, blk rpt w/gold stripes, 33½" 120.00
Side, bamboo Windsor, step-down crest, old rpt, 27¾" 105.00
Side, bamboo Windsor, 7-spindle bk, rpr seat, 36½" 55.00
Side, banister bk, half-trn spindles, shaped crest, 45" 415.00
Side, Belter, Rosalie, laminated rosewood, elaborate cvgs ** ..3,000.00
Side, cherry Chpndl, Gothic splat, shaped crest, 38" 1,100.00
Side, Co QA, vase splat, rpl rush seat, blk rpt, 39" 105.00
Side, Co QA, vase splat, Spanish ft, rush seat, dk rfn, 41½" 1,045.00
Side, Co QA, yoke crest, vase splat, rush seat, 41" 600.00
Side, Co Windsor, 7-spindle bow bk, saddle seat, 38" 250.00
Side, fruitwood Fr Provincial, floral cvg, uphl seat, 39" 125.00
Side, hardwood Flemish scroll, EX cvg, cane seat & bk, 52" 450.00
Side, mahog English Chpndl, rolled crest, uphl seat, 37", pr 330.00
Side, mahog English Co Chpndl, reuphl slip seat, 35" 175.00
Side, oak, 7-spindle bk w/shaped crest, depressed seat, 39" 135.00
Side, oak English Co, rush seat, rprs, 41" 400.00
Steer horn, crest/ams/legs of curled horn, reuphl, 30" 465.00
Wingbk, Chpndl, mahog base, old gr uphl, 47" 4,750.00
Wingbk, Chpndl style, c&b ft, old uphl, early 20th C, 46" 1,100.00
Wingbk, English Regency, plush uphl, trn ft w/castors, 47" 1,250.00

Chair Sets

Hitchcock type, red rpt w/gold & yel, rpl seats, 1 arm+5 side 990.00
Mahog Chpndl style, no seats, minor rprs, 31", 3 for 525.00
Mahog English Regency, striped reuphl, trn legs, 2 arm+4 side ..750.00
Mahog Hplwht, brocade reuphl, worn finish, 36", 2 arm+4 side .3,465.00
Mahog Sheraton style, shield bk, cvd, rfn, 6 for 1,000.00
Oak, Victorian, uphl seats, cvd bks, 6 side+2 arm 1,200.00
Side, arrowbk, dk brn pnt w/floral crest, 34", 6 for 1,500.00
Side, English, vase splat, rpl seats, blk/gold rpt, 33", 6 for 250.00
Side, ladderbk w/4 grad slats, rush seats, 20th C, 41", pr 165.00
Side, mahog Emp, sabre-leg, cvd slat, uphl seat, 4 for 990.00
Side, PA balloon bk, yel rpt w/blk & red striping, 32", 4 for 330.00
Side, walnut English QA, vase splats, reuphl seats, 42", pr 800.00
Side, Windsor, bow bk, blk w/yel striping, 38", 6 for ** 5,280.00

Chests

Chest, classical mahogany veneer, two short drawers over four, old brasses, refinished, Massachusetts, ca 1825, 50x39x20", $1,150.00.

Apothecary, pine & poplar w/mahog, red flame grpt, 40x36x13" ...**4,180.00**
Apothecary, pine Co, 16 nailed drw, old rfn, rprs, 36x33" **2,300.00**
Bachelor's, mahog English Chpndl, 3-drw, old rfn, 34" **1,550.00**
Bachelor's, mahog facade English Chpndl, mahog grpt, 35" L .**1,100.00**
Butler's, cherry Am Empire w/pull-out desk, 3-drw, 55x45x22" ..**1,980.00**
Camphor wood, dvtl, brass mts, rfn/rprs, 48" **425.00**
.Cherry & mahog veneer Fed, 4-drw, crest, rpl/rpr, 44x42" **600.00**
Cherry Am Co Sheraton, 4 dvtl drw, panel ends, rfn, 42" **550.00**
Cherry Co, 4 dvtl drw, molded edge top, rprs, 41x43x21" **1,200.00**
Cherry Co bowfront w/curly veneer, 4-drw, gallery, 45x42" **660.00**
Cherry Co Sheraton w/bookcase top, 4-dvtl drw, 92x40x19" ..**1,650.00**
Cherry Hplwht, 4 dvtl cockbeaded drw, rprs/rfn, 44x39x19" **440.00**
Cherry Hplwht w/inlay, Fr ft, 4 dvtl drw, 42x41x20" **880.00**
Cherry w/curly maple veneer Sheraton, 4 dvtl drw, rough, 44" ..**750.00**
Cherry/curly maple Sheraton w/inlay, 8-drw, 50x39x20" **3,190.00**
Cherry/pine, 2 short drw/4, beaded front, Fr ft, rfn, 47" **575.00**
Curly maple Co Emp, 2 short drw:3, paneled ends, 43x43x21" ..**990.00**
Figured veneer Fr Louis XV style, marquetry panel, 36x48x17" ..**1,800.00**
Mahog English Chpndl chest on chest, 6 drw:shelf:3 drw, 75" ..**4,290.00**
Mahog Fed, bowfront, 4 dvtl drw w/beading, rpl/rprs, 37x38" **880.00**
Mahog Fr style, serpentine facade, 5-drw, rfn/rpl, 47x42x22" **375.00**
Maple Co Chpndl, 4 dvtl drw, bracket ft, rprs, 38x36x20" **635.00**
Maple Co Chpndl, 6 grad drw, secret drw in cornice, 57x40" .**4,400.00**
Maple Co QA, pine sides, 6-drw, rpl brasses, 51x36" **4,180.00**
On fr, walnut Chpndl, 8-drw, cvd trifid ft, cornice, 76" ** ...**20,350.00**
On fr, walnut PA QA, 9 dvtl drw, molded cornice, 69x40x22" ..**5,500.00**
Pine English Co, 6-drw, worn rpt w/gr striping, 43x37" **600.00**
Walnut Chpndl, 2 drw:3, oval brasses, rprs, 45x40x22" **3,200.00**
Walnut Hplwht, 5 dvtl drw, Fr ft, orig brasses, 44x36" **2,750.00**

Commodes, See Chests

Cupboards (See Also Pie Safes)

Butternut Co, 2 do:2 drw:2 tin panel do, cornice, 83x42" **850.00**
Cherry Co, 2 panel do:3 drw:2 panel do, old varnish, 88x47" .**2,300.00**
Cherry Co, 2 panel do:3 dvtl drw:2 do, 2-pc, 84x52x20" **4,350.00**
Cherry/poplar Co, old brn grpt, 2 8-pane do:2 panel do, 86" ..**2,000.00**
Corner, ash Co, 4 panel do, nailed drw, pie shelf, 1-pc, 84" **1,100.00**
Corner, cherry Co, dbl do:drw:do, cornice, 1-pc, 79x49" **1,650.00**
Corner, Co Federal, grpt, ca 1820, 82x44", EX **1,760.00**
Corner, maple Co, 2 panel do, cut-out ft, 1-pc, 82x55" **1,450.00**
Corner, pine Co, 2 raised panel do, 1-pc, stripped, 86x45" **1,300.00**
Corner, pine Co, 9-pane do:panel do, 2-pc, rprs, 75x45" **2,100.00**
Corner, pine w/red flame grpt, reeded details, 1-pc, 54x32" **900.00**
Corner, poplar Co, dbl 8-pane do, pnt traces, 1-pc, 87" **2,600.00**
Corner, poplar Co Hplwht, 12-pane do:drw:panel do, 90" **5,170.00**
Corner, poplar Emp, 2 panel do:2 drw:2 panel do, stain, 85" ..**2,300.00**
Corner, poplar w/burl grpt, 2 arched do:3 drw:3 do, 85" **7,150.00**
Corner, poplar/cherry Co Chpndl, grpt, 12-pane do:2 do, 84" ..**4,950.00**
Hanging, cherry, panel do:dvtl drw, 21x13½ x13" * **330.00**
Hanging, mahog veneer, dvtl case, 4-pane do, OH, 26x24x10"* ..**378.00**
Hanging, mixed woods, raised panel do, red stain, 25x22x8" **745.00**
Hanging, pine, old red rpt, 26x19x12" **495.00**
Hanging, walnut PA, panel do in beaded fr, rfn, 27x22" **2,100.00**
Jelly, pine Co, panel do, cornice, old gray pnt, 62x36" **880.00**
Jelly, poplar, 4-panel do, molded cornice, old red, 72x38" **1,550.00**
Jelly, poplar Co, 2 dvtl drw:2 panel do, rfn, 53x44x19" **715.00**
Jelly, walnut Co, panel do, orange rpt int, scrubbed, 54x33" ...**1,595.00**
Oak Continental, molded/cvd details, 2-pc, rfn, 93x32x20" **3,025.00**
Pewter, poplar Co, dvtl drw, 2 panel do, 1-pc, 76x47x19" **7,350.00**
Pine & poplar, old red grpt, scrolled cornice, 2-pc, 84x41" **1,200.00**
Pine Co, 2 4-pane do:pie shelf:4 drw & 2 do, rfn, 76x61" **1,450.00**
Pine Co, 5-shelf, panel do, handmade, late, 1-pc, 75x30x14" **330.00**

Pine Co English, open top, 4-drw:3 false drw/2 do, 2-pc, 81" ..**1,045.00**
Pine Southern, stepbk top w/4 pane do:panel do, rprs, 30x26" ..**1,100.00**
Poplar Co, panel do:pie shelf:4 drw:panel do, 82x50x15" **2,100.00**
Poplar Co, 2 do:2 drw:2 panel do, 2-pc, rfn, 83x44x19" **1,375.00**
Poplar Co, 2 6-pane do:3 drw:2 panel do, 2-pc, 75x48x15" **1,450.00**
Poplar Co, 4 panel do, molded cornice, old pnt, 81x43" **600.00**
Poplar PA Co, 2 do:shelf:3 drw:2 do, rpl ft, 89x57x20" **3,750.00**
Walnut, 1 do, 1 shelf, nailed, appl molding, OH, 26x26x12" **770.00**
Walnut Co, 2 panel do, cornice, cut-out ft, 1-pc, 79x42" **935.00**
Walnut Co, 2 panel do:2 drw:2 panel do, old pnt, 2-pc, 81" **1,650.00**
Walnut Co, 2 panel do:2 drw:2 panel do, 2-pc, 81x48" **1,265.00**
Walnut Co, 2 6-pane do:2 drw:2 panel do, 2-pc, 85x52x17" ...**8,250.00**
Walnut Co, 2 6-pane do:2 panel do, cornice, 91x48" **2,425.00**

Desks

Desk, Federal cherry, slant lid, stepped valanced interior, replaced brasses, refinished, early 1800s, 44x40x18", $2,185.00. (Collector's hint: Drop front desks are more valuable if the writing surface is the proper height for a regular chair.)

Butler's, mahog Chpndl, 3 dvtl drw, fitted int, rfn, 48" **1,100.00**
Butler's, mahog veneer, 3-drw, Fr ft, fitted int, 41x46" **715.00**
Campaign, mahog English w/ebony line inlay, 2-drw, 38x49x22" .**990.00**
Cherry Co, slant top, dvtl case, 4 dvtl drw, rprs, 44x36x17" **2,200.00**
Cherry Co Chpndl, slant top, 4-drw, fitted int, 42x36" ** **4,675.00**
Cherry Co Hplwht w/walnut inlay, slant top, 4-drw, 47x41x21" .**1,980.00**
Cherry Hplwht w/inlay, slant top, 4-drw, fitted int, 43x39" **1,100.00**
Cherry/poplar Co Sheraton, dvtl drw, gallery, 33x31x25" **495.00**
Clerk's, walnut Co Emp, 2 dvtl drw, slant top, 51x29x26" **825.00**
Curly walnut W&M, slant top, fitted int, 4-drw, 44x37" ** .**18,700.00**
Lap, Tunbridgeware & walnut, 12", +later stand **200.00**
Lap, walnut, brass bound, Victorian, 20", on later stand **225.00**
Limbert #492 ½ , organizer on bk, long drw, arched apron, VG .**1,000.00**
Maple Co Chpndl, slant top, 4 dvtl drw, fitted int, 41x36" **3,300.00**
Pine Co Hplwht, on fr, dvtl drw, slant top, rstr, 38x38x20" **415.00**
Roll top, oak, well-fitted top, 4 drw ea side base, 45" W **1,650.00**
Walnut Am Vict, burl-panel roll top, brass gallery, 49x45" **1,300.00**
Walnut Co, slant top, 4 dvtl drw, fitted int, rfn, 43x40x19" **1,925.00**
Writing, mahog English Edwardian w/flame veneer, 2-drw, sm .**450.00**

Dressers

Henderon, mahog Victorian style, serpentine, mirror, cvgs, 72" .**850.00**

Oak, curved facade, swivel mirror, press/cvd decor **500.00**
Oak, lg swivel mirror in lyre fr, serpentine front, 3-drw **665.00**
Prudence Mallard, att; mahog, serpentine drw, cvd mirror fr ...**3,500.00**
Walnut Am Vict, rvtc/cvd fr on rnd-top mirror, marble top, 95" ..**1,200.00**
Walnut Renaissance Revival/Eastlake, marble top **900.00**

Dry Sinks

Cherry/butternut/poplar Co, panel do, dvtl drw, 33x32x15" **935.00**
Pine, yel grpt over dk, CI & brass thumb latches, 32x43x22" ..**1,400.00**
Pine Co, batten do, bl pnt traces, rpl latch, rfn, 34x44x25" **450.00**
Pine Co, 2 panel do, dvtl drw, red rpt, 33x52x24" **1,045.00**
Poplar Co, oak grpt over dk finish, dvtl drw, 35x42x20" **550.00**
Walnut Co, 2 panel do, dvtl well, bk shelf, rfn, 45x49x30" **1,500.00**

Highboys

Cherry Co QA, 3 drw:4 (top), 1 drw:3 (base), rprs, 76x38" **9,900.00**
Curly maple Co QA, flat top, scrolled apron, rpl, 67x36" **2,950.00**
Maple Co QA, 4-drw top, 1 drw:3 in base, rfn, mar, 64" **2,500.00**
Maple QA w/some curl, 4 drw:2 drw, cabriole legs, 73x36" **9,350.00**
Tiger maple QA, fan drop, flat top, rpl brasses/rfn, 72" ** ...**20,000.00**
Walnut PA Chpndl, 8 dvtl drw, ogee ft, molded cornice, 66½" ...**4,180.00**
Walnut PA Chpndl, 9 dvtl drw, ogee ft, cornice, 65x41x22" ** .**10,450.00**

Lowboys

Figured maple QA, heart-pierced apron, Spanish ft, 29x40" ...**6,000.00**
Mahog Am Chpndl, 4-drw, EX detail, ca 1900, 33x40x22" **1,015.00**
Mahog Chpndl style, old repro w/hand-cvd detail, 29x32x20" ..**2,860.00**
Walnut Philadelphia Chpndl style, 4-drw, b&c ft, 30x31x21" ..**3,575.00**

Pie Safes

Cherry/poplar Co, 24 star-punched tins, rfn, 70x39", EX **1,600.00**
Poplar Co, dbl do w/6 punched tin panels:2 drw:2 do, 84x44" **990.00**
Poplar Co, dvtl drw, 2 panel do, bl rpt, 1-pc, 39" W **500.00**
Poplar Co, tan grpt, rpt on punched tin, 2-drw, 63x48" **770.00**
Tin-covered wood w/old mc pnt, punched flower design, 27x40" .**225.00**
Walnut Co, single do w/5 punched tin panels, 76x32x18" ** .**2,860.00**

Secretaries

Burled walnut Victorian, much cvg, 98x44x22", EX **1,950.00**
Mahog Emp w/flame grain veneer, dvtl drws, slant lid, 87" **1,650.00**
Mahog Hplwht w/figured veneer & inlay, dbl do:3 drw, 77x39" ..**3,750.00**
Mahog w/flame grain veneer, bookcase, 99x46x24" **900.00**
Pine/poplar Co, 2 panel do:fall front lid:3 drw, 2-pc, 79" **2,750.00**
Walnut Co, 4 dvtl drw, drop lid, fitted int, 56x40x21" **1,100.00**

Settees

Fr style, cvd fr w/gold rpt, worn uphl, early 1900s, 50" **150.00**
Fr style, mahog fr, worn blk uphl, 46" **550.00**
Louis XVI style, tapestry uphl, old gold rpt, 52" W **700.00**
Pnt & decor Windsor, much stencil, ca 1830, 33x73" * **750.00**

Shelves

Corner, poplar, jigsaw work w/lattice & stars, blk pnt, 55" **660.00**
Hanging, hardwood, 3 stepbk w/trn posts, varnish, 21x23" **55.00**
Hanging, walnut, cvd rope detail w/tassels, sq nails, 11x13" **120.00**
Hanging, walnut, trn spindle gallery, 28x19" **450.00**
Hanging, walnut Co, chip-cvd, porc buttons, red rpt, 10x17" **530.00**

Hanging corner, walnut, jigsaw work w/stars, sq nails, 24" **75.00**

Sideboards

Cherry Hplwht style w/inlay, KY repro, 42x58x21" **1,100.00**
Cherry/mahog Emp, 3 drw:4 do, cvd ft, 43x71x25" **935.00**
Credenza, Fr Emp, brass & porc inlay, marble top, 44x68x18" ...**2,860.00**
Credenza, Fr style, exotic wood inlay, marble top, 54x56x25" .**1,265.00**
Huntboard, Southern pine Co, 2-drw, rpl brasses, 40x47x22" .**1,045.00**
Lifetime (att), 3 drw:1:2 do, orig hdw/finish, 60", EX **1,700.00**
Mahog & mahog veneer Classical, ca 1825, rfn, 42x59x23½" .**2,070.00**
Mahog & mahog veneer Classical, MA, 1820, 43x72x25", VG **925.00**
Mahog Am Empire, cvd fruits, 2 drw:2 bowfront do, paw ft **1,200.00**
Mahog Hplwht style, dvtl drws, repro, 39x72x27" **450.00**
Server, pine/poplar Co Hplwht, 3 dvtl drw, gallery, 39x37" **2,400.00**
Shop o/t Crafters #323, inlaid do ea side 3 drw, 57x54", G **1,200.00**
Wavy birch & mahog Fed, ca 1815, rstr, 39x69x21½" **3,025.00**

Sofas

Sofa, Classical-style carved mahogany veneer, rolled brass trim, red velvet upholstery, old refinish, 1850s, 35x84", $1,870.00.

Am Neoclassic Grecian, brass mts, cornucopias, paw ft, 88" **850.00**
Chinese Chpndl style, camel bk, uphl, 72" **330.00**
J&J Meeks, Stanton Hall, elaborate cvg on crest rail/apron **7,000.00**
Kittinger, Chpndl style camel bk, velvet uphl, repro, 88" **3,850.00**
Mahog Am Classical, leaf-cvd ends on str crest, paw ft, 99" **1,200.00**
Mahog Emp, highly cvd fr w/winged ball ft, rstr/reuphl, 57" **1,870.00**
Mahog Fed, reuphl, EX cvg, ca 1815, 35x77x29" **1,875.00**
Mahog Fed, trn/reeded legs, open arms, reuphl, 78" **2,500.00**
Mahog Sheraton w/inlay, reuphl, rstr, 73½" **1,775.00**
Mahog veneer Classical, much cvg, ca 1835, 48x37x15" **1,325.00**
Mahog veneer Classical w/brass, velvet uphl, 1820s, 35x84" ..**1,875.00**
Rococo Revival, rosewood fr, pk brocade uphl, rprs, 60" **850.00**

Stands

Cherry Classical, dvtl drw, pineapple-cvd legs, 27x19x19" **1,100.00**
Cherry Co, dvtl drw, scalloped base shelf, rpl top, 20x21" **195.00**
Cherry Co, dvtl drw, 2-brd top, trn legs, rprs, 29x21x21" **245.00**
Cherry Co, nailed drw, trn legs, 2-brd top, rfn, 31x20x20" **300.00**
Cherry Co, 2-drw (figured fronts), rpl pulls, 31x19x19" **440.00**
Cherry Co w/mahog veneer facade, 2 dvtl drw, rfn, 30x21x17" ..**440.00**
Cherry/birch/maple Co, 3-part base w/chip cvg, 25x19x15" **990.00**
Cherry/poplar Co, trn legs, nailed drw, rpl top, 29x19x17" **188.00**
Corner, cherry Classical w/figured veneer, 3-drw, 30x32" **1,400.00**
Curly maple & cherry Co, 2-drw, 2-brd, 29x21x19" **800.00**
Curly maple Sheraton, dvtl drw, 1-brd top, old rfn, 29x20x17" ..**935.00**
Drop leaf, cherry Co, 2 bird's-eye veneer drw, 27½" **715.00**
Drop leaf, mahog Emp, 2 dvtl drw, pull-out bin, 27x21x13" **335.00**
Drop leaf, cherry Co, 2-drw, 2-brd top, 29x19x13" **415.00**
Fr style w/mahog inlay, marble top, 1900s, 31x13x10½" **225.00**

Hardwood Co Hplwht, rpl bird's-eye maple top, drw, 30x28x25" ..220.00
Mahog Emp style, on castors, 20th C repro, 22x20"+leaves 250.00
Mahog Emp w/flame-grain veneer, 2 dvtl drw, 30x20x17" 350.00
Pine Co Hplwht, dvtl drw, 1-brd top, 38x17x17" 360.00
Pine Sheraton, 2 dvtl drw, orig flame grpt, 29x22x17" 1,925.00
Pine/poplar Co, dvtl drw, 1-brd top, trn legs, 27x19x19" 350.00
Poplar Co, trn legs, dvtl drw, 1-brd top, rfn, 29x21x18" 145.00
Poplar Co, 2-drw, 1-brd top, orig flame grpt, wear, 19x19" 550.00
Walnut Co Hplwht, dvtl drw, removable 2-brd top, 29x26x22" .385.00
Walnut Southern Hplwht, dvtl drw, 1-brd, 38x24x19" ** 1,550.00

Stools

Footstool, CI base w/old gold rpt, worn uphl, 14x10½" 250.00
Footstool, Co Windsor, pnt traces, branded P Mitchell, 16" 95.00
Footstool, mahog Am Fed, trn legs, 1815, sm 245.00
Footstool, Mission, arched sides, rpl leather top, 17x18x24" 260.00
Footstool, poplar Co Windsor, rectangular top, 6¾x13" 40.00
Footstool, walnut w/lt wood inlay, 5 trn legs, 12x12½" 145.00
Footstool, walnut w/old varnish, scalloped legs/apron, 6x7x14" 75.00

Tables

American Rococo carved walnut and laminated parlor table, marble top, pierced and carved apron, cabriole legs joined by cross pieces surmounted with urn-shaped finial, ca 1850s, 28x43x31", $3,300.00.

Banquet, mahog Emp, drop leaves, swing legs, 29½ x93x53" ..1,550.00
Banquet, mahog Fed Banded, orig hdw, old rprs, 3-pc 9,000.00
Banquet, mahog Fed style w/flame veneer apron, rprs, 91x48", pr .1,100.00
Breakfast, mahog English Regency tilt-top, brass ft, 60x48" 1,200.00
Card, cherry Chpndl demilune, tapered legs, rprs, 39x36" 2,860.00
Card, cherry Fed w/mahog veneer apron, rpl top, rfn, 35" 275.00
Card, mahog English Hplwht, folding leaf, swing leg 500.00
Card, satinwood English Hplwht style, swing top folds, rfn 375.00
Center, rosewood Rococo, turtle top, shell/foliage cvgs 1,300.00
Console, A Roux, cvd rosewood serpentine front/stretcher 1,800.00
Cricket tavern, oak English, do in apron, 28x23" dia 400.00
Cricket tavern, oak English, 2-brd top, rfn, 28½x26" dia 200.00
Cricket tavern, pine English, tripod base w/shelf, 30x31" 375.00
Dining, Arts & Crafts, quarter-sawn oak veneer, 48" dia 750.00
Dining, Arts & Crafts, 5-leg, veneered, minor chips, 54" dia 800.00
Dining, Berkey & Gay, Emp Revival, 3 ped, ea w/4 paw ft 5,500.00
Dining, mahog Hplwht style, banded, rfn, 96x46" 2,000.00
Dining, Victorian oak, split center ped, rfn, 58" dia+6 leaves .1,800.00
Dressing, mahog English Edwardian, 2-drw, mirror, 39x32" 450.00

Dressing, mahog English Hplwht, 3-drw, rprs, 22x30x42" 325.00
Dressing, pine Co, 3-drw, scalloped apron, rpl pulls, 37x18" 365.00
Drop leaf, cherry Co Hplwht, old rfn, rprs, 46x15"+2 leaves 550.00
Drop leaf, cherry Co Sheraton, 4-leg, rfn, 46x55" 250.00
Drop leaf, curly maple Co, trn legs, apron, 42x20"+12" leaves ...900.00
Drop leaf, curly maple Co Emp, rfn, 28x40x21"+16" leaves 500.00
Drop leaf, mahog Duncan Phyfe style, 2-drw, 1800s, 32x41" ..1,050.00
Drop leaf, mahog English QA, swing-leg, rfn, 48x16"+leaves 550.00
Drop leaf, walnut QA, cabriole legs, rstr, 42x14"+leaves 715.00
Gate leg, oak, old finish, late 1800s, 27x28x24" 350.00
Harvest, birch/pine Co, orig pnt, castors, 30x95x22"+leaves ...8,800.00
Harvest, pine Co, wide brd apron, 2-brd top, 33x105x29" 550.00
Lamp, Arts & Crafts, flared legs, sq shelf, no mk, 30x24" 250.00
Library, Limbert #1163, 2-drw, corbeled legs, 48", VG 900.00
Library, mahog & burl veneer, 3-drw, leather top, 30x38x32" ...1,500.00
Library, mahog Chpndl style, 4-drw, c&b ft, 30x72x40" 990.00
Library, mahog Renaissance Revival, 20th C repro, 54x28" 365.00
Pembroke, birch Co, trn legs, red traces, 39x42"+2 leaves 550.00
Pembroke, walnut Co Hplwht, 2-brd top, 28x36x17"+leaves 215.00
Sawbuck, pine & poplar Co, 2-brd top, rfn, 30x72x31" 385.00
Server, mahog Am Neoclassic, 2 side/frieze drw, cvgs/fluting ..1,750.00
Tavern, hardwood/pine Co QA, 1-brd top, rprs, 25x31x23" **..2,650.00
Tavern, pine Co Chpndl, 2-brd top, scalloped apron, 32x25" .1,650.00
Tea, walnut PA Chpndl, tilt top, tripod base, rprs, 30x36" ** ...6,875.00
Tea/tilt top, mahog Chpndl style, modern repro, 29" dia 495.00
Tea/tilt top, walnut Chpndl, tripod base, birdcage, 32" dia 2,200.00
Tilt top, cherry Fed, 1-brd top, scimitar legs, rfn, 21x19" 800.00
Tilt top, mahog Chpndl style, cvd details, worn, 30x27" 175.00
Tilt top, mahog English Chpndl style, tripod base, 31x22" 175.00
Tilt top, mahog Phila Chpndl, birdcage & pie crust top, 24" * ...700.00
Tilt top, walnut NY Fed w/curly maple & mahog, 26x23x17" 660.00
Work, cherry Emp w/mahog veneer, 2-drw, hinged top, 22x18" .385.00
Work, cherry Fed, drw, tripod legs w/scimitar legs, 18x17" 715.00
Work, mahog Emp w/figured veneer, 2 dvtl drw, paw ft, 21x16" ...525.00
Work, mahog Fed, 1 dvtl drw, pull-out shelves, 27x15" ** 6,380.00
Work, walnut Co QA, 2 dvtl drw, removable top, rfn, 48x32" ...770.00
Writing, mahog traditional style, trn/reeded legs, 34x22" 110.00

Wardrobes

Armoire, Alexander Roux, Am Rococo, cvd lions, mirror do .2,400.00
Kas, maple w/some curl, panel do, dvtl cornice, 79x71x24" 3,080.00
Kas, softwood, raised panels, molded cornice, rpt, 85x73" 1,950.00
Mahog English, panel do, bracket ft, cornice, 1900s, 79x45" 425.00
Poplar Co, 2 panel do, cut-out ft & apron, rfn, 74x48" 525.00
Poplar Co, 2 panel do:2 drw, cornice, red stain, 74x42x15" 450.00
Walnut Co, panel dbl-do, cornice, old varnish, rprs, 82x46" 525.00

Washstands

Co Sheraton, reddish rpt, rstr, 35x24x16" 200.00
Corner, mahog inlay Fed, New England, old rfn, 26x15x14" 690.00
Pine Co, dvtl gallery, trn legs & posts, 39x36x20" 415.00
Pine Co Emp, 1-drw, base shelf, gallery, rpt, 40x22x15" 275.00
Poplar Co Sheraton, fake drw, gallery, 31x17x17" 188.00
Walnut Am w/figured veneer, marble top:2 drw:2 do, 38x40x21" ...800.00
Walnut Co, dvtl drw, scalloped crest w/towel bar, rfn, 33" 385.00
Walnut Co Emp, dvtl drw w/Rockingham pull, rfn, 35x25x21" .300.00
Walnut Co Sheraton, dvtl drw & gallery, rpl/rfn, 28x19x17" 180.00

Miscellaneous

Armoire, Alexander Roux, Am Rococo, cvd lions, mirror do .2,400.00
Armoire, rosewood Rococo, ornate crest/floral-appl arch do ...5,200.00

Bin, pine Co, 2-part int, hinged lid, yel pnt, 47x39x20" **385.00**
Etagere, walnut Vict, 3-part mirror:shelf:fretwork:marble top .**1,400.00**
Lectern, Italian Rococo cvg, red leather top, 54½" **1,150.00**

Galena

Potteries located in the Galena, Illinois, area generally made plain utility wares with lead glaze often found in a pumpkin color with some slip decoration or splashes of other colors. These potteries thrived from the early 1830s until sometime around 1860. In the listings that follow, all items are made of red clay unless noted otherwise.

Bottle, pinch; gr-amber, wear/flakes, 7¾" **100.00**
Jar, gr-amber w/olive polka dots, wear/chips, 7¼" **195.00**
Jar, gr-orange, pebble look, hairline, 6¼" **185.00**
Jug, redware, gr-amber w/orange spots, ovoid, 9½", EX **195.00**
Pie plate, buff clay w/gr-amber spots, 9½" **85.00**

Galle

Emile Galle was one of the most important producers of cameo glass in France. His firm, founded in Nancy in 1874, produced beautiful cameo in the Art Nouveau style during the 1890s, using a variety of techniques. He also produced glassware with enameled decoration, as well as some fine pottery — animal figurines, table services, vases, and other objets d'art. In the mid-1880s he became interested in the various colors and textures of natural woods and as a result began to create furniture which he used as yet another medium for expression of his artistic talent. Marquetry was the primary method Galle used in decorating his furniture, preferring landscapes, Nouveau floral and fruit arrangements, butterflies, squirrels, and other forms from nature. It is for his furniture and his cameo glass that he is best known today. All Galle is signed.

In the listings below, 'fp' indicates items that have been fire polished. Our advisor for this category is Don Williams; he is listed in the Directory under Missouri.

Cameo

Atomizer, flower buds/foliage, lav on yel & frost, 8" **1,250.00**
Atomizer, poppies, 2-color, gold bulb & tassel, 6¼" **1,200.00**
Bottle, scent; floral, amethyst on yel frost, 8" **1,840.00**
Bowl, maple seed pods cvd w/in, leaf-cvd outside, 11½" **1,600.00**
Creamer, currants/leaves, red on frost/peach, 3¼x2¼" **1,495.00**
Inkwell, berries/leaves, red on yel cased, fp, squat, 2x6" **2,500.00**
Lamp, vines on yel & purple, slim std, 8" dome shade, 19" **8,000.00**
Plate, clematis, purple on frost, fp, 6¾" **900.00**
Toothpick holder, leaves/pods in gr, 2½" **525.00**
Vase, abstract flowers, bl/wht/gr on bl opal, 3-sided, 10" **850.00**
Vase, allover leaves/berries, orange on wht cluthra, 16x12" **3,000.00**
Vase, bleeding hearts, pk/gr on frost w/bl, long neck, 8" **2,000.00**
Vase, carnations, bl/purple on yel opal, 4½x6¾" **2,850.00**
Vase, floral, amethyst on bl, bottle form, 6¾" **1,045.00**
Vase, floral, bl/purple on pk, star mk, 9½" **1,000.00**
Vase, floral, brn on frosted, banjo form, 7" **1,200.00**
Vase, floral, brn on wht frost, bottle form, 6½" **1,000.00**
Vase, floral, brn on yel frost, baluster, 5" **700.00**
Vase, floral, brn to purple on yel frost, long can neck, 6" ...**1,000.00**
Vase, floral, brn/yel on rose/clear, waisted cylinder, 15" **2,350.00**
Vase, floral, dk brn on gr frost, str w/bulb base, 11" **1,150.00**
Vase, floral, fuchsia on lav frost, 2½x3" **500.00**
Vase, floral, orange on frost, 2½x2½" **800.00**
Vase, floral, pk on yel & wht frost, stick neck, 6½" **1,100.00**

Vase, floral, purple on bl, bulbous w/tapered neck, 3½" **275.00**
Vase, floral, purple on pk frost, flaring lip, 4½" **800.00**
Vase, floral, purple on yel-orange, banjo form, 6¾" **950.00**
Vase, floral, rust on shaded yel frost, trumpet neck, 4" **800.00**
Vase, floral cluster, purple/gray on pk opaque, 7" **1,200.00**
Vase, floral/lg leaves, brn/gr on yel, 5x2" **1,200.00**
Vase, floral/lg leaves, rust/red/gr on yel, 16x5½" **5,000.00**
Vase, fuchsia, brn on yel-brn, some fp, 6½" **525.00**
Vase, lg iris, purple on frost & purple, fp, 13½x3½" **3,500.00**
Vase, lilies/leaves, purple on yel opal, mk/France, 8½x5½" **5,250.00**
Vase, mtn scene, brn/gray on gray w/yel, baluster, 9" **4,000.00**
Vase, nasturtiums, tangerine on frosty opal, ovoid, 8¼" **2,500.00**
Vase, oak leaves/acorns/limbs, bl-gray on pk, 14x6½" **4,750.00**
Vase, orchids, purple on frost, flat-sided stick neck, 6" **1,000.00**
Vase, pansies, purple on yel, 5x3¼" **1,100.00**
Vase, pond lilies/pads, 3-color, vivid/well cut, 9x3½" **3,000.00**
Vase, poppies, orange on frost, fp, oval, 7" **1,900.00**
Vase, poppies, red on yel, U-form, 5" **1,000.00**
Vase, roses, red on citron/clear, EX cutting, fp, 8x7" **4,000.00**
Vase, roses, red/wine on gold-amber, slim, 12" **2,750.00**
Vase, wildflowers/grasses, brn on gray, tapered sides, 7" **1,000.00**
Vase, wisteria, amethyst on pk, 4½x6" **1,300.00**
Vase, wisteria, mulberry on frost, shouldered, 14" **2,000.00**
Vase, wisteria, red on yel to wine, allover cut/fp, 9x3" **1,750.00**

Enameled Glass

Vase, Nouveau-style flowering branches surround mantis on swirled form, ca 1890, 8", $1,430.00.

Bottle, etched shields/monks at table, mc/gilt on gray, 9½" **9,200.00**
Bowl, floral, mc/gold on gray, irregular rim, 4¾x8" **690.00**
Bowl, tulips/Dutch seascape on gray w/gr streaks, lid, 6" H **3,450.00**
Cordial, amber w/thistles on cup & stem, 3½" **425.00**
Ewer, poppy pods/ferns/dragonfly on lt amber, gilt, 7", EX **1,150.00**
Vase, etched Gothic motifs, appl flowers, gilt, cylinder, 7" ...**2,500.00**
Vase, fuchsia/gilt on gr, cylinder w/disk ft, 17½" **2,200.00**

Marquetry, Wood

Cabinet, mahog, cvd & inlaid florals & scenic, mk, 36x25" **4,250.00**
Stand, shaped 16x16" top/2nd tier w/inlay, thin arched legs ...**2,400.00**
Table, mahog, floral inlay, nesting set of 3, lg sz: 30x19" **4,000.00**
Table, 2-tier, butterfly/floral, serpentine legs, 28x25x16" **1,725.00**
Table, 2-tier, daffodils/grasses, scrolling legs, 32x36" **4,600.00**
Table, 2-tier, jonquils, curved y-legs, 30x30x20" **2,300.00**

Pottery

Centerpc, 3 geese w/necks joined, bodies form bowls, 7x15" ...**2,000.00**
Plate, landscape w/Oriental, floral border, 9¾", pr **275.00**

Plate, man in ragged cloak, icicle trim, shield form, 7x8½" 175.00
Tray, bachelor buttons emb/pnt on wht, 3x6" 200.00
Tureen, scenic, bud finial, 4 ft continue to form hdls, 10" 920.00
Vase, iris/butterfly, bl/gr/gold, ribs/dimples, drilled, 10" 500.00

Gambling Memorabilia

Gambling memorabilia from the infamous casinos of the West and items that were once used on the 'Floating Palace' riverboats are especially sought after by today's collectors.

Book, How To Play Poker, NY, 1929, 32-pg, EX 300.00
Book, Hoyle's Games, 1940s, 278-pg, VG 100.00
Book, Kid Canfield, GW Canfield, 1911, 48-pg, EX 140.00
Book, Practical Poker, Foster, NY, 1905, 253-pg, EX 80.00
Book, Webster's Poker Book, HT Webster, 1925, 126-pg, EX 45.00
Box, bird's-eye maple w/brass & MOP inlay, 1880s, 6x11x2½" ..200.00
Box, card & chip; rosewood w/brass inlay, '30s, 6½x8x2½" 60.00
Box, card; blk walnut & mahog w/aces inlay, 1885, 4½x8x2½" 80.00
Box, card; hammered copper w/4 aces on top, 1950, 6x8½", EX ...45.00
Box, card; mahog w/brass inlay, 1860s, 4½x7½x3¼", EX 120.00
Box, card/chip; leather covered, for 200 chips, 1900s, EX 75.00
Box, chip; celluloid, pnt/emb aces, lined, 1900s, 7x8½x2½" 160.00
Box, chip; mahog trunk form, pull-out rack, '20s, 5x10x6", EX 80.00
Box, chip; wood w/cards inlay, brass pips, 1930s, 10x8", EX 50.00
Box, gaming; mixed woods, MOP inlay, w/chips, 1880s, 8½x13x3" .150.00
Card press, mahog w/cvg, floral petit point, EX 375.00
Card press, maple w/MOP buttons, brass mts, EX 650.00
Card press, maple w/turq inlay roses, EX 275.00
Card press, pnt scene on maple, w/ivory finials, EX 700.00
Card press, rosewood, brass mts, ivory finial, EX 525.00
Card press, rosewood w/MOP floral inlay, EX 325.00
Chips, Catalin, Royal Band, A&L Mfg, MIB 65.00
Chips, clay, assorted advertising, 1900s, 30 for 150.00
Chips, ivory, scrimshaw floral, 1890s, 15 for 425.00
Cribbage board, spade shape, pnt cards in center, 5x7", EX 70.00
Dice cup, leather 40.00
Pharo box, rosewood w/brass inlay, w/chips/cards, 1865, EX .21,000.00
Pharo casekeeper, BC Wills Detroit, celluloid/maple, 1910, EX .600.00
Pharo casekeeper, Cowper, celluloid strips/maple, 1910, EX 550.00
Pharo casekeeper, F Grote & Co NYC, mahog & oak, ca 1900, EX .650.00
Pharo casekeeper, Geo Williams NYC, rosewood/ivory, 1860s, NM .1,050.00
Pharo casekeeper, Harris & Co NY, spades on veneer, 1900s 600.00
Pharo casekeeper, HC Evans Chicago, celluloid/walnut, 1915 ...475.00
Pharo casekeeper, Mason & Co Chicago, veneer, 1900, EX 400.00
Pharo casekeeper, Will & Fink, oak, clay markers, 1880s, NM .1,050.00

Pharo layout, nonfolding board in oak frame, F. Grote & Co., New York City, ca 1890, 17x41", EX, $1,500.00.

Pharo-dealing box, cut-out corner shows index, unmk, 1930s, EX ..400.00
Roulette watch, Monaco Roulette, enameled dial, 1890s, EX 250.00
Roulette watch, Roulette Ideal, beveled crystal, 1890s, EX 550.00

Roulette watch, St Louis Expo, enamel dial, 1904, EX in box 475.00
Table, bridge; inlaid woods, suit sign ea corner, 1940s, 31" sq 200.00
Trump indicator, brass disk, 1880s, 1" dia, 4 in brass box 170.00
Trump indicator, HP ivory disk, 1890s, 1½" dia, 4 in box 175.00
Watch, crown & anchor gaming dial of pnt metal, 1920s, EX 200.00
Wheel, wood w/brass pins, pnt dice pattern, 1900s, 28", EX 175.00
Whist scorer, cvd ivory hand w/pointing finger, 1870s, 7 for 850.00
Whist scorer, MOP w/silver & enamel, 1880s, 2" dia, EX 220.00

Game Calls

Those interested in hunting and fishing collectibles are beginning to take notice of the finer specimens of game calls available on today's market. Our advisor for this category is Randy Hilst; he is listed in the Directory under Illinois.

Black Duck, Whitting, Ind., rosewood with A&F logo carved in barrel, 1950s, complete in marked gift box, $1,000.00; Charles Perdew, Henry, Ill., walnut, made for U.L. & A., 1940s, exceptional in all respects, $2,900.00.

Crow, Charles Perdew, Henry IL, silver band, Pat Nov 2 1900 ..250.00
Crow, Charles Perdew, stamped, Pat 1909 ....150.00
Duck, AM Bowles, laminated Arkansas style, 1950s, EX 200.00
Duck, Bill Clifford, band on bbl & insert, EX 1,600.00
Duck, Glodo style, metal reed tone board, EX 750.00
Duck, Nat & Doug Porter, Reelfoot, cvd rings, ca 1900s, EX 235.00
Duck, Tom Dennison, metal reed, EX 125.00
Duck, William Burke, metal reed, cvgs on tiger maple, M 2,000.00
Duck (pintail), Tom Turpin, rosewood, EX 150.00
Goose, cedar, 2 metal eyes for hanging, 16½", NM 100.00
Goose, Jerry Reed, metal reed, 1940s, EX 100.00

Gameboards

Gameboards, the handmade ones from the 18th and 19th century, are collected more for their folk-art quality than their relation to games. Excellent examples of these handcrafted 'playthings' sell well into the thousands of dollars; even the simple designs are often expensive. If you are interested in this field, you must study it carefully. The market is always full of 'new' examples. Well-established dealers are often your best sources; they are essential if you do not have the expertise to judge the age of the boards yourself. Our advisor for this category is Louis Picek; he is listed in the Directory under Iowa.

Carom, 2-sided, mc pnt w/gold, early 1900s, 28½" sq 85.00

Checkers, blk pnt sqs on pine, gallery edge, primitive, 15½" **50.00**
Checkers, dk red & blk pnt w/yel stripes, wear, 24x18" **220.00**
Checkers, hardwood, worn blk, wht & red pnt, galleried, 17" **195.00**
Checkers, HP oilcloth on wooden fr, PA, 21x23" **525.00**
Checkers, pine, stencil, stain, & yel-pnt trim, 28x14" **160.00**
Checkers, pnt wood, faux marble sqs, stencil edge, 1900s, 18" ...**440.00**
Checkers, red & blk pnt w/mc striping & flowers, 24x15" **400.00**
Checkers, red & blk pnt wood, early nails, 19x25", EX **275.00**
Checkers, walnut w/blk-pnt sqs, rprs/cracks, 14x14" **150.00**
Checkers, walnut w/brn & blk sqs, 29x18" **440.00**
Checkers, yel & blk cb on pine bk w/walnut edge, 13x13¼" **140.00**
Checkers/backgammon, blk/gray/brn, buttons at edge, 18x19" **440.00**
Checkers/game, old red & gr rpt, primitive, 26x19" **140.00**
Checkers/geometric maze, pnt wood, appl gallery, 13x13" **195.00**
Checkers/parcheesi, pnt landscape border, oversz, 37x37" **1,100.00**
Oil on canvasboard, cattle in landscape on bk, 1880s, 19x25" ...**400.00**

Games

Game collectors are finding it more difficult to find their treasures at shows and flea markets. Most of the action these days seems to be through specialty dealers and auctions. The appreciation of the art on the boards and boxes continues to grow. You see many of the early games proudly displayed as art, and they should be. The period from the 1850s to 1910 continues to draw the most interest. Many of the games of that period were executed by well-known artists and illustrators. The quality of their lithography cannot be matched today. The historical value of games made before 1850 has caused interest in this period to increase. While they may not have the graphic quality of the later period, their insights into the social and moral character of the early 19th century are interesting.

20th-century games invoke a nostalgic feeling among collectors who recall looking forward to a game under the Christmas tree each year. They search for examples that bring back those Christmas-morning memories. While the quality of their lithography is certainly less than the early games, the introduction of personalities from the comic strips, radio and later TV created new interest. Every child wanted a game that featured their favorite character. Monopoly, probably the most famous game ever produced, was introduced during the Great Depression.

For further information, we recommend *Schroeder's Collectible Toys, Antique to Modern*, available from Collector Books. Our advisor for personality-related games is Norm Vigue; he is listed in the Directory under Massachusetts.

Across the Continent, Parker Bros, 1952, MIB **60.00**
Air Assault on Crete, Avalon, 1972, EX+ **32.00**
Alabama Coon, cb litho, Spear's, Bavaria, EX in box **200.00**
All-Star Basketball, Whitman, 1935, EX **65.00**
American Heritage Broadside, Milton Bradley, 1962, NM **25.00**
Amusing Game of Innocence Abroad, Parker Bros, 1888, VG- ..**210.00**
Authors, Parker Bros, 1943, VG **25.00**
Bagatelle, McLoughlin Bros, 1900, NM **450.00**
Baseball, bagetelle game, Marx, 1960s, 10x10", NMIB **65.00**
Blarney Stones, Parker Bros, 1940, VG **45.00**
Boy Hunter, target game, Marx, MIB **25.00**
Buckaroo, Milton Bradley, 1947, VG **30.00**
Bug-A-Boo, race game, Whitman, 1968, NM **30.00**
Bulls & Bears Stock Exchange Game, Parker Bros, 1936, EX **130.00**
Clown Ring Toss, wooden, 6" dia base, EX **35.00**
Collegiate Electric Basket, Electric Game Co, 1930s, EX **75.00**
Combat, board game, Ideal, 1963, NM **25.00**
Conflict, war game, Parker Bros, 1960, EX **45.00**
Contack, Parker Bros, 1939, MIB **45.00**

Cootie, Schaper, 1949, EX in box **25.00**
Crazy Clock, Ideal, 1964, EX **65.00**
Crossword Lexicon, Parker Bros, 1930s, EX **35.00**
Duck Pins, Samuel Gabriel, 1930s, EX **55.00**
Feeley Meeley, Milton Bradley, 1967, NM **25.00**
Five in One Game, pinball type, 1930s, EX **125.00**
Fumanchu Hidden Hoard, EX **35.00**
Funny Finger, Ideal, 1968, NM **15.00**

Game of Detective, board game, Bliss, 1890, complete in worn box, $2,950.00 at auction.

Game of Funny Conversation Cards, Milton Bradley, 1926, MIB ...**65.00**
Game of India, Milton Bradley, 1910, 15x15", EX+ **35.00**
Hickety Pickety, Parker Bros, 1930s, EX+ **28.00**
Jonah & Whale, Pat Pending, brass ball goes in hole, 2¾" sq **100.00**
Keno-Lotto, Selchow & Righter emb edition, 1930s **45.00**
Klix Dice Modern Crossword Game, Toy Creations, 1930s, MIB .**55.00**
Kooky Carnival, Milton Bradley, 1959, VG **15.00**
Lindy Hop-Off the New Airplane, Parker Bros, ca 1927, EX **375.00**
Merry Steeple Chase, Ottman, 1910, EX+ **35.00**
Monkey Target, paper litho, 14x9½x4½", G **25.00**
Old Maid, card game, Parker Bros, 1930s, complete, EX **15.00**
Ping Pong, J Jaques & Son Ltd, complete in 4x20x8" box **120.00**
Public Enemy, target game, Marx, 1950s, MIB **120.00**
Raffles, Sophisticated Game of Chance, 1939, EX **25.00**
Roulette, Milton Bradley, 1932, EX **45.00**
Satellite, target game, cb & plastic, USA, 1950s, MIB **60.00**
Snap Jacks, Samuel Gabriel, 1930s, EX **45.00**
Space Patrol, spinner type, tin & cb, Japan, 1950s, M **45.00**
Stagecoach, Milton Bradley, 1958, complete, EX **30.00**
Tiddle Tennis Jr, Schoenhut, 1930s, EX+ **35.00**
Tie 'N Tangle, Hasbro, 1967, EX **12.50**
Toppling Tower, Ideal, 1967, NM **22.50**
Train for Boston, Parker Bros, 1900, wooden box, EX **900.00**
Visit of Santa Claus, McLoughlin Bros, 1899, EX **495.00**
Wonder Multiplication Table, Ideal Bookbuilders, 1918, EX **35.00**
Yacht Race, Parker Bros, 1961, MIB **150.00**
Young Folks Geographical Game, McLoughlin Bros, 1880s, EX ...**50.00**

Personalities, Movies, and TV Shows

Addams Family, board game, Milton Bradley, 1974, MIB **30.00**
Alfred Hitchcock Presents Why, 1958, NM in EX box **30.00**
Alfred Hitchcock's Why, 1961, EX in box **25.00**
All in the Family, Milton Bradley, 1972, EX **15.00**
Annie Oakley, Milton Bradley, 1958, complete, EX **35.00**
Archie Bunker's Card Game, 1972, EX **12.00**
Around the World in 80 Days, board game, Transogram, 1957, EX ..**50.00**
Arrest & Trial, Transogram, photo cover box, 1963, VG **35.00**

Barbie Queen of the Prom, Mattel, 1960, NM 40.00
Barbie's Little Sister, Skipper; Mattel, 1964, EX 30.00
Barnie Google & Spark Plug, board game, 1923, EX 95.00
Battlestar Galactica, Parker Bros, #2534, 1978, NM 15.00
Bedknobs & Broomsticks, Whitman, 1971, NM 25.00
Beverly Hillbillies, board game, 1963, MIB 45.00
Blondie, Parker Bros, 1959, complete, EX in box 25.00
Blondie Goes to Leisureland, premium, 1953, M 30.00
Bringing Up Father, board game, '20s, EX in illus envelope 100.00
Bugs Bunny Adventure Game, board game, Milton Bradley, 1961, NM ..65.00
Burk's Law, Game of Who Killed; Transogram, 1963, NM 50.00
Captain Caveman & Teen Angels, M Bradley, 1980, NM 18.00
Captain Video, board game, M Bradley, complete, NMIB 125.00
Casper the Friendly Ghost, board game, Milton Bradley, 1959, EX ...20.00
Charlie McCarthy's Radio Party Game, 1938, M 50.00
Cherry Ames, Nursing Game; Parker Bros, 1959, NM 45.00
Combat, 1963, MIB 65.00
Dating Game, Hasbro, 3rd edition, 1968, EX 15.00
Davy Crockett, cards, Fess Parker illus box, 1955 ....45.00
Davy Crockett, horseshoe set, MIB 95.00
Dennis the Menace Baseball, MTP, 25" batting area, 1960, NM ..85.00
Detectives...Game of Deduction; R Taylor on box, '61, NM 65.00
Dick Tracy Super Detective, card game, 1941, FAS, NMIB 45.00
Dino the Dinosaur, missing spinner, Transogram, 1961, EX 35.00
Dukes of Hazzard, Ideal, 1981, EX 15.00
Felix the Cat, 1st version, Milton Bradley, 1960, EX 30.00
Felix the Cat's Dandy Candy Board Game, Built-Rite, 1957, NM ..45.00
Flintstones Big Hunt, 1962, EX 50.00
Godzilla, Mattel, 1978, EX 40.00
Gunsmoke, Lowell, 1955, NM in G box 65.00
Hardy Boys, cartoon art, Milton Bradley, 1969, NM 25.00
Hopalong Cassidy, Chinese checkers, NMIB 150.00
Hopalong Cassidy, dominoes, MIB 125.00
Hopalong Cassidy Lasso Game, w/Hoppy on Topper figure, EX .160.00
Hopalong Cassidy Target Game, tin, orig darts, MIB 275.00
Howdy Doody, bean bag game, EX 175.00
Howdy Doody, Visit to Howdy's...Studio, Milton Bradley, EX 85.00
I Dream of Jeannie, Milton Bradley, 1965, EX 45.00
James Bond, Thunderball; Milton Bradley, 1965, NM 40.00
Katzenjammer Kids Hockey, board game, 1950s, EX 42.00
Legend of Jesse James, Milton Bradley, 1966, NM 85.00
Lloyd Bridges in Underwater Adventures, 1961, MIB 85.00
Man From UNCLE, board game, Ideal, 1965, NM 40.00
Man From UNCLE, cards, Milton Bradley, 1965, EX 20.00
Margie Game of Whoopie, Milton Bradley, 1960s, NM 30.00
Marlin Perkins' Zoo Parade, board game, unused 38.00
Mary Poppins, Disney, Whitman, 1964, EX+ 35.00
Mash Golden Trivia, 1984, EX in box 7.00
McHale's Navy, Borgnine on box, Transogram, 1962, NM 40.00
Mickey Mouse, tiddly winks, Chad Valley, NMIB 275.00
Mickey Mouse Game Library, W Disney Productions, 1946, MIB .225.00
Mickey Mouse Party Game, permission of WDE, NMIB 100.00
Mork & Mindy, cards, Milton Bradley, MIB 10.00
Mr Novak, Transogram, 1963, EX 35.00
Munsters, cards, VG 30.00
Nancy Drew Mystery Game, Parker Bros, 1957, EX 45.00
Partridge Family, board game, Milton Bradley, EX in box 25.00
Patty Duke, board game, Milton Bradley, 1960s, EX 30.00
Pin the Tail on Mickey, Marx Bros, NMIB 115.00
Pink Panther, Milton Bradley, 1969, M 35.00
Popeye Ring Toss, Popeye & Olive figures, 1933, EX in box 175.00
Quick Draw McGraw Private Eye, Milton Bradley, 1960, NM 50.00
Raggedy Ann's Magic Pebble, Milton Bradley, 1941, EX 80.00
Restless Gun, John Payne on box, Milton Bradley, 1959, EX 45.00

Rifleman, board game, Milton Bradley, 1959, MIB 50.00
Rin Tin Tin, board game, Transogram, 1955, EX 45.00
Road Runner, Milton Bradley, 1968, EX 45.00
Robin Hood Robust Adventure, 1940s, EX 45.00
Rootie Kazootie, cards, 1953, EX in box 15.00
Scooby Doo, Milton Bradley, 1973, VG 22.00
Sea Hunt (Lloyd Bridges), board game, complete, EX 45.00
Six Million Dollar Man, Bionic Crisis, 1975, VG in box 7.50
Skeezix, cards, complete in EX box 45.00
Smokey Bear, Milton Bradley, 1968, NM 25.00
Smurf Card Game, 1982, NMIB 5.00
Snow White, board game, Cadaco, 1977, EX 10.00
Spanky & His Rascals Fun Game, board game, 1956, EX 60.00
Spanky & Little Rascals Clubhouse Bingo, Gabriel, 1958, NM 65.00
Spider Woman, board game, Hasbro, 1977, EX 15.00
Spiro Agnew History Game, 1971, NM 15.00
Stagecoach West, Wayne Rogers on lid, Transogram, 1961, EX 50.00

Star Trek Super Phaser Target Game, Paramount Pictures Corp., Made in Taiwan for Mega Corp., New York, NY, ca 1975, EX in box, $40.00.

Superman, board game, bright graphics, 1954, EX 115.00
Surfside 6, Lowell, 1961, EX 65.00
Tarzan, board game, Milton Bradley, 1977, MIB 15.00
Truth or Consequences, Lowell, 1962, NM 35.00
Twiggy, Milton Bradley, 1967, MIB 60.00
Untouchables, target game, Marx, 1950s, MIB 175.00

G. A. R. Memorabilia

The 'The Grand Army of the Republic' was first conceived by Chaplain W.J. Rutledge and Major B.J. Stephenson early in 1864 when they were tent-mates during our own Civil War. These men vowed to each other that if they were spared they would establish an organization that would preserve friendships and memories formed during this time. Shortly after the war ended, Rutledge and Stephenson made their desires a reality. The first National Convention of the Grand Army of the Republic was held in Indianapolis, Indiana, on November 20, 1866. The purpose of the organization was to provide aid and assistance to the widows and orphans of the fallen Union dead and to care for the hospitalized veterans as needed. The last comrade of the G.A.R. died in 1949.

Early encampments were held on both state and national levels, resulting in a wide variety of souvenir items being made. Many are now surfacing. Our advisor for this category is Richard Haussmann; he is listed in the Directory under Illinois.

Medal, election campaign; portrait on celluloid, ca 1900, VG 30.00
Medal, 18th Annual Encampment, aluminum, w/ribbon, 1892 ....35.00
Medal, 20th Nat'l Encampment, gilt bronze star, 1886, EX 50.00
Ribbon, 23rd Nat'l Encampment, wht silk, 1889, 10½", EX 25.00
Ribbon badge, celluloid panel w/crossed flags, 8½" 35.00
Spoon, 1894 Encampment, musket hdl 55.00
Spoon, 1898 Nat'l Encampment 30.00

Stein, Etruria-Mellor, hand w/cards/eagle/etc, 1861-66, 6" 260.00

Gas Globes and Panels

Gas globes and panels, once a common sight, have vanished from the countryside but are being sought by collectors as a unique form of advertising memorabilia. Early globes from the 1920s (some date back to as early as 1912), now referred to as 'one-piece globes,' were made of molded milk glass and were globular in shape. The gas company name was etched or painted on the glass. Few of these were ever produced, and this type is valued very highly by collectors today.

A new type of pump was introduced in the early 1930s; the old 'visible' pumps were replaced by 'electric' models. Globes were changing at the same time. By the mid-teens a three-piece globe consisting of a pair of inserts and a metal body was being produced in both 15" and 16½" sizes. Collectors prefer to call globes that are not one-piece or plastic 'three-piece glass' (Type 2) or 'metal body, glass inserts' (Type 3). Though metal-body globes (Type 3) were popular in the 1930s, they were common in the 1920s, and some were actually made as early as 1915. Though rare in numbers, their use spans many years. In the 1930s Type 2 and Type 3 globes became the replacements of the one-piece globe. The most recently manufactured gas globes are made with a plastic body that contains two 13½" glass lenses. These were common in the fifties but were actually used as early as 1932.

Note: Standard Crowns with raised letters are one-piece globes that were made in the 1920s; those made in the 1950s (no raised letters), though one-piece, are not regarded as such by today's collectors. Our advisor for this category is Scott Benjamin; he is listed in the Directory under Ohio.

Aero Mobilgas, type 3, new metal body, 15½", rare, $2,200.00; Aeropel, type 2, clear gill rippled body, 13½", rare, NM, $3,200.00.

Type 1, Plastic Body, Glass Inserts (Inserts 13½"), 1931–1950s

Ashland Diesel 175.00
Dixie, plastic band 200.00
DX Lubricating Gasoline, tan body 200.00
Frontier Gas, Rarin' To Go, w/horse 350.00
Hornet, Capcolite body, 13½", NM 225.00
Kendal Deluxe, Capcolite body w/red pnt, 13½" 200.00
Kendall Polly Power, Capcolite body, 13½", NM 195.00
Marathon, no runner 150.00
Never Nox Ethyl 250.00
Shamrock, oval body 200.00
Spur, oval body 200.00
Texaco Diesel Chief, Capcolite body, 13½", NM 600.00

Viking, pictures Viking ship 325.00
66 Flite Fuel, Phillips, shield shape, all plastic 350.00

Type 2, Glass Frame, Glass Inserts (Inserts 13½"), 1926-1940s

Aerio, gr gill ripple body, 13½", NM 5,000.00
Amaco, hull body, 12½", NM 350.00
American, hull body, 12½", NM 350.00
Amoco, gill body, 13½", NM 350.00
Atlantic, glass body, 13½" dia, NM 325.00
Atlantic Imperial, gill body, 13½", EX 375.00
Derby 375.00
Frontier Gas, Double Refined 325.00
Golden 97 Ethyl, hull glass body, 12½", NM 350.00
Gulf 375.00
Gulf, hull body, 13½", NM 425.00
Guyler Brand, milk glass, EX 650.00
Kanotex, w/sunflower, gill body 425.00
Koolmotor, clover shape 800.00
Pitman Streamlined, bl gill rippled body, 13½", NM 4,500.00
Red Crown, milk glass 350.00
Sinclair Dino, milk glass, EX 250.00
Sinclair Pennant 650.00
Skelly Anomarx w/Ethyl 450.00
Sky Chief, gill body, 13½", NM 400.00
Standard Crown, gr or orange, ea 800.00
Standard Flame 300.00
Texaco Diesel Chief 750.00
Texaco Ethyl 1,100.00
Texaco Star, blk outline on 'T' 400.00
White Rose, boy, glass body 1,200.00
WNAX, w/radio station pictured 900.00

Type 3, Metal Frame, Glass Inserts (Inserts 15" or 16½"), 1915-1930s

Aero Mobilgas, new metal body, rare, 15", NM 2,200.00
Atlantic White Flash, 16½" 500.00
Blue Sunoco, 15" 425.00
Crown, crown figural, 16½", EX 1,000.00
Esso Extra, 15" 425.00
Kendal Gasoline, metal body, rare, 15", NM 4,000.00
Mobil Gas, winged horse, 15" or 16½" metal fr, NM 600.00
Oil Creek Gas, drake well & derrick, 15" dia, NM 1,800.00
Phillips Benzo, low profile metal body, 15", NM 3,500.00
Pure, porc body, 15" 650.00
Purol Pep, porc body 700.00
Red Crown Ethyl 950.00
Richfield, w/eagle 600.00
Rocor, w/eagle 650.00
Signal, old stoplight, 15", VG 2,800.00
Socony, milk glass inserts on metal 1,000.00
Stanolined Aviation, rare, 16½", EX 3,750.00
Texaco Leaded, glass panels, pr 3,800.00
Tidex, 16½" 425.00
White Star, 15" fr, complete 850.00

Type 4, One-Piece Glass Globes, No Inserts, Co. Name Etched, Raised or Enameled, 1912–1931

Atlantic, chimney cap 2,400.00
Diamond 850.00
Dixie, etched 1,200.00

Musgo	**4,000.00**
Pierce Pennant, etched	**2,500.00**
Republic, 3-sided	**1,400.00**
Shell, rnd, etched	**750.00**
Sinclair, etched, milk glass	**1,000.00**
Sinclair Aircraft, etched	**3,500.00**
Skelly	**650.00**
Super Shell, clam shape	**1,500.00**
Super Shell, rnd, etched	**2,800.00**
Texaco, milk glass, emb letters, brass collar ...	**900.00**
That Good Gulf..., emb, orange & blk letters, EX ...	**900.00**
White Eagle, some feather detail, 20¾", EX ...	**1,500.00**
White Rose, boy pictured, pnt	**2,400.00**

Gaudy Dutch

Inspired by Oriental Imari wares, Gaudy Dutch was made in England from 1800 to 1820. It was hand decorated on a soft-paste body with rich underglaze blues accented in orange, red, pink, green, and yellow. It differs from Gaudy Welsh in that there is no lustre (except on Water Lily). There are seventeen patterns, some of which are: War Bonnet, Grape, Dahlia, Oyster, Urn, Butterfly, Carnation, Single Rose, Double Rose, and Water Lily. For further information we recommend *The Collector's Encyclopedia of Gaudy Dutch & Welsh* by John Shuman, available from Collector Books. Values are given for mint condition examples unless otherwise.

Butterfly, creamer	900.00
Butterfly, cup & saucer, butterfly in center ...	950.00
Butterfly, cup plate	800.00
Butterfly, plate, 6⅜"	575.00
Butterfly, teapot	2,300.00
Carnation, coffeepot	1,300.00
Carnation, cup & saucer	650.00
Carnation, plate, 8"	600.00
Carnation, teapot	1,350.00
Dahlia, creamer	900.00
Dahlia, plate, 8"	800.00
Dahlia, sugar bowl	900.00
Double Rose, cup & saucer	525.00
Double Rose, cup plate	700.00
Double Rose, plate, 10"	1,000.00
Double Rose, plate, 9"	900.00
Double Rose, teapot	725.00
Double Rose, waste bowl, 6"	625.00
Dove, creamer	700.00
Dove, plate, plain border, 6¼"	500.00
Dove, toddy plate	700.00
Grape, cup & saucer	475.00
Grape, cup plate	600.00
Grape, plate, 6¼"	300.00
Grape, plate, 7"	400.00
Grape, plate, 8¼"	525.00
Grape, soup plate, 8¾"	450.00
Grape, toddy plate, 4½"	375.00
Leaf, tea bowl & saucer	800.00
Oyster, creamer	400.00
Oyster, plate, orange pattern, 9¾"	1,300.00
Oyster, plate, 6⅜"	400.00
Oyster, teapot	500.00
Primrose, plate, mk Riley, 8¾"	550.00
Primrose, tea bowl & saucer	700.00
Single Rose, coffeepot	725.00

Single Rose, creamer	875.00
Single Rose, cup & saucer, EX	320.00
Single Rose, cup & saucer, NM	475.00
Single Rose, plate, 6½"	450.00
Single Rose, plate, 7¼"	500.00
Single Rose, plate, 9½"	550.00
Single Rose, soup plate	375.00
Single Rose, waste bowl, 6⅛"	550.00
Strawflower, plate, 9¼"	875.00
Strawflower, toddy plate, chip, mk Riley, 4¾" ...	525.00
Sunflower, plate, 7½"	550.00
Sunflower, sugar bowl, w/lid, EX	550.00
Urn, cup plate	425.00
Urn, plate, 8¼"	625.00
Urn, teapot	600.00

War Bonnet, pitcher, 5¾", $1,000.00.

War Bonnet, plate, 6⅜"	575.00
War Bonnet, soup plate	700.00
War Bonnet, sugar bowl, w/lid, hdl rpr ...	850.00
War Bonnet, toddy plate, faint mk, 5¼" ...	485.00
Zinnia, plate, deep, 9¾"	1,125.00

Gaudy Ironstone

Gaudy Ironstone was produced in the mid-1800s in Staffordshire, England. Some of the ware was decorated in much the same colors and designs as Gaudy Welsh, while other pieces were painted in pink, orange, and red with black and light blue accents. Lustre was used on some designs, omitted on others. The heavy ironstone body is its most distinguishing feature.

Key:
pc — polychrome   ug bl — underglaze blue

Cheese dish, Azalea, floral, cobalt/gold, Woods, w/tray ...	185.00
Cup & saucer, handleless; Morning Glory, ug bl, pc, EX ...	95.00
Mug, rabbits & frogs w/floral, blk transfer+4 colors, 5⅜" ...	1,325.00
Plate, floral, ug bl, pc w/lustre, Ironstone, 8⅜" ...	115.00
Plate, floral w/cornucopias, ug bl, pc, T Walker, 8¾" ...	200.00
Plate, Morning Glory, ug bl & lustre, 8⅜" ...	105.00
Plate, Morning Glory, ug bl w/red & gr, 8⅝", EX ...	105.00
Plate, Strawberry, ug bl, pc enamel & lustre, 8½" ...	150.00
Plate, tulips & berries, ug bl, pc, 8¾" ...	150.00
Plate, Urn, stains, 9¾" ...	200.00
Plate, vintage, ug bl w/red & gr & lustre, 9" ...	115.00
Platter, floral, ug bl w/purple & bl, 12½" ...	150.00
Platter, Imari floral in ug bl w/red & gold, 20¾", EX ...	225.00
Sugar bowl, floral, 3-color, w/lid, 4" ...	70.00

Tea set, floral, rprs, 9½" pot, 3-pc **500.00**

Gaudy Welsh

Gaudy Welsh was an inexpensive hand-decorated ware made in both England and Wales from 1820 until 1860. It is characterized by its colors — principally underglaze blue, orange-rust, and copper lustre — and by its uninhibited patterns. Accent colors may be yellow and green. (Pink lustre may be present, since lustre applied to the white areas appears pink. A copper tone develops from painting lustre onto the dark colors.) The body of the ware may be heavy ironstone, creamware, earthenware, or porcelain; even style and shapes vary considerably. Patterns, while usually floral, are also sometimes geometric and may have trees and birds. Beware! The Wagon Wheel pattern has been reproduced.

Our advisor for this category is Cheryl Nelson; she is listed in the Directory under Minnesota. For further information we recommend *The Collector's Encyclopedia of Gaudy Dutch and Welsh* by John Shuman, available from Collector Books.

Columbine, plate, 8¼" 95.00
Columbine, tea set, 17-pc 775.00
Cornflower, teapot 175.00
Daisy & Chain, creamer 80.00
Feather, cup & saucer 50.00
Flower Basket, cup & saucer 85.00
Flower Basket, plate, 9" 150.00
Glamorgan, pitcher, 4¾" 75.00
Grape & Lily, creamer & sugar bowl, w/lid 265.00
Grape & Lily, cup & saucer 90.00
Mask Spout, creamer, 2½" 75.00
Morning Glory, compote, 5¾x10¼" dia 285.00
Morning Glory, cup & saucer 95.00
Morning Glory, plate, 10" 135.00
Oyster, jug, 4½" 95.00
Oyster, pitcher, 5½" 120.00
Oyster, tea set, child's, 3-pc 225.00
Pagoda, pitcher, 5⅝" 100.00
Seeing Eye, cup & saucer 125.00
Shanghai, creamer 150.00
Strawberry, spill holder, 4⅜", pr 300.00
Sunflower, pitcher, snake hdl, 5" 200.00
Tulip, bowl, serving; 9" 50.00
Tulip, mug 85.00
Tulip, plate, 7¾" 75.00
Tulip, waste bowl, 6⅜" 110.00
Urn, tureen, ftd, 9½" W 275.00
Wagon Wheel, plate, 8¾" 110.00

Geisha Girl Porcelain

Geisha Girl Porcelain was one of several key Japanese china production efforts aimed at the booming export markets of the U.S., Canada, England, and other parts of Europe. The wares feature colorful, kimono-clad Japanese ladies in scenes of everyday Japanese life, surrounded by exquisite flora, fauna, and mountain ranges. Nonetheless, the forms in which the wares were produced reflected the late 19th- and early 20th-century Western dining and decorating preferences: tea and coffee services, vases, dresser sets, children's items, planters, etc.

Over a hundred manufacturers were involved in Geisha Girl production. This accounts for the several hundred different patterns, well over a dozen border colors and styles, and several methods of design execution. Geisha Girl Porcelain was produced in wholly hand-painted

versions and those that were hand painted over stencilled outlines. Be wary of Geisha ware executed with decals. Very few decalled examples came out of Japan. Rather, most were Czechoslovakian attempts to hone in on the market. Czech pieces have stamped marks in broad, pseudo-Oriental characters. Items with portraits of Oriental ladies in the bottom of tea or sake cups are *not* Geisha Girl Porcelain, unless the outside surface of the wares are decorated as described above. These lovely faces are formed by varying the thickness of the porcelain body and are called lithophanes.

The height of Geisha Girl production was between 1910 and the mid-1930s. Some post-World War II production has been found marked Occupied Japan. The ware continued in minimal production through the 1980s, but point of origin for the reproductions is Hong Kong. Modern productions are discerned by the pure whiteness of the porcelain; even, unemotional borders; lack of background washes and gold enameling; and overall sparseness of detail.

For further information we recommend *The Collector's Encyclopedia of Geisha Girl Porcelain* by Elyce Litts, available at your local bookstore, from Collector Books, or directly from the author. She is listed in the Directory under New Jersey.

Key:
#2 — Torii	#68 — SGK China, Occupied Japan
#4 — T in Cherry Blossom	J #1 — Yachi
#11 — diaper mk	J #6 — Tashiro
#12 — Royal Kaga	J #16 — Kutani
#16 — SNB	J #19 — Ozan
#19 — Japan	J #36 — Made by Kato
#20 — Made in Japan	J #46 — Yasutera
#35 — Plum Blossom	
#42 — Vantine	

Pancake server, So Big, red and gold edge with floral border, J #16, $135.00.

Basket vase, Bamboo Trellis, gr w/brn & gold, 8½", pr 150.00
Biscuit jar, Baskets of Mums B, red w/gold, 3-ftd 55.00
Biscuit jar, Court Lady, cobalt, J#1 ....65.00
Bonbon, Battledore, olive gr, mum shape 22.00
Bowl, berry; Boat Festival, cobalt, #35, ind 10.00
Bowl, Cherry Blossoms, red-orange edge, 7½" 40.00
Bowl, Dragonboat, bl w/gold, 6-lobed, 7" 35.00
Bowl, Pointing D, red-orange w/gold buds, 5¼" 10.00
Bowl, Porcelain Bench, red-orange w/gold buds, #19, 8" 35.00
Bowl, rice; Carp, red 12.00
Bowl, Stepping Stones, wavy red w/gold buds, #19, 6¾" 20.00
Box, Samisen Practice, gold rim, #68, 2x5x4" 50.00
Cocoa pot, Parasol B: Torii & Parasol, cobalt w/gold, #16 ....55.00
Cocoa set, Bamboo Trellis, gr, 13-pc, serves 6 ....160.00
Cocoa set, Chrysanthemum Garden, cobalt w/gold, #19, 9-pc 100.00
Creamer, Boy w/Scythe, cobalt w/gold, #20 ....15.00
Creamer, Long-Stemmed Peony, bl w/gold, slim, #20 ....10.00
Creamer & sugar bowl, Basket A, dk gr w/gold, scalloped 32.00

Creamer & sugar bowl, Ribbon Parasol, red-orange w/gold 28.00
Cup & saucer, demi; Basket A, curved sides, pattern w/in & w/out ..20.00
Cup & saucer, demi; Paper Carp, red-orange, #35 ....15.00
Cup & saucer, tea; Bamboo Trellis, red w/gold, floral int 22.00
Cup & saucer, tea; Bouncing Ball, bl-gr w/gold buds 25.00
Cup & saucer, tea; Flower Gathering A, bl w/gold lacing 18.00
Demitasse set, Temple A, mc, J#16, 15-pc, serves 6 ....185.00
Egg cup, Cherry Blossom Ikebana, red, #20 ....7.00
Egg cup, dbl; Mother & Son A, bl-gr 20.00
Hair receiver, Watching the Carp, cobalt w/gold, mk 30.00
Jar, condensed milk; Ikebana Party, cobalt w/gold, J#16 ....65.00
Jar, powder; Processional, mc border, J#16 ....37.00
Jug, Battledore, fluted edge & base, ribbed, 5" 35.00
Jug, Parasol C, wavy cobalt, #20, 5x4¾" 25.00
Lemonade set, Bellflower, #19, pitcher+5 mugs 140.00
Mug, Gardening, red w/gold line, 3" 45.00
Mug, lemonade; Geisha in Sampan B, cobalt w/gold, #19 ....12.00
Mustard, Garden Bench C, cobalt w/gold, #4 ....22.00
Pin tray, Boat Dance, gr w/gold lacing, 5x3" 14.00
Plate, Battledore, red w/gold, J#45, 9" 55.00
Plate, Bird Cage, pine gr w/wht, toy 12.00
Plate, Butterfly Dancers, red w/gold, 7" 28.00
Plate, Checkerboard, cobalt, scalloped, 6½" 20.00
Plate, Child Reaching for Butterfly, red, fluted, 7¼" 15.00
Plate, Duck Watching B, mk, 7" 15.00
Plate, Fan A, red-orange, #19, 4¼" 10.00
Plate, Flute & Koto, bl-gr w/gold buds, #19, 7" 24.00
Plate, Visitor to the Court, bl w/gold, scalloped, #19, 7¼" 15.00
Shakers, Blind Man's Bluff, lt apple gr, fluted, pr 25.00
Sugar shaker, Temple B, turq, thimble shape 45.00
Tea set, Bamboo Tree, #19, 16-pc, serves 6 ....125.00
Teapot, Garden Bench C, bl w/gold, #19, 4¾" 28.00
Teapot, Kite A, brn w/gold 25.00
Tray, dresser; Processional Parasol, mc, rectangular 65.00

German Porcelain

Unless otherwise noted, the porcelain listed in this section is marked simply 'Germany.' Products of other German manufactures are listed in specific categories. See also Bisque; Pink Pigs; Elfinware.

Figurine, 18th-Century figures toasting their glasses, Adolph Sache Factory, ca 1910, 11x19x12", $1,650.00.

Basket, appl roses on basketweave, thorn hdl, 8½" 165.00
Biscuit jar, pug dog w/monocle figural, unmk, 6" 260.00
Bookends, ea w/pr of lovers before garden wall, pr 250.00
Bowl, HP pk poppies, 9" 40.00

Candelabra, 2 3-D cherubs on floral-encrusted base, 12", pr ...1,050.00
Candle holder, blk cat figural, tail hdl, 5x4" 110.00
Candlesticks, figural std on scroll base, blk/wht, 12", pr 425.00
Creamer, alligator playing accordion figural, 3¾" 40.00
Creamer, squirrel eating acorn figural 65.00
Figurine, boy & girl dancing, older mk, 7" 95.00
Figurine, dancing boy & girl, pastels, C Scheidig mk, 7" 80.00
Figurine, equestrian Guarde Imperiale, 11½" 165.00
Figurine Girl extending toe, ENS Germany 55.00
Figurine Girl tying bonnet, ENS Germany 75.00
Figurine, Scottie dog, 1 sitting, 1 recumbent, Muller, 5", pr 45.00
Flower frog, Deco nude w/draped scarf, 4½x7" 40.00
Plate, floral bouquet, gold/gr beaded edge, hdls mk, 12" 50.00
Slipper, emb flowers, wht w/gold trim, 2½x4x1¼" 18.00
Vase, rose on mc, HP, sgn Madalin Land, 12" 90.00

Gladding McBean and Company

This company was established in 1875 in Lincoln, California. They first produced only clay drainage pipes, but in 1883 architectural terra cotta was introduced, which has been used extensively in the United States as well as abroad. Sometime later a line of garden pottery was added. They soon became the leading producers of tile in the country. In 1923 they purchased the Tropico Pottery in Glendale, California, where in addition to tile they also produced huge garden vases. Their line was expanded in 1934 to included artware and dinnerware.

At least fifteen lines of art pottery were developed between 1934 and 1942. For a short time they stamped their wares with the Tropico Pottery mark; but the majority was signed 'GMcB' in an oval. Later the mark was changed to 'Franciscan' with several variations. After 1937 'Catalina Pottery' was used on some lines. (All items marked 'Catalina Pottery' were made in Glendale.) For further information we recommend *The Collector's Encyclopedia of California Pottery*, by our advisor for this category, Jack Chipman. He is listed in the Directory under California.

Bowl, Capistrano Art Ware, coral satin, leaf form, 9¾x14" 24.00
Candle holders, Capistrano Art Ware, ivory/celadon, sq, pr 32.00
Candlestick, Coronado Art Ware, coral satin, 6½" 20.00
Cup & saucer, Ruby Art Ware 30.00
Lamp base, Ox Blood Art Ware 95.00

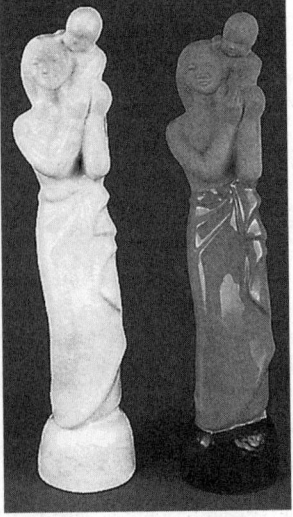

Samoan woman with child figures, Dorr Bothwell, ca 1937, satin white and terra cotta finished, 13", $150.00 to $250.00 each.

Vase, bud; Encanto Art Ware, celadon 22.00
Vase, Catalina Art Ware, ivory satin, turq int, shell form, 8" 45.00

Vase, Catalina Art Ware, periwinkle/bl texture, 6" 100.00
Vase, Garden Ware, bl-gr, bead relief at neck, 35" 550.00

Glass Animals and Figurines

These beautiful glass sculptures have been produced by many major companies in America, in fact, some are still being made today. Heisey, Fostoria, Duncan and Miller, Imperial, Paden City, Tiffin, and Cambridge made the vast majority, but there were many others involved on a lesser scale. Some, but not all, marked their animals.

As many of the glass companies went out of business, molds were often sold to others still active who used them to reproduce their own line of animals. While some are easy to recognize, others can be very confusing. For example, Summit Art Glass now owns Cambridge's 6½", 8½", and 10" swan molds. We recommend *Glass Animals of the Depression Era* by Lee Garmon and Dick Spencer, if you're thinking of starting a collection or wanting to identify and evaluate the glass animals you already have. Both are our advisors for this category and are listed in the Directory under Illinois. Note: Values are for clear unless noted color.

Cambridge

Bashful Charlotte, flower frog, gr, 11" 375.00
Bashful Charlotte, flower frog, gr, 6½" 145.00
Bashful Charlotte, flower frog, moonlight bl, 11" 525.00
Bashful Charlotte, flower frog, peachblo, 6" 150.00
Bashful Charlotte, flower frog, 11" 175.00
Bashful Charlotte, flower frog, 6½" 100.00
Bird, crystal satin, 2¾" L 30.00
Blue jay, flower holder 125.00
Bridge hound, ebony, 1¾" 35.00
Buddha, amber, 5½" 225.00
Draped Lady, flower frog, amber, 8½" 195.00
Draped Lady, flower frog, gr, 8½" 275.00
Draped Lady, flower frog, lt pk frost, 13" 300.00
Draped Lady, flower frog, pk, 8½" 275.00
Draped Lady, flower frog, 8½" 175.00
Eagle, bookend, 5½x4x4" 80.00
Frog, crystal satin 25.00
Heron, lg, 12" 125.00
Heron, sm, 9" 75.00
Lion, bookend, ea 125.00
Mandolin Lady, flower frog 250.00
Mandolin Lady, flower frog, dk amber 450.00
Mandolin Lady, flower frog, gr 400.00
Owl, lamp, ivory w/brn enamel, ebony base, 13½" 1,000.00
Pouter pigeon, bookend, milk glass, 5½" 70.00
Rose Lady, flower frog, dk amber, tall base, 9½" 275.00
Rose Lady, flower frog, gr, 8½" 200.00
Rose Lady, flower frog, tall base, 9½" 200.00
Scottie, bookends, hollow, pr 150.00
Scottie, frosted, hollow, ea 75.00
Sea gull, flower frog 50.00
Swan, candlestick, milk glass, 4½", ea 175.00
Swan, carmen, 6½" 200.00
Swan, carmen, 8½" 250.00
Swan, Crown Tuscan, 3½" 40.00
Swan, Crown Tuscan, 8½" 95.00
Swan, ebony, 10½" 250.00
Swan, ebony, 12½" 300.00
Swan, ebony, 3½" 60.00
Swan, ebony, 8½" 125.00
Swan, emerald, 3½" 35.00

Swan, emerald, 8½" 125.00
Swan, milk glass, 3½" 60.00
Swan, milk glass, 6½" 125.00
Swan, milk glass, 8½" 275.00
Turkey, bl, w/lid 550.00
Turkey, gr, w/lid 450.00
Turkey, pk, w/lid 400.00
Turtle, flower holder, ebony 225.00
Two Kids, flower frog 200.00
Two Kids, flower frog, amber satin 400.00

Duncan and Miller

Bird of paradise 700.00
Donkey, cart & peon, 3-pc set 475.00
Dove, head down, 11½" L 175.00
Duck, ashtray, red, 7" 70.00
Duck, cigarette box, red, 6" 170.00
Goose, fat, 6x6" 275.00
Heron, crystal satin, 7" 120.00
Mallard duck, cigarette box, #30, w/lid, 3½x4½" 45.00
Ruffled grouse, very rare 1,750.00
Swan, ashtray, crystal w/bl neck, 4" 35.00
Swan, bl opal, W&F, spread wings, 10x12½" 245.00
Swan, candle holder, red w/crystal neck, 7", ea 70.00
Swan, gr opal, W&F, spread wings, 10x12½" 225.00
Swan, open, 7" 45.00
Swan, solid, 3" 20.00
Swan, solid, 5" 30.00
Swan, solid, 7" 75.00
Swan, wht milk glass w/red neck, 10½" 450.00
Swordfish 300.00
Swordfish, bl opal, rare 500.00
Sylvan swan, bl or pk, 6½" 125.00
Sylvan swan, vaseline opal, 6½", ea 185.00
Sylvan swan, yel opal, 7½" 100.00
Sylvan swan, 12" 85.00
Tropical fish, ashtray, pk opal, 3½" 50.00
Tropical fish, candle holder, 5", ea 500.00

Fenton

Alley cat, teal marigold, 11" 65.00
Bear, blk, sitting 16.00
Bear, carnival, sitting 20.00
Bear, wht irid, sitting 15.00
Boy, blk, praying 12.00
Bunny, lt bl 16.00
Bunny, pale yel 16.00
Butterfly, candle holder, ruby carnival, 1989 souvenir, 7½", ea 85.00
Cardinal head, ruby, 6½" 95.00
Donkey, custard, HP daisies, 4½" 45.00
Elephant, flower bowl, blk satin, 6½x9" 400.00
Elephant, whiskey bottle, periwinkle, 8" 450.00
Fish, paperweight, red carnival, ltd ed 65.00
Fish, red w/amberina tail & fins, 2½" 55.00
Fish, vase, milk glass w/blk tail & eyes, 7" 425.00
Happiness Bird, red, 6½" 28.00
Peacock, bookends, crystal satin, 5¾", pr 175.00
Turtle, flower block, amethyst, 4" L 85.00

Fostoria

Bird, candle holder, 1½", ea 15.00

Fostoria miniatures, all in amber: Rabbit, 2⅛"; Cat, 3¾"; Frog, 1⅞", $30.00 each.

Cardinal head, Silver Mist, 6½"	125.00
Cat, lt bl, 3¾"	35.00
Chanticleer, blk, 10¾"	600.00
Chinese Lute, ebony w/gold, 12½"	300.00
Colts, sitting	40.00
Colts, standing, Silver Mist	45.00
Deer, sitting or standing, crystal or bl, ea	55.00
Deer, sitting or standing, milk glass	55.00
Deer, sitting or standing, Silver Mist	40.00
Dolphin, bl, 4¾"	25.00
Duck, mama	25.00
Duck w/3 ducklings, amber, set	50.00
Duckling, head bk (+)	20.00
Duckling, head down (+)	20.00
Duckling, walking (+)	15.00
Eagle, bookend, Silver Mist, NM, ea	150.00
Eagle, bookend, 7½", ea	150.00
Elephant, bookend, ebony, 6½", ea	85.00
Goldfish, horizontal, rare	125.00
Goldfish, vertical	95.00
Horse, bookend, 7¾", ea	45.00
Madonna, Silver Mist, orig issue, 10" (+)	50.00
Madonna, Silver Mist, w/base, orig issue, 11¾" (+)	80.00
Mermaid, 11½"	115.00
Pelican, amber, 1991 commemorative	55.00
Penguin, 4⅝"	75.00
Polar bear, topaz, 4⅝"	125.00
Polar bear, 4⅝"	65.00
Sea horse, bookend, 8", ea	115.00
Seal, topaz, 3⅞"	125.00
Squirrel, amber, running	35.00
Squirrel, amber, sitting	35.00
St Francis, Silver Mist, orig issue, 13½" (+)	325.00
Whale	20.00

Heisey

Airdale	500.00
Angelfish	120.00
Asiatic pheasant, 7½" L	300.00
Bull, sgn, 4x7½"	1,400.00
Bunny, head down, 2½"	200.00
Chick, head down or up, ea	65.00
Clydesdale, 7½x7"	400.00
Colt, kicking	185.00
Colt, kicking, amber	650.00
Colt, kicking, cobalt	950.00
Colt, rearing	195.00
Colt, rearing, amber	650.00

Colt, rearing, cobalt	950.00
Colt, standing	90.00
Colt, standing, amber	550.00
Colt, standing, cobalt	900.00
Cygnet, baby swan, 2½"	200.00
Doe head, bookend, 6¼", ea	800.00
Dolphin, candlesticks, #110, pr	250.00
Dolphin, candlesticks, Moongleam, #110, pr	700.00
Donkey	275.00
Duck, ashtray	80.00
Duck, ashtray, Flamingo	160.00
Duck, ashtray, Marigold	195.00
Duck, flower block	140.00
Duck, flower block, Flamingo	200.00
Duck, flower block, Hawthorne	295.00
Elephant, amber, lg or med, ea	1,850.00
Elephant, amber, sm	1,600.00
Elephant, lg or med, ea	400.00
Elephant, sm	195.00
Filly, head bkward, 8⅛x5¼"	1,400.00
Fish, bookend, ea	135.00
Fish, bowl, 9½"	425.00
Fish, candlestick, 5", ea	150.00
Fish, match holder, 3x2¾"	150.00
Flying mare	2,800.00
Flying mare, amber	3,500.00
Frog, cheese plate, Flamingo, #1210	145.00
Frog, cheese plate, Marigold	285.00
Gazelle, 10¾"	1,500.00
Giraffe, head bk	185.00
Giraffe, head forward	200.00
Giraffe, head to side	200.00
Goose, wings down	425.00
Goose, wings half	95.00
Goose, wings up	100.00
Hen, 4½"	400.00
Horse, bookend, ea	155.00
Horse head, bookend, frosted, ea	120.00
Horse head, box, 6½"	85.00
Horse head, cigarette box, #1489, 4½x4"	55.00
Horse head, cocktail shaker	85.00
Irish setter, ashtray	30.00
Irish setter, ashtray, Flamingo	45.00
Irish setter, ashtray, Moongleam	55.00
Kingfisher, flower block, Flamingo	175.00
Kingfisher, flower block, Moongleam	200.00
Mallard, wings down	325.00
Mallard, wings half	185.00
Mallard, wings up	150.00
Piglet, sitting	100.00
Piglet, standing	100.00
Plug horse	135.00
Plug horse, amber	600.00
Plug horse, cobalt	1,000.00
Pouter pigeon, 7½" L	700.00
Rabbit, paperweight, 2¾x3¾"	150.00
Rabbit mother, 4½x5½"	800.00
Ram head, stopper, 3½"	150.00
Ringneck pheasant, 11¾"	140.00
Rooster, amber, 5⅜"	2,500.00
Rooster, Fighting; crystal frost, 7½x5½"	200.00
Rooster, vase, 6½"	85.00
Rooster, 5½x5"	325.00
Rooster head, cocktail	50.00

Rooster head, cocktail shaker, 1-qt 65.00
Rooster head, stopper, 4½" 45.00
Scotty 100.00
Sea horse, cocktail 140.00
Show horse 1,250.00
Sow, 3x4½" 600.00
Sparrow 120.00
Swan, ind nut, #1503 ....20.00
Swan, master nut, #1503 ....45.00
Swan, pitcher 700.00
Swan, 7x8½" 800.00
Tiger, paperweight, 2¾x8" 1,100.00
Tropical fish, 12" 1,650.00
Wood duck 550.00

Imperial

Angelfish, bookend, amber (crystal or frosted), ea 150.00
Asiatic pheasant, amber 325.00
Bull, amber, very rare, 4" 685.00
Bulldog-type pup, milk glass, 3½" 65.00
Champ terrier, caramel slag, 5¾" 95.00
Chick, head down, milk glass 10.00
Chick, head up, milk glass 10.00
Clydesdale, amber 325.00
Clydesdale, Salmon 275.00
Clydesdale, Verde Gr 150.00
Colt, balking, amber 140.00
Colt, balking, caramel slag 45.00
Colt, kicking, Horizon Bl 35.00
Colt, standing, amber 140.00
Colt, standing, Sunshine Yel 85.00
Cygnet, blk, 2½" 55.00
Cygnet, caramel slag 55.00
Cygnet, Horizon Bl 25.00
Dog, Airedale, caramel slag 95.00
Dog, Airedale, Ultra Bl 65.00
Donkey, caramel slag 55.00
Donkey, Meadow Gr Carnival 95.00
Donkey, Ultra Bl 110.00
Duck, sitting, caramel slag, 4½" 45.00
Duck, standing, Ultra Bl, 2⅝" 45.00
Elephant, caramel slag, med 65.00
Elephant, caramel slag, sm 110.00
Elephant, Meadow Gr Carnival, #674, med 110.00
Elephant, Nut Brn, sm 120.00
Filly, head bkward, Verde Gr 145.00
Filly, head forward, blk, extremely rare 400.00
Filly, head forward, satin 75.00
Fish, bookend, ruby, ea 300.00
Fish, canape plate, amber 13.50
Fish, canape plate, cobalt 30.00
Fish, canape plate 12.50
Fish, candlestick, Sunshine Yel, 5", ea 40.00
Fish, match holder, Sunshine Yel satin, 3" 20.00
Flying Mare, amber, NI mk, extremely rare 1,800.00
Gazelle, blk, 11" 400.00
Giraffe, amber, ALIG mk, extremely rare 400.00
Horse head, bookend, pk, rare, ea 300.00
Jack, gr carnival, #506 ....110.00
Mallard, wings down, Horizon Bl, HCA, 4½" 75.00
Mallard, wings down, lt bl satin 22.50
Mallard, wings half, caramel slag 35.00
Mallard, wings up, caramel slag 35.00

Marmote Sentinel (woodchuck), caramel slag, 4½" 60.00
Owl, Hootless; caramel slag 50.00
Owl, jar, caramel slag, 16½" 65.00
Piglet, sitting, amber 75.00
Piglet, standing, amber 75.00
Piglet, standing, ruby, hole between legs 95.00
Plug horse, pk, HCA, 1978 ....40.00
Rabbit, paperweight, Horizon Bl, 2¾" 85.00
Ringneck pheasant, amber, extremely rare 260.00
Rooster, amber 425.00
Rooster, fighting, pk 175.00

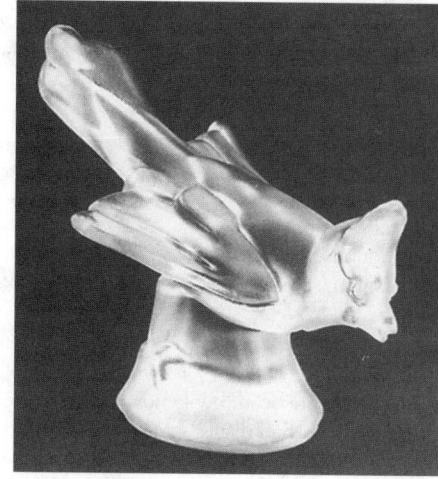

Imperial, Scolding Bird, Cathay Crystal, $175.00.

Scottie, milk glass, 3½" 45.00
Terrier, Parlour Pup, Sunshine Yel carnival 45.00
Terrier pup, amethyst carnival, 3½" 45.00
Tiger, paperweight, caramel slag, 8" L 85.00
Tiger, paperweight, jade marbleized, 8" L 150.00
Wood duck, caramel slag 45.00
Wood duck, Ultra Bl satin 45.00
Wood duckling, floating, Sunshine Yel satin 15.00
Wood duckling, standing, Sunshine Yel satin 15.00
Wood duckling, standing, Ultra Bl 45.00

L.E. Smith

Camel, recumbent, amber, 4½x6" 60.00
Cock, Fighting; bl, 9" 45.00
Elephant, 1¾" 12.00
Goose, 2½" 12.00
Goose Girl, gr or flame, 6", ea 50.00
Goose Girl, orig, 6" 25.00
Horse, bookend, rearing, amber, ea 38.00
Horse, bookend, rearing, blk, ea 65.00
Horse, bookend, rearing, emerald, ea 40.00
Horse, bookend, rearing, ruby, ea 40.00
Horse, recumbent, amberina, 9" L 125.00
King fish, aquarium, gr, 7¼x15" 265.00
Queen fish, aquarium, gr, 7x15" 225.00
Rooster, butterscotch slag, ltd ed, #208 ....85.00
Scottie, pipe rest, fired-on blk, 5½" L 10.00
Sparrow, head up, 3½" 15.00
Swan, milk glass, lg 45.00
Swan, milk glass w/decor, 8½" 45.00

New Martinsville

Bear, baby, head trn or str, 3", ea 60.00

Bear, mama, 4x6" 225.00
Bear, papa, 4x6½" 250.00
Chick, frosted, 1" 25.00
Duck, standing, Viking's Epic Line 35.00
Eagle, 8" 75.00
Elephant, bookend, 5½", ea 85.00
Gazelle, leaping, frosted base, 8¼" 65.00
German shepherd, 5" 75.00
Hen, 5" 65.00
Horse, head up, 8" 95.00
Nautilus shell, bookend, crystal frost, 6", ea 35.00
Piglet, standing 125.00
Porpoise on wave, orig 475.00
Rabbit, mama 350.00
Rooster w/crooked tail, 7½" 85.00
Seal, candlesticks, lg, pr 150.00
Seal w/ball, bookends, 7", pr 140.00
Seal w/ball, candle holder, 4½", ea 70.00
Tiger, head down, frosted, 7¼" 200.00
Tiger, head up, 6½" 200.00
Wolfhound, 7" 95.00
Woodsman, sq base, 7⅜" 95.00

Paden City

American eagle head, bookends, crystal frosted, 7½", pr 300.00
Bunny, cotton-ball dispenser, ears bk, bl frosted 90.00
Bunny, cotton-ball dispenser, ears bk, crystal frosted 60.00
Bunny, cotton-ball dispenser, ears bk, milk glass 95.00
Bunny, cotton-ball dispenser, ears up, pk frosted 150.00
Dragon swan, 9¾" L 215.00
Goose, lt bl, 5" 115.00
Pheasant, Chinese; 13¾" 85.00
Pheasant, Chinese; med bl, 13¾" 150.00
Pheasant, head turned, lt bl, 12" L 175.00
Polar Bear on ice, 4½" 65.00
Pony, blk, 12" 350.00
Pony, 12" 100.00
Pouter pigeon, bookend, 6¼", ea 85.00
Rooster, Barnyard; 8¾" 85.00
Rooster, Chanticleer; lt bl, 9¼" 200.00
Rooster, Elegant; lt bl, 11" 225.00
Rooster, head down, 8¾" 80.00
Squirrel on curved log, 5½" 65.00

Tiffin

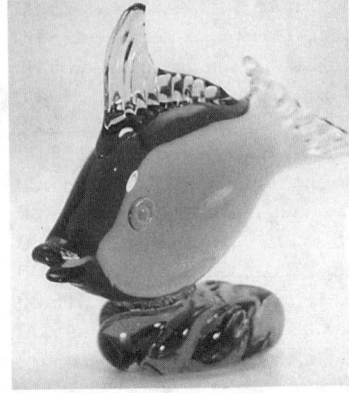

Tiffin, fish, Copen Blue, ca 1945, 8¾x9", $1,000.00 minimum value.

Cat, Sassy Susie, blk satin w/pnt decor, #9448, 11" 175.00
Fish, solid, 8¾x9" 350.00

Owl, lamp, cobalt, 1934-29 ....1,250.00

Viking

Angelfish, blk, 6½" 150.00
Angelfish, milk glass, 6½" 70.00
Bird, med dk bl, 9½" 25.00
Bird, moss gr, 12" 25.00
Bird, Orchid, 9½" 30.00
Cat, gr, 8" 55.00
Duck, dk teal, Viking's Epic Line, 9" 30.00
Duck, fighting, head up or down, Viking's Epic Line, ea 45.00
Duck, vaseline, 5" 25.00
Egret, orange, 12" 45.00
Horse, aqua bl, 11½" 95.00
Penguin, 7" 25.00
Rabbit, amber, 6½" 35.00
Rabbit (Thumper), 6½" 35.00
Rooster, Epic; red, 9½" (+) 60.00
Seal, persimmon, 9¾" L 15.00

Westmoreland

Bird in flight, Amber Marigold, wings out, 5" W 25.00
Bulldog, Crystal Mist, pnt collar, rhinestone eyes, 2½" 35.00
Butterfly, Gr Mist, 2½" 22.00
Butterfly, 4½" 27.00
Cardinal, Gr Mist 20.00
Owl, Crystal Mist, 5½" 30.00
Penguin on ice floe, Brandywine Bl Mist 35.00
Porky Pig, milk glass, hollow, 3" L 15.00
Pouter pigeon, any color, 2½", ea 25.00
Robin, 3¼" L 20.00
Starfish, candle holders, milk glass, 5", pr 45.00
Turtle, flower block, gr, 7 holes, 4" L 55.00
Turtle, paperweight, Gr Mist, no holes, 4" L 25.00

Miscellaneous

Horse head, bookends, milk glass, Indiana, 6", pr 35.00
Lady's leg, bookends, custard, Mosser, pr 175.00
Mopey dog, Federal, 3½" 10.00
Panther, walking, bl, Indiana, 3x7" 250.00
Pouter pigeon, bookend, Indiana, 5½", ea 40.00
Thrush, bl frost 40.00
Turtle, amber, LG Wright, 10" L 85.00

Glass Knives

Glass knives were manufactured from about 1920 to 1950, with distribution at its greatest in the late thirties and early forties. Colors generally followed Depression Glass dinnerware: crystal, light blue, light green, pink (originally called rose), and more rarely amber, forest green, and white (opal). Many glass knives were hand painted in fruit or flower designs. Knife blades were ground to a sharp edge. Today knives are usually found with blades nicked through years of use or bumping in silverware drawers or reground, which is acceptable to collectors as long as the original knife shape is maintained.

Many glass knives were engraved for gift-giving, personalized with the recipient's name and occasionally with a greeting. Originally presented in boxes, most glass knives were accompanied by a paper insert extolling the virtues of the knife and describing its care.

Boxes printed with World's Fair logos are fun to find, though not rare. Butter knives, which are smaller than other glass knives, typically were made in Czechoslovakia and sometimes match the handle patterns of glass salad sets. Knife lengths often vary slightly because the knives were snapped off the molded glass during manufacture.

Our advisor for this category is Adrienne Escoe; she is listed in the Directory under California. For information concerning the Glass Knife Collectors Club, see the Clubs, Newsletters, and Catalogs section of the Directory.

Values reflect knives with minor blade roughness or resharpening.

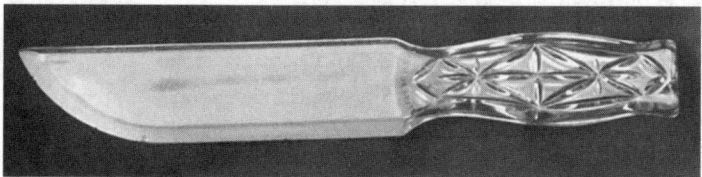

Aer-Flo (Grid), pink, 7½", $45.00.

Block, crystal, MIB	20.00
Block, gr	30.00
Dur-X 3-Leaf, bl, 9½", MIB	20.00
Dur-X 5-Leaf, bl, 9½", MIB	25.00
Grid, crystal	30.00
Rosespray, crystal	25.00
Stonex, crystal	45.00
Stonex, gr, 8¼", MIB	70.00
Thumbguard, crystal, M in plain box	20.00
Vitex (3-Star), bl, 9¼", MIB	32.00

Glass Shoes

Little shoes made of glass can be found in hundreds of styles, shapes, and colors. They've been made since the early 1800s by nearly every glasshouse, large and small, in America. To learn more about them, we recommend *Shoes of Glass* by our advisor Libby Yalom, who is listed in the Directory under Maryland.

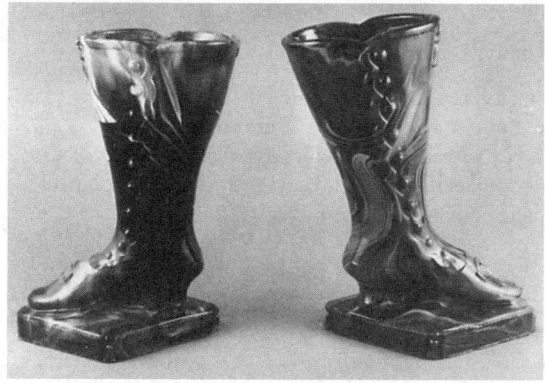

High-button shoes, slag glass, $160.00 each.

Baby's, crystal frost w/gold pnt laces/bow, '20s, 3⅞x2⅜"	30.00
Boot, cobalt w/pnt florals & gold, ca 1900, 6¾x4¾"	50.00
Boot, root beer frost, straps on sides, 3¼x2⅛"	30.00
Boot w/spur, Daisy & Button, cobalt, ca 1870-90, 5½x5¼"	120.00
Cane, crystal, fine mesh sole, solid heel, att US Glass, 4⅝"	45.00
Cat slipper, Winter Swirl, Boyd, 1986	14.00
Chinese shoe on toboggan, crystal, 1880s, 2¼x5⅛"	110.00

Crystal frost, laces & bow, Nat'l...Expo Philada 1899, 5⅜"	46.00
Daisy, cat at top, bl, ca 1887, 3x5⅞"	38.00
Daisy & Button, amber, clear heel, advertising, Duncan, 5¾"	55.00
Daisy & Button, milk glass, no scallop, 4⅞"	40.00
Daisy & Button, wht opal, Duncan, Patd Oct 19/86, lg	80.00
Dutch, crystal, 3 horizontal ridges on vamp, 3⅛x7"	45.00
Emb flower & trailing vine, ruby stain, souvenir, 2⅛x5"	32.00
Finecut, amber, holds Daisy & Button perfume bottle, 5⅞"	60.00
Finecut, bl, no laces, mk HTC, 1880s, 2¼x4"	23.00
High button, amethyst, mk Bouquet Holder, Pat Applied For	47.00
High top, blk amethyst, stippled top, bow at toe, 3⅝x4⅛"	50.00
Jockey boot, bl, hollow sole & heel, 1880s, 3⅛x4"	50.00
Kitten slipper, Daisy & Button, bl opal, Fenton, 2⅞x5⅝"	30.00
Knitted bootie, crystal, ribbon at top, 1880s, 2⅝x3⅝"	45.00
Man's bedroom slipper, amethyst, 1950s, 1½x5⅛"	20.00
Mc spatter, English, ca 1890, 3x5¾"	100.00
Roller skate, milk glass, mk Bottle Made in France	36.00
Rubina w/gold flakes, flowers & leaves across vamp, 2½x6"	95.00
Sandal, Daisy & Button sides, crystal, att Bryce Bros, 4½"	38.00
Spun glass, 2¼x2"	15.00
Yel & twisted pk w/yel latticinio & bl ribbed sole, 2x6½"	85.00
2-pc, milk glass, bow on removable front, 1890s, 4⅞x7⅝"	325.00

Glidden

Genius designer Glidden Parker established Glidden Pottery in 1940 in Alfred, New York, having been schooled at the unrivaled New York State College of Ceramics at Alfred University. Glidden pottery is characterized by a fine stoneware body, innovative forms, outstanding hand-milled glazes, and hand decoration which make the pieces individual works of art. Production consisted of casual dinnerware, artware, and accessories that were distributed internationally.

In 1949 Glidden Pottery became the second ceramic plant in the country to utilize the revolutionary Ram pressing machine. This allowed for increased production and for the most part eliminated the previously used slip-casting method. However, Glidden stoneware continued to reflect the same superb quality of craftsmanship until the factory closed in 1957. Although the majority of form and decorative patterns were Mr. Parker's personal designs, Fong Chow and Sergio Dello Strologo also designed award-winning lines.

Glidden will be found marked on the unglazed underside with a signature that is hand incised, mold impressed, or ink stamped. Interest in this unique stoneware is growing as collectors discover that it embodies the very finest of Mid-Century High Style. Our advisor is David Pierce; he is listed in the Directory under Ohio.

Ashtray, fish, Fred Press, #274, 5½" sq	20.00
Ashtray, leaves, Fred Press, #274, 5½" sq	18.00
Ashtray, Safex, dbl rectangle, 12½x6½"	30.00
Baker, Turq Matrix, #22, 2x11x9"	20.00
Bottle, dressing; Alfred Stoneware, #812, 5½x5½"	40.00
Bottles, liquor; Alfred Stoneware, #813/#814/#815, in basket	125.00
Bowl, cobalt, #15, 4x7x5¼"	25.00
Bowl, early pk, #17, 4¼x8"	25.00
Bowl, lug soup; Boston Spice, #467, 3½x7½x6"	15.00
Bowl, Sage & Sand, #38, 2x7¼x3¾"	15.00
Bowl, Turq Matrix, #26, 1¼x6½x5"	20.00
Canister, Garden, w/lid & bail, #601, 5x5½"	40.00
Canister, High Tide, w/lid & bail, #601, 5x5½"	35.00
Casserole, Counterpane, w/lid, #165, 5½x8½"	20.00
Casserole, Mexican Crock, w/lid, #165, 5½x8½"	25.00
Casserole, Pear, w/lid, #163, 6½x11"	30.00
Casserole, Turq Matrix, w/lid, #165, 5½x8½"	20.00

Casserole, Viridian, w/lid, #167, 4¼x5¼" 15.00
Coaster, Flourish, #19, 4" sq 8.00
Creamer, High Tide, #1430, 6x3½x3½" 25.00
Creamer, Sage & Sand, #1430, 6x3½x3½" 15.00
Creamer, Turq Matrix, #1430, 6x3½x3½" 20.00
Creamer & sugar bowl, Boston Spice, w/lid, #1430 & #1440 ....25.00
Creamer & sugar bowl, Pear, w/lid, #144 & #143 ....55.00
Cup & saucer, Flourish, #141 & #142 ....25.00
Cup & saucer, High Tide, #441A & #442 ....20.00
Cup & saucer, Sage & Sand, #141 & #142 ....12.00
Cup & saucer, Yellowstone, #141 & #142 ....15.00
Pitcher, Feather, #617, 3-qt 45.00
Pitcher, Glidden Bl, 3616, 2-qt 80.00
Planter, cobalt, #89, 4x4½" 25.00
Plate, Christmas Tree, #35, 5½" sq 30.00
Plate, Feather, #31, 10¼" sq 10.00
Plate, Mexican Cock, #31, 10¼" sq 15.00
Plate, Pear, #33, 8" sq 15.00
Plate, Snowdrop, #33, 8" sq 50.00
Spice set, Garden, 4 jars w/rack, #607, 2¾x3" 60.00
Tile, serving; Garden, #606, 12x4x7½" 45.00
Tray, Afrikans, #200, 8x6" w/stand 45.00
Tray, Tropical Fish, #200, 8x6" w/stand 45.00
Tumbler, Flourish, #5 ....20.00
Tumbler, Menagerie, Hippo, #1127, 5½" 25.00
Urn, coffee; Alfred Stoneware, Saffron, #816, w/stand 125.00
Vase, cobalt, #128, 4½x5½x2½" 20.00
Vase, cobalt, #58, 2½x5¾" 40.00
Vase, Early Pk, #49, 7x5¾" 50.00
Vase, Loop Artware, purple, #935, 2¼x5¾" 150.00
Vase, Turq Matrix, #40, 5x9½x6" 30.00

Goebel

F.W. Goebel founded the Hummelwork Porcelain Manufactory in 1871, located in Rodental, West Germany. They produced porcelain figurines, plates, and novelties, the most famous of which are the Hummel figurines (These are listed in a separate section.) There were many other series produced by Goebel — Disney characters, birds, animals, Art Deco figurines, and the Friar Tuck Monks that are especially popular. Our advisors for this category are Gale and Wayne Bailey; they are listed in the Directory under Georgia.

Creamer and sugar bowl, Golfers, M44 A&B, full bee mark, $75.00 for the pair.

Cardinal Tuck (Red Monk)

Condiment set & tray, stylized bee mk 250.00
Pitcher, S141/0, stylized bee mk, 4" 100.00
Sugar bowl, Z37, stylized bee mk 100.00

Charlot BYJ Figurines (Artist Signed)

A Child's Prayer, BYJ 17, Goebel bee mk 45.00
Atta Boy, BYJ 7, Goebel bee mk 40.00
Let It Rain, BYJ 51, Goebel bee mk 125.00
Little Miss Coy, BYJ 4, 3-line mk 45.00
Putting on the Dog, BYJ 25, Goebel mk 60.00

Co-Boy Figurines

Brad the Clockmaker (clock), Goebel mk 125.00
Brum the Lawyer, Goebel mk 75.00
Carl the Chef, Goebel bee mk 75.00
Chuck the Chimney Sweep, Goebel mk 85.00
Gerd the Diver, Goebel bee mk 85.00
Gil the Goalie, Goebel mk 65.00
Jim the Bowler, Goebel mk 55.00
Tommy Touchdown, Goebel mk 50.00

Friar Tuck (Brown Monk)

Ashtray, Z43/0, stylized bee mk 45.00
Bank, SD29, stylized bee mk, 4" 50.00
Condiment set & tray, stylized bee mk 75.00
Cookie jar, K29, full bee mk, 9" 350.00
Creamer & sugar bowl, w/tray, full bee mk 75.00
Mug, T74/0, stylized bee mk, 4" 35.00
Mug, T74/1, full bee mk 50.00
Mustard, S183, full bee mk, 4" 45.00
Pitcher, S141/0, stylized bee mk, 4" 35.00
Pitcher, S141/1, stylized bee mk, 5" 45.00
Shakers, P153, full bee mk, pr 35.00

Shakers

Orange rabbits, P133A&B, full bee mk, pr 40.00
Rabbit & carrot, P115 A&B, stylized bee mk, pr 30.00
Squirrel & acorn, P116 A&B, stylized bee mk, pr 30.00
Tyrolean boy & girl, P18 & P19, no trademark, pr 20.00

Miscellaneous

Ashtray, Scottie dogs, RT607, crown mk 50.00
Ashtray w/bird, RT216, Goebel bee mk 40.00
Condiment set, mushrooms, M2-D, crown mk 75.00
Decanter, boy w/mandolin, KL25, crown mk, 6" 65.00
Honey pot, yel beehive, H125/0, stylized bee mk 45.00
Perfume lamp, boy w/accordion, EF15, full bee mk 250.00

Goldscheider

The Goldscheider family operated a pottery in Vienna for many generations before seeking refuge in the United States following Hitler's invasion of their country. They settled in Trenton, New Jersey, in the early 1940s where they established a new corporation and began producing objects of art and tableware items. (No mention was made of the company in the Trenton City Directory after 1950, and it is assumed that by this time the influx of foreign imports had taken its toll.) In 1946 Marcel Goldscheider established a pottery in Staffordshire where he manufactured bone china figures, earthenware, etc., marked with a stamp of his signature. Larger artist-signed examples are the most valuable with the Austrian pieces bringing the higher prices.

A wide variety of marks has been found. Listed here are several that correspond with numbers in the listings that follow.

Key:
1 — Goldscheider USA Fine China
2 — Original Goldscheider Fine China
3 — Goldscheider USA
4 — Goldscheider-Everlast Corp.
5 — Goldscheider Everlast Corp. in circle
6 — Goldscheider Inc. in circle
7 — Goldcrest Ceramics Corp. in circle
8 — Goldcrest Fine China
9 — Goldcrest Fine China USA
10 — A Goldcrest Creation
11 — Created by Goldscheider USA

Anne Boleyn, gr/purple dress, Dorier, #1199, mk #7/#8, 10½"	...200.00
Beautiful Morning, lady in bl, Porcher, #272, mk #2/#6, 6½"	.......85.00
Bon Voyage, dog on suitcase, Jacobson	.........98.00

Figurine, Butterfly Girl, porcelain, dancer in short 'bat wing' tunic with web design and insects, Austria, marked, 19", $3,080.00.

Chinese Teahouse, Helen Lindoff, 2 figures on base	....................60.00
Gazelle, recumbent, gray, #703, mk #3, 6½x9½"	...........................75.00
German Shepherd's head, box, w/lid, 5½x4"	.................................95.00
Girl w/muff, bl & beige, 8"	....85.00
Henry VII, gr & purple, Dorier, #1198, mk #7/#8, 10½"	.............200.00
Juliet, doves, pk dress, Porcher, #745, #7/#9, 12¼"	...................350.00
Lady in hat holds muff, EX detail, 8¼"	.................................90.00
Lady seated & holding mirror, yel/wht dress, #811, mk #11, 7"	....75.00
Lady w/flower basket, teal dress, #801, mk #4/#11, 8"	...............75.00
Lady w/flowers in hair, wht floral dress, #257, mk #2/#6, 6½"	.......60.00
Lady w/speckled parasol, ermine trim, 11"	.............................175.00
Madame Pompadour, yel/wht dress, Porcher, #221, mk #2/#6, 6½"	..85.00
Madonna head, terra cotta face, gold hair, 10"	.........................185.00
Mother of Sorrow, sgn A Jacob, 10x5x4"	................................365.00
Nude, seated, terra cotta, #8726-15, 25"	................................460.00
Old Virginia, sgn Peggy Porcher, 8½"	...................................85.00
Pheasant, Goldcrest mk, 14"	....95.00
Rendezvous, lady in bl & pk, Porcher, #813, mk #9/#10, 8"	........85.00
Rendezvous, man in bl & gr, Porcher, #812, mk #9/#10, 8½"	........85.00
Rendezvous lamp, #812/#813 man/lady, marble base/cloth shade, pr	.300.00
Royal Blackamoor w/instrument, 15"	....................................195.00
Sing Lo, Oriental w/bird, pagoda & birdhouse, 7¼"	...................60.00
Southern belle, pk dress, holds yel hat, #506, mk #3/#5, 10½"	...100.00
Southern lady w/fan, pk/blk dress, #828, mk #3/#4, 10½"	..........125.00
Thai lady, gr sash/pk skirt, #708, mk #1/#5, 18¼"	.....................300.00

Gonder

Lawton Gonder grew up with clay in his hands and fire in his eyes. Gonder's interest in ceramics was greatly influenced by his parents who worked for Weller and a close family friend and noted ceramic authority, John Herold. In his early teens Gonder launched his ceramic career at the Ohio Pottery Company while working for Herold. He later gained valuable experience at American Encaustic Tile Company, Cherry Art Tile, and the Florence Pottery. Gonder was plant manager at the Florence Pottery until fire destroyed the facility in late 1941.

After years of solid production and management experience, Lawton Gonder established the Gonder Ceramic Art Company, formerly the Peters and Reed plant, in South Zanesville, Ohio. Gonder Ceramic Arts produced quality art pottery with beautiful contemporary designs which included human and animal figures and a complete line of Oriental pottery. Accentuating the beautiful shapes were unique and innovative glazes developed by Gonder such as flambe (flame red with streaks of yellow), 24k gold crackle, antique gold, and Chinese crackle.

All Gonder is marked with the company name and mold number. They include 'Gonder U.S.A' in block letters, 'Gonder' in script, 'Gonder Original' in script, and 'Gonder Ceramic Art' in block letters. Paper labels were also used. Some of the early Gonder molds closely resemble RumRill designs that had been manufactured at the Florence Pottery; and because some RumRill pieces are found with similar (if not identical) shapes, matching mold numbers, and Gonder glazes, it is speculated that some RumRill was produced at the Gonder plant. In 1946 Gonder started another company which he named Elgee (chosen for his initials LG) where he manufactured lamp bases until a fire in 1954 resulted in his shifting lamp production to the main plant. Operations ceased in 1957. Our advisors for this category are Marilyn and John McCormick; they are listed in the Directory under Kansas.

Bookends, horse head figural, brn, #582, pr	.................35.00
Bowl, console; wht, J-55, 5x12"	.................30.00
Candle holders, flower form, E-14, pr	.................20.00
Cookie jar, Ye Olde Oaken Bucket, #974, 8"	.................65.00
Ewer, gold crackle, J-25, 11"	.................65.00
Figurine, Chinese girl, #763, 13"	.................30.00

Figurine, panther, yellow with brown streaking, 5¼x14½", $85.00.

Lamp base, rearing horse, 12"	.................20.00
Tile, hunting dog decal, sq	.................20.00
Vase, cornucopia; gr, H-14, 10"	.................25.00
Vase, fish form, #522, 9"	.................85.00
Vase, gold crackle, hdls, H-56, 8½"	.................28.00
Vase, lav, H-86, 8½"	.................35.00
Vase, swan form, dk yel w/brn streaks, #802, 10"	.................35.00

Goofus Glass

Goofus was an inexpensive type of lustre-painted pressed glassware made by many companies during the first two decades of the 20th century. Bowls and trays are most common, and red and gold combinations are found more often than blues and greens. Our advisor for this category is Dan Gandolfo; he is listed in the Directory under Illinois.

Decanter, Basketweave, single rose on front, EX original paint, 10", $50.00.

Bottle, scent; pk tulips, orig pnt & stopper, 3½", EX 25.00
Bottle, water; grapes on crackle, no pnt, 7½" 40.00
Bowl, dahlia, scalloped, gold, ornate, 10x4" 55.00
Bowl, grapes on amethyst, scalloped, sq, orig pnt, 10", EX 82.00
Bowl, reindeer in center, orig pnt, EX 22.00
Box, powder; basketweave, milk glass, orig pnt, rare, NM 55.00
Coaster, flowers, orig pnt, rare, 3" dia, EX, set of 4 ....45.00
Lamp, fairy; roses, flash-fired gr, 3 holes for smoke, 7" 40.00
Lamp, oil; Nosegay, #2, EX orig pnt 165.00
Plate, holly, opal w/orig pnt, 10½", NM 50.00
Tumbler, grapes, gold on crackle, orig pnt, 4", NM 50.00
Vase, Cabbage Rose, EX orig pnt, 7" 50.00
Vase, dogwood blossoms, baluster, orig pnt, 15", EX 65.00
Vase, mixed fruit, rpt gold on clear, 10" 40.00
Vase, Rose in Snow, classic form, rpt, 10" 25.00
Vase, Statue of Liberty & Am Eagle, no pnt, 1880-1920, 12⅝" 98.00

Goss and Crested China

William Henry Goss received his early education at the Government School of Design at Somerset House, London, and as a result of his merit was introduced to Alderman William Copeland, who owned the Copeland Spode Pottery. Under the influence of Copeland from 1852-1858, Goss quickly learned the trade and soon became their chief designer. Little is known about this brief association, and in 1858 Goss left to begin his own business. After a short-lived partnership with a Mr. Peake, Goss opened a pottery on John Street, Stoke-on-Trent, but by 1870 he had moved to his business to a location near London Road. This pottery became the famous Falcon Works. Their mark was a spread-wing falcon (goss-hawk) centering a narrow, horizontal bar with 'W.H. Goss' printed below.

Many of the early pieces made by Goss were left unmarked and are difficult to discern from products made by the Copeland factory, but after he had been in business for about fifteen years, all of his wares were marked. Today unmarked items do not command the prices of the later marked wares.

Adolphus William Henry Goss (Goss's eldest son) joined his father's firm in the 1880s. He introduced cheaper lines, though the

more expensive lines continued in production. Shortly after his father's death in 1906, Adolphus retired and left the business to his two younger brothers. The business suffered from problems created by a war economy, and in 1936 Goss assets were held by Cauldon Potteries Ltd. These were eventually taken over by the Coalport Group, who retained the right to use the Goss trademark. Messrs. Ridgeway Potteries bought all the assets in 1954 as well as the right to use the Goss trademark and name. In 1964 the group was known as Allied English Potteries Ltd. (A.E.P.), and in 1971 A.E.P. merged with the Doulton Group. Now it remains to be seen if Goss ware will ever be produced again. Our advisor for this category is Patrick Herley; he is listed in the Directory under New York.

Figures, all rare: Boxer, Shelley, $135.00; Fisher Girl, Carlton, $55.00; Irish Colleen, Carlton, $115.00; Comical horse and jockey, Carlton, $110.00; Footballer, Grafton, $185.00.

Abbots cup, Fountains Abbey 16.00
Beer bowl, dragon 18.00
Bowl, Christ Church 13.50
Bucket, milk; Swiss 20.00
Creamer, Yarmouth, sm 24.00
Flask, Caerleon Tear 12.50
Jug, Litchfield, St Alban's Abbey 35.00
Jug, water; Egyptian 14.00
Lady Godiva, sm 48.00
Look Out House 110.00
Mortar, Bideford 14.00
Mortar, Hythe Gromwellian 15.00
Night light, R Burns Cottage, 6" 150.00
Pitcher, Devon Oak, Ipwich 35.00
Pot, Roman, Painswick 20.00
Shaker, Scarborough, early mk 35.00
Shakespeare bust, sm 35.00
Tobacco jar, terra cotta, 5½" 47.50
Urn, Minster 16.00
Vase, bud; sm 12.00
Vase, Exeter, Sheffield 24.00
Wall pocket, Christ Church, lg 30.00
Yorick's Skull, lg 140.00

Crested China

Arcadian, ewer, Wembly 18.00
Arcadian, figurine, Colonial man 67.50
Arcadian, figurine, submarine, E5 ....25.00
Arcadian, figurine, Tommy on Sentry Duty 57.50
Carlton, bust, Alexandra 60.00
Carlton, bust, Wordsworth 55.00
Carlton, figurine, Fisher girl 55.00
Carlton, pot, hdls, w/lid 22.50
Willow, figurine, Burns at the plough 75.00

Willow, model of Hay Castle, 3½" 47.50
Willow, Shakespeare Cottage 78.00

Gouda

Since the 18th century the main center of the pottery industry in Holland was in Gouda. One of its earliest industries, the manufacture of clay pipes, continues to the present day. The artware so easily recognized by collectors today was first produced about 1885. It was decorated in the Art Nouveau manner. Stylized florals, birds, and geometrics were favored motifs; only rarely is the scene naturalistic. The Nouveau influence was strong until about 1915. Art Deco was attempted but with less success. Though most of the ware is finished in a matt glaze, glossy pieces in both pastels and dark colors are found on occasion and command higher prices. Decoration on the glossy ware is usually very well executed. Most of the workshops failed during the Depression, though earthenware is still being made in Gouda and carries the Gouda mark. Until very recently Regina was still making a limited amount of the old Gouda-style pottery in a matt finish. Watch for the Gouda name, which is usually a part of the backstamp of the various manufacturers.

Dutch shoe, mc, glossy, Maas, 5½" 110.00
Inkwell/pen tray, Ivora, w/lid, 10½" 325.00
Jar, stylized decor, sgn, w/lid, 7½" 290.00
Jug, Ivora, floral, #120, 5¼" 300.00
Vase, allover realistic floral, mk Areo #3004, 20" 350.00
Vase, butterflies/florals, naturalistic, lg hdls, 16" 525.00
Vase, mc Art Deco sunburst, Arnhem, 2½" 45.00
Vase, mc stylized floral, hdls, BO Ivora, #213, 16½" 460.00

Vase, large stylized florals in violet, yellow, blue and green, #213 B.O. Ivora Gouda Holland, 17", $1,100.00.

Vase, stylized floral, classic form, 12½", EX 350.00
Vase, stylized floral, dbl-gourd neck on ovoid, 11½", pr, NM 400.00
Vase, stylized floral, 6x5" 135.00
Vase, stylized poppies, overhead hdl, sm neck, 9½x9½" 400.00

Graniteware

Graniteware, made of a variety of metals with enamel coatings, derives its name from its appearance. The speckled, swirled, or mottled effect of the vari-colored enamels may look like granite — but there the resemblance stops. It wasn't especially durable! Expect at least minor chipping if you plan to collect.

Graniteware was featured in 1876 at Phily's Expo. It was mass-produced in quantity, and enough of it has survived to make at least the common items easily affordable. Color, shape, and size are important considerations in evaluating an item; cobalt blue and white, green and

white, brown and white, and old red and white swirled items are unusual, thus more expensive. Pieces of heavier weight, seam constructed, riveted, and those with wooden handles and tin or matching graniteware lids are usually older.

For further study we recommend *The Collector's Encyclopedia of Graniteware, Colors, Shapes, and Values*, Books I and II, by our advisor, Helen Greguire. Both are available from the author. For information on how to order, see her listing in the Directory under New York. For the address of the National Graniteware Society, see the section on Clubs, Newsletters, and Catalogs.

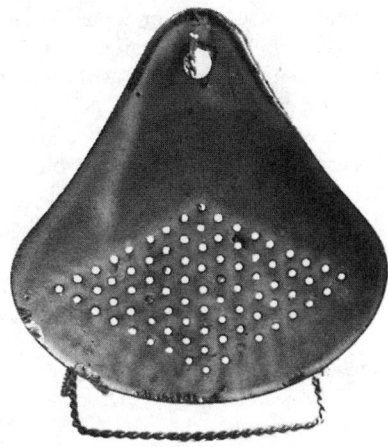

Hand skimmer, perforated, gray solid, 5½", VG, $350.00.

Basin, brn lg mottle w/blk, Onyx Ware, w/eyelet, EX 45.00
Basin, gray mottle, 4x14", EX 40.00
Bed pan, bl fine mottle w/cobalt trim, wht top, NM 85.00
Bowl, mixing; cobalt lg swirl w/blk trim, EX 175.00
Bowl, soup; Chrysolite swirl, 9½", EX 85.00
Bowl, vegetable; red lg swirl w/blk trim, oblong, VG 110.00
Bowl, vegetable; turq relish, rectangular, 10½x7½", NM 70.00
Bread box, red solid, brass hdl & hinges, oblong, NM 115.00
Bread riser, cobalt med mottle w/blk, ftd, sm, NM 395.00
Bread riser, gray mottle, ped base, tin lid, 15" dia, NM 135.00
Bread riser, turq swirl, strap hdl, tin lid, 16" dia, NM 395.00
Bread riser, wht w/bl trim, ped base, domed lid, lg, NM 65.00
Bucket, berry; turq swirl, tin lid, wood knob, 4x6", NM 155.00
Bucket, berry; turq swirl, tin lid, 4-qt, NM 145.00
Bucket, berry; wht w/blk trim, w/lid 40.00
Butter carrier, gray solid, oval, 6x7½x5", NM 250.00
Can, cream; Chrysolite lg swirl, bail hdl, EX 465.00
Can, cream; cobalt sm swirl, tin lid, strap hdl, 2-qt, NM 315.00
Can, cream; gray med mottle, bail hdl, tin lid, NM 25.00
Can, cream; turq swirl, tin lid, strap hdl, 2-qt, NM 250.00
Can, milk; bl lg mottle w/lt bl trim, Boston style, NM 145.00
Can, milk; gr lg swirl w/bl, Emerald Ware, bail hdl, NM 750.00
Can, water; bl lg swirl w/blk, wht int, sm, M 185.00
Churn, bl lg swirl w/blk hdls, dasher type, 17¾x8¼", EX 1,450.00
Coaster, dk gr & wht lg swirl w/blk trim, wht int, NM 195.00
Coffee biggin, bl med mottle, 4-pc, welded hdl, NM 485.00
Coffee biggin, gr med mottle, 4-pc, NM 395.00
Coffee biggin, red med mottle, 4-pc, NM 565.00
Coffee boiler, bl lg swirl, M 225.00
Coffee boiler, bl relish, tin lid, NM 295.00
Coffee boiler, brn fine mottle w/in & w/out (Onyx Ware), M 165.00
Coffee boiler, Chrysolite swirl, bail hdl, 10½", EX 495.00
Coffee boiler, gray mottle, bail hdl, NM 65.00
Coffee boiler, turq swirl, granite lid, bail hdl, lg, NM 195.00
Coffee flask, bl relish, seamed, metal screw top, 6¾", NM 310.00
Coffeepot, brn lg swirl, domed lid, 10½", EX 300.00
Coffeepot, cobalt med mottle, wood hdl & knob, NM 275.00

Coffeepot, gray med mottle, NM 125.00
Coffeepot, gray swirl, 4-cup, NM 75.00
Coffeepot, lg gray mottle, pewter trim, copper bottom, M 325.00
Coffeepot, sky bl swirl, domed lid, 11½", NM 155.00
Coffeepot, solid orange, EX 30.00
Coffeepot, turq swirl, domed & hinged lid, 9", NM ...155.00
Coffeepot, wht w/blk trim, matching domed lid, 10-cup, 11", NM ...22.00
Colander, gray solid, side hdls, 12" dia, NM 25.00
Colander, turq swirl, ped base, NM 145.00
Colander, wht w/cobalt hdls, ped base, 10", VG 20.00
Creamer, bl lg mottle, bl strap hdl, squatty, VG 325.00
Creamer, lt bl w/blk decor & gold, squatty, Germany, NM 100.00
Cup, custard; Apple gr w/tangerine int, advertising, NM 105.00
Cup & saucer, yel & wht lg swirl w/blk trim, 1960s, M 75.00
Cuspidor, cobalt lg swirl, rare, NM 475.00
Dipper, cobalt lg swirl w/blk trim, flat hook hdl, M 135.00
Dipper, cocoa; gray med mottle w/blk, wooden hdl, lg, EX 310.00
Dipper, Windsor; bl lg swirl, blk hollow hdl, EX 95.00
Dipper, Windsor; bl relish, hollow hdl, heavy, NM 65.00
Dish pan, cobalt lg swirl, riveted side hdls, 6x15", EX 110.00
Funnel, bl lg swirl w/blk trim, squatty, lg, NM 140.00
Funnel, dk gr fine mottle, wht int, Elite, lg, EX 125.00
Funnel, gray solid, 3¼", NM 37.50
Grater, cheese; sky bl swirl, curved top hdl, 12", NM 155.00
Grater, wht w/cobalt trim, Germany, sm, EX 75.00
Kettle, sky bl swirl w/blk trim, 6x12½", NM 90.00
Ladle, side snipe; turq swirl, triangular, 15", EX 125.00

Miniatures: Tray, turquoise mottle, 5" long, G, $95.00; Skillet, turquoise with white interior, 7½" diameter, VG, $120.00; Funnel, turquoise, 2½", G, $25.00.

Mold, corn; gray solid, oval, VG 95.00
Mold, gr relish, melon shape, tin lid w/hdl, #80, M 185.00
Mold, ice cream; Turk's head, cobalt med mottle, EX 125.00
Mold, pudding; turq swirl, oval, fluted, 7x5½", NM 235.00
Mug, cobalt lg swirl, wht int, NM 75.00
Mug, gr lg swirl w/blk trim, Emerald Ware, lg, EX 135.00
Mug, turq swirl, wide strap hdl, EX 55.00
Mush cup, turq swirl, strap hdl, 5x6", NM 125.00
Pail, chamber; bl lg swirl w/blk trim, bail hdl, NM 225.00
Pail, milk; gray solid, tin lid w/strap hdl, seamed, 2-qt, NM 75.00
Pail, water; cobalt lg swirl w/blk trim, lg, M 275.00
Pan, baking; Crysolite swirl, 2x16x8½", EX 195.00
Pan, bl lg swirl, Berlin style, 8½" 165.00
Pan, bread; gray lg mottle, oval, NM 145.00
Pan, gray solid, 1½x5", NM 30.00
Pan, jelly roll; bl relish, wht int, 1x10", M 55.00
Pan, jelly roll; turq swirl, wht int, 1x9¼", NM 45.00

Pan, lady finger; cobalt lg swirl, wht int, M 2,750.00
Pan, muffin; cobalt lg swirl w/in & w/out, 8-cup, NM 550.00
Pan, muffin; gray lg mottle, Turk's turban style, 9-cup, NM 145.00
Pan, muffin; gray lg mottle, 8-cup, in wire fr, EX 175.00
Pan, muffin; lt bl lg swirl, 6-cup, EX 325.00
Pan, pudding; lt bl fine mottled, Elite Austria, 12" 25.00
Pan, pudding; turq swirl, 2½x7", NM 37.50
Pan, sky bl swirl, convex, 2-cup, NM 160.00
Pan, utility; turq swirl, 16" dia, NM 100.00
Pie plate, bl relish, heavy, 10" dia, M 45.00
Pie plate, Chrysolite swirl, 9", NM 85.00
Pie plate, cobalt lg swirl w/blk trim, wht int, M 95.00
Pie plate, gray solid, 1x6½", NM 20.00
Pie plate, sky bl swirl, 9¾", EX 40.00
Pie plate, turq swirl, 9½", EX 35.00
Pitcher, milk; gray med mottle, 6¼", NM 165.00
Pitcher, milk; turq swirl, 5¾x5½", EX 255.00
Pitcher, milk; wht w/blk trim, 6", NM 36.00
Pitcher, water; bl & wht wavy mottle w/blk, 3-coated, M 575.00
Pitcher, water; bl relish, swirl hdl, 6x7½", NM 225.00
Pitcher, water; brn relish w/dk bl trim, NM 170.00
Pitcher, water; gr shaded, Shamrock Ware, EX 195.00
Pitcher, water; lt gr w/dk gr trim, 8", NM 38.00
Pitcher, water; old red lg swirl w/dk bl trim, wht int, EX 2,850.00
Pitcher & bowl, bl med mottle w/blk & gold, EX 225.00
Pitcher & bowl, gr & cream, 11", 4½x12", NM 70.00
Plate, gray solid, 9½", M 20.00
Plate, red lg swirl w/blk, 1960s, ltweight, M 35.00
Platter, Bl Diamond Ware, bl lg swirl, oval, M 375.00
Potty, turq swirl, wht int, 5x10", EX 75.00
Potty, wht w/blk trim, 10", NM 27.50
Roaster, cobalt lg swirl, oval, lg, 3-pc, NM 245.00
Roaster, solid bl, Savory, w/lid 45.00
Roaster, turq swirl, wht inset tray, 14" L, 3-pc, EX 125.00
Salt box, sky bl swirl, scalloped bk, hangs, 10x7", NM 275.00
Salt box, windmill scene, bl on wht, EX 195.00
Scoop, spice; gray med mottle, strap hdl, advertising, EX 325.00
Skillet, Emerald Ware, gr lg swirl, wht int, EX 395.00
Skillet, gr to cream shaded, wht int, blk hdl, CI, lg, M 170.00
Skillet, gray lg mottle, 1¼x5¾" dia, EX 75.00
Skillet, lav-bl lg swirl w/blk trim, med, EX 185.00
Skimmer, blk med mottle w/in & w/out, perforated, flat, hdld, EX .85.00
Skimmer, cobalt & gray lg mottle, perforated, flat, hdld, EX ....95.0_
Soap dish, wht w/no trim, fluted, 2" deep, NM ...._
Spatula, gray lg mottle, NM ...._
Spoon, basting; bl & wht lg mottle w/blk, wht int, EX ....55._
Spoon, bl relish, swirl in hdl, 11", VG 45.00
Spoon, tasting; wht w/bl fine veins ea side, side hdl, NM 60.00
Strainer ladle, turq swirl, flat hook hdl, 12½", NM 88.00
Syrup, wht w/NP lid & thumb rest, VG 195.00
Teacup, bl w/gray swirl, strap hdl, 2x4½", NM 32.50
Teacup, gray mottle, NM ....2_.0_
Teapot, apple gr fine mottle 40.00
Teapot, bl fine mottle, seamless Belle shape, VG 395.00
Teapot, bl lg swirl w/blk trim, Columbian Ware, NM 475.00
Teapot, bl relish, Landers Frary & Clark, 1897, NM 165.00
Teapot, gray solid, gooseneck spout, 2-cup, 6½", NM 165.00
Teapot, gray swirl, gooseneck spout, domed, 4-cup, 8½", NM ...60.00
Teapot, red med swirl, 1960s, M 125.00
Teapot, red/blk/orange/yel/bl lg swirl, squatty, VG 395.00
Teapot, sky bl swirl, gooseneck spout, domed lid, 8", NM 95.00
Teapot, wht w/pewter trim, copper-trim bottom, squatty, M 225.00
Tray, gray med mottle, oval, NM 145.00
Tray, red lg mottle w/dk bl trim, 1960s, rnd, lg, NM 55.00

Tumbler, dk bl solid w/blk trim, Ski Bl label, M 85.00
Washboard, cobalt, wooden fr, adult sz, NM 115.00
Water carrier, bl lg mottle, 2-pc hinged lid, oval, NM 695.00

Green Opaque

Introduced in 1887 by the New England Glass Company, this ware is very scarce due to the fact that it was produced for less than one year. It is characterized by its soft green color and a wavy band of gold reserving a mottled blue metallic stain. It is usually found in satin; examples with a shiny finish are extremely rare.

Basket, ruffled Hobnail amber rim, amber hdl, 8¾x9⅛" 550.00
Bowl, worn stain, 4x8" 300.00
Box, powder; NM gold mottling on bowl & lid, 4x6¼" 1,150.00
Cruet, orig stopper 1,150.00
Mug, 2¼" 500.00
Punch cup 350.00
Toothpick holder, gold trim 1,150.00
Tumbler, lemonade; w/hdl, 5" 900.00
Tumbler, M mottling 800.00
Tumbler, VG mottling 450.00
Vase, flared, M gold & mottling, 6" 900.00

Greenaway, Kate

Kate Greenaway was an English artist who lived from 1846 to 1901. She gained worldwide fame as an illustrator of children's books, drawing children clothed in the styles worn by proper English and American boys and girls of the 1800s. Her book, *Under the Willow Tree*, published in 1878, was the first of many. Her sketches appeared in leading magazines, and her greeting cards were in great demand. Manufacturers of china, pottery, and metal products copied her characters to decorate children's dishes, tiles, and salt and pepper shakers as well as many other items. See also Almanacs; Napkin Rings.

Biscuit jar, ceramic, boy w/tinted features, w/lid 165.00
Book, A Apple Pie, Greenaway illus, 1907, EX 150.00
Book, Almanac, Greenaway illus, London, 1888, VG 85.00
Book, Birthday Book for Children, Greenaway illus, 1880, VG .145.00
Book, Language of Flowers, Greenaway illus, morocco cover, VG ..250.00
Book, Marigold Garden, Greenaway illus, London, 1888, VG 55.00
Book, Pied Piper of Hamlin, Greenaway illus, NM 75.00

Child's tea set, pastel coloring with gilt, Vodrey Pottery, after 1879, serves six, EX, $175.00.

Engraving, Harper's Bazaar, Jan 1879, full pg 25.00
Inkwell, boy & girl, bronze 195.00
Match holder, ornate SP, girl in fancy clothes, Tufts 195.00
Pencil holder, pnt porc 20.00
Plate, ABC, girl in lg hat, Staffordshire, 7" 95.00
Stickpin holder, SP, girl figural, Meriden, 4" 125.00
Tea set, mc children scenes w/gold, child sz, 15-pc 465.00
Wall pocket, ceramic, 6 girls on open book form, 6x9x3" 125.00

Greentown Glass

Greentown glass is a term referring to the product of the Indiana Tumbler and Goblet Company of Greentown, Indiana, ca 1894 to 1903. Their earlier pressed glass patterns were #11, a pseudo-cut glass design; #137, Pleat Band; and #200, Austrian. Another line, Dewey, was designed in 1898. Many lovely colors were produced in addition to crystal. Jacob Rosenthal, who was later affiliated with Fenton, developed his famous chocolate glass in 1900. The rich, shaded opaque brown glass was an overnight success. Two new patterns, Leaf Bracket and Cactus, were designed to display the glass to its best advantage, but previously existing molds were also used. In only three years Rosenthal developed yet another important color formula, golden agate. The Holly Amber pattern was designed especially for its production. The Dolphin covered dish with a fish finial is perhaps the most common and easily recognized piece ever produced. Other animal dishes were also made; all are highly collectible. There have been many repros — not all are marked! The symbol (+) at the end of some of the following lines was used to indicate items that have been reproduced.

Our advisors for this category are Jerry and Sandi Garrett; they are listed in the Directory under Indiana. See the Pattern Glass section for clear pressed glass, only colored items are listed here.

Animal dish, bird w/berry, amber (+) 325.00
Animal dish, bird w/berry, emerald gr (+) 325.00
Animal dish, bird w/berry, Nile gr 1,950.00
Animal dish, cat on hamper, amber, tall 325.00
Animal dish, cat on hamper, canary, low 750.00
Animal dish, cat on hamper, chocolate, tall 475.00
Animal dish, cat on hamper, cobalt, tall 600.00
Animal dish, dolphin, beaded, amber 625.00
Animal dish, dolphin, beaded, golden agate 900.00
Animal dish, dolphin, sawtooth, amber (+) 625.00
Animal dish, dolphin, sawtooth, emerald gr (+) 550.00
Animal dish, dolphin, smooth, chocolate 450.00
Animal dish, fighting cocks, amber 1,400.00
Animal dish, fighting cocks, emerald gr 1,400.00

Animal dish, hen on diamond basketweave base, teal blue, $250.00.

Animal dish, fighting cocks, wht opaque 1,750.00
Animal dish, hen on nest, chocolate 800.00
Animal dish, hen on nest, cobalt 650.00
Animal dish, rabbit, emerald gr (+) 200.00
Animal dish, rabbit, teal bl 200.00
Animal dish, rabbit, wht opaque (+) 200.00
Austrian, bowl, canary, 8" 300.00
Austrian, butter dish, canary 425.00
Austrian, compote, canary, 4½" dia 200.00
Austrian, creamer, amber, child sz 225.00
Austrian, creamer, emerald gr, 4¼" 225.00
Austrian, nappy, canary, w/lid 265.00
Austrian, rose bowl, canary, lg 250.00
Austrian, sauce bowl, canary, 4⅝" 95.00
Austrian, vase, canary, 10" 350.00
Beehive, tumbler, chocolate 550.00
Beehive, vase, bud; amber 300.00
Bowl, cut glass type, chocolate, 6" 475.00
Brazen Shield, butter dish, bl 265.00
Brazen Shield, pitcher, bl 275.00
Brazen Shield, relish tray, bl 125.00
Brazen Shield, tumbler, bl 90.00
Button hook, chocolate 250.00
Cactus, bowl, chocolate, 5¼" 125.00
Cactus, butter dish, chocolate 200.00

Cactus, compote, chocolate,
footed, 8¼", $225.00.

Cactus, toothpick holder, chocolate (+) 90.00
Cactus, vase, chocolate, 6" 750.00
Cord Drapery, bowl, cobalt, fluted rim, 8¼" dia 250.00
Cord Drapery, cake plate, emerald gr, ftd 185.00
Cord Drapery, pitcher, amber 285.00
Cord Drapery, syrup, cobalt 425.00
Cord Drapery, tray, water; amber 280.00
Cupid, butter dish, Nile gr 480.00
Cupid, creamer, chocolate 400.00
Cupid, sugar bowl, wht opaque 130.00
Dewey, bowl, chocolate, 8" 285.00
Dewey, butter dish, canary, 5" 200.00
Dewey, butter dish, wht opaque, 4" 200.00
Dewey, serpentine tray, emerald gr, sm 60.00
Dewey, sugar bowl, cobalt, 2½" dia 185.00
Diamond Prisms, tumbler, chocolate 650.00
Early Diamond, dish, cobalt, rectangular, 8x5" 175.00
Early Diamond, tumbler, chocolate 190.00
Fleur-de-lis, celery holder, chocolate, 5¾" 365.00
Fleur-de-lis, pitcher, chocolate 1,100.00
Fleur-de-lis, spooner, chocolate 200.00
Greentown Daisy, butter dish, wht opaque 100.00
Greentown Daisy, mustard pot, chocolate 230.00

Herringbone Buttress, bowl, emerald gr, 6¼" 255.00
Herringbone Buttress, cordial, emerald gr, 3" 275.00
Herringbone Buttress, cordial, olive gr, 3⅜" 200.00
Herringbone Buttress, shaker, emerald gr, ea 300.00
Herringbone Buttress, vase, emerald gr, 6" 235.00
Holly, tumbler, chocolate 5,800.00
Holly Amber, bowl, oval, ped ft 1,700.00
Holly Amber, bowl, 7½" 675.00
Holly Amber, compote, jelly; w/lid, 4½" 1,450.00
Holly Amber, compote, w/lid, 7¼" 1,850.00
Holly Amber, cruet, w/stopper, 6" 2,250.00
Holly Amber, shaker, ea 600.00
Holly Amber, toothpick holder, lg 850.00
Holly Amber, vase, on ped, 8" 2,200.00
Leaf Bracket, bowl, chocolate, 8" 100.00
Leaf Bracket, butter dish, wht opaque 750.00
Leaf Bracket, cruet, chocolate 225.00
Leaf Bracket, toothpick holder, chocolate 325.00
Mug, indoor drinking scene, handleless, Nile gr 435.00
Mug, outdoor drinking scene, lt cobalt 340.00
Mug, Serenade, amber 135.00
Novelty, buffalo, wht opaque, dtd 1901 ....450.00
Novelty, Dewey bust w/base, wht opaque 215.00
Novelty, dustpan, canary 190.00
Novelty, mitted hand, Nile gr 600.00
Novelty, trunk, chocolate 1,100.00
Pattern #11, bowl, gr, rectangular, 8x6½" 90.00
Pattern #11, plate, gr, 8" sq 80.00
Pitcher, water; Paneled, chocolate 590.00
Pitcher, water; Ruffled Eye, amber 175.00
Pleat Band, compote, chocolate, plain stem, smooth rim, 4¼" ...185.00
Pleat Band, shaker, canary, ea 90.00
Pleat Band, shaker, chocolate, ea 235.00
Scalloped Flange, vase, chocolate 95.00
Shuttle, butter dish, chocolate 1,100.00
Shuttle, creamer, chocolate 650.00
Shuttle, mug, chocolate 90.00
Shuttle, mug, gr 450.00
Shuttle, pitcher, chocolate 3,800.00
Shuttle, sugar bowl, chocolate, w/lid 750.00
Shuttle, tumbler, canary 425.00
Teardrop & Tassel, compote, Nile gr, w/lid, 4⅝" 450.00
Teardrop & Tassel, pickle dish, chocolate 325.00
Teardrop & Tassel, shaker, amber, ea 300.00
Teardrop & Tassel, sugar bowl, wht opaque 135.00
Teardrop & Tassel, wine, Nile gr 450.00
Toothpick holder, dog's head, bl frost 400.00
Toothpick holder, Sheaf of Wheat, chocolate (+) 900.00
Tumbler, Paneled, chocolate 500.00
Tumbler, Uneeda Biscuit, chocolate, tall 145.00

Grueby

William Henry Grueby joined the firm of the Low Art Tile Works at the age of fifteen and in 1894, after several years of experience in the production of architectural tiles, founded his own plant, the Grueby Faience Company, in Boston, Massachusetts. Grueby began experimenting with the idea of producing art pottery and had soon perfected a fine glaze (soft and without gloss) in shades of blue, gray, yellow, brown, and his most successful, cucumber green. In 1900 his exhibit at the Paris Exposition Universelle won three gold medals.

Grueby pottery was hand thrown and hand decorated in the Arts and Crafts style. Vertically thrust stylized leaves and flowers in relief were the most common decorative devices. Tiles continued to be an important product, unique (due to the matt glaze decoration) as well as durable. Grueby tiles were often a full inch thick. Obviously incompatible with the Art Nouveau style, the artware was discontinued soon after 1910. The ware is marked in one of several ways: 'Grueby Pottery, Boston, USA'; 'Grueby, Boston, Mass.'; or 'Grueby Faience.' The artware is often artist signed. Our advisor for this category is David Rago; he is listed in the Directory under New Jersey.

Frieze, ship/birds, 3-color, in gilt fr, 4-tile, 27" L 1,900.00
Tile, bl/wht checks, 4x4", pr 90.00
Tile, cherub/cornucopia, 2-color, 6" 350.00
Tile, cherub w/flower cornucopia, bl/brn-mustard, 6x6" 650.00
Tile, galleon at sea, 3-color, glaze bubbles, unmk, 8" 900.00
Tile, knight on horsebk, 4-color, no mk, 6x6" 350.00
Tile, sailing ship/sea gulls, 3-color, 6x6" 500.00
Tile, St Matthew w/stylized angel, pumpkin/dk bl, unmk, 7¾" 975.00
Tile, tulip, yel/lt gr on dk gr, 6x6" 650.00
Tile, tulip/leaves, yel/lt gr on lt bl, late, 6x6" 450.00
Tile, waterspout; open-mouth fish, bl on red clay, 7½" 700.00
Vase, bl, bulb w/can neck, 4½" 400.00
Vase, bl, cylindrical w/closed-in mouth, 3½" 250.00
Vase, dk gr 'elephant skin,' cvd ribs, 5½x3¼" 425.00
Vase, feathery gr, full-length cvd leaves, 7x4" 900.00

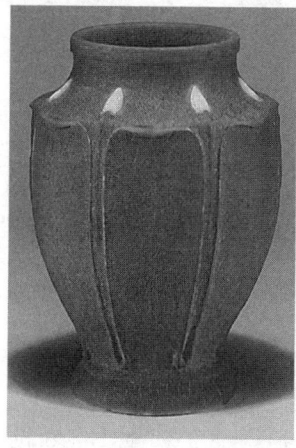

Vase, avocado green and yellow, leaf-molded ovoid with seven buds above the shoulder, signed E.R., #219, 12", $9,750.00.

Vase, gr, buds on long stems/appl leaves, sgn, 7x4½" 1,600.00
Vase, gr, bulbous, 2½" 450.00
Vase, gr, flower buds/long leaves, MA Seaman, EX mold, 12" .7,000.00
Vase, gr, leaves, sm neck, flat shoulder, 5x3¾" 1,800.00
Vase, gr, squat bulb form, 3½x6" 600.00
Vase, gr, wide vertical ribs, sm neck, fine glaze, 5x7" 1,700.00
Vase, gr, 5 scroll-top rim-to-shoulder hdls, 11" 4,500.00
Vase, gr broken glaze w/lg area of clay exposed, 13" 1,700.00
Vase, gr mottle, long/short leaves, bbl shape, 10x6" 2,000.00
Vase, gr w/yel buds, vertical stems, bulb bottom, 7½" 1,600.00
Vase, lt gr mottle, leaves/buds, bulbous body, 7¾x4½" 1,100.00
Vase, thick lt bl mottle, cvd ribs, sm rim, rpr, 4x4" 400.00
Wall pocket, gr, cvd decor, 6x7" 1,250.00

Gustavsberg

Gustavsberg Pottery, founded near Stockholm, Sweden, in the late 1700s, manufactured faience, creamware, and porcelain in the English taste until the end of the 19th century. During the 20th century, the factory has produced some inventive modernistic designs, often signed by their artists. Wilhelm Kage (1889-1960) is best

remembered for Argenta, a stoneware body decorated in silver overlay, introduced in the 1930s. Usually a mottled green, Argenta can also be found in cobalt blue and white. Other lines included Cintra (an exceptionally translucent porcelain), Farsta (copper-glazed ware), and Farstarust (iron oxide geometric overlay). Designer Stig Lindberg's work, which dates from the 1940s through the early 1970s, includes slab-built figures and a full range of tableware. Some pieces of Gustavsberg are dated.

Charger, Argenta, sea dragon o/l on gr mottle, mk/#d, '35, 14" ..1,350.00
Coasters, Argenta, gr w/silver inlay, 3½", set of 4 ....65.00
Cup & saucer, demitasse; floral, late 19th C 40.00
Dish, Argenta, gr w/silver inlay, scalloped, 4" dia 18.00

Urn, Argenta, silver decoration of lady in diaphanous gown holding torch (front and back), gold signature, Kage, angular stylized handles, standard green lid, #935, 1930, 9½", $1,380.00.

Figurine, abstract lion, terra cotta matt/gloss, 6x4x5" 175.00
Vase, Argenta, silver floral/butterflies, Grazia/#218DM, 6" 175.00
Vase, organic design, cobalt on cvd bl, Ekberg, 1920, 13" 550.00

Gutta Percha

Gutta percha is the plastic substance from the latex of several types of Malaysian trees. It resembles rubber but contains more resin. A patent for the use of this material in manufacturing an early type of plastic was issued in the 1850s, and it was used extensively for daguerreotype cases and picture frames.

See also Photographica.

Cup, mk Niles Drinking Cup, June 5, 1860, folds down 65.00
Inkwell, traveling bottle type, w/matching cap, 2" 75.00
Match safe, book figural, EX 75.00
Match safe, cross & dmn motif, flat-top book style, 2½x½" 85.00
Necklace, ornate cvd cameo on jet & blk enamel chain 150.00
Syringe, w/screw cap & looped plunger, 1860s 65.00

Hagen-Renaker

Best known for their line of miniature animal figures, Hagen-Renaker was founded in Monrovia, California, in 1946. In addition to the animals, they made replicas of characters from several popular Disney films under license from the Disney Studio. The firm relocated in San Dimas in 1966, where they remain active to the present time. Their wares are sometimes marked with an incised 'HR,' a stamped 'Hagen-Renaker' or part of the name, or paper labels. For more information, we recommend *The Collector's Encyclopedia of California Pottery* by Jack Chipman. Another source of information is *The Glass Menagerie* Newsletter listed in the Directory under Clubs, Newsletters and Catalogs.

Figurine, Pasha, baby elephant, 1955, 3½", $60.00; Miss Pepper, reclining Morgan foal, ca 1959, 2¾x4½", $125.00.

Alice in Wonderland, rare 355.00
English sheep dog, Mops, 3½" 40.00
Horse, Heather, 1953, 7" 375.00
Jock, from Lady & the Tramp, Disney 125.00
Peg, from Lady & Tramp, Disney, 1950s 150.00
Sealyham terrier 65.00
Siamese cat, Ching Wu, 1954 ....75.00

Hagenauer

Carl Hagenauer founded his metal workshops in Vienna in 1898. He was joined by his son Karl in 1919. They produced a wide range of stylized sculptural designs in both metal and wood.

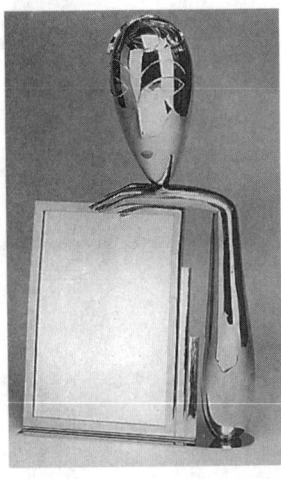

Dressing table mirror, stylized lady's head with applied curls, resting on bent arm, hand resting on mirror plate, chromium, signed, 24¾", $9,700.00.

African native shooting bow & arrow, blk/gold, 6½" 270.00
Baby, Blk, sitting, bronze, 3½" 275.00
Bowl, chrome, openwork base w/cats & dogs, ftd, 5½x9" 575.00
Candlesticks, slim cup & std, 10½", 8½", pr 150.00
Dancer, bronze w/ebonized wood skirt, stylized, 12" 2,000.00
Head of African woman, bronze on brass base, 8x7x3" 500.00
Head of African woman, bronze/brass w/blk finish, 7½" 550.00
Head of native girl, bronze/bronze/blk, by Rosenthal, 5½" 350.00
Horse, bronze w/blk finish, 1½" 55.00
Horse heads, stylized, patinated brass, 8x9x3" 375.00
Maid w/flowing skirt, wood/metal, elongated/stylized, 12" 1,150.00
Mirror, nude riding horse surmount, gilt metal, 19" 2,500.00
Native girl dancer, copper neck rings, blk finish, 10" 1,000.00
Nude dancer, on 1 toe, arms out, blk/gold on bronze, 11" 1,000.00
Nude walking (teak wood) panther w/silver metal collar, 10" .1,500.00

Table bell, chrome, str sided, hdl: 2 balls on rod, 4½" 200.00
Warrior w/shield/spear/headdress, bronze/brass, 6", pr 600.00
4 natives, bronze/brass, in mahog canoe, 5x20" 700.00

Hair Weaving

A rather unusual craft became popular during the mid-1800s. Human hair was used to make jewelry (rings, bracelets, lockets, etc.) by braiding and interlacing fine strands of hair into hollow forms with pearls and beads added for effect. Hair wreaths were also made, often using hair from deceased family members as well as the living. They were displayed in deep satin-lined frames along with mementoes of the weaver or her departed kin. The fad was abandoned before the turn of the century. See also Mourning Collectibles.

Bar pin, gold mt w/central ball of coiled hair 75.00
Bracelet, openwork, seed pearls/flowers in eng gold clasp 145.00

Brooch, blond and brown hair woven in bow, 1850s, 4½", $125.00.

Brooch, glass over braid, 32 seed pearls in gold fr, 1⅛" 80.00
Brooch, gold/blk enamel, woven garden scene, sm heart drop 265.00
Charm, cross from, woven over solid core, gold mts, 1870s, 1" 95.00
Cuff links, pr 125.00
Flowers on wht ribbon w/gilt paper trim, fr, 7¼x6½" 195.00
Necklace, 3 twisted coils of hair, 2 in lacy weave 110.00
Pendant, hair cords w/gold terminals & monogram plaque, lg 125.00
Ring, woven heart set in 14k gold band, 1860s 195.00
Stick pin, gold (?) mt w/finely woven initial 50.00
Watch chain, gold fittings & locket fob w/photo 70.00
Wreath, elaborate florals, 4-color hair, 27" fr, EX 200.00

Hall

The Hall China Company of East Liverpool, Ohio, was established in 1903. Their earliest product was whiteware toilet seats, mugs, jugs, etc. By 1920 their restaurant-type dinnerware and cookingware had become so successful that Hall was assured of a solid future. They continue today to be one of the country's largest manufacturers of this type of product.

Hall introduced the first of their famous teapots in 1920; new shapes and colors were added each year until about 1948, making them the largest teapot manufacturer in the world. These and the dinnerware lines of the thirties through the fifties have become popular collectibles. For more thorough study of the subject, we recommend *The Collector's Encyclopedia of Hall China* by Margaret and Kenn Whitmyer; their address may be found in the Directory under Ohio.

Blue Blossom, ball jug, #1	100.00
Blue Blossom, batter jug, Sundial	225.00
Blue Blossom, casserole, Thick Rim	50.00
Blue Blossom, shakers, hdls, pr	20.00
Blue Blossom, teapot, New York	200.00
Blue Bouquet, ball jug, #3	50.00
Blue Bouquet, bowl, Radiance, 9"	18.00
Blue Bouquet, bowl, salad; 9"	16.00
Blue Bouquet, bowl, Thick Rim, 7½"	16.00
Blue Bouquet, bowl, vegetable; rnd, 9¼"	18.00
Blue Bouquet, cake plate	18.00
Blue Bouquet, coffeepot, Five Band	50.00
Blue Bouquet, creamer, Modern	10.00
Blue Bouquet, cup	8.00
Blue Bouquet, gravy boat	22.00
Blue Bouquet, leftover, sq	50.00
Blue Bouquet, plate, 7¼"	7.00
Blue Bouquet, platter, oval, 11¼"	18.00
Blue Bouquet, pretzel jar	95.00
Blue Bouquet, saucer	2.00
Blue Bouquet, soup tureen	225.00
Blue Bouquet, spoon	75.00
Blue Bouquet, sugar bowl, w/lid, Modern	20.00
Cameo Rose, bowl, vegetable; rnd, 9"	22.00
Cameo Rose, butter dish, ¼-lb	75.00
Cameo Rose, tidbit tray, 3-tier	50.00
Caprice, ashtray	4.00
Caprice, bowl, celery; oval	20.00
Clover, bowl, Radiance, 6"	16.00
Clover, casserole, rnd, #70, 10"	45.00
Clover, jug, #5, Radiance	50.00
Clover, teapot, Windshield	150.00
Crocus, bowl, fruit; 5½"	6.00
Crocus, bowl, oval	24.00
Crocus, bowl, salad; 9"	18.00
Crocus, cake plate	30.00
Crocus, coffeepot, Meltdown	95.00
Crocus, creamer, Art Deco	18.00
Crocus, creamer, Meltdown	30.00
Crocus, cup	9.00
Crocus, custard	12.00
Crocus, jug, Simplicity	125.00
Crocus, pie baker	25.00
Crocus, plate, 6"	6.00
Crocus, plate, 9"	9.00
Crocus, platter, oval, 13½"	18.00
Crocus, shaker, Teardrop, ea	18.00
Crocus, sugar bowl, w/lid, Modern	12.00
Crocus, tidbit, 3-tier	75.00
Crocus, water bottle, Zephyr style	350.00
Fantasy, bean pot, New England, #4	100.00
Fantasy, cookie jar, Sundial	250.00
Fantasy, custard, Thick Rim	18.00
Fantasy, leftover, loop hdls	90.00
Frost Flowers, bowl, fruit; 5¼"	5.00
Frost Flowers, platter, 15"	18.00
Hallcraft, Fern, bowl, vegetable; divided	12.00
Hallcraft, Fern, butter dish	25.00
Hallcraft, Fern, ladle	6.00
Heather Rose, bowl, salad; 9"	11.00
Heather Rose, bowl, vegetable; w/lid	18.00
Heather Rose, gravy boat, w/underplate	14.00
Heather Rose, pickle dish, 9"	6.00
Mums, bowl, cereal; 6"	8.00
Mums, bowl, fruit; 5½"	6.00
Mums, bowl, salad	16.00
Mums, casserole, Medallion	35.00
Mums, creamer, Art Deco	12.00
Mums, cup	8.00
Mums, custard	7.00
Mums, mug, beverage	40.00
Mums, pie baker	25.00
Mums, plate, 8¼"	5.00
Mums, platter, oval, 11¼"	16.00
Mums, pretzel jar	90.00
Mums, saucer	2.00
Mums, sugar bowl, w/lid, Medallion	16.00
No 488, bean pot, #5	100.00
No 488, cookie jar, Five Band	125.00
No 488, cup	8.00
No 488, custard	10.00
No 488, drip jar & lid, Radiance	25.00
No 488, French baker	20.00
No 488, shakers, hdls, pr	16.00
No 488, sugar bowl, Art Deco, w/lid	30.00
No 488, teapot, Radiance	150.00
Orange Poppy, ball jug, #3	55.00
Orange Poppy, bowl, Radiance, 10"	25.00
Orange Poppy, bowl, Radiance, 7½"	14.00
Orange Poppy, bowl, soup; flat, 8½"	12.00
Orange Poppy, bread box	35.00
Orange Poppy, cake plate	18.00
Orange Poppy, casserole, oval, 11¼"	65.00
Orange Poppy, coffeepot, w/S-lid	45.00
Orange Poppy, cup	9.00
Orange Poppy, custard	6.00
Orange Poppy, match safe	20.00
Orange Poppy, plate, 6"	4.00
Orange Poppy, platter, oval, 11¼"	17.00
Orange Poppy, pretzel jar	85.00
Orange Poppy, saucer	2.00
Orange Poppy, shaker, Novelty Radiance, ea	25.00
Orange Poppy, sifter	35.00
Orange Poppy, spoon	50.00
Orange Poppy, waste basket	35.00
Pastel Morning Glory, bowl, fruit; 5½"	5.00
Pastel Morning Glory, bowl, rnd, 9¼"	25.00
Pastel Morning Glory, cake plate	18.00
Pastel Morning Glory, creamer, New York	10.00
Pastel Morning Glory, gravy boat	20.00
Pastel Morning Glory, pie baker	24.00
Pastel Morning Glory, plate, 7¼"	5.00
Pastel Morning Glory, platter, 11¼"	14.00
Primrose, cake plate	12.00
Primrose, cup	4.00
Primrose, plate, 7¼"	3.50
Red Poppy, bowl, cereal; 6"	10.00
Red Poppy, bowl, fruit; 5½"	5.00
Red Poppy, bowl, oval, 10¼"	20.00
Red Poppy, bowl, salad; 9"	14.00
Red Poppy, bread box, metal, 3 styles, ea	25.00
Red Poppy, cake plate	15.00
Red Poppy, coffeepot, Daniel	40.00
Red Poppy, creamer, modern	10.00
Red Poppy, cup	9.00
Red Poppy, cutting board, wooden	30.00
Red Poppy, dustpan, metal	35.00
Red Poppy, hot pad, metal	10.00

Red Poppy, mixer cover, plastic 20.00
Red Poppy, plate, 10" 25.00
Red Poppy, plate, 6" 3.50
Red Poppy, platter, oval, 13¼" 20.00
Red Poppy, pretzel jar 200.00
Red Poppy, saucer 1.50
Red Poppy, sifter, metal 30.00
Red Poppy, soap dispenser, metal 30.00
Red Poppy, sugar bowl, w/lid, Daniel 16.00
Red Poppy, tablecloth, cotton 60.00

Red Poppy, teapot, $95.00.

Red Poppy, toaster cover, plastic 14.00
Red Poppy, tray, rnd, metal 22.00
Red Poppy, waste can, rnd, metal 35.00
Sears' Arlington, gravy boat, w/underplate 12.00
Sears' Arlington, plate, 10" 5.00
Sears' Arlington, platter, oval, 15½" 16.00
Sears' Monticello, bowl, flat soup 10.00
Sears' Monticello, creamer 6.00
Sears' Monticello, gravy boat, w/underplate ...18.00
Sears' Monticello, plate, 9¼" 5.00
Sears' Monticello, sugar bowl, w/lid 14.00
Sears' Mount Vernon, bowl, cereal 6.00
Sears' Mount Vernon, casserole, w/lid 25.00
Sears' Mount Vernon, coffeepot, all china 95.00
Sears' Mount Vernon, pickle dish 6.00
Sears' Mount Vernon, plate, 10" 8.00
Sears' Richmond, bowl, fruit; 5¼" 3.00
Sears' Richmond, cup 4.50
Serenade, bowl, oval 16.00
Serenade, bowl, Radiance, 6" 8.00
Serenade, creamer, New York 8.00
Serenade, plate, 8½" 4.00
Serenade, sugar bowl, w/lid, Art Deco 16.00
Silhouette, baker, French; fluted 14.00
Silhouette, bowl, cereal; 6" 10.00
Silhouette, bowl, Medallion, 7½" 14.00
Silhouette, bowl, Radiance, 9" 16.00
Silhouette, bowl, vegetable; rnd, 9¼" 27.00
Silhouette, creamer, Medallion 10.00
Silhouette, cup, St Denis 30.00
Silhouette, jug, Medallion, #2 ....16.00
Silhouette, mug, beverage 40.00
Silhouette, platter, oval, 13¼" 18.00
Silhouette, saucer, St Denis 5.00
Silhouette, sugar bowl, w/lid, Medallion 16.00
Silhouette, tea tile, 6" 95.00
Teapot, Airflow, cobalt w/gold flowers 55.00
Teapot, Apple, blk w/gold trim 200.00

Teapot, Automobile, turq w/platinum, 6-cup 650.00
Teapot, Baltimore, red, 6-cup 200.00
Teapot, Basketball, turq, worn gold, 6-cup 550.00
Teapot, Boston, red, 2-cup 100.00
Teapot, Boston, red, 6-cup 125.00
Teapot, Damascus, turq, 6-cup 125.00
Teapot, Football, maroon, 6-cup 650.00
Teapot, French, cadet bl w/gold flowers 55.00
Teapot, Gamebirds, NY, 2-cup 125.00
Teapot, Gamebirds, Windshield, 6-cup 175.00
Teapot, Globe, turq w/gold, 6-cup 85.00
Teapot, Hollywood, maroon, 4-cup 30.00
Teapot, Hollywood, red, 8-cup 150.00
Teapot, Los Angeles, red, 4-cup 125.00
Teapot, Melody, red, 6-cup 250.00
Teapot, Moderne, turq w/gold, 6-cup 50.00
Teapot, New York, cobalt w/gold trim, 6-cup 45.00
Teapot, New York, red, 6-cup 125.00
Teapot, Parade, warm yel w/gold, 6-cup 45.00
Teapot, Pert, maroon w/gold, 6-cup 65.00
Teapot, Rhythm, Chinese red, 6-cup 175.00
Teapot, Star, Chinese red 175.00
Teapot, Streamline, canary w/platinum, 6-cup ..115.00
Teapot, Teataster, turq w/gold, oval, 6-cup 100.00
Teapot, Washington, marine, 12-cup 65.00
Teapot, Windshield, cobalt, 6-cup 125.00
Teapot, Windshield, cobalt w/gold, 6-cup 75.00
Teapot, Windshield, red, 6-cup 200.00
Teapot, Windshield, turq w/gold, 6-cup 55.00
Tulip, bowl, oval 18.00
Tulip, coffeepot, Perk 35.00
Tulip, gravy boat 20.00
Tulip, platter, 11¼" 14.00
Tulip, stack set, Radiance 75.00
Wild Poppy, ball jug, #3 ....125.00
Wild Poppy, cookie jar, Five Band 175.00
Wild Poppy, coquette, hdld 50.00
Wild Poppy, leftover, sq 75.00
Wild Poppy, tea tile 50.00
Wildfire, cake plate 16.00
Wildfire, custard 8.00
Wildfire, gravy boat 18.00
Wildfire, pie baker 25.00
Wildfire, platter, 13¼" 18.00
Wildfire, tidbit, 3-tier 50.00
Yellow Rose, bowl, fruit; 5½" 4.00
Yellow Rose, bowl, Radiance, 9" 12.00
Yellow Rose, creamer, Norse 10.00
Yellow Rose, cup 5.00
Yellow Rose, plate, 9" 6.00
Yellow Rose, saucer 2.00
Yellow Rose, stack set, Radiance 55.00

Zeisel Designs, Hallcraft

Bouquet, bowl, cereal; 6" 6.00
Bouquet, cup, AD 10.00
Bouquet, plate, 8" 7.00
Bouquet, shakers, pr 20.00
Caprice, bowl, coupe soup; 9" 9.00
Caprice, coffeepot, 6-cup 50.00
Caprice, egg cup 18.00
Caprice, plate, 11" 12.00
Fantasy, candlestick, 8", ea 25.00

Fantasy, cup & saucer 8.00
Fantasy, gravy boat 18.00
Fantasy, ladle 10.00
Fern, butter dish 27.50
Fern, gravy boat 12.50
Fern, platter, 13¾" 12.50
Fern, sugar bowl, w/lid 14.00

Flair, gravy boat, $35.00; Candle holder, $25.00.

Frost Flowers, creamer & sugar bowl, w/lid 22.50
Harlequin, bowl, fruit; ftd, lg 30.00
Harlequin, butter dish 60.00
Harlequin, coffeepot, 6-cup 50.00
Holiday, ashtray 6.00
Holiday, casserole, 2-qt 25.00
Holiday, creamer 8.00
Holiday, plate, 11" 5.00
Lyric, coffeepot, 6-cup 50.00
Lyric, egg cup 18.00
Mulberry, bowl, vegetable; 8¾" sq 16.00
Mulberry, candlestick, 4½", ea 20.00
Mulberry, marmite, w/lid 18.00
Mulberry, platter, 17" 20.00
Peach Blossom, bowl, salad; 14½" 27.50
Peach Blossom, candlestick, 8", ea 30.00
Peach Blossom, vinegar bottle 28.00
Pinecone, plate, E-style, 9¼" 7.50
Pinecone, tidbit tray, 3-tier, E-style 40.00
Spring, bowl, open baker, 11-oz 12.00
Spring, gravy boat 18.00
Spring, platter, 15" 18.00
Sunglow, casserole 20.00
Sunglow, ladle 9.00
Sunglow, teacup, 6-cup 60.00

Hallmark

Hallmark introduced a line of artplas (molded plastic) ornaments in 1973 that have quickly become popular with collectors. They also have produced miniature ornaments since 1988, which are very collectible, as well as limited edition ornaments produced for members of the Hallmark Keepsake Ornament Collectors' Club.

'Merry Miniatures' is a line of artplas 'Table Trimmers' made in 1973 which have become quite collectible as well, and collectors are avidly searching for these tiny figures in closets, children's toy boxes, and at flea markets.

The magazine, *The Ornament Collector,* edited by Rosie Wells, our advisor for this category, is available if you want more information on ornament collecting. Rosie also publishes a yearly official

Secondary Market Price Guide on Hallmark Ornaments, Merry Miniatures, Stocking Hangers, Lapel Pins, Cookie Cutters, etc. Her address is listed in the Directory under Clubs, Newsletters, and Catalogs and again under Illinois. Values are for ornaments in mint condition and with their originial boxes, while Merry Miniatures are assumed to be mint.

1973, Betsy Clark Series, XDH 110-2, 1st in series, 3¼" 135.00
1973, Manger Scene, XHD 102-2, wht glass ball, 3¼" 75.00
1974, Betsy Clark Series, QX 108-1, 2nd in series, 3¼" 80.00
1974, Raggedy Ann & Andy, QX 114-1, set of 4, 1¾" 90.00
1975, Adorable Adornments: Betsy Clark, QX 157-1, 3½" 260.00
1975, Adorable Adornments: Drummer Boy, QX 161-1, 3½" 250.00
1975, Adorable Adornments: Raggedy Andy, QX 160-1, 3½" ...350.00
1976, Betsy Clark Series, QX 195-1, 4th in series, 3¼" 100.00
1976, Happy Holidays Kissing Ball, QX 225-1, wht satin, 2½" ...230.00
1977, Angel Tree Topper, QSD 230-2, simulated wood angel 385.00
1977, Betsy Clark Series, QX 264-2, 5th in series, 3¼" 365.00
1978, Carousel Series, QX 146-3, 1st in series, handcrafted, 3" ..375.00
1978, Holiday Memories Kissing Ball, QHD 900-3, Mistletoe Ball .135.00
1978, Schneeberg Bell, QS 152-3, handcrafted, 3½" 200.00
1979, Here Comes Santa Series, QX 155-9, 1st in series, 3½" 600.00
1979, Holiday Scrimshaw, QX 152-7, handcrafted, 3½" 210.00
1980, Christmas Kitten Test Ornament, QX 353-4, handcrafted ...325.00
1980, Frosty Friends: A Cool Yule, QX 137-4, 1st in series 620.00
1981, Christmas Dreams, QX 437-5, panorama ball, 3¼" 205.00
1981, Thimble Series: Angel, QX 413-5, 4th in series, 1½" 125.00
1982, Holiday Wildlife: Cardinals, QX 313-3, wood & decofoam ..300.00
1982, Tin Locomotive, QX460-3, 1st in series, pressed tin 550.00
1983, Bellringer Series, QX 403-9, 5th in series 135.00
1983, Frosty Friends, QX 400-7, 4th in series 270.00
1984, Gift of Music, QX 451-1, musical, handcrafted 85.00
1984, Nostalgic Houses & Shops, QX 448-1, 1st in series 185.00
1985, Mr & Mrs Santa, QLX 705-2, lighted, handcrafted 85.00
1986, Reindeer Champs: Dasher, QX 422-3, handcrafted 135.00
1987, Rocking Horse, QX 482-9, 7th in series 45.00
1988, Kringle's Toy Shop, QLX 701-7, handcrafted 60.00
1989, Baby's First Christmas, QLX 727-2, lighted, musical 68.00
1990, Merry Olde Santa, QX 473-6, 1st in series, handcrafted 60.00
1991, Winnie the Pooh Collection: Tigger, handcrafted 100.00
1992, Tobin Fraley Carousel, QX 489-1, 1st in series 35.00
1993, Holiday Barbie, QX 572-5, 1st in series 90.00

Halloween

The origin of Halloween can be traced back to the ancient practices of the Druids of Great Britain who began their New Year on the 1st of November. The Druids were pagans, and their New Year's celebrations involved pagan rites and superstitions. They believed that as the old year came to an end the devil would gather up all the demons and evil in the world and take them back to Hell with him. Witches were women who had sold their souls to the devil and, with their black cat in attendance, flew up through their chimneys on brooms. When the Roman Catholic Church came into power in 700 A.D., they changed the holiday into a religious event called 'All Saints Day,' or 'Allhallows.' The evening before, October 31, became 'Allhallow's Eve' or 'Halloween.' Today Halloween is strictly a fun time, and Halloween items are fun to collect. Pumpkin-head candy containers of papier-mache or pressed cardboard, noisemakers, postcards with black cats and witches, costumes, and decorations are only a sampling of the variety available. See also Candy Containers.

Candy box, cat pulling cart, stenciled plywood, 9", EX 145.00

Costume, Sister Sally nun, adult sz, M 30.00
Costume, skeleton bones print on polished cotton, 1930s, EX 55.00
Diecut, bat on moon, emb cb, Germany, 5", EX 60.00
Diecut, pumpkin lady, emb cb, Germany, 7" 125.00
Diecut, witch, emb cb, Germany, 5" 75.00
Diecut, witch, emb cb, Germany, 7" 85.00
Diecut, witch & devil, emb cb standup, Germany, 16", EX, pr ...135.00
Figure, vegetable person w/lantern, compo, jtd limbs, 6", EX 500.00
Horn, cb & wood, HP carrot face, Germany, 7", EX 135.00
Jack-in-the-box, devil, compo head, 3½" box, VG 350.00
Jack-in-the-box, goblin, papier-mache/cloth, 3¾" box, VG 300.00
Jack-in-the-box, skull, compo w/squeaker, 3" box, EX 155.00
Jack-in-the-box, witch's compo head, squeaker, 3" box, EX 245.00
Jack-o'-lantern, papier-mache, not made w/insert, 4" 90.00
Jack-o'-lantern, papier-mache, orig insert, 8" 125.00
Jack-o'-lantern, pressed cb, crossed eyes, 3½", EX 110.00
Jack-o'-lantern, pressed cb, molded nose, paper insert, 5", VG ...125.00
Jack-o'-lantern, pressed cb, molded-on hat, 6", G (no hdl) 145.00
Jack-o'-lantern, pressed cb, paper insert, Germany, 5", VG 110.00
Jack-o'-lantern, pressed cb, paper insert, glasses, 5", EX 200.00
Jumping jack, pumpkin head, papier-mache & wood, 11", EX ...360.00
Lantern, cat, molded fiber, paper inserts, 6½", EX 250.00
Lantern, cat, papier-mache, rpl insert 145.00
Lantern, cat, pressed cb w/accordion body, 5", EX 125.00
Lantern, cat on fence, pressed cb, paper inserts, 7½", EX 135.00
Lantern, cat's head, pressed cb, gr eyes, 3¼", EX 330.00
Lantern, cat's head, pressed cb, paper insert, 3¾", EX 78.00
Lantern, cat's head, pressed cb, paper insert, 5", VG 110.00
Lantern, cat's head w/open mouth, papier-mache, 3", VG 95.00
Lantern, devil, compo, red, w/bail, 3" 250.00
Lantern, devil, egg-carton mache, orig insert, 9", EX 285.00
Lantern, devil's head, papier-mache w/insert, rare, 4", EX 500.00
Lantern, devil-faced witch, papier-mache, w/insert, 4", EX 525.00
Lantern, pumpkin man, celluloid, spring limbs, MIB 165.00
Lantern, pumpkin-head boy, papier-mache, Germany, 5", NM ..575.00
Lantern, skull, bsk w/gold, jaw moves, metal stand, Japan, 4" 85.00
Lantern, skull, papier-mache, 3", VG 165.00
Lantern, watermelon, pressed cb w/insert, 4", EX 550.00
Mask, Blk face, gauze 35.00
Mask, clown, papier-mache, 4-color, 5½x8" 60.00
Mask, donkey's head, papier-mache, HP, 15x9x5½" 45.00
Mask, mesh wire w/pnt features, w/fiber hair & beard, 12½" 75.00
Match holder, devil's head, china, Germany, 2½" 85.00
Nodder, blk cat, papier-mache, spring-mtd head, 6¼", EX 150.00
Nodder, cat, blk flocked w/wood neck, early, Germany, 5½" 190.00
Nodder, pumpkin-head figure, papier-mache, 5¼", EX 250.00
Nodder, pumpkin-head lady, papier-mache/cb, Germany, 9", EX .415.00
Nodder, pumpkin-head man, papier-mache, Germany, rare, 7", EX .550.00
Nodder, skeleton head, papier-mache, Germany, rare, 8", EX 360.00
Nodder, witch, cb & wood, 10", EX 185.00
Nodder, witch on cat, compo, Germany, 6½" 465.00
Noise maker, blk cat, paper on wood, ratchet, 1918, 6", VG 85.00
Noise maker, pumpkin head, cb & wood w/ratchet, 8", EX 125.00
Squeaker, pumpkin man, orange compo, gr felt robe, silent, 4" ..185.00

Candy Containers

Blk cat, fur on papier-mache, 7½" 350.00
Cabbage-head man, papier-mache, early, 6", VG 450.00
Cat, papier-mache, cone shape, Germany, 1950s, 7½" 65.00
Cat, papier-mache, US Zone, 2½" 65.00
Cat on pumpkin, compo, mc, early, Germany, 5" 350.00
Cat w/horn, papier-mache, Germany, 1950s, 7" 55.00
Devil on boot, compo & cb, 6", EX 110.00

Goblin on pumpkin w/cat, papier-mache, early, 6", EX 300.00
Melon head, pressed cb w/insert, early, 6½", EX 250.00
Melon head, pressed cb w/spring legs, early, 6", VG 220.00
Melon head w/bow tie, pressed cb, rare, 4", EX 440.00
Owl, papier-mache, blk w/orange, early, 7" 165.00
Pear-head man, papier-mache, early, 6½", VG 450.00
Pumpkin, papier-mache, Germany, 1950s, 4", M 35.00
Pumpkin, papier-mache, Germany, 1950s, 6", M 55.00
Pumpkin-head baby, cb & papier-mache, early, 3", VG 185.00
Pumpkin-head child, papier-mache, 3¾", G 110.00
Pumpkin-head lady, papier-mache, Germany, 6", M 250.00

Candy container, Pumpkin-head man in witch's hat, 8", M, $195.00.

Pumpkin-head man, compo, Germany, 4½", EX 175.00
Pumpkin-head man, papier-mache, Germany, early, 7", EX 150.00
Pumpkin-head man, papier-mache, Germany, 1950s, 5½", M 55.00
Skeleton, compo, crepe-paper attire, 4½" 145.00
Witch, crepe paper & compo, 6", EX 185.00
Witch, papier-mache, cone shape, Germany, 1950s, 7½", M 55.00
Witch, papier-mache, Germany, 1950s, 7½" 45.00

Hampshire

The Hampshire Pottery Company was established in 1871 in Keene, New Hampshire, by James Scollay Taft. Their earliest products were redware and stoneware utility items such as jugs, churns, crocks, and flowerpots. In 1878 they produced majolica ware which met with such success that they began to experiment with the idea of manufacturing art pottery. By 1883 they had developed a Royal Worcester type of finish which they applied to vases, tea sets, powder boxes, and cookie jars. It was also utilized for souvenir items that were decorated with transfer designs prepared from photographic plates.

Cadmon Robertson, brother-in-law of Taft, joined the company in 1904 and was responsible for developing their famous matt glazes. Colors included shades of green, brown, red, and blue. Early examples were of earthenware, but eventually the body was changed to semiporcelain. Some of his designs were marked with an M in a circle as a tribute to his wife, Emoretta. Robertson died in 1914, leaving a void impossible to fill. Taft sold the business in 1916 to George Morton, who continued to use the matt glazes that Robertson had developed. After a temporary halt in production during WWI, Morton returned to Keene and re-equipped the factory with the machinery needed to manufacture hotel china and floor tile. Because of the expense involved in transporting coal to fire the kilns, Morton found he could not compete with potteries of Ohio and New Jersey who were able to utilize locally available natural gas. He was forced to close the plant in 1923.

Interest is highest on examples in the monochrome glazes, and it is the glaze, not the size or form, that dictates value. The souvenir pieces are not particularly of high quality and tend to be passed over by today's collectors.

Bowl, gr mottle on brn, ochre gloss int, rtcl, #22/2, 3¼" H 130.00
Bowl vase, brn, incised arch design, 2x5" 180.00
Bowl vase, veined blk mottle on mocha, gr int, sgn King, 2¼" ...350.00
Candle shield, gr matt w/some crystalline, #22, 6¼", EX 90.00
Chamberstick, gr matt w/gray mottle int, shield bk, 7x4" 140.00
Creamer & sugar bowl, gr glossy, emb leaves, 3½", 2½", NM 40.00
Lamp base, dk gr matt, emb stylized tulips, squat, 6x11" 850.00
Pitcher, gr matt w/silvery streaks, mk, 11x11" 100.00
Pitcher, Salem Witch, 6½" 160.00
Vase, aqua to gray mottle, emb leaves, flaw, #124, 9¾" 350.00
Vase, bl & wht mottle on cobalt, emb panels, #129, 5½" 475.00
Vase, blk & gray mottle on aqua, squat, M in O mk, 4¼" 220.00
Vase, brn veined on teal gr, squat, early, 3½" 200.00
Vase, cobalt & aqua veins on wht, emb buds, gray int, #33, 6¾" ..500.00
Vase, dk brn, olive gr & teal mottle, wht int, #54, 3½" 170.00
Vase, gr, bulbous, 4½" 185.00
Vase, gr matt, emb buds & leaves, ovoid, M in O mk, 8¾" 750.00
Vase, gr matt, emb geometrics, bulbous, M in O mk, 7¾" 475.00
Vase, gr matt, incising at shoulder, bulbous, M in O mk, 6½" 150.00
Vase, gr mottle on brn, heavy drip at base, #118, 5¼" 180.00
Vase, gr w/exposed clay, cvd geometrics at shoulder, 4x4" 275.00
Vase, gray & mauve mottle on cobalt, ovoid, M in O mk, 7½" ..325.00
Vase, lav-pk mottle w/some lt gray, cylinder, mk, 4½x2½" 275.00
Vase, lt gr to blk flambe on gr, bulbous, 3½" 165.00
Vase, med cobalt & blk mottle, shouldered, M in O mk, 4¼" 130.00
Vase, red mocha mottle, bulging waist, M in O mk, 5½" 300.00
Vase, sea gr on aqua, 3 crimped sides (like Ohr), unmk, 3¾" 275.00
Vase, wht mottle on cobalt at shoulder, cobalt int, mk, 3½" 350.00

Handel

Philip Handel was best known for the art glass lamps he produced at the turn of the century. His work is similar to the Tiffany lamps of the same era. Handel made gas and electric lamps with both leaded glass and reverse-painted shades. Chipped ice shades with a texture similar to overshot glass were also produced. Shades signed by artists such as Bailey, Palme, and Parlow are highly valued.

China and glassware decorated by Handel are rare and command high prices on today's market. Teroma is a term used to describe glassware decorated on the exterior with paint that has a sandy finish. Many of Handel's chinaware blanks were supplied by Limoges. Our advisor for this category is Daniel Batchelor; he is listed in the Directory under New York.

Key: chp — chipped/lightly sanded

Lamps

Boudoir, Arts & Crafts-pnt 1-pc dome #5893 shade; mk base .2,200.00
Boudoir, gr floral-band 6-panel 1-pc #6361 shade; mk base 2,100.00
Boudoir, rvpt 7" hex landscape #6292 shade; unmk std, 14" 1,500.00
Boudoir, rvpt 7" windmill/night scene sgn/#d shade; mk std ...1,700.00
Boudoir, rvpt 8" scenic shade; ribbed std 1,500.00
Boudoir, rvpt/chp 7" lacy branch scenic #6150 shade; mk std .2,000.00
Candlestick, Teroma, winter scene, #5895 0389, 9½" 1,050.00
Chandelier, hammered copper, 4 tubes on rtcl copper straps ...1,300.00

Chandelier, 4-light, pnt 6-panel 6½" Prairie School shades 4,500.00
Desk, rvpt/chp cylinder shade w/peacocks; adjustable base 3,500.00
Floor, rvpt 10" mtn scene #6208 shade; metal harp fr; 59" 3,750.00
Floor, rvpt 10" sunburst #6977 shade; harp fr, 59" 2,800.00
Floor, rvpt/chp 10" rose-band #6872 shade; unmk harp std, 57" ...3,750.00
Floor, Steuben 10" shade w/in harp std, 52" 2,300.00
Hall, rvpt 10" ball shade w/2 parrots on gold, metal mts 2,500.00
Mantel, scenic Teroma cylinder shade; bronze ft/cap, 16" 1,200.00
Piano, ldgl 6¾" brickwork shade; organic base, sgn 2X 1,400.00
Piano, rectangular #6010½ shade, dk to lt brn texture 850.00
Sconce, 5½" ldgl 10-panel Arts & Crafts shade; 10½", EX 600.00
Table, acid-etch 18" gr-cased pine needle shade; 6-ftd std 2,200.00
Table, ldgl 16" water lilies shade; bronze std; 23" 2,750.00
Table, rvp 16" floral #6811 shade; mk bronze std, 24" 4,200.00
Table, rvpt 15" fruit tree #7140 sgn MW shade; tree std, M 2,900.00
Table, rvpt 16" water scene w/boats Venetian shade; mk std ..4,500.00
Table, rvpt 18" forest scene #6644 shade; baluster std; 26" 12,000.00
Table, rvpt 18" Nile river #6641 shade; unmk std, 26" 7,000.00
Table, rvpt 18" parrots #7128 dome shade; 3-strap std, EX 8,250.00
Table, rvpt 18" scenic shade #7024 sgn Bailey; vase std 4,000.00
Table, rvpt 18" tropical scene dome shade; sgn base 5,500.00
Table, rvpt/chp 15" multiflora dome shade; 3-strap unmk std .6,500.00
Table, rvpt/chp 18" butterflies/floral shade; 3-scroll std 8,500.00
Table, rvpt/chp 18" rose-border shade; unmk gilt-bronze std ...2,000.00
Table, rvpt/chp 18" scenic #6208 shade; buds/leaf unmk std ..4,250.00
Table, rvpt/chp 18" windmill etc #7035 shade; unmk std, EX .2,500.00
Table, rvpt/etched 18" #7719 shade w/birds; brass std, 25" 2,500.00
Table, sm slag glass lantern hangs from ring on L-shape std 2,200.00
Table, 16" tulip shade w/6 bent slag panels; vase std, EX 650.00
Torchiere, pnt gr/orange upright cone shade; unmk base, 16" 600.00

Miscellaneous

Bookends, seated gent reading book, eng John Burroughs, EX ...1,200.00
Bowl, bathing beauty portrait, metal hdls, #475/249, 6½" 1,100.00
Candlestick, Teroma, windmill/lake, sgn Gubisch, #4213, 8½" .1,500.00
Celery tray, china w/floral, sgn Runge, shield mk, 11" 600.00
Cigarette urn, Indian portrait, ormolu hdls, 3½", EX 450.00
Compote, ivory glass w/mc dragonflies & water lilies, 8" 250.00
Humidor, chipped opal w/matt gr pnt, bronze mts, knob lid, 8" .500.00
Humidor, chipped opal w/matt gr pnt, knob lid, 6" 300.00
Humidor, fisherman w/pipe, opalware, SP lid, 5" 650.00
Humidor, horse head on pnt opalware, #104/324, 6" 550.00
Humidor, horse/hound pnt on opalware, sqd, pipe on lid, 7" 600.00

Humidors: monk transfer on dark green, #204-279, NM, 6x3¼", $1,000.00; Owl on branch on green and brown, silverplated lid, #4038, M, $1,400.00.

Humidor, Teroma, sailing ship in bay, sgn Bedigie, #4207, 9" .2,950.00
Humidor, Tobacco/Indian, pnt gr ground on opal, knob lid, 8" ..1,000.00
Tazza, floral, gr & orange on yel opalware, #4122/C, 7½" 550.00
Vase, palms, brns on gray, sgn Bailey, ruffled/ftd, 11" 1,200.00
Vase, portrait of a young maid on china, sgn Parlow, 16" 3,600.00
Vase, simple floral on pnt texture, baluster, mk, 12", EX 1,000.00
Vase, Teroma, landscape, sgn Bedigie, 10" 2,000.00
Vase, Teroma, landscape, sgn Gubisch, #4209, 9¾" 1,800.00
Vase, Teroma, landscape, waisted cylinder, drilled, 11" 275.00
Vase, Teroma, snow-capped mtns/trees, sgn Bedigie, ftd, 9½" .1,400.00

Harker

The Harker Pottery was established in East Liverpool, Ohio, in 1840. Their earliest products were yellowware and Rockingham produced from local clay. After 1900 whiteware was made from imported materials. The plant eventually grew to be a large manufacturer of dinnerware and kitchenware, employing as many as three hundred people. It closed in 1972 after it was purchased by the Jeannette Glass Company. Perhaps their best-known lines were their Cameo wares, decorated with white silhouettes in a cameo effect on contrasting solid colors. Floral silhouettes are standard, but other designs were also used. Blue and pink are the most often found background hues; a few pieces are found in yellow. For further information we recommend *The Collector's Guide to Harker Pottery* by Neva Colbert.

Amy, bean pot, metal rack 75.00
Amy, cake plate 7.00
Amy, pie plate 8.00
Amy, plate, dinner 4.00
Calico Tulip, cake plate 17.50
Cameo, casserole, bl, w/lid, 7" 47.00
Cameo Rose, creamer & sugar bowl 12.50
Cameo Rose, cup 5.00
Cameo Rose, platter, 14" 12.00
Cameo Rose, rolling pin, bl 98.00
Cameo Rose, shakers, skyscraper shape, pr 15.00
Chesterton, cake set, pk floral, 8-pc 25.00
Chesterton, cake set, teal gr, 10-pc 27.50
Colonial Lady, bowl, batter 42.00
Colonial Lady, casserole, w/lid, 8½" 45.00
Colonial Lady, pie plate, 9" 30.00
Deco Dahlia, cake lifter 22.00
Deco Dahlia, cake tray, 10¾" 27.50

Deco Dahlia, individual casseroles, in wire holder, $35.00.

Deco Dahlia, pie plate, 10" 30.00
Gadroon, cup, charcoal 5.00
Mallo, rolling pin 85.00
Modern Tulip, bowl, 6" 5.00
Modern Tulip, teapot 18.00

Morning Glory, rolling pin 90.00
Pastel Tulip, gravy boat 14.00
Pastel Tulip, plate, dinner 8.50
Petit Point, casserole, w/lid, 8½" 22.00
Petit Point, pie plate, 9" 16.50
Poppy, bowl, utility; 11" 17.50
Rose II, cake lifter 16.50
White Rose, bowl, soup 12.00
White Rose, plate, 10" 12.00
White Rose, tile 28.00
Wood Song, plate, 7" 8.00

Harlequin

Harlequin dinnerware, produced by the Homer Laughlin China Company of Newell, West Virginia, was introduced in 1938. It was a lightweight ware made in maroon, mauve blue, and spruce green, as well as all the Fiesta colors except ivory (see Fiesta). It was marketed exclusively by the Woolworth stores, who considered it to be their all-time best seller. For this reason they contracted with Homer Laughlin to reissue Harlequin to commemorate their 100th anniversary in 1979. Although three of the original glazes were used in the reissue, the few serving pieces that were made were restyled, and collectors found the new line to be no threat to their investments.

The Harlequin animals, including a fish, lamb, cat, penguin, duck, and donkey, were made during the early 1940s, also for the dime-store trade. Today these are very desirable to collectors of Homer Laughlin china.

In the listings that follow, use the values designated 'high' for all colors other than turquoise and yellow. For medium green, double the 'high' values on all items other than flat items and small bowls. *The Collector's Encyclopedia of Fiesta* (values updated in 1994) by Sharon and Bob Huxford contains a more thorough study of this subject. It is available from Collector Books or your local library.

Animals, maverick, gold trim, ea 32.00
Animals, non-standard color, ea 158.00
Animals, standard color, ea 85.00
Ashtray, basketweave, high 45.00
Ashtray, basketweave, low 30.00
Ashtray, regular, high 42.50
Ashtray, regular, low 32.00
Bowl, '36s oatmeal; high 17.00
Bowl, '36s oatmeal; low 11.50
Bowl, '36s; high 26.50
Bowl, '36s; low 17.00
Bowl, cream soup; high 20.00
Bowl, cream soup; low 16.00
Bowl, fruit; high, 5½" 9.00
Bowl, fruit; low, 5½" 6.00
Bowl, ind salad; high 26.50
Bowl, ind salad; low 17.00
Bowl, mixing; Kitchen Kraft, mauve bl, 8" 110.00
Bowl, mixing; Kitchen Kraft, red or spruce gr, 6", ea ...72.00
Bowl, mixing; Kitchen Kraft, yel, 10" 110.00
Bowl, nappy; high, 9" 26.50
Bowl, nappy; low, 9" 16.50
Bowl, oval baker, high 25.00
Bowl, oval baker, low 18.00
Butter dish, high, ½-lb 90.00
Butter dish, low, ½-lb 75.00
Candle holders, high, pr 195.00
Candle holders, low, pr 162.00
Casserole, w/lid, high 95.00

Casserole, w/lid, low	58.00
Creamer, high lip, any color, ea	72.00
Creamer, ind; high	17.00
Creamer, ind; low	12.50
Creamer, novelty, high	23.00
Creamer, novelty, low	16.00
Creamer, regular, high	13.50
Creamer, regular, low	8.00
Cup, demitasse; high	46.00
Cup, demitasse; low	27.50
Cup, lg, any color, ea	92.00
Cup, tea; high	9.50
Cup, tea; low	7.50
Egg cup, dbl, high	20.00
Egg cup, dbl, low	14.00
Egg cup, single, high	21.00
Egg cup, single, low	16.50
Gravy boat, high	23.00
Gravy boat, low	16.00
Marmalade, any color, ea	125.00
Nut dish, basketweave, orig color	8.00
Perfume bottle, any color, ea	68.00
Pitcher, service water; high	55.00
Pitcher, service water; low	37.50
Pitcher, 22-oz jug, high	46.00
Pitcher, 22-oz jug, low	26.00
Plate, deep; high	20.00
Plate, deep; low	15.00
Plate, high, 10"	24.00
Plate, high, 6"	4.50
Plate, high, 7"	6.50
Plate, high, 9"	12.00
Plate, low, 10"	14.00
Plate, low, 6"	3.50
Plate, low, 7"	4.50
Plate, low, 9"	7.00
Platter, high, 11"	17.50
Platter, high, 13"	25.00
Platter, low, 11"	12.00
Platter, low, 13"	16.50
Saucer, demitasse; high	13.50
Saucer, demitasse; low	7.00
Saucer, high	3.50
Saucer, low	2.00
Saucer/ashtray, high	47.00
Saucer/ashtray, ivory	65.00
Saucer/ashtray, low	42.50
Shakers, high, pr	16.50
Shakers, low, pr	13.00
Sugar bowl, w/lid, high	17.00
Sugar bowl, w/lid, low	12.00
Syrup, any color	200.00
Teapot, high	88.00
Teapot, low	58.00
Tray, relish; mixed colors	200.00
Tumbler, high	40.00
Tumbler, low	30.00

Hatpin Holders

Most hatpin holders were made from 1860 to 1920 to coincide with the period during which hatpins were popularly in vogue. The taller types were required to house the long hatpins necessary to secure the large hats that were in style from 1890 to 1914. They were usually porcelain, either decorated by hand or by transfer with florals or scenics, although some were clever figurals. Glass examples are rare, and those of slag or Carnival Glass are especially valuable.

If you are interested in collecting or dealing in hatpins or hatpin holders, you will find that authority Lillian Baker has several fine books available on the subject, including her most recent publication, *Hatpins and Hatpin Holders*, complete with beautiful color illustrations and current market values. She is listed in the Directory under California. For information concerning the International Club for Collectors of Hatpins and Hatpin Holders, see the Clubs, Newsletters, and Catalogs section of the Directory. Our advisor for this category is Robert Larsen; he is listed in the Directory under Nebraska.

Austria, HP florals, saucer type	75.00
Carnival glass, Grape & Cable, purple, 7x2½"	355.00
Chocolate glass, emb florals, ca 1905, 7⅜"	375.00
Daisy & Button, clear, silver top w/pinholes, rare, 8"	355.00
Flow blue, Victorian scenes, Watteau	150.00
Nippon, berries, purple & bl w/gold	180.00

Royal Bayreuth, lily figural, yellow with green leaves, unmarked, sixteen pin holes, rare, 4½", $3,000.00 to $3,500.00.

Royal Bayreuth, man w/turkey, bl mk	350.00
RS Prussia, calla lilies, gr to dk gr	165.00
RS Prussia, floral decor, 3-hdld, red mk	750.00
Silver, etched & eng, 16 holes, unmk, 1880s, 5½x2¾"	225.00
Silver w/cherub figure at side, plush cushion, unmk, 4x2¾"	250.00
Silver w/plush velvet cushion, Art Nouveau, 6½x1¾"	165.00
Sterling golf bag form, 2 putters form legs, mk, 1895, 3"	185.00
Willow Art China, Jewish symbol transfer, Jerusalem, 5½"	80.00

Hatpins

A hatpin was used to securely fasten a hat to the hair and head of the wearer. Hatpins, measuring from 4" to 12" in length, were worn from approximately 1850 to 1920. During the Art Deco period, hatpins became ornaments rather than the decorative functional jewels that they had been. The hatpin period reached its zenith in 1913 just prior to World War I, which brought about a radical change in women's headdress and fashion. About that time, women began to scorn the bonnet and adopt 'the hat' as a symbol of their equality. The hatpin was made of every natural and manufactured element in a myriad of designs that challenge the imagination. They were contrived to serve every fashion need and complement the milliner's art. Collectors often concentrate on a specific type: hand-painted porcelains, sterling silver, commemoratives, sporting activities, Carnival Glass, Art Nouveau and/or Art Deco designs, Victorian Gothics with mounted stones, exquisite rhinestones, engraved and brass-mounted escutcheon heads, gold and gems, or simply primitive types made in the Victorian parlor. Some collectors prefer the long pin-shanks while others select only those on tremblants or nodder-type pin-shanks.

If you are interested in collecting or dealing in hatpins, see the information in the Hatpin Holders introduction concerning reference books and a national collectors' club. For further study we recommend *The Collector's Encyclopedia of Hatpins and Hatpin Holders*, available at your local bookstore or from Collector Books. Our advisor for this category is Robert Larsen; he is listed in the Directory under Nebraska.

Key: cab — cabochon

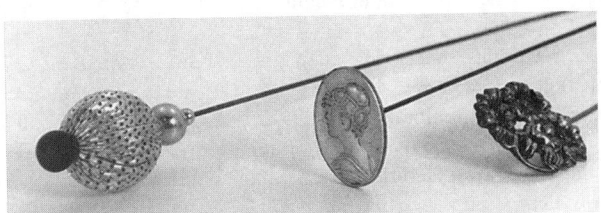

Gold-tone metal ball, 1" diameter on 10" pin, $45.00; 'The Girl of the Pingree Shoe,' Pingree Shoes advertising, 1¼" oval on 9¾" pin, $55.00; Sterling floral design with worn blue paint, 1¼" on 8" pin, $36.00.

Am Eagle head, silver w/red stone eye & rhinestones, 1¾" 145.00
Basse-taille enameled head over-pnt w/roses, gold trim, 1½" 110.00
Cab-cut garnet, 1" overall head, 5½" gilt pin 120.00
German silver scarab w/pnt wings & eyes, 1½x1¼" 85.00
HP Satsuma, birds & leaves, 1½", 10½" steel pin 135.00
HP Satsuma, Oriental ladies w/gold beads, 1¾", 10" pin 165.00
Ivory, hollow-cvd chrysanthemum, 1", 7⅜" steel pin 135.00
Mosaic set in brass mt w/gold-wire trim, ca 1875, 1", 8" pin 75.00
Nouveau brass fr w/faceted amethyst stones, 1½x2¾" 90.00
Nouveau brass w/4 topaz-colored stones, 2¾", 12" pin 90.00
Nouveau gilt on brass w/bezel-set pk faceted glass, 1½" 50.00
Peacock cab in 4-sided gilt-on-brass design, 1", 8" pin 55.00
Sterling Nouveau lady w/repousse work, ca 1905, 1", 9" pin 80.00
Vanity, Nouveau moth w/red faceted stone & rhinestones, 1½" .1,250.00
2-mold plastic circlet joined by brass tubular finding, 2" 45.00

Haviland

The Haviland China Company was organized in 1840 by David Haviland, a New York china importer. His search for a pure white, non-porous porcelain led him to Limoges, France, where natural deposits of suitable clay had already attracted numerous china manufacturers. The fine china he produced there was translucent and meticulously decorated, with each piece fired in an individual sagger.

It has been estimated that as many as 60,000 chinaware patterns were designed, each piece marked with one of several company backstamps. 'H. & Co.' was used until 1890 when a law was enacted making it necessary to include the country of origin. Various marks have been used since that time including 'Haviland, France'; 'Haviland & Co. Limoges'; and 'Decorated by Haviland & Co.' Various associations with family members over the years have resulted in changes in management as well as company name. In 1892 Theodore Haviland left the firm to start his own business. Some of his ware was marked 'Mont Mery.' Later logos included a horseshoe, a shield, and various uses of his initials and name. In 1941 this branch moved to the United States. Wares produced here are marked 'Theodore Haviland, N.Y.' or 'Made In America.'

Though it is their dinnerware lines for which they are most famous, during the 1880s and 1890s they also made exquisite art pottery using a technique of underglaze slip decoration called Barbotine, which had been invented by Ernest Chaplet. In 1885 Haviland bought the formula and hired Chaplet to oversee its production. The technique involved mixing heavy white clay slip with pigments to produce a compound of the same consistency as oil paints. The finished product actually resembled oil paintings of the period, the texture achieved through the application of the heavy medium to the clay body in much the same manner as an artist would apply paint to his canvas. Primarily the body used with this method was a low-fired faience, though they also produced stoneware. Numbers in the listings below refer to pattern books by Arlene Schleiger.

Biscuit jar, Moss Rose, 7x5" 150.00
Bowl, Clover, 6⅛" 15.00
Bowl, soup; Rosalinde, w/underplate 30.00
Box, powder; florals w/gold & gr, Star form, 1893-1930, 4½" 150.00
Butter pat, florals, Nenuphat blank, 1876-89, 3" sq 20.00
Butter tub, floral swags, 3½", +6½" plate 85.00
Cake set, birds/pk flowers, 16" platter, +10 9" plates 350.00
Celery dish, Clover, 12¼" 25.00
Chocolate set, carnations, dbl mk, pot, 6 c/s+tray 2,000.00
Chocolate set, floral sprays in pk & gr, 10" pot+4 c/s 310.00
Coffeepot, floral w/gold, Pompadour blank, 1888-96, 8½" 175.00
Coffeepot, Moss Rose 45.00
Compote, center medallion, ormolu mts, 1893-1930, 7x5½" 130.00
Creamer & sugar bowl, Autumn Leaf, w/lid 125.00
Cup & saucer, Arbor 38.00
Cup & saucer, bouillon; Silver Anniversary 26.00
Cup & saucer, Ganga 30.00
Cup & saucer, lav & pk roses w/gold, on blank #22 ....22.50
Cup & saucer, Ranson 30.00
Cup & saucer, Rosalinde, French 32.00
Ewer, rose & daisies HP over relief, 1865-75, 8" 165.00
Gravy boat, Gotham 40.00
Mayonnaise, gold trim on leaf shape, w/undertray, 1904-20 ....85.00
Pitcher, butterflies & floral on wht, mk H&C, 9" 100.00
Pitcher, water; emb florals w/gold, 1850-65, 10" 135.00
Plate, Arbor, 7½" 25.00
Plate, Clover, 7½" 16.50
Plate, Clover, 9¾" 25.00
Plate, deer couple, ornate border 95.00
Plate, Ladore, 10" 18.00
Plate, Marie de Medicis, ornate acorn/leaf borders, sgn, 9" 200.00
Plate, oyster; shell design, HP in factory, 1876-80, 9" 110.00
Plate, oyster; tiny florals, scrolled wells, 8", 4 for 275.00
Plate, Silver Anniversary, 7½" 22.00
Platter, Clover, 15¾" 115.00
Platter, lav & pk roses w/gold on blank #22, 14" 45.00
Platter, Louis XV, gold trim, 13⅝" 67.50
Platter, Princess, 16" 60.00
Platter, Ranson, 23" 195.00
Platter, Silver Anniversary, pk roses w/gold, 23" 100.00
Soup plate, Eden, mk Theo, 7½" 15.00
Teapot, tea rose sprays on bl, 4", +2" creamer 95.00
Tray, floral, mk, 14½x9½" 75.00
Vase, mums & fuchsia, purple on wht, 3-hdl, de Feure, 8" 500.00

Pottery

Jardiniere, stoneware, floral, tan/gr on brn, 7x9" 800.00
Pitcher, stoneware, cvd floral on brn w/gilt, att Dammouse, 6" ..550.00
Pitcher, stoneware, cvd wht flowers/gr leaves, AD, 7" 700.00

Stein, stoneware, seated boy reaching for apple, 8" 700.00
Vase, Barbotine, 2 wild fowl, sgn PLC, bulbous, 11" 650.00
Vase, Terra Cotta, sculpted florals, 12", pr 1,200.00

Hawkes

Thomas Hawkes established his factory in Corning, New York, in 1880. He developed many beautiful patterns of cut glass, two of which were awarded the Grand Prize at the Paris Exposition in 1889. By the end of the century, his company was renowned for the finest in cut glass production. The company logo was a trefoil form enclosing a hawk in each of the two bottom lobes with a fleur-de-lis in the center. With the exception of some of the very early designs, all Hawkes was signed.

Bowl, alternating miters/hobstars, deep, 8" 210.00
Bowl, Brazilian, +stand w/step-cut & pattern ring, 12½x14" ...1,150.00
Bowl, dmns w/X-hatching above dbl fans & hobstars, 10" 300.00
Bowl, flashed stars & fans, 8" 125.00
Bowl, hobstars & canes, sterling rim, 8" 160.00
Bowl, hobstars & fans, hobstar in base, shallow, 8½" 300.00
Bowl, Panel, 8" 1,000.00
Bowl, Queen's cutting, 10" 1,400.00
Box, handkerchief; hobstars & miters, hinged top, sqd, 6¾" 320.00
Candlesticks, eng florals, baluster stem, 12", pr 325.00
Carafe, hobstars & fans, honeycomb neck, squat, 7" 200.00
Cocktail, eng rooster on Steuben blank, sterling rim, sgn 275.00
Cocktail shaker, dmn band w/panels, sterling rim/lid, 11" 300.00
Compote, eng floral/leafy scrolls, 7¾", pr 200.00
Compote, Gravic, puffy blossoms/polished leaves, 5x8", EX 330.00
Compote, Radiant variation, full-length teardrop stem, 7½x6" ..200.00
Cordial, Queen's 200.00
Creamer & sugar bowl, brilliant cuttings, 4", 2½" 165.00
Cruet, geometrics, notched hdl, faceted stopper, 9" 140.00
Decanter, Flute, teardrop stopper, 7½" 200.00
Dessert set, Chrysanthemum, early, 9" bowl+8 5" sauces 900.00
Dish, Grecian, leaf shape, 6x8" 500.00
Jar, Venetian, faceted finial, 5½x3½", NM 300.00
Pitcher, Brunswick, stars/fans/mitres, 9", +8 tumblers 775.00
Plate, geometric & intaglio cuttings, 10" 275.00
Plate, Gladys, 8" 150.00
Powder jar, Paul Revere, 2¾" 250.00
Spooner, hobstars & strawberry dmns, 7½" 80.00
Sugar bowl, Teutonic, Steuben blank, no hdls, 2¼" 175.00
Tray, Carnation, oval, sgn, 10¼x7" 425.00
Tray, celery; Festoon, 10½x5" 150.00
Tray, celery; Festoon, 12" 250.00
Tray, dresser; Gravic, intaglio floral, 7x10" 100.00
Tray, Gravic, strawberries/leaves, 12" L 150.00

Ice cream tray, Gladys pattern, 16" long, $1,500.00.

Tray, Russian, rectangular w/hdls, 11½" 850.00
Vase, bl-gr w/wht branches etc, swirled crystal int, 7" 325.00
Vase, Brunswick, 12", pr 450.00
Vase, Carnation, fan form, 12" 500.00
Waste jar, flowers & swags, Celeste bl w/gold, sgn, 8½" 425.00

Head Vases

Vases modeled as heads of lovely ladies, delightful children, clowns, Madonnas — even some animals — were once popular as flower containers. Today they represent a growing area of collector interest. Most of them were imported from Japan, although some American potteries produced a few as well.

For more information, we recommend *Head Vases, Identification and Values*, by Kathleen Cole.

Girl marked 'Jean' and numbered, with unmarked matching boy, both 7", $42.50 each.

Baby in lg ruffled bonnet, Napco #C2643B, 1956, 5½" 42.50
Baby w/bow in hair, Inarco #E3156, 5½" 42.50
Baby w/kitten, unmk, 5½" 42.50
Benjamin Franklin, 6" 75.00
Clown in gr hat, smiling face, unmk, #9115, 6" 22.50
Clown in sm hat, lg bow at neck, Napcoware #C3321, 6" 32.50
Deco-style lady w/face raised, wide-brimmed hat, unmk, 9" 125.00
Girl in bonnet holding poodle, unmk, 6" 48.00
Girl in tam, gloved hand to face, Relpo #K1694/S, 5½" 38.00
Girl in wide-brimmed hat, pearl jewelry, Relpo #K1679, 7" 65.00
Girl w/curly hair, pearl necklace, ruffled collar, Parma, 7" ...62.50
Girl w/curly hair, pearl necklace & earrings, Lark, 7" 60.00
Girl w/flip hairdo, bsk, Inarco #E6211, 5¼" 48.00
Girl w/pearl jewelry, hand to face, Napco #C1615, 6" 32.50
Girl w/pigtails and yel scarf, Inarco #E2965, 7" 42.50
Girl w/red & wht hat & bow, Geo Z Lefton, 1955, 4½" 27.50
Girl w/telephone receiver, Inarco #E3548, 5½" 32.50
Girl winking, flat hat, bow at neck, unmk, 5" 32.50
Lady Aileen, tiara & necklace, Inarco #E1756, 5½" 37.50
Lady in bonnet w/hands to face, Lefton #2900, 6" 48.00
Lady in Derby-style hat, Rubens #530, rare, 6" 75.00
Lady in flat-rimmed hat w/appl rose, unmk, 5½" 47.50
Lady in flat-rimmed hat w/lg bow at side, unmk, 4" 32.50
Lady in flowered bonnet, pearl earrings, #C6018, 5½" 42.50
Lady in hat & coat, gold trim, Florence, 7" 55.00
Lady in pillbox hat, wht gloves, Relpo #A-1373S, 4½" 32.50
Lady in ruffled bonnet w/bow at side of chin, unmk, 5½" 42.50
Lady w/draped shawl, hand to face, Inarco #E240, 4½" 35.00
Lady w/flower in hair, pearl necklace, Rubens #497/M, 6½" 47.50

Lady w/gr bow in hair, pearl jewelry, Napcoware #6986, 9" **165.00**
Lady w/pearl earrings holding folded fan, Inarco #E1062, 6" **48.00**
Lady w/rose in hair, hand to face, Inarco #E193/M, 6" **42.50**
Lady w/side-swept hair, pearl jewelry, #3854, 6½" **48.00**
Mary w/Christ Child, Napcoware #E-7076, 6½" **42.50**
Oriental lady w/fan, Japan, 5" **42.50**
Teen girl w/bow in hair, Enesco paper label, 5½" **38.00**
Teen girl w/lg bow in hair, Japan, 5½" **38.00**
Teen girl w/ribbon in hair, Inarco #E2967, 5½" **38.00**

Heisey

A.H. Heisey began his long career at the King Glass Company of Pittsburgh. He later joined the Ripley Glass Company which soon became Geo. Duncan and Sons. After Duncan's death Heisey became half-owner in partnership with his brother-in-law, James Duncan. In 1895 he built his own factory in Newark, Ohio, initiating production in 1896 and continuing until Christmas of 1957. At that time Imperial Glass Corporation bought some of the molds. After 1968 they removed the old 'Diamond H' from any they put into use. In 1985 HCA purchased all of Imperial's Heisey molds with the exception of the Old Williamsburg line.

During their highly successful period of production, Heisey made fine handcrafted tableware with simple, yet graceful designs. Early pieces were not marked. After November 1901 the glassware was marked either with the 'Diamond H' or a paper label. Blown ware is often marked on the stem, never on the bowl or foot. For information concerning Heisey Collectors of America, see the Clubs, Newsletters, and Catalogs section of the Directory. See also Glass Animals.

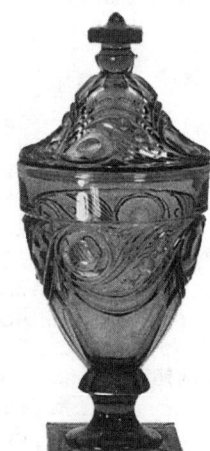

Ipswich, Sahara, candy dish, ½-lb, square base and finial, $235.00.

Candleblock, crystal; sq, 1-light 15.00
Charter Oak, crystal; bowl, finger; #3362 ....10.00
Charter Oak, flamingo; comport, #3362, ftd, 7" 55.00
Charter Oak, hawthorne; #3362, stem, parfait; 4½-oz 60.00
Charter Oak, marigold; tumbler, #3362, flat, 10-oz 10.00
Charter Oak, moongleam; pitcher, #3362, flat 95.00
Chintz, crystal; bowl, finger; #4107 ....8.00
Chintz, crystal; comport, oval, 7" 40.00
Chintz, crystal; cruet, oil, 4-oz 60.00
Chintz, crystal; ice bucket, ftd 85.00
Chintz, crystal; plate, dinner; sq, 10½" 40.00
Chintz, crystal; stem, wine; #3389, 2½-oz 17.50
Chintz, crystal; sugar bowl, 3-dolphin ftd 20.00
Chintz, crystal; tumbler, juice; #3389, 5-oz 11.00

Chintz, sahara; bowl, mint; ftd, 6" 30.00
Chintz, sahara; creamer, ind 25.00
Chintz, sahara; mayonnaise jar, dolphin ftd, 5½" 65.00
Chintz, sahara; plate, bread, sq, 6" 15.00
Chintz, sahara; platter, oval, 14" 65.00
Chintz, sahara; stem, parfait; #3389, 5-oz 35.00
Chintz, sahara; tray, celery; 10" 27.50
Crystolite, ashtray, sq, 4½" 4.50
Crystolite, basket, hdld, 6" 400.00
Crystolite, bowl, dessert; 5½" 12.00
Crystolite, bowl, preserve; 5" 12.00
Crystolite, bowl, punch; 7½-qt 120.00
Crystolite, candy box, swan shape, 6½" 35.00
Crystolite, cheese dish, ftd, 5½" 20.00
Crystolite, coaster, 4" 6.00
Crystolite, creamer, reg 20.00
Crystolite, cup, punch or custard 7.00
Crystolite, ice tub, w/SP hdls 75.00
Crystolite, mayonnaise ladle 9.00
Crystolite, plate, salad; 7" 9.00
Crystolite, plate, torte; 14" 35.00
Crystolite, urn, flower; 7" 75.00
Empress, alexandrite; ashtray 210.00
Empress, alexandrite; bowl, cream soup 65.00
Empress, cobalt; bowl, floral, dolphin ftd, 11" 400.00
Empress, cobalt; bowl, nappy, dolphin ftd, 7½" 275.00
Empress, cobalt; candy dish, w/lid, dolphin ftd, 6" 360.00
Empress, cobalt; plate, sq, 7" 55.00
Empress, cobalt; plate, 8" 70.00
Empress, flamingo; bowl, mint; dolphin ftd, 6" 20.00
Empress, flamingo; comport, ftd, 6" 50.00
Empress, flamingo; platter, 14" 35.00
Empress, flamingo; stem, sherbet; 4-oz 22.00
Empress, moongleam; plate, 12" 65.00
Empress, moongleam; sugar bowl, ind 40.00
Empress, moongleam; bonbon, 6" 30.00
Empress, moongleam; bowl, nappy, 4½" 12.50
Empress, moongleam; bowl, nappy, 8" 40.00
Empress, moongleam; bowl, salad; 2-hdld, sq, 10" 55.00
Empress, moongleam; mustard, w/lid 70.00
Empress, moongleam; plate, bouillon liner 15.00
Empress, sahara; comport, sq, 6" 75.00
Empress, sahara; creamer, ind 35.00
Empress, sahara; cup, AD 50.00
Empress, sahara; jug, ftd, 3-pt 200.00
Empress, sahara; saucer, AD 10.00
Empress, sahara; tray, celery; 13" 24.00
Empress, sahara; vase, ftd, 9" 110.00
Greek Key, crystal; bowl, banana split; flat, 9" 30.00
Greek Key, crystal; bowl, finger 20.00
Greek Key, crystal; bowl, nappy, 4½" 20.00
Greek Key, crystal; bowl, nappy, 5" 22.50
Greek Key, crystal; bowl, punch; ftd, 15" 225.00
Greek Key, crystal; candy dish, w/lid, 2-lb 195.00
Greek Key, crystal; coaster 12.00
Greek Key, crystal; creamer, oval, hotel sz 40.00
Greek Key, crystal; pitcher, 3-pt 165.00
Greek Key, crystal; plate, 6½" 20.00
Greek Key, crystal; shakers, pr 75.00
Greek Key, crystal; stem, cordial; ¾-oz 250.00
Greek Key, crystal; sugar bowl 35.00
Ipswich, crystal; bowl, finger; w/underplate 20.00
Ipswich, crystal; candy jar, w/lid, ¼-lb 150.00
Ipswich, gr; creamer 90.00

Ipswich, pk; cocktail shaker, strainer, #86 stopper, 1-qt 600.00
Ipswich, pk; pitcher, ½-gal 250.00
Ipswich, Sahara; plate, sq, 7" 25.00
Lariat, crystal; bowl, celery; 13" 22.00
Lariat, crystal; cheese dish, w/lid, 8" 50.00
Lariat, crystal; coaster, 4" 8.00
Lariat, crystal; plate, cookie; 11" 25.00

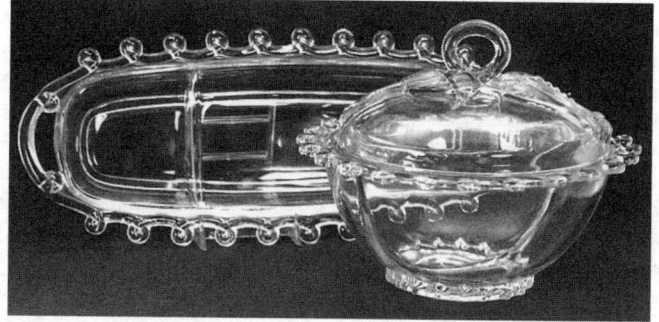

Lariat, crystal; Relish, three-compartment, $30.00; Candy dish, 7", $50.00.

Lariat, crystal; shakers, pr 200.00
Lariat, crystal; stem, wine; blown, 2½-oz 25.00
Lariat, crystal; tumbler, juice; ftd, 5-oz 15.00
Lodestar, dawn; ashtray 80.00
Lodestar, dawn; bowl, #1565, 6¾" 45.00
Lodestar, dawn; candy jar, w/lid, 5" 135.00
Lodestar, dawn; creamer 50.00
Lodestar, dawn; pitcher, #1626, 1-qt 150.00
New Era, crystal; bottle, rye; w/stopper 120.00
New Era, crystal; plate, bread & butter; 5½x4½" 15.00
New Era, crystal; saucer, AD 10.00
New Era, crystal; stem, claret; 4-oz 12.50
Octagon, crystal; basket, #500, 5" 85.00
Octagon, crystal; cup, #1231 ....5.00
Octagon, crystal; sugar bowl, hotel sz 10.00
Octagon, flamingo; bowl, cream soup; hdls 20.00
Octagon, flamingo; underplate, for cream soup 5.00
Octagon, hawthorne; creamer, hotel sz 30.00
Octagon, hawthorne; plate, 14" 50.00
Octagon, marigold; bowl, mint; #1229, 6" 30.00
Octagon, marigold; ice tub, #500 ....150.00
Octagon, moongleam; bowl, vegetable; 9" 30.00
Octagon, moongleam; plate, 10½" 35.00
Octagon, sahara; bowl, grapefruit; 6½" 22.00
Octagon, sahara; plate, luncheon; 8" 10.00
Octagon, sahara; tray, celery; 12" 17.00
Old Colony, cobalt; cigarette holder, #3390 ....100.00
Old Colony, crystal; bowl, nappy, 4½" 7.00
Old Colony, crystal; bowl, vegetable; oval, 10" 30.00
Old Colony, crystal; decanter, 1-pt 150.00
Old Colony, crystal; platter, oval, 14" 25.00
Old Colony, flamingo; bowl, grapefruit, 6" 23.00
Old Colony, flamingo; bowl, mint; dolphin ftd, 6" 22.00
Old Colony, flamingo; plate, rnd, 7" 14.00
Old Colony, flamingo; shakers, pr 80.00
Old Colony, marigold; bowl, finger; #4075 ....18.00
Old Colony, moongleam; bowl, salad; rnd, 2-hdld, 10" 65.00
Old Colony, moongleam; cup 38.00
Old Colony, moongleam; plate, sq, 10½" 70.00
Old Colony, moongleam; stem, wine; #3380, 2½-oz 50.00

Old Colony, sahara; bowl, cream soup; 2-hdld 22.00
Old Colony, sahara; bowl, nappy; 8" 40.00
Old Colony, sahara; ice tub, dolphin ftd 115.00
Old Colony, sahara; plate, sq, 8" 22.00
Old Colony, sahara; saucer, sq 10.00
Old Colony etch, crystal; stem, champagne; #3380, 6-oz 8.00
Old Colony etch, crystal; sugar bowl, dolphin ftd 17.50
Old Colony etch, flamingo; stem, tall soda; #3380, 10-oz 21.00
Old Colony etch, marigold; stem, short soda; #3380, 10-oz 30.00
Old Colony etch, moongleam; stem, champagne; #3390, 6-oz 30.00
Old Colony etch, moongleam; vase, ftd, 9" 175.00
Old Colony etch, sahara; stem, oyster/cocktail; #3390, 3-oz 20.00
Old Colony etch, sahara; tumbler, dolphin ftd 165.00
Old Sandwich, cobalt; stem, claret; 4-oz 150.00
Old Sandwich, crystal; cup 40.00
Old Sandwich, crystal; mug, beer, 12-oz 35.00
Old Sandwich, crystal; sugar bowl, oval 15.00
Old Sandwich, flamingo; bottle, catsup; w/#3 stopper 50.00
Old Sandwich, flamingo; parfait, 4½-oz 50.00
Old Sandwich, moongleam; creamer, oval 30.00
Old Sandwich, moongleam; saucer 25.00
Old Sandwich, moongleam; tumbler, 10-oz 45.00
Old Sandwich, sahara; candlestick, 6", ea 90.00
Orchid, crystal; ashtray, 3" 27.50
Orchid, crystal; bowl, crimped, 10" 70.00
Orchid, crystal; bowl, flared, 11" 57.50
Orchid, crystal; bowl, fruit or salad; ftd, 9" 125.00
Orchid, crystal; bowl, jelly; Waverly, ftd, 6½" 40.00
Orchid, crystal; bowl, nappy, Queen Anne, 4½" 37.50
Orchid, crystal; bowl, relish; rnd, 4-part, 9" 70.00
Orchid, crystal; bowl, salad; 7" 45.00
Orchid, crystal; butter dish, Waverly, w/lid, 6" 170.00
Orchid, crystal; candlestick, Flame, 2-light, ea 145.00
Orchid, crystal; candlestick, Waverly, 3-light, ea 87.50
Orchid, crystal; cigarette holder, #4035 ....60.00
Orchid, crystal; cocktail shaker, #4225, 1-pt 275.00
Orchid, crystal; mayonnaise, ftd, 5½" 40.00
Orchid, crystal; pitcher, 73-oz 450.00
Orchid, crystal; plate, cheese & cracker; 14" 135.00
Orchid, crystal; plate, demi-torte; 11" 50.00
Orchid, crystal; plate, salad; 7" 18.00
Orchid, crystal; plate, torte; Waverly, 14" 45.00
Orchid, crystal; shakers, pr 60.00
Orchid, crystal; sugar bowl, ind 25.00
Orchid, crystal; vase, ftd, 7" 85.00
Orchid, crystal; vase, 14" 650.00
Plantation, crystal; bowl, celery; 13" 35.00
Plantation, crystal; bowl, gardenia; 13" 45.00
Plantation, crystal; bowl, nappy, 5" 20.00
Plantation, crystal; bowl, salad; 9" 90.00
Plantation, crystal; candle block, 1-light 90.00
Plantation, crystal; candlestick, 3-light 80.00
Plantation, crystal; coaster, 4" 50.00
Plantation, crystal; cup 30.00
Plantation, crystal; plate, salad; 7" 20.00
Plantation, crystal; plate, sandwich; 14" 65.00
Plantation, crystal; saucer 7.00
Plantation, crystal; sugar bowl, ftd 30.00
Pleat & Panel, crystal; bowl, jelly; hdls, 5" 9.00
Pleat & Panel, crystal; bowl, vegetable; oval, 9" 35.00
Pleat & Panel, crystal; creamer, hotel style 10.00
Pleat & Panel, crystal; pitcher, ice lip, 3-pt 45.00
Pleat & Panel, crystal; platter, oval, 12" 15.00
Pleat & Panel, flamingo; bowl, lemon; w/lid, 5" 25.00

Pleat & Panel, flamingo; cup 15.00
Pleat & Panel, flamingo; saucer 5.00
Pleat & Panel, moongleam; marmalade, 4¾" 27.50
Pleat & Panel, moongleam; plate, bread, 7" 10.00
Pleat & Panel, moongleam; stem, 8-oz 25.00
Provincial, crystal; ashtray, sq, 3" 12.50
Provincial, crystal; bowl, flower; 12" 30.00
Provincial, crystal; cigarette box, w/lid 50.00
Provincial, crystal; coaster, 4" 10.00
Provincial, crystal; mustard jar 90.00
Provincial, crystal; plate, buffet; 18" 37.50
Provincial, limelight; bowl, nut/jelly; ind 35.00
Provincial, limelight; creamer, ftd 95.00
Provincial, limelight; tumbler, juice; ftd, 5-oz 50.00
Provincial, limelight; vase, violet; 3½" 95.00
Queen Ann, crystal; ashtray 30.00
Queen Ann, crystal; bonbon, 6" 10.00
Queen Ann, crystal; bowl, vegetable; oval, 10" 27.00
Queen Ann, crystal; candlestick, 3-ftd, 3", ea 45.00
Queen Ann, crystal; comport, sq, 6" 40.00
Queen Ann, crystal; jug, ftd, 3-pt 70.00
Queen Ann, crystal; mustard jar, w/lid 30.00
Queen Ann, crystal; plate, sq, 8" 10.00
Queen Ann, crystal; saucer, sq 3.00
Ridgeleigh, crystal; ashtray, sq 4.00
Ridgeleigh, crystal; bottle, cologne; 4-oz 85.00
Ridgeleigh, crystal; bowl, lemon; w/lid, 5" 35.00
Ridgeleigh, crystal; bowl, nappy, sq, 8" 22.00
Ridgeleigh, crystal; bowl, punch; 11" 90.00
Ridgeleigh, crystal; candle vase, 6" 30.00
Ridgeleigh, crystal; cheese dish, hdls, 6" 11.00
Ridgeleigh, crystal; coaster or cocktail rest 5.00
Ridgeleigh, crystal; cup, beverage 12.00
Ridgeleigh, crystal; plate, rnd, 6" 7.00
Ridgeleigh, crystal; saucer 5.00
Ridgeleigh, crystal; tray, celery; 12" 35.00
Rose, crystal; bell, dinner; #5072 ....150.00
Rose, crystal; bowl, flower; Waverly, 11" 67.50
Rose, crystal; bowl, honey; Waverly, ftd, 7" 60.00
Rose, crystal; bowl, mint; ftd, 5½" 35.00
Rose, crystal; bowl, salad; Waverly, 7" 55.00
Rose, crystal; butter dish, Waverly, w/lid, 6" 185.00
Rose, crystal; candlestick, Waverly, 3-light, ea 90.00
Rose, crystal; ice tub, Waverly, hdls 295.00
Rose, crystal; plate, demi-torte; Waverly, 11" 65.00
Rose, crystal; saucer, Waverly 15.00
Rose, crystal; stem, water; #5072, 9-oz 45.00
Rose, crystal; tray, celery; Waverly, 12" 60.00
Rose, crystal; vase, #4198, 10" 200.00
Saturn, crystal; bowl, celery; 10" 15.00
Saturn, crystal; bowl, whipped cream; 5" 15.00
Saturn, crystal; candelabrum, w/ball drops, 2-light 125.00
Saturn, crystal; saucer 5.00
Saturn, crystal; sugar bowl 17.00
Saturn, crytsal; vase, str sides, 8½" 25.00
Saturn, zircon/limelight; ashtray 150.00
Saturn, zircon/limelight; bowl, baked apple 65.00
Saturn, zircon/limelight; bowl, fruit; flared rim, 12" 100.00
Saturn, zircon/limelight; creamer 150.00
Saturn, zircon/limelight; pitcher, juice 300.00
Saturn, zircon/limelight; stem, parfait; 5-oz 110.00
Stanhope, crystal; ashtray, ind 20.00
Stanhope, crystal; bowl, salad; 11" 45.00
Stanhope, crystal; cup, w/ or w/o rnd knob 15.00

Stanhope, crystal; plate, 7" 7.50
Stanhope, crystal; saucer 5.00
Stanhope, crystal; stem, claret; #4083, 4-oz 25.00
Stanhope, crystal; vase, ball shape, 7" 50.00
Twist, crystal; baker, oval, 9" 10.00
Twist, crystal; plate, utility; 3-ftd, 10" 25.00
Twist, crystal; tumbler, iced tea; ftd, 12-oz 15.00
Twist, gr; bowl, mint; hdls, 6" 18.00
Twist, gr; grapefruit, ftd 35.00
Twist, gr; saucer 7.00
Twist, marigold/alexandrite; bowl, nasturtium; rnd, 8" 400.00
Twist, marigold/alexandrite; ice bucket 300.00
Twist, pk; bowl, nappy, 4" 12.00
Twist, pk; comport, tall, 7" 60.00
Twist, pk; platter, 12" 40.00
Twist, sahara; candlestick, 1-light, 2", ea 60.00
Twist, sahara; mustard jar, w/lid & spoon 100.00
Twist, sahara; sugar bowl, oval, hotel sz 50.00
Victorian, crystal; bowl, punch 250.00
Victorian, crystal; cigarette box, 4" 50.00
Victorian, crystal; creamer 25.00
Victorian, crystal; plate, cracker; 12" 75.00
Victorian, crystal; stem, wine; 2½-oz 20.00
Victorian, crystal; tumbler, bar; 2-oz 35.00
Victorian, crystal; vase, 4" 25.00
Waverly, crystal; bowl, fruit; 9" 20.00
Waverly, crystal; bowl, salad; 7" 17.00
Waverly, crystal; box, chocolate; w/lid, 5" 60.00
Waverly, crystal; box, trinket; lion cover 600.00
Waverly, crystal; candle holder, 3-light, ea 65.00
Waverly, crystal; cigarette holder 50.00
Waverly, crystal; creamer, ftd 20.00
Waverly, crystal; plate, salad; 7" 6.00
Waverly, crystal; plate, sandwich; 14" 35.00
Waverly, crystal; tray, celery; 12" 13.00
Waverly, crystal; vase, ftd, 7" 25.00
Yeoman, crystal; bowl, cream soup; hdls 12.00
Yeoman, crystal; creamer 10.00
Yeoman, crystal; plate, 14" 20.00
Yeoman, crystal; tray, celery; 9" 10.00
Yeoman, gr; bowl, vegetable; 6" 16.00
Yeoman, gr; stem, parfait; 5-oz 25.00
Yeoman, gr; stem cocktail; 3-oz 20.00
Yeoman, hawthorne; bowl, fruit; oval, 9" 55.00
Yeoman, hawthorne; sugar bowl, w/lid 40.00
Yeoman, marigold; cigarette box 100.00
Yeoman, marigold; plate, 7" 22.00
Yeoman, pk; bowl, finger 11.00
Yeoman, pk; cup 15.00
Yeoman, pk; salver, low ftd, 12" 25.00
Yeoman, pk; tumbler, whiskey; 2½-oz 8.00
Yeoman, sahara; bowl, jelly; low ftd, 5" 25.00
Yeoman, sahara; egg cup 32.00
Yeoman, sahara; saucer, AD 7.00
Yeoman, sahara; tumbler, str sides, 10-oz 20.00

Herend

Herend, Hungary, was the center of a thriving pottery industry as early as the mid-1800s. Decorative items as well as tablewares were made in keeping with the styles of the times. Items described in the following listings may be marked simply Herend, indicating the city, or with a manufacturer's backstamp.

Bowl, butterflies & insects, swirl scallops w/gold, 2x11½" 175.00
Creamer, Chinese Bouquet, sm 45.00
Figurine, Madonna, 11" 350.00
Figurine, school children playing, 8x10" 525.00
Pitcher, Queen Victoria pattern, 4½" 55.00
Plate, birds & butterflies on basketweave, 7¼" 47.50
Sugar bowl, Chinese Bouquet, sm 45.00
Teapot, Chinese Bouquet 225.00

Heubach

Gebruder Heubach is a German porcelain company that has been in operation since the 1800s, producing quality figurines and novelty items. They are perhaps most famous for their doll heads and piano babies, most of which are marked with the circular rising sun device containing an 'H' superimposed over a 'C.' Our advisor for this category is Grace Ochsner; she is listed in the Directory under Illinois.

Babies in pink and blue dresses, 5", $225.00 each.

Baby crawling on tummy, wht gown, bsk, 8" 350.00
Baby seated, wht gown w/bl trim, bl intaglio eyes, mk, 6" 250.00
Boy in dk bl sweater, tan pants, on tummy, holds ball, 5" L 300.00
Boy in gr knicker suit w/pocket linings trn out, 9" 375.00
Boy in tattered suit, broom resting between ft, 8" 350.00
Boy w/parasol, molded bsk, 5" 235.00
Dutch boy, seated, yoke on shoulders, basket ea side, 5" 225.00
Dutch boy & girl, seated, basket on bk, 5", pr 395.00
Dutch boy & girl stand bk to bk, bsk, unmk, 5¼x3" 150.00
Lad leans on bicycle, hand to forehead, mk, 12½" 650.00
Lady in lt gr dress w/floral design, lacy eyes, mk, 12" 300.00
Nude boy w/brn shoes, hand over eye, vase at bk, 4" 300.00
Nude boy w/clenched fists, pouty face, vase at bk, 6" 400.00
Nude boy w/legs crossed, patting tummy, 4½" 350.00
Pup w/muzzle, impressed mk, 5" 125.00
Snow baby dressed as bear, seated, 3" 225.00
Vase, anemones, pk on gray, gr mk, 8⅝x3" 88.00
Vase, roses, pk on gr w/gold, mk, 4x1½" 55.00

Hickman, Royal Arden

Born in Willamette, Oregon, Royal A. Hickman was a genius in all aspects of design interpretation. Mr. Hickman's expertise can be seen in the designs of the lovely Heisey figurines, Kosta crystal, Bruce Fox aluminum, Three Crowns aluminum, Vernon Kilns, and Royal Haeger Pottery (as well as handcrafted silver, furniture, and paintings).

Because Mr. Hickman moved around during much of his lifetime, his influence has been felt in all forms of the media. Designs from his independent companies include 'Royal Hickman Pottery and Lamps' (sold through Ceramic Arts Inc., of Chattanooga, Tennessee), 'Royal Hickman's Paris Ware,' 'Royal Hickman — Florida,' and 'California Designed by Royal Hickman.' The following listings will give examples of pieces bearing the various trademarks. Our advisors for this category are Lee Garmon and Doris Frizzell; both are listed in the Directory under Illinois. See also Royal Haegar; Vernon Kilns, Melinda pattern.

Bruce Fox Aluminum

Banana leaf, sgn Royal Hickman-RH 6, 22½" L 25.00
Dish, lobster, lg 50.00
Dish, 3-point leaf, sgn Royal Hickman, 15½" L 25.00
Ivy tray, #362, 13" 20.00
Oak leaf, 2 acorns, 14½" L 20.00
Platter, fish, EX detail, sgn Royal Hickman-RH 3, 13x9" 50.00
2-acorn oak tray, 14½" 25.00
5-point leaf tray, 14" 25.00
7-point leaf tray, sgn Royal Hickman, 14" 25.00

California, Designed by Royal Hickman

Bowl, red w/blk highlights, #607, 9½" 25.00
Figurine, deer, apple gr w/wht spots, appl eyes, 15" 45.00
Figurine, giraffe & young, pk w/blk spots 65.00
Punch bowl, Tom & Jerry, w/8 mugs 300.00
Swan, red w/blk highlights, #643, 17" 40.00

Miscellaneous Signatures

Sea horse vase, sgn Royal Hickman USA, #468, 8" 35.00
Vase, fish figurine, Petty Crystal Glaze, #467 ....25.00
Vase, lg heart, sgn Royal Hickman, Italy, #3774 ....45.00
Vase, rooster figurine, Petty Crystal Glaze, #565 ....95.00

Royal Hickman — Florida

Vase, free-form, #578, 14" 40.00
Vase, horse's head, gray w/wht mane, 13¾" 85.00
Vase, pouter pigeon, blk cascade, #599, 8½" 40.00
Vase, swan, head down, blk cascade, #624-R, 14" 60.00

Royal Hickman — Guadalajara, Mexico

Vase, 3 dolphin figures, 13" 95.00

Higgins

Contemporary glass artists Frances and Michael Higgins have been designing high-quality glassware since the late 1940s. Their designs are often created by fusing layers of glass together, though sometimes colored ground glass is used to 'paint' the decoration onto the surface. Molds are used, and through a process called 'slumping,' the glass is fired to a very high temperature, causing it to soften and take on the predetermined shape. Their work is ultramodern and is more readily found in metropolitan areas.

The earliest mark was an etched signature on the bottom — either 'Frances Stewart Higgins,' 'Michael Higgins,' or both, — which was dropped in favor of just 'Higgins' with a raised 'Higgins Man' figure, an H formed with a cup-like top and bottom superimposed over a vertical line. From approximately 1957 to 1964, the Higgins signature was embossed in gold on the top surface. Since 1964 up to the present the signature (no 'Higgins Man') has again been applied to the bottom, etched into the glass. Our advisor for this category is Dennis Hopp; he is listed in the Directory under Illinois.

Ashtray, orange & gr spikes w/gold rings, 10x12" 75.00

Ashtray set, blk & gold w/appl mc acrylic dots, 3-pc 95.00
Bowl, bl, sq, sgn, 2x7" 75.00
Bowl, centerpc; 4-color abstracts, flaring cone form, 4x17" 250.00
Clock, General Electric, dense int/ext decor, rnd face, 8" 550.00
Dish, abstracts, 3 slumped compartments, early mk, 15x12" 160.00
Dish, 5-color decor, slumped compartments, 2x13½" dia 100.00
Mobile, 14 sm pcs of mc fused glass, 20x22" 500.00
Vase, wht & gold int decor, 7" 200.00

Historical Glass

Glassware commemorating particularly significant historical events became popular in the late 1800s. Bread trays were the most common form, but plates, mugs, pitchers, and other items were also pressed in clear as well as colored glass. It was sold in vast amounts at the 1876 Philadelphia Centennial Exposition by various manufacturers who exhibited their wares on the grounds. It remained popular well into the 20th century.

In the listings that follow, L numbers refer to a book by Lindsey, a standard guide used by many collectors. Our advisor for this category is Darlene Yohe; she is listed in the Directory under Arkansas. See also Bread Plates; Pattern Glass.

Bottle, Granger, L-266 ....110.00
Bottle, Statue of Liberty, milk glass, rpr stopper 500.00
Bust, Dewey, Manila 1898, 5" 145.00
Compote, Washington Centennial, ftd, open 40.00
Covered dish, kitchen stove, flatiron hdl, L-149, 7" 300.00
Cup, McKinley, w/lid, L-355 ....60.00
Cup plate, Garfield, frosted intaglio 75.00
Flask, John Paul Jones 20.00
Glass, ale; Centennial 55.00
Goblet, Shield, 1876 Centennial 50.00

Goblet, Wilson and Grant, 6¼", $300.00.

Goblet, 3 Presidents, rare 325.00
Lamp, Emblem, L-62 ....195.00
Lamp chimney, Columbus, etched on floral band, L-9, 8" 250.00
Mug, Knights of Labor, L-513 ....50.00
Mug, Martyrs Lincoln & Garfield 50.00
Paperweight, Cleveland sulfide medallion, 3½" 195.00
Paperweight, Columbus intaglio figure, 1892 Expo 140.00
Paperweight, McKinley portrait, milk glass 125.00
Pin tray, bust of McKinley, frosted base, L-297 ....110.00
Pitcher, Dewey, L-400 ....55.00
Plaque, Lincoln Logs, L-278 ....55.00
Plate, Admiral Dewey, lattice-work rim, ca 1895, 5½" 110.00
Plate, Bryan, flag/eagle/star border, milk glass, L-359 ....85.00

Plate, General Fitshue Lee, lattice-work rim, 5½" 110.00
Plate, Harrison/Ft Meigs, amber 75.00
Plate, Liberty Bell, 10½" 80.00
Plate, Pope Leo, milk glass, L-240 ....25.00
Plate, Queen Victoria, L-435, 5¼" 25.00
Plate, Yankee Doodle, gr, open-work border, 5½" 35.00
Shaker, Benjamin Franklin, M-194 ....85.00
Shot glass, Bryan & McKinley, 1896, NM 130.00
Statue, Ruth the Gleaner, frosted, 1876 Phila Expo, Gillinder ...175.00
Syrup, Peace & Plenty, emb sailing ship & anchor, strap hdl 195.00
Toothpick holder, man w/hat, rare 225.00
Tumbler, America the Beautiful w/Eagle, L-458 ....35.00
Tumbler, flowers & religious motto 20.00
Tumbler, Lord's Prayer, blown & etched 35.00
Tumbler, Our Martyred President, McKinley & flags 30.00
Tumbler, Protection, Sound Currency, McKinley & Hobart 55.00
Tumbler, Rock of Ages, L-227 ....25.00
Wine, Washington Centennial 65.00

Hobbs, Brockunier, & Co.

Hobbs and Brockunier's South Wheeling Glass Works was in operation during the last quarter of the 19th century. They are most famous for their peachblow, amberina, Daisy and Button, and Hobnail pattern glass. The mainstay of the operation, however, was druggist items and plain glassware — bowls, mugs, and simple footed pitchers with shell handles. See also Frances Ware.

Bowl, Hobnail, rubena verde; Meriden SP fr w/leaves, 7½" 495.00
Carafe, Block, frosted w/amber flash, lg 145.00
Cheese dish, Hobnail, cranberry opal, rare 350.00
Cruet, Swirl, amber shaded to rust, polished pontil 350.00
Pitcher, clear cased cobalt w/silver mica, beehive form, 8½" 275.00
Pitcher, Hobnail, amberina rosy-fuchsia to amber, 7¾" 465.00
Pitcher, Honeycomb, bl opal, bl hdl, 9x7" 375.00
Pitcher, water; 'pnt' amberina T-print, hdl w/appl rosettes, 7" ...350.00
Vase, rubena, HP flowers w/gold, ruffled, 10" 150.00

Homer Laughlin

The Homer Laughlin China Company of Newell, West Virginia, was founded in 1871. The superior dinnerware they displayed at the Centennial Exposition in Philadelphia in 1876 won the highest award of excellence. From that time to the present, they have continued to produce quality dinnerware and kitchenware, many lines of which are becoming very popular collectibles. Most of the dinnerware is marked with the name of the pattern and occasionally with the shape name as well. The 'HLC' trademark is usually followed by a number series, the first two digits of which indicate the year of its manufacture. See also Fiesta; Harlequin; Riviera.

Amberstone, casserole 45.00
Amberstone, pie plate 35.00
Amberstone, plate, 10" 7.00
Amberstone, platter, oval 15.00
Americana, egg cup 14.00
Americana, plate, 8½" 12.00
Americana, teapot 65.00
Carnival, plate, cobalt or ivory, 6½", ea 3.00
Carnival, teacup, dk or lt gr, ea 2.00
Casualstone, bowl, jumbo salad; 10" 16.00
Casualstone, pitcher, disk type 32.00

Casualstone, plate, deep, gold trim 7.50
Casualstone, platter, oval, 13" 12.00
Conchita, casserole 125.00
Conchita, cup & saucer 18.00
Conchita, plate, 9" 15.00
Dogwood, bowl, mixing; Kitchen Kraft, 10½" 25.00
Dogwood, creamer 12.00
Dogwood, plate, scarce, 8" 10.00
Dogwood, sauce boat 18.00
Dreamland, plate, 10" 150.00
Dreamland, stein 120.00
Dreamland, tankard 220.00
Embossed Line, bowl, soup; tab hdls, 7" 10.00
Embossed Line, bowl, 4" 5.50
Embossed Line, casserole, 10" 38.00
Embossed Line, cup & saucer 14.00
Epicure, bowl, cereal/soup 15.00
Epicure, gravy bowl 20.00
Epicure, ladle, 5½" 25.00
Epicure, shakers, pr 15.00
Hacienda, bowl, vegetable; 8½" 23.00
Hacienda, plate, 7" 7.00
Hacienda, teapot, rare 125.00
Harmony, bowl, nappy, 9" 15.00
Harmony, casserole, Kitchen Kraft, 8" 32.00
Harmony, cup & saucer 9.00
Jubilee, bowl, mixing; Kitchen Kraft, 8" 100.00
Jubilee, cup & saucer 6.50
Jubilee, egg cup 11.00
Jubilee, plate, 9" 10.00
Laughlin Art China, chocolate pot, Currant 225.00
Laughlin Art China, mug, American Beauty 55.00
Laughlin Art China, plate, Currant, 9½" 45.00
Laughlin Art China, stein, White Pets 110.00
Laughlin Art China, sugar basket, Golden Fleece 160.00
Laughlin Art China, vase, Currant, slim form, 12" 115.00
Mexicana, bowl, lug soup; 4½" 25.00
Mexicana, egg cup, rolled edge 30.00
Mexicana, tumbler, fired-on design, 8-oz 15.00
Oven Serve, bowl, mixing; Kitchen Kraft, 10" 25.00
Oven Serve, cake plate, Kitchen Kraft 20.00
Oven Serve, platter, Kitchen Kraft 35.00
Pastel Nautilus, bowl, oatmeal; ftd, 6" 8.50
Pastel Nautilus, creamer 8.50
Pastel Nautilus, plate, 10" 12.00
Pastel Nautilus, plate, 7" 5.50
Pastel Nautilus, sugar bowl, w/lid 14.00
Priscilla, bowl, mixing; med, Kitchen Kraft, 8" 25.00
Priscilla, cup & saucer 9.50
Priscilla, plate, 7" 5.00
Priscilla, sugar bowl, w/lid 18.00
Rhythm, bowl, mixing; Kitchen Kraft, 8" 95.00
Rhythm, casserole 50.00
Rhythm, cup & saucer 10.00
Rhythm, pitcher, jug type, Kitchen Kraft 35.00
Rhythm, platter, 11½" 14.00
Rhythm, spoon rest, gr 245.00
Rhythm, underplate, Kitchen Kraft, 9" 13.00
Rhythm Rose, creamer 8.00
Rhythm Rose, cup & saucer 15.00
Serenade, pickle dish 12.00
Serenade, plate, 9" 8.00
Serenade, shakers, pr 13.00
Serenade, teacup & saucer 10.00

Serenade, teapot 65.00
Tango, bowl, fruit; 5¾" 6.50
Tango, casserole 50.00
Tango, creamer 9.00
Tango, plate, 10" 11.00
Virginia Rose, bowl, mixing; Kitchen Kraft, 6", 8", or 10", ea 25.00
Virginia Rose, butter dish, ½-lb 85.00
Virginia Rose, cup & saucer 9.50
Virginia Rose, mug, coffee 35.00
Virginia Rose, plate, 10" 12.00
Virginia Rose, platter, 15½" 35.00
Wells Art Glaze, bowl, oval baker, 9" 15.00
Wells Art Glaze, cup, bouillon; w/handles 15.00
Wells Art Glaze, egg cup, dbl 15.00
Wells Art Glaze, plate, 7" 8.00
Wells Art Glaze, platter, oval, 15½" 25.00
Wells Art Glaze, syrup 85.00
Wells Art Glaze, teapot 60.00

Hull

The A.E. Hull Pottery was formed in 1905 in Zanesville, Ohio, and in the early years produced stoneware specialities. They expanded in 1907, adding a second plant and employing over two hundred workers. By 1920 they were manufacturing a full line of stoneware, art pottery with both airbrushed and blended glazes, florist pots, and gardenware. They also produced toilet ware and kitchen items with a white semi-porcelain body. Although these continued to be staple products, after the stock market crash of 1929, emphasis was shifted to tile production. By the mid-thirties interest in art pottery production was growing, and over the next fifteen years, several lines of matt pastel floral-decorated patterns were designed, consisting of vases, planters, baskets, ewers, and bowls in various sizes.

The Red Riding Hood cookie jar, patented in 1943, proved so successful that a whole line of figural kitchenware and novelty items was added. They continued to be produced well into the fifties. (See also Little Red Riding Hood.) Through the forties their floral artware lines flooded the market, due to the restriction of foreign imports. Although best known for their pastel matt-glazed ware, some of the lines were high gloss. Rosella, glossy coral on a pink clay body, was produced for a short time only; and Magnolia, although offered in a matt glaze, was produced in gloss as well.

The plant was destroyed in 1950 by a flood which resulted in a devastating fire when the floodwater caused the kilns to explode. The company rebuilt and equipped their new factory with the most modern machinery. It was soon apparent that the matt glaze could not be duplicated through the more modern processes, however, and soon attention was concentrated on high-gloss artware lines such as Parchment and Pine and Ebb Tide. Figural planters and novelties, piggy banks, and dinnerware were produced in abundance in the late fifties and sixties. By the mid-seventies dinnerware and florist ware were the mainstay of their business. The firm discontinued operations in 1985.

Our advisor, Brenda Roberts, has compiled a lovely book, *The Collector's Encyclopedia of Hull Pottery*, with full-color photos and current values which has been recently reprinted. You will find her address in the Directory under Missouri. Another informative book is *Collector's Guide to Hull Pottery, The Dinnerware Lines*, by Barbara Loveless Gick-Burke, available from Collector Books or your local bookstore.

Advertising plaque, AE Hull Co Pottery, 1938, 5x11" 7,500.00
Blossom Flite, candle holder, pk, T-11, 3", ea 45.00
Blossom Flite, ewer, pk w/pk int, T-13, 13½" 155.00
Blossom Flite, honey pot, pk w/pk int, T1, 6" 70.00

Bow-Knot, cornucopia, pk/turq, B-5, 7½" 175.00
Bow-Knot, teapot, turq/bl, B-20, 6" 450.00
Bow-Knot, vase, pk/turq, B-11, 10½" 435.00
Bow-Knot, wall pocket, pitcher form, turq/bl, B-26, 6" 225.00
Butterfly, basket, 3-lobed shape, B-17, 10½" 285.00
Butterfly, lavabo, glossy; orig metal hanger, B-24/B-25, 16" 180.00
Butterfly, serving dish, center hdl, B-23, 11½" 95.00
Butterfly, vase, B-14, 3-ftd, 10½x6" 85.00
Butterfly, vase, bud; B-1, 6¾" 55.00
Calla Lily, bowl, console; pk/bl, single hdl, #590/32, 13" 140.00
Calla Lily, candle holder, cinnamon/gr, low, unmk, EA 75.00
Calla Lily, vase, bl/pk, angle hdls, #560/33, 13" 380.00
Camellia, basket, bl/pk, #142, 6¼" 325.00
Camellia, basket, hanging, bl/pk, #132, 7" 265.00
Camellia, vase, pk/bl, hdls, #102, 8½" 165.00
Camellia, vase, pk/bl, integral hdls, #138, 6¼" 90.00
Camellia, vase, pk/bl, low hdls, #130, 4¾" 65.00
Camellia, wall pocket, pk/bl, #125, 8½" 360.00
Cereal Ware, canister, Flying Bird, 8½" 95.00
Cereal Ware, canister, gold Grecian border, 8½" 80.00
Cereal Ware, spice jar, Bl Star & Lattice, 4¾" 55.00
Continental, ashtray, gr stripes, #52, 10¼" 35.00
Continental, basket, orange stripes, #55, 12¾" 165.00
Continental, vase, gr stripes, #53, 8½" 45.00
Cook 'N Serve, skillet tray, cold pnt decor, #27, 9¼x15½" 75.00
Dogwood, candle holder, ivory, #512, 3¾", ea 115.00
Dogwood, ewer, ivory, fancy rim & hdl, #519, 13½" 750.00
Dogwood, ewer, pk, #505, 8½" 270.00
Dogwood, vase, ivory/bl, angle hdls, #509, 6½" 100.00
Early Art, bottle, Shulton After Shaving Lotion, 5" 30.00
Early Art, jardiniere, Love Birds, brn, stoneware, unmk, 7½" 100.00
Early Art, vase, Crab Apple, ivory matt, stoneware, #65/33, 9" 100.00
Early Art, vase, stoneware, pk/bl stripes, matt, #32, mk, 8" 80.00
Early Art, vase, 2-color mottle, #40, H in circle, 7" 80.00
Early Banded Utility, bowl, ivory, stoneware, #428, mk, 6" 22.00
Early Banded Utility, bowl, ivory, stoneware, #428, mk, 9" 38.00
Early Utility, bowl, banded semiporc, unmk, 6½" 35.00
Early Utility, bowl, bl/pk bands, semiporc, E-1, 10" 40.00
Early Utility, casserole, teal bands, semiporc, w/lid, #113, 7½" ..60.00
Early Utility, pitcher, red bands, semiporc, unmk, 6½" 135.00
Early Utility, pitcher, Spring Gr bands, semiporc, 3½" 60.00
Ebb Tide, basket, shell form, E-11, 16½" 215.00
Ebb Tide, creamer, shell form, E-15, 4" 70.00
Ebb Tide, teapot, shell form, E-14, 6½" 190.00
Iris, bowl, console; pk/bl, #409, 12" 285.00
Iris, ewer, pk/bl, #401, 13½" 510.00
Iris, vase, ivory/pk, hdls, #404, 4¾" 65.00
Iris, vase, ivory/pk, ornate hdls, #403, 7" 95.00
Iris, vase, pk/bl, hdls, #404, 8½" 205.00
Lamp, Classic, floral on ivory, T-1, 1946, 7¾" 190.00
Lamp, Picture Frame, rose decal, L-2, 1940, 13" 275.00
Lamp, Rosella, floral on ivory, foil label, 1946, 6¾" 255.00
Magnolia, glossy; ewer, H-19, 13½" 400.00
Magnolia, glossy; vase, hdls, H-5, 6½" 42.00
Magnolia, matt; cornucopia, yel/Dusty Rose, #19, 8½" 120.00
Magnolia, matt; dbl cornucopia, pk/bl, #6, 12" 170.00
Magnolia, matt; teapot, yel/Dusty Rose, #23, 6½" 170.00
Magnolia, matt; vase, pk/bl, low hdls, #16, 15" 485.00
Mardi Gras/Granada, basket, ivory, #32, 8" 155.00
Mardi Gras/Granada, candle holder, ivory, unmk, 3¼", ea 35.00
Mardi Gras/Granada, vase, ivory, linear decor, hdls, #219, 9" 60.00
Mardi Gras/Granada, vase, ivory, 3-loop hdls, #216, 9" 52.00
Mirror Almond, bowl, vegetable; ivory w/caramel rim, hdls, 11" L ..12.00
Mirror Almond, French casserole, ivory w/caramel, w/lid, sm 10.00

Mirror Almond, plate, salad; ivory w/caramel rim, 6½" 3.00
Mirror Almond, stein, ivory w/caramel rim, 16-oz 7.00
Mirror Brown, baker, brn w/ivory foam, emb rooster, 13½" 40.00
Mirror Brown, bean pot, brn w/ivory foam, #510, 2-qt 26.00
Mirror Brown, bowl, salad; brn w/ivory foam, #569, 6½" 3.00
Mirror Brown, canisters, brn w/ivory foam, rnd, 6" to 9", 4 for ...400.00
Mirror Brown, carafe, brn w/ivory foam, 6¾" 32.00
Mirror Brown, duck-shaped casserole, brn w/ivory foam, 8" 42.00
Mirror Brown, pitcher, brown w/ivory foam, ice lip, 7½" 30.00
Mirror Brown, soup 'n sandwich, brn w/ivory foam, #553/#554 ....20.00
Morning Glory, basket, creme, #62, 8" 650.00
Novelty, Basket Girl, pk gloss, #954, 8" 40.00
Novelty, Caladium Leaf dish, 1957, 14" 35.00
Novelty, figurine, dancing girl, ivory/pk, #955, 1938, 7" 45.00
Novelty, figurine, elephant, ivory, unmk, 5¼" 32.00
Novelty, figurine, Swing Band instrumentalist, unmk, 6" 125.00
Novelty, planter, French poodle figural, #114, 8" 45.00
Novelty, planter, pig figural, #60, 1940-43, 8½" 45.00
Novelty, vase, flying goose figural, #96, 9¾" 75.00
Novelty, vase, poodle in bonnet figural, #38, 1955, 6½" 45.00
Nuline Bak-Serve, batter jug, Dmn Quilt, B-7, 5" 75.00
Nuline Bak-Serve, cookie jar, Dmn Quilt, red, B-20, 2-qt, 8" 110.00
Nuline Bak-Serve, teapot, Dmn Quilt, bl, B-5, 5½" 125.00
Orchid, basket, pk/ivory, #305 ....650.00
Orchid, bookends, pk/ivory, #316, pr 1,100.00
Orchid, bowl, console; pk/bl, #314 ....360.00
Orchid, jardiniere, bl, #310, 9½" 590.00
Orchid, lamp base, ivory/bl, unmk, 10" 600.00
Pagoda, flower bowl, ivory, ftd, P-2 ....12.00
Pagoda, flowerpot, attached saucer, P-12 ....35.00
Parchment & Pine, candle holder, Pearl Gray, S-10, 5", ea 25.00
Parchment & Pine, ewer, Pine Gr, blk int, S-7, 14½" 230.00
Parchment & Pine, teapot, Pine Gr/Pearl Gray, S-11, 6" 105.00
Pine Cone, vase, pk, angle hdls, #55, 6½" 155.00
Poppy, basket, ivory/pk, #601, 9" 755.00
Poppy, jardiniere, pk/bl, #603, 4¾" 140.00
Poppy, vase, ivory/pk, sm hdls, shaped rim, ftd, #606, 10½" 430.00
Poppy, vase, pk/bl, ruffled rim, angle hdls, ftd, #607, 10½" 430.00
Rosella, basket, floral on creme, R-12, 7" 275.00
Rosella, creamer, coral, R-3, 5½" 50.00
Rosella, vase, coral, low hdls, R-15, 8½" 120.00
Serenade, bowl, fruit; pk, ped ft, S-15, 7" 120.00
Serenade, candle holder, Regency Bl, 6½", ea 60.00
Serenade, teapot, yel, S-17, 5" 165.00
Sun-Glo, bowl, mixing; yel, #50, 9½" 40.00
Sun-Glo, grease jar, pk, #53, 5¼" 35.00
Sun-Glo, wall pocket, iron form, unmk, 6" 80.00
Thistle, vase, bl, angle hdls, ftd, #51, 6½" 95.00
Tile, boat, lt & dk bl w/wht, mk, 2¾x6" 110.00
Tile, HP floral on gr satin, #360, mk Faience, 4¼x4¼" 25.00
Tokay, cornucopia, pk grapes on gr/Sweet Pk, #10, 11" 65.00
Tokay, vase, pk grapes on lt gr/Sweet Pk, hdls, #8, 10" 95.00
Tropicana, ashtray, Caribbean figure on wht, T-52, 10" 375.00
Tropicana, basket, Caribbean figure on wht, T-55, 12¾" 715.00
Tropicana, vase, Caribbean figure on wht, T-53, 8½" 320.00
Tulip, ewer, creme/bl, #109-33, 13" 500.00
Tulip, flowerpot, bl, attached saucer, #116-33, 6" 155.00
Tulip, vase, bl, shaped rim, integral hdls, #105-33, 8" 160.00
Tulip, vase, creme/bl, integral hds, ftd, #107-33, 6" 110.00
Tuscany, basket, gr grapes on Milk Wht, twig hdl, #6, 8" 80.00
Tuscany, basket, gr grapes on Sweet Pk, #15, 12" 225.00
Tuscany, candy dish, gr grapes on Milk Wht, w/lid, #9, 8½" 130.00
Tuscany, ewer, gr grapes on Milk Wht, #13, 12" 255.00
Water Lily, glossy, vase, wht, low hdls, L-A, 8½" 168.00

Water Lily, matt; creamer, walnut/apricot, L-19, 5" 65.00
Water Lily, matt; teapot, walnut/apricot, L-18, 6" 170.00
Water Lily, matt; vase, turq/Sweet Pk, gold hdls, L-16, 12½" 385.00
Water Lily, matt; vase, turq/Sweet Pk, hdls, L-12, 10½" 205.00

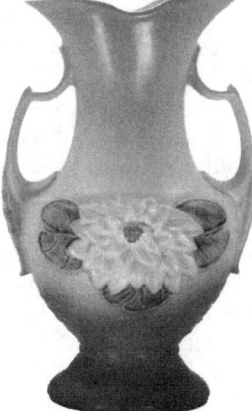

Water Lily, matt; vase, walnut/apricot, L-15, 12½", $435.00.

Wild Flower (# series), bowl, console; bl/pk, hdls, #70, 12" 390.00
Wild Flower (# series), teapot, russet/pk, #72, 8" 785.00
Wild Flower (# series), vase, pk/bl, hdls, #52, 5¼" 115.00
Wild Flower (# series), vase, russet/pk, low hdls, #67, 8½" 325.00
Wildflower (W series), basket, yel/Dusty Rose, W-16, 10½" 330.00
Wildflower (W series), cornucopia, yel/Dusty Rose, W-10, 8½" .115.00
Wildflower (W series), ewer, pk/bl, W-19, 13½" 435.00
Wildflower (W series), ewer, yel/Dusty Rose, W-2, 5½" 68.00
Woodland, glossy; creamer, bl/gr, W-27, 3½" 50.00
Woodland, glossy; dbl cornucopia, ivory w/gold, W-23, 14" 480.00
Woodland, glossy; ewer, 2-tone gr, W-6, 6½" 105.00
Woodland, glossy; jardiniere, rose/chartreuse, W-7, 5½" 75.00
Woodland, glossy; vase, ivory, W-1, 5½" 45.00
Woodland, matt; bowl, console; Dawn Rose, W-29, 14" 365.00
Woodland, matt; ewer, Dawn Rose, W-3, 5½" 95.00
Woodland, matt; ewer, Harvest Yel, W-6, 6½" 145.00
Woodland, matt; flowerpot, Dawn Rose, attached saucer, W-11 ..155.00
Woodland, matt; vase, Dawn Rose, ornate hdls, W-25, 12½" 485.00

Hummel

Hummel figurines were created through the artistry of Berta Hummel, a Franciscan nun called Sister M. Innocentia. The first figures were made about 1935 by Franz Goebel of Goebel Art Inc., Rodental, West Germany. Plates, plaques, and candy dishes are also produced, and the older, discontinued editions are highly sought collectibles. Generally speaking, an issue can be dated by the trademark. The first Hummels, from 1934-1950, were either incised or stamped with the 'Crown WG' mark. The 'full bee in V' mark was employed with minor variations until 1959. At that time the bee was stylized and represented by a solid disk with angled symmetrical wings completely contained within the confines of the 'V.' The three-line mark, 1964-1972, utilized the stylized bee and included a three-line arrangement, 'c by W. Goebel, W. Germany.' Another change in 1970 saw the 'stylized bee in V' suspended between the vertical bars of the 'b' and 'l' of a printed 'Goebel, West Germany.' Collectors refer to this mark as the 'last bee' or 'Goebel bee.' The current mark in use since 1979 omits the 'bee in V.' For a more thorough study of the subject, we recommend *Hummel Figurines and Plates, A Collector's Identification and Value Guide,* by Carl Luckey, available at your local book dealer. Idiosyncrasies in the numerical order of the following listings are due to computer sorting. See also Limited Edition Plates.

Key:
ce — closed edition	GB — Goebel bee
CM — crown mark	SB — stylized bee
FB — full bee	LB — last bee

#III/53, Joyful, candy box, FB, 6¼" 340.00
#III/63, Singing Lesson, candy box, CM, 5¼" 510.00
#1, Puppy Love, CM, 5" 450.00
#109/II, Happy Traveler, FB, ce, 8" 475.00
#112/I, Just Resting, FB, 3¾" 165.00
#114, Let's Sing, ashtray, LB, 3½x6¾" 110.00
#118, Little Thrifty, SB, 5" 145.00
#123, Max & Moritz, SB, 5¼" 130.00
#125, Vacation Time, plaque, FB, 4⅜x5¼" 310.00
#127, Doctor, CM, 4¾" 410.00
#128, Baker, FB, 4¾" 225.00
#13/0, Meditation, 3-line mk, 5" 185.00
#13 2/0, Meditation, 3-line mk, 4¼" 85.00
#132, Star Gazer, LB, 4¾" 160.00
#136/V, Friends, LB, 10¾" 1,000.00
#137/B, Child-in-Bed, plaque, rnd, FB, 2¾x2¾" 110.00
#141/I, Apple Tree Girl, FB, 6" 300.00
#142 3/0, Apple Tree Boy, CM, 4" 300.00
#145, Little Guardian, FB, 3¾" 170.00
#146, Angel Duet, font, CM, 2x4¾" 125.00
#150/0, Happy Days, FB, 5¼" 360.00
#152/B/II, Umbrella Girl, 3-line mk, 8" 850.00
#154/0, Waiter, LB, 6" 150.00
#16, Little Hiker, FB, 5½" 310.00
#164, Worship, font, SB, 2¾x4¾" 40.00
#165, Swaying Lullaby, plaque, LB, 4½x5¼" 125.00
#169, Bird Duet, FB, 4" 175.00
#17/0, Congratulations (no socks), FB, 6" 280.00
#172/II, Festival Harmony (Angel w/Mandolin), SB, 10¾" 380.00
#175, Mother's Darling, SB, 5½" 200.00
#176/I, Happy Birthday, CM, 6" 680.00
#179, Coquettes, FB, 5¼" 310.00
#18, Christ Child, CM, 2x6" 285.00
#180, Tuneful Goodnight, plaque, SB, 4x4¾" 240.00
#185, Accordion Boy, FB, 5¼" 215.00
#186, Sweet Music, 3-line mk, 5¼" 150.00
#188, Celestial Musician, FB, 7" 300.00
#192 Candlelight, (long candle), SB, 6¾" 325.00
#195/I, Barnyard Hero, 3-line mk, 5¾" 215.00
#196/0, Telling Her Secret, FB, 5¼" 350.00
#198/I, Home From Market, LB, 5¾" 155.00
#20, Prayer Before Battle, LB, 4¼" 130.00
#200/0, Little Goat Herder, FB, 4¾" 225.00
#203/I, Signs of Spring, CM, 5" 630.00
#204, Weary Wanderer, FB, 6" 285.00
#207, Heavenly Angel, font, 3-line mk, 2x4¾" 35.00
#21/I, Heavenly Angel, FB, 6¾" 280.00
#217, Boy w/Toothache, SB, 5½" 150.00
#219, Little Velma, FB, 4⅛" 4,500.00
#22/I, Angel w/Birds, font, FB, 3¼x4" 385.00
#220, We Congratulate, LB, 4" 110.00
#223, To Market, table lamp, 3-line mk, 9½" 250.00
#224/II, Wayside Harmony, table lamp, LB, 9½" 245.00
#229, Apple Tree Girl, table lamp, FB, 7½" 400.00
#23/I, Adoration, CM, 6¼" 725.00
#235, Happy Days, table lamp, SB, 7¾" 430.00
#240, Little Drummer, 3-line mk, 4¼" 90.00
#246, Holy Family, font, LB, 3x4" 28.00
#248, Guardian Angel, font, SB, 2¼x5½" 50.00

#25, Angelic Sleep, candle holder, SB, 3½x5" 125.00
#255, A Stitch in Time, SB, 6¾" 230.00
#256, Knitting Lesson, LB, 7½" 360.00
#258, Which Hand?, LB, 5¼" 150.00
#26/0, Child Jesus, font, FB, 1½x5" 30.00
#261, Angel Duet, 3-line mk, 5½" 165.00
#262, Heavenly Lullaby, SB, 3½x5" 285.00
#28/II, Wayside Devotion, FB, 7½" 460.00
#29/0, Guardian Angel, font, FB, 2½x5⅝" 880.00
#306, Little Bookkeeper, FB, 4¾" 5,500.00
#307, Good Hunting, LB, 5¼" 150.00
#319, Doll Bath, 3-line mk, 5¼" 160.00
#32/I, Little Gabriel, SB, 6" 2,300.00
#321, Wash Day, LB, 5¾" 160.00
#322, Little Pharmacist, SB, 6" 1,400.00
#328, Carnival, LB, 6" 150.00
#33, Joyful, ashtray, FB, 3½x6" 150.00
#332, Soldier Boy, 3-line mk, 6" 140.00

#334, Homeward Bound, last bee mark, 5", $250.00.

#337, Cinderella (eyes open), LB, 5½" 720.00
#344, Feathered Friends, LB, 4¾" 175.00
#346, Smart Little Sister, SB, 4¾" 1,400.00
#35/I, Good Shepherd, font, SB, 2¾x5¾" 150.00
#353/0, Spring Dance, LB, 4¾" 180.00
#355, Autumn Harvest, LB, 4¾" 150.00
#358, Shining Light, SB, 2¾" 60.00
#359, Tuneful Angel, LB, 2¾" 60.00
#363, Big Housecleaning, LB, 4" 210.00
#367, Busy Student, LB, 4¼" 110.00
#374, Lost Stocking, 3-line mk, 4⅜" 380.00
#42, Good Shepherd, CM, 6¼" 410.00
#43, March Winds, CM, 5" 350.00
#44/B, Out of Danger, table lamp, FB, 9½" 390.00
#47/0, Goose Girl, CM, 4¾" 530.00
#49 3/0, To Market, CM, 4" 375.00
#51 2/0, Village Boy, SB, 5" 90.00
#54, Silent Night, 3-line mk, 4¾x5½" 210.00
#55, St George, SB, 6¾" 240.00
#57/I, Chick Girl, CM, 4¼" 585.00
#59, Skier, FB, 5¼" 385.00
#6/0, Sensitive Hunter, CM, 4¾" 450.00
#60/A&B, Farm Boy & Goose Girl, bookends, FB, 6", pr 600.00
#62, Happy Pastime, ashtray, FB, 3½x6¼" 185.00
#63, Singing Lessons, SB, 2¾" 90.00
#65, Farewell, FB, 4¾" 310.00

#66, Farm Boy, LB, 5¼" 185.00
#67, Doll Mother, FB, 4¾" 265.00
#71, Stormy Weather, FB, 6¼" 480.00
#74, Little Gardener (gr dress), CM, 4¼" 430.00
#78/I, Infant of Krumbad (Blessed Child), CM, 2½" 110.00
#79, Globe Trotter, FB, 5" 230.00
#80, Little Scholar, LB, 5½" 175.00
#82 2/0, School Boy, CM, 4" 385.00
#84/0, Worship, CM, 5" 385.00
#86, Happiness, FB, 4¾" 150.00
#87, For Father, LB, 5½" 175.00
#88/II, Heavenly Protection, FB, 9¼" 875.00
#9, Begging His Share (w/hole), FB, 5½" 480.00
#9, Begging His Share (w/o hole), FB, 5½" 380.00
#92, Merry Wanderer, plaque, FB, 4¾x5⅛" 155.00
#93, Little Fiddler, plaque, CM, 4¾x5⅛" 385.00
#95, Brother, 3-line mk, 5½" 165.00
#96, Little Shopper, LB, 4¾" 155.00
#98/0, Sister, CM, 5¾" 380.00
#99, Eventide, FB, 4¾" 350.00

Hutschenreuther

The Porcelain Factory C.M. Hutschenreuther operated in Bavaria from 1814 to 1969. After the death of the elder Hutschenreuther in 1845, his son Lorenz took over operations, continuing there until 1857 when he left to establish his own company in the nearby city of Selb. The original manufactory became a joint stock company in 1904, absorbing several other potteries. In 1969 both Hutschenreuther firms merged, and that company still operates in Selb. They have distributing centers in both France and the United States. Our advisor for this category is Jack Gunsaulus; he is listed in the Directory under Michigan.

Figurine, bison fighting mtn lion, 9x14" 495.00
Figurine, boy & deer, wht, 4½" 98.00
Figurine, buck & doe, recumbent, Fitz, US Zone 1949, 10", pr ...165.00
Figurine, Don Quixote, MIB 450.00
Figurine, nude feeding fawn, brn/wht, sgn, ca 1946, 13x10" 595.00
Figurine, terrier on bk legs, 7¼" 175.00
Plate, boys in courtyard, brn/gilt border, titled, 9½" 860.00
Plate, queen's portrait, gilt/cobalt rim, 10", set of 4 ....3,100.00
Tray, flowers/gold on lt gr, 11", +pr sticks & 2 boxes 185.00

Imari

Imari is a generic term which covers a broad family of wares. It was made in more than a dozen Japanese villages, but the name is that of the port from whence it was shipped to Europe. There are several types of Imari. The most common features a design with panels of birds, florals, or people surrounding a central basket of flowers. The colors used in this type are underglaze blue with overglaze red, gold, and green enamels. The Chinese also made Imari wares which differ from the Japanese type in several ways — the absence of spur marks, a thinner-type body, and a more consistent control of the blue. Imari-type wares were copied on the continent by Meissen and by English potters, among them Worcester, Derby, and Bow. Unless noted otherwise, our values are for Japanese ware. Our advisor is Norma Angelo; she is listed in the Directory under New York.

Basin, 3 scenes: Jurojin/sages, fruit roundels, 1800s, 16" 800.00
Bowl, floral, 1800s, 8" 150.00
Bowl, floral panels, butterfly medallion, bl rim, 1850s, 7" 165.00

Bowl, floral/Greek Key motif, beaded, 6" **65.00**
Bowl, mtns/shishi/kylin/florals, ext: similar, 1880s, 12" H **350.00**
Bowl, octagonal, ea panel w/stylized flowerhead, Fukagawa, 5" ..**175.00**
Bowl, pk banding, gilt accents, att Spode, 1910, 7½" **275.00**
Bowl, rice; red reserves, very shallow, ring ft, mk, set of 4 ....**350.00**
Bowl, 3 conforming rows of reserve-pnt facets, 7½" **245.00**
Charger, birds/wise men/mtns, 1800s, 18" **650.00**
Charger, emb carp, foliage band on red, sgn Kakiemon, 24" **2,500.00**
Charger, ho-o medallion, panels w/sages, 1800s, 18", pr **1,250.00**

Charger, rabbits in low relief among geometric panels, reverse with stylized blossoms in underglaze blue, Meiji Period, 18½", $1,500.00.

Cup & saucer, Imari pattern, Coalport, set of 6 ....**200.00**
Dish, fluted w/wide paneled rim border, floral center, 12" **180.00**
Dish, wide floral border, thin inner border, scalloped, 10" L **160.00**
Dish, 4 floral border reserves, urn center, Karwachi mk, 13" **650.00**
Garden stool, birds/scenic medallions on floral ground, 21" **400.00**
Inkpot, red w/floral, waisted dome shape, Fukagawa mk **180.00**
Jar, florals, ribbed, w/lid, 1800s, 10½" **475.00**
Jardiniere, flowering tree reserves, much cobalt/red, 9½" **500.00**
Plaque, figural center, wide oval-paneled border, 18" **400.00**
Plaque, opposing red/bl rim panels, 8-sided, 10" **250.00**
Plate, figures on red, floral/scroll border, 1920s, 16" **125.00**
Plate, floral/foliage w/gold, scalloped, 1800s, Japan, 12" **125.00**
Platter, Imari pattern, Cauldon, 13" **275.00**
Punch bowl, floral, scalloped, 1800s, 11" **375.00**
Vase, bottle form, late, 7", pr **125.00**
Vase, crane/flowering tree reserves, flared rim, mk, 15", pr **700.00**
Vase, floral, ovoid, 1800s, 6½", pr **175.00**
Vase, flowering tree in lg panels, 12¾" **275.00**
Vase, flowering tree/fence in scroll reserves, lion finial, 14" **375.00**
Vase, red/bl floral panels alternate, dome lid, 12½" **400.00**

Imperial Glass Company

The Imperial Glass Company was organized in 1901 in Bellaire, Ohio, and started manufacturing glassware in 1904. Their early products were jelly glasses, hotel tumblers, etc., but by 1910 they were making a name for themselves by pressing quantities of Carnival Glass, the iridescent glassware that was popular during that time. In 1914 NuCut was introduced to imitate cut glass. The line was so popular that it was made in crystal and colors and was reintroduced as Collector's Crystal in the 1950s. From 1916 to 1920 they used the lustre process to make a line called Imperial Jewels, now referred to as stretch glass. Free-Hand ware, art glass made entirely by hand using no molds, was made from 1922 to 1928.

The company entered bankruptcy in 1931 but was able to continue operations and reorganize as the Imperial Glass Corporation. In 1936 Imperial introduced the Candlewick line, for which it is best known. In

the late thirties the Vintage Grape Milk Glass line was added, and in 1951 a major ad campaign was launched, making Imperial one of the leading milk glass manufacturers.

In 1940 Imperial bought the molds and assets of the Central Glass Works of Wheeling, West Virginia; in 1958 they acquired the molds of the Heisey Company and in 1960 the molds of the Cambridge Glass Company of Cambridge, Ohio. Imperial used these molds, and after 1951 they marked their glassware with an 'I' superimposed over the 'G' trademark. The company became a subsidiary of Lenox in 1973; subsequently an 'L' was added to the 'IG' mark. In 1981 Lenox sold Imperial to Arthur Lorch, a private investor (who modified the L by adding a line at the top angled to the left, giving rise to the 'ALIG' mark). He in turn sold the company to Robert F. Stahl, Jr., in 1982. Mr. Stahl filed for Chapter 11 to reorganize, but in mid-1984 liquidation was ordered, and all assets were sold. The few items that had been made in '84 were marked with an 'N' superimposed over the 'I' for 'New Imperial.' Our advisor is Joan Cimini; She is listed in the Directory under Ohio. See also Candlewick; Carnival Glass; Glass Animals and Figurines; Stretch Glass.

Box, sweetmeat; Cathay Crystal, signed, #5022, $250.00.

Ashtray, Cathay Crystal, plum blossom, #5007 ....**45.00**
Basket, Daisy, milk glass, Doeskin, #1950/40 ....**34.00**
Basket, Niagara, crystal, 8½" **45.00**
Bonbon, Pillar Flutes, bl, crimped, 7" **22.50**
Bowl, berry; Grape, milk glass, #1950/47, 8" **20.00**
Bowl, Cape Cod, crystal, ftd, #137B, 10" **77.00**
Bowl, cereal; Pillar Flutes, bl, 6" **30.00**
Bowl, cream soup; Monticello, crystal, 5½" **20.00**
Bowl, Daisy, Azalea, #464, 8¼" **35.00**
Bowl, Empire, crystal, flared, #7799W, 11" **22.00**
Bowl, fruit; Mount Vernon, crystal, 3-toed, 10" **22.00**
Bowl, Hobnail, milk glass, #1950/642, 10" **34.00**
Bowl, Katy, gr opal, #749B, 9¾" **125.00**
Bowl, Laced Edge, crystal, #7497F, 9½" **15.00**
Bowl, rose; caramel slag, #52C, 8" **45.00**
Bowl, salad; gr slag, #602, 11" **170.00**
Bowl, salad; Grape, Rubigold carnival, #1288, 11½" **95.00**
Cake plate, Cape Cod, crystal, low ftd, sq, #160/220, 10" **95.00**
Cake plate, Crochet Crystal, crystal **27.50**
Cake plate, Old Williamsburg, amber, ftd, #341/67D, 11" **45.00**
Candle holder, Corinthian, gr, #330, 7½" **15.00**
Candle holder, Dew Drop opal, #1886/643, 4" **24.00**
Candle holder, Hoffman House, amber, #46, 4¾" **15.00**
Candle holder, Milk House, ftd, hdl, #1950/81 ....**22.00**
Candle holder, Rose, Peacock carnival, #160, 3½" **15.00**
Candle holders, Cathay Crystal, dragon, #5009, pr **550.00**
Candlesticks, Katy, bl opal, 2-light, pr **250.00**
Candlesticks, Katy, cobalt, 2-light, pr **75.00**
Candy jar, Cathay Crystal, Shang, #5002 ....**325.00**

Celery tray, Mount Vernon, crystal, 10½" 18.00
Champagne, Cape Cod, gr, #1602 ....16.50
Claret, Cape Cod, gr, #1602 ....14.00
Compote, Cape Cod, crystal, #160/X wafer stem, 5¾" 35.00
Compote, Old English, crystal, #166, 4½" 10.00
Compote, Pillar Flutes, red, shallow, 7" 20.00
Creamer & sugar bowl, Cape Cod, crystal, #160/30 ....20.00
Creamer & sugar bowl, Molly, topaz, #725 ....15.00
Cruet, Cape Cod, crystal, #119 ....25.00
Cruet, Dew Drop opal, #1886/70, hdl 55.00
Cruet, purple slag, #3505 ....45.00
Cup & saucer, Katy, crystal 15.00
Decanter, Cape Cod, crystal, #160/163, 30-oz 70.00
Decanter, grape design, Peacock carnival, #163 ....65.00
Decanter, Niagara, crystal, 32-oz 42.50
Decanter, Peachblow, #P4038/1 ....190.00
Epergne, Cape Cod, crystal, #160/196, 2-pc 200.00
Flower bowl, Old English, crystal, #1346N, 7" 20.00
Flower bowl, Pillar Flutes, bl, 5" 25.00
Goblet, Cape Cod, Azalea, #1602, 11-oz 20.00
Goblet, Cape Cod, crystal, #160 ....10.00
Goblet, Cape Cod, red, wafer stem, #160 ....20.00
Goblet, Dew Drop opal, #1886 ....22.00
Goblet, Hoffman House, Heather, #46 ....14.00
Goblet, Scroll, amber, #322, 11-oz 12.00
Goblet, Turn O' the Century, Azalea, #612 ....22.00
Ivy ball, Early American Hobnail, amber, ftd, #742 .....24.00
Ivy ball, Spun, red w/crystal ft, 4" 65.00
Jar, Americana, amber, #282, lg, 2-pc 55.00
Jar, Americana, Helios carnival, #282/1, sm, 2-pc 55.00
Jar, Cathay Crystal, Ming, #5019 ....350.00
Jar, Ipswich, bl, #1405, 2-pc 45.00
Jar, mustard; 3-in-1 Diamond, crystal, #1, lg 65.00
Jar, pokal, gr slag, #464, 2-pc 95.00
Jar, pokal, purple slag, #464, 2-pc 85.00
Jelly dish, Beaded Block, bl opal, hdld 35.00
Lamp, Dew Drop opal, #1886/350 ....125.00
Lighter, Cape Cod, blk, #1602 ....35.00
Marmalade, Cape Cod, crystal, #89, 4-pc 45.00
Mayonnaise, Laurel, cut, Rose Pk, #256, w/ladle 30.00
Mug, Dumbo, gr, 1974 ....75.00
Nappy, Early American Hobnail, Ritz Bl, #7145B, 7" sq 26.00
Pickle dish, Pillar Flutes, bl, hdl, #682 ....25.00
Pitcher, Early American Hobnail, crystal, #742, 55-oz 30.00
Pitcher, iced tea; Tradition, crystal, ice lip, #165, 54-oz 60.00
Plate, Cape Cod, crystal, dinner sz 32.00
Plate, Cape Cod, red, #160/5D, 8" 24.00
Plate, Collector's Crystal, #5059D, 13" 30.00
Plate, Katy, bl opal, 6" 20.00
Plate, Laced Edge, crystal, 7½" 14.00
Plate, Mum, Peacock carnival, #524, 10½" 40.00
Plate, Niagara, crystal, 9½" 10.00
Plate, Old English, crystal, 7" 16.00
Plate, Pillar Flutes, bl, 8" 18.00
Plate, torte; Cape Cod, crystal, #150/75D, 14" 40.00
Plate, torte; Provincial, amber, #1506, 13" 35.00
Plate, Tradition, crystal, 8" 12.00
Punch bowl, Crocheted Crystal, +12 cups & ladle 130.00
Relish, Cape Cod, crystal, divided, #160/56, 9½" 35.00
Rose bowl, Spun, cobalt, metal fr 35.00
Sherbet, Cape Cod, amberina, #160 ....16.00
Sherbet, Cape Cod, Ritz Bl, tall 20.00
Sherbet, Early American Hobnail, ruby, #742, 9-oz 15.00
Tidbit tray, Laced Edge, crystal, 2-tier, #7432/86 .....30.00

Tumbler, big shot; shotgun shell, gr w/gold, #711, 14-oz 20.00
Tumbler, Crown Concord decor, Grape, #995, 10-oz 18.00
Tumbler, dbl old-fashioned; Cape Cod, crystal, #160, 14-oz 21.00
Tumbler, Gypsy Rings, Azalea, #116, 16-oz 14.00
Tumbler, iced tea; Dew Drop opal, #1886 ....18.00
Tumbler, iced tea; Tradition, crystal, 12-oz 12.50
Tumbler, juice; Cape Cod, Azalea, ftd, #1602, 6-oz 16.00
Tumbler, Niagara, crystal, 10-oz 10.00
Tumbler, old-fashioned; Cape Cod, crystal, #160, 7-oz 14.00
Tumbler, Shaeffer, cobalt, #4511, 9½-oz 12.50
Tumbler, sure shot; gr w/gold, #711, 11-oz 25.00
Tumbler, Voo Doo, bl/gold, #760, 16-oz 18.00
Vase, Cathay Crystal, Ku ribbon, #5012 ....800.00
Vase, Free-Hand, dk bl/wht swirl, orange int neck, 8x4½" 400.00
Vase, Free-Hand, drape decor, wht on mustard, orange int, 8½" 150.00
Vase, Free-Hand, hearts/vines, cobalt on opal, 6½" 375.00
Vase, Free-Hand, leaves/vines, purple on gr-tint opal, 4" 175.00
Vase, Free-Hand, red w/stretched tan & opal int, ruffled, 8" 300.00
Vase, Katy, bl opal, #743X, 4½" 45.00
Vase, Katy, red, #743B 45.00
Vase, marigold irid, flared, 8" 125.00
Vase, Monticello, crystal, 10½" 22.00
Vase, Pillar Flutes, bl, #682, 6" 45.00
Vase, Spun, red, 9" 65.00

Imperial Porcelain

The Blue Ridge Mountain Boys were created by cartoonist Paul Webb and translated into three-dimension by the Imperial Porcelain Corporation of Zanesville, Ohio, in 1947. These figurines decorated ashtrays, vases, mugs, bowls, pitchers, planters, and other items. The Mountain Boys series were numbered 92 through 108, each with a different and amusing portrayal of mountain life. Imperial also produced American Folklore miniatures, twenty-three tiny animals one inch or less in size, and the Al Capp Dogpatch series. Because of financial difficulties, the company closed in 1960.

American Folklore Miniatures

Cat, 1½" 40.00
Cow, 1¾" 35.00
Hound dogs, ea 35.00
Plaque, store ad, Am Folklore Porcelain Miniatures, 4½" 400.00
Sow 30.00

Blue Ridge Mountain Boys by Paul Webb

Dealer's sign, Handcrafted Paul Webb Mountain Boys in Porcelain, rare, 9", $650.00.

Ashtray, #101, man w/jug & snake 75.00
Ashtray, #103, hillbilly & skunk 75.00

Ashtray, #105, baby, hound dog, & frog 110.00
Ashtray, #106, Barrel of Wishes, w/hound 75.00
Ashtray, #92, 2 men by tree stump, for pipes 125.00
Box, cigarette; #98, dog atop, baby at door, sq 115.00
Decanter, #100, outhouse, man, & bird 75.00
Decanter, #104, Ma leaning over stump, w/baby & skunk 95.00
Decanter, man, jug, snake, & tree stump, Hispch Inc, 1946 ....75.00
Figurine, #101, man leans against tree trunk, 5" 90.00
Figurine, man on hands & knees, 3" 95.00
Figurine, man sitting, 3½" 95.00
Figurine, man sitting w/chicken on knee, 3" 95.00
Jug, #101, Willie & snake 75.00
Mug, #94, Bearing Down, 6" 95.00
Mug, #94, dbl baby hdl, 4¼" 95.00
Mug, #94, ma hdl, 4¼" 95.00
Mug, #94, man w/bl pants hdl, 4¼" 95.00
Mug, #94, man w/yel beard & red pants hdl, 4¼" 95.00
Mug, #99, Target Practice, boy on goat, farmer, 5¾" 95.00
Pitcher, lemonade 200.00
Planter, #100, outhouse, man, & bird 75.00
Planter, #105, man w/chicken on knee, washtub 110.00
Planter, #110, man, w/jug & snake, 4½" 65.00
Planter, #81, man drinking from jug, sitting by washtub 75.00
Shakers, Ma & Old Doc, pr 95.00

Miscellaneous

Items in this section that are designated 'IP' are miscellaneous novelties made by Imperial Porcelain; the remainder are of interest to Paul Webb collectors, though made by an unknown manufacturer. Prints on calendars and playing cards are signed 'Paul Webb.'

Artist board, babies or mtn women, sgn Paul Webb, 30x30" 275.00
Artist board, mtn boys only, sgn Paul Webb, 30x30" 225.00
Calendar, 1954, 12 sgn scenes, Brown & Bigelow, complete 48.00
Figurine, cat in high-heeled shoe, 5½" L 40.00
Hot pad, Dutch boy w/tulips, rnd, IP 30.00
Ink blotters, sgn scenes, ea 8.00
Mug, #29, man hdl, sgn Paul Webb, 4¾" 45.00
Planter, #106, dog sitting by tub, IP 75.00
Playing cards, ad: Rafe Oiling Gun, Brown & Bigelow, MIB 45.00
Shakers, pigs, 5", pr 95.00
Shakers, standing pigs, IP, 8", pr 95.00

Indian Tree

Indian Tree is a popular dinnerware pattern produced by various potteries since the early 1800s to recent times. Although backgrounds and borders vary, the Oriental theme is carried out with the gnarled, brown branch of a pink-blossomed tree. Among the manufacturers' marks, you may find represented such notable firms as Coalport, S. Hancock and Sons, Soho Pottery, and John Maddock and Sons.

Bowl, cream soup; Morley 17.00
Bowl, dog-feeding; shaped oval w/4 integral ft, Copeland 300.00
Bowl, fruit; Morley, sm 7.00
Bowl, Myott, 8" 18.00
Bowl, soup; rimmed, Maddock, 9" 20.00
Bowl, vegetable; rnd, Morley 22.00
Creamer & sugar bowl, Spode 60.00
Cup, Myott 4.00
Cup & saucer, Morley 14.00
Cup & saucer, Spode 32.00

Gravy boat, Maddock 32.00
Gravy boat, w/attached underplate, Spode 80.00
Pitcher, milk; Sadler, 4⅜" 15.00
Plate, luncheon; Morley, 8" 7.00
Plate, Maddock, 7¾" 8.00
Plate, Morley, 9½" 15.00
Plate, Spode, 7" 22.50
Plate, Spode, 9½" 30.00

Platter, 23", $225.00.

Platter, John Maddock & Son, 14" 32.00
Platter, Morley, 12" 22.00
Platter, Spode, 15" 165.00
Platter, well & tree, 21" 275.00

Inkwells and Inkstands

Receptacles for various writing fluids have been used since ancient times. Through the years they have been made from countless materials — glass, metal, porcelain, pottery, wood, and even papier-mache. During the 18th century, gold or silver inkstands were presented to royalty; the well-known silver inkstand by Philip Syng, Jr., was used for the signing of the Declaration of Independence, and impressive brass inkstands with wells and a pounce pot (sander) were proud possessions of men of letters. When literacy vastly increased in the 19th century, the dip pen replaced the quill pen; and inkwells and inkstands were widely used and produced in a broad range of sizes in functional and decorative forms from ornate Victorian to flowing Art Nouveau and stylized Art Deco designs. However, the acceptance of the ballpoint pen literally put inkstands and inkwells 'out of business.' But their historical significance and intriguing diversity of form and styling fascinate today's collectors.

Brass, imp's head, sm 75.00
Brass, sailing ship on raised 5½x3½" decor base 145.00
Brass, seated elephant between pineapple wells, w/tray 385.00
B3m, lt amber, GII-29, drum shape, flat collar, 2" dia 150.00
Ceramic w/pewter Nouveau whiplash floral o/l, Bigot, 4" 2,300.00
CI, leaping stag w/dogs in pursuit, glass wells, 5x9x5" 250.00
CI w/milk glass bulldog's head, self closing, 4½" 275.00
Copper/brass w/stylized forms set w/mc 'jewels,' Fr, sgn, 4½" ...500.00
Cut glass, bl, pyramid lid, 1" 125.00
Cut glass, cubed design, faceted lid, 2" sq 125.00
Cut glass, sq w/beveled corners, sterling lid, 2" 185.00
Cut glass w/matching lid, pk, brass mts, 4¾x2¾" 225.00
Faience, mc florals & ladies' faces, holds 4 accessories, 9½" ...150.00
Glass, gr irid w/brass lid, 4" dia 450.00
Glass, periwinkle bl, heavy bubbles, hinged lid, 4x4" 245.00
MOP & tortoise shell, 2 wells 400.00
Pnt bronze, Arab sits by camel, shading eyes, Austria, 7" L ..400.00
Porc, bl swirl, matching lid w/bird decor, 1¾" 85.00
Sheffield plate, beaded edges, 2 lift panels, claw ft 300.00

Sheffield plate, Rococo, 2 bottles, taperstick, 11½" **200.00**
Silver, Rococo style, London, 1896, 4" **650.00**
SP, cat on pillow w/tassels, glass insert, holder in ear **250.00**
SP, emb dragon on lid, dbl wells, scroll ft, 5x3" **175.00**
Sterling, bombe case, lion head/ring hdls, English, 10x6" **1,500.00**
Sterling, octagonal bombe shape on conforming tray, 39-oz **600.00**

Insulators

The telegraph was invented in 1844. The devices developed to hold the electrical transmission wires to the poles were called insulators. The telephone, invented in 1876, intensified their usefullness; and by the turn of the century, thousands of varieties were being produced in pottery, wood, and glass of various colors. Even though it has been rumored that red glass insulators exist, none have ever been authenticated. Many insulators are embossed with patent dates.

Of the more than 3,000 types known to exist, today's collectors evaluate their worth by age and rarity of color. Aqua and green are the most common colors in glass, dark brown the most common in ceramic. Threadless insulators, (for example, CD #701.1) made between 1850 and 1865, bring prices well into the hundreds, if in mint condition.

In the listings that follow, the CD numbers are from an identification system developed in the late 1960s by N.R. Woodward.

Those seeking additional information about insulators are encouraged to contact Line Jewels-Insulators (whose address may be found in the Directory under Clubs, Newsletters and Catalogs) or attend a club-endorsed show. For information, contact Len Linscott, listed in the Directory under Florida. In the listings below, items designated as OPEN have not been purchased/sold in large enough numbers to establish a value.

Key:
* — Canadian	SB — smooth base
** — Mexican	SDP — sharp drip points
*** — Australian	RB — rough base
CB — corrugated base	RDP — round drip points
CD — Consolidated Design	

Threaded Insulators

CD 102, NW & BIT Co, SB, lt gr **100.00**
CD 102.2, Westinghouse, SB, Peacock Bl **450.00**
CD 104, Brookfield, SB, aqua **30.00**
CD 104, National Insulator Co, SB, aqua **220.00**
CD 106*, Diamond, SDP, straw **6.00**
CD 107, Armstrong, SB, clear **3.00**
CD 109.9, JF Buzby, SB, squa....................**OPEN**
CD 112, Brookfield, SB, aqua **2.00**
CD 113, Hemingray, SDP, aqua **2.00**
CD 115, Brookfield, SDP, aqua **75.00**
CD 117, No Name, SB, aqua **20.00**
CD 120, CEW, SB, purple **200.00**
CD 121, Am Tel & Tel, SB, aqua **3.00**
CD 121, Hemingray, SDP, aqua **1.00**
CD 124.2, No Name, SB, aqua **15.00**
CD 127, WV, SB, aqua **75.00**
CD 128, Hemingray, SB, clear **1.00**
CD 131, No Name, SB, aqua **15.00**
CD 134, Am Ins Co, emb rim, aqua **12.00**
CD 139.9, McLaughlin, SB, aqua **100.00**
CD 143.5, T-HE, SB, lt aqua **55.00**
CD 143*, Canadian Pacific, SB, bl **5.00**
CD 151, HGCo, SB, aqua **8.00**

CD 152, B, SB, emerald gr **5.00**
CD 154, Hemingray, RDP, bluish-aqua **1.00**
CD 154*, Dominion, SB, gr **5.00**
CD 155**, Texcoco, SB, gr **40.00**
CD 160, Hawley, SB, aqua **50.00**
CD 162, R Good, SB, aqua **6.00**
CD 188, B, SB, aqua **7.00**
CD 196, Hemingray, SDP, aqua **30.00**
CD 200, California, SB, purple **200.00**
CD 210, Postal, SB, emerald gr **12.00**
CD 221, Whitall Tatum, SB, amber **200.00**
CD 233, Pyrex, SB, clear **3.00**
CD 250.7***, AGM, SB, straw **70.00**
CD 254, Hemingray, SB, aqua **18.00**
CD 257, Hemingray, RDP, aqua **7.00**
CD 260, Cable, SB, aqua **40.00**
CD 267, NEGMCo, SB, aqua **75.00**
CD 275, Locke, SB, aqua **30.00**
CD 283, VG Converse, SDP, aqua **24.00**
CD 288, Mershon, SB, lt gr **35.00**
CD 294, NEGM, SB, lt bl **30.00**
CD 308, No Name, SB, clear **30.00**
CD 327, Pyrex, SB, clear **14.00**

Threadless Insulators

CD 700, No Name, egg shape, SB, bl **195.00**

CD 701.1, no name, wide ridges, smooth base, lime green, OPEN (unestablished value).

CD 719, Tillotson, SB, gr milk glass....................**OPEN**
CD 728, No Name, SB, lt aqua **80.00**
CD 729.1, Milford & Biddle, SB, gr....................**OPEN**
CD 734*, McMicking, SB, lt aqua **60.00**
CD 736, ERW, SB, gr....................**OPEN**
CD 742.1*, MTC, rim emb, milk glass **245.00**

Irons

History, geography, art and cultural diversity are all represented in the collecting of antique pressing irons. The progress of fashion and invention can be traced through the ages by relics left in the form of pressing devices used in earlier times. Goffering irons, once needed for the frills and ruffles of the Victorian age, have been out of use so long that they are seldom recognized today. The fluter, essential for producing the yards of crimped ruffles demanded by 19th-century ladies, is now a quaint curiosity. Industrial technology can be traced through records left by centuries of irons.

The native character of nations is reflected by the geography where irons are found. Some countries lacked iron, so they made their pressing devices of other materials. And because an iron foundry represents a high form of investment and technology, less wealthy societies frequently used the easier-to-work brass.

A culture's priorities are reflected in the tools in daily use. Some value innovation while others are content with a standard generic product. There are degrees of ornamentation, depending on the country, the people, and their approach to life.

At times, to the pleasure of today's collectors, the work trancends proficiency and rises into the realm of art. Using a variety of materials — iron, brass, or wood — artisans built a monument to their inner vision. Their work survives, testifiying to the care, love, and attention lavished on household implements, elevating them in status to something that delights the eye.

In the listing that follows, prices are given for examples in very good to excellent condition. Damage, repairs, plating, excessive wear, rust and missing parts can dramatically reduce value. For further information we recommend *Irons By Irons* by our advisor Dave Irons; his address and information for ordering the book are listed in the Directory under Pennsylvania.

Upper left: English goffering, Queen Anne style, brass, with 4" barrel, EX, $350.00; Rear center: Smoothing stone, glass, 4" diameter, very early, $200.00; Center: Smoothing board, Danish, wood with carved stars, EX, $350.00; Front: Poking stick, English, brass, 14" long, EX, $175.00; Center right: Pan iron, Chinese, bronze with ivory handle, decorated with carvings, VG, $200.00.

Box, Salamander, porc knob, slug, EX	200.00
Detachable hdl, AC Williams slide latch, 3⅝", EX	150.00
Detachable hdl, Dover #912, str-sided hood, 4⅛", G	40.00
Detachable hdl, Potts type, EX NP, 3¾"	50.00
Detachable hdl, Sensible #0, rear latch, 4", VG	100.00
Electric, American Beauty, red inset in hdl, 7¾", EX	28.00
Electric, Eureka Cordless Automatic, Detroit, VG	48.00
Electric, Proctor Never Lift, 2-prong, 7¼", MIB	110.00
Electric, Silver Streak, Royal Blue, Pyrex shell, EX	850.00
Flower, Molla Tool Corp NYC, brass, makes 4⅝" flower, VG	90.00
Flower petal, brass & iron, makes 1¾" petal, VG	80.00
Fluter, Crown machine, March 23, 1880, EX	135.00
Fluter, English, fine-flute machine, 4" roller, bone grip, VG	265.00
Fluter, Geneva, rocker, Pat'd Aug 21, 1866 on base, 6x3⅞", EX	60.00
Fluter, North Bros Mfg, roller, EX pnt & NP, 7x3¾", EX	135.00
Goffering, European, wrought iron, spider base, w/4" bbl, G	300.00
Goffering, Kenrick 'S' upright, orig heater, VG	155.00
Liquid fuel, Am Gas Machine Co...#6664, blk porc, 7½", EX	90.00
Liquid fuel, Coleman #4A, bl, 8¼", w/trivet, EX	55.00
Liquid fuel, Wonder Pat'd Chicago Ill, front tank, 7", VG	90.00

Little, dmn grip, w/trivet, 3", EX	35.00
Little, Gem 2, wood grip, 2⅞", EX	50.00
Little, hexagonal block type, Roman numeral I on face, 2⅞", VG	45.00
Little, Lady Dover, gr pnt wooden hdl, red body, 3⅜"	45.00
Little, paneled cylinder grip, polishing top, NP traces, 4", EX	40.00
Little, Pearl, wood grip, EX pnt, 3¾"	110.00
Little, rnd heel, 0 on face, VG	60.00
Little, rope hdl, 2⅞", EX	30.00
Little, Swan, w/trivet, 2½", VG	125.00
Polisher, Geneva Star, star on face, mk hdl, 4⅞", EX	75.00
Polisher, Mahony, Morocco finish, 5", VG	30.00
Polisher, Marry Ann B Cook, Pat'd Dec 5, 1848, 5¼", EX	130.00
Sadiron, AC Williams, wire thumb latch, 2", EX	50.00
Sadiron, Enterprise, sq bk, 6¼", EX	45.00
Sadiron, Enterprise Star, ventilated hdl, 6⅞", EX	45.00
Sleeve, Sensible #5, 8", VG	50.00

Ironstone

During the last quarter of the 18th century, English potters began experimenting with a new type of body that contained calcinated flint and a higher china clay content, intent on producing a fine durable whiteware — heavy, yet with a texture that would resemble porcelain. To remove the last trace of yellow, a minute amount of cobalt was added, often resulting in a bluish-white tone. Wm and John Turner of Caughley, and Josiah Spode II were the first to manufacture the ware successfully. Others, such as Davenport, Hicks and Meigh, and Ralph and Josiah Wedgwood, followed with their own versions. The latter coined the name 'Pearl' to refer to his product and incorporated the term into his trademark. In 1813 a 14-year patent was issued to Charles James Mason, who called his ware Patented Ironstone. Francis Morley, G.L. Asworth, T.J. Mayer, and other Staffordshire potters continued to produce ironstone until the end of the century. While some of these patterns are simple to the extreme, many are decorated with in-mold designs of fruit, grain, and foliage on ribbed or scalloped shapes. In the 1830s transfer-printed designs in blue, mulberry, pink, green, and black became popular; and polychrome versions of Oriental wares were manufactured to compete with the Chinese trade. Our advise for this category comes from Home Place Antiques, whose address is listed in the Directory under Illinois. See also Mason's Ironstone.

Baker, Dmn T'print, Gelson Bros Henley, 7¼x5⅜"	60.00
Bowl, berry/sauce; Rolling Star, Edwards	30.00
Bowl, hot beverage; President, no hdl, Edwards, 4-pc, 10x9¾"	465.00
Bowl, sauce; Ceres, Elsmore & Forster, 5"	18.00
Bowl, sauce; Sharon Arch, Davenport, 4¾"	22.50
Bowl, soup; Boote's 1851, T&R Boote, 9½"	27.50
Bowl, soup; Mocho, T&R Boote, 8⅝"	20.00
Bowl, soup; Prairie Flowers, Livesley Powell & Co, 10"	30.00
Bowl, soup; Sharon Arch, Wedgwood, 9¾"	36.00
Bowl, vegetable; Boote's 1851, T&R Boote, 8⅞"	85.00
Bowl, vegetable; Dmn T'print, w/lid, Wedgwood, med	185.00
Bowl, vegetable; Gothic, w/lid, mk JF, 8¼x11¼x9¾"	145.00
Bowl, vegetable; Prize Bloom, w/lid, TJ&J Mayer,	195.00
Bowl, vegetable; Sydenham, w/lid, T&R Boote, 9" dia	245.00
Butter dish, Lily of the Valley, Shaw, 3-pc	235.00
Butter dish, Panelled Grape, 3-pc	235.00
Chamber pot, Boote's 1851, no lid, T&R Boote	95.00
Coffee cup & saucer, Scotia, F Jones & Co	65.00
Compote, New York, unmk, 5½x9½"	200.00
Creamer, Wheat & Clover, Turner & Tompkinson, 7⅜"	125.00
Cup & saucer, Western, Hope & Carter, mini	55.00

Pitcher, Ceres, Turner, Goddard & Co, 8¾" 165.00
Pitcher, Garibaldi, T&R Boote, 8¾" 98.00
Pitcher, Panelled Leaves, J&G Meakin, 8¾" 165.00
Pitcher, President, J Edwards, 8⅝" 155.00
Plate, Athenia, Adams, 8⅞" 22.00
Plate, Boote's 1851, 10-sided, T&R Boote, 9½" 32.00
Plate, cookie; Cherry Scroll, T&R Boote 50.00
Plate, Mocho, T&R Boote, 6½" 14.00
Plate, Rolling Star, Edwards, 9½" 27.50
Plate, Sharon Arch, Wedgwood, 10⅝" 32.00
Plate, Sydenham, T&R Boote, 10¼" 42.50
Plate, Sydenham, T&R Boote, 9½" 32.00
Plate, Virginia, Bougham & Mayer, 9½" 22.50

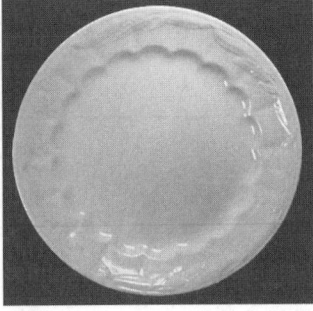

Plate, Wheat, W&E Corn, 9¾", 8 for $185.00.

Platter, De Soto, Thos Hughes, 11⅝x9" 50.00
Platter, Ribbed Raspberry, J&G Meakin, 12x9⅛" 65.00
Platter, Sharon Arch, Wedgwood, 16½" 50.00
Relish, Ceres, w/rope, Elsmore & Forster 78.00
Relish, Wheat, Meakin 28.00
Spittoon, lady's hand held, East Trenton Pottery, 4¼x4¾" 65.00
Sugar bowl, Tuscan, Edwards, 8x6½" 75.00
Tea set, Square Ridged, Johnson Bros, 3-pc 275.00
Teacup & saucer, Baltic, T Hulme 48.00
Teacup & saucer, Dmn T'print, Gelson Bros 32.00
Teapot, Ceres, Elsmore & Forster 245.00
Teapot, Poppy, poppy shape, J&C Wileman 200.00
Toothbrush holder, Columbia, vertical, unmk, 5" 100.00
Toothbrush holder, Wheat, vertical, unmk 100.00
Tureen, sauce; Cable & Ring, w/underplate & ladle, Bridgwood ..225.00
Tureen, sauce; President, oval, J Edwards, 3-pc 245.00
Tureen, sauce; Sevres, w/lid & underplate, J Edwards 265.00
Tureen, soup; Fluted Pearl, w/lid & underplate, J Wedgwood 395.00
Tureen, soup; Lafayette, w/lid, Clementson, 10x14x8" 215.00
Tureen, stew; Wrapped Sydenham, Maddock, 8x8¾" 225.00
Wash bowl, Leaf & Crossed Ribbon, Livesley Powell 125.00
Wash bowl & pitcher, Ceres, Elsmore & Forster, 14", 14" 345.00
Wash bowl & pitcher, Dallas shape, Clementson 375.00
Wash bowl & pitcher, Dmn T'print, Wedgwood 365.00
Wash bowl & pitcher, Fig, Wedgwood 395.00
Wash bowl & pitcher, Leaf & Crossed Ribbon, Livesley Powell ...285.00
Wash bowl & pitcher, Scalloped Decagon, Davenport 300.00
Wash bowl & pitcher, Wheat & Blackberry, Meakin 300.00
Wash pitcher, Boote's 1851, T&R Boote, 12" 140.00
Waste bowl, Ceres, bell shape, Elsmore & Forster (unmk) 120.00
Waste bowl, Tuscan, unmk, 3⅛x5¼" 80.00

Italian Glass

Throughout the 20th century, one of the major glassmaking centers of the world was the island of Murano. From the Stile Liberte work of Artisi Barovier (1890-1920s) to the early work of Ettore Sottsass in the 1970s, they excelled in creativity and craftsmanship. The 1920s to '40s featured the work of glass designers like Ercole Barovier for Barovier and Toso and Vittorio Zecchin, Napoleone Martinuzzi and Carlo Scarpa for Venini. Many of these pieces are highly prized by collectors.

The 1950s saw a revival of Italy as a world reknown design center for all of the arts. Glass led the charge with the brightly colored work of Fulvio Bianconi for Venini, Dino Martens for Aureliano Toso and Ercole Barovier for Barovier and Toso. The best of these pieces are extremely desirable. The '60s and '70s have also seen many innovative designs with work by the Finnish Tapio Wirkkala, the American Thomas Stearns and many other designers.

Unfortunately, amongst the great glass, there was a plethora of commercial ashtrays, vases and figurines produced that, though have some value, do not compare in quality and design as the great glass of Murano. These pieces are listed as 'Murano' glass rather than by maker.

Venini: The Venini company was founded in 1921 by Paolo Venini, and he led the company until his death in 1959. Major Italian designers worked for the firm, including Vittorio Zecchin, Napoleone Martinuzzi, Carlo Scarpa and Fulvio Bianconi. After his death, his son-in-law, Ludovico de Santillana, ran the factory and employed designers like Toni Zucchieri, Tapio Wirkkala and Thomas Stearns. The company is known for creative designs and techniques including Inciso (finely etched lines), Battuto (carved facets), Sommerso (controlled bubbles), Pezzato (patches of fused glass) and Fascie (horizontal colored lines in clear glass). Until the mid-60s, most pieces were signed with acid-etched 'Venini Murano ITALIA.' In the '60s they started engraving the signatures. The factory still exists.

Barovier: In the late 1920s, Ercole Barovier took over the Artisti Barovier and started designing many different vases. In the 1930s he merged with Ferro Toso and became Barovier and Toso. He designed many different series of glass including the Barbarico (rough, acid-treated brown or deep blue glass), Eugenio (free-blown vases), Efeso, Rotallato, Dorico, Egeo (vases incorporating murrine designs) and Primavera (white etched glass with black bands). He designed until 1974. The company is still in existence. Most pieces were unsigned.

Aureliano Toso: The great glass designer Dino Martens was involved with the company from about 1938 to 1965. It was his work that produced the very desirable Oriente vases. This technique consisted of free-formed patches of green, yellow, blue, purple, black and white stars and pieces of zanfirico canes fused into brilliantly colored vases and bowls. His El Dorado series was based on the same technique but was not opaque. He also designed pieces with alternating groups of black and white filigrana lines. Pieces are unsigned.

Seguso: Flavio Poli became the artistic director of Seguso in the late 1930s and remained until 1963. He is known for his Corroso (acid-etched glass) and his Valve series (elegant forms of two to three layers of colored glass with a clear glass casing).

Archimede Seguso: In 1946 Archimede Seguso left the Seguso Vetri D'Arte to open a new company and designed many innovative pieces. His Merlatto series (thin white filigrana suspended three dimensionally) is his most famous. The epitome of his work is where a colored glass (yellow or purple) is windowed in the merlotti. His Macchia Ambra Verde is yellow and spots on a gold base encased in clear glass. The A Piume series contained feathers and leaves suspended in glass. Pieces are unsigned.

Alfredo Barbini: Barbini was a designer known for his sculptures of sea subjects and his amorphic-shaped vases with an inner core of red or blue glass with a heavy layer of finely incised outer glass. He worked in the 1950s to 1960s, and some pieces are signed.

Vistosi: Although this glassworks was started in the 1940s, fame came in the 1960s and '70s with the birds designed by Allesandro Pianon and the early work of the Memphis school designer, Ettorre Sottsass. Pieces may be signed.

AVEM: This company is known for its work in the 1950s and '60s. The designer, Ansolo Fuga, did work using a solid white glass with inclusions of multicolored murrines.

Cenedese: This is a postwar company led by Gino Cenedese with Alfredo Barbini as designer. When Barbini left, Cenedese took over the design work and also used the free-lanced designs of Fulvio Bianconi. They are known for their figurines and vases with suspended murrines.

Cappellin: Venini's original partner (1921-25), Giacomo Cappellin, opened a short-lived company (1925-32) that was to become extremely important. His chief designer was the young Carlo Scarpa who was to create many masterpieces in glass both for Cappellin and then Venini.

Key:
c — controlled   som — sommerso
incl —inclusions   zan — zanfirico

Pezzato vase designed by Fulvio Bianconi in blue, amethyst and topaz gray squares, 8¼", $5,475.00. Photo courtesy of Skinner, Inc., Boston and Bolton, MA.

Aureliano Toso, ewer, Oriente, 4-color, appl hdl/clear ft, 11" .5,250.00
Aureliano Toso, vase, clear w/amethyst zan canes, 18" 3,300.00
Aureliano Toso, vase, Eldorado, single-hole, 12¼" 8,200.00
Aureliano Toso, vase, Oriente, free-form, 7" 600.00
AVEM, vase, wht w/2 turq windows of mc murrines, collar, 16¾" ..650.00
Barbini, lady swimmer, gold in clear on blk cube, 18¼" 1,850.00
Barbini, vase, clear battuto & som on yel & gray, 13¼" 2,650.00
Barbini, vase, clear teardrop som/inciso w/yel & bl, 8½" 900.00
Barbini, vase, clear teardrop w/bl, yel hollow core, 10¾" 1,000.00
Barbini, 3 ducks for VAMSA, gr core, clear w/bubbles, 16" L .1,100.00
Barovier, bird, wht w/pk & gold stripes, 16" 650.00
Barovier, bowl, clear & amber irid, Rugiadoso style, sgn, 8" 525.00
Barovier, bowl, Dorica, sqs of of bl & wht murrines, 4½" 1,850.00
Barovier, centerpiece, Primavera, blk & wht, 13" 30,000.00
Barovier, shell, clear irid, Rugiadoso style, sgn, 6½x17" 1,850.00
Barovier, shell, gr w/gold leak, 3" 60.00
Barovier, vase, Barbarico, pinched top, 8" 1,050.00
Barovier, vase, blk w/gold star murrines, sgn, 12" 5,750.00
Barovier, vase, Efeso, cobalt w/internal bubbles, 15¾" 1,400.00
Barovier, vase, gr irid w/c bubbles, appl clear ribbons, 11¼" 700.00
Barovier, vase, gr w/c bubbles, 10" 495.00
Barovier, vase, incl of bubbles & mica, 12" 425.00
Barovier, vase, jade gr w/blk & gr incl, 2-hdld, 6x14" 1,600.00
Cappellin, chalice, irid, 11½" 1,800.00
Cappellin, vase, irid w/lg air bubbles, cylindrical, 11" 1,875.00
Cappellin, vase, lemon yel w/appl fruit on lid, sgn, 10½" 1,050.00
Cappellin, vase, rose lattimo w/deep rose ft, 10" 1,350.00
Cenedese, bowl, owl form 110.00
Cenedese, bud vase, amethyst & blk 280.00

Cenedese, clown figure, 13" 550.00
Murano, birds (pr) on ped base, internal decor, 18½" 700.00
Murano, vase, blk cylinder, red & serpentine hdls, 10" 1,350.00
Murano, vase, blk w/red rim, 4½" 300.00
Seguso, Bullicante fish pr, amber core/random c bubbles, 14" L ..1,100.00
Seguso, fish, gr w/incised decor, sgn, 20½" 3,150.00
Seguso, vase, amethyst w/blk grillwork, 10½" 1,500.00
Seguso, vase, clear to gr w/inlaid leaves, heavy, 8" 1,400.00
Seguso, vase, gr irid som, ca 1940, 10½" 1,100.00
Seguso, vase, nastro richiamato clear, mc ribbons, label, 8½" ..1,650.00
Venini, aquatic bird, wht filigrana, matching base, 12½" 2,250.00
Venini, bottle, som, bl, sq form, sgn, 9½" 450.00
Venini, bottle, som, lt rose w/gold incl, sgn, 11" 1,500.00
Venini, bottle, wht w/gr & red bands, 14" 4,000.00
Venini, bottle & stopper, inciso, bl, label, 11¼" 975.00
Venini, bottle & stopper, inciso, bl, sgn, 8" 750.00
Venini, bottle & stopper, inciso, red, sgn, 7½" 700.00
Venini, bowl, murrine, hammered blk murrines, 11¼" 3,000.00
Venini, bowl, red & wht cvd murrines in clear, 6" dia 6,000.00
Venini, bowl, som, lt amethyst w/bubbles & gold, 1½x2" 130.00
Venini, candlesticks, inciso, 1 red/1 gr, sgn, 6½", 8", pr 1,500.00
Venini, carafe, inciso, amethyst w/Cristofle silver, sgn, 12" 1,500.00
Venini, compote, lattimo, amethyst cased, sgn, 6¾" 525.00
Venini, figurine, lady w/mc striped skirt, sgn, 13" 2,300.00
Venini, hourglass, translucent yel & amber, 7½" 1,000.00
Venini, lamp, yel, mushroom shape, 14" 500.00
Venini, mirror, pezzato, mc sqs, 3 cracks, 17x15" 2,800.00
Venini, pr of Commedia dell'Arte: Arlechinno/Arlechina, 13", 12" .5,175.00
Venini, pr of Commedia dell'Arte: Meneghino, label, 11" 2,750.00
Venini, rooster, wht w/mc stripes, sgn, rpr, 7½" 2,500.00
Venini, tumbler, gr & bl canes, 5½", 4 for 140.00
Venini, vase, battuto, peach, sgn, 18¾" 2,750.00
Venini, vase, battuto, red, sgn, 11" 4,500.00
Venini, vase, blk w/2 blk hdls, sgn, 8" 1,500.00
Venini, vase, clear w/abstract purple, bulbous, sgn, 10" 25,300.00
Venini, vase, Corroso, gr w/protruding points, sgn, 8" 7,100.00
Venini, vase, cream lattimo, brn/gold incl, hdls, '32, 10½" 2,250.00
Venini, vase, cream lattimo w/appl wht ft & ring at neck, 7" ..1,500.00
Venini, vase, Fasce, red & amber horizontal stripes, 5½" 400.00
Venini, vase, Forati, amethyst, single hole, sgn, 11½" 1,400.00
Venini, vase, Forati, bl w/pulled-out hole, 11½" 1,400.00
Venini, vase, Giada, coral w/copper incl, 8" 1,250.00
Venini, vase, Giada, olive gr, w/stopper, sgn, 12" 800.00
Venini, vase, handkerchief; clear, wht zan lacing, sgn, 11" 2,300.00
Venini, vase, handkerchief; latticinio, 8x9½" 800.00
Venini, vase, handkerchief; pk & wht zan, sgn, 9½" 1,050.00
Venini, vase, handkerchief; powder bl, wht cased, sgn, 8¼" 575.00
Venini, vase, handkerchief; wht opaque, garnet cased, sgn, 7½" ...575.00
Venini, vase, inciso, burnt orange, sgn, 17" 2,500.00
Venini, vase, latticinio & zan canes, 10" 425.00
Venini, vase, lattimo, lt bl, squat melon shape, 9½" 180.00
Venini, vase, lattimo, wht w/appl ring ft, 11½" 120.00
Venini, vase, mezza-filigrana, wht & clear, sgn, 11" 2,100.00
Venini, vase, mosaica filigrana, turq w/wht zan net, 14" 5,900.00
Venini, vase, occhi, amber & gr, 6½" 4,100.00
Venini, vase, pezzato, aubergine/gr/amber sqs, sgn, 11" 4,400.00
Venini, vase, pezzato, clear/turq/amethyst/gray sqs, sgn, 8¼" ...4,400.00
Venini, vase, Veronese, bl, 9½" 200.00
Venini, vase, violet (purple), 2-hole, sgn, 19" 2,250.00
Venini, vases, inciso, bl or amber, flared, sgn, 8", pr 1,150.00
Vistosi, bird, bl, metal ft, 7¼" 1,700.00
Vistosi, bird, bl w/metal ft, triangular shape, 7" 1,500.00
Vistosi, bird, gr, metal legs, 12¼" 1,250.00
Vistosi, bird, olive w/murrines, 2 metal ft, sq shape, 8½" 1,050.00

Vistosi, bowl, Palladia: Sottsass, wht w/red & blk, sgn, 8¾" 850.00
Vistosi, vase, bl w/blk & bl bands, pelzel, 7" 1,300.00
Vistosi, vase, Diodata: Sottsass, invt dbl gourd, gr/bl/blk 1,725.00
Vistosi, vase, Moceniga: Sottsass, yel w/blk, sgn, 8" 1,000.00

Ivory

Technically, true ivory is the substance composing the tusk of the elephant; the finest type comes from Africa. However, tusks and teeth of other animals — the walrus, the hippopotamus, and the sperm whale, for instance — are similar in composition and appearance and have also been used for carving. The Chinese have used this substance for centuries, preferring it over bone because of the natural oil contained in its pores, which not only renders it easier to carve but also imparts a soft sheen to the finished product. Aged ivory usually takes on a soft caramel patina, but unscrupulous dealers sometimes treat new ivory to a tea bath to 'antique' it! A bill passed in 1978 reinforced a ban on the importation of whale and walrus ivory. All examples listed here are Oriental in origin unless noted otherwise.

Carving of greengrocer and child, signed Koho, Meiji Period, 11½", $3,450.00; Carving of mother and child with tortoise, signed Koki, early 1900s, 13", $1,840.00.

Ancient w/staff, boy on goat beside, 12" 440.00
Chess men, tea stained, 16 pcs 250.00
Classical man (& woman), on oval ped, marble base, 12", pr ..3,300.00
Cormorant fisherman, treating his bird to a fish, Hozan, 9" 1,000.00
Emperor, seated, sgn, 7½", +teak stand 350.00
Frame, cvd dragon/scroll/heart, oval, easel bk, 5" 60.00
Kwan Yin, 11", +teakwood stand 200.00
Lady in flowing robe, infant to shoulder, holds rosary, 9" 800.00
Maid holding vase, 12½", +teakwood stand 385.00
Maid standing/playing 4-stringed mandolin, 12", +stand 300.00
Maid w/fan, teapot, cup & saucer, 11", +teakwood stand 465.00
Maid w/scroll & pen, 12½", +teakwood stand 240.00
Man w/fan, mask & bells, sgn, 6¾" 650.00
Mtn grove w/pines, eagles/macaques/etc, sgn Gyokumin, 8" ...1,800.00
Mystery ball, 2¼", +stand 130.00
Nude, billowing drapery, putto below, Dippe, 6½" 975.00
Okimono, figure & child on rocks, turtle on rope, sgn, 14" 2,200.00
Okimono, figure w/basket of crabs (& variation), 10", pr 700.00
Parasol hdl, rats & monkey on branch, 6¾" 150.00
Pipe, opium; comical bird bowl, pewter & copper mts, 1850s 325.00
Plaque, Guan Yin by censor, figures boating, 12", +stand 500.00
Quan Yin, stands & offers willow wand/flagon to dragon, 9" 875.00
Quan Yin holds bowl of fruit, 5½" 80.00
Tusk, gods climbing amidst foliage, Indian, 1800s, 9" 165.00

Tusk cvg: man, 6", & lady, 7", pr 150.00

Jack-in-the-Pulpit Vases

Popular novelties at the turn of the century, jack-in-the-pulpit vases were made in every type of art glass produced. Some were simple, others elaborately appliqued and enameled. They were shaped to resemble the lily for which they were named.

Chartreuse gr opal, ruffled edge, 7¼x4½" 65.00
Maroon opal to vaseline, ruffled edge, 7¼x4¼" 75.00
Orange opal to vaseline, emb ribs, vaseline leaf ft, 5½" 125.00
Sapphire bl, Dmn Quilt w/HP florals & gold, 9⅜x4⅝" 245.00
Spangle glass, bl/wht/amber w/silver flecks, 6½" 80.00
Wht opaque w/rose int, wishbone ft, 5x3¼" 75.00

Japanese Lustreware

Imported from Japan during the 1920s, novelty tableware items, vases ashtrays, etc. — often in blue, tan, and mother-of-pearl lustre glazes — were sold through five-and-dime stores or given as premiums for selling magazine subscriptions. The Occupied Japan Club is listed in the Directory under Clubs, Newletters, and Catalogs.

Ashtray, bathing beauty in orange on bl base, 2¾" 40.00
Ashtray, clown w/card suit decor, bridge set of 4 ....15.00
Ashtray, conch shell form, caramel, pk int 12.50
Astray, plunger in opening 14.00
Bowl, lotus flower shape, mk, 4½" dia 35.00
Condiment set, Deco florals w/aqua trim, 4-pc 25.00
Creamer & sugar bowl, floral, mc on orange, child sz 25.00
Incense burner, elephant w/monkey rider finial, bl & wht, 5" 30.00
Lemon dish, lemon decor, hdls 15.00
Pincushion, dog pulling cart, bl, tan & yel lustres, 3¼" 20.00

Pitcher, ships scene with lavender and tan lustre, black mark, 6", $40.00.

Shakers, yel chick in shell, hdl, 1929, pr 14.00
Sugar shaker, caramel top & base, mc flowers 15.00
Tea set, bluebirds, child sz, 13-pc, serves 4 ....65.00
Vase, HP sailing ship, 4½", pr 25.00
Vase, tan & purple w/mc castle scene, mk, 8" 30.00

Jervis

W.P. Jervis began his career as a potter in 1898. By 1908 he had his own pottery in Oyster Bay, New York. His shapes were graceful;

often he decorated his wares with sgraffito designs over which he applied a matt glaze. Many piece were incised 'Jervis' in a vertical arrangement. The pottery closed around 1912.

Bowl, bl w/some crystals, hdls, 2¼" H 150.00
Bowl, dk bl band w/cvd sqs on gray, 3x6", EX 450.00
Jardiniere, 6 lg leaf-cvd rim-to-base hdls, gr matt, 9x9" 1,200.00

Jewelry

Jewelry as objects of adornment has always been regarded with special affection. Whether it be a trinket or a costly ornament of gold, silver, or enameled work, jewelry has personal significance to the wearer. The art of the jeweler is valued as is any art object, and the names of Lalique or Faberge on collectible pieces bring prices demanded by the signed works of Picasso. Once the province of kings and noblemen, jewelry now is a legacy of all strata of society. The creativity reflected in the jeweler's art has resulted in a myriad of decorative adornments for men and women, and the modern usage of 'lesser' gems and base metals has elevated the value and increased the demand for artistic merit, so that now it is considered by collectors to be on a par with intrinsic value. Luxuriously appointed pieces of Victorian splendor and Edwardian grandeur now compete with the unique, imaginative renditions of jewelry produced in the exciting Art Nouveau period as well as the adventurous translation of jewelry executed in man-made materials versus natural elements. Today prices for gems and gemstones crafted into antique and collectible jewelry are based on artistic merit, personal appeal, pure sentimentality, and intrinsic value. Note: Diamond prices vary greatly depending on color, clarity, etc. Values given here are for diamond jewelry with a standard commercial grade of diamonds that are most likely to be encountered.

Our advisor for this category is Rebecca Dodds; her address may be found in the Directory under Florida. If you are interested in collecting or dealing in jewelry, you will find that authority Lillian Baker has several fine books available on the subject — *100 Years of Collectible Jewelry: 1850-1950; Art Nouveau and Art Deco Jewelry;* and *Fifty Years of Collectible Fashion Jewelry: 1925-1975.* These books are complete with beautiful full-color illustrations and current market values. Mrs. Baker is listed in the Directory under California. See also Plastics.

Key:

A/C — Arts and Crafts	gf — gold filled
AD — Art Deco	grad — graduated
AN — Art Nouveau	gp — gold plated
cab — cabochon	gw — gold washed
cl — clear	k — karat
comp — complementary	m/c — mine cut
ct — carat	plat — platinum
dmn — diamond	r/c — rose cut
dwt — penny weight	r/stn — rhinestone
Euro — European cut	rdm — rhodium
fl — filigree	stn — stone
g'el-plt — gold electroplate	tw — total weight
g-stn — gemstone	wg — white gold
g-t — gold-tone	yg — yellow gold

Bracelet, bangle; 14k yg w/21 sm opals, dbl safety lock 575.00
Bracelet, bangle; 9k gold, m/c dmn w/in scrolls & beadwork 260.00
Bracelet, charm; 14k yg, 12 charms, 50.0dwt 635.00
Bracelet, cuff; Spratling, sterling chevrons, amethyst cabs 1,000.00
Bracelet, cultured pearls, 3-row 5.5mm w/gold spacers 375.00
Bracelet, Geo Jensen, by Henning Koppel, shaped links, 8" 750.00
Bracelet, Los Ballesteros, sterling scroll/bead links, 1950s 230.00

Brooch, Levin, silver/14k shield w/gold o/l figures, 3" W 125.00
Brooch, Mexican silver flamenco dancer, 2½x2" 22.00
Brooch, 18k yg abstract w/.35 dmn, plat/dmn spray accent 690.00
Buckle, Tiffany, sterling, 1¼" W 150.00
Buckle, Tiffany, 14k yg, 1940s, 1" W 550.00
Buckle, Tiffany, 14k yg, 1940s, 2" W 750.00
Cuff links, Geo Jensen, sterling, by Henning Koppel, #83 ....135.00
Cuff links, Geo Jensen, 18k yg, by Henning Koppel, 1940s 650.00
Cuff links, Hans Hanson, 14k yg, pillow shape, pr 275.00
Cuff links, 10k yg w/.50 tw dmns, pr 125.00
Cuff links, 14k wg w/sapphires, pr 110.00
Cuff links, 18k yg w/5.8mm cultured pearl terminals 95.00
Earrings, jade, oval plaques mtd w/silver & dmn cross 150.00
Earrings, silver w/sq-cut gr stones & r/c dmn accents, Fr mk 375.00
Earrings, Tiffany, 14k yg, basketweave design, ½" W 1,200.00
Earrings, 14k yg, garnets, pr 85.00
Earrings, 14k yg fl w/9mm fiery opals, 2" L, pr 165.00
Earrings, 14k yg spray shape w/sm dmn & sapphire accents 345.00
Lavalier, sq peridot in scrolls, 4mm pearl+freshwater drop 78.00
Locket, baby's, eng 14k yg on 14k yg chain 65.00
Locket, gf 1½x1" eng heart on rope chain, ca 1940s 45.00
Necklace, Cartier, 14k yg snake links 1,430.00
Necklace, coral & fluted onyx beads/gold spacers, 14k clasp 230.00
Necklace, cultured pearls, 5.5mm, 14k wg clasp, 16" 100.00
Necklace, gf, heart slide w/seed pearl, Victorian 125.00
Necklace, yg, 9ct Bohemian garnets 195.00
Necklace, 1-strand 7½ -8mm cultured pearls, 20" 575.00
Pendant, Frank Gardner, lg teardrop citrine+3 aquas, 18k fr ...3,000.00
Pendant, Henry Steig, sterling, oval shape w/raised abstract 85.00
Pendant, lg Bohemian garnet in low-k yg on 14k chain 90.00
Pendant, Picasso, silver, rnd face form 775.00
Pendant, sterling chain & floral fr, bl-dyed agate, 21" 345.00
Pendant, 14k yg multistrand fine chain w/lg smoky topaz 345.00
Pendant, 14k yg rtcl mt w/onyx intaglio man's profile 175.00
Pin, Danecraft, sterling flower wreath, 1¼" dia 40.00
Pin, Geo Jensen, opposing poppies center dk bl cab, #236 ....175.00
Pin, Geo Jensen, stylized bird w/foliate surround, silver, 2" 175.00
Pin, Kramer, silver stylized human forms, ca 1950, 2" 200.00
Pin, Sigi, silver stylized fish w/purple cab eye, 2½" 100.00
Pin, Wm Spratling, silver/tortoise shell lover's knot, 2" 875.00
Pin, 18k yg starburst set w/sm r/c dmns centering pearl 345.00
Pin, 18k yg woven mesh circle designed as a bow, European 160.00
Ring, yg, 36 sm Bohemian garnets 75.00
Ring, 10k w/emerald-cut 10mmx8mm synthetic alexandrite 70.00
Ring, 14k, set w/sm synthetic ruby & dmn 145.00
Ring, 14k, 15 pave rubies 2.50 tw, 4 sm dmn ea side, modern 245.00
Ring, 14k wg, .40ct Euro dmn in eng mt 400.00
Ring, 14k wg, oval jade 17.5x11.6mm, +2 rows of sm dmns 300.00
Ring, 14k wg w/2 Euro dmn tw .60ct 600.00
Ring, 14k yg, heart-shape amethyst+19 dmns tw 1ct 1,200.00
Ring, 14k yg, 16x22mm topaz+18 4mm cultured pearls 450.00
Ring, 14k yg designed as a wizard, .50 ct dmn 575.00
Ring, 14k yg w/marquise sapphires & tw .50ct dmns 460.00
Ring, 14k yg w/1 lg & 4 sm tourmalines 500.00
Ring, 14k yg w/2 .10 dmns w/8 seed pearls, flower form 270.00
Ring, 14k yg w/7mm pearl amid bl enamel leaves 75.00
Ring, 18k plat, 7 sapphires w/8 sm dmns ea side 475.00
Ring, 18k wg, sq w/sm dmns surrounding center dmn .33ct 260.00
Ring, 18k yg, fluted dome mt, heavy 175.00
Ring, 18k yg, gr tourmaline cluster style 185.00
Ring, 18k yg bypass mt, 2 cultured pearls+sm dmn accents 150.00
Ring, 18k yg ram's head, textured finish 200.00
Ring, 18k yg w/lg faceted smoky topaz 135.00
Stickpin, amethyst 8x6mm in wg, .03ct dmn 95.00

Tie bar, Geo Jensen, sterling, #51 ....175.00

Costume Jewelry

Bracelet, Lanvin Paris, gp w/geometric blk/purple/wht, 1½" 40.00
Bracelet, Les Bernard (unsgn), gp w/blk enamel & r/stns 35.00
Bracelet, pave set r/stns on wht metal links, ¾" W 45.00
Bracelet, Weiss, r/stns, dbl row sq links, ⅜" W 50.00
Bracelet, Weiss, 19 r/stns, ea 7mm, single row 18.00
Brooch, Miriam Haskell, 1 lg pearl & 17 seed pearls 125.00
Brooch, Weiss, lg rnd gr crystal w/in 5 rows of stns, 2" dia 22.00
Brooch, Weiss, openwork flowers w/mc rnd & marquise r/stns 38.00
Charm, Cini, sterling owl on branch, 1" 25.00
Choker, Carnegie, 13-strand crystal beads 60.00
Earrings, Carnegie, 2-sections: ea w/2 'pearls'+5 r/stns 15.00
Earrings, Kramer, Aurora Borealis, ¾" dia 20.00
Earrings, Marino, chrome bows, 1" 10.00
Earrings, Marvella, lg gray baroque pearls on gold leaf, ⅞" 15.00
Earrings, sterling w/marcasites, 3 curved rows, 1⅛" 55.00
Necklace, Accessocraft, long flat chrome links, 15" 20.00

Necklace, Hattie Carnegie, butterfly form with purple and red cabochons, 5½x7" on chain, $350.00.

Necklace, Bogoff, r/stns, ½-rnd front designs, lg marquise 65.00
Necklace, Fr SP, ornate links w/12 hanging flowers & leaves 35.00
Necklace, gp sq links w/mc faux gems, +bracelet 45.00
Necklace, Miriam Haskell, pearl & 'gold' rope 75.00
Necklace, Miriam Haskell, pearls w/butterfly, choker style 75.00
Necklace, Trifari, 14 sections, ea w/leaves & grad r/stns 45.00
Pin, Austria, brn r/stns & faux gems, moonstone center, 2" 35.00
Pin, bar; Kenneth Lane, gr plastic & r/stns 50.00
Pin, cameo, wht on blk celluloid, 1⅞" 30.00
Pin, cvd bone, flowers on leaves, 2" 22.00
Pin, David Anderson, bl enameled leaf form 55.00
Pin, Eisenberg, gr & wht r/stns form bouquet, 1940s 150.00
Pin, Eisenberg Ice, red & wht r/stns 100.00
Pin, flower bouquet set w/r/stns, red cab center stns, 3" 35.00
Pin, Kim, copper, Art Moderne seated cat, 3" 20.00
Pin, Krementz, r/stn flowers, SP, 1¾" dia 20.00
Pin, LJM, brn tortoise glass cameo, ornate gp fr, r/stns 20.00
Pin, Scotty dog, wht glass on gold metal, mc r/stn trim, 2" 25.00
Pin, Sterlingcraft by Coro, gold on sterling, birds/branch 40.00
Pin, Weiss, marquise r/stns, 5 sm r/stn flowers, 2" 30.00
Sweater guard, pearl chain, palm trees over bl butterfly wings 8.00

Josef Originals

Josef Original figurines were designed by Muriel Joseph George of

Arcadia, California, from 1946 until she retired in 1982. (The spelling Josef was a printer error in the first labels for Pitty Sing. The first retail sale and time did not permit them to correct it, so it remains 'Josef Originals.) They were made in California until the early 1960s, at which time George Good (her representative and soon-to-be partner) convinced her to go to Japan to remain competive in the marketplace. All figures produced in Japan were made to her exact specifications, and the quality continued to be very high. After she retired, her partner, George Good, retained the Josef name and produced figurines until 1985 (she still designed some things for him), when he sold the company to Applause. They continue to make Josef figurines, though pieces are limited and not of the same quality. Examples below are from the period of the 1940s through the 1980s (before Muriel's retirement), when the girls were all made with black eyes and a glossy finish, the animals with a semigloss finish. Prices are for figurines in perfect condition; one with repair or damage is not considered collectible. Caution: we have found figurines that have Josef labels, but are not Josef Originals. All Josef Originals are marked with an oval sticker, either with the California or Japan designation, and all (except the animals) carry either an incised or ink-stamped mark, 'Josef Originals©'. Our advisors for this category are Jim and Kaye Whitaker (Eclectic Antiques), authors of *Josef Originals*; their address is in the Directory under Washington.

Birthday Girl #12, holds mirror, pk gown, blk eyes 35.00
Birthday Girl #3, w/bucket, bl gown, blk eyes, Japan 30.00
Birthstone Doll, March, aqua dress & stones, Japan 22.00
Birthstone Doll, November, orange dress & stones, Japan 22.00
California Belle, Chapel Belle, pk gown w/hymnal, CA bsk, 7" ...32.00
Camel, standing, Japan, 6¾" 60.00

Christmas lady music box, fur collar, 6½", $85.00.

Doll of the month, w/birthstones, California, 3¼", ea 35.00
Frogs, various poses & szs, gr, ea 14.00
Gigi series, w/tennis racket, wht & gray dress, Japan 90.00
Impossible Dream music box boy & girl, rose/bl, Japan, 6½" 90.00
Little Internat'l, Africa, girl in wht, pk feather, Japan, 4" 33.00
Little Internat'l, America, Indian girl, Japan, 4" 33.00
Little Internat'l, Hungary, mauve/wht/bl w/gold, Japan, 4" 33.00
Little Internat'l, Russia, rose dress, wht hat, Japan, 4" 33.00
Little Internat'l, Sweden, gray & wht, w/flowers, Japan, 4" 33.00
Little TV, cowboy w/lg hat, rope, chaps & guns, Calif '53, 5¼" 75.00
Mama, pk gold, holds hat, California, 7¼" 80.00
Mary Ann, pk gown (matches Mama's), holding flower 35.00
Mice, various poses & costumes, semigloss, Japan, ea 17.00
Monkeys, various poses & szs, Japan, ea 18.00
Pitty Sing, Chinese boy w/lg hat & kitten, California 50.00
Rabbits, various poses, 3" to 5", ea 16.00

Robin, Musicale series, bl gown, w/harp, Japan, 6" 65.00

Judaica

The items listed below are representative of objects used in both the secular and religious life of the Jewish people. They are evident of a culture where silversmiths, painters, engravers, writers, and metal workers were highly gifted and skilled in their art. Most of the treasures shown in recently displayed exhibits of Judaica were confiscated by the Germans during the late 1930s up to 1945; by then eight Jewish synagogues and fifty warehouses had been filled with Hitler's plunder. Judaica is currently available through dealers, from private collections, and the annual auction held in Israel.

Belt buckle, silver, Moses/Aron/putti/etc, Shreve & Low, 7" **700.00**
Candelabra, brass, 3-arm, lions support Star of David, 14", pr **500.00**
Candelabrum, Polish brass, 7-light, scrollwork, 1800s, 12" **175.00**
Case, metal w/eng silver front; holds counting of Omer scroll **700.00**
Hanukkah dreidl, Schor, silver, sq, rtcl/eng sides, stemmed, 2" ...**3,500.00**

Hanukkah lamp, German silver, flower heads and classical swags, eight arms, early 1900s, 8⅜", $800.00.

Hanukkah lamp, Am SP, 8-socket, branches/foliage, 11" **325.00**
Hanukkah lamp, Polish brass, architectural w/lions, 13" **2,400.00**
Hanukkah lamp, Polish SP, eng lions/peacock, 8-font, 13" **985.00**
Hanukkah lamp, Polish SP, 1800s, 9x9½" **275.00**
Hat, deeply cupped, mc woven yarns w/appl metal pcs, 1920 .....**435.00**
Kiddush cup, Moscow, eng silver, cylindrical, 1874, 2½" **225.00**
Kiddush cup, Russian silver, bright-cut eng, 1890s, 2" **275.00**
Kiddush goblet, silver Augsburg type, flowers/scrolls, 5" **300.00**
Menorah, brass, arms adjust, 16¾x15½" **175.00**
Menorah, Portugal, Continental silver, emb foliage, 19" **1,250.00**
Mezuzah, Am silver, eng zodiac rondells, allover rtcl, 7" **4,800.00**
Necklace, bride's, silver filigree pendants/balls, Yemen, 1800s ...**385.00**
Passover decanter, ruby etch/pnt glass, vintage motif, 12" **325.00**
Passover Matzah plate, ceramic, wht w/blk text, 1920s, 10" **275.00**
Passover Seder plate, pewter, 1708, w/20th-C inscriptions, 15" ..**600.00**
Passover Seder plate, silver, eng text/symbolic foods, 13" **700.00**
Plaque, brass, Shatz monogram/verse, fr w/appl plaques, 24" ...**1,100.00**
Sabbath candlesticks, silver, eng leaves, Warsawie, 14", pr **1,100.00**
Sabbath plate, Schor, wood w/silver plaque, 13", +knife **13,200.00**
Shavuot vase, ruby glass w/eng lions & flowers, 9", VG **165.00**
Shawl, blk cotton net w/silver strip embr w/house, 1920 ....**120.00**
Spice container, silver fish form, garnet eyes, mk, 7½" **550.00**
Spice tower, Austro-Hungarian silver, 3-tier, filigree, 10" **875.00**
Spice tower, Continental silver, revolving finial, 7½" **500.00**
Sugar tongs, delicate filigree, appl flowers, Bazael label **190.00**
Synagogue paddle, wooden hand shape w/admonishment, 1800s, 14" .**2,640.00**
Torah breast plate, English silver, 1923, 12" **2,000.00**
Torah pointer, Russian silver, chased florals, 1827 mk, 7½" **375.00**

Vase, brass, 3 Stars of David enclosing scenes, 1913, 8" **525.00**
Woodcut print, Hanukkah, Forst Siegmond, 12x9" **75.00**

Jugtown

The Jugtown Pottery was started about 1920 by Juliana and Jacques Busbee, in Moore County, North Carolina. Ben Owen, a young descendant of a Staffordshire potter, was hired in 1923. He was the master potter, while the Busbees experimented with perfecting glazes and supervising design and modeling. Preferred shapes were those reminiscent of traditional country wares and classic Oriental forms. Glazes were various: natural-clay oranges, buffs, 'tobacco-spit' brown, mirror black, white, 'frog-skin' green, a lovely turquoise called Chinese blue, and the traditional cobalt-decorated salt glaze. The pottery gained national recognition, and as a result of their success, several other local potteries were established. Jugtown is still in operation; however, they no longer use their original glaze colors which are now so collectible.

Candlestick, thick wht w/exposed clay, cupped top, 11" **125.00**
Vase, blk gloss, pear shape, 3¾x3½" **125.00**
Vase, brn & gr, 6" **90.00**

Vases, Chinese Blue with areas of exposed red clay: Ovoid, 7", $565.00; Inkwell form, 3½", $245.00.

Vase, brn w/drippy yel, 3-hdl, circular mk, 6" **95.00**
Vase, Chinese bl, 6x7" **600.00**
Vase, Chinese bl drip on red/brn clay, 5½x5" **500.00**
Vase, dk bl mottled matt, ovoid, 5x3½" **475.00**
Vase, gr, 4" **75.00**
Vase, gr/brn matt, ogee sides, 11" **190.00**
Vase, opaque wht matt, bulbous w/4 strap neck hdls, 9x6" **400.00**
Vase, robin's egg bl/red gloss, pear form, 6¼x4¾" **325.00**

K. P. M. Porcelain

Under the tutelage of Frederick the Great, King of Prussia, porcelain manufacture was instituted in Berlin in 1751 by William K. Wegeley. In jealous competition with Meissen, hard-paste porcelain was produced (dinnerware, figurines, vases, etc.), some of which were undecorated while other pieces were hand painted in Watteau scenes, landscapes, or florals. It soon became evident that the factory was unable to offer serious competition. The King withdrew his support, and the factory failed in 1757. In 1761 Johann Ernst Gotzkowsky bought the rights and attempted a similar operation which soon failed due to financial difficulties. Still determined to gain the same recognition enjoyed by Meissen, the King bought the plant in 1763 and ruled the operation with an iron hand, often assuring his success by taking advantage of his position. The King died in 1786, but production has continued and quality tableware and decorative porcelains are still being made on a commercial basis. Earliest marks were simply 'G' or 'W,' followed by the scepter mark. After 1830 'K.P.M.' with an orb or eagle was adopted. Our advisor for this category is Don Williams; he is listed in the Directory under Missouri.

Basket, fruit; rtcl, HP floral center, w/gilt, hdls, 13" L **700.00**
Compote, putti/seashell on mermaid std, sea horse base, 12" ...**1,500.00**
Figurine, boy w/flute & birdcage **245.00**
Fruit bucket, floral, rtcl, pk & gold knob, 1800s, 12" **1,000.00**
Plaque, draped nude, sgn Wagner, 6½x4½" **2,500.00**

Plaque, Daphne with laurel crown, signed Wagner, scepter mark, gilt frame, 9" diameter, $4,400.00.

Plaque, Gute Nacht, girl w/chamberstick, sgn Gross, 7½x5" ...**2,500.00**
Plaque, mtn scene, sgn STB/DIE Wand, 11x9" **635.00**
Plaque, reclining maid reads book propped up w/skull, 6x9" ...**2,500.00**
Plaque, Solitude, seated seminude, gesso & gilt fr, 9x6" **4,800.00**
Plaque, Yum-Yum, from Mikado, sgn Wagner Wien, fr, 13x9" .**6,800.00**
Tureen, soup; floral, putti finial, scroll hdls, +tray **935.00**
Vase, 2 floral reserves on encrusted gold, 8" **675.00**

Kayserzinn Pewter

J.P. Kayser Sohn produced pewter decorated with relief-molded Art Nouveau motifs in Germany during the late 1800s and into the 20th century. Examples are marked with 'Kayserzinn' and the mold number within an elongated oval reserve. Items with dimensional animals, insects, birds, etc., are valued much higher than bowls, plates, and trays with simple embossed florals, which are usually priced at $100.00 to about $200.00, depending on size.

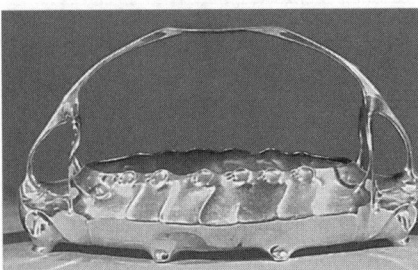

Cake basket, chased vines and berries, handle attached to three stems at each end, six small feet, #4529, marked, 17¼" long, $1,000.00.

Bonbon, shell form w/Art Nouveau nude, sgn/#4136, 8x6¾" **195.00**
Bowl, appl floral, hdls, #4227, 13½" **100.00**

Bowl, serving; sunflowers & dragonfly, oval, #4120, 10¼x6" **130.00**
Candelabrum, 2-arm, T-form std, #4531, 10½" **1,200.00**
Chamberstick, stylized sunflowers, 2-pc, #4144 ....**230.00**
Flagon, acorns & leaves, squirrel finial, 13" **465.00**
Pitcher, satyr's face & iris mold, #4061, 12½" **385.00**
Sugar bowl, Dragon Ship form, open, 8" L **165.00**
Tray/inkwell, lotus lilies, dragonfly, #4256, 9x14" **500.00**
Vase, emb skull & horn motif, chalice form, #4500 ....**900.00**
Vase, emb vintage, #49, 12" **200.00**

Keen Kutter

Keen Kutter was a brand name of E.C. Simmons Hardware, used from about 1870 until the mid-1930s. In 1923 Winchester merged with Simmons but continued to produce Keen Kutter-marked knives and tools. The merger dissolved, and in 1940 the Simmons Company was purchased by Shapleigh Hardware. Older items are very collectible. For further study we recommend *Keen Kutter*, an illustrated price guide by Jerry and Elaine Heuring, available at your favorite bookstore or public library.

In the following listings, values are for examples in excellent condition, unless otherwise noted. See also Knives.

Awl, brad; K110 ....**15.00**
Axe, broad; KP67 ....**75.00**
Axe, camp; K30 ....**30.00**
Axe, Dayton pattern; KD113 ....**40.00**
Axe, house; KHA **25.00**
Axe, New Yankee pattern; KY300 ....**40.00**
Axe, Scout; K20, w/sheath **45.00**
Axe, western pattern; KR360 ....**50.00**
Axe, Wisconsin pattern; KW304 ....**40.00**
Bit, auger; K3-20, 16 szs, ea **10.00**
Bit, electrician's, KE60, 6 szs, ea **10.00**
Bit, extension; K180, 18-24", ea **25.00**
Blower, K1900 ....**75.00**
Brace, bit; K10, 10" **25.00**
Brace, bit; K16, 6" **50.00**
Brace, corner; K500 ....**100.00**
Brace, drill; KD10 ....**150.00**
Chisel, butt; KFB ¼-2, 10 szs, ¼"-2", ea **20.00**
Chisel, butt; KF5, 5-pc **100.00**
Chisel, firmer; KSA8, 8-pc set **150.00**
Chisel, gouge; KOB⅛, 12 szs, ⅛"-2" **20.00**
Draw knife, K8, 8" **45.00**
Drill, hand; K5, 13½" **40.00**
File, KM4 ....**15.00**
Gauge, marking; K26 ....**25.00**
Glass cutter, dmn point, mk leather case **75.00**
Hammer, bill poster's, K55, 5-oz **25.00**
Hammer, blacksmith's, KBB3, 48-oz **45.00**
Hammer, nail; K1½ , 16-oz **25.00**
Hammer, saw-setting; KBSS, 7-oz **25.00**
Hammer, tack; K500, 8-oz **25.00**
Hatchet, broad; KBB5 ....**30.00**
Hatchet, flooring; KCB0 ....**30.00**
Hatchet, rig builder's, KRBG **30.00**
Hatchet, shingling; KBS51 ....**25.00**
Level, iron, K624, 24" **100.00**
Level, iron, K69, 9" **100.00**
Level, wooden, KO/30, 30" **25.00**
Level, wooden, K5/26, 26" **40.00**
Mallet, K216 ....**25.00**

Measuring tape, pocket model, K48, 8-ft 25.00
Nippers, cutting; K6 ....25.00
Outside caliper, K34 ....25.00
Pincers, carpenter's, K812 ....25.00
Plane, block; K120, 7½" 25.00
Plane, block; K19, 7" 30.00
Plane, block; K65, 7" 30.00
Plane, circular; K200, 10" 250.00
Plane, combination; K64, 21 cutters 350.00
Plane, fore; K6C, 18" 40.00
Plane, jack; KJ, 15" 45.00
Plane, jack; K26, 15" 45.00
Plane, jack; K5½ , 15" 50.00
Plane, rabbet & fillester; K78, 8½" 50.00
Plane, rabbet; K10, 13" 200.00
Plane, scrub; K240, 9½" 60.00
Plane, smooth; KHS, 9½" 45.00
Plane, smooth; K35, 9" 45.00
Plane, smooth; K4½ C, 10" 60.00
Pliers, chain-nose; K65 ....25.00
Pliers, combination; K160 ....25.00
Pliers, flat-nose; K16 ....25.00
Pliers, lineman's, K966 ....25.00
Pliers, milliner's, K51 ....25.00
Plumb bob, K60 ....45.00
Router, K171, 7½" 50.00
Rule, steel, K312, 12" 25.00
Rule, 2-fold, K360, w/caliper, 6" 40.00
Rule, 4-fold, K620, 24" 30.00
Rule, 6-fold, K503, 36" 50.00
Saw, back; K44 ....30.00
Saw, back; K97, adjustable 40.00
Saw, compass; K95 ....30.00
Saw, crosscut; K1006 ....40.00
Saw, hack; K48 ....25.00
Saw, hand; K816 ....25.00
Saw set, K195 ....25.00
Scraper, cabinet; K79, 11" 25.00
Scraper, cabinet; K90, 11" 45.00
Screwdriver, cabinet; K45, 6 szs, 3"-10", ea 15.00
Screwdriver, offset; K7, 7" 20.00
Spoke shave, K95 ....25.00
Square, carpenter's, K3, steel, 24" 25.00
Square, takedown; KTR100, 24" 100.00
Square, try; K226, 6" 40.00
Staple puller, K700 ....25.00
Tack puller, K5 ....15.00
Work bench, K15 ....300.00
Wrecking bar, KWC, 18" 25.00
Wrench, dbl-end; K23, 9 szs, 4"-13", ea 20.00
Wrench, monkey; KB6, 6" 50.00
Wrench, pipe; KW14, 14" 30.00

Kelva

Kelva was a trademark of the C.F. Monroe Company of Meriden, Connecticut; it was produced for only a few years after the turn of the century. It is distinguished from the Wave Crest and Nakara lines by its unique Batik-like background, probably achieved through the use of a cloth or sponge to apply the color. Large florals are hand painted on the opaque milk glass; and ormolu and brass mounts were used for the boxes, vases, and trays. Most pieces are signed. Our advisors for this category are Dolli and Wilfred Cohen; they are listed in the Directory under California.

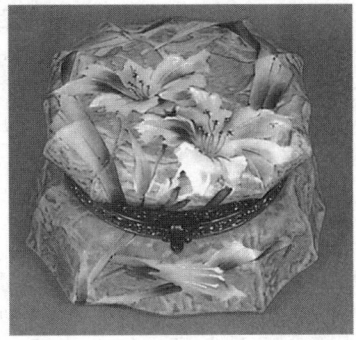

Box, exotic flowers on blown-out hexagon, ormolu collar, original lining, 3" high, $365.00.

Biscuit jar, floral, wht on peach, SP lid & hdl, rare 850.00
Box, floral, bl-gray on red, 3½x6" dia 695.00
Box, floral, pk on bl-gray, mirror in lid, 3¾x4½" 595.00
Box, metal filigree, glass lid w/floral, 3x3¼" 450.00
Box, petunias, pk on gr, 3¾x8" dia 895.00
Box, wild roses, pk on gr, sq, hinged lid, 2¾x4" 425.00
Ferner, floral, bl & wht on dk pk, ftd, 6¼x7¾" 575.00
Humidor, floral & Cigars on gr, cylindrical, 4¾" 695.00
Shakers, floral, pk on gr, 3", pr 325.00
Tray, Crown Mold, floral on gr, 6" dia 300.00
Tray, daisies on maroon, rnd w/emb metal rim, rope hdl, 3½" 195.00
Tray, floral, pk on gr, hexagonal, 4" 215.00
Vase, daisies, wht on burgundy mottle, squat hex base, 13" 750.00
Vase, floral on red, emb wht ribbons wrap base, ftd, 8x3" 595.00
Vase, floral on rose, trumpet form w/4 ormolu ft, 6x2" 495.00
Whisk broom holder, floral, pk on bl 895.00

Kenton Hills

Kenton Hills Porcelain was established in 1940 in Erlanger, Kentucky, by Harold Bopp, former Rookwood superintendent, and David Seyler, noted artist and sculptor. Native clay was used; glazes were very similar to Rookwood's of the same period. The work was of high quality, but because of the restrictions imposed on needed material due to the onset of the war, the operation failed in 1942. Much of the ware is artist signed and marked with the Kenton Hills name or cipher and shape number.

Vase, bl gloss, HB mk, #111, 6" 180.00
Vase, daisies, pk & bl on wht, sgn Brunner, #168, 5½x3½" 350.00
Vase, dk gr tiger-eye glaze, tiny rim, 8½" 450.00
Vase, floral spray, butterfat glaze, Dickman, #188, 5x3½" 275.00
Vase, leaves & flowers, peach & bl, Wm Hentschel, 12" 450.00
Vase, red aventurine, squat, 3¼x4" 250.00

Kew Blas

Kew Blas was a trade name used by the Union Glass Company of Summerville, Massachusetts, for their iridescent, lustered art glass produced from 1893 until about 1920. The glass was made in imitation of Tiffany and achieved notable success. Some items were decorated with pulled leaf and feather designs, while others had a monochrome lustre surface. The mark was an engraved 'Kew Blas' in an arching arrangement.

Candlestick, gold, swirled baluster stem, wide base, 8" 250.00
Candlesticks, mc irid, wide flat ft, sgn, 8x5", pr 675.00
Compote, gold ribbed bowl, sgn, 4x5½" 300.00
Goblet, amber irid, raised rim, 5" 115.00
Vase, feathers on wht, gold int, waisted, 8x4" 1,275.00
Vase, gold irid w/gr 'snakeskin,' scalloped, 4½" 650.00

Vase, veins on gold irid, slender, 12" 1,000.00
Vase, zippered pattern, gr & gold, rose bowl form, sgn, 4½" 625.00

King's Rose

King's Rose is a soft-paste ware that was made in Staffordshire, England, from about 1820 to 1830. It is closely related to Gaudy Dutch in body type as well as the colors used in its decoration. The pattern consists of a full-blown, orange-red rose with green, pink, and yellow leaves and accents. When the rose is in pink, the ware is often referred to as Queen's Rose.

Cake plate, Queen's, floral rim band, rose in center, 10" 165.00
Creamer, minor wear & stain, 4¾" 190.00
Cup & saucer, handleless; pk border, wear 85.00
Cup & saucer, line border, wear 85.00
Cup & saucer, Queen's, swirl mold, saucer w/bl dot border 225.00
Cup & saucer, red rose, vine border, NM 200.00
Cup plate, 3½", EX 110.00

Plates, solid border, 9¾", EX, four for $500.00.

Plate, minor flaking, 8½" 105.00
Plate, pearlware, major rpr to polychrome, 10" 85.00
Plate, pk rose, vine border, shaped rim, 7", NM 160.00
Plate, sectional border, lt wear, 9¾" 165.00
Plate, toddy; Queen's, scalloped, 5½" 110.00
Plate, 8½" 165.00
Teapot, prof rpr, 6" 300.00
Teapot, sectional border, lt wear, 6" 425.00
Waste bowl, solid border, lt wear, 2¾x5⅝" 200.00

Kitchen Collectibles

During the last half of the 1850s, mass-produced kitchen gadgets were patented at an astonishing rate. Most were ingeniously efficient. Apple peelers, egg beaters, cherry pitters, food choppers, and such were only the most common of hundreds of kitchen tools well designed to perform only specific tasks. Today all are very collectible.

We should note here that cast-iron counterfeit production is on its way up. Phony production numbers, finishes, etc., are being made at this time. Many of these new pieces are the popular cornstick pans. Buyer beware! Our advisor for Cast Kitchen Ware is Denise Harned, who is the author of *Griswold Cast Collectibles*. She is listed in the Directory under Connecticut. We also recommend *Kitchen Glassware of the Depression Years* by Gene Florence and *Kitchen Antiques, 1790-1940*, by Kathryn McNerney. See also Appliances; Fry; Glass Knives; Molds; Primitives; Reamers; Tinware; Wooden Ware.

Cast Kitchen Ware

Aebleskiver pan, Griswold #32 ....75.00
Bundt pan, Frank Hay #965 (made by Griswold) 300.00
Bundt pan, Griswold, rare 1,250.00
Cake mold, lamb, Griswold #866 ....185.00
Cake mold, Santa, Griswold 550.00
Cornbread pan, Wagner, tea sz 75.00

Crispy cornstick pan, Griswold #262, miniature, 4x8½", $125.00.

Cornstick pan, Griswold #273 ....115.00
Cornstick pan, Krusty Korn Kob Jr, Wagner, 1920 ....50.00
Dutch oven, Griswold #10, Tite Top, lg emblem 75.00
Dutch oven, Griswold #10 Chuckwagon, 3-leg, lg emblem 145.00
Dutch oven, Griswold #8, w/trivet, sm emblem 60.00
Golf ball pan, Griswold #9, 10⅜x7" 115.00
Griddle, Griswold #8, bail hdl 120.00
Griddle, Griswold #9, rectangular 125.00
Kettle, Griswold #3, Erie, 8" 100.00
Kettle, Griswold #8, Maslin shape, 6-qt 125.00
Muffin pan, Griswold #17 ....75.00
Muffin pan, Reids Pan Dec 1870, 13 muffins, 16¾x9" 160.00
Muffin pan, 6 fruit-shaped muffins, unmk, 9½x6¾" 78.00
Popover pan, Griswold #10, 11⅛x7⅝" 75.00
Popover pan, Griswold #18 ....75.00
Roaster, Wagner #5, no lid 95.00
Skillet, egg; Griswold, sq w/hdl on corner 90.00
Skillet, Griswold #0, lg emblem, no smoke ring 85.00
Skillet, Griswold #10, lg emblem, no smoke ring 70.00
Skillet, Griswold #12, Erie, lg emblem, heat ring 80.00
Skillet, Griswold #14, lg emblem, no smoke ring 150.00
Skillet, Griswold #2, sm emblem 65.00
Skillet, Griswold #8, deep, w/lid 150.00
Skillet, Jos Bell & Co, Wheeling WV, pitting, 11½" 85.00
Skillet, Victor #8 ....55.00
Skillet, Wagner #10 ....45.00
Skillet, Wapak Indian #9 ....105.00
Skillet/griddle, Griswold #109 ....115.00
Teakettle, George Starrett...1868 on lid, gooseneck spout 100.00
Teakettle, Wagner, child sz 95.00
Vienna roll pan, Griswold #2 ....95.00
Waffle iron, Detroit Iron & Brass Co #7 & 8, Pat...1877 ....75.00
Waffle iron, GF Filley 75.00
Waffle iron, Griswold #11, sq, w/stand 135.00
Waffle iron, Heart & Star, Griswold 160.00
Waffle iron stand, Wagner 65.00
Wheat stick pan, Griswold #27 ....185.00

Egg Beaters

Egg beaters are an unbeatable collectible. Ranging from handhelds to rotary cranks, to squeeze power, to Archimedes up-and-down models, egg beaters are America's favorite kitchen gadget. A mainstay of any kitchenware collection, egg beaters in recent years have come into their own — nutmeg graters, spatulas and can openers will have to scramble to catch up. At the turn of the century, everyone in America owned an egg beater. Every household did its own mixing and baking — there were no pre-processed foods. And every inventor thought he/she could make a better beater. Thus American ingenuity produced more than 1,000 egg beater patents, dating back to 1856, with several hundred different models being manufactured over the years. As a true piece of Americana, the egg beater has risen in value over the past couple of years, with a half dozen mixers valued at $1,000.00. But the vast majority are in the under $20.00 range. And just when you think you've seen them all, new ones always — always — turn up, usually at flea markets or garage sales. For further information, we recommend our advisor (author of the definitive book on egg beaters) Don Thornton, who is listed in the Directory under California. See also Clubs and Newsletters for Kollectors of Old Kitchen Stuff (KOOKS).

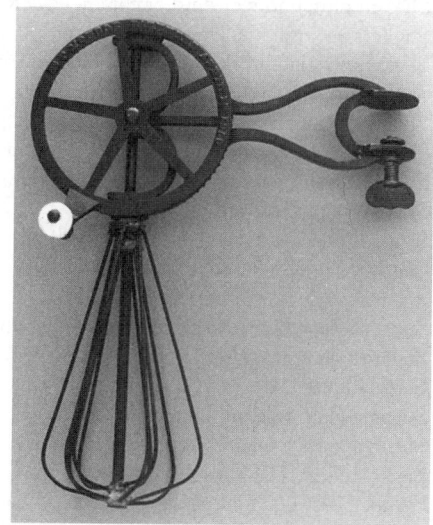

E.P. Monroe, Patented April 19, 1859, 10½", $165.00.

Aluminum Beauty Pat'd April 20, 1920..., rotary crank, 10½" **15.00**
Another Androck Product Pat No 2210910, rotary crank, 10¾" ..**15.00**
Beats Eggs, Cream...No 825 Androck, hand-held fan type, 11" **5.00**
Biltrite...Pat Stuber & Kuck..., rotary crank, wood hdl, 10½" **30.00**
Dover...Patd May 6th 1873...1891..., CI rotary crank, 11¼" **50.00**
Horlicks, Archimedes, all-wire drink mixer, 9¼" **30.00**
Jiffy Whip...Krasbert & Sons' Mfg, rotary crank turbine, 11¾" **25.00**
Patent No 2906510, hand held, plastic hdl **5.00**
Quik Whip Reg US Pat Off...Pending, metal, squeeze power, 11¼" ..**80.00**
Super Speed A&J Spinnit..., rotary turbine, wood hdl, 11½" **30.00**
Turbine Beater Androck Made in USA, rotary crank, 11½" **18.00**
Twin Speed Mixer, rotary crank, plastic hdl, 11½" **20.00**
Vandeusen Egg Whip, CA Chapman...1894, all metal, hand held, 11" ..**15.00**
WB-over-W Made in USA, Wallace Bros rotary, wood hdl, 11" **10.00**
Whipwell...USA Pat Mch 23, 1920..., rotary crank, wood hdl, 11" ..**20.00**
Zip Whit S, J&H Dist...Cal, rotary crank, plastic hdl, 13½" **45.00**

Glass

Ashtray, Jadite, Jeannette **8.00**
Baker, Jadite, oval, McKee, 5x3½" **12.00**
Batter bowl, gr, ribbed, Anckor Hocking **30.00**
Batter bowl, Mayfair bl, Anckor Hocking **150.00**
Batter jug, amber, McKee **65.00**

Batter jug, blk, Fenton **125.00**
Batter jug, blk, Paden City **225.00**
Batter jug, gr, Jenkins **300.00**
Batter jug, gr, New Martinsville **65.00**
Batter jug, gr, Paden City **40.00**
Beater bowl, Jadite, w/beater, Jeannette **25.00**
Bottle, oil & vinegar; gr, Paden City **42.50**
Bottle, oil & vinegar; Twist, pk, Heisey **85.00**
Bowl, bl, Hazel Atlas, 10⅝" **55.00**
Bowl, bl, Hazel Atlas, 6" **17.50**
Bowl, bl, Hazel Atlas, 6⅝" **20.00**
Bowl, bl, Hazel Atlas, 8½" **27.50**
Bowl, bl, horizontal rib, Jeannette, 9¾" **75.00**
Bowl, bl, LE Smith, 7¼" **40.00**
Bowl, bl, w/metal beater, Jeannette **50.00**
Bowl, custard or caramel, McKee, 8", ea **18.00**
Bowl, custard or caramel, McKee, 9", ea **20.00**
Bowl, egg beater; Jadite, w/spout, McKee **12.00**
Bowl, Jadite, McKee, 9" **18.00**
Bowl, Jennyware, crystal, 6" **8.00**
Bowl, mixing; amber, McKee, 7⅜" **30.00**
Bowl, mixing; blk, 8⅜" **35.00**
Bowl, mixing; gr, panelled, Hocking, 10¼" **18.00**
Bowl, pk, mk Cambridge, 9¾" **22.00**
Bowl, Restwell, bl, Hazel Atlas, 5¾" **17.50**
Bowl, Tom & Jerry, Jadite, McKee **75.00**
Butter dish, amber, ¼-lb, Federal **25.00**
Butter dish, Block Optic, gr, Hocking **40.00**
Butter dish, Clambroth, gr, Hocking **65.00**
Butter dish, cobalt, emb lid, Hazel Atlas, 1-lb **200.00**

Crisscross cobalt butter dishes by Hazel Atlas: 1-lb, $95.00; ¼-lb, $95.00.

Butter dish, custard, McKee **35.00**
Butter dish, Delphite bl, emb Butter on lid, Jeannette **200.00**
Butter dish, gr, Block Optic **40.00**
Butter dish, gr, emb B on lid, 2-lb, Jeannette **150.00**
Butter dish, pk, emb B, Jeannette, 2-lb **125.00**
Butter dish, pk, emb Butter on lid, Jeannette **55.00**
Butter dish, Seville yel, McKee **65.00**
Butter tub, amber, Federal **25.00**
Cake plate, Snowflake, pk **20.00**
Canister, Chalaine bl, rnd, w/lid, 48-oz **85.00**
Cocktail shaker, gr, Imperial **30.00**
Cocktail shaker, red, Duncan Miller **50.00**
Cookie jar, gr, ribbed, w/coffee lid, Anchor Hocking **40.00**
Crock, gr, Hocking, 8" **40.00**
Crock, Jadite, rnd, knob on top, Jeannette, 40-oz **40.00**
Cruet, bl, New Martinsville **55.00**
Cruet, pk, Hazel Atlas **40.00**
Cruet, yel, Lancaster Glass **75.00**
Cup, Tom & Jerry, Jadite, McKee **10.00**

Curtain rings, forest gr, ea	10.00
Decanter, gr, pinched-in, Hocking	40.00
Dispenser, water; clear w/jade gr top	45.00
Dispenser, water; jade gr, McKee	95.00
Dripolator, clear w/emb ribs, Silex, 2-cup	22.00
Dripolator, red, Silex	175.00
Funnel, crystal, 9"	15.00
Gravy boat, gr, Cambridge	50.00
Gravy boat, pk, dbl, Cambridge	22.00
Ice bucket, Black Forest, pk, Van Deman	65.00
Ice bucket, gr, Fenton	50.00
Ice bucket, gr, w/lid, Fenton	95.00
Ice bucket, Party line, pk, Paden City	30.00
Ice bucket, pk, w/etched flower & sq bottom, Fenton	30.00
Ice bucket, pk, w/sterling bear	50.00
Ice bucket, yel, Fenton, w/lid	125.00
Jell-O mold, pk, Tufglas	25.00
Ladle, amber	8.00
Ladle, blk, rnd bottom	30.00
Ladle, Festive, bl, Duncan	15.00
Ladle, pk or gr	10.00
Match holder, bl, Jeannette	75.00
Measure, amber, w/o hdl, 3-spout, Federal	35.00
Measure, bl, 3-spout, Fire-King	18.00
Measure, Chalaine bl, ftd, w/hdl, 4-cup	200.00
Measure, clear, advertising, Armour, Westmoreland	25.00
Measure, clear, advertising, Owens & Co, Westmoreland	30.00
Measure, clear, Jeannette, ⅓-cup	20.00
Measure, Delphite, Jeannette, ¼-cup	27.50
Measure, Glasbake, fired-on red, McKee	30.00
Measure, gr, Hocking, 1-cup	150.00
Measure, Jadite, Jeannette, set	50.00
Measure, pk, Jeannette, ½ -cup	40.00
Measure, pk, 1-spout, Cambridge, 1-cup	225.00
Measure, ultramarine, Jeannette, 1-cup	45.00
Measure, wht w/trim, 3-spout, Hazel Atlas	65.00
Measure, yel, 3-spout, Hazel Atlas	225.00
Measure pitcher, custard w/red trim, McKee, 2-cup	20.00
Measure pitcher, gr, ribbed, Hocking, 2-cup	45.00
Measure pitcher, gr, sunflower in bottom, Jeannette, 2-cup	95.00
Measure pitcher, wht opaque, floral decal, McKee, 2-cup	22.50
Milk jug, bl, Paden City	40.00
Mug, Adams Rib, pk	18.00
Mug, forest gr, Cambridge	45.00
Mug, Moondrops, cobalt, New Martinsville	35.00
Mug, pk or gr, ftd, Jeannette, ea	25.00
Mug, red, New Martinsville	25.00
Napkin holder, frosted, Nar-O-Fold	35.00
Napkin holder, Paramount, pk, US Glass	350.00
Napkin holder, Party Line, blk, Paden City	135.00
Napkin holder, Party Line, gr, Paden City	85.00
Napkin holder, wht, Slen-Dr-Fold	50.00
Pretzel jar, pk, Hocking	55.00
Refrigerator dish, amber, Federal, rnd, 4½" dia	8.00
Refrigerator dish, bl, Pyrex, 4¼x6¾"	15.00
Refrigerator dish, Chalaine bl, 7¼" sq	110.00
Refrigerator dish, cobalt, flat knob, rnd, 5¼" dia	60.00
Refrigerator dish, gr, oval, Hocking, 8"	35.00
Refrigerator dish, gr, Tufglas, 5⅞" sq	25.00
Refrigerator dish, Jennyware, pk, 4x4"	25.00
Refrigerator dish, Kompakt, gr, Hocking, 4x4"	17.00
Refrigerator dish, pk, Federal, 4x8"	20.00
Refrigerator dish, pk, rnd, Hocking, 4½"	15.00
Rolling pin, Chalaine bl, blown	400.00
Rolling pin, clear w/mc splotches, 1875-1900, 17"	170.00
Rolling pin, cobalt, hdls attached to metal rod inside	400.00
Rolling pin, cobalt, pontiled end, 1870-1900, 18", M	275.00
Rolling pin, custard, McKee	200.00
Rolling pin, Delphite bl, smooth & shaker top ends, McKee	425.00
Rolling pin, forest gr, blown	150.00
Rolling pin, gr, hdls attached to wooden dowel pin	400.00
Rolling pin, milk glass, pnt British flags, 14"	90.00
Rolling pin, Nailsea, red & wht loopings on clear, 15"	210.00
Rolling pin, olive gr w/wht flecks, 1850-70, 15"	125.00
Salad fork & spoon, amber, striped hdl, flattened, set	40.00
Salad fork & spoon, bl, lg pointed hdl	60.00
Salad fork & spoon, bl, set	55.00
Salad fork & spoon, blk, Cambridge, set	110.00
Salad fork & spoon, forest gr, flattened hdl, set	55.00
Salad fork & spoon, red, teardrop hdl, set	60.00
Salad fork & spoon, yel, sm pointed hdl, set	40.00
Salt box, gr, rnd, emb Salt on lid, Jeannette	165.00
Salt box, Jadite, Jeannette	225.00
Sanitary refrigerator jar, gr	150.00
Shaker, cinnamon; custard or caramel, McKee, ea	25.00
Shakers, gr, rnd, metal lid, Hocking, pr	25.00
Shakers, gr clambroth, panelled, Hocking, pr	17.50
Shakers, opaque yel, emb Salt, Hocking, pr	12.00
Shakers, Roman Arch, Delphite bl, McKee, pr	110.00
Shakers, Scotty dog, blk & wht, Hocking, pr	15.00
Shakers, Sombrero Sam, red & wht, metal lid, Hocking, pr	25.00
Shakers, sq, wht, McKee, 16-oz, pr	90.00
Straw holder, pattern glass, crystal, w/lid	275.00
Sugar shaker, amber, Paden City	150.00
Sugar shaker, bl, Cambridge	150.00
Sugar shaker, Delphite bl, sq, metal lid, Jeannette	75.00
Sugar shaker, gr, bullet-shaped, dots on top, McKee	120.00
Sugar shaker, pk	45.00
Sugar shaker, red, mk Hawkes	350.00
Sugar shaker, Roman Arch, custard, McKee	30.00
Sugar shaker, Tilt-a-spoon, cobalt, Paden City	400.00
Syrup, #198, gr, Paden City, 8-oz	35.00
Syrup, #198, gr, w/liner, Paden City, 12-oz	45.00
Syrup, bl, Paden City	35.00
Syrup, clear, w/lid, Paden City	35.00
Syrup, forest gr, New Martinsville	55.00
Syrup, gr, w/liner, Paden City	45.00
Syrup, pk, New Martinsville	40.00
Syrup, pk, Paden City	35.00
Syrup, pk, pnt flowers, Paden City	40.00
Syrup, pk, slotted lid, Imperial	70.00
Syrup, pk Hazel Atlas	45.00
Towel bar, gr, twisted	25.00
Towel bar holder, gr, pr	25.00
Tumbler, amber, McKee	18.00
Tumbler, bl, mk HA (Hazel Atlas)	15.00
Tumbler, gr, ftd, Paden City	10.00
Tumbler, Rena, gr, Paden City	10.00
Water bottle, Crisscross, crystal	5.00
Water bottle, forest gr, Duraglas	25.00
Water bottle, forest gr, Owens-Illinois	15.00
Water bottle, gr, 2-styles, Hocking, 32-oz	20.00
Water bottle, lattice design, crystal, w/lid	50.00

Miscellaneous

Apple & peach peeler, Sinclair Scott Reading, CI, EX	110.00
Apple corer, T-shaped, tin, handmade	22.00

Apple peeler, Goodell, CI, 1898, complete 70.00
Apple peeler, Lockley & Howland, Pat...& Dec 5, 1856, CI 75.00
Apple peeler, Sargent & Foster label, mtd on brd 295.00
Apple peeler, Wht Mtn #3, Goodell, CI, ca 1898, EX 50.00
Apple peeler/corer/slicer, Wht Mountain, MIB 125.00
Apple segmenter, Apple Cutter, Rollman Mfg..., iron & tin 75.00
Biscuit tin, Ivins Bakers of Good...1846, 5¼x5" sq 32.00
Can, Rumford Baking Powder, never opened, 4-oz 22.00
Can opener, Home, CI, dtd Feb 11, '90 ....16.00
Can opener, Iron Marvel, pnt CI, ca 1919, 7¼" 42.00
Can opener, Never Slip, CI, loop hdld, Pat Nov 12, '02 ....14.00
Can opener, wrought iron, bull head, tail forms hdl, 6½" 95.00
Cheese slicer, tin blade w/long wood hdl on pine brd 45.00
Cherry seeder, Goodel Co Antrim NH, CI, ca 1895 ....55.00
Cherry seeder, Home Cherry Stoner...1917...USA, CI, EX 50.00
Cherry seeder, unmk, CI & wood, Pat April 9, 1867 ....70.00
Chopper, wood hdl w/riveted curved metal blade, 5x6½" 20.00
Chopper, wrought-iron blade w/wooden hdl ea end, 1850s, lg 70.00
Churn, Dazey, #10, 1-qt 1,000.00
Churn, Dazey, #20, 2-qt 125.00
Churn, Dazey #30, 3-qt 95.00
Churn, Dazey #40, 1-gal 80.00
Churn, Lightning Butter Machine, Pat 1917, #20 ....89.00
Churn, Universal Butter Merger & Family Churn, #125 ....450.00
Churn, unmk, glass, 1-qt 195.00
Coconut shredder, CI, clamps on, ca 1920 ....90.00
Cream remover, Elgin, Pat 5-1-23, MIB w/instructions 8.50
Cream whipper, Fries, tin, side crank, 11" 110.00
Crimper, brass wheel, waffle design on tamper end 42.00
Crimper, tin wheel, shaped wooden hdl, 6¾" 35.00
Crimper, wht pottery blade, trn wood hdl, 7" 75.00
Cutter, biscuit; Jenny Wren Flour, tin w/strap hdl, sm 7.50
Cutter, biscuit; Kreamer, strap hdl, sm 8.00
Cutter, doughnut; Horsford's Baking Powder, tin 25.00
Cutter, doughnut; Rumford 27.50
Cutter, kraut; cherry w/lollipop crest, old patina, 18" 75.00
Cutter, kraut; walnut w/iron blade, dk patina, 20x7¾" 65.00
Cutter, marmalade; Universal, CI, clamp type 145.00
Dough scraper, hand wrought w/heart cutout on blade, 4x3" 120.00
Egg separator, JA Frost Grocer, tin 12.50
Egg separator, Use Boss Flour, tin, EX 12.50
Grater, Gentleman's, CI, ca 1880, EX 215.00
Grater, horseradish; Houghin Mfg Co NY, CI, crank hdl, 1872 .230.00
Grater, nutmeg; Bogar, ca 1896, EX 110.00
Grater, nutmeg; CI, Pat June 7, 1870 on lid, trn hdl, 6" 260.00
Grater, nutmeg; Edgar, dk tin w/wood, Pat Nov 10, 1896 ....90.00
Grater, nutmeg; Gem, Caldwell, CI & tin w/wood hdls, 1890s ..125.00
Grater, nutmeg; tin & wood, 4½" 105.00
Grater, punched tin, half-circle shape 35.00
Grater, punched tin, pegged wooden fr, 1840s, 14x4¾" 80.00
Grater, punched tin in wooden box fr, 9¾"+4" hdl 150.00
Grater, tin w/crank hdl, wooden pusher, table clamp 25.00
Grinder, Griswold #1, NMIB 45.00
Grinder, handmade, spiked rollers in wood box, 1860s, 11x7x7" ..150.00
Grinder, Landers Frary & Clark, CI, crank hdl, 11" 125.00
Grinder, nut; Androck, glass bottom 20.00
Ice cube breaker, Lightning 80.00
Jar lifter & opener, Iron Hottongs, lg 15.00
Juicer, Easley's Pat 3/10/88, cobalt glass, 2½x4½" 160.00
Juicer, Handy Andy 35.00
Lemon squeezer, CI, fluted bowl, 8" L 20.00
Lemon squeezer, iron w/wht ironstone ball & cup, Pat...1868 ......65.00
Lemon squeezer, Little Giant, CI fr, dtd May 3, 1881 ....100.00
Mayonnaise maker, Wesson Oil 75.00

Measure, Maytag, aluminum, mini 11.00
Mixer, margarine; Nucoa Marg, wooden, '20s, 5¾x1½" dia 40.00
Mixer, mayonnaise; Hutchinson 425.00
Mixer, mayonnaise; Universal, no funnel 395.00
Mixer, Robert's Lightning, Pat...1913, glass & tin 32.00
Mold, pudding; Kreamer, tin, 2-pc 35.00
Pan, angel food cake; Swan's Down Cake Flour, tin 30.00
Pan, cake; Calumet Baking Powder, tin, rnd 12.00
Pan, lady finger; Kreamer, 6 riveted cups 25.00
Platter, meat; Griswold, cast aluminum 95.00
Potato masher, dbl wire fulcrum action, wooden hdl, 11½" 50.00
Potato masher, heavy wire w/wooden hdl 12.50
Potato peeler, mk Hamlinite, tin bk w/grit bottom, 1920 ....55.00
Potato ricer, ironstone & metal, late 1800s 135.00
Press, Improved Fruit & Jelly...Aug 12, 1873, CI, 2-pc, EX 95.00
Raisin seeder, Boss, AC Williams, Ravenna OH, clamps on 130.00
Raisin seeder, Everett, wooden, last Pat May 2, '93 ....75.00
Raisin seeder, Gem, dtd Dec 24, 1895, 6" 80.00
Raisin seeder, Landers Frary Clark, clamps on 50.00
Raisin seeder, X-Ray, CI, table clamp, 1880s, 7" 78.00
Scoop, flour; Dover, tin hooded shape w/stick hdl 30.00
Scoop, flour; Jenny Wren Ready Mixed Flour 10.00
Sifter, Androck, tin w/red bands & wooden hdl 20.00
Sifter, Blood's Pat...1861, Dover, wooden, w/stencil & label 350.00
Sifter, Gem Sifter...JL Clark...Rockford IL, tin 22.50
Sifter, Necco, tin, 1-cup 12.50
Slicer, vegetable; iron blade in pine fr, handmade, 11x6½" 22.00
Slicer, vegetable; Specialty Mfg...PA, 6-blade, 1898, EX 85.00
Slicer, vegetable; tin w/slanting cutting blades, 7x18", EX 35.00
Spoon, mixing; Fidelity The Flour Supreme, opener end 10.00
Spoon, stuffing; Gerighty Co, Toledo OH, heavy plate, 1948 ......45.00
Sprinkler bottle, cat w/bl marble eyes, curled tail, 8" 80.00
Sprinkler bottle, clothespin, 8", from $45 to 65.00
Sprinkler bottle, sadiron, girl ironing 46.50
Sprinkler bottle, sadiron, gr 35.00
Sprinkler bottle, Siamese cat, from $75 to 85.00
Sprinkler bottle, Sprinkle Plenty, Chinese man, red & blk 45.00
Sprinkler bottle, Victorian lady w/purse 120.00
Strainer, tea; Compliments of Belmont Realty...RI, tin 15.00
Strainer, tea; SP, on stand, hook side hdl, sm 15.00
Strawberry huller, Boston Huller, brass, Pat Oct 30, '94 ....20.00
Sugar devil/fruit auger, wood hdl, Pat July 27, 1875, 16x10" 110.00
Sugar nippers, iron, scissors shape, dbl crescent blades, 9" 150.00
Wrench, fruit jar; Triumph, dtd Nov 3, '03 ....10.00

Knives

Knife collecting as a hobby began in earnest during the 1960s when government regulations required for the first time that knife companies mark their product with the country of origin. The few collectors and dealers cognizant of this change at once began stockpiling the older knives made before this law was enacted. Another impetus to the growing interest in this area came with the Gun Control Act of 1968, which severely restricted gun trading. Frustrated gun dealers transferred their attention to knives. Today there are collectors clubs in many of the states.

The most sought-after pocketknives are those made before WWII. However, Case, Schrade, and Primble knives of a more recent manufacture are also collected. Most collectors prefer knives 'as found.' Do not attempt to clean, sharpen, or in any way 'improve' on an old knife.

The prices quoted here are for knives in mint condition (except for those in the Miscellaneous section). If a knife has been used, sharpened, or blemished in any way, its value decreases. The newer the knife, the greater the reduction in value. For further information refer to *The*

Standard Knife Collector's Guide, 2nd Edition, by Ron Stewart and Roy Ritchie and *Sargent's American Premium Guide to Knives and Razors, Identification and Values, 3rd Edition*, by Jim Sargent. Our advisor for this category is Bill Wright; he is listed in the Directory under Indiana.

Key:
bd — blade
Cut — Cutlery
jack — jackknife
imi — imitation
lp — long pull

N/S — nickel silver
p/b — push button
s/b — switchblade
w/b — winterbottom

Case, B1025, waterfall hdl, 1-bd, Tested XX, 3" 225.00
Case, Dr's, yel compo hdl, 1-bd, USA, 1965-69, 3⅝" 70.00
Case, Muskrat, red bone hdl, 2-bd, XX, 1940-64, 3⅞" 175.00
Case, RM1097, leg, candy stripe hdl, Tested XX, 1920-30, 5" 400.00
Case, R1051L, candy stripe hdl, 1-bd, Tested XX, 1920-40, 3⅞" ..500.00
Case, W1216, wire hdl, 1-bd, Tested XX, 1920-40, 3⅛" 150.00
Case, 06221, gr bone hdl, 2-bd, Tested XX, 1920-40, 3¼" 350.00
Case, 06244, gr bone hdl, 2-bd, XX, 3¼" 90.00
Case, 11031SH, walnut hdl, 1-bd, Tested XX, 1920-40, 3⅛" 110.00
Case, 11031SH, walnut hdl, 1-bd, XX, 1940-64, 3" 35.00
Case, 1116SP, walnut hdl, 1-bd, XX, 3½" 45.00
Case, 2103SP, slick blk hdl, 1-bd, Tested XX, 1920-40, 3¼" 260.00
Case, 22024SP, slick blk hdl, 2-bd, XX, 3" 225.00
Case, 2217, slick blk hdl, 2-bd, Tested XX, 3⅞" 250.00
Case, 2231½SAB, slick blk hdl, 2-bd, Tested XX, 3¾" 125.00
Case, 2234LP, doctor's, slick blk hdl, 2-bd, Tested XX, 3⅝" 450.00
Case, 2245SHSP, slick blk hdl, 2-bd, XX, 3¾" 135.00
Case, 3232, yel compo hdl, 2-bd, XX, 3⅝" 125.00
Case, 3246RSS, rigger's, yel compo hdl, 2-bd, XX, 4⅜" 85.00
Case, 4100SS, melon tester, compo, 1-bd, USA, 1965-69, 5½" 75.00
Case, 5205½, gr bone hdl, 2-bd, Tested XX, 1920-40, 3⅜" 450.00
Case, 5206½, stag hdl, 2-bd, XX, 1920-40, 2⅝" 225.00
Case, 5207, stag hdl, 2-bd, Tested XX, 1920-40, 3½" 450.00
Case, 5214½, stag hdl, 2-bd, Tested XX, 1920-40, 3⅜" 150.00
Case, 5220, stag hdl, 2-bd, 10 Dot, 2⅞" 55.00
Case, 5238, Rogers bone hdl, 2-bd, Case Bradford PA, 3⅝" 300.00
Case, 5247JLP, red stag hdl, 2-bd, Tested XX, 3⅞" 750.00
Case, 61011, hawkbill, gr bone hdl, 1-bd, Tested XX, 1920-40, 4" ..150.00
Case, 61093, toothpick, red bone hdl, 1-bd, XX, 1940-64, 5" 150.00
Case, 61098, Rogers bone hdl, 1-bd, Tested XX, 1920-40, 5½" ..400.00
Case, 6124½, gr bone hdl, 1-bd, Tested XX, 1920-40, 3" 125.00
Case, 6125½, Rogers bone hdl, 1-bd, Tested XX, 1920-40, 5" 850.00
Case, 6151SAB, gr bone hdl, 1-bd, Tested XX, 5¼" 600.00

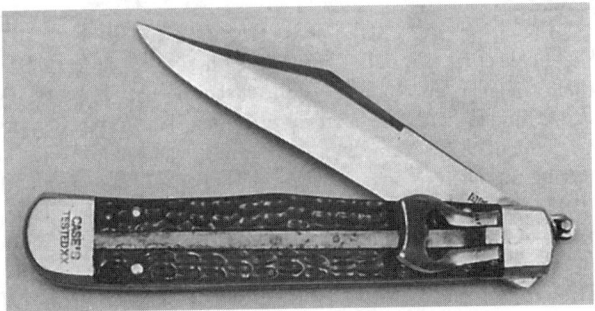

Case, #6161L, green bone handle, hinge-type release, Tested XX, 4⅜", $1,100.00.

Case, 6165, bone hdl, 1-bd, USA, 1965-69, 5¼" 250.00
Case, 6165SAB, bone stag hdl, 1-bd, XX, 1940-64, 5¼" 150.00

Case, 6165SAB, gr bone hdl, 1-bd, Tested XX, 1920-40, 5¼" 400.00
Case, 6172, gr bone hdl, 1-bd, Tested XX, 5½" 1,400.00
Case, 6200LP, gr bone hdl, 2-bd, Tested XX, 1920-40, 4" 700.00
Case, 62009, gr bone hdl, 2-bd, XX, 1940-55, 3¼" 150.00
Case, 62024½, bone hdl, 2-bd, XX, 3" 45.00
Case, 62042, rough blk bone hdl, 2-bd, XX, 2⅞" 40.00
Case, 6209X, rough blk hdl, 2-bd, XX, 1940-50, 3⅛" 140.00
Case, 6214, bone stag hdl, 2-bd, XX, 1940-64, 3 ⅜" 40.00
Case, 6214½, bone hdl, 2-bd, XX, 1940-64, 3⅜" 40.00
Case, 6217R, gr bone hdl, 2-bd, Tested XX, 4" 250.00
Case, 6225½, coke bottle, gr bone hdl, Tested XX, 3" 225.00
Case, 6228LP, easy open, gr bone hdl, Case Brad PA, 3⅝" 200.00
Case, 6233LP, gr bone hdl, 2-bd, Tested XX, 2⅝" 200.00
Case, 6235, gr bone hdl, 2-bd, Tested XX, 3¼" 150.00
Case, 6240SP, gr bone hdl, 2-bd, Tested XX, 4½" 600.00
Case, 6247JLP, rough blk hdl, 2-bd, Tested XX, 3⅞" 450.00
Case, 6249, Copperhead, blk hdl, 2-bd, Tested XX, 1920-40, 4" ..375.00
Case, 7201, tortoise shell hdl, 2-bd, Tested XX, 1920-40, 2⅝" ...225.00
Case, 8151LSAB, pearl hdl, 1-bd, Tested XX, 5¼" 1,200.00
Case, 8233, letter opener, pearl hdl, 2-bd, 6¾" 225.00
Case, 9165SAB, cracked ice hdl, 1-bd, Tested XX, 1920-40, 5¾" ..500.00
Case, 9201, imi pearl hdl, 2-bd, 10 Dot, 1970, 2⅝" 30.00
Case, 92027½LP, imi pearl hdl, 2-bd, Tested XX, 2¾" 125.00
Case, 9220LP, peanut, cracked ice hdl, 2-bd, Tested XX, 2⅞" 250.00
Case, 92210, dbl s/b, cracked ice hdl, 2-bd, Tested XX, 3⅜" 500.00
Keen Kutter, Congress, brn bone hdl, 4-bd, EC Simmons, 3¼" ..100.00
Pal, penknife, candy stripe hdl, 1-bd, Pal Cutlery, 3" 22.50
Queen, 10, jack, w/b bone hdl, 2-bd, 3½" 28.00
Queen, 11EO, w/b bone hdl, 1-bd, 4" 25.00
Queen, 14, peanut, w/b bone hdl, 3-bd, 2¾" 25.00
Queen, 15, Congress, Rogers bone hdl, 2-bd, 3½" 40.00
Queen, 19, trapper, w/b bone hdl, 2-bd, 4⅛" 85.00
Queen, 2, serpentine jack, imi burnt orange hdl, 2-bd, 3¼" 30.00
Queen, 20, Texas toothpick, Rogers bone hdl, 1-bd, 1200 made, 5" ...45.00
Queen, 22, Barlow, brn bone hdl, 2-bd, 3½" 45.00
Queen, 25, Barlow, brn bone hdl, 2-bd, 3½" 60.00
Queen, 26, serpentine, w/b bone hdl, 3-bd, 3¼" 35.00
Queen, 32, Congress, w/b bone hdl, 4-bd, 4" 55.00
Queen, 33, Congress, w/b bone hdl, 4-bd, 3½" 40.00
Queen, 36, lockbk, Rogers bone hdl, 1-bd, 4½" 75.00
Queen, 36, lockbk, w/b bone hdl, 1-bd, 4½" 60.00
Queen, 46, fisherman's, w/b bone hdl, 2-bd, 5" 35.00
Queen, 49, stockman, w/b bone hdl, 3-bd, 4¼" 40.00
Queen, 5, Senator, w/b bone hdl, 2-bd, 2½" 20.00
Queen, 54, pearl hdl, 3-bd, 2⅝" 25.00
Queen, 57, smoked pearl hdl, 3-bd, 3⅜" 125.00
Queen, 6105, swell center, stag hdl, 2-bd, 3½" 35.00
Queen, 6120, jack, stag hdl, 2-bd, Queen, 4½" 40.00
Queen, 8145, jack, stag hdl, 2-bd, 4½" 35.00
Queen, 8150, folding hunter's, stag hdl, 2-bd, rare, 5¼" 50.00
Queen, 8415, canoe, stag hdl, 2-bd, 3⅝" 35.00
Queen, 8420, mini-trapper, stag hdl, 2-bd 35.00
Queen, 9, stockman's, w/b bone hdl, 3-bd, 4" 35.00
Remington, RB45, Barlow, brn bone hdl, 2-bd, 3⅜" 175.00
Remington, RH73, jack, brn bone hdl, 2-bd, 3⅛" 130.00
Remington, R1071, cocobolo hdl, acorn shield, 2-bd, 3⅜" 125.00
Remington, R1103, brn bone hdl, 2-bd, 3⅜" 135.00
Remington, R1123, brn bone hdl, bullet shield, 2-bd, 4½" 1,200.00
Remington, R1153, jack, brn bone hdl, 2-bd, 4½" 400.00
Remington, R1173, brn bone hdl, baby bullet shield, 2-bd, 3½" ..2,200.00
Remington, R1285, swell center, tortoise shell hdl, 2-bd, 3" 160.00
Remington, R1303, lockbk, bone hdl, bullet shield, 1-bd, 4½" ..1,400.00
Remington, R1339, metal hdl, 2-bd, 3" 65.00
Remington, R1383, fish scaler, brn bone hdl, 1-bd, 4¼" 450.00

Remington, R1535, florist's, imi ivory hdl, 1-bd, 3¾" 100.00
Remington, R1582, slick blk hdl, 2-bd, 3" 90.00
Remington, R1613, bone hdl, rnd shield, 1-bd, 5" 900.00
Remington, R165, jack, yel scale hdl, 2-bd, 3½" 125.00
Remington, R1653, peanut, brn bone hdl, 2-bd, 2⅞" 125.00
Remington, R1783, jack teardrop, brn bone hdl, 2-bd, 3½" 125.00
Remington, R1823LP, brn bone hdl, 2-bd, 3⅝" 125.00
Remington, R1825LP, imi tortoise shell hdl, 2-bd, 3⅝" 125.00
Remington, R1915LP, candy stripe hdl, 2-bd, 3⅜" 150.00
Remington, R1957, florist's, imi ivory hdl, 1-bd, 4¼" 100.00
Remington, R203, jack/easy open, brn bone hdl, 2-bd, 3⅝" 200.00
Remington, R2095, blk & wht compo hdl, 2-bd, 3⅛" 90.00
Remington, R219LP, solid brass hdl, 2-bd, 3⅝" 175.00
Remington, R2215, jack, red & blk pyremite hdl, 2-bd, 3⅜" 125.00
Remington, R273, Texas jack, bone hdl, acorn shield, 2-bd, 4" .300.00
Remington, R3054, stockman's, pearl hdl, 3-bd, 4" 500.00
Remington, R3059, stockman's, metal hdl, 3-bd+punch, lp, 4" ..240.00
Remington, R3070, stockman's, buffalo horn hdl, 3-bd, 4" 250.00
Remington, R313, trapper's, brn bone hdl, 2-bd, 3⅞" 250.00
Remington, R333, brn bone hdl, 2-bd, 3¾" 300.00
Remington, R365, jack, gold swirl pyremite hdl, 2-bd, 3⅜" 200.00
Remington, R378, cocobolo hdl, acorn shield, 3¾" 150.00
Remington, R603, sm serpentine jack, bone hdl, 2-bd, 3⅜" 110.00
Remington, R629, lobster, metal hdl, 3-bd, w/bail, 2¾" 90.00
Remington, R64, lobster, metal hdl, 3-bd, 3⅜" 75.00
Remington, R645, s/b, candy stripe hdl, 1-bd, 4" 500.00
Remington, R653, bow tie, bone hdl, 2-bd, 3⅞" 400.00
Remington, R683LP, gunstock, brn bone hdl, 3-bd, 3" 500.00
Remington, R698, Hawkbill, cocobolo hdl, 1-bd, 4" 110.00

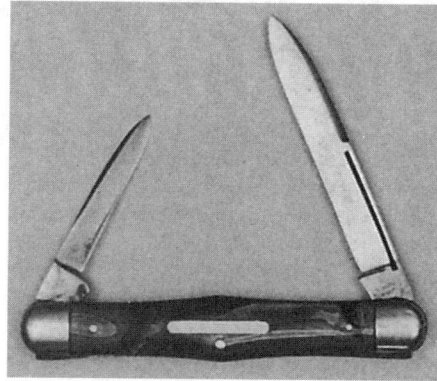

Remington, R7225, green swirl pyremite handle, swell center, long pull, 2-blade, 3", $130.00.

Western States, 1235, genuine horn hdl, w/shield, 2-bd, 3½" 60.00
Western States, 6130, bone hdl w/oval shield, 1-bd, 4½" 280.00
Winchester, Texas jack, ebony hdl, 2-bd, 4½" 300.00
Winchester, 1605, cocobolo hdl, 1-bd, 3½" 75.00
Winchester, 1920, folding hunter, bone hdl, 1-bd, 5⅜" 1,100.00
Winchester, 1921, stag hdl, 1-bd, 3⅜" 140.00
Winchester, 1936, brn bone hdl, 1-bd, 5" 350.00
Winchester, 1938, brn bone hdl, 1-bd, 3⅜" 125.00
Winchester, 1950, lockbk, stag hdl, 1-bd, 5¼" 1,200.00
Winchester, 2037, jack, celluloid hdl, 1-bd, 3" 115.00
Winchester, 2084, sleeveboard, bl celluloid hdl, 1-bd, 3⅜" 185.00
Winchester, 2099, jack, pk celluloid hdl, 2-bd, 3⅜" 150.00
Winchester, 2202, serpentine jack, smooth hdl, 2-bd, 3" 100.00
Winchester, 2205, pen, metal hdl, 2-bd, 3¼" 125.00
Winchester, 2303, sm Senator, pearl hdl, 2⅝" 125.00
Winchester, 2312, Wharncliffe, pearl hdl, 2-bd, 2⅞" 150.00
Winchester, 2324, pen, pearl hdl, 2-bd, 3" 145.00
Winchester, 2608, stabber, cocobolo hdl, 2-bd, 3⅝" 125.00
Winchester, 2613, sleeveboard, ebony hdl, 2-bd, 3⅜" 110.00

Winchester, 2627, slim jack, cocobolo hdl, 2-bd, 3¼" 125.00
Winchester, 2640, Coke bottle, ebony hdl, 2-bd, 3¾" 250.00
Winchester, 2853, gunstock, brn bone hdl, 2-bd, 3½" 425.00

Hunting Knives

Case Knife-Axe Combo, stag hdl, USA, 1965-70, M 325.00
Case XX, stag hdl, skinning bd, 8½", M 75.00
Case XX, USA, blk compo hdl, skinning bd, 9½", M 30.00
Keen Kutter, dk bone hdl, 6" Bowie bd, EX 375.00
Marbles Ideal, leather hdl, str 5" bd, EX 75.00
Marbles Ideal, stag hdl, str 8" bd, EX 500.00
Marbles Trailmaker, leather hdl, 10" Bowie bd, M 600.00
Marbles Woodcraft, leather hdl, 4½" skinning bd, EX 85.00
Marbles Woodcraft, stag hdl, 4½" skinning bd, EX 175.00
Remington, RH28, blk hdl, 4½" bd, M 125.00
Remington, RH32, leather washer hdl, 4½" skinning bd, M 125.00
Remington, RH40, fancy notches top of 10" bd, EX 1,000.00
Remington, RH73, stag hdl, etch deer scene on bd, M 150.00
Winchester, dk bone hdl, 6" Bowie bd, EX 500.00
WR Case, Rogers bone hdl, Bowie bd, 10", EX 170.00

Miscellaneous

Bowie, Arkansas toothpick type, staghorn grips, 14½", EX 950.00
Bowie, Corsan & Denton, emb N/S hdl, 10½", EX 100.00
Bowie, G Woodhead, pearl hdl, emb N/S collar, 4" dirk bd, EX .250.00
Bowie, IXL 8" clip point, stag horn hdl, 1850-60, EX 750.00
Bowie, J Rogers, stag horn hdl, 9" clip point, 1860-70, EX 700.00
Bowie, James Rodgers, stag hdl, 7" spear point bd, 1850s, EX 600.00
Bowie, Joseph Allen & Son Sheffield England, 6½" bd, 11" 85.00
Bowie, Joseph Rogers, 6" bd mk England, 1890-1920, EX 200.00
Bowie, SC Wragg, emb N/S hdl, 6" clip point, 1840s, EX 475.00
Bowie, SC Wragg, pearl hdl w/emb N/S ends, 9" bd, EX 3,000.00
Bowie, WF Jackson, 10 " bd mk Rio Grande Camp Knife, EX ..1,500.00
Buck sheath, David Yellowhorse, brass hdl w/inlay, 4" bd, M 250.00
Folding, wrought hooked bd, mk LU, iron ferrule, 1790s, 10" 165.00
Merchant Marines seaman's, rosewood hdl, WWII era, 5", EX ...30.00
Trench, Italian Fascist, blk pnt, 8½" blade, +scabbard, EX 225.00
Woodell's Star Hunter, wood hdl w/pewter fittings, 6½" bd 70.00

Kosta

Kosta glassware has been made in Sweden since 1742. Today they are one of that country's leading producers of quality art glass. Two of their most important designers were Elis Bergh (1929-1950) and Vicke Lindstrand, artistic director from 1950 to 1973. Lindstrand brought to the company knowledge of important techniques such as Graal, fine figural engraving, Ariel, etc. He influenced new artists to experiment with these techniques and inspired them to create new and innovative designs. Today's collectors are most interested in pieces made during the 1950s and '60s. Our advisor for this category is Abby Malowanczyk; she is listed in the Directory under Texas.

Bowl, cameo doves, gr on clear irid, ftd, Vallien, 5½x6" 400.00
Bowl, free-form, clear w/red & bl swirl base, Unik #5 Warff, 7" .200.00
Obelisk, cased bl crackle, 1 side w/etched birds, Warff, 9½" 375.00
Paperweight, bubbles/gr & bl swags in knob form, Warff, 5½" 180.00
Vase, bl striped, controlled air bubbles, ovoid, #47824 ....350.00
Vase, bud; mushroom shape, #1029, 4" 30.00
Vase, clear-cased red w/red & wht swirls, Lindstrand, 7½" 550.00
Vase, clear w/bl powders, appl blk/wht canes, sqd, 7½" 130.00
Vase, eng feathers, teardrop shape, sgn LG, #382, 6" 200.00

Vase, eng fishermen w/nets, conical, Lindstrand/#26134, 9½" ...**450.00**
Vase, eng kneeling nude, paperweight base, sgn/#d, 5" **60.00**
Vase, eng matador, Vicke Lindstrand, 1950s, 10x8" **850.00**
Vase, int seaweed/bubbles, teardrop, Lindstrand/#1803, 8" **175.00**
Vase, int yel free-form in clear, Lindstrand/#1119, 13½" **375.00**
Vase, irid purple on clear, Artisten B Vallien, dbl gourd, 8" **300.00**

Kutani

Kutani, named for the Japanese village where it originated, was first produced in the 17th century. The early ware, Ko Kutani, was made for only about thirty years. Several types were produced before 1800, but these are rarely encountered. In the 19th century kilns located in several different villages began to copy the old Kutani wares. This later, more familiar type has large areas of red with gold designs on a white ground decorated with warriors, birds, and flowers in controlled colors of red, gold, and black.

Jardiniere, panels with figures in landscapes, scrollwork borders, iron red, navy and gold, 1800s, 14x16½ ", $2,000.00.

Bowl, trees/boats/houses/etc, w/lid, 1900s, 5x4" **45.00**
Censor, supported by 3 karako, bird/floral panels, 10", VG **190.00**
Compote, figures & florals, 1890s, 5½x8" **165.00**
Ewer, butterflies, birds & flowers, mc, 1920s, 12" **100.00**
Figurine, beggar w/staff on rockwork, sgn, ca 1920, 7¼" **325.00**
Teapot, figures in scene, cobalt & gold, ftd, squat, mk, 8" **625.00**
Vase, figures & scenes in rnd reserves, egg form, 5", pr **385.00**
Vase, floral, 5" **58.00**
Vase, 100 Lohan design on rust red, cylindrical, 12" **150.00**

L. E. Smith

Perhaps best known for their line of black glass vases and novelty items, this 20th-century American glass company located in Mt. Pleasant, Pennsylvania, also made several patterns of colored Depression-type dinnerware as well as some glass animals. They reproduced the Moon and Star pattern during the 1960s which proved so successful that they continue to make a few pieces yet today, though the colors now in production (crystal, pink, cobalt, and teal green) are of little interest to collectors. See also Black Glass; Moon and Star.

Bowl, cobalt, 8¼" **45.00**
Bowl, fruit; Mt Pleasant, amethyst, ftd, sq, 9¼" **30.00**
Bowl, rose; Mt Pleasant, pk or gr, 4" **18.00**
Candlesticks, Mt Pleasant, pk or gr, single, pr **20.00**
Compote, Vintage Grape, milk glass, 5½" **15.00**
Cookie jar, blk **60.00**
Cup, Mt Pleasant, amethyst, blk or cobalt, ea **12.00**
Dispenser, water; cobalt **395.00**
Napkin holder, horizontal ribs **42.50**

Plate, grill; Mt Pleasant, amethyst, blk or cobalt, 9", ea **12.00**
Saucer, Mt Pleasant, pk or gr, ea **2.50**
Sugar shaker, emb bands, metal lid w/integral hdl **37.50**
Vase, Bruno, gr, emb flowers, 7" **15.00**
Vase, Mt Pleasant, amethyst, blk or cobalt, 7¼", ea **30.00**

Labels

Before the advent of the cardboard box, wooden crates were used for transporting products. Paper labels were attached to the crates to identify the contents and the packer. These labels often had colorful lithographed illustrations covering a broad range of subjects. Eventually the cardboard box replaced the crate, and the artwork was imprinted directly onto the carton. Today these paper labels are becoming collectible — primarily for the art, but also for their advertising appeal. Our advisor for this category is Cerebro; their address is listed in the Directory under Pennsylvania.

Unless otherwise noted, values are given for examples in excellent to near-mint condition.

Apples, Uncle Sam, Wapato, Washington, EX, $5.00.

Apple, Antler, 12-point buck, 9x10½" **45.00**
Apple, Boy Blue, boy w/horn, Okanogan, 9x11" **3.00**
Apple, Good Pickens, boy in overalls **5.00**
Apple, Jackie Boy, sailor boy **10.00**
Apple, wht setter dog **12.00**
Asparagus, Caligras, man & horse-drawn wagon **3.00**
Asparagus, Kingfish, crowned fish leaps out of water **3.00**
Cigar box, American Kid, Indian woman, M **18.00**
Cigar box, Big Wolf, JW Smith, M **7.50**
Cigar box, Bulldog, 4½" sq **8.00**
Cigar box, Christy girl, 2 sm side vignettes, M **16.00**
Cigar box, Cigarros Primeros, Grecian man wrestling, M **22.00**
Cigar box, Concurrencia, Am flag, train & ship, 4½" sq **18.00**
Cigar box, Corso, Napoleon, 6x9", M **35.00**
Cigar box, Dulcior, old man smoking cigar, 4½" sq, M **12.00**
Cigar box, El Arabe, Arab riding stallion, 6x9", M **25.00**
Cigar box, Elsedor, woman riding horse, M **35.00**
Cigar box, Epochal, 3 men smoking cigars, 4½" sq, M **20.00**
Cigar box, Extra Fein, little boy & dog, 6x9", M **18.00**
Cigar box, Flora, woman & clipper ship, 4½" sq **10.00**
Cigar box, Fuchsel #8, 2 foxes in forest, 6x9", M **45.00**
Cigar box, Jay-Bee's, bl jay & beehive, 6x9", M **18.00**
Cigar box, Judge Kent, man, eagle & scales, 6x9", M **8.00**
Cigar box, La Mareva, woman in feathered hat, 6x9", M **6.00**
Cigar box, La Sultana, gold eagle, M **4.00**
Cigar box, Lord Shelburne, lg brn horse, 6x9", M **50.00**
Cigar box, Moro Light, lighthouse, 6x9", M **1.00**
Cigar box, New Day, sunrise over tobacco field, 6x9", M **4.00**
Cigar box, Porto-Vana, tobacco plantation, 6x9", M **2.00**

Cigar box, Single Kay, trotter horse, 6x9", M 15.00
Cigar box, War Horse, knight on horse, 4¼x4½", EX 7.50
Citrus, Blue Heron, bird & cattails, FL, 9" sq 3.00
Citrus, Jolly Roger, pirate & ship, FL, 9" sq 3.00
Cranberry, Arrow, Indian shooting buffalo, 10x7" 12.00
Cranberry, Paul Revere, man on horse, 7x10" 45.00
Cranberry, Puritan, Quaker man w/Bible, 7x10" 15.00
Firecracker pack, Red Fox 20.00
Grapefruit, Arizona Star, grove & mtns, Sacramento 6.00
Grapefruit, Yuma Chief, Indian chief, 11x10" 85.00
Hotel/Luggage, El Tovar, Grand Canyon, 1930s 4.00
Lemon, Bridal Veil, falls in Yosemite, Santa Paula, 12½x8¾" 6.00
Lemon, Green Head, gr duck's head 2.00
Lemon, Kaweah Maid, Indian lady, 11x10" 3.00
Orange, Carefree, laughing blond on bl, Redlands, 10x11" 3.00
Orange, Gander, wild goose, 11x10" 55.00
Orange, Memory, silhouette of girl & rose in fr, 10x11" 9.00
Pear, Big Game, football player & stadium, Wenatchee, 8x11" 9.00
Pear, Duckwall, Wood Duck by brick wall, 10¾x7¼" 3.00
Pear, Lake Ridge, lake & mtns, 10½x7½" 3.50
Pear, Old Orchard, 2 little girls, gilt trim, 10¾x7¼" 3.00
Tobacco, Black Oak, Hoen litho, 6¼x12⅜" 32.00
Tobacco, Juno 17.50
Tobacco, Victory Brand, Hoen litho, 6½x13" 48.00
Vegetable, Gay Johnny, barefoot boy in cowboy hat, 6½x5" 4.00
Whiskey bottle, Old Crow, distillery 1.00
Yam, Sho-Am-Sweet, Blk chef, 7x4" 2.00

Labino

Dominick Labino was a glass blower who until mid-1985 worked in his studio in Ohio, blowing and sculpting various items which he signed and dated. A ceramic engineer by trade, he was instrumental in developing the heat-resistant tiles used in space flights. His glassmaking shows his versatility in the art. While some of his designs are free-form and futuristic, others are reminiscent of the products of older glasshouses. Because of problems with his health, Mr. Labino became unable to blow glass himself; he died January, 10, 1987. Work coming from his studio since mid-1985 has been signed 'Labino Studios, Baker,' indicating ware made by his protegee, E. Baker O'Brien. In addition to her own compositions, she continues to use many of the colors developed by Labino.

Bottle, silver schmelz, knopped neck, 1978, 7" 750.00
Bowl, red-orange copper w/cadmium orange designs, 1985, 5½" ...500.00
Decanter, copper red, appl prunts, 1971, 10", +7 glasses 1,400.00

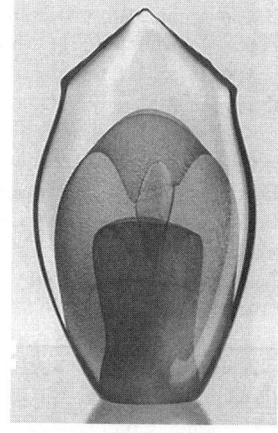

Emergence sculpture, pointed oviform with iridescent copper, pink and purple, signed and dated 7-1981, 8¾", $3,900.00.

Fountain, pk/purple int emerging forms in clear, 1983, 9" 3,000.00
Jar, vaseline, bulbous w/rnd ft, rnd finial, 1974, 6" 500.00
Lamp, oil; bl w/appl threading on shaft, wide ft, 1972, 12" 1,200.00
Paperweight, bl w/purple clouds, opal/brn swirls, conical, 4" 325.00
Sculpture, fish on rnd ped, copper schmelz, bl eyes, '82, 6" 550.00
Sculpture, Neutron Collision, lt int irid, clear cased, 4½" 1,500.00
Vase, clear-cased cobalt w/3-color pull-ups, 1979, 5½" 1,200.00
Vase, cobalt-cased copper schmelz, int free-form, 1975, 6x4" 900.00
Vase, copper schmelz, bulbous w/lt ribbing, 1966, 10" 550.00
Vase, copper w/red/bl/wht/orange design, ovoid, 1983, 4½" 500.00
Vase, owl form, silver schmelz, 1967, 5" 575.00
Vase, red/bl looping swirls in smoke, baluster, 1978, 11" 700.00

Lace, Linens, and Needlework

It has been recorded that lace was found in the tombs of ancient Egypt. Lace has always been a symbol of wealth and fashion. Italian laces are regarded as the finest ever produced, but the differences between them and the laces of France are nearly indistinguishable. Needlework was revived during the 18th century and became the favorite of feminine pastimes. Examples of many forms (tatting, embroidery, needlepoint, and crochet, for instance) are available today; and, though fragile in appearance, have withstood the ravages of time with remarkable durability.

Key:
embr — embroidered   ms — machine sewn
hs — hand sewn

Back splash, linen, ecru, silk-embr girls, fringed, 34x18" 125.00
Bed tick, homespun linen, embr initials, 67x61" 85.00
Bedspread, cotton w/embr lady & men, 1930s, ¾-sz 150.00
Bedspread, crochet, Snow Flake w/popcorn stitch, fringe, lg 375.00
Bedspread, homespun linen, natural on wht, 99x69" 215.00
Bedspread, Marseilles lace, woven-in nursery rhymes, crib sz 200.00
Bolster cover, Irish linen, floral embr, scalloped, 32x86" 150.00
Bun warmer, linen w/Battenburg border, ecru, standard sz 45.00
Centerpiece, Battenburg lace, scalloped edge, 14" dia 125.00
Centerpiece, Battenburg lace scalloped border, 12" dia 110.00
Centerpiece, crochet, eagle, shields in corners, 15x18" 95.00
Crochet panel, Sunbonnet Girl, 11x16" 65.00
Doily, crochet, initial in center, 10x17" 37.50
Doily, crochet, Masonic emblem w/G in center, ecru, 17x15" 65.00
Doily, crochet, stars w/scalloped border, ecru, 13" dia 48.00
Doily, crochet, Statue of Liberty & flag, 18x22½" 130.00
Drapes, 1920s floral, 3-panel, 106x42" 110.00
Handkerchief, wht linen w/lace trim 35.00
Linen pc, homespun, bl/wht plaid, 39x40" 95.00
Mat, crochet, 'Baby' filet, 5x8" 55.00
Napkin, linen, embr flower basket, 6 corners, crochet edge 35.00
Needlework panel, children on teeter totter, sgn/1864, 21x19" 250.00
Needlework panel, lady in garden w/dog, fr, 16x15" 175.00

Needlework picture, Rebecca at the well, multicolor threads on linen, signed, ca 1770, 14½x10½", $7,000.00 at auction.

Pillow sham, red embr wreath w/MA, 3¼" ruffle, 28x30" **62.00**
Runner, Battenburg border, 18x70" **65.00**
Runner, Battenburg fleur-de-lis, 19x74" **110.00**
Runner, Cluny lace 4" border, 8" at corners, 17x42" **135.00**
Runner, crochet, Bread in center, 4½x11" **55.00**
Shams, Good Morning/Good Night embr w/scenes, pr **125.00**
Shams, Irish linen, ruffles, pr **70.00**
Sheet, homespun linen, hs hem/central seam, 74x76" **135.00**
Sheets, homespun wool, hs center seam, 84x70", pr **110.00**
Show towel, homespun, mc embr, name/1844, 54x20", VG **140.00**
Show towel, red & bl X-stitch flowers/etc/1883, 58", EX **425.00**
Tablecloth, Battenburg, 90x68" **285.00**
Tablecloth, Battenburg grapeleaf pattern w/inserts, 68" dia **265.00**
Tablecloth, Battenburg lace, English, ca 1910, 52" dia **250.00**
Tablecloth, Battenburg lace, grape clusters, 55" dia **175.00**
Tablecloth, Battenburg lace, grape clusters, 66" dia **200.00**
Tablecloth, Battenburg lace, scalloped edge, 14" dia **95.00**
Tablecloth, bl & wht cotton homespun, center seam, 78x58" **215.00**
Tablecloth, bobbin lace, 44" dia **115.00**
Tablecloth, crochet flowers, 96x115" **135.00**
Tablecloth, ecru linen w/cutwork, hand embr & crochet, 64x80" ...**100.00**
Tablecloth, ecru needlepoint lace, 140" L, +12 napkins **800.00**
Tablecloth, homespun linen, bl/wht, fringed, 36x36" **110.00**
Tablecloth, homespun linen, wht-on-wht stripes, hs, 44x62" **90.00**
Tablecloth, linen, appl golfers, etc, 104x68", +12 napkins **175.00**
Tablecloth, linen, appliqued flowers, 48x52", EX **135.00**
Tablecloth, linen, monogram, 72x108", M **125.00**
Tablecloth, linen, openwork & embr flowers, 54x54" **125.00**
Tablecloth, linen, ornate Venetian needle lace, 98x92" **525.00**
Tablecloth, linen, wide tatted border, 42" dia **135.00**
Tablecloth, linen w/embr & lace, 120x80", +12 napkins **400.00**
Tablecloth, linen w/6" tatted edge, 50x42" **125.00**
Tablecloth, machine lace, floral, scalloped, 82x68" **85.00**
Tablecloth, machine lace, wht, 62" dia, M **100.00**
Tablecloth, picot work, 120" L, +12 napkins **500.00**
Tea cozy, Battenburg lace, flower, 12x16" **150.00**
Throw, chenille, flowers, red on tan, Victorian, 40" sq, EX **98.00**
Towel, filet crochet trim **50.00**
Towel, PA German homespun, cutwork panels, wear, 55x15" ...**300.00**

Lacy Glassware

Lacy glass became popular in the late 1820s after the development of the pressing machine. It was decorated with allover patterns — hearts, lyres, sheaves of wheat, etc. — and backgrounds were completely stippled. The designs were intricate and delicate, hence the term 'lacy.' Although Sandwich produced this type of glassware in abundance, it was also made by other eastern glassworks as well as in the midwest. By 1840 its popularity on the wane and a depressed economy forcing manufacturers to seek less expensive modes of production, lacy glass began to be phased out in favor of pressed pattern glass.

Reference numbers correspond with *Sandwich Glass* by Ruth Webb Lee. When no condition is indicated, the items listed below are assumed to be without obvious damage; minor roughness is normal. See also Salts, Open.

Bowl, Beehive, octagonal, shallow, sm chips, 9¾" **75.00**
Bowl, Peacock Eye, L-132, chips, 8⅞" **145.00**
Bowl, Peacock Eye, Sandwich, rim chips, 9" **55.00**
Bowl, Princess Feather, Sandwich, 1⅝x7½" **75.00**
Dish, Gothic, oblong, minor chips, 8x6" **40.00**
Dish, Princess Feather, chips, 6⅝" **25.00**
Plate, floral, 7¾" **30.00**

Plate, Peacock Eye, 5¼" **30.00**
Plate, Peacock w/Thistle center, chips, 8" **40.00**
Plate, Roman Rosette, Sandwich, opal, 5½", EX **75.00**
Plate, swag & thistle rim, chips, 7" **35.00**
Plate, 12-sided, L-112, chips, 7¼" **130.00**
Relish, Gothic, L-101, chips, 9" **205.00**
Sugar bowl, Gothic, clambroth, Sandwich, 5", EX **200.00**
Toddy, Gladstone for the Million, sm chips, 5" **30.00**
Wash bowl & pitcher, L-80-1, Sandwich, mini, EX **245.00**

Lalique

Beginning his lengthy career as a designer and maker of fine jewelry, Rene Lalique at first only dabbled in glass, making small panels of pate-de-verre (paste-on-paste) and cire perdue (wax casting) to use in his jewelry. He also made small flacons of gold and silver with his glass inlays, which attracted the attention of M.F. Coty, who commissioned Lalique to design bottles for his perfume company. The success of this venture resulted in the opening of his own glassworks at Combs-la-Ville in 1909. In 1921 a larger factory was established at Wingen-sur-Moder in Alsace-Lorraine. By the thirties Lalique was world renown as the most important designer of his time.

Lalique glass is lead based, either mold blown or pressed. Favored motifs during the Art Nouveau period were dancing nymphs, fish, dragonflies, and foliage. Characteristically the glass is crystal in combination with acid-etched relief. Later some items were made in as many as ten colors (red, amber, and green among them) and were occasionally accented with enameling. These colored pieces, especially those in black, are highly prized by advanced collectors.

During the twenties and thirties, Lalique designed several vases and bowls reminiscent of American Indian art. He also developed a line in the Art Deco style decorated with stylized birds, florals, and geometrics. In addition to vases, clocks, automobile mascots, stemware, and bottles, many other useful objects were produced. Most items made before his death in 1945 were marked 'R. Lalique'; later the 'R' was deleted even though some of the original molds were still used. Numbers found on the bases of some pieces are catalog numbers. Beware of fraudulent pieces that have began to surface in increasing numbers. Our advisor for this category is John Danis; he is listed in the Directory under Illinois.

Key:
cl/fr — clear and frosted   RL — signed R. Lalique
L — signed Lalique   RLF — signed R. Lalique, France

Bottle, scent; Arys, Ovoide Feuilles, heart motif, mk, 4½" **625.00**
Bottle, scent; Cactus, fr w/blk enamel dots, eng mk, 3¾" **220.00**
Bottle, scent; Camille, dk bl, shell design, RL, 2¼" **2,500.00**
Bottle, scent; Deux Fleurs, blossoms, fr, LF, 3½" **150.00**
Bottle, scent; Epines, cl/fr, thorny branches, brn patina, RL, 3½" ..**600.00**
Bottle, scent; Hirondelles, birds, bl wash, RL, 3½" **1,500.00**
Bottle, scent; Les Infants, fr, brn stain, sgn, 4" **700.00**
Bottle, scent; Lotus, fr, brn stain, RL #522, 2½" **1,000.00**
Bottle, scent; Petites Feuilles, fr, gr stain, RL, 4¼" **1,200.00**
Bottle, scent; Phalene, winged maiden, yel/amber, RLF, 4" **2,000.00**
Bottle, scent; Violette D'orsey Baccarat in RL metal fr, 5½" ...**2,800.00**
Bowl, Calypso, 5 mermaids, opal, shallow, LF, 15", NM **2,100.00**
Bowl, Coquilles, shells, deep bl opal, RLF/#3200, 10" **500.00**
Bowl, Tournon, 12 relief flowers, cl/opal, RL, 4¾x12" **650.00**
Box, powder; Chantilly, 6 deer, sepia wash on lid, RL, 3" **600.00**
Box, Rosaces, lappets, sepia wash, RLF, 6½" dia **660.00**
Card holder, acanthus ends, cl/fr, LF, 4½" **135.00**
Chandelier, Charmes, leafy branches, amber, RLF, 13½" dia ..**4,300.00**

Clock, Moineaux, fr dome case w/birds & berries, RLF, 6x9" ..1,500.00
Collector plate, 1965 ....1,000.00
Collector plate, 1966 ....325.00
Collector plate, 1967 ....200.00
Collector plate, 1968 ....100.00
Collector plate, 1969 ....100.00
Collector plate, 1970 ....80.00
Collector plate, 1971 ....80.00
Collector plate, 1972 ....75.00
Collector plate, 1973 ....100.00
Collector plate, 1974 ....100.00
Collector plate, 1975 ....100.00
Collector plate, 1976 ....150.00
Goblet, Langeais, fr ribbed stems, 5", set of 8 ....230.00
Jardiniere, St Hubert, lg antelope hdls, cl/fr, RL, 19" L 1,950.00
Light shade, Dahlias, relief flowers, fr, RL, 12" 1,725.00
Light shade, Soleil, sun elements, opal, RLF 12" 1,725.00
Luminaire, Veronique, flowering branches, brn patina, 8½" .16,000.00
Mascot, dragonfly, cl/fr, sgn, 3x7" 2,200.00
Mascot, Longchamp, horse head, gray fr, RLF, 6x5" 2,875.00
Mascot, Victorie, stylized head, fr, RL, 6x10", EX 5,000.00
Necklace, fuchsia flower beads+ovals & balls, 18" 2,000.00
Ornament, Tete de Belier, ram head, cl/fr, RLF, 3¾", EX 2,500.00
Paperweight, Longchamp, horse head, RLF, 5" 2,300.00
Pendant, Libellules, dragonflies, gr, 1⅝", NM 690.00
Pendant, Lys, 2 lilies, triangular, L, 2" 700.00
Pendant, Northwind motif against foil, gilt mt, L, 2½" dia 1,100.00
Plaque, Vierge a l'enfant, mother/child, wood base, RL, 14" ...1,150.00
Plate, Chardon, thistle pods/thorny branches, LF, 8" 345.00
Plate, Coquilles #2, 4 emb shells, opal, RL, 10½" 660.00
Sculpture, Tete de Cheval, horse head, lighted base, L, 9" 4,950.00
Sherbet, crystal w/lav bird stem, RLF, 4½" 110.00
Statuette, seated nude w/hair of flowers, blk base, LF, 4" 260.00
Statuette, Suzanne, nude w/drapery, amber w/base, RL, 11" .11,000.00
Vase, Albert, lg eagle head hdls, gray, U-form, RLF, 6¾" 980.00
Vase, Bacchantes, nudes, dk amber, RLF, 10" 10,350.00

Vase, Baies, berries and vines in relief with black enameling, R. Lalique, 10½", $6,900.00.

Vase, Beliers, crouching rams as hdls, smoke fr, ftd, RLF, 7" ...1,495.00
Vase, Biskra, palm leaves, lt gr, bulbous, RLF, 12" 2,900.00
Vase, Boulouris, birds on fence ribbing, LF, 6" 275.00
Vase, Chevaux, 5 horses/grasses, fr, flared U-form, RLF, 7" 2,200.00
Vase, Courlis, sea gulls/waves, red amber/fr, RLF, 7x6" 3,500.00
Vase, Dahlias, lg fr flowers w/blk centers, RLF, 5x7" 1,980.00
Vase, Danaides, 6 nudes, bl wash, RLF, str sides, 7" 2,750.00
Vase, Domremy, thistle pods, emerald, RLF, 8½x7" 1,800.00
Vase, Ecailles, allover scales, red amber, RLF, 12x9" 4,800.00
Vase, Esterel, leaves, lt gr patina on opal, RLF, 7x7" 690.00
Vase, Formose, stylized fish, opal, spherical, RL, 7" 1,265.00

Vase, Grenade, lappets, amethyst, RLF, 8x10" 925.00
Vase, Grignon, stylized wheat sheaves, brn patina, 7½" 460.00
Vase, Grives, thrushes on branches, fr, V-form, L, 7" 260.00
Vase, Gui, mistletoe emb on fr, spherical, RL, 7" 1,000.00
Vase, Guirlande de Roses, rose garlands, fr w/bl, RLF, 5½" 460.00
Vase, Mossaic, leaves in high relief, topaz gray, RL, 5" 2,200.00
Vase, Mossi, allover knop design, cl/fr, cylindrical, RL, 8½" 800.00
Vase, Oran, peonies/leaves, opal, RLF, 14" 7,500.00
Vase, Ormeaux, elm leaves, red amber fr, RLF/#984, 6½x6½" ...2,500.00
Vase, Ornis, lg birds as hdls, opal, RFL/#976, ftd, 7½" 1,725.00
Vase, Palissy, stylized snails, opal, spherical, RLF, 7" 1,375.00
Vase, Penthievre, fantasy fish, gr, RLF, 10x10" 5,750.00
Vase, Perruches, parakeets, red w/fr, RL, 10x9" 6,900.00
Vase, Piriac, raised fish band above waves, fr, RLF, 7" 1,200.00
Vase, Poisson, lg fish, dk amber, spherical, RL, 9½" 7,400.00
Vase, Raisins, grape clusters, fr, RLF, 6x3" 330.00
Vase, Rampillon, dmn motifs/florals, opal, conical, RLF, 5" 900.00
Vase, Ronces, bramble thorns, red opal/yel, RL, 9" 3,850.00
Vase, Rounesols, sunflowers w/emb centers, electric bl, 5" 2,300.00
Vase, Sauge, leaves, bright gr, teardrop form, RLF/#935, 10" 990.00
Vase, Serpent, coiled snake, red-brn, RLF, spherical, 10" 10,900.00
Vase, Sophora, lg leaves, gray w/fr in recesses, RL, 10x10" 4,400.00
Vase, Teheran, 4 etched bird/trees reserves, fr, RLF, 2½" 935.00
Wine, winged berry stem, RL, 4¾", set of 6 ....215.00

Lamps

The earliest lamps were simple dish containers with a wick that hung over the edge or was supported by a channel or tube. Grease and oil from animal or vegetable sources were the first fuels used. Ancient pottery lamps, crusie, and Betty lamps are examples of these early types. In 1784 Swiss inventor Ami Argand introduced the first major improvement in lamps. His lamp featured a tubular wick and a glass chimney. During the first half of the 19th century, whale oil, burning fluid (a highly explosive mixture of turpentine and alcohol), and lard were the most common fuels used in North America. Many lamps were patented for specific use with these fuels.

Kerosene was the first major breakthrough in lighting fuels. It was demonstrated by Canadian geologist Dr. Abraham Gesner in 1846. The discovery and drilling of petroleum in the late 1850s provided an abundant and inexpensive supply of kerosene. It became the main source of light for homes during the balance of the 19th century and for remote locations until the 1950s.

Although Thomas A. Edison invented the electric lamp in 1879, it was not until two or three decades later that electric lamps replaced kerosene household lamps. Millions of kerosene lamps were made for every purpose and pocketbook. They ranged in size from tiny night or miniature lamps to tall stand or piano lamps. Hanging varieties for homes commonly had one or two fonts (oil containers), but chandeliers for churches and public buildings often had six or more. Wall or bracket lamps usually had silvered reflectors. Student lamps, parlor lamps (now called Gone-with-the-Wind lamps), and patterned glass lamps were designed to complement the popular furnishing trends of the day. Gaslight, introduced in the early 19th century, was used mainly in homes of the wealthy and public places until the early 20th century. Most fixtures were wall or ceiling mounted, although some table models were also used.

Few of the ordinary early electric lamps have survived. Many lamp manufacturers made the same or similar styles for either kerosene or electricity, sometimes for gas. Top-of-the-line lamps were made by Pairpoint, Phoenix, Tiffany, Bradley and Hubbard, and Handel. See also these specific sections.

Currently values of peg lamps are up by about 30% to 40%, and pattern glass lamps in some of the standard lines have jumped from 25% to 100%. When buying lamps that have been converted to electricity, inspect them very carefully for any damage that may have resulted from the alterations; such damage is very common, and when it does occur, the lamp's value may be lessened by as much as 50%. Lamps seem to bring much higher prices in some areas than others, especially the larger cities. Conversely, in rural areas they may bring only half as much as our listed values. One of our advisors for lamps is Ruth Osborne; she is listed in the Directory under Ohio.

Key:
ac — acorn burner   pb — pinafore burner
hb — hornet burner   SIA — Scenes in Action
nb — nutmeg burner   Vb — P&A Victor burner
Ob — O burner

Aladdin Lamps, Electric

From 1908 Aladdin lamps with a mantle became the mainstay of rural America, providing light that compared favorably with the electric light bulb. They were produced by the Mantle Lamp Company of America in over eighteen models and more than one hundred styles. During the 1930s to the 1950s, this company was the leading manufacturer of electric lamps as well. Still in operation today, the company is now known as Aladdin Industries Inc., located in Nashville, Tennessee. For those seeking additional information on Aladdin Lamps, we recommend *Aladdin — The Magic Name in Lamps*; *Aladdin Electric Lamps*; and *A Collector's Manual and Price Guide*, all written by our advisor for Aladdins, J. W. Courter; he is listed in the Directory under Kentucky. Mr. Courter has also published a book called *Angle Lamps, Collector's Manual and Price Guide*.

Bed, #2305-SS, Whip-o-lite fluted & flocked shade, EX 200.00
Bed, #909-SS, Whip-o-lite fluted shade, EX 200.00
Bedroom, M-59, Colonial, modern candlestick, EX 50.00
Bedroom, P-51, ceramic, EX 25.00
Boudoir, G-1, plain color, early, EX 50.00
Boudoir, G-36, Alacite, floral base, EX 75.00
Boudoir, M-91, metal, EX 50.00
Figurine, G-16, lady, crystal, etched, EX 600.00
Figurine, G-234, pheasant, EX 200.00
Figurine, G-333, bride & groom, EX 200.00
Figurine, G-79, rooster, EX, minimum value 1,200.00
Glass Urn, G-213A, Alacite, closed urn, EX 225.00
Glass Urn, G-377, Alacite, tall ribbed urn, EX 110.00
Pinup, G-351, wall medallion, Alacite, EX 85.00
Pinup, P-57, gun-n-holster, creamic, EX 125.00
Ranch House, G-378C, Alacite Bullet, illuminated urn, EX 300.00
Table, #785, Lg Vase, tan, EX 225.00
Table, E-300, Vogue Vase, gr, EX 325.00
Table, G-120, moonstone, EX 70.00
Table, G-179, Opalique, EX 100.00
Table, G-208, Alacite, illuminated base, EX 60.00
Table, G-297C, Alacite, certified, EX 50.00
Table, G-60, short harp, EX 100.00
Table, G-7, marble-like glass, EX 300.00
Table, G-84, Velvex, EX, minimum value 450.00
Table, M-3, metal, EX 100.00
Table, M-367, metal, iron base, spun glass shade, EX 15.00
Table, M-495, brass metal, EX 20.00
Table, P-401, ceramic, EX 40.00
TV lamp, M-367, blk iron base w/shade 30.00
TV lamp, TV-426, metal w/foil shade, EX 25.00

Aladdin Lamps, Kerosene

Model #12, Crystal Vase, #1240, variegated verde, 12", M 200.00
Model #12, Crystal Vase, #1247, Red Venetian Art-Craft, EX ...400.00

Model #12, Florentine Vase, #1222, Rose Moonstone, 8½", EX ..1,800.00
Model #2, parlour lamp, Old English or Jap bronze, EX 650.00
Practicus, table lamp, polished brass, NM 375.00
Table Model A, Venetian, #103, Rose, EX 165.00
Table Model B, Beehive, #B-81, gr crystal, EX 120.00
Table Model B, Cathedral, #B-112, Rose Moonstone, EX 300.00
Table Model B, Corinthian, B-105, clear font, gr ft, EX 120.00
Table Model B, Quilt, #B-91, wht & rose moonstone, NM 325.00
Table Model B, Short Lincoln Drape, #B-60, Alacite, EX 425.00
Table Model B, Victoria, #B-25, china w/decor, w/oil fill, NM ..500.00
Table Model B, Washington Drape, #B-52, amber crystal, EX 135.00
Wall Bracket Model #4, NM 385.00

Angle Lamps

The Angle Lamp Company of New York City developed a unique type of kerosene lamp that was a vast improvement over those already on the market; they were sold from about 1896 until 1929 and were expensive for their time. Our Angle lamp advisor is J.W. Courter; he is listed in the Directory under Kentucky. See the narrative for Aladdin Lamps for information concerning popular books Mr. Courter has authored.

No 101, wall cone, single burner, pnt tin, no glass, VG 225.00

Single wall lamp, #103, nickel-plated tin, ruby petal-top shade, kerosene burner, EX, $800.00.

No 115, barn lantern, tin, complete, EX 1,000.00
No 125, wall, pinwheel emb, 1-burner, NP brass, no glass, EX ...275.00
No 203, hanging, 2-burner, NP tin, wht chimney tops, EX 350.00
No 465, chandelier, 4-arm, polished brass, wired, plain glass ..3,500.00

Chandeliers

Brass w/crimped pan, 4 sockets, hanging loop, dk patina, EX 300.00
CI ornate fixture, 3 Lomax star fonts/milk glass 10" shades 425.00
Crystal, 10-arm, w/prisms & drops, 32x29" 700.00
Gilt metal, 6-light, Renaissance style, 34" 2,250.00

Decorated Kerosene Lamps

Bl opal font, clear ringed stepped ped, sq ft, 8" 450.00
Cobalt cut to clear, marble base, fluted brass stem, 16½" 825.00
Cobalt cut to clear flowers, 7" cut/frosted ball shade, 22" 900.00
Cranberry cut to clear, wht opaque base w/gilt, 12½" 385.00
Cranberry opal, lg ribbed font on rnd flattened ft, 6¾" 100.00
Cranberry ribbed ball shade, Dmn Quilt font, spatter stem 750.00
Dk bl cut to clear paw prints, brass stem, marble ft, 12" 700.00
Fiery opal cut to clear, marble base, brass stem, 7¾" 300.00
Pnt milk glass fringed 14" shade & bulbous font, metal ft 250.00
Rubena frost w/floral 6" shade/font; orig burner, NP std, 15" 495.00

Sanded clambroth font w/acanthus decor, marble base, 11½" **100.00**
Wht cut to clear floral font, mercury stem, slate ft, 8½" **425.00**
Wht cut to clear w/t'prints & quatrefoils, marble base, 26" **450.00**

White cut to clear font on matching stem, double-stepped marble base, fancy gold scroll decoration, 20⅜", $500.00; White cut to clear font and shade on milk glass base, worn gold decoration, P&A Victor burner, 17¼", $550.00.

Fairy Lamps

Amber Dmn Quilt, clear Clarke base, 5", EX **75.00**
Bl opal to clear w/emb medallions, ruffled bl base, 7" **395.00**
Bl pastel w/wht ruffle on base & shade, Clarke base, 6" **425.00**
Bl verre moire, clear Clarke base, 4¾x4" **200.00**
Burmese, berries & leaves, clear Clarke base, 4¾x4" **650.00**
Burmese, Clarke flower bowl base, Webb, 4¼x5" **245.00**
Burmese, clear Clarke base, pyramid sz, 3¾" **125.00**
Burmese, floral, burmese Clarke cup, sqd/folded base, 6" **2,200.00**
Burmese, frilly pleated skirt, Cricklite sz, 5½x7½" **950.00**
Burmese, ivy, sq base w/rolled rim, frosted cup, 6x6" **2,100.00**
Burmese, prunus blossoms, Clarke's Cricklite, 6½" **985.00**
Burmese, prunus blossoms, Webb, Clarke insert, 5¼x3¾" **1,250.00**
Burmese, Queen's, pyramid, Clarke base, 4½x5" **1,150.00**
Burmese (shiny), pk/gold Clarke ceramic base w/3 c'holders ...**1,100.00**
Cased gr satin, Webb, Clarke base, 4¾" **245.00**
Cat's head figural, bsk w/amber eyes, 3¼" **250.00**
Cinnamon MOP shade, clear Clarke base, 4½" **100.00**
Cranberry overshot shade w/appl clear ruffles, brass base **300.00**
Cranberry verre moire, clear Clarke base, 5¾x6" **225.00**
Cranberry verre moire, clear Clarke cup, pyramid sz, 3¾" **145.00**
Cranberry verre moire, matching crimped bowl base, 5x6" **650.00**
Cranberry verre moire frost, matching ruffled base, 6x9" dia **795.00**
Cranberry w/appl petals, clear petal base, 4½" **350.00**
Gr & wht swirl stripes on frost, Clarke base, 2-pc, 6x4¼" **155.00**
Gr verre moire, clear Clarke cup, 6x8" **500.00**
Jeweled brass w/finger hold, 4⅝" **80.00**
Owl's head, cranberry, purple eyes, Clarke cup, 4" **195.00**
Owl's head, 2-faced, gr frosted, clear Clarke base, 4¼" **295.00**
Peachblow, Clarke pyramid-sz cup, 6½" **200.00**
Peacock bl satin w/matching ruffled saucer, Clarke base, 5½", EX ...**550.00**
Pekinese dog's head figural, bsk w/amber eyes, 3⅜" **200.00**
Pk o/l w/flowers, petal base, Clarke cup, 6", NM **620.00**
Pk opal 5-petal top on pressed tall stem clear base, 10x3" **225.00**
Pk satin, clear Clarke base, 4¾", NM **150.00**
Pk shaded w/clear ruffled rim, scalloped base, 5½" **195.00**
Pk Swirl MOP satin, 5x5½" **535.00**
Rainbow Dmn Quilt MOP, Clarke top/base, crimped, 6¾" **5,000.00**
Red o/l, clear cup, red o/l crimped base, 5x7" **500.00**
Red/gr striped flower form w/rigaree, ornate base, pyramid sz **250.00**

Sapphire bl overshot, clear Clarke pyramid base, 4½" **70.00**
Spatter, gr/wht o/l swirl, appl clear drips/ft, 4½" **395.00**
Spatter, mc, unmk crystal base, 3¾" **150.00**
Vaseline, emb florals, 2 clear inserts, 6¾x5" **165.00**
Vaseline opal, melon ribs, clear Clarke base, 2-pc, 4x2¾" **145.00**
Vaseline T'print, matching base, 5½" **175.00**
Wht bsk w/cottage scene, 4¼" **250.00**
Wht satin w/HP flowers, faceted mc stones, Clarke cup, 5" **175.00**
Yel satin Dmn Quilt, clear Clarke base, 5x4¼" **150.00**
3-face (lion/monkey/unknown animal) figural, wht bsk, 3⅞" **500.00**

Gone-With-the-Wind and Banquet Lamps

Artichoke, lav/gr pnt on milk glass ball/font, metal ft, 24" **250.00**
Banquet-type, mercury & bristol, ball shade, stick base, 20" **240.00**
Daisy & Button, Alice Bl & amber, complete, lg **485.00**
Lg roses on globe & pear-shaped base, 32" **650.00**
Lime cut to clear, ribbed/ruffled shade; NP/marble std, 23" **495.00**
Mums emb on red satin, brass-plated CI base, 22", EX **300.00**
Roses on pk ball shade/bulbous oval base, ormolu ft, 27" **350.00**

Roses hand painted on milk glass, all original, EX brass plating, 30", $600.00.

Vaseline opal striped/ruffled 8½" shade; brass std, 24" **765.00**
Victoria red satin ball shade & font, brass base, 27", EX **475.00**

Hanging Lamps

Blown, Empire style, soot cover, gilt brass fr w/swan's heads ...**1,000.00**
Coin Spot red satin, ball shade, brass fr, pressed font, 27" **250.00**
Cranberry dome shade, rtcl brass fr, prisms, smoke bell **660.00**
Cranberry Hobnail 14" shade/font, ornate brass fr, prisms **1,000.00**
Cranberry Hobnail 14" shade/font; butterfly-brace fr, prisms ..**1,400.00**
Cranberry swirl cylinder shade, emb/scrollwork brass mts **140.00**
Iron Horse, blk CI fr w/milk glass shade, clear font, EX **275.00**
Opal pk bell-shape shade, clear orig font, brass fr, 14" **225.00**
Peachblow 14" ribbed shade/font, ornate brass fr w/prisms **750.00**
Store, brass Rochester font, 2 chimneys, pnt tin shade, 27" **100.00**

Lanterns

Barn, wood fr, tin top/bottom, 4 glass sides, 13½", EX **285.00**
Brass w/clear bull's-eye globe, whale oil burner, 9" **500.00**
Dietz #8 Gem, Pat Jan 28 1868, kerosene model, VG **88.00**
Dietz Racket, brass w/clear globe, 8" **75.00**
Revere type, punched tin w/hearts/dmns/circles/etc, 12" **495.00**
Skater's, brass w/sandy ruby globe, 7", EX **245.00**

Skater's, tin w/glass panes, rtcl top, smoke shield, 8" **65.00**
Tin, beveled-edge glass, Holmes, Booth & Hayden burner, 8¾" ...**215.00**
Tin, punched cylinder w/cone top, rpr ring hdl, pnt, 12" **195.00**
Tin, red, bl & gr glass in 3 sides, hinged door, 10" **75.00**
Tin, rpt, gr glass, heart-shaped vents, takes candle, 12" **275.00**
Tin blk-out type w/copper band, spring-loaded tube, 9½" **195.00**
Tin w/brass trim, kerosene burner, clear globe, 12½" **130.00**
Tin w/clear globe, NE Glass Co, Pat Oct 14, 1861, 12" **220.00**
Tin w/pressed glass globe, blk pnt, ring hdl, 11", EX **285.00**

Lard Oil/Grease Lamps

Betty, iron, open front, hanger, simple **130.00**
Betty, miner's, wrought w/heart finial, gold pnt, 4"+hanger **195.00**
Betty, sheet copper, homemade, 4½"+hanger & pick **55.00**
Betty, tin, crimped edge shelf, rnd, pan, 7" **360.00**
Betty, tin, lg saucer base, tube supports oval lamp, 7x8" **65.00**
Betty, tin w/orig crimped stand, 12½" overall **600.00**
Betty, wrought iron, brass lid w/chicken finial, 7¼" **360.00**
Betty, wrought iron, brass lid w/iron finial, 5¼" **155.00**
Betty, wrought iron w/brass spade-shaped ornament, 4½" **300.00**
Betty, wrought iron w/polished brass lid w/heart finial, 4" **165.00**
Cruise, dbl, wrought iron, twisted hanger, 11½"; 13", pr **75.00**
Kettle, brass, heavy iron gimbal hanger, 6½" **215.00**
Pan, iron, twisted hanger, 1700s, 20" **215.00**
Rush, iron, candle socket counterbalance, 7¾" **335.00**

Miniature, Kerosene Lamps

Beaded Drape, white opalescent with ruby thumbprints, nutmeg burner, 9¾", EX, $250.00; Red satin glass, nutmeg burner, 8½", EX, $275.00; Artichoke, hand-painted decoration on milk glass, 7¾", EX, $275.00.

Amber, glass burner, 5" **125.00**
Amber, ribbed swirl pattern, nb, 8" **450.00**
Amber & honey swirl, amber ped, nb, 9" **3,750.00**
Amber Log Cabin, hb, 3½" **725.00**
Amber shoe form, hb, 3", EX **800.00**
Amber w/emb circles, ftd/shouldered, ab, 4¾" **135.00**
Amethyst, emb beaded pleats, chimney-shape shade, ab, 6", EX ..**150.00**
Artichoke, amber satin, nb, 8" **800.00**
Artichoke, bl satin, nb, 8" **800.00**
Bl, paneled, ab, 3½" **150.00**
Bl match-holder form, nb, 7¾", EX **750.00**
Bl opal, clear ft, foreign burner, 7" **4,000.00**
Bl opaque, emb scrolls on base & ball shade, nb, 8½", EX **230.00**
Bl opaque Defender style, nb, 8½" **200.00**

Bulging Loops, pk o/l, orig brass burner, complete, 7¾x4" **650.00**
Candy-striped pk & wht over wht int, foreign burner, 8" **3,750.00**
Cathedral, amber, inverted shade, ped base, nb, 10", NM **210.00**
Chartreuse o/l satin cone shade/ball base, wafer ft, 7½" **850.00**
Cobalt, glass burner, 4¾", EX **125.00**
Coin Spot, cranberry opal, clear ped, nb, 7½" **3,400.00**
Cranberry angular shade, gourd-shape base, 9" **275.00**
Cranberry Beaded Swirl bulbous shade/base, complete, 8½" **450.00**
Cranberry emb swirl w/medallions cylinder shade/base, petal ft .**750.00**
Cranberry ruffled shade, base w/appl clear garlands/ft, 9" **850.00**
Cranberry swirl umbrella shade/pedestal base, complete, 8" **695.00**
Custard, emb ribs on umbrella shade & base, 7½", EX **130.00**
Cut Velvet Dmn Quilt, amber, frosted ft, ab, 7½" **750.00**
Daisy & Cube, nb, 8" **225.00**
Delft windmill porc ball shade/sq base, complete, 6" **250.00**
Glow, emerald gr, glass burner, 5¼" **125.00**
Glow, med bl, glass burner, 5¼" **125.00**
Glow, milk glass, glass burner, 4¾" **225.00**
Gr irid w/irregular red threads, brass base w/spider, 6x4" **325.00**
Greek Key, ab, 8½" **115.00**
Leon's Ribbed, bl opaque, ribs/dmns, ac, P&A on knob, 6", EX ...**65.00**
Log cabin, clear, hb, 3½", EX **350.00**
Milk glass, ribbed base/cone shade/hdld match cup, 8" **100.00**
Milk glass beehive shade, clear base, 8" **175.00**
Milk glass log cabin shade, hb, Pat date, 3¾" **575.00**
Milk glass tulip shade w/pnt decor, nb, 8½" **400.00**
Milk glass w/emb florals, nb, 7" **200.00**
Milk glass w/HP farm snow scene, ball shade/cylinder base, 9" ...**350.00**
Milk glass w/HP floral ball shade/gourd base, complete, 7" **295.00**
Milk glass w/HP floral 4" ball shade/base, complete, 8½" **295.00**
Milk glass w/mc pnt Artichoke base & shade, complete, 7¾" **450.00**
No 420 (Westmoreland), umbrella shade, flaring base, hb, 7" **160.00**
Owl head, bsk, gray w/bl neck ribbon, 3½x3" **275.00**
Pan-American Expo 1901, continents on ball shade/base, 10" **545.00**
Pineapple in Basket, milk glass w/fired-on brn, nb, 7½", EX **180.00**
Pk o/l rose petal shade on ribbed base, nb, 7" **550.00**
Pk o/l satin ball shade on melon-ribbed base, 6¾", EX **400.00**
Pk o/l w/emb panels, matching chimney shade, 8", EX **650.00**
Pk opal w/appl gr glass leaves & ft, nb, 8¼" **2,250.00**
Pk satin Drape ball shade/sq base, complete, 8¾" **450.00**
Red satin flower form shade, matching base, 8¾", EX **200.00**
Red satin w/emb beaded shells on shade & base, 8¾", NM **475.00**
Red satin w/emb wide leaf pattern, nb, 8¾" **450.00**
Santa figural, milk glass w/mc pnt, nb, 9½" **1,500.00**
Shoe, zero burner & chimney, dtd, 3", EX **1,300.00**
Skeleton head/shoulders, bsk w/pastel trim, glass eyes, 7" **5,000.00**
Spatter glass, emb swirls, nb, 6¾", EX **400.00**
Spatter ruby & wht swirl, nb, 8¼", EX **1,750.00**
Teal w/cut-bk floral ball shade/cylinder base, complete, 11" **895.00**
Twinkle, gr, ab, 7" **250.00**
Vaseline opal overshot flared shade/waisted base, 10½" **850.00**
Wht to bl bird/floral Bristol fluted fan shade/ftd sq base **850.00**

Motion Lamps

Animated motion lamps were popular from the 1920s to the early 1960s. They are characterized by action created by heat from a light bulb which causes a cylinder to revolve and create the illusion of an animated scene. Most were probably designed after the burning candle type in early days that rang bells and had hanging designs. Some of the better-known manufacturers were Econolite Corp., Scene in Action Corp., and L.A. Goodman Mfg. Company. As with many collectible items, prices are guided by condition, availability and collector demand, which seems to be more intense on the west and east coast, often resulting in higher prices there than in the midwest. Values are given for lamps in mint condition. Any damage or flaws seriously reduce the price. Our advisors for motion lamps are Kaye and Jim Whitaker; they are listed in the Directory under Washington.

Airplanes, Econolite, plastic, 1958, 11" 125.00
Antique cars, Econolite, plastic, 1957, 11" 125.00
Christmas tree, Econolite, paper, 1951, 15" 90.00
Fire fighters, LA Goodman, plastic, 1957, 11" 175.00
Forest fire, Econolite, plastic, 1955, 11" 100.00
Forest fire, LA Goodman, plastic, 1956, 11" 95.00
Fountain of Youth, Econolite, Roto-Vue Jr, 10" 115.00
Hopalong Cassidy, Econolite, Roto-Vue Jr, 1949, 10" 525.00
Marine scene, SIA, ship/lighthouse, glass, 1930s 175.00
Merry-Go-Round, Econolite, Disney, red plastic, 1955 ....225.00
Mill scene, Econolite, plastic, 1956, 11" 100.00
Miss Liberty, Econolite, 1957, 11" 125.00
Mountain waterfall & campers, LA Goodman, 1956, 11" 120.00
Niagara Falls, Econolite, plastic, 1955, 11" 95.00
Niagara Falls, LA Goodman, plastic, 1957, 11" 85.00
Niagara Falls, SIA, glass/metal, 1930s, 10" 175.00
Ocean creatures, LA Goodman, plastic, 1955, 11" 125.00
Oriental fantasy, LA Goodman, plastic, 1957, 11" 115.00
River boats, Econolite, plastic, 1947, 11" 125.00
Santa & reindeer, LA Goodman, plastic, 1955, 11" 130.00
Seattle World's Fair, Econolite, plastic, 1962, 11" 125.00
Ships, Rev-O-Lite, bronze & plastic, 1930s, 10" 125.00
Snow scene w/church, Econolite, plastic, 1957, 11" 115.00
Truck & bus, Econolite, plastic, 1957, 11" 150.00
Water skiers, Econolite, plastic, 1958, 11" 150.00

Pattern Glass Lamps

Angela, wht opal, bl ft & hdl, finger lamp, 5¼", EX 75.00
Aquarius, amber, stem lamp, #2 burner, 10" 125.00
Bull's Eye, clear font, bl opaque stem & ft, #2, 11", EX 350.00
Bull's Eye, emerald gr, stand lamp, 8½" 100.00
Bull's Eye, gr, #1 burner & chimney, finger lamp, 3½" 70.00
Bull's Eye, gr, Safety hdl, finger lamp, ftd, 5¾" 95.00
Cathedral font, bl w/clear 3-part stem, Daisy & Button shade 375.00

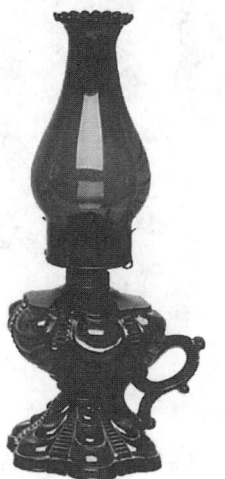

Coolidge Drape, cobalt with matching tulip-top chimney, #1 burner, 6", EX, $400.00.

Daisy & Button Panel, amber, #0 lock-on burner, EX 95.00
Daisy & Fern bl satin font, milk glass stem & ft, 17½" 225.00
Dmn & Fan, amber, finger lamp, flat, 3¾", EX 55.00
Eason, clear opal w/blk ft & hdl, finger lamp, 5⅜" 350.00

Emma, clear opal, #0 burner & chimney, finger lamp, EX 50.00
Empress, gr, #1 burner & chimney, finger lamp, 5¼" 125.00
Erin Fan, gr, #1 burner & chimney, finger lamp, 5¼" 150.00
Heart, gr opaque, stem lamp, #2 burner, 9¾", EX 175.00
Heart, yel custard, #1 burner & chimney, finger lamp, 5" 275.00
Hobbs Coin Dot, bl opal, #1 burner & chimney, finger lamp 350.00
Hobbs Coin Dot, cranberry opal, #1 burner & chimney, finger ..250.00
Hobbs Coin Dot, wht opal, #0 burner & chimney, finger lamp ..200.00
Janice, bl, #1 pb, finger lamp, ftd, 6½", EX 120.00
Markham Swirl Band, wht opal, #0 burner & chimney, finger ...150.00
Peacock Feather, amber, #1 burner, stem lamp, 8" 190.00
Peacock Feather, bl, finger lamp, ftd, 6", EX 150.00
Primrose, wht opal, #0 burner & chimney, finger lamp 250.00
Prince Edward, emerald gr, finger lamp, 5¾" 250.00
Prince Edward, milk glass, #1 burner & chimney, finger lamp 200.00
Princess Feather, cobalt, #1 burner, stem lamp, 8", EX 300.00
Queen Heart, emerald gr, #1 burner & chimney, finger lamp 125.00
Sandwich Blackberry, bl opaque on gold-veined stem, blk ft 250.00
Sheldon Swirl, bl opal, #1 burner & chimney, finger lamp, 5" ...375.00
Sheldon Swirl, vaseline, #1 burner, stem lamp, 8", EX 225.00
Sheldon Swirl, vaseline, #1 burner & chimney, finger lamp, 6" 60.00
Snowflake, bl opal, #0 burner & chimney, finger lamp 400.00
Snowflake, bl opal, #1 burner & chimney, finger lamp 650.00
Snowflake, cranberry opal, #0 burner & chimney, finger lamp ...450.00
Snowflake, cranberry opal, #1 burner & chimney, finger lamp ..1,300.00
Swirl, bl opal, #0 burner & chimney, finger lamp 325.00
Venetian, bl opal, #1 burner & chimney, finger lamp, 6", NM ...250.00
Wild Rose & Bow Knot, chocolate, stand lamp, 8⅝" 400.00

Peg Lamps

Bl Dmn Quilt MOP sq ruffle shade/bulb font; fluted std, 17" 695.00
Blown, pewter collar, brass & pewter burner, 5¾" 220.00
Clear w/gold floral shade/font; brass twist stick, 20" 400.00
Pk ribbed Bristol o/l ruffled 6" shade; brass std, 17" 590.00
Pk Swirl MOP fluted shade, gold dore base, 13" 575.00
Stippled cranberry w/gold cherries on shade/font, 11" 550.00

Reverse-Painted Lamps

Classique, 16" egrets/water lilies shade; Arts & Crafts std 2,100.00
Classique, 16" snow scene cone shade; Arts & Crafts std, M ...1,300.00
Classique, 8" macaws/cockatoos #2011 shade; ornate std, 14" .1,200.00
Jefferson, 16" rose blossom 6-panel shade; glass/metal std 1,375.00
Jefferson, 16" scenic sanded/chipped dome shade; mk base 1,200.00

Moe Bridges, geese in wooded landscape 18" conical shade, signed bronzed metal Grecian urn base with paw feet, 23", $3,250.00.

Moe Bridges, 16" scenic sgn #251 shade; bronzed std, M 1,300.00
Moe Bridges, 18" scenic #186H shade; vase std w/gr patina 2,200.00
Moe Bridges, 8" floral swag cone shade; pnt metal std, EX 150.00

Phoenix, 16" lake/mill dome shade; floral-emb metal base 450.00
Pittsburgh, 18" tepee/lake dome shade w/label; unmk vase std ...1,800.00
Unmk, 16" seascape dome shade; bronze metal base, 26" 450.00
Unmk, 16" woods/river dome DiOrio shade; metal std, 20" 300.00

Student Lamps, Kerosene

Brass, dbl cased gr shades, electrified, 22½x27", EX 400.00
Brass, milk glass shade, Kosmos Brenner, 18" 350.00
Brass w/fleur-de-lis on font & reservoir, rpr, 21" 350.00
Brass w/yel-cased umbrella shade, urn font, adjusts, 22" 590.00
NP, Miller syphon-style, wht shade, cut/frosted font, 21" 1,150.00
NP brass, dbl, GA Kleemann, NY, 19½" 550.00
NP brass, Manhattan, repro 7" milk glass shade, orig, 21" 350.00

Whale Oil/Burning Fluid Lamps

Blown, amber, hand-tooled ped, brass neck ring, 1830s, 7" 825.00
Blown cone form on rnd ft, appl hdl, repro burner, 2⅝" 230.00
Blown petticoat globe, saucer base, 3-knop stem, 5¾x4½" 990.00
Canary flint, hex base, 4-pruntie font, 11", EX 770.00
Flint, hex base, wafer & Dmn Quilt font w/T'print, 9½" 100.00
Flint, hex base, wafer & Sandwich Star font, 10½" 100.00
Flint, pressed base, blown pear-shaped font w/wafer, 7½" 300.00
Flint, rnd base, hex stem, rnd font, 7½" 85.00
Free-blown font w/pressed base, dbl burners, 9¼", NM 150.00
Periwinkle bl opaque w/sapphire bl font w/wht loops, 10", EX ...165.00
Pressed, flattened dmn pattern w/wafers, pewter collar, 10½" 150.00
Pressed, fleur-de-lis & star base, blown font, 8¾" 265.00
Pressed, hex baluster base w/gr to clear font, 11¼" 2,850.00
Pressed cobalt base, clear blown font w/bl & wht loops, 10" ...2,475.00
Pressed lemon-squeezer base, blown conical font, 9¼", EX 360.00
Pressed lemon-squeezer base w/hollow stem, bulbous font, 8½" ..470.00
Pressed quatrefoil base w/engr bulb-form font, 11", EX 360.00
Pressed sq ft w/baluster stem, blown/panel-cut font, 9" 125.00
Pressed stepped base, blown font, 6½" 140.00
Sapphire bl flint, Arch font, hex base, 10" 2,695.00

Miscellaneous

Astral, brass w/marble base, clear cut prisms, 22½" 600.00
Astral, dbl; gilt brass w/frosted globes, cut prisms, 17" 520.00
Astral, gilt brass, etched & cut shade, 1850s, 25½" 460.00
Bronze dragon atop jeweled ball holds glass shade, 28" 1,700.00
Lace maker's, blown, pressed lacy base, tin/cork burner, 9½" 550.00
Lace maker's, cranberry overshot, brass base, 16¼" 395.00
Sparking, pewter, cast ear hdl, single burner, unmk Am, 4" 50.00
Sparking, pewter, ring hdl, M Hyde, 4¼" 280.00
Table, Nouveau, metal w/3 sm hanging jeweled shades w/fringe ..650.00
Watch Pocket Lamp, NP brass, in wood box w/extra lights 450.00

Lang, Anton

Anton Lang was a German studio potter and an actor in the cast of the Oberammergau Passion Plays early in the 20th century. Because he played the role of Christ three times, his pottery was purchased by tourists overseas and brought back to the U.S. in suitcases, which accounts for the prevalence of smaller examples today. During 1923 when the play was being threatened with extinction due to Germany's postwar Depression, Anton Lang and the other 'Passion Players' toured the U.S. performing scenes from the play and selling their crafts. Lang would occasionally throw pottery when the cast passed through a pottery center such as Cincinnati, where Rookwood was located. His pot-

tery, marked with his name in script, is fairly scarce and highly valued for its artistic quality. Postcards, programs, and photographs depicting Lang are also collectible.

Figurine, cat & ball, gun-metal irid, Deco style, 8" 550.00
Flowerpot, aqua irid, mini, 2" 50.00
Pitcher, cobalt irid, HP Deco flowers & dots, yel int, 5" 150.00
Postcard, German, depicting Lang in formal dress 30.00
Vase, brn glossy, squeezebag edelweiss, Oberammergau, 4" 150.00
Vase, HP stripes in color on overall milky ground, mini, 2" 45.00
Vase, oxblood, 2¾" 200.00

Le Verre Francais

Le Verre Francais was produced during the 1920s by Schneider at Epinay-sur-Seine in France. It was a commercial art glass in the cameo style composed of layered glass with the designs engraved by acid. Favored motifs were stylized leaves and flowers or geometric patterns. It was marked with the name in script or with an inlaid filigrane. Our advisor for this category is Don Williams; he is listed in the Directory under Missouri.

Key: fp — fire polished

Cameo

Bowl, lg daisies on rose mottle, ftd, 5½x12" 850.00
Bowl, 5 scarabs, tortoise shell on orange, 4x10" 1,500.00
Ewer, sq Deco floral, brn/orange on yel mottle, bun ft, 12" 2,000.00
Lamp, elephants/palms on top & base, 2-tone lav/rust, 21x12" ...10,000.00
Pitcher, lg stylized floral, rust/bl on yel, Charder, 13" 2,000.00
Vase, bellfowers/leaves, red/wine on pk/wht, slim, ftd, 14" 1,200.00
Vase, berries/paneled neck, lav-brn on rust, slim, hdld, 18" 2,500.00
Vase, bird on pine cone branch (3 repeats), ovoid, 8½" 2,000.00
Vase, Deco floral, red on yel-rust, hdld/ftd, Charder, 19" 2,000.00

Vase, fish swimming in underwater scene, orange with green and brown, signed Charder, 12x9", $3,500.00.

Vase, floral, bl on topaz, inlaid filigrane, mk, 3x4" 350.00
Vase, floral/lg leaves, lav/wine on rose mottle, slim, ftd, 14" ...1,000.00
Vase, roses, red/gr on pk mottle, stick neck, 10½" 1,200.00
Vase, scarabs/geometrics, brn mottle on orange, ftd, 9½" 2,000.00
Vase, sq Deco floral, brn/rust on yel, slim, bun ft, 14" 850.00
Vase, stylized leaves, orange on wht fr, purple hdls, 10" 1,500.00
Vase, wavy ribs/disks, brns/gr on amber mottle, Charder, 16" ..1,870.00

Leach, Bernard

Bernard Leach was an artist who became a potter. From 1909 to 1920, he stayed in China and Japan where he became fascinated with traditional Oriental pottery and became a master of it. After returning to his native England, he became the most influential potter of the 20th century. Leach's methods and materials revolutionized modern art pottery. His ceramics are marked with a 'BL' seal and a 'S' seal for St. Ives, where his pottery was located in England.

Bottle, tenmoku, slab sides w/rnded shoulders, 7½" 1,200.00
Bowl, tenmoku w/rust, paneled sides, short ft, St Ives, 8" 1,200.00
Tea bowl, brn khaki on gray stoneware, 3" 215.00
Vase, bottle; celadon/bl w/iron red 'tree of life,' 7½" 1,250.00
Vase, iron red/oxide on cream, St Ives, ovoid, 10" 1,200.00
Vase, oatmeal glaze w/pnt salmon, stoneware, 15½" 1,850.00

Leeds, Leeds Type

The Leeds Pottery was established in 1758 in Yorkshire and under varied management produced fine creamware, often highly reticulated and transfer printed, shiny black-glazed Jackfield wares, polychromed pearlware, and figurines similar to those made in the Staffordshire area. Little of the early ware was marked; after 1775 the impressed 'Leeds Pottery' mark was used. From 1781 to 1820, the name 'Hartley Greens & Co.' was added. The pottery closed in 1898.

Today the term 'Leeds' has become generic and is used to encompass all polychromed pearlware and creamware, wherever its origin. Thus similar wares of other potters (Wood for instance) is often incorrectly called 'Leeds.' Unless a piece is marked or can be definitely attributed to Leeds by confirming the pattern to be authentic, 'Leeds-Type' would be a more accurate nomenclature.

Key:
cw — creamware   pw — pearlware

Bowl, cw, fluted, rtcl lid, floral finial, 7", w/ladle, VG 350.00
Candlestick, sq/rtcl, 12 sm rods support cup, mk, 9½" 550.00
Charger, pw, bl & wht Leeds floral, scalloped rim, 13¾", EX 165.00
Charger, pw, bl feather edge, bl & wht floral, 14¼", NM 415.00
Cup & saucer, rose in orange/bl, yel/bl flowers, blk bands, NM ..350.00
Dish, bl feather edge, mk Best Goods, rectangular, 5x4" 100.00
Jug, pw, gaudy floral in bl/orange, leaf hdl, flake, 6" 335.00
Plate, cw, swag-emb/rtcl rim, mk, stains, 8¾" 250.00
Platter, eagle, mc w/bl feather edge, 1800s, 16¼" 1,495.00
Saucer, pw, gaudy floral, 4-color, 4¼" 85.00
Tea caddy, pw, floral, 3-color, 5¼", EX 1,010.00
Teapot, cw, Chintz in iron red/blk, floral finial, 5", NM 1,875.00
Teapot, cw, festoons/floral sprigs, twist hdl, 3½", VG 600.00
Teapot, cw, house scene, blk transfer+3 colors, 4½x8", VG 365.00
Tray, rtcl dmn shape, emb scrolls, twist hdl, 8" L 400.00

Lefton China

In 1940 the Lefton China Co. was founded by George Zoltan Lefton, a native of Hungary, who in the 1930s was in the designing and manufacturing of sportswear. His hobby of collecting fine porcelains led him to the creation of his own ceramic business. Today the company is a leading producer of ceramic giftware, and the products are found in gift shops throughout the world.

Important to collectors are Lefton trademarks which aid in the dating of pieces. Most Lefton items are identified by a fired-on trademark or a paper label found on the bottom of each piece. These marks are found in both single and multicolor styles. Usually any number found below the marks are the item identification numbers and, if preceded by letters, will be the factory identification numbers. Older and discontinued items such as a vase formed as hands, parakeets, Little Adorables (Limited Edition), flamingo with baby, cherubs on trees, Huckleberry Finn and dog set, Holy Family, Napoleon, and swan candy dishes are eagerly sought after by collectors. As with any antique or collectible, the prices vary, depending on location, condition, and availability. For more information, we recommend *Collector's Encyclopedia of Lefton China* by our advisor, Loretta DeLozier; she is listed in the Directory under Iowa.

Angel, Kewpie of the Month, #130, 4½" 30.00
Animal, French poodle w/stones & 2 puppies, #80063, 6" 45.00
Animal, lamb w/china flowers & stones, #80551, 5" 33.00
Animal, sheep family, #117, 3-pc 21.00
Bank, nest house w/stones, #90338, 5" 41.00
Bank, owl w/rhinestone eyes, #90195, 6½" 50.00
Bank, Piggy, blk w/stones, #90199, 5¼" 25.00
Bell, Candy Cane Girls, #90401, 4" 13.00
Bell, Christmas, #80109, 4½" 20.00
Bookends, Cardinals, #90581, 5", pr 50.00
Bowl, sleigh shape, wht w/sponged gold, pk roses, #321 ....95.00
Butterfly, w/clip, #80578 ....11.00
Cigarette set (holder+2 trays), flower or bird design, #40133 ....27.00
Compote, grape design, #20053 ....28.00
Cookie jar, apple, w/lid, #20487, 6" 60.00
Cookie jar, winking Santa Claus, #90148, 10" 200.00
Cup & saucer, fruit pattern, #911 ....35.00
Dish, latticed w/lilac & stones, #232, 6" 30.00
Dish, pk w/feather, #20567, 5" 27.00
Ewer, bsk w/cameo & gold trim, #1875, 8" 28.00
Figurine, boy, James, #374, 10" 55.00
Figurine, Chinese sitting, #1008, 4½", pr 38.00
Figurine, Chinese w/umbrella & stones, #2175, 9", pr 60.00
Figurine, fisherman, bsk, #767, 7½" 52.00
Figurine, lady w/sm girl, #398, 6", pr 60.00
Figurine, Modern Dancers, #80103, 5½", pr 60.00
Figurine, Pussy Cat, Pussy Cat, #1474, 5" 45.00
Figurine, Rock-a-Bye in the Tree Top, #1104, 8" 55.00
Jam jar, Mr Santa, #1651, 6½" 24.00
Mug, bl aster, #6496, 4" 8.00
Mug, Teddy Roosevelt, #2191, 4½" 25.00
Planter, Gingham Elephant, #50090 ....22.00
Planter, girl pushing cart, #50584, 4½" 24.00
Planter, girl w/cart, #50048, 5" 30.00
Plaque, My Guests Like My Kitchen Best, #60329, 8" 28.00

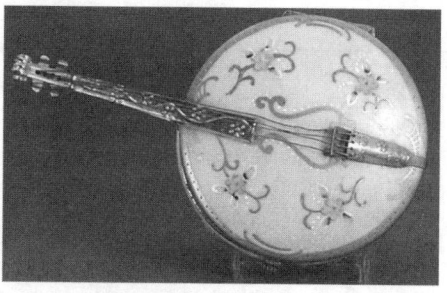

Powder box, banjo form, pink with metal handle, 7½", $50.00.

Shakers, Christy, #441, 2½", pr 8.00
Shakers, comical animal, #30404, 3½", pr 18.00
Snack set, Tree of Life, #20227 ....22.00
Spice set, frying pan shape w/rooster design, #20601, 6-pc 40.00
Spoon rest, Blk Chef, nodder, #90413, 5" 135.00
Teapot, Golden Lily design, #20027 ....65.00
Tray, single tidbit; Brn Heritage Floral, #20131 ....24.00
Vase, #124, mini, 2¾" 18.00
Vase, head, blk/wht/gold, #5057, 6½" 60.00
Vase, lilacs & stones, #153, 5" 40.00
Vase, rabbit head in pk w/stones, #70244, 7½" 25.00
Wall pocket, fruit design, #50574, 4½" 22.00
Wall pocket, girl w/striped bow around neck, #6767, 5" 40.00

Legras

Legras and Cie was founded in St. Denis, France, in 1864. Production continued until the 1930s. In addition to their enameled wares, they made cameo art glass decorated with outdoor scenes and florals executed by acid cuttings through two to six layers of glass. Their work is signed 'Legras' in relief and in enamel. Our advisor for this category is Don Williams; he is listed in the Directory under Missouri.

Cameo

Bowl, stylized mums, cut/pnt on textured frost, 4x8½" 625.00
Compote, foliage, gr on clear, etched ft, 10x16" 1,150.00
Lamp, grapes, purple on frosted dome shade, glass base, 19" 6,500.00
Lamp, grapes, purple on frosted dome shade/metal base, 19" ...2,000.00
Vase, apple blossoms, cut/pnt on frost, ovoid, 8" 300.00
Vase, aquatic scene cut/pnt, 6" 295.00
Vase, birds/vines/trees on textured bl, tapered, 8" 550.00
Vase, coral/shells cut/pnt on yel, baluster, 7" 150.00
Vase, floral stem, cut/pnt on textured clear, 12½" 825.00
Vase, leaves, cut/pnt, red on pk, 9" 1,175.00
Vase, lg birds/geometrics at shoulder, brn on frost, 16" 1,800.00
Vase, Queen Anne's lace, cut/pnt on rose, slim, 26" 2,500.00
Vase, sea plants/clam, wine/brn on shaded apricot, slim, 14" ..1,600.00
Vase, shepherd/flock/mtn, tricorner, 4" 750.00
Vase, stylized grapevines, cut/pnt on wht, ovoid, 9½" 575.00
Vase, V-shaped band w/birds, brn/wht, cylindrical, 15" 1,200.00

Enameled Glass

Box, snowy trees/birds pnt on orange sky, cylindrical, 2¾" 775.00
Vase, floral, mc on coral to yel frost, sgn, 9" 285.00
Vase, ships/trees, cylindrical w/irregular rim, 5¼" 225.00
Vase, Star of David medallion pnt on orange mottle, 14½" 850.00

Lenox

Walter Scott Lenox, former art director at Ott and Brewer, and Jonathan Coxon founded The Ceramic Art Company of Trenton, New Jersey, in 1889. By 1906 Cox had left the company and to reflect the change in ownership, the name was changed to Lenox Inc. Until 1930 when the production of American-made Belleek came to an end, they continued to produce the same type of high-quality ornamental wares that Lenox and Coxon had learned to master while in the employ of Ott and Brewer. Their superior dinnerware made the company famous, and since 1917 Lenox has been chosen the official White House China. Our advisor for this category is Mary Frank Gaston; she is listed in the Directory under Texas. See also Ceramic Art Company.

Creamer and sugar bowl, pink flowers and narrow gold lines, gold angular handles, with lid, Belleek, 6¼", 6", $250.00 for the pair.

Bowl, fruit; Blue Tree 35.00
Bowl, ivory w/gold trim, triangular, 7" 35.00
Bowl, vegetable; Olympia, oval, platinum trim 87.50
Butter tub, lav violets, pierced gold hdls, hexagonal, 3½" 110.00
Cake plate, Lenox Rose, low ped 140.00
Cake plate, Ming, hdls 115.00
Coffeepot, cobalt w/sterling o/l flowers, 8", +cr/sug 300.00
Compote, Lenox Rose, 4x9" 136.00
Compote, Ming, sm 97.50
Cordial, rtcl silver ftd holders, 2", set of 6 ....100.00
Creamer, Ming 60.00
Creamer & sugar bowl, Blue Ribbon 35.00
Cup & saucer, Bellevue Sea Green 35.00
Cup & saucer, Biltmore 40.00
Cup & saucer, bouillon; Empress 47.50
Cup & saucer, Brookdale, old style 37.50
Cup & saucer, Caribee 40.00
Cup & saucer, Country Garden 37.50
Cup & saucer, demitasse; Rhodora 47.50
Cup & saucer, Empress 38.00
Cup & saucer, Flirtation 38.00
Cup & saucer, Jefferson 32.00
Cup & saucer, Lenox Rose 36.00
Cup & saucer, Mansfield, old style 36.00
Cup & saucer, Musette 42.00
Cup & saucer, Olympia, platinum trim 37.50
Cup & saucer, Sachet 36.00
Cup & saucer, Springdale 40.00
Cup & saucer, Tuxedo, old style 47.50
Cup & saucer, Wyndcrest 36.00
Dove dish, ivory w/gold, 7" 34.00
Figurine, swan, pk, gr mk, 3x4½" 35.00
Gravy boat, Kingsley 150.00
Plate, bread & butter; Caribee 20.00
Plate, bread & butter; Glendale 10.00
Plate, bread & butter; Rhodora 18.00
Plate, chop; Olympia, platinum trim 135.00
Plate, dinner; Blue Ridge 37.50
Plate, dinner; Buchanan 27.50
Plate, dinner; Empress 36.00
Plate, dinner; Glendale, 10½" 25.00
Plate, dinner; Kinglsey 40.00
Plate, dinner; Meadow Song 37.50
Plate, dinner; Ming 36.00
Plate, dinner; Olympia, platinum trim 42.00
Plate, dinner; Repetoire 37.50
Plate, dinner; Snow Flower 40.00

Plate, dinner; Wheat 32.00
Plate, luncheon; Lenox Rose 30.00
Plate, luncheon; Ming 31.00
Plate, salad; Autumn 50.00
Plate, salad; Brookdale 22.50
Plate, salad; Buchanan 25.00
Plate, salad; Caribee 24.50
Plate, salad; Country Garden 25.00
Plate, salad; Empress 25.00
Plate, salad; Flirtation 25.00
Plate, salad; Jefferson 25.00
Plate, salad; Lenox Rose 20.00
Plate, salad; Olympia, platinum trim 25.00
Plate, salad; Wheat 25.00
Platter, Empress, 19" 155.00
Platter, Kingsley, 13¾" 150.00
Platter, Kingsley, 16¾" 175.00
Platter, Lenox Rose, 11" 110.00
Platter, Ming, oval, 16¾" 230.00
Platter, Ming, 12½" dia 210.00
Platter, Wyndcrest, lg 130.00
Platter, Wyndcrest, sm 120.00
Soup, Imperial, rimmed 45.00
Soup, Kingsley, rimmed 48.00
Soup, Wakefield, rimmed 30.00
Soup, Washington, rimmed 30.00
Sugar bowl, Kingsley 97.50
Teapot, Lenox Rose 230.00
Vase, belleek, Arts & Crafts banded decor, mc on cream, 8x5" ..175.00
Vase, poppies, red on mc ground, NM Drummer, 10", EX 60.00
Vase, Rose Manor, globular, 4½" 42.00

Letter Openers

Made in a wide variety of materials and designs, letter openers make for an interesting collection that is easy to display and easy on the budget as well. Our advisor for this category is Ron Damaska; he is listed in the Directory under Pennsylvania.

Bone, scrimshaw leaves, red/blk stain, cut-out hearts, 5¼" 80.00
Brass, nude man in bbl, advertising 25.00
Celluloid, Railway Express Agency on hdl, 9", EX 6.50
Ivory, dagger shape, ebony & abalone hdl, old 65.00
Metal, Gulf Oil 10.00
Plastic, Fuller Brush man figural, pk 9.50
Pot metal w/brass blade, cowboy on rearing horse, blk pnt, 8" 12.00
SP, Reed & Barton, cherubs in grape arbor hdl, ornate 35.00
Whalebone, Naughty Nellie leg hdl, 5½" 25.00
Whalebone, sword form, 4¼", EX 25.00

Libbey

The New England Glass Company was established in 1818 in Boston, Massachusetts. In 1892 it became known as the Libbey Glass Company. At Chicago's Columbian Expo in 1893, Libbey set up a ten-pot furnace and made glass souvenirs. The display brought them worldwide fame. Between 1878 and 1918 Libbey made exquisite cut and faceted glass, considered today to be the best from the brilliant period. The company is credited for several innovations — the Owens bottle machine that made mass-production possible and the Westlake machine which turned out both electric light bulbs and tumblers automatically. They developed a machine to polish the rims of their tum-

blers in such a way that chipping was unlikely to occur. Their glassware carried the patented Safedge guarantee. Libbey also made glassware in numerous colors, among them cobalt, ruby, pink, green, and amber. Our advisor for this category is Mike Roscoe; he is listed in the Directory under Ohio.

Bowl, amberina, triangular w/vertical ribs, 2½x5½" 285.00
Bowl, clear w/opal elephant stem, 8x11" 385.00
Bowl, cut, hobstars/swirls, shallow, 10" 975.00
Bowl, cut, Stratford, incurvate, sgn, 9", NM 200.00
Bowl, cut, triple sq design, 9½" 350.00
Bowl, cut flowers/thistles, ped ft, 6½x7" 400.00
Bowl, cut ovals, flared on sm rnd ft, 10" 60.00
Bowl, fruit; cut, pattern '69,' hobstars/fans, 7", set of 6 ....900.00
Bowl, intaglio fruits/leaves, flared/scalloped, 6x11" 880.00
Bowl, nut; cut, lovebirds, cherry blossoms & ferns, 3x5¼" 145.00
Candlesticks, cut, gr-cut-to clear flowers, 12", pr 325.00
Candlesticks, facet-cut std w/int bubble, hobstar ft, 9", pr 290.00
Candlesticks, floral intaglio, bulbous base, 12", pr 400.00
Celery tray, cut, Glenda, sgn, 12" 325.00
Chalice, gr-cut-to clear panels, deer in forest scene 150.00
Cordial, monkey stem, opal, Nash 145.00
Decanter, eng wheat/grasses, monogram, hollow stopper, 13" 575.00
Jug, cut, Princess, 1896 signature 550.00
Maize, celery, clear w/amber staining & bl leaves, 6" 235.00
Maize, pickle castor, gr husks on custard, SP fr 500.00
Maize, pitcher, bl husks on clear w/amber irid, clear hdl, 9" 585.00
Maize, shakers, gold-edged bl husks on custard, pr 250.00
Maize, sugar shaker, gold-edged yel husks on custard, 6" 235.00
Maize, syrup, gr husks on custard, scarce, 6" 350.00
Maize, toothpick holder, gold-edged gr husks on custard 400.00
Maize, tumbler, bl husks on irid 235.00
Pitcher, cut, Princess, bulbous, 1896 mk, lg 225.00
Pitcher, cut stars/fans/strawberry dmns, 9", +6 tumblers 1,200.00
Pitcher, tankard, cut, Star & Feather, notched hdl, 8½" 400.00
Plate, cut, Imperial, 7", NM 200.00
Platter, cut, hobstars/X-hatching/cane, 14", NM 800.00
Platter, ice cream; cut strawberries, 17" 700.00

Punch bowl, cut Strawberry Diamond pattern with hobstars and fans, 14", with twenty-three near-matching cups and fitted wooden case, $1,000.00.

Rose bowl, swirl mold, 8" 110.00
Toothpick holder, floppy hat shape, Columbian Expo 1893 ....225.00
Toothpick holder, Knickerbocker, sgn, ca 1920 ....55.00
Tray, bread; cut, Sultana, 11½" L 165.00
Vase, amberina, lily form, ribbed, no mk, 8" 650.00
Vase, amberina, ribbed, slender/ftd, sgn, 11" 1,075.00
Vase, blue-cut-to clear geometrics & buds, baluster, 9" 625.00
Vase, cut, floral, paperweight base, 4x1¾" 85.00

Vase, cut, lovebirds/wisteria, waisted, sgn, 12" 800.00
Wine, eng flowers, 4½", set of 6 ....60.00
Wine, frosted sitting bear stem, 5½", pr 250.00
Wine, kangaroo stem, opal, Nash 165.00

Lightning Rod Balls

Used as ornaments on lightning rods, the vast majority of these balls were made of glass, but ceramic examples can be found as well. Their average diameter is 4½" but can vary from 3½" up to 5½". Only a few of the many available pattern-and-color combinations are listed here. The most common measure 4½" and are found in sun-colored amethyst and milk glass. Our advisor is Mike Bruner, author of a book on this subject. Anyone interested in receiving a hobby-related newsletter may write to him for more information; he is listed in the Directory under Michigan.

Amber, Mast 125.00
Amethyst, sun-colored, plain, rnd 8.00
Bl, ceramic, rnd 100.00
Bl opaque, Mast 30.00
Bl opaque, Nat'l 23.00
Cobalt, Nat'l 55.00
Cobalt, plain, rnd 50.00
Gray-gr, ribbed grape 175.00
Milk glass, Moon & Star 45.00
Milk glass, plain, rnd 7.50
Pk, rnd 425.00
Red, Electra, cone 90.00
Red, Moon & Star 125.00
Silver, Nat'l 400.00
Teal bl, rnd 280.00

Limited Edition Plates

Currently values of some limited edition plates have risen dramatically while others have drastically fallen. Prices charged by plate dealers in the secondary market vary greatly; we have tried to suggest an average.

Bing and Grondahl

1895, Behind the Frozen Window 6,250.00
1896, New Moon 1,950.00
1897, Christmas Meal of Sparrows 1,100.00
1898, Roses & Star 685.00
1899, Crows Enjoying Christmas 1,500.00
1900, Church Bells Chiming 850.00
1901, 3 Wise Men 425.00
1902, Gothic Church Interior 395.00
1903, Expectant Children 395.00
1904, View of Copenhagen From Fredericksberg Hill 195.00
1905, Anxiety of the Coming Christmas Night 195.00
1906, Sleighing to Church 155.00
1907, Little Match Girl 195.00
1908, St Petri Church 105.00
1909, Yule Tree 105.00
1910, Old Organist 105.00
1911, Angels & Shepherds 105.00
1912, Going to Church 105.00
1913, Bringing Home the Tree 105.00
1914, Amalienborg Castle 100.00
1915, Dog on Chain Outside Window 175.00

1916, Prayer of the Sparrows 105.00
1917, Christmas Boat 105.00
1918, Fishing Boat 105.00
1919, Outside the Lighted Window 95.00
1920, Hare in the Snow 95.00
1921, Pigeons 85.00
1922, Star of Bethlehem 87.00
1923, Hermitage 82.00
1924, Lighthouse 105.00
1925, Child's Christmas 95.00
1926, Churchgoers 95.00
1927, Skating Couple 145.00
1928, Eskimos 95.00
1929, Fox Outside Farm 105.00
1930, Tree in Town Hall Square 115.00
1931, Christmas Train 115.00
1932, Lifeboat at Work 110.00
1933, Korsor-Nyborg Ferry 105.00
1934, Church Bell in Tower 95.00
1935, Lillebelt Bridge 105.00
1936, Royal Guard 105.00
1937, Arrival of Christmas Guests 135.00
1938, Lighting the Candles 165.00
1939, Old Lock-Eye, The Sandman 215.00
1940, Delivering Christmas Letters 245.00
1941, Horses Enjoying Meal 265.00
1942, Danish Farm on Christmas Night 205.00
1943, Ribe Cathedral 145.00
1944, Sorgenfri Castle 115.00
1945, Old Water Mill 175.00
1946, Commemoration Cross 105.00
1947, Dybbol Mill 145.00
1948, Watchman 105.00
1949, Landsoldaten 170.00
1950, Kronborg Castle at Elsinore 155.00
1951, Jens Bang 145.00
1952, Old Copenhagen Canals & Thorsvaldsen Museum 135.00
1953, Royal Boat 135.00
1954, Snowman 135.00
1955, Kaulundborg Church 130.00
1956, Christmas in Copenhagen 160.00
1957, Christmas Candles 175.00
1958, Santa Claus 135.00
1959, Christmas Eve 145.00
1960, Village Church 150.00
1961, Winter Harmony 105.00
1962, Winter Night 85.00
1963, Christmas Elf 110.00
1964, Fir Tree & Hare 65.00
1965, Bringing Home the Tree 55.00
1966, Home for Christmas 55.00
1967, Sharing the Joy 42.00
1968, Christmas in Church 33.00
1969, Arrival of Guests 30.00
1970, Pheasants in Snow 24.00
1971, Christmas at Home 24.00
1972, Christmas in Greenland 21.00
1973, Country Christmas 29.00
1974, Christmas in the Village 28.00
1975, The Old Water Mill 28.00
1976, Christmas Welcome 27.00
1977, Copenhagen Christmas 27.00
1978, A Christmas Tale 27.00
1979, White Christmas 27.00

1980, Christmas in the Woods 27.00
1981, Christmas Peace 30.00
1982, The Christmas Tree 40.00
1983, Christmas in Old Town 40.00
1984, Christmas Letter 43.00
1985, Christmas Eve, Farm 40.00
1986, Silent Night 40.00
1987, Snowman's Christmas 50.00
1988, In King's Garden 36.00
1989, Christmas Anchorage 46.00
1990, Changing Guards 52.00
1991, Copenhagen Stock Exchange 73.00
1992, Pastor's Christmas 73.00
1993, Father Christmas in Copenhagen 73.00

M. I. Hummel

The last issue for M.I. Hummel annual plates was made in 1995.

1971, Heavenly Angel 525.00
1972, Hear Ye, Hear Ye 50.00
1973, Globe Trotter 95.00

1974, Goose Girl, $50.00.

1975, Ride Into Christmas 50.00
1976, Apple Tree Girl 50.00
1977, Apple Tree Boy 60.00
1978, Happy Pastime 45.00
1979, Singing Lesson 35.00
1980, School Girl 45.00
1981, Umbrella Boy 50.00
1982, Umbrella Girl 80.00
1983, The Postman 165.00
1984, Little Helper 60.00
1985, Chick Girl 75.00
1986, Playmates 140.00
1987, Feeding Time 105.00
1988, Little Goat Herder 95.00
1989, Farm Boy 110.00
1990, Shepherd's Boy 185.00
1991, Just Resting 115.00
1992, Meditation 130.00
1993, Doll Bath 150.00
1994, Doctor 200.00
1995, Come Back Soon 250.00

Royal Copenhagen

1908, Madonna & Child 3,200.00
1909, Danish Landscape 195.00
1910, Magi 150.00
1911, Danish Landscape 160.00

1912, Christmas Tree 145.00
1913, Frederik Church Spire 145.00
1914, Holy Spirit Church 165.00
1915, Danish Landscape 175.00
1916, Shepherd at Christmas 125.00
1917, Our Savior Church 105.00
1918, Sheep & Shepherds 105.00
1919, In the Park 105.00
1920, Mary & Child Jesus 105.00
1921, Aabenraa Marketplace 105.00
1922, 3 Singing Angels 95.00
1923, Danish Landscape 100.00
1924, Sailing Ship 145.00
1925, Christianshavn Street Scene 105.00
1926, Christianshavn Canal 95.00
1927, Ship's Boy at Tiller 175.00
1928, Vicar's Family 105.00
1929, Grundtvig Church 105.00
1930, Fishing Boats 130.00
1931, Mother & Child 130.00
1932, Frederiksberg Gardens 135.00
1933, Ferry & Great Belt 160.00
1934, Hermitage Castle 165.00
1935, Kronborg Castle 215.00
1936, Roskilde Cathedral 185.00
1937, Main Street of Copenhagen 255.00
1938, Round Church of Osterlars 310.00
1939, Greenland Pack Ice 405.00
1940, Good Shepherd 400.00
1941, Danish Village Church 345.00
1942, Bell Tower 395.00
1943, Flight Into Egypt 550.00
1944, Danish Village Scene 290.00
1945, Peaceful Scene 450.00
1946, Zealand Village Church 190.00
1947, Good Shepherd 250.00
1948, Nodebo Church 220.00
1949, Our Lady's Cathedral 235.00
1950, Boeslunde Church 235.00
1951, Christmas Angel 365.00
1952, Christmas in Forest 145.00
1953, Frederiksberg Castle 155.00
1954, Amalienborg Palace 170.00
1955, Fano Girl 195.00
1956, Rosenborg Castle 195.00
1957, Good Shepherd 125.00
1958, Sunshine Over Greenland 120.00
1959, Christmas Night 120.00
1960, Stag 145.00
1961, Training Ship 155.00
1962, Little Mermaid 215.00
1963, Hojsager Mill 75.00
1964, Fetching the Tree 65.00
1965, Little Skaters 70.00
1966, Blackbird 40.00
1967, Royal Oak 40.00
1968, Last Umiak 39.00
1969, Old Farmyard 39.00
1970, Christmas Rose & Cat 45.00
1971, Hare in Winter 24.00
1972, In the Desert 24.00
1973, Train Home Bound 28.00
1974, Winter Twilight 28.00
1975, Queen's Palace 24.00

1976, Danish Watermill **31.00**
1977, Immervad Bridge **24.00**
1978, Greenland Scenery **24.00**
1979, Choosing the Tree **52.00**
1980, Bringing Home the Tree **37.50**
1981, Admiring the Tree **39.00**
1982, Waiting for Christmas **72.00**
1983, Merry Christmas **52.00**
1984, Jingle Bells **52.00**
1985, Snowman **59.00**
1986, Wait for Me **59.00**
1987, Winter Birds **59.00**
1988, Christmas Eve Copenhagen **69.00**
1989, Old Skating Pond **75.00**
1990, Christmas in Tivoli **72.00**
1991, St Lucia Basilica **52.00**
1992, Royal Coach **59.00**
1993, Arrival Guests by Train **59.00**

Limoges

From the mid-18th century, Limoges was the center of the porcelain industry of France, where at one time more than forty companies utilized the local kaolin to make a superior quality china, much of which was exported to the United States. Various marks were used; some included the name of the American export company (rather than the manufacturer) and 'Limoges.' After 1891 'France' was added. Pieces signed by factory artists are more valuable than those decorated outside the factory by amateurs. For a more thorough study of the subject, we recommend you refer to *The Collector's Encyclopedia of Limoges Porcelain, 2nd Edition,* by our advisor, Mary Frank Gaston, who is listed in the Directory under Texas. Her book has beautiful color illustrations and current market values.

Biscuit jar, red poppies w/gold, poppy finial, 7½" **250.00**
Bowl, bell flowers w/much gold, artist sgn, 10" **160.00**
Bowl, chestnuts & burrs on branch, sgn, T&V, 2¼x10" **150.00**
Bowl, cream soup; Florale, ivory w/gold, w/liner **50.00**
Bowl, floral w/gold, scalloped rectangle, 9x4" **45.00**
Bowl, gold flowers & branches, 3-compartment, hdls, 11½" **165.00**
Bowl, mc floral w/gold scrolls, scalloped, LS&S, 8½" **125.00**
Bowl, punch; grapes, purple/gr on yel, sgn MGH 1915, 12" **280.00**
Bowl, wild roses w/gold, flower ring hdl, 4-lobed, 11x6¾" **150.00**
Box, floral reserve, gold vines allover, 1x2¼x2½" **90.00**
Box, floral/gilt on gr, scalloped shell shape, sgn MR, 6" **75.00**
Box, jewel; Empress Louise, gilt/jeweled, T&V, 3x6½" dia **225.00**
Box, purple flowers & gold scrolls, sgn MO, 5¾" dia **135.00**
Box, stamp; floral, gold trim, red mk, 3¾x1¾" **45.00**
Cake plate, orchids w/gold, emb scrolls, open hdls, sgn **95.00**
Casserole, wht w/gold rope hdls & anchor, w/lid, 1870s, lg **200.00**
Chocolate pot, daisies/gold on lt gr, mk American, +4 c/s **110.00**
Chocolate pot, lav flowers w/gr & gold, ovoid, JPL, 10½" **125.00**
Coffee set, owl & forest scenic bands, 9" pot+18 pcs **595.00**
Game set, birds, gilt scalloped edge, 17" platter+12 plates **825.00**
Jar, powder; gold leaf fronds on eggshell, sgn **75.00**
Mug, vintage on pastel gr to tan, gold hdl, T&V, 5⅝x4" **98.00**
Panel, lady in feathered hat (touch-up), gilt fr, 5x3½" **200.00**
Pitcher, cider; roses & vines w/gold, mk, 5¾x6¾" **155.00**
Plaque, pastoral scene, prof decor, sq, ca 1890, 10½" **350.00**
Plate, bird pr, artist sgn, 13" **265.00**
Plate, bldg/trees, heavy shaped gold edge, no mk, 13½", pr **395.00**
Plate, fruit, Dubois, 10¼" **295.00**
Plate, game bird, L Courdert, much gold, Coronet, 10⅛", pr **325.00**

Plate, game birds, gold Rococo rim, 9½", pr **265.00**
Plate, golden pheasant, artist sgn, much gold, Coronet, 9" **165.00**
Plate, lady/equestrian, sgn Picat, gold Rococo rim, 13" **295.00**
Plate, mini flowers w/gold, sgn, scalloped, 9⅝" **48.00**
Plate, pk florals w/gold & bl ribbon, hdls, GDA, 13" **175.00**
Plate, pk roses w/gr foliage & gold Rococo, T&V, 12¾" **190.00**
Plate, quail pr/flowers on pastels, sgn Bay, gold rim, 14" **225.00**
Plate, roses, irregular edge, pierced for hanging, mk, 10⅜" **135.00**
Plate, roses, sgn Broumiller, gold Rococo rim, no mk, 14" **250.00**
Plate, roses, sgn Marcell, irregular gold rim, mk, 10¼" **135.00**
Platter, fish; fish amidst leafage, +12 plates **525.00**
Platter, mc floral w/gold, T&V, 14" **75.00**
Platter, pheasant pr, sgn Luc, gold hdls, oval, 14½" **225.00**
Platter, pk forget-me-nots, scroll rim, Elite, 16¾" **130.00**
Tankard, floral, Gutret, 13" **300.00**
Tankard, monk portrait medallion w/gold scrolls, sgn, 14½" **425.00**
Teapot, wht w/elaborate floral & scroll silver o/l, 2¼x5½" **100.00**
Tray, dresser; floral sprays, beaded & scalloped, 10½x8¼" **65.00**
Tray, dresser; red roses w/gold scrolls, scalloped, 11¾x8" **67.50**
Trivet, roses, sgn E Thau, T&V, 6½" dia **50.00**
Tureen, forget-me-nots & gold scrolls, w/lid, Elite **155.00**

Lithophanes

Lithophanes are porcelain panels with relief designs of varying degrees of thickness and density. Transmitted light brings out the pattern in graduated shading, lighter where the porcelain is thin and darker in the heavy areas. They were cast from wax models prepared by artists and depict views of life from the 1800s, religious themes, or scenes of historical significance. First made in Berlin about 1803, they were used as lamp shade panels, window plaques, or candle shields. Later steins, mugs, and cups were made with lithophanes in their bases. Japanese wares were sometimes made with dragons or geisha lithophanes. Our advisor for this category is Lucille Malitz; she is listed in the Directory under New York. See also Dragon Ware; Steins.

Table lamp, yellow brass with six-panel scenic lithograph shade, original gas burner, 20¾", $1,400.00.

Candle shield, children read, PR, brass holder, 3¼x2½" **120.00**
Candle shield, lovers in boat, wood-caned fr, 9x7" **400.00**
Candle shield, maid feeds birds, wood fr, KPM, 10x12" **600.00**
Fairy lamp, genre scenic in domed shade, Clarke cup, 5" **750.00**
Fairy lamp, mc landscape w/fox & deer, Clarke cup, 4½" **550.00**
Fairy lamp, wooded landscape & children, mc, Clarke cup, 4½" ..**1,000.00**
Lamp, 4 7x5" scenic panels **650.00**
Lamp, 6 scenic panels in shade; 3-strap std w/bun base, 21" **1,400.00**
Lamp, 6½x9" 5-panel scenic shade; silver base, 17", pr **1,900.00**
Lantern, 4 mini panes w/children scenes, ea pane: 1x¾" **200.00**
Panel, blond boy playing dominoes, sgn, 8x10" **275.00**

Panel, couple in woods/children at well, PPM, 7x5¾", pr **210.00**
Panel, lady dressing, mk PR, cracked, 4½x3¾" **70.00**
Panel, man gives lady gift, child sleeps, PPM, 5x4¼" **350.00**
Panel, medieval lady leaving church, KPM, 12½x10" **275.00**
Panel, moonlit rocky mtns coast, metal hanger mk Paris, 4x5" **75.00**
Panel, peasants working by lake, mk, #d, 7x5½", pr **150.00**
Panel, young maiden, KPM, wood fr, 6x4" **200.00**
Panel in plique-a-jour fr, figures on river, PR, 10x9", pr **900.00**
Tea set, Arita, blk w/gold, 18-pc **75.00**

Little Red Riding Hood

Though usually thought of as a product of the Hull Pottery Company, research has shown that a major part of this line was actually made by Regal China. The idea for this popular line of novelties and kitchenware items was developed and patented by Hull, but records show that to a large extent Hull sent their whiteware to Regal to be decorated. Little Red Riding Hood was produced from 1943 until 1957. Values have risen sharply over the past several months. For further information we recommend *Collecting Hull Pottery's Red Riding Hood* by Mark Supnick. Watch for the announcement of another book on this subject by Joyce and Fred Roerig, authors of *The Collector's Encyclopedia of Cookie Jars*. Our advisors for this category are Rose and Charlie Snyder; they are listed in the Directory under Kansas.

Bank, standing **550.00**
Bank, wall hanging, M **1,500.00**
Batter pot **425.00**
Butter dish **395.00**
Canister, cereal, M **850.00**
Canister, salt **800.00**
Canisters, coffee, sugar or flour; ea **650.00**
Cookie jar, closed basket, minimum **350.00**
Cookie jar, open basket, gold flowers on apron, minimum **300.00**
Cookie jar, open basket, red shoes **575.00**
Cookie jar, poinsettia **1,050.00**
Cookie jar, red spray w/gold bows, red shoes **850.00**
Cookie jar, wht **200.00**
Cracker jar, unmk **550.00**
Creamer, top pour, no tab hdl **350.00**
Creamer, top pour, tab hdl **300.00**
Creamer & sugar bowl, side pour **300.00**
Grease jar, flower basket, gold trim **1,050.00**
Match holder, wall hanging **800.00**
Mug, emb figure, wht (no color), minimum value **650.00**
Mustard, w/spoon **375.00**
Pitcher, batter **375.00**
Pitcher, milk; standing, 8" **265.00**
Planter, hanging **475.00**
Shakers, Pat Design 135889, med sz **850.00**
Shakers, 3¼", pr **125.00**
Shakers, 5½", pr **175.00**
Spice jar, sq base **650.00**
Sugar bowl, crawling, unmk **275.00**
Sugar bowl, side pour **175.00**
Sugar bowl lid **225.00**
Teapot **365.00**
Wolf jar, yel **900.00**

Liverpool

In the late 1700s Liverpool potters produced a creamy ivory ware, sometimes called Queen's Ware, which they decorated by means of the newly perfected transfer print. Made specifically for the American market, patriotic inscriptions, political portraits, or other States themes were applied in black with colors sometimes added by hand. (Obviously their loyalty to the crown did not inhibit the progress of business!) Before it lost favor in about 1825, other English potters made a similar product. Today Liverpool is a generic term used to refer to all ware of this type. Our advisor for this category is William Kurau; he is listed in the Directory under Pennsylvania.

Jugs: Washington transfer with enameled 'First President of the U.S. of America on front, Amelia ship with American flag on back, black transfer with multicolor details, 10", NM, $4,950.00; Independence and flags on front, Washington, Justice, Liberty, and Victory on back, black transfer, ca 1800, 8", $1,650.00.

Bowl, Rocks & Sands & Every Ill..., gr, 7" dia **1,400.00**
Jug, Am schooner/Independence, mc, eagle spout, 9½" **1,850.00**
Jug, Am 3-masted ship/pastoral scene, 1800s, 6¾", NM **660.00**
Jug, City of Washington/Washington in Glory, rprs, 9" **865.00**
Jug, East India man/Frigate, blk transfer, 8½", EX **595.00**
Jug, L'Insurgent & Constellation, mc w/gold, 9½" **980.00**
Jug, Masonic symbols/Mason w/coat of arms, mulberry, 8½" **750.00**
Jug, Masonic symbols/wreath & verse, blk, 10¾", EX **1,150.00**
Jug, Success to Trade/Coopers's Arms, mc, 8½", VG **635.00**
Jug, Washington & map/Independence, early 1800s, 10" **1,200.00**
Jug, 3-masted Am ship, mc w/gold, 9¼" **1,095.00**
Mug, Success to Duke of York...Army, equestrian, blk, 6", VG ..**385.00**
Plaque, Geo Washington portrait medallion, 1800s, 5", EX+ ..**1,550.00**
Platter, 3-masted ship, mc, 18½" **800.00**

Lladro

Lladro porcelains are currently being produced in Labernes Blanques, Spain. Their retired and limited edition figurines are popular collectibles on the secondary market.

Angel behind sleeping child, finger to lips, 7" **80.00**
Attentive Dogs, #4657, discontinued 1981 ....**665.00**
Bar Mitzvah Boy **250.00**
Boy Tennis Player, #4894 ....**295.00**
Brave Knight, #1385 ....**685.00**
Claudette, 35755 ....**285.00**
Cobbler, #4853 ....**550.00**
Daddy's Girl, #5584 ....**350.00**
Dancing Partner, #5093 ....**290.00**
Dog playing bongos, #1156 ....**500.00**
Dressmaker, #4700 ....**360.00**

Feeding the Pigeons, #5428 ....630.00
Flower Song 400.00
Garden Song 395.00
Gentleman Equestrian, #5329 ....345.00
Girl w/Goose, #4815 ....295.00
Girl w/Turkey, #4569, discontinued 1981 ....400.00
Horse, #1203, discontinued 1981 ....300.00
Indian Brave, Am West Series 1,250.00
It's Your Turn, #5959 ....325.00
Jester's Serenade, ltd ed 1,400.00
Kissing Doves, #1170, discontinued 1988 ....200.00
Little Eagle Owl, #2020 ....425.00
Love Letter, Rockwell, #1406 ....785.00
Mother, Child & Lamb, #5297 ....230.00
Nap Time, #5448 ....225.00
New Hat, #5345 ....270.00
Nostalgia, #5071 ....310.00
On the Farm, #1306 ....240.00
Peter Pan 1,300.00
Pick of the Litter 345.00
Pilar, #5410 ....315.00
Red Riding Hood, #4965 ....650.00
Shall We Dance, #5799 ....500.00
Snow White, Armani 1,200.00
St Nick, #5427 ....635.00
Summer Stroll 245.00
Suzy & Doll, Rockwell, #1378 ....450.00
Talk to Me, #5987 ....140.00
Time To Rest, #5399 ....295.00
Tinkerbell, ltd edition, 1992, 10" 2,450.00
Tricycle, #5031 ....1,725.00
Veterinarian, #4825 ....435.00
Voyage of Columbus, limited edition 1,450.00
1742 Onward 1,650.00

Lobmeyer

J. and L. Lobmeyer, contemporaries of Moser, worked in Vienna, Austria, during the last quadrant of the 1800s. Most of the work attributed to them is decorated with distinctive enameling; favored motifs are people in 18th-century garb.

Bowl, couple in mc enamel, quatrefoil, 4", +underplate 975.00
Bowl, mythical creatures/humans/chariots/etc, oval, 4x4" 1,500.00
Box, intaglio lid w/nude & cornucopias, clear, 6" dia 750.00
Tumbler, lady & florals, 12-panel, sgn 400.00
Vase, gr patina w/gold & mc enameling, sgn, 1890, 8" 725.00

Locke Art

Joseph Locke already had proven himself many times over as a master glassmaker, working in leading English glasshouses for more than seventeen years. He came to America where he joined the New England Glass Company. There he invented processes for the manufacture of several types of art glass — amberina, peachblow, pomona, and agata among them. In 1898 he established the Locke Art Glassware Co. in Mt. Oliver, Pittsburgh, Pennsylvania. Locke Art Glass was produced using an acid-etching process by which the most delicate designs were executed on crystal blanks. Most examples are signed simply 'Locke Art,' often placed unobtrusively near a leaf or a stem. Other items are signed 'Jo Locke,' some are dated, and some are unsigned. Most of the work was done by hand. The business continued into the 1920s. For further study we recommend *Locke Art Glass, Guide for Collectors*, by Joseph and Janet Locke, available at your local bookstore.

Bowl, Poppy, 2¼x4½" 125.00
Champagne, Poppy, 6" 150.00
Fruit cup, Poppy, saucer ft, sgn, 3x3½" 125.00
Goblet, Ivy etch, sgn 150.00
Pitcher, Poinsettia, sgn, 8½" 650.00
Salt cellar, Vintage, sgn, ped ft, 2¼x1¼" 125.00
Tray, ice cream; floral eng, 16x8" 550.00
Tumbler, Roses, hdl, sgn, 4" 125.00
Vase, butterflies/sheaves of wheat, sgn, ftd/ruffled, 6x5" 750.00
Vase, Peonies, sgn, ruffled, 5" 650.00

Locks

The earliest type of lock in recorded history was the wooden cross bar used by ancient Egyptians and their contemporaries. The early Romans are credited with making the first key-operated mechanical lock. The ward lock was invented during the Middle Ages by the Etruscans of Northern Italy; the lever tumbler and combination locks followed at various stages of history with varying degrees of effectiveness. In the 18th century the first precision lock was constructed. It was a device that utilized a lever-tumbler mechanism. Two of the best-known of the early 19th century American lock manufacturers are Yale and Sargent, and today's collectors value Winchester and Keen Kutter locks very highly. Factors to consider are rarity, condition, and construction. Brass and bronze locks are generally priced higher than those of steel or iron. Our advisor for this section is Joe Tanner; he is listed in the Directory under Washington.

Key:
bbl — barrel   st — stamped

Top row all Winchester, left to right: Iron, push key, $150.00; Iron, lever, $150.00; Brass, lever, $175.00; Tin, double lever, $125.00; Bottom row: Commemorative, brass, lever, George Worthington Co., 1829-1929, $150.00; Norvel Shapleigh Hdw. Co., brass, lever, $175.00; BBB, Bingham's Best Brand, brass, lever, $150.00; Mercury, iron, story lock, push key, $250.00.

Brass Lever Tumbler

Ames Sword Co, Perfection st on shackle, 2¾" 60.00
Automatic, emb, flat key, 2⅛" 15.00
Bingham's Best Brand, BBB emb on front, 3¼" 150.00
Cleveland 4 Way, Cleveland 4 Way emb on front, 3⅝" 90.00
Cotterill, stamped High Security key, 5⅛x3⅛" 275.00

Crusader, shield, swords emb on body, 2¾" **45.00**
Eagle Lock Co, word Eagle emb on front, scrolled, 3" **60.00**
Jackson's, st Jackson's on front, 2½" **20.00**
JWM, emb, bbl key, 2⅝" **25.00**
Keen Kutter, shape of KK emblem, KK emb on front, 4¾" **125.00**
Mercury, Mercury emb on body, 2¾" **75.00**
Motor, Motor emb on body, 3¼" **35.00**
Our Very Best, OVB emb on body, 2⅞" **150.00**
Roeyonoc, Roeyonoc st on body, 3¼" **30.00**
Romer & Co, Romer & Co st on dust cover, 3" **55.00**
Ruby, Ruby emb in scroll on front, 2¾" **20.00**
Safe, Safe emb in scroll on front, 2⅜" **20.00**
Siberian, Siberian emb on shackle, 2½" **110.00**
Sphinx, sphinx & pharaoh head emb on front, 2¾" **35.00**
W Bohannan & Co, SW emb in scroll on front, 2⅜" **30.00**
Watch, emb, flat key, 3" **30.00**
Winchester, Winchester emb on front, 3" **160.00**

Combinations

Chicago Combination Lock Co, st on front, brass, 2¾" **60.00**
Corbin Sesamee 4-Dial Brass Lock, st Sesamee, 2¾" **12.00**
Edwards Mfg Co No-Key, st on lock, brass, 2¾" **60.00**
Junkunc Bros Mfrs, all st on bk, brass, 1⅞" **25.00**
Karco st on body, 2½" **50.00**
Number or letter disk type (4 disks), brass, 2¾" **130.00**
Quaint Mfg Co, st on lock case, 4¼" **200.00**
Sq lock case of steel, st Pat Germany, 4-wheel, 3¼" **110.00**
Sutton Lock Co st on body, 3" **200.00**
Vulcana Push Lock Corp, st on lock case, 3¼" **50.00**
Your Own st on body, 3⅞" **325.00**

Eight-Lever Type

Armory, brass, Armory 8-Lever st on front **25.00**
Electric, steel, Electric st on front **25.00**
Goliath, steel, Goliath 8-Lever st on front **20.00**
Miller, steel, Miller 8-Lever st on front **18.00**
Samson, brass, 8-Lever st on front **18.00**

Iron Lever Tumbler

Bull, word Bull emb on front, 2⅝" **30.00**
Bulldog, word Bulldog & face of dog emb on front, 2¾" **30.00**
Dan Patch, Dan Patch emb on front, horseshoe on bk, 2¾" **130.00**
Dragon, word Dragon & dragon emb on front, 2⅞" **25.00**
Eagle, word Eagle emb on body, 4⅜" **40.00**
Indian Head, Indian head emb on front, 3" **90.00**
Jupiter, word Jupiter/star & moon emb on front, 3¼" **18.00**
Karo, word Karo emb on front, CI, 3⅛" **25.00**
King Korn, words King Korn emb on body, 2⅞" **40.00**
Nineteen O Three, 1903 emb on front, iron, 3⅞" **90.00**
Red Chief, words Red Chief emb on body, 3¾" **80.00**
Rugby, football emb on body, 3" **20.00**
Unique, word Unique emb on front, 3¼" **120.00**
Yale & Towne, lion face emb on front, shackle mk Y&T, 3" **110.00**

Lever Push Key

Aztec, emb 6-Lever, 2⅛" **50.00**
Celtic Cross, emb cross on face, brass, 2¼" **125.00**
Champion, emb Champion 6-Lever, brass push-key type, 2¼" **25.00**
Climax, emb Climax 6-Lever, iron push-key type, 2¼" **35.00**
Columbia, emb Columbia 6-Lever, brass push-key type, 2¼" **35.00**

Dash, emb Dash 6-Lever, iron push-key type, 2¼" **25.00**
Duke, emb 6-Lever, 2⅛" **45.00**
Excelsior, emb Excelsior 6-Lever, brass push-key type, 2¼" **25.00**
Harvard, emb Harvard 4-Lever, brass push-key type, 2" **50.00**
IXL, emb IXL on body, 2¼" **75.00**
Jewett Buffalo, emb, brass, 2¼" **150.00**
Keystone, emb Keystone 6-Lever, brass push-key type, 2¼" **40.00**
McIntosh, emb McIntosh on body, 2¼" **90.00**
SB Co, emb SB Co on body, 3¼" **60.00**
Smith & Egge Mfg Co, Smith & Egge st on front, 3" **75.00**
Ten Star, emb Ten Star 6-Lever, 2¼" **45.00**

Logo — Special Made

Brass pancake push key emb US Internal Revenue, 2¼" **185.00**
Heart-shape brass lever type emb Shults Co, bbl key, 2¾" **55.00**
Heart-shape brass lever type st Board Education, bbl key, 3½" **60.00**
Sq brass pin-tumbler case st Regd US Mail, int counter, 2¾" **140.00**
Sq Yale-type brass pin tumbler, emb w/Texaco & star, 3" **25.00**
Sq Yale-type brass pin tumbler, st Shell Oil Co on body, 3⅛" **20.00**
Sq Yale-type brass pin tumbler, st US/A/tree/Forest Svc, 2⅞" **125.00**

Pin-Tumbler Type

Corbin, brass, Corbin in oval st on body, 3⅝" **25.00**
Eagle, brass, Eagle st on body, 2⅞" **20.00**
Fulton, emb Fulton on body, 2⅝" **30.00**
Il-A-Noy, emb Il-A-Noy on body, 2½" **40.00**
Pearl, brass, emb Pearl on body, 2⅛" **16.00**
Sargent, brass, emb Sargent on body, 3" **15.00**
Segal, iron, emb Segal on shackle, 3¾" **40.00**
Shapleigh, emb Shapleigh on body, 2⅝" **40.00**
Yale, brass, emb Yale on body, Made in England on shackle, 3" ...**40.00**
Yale, brass, emb Yale on body, Yale & Towne on shackle, 2⅝" **25.00**

Scandinavian (Jail House) Type

JHW Climax Co, iron, 2⅞" **50.00**
Star, emb line on bottom, iron, 3¾" **100.00**
Star, iron, 2½" **70.00**
99 Miller, emb 99, brass, 1¾" **80.00**
999 Miller, emb 999, brass, 2½" **70.00**

Six-Lever Type

Eagle, brass, Eagle Six Lever st on body **15.00**
Edwards, iron, Edwards st on body **15.00**
Safe, brass, Safe st on body **18.00**
Yale, brass, Yale emb on front **12.00**

Story and Commemorative

AYPEX Seattle (Alaska Yukon Pacific Expo), emb tin/iron, 3" .**225.00**
Canteen, US emb on lock, lock: canteen shape, 2" **500.00**
CI, emb ornate scroll motif throughout body of lock, 3½" **170.00**
CI, emb skull/X-bones w/florals, NH Co on bk, 3¼" **200.00**
CQD/sinking ship Titanic & SOS waves emb on brass, 2¾" **120.00**
Eagle/stars/shield & stars, emb CI, Eagle Liberty, 2½" **300.00**
Mail Pouch, emb on lock, lock in shape of a mail pouch, 3⅛" **225.00**
1901 Pan Am Expo, brass, emb w/buffalo, 2⅝" **175.00**

Warded Type

Army, iron pancake ward key, emb letters, 2½" **35.00**

Globe, iron sq lock case, emb US on bk, 2⅜" 20.00
Hex, iron, sq lock case, emb US on bk, 2⅛" 95.00
Navy, iron pancake ward key, bk: scrolled emb letters, 2½" 35.00
Red Cross, brass sq case, emb letters, 2" 10.00
Rex, steel case, emb letters, 2⅝" 18.00
Safe, brass sq case, emb letters, 1⅞" 8.00
Safety First, brass pancake type, emb letters, 2¾" 15.00
Secure, iron pancake type, emb letters, 2⅝" 20.00
Sprocket, brass oval shape, emb letters, 2⅛" 50.00
Try Me, iron pancake type, emb letters, 2½" 25.00
Winchester, brass sq case, stamped letters, 2¾" 125.00

Wrought Iron Lever (Smokehouse) Type

DM&Co, bbl key, 4¼" 15.00
MW&Co, bbl key, 2⅝" 10.00
MW&Co, flat key, 3½" 20.00
S&Co, bbl key, 3" 8.00

Loetz

The Loetz Glassworks was established in Klostermule, Austria, in 1840. After Loetz's death the firm was purchased by his grandson, Johann Loetz Witwe. Until WWII the operation continued to produce fine artware, some of which made in the early 1900s bears a striking resemblance to Tiffany's, with whom Loetz was associated at one time. In addition to the iridescent Tiffany-style glass, he also produced threaded glass and some cameo. The majority of Loetz pieces will have a polished pontil. Our advisor for this category is Don Williams; he is listed in the Directory under Missouri.

Basket, rubena verde irid w/raindrops, hdl w/prunts, 16x9" 700.00
Bowl, gr irid, 6-lobe, in bronze Deco armature, 4x7" 175.00
Bowl, yel w/gr waves & gold irid, 4½" 1,700.00
Compote, gr w/fuchsia waves, gr borders, hollow std, 10" 2,500.00
Inkwell, gr irid, on attached rtcl brass tray 265.00
Inkwell, silver o/l lotus on gr irid, sqd, metal top, 3x3" 350.00
Loving cup, bl raindrop irid w/silver o/l florals, 3-hdld, 5" 2,100.00
Rose bowl, silver o/l scrolls on bl irid w/oil spots 850.00
Syrup, dk bl-gr w/appl heavy lines, 7½" 595.00

Vases: light green with brownish iridescent swirls and raindrops on melon-ribbed form with Nouveau-style silver overlay, 7¼x5", $800.00; Gold peppering on iridescent raindrop finish with blue and pink iridescent highlights on gooseneck form with Nouveau-style iris silver overlay, 8¾x3½", NM, $1,000.00.

Vase, amber w/gold feathers, quatralobe rim, 5" 1,200.00
Vase, amethyst, copper Art Moderne o/l, 10" 250.00
Vase, amethyst irid w/allover threading, cylindrical, 8" 150.00
Vase, amethyst w/wine irid irregular ribs, lobed top/base, 12" 250.00
Vase, bl irid on bubbly clear, flaring U-form, 8" 575.00
Vase, bl-gold irid w/oil spots, shouldered, sm neck, 5" 770.00
Vase, blk amethyst w/bl & gold oil spots, ruffled, 4½" 150.00
Vase, dk gr, bottle form w/flat lip, 13" 275.00
Vase, gold w/bl irid swagged threads, corset form w/ribs, 7" 200.00
Vase, gold w/bl waves, in bronze fr w/grapes & owls, 12½" 1,800.00
Vase, gold w/EX irid, lg appl loops, bottle form, 11½" 1,200.00
Vase, gold w/oil spots, bl irid trellis at waist, 8" 1,380.00
Vase, gold w/oil spots, ruffled, polished pontil, 14" 250.00
Vase, gr irid, fire-polished rim, polished pontil, 10" 125.00
Vase, gr irid w/brass rim, str sides, 5" 185.00
Vase, gr irid w/oil spots, bent neck, bell-shape body, 11" 400.00
Vase, gr textured w/pk & gr irid, in metal fitting, att, 15" 1,400.00
Vase, gr w/allover rainbow irid, embedded threads, 6½" 225.00
Vase, gr w/bl & gold swirls, fluted, att, 4x4" 275.00
Vase, gr w/bl/purple oil spots, fluted, dimpled, att, 6" 100.00
Vase, gr w/EX irid, oil spots & random threads, 9" 2,100.00
Vase, gr w/oil spots, dimpled at waist, 8" 375.00
Vase, gr w/red oil spots, ruffled, ground pontil, 12" 200.00
Vase, gr w/silver oil spots, ogee sides, flat rim, 10" 250.00
Vase, gray-gr w/dimples, ribbed w/tri-pulled rim, 14" 250.00
Vase, jack-in-pulpit; gold & purple irid w/appl vines, 16" 485.00
Vase, lav bl w/oil spots, swirled, 3-fold rim, 7" 250.00
Vase, lt gold w/dk gold zipper decor, 6-sided, 8" 450.00
Vase, navy w/irid waves, flared rim, 4" 800.00
Vase, olive irid, conical w/fan-shaped rim, 10" 120.00
Vase, pk w/bl & platinum irid, wavy ridges, 3½" 210.00
Vase, purple w/gr irid ribs, twisted/shaped cylinder, 12" 350.00
Vase, red w/silvery bl crackle, M Kirschner, Argentan, 11" 650.00
Vase, rubena verde w/irregular gr threads, fan form, 7" 350.00
Vase, silver o/l bleeding hearts on bronze irid w/spots, 10" 2,000.00
Vase, silver o/l carnations/scrolls on gold w/oil spots, 4½" 550.00
Vase, silver o/l floral on bl, 4½x4" 750.00
Vase, silver o/l floral on EX oil-spotted peacock bl, 11" 2,450.00
Vase, silver o/l floral on gr frost, squatty, 4x5" 195.00
Vase, silver o/l iris, oil spots, irid w/gold specks, 9x3½" 1,000.00
Vase, silver o/l lotus & pod on gr, twist/pinched, 4" 200.00
Vase, silver o/l swirls on lt gr w/swirls & raindrops, 7x5" 800.00
Vase, silvery irid, drapery design, 6" 195.00
Vase, verre de soie, appl florals, squat w/trifold rim, 4" 150.00
Vase, yel cased w/gold spots, pinched rim, lg dents, 7" 1,400.00

Lomonosov Porcelain

Founded in Leningrad in 1744, the Lomonosov porcelain factory produced exquisite porcelain miniatures for the Czar and other Russian nobility. One of the first factories of its kind, Lomonosov made a line that consisted largely of vases and delicate sculptures. In the 1800s Lomonosov became closely involved with the Russian Academy of Fine Arts, a connection which has continued to this day as the company continues to supply the world with these fine artistic treasures. In 1992 the backstamp was changed to read 'Made in Russia,' instead of 'Made in USSR.' Some dealers may be pricing items marked 'Made in USSR' at 50% or more above prices listed below.

Bullock, #6490 ....24.50
Doe, #6546 ....103.00
Donkey, #6498 ....18.50
Elephant, #6573 ....24.50

Foal, wht, #6414 ....**21.50**
Foal, wht, #6512, lg **51.00**
Fox, #6541 ....**13.50**
Leopard, #6552 ....**123.00**
Lion Cub, recumbent, #6441 ....**11.50**
Otter, #6538 ....**26.50**
Polar Bear, #6449, lg **125.00**
Redstart, #6559 ....**10.00**
Robin, #2479, sm **14.50**
Wild Cat, #6563 ....**32.50**

Longwy

The Longwy workshops were founded in 1798 and continue today to produce pottery in the north of France near the Luxembourg-Belgian border under the name 'Societe des Faienceries de Lonswy et Senelle.' The ware for which they are best known was produced during the Art Deco period, decorated in bold colors and designs. Earlier wares made during the first quarter of the 19th century reflected the popularity of Oriental art, cloisonne enamels in particular. The designs were executed by impressing the pattern into the moist clay and filling in the depressions with enamels. Examples are marked 'Longwy,' either impressed or painted under glaze.

Box, Deco, concentric circles, mc on cream crackle, 3x6" **325.00**
Box, floral, mc/wht, bow-tie form, ca 1930s, 5½" W **280.00**
Box, florals in strong mc, rectangular, ca 1930s, 4" L **175.00**
Box, mc slip flowers w/gold, ftd, 5" **125.00**

Charger, stylized elephants and maiden in jungle scene, brilliant colors, stamped mark, 15", $2,000.00.

Tile, birds, metal mt **225.00**
Tile, Deco lady in garden, for Primavera, 8" sq **400.00**
Tile, stylized flowers **100.00**
Trivet, bird, metal mt, 6" **280.00**
Vase, nudes/bird/ram, vivid tones, widens toward base, 12" **1,150.00**
Vase, rows of cvd/pnt overlapping devices, mc, 10x3", pr **700.00**
Vase, triangular mc Deco floral panels on wht crackle, 12" **900.00**

Lonhuda

William Long was a druggist by trade who combined his knowledge of chemistry with his artistic ability in an attempt to produce a type of brown-glazed slip-decorated artware similar to that made by the Rookwood Pottery. He achieved his goal in 1889 after years of long and dedicated study. Three years later he founded his firm, the Lonhuda Pottery Company. The name was coined from the first few letters of the last name of each of his partners, W.H. Hunter and Alfred Day. Laura Fry, formerly of the Rookwood company, joined the firm in 1892, bring-

ing with her a license for Long to use her patented airbrush-blending process. Other artists of note, Sarah McLaughlin, Helen Harper, and Jessie Spaulding, joined the firm and decorated the ware with nature studies, animals, and portraits, often signing their work with their initials. Three types of marks were used on the Steubenville Lonhuda ware. The first was a linear composite of the letters 'LPCO' with the name 'Lonhuda' impressed above it. The second, adopted in 1893, was a die-stamp representing the solid profile of an Indian, used on ware patterned after pottery made by the American Indians. This mark was later replaced with an impressed outline of the Indian head with 'Lonhuda' arching above it. Although the ware was successful, the business floundered due to poor management. In 1895 Long became a partner of Sam Weller and moved to Zanesville where the manufacture of the Lonhuda line continued. Less than a year later, Long left the Weller company. He was associated with J.B. Owens until 1899, at which time he moved to Denver, Colorado, where he established the Denver China and Pottery Company in 1901. His efforts to produce Lonhuda utilizing local clay were highly successful. Examples of Denver Lonhuda are sometimes marked with the LF (Lonhuda Faience) cipher contained within a canted diamond form.

Bowl, banana boat; tiny blossoms, 4-ftd, hdls, 5½x9½" **175.00**
Ewer, dogwood blossoms, mc on brn to gr, ADF, #215, 7" **375.00**
Napkin ring, floral on brn, 2x2" **95.00**
Vase, floral on brn, ruffled rim, 5x5½" **225.00**
Vase, floral on brn, sgn Jessie Spaulding, faience, 7½" **400.00**
Vase, grapes, gray-bl w/gr & rust vine on brn bsk, 9½" **285.00**
Vase, thistles/leaves, bk: flower, mk Denver-Lonhuda, 7½" **265.00**
Vase, tulips on brn, integral hdls, 6x9" **650.00**

Lotton

Charles Lotton is a contemporary glass artist. He began blowing glass and developing original designs nearly thirty years ago. He now has work on display in many major glass museums and collections, among them the Smithsonian, the Art Institute of Chicago, the Museum of Glass, and the Chrysler Museum. He has become famous for his unique lamps. Each piece is signed and dated. His three sons, David, Daniel and John, each work in their own studios. All four artists produce distinctive work. They sell their glass at antique shows and in their showroom in Lansing, Illinois. For further information read *Lotton Art Glass* by Charles Lotton and Tom O'Conner; see the Directory under Illinois.

Table lamp, Multi-Flora, cased cobalt 20" shade & base, 26" ..**3,400.00**
Vase, floral, pk & opal on bl & gr stems, John, 1992, ftd, 8" **245.00**
Vase, hooked feathers on opal, red int, 8" **800.00**
Vase, leaves/vines, pk on cobalt, 5" **200.00**
Vase, Multi-Flora, pk flowers on verre de soie, 10" **750.00**
Vase, split leaf/vines on selenium red, 6" **600.00**
Vase, split leaves on gr irid, 10½" **600.00**
Vase, split leaves/vines on cobalt, 12" **750.00**
Vase, split leaves/vines on opal w/red int, 5" **450.00**

Lotus Ware

Isaac Knowles and Issac Harvey operated a pottery in East Liverpool, Ohio, in 1853 where they produced both yellow ware and Rockingham. In 1870 Knowles brought Harvey's interests and took as partners John Taylor and Homer Knowles. Their principal product was ironstone china, but Knowles was confident that American potters could produce as fine a ware as the Europeans. To prove his point, he hired Joshua Poole, an artist from the Belleek Works in Ireland. Poole quickly perfected a Belleek-type china, but fire destroyed this portion of the company. Before it could function again, their hotel china business had grown to the point that it required their full attention in order to meet market demands. By 1891 they were able to try again. They developed a bone china, as fine and thin as before, which they called Lotus. Henry Schmidt from the Meissen factory in Germany decorated the ware, often with lacy filigree applications or hand-formed leaves and flowers to which he added further decoration with liquid slip applied by means of a squeeze bag. Due to high production costs resulting from so much of the fragile ware being damaged in firing and because of changes in tastes and styles of decoration, the Lotus Ware line was dropped in 1896. Some of the early ware was marked 'KT&K China'; later marks have a star and a crescent with 'Lotus Ware' added. Our advisor for this category is Mary Frank Gaston. She is listed in the Directory under Texas.

Vase, double gourd shape with step handles, gold-beaded florals, marked, 8¼", $800.00; Jar, twisted and fluted cylinder with floral and fishnet panels and gilt decoration, marked, 7", $600.00.

Bowl, 2 rtcl aqua medallions, mc roses, beaded oval rim, 4x6" ...450.00
Ewer, rtcl, melon ribs, beaded slim neck, 10" 1,850.00
Jardiniere, yel roses/gold on wht, scrolled edge, 7" 800.00
Pitcher, fishnet, mc scattered flowers, squatty, 3" 250.00
Planter, emb pk floral w/gold leaves, pk lustre int, mk, 4x4½" 625.00
Rose jar, bl floral sprays w/gold, openwork lid, mk, 7½" 900.00
Rose jar, 2 rtcl ovals, dbl-bead rim, rtcl lid, 4½" 700.00
Teapot, HP bows & gold paste w/fishnet decor, bamboo hdl, 5" ...700.00
Vase, appl floral & leaf decor, scroll hdls, mk, 8½" 1,200.00
Vase, appl jewel medallions, gold Nouveau hdls, mk, 10" ...1,300.00
Vase, flowers in relief, sawtooth rim, wht ovoid form, 4¼" 200.00
Vase, mc florals, appl gilt hdls, sgn TBJ, 9" 400.00
Vase, mc roses, emb decor on neck, ornate gold hdls, mk, 10" ...900.00
Vase, 2 rtcl ovals, beaded florals, ftd/scroll hdls, 9½" 1,250.00

Lu Ray Pastels

Lu Ray Pastels dinnerware was introduced in the early 1940s by Taylor, Smith, and Taylor of East Liverpool, Ohio. It was offered in assorted colors of Persian Cream, Sharon Pink, Surf Green, Windsor Blue, and Gray in complete place settings as well as many service pieces. It was a successful line in its day and is once again finding favor with collectors of American dinnerware. For further information we recommend *Collector's Guide to Lu Ray Pastels* by Bill and Kathy Meehan.

Bowl, cream soup 37.50
Bowl, fruit; 5½" 4.50

Bowl, mixing; lg 75.00
Bowl, salad; lg 40.00
Bowl, soup; 8" 12.50
Bowl, tab hdl, 6" 13.50
Bowl, vegetable; oval 15.00
Bowl, vegetable; 9" 10.00
Bowl, 36's 25.00
Butter dish, w/lid, ¼-lb 30.00
Calendar plate, 1958-61, ea 22.50
Casserole, w/lid 65.00
Coffeepot, demi; ovoid, w/lid 120.00
Coffeepot, demi; str sides, w/lid 200.00
Creamer 5.00
Creamer, demi; ovoid 22.00
Creamer, demi; str sides 40.00
Cup & saucer 7.50
Cup & saucer, demi 18.00
Cup & saucer, demi; str sides 35.00
Egg cup 17.50
Egg cup, Chatham Gray, rare color 25.00
Epergne 95.00
Muffin cover, w/8" underplate 95.00
Nut dish 35.00
Pitcher, bulbous w/flat bottom 45.00
Pitcher, ftd 50.00
Pitcher, juice; ovoid 110.00
Pitcher, syrup 40.00
Plate, cake 25.00
Plate, Chatham Gray, rare color, 7" 10.00
Plate, chop; 14" 27.50
Plate, divided 20.00
Plate, very rare, 8" 15.00
Plate, 10" 12.50
Plate, 6" 2.00
Plate, 7" 6.00
Plate, 9" 7.50
Platter, #1040, 9½" 8.00
Platter, oval, 11½" 10.00
Platter, oval, 12" 9.00
Platter, oval, 13" 10.00
Relish, 4-part 60.00
Sauce boat, fast-stand 17.50
Sauce pitcher 22.50
Saucer, cream soup 20.00
Shakers, pr 10.00
Sugar bowl, demi; ovoid, w/lid 24.00
Sugar bowl, demi; str sides, w/lid 40.00
Sugar bowl, w/lid 9.00
Teapot, w/lid, curved spout 45.00
Teapot, w/lid, flat-top spout 50.00
Tidbit, 2-tier 40.00
Tray, pickle 18.00
Tumbler, juice 22.50
Tumbler, water 45.00
Vase, bud; 2 styles, ea 175.00

Lunch Boxes

Early 20th-century tobacco companies such as Union Leader, Tiger, and Dixie sold their products in square, steel containers with flat, metal carrying handles. These were specifically engineered to be used as lunch boxes when they became empty. (See Advertising, specific companies.) By 1930 oval lunch pails with colorful lithographed decorations on tin were being manufactured to appeal directly to children. These were made by Ohio Art, Decoware, and a few other companies. In 1950 Aladdin Industries produced the first 'real' character lunch box — a Hopalong Cassidy decal-decorated steel container now considered the beginning of the kids' lunch box industry. The other big lunch box manufacturer, American Thermos (later King Seely Thermos Company) brought out its 'blockbuster' Roy Rogers box in 1953, the first fully lithographed steel lunch box and matching bottle. Other companies (ADCO Liberty; Landers, Frary & Clark; Ardee Industries; Okay Industries; Universal; Tindco; Cheinco) also produced character pails. Today's collectors often tend to specialize in those boxes dealing with a particular subject. Western, space, TV series, Disney movies, and cartoon characters are the most popular. There are well over five hundred different lunch boxes available to the astute collector. For further information we recommend *The Illustrated Encyclopedia of Metal Lunch Boxes* by Allen Woodall and Sean Brickell and *A Pictorial Price Guide to Lunch Boxes and Thermoses* by Larry Aikins. Our advisor for this category is Allan Smith; he is listed in the Directory under Texas. In the following listings, lunch boxes are metal unless noted vinyl or plastic, and values include thermoses only when they are mentioned within the descriptions.

Airline Stewardess, Ardee, vinyl, w/thermos, 1972, EX **175.00**
America, Aladdin, 1958, NM **460.00**
Back to School, Aladdin, plastic, w/thermos, 1980, EX **50.00**
Banana Splits, w/thermos, NM **400.00**
Barbie & Midge, EX **110.00**
Batman, Aladdin, w/thermos, 1966, EX **275.00**
Beany & Cecil, King Seely, vinyl, brn, 1963, EX **475.00**
Beatles, Aladdin, 1966, VG+ **200.00**
Beverly Hillbillies, Aladdin, 1963, G **110.00**
Bonanza, Canadian, EX **120.00**

Bonanza, 1965, VG, $75.00.

Boston Bruins, Okay, 1973, NM **475.00**
Brave Eagle, red band, w/thermos, 1957, VG+ **175.00**
Bread Loaf, Italy, plastic, 1980, EX **110.00**
Bullwinkle & Rocky, Universal, 1962, EX **400.00**
Captain Astro, Ohio Art, 1966, VG+ **275.00**
Captain Kangaroo, unknown, vinyl, 1964, EX **425.00**
Circus Wagon, American, dome top, 1958, EX **340.00**
Coca-Cola, Aladdin, vinyl, w/thermos, 1980, EX **155.00**
Daniel Boone, Aladdin, 1955, EX **360.00**
Dick Tracy, Aladdin, plastic, 1989, EX **10.00**
Dick Tracy, Aladdin, w/thermos, 1967, EX **210.00**
Disney Fire Fighters, 1969, EX **100.00**
Dr Doolittle, Canadian, EX **110.00**
Fess Parker, King Seely, w/thermos, 1965, VG **230.00**
Frontier Days, Ohio Art, 1957, VG+ **260.00**
Giant Eagle, Taiwan, plastic, 1978, EX **30.00**

Gigi, Aladdin, vinyl, w/thermos, 1962, EX **340.00**
Gunsmoke, w/dbl LL's, 1959, EX **450.00**
Harley-Davidson, Taiwan, plastic, 1978, EX **25.00**
Howdy Doody, Adco, 1954, VG+ **310.00**
HR Pufnstuf, Aladdin, 1970, VG- **90.00**
Jet Patrol, 1957, EX **270.00**
Jetsons, Aladdin, dome top, 1963, EX **850.00**
Jungle Book, Aladdin, w/thermos, 1968, EX **120.00**
Keebler, Taiwan, plastic, w/thermos, 1978, EX **55.00**
Lawman, King Seely, 1961, VG **100.00**
Levi's, Taiwan, plastic, w/thermos, 1985, EX **45.00**
Lone Ranger, bl band, 1954, NM **475.00**
Mermaid, Thermos, plastic, w/thermos, 1989, EX **25.00**
Mickey Mouse, Mexico, vinyl, EX **160.00**
Munsters, King Seely, 1965, VG **160.00**
NHL, Okay, 1970, NM **525.00**
Open for Lunch, Taiwan, plastic, 1987, EX **30.00**
Peanuts, King Seely, vinyl, gr, w/thermos, 1971, EX **145.00**
Peter Pan Sandwich, unknown, 1974, VG+ **185.00**
Pets & Pals, King Seely, 1961, VG **85.00**
Pickle, Fesco, plastic, 1972, EX **175.00**
Police Patrol, Aladdin, 1978, VG **140.00**
Pony Tail, King Seely, vinyl, 1960, EX **185.00**
Rifleman, Aladdin, 1961, EX **330.00**
Rocky, Thermos, plastic, w/thermos, 1977, EX **35.00**
Rocky, Thermos, plastic, 1977, EX **25.00**
Sabrina, Aladdin, vinyl, 1972, EX **230.00**
School Days, King Seely, 1960, VG **120.00**
Smokey Bear, Okay, 1975, VG+ **175.00**
Smurfs, King Seely, 1983, VG+ **160.00**
Steve Canyon, Aladdin, 1959, VG+ **185.00**
Super Heroes, w/thermos, NM **60.00**
Tom Corbet Space Cadet, w/thermos, EX **350.00**
Toppie, American, 1957, M **1,600.00**
Traveler, Ohio Art, brn, 1964, EX+ **95.00**
Treasure Chest, Aladdin, dome top, 1961, VG+ **275.00**
Wrangler, Aladdin, vinyl, 1962, EX **325.00**
Yel Submarine, King Seely, 1968, VG+ **395.00**

Lutz

From 1869 to 1888, Nicholas Lutz worked for the Boston and Sandwich Glass Company where he produced the threaded and striped art glass that was popular during that era. His works were not marked; and, since many other glassmakers of the day made similar wares, the term Lutz has come to refer not only to his original works but to any of this type.

Cup & saucer, yel/wht/gold striping, gold in hdl, 2½", 4½" **80.00**
Finger bowl, bl/wht/gold striping, 5¾", +underplate **100.00**
Flask, bl/wht/gold striping, ovoid w/flattened sides, 4¾" **130.00**
Oil lamp font, wht/bl striping, clear stem, 5½" **115.00**
Smoke bell, pk/wht/gold striping, ruffled, triangular, iron mt **100.00**
Wine, pk/wht/gold striping, trumpet-shape base, 4⅛" **115.00**

Maastricht

Maastricht, Holland, was the site of the De Sphinx Pottery, founded in 1836 by Petrus Regout. They made earthenware decorated with transfer prints as well as dinnerware with gaudy hand-painted designs. Potteries are still working in this area today.

Bowl, gaudy stick spatter, mc florals, 9", EX **40.00**

Bowl, Oriental decor, mk, 6" **45.00**
Bowl, Oriental decor, 4¼x8" **70.00**
Bowl, vegetable; gaudy stick spatter, mc florals, 8¼" **75.00**
Creamer & sugar bowl, gaudy stick spatter, 3-color flower **165.00**
Plate, Abraham Lincoln, Petrus Regout, 9" **55.00**
Plate, gaudy stick spatter, blk rim, mc flower, 8⅜" **65.00**
Plate, gaudy stick spatter, mc florals, wear, 11½" **75.00**
Plate, parakeets, bl transfer, Petrus Regout, 8" **40.00**

Maddux of California

One of the California-made ceramics now so popular with collectors, Maddux was founded in the late 1930s and during the years that followed produced novelty items, TV lamps, figurines, planters, and tableware accessories. Our advisor for this category is Doris Frizzell; she is listed in the Directory under Illinois.

#1019, swan console bowl (set), porc wht, 11½" **20.00**
#1047, Contempo bowl (set), wht satin, 16½" **15.00**
#1067, shell console bowl (set), pk, 16" **15.00**
#2108, cookie jar, Raggedy Andy **300.00**
#2113, cookie jar, Humpty Dumpty **300.00**
#221, vase, swan, wht, 12" **20.00**
#225, vase, horse's head top, str-sided body, aqua, 12" **18.00**
#3017, seashell bowl, wht **15.00**
#3275, gr pepper relish, w/lid **20.00**
#400/#401, flamingo, pr **35.00**
#510, planter, swan, blk, 11" **18.00**
#515, planter, flamingo, pk, 10½" **45.00**
#809, TV lamp, shell, Pearltone, 13" **20.00**
#810, TV lamp, stallion, prancing, on base, 12" **30.00**

#826, TV lamp, cockatiels, $50.00.

#828, TV lamp, swan planter, wht porc, 12½" **20.00**
#829, TV lamp, deer (2), running, natural, 10½" **35.00**
#839, TV lamp, mallard, flying, natural colors, 11½" **35.00**
#841, TV lamp, head of Christ, 3-D planter **25.00**
#844, TV lamp, prairie schooner (covered wagon), 11" **40.00**
#846, TV lamp, nativity scene, 3-D planter, 12" **25.00**
#859, TV lamp, Toro (bull), ft on mound, 11½" **20.00**
#887, TV lamp, Persian Glory (horse head), 11½" **20.00**
#889, TV lamp, Malibu shell, Pearltone, 10¼" **20.00**
#892, TV lamp, Colonial ship, 10½" **30.00**
#894, TV lamp, Toro (bull), charging, walnut, 11½" **20.00**
#896, TV lamp, bassett hound, 12½" **45.00**
#897, TV lamp, mare & foal, wht porc **35.00**
#907, doe, walnut, wht porc, tangerine, 12½" **15.00**
#912/#913, Chinese pheasants, air-brushed colors, 11", pr **30.00**

#914, stag, standing, natural colors, 12½" **15.00**
#923, swans (2), blk matt, 10½" **25.00**
#924, stag, standing, natural colors, 12½" **15.00**
#925/#926, horses, rearing/charging, pr **20.00**
#928/#929, mallards, male/female, natural, 9½", pr **40.00**
#932, rooster, 10½" **30.00**
#969, Early Birds, blk matt, tangerine, 14½", pr **25.00**
#970, flamingo, flying, natural, 11" **45.00**
#971, flamingo, winging, natural, 12" **45.00**
#972/#973, bull, red, head up/head down, 11" L, pr **150.00**
#982, horse, prancing **20.00**
Ashtray, red or yel, metal caddy w/6 ind trays **20.00**
Cats, Deco style, blk matt, 12½", facing pr **45.00**
Cockatiel, on branch w/appl flower, 11" **25.00**
Cookie jar, clown, very lg **325.00**
Deer & doe, stylized, elongated, 12", pr **35.00**
Ducklings, 3 on grassy base **20.00**
Flamingo Line, dbl flamingo vase, 5" **40.00**
Flamingo Line, single flamingo planter, 6" **40.00**
Planter, rearing horse, 10x7½" **22.00**
Squirrel, Maddux of Calif **225.00**

Magazines

Magazines are collected for their cover prints and for the information pertaining to defunct companies and their products that can be gleaned from the old advertisements. In the listings that follow, items are assumed to be in very good condition unless noted otherwise. See also Movie Memorabilia; Parrish, Maxfield.

Key:
 M — mint condition, in original wrapper
 EX — excellent condition, spine intact, edges of pages clean and
      straight
 VG — very good condition, the average as-found condition

Avante Garde, 1968, Monroe cover & photo art, M **140.00**
Fortune, 1948, railroad cover, EX **30.00**
Harper's Weekly, 1865, October 28, Fenians cover, EX **22.00**
Harper's Weekly, 1870, December 24, Anxious Times...cover, EX .**12.50**
Illustrated London News, 1856, October 18, Czar Alexander II ...**12.00**
Illustrated London News, 1874, March 7, Ashantee War, EX **12.00**

Ladies' Home Journal, 1961, February, Jacqueline Kennedy cover, EX, $10.00.

Ladies' Home Journal, 1971, August, Rose Kennedy cover, VG **6.00**
Ladies' Home Journal, 1971, January, Sophia Loren cover, EX **10.00**
Ladies' Home Journal, 1972, April, Elizabeth Taylor cover, EX **7.50**
Ladies' Home Journal, 1972, December, Bob Hope cover, EX **10.00**

Ladies' Home Journal, 1972, June, Nixon cover, EX **8.50**
Ladies' Home Journal, 1973, March, Joan Kennedy cover, EX **7.50**
Ladies' Home Journal, 1973, May, Princess Grace & daughter, EX ..**10.00**
Leslie's, 1860, January 7, Wm Seward cover, EX **16.50**
Leslie's, 1860, October 13, Prince of Wales cover, EX **12.00**
Leslie's, 1876, August 19, Centennial cover, EX **12.50**
Leslie's, 1882, October 7, Political Circus Leap cover, EX **17.50**
Leslie's, 1884, February 2, Massachusetts cover, G **12.50**
Liberty, 1941, August 18, Nazi cover, EX **6.50**
Life, 1937, September 27, Nelson Eddy cover, EX **12.50**
Life, 1940, July 15, Rita Hayworth cover, EX **14.00**
Life, 1940, September 2, Dionne Quints cover, EX **12.50**
Life, 1942, March 30, Shirley Temple cover, EX **15.00**
Life, 1943, Roy Rogers & Trigger cover, EX **45.00**
Life, 1945, October 1, Shirley Temple's Wedding, EX **10.00**

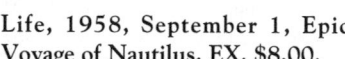
Life, 1958, September 1, Epic Voyage of Nautilus, EX, $8.00.

Life, 1960, January 18, Speaker of House, Ghana Africa cover **4.00**
Life, 1962, July 17, Bing Crosby & family cover, EX **16.00**
Life, 1967, November 17, Jackie Onassis in Cambodia, EX **3.50**
Literary Digest, 1934, polo cover, EX **30.00**
Look, 1963, May 21, Bobby Kennedy cover, EX **12.00**
Look, 1964, February 25, Pope Paul cover, EX **7.00**
Look, 1970, December 15, Christmas for POWs cover, EX **8.50**
Look, 1971, September 21, 16th Annual Auto Show cover, EX ...**18.00**
Modern Man, 1956, Monroe cover & centerfold, M **75.00**
Newsweek, 1933, February 17, much prewar news **15.00**
Newsweek, 1937, September 20, Justice Black cover, EX **6.00**
NY Times, 1959, March 29, Eisenhower cover, EX **4.50**
NY Times, 1962, November 18, Russians parade in West Berlin **3.50**
Official Detective Stories, 1946, 5 for **35.00**
Playboy, 1953, 1st edition, Monroe nude cover, 42-pg, EX+ ...**1,000.00**
Playboy, 1956, November, Betty Blue, NM **60.00**
Playboy, 1960, January, Stella Stevens, NM **32.00**
Playboy, 1963, July, Carrie Enwright, NM **23.00**
Playboy, 1969, Fifteenth Holiday Anniversary Issue, EX **24.00**
Playboy, 1971, December, Karen Chrysty, EX **14.00**
Saturday Evening Post, 1903, Blks picking cotton cover, EX **40.00**
Saturday Evening Post, 1903, lady golfer cover, EX **50.00**
Saturday Evening Post, 1917, Leyendecker soldier cover **45.00**
Saturday Evening Post, 1936, February 15, Leyendecker cover **12.00**
Saturday Evening Post, 1952, golf driving range cover, NM **30.00**
Saturday Evening Post, 1954, October, 31, LBJ campaign, EX **6.00**
Saturday Evening Post, 1957, June 29, Rockwell cover, EX **12.50**
Saturday Evening Post, 1959, Family Tree Rockwell cover, EX **35.00**
Saturday Evening Post, 1962, baseball teams, Playboy item **30.00**
Saturday Evening Post, 1963, December 14, JFK by Rockwell, EX ...**16.50**
Sport Magazine, 1950, Stan Musial cover, EX **30.00**
Sports Album, 1940, R Kiner baseball cover, NM **35.00**

Sports Illustrated, 1950, Palmer, Venturi, Finsterwald cover **27.00**
Sports Illustrated, 1964, Koufax cover, EX **32.00**
Sports Illustrated, 1964, Stengel & Berra cover, EX **25.00**
Sports Stars, 1952, Durocher cover, Ty Cobb story, EX **35.00**
Sports Stars, 1952, Robinson & Reese cover, EX **35.00**
Sportsman's Review, 1908, September 19, EX **10.00**
Tempo, 1953, Elizabeth Taylor cover, EX **20.00**
Time, 1938, Frank Capra cover, EX **28.00**
Time, 1941, June 9, Mussolini cover, EX **17.00**
Time, 1946, April 8, Sir Lawrence Olivier cover, EX **12.50**
Time, 1948, Eddie Arcaro cover, horse racing feature, EX **30.00**
True Story, 1928, Joan Crawford cover, EX **15.00**
TV Guide, 1953, July 24, Groucho cover, EX **115.00**
TV Guide, 1956, July 7, Lassie cover, EX **43.00**
TV Guide, 1959, May 30, Steve McQueen cover, EX **47.00**
TV Guide, 1964, September 26, Dan Blocker cover, EX **21.00**
TV Guide, 1968, August 24, Cast of Star Trek cover, EX **100.00**
TV Guide, 1969, July 19, First Telecast From the Moon, EX **15.00**
TV Guide, 1970, April 4, Cast of Brady Bunch cover, EX **80.00**
TV Guide, 1972, June 10, Doris Day cover, EX **13.00**
TV Guide, 1975, David Janssen cover, EX **17.00**
TV Guide, 1979, December, Cast of Charlie's Angels cover, EX ..**15.00**
TV Guide, 1980, July 12, Cast of Dukes of Hazzard cover, EX **10.00**
TV Guide, 1984, April 24, Cast of Knight Rider cover, EX **7.00**
Vogue, 1924, woman w/butterfly net illus cover by Brissaud **55.00**
Yachtsman's Magazine, 1942, May, EX **20.00**

Majolica

Majolica is a type of heavy earthenware, design-molded and decorated in vivid colors with either a lead or tin type of glaze. It reached its height of popularity in the Victorian era; examples from this period are found in only the lead glazes. Nearly every potter of note, both here and abroad, produced large majolica jardinieres, umbrella stands, pitchers with animal themes, leaf shapes, vegetable forms, and nearly any other design from nature that came to mind. Few, however, marked their ware. Among those who did were Minton, Wedgwood, Holdcroft, and George Jones in England; Griffin, Smith and Hill (Etruscan) in Phoenixville, Pennsylvania; and Chesapeake Pottery (Avalon and Clifton) in Baltimore.

Color and condition are both very important worth-assessing factors. Pieces with cobalt, lavender, and turquoise glazes command the highest prices. For further information we recommend *The Collector's Encyclopedia of Majolica* by Mariann Katz-Marks (see Directory, Pennsylvania). Our advisor for this category is Hardy Hudson; he is listed in the Directory under Florida.

Asparagus server, asparagus spears on sq tray, Minton, 9" **650.00**
Basket, floral limb, Oriental ft & hdl detail, lav int, 15" **450.00**
Bowl, salad; Shell & Seaweed, Etruscan, ftd, 8¼" **550.00**
Bowl, strawberry leaf/fruit/floral on wht, Wedgwood, 8" **300.00**
Bowl, Sunflower, textured bl ground, lav int, Wardle, 10½" **350.00**
Box, match; oak leaves/acorns, gr/tan, lav int, G Jones, 4" L **450.00**
Box, sardine; floral & fence **350.00**
Box, sardine; Pond Lily, fish/florals on med bl, Holdcroft **800.00**
Box, sardine; Rope Edge, Xd fish on lid, rustic style, 8x8" **800.00**
Box, Yel Basketweave, fish on lid, brn rope bands, 5½x5½" **500.00**
Butter dish, Bamboo, Etruscan **500.00**
Butter dish, Basketweave & Bamboo, Banks & Thorley, 8" dia ..**300.00**
Butter dish, Shell & Seaweed, Etruscan **1,300.00**
Butter pat, Astor, centered in bl field w/feathered wht edge **65.00**
Butter pat, Butterfly, bl on wht, Fielding, 3" **85.00**
Butter pat, Horseshoe, Wedgwood **95.00**

Cake stand, New England Astor on wht, att Hampshire, 2x9" ...300.00
Cake stand, Shell & Seaweed, 9" dia 1,100.00
Candlestick, 2 dolphins on curving base, Worcester, 4" 450.00
Centerpc, cabbage leaf on leafy base w/2 rabbits, Minton, 8" .3,800.00
Centerpc, putto ea side lg shell, Minton, 8" 2,000.00
Cheese keeper, Heron on cobalt 3,200.00
Cheese keeper, Lily, cobalt, swan finial, Etruscan, 7½" 3,300.00
Cheese keeper, Pond Lily, wht on dk gr, Holdcroft, 9" 1,000.00
Compote, wicker/floral bowl, 3 twig ft, Brn Westhead Moore, 7" ..550.00
Creamer, Butterfly & Floral on bl wicker, sq, 3½" 100.00
Creamer, Shell, assorted seashells on wht, Fielding, 4" 165.00
Creamer, Shell & Seaweed, Etruscan, 4" 360.00
Cup & saucer, Bamboo & Floral on bl 225.00
Cup & saucer, coffee; Water Lily on textured wht 245.00
Cup & saucer, Pineapple, gr leaves, lav int, yel fruit 250.00
Cup & saucer, Rose & Rope on brn w/yel bands, GS&H 300.00
Cuspidor, Fan, 6½" 300.00
Cuspidor, Sunflower, cobalt, Etruscan, 7" 1,200.00
Dish, dessert; Fan & Bow, pk flower/bow on 2-tone bl/yel, 7" 175.00
Dish, sauce; 3 mc fans on wht texture, Shorter & Boulton, 5" 150.00
Egg basket, Morning Glory, 6", w/4 egg cup inserts 550.00

Garden seat, fern and leaf with floral decoration in brown, green and yellow, pierced sides, John Adams, ca 1870, $3,500.00.

Garden seat, banana leaves about bamboo bundle, Minton, 19" ..3,800.00
Humidor, crocodile w/cape figural 400.00
Humidor, man w/beanie hat & goggles figural 300.00
Humidor, monkey figural 440.00
Humidor, potbellied man figural 250.00
Humidor, Sunny Bank, Spaulding & Merrick, Avalon, 9" 450.00
Match holder, standing monkey wearing loincloth, 7¾" 300.00
Mug, Frog & Fern on Bamboo, 2 frogs inside, 4½" 300.00
Pitcher, Albino Sunflower, lg flower on texture, Etruscan, 6" ...250.00
Pitcher, Basketweave & Bamboo, lg leaves, Banks & Thorley, 8" ..250.00
Pitcher, Bird & Pond Lily on wht texture, bulbous, sq top, 8" ...350.00
Pitcher, Blackberry on wht texture, twig hdl, 7½" 245.00
Pitcher, Court Jester (finial), grapes/revelers, Minton, 13" 1,600.00
Pitcher, Dogwood & Lilac w/bbl staves, yel rope trim, 8" 325.00
Pitcher, Fan, Butterfly & Cricket, 2 fans on yel, 8¾" 300.00
Pitcher, Fern & Bamboo, lg wraparound leaf, Wardle, 7½" 200.00
Pitcher, figural shell body, ocean waves at base, Fielding, 8" 375.00
Pitcher, Fish, wht above, waves below, lav int, mk, 7½" 450.00
Pitcher, Fish on Waves on spherical body, flared bl top, 8" 350.00
Pitcher, Floral Turq Banded on wht 'slats,' brn hdl, 8" 250.00
Pitcher, Fruit, cluster/leaves on veined wht, Clifton, 6½" 150.00
Pitcher, Hawthorne, Etruscan, 8¼" 415.00
Pitcher, Hummingbird, bl 'caned' neck band/bottom, 9" 325.00
Pitcher, Leaf Spout, Rose & Basketweave, cobalt bands, 9" 200.00
Pitcher, lily w/insects forms body, Adams & Bromely, 8" 300.00

Pitcher, Little Girl & Dog on wide cobalt band, 8" 400.00
Pitcher, Peas in Pod, brn basketweave bottom, pewter lid, 5½" ..275.00
Pitcher, Pelican, 1 under spout, 1 as hdl, 9" 900.00
Pitcher, Pig Waiter figural 500.00
Pitcher, Robin on Branch, brn band top/bottom, 7½" 200.00
Pitcher, Rustic, Etruscan, 8½" 330.00
Pitcher, Rustic Blackberry on wht, tree knurl base, 5½" 165.00
Pitcher, Shell & Seaweed, cobalt, Wedgwood, 7" 495.00
Pitcher, Shell & Seaweed, Etruscan, 5½" 550.00
Pitcher, Stork in Marsh w/Overhead Fish on bl, cobalt hdl, 9" ..600.00
Pitcher, Sunflower on cobalt texture, Etruscan, 6½" 400.00
Pitcher, tankard; Baseball/Soccer Players, colorful, GS&H, 8" ..3,000.00
Pitcher, Woman Feeding Dogs, hound hdl, 6" 275.00
Plate, Apple & Strawberry on wht w/cobalt edge, Etruscan, 9" ..300.00
Plate, bird, yel/brn, over floral twig on wht, bl edge, 8" 200.00
Plate, Bird in Flight on textured bl w/wht floral, 8½" 225.00
Plate, Cauliflower, Etruscan, 9" 275.00
Plate, Crane, w/cattails on wht, scalloped/rtcl, Wedgwood, 9" ..300.00
Plate, Dogwood w/lg leaves on cobalt w/scalloped edge, 8" 200.00
Plate, Fern & Floral, lush gr leaves/lav blossoms, 8" 175.00
Plate, oyster; Fish, 6 sm wells, lg fish at side, 10" 550.00
Plate, oyster; half-moon, Copeland 400.00
Plate, oyster; Seaweed, 5 lav wells, ½-moon shape, 8" 400.00
Plate, Parrot, Butterfly & Bamboo, mk Rd No 3119, 9" 200.00
Plate, Rose, mottled center, Etruscan, 7" 150.00
Plate, Water Lily on dk gr, Holdcroft, 8" 175.00
Plate, Wild Rose on wht, bl border, 8¾" 150.00
Platter, Bamboo & Bow, yel w/cobalt center, 13" 300.00
Platter, Begonia Leaf on wht basketweave w/yel edge, 13" 300.00
Platter, bread; Shell & Seaweed, Etruscan 1,000.00
Platter, Fern, Floral & Bow (sm bow on ferns), oval, 14" 300.00
Platter, Geometric, lav/gr/wine stripes, daisy hdls, 13" 300.00
Platter, Oriental, bamboo/flowers on wht, Wedgwood, 13" 375.00
Platter, Rose on Basketweave, cobalt outer border, hdls, 13" 350.00
Platter, swan hdl, woven bl w/yel wrapped border, 13" 325.00
Relish, 3-lobe leaf w/bl flower, center twig hdl, G Jones, 12" 900.00
Salt dip, child in bl drape holds wicker basket, Wedgwood 450.00
Shakers, Coral, mk L15, Etruscan, 4", pr 800.00
Spoon holder, Fan, yel/bl on brn, 5" 200.00
Sugar bowl, Parrot on Branch on bl basketweave, 5½" 180.00
Syrup, Albino Coral on textured wht, pewter mts, Etruscan, 7" .300.00
Syrup, Argenta, Wedgwood 415.00
Syrup, Dogwood on irregular tan 'slats,' Holdcroft, 4" 325.00
Syrup, Sunflower, cobalt, Etruscan 550.00
Teapot, Bird & Iris on wht, Etruscan, 6", +cr/sug 700.00
Teapot, Clifton Decor Blackberry on wht, brn spout/hdl, 6" 250.00
Teapot, Drum Shape w/floral on bl wicker, 6½", +sug/cr 650.00
Teapot, Fish Swallowing Fish 800.00
Teapot, Floral & Basketweave, bl ground, yel collar/base, 5" 300.00
Teapot, Isle of Man, 3-legged man figural, mk Broughton, 8" .1,500.00
Teapot, Shell & Seaweed, Griffin Smith & Hill, 6" 985.00
Teapot, Sunflower & Classical Urn on wht w/bl band, Lear, 6" .350.00
Tray, ice cream; Fan, scroll beside, bow hdls, Fielding, 15" 500.00
Tray, Pond Lily chain on brn, lily pad border, oval, 13" 325.00
Tray, relish; Onion & Pickle, +assorted vegetables, Wedgwood .300.00
Umbrella stand, Stork in Rushes on cobalt 1,800.00
Vase, Classical Harp, masthead-like winged mermaid, 6" 350.00
Vase, wht long-horned ram on mottled brn, gr int, Shirley, 6" ...325.00
Wine caddy, dbl, putto/rtcl vintage, spoked wheels trn, 13" 4,000.00

Malachite Glass

Malachite is a type of art glass that exhibits strata-like layerings in shades of green, similar to the mineral in its natural form. Some examples have an acid-etched mark of Moser/Carlsbad, usually on the base. However, it should be noted that in the past fifteen years there have been reproductions from Czechoslovakia with a paper label.

Basket, woman & cherubs, loop hdl, 6x6½" 150.00
Box, nudes on lid & base, 2x3½" dia 100.00
Box, Oriental lady's portrait 90.00
Cat, seated, tail around ft, 4½" 50.00
Dresser set: box, bottle, atomizer, emb roses, Czech 500.00
Fish dish, Deco figural, Moser 135.00
Vase, nudes & grapes, Moser/Carlsbad, 9½" 200.00

Mantel Lustres

Mantel lustres are decorative vases or candle holders made from all types of glass, often highly decorated, and usually hung with one or more rows of prisms. In the listings that follow, values are given for a pair.

Three-light girandoles with spaniel figural bases, each with prism-hung coronas on foliate arms, marble plinths, ca 1845-60, $550.00 for the pair.

Cobalt, triple o/l, elaborate cutting/HP, prisms, 26" 2,800.00
Cobalt to clear w/gold, clear prisms, 14¾" 1,100.00
Cranberry cut to clear, prisms, slender, 11" 475.00
Dk gr w/gilt trim, prisms, 14" 425.00
Gr cut to wht, medallions, HP florals/gold, 8 prisms, 11" 295.00
Gr w/portrait medallions & gold, prisms, Bohemian, 14½" 1,400.00
Pk o/l w/wht roses & mc leaves, prisms, 11" 300.00
Pk w/enamel, waisted top, 2 rows prisms w/ball drops, 15" 600.00
Ruby w/gold bands & florals, appl snake, prisms, 12" 450.00
Wht cut to ruby w/florals, prisms, now lamps 385.00

Maps and Atlases

Maps are highly collectible, not only for historical value but also for their sometimes elaborate artwork, legendary information, or data that since they were printed has been proven erroneous. There are many types of maps including geographical, military, celestial, road, and railroad. The most valuable are those made before the mid-1800s. Our advisor for this category is Murray Hudson; he is listed in the Directory under Tennessee.

Key:
hc — hand colored   CW—Civil War

Atlases

Colton's Gen, 170+ maps/plans, red leather w/gilt, 1857 ....1,600.00

Colton's Gen, 180 maps, Imperial folio sheets, 1873, EX 675.00
Mitchell's New Gen, 147+ hc maps/plans, eng grapes, 1880, EX .515.00
New Gen...of the Globe, 60 maps, Phila, A Finley, 1824 ....1,700.00
New Internat'l Atlas of World, Geographical Publishing, 1923 ....50.00
OW Gray National, 50+ maps, some dbl, city maps, 1875, folio ..525.00
Rand McNally, 2-vol, mc, some dbl pgs, 1896, 21x14", G 250.00

Maps

Atlanta, houses/line of battle, gov't issue, CW era, 18x27" 35.00
Battlefields of Chattanooga TN, 2 maps on 1, CW era, 18x28" ...35.00
CA, hc, Frisco inset, gold mine info, Mitchell, 1882, 15x22" 60.00
CO, from atlas, RR/mining camps, ID/WY on bk, hc, 1900, 10x14" ..25.00
Cornwall, England; inset of island areas, 1788, 13x11" 35.00
CW Campaigns GA/NC/SC; mc lines: Fed marches, 1875, 9x12" ..30.00
Dutch & Austrian Flanders & Holland, Murray, 1785, 15x18" 32.50
Heavens, hc, w/Andromeda/Swan/Lizard/etc, 1835, 14x16" 50.00
IO, MO; hc, towns/RRs, bk: St Louis w/streets, 1884, 15x24" 40.00
MI, WI; hc, upper areas unsettled, Mitchell, 1866, 12x15" 35.00
Military, hc, ships in water areas, Colton, 1862, 15x18" 75.00
MO, some of KS, RRs/depots, Asher & Adams, 1872, 16x22" 40.00
Modern Africa, hc, settlements, 1800, 14x20", EX 35.00
MS Bay to Nova Scotia, J Murray, VT nonexistant, 1785, 18x23" ..65.00
N Am, watercolor on paper, sgn/dtd 1826, fr, 23½x18" 575.00
New Orleans, hc areas, w/Algiers/Belleville/etc, 1866, 12x15" 35.00
NY City, sts/points of interest, fancy borders, 1866, 12x15" 30.00
OH River Valley & NE US, dtd 1755, 27x20", EX 650.00
Petersburg, Grant's war zone, Tomlinson, 1864, 19x14" 150.00
Plan for gunboat attack on Forts Strong & Lee, CW, 1865, 14x7" ..30.00
Political Map of N Am, Indian areas, hc, 1843, 10x12" 35.00
RR map of KS, w/Wells Fargo/Pacific Express, 1888, 20x26" 40.00
RR Map of NW States, central IN/IL/MI/WI/IO, 1849, 13x16" ...35.00
RR map of WA, mtns/passes/Indian reservations, 1892, 20x26" ...30.00
Seat of War 1861, hc cannons illus battles, FL inset, 23x30" 95.00
Sweden, Denmark & Norway, blk & wht, 1787, 8x9", EX 65.00
US, fancy borders, RR/rivers/reservations/etc, 1882, 15x22" 50.00
US, mc litho, Pony Express rts/etc, Gov't issue, 1880s, 18x27" 35.00
UT, NV; hc, towns/forts/Indians, Mitchell, 1881, 15x22" 50.00
War Dept Weather, 2 lg red insets, US in lt gr, 1876, 18x24" 25.00
World, from pg of Navigation of Portingales..., 1598, 7x11" 45.00

Marblehead

What began as therapy for patients in a sanitarium in Marblehead, Massachusetts, has become recognized as an important part of the Arts and Crafts movement in America. Results of the early experiments under the guidance of Arthur E. Baggs in 1904 met with such success that by 1908 the pottery had been converted to a solely commercial venture. Simple vase shapes were often incised with stylized animal and floral motifs or sailing ships. Some were decorated in low relief; many were plain. Simple matt glazes in soft yellow, gray, wisteria, rose, tobacco brown, and their most popular, Marblehead blue, were used alone or in combination. The Marblehead logo is distinctive — a ship with full sail and the letters 'M' and 'P.' The pottery closed in 1936.

Bowl, bl, 1¼x3¼", +frog 225.00
Bowl, bl/brn matt, 2x4½" 175.00
Bowl, dk bl, closed-in mouth, minor rpr, 4x9" 200.00
Bowl, leaf/vine band, 2-tone bl on gray, H Tutt, 2x6½" 1,100.00
Bowl, pk/gr mottle, incurvate, 1¼x9" 225.00
Bowl, textured w/2-tone gr semigloss, str/flared, 5x7" 200.00
Bowl vase, lav, 1¾x3½" 150.00
Candlestick, gray, long loop hdl, 7¼" 225.00

Chamberstick, dk bl, early, 6x4¾"	450.00
Pitcher, gray-wht broken glaze, bulbous, early, 7"	200.00
Plaque, lg sailing shop in rope surround, tan/yel, fr, 9"	1,500.00
Teapot, Arts & Crafts geometrics, brn/gr, fiber hdl, 7½"	2,300.00
Tile, excised flower, mottled yel/brn satin, mk, 6½" sq	325.00
Tile, flying fish, mc matt vellum, nicks, 4½" sq	675.00
Tile, galleon, wht on bl, crackled matt, mk, fr, 4½"	475.00
Vase, birds flying, dk gray on speckled gray, MT, 9x5", NM	600.00
Vase, bl, ovoid, 3½"	170.00
Vase, bl, swollen cylinder, 5"	350.00
Vase, bl, trumpet form, 4½"	245.00
Vase, bl gloss, bulbous, short neck, 5"	275.00
Vase, brn matt, 9x6"	800.00
Vase, bud; lav, cylinder w/wide base, 5¾"	150.00
Vase, cvd Arts & Crafts leaves, brn on dk gr, MT, 10x6"	1,800.00
Vase, dk bl, pear shape w/flaring rim, 6½x5"	450.00
Vase, gr, beehive shape, 5¾"	385.00
Vase, gr, flared, 3"	230.00
Vase, gray, cylindrical w/closed-in mouth, 5"	270.00
Vase, gray, flared lip, 2½"	90.00
Vase, gray w/bl int, ovoid, 9x4½"	650.00
Vase, lav, flared, 7½x4"	550.00
Vase, lav, shouldered, 2½x3½"	150.00
Vase, leafy trees on pencil trunks, 3-color, spherical, 6½"	1,385.00
Vase, mottled mustard & brn shading to gr, ovoid, 5⅛"	230.00
Vase, purple & bl, cylindrical w/rolled-in rim, 8"	850.00
Vase, stylized floral, 3-color on gray, swollen can form, 5"	1,600.00
Vase, stylized flower buds, 4-color, H Tutt, 4x4"	2,100.00
Vase, stylized pine cones on long stems, rust on dk bl, 5x3"	1,000.00
Vase, Viking ships/waves, 6-color, EX art, 14"	16,000.00
Vase, yel, ovoid, 5¼"	300.00

Marbles

Marbles have been popular with children since the mid-1800s. They've been made in many types from a variety of materials. Among some of the first glass items to be produced, the earliest marbles were made from a solid glass rod broken into sections of the proper length which were placed in a tray of sand and charcoal and returned to the fire. As they were reheated, the trays were constantly agitated until the marbles were completely round. Other marbles were made of china, pottery, steel, and natural stones.

Below is a listing of the various types, along with a brief description of each. When size is not otherwise indicated, prices are listed for mint condition marbles of average size, ½" to 1".

Agates: stone marbles of many different colors — bands of color alternating with white usually encircle the marble; most are translucent.

Ballot Box: handmade (with pontils), opaque white or black, used in lodge elections.

Bloodstone: green chalcedony with red spots, a type of quartz.

China: with or without glaze, in a variety of hand-painted designs — parallel bands or bull's-eye designs most common.

Clambroth: opaque glass with outer evenly spaced swirls of one or alternating colors.

Clay: one of the most common older types; some are painted while others are not.

Comic Strip: a series of twelve machine-made marbles with faces of comic strip characters, Peltier Glass Factory, Illinois.

Crockery: sometimes referred to as Benningtons; most are either blue or brown, although some are speckled. The clay is shaped into a sphere, then coated with glaze and fired.

End of the Day: single-pontil glass marbles — the colored part often appears as a multicolored blob or mushroom cloud.

Goldstone: clear glass completely filled with copper flakes that have turned gold-colored from the heat of the manufacturing process.

Indian Swirls: usually black glass with a colored swirl appearing on the outside next to the surface, often irregular.

Latticinio Core Swirls: double-pontil marble with an inner area with net-like effects of swirls coming up around the center.

Lutz Type: glass with colored or clear bands alternating with bands which contain copper flecks.

Micas: clear or colored glass with mica flecks which reflect as silver dots when marble is turned. Red is rare.

Onionskin: spiral type which are solidly colored instead of having individual ribbons or threads, multicolored.

Peppermint Swirls: made of white opaque glass with alternating blue and red outer swirls.

Ribbon Core Swirls: double-pontil marble — center shaped like a ribbon with swirls that come up around the middle.

Rose Quartz: stone marble, usually pink in color, often with fractures inside and on outer surface.

Solid Core Swirls: double-pontil marble — middle is solid with swirls coming up around the core.

Steelies: hollow steel spheres marked with a cross where the steel was bent together to form the ball.

Sulfides: generally made of clear glass with figures inside. Rarer types have colored figures or colored glass.

Tiger Eye: stone marble of golden quartz with inclusions of asbestos, dark brown with gold highlights.

Vaseline: machine-made of yellowish-green glass with small bubbles.

For a more thorough study of the subject, we recommend *Antique and Collectible Marbles, 3rd Edition; Machine-Made and Contemporary Marbles, 2nd Edition;* and *Big Book of Marbles,* all by our advisor, Everett Grist; you will find his address in the Directory under Illinois.

Onionskin with mica, ¾", $110.00 (1¾", $900.00).

Agate, contemporary, carnelian, 1¾"	160.00
Banded Opaque, gr & wht, 2"	1,200.00
Banded Opaque, red & wht, 1¾"	1,200.00
Banded Opaque, red & wht, ¾"	95.00
Banded Transparent Swirl, bl, ¾"	75.00
Banded Transparent Swirl, lt gr, 1¾"	600.00
Bennington, bl, 1¾"	40.00
Bennington, bl, ¾"	3.00
Bennington, brn, 1¾"	30.00
Bennington, fancy, 1¾"	80.00
Bennington, fancy, ¾"	5.00
China, decorated, glazed, apple, 1¾"	800.00
China, decorated, glazed, rose, 1¾"	800.00
China, decorated, glazed, wht w/geometrics, 1¾"	125.00
China, decorated, unglazed, geometrics & flowers, ¾"	200.00
Clambroth, opaque, bl & wht, 1¾"	2,600.00
Clambroth, opaque, bl & wht, ¾"	250.00
Clambroth Swirl, red/wht, Germany, 1900, ⅞"	375.00

Comic, Andy Gump **90.00**
Comic, Betty Boop **150.00**
Comic, Cotes Bakery, advertising **700.00**
Comic, Kayo, rare **150.00**
Comic, Little Orphan Annie **100.00**
Comic, Moon Mullins **175.00**
Comic, Popeye **70.00**
Comic, set of 12 ....**1,500.00**
Comic, Skeezix **100.00**
Comic, Tom Mix **1,800.00**
Cork Screw, machine-made **5.00**
End of Day, bl & wht, 1¾" **1,100.00**
Goldstone, ¾" **35.00**
Indian Swirl, 1¾" **1,500.00**
Indian Swirl Lutz-type, gold flakes, ¾" **600.00**
Line Crockery, clay, 1¾" **125.00**
Mica, bl, ¾" **25.00**
Mica, gr, 1¾" **600.00**
Onionskin, 16-lobe, unusual, 1¾" **1,800.00**
Onionskin, ¾" **90.00**
Onionskin, 4-lobe, 1¼" **450.00**
Opaque Swirl, gr, ¾" **75.00**
Opaque Swirl Lutz-type, bl, yel, gr, ¾" **325.00**
Peppermint Swirl, opaque, red, wht, & bl, 1¾" **3,000.00**
Peppermint Swirl, opaque, red, wht, & bl, ¾" **125.00**
Pottery, 1¾" **45.00**
Ribbon Core Lutz-type, red, 1¾" **1,800.00**
Slag, machine-made, sm **3.00**
Slag, machine-made, 1½" **150.00**
Solid Opaque, gr, 1¾" **600.00**
Solid Opaque, ¾" **50.00**
Sulfide, alligator, 1¾" **160.00**
Sulfide, bird, 2", EX **150.00**
Sulfide, boar, 1⅞", EX **160.00**
Sulfide, bust of George Washington, 2⅜", NM **650.00**
Sulfide, cat, 1¼" **100.00**
Sulfide, child sitting, 1¾" **600.00**
Sulfide, child w/hammer, 1¾" **600.00**
Sulfide, child w/sailboat, 1¾" **650.00**
Sulfide, crucifix, 1¾" **600.00**
Sulfide, dbl eagle, rare, 1¾" **675.00**
Sulfide, dog, 1¾" **125.00**
Sulfide, dog w/bird in mouth, 1¾" **900.00**
Sulfide, dove, 1⅝", M **160.00**
Sulfide, elephant, 1¾" **300.00**
Sulfide, face of angel w/wings, 1¾" **1,000.00**
Sulfide, fox, 1½", EX **130.00**
Sulfide, goat, 1¾" **125.00**
Sulfide, hen, 1⅛" **100.00**
Sulfide, lamb, lt amber, 1¾" **1,600.00**
Sulfide, lamb, 1¾", NM **125.00**
Sulfide, lion, 2", NM **175.00**
Sulfide, Little Boy Blue, 1¾" **700.00**
Sulfide, otter, 1½" **135.00**
Sulfide, owl w/wings spread, 1¾" **375.00**
Sulfide, papoose, 1¾" **700.00**
Sulfide, pig, 1¾" **150.00**
Sulfide, pig, 2", M **180.00**
Sulfide, pony, 1¾" **200.00**
Sulfide, rabbit, 1¾" **150.00**
Sulfide, raccoon, 2" **200.00**
Sulfide, rooster, 1¾" **150.00**
Sulfide, Santa Claus, 1¾" **1,200.00**
Sulfide, sheep, 1¾" **150.00**

Sulfide, squirrel, standing, 1¾", EX **170.00**
Sulfide, squirrel w/nut, 2", EX **200.00**

Marine Collectibles

See also Steamship Collectibles; Telescopes; Scrimshaw; Tools.

Backstaff Davis Quadrant, fruit wood/boxwood, 1750s, 22", EX .**4,000.00**
Bag, chart; hand-sewn sailcloth, +3 charts, ca 1850s, EX **150.00**
Bag, ditty; complete w/deck outfit/tools/needle case, EX **325.00**
Barograph, brass movement, 1920s, 11", w/orig dvtl case **200.00**
Bell, M/V Frontier 1978, polished bronze, 10½" dia **150.00**
Binnacle, brass, orig burner, mahog base, 13", EX **425.00**
Binnacle, ELWA, brass cased, wooden base, 13", EX **235.00**
Binnacle, John Bliss...NY USA, brass, liquid compass, 15", EX ..**650.00**
Binnacle, Kelvin-White Nautical...NY, brass, 10", EX **425.00**
Chart, entrance to San Francisco Bay, Alden, 1859, fr **350.00**
Chronometer, Russian, brass, dbl gimbal, w/key, EX **1,000.00**
Chronometer, Waltham Watch Co, cased, EX **425.00**
Clock, helm; Chelsea, Geo Butler San Francisco, 13½" **1,100.00**
Clock, ship's bell; Salem, brass, 8-day, 4¾" dia, EX **150.00**
Desk, captain's traveling; 3 sm drw, w/key, 6x18x10", EX **800.00**
Harpoon, presentation, mtd on brd w/plaque dtd 1966, 9x36" ...**175.00**
Hook, halibut; cvd wood w/bone barb & copper wire, 5¼" **275.00**
Horn, fog; Magnavox, ft-pumped dbl bellows, minor rstr **175.00**
Hygrograph, L Maxant, pnt metal case, ca 1920, 11", EX **125.00**
Hygrometer, France, curved thermometer, ventilated case, 4¼" .**100.00**
Inclinomoter, pilot house; German, brass w/teak, 1920s, 14" W ..**120.00**
Lamp, anchor; Ahlemann & Schlatter, copper & brass, 17", EX ..**300.00**
Lamp, ship's breakdown; orig oil font & chimney, 23", NM **475.00**
Lamp, stern, brass, orig oil font & chimney, 19", NM **400.00**
Lantern, masthead; copper, clear lense, 13½", G **120.00**
Lantern, masthead; solid brass, clear lens, 10½", EX **150.00**
Lights, port & starboard running; brass, 10", matched pr **250.00**
Log book, Spanish-Am warship, ca 1899, EX **350.00**
Octant, ebony fr, ivory scales, brass mts, 1800s, w/case **900.00**
Octant, Samuel Thaxter...Boston, ebony/ivory/brass, 1800s **750.00**
Octant, Spencer Browning & Rust London, mahog fr, 17" **750.00**
Oil can, US Lighthouse Depot...NY, brass, rprs, 6½x12" **775.00**
Propeller, brass, 4-bladed, 26" dia **50.00**
Scales, GeGrave &Co...London, British Navy, cased set **125.00**
Sextant, C Plath Hamburg, 3-circle fr, VG in mahog box **300.00**
Sextant, David O White...US Navy Mark II, 1944, EX in case ..**415.00**
Sextant, Heath & Co...London, silver & rosewood, EX in box ..**500.00**
Sextant, Schwalb Hermanos Lima y Valparaiso, NMIB **900.00**
Sextant, Worthington & Allen London, pillar fr, 1800s, EX ..**1,000.00**
Sternboard, cvd & pnt w/lion's head & motto, 1800s, 57" **865.00**
Swab, cloth w/6½" trn ivory hdl, 10", EX **140.00**
Trumpet, captain's speaking; brass, 1800s, 14", EX **300.00**
Wheel, mahog w/brass hub & ring, 16" dia, EX **350.00**
Wheel, wood w/brass hub & wide bands, heavy, 36" **400.00**

Martin Bros.

The Martin Bros. were studio potters who worked from 1873 until 1914, first at Fulham and later at London and Southall. There were four brothers, each of whom excelled in their particular area. Robert, known as Wallace, was an experienced stonecarver. He modeled a series of grotesque bird and animal figural caricatures. Walter was the potter, responsible for throwing the larger vases on the wheel, firing the kiln, and mixing the clay. Edwin, an artist of stature, preferred more naturalistic forms of decoration. His work was often incised or had relief designs of seaweed, florals, fish, and birds. The fourth brother, Charles, was their business manager. Their work was incised with their names, place of production, and letters and numbers indicating month and year.

Bird, lid is head, gr/bl/brn, sgn/dtd, 9" **7,000.00**
Bird couple, mc slips, sgn/dtd, 8½" **8,500.00**

Bulldog, grotesque, ruffle around neck, removable head, restored base, 11¼", $9,400.00.

Clock case, Gothic style w/bizarre creature over dial, 11" **4,400.00**
Jug, smiling face w/exposed teeth ea side, brn/tan/wht, 9" **2,700.00**
Pitcher, raised/etched floral, 3 bl shades, 10" **750.00**
Spoon warmer, cylinder modeled as cockerel head, comb as hdl ..**800.00**
Vase, allover cvd jellyfish w/appl centers, copper, 9x5" **900.00**
Vase, coral-like branches in sgraffito on brn, hdls, 9x4" **1,100.00**
Vase, dragons cvd on brn, 4 snake hdls, rstr, 9" **1,450.00**
Vase, hummingbirds/orchids, bl/brn on tan, dtd 1897, 7x7" **1,600.00**
Vase, 5 cvd grotesque dragons, gr/brn on tan & bl, 10x8" **4,750.00**

Mary Gregory

Mary Gregory glass, for reasons that remain obscure, is the namesake of a Boston and Sandwich Glass Company employee who worked for the company for only two years in the mid-1800s. Although no evidence actually exists to indicate that glass of this type was even produced there, the fine colored or crystal ware decorated with figures of children in white enamel is commonly referred to as Mary Gregory. The glass, in fact, originated in Europe and was imported into this country where it was copied by several eastern glasshouses. It was popular from the mid-1800s until the turn of the century. It is generally accepted that examples with all-white figures were made in the U.S.A., while gold-trimmed items and those with children having tinted faces or a small amount of color on their clothing are European. Though amethyst is rare, examples in cranberry command the higher prices. Blue ranks next; and green, amber, and clear items are worth the least. Watch for new glass decorated with screen-printed children and a minimum of hand painting. The screen effect is easily detected with a magnifying glass.

Key: R & B—Reed and Barton

Atomizer, cranberry, boy & girl, 5" 360.00
Atomizer, lt bl, girl w/umbrella, sq, 5¼x2½" 365.00
Bottle, barber's; cobalt, girl playing tennis, 8" 195.00
Bottle, scent; ruby, girl, clear stopper, 4½" 250.00
Box, amber, boy by fence, 3½x3¾" dia 275.00

Box, blk amethyst, 2 girls making rose wreaths, 3¼x7" dia **1,000.00**
Box, cobalt, girl on lid, 2½x3½" dia 285.00
Box, dresser; amber, boy w/violin, 3x5" dia 250.00
Box, emerald gr, boy in grass, 6½x3⅞" 215.00
Box, pale amber, boy drinking from pump, metal ft, 3¾x2½" 325.00
Box, patch; bl, girl 150.00
Candy dish, emerald, boy w/butterfly, 6½x4" 225.00
Carafe, wine; clear, girl w/flowers, tinted detailing 265.00
Carafe, wine; lime gr, boy in chair, Optic pattern, 9¾x5" 235.00
Centerpc, lady, cased pk; rfn SP R&B base w/2 storks, 18" 900.00
Cheese dish, cranberry, 3 figures, 9" dome 365.00
Creamer & sugar bowl, sapphire bl, boy, 3¾", 2" 235.00
Cruet, amber, boy, amber bubble stopper, 9½x3" 245.00
Lustres, cranberry, girl, pastels & gold, 6 prisms, 10½", pr **2,025.00**
Pitcher, amethyst, girl w/butterfly net, gold trim, 12¼" 450.00
Pitcher, gr, boy w/flowers, 3-lobed, gold trim, 5" 170.00
Pitcher, ruby, girl, 2½" 225.00
Pitcher, sapphire bl, girl, 2" 225.00
Rose bowl, cranberry, girl w/flower, 2½" 300.00
Tray, cobalt, boy w/staff, girl feeding deer, 10¾x8½" 375.00
Tray, cranberry, 2 boys fishing, rectangular, 7x9½" 375.00
Tumbler, amber, boy w/hat & cane, 4⅛x2¾" 40.00
Tumbler, amber, girl, 4⅞x2¾" 55.00
Tumbler, amber, girl w/balloon, 4x2½" 40.00
Tumbler, bl, girl, tinted face & hair, ftd, 6" 198.00
Tumbler, cranberry, boy & butterfly, gold trim, 5⅝" 135.00
Tumbler, cranberry, boy on rick, 3½" 125.00
Tumbler, gr, boy, 3⅝x2¼" 42.00
Tumbler, lime gr, boy w/flowers, 4½x2¾" 45.00
Tumbler, vaseline, girl, 4¼x2½" 45.00
Vase, bl Bristol, ewer form, 5x3" 175.00
Vase, bl Bristol, girl, ped ft, 9½" 225.00
Vase, bud; amber, cupid & owl, 7" 290.00
Vase, gr, boy running w/flower, 11x3½" 145.00
Vase, gr, lady on bench in garden, ribbed, slender, 14" 195.00
Vase, gr, lady w/hoop & birds, 12½" 330.00
Vase, turq, boy (& girl), facing pr, 10⅜x4½" 550.00

Mason's Ironstone

In 1813 Charles J. Mason was granted a patent for a process said to 'improve the quality of English porcelain.' The new type of ware was in fact ironstone which Mason decorated with colorful florals and scenics, some of which reflected the Oriental taste. Although his business failed for a short time in the late 1840s, Mason re-established himself and continued to produce dinnerware, tea services, and ornamental pieces until about 1852 at which time the pottery was sold to Francis Morley. Ten years later, Geo. L. and Taylor Ashworth became owners. Both Morley and the Ashworths not only used Mason's molds and patterns but often his mark as well. Because the quality and the workmanship of the later wares do not compare with Mason's earlier product, collectors should take care to distinguish one from the other. Consult a good book on marks to be sure. The Wedgwood Company now owns the rights to the Mason patterns and is reproducing the Vista pattern under its Franciscan trademark. Note: Blue Vista is generally valued at 15% to 20% above prices for pink/red. Our advisor for this category is Susan Hirshman; she is listed in the Directory under Oregon.

Basket, fruit; mk, early 1800s, 9" dia 250.00
Bowl, cereal; Stratford 15.00
Bowl, vegetable; Vista, pk, oval 40.00
Butter dish, Vista 48.00
Chop plate, Vista 57.50

Coffeepot, Vista, pk	100.00
Cream soup & saucer, Vista, pk	40.00
Creamer, Stratford	30.00
Gravy boat, Fruits	38.00
Pitcher, milk; Fruits	42.50
Plate, dinner; Vista, pk	20.00
Plate, Imari colors, mk, deep, 8"	100.00
Plate, luncheon; Vista	12.50
Platter, Vista, pk, 15"	80.00
Shakers, Vista, pr	50.00
Teapot, Fruits	80.00
Teapot, Stratford	85.00
Teapot, Vista	80.00
Tray, sandwich; Vista, pk	65.00

Massier

Clement Massier was a French artist-potter who in 1881 established a workshop at Golfe Juan, France, where he experimented with metallic lustre glazes. (One of his pupils was Jacques Sicardo, who brought the knowledge he had gained through his association with Massier to the Weller Pottery Company in Zanesville, Ohio.) The lustre lines developed by Massier incorporated nature themes with allover decorations of foliage or flowers on shapes modeled in the Art Nouveau style. The ware was usually incised with the Massier name, his initials, or the location of the pottery. Massier died in 1917.

Vase, grasshoppers among wheat on green with pink iridescence, oviform, painted signature, incised mark, 12¾", $2,500.00.

Bowl, mc irid, molded as sirens in ocean waves, rstr, 14"	2,400.00
Lamp base, berries/leaves, mc irid, baluster, wood base	1,000.00
Vase, abstract fruit, mc irid, long sq neck, 9"	1,300.00
Vase, butterflies, gold irid, flaring toward base, 9"	900.00
Vase, daisies, mc on gold lustre, gilt, hdls, 19"	600.00
Vase, floral, irid on gr mottle, cylindrical, 5"	400.00
Vase, floral, purple/gold irid, dbl gourd, sgn, 10x3½"	700.00
Vase, palm motif, mc irid, cone shape w/sm low hdls, 7½"	1,600.00

Match Holders

Before the invention of the safety match in 1855, matches were kept in matchboxes and carried in pocket-size match safes because they ignited so easily. John Walker, an English chemist, invented the match more than one hundred years ago, quite by accident. Walker was working with a mixture of potash and antimony, hoping to make a combustible that could be used to fire guns. The mixture adhered to the end of the wooden stick he had used for stirring. As he tried to remove it by scraping the stick on the stone floor, it burst into flames. The invention of the match was only a step away! From that time to the present, match holders have been made in amusing figural forms as well as simple utilitarian styles and in a wide range of materials. Both table-top and wall-hanging models were made — all designed to keep matches conveniently at hand. Our advisor for this category is Ron Damaska; he is listed in the Directory under Pennsylvania. See also Advertising.

Brass, work-type sleigh with two sap buckets, 3x6", $150.00.

Brass, pig form, short legs, open top, 1800s, 2x4½"	145.00
China, boy w/rabbits & game birds, 5½"	125.00
China, girl feeding chicks, boy w/pig, 4", pr	240.00
China, Greek figure in toga w/horn, 5¼"	125.00
China, saucer type, box holder, Mayer	25.00
China, shoe form, striker on sole	25.00
CI, Bacchus face, grotesque, EX orig	150.00
CI, high-button shoe form, rectangular base, 4x5"	50.00
CI, lady's high-button shoe, 2-tiered base, Riche 1887, 5"	60.00
CI, rtcl bkplate, 2-compartment, 7"	45.00
Glass, Am Shield, shield form, 1492/1892, 4"	165.00
Glass, amber, hand holding container	80.00
Jasper, elephant head, hat & eyeglasses, chamberstick shape	95.00
Pottery, bust of Indian warrior, no mk, 6x4"	65.00
Pressed wood, Scottie figural front, wall-hanging	25.00
Tin, Compliments JN Jordan, Ely IO, EX	65.00

Match Safes

Match safes, aptly named cases used to carry matches in the days before cigarette lighters, were used during the last half of the 19th century until about 1920. Some incorporated added features (hidden compartments, cigar cutters, etc.), some were figural, and others were used by retail companies as advertising giveaways. They were made from every type of material, but silverplated styles abound. Both the advertising and common silverplated cases generally fall in the $50.00 to $100.00 price range. Those listed below are representative of the more desirable, harder-to-find examples. Our advisor for this category is Ron Damaska; he is listed in the Directory under Pennsylvania. See also Advertising.

Advertising, CI rabbit figural	150.00
NP brass, camera case form, 2½x1¼"	135.00
NP brass, figural Gladstone bust, 2¼x1"	265.00
NP brass, man on potty figural, 1¾"	375.00
NP brass, outhouse figural, door opens to show man w/in, 2"	265.00
Silver, enamel, HP hand w/cards, I'll Try Solo, 1890s, EX	250.00
Silver, enamel, HP royal flush in spades, 1890s	900.00
Silver, roulette wheel w/enameling, ca 1900, EX	500.00
Sterling, couple dancing among gambling symbols, 1890s	250.00
Sterling, emb smoking lady, serpent at bottom, 1890s	350.00
Sterling, playing cards relief, Tiffany, 1890s, EX	900.00

Sterling, wishbone relief, 4-leaf clover/etc, 1890s 350.00
14k gold, fancy, Victorian 400.00

McCoy

The third generation McCoy potter in the Roseville, Ohio, area was Nelson, who with the aid of his father, J.W., established the Nelson McCoy Sanitary Stoneware Company in 1910. They manufactured churns, jars, jugs, poultry fountains, and foot warmers. By 1925 they had expanded their wares to include majolica jardinieres and pedestals, umbrella stands and cuspidors, and an embossed line of vases and small jardinieres in a blended brown and green matt glaze. From the late twenties through the mid-forties, a utilitarian stoneware was produced, some of which was glazed in the soft blue and white so popular with collectors today. They also used a dark brown mahogany color and a medium to dark green, both in a high gloss. In 1933 the firm became known as the Nelson McCoy Pottery Company. They expanded their facilities in 1940 and began to make the novelty artware, cookie jars, and dinnerware that today are synonomous with 'McCoy.' More than two hundred cookie jars of every theme and description were produced.

Stimulated by the high prices commanded by desirable cookie jars, a broad spectrum of 'new' cookie jars are flooding the marketplace in three categories: 1) Manufacturers have expanded their lines with exciting new designs to attract the collector market. 2) Limited editions and artist-designed jars have proliferated. 3) Reproductions, signed and unsigned, have pervaded the market, creating uncertainty among new collectors and inexperienced dealers.

More than a dozen different marks have been used by the company; nearly all incorporate the name 'McCoy,' although some of the older items were marked 'NM USA.' For further information consult *The Collector's Encyclopedia of McCoy Pottery* (with recently updated values) by Sharon and Bob Huxford, available at your local bookstore or public library. Numbers in listings below refer to this book.

Alert! It should be noted that the original Nelson McCoy Pottery has closed its doors. Now an entrepreneur has emerged and has adopted the McCoy Pottery name and mark. This company is reproducing old McCoy designs as well as some classic designs of other defunct American potteries. Their wares are signed 'McCoy' with a mark which very closely approximates the old McCoy mark. Our McCoy cookie jar advisor is Judy Posner; she is listed in the Directory under Pennsylvania.

Cookie Jars

Animal Crackers 95.00
Apollo Age, minimum value 1,000.00
Apple, 1950-64 ....50.00
Apple on Basketweave 50.00
Astronauts 650.00
Bananas 125.00
Barnum's Animals 350.00
Baseball Boy 195.00
Bear, cookie in vest, no 'Cookies' 75.00
Betsy Baker 250.00
Black Kettle, w/immovable bail, HP flowers 35.00
Black Vase, w/flowers on lid 185.00
Bobby Baker 85.00
Bugs Bunny, cylinder 225.00
Caboose 165.00
Cat on Coal Scuttle 175.00
Chairman of the Board, minimum value 400.00
Chef 125.00

Chinese Lantern 75.00
Chipmunk 120.00
Circus Horse 250.00

Clown Bust, $100.00.

Clown in Barrel 130.00
Clyde Dog 150.00
Coalby Cat 400.00
Coffee Grinder 45.00
Coffee Mug 40.00
Colonial Fireplace 95.00
Cookie Barrel 40.00
Cookie Boy 225.00
Cookie Cabin 125.00
Cookie Jug, dbl loop 30.00
Cookie Jug, single loop, 2-tone gr rope 25.00
Cookie Jug, w/cork stopper, brn & wht 25.00
Cookie Log 65.00
Cookie Safe 65.00
Cookstove 50.00
Corn 150.00
Covered Wagon 150.00
Cylinder, w/red flowers 35.00
Dalmations in Rocking Chair 450.00
Dog on Basketweave 85.00
Drum 75.00
Duck on Basketweave 75.00
Dutch Boy 55.00
Dutch Girl, boy on reverse, rare 150.00
Dutch Treat Barn 65.00
Elephant w/Split Trunk, rare, minimum value 425.00
Engine, blk 175.00
Flowerpot, plastic flower on top, minimum value ..500.00
Football Boy 195.00
Forbidden Fruit 65.00
Freddy Gleep 500.00
Friendship 200.00
Frontier Family 50.00
Fruit in Bushel Basket 80.00
Gingerbread Boy 75.00
Globe 325.00
Grandfather Clock 85.00
Granny 85.00
Granny, gold trim 125.00
Hamm's Bear 225.00
Happy Face 75.00
Hen on Nest 95.00
Hillbilly Bear, rare, minimum value 900.00
Hobby Horse 150.00

Honey Bear 85.00

Indian, $350.00.

Jack-O'-Lantern, minimum value 500.00
Kangaroo, bl 300.00
Kettle, jumbo sz 40.00
Kissing Penguins 85.00
Kitten on Basketweave 85.00
Kittens (2) on Low Basket, minimum value 800.00
Kittens on Ball of Yarn 120.00
Kookie Kettle, blk 35.00
Lamb on Basketweave 65.00
Leprechaun, minimum value 1,200.00
Liberty Bell 60.00
Little Clown 85.00
Lollipops 85.00
Mac Dog 95.00
Mammy, Cookies on base 225.00
Mammy w/Cauliflower, G pnt, minimum value 1,100.00
Modern 45.00
Monk 45.00
Mother Goose 150.00
Mr & Mrs Owl 110.00
Nursery, decal of Humpty Dumpty 100.00
Oaken Bucket 35.00
Old Churn 35.00
Pears on Basketweave 50.00
Pelican 175.00
Picnic Basket 75.00
Pineapple 65.00
Pineapple, Modern 60.00
Pirate's Chest 90.00
Popeye Cylinder 225.00
Potbelly Stove, blk 40.00
Puppy, w/sign 95.00
Quaker Oats, rare, minimum value 800.00
Red Barn, cow in door, rare, minimum value 350.00
Rooster, wht, 1970-1974 ....65.00
Rooster, 1955-1957 ....125.00
Round w/HP Leaves 55.00
Sad Clown 75.00
Snoopy on Doghouse 295.00
Snow Bear 85.00
Spaniel in Doghouse, pup finial 295.00
Stagecoach, minimum value 1,000.00
Strawberry, 1955-57 ....45.00
Strawberry, 1971-75 ....55.00
Teapot, 1971 ....50.00
Tepee, str top 325.00
Tilt Pitcher, blk w/roses 40.00
Tomato 35.00

Touring Car 125.00
Tudor Cookie House 125.00
Tulip on Flowerpot 185.00
Turkey, gr, rare color 300.00
Upside Down Bear, panda 75.00
WC Fields 225.00
Wedding Jar 110.00
Windmill 150.00
Wishing Well 45.00
Woodsy Owl 250.00
Wren House 150.00
Yosemite Sam, cylinder 225.00

Miscellaneous

Basket, pine cones, Rustic glaze, 1945 ....35.00
Bean pot, Kathy Kale, HP apple on yel ware, 2-qt 75.00
Bowl, horizontal ribs on gr gloss, #11 in shield 40.00
Figurine, blk panther, no mk, 1950s, lg 40.00
Flowerpot, lg leaves emb at base of ribbed U-form, gr gloss 20.00
Grease jar, Cabbage, lg gr cabbage head on red base 55.00
Hanging basket, basketweave w/emb 'ring' hdls, aqua, 7½" 32.50
Jardiniere, butterfly band, gr on tan matt, sm 30.00
Ladder pc, duck, head down, on tall base, no mk, sm 30.00
Ladder pc, hillbilly, seated, in lg hat, mk USA 75.00
Lamp base, rearing horse, textured gold 85.00
Pitcher, stylized chicken form, wht semigloss, ca 1943 ....25.00
Pitcher, tankard; Buccaneer, pirate emb on gr gloss 100.00
Pitcher, tilt type w/ice lip, yel gloss, no mk 30.00
Pitcher, Water Lily, fish hdl, gr gloss, no mk 55.00
Planter, Butterfly, lg figural, 1940 ....28.00
Planter, carriage w/separate umbrella, movable wheels 90.00
Planter, cat w/gr bow, crouching, looking right, unmk, 1953 ....30.00
Planter, rolling pin, boy seated on top, no mk, 1952 ....65.00
Planter, spinning wheel, gr & tan gloss, 1953 ....20.00
Planter, stork by basket, 1956 ....40.00
Planter, stretch doggie, no mk, 1941, sm 100.00
Planter, 2 fawns, beige gloss w/blk accents, sm 20.00
Planter, 3 fawns by fence, trees in bkground, 1954, lg 165.00
Planter bookends, hunting dog w/fowl in mouth, 1955, pr 85.00
Tea set, Pine Cone, 3-pc 70.00
Tray, cupped hands w/leaves & berries at wrist, 1940s 30.00
Vase, Blossomtime, appl flowers, 5" 25.00
Vase, emb birds, bk cherries, ftd, yel gloss, 8" 22.00
Vase, heart shape w/emb roses, pk gloss 25.00
Vase, leaf band emb at shoulder, closed hdls, yel, 9" 23.00
Vase, lily, lg flower w/leaves at base, 1947 ....30.00
Vase, Onyx, bulbous w/hdls, 7" 65.00
Vase, poppies, 3 lg flowers & leaves, 1955 ....100.00
Vase, Springwood, dogwood spray, wht on pk, pillow form 25.00
Wall pocket, clock, weights on chains 55.00
Wall pocket, orange, leaf bkground 40.00
Wall pocket, owls on trivet 40.00
Window planter, Grecian, gold swags w/gr highlights on wht 40.00

McCoy, J. W.

The J.W. McCoy Pottery Company was incorporated in 1899. It operated under that name in Roseville, Ohio, until 1911 when McCoy entered into a partnership with George Brush, forming the Brush-McCoy Company. During the early years, McCoy produced kitchenware, majolica jardinieres and pedestals, umbrella stands, and cuspidors. By 1903 they had begun to experiment in the field of art pottery and, though never involved to the extent of some of their contemporaries, nevertheless produced several art lines of merit. Their first line was Mt. Pelee, examples of which are very rare today. Two types of glazes were used, matt green and an iridescent charcoal gray. Though the line was primarily mold formed, some pieces evidence the fact that while the clay remained wet and pliable it was pulled and pinched with the fingers to form crests and peaks in a style not unlike George Ohr.

The company rebuilt in 1904 after being destroyed by fire, and other artware was designed. Loy-Nel Art and Renaissance were standard brown lines, hand decorated under the glaze with colored slip. Shapes and artwork were usually simple but effective. Olympia and Rosewood were relief-molded brown-glaze lines decorated in natural colors with wreaths of leaves and berries or simple floral sprays. Although much of this ware was not marked, you will find examples with the die-stamped 'Loy-Nel Art, McCoy,' or an incised line identification.

Ewer, Mt Pelee, blk, 7" 1,000.00
Loy-Nel-Art, bowl, flat, w/hdls, lg 150.00
Loy-Nel-Art, spittoon, pansies, 4½" 195.00
Loy-Nel-Art, vase, daffodils, 5" 145.00
Loy-Nel-Art, vase, pansies, hdls, 8" 250.00
Olympia, pretzel bowl, emb leaves & pods 400.00
Olympia, vase, emb corn, cylindrical, 1905, 11" 350.00
Rosewood, ewer, emb grapes & leaves, 10" 350.00
Rosewood, vase, emb flowers, tiny rim, 1905, 5" 200.00
Rosewood, vase, rusty red streaks on brn gloss, pre-1903, 6" 150.00
Tankard, Corn, majolica-type glaze, 1910 .... 350.00
Umbrella stand, Liberty Bell, sgn Cusick, 23" 795.00

Medical Collectibles

The field of medical-related items encompasses a wide area from the primitive bleeding bowl to the X-ray machines of the early 1900s. Other closely related collectibles include apothecary and dental items. Many tools that were originally intended for the pharmacist found their way to the doctor's office, and dentists often used surgical tools when no suitable dental instrument was available. A trend in the late 1700s toward self-medication brought a whole new wave of home-care manuals and 'patent' medical machines for home use. Commonly referred to as 'quack' medical gimmicks, these machines were usually ineffective and occasionally dangerous. Our advisor for this category is Jim Calison; he is listed in the Directory under New York.

Apothocary jars, Pulvis, Salsus, 8½", $165.00 for the pair.

Book, Encyclopedia of Obstetrics, 1890, rebound 95.00
Book, Gray's Anatomy, 1878, EX 20.00
Book, Maidenhood & Motherhood, West, 1888, EX 35.00
Book, Practical Treatise/Diseases of Women, Scudder, 1859 .... 65.00
Chisel, bone; W&H Hutchinson Sheffield, 1860s, 1¼" blade 60.00
Compressor, cork; Enterprise Mfg, Pat Aug 7, 1867, CI, EX 120.00

Dental scraper, steel shaft w/ivory hdl, 4½" 50.00
Eye cup, amber, 8-sided, 2½" 75.00
Eye cup, clear, blown glass, pontil scar, 2⅞" 40.00
Eye cup, clear, fish bowl shape 18.00
Eye cup, clear, John Bull, 1917 .... 20.00
Eye cup, cobalt, bucket shape w/indented sides, 1⅜" 24.00
Eye cup, cobalt, emb on 2 sides: Wyeth, 1¼x1⅝" 12.50
Eye cup, cobalt, ped ft, mk WT Co 20.00
Eye cup, wht porc, bucket shape, Boots Chemists, 1⅝" 55.00
Fleam, brass w/3 hinged iron blades, in case, 3½" 170.00
Forceps, extracting; NP steel, Clev-Dent #150A 10.00
Forceps, unplated steel, Charriere, 1860s, 4⅝" 45.00
Jar, clear w/cobalt bands, free-blown, 1860s, 9¾" 300.00
Jar, Foley's Kidney Pills, label under glass, 1890s, 11" 275.00
Jar, golden amber globe w/clear glass lid, 1890s, 12½" 275.00
Jar, leach; stoneware, AD Patent Leech Jar...Lambeth, 6" 1,850.00
Kit, surgeon's; gutta-percha hdld instruments, 1800s, EX 550.00
Needle, arterial; ribbed ivory hdl, Lariviere, 1840s, 7" 60.00
Opthalmoscope, Morton type, Curry & Paxton London, EX ... 165.00
Pill cutter, hdld blade on wooden base w/brass hinge, 12½" 190.00
Pill roller, walnut & brass, early 325.00
Quack machine, Davis & Kidder 350.00
Saw, amputation; pistol grip type, Civil War era, 14½", EX 225.00
Scalpel, ebony hdl mk Charriere, 1860s, 6", EX 30.00
Scalpel, folding type, ivory covers, 5½" 45.00
Spoon, medicine; crystal, emb Phillips Milk of Magnesia, 4" L 20.00
Stethoscope, binaural; bell shape, plated brass chest pc 35.00
Stethoscope, monaural; hard rubber, removable shaft, 6¾" 155.00
Tenaculum, ribbed ivory hdl, Tiemann, 1850s, 6¼" 67.50
Tongue depressor, ivory, 5¼" 27.50
Tooth key, steel shaft, 1-claw, bone hdl, 1840s, 5" 200.00
Tweezers, spring steel, Sheffield, ca 1890s, 4" 35.00
Vaccinator, plated metal, 5-pronged, 3½" 40.00
Yearbook, Hahnemann Medical College, 1934, 259-pg, EX 30.00

Meissen

The Royal Saxon Porcelain Works was established in 1710 in Meissen, Saxony. Under the direction of Johann Frederick Bottger, who in 1708 had developed the formula for the first true porcelain body, fine ceramic figurines with exquisite detail and tableware of the highest quality were produced. Although every effort was made to insure the secrecy of Bottger's discovery, others soon began to copy his ware; and in 1731 Meissen adopted the famous crossed swords trademark to identify their own work. The term 'Dresden ware' is often used to refer to Meissen porcelain, since Bottger's discovery and first potting efforts were in nearby Dresden. See also Onion Pattern.

Box, powder; roses, pk on wht, Xd swords 175.00
Charger, florals in relief, gold on gr, Xd swords, 11" 275.00
Compote, birds/florals, rtcl basketweave border, 11" W 430.00
Compote, Indian Purple, rtcl rim, knob ped, 8½x9" 550.00
Figurine, boy drinking bowl of milk, 6½" 1,975.00
Figurine, boy on play horse, newspaper cap, long gown, 7" 1,000.00
Figurine, boy w/flute & dog, #22, 1800s, 5½" 580.00
Figurine, cherub w/scythe & wheat, Xd swords, 5" 575.00
Figurine, Europa & Bull, 1800s, 8" 1,400.00
Figurine, girl on goat w/grape garland, boy w/horn beside, 6" 900.00
Figurine, Gnaga, carrying infant & basket, 1920s, rpr, 7" 750.00
Figurine, Good Mother, seated lady w/3 children, 8¾" 1,650.00
Figurine, Grape Harvest (group), #F92, 6" 875.00
Figurine, Happy Family, couple admiring baby, 8½" 1,800.00
Figurine, lady at table w/basket of flowers, 1800s, #43, 6" 1,100.00

Figurines: Seated lady with two children, playing cards falling to floor, restored, 8⅝", $1,495.00; Two women by urn, arrows, and quiver, lovebirds and letter at their feet, minor restoration, 9¾", $1,600.00.

Figurine, lady seated at dressing table, 5¾" 1,200.00
Figurine, lady w/basket of flowers, #668-12, 1800s, 8", EX 1,200.00
Figurine, maid w/grapes (losses), 1800s, 3¾" 285.00
Figurine, man in fur/maroon cloak stands by lamp, #7801, 8" 500.00
Figurine, man in yel coat/floral vest, 5½", EX 465.00
Figurine, peasant maid w/flowers/man w/carafe, keg behind, 6" ..495.00
Figurine, swan trn to right on foliate base, 9", EX 1,150.00
Figurine, 18th-C man reading book, Xd swords 650.00
Leaf plate, red, wht & gold, raised beading, ca 1860, 9¾" 250.00
Plate, floral medallions on cobalt & wht, 11½" 575.00
Platter, wide cobalt border w/gilt crest, serpentine, 21" 350.00
Vase, appl bl flowering vine, bird hdls on rtcl lids, 9", pr 1,700.00
Vase, cobalt w/wht & gold, serpent hdls, 11" 230.00
Vase, flowers, snake/leaf hdls, scroll band, gilt, 19" 2,500.00

Mercury Glass

Mercury glass was popular during the 1850s and enjoyed a short revival at the turn of the century. It was made with two thin layers, either blown with a double wall or joined in sections, with the space between the walls of the vessel filled with a mixture of tin, lead, bismuth, and mercury. The opening was sealed to prevent air from dulling the bright color. Though most examples are silver, blue and gold can be found on occasion. Remember that the value of this type of glass hinges greatly upon condition of the mercury lining. In the listings that follow, all examples are silver unless noted another color.

Bowl, 3 clear appl ft, 4¾x9½" 115.00
Candlestick, gold w/wht floral, baluster, 11", pr 95.00
Mug, clear hdl, 3" 36.00
Rolling pin 110.00
Rose bowl, gold, Czechoslovakia, 10" 200.00
Toothpick holder 45.00
Urn, gold int, ped base, 3" 125.00
Vase, teal bl, spittoon shape, M 225.00
Wig stand, 10½" 225.00

Merrimac

Founded in 1897 in Newburyport, Massachusetts, the Merrimac Pottery Company primarily produced gardenware. In 1901, however, they introduced a line of artware that is now attracting the interest of collectors. Marked examples carry an impressed die-stamp or a paper label, each with the firm name and the outline of a sturgeon, the Indian word for Merrimac.

Vase, curdled gr matt, bulbous w/can neck, label, 8x5½" 900.00
Vase, cvd/appl upright Arts & Crafts leaves on 2-tone gr, 6" ..1,700.00
Vase, gr matt, spherical tapering toward base, 6½x6¾" 450.00
Vase, gr mottle, hdls, narrow neck, no mk, 4x3¾" 250.00
Vase, long-stem stylized floral, gr/gun metal, 6x5" 900.00

Metlox

The Metlox Manufacturing Company was founded in 1927 in Manhattan Beach, California. Before 1934 when they began producing the ceramic housewares for which they have become famous, they made ceramic and neon outdoor advertising signs. The company went out of business in 1989.

Well-known sculptor Carl Romanelli designed artware in the late 1930s and early 1940s (and again briefly in the 1950s). His work is especially sought after today. Some pattern lines can be confusing. There are two 'rooster' lines, Red Rooster (red, orange and brown) and California Provincial (dark green and burgundy), and there are two 'homestead' lines, Colonial Homestead (red, orange and brown like the Red Rooster pieces) and Homestead Provincial (dark green and burgundy like California Provincial). For further information we recommend *The Collector's Encyclopedia of California Pottery* by Jack Chipman, and *Collector's Encyclopedia of Metlox Potteries* by our advisor Carl Gibbs, Jr.; he is listed in the Directory under Texas.

Cookie Jars

Ballerina Bear 135.00
Bluebird on Pine Cone 225.00
Broccoli 175.00
Calf, 'Moo' 400.00
Candy Girl, head jar 395.00
Clown, wht w/bl details 275.00
Clown, wht w/blk details 225.00
Cookie Girl, sandstone 50.00
Corn 135.00
Cow, yel 425.00
Daisy Topiary 75.00
Dina, bl 175.00
Drummer Boy 650.00
Flamingo 800.00
Frosty Penguin 165.00
Gingham Dog, cream 150.00
Grapes 300.00
Hen, wht 325.00
Humpty Dumpty, no ft 325.00
Kaola Bear 125.00
Katy Cat 125.00
Kitten, 'Meow' 165.00
Lucy Goose 175.00
Mammy Cook, bl 550.00
Mother Goose 350.00
Panda Bear 145.00
Pineapple 100.00
Pinocchio 425.00
Puddles 75.00
Pumpkin, boy on lid 525.00
Rabbit, clover bloom finial 325.00
Raggedy Boy or Girl, ea 225.00

Roller Bear	165.00
Rose	435.00
Salty Pelican	225.00
Scottie, blk	150.00
Scottie, wht	225.00
Sombrero Bear	95.00
Squash	195.00
Strawberry	195.00

Dinnerware

Antique Grape, coffeepot	85.00
Antique Grape, comport	45.00
Antique Grape, mug	20.00
Antique Grape, plate, dinner	15.00
Antique Grape, salad set	65.00
California Geranium, bowl, vegetable; 10" dia	24.00
California Geranium, bowl, 5¾"	9.00
California Geranium, creamer & sugar bowl, w/lid	33.00
California Geranium, cup & saucer	11.00
California Geranium, plate, 10½"	10.00
California Geranium, plate, 8¼"	7.00
California Geranium, server, oblong, divided, 16"	29.00
California Geranium, shakers, pr	20.00
California Ivy, bowl, salad	55.00
California Ivy, bowl, vegetable; 11¼"	30.00
California Ivy, bowl, 5¼"	9.00
California Ivy, bowl, 6¾"	12.00
California Ivy, casserole; w/lid	60.00
California Ivy, chop plate, 13"	30.00
California Ivy, cup & saucer	11.00
California Ivy, cup & saucer, demitasse	25.00
California Ivy, pitcher, 10"	49.00
California Ivy, plate, 10¼"	13.00
California Ivy, plate, 6¼"	6.00
California Ivy, plate, 9¼"	11.00
California Ivy, platter, 13"	29.00
California Provincial, bean pot w/lid	75.00
California Provincial, bread server, 9½"	49.00

California Provincial, canister, 10", $95.00.

California Provincial, creamer & sugar bowl	45.00
California Provincial, cup & saucer	16.00
California Provincial, gravy, hdl, 6¼"	32.00
California Provincial, jam & mustard	45.00
California Provincial, plate, 10"	15.00
California Provincial, plate, 6½"	7.50
California Provincial, salt box, w/lid	95.00
California Provincial, shakers, figural, pr	49.00

California Strawberry, bowl, divided vegetable	35.00
California Strawberry, bowl, salad; lg	55.00
California Strawberry, bowl, soup; 6¾"	12.00
California Strawberry, bowl, vegetable; 8"	29.00
California Strawberry, butter dish	45.00
California Strawberry, casserole, w/lid	55.00
California Strawberry, creamer	18.00
California Strawberry, cup & saucer	14.00
California Strawberry, gravy boat	32.00
California Strawberry, plate, 6"	7.00
California Strawberry, platter, oval, 11"	30.00
California Strawberry, platter, oval, 9½"	25.00
California Strawberry, salad fork	25.00
California Strawberry, shakers, pr	20.00
Geranium, bowl, vegetable; 10" dia	25.00
Geranium, creamer	15.00
Geranium, cup & saucer	10.00
Geranium, plate, 10½"	10.00
Geranium, server, divided; oblong, 16"	25.00
Geranium, shakers, pr	16.00
Happy Days, bowl, divided vegetable; w/hdl	45.00
Homestead Provincial, bowl, divided vegetable	45.00
Homestead Provincial, bowl, salad; 11"	75.00
Homestead Provincial, bread server	49.00
Homestead Provincial, butter dish	49.00
Homestead Provincial, casserole, hen shape, ind	110.00
Homestead Provincial, chop plate, 12¼"	55.00
Homestead Provincial, coffeepot	95.00
Homestead Provincial, creamer & sugar bowl	45.00
Homestead Provincial, cup & saucer	16.00
Homestead Provincial, gravy, hdl	32.00
Homestead Provincial, jam & mustard	45.00
Homestead Provincial, kettle casserole, no hdl	90.00
Homestead Provincial, mug	22.00
Homestead Provincial, plate, 10"	15.00
Homestead Provincial, plate, 6"	7.50
Homestead Provincial, platter, oval, 14"	49.00
Homestead Provincial, shakers, hen, pr	50.00
Homestead Provincial, shakers, pr	24.00
Homestead Provincial, sugar bowl	25.00
Homestead Provincial, tankard	30.00
Homestead Provincial, vinegar cruet	26.00
Homestead Provincial, wall pocket/match holder	65.00
Pepper Tree, bowl, fruit	9.00
Pepper Tree, casserole, w/lid, 8¾"	45.00
Pepper Tree, cup & saucer	14.00
Pepper Tree, plate, dinner	12.00
Pepper Tree, plate, salad	9.00
Provincial Blue, coffeepot	95.00
Provincial Blue, cup & saucer	16.00
Provincial Blue, tankard	30.00
Provincial Fruit, bowl, cereal; 7"	13.00
Provincial Fruit, bowl, lug; 5"	18.00
Provincial Fruit, bowl, serving; 10"	35.00
Provincial Fruit, cup & saucer	14.00
Provincial Fruit, plate, 10½"	13.00
Provincial Fruit, plate, 7½"	10.00
Provincial Fruit, sugar bowl	22.00
Red Rooster Provincial, bowl, cereal	14.00
Red Rooster Provincial, bowl, salad; lg	75.00
Red Rooster Provincial, bowl, vegetable; w/lid	65.00
Red Rooster Provincial, bowl, vegetable; 10"	40.00
Red Rooster Provincial, canister, sugar or tea; ea	32.00
Red Rooster Provincial, chop plate, 12"	65.00

Red Rooster Provincial, coffeepot 95.00
Red Rooster Provincial, cruet set, 5-pc+lids+wooden holder 165.00
Red Rooster Provincial, cup & saucer 15.00
Red Rooster Provincial, lazy susan 165.00
Red Rooster Provincial, pitcher, sm 45.00
Red Rooster Provincial, platter, 13½" 40.00
Red Rooster Provincial, platter, 16" 95.00
Red Rooster Provincial, tumbler 28.00
Sculptured Daisy, bowl, cereal; 7" 14.00
Sculptured Daisy, bowl, fruit; 6" 10.00
Sculptured Daisy, bowl, vegetable; sm 29.00
Sculptured Daisy, butter dish, ¼-lb 45.00
Sculptured Daisy, casserole, w/lid 45.00
Sculptured Daisy, cup & saucer 14.00
Sculptured Daisy, gravy boat 35.00
Sculptured Daisy, plate, dinner; 10½" 13.00
Sculptured Daisy, plate, 6" 6.50
Sculptured Daisy, plate, 7½" 10.00
Sculptured Daisy, platter, 11" 35.00
Sculptured Daisy, platter, 14" 39.00
Sculptured Daisy, shakers, pr 22.00
Sculptured Daisy, sugar bowl, w/lid 24.00
Sculptured Grape, cup & saucer 16.00
Sculptured Zinnia, cup & saucer 14.00
Sculptured Zinnia, plate, salad; 7½" 10.00
Woodland Gold, bowl, vegetable; rnd, 9" 35.00
Woodland Gold, cup & saucer 14.00
Woodland Gold, plate, dinner 13.00
Woodland Gold, plate, 8" 10.00
Woodland Gold, platter, 13" 35.00

Romanelli Artware

Bookends, nude w/dogs, mc, pr 375.00
Figurine, flamingo, 6" 50.00
Figurine, Indian brave, 9" 250.00
Figurine, 2 birds on branch, satin bl, #1826 ....85.00
Flower holder, draped nude before triple vase, ivory, 8¾" 200.00
Miniature, crocodile 80.00
Miniature, elephant 95.00
Miniature, monkey on all fours, turq & brn, 4½" 85.00
Miniature, Scottie dog 45.00
Vase, angelfish form, 8½" 100.00
Vase, sea horse, satin bl, #1809, 9¼" 175.00
Vase, swordfish form, bl matt, 9" 125.00
Vase, Zodiac sign, 8" 110.00

Mettlach

   In 1836 Nicholas Villeroy and Eugene Francis Boch, both of whom
were already involved in the potting industry, formed a partnership and
established a stoneware factory in an old restored abbey in Mettlach,
Germany. Decorative stoneware with in-mold relief was their specialty,
steins in particular. Through constant experimentation, they developed
innovative methods of decoration. One process, called chromolith,
involved inlaying colorful mosaic designs into the body of the ware.
Later underglaze printing from copper plates was used. Their stoneware
was of high quality, and their steins won many medals at the St. Louis
Expo and early world's fairs. Most examples are marked with an incised
castle and the name 'Mettlach.' The numbering system indicates size,
date, stock number, and decorator. Production was halted by a fire in
1921; the factory was not rebuilt. Our advisor for this category is Ron
Fox; he is listed in the Directory under New York.

Key:
L — liter   PUG — print under glaze
POG — print over glaze   tl — thumb lift

#2416, vase, etched: Art
Nouveau, 16", $1,375.00;
#2976, vase, etched: Art
Nouveau, rare colors,
14½", $1,200.00.

#1005, stein, relief: tavern scene, inlaid lid, 1-L 320.00
#1044/221 & 222, plaques, PUG: Nurnberg/Munchen, 14", pr ..965.00
#1044/291, plaque, PUG: Stadthor Esslingen, 12" 200.00
#1044/94, plaque, PUG: Cochem, 12" 175.00
#1044/96, plaque, PUG: Schlossberg bei Zeltingen, 12" 135.00
#1062, stein, mosaic, inlaid lid, ½-L 550.00
#1078/1909, stein, PUG: frogs, pewter lid, ½-L 600.00
#1095, stein, mosaic, inlaid lid, ½-L 440.00
#1145/1526, stein, PUG/relief: barmaid, pewter lid, ½-L 285.00
#1159, stein, etched: musicians, inlaid lid, rpr, 6.2-L 715.00
#1171/2842, beaker, PUG: dwarf, ¼-L 175.00
#1189/2327, beaker, PUG: lady at shore, w/hdl, ¼-L 100.00
#1191/2327, beaker, PUG: fisherman, ¼-L 100.00
#1192/2327, beaker, PUG: man w/net, ¼-L 110.00
#1281/1526, stein, PUG: man drinking, pewter lid, ½-L 200.00
#1338/3257, stein, PUG: dressed frogs, pewter lid, 1.6-L 580.00
#1385, plaque, etched: man w/shield & club, 1910, 14¾" 800.00
#1501, cup, PUG: soldier, chip, ¼-L 85.00
#1526, stein, POG: Rothenburg, pewter lid, ½-L 220.00
#1526, stein, PUG: Princeton University, no lid, 1899, ½-L 80.00
#1562, stein, etched: portrait medallion, hairline, 5.6-L 900.00
#1566, stein, etched: highwheeler, pewter lid, ½-L 900.00
#1578, stein, etched: drinking scene, pewter lid, 4½-L 1,760.00
#1675, stein, etched: Heidelberg, inlaid lid, sm rpr, ½-L 415.00
#1695, stein, etched: hunters, inlaid lid, ½-L 770.00
#1725, stein, etched: couple & crest, inlaid lid, ¼-L 375.00
#1732, stein, etched: crest, pewter lid, missing tl, ½-L 470.00
#1733, stein, etched: jockey occupational, inlaid lid, ½-L 2,200.00
#1786, stein, etched: St Florian, rpl dragon finial, ½-L 525.00
#1816, stein, mosaic, inlaid lid, pewter rim, ½-L 440.00
#1922, stein, mosaic/etched: spiral design, 2½-L 1,100.00
#1932, stein, etched: cavaliers, barmaid pewter lid, ½-L 495.00
#1932, stein, etched: cavaliers, pewter lid, 1-L 635.00
#1995, stein, etched: man drinking, inlaid lid, ½-L 470.00
#2005, stein, etched: interior scene, inlaid lid, ½-L 550.00
#2024, stein, etched: Berlin shield, inlaid lid, ½-L 690.00
#2025, stein, etched: cherubs, inlaid lid, ½-L 415.00
#2068, stein, etched: drinking scene, inlaid lid, rpr, ½-L 360.00
#2075, stein, etched: telegrapher, new lid, rpr, ½-L 715.00
#2077, stein, relief: 3 panels, bl, inlaid lid, .3-L 175.00
#2077, stein, relief: 3 panels on terra cotta, rpr, ½-L 75.00
#2082, stein, etched: Wm Tell, inlaid lid, 1-L 1,870.00
#2083, stein, etched: boar hunt, inlaid lid, ½-L, NM 660.00

#2090, stein, etched: man at table, inlaid lid, ½-L 690.00
#2092, stein, etched: dwarf, inlaid lid, ½-L 910.00
#2093, stein, etched: suit of cards, inlaid lid, ½-L 800.00
#2100, stein, etched: warriors, inlaid lid, ½-L 880.00
#2134, stein, etched: dwarf, inlaid lid, ½-L 2,365.00
#2204, stein, relief: Imperial Eagle, inlaid lid, 1-L 1,350.00
#2205, stein, etched: hunters, inlaid lid, sm rpr, 5.2-L 1,650.00
#2235, stein, etched: targets/barmaid, inlaid lid, rpr, ½-L 275.00
#2235, stein, etched: targets/barmaid, inlaid lid, 1-L 880.00
#2263, stein, relief: cavaliers, inlaid lid, ½-L 440.00
#2322, plaque, etched: cavalier & bar maid, bl, 1909, 14½" 1,200.00
#2373, stein, etched: St Augustine FL, inlaid lid, ½-L 660.00
#2382, stein, etched: Thirsty Knight, inlaid lid, ½-L 800.00
#24, stein, relief: cavaliers, inlaid lid, ½-L 350.00
#2402, stein, etched: Siegfried's Courting, inlaid lid, ½-L 1,045.00
#2443, plaque, cameo: lady & attendants, Castle mk, 18¼" 1,250.00
#2526, stein, relief: Creussan type, pewter lid, ½-L, NM 935.00
#2530, stein, cameo: boar hunt, inlaid lid, new base, .3-L 255.00
#2580, stein, etched: De Kannenburg, inlaid lid, ½-L 770.00
#2592, plaque, etched: owl on limb, gold wear, 17½" 1,760.00
#2634, stein, cameo: Rodenstein, inlaid lid, rpr, 2½-L 770.00
#2686, stein, cameo: male figures, inlaid lid, rpr, 2½-L 1,100.00
#2692, stein, etched: drinking scene, inlaid lid, chip, 3-L 715.00
#2693, stein, etched: drinking scene, inlaid lid, flaw, ½-L 525.00
#2718, stein, etched: David & Goliath, inlaid lid, 1-L 2,300.00
#2721, stein, occupational: cabinetmaker, inlay lid, ½-L 1,500.00
#2755, stein, cameo: drinking scenes, inlaid lid, rpr, ½-L 340.00
#2765, stein, etched: knight on wht horse, inlaid lid, 1-L 3,625.00
#2765, stein, etched: knight on wht horse, inlaid lid, ½-L 2,255.00
#2766, stein, etched: man drinking, inlaid lid, ½-L 690.00
#2789/5145, stein, Rookwood type: portrait, pewter lid, ½-L 525.00
#2791/6136, stein, Rookwood type: portrait, pewter lid, ½-L 470.00
#2814, punch bowl, cvd/pnt: maids/vintage band, hdls, 10x11" ..1,265.00
#2833B, stein, etched: man sitting by tree, inlaid lid, ½" 525.00
#2833F, stein, etched: toasting scene, ½-L 495.00
#2844, stein, etched: harvest scene, inlaid lid, ½-L 1,265.00
#2880, stein, etched: dining scene, inlaid lid, ½-L 495.00
#2886, stein, etched: men at table, pewter lid, 1-L 635.00
#2948, creamer & sugar bowl, etched: Art Nouveau, 4", NM 360.00
#2958, stein, etched: bowling scene, inlaid lid, 2.8-L, EX 330.00
#2959, stein, etched: bowling scene, inlaid lid, 1-L 660.00
#3099, stein, etched: Diogenes, inlaid lid, 3-L 2,500.00
#3135, stein, etched: eagle, inlaid lid, ½-L 1,325.00
#3250, stein, etched: man dining, inlaid lid, flake, ½-L 470.00
#3322, pitcher, etched: Art Nouveau, 8" 415.00
#3341, gravy pitcher, etched: Art Nouveau, 6½" 350.00
#5006, stein, faience: Salzburg, pewter lid, rare sz, .3-L 300.00
#5010/1044, plaque, faience: floral, hairline, 13½" 110.00
#5021, stein, faience: medallions, pewter lid, rpr, 5-L 715.00
#5024, stein, faience: floral, pewter lid, hairline, 1-L 500.00
#5038/1044, plaque, Delft type: Rathaus in Koln, 17½" 285.00
#5189, stein, Delft type: portrait, pewter lid, rpr, ½-L 275.00
#5442, stein, faience: man on keg, rpr, rpl ft ring, 1-L 850.00
#603/1526, stein, PUG: men at table, pewter lid, ½-L 200.00
#675, stein, relief: bbl shape, brn, inlaid lid, ½-L 145.00
#7037, plaque, phanolith: dancing figures, rpr, 17½", EX 360.00
#983/1909, stein, PUG: Falstaff, pewter lid, ½-L 285.00

Microscopes

The microscope has taken on many forms during its 250-year evolutionary period. The current collectors' market primarily includes examples from England, those surplused from institutions, and continental beginner and intermediate forms which sold through Sears Roebuck & Company and other retailers of technical instruments. Earlier examples have brass maintubes which are unpainted. Later, more common examples are all black with brass or silver knobs and horseshoe-shaped bases. Early and more complex forms are the most valuable; these always had hardwood cases to house the delicate instruments and their accessories. Instruments were never polished during use, and those that have been polished to use as decorator pieces are of little interest to most avid collectors. Our advisor for this category is Dale Beeks; he is listed in the Directory under Idaho.

Bausch & Lomb, all brass, horseshoe base, 1897, 14", EX 350.00
Bausch & Lomb, blk base, brass tube, 1897, 14", EX 325.00
Bausch & Lomb, brass, tripod base, 1885, 16", EX, +case 425.00
Bausch & Lomb, ca 1915, EX orig 200.00
Bausch & Lomb, laboratory, blk & brass, 1915, +fitted case 225.00
Bausch & Lomb, laboratory style, 1937, 14¾", +case 175.00
English, student, brass, ca 1870, 12", +case/accessories 325.00
English, Watson, binocular form, 1880, 18", EX, +case 875.00
French, drum or furnace form, 5", EX, +case 60.00
Grunow, New York, iron & brass, 15", EX, +case 900.00
Gundlach, brass, Y base, 1879, 14", EX 325.00
Hand-held, simple form, 1890, 3", G 45.00
McAllister, chain-drive focus, brass, 14", G, +case 325.00
R&J Beck Ltd London, 12", EX 225.00
Stamp magnifier, brass, 3-leg, 1½", G 55.00
Tighe, brass, 12", EX, +case 450.00
Tolles, Boston, brass, Y base, 1880s, 15", G, +case 450.00
Watson, English binocular form, 1880, 18", EX, +case 900.00
Zentmeyer, brass, complex, dbl pillar, tripod base, 18", G 1,400.00

Midwestern Glass

As early as 1814, blown glass was made in Ohio. By 1835 glasshouses in Michigan were producing similar pattern-molded types that have long been highly regarded by collectors. During the latter part of the 19th century, all six of the states of the Northwest Territory were mass-producing the pressed glass tableware patterns that were then in vogue. Various types of art glass were produced in the area until after the turn of the century. Items listed here are attributed to the Midwest by certain physical characteristics known to be indigenous to that part of the country. See also Findlay Onyx; Greentown Glass; Libbey; Zanesville Glass. Our advisor for this category is Mark Vuono; he is listed in the Directory under Connecticut.

Bottle, aqua, 16 swirled ribs, flared lip, 7⅛" 165.00
Bottle, aqua, 18 melon ribs, club shape, 7⅞" 175.00
Bottle, aqua, 22 swirled ribs, pontiled, flared lip, 5" 375.00
Bottle, nursing; aqua, Ogival pattern, sheared lip, 5½" 30.00
Bottle, nursing; aqua, 12 Dmn, pontiled, fire-polished lip, 8" 40.00
Bottle, nursing; aqua, 19 vertical ribs, 6⅝" 60.00
Creamer, 15 vertical ribs, appl hdl, broken blister, 5" 60.00
Flask, chestnut; amber, 16 ribs, pontiled, stain, 4¾" 120.00
Flask, chestnut; aqua, 16 Dmn, fire-polished lip, 6" 220.00
Flask, chestnut; aqua, 18 swirled ribs, sheared lips, 6" 165.00
Flask, chestnut; golden olive-amber, 16 vertical ribs, 7" 270.00
Flask, chestnut; honey-amber, 18 swirled ribs, blister, 6⅛" 275.00
Flask, chestnut; lt gr, 18 broken swirl ribs, pontiled, 6⅜" 165.00
Flask, chestnut; lt gr, 18 vertical ribs, lt wear, 7" 127.50
Pan, aqua, 18 swirled ribs, folded rim, 1½x6¼" 550.00
Pan, golden amber, folded rim, 5⅞" 550.00
Tumbler, lt gr, 18 broken swirl ribs, 4¼" 3,900.00

Militaria

Because of the wide and varied scope of items available to collectors of militaria, most tend to concentrate mainly on the area or areas that interest them most or that they can afford to buy. Some items represent a major investment and because of their value have been reproduced. Extreme caution should be used when purchasing Nazi items. Every badge, medal, cap, uniform, dagger, and sword that Nazi Germany issued is being reproduced today. Some repros are crude and easily identified as fakes, while others are very well done and difficult to recognize as reproductions. Purchases from WWII veterans are usually your safest buys. Reputable dealers or collectors will normally offer a money-back guarantee on Nazi items purchased from them. There are a number of excellent Third Reich reference books available in bookstores at very reasonable prices. Study them to avoid losing a much larger sum spent on a reproduction. Our advisor for this category is Ron Willis; he is listed in the Directory under Oklahoma.

Key: insg — insignia

Imperial German

Badge, Flight troops; Bavarian Army Observer, silver, 2-pc, EX ..625.00
Badge, wound; Navy, Xd swords & anchor, NM finish, rpr, EX ..200.00
Badge, wound; WWI, blk, hollow, stamped type, EX pnt 17.50
Buckle, WWI, Prussian, field-gray pnt finish, M 22.50
Epaulettes, pre-WWI, red w/brass trim, silver/blk piping, pr 67.50
Helmet, Baden Guard Grenadier, silver trim/spike, EX 500.00
Medal, Chino 1900 Combat, Boxer Rebellion, bronze 85.00
Medal, Franco-Prussian Commemorative, bronze, no ribbon 18.00
Medal, Iron Cross, 1st class, silver, 1914, EX 85.00
Medal, Wilhelm I Centennial, bronze, no ribbon 15.00
Military pass, WWI, Kriegsmarine, 1917-18, EX 35.00
Shako, Marine Officer, leather w/brass, horsehair plume, EX ..1,450.00
Shoulderboards, Medical Staff, silver w/blk, slip-on, pr 40.00
Tunic, WWI, Air Service, field gray, concealed buttons, EX 495.00

Third Reich

Armband, Armed Forces Personnel, blk embr eagle on wht 25.00
Armband, Asst Stretcher Bearer, blk embr on wht, EX 20.00
Armband, Hitler Youth, embr & sewn cloth, EX 25.00
Armband, SA Leader, gold bullion on red-orange cotton, EX 200.00
Armband, SS, sewn, wht satin swastika, red wool, blk trim 100.00
Badge, Army Motor Vehicle Driver, gilt on gray wool, EX 20.00
Badge, combat; Navy Auxiliary Cruiser, worn gold plate, VG 150.00
Badge, combat; Navy Mine Sweeper, gilt wreath, solid bk, G 90.00
Badge, DRL Sport Assoc, gold, w/swastika, EX 45.00
Badge, lanyard; Army Tank Marksmanship, eagle & tank, metal .25.00

Badge, Luftwaffe Wireless Operator, pot metal, EX, $150.00.

Badge, Luftwaffe Flak Artillary, SP, solid bk, hallmk, EX 75.00
Badge, Luftwaffe Ground Combat, gray metal, solid bk, VG 125.00
Badge, Luftwaffe Pilot, silvered eagle, hallmk, early, EX 300.00
Badge, Navy Sr Administration Petty Officer, yel embr on bl 22.00
Badge, Reich Party Day, brass eagle, 1933, EX 15.00
Badge, Tank Assault, SP, solid bk, hallmk, EX 45.00
Badge, wound; blk finish, stamped style, NM 15.00
Badge, wound; blk finish, stickpin style, EX 15.00
Badge, wound; gold finish, solid-bk style, hallmk, NM 125.00
Bandoleer, ammunition; Luftwaffe, camo, 12-pocket, 1943, EX .250.00
Banner, Hitler Youth, swastika, red on wht, 115x46", EX 300.00
Bar, Army Close Combat, EX gold plate, hallmk, EX 225.00
Bath, Luftwaffe Observer, gray embr on gray wool, NM 35.00
Belt buckle, German Youth, brass tunic on NP field, RZM hallmk ..35.00
Belt buckle, Luftwaffe, pebbled aluminum, brn leather belt 30.00
Belt buckle, SA Enlisted, brass, rotated swastika 25.00
Brooch, Red Cross Nurse, enameled oval, EX 95.00
Cap, Kriegsmarine, gold embr on bl wool, blk ribbon, EX 50.00
Cap, visor; Allgemeine SS, coffee-can style, blk wool, EX 1,250.00
Collar tabs, flight; Luftwaffe Lieutenant, silver bullion 30.00
Collar tabs, SS, gray embr skull on blk wool, EX 125.00
Dog tag, Stalog POW for Am POW, rare 150.00
Flashlight, Army, field gray, rectangular body, EX 18.00
Frontplate, shako; Police, SP eagle, EX 20.00
Gas mask, Reichswehr, field gray finish, filter dtd 1925, EX 75.00
Greatcoat, Luftwaffe Artillery Officer, wool, dbl-breasted 130.00
Helmet, flight; Luftwaffe, brn leather, fleece lined, EX 105.00
Helmet, Luftschutz M34 'Sq Dip,' dull bl, cloth liner, EX 350.00
Helmet, Luftwaffe Paratrooper, field gray, eagle insg, EX 900.00
Insignia, cap; Army Field Officer, embr eagle on gr 25.00
Insignia, knife grip; Hitler Youth, enamel dmn, RZM mk 30.00
Insignia, Luftwaffe Flight Personnel, propeller on gray, EX 15.00
Insignia, sleeve; Africa Corps Mtn Troop, edelweiss on tan, M 25.00
Knife, Hitler Youth, Eickhorn, squirrel trademk, w/scabbard 450.00
Leggings, Army, field gray canvas & blk leather, EX 30.00
Letter opener, Luftwaffe, NP finish, eagle & swastika, EX 200.00
Medal, Army, 12-Year Long Service, gilt metal, eagle device 30.00
Medal, Honor Cross, bronze, w/swords & ribbon, 1914-18, EX 15.00
Medal, Iron Cross, 2nd class, w/ribbon, 1939, EX 35.00
Medal, Luftwaffe, 4-Yr Long Service, SP w/ribbon, EX 45.00
Medal, Mother's Cross, silver, w/ribbon, M 30.00
Medal, War Service Cross, 1st class, w/o swords, silver, EX 35.00
Pamphlet, Nazi propaganda, dtd 1938, EX 35.00
Pennant, Army vehicle, 2-sided, embr eagle on gray, metal fr 150.00
Pin, Hitler Youth 1935 Commemorative, aluminum wreath 15.00
Shield, Demjansk; Army, gray metal on wool, EX 85.00
Shorts, Army tropical, olive cotton twill, NM 150.00
Shoulderboard, Army Administration Feldwebel, silver & gr 20.00
Shoulderboard, Navy Coast Artillery, Xd anchors on wool, EX 15.00
Sign, Nazi, enameling, eagle & swastika, much writing, rare 400.00
Stickpin, Cross Badge of Honor, red & blk eagle, SP wreath 85.00
Stickpin, RAD Membership, enamel on silver, hallmk 55.00
Suspenders, Army, gray w/gray metal, scarce 27.50
Trousers, Waffen SS, summer camo, EX 650.00
Tunic, parade dress; Army Artillery NCO, gray wool, EX 250.00
Uniform, Luftwaffe Flight Troop, wool, tunic & breeches 300.00
Uniform, SS Panzer, wraparound tunic & breeches, EX 2,300.00

Japanese

Armband, WWII, red & yel linen w/Japanese characters 25.00
Armband, WWII, wht linen w/Japanese characters, EX 35.00
Badge, Army Spotter's Proficiency, alumimum, blossom & scope .50.00
Badge, Order of Golden Kite, 7th class, silver, w/ribbon 155.00

Badge, WWII, Machine Gun Marksman, 2nd class, aluminum 50.00
Box, field equipment; WWII, wood w/metal tags, 10x3½x3" ...15.00
Buckle, WWII, NCO, NP brass, 2-pc, EX 75.00
Canteen, WWII, Cavalry, aluminum bottle shape, worn pnt 35.00
Cap, visor; WWII, khaki wool, yel wool star insg, EX 50.00
Cape, Army Officer's, waterproof, w/hood & collar tabs, EX 65.00
Coat, WWII, Army, twill w/fur lining, compo buttons, EX 100.00
Collar tabs, WWII, Navy Captain, lg pattern on bl navy 25.00
Flag, battle; WWII, printed linen, rising sun, 50x34", EX 100.00
Gas mask, WWII, civilian's, complete w/straps & filter, EX 15.00
Hat, visor; WWII, Army Officer, khaki wool w/red piping 125.00
Helmet, WWII, Home Guard, brn khaki finish, wht crown band ..110.00
Medal, Order of Rising Sun, 7th class, silver w/enameling 185.00
Medal, WWII era, Red Cross, silver, w/ribbon 40.00
Medallion, China War, gilt bronze, battle scene, +case 75.00
Telescope, Artillery spotting; 25x2 power, Nikko, +case 275.00
Wings, WWII, pilot's, yel/silver embr on bl, EX 55.00

United States

Badge, Utah Indian Reservation Police, coin silver, ca 1900 ......125.00
Badge, WWI, Marksman, bronze star w/target motifs, NM 15.00
Badge, WWII, Army Glider, Sterling hallmk, pin-bk 75.00
Badge, WWII, Army Police, brass w/silver traces, w/eagle 15.00
Badge, WWII, Ship Building Identification, SP w/eagle, EX 45.00
Bullet mold, Civil War, for .44 cal revolver, steel, Colt's 135.00
Caltrap, Civil War, iron spike, EX 25.00
Canteen, Civil War, Confederate, tin drum type, 5½" dia 450.00
Chevrons, Army Chief Trumpeter, horn on bl, ca 1885, EX 27.50
Chevrons, Army Ordnance Sergeant, bl wool, 1901-02, EX 22.50
Field glasses, Civil War, Fr made, brass & leather 125.00
Gloves, WWI, Army, khaki wool w/brn leather, EX, pr 15.00
Greatcoat, WWI, Army, khaki blanket wool, roll collar, EX 20.00
Hat, campaign; WWI, khaki felt wool, leather band & strap, EX .25.00
Hat, visor; Army Infantry Model 1902 Officer, rifles insg 75.00
Hat, visor; WWII, Army Officer, khaki wool, eagle insg, EX 40.00
Hat, WWII, Infantry Campaign, khaki wool, leather band, EX 20.00
Hat device, Civil War, Union Artillery, brass, Xd cannons, 2" 60.00
Haversack, brn khaki canvas, brass buckle, 1906, EX 15.00
Helmet, Indian War era, Cavalry, spike style, eagle front, EX 100.00
Helmet, Viet Nam War era, camo net over khaki pnt, EX 45.00
Helmet, Viet Nam War era, Helicopter Pilot, khaki pnt, NM 125.00
Helmet, WWI, Marine Corps, w/insg, liner & strap, VG 65.00
Insignia, cap; WWII, Navy 'Mosquito Boat,' bl on wht, EX 15.00
Insignia, hat; Civil War, brass, Xd cannons, G 65.00
Insignia, shoulder; Infantry Mechanic, hammers on wool, 1880s .150.00
Insignia, shoulder; WWI, Tank Corps, red/wht/bl on khaki 40.00
Insignia, shoulder; WWI, 3 Corps, embr caltrap on khaki 15.00
Insignia, shoulder; WWII, Navy PT Boat, wht on dk bl wool 15.00
Insignia, sleeve; WWI, Army Artillery Master Gunner 50.00
Insignia, WWII, Air Transport Command, mc on leather 40.00
Jacket, Civil War, VA Confederate, gray w/blk & gr trim, VG ..550.00
Jacket, flight; WWII, Navy GI, brn leather, zipper front, EX 250.00
Jacket, WWII, A-2, brn leather, knit cuffs, Major insg, EX 300.00
Lance point, Civil War, Confederate, wrought blade, 14½" 125.00
Medal, Civil War, Naval Veteran, bronze w/gilt medallion, '07 .125.00
Medal, Indian War Veteran, Maltese Cross, bronze, 1890s, EX ..400.00
Medal, Naval Reserve Meritorious Service, w/ribbon, 1980, M 18.00
Pistol, flare; WWI, Navy Mk III, brass w/wood grips, 9" bbl 225.00
Plate, mess; Navy Commodore, wht porc, pennant border, 1912 ..30.00
Shirt, Viet Nam War Era, Marine Corps, camo fatigue, 4-pocket .15.00
Shirt, WWII, Army, tan khaki cotton, 2 flap pockets, EX 15.00
Surgeon's kit, Civil War, walnut case w/5 implements, 7½", EX ..450.00
Trousers, WWII, Army, khaki wool, EX 15.00

Tunic, Army dress, khaki wool twill, brass buttons, 1930s, EX 20.00

Miscellaneous

Austrian, canteen, WWII, field gray enamel, cork stopper 45.00
Belgium, medal, Resistance, bronze, 1945, w/ribbon 15.00
Croatia, badge, Pilot, silver w/mc enamel, pin-bk, EX 90.00
E Germany, banner, nation's colors, inscription, 19880s, 9x7" 15.00
France, armband, WWI, Inductee, brn twill w/brass badge 25.00
France, helmet, WWII, Army, worn khaki finish, VG 20.00
Israel, helmet, Tanker, khaki finish, leather flaps, 1960s 175.00
Italy, badge, WWII, Tank Driver, SP on bronze, pin-bk, EX 95.00
Italy, fez, WWII, Fascist GIL Youth Leader, blk beaver, EX 350.00
Italy, hat, visor; Army Medical Officer, khaki wool, '50s 55.00
Italy, medal, WWI, War Cross, bronze, w/ribbon, EX 25.00
Italy, medal, WWII, Annexation of Fiume, w/ribbon 65.00
Italy, medal, WWII, Fascist Youth Cross of Merit, silver 85.00
Poland, badge, breast; Balloon Observer, gilt/silver, '33, EX 100.00
Poland, badge, breast; Central Lithuanian, brass, 2-pc, 1920 ....85.00
Poland, badge, breast; Parachute Instructor, silver eagle 45.00
Portugal, WWI, Army, fluted 'Maximilian' style, dk bl-gr finish ..30.00
Russia, badge, Communist Air Squadron Training, 1920s 175.00
Russia, medal, Fire Service, silver, w/ribbon, 1980s 55.00
Russia, medal, Liberation of Warsaw, brass, w/ribbon, 1945 ....35.00
Russia, medal, WWII, Victory Over Germany, bronze, w/ribbon .15.00

Milk Glass

Milk glass is the current collector's name for milk-white opaque glass. The early glassmaker's term was Opal Ware. Originally attempted in England in the 18th century with the intention of imitating china, milk glass was not commercially successful until the mid-1800s. Pieces produced in the U.S.A., England, and France during the 1870-1900 period are highly prized for their intricate detail and fiery, opalescent edges.

For further information we recommend *Collector's Encyclopedia of Milk Glass, An Identification & Value Guide*, by Betty and Bill Newbound. Our advisor for this category is Rod Dockery; he is listed in the Directory under Texas. Several standard collectors' books have been referenced in our listings: Belknap (B), Collector's Encyclopedia by Newbound (CE), Ferson (F), Grist (G), Imperial's Vintage Milk Glass (I), Millard (M), and Warman (W). See also Animal Dishes with Covers; Bread Plates; Historical Glass; Westmoreland.

Plate, Three Kittens, worn paint, B-10C, $35.00.

Bottle, Klondike Nugget, B-238B 78.00
Box, Moses in Bulrushes on lid, w/rush base, CE-162 ....225.00
Covered dish, Baseball, G-100C 30.00
Covered dish, Battleship, Wheeling, F-39, sm 70.00

Covered dish, Cabbage, Vallerysthal, F-212, EX 70.00
Covered dish, Cruiser Battleship, M-300B 90.00
Covered dish, Football, G-100 ....65.00
Covered dish, Little Red Schoolhouse, F-171, EX pnt 100.00
Creamer, owl form w/glass eyes, F-587, sm 37.50
Creamer & sugar bowl, Imperial, 3-toed, I-31 ....28.00
Creamer & sugar bowl, Imperial Grape, I-831 ....30.00
Egg, emb horseshoe, decor, 6¼" 40.00
Egg, emerging chick, flat base, CE-427, 2½" 40.00
Match holder, Hand & Fan, EX pnt, F-208 ....22.00
Match holder, Indian head, mk K, W-25B 25.00
Pin dish, Star of David w/bl florals & gold trim, 4" 15.00
Pitcher, Fish, Atterbury, F-328, 7¼" 150.00
Plate, ABC, B-8E 50.00
Plate, Anchor & Belaying Pin, F-683 ....30.00
Plate, Anchor & Yacht, B-13A 35.00
Plate, Ancient Castle, B-12A, 7" 35.00
Plate, Angel & Harp, B-11C 40.00
Plate, Angel Head, B-7F, 9" 30.00
Plate, Beaded Loop Indian Head, B-8F 45.00
Plate, Block Border Fancy, HP decor, CE-259 ....45.00
Plate, Columbus, B-5A 45.00
Plate, Contrary Mule, B-12B 40.00
Plate, Cupid & Psyche, B-6B 35.00
Plate, Diamond & Shell Border, HP, B-8D, 7¼" 20.00
Plate, Dogs & Cats, B-20D 100.00
Plate, Easter Bunny & Egg, B-3C 60.00
Plate, Easter Chicks, F-492 ....37.50
Plate, Easter Lay, W-119C 75.00
Plate, Easter Sermon, B-7C 75.00
Plate, Lacy Indian, B-4F 65.00
Plate, Little Red Hen, B-21A 45.00
Plate, No Easter Without Us, B-3E 45.00
Plate, Owl Lovers, B-7B 45.00
Plate, Rabbit & Horseshoe, B-7A, 7" 40.00
Plate, Serenade, B-9E 40.00
Plate, Setting Hen & Chicks, B-14 ....45.00
Plate, Spring Meets Winter, B-24A 60.00
Plate, Sunken Rabbit, B-6E 45.00
Plate, Washington/13 Stars, B-1, 8¼" 55.00
Plate, Woof Woof, B-13F 50.00
Plate, 3 Bears, F-473 ....40.00
Plate, 3 Dogs, F-397 ....85.00
Plate, 3 Owls, B-10D 35.00
Plate, 3 Puppies w/squirrel, B-20C 88.00
Salt cellar, Basket, dtd, F-352 ....30.00
Sherbet, Rooster, red pnt details, B-274E 12.50
Sugar bowl, Wild Iris, orig gold pnt, F-300 ....60.00
Swan, closed neck, basketweave base, B-155B 65.00
Tumbler, Louisiana Purchase, M-193B 20.00

Millefiori

Millefiori was a type of art glass first produced during the late 1800s. Literally, the term means 'thousand flowers,' an accurate description of its appearance. Canes, fused bundles of multicolored glass threads such as are often used in paperweights, were cut into small cross sections, arranged in the desired pattern, refired, and shaped into articles such as cruets, lamps, and novelty items. It is still being produced, and many examples found on the market today are of fairly recent manufacture. See also Paperweights.

Coffeepot, appl bl hdl & spout, 5¾x3" 225.00
Cup & saucer, cylindrical, angle hdl, 2½x2" 45.00

Lamp, globe shade, invt trumpet base, 14" 765.00
Lamp, 9" dome shade, bottle-form base, 19" 880.00
Sugar shaker, frosted hdl, 4½" 100.00
Vase, satin finish, appl swirl at base/neck/shoulder, 3½" 50.00
Vase, stick neck, 8" 100.00

Miniatures

There is some confusion as to what should be included in a listing of miniature collectibles. Some feel the only true miniature is the salesman's sample; other collectors consider certain small-scale children's toys to be appropriately referred to as miniatures, while yet others believe a miniature to be any small-scale item that gives evidence to the craftsmanship of its creator. For salesman's samples, see specific category; other types are listed below. See also Dollhouses and Furnishings; Children's Things.

Ranking at the top of today's leading collectibles, scaled 1:12" miniatures represent the work of hundreds of artisans who supply local shops with highly prized one-of-a-kind articles and specialties, all scaled one inch to the foot. Many leading producers and distributors of collectibles have entered the field as well. Clubs for miniature enthusiasts have sprung up throughout the United States, Canada, and abroad.

Blanket box, gr pnt wood, 1800s, 4¾x9¾", EX 440.00
Blanket chest, pine, trn ftd, dvtl case & till, repro, 9¾" 95.00
Blanket chest, poplar w/old red-brn finish, dvtl, 24¼" 495.00
Blanket chest, poplar w/orig red flame grpt, rprs, 13" 300.00
Box, dome top, sliding puzzle-type lid, curly hardwood, 3½" 300.00
Chest, cherry Hplwht style, 4 dvtl drw, 22x20x12" 300.00
Chest, cherry Hplwht style w/inlay, 4 dvtl drw, 30x26x16" 495.00
Chest, cherry Hplwht style w/inlay, 4-drw, repro, 23x18½" 260.00
Chest, cherry w/inlay, 2 dvtl drw, rpr, 9½x11x7¼" 2,200.00
Chest, hardwood, 6-drw, nail construction, 3x6x7", EX 150.00
Chest, poplar, 3-drw, red & blk grpt w/gold stencil, 18" 525.00
Chest, walnut, 3 nailed drw, porc pulls, cut-out ft, 19x17" 715.00
Chest, walnut & pine, 3-drw, old alligatored blk pnt, 8¾" 140.00
Chest, walnut Hplwht, 4 dvtl drw, Fr ft, needs rstr, 21x15" 6,000.00
Chest, walnut Hplwht style, 4 dvtl drw, 23x20x12" 385.00
Desk, cherry Hplwht style w/inlay, slant front, 29x21" 330.00

Dresser, six drawers, quarter columns, turned legs, carved skirt, English, ca 1920s, 12x12½x6¼", EX, $450.00.

Hearth toaster, wrought iron, rotating hdl, 4½x6x14" 140.00
Mandolin, olive wood & silver, Continental, 5" 120.00
Parlor suite, sterling, scrollwork bk, 1910, 1¾", 3-pc 175.00
Pitcher, free blown, pontil scar, Am, 1840-70, 2½" 75.00
Trunk, orig leather covering w/brass studs, w/key, 6" 195.00

Minton

Thomas Minton established his firm in 1793 at Stoke on Trent and within a few years began producing earthenware with blue-printed patterns similar to the ware he had learned to decorate while employed by the Caughley Porcelain Factory. The Willow pattern was one of his most popular. Neither this nor the porcelain made from 1798 to 1805 was marked (except for an occasional number series), making identification often impossible.

After 1805 until about 1816, fine tea services, beehive-shaped honey pots, trays, etc., were hand decorated with florals, landscapes, Imari-type designs, and neoclassic devices. These were often marked with crossed 'L's. It was Minton that invented the acid gold process of decorating (1863), which is now used by a number of different companies. From 1816 until 1823, no porcelain was made. Through the twenties and thirties, the ornamental wares with colorful decoration of applied fruits and florals and figurines in both bisque and enamel were usually left unmarked. As a result, they have been erroneously attributed to other potters. Some of the ware that was marked bears a deliberate imitation of Meissen's crossed swords. From the late twenties through the forties, Minton made a molded stoneware line (mugs, jugs, teapots, etc.) with florals or figures in high relief. These were marked with an embossed scroll with an 'M' in the bottom curve. Fine parian ware was made in the late 1840s, and in the fifties Minton experimented with and perfected a line of quality majolica which they produced from 1860 until it was discontinued in 1908. Their slogan was 'Majolica for the Millions,' and for it they gained widespread recognition. Leadership of the firm was assumed by Minton's son Herbert sometime around the middle of the 19th century. Working hand in hand with Leon Arnoux, who was both a chemist and an artist, he managed to secure the company's financial future through constant, successful experimentation with both materials and decorating methods. During the Victorian era, M.L. Solon decorated pieces in the pate-sur-pate style, often signing his work; these examples are considered to be the finest of their type. After 1862 all wares were marked 'Minton' or 'Mintons,' with an impressed year cipher.

Many collectors today reassemble the lovely dinnerware patterns that have been made by Minton. Perhaps one of their most popular lines was Minton Rose, introduced in 1854. The company itself once counted forty-seven versions of this pattern being made by other potteries around the world. In addition to less expensive copies, elaborate hand-enameled pieces were also made by Aynsley, Crown Staffordshire, and Paragon China. Solando Ware (1937) and Byzantine Range (1938) were designed by John Wadsworth. Minton ceased all earthenware production in 1939.

Dinnerware values given in the following listings are for items that were produced from 1870-1950. Current production pieces bring lower prices on the resale market. Advice for this category comes from Old China Patterns Ltd., they are listed in the Directory under Canada. See also Majolica; Minton; Pate-Sur-Pate.

Bouillon cup & saucer, Pattern #B898	45.00
Bouillon cup & saucer, Pink Cockatrice	50.00
Bowl, rim soup; Pattern #B898	36.00
Bowl, salad; Pink Cockatrice	45.00
Bowl, vegetable; Kent, oval	125.00
Bowl, vegetable; Minton Rose, oval, w/lid	130.00
Butter pat, Ancestral	24.00
Cake plate, Kent	75.00
Charger, Secessionist, floral border, gr/wine, 15"	850.00
Coffee cup & saucer, Pattern #B898, lg	45.00
Coffeepot, Cockatrice, 8", +6 cup & saucers	750.00
Cup & saucer, Ashton	48.00
Cup & saucer, Gold Laurentian	90.00
Cup & saucer, Greenwich	48.00
Cup & saucer, Haddon Hall	40.00
Cup & saucer, Kent	45.00

Demitasse pot, Birds of Paradise, 1863, +6 c/s	285.00
Plate, bread & butter; Buckingham	24.50
Plate, bread & butter; Gold Laurentian	25.00
Plate, dinner; Ardmore	36.00
Plate, dinner; Ashton	45.00
Plate, dinner; Greenwich	47.50
Plate, dinner; Kent	36.00
Plate, lady in apron/flowers, rtcl, sgn Boullemeier, 9½"	650.00
Plate, salad; Ardmore	32.00
Plate, salad; Greenwich	32.00
Plate, salad; Kent	32.00
Platter, Ashton, 14"	125.00
Platter, Kent, 14"	98.00
Sugar shaker, flower form, yel & orange petals, gr leaves, 5"	45.00
Teapot, Cheviot	145.00
Teapot, Haddon Hall	195.00
Vase, bud; floral, gr/wine, tiny neck/bulbous body, 7½"	400.00

Mirrors

The first mirrors were made in England in the 13th century of very thin glass backed with lead. Reverse-painted glass mirrors were made in this country as early as the late 1700s and remained popular throughout the next century. The simple hand-painted panel was separated from the mirrored section by a narrow slat, and the frame was either the dark-finished Federal style or the more elegant, often-gilded Sheraton.

Mirrors changed with the style of other furnishings; but whatever type you purchase, as long as the glass sections remain solid, even broken or flaking mirrors are more valued than replaced glass. Careful resilvering is acceptable if excessive deterioration has taken place. In the listings that follow, the term 'style' (example: Federal style) is used to indicate a mirror reminiscent of but made well after the period indicated. Obviously these repro styles are valued much lower than their original counterparts. Our advisor for this category is Michael Hinton; he is listed in the Directory under Pennsylvania.

Key:
Chpndl — Chippendale   Fed — Federal
Emp — Empire   QA — Queen Anne

Wall mirror, French mahogany and gilt with carved florals and garlands over eglomise militia panel, twin column sides, 62x29", $1,600.00.

Architectural, Emp mahog, 2-part, rvpt ship, 30x19"	275.00
Architectural, Emp pine w/mahog veneer, 2-part, rvpt, 36x19"	265.00
Architectural, Emp walnut, rvpt ship/stars/etc, rfn, 40x21"	385.00

Architectural, Fed pine, 2-part, rvpt landscape, 21x14" 360.00
Architectural, pine, 2-part, rvpt top, rfn, rprs, 22x13" 165.00
Architectural, 2-part, rvpt ship w/Am flag, gold rpt, 24x15" 110.00
Arts & Crafts, X design ea side, beveled, 4 hooks, 22x39" 300.00
Brass, oval Gothic fr, rectangular base, Victorian, 14" 275.00
Cheval, beveled mahog fr, shoe ft, trn posts, 46x24" 325.00
Cheval, hardwood English, brass & glass ball & claw ft, 81x29" ..650.00
Chinese gilt Chpndl-style, pagoda cartouch, rtcl sides, 64x33" ..935.00
Chinoiserie decor on blk enamel QA style, beveled, 58x24" 440.00
Chpndl mahog & gilt gesso, rstr, ca 1770, 20½" 1,100.00
Chpndl scroll curly maple, Prince of Wales feather, 35" 475.00
Chpndl scroll mahog, old finish w/gold trim, 29x15" 165.00
Chpndl scroll mahog, phoenix in crest, worn finish, 35x17" 330.00
Chpndl scroll mahog on pine, phoenix in crest, 37x21", M 1,325.00
Chpndl scroll walnut, gold-pnt compo eagle, 21x13" 325.00
Chpndl scroll walnut, rprs, rpl glass, 20x12" 300.00
Chpndl-style scroll bird's-eye maple, repro, 28x17" 85.00
Chpndl-style scroll mahog, gold compo eagle & fruit, 40x20" 275.00
Country Chpndl mahog, molded fr, old rfn, 20x12" 300.00
Curly maple, worn silvering, 19x12½" 195.00
Emp, convex, gilt fr w/scrolled foliage, eagle atop, 46" 990.00
Emp, gilt/gesso floral block/ring trn fr, 3-part, '20, 60x25" 500.00
Emp, half-turnings w/corner blks, old gold & blk rpt, 23x13" 75.00
Emp, pine w/half-trnings & corner blocks, rfn, 23x16" 95.00
Emp, rpt blk w/gold, minor edge damage, 43x25" 625.00
Emp, worn blk pnt & gilt, rvpt scene, 2-part, Am, 41x20" 165.00
Emp over-mantel, EX details w/orig gilt, 20x37" 275.00
Emp over-mantel mahog/gilt/ebonized triptych, 31x60" 675.00
Fed, rpt, rpl mirror, 2-part, Am, 21x14" 95.00
Fed cvd gilt/gesso, acorn drops, rvpt scenic, 1820, 55x34" 2,800.00
Fed cvd giltwood convex w/2-arm candelabra & eagle, 40x30" ..3,600.00
Fed mahog w/ebony pilasters, stenciling, 2-part, 22x11" 110.00
Fed scroll mahog w/string inlaid liner, 36¼x19" 550.00
Gilt fr w/oval rose rvpt panel, rectangular, 53" 550.00
Gilt gesso & walnut, N Europe, late 1700s, 25x11¼" 550.00
Giltwood, oval floral fr w/2 scroll ft, 20" 275.00
Giltwood, wide ornately cvd/rtcl fr, 72x48" 1,500.00
Giltwood convex, cvgs top/below, eagle/23 balls (states), 56" .2,500.00
Giltwood girandole, ca 1800, 36x30" 1,100.00
Grpt pine w/orig red & blk, faded yel stencil, 17x14" 140.00
Mission-style oak, 7 hooks at top, rfn, 25x42" 600.00
Neoclassic giltwood convex w/cvd eagle atop, 16" dia, 25" 475.00
Neoclassic giltwood convex w/cvd eagle atop, 21" dia, 36" 900.00
Plateau, SP, octagonal, molded fr w/central ornament, 27x19" ..275.00
Plateau, SP w/cut-out floral sides & ft, 12" 90.00
QA giltwood & walnut veneer, 1700s, rfn, 19x10" 350.00
QA scroll mahog veneer on pine, EX gilt, 15x10½" 335.00
QA scroll mahog w/gilt liner, rstr, 32x17" 250.00
QA scroll walnut veneer, English, rfn, 21x12" 300.00
QA-style w/chinoiserie decor, Wmsburg repro, 44x18" 350.00
Regency, giltwood w/appl row of spheres, 1820, 37" dia 770.00
Shaving, mahog on pine English w/lt wood inlay, 3-drw, 23" 220.00
Shaving, mahog veneer Hplwht, bow front, dvtl drw, 17x14" 220.00
Shaving, mahog veneer on pine w/inlay, dvtl drws, 20x15x7" 175.00
Shaving, QA mahog, old finish, rpr, 15", EX 110.00
Sponge pnt, half column/corner blocks, rvpt, 2-part, 22x12" 85.00
Tramp-art type, comb box at bottom, rtcl bkbrd, 19x14", EX 130.00
Wedding, brass w/arched emb panel, Dutch, 18/19th C, 23" 325.00

Mocha

Mocha Ware is utilitarian pottery made principally in England (and to a lesser extent in France) between 1780 and 1840 on the then prevalent creamware and pearlware bodies. Initially, only those pieces decorated in the seaweed pattern were called 'Mocha,' while geometrically decorated pieces were referred to as 'Banded Creamware.' Other types of decorations were called 'Dipped Ware.' During the last thirty to forty years the term 'Mocha' has been applied to the entire realm of 'Industrialized Slipware' — pottery decorated by the turner on his lathe using coggle wheels and slip cups.

Mocha was made in numerous patterns — Tree, Seaweed or Dandelion, Rope (also called Worm or Loop), Cat's-eye, Tobacco Leaf, Lollypop or Balloon, Marbled, Marbled and Combed, Twig, Geometric or Checkered, Banded, and slip decorations of rings, dots, flags, tulips, wavy lines, etc. It came into its own as a collectible in the latter half of the 1940s and has become increasingly popular as more and more people are exposed to the rich colorings and artistic appeal of its varied forms of abstract decoration.

The collector should take care not to confuse the early pearlware and creamware Mocha with the later kitchen yellow ware, graniteware, and ironstone sporting mocha-type decoration that was produced in America by such potters as J. Vodrey, George S. Harker, Edwin Bennett, and John Bell. This type was also produced in Scotland and Wales and was marketed well into the 20th century.

Bowl, earthworm, 3-color on bl-gray band w/bl stripe, 7¼" 400.00
Bowl, earthworm w/bl band & blk stripes, 3¼x6¼" 275.00
Bowl, seaweed, bl on wht band, bl stripes, 6x12¼" 360.00
Bowl, seaweed, brn on wht band w/brn stripes, 4x9¼" 245.00
Bowl, seaweed, gr on wht band, brn stripes, stain, 5¾x12⅝" 385.00
Chamber pot, blk earthworm, bl bands, blk stripes, 5½x8¾" 275.00
Creamer, seaweed, blk on beige w/olive, wht leaf hdl, 4¼" 855.00
Creamer, seaweed, gr on wht band, brn stripes, chip, 4" 415.00
Creamer, seaweed on gray band w/bl & blk stripes, rprs, 4", G ...135.00
Mug, alternating bands of dicing, mc seaweed, rstr, 5¾" 230.00
Mug, checkered decor, Wood & Caldwell, early 1800s, 6" 635.00
Mug, earthworm, 1800s, 5" 600.00
Mug, seaweed on orange-tan bands w/blk stripes, gr rim, 6" 475.00
Pitcher, earthworm, emb bands, 4-color, minor rprs, 6¾" 605.00
Pitcher, seaweed, bl on wht band w/brn stripes, 4¾" 580.00
Pitcher, seaweed, brn & bl on wht band w/blk stripes, 9½" 1,320.00
Pitcher, seaweed, brn on wht band w/brn stripes, 9¼" 1,200.00
Salt cellar, seaweed, gr on wht band, wear/stains, 2⅛x2¾" 360.00
Shaker, earthworm, 3-color w/bl & blk bands, bl dome top, 5" ..635.00
Shaker, earthworm on tan w/brn & bl stripes, 5" 635.00
Sugar bowl, seaweed, blk on wht band w/bl stripes, 5¾", EX 990.00
Waste bowl, earthworm, bl/tan/wht/dk brn, beaded bands, 6½" .365.00

Molds

Food molds have become popular as collectibles — not only for their value as antiques, but because they also revive childhood memories of elaborate ice cream Santas with candy trim or barley sugar figurals adorning a Christmas tree. Ice cream molds were made of pewter and came in a wide variety of shapes and styles. Chocolate molds were made in fewer shapes but were more detailed. They were usually made of tin, copper, and occasionally of pewter. Hard candy molds were usually metal, although primitive maple sugar molds (usually simple hearts, rabbits, and other animals) were carved from wood. (Unless otherwise indicated, those in our listings are cast aluminum or stainless steel.) Cake molds were made of cast iron or cast aluminum and were most common in the shape of a lamb, a rabbit, or Santa Claus. Our advisors for this category are Dale and Jean Van Kuren; they are listed in the Directory under New York.

Chocolate Molds

Bishop on horse over house top, 2-pc w/clamps, 6x4½" 98.00

Boy w/big cap & knickers, 2-pc w/clamps, 6¼x4" 98.00
Cat, sitting, much detail, 2-pc w/clamps, 3⅞x3¾" 110.00
Chick, SJCo, Made in Germany, w/clip, 3x4½" 65.00
Dog, seated, 2-pc, 3⅜" 28.00
Dog, seated, 2-pc, 4⅝" 50.00
Duck, 2-pc, 7¾" 85.00
Elephant, much detail, 2-pc w/clamps, 4x2½" 90.00
Father Christmas on donkey, 2-pc w/clamps, 3⅛x3⅛" 95.00

Harp with fancy frame of woman's
head with flowing hair, two-piece
with clamps, 4", $95.00.

Hen on nest, Germany, 2-pc, 3⅞" 28.00
Hen on nest, 2¾" 25.00
Horse, G detail, 2-pc w/clamps, 3¾x3" 90.00
Jack-o'-lantern, 2-pc, folding 66.00
Kewpie, 2-pc w/clamps, 8½" 55.00
Lamb, recumbent, face out, oval base, 2-pc w/clamps, 7x8½" 150.00
Lion, France, 2-pc, 4⅜" 40.00
Lion, 2-pc, 6½" 65.00
Model A Ford, 2-pc, 3x5¼" 90.00
Mule w/saddle bags & bridle, 2-pc w/clamps, 8½x9½" 150.00
Owl, 2-pc, 4⅜" 50.00
Pig, standing, 2-pc w/clamps, 6¼x3" 87.00
Pig, upright, Made in Germany, 2-pc, 3⅛" 70.00
Prizefighting bunny, 2-pc, 6¼" 48.00
Rabbit, running, Made in USA, 10½" 110.00
Rabbit, sitting, 2-pc w/clamps, 7¾x7½" 85.00
Rabbit, 2-part, hinged, 4½" 115.00
Rabbit, 3½" 30.00
Rabbit w/basket, 2-pc, Made in Germany, 7½" 105.00
Rooster, 10½" 105.00
Rooster, 2-pc, 6" 60.00
Rooster, 2-pc w/clamps, 3x2¾" 45.00
Santa Claus, 2-pc, 7½" 165.00
Santa Claus w/basket, 2-pc, 6½" 120.00
Soccer player, 2-pc w/clamps, 4½x3½" 54.00
Turkey, 2-pc, no clamps, 4" 22.00
Wild boar, 2-pc, 4⅝" 70.00

Hard Candy Molds

Castle w/flag, groove for stick, 1¾x1½" 78.00
Elephant, TM-138, groove for stick, 1¾x1¼" 62.50
Leaf designs, 2-pc, 11¾" L 30.00
Pipe, TM-88, groove for stick, 3½x¾" 45.00
Rabbits w/baby in cart, T-41, groove for stick, 4½x3½" 110.00

Rat, TM-238, groove for stick, 2½x1" 80.00
Steamboat w/paddle wheel, groove for stick, 1¼x2¼" 90.00
3 eagles w/shield, cast lead, 2-pc, 8¼" 185.00

Ice Cream Molds

American Eagle, pewter, 2-pc, hinged, 4½x4" 85.00
Basket, octagon, E-1013, 2-pc 37.50
Basket, 3-pc, hinged, E&Co NY 60.00
Bell, #605 ....35.00
Christmas bells, 5 in mold, 2-pc, hinged, 1900s 48.00
Cupid in rose, E-959 ....50.00
Engagement ring 85.00
Father Christmas, E&Co #166, 2-part, hinged, 5x2¼x3¼" 155.00
Football, E-1159 ....27.50
Goose egg, #298 ....27.50
Harp, aluminum, K-361, 1940s 34.00
Lilacs & leaves, 4¼x3x2¼" 46.00
Medallion, passion flower relief, E-270 ....34.00
Melon, E-204 ....16.00
Petunia, 3" 22.50
Potato, #245, sm 27.50
Potato, K-154 ....37.50
Rose, E-295 ....35.00
Shriner emblems, E-1081 ....32.50
Slipper, 3-part, #570 ....32.50
Stork w/baby, standing, E-1151 ....57.50
Strawberry, E-316 ....32.50
Tulip, E-352 ....32.50
Victorian girl, #286, 5" 55.00

Maple Sugar Molds

Cow in 2 parts, varnished, 4½x7" 67.50
Heart, spade, dmn; deep-cvd pine, ca 1835, 16x4x2" 250.00
Heart, wood w/iron hinge, pouring hole at top, 1890s, 5" 88.00
Heart & clover, primitive, 5x17½" 60.00
Hearts (3), primitive cvg, pegged 3-pc board, 1¾x12x4¼" 110.00
Openwork on rnd fluted cups, CI, 1840s, 12 in 11x16" fr 115.00

Miscellaneous

CI, fish, 13¼" 85.00
Copper, fish, MIG, 10¾" 30.00
Copper, fish, 10" W 220.00
Copper, fruit, 8½" 220.00
Copper, geometric design, 7¼" dia 85.00
Copper, geometric design w/star center, 10" dia 165.00
Copper, Prince of Wales feather, 5½" 80.00
Copper, shell, 9" 250.00
Copper/tin, ear of corn, 3¾x5¼" 80.00
Copper/tin, fancy design in oval shape, 2¾x7½x5¾" 95.00
Copper/tin, fish, 4¼x5¼" 99.00
Copper/tin, grapes, 5½x3¾" 80.00
Copper/tin, pear, oval, polished, 5¼" 35.00
Copper/tin, pears, rpr, 6½" 35.00
Copper/tin, rose, 6½" 75.00
Copper/tin, sheaf, 6½" 75.00
Copper/tin, sheaf, 7¼x5½" 90.00
Pottery, heart center, swirled ribs, gr glaze, 4½x10½" 35.00
Stoneware, cow, oblong, tan, sm flakes, 5¼" 95.00
Stoneware, fish, oval, chips, 7¾" 30.00
Stoneware, fruit cluster, scalloped sides, 4¼x7¾" 70.00
Stoneware, quail, tan w/gray int, oval, flakes, 5¾" 85.00

Stoneware, Turk's head, molded decor, Albany slip, 12¾" 330.00
Tin, crown, scalloped sides, 6½" 40.00
Tin, emb fruit, removable flat bottom, Kreamer, 4x8¼x6½" 55.00
Tin, fish, EX details, 11x4½" 42.00
Tin, lion, 5¼" 45.00
Tin, melon shape, 2-pc, ring to lift on top, 4x6½" 28.00

Monmouth

The Monmouth Pottery Company was established in 1892 in Monmouth, Illinois. Their primary products were salt-glazed stoneware crocks, churns, jugs, Bristol, spongeware, and brown glaze. In 1906 they were absorbed by a conglomerate called the Western Stoneware Company. Monmouth became their #1 plant and until 1930 continued to produce stoneware marked with their maple leaf logo. Items marked 'Monmouth Pottery Co.' were made before 1906; after the merger, 'Co.' was dropped and 'Ill.' was substituted.

Ashtray, advertising, 3 sets of ftprints, 9" 10.00
Cookie jar 50.00
Jardiniere, Aztec, 7" 75.00
Jardiniere, Egyptian motif, brn-glazed int, 7" 75.00
Pitcher, cobalt, water sz 17.50
Vase, brn, rope-trimmed hdls, 12" 65.00
Vase, emb floral neck band, lt bl/gr mottled matt, 18" 125.00
Water cooler, Egyptian motif, 9¼x11", M 300.00

Monot and Stumpf

The firm of Monot and Stumpf was organized in 1868, the merger of the E.S. Monot and F. Stumpf glassworks. It was located in Pantin, France. They produced fine art glass of various types until ca 1892, when the company reorganized and became known as the Cristallerie de Pantin.

Banquet lamp, pk opal swirl shade/font; brass swirl std, 27" 750.00
Lamp, miniature; emb swirl on pk opal, Pantin, 10x4", M 850.00
Oil lamp, amber-pk opal swirl shade/font, marble std, 19" 325.00
Salt cellar, lav-pk oval, gold lustre int, fluted, 1⅝" 75.00
Shade, pk irid, gold lustre int, 4¾x7⅞" 175.00
Shade, pk opal, swirled ribs, ruffled/flared, 6½x8½" 225.00
Vase, pk opal to clear w/gold irid, HP florals, hdls, 10¾" 165.00

Mont Joye

Mont Joye was a type of acid-cut French cameo glass produced by Cristallerie de Pantin in Paris around the turn of the century. It is accented by enamels. Our advisor for this category is Don Williams; he is listed in the Directory under Missouri.

Bowl, iris int, turned-in rim, ftd, 3½x9¾x7" 435.00
Rose bowl, violets/leaves on gr, 4¾x5½" 300.00
Vase, floral/leaves, gr/gold on brn texture, long neck, 19" 1,500.00
Vase, leaves & buds on hammered topaz, gold stamp, 6½" 625.00
Vase, lg floral/gilt on gr, wht-lined flaring neck, 20" 2,000.00
Vase, peonies, cut/pnt, 4-sided, 8½", EX 750.00
Vase, poppies/pods, gold on amethyst w/gold texture, sqd, 7" 700.00

Moon and Star

Moon and Star was originally produced in the 1880s by John

Adams & Company of Pittsburgh. In the 1960s, Joseph Weishar of Wheeling, West Virginia, owner of the Island Mould & Machine Company, reproduced some of the original molds and incorporated the pattern into approximately forty new and different items. Two of the largest distributors of this line were L.E. Smith of Mt. Pleasant, Pennsylvania, who pressed their own glass, and L.G. Wright of New Martinsville, West Virginia, who had theirs pressed by Fostoria, Fenton, and Westmoreland. Both companies carried a large and varied assortment of shapes and colors. Several other companies were involved in its manufacture as well, especially of the smaller items.

Over the years the glassware has been pressed in amberina (yellow shading to orange- or ruby-red), green, amber, crystal, light blue, and ruby. Pieces in ruby and light blue are most collectible and harder to find than the other colors, which seem to be abundant. Purple, pink, cobalt, amethyst, tan slag, and light green and blue opalescent were made, too, but on a lesser scale.

Current L.E. Smith catalogs contain a small assortment of pieces that are still available in crystal, pink, cobalt (lighter than the old shade), and these colors with an iridized finish. A new color, teal green, was introduced in 1992, a water set in sapphire blue opalescent was pressed in 1993, and the new color in 1994 was cranberry ice. Our values are given for ruby and light blue. For amberina, green, and amber, deduct 30%.

Ashtray, moons at rim, star in base, 6-sided, 5½" 12.00
Butter dish, allover pattern, scalloped ft, 6x5½" dia 45.00
Candle holders, allover pattern, flared & scalloped ft, 6", pr 35.00
Compote, allover pattern, ftd, scalloped rim, 5½x8" 35.00
Compote, allover pattern, ftd, scalloped rim, 7x10" 45.00
Compote, allover pattern, w/lid, 10x8" 50.00

Creamer and sugar bowl, ruby, with lid, 5¾", 6", $65.00 for the pair.

Creamer & sugar bowl, open, disk ft, sm 25.00
Decanter, bulbous w/allover pattern, plain neck, 32-oz, 12" 50.00
Goblet, water; plain rim & ft, 5¾" 14.00
Jelly dish, plain flat rim, disk ft, patterned lid, 6¾x3½" 30.00
Nappy, allover pattern, crimped rim, 2¾x6" 18.00
Relish bowl, 6 lg scallops form allover pattern, 1½x8" 16.00
Salt cellar, allover pattern, scalloped, sm flat ft 8.00
Shakers, allover pattern, metal lids, 4x2", pr 25.00
Sherbet, plain rim & stem, 4¼x3¾" 15.00
Soap dish, allover pattern, oval, 2x6" 12.00
Sugar bowl, allover pattern, sm flat ft, w/lid, 5¼x4" 35.00
Sugar shaker, allover pattern, metal lid, 4½x3½" 35.00
Syrup, allover pattern, metal lid, 4½x3½" 30.00
Toothpick holder, allover pattern, scalloped rim, ftd 9.00
Tumbler, iced tea; no pattern at rim or on ft, 11-oz, 5½" 20.00
Tumbler, juice; no pattern at rim or on disk ft, 5-oz, 3½" 10.00

Tumbler, no pattern at rim or disk ft, 7-oz, 4½" 12.00

Moorcroft

William Moorcroft began to work for MacIntyre Potteries in 1897. At first he was the chief designer, but very soon took over their newly created Art Pottery department. His first important design was the Aurelian Ware, part transfer and part hand painted. Very shortly thereafter, around the turn of the century, he developed his famous Florian Ware, with heavy slip and done in mostly blue and white. Since the early 1900s there has been a sucession of designs, most of them very characteristic of the company. Moorcroft left MacIntyre in 1913 and went out on his own. He had already well established his name, having won prizes and gold medals at the St. Louis World's Fair as well as in Paris. In 1929 Queen Mary, who had been collecting his pottery, made him 'Potter to the Queen,' and the pottery was so stamped up until 1949. William Moorcroft died in 1945, and his son Walter ran the company until recent years. The factory is still in existence. They now produce different designs but continue to use the characteristic slipwork. Moorcroft pottery was sold abroad in Canada, the United States, Australia, and Europe as well as in specialty areas such as the island of Bermuda.

Moorcroft went through a 'Japanese' stage in the early teens with his lovely lustre glazes, Oriental shapes and decorations. During the mid-teens he began to produce his most popular Pomegranate Ware, as well as Wisteria (often called 'Fruit'). Around that time he also designed the popular Pansy line as well as Leaves and Grapes. Soon he introduced a beautiful landscape series called variously Hazeldine, Moonlit Blue, Eventide and Dawn. These wonderful designs along with Claremont (Mushrooms) seem to be the most sought after by collectors today. It would be possible to add many other designs to this list.

During the 1920s and '30s, Moorcroft became very interested in highly fired Flambe (red) glazes. These could only be achieved through a very difficult procedure which he himself perfected in secret. He later passed the knowledge on to his son.

Dating of this pottery is done by knowledge of the designs, shapes, signatures and marks on the bottom of each piece; an experienced person can usually narrow it down to a short time frame. Prices escalated for this 'rediscovered' pottery in the late 1980s but has now leveled off. This is true mainly for the pre-1935 designs of William Moorcroft, which is the era most sought after by collectors. Prices in the listings below are for pieces in mint condition unless noted otherwise; no reproductions are listed here. Advisors for this category are Wilfred and Dolli Cohen; they are listed in the Directory under California.

Biscuit jar, wisteria, yel/wine/plum on lt to dk bl, SP lid 1,200.00
Bottle, dresser; orchids, bl/wht/yel/gr on wht matt, 6" 230.00
Bowl, columbine, orange/rust on flambe, 1¾x4½" 90.00
Bowl, Eventide, trees/sunset on brn to tan, incurvate, 3x8" 1,400.00
Bowl, Flamminian, bl flowers in gr circles on med gr, 6x9" 650.00
Bowl, hibiscus, red/yel/gr on gr int & ext, 3x6" 150.00
Bowl, Landscape, int/ext scenic on yel-gr w/rose tint, 4x9" 1,600.00
Bowl, magnolias, pk/purple on ivory, 3¾x8" 200.00
Bowl, Moonlit Bl, int/ext: turq trees on cobalt, 3x8" 1,400.00
Bowl, wisteria, red/plum/yel on cobalt, hdls, 5x7" 425.00
Bowl vase, int/ext: pomegranates, 4x8" 675.00
Box, anemones, lav/mauve/bl on wht matt, 4" dia 120.00
Box, fruit & leaf, 3½x6" dia 220.00
Box, orchids, red/yel/gr flambe, 3¾" dia 275.00
Box, pansies on dk bl, #107, 4x4" dia 325.00
Butter pats, assorted flowers, set of 6 ....150.00
Cache pot, columbines, red on off-wht, 6½" 140.00
Candlesticks, pomegranates, red on cobalt, 7½", NM, pr 850.00
Chalice, Nouveau floral/gilt, MacIntyre, rim hdls, 7½" 1,700.00

Charger, leaves & berries on rouge flambe, 11" 500.00
Compote, anemones, wine/red/bl on teal to dk bl, 5x6" 375.00
Cup & saucer, cornflowers, Florian type, yel/wine on yel-gr 525.00
Cup & saucer, Spanish, wine/rose/tan on tan & gr 700.00
Dealer's sign, Moorcroft Pottery in gr on wht, 4½x8" 100.00
Humidor, Spanish design, brn/red floral on gr to bl, 4½" 1,800.00
Jar, wisteria on dk bl, ginger jar form, #769Y, 8½" 750.00
Jardiniere, lustre ware, grapes on gr-yel, hdls, 9x9" 2,600.00
Lamp, flowers, mc on red flambe, dk red rim/base, 18½" 1,400.00
Lamp base, grapes & leaves on red flambe, 12" 300.00
Lamp base, Moonlit Bl, trees w/lime tinge on dk bl/teal, 11" ..2,400.00
Mug, commemorative, Peace June 28, 1919, 3⅝" 320.00
Pitcher, anemones, purple/red/wht on dk bl, 7" 285.00
Pitcher, Dura Ware, floral, cobalt/wht squeezebag on teal, 6" 325.00
Pitcher, rose, pk w/gr leaves, mk Collector's Club, 6" 180.00
Planter, anemones, wine/purple on dk bl, 2¾x8" 170.00
Plate, Claremont, toadstools on teal bl/gr, 9" 1,150.00
Plate, pomegranates, wine/dk bl, teal underside, 8", 8 for 1,000.00
Sugar bowl, anemones, wine on dk bl, 3¼" 130.00
Tea tile, Florian, floral, wht-lined dk bl on teal, 6" dia 275.00
Vase, anemones on dk bl, shouldered, 5" 220.00
Vase, anemones on med gr, bl int/base rim, slim neck, 12½" 600.00
Vase, Aurelian, transfer floral/gilt, ball top, MacIntyre, 9" 550.00
Vase, Claremont, mushrooms on dk to lt bl, #45, 4" 575.00
Vase, Claremont, toadstools, red/gr/wine on gr to dk bl, 3½" 575.00
Vase, Claremont, toadstools on gr to cobalt, 10" 2,900.00
Vase, clematis, purple/rose/wine on gr to teal to dk bl, 11" 775.00
Vase, clematis, 4-color on dk bl, bulbous, 3¾" 150.00

Vase, five blue cornflowers on powder blue with dark blue specks, script signature, #101, 14½", $1,900.00.

Vase, cornflowers, 3 stems in shaped wht reserve on bl, 8½" 450.00
Vase, Dawn, landscape/geometric band, 3 tones of bl/yel, 7" 750.00
Vase, Eventide, yel/gr trees on gr to wine to teal, #376, 6" 975.00
Vase, Florian, cornflowers, dk on lt bl to cobalt, 5" 750.00
Vase, Florian, floral, yel/gr/wht tracing on wht to dk bl, 5" 750.00
Vase, Florian, poppies/forget-me-nots, MacIntyre, 12" 1,700.00
Vase, Florian, stylized floral on lt gr, chalice form, 9" 675.00
Vase, Florian, yel/gr on lt/dk bl, MacIntyre, stick neck, 5" 725.00
Vase, freesia, wht at top, cobalt below, 9" 650.00
Vase, grapes & leaves, red/yel flambe, shouldered, 9½" 850.00
Vase, grapes on wht, mk Collector's Club, 7¾" 200.00
Vase, Hazeldene, gr trees on lt gr w/dk gr hills, 7x4½" 1,950.00
Vase, hibiscus, mc on cobalt, bulbous, 5½x4" 195.00
Vase, hibiscus, wine/bl/yel on dk bl, 8½" 200.00
Vase, leaves & berries, mc on cobalt, 6" 220.00
Vase, lustre, poppies, bl/gr on ivory, mk Liberty, 10" 1,400.00

Vase, orchids, mc on dk bl, bulbous w/can neck, 10" **650.00**
Vase, orchids & spring flowers, red/yel/bl on med gr, 7¾" **350.00**
Vase, orchids & spring flowers on gr to dk bl, 13" **800.00**
Vase, pansies, cobalt/yel/plum on cobalt, #M74, 7½" **475.00**
Vase, pansies, strong mc on dk bl, 14½" **1,050.00**
Vase, pomegranates, red w/dk bl & red berries, hdld U-form, 6" ..**750.00**
Vase, pomegranates, red w/purple berries on dk bl, 8x6" **650.00**
Vase, pomegranates, red/yel/brn on dk bl, '55, 13x8" **1,100.00**
Vase, pomegranates, wine on cobalt mottle, 6x7" **425.00**
Vase, pomegranates, wine on dk bl, 11" **525.00**
Vase, pomegranates on bl, incurvate rim, cylindrical, 12" **650.00**
Vase, Tudor Rose, cobalt/wine on lt aqua, 8½", NM **1,595.00**
Vase, Tudor Rose, florals on gr w/purple lustre, 10½" **2,700.00**
Vase, Tudor Rose, squeezebag floral on lime, ca '05, 8x6" **1,900.00**
Vase, wisteria, mauve/dk bl/gr on ivory, hdls, early, 10" **2,200.00**
Vase, wisteria, yel/wht/dk bl/purple on cobalt, 10" **575.00**
Vase, wisteria on dk bl, shouldered, 9½" **400.00**

Moravian Pottery & Tile Works

Dr. Henry Chapman Mercer was an author, anthropologist, historian, collector, and artist. One of his diversified interests was pottery. In 1898 he established the Moravian Pottery and Tile Works in Doylestown, Pennsylvania, the name inspired by his study and collection of decorative stove plates made by the early Moravians. Because the red clay he used there proved to be unfit for tableware, he turned to the production of handmade tile which he himself designed. Though he never allowed it to become more than a studio operation, the tile works was nevertheless responsible for some important commercial installations, one of which was in the capitol building at Harrisburg.

Mercer died in 1930. Business continued in the established vein under the supervision of Mercer's assistant, Frank Swain, until his death in 1954. Since 1968 the studio has been operated by The Bucks County Commission, and tiles are still fashioned in the handmade tradition. They are marked 'Mercer' and are dated.

Tile, Flying Dutchman,
4x4", $110.00.

Inkwell, cvd tree of life/inscriptions, gr, 4x4", NM **450.00**
Tile, Adam & Eve, 4" sq **50.00**
Tile, Doctor, from Canterbury Tales, bl & wht, 4" **75.00**
Tile, grapes & leaves on bl, 2¾" **15.00**
Tile, medieval musician, mc gloss, 6½", set of 12 ....**1,200.00**

Morgantown Glass

Incorporated in 1899, the Morgantown Glass Works experienced many name changes over the years. Today 'Morgantown Glass' is a generic term used to indicate all glass produced there. Purchased by Fos-

toria in 1965, the factory was permanently closed in 1971. Our advisor for this category is Jerry Gallagher, longtime researcher of the company and author of *A Handbook of Old Morgantown Glass, Volume I.* He is listed in the Directory under Minnesota. See Clubs, Newsletters, and Catalogs for information concerning Mr. Gallagher's book, The Morgantown Collectors of America (a research society founded by him), and *The Morgantown Newscaster,* a triannual M.C.A. journal with research updates and reports of current trends.

Adonis etch, crystal; stem, goblet; 7604½ Heirloom, 9-oz **45.00**
Adonis etch, crystal/gr; stem, goblet; 7606½ Athena, 9-oz **95.00**
Adonis etch, gr; stem, parfait; #7604½ Heirloom, 5-oz **55.00**
Adonis etch, rose; stem, goblet; #7604½ Heirloom, 9-oz **60.00**
Adonis etch, topaz; stem, goblet; #7604½ Heirloom, 9-oz **58.00**

Alexandra, candy box,
Duo-tone Randall Blue to
Crystal, 5¼x6" diameter,
#7643-1, rare, $235.00.

Am Beauty etch, crystal; jug, no lid, #19 Flemish, 34-oz **245.00**
Am Beauty etch, crystal; jug, no lid, #2 Acadia, 54-oz **310.00**
Am Beauty etch, crystal; stem, champagne; #7668 Galaxy, 5-oz ..**45.00**
Am Beauty etch, crystal; stem, goblet; #7668 Galaxy, 10-oz **48.00**
Am Beauty etch, crystal; stem, goblet; #7695 Trumpet, 10-oz **58.00**
Am Beauty etch, rose; finger bowl, #2927, 4¼" **62.50**
Am Beauty etch, rose; jug, no lid, #39 Milton, 54-oz **280.00**
Am Beauty etch, rose; stem, goblet; #7565 Astrid, 10-oz **62.50**
Am Beauty etch, rose-amber; jug, w/lid, #39 Milton, 54-oz **335.00**
Aquaria etch, crystal/gr; champagne, #7643 Oceana, 6-oz **87.50**
Aquaria etch, crystal/gr; goblet, #7643 Oceana, 9-oz **95.00**
Art Moderne, cobalt w/crystal; candlesticks, #7640½, pr **335.00**
Art Moderne, cobalt w/crystal; stem, cordial; #7640, 1½-oz **145.00**
Art Moderne, cobalt w/crystal; stem, goblet; #7640, 9-oz **95.00**
Art Moderne, crystal w/blk; stem, goblet; #7640, 9-oz **100.00**
Art Moderne, crystal w/frost; stem, icer; sgn DC Thorpe, 2-pc ...**245.00**
Art Moderne, crystal w/pastel; stem, goblet, #7640, 9-oz **58.00**
Art Moderne, pastel w/crystal; stem, goblet; #7640, 9-oz **90.00**
Baden etch, blk filament; stem, goblet; #7606½ Athena, 9-oz **95.00**
Barry #37, crystal/rose; jug, Palm Optic, 48-oz **335.00**
Barry #37, Meadow Gr-cased Alabaster/gr; jug, 48-oz **595.00**
Barry #37, Meadow Gr/Jade; jug, 48-oz **495.00**
Barry #37 AN, gr-cased Alabaster/gr; tumbler, ftd, 13-oz **95.00**
Biscayne etch, crystal w/gold; goblet, #7587 Kingsley, 9-oz **57.50**
Biscayne etch, crystal w/gold; bar tumbler, #9715, 2½-oz **68.00**
Bramble Rose etch, crystal; champagne, #7577 Venus, 5½-oz **58.00**
Bramble Rose etch, crystal; goblet, #7577 Venus, 9-oz **58.00**
Bramble Rose etch, rose; plate, luncheon; #1500, 8½" **32.00**
Carlton, platinum Marco; bowl, flared, #4355 Janice, 13" **215.00**
Carlton, platinum Marco; stem, goblet; #7653 Cantana, 9-oz **78.00**
Carlton etch, crystal/blk; goblet, #7606½ Athena, 9-oz **87.50**
Carlton etch, crystal/blk; sherbet; #7606½ Athena, 5½-oz **65.00**
Carlton Frostie etch, crystal; punch bowl, #21, 12" **465.00**

Carlton Madrid, topaz/crystal; stem, goblet; #7665 Laura, 9-oz **65.00**
Carlton Milan, crystal; stem, goblet; #7668 Galaxy, 10-oz **32.50**
Cathay etch, crystal; stem, champagne; #7711 Callahan, 5½-oz ...**50.00**
Cathay etch, crystal; stem, goblet; #7711 Callahan, 9-oz **65.00**
Continental Line, Old Amethyst/crystal; basket, #4357, 9" **360.00**
Continental Line, Spanish Red/crystal; basket, #20, 4½" **345.00**
Continental Line, Stiegel Gr/crystal; basket, #4358, 6" **275.00**
Corinth etch, crystal w/gold; stem, goblet; #7654 Lorna, 9-oz **58.00**
Corinth etch, crystal w/gold; stem, wine; #7654 Lorna, 3-oz **68.00**
Crinkle, amberina; tumbler, water; flat, #1962, 10-oz **68.00**
Crinkle, amethyst; tankard, lemonade; #1962, 64-oz, 9" **75.00**
Crinkle, amethyst; tumbler, iced tea; ftd, #1962, 13-oz **27.50**
Crinkle, crystal; pitcher, juice; #1962, 34-oz, 6½" **50.00**
Crinkle, gr; Ockner jug, #1962, 54-oz **72.00**
Crinkle, gr; tumbler, iced tea; ftd, #1962, 13-oz **24.00**
Crinkle, lt bl; tumbler, flat, frosted, #1962, 20-oz **38.00**
Crinkle, peacock bl; Ockner jug, #1962, 54-oz **98.00**
Crinkle, peacock bl; tumbler, iced tea; ftd, #1962, 13-oz **27.50**
Crinkle, peacock bl; tumbler, juice; flat, #1962, 6-oz **22.00**
Crinkle, peacock bl; tumbler, water; flat, #1962, 10-oz **22.00**
Crinkle, pk; sherbet, ftd, #1962, 6-oz **20.00**
Crinkle, ruby; Ockner jug, #1962, 54-oz **135.00**
Crinkle, ruby; Owl tumbler, highball; flat, #1969, 16-oz **85.00**
Crinkle, ruby; tumbler, zombie; flat, #1962, 20-oz **38.00**
Elizabeth, azure; stem, goblet; #7630 Ballerina, 9-oz **87.50**
Elizabeth, azure; stem, goblet; #7664 Queen Anne, 9-oz **105.00**
Elizabeth, crystal; stem, wine; #7630 Ballerina, 2¾-oz **65.00**
Fairwin, bl filament; stem, goblet; #7673 Lexington, 9-oz **110.00**
Fairwin, bl filament; stem, juice; #7673 Lexington, 5-oz **75.00**
Faun etch, crystal/blk; champagne, #7640 Art Moderne, 5½-oz .**160.00**
Faun etch, crystal/blk; goblet, #7640 Art Moderne, 9-oz **185.00**
Fernlee, blk filament; stem, goblet; #7672 Octette, 9-oz **78.00**
Fernlee, crystal/blk; stem, goblet; #7640 Art Moderne, 9-oz **135.00**
Florence etch, crystal; stem, cocktail; #300 Touraine, 3-oz **45.00**
Florence etch, crystal; stem, goblet; #300 Touraine, 9-oz **42.50**
Floret etch, crystal; stem, goblet; #7684 Yale, 9-oz **85.00**
Floret etch, crystal; stemmed icer & insert, unknown # **65.00**
Fontinelle, blk filament; candlesticks, low, #7620, pr **255.00**
Fontinelle, blk filament; stem, goblet; #7620 Fontanne, 9-oz **150.00**
Fontinelle, gr/crystal; stem, goblet; #7620 Fontanne, 9-oz **155.00**
Golf Ball, cobalt/crystal; candlesticks, #7643, 4", pr **195.00**
Golf Ball, cobalt/crystal; candy dish, flat, #1212 Michael, 7" **300.00**
Golf Ball, cobalt/crystal; stem, champagne; #7643, 5½-oz **47.00**
Golf Ball, cobalt/crystal; stem, goblet; #7643, 9-oz **55.00**
Golf Ball, crystal; pilsner, #7643, 10-oz, rare, 9" **145.00**
Golf Ball, pastel/crystal; stem, goblet; from $48 to **60.00**
Golf Ball, rose/gr finial; candy dish, flat, #2938 Helga, 5" **660.00**
Golf Ball, ruby/crystal; candy dish, #7858 Leora, 5½" **375.00**
Golf Ball, ruby/crystal; candy dish, #9074 Maureen, 4½" **360.00**
Golf Ball, ruby/crystal; candy dish, flat, #1212 Michael, 7" **275.00**
Golf Ball, ruby/crystal; candy dish, flat, #2938 Helga, 5" **250.00**
Golf Ball, ruby/crystal; compote, low, w/lid, #643 Celeste **350.00**
Golf Ball, ruby/crystal; stem, goblet; #7643, 9-oz **48.00**
Golf Ball, Stiegel/crystal; candy dish, LeRoy decor, #2938, 5" **290.00**
Guest set, Anna Rose; Palm Optic, #25 Trudy, 2 pcs **60.00**
Guest set, Azure; Festoon Optic, #25 Trudy, 2 pcs **80.00**
Guest set, Azure; Peacock Optic, #24 Maria, 4 pcs, rare **465.00**
Guest set, Baby Bl opaque; Hollyhock decor, #23 Margaret **165.00**
Guest set, Golden Iris; hdld, pulled spout, #23 Margaret **250.00**
Guest set, Jade Gr opaque; #25 Trudy, 2 pcs **78.00**
Guest set, yel opaque bottle/blk tumbler; #25 Trudy **210.00**
Hollywood, blk band; tumbler, highball; flat, #8701, 12-oz **38.00**
Hollywood, red band; jug, cocktail; #548 Fairbanks, 36-oz **245.00**
Labelle etch, crystal/blk; champagne, #7640 Art Moderne **68.00**

Labelle etch, crystal/gold band; goblet, #7640 Art Moderne **95.00**
LeMons, cobalt/gold; stem, goblet; #7640, 9-oz **195.00**
LeMons, cobalt/platinum; stem, goblet; #7640, 9-oz **145.00**
LMX (El Mexicano), Hyacinth; Ockner jug, #1933, 54-oz **350.00**
LMX (El Mexicano), Ice; candle holders, bulbous, 4", #1933, pr .**280.00**
LMX (El Mexicano), Ice; sherbet, ftd, #1933, 7-oz **25.00**
LMX (El Mexicano), Rose Quartz; ice tub, #1933 ....**295.00**
LMX (El Mexicano), Rose Quartz; Ockner jug, #1933, 54-oz **340.00**
LMX (El Mexicano), Rose Quartz; sherbet, ftd, #1933, 7-oz **57.00**
LMX (El Mexicano), Rose Quartz; tumbler, ftd, #1933, 13-oz **68.00**
LMX (El Mexicano), Seaweed; decanter, liquor; w/stopper, #1933 ..**225.00**
LMX (El Mexicano), Seaweed; relish, 3-part, #1933 ....**115.00**
Mayfair etch, crystal; stem, champagne; #7668 Galaxy, 6-oz **27.00**
Mayfair etch, crystal; stem, goblet; #7668 Galaxy, 10-oz **38.00**
Melon, alabaster/cobalt; beverage set, #20069, 7-pc **850.00**
Melon, frosted/blk; Aurora etch, jug, #20069 ....**695.00**
Mikado etch, crystal; stem, champagne; #7711 Callahan, 6-oz **37.50**
Mikado etch, crystal; stem, goblet; #7711 Callahan, 10-oz **48.50**
Monroe #7690, cobalt or ruby/crystal; stem, champagne, 6-oz **75.00**
Monroe #7690, cobalt or ruby/crystal; stem, goblet; 9-oz **87.50**
Monroe #7690, Golden Iris/crystal; stem, cordial; 1½-oz **110.00**
Monroe #7690, Old Amethyst/crystal; stem, cordial; 1½-oz **140.00**
Monroe #7690, Old Amethyst/crystal; stem, goblet; 10-oz **110.00**
Morgantown Square #77942, champagne, flared, 5½-oz **140.00**
Morgantown Square #77942, goblet, flared, 10-oz **200.00**
Morgantown Square #77943, champagne, DC Thorpe decor, 5-oz .**195.00**
Morgantown Square #77943, claret, DC Thorpe decor, 4½-oz ...**255.00**
Nantucket etch, crystal; stem, goblet; Queen Anne, 10-oz **95.00**
Nantucket etch, crystal/gr; stem, goblet; #7654 Lorna, 9-oz **78.00**
Nasreen, blk/filament; sherbet, #7606½ Athena, 5½-oz **75.00**
Nasreen, crystal/blk; tumbler, #9074 Belton, 9-oz **58.00**
Nasreen etch, topaz/crystal; stem, claret; #7665 Laura, 5-oz **95.00**
Old Bristol, cobalt w/opal; candlesticks, 4", pr **330.00**
Old Bristol, cobalt w/opal; plate, unknown #, 7½" **88.00**
Old English #7678, cobalt/crystal; stem, champagne; 6½-oz **50.00**
Old English #7678, cobalt/crystal; stem, goblet; 10-oz **62.00**
Old English #7678, ruby/crystal; stem, goblet; 10-oz **65.00**
Old English #7678, Steigel Gr/crystal; stem, goblet; 10-oz **55.00**
Old English #7678, Stiegel Gr/crystal; stem, iced tea; 12-oz **55.00**
Old English #7678, Stiegel Gr/crystal; stem, sherbet; 6½-oz **45.00**
Palm Optic, alexandrite; iced tea, #7667 Georgian, 12-oz **165.00**
Palm Optic, Anna Rose; goblet, #7577 Venus, 9-oz **40.00**
Palm Optic, Anna Rose/gr; goblet, #7614 Hampton, 9-oz **87.50**
Palm Optic, Anna Rose/gr; goblet, #7646 Sophisticate, 9-oz **90.00**
Palm Optic, Anna Rose/gr; wine, #7614 Hampton, 3-oz **95.00**
Palm Optic, azure; champagne, #7536 Alycia, 9-oz **45.00**
Palm Optic, azure; goblet, #7536 Alycia, 5½-oz **50.00**
Palm Optic, azure; ice bucket, SP metal rim/bail **295.00**
Palm Optic, azure; salver, ftd, unknown #, 7" **145.00**
Palm Optic, crystal; goblet, #7577 Venus, 9-oz **38.00**
Palm Optic, crystal/Anna Rose; jug, #37 Barry, 48-oz **275.00**
Palm Optic, Venetian Gr; goblet, #7577 Venus, 9-oz **48.00**
Palm Optic, 14k Topaz; goblet, #7577 Venus, 9-oz **38.00**
Paragon #77943½, crystal/blk; stem, goblet; 9-oz **145.00**
Paragon #77943½, crystal/blk; stem, sherbet; 5½-oz **85.00**
Peacock Optic, gr or rose; stem, goblet; #7638 Avalon, 9-oz **40.00**
Peacock Optic, gr; decanter, crystal stopper, #10½ Lynwood **355.00**
Peacock Optic, gr; tumbler, bar; flat, #9051, 1½-oz **85.00**
Picardy etch, crystal; champagne, #7646 Sophisticate, 5½-oz **35.00**
Picardy etch, crystal; goblet, #7646 Sophisticate, 9-oz **48.00**
Pineapple Optic, amber; goblet, #7644½ Vernon, 9-oz **45.00**
Pineapple Optic, gr; champagne, #7644½ Vernon, 5½-oz **38.00**
Pineapple Optic, gr; goblet, #7644½ Vernon, 9-oz **52.00**
Priscilla, blk filament; champagne, #7620 Fontanne, 6-oz **87.50**

Priscilla, blk filament; goblet, #7620 Fontanne, 9-oz **115.00**
Pygon #77942, crystal/blk; sherbet, 5-oz **65.00**
Pygon #77942, crystal/frosted; champagne, Thorpe, 5½-oz **135.00**
Pygon #77942, crystal/frosted; wine, sgn Thorpe, 3½-oz **150.00**
Pygon #77942, frosted; wine, Thorpe HP bird decor, 3½-oz **195.00**
Richmond, crystal; stem, goblet; #7570 Horizon, 10-oz **27.00**
Richmond, crystal; stem, goblet; #7589 Laurette, 9-oz **32.00**
Rosalie etch, crystal; bowl, console; #4355 Janice, 13" **185.00**
Rosalie etch, topaz/crystal; stem, goblet; #7662 Majesty, 10-oz **95.00**
Saranac etch, crystal; stem, champagne; #7690 Monroe, 5½-oz **48.00**
Saranac etch, crystal; stem, goblet; #7690 Monroe, 10-oz **68.00**
Sea Gulls, enamel decor; jug, #545 Pickford, 60-oz **395.00**
Sea Gulls, enamel decor; tumbler, ftd, #9093, 12-oz **75.00**
Sear's Lace Bouquet, crystal; champagne; #7668 Galaxy, 6-oz **38.00**
Sear's Lace Bouquet, crystal; goblet; #7668 Galaxy, 10-oz **47.50**
Sonoma etch, crystal; stem, champagne; #7569 Cynthia, 6-oz **55.00**
Sonoma etch, crystal; stem, goblet; #7659 Cynthia, 10-oz **65.00**
Sonoma etch, topaz; stem, goblet; #7659 Cynthia, 10-oz **78.00**
Superba, blk/filament; champagne, #7664 Queen Anne, 6½-oz .**138.00**
Superba, blk/filament; goblet, #7664 Queen Anne, 10-oz **195.00**
Superba, crystal/blk; champagne, #7654½ Legacy, 6½-oz **135.00**
Superba, crystal/blk; champagne, 7654½ Legacy, 10-oz **185.00**
Superba, crystal/blk; goblet, #7654½ Legacy, 10-oz **185.00**
Tinker Bell, azure; tumbler, ftd, #9069, 12-oz **70.00**
Tinker Bell, crystal; goblet, #7631 Jewel, 10-oz **145.00**
Tinker Bell, crystal; guest set, #24 Maria, 4-pc, very rare **650.00**
Tinker Bell, gr; vase, bud; ftd, #53 Serenade, 10" **320.00**
Versailles, crystal; stem, goblet; #7688 Jamestown, 9-oz **48.00**
Versailles, crystal; stem, goblet; #7711 Callahan, 10-oz **48.00**
Victoria, crystal; goblet, #300 Touraine, 9-oz **45.00**
Victoria Regina, crystal/blk; goblet, #7640 Art Moderne, 9-oz **97.50**
Virginia etch, amber; stem, goblet; #7614 Hampton, 9-oz **50.00**
Virginia etch, crystal; stem, goblet; #7587 Kingsley, 9-oz **40.00**
Virginia etch, crystal; stem, goblet; #7711 Callahan, 10-oz **48.00**
Yale #7684, cobalt or ruby; stem, goblet; 9-oz **110.00**
Yale #7684, crystal; stem, goblet; 9-oz **90.00**
Yale #7684, Stiegel gr; stem, goblet; 9-oz **98.00**

Continental Line

Ashley #4354, Stiegel/crystal; basket, ftd, 8-crimp, 10" dia **265.00**
Clayton #4357½, Ritz Bl/crystal; basket, canoe rim, 10" **325.00**
Electra #35½, Ritz Bl; vase, flower; hdld, 10" **285.00**
Irene #4356, amber/crystal; basket, 8-crimp, 10½" **315.00**
Irene #4356, Spanish Red/crystal; basket/bowl, 6-crimp, 10½" ...**285.00**
Janet, 34355, Spanish Red/crystal; basket/bowl, 8-crimp, 13" **290.00**
Jennie #20, Anna Rose/crystal; basket, bonbon; 4½" dia **385.00**
Jupiter #71, Stiegel/crystal; vase, flower; Italian base, 6" **275.00**
Lyndale #64, Confetti; kerosene lamp, Italian base, 6" **450.00**
Naples #35½, Venetian Gr; vase, flower; Italian base, 12" **395.00**
Neopolitan #64, Ritz Bl; ivy ball, Italian base, 6" **235.00**
Patrick #4358, crystal; basket, flower; 8-crimp, 10" **345.00**
Patrick #4358, Randall Bl/crystal; basket, flower; 8-crimp, 8" **295.00**
Patrick #4358, Stiegel/crystal; basket, flower; 8-crimp, 8" **285.00**
Rima #68, Ritz Bl; vase, flower; Italian base, 10" **310.00**
Trindle #4357, Old Amethyst; basket, 8-crimp, 9" **340.00**
Vienna #71, Stiegel Gr; bowl, console; Italian base, 12" **785.00**
Ziegfield #61, Stiegel Gr; witch ball, Italian base, 8" **825.00**

Silk-Screen Color Printing on Crystal

Manchester Pheasant, champagne, #7664 Queen Anne, 6½-oz .**148.00**
Manchester Pheasant, goblet, #7664 Queen Anne, 10-oz **210.00**
Manchester Pheasant, sherbet, #7664 Queen Anne, 6½-oz **135.00**

Queen Louise, crystal/rose; stem, cocktail; #7614 Hampton, 6-oz .**145.00**
Queen Louise, crystal/rose; stem, goblet; #7614 Hampton, 9-oz .**180.00**
Queen Louise, crystal/rose; stem, wine; #7614 Hampton, 6-oz ...**155.00**

Sunrise Medallion Etch

#37 Barry, azure; jug, ftd, 48-oz **585.00**
#37 Barry, crystal; jug, ftd, 80-oz **460.00**
#45 Catherine, azure; vase, bud; ftd, 10" **280.00**
#45 Catherine, gr or rose; vase, bud; ftd, 10" **270.00**
#53 Serenade, azure; vase, bud; bulbous, ftd, 10" **370.00**
#53 Serenade, rose; vase, bud; bulbous, ftd, 10" **360.00**
#7630 Ballerina, azure; stem, goblet; 9-oz **75.00**
#7630 Ballerina, crystal; stem, goblet; 9-oz **62.00**
#7630 Ballerina, gr; stem, goblet; 9-oz **65.00**
#7630 Ballerina, rose; stem, goblet; 9-oz **70.00**
#7630 Ballerina, topaz; stem, goblet; 9-oz **62.00**
#7654½ Legacy, crystal w/moonstone; champagne, 6-oz **135.00**
#7654½ Legacy, crystal w/moonstone; cocktail, 3-oz **135.00**
#7654½ Legacy, crystal w/moonstone; goblet, 9-oz **190.00**
#7664 Queen Anne, azure; stem, goblet; 10-oz **90.00**
#7664 Queen Anne, crystal; stem, goblet; 10-oz **78.00**

Moriage

The term 'moriage' refers to certain Japanese wares decorated with applied slipwork designs. There are several methods used to achieve the characteristic relief effect. The decorative devices may be designed separately and applied to the vessel, piped on in narrow ribbons of clay (slip-trailed), or built up by brushing on successive layers of liquified slip. See also Dragon Ware; Nippon.

Powder box, allover Nouveau florals on green, 2½x5", $125.00.

Ashtray, floral, 4¾" **50.00**
Chocolate pot, mc florals, heavy moriage, 9½" **150.00**
Cracker jar, wide floral band on wine, 4-ftd, 7" **300.00**
Cup & saucer, demitasse; wht wisteria **50.00**
Humidor, EX slipwork, 7" **200.00**
Plaque, fronds & pods, ornate border, 8½" **210.00**
Sugar shaker, roses on green, bbl form **95.00**
Vase, florals in reserves on gr, ftd, 9" **245.00**
Vase, mc floral panels, 3-hdld, 7x5½" **240.00**
Vase, pastel florals over shadow flowers, flared rim, 4½" **235.00**

Mortars and Pestles

Mortars are bowl-shaped vessels used for centuries for the purpose of grinding drugs to a powder or grain into meal. The masher or grinding device is called a pestle.

Gray and green marble, 4½" mortar with 5½" pestle, $150.00.

Brass, side hdls, 1¾", w/pestle	120.00
Brass, side hdls, 3⅝", w/pestle	40.00
Brass, 3x4½", w/pestle	95.00
Burl, EX figure, old soft patina, 7¾", w/pestle	275.00
Burl, rfn, 8", w/plain wood pestle	140.00
CI, EX detail, 8¾", w/pestle	60.00
CI, flared ft, 6¾", w/pestle	55.00
Maple, 7", w/pestle	98.00
Trn wood, red pnt traces, 8", w/pestle	85.00
Trn wood, red stain, 7¾", w/pestle	215.00
Wooden, 6", +10" pestle	110.00
Wooden bowl shape, figured, dk finish, 3¾x7", w/pestle	165.00

Mortens Studio

Oscar Mortens was already established as a fine sculptural artist when he left his native Sweden to take up residency in Arizona. During the 1940s he developed a line of detailed animal figures which were distributed through the Mortens Studios, a firm he co-founded with Gunnar Thelin. Thelin hired and trained artists to produce Mortens' line, which he called Royal Designs. More than two hundred dogs were modeled and over one hundred horses. Cats and wild animals such as elephants, panthers, deer, and elk were made, but on a much smaller scale. Bookends with sculptured dog heads were shown in their catalogs, and collectors report finding wall plaques on rare occasions. The material they used was a plaster-type composition with wires embedded to support the weight. Examples were marked 'Copyright by the Mortens Studio' either in ink or decal. Watch for flaking, cracks, and separations. Crazing seems to be present in some degree in many examples. When no condition is indicated, the items listed below are assumed to be in near-mint condition, allowing for minor crazing.

Airedale	95.00
Boston Terrier pup sitting, #838	55.00
Boxer, #551, mini	60.00
Boxer, standing, 5½x5½"	80.00
Boxer pup, ears down, bkside up	40.00
Boxer pup, playing	55.00
Boxer pup, recumbent	78.00
Boxer pup, scratching, #508	55.00
Boxer pup, sitting, #823	55.00
Champs Wire-Hair Terrier, begging, mini	45.00
Cocker Spaniel, blk & wht, #763	55.00
Cocker Spaniel pup, recumbent, brn, #515	65.00
Cocker Spaniel pup w/paw up, #841	55.00
Collie pup, recumbent	50.00

Collie pup, sitting, #818	55.00
Dachshund, recumbent	48.00
Dalmation pup, sitting, #812	55.00
English Setter pup, sitting	45.00
Fox Terrier, show stance	75.00
German Shepherd, sitting, #789	95.00
Horse, mane erect	110.00
Pekinese, standing, #740, 3½x4½"	85.00
St Bernard, #778, 6½x8½"	150.00
Wire-Hair Terrier, sitting, #829	55.00

Morton Pottery

Six potteries operated in Morton, Illinois, at various times from 1877 to 1976. Each traced its origin to six brothers who immigrated to America to avoid military service in Germany. The Rapp brothers established their first pottery near clay deposits on the south side of town where they made field tile and bricks. Within a few years, they branched out to include utility wares such as jugs, bowls, jars, pitchers, etc. During the ninety-nine years of pottery operations in Morton, the original factory was expanded by some of the sons and nephews of the Rapps. Other family members started their own potteries where artware, gift-store items, and special-order goods were produced. The Cliftwood Art Pottery and the Morton Pottery Company had showrooms in Chicago and New York City during the 1930s. All of Morton's potteries were relatively short-lived operations with the Morton Pottery Company being the last to shut down on September 8, 1976. For a more thorough study of the subject, we recommend *Morton's Potteries: 99 Years, Vols. I and II*, by Doris and Burdell Hall; their address can be found in the Directory under Illinois.

Morton Pottery Works – Morton Earthenware Co. (1877-1917)

Chamber pot, yel ware, mini	25.00
Cuspidor, bl, rare, 7"	75.00
Cuspidor, brn, 7"	50.00
Food mold, Turk's hat, brn Rockingham	70.00
Jardiniere, brn Rockingham, 7"	30.00
Jardiniere, gr, 5"	20.00
Jug, brn Rockingham, mini	45.00
Mug, yel ware, ½-pt	65.00
Stein, German motto, gr, rare	80.00
Teapot, restaurant, brn, nesting, ind, set of 2	40.00

Cliftwood Art Potteries, Inc. (1920-1940)

Beer set, brn drip, bbl shape, pitcher+6 steins	180.00
Bowl, batter; pk/orchid on wht, ribbed, hdld	45.00
Figurine, bald eagle, natural colors, 8½"	85.00
Figurine, buffalo, natural colors, 6¼x10"	200.00
Figurine, bulldog, gray, seated, 11"	80.00
Figurine, lion, natural colors, solid cast, 16" L	125.00
Figurine, police dog, brn drip, 5x8½"	55.00
Flower frog, frog, pk, 5½"	22.00
Flower frog, lily pad, bl, 4"	14.00
Flower frog, lily pad, brn drip, 6"	20.00
Flower frog, turtle, bl/mulberry drip, 5½"	18.00
Flower frog, turtle, gr, 4"	14.00
Jar, Pretzels emb on brn drip, bbl shape, w/lid	60.00
Matchbox holder, pk/turq over wht, wall mt	50.00

Midwest Potteries, Inc. (1940-1944)

Figurine, Afghan hound, wht w/gold decor, 7"	35.00

Figurine, camel, tan, 8½" 20.00
Figurine, cockatoo on ped, yel w/gr drip, 6" 15.00
Figurine, deer, wht w/gold decor, 8-point antlers, 12" 40.00
Figurine, Irish setter, natural colors, 5" 35.00
Figurine, lady w/Russian wolfhound, wht w/gold decor, 11" 125.00
Figurine, pony, yel w/gold decor, 3½" 18.00
Figurine, tiger, yel w/brn stripes, 6x10" 40.00
Miniature, boat, yel w/bl sails, 2" 8.00
Miniature, camel, brn, 2½" 8.00
Miniature, goose, wht matt, 1¾" 7.00
Miniature, polar bear, wht, 1¾" 8.00
Miniature, rabbits kissing, wht w/gold decor, rare, 2½" 25.00
Miniature, squirrel, brn, 2" 10.00

Morton Pottery Company (1922-1976)

Bank, acorn, brn 25.00
Bank, bulldog, gr 20.00
Bank, church, brn 25.00
Bank, log cabin school, brn 25.00
Bank, pig, blk w/wht stripe 40.00
Bank, shoe house, yel w/gr roof 25.00
Figurine, cat, reclining, wht w/gray spots 18.00
Figurine, horse & colt by pump & bbl, natural colors 40.00
Figurine, John Kennedy Jr, age 3, saluting, rare 30.00
Figurine, oxen, brn, pr 30.00
Grass grower, Christmas tree 15.00
Grass grower, GI, Hi Buddy 25.00
Grass grower, Jiggs 30.00
Grass grower, Jolly Jim 20.00
Grass grower, pig 20.00
Lamp, Irish setter, bird in mouth 70.00
Lamp, teddy bear 25.00
Lamp, TV; buffalo, natural colors 100.00
Lamp, TV; horse head, brn 40.00
Lamp, TV; panther, blk 30.00

American Art Potteries (1947-1961)

Figurine, Afghan hounds, blk, 15", pr 50.00
Figurine, deer, leaping, brn w/gr spray, 6" 18.00
Figurine, horse, rearing, brn w/gr spray, 6" 15.00
Figurine, parrot on stump, wht w/gold decor, 8" 20.00
Figurine, wild horse, brn spray, 11½" 35.00
Planter, deer reclining by stump, gr w/brn spray 18.00
Planter, fish, pk & purple on wht 14.00
Planter, pig, blk w/wht stripe 20.00
Planter, quail, natural colors 25.00
Planter, wheelbarrow, parrot shape, pk w/gray spray 12.00

Mosaic Tile Co.

The Mosaic Tile Company was organized in 1894, in Zanesville, Ohio, by Herman Mueller and Karl Langenbeck, both of whom had years of previous experience in the industry. They developed a faster, less-costly method of potting decorative tile, utilizing paper patterns rather than copper molds. By 1901 the company had grown and expanded with offices in many major cities. Faience tile was introduced in 1918, greatly increasing their volume of sales. They also made novelty ashtrays, figural boxes, bookends, etc., though not to any large extent. Until they closed during the 1960s, Mosaic used various marks that included the company name or their initials 'MT' superimposed over 'Co.' in a circle.

Brush holder, lav, fireplace form, mk 55.00
Figurine, German Shepherd, tan, 10½" 125.00
Paperweight, Abraham Lincoln 45.00

Pointer dog stands beside tray, 8" long, $125.00.

Tile, African boy profile w/yel halo on cobalt, 5¾"+fr 275.00
Tile, General Pershing bust, jasper, wht on bl 50.00
Tile, Mary & lamb 25.00
Tile, Medusa head, 4" 95.00
Tile, Teddy Roosevelt, mc transfer, 4¼" 125.00
Tile, Vice President Marshall, wht on bl, hexagonal, 1916 ....45.00

Moser

Ludwig Moser began his career as a struggling glass artist, catering to the rich who visited the famous Austrian health spas. His talent and popularity grew and in 1857 the first of his three studios opened in Karlsbad, Czechoslovakia. The styles developed there were entirely his own; no copies of other artists have ever been found. Some of his original designs include grapes with trailing vines, acorns and oak leaves, and richly enameled, deeply cut or carved floral pieces. Sometimes jewels were applied to the glass as well. Moser's animal scenes reflect his careful attention to detail. Famed for his birds in flight, he also designed stalking tigers — even elephants — all created in fine enameling.

Moser died in 1916, but the business was continued by his two sons who had been personally and carefully trained by their father. The Moser company bought the Meyr's Neffe Glassworks in 1922, and continued to produce quality glassware.

When identifying Moser, look for great clarity in the glass; deeply carved, continuous engravings; perfect coloration; finely applied enameling (often covered with thin gold leaf); and well-polished pontils. Our advisor for this category is Don Williams; he is listed in the Directory under Missouri. Items described below are enameled unless noted otherwise.

Bottle, scent; cane cuttings w/gold, cut stopper, 5½" 175.00
Bowl, amber, mc/gold grapevines, scroll ft, sq, 1½x4¾" 250.00
Bowl, cameo floral on smoke texture, 4x6½" dia 425.00
Bowl, cameo tulips, cranberry on clear, 8" 575.00
Bowl, cranberry w/mc florals & swags, 3½x5", +underplate 260.00
Bowl, cut, amber, paneled, scalloped, Karlsbad, 6½" 300.00
Bowl, vivid bl w/florals, 6 clear ft/rim trim, 4x8" 225.00
Box, Prussian bl w/allover flowers & leaves, 5½" dia 140.00
Cruet, bl w/wht & gold floral, clear hdl/stopper, no mk, 9" 590.00
Cruet, cranberry, allover gold, clear faceted stopper, 9x5" 750.00
Cup & saucer, emerald gr w/gold & HP decor, 2¾" 75.00
Decanter, appl acorns/gilt/mc leaves, 8", +tray & 4 wines 2,000.00
Decanter, moss gr w/allover floral, ribbed, 8½", pr 1,150.00
Ewer, gr, allover gold design, str sides, 12" 200.00
Jardiniere, pk opal w/glass jewels & gold, 7½x9½" 975.00
Pitcher, bl w/mc enamel, appl reed hdl, 9", +2 tumblers 750.00
Pitcher, Coin Spot, sapphire bl, mc scrolls etc, bulbous, 8" 745.00

Pitcher, cranberry w/mc enameling, 10¼", +2 4" tumblers 3,000.00
Pitcher, Invt T'print, amberina, appl grapes & bird, 6¾" 3,000.00
Pitcher, ruby, portrait decal w/mc enamel, gold rim, 5½" 225.00
Ring tree, blk amethyst w/HP florals & gold, 4x3¾" 110.00
Shot glass, acid cut-bk gilt cocks, floral paperweight base 195.00
Tazza, cobalt w/gold floral, 4¾x5¾" 400.00
Tumbler, allover gold oak leaves/appl silver acorns 700.00
Vase, amber, intaglio florals w/gold, 9" 125.00
Vase, amber, roses/gold stems/ferns, pr appl fish, ftd, 8" 300.00
Vase, amethyst, gold/yel butterfly/leaves, appl acorns, 4" 500.00
Vase, amethyst shaded, intaglio cutting, octagonal, 4½" 195.00
Vase, apricot to clear w/enameling, scalloped fan form, 9" 325.00
Vase, bl crackle w/2 mc fish & seaweed, 8" 425.00
Vase, bud; cranberry, gold floral & 2 moths, 7½" 350.00
Vase, cameo elephants/palm trees, gilt/gr on amethyst, 11" 850.00
Vase, cameo floral, lav/gr on wht frost, sqd, 10" 650.00
Vase, cameo leaves, ovoid, 2¾" 150.00
Vase, cranberry, gold coralene florals/pnt scene, 11" 575.00
Vase, cranberry, mc ferns/berries/bugs, appl branch, gilt, 3" 625.00
Vase, cranberry w/clear ft, florals, 6x1½" 165.00
Vase, cream cased, ruby florals/gilt, bottle form, 10" 125.00
Vase, gr to clear, gold vines/yel scrolls, dbl-lobed, 7½" 200.00
Vase, gr to clear cut w/tulips, 4-sided, 12" 275.00
Vase, red w/pk florals & gold branches, 8-panel, 8" 225.00
Vase, smoke, crane/lotus/dragonfly, heart hdls, 8x6" 225.00
Vase, wht cut to cobalt, florals w/gold, trumpet shape, 13" 275.00
Vase, yel & purple w/gold enameling, Karlsbad, 15" 900.00
Vase, yel opal w/gold leaves, appl grapes/ft, 6", pr 1,200.00
Wine, gr cup, clear hollow stem, etched, 5½" 50.00

Moss Rose

Moss Rose was a favorite dinnerware pattern of many Staffordshire and American potters from the mid-1800s. In America the Wheeling Pottery of West Virginia produced the ware in large quantities, and it became one of their best sellers, remaining popular well into the nineties. See also Haviland.

Bowl, HP, gold rim, ped ft, unmk, 5x9¾" 22.00
Cake plate, open hdls, unmk 60.00

Coffeepot, dolphin handle, 7", $75.00.

Creamer, Meakin 35.00
Creamer & sugar bowl, late, unmk 28.00
Cup & saucer, demitasse; ornate hdl & ft 10.00
Cup & saucer, Meakin 26.50
Plate, lt wear, 9" 20.00
Plate, unmk, 7½" 9.00
Shaving mug, unmk 30.00
Tea set, Japan, 16-pc+lids 60.00
Toothbrush holder, w/drain 75.00
Wash set, unmk, 11" pitcher+13½" bowl 295.00

Mother-of-Pearl Glass

Mother-of-Pearl glass was a type of mold-blown satin art glass popular during the last half of the 19th century. A patent for its manufacture was issued in 1886 to Frederick S. Shirley, and one of the companies who produced it was the Mt. Washington Glass Company of New Bedford, Massachusetts. Another was the English firm of Stevens and Williams. Its delicate patterns were developed by blowing the gather into a mold with inside projections that left an intaglio design on the surface of the glass, then sealing the first layer with a second, trapping air in the recesses. Most common are the Diamond Quilted, Raindrop, and Herringbone patterns. It was made in several soft colors, the most rare and valuable is rainbow — a blend of rose, light blue, yellow, and white. Occasionally it may be decorated with coralene, enameling, or gilt. Watch for 20th-century reproductions, especially in the Diamond Quilted pattern. Our advisors for this category are Betty and Clarence Maier; they are listed in the Directory under Pennsylvania.

Bottle, scent; Dmn Quilt, pk, crystal cut stopper, 6¼" 650.00
Bottle, Swirl, bl to gr w/yel, Stevens & Wms, 12" 900.00
Bowl, Dmn Quilt, bl, frosted thorny ft, 4¾x6½" 450.00
Bowl, Rivulet, rainbow, 8-crimp, 3-ftd, 4x5" 695.00
Bowl, Swirl, tan to aqua, bl int, Stevens & Wms, 3⅝x7⅜" 850.00
Creamer & sugar bowl, Ribbon, bl, 2½", 2½" 395.00
Cruet, perfume; Dmn Quilt, apricot, frost hdl/stopper, 4" 600.00
Cup, punch; Dmn Quilt, rainbow, frost hdl, firing line, 3" 200.00
Ewer, Herringbone, bl, 11½" 485.00
Ewer, Swirl, peach shaded, ftd, twist hdl wraps neck, 15" 795.00
Ewer, Swirl, pk shaded, appl florals, rope hdl, 15" 1,220.00
Finger bowl, Dmn Quilt, pk, ruffled, 3x5⅜" 245.00
Finger bowl, Dmn Quilt, rainbow, triangular rim, mk Pat, 4½" ..750.00
Finger bowl, Herringbone, red to pk, 3x4¼" 165.00
Lamp base, Melon Rib, rainbow, glossy, 7¾x3¾" 795.00
Pitcher, Dmn Quilt, pk to orange to pk, reeded shell hdl, 9" 300.00
Pitcher, Dmn Quilt, yel, sq top, 6½x3" 375.00
Rose bowl, concentric circles, rainbow, mk Pat, 2⅜x4⅜" 850.00
Rose bowl, Dmn Quilt, bl, dimpled sides, 4¾x5" 325.00
Rose bowl, Dmn Quilt, pk, 8-crimp top, 3¼x4" 195.00
Rose bowl, Dmn Quilt, wht w/amber & wht matsu-no-ke, 3-ftd ..750.00
Rose bowl, Herringbone, bl, egg shape, 6-scallop, 3¾x3⅜" 165.00
Rose bowl, Herringbone, bl, HP bird on branch, Webb, 3" 275.00
Rose bowl, Herringbone, peach, 6-crimp, 3⅝" 165.00
Rose bowl, Herringbone, pk, egg shape, crimped, 3¾x3" 175.00
Rose bowl, Ribbon, wht, 3-pinch top, wafer ft, 3x2¾" 125.00
Rose bowl, Rivulet, gr, 8-crimp, ruffled ft, 3⅞x3¼" 295.00
Sugar shaker, Herringbone, bl, mk Pat, 6¼" 650.00
Tray, card; apricot, heart hdl, ftd, berry pontil, 6½" dia 500.00
Tumbler, Moire, bl, 4" 145.00
Vase, Basketweave, pk, J Northwood, 5¾" 950.00
Vase, Dmn Quilt, amberina, ruffled, 8¼x5" 1,250.00
Vase, Dmn Quilt, bl, frost at rim, 8x3½" 475.00
Vase, Dmn Quilt, bl, gold decor, Webb, 9¼x4⅛" 895.00
Vase, Dmn Quilt, bl, mc flowers & yel branches, 4x3" 195.00
Vase, Dmn Quilt, bl, 4-petal top, 5x3⅜" 165.00
Vase, Dmn Quilt, brn shaded, forget-me-nots, 6½" 825.00
Vase, Dmn Quilt, pk, slim, 10" 275.00
Vase, Dmn Quilt, rainbow, egg w/shell ft/wishbones, Pat, 8½" ...950.00
Vase, Herringbone, bl, ewer form, frosted thorn hdl, 6x4" 245.00
Vase, Herringbone, peach, frosted streamer around neck, 6⅛" ...195.00

Vase, Herringbone, pk, ribbed w/hdl, 11x4" 175.00
Vase, Raindrop, bl, ruffled rim, 7⅝x4¼" 185.00
Vase, Raindrop, butterscotch, bulbous, Mt WA, 8x7½" 425.00
Vase, Raindrop, lt bl, str panel sides, ruffled, Mt WA, 8x5" 200.00
Vase, Ribbon, chartreuse, rectangular top, ftd, 2¾x2⅞" 195.00
Vase, Ribbon, lt brn, tricorner top, 6¼x4½" 325.00
Vase, Ribbon, pk, ruffled 3-petal rim, SP base, 7¾" 165.00
Vase, Swirl, bl, melon sections, ormolu ft, 6½" 425.00
Vase, Swirl, bl-gr, long neck/shaped body, Stevens & Wms, 8" ..1,400.00
Vase, Swirl, gr to rose, Stevens & Williams, 5⅜x4⅝" 850.00
Vase, Swirl, pk, melon ribs, ruffled, 6¼x2⅞" 195.00
Vase, Swirl, rubena verde, stick neck, Stevens & Wms, 10" 250.00
Vase, Swirl, yel to bl, bulb w/long neck, Stevens & Wms, 12" .1,000.00

Mourning Collectibles

During the 18th and early 19th centuries, ladies made needlework pictures, samplers, paintings on ivory plaques, watercolor drawings, etc., to commemorate the death of a loved one. Elements contained in nearly all examples are the tomb, mourners, a weeping willow tree, and data relating to the deceased. Often plaits of hair were included. Today these are recognized and valued as a valid form of folk art. Our advisor for this category is Steve DeGenaro; he is listed in the Directory under Ohio. See also Hair Weaving.

Funeral plate, baby in silk- & flower-draped casket, Victorian 75.00
Memorial, needlework/watercolor/ink, late 1700s, 16x19", EX .1,150.00
Memorial, pnt & ink on paper, monument w/obit, 1849, 10x13" ..248.00
Memorial, watercolor & silk embr, willow, lady & tomb, 1820s .2,500.00
Pendant, portrait on ivory, hair on reverse, 1½x2" 600.00

Movie Memorabilia

Movie memorabilia covers a broad range of collectibles, from books and magazines dealing with the industry in general to the various promotional materials which were distributed to arouse interest in a particular film. Many collectors specialize in a specific area — posters, pressbooks, stills, lobby cards, or souvenir programs (also referred to as premiere booklets). In the listings below, a one-sheet poster measures approximately 27" x 41", three-sheet: 41" x 81", and six-sheet: 81" x 81". See also Autographs; Cartoon Art; Paper Dolls; Personalities.

Poster, *The Singing Vagabond*, Gene Autry and Champion, Republic, 1935, 42x27", NM, $685.00.

Banner, Affair to Remember, Grant & Kerr, 1957, 24x82", NM .225.00
Book, Alice Faye, all her movies w/cast photos etc, 194-pg 12.50
Book, Marilyn Monroe, Destruction of Am Dream, Hembus, EX ..200.00
Book, Marilyn Monroe, MM Story, Franklin/Palmer, hardbk, EX .550.00

Book, Marilyn Monroe, That Girl Marilyn, Jane Russell, EX 125.00
Book, Marilyn Monroe, The Girl, paperbk, EX 25.00
Calendar top, Jayne Mansfield, 1950s, lg 45.00
Car scent holder, Marilyn Monroe, 4 cards, 1950s 200.00
Cigarette card, Poppy, Fields/Hudson, blk/wht, 1⅜x2⅝" 5.00
Cigarette card, Rags, M Pickford, blk/wht, 4x2¾" 7.50
Cigarette card, Roberta, Astaire/Rogers, blk/wht, 3x2½" 8.00
Doll, Marilyn Monroe, 7 Year Itch, 1982, 11½", MIB 90.00
Folder, La Dolce Vita, Anita Ekberg, late 1950s 30.00
Insert, Birds, Fr reissue, 1983, 47x64" 75.00
Insert, Birds, Tippi Hedren, Hitchcock, 1963, 36x14", NM 250.00
Insert, Branded, Buck Jones, 1928, 36x14", VG 250.00
Insert, Die Die My Darling, Bankhead, 1965, 36x14" 30.00
Insert, Dr Terror's House of Horrors, Lee/Cushing, 36x14" 30.00
Insert, High Noon, Cooper, 1952, 36x14", NM 325.00
Insert, Red Planet Mars, 1952, 36x14" 30.00
Insert, Revenge of the Creature, J Agar, 1955, 36x14" 250.00
Insert, Tarzan & Leopard Woman, Weissmuller, '46, 36x14", VG .200.00
Insert, Terror Is a Man, Lederer/Derr, 1959, 36x14", NM 16.50
Lobby card, At the Circus, Marx Bros, 1939, 11x14", EX 175.00
Lobby card, Billy the Kid Trapped, Crabbe, 1942, 11x14", NM ...16.00
Lobby card, Bus Stop, Monroe, 1956, 11x14", set of 8 ....375.00
Lobby card, Citizen Kane, Welles, 1941, 11x14", VG 400.00
Lobby card, Devil Dogs of the Air, Cagney, 1955, 11x14", EX ...225.00
Lobby card, Every Day's a Holiday, Mae West, 1938, 11x14", EX ..250.00
Lobby card, Farewell to Arms, Hays/Cooper, 1932, 11x14", EX .500.00
Lobby card, Fugitive at Large, Jack Holt, 1939, 11x13" 32.00
Lobby card, Garden of Allah, Detriech/Boyer, 1936, 11x14", EX ..125.00
Lobby card, Lucky Texan, Wayne, 1934, 11x14", NM 225.00
Lobby card, Made for Each Other, Lombard/Stewart, '39, 11x14" .50.00
Lobby card, Mata Hari, Garbo/Novarro, 1932, 11x14" 800.00
Lobby card, Out of the Past, Mitchum/Greer, 1947, 11x14", EX .550.00
Lobby card, Public Enemy, James Cagney, 1944, 11x14", VG 75.00
Lobby card, Sergeant York, Cooper, 1941, 11x14", EX, pr 125.00
Lobby card, Sex, Louise Glaum, 1920, 11x14", set of 8 ....250.00
Lobby card, Task Force, Gary Cooper, 1956, 11x14", EX 35.00
Lobby card, Top Hat, Astaire/Rogers, 1955, 11x14", EX 400.00
Lobby card, Wild Angels, P Fonda, 1966, NM, 8 for 95.00
Magazine, Confidential, Monroe/Elvis/etc cover, 1957, EX 25.00
Magazine, Modern Screen, Kim Novak cover, July 1956, EX 25.00
Magazine, Modern Screen, Marilyn Monroe cover, 1953, EX 50.00
Magazine, Modern Screen, Myrna Loy cover, 1939, EX 35.00
Magazine, Motion Picture, Marilyn Monroe cover, Jan 1953, NM ..75.00
Magazine, Motion Picture, Monroe/Taylor cover, 1973, NM 30.00
Magazine, Movie Life, Janet Leigh cover, Sept 1953, EX 16.50
Magazine, Movie World, Patricia Neal cover, Mar 1952, M 15.00
Magazine, Movieland, Marilyn Monroe cover, July 1952, NM ...100.00
Magazine, Photoplay, Bette Davis cover, 1941, EX 28.00
Magazine, Photoplay, Jayne Mansfield cover, 1957, EX 22.00
Magazine, Photoplay, Madge Evans cover, June 1932, EX 45.00
Magazine, Photoplay, Marilyn Monroe cover, Apr 1954, NM 65.00
Magazine, Photoplay, Marilyn Monroe cover, 1956, EX 48.00
Magazine, Screen Stories, Marilyn Monroe cover, Nov 1954, NM ..35.00
Magazine, Screenland, Janet Gaynor cover, May 1931, NM 45.00
Photo, Rudolph Valentino at RR station 35.00
Poster, All President's Men, Redford/Hoffman, 1975, 41x27", EX .12.00
Poster, Amazing Transparent Man, 1959, 22x28" 50.00
Poster, Behave Yourself, Winters/Granger, Vargas, '51, 41x27" .300.00
Poster, Breakfast at Tiffany's, Hepburn, Italy, '61, 78x55", EX .1,600.00
Poster, Bronze Venus, Lena Horn, 1943, 81x41", EX 1,200.00
Poster, Camille, Greta Garbo, Fr, 1946, 63x47", NM 935.00
Poster, Catered Affair, Davis/Reynolds/Borgnine, '56, 22x28" 50.00
Poster, Damn Yankees, Vernon, 1958, 22x28" 50.00
Poster, Fancy Pants, Hope/Ball, 1962 reissue, 41x27", EX 20.00

Poster, Flying Down to Rio, Astaire/Rogers, on linen, 43x29" ...**150.00**
Poster, Goldfinger, Connery, Fr, 1964, 63x47", NM **150.00**
Poster, Gun Crazy, Peggy Cummins, 1949, 40x30", EX **600.00**
Poster, Hellcats of Navy, Reagan/Davis, 1957, 41x27", M **78.00**
Poster, Hush...Sweet Charlotte, Davis/DeHaviland, '65, 27x41" .**100.00**
Poster, Lady & Tramp, Disney, linen bk, 1955, 42x27", EX **500.00**
Poster, Lady From Nowhere, Mary Aster, 1936, 41x27", EX **400.00**
Poster, Last Tango in Paris, Marlon Brando, 1973, 27x41", NM ..**200.00**
Poster, Letter to 3 Wives, Crain/Darnell/Southern, 1949, 22x28" .**50.00**
Poster, Love Me Tender, Elvis Presley, 1-sheet, 1956, 2x741" ...**300.00**
Poster, Phone Call From Stranger, Davis, 27x41", M **75.00**
Poster, Pride of St Louis, Dizzy Dean, 1952, 14x22" **85.00**
Poster, Texas Masquerade, Hopalong Cassidy, 80x80", NM **400.00**
Poster, Torch Song, Crawford, 1953, 27x41", M **75.00**
Poster, Wind, L Gish/Lars Hanson, linen bk, 1928, 41x27", EX ..**5,500.00**
Poster, 101 Dalmations, Disney, 1961, 3-sheet, EX **325.00**
Pressbook, Rebel w/o a Cause, Dean, 1955, 19-pg, EX **100.00**
Program, Bus Stop, Marilyn Monroe illus, Roxy Theatre **65.00**
Sheet music, Marilyn Monroe, Ladies of Chorus, fr **200.00**
Souvenir book, Judy Garland, Palace, 1954 ....**35.00**
Window card, Bell of the Nineties, M West, 1934, 22x14", EX .**125.00**
Window card, Dumbo, Belgian, Disney, 1941, 22x14", EX **450.00**
Window card, Jungle Book, Disney, 1967, 22x14", NM **100.00**
Window card, Lady of Tropics, R Taylor/H Lamar, 1939, 28x22" ..**75.00**
Window card, Little Foxes, Bankhead, 1940, 22x14", NM **125.00**
Window waver, Marilyn Monroe, Starpool, M **125.00**

Mt. Washington

The Mt. Washington Glass Works was founded in 1837 in South Boston, Massachusetts, but moved to New Bedford in 1869 after purchasing the facilities of the New Bedford Glass Company. Frederick S. Shirley became associated with the firm in 1874. Two years later the company reorganized and became known as the Mt. Washington Glass Company. In 1894 it merged with the Pairpoint Manufacturing Company, a small Brittania works nearby, but continued to conduct business under its own title until after the turn of the century. The combined plants were equipped with the most modern and varied machinery available and boasted a working force with experience and expertise rival to none in the art of blowing and cutting glass. In addition to their fine cut glass, they are recognized as the first American company to make cameo glass, an effect they achieved through acid-cutting methods. In 1885 Shirley was issued a patent to make Burmese, pale yellow glassware tinged with a delicate pink blush. Another patent issued in 1886 allowed them the rights to produce Rose Amber, or amberina, a transparent ware shading from ruby to amber. Pearl Satin Ware and Peachblow, so named for its resemblance to a rosy peach skin, were patented the same year. One of their most famous lines, Crown Milano, was introduced in 1893. It was an opal glass either free-blown or pattern-molded, tinted a delicate color and decorated with enameling and gilt. Royal Flemish was patented in 1894 and is considered the rarest of the Mt. Washington art glass lines. It was decorated with raised, gold-enameled lines dividing the surface of the ware in much the same way as lead lines divide a stained glass window. The sections were filled in with one or several transparent colors and further decorated in gold enamel with florals, foliage, beading, and medallions.

Our advisors for this category are Betty and Clarence Maier; they are listed in the Directory under Pennsylvania. See also Amberina, Cranberry; Salt Shakers; Burmese; Crown Milano; Royal Flemish; etc.

Biscuit jar, lilacs in wht reserve on lt gr, squat, 8" dia **300.00**
Biscuit jar, yel mums on gr, paneled w/emb scrolls, SP mts **625.00**
Biscuit jar, 4 sq reserves w/portraits on gr w/gold, 10½" **385.00**

Condiment set, daisies on bl, 3-pc in Wilcox SP fr **225.00**
Creamer, emb/gilt flowers/scrolls/leaves, ribbed, SP mts **475.00**
Lamp, cameo birds/flowers, wht on yel 10" shade/bulb base **3,500.00**
Mustard jar, roses/moss on opal w/tan finish, ribbed, 2x2½" **350.00**
Pitcher, amethyst w/florals, 11½" **225.00**
Ring holder, florals, saucer base w/beaded ring stick **85.00**
Rose bowl, Verona, gold pond lilies, 6½" **295.00**
Salt shaker, pk apple blossoms on lay-down egg form **125.00**
Shakers, egg form, holly/berry/floral on yel, 2½", pr **175.00**
Shakers, floral on melon shape, orig tops, pr **150.00**
Shakers, 5 Lobe, w/decor, orig lids, pr **95.00**
Syrup, roses on wht opal, orig SP top, 5¾" **245.00**
Toothpick holder, fig shape w/mc florals, SP lids, pr **175.00**
Tumbler, cameo acanthus/arches/ovals, pk/wht, ribbed, 4¾" ..**1,100.00**
Vase, floral, mc on lt gr, slender, fluted top, 10⅝" **475.00**
Vase, floral, yel & bl on bl, scalloped egg shape, ftd, 7" **395.00**
Vase, Lava, blk w/gold/mc inclusions, stick neck, 4½" **1,750.00**
Vase, Napoli, gold floral tracery, gr flowers on rim, 5x6" **1,375.00**
Vase, Napoli, mums, gold sponging/blk enamel, T'print, 12" ..**1,600.00**

Mulberry China

Mulberry china was made by many of the Staffordshire area potters from about 1830 until the 1850s. It is a transfer-printed earthenware or ironstone named for the color of its decorations, a purplish-brown resembling the juice of the mulberry. Some pieces may have faded out over the years and today look almost gray with only a hint of purple. (Transfer printing was done in many colors; technically only those in the mauve tones are 'mulberry'; color variations have little effect on value.) Some of the patterns (Corean, Jeddo, Pelew, and Formosa, for instance) were also produced in Flow Blue ware. Others seem to have been used exclusively with the mulberry color. Our advisor for this category is Mary Frank Gaston; she is listed in the Directory under Texas.

Temple, plate, Podmore Walker, 8¾", $75.00.

Abbey, creamer, Adams **175.00**
Abbey, creamer & sugar bowl, w/lid **325.00**
Abbey, pitcher, 8-sided, 7¼" **265.00**
Athens, plate, Adams, 10½" **55.00**
Athens, platter, Meigh, 15½" **175.00**
Bluebell & Leaf, creamer **285.00**
Bochara, plate, Edwards, 10" **75.00**
Bochara, plate, Edwards, 10¾" **85.00**
Bochara, platter, Edwards, 15¼" **235.00**
Bochara, sauce tureen, w/undertray, Edwards **635.00**
Castle Scenery, pitcher, Furnival, 8" **415.00**
Castle Scenery, sugar bowl, w/lid, Furnival **275.00**

Corean, bowl & pitcher, NM 985.00
Corean, creamer 165.00
Corean, cup & saucer 75.00
Corean, cup & saucer, lg 90.00
Corean, cup plate 50.00
Corean, pitcher, 1½-pt, 6¾" 300.00
Corean, pitcher, 1½-qt, 8¾" 425.00
Corean, pitcher, 1-qt, 7¾" 400.00
Corean, plate, 7" 35.00
Corean, plate, 7¾" 45.00
Corean, plate, 8" 50.00
Corean, plate, 9" 80.00
Corean, plate, 9⅞" 88.00
Corean, platter, Podmore Walker, 13½" 225.00
Corean, platter, 15¾x12¼" 285.00
Corean, sauce boat 100.00
Corean, sauce plate, 4¼" 55.00
Corean, sugar bowl, 6-sided, w/lid 350.00
Corean, teapot, rpr 550.00
Corean, waste bowl, 4x6½" 200.00
Cyprus, creamer, Davenport 225.00
Cyprus, honey dish, 4¼" 70.00
Cyprus, plate, Davenport, 9¼" 65.00
Cyprus, platter, Davenport, 16" 275.00
Cyprus, sugar bowl, w/lid 195.00
Cyprus, teapot, 8-sided, ped ft 425.00
Dresden, pitcher, Challinor, 8¼" to spout 275.00
Flora, platter, Walker, 15⅜" 225.00
Foliage, plate, Wally, 9" 75.00
Heath's Flower, platter, 13½" 335.00
Hong, pitcher, 2-qt, 9⅞" 500.00
Hyson, sugar bowl, Clementson 275.00
Jeddo, bowl, vegetable; Gothic shape, w/lid, Adams ...535.00
Jeddo, cup & saucer, Adams 85.00
Jeddo, cup plate, Adams, 4" 65.00
Jeddo, gravy boat, Adams 175.00
Jeddo, pitcher & bowl, Adams 675.00
Jeddo, plate, Adams, 6" 35.00
Jeddo, plate, Adams, 7½" 38.00
Jeddo, sugar bowl, w/lid, Adams 230.00
Jeddo, teapot, Adams 475.00
Jeddo, waste bowl & pitcher, Adams 750.00
Kyber, cup plate 70.00
Marble, creamer, child sz 200.00
Marble, pitcher, 8" 315.00
Moresque, cake stand, Wedgwood, gilt lustre, ftd, 2½x11¾" 425.00
Nankin, bowl, vegetable; 8-sided, w/lid, Davenport, lg ...350.00
Ning-Po, creamer, Hall 275.00
Ning-Po, plate, Hall, 9½" 70.00
Ning-Po, platter, Hall, 15½" 240.00
Panama, creamer, Challinor 245.00
Pelew, bowl, vegetable; w/lid, Challinor 525.00
Pelew, bowl, vegetable; 9¼" 175.00
Pelew, plate, Challinor, 7½" 38.00
Pelew, plate, Challinor, 9¾" 80.00
Pelew, sauce plate, 4¼" 55.00
Pelew, waste bowl, Challinor, 5½" 215.00
Peruvian, cup, handleless; Wedge Wood 66.00
Peruvian, honey dish, Wedge Wood 75.00
Peruvian, pitcher, Wedge Wood, 8½" 385.00
Rhone Scenery, cup & saucer 70.00
Rhone Scenery, plate, 9¾" 75.00
Rose, creamer, Walker 285.00
Rose, fish sauce boat, hdls, Walker, rare 325.00

Rose, plate, Walker, 9½" 70.00
Rose, platter, Walker, 13½" 225.00
Strawberry, platter, rare, 12⅜x9¾" 185.00
Sydenham, platter, Clementson, 16x12⅝" 285.00
Tavoy, plate, 10" 80.00
Temple, bowl, vegetable; Podmore Walker, 7" 170.00
Temple, plate, Podmore Walker, 9¾" 80.00
Udina, platter, Clementson, 18" 195.00
Washington Vase, creamer, Podmore Walker 225.00
Washington Vase, cup & saucer, Podmore Walker 75.00
Washington Vase, plate, Podmore Walker, 6½" 40.00
Washington Vase, plate, Podmore Walker, 7¾" 45.00
Washington Vase, plate, Podmore Walker, 8½" 65.00
Washington Vase, plate, Podmore Walker, 9" 75.00
Washington Vase, plate, Podmore Walker, 10" 80.00
Washington Vase, platter, Podmore Walker, 13½x10" ...150.00
Washington Vase, sauce bowl, Podmore Walker, 5½" 35.00
Washington Vase, teapot, Podmore Walker 525.00
Washington Vase, waste bowl, Podmore Walker 200.00
Whampoa, sugar bowl 225.00

Muller Freres

Henri Muller established a factory in 1900 at Croismare, France. He produced fine cameo art glass decorated with florals, birds, and insects in the Art Nouveau style. The work was accomplished by acid engraving and hand finishing. Usual marks were 'Muller,' 'Muller Croismare,' or 'Croismare, Nancy.' In 1910 Henri and his brother Deseri formed a glassworks at Luneville. The cameo art glass made there was nearly all produced by acid cuttings of up to four layers with motifs similar to those favored at Croismare. A good range of colors was used, and some later pieces were gold flecked. Handles and decorative devices were sometimes applied by hand. In addition to the cameo glass, they also produced an acid-finished glass of bold mottled colors in the Deco style. Examples were signed 'Muller Freres' or 'Luneville.' Our advisor for this category is Don Williams; he is listed in the Directory under Missouri.

Key: fp — fire polished

Vase, large pine trees frame foggy mountain scene with waterfall, gray with pink, blue, and black, signed, 16", $6,500.00.

Cameo

Bottle, atomizer; ships/trees, 8½" 2,500.00
Bottle, scent; roses, 3-color, bud stopper, 4½" 1,325.00
Vase, blk birds on branch/water/trees, stick neck, 13" 3,000.00
Vase, blossoms/seed pod, ovoid, 5" 900.00

Vase, floral branches on orange mottle, fp, 6½" 1,100.00
Vase, forest/sun/snake, brn on yel, baluster, 11" 3,500.00
Vase, irises, gr on milky wht, flattened, fp, 6¾" 920.00
Vase, lady seated by waterway, mtns/village, bl tones, 15" 4,000.00
Vase, leaves on lava-like texture, 4" 800.00
Vase, leopards, baluster, 9" 2,500.00
Vase, lg flowers on yel, bulbous, 6½" 900.00
Vase, peonies, orange/brn on gold-tan, flared/ftd, 13½" 4,500.00
Vase, pine grove/mtns, brn on bl/amber frost, ftd, 5½" 1,200.00
Vase, pine trees/lake/mtns, classic form, 11" 4,000.00
Vase, poppies on textured opal, 4-color, trumpet form, 13½" ..4,000.00
Vase, river scene, blk/teal on 3-color ground, 8½" 1,600.00
Vase, water lilies/dragonfly/bug, gr on lt peach, 12¾" 2,500.00
Wine, violets w/gold outlines on gr texture, 5½" 1,100.00

Miscellaneous

Bowl, yel/red/bl acid finish, Luneville, 3x8" 425.00
Shade, conical, w/6 angle ribs & panels w/rings, 14" dia 290.00
Vase, bl & gr w/silver foil, Luneville, 14" 1,500.00
Vase, cased/mottled, top/base border, 8¾" 350.00
Vase, yel/red/bl acid finish, Luneville, 7" 550.00

Muncie

Muncie Pottery, established in Muncie, Indiana, by Charles O. Grafton, was produced from 1922 until about 1935. It is made of a heavier clay than most of its contemporaries; the styles are sturdy and simple. Early glazes were bright and colorful. In fact, Muncie was advertised as the 'rainbow pottery.' Later most of the ware was finished in a matt glaze. The more collectible examples are those modeled after Consolidated Glass vases — sculptured with lovebirds, grasshoppers, and goldfish. Their line of Art Deco-style vases bear a remarkable resemblance to the Consolidated Glass company's Ruba Rombic line. Vases, candlesticks, bookends, ashtrays, bowls, lamp bases, and luncheon sets were made. A line of garden pottery was manufactured for a short time. Items were frequently impressed with MUNCIE in block letters. Letters such as A, K, E, or D and the numbers 1, 2, 3, 4, or 5 often found scratched into the base are finishers' marks.

Lamp base, fan shape, Ruba Rombic, gloss dark green drip over peachskin, 8¼", $295.00.

Vase, dbl bud; gate form, matt bl/rose, 4½" 110.00
Vase, fan shape, matt gr/rose, 8" 72.50
Vase, Fish mold, gloss lt bl, 8½" 245.00
Vase, folded-brim hat, matt lt gr, 5" 125.00
Vase, Katydid mold, matt gr/rust, 6½" 187.50
Vase, molded, ruffled top, matt gr/rose, 4" 40.00
Vase, pillow form w/lovebird mold, matt gr/gr, 9" 265.00
Vase, Ruba Rombic, matt gr/lav, 6" 185.00

Vase, ruffled top, matt wht/bl, 6" 55.00
Vase, stick form, gloss bl/wht, 8" 50.00
Vase, trn, ruffled top, matt wht/pk, 4" 47.50
Wall pocket, rectangular, matt gr w/emb vines, 9" 165.00

Musical Instruments

The field of automatic musical instruments covers many different categories ranging from watches and tiny seals concealing fine early musical movements to huge organs and orchestrions which weigh many hundreds of pounds and are equivalent to small orchestras. Music boxes, first made in the early 19th-century by Swiss watchmakers, were produced in both disk and cylinder models. The latter type employs a pinned cylinder with tiny pins that lift the teeth in the comb of the music box (producing a sound much like many individual tuning forks), and music results. The value of a cylinder music box depends on the length and diameter of the cylinder, the date of its manufacture, the number of tunes it plays (four or six is *usually* better than ten or twelve), and its manufacturer. Nicole Freres, Henri Capt, LeCoultre, and Bremond are among the most highly regarded, and the larger boxes made by Mermod Freres are also popular. Examples with multiple cylinders, extra instruments (such as bells or an organ section), and those in particularly ornate cabinets or with matching tables bring significantly higher prices. While smaller cylinder boxes are still being made, the larger ones (over 10" cylinders) typically date from before 1900. Disk music boxes were introduced about 1890 but were replaced by the phonograph only twenty-five years later. However, during that time, hundreds of thousands were made. Their great advantage was in playing inexpensive interchangeable disks, a factor that remains an attraction for today's collector as well. Among the most popular disk boxes are those made by Regina (USA), Polyphon, Mira, Stella, and Symphonion. Relative values are determined by the size of the disks they play, whether they have single or double combs, if they are upright or table models, and how ornate their cases are. Especially valuable are those that play multiple disks at the same time or are incorporated into tall case clocks.

Player pianos were made in a wide variety of styles. Early varieties consisted of a mechanism which pushed up to a piano and played on the keyboard by means of felt-tipped fingers. These use sixty-five note rolls. Later models have the playing mechanism built in, and most use eighty-eight note rolls. Upright pump player pianos have little value in unrestored condition because the cost of restoration is so high. 'Reproducing' pianos, especially the 'grand' format, can be quite valuable, depending on the make, the size, the condition, and the ornateness of the case. 'Reproducing' pianos have very sophisticated mechanisms and are much more realistic in the reproduction of piano music. They were made in relatively limited quantities. Better manufacturers include Steinway and Mason & Hamlin. Popular roll mechanism makers include Ampico, Duo-Art and Welte. The market for all types of player pianos has been weak for several years.

Coin-operated pianos (Orchestrions) were used commercially and typically incorporate extra instruments in addition to the piano action. These can be very large and complex, incorporating drums, cymbals, xylophones, bells, and hundreds of pipes. Both American and European coin pianos are very popular, especially the larger and more complex models made by Wurlitzer, Seeburg, Cremona, Weber, Welte, Hupfeld and many others. These companies also made automatically playing violins (Mills Violin Virtuoso, Hupfeld), banjos (Encore) and harps (Whitlock); these are quite valuable.

Mechanical organs range all the way from parlor pump organs and roll-operated reed organs to band organs found on carousels and giant fairground and dance hall organs. Pump organs made by Estey, Willcox and others are often very ornate but also very common and bulky; as a result, the market is very limited. The more sophisticated roll-playing reed organs are collectible but still find a limited market due to the cost of restoration. They are very undervalued and have been for a long time. Carousel-type band organs, especially those made by well-known manufacturers such as Wurlitzer and Artizan, continue to sell well. The highest values are reserved for the larger Welte, Gavioli, Bruder, and other organs used in fairgrounds, dance halls, and private residences that incorporate hundreds of pipes. With a harder-to-find larger instrument, a good supply of rolls contributes much to its value, since in many cases rolls cannot be found.

Unless noted, prices given are for instruments in fine condition, playing properly, with cabinets or cases in well-preserved or refinished condition. In all instances, unrestored instruments sell for much less, as do those with broken or missing parts, damaged cases, and the like. On the other hand, particularly superb examples in especially ornate case designs and those that have been particularly well kept will often command more. Our advisor for mechanical instruments is Martin Roenigk; he is listed in the Directory under Connecticut. Fred Oster advises us on non-mechanical instruments; he is listed under Pennsylvania.

Key:

c — cylinder   d — disk

Box, inlaid rosewood with three 13" cylinders, thirty tunes, single comb, tune card, EX, $4,180.00.

Mechanical

Accordion, Tanzbar 850.00
Box, B&M Etouffoirs en Acier, 10¾" c, 6-tune 800.00
Box, Baker, Troll & Fils, 17¼" c, 12-tune, 31" case 2,400.00
Box, Criterion 15½", dbl combs, w/matching base, EX 5,500.00
Box, German Symphonion, 13¾" d, walnut veneer 22" case ...2,300.00
Box, Imperial Symphonion 17⅝" upright, 2 c, EX 7,000.00
Box, interchangeable 11" c, w/writing table, EX 6,500.00
Box, Langdorf & Fils, 17¼" c, 6-tune, 29" case 3,500.00
Box, Langdorf Longue Marche, 7 12½" c, EX 12,000.00
Box, Lochmann Orig 24½" c, tubular bells, upright, EX 18,000.00
Box, Mandoline Quatuor, 17¼" c, ornate 28" case 5,000.00
Box, Mermod Freres, 11¼" c, 2½" d, 10-tune 1,500.00
Box, Mermod Freres, 17½" c, 8-tune, 35" case 4,500.00
Box, Mermod Freres Ideal Soprano, 14¾" c, 6-tune 3,400.00
Box, Mermod Freres Interchangeable, 4 13" c, rprs/rstr 5,000.00
Box, Nicole Freres, 13¼" c, 8-tune, ebony wood case 1,700.00
Box, Nicole Freres (att), 10¾" c, 6-tune, VG 1,300.00
Box, Perfection 14" single comb, 4 d, EX orig 1,800.00
Box, Regina, 11" d, oak case, VG, +16 d 1,100.00
Box, Regina, 12" d, mahog cabinet 1,600.00

Box, Regina, 15½" d, curved front, changer, oak case, EX 16,500.00
Box, Regina, 15½" d, cvd mahog case, 10½x21x19", +60 d 5,700.00
Box, Regina, 15½" d, single comb, pinstriped case, EX 2,400.00
Box, Regina, 20¾" d, dbl comb, oak desk case, ca 1910 ....12,000.00
Box, Regina, 20¾" d, walnut 29" case 4,500.00
Box, Regina, 27" d, 2 c, eng mahog case 8,000.00
Box, Regina, 27"d, oak folding-top style, rstr 9,500.00
Box, Stella, 17¼" d, table model, dbl comb, mahog case, EX ..5,000.00
Box, Stella Concert, 15½" d, w/table 4,000.00
Box, Swiss, sewing necessaire, 2½" c, single comb, 1830s 2,200.00
Box, Swiss, 11⅛" c, 3-tune, key wind, 1850s 1,700.00
Box, Swiss, 12⅞" c, 4-tune, ca 1850, 21" case 1,600.00
Box, Swiss, 13" c, 6-tune, Louis XV case, 43x29" 2,000.00
Box, Swiss, 6½" c, 3-tune, veneer case, 21" case 850.00
Box, Swiss, 7¼" c, single comb, fruitwood case, 1830s 1,400.00
Box, Swiss Bells & Drum in Sight, 13" c, 8-tune, 24" 2,400.00
Box, Swiss Flutes Voix Celestes, 11" c, 6-tune, 20¾" 2,200.00
Box, Swiss Sublime Harmony, 8⅛" c, dbl comb, 17" case 1,100.00
Box, Swiss Sublime Harmony Piccolo Zither, 18½" c, 10-tune ..3,700.00
Box, Symphonium, 17⅝" d, table model, dbl comb, mahog case ...5,800.00
Box, Troll & Baker, 13 c, brass & silver inlay, 9 bells, EX 55,000.00
Calliope, Tangley, roll operated, EX 7,500.00
Nickelodeon, Capital, oak case w/violin pipes & rolls, EX 8,000.00
Nickelodeon, Coinola CX, walnut case, w/xylophone, EX orig ..7,000.00
Nickelodeon, Seeburg A, EX orig 3,500.00
Nickelodeon, Seeburg C, oak w/beveled glass panels, EX orig .5,000.00
Nickelodeon, Seeburg E, w/xylophone, rstr 10,500.00
Nickelodeon, Seeburg G look-alike, EX orig 11,000.00
Nickelodeon, Seeburg K, w/flute pipes, EX orig 12,000.00
Nickelodeon, Seeburg K, w/xylophone, eagle front 12,000.00
Nickelodeon, Seeburg L, EX orig 6,000.00
Nickelodeon, Wurlitzer CX, Grecian style, rstr 23,500.00
Orchestrelle, Aeolian, heavily cvd mahog, EX orig 2,000.00
Orchestrelle, Aeolian V, oak, EX orig 3,500.00
Orchestrelle, Aeolian W, EX, +200 rolls 4,900.00
Orchestrion, Coinola C-2, EX 27,000.00
Orchestrion, Cremona J, rstr 45,000.00
Orchestrion, Seeburg G, NM 55,000.00
Orchestrion, Wurlitzer B, EX orig 2,750.00
Organ, band; Artizan, 46-key, +15 rolls 16,000.00
Organ, band; Wellershaus, 56-key/191 pipes/2 drums, 1875 ..18,000.00
Organ, band; Wurlitzer #146, rstr 18,000.00
Organ, band; Wurlitzer #153, rstr 40,000.00
Organ, concert; Cabinetto, walnut case w/gilt, 17½" 550.00
Organ, dance; Arburo, rstr 15,000.00
Organ, dance; Bursen, rstr 17,500.00
Organ, Dutch street; Limonaire, 34-key, w/music book/1 figure ..22,000.00
Organ, fairground; Gavioli, 65-key, 240 pipes, EX 42,000.00
Organ, monkey; Molinari, 26-key, EX 4,000.00
Organ, monkey; Molinari, 47-key, w/orig cart, EX 17,500.00
Organ, Nelson Wiggins style 8, rstr 11,000.00
Organ, Wilcox & Wht Symphony, oak, w/shutters, rstr 1,500.00
Organette, Organina, walnut case, paper rolls 375.00
Piano, grand; Ampico, art case, 74", EX orig 22,000.00
Piano, grand; Chickering Ampico #65, 77", EX orig 16,000.00
Piano, grand; Knabe Ampico, 62", EX orig 1,200.00
Piano, grand; Marshall & Wendall Ampico, 60", EX orig 1,200.00
Piano, grand; Steinway Louis XV Duo-Art XR, mahog, 73", rstr ..18,500.00
Piano, grand; Wurlitzer Recordo, retubed, rfn, 56" 1,500.00
Piano, push-up; Harrand Cecilian, EX 500.00
Piano, upright; Ampico B, Marshall & Wendall, EX 2,200.00
Piano, upright; Ampico Marshall & Wendall, rstr 3,700.00
Piano, upright; Charles Steiff Welte, M orig 1,200.00
Piano, upright; Chickering Ampico, EX orig 1,500.00

Piano, upright; George Steck Duo-Art, EX 1,400.00
Piano, upright; Steinway Duo-Art, rstr 6,000.00
Piano/pipe organ, Reproduco, EX orig 6,500.00
Piano/pipe organ, Reproduco, orig Seeburg Swan Glass, rstr ...9,500.00
Pianocorder, Marantz, w/50 cassettes, EX 3,000.00
Violano-Virtuoso, Mills, oak case, ca 1920 ....18,000.00

Non-Mechanical

Banjo, J Rickett, 5-string, w/inlay, 1890s, EX 575.00
Banjo, SS Stewart Orchestra #2c, 5-string, inlay, ca 1892, EX .1,250.00
Banjo, Vega Senator, 5-string, 1929, 11" rim, EX 750.00
Baritone horn, Fr, brass, 3 piston valves, ca 1885, EX 150.00
Baritone horn, Pierre Sartel, SP, 3 piston valves, EX 200.00
Bass horn, B Barrett, ca 1790, EX 2,000.00
Cornet, Imperial London, brass, 3 piston valves, 1890s, EX 60.00
Dulcimer, Pennsylvania German, hammered, 1800s 450.00
Fife, Crosby, rosewood, NP ferrules, 12", EX 60.00
Flute, AR Jollie, cocuswood, nickel keys, pewter plugs, 18", VG .450.00
Flute, C Peloubet, cocuswood, ivory mts, silver keys, 21", EX 600.00
Flute, Firth Hall & Pond, cocuswood, ivory mts & cap, 21" 600.00
Flute, unstamped Am, boxwood, bone mts, brass key, 1835, 17" .175.00
Flute, Wm Hall & Son, boxwood, ivory mts, less end cap, 21" ...500.00
French horn, C Mahillon Brussels, brass, 3 piston valves, EX 650.00
Guitar, CF Martin #4-21, ca 1880, w/orig wood coffin case, EX .1,000.00
Guitar, Gibson LG-1c, sunburst, flat top, 1948, VG 275.00
Guitar, Martin D-18, flat top, rpl bridge, 1944, EX+case 3,400.00
Guitar, Martin 0-18T Tenor, 1953, G- 350.00
Guitar, Martin 00-21, flat top, 1963, VG+, w/soft case 1,800.00
Guitar, steel; Epiphone Electar Zephyr, '40s, w/case & pedal 375.00
Guitar, steel; Gibson Model BR-4, sunburst, mahog, 1946, EX ..300.00
Piano, grand; Kurtzmann, 1885, EX orig 6,000.00
Piano, upright; J Browne London, burled walnut, 1870s, EX ...1,800.00
Piano, upright; Steinway Ampico, mahog case, 1911, rstr 12,000.00
Soprano uke, Hawaiian, koa body, EX 160.00
Tiple, Martin T-17, 1931, G 400.00
Tuba, I Stowasser, brass & German silver, ca 1855, EX 850.00
Violin, Am, baroque neck, pnt-on stars, early 1800s, child's 300.00
Violin, Am, orig baroque setup, early 1800s 300.00
Violin, CW Gates VT, ivory inlay, 1935, orig case 250.00
Zither, Am Concert, floral marquetry, ca 1890s 350.00

Mustache Cups

Mustache cups were popular items during the late Victorian period, designed specifically for the man with the mustache! They were made in silverplate as well as china and ironstone. Decorations ranged from simple transfers to elaborately applied and gilded florals. To properly position the 'mustache bar,' special cups were designed for the 'lefties.' These are the rare ones!

Clydesdale mare & gold w/gold, left handed 125.00
Floral, HP w/much gold on wht, #d, 3¾" 70.00
Floral spray w/pk ribbon, decaled, scrolled blank & hdl 36.00
Oriental motif, HP, 2¾x3", +saucer 55.00
Pk lustre w/gold leaves 55.00
SP, cut/beaded decor, Eureka Silver, 1901, +saucer 115.00
SP, floral eng, Barbour, EX 75.00

Nailsea

Nailsea is a term referring to clear or colored glass decorated in contrasting spatters, swirls, or loops. These are usually white but may also be pink, red or blue. It was first produced in Nailsea, England, during the late 1700s but was made in other parts of Britain and Scotland as well. During the mid-1800s a similar type of glass was produced in this country. Originally used for decorative novelties only, by that time tumblers and other practical items were being made from Nailsea-type glass. See also Lamps; Witch Balls.

Bottle, bellows; wht w/rose loopings, rigaree, 11" 245.00
Creamer, aqua opaque w/rose & bl loopings, pour spout, 4⅜" 385.00
Flask, clear w/wht loopings, pontil scar, 7¾" 55.00
Flask, cobalt w/wht loopings, 7¼" 245.00
Flask, cranberry red cased w/wht loopings, 6⅞" 175.00
Flask, orange/wht striping, molded swirl below neck, 6x4½" 80.00
Flask, wht w/pk loopings, 8" 210.00
Flask, wht w/red & bl loopings, 7½" 285.00
Tumbler, wht w/rose loopings, 4" 95.00
Vase, clear w/wht loopings, 7¾" 150.00

Nakara

Nakara was a line of decorated opaque milk glass produced by the C.F. Monroe Company of Meriden, Connecticut, for a few years after the turn of the century. It differs from their Wave Crest line in several ways. The shapes were simpler; pastel colors were deeper and covered more of the surface; more beading was present; flowers were larger; and large transfer prints of figures, Victorian ladies, cherubs, etc., were used. Ormolu and brass collars and mounts complemented these opulent pieces. Most items were signed; however, this is not important since the ware was never reproduced. Our advisors for this category are Dolli and Wilfred R. Cohen; their address is listed in the Directory under California.

Ashtray, floral on gr hexagonal bowl, ormolu mts, sm 200.00
Bonbon, geometric scrolls & beads, ormolu collar, mk 475.00

Bonbon, pink florals on green, tiny white flowers on yellow sections, open type with handle, 6½", $400.00.

Box, cartouch of 2 ladies in garden on gr, 8½" 1,395.00
Box, Collars & Cuffs; lilies on pnt 'burmese' coloring 1,750.00
Box, Crown mold, peonies on moss gr, 8½" dia 1,350.00
Box, dk bl & tan w/wht beading, hexagonal, hinged, 4" dia 470.00
Box, ferns in gr/gold on shaded bl, 3" H 300.00
Box, floral on moss gr, mirror in lid, 4½" dia 575.00
Box, Greenaway figures & beading, unemb form, 6" dia 895.00
Box, lady's portrait, rococo, mk, 5½x8¼" 1,395.00
Box, lady's portrait on gr, beaded border, 4½" dia 695.00
Box, roses, red & wht on pk & gr, bl & wht beads, mk, 6" dia 635.00
Hair receiver, children have tea, wht beadwork, dmn shape 585.00

Humidor, frog reading newspaper on bl, metal lid, 6¾" 1,050.00
Match holder, floral on pk, ormolu rim & hdls 325.00
Tray, daises/scrolls, hexagonal, metal rim, 4" 200.00
Vase, daisies in pk fr, lav/tan Nouveau decor, cylindrical, 11" 875.00
Vase, iris, purple on burnt orange, ftd, 13½" 1,050.00

Napkin Rings

Napkin rings became popular during the late 1800s. They were made from various materials. Among the most popular and collectible today are the large group of varied silverplated figurals made by American manufacturers. Recently the larger figurals in excellent condition have appreciated considerably. Only those with a blackened finish, corrosion, or broken and/or missing parts have maintained their earlier price levels. When no condition is indicated, the items listed below are assumed to be all original and in very good to excellent condition. Check very carefully for missing parts, solder repairs, or marriages.

A timely warning: inexperienced buyers should be aware of excellent reproductions on the market, especially the wheeled pieces. However, these do not have the fine detail and patina of the originals and tend to have a more consistent, soft pewter-like finish. These are appearing at the large, quality shows at top prices, being shown along with authentic antique merchandise. Beware!

Key:
gw — gold washed   SH&M — Simpson, Hall, &
R&B — Reed & Barton   Miller

Acorn & leaf ea side of ring on rnd base, Toronto #129 ....60.00
Boy beside ring removing shoes & shocks, Derby 375.00
Boy in harness pulls wheeled ring 400.00

Boy stealing eggs from nest atop ring, bird on oval base, Meriden #274, 2¼", $395.00.

Bud vase atop ring resting on rnd base w/flowers, Webster #168 ...125.00
Bud vase w/spout atop ring, sailor w/anchor, R&B #1357 ....300.00
Bulldog stands before ring 225.00
Cat pulls wheeled base that supports ring 425.00
Cat w/glass eyes sits, decor ring in body, Meriden #4210 ....400.00
Cherries on branch lean against ring on lg leafy base 150.00
Cherub (lg) beside bbl ring on branch base 300.00
Cherub on wild turtle, stationary wheels, ring on top, SH&M ...400.00
Cherub paints ring, leafy base, Middletown #113 ....200.00
Cherub sits ea side of bbl-shaped ring, Meriden #147 ....150.00
Cherub w/feather in hat sits atop ring 225.00
Cherubs (2) on fancy base, Webster #170 ....200.00
Chick by ornate ring on wishbone 75.00
Deer stands by ring on leafy base, flower at side 80.00
Deer w/forelegs on ring, rectangular base, Acme 85 ....225.00

Dog ea side of ring on trunk base, bird atop, Meriden #366 ....200.00
Dog w/glass eyes sits & holds bone, Tufts 350.00
Draped lady w/torch bud base beside ring, R&B #1365 ....500.00
Eagle ea side of ring, Meriden 70.00
Eagle w/wings spread, ring on bk, Rogers #203 ....475.00
Egyptian kneels & holds ring behind, R&B #1508 ....175.00
Fairy w/butterfly, Wilcox #2206 ....220.00
Fan ea side of butterfly under ring, sq base, Meriden 75.00
Flower at side of ring on leafy base 60.00
Fox ea side of oblong base, Meriden 250.00
Fox ea side of ring, Rockford #174 ....275.00
Frog rests on ring, rocky base 125.00
Giraffe under palm, rectangular base, Racine #145 ....350.00
Girl by bbl-shape ring w/in branches w/owl family, #205 ....500.00
Goat by 6-sided ring 125.00
Goat in harness pulls wheeled ring, Meriden #214 ....400.00
Greenaway baby on chair & baby in canoe on fork-shape base ..400.00
Greenaway boy & girl by fence, rectangular base, JW Tufts 375.00
Greenaway boy by fence, raised base, Tufts #1593 ....350.00
Greenaway boy feeds dog on rectangular base, Meriden #199 ....450.00
Greenaway boy on wooden horse w/stick & reins, Derby #378 ...245.00
Greenaway boy w/bat & ball before ring 475.00
Greenaway boy w/drumstick on hands & knees, ring on bk, #243 .350.00
Greenaway girl climbs ring, goose pecks from behind 250.00
Greenaway girl pushes boy on sled, sq holder, SH&M #037 ....350.00
Horse prances w/ring on bk, leafy base, ftd 185.00
Horse rearing/pulling wheeled ring, Meriden #219 ....550.00
Lily pad, curved hdl on eng base, Meriden #168 ....60.00
Lion reclines w/ring on bk 150.00
Man in top hat w/cane, 8-sided base, Wilcox #4300 ....165.00
Mastiff dog w/paw on ball, rectangular base 250.00
Oriental fans ea side w/bee beneath ring, Meriden #208 ....150.00
Owl & violin on base next to fancy ring, Wilcox 350.00
Owl on branch over ring, #028 on base 250.00
Peacock sits atop decor ring, Meriden #151 ....295.00
Pear & leaf ea side of ring 150.00
Rabbit sitting on 8-sided base 120.00
Rip Van Winkle w/rifle, bbl ring on bk, dog beside, Meriden 895.00
Rooster beside ring, Rogers #11 ....125.00
Sailor boy leans on ring on top of anchor, SH&M #706 ....425.00
Sailor boy on triangle base w/poles behind, Tufts #2590 ....350.00
Sailor boy w/ring on his bk 325.00
Sailor boy w/rope & anchor beside ring & bud vase, R&B 600.00
Squirrel w/glass eyes blows horn 185.00
Stork harnessed to fancy cart w/ring, SH&M, 6" L 600.00
Strawberry hanging from ring on leafy base 60.00
Wheelbarrow on shield base 225.00

Nash

A. Douglas Nash founded the Corona Art Glass Company in Long Island, New York. He produced tableware, vases, flasks, etc., using delicate artistic shapes and forms. After 1933 he worked for the Libbey Glass Company.

Bowl, Chintz, bl swags w/gr, 2¾x4¼" 200.00
Bowl, gold w/bl highlights, ruffled, 2⅜x3" 95.00
Bowl, raised 'veins,' gold irid w/bl highlights, 2½x3" 350.00
Compote, gold Favrille, scalloped, low ft, sgn, 3¼x6¼" 475.00
Cordial, Chintz, red w/silver stripes, sgn, 6 for 950.00
Vase, amber, Cypriot type, trumpet neck, 9" 500.00
Vase, Chintz, red w/silver stripes, wide body, mk/#d, 5½" 975.00
Vase, mold-blown decor w/gold irid, disk ft, #544, 4", pr 750.00

Natzler, Gertrude and Otto

The Natzlers came to the United States from Vienna in the late 1930s. They settled in Los Angeles where they continued their work in ceramics, for which they were already internationally recognized. Gertrude created the forms; Otto formulated a variety of interesting glazes, among them volcanic, crystalline, and lustre. Our advisor for this category is Abby Malowanczyk; she is listed in the Directory under Texas.

Bowl, canary yel gloss, shallow, sgn, 5", pr 550.00
Bowl, copper w/gr & purple highlights, shallow, 5" 180.00
Bowl, pk/bl/purple/tan mc, shallow, 4" 250.00
Bowl, yel over slightly ribbed natural tan, rim folded, 4" H 975.00
Vase, bl/gold crystalline matt, bulbous, 4½" 700.00
Vase, canary yel, flaring cylinder, sgn, 6¾" 1,300.00
Vase, dk yel gloss w/touches of yel, flaring form, 4x8" 900.00
Vase, thick bl/gr on dk brn clay, flattened form, 4x6x9" 950.00

New England Glass Works

Founded in 1818 by Deming Jarves in Boston, Massachussetts, the New England Glass Company produced cut, blown three-mold, free-blown, and pressed glass of the highest quality. They were recognized for their fine decorative accomplishments, using etching, gilding, and engraving to emphasize their wares. For more than fifty years, they produced prize-winning pressed glass dinnerware sets. Because they refused to compromise the quality of their product by using the cheaper lime-based glass that flooded the market in the 1860s, the company fell into financial trouble and by 1877 was forced to close. However, William Libbey, who had been the sales manager there since 1870, leased the premises and resumed operations with his father, Edward Drummond Libbey, as full partner. In 1892 the firm became known as The Libbey Glass Company. See also Amberina; Libbey.

Bottle, scent; Buttons & Panels, cruciform stopper, 6" 375.00
Candlestick, crucifix shape, canary, pinpoint flakes, 9¾" 120.00
Lamp, milk glass, monument base w/emb lion & flowers, 7¼" 800.00
Mug, eng initials & wreath, swirl ribs at base, appl ft, 4¾" 1,550.00

New Geneva

In the early years of the 19th century, several potteries flourished in the Greensboro, Pennsylvania, area. They produced utilitarian stoneware items as well as tile and novelties for many decades. All failed well before the turn of the century.

Flowerpot, brown florals and foliage with scallops and dots on grayish red clay, attached saucer base, 8½", NM, $850.00.

Flowerpot, attached base, 2 names & floral in brn, 8", EX 550.00
Jar, red clay w/brn floral & foliage, appl hdls, 10", NM 795.00
Pitcher, brushed floral in Albany slip on tan clay, chips, 6" 275.00
Pitcher, brushed floral in Albany slip on tan clay, 7¾" 525.00
Pitcher, brushed floral on gray clay, 6½", NM 525.00
Pitcher, detailed brn-brushed floral on red clay, 5¾" 675.00

New Martinsville

The New Martinsville Glass Company took its name from the town in West Virginia where it began operations in 1901. In the beginning years, pressed tablewares were made in crystal as well as colored and opalescent glass. Considered an innovator, the company was known for their imaginative applications of the medium in creating lamps made entirely of glass, vanity sets, figural decanters, and models of animals and birds. In 1944 the company was purchased by Viking Glass, who continued to use many of the old molds, the animals molds included. They marked their wares 'Viking' or 'Rainbow Art.' Viking recently ceased operations and has been purchased by Kenneth Dalzell, President of the Fostoria Company. They, too, are making the bird and animal models. Although at first they were not marked, future productions are to be marked with an acid stamp. Dalzell/Viking animals are in the $50.00 to $60.00 range. Values for cobalt and red items are two to three times higher than for the same item in clear. See also Depression Glass; Glass Animals and Figurines.

Banana boat, Janice, red, low ft, 12" 125.00
Basket, Janice, 8¼" 60.00
Bookends, lady's head, pr 200.00
Bottle, scent; Geneva, w/blk stopper 40.00
Bowl, Prelude, ruffled, lg 45.00
Candlesticks, dbl; Florentine etch, #4429, pr 35.00
Champagne, Prelude 22.00
Cordial, Prelude 37.00
Creamer, Georgian, gr, 4" 16.00
Creamer & sugar bowl, Janice, lt bl 55.00
Cup & saucer, Janice, lt bl 17.00
Goblet, Mt Vernon, red, golf-ball stem, 6" 9.00
Pitcher, Oscar, amber, +2 tumblers 40.00
Pitcher, Oscar, red, +2 tumblers 90.00
Plate, luncheon; Radiance, amber, 8" 12.00
Plate, luncheon; Radiance, red, 8" 80.00
Plate, sandwich; Prelude, 14" 45.00
Punch cup, Mardi Gras 10.00
Tumbler, Addie, blk, ftd, 4¾" 12.00
Tumbler, iced tea; Prelude, ftd 30.00
Tumbler, Oscar, amber, platinum trim 5.50
Vanity set, 2 bottles, puff box & triangular tray, bl 120.00
Wine, Hostmaster, red, 4x2½" 14.00

Newcomb

The Newcomb College of New Orleans, Louisiana, established a pottery in 1895 to provide the students with first-hand experience in the fields of art and ceramics. Using locally dug clays — red and buff in the early years, white-burning by the turn of the century — potters were employed to throw the ware which the ladies of the college decorated. Until about 1910 a glossy glaze was used on ware decorated by slip painting or incising. After that a matt glaze was favored. Soft blues and greens were used almost exclusively, and decorative themes were chosen to reflect the beauty of the South. 1930 marked the end of the matt-glaze period and the art-pottery era.

Various marks used by the pottery include an 'N' within a 'C,' sometimes with 'HB' added to indicate a 'hand-built' piece. The potter often incised his initials into the ware, and the artists were encouraged to sign their work. Among the most well-known artists were Sadie Irvine, Henrietta Bailey, and Fannie Simpson.

Newcomb pottery is evaluated to a large extent by two factors: design and condition. In the following listings, items are assumed matt unless noted otherwise. Our advisor for this category is Dave Rago; he is listed in the Directory under New Jersey.

Vase, thistles, green and blue on dark and light blues, signed MI, 1902, 8½x5", $10,500.00; Bowl, flowers, light blue and yellow on dark blue gloss, Leona Nicholson, 1908, 2x5¾", $3,250.00; Tile, nasturtium band, yellow with green vines on light blue, Desiree Roman, 1904, 5¾" diameter, $2,200.00.

Bowl, floral, AF Simpson, incurvate rim, early, 3½" 600.00
Bowl, floral, wht on lt bl w/dk bl rim, Horner, 2x6" 750.00
Bowl, irises/foliage on shoulder, Irvine, 1924, 4½x6¾" 1,000.00
Bowl, sm floral band on bl to violet, Irvine, 1919, 2x8" 800.00
Pitcher, wide crocus band, glossy, Benson, 8½" 4,000.00
Tile, house in landscape, Irvine, 1910, 4¾" dia 1,500.00
Tile, sailing ship, bl/ivory gloss, H Bailey, 1902, 5¾" 600.00
Vase, arrow leaves/long-stem flowers, Roman, early, 9x3½" 5,000.00
Vase, blk/gr/brn drip glaze, flaring toward base, early, 11" 800.00
Vase, cvd leaf base band, glossy, Roman, 1903, hairline, 7x4"...1,100.00
Vase, daffodils at top, flared cylinder, EX art, Irvine, 11" 2,500.00
Vase, dk gr matt drip over emerald matt, Meyer, 5x4" 350.00
Vase, floral, wht w/gr stems on bl, Simpson, 1910, 4¾x3" 1,400.00
Vase, floral at rim band, Irvine, ovoid, 4½" 500.00
Vase, floral at shoulder, purple/rose/gr on rose, Irvine, 8" 1,400.00
Vase, floral ribs, gr/cream on bl, Irvine, 6x6" 1,400.00
Vase, full-length trees, gr/bl/purple, Irvine, 14" 4,750.00
Vase, gr matt w/brn drip, sgn JM, imp mk, 5" 300.00
Vase, indistinct floral, Irvine, ovoid, 5½" 700.00
Vase, irises/leaves cvd on gr matt, hdls, Palfrey, '09, 4x5" 600.00
Vase, leaves, gr on lt bl, MC Chalaron, 1919, 8½x3" 1,600.00
Vase, lg upright thistles, cvd/cut bk, sgn MI, 1902, 9x5"........11,000.00
Vase, long-stem floral, Bailey, 1915, 7x3¾" 2,800.00
Vase, long-stem narcissus, slim/concave, Mason, 1913, 11" 3,500.00
Vase, moon/moss/oak trees, EX color/cvg, Irvine, 1927, 9x4" .3,000.00
Vase, moon/moss/trees, EX art, Irvine, 1918, 7½x3½" 3,250.00
Vase, moon/moss/trees, Irvine, 5x4" 1,500.00
Vase, moon/moss/trees, Irvine, 6½" 2,000.00
Vase, moon/moss/trees, Simpson, flared cylinder, 1922, 7" 1,800.00
Vase, moss/oak trees, 1923, 8¾x3½" 2,500.00

Vase, olive gloss on red clay, 3½" 200.00
Vase, pine cones/needles at shoulder, Bailey, 1929, 5x4" 1,400.00
Vase, sm floral at top, EX art, Simpson, #223, 9x3½" 2,250.00
Vase, stylized blossoms on dk bl, Irvine, 1932, 2x2¼" 700.00
Vase, stylized floral/leaves, Irvine, 1925, 4½x2" 800.00
Vase, stylized flowers HP on cream, Sliger, 1901, 5x6" 3,500.00

Newspapers

In addition to historic content, there are other factors that can add or take away from the value of an old newspaper. These factors are: whether or not the account is a 'first report' (the first time that the news appeared — a 'later-report' is a subsequent reporting); location of articles on the event (those with front-page articles are more highly valued); displayability (size of headlines, presence of photos or graphics to illustrate the event, etc.); whether the paper is from a small or large town; a daily or weekly; and charisma of the paper or event. Prices listed here are for a typical mid-sized town paper with front-page coverage and medium-size headlines.

Papers that do not cover a specific event are called 'atmosphere' newspapers. While these are not as valuable, they offer interesting insight into a particular era through ads for runaway slaves, ships' schedules, jobs wanted, etc. Many have interesting articles on topics such as mermaids, hangings, sea voyages, and a host of other topics.

For a more complete price guide and information on how to determine values as well as how to grade historic newspapers, detect reprints, where to buy and sell originals and much more, the Newspaper Collectors Society of America offers a *Free Mini-Course About Historic Newspapers*. To obtain your copy of the 24-page primer and extensive price guide, send $1.00 and an SASE to NCSA, Box 19134-S, Lansing, MI 48901. From it you will learn, for instance, how to recognize the original April 15, 1865, *New York Herald* version of the report of Lincoln's assassination from among the thousands of reprints which abound today. This booklet could save collectors from making bad investments and prevent dealers from loosing their honest reputation. Our advisor for this category is Rick Brown; his name, address, and phone number are listed in the Directory under Michigan.

1784-1799, Atmosphere papers 30.00
1800-1820, Atmosphere papers 8.00
1821-1859, Atmosphere papers 6.00
1861, Civil War opens, first Confederate reports 250.00
1861, Civil War opens, first Union reports 125.00
1861, Civil War opens, later Confederate reports 150.00
1861, Civil War opens, later Union reports 40.00
1861-1865, Atmosphere papers, Confederate 125.00
1861-1865, Atmosphere papers, Union 8.00
1861-1865, Major battles of Civil War, Confederate titles 250.00
1861-1865, Major battles of Civil War, first Union reports 75.00
1861-1865, Major battles of Civil War, later Union reports 35.00
1862, Emancipation Proclamation 135.00
1863, Battle of Gettysburg, first Union reports 125.00
1863, Battle of Gettysburg, later Union reports 60.00
1863, Gettysburg address 200.00
1865, Capture & death of J Wilkes Booth 115.00
1865, End of Civil War, first Union reports 125.00
1865, End of Civil War, later Union reports 60.00
1865, Fall of Richmond 175.00
1865, Harper's Weekly, Apr 29 edition 250.00
1865, Leslie's Illustrated Newspaper, Apr 29 edition 300.00
1865, Lincoln assassination, NY Herald, Apr 15 ....900.00
1865, Lincoln assassination, other titles, first reports 200.00

1865, Lincoln assassination, other titles, funeral reports 50.00
1866-1900, Atmosphere papers 4.00
1871, Chicago fire, Chicago paper, first reports 75.00
1871, Chicago fire, later reports 35.00
1876, Custer's Last Stand, first reports 200.00
1876, Custer's Last Stand, later reports 75.00
1881, Billy the Kid killed 200.00
1881, Garfield assassinated 50.00
1881, Gunfight at OK Corral 250.00
1882, Jesse James killed, first reports 225.00
1882, Jesse James killed, later reports 75.00
1892, Lizzie Borden crime & trial 40.00
1898, Sinking of Maine 40.00
1898, Spanish American War begins 20.00
1898, Spanish American War ends 30.00
1900-1945, Atmosphere papers 3.00
1901, McKinley assassinated 65.00
1903, Wright Brother's flight, front page 250.00
1906, San Francisco earthquake, other titles 30.00
1906, San Francisco earthquake, San Francisco paper 350.00
1912, Sinking of Titanic, first reports 350.00
1912, Sinking of Titanic, later reports 75.00
1914, WWI begins 25.00
1915, Lusitania sunk, first reports 75.00
1917, US declares war 30.00
1918, Armistice 40.00
1927, Babe Ruth hits 60th home run 75.00
1927, Lindbergh in Paris, first reports 75.00
1927, Lindbergh in Paris, later reports 30.00
1929, St Valentine's Day Massacre 135.00
1929, Stock Market crash 100.00
1931, Jack 'Legs' Diamond killed 28.00
1932, Lindbergh baby found dead 65.00
1933, Machine Gun Kelley captured 30.00
1934, Baby Face Nelson killed 35.00
1934, Bonnie & Clyde killed 135.00
1934, Dillinger killed 100.00
1934, Pretty Boy Floyd killed 30.00
1935, Will Rogers & Wiley Post in plane crash 35.00
1937, Hindenbergh explodes, first reports 65.00
1937, Hindenbergh explodes, later reports 35.00
1939-1945, Major battles in the war 25.00
1941, Pearl Harbor attacked, Honolulu Star-Bulletin (+) 850.00
1941, Pearl Harbor attacked, Dec 8 issues, first reports 30.00
1941, Pearl Harbor attacked, other titles w/lg headlines 35.00
1944, D-Day 30.00
1945, FDR dies 20.00
1945, First atomic bomb dropped 30.00
1945, VE-Day or VJ-Day 30.00
1948, Dewey Defeats Truman, Chicago Daily Tribune 800.00
1950, US enters Korean War 20.00
1957, Soviets launch Sputnik 10.00
1958, Alaska joins Union 15.00
1959, Hawaii joins Union 15.00
1962, Death of Marilyn Monroe 30.00
1962, John Glenn orbits Earth 18.00
1963, JFK assassination, Nov 22, Dallas title 75.00
1963, JFK assassination, Nov 22 or 23, other titles 15.00
1968, Bobby Kennedy assassination 15.00
1968, Martin Luther King assassination 22.00
1969, Moon landing 18.00
1974, Nixon resigns 15.00
1977, Death of Elvis, Memphis paper 30.00
1986, Challenger explodes 6.00

Nicodemus

Chester Nicodemus moved from Dayton, Ohio, to Columbus in 1930 and started teaching at the Columbus Art School. During this time he made vases and commissioned sculptures, water fountains, and limestone and wood carvings. In 1941 Chester left the field of teaching to pursue pottery making full time, using local red clay containing a large amount of iron. Known for its durability, he called the ware Ferro-stone. He made teapots and other utility wares, but these goods lost favor, so he started producing animal and bird sculptures, nativity sets, and Christmas ornaments, some bearing Chester's and Florine's names as personalized cards for his customers and friends. Chester died in 1990.

His glaze colors were turquoise or aqua, ivory, green mottle, (pink) pussy willow, and golden yellow. The glaze was applied so that the color of the warm red clay would show through, adding an extra dimension to each piece. Examples are usually marked with his name incised in the clay, but paper labels were also used. Our advisor for this category is James Riebel; he is listed in the Directory under Ohio.

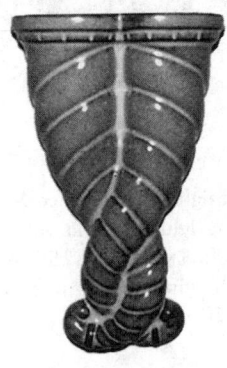

Wall pocket, double cornucopia, $350.00.

Ashtray, fraternity, 4" 25.00
Bookends, camel, pr 400.00
Bookends, dryad (kneeling nude), pr 250.00
Christmas card 100.00
Christmas decoration 40.00
Coffeepot, ind 100.00
Figurine, bull, 7" 275.00
Figurine, cardinal 250.00
Figurine, collie, 6" 150.00
Figurine, dachshund 150.00
Figurine, kangaroo 250.00
Figurine, Madonna of the Flowers 150.00
Figurine, robin, 4½" 175.00
Figurine, St Francis, w/bowl 300.00
Figurine, St Francis, w/stand, no bowl, 14" 450.00
Nativity set, 9-pc 500.00
Pitcher, bl, 3" 50.00
Pitcher, mustard, sm 50.00
Planter, elephant 55.00
Pottery festival ornament, 1986-87, ea 50.00
Vase, hdls, 4" 125.00
Vase, mauve, hdls, w/sticker, 4" 160.00
Vase, w/fish & sea horse 400.00
Water fountain, boy w/frog, 21" 3,500.00

Niloak

During the latter part of the 1800s, there were many small utilitarian potteries in Benton, Arkansas. By 1900 only the Hyten Brothers Pottery remained. Charles Hyten, a second generation potter, took control of the family business around 1902. Shortly thereafter he renamed it the Eagle Pottery Company. In 1909 Hyten and former Rookwood potter Arthur Dovey began experimentation on a new swirl pottery. Dovey previously worked for the Ouachita Pottery Company of Hot Springs and produced a swirl pottery there as early as 1906. In March 1910 the Eagle Pottery Company introduced Niloak, kaolin spelled backwards. During 1911 Benton businessmen formed the Niloak Pottery corporation. Niloak, connected to the Arts and Crafts Movement and known as 'mission' ware, had a national representative in New York by 1913. Niloak's production centered on art pottery characterized by accidental, swirling patterns of natural and artificially colored clays. Many companies through the years have produced swirl pottery, yet none achieved the technical and aesthetic qualities of Niloak. Hyten received a patent in 1928 for the swirl technique. Although most examples have an interior glaze, some early Mission Ware pieces have an exterior glaze as well; these are extremely rare. Swirl/Mission Ware production continued steadily until the Depression when hard times and sagging sales caused Hyten to produce more traditional wares. In 1931 Niloak introduced Hywood Art Pottery, a glazed ware (sometimes similar in shape to Weller's Nile) of mostly hand-thrown vases. Soon thereafter, Niloak introduced castware as its primary production and renamed the line Hywood by Niloak. Throughout its existence, the company produced utilitarian items as well as artware. In 1934 Hyten's company found itself facing bankruptcy. Hardy L. Winburn, Jr., along with other Little Rock businessmen, raised the necessary capital and were able to provide the kind of leadership needed to make the business profitable once again. Both lines (Eagle and Hywood) were renamed 'Niloak' in 1937 to capitalize on this well-known name. The pottery continued in production until 1947 when it was converted to the Winburn Tile Company, which exists to this day in Little Rock. Be careful not to confuse the swirl production of the Evans Pottery of Missouri with Niloak. The significant difference is the dark brown matt interior glaze of Evans pottery.

Our co-advisors for this category are Lila and Fred Shrader (see the Directory under California) and David Edwin Gifford (see Arkansas), author of *The Collector's Encyclopedia of Niloak*.

Mission Ware

Hatpin holder, 6", $700.00.

Ashtray, 5½" dia	145.00
Ashtray/match holder, 5½" dia	175.00
Bookend, 4x4" tiles w/weighted castware 'razorbk'	285.00
Bowl, flat 'float' type, 11"	195.00
Bowl, flower; perforated flared rim, 3x8"	265.00
Bowl, rose-bowl style, 5x6"	150.00
Candlestick, flared base, 9"	185.00
Candlesticks, saucer base, 3½", pr	335.00

Candlesticks, 10", pr	400.00
Chamberstick, hdl, 4"	175.00
Cigarette jar, w/lid, 3½x4½"	235.00
Compote, ped ft, 8x6½"	315.00
Ewer, att, no mk, 8½"	350.00
Humidor, w/lid, 6½"	350.00
Inkwell, 2½"	165.00
Jar, cookie or cracker; w/lid, 6½"	400.00
Jar, ginger; w/lid, 8"	190.00
Jar, powder; w/lid, 5½x3"	280.00
Mug, bbl shape, 4"	145.00
Pedestal, brn, cream & bl swirl, impressed mk, 9"	210.00
Pitcher, bulbous, 7½"	195.00
Pitcher, cylindrical, 6½"	145.00
Tankard, flared base, 12x5"	495.00
Tile, 4½x4½"	185.00
Toothpick holder, flared neck, 1¾"	85.00
Tumble-up (7½" water bottle+4" tumbler)	445.00
Tumbler, 4"	55.00
Vase, bud; slim ringed cylinder w/wide base, 6½"	200.00
Vase, bud; slim ringed cylinder w/wide base, 8½"	250.00
Vase, can form, 2"	75.00
Vase, classic form, unusual swirl, 10"	400.00
Vase, classic form, 10"	250.00
Vase, classic form, 13"	450.00
Vase, cone shape w/3" wide ft, 9½"	235.00
Vase, cylindrical, mini, 1¾"	95.00
Vase, cylindrical, w/slight flared base, 8½"	175.00
Vase, fan shape w/3" wide base, 8"	195.00
Vase, med/dk brn/cream/bl, 16"	1,500.00
Vase, pear shape, 7½"	175.00
Vase, rose bowl shape, 5½x3"	135.00
Vase, slightly pear shaped, unusual drip effect, 9½"	325.00
Vase, wide flared top, 11½"	350.00
Vase, wide shoulders, narrow neck, 11"	370.00
Wall pocket, 6½"	250.00

Miscellaneous

Ashtray, bunny, hi-gloss, 4½"	20.00
Ashtray, swan, matt, 5½"	30.00
Ashtray, Wilson's Cafe, Tulsa, hi-gloss, 5x4"	45.00
Basket, emb flowers on deep yel, emb mk, 6"	40.00
Basket, hanging; emb florals, 3-hdl, incised mk, 3¼"	40.00
Bowl, berry; hi-gloss, 8½", +6 4½" bowls	165.00
Bowl, cuspidor form, matt, 3x5"	25.00
Bowl, flower form, 3½x10", +5½" duck flower frog	80.00
Bowl, oblong, matt, 3x14"	75.00
Candlestick, low, matt, 1½x5"	20.00
Candlesticks, flared base, matt, 7", pr	110.00
Cookie jar, tab hdls, matt, w/lid, 6½"	80.00
Cup & saucer, bl, petal design, 3", 6"	40.00
Figurine, deer, standing, matt, 5½"	28.00
Figurine, elephant, bl, incised mk, 3½x6½"	80.00
Figurine, elephant, matt, 3½x6½"	65.00
Figurine, razorback hog w/ or w/o U of A, matt, 3¾"	80.00
Figurine, Scottie dog resting, hi-gloss, 3¾"	35.00
Figurine, Southern Belle, seated, matt, 5"	60.00
Figurine, Southern Belle, skirt held wide, lg hat, 7¼"	100.00
Figurine, Trojan horse, gloss, 8½"	120.00
Figurine, wooden shoe, matt, 2½x5"	15.00
Jug, hi-gloss, mini, 3½"	20.00
Jug, syrup; remnants of orig label, matt, 6"	40.00
Mug, hand-thrown, matt, 5½"	65.00

Mug, hi-gloss, 3½"	12.00
Pitcher, castware, angle hdl, unmk, 2¾"	20.00
Pitcher, ewer style, matt, 16½"	95.00
Pitcher, ewer style, matt, 8"	30.00
Pitcher, flat ball shape w/cork-wrapped stopper, matt	110.00
Pitcher, Ozark Dawn II, Deco ball form, unmk, 8"	60.00
Pitcher, Ozark Dawn II, pk w/gr overspray, ball form, 7¾"	60.00
Pitcher, petal design, mottled semigloss, 8"	90.00
Pitcher, pnt flowers & Ozarks decor, sticker, 3½"	20.00
Pitcher, streamlined wedge shape w/flat seated lid, 6"	100.00
Planter, cart, matt, 4½"	20.00
Planter, deer, free standing, emb mk, 10"	100.00
Planter, elephant (from Circus Planter group), matt, 7"	40.00
Planter, emb swags on ftd rectangle form, 3½x5½x3"	40.00
Planter, fish, hi-gloss, 4½x5x9"	30.00
Planter, goat, dk pk, incised mk, 4¼"	100.00
Planter, kangaroo, matt w/HP highlights, 5"	45.00
Planter, polar bear before rectangular form, mk, 3½"	45.00
Planter, Southern Belle w/ruffled skirt, matt, 10"	100.00
Planter, squirrel, opening between arms, mk, 5"	50.00
Planter, wishing well, open overhead structure, hi-gloss	40.00
Shakers, ball shape w/'S' & 'P' hdls, matt, 2¼", pr	25.00
Shakers, bird (cute), matt, 2¼", pr	40.00
Shakers, goose, Ozark Dawn II, sticker, 2", pr	50.00
Shakers, penguin, matt, 2¾", pr	40.00
Shakers, Scottie dog, hi-gloss, 3¼", pr	30.00
Toothpick holder, cannon (pointed upward), matt, 3½"	20.00
Toothpick holder, conch shell, hi-gloss, 2¾"	15.00
Toothpick holder, military tank, hi-gloss, 2½"	20.00
Toothpick holder, open-mouth frog, matt, 2¾"	30.00
Vase, bl, squat w/shaped rim, incised Hywood, 2½"	25.00
Vase, cornucopia; bl Lewis glaze, 2nd Hywood, 7"	40.00
Vase, cornucopia; hi-gloss, 3½"	15.00
Vase, emb decor on urn form w/sq rim & hdls, 8"	35.00
Vase, fan form, matt, 7"	30.00
Vase, gr to wht, sm flared rim, unmk, 5¾"	40.00
Vase, gr waisted form, 2nd Hywood, 5"	60.00
Vase, hand-thrown, 3 appl hdls, Stoin glaze, 8"	120.00
Vase, hdld w/well-formed leaves & flowers at base, 7"	45.00
Vase, inverted shaped rim, Stoin glaze, Hywood, 6⅛"	60.00
Vase, Ozark dawn II, trumpet neck, mk, 7"	40.00
Vase, Peacock Blue II, trumpet neck, hdls, Hywood, 6"	60.00
Vase, pk w/bl overspray, Hywood, 5"	40.00
Vase, Stoin glaze, appl hdls, unmk, 11¼"	120.00
Vase, trifluted & emb (3 cylinders 1¾" W), 7½"	55.00
Vase, trophy shape w/hdls, hi-gloss, 8"	40.00
Wall pocket, overlapping leaves, matt, 8½"	85.00

Nippon

Nippon generally refers to Japanese wares made during the period from 1891 to 1921, although the Nippon mark was also used to a limited extent on later wares (accompanied by 'Japan'). Nippon, meaning Japan, identified the country of origin to comply with American importation restrictions. After 1921 'Japan' was the acceptable alternative. The term does not imply a specific type of product and may be found on items other than porcelains. For further information we recommend *The Collector's Encyclopedia of Nippon Porcelain* (there are three in the series) by our advisor, Joan Van Patten; you will find her address in the Directory under New York. In the following listings, items are assumed hand painted unless noted otherwise. Numbers included in the descriptions refer to these specific marks:

Key:
#1 — China E-OH	#5 — Rising Sun
#2 — M in Wreath	#6 — Royal Kinran
#3 — Cherry Blossom	#7 — Maple Leaf
#4 — Double T Diamond in Circle	#8 — Royal Nippon, Nishiki
	#9 — Royal Moriye Nippon

Bottle, cologne; river scenic w/cobalt, bulbous, #2, 5"	200.00
Bowl, floral band along scalloped rim w/gold, mk, 7¾"	85.00
Bowl, floral w/gold geometric band, 6-sided, 3-ftd, #2, 7¼"	80.00

Bowl, floral center and reserves on red with much gold, pierced and scalloped rim, green mark, 11", $225.00.

Bowl, master nut; sm floral on wht, #2, 9½", +4 sm	135.00
Bowl, peanuts in relief int, twig hdls, gr #2, 7"	100.00
Bowl, reserves in gr band w/gold, w/underplate, #7, 8¾"	175.00
Bowl, roses w/gold on wht, 3-part, center hdl, #7, 7½"	100.00
Bowl, Wedgwood, cream on lav, oval, hdls, gr #2, 9½"	300.00
Box, cigarette; sampan scene on lid, gr #2, 4¾"	200.00
Box, trinket; florals on heart shape, gr #2	85.00
Butter dish, floral on cream w/gold, gr #2, 7½"	150.00
Cake plate, wide floral band w/gold, open hdls, #7, 11¼"	250.00
Candlesticks, Deco floral w/gold, 6-sided base, #2, 8", pr	300.00
Candlesticks, florals on cobalt w/gold, #2, 8", pr	350.00
Celery tray, mc florals w/gold at rim, gr #2, 12"	65.00
Chocolate pot, Deco floral on wht, fancy hdl, #2, 9¾"	125.00
Chocolate pot, iris on shaded brn, bl #7, 10"	325.00
Cookie jar, mc roses on cobalt w/gold, 3-ftd, bl #7, 7¾"	500.00
Creamer & sugar bowl, roses on wht w/gold, melon ribs, mk	100.00
Cup & saucer, cobalt w/gold trim, unmk	70.00
Cup & saucer, gold o/l on wht, #7	60.00
Egg cup, Doll Face pattern, Morimura sticker, 3½"	80.00
Ewer, fox hunt tapestry, Greek Key band, bulbous, #7, 7"	850.00
Ewer, landscape tapestry, angle hdl, bl #7, 10¾"	1,000.00
Ferner, river scenic, canted corners, ftd, #7, 8" L	175.00
Ferner, Wedgwood, cream on bl, gr #2, 3½x7"	425.00
Hair receiver, mc roses on gr w/gold, bl #7, 5"	75.00
Hatpin holder, floral on wht, 6-sided underplate, #2, 4½"	85.00
Humidor, bright Deco designs, 6-sided, #2, 5½"	375.00
Humidor, dogs in relief, Greek Key band, #2, 6"	900.00
Humidor, floral w/much gold & beading, bl #7, 5½"	700.00
Humidor, Indian on running horse in relief, brn tones, #2, 6"	1,100.00
Humidor, lady's portrait reserve, beading, 6-sided, #7, 7¾"	925.00
Humidor, man on camel in relief, gr #2, 7"	1,000.00
Humidor, mc roses w/gold beading, cylindrical, #7, 8¼"	500.00
Humidor, moriage pipes, bl #7, 7"	700.00
Humidor, river scenic, 6-sided, ftd, bl #2, 9¾"	550.00
Incense burner, geisha figural, mk, 5"	245.00
Jar, potpourri; Deco-style florals on wht w/bl trim, #2, 5½"	150.00
Jug, whiskey; river reserve on keg form, gr #2, 5½"	700.00
Jug, wine; river scenic w/figures, earth tones, #2, 9½"	750.00

Lamp, river scenic reserve on cobalt, mk, 17" 275.00
Lemon dish, bl birds on wht w/gold, open hdls, bl #5, 5½" 25.00
Luncheon set, pk blossoms on wht w/gold band, 72-pc 1,000.00
Matchbox holder, gold o/l on wht, hanging, #2, 4½" 100.00
Mug, man on camel, earth tones, moriage trim, #2, 4¾" 275.00
Mustache cup, river scenic w/gold, #2 ....195.00
Pitcher, floral, brns & gr on cream, simple shape, #7, 5½" 145.00
Pitcher, lemonade; mc roses w/gold, bl #7, 6" 175.00
Plaque, blown-out fish hang from nail, wood ground, 9x18" ...1,400.00
Plaque, fish on shelf, gr #2, 12" dia 325.00
Plaque, lions in relief, earth tones, gr #2, 10½" 700.00
Plaque, man on camel in relief, gr #2, 10½" 1,000.00
Plaque, river & mtn scene, floral border, #2, 8¾" 185.00
Plaque, shepherd w/flock, earth tones, gr #2, 10" 300.00
Plate, fishing scene on cobalt w/gold rim, gr #2, 10" 245.00
Plate, floral w/gold, ruffled rim, #7, 11" 300.00
Punch bowl, roses w/cobalt & gold, #2, 6¾x10" 425.00
Stein, floral cloisonne on porc, gr #2, 7" 525.00
Stein, monk drinking, vintage border, gr #2, 7" 600.00
Sugar shaker, roses, pk on wht w/gold, 7", 4" 100.00
Syrup, roses w/gold, w/underplate, gr mk, 6" 125.00
Tankard, elk in relief, #2, 11½", +4 5" mugs 4,000.00
Tea set, bl butterflies on wht, bl #5, child sz, 15-pc 250.00
Tea set, river scene w/gold, #2, 6½" pot+11 pcs 400.00
Teapot, scenic medallion on cobalt w/gold, #2, 6" 275.00
Tile, windmill scene, octagonal, #2, 5½" 70.00
Tray, dresser; portrait reserves, gold o/l on wht, #7, 12" 400.00
Tray, scenic reserves on cobalt w/gold, #7, 11¼" L 275.00
Urn, mc roses on cobalt w/gold, bl #7, w/lid, 13" 1,000.00
Urn, river scenic reserve w/gold, uptrn hdls, gr #1, 13¾" 800.00
Vase, Anna Potocka medallion, much gold, hdls, #7, 7½" 600.00
Vase, floral, mc on cobalt, low hdls, wide base, #7, 9½" 225.00
Vase, floral, mc on wht w/gold, gourd shape, hdls, #7, 7½" 600.00
Vase, floral in relief, hdls, beading, bulbous, #7, 9½" 550.00
Vase, floral reserve & band on cobalt w/much gold, #2, 7½" 525.00
Vase, floral w/coralene beading, classic form, mk, 7" 325.00
Vase, floral w/gold, uptrn hdls, gr #7, 10" 300.00
Vase, gold o/l leaves on brn, cylindrical, #7, 7½" 200.00
Vase, gold on cobalt, basket form, gr #2, 7¾" 365.00
Vase, gold scenic medallion & band on cobalt, hdls, #7, 7½" 500.00
Vase, grapes, scalloped rim, low hdls, gr #7, 9¼" 275.00
Vase, hyacinths, classic form, hdls, bl #7, 10¾" 295.00
Vase, lady's portrait reserve w/gold on turq, bl #7, 18¼" 1,800.00
Vase, lg open florals on gr w/gold, hdls, flared ft, #7, 11" 300.00
Vase, moriage gulls on earth tones, hdls, bl #7, 4½" 235.00
Vase, moriage trees, bulbous, hdls, bl #7, 9" 450.00
Vase, moriage trees & landscape in relief, gr #2, 9½" 550.00
Vase, ostrich reserve, cobalt w/gold, hdls, #2, 13" 550.00
Vase, pk roses, tub hdls, flared ft, gr #2, 7" 225.00
Vase, rose medallion, much gold, integral hdls, unmk, 8½" 375.00
Vase, rose tapestry, sm gold hdls, squat, #7, 6" 525.00
Vase, roses, sm gold hdls, 6-sided, #7, 7¾" 275.00
Vase, roses & much gold, basket form, unmk, 7" 350.00
Vase, scenic sponge tapestry, cylindrical, hdls, unmk, 8½" 400.00
Vase, scenic tapestry, cylindrical, #7, 6¼" 465.00
Vase, silver floral o/l on cobalt, shouldered, gr mk, 6½" 450.00
Vase, swan scenic w/moriage, bulbous, hdls, #7, 9" 375.00
Vase, Wedgwood, cream on bl, hdls, gr #2, 8" 550.00
Vase, windmill scenic, loving cup form, #2, 5½" 85.00

Nodders

So called because of the nodding action of their heads and hands,

nodders originated in China where they were used in temple rituals to represent deity. Early in the 18th century, the idea was adopted by Meissen and by French manufacturers who produced not only china nodders but bisque as well. Most nodders are individual; couples are unusual. The idea remained popular until the end of the 19th century and was used during the Victorian era by toy manufacturers.

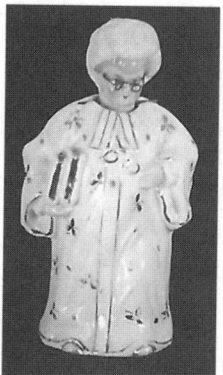

Old lady with granny glasses, white gown with gold trim, 6", $110.00.

Blk couple, she undressing, HP bsk, Japan, 6", pr 315.00
Duck, compo, mc pnt, cb candy container base, 6½", VG 35.00
German playing accordion, 7" 65.00
Girl w/basket, bsk, mc w/gold 155.00
Goose, celluloid, worn pnt, 8", EX 185.00
Santa, celluloid on tin base, Japan, 7" 130.00
Santa, papier-mache & cb w/compo head, clockwork, 28", EX ..1,265.00
Santa on elephant, papier-mache, Germany, 10½", VG 745.00
Space Man, 5" 75.00

German Comic Characters

During the early 1930s, Germany produced a collection of small figure dolls, approximately 2" to 4" high, representing the most popular comic strip and cartoon characters of that time. They were made of bisque with brightly painted details and clearly stamped with their appropriate names and 'Germany' on their backs. Generally, their movable heads were attached with an elastic string going through their bodies, hence the name 'nodders,' but there were some characters produced earlier that were frozen with no movable parts. The most popular ones came in boxed sets, but the lesser-known characters were sold separately, making them rarer and harder to find today. We have listed the most valuable characters from the series here; those not mentioned below are valued at $125.00 and under. Our advisor for German character nodders is Doug Dezso; he is listed in the Directory under New Jersey.

Ambrose Potts 350.00
Aunt Mamie or Uncle Willie, ea 350.00
Auntie Blossom 150.00
Bill, Dock, Avery, Max or Pop Jenks, ea 200.00
Buttercup 250.00
Chubby Chaney 250.00
Corky 475.00
Ferina 350.00
Grandpa Teen 350.00
Happy Hooligan 600.00
Harold Teen 150.00
Junior Nebbs 500.00
Lillums 150.00
Little Annie Rooney, arm moves 250.00
Little Egypt 350.00
Lord Plushbottom 150.00

Ma or Pa Winkle, ea	350.00
Marjory, Patsy, Lilacs or Josie, ea	400.00
Mary Ann Jackson	250.00
Min Gump	150.00
Mr Bailey	150.00
Mr Bibb	400.00
Mr Wicker	250.00
Mushmouth	350.00
Mutt or Jeff, ea	250.00
Nicodemus	350.00
Old Timer	350.00
Pat Finnegan	400.00
Pete the Dog	150.00
Rudy or Fanny Nebbs, ea	250.00
Scraps	250.00
Widow Zander	400.00
Winnie Winkle	150.00

Noritake

The Noritake Company was first registered in 1904 as Nippon Gomei Kaisha. In 1917 the name became Nippon Toki Kabushiki Toki. The 'M' in wreath mark is that of the Morimura Brothers, distributors with offices in New York. It was used until 1941. The tree crest mark is the crest of the Morimura family.

The Noritake Company has produced fine porcelain dinnerware sets and occasional pieces decorated in the delicate manner for which the Japanese are noted. Their Azalea pattern was produced exclusively for the Larkin Company, who gave the lovely ware away as premiums to club members and their home agents. From 1916 through the thirties, Larkin distributed fine china which was decorated in pink azaleas on white with gold tracing along edges and handles. Early in the thirties, six pieces of crystal hand painted with the same design were offered: candle holders, a compote, a tray with handles, a scalloped fruit bowl, a cheese and cracker set, and a cake plate. All in all, seventy different pieces of Azalea were produced. Some, such as the fifteen-piece child's set, bulbous vase, china ashtray, and the pancake jug, are quite rare. One of the earliest marks was the Noritake M in wreath with variations. Later the ware was marked 'Noritake, Azalea, Hand Painted, Japan.' Authority Joan Van Patten has compiled two lovely books, *The Collector's Encyclopedia of Noritake, Vols. I and II*, with many full-color photos and current prices; you will find her address in the Directory under New York. Our advisor for Azalea is Alton Parker; he is listed in the Directory under Florida. In the following listings, examples are hand painted unless noted otherwise. Numbers refer to these specific marks:

Key:
#1 — Komaru   #3 — N in Wreath
#2 — M in Wreath

Azalea

Butter dish, #25, $150.00.

Basket, mint; Dolly Varden, #193	195.00
Bonbon, #184, 6¼"	50.00
Bowl, #12, 10"	42.50
Bowl, deep, #310	68.00
Bowl, fruit; shell form, #188, 7¾"	385.00
Bowl, oatmeal; #55, 5½"	28.00
Bowl, vegetable; divided, #439, 9½"	295.00
Bowl, vegetable; oval, #101, 10½"	60.00
Bowl, vegetable; oval, #172, 9¼"	58.00
Butter chip, #312, 3¼"	145.00
Butter tub, w/insert, #54	48.00
Cake plate, #10, 9¾"	40.00
Candy bowl, #185	195.00
Candy jar, #313	695.00
Casserole, gold finial, w/lid, #372	540.00
Casserole, w/lid, #16	125.00
Celery/roll tray, #99, 12"	55.00
Cheese/butter dish, #314	135.00
Child's set, #253, 15-pc	2,500.00
Coffeepot, AD; #182	595.00
Compote, #170	98.00
Condiment set, #14, 5-pc	65.00
Creamer & sugar bowl, #122	158.00
Creamer & sugar bowl, #449, ind	395.00
Creamer & sugar bowl, #7	45.00
Creamer & sugar bowl, AD; open, #123	140.00
Creamer & sugar bowl, gold finial, #401	155.00
Cruet, #190	195.00
Cup & saucer, #2	17.50
Cup & saucer, AD; #183	150.00
Cup & saucer, bouillon; #124, 3½"	24.50
Egg cup, #120	60.00
Gravy boat, #40	48.00
Jam jar set, #125, 3-pc	155.00
Match/toothpick holder, #192	130.00
Mayonnaise set, scalloped, #453, 3-pc	495.00
Mustard jar, #191	60.00
Pickle/lemon set, #121	24.50
Pitcher, milk jug; #100, 1-qt	195.00
Plate, #4, 7½"	10.00
Plate, bread & butter; #8, 6½"	10.00
Plate, cream soup; #363	175.00
Plate, dinner; #13, 9¾"	28.00
Plate, grill; 3-compartment, #338, 10¼"	165.00
Plate, scalloped sq, salesman's sample	950.00
Plate, soup; #19, 7⅛"	25.00
Plate, sq, #315, 7⅝"	85.00
Platter, #17, 14"	60.00
Platter, #186, 16"	475.00
Platter, #56, 12"	58.00
Platter, cold meat; #311, 10¼"	215.00
Refreshment set, #39, 2-pc	48.00
Relish, #194, 7⅛"	85.00
Relish, loop hdl, 2-part, #450	425.00
Relish, oval, #18, 8½"	20.00
Relish, 2-part, #171	58.00
Relish, 4-part, #119, rare, 10"	150.00
Saucer, fruit; #9, 5¼"	10.00
Shakers, #126, ind, pr	27.50
Shakers, bell form, #11, pr	30.00
Shakers, bulbous, #89, pr	30.00
Spoon holder, #189, 8"	115.00
Spoon holder, #339, 2-pc	35.00
Syrup, #97, w/underplate	135.00

Tea tile, #169, 6" **48.50**
Teapot, #15 ....**110.00**
Teapot, gold finial, #400 ....**495.00**
Toothpick holder, #192 ....**130.00**
Vase, bulbous, #452 ....**1,150.00**
Vase, fan form, ftd, #187 ....**185.00**
Whipped cream set, #3, 3-pc **38.50**

Ashtray, lady w/sweeping tray skirt, gr #2, 4" **325.00**
Bowl, berry; Tree in Meadow, 10½", +6 5½" bowls **150.00**
Bowl, Deco floral, bl & cream on red, #2, 9" **85.00**
Bowl, figures join hands to form hdls, red #2, 6" H **1,250.00**
Bowl, floral on wht w/orange lustre, 6-sided, hdls, #2, 8¼" **65.00**
Bowl, parrot on branch, bl lustre rim, hdls, #2, 8¾" **65.00**
Bowl, river scenic, gold hdls, oval, #2, 10½" **60.00**
Bowl, sauce; swan scenic on bl, w/underplate, #2, 3½" H **50.00**
Bowl, sunflower on wht, red rim, hdls, #2, 6" L **50.00**
Bowl, toucan perched at rim, red #2, 7" **145.00**
Box, lady in plumed hat sits on lid, #2, 10¼" H **1,300.00**
Box, puff; Deco lady w/red hat & scarf on bl, #2, 4" **250.00**
Box, puff; Spanish lady on gr, red 2, 3½" **250.00**
Box, trinket; lady w/whippet on heart form, #2, 3½" **250.00**
Cake plate, 4 floral medallions in geometric band, #2, 9½" **35.00**
Candlesticks, florals & butterfly on tulip form, #2, 5½", pr **165.00**
Candy dish, Deco floral, yel & brn on wht, red #2, 5¾" **75.00**
Candy dish, exotic birds & flowers, basket form, #2, 5½" **60.00**
Candy dish, floral on red, fleur-de-lis finial, #2, 7½" **110.00**
Candy dish, river scenic, center hdl, red #2, 8½" L **80.00**
Cheese dish, floral reserve, bl lustre, slant lid, #2, 8" **85.00**
Cheese dish, windmill & river scenic, slant lid, #2, 8" **80.00**
Chocolate pot, lady w/whippets, gold hdl & finial, #2, 8¼" **220.00**
Condiment set, comical fish, orange lustre, #2, 3-pc on tray **100.00**
Condiment set, Tree in Meadow, 4-pc **45.00**
Creamer & sugar bowl, bl & wht w/rose bud finial, #2, 4" **55.00**
Creamer & sugar bowl, Oriental scene w/figures & gold, #2 ....**55.00**
Creamer & sugar bowl, Tree in Meadow **38.00**
Creamer & sugar shaker, sampan scenic, red #2, 6½" shaker **85.00**
Cup & saucer, Tree in Meadow **18.00**
Demitasse pot, Tree in Meadow **125.00**
Demitasse set, floral reserve w/gold, #1, 7" pot+15 pcs **275.00**
Dresser doll, clown w/wide ruffle at neck, #2, 8½" **415.00**
Dresser doll, girl w/hands to chin, bow finial, #2, 6½" **500.00**
Dresser doll, lady w/hands to head, gr/blk/wht dress, #2, 7" **350.00**
Egg warmer, floral medallion on bl & wht, #2, 6" dia **90.00**
Flower frog, mermaid at side of flower form, #2, 3½" **275.00**
Honey jar, roses on hive form w/red band, appl bees, #2, 4½" **75.00**
Humidor, Deco florals on blk w/cream bands, gr #2, 6½" **210.00**
Humidor, lion & palm trees, earth tones, gr #2, 5¾" **250.00**
Humidor/candy dish, Tree in Meadow **400.00**
Inkwell, lady figural, red #2, 4½" **325.00**
Jam jar, Tree in Meadow, w/underplate & spoon **100.00**
Lamp, Colonial lady figural, gr #2, 9" **1,150.00**
Lemon dish, Tree in Meadow **20.00**
Match holder, lady w/whippet, red #2 ....**125.00**
Muffineer set, Tree in Meadow **125.00**
Pin dish, dog sits at side of tray, red #2, 2¾" **50.00**
Pin dish, recumbent clown figural, red #2, 4" L **300.00**
Pitcher, river scenic, gold trim at rim & hdl, #2, 5½" **35.00**
Planter, Deco florals w/bl trim, hanging, #2, 5" **175.00**
Plate, Deco floral on yel, hdls, #2, 10¼" **85.00**
Plate, Deco lady in landscape, #2, 8½" **225.00**
Plate, sandwich; Colonial lady in landscape, bl rim, #2, 8" **125.00**
Plate, serving; Tree in Meadow, pierced hdls, 9½" **65.00**

Plate, Tree in Meadow, 7½", 6 for **75.00**
Relish, Tree in Meadow, 2-part **45.00**
Serving dish, orchid on blk, bl rim, side hdl, #2, 7¾" **65.00**
Sugar shaker, owl figural, bl lustre, gr #2 ....**125.00**
Syrup, floral on wht w/gold, w/undertray, #2, 4½" **55.00**
Tea set, Tree in Meadow, 15-pc **225.00**
Toothpick holder, Tree in Meadow, mk **45.00**
Tray, dresser; lady on skis, red #2, 8½" L **300.00**
Trivet, flower basket on wht, gr rim, gr #2, 5¾" dia **50.00**
Vase, floral on wht, basket form w/gold twig hdl, #2, 10" **225.00**
Vase, jack-in-pulpit; Deco floral, pk int, #2, 6¾" **155.00**
Vase, landscape panels w/Wedgwood trim, gr #2, 10" **375.00**
Vase, parrot perched between 2 lily forms, #2, 7" **215.00**
Vase, river scenic band on gr w/gold, hdls, #1, 9¼", pr **340.00**
Vase, sampan scenic band, gold angle hdls, #1, 8½" **250.00**
Wall pocket, exotic bird on red w/gold, gr #2, 8" **125.00**
Wall pocket, lg pk rose, orange lustre, 9" **80.00**
Wall pocket, mc florals w/bl lustre at top, #2, 8" **85.00**

Norse

The Norse Pottery was established in 1903 in Edgerton, Wisconsin, by Thorwald Sampson and Louis Ipson. A year later it was purchased by A.W. Wheelock and moved to Rockford, Illinois. The ware they produced was inspired by ancient bronze vessels of the Norsemen. Designs were often incised into the red clay body. Dragon handles and feet were favored decorative devices, and they achieved a semblance of patina through the application of metallic glazes. The ware was marked with a stylized 'N' containing a vertical arrangement of the remaining letters of the name. Production ceased after 1913.

Pitcher, incised decoration, 10", $795.00.

Pitcher, abstract cvg, gr on blk matt, stoppered, 7", NM **350.00**
Vase, flat shoulder w/cvd geometrics, zigzags, hdls, 7x3" **170.00**
Vase, incised geometrics, gr on blk matt w/gold, 4½x4" **220.00**
Vase, lg dragons around middle, blk matt, ftd, 12x6½" **850.00**
Vase, owls relief, gr patina on blk matt, ftd, 4x5½" **425.00**

North Dakota School of Mines

The School of Mines of the University of North Dakota was established in 1890; but due to a lack of funding it was not until 1898 that Earle J. Babcock was appointed as Director, and efforts were made to produce ware from the native clay he had discovered several years earlier. The first pieces were made by firms in the east from the clay Babcock sent them. Some of the ware was decorated by the manufacturer; some was shipped back to North Dakota to be decorated by native artists. By 1909 students at the University of North Dakota were producing utilitarian items such as tile, brick, shingles, etc., in conjunction with a ceramic course offered through the Chemistry

Department. By 1910 a ceramic department had been established, supervised by Margaret Kelly Cable. Under her leadership, fine artware was produced. Native flowers, grains, buffalo, cowboys, and other subjects indigenous to the state were incorporated into the decorations. Some pieces have an Art Nouveau – Art Deco style easily attributed to her association with Frederick H. Rhead, with whom she studied in 1911. During the twenties the pottery was marketed on a limited scale through gift and jewelry stores in the state. From 1927 until 1949 when Miss Cable announced her retirement, a more widespread distribution was maintained with sales branching out into other states. The ware was marked in cobalt with the official seal — 'Made at School of Mines, N.D. Clay, University of North Dakota, Grand Forks, N.D.' in a circle. Very early ware was sometimes marked 'U.N.D.' in cobalt by hand.

Bowl, abstract spokes, 3-color on dk rose, SIG, '58, 9" 150.00
Bowl, dk bl, sgn PB, 2x7" 300.00
Bowl, olive gr, sgn Patten & Huck, #4909, 2½x3½" 125.00
Bowl, pk & gr floral, sgn Huck & JM, #4592, 3½x4½" 175.00
Bowl, stylized flowers, Daker, Bentonite clay, 3" 250.00
Curtain pull, lav prairie rose, mk, 1½" dia, EX......................35.00
Decanter, cvd Indian-motif band on med bl, Mattson, 9x5" 425.00
Dish, HP floral & butterfly, w/lid 395.00
Ewer, floral, Cable, 5" 325.00
Lamp base, cvd palm trees, gr matt, Peterson, 1951, 9x5" 300.00
Pitcher, cornflower bl, #86H 150.00
Tile, Dutch lady, mc on ivory, glossy, HE/1935, 5¼x2½", NM ...425.00
Tile, ship, 3-color, Hazel Rhode/1933, 4½x4" 475.00
Vase, birds incised, Lein, 1938, 5½" 425.00
Vase, birds/bands cvd/pnt on aqua, cut bk, Mary E, 8x7" 4,000.00
Vase, blk/bl bands on lt bl gloss, sgn, 7¾x4" 375.00
Vase, buffalo band, blk on rust matt, Mattson, 3x4½" 600.00
Vase, crocus cvd/pnt allover, cut bk, 2-tone gr, Huck, 6½" 1,300.00
Vase, daffodils cvd on yel to wht, sgn JT, 5½x5" 425.00
Vase, daisies cvd on wht speckled, M Youngs, 1938, 5½x3¾" 275.00
Vase, diagonal leaves, lt yel-gr semimatt, 4x4" 150.00
Vase, floral band cog, pk/gr on pk matt, 3¼x3¼" 350.00
Vase, floral cvg, sgn Mattson, 3" 275.00
Vase, floral shoulder band cvd/pnt on gr/brn matt, Huck, 4x6" ..550.00
Vase, geometric leaves cvd on ivory gloss, Cable, 6x2¾" 250.00
Vase, Indian designs, tan/blk on dk red, Gregorie, 4½x6" 475.00
Vase, lav gloss w/yel & lav floral int, funnel shape, 4x6" 275.00
Vase, lg cvd leaves, yel/tan outlines on bl gloss, Mattson, 4" 500.00
Vase, oxblood red, sgn PB, 6" 395.00
Vase, rose shoulder band cvg, pk/gr on lt brn, Cable, 3x5" 550.00
Vase, rose/brn matt, Mattson, 6x6" 300.00
Vase, roundels cvg, gr/brn, Huck, #3285, 1934, 7x5" 950.00
Vase, wheat stalks cvd on celadon, Cable, 7¾x4¾" 700.00

North State

In 1924 the North State Pottery of Sanford, North Carolina, began small-scale production, the result of the extreme fondness Mrs. Rebecca Copper had for potting. With the help of her husband and the abundance of suitable local clay, the pottery flourished and became well known for lovely shapes and beautiful glazes. The pottery was in business for thirty-five years; most of its ware was sold in gift and craft shops throughout North Carolina.

Ashtray, burnt orange/gr, imp mk, 1¾" H, NM 25.00
Ewer, bl over red clay, 8½" 95.00
Pitcher, copper lustre, slender form, 6½" 50.00
Vase, beige, fan form, 3¾" 25.00

Ewer, 8½", $95.00; Puzzle jug, 4½", $18.00.

Vase, gr & gun-metal drip, shouldered, 9" 375.00
Vase, oxblood w/gr patches, shouldered, 10½" 750.00

Northwood

The Northwood Company was founded in 1896 in Indiana, Pennsylvania, by Harry Northwood, whose father, John, was the art director for Stevens and Williams, an English glassworks. Northwood joined the National Glass Company in 1899 but in 1901 again became an independent contractor and formed the Harry Northwood Glass Company of Wheeling, West Virginia. He marketed his first carnival glass in 1908, and it became his most popular product. His company was also famous for its custard, goofus, and pressed glass. Northwood died in 1923, and the company closed. See also Carnival; Custard; Goofus; Opalescent; Pattern Glass.

Bowl, berry; Royal Ivy, frosted rubena, 7-pc set 315.00
Bowl, master berry; Royal Ivy, satin rainbow spatter 145.00
Butter dish, Cherry T'print, crystal w/ruby & gold 100.00
Butter dish, Intaglio, gr w/M gold 110.00
Butter dish, Strawberry & Cable, crystal w/ruby & gold 125.00
Celery vase, Leaf Umbrella, cased spatter 225.00
Creamer, Peach, gr w/gold 70.00
Creamer, Royal Ivy, frosted rubena 195.00
Creamer & sugar bowl, Royal Oak, rubena frost, w/lid, 6" 250.00
Cruet, Royal Ivy, rubena, tricorn spout, faceted stopper, 7" 450.00
Pickle castor, Royal Ivy, satin rubena; EX SP fr 350.00
Pickle castor, Windows, bl opal; EX SP fr 350.00
Pitcher, water; Cherry & Plum, crystal w/ruby stain & gold 125.00
Pitcher, water; Gothic Arches, gr w/gold, +4 tumblers 225.00
Pitcher, water; Invt Rib, wht agate 150.00
Pitcher, water; Leaf Mold, vaseline spatter, 8x6" 275.00
Pitcher, water; Oriental Poppy, gr 250.00
Pitcher, water; Royal Ivy, rainbow craquelle frost 595.00
Pitcher, water; Waving Quilt, gr w/gold, +6 tumblers 225.00
Plate, pinwheels/swirls, mauve & red on bl, mk Pat, 6½" 1,000.00
Rose bowl, pull-ups, chartreuse/aqua/gr on wht satin, 3x3" 295.00
Rose bowl, pull-ups, rose on yel, threaded, pk int, 4" 1,200.00
Shakers, Cactus, amethyst, pr 140.00
Shakers, Royal Oak, pastel gr opaque, cased, 2⅝", pr 90.00
Spoon holder, Gothic Arches, gr w/gold 40.00
Spooner, Cherry T'print, crystal w/ruby & gold 60.00
Sugar bowl, Cherry T'print, crystal w/ruby & gold, w/lid 75.00
Sugar bowl, Memphis, gr w/M gold, w/lid 80.00
Sugar shaker, Leaf Mold, cranberry spatter w/mica 395.00
Sugar shaker, Leaf Umbrella, bl cased 300.00
Sugar shaker, Leaf Umbrella, cranberry 365.00
Sugar shaker, Ring Neck Optic, cranberry 195.00
Sugar shaker, Royal Ivy, rubena 185.00
Sugar shaker, Royal Ivy, rubena frost 300.00

Syrup, Leaf Mold, cranberry spatter w/mica 600.00
Toothpick holder, Royal Ivy, rubena 125.00
Tumbler, Cherry & Plum, crystal w/ruby & gold 30.00
Tumbler, Leaf Umbrella, bl cased 85.00
Tumbler, Royal Ivy, cased spatter 70.00
Tumbler, Strawberry & Cable, crystal w/ruby & gold 35.00
Vase, abstract birds (Vs) on celadon gloss, sqd, 6", pr 600.00

Norweta

Norweta pottery was produced by the Northwestern Terra Cotta Company of Chicago, Illinois. It was made for approximately ten years, beginning sometime before 1907. Both matt and crystalline glazes were employed, and terra cotta vases were also produced. Not all was marked.

Doorstop, seated elf reading a book, 5-color, 9x5" 350.00
Vase, bl crystalline on cream, classic form, no mk, 8" 395.00
Vase, bl crystalline on pk gloss, flat shoulder, 4½x2¾" 550.00

Nutcrackers

The nutcracker, though a strictly functional tool, is a good example of one to which man has applied ingenuity, imagination, and engineering skills. Though all were designed to accomplish the same end, hundreds of types exist in almost every material sturdy enough to withstand sufficient pressure to crack the nut. Figurals are popular collectibles, as are those with unusual design and construction. Patented examples are also desirable. Our advisor for this category is Earl MacSorley; he is listed in the Directory under Connecticut. For more information, we recommend *Ornamental and Figural Nutcrackers* by Judith A. Rittenhouse.

Bear, sitting, wooden, glass eyes, Germany, 1870-90, 8¾" 175.00
Bears on seesaw, wooden, glass eyes, Russian, 1950s, 11" 150.00
Cat, screw-type, brass, mk Austria, ca 1910, 4¾" 450.00
Cat, wooden, glass eyes, Swiss or Tyrolean, 1900s, 6½" 135.00
Clown, CI, pnt, English, 1920s, 5¾" 75.00
Dog, CI, worn blk pnt w/orange base, Harper Supply Co, 13" 95.00
Dragon, CI, gold pnt, English, 1900-10, 14" 275.00
Eagle, wooden, glass eyes, 1900s, 7½" 150.00
Elephant, pnt CI, Am, 1920-30, 4¾" 150.00
Fish, olive wood, eye is hinge, Greek, 1950s, 8" 25.00
Folk art head, wooden, red pnt in mouth, Am, 1800-50, 11" ..1,200.00
Frog, wrought iron, glass eyes, mk Germany, 1800s, 6¼" 250.00
Grandfather's clock, brass, mk Made in England, ca 1925, 5½" 75.00
Jester, brass, dbl-faced, English, early 1900s, 7¼" 50.00
Kangaroo, brass-plated CI, mk Nester, English, 1930s, 5½" 150.00
Lady in hoop skirt, screw-type, brass, English, 3¾" 125.00
Laughing elf, wooden, 1900s, 11" 215.00
Lion's head w/crown, brass, English, 1880-1920, 5⅝" 65.00
Man in stocking cap, wooden, Swiss or Tyrolean, 1900s, 8" 150.00
Mermaid, brass, seashell w/ocean waves, mk Made in England, 5"...75.00
Nut, aluminum, sticker mk Made in Taiwan, recent, 5" 10.00
Ram, wooden, intricate cvg, Swiss or Tyrolean, 1800-50, 8¼" ...200.00
Squirrel, CI, blk pnt, Am, ca 1900, 4½x5½x2" 30.00
Squirrel, screw-type, wooden, English, 1850-80, 6⅝" 100.00
Wild boar, wooden, glass eyes, 1900s, 9½" 175.00
Woodsman, wooden, fur hair, East Germany, 1989, 10½" 150.00

Occupied Japan

Items marked 'Occupied Japan' have become popular collectibles in

the last few years. They were produced during the period from the end of World War II until April 18, 1952, when the occupation ended. By no means was all of the ware exported during that time marked 'Occupied Japan'; some was marked 'Japan' or 'Made In Japan.' It is thought that because of the natural resentment felt by the Japanese toward the occupation, only a fraction of these wares carried the 'Occupied' mark. Even though you may find identical 'Japan'-marked items, because of its limited use, only those with the 'Occupied Japan' mark are being collected to any great extent. Values vary considerably, based on the quality of workmanship. Generally, bisque figures command much higher prices than porcelain, since on the whole they are of a finer quality.

For those wanting more information, we recommend *The Collector's Encyclopedia of Occupied Japan Collectibles* by Gene Florence; he is listed in the Directory under Kentucky. Our advisor for this category is Florence Archambault; she is listed in the Directory under Rhode Island. She represents the Occupied Japan Club, whose mailing address may be found under Clubs, Newsletters, and Catalogs. All items described in the following listings are assumed ceramic unless noted otherwise.

Toy, green celluloid bear, painted details, string jointed, 5½", $35.00.

Ashtray, curled leaf, lt & dk gr 4.50
Ashtray, Indian in canoe form, 2¼x4¼" 22.50
Ashtray, metal w/emb Statue of Liberty, NY City souvenir 12.50
Ashtray, nude Blk baby by clothesline, 2½" 27.50
Bookends, penguins, blk, bl, orange & wht, 4", pr 35.00
Box, bl Wedgwood type, 1¼x2½x2¾" 20.00
Bracelet, rhinestones in stretch metal band, Lady Patricia 35.00
Butter dish, gr basketweave, rectangular 20.00
Cigarette lighter, alligator on metal, 1¼x¾" 15.00
Clock, wooden owl form, eyes move, 6" 250.00
Creamer, bull's head form, Ugaco, 4½" 25.00
Creamer, collie's head form, Ugaco, 4½" 25.00
Creamer, cow figural, brn & beige, 5¼x8" 35.00
Creamer, cow figural, brn & wht, 3⅜x5¼" 30.00
Creamer & sugar bowl, chicken forms, +matching shakers 20.00
Cup & saucer, demitasse; mc flowers w/gold, porc 20.00
Cup & saucer, pk & red flowers, Trimont Co 15.00
Cup & saucer, red flower on blk, Chugai Co 20.00
Cup & saucer, river scene w/gold trim, Auger design, mk 22.50
Doll, Dutch girl w/instrument, celluloid, 8⅝" 48.00
Doll, football player, celluloid, jtd arms, 6" 25.00
Figurine, Balinese lady dancer, gold trim, 8¾" 38.00
Figurine, ballerina, net dress, 5¾" 40.00
Figurine, bellboy w/luggage, EX colors, 4" 20.00
Figurine, Blk fiddler in red & bl, 6" 40.00
Figurine, boy w/guitar & dog, 4½" 20.00
Figurine, boy w/umbrella, 6x4" 35.00
Figurine, bride & groom, bsk, 6" 45.00
Figurine, cat playing sax, bsk, 4" 32.00
Figurine, cherub w/sax on ball, bsk, 3½" 20.00
Figurine, Chinese boy in blk & wht, 6½" 27.50
Figurine, collie, porc, 5" 27.50
Figurine, Colonial man, bl coat, tricorner hat, 10½" 65.00

Figurine, couple at piano, 4" 15.00
Figurine, cowboy & cowgirl, bsk, 6½", pr 40.00
Figurine, Dutch boy & girl w/detachable buckets, bl, 4¼", pr 30.00
Figurine, elf on butterfly, 3¾" 20.00
Figurine, elf on snail, 4½x4" 25.00
Figurine, girl w/basket, Hummel type, 6¼" 35.00
Figurine, girl w/bird, Hummel type, bsk, 4" 20.00
Figurine, Hawaiian boy, 8" 50.00
Figurine, Indian chief w/tomahawk, 6" 40.00
Figurine, Indian w/bow & arrow, 5⅞" 30.00
Figurine, lady playing violin, 3-D flower on base, 7" 30.00
Figurine, lady w/feathers in hair, fancy gown, 10½" 35.00
Figurine, Little Red Riding Hood, 4" 15.00
Figurine, man w/hands in pockets, bsk, 2½" 8.50
Figurine, Mary & lamb, bsk, 8" 57.50
Figurine, Oriental dancer w/gr headdress holds fan, 6¼" ...20.00
Figurine, Oriental musical couple, 4", pr 20.00
Figurine, Oriental warrior, bsk, 8" 50.00
Figurine, Scottish lass in bl & red, bsk, 4½" 25.00
Figurine, Victorian man in high-bk chair, bl coat, 3" 14.00
Figurine, youth in knickers, hat in hand, 5" 16.50
Incense burner, elephant w/howdah lid, gold trim, Ucagco ...35.00
Incense burner, Indian holding burner, 6" 22.50
Lamp, Colonial couple, new silk shade, 15" 75.00
Lamp, parrot/tree trunk, pnt parrot on orig shade, 10" 60.00
Mug, elephant figural, trunk forms hdl, 4¾" 20.00
Pin, Scottie head, red bow at neck, celluloid, incised mk ...12.50
Planter, duck w/top hat, 6¾x5" 18.00
Planter, farmer & cart 15.00
Planter, kitten on slipper, 2½x5¼" 15.00
Planter, shoe house, red roof, bl shoestring, 4¼x5" 14.00
Planter, wheelbarrow, 2½" 10.00
Plaque, boy in blk hat & pants, Yamaka, 6¼" 22.50
Plaque, cup & saucer form, 4" 15.00
Plaque, Dutch lady, 6" 25.00
Plaque, girl in red hat & blouse, wht apron, 5¼" 15.00
Plaque, man in red hat & yel robe, Yamaka, 7½" 25.00
Plate, flamingos, Souvenir of Miami Florida, rtcl rim, 7¼" ...35.00
Plate, German Shepherd, 4" 25.00
Plate, old mill scene, 5¼" 25.00
Powder jar, appl gold flower on wht, 4x4½" 42.50
Shakers, cabbage form, 3¼x4⅛", pr 18.00
Shakers, chef & stove, 5", pr 37.50
Shakers, coffeepot form, metal w/emb florals, pr 17.50
Shakers, cowboy boots w/spurs, metal, mk in heel, pr 17.50
Shakers, mc florals w/gold top, 5½", pr 22.50
Shakers, red bird, 3¼", pr 20.00
Shelf, corner; lacquerware, folds flat, 9¼" 42.50
Sugar bowl, florals, ornate hdls, w/lid 12.00
Tea set, windmill forms, teapot+6 c/s 135.00
Teapot, floral on brn, sm 20.00
Teapot, tomato form, Maruhon Ware, mk, 4½" 35.00
Toby jug, preacher, 7" 55.00
Toby mug, devil bust, 2" 25.00
Tray, Indian's head, EX colors, 4¾x5" 47.50
Vase, florals on gr, maroon trim, 3" 10.00
Vase, fluted scalloped lip, hdls, metal, 5¾" 8.50
Wall pocket, iris form, mc 15.00
Wall pocket, teapot form w/flower decor, 6x8" 38.00

Ohr, George

George Ohr established his pottery around 1893 in Biloxi, Missis-

sippi. The unusual style of the ware he produced and his flamboyant personality earned him the dubious title of 'the mad potter of Biloxi.' Though acclaimed by some of the critics of his day to be perhaps the most accomplished thrower in the history of the industry, others overlooked the eggshell-thin walls of his vessels, each a different shape and contortion, and saw only that their 'tortured' appearance contradicted their own sedate preferences.

Ohr worked alone. His work was typically pinched and pulled, pleated, crumpled, dented, and folded. Lizards and worms were often applied to the ware, each with detailed, expressive features. He was well recognized, however, for his glazes, especially those with a metallic patina. The ware was marked with his name, alone or with 'Biloxi' added. Ohr died in 1918. Our advisor for this category is Fer-Duc, Inc.; whose address is listed in the Directory under New York.

Chalice, burnt gray w/ruffled cup on pocked gr flared base 900.00
Hat, khaki brn/gun-metal blk, free-form w/ripped edge, 2x6" ..1,700.00
Inkwell, house w//Am flag as base, ochre/gr specks, EX 1,700.00
Mug, buff bsk, in-body twist, 3 strap hdls, 4¾" 850.00
Mug, leathery bl to yel & gr, in-body twist, firing line, 4" 1,100.00
Pitcher, buff bsk, manipulated to form rim & cut-out hdl, 5" ..1,000.00
Pitcher, gun-metal, flaring sides, strap hdl, 10½" 1,200.00
Pitcher, gun-metal blk drip, dimpled/folded rim, Xd hdl, 4x7"....2,000.00
Pitcher, midnight bl/gr, ruffled rim, ftd, 6x5½" 1,900.00
Pitcher, sponged bl/rust/yel, folded rim, contrived hdl, 5" 3,250.00
Plaque, lg appl crab, dk gr gloss, 8x8½" 4,500.00
Teapot, brn speckled, in-body twist, 4x6" 2,750.00
Teapot, orange/brn gloss, gooseneck spout, minor flake, 4" 1,900.00
Teapot, red w/gr sponging, str sides, S-spout, 5x8" 8,800.00
Vase, beige/orange bsk, spherical w/central twist, 4x3½" 650.00
Vase, bl gloss, ftd ridged cylinder w/sloping shoulder, 4" 550.00
Vase, bl gloss, pear shape w/2 pinched necks, 4½x2¾" 1,050.00
Vase, bl/blood-red gloss, pleated rim, pear shape, 4½" 5,250.00
Vase, bl/gr, lav/bl matt int, under-rim twist, dents, 4x5" 3,000.00
Vase, blistered pk/bl, ftd, 4¾x2½" 650.00
Vase, blk aventurine/metal flakes, lg body dents, 4x2½" 700.00
Vase, blood red/gr gloss, ftd w/trumpet neck, 4½x2¾" 1,000.00
Vase, brn on yel specked, can neck, in-body twist, 3½x4" 1,650.00
Vase, brn/ochre gloss, bulbous, 2½x3" 350.00
Vase, buff bsk, folded/crimped-top cylinder w/base twist, 7" 800.00
Vase, gr/gun-metal blk, 3-step neck w/twist, 6x5" 2,750.00
Vase, gr/yel mottle, in-body twist, bulbous w/hdls, rpr, 6" 3,000.00
Vase, gun-metal blk, sm rim, joined at waist w/scallops, 3x5" .1,100.00
Vase, gun-metal blk matt, lily neck, 3-lobe ribbon hdls, 4½" ..1,800.00
Vase, half brn/half yel speckled, ridged, folded rim, 4x4½" 1,400.00
Vase, khaki gr, cylinder w/ear hdls (1 at rim/1 at base), 5" 700.00
Vase, khaki gr/brn gloss, goblet neck w/twist, 9x3" 3,400.00
Vase, khaki gr/maroon gloss w/blk specks, scroll hdls, 4x3" 2,000.00
Vase, lav speckled gloss, lg dents, folded rim, 5x5" 3,250.00
Vase, lt red bsk, rim fluted/flattened, pushed-in base, 5x5" 1,000.00
Vase, orange/buff bsk, folded rim, in-body base twist, 4½x3¾" ..1,000.00
Vase, pocked pk/bl matt, yel/gr speckled int, bbl shape, 5" 800.00
Vase, red bsk, folded rim/in-body twist, inscription, 3½" 1,000.00
Vase, red/cream swirl bsk, lengthy inscription, folded, 5" 3,100.00
Vase, royal bl gloss w/pinched 'faces,' sqd rim, 2¼x4" 850.00
Vase, wht bsk, flaring neck, dimpled, 5x3¼" 500.00
Vase, yel/gr flaring neck, leathery bl waist, 2¾x3" 600.00
Vessel, gun-metal blk bsk, folded rim, 3x6" 550.00
Vessel, lt bsk clay, closed-in folded rim, 4½x6" 675.00

Old Ivory

Old Ivory dinnerware was produced during the late 1800s by Herman Ohme, of Lower Salzbrunn in Silesia. The patterns are referred to by the numbers stamped on the bottom of many items. (Though not every piece is numbered, the vast majority bears the tiny blue fleur-de-lis/crown mark with Silesia or Germany beneath. Handwritten numbers signify something other than pattern.) Patterns #16 and #84 are the easiest to find and come in a wide variety of table items. Values are about the same for both patterns. Other floral designs include pink, yellow, and orange roses; holly; and lavender flowers — all on the same soft ivory background. The ware was not widely distributed; its two main distribution points were in Maine and, to a lesser extent, Chicago. Our prices are intended to represent a nationwide average, though you may have to pay a little more in some areas. Novice collectors should be aware of copy-cat versions from the turn of the century that are much heavier and of a coarser material. They are marked 'Old Ivory' without the blue trademark. They are not included in this listing.

Bowl, berry; #82, 5½" 25.00
Bowl, berry; Holly, #17, 5¾" 40.00
Cake plate, #15, 10" 125.00
Chocolate pot, #16 or #84 ....450.00
Chocolate pot, #75, yel roses 450.00
Chocolate pot, no #, 'Etoile,' gr roses & trim 595.00
Chocolate set, #16 or #84, pot+6 c/s 800.00
Chop plate, #15, rnd, worn gold 150.00
Cracker jar, #16 or #32, fleur-de-lis finial, tall 495.00
Cracker jar, #16 or #84, squatty, w/hdls 425.00
Cracker jar, #33, squat, hdls 375.00
Creamer & sugar bowl, #16 or #84, w/lid 225.00
Cup & saucer, chocolate; #7 ....50.00
Demitasse pot, #16 or #84, very rare, +6 c/s 975.00
Hair receiver, very rare, EX 150.00

Master berry bowl with four individual bowls (one shown), Holly pattern, $400.00.

Mayonnaise & tray, #16 or #84 ....250.00
Plate, #145, 6¼" 30.00
Plate, #16 or #84, 6¼" 25.00
Plate, #16 or #84, 7½" 45.00
Plate, serving; no #, 'Etoile,' gr roses, hdls, 10" sq 275.00
Platter, #21, orchid & wht flowers, 12x9½" 150.00
Platter, cold meat; #90, 11½x8¼", +8 7¾" plates 350.00
Shakers, #16 or #84, pr 135.00
Toothpick holder, #16 or #84 ....250.00
Tray, celery; #15, 11½" 95.00
Waste bowl, mk Silesia & Ohme 225.00

Old Paris

Old Paris porcelains were made from the mid-18th century until

about 1900. Seldom marked, the term refers to the area of manufacture rather than a specific company. In general, the ware was of high quality; characterized by classic shapes, colorful decoration, and gold application.

Candlestick, Chinaman in floral robe supports lily, 20", EX 1,000.00
Censer, maids as 4 seasons on bl & wine w/gilt, rstr, 9" 660.00
Cup, cylindrical w/scenes, gilt trim & paw ft, 4" 145.00
Cup & saucer, SS Dexter w/gold, RT Lux, 3¼", 6¼" 2,695.00
Cup & saucer, SS Ruth, RT Lux, wear/sm chip, 3½", 6¾" 1,700.00
Figurine, Diane (& Hercules), on floral-pnt plinth, 19", pr 1,200.00
Figurine, man (& lady) carry game birds, 13", pr 1,200.00
Plate, SS Ruth, RT Lux, gold trim, 9⅜" 240.00
Quill holder, figural seated hunter, chin to cheek, 9" 175.00
Urn, hunt scenes on cobalt w/gilt, scroll hdls, 14", EX 1,100.00
Urn, lg mc floral on blk body/sq base, gold swan hdls, 17" 800.00
Vase, bsk lady on base/floral, leaf hdls, fan top, 16", pr 500.00
Vase, lg figural panel on cobalt w/gold, classic form, 22" 500.00
Vase, maroon, cornucopia w/eagle head end, plinth, 8", pr 400.00
Vase, roses/gilt foliage on blk, scalloped, 9" 135.00
Vase, scenic on yel, flared, hdld/ftd, 1820s, 10", pr 1,000.00
Vase, Turkish slaves top/sq base, gold trim/hdls, 13", pr 4,000.00
Vase, wedding scene on purple, gr dragon hdls, 17", pr 850.00
Vase, wine w/floral, cylinder w/appl leaves/flowers, 14", pr 440.00

Old Sleepy Eye

Old Sleepy Eye was a Sioux Indian chief who was born in Minnesota in 1780. His name was used for the name of a town as well as a flour mill. In 1903 the Sleepy Eye Milling Company of Sleepy Eye, Minnesota, contracted the Weir Pottery Company of Monmouth, Illinois, to make steins, vases, salt crocks, and butter tubs which the company gave away to their customers in each bag of their flour. A bust profile of the old Indian and his name decorated each piece of the blue and gray stoneware. In addition to these four items, the Minnesota Stoneware Company of Red Wing made a mug with a verse which is very scarce today.

In 1906 Weir Pottery merged with six others to form the Western Stoneware Company in Monmouth. They produced a line of blue and white ware using a lighter body, but these pieces were never given as flour premiums. This line consisted of pitchers (five sizes), steins, mugs, sugar bowls, vases, trivets, and mustache cups. These pieces turn up only rarely in other colors and are highly prized by advanced collectors. Advertising items such as trade cards, pillow tops, thermometers, paperweights, letter openers, postcards, cookbooks, and thimbles are considered very valuable. The original ware was made sporadically until 1937. Brown steins and mugs were produced in 1952.

Barrel, flour; orig paper label, 1920s 1,800.00
Barrel, grapevine-effect banding 3,500.00
Barrel, oak w/brass bands 4,500.00
Butter crock, Flemish 625.00
Calendar, 1904, NM 375.00
Calendar, 1904, VG 150.00
Cookbook, EX 185.00
Cookbook, Indian on cover, Sleepy Eye Milling Co, 4¾x4" 300.00
Cookbook, loaf of bread shape, EX 115.00
Cookbook, loaf of bread shape, NM 210.00
Coupon, for ordering cookbook 250.00
Coupon, for ordering pillow top 200.00
Dough scraper, tin/wood, To Be Sure, EX 435.00
Fan, Indian chief, die-cut cb, 1900 ....220.00
Flour sack, cloth, mc Indian, red letters 345.00
Flour sack, paper, Indian in blk, blk lettering, NM 125.00

Ink blotter 125.00
Label, barrel end; mc Indian portrait, 16", NM 160.00
Label, egg crate; Indian chief in color, 1930s, 9x11" 32.00
Letter opener, bronze 900.00
Match holder, pnt 1,875.00
Match holder, wht 1,050.00
Mug, bl & gray, 4¼" 360.00
Mug, bl & wht, 4¼" 220.00
Mug, verse, Red Wing, EX 1,625.00
Paperweight, bronzed company trademk 560.00
Pillow cover, Sleepy Eye & tribe meet President Monroe 750.00
Pillow cover, trademk center w/various scenes, 22", NM 850.00
Pin-bk button, Indian, rnd face 350.00
Pitcher, #1, 4" 185.00
Pitcher, #2 ....250.00
Pitcher, #3 ....315.00
Pitcher, #3, w/bl rim 1,375.00
Pitcher, #4 ....400.00
Pitcher, #5 ....435.00
Pitcher, bl & gray, 5" 235.00
Pitcher, bl on cream, 8", M 345.00
Pitcher, gold & brn, 1981 ....160.00
Pitcher, standing Indian, good color, #5 size 1,560.00
Plaque, plaster bust of Old Sleepy Eye in wood fr, 33x25" 385.00
Postcard, colorful trademk, 1904 Expo Winner 185.00
Ruler, wooden, 15" 500.00
Salt crock, Flemish, 4x6½" 560.00
Sheet music, in fr 300.00
Sign, self-fr tin, Old Sleepy Eye Flour, 20x24" 2,500.00
Sign, tin litho die-cut Indian, ...Flour & Cereals, 13½" 1,650.00
Spoon, demitasse; emb roses in bowl, Unity SP 105.00
Spoon, Indian-head hdl 125.00
Stein, bl & wht, 7¾" 625.00
Stein, brn, 1952, 22-oz 300.00
Stein, brn & wht 1,125.00
Stein, brn & yel, Western Stoneware 1,125.00
Stein, cobalt 1,000.00
Stein, Flemish 595.00
Stein, ltd edition, 1979-84, ea 125.00
Sugar bowl, bl & wht, 3" 750.00
Thermometer, front rpl 400.00
Vase, cattail, all cobalt 1,450.00
Vase, cattails, bl & wht, good color, 9" 530.00
Vase, cattails, brn on yel, rare color 1,000.00
Vase, Indian & cattails, Flemish, 8½" 470.00

O'Neill, Rose

Rose O'Neill's Kewpies were introduced in 1909 when they were used to conclude a story in the December issue of *Ladies' Home Journal*. They were an immediate success, and soon Kewpie dolls were being produced worldwide. German manufacturers were among the earliest and also used the Kewpie motif to decorate chinaware as well as other items. The Kewpie is still popular today and can be found on products ranging from Christmas cards and cake ornaments to fabrics and wallpaper.

Our advisor for this category is Denis C. Jackson who is listed in the Directory under Washington. In the following listings, 'sgn' indicates that the item is signed Rose O'Neill. Unsigned items are of little interest to collectors. Items marked 'Germany' are sometimes reproductions.

Bell, brass, Kewpie figural, 3" 98.00
Book, Kewpies Book, 1983, M 24.00
Box, bsk, Kewpie on bk, kicking, on lid, 2½" 365.00

Cake top, Huggers, 3½" 245.00
Creamer, gr jasper w/pk Kewpies & flowers, Germany, 2½" 315.00
Cup, Kewpies on milk glass 32.00
Kewpie, bsk, arms folded, 4½" 550.00
Kewpie, bsk, Doodle Dog, 1½" 550.00
Kewpie, bsk, Doodle Dog, 4" 2,000.00
Kewpie, bsk, Farmer, 4" 445.00
Kewpie, bsk, Governor, 2½" 315.00
Kewpie, bsk, Governor, 4" 445.00
Kewpie, bsk, Guitar Player, 3½" 390.00
Kewpie, bsk, Hottentot, Blk, 3½" 440.00
Kewpie, bsk, Huggers, 3½" 315.00
Kewpie, bsk, Japan, 2" 50.00
Kewpie, bsk, Japan, 6" 130.00
Kewpie, bsk, jtd hips & shoulders, pnt shoes & socks, 4" 445.00
Kewpie, bsk, jtd hips & shoulders, pnt shoes & socks, 7" 1,000.00
Kewpie, bsk, jtd hips & shoulders, 12" 1,150.00
Kewpie, bsk, jtd hips & shoulders, 4" 485.00
Kewpie, bsk, reclining on stomach, label, 3" 475.00

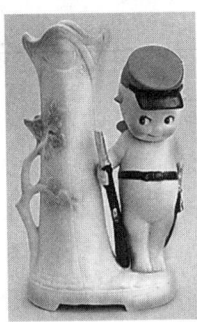

Kewpie, bisque, Soldier, Germany, ca 1913, 6½", M, $970.00.

Kewpie, bsk, Thinker, 6" 440.00
Kewpie, bsk, Traveler, 3½" 360.00
Kewpie, bsk, Traveler w/Doodle Dog, Japan, 2½" 425.00
Kewpie, bsk, 1-pc body & head, jtd shoulders, clothing, 3" 260.00
Kewpie, bsk, 1-pc body & head, jtd shoulders, clothing, 7" 365.00
Kewpie, bsk, 1-pc body & head, jtd shoulders, 10" 655.00
Kewpie, bsk, 1-pc body & head, jtd shoulders, 2½" 130.00
Kewpie, bsk, 1-pc body & head, jtd shoulders, 6" 235.00
Kewpie, bsk head, glass eyes, cloth body, 16", minimum value ..4,700.00
Kewpie, bsk head, glass eyes, toddler body, JDK, 10" 4,300.00
Kewpie, bsk head, pnt eyes, cloth body, 10" 2,300.00
Kewpie, bsk head, pnt eyes, cloth body, 14" 2,400.00
Kewpie, celluloid, Blk, 5" 150.00
Kewpie, celluloid, jtd shoulders, 12" 260.00
Kewpie, celluloid, jtd shoulders, 22", minimum value 945.00
Kewpie, celluloid, jtd shoulders, 3" 75.00
Kewpie, celluloid, Soldier or Action figure, 4", minimum 100.00
Kewpie, celluloid, 2" 42.50
Kewpie, celluloid, 9" 170.00
Kewpie, cloth, 1-pc body, orig dress & bonnet, 12", M 275.00
Kewpie, cloth, 1-pc body forms clothes, mask face, 26", M 1,150.00
Kewpie, cloth, 1-pc body forms clothes, mask face, 8", M 185.00
Kewpie, shoulder head, cloth or stockinette body, 7" 685.00
Kewpie driving chariot, bsk, minimum value 2,950.00
Kewpie in basket w/flowers, bsk, 3½" 575.00
Kewpie in chair w/arms crossed, bsk, 3½" 500.00
Kewpie on inkwell, bsk, 3½" 575.00
Kewpie on tummy, tiny bl wings, bsk, 4", minimum value 515.00
Kewpie perfume bottle, bsk, 3½" 395.00
Kewpie w/broom, bsk, 4" 480.00
Kewpie w/pumpkin, bsk, 4" 365.00

Kewpie w/turkey, bsk, 2" 350.00
Kewpies, bsk, 2 reading book, sgn, 3½" 895.00
Paperweight, Kewpie center, pnt-on wings, Gibson 1935, 4½" ...345.00
Pitcher, cook jumping over other Kewpie, sgn 245.00
Postcard, Action Kewpies, M 12.00
Postcard, Kewpies, Christmas, ca 1920s 38.00
Sifter, flour; Kewpie pnt on tin 48.00
Soap, Kewpie figural, 4", set of 5, MIB 550.00
Spoon, SP, Kewpie hdl 100.00

Onion Pattern

The familiar pattern known to collectors as Onion acquired its name through a case of mistaken identity. Designed in the early 1700s by Johann Haroldt of the Meissen factory in Germany, the pattern was a mixture of earlier Oriental designs. One of its components was a stylized peach, which was mistaken for an onion; as a result, the pattern became known by that name. Usually found in blue, an occasional piece may also be found in pink and red. The pattern is commonly associated with Meissen, but it has been reproduced by many others including Villeroy and Boch and Royal Copenhagen.

Blue Danube is a modern line of Onion-patterned dinnerware produced in Japan and distributed by Lipper International of Wallingford, Connecticut. 125 items are available in porcelain; it is sold in most large stores with china departments.

Basket, rtcl, shallow, Meissen, 1890s, 7" 150.00
Bowl, notched corners, Xd swords, sq, 9" 275.00
Butter pat, Germany 23.00
Cake plate, 10" dia 155.00
Canister, Zucker, stenciled, ped base 65.00
Chamberstick, 6" 75.00
Coffeepot, graniteware 50.00
Creamer, Meissen, 3½" 60.00
Cup & saucer, Germany 30.00
Cup & saucer, Hutschenreuther 26.00
Cup & saucer, Meissen Xd swords 85.00
Cup & saucer, no mk 25.00
Funnel, loop hdl 75.00
Infant feeder, 6¼x2½" 60.00
Jar, instant coffee; Japan 20.00
Letter opener, brass blade, Germany 35.00
Masher, lg 175.00
Plate, bread & butter; Hutschenreuther 15.00
Plate, dinner; Hutschenreuther, 10½" 24.00
Plate, lattice edge, Meissen, 11½" 165.00
Plate, Meissen Xd swords, 10" 70.00
Plate, salad; Hutschenreuther 16.50
Plate, sq, Meakin, 7" 30.00
Platter, Germany, 10x7¼" 60.00
Rolling pin, heavy porc, unmk Germany, 18" 275.00
Salt box, rnd, wooden lid, wall mt, Made in Japan, 7" 95.00
Spoon, 10" 85.00
Tureen, rnd, hdls, Japan, w/underplate, 9" 30.00
Vase, ftd, Xd swords, 5" 130.00

Opalescent Glass

First made in England in 1870, opalescent glass became popular in America around the turn of the century. Its name comes from the milky-white opalescent trim that defines the lines of the pattern. It was produced in table sets, novelties, toothpick holders, vases, and lamps.

Acorn Burrs (& Bark), bowl, sauce; bl 40.00
Alaska, banana boat, vaseline 185.00
Alaska, butter dish, vaseline 225.00
Alaska, creamer, bl 75.00
Alaska, creamer, emerald 55.00
Alaska, creamer, vaseline 65.00
Alaska, cruet, emerald 195.00
Alaska, pitcher, water; bl 385.00
Alaska, pitcher, water; vaseline 370.00
Alaska, shakers, bl, pr 100.00
Alaska, shakers, bl w/HP decor, pr 110.00
Alaska, shakers, vaseline, pr 90.00
Alaska, spooner, bl 75.00
Alaska, spooner, vaseline 65.00
Alaska, sugar bowl, bl, w/lid 160.00
Alaska, sugar bowl, vaseline, w/lid 135.00
Alaska, tray, bl 180.00
Alaska, tumbler, vaseline 65.00
Arabian Nights, pitcher, water; bl 275.00
Arabian Nights, pitcher, water; vaseline 265.00
Arabian Nights, pitcher, water; wht 210.00
Arabian Nights, tumbler, cranberry 100.00
Argonaut Shell, butter dish, bl 295.00
Argonaut Shell, compote, jelly; vaseline 85.00
Argonaut Shell, cruet, wht 150.00
Argonaut Shell, spooner, bl 150.00
Argonaut Shell, sugar bowl, bl, w/lid 225.00
Argonaut Shell, tumbler, vaseline, rare 125.00
Beaded Ovals in Sand, butter dish, bl 270.00
Beaded Ovals in Sand, creamer, gr 70.00
Beads & Bark, vase, gr, ftd 55.00
Beatty Rib, creamer, wht, ind 25.00
Beatty Rib, sugar bowl, bl 125.00
Beatty Swirl, butter dish, bl 160.00
Beatty Swirl, mug, bl 50.00
Beatty Swirl, pitcher, water; vaseline 170.00
Beatty Swirl, tray, water; bl 80.00
Beatty Swirl, tumbler, vaseline 45.00
Blown Drape, tumbler, gr 40.00
Boggy Bayou, vase, amethyst 45.00
Bubble Lattice, butter dish, gr 150.00
Bubble Lattice, cruet, vaseline 160.00
Bubble Lattice, finger bowl, gr 30.00
Bubble Lattice, spooner, bl 50.00
Bubble Lattice, sugar bowl, wht 65.00
Bubble Lattice, toothpick holder, gr 240.00
Bubble Lattice, tumbler, cranberry 95.00
Buttons & Braids, bowl, wht 35.00
Buttons & Braids, pitcher, water; bl 175.00
Buttons & Braids, pitcher, water; gr 175.00
Buttons & Braids, tumbler, bl 40.00
Buttons & Braids, tumbler, cranberry 100.00
Christmas Pearls, shakers, gr, pr 90.00
Christmas Snowflake, tumbler, bl 85.00
Christmas Snowflake, tumbler, cranberry 100.00
Chrysanthemum Base Swirl, bowl, sauce; wht 25.00
Chrysanthemum Base Swirl, butter dish, bl 300.00
Chrysanthemum Base Swirl, pitcher, water; bl 395.00
Chrysanthemum Base Swirl, straw holder, bl 350.00
Chrysanthemum Base Swirl, sugar shaker, bl 175.00
Chrysanthemum Base Swirl, tumbler, bl 80.00
Circle Scroll, compote, jelly; bl 145.00
Circle Scroll, spooner, gr 80.00
Circle Scroll, sugar bowl, gr 175.00

Circle Scroll, tumbler, bl 90.00
Coin Spot, bowl, berry; cranberry, master 60.00
Coin Spot, celery vase, gr 110.00
Coin Spot, compote, bl 50.00
Coin Spot, pitcher, water; gr 130.00
Coin Spot, pitcher, water; rubena 170.00
Coin Spot, pitcher, water; wht 90.00
Coin Spot, sugar shaker, gr 95.00
Coin Spot, tumble-up, cranberry 235.00
Coin Spot, tumbler, bl 40.00
Criss Cross, pitcher, water; cranberry, Consolidated 1,200.00
Criss Cross, sauce, wht, Consolidated 45.00
Daisy & Fern, bottle, scent; cranberry 135.00
Daisy & Fern, creamer, cranberry 195.00
Daisy & Fern, mustard pot, bl 85.00
Daisy & Fern, pitcher, water; bl 225.00
Daisy & Fern, pitcher, water; wht 135.00
Daisy & Fern, shakers, cranberry, 2¾", pr 170.00
Daisy & Fern, sugar bowl, bl 125.00
Daisy & Fern, tumbler, gr 50.00
Daisy & Fern, vase, cranberry 135.00
Diamond Spearhead, celery vase, wht 75.00
Diamond Spearhead, compote, gr, tall 125.00
Diamond Spearhead, compote, jelly; vaseline 100.00
Diamond Spearhead, creamer, bl 90.00
Diamond Spearhead, cup & saucer, vaseline 80.00
Diamond Spearhead, mug, cobalt 70.00
Diamond Spearhead, pitcher, water; bl or vaseline, ea 395.00
Diamond Spearhead, pitcher, water; wht 225.00
Diamond Spearhead, spooner, gr 100.00
Diamond Spearhead, sugar bowl, bl 200.00
Dolly Madison, creamer, gr 90.00
Dolly Madison, spooner, bl 70.00
Dolly Madison, spooner, wht 55.00
Dolly Madison, sugar bowl, bl, w/lid 125.00
Dolly Madison, tumbler, gr 80.00
Double Greek Key, butter dish, wht 160.00
Double Greek Key, celery vase, bl 120.00
Double Greek Key, creamer, bl 110.00
Double Greek Key, shakers, wht, pr 150.00
Double Greek Key, spooner, bl 75.00
Double Greek Key, sugar bowl, bl, w/lid 155.00
Double Greek Key, tumbler, bl 65.00
Drapery, creamer, bl 75.00
Drapery, pitcher, water; bl 175.00
Everglades, bowl, sauce; bl, oval 40.00
Everglades, butter dish, bl 250.00
Everglades, butter dish, vaseline 280.00
Everglades, compote, jelly; gr 100.00
Everglades, compote, jelly; vaseline 115.00
Everglades, creamer, bl 95.00
Everglades, pitcher, water; vaseline 375.00
Everglades, shakers, vaseline, pr 220.00
Everglades, sugar bowl, bl 135.00
Everglades, tumbler, bl 70.00
Fan, butter dish, gr 350.00
Fan, gravy boat, wht 35.00
Fern, finger bowl, bl 55.00
Fern, mustard pot, bl 130.00
Fern, pitcher, bl 225.00
Fern, pitcher, water; cranberry, 8½" 450.00
Fern, shakers, wht, pr 90.00
Fern, toothpick holder, cranberry, rare 450.00
Fern, tumbler, cranberry 90.00

Fern, tumbler, wht 30.00
Flora, butter dish, wht 135.00
Flora, compote, jelly; vaseline 115.00
Flora, creamer, vaseline 80.00
Flora, cruet, bl 650.00
Flora, pitcher, water; bl 475.00
Flora, shakers, vaseline, pr 400.00
Flora, shakers, wht, pr 250.00
Flora, spooner, vaseline 90.00
Flora, sugar bowl, bl, w/lid 120.00
Flora, toothpick holder, vaseline 310.00
Flora, toothpick holder, wht 200.00
Flora, tumbler, bl 75.00
Fluted Scrolls, butter dish, bl 145.00
Fluted Scrolls, cruet, bl 150.00
Fluted Scrolls, pitcher, water; bl 200.00
Fluted Scrolls, pitcher, water; vaseline 195.00
Fluted Scrolls, puff box, vaseline 50.00
Frosted-Leaf & Basketweave, butter dish, vaseline 240.00
Frosted-Leaf & Basketweave, creamer, vaseline or canary, ea 125.00
Frosted-Leaf & Basketweave, spooner, bl 130.00
Frosted-Leaf & Basketweave, sugar bowl, bl 170.00
Gonterman Swirl, butter dish, amber 325.00
Gonterman Swirl, celery vase, bl or amber, ea 185.00
Gonterman Swirl, creamer, bl 80.00
Gonterman Swirl, cruet, bl 300.00
Hobnail, butter dish, bl 250.00
Hobnail, butter dish, cranberry 290.00
Hobnail, celery, vaseline, 6½" 150.00
Hobnail, creamer, vaseline 95.00
Hobnail, finger bowl, cranberry 90.00
Hobnail, syrup, rubena 325.00
Hobnail, tray, water; bl 135.00
Hobnail, tumbler, cranberry 85.00
Honeycomb, cracker jar, bl 265.00
Honeycomb, pitcher, amber 275.00
Honeycomb & Clover, bowl, master berry; bl 60.00
Honeycomb & Clover, bowl, novelty, wht 26.00
Honeycomb & Clover, butter dish, bl 325.00
Honeycomb & Clover, tumbler, gr 75.00
Idyll, butter dish, gr 375.00
Idyll, creamer, gr 85.00
Idyll, spooner, bl 130.00
Idyll, sugar bowl, gr 200.00
Idyll, toothpick holder, bl 300.00
Idyll, tumbler, bl 80.00
Intaglio, bowl, novelty, bl 45.00
Intaglio, butter dish, bl 400.00
Intaglio, compote, jelly; wht 30.00
Intaglio, creamer, bl 60.00
Intaglio, cruet, vaseline 175.00
Intaglio, shakers, bl, pr 150.00
Intaglio, spooner, wht 35.00
Intaglio, sugar bowl, wht 85.00
Intaglio, tumbler, wht 50.00
Inverted Fan & Feather, creamer, bl 140.00
Inverted Fan & Feather, shakers, bl, pr 250.00
Inverted Fan & Feather, tumbler, bl 85.00
Iris w/Meander, bowl, master berry; gr 80.00
Iris w/Meander, butter dish, bl 300.00
Iris w/Meander, compote, jelly; bl or vaseline, ea 45.00
Iris w/Meander, creamer, bl or vaseline, ea 95.00
Iris w/Meander, pickle dish, wht 40.00
Iris w/Meander, pitcher, water; bl 375.00

Iris w/Meander, spooner, bl	75.00
Iris w/Meander, sugar bowl, gr, w/lid	125.00
Iris w/Meander, toothpick holder, wht	45.00
Iris w/Meander, tumbler, wht	55.00
Iris w/Meander, vase, vaseline	60.00
Jackson, candy dish, vaseline	40.00
Jackson, creamer, bl	75.00
Jackson, pitcher, water; bl	250.00
Jackson, spooner, vaseline	60.00
Jackson, sugar bowl, bl	115.00
Jackson, sugar bowl, vaseline	110.00
Jackson, tumbler, wht	60.00
Jewel & Flower, bowl, novelty, bl	35.00
Jewel & Flower, butter dish, bl	300.00
Jewel & Flower, creamer, wht	55.00
Jewel & Flower, cruet, vaseline	350.00
Jewel & Flower, pitcher, water; bl	650.00
Jewel & Flower, pitcher, water; vaseline	450.00
Jewel & Flower, spooner, bl	95.00
Jewel & Flower, tumbler, vaseline	70.00
Jeweled Heart, bowl, sauce; wht	25.00
Jeweled Heart, butter dish, bl	300.00
Jeweled Heart, compote, gr	120.00
Jeweled Heart, plate, bl, sm	40.00
Jeweled Heart, sugar bowl, gr, w/lid	155.00
Jeweled Heart, tumbler, gr	55.00
Lords & Ladies, butter dish, bl	85.00
Lords & Ladies, creamer, bl	55.00
Lustre Flute, bowl, sauce; bl	25.00
Lustre Flute, butter dish, bl	285.00
Lustre Flute, pitcher, bl	325.00
Lustre Flute, spooner, bl	90.00
Lustre Flute, tumbler, wht	40.00
Over-All Hob, creamer, bl	50.00
Over-All Hob, pitcher, water; vaseline	175.00
Palm Beach, pitcher, water; vaseline	350.00
Palm Beach, spooner, vaseline	125.00
Palm Beach, sugar bowl, bl	175.00
Palm Beach, tumbler, bl	95.00
Palm Beach, wine, vaseline, rare	350.00
Paneled Holly, bowl, master berry; bl	85.00
Paneled Holly, butter dish, bl	300.00
Paneled Holly, shakers, bl, pr	250.00
Paneled Holly, spooner, wht	60.00
Paneled Holly, sugar bowl, bl	225.00
Paneled Holly, tumbler, wht	45.00
Paneled Sprig, cruet, wht	115.00
Paneled Sprig, cruet, wht opal lattice, scarce	165.00
Paneled Sprig, toothpick holder, wht	70.00

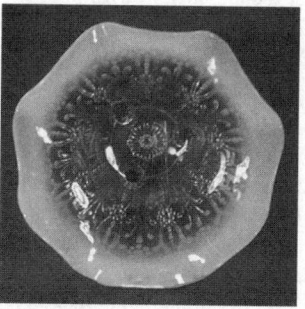

Pearl Flowers, bowl, blue ruffled rim, three-footed, 9", $62.50.

Poinsettia, bowl, fruit; bl	70.00
Poinsettia, pitcher, water; bl, either shape	275.00
Poinsettia, sugar shaker, gr	200.00
Poinsettia, syrup, cranberry	350.00
Poinsettia, tumbler, bl	95.00
Polka Dot, pitcher, water; cranberry	700.00
Princess Diana, butter dish, bl	90.00
Princess Diana, compote, bl, metal base	120.00
Princess Diana, pitcher, water; vaseline	90.00
Regal, butter dish, bl	200.00
Regal, celery vase, bl	165.00
Regal, celery vase, gr	140.00
Regal, pitcher, gr	195.00
Regal, sugar bowl, bl	195.00
Reverse Swirl, bottle, water; bl	140.00
Reverse Swirl, butter dish, vaseline	165.00
Reverse Swirl, cruet, cranberry	450.00
Reverse Swirl, custard cup, bl	45.00
Reverse Swirl, lamp, cranberry, mini	290.00
Reverse Swirl, pitcher, water; bl	195.00
Reverse Swirl, sugar shaker, vaseline	135.00
Reverse Swirl, tumbler, wht	26.00
Ribbed Spiral, creamer, vaseline	55.00
Ribbed Spiral, pitcher, water; bl	600.00
Ribbed Spiral, shakers, bl, pr	195.00
Ribbed Spiral, toothpick holder, bl	95.00
Ribbed Spiral, vase, vaseline, lg	35.00
Ruffles & Rings, bowl, nut; gr	30.00
Ruffles & Rings, rose bowl, bl	35.00
Scroll w/Acanthus, bowl, master berry; bl	40.00
Scroll w/Acanthus, butter dish, bl	350.00
Scroll w/Acanthus, compote, jelly; gr	40.00
Scroll w/Acanthus, pitcher, water; gr	400.00
Scroll w/Acanthus, shakers, gr, pr	80.00
Scroll w/Acanthus, sugar bowl, gr	135.00
Scroll w/Acanthus, toothpick holder, bl	200.00
Scroll w/Acanthus, tumbler, gr or vaseline, ea	70.00
Seaweed, butter dish, cranberry	350.00
Seaweed, pitcher, water; bl	310.00
Seaweed, syrup, wht	115.00
Shell, Beaded; sugar bowl, bl	185.00
Shell, Beaded; toothpick holder, gr	500.00
Shell, Beaded; tumbler, gr	85.00
Spanish Lace, bottle, scent; bl	175.00
Spanish Lace, bride's basket, cranberry, 2 sizes, ea	160.00
Spanish Lace, creamer, bl	80.00
Spanish Lace, cruet, bl	230.00
Spanish Lace, jug, liqueur; cranberry	750.00
Spanish Lace, pitcher, water; cranberry	500.00
Spanish Lace, rose bowl, vaseline	45.00
Spanish Lace, shakers, vaseline, bulbous, 2⅞", pr	160.00
Spanish Lace, sugar shaker, cranberry	180.00
Spanish Lace, tumbler, vaseline	60.00
Stars & Stripes, pitcher, water; cranberry	975.00
Stars & Stripes, pitcher, water; cranberry, tankard form, 8½"	1,500.00
Stars & Stripes, tumbler, wht	60.00
Stripe, pitcher, bl	250.00
Stripe, shakers, vaseline, pr	95.00
Stripe, tumbler, bl	45.00
Sunburst on Shield, bowl, master berry; bl	60.00
Sunburst on Shield, cruet, bl, rare	500.00
Sunburst on Shield, pitcher, water; bl	500.00
Sunburst on Shield, spooner, bl	125.00
Sunburst on Shield, sugar bowl, vaseline	175.00

Sunburst on Shield, tumbler, bl 100.00
Swag w/Brackets, bowl, novelty, vaseline 40.00
Swag w/Brackets, bowl, sauce; gr 26.00
Swag w/Brackets, butter dish, bl 165.00
Swag w/Brackets, compote, jelly; bl 48.00
Swag w/Brackets, creamer, bl 75.00
Swag w/Brackets, creamer, vaseline 70.00
Swag w/Brackets, shakers, vaseline, pr 200.00
Swag w/Brackets, spooner, bl 85.00
Swag w/Brackets, toothpick holder, gr 270.00
Swag w/Brackets, tumbler, gr 60.00
Swirl, pitcher, water; bl 125.00
Swirl, pitcher, water; cranberry 595.00
Swirl, sugar bowl, bl, w/lid 85.00
Swirl, toothpick holder, gr 100.00
Tokyo, compote, jelly; bl 40.00
Tokyo, plate, wht 30.00
Tokyo, sugar bowl, bl 110.00
Tokyo, vase, gr 45.00
Water Lily & Cattails, bowl, master berry; bl 55.00
Water Lily & Cattails, relish, gr, hdls 35.00
Water Lily & Cattails, spooner, amethyst 65.00
Water Lily & Cattails, sugar bowl, gr 175.00
Water Lily & Cattails, tumbler, bl 55.00
Wild Bouquet, bowl, sauce; bl 35.00
Wild Bouquet, butter dish, bl 450.00
Wild Bouquet, compote, jelly, gr 135.00
Wild Bouquet, compote, jelly; bl 150.00
Wild Bouquet, creamer, gr 70.00
Wild Bouquet, shakers, bl, pr 135.00
Wild Bouquet, toothpick holder, gr 400.00
Wild Bouquet, tumbler, bl, rare 125.00
Windows (Swirled), celery vase, bl 75.00
Windows (Swirled), mustard, cranberry 100.00
Windows (Swirled), pitcher, water; cranberry 695.00
Windows (Swirled), plate, cranberry, either sz 200.00
Windows (Swirled), toothpick holder, bl 275.00
Wreath & Shell, bowl, master berry; bl 85.00
Wreath & Shell, bowl, novelty; vaseline 50.00
Wreath & Shell, bowl, sauce; bl 30.00
Wreath & Shell, butter dish, bl 225.00
Wreath & Shell, celery vase, bl 165.00
Wreath & Shell, pitcher, water; wht 170.00
Wreath & Shell, rose bowl, bl 80.00
Wreath & Shell, sugar bowl, cranberry, w/lid 130.00

Opaline

A type of semiopaque opal glass, opaline was made in white as well as pastel shades and is often enameled. It is similar in appearance to English bristol glass, though its enamel or gilt decorative devices tend to exhibit a French influence.

Bottle, scent; pk, gold filigree scrolls, 2¾x1½" 110.00
Box, bl, brass mts/paw ft, 4½x7½x5" 190.00
Box, wht, Greek Key cast gilt metal hinge, 4x5½" 145.00
Ring tree, gold & wht decor on bl, 2½" 48.00
Vase, pk w/floral, elongated U-form in SP base w/flower mt 150.00

Orientalia

The art of the Orient is an area of collecting currently enjoy-

ing strong collector interest, not only in those examples that are truly 'antique' but in the 20th-century items as well. Because of the many aspects involved in a study of Orientalia, we can only try through brief comments to acquaint the reader with some of the more readily available examples. We suggest you refer to specialized reference sources for more detailed information. See also specific categories.

Key:
Ch — Chinese	FV — Famille Verte
ctp — contemporary	gb — guard border
cvg — carving	hdwd — hardwood
drw — drawer	Jp — Japan
Dy — Dynasty	Ko — Korean
E — export	lcq — lacquer
FJ — Famille Juane	mdl — medallion
FN — Famille Noire	rswd — rosewood
FR — Famille Rose	tkwd — teakwood

Blanc de Chine

Figurine, Kuan Ti, robes over his armor, 15", +stand 600.00
Figurine, lady w/long-stem flower on rockwork base, 8½" 65.00
Figurine, Quan Yin w/scroll, seated by table, rstr, 9" 1,400.00
Teapot, molded as a laughing Buddha, Qianlong period, 6" 400.00

Blue and White Porcelain

Bottle, 3 Friends (pine/plum/bamboo) ea side, Choson Dy, 10" .11,000.00
Bottle, 3-claw dragon/flaming pearl, Choson Dy, 11" 5,200.00
Bowl, landscape panels, archaic-style mk, 1600s, 6½" 375.00
Garden seat, rtcl bl ground w/wht florals, hexagonal, 19" 395.00
Jar, dragons/phoenix, shouldered sq, rtcl lid, Wan Li mk, 7" ...3,500.00
Jar, 4 mum medallions between scrolls, 1700s, 7", NM 1,350.00
Vase, cranes in relief on bl cloud ground, cylindrical, 12" 375.00

Bronze

Figure, female buffalo with hoof raised, mouth open in mid-cry, signed Sui-u-ken, Meiji Period, 8⅝" long, $250.00.

Bowl, 3-lobe, 3 cylinder ft, loop hdls, Han Dy style, 8" H 275.00
Devil's mask, cat head in ornate headdress, 1900, 17" 400.00
Figure, many-armed deity, ornate headdress, lotus base, 18" 1,100.00
Figure, seated Hotei, Ch, 2¾" 120.00
Jar, bird reserves, foo lion finials, Jp, 1800s, 16", pr 600.00
Jar, dragon relief, dragon finial, ftd, spherical, 6", EX 110.00
Letter opener, figural hdl, Jp 55.00
Pen case, simple silver inlay, gourd form w/hdl, Jp, 6¾" 50.00
Sculpture, dragon holding 3¾" crystal ball, Jp, 11" 425.00
Sculpture, warrior w/sword, Jp, 15", pr 1,485.00

Tsuba, gold inlay, 2 figures & trees, 1800s, 2½x2" **375.00**
Urn, bird reserves, bird/elephant legs, monkey finial, 38" **2,500.00**
Vase, intricate relief motifs, 3-sided/ftd, Jp, 1800s, 17" **325.00**

Celadon

Celadon, introduced during the Ching Dynasty, is a green-glazed ware developed in an attempt to imitate the color of jade. Designs are often incised or painted on over glaze in heavy enamel applications.

Bowl, dense sm/random lg crackle, Koryo Dy, 12/13th C, 7" ...**6,900.00**
Bowl, eng floral spray, ftd, Ming Dy, 6½", pr **500.00**
Bowl, notched lip, Ko, 1200s, kiln adhesion, 7½" **200.00**
Bowl, 4 floral rnds/string courses, int: 4 phoenixes, 1200, 8" **700.00**
Brush pot, carp/waves, cylindrical, 1800s, 6" **325.00**
Charger, peony band, 2 petal rings, 1700s, 16" **440.00**
Dish, cvd lotus petals, clouds/emb dragon, 1300, rstr, 16" **650.00**
Dish, shallow, on thick ring ft, Ming Dy, about 14th C, 10" **220.00**
Tazza, butterflies, in ornate Fr ormolu holder, 5" dia **220.00**
Vase, appl brn foliate/geometric borders, dbl gourd, 13", pr **1,100.00**
Vase, emb foliage, late Ming Dy, now lamp, vase: 8" **275.00**
Vase, inlaid blk/wht strands of mums, pear form, 1100s, 13" .**21,850.00**

Furniture

Armchair, tkwd, dragon arms/bk support, cvd legs, Ch **365.00**
Breakfront, hdwd w/inlay, rtcl crest, figural surmount, 96" **1,300.00**
Cabinet, blk lcq w/decor, Meiji, 42", +lcq stand **2,300.00**
Cabinet, lcq, pagoda top, doors, several drw, Ch E, 23" **995.00**
Cabinet, red lcq/parcel gilt, cvd/rtcl doors, Ch, 90x36" **700.00**
Stand, hdwd w/marble inset, cvgs, 4-legs, 1880s **600.00**
Table, hdwd, fr/legs/apron w/extensive inlay, 48" marble top ..**2,000.00**
Table, 4 ferocious dragon legs, rnd w/center ped, Ch, 59" **2,550.00**

Hardstones

Cornelian, bowl, rtcl rswd stand w/berries/floral, 3½x4" **175.00**
Crystal quartz, Ho-Ti, 1880s, 2½", tkwd stand **75.00**
Jade, celadon, group of 3 intricately cvd hairpins, 1800s **1,800.00**
Jade, gr, brush washer, cvd lotus pods, rswd stand, 2¾x4" **100.00**
Jade, gr, medallion, rtcl floral/bird, 2¼" dia, tkwd stand **65.00**
Jade, gr & wht, dbl dish, cvd as joined leaves, 8¾" **150.00**
Jade, lt gr w/mutton fat & rust, brush pot, cylindrical **385.00**
Jade, muttonfat, mtn w/3 immortals & pavilion, 1700s, 3½" **800.00**
Jade, nephrite, vase w/loose ring hdls on cvd tabs, 2½" **50.00**
Jade, spinach, vase, mask/ring hdls, cvgs, lid, 1700s, 6", NM ...**1,495.00**
Jade, wht, dragon group joined by rtcl link chain, 5" **2,000.00**
Jade, wht, plaque, rtcl/cvd w/cranes & ju-i in clouds, 5x1¾" **250.00**
Jadeite, wht/gr, pendant, bird/prunus, jadeite/crystal beads **190.00**
Lapis lazuli, seated lady, 3¼", +stand **165.00**
Lapis lazuli, vase, foo dog finial, masks/lappets, lid, 8" **875.00**
Malachite, lady w/basket of flowers, 4", tkwd base **200.00**
Nephrite, boy w/fungus branch stands on carp in waves, 4" **1,700.00**
Rose quartz, exotic bird, 8", +stand **110.00**
Rose quartz, maid w/scroll, 9", +tkwd stand **175.00**

Inro

Bronze, w/cord ojime & bronze gourd netsuke, 2-case **375.00**
Lcq, blk w/gilt house, bk: running demon, netsuke, 5-case **1,200.00**
Lcq, blk w/gilt landscape, 4-case, 1¾x3½" **650.00**
Lcq, blk w/gilt landscape, 5-case, 2x3½" **1,900.00**
Lcq, brn w/inlaid gold shells, 4-case, 3x3¼" **850.00**
Lcq, gold, floral & zoomorphic mon, 4-case, 1800s **865.00**

Lcq, gold & silver, sage in boat, 1800s, 2⅝" **1,725.00**
Lcq, rainstorm & boats landscape, 5-case, 1800s, 3¾" **3,100.00**
Lcq, silver ojime, red lcq netsuke, 5-case **550.00**
Mixed metal, gold & silver, blossoms/geese/bamboo, 4-case, 2½" ..**175.00**
Porc, bl/wht, 2-case, 2x2" **125.00**
Silver/bronze, silver bead ojime, ivory mask netsuke, 2-case **260.00**

Lacquer

Lacquerware is found in several colors, but the one most likely to be encountered is cinnabar. It is often intricately carved, sometimes involving hundreds of layers built one at a time on a metal or wooden base. Later pieces remain red, while older examples tend to darken.

Sewing box, gilt and black landscape decoration on red with palace scene on lid, black interior, Chinese, 9x15½", $700.00.

Box, aquatic plants, gilt hiramaki-e & aogai, Meiji, 5x9x6" **1,265.00**
Box, blk detailed decor, 1800s, 5½x15x12" **495.00**
Box, food; woven panels w/cvd giltwood borders, stacking, 32" ..**825.00**
Box, gold & silver hiramaki-e on red, Edo, ca 1800, 5¼" **700.00**
Box, lcq bronze w/carp decor, sgn, Jp, 7" **100.00**
Box, peacocks on rocks, diapering w/gilt, 1800s, 12½" dia **750.00**
Box, scroll; peony blossoms, gold & silver, ca 1800, 17¾" **1,495.00**
Kogo, plum branch on wall, gold & silver on red, 2⅝" dia **925.00**
Shodana, tortoise-shell veneer w/gilt, Meiji, 13x11x7" **1,150.00**
Tea box, blk w/gold court scenes ea panel, 1800s, 8¾" L **275.00**
Tea caddy, bldgs on blk, claw ft, octagonal, 1850s, 8¾" **195.00**
Tea caddy, blk/gold w/figural panels, serpentine, 1850s **400.00**
Tray, gold mums/foliage, int/ext walls w/kiri on gold, 8" **425.00**

Netsukes

A netsuke is a miniature Japanese carving made with two holes called the Himitoshi, either channeled or within the carved design. As kimonos (the outer garment of the time) had no pockets, the Japanese man hung his pipe, tobacco pouch, or other daily necessities from his waist sash. The most highly valued accessory was a nest of little drawers called an Inro, in which they carried snuff or sometimes opium. The netsuke was the toggle that secured them. Although most are of ivory, others were made of bone, wood, metal, porcelain, or semiprecious stones. Some were inlaid or lacquered. They are found in many forms – figurals the most common, mythological beasts the most desirable. They range in size from 1" up to 3", which was the maximum size allowed by law. Many netsukes represented the owner's profession, religion, or hobbies. Scenes from the daily life of Japan at that time were often depicted in the tiny carvings. The more detailed the carving, the greater the value.

Careful study is required to recognize the quality of the netsuke. Many have been made in Hong Kong in recent years; and even though some are very well carved, these are considered copies and avoided by the serious collector. There are many books that will help you learn to recognize quality netsukes, and most reputable dealers are glad to assist you. Use your magnifying glass to check for repairs. In the listings that follow, netsukes are ivory unless noted otherwise; 'stain' indicates a color wash.

Shoki (demon queller) kneels and sharpens sword, sepia wash and black pigment on ivory, signed Doraku, Meiji period, 1¾", $460.00.

Boy & Hotei's sack, sgn Ryoto, sgn 130.00
Boys (2) w/Hotei's sack, triangular, probably Kyoto 150.00
Crab climbing atop monkey's head, 1½" 195.00
Dog & skeleton, 1¼" 325.00
Dragon standing on head, triangular, sgn Ikko, 1820s 280.00
Dragon w/flames, coiled, probably Kyoto, sgn Tomoto, 1800 .....525.00
Elephant, seated, cvd bone, 1¼" 45.00
Figs (2), wood, 2" 175.00
Foo dog, reclining, puppy on its bk, 2" L 320.00
Foo dog, reclining, 1¾" 200.00
Gama Sennin in cloak, holding 3-toed frog on shoulder, 1700s .425.00
Gama Sennin on toad, sgn Masakazu, sepia wash, 1⅜" 800.00
Horse, reclining, 2" 300.00
Hotei, porc, sgn Masakazu, 1800s 200.00
Hotei in brocade robes, leaning on left handl, sgn Nobumasa ...180.00
Jurojin, seated, monkey shaving his head, glazed pottery 110.00
Kikujido (Chrysanthemum Boy) leans on cushion, Tomochika .270.00
Lion-dog in curled position, sgn Kukenaga, 1800s, 1¾" 1,585.00
Lioness & cubs, sepia wash, 1800s, 1⅞" 575.00
Male shishi crouching over silk ball, 1800s 160.00
Man, kneeling w/abacus, 2" 185.00
Man, reclining, w/dog, 2" 250.00
Man, seated, w/crooked cane, 1½" 275.00
Man, seated w/theatre mask, wood, 1½" 125.00
Man, seated/howling, wood w/ivory teeth & eyes, 1½" 250.00
Man & dog, triangular, sgn Tomomitsu, early 19th C 230.00
Man & oni arm wrestle atop lotus leaf, sgn Tomotada, 1700s .1,000.00
Man carrying 2 children on his head, 2½" 125.00
Man seated on clam shell, brn stain, late 1700s, 2⅛" 1,725.00
Man w/rat, 1¼" 180.00
Men wrestling, cvd ebony, 1½" 175.00
Monkey & deer, triangular, lg himitoshi, sgn Kunimitsu 350.00
Monkey climbing lg squash, 1½" 150.00
Oni on 1 leg, in tigerskin lioncloth, triangular, Hidekazu 240.00
Ox w/rope halter, late 1700s, 2⅞" 975.00
Pea pod, wood, w/ivory worm emerging, 2" 225.00
Puppies (2), wrestling, porc, 1800s 80.00
Puppy w/pawson shell, inlaid eyes, early 1800s, 1¾" 550.00
Rabbits (2), 1½" 165.00
Ransaika seated on lg pouch, triangular, 1700s 425.00
Rat climbing on clam shells, inlaid eyes, stain, 1790s, 2" 865.00
Rat perched on candle, sepia stain, 1800s, 2" 975.00
Sage, stroking beard, standing over tiger, holding his tail 400.00
Snail on persimmon, shaded stain, 1800s, 1½" 1,265.00
Squirrel on grapes, blk pigment, sepia wash, 1800s, 2½" 800.00
Woman's face, wood, 2" 200.00
Woman w/children, 1½" 280.00

Porcelain

Chinese export ware was designed to appeal to Western tastes and was often made to order. During the 18th century, vast amounts were shipped to Europe and on westward. Much of this fine porcelain consisted of dinnerware lines that were given specific pattern names. Rose Mandarin, Fitzhugh, Armorial, Rose Medallion, and Canton are but a few of the more familiar.

Bowl, E, crest & floral sprays, 1820s, 5½" 275.00
Bowl, E, floral garlands around noble crest, 1800, 8¾" 300.00
Bowl, FN, phoenix bird center, 1850s, 8½" 85.00
Bowl, FR, ladies in garden, ring hdls, 1800s, 4" 115.00
Bowl, fruit; deities & flowers, gr int, 7" 140.00
Bowl, punch; E, hunting scenes, late 1700s, 11¼" 1,955.00
Bowl, punch; E, mandarin subjects, late 1700s, 11⅜" 3,165.00
Bowl, red/gold dragon/cloud/bird, bl floral int, 1780s, 5½" 450.00
Bowl, vegetable; Brn Fitzhugh, w/lid, 1800s, 9½" 975.00
Charger, FR, butterflies/florals, diapered edge, 1840s, 12" 135.00
Coffeepot, Nanking, lighthouse style, gold trim, 1800s, 9¾" 865.00
Figurine, bird on rocky plinth, gr/yel/gray, 7", pr 425.00
Jar, figures/dragon/boat, spherical, w/lid, tkwd stand, 12" 375.00
Jug, cider; E, Masonic, mc w/gold, 1800s, 11" 925.00
Jug, cider; E, Masonic, Nanking, w/lid, 1850s, 11" 2,200.00
Jug, cider; E, Success to Bombay, ship & lighthouse, 11¼" 2,500.00
Jug, cider; Nanking, gold decor, 1800s, 9¼" 980.00
Pillow, FR, cat form, bl/yel cushion w/coverlet, 1820s, 10" 1,265.00
Plate, E, bl & wht, bull/stream, armorial rim, 8-sided, 8¼" 300.00
Plate, E, Embroideress, blk w/gold & red, 1700s, 9", pr 800.00
Plate, E, foo lions/still life in shaped panels, 1880s, 10" 375.00
Plate, E, Judgment of Paris, gilt & mc enamel, 1750s, 9", pr 1,380.00
Plate, FR, 1800s, 9¾", 10 for 450.00
Plate, meat; E, floral, pk border w/gold & red edge, 1820s 300.00
Plate, Orange Fitzhugh, 1800s, 9¾" 4,180.00
Plate, soup; Nanking, Arms of Boyd, 1800s, 9½", EX 800.00
Platter, Bl Fitzhugh, 20x16" 745.00
Platter, E, Arms of Cooke, eagle crest, 17¾" 1,600.00
Platter, E, floral sprays, serpentine, 1820s, 13" 675.00
Platter, E, Nanking decor w/floral border, 1820s, 16" 550.00
Platter, Gr Fitzhugh, armorial, rtcl insert, rim rpr, 15x18" 2,100.00
Platter, Gr Fitzhugh, armorial, 1800s, 13" 1,750.00
Platter, Orange Fitzhugh, early 19th C, firing blemish, 16" 1,100.00
Tea bowl & saucer, floral int, brn ext, 1700s 100.00
Tea caddy, E, floral, scroll/gilt base, 1820s, 5" 200.00
Tea set, E, red monochrome w/gilt, 1700s, 14-pc 3,335.00
Teapot, E, lav floral sprays, 18/19th C 130.00
Teapot, FR, floral, cylindrical, 7" 75.00
Teapot & sugar bowl, Nanking, gold decor, 1800s, 6" pot 460.00
Tureen, sauce; Bl Fitzhugh, strap hdls, 8" L 425.00
Tureen, sauce; E, 1000 Butterfly, gilt hdls, 1800s, 7½", pr 965.00
Tureen, soup; E, 1000 Butterfly, 1800s, 12" 745.00
Urn, E, sepia medallions w/gold, 1700s, 16½", pr 2,300.00
Vase, deity on swan & elder statesman, butterfly hdls, 27" 880.00
Vase, FR, figures/dignitary, hexagonal baluster, 1880s, 22" 465.00

Pottery

Bowl, bird & floral on crackle glaze, low, early, 12¾" 200.00
Bowl, floral, wht on chalky bl, Ming Dy, shallow, 15" 325.00
Bowl, gr/brn/ochre splashed over buff, Tang Dy, 3", +box 525.00
Bowl, gray crackle, Ko, 18th/19th C, 8¾" 130.00
Bowl, thin gray-wht, ring ft, incurvate, Song Dy, 5" 350.00
Figurine, elder in bl/rose, floral base, 1800s, mk, 9½" 125.00
Figurine, horse/rider, straw glaze, Tang, 7/8th C, rpr, 11" 965.00
Figurine, saddled horse w/neck bent, red traces, rpr, 14" 1,265.00
Garden stool, butterflies/mums/gold bird band/lion masks, 19" ..275.00
Plaque, figures & horse in relief, earthenware, early, 7x10" 100.00
Sake bottle, blk, undecorated, teardrop form, 1800s, 13" 135.00

Tea bowl, lt bl w/streaks, Jun Yao, cut ring ft, 14th C, 4" 825.00
Teapot, terra cotta, gr enamel spout/hdl, branch on lid, 4x7" 45.00
Teapot, terra cotta w/eng scene, Jp, 5½x7½" 90.00
Vase, crazed orange-yel, 13", pr 385.00
Vase, phoenix birds/beading on crackleware, 1880s, 10" 45.00
Vase, terra cotta, Greek Key top/bottom, 1850s, Jp, 9¾" 90.00

Rugs

The 'Oriental' or Eastern rug market has enjoyed a renewal of interest in recent years as collectors have become aware of the fact that some of the semiantique rugs (those sixty to one hundred years old) may be had at a price within the range of the average buyer.

Afshar, blue and red Greek cross central medallion, tree shapes and medallions, three borders, 75x56", $800.00.

Afghanistan, geometrics, blk/cream on red, wear, 70x38" 210.00
Afghanistan, geometrics, blk/cream on red, 83x52" 400.00
Bidjar, red w/mc dk bl mdl, band border, 84x55" 325.00
Bokar, geometrics on dk bl, 140x109" 525.00
Chinese, bl w/sculptured mc sea/cloud/dragon, 150x115" 875.00
Chinese, gr w/floral, gold/wine floral border, 144x100" 550.00
Chinese, open gr ground w/mc floral sprays, 140x107" 1,900.00
Chinese, 6 sqs w/animals, floral border, sculpted, 120x144" 500.00
Dozar, red w/mc floral sprays, 135x72" 1,300.00
Herati, pk w/bl/ivory/rust floral, geometric gb, 150x120" 2,800.00
Heriz, red w/floral, ivory corners, band border, 150x120" 2,400.00
Heriz, red w/mc geometric mdl, conforming gb, 144x120, VG ..2,800.00
Heriz, red w/mc geometrics, ivory corners, bl gb, 120x84", VG ...1,400.00
Indo-Persian Tabriz, floral, 4-color on red, 106x67" 380.00
Kashan, floral, 7-color on cream, 200x120" 950.00
Kazak, geometrics, Greek Keys, minor rpr, 46x68", VG 750.00
Kirman, beige w/floral, 59x24" 110.00
Kirman, ivory w/allover mc floral, floral/pk gb, 144x120" 1,800.00
Kirman, ivory w/allover mc floral, 180x120" 3,000.00
Kirman, ivory w/allover mc florals, floral border, 240x140" 3,600.00
Kirman, ivory w/pastel floral, conforming band, 55x150" 900.00
Kirman, mc floral tiles w/dk bl floral gb, 144x108" 2,300.00
Kirman, red w/florals, floral reserve border, 160x120" 2,400.00
Pakistani Jaldar runner, geometrics, 5-color, fringe, 94x42" 160.00
Sarouk, wine w/floral, conforming border, 144x106" 2,600.00
Sparta, gr w/geometrics, ivory corners, worn border, 144x100" ...660.00
Sumac Caucasian, geometrics in red/bl/wht/blk, 1950s, 95x145" ..450.00
Turkish, dk bl w/9 mc mdls, geometric ivory gb, 158x60" 2,000.00

Snuff Bottles

The Chinese were introduced to snuff in the 17th century, and their carved and painted snuff bottles typify their exquisite taste and workmanship. These small bottles, seldom measuring over 2½", were made of amber, jade, ivory, and cinnabar; tiny spoons were often attached to their stoppers. By the 18th century, some were being made of porcelain, others were of glass with delicate interior designs tediously reverse painted with minuscule brushes sometimes containing a single hair. Copper and brass were used but to no great extent.

Agate, banded, EX color, 2½" 500.00
Agate, blk w/gray flowers, malachite cap, 2½" 300.00
Agate, cvd duck/lotus, bk: lotus, gr glass stopper, 1800 ....200.00
Burl wood, flat oblong flask form, bone stopper 2¾" 110.00
Coral, cvd goldfish/birds/bats/bamboo, cvd cap, 2½" 450.00
Glass, yel w/cvd peonies & rocks, amethyst stopper, 1800s 1,265.00
Ivory, court scene ea side, vines/lappets, 1800-80 ....900.00
Ivory, ring-hdld urn w/figural cvgs, 3⅛" 140.00
Jade, lt gr, rtcl moth ea side, tkwd stand, 3" 325.00
Jade, wht nephrite, allover basketweave, 3" 200.00
Jadeite, mtd horsemen in battle cvg, even gr color, 1800s 5,500.00
Lapis, cvd crane/ferns, coral cap, 2¼" 340.00
Malachite, cvd bird of paradise, malachite cap, 2¾" 300.00
Malachite, 2 cvd fish, EX color, 2⅛" 125.00
Opal, 2 cvd birds & flowering tree, 2" 800.00
Opal glass, cvd floral branches, loose ring hdls, EX 300.00
Peking glass, cranberry o/l, cvd ritual vessels, 1800s, EX 290.00
Peking glass, gray/pk mottle molded/cvd as lotus bud, 1800s ...2,185.00
Peking glass, red, cylindrical, opaque stopper, 4" 60.00
Rhodonite, pk w/blk, cvd bird of paradise, matching cap, 2½" ...300.00
Rvpt, dbl sections, ea w/figural scenes, sgn/dtd 1928 ....1,200.00
Rvpt, lotus/floral, clear w/lt bl cap, 3" 150.00
Tiger eye, cvd dragon, 2½" 150.00
Tiger eye, raised scrolls, close-to-body hdls, dome lid, 2¾" 300.00
Turq, cvd bats/figures, coral stopper, on teak stand, 3½" 300.00

Sumida

Basket, 3 people at front, 1 at open hdl, Gawa, 9" 395.00
Mug, appl monkey, enamel drip at top, 4½" 90.00
Mug, wise man appl at center, seal signature, Gawa, 5½" 150.00
Tankard, 2 boys in center, drip at top, imp mk, 9¼" 275.00
Vase, boy w/rock relief, mc mottle, 7x2⅞" 135.00
Vase, floral branches, ca 1885, 12" 600.00

Textiles

Jacket, bl floral embr on yel silk, genre/floral bands, 1880s 225.00
Obi shash, red, bl & gold, M 125.00
Painting on silk, wooded mtn scene w/figures, 1800s, 67x42" .1,100.00
Panel on silk, HP exotic birds/foliage, fr, 56x32" 330.00
Panel on silk, woven landscape, Kesi, 1880s, 70x32" 690.00
Robe, bird/floral embr, gold/blk/red/gr 300.00
Robe, dragons/cranes/clouds/symbols on bl silk, 1920, 58" 500.00
Robe, floral/figural embr on blk satin, earlier trim, 1800s 330.00
Robe, gold dragons, bl clouds/bats on brn silk, 1800s, 54" 1,000.00
Tapestry, battle on gr floral, gold bullion, 1800s, 81x55" 1,400.00

Woodblock Prints, Japanese

Framed prints are of less value because one can not inspect their condition or tell if they have borders or are trimmed.

Courtyard w/flowering sakura, Hiroshige, oban triptych, VG 935.00
Crowd at Nihonbashi fireworks, Toyokuni I, oban triptych, EX .465.00
Fuji From Sea of Miura, Hiroshige, oban tat-e 500.00
Kabuki Actors, Utagawa Toyokuni, 1850, oban 125.00
Landscape w/diving wild geese, Hiroshige, fr, 17½x12¾" 195.00
Samurai battle/castle, Kuniyoshi, trimmed, oban triptych 750.00

Tenzen Ohno, Toyohara Kunichika, 1st impression, oban 125.00
Village scene, Hiroshige, fr, 16½x21½" 120.00

Miscellaneous

Box, tobacco; cvd bone, w/ojime & pipe holder, Jp 275.00
Cvg, wood, deified soldier stands over monkey, some pnt, 17" ...120.00
Cvg, wood, Quan Yin on lotus & rock base, pnt traces, 22", pr ..550.00
Cvg, wood, war lord on throne, gilt robe, Jp, 1850s, 17" 300.00
Pipe, silver & bamboo, Jp, 9" 100.00
Pocket shrine, wood/lcq, sleeping Buddha, 4¾" 650.00

Orrefors

Orrefors Glassworks was founded in 1898 in the Swedish province of Smaaland. Utilizing the expertise of designers such as Simon Gate, Edward Hald, Vicke Lindstrand, and Edwin Ohrstrom, it produced art glass of the highest quality. Various techniques were used in achieving the decoration. Some were wheel engraved; others were blown through a unique process that formed controlled bubbles or air pockets resulting in unusual patterns and shapes. Our advisor for this category is Abby Malowanczyk; she is listed in the Directory under Texas.

Bowl, clear w/int red stripe & blk line, #4085/426, 4x6½" 145.00
Bowl, eng scroll-fr panels w/nudes, Gate, 7¾", +underplate 1,800.00
Bowl, Sailor's Dream, mc pnt, Gunnar Cyren, 7x9" 1,500.00
Goblet, Tulpenglaser, gray layers, thin/elongated, '57, 17" 850.00

Vase, Ariel, fantasy figures, clear with internal bubbles, smoky internal layer, Edwin Ohrstrom, #2035E, 1954, 6½", $5,000.00 at auction; Vase, Ariel, geometric bubble pattern, deep blue cased with clear with internal amber layer, Indeborg Lundin, #332E4, 1974, 8½", $1,300.00 at auction.

Vase, Ariel, 6-petal airtrap flowers, Ohrstrom #335, 5x5" 1,150.00
Vase, Ariel, arched bl inclusions in crystal, Lundin, '67, 6" 850.00
Vase, Ariel, cobalt layer w/bubble stripes, Lundin #351K, 5" 440.00
Vase, Ariel, female face/bird, bl/clear, Ohrstrom #404, 6" 3,300.00
Vase, Ariel, leaves, yel/bl ground, Alberius #5644-51, 7½" 2,100.00
Vase, Ariel, male profile, gr core, Ohrstrom, cylinder, 6¾" 700.00
Vase, Ariel, nudes under still life, Ohrstrom #573, 6" 5,175.00
Vase, charcoal/clear, slender bottle form, #3538, 8½" 80.00
Vase, eng vineyard/nudes, thick, Landberg/Expo 1950, 10" 545.00
Vase, Graal, fish/seaweed, Hald, spherical, 5" 550.00
Vase, man w/harp, blk ft, Lindstrand #1048, 1932, 7½" 1,850.00
Vase, mc face in clear, cylinder, Nilsen #972878, 7½" 2,400.00
Vase, seated nude child blows bubbles, Lindstrand #1382, 8" 550.00
Vase, 3 nude male divers, blk disk ft, Lindstrand, 14" 3,680.00

Ott and Brewer

The partnership of Ott and Brewer began in 1865 in Trenton, New Jersey. By 1876 they were making decorated graniteware, parian, and 'ivory porcelain' — similar to Irish belleek though not as fine and of different composition. In 1883, however, experiments toward that end had reached a successful conclusion, and a true belleek body was introduced. It came to be regarded as the finest china ever produced by an American firm. The ware was decorated by various means such as hand painting, transfer printing, gilding, and lustre glazing. The company closed in 1893, one of many that failed during that depression. In the listings below, the ware is belleek unless noted otherwise. Our advisor for this category is Mary Frank Gaston; she is listed in the Directory under Texas.

Basket, pk flowers w/gold, cactus-shaped hdl w/appl tulips, mk .1,100.00
Bowl, gold paste florals & leaves, scalloped, mk, 2x4¾" 475.00
Chocolate pot, floral w/gold dragon-shape spout & hdl, mk, 13" .1,000.00
Chocolate set, poppies w/gold sponging, 16-pc, NM 1,500.00
Compote, shell on branch-form base, lt bl lustre, 3½x5¾" 425.00
Creamer & sugar bowl, HP floral, scalloped, mk, 3¼", 2" 500.00
Cup & saucer, HP red flowers w/gold leaves & lav sprigs, unmk ..125.00
Ewer, gold paste florals & leaves, curved rim & hdl, mk, 5¼" 650.00
Pitcher, gold paste thistles on panel, emb sides, mk, 8" 725.00
Shoe, sponged gold decor on bow, mk, 7½" 750.00
Sugar bowl, Tridacna design w/gold florals, mk, 4½" 300.00
Teapot, HP poppies w/gold, bark top & branch hdl, mk, 8½" 800.00
Tray, HP wild duck, sq w/scalloped border, mk, 8" 900.00
Vase, gold paste leaves & butterfly, uptrn hdls, 5½" 625.00

Overbeck

The Overbeck Studio was established in 1911 in Cambridge City, Indiana, by four Overbeck sisters. It survived until the last sister died in 1955. Early wares were often decorated with carved designs of stylized animals, birds, or florals with the designs colored to contrast with the background. Others had tooled designs filled in with various colors for a mosaic effect. After 1937, Mary Frances, the last remaining sister, favored handmade figurines with somewhat bizarre features in fanciful combinations of color. Overbeck ware is signed 'OBK,' frequently with the designer's and potter's initials under the stylized 'OBK.'

Figurine, Colonial girl, hoop skirt, mc 325.00
Figurine, squirrel, brn tones, minor chips, 3" 120.00
Vase, geometric cvg, gray/brn matt, cylindrical, 2¾" 90.00
Vase, pine cones cvd in panels, pk-gr ground, sgn EF, 4¾" 1,100.00
Vase, stylized cattails, 2-tone mustard, sgn E&H, 5¾x3½" 2,100.00
Vase, 3 cvd floral panels, brn on dk brn, cylinder, EF, 7" 2,100.00

Overlay Glass

Art glass having layers of more than one type or color of glass is sometimes called overlay or cased glass. Very often glassware of this type has applied decorations such as fruit, flowers, leaves, or ruffles (rigaree), such as is commonly identified with Stevens and Williams.

Bottle, scent; wht over clear, elaborate gold decor, 5½" 200.00
Decanter, pk shaded to wht, clear hdl & stopper, 9¼x4" 245.00
Rose bowl, bl, HP florals, frosted ft, crimped, 4¾" 135.00
Rose bowl, bl, HP mc bird & flowers, frosted ft, 6¼x4" 135.00
Rose bowl, bl, HP morning glories, frosted ft, 5x4½" 135.00
Rose bowl, bl, 8-crimp, 3¾x3¾" 45.00

Rose bowl, lt gr, HP florals/gold buds, egg shape, 4½x3½" 85.00
Rose bowl, pk, HP florals w/gold, 8-crimp, frosted ft, 5x4⅛" 135.00
Tumbler, pk, 4¼x2½" 45.00
Vase, bl, petit-point decor w/gold trim, 9x4½", pr 350.00
Vase, bl w/clear leaves & points at rim, more at base, 6" 225.00
Vase, chartreuse gr, appl vaseline scallop & ft, 8x4" 95.00
Vase, cream opaque, appl bl plums, amber ft/leaves/hdl, 6" 138.00
Vase, dk orange, gold flowers (Webb style), 6½" 175.00
Vase, dk rose w/crystal rigaree, 6½x3", pr 145.00
Vase, peach shaded satin, HP florals, frosted hdl, 10⅜" 135.00
Vase, pk, appl clear flowers/leaves/ruffle, 4¾x3" 120.00
Vase, pk, HP florals, 3-petal top, clear hdl, 5¼x4" 85.00
Vase, pk satin w/HP florals, 3-petal top, ewer form, 8¼" 110.00
Vase, pk shaded satin, HP floral w/jewels & gold, hdls, 7¼" 100.00
Vase, purple, emb swirls & dmns, clear frosted ft, 4x5" 120.00
Vase, red, HP florals, gold hdls, 8½x3¾" 150.00
Vase, yel, tomato red int, sq top, 4¼x3½" 65.00
Wall vase, peach to wht, HP florals, bamboo shape, 12" 125.00

Overshot

Overshot glass is characterized by the beaded or craggy appearance of its surface. Earlier ware was irregularly textured, while 20th-century examples tend to be more uniform.

Bowl, rubena, on wht metal ped ft, 6½x8½" 180.00
Decanter, cranberry, w/ice bladder, bubble stopper, 12" 355.00
Jug, claret; rubena w/pewter mts, 12", +4 wines w/pewter bases ..475.00
Pitcher, cranberry, petal top, clear rope hdl, 9¾x4½" 295.00
Pitcher, gr w/amber shell hdl, Sandwich, 1875, 8¼" 225.00
Pitcher, tankard; cranberry, clear reed hdl, 9" 165.00
Tumbler, cranberry 45.00

Owen, Ben

Ben Owen worked at the Jugtown Pottery of North Carolina from 1923 until it closed in 1959. He continued in the business in his own Plank Road Pottery, stamping his ware 'Ben Owen, Master Potter.' His pottery closed in 1972. He died in in 1983 at the age of 81.

Candlesticks, blk, 13", pr 150.00
Tile, goose in flight, low relief, mc faience, 11½x17½" 375.00
Vase, Aqua Verdi, 6" 200.00
Vase, blk-flecked gr gloss, high shoulder w/4 loop hdls, 5" 265.00
Vase, Chinese bl curdled w/wht, 7" 235.00

Owens Pottery

J.B. Owens founded his company in Zanesville, Ohio, in 1891, and until 1907, when the company decided to exert most of its energies in the area of tile production, made several quality lines of art pottery. His first line, Utopian, was a standard brown ware with underglaze slip decoration of nature studies, animals, and portraits. A similar line, Lotus, utilized lighter background colors. Henri Deux, introduced in 1900, featured incised Art Nouveau forms inlaid with color. (Be aware that the Brush McCoy Pottery acquired many of Owens' molds and reproduced a line similar to Henri Deux, which they called Navarre.) Other important lines were Opalesce, Rustic, Feroza, Cyrano, and Mission, examples of which are rare today. The factory burned in 1928, and the company closed shortly thereafter. Values vary according to the quality of the artwork and subject matter. Examples signed by the artist bring higher prices than those that are not signed.

Henri Deux, vase, 7" 450.00
Lotus, vase, floral, mc on gray to wht, #1243, rpr, 10½" 300.00
Lotus, vase, toadstools, mc on lav to gray, hdls, #235, 5x7½" 450.00
Matt, vase, floral, mc on bl to gray, unmk, 13x8½" 750.00
Matt, vase, floral, mc on gr & brn, twisted form, #117, 4½" 175.00
Matt Gr, vase, cvd berries/leaves, lg hdls, #235, 5" 175.00
Matt Gr, vase, emb stylized roses, angle hdls, 9¾x4¼" 450.00
Matt Gr, vase, Greek Key design, ovoid, 9½x3½" 400.00
Matt Gr, vase, stylized Arts & Crafts, gourd form, 4½" 225.00
Opalese, vase, floral, gr/gold coralene, 11x4" 850.00

Plaque, trees and mountain landscape in bold colors, 9x11", in oak frame, $900.00.

Plaque, stylized scene w/mtns & trees, 3-color matt, 13x13" ...1,300.00
Tile, Egyptian style lotus blossom relief, mc, 6" sq 175.00
Tile, geese/clouds in low relief, no mk, 11½x17½" 550.00
Tile, lg red oak leaves, brn acorns on mustard, mk, 5¾" 175.00
Utopian, humidor, cigar & matches, 7½" 325.00
Utopian, vase, floral, hdls, #980, 7x4" 125.00
Utopian, vase, florals, sgn ST, bulbous, 10" 295.00
Utopian, vase, Indian profile, 12" 1,800.00
Utopian, vase, kitten portrait, bulbous, mk JB Owens, 8" 1,800.00
Utopian, vase, Nouveau lady, mc on beige, #1114, 6" 1,400.00
Utopian, vase, poppies, mc on orange to yel, #1055, 13" 400.00
Utopian, vase, vintage, hdls, 7x6" 250.00

Pacific Clay Products

The Pacific Clay Products Company got its start in the 1920s as a consolidation of several smaller southern California potteries. The main Los Angeles plant had been founded in 1890 to make kitchen stoneware, ollas, and similar items. Terra cotta and brick were later produced.

In 1932 Hostess Ware, a vividly colored line of dinnerware, was introduced to compete with Bauer's Ring Ware. Coralitos, a lighter-weight, pastel-hued dinnerware line was first marketed in 1937, and a similar but less expensive line called Arcadia soon followed. Art ware including vases, figurines, candlesticks, etc., was produced from 1932 to 1942, at which time the company went into war-related work and pottery manufacture ceased. A limited amount of hand-decorated dinnerware was also made. For further information we recommend *The Collectors Encyclopedia of California Pottery* (with 1995 values) by our advisor, Jack Chipman; he is listed in the Directory under California.

Bowl, Ring-style, 8½" 30.00
Casserole, Ring, orange, w/lid, in metal rack 65.00
Chop plate, Ring-style, 12" 40.00
Coffeepot, demitasse; Ring-style, wht 100.00
Creamer, demitasse; Ring, gr 20.00

Cup & saucer, demitasse; Ring-style **25.00**
Egg cup, early design, flat ft **45.00**
Pie plate, delphinium blue, wooden hdl, 11" **95.00**
Teapot, Ring-style, turq, ftd, lg **100.00**
Tumbler, Ring-style **22.00**
Vase, Art Deco, bl, 7" **35.00**

Paden City

The Paden City Glass Company began operations in 1916 in Paden City, West Virginia. The company's early lines consisted largely of the usual pressed tablewares, but by the 1920s production had expanded to include colored wares in translucent as well as opaque glass in a variety of patterns and styles. The company maintained its high standards of handmade perfection until 1949, when under new management much of the work formerly done by hand was replaced by automation. The Paden City Glass Company closed in 1951; its earlier wares, the colored patterns in particular, are becoming very collectible.

Paden City Glass is not always easily recognized by collectors or dealers, as it was almost never marked. It is believed this was so the glass could be sold to decorating companies. The company assigned both line numbers and names to many of its blanks or sets of glassware. Colors were sometimes given more than one name, and etchings were named as well. All this makes identification of items offered for sale through mail order difficult, and labels prepared by dealers are often confusing.

A review of literature available on Paden City reveals the following names for the company's plate etchings: Ardith; California Poppy; Cupid; Delilah Bird (Peacock Reverse); Eden Rose; Frost; Gazebo; Gothic Garden; Lela Bird; Nora Bird; Orchid (three variations); Peacock and Rose (Peacock and Wild Rose); Samarkand; Trumpet Flower; Utopia. Names given to cuttings made on Paden City blanks are Yorktown and Lazy Daisy. It is not clear whether the names originated with Paden City or with secondary decorating companies.

Our advisors for this category are George and Mary Hurney; they are listed in the Directory under Illinois. (Note: their interest is only in Paden City glassware, not the pottery.) See also Glass Animals and Figurines; Kitchen Collectibles, Glass.

This list gives company line numbers with corresponding line names:

#69, #69½ — Georgian
#191 — Party
#210 — Regina
#215 — Hotcha
#220 — Largo
#221 — Maya
#300 — Wotta
#411 — Mrs B
#412 — Crow's Foot Square
#890 — Crow's Foot Round
#895 — Lucy
#991 — Penny
#994 — Popeye and Olive
#1503 — Trance

And, finally, a listing of colors with alternate names or descriptive phrases:

Amber — (dull)
Cheriglo — (delicate) pink
Cobalt Blue — Royal Blue
Crystal — (clear, no tint)
Dark Green — forest green
Dark Amber — (honey color)
Light Blue — Copen, Neptune

Mulberry — amethyst
Opal — opaque white
Primrose — (amber with reddish tint)
Red — ruby
Rose — (dark pink)
Yellow — (pale, soft)

Basket, Trance, forest gr, #1503, 7½" **22.00**
Batter jug, Black Forest **125.00**

Batter jug, clear with black lid, $60.00; Syrup, clear with black lid, $50.00.

Bowl, centerpc; Wotta Line, silver o/l, 12" **50.00**
Bowl, cereal; Georgian, gr, 5¾" **22.00**
Bowl, console; Luli #300 Line, flat rim, floral etch, 12½" **30.00**
Bowl, cream soup; Crow's Foot, amber **9.00**
Bowl, cream soup; Crow's Foot, red **18.00**
Bowl, fruit; Black Forest, blk, 11" **30.00**
Bowl, Hotcha, amber, 3-ftd, 12" **35.00**
Bowl, Maya #221, lt bl, hdls, 12" **55.00**
Bowl, mayonnaise; Wotta Line w/Irwin etch **18.00**
Cake plate, Peacock & Wild Rose, gr, ftd **185.00**
Candlesticks, Wotta Line, silver o/l, 6¼", pr **55.00**
Candy dish, Vale, red, ball stem, floral etch, #900 ....**70.00**
Cheese stand, Crow's Foot **10.00**
Cocktail, Cerise **18.50**
Cocktail, Fuchsia **20.00**
Compote, First Love, 5½" **32.00**
Compote, Luli, red, 7½" **75.00**
Console set, Ardith, blk, bowl+2 candlesticks **125.00**
Cordial, Fuchsia **45.00**
Cordial, Penny Line, red **24.00**
Creamer, Black Forest, blk **55.00**
Creamer & sugar bowl, Crow's Foot, blk **30.00**
Creamer & sugar bowl, Mrs B, red **25.00**
Creamer & sugar bowl, Popeye & Olive, red **35.00**
Cup, Luli, red **12.00**
Cup & saucer, Crow's Foot, amber **5.00**
Cup & saucer, Crow's Foot, red, rnd **17.00**
Cup & saucer, Georgian, gr **13.00**
Cup & saucer, Mrs B, red **10.00**
Cup & saucer, Penny Line, red **10.00**
Cup & saucer, Popeye & Olive, red **15.00**
Goblet, Cerise, 8" **24.00**
Goblet, Georgian, red, high ft, 9-oz **18.50**
Goblet, Penny Line, gr, 6" **12.00**
Goblet, Penny Line, high ftd, floral cutting, 12-oz **12.00**
Goblet, Penny Line, red, water sz **18.50**
Goblet, Penny Line, red, 6" **20.00**
Ice bucket, Black Forest, amber **90.00**
Ice bucket, Hotcha Glades, etched clear w/platinum **35.00**
Pitcher, Black Forest, pk, 72-oz, 10½" **400.00**
Plate, Black Forest, red, 8" **30.00**
Plate, Crow's Foot, amber, sq, 6" **1.00**
Plate, Crow's Foot, amber, sq, 8½" **3.50**
Plate, Georgian, gr, 6" **6.00**
Plate, Peacock Reverse, red, 10" sq **60.00**

Plate, Popeye & Olive, red, 8" 7.50
Plate, Spire, hdls, 11½" 12.00
Server, Mrs B, red, center hdl 35.00
Shakers, Party Line, amber, pr 10.00
Sherbet, Cerise, tall, 6" 18.50
Sherbet, Fuchsia, 5⅜" 24.00
Sherbet, Georgian, red, stem 12.50
Sherbet, Penny Line, high ft, floral cutting 8.00
Sherbet, Penny Line, red 12.50
Tumbler, Georgian, red, ftd V-shape, 3½" 10.00
Tumbler, ice cream soda; Party Line, amber, ftd, 7" 18.50
Tumbler, ice cream soda; Party Line, pk 25.00
Tumbler, iced tea; Georgian, red, 11-oz 15.00
Tumbler, Party Line, red, 3¼" 8.00
Tumbler, Party Line, red, 4" 8.00
Tumbler, Party Line, red, 4⅛" 10.00
Tumbler, Party Line, red, 5¼" 12.00
Tumbler, Party Line, red, 6" 12.50
Vase, Ardith, blk, 8" 95.00
Vase, bud; Peacock Reverse 195.00
Vase, California Poppy, gr, 12" 150.00
Vase, Orchid, red, 9" 120.00
Vase, Peacock & Wild Rose, pk, 10" 130.00
Vase, Peacock & Wild Rose, pk, 12" 195.00
Vase, Peacock Reverse, blk, 9" 130.00
Vase, Utopia, blk amethyst, paneled, 10½" 195.00
Whipped cream pail, Black Forest, gr 65.00
Wine, Futura, red, 3-oz 12.00

Paintings on Ivory

Miniature works of art executed on ivory from the 1800s are assessed by the finesse of the artist, as is any fine painting. Signed examples and portraits with an identifiable subject are usually preferred.

Portrait of small girl, watercolor, unsigned, gilt locket frame with twist of hair attached to the back, American School, 1800s, 1⅞x1⅝", $900.00.

Am militia officer, sgn Forbes Boston, 5½x4½" 395.00
Dbl-sided, Naval officer, child, 2¼x2" 500.00
French lady, sgn J Arele, oval brass fr, 3¼x2½" 135.00
French lady, sgn Lebrun, decor oval brass fr, 3¼x2½" 220.00
George Washington, in manner of Ramage, 1¾x2¼" 3,600.00
Girl in lacy bonnet, sgn Reynolds, ca 1880, later fr, 3x2⅜" 245.00
Lady, lace cap/work dress, CP Newell 03, gold case, 2¾" 165.00
Lady & child, watercolor, Am school, 19th C, 3⅛x2¼", VG 330.00
Lady in bl gown, fr, 5¾x5" 200.00
Lady in bl gown, primitive, brass fr, 4⅝" 120.00
Lady in high lace collar, gold-filled oval case, 2½" 715.00
Lady in plumed hat, sgn Lebrun, ivory fr, 5⅜x4¾" 165.00
Man, primitive style, gilt case, 2¾" 275.00
Man, watercolor, silver-colored metal fr, 2¼" 300.00
Man w/long sideburns, gold-filled oval case, 2½" 578.00

Napoleon, sgn Delaroche, oval brass fr, 3⅜x2⅝" 350.00
2 girls w/open book, pastels, gilt brass fr, 2¾x2¼" 275.00

Pairpoint

The Pairpoint Manufacturing Company was built in 1880 in New Bedford, Massachusetts. It was primarily a metalworks whose chief product was coffin fittings. Next door, the Mt. Washington Glassworks made quality glasswares of many varieties. (See Mt. Washington for more information concerning their artware lines.) By 1894 it became apparent to both companies that a merger would be to their best interest.

From the late 1890s until the 1930s, lamps and lamp accessories were an important part of Pairpoint's production. There were three main types of shades, all of which were blown: puffy — blown-out reverse-painted shades (usually floral designs); ribbed — also reverse painted; and scenic — reverse painted with scenes of land or seascapes (usually executed on smooth surfaces, although ribbed scenics may be found occasionally). Cut glass lamps and those with metal overlay panels were also made. Scenic shades were sometimes artist signed. Every shade was stamped on the lower inside or outside edge with 1) The Pairpoint Corp., 2) Patent Pending, 3) Patented July 9, 1907, or 4) Patent Applied For. Bases were made of bronze, copper, brass, silver, or wood and are always signed.

Because they produced only fancy, handmade artware, the company's sales lagged seriously during the Depression; and, as time and tastes changed, their style of product was less in demand. As a result, they never fully recovered; consequently part of the buildings and equipment was sold in 1938. The company reorganized in 1939 under the direction of Robert Gundersen and again specialized in quality hand-blown glassware. Isaac Babbit regained possession of the silver departments, and together they established Gundersen Glassworks, Inc. After WWII, because of a sharp decline in sales, it again became necessary to reorganize. The Gundersen-Pairpoint Glassworks was formed, and the old line of cut, engraved artware was reintroduced. The company moved to East Wareham, Massachusetts, in 1957. But business continued to suffer, and the firm closed only one year later. In 1970, however, new facilities were constructed in Sagamore under the direction of Robert Bryden, sales manager for the company since the 1950s.

In 1974 the company began to produce lead glass cup plates which were made on commission as fund-raisers for various churches and organizations. These are signed with a 'P' in diamond and are becoming quite collectible. Our advisor for Pairpoint lamps is Daniel Batchelor; he is listed in the Directory under New York. See also Napkin Rings.

Key: pwt — paperweight

Glass

Biscuit jar, teal Invt T'print, 7½x5" 435.00
Bowl, cut/eng floral, 3¼x12" 185.00
Candlesticks, cut, red to clear, baluster, 10½", pr 300.00
Carafe, cut w/ovals & miters, 7½" 200.00
Compote, cobalt, in SP fr, 9" 135.00
Mantel urn, cut, Urn & Flame, w/lid, 12" 200.00
Vase, cut, red to clear w/flowers & leaves, 11" 275.00

Lamps

Puffy 13" yel rose shade; SP Nouveau base #3083 ....7,150.00
Puffy 14" apples/etc shade; bronze trunk std, 20" 15,000.00

Puffy 14" dogwood/butterflies shade; SP tripod std #D3084, EX ...**6,250.00**
Puffy 14" hummingbird/mum Stratford shade; fluted SP std **6,750.00**
Puffy 14" roses/butterfly Oxford shade; rose-pnt glass std **11,825.00**
Puffy 15" hummingbird/rose shade, 22" **5,500.00**
Puffy 18" Pilgrims Landing Ravena shade; floral-emb SP std ...**8,000.00**
Puffy 8" dogwood/latticinio Stratford shade; #C3057 std, EX ..**2,600.00**
Puffy 8" rose/butterfly shade; SP std w/wide base on paw ft **3,500.00**
Puffy 8" roses/butterflies on blk shade; #C3064 std, 15", EX **4,000.00**
Puffy 8½" floral-border Stratford shade; SP #C3064 std **2,500.00**
Rvpt 12" Italian garden Berkley shade, 22" **3,000.00**
Rvpt 12" lotus shallow shade; gilt foliate Nouveau base, 12" ...**8,800.00**
Rvpt 13" tulip shade outlined on ext w/blk; gilt std #3309 ......**1,760.00**
Rvpt 15" scenic Carlisle shade; trn std on sq base w/paw ft **2,250.00**
Rvpt 16" farm scene shade w/farmer & horse; hdld vase std **1,800.00**
Rvpt 16" multiflora Directorie shade; 3-stick std on marble ...**5,750.00**
Rvpt 17½" exotic birds Exeter shade; SP std, 22" **6,500.00**
Rvpt 18" peacocks in garden Carlisle shade; 3-part urn std **3,600.00**
Rvpt 18" whaling ships Exeter shade; unmk std, 23" **5,000.00**
Rvpt 7" hex floral shade; vasiform std, 14" **1,200.00**
Rvpt 7" 4-panel floral Vassar shade; SP/onyx cherub std **880.00**
Rvpt 8½" butterfly panel shade; slim std #C3020, 12", EX **900.00**
Rvpt 8½" river scene shade; NP std, 16" **1,200.00**
Rvpt 9" palm shade w/fishing fillage; paneled vase std, 14" **3,600.00**
Rvpt 9" palm shade w/fishing village; tree trunk std, 16" **3,750.00**
SP rtcl 18" cone shade w/prisms; SP/onyx candlestick base, EX ..**1,700.00**

Paper Dolls

No one knows quite how or when paper dolls originated. One belief is that they began in Europe as 'pantins' (jumping jacks) and were frequently worn as part of the costume. By the late 1790s, they were being mass-produced. During the 19th century, most paper dolls portrayed famous dancers and opera stars such as Fanny Elssler and Jenny Lind. In the late 1800s, the Raphael Tuck Publishers of England produced many series of beautiful paper dolls; retail companies used them as advertisements to further the sale of their products. Around the turn of the century, many popular women's magazines began featuring a page of paper dolls.

Most familiar to today's collectors are the books with dolls on cardboard covers and clothes on the inside pages. These made their appearance in the late 1920s and early thirties. The most collectible (and the most valuable) are those representing celebrities, movie stars, and comic-strip characters of the thirties and forties.

For further information we recommend *Schroeder's Collectible Toys, Antique to Modern*, by Sharon and Bob Huxford. When no condition is indicated, the dolls listed below are assumed to be in mint, uncut, original condition. Cut sets will be worth about half price if all dolls and outfits are included and pieces are in very good condition. If dolls were produced in die-cut form, these prices reflect such a set in mint condition with all costumes and accessories.

Airline Hostess & Pilot, Merrill, 1950s, NM **25.00**
Annie Oakley, Whitman #2043, 1954, partially cut, complete **30.00**
Annie Oakley (Gail Davis) w/Tagg & Lofty, #2056, 1955, uncut, M .**78.00**
Archies, Whitman #1987, 1969, partially cut **12.00**
Ava Gardner, Whitman, 1953, 1 doll & 22 items, cut, EX **22.50**
Baby Sparkle Plenty, Saalfield #2500, 1948, unused **65.00**
Ballet Dancers, M-3447, 1947, M **50.00**
Barbie Has a New Look, 2 dolls, Whitman #1976, 1967, M **35.00**
Bells of the Civil War, Platt & Munk, 1962, EX **15.00**
Blondie, Whitman #987, 1945, M **125.00**
Charlie's Angels Jill, Farrah Fawcett, 1976, NM **30.00**
Christmas Twins in Santa Claus Land, jointed cutouts, 1920, EX ..**65.00**

Claudette Colbert, Authorized Edition, Saalfield #2451, 1943, EX, $180.00.

Cinderella, Hallmark, 1947, EX **16.50**
Commodore Nut, McLoughlin, ca 188, cut, nearly complete **55.00**
Cowboy Joe & Cowgirl Jill, Merrill, 1950, cut, complete **16.50**
Dinah Shore, Whitman #2042, 1954, cut, nearly complete **25.00**
Dodie of My Three Sons, uncut, M **35.00**
Dolly Delight, Tuck Our Pets Series #3, cut, VG **16.50**
Dolly Dingle, April 1931, uncut, EX **13.00**
Esther Williams, 3 dolls, Merrill #1563, 1950, uncut, EX **42.50**
Flying Nun, 1960s, MIB **45.00**
Hedy Lamar, S-2600, 1951, uncut, M **185.00**
It's a Date, Whitman #1976, 1956, NM **30.00**
Jack & Jill's New Frocks & Frills, Regensteiner, 1925, uncut **35.00**
Jane Powell, Whitman #1171, 1953, 2 dolls, uncut, EX **120.00**
Lana Turner, Whitman #982, 1942, uncut **200.00**
Lizzie, McLoughlin, cut, G **42.00**
Malibu Skipper, Whitman #1952, 1973, cut, EX in folder **15.00**
Mary Jane, 1972, complete w/magnets, VG **15.00**
Mickey & Minnie Mouse, 4 outfits ea, Saalfield, 1933, EX **125.00**
Nanny & the Professor, uncut **35.00**
Paper Dolls w/Glamour Gowns, Saalfield, 1954, cut, EX **10.00**
Partridge Family, Saalfield #5137, 1971, M **40.00**
Sally, Sandra & Sue, Merrill, 1955, partially cut, EX **15.00**
Sandy & Sue, Whitman #1956, 1963, M **22.00**
Shirley Temple, Gabriel, uncut, 40", MIB **250.00**
Shirley Temple, Saalfield, 1958, partially cut, complete **30.00**
Snow White, Whitman #1974, 1950, M **20.00**
Sunny & Sue Paper Doll Book, 1950s, unused **15.00**
Sunshine Family, Whitman #1976, 1974, M **12.00**
Susan Dey of Partridge Family, uncut in box **20.00**
Susan Doll Book, Merrill, 1954, partially cut, incomplete **8.00**
Tricia Nixon, Whitehouse cover, 1970, M **25.00**
Wishnik (Trolls), Whitman #1965, 1965, M **25.00**

Paperweights

All paperweights listed here are made totally of glass (including the lampwork flowers, fish, birds, snakes, lizards, and millefiori rods). The only elements that are not glass are the clay sulfides encased within some of the Baccarat and St. Louis weights. Today, antique weights (1845 to ca 1870s) and those made by contemporary artists attract the most attention and are the most expensive. Lower-priced 'gift' weights come from American glasshouses and studios, China, Murano, Italy, and Scotland. But because of the expenses involved in their manufacture (fuel, material, and labor), even they are not cheap. There is an international association of paperweight collectors with many state and regional chapters. (For information see Clubs, Newsletters, and Catalogs in the Directory.) Many books are currently available on the subject of paperweights. For the beginner we recommend *All About Paperweights* by L.H. Selmen.

Probably inspired by the work of Pierre Bigaglia (Venice), the

French factories of Baccarat, Clichy, and St. Louis turned their attention to paperweight-making in the 1840s. They first made millefiori paperweights, the technique a revival of methods used in Alexandria, Damascus, Rome, and Byzantium before the time of Christ. (This art form had faded out but had been revived in 16th-century Venice.) The French Classic period was 1845 to 1860; English (Whitefriars and Bacchus) and American (Sandwich and New England) glasshouses followed their lead about ten years later. Gradually, as the paperweight's popularity declined, production began to wane; Clichy closed in the 1880s, as did a few American factories. Baccarat made weights as late as 1910; in the '20s and '30s, a worker by the name of Dupont revived the art. Then in the 1950s St. Louis and Baccarat sparked a renewal of interest in weight-making that is still going strong today. Some of the most desirable weights from American artists were made by the Banfords, Randall Grubb, Rick Ayotte, Chris Buzzini, Ken Rosenfeld, Gordon Smith, Paul Stankard, Charles Kaziun (d), Del (d) and Debbie Tarsitano, and the Trabuccos. From Scotland, Paul Ysart (d), Perthshire and Caithness/Whitefriars are also well known.

Note: Prices do not reflect the usual buyer's fee charged by most auction houses. Furthermore, there are many factors which determine value, particularly of antique weights. Auction-realized prices of contemporary weights are usually different from issue price; 'list price' may be for weights issued earlier and reduced for clearance or influenced by market demand and other factors. The competition for antique weights has been increasing dramatically over the last five years. New collectors entering the field have greatly influenced prices. As the numbers of collectors increase, available antique weights decrease per capita, forcing prices upwards. Since the 1930s antique paperweights have steadily increased in value making them one of today's best investments. The dimension given at the end of the description is diameter.

Key:
A — antique
con — concentric
fct — faceted
gar — garland
grd — ground
jsp — jasper
latt — latticinio

LE — limited edition
mill — millefiori
o/l — overlay
pm — pastry mold
pwt — paperweight
sil — silhouette

Ayotte, Rick

Cardinal on leafy branch on lt bl grd, 1981, 2½" 400.00
Meadowlark on branch on clear grd, 1980, 2½" 375.00
Summer, carnations/daisies/freesia/mums 950.00
Summer (2nd or 4), carnations, daisies, freesia, mini mums 950.00
Summer Bouquet illusion, upright, 4½" W 1,350.00
2 parrots on branches on clear grd, compound, 1980, 2¾" 500.00
2 purple-throated sapphire hummingbirds w/fuchsia, 3" 850.00

Baccarat, Antique

Bl & wht primrose w/starburst center on star-cut grd, 3" 950.00
Closepack mill w/6 sil canes & complex canes on muslin, 3⅛" ..2,000.00
Dbl o/l mushroom on star-cut grd w/mc complex canes, 3" 7,500.00
Fct clematis & buds w/twist stems on clear star-cut grd, 2⅝" ...1,000.00
Fct gar wallflower bouquet on clear star-cut grd, 3⅛" 8,000.00
Fct pansy w/garland on clear star-cut grd, 2¾" 2,000.00
Fct primrose w/cobalt tips & gr leaves on star-cut grd, 2⅞" ...1,300.00
Fct primrose w/starburst center on star-cut grd, 2⅛" 900.00
Flat bouquet w/3 flowers & bud 9,350.00
Gar butterfly w/mc wings on clear star-cut grd, 3⅛" 2,000.00
Joan of Arc sulfide on gr flash grd, 1 top fct, 3½" 2,000.00
Mc patterned mill w/6 complex canes on upset muslin grd, 3⅛" .4,000.00

Spaced con mill over translucent gr grd, starburst center, 2" 550.00
Wild strawberry on clear grd, slightly off center, 2¾" 1,500.00
3-flower flat bouquet on clear grd, 15 leaves, 3⅛" 8,500.00

Baccarat, Modern

Bonsai tree w/gr foliage on red, 1987, 3¼", MIB 400.00
Butterscotch & wht clematis w/buds & leaves on wht opaque, 3⅛" .400.00
Geo Washington sulfide on emerald gr, MIB 160.00
H Hoover sulfide on bl cut to wht to clear, 6 fcts, 3⅛" 80.00
JF Kennedy sulfide on brn star-cut grd, acid etch, 2¾" 175.00
John F Kennedy sulfide on latticed emerald gr, MIB 200.00
Kennedy sulfide on ruby X-hatched grd, MIB 200.00
King Edward & Queen Elizabeth sulfide on rayed grd, MIB 150.00

Buzzini, Chris

Harlequine Lupine w/pk & yel blooms & buds, LE 10, 3⅜" 800.00
Sierra Lessingia w/bud bulbs & roots, LE 10, 3⅜" 700.00
3 wht Mock Orange on branches, 3 buds/long leaves, LE 10, 3½" ...900.00
3 Yosemite Aster & 2 buds, brn stem, speckled leaves, LE 10, 3⅜" ...800.00

Clichy, Antique

Clichy, central rose, patterned multicolored millifiori canes on cushion of white lacy twists, 2½", $900.00.

Con canes w/outer row of 6 wht roses on cobalt grd, 2⅜" 1,500.00
Con mill piedouche, star/pastry mold/flower canes, 2⅜x3" 4,750.00
Daisy on wht swirling latt grd, 5 red petals, 2¾" 9,500.00
Fct chequer w/17 canes over latt grd, 2⅝" 2,300.00
Gr & wht whorl w/stars amid wht latt/red ribbon spokes, 3¼" ...3,750.00
Lime gr checquer 5,225.00
Pk rose nosegay w/5 gr leaves on clear grd, 2¾" 3,750.00
Red daisy over latt grd 10,450.00
Rose cane amid spaced con pattern of 6 canes w/in 12, 2⅛" 950.00
Spaced mill w/9 canes, minor scratches, 2" 450.00
32 mill canes in gr latt chequer brd on wht latt grd, 2¾" 4,750.00

Donofrio, Jim

Wolf on snowy grd w/foliage on tree trunk & branch 800.00
2 tree frogs on bamboo, 3⅜" 1,000.00

Ebelhare, Drew

Mc mill & canes in red & wht stave basket, 2½" 230.00
Pk & wht swirl, bl complex center cane, E cane/etch sgn, 2½" ...175.00
Red, wht & bl close con canes in red & wht stave basket, 2½" ..215.00
Red, wht & bl close con mill in red & wht stave basket, 2¼" 215.00
Spaced con fireworks from long canes in red & bl basket, 2¼" ...300.00

Grubb, Randy

Mauve shooting stars w/gr leaves & stems 400.00

Plum blossom+wht flowers w/yel stamens on branch 435.00
2 dahlias, flowers & buds w/gr leaves, magnum 1,200.00
2 dahlias (1 red/1 lav)+2 violets & yel floral spray, 3¼" 400.00
2 fuchsia blossoms w/red-rimmed gr leaves, 1994, 3⅛" 375.00

Kaziun, Charles

Mill on bl w/7 canes, K w/heart canes, 1⅞" 525.00
Pk crimp rose w/4 leaves, K cane w/in heart canes, 2⅞" 1,400.00
Red crimp rose, K cane w/in heart canes, 3¼" 1,600.00
Rose w/4 aventurine leaves on clear, sgn, upright ped, 2¼" 800.00
Spider lily, purple & wht on yel jsp grd, sgn w/gold K, 1⅞" 425.00
Spider lily, yel & orange on bl & wht jsp grd, 1⅞" 425.00
Tiger lily on pk w/gold aventurine grd, fct & ftd, 1x⅞" 400.00

Lundberg Studios

Lundberg, Steven; dragonfly & yel water flower & bud 380.00
Lundberg, Steven; parrot on branch on bl grd w/wht moon, 2⅞" ..250.00
Lundberg, Steven; Pine Moon, branches & moon 280.00
Lundberg, Steven; Queen of the Night w/cactus 300.00
Lundberg, Steven; seascape on cobalt grd, 1982, 3" 250.00
Salazar, Daniel; fish, rocks & shells on rainbow irid, 2¾" 325.00
Salazar, Daniel; fish, starfish & sea life, w/stand 400.00
Salazar, Daniel; Golden Clematis w/butterfly 320.00
Salazar, Daniel; mc candle amid gr wreath, 1988, 3" 100.00

New England Glass, Antique

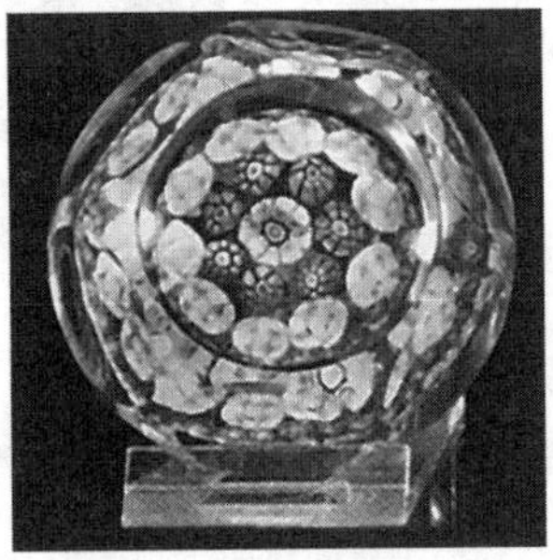

Faceted with four concentric millefiori rings surrounding a pink, blue
and white cane, 2¾", $650.00.

Fct scramble w/tightly packed ribbons/canes/tubes, 2⅞", NM 325.00
Fruits on swirl latt basket, slightly clouded dome 550.00
Pattern mill w/X & 4 canes amid X lines, 2¾" 350.00
Pk, wht & gr dominate in scramble, 2⅞" 250.00
Yel apple w/gr highlights on clear 'cookie' base, 3¼" 1,185.00
5 pears & 4 cherries w/gr leaves on wht swirl latt grd, 2⅝" 500.00

Orient & Flume

Blk music note & scale on wht, LE 250, Braley, 3" 130.00
Blk widow spider by pk dahlia, LE 250, S Beyers, 3½" 270.00
Golden carp & lily pads, LE 250, S Beyers, 3⅝" 290.00

Parabelle

Complex canes/pansies/roses in basket/2 torsades, LE 10, 3¼" ...1,250.00
Con complex canes w/wht & gr rose cane on red opaque, LE 10, 3" .400.00
Con mc mill on gr irid grd, 1991, 2¾" 150.00
Pk & gr rose center cane w/bl & wht swirl gr, LE 10, 3⅝" 500.00

Rose & pansy canes, bl checquer on sodden snow grd, LE 10, 3" ..700.00
Upright flowers in latt basket, latt/ribbon hdl, LE 10, 2⅞" 1,000.00

Parsley, Johne

2 yel flowers & buds w/frond leaves on translucent bl, 2" 650.00
3 pk flowers w/red tips & stamens, lt & dk gr leaves, 2½" 600.00
3 ripe peaches & cherries, veined gr leaves, bl grd, 2¼" 675.00

Perthshire

Bouquet on royal bl webbed cushion grd, 3¼" 440.00
Floral vines on yel trellis on gr grd, P cane, 3" 260.00
Mc patterned mill & twisted ribbons on pk grd, 1978, 3" 120.00
Pattern mill w/9 sil canes, ltd ed of 350, 3" 240.00
Pk flower w/various canes (3 ea sil & colored picture), 2½" 170.00
Red, wht & bl crown, 1969 ....550.00
Scottish thistles w/in wht stardust canes w/6 mill canes, 3¼" 385.00
Shepherd w/lamb on starry blk grd, 1 top fct, 1982, 3" 400.00
Spanish Armada, ship sil amid canes w/'400' anniversary cane ..190.00
Turtle dove w/in ring of wht stars on cobalt grd, 1991, 3" 300.00
5 pastel canes w/sils w/in garland on muslin grd, 1990, 2" 160.00

Rosenfeld, Ken

Bouquet w/7 mc flowers & 2 buds on star-cut grd, 1987, 3¼" 300.00
Half-circle bouquet w/9 flowers on clear grd, 1984, 2⅛x3⅛" 250.00
Purple, bl & yel flowers on sandy grd, 1992, 3¼" 325.00
Red flower w/opening bud & 3 sm buds w/leaves, med sz 250.00
Thistle w/leaves, med sz 250.00
3 lg mc flowers & leaves on clear grd, R cane, 2¾" 250.00
4 lg mc flowers w/buds & vines on clear grd, R cane, 3½" 255.00

St Louis, Antique

Bl pansy w/brn & yel details on wht upset muslin grd, 2" 1,500.00
Carp sulfide w/red tongue on cobalt & wht jsp grd, 2¾" 1,100.00
Chamomile flower over salmon swirling latt grd, 3" 2,250.00
Clematis on wht swirl latt grd, wht starburst center, 2" 1,100.00
Dahlia on swirl latt basket, 2⅝" 1,000.00
Devil dancing sil cane amid mc con mill canes, 2¾" 3,000.00
Fct gar bouquet on clear, wht/pk/bl/ochre/gr, 3", EX 4,000.00
Mc bouquet on red o/l cut to wht to clear, 13 fcts, '77, 3" 550.00
3 lampwork mc flowers w/gr leaves on star-cut grd, 3" 3,500.00
4-color crown w/strips of latt w/red/wht/bl cane, 2¼" 1,750.00

Stankard, Paul

Blkberries/leaves w/wht buds, 2-layer, 2¾" 1,870.00
Dogwood on bright bl grd, 2¾" 770.00
Lady slipper, pk on bl grd, 1972, 2¼" 600.00
Pk, yel & wht flowers w/blk currants, 1979, S cane, 3" 1,855.00
Poinsettia, red/floating, PS cane, 1973, 2¼" 715.00
6 roses w/gr leaves on clear grd, S cane, 1978, 2⅞" 1,455.00

Trabucco, Jon and David

Pk rose w/pk buds & 6 sm bl buds, 1992, 3" 325.00
Purple rose & bud w/7 gr leaves on clear grd, 1988, 2⅞" 160.00
8 blueberries w/pk flowers & buds, 1992, 3½" 425.00

Trabucco, Victor

Morning-glory bouquet on clear grd, 1992, 3¼" 625.00

Pk & bl flowers, magnum **950.00**
Pk rose+bud, buttercup+bud & 2 morning glories on clear, 14" ...**975.00**
Red flower & bud w/sm wht flower & 2 buds on dirt grd **650.00**

Whitefriars

Bl, wht & pk con mill canes, 1 top/6 side fcts, 1982, 3" **130.00**
Butterfly w/in mc gar, 1 top/6 side fcts, sgn/1982, 2⅞" **140.00**
Con mill w/yel center cane amid mc canes, dtd 1848, 3¾" **375.00**
Con pk, wht & bl mill canes, dtd 1848, 3" **400.00**
Liberty bell sil cane amid 13 star canes w/in mc ring, 3" **325.00**
Mc patterned mill, 1 top & 5 side fcts, 1973, 3" **350.00**
Red & wht heart cane amid mc mill canes, sticker, 3¼" **180.00**

Miscellaneous

Bacchus, pk & wht con mill in stave basket, 3¼" **1,800.00**
Banford, Bob; lilies of valley w/wide leaves on cranberry grd **600.00**
Banford, Bob; 5-flower bouquet in fct column, 3¾" **1,000.00**
Banford, Ray; pk iris w/bud & gr leaves on clear, B cane, 3" **275.00**
Banford, Ray; purple iris & bud w/leaves on wht opaque, sgn, 3" ..**450.00**
Bohemian, close-pack mc mill on upset muslin grd, 1850s, 2½" .**1,300.00**
Bohemian, hunter/rabbit sulfide fct on pebble grd, 3¼" **400.00**
Caithness, Comet, bl, wht & clear on blk grd, 3" **115.00**
Caithness, Moonflower, blk grd w/bl, bubbles, 3¼" **50.00**
Millville, wht crimped umbrella w/mc pebbles in clear, 3¼" **140.00**
Pairpoint, fct rose w/4 gr leaves on bl grd, 3" **275.00**
Somerville, 2 red birds & nest w/2 eggs on clear grd, 4⅛" **500.00**
Tarsitano, Debbie; 7-petal wht flower w/bud & gr leaves, 2¾" ...**850.00**
Tarsitano, Delmo; cherries w/leaves on clear star-cut, sgn, 2¼" ..**500.00**
Ysart, Paul; gar butterfly on lime opaque grd, PY cane, 3" **750.00**
Ysart, Paul; gar 5 mc flower bouquet on bl denim opaque, 3" **750.00**

Paragon

The Paragon China Company has operated in Longton, England, from about 1920 to the present. Their line of finely modeled figurines in particular are attracting favorable collector interest.

Cup & saucer, red, cream & wht w/much gold, ca 1939, set of 8 ..**275.00**
Cup & saucer, wine w/gold **38.00**
Figurine, flower girl, #8, 6" **70.00**
Figurine, Lady Melanie **135.00**
Plate, fox terrier, sgn Johnson, gr border w/gold, 10½" **175.00**

Parian Ware

Parian is hard-paste unglazed porcelain made to resemble marble. First made in the mid-1800s by Staffordshire potters, it was soon after produced in the United States by the U.S. Pottery at Bennington, Vermont. Busts and statuary were favored, but plaques, vases, mugs, and pitchers were also made.

Bust, Abraham Lincoln, beardless & in toga, rprs, 12¾" **200.00**
Bust, Abraham Lincoln, minor damage to plinth, 15¾" **600.00**
Bust, General Lee, 11¾" **575.00**
Bust, Greek youth, 5⅞" **50.00**
Bust, Napoleon, after Houdon, sgn under shoulder, 18" **825.00**
Bust, US Grant, 11½" **325.00**
Clock, cherubs, enameling & gilt, rprs, 16" **350.00**
Dogs: Retribution & Imposing on Good Nature, Chester, 6", pr ..**4,100.00**
Figurine, Adriadne on panther, after Dannecker, 1800s, 10" **350.00**

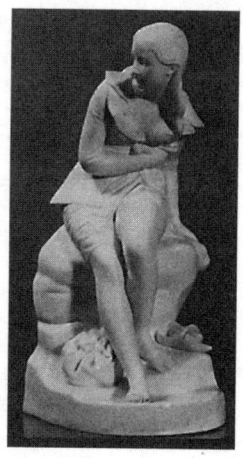

Figure, Dorothea, John Bell, Minton, model #189, dated 1870, 13½", $295.00.

Figurine, girl praying, kneeling, book on 1 knee, 9" **175.00**
Figurine, lady seated, feeding bird, English, 1850s, 12" **165.00**
Figurine, Miranda, seated, imp John Bell mk, 15" **220.00**
Pitcher, corn stalks emb, 11" **195.00**
Pitcher, emb foliage & medallions, 8" **140.00**
Pitcher, emb reeds & berries, ornate hdl, 10¾" **195.00**
Plaque, youth pushing Cupid in wheelbarrow, wht & gr, 9" **25.00**

Parrish, Maxfield

Maxfield Parrish was a painter and illustrator who began his career in the last decade of the 19th century. His work remained prominent until the early 1940s. His most famous painting, *Daybreak*, was published in print form and sold nearly two thousand copies between 1910 and 1930. All prices are for framed prints except for those from the 1960s.

Ad, Companion, Peter Peter Pumpkin Eater, full sheet, 1919 ....**150.00**
Ad, glass slide, Edison/Mazda Lamps, 4x3¼", EX **300.00**
Ad, Saturday Evening Post, Edison/Mazda Lamps, full sheet, '24 .**85.00**
Ad, Silent Night, Xmas card, Sunstrand Tool Co, 1942, EX **50.00**
Book, Arabian Nights, 1909, EX **150.00**
Book, Italian Villas **295.00**
Book, King Albert's Book, Dieserai, NM **125.00**
Book, Knave of Hearts, hard-bound, NM **1,050.00**
Book, Knave of Hearts, slightly scuffed, EX **900.00**
Book, Poems of Childhood, Parrish illus, 1904, EX **225.00**
Book, Tanglewood Tales, 1910, EX **125.00**
Book plate, Lady Violetta w/milk pitcher, fr, 1925 ....**90.00**
Book plate, Page, Knave of Hearts, fr, 1925, EX **75.00**
Booklet, Jell-O, Parrish front & bk covers, NM **50.00**
Calendar, Ecstasy, Mazda, 1930, 20x10", NM **750.00**
Calendar, of Friendship; Dodge, 1927, complete, 8x5¾", EX **85.00**
Calendar, Old Glen Mill, 1954, 21½x16½", EX **250.00**
Calendar, Sheltering Oaks, complete, 1960, 10½x5¼", EX **150.00**
Calendar, Sunlight, complete, 1958, 8½x6¾", EX **180.00**
Calendar, Sunlit Valley, 1950, 22x17", VG **350.00**
Calendar, Waterfall, Mazda, complete, 1931, 20x10", NM **900.00**
Calendar print, Golden Hours, sm, EX **200.00**
Calendar print, Moonlight, Edison/Mazda, 1934, 9x12" **195.00**
Calendar print, Reveries, antique fr, 1927, 10¼x6½", EX **175.00**
Calendar print, Sunrise, 20½x15" **525.00**
Magazine cover, man & son in snow, Collier's, Nov 1906, EX **35.00**
Playing cards, Ecstasy, Edison/Mazda, full deck, EX **250.00**
Playing cards, Spirit of Night, Edison/Mazda, full deck, EX **275.00**
Playing cards, Waterfall, Edison/Mazda, full deck, EX **250.00**
Poster, Century, nude in forest, orig fr, 1898, 13x18" **775.00**
Print, Air Castles, nymph, castles in sky, 1904, 14x18" **285.00**

Print, Ancient Tree, massive oak, mtns beyond, 1952, 17x21" ..350.00
Print, Arabian man in blk watches smoke emit from lamp, 8x10" .195.00
Print, Bl & Yel Hose, chefs in kitchen, 1925, 12x14" 95.00
Print, Centaur, fr, 12x9", VG 175.00
Print, Cleopatra, 21½x27½"+gold fr 1,800.00
Print, Contentment, lg 900.00
Print, Daybreak, nymph awakens lady, 1923, 13x21" 250.00
Print, Dream Castles, youth looks toward castle, 1912, 8x11" 140.00
Print, Dreaming, lg 650.00
Print, Dreamlight, lady sits in forest, Mazda, 1925, 9x13" 350.00
Print, Easter, nymph on wall w/lilies, 1911, 7½x10½" 110.00
Print, Enchantment, sm 325.00
Print, Errant Pan, hand-cvd fr, 1910, 11x9", NM 195.00
Print, Evening Shadows, farm scene, fr, 1940, 16x12", EX 175.00
Print, Fisherman & Genie, orig label, 11x8¾", NM 125.00

Triptych from Florentine Fete mural, original frame, 8x9½", $85.00.

Print, Gardan of Allah, 9x18" 200.00
Print, Garden of Allah, 3 ladies by pool, 1918, 19x34" 465.00
Print, Hilltop, Art Nouveau fr, scarce, 12x20", EX 400.00
Print, Hilltop, 2 ladies under fir tree, 1926, 9x13" 150.00
Print, Lady Ursala, lady before king on throne, 1925, 12x14" 95.00
Print, Lights of Welcome, matted, 8x10½", NM 225.00
Print, Lonesome Princess, fr, 7x5", EX 50.00
Print, New Moon, night farm scene, 1958, 12x15" 225.00
Print, Old King Cole, J Lane, NY & London, 1910, 3x11½ , M ..325.00
Print, Old King Cole, 6¼x23" 950.00
Print, Page, knave on wall looking to village, 1925, 12x14" 250.00
Print, Peaceful Valley, farm scene, 1964, 12x12" 150.00
Print, Pied Piper, early fr, 6¾x21", scarce, VG 875.00
Print, Polly Put the Kettle On, Jell-O, 1924, 10x14" 50.00
Print, Prince Codedad, fr, 9x11", VG 135.00
Print, Reveries, ladies by fountain, Mazda, 1927, 6x10" 125.00
Print, Reveries, 12x15" 575.00
Print, Romance, House of Art, orig fr & label, 14x23½", NM+ ..950.00
Print, Stars, 18x30", NM 1,000.00
Print, Sunrise, 6x8" 225.00
Print, Twilight, old barn, fr, 11x8" 110.00
Print, Violetta & Knave, tarts in oven, 1925, 12x14" 97.50
Print, Waterfall, 7x10", EX 250.00
Print, Wild Geese, lady on rocks, mtns beyond, 1924, 13x16" ...285.00
Print, Winter Twilight, 8½x11" 150.00

Pate-De-Verre

Simply translated, pate-de-verre means paste of glass. In the manufacturing process, lead glass is first ground, then mixed with sodium silicate solution to form a paste which can be molded and refired. Some of the most prominent artisans to use this procedure were Almaric Walter, Daum,

Argy-Rousseau, and Decorchemont. See also specific manufacturers.

Bust of satyr, amethyst, mk Despret/#1099, 6½" 1,100.00
Dish, clear/red streaked, cvd w/flowers, 8-side lip, 8" L 2,100.00
Pendant, lady w/flowing hair, amethyst, gilt mt, 1¼" dia 385.00
Sculpture, lady's head, yel, sgn Despret, 4" L 550.00
Vase, rim decor, gr/rust/purple mottle, Decorchemont, 4" 1,400.00

Pate-Sur-Pate

Pate-sur-pate, literally paste-on-paste, is a technique whereby relief decorations are built up on a ceramic body by layering several applications of slip, one on the other, until the desired result is achieved. Usually only two colors are used, and the value of a piece is greatly enhanced as more color is added.

Lamp base, maid/arabesques on gr, gilt bronze base, 19" 350.00
Panel, maids dancing, sgn Crelerot, gilt metal fr, 7x4½", pr 650.00
Pitcher, Romans on red/brn, Roman finial, Geo Jones, 9", EX ...385.00
Vase, bird/wheat on dk gr, gilt borders, mask hdls, 14½", EX 500.00
Vase, girl, wht on brick red, gilt elephant hdls, sqd, 10", EX 300.00
Vase, lady/child w/fish, wht in lav oval on bl, Germany, 6" 450.00

Pattern Glass

Pattern Glass was the first mass-produced fancy tableware in America and was much prized by our ancestors. From the 1840s to the Civil War, it contained a high lead content and is known as 'Flint Glass.' It is exceptionally clear and resonant. Later glass was made with soda lime and is known as non-flint. By the 1890s pattern glass was produced in great volume in thousands of patterns, and colored glass came into vogue. Today the highest prices are often paid for these later patterns flashed with rose, amber, canary, and vaseline; stained ruby; or made in colors of cobalt, green, yellow, amethyst, etc. Demand for pattern glass declined by 1915, and glass fanciers were collecting it by 1930. No other field of antiques offers more diversity in patterns, prices, or pieces than this unique and historical glass that represents the Victorian era in America.

Our advisor for this category is Darlene Yohe; she is listed in the Directory under Arkansas. For a more thorough study on the subject, we recommend *The Collector's Encyclopedia of Pattern Glass*, by Mollie Helen McCain, available from Collector Books. See also Bread Plates; Cruets; Historical Glass; Salt and Pepper Shakers; Salts, Open; Sugar Shakers; Syrups; specific manufacturers such as Northwood.

Note: Values are given for open sugar bowls and compotes unless noted 'w/lid.'

Actress, bowl, w/lid 115.00
Actress, compote, 11x6" 125.00
Actress, creamer, frosted base 75.00
Actress, goblet, frosted bowl 120.00
Admiral Dewey, See Dewey; See Also Greentown Dewey
Alabama, creamer, ruby stained 60.00
Alabama, jelly compote 62.50
Allover Diamond, cordial 36.00
Allover Diamond, goblet 27.50
Allover Diamond, tumbler 15.00
Almond Thumbprint, cordial 42.50
Almond Thumbprint, creamer, non-flint 40.00
Almond Thumbprint, tumbler, ftd 38.00
Amazon, cake stand, plain, lg 55.00
Amazon, creamer 38.00

Amazon, egg cup 12.50
Amberette, See Klondike
Apollo, bread tray, sq 30.00
Apollo, goblet, frosted 48.00
Apollo, salt cellar 20.00
Apollo, toothpick holder 27.50
Arched Ovals, bowl, berry 12.50
Arched Ovals, pitcher, water, gr 42.50
Argus, bottle, bitters 57.50
Argus, champagne 75.00
Argus, sugar bowl, w/lid 68.00
Art, bowl, 9¾" 40.00
Art, compote, w/lid, 9x9½" 50.00
Art, tumbler 32.50
Ashburton, goblet, short, flint 42.50
Ashburton, vase, ped base, flint, 9¼" 82.50
Ashburton, whiskey, hdld, flint 95.00
Atlas, cordial 46.00
Atlas, tumbler 27.50
Atlas, whiskey, ruby stained 42.50
Aurora, mug, hdld, ruby stained 62.50
Aurora, pitcher, water 45.00
Austrian, butter dish, canary 325.00
Austrian, goblet 38.00
Austrian, punch cup, amber 145.00
Balder, See Pennsylvania
Baltimore Pear, goblet 36.00
Baltimore Pear, jelly bowl 27.50
Baltimore Pear, pitcher, water 98.00
Bar & Diamond, tumbler 22.50
Barberry, bowl, oval, 6" 20.00
Barberry, plate, bl, 6" 48.00
Barberry, tumbler, ftd 22.50
Barley, butter dish 45.00
Barley, goblet 35.00
Barley, wine 38.00
Barrel Huber, See Huber
Basket Weave, cordial, apple gr 42.50
Basket Weave, mug, 3" 20.00
Basket Weave, tumbler 17.50
Beaded Band, goblet 32.00
Beaded Band, relish, sm 15.00
Beaded Band, spooner 25.00
Beaded Grape, butter dish, gr, sq 85.00
Beaded Grape, celery tray 35.00
Beaded Grape Medallion, compote, collared base, w/lid 88.00
Beaded Grape Medallion, goblet, buttermilk 32.00
Beaded Medallion, compote, low std, w/lid, 8¼" 88.00
Beaded Medallion, pitcher, water 115.00
Beaded Medallion, sugar bowl, open 30.00
Beaded Mirror, See Beaded Medallion
Beaded Swirl, butter dish 36.00
Beaded Swirl, compote, high std, gr 48.00
Beaded Tulip, goblet 32.50
Beaded Tulip, plate, 6" 24.00
Bearded Head, See Viking
Bellflower, champagne, fine rib, dbl vine, cut flowers 245.00
Bellflower, compote, 4½x8½" 95.00
Bellflower, cordial, knob stem 120.00
Bigler, celery vase 90.00
Bigler, decanter, bar lip, 1-pt 60.00
Bird & Strawberry, bowl, 10½" 95.00
Bird & Strawberry, creamer 55.00
Bird & Strawberry, pitcher, water 240.00

Bleeding Heart, butter dish 80.00
Bleeding Heart, creamer, molded hdl 32.00
Bleeding Heart, relish, oval 36.00
Block & Fan, creamer, ruby stained, ind 37.50
Block & Fan, finger bowl 50.00
Block & Fan, waste bowl 35.00
Blue Jay, See Cardinal Bird
Bohemian, butter dish, gr w/gold 127.50
Bohemian, mug, rose stained w/gold 80.00
Bow Tie, creamer 55.00
Bow Tie, sugar bowl 37.50
Broken Column, cake stand 75.00
Broken Column, carafe 80.00
Broken Column, champagne 110.00
Buckle, egg cup, non-flint 30.00
Buckle, sugar bowl, w/lid, flint 95.00
Buckle, wine, flint 125.00
Buckle w/Star, butter dish 42.50
Buckle w/Star, mug 30.00
Bull's Eye, decanter, bar lip, 1-qt 125.00
Bull's Eye, mug, appl hdl, 3½" 100.00
Bull's Eye, sugar bowl, w/lid 125.00
Bull's Eye & Fan, relish 22.50
Bull's Eye & Fan, sugar bowl, w/lid 36.00
Bull's Eye & Fan, wine, emerald gr 42.50
Bull's Eye Band, See Reverse Torpedo
Bull's Eye in Heart, See Heart w/Thumbprint
Bull's Eye w/Diamond Point, celery vase 150.00
Bull's Eye w/Diamond Point, tumbler, water 110.00
Bull's Eye w/Diamond Point, wine 125.00
Button Arches, goblet 27.50
Button Arches, pitcher, milk; ruby stained 110.00
Button Arches, salt cellar, ind 17.50

Cabbage Rose

Cabbage Rose, basket, 12" 120.00
Cabbage Rose, butter dish 65.00
Cabbage Rose, tumbler 42.50
Cable, creamer 195.00
Cable, plate, 6" 75.00
California, See Beaded Grape
Cane, goblet, amber 35.00
Cane, pitcher, water; bl 75.00
Cane, spooner, apple gr 38.00
Cape Cod, marmalade jar 88.00
Cape Cod, pitcher, milk 60.00
Cardinal Bird, goblet 38.00
Cardinal Bird, honey dish, 3½" 35.00
Cardinal Bird, sugar bowl, w/lid 60.00
Cathedral, cake stand, bl 65.00

Cathedral, creamer, amber, flat, sq 48.00
Cathedral, sugar bowl, w/lid 65.00
Centennial, See Liberty Bell
Chain, bread plate 32.00
Chain, sugar bowl, w/lid 35.00
Chain & Shield, goblet 30.00
Chain & Shield, platter, oval 27.50
Chain w/Diamonds, See Washington Centennial
Chain w/Star, jelly compote 18.00
Chandelier, goblet, etched 58.00
Chandelier, salt cellar master 32.00
Classic, butter dish, open log ft 245.00
Classic, celery vase 120.00
Classic, plate, President Cleveland 185.00
Cleat, pitcher, water; flint 125.00
Coin, See US Coin
Colorado, banana stand, gr 42.50
Colorado, calling card tray 27.50
Colorado, custard cup, gr, lg 27.50
Columbian Coin, compote, w/lid, frosted coins, 8" ...165.00
Columbian Coin, goblet, clear w/gold 62.50
Columbian Coin, toothpick holder, clear w/gold 130.00
Comet, goblet 88.00
Comet, pitcher, water 525.00
Comet, sugar bowl, w/lid 175.00
Compact, See Snail
Connecticut, pitcher, water 50.00
Connecticut, tumbler, lemonade; hdl 20.00
Cord & Tassel, compote, low, 8" 30.00
Cord & Tassel, goblet 38.00
Cord Drapery, butter dish 75.00
Cord Drapery, pitcher, water; cobalt 245.00
Cord Drapery, wine 88.00
Cordova, celery vase 45.00
Cordova, compote, high std, w/lid 42.50
Cordova, tumbler 17.50
Cottage, celery vase, amber 87.50
Cottage, plate, 7" 22.50
Cottage, sauce bowl 12.00

Croesus

Croesus, bowl, ftd, amethyst, 4x7" 70.00
Croesus, creamer, gr, 3" 195.00
Croesus, pitcher, water; amethyst w/gold, ftd, 11" ..160.00
Croesus, pitcher, water; gr 200.00
Croesus, salt cellar, amethyst, ftd 40.00
Crow's Foot, See Yale
Crown Jewels, See Chandelier
Crystal Wedding, goblet, ruby stained 88.00
Crystal Wedding, nappy 27.50
Crystal Wedding, plate, ruby stained, 10" 50.00
Crystal Wedding, tumbler, ruby stained 48.00

Cube w/Fan, See Pineapple & Fan
Cupid & Venus, bread plate 42.50
Cupid & Venus, cordial, 3½" 88.00
Cupid & Venus, goblet 78.00
Cupid & Venus, pitcher, water 70.00
Currant, relish 15.00
Currant, wine 20.00
Currier & Ives, bowl, oval, 10" 32.50
Currier & Ives, pitcher, milk 36.00
Currier & Ives, tumbler 42.50
Curtain, spooner 25.00
Curtain, sugar bowl, w/lid 40.00
Curtain Tie-Back, relish 12.50
Cut Log, compote, high std, 7¼" dia 100.00
Cut Log, salt cellar, master 68.00
Cut Log, sugar bowl, w/lid 65.00
Dahlia, champagne, amber 62.50
Dahlia, creamer 20.00
Dahlia, sugar bowl, vaseline, w/lid 65.00
Daisy & Button, banana boat, 14" 48.00
Daisy & Button, cake stand 50.00
Daisy & Button, goblet, apple gr 48.00
Daisy & Button w/Crossbar, butter dish, canary yel ...70.00
Daisy & Button w/Crossbar, goblet 27.50
Daisy & Button w/Crossbar, wine 27.50
Daisy & Button w/Thumbprint Panels, butter dish, w/lid ...185.00
Daisy & Button w/Thumbprint Panels, cake stand 55.00
Daisy & Button w/V Ornament, finger bowl 20.00
Daisy & Button w/V Ornament, toothpick holder, bl 42.50
Dakota, basket, plain 235.00
Dakota, compote, high standard, 5" 65.00
Dakota, pitcher, water; etched, ½-gal 95.00
Dakota, plate, 10" 88.00
Dakota, waste bowl, plain 47.50
Deer & Dog, butter dish, dog finial 150.00
Deer & Dog, wine 80.00
Deer & Pine Tree, butter dish, bl 135.00
Deer & Pine Tree, goblet 60.00
Deer & Pine Tree, sugar bowl, w/lid 60.00
Delaware, bowl, 9" 27.50
Delaware, dresser tray 32.00
Delaware, finger bowl, clear w/gold 22.50
Delaware, punch cup, gr w/gold 32.50
Dew & Raindrop, pitcher, water 50.00
Dew & Raindrop, punch cup 9.00
Dewdrop, egg cup, dbl 25.00
Dewdrop w/Star, cake stand, 11" 45.00
Dewdrop w/Star, relish, 9" 12.50
Dewey, butter dish, amber 88.00
Dewey, mug 37.50
Dewey, tray, serpentine shape 30.00
Diagonal Band, cake stand 40.00
Diagonal Band, marmalade, orig lid 47.50
Diagonal Band, sugar bowl 16.00
Diamond Horseshoe, See Aurora
Diamond Medallion, See Grand
Diamond Point, creamer, flint 120.00
Diamond Point, pitcher, water; flint 450.00
Diamond Point, whiskey, hdl, flint 88.00
Diamond Quilted, bowl, vaseline, 7" 24.00
Diamond Quilted, champagne 22.50
Diamond Quilted, goblet, amethyst 37.50
Diamond Quilted, tumbler, amber 32.50
Diamond Thumbprint, compote, low std, 8" 70.00

Diamond Thumbprint, honey dish 20.00
Diamond Thumbprint, whiskey, flint 150.00
Dinner Bell, See Cottage
Doric, See Feather
Double Leaf & Dart, See Leaf & Dart
Drapery, creamer 36.00
Drapery, goblet 27.50
Egg in Sand, platter, 12½" 45.00
Egg in Sand, relish 12.50
Egg in Sand, tumbler 32.00
Egyptian, creamer 45.00
Egyptian, plate, 12" 88.00
Elephant, See Jumbo
Emerald Green Herringbone, See Florida
Empress, butter dish 60.00
Empress, tumbler, gr w/gold 50.00
English Hobnail Cross, See Klondike
Esther, cake stand, gr 110.00
Esther, creamer, gr 120.00
Esther, tumbler, gr 88.00
Etched Dakota, See Dakota
Eureka, sugar bowl, flint 25.00
Eureka, tumbler 28.00
Excelsior, claret 48.00
Excelsior, cordial 45.00
Excelsior, pickle jar, w/lid 50.00
Excelsior, sugar bowl, w/lid 135.00
Eyewinker, banana stand 130.00
Eyewinker, celery vase, 6½" 60.00
Eyewinker, goblet 28.00
Eyewinker, sugar bowl, w/lid 55.00
Fairfax Strawberry, See Strawberry
Feather, champagne 60.00
Feather, cordial 120.00
Feather, plate, 10" 45.00
Festoon, creamer 40.00
Festoon, plate, 8" 40.00
Fine Cut, pitcher, water; amber 78.00
Fine Cut, plate, 10" 20.00
Fine Cut & Block, cordial 65.00
Fine Cut & Block, pitcher, water; amber blocks 90.00
Fine Cut & Block, tumbler 18.00
Fine Cut & Diamond, See Grand
Fine Cut & Feather, See Feather
Fine Cut & Panel, goblet 22.00
Fine Cut & Panel, plate, amber, 6" 25.00
Fine Cut & Panel, shaker, amber, orig top 38.00
Fine Rib, egg cup, dbl, flint 36.00
Fine Rib, spoon holder 55.00
Fingerprint, See Almond Thumbprint

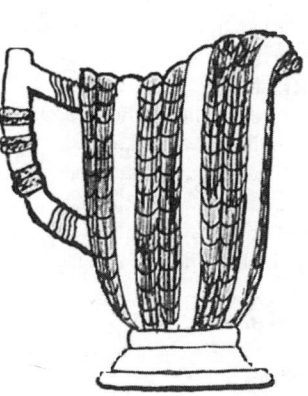

Fishscale

Fishscale, bowl, 10" 25.00
Fishscale, creamer 25.00
Fishscale, tumbler 98.00
Flamingo Habitat, compote, w/lid, 6½" 98.00
Flamingo Habitat, sugar bowl, w/lid 55.00
Florida, creamer, emerald gr 50.00
Florida, plate, 7½" 12.00
Florida Palm, tumbler 30.00
Flower Pot, butter dish 50.00
Flower Pot, goblet 45.00
Flute, bottle, bar; flint, 1-qt 75.00
Flute, claret 25.00
Frosted Circle, punch cup 18.00
Frosted Circle, wine 42.50
Frosted Leaf, egg cup 87.50
Frosted Leaf, goblet 120.00
Frosted Leaf, tumbler, ftd 100.00
Frosted Lion, See Lion
Frosted Ribbon, See Ribbon
Frosted Roman Key, champagne 75.00
Frosted Roman Key, sugar bowl, w/lid 85.00
Frosted Stork, platter, oval, 11½" 75.00
Frosted Stork, sauce bowl 30.00
Galloway, basket 80.00
Galloway, goblet 60.00
Galloway, sauce bowl, flat, 4¼" 17.50
Garfield Drape, butter dish 80.00
Garfield Drape, pitcher, water 105.00
Gem, See Nailhead
Georgia, mug 30.00
Georgia, spooner 35.00
Georgia, tumbler 32.50
Good Luck, See Horseshoe
Grand, butter dish 38.00
Grand, spooner 20.00
Grape & Festoon w/Shield, mug, sapphire bl, 2½" 50.00
Grape & Festoon w/Shield, pitcher, water 75.00
Grasshopper, bowl, ftd, w/lid, 7" 55.00
Grasshopper, butter dish, amber 100.00
Grasshopper, compote, w/lid, 8¼" dia 67.50
Greek Key, goblet, buttermilk 50.00
Greek Key, pitcher, tankard, 1½-qt 245.00
Guardian Angel, See Cupid & Venus
Hairpin, goblet 42.50
Hairpin, tumbler 55.00
Halley's Comet, pitcher, water tankard, eng 110.00
Halley's Comet, tumbler 27.50
Hamilton, goblet 40.00
Hamilton, goblet, flint 55.00
Hawaiian Lei, cake stand, 9¼" 32.00
Hawaiian Lei, cup & saucer 40.00
Heart w/Thumbprint, bowl, sq, 7" 36.00
Heart w/Thumbprint, goblet, gr w/gold 88.00
Heart w/Thumbprint, wine, gr w/gold 140.00
Herringbone Band, See Ripple
Herringbone Buttress, See Greentown, Herringbone Buttress
Hickman, goblet 42.00
Hidalgo, celery vase, amber stain 50.00
Hidalgo, tumbler 27.50
Hinoto, tumbler, ftd 47.50
Hinoto, wine 65.00
Holly, egg cup 58.00
Holly, goblet 98.00
Holly, sugar bowl, w/lid 130.00

Holly Amber, See Greentown, Holly Amber
Honeycomb, cordial, flint, 3½" 27.50
Honeycomb, honey dish, w/lid, non-flint 24.00
Honeycomb, tumbler, bar; flint 37.50
Hops & Barley, See Wheat & Barley
Horn of Plenty, butter dish, acorn finial, flint 130.00
Horn of Plenty, champagne, flint 225.00
Horn of Plenty, sweetmeat, flint 325.00
Horn of Plenty, tumbler, water; flint 88.00
Horseshoe, bowl, vegetable; oblong 32.50
Horseshoe, cake stand 100.00
Horseshoe, doughnut stand 78.00
Horseshoe, goblet, plain 32.00
Huber, champagne, flint 32.00
Huber, egg cup 30.00
Hummingbird, butter dish 45.00
Hummingbird, wine 95.00
Idaho, See Snail
Illinois, creamer, ind 32.00
Illinois, relish 15.00
Illinois, tumbler, emerald gr 45.00
Iowa, creamer 32.50
Iowa, olive dish 18.00
Iris w/Meander, See Opalescent Glass
Ivy in Snow, goblet 32.00
Ivy in Snow, mug, ruby stained 48.00
Ivy in Snow, tumbler 35.00
Jacob's Ladder, bottle, cologne; Maltese cross stopper ...90.00
Jacob's Ladder, creamer 33.00
Jersey Swirl, butter dish, bl 70.00
Jersey Swirl, salt cellar, bl, ind 22.50
Jewel Band, goblet 36.00
Jewel Band, pitcher, milk 48.00
Jewel w/Dewdrop, cake stand, 8" 48.00
Jewel w/Dewdrop, relish, oval, 8½" 24.00
Jewel w/Dewdrop, sugar bowl, w/lid 65.00
Jewel w/Dewdrop, sugar bowl, w/lid 20.00
Jewel w/Festoon, punch cup 12.50
Jewel w/Festoon, sauce bowl 65.00
Jewel w/Moondrop, pitcher, water 65.00
Jewel w/Moondrop, tumbler 42.50
Jewelled Moon & Star, goblet 45.00
Jewelled Moon & Star, platter 45.00
Job's Tears, See Art
Jumbo, butter dish, frosted elephant finial 675.00
Jumbo, compote, frosted elephant finial, 12" 435.00
Jumbo, goblet 695.00
Jumbo, spooner 98.00
Kentucky, olive dish 27.50
Kentucky, pitcher, water 60.00
Kentucky, punch cup, gr 20.00
King's Crown, claret, ruby stained 55.00
King's Crown, cordial 30.00
King's Crown, creamer, eng 88.00
King's Crown, custard cup, ruby stained 27.50
King's Crown, tumbler, ruby stained 37.50
Klondike, butter pat, amber stained 35.00
Klondike, punch bowl, tulip shape 500.00
Klondike, tumbler 27.50
Klondike, tumbler, amber stained 140.00
Kokomo, tumbler 20.00
La Clede, See Hickman
Lace, See Drapery
Lawrence, See Bull's Eye
Leaf, See Maple Leaf

Leaf & Dart, butter dish, ped base 98.00
Leaf & Dart, wine 28.00
Leaf Bracket, See Greentown, Leaf Bracket
Leaf Medallion, See Northwood, Leaf Medallion
Liberty Bell, butter dish, mini 165.00
Liberty Bell, plate, closed hdls, 6" 78.00
Liberty Bell, salt cellar 27.50

Lily of the Valley

Lily of the Valley, champagne 37.50
Lily of the Valley, sugar bowl, 3-ftd 25.00
Lincoln Drape, creamer, flint 185.00
Lincoln Drape, sugar bowl, w/lid, flint 120.00
Lincoln Drape, sweetmeat, flint 375.00
Lion, bowl, 8x5" 57.50
Lion, champagne 195.00
Lion, cordial 195.00
Lion, wine 215.00
Log Cabin, bowl, w/lid 425.00
Log Cabin, creamer, 4½" 125.00
Log Cabin, marmalade jar 285.00
Long Spear, See Grasshopper
Loop, cordial, non-flint, 2¾" 34.00
Loop, goblet, flint 22.50
Loop & Dart, compote, high std, 6½" 95.00
Loop & Dart, spooner 35.00
Loop w/Stippled Panels, See Texas
Maine, butter dish 60.00
Maine, pitcher, water 100.00
Manhattan, carafe, water; pk stained 90.00
Manhattan, creamer, ind 25.00
Manhattan, plate, 6" 12.00
Maple Leaf, butter pat 15.00
Maple Leaf, tumbler 37.50
Maryland, bowl, berry; ruby stained 40.00
Maryland, relish, ruby stained 50.00
Maryland, shaker, clear w/gold 32.00
Mascotte, butter pat 18.00
Mascotte, cheese dish 67.50
Massachusetts, cordial 58.00
Massachusetts, pitcher, water 70.00
Medallion, goblet, amber 45.00
Medallion, sugar bowl, amber, w/lid 45.00
Melrose, pitcher, milk 50.00
Melrose, plate, 6" 12.00
Melrose, wine 20.00
Michigan, bowl, 8" 42.00
Michigan, spooner, pk stained 75.00
Michigan, vase, 6" 18.00
Michigan, wine, bl stained 60.00
Minerva, creamer 55.00
Minerva, honey dish 20.00

Minnesota, butter dish 60.00
Minnesota, nappy, 4½" 15.00
Minnesota, toothpick holder, 3-hdld, ruby stained 158.00
Minnesota, tumbler, water 20.00
Minor Block, See Mascotte
Mirror, See Galloway
Missouri, cordial 62.50
Missouri, doughnut stand, 6" 40.00
Missouri, spooner 30.00
Missouri, tumbler, gr 36.00
Moon & Star, bowl, w/lid, 6" 24.00
Moon & Star, claret 45.00
Moon & Star, pitcher, water 175.00
Moon & Star, sugar bowl, w/lid 60.00
Morning Glory, champagne, flint 385.00
Morning Glory, salt cellar, ped ft, flint, master 230.00
Nail, decanter 37.50
Nail, pitcher, water 80.00
Nailhead, relish 12.00
Nailhead, spooner 20.00
Nestor, tumbler, gr 32.00
New England Pineapple, goblet, flint 70.00
New England Pineapple, pitcher, water 325.00
New Jersey, cake stand, 8" 70.00
New Jersey, goblet 42.50
O'Hara Diamond, goblet, ruby stained 48.00
O'Hara Diamond, plate, 7" 22.00
One Hundred & One, butter dish 65.00
One Hundred & One, goblet 50.00
One-O-One, See One Hundered & One
Oregon #1, carafe, water 38.00
Oregon #1, mug 37.50
Oregon #1, tumbler 28.00
Orion, See Cathedral
Palmette, cup plate 45.00
Palmette, goblet 38.00
Panelled Daisy, goblet 27.50
Panelled Daisy, plate, sq, 9" 28.00
Panelled Forget-Me-Not, creamer 35.00
Panelled Forget-Me-Not, spooner 27.50
Panelled Herringtone, See Florida
Panelled Star & Button, mug, mini 16.50
Panelled Star & Button, salt cellar, master 15.00
Panelled Thistle, plate, w/bee, sq, 7" 25.00
Panelled Thistle, sugar bowl, w/lid 42.50
Pavonia, celery vase, eng 40.00
Pavonia, creamer, eng 40.00
Pavonia, pitcher, water 55.00
Pavonia, tankard, etched 48.00
Pavonia, tumbler, ruby stained 40.00
Pennsylvania, creamer, clear w/gold, 3" 18.00
Pennsylvania, pitcher, water 75.00
Pennsylvania, relish 10.00
Pennsylvania, tumbler, water; clear w/gold 25.00
Pigmy, See Torpedo
Pillow Encircled, mug 30.00
Pillow Encircled, tumbler 30.00
Pillow Encircled, tumbler, ruby stained 40.00
Pineapple & Fan, pitcher, water 80.00
Pineapple & Fan, vase, trumpet form, 10" 32.00
Pineapple Stem, See Pavonia
Pioneer, See Westward Ho
Pleat & Panel, butter dish 55.00
Pleat & Panel, goblet 35.00

Plume, celery vase 35.00
Plume, compote, collared base, 6" 38.00
Polar Bear, goblet 100.00
Polar Bear, tray, water; frosted 225.00

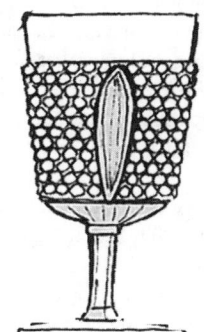

Popcorn

Popcorn, butter dish 57.50
Popcorn, pitcher, water 85.00
Popcorn, wine 32.00
Portland, goblet, clear w/gold 35.00
Portland, toothpick holder 24.00
Portland, wine 25.00
Powder & Shot, creamer, flint 100.00
Powder & Shot, egg cup, flint 60.00
Powder & Shot, sugar bowl, w/lid, flint 88.00
Prayer Rug, See Horseshoe
Pressed Leaf, pitcher, water 90.00
Pressed Leaf, spooner 22.50
Primrose, pitcher, milk; bl 60.00
Primrose, plate, amber, 7" 20.00
Primrose, wine 17.50
Princess Feather, bowl, oval, 8" 30.00
Princess Feather, goblet 45.00
Princess Feather, plate, 8" 35.00
Priscilla, butter dish 88.00
Priscilla, creamer, ind 25.00
Priscilla, creamer, lg 40.00
Priscilla, mug 17.50
Psyche & Cupid, celery vase 30.00
Psyche & Cupid, pitcher, water 80.00
Recessed Pillared Red Top, See Nail
Red Block, bowl, 8" 80.00
Red Block, mug 57.50
Red Top, See Button Arches
Reverse Torpedo, compote, high std, 6" 88.00
Reverse Torpedo, relish, oval, ruby stained, 9" 38.00
Reverse Torpedo, tumbler 32.00
Ribbed Ivy, butter dish 90.00
Ribbed Ivy, sugar bowl, w/lid 120.00
Ribbed Palm, celery vase, flint 68.00
Ribbed Palm, honey dish, flint 15.00
Ribbed Palm, wine, flint 75.00
Ribbon, compote, w/lid, 8" 72.50
Ribbon, creamer, frosted 40.00
Ribbon, platter, 13" 55.00
Ribbon Candy, cordial 44.00
Ribbon Candy, goblet 92.50
Ripple, ice tub 55.00
Ripple, sugar bowl 20.00
Ripple, wine 35.00
Ripple Band, See Ripple
Rochelle, See Princess Feather

Roman Key, champagne, frosted, flint 80.00
Roman Key, goblet, frosted, flint 55.00
Roman Key, sugar bowl, w/lid, flint 120.00
Roman Rosette, creamer 30.00
Roman Rosette, shakers, pr 35.00
Roman Rosette, tumbler 32.00
Rose in Snow, butter dish, sq 48.00
Rose in Snow, pitcher, water; amber 160.00
Rose in Snow, tumbler 32.50
Rose Sprig, pitcher, milk 45.00
Rose Sprig, pitcher, milk; bl 88.00
Rosette, bowl, 7½" 15.00
Rosette, jelly compote 20.00
Rosette, sugar bowl, w/lid 30.00
Royal Ivy, See Northwood, Royal Ivy
Royal Oak, See Northwood, Royal Oak
Ruby Thumbprint, See King's Crown
S-Repeat, carafe, water 500.00
S-Repeat, wine, gr 45.00
Sandwich Star, butter dish 180.00
Sandwich Star, decanter, bar lip, 1-pt 75.00
Sawtooth, cake stand, non-flint 60.00
Sawtooth, tumbler, bar; non-flint 25.00
Sawtooth, wine, non-flint 22.50
Sawtooth Band, See Amazon
Scalloped Daisy Red Top, See Button Arches
Scroll w/Flowers, mustard jar 50.00
Scroll w/Flowers, sugar bowl, w/lid 55.00
Sedan, See Panelled Star & Button
Seneca Loop, See Loop
Shell & Jewel, bowl, 10" 28.00
Shell & Jewel, sugar bowl, w/lid 45.00
Shell & Jewel, tumbler, gr 38.00
Shell & Tassel, butter dish, dog finial 160.00
Shell & Tassel, oyster dish 225.00
Shell & Tassel, platter, oval, 13" 57.50
Sheraton, plate, sq, 8½" 14.00
Sheraton, relish, hdld, bl 22.50
Sheraton, wine 22.00
Shoshone, jelly compote 78.00
Shoshone, mug 25.00
Shoshone, tumbler, ruby stained 32.50
Shrine, sugar bowl, w/lid 50.00
Shuttle, creamer, tall 30.00
Shuttle, tumbler 48.00
Skilton, compote, 7" 27.50
Skilton, relish 18.00
Snail, cheese dish 120.00
Snail, custard cup 30.00
Snail, shaker, orig top 65.00
Snail, tumbler 42.50
Spades, See Medallion
Spirea Band, bowl, flat, amber, 8" 35.00
Spirea Band, creamer 25.00
Spirea Band, wine, bl 25.00
Sprig, butter dish 62.50
Sprig, goblet 35.00
Sprig, wine 38.00
Star & Feather, plate, amber, 7" 18.00
Star Rosetted, compote, 7½" 18.00
Star Rosetted, plate, bl, 7" 14.00
Star Rosetted, plate, 7" 12.00
Stars & Stripes, cordial 20.00
Stars & Stripes, wine 17.50

States, creamer, ind 22.00
States, goblet, clear w/gold 38.00
States, plate, 10" 30.00
States, tray 22.00
Stedman, champagne 40.00
Stedman, spooner 17.50
Stippled Chain, cake stand 50.00
Stippled Chain, egg cup 30.00
Stippled Forget-Me-Not, butter dish 50.00
Stippled Forget-Me-Not, sugar bowl, w/lid 40.00
Stippled Grape & Festoon, goblet 35.00
Stippled Grape & Festoon, pitcher, water 100.00
Stippled Ivy, spooner 30.00
Stippled Ivy, sugar bowl, w/lid 38.00
Stippled Panelled Flower, See Maine
Strawberry, spooner 35.00
Strigil, plate, 11" 27.50
Strigil, punch cup 15.00
Sunk Honeycomb, cracker jar, ruby stained 450.00
Sunk Honeycomb, cup & saucer, ruby stained 37.50
Sunk Honeycomb, goblet, ruby stained 47.50
Sunken Primrose, See Florida

Swan

Swan, celery vase, etched 35.00
Swan, goblet, canary yel 62.50
Swan, sauce bowl 12.50
Swan, sugar bowl, w/lid 195.00
Tarentem's Thumbprint, pitcher, water; etched 45.00
Teardrop & Tassel, compote, 6" 30.00
Teardrop & Tassel, goblet 145.00
Teardrop & Tassel, See Also Greentown Teardrop & Tassel
Teardrop & Tassel, spooner 42.50
Tennessee, cake stand, 8½" 35.00
Tennessee, mug 38.00
Tennessee, tray, oval, 14" 57.50
Texas, compote, scalloped lid, 6" 250.00
Texas, goblet, clear w/gold 68.00
Texas, wine, ruby stained 115.00
Theatrical, See Actress
Thousand Eye, bowl, amber, ftd, 8" 32.00
Thousand Eye, butter dish, bl 38.00
Thousand Eye, egg cup, bl 62.50
Thousand Eye, pitcher, milk; bl, w/lid, 7" 100.00
Thousand Eye, plate, amber, 6" 20.00
Thousand Eye, plate, 10" 35.00
Three Face, butter dish 145.00
Three Face, champagne, saucer type 150.00
Three Face, claret 125.00
Three Face, goblet, eng 135.00
Three Face, spooner 80.00

Three Face, wine 175.00
Three Panel, bowl, amber, 7" 27.50
Three Panel, sugar bowl, vaseline, w/lid 65.00
Three Panel, tumbler 24.00
Thumbprint, See Argus
Thumbprint Band, See Dakota
Thunderbird, See Hummingbird
Torpedo, banana stand 57.50
Torpedo, creamer, ftd 32.50
Torpedo, jelly compote, w/lid 40.00
Tree of Life, See Portland
Tree of Life w/Hand, butter dish 110.00
Tree of Life w/Hand, creamer, w/hand & ball hdl 67.50
Tree of Life w/Hand, spooner 38.00
Triangular Prism, spooner, flint 55.00
Tulip w/Sawtooth, creamer, flint 88.00
Tulip w/Sawtooth, goblet, flint 65.00
Tulip w/Sawtooth, salt cellar, petal rim, flint 45.00
Two Panel, goblet 20.00
Two Panel, pitcher, water; gr 65.00
US Coin, bowl, clear, 6" 178.00
US Coin, cake stand, frosted 435.00
US Coin, compote, frosted, w/lid, 7" 450.00
US Coin, creamer, frosted 595.00
US Coin, epergne, frosted 700.00
US Coin, sauce bowl, frosted, flat, 4" 135.00
US Coin, sugar bowl, clear, w/lid 235.00
US Coin, sugar bowl, frosted 350.00
US Coin, syrup, frosted 350.00
US Coin, waste bowl, clear 235.00
Utah, goblet 25.00
Utah, sugar bowl, w/lid 37.50
Utah, tumbler 17.50
Valencia Waffle, butter dish, gr 48.00
Valencia Waffle, goblet, bl 32.00
Vermont, basket, clear w/gold 37.50
Vermont, pitcher, water; gr w/gold 130.00
Vermont, tumbler, clear w/gold 22.50
Viking, butter dish 80.00
Viking, celery vase 40.00
Viking, egg cup 40.00
Viking, sugar bowl, w/lid 57.50
Waffle, goblet, flint 95.00
Waffle, sugar bowl, flint, w/lid 98.00
Waffle & Thumbprint, decanter, blown, flint, 1-qt 175.00
Waffle & Thumbprint, goblet, flint 95.00
Washington, champagne 130.00
Washington, honey dish, 3½" 30.00
Washington, wine 120.00
Washington Centennial, egg cup 42.50
Washington Centennial, wine 45.00
Wedding Bells, goblet 45.00
Wedding Bells, spooner 40.00
Wedding Ring, tumbler 82.50
Westward Ho, butter dish 195.00
Westward Ho, marmalade, w/lid 188.00
Westward Ho, pitcher, water 250.00
Wheat & Barley, jelly compote 20.00
Wheat & Barley, mug 25.00
Wheat & Barley, pitcher, water; amber 80.00
Wildflower, champagne, bl 78.00
Wildflower, creamer 45.00
Wildflower, creamer, bl 37.50
Wildflower, tumbler 30.00

Willow Oak, butter dish, bl 75.00
Willow Oak, plate, 9" 24.00
Willow Oak, waste bowl, canary 45.00
Windflower, goblet 32.50
Windflower, sugar bowl, w/lid 55.00
Wisconsin, compote, triangular, high std, 6" 42.00
Wisconsin, cup & saucer 48.00
Wooden Pail, spooner, amber 45.00
Wooden Pail, sugar bowl, amethyst, mini 24.00
Wooden Pail, tumbler 20.00
Wyoming, bowl, 8" 16.00
Wyoming, creamer 48.00
Wyoming, pitcher, water 82.50
X-Ray, butter dish, gr 80.00
X-Ray, rose bowl, emerald gr w/gold 70.00
X-Ray, sugar bowl, w/lid, regular 37.50
Yale, tumbler 20.00
Zipper, creamer 20.00
Zipper, wine 32.50

Paul Revere Pottery

The Saturday Evening Girls were a social group of young Boston ladies who met to pursue various activities, among them pottery making. Their first kiln was bought in 1906, and within a few years it became necessary to move to a larger location. Because their new quarters were near the historical Old North Church, they chose the name Paul Revere Pottery. With very little training, the girls produced only simple ware. Until 1915 the pottery operated at a deficit; then a new building with four kilns was constructed on Nottingham Road. Vases, miniature jugs, children's tea sets, tiles, dinnerware, and lamps were produced, usually in soft matt glazes often decorated with incised, hand-painted designs from nature. Examples in a dark high gloss may also be found on occasion.

Several marks were used: 'P.R.P.'; 'S.E.G.'; or the circular device, 'Boston, Paul Revere Pottery' with the horse and rider.

The pottery continued to operate; and even though their product sold well, the high production costs of the handmade ware caused the pottery to fail in 1946.

Booklet, lists 90 different pcs, mc/blk & wht, 4-pg, 9x6" 80.00
Bowl, band, wht on yel, flared rim, SEG/FL/10-22, 2¼x12½" 130.00
Bowl, bl to whitish band w/blk on steel bl, PRP, 1½x3¼" 70.00
Bowl, chrome yel, SEG/2-13-19, 3x8" 120.00
Bowl, dogwood flower band on mc, SEG/AM/11-20, 2¼x8¼" ..1,200.00
Bowl, dragon's-blood red, aqua int, PRP/LS/11-37, 3¼x9¾" 160.00
Bowl, geometric bands mc on chicory bl, SEG/LS/5-6-20, 3½" ..190.00
Bowl, grape clusters band on brn-purple, SEG, 1½x4¾" 220.00

Bowl, incised camels, artist signed, marked SEG, ca 1909, 2½x5", $1,100.00.

Bowl, incised rosettes, wht on bl, SEG/RB/SW/6-2-11, 2x4¼" ...300.00
Bowl, lotus band, yel on ivory, SEG/TM, 1½x4¾" 210.00
Bowl, lt chocolate brn, low, SEG/TM/4-4-17, 2½x8¼" 100.00
Bowl, mc mottle, bl rim, SEG/1-26, 3x4", +mk gray frog, 1¾" ...120.00
Bowl, yel, PRP/FL/16, 2¼x5½" 150.00
Box, floral band, bl/blk on wht, SEG/JG/15, 1½x3" dia 350.00
Calendar holder, scenic view, SEG/JM/4-20, label, 3¼" 120.00
Candle holder, floral, bl & gr on blueberry, SEG/19-26, 4" 200.00
Cookie jar, blk metallic/aqua drip on gr/gray, PRP/7-40, 5x6" ...170.00
Creamer, rabbits w/lettuce band on mocha mottle, SEG/AM, 2¾" .250.00
Creamer, tree band, early form, SEG/JG/3-4-14, 3¼" 200.00
Cup, dressed rabbit, rosettes band, SEG/XMAS 1914, 3x3", NM ...1,500.00
Cup & underplate, swan reserve, wide bl band, SEG/EG/8-18 ...250.00
Egg cup, lotus band, yel on ivory, SEG/SG/12-12, 1½x1¾" 600.00
Egg cup, tulips & geometrics on ivory, SEG/IG/IH, 1¾" 150.00
Egg cup & plate, chick on bl, RTP on plate, SEG/EG/5-22 & 015 ..230.00
Jar, monogram/rabbit reserve on cream, bl top, 6-sided, 5" 550.00
Jar, tree band, 4-color on wht, SEG/TM/13, w/lid, 5" 700.00
Lamp, chicory bl to aqua at crest & shoulder, SEG, 10x6" 220.00
Nut dish, squirrels band on ivory, SEG/JG/1-6-14, 3" 500.00
Paperweight, swan, 3-color on yel, octagonal, 1x2¾", EX 150.00
Paperweight, swan on bl, octagonal, PRP, ½x2½" 180.00
Pitcher, band, wht on yel, bulbous, SEG/JM/3-20, 4x4" 100.00
Pitcher, hens & chicks band, yel on ivory, SEG/JG/4-16, 4¼" ...550.00
Pitcher, lotus band on mustard yel, PRP label, 6½x7", NM 275.00
Plate, buttercup yel allover, PRP/1-24, 6¼" 30.00
Plate, chicks in 3 groups on yel band, SEG/EG/6-16, 7¾" 375.00
Plate, Eate Thy Breade in... in band on yel, PRP/9-34, 9¾" 350.00
Plate, Greek Key band on ivory, SEG/IG/4-2-14, 7¾" 190.00
Plate, hens & chicks band on yel matt, SEG/FL/9-7-11, 6¼" 850.00
Plate, narrow band, wht on yel, SEG/FL/10-14, 6¼", 4 for 140.00
Plate, pigs band on ivory, SEG/LS/07-12-10, 8½" 2,000.00
Plate, pine cones band on tan semimatt, SEG/EG/9-14, 8¼" 190.00
Plate, rabbit reserve, wide bl band, SEG/FL/8-18, 6¼" 230.00
Plate, rosettes band, wht on yel, SEG/JMD/3-19, 7½" 220.00
Plate, tree landscape band, ivory on yel, SEG/FL/5-19, 8¼" 350.00
Tea set, tree landscape band, stacking, SEG/EG/9-12-11, 3-pc ..650.00
Tile, Old State House..., lav/gr/brn/bl, PRP, 3¾x3¾" 600.00
Tray, tree band on yel, SEG/FL/4-19, 10½x7¾" 450.00
Trivet, Greek Key band on yel, SEG/IG/12-13, 5½" dia 160.00
Trivet, steel bl, low lustre, PRP, label, 5¼x5¼" 40.00
Trivet, tree scene on yel, SEG, 4½" dia 200.00
Vase, blk textured, PRP, 4½x3½" 200.00
Vase, bud; mc speckles on ochre, SEG/9-11-11, 5⅛" 150.00
Vase, gr, bl, red blend w/silver crystals on lt gr, 3¾" 130.00
Vase, Greek Key border, 3-color, SEG/FL/25, 4¼x5" 400.00
Vase, ochre/tan/gr mottle on burnt orange, PRP/11-32, 3¾" 120.00
Vase, sky bl gloss, PRP, 4½" 65.00
Vase, tree band, gr/lt bl on dk bl, ovoid, no mk, 4½" 900.00
Vase, turq flecks on royal bl, PRP/LS, 6½" 180.00
Vase, turq satin, rolled rim, shouldered, PRP, 4¼" 60.00
Vase, volcanic 4-color drip, SEG/1-20, 10½" 475.00

Pauline Pottery

Pauline Pottery was made form 1883 to 1888 in Chicago, Illinois, from clay imported from the Ohio area. Its founder was Mrs. Pauline Jacobus, who had learned the trade at the Rookwood Pottery. Mrs Jacobus moved to Edgerton, Wisconsin, to be near a source of suitable clay, thus eliminating shipping expenses. Until 1905 she produced high-quality wares, able to imitate with ease designs and styles of such masters as Wedgwood and Meissen. Her products were sold through leading department stores, and the names of some of these firms may appear on the ware. Not all were marked; unless signed by a noted local artist, positive identification is often impossible. Marked examples carry a variety of stamps and signatures: 'Trade Mark' with a crown, 'Pauline Pottery,' and 'Edgerton Art Pottery' are but a few.

Pitcher, applied peach florals on gold and black, 5", $385.00.

Bowl, roses, yel on yel semigloss, 3½x9½" 275.00
Ewer, floral & butterfly, Limoges style, mk, 9½" 435.00
Vase, cobalt gloss, bottle shape, 5½x3½" 200.00
Vase, sm flowers on dk brn, sgn, 1880, 8" 535.00

Peachblow

Peachblow, made to imitate the colors of the Chinese Peachbloom porcelain, was made by several glasshouses in the late 1800s. Among them were New England Glass; Mt. Washington; Webb; and Hobbs, Brockunier and Company (Wheeling). Its pink shading was achieved through action of the heat on the gold content of the glass. While New England's peachblow shades from deep crimson to white, Mt. Washington's tends to shade from pink to blue-gray. Many pieces were enameled and gilded. While by far the majority of the pieces made by New England had a satin (acid) finish, they made shiny peachblow as well. Wheeling glass, on the other hand, is rarely found in satin. In the 1950s Gundersen-Pairpoint Glassworks initiated the reproduction of Mt. Washington peachblow using an exact duplication of the original formula. Though of recent manufacture, this glass is very collectible. Our advisors for this category are Betty and Clarence Maier; they are listed in the Directory under Pennsylvania.

Biscuit jar, gold prunus, SP lid/hdls, Webb, 5½" 750.00
Bowl, acid, ftd/ruffled, NE Glass, 2¼x6¼" 200.00
Bowl, gold prunus/pine needles, Webb, 3¾x2¾" 365.00
Compote, ruffled, Gundersen, 5x10" 350.00
Creamer, Mt WA, 2½" 2,050.00
Creamer, sqd top, amber hdl, Wheeling, 4½" 700.00
Creamer, sqd top, amber hdl, Wheeling, 4½" 700.00
Creamer & sugar bowl, Libbey, 1893 World's Fair decor 850.00
Cruet, cut amber stopper, Wheeling, 6½" 900.00
Cruet, Wheeling, 6¾" 1,085.00
Cup, clear hdl, Webb 75.00
Cup, punch; reeded hdl, NE Glass 275.00
Darner, NE Glass, 6" 155.00
Darner, World's Fair 1893, NE Glass 175.00
Ewer, amber rigaree, petticoat form, Wheeling, 10x5" 1,950.00
Finger bowl, gold prunus/butterfly, tricorner, Webb, 3x4½" 275.00
Jar, acid, gold pine needles, butterfly on lid, Webb, 5" 695.00
Mustard pot, bulbous, hinged metal lid w/hdl, Wheeling 450.00
Pitcher, acid, amber hdl, outstanding color, Wheeling, 8x6½" ..1,600.00
Pitcher, acid, draped mold, crimped top, Wheeling, 5¼" 375.00
Pitcher, cider; bird/butterfly/floral, camphor hdl, 7" 475.00
Pitcher, sq top, amber hdl, Wheeling, 8x6½", EX 1,250.00
Pitcher, tankard; acid, daisies/butterfly/poem, Mt WA, 8¾" .24,500.00
Pitcher, tankard; acid, reeded amber hdl, Wheeling, 10½" 2,300.00

Rose bowl, gold branched florals, Webb, 2½" dia 450.00
Shakers, bulbous, Wheeling, 2½", pr 600.00
Spooner, acid, crimped, NE Glass, 4½" 500.00
Sugar shaker, dainty floral, ovoid, Mt WA, 4" 500.00
Toothpick holder, sq top, Mt WA, 2¾" 2,250.00
Tumbler, acid, Wheeling, 3¾" 500.00
Tumbler, Drape, Wheeling, 3¾" 350.00
Tumbler, Gundersen, 3¾" 140.00
Tumbler, lemonade; Wheeling, 5½" 800.00
Tumbler, Wheeling, 3¾" 300.00
Vase, acid, gold prunus/leaves, Webb, 10½x7" 800.00
Vase, acid, lily form, NE Glass, 6" 500.00
Vase, acid, lily form, NE Glass, 8" 600.00
Vase, bird/flowers, Sandwich, 11⅜x4⅜" 225.00
Vase, draped mold, ruffled, Wheeling, 7" 650.00
Vase, floral, dbl bulb w/stick neck, Mt WA, 8" 3,000.00
Vase, floral/beetle, ruffled, Webb, 3¼", pr 300.00
Vase, gold floral/butterfly, Webb, 3⅜x2⅝" 365.00
Vase, gold floral/foliage, Webb, 7½x3⅝" 325.00
Vase, gold flowers/dragonfly, hdls, Webb, 7½x5" 395.00
Vase, gold leaves & silver flowers, 5⅛x3¼" 295.00
Vase, Morgan, amber griffin holder, Wheeling, 7¾" 1,200.00
Vase, stick neck, Wheeling, 8½" 950.00

Pearlware

Developed by Wedgwood in the late 1770s primarily for their dinnerware lines, pearlware was soon being made by many other Staffordshire potteries as well. Much of it made for export to America. It is characterized by its blue-white body, similar in appearance to true porcelain. During the first decade of the 1800s, pearlware with chinoiserie decorations and hand-painted flowers became popular.

Key: ug — underglaze

Bowl, Adam's Rose type, floral/bands, Wood, 10½", VG 200.00
Bowl, gr feathered edge, rectangular, 10½", NM 120.00
Bowl, ug bl/yel flower & foliage, bl bands/vines, 11" 700.00
Creamer, floral, 4-color, wear/stain, 4¼" 140.00
Cup & saucer, floral, ug bl w/yel accent, ftd cup, VG 90.00
Cup & saucer, handleless; bl & wht Oriental transfer 45.00
Cup & saucer, handleless; mother & children, bl transfer 85.00
Cup & saucer, handleless; strawberries, flakes, NM 110.00
Cup & saucer, handleless; strawberry & rose, EX 75.00
Invalid feeder, bl Oriental transfer, stain, 2¼" 95.00
Mug, boy & sheep, med bl transfer, stain/chips, 2½" 60.00
Mug, Cornwallis, blk transfer, pk lustre striping, 2⅛" 470.00
Mug, Liberty & allegorical figures, mc, 6" 350.00
Mug, Love Feast, blk rings top/base, 2 hdls, 1850s, 5" 325.00
Mug, Pretty Bird, blk transfer w/mc enameling, 2" 100.00
Mug, West View...Bridge...at Sutherland, transfer/HP, 5½" 375.00
Pepper pot, mc floral/striping, helmet-shaped top, ftd, rpr 110.00
Pitcher, mc floral w/brn striping, 4⅝" 75.00
Pitcher, silver lustre florals & rust enamel, rpr, 5¾" 330.00
Plate, Adam's Rose-type flower, scalloped, 9" 35.00
Plate, bl feather edge, scalloped, mk Turner, 10", NM 65.00
Plate, gr feather edge, mk Reid, 8½", 8 for 490.00
Plate, hot water; bl sprig & rim, crown mk, 8⅜" 95.00
Plate, mc floral, gr feather edge, wear/chips, 9" 105.00
Platter, shaped emb rim, ug bl sunflower w/rose, 15" 725.00
Platter, ug bl floral, emb fishscale/leaf border, 17½" 650.00
Shaker, bl & wht, dome top, prof rpr, 4¼" 110.00
Sugar bowl, mc floral band, acorn finial, shell hdl, VG 300.00

Tea set, New Hall-type decor w/swags & mc florals, 6-pc 600.00
Teapot, yel/gr floral & bands, bl striping, 5x10", EX 450.00
Waste bowl, bl & wht Oriental decor, prof rpr, 3x6¼" 165.00

Peking Cameo Glass

The first glasshouse was established in Peking in 1680. It produced glassware made in imitation of porcelain, a more desirable medium to the Chinese. By 1725 multilayered carving that resulted in a cameo effect lead to the manufacture of a wider range of shapes and colors. The factory was closed from 1736 to 1795, but glass made in Po-shan and shipped to Peking for finishing continued to be called Peking glass. See also Orientalia.

Bottle, scent; floral, turq on wht, disk stopper, 5¼" 150.00
Bowl, yel w/relief peony branch panels, ftd, 6" 800.00
Cup, yel, relief dragon panels, tall ft, 1800s, 4½" W 800.00
Vase, cranes/peonies, gr on wht, Ching Dynasty, 14" 950.00
Vase, rams in landscape, lappet bands, cobalt/wht, 1800, 9" 1,750.00
Vase, turq w/cvd dragons in panels, stick neck, 1800s, 9" 1,300.00

Peloton

Peloton glass was first made by Wilhelm Kralik in Bohemia in 1880. This unusual art glass was produced by rolling colored threads onto the transparent or opaque glass gather as it was removed from the furnace. Usually more than one color of threading was used, and some items were further decorated with enameling. It was made with both shiny and acid finishes.

Bowl, wht cased, mc strings, 4-crimp, 3¾x3½" 295.00
Box, powder; mc strings, Pairpoint metal lid, 3x5½" 225.00

Pitcher, enameled floral, green stringing on clear, gilt trim, 5", $245.00.

Pitcher, bl w/mc leaves/flowers/butterfly, 8" 450.00
Pitcher, clear overshot w/mc strings, 6⅝x3⅝" 165.00
Rose bowl, lav, ribbed, crystal pulled ft, 3" H 175.00
Rose bowl, wht w/pastel strings, clear rim, scalloped ft, 4" 295.00
Vase, lav to wht w/pastel strings, waisted/ruffled, 5¾" 265.00
Vase, wht cased, mc strings, bulbous, tricorn top, 3¾x4¾" 295.00

Pennsbury

Established in the 1950s in Morrisville, Pennsylvania, by Henry Below, the Pennsbury Pottery produced dinnerware and novelty items, much of which was sold in gift shops along the Pennsylvania Turnpike. Henry and his wife, Lee, worked for years at the Stangl Pottery before striking out on their own. Lee and her daughter were the artists responsible for many of the early pieces, the bird figures among them. Pennsbury pottery was hand painted, some in blue on white, some in multi-color on caramel. Pennsylvania Dutch motifs, Amish couples, and barbershop singers were among their most popular decorative themes. Sgraffito (hand incising), was used extensively. The company marked their wares 'Pennsbury Pottery' or 'Pennsbury Pottery, Morrisville, PA.'

In October of 1969 the company closed. Contents of the pottery were sold in December of the following year; and in April of 1971, the buildings burned to the ground. Items marked Pennsbury Glenview or Stumar Pottery (or these marks in combination) were made by Glenview after 1969. Pieces manufactured after 1976 were made by the Pennington Pottery. Several of the old molds still exist, and the original Pennsbury Caramel process is still being used on novelty items, some of which are produced by Lewis Brothers (New Jersey). Production of Pennsbury dinnerware was not resumed after the closing. Our advisor for this category is Shirley Graff; she is listed in the Directory under Ohio. Note: prices may be higher in some areas of the country — particularly on the East Coast, the southern states, and Texas.

Ashtray, Bordentown Yacht Club, 8"	30.00
Ashtray, Fairless Works, gray	30.00
Ashtray, It's Makin' Down	18.00
Ashtray, Outen the Light	20.00
Ashtray, Such Smootzers	20.00
Bowl, pretzel; Barber Shop Quartet	65.00
Coffee mug, Blk Rooster	20.00
Cruets, PA Dutch, pr	120.00
Egg cup, Folk Art	20.00
Figurine, bluebird	125.00
Figurine, chickadee	90.00
Figurine, goldfinch	125.00
Figurine, hen, 11"	185.00
Figurine, magnolia warbler	95.00
Figurine, nuthatch	125.00
Figurine, redstart	75.00
Figurine, rooster, 12"	185.00
Figurine, wren, wht, sm	75.00
Lamp, Hex, #20XG	190.00
Mug, Blk Rooster	22.00
Mug, Sweet Adeleine, barbershop quartet	12.50
Pie plate, boy & girl, 9"	80.00
Pitcher, Blk Rooster, 2-qt	80.00
Pitcher, Blk Rooster, 4"	22.00
Pitcher, Eagle, 1-qt	60.00
Plaque, eagle, 12½"	70.00
Plaque, eagle, 6½"	40.00
Plaque, PA family wagon, 8"	40.00
Plaque, Such Smootzers, 4"	20.00
Stein, Looking at You	24.00

Pens and Pencils

The first metallic writing pen was patented in 1809, and soon machine-produced pens with steel nibs gradually began replacing the quill. The first fountain pen was invented in 1830; but due to the fact that a suitable metal for the tips had not yet been developed, they were not manufactured commercially until the 1880s. The first successful commercial producers were Waterman in 1884 and Parker with the Lucky Curve in 1888.

The self-filling pen of 1890 featured the soft, interior sack which filled with ink as the metal bar on the outside of the pen was raised and lowered. Variations of the pumping mechanism were tried until 1932 when Parker introduced the Vacuumatic, a sackless pen with an internal pump. Our advisors for this category are Judy and Cliff Lawrence; they are listed in the Directory under Florida. For those seeking additional information, a catalog is published monthly by the Pen Fancier's, whose address can be found in the Directory under Clubs, Newsletters, and Catalogs. In the listings that follow, all pens are lever-filled unless otherwise noted.

Key:

AF — aeromatic filler	GPM — gold-plated metal
BF — button filler	GPT — gold-plated trim
CF — cartridge filler	HR — hard rubber
CPT — chrome-plated trim	NPT — nickel-plated trim
ED — eyedropper filler	PF — plunger filler
GFM — gold-filled metal	TD — touchdown filler
GFT — gold-filled trim	VF — vacuumatic filler

Ballpoint Pens

Everhard Faber, 1945, brn/GF cap, EX	65.00
Eversharp, CA, 1945, bl/GF cap, M	95.00
Eversharp, CA, 1947, GFM, EX	125.00
Eversharp, Skyline, CA, 1944, maroon w/striped cap, EX	50.00
Eversharp, Skyline, CA, 1948, brn/gold striped cap, M	50.00
Reynold's, Internat'l, 1945, aluminum, GF clip, EX	125.00
Reynold's, Internat'l, 1945, aluminum, M	250.00
Sheaffer, Stratowriter, 1946, GFM, M	95.00

Dip Pens

ES Johnson, MOP & GFM (seamless), #4 nib, EX	165.00
Grieshaber, orange & wht glass holder & GFM, worn nib holder	65.00
HM Smith, 1867, retractable, pencil combo, blk HR, GFT, EX	125.00
LeRoy W Fairchild Regal, reverse holder, blk HR, GFT, EX	150.00
Spencer, MOP & GFM (seamless), #3 nib, EX	150.00

Fountain Pens

Eversharp, #64, 1944, blk, 14k gold cap & trim, LF, EX	300.00
Eversharp, Presentation Skyline, blk, GFM cap, GFT, LF, M	95.00
Eversharp, Skyline, 1943, blk, GFT, LF, EX	70.00
Eversharp, Skyline, 1944, gray, GFT, LF, EX	70.00
Parker, #51, 1947, blk w/GF cap, GFT, VF, demi-sz, EX	80.00
Parker, #51 Flighter, 1952, stainless steel, GFT, AF, EX	175.00
Parker, #51 Special, 1951, burgundy, chrome cap, CPT, AF, M	45.00
Parker, #75 Presidential, 1980, 14k gold, AF, EX	795.00
Parker, #75 Spanish Treasure, 1966, sterling, GFT, EX	1,000.00
Parker, Bl Dmn Heirloom 51, 1945, blk, gold cap/trim, VF, EX	995.00
Parker, Bl Dmn Vacuumatic, 1945, silver stripes, wht GFT, EX	70.00
Parker, Bl Dmn Vacuumatic, 1946, bl stripes, GFT, VF, EX	70.00
Parker, Bl Dmn 51, 1943, blk, GF cap, GFT, VF, EX	100.00
Parker, Debutante Vacuumatic, 1946, bl stripes, GFT, VF, EX	75.00
Parker, Duette Depression, 1932, cherry red, GFT, BF, EX	150.00
Parker, Duofold Sr, 1931, blk, GFT, initialed, BF, EX	350.00
Parker, Lucky Curve, 1920, GFM, initialed, BF, EX	400.00
Parker, Lucky Curve Vest Pocket, 1922, GFM, GFT, BF, EX	550.00
Parker, Oversz Vacuumatic, 1934, blk, GFT, initialed, VF, EX	695.00
Parker, Parkette Deluxe, 1934, gr pearl marbleized, LF, EX	65.00
Parker, Royal Challenger, 1939, red marbled, sword clip, BF, EX	295.00
Parker, Sr Maxima Vacuumatic, 1937, pearl stripes, NPT, VF, EX	695.00
Parker, Vacuumatic, 1935, emerald pearl stripes, GFT, EX	185.00
Parker, Vacuumatic, 1940, silver pearl stripes, NPT, VF, EX	70.00
Sheaffer, Lifetime, 1924, gr jade marbleized, GFT, LF, EX	299.00
Sheaffer, Lifetime, 1929, pearl & blk marbleized GFT, LF, EX	250.00
Sheaffer, Lifetime, 1932, gr & blk marbleized, GFT, LF, EX	400.00

Sheaffer, Lifetime, 1937, gold pearl stripes, GFT, PF, EX **150.00**
Sheaffer, Self-Filling #2, 1918, blk chased HR, NPT, EX **125.00**
Sheaffer, Sovereign Snorkel, 1952, gr, chrome cap, GFT, TD, M .**45.00**
Sheaffer, Univer, 1934, pearl & blk marbleized, GFT, LF, EX **60.00**
Sheaffer, Wht Dot Clipper Snorkel, 1952, blk, GFT, TD, M **75.00**
Sheaffer, Wht Dot Crest Triumph TM, 1951, maroon, GFT, TD, M .**100.00**
Sheaffer, Wht Dot Statesman, 1949, blk, GFT, TD, EX **60.00**
Swan, #48 ETN, 1927, blk HR, GFT, LF, EX **350.00**
Wahl-Eversharp, Gold Seal, 1928, coral marbleized, LF, G **250.00**
Waterman, Ideal, #52½ V, 1925, blk HR, GFT, LF, EX **70.00**
Waterman, Ideal #13 (Canada), 1911, blk HR, GFT, ED, NM ..**350.00**
Waterman, Ideal #42 Safety, 1920, 18k rolled gold ED, EX **750.00**
Waterman, Ideal #452, 1927, sterling filigree, LF, G **580.00**
Waterman, Ideal #552½ V, 1925, solid 14k gold, LF, EX **580.00**
Waterman, Ideal #554 LEC, 1925, 14k gold, LF, G **650.00**
Waterman, 1948, blk, GFT, LF, EX **105.00**

Mechanical Pencils

Eversharp, Repeater, 1949, blk, chrome-gold band, GFT, M **65.00**
Eversharp, Skyline Repeater, 1944, bl, GFT, M **70.00**
Eversharp, 5th Ave, 1944, brn, 14k gold top & trim, M **120.00**
Parker, Duofold Sr, 1925, red HR, GFT, EX **195.00**
Parker, Repeater, 1981, GFM, GFT, EX **40.00**
Parker, True Bl, 1930, GFT, EX **90.00**
Parker, 1973, bronze lacquer, GFT, M **30.00**
Parker, 51 Liquid Lead, 1958, gr w/Lustraloy top, CPT, EX **50.00**
Parker, 51 Special, 1954, maroon, chrome top, CPT, M **35.00**
Sheaffer, TM, 1953, blk w/solid gold 14k band, M **40.00**
Sheaffer, Tuckaway, 1947, brn w/GFM top, GFT, G **20.00**
Sheaffer, Wht Dot, 1948, bl, GFT, EX **22.00**
Sheaffer, Wht Dot, 1954, blk, GFT, M **29.00**
Sheaffer, 1920, GFM, GFT, EX **16.00**
Wahl-Eversharp, 1920, GFM, initialed, EX **50.00**
Wahl-Eversharp, 1920, solid gold, initialed, EX **375.00**
Wahl-Eversharp, 1922, GFM & GFT, EX **22.00**
Wahl-Eversharp, 1928, red HR, NPT, EX **70.00**
Waterman, Ideal, 1926, sterling filigree, EX **425.00**
Waterman, Ideal, 1927, sterling, NM **495.00**
Waterman, 1935, red-specked silver-pearl marbleized, CPT, EX ...**100.00**

Sets

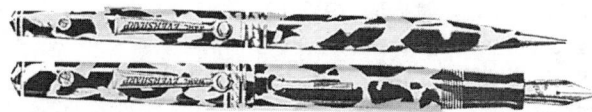

Wahl-Eversharp, 1931, Gold Seal Personal Point Standard Equipoise pen in pearl and black, gold-filled trim, lever filler, M, $350.00; Matching pencil, M, $120.00.

Parker, 61, 1959, gray, Lustraloy caps, capillary filler, EX **90.00**
Sheaffer's, Lifetime Crest, '37, gold stripes, GFT, LF, EX **250.00**
Sheaffer's, Lifetime Crest, '46, blk w/GFM caps, GFT, LF, NM ..**295.00**
Sheaffer's, Lifetime Sentinel, blk & gold caps, GFT, LF, EX **285.00**
Waterman, Supersize 100 Year, 1941, burgundy, GFT, EX **895.00**

Personalities, Fact and Fiction

One of the largest and most popular areas of collecting today, if tradepaper ads and articles be any indication, is character-related memorabilia. Everyone has favorites, whether they be comic-strip personali-

ties or true-life heroes. The earliest comic strip dealt with the adventures of the Yellow Kid, the smiling, bald-headed Oriental boy always in a nightshirt. He was introduced in 1895, a product of the imagination of Richard Fenton Outcault. Today, though very hard to come by, items relating to the Yellow Kid bring premium prices.

In 1902 Buster Brown and Tige, his dog and constant companion (more of Outcault's progenies), made it big in the comics as well as in the world of advertising. Shoe stores appealed to the younger set through merchandising displays that featured them both. Today items from their earlier years are very collectible.

Though her 1923 introduction was unobtrusively made through only one newspaper, New York's *Daily News*, Little Orphan Annie, the vacant-eyed redhead in the inevitable red dress, was quickly adopted by hordes of readers nationwide; and before the demise of her creator, Harold Gray, in 1968, she had starred in her own radio show. She made two feature films, and in 1977 'Annie' was launched on Broadway.

Other early comic figures were Moon Mullins, created in 1923 by Frank Willard; Buck Rogers by Philip Nowlan in 1928; and Betty Boop, the round-faced, innocent-eyed, chubby-cheeked Boop-Boop-a-Doop girl of the early 1930s. Bimbo was her dog and KoKo her clown friend.

Popeye made his debut in 1929 as the spinach-eating sailor with the spindly-limbed girlfriend, Olive Oyl, in the comic strip *Thimble Theatre*, created by Elzie Segar. He became a film star in 1933 and had his own radio show that during 1936 played three times a week on CBS. He obligingly modeled for scores of toys, dolls, and figurines, and especially those from the thirties are very collectible.

Tarzan, created around 1930 by Edgar Rice Burroughs, and Captain Midnight, by Robert Burtt and Willfred G. Moore, are popular heroes with today's collectors. During the days of radio, Sky King of the Flying Crown Ranch (also created by Burtt and Moore) thrilled boys and girls of the mid-1940s. Hopalong Cassidy, Red Rider, Tom Mix, and the Lone Ranger were only a few of the other 'good guys' always on the side of law and order.

But of all the fictional heroes and comic characters collected today, probably the best loved and most well known is Mickey Mouse. Created in the late 1920s by Walt Disney, Micky (as his name was first spelled) became an instant success with his film debut, Steamboat Willie. His popularity was parlayed through wind-up toys, watches, figurines, cookie jars, puppets, clothing, and numerous other products. Items from the 1930s are usually copyrighted 'Walt Disney Enterprises'; thereafter, 'Walt Disney Productions' was used.

For more information we recommend *Schroeder's Collectible Toys, Antique to Modern*, by Sharon and Bob Huxford. For those interested in Disneyanna, we recommend *Stern's Guide to Disney Collectibles*; *Character Toys and Collectibles* (there are two volumes); and *The Collector's Encyclopedia of Disneyana*. All are available from Collector Books. Our advisor for this category is Norm Vigue; he are listed in the Directory under Massachusetts. See also Autographs; Banks; Big Little Books; Cartoon Books; Children's Books; Comic Books; Cookie Jars; Dolls; Games; Lunch Boxes; Movie Memorabilia; Paper Dolls; Pin-Back Buttons; Posters; Puzzles; Rock 'N Roll Memorabilia; Toys.

Abbott & Costello, wristwatch, quartz, Bradley, 1986, MIB **25.00**
Addams Family, Lurch Doll, Filmways TV, 1964 ....**125.00**
Alice in Wonderland, chocolate tin, Mad Tea Party, 1930s **150.00**
Alice in Wonderland, figure, ceramic, Disney, 1960s **25.00**
Alice in Wonderland, overnight case, Disney, M **125.00**
Alice in Wonderland, paint book, Disney, 1951, W-2167, M **55.00**
Alice in Wonderland, record album, Disney art cover, 1944 ....**55.00**
Alvin Chipmunk, Soaky, 1963, M **15.00**
Amos 'n Andy, map, M in mailer **60.00**
Amos 'n Andy, poster, Campbell's Soup, EX **145.00**
Amos 'n Andy, record album, photo cover, 1947, EX/NM **100.00**

Annie Oakley, wristwatch, MIB 345.00
Archie Bunker, ashtray 15.00
Babe Ruth, pin, Quaker Oats, 1920s 30.00
Bambi, figurine, porc, mc pnt, Am Pottery, 1949, 10x9" 120.00
Bambi, Flower figurine, porc, mc, Am Pottery, 1949, 5x3", M ...120.00
Bambi, planter, porc, mc pnt, Am Pottery, 1949, 10x7x6" 90.00
Bambi, scent lamp, porc figural, Goebel, 1940s 295.00
Barney Google & Spark Plug, platform racer, pnt tin, 1924, EX ..3,600.00
Batman, Batcave desk lamp, 1966, M 55.00
Batman, bicycle handle-bar ornament, 8", M in pkg 50.00
Batman, Joker wristwatch, DABS, 1977, MIB 300.00
Batman, light switch plate 10.00
Batman, record set, cb & vinyl, 45 rpm disks, 9x9", M in pkg 75.00
Batman, Robin the Boy Wonder wristwatch, Timex, 1976, M 65.00
Batman, Robin wristwatch, Timex, 1978, M 65.00
Batman, spoon & fork, M on card 35.00
Batman, Thingmakers, illus, 1966, M on card 85.00
Batman, wristwatch, DABS, 1977, NM 125.00
Beany & Cecil, Cecil hand puppet, talks, Mattel, 1961, M 60.00
Beany & Cecil, Dishonest John talking puppet, pull string, M ...125.00
Beany & Cecil, tea set, 6-place, Worchester, 1960, M 45.00
Betty Boop, figure, bsk, playing accordion, 3¼", M 85.00
Betty Boop, mask, theater giveaway, 1931 ....125.00
Betty Boop, wall vase, figural, Fleischer Studios 125.00
Big Bird, clock, animated arms, Bradley 40.00
Bobby Benson, tie clasp, enameled, NM 60.00
Bozo the Clown, hand puppet, talker, EX 45.00
Buck Jones, guitar, wood, professional, EX graphics, '31, NM 225.00
Buck Jones, Ranger chaps, NM 135.00
Buck Rogers, Galactic playset, M, sealed 40.00
Buck Rogers, helmet, M 150.00
Buck Rogers, Solar Scout badge, premium, EX 95.00
Buck Rogers, Strato kite, 1946, NM 38.00
Buck Rogers, water pistol, steel litho, 7½", VG 100.00
Bugs Bunny, Kool-Aid packs (2), illus of Bugs, 1960s, M, pr 30.00
Bugs Bunny, Talking Alarm Clock, battery op, Janex, 6", NM 35.00
Bugs Bunny, theater, Sawyer Viewmaster, complete, w/box 55.00
Bullwinkle, Soaky, 11", NM 25.00
California Raisin, figure, chalkware, 5", NM 12.50
Captain Crunch, Sea Cycle, cereal premium, MIB 35.00
Captain Hook, marionette, compo & cloth, Disney, 1930s, 16", MIB ..160.00
Captain Marvel, Buzz Bomb, M 20.00
Captain Marvel, club order form for premiums, 1940s, 8x10", M .30.00
Captain Marvel, Shazam membership card w/message, '45, NM ...68.00
Captain Midnight, manual & code book, Ovaltine, 10-pg, NM+ ..135.00
Captain Midnight, mug, Ovaltine, no lid, M 28.00
Captain Video, ring, Secret Seal, 1950s, M 120.00
Casper & Wendy, Ghost slate, 1950s, EX 14.50
Cat in the Hat, wristwatch, Lafayette Watch Co, 1972 ....75.00
Charlie Chaplin, lead figure 48.00
Charlie Chaplin, terra cotta figure, Elastolin, Germany, 2½" 135.00
Charlie Horse, hand puppet, Shari Lewis, 1960 ....25.00
Charlie McCarthy, alarm clock, 1938, EX 400.00
Charlie McCarthy, egg cup, ceramic, lustreware, NM 100.00
Charlie McCarthy, soap figure, 1940s, NMIB 65.00
Cinderella, planter, ceramic, mc pnt, WD USA, 7x6", NM 96.00
Cinderella, Soaky, NM 15.00
Cinderella, wristwatch, Ingersoll, 1950, NM 65.00
Cisco Kid, face mask, Butternut Bread, EX 35.00
Cisco Kid, scarf slide 45.00
Clarabell the Clown, marionette, NM 175.00
Daffy Duck, handkerchief, ring-neck Daffy, 1940s 45.00
Dale Evans, cowgirl outfit, 1953, EX 125.00
Dale Evans, wristwatch, Bradley, w/Buttercup, 1950, MIB 445.00

Davy Crockett, bank, metal figure w/copper finish, 6" 35.00
Davy Crockett, belt, metal arrow buckle, NM 26.00
Davy Crockett, Flying Arrow, unassembled, 1955, M in cb pkg ...50.00
Davy Crockett, Frontier Kit, leather powder horn & belt, MIB 75.00
Davy Crockett, gloves, Walt Disney, pr 95.00
Davy Crockett, holster set, leather w/Buck cap gun, MIB 95.00
Davy Crockett, lamp, w/shade, Remco, 1955 ....160.00
Davy Crockett, loose-leaf binder, White House & Alamo, 1950s ..65.00
Davy Crockett, outfit, 1950s, M on card 75.00
Davy Crockett, ring, gold plated, Cracker Jack, M 12.00
Davy Crockett, string tie, clips on, M in pkg 23.00
Davy Crockett, sunglasses display, w/6 pr glasses, MIB 160.00
Davy Crockett, wristwatch, Liberty, 1" dial w/pistol, NMIB 635.00
Dick Tracy, badge, Crime Stoppers, enameled brass, ID card, M .32.00
Dick Tracy, badge, Secret Service, tin w/silver pnt 75.00
Dick Tracy, book, Celebrated Cases of DT, 1st ed, M 75.00
Dick Tracy, candy bar wrapper, 1950s 75.00
Dick Tracy, Comicooky set, M 75.00
Dick Tracy, fingerprint set, DT Detective, 1933, NM ...75.00
Dick Tracy, holster set, plastic & metal, J Henry, M on card 70.00
Dick Tracy, iron-on patch, Crime Stoppers 20.00
Dick Tracy, kit, Crime Stoppers, unused, 1961 ....38.00
Dick Tracy, penny book, DT Gets His Man, 1938 ....30.00
Dick Tracy, pin-bk, DT Detective, paper label, NM 39.00
Dick Tracy, ring, secret compartment 215.00
Dick Tracy, Soaky, M 35.00
Dick Tracy, suspenders, NM on card 75.00
Dionne Quintuplets, book, We'll Be Three, 1936, EX 18.00

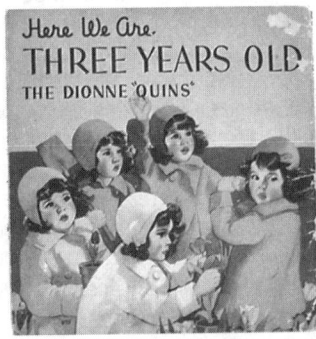

Dionne Quintuplets, book, *Here We Are Three Years Old*, Whitman, #1937, NM, $28.00.

Dionne Quintuplets, calendar, 1937, EX 30.00
Dionne Quintuplets, dolls, compo, all orig, 1937, 7", 5 for 800.00
Dionne Quintuplets, hair ribbon, 1935, M on card 75.00
Donald Duck, creamer, Disney 75.00
Donald Duck, figure, American Pottery, 6½", NM 85.00
Donald Duck, figure, bsk, on scooter, 1930s, 3¾", NM 165.00
Donald Duck, figure, compo, WDE, 6", VG 725.00
Donald Duck, figurine, Seiberling rubber, movable head, lg 225.00
Donald Duck, fork, stainless steel, 1959 ....20.00
Donald Duck, nodder, orig tag 850.00
Donald Duck, paint box, tin litho, Transogram, 1946, used, EX ...38.00
Donald Duck, Piston Race Car, plastic, battery op, 9", MIB 140.00
Donald Duck, ramp walker, pushing wheelbarrow, EX 25.00
Donald Duck, tea set, tin litho, Ohio Arts, 1939, serves 3 ....295.00
Donald Duck, toothbrush holder, single figure, 5¼", EX 175.00
Donald Duck, warming dish, DD figural, Am pottery 115.00
Donald Duck, wristwatch, 50th b'day, Bradley, Registered Ed, MIB ..225.00
Dopey, hand puppet, compo head, WDE, 1940s, EX 65.00
Dopey, Soaky, EX 15.00
Elmer Fudd, Soaky, EX 25.00
Elsie the Cow, tablecloth, w/Elmer & children, EX 135.00

ET, rubber mask, M 15.00
Evel Knievel, wristwatch, 1976, NM 85.00
F-Troop, pin-bk button 6.00
Felix the Cat, ashtray, Wilton Crested China, 1920s 275.00
Felix the Cat, bottle, ginger ale; Canada, 1930s, 9" 250.00
Felix the Cat, figure, chalkware, England, 1920s, 7" 275.00
Felix the Cat, figure, pnt plaster, 13", EX 400.00
Felix the Cat, figure, wooden, w/pipe, Fun-o-flex, 1930s 195.00
Felix the Cat, pin, enameled, 1920s 80.00
Felix the Cat, plate, baby's, 1930s 295.00
Felix the Cat, postcard, 1920s 20.00
Felix the Cat, rattle & whistle, tin, European, NM 225.00
Flintstones, Bamm Bamm doll, Ideal, 1964, 12", NM 85.00
Flintstones, clock, windup, 1991, MIB 50.00
Flintstones, Dino push puppet, Kohner, M 40.00
Flintstones, Fred bank, plastic, 10", M 45.00
Flintstones, Fred camera, figural, M on card 30.00
Flintstones, Pebbles bank, ceramic, on Dino 50.00
Flying Nun, bagatelle game, M in pkg 55.00
Frankenstein, Soaky 85.00
G-Man, pencil box, cb litho, 1930s, 10½x5¼", EX 60.00
G-Man, siren, picket-type signal, tin, crank wind 65.00
Gene Autry, counter display, from winter 1936 tour, 11x14" 45.00
Gene Autry, covered wagon lamp, GA on Champ, etc, EX 425.00
Gene Autry, pennant, cloth, Bk in Saddle Again, w/Champion ..45.00
Gene Autry, wristwatch, Always Your Pal, Swiss, 1948 ....125.00
Gene Autry, wristwatch, GA on rearing horse, Wiland, 1948 ....125.00
Goofy, wristwatch, Pedre, MIB 125.00
Green Hornet, pin-bk, Adventure Club, celluloid, early, EX 375.00
Happy Hooligan, pipe, clay, HH in relief, policeman on stem 175.00
Happy Hooligan, whistle, HP ceramic figural, 1920s 80.00
Happy Hooligan & the Cop, mechanical card, cb, 5½x6¾", EX ...85.00
Hoky Poky, wristwatch, animated, MIB 345.00
Holly Hobbie, wristwatch, Bradley, M 45.00

Hopalong Cassidy, School Slate Outfit, Willam Boyd graphics, Transogram, ca 1950, 9x11" slate with chalks and pencils, NM in box, $285.00.

Hopalong Cassidy, alarm clock, blk, US Time, EX in orig box ...475.00
Hopalong Cassidy, album, leather cover, holds 2 5x7" pictures ..165.00
Hopalong Cassidy, ballpoint pen refill, MIB 27.00
Hopalong Cassidy, banner, felt, 1950, EX 20.00
Hopalong Cassidy, bedspread, gr chenille, NM 250.00
Hopalong Cassidy, birthday postcard, Savings Club 10.00
Hopalong Cassidy, cabinet card, blk & wht, 5¼x3¼", M 30.00
Hopalong Cassidy, coloring set, figural pnts/crayons/etc, MIB 250.00
Hopalong Cassidy, decanter, Sunshine straws 30.00
Hopalong Cassidy, exploitation manual, United Artists, 1950 .....45.00
Hopalong Cassidy, hair trainer, 1950s, full 5½" bottle, M 28.00
Hopalong Cassidy, jug, milk; 1-gal, rare 495.00
Hopalong Cassidy, photo card, fan club, blk & wht, 6½x6½" 15.00

Hopalong Cassidy, pop-up book, lg, unused 50.00
Hopalong Cassidy, poster, Sunny Spread, 1950s, 16x20", M 25.00
Hopalong Cassidy, radio, blk or red, ea 650.00
Hopalong Cassidy, ring binder, hardcover, loose-leaf book 125.00
Hopalong Cassidy, target, tin litho, tall, EX 145.00
Hopalong Cassidy, wood-burning set, unused, NMIB 250.00
Hopalong Cassidy, wristwatch, saddle, plastic, MIB 325.00
Hopalong Cassidy, wristwatch, US Time, 1951, lg, EX 95.00
Horace Horsecollar & Donald Duck, WWII poster, 1943, NM ..125.00
Howdy Doody, bandages, MIB 25.00
Howdy Doody, bandanna, 1950s, 20" sq, M 75.00
Howdy Doody, bank, head figural, Vandor 35.00
Howdy Doody, bank, TV set, ceramic 50.00
Howdy Doody, bookends, Vandor, pr 125.00
Howdy Doody, ceiling shade, glass, NM 265.00
Howdy Doody, Christmas stocking, 19" 110.00
Howdy Doody, doll, cloth, 12", M 20.00
Howdy Doody, doll, stuffed, 40th birthday, w/tag, M 25.00
Howdy Doody, figure, flexible cb, Wonder Bread, M 40.00
Howdy Doody, key puzzle, w/instructions, NM 15.00
Howdy Doody, merchandise catalog, 1947-55, reprint 15.00
Howdy Doody, music box, HD playing piano 125.00
Howdy Doody, Ovaltine shaker, w/top, orig shakers 45.00
Howdy Doody, paint set, box only 30.00
Howdy Doody, pencil holder, face, all orig parts, M 120.00
Howdy Doody, Phonodoodle record player, EX 200.00
Howdy Doody, push puppet, Kohner, M 100.00
Howdy Doody, store hanger, Wonder Bread, 12", NM 35.00
Howdy Doody, store hanger, Wonder Bread, 6" 28.00
Howdy Doody, table lamp, figural, EX 165.00
Howdy Doody, talking alarm clock, MIB 125.00
Howdy Doody, tool box, Official Ranch House, metal, EX 95.00
Howdy Doody & Clarabell, ukelele 95.00
Howdy Doody & Santa, wall lamp, HD on chimney, rare version ..175.00
Jack Armstrong, Magic Answer Box 40.00
Jack Armstrong, Ped-O-Meter, bl or silver, M 30.00
Jack Armstrong, whistle-ring, 1940s, NM+ 95.00
James Bond, wristwatch, musical, M on card 45.00
Jerry Mahoney, wiffle ball, NBC premium, MIB 75.00
Jiggs, Syroco figure 60.00
Jiminy Crickett, fiddle, Disney, M w/bow 25.00
Junior G-Man, Special Investigator badge, tin, EX 12.00
Ken Maynard, stationery, 4 pgs, 8½x11", M 15.00
Ken Maynard, story record, 1940s, 8" 20.00
Kit Carson (Bill Williams), TV costume, 1950s, NM 125.00
Krazy Kat, pin, enamel w/orange rhinestones, 1920s 38.00
Laugh-In, sleeping bag, characters from show, 1969, EX 75.00
Laurel & Hardy, figures, chalk, Esso, 1972, 18", pr 45.00
Little Orphan Annie, ashtray, lustreware 130.00
Little Orphan Annie, decoder, Speedomatic, brass, 1940 ....50.00
Little Orphan Annie, electric stove, lg, cord removed 50.00
Little Orphan Annie, ID bracelet 24.00
Little Orphan Annie, mug, beige, Ovaltine, NM decal 22.00
Little Orphan Annie, mug, gr, Shake-Up, w/lid, NM 50.00
Little Orphan Annie, whistle, premium 60.00
Little Orphan Annie, wristwatch, Harold Gray, EX 85.00
Little Orphan Annie, wristwatch, MIB 295.00
Lone Ranger, badge, Chief Scout, M 90.00
Lone Ranger, bank, strong box, leather covered, w/key, 1938 ....250.00
Lone Ranger, color book, uncolored, 1951, NM 35.00
Lone Ranger, crayon box, tin litho, 1950s, EX 35.00
Lone Ranger, illus coupon for comic book, 1939 ....10.00
Lone Ranger, Jail House keys, M on card 55.00
Lone Ranger, pencil case, brn cb 60.00

Lone Ranger, pin, bl & gold, circular, 1938 ....52.00
Lone Ranger, pocketknife, Camco USA, EX 30.00
Lone Ranger, postcard, Bond Bread, Safety Club, 1939, M 25.00
Lone Ranger, push puppet, wood & plastic, Kohner, 1940s, 7" ..160.00
Lone Ranger, radio, Airline, wht plastic case, lights up, EX 625.00
Lone Ranger, ring, saddle, w/film strip, M 155.00
Lone Ranger, ring, Six-Shooter, EX 125.00
Lone Ranger, sign, counter; Six-Shooter Ring, diecut, 7½x6" 135.00
Lone Ranger, tent, MIB 175.00
Lone Ranger, Wheaties box, Texas Ed mask on bk, 1958 ....50.00
Lum & Abner, almanac, 1936, EX 22.50
Mad Hatter, figure, WDP, 4" 18.00
Maggie & Jiggs, Christmas card, 1930s, EX 15.00

Mammy Yokem, Baby Barry Toy Co., NY, 20", NM, $85.00.

Man from UNCLE, Ilia Kuryakin doll, Gilbert, 12", EX 40.00
Man from UNCLE, Napoleon Solo doll, 12", MIB 235.00
Mary Marvel, wristwatch, MIB 345.00
Mary Poppins, dot/color book, unused 16.50
Mickey, Minnie & Pluto, tea set, Disney, 1940s, 7-pc, MIB 225.00
Mickey & Minnie Mouse, tea set, lustreware, 23-pc, serves 6 .....300.00
Mickey Mouse, alarm clock, Lorus, Japan, EX 20.00
Mickey Mouse, badge, Fire Department, 1930s, rare, NM 250.00
Mickey Mouse, ballpoint pen, early, scarce 48.00
Mickey Mouse, bank, compo house, 1960s 30.00
Mickey Mouse, bracelet, SP 185.00
Mickey Mouse, bridge pad, full-bodied MM on cover, WD 65.00
Mickey Mouse, Bubble Buster, Kilgore, 1930s, 8", EX 175.00
Mickey Mouse, charm, hard celluloid 17.50
Mickey Mouse, clock, Elgin, 1971, 11", VG 10.00
Mickey Mouse, clock, pie-eyed, walking, Bradley, MIB 225.00
Mickey Mouse, color book, colored in, 1935 ....60.00
Mickey Mouse, color book, 1931, lg, EX 50.00
Mickey Mouse, creamer, china, rat-faced figural, 1930s 140.00
Mickey Mouse, figure, bsk, w/sword, 1930s, 3¼", VG 75.00
Mickey Mouse, figure, Seiberling Rubber, ca 1930, 3½", EX 55.00
Mickey Mouse, figure, Seiberling Rubber, 6", EX 175.00
Mickey Mouse, film, paper, 1930s 25.00
Mickey Mouse, game, Snap, Silly Symphonies, Chad Valley, MIB .110.00
Mickey Mouse, map, Globe Trotter, w/12 cards, M in envelope ...375.00
Mickey Mouse, map, Treasure Island, Standard Oil, '38, 25x20" ..125.00
Mickey Mouse, pin-bk, celluloid, blk/wht, ca 1929, EX 150.00
Mickey Mouse, pin-bk, celluloid, Good Teeth, 1930s, NM 125.00
Mickey Mouse, pin-bk, celluloid, 1938, NM 125.00
Mickey Mouse, plate, cup & saucer, aluminum, 1930s 185.00
Mickey Mouse, playing cards, Shuffled Symphonies, England, MIB ..75.00
Mickey Mouse, pocket watch, Ingersoll, w/orig fob, 2" dia, NM .450.00
Mickey Mouse, projector, Keystone, 1930s, MIB 495.00
Mickey Mouse, radio, Emerson, molded faux wood case, 7½", G ..300.00
Mickey Mouse, ramp walker, pushing roller, 1960s 25.00

Mickey Mouse, sand pail, Happynak, mc, England, 1940s, EX 85.00
Mickey Mouse, spoon, emb SP, 1930s 28.00
Mickey Mouse, Sunshine Straws, MIB 20.00
Mickey Mouse, tablecloth, orange paper, 1930s, EX 150.00
Mickey Mouse, tea set, Magic Kingdom, child's, MIB 30.00
Mickey Mouse, watch fob, Ingersoll, brass link chain 300.00
Mickey Mouse, world globe, 1950, MIB 175.00
Mickey Mouse, wristwatch, celebrating 50th year, MIB 165.00
Mickey Mouse, wristwatch, digital, Bradley, 1970s, MIB 150.00
Mickey Mouse, wristwatch, Ingersoll, 1933, EX in box 700.00

Mickey Mouse, wristwatch, Ingersoll, ca 1933, MIB with original papers, $900.00.

Mickey Mouse, wristwatch, Ingersoll, 1950s, MIB 125.00
Mickey Mouse, wristwatch, M in emb 1992 Convention container .300.00
Mickey Mouse, wristwatch, US Time, vinyl band, '47, box, EX .275.00
Mickey Mouse & Goofy, alarm clock, WDP, 1960s, 5½", NM ...125.00
Mickey Mouse & Pluto, alarm clock, dbl bell, WDP, 1950s, NM ..150.00
Mickey Mouse & Pluto, plate, child's, 3-part, Patriot China 115.00
Mickey Mouse Club, coloring set, numbered pencils, 1950s, M 40.00
Mickey Mouse Club, harmonica, NM 20.00
Mickey Mouse Club, projector, NMIB 40.00
Mighty Mouse, alarm clock, tin litho, Japan, 1960s, NM 78.00
Minnie Mouse, cup, ceramic, Bavaria, 3¾" 150.00
Minnie Mouse, earring holder, metal 10.00
Minnie Mouse, ramp walker, pushing carriage, 1960s 25.00
Minnie Mouse, travel clock, Bradley, MIB 275.00
Minnie Mouse, wristwatch, Bradley, 1975, M 60.00
Mother Goose, Playbox, paper pop-up, McLoughlin, 1950, NM ..75.00
Mr Magoo, Soaky, EX 22.00
Mr Magoo, wall decoration, vinyl, 1975, M 12.50
Ms Pac Man, wristwatch, Bradley, MIB 40.00
Mutt & Jeff, bank, CI 90.00
Mutt & Jeff, lapel stud button, emb characters w/names, oval 65.00
Mutt & Jeff, stickpins, brass, 1920s, pr 130.00
Oliver, punch-out/sticker book, Disney, 1968, EX 16.50
Our Gang, Fatty Arbuckle photo, premium 12.00
Peanuts, Snoopy, bank, ceramic, 40th Anniversary 25.00
Peanuts, Snoopy music box, Schmid, 1963, M 50.00
Peanuts, Snoopy nodder, dog-fighter pilot 40.00
Peanuts, Snoopy Rock Around the Clock clock, MIB 90.00
Peanuts, Snoopy Sno-Cones machine 5.00
Peanuts, Snoopy telephone, 7½", EX 25.00
Peanuts, Snoopy wristwatch, Timex, 1970s, VG 75.00
Peanuts, Snoopy wristwatch, United Features, Swiss, 1988, M 85.00
Peanuts, Woodstock bank, Swiss, rare 25.00
Peter Max, fondue set 250.00
Peter Rabbit, safety pins, 1930s, M on card 55.00
Pinocchio, bank, ceramic, head form 65.00
Pinocchio, lamp shade, NM 65.00
Pinocchio, Paper Circus, uncut, 1939, 20x18", NM 125.00
Pinocchio, pin-bk, celluloid, Good Teeth, 1930s, NM 145.00
Pinocchio, Soaky, EX 15.00

Planet of the Apes, Dr Zaius hand puppet, M in pkg 29.00
Planet of the Apes, Galen figure Dangle, M in pkg 23.50
Planet of the Apes, gum cards, Topps, 1975, set of 66, NM 75.00
Pluto, alarm clock, Bayard, WDP, 1964, 5x4½", NM 175.00
Pluto, ramp walker, NM 30.00
Popeye, animated book, King Features, 9½x13", EX+ 60.00
Popeye, bank, dime registering, 1929, EX 75.00
Popeye, bank, head figural, chalkware, EX 125.00
Popeye, bubble set, King Features, 1936, 7x5", MIB 80.00
Popeye, bubble set, pnt wood, Transogram, VG 15.00
Popeye, Christmas card, Hallmark, 1934, EX 45.00
Popeye, Christmas shade, Cheers, 1929, MIB 150.00
Popeye, clock, animated, Smith, England, 1960s, M 175.00
Popeye, color book, Color & Recolor w/Crayons, 1957, unused ...25.00
Popeye, doll, rubber foam, 13", EX 100.00
Popeye, figure, carnival chalk, 1930s, 11", NM 75.00
Popeye, figure, Syroco, KFS, 1944, 5" 110.00
Popeye, harmonica, 1929, EX 65.00
Popeye, lamp, metal, orig tin pipe, dtd 1935, EX 150.00
Popeye, Lite Up pipe, 1948, M on card 50.00
Popeye, musical pillow, mc scene on plastic, 1948, M, sealed 250.00
Popeye, napkin holder, Bakelite 45.00
Popeye, paint set, Am Crayon, MIB 80.00
Popeye, pencil, Eagle, 1929, 10½", EX 30.00
Popeye, pencil box, 1929, EX 30.00
Popeye, pencil sharpener, 1929 ....125.00
Popeye, printer set, 1935, MIB 85.00
Popeye, soap mold, tin 25.00
Popeye, Sweetpea mask, cb, 1940s, NM 15.00
Porky Pig, Soaky, EX 20.00
Prince Valiant, bank, dime registering, KFS, 1954, EX 115.00
Raggedy Ann, talking alarm clock, Janex, 6¼", EX 25.00
Raggedy Ann & Andy, talking alarm clock, Janex, NMIB 35.00
Red Riding Hood, baby's plate, England, 1920s 55.00
Rex Mars, wristwatch, MIB 895.00
Rin Tin Tin, ring, plastic, NM 17.50
Robin Hood, wristwatch, M in 3-D box 375.00
Rocky, balancing toy, 1969, M on card 15.00
Ronald McDonald, wristwatch, crew, MIB 110.00
Ronald McDonald, wristwatch, Criperion, 17-jewel, MIB 185.00
Roy Rogers, alarm clock, Ingraham, 1950s, NMIB 375.00
Roy Rogers, archery set, MIB 125.00
Roy Rogers, bank, porc figural on Trigger, M 245.00
Roy Rogers, bedspread, embr cotton, EX 175.00
Roy Rogers, binoculars, 2-power, MIB 85.00
Roy Rogers, book, Dbl-R Ranch, orig dust jacket, 1951 ....12.50
Roy Rogers, book, Rodeo Sticker Fun, uncut, NM 75.00
Roy Rogers, Fix It Stagecoach, w/gun & whip, NMIB 245.00
Roy Rogers, guitar, red, EX graphics, 28", EX 125.00
Roy Rogers, harmonica, 1950s, EX 35.00
Roy Rogers, loose leaf notebook, RR on Trigger cover, EX 65.00
Roy Rogers, Lucky Horseshoe, red rubber, EX 23.00
Roy Rogers, moccasins, MIB 100.00
Roy Rogers, nodder, rpt hat 140.00
Roy Rogers, pencil, King of Cowboys, M 3.00
Roy Rogers, photo, movie theatre giveaway 10.00
Roy Rogers, pocketknife, 1950s, M 65.00
Roy Rogers, ring, Saddle, sterling silver, sgn 250.00
Roy Rogers, scarf, silk, w/hat slide, 1945 ....60.00
Roy Rogers, scarf, w/gun & holster slide, 1950s, sm 60.00
Roy Rogers, wristwatch, Bradley, quartz, 1985, MIB 95.00
Roy Rogers, youth saddle, w/martingale, tooled leather, EX 875.00
Sgt Preston, distance finder, NM 40.00
Shirley Temple, badge, Police, 1937 ....25.00

Shirley Temple, book, How I Raised ST, 1935, EX 25.00
Shirley Temple, book, Real Little Girl, EX 50.00
Shirley Temple, book, ST's Favorite Poems, hardcover, EX 45.00
Shirley Temple, color box, ST on top, 1937 ....140.00
Shirley Temple, creamer, portrait on cobalt glass 32.00
Shirley Temple, Great Big Coloring Book, 1936, NM 75.00
Shirley Temple, mug, portrait on cobalt glass 40.00
Shirley Temple, pin, ST League, portrait, England, 1930s, M 85.00
Shirley Temple, pitcher, cobalt glass, EX 45.00
Shirley Temple, postcard, as Little Colonel, England, 1930s, M ...20.00
Shirley Temple, sewing card set, Saalfield, NMIB 30.00
Shirley Temple, song album #2, 1936, EX 35.00
Shirley Temple Club, ring, face, sterling, 1930s, rare 300.00
Six Million Dollar Man, astronaut outfit, M in pkg 25.00
Skeezix, pin-bk button, celluloid, I Like...Sweaters, NM 45.00
Skippy, doll, oilcloth, w/hat, 12", NM 75.00
Smitty, doll, oilcloth, 9¾", NM 60.00
Smokey Bear, badge, Jr Forest Ranger, chrome-plated brass, M 35.00
Smokey Bear, pocket watch 65.00
Smokey Bear, poster, 1947 ....60.00
Smokey Bear, Soaky 25.00
Sniffles, bank, standing beside stump, HP metal, '40, NM 125.00
Snow White, bank, dime registering, WDE, 1938, EX 150.00
Snow White, book, hardbk, from Disney movie, 1938 ....65.00
Snow White, paint box, tin, WDE, Belgium 75.00
Snow White, sheet music, 1938, M 30.00
Snow White, tumbler, 1930s 22.00
Snow White, wristwatch, Magic Mirror, MIB 295.00
Snow White & 7 Dwarfs, figural soap set, MIB 120.00
Snow White & 7 Dwarfs, linen book, Disney, 1938, EX 30.00
Speedy Gonzalez, Soaky, EX 22.00
Spiderman, emblem, Bike Patrol, mc, 1978 ....10.00
Spiderman, Super Hero rubber wind-up figure, Marx, '68, 5", MIB .120.00
Spiderman, wristwatch, DABS, 1977, sm, NM 75.00
Spiro Agnew, alarm clock, MIB 55.00
Spiro Agnew, wristwatch, NM 50.00
Stan Laurel, decanter, Heritage China, 1976, 10x7", NM 95.00
Star Wars, R2-D2 model kit, sealed 20.00
Starsky & Hutch, costumes, 1976, MIB, pr 25.00
Superman, Coloring Set, Transogram, 1954, 11x10", MIB 175.00
Superman, folder, Secret Code, Action Comics premium 30.00
Superman, Kryptonite rock, 1977, MIB 15.00
Superman, lamp, figural 45.00
Superman, paint set, Sparkle, Kenner, 1966, 11x8", MIB 65.00
Superman, pocket watch, Bradley 150.00
Superman, sun suit, child's, 1940s, EX 125.00
Superman, suspenders, M on card 25.00
Superman, whistle/flashlight, EX 30.00
Sylvester, Dakin figure, EX 12.00
Terry & Pirates, color book, Saalfield, 1946, M 30.00
Three Stooges, doll set, stuffed cloth, Collins, 1982, M on card .140.00
Three Stooges, pocket watch, mk FTCC, clockwork, 2" dia, EX ..75.00
Thumper, figure, ceramic, Am Pottery, scarce, 7", NM 65.00
Tom & Jerry, bank, ceramic, figural, England, 1970 ....50.00
Tom & Jerry, egg cup, plastic, 1970 ....18.00
Tom Mix, belt buckle, secret compartment, radio premium 75.00
Tom Mix, compass, Glow in the Dark, NM 70.00
Tom Mix, ID bracelet, Ralston Strait Shooters 65.00
Tom Mix, mask, cb, NM 60.00
Tom Mix, rocket parachute, M in mailer 155.00
Tom Mix, telephone set, premium 125.00
Tom Mix, wristwatch, Ralston, 1984 ....150.00
Tony the Tiger, baseball, MT 18.00
Top Cat & Benny, ramp walker, Marx, 1960, EX+ 45.00

Uncle Willie & Emmy, planter, bsk, 1930s **125.00**
Walrus & Carpenter, plate, baby's, England, 1920s **225.00**
Welcome Back Kotter, bank, mechanical **35.00**
Winnie the Pooh, push puppet, EX **25.00**
Winnie the Pooh, Tricky Trapeze, Kohner, 1964, NM **19.50**
Wonder Woman, dress-up kit, lip gloss, blush, tiara, 1988 ....**10.00**
Wonder Woman, wristwatch, DABS, 1977, sm, NM **65.00**
Wonder Woman, wristwatch, DC Comics, 1975, M **150.00**
Woody Woodpecker, book, punch-out color album, 1972, M **30.00**
Woody Woodpecker, clock, animated, 1960s, MIB **400.00**
Woody Woodpecker, hand puppet, Mattel, 1962 ....**35.00**
Wyatt Earp, badge, Marshall, NM **25.00**
Wyatt Earp, gun set, cowhide holsters, Hubley, 1959, VG **350.00**
Yellow Kid, hand puppet, dtd 1896, 6" **250.00**
Yellow Kid, punch board, YK w/umbrella, 1930s, M **95.00**
Yogi Bear, lamp, porc, figural, 1980, MIB **30.00**
Ziggy, bank, ceramic, holding piggy **35.00**
Zorro, Paint-By-Number set, NMIB **140.00**
Zorro, pencil sharpener, ceramic, figural, 6" **225.00**
Zorro, table lamp, Zorro w/sword figural, porc, 8" **195.00**
3 Little Pigs & Big Bad Wolf, clock, Ingersoll, MIB **600.00**

Peters and Reed

John Peters and Adam Reed founded their pottery in Zanesville, Ohio, just before the turn of the century, using the local red clay to produce a variety of wares. Moss Aztec, introduced about 1912, has an unglazed exterior with designs molded in high relief and the recesses highlighted with a green wash. Only the interior is glazed to hold water. Pereco (named for Peters, Reed and Company) is glazed in semimatt blue, maroon, or cream. Orange was also used very early, but such examples are rare. Shapes are simple with in-mold decoration sometimes borrowed from the Moss Aztec line. Wilse Blue is a line of high-gloss medium blue with dark specks on simple shapes. Landsun, characterized by its soft matt multicolor or blue and gray combinations, is decorated either by dripping or by hand brushing in an effect sometimes called Flame or Herringbone. Chromal, in much the same colors as Landsun, may be decorated with a realistic scenic, or the swirling application of colors may merely suggest one. (Brush-McCoy made a very similar line called Chromart. Neither will be marked; and due to the lack of documented background material available, it may be impossible make a positive identification. Collectors nearly always attribute this type of decoration to Peters and Reed.) Shadow Ware is a glossy, multicolor drip over a harmonious base color. When the base is black, the effect is often iridescent.

Perhaps the most familiar line is the brown high-glaze artware with the 'sprigged'-type designs. Although research has uncovered no positive proof, it is generally accepted as having been made by Peters and Reed. It is interesting to note that many of the artistic shapes in this line are recognizable as those made by Weller, Roseville, and other Zanesville area companies. Other lines include Mirror Black, Persian, and an unidentified line which collectors call Mottled Colors. In this high-gloss line, the red clay body often shows through the splashed-on multicolors.

In 1922 the company became known as the Zane Pottery. Peters and Reed retired, and Harry McClelland became president. Charles Chilcote designed new lines, and production of many of the old lines continued. The body of the ware after 1922 was light in color. Marks include the impressed logo or ink stamp 'Zaneware' in a rectangle.

Bowl, floral emb on gr matt, 3-ftd, 3½x7" **45.00**
Bowl, Landsun, bl, 9" **40.00**
Bowl, Landsun, brn tones, 10" **45.00**

Bowl, Pereco, 3x7", $45.00.

Bowl, Zaneware, yel, flared **25.00**
Candlesticks, yel, twisted, Zaneware mk, 9", pr **90.00**
Cuspidor, Moss Aztec, rose relief, gr on red clay, 4¾" **75.00**
Ewer, Brn Ware, wreath, squat, 5" **45.00**
Flowerpot, Brn Ware, grapes, 5" **60.00**
Flowerpot, Florentine **35.00**
Jardiniere, Persian, lion, brn, 6" **60.00**
Jug, Brn Ware, cavalier, 6" **80.00**
Jug, Brn Ware, wreath, 5" **60.00**
Mug, Brn Ware, cavalier, 5" **50.00**
Pitcher, Brn Ware, grapes, 11" **125.00**
Pitcher, mc drip on rust, glossy, unmk, 5", EX **50.00**
Sugar bowl, Florentine **20.00**
Umbrella stand, vines/flowers at top, gr w/brn, 21" **300.00**
Vase, blk & yel drip swirls on bl, glossy, 6-sided, unmk, 9" **90.00**
Vase, Brn Ware, flowers, 6" **45.00**
Vase, bud; Landsun, 6" **35.00**
Vase, bud; Wilse Bl, 6" **20.00**
Vase, Chromal, cabin in landscape, bulbous, 7" **350.00**
Vase, Chromal, landscape, yel & earth tones, 7½" **300.00**
Vase, emb roses/vines, lt bl matt, 14" **140.00**
Vase, Florentine, HP flowers, bulbous, 5" **35.00**
Vase, Landsun, bl & brn, bulbous, flared lip, 5" **50.00**
Vase, Landsun, gr, brn & bl, flared lip, 6" **60.00**
Vase, Landsun, gr & bl, shape 40B, 8" **60.00**
Vase, Shadow Ware, beige w/bl drips, 4" **60.00**
Vase, Shadow Ware, brn w/bl drips, bulbous, 8" **90.00**
Vase, Shadow Ware, gr drip on mirror blk, unmk, 13½" **250.00**
Wall pocket, Moss Aztec **95.00**
Wall pocket, Wilse Bl, sunflower, NM **50.00**

Pewabic

The Pewabic Pottery was formally established in Detroit, Michigan, in 1907 by Mary Chase Perry Stratton and Horace James Caulkins. The two had worked together since 1903, firing their ware in a small kiln Caulkins had designed especially for use by the dental trade. Always a small operation which relied upon basic equipment and the skill of the workers, they took pride in being commissioned for several important architectural tile installations.

Some of the early artware was glazed a simple matt green; occasionally other colors were added, sometimes in combination, one over the other in a drip effect. Later Stratton developed a lustrous crystalline glaze. (Today's values are determined to a great extent by the artistic merit of the glaze.) The body of the ware was highly fired and extremely hard. Shapes were basic, and decorative modeling, if used at all, was in low relief. Mary Stratton kept the pottery open until her death in 1961. In 1968 it was purchased and reopened by Michigan State University. Several marks were used over the years: a triangle with 'Revelation Pottery' (for a short time only); 'Pewabic' with five maple leaves; and the impressed circle mark.

Bookends, frontal view of rabbit, bl/gr w/clear lustre, pr 550.00
Bowl, gray/bl irid, 3x4" 300.00
Candlesticks, pk irid to bl, low flower form, 1½x3½", pr 100.00
Tile, putti medallion, gun metal & brn, unmk, 3¼" dia 290.00
Vase, bl metallic w/platinum highlights, shouldered, 5" 500.00
Vase, bl/purple semimatt lustre, bulb w/sloped shoulder, 5" 400.00
Vase, blk/turq/bl lustre, hammered texture, ovoid, 8x5½" 1,400.00
Vase, cvd swirling lines, celadon/gold w/int lustre, 2½x2½" 375.00
Vase, flower frog; purple/red irid, horizontal ridges, 2x3" 100.00
Vase, flowing sky bl flambe exposing clay, 6x6" 600.00
Vase, gr/purple/bl metallic, hdls, hand thrown, 8½" 1,900.00
Vase, irid cobalt/silver/gr drip glaze, flat shoulder, 4x4" 700.00
Vase, purple/bl/turq flowing irid, flared neck, 5x4" 600.00
Vase, shaded lt gr matt drip, shouldered, 10¾x5" 450.00
Vase, silver volcanic irid over bl translucent, 10" 2,975.00
Vase, turq over copper lustre, 3½x3½" 350.00
Vase, turq over metallic copper, early, 4" 575.00
Vase, turq w/brn specks & crystals, glossy, bulbous, 6" 375.00
Vase, turq w/brn specks & fine specks, bulbous, 6" 350.00
Vase, violet/copper/gold irid flambe, ridged body, 5x4" 650.00
Vase, yel/brn matt, early signature, 7" 425.00

Pewter

Pewter is a metal alloy of tin, copper, very small parts of bismuth and/or antimony, and sometimes lead. Very little American pewter contained lead, however, because much of the ware was designed to be used as tableware, and makers were aware that the use of lead could result in poisoning. (Pieces that do contain lead are usually darker in color and heavier than those that have no lead.) Most of the fine examples of American pewter date from 1700 to the 1840s. Many pieces were melted down and recast into bullets during the American Revolution in 1775; this accounts to some extent why examples from this period are quite difficult to find. The pieces that did survive may include buttons, buckles, and writing equipment as well as the tableware we generally think of.

After the Revolution, makers began using antimony as the major alloy with the tin in an effort to regain the popularity of pewter, which glassware and china was beginning to replace in the home. The resulting product, known as britannia, had a lustrous silver-like appearance and was far more durable. While closely related, britannia is a collectible in its own right and should not be confused with pewter.

Key: tm — touch mark

Teapot, Eben Smith, pear-shaped Queen Anne style, 7", EX, $1,550.00; Coffeepot, George Richardson, Cranston marks, 8¾", NM, $550.00.

Basin, Gershom Jones eagle tm, Providence RI, 7¾", EX 275.00

Basin, unmk Am, polished, pitting, 1⅞x6¼" 165.00
Basin, unmk Am, split in rim, 2x8" 50.00
Beaker, Boardman & Hart tm, ca 1828-53, 3⅛" 350.00
Beaker, John Carpenter tm, 1760-63, 4¼" 315.00
Beaker, John Will tm, 1750-64, 4x4¾" 1,600.00
Beaker, Timothy Boardman tm, ca 1820s, 5¼" 600.00
Candlestick, R Gleason tm, 7" 330.00
Chalice, communion; unmk Am, 6¼", pr 275.00
Chalice, unmk Am, 5¾" 195.00
Charger, angel tm, Continental, rpr/wear, 15¾" 250.00
Charger, English rose tm, wear/scratches, 16½" 250.00
Charger, London tm, wear, old rpr, 12¼" 100.00
Charger, Robert Palethorp eagle tm, Phila, 13" 360.00
Coffeepot, Freeman Porter tm, lighthouse style, 10⅝" 200.00
Coffeepot, G Richardson tm, bulbous, domed lid, rprs, 11" 360.00
Coffeepot, Oliver Trask tm, bright-cut decor, 12" 460.00
Coffeepot, Smith & Co tm, 10" 330.00
Creamer, Edward Quick tm, 3-ftd, 3½" 1,850.00
Creamer, unmk Am, well-shaped ear hdl, 5¾" 185.00
Flagon, communion; Roswell Gleason tm, 10" 495.00
Flagon, communion; Smith & Feltman Albany tm, 10½" 500.00
Flagon, communion; unmk, decorative details, dents, 14" 110.00
Flagon, Engish tm (partial), battered/rpr, 9" 105.00
Flagon, rose tm, wear/scratches, 13¼" 160.00
Goblet, unmk English, eng monogram, 4⅞" 35.00
Ladle, Thomas Danforth Boardman tm, 13½" 260.00
Lamp, R Dunham tm, 5⅝"+whale-oil burner 330.00
Measure, England, bellied tankard form, 5½" 150.00
Measure, James Birch tm, tankard form, qt, 6¼" 165.00
Mold, int flutes & fruit-design top, 6" 75.00
Mug, Robert Bush Sr tm, 1870s, 6¼" 290.00
Mug, Robert Iles tm, tulip shape, 1-pt, 4¾" 375.00
Mug, tankard, TDB (Thomas D Boardman) tm, rprs, 4" 495.00
Nursing bottle, England, 1700s, scarce, rprs, 6¼" 435.00
Pitcher, rum; England, 1800s, 8¼" 315.00
Pitcher, unmk, battered, 7½" 75.00
Pitcher, water; Flagg & Homan tm, ear hdl, 9" 250.00
Pitcher, water; Sellew & Co Cincinnati tm, hinged lid, 9¼" 400.00
Pitcher, water; unmk Am, battering, resoldered, 10" 275.00
Plate, angel tm, eng rim, wear & dents, 8⅞" 60.00
Plate, Boardman group lion tm, 9⅜" 260.00
Plate, Brob Zinn tm, Continental, 8" 78.00
Plate, Compton tm, minor wear, 8" 116.00
Plate, crowned rose tm & London, wear, 9" 150.00
Plate, Edward Danforth lion tm, wear, 8" 176.00
Plate, London tm, wear/scratches, 8⅞" 55.00
Plate, London tm, 9¼" 95.00
Plate, London tm (partial), wear/scratches, 7⅞" 75.00
Plate, Love tm, 8½" 375.00
Plate, Parks Boyd eagle tm, Phila, wear, 7⅞" 250.00
Plate, Roswell Gleason tm, 10⅞" 250.00
Plate, Sheldon & Feltman Albany tm, 10¼" 185.00
Plate, soup; angel tm, scratches, 11½" 170.00
Plate, soup; unmk, battered, 10½" 130.00
Plate, Thomas Danforth Philadelphia eagle tm, 7¾" 415.00
Plate, Townsend & Compton tm, wear, 7¾" 95.00
Plate, unmk Am, 10¼" 115.00
Plate, Wm Billings tm, 8¼" 400.00
Plate, Wm Danforth eagle tm (partial), wear, 8¾" 195.00
Platter, Samuel Danforth tm, 7⅞" 200.00
Porringer, cast crown hdl, 4½" 245.00
Porringer, cast flower hdl, 5½" 250.00
Porringer, cast flower hdl w/Boardman tm, ca 1810-30, 5½" 600.00
Porringer, Old English hdl, Am, battered, 3⅜" 195.00

Porringer, Old English hdl, 4½" 415.00
Porringer, solid hdl, 5½" dia 965.00
Pot, Continental, w/spout & hinged lid, dents/rprs, 7¾" 75.00
Shaker, unmk Am, 5¾" 130.00
Spoon, Thomas Danforth Boardman tm, 8" 290.00
Syrup, unmk Am, ear hdl, shell thumb pc, 8⅛" 100.00
Tall pot, Boardman & Hart NY tm, 11⅜" 330.00
Tall pot, Boardman eagle tm, minor heat damage, 12" 250.00
Tall pot, Calder tm, 11" 360.00
Tall pot, I Trask tm, lighthouse style, rprs, 12" 415.00
Tall pot, R Gleason tm, lighthouse style, minor dents, 10⅝" 685.00
Tall pot, Sellew & Co Cincinnati tm, 10½" 385.00
Tall pot, unmk Am, dents, rpr, 11½" 130.00
Tall pot, unmk Am, 10" 330.00
Tankard, Edward Quick tm, dome lid, 1735-60, 1-qt, 7" 1,600.00
Tankard, SM in circle tm, tulip shape, England, 1750s, 6" 1,035.00
Tankard, Wm Eddon tm, dome top, ca 1720, 7¼" 1,500.00
Tea set, Homan & Co Cincinnati, cast flower finials, 4-pc 300.00
Tea set, Sellew & Co Cincinnati tm, 11" pot+cr & sug 500.00
Teapot, Boardman & Hart NY tm, tiny split, 7½" 330.00
Teapot, Calder, Providence tm, resoldering, 9¼" 275.00
Teapot, Eben Smith tm, bright-cut eng, 8½" 290.00
Teapot, G Richardson tm, minor dents, 7⅝" 495.00
Teapot, J Munson tm, minor battering, 8" 250.00
Teapot, James Dixon & Sons tm, octagonal w/wood hdl, 8" ...160.00
Teapot, RC Wilcox & Co, dents/battering, 8¾" 105.00
Teapot, Robert Bush Jr tm, egg shape, late 1700s, 7¼" 490.00
Teapot, S Simpson tm, 7¾" 320.00
Teapot, Samuel Ellis tm, 3-ftd, pear shape, wood hdl, 6¾" 3,000.00
Teapot, Smith & Co tm, 8" 300.00
Teapot, Thomas Boardman, pear shape, extended base, 9" 1,500.00
Teapot, unmk, att Boardman group, minor dents, 5½" 545.00
Teapot, unmk Am, EX detail, 6½" 300.00
Teapot, unmk Am, minor damage to hinge, 6⅝" 140.00
Teapot, unmk Am, 8½" 165.00
Tumbler measure, Half Pint, English, 4" 40.00

Pfaltzgraff

Pfaltzgraff has operated in Pennsylvania since the early 1800s making redware at first, then stoneware crocks and jugs, yellow ware and spongeware in the twenties, artware and kitchenware in the thirties, and stoneware kitchen items through the forties. To collectors, they're best known for their Gourmet Royal (circa 1950s), a high-gloss dinnerware line of solid brown with frothy white drip glaze around the rims, and their giftware line called Muggsy, comic-character mugs, ashtrays, bottle stoppers, children's dishes, a pretzel jar, a cookie jar, etc. It was designed in the late 1940s and continued in production until 1960. The older versions have protruding features, while the features of later examples were simpy painted on.

For more information on Gourmet Royal dinnerware, we recommend *The Flea Market Trader* (Collector Books) and *The Garage Sale and Flea Market Annual* (Nostalgia Publishing Co.).

Ashtray, Muggsy 125.00
Cigarette server, Muggsy 125.00
Clothes sprinkler bottle, Muggsy, Myrtle, wht, from $125 to 175.00
Cookie jar, Muggsy, character face, minimum value 250.00
Jar, utility; Muggsy, Blk action figure 125.00
Mug, Muggsy, any action figure, from $65 to 80.00
Mug, Muggsy, any character face, from $35 to 40.00
Tumbler, Muggsy 60.00

Phoenix Bird

Blue and white Phoenix Bird china has been produced by various Japanese potteries from the early 1900s. With slight variations the design features the Japanese bird of paradise and scroll-like vines of Kara-Kusa, or Chinese grass. Although some of their earlier ware is unmarked, the majority is marked in some fashion. More than one hundred different stamps have been reported, with 'Made in Japan' the one most often found. Coming in second is Morimura's/wreath and/or crossed stems (both having the letter 'M' within). The cloverleaf with 'Japan' below very often indicates an item having a high-quality transfer-printed design. Among the many categories in the Phoenix Bird pattern are several shapes; therefore (for identification purposes), each has been given a number, i.e. #1, #2, etc. Newer items, if marked at all, carry a paper label. Compared to the older ware, the coloring of the new is whiter and the blue more harsh; the design is sparse with more ground area showing. Although collectors buy even 'new' pieces, the older is of course more highly prized and valued.

For further information we recommend *Phoenix Bird Chinaware, Books I — IV*, written and privately published by our advisor, Joan Oates; her address is in the Directory under Michigan. Join Phoenix Bird Collectors of America (PBCA) and receive the *Phoenix Bird Discoveries* newsletter, an informative publication that will further your appreciation of this chinaware. See Clubs, Newsletters and Catalogs for ordering information.

Bowl, cereal; 6" 15.00
Bowl, Made in Japan, 4¾" 7.50
Bowl, oval, Made in Japan, 7¾x6" 30.00
Bowl, vegetable; oval, 2x9¾x7½" 65.00
Cake tray, rnd w/hdls, #3 ....55.00

Casserole, #2, round, mark 17 (on inside of lid), $145.00.

Condensed milk container, #2, w/underplate 125.00
Creamer, Made in Japan 12.50
Creamer & sugar bowl, squatty, Made in Japan 32.00
Cup & saucer, bouillon 25.00
Cup & saucer, demitasse; Occupied Japan 22.50
Cup & saucer, Japan 9.50
Egg cup, dbl, 3¼" 16.50
Gravy boat, #2, Nippon 75.00
Mustard pot, w/lid, #2 ....55.00
Plate, dinner; 9¾" 45.00
Plate, grill; 3-section, heavy, 10½" 55.00
Plate, Made in Japan, 7¼" 9.00
Plate, tea/toast; kidney shape, #1, 7¾" W 28.00
Plate, 6" 7.00
Platter, 12" 50.00
Shakers, 6-sided, pr 25.00
Soup plate 'A,' thin flange, 8⅛" 35.00
Sugar bowl, Nippon, #11 ....25.00
Teapot, w/lid, #10 ....55.00
Tureen, vegetable; oval, w/lid 135.00

Phoenix Glass

Founded in 1880 in Monaca, Pennsylvania, the Phoenix Glass Company became one of the country's foremost manufacturers of lighting glass by the early 1900s. They also produced a wide variety of utilitarian and decorative glassware, including art glass by Joseph Webb, colored cut glass, Gone-with-the-Wind style oil lamps, hotel and bar ware, and pharmaceutical glassware. Today, however, collectors are primarily interested in the 'Sculptured Artware' produced in the 1930s and 1940s. These beautiful pressed and mold-blown pieces are most often found in white milk glass or crystal with various color treatments or a satin finish.

Phoenix did not mark their 'Sculptured Artware' line on the glass; instead, a silver and black or gold and black foil label in the shape of the mythical phoenix bird was used.

Quite often glassware made by the Consolidated Lamp and Glass Company of nearby Coraopolis, Pennsylvania, is mistaken for Phoenix's 'Sculptured Artware.' Though the style of the glass is very similar, one distinguishing characteristic is that perhaps 80% of the time Phoenix applied color to the background leaving the raised design plain in contrast, while Consolidated generally applied color to the raised design and left the background plain. Also, for the most part, the patterns and colors used by Phoenix were distinctively different from those used by Consolidated.

In 1970 Phoenix Glass became a division of Anchor Hocking which in turn was acquired by the Newell Group in 1987. Phoenix has the distinction of being one of the oldest continuously operating glass factories in the United States. For more information refer to *Phoenix and Consolidated Art Glass, 1926-1980*, written by our advisor, Jack D. Wilson, who is listed in the Directory under Illinois. See also Consolidated Glass.

Key: mg — milk glass

Ashtray, Phlox, deep burgundy pearlized 60.00
Banana boat, Diving Girl, orange w/frost 325.00
Bowl, Tiger Lily, purple & clear satin 350.00
Candle holders, Strawberry, bl on mg, 4¼", pr 150.00
Cigarette box, Phlox, deep burgundy pearlized 180.00
Compote, Lacy Dewdrop, pk decor on mg 145.00
Pitcher, Lacy Dewdrop, gray highlights on mg 175.00
Platter, Jonquil, yel wash, overall satin, 14" 275.00
Umbrella vase, Thistle, lime gr pearlized 425.00
Vase, Aster, slate gray pearlized, 7" 95.00
Vase, Bluebell, rose pearlized, 7" 125.00
Vase, Cosmos, lt yel w/frost, 7½" 150.00
Vase, Daisy, bl on mg, 9x9" 200.00
Vase, Daisy, tan on frosted, 9x9" 200.00
Vase, Dancing Girl, gr on mg, 12" 350.00

Vase, Figured, frosted design on yellow, 6", $80.00.

Vase, Fern, lt tan pearlized, 7" 125.00
Vase, Freesia, bl & frosted, 8" 295.00
Vase, Jewel, med gr on mg, 5" 100.00

Vase, Madonna, deep burgundy pearlized, 10" 250.00
Vase, Philodendron, burgundy pearlized, 11½" 185.00
Vase, Primrose, mg on gr, 8¾" 375.00
Vase, Star Flower, blk stain on crystal, 7" 300.00
Vase, Wild Geese, mg on gr, 9" 175.00
Vase, Wild Rose, rose-wash frosted, 10½" 175.00
Vase, Zodiac, dk rose on mg, 10½" 650.00

Phonographs

The phonograph, invented by Thomas Edison in 1877, was the first practical instrument for recording and reproducing sound. Sound wave vibrations were recorded on a tinfoil-covered cylinder and played back with a needle that ran along the grooves made from the recording, thus reproducing the sound. Other companies further improved Edison's invention; Victor, Edison, Columbia, Zonophone, and Vitaphone; among them there were others. Wooden-horn phonographs with outside horns are the most valuable. Spring models were produced until 1929 (and later); after 1929, most were electric (though some electric motor models were produced as early as 1910.)

Unless another condition is noted, prices are for complete, original phonographs in at least fine to excellent condition. Note: Edison coin-operated cylinder players start at $7,000.00 and may go up to $20,000.00 each. All outside horn Victor phonographs are worth at **least** $1,000.00 or more if in excellent original condition. Our advisor for this category is J.R. Wilkins; he is listed in the Directory under Texas.

Key:
mg — morning glory   rpd — reproducer
NP — nickel plated

Busy Bee Grand, disk, red mg horn 400.00
Busy Bee Grand, disk, 18½" red & gold horn 425.00
Columbia A, cylinder, oak, floating rpd, nickel horn 600.00
Columbia A, disk, NY decal 275.00
Columbia A, disk, Washington decal 345.00
Columbia AB, cylinder, 2 mandrels 1,250.00
Columbia AJ, disk, brass bell horn 950.00
Columbia AQ, cylinder, sm horn, key wound, complete 400.00
Columbia AT, cylinder, flowered horn, floor crane 600.00
Columbia AZ, cylinder, lyre rpd 425.00
Columbia B (Eagle), cylinder, orig aluminum horn 375.00
Columbia B (Eagle), floating rpd, brass bell horn, key wind 550.00
Columbia BC, cylinder, 4" Higham rpd, brass horn 1,100.00
Columbia BE (Leader), lyre rpd, lg horn, long mandrel 1,500.00
Columbia BE (Leader), serpentine, lyre rpd, brass bell horn 700.00
Columbia BF, cylinder, oak, 14" brass bell, 6" mandrel 525.00
Columbia BI (Sterling), disk, nickel horn 1,500.00
Columbia BJ (Imperial), disk, nickel mg horn, NM 525.00
Columbia BK, cylinder, 2 min, lg brass bell/crane 250.00
Columbia BQ (Rex), orig mg horn 975.00
Columbia HG (Home Grand), 5" cylinder, AT type cabinet 850.00
Columbia P (Premium), disk, 24" horn 300.00
Columbia Q, cylinder, key wind 350.00
Columbia Q, floating rpd, 12" NP horn, key wind 375.00
Columbia Q (Busy Bee), floating rpd, 10" blk cone horn 275.00
Columbia QQ, cylinder, 14" aluminum horn, key wind 275.00
Edison 'Suitcase' Standard, Model A, automatic rpd, 2-clip 800.00
Edison 'Suitcase' Standard, Model A, automatic rpd, 4-clip 700.00
Edison Amberola X, cylinder, oak, inside horn 400.00
Edison Amberola 30, cylinder, oak, Dmn C rpd, inside horn 350.00
Edison Amberola 50, cylinder, Dmn C rpd, inside horn 375.00
Edison Amberola 75, cylinder, mahog, Dmn C rpd, inside horn ...600.00

Edison Concert, Model D rpd, lg brass horn/stand, early 3,000.00
Edison Fireside, cylinder, Gem mg horn 450.00
Edison Fireside, cylinder, N rpd, metal cygnet horn 900.00
Edison Fireside, cylinder, 2/4 min, H rpd, fireside horn 750.00
Edison Fireside A, cylinder, Dmn B rpd, repro horn 400.00
Edison Gem, cylinder, C rpd, repro maroon horn, crank wind ...475.00
Edison Gem, cylinder, C rpd, 20" repro blk horn, crank wind 450.00
Edison Gem A, cylinder, orig rpd, sm blk horn, oil pan model ...675.00
Edison Gem B, cylinder, B rpd, key wind 500.00
Edison Home, cylinder, C rpd, brass mg horn 900.00
Edison Home, cylinder, H rpd, 30" flower horn 775.00
Edison Home, cylinder, ribbon decal, C rpd, 14" brass bell 650.00
Edison Home (suitcase), cylinder, automatic rpd, 14" bell horn .750.00
Edison Home A, cylinder, oak, C rpd, lg brass bell horn 600.00
Edison Maroon Gem D, cylinder, K rpd, maroon fireside horn ..1,500.00
Edison Opera, cylinder, oak, oak cygnet horn 4,500.00
Edison Standard, cylinder, C rpd, mg horn 600.00
Edison Standard, cylinder, H rpd, flowered mg horn 750.00
Edison Standard, Model D or E, cylinder/4-min, H rpd, mg horn .500.00
Edison Standard (Sq), cylinder, C rpd, no horn 300.00
Edison Standard A, cylinder, low case, C rpd, repro bell horn 450.00
Edison Standard C, cylinder, C rpd, 14" brass bell 450.00
Edison Standard E, cylinder, 4-min, H rpd, metal cygnet horn ...750.00
Edison Triumph, cylinder, 2/4-min, H rpd, #10 cygnet horn, VG ..875.00
Edison Triumph, cylnder, H rpd, no horn 850.00
Edison Triumph D, cylinder, 2/4-min, H rpd 725.00
Harmony, disk, oak, bl-trimmed horn 500.00
Little Wonder, disk, orig rpd, repro horn 600.00
Puck Lyre, cylinder, sm NP horn, key wind 320.00
Regina Hexaphone, Model 103, cylinder, wood horn, coin-op ..8,000.00
Standard, disk, open works, orig horn, ¾" center post 500.00
Standard A, disk, orig rpd, blk mg horn w/gold 600.00
Standard A, disk, red mg horn 700.00
Standard X, disk, blk mg horn w/gold trim 700.00
Standard X2, disk, front mt, orig rpd, blk horn 700.00
Victor E, disk, brass bell horn 1,150.00
Victor E, disk, pre-dog model, Concert rpd, brass bell horn 1,000.00
Victor E (Monarch Jr), disk, Exhibition rpd, brass bell horn ...1,200.00
Victor I, disk, brass bell horn 500.00
Victor II, disk, Exhibition rpd, oak horn 2,000.00
Victor II, disk, Exhibition rpd, 11½" brass bell horn 1,200.00
Victor III, disk, blk mg horn 1,400.00
Victor Junior, disk, oak, orig rpd, blk horn 17.00
Victor M (Monarch), disk, Exhibition rpd, 18½" brass bell 1,200.00
Victor MS (Monarch Special), disk, Exhibition rpd, bell horn ..2,000.00
Victor R (Royal), disk, Concert rpd, brass bell horn 1,200.00
Victor R (Royal), disk, Exhibition rpd, 9½" brass bell 900.00
Victor V, disk, Exhibition rpd, blk mg horn 1,750.00
Victor VI, disk, mahog w/gold, Exhibition rpd, mahog horn ...5,500.00
Victor VV-XIV, mahog, all orig 450.00
Victor VV-XIV, oak, all orig 550.00
Zonophone A, disk, beveled glass, Concert rpd, brass horn 1,500.00
Zonophone Grand Opera, disk, orig rpd, lg brass bell horn 2,000.00

Photographica

Photographic collectibles include not only the cameras and equipment used to 'freeze' special moments in time but also the photographic images produced by a great variety of processes that have evolved since the daguerrean era of the mid-1800s. For the most part, good quality images have either maintained or increased in value. Poor quality examples (regardless of rarity) are not selling well. Interest in cameras and stereo equipment is down, and dealers report that often average-

priced items that were moving well are often completely overlooked. Though rare items always have a market, collectors seem to be buying only if they are bargain priced.

Our advisor for this category is John Hess; he is listed in the Directory under Massachusetts.

Albumens

Abraham Lincoln portrait, JE McClees...Philadelphia, EX 300.00
Cavalry inspection scene, FT Riley KS, 1900, 9½x7½" 40.00
Cowboys branding steer, 1 on horse, cattle beyond, 6x9" 50.00
Evansville Wharf during 1884 flood, fr, 16x19", pr 100.00
Gen Grant's cottage, Mt McGregor NY, couple on porch, 9x12" .10.00
Golden Gate from San Fransisco Bay CA, Taber, 9x12" 22.50
Gunboat General Grant, Brady, matted/fr, 12x15" 300.00
Hay wagon in front of home, farmer/horses/women, 1860s, 7x9" ..10.00
Steamer Clinch w/Matthew Brady in foreground, fr, 14x17" 330.00
Steamer Jacob Strader, some fading, 12x14" 85.00
Steamship City of Owensboro, Jeffersonville IN, 15x18" 260.00
Waterfront view of Oswego harbor, Austen, 1869, 13¼x16¼" ...170.00
Workers on dry-docked snag boat, Boehl & Koenig, 8¾x12½" ..130.00
1-room schoolhouse w/36 students at desks, 6½x8½" 40.00

Ambrotypes

An ambrotype is a type of photograph produced by an early wet-plate process whereby a faint negative image on glass is seen as positive when held against a dark background.

Half plate, children seated on sled, EX 250.00
Half plate, Freemason w/vest & apron, EX 200.00
Whole plate, Old Harpswell, Maine Meeting House, exterior 450.00

6th plate, Chief Maungwudaus of Ojibway tribe of Pennsylvania, in full regalia, tinted, rare, EX, $2,900.00.

6th plate, girl w/puppy on nearby table, VG 130.00
6th plate, man sawing wood, w/case, EX 400.00
6th plate, mason wearing vestment w/tassels, VG in ½-case 17.00
6th plate, Zouave in red pantaloons w/musket, +case 165.00
9th plate, sleeping blk & wht pointer (dog), EX in full case 32.50
9th plate, 1700s gentleman, from primitive painting, +case 20.00
9th plate, 2 Civil War soldiers on horsebk, VG in case 145.00

Cabinet Photos

Banjo-playing family of 5 women, full views of 5 banjos 40.00
Bartlett Family Trick Shot Performers, 3 w/rifles 32.50
Blk mammy holding wht baby on her lap, ca 1888 ....32.50
Casements of Fort Monroe VA, Baulch, over-sz, VG 15.50
Chang-Yu Sing Chinese Giant, w/3 ladies in garden, Bogardus 30.00
Greely Arctic Expedition Seasons of 1881-84, oversz, VG 40.00
Jason & Owen Brown (sons of John) by cabin, Jarvis, oversz 40.00
Jolly Joe, circus fat man, Frank Wendt, VG 16.50

Laguna Indian Pueblo in NM, N Brown, oversz **50.00**
Libby Prison shortly after liberation, Cook, VG **30.00**
Man playing guitar, Curtis & Ross, Lewiston ME **12.50**
Military musician at Fort Wingate NM, flute on table **32.50**
Packet ships at wharf in Tacoma WA, Rutter, 1880s, oversz **26.00**
Postmortem, man w/eyes open, vignetted chest pose, flowers **18.50**
SA Shields & Wife, height 7'7", Weight 290-Lbs, Eisenmann **26.50**
Sitting Bull in buckskin 10-gal hat, chest view, lt image, rare **80.00**
Spanish Am War bugler w/bugle, tents beyond, oversz, EX **20.00**
Spanish Am War soldier w/Springfield rifle & bayonet **25.00**
Tejon St, Colorado Springs, exterior view, FA Nims, EX **35.00**
Trapeze artist w/bar in hand, wht leotards, Chickering **12.50**
US Marine Corp Sergeant, insignia on kepi, half-view **50.00**

Cameras

Among the earliest daguerrean cameras was the sliding box-on-a-box camera. It was focused by sliding one box in and out of the other, thus adjusting the distance of the lens to the ground glass. This was replaced on later models with leather bellows. These were the forerunners of the multilens cameras developed in the late 1870s, which were capable of recording many small portraits on a single plate. Double-lens cameras produced stereo images which, when viewed through a device called a stereoscope, achieved a 3-dimensional effect. In 1888 George Eastmann introduced his box camera, the first to utilize roll film. This greatly simplified the process, making it possible for the amateur to enjoy photography as a hobby. Detective cameras, those disguised as books, handbags, etc., are among the most sought after by today's collectors.

Ansco Buster Brown #2, MIB **50.00**
Blair Hawk-Eye Stereo, red leather bellows, ca 1904, EX **300.00**
Bosley B-2, USAF model, 35mm, AF legend on top, EX **115.00**
Dan 35 Model I, removable top, ca 1946-48, EX **75.00**
Eastman Kodak Premo, red bellows, brass lens, 1903, +case **85.00**
Gnome Pixie, metal box style, blk enamel, M **12.50**
Graflex Graphic 35 Electric, 35mm, ca 1959, EX **125.00**
Herbert George Imperial Debonair, Bakelite box style, EX **5.00**
Houghton Ensign Special Reflex, brass mts, 1930s, EX **465.00**
Keystone Wizard XF1000, holds Poloroid SX-70 film, 1978, M **16.50**
Kodak Brownie Cresta, blk plastic, box style, ca 1955, NM **15.00**
Kodak Girl Scout, 127 film, bright gr w/emblem, 1929-34 ....**120.00**
Konishiroku Konica F, 35mm SLR, ca 1960, NM **525.00**
Kuribayashi Petriflex, 1953, EX **165.00**
Leica R3 Electronic, 35mm, old style flash, VG, w/tripod **335.00**
Minolta Super A, 35mm, normal lens, 1957, NM **135.00**
Monroe Pocket Poco, folding, 1890s, 3x4" **225.00**

Pathe 35mm movie camera, rectangular, with shield of United Society of Cinematographers, early, 12", in case with two magazines, $1,350.00 at auction.

Pocket Magda, metal folding style, ca 1920, EX **200.00**
Polaroid Land Camera Speedliner #941, MIB **25.00**
Ricoh Singlex, 35mm, ca 1964-66, EX **110.00**
S Wing, 4-tube lens set, wet plate type, ca 1870, EX **1,750.00**
Samoca 35 Super, 35mm, 36 exposures, 1956, EX **42.00**

Sears Tower 37 by Mamiya, ca 1961, EX **65.00**
Thornton Special Ruby, wood w/brass trim, ca 1905, EX **235.00**
Voigtlander Vito II, 35mm, Compur shutter, EX **35.00**
Welta Radial, folding bed, 120 roll film, 1930s, EX **45.00**
Zeiss Ikon Bobette I, folding type, ca 1929, EX **130.00**
Zeiss Ikon Stereo Nettel, leather covered, 1927-30, VG **200.00**

Carte De Visites

Among the many types of images collectible today are carte de visites, known as CDVs, which are 2¼" x 4" portraits printed on paper and produced in quantity. The CDV fad of the 1800s enticed the famous and the unknown alike to pose for these cards, which were circulated among the public to the extent that they became known as 'publics.' When the popularity of CDVs began to wane, a new fascination developed for the cabinet photo, a larger version measuring about 4½" x 6½". Note: A common portrait CDV is worth only about 50¢ unless it carries a revenue stamp on the back; those that do are valued at about $1.00 each.

Abraham & Mary T Lincoln, oval portraits, gem sz **22.50**
Abraham & Tad Lincoln reading book, Berger copy, VG **15.00**
Abraham Lincoln on balcony of Wht House, HF Warren **125.00**
Abraham Lincoln w/left arm at bk, Brady, 1864, VG **400.00**
Blk Mammy w/wht boy, J&W Vincent Cincinnati, EX **40.00**
Boston Corbett of 5th NY Cavalry in oval, rare **195.00**
Brigadier Gen Geo A Custer, waist-up view, Anthony, 1864, EX ..**450.00**
Canton Girl, stands by chair w/umbrella, wearing coat **12.50**
Capital building in WA DC, trolley at side, MB Brady & Co **40.00**
Carlotta Williamson Infant Pianist Aged 5 Yrs, by piano, 1870s ..**16.00**
Chang the Chinese Giant, 9' tall, 360-lbs **30.00**
Charles Dickens in meditating pose, from engraving **10.00**
Che-Mah the Chinese Dwarf beside normal-sz man, Eisenmann ..**25.00**
Child riding wooden rocking horse, VG **16.50**
Chinese merchant in silk robe, seated w/scrolls on lap, G **10.00**
Circus Albino Towie & parrot Iboina, Bogardus, NY, VG **15.00**
Civil War dbl amputee in civilian attire, EX **30.00**
Civil War Naval captain seated by friend, sleeve insignia **22.50**
Eli Bowen (legless acrobat) w/wife & child, EX **30.00**
Eng & Chang, Orig Siamese Twins; w/2 sons, EX **30.00**
Falls of St Croix, Whitney's Gallery, MN **35.00**
Federal Lieutenant in frock coat, Brady, VG **22.50**
Girl holding china-head doll in her lap, EX detail **10.00**
Jesse James' death portrait, advertising on bk, EX **3,500.00**
John Wilkes Booth, arm on hip, cane in hand, VG **40.00**
Landon Middlecoff (giant) beside normal-sz man, Eisenmann **25.00**
Lincoln Park Portland ME, people on benches, AM McKenney ..**20.00**
Maori chief in feathered robe smoking pipe, VG **40.00**
Mary Todd Lincoln, age 42, ca 1850, EX **55.00**
Miss Zoe Zolenda, circus performer in fancy dress, Eisenmann **12.50**
Mrs Morgan (Maori Indian) in ethnic robe **20.00**
Napoleon Sarony in Turkish dress, c 1866, trimmed, EX **150.00**
Postmortem, baby in bassinet, hands clasped, EX **22.50**
PT Barnum, chest-up view, looking to right **20.00**
Soochow girl in robe by table w/flowers & Oriental pipe **12.50**
Union soldier w/Remington revolver, GM Green of IL, 1870s, VG ..**40.00**
Union 1st Sergeant, 9-button coatee, M1851 eagle buckle **32.50**
Waino & Plutano Wild Men of Borneo, midgets portrait **32.50**
Yuma girl in blanket w/infant in cradle wrap, EX **100.00**
Yuma man, full figure, wrapped in blanket, EX **60.00**
2 men standing by wooden 'bone-shaker' bicycle, ca 1850s, EX **36.00**

Daguerreotypes

Among the many processes used to produce photographic images are the daguerreotypes (made on a plate of chemically treated metal) — the most-valued examples being the 'whole' plate which measures 6½" x 8½". Other sizes include the 'half' plate, measuring 4½" x 5½", the 'quarter' plate at 3¼" x 4¼", the 'sixth' plate at 2¾" x 3¼", the 'ninth' at 2" x 2½", and the 'sixteenth' at 1⅜" x 1⅝". (Sizes may vary slightly, and some may have been altered by the photographer.)

Half plate, bull w/outbuilding beyond, w/leather case 3,500.00
Half plate, family of 6, ca 1850s, matted, w/case 250.00
Half plate, Mexican War officer seated w/sword, cased, EX 2,200.00
Half plate, postmortem, parents & children w/dead baby 575.00
4th plate, cigar salesman w/box at table, w/case 2,500.00
4th plate, man in winter coat & tall blk hat on sofa, +case 85.00
4th plate, Odd Fellow in gilt vest & apron, w/case, EX 450.00
4th plate, parents w/baby & toy dog, in full case, EX 110.00
6th plate, child's postmortem, hand-colored, cased, EX 380.00
6th plate, child w/dog on chair at side, w/case, EX 450.00
6th plate, child w/Staffordshire dog, cased, EX 100.00
6th plate, cross-eyed man seated, half-view, +case 40.00
6th plate, Eastern Indian in ornate headdress, EX 2,500.00
6th plate, fireman in uniform, tinted, cased, EX 400.00
6th plate, Genessee River Bank, street view, cased, EX 950.00
6th plate, girl in bonnet, tinted dress, lace gloves, +case 25.00
6th plate, identical twin sisters, metal mat, +case 60.00
6th plate, lady in blk satin, Marsters Balto, +case 50.00
6th plate, lady in blk satin w/lg cameo under collar, +case 20.00
6th plate, married couple, blk suit, print dress, +case 16.50
6th plate, old lady in bonnet, holds pipe & book, EX 200.00
6th plate, rattlesnake w/rattle clearly seen, VG 1,300.00
6th plate, seated couple, identified missionaries, 1840s, EX 90.00
6th plate, sm girl on sofa looking grumpy, +½ case 22.50
6th plate, sulky & driver, cased, EX 300.00
6th plate, teacher w/pointer, man in blk w/lg tie, EX 65.00
6th plate, 2 ladies seated & holding hands, +case 20.00
9th plate, fireman in uniform, w/leather case, VG 550.00
9th plate, head view of lady w/long curls, vignetted, Boston 22.50
9th plate, lady in plaid dress w/lace collar, +case 18.50
9th plate, lady seated, satin shawl, beaded purse, +case 18.50
9th plate, man w/lg blk cravat, Eastman on mat, +case 20.00

Photos

Ozobrome, Rainy Day, Dr R Lovejoy, ca 1905, 7x9" 360.00
Photogravure, Every Wind, Ojibway lady's portrait 200.00
Silverprint, A Lincoln portrait, GB Ayres, ca 1888, 8¾x7", VG ..380.00
Silverprint, Babe Ruth, B Heller, 1930s, 8x9" 440.00
Silverprint, baseball team w/equipment, 1890s, 6½x9", EX 70.00
Silverprint, Chief Low Dog in battle dress, DF Barry, EX 220.00
Silverprint, child worker, pre-teen, 1910s, LW Hine, 5x7" 880.00
Silverprint, Prisoners in Potter's field, Riis, 1880s, 10x9" 800.00

Stereoscopic Views

Stereo cards are photos made to be viewed through a device called a stereoscope. The glass stereo plates of the mid-1800s and photo prints produced in the darkroom are among the most valuable. In evaluating stereo views, the subject, date, and condition are all-important. Some views were printed over a thirty- to forty-year period; 'first generation' prices are far higher than later copies. Right now, quality stereo views are at a premium.

American Falls, Anthony, 1859, EX 25.00
Black Hills Gold Region, WY Territory, 4 for 300.00
Cincinnati wharf, set of 8 ....280.00

Gen Custer at His Headquarters, Brady, JC Taylor pub, 1865 ....920.00
Lincoln & McClellan in conference, orange mt, Anthony, 1862 ..925.00
Louisiana Purchase Expo, 1904, 6 for 32.00
Major General Fitzhugh Lee, Havana, 1898 ....20.00
PA landscape, TH Johnson, ivory mt, 6 for 80.00
Southern views, JA Palmer, set of 18, EX 400.00
Union Meeting, Anthony #909, 1861, EX 17.50
War Chief of the Zuni Indians, O'Sullivan 60.00
WWI troups, prisoners, landscapes, Keystone, 20 for 50.00
Zuni Indian Girl w/water olla, O'Sullivan 60.00

Tintypes

Tintypes, contemporaries of ambrotypes, were produced on japanned iron and were not as easily damaged.

Half plate, Blk man & 10 wht men on overhead walkway, VG 16.50
Half plate, farmer w/horse team & logging cart, EX 65.00

Whole plate, family group including man with camera, early sewing machine and fancy Victorian table, EX, $125.00.

Whole plate, outdoor scene of business building, 8½x6½" 150.00
Whole plate, 3 men w/beer glasses & bottle, 8x6", EX 110.00
4th plate, girl w/doll beside grandmother, VG 9.50
6th plate, Blk child w/wht baby in lg dress, VG 110.00
6th plate, Blk lady w/feather in hat, ca 1860s 16.00
6th plate, Civil War Sergeant w/M1850 staff & sword, +case 140.00
6th plate, GAR drum major w/baton, medal on chest, rare 60.00
6th plate, Indian Wars soldier w/bayonetted Springfield rifle 95.00
6th plate, lady by stereo viewer & cards 16.50
6th plate, man in frock coat w/cornet/M1840 sword, EX, +case .400.00
6th plate, man on 'bone-shaker' bicycle, plants on floor 70.00
6th plate, Scotsman in full costume of kilt, tam & purse 15.00
6th plate, Spanish Am soldier w/Springfield rifle & bedroll 95.00
6th plate, Spanish Am war soldier in greatcoat, campaign hat 35.00
6th plate, Zouave in dress uniform w/rifle & bayonet, early 250.00
6th plate, 1800s bicyclist w/bike, tool kit strapped to fr 12.50
6th plate, 1870s militiaman, M-1872 shako 35.00
6th plate, 2 baseball players, 1880s, cased, VG 150.00
6th plate, 5 nurses & 4 women wearing sailor dresses 16.00
9th plate, gold miners w/equipment in landscape, +full case 75.00
9th plate, Union infantryman w/bayonetted musket, +case 130.00

Union Cases

From the mid-1850s until about 1880, cases designed to house these early images were produced from a material known as thermoplastic, a man-made material with an appearance much like gutta percha. Its innovator was Samuel Peck, who used shellac and wood fibers to create a composition he called Union. Peck was part owner of the Scoville Company, makers of both papier-mache and molded leather cases, and he used the company's existing dies to create his new line. Other companies, among them A.P. Critchlow & Company; Littlefield, Parsons & Company; and Holmes, Booth, & Hayden soon duplicated his material and produced their own designs. Today's collectors may refer to cases made of this material as 'thermoplastic,' 'composition,' or 'hard cases,' but the term most often used is 'Union.' It is incorrect to refer to them as gutta-percha cases.

Sizes may vary somewhat, but generally a 'whole' plate case measures 7" x 9⅛" to the outside edges, a 'half' plate 4⅞" x 6", a 'quarter' plate 3¾" x 4¾", a 'sixth' 3⅛" x 3⅝", a 'ninth' 2⅜" x 2⅞", and a 'sixteenth' 1¾" x 2". Clifford and Michele Krainik and Carl Walvoord have written a book, *Union Cases*, which we recommend for further information.

Chess players, Littlefield Parsons & Co, 6th plate	125.00
Deer & cherub, 4th plate, w/flaked prints	110.00
Fruit/floral cluster, oval, 9th plate, EX	40.00
Hanging pot of flowers, 4th plate, +tintype of lady	105.00
Lady on horse w/boy & dog, 4th plate	85.00
Medallion w/waffle center, octagonal, 6th plate	60.00
Strawberries, 9th plate, +ambro portraits, EX	50.00
Washington profile, First in Peace, 6th plate	330.00
4 figures & horse, 4th plate	95.00
4-lobe device centers oval w/in star-filled sq, 9th plate	40.00

Miscellaneous

Album, celluloid, lg slip cover	135.00
Album, leather w/brass latch, rvpt glass insert, 6x7½"	45.00
Ferrotype, Geo B McClellan in uniform, brass fr, 1x¾", EX	150.00
Graphoscope, walnut veneer on hardwood base, 1870s, EX	200.00
Stanhope, celluloid umbrella hdl, unscrews, 4"	165.00
Stanhope, charm, church form, Lord's Prayer	45.00
Stanhope, cross, 5 rhinestones, Lord's Prayer, MIB	45.00
Stanhope, manicure set, 3 implements, 6 Niagara Falls views	45.00
Stanhope, needle case, cvd ivory umbrella form, French views	150.00
Stanhope charm, bbl shape, wht plastic, 7 Niagara Falls views	22.00

Piano Babies

A familiar sight in Victorian parlors, piano babies languished atop shawl-covered pianos in a variety of poses: crawling, sitting, on their tummies or on their backs playing with their toes. Some babies were nude, and some wore gowns. Sizes ranged from about 3" up to 12". The most famous manufacturer of these bisque darlings was the Heubach Brothers of Germany, who nearly always marked their product; see Heubach for listings. Watch for reproductions.

Baby w/animal, pot, flowers, on chair, etc, 12", ea, minimum	625.00
Baby w/animal, pot, flowers, on chair, etc, 4", ea	225.00
Black, fine quality, 4"	325.00
Black, med quality, 16"	550.00
Black, med quality, 4"	165.00
Black, 12"	625.00
Med quality, may be unpnt on bk side, 12"	350.00
Med quality, may be unpnt on bk side, 16"	495.00
Med quality, may be unpnt on bk side, 4"	125.00
Protruding ears, open/closed mouth, Germany, 6x9½"	595.00

Picasso Art Pottery

Pablo Picasso created some distinctive pottery during the 1940s, marking the ware with his signature.

Bowl, bird, blk/gr on wht, 6½", NM	400.00
Bowl, Face, blk/gr/red on wht, 1955, 5¼"	1,200.00
Charger, Sun, blk/yel/gr, 16½"	1,150.00
Pitcher, sun-like face/bands/dots, blk on terra cotta, 10"	2,300.00
Pitcher, woman's face, blk/brn on wht, 11½"	2,300.00
Vase, stylized pnt owl, blk/purple on wht, 10x4", NM	700.00

Pickard

Founded in 1893 in Edgerton, Illinois, the Pickard China Company was originally a decorating studio, importing china blanks from European manufacturers. Some of these early pieces bear the name of those companies as well as Pickard's. Trained artists decorated the wares with hand-painted studies of fruit, florals, birds, and scenics and often signed their work. In 1915 Pickard introduced a line of 23k gold over a dainty floral-etched ground design. In the 1930s they began to experiment with the idea of making their own ware and by 1938 had succeeded in developing a formula for fine translucent china. Since 1976 they have issued an annual limited edition Christmas plate. They are now located in Antioch, Illinois.

The company has used various marks. The earliest (1893-1894) was a double-circle mark, 'Edgerton Hand Painted' with 'Pickard' in the center. Variations of the double-circle mark (with 'Hand Painted China' replacing the Edgerton designation) were employed until 1915, each differing enough that collectors can usually pinpoint the date of manufacture within five years. Later marks included the crown mark, 'Pickard' on a gold maple leaf, and the current mark, the lion and shield. Work signed by Challinor, Marker, and Yeschek is especially valued by today's collectors. Our advisor for this category is Milt Steinfeld; he is listed in the Directory under New Jersey.

Tankard pitcher, Falstaff with jug of ale, signed P. Gasper, gilt rim and handle, 15", $1,400.00.

Bowl, grapes/gilt w/in & w/out, sgn Coufall, claw ft, 14"	800.00
Bowl, Tree of Life, Samuelson, hdls, 1919 mk, 8½"	115.00
Cake plate, HP trumpet flowers w/gold, Limoges blank, 11"	175.00
Candy dish, sunflowers w/gold, Nessy, 1910-12 mk, 8¾"	165.00
Charger, red poppies w/gold, 1910 mk, 12½"	225.00
Creamer & sugar bowl, encrusted gold, maple leaf mk, lg	65.00
Creamer & sugar bowl, lilies w/cobalt & gold, sgn Richter	150.00
Pitcher, cherries on gr, gold neck band/hdl, Lind, 5¾"	395.00
Pitcher, pine cones w/gold on rust, sgn Renir, 8"	695.00
Pitcher, water lily, gr & gold, 5"	395.00
Plate, acorns on branch, gold rim, Wright, 1905-10, 7⅝"	75.00
Plate, blackberries, artist sgn, 1910 mk, 8¾"	125.00
Plate, Dutch girls, windmills & tulips, Rawlins, 8½"	195.00
Plate, floral, octagonal, 1912-19 mk, 10½"	125.00
Plate, floral, sgn Keates, 1910 mk, 6½"	60.00
Plate, floral, trees & water, sgn F James, 1912-19 mk, 8¾"	200.00

Plate, fruit, sgn Reau, 9" **115.00**
Plate, mc berries & blooms, gold rim, sgn, 1898-1904 mk, 8⅝" ..**155.00**
Plate, mc lilies, gold rim, sgn Wright, 1905-10 mk, 8¼" **92.50**
Plate, mixed flowers w/gold, sgn F James, 1910-12 mk, 8¾" **100.00**
Plate, pk carnations, 1905 mk, 8½" **135.00**
Plate, poinsettias, sgn J Nessy, maple leaf mk, 8¾" **145.00**
Plate, temple & moon over water, sgn, matt, 1912-19 mk, 8¼" ..**200.00**
Plate, Yosemite, sgn Marker, 8½" **295.00**
Sugar bowl, roses, sgn Wagner **85.00**
Sugar bowl, stylized Deco design, sgn Efdon **65.00**
Vase, Chinese peacock, gold hdls, sgn Marker, 9½" **225.00**
Vase, mc mums w/scrolls & dots, LeRoy, 1898-1904, 5¼" **400.00**

Pickle Castors

Pickle castors, which were both functional and decorative, became popular after the Civil War, reaching their peak about 1885. By 1900 they had virtually disappeared from factory catalogs. Numerous styles were available. They consisted of a decorated, silverplated frame that held either a fancy clear pressed-glass insert or one of decorated colored art glass — the latter being popular in the more affluent Victorian households and more desirable with collectors today.

In the listings below, the description prior to the semicolon refers to the jar (insert), and the remainder of the line describes the frame. When no condition is indicated, the silverplate is assumed to be in very good to excellent condition; glass jars are assumed near-mint.

Key:
rsl — resilvered   3-D — three-dimensional

Amberina, melon shape; ornate SP fr, +tongs **495.00**
Bl satin w/enameling, egg shape; Tufts rsl fr **550.00**
Bluerina, HP floral, 2" mini; ped SP base & bail, +mini tongs **250.00**
Broken Column, ruby stain; EX SP fr **350.00**
Cane & Rosette; rsl fr **175.00**
Cased spatter; EX SP fr **395.00**
Clear pressed castle on sculptured glass base, SP bail/lid **350.00**
Cobalt w/florals & gold; rsl Benedict fr, 10½" **450.00**
Cone, pigeon blood; ornate SP fr, +tongs **550.00**
Cranberry, Invt T'print w/HP florals; Meriden fr, +tongs **425.00**
Cranberry; ornate ftd SH&M SP fr, mini, 5½", +tongs **395.00**
Cupid & Venus; EX SP fr **285.00**
Cut velvet, butterscotch; orig SP fr **425.00**
Daisy & Button, amber; rsl fr **275.00**
Daisy & Button, cranberry opal; orig worn SP fr **110.00**
Dmn, sapphire bl; Meriden ftd fr w/side loops, +tongs **295.00**
Dmn Point, honey amber; Forbes SP fr, +tongs **210.00**
Fine Cut, vaseline; EX SP fr **295.00**
Frosted pumpkin jar w/bird finial; Wilcox #0675 fr w/pickles **450.00**
Herringbone, frosted wht to pk; Rogers sq ruffled fr, +tongs **650.00**
Hobnail, bl opal; Meriden twig-ftd fr w/etched birds, +tongs **365.00**
Hobnail, cranberry; SH&M fr w/3-D cherries, +tongs, 12½" **550.00**
Invt Rubena HP floral; ftd Wilcox fr w/girl jumping rope **550.00**
Invt T'print, cranberry, florals; rsl Toronto fr **495.00**
Invt T'print, cranberry w/coralene beading; ornate fr **675.00**
Invt T'print, cranberry w/gold; Barbour SP fr, +tongs **495.00**
Invt T'print, cranberry; SP Loop fr w/tube top ornament **350.00**
Invt T'print, gr w/HP floral; 13" Meriden fr, bail w/flowers **650.00**
Invt T'print, orange w/HP floral; Meriden fr w/leaves, side bail .**650.00**
Invt T'print, rubena w/HP floral; Pairpoint fr, butterfly lid **550.00**
Invt T'print, sapphire bl w/mc florals; orig SP fr, +tongs **550.00**
Open Heart & Arches, pigeon blood; EX SP fr **395.00**
Optic, bl w/floral, corset shape; Wilcox SP fr w/insects **525.00**

Optic Rib, cranberry w/daisies; SP fr **350.00**

Paneled Diamond Point, vaseline; ornate Pairpoint silverplated frame (worn), 12¼", $125.00.

Peachblow w/floral; birds on base of fr, ornate finial, 9" **425.00**
Pk opal w/florals; rsl SP fr & tongs **450.00**
Polka Dot, cobalt; EX SP fr **425.00**
Pressed w/etched leaves; new SP fr **275.00**
Ribbed Pillar, frosted pk spatter, Northwood; orig SP fr **450.00**
Rose Dmn Quilt MOP, wht int; ornate Reed & Barton SP fr **450.00**
Royal Oak, rubena, Northwood; rstr sgn fr w/fretwork, +tongs ...**425.00**
Rubena w/daisies; ornate 2-hdl fr, w/fork **295.00**
Swirled Windows, bl opal; orig rsl fr, +tongs **345.00**
Van Dyke, amber; ftd Wilcox fr, fancy bail, +fork **325.00**
Zipper Slash, amber, etched decor; rsl fr **350.00**

Pie Birds

A Pie Bird (also known as a pie vent or pie funnel) is placed in the middle of a pie to serve the dual purpose of supporting the pastry (to prevent sogginess) and acting as a vent that allows the steam to escape, thus avoiding runover. They are open-bottomed, hollow, and glazed inside and out. They are designed with a top vent, and most have two arches around the base. The steam enters the pie bird via the arches and exits through the top vent. In Victorian times pie funnels were first used in deep-dish meat pies. Bird-shaped vents were made as early as 1910 in England and from 1930 until the '60s in America. Later, figural pie vents were made in England. In the past two years, over 100 new U.S.-made pie vents have flooded the collectibles market. Incense burners, one-hole pepper shakers, and a dated brass toy bird whistle that you may encounter should not be mistaken for pie vents.

Our advisors for this category are Alan Pedel (representing the English market; see England in the Directory) and Lillian Cole (listed under New Jersey).

Angel w/hands together in front, wht, England, 4" **50.00**
Bird, cobalt, stoneware, NH pottery, new, 4¼" **10.00**
Bird, yel w/blk & brn details, England, 4" **48.00**
Bl salt glazed, mk Rowe Pottery **12.00**
Blackbird on wht base, mk Royal Worcester **45.00**
Blackbird w/brn base & beak **16.50**
Blk boy in bl overalls w/banjo, England, 4" **57.50**
Blk chef, yel/red/wht attire, brn spoon, Taiwan, 4½" **10.00**
Blk lady, in red/wht, yel-dot turban, brn spoon, Taiwan, 4½" **10.00**
Bobby w/nightstick, plump, ceramic **50.00**
Chef holding pie, ceramic **50.00**
Chick, yel w/pk, Josef Originals **18.00**
Dragon, copper lustre or gray mottled, bl eyes, Welsh, 4¼", ea **80.00**
Funnel, wht, mk Synab Vit-Porcelain, Australian **45.00**
Pelican on stump, yel bill & ft, England **52.50**

Pig chef, pk w/polka-dot kerchief, high hat, England, 4¼" 50.00
Rooster, Bl Willow 20.00
Rooster, Cleminson, mc, mk w/pottery bkstamp or incised Cb 18.00
Songbird, bl & gray w/blk wings 22.50

Pierce, Howard

Howard Pierce, having begun his studio pottery in 1941 in Claremont, California, was a talented artist who found a special niche in creating porcelain wildlife pieces. His formal training encompassed three years, one each at the Chicago Art Institute, California's Pomona College and the University of Illinois. Howard, along with his wife, Ellen Van Voorhis, produced a large number of varied pieces over a half century.

While wildlife held a special interest for Mr. Pierce, his initial products were vases, wall pockets, bowls, jewelry and other art and dinner wares. Throughout his career, he took special interest in a variety of materials: polyurethane, which he discovered caused an allergic reaction for him, ultimately forcing him to discontinue its use; bisque in a Jasperware style, mostly in mint or pink glazes; porcelain bisques which he used to model animals and plants that were positioned in or near open areas of his high-gloss vases and candle holders; a lava treatment that he best describes as, '...bubbling up from the bottom'; gold leaf which is scarce today but should not be confused with 'Sears gold'; a rough-textured Mt. St. Helens glaze which he obtained by using some of the ash from the volcano when it erupted; and cement. By the time Mr. and Mrs. Pierce had moved to Joshua Tree, California, he was concentrating almost all his talents on animals and wildlife. He experimented with glazes, recording the glaze numbers in a book and, on occasion, incising that number into the bottom of a creation. His earliest mark is the 'Claremont, CA,' underglaze mark which most often included a stock number. Next he used a rubber stamp-type mark that read 'Howard Pierce Porcelain.' Later the word 'Porcelain' was dropped. Not all of his pieces are marked, especially the smaller two pieces in a three-piece set or the smaller item in a two-piece set. Near the end of 1992, due to failing health, Howard and Ellen Pierce destroyed all the molds they had ever created. When his health improved, Mr. Pierce began working a few hours a week making smaller pieces of his past work. He also was able to create a few new molds, but again, they were smaller in size. The small pieces carry 'Pierce' in a stamp-like mark. Howard Pierce passed away in February, 1994. Our advisor for this category is Susan N. Cox; she is listed in the Directory under California.

Bowl, bl & blk, fluted, 9" 98.00
Figurine, boy & girl hold hands on base, Blk faces, 4" 65.00
Figurine, dolphin on base, experimental gr, 10" L 185.00
Figurine, ermine, seated upright, wht w/brn, ca 1950s, 9" 155.00
Figurine, heron on base, experimental bl, 9½" 145.00
Figurine, heron on base, gray, 9½" 105.00
Figurine, horse, brn w/tan & mottled tail, 9" 155.00
Figurine, monkey, brn body, wht head, sgn, 3" 125.00
Figurine, monkeys (3), totem-pole type, blk, 15" 78.00
Figurine, pheasant pr in tree, brn w/wht, 10¾" 165.00
Figurine, porcupine, rough-textured blk w/wht, 4" 95.00
Figurine, quail pr in tree, brn w/wht, 10¾" 150.00
Figurine, roadrunner, wire legs, tail up, polyurethane 185.00
Pencil holder, nude obese women, brn, 4¼" 40.00
Pin, lapel; bird, pewter, 2" 50.00
Planter, duck w/open bk, Sears gold 50.00
Vase, bud; brn, stamp mk, 3½" 30.00
Vase, bud; experimental bl w/blk 62.00
Wall hanging set, birds in flight, varied szs, set of 5 ....335.00
Wall pocket, Jasperware pk & tan w/5 wht deer, 8" L 160.00

Pigeon Blood

Pigeon blood glass, produced in the late 1800s, may be distinguished from other dark red glass by its distinctive orange tint.

Biscuit jar, Torquay 475.00
Bowl, Invt T'print, 2⅝x4½" 175.00
Bowl, Torquay, SP rim, 9" 195.00
Cookie jar, Florette, SP hdl, rim & lid 200.00
Lamp, Invt T'print ball shade w/gold, hanging, mini, 6" 550.00
Pitcher, appl clear hdl, 7" 200.00
Rosebowl, HP floral w/gilt, 5" dia...70.00
Shakers, Bulging Loop, pr 185.00
Sugar shaker, hairpin-like emb, tin top, 5½", EX 250.00
Syrup, Torquay 275.00
Wine, 6" 40.00

Pigeon Forge

Douglas J. Ferguson and Ernest Wilson started their small pottery in Pigeon Forge, Tennessee, in 1946. Using red-brown and gray locally dug clay and glazes which they themselves formulate, bowls, vases, and sculptures are produced there. Their primary target is the tourist trade.

Bowl, teal & brn, D Ferguson, 10" 45.00
Figurine, blk bear, sitting or walking, 4", ea 22.50
Figurine, speckled owl, 1½" 26.50
Tile, wild plants, yel on turq mottle, Ferguson, 6" sq 125.00

Pilkington

Founded in 1892 in Manchester, England, the Pilkington pottery experimented in wonderful lustre glazes that were so successful that when they were diplayed at exhibition in 1904, they were met with critical acclaim. They soon attracted some of the best ceramic technicians and designers of the day who decorated the lustre ground with flowers, animals, and trees; some pieces were more elaborate with scenes of sailing ships and knights on horseback. Each artist signed his work with his personal monogram. Most pieces were dated and carried the company mark as well. After 1913 the company became known as Royal Lancastrian.

Their Lapis Ware line was introduced in the late 1920s, featuring intermingling tones of color under a matt glaze. Some pieces were very simply decorated while others were painted with designs of stylized leafage, scrolls, swirls, and stripes. The line continued into the thirties. Other pieces of this period were molded and carved with animals, leaves, etc., some of which were reminescent of their earlier wares.

The company closed in 1938 but reopened in 1948. During this period their mark was a simple P within the outline of a petaled flower shape. Our advisor for this category is David Erhard; he is listed in the Directory under California.

Bowl, $275.00; Vase, $425.00; Candle holder, $95.00.

Figurine, bear, Richard Joyce, 3½" 300.00
Vase, Deco design, gr & bls, matt, 6½x6½" 350.00
Vase, fish/seaweed, gold on bl, Richard Joyce, 6½x5½" 2,000.00
Vase, Lapis, Richard Joyce, dbl gourd shape, bold design 450.00
Vase, matt gr, rnded shoulder, flared neck, emb decor 300.00
Vase, matt orange, 10" 275.00
Vase, matt orange, 6" 150.00

Pillin

Polia Pillin was born in Poland in 1909; many of her family were artisians and craftsmen. Except for a few weeks of formal instruction at the Hull House in Chicago, Pillin is self-taught in the arts. Her work has been shown in many exhibits, and she has received awards from the Los Angeles County Art Institute, Syracuse Museum, Los Angeles County Fair, and the California State Fair. First interested in oils and watercolors, she has carried the same Byzantine quality over to her pottery. All of her work is signed 'Pillin' or 'W&P Pillin,' both with the loop of the P extended in an arc over the remaining letters of her name.

Bowl, ladies' portraits, brn/blk, bulbous, 4x7" 450.00
Bowl, lady & tree, 3¾x5" 350.00
Bowl, punch; mc yel, rare, 16" 1,750.00
Cordial set, horses decor, 7-pc 1,200.00
Jug, blistered yel/brn gloss, sgn, 7¾x5" 275.00
Vase, abstract figure on all 4 sides, 11½x3¾" 975.00
Vase, horse & 2 ladies, wht on peacock & rust, 9x7" 850.00
Vase, horses, 7" 395.00
Vase, horses (2), 2" 150.00
Vase, lady w/birds, ball form, 6" 425.00
Vase, lady w/flower & bird, 6" 425.00
Vase, lt to dk gr, glossy, bulbous w/sm opening, 6½" 200.00
Vase, scarlet flambe gloss, spherical w/short neck, 9½x7" 425.00

Pin-Back Buttons

Buttons produced up to the early 1920s were made of a celluloid covering held in place by a ring (or collet) to the back of which a pin was secured. Manufacturers used these 'cellos' to advertise their products. Mnay were of exceptional quality in both color and design. Buttons in sets were produced that featured a variety of subjects. These were given away by tobacco, chewing gum and candy manufacturers, who often packed them with their product as premiums. Usually the name of the button maker or the product manufacturer was printed on a paper placed in the back of the button. Often these 'back papers' are still in place today. Much of the time the button maker's name was printed on the button's perimeter, and sometimes the copyright was added. Beginning in the 1920s, a large number of buttons were lithographed on tin; these are referred to as tin 'lithos.' Nearly all pin-back buttons are collected today for their advertising appeal or graphic design. There are countless categories to base a collection on.

The following listing contains non-political buttons representative of the many varieties you may find. All are celluloid unless described otherwise. Values reflect buttons in excellent, well-centered condition, with bright color and only the very slightest of wear, if any.

Aunt Jemima (smiling), I'se in Town Honey!, mc on wht, ⅞" ...125.00
Babe Ruth, baseball, Club Member, blk on wht, ⅞" 50.00
Best Buick Yet, tin litho, red/wht on bl, 1½" 30.00
Big Brother & the Holding Co, blk/red on orange, 1½" 12.00

Black Cat Stove & Shoe Polish, cat, red/yel/blk/wht, 1¼" 25.00
C-Er-Lay Poultry Feed, chicken, blk/yel/wht/red, 1¼" 15.00
California Raisin (running), 1987 Calrab, mc on wht, 1½" 10.00
Campbell Kid, I'm a, kid chef, mc w/bl rim, ⅞" 50.00
Campbell Kid, I'm a, kid cowboy, mc w/red rim, ⅞" 50.00
Campbell Kid, I'm a, kid milkmaid, mc w/yrl rim, ⅞" 50.00
Capt Chas A Lindbergh, Our Hero, blk/wht, 1¼" 25.00
Cupid Brand Pickles & Preserves, Cupid, mc on dk bl, ⅞" 25.00
Ducks Unlimited, sgn Maass, mc on wht, 1974, 2¼" 25.00
Duffy's Pure Malt Whiskey, chemist at work, mc, 1¾" 40.00
Elks Mardi Gras, $10 Reward, clown, mc on wht, 1¼" 22.50
Fischer's Pan-Tan Bread, egg & cream, red/wht/bl, 1" 12.00
Gen MacArthur w/in patriotic V, tin litho, red/wht/bl, 1¼" 15.00
Girl Scout (picture), mc on yel, ⅞" 15.00
Gluek's Beer, trademark, bl on wht, 1" 25.00
Green-Marshall Paints, cop, gr/blk/wht, 1¼" 18.00
Hagerstown Brewing Co, brewery scene, mc, ⅞" 70.00
Hart-Parr Oil Tractors, tractor, yel/red/blk/wht, 1¼" 200.00
Jockey Sweaters, jockey on horse, red/lime, 1" horizontal oval 15.00
Leader Thrashing Machinery, lion, mc w/red & gold rim, 1" 75.00
McCormick OK Line, world globe, bl/red/gr, ⅞" 30.00
Michael Jordan, It'll Be Sweet 2 Repeat, mc, 3" 15.00
National Cycle, eagle atop shield, spoked wheel, mc, 1½" 35.00
New Idea Manure Spreader, farm scene, mc, 1" 75.00
New York Central Lines, wht/blk, 1" horizontal oval 15.00
Old Trusty Incubator, dog, mc, 1½" 80.00
Pat Paulsen for President, tin litho, blk/red/wht/bl, 2¼" 12.50
Patton's Sun-Proof Paints, sunflower, yel/brn/wht, ⅞" 10.00
Peters Referee Shells, gun shell & P, mc w/red rim, ⅞" 50.00
Popeye, Penney's Back to School, red/blk/wht, 1935, ⅞" 30.00
Pyro-Action Spark Plugs, crusader, mc, ⅞" 30.00
Reddy Kilowatt, The Mighty Atom, red/wht on dk bl, ⅞" 25.00
Santa, flying biplane, w/store advertising, mc, 1¼" 150.00
Santa, holly around hat, w/store advertising, mc on dk bl, 1¼" 80.00

Shmoo, white on dark green, late 1940s, 2⅛", $40.00.

St Charles Evaporated Milk, unsweetened on cow, mc, 1¼" 30.00
The Boston Herald, newsboy running, mc, 1¼" 85.00
The Lambert, Shore & Beach, auto, blk/red on wht, 1" 50.00
Weilands Pork Products, Willie pig, yel/dk bl on wht, 1¼" 25.00
Yellow Label Club, syrup can on table, yel/wht/dk bl, 1" 15.00

Pink Lustre Ware

Pink lustre was produced by nearly every potter in the Staffordshire district in the late 18th and first half of the 19th centuries. The application of gold lustre on white or light-colored backgrounds produced pinks, while the same over dark colors developed copper. The wares ranged from hand-painted plaques to transfer-printed dinnerware. Design features in the phrase immediately following the item (i.e. cup, plate, etc.) are in pink lustre unless otherwise specifically described within the line.

Cup & saucer, bird on floral branch/rim band, mc decor 110.00
Cup & saucer, foliage/band, yel/red sunbursts etc, mk Wood 110.00
Cup & saucer, handleless; schoolhouse, EX 42.00
Cup & saucer, house pattern, rosette mk, VG 35.00
Mug, child's; name & birth date, 1850s, 3¼" 100.00
Pitcher, grapevine border, horses & cows, 1830, 5½" 200.00
Pitcher, house, W View of Iron Bridge/Farmers Arms, 8" 325.00
Pitcher, strawberry decor in bas-relief, 8¾" 335.00
Plate, red Adam's Rose-type flowers, pk lustre leaves, 8" 90.00
Plate, 4-color floral border, pk lustre leaves & rim, 7½" 50.00
Punch bowl, florals & house scene, scenic int, 11" 445.00
Tea set, England, 1800s, 7-pc 460.00

Pink Paw Bears

These charming figural pieces are very similar to the Pink Pigs described in the following category. They were made in Germany during the same time frame. The cabbage green is identical; the bears themselves are whitish-gray with pink foot pads. You'll find some that are unmarked while others are marked 'Germany' or 'Made in Germany.' In theory, the unmarked bears are the oldest, made prior to 1890 when the McKinley Tariff Act required imports to be marked with the country of origin. Those marked 'Made In' were probably produced after the revision of the Act in 1914.

1 by bean pot 135.00
1 by graphophone 135.00
1 by honey pot 125.00
1 by top hat 110.00
1 in roadster (car identical to pink pig car) 145.00
1 on binoculars 135.00
1 peeking out of basket 115.00
1 sitting in wicker chair 150.00
2 in purse 135.00
2 in roadster 150.00
2 on pin dish 120.00
2 peering in floor mirror 150.00
2 sitting by mushroom 125.00
3 on pin dish 130.00

Pink Pigs

Pink Pigs on cabbage green were made in Germany around the turn of the century. They were sold as souvenirs in train depots, amusement parks, and gift shops. 'Action pigs' (those involved in some amusing activity) are the most valuable, and prices increase with the number of pigs. Though a similar type of figurine was made in white bisque, most serious collectors prefer only the pink ones. They are marked in two ways: 'Germany' in incised letters, and a black ink stamp 'Made in Germany' in a circle.

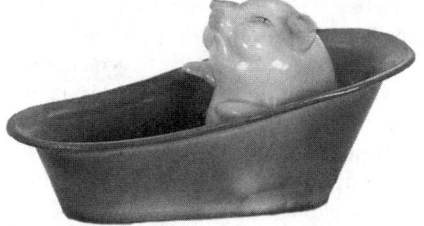

Pig sitting in bathtub, $95.00.

1 beside gr drum, wall-mt match holder 60.00

1 beside stump, camera around neck, toothpick holder 120.00
1 coming out of cup 85.00
1 coming out of suitcase 85.00
1 coming through gr fence, post at sides, open for flowers 95.00
1 driving touring car 165.00
1 in case looking through binoculars 145.00
1 in gr Dutch shoe 50.00
1 in gr suitcase bank, head 1 side, bk other, gold trim 75.00
1 in Japanese submarine, Japan imp on both sides 125.00
1 in jaws of trap, rare, unmk, 5" L 125.00
1 in money sack bank 85.00
1 in roadster 145.00
1 lg pig sitting behind 3" trough 95.00
1 napping on side, Schlite Patent, 5" L 98.00
1 on binoculars, gold trim 125.00
1 on horseshoe-shaped dish w/raised 4-leaf clover 75.00
1 on keg playing piano 150.00
1 on shoulder of gr ink bottle 75.00
1 plays accordion on side of tray, wht bear ea side 125.00
1 pushing head through wooden gate 75.00
1 putting letter in mailbox 95.00
1 reclining on horseshoe ashtray 70.00
1 riding train, 4½" 150.00
1 sits, holds orange Boston Baked Beans pot match holder 85.00
1 sits by high-top boot 75.00
1 sitting on log, mk Germany 80.00
1 w/attached toothpick holder 65.00
1 w/front ft in 3-part dish containing 3 dice, 1 ft on dice 75.00
1 w/tennis racket stands beside vase, Lawn Tennis, 3¾" 95.00
1 wearing chef's costume, holds frypan, w/basket 95.00
2, mother & baby in bl blanket in tub, rabbit on board atop 110.00
2, mother in tub gives baby a bottle, lamb looks on, 4x3½" 85.00
2, 1 at telephone booth, 1 inside, 4½" 110.00
2 at confession, 4½" 90.00
2 behind trough, unmk 75.00
2 by eggshell 80.00
2 by lg gr telephone 95.00
2 dancing, in top hat, tux & cane 110.00
2 holding hands in roadster, 4½" L 160.00
2 in basket, Merry Squeelers, 3½x3" 90.00
2 in bed, Good Night on footboard, 4x3x2½" 145.00
2 in carriage 95.00
2 in love sit on lg log, 2 openings on tree stump, 7" L 75.00
2 in open trunk, 3¾" 95.00
2 in purse 75.00
2 on basket, head raising lid, plaque on front 80.00
2 on binoculars, gold trim 140.00
2 on cotton bale, 1 peers from hole, 1 over top 110.00
2 on seesaw on top of pouch bank 75.00
2 on top hat 95.00
2 on tray hugging, 3x4½" 65.00
2 sitting at table playing card game 'Hearts' 170.00
3, 1 on lg slipper playing banjo, 2 dancing on side 145.00
3, 2 sit in front of coal bucket, 3rd inside 125.00
3 at trough, 4½" L 98.00
3 dressed up on edge of dish 80.00
3 sm pigs behind oval trough, mk, 2¾x2½x1¾" 95.00
3 w/baby carriage, father & 2 babies, Wheeling His Own 125.00
3 w/carriage, mother & 2 babies, Germany 95.00

Pisgah Forest

The Pisgah Forest Pottery was established in 1920 near Mount Pisgah in Arden, North Carolina, by Walter B. Stephen, who had worked in previous years at other locations in the state — Nonconnah and Skyland (the latter from 1913 until 1916). Stephen, who was born in the mountain region near Asheville, was known for his work in the Southern tradition. He produced skillfully executed wares exhibiting an amazing variety of techniques. He operated his business with only two helpers. Recognized today as his most outstanding accomplishment, his Cameo line was decorated by hand in the pate-sur-pate style (similar to Wedgwood Jasper) in such designs as Fiddler and Dog, Spinning Wheel, Covered Wagon, Buffalo Hunt, Mountain Cabin, Square Dancers, Indian Campfire, and Plowman. Stephen is known for other types of wares as well. His crystalline glaze is highly regarded by today's collectors.

At least nine different stamps mark his wares, several of which contain the outline of the potter at the wheel and 'Pisgah Forest.' Cameo is sometimes marked with a circle containing the line name and 'Long Pine, Arden, NC.' Two other marks may be more difficult to recognize: 1) a circle containing the outline of a pine tree, 'N.C.' to the left of the trunk and 'Pine Tree' on the other side; and 2) the letter 'P' with short uprights in the middle of the top and lower curves. Stephen died in 1961, but the work was continued by his associates. Our advisor for this category is R.J. Sayers; he is listed in the Directory under North Carolina.

Bowl, Cameo, wagon train, wht on gr, sgn Stephen, 2¾x6¾" 200.00
Creamer, Cameo, wagon train, wht on gr, bl gloss body, 5" 200.00
Creamer & sugar bowl, Cameo, wagons, wht on gr, 4½", 5" 350.00
Creamer & sugar bowl, crackle, w/lid, 1942, 2¼" 70.00
Creamer & sugar bowl, gr, pk int 55.00
Jar, pk satin, hdls, Stephen, 1934, 6x5" 100.00
Jug, bl to red, hi-glaze, 6" 50.00
Mug, Cameo, covered wagon, Stephen, 1949 ....150.00
Mug, Cameo, lady at spinning wheel, wht on bl, sgn, 3¼" 150.00
Teapot, crackle, Stephen, 4" 80.00
Teapot, rose speckled, 1935, 6½" 55.00
Vase, bl crackle hi-glaze, wht int, Stephen, 8½" 50.00
Vase, bl crystalline w/wht over caramel, 1941, 7x6" 500.00
Vase, bl/gr crystalline over cream, dtd 1948, 6x6" 425.00
Vase, bl/wht crystalline over gold to caramel, sgn/'40, 7x5" 500.00
Vase, bl/wine crackled flambe, pk int, horizonal ribs, 10" 200.00
Vase, Cameo, wagon scene/mtns, wht on gr, pk int, dtd, 6x4" ...300.00
Vase, caramel crystalline over wht w/bl showing, sgn, 8x6" 495.00
Vase, celadon gloss, 3-hdl, sgn Aunt Nancy, 7½x6" 150.00
Vase, grape hi-glaze, classic form, mk, 1950, 8" 70.00
Vase, grape hi-glaze, squat, raised mk, 1937, 3½x6" 40.00
Vase, lt teal gr speckled, hdls, no date, 7" 35.00
Vase, maroon hi-glaze, wht int, raised mk, 5½" 30.00
Vase, purple hi-glaze, classic form, raised mk, 1950, 8" 60.00
Vase, turq crackle, pk int, incurvate, sgn Stephen/1946, 6½" 45.00
Vase, turq gloss, baluster, 15x8½" 700.00
Vase, wht crystals scattered on cream to gr, pk int, sgn, 6" 100.00
Vase, yel/wht crystalline, 5½x5½" 400.00

Pittsburgh Glass

As early as 1797, utility window glass and hollowware were being produced in the Pittsburgh area. Coal had been found in abundance, and it was there that it was first used instead of wood to fuel the glass furnaces. Because of this, as many as 150 glass companies operated there at one time. However, most failed due to the economically disastrous effects of the War of 1812. By the mid-1850s those that remained were producing a wide range of flint glass items including pattern-molded and free-blown glass, cut and engraved wares, and pressed tableware patterns. Our advisor for this category is Mark Vuono; he is listed in the Directory under Connecticut.

Pillar mold pitcher, clear, swirled ribs, polished pontil, ca 1830-1850, 8¼", $450.00; Pitcher, blown, aqua, ribbed, hollow blown handle, folded-in lip, ca 1830-1850, 8", $350.00.

Candlesticks, flint, hexagonal, 9¾", pr 150.00
Candlesticks, flint, hexagonal w/pewter inserts, 9¾", pr 420.00
Compote, cut florals, folded rim, pressed base, 8⅜x8⅛" 300.00
Compote, cut strawberry dmns & fans, ftd, knop stem, 6¾x8" ...300.00
Compote, eng vintage, appl ft, 8⅞x9½" 225.00
Decanter, cut strawberry dmns & fans, w/stopper, 8½" 625.00
Decanter, Pillar mold, flint, 10¾" 85.00
Jar, appl cobalt rings, lid w/cobalt ring, 10⅞" 660.00
Jar, flint, baluster stem & bowl, galleried rim, w/lid, 11¾" 200.00
Jar, 2 appl rings & lid finial, 11¾" 165.00
Jigger, cobalt, 6 panels, 2⅜" 30.00
Lamp, blown onion-form font w/dbl-knop stem, w/burner, 5¾" .285.00
Pitcher, cobalt, spiral tooling at neck, appl hdl, 7⅝" 2,035.00
Pitcher, cut dmn-point rings & panels, flint, chips, 6¼" 150.00
Pitcher, cut panels, edge flakes, 8⅜" 115.00
Pitcher, cut rings, ribs, strawberry dmns, flint, 5⅛" 200.00
Pitcher, Pillar mold, flint, appl ft & hdl, 10½" 600.00
Sugar bowl, Pillar mold, 6¼" 85.00
Tumbler, cobalt, 8 panels, 3¼" 95.00
Tumbler, cut panels, strawberry dmns & fans, 3½" 140.00
Tumbler, electric bl, flint, 5 panels, flakes, 3" 60.00
Tumbler, gray-amethyst, flint, 6 panels, sm flakes, 2⅞" 50.00
Tumbler, pale bl, 5 panels, 2⅛" 12.00
Tumbler, pale bl, 7 panels & 7 arches, flakes, 3⅜" 20.00
Tumbler, sapphire bl, 8 panels, 2¼" 50.00
Urn, cut rings & strawberry dmns, rayed base, flint, 7⅛" 350.00
Vase, cut dmn point & panels, urn shape, 7⅛", pr 320.00
Vase, cut strawberry dmns & panels, appl ft, 9½" 275.00
Vase, cut strawberry dmns/panels/fans, rayed ft, ball stem, 9" 425.00
Vase, deep aqua, blown, trumpet neck, folded lip, stain, 6¼" ..1,325.00
Vase, Pillar mold, wide appl ft, baluster stem, flint, 11" 150.00
Wine, cut strawberry dmns & fans, 4⅛" 105.00
Wine, cut strawberry dmns/panels/fans, flint, ftd, 4" 90.00

Plastics

The term 'collectible plastics' is defined as those types produced between 1868 (when synthetic plastics were invented) and the period immediately following WWII. There are several, and we shall mention each one and attempt briefly to acquaint you with their characteristics:

1) Pyroxylin (Celluloid, Loalin, French Ivory, Pyralin). Chemical name: cellulose nitrate. Earliest form, invented in 1868 by John Wesley Hyatt; highly flammable; yellows with age; much used in toiletry articles. Fairly lightweight, many articles of pyroxylin were made by heating and molding thin sheets.

2) Cellulose Acetate (Tenite, Similoid). Made in attempt to produce a product similar to cellulose nitrate but without the flammability. Had limited use in the costume jewelry trade; most often encountered

as car knobs and handles of the thirties and forties. Surfaces tend to crack with age and exposure to light. Always molded, never cast. Colors varied; imitation horn and marble were most popular.

3) Casein Plastics (Ameroid, Galalith, Dorcasine, Casolith). Invented in 1904 using milk proteins. Use limited to buttons and buckles due to warping and lengthy curing time. Made in a wide range of colors; very easy to laminate or to carve from stock rods or sheets, but never molded.

4) Phenol Formaldehyde (Bakelite, Catalin, Marblette, Agatine, Gemstone, Durite, Durez, Prystal). Invented by L.H. Baekland in 1908; used extensively in the thirties. There are two major types: cast and molded. Molded types include Durez and Bakelite, dark-toned, wood flour-filled plastics that were used extensively for early telephones (still used when non-conductivity of heat and electricity is vital). The most popular name in cast phenolics was Catalin, trade name of the American Catalin Corporation of New York. Made in a wide range of colors; widely used for costume jewelry, cutlery handles, decorative boxes, lamps, desk sets, etc. Heavyweight material with a slightly 'greasy' feel; very hard but can be carved with files, grinding tools, and abrasive cutters. Buffs to high, durable polish. Cast phenolics were used primarily from 1930 to around 1950 when they proved too labor-intensive to be economical.

5) Urea Formaldehyde (Beetleware, Plaskon, Duroware, Hemocoware, Uralite). Invented around 1929, this was lighter in color than phenol formaldehyde, thus used for injection-molded products in pastel colors. Lightweight, not strong; shiny rather than glossy. It cannot be carved and was used mainly for cheap radio and clock cases, never for jewelry.

The period between the two World Wars produced acrylic resins such as Lucite and vinyl. Polystryene made its appearance then, and furfural-phenols were in use in industrial applications. Though a great future was predicted for ethyl cellulose, by the late thirties it was still in the experimental phase. For most purposes the field of decorative plastics from the first half of the century can be narrowed down to the five major types listed above. Of these, cellulose acetate is rarely encountered. Casein is limited to button and belt buckle manufacture; urea is easily identifiable as a cheap, brittle material. Pyroxylin is the celluloid of which so many vanity sets were made. Molded phenolics such as Bakelite were dark in color and used for utilitarian objects; cast phenolics such as Catalin were used most notably for jewelry (Please don't call it Bakelite.), cutlery handles, desk sets, and novelties.

Dealers and collectors should be aware of '70s reproduction Marblette animal napkin rings (they have no eye rods and no age patina) and molded acrylic bracelets in imitation of carved Catalin ones (look for a seam line or lack of definition in carved areas). As prices rise, copies become more common. 1986 saw the mass-production of inlaid polka-dot bracelets using old-stock findings but without the precision fit (or patina) of the originals.

In 1988 and continuing to the present, a large number of 'collage' pieces appeared in vintage clothing and antique stores on the West and East Coasts. These are over-sized, glued-together assemblages of old Catalin stock parts including buttons with the shanks filed off, poker chips, etc., made into brooches or pendants, sometimes hung on necklaces of re-strung Catalin beads. They can be recognized by their aesthetically jumbled, 'put-together' look; and although some may claim they are old, they are not.

Our advisor for this category is Catherine Yronwode, who also publishes an informative newsletter, *The Collectible Plastics*; she is listed in the Directory under California.

Bakelite

Cigarette box, half-cylinder, rotates open, dk brn 45.00
Clock, electric, alarm, Deco design, blk or dk brn 65.00
Clock, mantel, wind-up alarm, Deco design, dk brn 60.00
Inkwell, streamlined, blk, w/lid 25.00
Penholder, streamlined, blk 22.50

Radio, Majestic #55, dk brn, 1939 ....250.00
Radio, Silvertone Compact, Sears, dk brn, 1936-1937 ....250.00
Radio, Stewart Warner Varsity College, dk brn, 1938-1939 ....250.00
Roulette wheel, dk brn, 1930s 80.00
Roulette wheel, mc Catalin chips, wood rack, w/box, 1930s 200.00
Watch, lady's handbag; Westclox, blk, 2¾" dia 100.00

Catalin

Ashtray, marbleized lt gr, sq, 4½" 30.00
Barometer, Taylor, amber & dk gr, rectangular, 4" 45.00
Blotter, Carvacraft, Great Britain, amber/blk 45.00
Bottle opener, chrome plate, red, gr, or amber hdl 10.00
Bracelet, bangle; apple-juice clear, figural bk-cvg 175.00
Bracelet, bangle; apple-juice clear, floral bk-cvg 150.00
Bracelet, bangle; apple-juice clear, geometric bk-cvg 130.00
Bracelet, bangle; deep cvg, w/rhinestones 80.00
Bracelet, bangle; elaborate floral cvg, narrow 40.00
Bracelet, bangle; elaborate floral cvg, wide 65.00
Bracelet, bangle; lt geometric cvg, narrow 28.00
Bracelet, bangle; lt geometric cvg, wide 45.00
Bracelet, bangle; novelty, mc, figural or animal cvg 250.00
Bracelet, bangle; scratch cvd, narrow 20.00
Bracelet, bangle; scratch cvd, w/rhinestones 27.00
Bracelet, bangle; scratch cvd, wide 27.00
Bracelet, bangle; stylized floral cvg, narrow 28.00
Bracelet, bangle; stylized floral cvg, wide 45.00
Bracelet, bangle; uncvd, narrow 6.00
Bracelet, bangle; uncvd, wide 10.00
Bracelet, bangle; 12 inlaid polka dots, wide 200.00
Bracelet, bangle; 2-color stripes 70.00
Bracelet, bangle; 3-color stripes 90.00
Bracelet, bangle; 4-color (or more) stripes 125.00
Bracelet, bangle; 6 inlaid polka dots, narrow 180.00
Bracelet, cellulose acetate chain, 7 cvd figural charms 250.00
Bracelet, clamper; figural, animal, or novelty applique 225.00
Bracelet, clamper; inlaid geometric designs 150.00
Bracelet, clamper; stylized floral cvg 60.00
Bracelet, clamper; w/inlaid rhinestones 50.00
Bracelet, curved/flat links, deeply cvd 65.00
Bracelet, curved/flat links, uncvd 45.00
Bracelet, stretch; orig elastic, Catalin & metal 50.00
Bracelet, stretch; orig elastic, deeply cvd 65.00
Bracelet, stretch; orig elastic, mc, uncvd 50.00

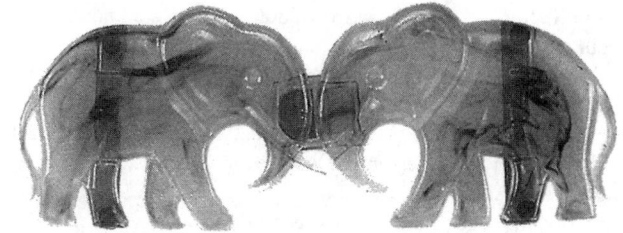

Buckle, two-piece latch type, carved elephants, ca 1935, $55.00.

Buckle, latch type, mc, novelty or figural applique 40.00
Buckle, latch type, mc, stylized floral or geometric, cvd 40.00
Buckle, latch type, mc, uncvd 25.00
Buckle, latch type, 1-color, novelty or figural applique 25.00
Buckle, latch type, 1-color, stylized floral or geometric 10.00
Buckle, latch type, 1-color, uncvd 5.00

Buckle, latch type, 1-color w/rhinestones, Deco 25.00
Buckle, slide type, mc, stylized floral or geometric, cvd 35.00
Buckle, slide type, mc, uncvd 12.50
Buckle, slide type, 1-color, stylized floral or geometric, cvd 8.00
Buckle, slide type, 1-color, uncvd 4.00
Butter mold, gr/amber/brn, floral cvg, 2½" 35.00
Buttons, card of 6, red or blk laminated, 1½" rod 18.00
Buttons, card of 6, Scotty, fruit, or cvd floral figural 28.00
Buttons, card of 6, uncvd octagonal, amber, 1" dia 10.00
Cake breaker, CJ Schneider, red, gr, or amber hdl 4.00
Carving set, knife, fork, steel 30.00
Carving set, 3-pc w/wood wall rack 40.00
Checkers, red & blk, full set, in box 32.00
Cheese slicer, Scotty hdl, wood & chrome base 15.00
Chess set, hand cvd, red & blk, leather box 250.00
Chopsticks, ivory, pr 5.00
Cigarette box, chrome inserts, cylindrical, 4½" 40.00
Cigarette box, lt gr, wood bottom, rectangular, 5½x3¾" 30.00
Cigarette holder, imitation amber, sterling tip, orig case 25.00
Cigarette holder, long, mc or w/rhinestones 25.00
Cigarette lighter, Arco-Lite devil's head, red or blk 175.00
Cigarette lighter, mc stripes or inlay 45.00
Clock, New Haven, wind-up alarm, amber, Deco, 3⅝" 60.00
Clock, Sessions, electric alarm, scalloped case, 4¼" dia 60.00
Clock, Seth Thomas, wind-up alarm, maroon case, 3½" 50.00
Clock, Westclox, Moonbeam, electric flashing light alarm 80.00
Clothesline, Jigger, red anchors, 10 pins, metal box 10.00
Cocktail recipes, Ben Hur, mtd on drunk, red w/blk base 45.00
Cocktail recipes, Ben Hur, mtd on fighting roosters 45.00
Cork, Ben Hur, w/red fighting roosters, blk base 25.00
Corkscrew, chrome, red, gr, or amber hdl 12.50
Corn holder, Kob Knobs, diamond shape or lathe trn, 8 +box 40.00
Crib toy, Tykie Toy, boy, girl, clown, kitten, etc, ea 100.00
Crib toy, Tykie Toy, clown, Laolin head/Catalin body 60.00
Crib toy, Tykie Toy, elephant, Laolin head/Catalin body 60.00
Crib toy, Tykie Toy, 11 mc spools on string, 1940s 60.00
Crib toy, Tykie Toy, 12-1½" rings on 2⅞" ring, 1940s 60.00
Crib toy, Tykie Toy catalog, 1946 ....25.00
Crib toy, Tykie Toy Tales (book about these toys), 1946 ....45.00
Dice, ivory or red, 2½", pr 15.00
Dice, ivory or red, ¾", pr 2.00
Dice cage, metal/red Catalin, blk Lucite base, w/dice 75.00
Dice cup, leather or cork lined 30.00
Dominoes, ivory or blk, full set, w/wood box 30.00
Dominoes, red or gr, full set, w/wood box 40.00
Drawer pull, 1-color, w/pnt inlay stripe 2.00
Drawer pull, 2-color, octagon, w/inlaid dot 3.00
Dress clip, mc inlaid Deco design 20.00
Dress clip, novelty, figural animal or vegetable, ea 50.00
Dress clip, scratch cvd 15.00
Dress clip, stylized floral cvg 20.00
Dress clip, 1-color, w/rhinestones, Deco design 20.00
Earrings, lg drop style, pr 10.00
Earrings, novelty, figural animal or vegetable, pr 35.00
Earrings, stylized floral cvg, pr 15.00
Earrings, uncvd disks, pr 8.00
Egg beater, red, gr, or amber hdl 16.00
Flatware, chrome plate, 1-color hdl 2.00
Flatware, chrome plate, 3-pc matched place setting 8.00
Flatware, stainless, 1-color hdl 2.50
Flatware, stainless, 1-color hdl, leatherette box, 36-pc 180.00
Flatware, stainless, 1-color hdl, 3-pc matched place setting 7.50
Flatware, stainless, 2-color hdl 3.50
Flatware, stainless, 2-color hdl, wood box, 36-pc 225.00

Flatware, stainless, 2-color hdl, 3-pc matched place setting 12.00
Gavel, lathe turned, ivory 20.00
Gavel, lathe turned, red, blk, & ivory 25.00
Gavel, lathe turned, red, w/presentation box, dtd 1946 ....30.00
Ice cream scoop, stainless, red hdl 20.00
Inkwell, Carvacraft Great Britain, amber, dbl well 90.00
Inkwell, Carvacraft Great Britain, amber, single well 70.00
Knife, cvd red, gr, or amber hdl 6.00
Lamp base, brass & amber, Deco design, 10" 30.00
Lamp base, red, amber, & blk, Deco design, 8" 44.00
Letter opener, blk & amber stripes, Deco design 20.00
Letter opener, chrome/Catalin, Deco design 14.00
Letter opener, marbleized gr, dagger shape 20.00
Mah-Jong set, tiles, rails, 6-color, complete, w/box 45.00
Memo pad, Carvacraft Great Britain, amber 45.00
Nail brush, Ducky, duck shape, translucent eye rod 40.00
Nail brush, marbleized lt gr, 2½x1½" 8.00
Nail brush, Masso, amber octagon, 2" dia 8.00
Nail brush, turtle shape, dark amber, 3½" 16.00
Napkin ring, amber, red, or gr, 2" dia band 8.00
Napkin ring, animal or bird, no inlaid eye or ball on head, ea 30.00
Napkin ring, chicken w/inlaid beak 35.00
Napkin ring, elephant w/ball on head 35.00
Napkin ring, lathe turned, amber, red, or gr, 1¾" dia 8.00
Napkin ring, Mickey Mouse or Donald Duck shape w/decal 58.00
Napkin ring, rabbit w/inlaid eye rod 35.00
Napkin ring, rocking horse or camel w/inlaid eye rod, ea 66.00
Napkin ring, Scotty, w/inlaid eye rod 40.00
Napkin ring set, 6-colors, 2" band, orig box 40.00
Necklace, cellulose acetate chain, animal figurals 250.00
Necklace, cellulose acetate chain, Deco dangling pcs 175.00
Necklace, cvd red & amber beads, 18" 65.00
Necklace, uncvd gr beads, 20" 40.00
Ozone generator, Air-Clear, dk amber, streamlined case 70.00
Pencil sharpener, Disney character decal, silhouette shape 40.00
Pencil sharpener, gun, tank, or plane shape w/decal, ea 35.00
Pencil sharpener, orange, no decal, ¾x1" 8.00
Pencil sharpener, red, Mickey Mouse decal, ¾x1" 30.00
Pencil sharpener, Scotty, red, cvd details, blk base 30.00
Pencil sharpener, Scotty, yel, silhouette shape 20.00
Pencil sharpener, Trylon & Perisphere, 1939 World's Fair 50.00
Penholder, amber & blk striped, Deco design 35.00
Penholder, marbleized amber, Deco design 25.00
Penholder, Scotty, red w/blk base 45.00
Picture frame, amber & red Deco design, 6x7" 45.00
Picture frame, red, gr, or amber, sq, 6" 35.00
Pin, animal, resin wash w/glass eye, lg 110.00
Pin, animal, resin wash w/glass eye, sm 75.00
Pin, animal or vegetable, inlaid or appl in several colors, lg 170.00
Pin, animal or vegetable, inlaid or appl in several colors, sm 95.00
Pin, animal or vegetable, 1-color, lg 80.00
Pin, animal or vegetable, 1-color, sm 70.00
Pin, mc Deco design, lg 70.00
Pin, mc Deco design, sm 50.00
Pin, novelty or patriotic figural, resin wash/inlay/appl, lg 185.00
Pin, novelty or patriotic figural, resin wash/inlay/appl, sm 120.00
Pin, novelty or patriotic figural, 1-color, lg 95.00
Pin, novelty or patriotic figural, 1-color, sm 65.00
Pin, stylized floral cvg, lg 45.00
Pin, stylized floral cvg, sm 40.00
Pin, w/danglers, animal or vegetable, resin wash/inlay/appl 195.00
Pin, w/danglers, animal or vegetable, 1-color 100.00
Pin, w/danglers, geometric form, mc 60.00
Pin, w/danglers, geometric form, 1-color 50.00

Pin, w/danglers, novelty or patriotic, resin wash/inlay/appl 210.00
Pin, w/danglers, novelty or patriotic, 1-color 110.00
Pipe, amber & gr, bowl lined w/clay 28.00
Pitcher, glass, red, gr, or amber hdl, syrup size 18.00
Pocket watch, Debonaire, yel Deco case, 1⅞" dia 60.00
Poker chip rack, cylindrical, w/50 chips, 2½" 85.00
Poker chip rack, rectangular, w/200 chips, 4" 120.00
Powder box, amber & blk fluted cylinder, 2½" 50.00
Powder box, amber & gr fluted cylinder, 4" 60.00
Radio, AMC 'Peaktop,' amber, maroon trim 2,500.00
Radio, Emerson Cathedral (AU190), amber 1,200.00
Radio, Emerson Cathedral (AU190), gr marbled 2,200.00
Radio, Emerson College model, amber or gr, 1938 ....1,000.00
Radio, Emerson College model, red, 1938 ....1,200.00
Radio, Fada Streamliner, amber, amber knobs/bezel, 1941 ......1,000.00
Radio, Fada Streamliner, amber, red knobs/bezel, 1941 ....1,100.00
Radio, Fada Streamliner, red, amber knobs/bezel, 1941, rare ...9,800.00
Radio, Kadette Klockette, amber, gr, or maroon, 1937 ....1,200.00
Radio, Kadette Klockette, red, 1937 ....1,500.00
Ring, inlaid Deco stripe design, 2-color 45.00
Ring, stylized floral cvg, 1-color 35.00
Ring, uncvd, 1-color 15.00
Ring, uncvd, 2-color 25.00
Ring case, hinged-lid style, amber or maroon 100.00
Ring case, open-top style, amber, red, or blk, Deco design 85.00
Safety razor, Schick Injector, amber hdl 12.00
Safety razor, Schick Injector, extra blades, orig box, 1939 ....40.00
Salad servers, Chase chrome, ivory, blk, or brn, pr 30.00
Salad servers, chrome, red, gr, or amber hdls, pr 12.00
Shakers, ball shape or half-cylinder shape, 1½", pr 25.00
Shakers, glass, in 3⅛" Catalin holder, pr 25.00
Shakers, mushroom shape, amber & ivory, 1⅞", pr 30.00
Shakers, stepped cylinder shape, 3½", pr 25.00
Shakers, Washington Monument, 3¼", pr 30.00
Shaving brush, red, gr, or amber 18.00
Shaving brush, red, gr, or amber, w/holder 30.00
Spatula, stainless, red, gr, or amber hdl 4.50
Spoon, iced tea, chrome, w/Catalin knob, 6-pc set 18.00
Spoon, slotted, stainless, red, gr, or amber hdl 4.50
Steering knob, chrome clamp 18.00
Stirrer, iced tea; Chase, chrome ball/mint leaf, 6-pc set 26.00
Stirrer, iced tea; shovel blade, Catalin hdl, 6-pc set 36.00
Strainer, red, gr, or amber hdl, 2¾" dia 4.00
Strainer, red, gr, or amber hdl, 5" dia 6.00
Swizzle stick, baseball-bat shape, amber or red 4.00
Swizzle stick holder, amber or red, Rheingold Lager decal 70.00
Thermometer, BT Co, amber & blk, 2¾" dia 45.00
Thermometer, Taylor, amber & dk gr, rectangular, 4" 45.00
Writing set, blk, amber, or gr marble, Deco, 5-pc, orig box 150.00

Celluloid

Bracelet, imitation tortoise w/inlaid rhinestones 40.00
Bracelet, snake w/inlaid rhinestones 48.00
Bridge marker, pnt ivoroid animal or figure, France 20.00
Bridge pencil holder, animal, pearlescent ivory on blk 60.00
Buttons, ivoroid or pearlescent, ¾" dia, card of 6 ....8.00
Carving set, ivoroid, knife/fork/steel, eng blade 30.00
Clock, Greek temple facade, wind-up alarm, ivoroid 45.00
Dresser set, amberoid & gr marbleized, 7-pc 70.00
Dresser set, ivoroid, 10-pc, w/9" bevel glass mirror 100.00
Dresser set, ivory pearlescent or amberoid, 5-pc 50.00
Flatware, gr pearl on blk hdl, 3-pc set 9.00
Flatware, ivoroid hdl, table knife, fork, or spoon, ea 2.00

Hair receiver, ivoroid, pearlescent or amberoid, w/2-part lid 12.00
Manicure set, ivoroid, pearlescent or amberoid, 10-pc, +case 30.00
Manicure set, ivoroid, 18-pc, roll-up leather case 25.00
Manicure set, 4 mini-tools in coral-color tube, Germany 22.00
Manicure set, 4 mini-tools in tube holder w/pnt florals 35.00
Mirror, dresser; ivoroid, cut-out hdl, bevel glass, 8" 20.00
Mirror, dresser; ivoroid, oval bevel glass, 13" 28.00
Mirror, dresser; pearlescent or amberoid, bevel glass, 12" 24.00
Picture frame, easel bk, ivoroid, 2" dia 12.00
Powder box, ivoroid, pearlescent or amberoid 12.00
Shaving stand, ivoroid, 5-pc, w/razor 75.00

Lucite

Bottle, perfume; w/atomizer, rose inclusion 10.00
Bracelet, stretch, orig elastic, clear, bk-cvd 25.00
Picture frame, Deco, clear, sq, 6" 14.00
Purse, box style, clear, pearl, ivory, or tortoise 45.00
Shakers, translucent red, 4", pr 12.00

Playing Cards

    Playing cards can be an enjoyable way to trace the course of history. Knowledge of the art, literature, and politics of an era can be gleaned from a study of its playing cards. When royalty lost favor with the people, Kings and Queens were replaced by common people. During the periods of war, generals, officers, and soldiers were favored. In the United States, early examples had portraits of Washington and Adams as opposed to Kings, Indian chiefs instead of Jacks, and goddesses for Queens.

    Tarot cards were used in Europe during the 1300s as a game of chance, but in the 18th century they were used to predict the future and were regarded with great reverence.

    The backs of cards were of no particular consequence until the 1890s. The marble design used by the French during the late 1800s and the colored wood-cut patterns of the Italians in the 19th century are among the first attempts at decoration. Later the English used cards printed with portraits of royalty. Eventually cards were decorated with a broad range of subjects from reproductions of fine art to advertising.

    Although playing cards are becoming popular collectibles, prices are still relatively low. Complete decks of cards printed earlier than the first postage stamp can still be purchased for less than $100.00. Our advise for this category comes from the American Antique Deck Collectors Club, 52 Plus Joker; see Directory under Clubs, Newsletters, and Catalogs.

Key:
C — complete   OB — original box
cts — courts   SC — score card
hc — hand colored   std — standard
J — joker   XC — extra card

Union Playing Cards, American Playing Card Co., New York, colored lithography, 1862, EX in partial box, $700.00 at auction.

Advertising

Anheuser-Busch Spanish Am War #1, officer cts, 1898, VG- .1,270.50
Anheuser-Busch Spanish Am War #2, officer cts, 1900, MIB 685.00
Black Velvet, reclining ladies on blk, dbl deck, 1974, EX, OB 25.00
Budweiser Girl, lady in yel, M, sealed 17.00
Detroit-Scripps Motor Co, ship & flags, ca 1916, 52+J, VG 225.00
Dirty Dicks, wide, Bahamas, 52+J, NM in partial OB 35.00
Edison Mazda Lamps, Parrish Waterfall bks, NM, OB 187.50
El Benedicto Cigars, wide, couple by fire, early 1900s, G 35.00
English Ovals, gold birds in circle on red, 52+J+XC, MIB 20.00
Evinrude Motors, lady in boat/boy in boat, dbl deck, VG, OB 22.50
Frontenac Ale, wide, Contains Alcohol..., 52+J, EX+, OB 85.00
GE Refrigerators, Sphinx & refrigerator, 52+J, EX, OB 12.00
Greenpeace, non-std dolphin hearts, etc, special J, MIB 18.00
Guckenheimer, Am whiskey, blk/wht, USPC, 52+2J, MIB 15.00
Hiram Walker, London Dry Gin, 3 '20s-style people, 52+J+XC, VG .17.50
Kent, King Sz, military cartoons, 1970, 52+J, MIB 45.00
Kool, Jazz Festival on blk, 52+2J, MIB 6.00
Ohio Knife Co, wide, plant on bl, 1926, 52+J+SC, VG, OB 66.00
Premier Malt Products, wide, Wht Banner Malt Extract, '31, MIB ..95.00
Shriner-Mason, narrow, logo on blk, 1930s, C, MIB 32.50
1955 Chevrolet, narrow, turq w/wht top, Congress, MIB 23.00

Modern Decks

Aircraft Spotter, wide, aircraft, 1942, 52+J+fact card, NMIB 22.00
Butch, stealing golf ball, Staehle, 52+2J, M 4.00
Elvgren, girl on beach w/basket on head, Brn & Bigelow, MIB 45.00
Esquire, redhead on bl, poem, 1944, 52+J+XC, G+ 12.50
Florentine, risque love scenes, Philibert, Fr, 1955, M 82.50
France-Gran Prix Grimaud, Lirola, 1973, 52+2J+fact card, MIB ..20.00
Vargas, 52 pinups, 1953, 52+J+bio card, NMOB 140.00
Vargas, 52 pinups on faces, bl bks, 1953, 54C, VG, OB 105.00
Victory, pinochle, nonstd cts, after VE Day, 48, NM 35.00
Waddington, Polar Bear/Panther, dbl deck, 104+2J, MIB 56.00

Older Decks, Narrow, Odd Sizes or Shapes

Arpak, eagle w/shield, 52C, VG 28.00
Clark's Tiles, cards on tiles, 1972, 52+J+XC+5, VG, OB 35.00
Fan-C-Pack, Pastel Eze, 1935, 6 M decks in leather box 250.00
Gaigel #3, USPC, pinochle, ca 1900-48, C, M in torn box 55.00
Globe, circular, 'waterproof,' ca 1890, 52+J, G 99.00
Golden Dmn, Hanzel, gold edges, 1925, 52+J+XC, M, sealed 82.50
New Index, USPC, sorting feature, 1928, 52+J, EX, OB 22.00
Royal Revelers, dbl deck, anti-prohibition, 1932, EX/EX-, OB 86.00

Older Decks, Wide

Bicycle #808, League, red bks, 1895, 52+J, VG 50.00
Bicycle #808, Model #1, red bks, 52, VG+ 30.00
Bicycle #808, safety, red bks, 52, EX 47.00
Capitol #188, cherub bks, 52+Capitol J, G 50.00
Congress #606, Liberty, Allied flags, 52+J, NMIB 50.00
Kalamazoo, Old Oaken Bucket, gr phototone, 52+J+SC, EX- 157.00
NYCC Squeezers #34, gr bks, 52C, EX+ 22.00
Piatnik, Austrian, German suits, ca 1887, 31 of 32, EX- 2.50

Souvenir and Expositions

Alaska, narrow, totem pole bks, 52 photos, 1950s, 52+J, M 20.00
Alaska Yukon, 52 photos, 1909, 52+Chief J, VG, ½ OB 65.00
CA, wide, Bullock's Orange Grove, 1927, 52+J+booklet, MIB 50.00

Canada, flag bks w/beaver center, DeLaRue, 52+J+XC, EX, OB ..10.00
Chicago, narrow scenic w/globe, 1933, 52, G- 12.00
Dallas Cheerleaders, 52 action photos, 1981, 52+J+2XC, VG, OB ...2.50
Elvis, dk suit w/rhinestones, Sincerely Elvis, MIB 12.00
Hawaii, wide, Kamehameha I, gold fr, 52+J+ad card, VG, OB 60.00
Niagara Falls, wide, corner indices, 1901, 52+J+XC, EX, OB 52.00
Norway, photo bks, Olympic promos for Lillehammer, 1994, MIB ..28.00
NY, dbl deck, color sketches, 1964, 52C, MIB 17.50
O'Callaghan's Chicago, gr border, 1930, 52+J+XC, VG-, OB 60.00
Pan-Am Expo, wide, 52 photos, 1901, 52+J, EX, broken OB 40.00
Sea To Summit, ME & NH views, 1900, 52+J+XC, EX, broken OB .45.00
Vermont, State Capitol bks, 52+scenic J+SC, EX, OB 32.50
WA State, Mt Ranier bks, 1910, rare, 52+Geo WA J, NM- 170.00
White Mtns, NH views, Chisolm Bros, 52+J+SC+XC, EX-, OB .45.00
Yellowstone, flower bks, park logo, 1911, 52+J+SC, EX+, OB 85.00
Yellowstone, photo center on bl, 1925, 52+J, MIB 22.00

Tarot and Fortune Telling

Bond 007 Tarot, Live & Let Die, Hall, 78+2XC+booklet, NMIB ..7.00
Egyptian, repro of 1870 tarot deck, 78+booklet, NM, OB 25.00
Le Normand, Cerraras of London, 1925, 36C, VG- 25.00
Military, nonstd cts & Aces, 1918, 56C, NM, taped OB 50.00
Professor Seward, Gypsy Witch, river bks, 52+J, EX, OB 12.50
Tarot, PC Smith & University Books, 78, NM, torn box 15.00
Voyager Tarot, Wanless & Knutson, 1st ed, 1984, MIB 35.00

Transformations

Harlequin, Tiffany, Carryl, no indices, 1879, 49 of 52, VG+ 175.00
Hustling Joe I, USPC, comical, 1895, 52C, broken box 385.00
Murphy Varnish, cartoon pips, 1883, 52+J, G- 600.00
Vanity Fair, USPC, comical, 1895, 52+J, NM, partial OB 500.00

Transportation: Airline, Steamship, Railroad

Alaska, 727 plane, Fly w/Happy Face, MIB 7.00
Am Export, dbl deck, sailing ship logo, 52+2J, MIB 8.00
American, bl bkground, special Aces, 1959, 52+2J, NM, OB 15.00
C&O, Chessie/Peake, cream/turq, 52+2J, MIB 28.00
CN Rail, wide scenic, 52 photos, 1905, 52+J, G to VG, OB 30.00
CP Rail, wide scenic, trees/red leaves, 1910, 52+J+XC, EX, OB ..37.50
French Line, wide, non-std, M Marie, 1961, 52+2J, EX- 40.00
Iberia Airlines, Fournier, gr & gold painting, 1973, MIB 13.00
Milwaukee Rd, wide scenic, Minnehaha Falls, 52+J, EX-, OB 145.00
Northwest Airlines, logo center on yel, 1944, M, sealed 25.00
Pan Am, mc photos, 1950s, 52+2J, NMIB 32.00
Silja Line, non-std, fantasy cts, 52+4J, M 12.00
TWA, Collector Series, Lockheed 1049, 1952, 52+2J, EX, OB 10.00
Union Pacific, wide, Devil's Slide, 1915, 52+J+XC, VG, OB 105.00
US Air, horizontal red US & brn Air, MIB 6.00

Political

The most valuable political items are those from any period which relate to a political figure whose term was especially significant or marked by an important event or one whose personality was particularly colorful. Posters, ribbons, badges, photographs, and pin-back buttons are but a few examples of the items popular with collectors of political memorabilia.

Political campaign pin-back buttons were first mass-produced and widely distributed in 1896 for the president-to-be William McKinley and for the first of three unsuccessful attempts by William Jennings Bryan. Pin-back buttons have been used during each presidential campaign ever since and are collected by many people. The most scarce are those used in the presidential campaigns of John W. Davis in 1924 and James Cox in 1920. Our advisor for this category is Paul J. Longo; he is listed in the Directory under Massachusetts. See also Autographs; Broadsides; Historical Glass; Watch Fobs.

Badge, Member of Brackette Republican Club, sepia celluloid 25.00
Balloon, Wallace for President, unused, 1972 ....5.00
Ballot, Nat'l Republican Ticket; Grant/Colfax, 1868, EX 50.00
Bandanna, Wm Henry Harrison on horsebk, 1840, 26x26½", EX ...500.00
Bar pin, FD Roosevelt, cloth covered, red/wht/bl, EX 12.00
Bar pin, George Bush for President, plastic, red/wht/bl 3.00
Book, Bull Moose Party, w/songs, 1912, 62-pg, EX 35.00
Bridle rosettes, Cleveland/Thurman portraits, w/gold/silver, pr ..500.00
Bumper sticker, Kennedy/Johnson jugate, orange/blk, NM 15.00
Button, clothing; Hancock/English jugate, 2-pc, 1880 ....36.00
Button, Geo WA inaugural, eagle w/shield, 1789, EX 300.00
Button, Mondale/Ferraro jugate, 1984, 1¾" 6.00
Button, Nixon/Agnew jugate, 1968, 3½" 10.00
Button, Reagan/Bush jugate, mc photo, 1985 inauguration 4.00
Button, T Roosevelt & playing cards, Stand Pat, 1¼", EX 200.00
Button, Write in Dick Gregory President, M 7.00
Car window attachment, Reagan for President, plastic elephant ..10.00
Card, Martin Van Buren, mechanical metamorphic, VG 125.00
Coin, Roosevelt/Garner jugate, portraits, swastika, 1¼" 20.00
Dollar token, Senator Goldwater, 1964 ....5.00
Ferrotype, GB McClellan for President 1864, brass shell 200.00
Handkerchief, Harrison/Morton jugate, 19¼x20½", EX 95.00
Key chain viewer, ML King/JF Kennedy, Immortal Americans 10.00
Lapel device, B Harrison, 3-D log cabin, wht metal, 1888 ....50.00
License plate, Al Smith the Happy Warrior, EX 100.00
License plate, Hoover, blk & cream, lt rust 30.00
License plate, LBJ for the USA, red/wht/bl, EX 25.00
Magic lantern slide, US Grant, mc, late 1800s, EX 75.00
Match holder, Horace Greeley portrait, 1872, 6x4¼", EX 140.00
Medal, A Lincoln Railsplitter of West, brass, 1860, M 75.00
Medal, Genl Andrew Jackson/Hero of New Orleans, brass, 1824 .40.00
Medal, Geo WA Birth & Death, wht metal, edge clip, NM 30.00
Medal, Henry Clay & Am System, copper, 1840, EX 50.00
Medal, James Buchanan No Sectionalism, brass, 1856 ....35.00
Medal, John Bell Union Candidate...1860, brass, NM 65.00
Medal, Martin Van Buren Fearless Democrat, wht metal 50.00
Medal, Millard Fillmore for Whole Country, brass, 1856 ....60.00
Medal, Ulysses S Grant, gilt brass, 1879, M 40.00
Medal, WH Harrison People's Choice, copper, 1840, NM 40.00
Memorial proclamation, A Lincoln, NH, 1865, 4-pg 70.00
Pamphlet, Blain the Proscriptionist..., mud slinging, 8-pg 38.00
Pamphlet, WH Harrison, New Sepulchre..., 1841, 31-pg, EX 22.50
Pennant, Grover Cleveland, portrait, felt, soiled, VG 45.00
Pennant, Teddy Roosevelt for President, portrait, VG 100.00
Pin tray, T Roosevelt portrait, EX 75.00
Pin-bk, Bobby Baker for Secretary of Treasury, anti-LBJ 10.00
Pin-bk, Escalate Viet Nam, Vote Nixon, red & wht 4.00
Pin-bk, H Hoover, portrait w/sm elephant below, 1928, EX 12.00
Pin-bk, I'm for Nixon/Lodge, M 4.00
Pin-bk, Let's Back Ike/Dick, Eisenhower/Nixon jugate 15.00
Pin-bk, Nobody Drowned at Watergate, M 4.00
Pin-bk, Win w/Taft, EX 5.00
Pin-bk, Wm McKinley, Is This Imperialism, 1900 ....1,000.00
Postcard, T Roosevelt portraits (1 Rough Rider) & Wht House ...15.00
Postcard, Western Wht House, Nixon estate 4.00
Poster, William Jennings Bryan, portrait, 19½x13½", EX 75.00
Poster, WJ Bryan, The Issue..., portrait/mc scene, 29x18", EX ...700.00
Pot holder, Kennedy for President, M 30.00

Razor, John Adams, portrait & eagle on horn hdl, Paris, EX ...1,000.00
Ribbon, B Harrison portrait & flags, woven, red/wht/bl 75.00
Ribbon, Elect Dewey & Warren, Vote Republican, eagle, EX 32.00
Ribbon, Garfield memoriam, Republican Invincibles, M 65.00
Ribbon, McKinley/Hobart jugate, yel, 7½x2¼", EX 75.00
Ribbon, Ohio for Hayes 1876 on pk, EX 135.00
Ribbon, Remember the Maine, blk letters on red, EX 25.00

Scarf, Win With Ike for President, red, white and blue, 26" square, EX, $45.00.

Sticker, Kennedy for US Senator, red/wht/bl, M 40.00
Stickpin, Bryan, celluloid oval, mc 25.00
Stickpin, Harrison/Morton jugate, log cabin on shield 65.00
Stud, Cleveland in relief, lt bl 35.00
Textile, Taylor on horse leading troops, fr, 8x20" 200.00
Ticket, Democratic Nat'l Convention, FDR portrait, 1936 ....20.00
Ticket, Republican Nat'l Convention, Lincoln portrait, 1940 ......20.00
Token, anti-Andrew Jackson, running boar, brass, 1834 ....60.00
Token, Senator Birch Bayh 4.00
Token, WH Harrison/log cabin emb, pewter, 1840 campaign 30.00
Watch fob, Willkie/McNary jugate, brass bell form 30.00

Pomona

Pomona glass was patented in 1885 by the New England Glass Works. Its characteristics are an etched background of crystal lead glass often decorated with simple designs painted with metallic stains of amber or blue. The etching was first achieved by hand cutting through an acid resist. This method, called first grind, resulted in an uneven feather-like frost effect. Later, to cut production costs, the hand-cut process was discontinued in favor of an acid bath which effected an even frosting. This method is called second grind. Our advisors for this category are Betty and Clarence Maier; they are listed in the Directory under Pennsylvania.

Bowl, 2nd grind, folded & crimped rim, 4" 50.00
Bowl, 2nd grind, pansies/bl butterfly, crimped, 4x10" 300.00
Celery, 1st grind, bl cornflowers, pinched rim, petal ft, 7" 485.00
Creamer, 2nd grind, amber stain, mini 250.00
Creamer & sugar bowl, 1st grind, wishbone ft, crimped, 4" 675.00
Finger bowl, 1st grind, amber stain, 4½", pr 345.00
Finger bowl, 2nd grind, blueberries, ruffled, 2½x5" 90.00
Finger bowl, 2nd grind, blueberries, 3½", +underplate 150.00
Finger bowl, 2nd grind, cornflowers, 5½" 115.00
Goblet, 1st grind, no decor, 6" 115.00
Pitcher, tankard; 1st grind, gold grass/bl butterflies, 12" 745.00
Pitcher, tankard; 2nd grind, butterfly/pansies, Dmn Quilt, 8" 250.00
Pitcher, water; 2nd grind, bl cornflowers, 7" 200.00
Pitcher, water; 2nd grind, Dmn Quilt, 6½", +4 tumblers 700.00
Pitcher, water; 2nd grind, pansies/butterflies, 7½" 275.00
Rose bowl, 2nd grind, bl cornflowers, 3¾" 120.00
Toothpick holder, 1st grind, amber ruffled rim, hdl, 3½" 335.00

Tumbler, 1st grind, bl cornflower, 3¾" 125.00
Tumbler, 2nd grind, pansies, 3¾" 145.00
Tumbler, 2nd grind, pansies/butterfly on Dmn Quilt, 3¾" 175.00
Vase, 1st grind, ovoid w/sq fluted rim, 7" 300.00

Porcelier

The Porcelier Company, originally from East Liverpool, Ohio, started business in the late 1920s and moved to Greensburg, Pennsylvania, in the early 1930s. The company flourished until the late 1940s and finally closed its doors due to labor disputes in 1954.

They produced an endless line of vitrified porcelain products including furniture coasters, electric appliances, dripolators and light fixtures.

The prices below are for items in excellent condition. If you have any questions or information regarding Porcelier, please contact our advisor, Jim Barker; he is listed in the Directory under Pennsylvania.

Casserole dish, Moderne, w/lid 45.00
Ceiling light fixtrue, basketweave, 2-light 35.00
Coffee/teapot, NY World's Fair, 6-cup 95.00
Creamer & sugar bowl, Mexican & cactus 35.00
Dripolator coffee/teapot, hearth, 6-cup 35.00
Dropolator coffee/teapot, Flamingo, 8-cup 65.00
Furniture coasters, set of 4 ....25.00
Percolator, electric, #410 ....55.00
Pitcher, ducks in flight 35.00
Teapot, tomato shape 50.00
Water cooler, bbl shape 75.00

Postcards

Postcards are distinguished from almost any other collectible due to the fact that nearly any topic can be found represented on cards! For this reason, postcard collecting is considered the 'all-encompassing hobby'! A German by the name of Emmanuel Herrman is credited for inventing the postcard, first printed in Austria in 1869. They were eagerly accepted by the Continentals and the English alike, who saw them as a more economical way to send written messages.

The first to be printed in the United States were on U.S. government postals. The Columbian Exposition of 1892-1893 served as the spark that ignited the postcard phenomenon. Souvenir cards by the thousands were sent to folks back home — expo scenes, transportation themes, animals, birds, and advertising messages became popular. There were patriotic themes, Black themes, and cards for every occasion and holiday. Scenics, cards with small-town railroad depots, and views of U.S. towns (especially photos) are very sought after.

Some of the earliest postcard publishers were Raphael Tuck, Nister, and Gabriel. Early 20th-century illustrators such as Frances Brundage and Ellen Clapsaddle designed cards that are especially collectible today.

Although the postcard rage waned at the onset of WWI, they rank today among the most sought-after items of ephemera, second only to stamps.

Even though postcards may be sixty to ninety years old, they must be in excellent condition. As a worth-accessing factor, condition is second only to subject matter. When no condition is indicated, the items listed below are assumed to be in excellent condition whether used or unused. Our advisor for this category is Ronald D. Millard; he is listed in the Directory under Florida.

Key:
p/ — publisher   s/ — signed

Hurrah, A Bully Fourth, Roosevelt era, 1¢ stamp, EX, $8.00.

Advertising, City Brewery, Juneau AK, factory photo, EX 35.00
Advertising, Cracker Jack Bears, 1907, EX 22.50
Advertising, DH Bakers Bottling Works, interior, EX 27.50
Advertising, Royal Coffee, cats, 1912 ....6.00
Advertising, Sodium Nitrate, Germany, 1930, M 35.00
Advertising, Warner Corsets, Mucha girl, EX 700.00
Aviation, Curtiss Flying Boat at Cambden Harbor ME, 1930, EX ..60.00
Aviation, Italian Air Force, Mussolini quote, VG 30.00
Aviation, Lindbergh photo portrait, EX 70.00
Aviation, Zeppelin photo, early 24.00
Black, girl's photo portrait, hand colored, USA, 1910, VG 32.00
Black, Jes...Luck, Tuck Happy Darkies #2363, G 20.00
Black, Josephine Baker nude photo portrait, EX 125.00
Black, Uncle Joe's Express, sepia tone, VG 45.00
Black, Uncle Remus, Cole Book Co, 1906, G 15.00
Boileau, Philip; couple kissing, MJS, Russia, EX 55.00
Christmas, Looking for Santa, children in plane, 1908, EX 8.50
Christmas, Santa hold-to-light, Germany, 1901 ....200.00
Christmas, Winch girl w/mistletoe kisses boy w/holly, 1910, G 27.50
Christy, Earl; lady's portrait, EX 3.50
Clapsaddle, Best Christmas Wishes, children in snow, EX 22.00
Clapsaddle, Christmas Cheer, 1890, G- 15.00
Clapsaddle, Halloween, blk cat, EX 22.00
Easter, Angel hold-to-light, NY, 1906, EX 60.00
Exposition, Columbian Expo Official, 1893, 8 for 120.00
Exposition, Dusseldorf, Germany, 1902, VG 45.00
Exposition, St Louis, Buston & Skinner, 1940, M, 6 for 50.00
Exposition, Vienna Jubilee 1898, mixed set of 25 ....500.00
Fantasy, fairies & elves, Tarrant, Haig, etc, 50 for 220.00
Fisher, Harrison; Following the Race, horsewoman, EX 25.00
Fisher, Harrison; Her Future, Series C, VG 55.00
Golliwog, booklet type 35.00
Halloween, goblins & lady w/candle, Winsch, 1911, EX 40.00
Halloween, Is This Your Pussy?, Wall, VG 15.00
Halloween, mechanical, Blk boy behind jack-o'-lantern 150.00
Hold-to-light, comic, lady takes man's wallet, EX 30.00
Hold-to-light, WWI scene, EX 25.00
Kirchner, Raphael; bicyclists, France, 1901, VG 35.00
Kirchner, Raphael; Geisha, gr border, France, 1901, EX 50.00
Kirchner, Raphael; Nouveau girl fishing, France, 1902, EX 45.00
Leather, Turkish man smoking water pipe, 1909, EX 12.50
Lessieux, Louis; Emerald, ca 1920, NM 48.00
Linen, Remember Pearl Harbor, Kropp, 1943, VG 12.50
Mechanical, Punch & Judy, PFB series #6015, NM, pr 220.00
Metamorphic, Devil Laughs at It, nightclubs, Germany, NM 40.00
Metamorphic, Turkey at the Farce (stuffing), Gilbert, 1915, EX ..78.00
O'Neill, Rose; Coontown Kids, Tuck, pr 200.00
Photo, Amos 'n Andy, sepia, 1953, EX 35.00
Photo, child playing violin, 1907 ....15.00
Photo, Coney Island view, early, VG 2.00

Photo, Eddie Cantor, 1933, G **35.00**
Photo, JG Carpenter's...Store, Coldbrook NY, Beach, 1936, EX ..**32.00**
Photo, Life Saving Club, 1909, M **10.00**
Photo, Major Mite, smallest man in 'The Circus' w/Chaplin **35.00**
Photo, Overland 5-seater touring car, text on bk, EX **65.00**
Photo, Potato Days, Reinbeck IA, eating contest, sepia, 1910 ......**30.00**
Photo, sluicing gold in Yukon, VG **22.00**
Photo, Union Depot, IL, CR Childs, sepia, 1915, EX **45.00**
Photo, 2 ladies in mermaid dresses, emb, ca 1907 ....**18.00**
Poster type, Hungarian monument, Kanitz, unused **4.00**
Russian street views, country, costumes, etc, 35 for **50.00**
Schmucker, Samuel; Champagne, Cocktail Girl series, M **150.00**
Sports, Cherokee Baseball Club, w/Jim Thorpe, unused **275.00**
Sports, Dan Patch, champion race horse, blk & wht, EX **45.00**
Stern, Roosevelt Bears, EX to NM, 10 for **120.00**
Tuck, Army Service Corps, Series #9167, 6 for **24.00**
Tuck, Auld Lang Syne gramaphone record, Series A, VG **35.00**
Tuck, Buster Brown, Outcault, 1908, 4 for **45.00**
Tuck, little Blk boy, Outcault, 1903, M **25.00**
Valentine, mechanical, cherub & trunk, Winsch, 1912, VG **75.00**
Valentine, Nouveau lady, EX color & gold, USA, 1907, EX **35.00**
Woven in silk, Dunkerque 1915, Flame Series, p/Deffrene, EX **40.00**
Woven in silk, RMS Saxonia, ship at sea, raised border **75.00**

Posters

Advertising posters by such French artists as Cheret and Toulouse-Lautrec were used as early as the mid-1800s. Color lithography spurred their popularity. Circus posters by the Strobridge Lithograph Co. are considered to be the finest in their field, though Gibson and Co. Litho, Erie Litho, and Enquirer Job Printing Co. printed fine examples as well. Posters by noted artists such as Mucha, Parrish, and Hohlwein bring high prices. Other considerations are good color, interesting subject matter and, of course, condition. The WWII posters listed below are among the more expensive examples; 80% of those on the market bring less than $50.00. See also Movie Memorabilia; Political.

Key:
B&B — Barnum and Bailey   RB — Ringling Bros.

Advertising

American Stores Co, Younger Generation, farm scene, 18x14", EX ..**90.00**
Columbus Buggy, Columbus/King & Queen of Spain, 25x38", G ..**400.00**
Ferry's Seeds, owl, DM Ferry & Co, 1907, 36x27", VG **425.00**
Goodyear Tires, pinup girl in tire tube, 1900, 38x31", G **200.00**
Ingersoll Watches, pocket watch, 1930s, 8-sheet on linen mt .**1,600.00**
Levis, bunkhouse scene w/men & skunk, 34x84", EX **750.00**
Lion Coffee, lion smoking pipe, fr, 31x20", EX **400.00**
Pierce Arrow, sepia tones, unsgn, 37¼x27¼", EX **1,000.00**
Runkel Cocoa, couple at breakfast, mc, 24x24", EX **700.00**
Simonize Your Car, scantily clad lady w/sword, 26x23", NM **80.00**
Texaco Motor Oil, early car on rack & 2 pumps, 25x19½", EX ..**1,350.00**

Circus

Anthropoid Apes, ape behind bars, 20x28", VG **100.00**
Bartok, elephants/clowns/etc, 1969, 20x28" **25.00**
Beatty-Cole Bros, Beatty & lions, 1967, 14x46" **25.00**
Beatty-Cole Bros, elephants, 1957, 28x28" **30.00**
Buffalo Ranch Real Wild West, mc scenes, 56x21", EX **800.00**
Christy Bros Wild Animal Show, lion & horse, 106x41", EX **800.00**

Christy Bros. Wild Animal Show, color litho, dry mounted on heavy backing, 28x42", EX, $100.00. (If not dry mounted the value is $325.00.)

Cirque Nat'l, wrestlers, mc, Paris, 47x63", NM **500.00**
Cole Bros, caged animals, Erie Litho, 21x28", G **110.00**
Cole Bros, Something New - Boxing Horses, mc, 28x21", EX **55.00**
Cole Bros, 3 freight trains, 1930s, 18x26", EX **160.00**
Cristiani-Wallace Bros, clowns, 1962, 20x28" **25.00**
Mills Bros 3-Ring..., clowns/etc, 1963, 14x40" **25.00**
Olympia, clown w/ball, bright colors, 32x23", EX **60.00**
RB B&B, Mister Mistin Jr Child Wonder, mc, 1930 ....**110.00**
RB B&B, tigers & lions, 28x19", EX **450.00**
RB B&B, Ubangi Savages, 3-color, 23x15", NM **150.00**
RB Greatest Show..., elephants/clown, 19x28", NM **600.00**
Tim McCoy's Wild West, horse & trainer, 54x20½", EX **250.00**

Literary

About Paris, red windmill & bl cats, 1895, 15x10", EX **250.00**
Bradley His Book, Christmas 1896, rstr, 42x29", EX **715.00**
Century August, lady w/poppies, Leyendecker, 1896, 21x15", EX ..**660.00**
Harper's Christmas, lady in bl, Penfield, 1894, 18x12½", EX **330.00**
Harper's March, lady in blk gown, Penfield, 1896, 18x11", EX ...**300.00**
Lippincott's December, lady w/book, mc, 1895, 14x9", EX+ **360.00**
Lippincott's June, lady in red w/book, 1895, 19x12½", EX **300.00**
London Letter, lady in bl & gr, Rogers, 1900, 30x20", NM **275.00**
Martian, man gazing out window, Harper & Bros, 1897, 21x13, EX ..**440.00**
Saturday Evening Post, soldiers dining & dancing, 1945, 28x22" .**100.00**

Magic

Alexander the Man Who Knows, blk & wht on red, 42x28", VG .**150.00**
Alexander the Man Who Knows, red ground, 41x28", EX **250.00**
Carter the Great, Otis Litho, 3-part, 78x42", EX **500.00**
George Triumphant Am Tour, sphinx/pyramids, Otis, 41x27", EX ..**250.00**
Maro Prince of Magic, portrait & flags, 1905, 13x37", NM **165.00**

Minstrel

Messett's Musical Entertainers, mc, Quigley Litho, 41x13", EX .**275.00**
New Orleans Minstrels, Lillypop & Sparky, 30x22", G **60.00**
Quartet scene, Donaldson #44879, 26x22", EX **185.00**
Ragtime Jubilee, cb litho, 1930s, 22x14", M **140.00**

Theatrical

Ben-Hur, scene from play, 1906, 22x28", VG **450.00**
Held by the Enemy, man on horsebk, Springer, 81x40", EX **360.00**
Humorous Blk scene, mc, Enquirer, Job Printing, 20x27", NM ...**275.00**
Iolanthe, young girl, ca 1930, 20x30", EX **20.00**
Uncle Tom's Cabin, Ackermann Quigley, 28x42", EX **100.00**

Travel

American Airlines to Boston, red/wht/bl flag, 1953, 39x29", EX 250.00
Bruxelles Expo, couple overlook fair, 1897, 41x60", EX 1,200.00
Cote D'Azur, lady & landscape, mc, Dellepiane, 41x30", NM ...715.00
Georges de la Diosaz, canyon & waterfall, mc, 39x24½", NM ...330.00
Holland-America Line, cruise ship, Dirksen, 37x24", EX 600.00
Le Mont Revard, hotel view, Dupey, Paris, 42½x31", EX 500.00
Nat'l Parks, deer at sunset, 3-color, Waugh, 1935, 40x27", EX ...850.00
Red Star Line Antwerpen NY, sailor & ship, 1898, 33x21", EX .500.00
Ski in Canada, skier, mc, Vickery, 35x24½", EX 465.00
Sports D'Hiver Dans Les Vosges, skiers, Paris, 40x24", NM 1,600.00
Vichy, chair w/figures beyond, mc, Courbet, 40x25", EX+ 330.00

War

WWI, Buy War Savings Stamps, Joan of Arc, 1918, 28x18", EX+ ...225.00
WWI, Gee! I Wish I Were a Man, Christy, 1918, 40x25", EX ...900.00
WWI, Hun or Home?, Hun stalks mother & child, 30x19½" 35.00
WWI, I Want You for the Navy, Christy, 1917, 41x27½", EX ...400.00
WWI, L'Emprunt de Liberation, allied flags, Faivre, 21x45", NM ..150.00
WWI, Remember Belgium, blk silhouettes, E Young, 20x20", NM ..165.00
WWI, Seeds of Victory..., color litho, 1918, 32¾x21¾", EX 75.00
WWI, Together We Win, color litho, 38½x28½", EX 90.00
WWI, Your Work Means Victory..., color litho, 37x28", EX 185.00
WWI, 2nd Liberty Loan of 1917, Uncle Sam, 19¾x30", NM 130.00
WWII, US Marines Want You!, full color, 28x18", EX 160.00
WWII, Your Duty Buy...Bonds, Liberty/immigrants, 20x30", NM ..130.00

Miscellaneous

Blk man in overcoat & top hat, Am Show Print, 1915, 56x44" .450.00
Concert, (Bob) Dylan, Milton Glaser, mc, late 1960s, 22x33" 35.00
Concert, Willie Nelson, Rushmore Plaza, 1970s, 17x13", VG 50.00
March Against Death...WA Nov 13-15, 1969, Picasso, 15x23" .385.00
Racing, Donaldson Fair...KY, trotter, mc, 1910, 30x20¼", EX ...450.00
Sports, Dick Mayer US Open Champ, cb, Chesterfield, 21x22", NM ..75.00
Sports, Ralph Kliner, Red Man, 1952, 11x15", EX 75.00
Sports, Sam Snead Ace Golfer, Granger Tobacco, 14x19", EX ..145.00
Wanted, James Earl Ray, 3 photos of Ray, 1968, EX 350.00

Pot Lids

    Pot lids were pottery covers for containers that were used for hair dressing, potted meats, etc. The most desirable were decorated with colorful transfer prints under the glaze in a variety of themes, animal and scenic. The first and probably the largest company to manufacture these lids was F & R Pratt of Fenton, Staffordshire, established in the early 1800s. The name or initials of Jesse Austin, their designer, may sometimes be found on exceptional designs. Although few pot lids were made after the 1880s, the firm continued into the 20th century.

    American pot lids are very rare. Most have been dug up by collectors searching through sites of early gold rush mining towns in California. Minor rim chips are expected and normally do not detract from listed values.

American

Amadine for Cure & Prevention of Chapped..., blk on wht, 3", EX ...100.00
Angell's Dandruff Eradicator..., pheasants, blk on wht, 3" 350.00
Areka Nut Tooth Paste...London & NY, palms, blk/wht, 3¼", EX .210.00
Caswell, Massey...Cold Cream of Cucumbers, gr & wht, 2½", EX .525.00
Celebrated Alexandra Cherry Paste..., brn on wht, 1½", EX ...2,200.00

Dr Harvey's Pomade, lizard, blk on wht, chip, rare, 3" 600.00
Formodenta...By Caswell, Hazard...RI; blk on wht, 2½", EX 425.00
Genuine Beef Marrow...Hauel..., bull, blk on wht, 3", EX 350.00
Jules Hauel..., river scene, blk on wht, 4⅛", EX 900.00
Liston's Extract of Beef Chicago IL, blk on wht, 2", EX 100.00
Rousel's Premium Shaving Cream..., purple on wht, 3¼", EX 475.00
Williams Swiss Violet Shaving Cream..., mc on wht, 3¾", EX ...160.00

English

Lady with three sheep and dog, multicolored, Pratt, ca 1840-1860, 4", EX, $200.00.

Am Indians Hunting Buffalo, mc, Pratt, 4½", EX 260.00
Areca Nut Tooth Paste..., palace & courtyard, blk on wht, 2⅝" .140.00
Bears on Rock Cliff, mc, Pratt, 3½", EX 110.00
Chen Chew River, Pratt, 4" 125.00
Cherry Toothpaste...F Newbury..., sailboat, blk on wht, 2¾", EX .75.00
Enthusiast, man fishing, Pratt, mc, fr, 4⅛", EX 110.00
Faithful Shepherd, Pratt, mc, fr, 2¾" 150.00
Kettle of Fish, dogs spill kettle, Pratt, mc, 4", EX 130.00
Napoleon III & Empress Eugenia, Pratt, mc, wood fr, 4¾" 260.00
Napoleon Price...Tooth Paste, profiles, yel & blk on wht, 2¾" ...200.00
New St Thomas's Hospital, Pratt, mc, fr, 4¼", EX 160.00
Oriental Rose Tooth Paste..., lady, blk on wht, 3½", EX 1,200.00
Queen's Own Cherry Tooth Paste, queen, red on wht, 3⅜", VG ..350.00
Ross & Son's Genuine Bears Grease...London, mc w/gold, 3⅞" ..1,000.00
School for Boys/Bear Inn/Alas Poor Bruin, mc, Pratt, chip, 2⅞" ..190.00
Shakespeare House, Henly St, Stratford on Avon, Pratt, 4" 125.00
Shirtliff's...Tooth Paste..., blk on wht, rectangular, 3¾" 150.00
Tatnell & Son, Pegwell Bay Ramsgate, Pratt, mc, 5", EX 100.00
Transplanting Rice, Pratt, 4" 105.00
Uncle Toby, Pratt, 4" 105.00
Village Wedding, Pratt, 4" 118.00
War, Pratt, 4" 125.00
White Clove Tooth Paste..., floral, blk on wht, 2⅝", EX 150.00

Powder Horns and Shot Flasks

    Though powder horns had already been in use for hundreds of years, collectors usually focus on those made after the expansion of the United States westward in the very early 1800s. While some are basic and very simple, others were scrimshawed and highly polished. Especially nice carvings can quickly escalate the value of a horn that has survived intact to as high as $400.00. Those with detailed maps, historical scenes, etc., bring even higher prices.

    Metal flasks were introduced in the 1830s; by the middle of the century they were produced in quantity and at prices low enough that they became a viable alternative to the powder horn. Today's collector regards the smaller flasks as the more desirable and valuable, and those made for specific companies bring premium prices.

Flask, brass, appl game decor, Dixon & Sons, 8¾", EX 125.00
Flask, brass, Batty 1854 Peace, clasped hands, 9¾", G 235.00

Flask, brass, emb hunt scene ea side, 8¾", VG 75.00
Flask, brass, emb hunter & dog ea side, 6½", EX 65.00
Flask, brass, emb scene w/dog & vines, 7½", EX 125.00
Flask, brass, emb shells, w/measuring spout, 9¾", VG 50.00
Flask, brass, ornate decor, Hawksley, 10", EX 95.00
Flask, copper, Dix & Sons, w/measuring tip, 5¼" 60.00
Flask, copper, emb hunt scenes, Batty, 7½", EX 150.00
Flask, copper, fluted, Am Flask & Cap Co, 9¾", VG 50.00
Flask, copper w/brass ends, compartments, 4½", EX 50.00
Flask, leather, emb stag, leaves & squirrel, 8", EX 50.00
Horn, Am eagle w/branches, crude cvg, 22", EX 100.00
Horn, cvd nozzle end, wood plug, 7" 75.00
Horn, eagle/sailing ship/flag cvgs, dtd 1813, 15", EX 825.00
Horn, fish-shaped spout, fish & Masonic eng, 11", EX 450.00
Horn, name/soldier/cannon/etc, allover eng, 13" 350.00
Horn, ship cvgs, wood cap, 1811, 14" 400.00
Horn, ships, buildings & geometric engr, sgn/dtd 1776, 13" 4,950.00
Horn, silver mts, Scottish hallmk, 13" 500.00
Horn, WA initials & floral eng, 1800s, 11", VG 105.00

Pratt

Prattware is a type of relief-molded earthenware with polychrome decoration. Scenic motifs with figures were popular; sometimes captions were added. Jugs are most common; but teapots, tableware, even figurines were made. The term 'Pratt' refers to Wm. Pratt of Lane Delph, who is credited with making the first of this type, though similar wares were made later by other Staffordshire potters.

Box, Royal Harbor scenic lid, ca 1880, 5" dia 225.00
Figurine, mother & child, 1800s, 8½", EX 460.00
Figurine, Peace, lady w/dove, mc, 1800, 7", NM 165.00
Jar, Albert Memorial, edge chips, 4¼" 80.00
Jar, Cavalier, mc, later repro of earlier jar, sgn, 4¼" 125.00
Jar, War, fallen soldier & horse, 4" dia, EX 140.00
Jug, Lord Wellington & General Hill, ca 1810, 5¼" 430.00
Jug, Royal Sufferers & Duke of York, Hawley, 1795, 7½", EX 700.00
Model of a clock, mc decor, rnd on sq base, 4½" 400.00
Pitcher, soldier w/rifle in relief, 7" 195.00
Plate, discus thrower, serpentine rim, mk Old Greek, 9" 40.00
Plate, Lend a Bite 125.00
Teapot, sq hdl, mk Old Greek, 6¾", NM 90.00

Precious Moments™

Known as 'America's Hummels,' Precious Moments™ are a line of well-known collectibles created by Samuel J. Butcher and produced by Enesco, Inc. These pieces have endeared themselves to many because of the inspirational messages they portray. Over 300,000 Club Members have joined the National Club in fourteen years.

The collection was fifteen years old in 1993. Each piece is produced with a different mark each year. This mark, not the date, is usually the link to the value of the piece. Most mold changes result in increased values; and when a piece is retired or suspended, its price increases as well. As an example, 'God Loveth a Cheerful Giver' retailed for $9.50 in 1980; it was retired in 1981 and has a secondary market price now of $750.00. The majority of the collection has increased in value from its original retail.

Rosie Wells Enterprises, Inc., our advisor for this category, has published the Precious Moments™ collector magazine, *Precious Collectibles*,® as well as a secondary market price guide. She has hosted International Conventions for Precious Moments™ collectors since

1983. Her address is in the Directory under Clubs, Newsletters, and Catalogs. Items listed below are assumed to be in mint condition with the original box.

Baby's First Trip, angel pushes buggy, 16012, Dove mk 250.00
Bless Those Who Serve..., Navy, 526568, Flag mk 95.00
Bless You Two, bride & groom, E-9255, Cross mk 40.00
Faith Is a Victory, girl/boxing gloves, 521396, Bow & Arrow mk .170.00
Good Lord Has Blessed..., couple/dogs, 114022, Cedar Tree mk ..155.00
His Sheep Am I, boy & lamb, E-7161, Hourglass mk 80.00
I Get a Kick..., girl & cow, E-2827, Fish mk 150.00
I'm Sending...Christmas, musical, girl/snowball, Cedar Tree mk ..145.00
I'm So Glad You..., angel w/butterfly, 520640, Flower mk 140.00
Its Better To Give Than Receive, Policeman, 12297 ....120.00
Jesus Loves Me, container, girl w/bunny, E-9281, Fish mk 50.00
Let the Heavens..., dtd '81 ornament, angel, E-5629, no mk 230.00
Let the Whole World Know, boy & girl in tub, E-7165, Fish mk .85.00
Lord Help Us Keep Our Act..., clown on unicycle, Dove mk 180.00
Lord Keep My Life in Tune, boy w/paino, 12165, Dove mk 135.00
Lord Keep My Life in Tune, girl/piano, 12580, Olive Branch mk .140.00
Love Is Patient, boy w/teacher, E-9251, Cross mk 80.00
Love One Another, boy & girl on stump, E-1376, no mk 135.00
Make a Joyful Noise, goose girl, 520322, Butterfly mk 955.00
No Tears Past the Gate, angel/girl, 101826, Olive Branch mk ...120.00

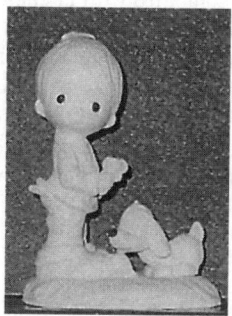

Praise the Lord Anyhow, ice cream cone boy, E-1374B, no mark, $130.00.

Sam Butcher, Sam w/population sign (5), 529567, G Clef 90.00
Seek Ye the Lord, girl graduate, E-9262, Fish mk 55.00
Smile Along the Way, clown on drum, 101842, no mk 180.00
Smile Along the Way, ornament, clown, 101842, Flower mk 40.00
Winter's Song, girl w/birds, limited ed, #12092, Flower mk 175.00
Your As Pretty...Christmas Tree, ornament, girl in tree dress 40.00
15 Happy Yrs... What a Tweet, angel & bird choir, G Clef mk ..120.00

Pre-Columbian Artifacts

The term 'pre-Columbian' loosely refers to some time prior to 1492, when Columbus arrived in America. In particular, it indicates pre-1492 artifacts of Central and South America, some of which can be dated as early as 4000 B.C. Artifacts representing the cultures of the Inca, Maya, and Aztec Indians are avidly sought by the collector. These may be made of precious metals, hardstones, or pottery. Some were used in rituals and religious rites; some such as bowls and other utensils, though strictly utilitarian, nevertheless convey through form and decoration the craftsmanship of these early tribes.

Axe, copper, Aztec, 1400-1500, 2" 145.00
Bowl, ceremonial; 3 legs, relief decor, Mayan, 3½x8½" 150.00
Bowl, ext pnt red, 3 legs, Mayan, 4½x11" 100.00
Bowl, mc, 3-leg, Aztec, 1200-1300, intact, 8½" 725.00
Bowl, pnt dmns/Xs, Mayan, 3½x7" 145.00

Canteen, hdls, Mayan, 13½x13½" 185.00
Celt, stone, 14000-1500, Aztec 50.00
Figure, brn/cream stone, cvd adornments, cracked, 10½" 575.00
Knife, obsidian, Tlaxcala area, Aztec, 4" 285.00
Mask, Olmec, mottled jadeite, from Michoacan, 6x6" 325.00
Plate, redware, Azetc, 1200-1300, intact, 8½" 110.00

Primitives

Like the mouse that ate the grindstone, so has collectible interest in primitives increased, a little bit at a time, until demand is taking bites instead of nibbles into their availability. Although the term 'primitives' once referred to those survival essentials contrived by our American settlers, it has recently been expanded to include objects needed or desired by succeeding generations — items representing the cabin-'n-cornpatch existence as well as examples of life on larger farms and in towns. Through popular usage, it also respectfully covers what are actually 'country collectibles.'

From the 1600s into the latter 1800s, factories employed carvers, blacksmiths, and other artisans whose handwork contributed to turning out quality items. When buying, 'touchmarks,' a company's name and/or location and maker's or owner's initials, are exciting discoveries.

Primitives are uniquely individual. Following identical forms, results more often than not show typically personal ideas. Using this as a guide (combined with circumstances of age, condition, desire to own, etc.) should lead to a reasonably accurate evaluation. For items not listed, consult comparable examples. Authority Kathryn McNerney has compiled several lovely books on primitives and related topics: *Primitives, Our American Heritage*; *Collectible Blue and White Stoneware*; and *Antique Tools, Our American Heritage*. You will find her address in the Directory under Florida. See also Butter Molds and Stamps; Boxes; Copper; Farm Collectibles; Fireplace Implements; Kitchen Collectibles; Molds; Tinware; Weaving; Woodenware; and Wrought Iron.

Clothes wringer, corrugated wooden roller, factory stamped Home Washer, cast-iron handle, gears, adjustable side springs, clamps to tub, EX, $65.00.

Bed warmer, brass w/simple floral eng, trn wooden hdl, 44" 250.00
Bed warmer, brass w/well-tooled floral, trn wood hdl, 43", EX 385.00
Bed warmer, copper eng, pnt traces, 41" 195.00
Box, candle; tin, cylindrical, gr-gray rpt, 11" 150.00
Box, dough; dvtl pine & hardwood, 2-brd top, rprs, 29x26x51" .360.00
Candle mold, pewter, 12-tube, walnut fr, 16", EX 750.00
Candle mold, redware, 24-tube, in pine fr, old rpr, 22¼" 1,300.00
Candle mold, tin, 10-tube, w/hdl, 11" 120.00
Candle mold, tin, 12-tube, minor battering, 11½" 85.00
Candle mold, tin, 12-tube, 10¾" 140.00
Candle mold, tin, 12-tube, 11¼" 150.00
Candle mold, tin, 2-tube, crimped edge, 10¼" 75.00
Candle mold, tin, 24-tube, ear hdls, 8½" 295.00

Candle mold, tin, 36-tube, resoldered hdl, 11½" 360.00
Candle mold, tin, 36-tube, 9" 300.00
Candle mold, tin, 6-tube, center strap hdl, EX 95.00
Candle mold, tin, 8-tube, resoldered, 10½" 100.00
Candle snuffer/wick trimmer, iron, scissors form, ftd, 7" 95.00
Carrier, dvtl pine, no dividers, 1" wide open hdl, 4x16x10" 65.00
Cheese mold, dk tin heart shape, ftd, strap hdl 300.00
Cheese press, pine & hardwood, old patina, 45¾" 85.00
Churn, rocking style, pine w/worn red, 32x34x12" on legs 275.00
Churn, staved construction, old finish, 24"+dasher 275.00
Churn, tin, cylindrical w/wooden dasher, strap hdls, 16" 198.00
Churn, tin, pnt, worn flower decal, 19"+wooden dasher, VG 125.00
Churn, tin, rectangular, 4-legged, strap hdls, cranks, lg 225.00
Clothes wash fork, cvd maple, open 'D' hdl, 2-prong, 30" 55.00
Cookie board, CI, bird on branch in oval, 3x4⅞" 165.00
Cookie board, CI, pineapple on oblong, 4½x6" 150.00
Dipper, wrought iron & brass, 2½" dia, 8" hdl 75.00
Dough scraper, wrought blade, wooden hdl, 1870s, 4½x4½" 75.00
Dough scraper, wrought iron 40.00
Drain board, handmade w/tin bk, 23½x15¾" 150.00
Foot warmer, Goodwill's Bed &...1895, stoneware, 10½" 175.00
Foot warmer, punched tin, mortised & pinned cherry fr, 8x9" ...200.00
Foot warmer, punched tin w/mortised walnut fr, 6x9x8" 330.00
Foot warmer, skater's, wooden, cutouts on top, 5⅝x11x7½" 120.00
Funnel, keg; hand cvd, 1-pc, early, 8½x6" 75.00
Glove stretcher, wire hand shape, 1930s, 12¾x4¼", pr 30.00
Glove stretcher, wooden, 4-fingered, ca 1900, 11½x3¾" 65.00
Grape crusher, wood fr w/iron rollers, hand crank, EX 145.00
Lamp filler, tin w/hinged lid, strap hdl, tapered spout, VG 35.00
Lard squeezer, cvd corrugated surfacing inside, 1870s, 14" 50.00
Mold, springerle, wood, designs ea side, 1x5⅜x4½" 250.00
Rack, drying; pine, red pnt traces, 48x44x13" 175.00
Rack, drying; pine, shoe ft, mortised & pinned, 45x38" 300.00
Rack, drying; pine, 2-part ea w/3 bars, 36x78" 115.00
Rack, drying; poplar, dbl trefoil crest, 33"+arms, EX 400.00
Rack, spoon; oak, some renailing, old dk finish, 15" 270.00
Rack, towel; maple, 3 12" movable arms w/acorn finial, EX 52.00
Sander, boxwood w/old varnish, minor age crack, 2½" 105.00
Sausage stuffer, tin cylinder w/wood plunger, 23½x3½" 40.00
Shoe last, wood, infant's, 4½" 25.00
Skimmer, tallow; punched tin dipper w/long iron hdl, 1850s 75.00
Skimmer, tin almond-shaped bowl, CI hdl, Perfection, 9¼" 60.00
Soap dish, trn wood, old dk patina, 1½x3" dia 35.00
Spigot, sap; wood & pewter 12.00
Spile, cvd maple 10.00
Sugar nippers, wrought steel, simple tooling, 9½" 125.00
Tray, cutlery; pine, rnd hdl on divider, 12½x9¼" 65.00
Tub, staved pine, dk tin bands, wooden hdls, 1850s, 11x14" 110.00
Washboard, Little Darling, wood & tin, 17½x8¼" 35.00
Washboard, Midget, wood fr w/metal wash surface, 18", M 15.00
Washboard, wood w/tin ribbed surface, mk Pail, sm 22.50
Wick trimmers, steel, scissors style, 6¾" 55.00
Wood box, hutch type, pine w/bl/gr pnt, OH, 41x40x20" 770.00
Yoke, human, wooden, scorped to fit neck & shoulders, 34½" 50.00

Prints

The term 'print' may be defined today as almost any image printed on paper by any available method. Examples of collectible old 'prints' are Norman Rockwell magazine covers and Maxfield Parrish posters and calendars. 'Original print' refers to one achieved through the efforts of the artist or under his direct supervision. A 'reproduction' is a print produced by an accomplished print maker who reproduces another artist's print or original work. Thorough study is required on the part of the collector to recognize and appreciate the many variable factors to be considered in evaluating a print. Prices vary from one area of the country to another and are dependent upon new findings regarding the scarcity or abundance of prints as such information may arise. Although each collector of old prints may have their own varying criteria by which to judge condition, for those who deal only rarely in this area or newer collectors, a few guidelines may prove helpful. Staining, though unquestionably detrimental, is nearly always present in some degree and should be weighed against the rarity of the print. Professional cleaning should improve its appearance and at the same time help preserve it. Avoid tears that affect the image; minor margin tears are another matter, especially if the print is a rare one. Moderate 'foxing' (brown spots caused by mold or the fermentation of the rag content of old paper) and light stains from the old frames are not serious unless present in excess. Margin trimming was a common practice; but look for at least ½" to 1½" margins, depending on print size.

When no condition is indicated, the items listed below are assumed to be in very good to excellent condition. See also Parrish, Maxfield.

Audubon, John J.

Audubon is the best known of American and European wildlife artists. His first series of prints, 'Birds of America,' was produced by Robert Havell of London. They were printed on Whitman watermarked paper bearing dates of 1826 to 1838. The Octavo Edition of the same series was printed in seven editions, the first by J.T. Bowen under Audubon's direction. There were seven volumes of text and prints, each 10" x 7", the first five bearing the J.J. Audubon and J.B. Chevalier mark, the last two, J.J. Audubon. They were produced from 1840 through 1844. The second and other editions were printed up to 1871. The Bien Edition prints were full size, made under the direction of Audubon's sons in the late 1850s. Due to the onset of the Civil War, only 105 plates were finished. These are considered to be the most valuable of the reprints of the 'Birds of America Series.'

In 1971 the complete set was reprinted by Johnson Reprint Corp. of New York and Theaturm Orbis Terrarum of Amsterdam. Examples of the latter bear the watermark G. Schut and Zonen. In 1985 a second reprint was done by Abbeville Press for the National Audubon Society.

Although Audubon is best known for his portrayal of birds, one of his less-familiar series, 'Vivaparous Quadrupeds of North America,' portrayed various species of animals. Assembled in corroboration with John Bachman from 1839 until 1851, these prints are 28" x 22" in size. Several octavo editions were published in the 1850s. In the following listing, all measurements are actual print size unless stated otherwise.

Am Coot, #305, Bowen, 1850s, 6½x10" 125.00
Am Crow, Bien 2,000.00
Artic Fox, #121, JT Bowen, 1844, 21x25" 2,500.00
Belted Kingfisher, Havell, #77, 34x25", EX 6,500.00
Booby, #207, Amsterdam Edition, 39x26" 400.00
Burgomaster Gull, #396, Havell, 26x28½" 2,900.00
Cardinal, #203, Bowen, 1st edition, 6½x10" 650.00
Common Puffin, #454, Bien, fr 600.00
Duck Hawk, #16, Amsterdam Edition, 39x26" 500.00
Fish Crow, #226, Bowen, 1850s, 6½x10" 150.00
Florida Comorant, #252, Havell, 1835, 19½x26½" 2,500.00
Golden Eagle, #181, Havell, 39x26" 7,500.00
Golden-Winged Woodpecker, #273, Bowen, 1850s, 6½x10" 125.00
Great Am Hen & Young, #6, 26¾x39¾" 25,000.00
Greenshank, #269, Havell, ca 1826-38, 18x25" 3,000.00
Key-West Dove, #167, Havell, 25x38" 5,000.00
Lincoln's Finch, #277, Bien, 18x25" 365.00
Mountain Mockingbird, #139, Bowen, 1850s, 6½x10" 125.00

Musk Ox, Males; #111, Bowen, 1847, 21⅝x27⅛" 2,000.00
Osprey, #381, Amsterdam Edition, 39x26" 2,000.00
Oyster Catcher, #223, Havell, 26x38" 4,500.00
Red-Breasted Sandpiper, #315, Havell, 1836, 12¼x19½" 750.00
Red-Shouldered Hawk, #56, Havell, 26x38" 15,000.00
Robin, #131, Amsterdam Edition, 39x26" 725.00
Shoveller Duck, #394, Bowen, 1st edition, 6½x10" 400.00
Swamp Hare, #37, Bowen, 1850s, 7x10" 150.00
Velvet Duck, Male & Female; #247, Havell, 1835, 24x38⅛" ..4,500.00
White Ibis, #222, Havell, 1833, 26x28" 9,000.00
White-Crowned Pigeon, #280, Bien, ca 1858-60, 39x26" 2,500.00

Currier and Ives

Nathaniel Currier was in business by himself until the late 1850s when he formed a partnership with James Merrit Ives. Currier is given credit for being the first to use the medium to portray newsworthy subjects, and the Currier and Ives views of 19th-century American culture are familiar to us all. In the following listings, 'C' numbers correspond with a standard reference book by Conningham. Values are given for prints in very good condition; all are colored unless indicated black and white. Unless noted 'NC' (Nathaniel Currier), all prints are published by Currier and Ives. Our advisors for this category are John and Barbara Rudisill (Rudisill's Alt Print Haus); they are listed in the Directory under Maryland.

The Levee — New Orleans, 1884, C-3480, large folio, $12,000.00.

Abigail, NC, 1846, C-9, sm folio 85.00
Alnwick Castle, Scotland; undtd, C-87, med folio 125.00
Am Farm Scenes/No 3, NC, 1853, C-133, lg folio 4,000.00
Am Fireman, Prompt to the Rescue; 1858, C-154, med folio ..1,200.00
Am Game, 1866, C-163, lg folio 1,000.00
Am Prize Fruits, 1862, C-183, lg folio 1,900.00
Arkansas Traveler, 1870, C-270, sm folio 275.00
Autumn on Lake George, undtd, C-324, sm folio 250.00
Battle of Gettysburg, undtd, C-407, sm folio 275.00
Beautiful Persian, undtd, C-457, sm folio 75.00
Belle of New York, undtd, C-490, sm folio 75.00
Ben Franklin, Statesman...; NC, 1847, C-499, sm folio 500.00
Bird's Nest, undtd, C-533, sm folio 110.00
Black-Eyed Beauty, undtd, C-549, sm folio 75.00
Black-Eyed Susan, NC, 1848, C-551, sm folio 300.00
Blue Fishing, undtd, C-578, sm folio 950.00
Bound To Smash, 1877, C-633, sm folio 250.00
Brook Trout Fishing, 1872, C-704, sm folio 900.00
Burning of Chicago, 1871, C-738, sm folio 450.00
Camping Out, Some of Right Sort; NC, 1856, C-777, lg folio ...3,500.00
Canal Scene, Moonlight; undtd, C-781, sm folio 300.00
Cares of a Family, NC, 1856, C-814, lg folio 3,500.00
Cause & Effect, A Natural Result; 1887, C-866, sm folio 225.00
Champion Pacer Direct, 1891, C-966, sm folio 300.00
Chicky's Diner, undtd, C-1029, sm folio 150.00
Christ Walking on the Sea, undtd, C-1071, sm folio 30.00

Clipper Ship in a Hurricane, 1855, C-1154, med folio **2,000.00**
Clipper Ship in a Snow Squall, undtd, C-1157, sm folio **1,000.00**
Cork Castle & Blk Rock Castle, undtd, C-1253, sm folio **90.00**
Cottage Door Yard, Evening; NC, 1855, C-1265, med folio **400.00**
Cozzen's Dock, West Point, undtd, C-1277, med folio **775.00**
Crack Team at the Crashing Gate, 1869, C-1282, lg folio **1,600.00**
Daisy & Her Pets, 1876, C-1346, sm folio **90.00**
Darktown Yacht Club, Hard...Breeze; 1885, C-1439, sm folio **230.00**
Day Before Marriage, NC, 1847, C-1459, sm folio **100.00**
Death of President Lincoln, 1865, C-1500, sm folio **110.00**
Dreadful Wreck of Mexico on Hempstead..., NC, undtd, C-1624 ..**2,400.00**
Dude Belle, 1883, C-1634, sm folio **230.00**
Dude Swell, 1883, C-1635, sm folio **230.00**
Dutchman & Hiram Woodruff, 1871, C-1640, sm folio **700.00**
Easter Flowers, 1869, C-1655, sm folio **50.00**
Emma, NC, 1849, C-1727, sm folio **90.00**
Express Train, 1870, C-1792, sm folio **2,000.00**
First Ride, NC, 1849, C-1987, sm folio **130.00**
First Trot of the Season, 1870, C-1998, lg folio **2,000.00**
Fording the River, NC, undtd, C-2081, med folio **550.00**
Fox Chase, Gone Away; NC, 1846, C-2103, sm folio **350.00**
Fruit & Flowers Piece, 1863, C-2160, med folio **400.00**
Fruits of Temperance, 1870, C-2195, sm folio **200.00**
Fruits of the Season, 1870, C-2198, sm folio **150.00**
Georgie, Quite Tired; undtd, C-2359, sm folio **90.00**
God Bless Our Home, undtd, C-2392, sm folio **200.00**
Going to the Trot, Good Day; 1869, C-2409, lg folio **1,800.00**
Grand National Whig Banner, NC, 1844, C-2511, sm folio **200.00**
Grand Pacer Richball, 1890, C-2519, sm folio **300.00**
Great Salt Lake, undtd, C-2649, sm folio **400.00**
Happy Family, NC, undtd, C-2708, sm folio **130.00**
Harvesting, The Last Load; undtd, C-2750, sm folio **325.00**
High Bridge at Harlem NY, NC, 1849, C-2810, sm folio **550.00**
Home of the Deer, 1870, C-2866, med folio **500.00**
Home on the Mississippi, 1871, C-2876, sm folio **575.00**
Hooked!, 1874, C-2928, sm folio **500.00**
Hudson From West Point, 1862, C-2972, med folio **1,050.00**
Hues of Autumn on Racquet River, undtd, C-2982, sm folio **300.00**
Impending Crisis, Caught in the Act; 1860, C-3033, med folio .**250.00**
Imported Messenger, 1880, C-3042, sm folio **300.00**
In the Mountains, undtd, C-3071, sm folio **275.00**
Inviting Dish, 1870, C-3124, sm folio **150.00**
Jane, undtd, C-3181, sm folio **80.00**
John Adams, 2nd President of US; NC, undtd, C-3251, sm folio ...**175.00**
Just Married, undtd, C-3321, sm folio **100.00**
Lake George, NY; undtd, C-3407, sm folio **250.00**
Lakeside Home, 1869, C-3423, med folio **350.00**
Leaders, 1888, C-3471, lg folio **1,000.00**
Life in the Country, Evening; 1862, C-3508, med folio **850.00**
Life in the Woods, Returning; 1860, C-3513, lg folio **3,500.00**
Life of a Fireman, Race; NC, 1854, C-3519, lg folio **3,000.00**
Life on the Prairie, Buffalo Hunt; 1862, C-3527, lg folio **5,500.00**
Little Ellen, undtd, C-3614, sm folio **95.00**
Little Mary & the Lamb, 1877, C-3670, sm folio **150.00**
Little May Blossom, 1874, C-3671, sm folio **90.00**
Little Sisters, 1875, C-3710, sm folio **95.00**
Loss of Steamship Swallow, NC, 1845, C-3779, sm folio **425.00**
Lucy, NC, undtd, C-3835, sm folio **95.00**
Mama's Rosebud, 1858, C-3949, med folio **140.00**
May Queen, NC, undtd, C-4089, sm folio **90.00**
Midnight Race on Mississippi, 1875, C-4117, sm folio **775.00**
Mill-Cove Lake, undtd, C-4123, sm folio **350.00**
Mixed at the Finish, 1880, C-4162, sm folio **300.00**
Moose & Wolves, A Narrow Escape; undtd, C-4185, sm folio ...**300.00**

Mother's Wing, 1866, C-4239, med folio **250.00**
My Boyhood's Home, 1872, C-4276, sm folio **200.00**
My Three White Kitties, ...Their ABCs; undtd, C-4357, sm folio ...**150.00**
Narrows From Stanten Island, NC, undtd, C-4380, sm folio **375.00**
Naval Heroes of US #3, NC, 1846, C-4399, sm folio **550.00**
New England Home, undtd, C-4417, sm folio **225.00**
New Fashioned Girl, undtd, C-4422, sm folio **225.00**
New Suspension Bridge, Niagara Falls; undtd, C-4432, sm folio .**300.00**
Niagara Falls From Goat Island, undtd, C-4457, med folio **350.00**
October Landscape, undtd, C-4529, med folio **550.00**
Old Farm House, 1872, C-4557, sm folio **1,100.00**
Old Mill in Summer, undtd, C-4571, sm folio **300.00**
On a Point, NC, 1855, C-4592, med folio **600.00**
On the Owago, undtd, C-4608, sm folio **200.00**
On the St Lawrence, Indian Encampment; undtd, C-4609, sm folio .**325.00**
Partridge Shooting, 1870, C-4718, sm folio **400.00**
Patriot of 1776, 1876, C-4725, sm folio **200.00**
Peaceful River, undtd, C-4736, sm folio **175.00**
Pigeon Shooting, Playing the Decoy; 1862, C-4780, lg folio ...**2,975.00**
Popping the Question, NC, 1847, C-4846, sm folio **95.00**
Pride of the Garden, 1873, C-4914, sm folio **150.00**
Puzzled Fox, 1872, C-4984, sm folio **300.00**
Rabbits in Woods, undtd, C-5036, sm folio **250.00**
Raspberries, 1870, C-5065, sm folio **150.00**
Rising Family, 1857, C-5151, lg folio **4,500.00**
Riverside, undtd, C-5162 ....**200.00**

The Road, Summer; 1853, C-5165, large folio, $5,000.00.

Robinson Crusoe..., 1874, C-5189, sm folio **175.00**
Roses of May, 1870, C5215, sm folio **100.00**
Royal Mail Steamship Persia, NC, 1856, C-5240, lg folio **1,150.00**
Safe Sailing, undtd, C-5292, sm folio **175.00**
Scenery of the Catskills, undtd, C-5419, sm folio **300.00**
Shooting on the Prairie, undtd, C-5498, sm folio **650.00**
Silver Cascade, Wht Mountains; undtd, C-5521, sm folio **300.00**
Soldier's Adieu, NC, 1847, C-5593, sm folio **125.00**
Southern Beauty, undtd, C-5630, sm folio **75.00**
Spaniel, NC, 1842, C-5637, sm folio **275.00**
Split Rock, St John River; undtd, C-5663, sm folio **275.00**
Steamer Penobscot, 1883, C-5736, lg folio **1,500.00**
Stella & Alice Grey, ...Whalebone; NC, 1855, C-5811, lg folio .**1,750.00**
Striped Bass, 1872, C-5844, sm folio **375.00**
Summer Time, undtd, C-5878, med folio **400.00**
Sunrise on Lake Saranac, 1860, C-5895, lg folio **2,600.00**
Sylvan Lake, undtd, C-5940, sm folio **200.00**
Tomb of Kosciusko, NC, undtd, C-6103, sm folio **125.00**
Trolling for Bluefish, 1866, C-6158, lg folio **10,000.00**
Under Cliff, On the Hudson; undtd, C-6282, sm folio **250.00**
Valley Forge VA, undtd, C-6355, sm folio **250.00**

Velocipede, 1869, C-6365, sm folio **1,400.00**
View of Astoria, LI, 1862, C-6388, med folio **1,200.00**
View on Rondout, undtd, C-6451, med folio **600.00**
Village Blacksmith, 1864, C-6462, lg folio **3,000.00**
Virginia Water Windsor Park, undtd, C-6475, sm folio **125.00**
Washington As a Mason, 1868, C-6513, sm folio **175.00**
Washington at Prayer, NC, undtd, C-6517, sm folio **125.00**
Washington's Reception by Ladies..., NC, 1845, C-6555, sm folio .**125.00**
Water Jump at Jerome Park, undtd, C-6564, sm folio **465.00**
Water Rail Shooting, NC, 1855, C-6567, sm folio **800.00**
White Squadron US Navy, 1893, C-6644, lg folio **1,200.00**
Wild Duck Shooting, On the Wing; 1870, C-6671, sm folio **600.00**
Winter Morning, 1861, C-6740, med folio **2,100.00**
Woodcock Shooting, 1870, C-6775, sm folio **550.00**
Wooding Up on the Mississippi, 1863, C-6776, lg folio **9,500.00**
Woodlands in Summer, undtd, C-6778, sm folio **250.00**
Wreck of the Atlantic, 1873, C-6787, sm folio **300.00**
Young Brood, 1870, C-6840, sm folio **250.00**

Fox, R. Atkinson

A Canadian who worked as an artist in the 1880s, R. Atkinson Fox moved to New York about ten years later, where his original oils were widely sold at auction and through exhibitions. Today he is best known, however, for his prints, published by as many as twenty printmakers. More than thirty examples of his work appeared on Brown and Bigelow calendars, and it was used in many other forms of advertising as well. Though he was an accomplished artist able to interpret any subject well, he is today best known for his landscapes. Fox died in 1935. Our advisor for Fox prints is Pat Gibson whose address is listed in the Directory under California.

Aces All, 1929, 10x8" **245.00**
Andrew Jackson, 1923 calendar, #742, 8x5" **80.00**
Artist Supreme, #360, 10x8" **145.00**
At the Foothills of Pikes Peak, #332, 9x7" **90.00**
At the Pool, cows, #579, 7½x10" **175.00**
Birch Bordered Waters, #660, 10x7" **95.00**
Dawn, #1, 18x10" **125.00**
Day Dreams, #410, 10x14" **250.00**
Day's Work Done, 2 horses at stream, #626, 9x7", M **185.00**
Departure of Columbus, #544, 8½x12" **195.00**
Discovery of the Mississippi, sgn, #395, 12x16" **185.00**
Dreamy Paradise, 9x7" **95.00**
Edge of the Meadows, #117, 16½x10" **225.00**
English Garden, garden w/brn stone path, #57, 14x20" **95.00**
Faithful & True, old couple, #533, 7½x5½" **265.00**
Fallen Monarch, train w/logs, #98, 10x13" **95.00**
Garden Gate, #679, 22x12" **165.00**
Garden of Love, fountain, #42, orig fr, 10x12" **100.00**
Garden Retreat, #81, 20x10" **100.00**
Girl of the Golden West, sgn Geo White (pseudonym), 6x8" **85.00**
Golden West, #567, 1934, 13x15" **175.00**
Good Shepherd, #29, 12x20" **145.00**
Good Ship Adventure, #17, 16x10" **125.00**
Guardian of the Valley, mountain puzzle, #591 ....**80.00**
Harvesting, 1912 calendar, #451, unfr, 6x8" **195.00**
In New York Bay, calendar top, #522, 6x4" **125.00**
Land of Dreams, #14, 10x8" **65.00**
Monarch of the North, polar bears, #613, 14½x10" **250.00**
Monarchs, lions, #442, 6x8" **225.00**
Moonlight on the Camp, #560, 10x8" **100.00**
Mount Hood, pastel colors, #136, 8½x11" **95.00**
Mount Rainier, #524, 16x10" **180.00**

Mountain Lake, #301, 8x11" **70.00**
October Days, birch trees & flowers, #44, 6x8" **65.00**
Old Faithful, sheep & dog, #620, 13x18" **150.00**
Old Mill, #538, 10x7" **90.00**
On Guard (dog & sheep), #588, 6x4" **150.00**
Prize Winners, cows, #415, 8x10" **150.00**
Ready for All Comers, horse's head, #428, 14x19" **250.00**
Repairing of All Kinds, blksmith, #640, 13x10" **375.00**
Sapphire Seas, #158, 14x20" **150.00**
Seeking Protection, horses & fire, #363, 9½x8" **195.00**
Sentinels of the Pass, pseudonym used, 6x8" **45.00**
Sentry, bear, sgn, #373, 16x12" **170.00**
Silent Rockies, bears, #318, 7x9" **85.00**
Silvery Divide, pseudonym used, 6x8" **50.00**
Spirit of Youth, #4, 18x10" **95.00**
Sunset Dreams, sgn, #23, orig fr, 18x10" **100.00**
When Evening Calls Them Home, cows by stream, #353, 9x7" .**175.00**
White Feather, Indian maiden, #309, 15x11" **350.00**

Gutmann, Bessie Pease

Delicately tinted prints of appealing children sometimes accompanied by their pets, sometimes asleep, often captured at some childhood activity are typical of the work of Gutmann; she painted lovely ladies as well and was a successful illustrator of children's books. Her career spanned the earlier decades of this century. Our advisor for this category is Earl MacSorley; he is listed in the Directory under Connecticut.

Afternoon Tea, Colonial **55.00**
Always, #774, 1913, 18½x13½" **950.00**
Awakening, #664 ....**75.00**
Baby's 1st Christmas, #158 ....**150.00**
Butterfly, fr, 14x19" **150.00**
Contentment, #781, oval fr, 4½x8" **85.00**
Daddy's Coming, #644 ....**300.00**
Dancing Lesson, Grimball, fr, 7x5" **95.00**
Feeling, #19, circular fr **125.00**
Girl of My Dreams, Doench, #682 ....**200.00**
Goldilocks, #771 ....**400.00**
Good Morning, #801 ....**100.00**
Harmony, #802 ....**125.00**
Hearing, #22, circular fr **125.00**
In Disgrace, #792, fr **150.00**
In Slumberland, 21x14" **50.00**
Kitty's Breakfast, #805 ....**85.00**
Lavender & Old Lace, Colonial **75.00**
Message of the Roses, #641 ....**250.00**
Miss Flirt, unfr, 11x14" **40.00**
Reward, #794 ....**150.00**
Sonny Boy, #784 ....**100.00**
Touching, #210 ....**85.00**
Wedding Breakfast, Colonial **75.00**
Winged Aureole, #700 ....**275.00**

Homer, Winslow

Key:
AJ — Appleton's Journal   HW — Harper's Weekly

Approach of the British Pirate Alabama, HW, 1863 ....**40.00**
Aquarial Gardens Bromfield St Boston, 1859, 6½x9½" **100.00**
Artist in the Country, AJ, 1870 ....**35.00**
At Sea, Signalling a Passing Steamer, HW, 1871 ....**35.00**
Bathing at Long Beach..., wood eng, 1871 ....**90.00**

Bivouac Fire on the Potomac, HW, dbl sheet, 1861 ....40.00
Camping Out on the Irondacks, HW, 1874 ....75.00
Charge of the First MA Regiment..., HW, 1862 ....15.00
Chinese in New York, opium-smoking scene, HW, 1874 ....25.00
Cricket Players on Boston Common, 1859, 5½x9½" 100.00
Filling Cartridges, HW cover, complete issue, 1861 ....45.00
Fourth of July Scene on Boston Common, 1859, 5½x9½" 120.00
Gen Beauregard, HW, 1861 ....30.00
Gen Thomas Swearing In the Volunteers..., HW cover, 1861 ......15.00
Gloucester Harbor, HW, complete issue, 1873 ....175.00
Great Fair Given at the City..., HW, dbl sheet, 1861 ....35.00
Great Sumter Meeting..., 1863 ....25.00
Jurors Listening to Counsel..., HW, 1869 ....50.00
Last Days of Harvest, HW, 1873 ....55.00
Morning Bell, HW, 1873 ....45.00
New Town of Belmont Massachusetts, 5x9½" 130.00
Nooning, HW, 1872 ....140.00
On the Beach, 2 Are company, 3 Are None; HW, 1872 ....95.00
On the Beach at Long Branch, HW, 1874 ....85.00
Our Army Before Yorktown VA, centerfold, HW, 1862 ....30.00
Our Next President, HW cover, 1868 ....40.00
Our Outlying Picket in the Woods, HW, 1862 ....30.00
Parsonage, HW, complete issue, 2 illus, 1860 ....30.00
Perilous Leap, full page in HW, 1890 ....35.00
Quiet Day in the Woods, AJ, 1870 ....50.00
Scene on the Back Bay Lands, Boston; 1859, 5½x9½" 125.00
Sea-Side Sketches, A Clam Bake; HW, 1873 ....110.00
Seesaw - Gloucester Harber, 1874, 5½x9½" 125.00
Shell in the Rebel Trenches, HW, 1863 ....35.00
Skating on Jamaica Pond Near Boston, 1859, 5½x9½" 100.00
Skating Season 1862, HW, 1862 ....80.00
Spring in the City, HW, 1858 ....75.00
Straw Ride, Harper's Bazaar, 1869 ....100.00
War-Making Havelocks..., HW, 1861 ....30.00
Watch Tower, Corner of Spring & Varick Streets, NY: 1874 ....35.00
Winter, skating scene, HW, 1868 ....85.00

Icart, Louis

Louis Icart was a Parisian artist who immortalized the women of France through his etchings, which were widely produced in the 1920s. During the thirties and forties, his popularity waned, and etchings from this period are harder to find. He also produced a few lithographs and about four hundred oils. Most etchings made after 1925 have Icart's embossed 'windmill' seal at the lower left. Be skeptical of watercolors and sketches that look similar in subject to one of the etchings. Prices appear to be stabilizing, as the art market adjusts to American recession and Japanese lethargy. Our Icart advisor is William Holland, author of *Louis Icart: The Complete Etchings*; and *The Collectible Maxfield Parrish*; he is listed in the Directory under Pennsylvania.

Bathers, 2 ladies beneath tree, 3rd wading, ca 1926, 21x17" ...2,000.00
Blossom Time, 1926, 14¾x19½" 1,380.00
Carmen, 1927, 20¼x13⅞" 1,000.00
Casanova, 1928, 21x14" 1,200.00
Chronicles of Women: Strategist; 1917, 10x6⅞" 700.00
Eve, 1928, 13x19" 1,400.00
Forsythia, 1925, 19½x15½" 1,265.00
French Doll, lady smoking, admiring doll, 14x18" 1,150.00
Gay Trio, 1936, 18½x11" 4,800.00
Hydrangeas, 1929, 16⅞x21" 1,800.00
Lilies, lady seated, arms full of flowers, 28x19" 3,500.00
Little Thieves, ca 1926, 16½x12" 1,600.00
Louise, 1927, 20x13¼" 1,980.00

Madame Butterfly, 1927, 20x13¼" 1,000.00
Minuet, 1929, 20¼x13¼", EX 1,200.00
Miss California, 1927, 21x16¾" 1,725.00
On the Green, lady lying on grassy knoll w/parasol, 10½x15" .1,400.00
Pierrot by the Moonlight, 1927, 20¼x13" 1,365.00
Pink Alcove, 1929, 10¼x12½" 1,200.00
Puff of Smoke, 1922, 19¼x13½" 1,265.00
Red Riding Hood, 1927, 21⅛x14" 1,800.00
Repose, 1934, 19¾x46½" 8,000.00
Salome, standing by doorway, 20x14" 1,400.00
Smoke, seminude w/cigarette, ca 1926, 19½x14¼" 2,200.00
Speed, woman w/3 greyhounds, ca 1927, 15x25" 3,000.00
Speed II, 1933, 15x24½" 3,000.00
Spilled Milk, 1925, 17x21½" 1,400.00
Spring Blossoms, 1932, 24½x16" 2,300.00
Springtime Vision, 1914, 11¼x18½" 1,955.00
Swallows, ca 1926, 18½x10½" 1,200.00
Symphony in Blue, lady seated by lg vase of flowers, 22x19" ...1,650.00
Werther, lady by garden wall, 1928, 21x14" 2,000.00

Kellogg

Cares of a Family, girl w/chicks 85.00
City Hall, New York 375.00
Dogs of High Degree, funny canines 110.00
Duck Shooting, sm folio 385.00
Little Hero, boy playing soldier 75.00
Little Minnie 75.00
Margaret 85.00
Prodigal Son Returns to His Father 85.00

Kurz and Allison

Louis Kurz founded the Chicago Lithograph Company in 1833. Among his most notable works were a series of thirty-six Civil War scenes and one hundred illustrations of Chicago architecture. His company was destroyed in the Great Fire of 1871, and in 1880 Kurz formed a partnership with Alexander Allison, an engraver. Until both retired in 1903, they produced hundreds of lithographs in color as well as black and white.

Battle of Champion Hills, lg folio 130.00
Battle of Fort Donnelson, lg folio, EX 185.00
Battle of Nashville, on brd, rstr tears, 17½x25" 275.00
Battle of New Orleans, on brd, 17½x25", EX 325.00
Colonel T Roosevelt, USV, blk/wht, w/Rough Riders, lg folio ...160.00
Daniel in Lions' Den, blk/wht, stands by lions, lg folio 90.00
General Joseph Hooker, blk/wht, bust view, lg folio 90.00
Great Connemaugh...Disaster (Johnstown flood), lg folio 335.00
Last Charge & Capture of Port Arthur, lg folio 200.00
Trial of Robert Emmett, His Closing Remarks; lg folio 200.00
Wm McKinley, blk/wht, bust view w/facsimile sgn, lg folio 90.00

McKenney and Hall

Wa-Pel-La, Chief of Musquakees, hand colored, 1838, folio edition, 18x13", $1,100.00.

Ap-Pa-Noo-Se, Sauke chief, 1838, 18x13" 825.00
Chou-Ca-Pe, 1837, 18x13" 500.00
Keokuk Chief of Sacs & Foxes, Bowen, 1838, lg folio 900.00
Ki-On-Twog-Ky, Cornplant, 1836, 18x13" 1,045.00
Pow-A-Sheek, Fox chief, 1838, 18x13" 935.00
Push-Ma-Ta-Ha, Choctaw warrior, 1838, 18x13" 935.00
Red Jacket, A Seneca War Chief; 1837, 18x13" 1,300.00

Mucha, Alphonse

Mucha became famous for his beautiful Art Nouveau lithographs featuring Sarah Bernhardt and Job cigarette papers, which he issued in the 1890s. Born in Prague in 1860, he studied there as well as in Paris and for a time taught at the New York School of Applied Design for women before returning to Prague.

Automne, 1903, 27¾x12" 6,300.00
Biscuite Lefevre-Utile, blond w/plate of biscuits, 24x17" 7,450.00
Flirt, linen-bk, 1900, 23x10", EX 2,500.00
Jardin du Luxembourg, 1890, 24x34" 345.00
Job, lady w/blk hair on mc ground, fr, 1898, 57x38", EX 7,000.00
L'Illustration Noel, ladies on mc ground, 1896, 16x12", EX 600.00
La Plume, lady in gr on red Nouveau ground, fr, 9½x7", NM 665.00
Leslie Carter, lady in gr & bl on mc ground, 1908, 83x31½", EX .3,960.00
Monaco Monte-Carlo, maid w/in floral halo, 42x29" 7,500.00

Reverie, color lithograph, 1896, 25x18¾", $1,200.00.

Russian Restituenda, 1922, 30x17" 1,000.00
Sarah Bernhardt as Photina, 1897, 68½x22½" 7,400.00
Wiener Chic, lady in wht, 1900, 15x11", EX 1,000.00
Zodiaque, lady encircled by signs, 1897, fr, 25x18½", NM 9,350.00

Nutting, Wallace

Born in 1862, Nutting pursued many careers. His hand-tinted photographs of landscapes and interior scenes are prized by collectors today. He was also a writer, minister, farmer, and a furniture maker, designing reproductions of early American pieces. Collectors of his prints should be aware of rosy-hued, inconsistently bright or dark examples — especially large prints of An Elaborate Dinner and A Chair for John; these have been reproduced. Prices for large interior prints have recently been on the increase. Those with animals have risen at least 50% in the past few years, and prints with men are commanding extremely high prices. Those with babies and/or adolescent children bring very high prices as well. Our advisor for this category is Milt Steinfeld; he is listed in the Directory under New Jersey.

All Smiles, lady looks in mirror, 7½x9¼" 250.00
Apple Tree Bend, 11x13" 105.00
Birch Grove, trees on hill by lake, 4½x6¼" 75.00

Breakfast Hour, 11x7" 110.00
Call for More, interior scene, 1916, fr, 16x21" 235.00
Cobb's Creek Banks, matted & fr, 28⅝x22½" 110.00
Corner Cupboard, girl gets china from cupboard, 11x17" 175.00
Cottages on the Old Sod, 11x14" 625.00
Equinox Pond 50.00
Farmstead Entrance, matted & fr, 14¾x17¾" 85.00
Floral Arrangement, rare 800.00
Garden Steps 60.00
Home Room, girl in rocker sips tea, 13x16" 195.00
LaJolla 300.00
Newton Autumn, 15x16½" 135.00
Old Parlor Idyl, couple beside fireplace, 7½x9½" 595.00
Old Time Romance, lady reading, 1914, in orig 12x15" fr 195.00
Parson's Gate 200.00
Patriarch in Bloom, trees over walls in country, 10x13" 110.00
Primrose Cottage, roses on thatched cottage, 7¼x9¼" 150.00
Quilting, 3 ladies in bedroom, 12x6" 215.00
Solitude Moments, 21x25½" 170.00
Tea for Two, 2 girls seated have tea in house, 11x14" 175.00
Untitled, girl in bed looks in mirror, 5x7" 95.00
Untitled, girl sews by fire, 7x9" 110.00
Untitled, lady heating water at fireplace, fr, 7¾x9⅝" 115.00
Untitled, lady making dough before fireplace, 7¾x9⅝" 105.00
Untitled, road along stream, 8x10" 48.00
Yosemite Waters, orig 13x11" fr 215.00

Picasso

Exposition Vallauris 1962, wove paper, sgn, fr, 25¼x21" 2,200.00
Figure, litho, sgn, 1949, 26x20" 9,200.00
L'Entreinte, Arches paper, sgn, 1963, fr, 24½x29½" 6,500.00
Nature Morte aux Poires, sgn, 1961, fr, 19½x23½" 2,200.00
Untitled, 156 Series; sgn, 1971, fr, 14½x20" 2,200.00
Visage de Femme (Pomone), sgn, fr, 12x12" 2,200.00

Prang, Louis

Battle of Antietam, lg folio 150.00
Battle of Chattanooga, 15x21½" 120.00
Battle of Manila, 1896, 16x20" 150.00
Battle of Port Hudson, View of Big Guns; lg folio 185.00
Capture of New Orleans, chromolitho, naval battle, lg folio 395.00
Fruits, sgn, 22x14" 850.00
Salome, paper poster, 16x13" 375.00
Sheridan's Final Charge at Winchester, 15x21½" 185.00
Vient de Pariatre, poster paper, linen bk, 30x18" 600.00

Yard Longs

Values for yard-longs are given for examples in **near mint** condition, full length, nicely framed, and with the original glass. To learn more about this popular area of collector interest, we recommend Those Wonderful Yard-Long Prints and More, and More Wonderful Yard-Long Prints by our advisors W.D. and M.J. Keagy, and C.G. and J.M. Rhoden. They are listed in the Directory under Indiana and Illinois respectively. A word of caution: watch for reproductions; know your dealer.

A Shower of Pansies, Muller Luchsinge & Co 200.00
A Yard of Mixed Flowers, Guy Bedford 225.00
A Yard of Roses, Newton A Wells, c 1898 ....225.00
Barbara, sgn C Allan Gilbert, 1912 ....285.00
Chrysanthemums, C Klein 195.00
Grandmother's Garden 325.00

Hula Girl dancing by firelight, sgn Gene Pressler 350.00
Hula Girl on surfboard, sgn Gene Pressler 350.00
Spring Is Here, Cambril, c 1907 ....225.00
The Pride of America, J Califano 225.00
White & Purple Lilacs, Paul DeLongpre, c 1896 ....225.00
Yard of assorted fruit, Guy Bedford 225.00
Yard of Poppies, Guy Bedford 275.00
Yard of violets in crystal bowl, sgn LeRoy 225.00
1911 Pabst Extract American Girl calendar 375.00
1929 Selz Good Shoes, sgn Earl Chambers 300.00

Purinton

Founded in 1936 in Wellsville, Ohio, Purinton Pottery relocated in 1941 in Shippenville, Pennsylvania, and began producing hand-painted wares that are today attracting the interest of collectors of 'country-type' dinnerware. Using bold brush strokes of vivid color, simple yet attractive patterns such as Apple, Fruits, Tea Rose, and Pennsylvania Dutch were manufactured in tableware sets and accessory pieces. For more information we recommend *Purinton Pottery* by Susan Morris; she is listed in the Directory under Iowa. Our advisor for this category is Pat Dole; she is listed in the Directory under Alabama.

Palm Tree, canister, $200.00; Matching range shakers, 75.00.

Bowl, cereal; Apple, 5¼" 10.00
Bowl, cereal; Normandy Plaid, 5¼" 10.00
Bowl, cereal; Pennsylvania Dutch, 5¼" 20.00
Bowl, divided vegetable; Brn Intaglio, oval, 10½" 30.00
Bowl, fruit; Intaglio, 12" 40.00
Bowl, salad; Maywood, 11" 25.00
Bowl, vegetable; Normandy Plaid, 8½" 25.00
Bowl, vegetable; Peasant Garden, 8½" 80.00
Canisters, Apple, oval, red trim, 9", set of 4 ....200.00
Chop plate, Peasant Garden, 12" 150.00
Coffeepot, Fruit 65.00
Cookie jar, Apple, pottery lid, 9½" 75.00
Creamer & sugar bowl, Apple 50.00
Creamer & sugar bowl, Fruit 40.00
Creamer & sugar bowl, Normandy Plaid 40.00
Cup & saucer, Apple 15.00
Cup & saucer, Maywood 20.00
Cup & saucer, Normandy Plaid 15.00
Grease jar, Fruit, red trim 45.00
Grease jar, Ivy 45.00
Honey jug, Ivy 25.00
Jug, Apple, Dutch, 2-pt 45.00
Jug, Apple, Dutch, 5-pt, 8" 65.00
Jug, Apple, Kent, 6¼" 30.00
Jug, Fruit, Dutch, 2-pt 45.00
Jug, Fruit, Kent, 1-pt 30.00
Jug, Fruit, Oasis, 9½", minimum value 1,200.00
Jug, Ivy, Kent, 4½" 30.00
Mug, beer; Intaglio, 16-oz, 4¾" 60.00

Mug, Heather plaid, 8-oz, 4" 40.00
Mug, Intaglio, 8-oz, 4" 60.00
Night bottle, Fruit, 7½" 55.00
Plate, Apple, 8½" 20.00
Plate, Apple, 9¾" 22.00
Plate, Intaglio, 8½" 20.00
Plate, Normandy Plaid, 6¾" 10.00
Plate, Normandy Plaid, 9¾" 15.00
Plate, Pennsylvania Dutch, 9¾" 40.00
Platter, Heather Plaid, 12" 30.00
Platter, Maywood, 12" dia 40.00
Relish, Pennsylvania Dutch, 3-part, 10" 75.00
Shakers, Apple, range sz, 4", pr 50.00
Shakers, Fruit, range sz, 4", pr 40.00
Shakers, Heather Plaid, jug style, 2½", pr 20.00
Shakers, Normandy Plaid, 4¼", pr 60.00
Soup & sandwich set, Intaglio 50.00
Soup & sandwich set, Pennsylvania Dutch 75.00
Teapot, Apple, 2-cup 40.00
Teapot, Apple, 6-cup 70.00
Teapot, Fruit, 4-cup 45.00
Teapot, Ivy, 2-cup 45.00
Teapot, Ivy, 6-cup 55.00
Teapot, Mountain Rose, 6-cup 85.00
Tumbler, Apple, 5" 20.00
Tumbler, Fruit, 5" 20.00
Tumbler, Normandy Plaid, 12-oz, 5" 20.00
Tumbler, Sunflower, 12-oz, 5" 30.00

Purses

Beaded purses and bags represent an area of collecting interest that is very popular today. Purses from the early 1800s are often decorated with small, brightly colored glass beads. Cut steel beads were popular in the 1840s and remained stylish until about 1930. Mesh purses are also popular. In the 1820s mesh was woven. Chain-link mesh came into usage in the 1890s, followed by the enamel mesh bags carried by the flappers in the 1920s. Purses are divided into several categories by (a) construction techniques — whether beaded, embroidered, or a type of needlework; (b) material — fabric or metal; and (c) design and style. Condition is very important. Watch for dry, brittle leather or fragile material. For those interested in learning more, we recommend *Antique Purses, A History, Identification, and Value Guide, Second Edition*, by Richard Holiner; *More Beautiful Purses*, and *Combs and Purses*, both by Evelyn Haertigi of Carmel, California. Our advisor for this category is Veronica Trainer; she is listed in the Directory under Ohio.

Beaded, blk & silver, allover loopy fringe, drawstring, 5x10" 70.00
Beaded, floral tapestry, ornate fr, fringe, chain hdl, 8x14" 475.00
Beaded, gold & silver floral, gilt fr, fringe, France, 4x7" 70.00
Beaded, gr & blk grid on wht, blk & wht fringe, Czech, 7x9" 90.00
Beaded, mc peacock on blk, SP fr, 8x9½" 250.00
Beaded, mc river scene, ornate fr, fringe, Germany, 8x13" 350.00
Blk satin w/vanity case top, dmn shape, Evans, 6½x6" 400.00
Blk silk, ornate 800 silver fr, chain hdl, 10½x10¼" 340.00
Cloisonne, florals on bl, cord hdl, 4x4½" 600.00
Crochet, wht, lined, w/zipper, 1930s, 4x7" 15.00
Leather, alligator's paw, cord hdl, 7¾x5¾" 65.00
Leather, tooled, blk & brn, strap hdl, Jemco, 6¾x5½" 82.50
Leather, tooled, brn, Deco style, w/mirror, 7x7" 55.00
Leather, tooled, clutch type, Meeker, 5¼x9¼" 70.00
Leather, tooled, strap hdl, Jemco, 6¾x5¾" 100.00
Leather, vanity type w/mirrored lid, Lili-Staly, 4x6½x4½" 300.00

Lucite, tortoise, envelope closure, swing hdls, 4x7x3" **250.00**
Mesh, birds on branches, red/blk/wht, Mandalian, 8x5" **265.00**
Mesh, blk & gold geometrics, Mandalian, 6x3½" **125.00**
Mesh, blk & silver, Whiting & Davis fr, 7¼x4" **100.00**
Mesh, blk web on silver, Whiting & Davis fr, 7x5½" **200.00**
Mesh, gold, fringe, Whiting & Davis fr, 7x4" **65.00**
Mesh, mc floral, Whiting & Davis fr, 3¾x2½" **90.00**
Mesh, mc floral, Whiting & Davis fr, 6½x4" **175.00**
Mesh, red, lg red enameled floral, Whiting & Davis fr, 7½x5½" **175.00**
Mesh, yel & blk dmns on bl, gilt fr, Mandalian, 7x4½" **175.00**
Mesh, 10k, 3 sm dmns/4 sm oval sapphires in fr **500.00**
Nylon, yel & brn drawstring bag, 1930s 12x10", EX **15.00**
Plastic, clear w/gold tulle & sparkles, Wilardy, 3¾x7x3¼" **350.00**
Rhinestones, hand set, Czechoslovakia, sm **75.00**
Suede, blk & gold vanity w/hdls, fitted int, France, 3x4x2" **125.00**
Suede, clutch w/sterling & chrysoprase accents, Spaulding **265.00**
Velvet, blk w/pearlized stripes, mirror & comb w/in, Ingber **25.00**

Puzzles

'Jigsaw' puzzles have been around almost as long as games. The first examples were handcrafted from wood, and they are extremely difficult to find. Most of the early examples featured moral subjects just as the board games did. By the 1890s jigsaw puzzles had become a major form of home entertainment. During the Depression years jigsaw puzzles were set up on card tables in almost every home. The early wood examples are the most valuable.

Cube puzzles, or blocks, were often made by the same companies as the board games. Again, early examples display the finest quality lithography. While all subjects are collectible, some (such as Santa blocks) often command prices higher than games from the same period. Our advisor for this category is Norm Vigue; he is listed in the Directory under Massachusetts. In the listings all items are jigsaw puzzles unless noted otherwise.

Washington Crossing the Delaware, McLoughlin Bros., EX in 16x11" color-lithographed box, $300.00.

Miscellaneous

Campbell's Tomato Soup can, M in orig can **20.00**
Chase, fox-hunt scene, Bradley-Piedmont, 1930s, EX in box **12.00**
Columbia Space Shuttle, MIB, sealed **20.00**
Cross Country Marathon, Milton Bradley, carly 1900s, EX in box ..**42.50**
Fire Engine Picture Puzzle, McLoughlin Bros, 12" box, VG **80.00**
Horse-drawn steam fire engines, Milton Bradley, 1904, EX **165.00**
Horse-drawn steamer w/fire beyond, McLoughlin Bros, 16x23" .**170.00**
Little Workers Picture Cubes, McLoughlin Bros, 10½x8x3" **550.00**
N&S America, wood litho, Rand McNally, ea: 8¾x11¾", pr **55.00**
NY Times Historic, Parker Bros, Edward VII abdication, EX **15.00**
Piccadilly Jig, early 1900s **30.00**
Playboy, jigsaw, 1973, M **20.00**
Roadside Mill, Madmar Blue-Ribbon, 1930s, 200-pc, EX in box ..**25.00**

Village Pond, winter scene, Straus, 1950s, 500-pc, EX in box **25.00**
Washington Crossing Delaware, McLoughlin Bros, EX in box ...**300.00**

Personalities, Movies, and TV Shows

Alice in Wonderland, Tenniel illus, '30s, set of 4, EX **75.00**
Aquaman, MIB **20.00**
Batman, moon behind him, 1970s, 81-pc, EX in VG box **7.50**
Batman Returns, Penguin on Penguinmobile, 200-pc, NM **10.00**
Broken Arrow, Lupton & Ansara, Built-Rite, 1958, EX **35.00**
Brothers Grimm, dragon, from G Pal film, 1962, EX **15.00**
Bugs Bunny, Whitman, 1975, EX **10.00**
Cheyenne, set of 3, 1 Walker photo, Milton Bradley, 1957, NM ..**85.00**
Chilly Willy, fr-tray, 1963, 8x10", EX **10.00**
Combat, tank corps pictured, Jaymar, 1966, M, sealed **24.50**
Daniel Boone, fr-tray, Fess Parker Wilderness Scout, 1960s **17.50**
Dark Shadows, Barnabas in catacombs, 1969, MIB **85.00**
Emergency, Casse-Tete, 1972, EX in can **7.50**
Gabby Gator, Lantz art, 1963, 8x10", NM **12.00**
Little Lulu, fr-tray, 1973, 11x13", M, sealed **17.50**
Peter Potamus, fr-tray, Whitman, 1964, EX **15.00**
Rock Hudson, Man's Favorite Sport movie promo **25.00**
Suzanne Sommers as Chrissy, Casse-Tete, 1978, EX in box **9.00**
Wild Bill Hickok, Guy Madison, Built-Rite, 1955, NM **25.00**

Pyrography

Pyrography, also known as burnt wood, Flemish art or poker work, is the art of burning designs into wood or leather and has been practiced over the centuries in many countries.

In the late 1800s pyrography became the hot new hobby for thousands of Americans who burned designs inspired by the popular artists of the day including Mucha, Gibson, Fisher and Corbett. Thousands of wooden boxes, wall plaques, novelties and pieces of furniture that they purchased from local general stores or from mail-order catalogs were burned and painted. These pieces were manufactured by companies such as The Flemish Art Company of New York and Thayer & Chandler of Chicago, who printed the designs on wood for the pyrographers to burn.

This Victorian fad developed into a new form of artistic expression as the individually burned and painted pieces reflected the personality of the pyrographers. The more adventurous started to burn between the lines and developed a style of 'all-over burning' that today is known as Pyromania. Others not only created their own designs but even made the pieces to be decorated. Both these developments are particularly valued today as true examples of American folk art.

By the 1930s its popularity had declined and, like Mission furniture, was neglected by generations of collectors and dealers. The recent appreciation of Victoriana, the Arts and Crafts Movement, the American West and the popularity of turn-of-the-century graphic art has rekindled interest in pyrography which embraces all these styles.

A new book, *The Burning Passion — Antique and Collectible Pyrography*, by Carole and Richard Smyth, our advisors for this category, is currently available from the authors; they are listed in the Directory under New York.

Key: hb — hand burned

Box, handkerchief; unpnt fruit & roses, factory stamp, EX **25.00**
Chair/table, hb/pnt poinsettias, Rest Ye..., velvet on top, EX **950.00**
Fr, hb/pnt cherries, oval opening, stands, 7½x6", EX **85.00**
Fr, hb/pnt mums, Thayer & Chandler, stands, 7½x6", EX **85.00**
Match holder, burned/pnt Uncle Sam silhouette, 10¾", EX **185.00**
Match holder, Gibson girl w/flowers, hb/pnt flowers, 5¾", EX **95.00**
Match holder, hb/pnt sun & 'Help Yourself,' hinged, 4¾x4" **95.00**

Mirror, hb/pnt Gibson girl, orig Fr beveled glass, 8½" L **95.00**
Pipe rack, hb/pnt, 5x8", EX **145.00**
Plaque, hb w/3-ply pnt & cvd birds & nest, 5½" dia, EX **65.00**
Plaque, hb/pnt Indian Chief, Flemish Art Co #953, 20½x9", EX ...**200.00**
Umbrella stand, deeply burned/pnt iris, metal tray, 28", EX **365.00**

Quezal

The Quezal Art Glass and Decorating Company of Brooklyn, New York, was founded in 1901 by Martin Bach. A former Tiffany employee, Bach's glass closely resembled that of his former employer. Most pieces were signed 'Quezal,' a name taken from a Central American bird. After Bach's death in 1920, his son-in-law, Conrad Vohlsing, continued to produce a Quezal-type glass in Elmhurst, New York, which he marked 'Lustre Art Glass.' See also that particular category. Examples listed here are signed unless noted otherwise.

Bottle, scent; gold, matching stopper, 5" **550.00**
Bowl, nut; gold, ribbed, shouldered, 2½" **135.00**
Chandelier, feathers, wht on yel, gold int, SP mts, 42" **2,750.00**
Decanter, feathers, gr/gold on gr, gold neck, 11½" **3,850.00**
Desk lamp, feather shade, gooseneck gilt-metal base, 12" **300.00**
Lamp, honeycomb shade, brass stick std, 4½x4½" **500.00**
Shade, feathers, gr/gold, 8x6½", EX **900.00**
Shade, gold irid w/ribs, 6½", pr **225.00**
Shade, pulled/trailed decor, gold irid, fluted, 4" dia, pr **325.00**
Sherbet, leaves, gr/wht/gold on opal, lustre int, 3¾x3" **1,350.00**
Vase, hooked waves, gr irid on opal, gold int, 3x4" **7,000.00**
Vase, hooks/feathers, gold/platinum on gr, 10" **2,700.00**
Vase, jack-in-pulpit; feathers, gold/gr irid, gold int, 16" **5,500.00**
Vase, jack-in-pulpit; gold face, gr/gold feather stem, 12" **2,400.00**
Vase, King Tut, elongated flared neck, hdls, disk ft, 12x4" **1,650.00**
Vase, King Tut variant, gr/yel/silver w/purple on opal, no mk, 9" .**550.00**

Quilts

Quilts, while made of necessity, nevertheless represent an art form which expresses the character and the personality of the designer. During the 17th and 18th centuries, quilts were considered a necessary part of a bride's hope chest; the traditional number required to be properly endowed for marriage was a 'baker's dozen'! Quilts were used not only for bed coverings but for curtains, extra insulation, and mattresses as well. The early quilts were made from pieces salvaged from cloth items that had outlived their original usefulness and from bits left over from sewing projects. Regardless of shape, these scraps were fitted together following no organized lines. The resulting hodge-podge design was called a crazy quilt.

In 1793 Eli Whitney developed the cotton gin; as a result, textile production in America became industrialized. Soon inexpensive fabrics were readily available, and ladies were able to choose from colorful prints and solids to add contrast to their work. Both pieced and appliqued work became popular. Pieced quilts were considered utilitarian, while appliqued work was shown with pride of accomplishment at the fair. Today many collectors prize pieced quilts and their intricate geometric patterns above all other types. Many of these designs were given names: Daisy and Oak Leaf, Grandmother's Flower Garden, Log Cabin, and Ocean Wave are only a few. Appliqued quilts involved stitching one piece — carefully cut into a specific form such as a leaf, a flower, or a stylized device — onto either a large one-piece ground fabric or an individual block. Often the background fabric was quilted in a decorative pattern.

Amish women scorned printed calicos as 'worldly' and instead used colorful blocks set with black fabrics to produce a stunning pieced effect. During the Victorian era, the crazy quilt was revived, but the ladies of the 1870s used plush velvets, brocades, silks, and linen patches and embroidered along the seams with feather or chain stitches.

Another type of quilting, highly prized and rare today, is trapunto. These quilts were made by first stitching the outline of the design onto a solid sheet of fabric which was backed with a second having a much looser weave. White was often favored, but color was sometimes used for accent. The design (grapes, flowers, leaves, etc.) was padded through openings made by separating the loose weave of the underneath fabric; a backing was added and the three layers quilted as one.

Besides condition, value is judged on intricacy of pattern, color effect, and craftsmanship. Examine the stitching. Quality quilts have from ten to twelve stitches to the inch. In the listings that follow, examples rated excellent have minor defects. Values given here are auction results; retail may be somewhat higher.

Key:
dmn — diamond
embr — embroidered
hs — hand sewn
hq — hand quilted, quilting
mp — machine pieced
ms — machine sewn
X — cross

Red and green cotton patches on white, finely quilted, 1800s, 90x90", EX, $1,250.00.

Amish

Bow Tie, bright mc, ms binding, EX hq, 72x88", EX **850.00**
Octagons & 9-Patch, bl shades w/gr border, full sz, EX **525.00**
Star, dk colors, bl border/binding, EX work, crib sz, 34x44" **385.00**
Star center, blk on orange, contemporary, 90x94", M **725.00**
Sunshine & Shade, purple/gr/red/pk/blk, 20th C, 80x86" **850.00**
Urn of Flowers, pk/tan/rose/gr, 1930s, 96x75", M **425.00**
Weathervane, blk/dk & lt bl/lav, 1940s, 80x102", EX **325.00**

Appliqued

Butterfly, mc prints on wht, 1930s, 72x60", M **300.00**
Dogwood, mc cottons, hs, from kit, 94x74", NM **400.00**
Dogwood flowers & branches on gr, dmn quilted, 77x94", EX ...**350.00**
Eagle & stars, red & gr on wht, 1850s, 86x78", VG **695.00**
Eagle center w/florals, mc calico/solid red, wear, 80x91" **850.00**
Floral center w/tree & bud border, mc calico/wht, 90x91", EX ...**935.00**
Floral medallions, red & gr calico on wht, 1800s, 101x84" **500.00**
Floral medallions (9), mc swag border, EX work, 81x86", EX **935.00**
Florals w/oak leaves, yel/gr calico on wht, 85x82" **415.00**
Flower urns & puffed berries, fine quilting, 78x75" **635.00**
Flowers, mc pastels on wht, EX quilting, 90x82", M **500.00**
Folky floral, red/gr/wht, fine quilting, 88x83" **880.00**
Leaves, gr/brn/orange/wht, EX quilting, 90x80", EX **225.00**
Oak leaf, pinwheels & stars, tan & gr on wht, ms/hq, 107x80" ..**400.00**

Oak leaf medallions (9), sawtooth border, fading, 82x83" **350.00**
Oak leaf medallions & tulips, mc on wht, wear, 88x80" **465.00**
Ohio Rose, mc solids on wht, 12 blocks, 1920s, 77x62", EX **325.00**
Poppies, red & gr on wht, EX quilting, hs, 83x72", VG **250.00**
Rose medallions, 3-color in red grid, ltweight, 97x83" **715.00**
Sunbonnet Sue, mc prints & solids, blk embr, 98x76", M **425.00**
Tulips, mc w/gr on wht, EX quilting, 1950s, 84x72", NM **325.00**
Tulips in urn, hearts in center, dmn border, wear, 86x76" **600.00**
Water Lily, peach/gr/wht, gr binding, 90x68", EX **325.00**

Mennonite

Carolina Lily, lt & dk gr/pk/bl, embr stems, 80x74", NM **935.00**
Chinese Coin, solid bls & grays, ms/hs/hq, 80x66" **600.00**
Friendship, wool/cottons, embr names, dtd 1916, 81x69" **330.00**
Star, yel & bl, ms/hs/hq, lt overall wear, 87x74" **500.00**
9 Patch, reds w/lt gr, beige & gr border, bl binding, 84x78" **275.00**

Pieced

Basket, mc pastels on gr, 1930s, 78x72", EX **315.00**
Baskets of lilies, bl/beige/wht, hs, 86x68" **360.00**
Blazing Star, mc pastels, lav & wht border, 1930s, 76x68", EX ...**300.00**
Blocks, gr & wht w/much embr, ms/hs, 84x66", EX **235.00**
Boxed Ts, red/wht/gray ginghams, 1930s, 82x68", EX **355.00**
Broken Star, bl on wht w/bl binding, 1930s, 92x78", M **385.00**
Double Irish Chain, bl & wht, 1920s, 76x66", EX **325.00**
Double Irish Chain, Turkey red/navy/wht, ca 1900, 86x76", EX ..**400.00**
Double Wedding Ring, pk/bl/wht, 1930s, 80x72", EX **500.00**
Dresden Plate, mc prints/gr/wht, 1930s, 78x80", M **500.00**
Drunkard's Path, mc & red calico, 1870s, 78x77", EX **500.00**
Field of Diamonds, mc w/yel centers, 1930s, 88x80", M **325.00**
Floral medallions, mc prints, sgn/dtd 1854, faded, 92x68" **250.00**
Flower Garden, mc & wht hexagon blocks, 1940s, 102x88", EX ...**395.00**
Flying Geese, mc prints & solids w/red calico, 90x80", EX **450.00**
Grandmother's Flower Garden, mc cottons, 1920s-30s, 76x64", EX .**285.00**
Grandmother's Flower Garden, mc cottons, 1930s, 110x69", EX ..**325.00**
Improved 9-Patch, mc prints & wht muslin, 1930s, 82x70", EX .**350.00**
Irish Chain, bl & wht, feather quilting, 92x82", EX **440.00**
Jacob's Ladder, red & print cottons, EX quilting, 88x68", EX **285.00**
King's Cross, mc calico & wht, 78x70", EX **285.00**
LeMoyne Star, mc pastels, wht binding, 1920s, 85x70", NM **450.00**
Log Cabin, mc prints w/solid red center, 80x80", M **770.00**
Log Cabin, mc prints/calico w/pk & red, 75x75" **575.00**
Log Cabin Medallion, mc prints/solids, lt wear, 71x70" **300.00**
Lone Star, brn & gold tones, EX quilting, 82x74", EX **275.00**
Lone Star, pastels & solids, EX quilting, 1930s, 94x84", EX **450.00**
Lone Star, red/wht/bl, bl binding, EX quilting, 80x76", M **375.00**
Maple Leaf, mc 8" blocks, wide border, 1930s, 92x66", EX **200.00**
Optical, red/bl/wht, ms binding, 82x68", EX **250.00**
Patchwork, ginghams & chambrays, red sash, 1930s, 82x66", EX ..**315.00**
Pincushion, feed sacks & lt yel, 1930s, 76x68", NM **300.00**
Pine Tree, gr calico on wht, 110x92", EX **715.00**
Pinwheel, red/wht/bl cotton, ms border, 1930s, 84x68", EX **325.00**
Pinwheel (16 sqs), goldenrod/gr/red calico, 75x76", EX **500.00**
Railroad, dk ginghams, 1920s, 76x64", M **300.00**
Rising Sun, mc calico, ca 1890-1900, rprs, 84x60", VG **300.00**
Snail's Trail, lav & bleached muslin, ms binding, 72x66", EX **325.00**
Snowball, pk & wht octagons, 80x62", EX **235.00**
Spider Web, mc solids & prints, 1940s, 82x62", M **325.00**
Star, yel/red/pk/gr, quilted flower designs, 82x82" **300.00**
Star of Bethlehem, mc, 1800s, 87x89", EX **650.00**
Stars (4), gingham & polished cotton, 92x82", M **325.00**
Stars w/in grid, gr/red/wht, wear/spots, 87x89" **450.00**

Triple Irish Chain, rose & wht, pk binding, 90x78", NM **385.00**
Wedding Ring, peach & wht, scalloped border, 90x72", NM **325.00**
Wild Goose Chase, red/wht/gray, 1920s, 84x68", NM **365.00**
Windmill, red & wht, EX quilting, 85x70", M **300.00**
Yo-Yo, cotton prints, 1920s-30s, EX quilting, 88x84", EX **285.00**
Yo-Yo, mc pastels & solids, 1930s, ltweight, 88x88", EX **225.00**
4-Patch, mc calicos & ginghams, 1920s, 81x66", EX **265.00**
6-Pointed Star, mc w/wht hexagons, 1930s, 86x68", EX **315.00**
9-Patch, linsey woolsey, blk & salmon, 98x86", EX **600.00**

Quimper

    Quimper is a type of pottery produced in Quimper, France. A tin enamel-glazed earthenware pottery with hand-painted decoration, it was first produced in the 1600s by the Bousquet and Caussy Factories. Little of this early ware was marked. By the late 1700s, three factories were operating in the area, all manufacturing the same type of pottery. The Grande Maison de HB, a company formed as a result of a marriage joining the Hubaudiere and Bousquet families, was a major producer of Quimper pottery. They marked their wares with various forms of the 'HB' logo; but of the pottery they produced, collectors value examples marked with the 'HB' within a triangle most highly.

    Francois Eloury established another pottery in Quimper in the late 1700s. Under the direction of Charles Porquier, the ware was marked simply 'P.' Adolph Porquier replaced Charles in the 1850s, marking the ware produced during that period with an 'AP' logo. 'PB' (for Porquier-Beau) was used ca 1875 until 1900.

    Jule HenRiot began operations in 1886, using molds he had purchased from Porquier. His mark was 'HR,' and until the 20th century he was in competition with The Grande Maison de HB. In 1926 he began to mark his wares 'HenRiot Quimper.' In 1968 the two factories merged. They are still in operation under the name Les Faenceries de Quimper. The factory sold in the fall of 1983 to Sarah and Paul Janssens from the United States, making it the first time the owners were not French. For those interested in learning more about Quimper, we recommend *Quimper Pottery: A French Folk Art Faience* by Sandra V. Bondhus, our advisor for this category, whose address can be found in the Directory under Connecticut.

Teapot, lady with flowers, blue trim, flat canteen type, HB Quimper, 9x10", restored, lid missing, $180.00. (Mint value with lid, $450.00.)

Bell, peasant man, bagpipe form, unglazed clapper, HQF, 3½" ...**110.00**
Bowl, lady w/bud sprigs, HBQ, 2½x5¼" sq **25.00**
Bowl, lady w/floral sprays, pierced, canted corners, HQF, 8" **120.00**
Bowl, vegetable; man & lady, horseshoe hdls, w/lid, HQ, 6" **120.00**
Butter dish, man w/bagpipes, Decor Riche, HBQ, 4x7" **300.00**
Cache pot, rooster & florals, HBQF, flake, 3" **90.00**
Candlesticks, man & lady, yel/red/bl details, HBQ, 8", pr **625.00**
Chamberstick, peasant man, ruffled, HQF, 5" dia **160.00**
Cheese dish, lady on lid, butterfly finial, HR Quimper, 7¼" **325.00**
Coffeepot, man & lady, hexagonal, HQF, 8", EX **140.00**

Compote, man w/walking stick, scalloped, HR Quimper, 4x8½" ..185.00
Coupe, Porquier Beau Botanical decor, sgn, 8¼" 800.00
Cup & saucer, demitasse; peasant man, HQF, 2", 4" 40.00
Egg cup, man & lady, Ordinaire, HQF, 4¼", pr 55.00
Egg cup, man & lady w/garlands, HB Quimper, 2¼", pr 100.00
Inkstand, dbl wells/stamp compartment, cherub, HB, 19th C 700.00
Inkwell, dbl, man w/florals, inserts & lids, HQF, 2x7" L 245.00
Jam pot, peasant man & fir tree, straw hdl, HB, rstr, 2½" 65.00
Knife rest, lady or man, 1800s, 3⅛", pr 110.00
Match holder, man, latticework, HQF, #89, 3x3¼" 195.00
Mug, lady w/florals, HQF, 6" 75.00
Mustard jar, man w/sprigs, w/lid & undertray, HQF, 4½x4" 130.00
Pin tray, lady & fir tree, red S design, HBQ, 4⅞x3" 40.00
Pitcher, cider; man w/walking stick, HQ, 4½" 120.00
Pitcher, lady, geometric panels, HRQ, fading/wear, 6" 130.00
Pitcher, lady & florals, striped hdl, HQF, flakes, 4" 55.00
Pitcher, lady's portrait, floral garland, HQ, 5¼", NM 50.00
Pitcher, man & fir tree, Breton Quimper, 5" 55.00
Pitcher, man & florals, HQF, 6¼" 125.00
Pitcher, peasant man w/whip, florals, HBQ, 6½" 90.00
Plate, boy's portrait, Ivoire Corbeille, HQ, 8¼" 50.00
Plate, lady, a la touch floral sprig, scalloped, HRQ, 6", NM 50.00
Plate, lady, Demi-Fantasie pattern, fish form, HQF, 10" 210.00
Plate, lady by fence, Malicorne, PBX, 4¾" 85.00
Plate, man in yel beret, rolled rim, HR Quimper, 7" sq 230.00
Plate, man w/walking stick & fir tree, HBQF, 9" 45.00
Plate, peasant lady, Ordinaire, HQF, 5¾", 4 for 120.00
Plate, 3 yel roses, floral garlands, sponged rim, HQ, 8" 65.00
Platter, lady, garland border, HQF, 13¾x9" 225.00
Porringer, lady knitting, Malicorne, pierced, PBX, 7½" 45.00
Powder jar, lady's portrait, Ivoire Corbeille, HQ, 4" dia 55.00
Salt cellar; dbl; shoes form w/ring hdl, HB, 4" L 65.00
Snuff bottle, peasant man, bagpipe shape, Malicorne, 3" 150.00
Statue, Ste Anne w/child Mary at side, HRQ, 13" 220.00
Statue, Ste Vierge w/Christ Child, HQF, recent, 6¼" 35.00
Sugar bowl, lady, Ordinaire pattern, w/lid, HQF, 4x5½" 40.00
Sugar bowl, peasant lady & fir tree, hdls, HBQ, 4¼x5¼" 50.00
Tea bag holder/spoon rest, peasant man, bagpipe shape, HQ, 3" ..55.00
Teapot, man & lady, bl striped hdl, HQ, 8" 200.00
Tile, man's portrait, sunflowers, Ivoire Corbeille, HQ, 9" dia 175.00
Tulipiere, lady w/distaff, 6 openings, HQF, 7¼x5½" 375.00
Tulipiere, Normandie man, heart shape, 8 openings, sgn, 10" 525.00
Tureen, lady & floral on lid, garland base, HQF, 5½x8" 85.00
Tureen, peasant lady, Ordinaire, new, HQF, 9½x10¼" 100.00
Tureen, yel band w/bl circlets & red dots, hdls, HQ, 4x4" 65.00
Vase, bud; lady, a la touche sprays, HBQ, 6x5" 55.00
Vase, bud; lady & florals, cornucopia form, HQ, 3½" 55.00
Vase, bud; peasant man & florals, hdls, HB Quimper, 6½" 110.00
Vase, florals & geometrics, Henriot Quimper, recent, 10x5" 30.00
Vase, lady spinning, geometrics, shell hdls, sgn HQ, 12x8¼" 450.00
Vase, lady w/basket, garland spray, hdls, HR Quimper, 7¼" 200.00
Vase, man/lady/moon crescent, dolphin support, HR, 19th C, 6", pr .650.00
Vase, quintal; lady w/flower, 5 openings, HQF, 6" 140.00
Vase, quintal; man w/flute, 5 openings, HQ, 3½", EX 55.00
Wall pocket, lady at fence, Malicorne, unsgn, 11½" 195.00
Wall pocket, lady w/basket, cone form, HQF, #118, 10½" 200.00
Wall pocket, man & lady, dbl-cone form, Belle-Ile, HQF, 10" ...220.00
Wall pocket, man & lady, Malicorne, lyre form, PBX, 7½" 375.00
Wall pocket, man w/horn, bagpipe shape, HR Quimper, 8½", EX .120.00

Radford

Pottery associated with Albert Radford (1882-1904) can be cate-gorized by three periods of production. Pottery produced in Tiffin, Ohio, (1896-1899) consists of bone china (no marked examples known) and high-quality jasperware with applied Wedgwood-like cameos. Tiffin jasperware is often impressed 'Radford Jasper' in small block letters. At Zanesville, Ohio, Radford jasperware was marked only with an incised, two-digit shape number, and the cameos were not applied but rather formed within the mold and filled with a white slip. Zanesville Radford ware was produced for only a few months before the Radford pottery was acquired by the Arc-en-Ciel company in 1903. Production in Zanesville was handled by Radford's father, Edward (1840-1910), who remained in Zanesville after Albert moved to Clarks-burg, West Virginia, where the Radford Pottery Co. was completed shortly before Albert's death in 1904. Jasperware was not produced in Clarksburg, and the molds appear to have been left in Zanesville, where some were subsequently used by the Arc-en-Ciel pottery. The Clarks-burg, West Virginia, pottery produced a standard glaze, slip-decorated ware, Ruko; Thera and Velvety, matt glazed ware often signed by Albert Haubrich, Alice Bloomer, and other artists; and Radura, a semi-matt green glaze developed by Albert Radford's son, Edward. The Clarksburg plant closed in 1912. Our advisor for this category is James L. Murphy; he is listed in the Directory under Ohio.

Vase, winged figures with instruments, #14, 7", $310.00.

Jasper

Ewer, grapes/blkberries, lt bl, face on hdl, #17, 9" 285.00
Mug, floral relief, lt bl, 4½" 150.00
Vase, cherubs on flying eagles, #23, 9½" 475.00
Vase, lady sits, trees & dog, bark trim, #14, 7" 310.00
Vase, lady w/flowers, bk: grapes, #59, 4" 150.00

Miscellaneous

Jardiniere, Ruko, tulips, 8½x9" 250.00
Jardiniere & ped, winged creatures/foliage, streaky gr, 34" 500.00
Mug, grape & floral relief, wht on bl, #25, 5" 225.00
Vase, Thera, floral, red on gr matt, rare, 12" 450.00
Vase, Thera, gr bsk w/pk floral, 8", NM 160.00
Vase, 2 children & lion, wht & lt brn, #15, 7" 225.00

Radios

Vintage radios are becoming very collectible. There were thou-sands of styles and types produced, the most popular of which today are the breadboard and the cathedral. Consoles are usually considered less marketable, since their size makes them hard to display and store. For those wishing to learn more about antique radios, we recommend *The Collector's Guide to Antique Radios*, by Sue and Marty Bunis, available from your local bookstore or Collector Books. They are also the authors of *A Collector's Guide to Transistor Radios*. For information on novelty radios, refer to *Collector's Guide to Novelty Radios* by Marty Bunis and Robert Breed. Values are given for radios in near mint to mint condition.

Key:

phono — phonograph   tbl/m — table model

A-C Dayton XL-71 Navigator, wood, battery, tbl/m, 1929 ....85.00
Addison B2E, plastic, left grill bars, right dial, tbl/m 300.00
Admiral #303, wood, upper grill, AM/FM, tbl/m, 1959 ....20.00
Admiral 14-B5, ivory plastic, 2 bands, hdl, tbl/m, 1941 ....40.00
Admiral 6R11, plastic, lift top, tbl/m, 1949 ....25.00
Air Castle #751, wood, blk slide rule dial, blk top, tbl/m 35.00
Airline, #62-553, wood, push buttons, left Deco grill, tbl/m 125.00
Airline #14BR-521A, plastic, lower front dial, sm case, tbl/m 35.00
American Bosch #470-G, wood, cutouts in grill, console, 1935, .120.00
Apex #160, wood, highboy, stretcher base, console, 1930 ....140.00
Arvin #160T, plastic, metal grill, ribbed top, tbl/m, 1948 ....35.00
Arvin #247D, wood, 3-shelf bookcase ea side, 1938 ....175.00

Atwater Kent #9A, breadboard type, rectangular wooden board, one left and one center dial, four tubes, battery, 1923, $650.00.

Atwater Kent #20C, wood, rectangular, battery, tbl/m, 1925 .....100.00
Atwater Kent #387, Cathedral, wood, cloth grill, 1934 ....275.00
Atwater Kent #854, Tombstone, wood, cloth grill, 1935 ....145.00
Automatic TT-600, plastic, tubes & transistors, portable, '57 ......75.00
Belmont #1170, wood, tuning eye, cloth grill, console, 1936 ......135.00
Bremer-Tully #7-70, wood, rectangular, tbl/m, 1928 ....100.00
Brunswick #4689, wood, Queen Anne-style console, 1939 ....200.00
Chancellor #35P, leatherette, AC/DC/battery, portable, '47 ....25.00
Cleartone #60 Goldcrest, wood, rectangular, battery, tbl/m 100.00
Crosley #5-75, mahog highboy, battery, console, 1926 ....160.00
Crosley #50, wood, Bakelite panel, battery, tbl/m, 1924 ....120.00
Crosley Ace 3C, wood, rectangular, dbl doors, battery, tbl/m 175.00
Day-Fan Dayroyal, mahog, desk-style console, battery, 1926 ......150.00
Dewald #562 Jewel, Catalin, hdl, tbl/m, 1941, minimum value ..750.00
Electro S-5, Cathedral, walnut, ornate grill, 1930 ....295.00
Emerson #365, walnut, tuning eye, hifi, tbl/m, 1940 ....75.00
Emerson #516, plastic, slanted side rule dial, tbl/m, 1947 ....45.00
Emerson #713, wood, sunburst front, rayed grill, tbl/m, '52 ....70.00
Eveready #32, wood, sliding doors, 7 tubes, console, 1929 ....175.00
Fada #252 Temple, Catalin, tbl/m, 1941, minimum value 550.00
Fada #605, plastic, horizontal louvers, tbl/m, 1946 ....55.00
Farnsworth GT-050, plastic, Deco style, tbl/m, 1948 ....60.00
Firestone #4-A-37, wood, pull-out phono, console, 1947 ....100.00
General Electric #114, brn plastic, 2 knobs, tbl/m, 1946 ....55.00
General Electric H-634, wood, push buttons, tbl/m, 1939 ....60.00
General Electric S-22, Tombstone, wood, w/stand, 1931 ....250.00
Grebe #80, Tombstone, walnut, cutouts in grill, 1933 ....160.00
Hoffman C-1007, wood, pull-out phono, console, 1949 ....125.00
Howard #40, wood, lowboy console w/stretcher base, 1931 ....135.00
Jewel #5050, plastic, checkered grill on top, portable, 1951 ....45.00
Knight #5F-565, leatherette, AC/DC/battery, portable, 1949 ....40.00

Magnavox TRF-50, wood, cvd dbl doors, battery, tbl/m, '24 ......230.00
Majestic #161, Tombstone, wood, chrome cutouts on grill 195.00
Midwest #16-37, wood, Deco case w/cloth grill, console, 1937 ...125.00
Motorola #52, Catalin, vertical louvers, tbl/m, 1939, minimum .550.00
Motorola 78F11, wood, console w/pull-out phono, 1949 ....90.00
Olympic #7-925, wood, console w/pull-out phono, 1948 ....70.00
Packard-Bell #880, wood, console w/left phono, 1948 ....90.00
Philco #37-61, Tombsone, wood, cloth grill, 1937 ....130.00
Philco #39-55, wood, fold-up front, remote control console 195.00
Philco #46-1217, wood, pull-out phono, console, 1946 ....150.00
Philco #60, Cathedral, wood, cloth grill, 1936 ....250.00
Philco PT-61 Transitone, 2-tone wood, tbl/m, 1940 ....50.00
RCA #77V1, wood, lift top, left phono, console, 1948 ....65.00
RCA #9X11, Catalin, grill w/cutout, tbl/m, 1939, minimum 700.00
RCA Radiola #24, leatherette, battery, portable, 1925 ....325.00
Roland #8FT1M, plastic, woven grill, tbl/m, 1953 ....25.00
Silvertone #1580, wood, lowboy, 7 tubes, console 145.00
Silvertone #7038, wood, horizontal grill bars, tbl/m, 1941 ....60.00
Sparton #7AM46, wood, slide rule dial, Police console, '46 ....100.00
Stewart-Warner #1264, wood, lowboy, cloth grill, console, '34 ..140.00
Stromberg-Carlson #1235-PLM, wood, console w/pull-out phono .125.00
Stromberg-Carlson #61-L, wood, 8-sided dial, console, 1936 .....140.00
Trav-Ler #135-M, wood, rnd dial, 7 tubes, console, 1937 ....90.00
Truetone D2018, plastic, Modern style, tbl/m, 1950 ....125.00
Western Electric #4B, wood, rectangular, battery, tbl/m, '23 ......450.00
Westinghouse WR-336, wood, tuning eye, console, 1939 ....140.00
Zenith #14-H-789, wood, console w/fold-down phono door, '48 ..120.00
Zenith #4-S-220V, ebony finish, ftd tbl/m, 1937 ....175.00
Zenith #5-J-247, wood, lower storage, chair-side, 1937 ....140.00
Zenith #6-S-254Y, ebony finish, triangular dial, console, '37 .....230.00

Novelty

All laundry detergent box form, AM, MIB 65.00
Annie & Sandy 40.00
Atlas Battery 30.00
Bon Ami cleanser, can form, AM, MIB 20.00
Delco Freedom Battery 20.00
Heinz Ketchup, bottle form, MIB 40.00
John Player race car 30.00
Mork Eggship, AM, MIB 35.00
Popeye, transistor, 1973, MIB 50.00
Pratt & Lambert, paint can 30.00
Radio Shack Robot, MIB 30.00
Sesame Street Trash Can 25.00
Smurf head figural, AM, 1982, EX 20.00
Sprout figural, AM 20.00
Stutz Bear Cat, Japan 60.00
Tony the Tiger figural, AM, 1980, MIB 30.00

Transistor

Post-World War II baby boomers, now approaching their fiftieth year, are rediscovering prized possessions of youth, their pocket radios. The transistor wonders, born with rock 'n roll, were at the vanguard of miniaturization and futuristic design in the decade which followed their introduction to Christmas shoppers in 1954. The tiny receiving sets launched the growth of Texas Instruments and shortly to follow abroad, Sony and other Japanese giants.

The most desirable sets include the 1954 four-transistor Regency TR-1 and colorful early Sony and Toshiba models. Certain pre-1960 models by Hoffman and Admiral represented the earliest practical use of solar technology and are also highly valued. To avoid high tariffs, scores of two-transistor sets, boys' radios, were imported from Japan with names like Pet and Charmy. Many early inexpensive transistor sets could be heard only with an earphone. The smallest sets are known as shirt-pocket models while those slightly larger are called coat pockets. Early collectible transistor radios all have civil defense triangle markings at 640 and 1240 on the frequency dial and nine or fewer transistors. Very few desirable sets were made after 1963. Model numbers are most commonly found inside sets. Our advisor for this category is Mike Brooks; he is listed in the Directory under California and welcomes questions. Please include a SASE.

Bulova #250	200.00
De Wald K-544	100.00
Dick Tracy, 2-transistor	60.00
Disasteradio B-1	55.00
Global GR-711	65.00
Honeytone #604	50.00
Jupiter #6T330	55.00
Mantola, all transistor	125.00
National Pocket Super	60.00
Philco T-7	50.00
Sceptre, 2-transistor	45.00
Sony ICR-120	150.00
Tiny Tim	55.00
Top Flight, 2-transistor	40.00
Toshiba #5-TR	110.00
Zephyr ZR-620	45.00
Zohar Z Transistor	45.00

Railroadiana

Collecting railroad-related memorabilia has become one of America's most popular hobbies. The range of collectible items available is almost endless, considering the fact that more than 175 different railroad lines are represented. Some collectors prefer to specialize in only one, while others attempt to collect at least one item from every railway line known to have existed. For the advanced collector, there is the challenge of locating rarities from short-lived railroads; for the novice there are abundant keys, buttons, passes, and playing cards. Among the most popular specializations are dining-car collectibles — flatware, glassware, dinnerware, etc., in a wide variety of patterns and styles.

Almost anything from the Rock Island Line has become very collectible, and good lanterns are appreciating on today's market. The Denver & Rio Grande Railroad lantern manufactured by Handlan-Buck, top marked and with a red cast (embossed) melon globe now commands about $1,400.00. Lantern prices are based on the scarcity of the railroad, the color and shape of the globe, and whether the railroad name is embossed rather than being simply acid etched. Note: Two-color lantern globes are now being reproduced.

Since we've mentioned reproductions, collectors should be made aware that there is a spittoon currently out of Taiwan that is brass, about 12" high, could be in two sections, and has a pinched waist. The wording 'Union Pacific Railroad' and a train are embossed on the front and the back. Unscrupulous dealers are passing these off as old and asking exorbitant prices. Buyer beware! To continue this sad story, railroad police badges have given the trade the jitters; so many are reproduced (so well!). Remember the 11th commandment: Know Thy Dealer. (Prices stated below are for authentic badges.)

For a more thorough study, we recommend *Railroad Collectibles, Third Revised Edition*, by Stanley L. Baker, available at your local library or bookstore. Because prices are so volatile, the best pricing sources are often monthly or quarterly 'For Sale' lists. Two you may find helpful may be ordered from Golden Spike, P.O. Box 422, Williamsville, NY 14221, and Grandpa's Depot and Caboose, 1616 17 St., Suite 267, Denver, CO 80202. Our advice for the dinnerware section comes from Shrader's Antiques (see Directory, California), while Grandpa's Depot (see Colorado) advises us for the remainder.

Key:
BL — bottom logo	SL — side logo
BS — bottom stamped	SM — side marked
NBS — no bottom stamp	TL — top logo
R&B — Reed and Barton	TM — top marked

Dinnerware

Plate, Pullman, Indian Tree, Buffalo China, 10½x7⅛", $98.00.

Ashtray, GN, Glory of the West, BS, 4"	135.00
Ashtray, GN, Mtns & Flowers, BS, 4" dia	85.00
Bowl, baked apple; PRR, Keystone, NBS, 4x5¾"	125.00
Bowl, baker; B&O, Capitol, BS, 5x6"	75.00
Bowl, baker; SP, Sunset, BS, 6x8"	135.00
Bowl, berry; B&O, Centenary, BS, 5½"	85.00
Bowl, berry; C&O, Staffordshire, BS, 5½"	110.00
Bowl, berry; CMStP&P, Galatea, NBS, 4½"	55.00
Bowl, berry; GN, Mtns & Flowers, BS, 5½"	65.00
Bowl, berry; Pullman, Indian Tree, TM, NBS, 5½"	100.00
Bowl, berry; UP, Challenger, TL, NBS	35.00
Bowl, bouillon; ATSF, CA Poppy, dbl hdld, NBS	95.00
Bowl, bouillon; NYC, Mercury, NBS	55.00
Bowl, bouillon; PRR, Purple Laurel, NBS	25.00
Bowl, bouillon; SP, Prairie Mtn Wildflowers, BS	85.00
Bowl, cereal; Alaska RR, McKinley, SL, NBS, 6½"	275.00
Bowl, cereal; ATSF, Adobe, TL, NBS, 6"	50.00
Bowl, cereal; CMStP&P, Traveler, NBS, 6½"	65.00
Bowl, cereal; CRI&P, Golden Rocket, TL, NBS, 6½"	125.00
Bowl, cereal; D&RGW, Prospector, TL, NBS, 6½"	67.00
Bowl, cereal; GN, Glacier, BS, 6½"	110.00
Bowl, cereal; UP, Historical, TL, NBS, 6½"	210.00
Bowl, flat salad; B&O, Capitol, TL, NBS, 7½"	95.00
Bowl, master salad; GN, Glory of the West, 9x3½"	400.00
Bowl, soup; B&O, Centenary, BS, 9"	150.00
Bowl, soup; GM&O, Rose, TL, NBS, 9"	235.00
Bowl, soup; NYC, Hudson, Haviland, BS, 8½"	75.00
Bowl, soup; PRR, Keystone, TL, NBS, 9"	82.00
Bowl, vegetable; B&O, Capitol, TL, NBS, 5x6½"	45.00
Butter pat, ATSF, CA Poppy, NBS	32.00
Butter pat, B&O, Centenary, Lamberton, BS	75.00
Butter pat, CMStP&P, Traveler, NBS	75.00
Butter pat, CRI&P, Golden State, TL, NBS	140.00
Butter pat, D&H, Canterbury, NBS	35.00
Butter pat, FEC, Mistic, BS	155.00
Butter pat, Fred Harvey, Trend, rnd, NBS	55.00
Butter pat, GM&O, Rose, NBS	35.00
Butter pat, MKT, Shirley, NBS	25.00
Butter pat, MP, Jefferson, NBS	85.00
Butter pat, N&W, Cavalier, NBS	100.00

Butter pat, N&W, Pinehurst, NBS 50.00
Butter pat, Pullman, Calumet, TM, NBS 185.00
Butter pat, Pullman, Indian Tree, TM, NBS 85.00
Butter pat, SP, Harriman Blue, TL, BS 165.00
Butter pat, UP, Blue & Gold, NBS 25.00
Celery tray, UP, Historical, TL, BS, 10x4½" 275.00
Chocolate pot, ATSF, Griffon, NBS, w/lid 450.00
Compote, MStP&SSM, Logan, NBS, 3½x7" 210.00
Creamer, ACL, Flora of the South, ind, 2" 175.00
Creamer, CN, Bonaventure, no hdl, ind, 2" 65.00
Creamer, CN, Bonaventure, SL, NBS 85.00
Creamer, CN, Mustard Gold, BS, 3¾" 25.00
Creamer, CP, Bows & Leaves, BS 35.00
Creamer, Fred Harvey, Cactus logo, no hdl, ind, 2" ...135.00
Creamer, MKT, Katy Ornaments, NBS, 4¼" 65.00
Creamer, NYC, DeWitt Clinton, SL, NBS, 4" 50.00
Creamer, NYNH&H, Blue Platinum, no hdl, SL, ind, 2" ...125.00
Creamer, SP, Prairie Mtn Wildflowers, SL, BS, ind, 3" ...150.00
Creamer, T&P, T&P Arrow, no hdl, SL, NBS, ind, 2¾" ...385.00
Creamer, UP, Winged Streamliner, SL, NBS, 4½" 85.00
Cup & saucer, ACL, Flora of the South, BS 235.00
Cup & saucer, CN, Queen Elizabeth, SL, NBS 75.00
Cup & saucer, CP, Bows & Leaves, BS 85.00
Cup & saucer, D&RGW, Blue Adam, NBS 70.00
Cup & saucer, demi; ACL, Carolina, BS 90.00
Cup & saucer, demi; C&EI, Dixieland, NBS, no logo ...65.00
Cup & saucer, demi; CMStP&P, Peacock, NBS 135.00
Cup & saucer, demi; CP, Blue Maple Leaf, SL 110.00
Cup & saucer, demi; Fred Harvey, Webster, NBS 95.00
Cup & saucer, demi; NYC, DeWitt Clinton, SL, NBS ...110.00
Cup & saucer, demi; UP, Blue & Gold 50.00
Cup & saucer, Dominion, SL, NBS 95.00
Cup & saucer, EH&A, Hampton, SL, NBS 275.00
Cup & saucer, NP, Yellowstone, SL, NBS 345.00
Cup & saucer, PRR, Mtn Laurel, NBS 55.00
Cup & saucer, SRR, Piedmont, BS 45.00
Cup & saucer, Wabash, Banner, SL, NBS 225.00
Egg cup, ATSF, Adobe, NBS 12.00
Egg cup, C&NW, Flambeau, NBS 25.00
Egg cup, D&H, Canterbury, SL, NBS 165.00
Egg cup, UP, Portland Rose, BS, sm 285.00
Gravy boat, C&NW, Depot Ornaments, NBS 135.00
Gravy boat, CB&Q, Violets & Daisies, BS 325.00
Gravy boat, CM&PS, Puget, SL, NBS 295.00
Gravy boat, SMStP&P, Galatea, NBS 275.00
Gravy boat, UP, Desert Flower, BS 135.00
Hot food cover, B&O, Capitol, SL, NBS, 6½" 185.00
Hot food cover, B&O, Derby, NBS, 6½" 30.00
Hot food cover, CMStP&P, Galatea, NBS, 6" 150.00
Ice cream shell, B&O, Camden, NBS, 5½x6" 35.00
Ice cream shell, L&N, Regent, NBS, 5x6" 55.00
Ice cream shell, UP, Winged Streamliner, NBS, 4½x4" ...55.00
Match holder/ashtray, T&P, Cobalt Blue, SL, NBS 365.00
Mustard pot, Fred Harvey, Cactus, w/lid, SL, NBS, 3x2½" ...145.00
Mustard pot, NYNH&H, Platinum Blue, w/lid, SL, NBS, 3x2½" ..185.00
Pitcher, B&A, Berkshire, SL, NBS, 6" 385.00
Pitcher, CP, Baker Green, BS, 5½" 65.00
Pitcher, SP, Imperial, no oranges, BS, 6½" 325.00
Plate, ACL, Flora of the South, BS, 9" 95.00
Plate, Alaska RR, McKinley, TL, NBS, 7½" 350.00
Plate, ATSF, Bleeding Blue, TL, NBS, 7½" 175.00
Plate, ATSF, Mimbreno, BS, 6½" 75.00
Plate, B&O, Centenary, BS, 10½" 145.00
Plate, B&O, Centenary, divided, BS, 10½" 195.00

Plate, C&O, Chessie, TL, NBS, 9½" 265.00
Plate, C&O, Homestead, NBS, 9½" 45.00
Plate, CN, Windsor, children's ware, TL, NBS, 8½" ...125.00
Plate, CN, Windsor, TL, NBS, 8½" 35.00
Plate, CP, Blue Maple Leaf, TL, NBS, 9¼" 65.00
Plate, CRI&P, LaSalle, TL, NBS, 5½" 125.00
Plate, D&H, Adirondack, TL, NBS, 5½" 45.00
Plate, D&H, Vermont, TL, NBS, 9½" 225.00
Plate, DL&W, St Albans, BS, 9½" 235.00
Plate, Fred Harvey, Cactus logo, TL, NBS, 10" 95.00
Plate, Fred Harvey, Southwest, TL, NBS, 10" 165.00
Plate, GN, Empire, grill type, BS, 9½" 195.00
Plate, GTW, City of Grand Rapids, TL, NBS, 9" 235.00
Plate, IC, Creole, TL, BS, 10¼" 235.00
Plate, Interstate News Service, Interstate, TL, NBS, 9¼" ...165.00
Plate, MKT, Alamo, cobalt band, NBS, 10½" 350.00
Plate, NYNH&H, Merchants, TL, BS, 8½" 165.00
Plate, SL&SF, Denmark, NBS, 9½" 65.00
Plate, SP, Harriman Blue, TL, BS, 9" 135.00
Plate, SP, Prairie Mtn Wildflowers, NBS, 9½" 55.00
Plate, SP&S, Red Leaves, NBS, 8" 55.00
Plate, SPLA&SL, Harriman Blue, TL, NBS, 7" 465.00
Plate, SRR, Peach Blossom, BS, 9¼" 195.00
Plate, UP, Challenger, TL, NBS, 9½" 65.00
Plate, UP, Desert Flower, BS, 9½" 95.00
Plate, UP, Portland Rose, BS, 8" 265.00
Plate, WP, Feather River, TL, NBS, 5¼" 65.00
Plate, WP, Meridale, BS, 7½" 75.00

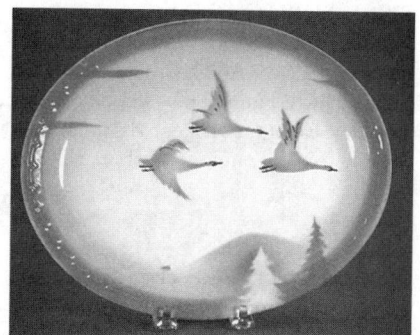

Platter, Milwaukee Railroad, Traveler, pink on white with black details, 9¾x7¾", $75.00.

Platter, C&NW, Rockford, BS, 8x12" 110.00
Platter, C&O, Staffordshire, BS, 10½x8" 235.00
Platter, CMStP&P, Galatea, NBS, 5½x7½" 50.00
Platter, CMStP&P, Peacock, NBS, 6½x8" 55.00
Platter, CN, Rupert, TL, NBS, 9½x7½" 45.00
Platter, GTW, City of Grand Rapids, TL, NBS, 10½x7½" ...85.00
Platter, IC, Coral, NBS, 5½x7" 25.00
Platter, MStP&SSM, Robinson Baker, NBS, 6½x4½" ...75.00
Platter, Parker Railway News, Albany-Macon, TL, NBS, 12x8½" .195.00
Platter, Pullman, Calumet, TM, NBS, 12x8½" 100.00
Platter, Purple Laurel, BS, 7½x11½" 60.00
Platter, SP, Prairie Mtn Wildflowers, BS, 8½x12½" ...145.00
Platter, WP, Feather River, TL, NBS, 9x11" 265.00
Relish, CB&Q, Violets & Daisies, NBS, 3½x7½" 65.00
Relish, CMStP&P, Galatea, NBS, 3½x7½" 70.00
Relish, CMStP&P, Traveler, NBS, 4x9½" 50.00
Relish, UP, Historical, TL, BS, 7½x3½" 225.00
Sherbet, Reading, Stotesbury, ped ft, NBS 165.00
Sugar bowl, AFSF, CA Poppy, BS, w/lid 165.00
Sugar bowl, Amtrak, National, NBS 32.00
Teapot, CN, Verde Green (cube), SL, NBS, w/lid 200.00
Teapot, NYNH&H, Platinum Blue, SL, BS, w/lid 260.00

Toothpick holder, MKT, Katy Ornaments, NBS, 2" 45.00

Glass

Ashtray, SCL, red & bl logo, 6-sided 10.00
Champagne, Southern Ry, gr logo, 4½" 25.00
Glass, martini; Southern Ry, gr logo 10.00
Goblet, water; UP, stemmed, wht shield, 5½" 18.00
Roly poly, Wabash, flag & train, red & bl, 3¼" 12.00
Tumbler, NYC, flanged heavy base, 5¼" 7.50
Tumbler, PRR, Madison Sq Garden history, 5½" 5.50
Tumbler, Santa Fe in wht, 4", 4 for 20.00
Tumbler, water; NYC, wht logo, flanged base, 5" 10.00

Keys

Switch keys are brass with a hollow barrel and a round head with a hole in the center. The initials or the name of the railroad company that used it are incised on the head. Examples representing common railroads are valued at $15.00 and up, while those from the Colorado & Southern Ry are now selling for $65.00, as are some of the early predecessors.

Car, D&RGW, steel 10.00
Switch, AT&S, Adlake S 22.00
Switch, D&H, Slaymaker 32.00
Switch, D&RGW, Adlake 25.00
Switch, L&N, brass, fat bbl type 20.00
Switch, LS&MS, A&W, Chicago 37.50
Switch, MK&T, brass, fat bbl type 20.00
Switch, MOPAC, FS Hdw 17.50
Switch, NYC, FS Hdw, brass 22.50
Switch, P&WV, Adlake 37.50
Switch, PRR, Fraim, brass, knobby style, EX patina 35.00
Switch, Seabord, Adlake, brass 32.00
Switch, Y&N, Fraim, brass, short bbl 32.50

Lamps

Inspector's, CMStP&P, clear lens, EX 65.00
Marker, tail end; CMStP&P, 4-lens, EX 185.00
Marker, tail end; Omaha Ry, 4-lens, wall mt 150.00
Semaphore, CNWRR, 2-lens, EX 88.00
Switch stand lamp, B&A, 4-lens, electrified, EX 100.00
Track walker's, hand type, unmk, EX 75.00

Lanterns

Before 1920 kerosene brakemen's lanterns were made with tall globes, usually 5⅜" tall. These are the most desirable and are usually found at the top of the price scale. Short globes from 1921 through 1940 normally measure 3½" in height, except for those manufactured by Dietz, which are 4" tall. (Soon thereafter, battery brakemen's lanterns came into widespread useage; these are not popular with collectors and are generally not railroad marked.)

All should be marked with the name or initials of the railroad. Look on the top, the top apron, or the bell base (if it has one). Globes may be found in these colors (listed in order of popularity): clear, red, amber, aqua, cobalt, and two-color.

B&O, Adlake Kero, short amber globe, EX 150.00
CB&Q, Adams & Westlake, short red unmk globe 75.00
CC&O, Adlake Reliable, bl etched tall globe 555.00
CC&O, Keystone Casey, tall etched globe, brass burner 435.00
CRR on dome, Adlake Reliable, clear etched tall globe, EX 485.00
D&RGW, tin, sm 88.00
L&N, Armspear, red mk 5⅜" globe 175.00

Lehigh Valley, Armspear, clear 5⅜" mk globe 150.00
N&W, Adams & Westlake, cast tall mk globe, Pat, EX 225.00
N&W, Armspear, clear short globe 115.00
NYC, Dietz, clear mk 4" globe 60.00
NYC, Dietz #5, clear tall unmk globe, brass burner 225.00
NYC, Dietz #6, clear tall cast globe, brass burner, EX 435.00
NYNH&H, Adlake Adams, clear emb tall globe, EX 250.00
Presentation, Adams & Westlake, etched globe, 1880, 11" 1,775.00
Presentation, Adams & Westlake Queen, NP on brass, 10¾" .1,675.00
Presentation, CT Hamm 39, NP w/gr-over-clear globe, 12" 1,500.00
Pullman, Adams-Westlake, brass fr, clear lens 330.00
SCL, red short globe 115.00
Southern Ry, Adlake Reliable, tall mk globe 150.00
TC, Adlake Reliable, clear tall unmk globe, brass burner 250.00

Linens

Apron, bartender's, UP, plum, Overland logo 6.50
Apron, cook's, UP, wht, Overland logo 10.00
Bag, package shipping; Ry Express Agency, 40x32" 10.00
Blanket, Burlington Northern, brn & blk wool, full sz 100.00
Blanket, C&O, lt bl, Chessie & kittens on binding, twin sz 195.00
Blanket, Canadian Nat'l, tan wool, maple leaf logo, twin sz 85.00
Blanket, NP, royal bl wool, stamped logo, twin sz 175.00
Blanket, NP/Pullman, bl cross-stitch pattern woven in, twin sz ..150.00
Headrest cover, Denver Zephyr, brn on tan, 20x14" 35.00
Headrest cover, N&W, red logo & stripe, 22x15", EX 17.00
Headrest cover, SCL, beach scene, 15x16" 15.00
Napkin, NRPC, royal bl, 18", M 5.00
Napkin, Rock Island, 18" sq 15.00
Napkin, UP, wht on wht, 18" sq 7.00
Pillowcase, C&O for Progress, bl dome on wht, M 12.00
Tablecloth, CA Zephyr logo, 42x44" 20.00
Tablecloth, Frisco, old logo, wht on wht, 33x51", EX 40.00
Tablecloth, Rock Island, damask, bearskin wht on wht, 51x33" ..45.00
Tablecloth, Rock Island, ecru, floral design, 56x43", EX 45.00
Towel, CA Zephyr, red logo & stripe on wht, 22x16" 15.00
Towel, NYC, red stripe on wht cotton, 22x16" 20.00
Towel, Penn Central, gr logo & stripe on wht 8.00
Towel, Pullman, bl logo & stripe, 1918, 22x16" 15.00
Towel, Southern Ry/Pullman, bl stripe, 22x16" 10.00
Towel, UP/Pullman, woven logo w/bl stripe, 22x16" 12.00
Wiping cloth, Axy-Dent & Wipe Out Accidents on Santa Fe 4.00

Locks

Brass switch locks (pre-1920) were made in two styles: heart-shaped and Keen Kutter style. Values for the heart-shaped locks are determined to a great extent by the railroad represented and just how its name appears on the lock. Most in demand are those with large embossed letters; if the letters are small and incised, demand is minimal. For instance, one from the Union Pacific line (even with heavy embossed letters) may go for only $45.00, while the same from the D&RG railroad could go easily sell for $250.00. Old Keen Kutter styles (brass with a 'pointy' base) from Colorado & Southern and Denver & Rio Grande could range from $600.00 to $1,200.00.

Steel switch locks (circa 1920 on) with the initials of the railroad incised in small letters — for example BN, L&H, and PRR — are usually valued at $12.00 to $15.00.

BNR, Keline, steel, w/chain, EX 15.00
N&W, Adlake, brass, w/N&W Slaymaker key 98.00
NC&STL, brass, dust cover, no spring, ca 1905 ....230.00
P&R, Fraim, ornate casting, brass, 1920, M 265.00
Switch, CRR, Adlake, steel, w/chain 17.50

Switch, CRR, Keline, w/chain, unused 17.00
Switch, NGI, brass 120.00
Switch, SA&O, brass 225.00
Switch, UP, cast brass, EX 145.00

Lock and key, Illinois Central, brass, Remove Key When Locking embossed on front, $150.00.

Silverplate

The value of a hollowware item is affected by where the logo and/or railroad name was stamped; a side-marked piece is much preferred to one with the mark on the bottom. Note: Some railroad silver from early private cars has recently surfaced. Marks such as Denver & Salt Lake car 101 (called the 'Pheasant') and FECRy's 'Alicia' (Henry Flagler's car) are good examples and might today be considered 'museum quality' by railroadiana buffs.

Bowl, ice cream; Pullman; Meriden, early BS, 4½" 65.00
Bowl, melon; Pullman, sets on flange, BS, 1929, 6½" 75.00
Bowl, vegetable; Canada Pacific, w/lid, 7" dia 78.00
Finger bowl, GN, Internat'l 45.00
Fork, cocktail; GN, Hutton 20.00
Fork, luncheon; GN, Hutton 18.00
Fork, place; C&NW, Windsor, TM 22.00
Fork, place; D&RG, Tiffany, 1889 ....50.00
Fork, place; Seaboard Coast Line, Zephyr, TM 12.00
Fork, place; UP, Savoy 10.00
Fork, place; UP, Zephyr, BM 12.00
Fork, salad; SF, Cromwell, TM, EX 12.00
Gravy ladle, UP, Westfield, BM, 8½" 85.00
Hot food cover, D&RG, Internat'l, TM, 1947, 6½" dia 95.00
Knife, butter; GN, Hutton 20.00
Knife, butter; NYC, Clovelly 18.00
Knife, place; D&RG, Am pattern, TM 18.00
Knife, place; Fred Harvey, Albany, Internat'l 18.00
Knife, place; NYC, Century, BS 12.00
Knife, place; SF, Albany, MIE 18.00
Knife, viande; PRR, Broadway, BM 15.00
Knife, viande; Pullman, Roosevelt 15.00
Pitcher, cream; NYNH&H, Reed & Barton, BM, 8-oz 65.00
Plate, service; Pullman, octagon, Internat'l, BS, 10" 125.00
Spoon, demitasse; UP, Westfield, BM 28.00
Spoon, grapefruit; UP, Westfield, Meriden, BM 20.00
Spoon, iced tea; CA Zephyr, BM 18.00
Spoon, iced tea; D&RG, Am pattern 18.00
Spoon, place; Burlington Rte, Modern, lt wear 12.00
Spoon, place; CA Zephyr, BM 15.00
Spoon, place; PRR, Broadway, TM 18.00
Spoon, place; Seaboard, Century 12.00
Spoon, serving; Fred Harvey, Albany, Internat'l 18.00
Spoon, serving; GN, Hutton, TM 15.00
Spoon, serving; SCL, Zephyr 12.00
Spoon, serving; UP, Savoy, BM 12.00
Spoon, soup; CA Zephyr, BM 18.00
Spoon, soup; Milwaukee, Ambassador, BS 12.00

Spoon, soup; NYC, Century, BS 12.00
Spoon, soup; Pullman, Roosevelt 15.00
Sugar bowl, NYNH&H, BM 65.00
Sugar tongs, NYNH&H, Wallace 65.00
Sugar tongs, UP, Sierra, Reed & Barton, TM 65.00
Teaspoon, CA Zephyr, BM 18.00
Teaspoon, MPTP, Century, BS 15.00
Tray, serving; Pullman, Internat'l, BS, 1930, 12x9" 95.00

Miscellaneous

Annual passes are skyrocketing in popularity (as opposed to trip or one-time passes, which are not very desirable in the field of pass collecting). Their values are contingent upon the specific railroad, its length of run (whether it was a short one or a major line), and their appearance. Many were tiny works of art lettered with fancy calligraphy and decorated with vignettes.

Timetables are climbing rapidly in popularity, and pins with the names of railroad companies are very good right now. On the other hand, 'Brotherhood' pins (or any item) hold little interest for collectors. Watch for reproductions signs; most are small in size, about 5" x 12", on aged cardboard under glass in black frames. These will read 'Public Telephone,' 'Waiting Room,' etc.

Almanac, Rock Island, 1883, 48-pg, 6x8", EX 40.00
Ashtray, CRR, ceramic, Royal China, gold trim, 5⅜" 57.50
Badge, breast; CB&Q RR Watchman, silver star shape 235.00
Badge, breast; Wells Fargo RR Division, brass, 6-pointed star 200.00
Badge, hat; C&NW Freight Brakeman, EX 35.00
Badge, Reading Police, eagle atop circle, silver, screw bk 225.00
Baggage check, Montgomery to Lynchburg VA, brass, 2⅛x1¾" ...75.00
Baggage label, C&O, bl circle on wht sq, 4" 10.00
Baggage label, GN, wht w/bl letters, goat on red circle, 5" 10.00
Baggage label, NP, Yellowstone Park logo, 2" dia 10.00
Blotter, ABC on Radio w/Gordon MacRae, RR Hour, 3x5½", M ...10.00
Blotter, Burlington Rte, Glacier Nat'l Park, 4x9" 7.00
Blotter, MKT, wht w/Katy & logo in red 7.00
Blotter, North Coast Ltd, Yellowstone Park logo & locomotive 7.00
Blotter, NP, Salmon, Yellowstone Park logo, M 7.00
Book, cash; IL Central, hardbound, 1946, 13x17", NM 10.00
Book, Rail, Sagebrush & Pine; Ferrell, 1967, EX 28.00
Book, record of ticket sales, IL Central, 1947, 13x12" 20.00
Book, Virginian Ry, H Reid, 1961, EX 45.00
Booklet, D&RG, Around the Corner, 1907, 6x9", EX 40.00
Booklet, NP, Storied Northwest, color cover, 1916, 11-pg 10.00
Booklet, pass rules; L&N, 1920, 34-pg, 3⅛x6", EX 22.00
Booklet, Pullman, Pioneers' Centennial, gold emb cover, 1931 ......7.50
Calendar, C&O, 4-pg, 1927, EX 85.00
Calendar, IL Central, wall type, folds out, 1970, 10x15", M 15.00
Calendar, PA RR, night scene, partial pad, 1939, EX 150.00
Calendar, Santa Fe, Grand Canyon, mc, 1983, 24x14", VG 17.50
Calendar top, NYC, 1928, EX 5.00
Cap, conductor's, MO-KS-TX, blk w/gold Katy buttons, w/visor ..95.00
Cap, conductor's, NP, blk w/visor, gold cord & buttons 50.00
Chisel, C&NW, alloy, 7" 7.00
Chisel, UP, 7" 7.00
Coat, waiter's, Amtrak, wht w/blk piping, EX 15.00
Coat hanger, CA Zephyr, wooden 17.00
Coat hanger, Pullman, Travel & Sleep..., wooden 12.50
Gauge, NY Air Brake Co, brass, red hand, M 60.00
Gauge, Westinghouse, brass, red & blk enamel, M 150.00
Globe, B&O, clear w/Capital Dome logo, tall 78.00
Globe, NYC, clear, 6" 47.50
Globe, PA Lines, clear, 5½" 45.00
Globe, unmk, amber, short 40.00

Globe, unmk, clear, short	20.00
Globe, unmk, gr or red, 5½", ea	40.00
Globe, unmk, red, short	20.00
Globe, WTCo, red, 5½"	55.00
Grab bar, Caboose, steel, 35"	15.00
Hat, Amtrak, no badge, M	35.00
Hat, Milwaukee, bl w/2 wht bands, 2 silver cap buttons, G	95.00
Hat, Reading, summer wicker, silver buttons, blk cord	95.00
Hook, dbl mail bag; C&NW, 8"	10.00
Lapel pin, Rio Grande, yel enamel, M on card	5.00
Lapel pin, Rock Island, bearskin logo, screw bk	18.00
Menu, breakfast; Amtrak, dbl fold, 1972, 11x20"	1.25
Menu, CA Zephyr Italian Dinner, glossy card, 1950s, 6x7"	10.00
Number plate, brass, Locomotive #, 6x14"	700.00
Oil can, RR mks, long spout, unused, 30"	65.00
Oil can, unmk, long spout, unused, 30"	36.00
Pail, C&NW, Belson, Galvanized, 10x30", VG	25.00
Paperweight, CM&StP, walking bear figural, 4½"	250.00
Paperweight, NYC, Hudson-type steam locomotive #5200, 9⅜"	175.00
Pass, annual; Burlington & MO River RR in NE, 1889, M	100.00
Pass, annual; Pullman, bl, 1912	10.00
Pass, Houston & Shreveport, aqua, 1909	40.00
Pass booklet, N&W, 25 slips inside, cb cover, 2⅝x5", M	25.00
Photo, crew in St Paul, 1901, 8x10"	135.00
Pincers, D&RGW, CI, 12½"	15.00
Poster, UP, City of Portland, 18x15", EX	15.00
Recipe book, Recipes from Frisco Land, 96-pg, 6x9", EX	10.00
Ruler, CGW, metal, 2 logos in orange, worn	2.00
Schedule, NYNH&H, 1910, 62-pg, EX	22.00
Sign, Chessie, Quiet Is Requested..., heavy cb, 6x9", EX	17.00
Sign, gate; NYC Grand Central Terminal, canvas, 1920-30, 29x72"	25.00
Sign, No Smoking..., pnt steel, red & blk on wht, 6x9"	10.00
Sign, NYC System, pnt steel, yel & bl, oval, 32x47"	195.00
Sign, RR Crossing, porc, wht w/blk cross & border, 24" dia	85.00
Sign, Ry Express, heavy metal, 2-pc, mc pnt, 5¾x10", M	130.00
Sign, Union Station, pnt heavy-gauge metal, 2-sided, 9x44"	150.00
Spike & mallet head, BR&P, 9"	10.00
Step stool, IC, gray w/silver top, 9½x14½"	190.00
Step stool, passenger; NYC, gray w/silver top, 13½x15¾"	240.00
Stove, B&M #5 RR, depot potbelly, 1915, 48x32x32"	375.00
Stove, Union Stove Works, NY, Station Agent, CI, potbelly, 46"	435.00
Ticket, Clinchfield, cb, 1¼x2¼"	3.00
Ticket, D&SL, 1910, dbl, unissued, 4x9"	4.25
Ticket, N&W, 3-part, cb stock, 2¾x3¼", M	3.25
Ticket, Yazoo & MS Valley, cb, 2¼x3⅛"	5.50
Timetable, ATSF, 1933 World's Fair ads, 1933, VG	25.00
Timetable, Chicago Great Western, 1912, VG	40.00
Timetable, Cotton Belt Rte, 1933 World's Fair ad, 1933, G	16.00
Timetable, FL East Coast, 1932, EX	18.00
Timetable, Lehigh Valley, Blk Dmn route, photos, 1930, EX	25.00
Timetable, MP, diesel & steam locomotives on cover, 1942	22.50
Timetable, MP, w/lg map, 1893, VG	57.50
Timetable, MP Passenger Train Service, 1923, EX	25.00
Timetable, Rutland RR, Montreal-NY-Boston, 1932, VG	18.00
Timetable, Salt Lake Route, 1921, EX	20.00
Timetable, Soo Line, 1926, VG	26.50
Timetable, Southern Ry, photo cover, route map, 1914, EX	27.50
Timetable, UP, 1947	7.00
Timetable, Wabash, flag cover, 1954	5.00
Torch, unmk candle type, heavy iron, 13½", EX	50.00
Vest, bartender's, Amtrak, 5 gold buttons, mc piping, EX	17.00
Window lifter, CB&Q, solid oak, leather & steel plate, 13½"	40.00
Wrench, dbl open-end; C&NW, 22", EX	25.00
Wrench, single open-end; C&NW, 15"	20.00

Razors

As straight razors gain in popularity, prices increase. And with the lure of investment appreciation, the novice or the speculator sometimes find themselves making purchases that later prove to be unwise. It is important to be able to recognize the material of which the handle is made. This has a great bearing on value, and imitations abound. Learn to distinguish between celluloid and genuine ivory. Razors with plain celluloid handles are practically worthless unless the blade carries a desirable trademark. Those with decorations of scrollwork, leaves and vines, or decorative metal on each end fall into the $8.00 to $12.00 price range. Even plain ivory-handled razors are not especially valuable unless the blade is well marked and from a good manufacturer. On a more positive note, celluloid-handled razors with designs such as castles, windmills, nudes, deer, alligators, automobiles, horses, cowboys, peacocks, and various kinds of birds, etc., are very desirable (some more than others) and are usually worth from $25.00 to $50.00 to collectors. Those with a figural handle such as a fish, shotgun, eagle, or a barber pole might be worth in excess of $100.00 for an especially nice example. Ivory, on the other hand, is rarely found; if the carvings are well done, clean, undamaged specimens should start at about $100.00 and escalate according to the intricacy of the design.

Buffalo horn is sometimes mistakenly called bone. It is usually black, translucent tan, or gray. Though plain handles are worth very little, the early heat-molded examples with a motif such as mentioned above often sell for more than $100.00. In the same range are mother-of-pearl and stag (deer horn) handles; very elaborate designs go even higher, but watch for imitations.

There is one imitation, however, that is highly desirable. That is jigged bone made to look like stag. This material is rough textured and dyed a handsome tan or brown; usually examples with these handles sell in the $40.00 to $75.00 range. Razors with wooden handles are very rare, but even those from the 1800s are worth only about $35.00, since they are usually very plain. 20th-century examples are only valued at around $15.00. Don't be fooled by buffalo horn colored in imitation of tortoise — and you'll find celluloid imitations, too. Genuine tortoise handles are worth from $25.00 to $100.00 depending on age, condition, and workmanship. Sterling razors are valued at $75.00 and up, but make sure they are marked 'sterling.' Even if you were to mistake aluminum for silver, those with relief-cast designs are worth $50.00 to $75.00, but only $20.00 or so if the design is incised.

Corn razors were made to pare troublesome corns on the feet. They are a bit smaller and if plain worth a little more than plain full-size razors. Fancy examples are generally not worth as much as their full-size couterparts.

The older blades are wedge-shaped (flat-sided) in cross-section; hollow-ground blades (made after 1880) are concave. Generally speaking, those etched with words are only worth a little more than a plain, common blade. Try to find those with people, places, and things — the more famous, the better.

Key:
bd — blade   cell — celluloid

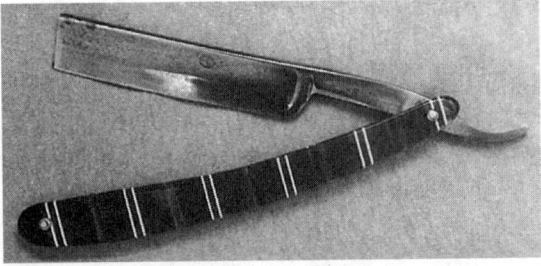

Case Bros., Tested XX, Little Valley, N.Y. Square Point, candy-stripe handle, $225.00.

Beverwyck #10, pick bone hdl, Germany, EX 33.00
Bigelow Parkin Co Pat May 11, 1921, w/advertising 22.50
Blue Steel Special, blk faux stag hdl, EX 25.00
Burham, hollow twist pattern hdl, before 1909, NM 14.00
Cattaraugus Cutlery, faux tortoise bamboo hdl, travel sz, VG 43.00
Clauss Fremont O, ivory cell hdl w/Indian in headdress, EX 90.00
David Everts, crossed flag logo, cell hdl: nude w/roses, NM 75.00
Dixie, gr & blk striped hdl, EX 28.00
E Weck & Son, blk emb hdl, removable bd/guard, 1909, NM 16.00
Ern , #2611, blk hdl w/etched map of Cuba, w/box, EX 55.00
Fox Cutlery, yel mottled rnd hdls, etched bd/shank, Germany, EX .18.00
Fredrick Reynolds, honey horn hdl, wedge bd, EX+ 38.00
Fulton Cutlery, mottled mc butterscotch flat hdl, VG+ 12.00
Gem Micromatic, gold-tone, early 6.00
Genco, woodgrain hdl w/facing Grecian heads, NM 45.00
Geneva, silver/gr hdl w/molded ribs, tulip-shape ends, NM 55.00
Griffon, ivory hdl, MOP tang, NM 38.00
H Broker & Co, etched bd w/early ship, blk hdl, Germany, EX 35.00
Hatch Cutlery, lt yel mottled hdl, NM 14.00
Henry Sears & Son, goddess w/long hair, NM 75.00
Imperial, blk hdl, etched bd w/horseless carriage, VG 28.00
Imperial, blk hdl, etched bd w/2 men on tandem bike, NM 35.00
Internat'l Saftey Razor Co, blk hdl w/wht spacer, w/case, NM 30.00
J Eccleston's, dk horn hdl, etched bd w/steamer & 2 cars, VG 75.00
J Wiss & Sons, ray-pattern cvd bone hdl, tang N 65, VG+ 35.00
JA Henckels, scrolled hdl w/Emperor emb, Germany, VG+ 35.00
Joseph Elliot, cvd ivory bone hdl, VG+ 70.00
JR Torrey, molded hdl w/cherub's head under scroll, VG 22.00
Keen Kutter, emb shank & ivory cell hdl, K743, EX 32.00
Keen Kutter, woodgrain hdl, etched bd w/logo, K17, NM 45.00
Lehrking & Daevel Co, checkered cell hdl w/scroll ends, NM 33.00
Linder & Co, purple-stained horn hdl, gold emb, crown mk, EX+ ..38.00
Logan, Gregg & Co; yel cell w/fishscale pattern, EX 45.00
Rheinsche Cutlery, cell hdl w/nude picking grapes, Germany, EX ..110.00
Robert Klass, inlay in amber hdl, gold crane logo on bd, NMIB ...45.00
Robeson Shuredge, vines, berries & wreath, Germany, VG 25.00
Rolls Razor, stone hdl, MIE, M in case w/extra bds 16.50
Star Safety, gutta percha hdl, corn knife, EX 30.00
Supplee Hdwe Co, faux tortoise shell hdl, etched bd, Germany, NM .23.00
Trusteel, blk hdl, EX 22.00
Wade & Butcher Sheffield, blk horn hdl, 3 pewter-like inlays, EX ..65.00
WH Morley...Clover Brand, Nouveau nude on hdl, Germany, EX ..85.00
Wilbert Cutlery, cell hdl w/emb leaves & berries, Germany, EX ...25.00
Winchester, ivory cell hdl, #8532 on tang, EX 60.00
Wostenholm & Son, flat ivory cell hdl, scroll w/gold, EX+ 30.00

Reamers

Reamers have been made in hundreds of styles and colors and by as many manufacturers. Their purpose is to extract the juices from lemons, oranges, and grapefruits. The largest producer of glass reamers was McKee, who pressed their products from many types of glass — custard; delphite and Chalaine blue; opaque white; Skokie green; black; caramel and white opalescent; Seville yellow; and transparent pink, green, and clear. Among these, the black and the caramel opalescents are the most valuable.

The Fry Glass Company also made reamers that are today very collectible. The Hazel Atlas Crisscross orange reamer in pink often brings in excess of $300.00; the same in blue, $275.00. Hocking produced a light blue orange reamer and, in the same soft hue, a two-piece reamer and measuring cup combination. Both are considered rare and very valuable with currently-quoted estimates at $400.00 and up for the former and $800.00 and up for the latter. In addition to the colors mentioned, red glass examples — transparent or slag — are rare and costly.

Among the most valuable ceramic reamers are those made by American potteries. The Spongeband reamer by Red Wing is valued in excess of $500.00; Coorsite reamers with gold or silver trim are worth $300.00 and up. Figurals are popular — Mickey Mouse and John Bull may bring $600.00 to $1,000.00. Others range from $55.00 to $350.00. Fine china one- and two-piece reamers are also very desirable and command very respectable prices.

A word about reproductions: A series of limited edition reamers is being made by Edna Barnes of Uniontown, Ohio. These are all marked with a 'B' in a circle. Other repoductions have been made from old molds. The most important of these are: Anchor Hocking two-piece, two-cup measure and top, Gillespie one-cup measure with reamer top, Westmoreland with flattened handle, Westmoreland four-cup measure embossed with orange and lemons, Duboe (hand-held darning egg), and Easley's diamonds one-piece.

Our advisor for this category is Dee Long; she is listed in the Directory under Illinois. For more information concerning reamers and reproductions, contact our advisor or the National Reamer Collectors Association (see Clubs, Newsletters, and Catalogs). Be sure to include an SASE when requesting information.

Ceramic

Baby's, chicks jumping rope, 2-pc 55.00
Baby's, dog w/orange juice sign 60.00
Baby's, mouse angel, pk, gr or bl, ea 65.00
Baby's, orange, dog & cat w/umbrella 60.00
Baby's, orange & lemon boxing 60.00
Baby's, teapot shape, child on horse, Goebel 110.00
Baby's orange, red & wht, Japan 50.00
Clown face, red lips, 2-pc 60.00
Clown figural, maroon/gr/blk/wht, Japan, 6½" 75.00
Clown figural w/yel hat on gr leaf, 3½" 80.00
Cottage form w/mc details, twig hdl, Japan, 5½" 60.00
Duck figural cup w/reamer top, decal, Japan, 2¾" 85.00
Elephant figural, reamer hat, bl & wht, Goebel, 4⅛" 350.00
Germany, floral, 3", 2-pc 90.00
Orange opens to clown reamer w/flower cap, lustre, Japan, 5½" ...65.00
Pail form w/hdl, tan & yel, Japan, 7¾" 65.00
Pear form, tan w/brn hdl & gr leaves 45.00
Pelican figural, reamer on bk, mc, Japan, 2¾" 125.00
Pitcher form, mc florals, Austria, 3¼" 65.00
Pitcher form, yel fruit w/tan & gr, 2-pc, 3¼" 57.50
Puddinhead figural, gr hat, 6¼" 150.00
Royal Rudolstadt, floral, 2-pc 125.00
Saucer form, rust leaves, dk bl trim, 3½" 35.00
Saucer form w/Negro head reamer, Japan, 3½" 275.00
Toy, lustre, from tea set, 2"-3" tall, ea 95.00

Glass

Jennyware, pink, $90.00.

Cambridge, amber, loop hdl, Rockwell 750.00
Darning egg, hand held, crystal only, all others are repros 70.00
Duboe, hand held, crystal only, all others are repros 80.00
Federal, pk, ribbed, loop hdl 35.00
Federal, pk, tab hdl, ribbed, seed dam 50.00
Fenton, pitcher & reamer set, red 1,000.00
Hazel Atlas, cobalt, pitcher & reamer set, 2-cup (+) 250.00
Hazel Atlas, cobalt, sm tab hdl 300.00
Hazel Atlas, cobalt, tab hdl, lg 275.00
Hazel Atlas, Crisscross, pk, lg 325.00
Hazel Atlas, gr, ftd, tall, 4-cup 35.00
Hazel Atlas, pk, tab hdl, sm 40.00
Hocking, Circle, pitcher w/reamer top 50.00
Hocking, gr, loop hdl, orange sz 15.00
Hocking, Vitrock, wht, tab hdl 40.00
Indiana Glass, amber, 6-sided cone, vertical hdl 250.00
Jeannette, Delphite bl, lg 1,200.00
Jeannette, gr, loop hdl, lg 20.00
Jeannette, gr, reamer pitcher, 2-cup 45.00
McKee, Chalaine bl, well in cone, grapefruit sz 500.00
McKee, custard, well in cone, grapefruit sz 350.00
McKee, Glasbake, crystal 125.00
McKee, ultramarine, well in cone, grapefruit sz 650.00
Radnt, gr 450.00
Radnt, pk 450.00
Re-Go, gr, 2-pc w/wood post 600.00
Sunkist, chocolate 600.00
Sunkist, gr opal (much opal) 400.00
Sunkist, gray 150.00
Sunkist, Jadite 40.00
US Glass, amber, pitcher form, 4-cup 500.00
US Glass, bl, pitcher form, 2-cup 750.00
US Glass, bl-gr, slick hdl, grapefruit sz 600.00
US Glass, pk, pitcher form, w/lid, 3-pc 250.00
Valencia, wht opal 85.00
Westmoreland, crystal w/decor, baby's 50.00
Westmoreland, frosted pk, baby's 125.00
Westmoreland, pk, baby's, 2-pc 160.00
Westmoreland, wht, flattened loop hdl 250.00

Records

Records of interest to collectors are often not the million-selling hits by 'superstars.' Very few records by Bing Crosby, for example, are of any more than nominal value, and those that are valuable usually don't even have his name on the label! Collectors today are most interested in records that were made in limited quantities, early works of a performer who later became famous, and those issued in special series or aimed at a limited market. Vintage records are judged desirable by their recorded content as well; those that lack the quality of music that makes a record collectible will always be 'junk' records in spite of their age, scarcity, or the obsolescence of their technology.

Records are usually graded visually rather than by audio quality, since it is seldom if ever possible to first play the records you buy at shows, by mail, at flea markets, etc. Condition is one of the most important value-assessing factors. For example, a truly mint-condition Elvis Presley 45 of Milk Cow Blues (Sun 215) has a potential value of over $1,000.00. If that same 45 had a sticker on it that was one-eighth of an inch square, it could lose up to half of that value! To be judged mint, a record and sleeve must be in original, unsealed condition. It must show NO evidence of use. Excellent condition is a rating applied to a record that may show slight signs of wear and use but will have almost no audible defect.

While the value of most 78s does not depend upon their being in appropriate sleeves or jackets (although a sleeveless existence certainly contributes to damage and deterioration!), this is not the case with many 45s, most EPs (extended play 45s) and LPs (long-playing 33⅓s). Often, common and otherwise minimally valued 45s might be collectible if they are in appropriate 'picture sleeves' (special sleeves that depict the artist/group or other fanciful or symbolic graphic and identify the song titles, record label and number), e.g. many common records by Elvis Presley, The Beatles and The Beach Boys. In order for most EPs and LPs to be saleable, they *must* be in their original jackets and in nice condition — indeed, excellent or better — unless they are very scarce and sought-after. Sleeves may show marginal deterioration but no repairs, pen or pencil marks, stickers, or physical damage. A Good record has both visual and audible distractions but is still playable. Sleeves will show ring wear but will not be physically damaged, and Fair indicates a record that is both visually and audibly distracting, one that has obvious damage — no skips, but possible 'play through' scratches. It can still be usable. Sleeves will show heavy ring wear and some minor physical damage. A Poor record may or may not play. Sleeves are faded, torn, marked, or otherwise damaged beyond pleasurable viewing.

Many promo records being discarded by radio stations today are finding their way into collections. These may say 'Not for Sale,' 'Audition Copy,' 'D.J.,' etc. These radio station versions are sometimes different than commercial issues and sometimes more sought after than their commercial twins. Promos by certain 'hot artists,' such as Elvis Presley and The Beach Boys are usually premium disks.

Our advisor for this category is L.R. Docks, author of *American Premium Record Guide*, which lists 60,000 records by over 7,000 artists, now in its fourth edition. He is listed in the Directory under Texas. In the listings that follow, prices are suggested for records that are in excellent condition.

Key:

Bru — Brunswick	Para — Paramount
Ch — Champion	Orch — Orchestra
Col — Columbia	Vi — Victor
Edi — Edison	Vo — Vocalion

Blues, Rhythm and Blues, Rock 'N Roll, Rockabilly

Adventurers, Rock & Roll Uprising, Co 42227, 45 rpm 8.50
Allen, Rex; Under Western Skies, Decca 8402, LP 12.50
Anka, Paul; Diana, ABC Paramount 9831, 78 rpm 18.00
Bachelors, Delores, Earl 101, 45 rpm 22.50
Baker, Katherine; Chicago Fire Blues, Gennett 6157, 78 rpm 175.00
Baker, Laverne; Sings Bessie Smith, Atlantic 1281, LP 35.00
Barons, Forget About Me, Decca 29293, 45 rpm 17.50
Bentley, Gladys; Ground Hog Blues, Okeh 8610, 78 rpm 17.50
Berry, Chuck; Maybelline, Chess 1604, 78 rpm 12.50
Black Boy Shine, Crazy Woman Blues, Vo 03454, 78 rpm 25.00
Blind Mack, Rootin' Ground Hog Blues, Vo 03167, 78 rpm 65.00
Blue Dots, Save All Your Love for Me, De Luxe 6061, 45 rpm 25.00
Bradix, Big Charley; Wee Wee Hours, Aristocrat 418, 78 rpm ...100.00
Brown, Charles; My Last Affair, Aladdin 3120, 45 rpm 12.50
Brown, Lee; Low Down Feelin', Decca 7626, 78 rpm 8.50
Burley, Dan; South Side Shake, Circle 1020, 78 rpm 15.00
Butterbeans & Susie, Kiss Me Sweet, Okeh 8182, 78 rpm 100.00
Cadillacs, White Gardenia, Capitol 4825, 45 rpm 12.50
Cardinals, I'll Always Love You, Atlantic 952, 45 rpm 40.00
Carter, Bo (& Walter Jacobs); Beans, Bluebird 5629, 78 rpm 35.00
Cellos, You took My Love, Apollo 510, 45 rpm 12.50
Chantels, I Love You So, End 1020, 45 rpm 6.00
Checkers, Over the Rainbow, King 4719, 45 rpm 25.00

Cline, Patsy; Patsy Cline, Coral 8611, LP **25.00**
Cochran, Eddie; Teenage Heaven, Liberty 55177, 45 rpm **8.50**
Collins, Vie; Nobody Knows, Silvertone 3518, 78 rpm **85.00**
Copeland, Ken; Fanny Brown, Lin 5017, 45 rpm **17.50**
Curtis, Mac; Grandaddy's Rockin' King 4949, 45 rpm **30.00**
Daily, Dusky; Miss Georgia Blues, Vo 04963, 78 rpm **20.00**
Davis, Link; Bayou Buffalo, Starday 275, 45 rpm **12.50**
Davis, Walter; Sloppy Drunk Again, Bluebird 5879, 78 rpm **35.00**
Day, Bobby; Rockin' Robin, Class 229, 78 rpm **25.00**
Deep River Boys, Truthfully, Jay-Vee 788, 45 rpm **6.50**
Donner, Ral; Takin' Care of Business, Gone 2002, LP **85.00**
Dreamers, Because of You, Cousins 1005, 45 rpm **8.50**
Dylan, Bob; Corina Corina, Co 42656, 45 rpm, minimum value ..**50.00**
Eddie & Oscar, Flying Crow Blues, Vi 23324, 78 rpm **325.00**
Escorts, My First Year, Judd 1014, 45 rpm **10.00**
Everly Brothers, Folk Songs, Cadence 3059, LP **25.00**
Fender, Freddy; Little Mama, Duncan 1004, 45 rpm **12.50**
Five Crowns, If I Were King, Alana 576, 45 rpm **8.00**
Five Satins, To the Aisle, Ember 1019, 45 rpm **6.50**
Flamingos, Would I Be Crying, Checker 853, 45 rpm **17.50**
Foster, Jim; Riverside Blues, Ch 15301, 78 rpm **200.00**
Four Lovers, Pucker Up, Epic 9255, 45 rpm **32.50**
Fuller, Johnny; Too Late To Change, Hollywood 1077, 45 rpm ...**12.50**
George & Earl, Got Anything Good?, Mercury 70605, 45 rpm **5.00**
Gibson, Clifford; Jive Me Blues, Bluebird 5110, 78 rpm **85.00**
Griffin, Floyd; Back-Biter Blues, Supertone 9523, 78 rpm **150.00**
Guitar Slim, Broke & Lonely, Diamond 204, 45 rpm **12.50**
Haley, Bill & Comets; Rock w/Bill..., Essex 117, EP **65.00**
Hamilton, George; Atlanta Rag, Ch 15726, 78 rpm **175.00**
Hearts, Lonely Nights, Baton 208, 45 rpm **7.50**
Hickey, Ersel; What Do You Want; Epic 9320, 45 rpm **8.50**
Hill, King Solomon; Tell Me Baby, Ch 50022, 78 rpm **125.00**
Hooker, John Lee; Wobbling Baby, Chart 609, 45 rpm **12.50**
Hunter, Alberta; My Particular Man, Co 14450-D, 78 rpm **65.00**
Inspirations, Raindrops, Apollo 494, 45 rpm **25.00**
Jackson, Wanda; My Destiny, Capitol 4354, 45 rpm **8.50**
Jammin' Jim, Shake Boogie, Savoy 1106, 78 rpm **8.00**
Jenkins, Bo Bo; Democrat Blues, Chess 1565, 45 rpm **50.00**
Johnson, Lonnie; Lonesome Road, King 520, LP **65.00**
Johnson, Stovepipe; Devilish Blues, Vo 1203, 78 rpm **175.00**
Kansas Katie, Deep Sea Diver, Bluebird 8944, 78 rpm **12.50**
King, BB; King of the Blues, Crown 5167, LP **17.50**
Lamplighters, Tell Me You Care, Federal 12176, 45 rpm **30.00**
Larks, My Lost Love, Apollo 435, 45 rpm **200.00**
Liggins, Jimmy; Low Down Blues, Specialty 427, 45 rpm **12.50**
Lightnin' Hopkins, Mussy Haired Woman, Chart 636, 45 rpm **10.00**
Lightnin' Slim, Sugar Plum, Excello 2075, 45 rpm **12.50**
Little Son Joe, My Black Buffalo, Vo 04978, 78 rpm **12.50**
Love Notes, Surrender Your Heart, Imperial 5254, 45 rpm **125.00**
Magnificents, My Heart Is Calling, Dee Gee 3008, 45 rpm **8.50**
Marvin & Johnny, Baby Doll, Specialty 479, 45 rpm **7.00**
Mary & Mack, Black, Bluebird 7908, 78 rpm **35.00**
McCoy, Robert/Lee; Tough Luck, Bluebird 7115, 78 rpm **17.50**
McTell, Kate; Ticket Agent Blues, Decca 7078, 78 rpm **65.00**
Miles, Josie; Sweet Man Joe, Ajax 17076, 78 rpm **40.00**
Miracles, You're an Angel, Cash 1008, 45 rpm **25.00**
Monkey Joe &...Music Grinders, That Same Cat, Vo 05274, 78 rpm .**12.50**
Muddy Waters, Best of..., Chess 1427, LP **65.00**
Muddy Waters, Train Fare Home, Aristocrat 1306, 78 rpm **17.50**
Nixon, Elmore; Playboy Blues, Mercury 70061, 78 rpm **7.50**
Nutmegs, Whispering Sorrows, Herald 466, 45 rpm **10.00**
Penguins, Sweet Love, Dooto 432, 45 rpm **12.50**
Platters, Give Thanks, Federal 12153, 45 rpm **65.00**
Potter, Nettie; Meat Man Blues, Pathe-Actuelle 032124, 78 rpm ..**12.50**

Preston, Johnny; Running Bear, Mercury 20592, LP **35.00**
Quarter Notes, My Fantasy, De Luxe 6129, 45 rpm **7.00**
Reed, Jimmy; High & Lonesome, Chance 1142, 45 rpm **125.00**
Roberts, Sally; Gonna Ramble Blues, Okeh 8485, 78 rpm **50.00**
Rockets, Be Lovey Dovey, Modern 992, 45 rpm **10.00**
Rucker, Laura; Little Joe, Para 13075, 78 rpm **175.00**
Rush, Otis (& Band); Groaning the Blues, Cobra 1010, 45 rpm ...**12.50**
Safaris, Image of a Girl, Eldo 101, 45 rpm **12.50**
Serenaders, Tomorrow Night, J V-B 2001, 45 rpm **85.00**
Sloppy Henry, Traveling Blues, Okeh 8305, 78 rpm **45.00**
Smith, Bessie; After You've Gone, Co 14197-D, 78 rpm **40.00**
Smith, Clara; Courthouse Blues, Co 14073-D, 78 rpm **40.00**
Smokehouse Charley, My Texas Blues, Ch 15794, 78 rpm **125.00**
Snow, Hank; Old Doc Brown, RCA Victor 1156, LP **25.00**
Squires, Heavenly Angel, Vita 116, 45 rpm **35.00**
Stewart, Priscilla; Biscuit Roller, Para 12402, 78 rpm **125.00**
Swan, Jimmy; Losers Weepers, Trumpet 197, 45 rpm **12.50**
Sylvester, Hannah; Farewell Blues, Famous 3237, 78 rpm **50.00**
Teardrops, My Inspiration, King 45004, 45 rpm **17.50**
Temptations, Mister Juke Box, Savoy 1532, 45 rpm **8.50**
Thornton, Willie Mae; Hound Dog, Peacock 1612, 45 rpm **45.00**
Trammell; Bobby Lee; Shirley Lee, ABC Para 9890, 45 rpm **17.50**
Turner, Ike; I'm Lonesome Baby, Chess 1459, 78 rpm **7.50**
Uncle Skipper, Cutting My ABCs, Decca 7353, 78 rpm **25.00**
Voices, Why, Cash 1011, 45 rpm **17.50**
Washboard Walter & Band, Wuffin' Blues, Para 13100, 78 rpm .**250.00**
Wheeler, Onie; Too Hot To Handle, K-Ark 671, 45 rpm **12.50**
White, Georgia; Tell Me Baby, Decca 752, 78 rpm **10.00**
Williams, Hank; Ramblin' Man, MGM 3219, LP **55.00**
Williams, Johnny; Prison Bound, Staff 718, 78 rpm **12.50**
Yates, Blind Richard; Sore Bunion Blues, Ch 15281, 78 rpm **125.00**
Zircons, Return My Love, Winston 1022, 45 rpm **17.50**

Country and Western

Anderson, Les; He's Just a Hobo, Cormac 1108, 78 rm **10.00**
Asparagus Joe, Nutty Song, Ch 16012, 78 rpm **8.00**
Baker, Buddy; Box Car Blues, Vi 21549, 78 rpm **12.50**
Baldwin, Luke; Daddy & Home, Ch 15811, 78 rpm **12.50**
Bird, Connie; Little Mamie, Gennett 6929, 78 rpm **40.00**
Bob & Monte, Utah Trail, Vo 5279, 78 rpm **5.00**
Boone, Jimmy; Brakeman's Reply, Superior 2638, 78 rpm **25.00**
Branch & Coleman, Telegraph Shack, Okeh 45561, 78 rpm **25.00**
Burnett Brothers, Countin' Cross Ties, Vi 23730, 78 rpm **17.50**
Butcher, Dwight; Pistol Pete, Vi 23819, 78 rpm **30.00**
Carolina Buddies, Work Don't Bother Me, Co 15663-D, 78 rpm .**12.50**
Carolina Tar Heels, Farm Girl Blues, Vi 23516, 78 rpm **40.00**
Cartwright Brothers, Kelly Waltz, Co 15220-D, 78 rpm **7.50**
Carver Boys, Simpson County, Para 3233, 78 rpm **85.00**
Childers & White, Red River Valley, Okeh 45208, 78 rpm **8.50**
Clifford, Bob; My Two Time Mama, Vo 5488, 78 rpm **17.50**
Colt Brothers, Somethin' I Et, Melotone 12483, 78 rpm **7.00**
Cramer Brothers, Sara Jane, Broadway 8059, 78 rpm **25.00**
Dalhart, Vernon; Great Titanic, Buddy 8037, 78 rpm **65.00**
Dixon Brothers, Weave Room Blues, Bluebird 6441, 78 rpm **7.50**
East Texas Serenaders, Deacon Jones, Bru 298, 78 rpm **12.50**
Fletcher & Foster, Travelin' North, Ch 16121, 78 rpm **45.00**
Georgia Crackers, Diamond Joe, Okeh 45098, 78 rpm **25.00**
Great Cap Entertainers, Pussy Cat Rag, Broadway 8140, 78 rpm ..**12.50**
Hackberry Ramblers, Jolie Blonde, Bluebird 2003, 78 rpm **10.00**
Hamblen, Stuart; Boy in Blue, Bluebird 5242, 78 rpm **10.00**
Hillard, Harry; Blue Yodel No 9, Ch 16337, 78 rpm **75.00**
Horton, Johnny; Birds & Butterflies, Abbott 103, 78 rpm **10.00**
Hughey, Dan; Sweet Kitty Wells, Ch 15502, 78 rpm **8.00**

Johnson, Smilin' Tubby; Oh Suzanna, Ch 15278, 78 rpm **7.00**

Justice, Dick; Brown Skin Blues, Bru 336, 78 rpm **17.50**

Kentucky Thorobreds, Mother's Advice, Para 3011, 78 rpm **17.50**

Kincaid, Bradley; Little Mohee, Gennett 6856, 78 rpm **17.50**

Log Cabin Boys, Ole Bill Jackson Brown, Banner 32903, 78 rpm ...**7.00**

Lookout Mtn Revelers, Dreaming of Mother, Para 3123, 78 rpm .**12.50**

Mack, Bill; Big Bad Daddy, Imperial 8151, 78 rpm **8.00**

Mainer, JE; Leaf From the Sea, Bluebird 6347, 78 rpm **8.50**

Martin & Roberts, Hot Corn, Ch 16520, 78 rpm **25.00**

Marvin, Johnny; Seven Come Eleven, Vi 23708, 78 rpm **15.00**

McGhee & Coger, He Included Me, Gennett 6795, 78 rpm **20.00**

Monroe Brothers, New River Train, Bluebird 6645, 78 rpm **10.00**

Moreland, Peg; Cowboy Jack, Vi 23593, 78 rpm **12.50**

Narmour & Smith, Little Star, Okeh 45276, 78 rpm **30.00**

Oaks, Charlie; Kaiser & Uncle Sam, Vo 5073, 78 rpm **7.00**

Parker, Dan & Bill; Fifty Years Repentin', Crown 3266, 78 rpm ...**12.50**

Pickard Family, Down in Arkansas, Banner 6283, 78 rpm **7.00**

Pie Plant Pete, Boston Burglar, Gennett 6748, 78 rpm **12.50**

Reneau, George; Prisoner's Song, Vo 5056, 78 rpm **8.00**

Ritter, Tex; High Wide & Handsome, Decca 5315, 78 rpm **8.50**

Rodgers, Jessie; Rattlesnake Daddy, Bluebird 5839, 78 rpm **8.50**

Scottsdale String Band, Silver Bell, Okeh 45279, 78 rpm **17.50**

Southern Moonlight Entertainers, Buckin' Mule, Vo 5407, 78 rpm .**17.50**

Stripling Brothers, Coal Mine Blues, Vo 02739, 78 rpm **40.00**

Tennessee Ramblers, Fiddlers Contest, Bru 257, 78 rpm **12.50**

Virginia Possum Tamers, Turkey in Straw, Ch 15522, 78 rpm **12.50**

Welling & McGhee, At the Cross, Para 3115, 78 rpm **12.50**

Weston, Don; Dying Cowgirl, Ch 16764, 78 rpm **17.50**

Wooten, Kyle; Lumber Camp Blues, Okeh 45511, 78 rpm **40.00**

Young, Clarence; Little Pal, Ch 15924, 78 rpm **12.50**

Jazz, Dance Bands, Personalities

Arcadian Serenaders, Yes Sir Boss, Okeh 40562, 78 rpm **35.00**

Bailey's Lucky Seven, Smile All..., Gennett 3075, 78 rpm **10.00**

Bargy, Roy; Jim-Jams, Vi 19537, 78 rpm **12.50**

Broadway Bell-Hops, Leonora, Harmony 450-H, 78 rpm **7.00**

Broadway Broadcasters, Wob-A-Ly Walk, Romeo 625, 78 rpm **8.50**

Brunies, Merritt (Orch); Flamin' Mamie, Okeh 40579, 78 rpm **50.00**

California Ramblers, Black & Blue Rhapsody, Edi 11042, 78 rpm ..**50.00**

Candullo, Joe (Orch); Phantom Blues, Perfect 14874, 78 rpm **10.00**

Candullo, Joe (Orch); She's Still My..., Gennett 3385, 78 rpm **15.00**

Cantor, Eddie; Modern Maiden's Prayer, Aeolian Vo 1220, 78 rpm ..**17.50**

Chapman, Jack (Orch); Carolina Blues, Vi 19775, 78 rpm **100.00**

Coon-Sanders Orig Nighthawk, Louise You..., Vi 19958, 78 rpm .**25.00**

Crosby, Bing; I Apologize, Bru 6179, 78 rpm **10.00**

Dixie Jazz Band, Dixie Drag, Jewel 5446, 78 rpm **10.00**

Dixie Jazz Band, Hot Aire, Oriole 517, 78 rpm **10.00**

Etting, Ruth; Close Your Eyes, Bru 6657, 78 rpm **10.00**

Frankie & Johnnie Orch, Stompin', Bluebird 6499, 78 rpm **12.50**

Georgia Strutters, Georgia Grind, Harmony 231-H, 78 rpm **17.50**

Gold, Lou (Orch); I Wish't I Was..., Perfect 14549, 78 rpm **10.00**

Golden, Ernie (Orch); Golden Gate, Harmony 578-H, 78 rpm **7.50**

Golden Gate Orch, Red Hot Henry Brown, Perfect 14500, 78 rpm .**10.00**

Gorman, Ross & Virginians; I'd Rather Be..., Col 615-D, 78 rpm **10.00**

Gresh, Earl (Orch); Where...Wild Flowers..., Col 1031-D, 78 rpm .**12.50**

Hall, Fred (Jazz Band); West End Blues, Regal 8655, 78 rpm **10.00**

Hall, Fred (Sugar Babies); Sobbin' Blues, Okeh 40437, 78 rpm **20.00**

Hallet, Mal (Orch); Boomerang, Edi 14080, 78 rpm **100.00**

Harlem Footwarmers, Sweet Chariot, Co 1467-D, 78 rpm **65.00**

Harmonians, I Can't Maker Her Happy, Harmony 746-H, 78 rpm .**6.00**

Jazz Pilots, She Knows Her Onions, Okeh 40688, 78 rpm **10.00**

Joy, Jimmy (Orch); Stomp It Mr Kelly, Okeh 40627, 78 rpm **75.00**

Kahn, Art (Orch); Hobo's Prayer, Col 624-D, 78 rpm **12.50**

Kirby's Kings of Jazz, Oh! Daisy; Bell 589, 78 rpm **35.00**

Knickerbockers, Sweet & Low Down, Col 549-D, 78 rpm **7.50**

Lanin, Sam (Orch); Say Who Is...Doll?, Perfect 14544, 78 rpm **7.50**

Lee, Ruth; Maybe Someday, Nordskog 3008, 78 rpm **225.00**

Lown, Bert (Orch); My Castle in Spain..., Harmony 853-H, 78 rpm .**12.50**

Mandello's Dance Orch, Dixie Drag, Banner 6214, 78 rpm **10.00**

Manhattan Dance Makers, I'm Gonna..., Harmony 413-H, 78 rpm .**7.50**

Markel, Mike (Orch); Deep Henderson, Okeh 40625, 78 rpm **12.50**

McKinney's Cotton Pickers, Plain Dirt, Vi V-38097, 78 rpm **35.00**

Meyers, Vic (Orch); Africa, Cameo 576, 78 rpm **10.00**

Meyers, Vic (Orch); Blow the Smoke Away, Col 1516-D, 78 rpm .**6.00**

Okeh Syncopators, Jig Walk, Okeh 40614, 78 rpm **10.00**

Original Indiana Five, Sittin' Around, Perfect 14601, 78 rpm **10.00**

Original Memphis Five, I'm More..Satisfied, Vo 15712, 78 rpm ...**75.00**

Pennsylvania Syncopators, Black Bottom, Bell 439, 78 rpm **10.00**

Red Hot Dogs, Blame It on Black Bottom..., Banner 6057, 78 rpm ..**12.50**

Red Onion Jazz Babies, Terrible Blues, Gennett 5607, 78 rpm ...**125.00**

Rich, Fred (Orch); She's Got 'It,' Col 1036-D, 78 rpm **10.00**

Robison, Willard (Orch); Rosy Cheeks, Perfect 14803, 78 rpm **12.50**

Siegel, Al (Orch); Sooke Hey Hey, Para 20314, 78 rpm **30.00**

Six Black Diamonds, Dixie Flyer Sam, Banner 1428, 78 rpm **20.00**

Six Brown Brothers, Walkin' the Dog, Vi 18140, 78 rpm **7.00**

Six Jelly Beans, I Scream, You Scream...; Challenge 571, 78 rpm .**15.00**

Southern Melody Serenaders, Oh You..., Marathon 221, 78 rpm .**17.50**

Specht, Paul (Orch); Static Strut, Col 627-D, 78 rpm **12.50**

Steele, Joe (Orch); Coal Yard Shuffle, Vi V-38066, 78 rpm **125.00**

Straight, Charley (Orch); Bathing Beauty..., Para 20264, 78 rpm ...**30.00**

Van's Hotel Half Moon Orch, Cornfed, Perfect 14860, 78 rpm **10.00**

Volunteer Firemen, Keep Your Skirts Down..., Bru 3041, 78 rpm ...**7.50**

Voorhees, Don (Orch); Pardon the Glove, Cameo 1134, 78 rpm .**15.00**

Williams, Ralph (Orch); I Could Fall in..., Vi 19958, 78 rpm **25.00**

Williams Fess & Joy Boys; Dixie Stomp, Vo 15690, 78 rpm **100.00**

Wintz, Julie; Spanish Mamma, Perfect 14641, 78 rpm **10.00**

Wirges, Bill (Orch); KY's Way of..., Perfect 14541, 78 rpm **10.00**

Red Wing

The Red Wing Stoneware Company, founded in 1878, took its name from its location in Red Wing, Minnesota. In 1906 the name was changed to the Red Wing Union Stoneware Company after a merger with several of the other local potteries. For the most part they produced utilitarian wares such as flowerpots, crocks, and jugs. Their early 1930s catalogs offered a line of art pottery vases in colored glazes, some of which featured handles modeled after swan's necks, snakes, or female nudes. Other examples were quite simple, often with classic styling. After the addition of their dinnerware lines in the 1935, 'Stoneware' was dropped from the name, and the company became known as Red Wing Potteries, Inc. They closed in 1967. For further study we recommend *Red Wing Stoneware, An Identification and Value Guide*, and *Red Wing Collectibles* by Dan and Gail DePasquale and Larry Peterson, available at your bookstore or from Collector Books. Our advisor for the general dinnerware lines is Doug Podpeskar; he is listed in the Directory under Minnesota. Karen Silvermintz (see Texas) and Charles Alexander (see Indiana) advise on the Town and Country dinnerware.

Key:
c/s — cobalt on stoneware	RW — Red Wing
MN — Minnesota	RWUS — Red Wing Union
NS — North Star	Stoneware

Commercial Art Ware and Miscellaneous

Ashtray, wing form, emb feathers **38.00**

Figurine, draped female lute player w/doe, #2507 .... 125.00
Figurine, Tambourine Lady, #81416 .... 120.00

Toothpick holder, monk's face in relief, cobalt, 3", $350.00.

Vase, gr/ochre matt, trumpet neck, squat base, #186, 10½" 275.00
Vase, gr/ochre mottled matt, ovoid, 10½x6" 250.00
Vase, wht, #1583, 7" 95.00
Vase, wht, gr int, #512, 10½" 200.00
Vase, yel, gr, gray & tan, low waist, flared neck, #196, 10½" 110.00

Cookie Jars

Bob White, unmk 80.00
Carousel, unmk 350.00
Crock, wht 25.00
Dutch Girl, yel w/brn trim 75.00
Friar Tuck, cream w/brn trim, mk 85.00
Friar Tuck, gr, mk 150.00
Friar Tuck, yel, unmk 75.00
Grapes 85.00
Grapes, cobalt or dk purple, ea 225.00
Jack Frost, unmk 600.00
King of Tarts, mc, mk 500.00
King of Tarts, pk w/bl & blk trim, mk 475.00
King of Tarts, wht, unmk 350.00
Peasant design, emb/pnt figures on brn 60.00
Pierre (chef), brn, unmk 125.00
Pierre (chef), gr, unmk 275.00
Pierre (chef), pk, mk 350.00
Pineapple, yel 100.00

Dinnerware

Blossomtime, bowl, Concord shape, 8½" 10.00
Blossomtime, cup & saucer, Concord shape 5.00
Blossomtime, plate, Concord shape, 10½" 6.00
Blossomtime, platter, Concord shape, 13¼" 12.00
Bob White, bowl, salad; bird int, 12" 60.00
Bob White, casserole, w/lid, 2-qt 45.00
Bob White, cup & saucer 20.00
Bob White, plate, 10½" 12.50
Bob White, platter, 13½" 27.50
Bob White, shakers, quail form, pr 40.00
Bob White, sugar bowl, w/lid 25.00
Bob White, teapot 70.00
Bob White, tumbler, rare 115.00
Brittany, buffet bowl 42.50
Brittany, plate, dinner 7.50
Brittany, shakers, pr 12.00
Capistrano, bowl, divided vegetable 20.00
Capistrano, plate, dinner; 10" 10.00
Capistrano, plate, 6½" 5.00
Crazy Rhythm, creamer & sugar bowl 25.00
Crazy Rhythm, tid-bit tray, 2-tier 20.00

Damask, plate, dinner 10.00
Damask, sugar bowl, w/lid 12.00
Frontenac, bowl, cereal 5.50
Frontenac, butter dish 16.50
Frontenac, creamer 10.00
Frontenac, plate, dinner 8.00
Frontenac, plate, salad 5.00
Frontenac, trivet 50.00
Kermis, bowl, salad; lg 400.00
Kermis, plate, salad 110.00
Lotus, bowl, vegetable 12.00
Lotus, casserole, w/lid 25.00
Lotus, creamer & sugar bowl 25.00
Lotus, cup & saucer 10.00
Lotus, dinner service for 6, 70 pcs 450.00
Lotus, egg plate, w/lid 85.00
Lotus, plate, dinner; 10½" 10.00
Lotus, plate, 6¼" 12.00
Lotus, platter, oval, 13" 25.00
Lotus, sugar bowl, w/lid 15.00
Magnolia, bowl, fruit; 5¼" 5.00
Magnolia, cup & saucer 10.00
Magnolia, gravy boat w/attached underliner 20.00
Magnolia, plate, 10" 12.50
Magnolia, rim soup 15.00
Normandy, tidbit tray, 2-tier 20.00
Pompeii, bowl, divided vegetable 17.00
Pompeii, creamer 6.50
Pompeii, plate, 10" 8.50
Random Harvest, bowl, salad; lg 85.00
Random Harvest, cup & saucer 15.00
Random Harvest, plate, dinner 10.00
Random Harvest, sugar bowl, w/lid 12.50
Reed, custard 10.00
Round-Up, bowl, salad; sm, 6" 40.00
Round-Up, casserole, lg 195.00
Round-Up, coffee mug 100.00
Round-Up, cruets, pr 250.00
Round-Up, cup & saucer 40.00
Round-Up, plate, dinner 30.00
Round-Up, shakers, pr 90.00
Round-Up, teapot 220.00
Smart Set, bread tray, 24" 100.00
Smart Set, casserole, 2-qt 70.00
Smart Set, creamer & sugar bowl 75.00
Smart Set, pitcher, water; 112-oz 125.00
Smart Set, teapot 250.00
Tampico, gravy boat w/attached underplate 22.50
Tampico, mug, coffee 45.00
Tampico, relish tray 75.00
Village Green, bowl, cereal 15.00
Village Green, casserole stand, 8" 12.00
Village Green, shakers, pr 20.00
Vintage, gravy boat 22.00

Stoneware

Bean pot, Albany slip, Boston style, RW, 1-gal 200.00
Bean pot, Albany slip, short neck, NS, 1-gal 125.00
Bean pot, Saffron w/band, RWUS, 1-gal 85.00
Bowl, mixing; bl bands on wht, 6" 50.00
Bowl, red & bl bands on yel, 10" 50.00
Bowl, shoulder; wht, sm 60.00
Butter crock, low style, c/s, RW, 10-lb 75.00

Casserole, bl bands on wht, emb ribs, RWUS, sm 100.00
Chamber pot, Albany slip w/wht band on lid, NS, lg 500.00
Chamber pot, wht, fancy hdl, w/lid, RW, 7" 100.00
Churn, leaf/#4, c/s, RW, 4-gal 700.00
Churn, molded seam, parrot/#3, c/s, MN, 3-gal 2,600.00
Churn, red wing/#2/Union oval, c/s, 2-gal 225.00
Churn, 2 leaves/#8, c/s, 8-gal 350.00
Combinette, bl bands & emb lily on wht, w/lid 225.00
Cooler, butterfly/#6, c/s, RW, 6-gal 1,700.00
Cooler, daisy/#6, c/s, RW, 6-gal 1,600.00
Cooler, red wing/Ice Water/#5/Union oval, c/s, 5-gal 400.00
Cooler, 2 leaves/#4, c/s, Albany slip on lid, RW, 4-gal 1,700.00
Crock, 'drop 8'/#3, c/s, RW, 3-gal 275.00
Crock, butter; #20, cobalt on wht ware, early, MN, 20-lb 425.00
Crock, butter; high style, Albany slip, NS, 1-pt 125.00
Crock, butter; high style, wht, MN, 1-gal 35.00
Crock, butter; low style, Albany slip, MN, 3-lb 60.00
Crock, butter; low style, Albany slip, RW, 1-lb 80.00
Crock, butter; low style, salt glaze, MN, 5-lb 65.00
Crock, butter; low style, wht, MN, 3-lb 30.00
Crock, butter; low style, wht, RW, 2-lb 40.00
Crock, butterfly/#20, c/s, RW, 20-gal 450.00
Crock, butterfly/#6, c/s, RW, 6-gal 375.00
Crock, dbl 'P'/#3, c/s, MN, 3-gal 350.00
Crock, leaf/#10, c/s, MN, 10-gal 375.00
Crock, red wing/#20 on wht, RWUS, 20-gal 80.00
Crock, red wing/#40 on wht, RWUS, 40-gal 250.00
Crock, 2 birch leaves/#2, c/s, MN, 2-gal 50.00
Crock, 2 elephant-ear leaves/#5, c/s, ca 1900, 5-gal 70.00
Crock, 2 leaves/#25, c/s, hand-trn, transitional, 25-gal 275.00
Cuspidor, molded seam, wht w/Albany slip top 125.00
Jar, ball lock; red wing/#5/Union oval, c/s, 5-gal 175.00
Jar, beater; Albany slip, emb ribs, 1930s, RW 85.00
Jar, fruit; Stone Mason, blk or bl labels on wht, 1899, ½-gal 185.00
Jar, packing; red wing/#3/Union oval, c/s, bail hdl, 3-gal 250.00
Jar, preserve/snuff; Albany slip, MN, 1-gal 55.00
Jar, preserve/snuff; Albany slip, MN, ½-gal 200.00
Jar, preserve/snuff; Albany slip, RW, 4-gal 175.00
Jar, preserve/snuff; wht, RW, 1-gal 70.00
Jar, preserve/snuff; wht, RW, 1-qt 100.00
Jug, beehive threshing; birch leaf/#5, c/s, hand-trn, 5-gal 450.00
Jug, beehive; #4 etched on Albany slip, hand-trn, RW, 5-gal 700.00
Jug, beehive; birch leaf/#4/Union oval, c/s, 4-gal 400.00
Jug, common, Albany slip, cone top, MN, 1-qt 70.00
Jug, common, Albany slip, dome top MN, 1-gal 175.00
Jug, common, Albany slip, molded seam, dome top, NS, 1-qt 175.00
Jug, common, wht, standard top, MN, 1-gal 70.00
Jug, fancy, bl bands on wht w/brn ball top, MN, 1-pt 650.00
Jug, fancy, wht w/brn ball top, MN, ⅛-pt 225.00
Jug, fancy, wht w/brn ball top, RW, 1-qt 100.00
Jug, molded seam, Albany slip, bail hdl, RW, 1-gal 325.00
Jug, molded seam, wht, bail hdl, ca 1895, 1-gal 150.00
Jug, molded seam, wht, bail hdl, RW, 1-qt 125.00
Jug, molded seam, wht, wide mouth, MN, ½-gal 100.00
Jug, molded seam, wht, wide mouth, RW, 1-qt 45.00
Jug, shoulder; brn & salt glaze, ball top, RW, 1-gal 200.00
Jug, shoulder; brn & salt glaze, cone top, RW, 2-gal 125.00
Jug, shoulder; brn & salt glaze, funnel top, MN, 2-gal 125.00
Jug, shoulder; brn & salt glaze, standard top, RW, 1-gal 125.00
Jug, shoulder; brn & salt glaze, wide mouth, NM, 1-gal 350.00
Jug, shoulder; brn top, wing/#5 on wht, 5-gal 325.00
Jug, shoulder; wht, funnel top, MN, 2-gal 75.00
Jug, shoulder; wht, standard top, MN, 1-gal 85.00
Jug, shoulder; wht, standard top, RW, 2-gal 50.00

Jug, shoulder; wht, standard top, short, MN, 1-qt 150.00
Jug, shoulder; wht, standard top, wide mouth, MN, 1-gal 30.00
Jug, shouldered syrup; wht, cone top, MN, 1-gal 70.00
Meat roaster, shouldered base, emb rings on lid, bail hdl, MN ...175.00
Mug, Saffron w/band decor, RWUS 350.00
Pan, milk; bl (uncommon color), RW, 7" 125.00
Pie plate, Albany slip, RW, 9" 125.00
Pitcher, Albany slip, bbl form, RWUS 125.00
Pitcher, Albany slip w/emb irises, ca 1940, RW 125.00
Pitcher, Spongeband & Saffron, RWUS, lg 175.00
Spittoon, bl bands on salt glaze, German style, MN, rare 650.00
Spittoon, bl bands on wht, German style 350.00
Spittoon, cobalt bands on salt glaze, German style 400.00

Town and Country

Produced by Red Wing for one year only in the late 1940s, Town and Country was designed by Eva Zeisel as an informal or semiformal dinnerware. Irregular, often eccentric shapes characterize the line, as handles of pitchers and serving pieces are usually extensions of the rim. Bowls and platters are free-form comma shapes or appear tilted, with one side slightly higher than the other. Although the ware is unmarked, it is recognizable by its distinctive shapes and glazes. White is often used to complement exteriors of bowls and cups; bronze (metallic brown) enjoys favored status, while gray is unusual. Other colors include rust, dusk blue, sand, chartreuse, peach, and forest green.

Bean pot, rust, w/lid 400.00
Bowl, mixing; dusk bl 100.00
Bowl, vegetable; sand, 8" 35.00
Bowl, 5" 15.00

Casserole, sand, stick handle, $75.00.

Casserole, marmite, chartreuse, ind 35.00
Casserole, peach, stick hdl 75.00
Creamer, rust 35.00
Creamer & sugar bowl, w/lid, minimum value 50.00
Cruets, oil & vinegar; mixed colors, orig stoppers, sm, pr 150.00
Cup & saucer, forest gr w/wht int 27.50
Pitcher, peach, 3-pt 125.00
Pitcher, sand, 2-pt 85.00
Plate, bronze, 10" 45.00
Plate, gray, 8" 15.00
Plate, 10½" 20.00
Plate, 6½" 5.00
Platter, peach, comma shape, 9" 35.00
Shaker, lg 15.00
Shakers, Shmoo shape, bronze, pr 65.00
Shakers, Shmoo shape, same-color other than bronze, pr 45.00
Sugar bowl, bronze, w/lid 65.00
Syrup, chartreuse 95.00

Teapot, sand **250.00**

Redware

The term redware refers to a type of simple earthenware produced by the Colonists as early as the 1600s. The red clay used in its production was abundant throughout the country, and during the 18th and 19th centuries redware was made in great quantities. Intended for utilitarian purposes such as everyday tableware or use in the dairy, redware was simple in design and decoration. Glazes of various colors were used, and a liquid clay referred to as 'slip' was sometimes applied in patterns such as zigzag lines, daisies, or stars. Plates often have a 'coggled' edge, similar to the way a pie is crimped or jagged, which is done with a special tool. In the following listings, EX (excellent condition) indicates only minor damage. Our advisor for this category is Barbara Rosen; she is listed in the Directory under New Jersey.

Baking pan, brn, fluted edges, appl hdls, 13" **60.00**
Bank, apple form, old red finish, 3½" **150.00**
Bank, chest-of-drawers form w/yel slip knobs, 7½" **140.00**
Bank, onion form, brn w/yel slip decor, Schofield, 4½" **400.00**
Bowl, brn sponging, appl ribbed hdls, wear, 5¼x8¼" **105.00**
Bowl, gr w/orange spots, oblong, wear, 11½" **275.00**
Bowl, milk; dk brn int, 3¾x15" **195.00**
Bowl, milk; gr-amber w/wht slip, 3x9" **250.00**
Bowl, milk; gr-tan, 14¾" **85.00**
Bowl, yel slip w/brn wavy & str lines, chips, 3¼x10" **280.00**
Butter tub, orange, horizontal ribs, w/hdls, 5x8", EX **700.00**
Charger, emb Washington bust in medallion, coggled rim, 13" ..**470.00**
Charger, 2-line yel slip, coggled rim, wear, 11¼" **220.00**
Charger, 3-line yel slip, coggled rim, wear, 11¾" **700.00**
Cookie brd, 6 designs w/EX detail, 8½x5¾" **440.00**
Creamer, gr-clear w/brn splotches, sm chips, 3⅝" **95.00**
Cup, amber w/brn flecks, 3x4½" **85.00**
Figurine, dog, seated, brn, minor damage, 3" **95.00**
Flask, clear w/red tones & dk brn splotches, 7¼" **170.00**
Flask, 2-tone dk brn, 6⅜" **110.00**
Flowerpot, gr-amber, tooled foliage, saucer base, 5½" **140.00**
Flowerpot, gr-amber w/brn spots, mismatched saucer, 9" **110.00**
Flowerpot, gr/yel/rust mottle, Shenandoah, attached tray, VG ...**170.00**
Inkwell, molded florals, dk pnt, glazed int, chip, 4⅝" **75.00**
Jar, apple butter; gr-amber & brn, ribbed strap hdl, 5x6" **130.00**
Jar, apple butter; tan flecks, chips, 7" **30.00**
Jar, brn matt ext, glossy int, John Bell, Waynesboro, 7¼" **85.00**
Jar, dk brn splotches, tooled lines, shoulder hdls, ovoid, 9" **165.00**
Jar, gr alkaline, 1800s, flakes, 10¼" **165.00**
Jar, gr-amber w/dk orange spots, chip, 3⅝" **45.00**
Jar, gr-tan mottle, 4¾" **30.00**
Jar, preserve; gr-beige w/brn flecks & red highlights, 6¼" **50.00**
Jar, tan flecks, ovoid, W Smith Womelsdorf, chips, 5½" **195.00**
Jug, brn splotches, strap hdl, ovoid, 7" **100.00**
Jug, dk brn, glossy, att Boughner, Greensboro PA, 13¼" **275.00**
Jug, dk brn speckles, ovoid, early, 7" **75.00**
Jug, dk gr metallic, ovoid, 8" **150.00**
Jug, dk gr speckles, ovoid, 12" **150.00**
Jug, olive gr w/orange spots, ovoid, strap hdl, 6" **140.00**
Loaf pan, yel slip decor, coggled rim, prof rpr, 14" **425.00**
Milk pan, brn & yel slip decor, flakes, 4x14" **140.00**
Mold, fish, clear w/brn flecks & splotches, chips, 11⅝" **440.00**
Mold, Turk's head, blk sponging, edge chips, 7" **75.00**
Mold, Turk's head, brn sponging, shiny, scalloped, 4½x11" **75.00**
Mold, Turk's head, dk brn, chips, 7" **35.00**

Mold, Turk's head, red w/brn flakes, wht slip at rim, 1½x6" **95.00**
Mold, Turk's head, swirled ribs, wht slip rim, chip, 12" **75.00**
Mold, Turk's head, yel slip wavy line w/polka dots, 9½" **1,565.00**
Mug, brn splotches, strap hdl, minor wear, 5" **250.00**
Mug, dk amber, mk WWC 1906, 2⅝" **25.00**
Mug, 2-tone brn, w/hdl, oversz, 8" **195.00**
Pie plate, amber w/brn flecks, 7⅞" **95.00**
Pie plate, yel slip crow's ft, coggled rim, chips, 7½" **188.00**
Pie plate, yel slip 1908, coggled rim, wear/chips, 8¾" **165.00**
Pie plate, 3-line yel slip, coggled rim, wear, 8" **360.00**
Pie plate, 3-line yel slip, coggled rim, wear, 9" **220.00**
Pie plate, 3-line yel slip, coggled rim, 9⅝" **385.00**
Pitcher, amber w/brn swirls, impressed leaf at base, 7¾" **85.00**
Pitcher, lt gr slip w/brn splotches, 7¾" **250.00**
Pitcher, manganese splotches, 1800s, 10½" **360.00**
Pitcher, wht slip on amber matt w/dk brn splotches, 7¼" **95.00**
Stew pot, gr, ribbed body, 1800s, 8½", EX **400.00**
Sugar bowl, dk w/blk splotches, tooled bands, appl hdls, 5½" **105.00**

Regal China

Located in Antioch, Illinois, the Regal China Company began its business in 1938. Products of interest to collectors are James Beam decanters, cookie jars, salt and pepper shakers, and similar novelty items. The company closed its doors sometime in 1993. The Old MacDonald Farm series listed below is becoming especially collectible. See also Cookie Jars; Decanters.

Shakers

Alice in Wonderland, rare, pr **625.00**
Bendel, bears, wht w/brn & pk trim, pr **125.00**
Bendel, kissing pigs, gray w/pk trim, lg, pr **275.00**
Bendel, love bugs, burgundy, lg pr **140.00**
Bendel, love bugs, burgundy, sm, pr **70.00**
Bendel, love bugs, gr, sm, pr **55.00**
Dutch girls (matches cookie jar), rare, pr **275.00**
Goldilocks, pr **150.00**
Van Telligen, bears, yel w/rose accents, pr **18.00**
Van Telligen, dogs, blk, pr **85.00**
Van Telligen, dogs, wht, pr **50.00**
Van Telligen, ducks, yel w/blk spots, pr **35.00**
Van Telligen, Dutch boy & girl, pr **35.00**
Van Telligen, Peek-a-Boo, peach trim, sm, pr **250.00**
Van Telligen, Peek-a-Boo, red dots, lg, pr **425.00**
Van Telligen, Peek-a-Boo, wht, lg, pr **325.00**
Van Telligen, Peek-a-Boo, wht, sm, pr **165.00**
Van Telligen, Peek-a-Boo, wht w/gold trim, lg, pr **425.00**

Old MacDonald's Farm

Assorted spice jars, $100.00 each.

Butter dish, cow's head 225.00
Canister, flour, cereal, coffee, or cookie; med, ea 235.00
Canister, pretzels, peanuts, pocpcorn, chips, tidbits; lg, ea ...325.00
Canister, salt, sugar, or tea, med, ea 235.00
Canister, soap, lg 325.00
Cookie jar, barn 275.00
Creamer, rooster 110.00
Grease jar, pig 175.00
Jar, spice; sm 100.00
Pitcher, milk 400.00
Shakers, boy & girl, pr 75.00
Shakers, churn, pr 65.00
Shakers, feed sacks w/sheep, pr 165.00
Sugar bowl, hen 125.00
Teapot, duck's head 250.00

Relief-Molded Jugs

Early relief-molded pitchers (ca 1830s-40s) were made in two-piece molds into which sheets of clay were pressed. The relief decoration was deep and well defined, usually of animal or human subjects. Most of these pitchers were designed with a flaring lip and substantial footing. Gradually styles changed, and by the 1860s the rim had become flatter and the foot less pronounced. The relief decoration was not as deep, and foliage became a common design. By the turn of the century, many other types of pitchers had been introduced, and the market for these early styles began to wane.

Watch for recent reproductions; these have been made by the slip-casting method. Unlike relief-molded ware which is relatively smooth inside, slip-cast pitchers will have interior indentations that follow the irregularities of the relief decoration. Our advisor for this category is Kathy Hughes; she is listed in the Directory under North Carolina.

'Wedgwood' white smear glaze, Old Hall Earthenware Co., Ltd., ca 1870, $400.00.

Apostle, 8 figures, 8 sides, 1842, 11" 550.00
Argos, gr, Brownfield, Apr 29, 1864, 8" 175.00
Ariadne, Samuel Alcock & Co, ca 1850, 9" 500.00
Calla Lily & Wire, wht, Dudson, ca 1865, 7", EX 175.00
Chrysanthemum, gr & wht, Ridgway, ca 1860, 9¼" 275.00
Distin family/instruments, bl smear/gilt, Alcock, 1840s, 7" ...475.00
Equestrian hunters, grapevines, lt gr, branch hdl, unmk, 6" 125.00
Good Samaritan, buff/tan, Jones & Walley, 1841, 8" 375.00
Gothic Floral, bl/brn/wht, Beech & Hancock, July 14, 1862, 8" .200.00
Rose, parian, unmk, ca 1850, 6½" 150.00
Sir Walter Scott commemorative, gray-gr, Minton, 8" 350.00

Sleeping Beauty, teal/wht, Dudson, ca 1860, 5¼" 185.00
Tam O'Shanter, bl stoneware, Ridgway, Oct 1, 1835, 6" ...200.00
Toby Philpot, tan, 8" 375.00

Restraints

Since the beginning of time, many things from animals to treasures have been held in bondage by hemp, bamboo, chests, chains, shackles, and other constructed devices. Many of these devices were used to hold captives who awaited further torture, as if the restraint wasn't torturous enough. The study and collecting of restraints enables one to learn much about the advancement of civilization in the country or region from which they originated. Such devices at various times in history were made of very heavy metals — so heavy that the wearer could scarcely move about. It has only been in the last sixty years that vast improvements have been made in design and construction that afford the captive some degree of comfort. Our advisor for this category is Joseph Tanner; he is listed in the Directory under Washington.

Key:
bbl — barrel
d-lb — double lock button
K — key
Kd — keyed
lc — lock case
NST — non-swing through
ST — swing through
stp — stamped

Foreign Handcuffs

Adams, teardrop lc, bbl Kd, NST, usually not stp 170.00
Australian, Saf Lock, ST, takes pin-tumbler K in side, stp ...140.00
Deutsche Polizei, ST, middle hinge, folds, takes bbl-bit K 80.00
East German, aluminum, single lg hinge, ST, bbl key 50.00
East German, heavy steel, NP single lg hinge, NST, bbl key 80.00
English, Chubb, NST, hi-security 10-slider lock mechanism ...275.00
English, Chubb Arrest, steel, ST, multi-bit solid K 225.00
English, Latrobe, aluminum alloy, center chain, ST, dbl-bit K ...160.00
French Lapegy, ST, aluminum alloys, takes flat bitted K 75.00
French Revolved, oval, ST, takes 2 Ks: bbl & pin tumbler 150.00
German, 3-lb steel set, 2⅝" thick, center chain, bbl K 175.00
German Clejuso, oval design, ST, dbl-cuff weight, 22-oz 100.00
German Clejuso, sq lc, adjusts/NST, d-lb on side, bbl K 100.00
German Darby, adjusts, well finished, NST, sm 120.00
German Hamburg 8, non-adjust NST, center bar/post w/K-way ..250.00
Hiatt, English Darby, like US CW Darby, stp Hiatt & #d 75.00
Hiatt, solid state, 2 separate cuffs joined bk to bk, stp/#d 165.00
Hiatt English non-adjust screw K Darby style, uses screw K ..100.00
Hiatt Figure 8, swings open to insert/withdraw wrists 125.00
Italian, stp New Police, modern Peerless type, ST, sm bbl K ...35.00
Plug 8, remove plug before inserting external threaded K 200.00
Spanish, stp Alcyon/Star, modern Peerless type, flat K 65.00
Spanish, stp Alcyon/Star, modern Peerless type, ST, sm bbl K ...45.00

Foreign Leg Shackles

East German, aluminum, lg hinge, cable amid 4 cuffs, bbl key ...80.00
German Clejuso, sq lc, adjusts/NST, d-bl on side, bbl K 125.00
German Clejuso Darby type, adjusts/NST/plated, uses screw K ..160.00
Hiatt English combo manacles, handcuff/leg irons w/chain 275.00
Hiatt English non-adjust screw K Darby style, uses screw K ...100.00
Hiatt Plug leg irons, same K-ing as Plug-8 cuffs, w/chain 225.00

U.S. Handcuffs

American Munitions, modern/rnd, sm bbl Kd, ST bow, stp 45.00

Bean Giant, sideways figure 8, solid center lc, dbl-bit K 400.00
Bean Patrolman, kidney-bean form, d-lb on lc, NST, stp T 100.00
Bean-Cobb, sm rnd lc, removable cylinder, d-lb, NST, 1899 ....80.00
Cavenay, looks like Marlin Daley but w/screw K, NST 160.00
Civil War padlocking type, various designs w/loop for lock 170.00
Colt, modern ST bow, sm bbl Kd, stp w/Colt & Co name 150.00
Flash Action Manacle, like Bean Giant w/ST, K-way center 200.00
Flexibles, steel segmented bows, NST Darby type, screw K 150.00
H&R Super, ST, shaft-hinge connector takes hollow titted K ...100.00
Harvard, takes sm bbl K, ST, stp Harvard Lock Co 65.00
Judd, NST, used rnd/internally triangular K, stp Mattatuck 120.00
Lilly Hand Iron, 2" strap iron (8" L), oval bands, NST, sq K 400.00
Marlin Daley, NST, bottle-neck form, neck stp, dbl-titted K 200.00
Mattatuck, NST, propeller-like K-way, stp Mattatuck/etc 90.00
Palmer, 2" steel bands, 2 K-ways (top & center), NST stp 300.00
Peerless, ST, takes sm bbl K, stp Mfg'ered by Peerless Co 40.00
Peerless, ST, takes sm bbl K, stp Mfg'ered by S&W Co 75.00
Phelps, NST, twist chain between cuffs, Tower Look-alike 200.00
Pratt combo, 1 cuff connnects w/nipper/claw, ST, mk Pratt 225.00
Providence Tool Co, stp, NST, Darby screw K style 120.00
Rankin, steel NST, mk screw K 225.00
Romer, NST, takes flat K, resembles padlock, stp Romer Co 250.00
S&W 94 Maximum Security, ST, takes Ace-type K, stp S&W 80.00
Strauss, ST, takes lg solid bitted K, stp Strauss Eng Co 85.00
Tower, NST, bottom K, solid/flat fitted K goes in cuff edge 100.00
Tower bar cuffs, cuffs separate by 10-12" steel bar 120.00
Tower Dbl Lock, NST, takes bbl-bitted K, usually stp Tower 60.00
Tower Detective Pinkerton, NST, sq lc, bbl-bitted K, no stp 120.00
Tower Single Lock, NST, bbl-bit K, K-way slanted on lc, sm 70.00
Tower-Bean, NST, sm rnd lc, takes tiny bbl-bitted K, stp 75.00
Tri-lock, heavy polymer & stainless steel, ST, triple lock 60.00
Walden 'Lady Cuff,' NST, takes sm bbl K, lightweight, stp 250.00

U.S. Leg Shackles

American Munitions, as handcuffs 55.00
Civil War or prison ball & chain, padlocking or rivet type 250.00
Cloc spike, 30" L opening for ankle w/padlock & 2 spikes 500.00
H&R Supers, as handcuffs 400.00
Harvard, as handcuffs 75.00
Judd, as handcuffs 135.00
Leg lock brace, metal brace, ankle to knee, lever locked 225.00
Oregon boot, break-apart shackle on above ankle support 400.00
Palmer, as handcuffs but w/detachable chain, NST 400.00
Providence Tool Co, stp, NST 150.00
Strauss, as handcuffs 125.00
Tower, bottom K, as handcuffs 100.00
Tower ball & chain, leg iron w/chain & 6-lb to 50-lb ball 200.00
Tower Dbl-Lock, as handcuffs 90.00
Tower Detective, as handcuffs 150.00

Various Other Restraining Devices

African slave Darby-style cuffs, heavy iron/chain, handmade 130.00
African slave Darby-style leg shackles, heavy/hand forged 160.00
African slave padlocking or riveted forged iron shackles 135.00
Argus iron claw, twist T to open & close 40.00
Darby neck collar, rnd steel loop opens w/screw K 150.00
English figure-8 nipper, claws open by lifting top lock tab 80.00
Gale finger cuff, knuckle duster, non-K, mk GFC 125.00
German nipper, twist hdl opens/closes cuff, stp Germany/etc 75.00
Jay Pee, thumb cuffs, mk solid body, bbl K 15.00
Mighty-Mite, thumb cuffs, solid body, ST, mk, bbl K 75.00
Phillips nipper, claw, flip lever on top to open 80.00

Thomas nipper, claw, push button top to open 80.00
Tower Lyon, thumb cuffs, solid body, NST, dbl-bit center K 150.00

Reverse Painting on Glass

Verre eglomise is the technique of painting on the underside of glass. Dating back to the early 1700s, this art became popular in the 19th century when German immigrants chose historical figures and beautiful women as subjects for their reverse glass paintings. Advertising mirrors of this type came into vogue at the turn of the century.

Emilie, puff sleeves/lace bodice, red ribbon, rpr, 13x10" 250.00
Equestrian w/angel & castle, faux marble fr, 17x14" 900.00
Geo WA silhouette, intricate border, fr w/gilt liner, 13x11" 250.00
Interior w/2 ladies, musicians & students, China, 22x16", pr 650.00
Man in wht uniform, 3-color trim, 'F Napoleon,' 15x12" 275.00
Oriental lady in bl kimono, cvd fr, 19x15½", EX 450.00
Side-wheeler Steamship Ohio, EX color, fr, 10½x12½" 275.00
Vase of flowers, mc/tinsel on blk, rpt gold fr, 19x22½" 235.00

Richard

Richard, who at one time worked for Galle, made cameo art glass in France during the 1920s. His work was often multilayered and acid cut with florals and scenics in lovely colors. The ware was marked with his name in relief. Our advisor for this category is Don Williams; he is listed in the Directory under Missouri.

Vase, coastal village land-scape, black on fire-orange, 19½", $1,600.00.

Cameo

Goblet, river scene w/stone tower in fuchsia, knob std, 8" 425.00
Vase, floral, amethyst on frost, bulging on 4 sides, 4x8" 550.00
Vase, floral, brn on yel, twin-peaked rim, 4x4" 495.00
Vase, floral, violet on lime gr, 6" 625.00
Vase, floral w/butterfly & dragonfly, violet on bl, 5" 650.00
Vase, mtn village, pumpkin/brn on lemon yel, elongated, 16" ...1,300.00
Vase, pine cone limbs, brn on rubena verde, tapered, 11½" 900.00

Ridgway

As early as 1792, the Ridgway brothers, Job and George, produced fine quality earthenwares in Shelton, Staffordshire, marking their products 'Ridgway, Smith, & Ridgway' and later 'Job & George Ridgway.' Around 1800 the brothers split, and each had his own firm, both in Shelton. They were joined in the business by various members of the Ridgway family, and in fact their descendants still operate there today.

The two firms created by the split were the Bell Works and the Cauldon Pottery. Bell produced stone china and earthenware decorated with blue transfer printing. Their mark was 'J. & W. Ridgway' or 'J. & W.R.' (John and William) until 1848 when 'William Ridgway' was used. The Cauldon Pottery made earthenware, stone china, and high-quality porcelains fine enough to win them the distinction of being appointed potters to the Queen. From 1830 their wares attest to this fact, bearing the Royal Arms mark with 'J.R.' within the crest. In 1840 '& Co.' was added. Most examples of Ridgway's wares found today are transfer-printed historical scenes. See also Staffordshire, Historical; and Flow Blue.

Ashtray, Coaching Days, metal box for matches 60.00
Bowl, Coaching Days, 10" 55.00

Bowl, Tyrolean, red transfer, 9" long, $30.00.

Coffeepot, Coaching Days, 8" 110.00
Creamer, Coaching Days, EX 40.00
Cup & saucer, Coaching Days 37.50
Mug, Coaching Days, Broken Trade, 4" 35.00
Mug, Coaching Days, 2-hdld, 5" 65.00
Mug, Columbus Cathedral, Havana Cuba, 4¾" 35.00
Mug, Mormon Sq, Salt Lake City, 4½" 45.00
Mug, Polar Bear & Cat, silver lustre trim, 4½" 50.00
Pitcher, stoneware, bl w/emb band, HP flowers, 1835, 11" 175.00
Pitcher, tankard; Mr Pickwick, silver lustre trim, 9½" 115.00
Plate, Coaching Days, 10" 45.00
Plate, Coaching Days, 9" 35.00
Punch bowl, flowers & birds, blk transfer w/mc, 7x16" 135.00
Tray, Coaching Days, oval, 12½" 80.00
Vase, Coaching Days, 5" 70.00

Riviera

Riviera was a line of dinnerware introduced by the Homer Laughlin China Company in 1938. It was sold exclusively by the Murphy Company through their nationwide chain of dime stores. Riviera was unmarked, lightweight, and inexpensive. It was discontinued sometime prior to 1950. Colors are mauve blue, red, yellow, light green, and ivory. On rare occasions, dark blue pieces are found, but this was not a standard color. For further information we recommend *The Collector's Encyclopedia of Fiesta* (1994 values) by Sharon and Bob Huxford, available from Collector Books.

Batter set, complete 225.00
Batter set, ivory, w/decals, complete 145.00
Bowl, baker; 9" 18.00
Bowl, cream soup; w/liner, ivory 80.00
Bowl, fruit; 5½" 9.00

Bowl, nappy; 9¼" 20.00
Bowl, oatmeal; 6" 28.00
Butter dish, cobalt, ¼-lb 200.00
Butter dish, colors other than cobalt or turq, ¼-lb 100.00
Butter dish, turq, ¼-lb 185.00
Butter dish, ½-lb 90.00
Casserole 85.00
Creamer 8.00
Cup & saucer, demitasse; ivory 50.00
Jug, open ivory, 4½" 85.00
Jug, w/lid 100.00
Pitcher, juice; mauve bl 175.00
Pitcher, juice; yel 90.00
Plate, deep 18.00
Plate, 10" 35.00
Plate, 6" 7.00
Plate, 7" 8.00
Plate, 9" 12.50
Platter, closed hdls, 11¼" 18.00
Platter, cobalt, 12" 50.00
Platter, 11½" 14.00
Sauce boat 17.50
Saucer 3.00
Shakers, pr 18.00
Sugar bowl, w/lid 16.00
Teacup 8.50
Teapot 100.00
Tidbit, ivory, 2-tier 70.00
Tumbler, hdl 55.00
Tumbler, hdl, ivory 115.00
Tumbler, juice 42.00

Robertson

Fred H. Robertson, clay expert for the Los Angeles Brick Company and son of Alexander Robertson of the Roblin Pottery, experimented with crystalline glazes as early as 1906. In 1934 Fred and his son George established their own works in Los Angeles, but by 1943 they had moved operations to Hollywood. Though most of their early wares were turned by hand, some were also molded in low relief. Fine crackle glazes and crystallines were developed. Their ware was marked with 'Robertson,' 'F.H.R.,' or 'R.,' with the particular location of manufacture noted. The small pottery closed in 1952.

Pitcher, emb flying geese, gr matt, angle hdl, mk FHR/LA, 6" 225.00
Tile, bearded man's portrait, bsk, 1895, 9¼x8", NM 850.00
Vase, bl, mk R, 3" 75.00
Vase, bl, pillow form, Hollywood mk, 4½" 95.00
Vase, bl crackle, flattened ftd dish form, sgn, 4½" 95.00
Vase, bl hi-glaze, hdls, 3" 75.00
Vase, Chinese bl gloss, bottle form, 3" 65.00

Robineau

After short-term training in ceramics in 1903, Adelaide Robineau (with the help of her husband Samuel) built a small pottery studio at her home in Syracuse, New York. She was adept at mixing the clay and throwing the ware, which she often decorated by incising designs into the unfired clay. Samuel developed many of the glazes and took charge of the firing process. In 1910 she joined the staff of the American Women's League Pottery at St. Louis, where she designed the famous Scarab Vase. After this pottery failed, she served on the faculty of Syracuse University. Her work was and is today highly acclaimed for the high standards of excellence to which she aspired.

Vase, bl crystalline over gr on porc, sgn RP/#153, 5", NM **2,860.00**
Vase, celadon gloss to yel matt flambe over wht porc, 2" **1,200.00**

Robj

Robj was the name of a retail store that operated in Paris for only a few years, from about 1925 to 1931. Robj solicited designs from the best French artisans of the period to produce decorative objects for the home. These objects were produced mostly in porcelain but also in glass and earthenware. The most well known are the figural bottles which were particularly popular in the United States. However, Robj also produced tea sets, perfume lamps, chess sets, ashtrays, bookends, humidors, powder jars, cigarette boxes, figurines, lamps, and milk pitchers. Robj objects tend to be whimsical, and all embody the Art Deco style. Items listed below are ceramic unless noted otherwise. Our advice for this category comes from Randall Monsen and Rod Baer, their address is listed in the Directory under Virginia.

Atomizer, 4 Seasons, glass, gilt eng top, ca 1925, 6" **600.00**
Decanter, preacher in blk robe, hands at waist, 11" **175.00**
Figurine, bespectacled wht-haired witch w/cane, 10" **325.00**
Figurine, seated Deco-style lady, 1 knee bent, gray, 11x10" **750.00**
Lamp base, porc, gr leaves & red berries, appl wht balls, 7" **225.00**
Tray, Arab figural **325.00**
Vase, enameled glass, medallion ea side, ovoid, 9" **800.00**

Rock 'N Roll Memorabilia

Memorabilia from the early days of Rock 'n Roll recalls an era that many of us experienced firsthand; these listings are offered to demonstrate the many and various aspects of this area of collecting. Values are for mint condition examples. Items indicated by this symbol (+) have been reproduced. Beware! Many are so well done even a knowledgeable collector will sometimes be fooled.

Our advisor for Elvis memorabilia is Rosalind Cranor, author of *Elvis Collectibles* and *Best of Elvis Collectibles* (Overmountain Press); she is listed in the Directory under Virginia. The remainder is under the advisement of Bojo (Bob Gottuso); see Pennsylvania.

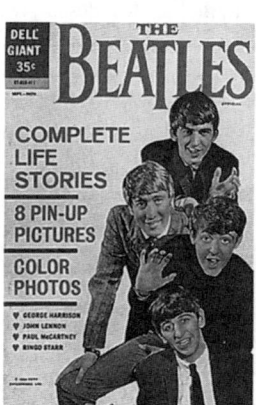

Beatles, comic book, Dell #1, 1964, NM, $250.00.

Beatles, album, Yesterday & Today, butcher cover, mono **375.00**
Beatles, balloon, various colors, sealed in pkg **65.00**
Beatles, bamboo plate, group mc picture, 12" **75.00**

Beatles, banjo, plastic, Mastro, 22", EX **700.00**
Beatles, beach towel, Cannon, NM **140.00**
Beatles, binder, vinyl, various colors, 3-ring **90.00**
Beatles, biscuit plate, UK pottery w/mc decal & lip ext, NM **90.00**
Beatles, blanket, UK, tan w/red & blk, photos/names, NM **350.00**
Beatles, blow-up dolls, set of 4, EX **85.00**
Beatles, bongo drums, Mastro, EX **750.00**
Beatles, book, In His Own Write, J Lennon, Signet, 1965, EX **15.00**
Beatles, bowl, cereal; UK Washington Pottery, NM **100.00**
Beatles, box, Lux soap offer, w/insert **200.00**
Beatles, brooch, photo disk on brass bking, 1¾" **40.00**
Beatles, brunch bag, vinyl, zippered top, 8" **350.00**
Beatles, button, I'm Bugs About the Beatles, 3½", M **16.00**
Beatles, candy dish, Paul, pottery, gilt edge, UK **110.00**
Beatles, cartoon Colorforms, complete & NMIB w/instructions .**325.00**
Beatles, charm, oval plastic w/faces, set of 4 ....**24.00**
Beatles, clutch purse, cloth w/leather strap & pics all over **160.00**
Beatles, clutch purse, vinyl w/leather strap, group photo (+) **140.00**
Beatles, commemorative coin, 1964 US Tour, M in sealed pkg **12.50**
Beatles, concert book, 1964, 12x12" **18.00**
Beatles, concert book, 1965, 12x12" **19.00**
Beatles, concert ticket, complete, minimum value **40.00**
Beatles, cup, fired decal, UK Washington Pottery **85.00**
Beatles, Disk Go case, plastic 45 record holder **85.00**
Beatles, doll, vinyl, John or George w/guitar, Remco, 4", ea **85.00**
Beatles, dress, Holland, any of 3 styles, NM **600.00**
Beatles, drum, Ringo, w/stand, sticks, etc, UK **350.00**
Beatles, flasher pin, various styles, 2½", ea (+) **15.00**
Beatles, flasher ring, silver coated (+) **15.00**
Beatles, guitar, Beatleist, 6-string, Mastro, 20", NM **450.00**
Beatles, guitar, electric; Selco/Red Jet, NMIB **1,400.00**
Beatles, guitar, JR, pk & red, Mastro, 21", NM **290.00**
Beatles, guitar, Yeah Yeah, 6-string, Mastro, 21", NM **450.00**
Beatles, guitar, 4 Pop, Mastro, 21", NM **290.00**
Beatles, guitar string, Hofner, Selmer, in orig pkg **70.00**
Beatles, gum card, set from 1960s, complete, NM **90.00**
Beatles, gum cards, blk & wht or mc, NM, ea card **1.50**
Beatles, Halloween costume, w/mask, ea **200.00**
Beatles, handbag, group photo, brass hdls, NM **275.00**
Beatles, handbag, pictures all over, brass hdls, NM **275.00**
Beatles, harmonica, Hohner, NMIB **90.00**
Beatles, hummer, cb tube, 11", +2 plastic tips **80.00**
Beatles, locket, leather, w/11 photos inside **35.00**
Beatles, lunch box, bl, EX **250.00**
Beatles, lunch box, Yel Submarine, EX **225.00**
Beatles, model kit, Ringo, Revel, EX in box **150.00**
Beatles, mug, photo under clear, thermal, 4" (+) **85.00**
Beatles, nylons, Ballito, UK, sealed in pkg **125.00**
Beatles, paint-by-number, 1 of ea, complete, NM **450.00**
Beatles, pencil case, zippered top, SPP **100.00**
Beatles, pennant (wide variety), 1960s, miniumum value, ea **25.00**
Beatles, phonograph, group picture on top & inside, EX **1,200.00**
Beatles, pin, 9 available, by Green Duck, 1", ea (+) **10.00**
Beatles, postcard, individual portrait, EX, set of 4 ....**10.00**
Beatles, scarf, mc pictures on wht, fringed, NM (+) **35.00**
Beatles, sheet music, Day Tripper, 1964, M **9.00**
Beatles, shoulder bag, vinyl w/cord strap, group picture **275.00**
Beatles, Soakie bubble bath container, Paul or Ringo, NM, ea **90.00**
Beatles, switchplate cover, Yel Submarine, 10½x6", M **25.00**
Beatles, talcum powder, Margo of Mayfair, UK, NM **400.00**
Beatles, tumbler, juice; red & blk photo & music notes **90.00**
Beatles, tumbler, rubber coated, group photo **100.00**
Beatles, tumbler, thermal, picture under clear plastic (+) **75.00**
Beatles, writing tablet, Vernon Royal, unused, NM **55.00**

Beatles, Yel Submarine, die cast, Corgi, 5", EX 200.00
Bee Gees, phonograph 35.00
Bobby Sherman, record, from Rice Krispies box 15.00
Boy George, doll, LJN, 1984, MIB 100.00
Donnie & Marie, record player, 1977 ....30.00
Elvis Presley, guitar, Love Me Tender, Emenee, M in case 1,700.00
Elvis Presley, music box, clockwork, figure dances, 8x5", EX 65.00
Elvis Presley, photo album, vinyl, 1950s 675.00
Elvis Presley, pin-bk button, Love Me Tender, celluloid, lg 50.00
Elvis Presley, pocket mirror, England, late 1960s 35.00
Elvis Presley, polo shirt, crew neck, wht w/blk trim, 1956, NM ..440.00
Elvis Presley, postcard, portrait, Christmas 1967, 3½x5½" 15.00
Elvis Presley, poster, youthful portrait, blk/wht, RCA, 8x10" 60.00
Elvis Presley, skimmer pump shoe, Faith Show, EX, pr 950.00
Elvis Presley, souvenir menu, Sahara Taho, mc, 1974, M 30.00
Elvis Presley, standee, wht rhinestone suit, EX 200.00
Elvis Presley, wallet, 1950s, EX, minimum value 500.00
Kiss, bedspread, sealed in bag w/insert 100.00
Kiss, board game, complete, EX 50.00
Kiss, Colorforms, 1979, unused 45.00
Kiss, comb, Australian 9.00
Kiss, guitar, plastic, 24", EX 80.00
Kiss, Halloween costume, w/mask, EX in box 50.00
Kiss, make-up kit, Kiss Your Face, sealed 85.00
Kiss, note book, group pose, unused 20.00
Kiss, pencils, 4 in pkg 35.00
Kiss, puzzles, group photo, complete 18.00
Kiss, record player, Tiger, EX 135.00
Kiss, transistor radio, w/box 70.00
Kiss, trash can, EX 90.00
Kiss, Viewmaster, 3 reels w/booklet, in pkg 25.00
Madonna, doll, as Breathless Mahoney, 18" 25.00
Michael Jackson, Deluxe Colorforms, 1984, M 27.50
Michael Jackson, Dress-Up Set, 1984, MIB 20.00
Michael Jackson, microphone, LJN, 1984 ....25.00
Michael Jackson, spiral notebook, unused 6.00
Monkees, bracelet, 4 charms, 1967, EX 25.00
Monkees, guitar, paper photos, 20" 75.00
Monkees, Halloween costume, boy's or girl's style, w/box 80.00
Monkees, model kit, plastic, MPC, complete 125.00
Monkees, Monkeemobile, Corgi, 3", EX 50.00
Monkees, playing cards, 52 w/40 photo bks, Ed-U, 1966, NM 35.00
Monkees, sunglasses, 1960s style w/chain & mfr tag 25.00
Monkees, tambourine, Raybert, 1967 ....75.00
Monkees, Viewmaster, 3 reels, w/instructions & pkg 25.00
Partridge Family, Colorforms, David Cassidy 30.00
Pat Boone, bracelet, on card 65.00
Paul Revere & Raiders, model kit, M, sealed 350.00
Rolling Stones, cup, 7-11, 1990 ....18.00
Rolling Stones, lips keychain, sealed 8.00
Rolling Stones, pin-bk button, blk & wht, 3" 25.00

Rockingham

In the early part of the 19th century, American potters began to favor brown- and buff-burning clays over red because of their durability. The glaze favored by many was Rockingham, which varied from a dark brown mottle to a sponged effect sometimes called tortoise shell. It consisted in part of manganese and various metallic salts and was used by many potters until well into the 20th century. Over the past two years, demand and prices have risen sharply, especially in the east. See also Bennington.

Bottle, book form, chip, 6" 250.00

Bottle, fish form, kiln flaw, 11" 385.00
Bottle, mermaid shape, chip on lip, 7¼" 75.00
Bowl, fish & peacock eye, rare pattern, chips, 2x7½" 215.00
Bowl, mixing; wear, 4¾x10½" 40.00
Bowl, octagonal, 12½" 175.00
Bowl, oval, wear/scratches, 13½" 170.00
Bowl, str fluted sides, 5¾x9¼" 100.00
Bowl, 2¾x10½" 95.00
Bowl, 3½x8½" 60.00
Creamer, molded fern decor, 4⅜" 145.00
Creamer, molded wreath, 5½" 145.00
Dog, coleslaw coat & tooling, chips, 7¾" 935.00
Dog, seated, brn & bl-gr, flakes, 12½" 855.00
Flask, mermaid form, 8" 300.00
Inkwell, boy asleep, 5¾" 150.00
Jar, w/lid, 8" dia, EX 88.00
Mug, tooled rim, 2¾" 65.00
Mug, wear & minor flake on base, 3¾" 45.00
Pie plate, 11¼" 135.00
Pie plate, 8⅜" 95.00
Pie plate, 9⅜" 95.00
Pig bank, marbleized olive-brn, tan & gr, 6⅜" 55.00

Pitcher, animals in relief on brown, 9½", EX, $325.00.

Pitcher, att to Cincinnati, hairline, 7¼" 85.00
Pitcher, deer & hanging game, 9" 275.00
Pitcher, hanging game hdl, eagle spout, 9½", EX 295.00
Pitcher, hound hdl, 3⅛" 285.00
Pitcher, molded Gothic arch, 6⅜" 225.00
Pitcher, squat, 4⅜" 75.00
Pitcher, tooled band, beaded trim, rpr, 7½" 110.00
Pot, w/lid & hdl, 4⅝" 280.00
Soap dish, molded leaf design, rectangular, 4x6¼", EX 75.00
Soap dish, 5¼" 85.00
Soap dish, 7¼" 95.00
Teapot, mc florals, 1874, rpr, 14" 330.00
Toby creamer, 5" 95.00
Toby pitcher, tricorner hat rpr, 9¼" 110.00
Whistle, frog figural 50.00

Rogers, John

John Rogers (1829-1904) was a machinist from Manchester, New Hampshire, who turned his hobby of sculpting into a financially successful venture. From the originals he meticulously fashioned of red clay, he had bronze master molds made from which plaster copies were cast. He specialized in five different categories: theatrical, Shakespeare, Civil War, everyday life, and horses. His large detailed groupings portrayed the life and times of the period between 1859 and 1892. When no condition is indicated, examples are assumed to be in very good to excellent condition. Our advisor for this category is George Humphrey; he is listed in the Directory under Maryland.

Bath **2,000.00**
Bushwacker **2,000.00**
Chess **825.00**
Country Post Office **750.00**
Faust & Marguerite, Leaving the Garden **1,200.00**
Fetching the Doctor **750.00**
Fighting Bob, ca 1889 ....**1,100.00**
Football, inscr, 16x11" **1,000.00**
Frolic at the Old Homestead, 1887, 22½" **800.00**
Hide & Seek **2,000.00**
Home Guard **800.00**
Madam Your Mother Craves a Word **700.00**
Matter of Opinion **600.00**
Neighboring Pews **475.00**
Picket Guard **750.00**
Referee **600.00**
Rip Van Winkle at Home, 18½" **425.00**
School Days **600.00**
Slave Auction **2,000.00**
Speak for Yourself John **600.00**
Village Schoolmaster **850.00**
Washington **1,250.00**
Watch for the Santa Maria **700.00**
Wounded Scout, ca 1864 ....**750.00**

Rookwood

The Rookwood Pottery Company was established in 1879 in Cincinnati, Ohio. Its founder was Maria Longworth Nichols Storer, daughter of a wealthy family who provided the backing necessary to make such an enterprise possible. Mrs. Storer hired competent ceramic workers who through constant experimentation developed many lines of superior art pottery. While in her employ, Laura Fry invented the airbrush-blending process for which she was issued a patent in 1884. From this, several lines were designed that utilized blended backgrounds. One of their earlier lines, Standard, was a brown ware decorated with underglaze slip-painted nature studies, animals, portraits, etc. Iris and Sea Green were introduced in 1894 and Vellum, a transparent mat-glaze line, in 1904. Other lines followed: Ombroso in 1910 and Soft Porcelain in 1915. Many of the early artware lines were signed by the artist. Soon after the turn of the 20th century, Rookwood manufactured 'production' pieces that relied mainly on molded designs and forms rather than freehand decoration for their esthetic appeal. The Depression brought on financial difficulties from which the pottery never recovered. Though it continued to operate, the quality of the ware deteriorated, and the pottery was forced to close in 1967.

Unmarked Rookwood is only rarely encountered. Many marks may be found, but the most familiar is the reverse 'RP' monogram. First used in 1886, a flame point was added above it for each succeeding year until 1900. After that a Roman numeral added below indicated the year of manufacture. Impressed letters that related to the type of clay utilized for the body were also used — G for ginger, O for olive, R for red, S for sage green, W for white, and Y for yellow. Artware must be judged on an individual basis. Quality of the artwork is a prime factor to consider. Portraits, animals, and birds are worth more than florals; and pieces signed by a particularly renowned artist are highly prized. Our advice for this category comes from Fer-Duc Inc., whose address is listed in the Directory under New York.

Aventurine

Compote, 2 elephants support bowl, gr & brn, 16½" dia **1,900.00**
Vase, brn to gr in walnut brn on 4-sided shape, 1916, 5" **275.00**
Vase, caramel to chocolate drip in orange to red, 1932, 6½" **700.00**
Vase, 1920, butterflies/floral on gr, Lincoln, 10" **1,000.00**

Cameo

Plate, white roses on peach, crimped edges, #205B, 10", $275.00.

Cup & saucer, daisies on lt gr, AB Sprague, 1887, #291 ....**400.00**
Pitcher, dogwood blossoms, Valentien, 1890, #547, 3" **225.00**
Pitcher, lilies on gray, A Van Briggle, 1888, #246, 9" **400.00**
Plate, roses, wht & brn on peach to cream, Wilcox, 1889, 10" ...**150.00**
Teapot, floral, wht & brn on peach & cream, Valentien, 8" **500.00**

Iris

Vase, apple blossoms on bl to cream, S Sax, 1907, #935C, 9" .**2,200.00**
Vase, apple blossoms on gray/wht/pk, Coyne, 1906, 8x4" **1,400.00**
Vase, autumn oak leaves on pk to bl, Van Horne, 1909, 7" **950.00**
Vase, Canadian geese in landscape, Shirayamadani, 1910, 9" .**10,000.00**
Vase, crocus on violet to cream, E Diers, 1903, #614F, 6" **1,100.00**
Vase, daisies & buds on bl to peach, E Noonan, 1909, 7½" **3,200.00**
Vase, dogwood flowers on bl to gray, Baker, '02, #S1717, 6" ...**1,100.00**
Vase, floral, gray w/gr on lav to wht, Wareham, 1898, 6" **650.00**
Vase, floral, mc on blk to pk, EN Lincoln, 1911, 9½" **1,600.00**
Vase, floral, mc on yel to lav, Rothenbusch, '05, #913D, 7" **1,600.00**
Vase, floral, pk/gr on periwinkle, Rothenbusch, 1901, 4½" **450.00**
Vase, gulls (4) on pk to bl, AB Sprague, 1898, #852E, 4½x5" .**1,100.00**
Vase, harbor scene w/dinghies, Coyne, 1911, #950D, 9" **2,500.00**
Vase, iris (15) on slate gray, Schmidt, 1910, 8½" **2,600.00**
Vase, iris on gray to lav to wht, Schmidt, 1904, 12" **4,750.00**
Vase, irises, purple on blk to lav & gr, Coyne, 1907, 11x4" **3,250.00**
Vase, leaves & branches, mc on bl, Sax, 1902, #922D, 7" **1,800.00**
Vase, lilies, mc on pk to gray, S Sax, 1906, #941C, 9½" **2,200.00**
Vase, oak leaves/acorns on gray to cream, Asbury, 1908, 7x5" ...**1,200.00**
Vase, orchids, mc on lav to wht, S Coyne, '07, #925C, 9½" **900.00**
Vase, pansies, mc on wht to bl, L Asbury, 1907, #732, 8½" **900.00**
Vase, pansies on blk to wht, S Sax, 1902, #741C, 5½" **1,400.00**
Vase, peacock feather on bl to blk, Schmidt, '11, #907F, 8" **6,000.00**
Vase, rooks in flight w/pine needles beyond, Coyne, 1906, 9" .**3,750.00**
Vase, roses & buds, OG Reed, 1902, #905C, 9½" **3,500.00**
Vase, snapdragons on bl to gr, C Schmidt, 1904, #654E, 3½" .**1,600.00**
Vase, swans on gray to wht, Schmidt, 1907, #950, 9½" **15,000.00**
Vase, sweet peas, lav on ivory to lav, Asbury, 1906, 8½" **1,200.00**
Vase, tulips, pk & brn on tan to wht, M Nourse, 1904, 7½" **1,100.00**

Jewel Porcelain

Bowl, centerpc; floral band, yel on yel, Sax, 14" **1,300.00**

Jardiniere, fruit/flower band, mc on bl, Conant, 1920, 8x8" **450.00**
Vase, abstract decor, lt/dk bl & gr, Jensen, 1930, 6x3½" **575.00**
Vase, anemones on lt bl to wht, Shirayamadani, 1945, 7x5" ...**1,200.00**
Vase, mum garland, ivory w/blk outlines on wine, HEW, 7½" ..**800.00**
Vase, wht birds in landscape, Conant, 1929, rstr rim, 7" **750.00**
Vase, wispy floral on gray to pk, Shirayamadani, 1921, 6x3" ...**2,500.00**

Limoges

Pitcher, bamboo & butterfly, gold-flecked, Retting, 1885, 5½" ..**350.00**
Pitcher, bees & flowers, A Humphreys, 1882, 6" **500.00**
Pitcher, birds, blk/gold/wht/brn, McDonald, 1882, 6½" **550.00**
Pitcher, butterflies, mc w/gold, Rettig, 1882, #65, 9½" **800.00**
Pitcher, Oriental grass & butterflies, brns/gr/gilt, ARV, 7" **495.00**
Pitcher, swallows, mc w/gold, Humphreys, 1882, 8½x8" **550.00**
Vase, seascape w/appl bronze crabs, ML Nichols, 1883, 10" **5,500.00**
Vase, 3 rose blossoms, mc on dk gr, AR Valentien, 1882, 11" .**1,600.00**
Vessel, beetles w/gold, 2-spout, Valentien, 1883, #108 ....**2,100.00**

Mat

Note: Both incised mat and painted mat are listed here. Incised matt descriptions are indicated by the term 'cvd' within the line; the others are for the hand-painted mat ware.

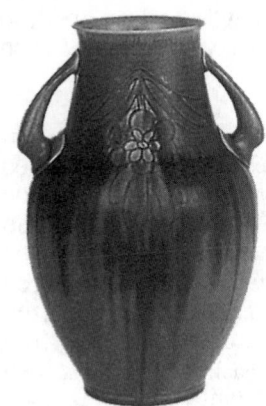

Vase, stylized florals carved on two-tone green mat, signed Elizabeth Lincoln, #339B, 1920, 14x8", $2,000.00.

Bowl, chevron rim design, 2-tone bl, #957DD, 1909, 2x5½" **210.00**
Candle holder, lily-pad base w/hand-formed stem, Valentien **325.00**
Jar, cvd/pnt peacock feather on gr, S Coyne, 1905, 5½" **800.00**
Pitcher, cvd/pnt Greek Key band, red on gr, Valentien, 4x5" **275.00**
Pitcher, medallion/head of owl, gr, Pons, #259D, 1907, 5" **200.00**
Umbrella stand, dk brn to dk gr, cylindrical, 1909, 24", EX **750.00**
Vase, apple blossom branch on gr to pk, Reed, 1907, 11x4" **2,100.00**
Vase, berries & leaves on rose w/blk, Tischler, 1922, 6½" **850.00**
Vase, bud; autumn leaves, Steinle, 1900, #172, 8x3½" **400.00**
Vase, cvd decor on brn w/bl crystals, #2913, 1906, 6" **130.00**
Vase, cvd floral, dk bl/purple, Hentschel, 1912, 10" **1,200.00**
Vase, cvd floral, gr w/red, Pons, 3 lg hdls, 1907, 6½" **650.00**
Vase, cvd floral band, 4-color on yel/pk, Todd, 1902, 5½" **600.00**
Vase, cvd floral/leaves, gr/bl/brn on wine, Todd, 1912, 8½" **800.00**
Vase, cvd leaves/thistle, gr/red on wine, Coyne, 1904, 6" **425.00**
Vase, cvd mushroom band, bl/wine, corseted, Hentshel, '11, 9" .**325.00**
Vase, cvd peacock feathers, brn/bl/crystalline brn, Todd, 6" **750.00**
Vase, cvd peacock feathers, gr/bl, Lincoln, 1920, 9x3" **500.00**
Vase, cvd peacock feathers, turq/brn on turq, Todd, Xd, 11" **750.00**
Vase, cvd stems/flowers at shoulder, gr/brn, Toohey, 1904, 6" .**1,000.00**
Vase, cvd swirling leaves, dk red/gr, #1064, 1913, 4" **240.00**
Vase, cvd tulips, bl/gr, #1907, 1917, 5" **160.00**

Vase, dragonflies, bl on rose, S Toohey, 1904, #66Z, 3" **1,100.00**
Vase, lg/sm brn & teal dots, Barrett, 1929, 5¾x5" **600.00**
Vase, mums, mc on gr, Jens Jensen, 1930, #2969, 7½" **900.00**
Vase, Nouveau floral on purple, CS Todd, 1921, #900D, 7" **600.00**
Vase, stylized tulips, pk/gr, #2424, 1919, 8" **220.00**
Vase, stylized upright floral/leaf, gr, #2413, Xd, 8" **280.00**
Vase, whiplash lines extend from hdls, red/gr, 1913, 11" **650.00**
Wall pocket, ivy relief, gr on brn butterfat, 1921, 8½x6" **300.00**

Porcelain

Vase, birds & blossoms, A Conant, 1919, #2, 6" **950.00**
Vase, daisies, lt bl on lav butterfat, Jensen, 1944, 5¾x3¾" **475.00**
Vase, daisies on powder bl, pk int, S Sax, 1920, #2032E, 8" **1,900.00**
Vase, delicate floral on peach to cream, McDonald, 1943, 3½" ..**450.00**
Vase, floral, mc on cream, J Jensen, 1945, 9½" **600.00**
Vase, floral, mc on dk bl, S Sax, 1924, #2726, 6" **4,000.00**
Vase, floral, mc on wht, L Holtkamp, 1953, 6½" **350.00**
Vase, floral branches on gray to bl, P Conant, 1917, #2061, 7" ..**900.00**
Vase, flowers & berries, Rothenbusch, 1924, #1325, 5½" **900.00**
Vase, geometric floral, aqua/gray-gr, Sax, 1916, #2293, 11½" ..**1,300.00**
Vase, lg abstract floral, bl/ivory on brn, Jensen, 1945, 6x5½" **650.00**
Vase, mice, brn & wht on gray w/bl neck, Jensen, 1934, 5" **2,500.00**
Vase, Oriental birds & leaves, A Conant, 1919, #2120, 7" **900.00**
Vase, peonies, brn/tan/blk on lt brn, Jensen, 1945, 13x9" **1,300.00**
Vase, pigeon feathers, wht on lt yel, Hentschel, 1931, 6x3" **100.00**
Vase, pussy willows on brn, gr int, S Sax, 1920, #2040E, 7½" **900.00**
Vase, trees w/blossoms & mtns, A Conant, 1922, #913E, 6½" ..**3,750.00**
Vase, tulips, cvd/pnt on wht, orange int, Epply, '27, 6½" **1,000.00**

Sea Green

Pitcher, grapes & leaves cvd & pnt on blk, Baker, 1900, 10" ..**2,500.00**
Vase, daffodils, yel & gr on bl, Toohey, 1900, #732B, 10" **3,500.00**
Vase, iris buds, lav on lt gr, Matt Daly, 1897, #532, 9½" **3,500.00**
Vase, poppies in heavy relief, LN Lincoln, 1905, #907DD, 9" .**7,500.00**
Vase, ship on wavy sea w/moon, S Laurence, 1901, 11" **11,000.00**
Vase, underwater scene w/fish, ET Hurley, 1903, #940D, 9" ...**3,750.00**
Vase, 2 sea gulls w/open wings, ET Hurley, 1900, #46, 9" **3,000.00**

Standard

Bowl, buds & blossoms, Reed, #536, 1892, 3x4¼" **275.00**
Chocolate pot, leaves/acorns, Asbury, cylindrical, 1904, 10" **450.00**
Creamer, clover blossoms, Markland, #692, 1894, 4x5" **200.00**
Creamer, violets, butterfly hdl, Markland, #829, 1894, 2¾" **150.00**
Ewer, cherries, Asbury, 1899, 10" **500.00**
Ewer, floral, mc on brn & orange, 1889, #40W, 5½", EX **240.00**
Ewer, hibiscus, Daly, #381, 1888, 9" **550.00**
Ewer, mums, yel on orange & brn, S Toohey, 1890, #433, 7" **450.00**
Ewer, roses, AM Valentien, #537D, 1892, 10" **450.00**
Ewer, silver o/l & mc floral on yel to brn, Zettel, #499W, 7" ...**1,500.00**
Ewer, silver o/l floral sgn Gorham, dandelions, 6" **1,800.00**
Jardiniere, wild roses, Sprage, hdls, 7x8" **700.00**
Jug, silver o/l filigree on 1 side over corn, SE, 1897, 7" **2,500.00**
Jug, silver o/l vintage over ear of corn, Strafer, 1893, 8" **1,400.00**
Mug, Black-Eye (Indian), Swing, 1900, 4½" **1,100.00**
Mug, Chief Goes to War Sioux, Felten, 1900, 5" **1,150.00**
Mug, clover blossoms, mc on brn shaded, sgn, 1890s, #328S, 6" ...**225.00**
Mug, ear of corn, Nourse, #587C, 1896, 5" **225.00**
Mug, mums, McDonald, 1889, 6" **350.00**
Vase, berries & leaves, Dibowski, 1893, #442C, 6½" **1,100.00**
Vase, butterflies w/some crystalline, WH, 1906, 6½x2½" **450.00**
Vase, clover, Schmidt, 1900, 5½x4" **225.00**

Vase, daffodils, Steinle, 1905, 8½x3½" 550.00
Vase, daisies, Asbury, long flared neck, #846C, 1902, 11" 525.00
Vase, daisy cluster, Hurley, #904CC, 1903, 9¾" 600.00
Vase, dogwood, Nourse, 1894, 6x5¾" 425.00
Vase, floral, mc on gr to bl-gr, Zettel, 1894, #763C, 5½x5" 450.00
Vase, floral, Steinle, hdls, #459D, 1900, 6" 325.00
Vase, hibiscus, Steinle, #800, 1899, 5½x5½" 250.00
Vase, leaves/berries, Zettel, bulbous w/trumpet neck, 1898, 9" ...300.00
Vase, nasturtiums, unsgn, trumpet neck, 1898, 12½" 400.00
Vase, tulips, CA Baker, elongated ovoid, #796B, 1900, 10" 400.00
Whiskey jug, ear of corn/wheat, Nourse, bulbous, 1899, 8" 400.00

Tiger Eye

Candlestick, wild rose, yel on red-brn, Wilcox, 1889, #508 ....240.00
Pitcher, lilies, yel & brn on brn & orange, Valentien, 1886, 5" ..325.00
Vase, brn & blk w/gold highlights, 1885, #1726, 8½" 800.00
Vase, dk brn & gold, tapered classic form, 1887, #533, 7" 700.00
Vase, serpents, EX detail, Shirayamadani, 1893, #644, 18½" ..10,000.00

Vellum

Plaque, lake viewed through trees, SE Coyne, 1900, 12x14" ...4,300.00
Plaque, Not a Breeze, Sarah Sax, orig fr, 5½x7¼"+fr 950.00
Plaque, trees shadowed in water, C Schmidt, fr, 5x9½", EX 1,700.00
Vase, autumn leaves, pastels, Lincoln, 1905, 8x4" 600.00
Vase, berries, wine/gr/russet on dk bl, Sax, 1914, 12x6" 2,000.00
Vase, Canadian geese, Shirayamadani, 1911, 7½x3½" 6,500.00
Vase, cvd abstract floral on bl-gray/gr matt, 1908, 7x3" 250.00
Vase, daffodils, Steinle, #839B, 1907, 9" 650.00
Vase, daisies, cvd & pnt on ivory w/gray band, Sax, '05, 7" 1,700.00
Vase, floral, mc on gray, silver o/l, Hurley, 1912, 10½" 1,900.00
Vase, floral, mc w/blk on cream, Holtkamp, 1942, 8" 600.00
Vase, landscape, pk/ivory, van Horn, cylindrical, 1911, 7" 900.00
Vase, lg tulips, yel/wht/blk on celadon, S Sax, 1904, 10x5" 1,200.00
Vase, lily of the valley on lav, Sax, '15, 1939, 4½x7½" 950.00
Vase, long-stem daisies on bl to gr, Noonan, 1908, 7" 825.00
Vase, mums on bl/brn/cream, Rothenbusch, 1925, 10x5½", M .3,800.00
Vase, Queen Anne's Lace, L Asbury, 1911, #900A, 13" 2,500.00
Vase, roses, pk on bl to ivory, Rothenbusch, 1927, 11x4" 2,750.00
Vase, roses w/thorny stems, Rothenbusch, 1905, 5¾x2¾" 750.00
Vase, stylized dandelions, yel/gr on ivory/gr, Epply, '07, 6" 1,100.00
Vase, stylized floral band on celadon, van Horn, 1915, 11" 850.00
Vase, tree scene, lav/ivory, van Horn, 1911, 7¾x3" 800.00
Vase, tree/river, Diers, uncrazed, 1930, 8x4" 2,100.00
Vase, trees, gray/pk/cream/lav/bl, Rothenbusch, 1915, 11" 1,500.00
Vase, trees/lake, ET Hurley, 1930, 11x5" 2,500.00

Wax Mat

Vase, abstract floral, intense color, Jensen, 4½x4" 500.00
Vase, abstract floral, intense color, Tischler, 1923, 10x7" 750.00
Vase, abstract floral/leaf on lt bl, #2639E, 1929, 8" 350.00
Vase, abstracts on shoulder on mustard, #356F, 1929, 5½" 250.00
Vase, daffodils on yel to gr, Lincoln, 1927, 11x4" 1,000.00
Vase, lg pk floral/gr leaves on yel mottle, Barrett, 1926, 9" 700.00
Vase, panoramic scenic, EX art, Patty Conant, 1916, 7½x3½" ..2,500.00
Vase, peacock feather band, bl/gr on pk, Lincoln, 1920, 9x4" .1,200.00
Vase, water lilies/pads on salmon-pk butterfat, 1930, 7x4" 750.00

Miscellaneous

Bookends, fish leaping from stream, bronze, ET Hurley, 6", EX ..900.00
Bowl, conch shell, gun metal on gr w/yel, Epply, '28, #6061, 4" .450.00

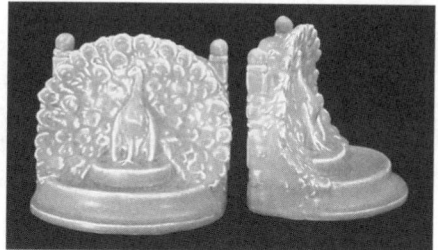

Bookends, peacock form, rose color,
XIX/#2445, 4½x5", $350.00 for the pair.

Sculpture, lady on horse, att L Abel, 1940, #6177, 8x12" 650.00
Soap dish, 1955, nude lying on side of rim, pk gloss, 1¾x4½" ...100.00
Tile, Arts & Crafts tree, gr/brn on bl & cream, oak fr, 6" 1,000.00
Tile, duck w/ducklings, #442, 6" sq+wood fr 850.00
Tile, Faience, exotic birds bk to bk on purple, 5½"+wood fr 750.00
Tile, parrot among blossoms, #442, 6" sq+fr 350.00
Tile, Viking ship & lg fish, 7-color, #442, 6" sq+fr 600.00
Tile, 1902, Faience, river scene w/mtns, 12" sq+oak fr 3,250.00
Tile, 1905, Arts & Crafts rose/leaves, 5½"+oak fr 475.00
Tile, 1905, 3 sea horses cut bk on gr mat, 9"+fr 1,000.00
Umbrella stand, gr matt cylinder w/cut-out hdls, 24" 800.00
Vase, floor; unglazed, #307GY/466, 26x18", pr (1 EX) 600.00
Vase, 1922, emb upright leaves, pk/gr mat, #1822, 6" 220.00
Vase, 1923, oxblood, lg dk red patch on wht (trial), 8x4" 375.00
Vase, 1924, Arts & Crafts geometric, rose mat, #2135, 6" 200.00
Vase, 1926, berries/leaves around neck on bl mat, 4½x3½" 125.00
Vase, 1927, emb floral on dk bl, #2108, 6½" 100.00
Vase, 1928, ivory mat, modernistic, 4-sided, 8" 75.00
Vase, 1928, swirls from hdls, dk/lt bl crystalline, #2331, 8" 425.00
Vase, 1928, 3 emb wide upright leaves, gr/pk mat, #2091, 7" 200.00
Vase, 1929, emb leaves/buds, brn w/bl crystals, #1811, 5" 350.00
Vase, 1930, cvd grapes/leaves, turq semi-mat, #2604 ....200.00
Vase, 1930, emb fish/seaweed, squeezebag decor, Hentschel, 9" .1,500.00
Vase, 1932, violet bl to lt brn metallic, 4x2¾" 175.00
Vase, 1933, bl mat, sq w/2 dimples ea side, #2003, 4½" 120.00
Vase, 1934, yel mat, 3 integral rim-to-shoulder hdls, 5½" 275.00
Vase, 1938, red over caramel crystalline, #6331, 7½x7½" 550.00
Vase, 1945, emb leaves, red on lt bl semi-mat, Rehm, 4¾" 350.00
Wall pocket, 1921, emb leaves & buds on U-form, #1391, 6½" .250.00

Rorstrand

The Rorstrand Pottery was established in Sweden in 1726 and is today Sweden's oldest existing pottery. The earliest ware, now mostly displayed in Swedish museums, was much like old Delft. Later types were hard-paste porcelains that were enameled and decorated in a peasant style. Contemporary pieces are often described as Swedish Modern. Rorstrand is also famous for their Christmas plates.

Statue, Ekeby, Lindstrom, 1940s, 12" 350.00
Vase, appl leaves on oxblood, 19th C, 10" 750.00
Vase, crackle, Kathler, 5" 125.00
Vase, Deco figures, 8" 185.00
Vase, oxblood w/appl gr leaves, 19th C, 10" 750.00
Vase, sgraffito fish, 1950s, 8" 450.00

Rose Mandarin

Similar in design to Rose Medallion, this Chinese Export porcelain features the pattern of a robed mandarin, often separated by florals, ladies, genre scenes, or butterflies in polychrome enamels. It is sometimes trimmed in gold. Elaborate in decoration, this pattern was popular from the late 1700s until the early 1840s.

Basin, 16¼" 865.00

Bough pots, 1800s, one lid repaired, 8½", $4,300.00 for the pair.

Bowl, sq, 1800s, 8¾", pr 1,095.00
Coffeepot, 1800s, 10¼" 1,500.00
Garniture, 3-pc, early 1800s, 12" 1,850.00
Hot water dish, 9¾" 625.00
Plate, 9½" 100.00
Platter, 1800s, 14¼" 500.00
Platter, 1800s, 14¾x18" 600.00
Platter, 1800s, 20" 1,980.00
Shrimp dish, 1800s, 10⅝" dia 700.00
Soap dish, 1800s, imperfections, 3-pc, 5½" L 400.00
Tazza, 1800s, 4x10" 900.00
Vase, gold decor, 1800s, 12", 3 for 2,300.00
Vegetable dish, 1800s, w/lid, 9½" L 700.00

Rose Medallion

Rose Medallion is one of the patterns of Chinese export porcelain produced from before 1850 until the second decade of the 20th century. It is decorated in rose colors with panels of florals, birds, and butterflies that form reserves containing Chinese figures. Pre-1850 ware is unmarked and is characterized by quality workmanship and gold trim. From about 1850 until circa 1860, the kilns in Canton did not operate, and no Rose Medallion was made. Post-1860 examples (still unmarked) can often be recognized by the poor quality of the gold trim or its absence. In the 1890s the ware was often marked 'China'; 'Made in China' was used from 1910 through the 1930s.

Bowl, chop; 15½" dia 400.00
Bowl, deep w/str sides, flared rim, w/lid, 5½" 475.00
Bowl, gilt ground, 8" 300.00
Bowl, potpourri; cylindrical, flared rim, 4½" 80.00
Bowl, vegetable; octagonal oval, w/lid, 1800s, pr ... 585.00
Bowl, 10", on 4" tubular base, rare 650.00
Bowl, 14¾" 1,200.00
Bowl, 1800s, 10" 300.00
Bowl, 3 figures, deep, Made in China, 7½" 67.50
Brush pot, 4½", pr 200.00
Candle cup, flared top, 2⅜" 70.00
Charger, floral band around lg figural scene, 15" ... 300.00
Creamer, tall ovoid w/scalloped rim, wht hdl, 5" 225.00
Creamer & sugar bowl, bulbous, Made in China, 5½" ... 150.00

Cup & saucer, China 40.00
Cup handleless; ped ft, 20th C, 2⅜x3¼" 25.00
Dish, shallow, 12" 200.00
Lamp base, cylindrical, gold hdls/chinoiserie ft, 12½" ... 475.00
Lamp base, 6 appl salamanders around neck, 30" ... 990.00
Planter, flaring hexagon, 5¼x7¼" 200.00
Plate, deep, 18 scallops, lemon peel glaze, 8¼" 195.00
Plate, fluted rim, 8½" 150.00
Plate, hot water; armorial, 9⅜" 1,725.00
Plate, hot water; chip, 10¼" 350.00
Plate, Made in China, 9½" 57.50
Plate, ornate border w/4 panels, 8" 95.00
Plate, ribbon & flower borders, 8½" 145.00
Plate, rtcl rim, 6" 85.00
Plate, rtcl rim, 8½" 95.00
Plate, rtcl rim, 9½" 125.00
Plate, spitting dragons, 7½" 90.00
Plate, 1870s, 9½" 235.00
Plate, 2 border designs, 7¾" 85.00
Plate, 4 medallions, gold curlique border, 8¼" 95.00
Platter, ftd, shaped edge, 14" 375.00
Platter, oval, 16¼" 300.00
Platter, rtcl, w/gold, early, 10x9" 425.00
Platter, scenic, 1800s, w/strainer, 16½" 875.00
Platter, w/strainer, 20x13½" 1,035.00
Platter, well & tree, 19" 750.00
Platter, 18" 600.00
Punch bowl, 1800s, 15⅝" 1,375.00
Shaker, dome top, 2¾x1⅞" sq 70.00
Sugar bowl, bulbous, Made in China, 4x6" 100.00
Teapot, cylindrical, 4¾x3¾" 110.00
Teapot, 6¼x5" 275.00
Tureen, soup; w/lid, 15½" 2,600.00
Tureen, w/dbl-vine hdls, 6½x8", EX, +undertray 775.00
Umbrella stand, 23½" 1,400.00
Vase, bottle form, 6½", pr 300.00
Vase, Ku form, landscape panels, 13" 375.00
Vase, slim form w/salamander hdls, 10½", pr 450.00
Vase, spherical, 9x8½", pr 750.00
Vase, 1800s, 13½", pr 920.00

Roselane

Founded in California in 1938 by William and Georgia Fields, the Roselane company at first produced only figurines for the local florist. But by the forties they offered candle holders, wall pockets, vases, and a line of modernistic animals mounted on wooden bases. In the fifties their 'Sparklers' became popular — small stylized animal and bird figures with rhinestone eyes. (Today these are worth from $10.00 to $25.00, depending on size.) The company closed in 1977. A variety of marks was used; all incorporate the Roselane name.

Bowl, console; pk & gray, A-20, 20" L 35.00
Bowl, fish design, turq & blk, w/stand, 13" dia 65.00
Candle holders, Chinese Modern, dove gray gloss, pr ... 75.00
Figurine, Balinese dancers, gray & mauve, 10x8", pr ... 75.00
Figurine, boy w/dog, 5½" 12.00
Figurine, egret, 9", +matching bowl 45.00
Figurine, mama & baby quail 45.00
Figurine, owl, sgraffito feathers on tan, 6½" 60.00
Planter, Chinese Coolie atop rectangular form 22.50
Vase, Chinese Modern, emb decor base, ftd, 9¾" 25.00

Rosemeade

Rosemeade was the name chosen by Wahpeton Pottery Company of Wahpeton, North Dakota, to represent their product. The founders of the company were Laura A. Taylor and R.J. Hughes, who organized the firm in 1940. It is most noted for small bird and animal figurals, either in high gloss or a Van Briggle-like matt glaze. The ware was marked 'Rosemeade' with an ink stamp or carried a 'Prairie Rose' sticker. The pottery closed in 1961. Our advisor for this category is Bryce L. Farnsworth; he is listed in the Directory under North Dakota.

Ashtray, Ashley ND Dmn Jubilee 60.00
Ashtray, Chicago Equipment Co 60.00
Ashtray, crouching pheasant 275.00
Ashtray, DeKalb Chix 155.00
Ashtray, Illinois state form 30.00
Ashtray, mallard duck 125.00
Bank, Jamestown buffalo 180.00
Bookends, wolfhounds, pr 235.00
Figurine, fighting cocks, mini, pr 275.00
Figurine, fighting cocks, pr 200.00
Figurine, fox, mini, pr 250.00
Figurine, geese, gray, mini, pr 120.00
Figurine, mountain goat 160.00
Figurine, panda bear 425.00
Figurine, turkeys, mini, pr 175.00
Figurine, walrus, bronze lustre 650.00
Flower frog, heron 40.00
Flower frog, leaping deer 50.00
Flower frog, pheasant 95.00
Flower frog, turkey 90.00
Pin tray, Teddy Roosevelt bear 190.00
Planter, elephant 50.00
Planter, sleigh 105.00
Shakers, bear cubs, sitting, pr 65.00
Shakers, buffalo, pr 140.00
Shakers, cucumbers, pr 62.50
Shakers, dog heads, bloodhounds, pr 32.00
Shakers, dog heads, chow chows, pr 35.00
Shakers, dog heads, English setters, pr 30.00
Shakers, dog heads, Scotties, pr 32.50
Shakers, dog heads, terriers, pr 30.00
Shakers, donkey heads, pr 65.00
Shakers, ducklings, pr 75.00
Shakers, elephants, pr 55.00
Shakers, flamingos, pr 105.00
Shakers, gophers, paws crossed, pr 42.50
Shakers, horse heads, palominos, pr 57.50
Shakers, leaping deer, pr 160.00
Shakers, mallards, standing drake & hen, pr 90.00
Shakers, ponies, pr 75.00
Shakers, Prairie Roses, pr 30.00
Shakers, quail, pr 45.00
Shakers, roadrunners, pr 225.00
Shakers, Siamese cats, pr 70.00
Shakers, skunks, lg, pr 40.00
Shakers, tulips, pr 22.00
Spoon rest, cactus 55.00
Spoon rest, elephant 70.00
Sugar bowl, mallard hen 55.00
Sugar bowl, turkey hen 55.00
Tidbit tray, turkey 150.00
TV lamp, horse, blk stallion 485.00

TV lamp, horse, palomino 380.00
TV lamp, panther, gr 420.00
TV lamp, pheasant 400.00
Vase, deer, turq matt, 7½" 45.00
Wall pocket, deer 40.00

Rosenthal

In 1879 Phillip Rosenthal established the Rosenthal Porcelain Factory in Selb, Bavaria. Its earliest products were figurines and fine tablewares. The company has continued to operate to the present decade, manufacturing limited edition plates.

Bowl, soup; Devonshire 20.00
Bowl, vegetable; Devonshire, w/lid 65.00
Cigarette urn, rose buds w/gold, 2½", +4" underplate 25.00
Creamer, Devonshire 30.00
Cup & saucer, Devonshire 20.00
Figurine, bird on branch, #1648, 6" 150.00
Figurine, boy feeding bird, wht, 4" 120.00
Figurine, boy feeding fawn, wht, 6½" 145.00
Figurine, boy sits & feeds squirrel, wht, 4½" 125.00
Figurine, boy w/lamb 225.00
Figurine, boy w/4 birds, wht, 5" 130.00
Figurine, chickadee, #1648, 6" 130.00
Figurine, child w/chicks, US Zone Germany, #1040 ....95.00
Figurine, Cocker Spaniel pup w/sad face, Kuspert, 4" 145.00
Figurine, frog on leaf, #1080, 2½" 90.00
Figurine, girl feeding pigeons, sgn Claire Weiss 75.00
Figurine, Great Dane, brindle, 8¾x9" 400.00
Figurine, lady w/Borzoi, sgn, US Zone, #1553, 4¾x7x11" 550.00
Figurine, narrow angular face, in tunic & drape, wht, 19" 900.00
Figurine, nude on bench w/parrot, #K288, 6¼x7¼" 325.00
Figurine, peacock, #978, 5x10" 295.00
Figurine, sea gull, sgn Heidenreich, 9x12" 250.00
Figurine, sea gulls, sgn Meisel, 18½" 1,450.00
Figurine, Wire Fox Terrier, M-52, 3½" 148.00
Gravy boat, Devonshire 50.00
Pitcher, tankard; lilies, gold hdl, sgn Hayes 1912, 12½" 200.00
Plate, dinner; Devonshire 18.00
Plate, mc flowers on shaded ground, 8½" 27.50
Plate, mixed fruit w/gold, JZ Selb, 8", 4 for 195.00
Platter, Devonshire, 11½" 35.00
Platter, Devonshire, 13" 45.00

Sculpture, Heidi and Margot Hopfner dancing, hand painted in burnt orange on white, signed H.L. Zimmerman, 12½", $1,320.00.

Sugar bowl, Devonshire 40.00
Tankard, kneeling nude, HP decor, 6" 125.00
Tray, Delft-style windmill scene, St Cloud, 8x10" 95.00
Vase, birds on abstract gr, sgn Wiinblad, ovoid, 5¾x5¾" 120.00

Roseville

The Roseville Pottery Company was established in 1892 by George F. Young in Roseville, Ohio. Finding their facilities inadequate, the company moved to Zanesville in 1898, erected a new building, and installed the most modern equipment available. By 1900 Young felt ready to enter into the stiffly competitive art pottery market. Roseville's first art line was called Rozane. Similar to Rookwood's Standard, Rozane featured dark blended backgrounds with slip-painted underglaze artwork of nature studies, portraits, birds, and animals. Azurean, developed in 1902, was a blue and white underglaze art line on a blue blended background. Egypto (1904) featured a matt glaze in a soft shade of old green and was modeled in low relief after examples of ancient Egyptian pottery. Mongol (1904) was a high-gloss oxblood red line after the fashion of the Chinese Sang de Boeuf. Mara (1904), an iridescent lustre line of magenta and rose with intricate patterns developed on the surface or in low relief, successfully duplicated Sicardo's work. These early lines were followed by many others of highest quality: Fudjiyama and Woodland (1905-06) reflected an Oriental theme; Crystalis (1906) was covered with beautiful frost-like crystals. Della Robbia, their most famous line (introduced in 1906), was decorated with designs ranging from florals, animals, and birds to scenes of Viking warriors and Roman gladiators. These designs were accomplished by sgraffito with slip-painted details. Very limited but of great importance to collectors today, Rozane Olympic (1905) was decorated with scenes of Greek mythology on a red ground. Pauleo (1914) was the last of the artware lines. It was varied — over two hundred glazes were recorded — and some pieces were decorated by hand, usually with florals.

During the second decade of the century until the plant closed forty years later, new lines were continually added. Some of the more popular of the middle-period lines were Donatello, 1915; Futura, 1928; Pine Cone, 1931; and Blackberry, 1933. The floral lines of the later years have become highly collectible. Pottery from every era of Roseville production — even its utility ware — attest to an unwavering dedication to quality and artistic merit.

Examples of the fine art pottery lines present the greatest challenge to evaluate. Scarcity is a prime consideration. The quality of artwork varied from one artist to another. Some pieces show fine detail and good color, and naturally this influences their values. Studies of animals and portraits bring higher prices than the floral designs. An artist's signature often increases the value of any item, especially if the artist is one who is well recognized. For further information consult *The Collector's Encyclopedia of Roseville Pottery, First and Second Series,* by Sharon and Bob Huxford, available at your local library or bookstore. Our advisors for this category are Jeanette and Marvin Stofft; they are listed in the Directory under Indiana.

Futura vases: Art Deco neck with triangular design in light blue and green, 10", $700.00; Bulbous form with terraced neck, gun metal to green, glossy, 12", $950.00; Deco form with four buttresses, brown with yellow drip at top, 10", NM, $500.00.

Apple Blossom, jardiniere, #342-6, 6"	125.00
Artwood, vase, #1057-8, 8"	75.00
Autumn, mug, shaving; no mk, 4"	275.00
Autumn, wash pitcher, 12½"	500.00
Aztec, vase, stylized floral, waisted w/flat rim, 11"	500.00
Azurean, vase, slim form, flared rim, #865, RPCO, 18"	1,250.00
Baneda, vase, cylindrical, ftd, hdls, silver paper label, 7"	250.00
Bittersweet, basket, #807-8, 8½"	110.00
Bittersweet, planter, #828-10, 10½"	100.00
Blackberry, hanging basket, leaves & berries, 4½x6½"	550.00
Blackberry, vase, ring hdls, 8"	335.00
Bleeding Heart, bowl, #377-4, 4"	75.00
Bleeding Heart, vase, #969-8, 8"	150.00
Bushberry, bowl, ring hdls, #411, 4"	60.00
Bushberry, planter, #383-6, 6½"	110.00
Capri, ashtray, #598-9, 9"	35.00
Carnelian I, vase, fan; hdld, ink stamp, 8"	60.00
Carnelian II, ewer, ear hdls, flared ft, 12½"	175.00
Carnelian II, vase, classic form, no mk, 7"	100.00
Cherry Blossom, candle holders, ring hdls, 4", pr	250.00
Cherry Blossom, hanging basket, floral over ribs, no mk, 8"	500.00
Cherry Blossom, vase, hdls, 10"	325.00
Chloron, vase, gr, integral hdls, gourd shape, 9"	450.00
Clemana, flower frog, floral #23, 4"	75.00
Clemana, vase, floral, #280-6, 6½"	125.00
Clematis, flowerpot, #668-5, 5½"	110.00
Clematis, vase, cornucopia; #140, 6"	45.00
Clematis, vase, floral, gr, 8"	60.00
Columbine, vase, #17-7, 7½"	90.00
Columbine, vase, cornucopia; #149-6, 5½"	60.00
Corinthian, bowl, concave ribs, floral neck, ftd, no mk, 4½"	70.00
Corinthian, wall pocket, concave ribs, floral neck, no mk, 8"	175.00
Cornelian, jardiniere, #119, base dia: 4"	75.00
Cornelian, pitcher, emb wild rose on yel, no mk, 9"	100.00
Cornelian, toothbrush holder, hdls, no mk, 5"	85.00
Cosmos, flower frog, hdld, no mk, 3½"	75.00
Cosmos, vase, #945-5, 5"	75.00
Creamware, candlestick, decor/gold traced, 3-sided, no mk, 8½"	125.00
Creamware, candlestick, Good Night, no mk, 7"	350.00
Creamware, mug, Quaker men motif, 5"	175.00
Creamware, mug, strawberry decal, 5"	100.00
Creamware, pot/liner, 6-sided, 3½"	85.00
Creamware, tankard, Indian decal, 10½"	350.00
Creamware, trivet, cherries, no mk, 6"	110.00
Cremona, vase, floral, ftd, fan shape, no mk, 5"	35.00
Crystalis, vase, gr w/bl crystals, shouldered, no mk, 11"	1,450.00
Dahlrose, hanging basket, floral, no mk, 7½"	175.00
Dahlrose, vase, pillow; hdls, no mk, 5x7"	125.00
Dawn, ewer, #834-16, 16"	400.00
Della Robbia, pitcher, horse & chariot w/rider, 8"	4,000.00
Della Robbia, teapot, 6-sided, 8"	1,500.00
Della Robbia, vase, daisies, bulbous, 8"	4,000.00
Della Robbia, vase, pine cone band/leaves, cylindrical, 7½"	2,000.00
Della Robbia, vase, swimming swans, classic, 11½"	7,000.00
Dogwood I, jardiniere, floral, ink stamp, 8"	125.00
Dogwood II, vase, dbl bud; floral, 8"	135.00
Dogwood II, window box/liner, floral, no mk, 5½x13½"	135.00
Donatello, ashtray, flared rim, no mk, 3"	75.00
Donatello, comport, ftd, no mk, 5"	80.00
Donatello, vase, no mk, 12x7"	200.00
Dutch, humidor, w/lid, children fishing, knob finial, 6"	250.00
Egypto, lamp base, gr, 3 elephant-trunk hdls, no mk, 10"	750.00
Egypto, vase, emb lily pads & buds on scrolling stems, 8"	485.00
Egypto, vase, iris, overlapping leaves at bottom, 13x10"	4,500.00

Falline, candle holder, loop hdls, brn-gr-bl glaze, no mk, 4" 150.00
Falline, vase, bulbous, ftd, hdls, sm silver label, 6" 275.00
Ferella, vase, brn, ftd, hdls, no mk, 6" 275.00
Florane, bowl, hdls, ink stamp, 12½" 50.00
Florane, vase, dbl bud; ink stamp, 5" 60.00
Florentine, ashtray, emb grapes, no mk, 5" 60.00
Florentine, lamp base, emb grapes, hdls, ftd, no mk, 8" 200.00
Florentine, vase, dbl bud; emb grapes, no mk, 4½" 75.00
Foxglove, flower frog, #46, 4" 75.00
Foxglove, vase, fan shape, #47-8, 8½" 175.00
Freesia, basket, #390-7, 7" 120.00
Freesia, vase, angle hdls, #121-8, 8" 68.00
Freesia, window box, #1392-8, 10½" 100.00
Fuchsia, candlesticks, #1133-5, 5½", pr 150.00
Fuchsia, vase, #893-6, 6" 150.00
Fudji, vase, cyindrical form, no mk, 9" 1,500.00
Fudji, vase, Oriental stylized floral, shouldered, 10½" 1,500.00
Futura, pillow vase, lt/dk bl triangle panels, label, 5x6" 200.00
Futura, vase, bullet form in 4-buttress support, gr/bl, 8" 650.00
Futura, vase, long stepped neck, long hdls, #382-7 ....200.00
Futura, vase, lt gr horizontal ribs, no mk, 10" 1,250.00
Futura, vase, 4 Deco buttresses on cone shape, #401-8 ....450.00
Futura, vase, 4-sided tapered top on lobed ball, #393-12 ....750.00
Futura, vase, 6-sided twist w/abstract geometrics, #425-8 ....375.00
Futura, window box, cream over bl, no mk, 5x15½" 650.00
Gardenia, basket, #610-12, 12" 170.00
Gardenia, bowl, ring hdls, ruffled rim, #641-5", 5" 55.00
Holland, powder jar, no mk, 3" 95.00
Holly, teapot, leaves & berries, hdld, 4½" 250.00
Imperial I, planter, no mk, 14x16" 150.00
Imperial II, bowl, brn over bl, flared, ftd, no mk, 5x12½" 200.00
Imperial II, cream over brn, rim-to-shoulder hdls, no mk, 8" 200.00
Iris, basket, hdld, #355-10, 9½" 300.00
Iris, bowl, console; #361-8, 3x10" 125.00
Ivory II, candlestick, #1122-5, 5½", ea 40.00
Ivory II, vase, ftd, #271-6, 6½" 75.00
Ixia, basket, hanging, 7" 225.00
Ixia, bowl, console; #330-7, 3½x10½" 100.00
Jonquil, vase, gourd shape, hdls, no mk, 4½" 125.00
Jonquil, vase, hdls, no mk, 12" 600.00
Juvenile, creamer, bears, gr bands, no mk, 4" 200.00
Juvenile, creamer, chicks, side pour 200.00
Juvenile, creamer, chicks, 3" 100.00
Juvenile, creamer, Santa Claus, hdld, 3½" 200.00
Juvenile, dish, pudding; chicks, no mk, 7" 100.00
Juvenile, mug, dog, ink stamp, 3" 100.00
Juvenile, mug, fancy cat, 3" 150.00
Juvenile, mug, rabbit, 3" 75.00
Juvenile, plate, divided; fancy cat, 8½" 300.00
Juvenile, plate, pigs on circle, rolled edge, 8" 250.00
Juvenile, plate, rabbits on circle, rolled edge, 8" 150.00
Juvenile, teapot, duck, no mk, 4" 225.00
La Rose, bowl, ink stamp, 3" 65.00
La Rose, jardiniere, ink stamp, 6½" 110.00
Laurel, bowl, wide, no mk, 3½" 125.00
Lombardy, vase, bl, melon ribs, flared rim, 3-ftd, no mk, 6" 200.00
Lotus, pillow vase, #L4-10, 10½" 150.00
Luffa, lamp, bl/gr glaze, floral, no mk, 9½" 500.00
Luffa, vase, floral, sm angle hdls, flared ft, 13" 300.00
Luffa, vase, floral, sm angle hdls, unmk, 8½" 125.00
Lustre, basket, flared rim, hdl, no mk, 6" 150.00
Magnolia, ashtray, #28, 7" wide 80.00
Magnolia, basket, #386-12, 12" 175.00
Magnolia, planter, #388-6, 8½" 90.00

Mara, bowl, hdlds, 4" 1,300.00
Matt Green, gate, gr, no mk, 5x8" 45.00
Matt Green, tobacco jar, gr, w/lid, no mk, 6" 200.00
Mayfair, pot, #71-4, 4½" 40.00
Ming Tree, bowl, tub form, twig hdls, #526-9, 4x11½" 55.00
Ming Tree, conch shell, #563, 8½" 50.00
Ming Tree, vase, twig hdls, #582, 8" 60.00
Mock Orange, bowl, #900, 4" 37.50
Mock Orange, planter, #931-8, 3½x9" 45.00
Moderne, comport, #295, 5" 125.00
Moderne, vase, ftd ball shape, #299, 6½" 150.00
Mongol, vase, cylindrical, flared bottom & neck, w/seal, 16" ..1,150.00
Mongol, vase, cylindrical, no mk, 10½" 950.00
Mongol, vase, wide gourd shape w/3 extended ft, 7¾x4¾" 475.00
Monticello, vase, brn, classic shape, hdls, no mk, 5" 140.00
Morning Glory, basket, floral, hdld, sm label, 10½" 500.00
Morning Glory, vase, wht, angle hdls, 14½x10" 1,100.00
Moss, vase, ftd, #290-6, 6" 150.00
Mostique, hanging basket, 7" 225.00
Mostique, jardiniere, floral, no mk, 8" 150.00

Mostique, jardiniere and pedestal, dark grays, 28", $650.00; Florentine, umbrella stand, 20", $550.00; Magnolia, jardiniere and pedestal set: with blue 10" jardiniere, $1,200.00; with 8" brown, $850.00; with 8" green, $750.00.

Old Ivory, planter, 4" 60.00
Olympic, pitcher, Pandora Brought to Earth, 7" 2,150.00
Orian, comport, bl/gr, #272-10, 4½x10½" 90.00
Orian, vase, #733-6, 6½" 90.00
Pauleo, vase, lg iris, maroon on bl, bulb w/flared neck, 17" 1,350.00
Pauleo, vase, maroon, classic, 18½" 1,250.00
Pauleo, vase, trees in foreground, hills/trees, 17x7½" 1,600.00
Peony, bookends, #11, 5½", pr 200.00
Peony, vase, #169-8, 8" 90.00
Persian, hanging basket, no mk, 9" 250.00
Pine Cone, ashtray, shell shaped, #499, 4½" 70.00
Pine Cone, boat dish, #427-8, 9" 250.00
Pine Cone, planter, #124, 5" 125.00
Pine Cone, tray, dbl; leaves in middle form hdl, no mk, 13" 275.00
Pine Cone, vase, ftd, twig hdls, gr, #908-8, 8" 185.00
Poppy, ewer, #880-18, 18½" 500.00
Poppy, vase, #346-6, 6" 125.00
Primrose, vase, #761-6, 6½" 150.00
Raymor, bowl, salad; #161, 11½" 40.00
Rosecraft Panel, window box, ink stamped, 6x12" 250.00
Rozane, letter holder, Royal seal, 3½" 200.00
Rozane, vase, floral, classic form, #891, RPCO mk, 14" 450.00

Rozane, vase, floral, 3-hdld, cylindrical w/flared base, 14" 950.00
Rozane Light, sugar bowl, floral, hdld lid, 4½" 200.00
Rozane Light, vase, floral, 3-hdld, 3-ftd, can neck, 8½" 1,500.00
Rozane 1917, basket, bl, hdl, ink stamp, 11" 150.00
Rozane 1917, bowl, ftd, hdls, ink stamp, 3½" 60.00
Rozane 1917, bowl, gr, ink stamp, 3" 60.00
Rozane 1917, comport, tall ft, hdls, no mk, 8" 125.00
Rozane 1917, vase, gr glaze, ftd, ink stamp, 10" 110.00
Rozane 1917, vase, pk glaze, ink stamp, 6½" 50.00
Russco, vase, triple cornucopia; sm silver paper label, 8x12½" ...120.00
Silhouette, vase, #780-6, 6" 55.00
Silhouette, vase, nude, fan form, #783, 7" 250.00
Snowberry, ashtray 45.00
Snowberry, tray, #1BL-12, 14" 125.00
Snowberry, vase, pillow form, #1-FH-6, 6½" 55.00
Sunflower, bowl, console; hdls, sm blk paper label, 3x12½" 325.00
Sunflower, vase, ftd, no mk, 5" 325.00
Sylvan, jardiniere, squirrels, no mk, 9" 300.00
Teasel, vase, #881-6, 6" 80.00
Thornapple, vase, #820-9, 9½" 200.00
Thornapple, vase, bud; triple, #1120, 6" 150.00
Topeo, bowl, red glaze, silver paper label, 7" 200.00
Topeo, vase, gourd shape, red glaze, no mk, 14" 550.00
Tourist, window box, no mk, 8½x19" 1,500.00
Tourmaline, vase, bl, sq, silver paper label, 8" 90.00
Tourmaline, vase, gr, 6-sided, no mk, 10" 150.00
Tuscany, vase, ornate hdls, blk paper label, 4" 50.00
Velmoss, vase, leaf design from top, hdls, no mk, 9½" 125.00
Velmoss Scroll, vase, floral, shouldered, no mk, 5" 150.00
Venetian, bake pan, no mk, 9" 30.00
Vista, basket, flared rim, hdld, no mk, 9½" 275.00
Vista, vase, slim w/buttress hdls, #134-18, 15" 500.00
Water Lily, vase, #78-9, 9 " 150.00
White Rose, vase, #980-6, 5" 75.00
White Rose, vase, dbl bud; #148, 4½" 90.00
Wincraft, bookends, #259, 6½", pr 125.00
Wincraft, vase, floral on turq, ftd cylinder, #285, 10" 85.00
Windsor, lamp base, ball shape w/hdls, no mk, 7" 400.00
Windsor, vase, floral on bl, hdls, paper label, 9" 350.00
Wisteria, vase, bl floral, waisted, hdls, silver paper label, 10" 900.00
Zephyr Lily, vase, #135-9, 9" 100.00
Zephyr Lily, vase, fan shape, #205-6, 6½" 90.00

Rowland and Marsellus

Though the impressive back stamp seems to suggest otherwise, Rowland and Marsellus were not Staffordshire potters but American importers who commissioned various English companies to supply them with the transfer-printed historical ware that had been a popular import item since the early 1800s. Plates (both flat and with a rolled edge), cups and saucers, pitchers, and platters were sold as souvenirs from 1890 through the 1930s. Though other importers — Bawo & Dotter, and A. C. Bosselman & Co., both of New York City — commissioned the manufacture of similar souvenir items, by far the largest volume carries the R. & M. mark, and Rowland and Marcellus has become a generic term that covers all 20th-century souvenir china of this type. Their mark may be in full or 'R. & M.' in a diamond. Though primarily made with blue transfers on white, other colors may occasionally be found as well. Our advisor for this category is David Ringering; he is listed in the Directory under Oregon.

Key:
r/e — rolled edge   v/o — view of
s/o — souvenir of

Cup & saucer, Albany, s/o 75.00
Cup & saucer, farmer's 75.00
Cup & saucer, Lenox MA, s/o 75.00
Cup & saucer, Portland ME, s/o 75.00
Plate, Albany (NY) State Capitol, v/o, 9" 30.00
Plate, Albany NY, Fort Frederick, s/o, r/e, 10" 55.00
Plate, Baltimore IN, Courthouse, s/o, r/e, 10" 55.00
Plate, Battle of Lake Erie, fruit & flower border 50.00
Plate, Bethleham PA, Moravian College, v/o, 9" 30.00
Plate, Boston MA, Tremont St Mall, s/o, r/e, 10" 50.00
Plate, coupe; American Poets, 7 portraits, v/o, 10" 50.00
Plate, coupe; Chicago IL, v/o, 6" 30.00
Plate, coupe; Denver, v/o, 10" 50.00
Plate, coupe; Harrisburg New Capitol Building, s/o, 10" 50.00
Plate, coupe; Jamestown Expo, Expo building, s/o, 1907, 6" 45.00
Plate, coupe; Miami, Chief Osceola, s/o, 10" 60.00
Plate, coupe; Plymouth MA, 5 scenes, v/o, 6" 30.00
Plate, coupe; San Antonio TX, 6 scenes, s/o, 10" 50.00
Plate, coupe; San Francisco Harber Scene, v/o, 10" 50.00
Plate, coupe; Washington DC Capitol, v/o, 6" 35.00
Plate, Detroit MI, Entrance to Detroit River Tunnel, s/o, 9" 30.00
Plate, Golden Rule, Company Store, mc, s/o, r/e, 10" 85.00
Plate, Hermitage, fruit & flower border 50.00
Plate, Jackson MI, New Capitol Building, s/o, r/e, 10" 75.00

Plate, John Alden and Priscilla, fruit and flower border, dark blue, $50.00.

Plate, Lookout Mtn TN, Moccasin Bend & Lookout, s/o, r/e, 10" ..60.00
Plate, Newark NJ, City Hall, v/o, 9" 30.00
Plate, Niagara Falls (NY), general view, v/o, 9" 30.00
Plate, Onset MA, Meet Me on Cape Cod, v/o, r/e, 10" 70.00
Plate, Thousand Islands, v/o, r/e, 10" 65.00
Plate, Whirlpool Rapids, fruit & flower border 50.00
Plate, Woonsocket RI, US Post Office, v/o, 9" 30.00
Plate, Zanesville OH, New Y Bridge, s/o, r/e, 10" 60.00
Tumbler, Fall River MA 75.00
Tumbler, Plymouth, v/o 65.00

Royal Bayreuth

Founded in 1794 in Tettau, Bavaria, the Royal Bayreuth firm originally manufactured fine dinnerware of superior quality. Their figural items, produced from before the turn of the century until the onset of WWI, are highly sought after by today's collectors. Perhaps the most abundantly produced and easily recognized of these are the tomato and lobster pieces. Fruits, flowers, people, animals, birds, and vegetables shapes were also made. Aside from figural items, pitchers, toothpick holders, cups and saucers, humidors and the like were decorated in florals and scenic motifs. Some, such as the very popular Rose Tapestry line, utilized a cloth-like tapestry background. Transfer prints were used as well. Two of the most popular are Sunbonnet Babies and Nursery

Rhymes (in particular, those decorated with the complete verse).

Caution: Many pieces were not marked; some were marked 'Deponiert' or 'Registered' only. While marked pieces are the most valued, unmarked items are still very worthwhile. Our advisors for this category are Larry Brenner from New Hampshire and Dee Hooks from Illinois; they are listed in the Directory under their home states.

Figurals

Ashtray, clown, wht pearl lustre, bl mk	425.00
Ashtray, devil, red, bl mk	385.00
Ashtray, elk, bl mk	315.00
Bowl, poppy, red, bl mk, 8"	295.00
Bowl, shell, bl mk, 8½"	335.00
Cake plate, Devil & Cards, full devil center, bl mk, 7"	725.00
Candlestick, elk, low, bl mk	450.00
Candlestick, poppy, red, bl mk	685.00
Candlestick, Santa Claus, bl mk	4,000.00
Cracker jar, tomato, bl mk	550.00
Cup, demitasse; tomato, unmk	65.00
Cup & saucer, shell, bl mk	200.00
Hatpin holder, poppy, red, bl mk	635.00
Humidor, lobster, bl mk	665.00
Marmalade, orange, bl mk	375.00
Match holder, chimpanzee, bl mk, wall hanging	875.00
Match holder, Devil & Cards, full devil, bl mk	3,250.00
Match holder, Santa Claus, bl mk	5,250.00
Mustard, grapes, pearlized, bl mk	300.00
Mustard, lobster & leaf, bl mk	125.00
Mustard, poppy, red, bl mk	200.00
Mustard, shell, bl mk	135.00
Nappy, lettuce leaf, bl mk	48.00
Nappy, lobster & leaf, bl mk	55.00
Nappy, poppy, pearlized, bl mk	150.00
Pipe rest, bassett, bl mk	375.00
Pitcher, apple, bl mk, lemonade sz	875.00
Pitcher, bell ringer, bl mk, milk sz	500.00
Pitcher, buffalo, gray, bl mk, water sz	315.00
Pitcher, bull, blk, bl mk, cream sz	300.00
Pitcher, bull, gray, bl mk, cream sz	300.00
Pitcher, butterfly, open wings, bl mk, cream sz	335.00
Pitcher, cat, blk, bl mk, cream sz	250.00
Pitcher, cat, gray stripes, bl mk, cream sz	275.00
Pitcher, clown, red, bl mk, cream sz	350.00
Pitcher, coachman, bl mk, cream sz	300.00
Pitcher, coachman, bl mk, water sz	1,000.00
Pitcher, cow, brn, bl mk, cream sz	250.00
Pitcher, cow, red, bl mk, cream sz	315.00
Pitcher, dachshund, bl mk, cream sz	300.00
Pitcher, devil, red, bl mk, milk sz	500.00
Pitcher, Devil & Cards, bl mk, cream sz	235.00
Pitcher, Devil & Cards, bl mk, water sz	600.00
Pitcher, duck, bl mk, cream sz	300.00
Pitcher, eagle, bl mk, water sz	800.00
Pitcher, eagle, gray, bl mk, cream sz	300.00
Pitcher, elk, bl mk, cream sz	200.00
Pitcher, fish, open mouth, bl mk, milk sz	500.00
Pitcher, fish, unmk, cream sz, 3½"	300.00
Pitcher, frog, gr & bl, bl mk, cream sz	285.00
Pitcher, lemon, bl mk, cream sz	285.00
Pitcher, lobster, bl mk, cream sz	150.00
Pitcher, lobster, bl mk, water sz	500.00
Pitcher, lobster, red w/gr hdl, unmk, cream sz	65.00
Pitcher, melon, bl mk, milk sz	325.00

Pitcher, milkmaid, red, bl mk, cream sz	650.00
Pitcher, mountain goat, bl mk, cream sz	335.00
Pitcher, oak leaf, bl mk, cream sz	300.00
Pitcher, oak leaf, pearlized, bl mk, cream sz	325.00
Pitcher, Old Man of the Mountain, bl mk, cream sz	150.00
Pitcher, orchid, bl mk, water sz	2,500.00
Pitcher, oyster & pearl, bl mk, cream sz	195.00
Pitcher, pansy, bl mk, cream sz	355.00
Pitcher, parakeet, bl mk, cream sz	285.00
Pitcher, parrot, red, bl mk, milk sz	550.00
Pitcher, pelican, bl mk, cream sz	350.00
Pitcher, perch, bl mk, water sz	1,100.00
Pitcher, robin, bl mk, cream sz	200.00
Pitcher, robin, bl mk, milk sz	400.00
Pitcher, robin, bl mk, water sz	880.00
Pitcher, rooster, dk gray, bl mk, cream sz	350.00
Pitcher, Santa Claus, bl mk, cream sz	2,500.00
Pitcher, Santa Claus, bl mk, water sz	5,000.00
Pitcher, seal, bl mk, cream sz	300.00
Pitcher, shell, bl mk, tall, cream sz	180.00
Pitcher, shell, lobster hdl, bl mk, water sz	600.00
Pitcher, St Bernard, bl mk, cream sz	255.00
Pitcher, St Bernard, blk, bl mk, cream sz	400.00
Pitcher, strawberry, bl mk, cream sz	250.00
Pitcher, tomato, bl mk, cream sz	150.00
Plate, lobster & leaf, bl mk, 5"	70.00
Pot, demitasse; poppy, red, bl mk	595.00
Relish, poinsettia, bl mk	500.00
Shakers, grapes, pearlized, bl mk, pr	200.00
Shakers, shell, bl mk, pr	150.00
Shakers, strawberry, bl mk, pr	400.00
Shoe, lady's, high top, bl mk	215.00
Shoe, man's, wht, bl mk	335.00
Sugar bowl, apple, bl mk	200.00
Sugar bowl, grapes, purple, bl mk	180.00
Sugar bowl, tomato, bl mk	150.00
Tea set, murex shell, bl mk, 3-pc	425.00
Tea strainer, anemone, bl mk, rare	275.00
Teapot, orange, bl mk	250.00
Teapot, strawberry, bl mk	385.00
Teapot, tomato, bl mk	200.00
Toothpick holder, lamplighter, bl mk	475.00
Tray, dresser; Devil & Cards, bl mk	675.00

Nursery Rhymes

Bell, Ring Around the Rosies, bl mk	315.00
Bowl, Jack & the Beanstalk, bl mk, ftd	265.00
Box, trinket; Jack & the Beanstalk, sq, bl mk, 2½"	135.00
Cake plate, Ring Around the Rosies, bl mk	265.00
Candlestick, Jack & Jill, bl mk, w/underplate	300.00
Candlestick, Jack & the Beanstalk, bl mk	235.00
Chamberstick, Little Jack Horner, bl mk	185.00
Coffeepot, Jack & Jill, bl mk	365.00
Cup & saucer, Jack & the Beanstalk, bl mk	215.00
Dish, Little Jack Horner, bl mk, leaf shape	165.00
Pin dish, Jack & the Beanstalk, bl mk	115.00
Pitcher, Jack & Jill, bl mk, cream sz	215.00
Pitcher, Little Jack Horner, bl mk, cream sz	135.00
Pitcher, Little Jack Horner, bl mk, milk sz	215.00
Plate, Jack & Jill, bl mk, 7½"	175.00
Plate, Little Bo Peep, bl mk, 6¼"	95.00
Plate, Little Boy Blue, bl mk, 7"	135.00
Plate, Little Boy Blue, bl mk, 7⅝"	185.00

Plate, Ring Around the Rosies, bl mk, 6" 115.00
Sugar bowl, Little Boy Blue, bl mk 215.00
Sugar bowl, Little Miss Muffett, bl mk 215.00

Scenics and Action Portraits

Ashtray, Dutch boy & girl, bl mk 85.00
Bowl, Snow Baby, bl mk, 6" 215.00

Bowl, girl with muff, blue mark, 3x10¾", $550.00.

Box, trinket; Sand Babies, bl mk 200.00
Chamberstick, Snow Baby, funnel shape, bl mk 295.00
Humidor, castle scene, bl mk 385.00
Humidor, fox hunt, sq shape, bl mk, 6¼" 400.00
Match holder, Snow Baby, bl mk 275.00
Match holder, tavern scene, bl mk 200.00
Pitcher, hunt scene, bl mk, cream sz, 3½" 110.00
Pitcher, man w/pipe, bl mk, cream sz 135.00
Pitcher, Snow Baby, bl mk, cream sz 235.00
Shaker, lady feeding chickens, unmk 65.00
Toothpick holder, Blk Corinthian, ftd, hdls, bl mk 110.00
Toothpick holder, penguin ea side, triangular shape, bl mk 235.00
Vase, castle scene, hdls, 6½" 225.00
Vase, hunter w/dog at side, bl mk, 5¼" 270.00

Sunbonnet Babies

Bell, babies fishing, bl mk 385.00
Bowl, cereal; babies sweeping, bl mk, 5¼" 335.00
Cake plate, 2 hdls, bl mk 350.00
Candlestick, shield bk, bl mk 500.00
Chamberstick, ring hdl, bl mk 375.00
Cup & saucer, babies fishing, bl mk 350.00
Hair receiver, babies sewing, bl mk 450.00
Pitcher, babies cleaning, cream sz, 3" 275.00
Pitcher, babies ironing, bl mk, 4" 350.00
Pitcher, babies sewing, bl mk, cream sz 250.00
Plate, babies cleaning, bl mk, 6" 210.00
Plate, babies ironing, bl mk, 6" 175.00
Plate, babies sweeping, bl mk, 6" 75.00
Plate, babies washing, bl mk, 10¼" 395.00
Plate, babies washing, bl mk, 9" 295.00
Rose bowl, babies fishing, bl mk 395.00
Rose bowl, babies washing, bl mk 375.00
Sugar bowl, babies fishing, bl mk 275.00
Teapot, babies cleaning, bulbous, bl mk 450.00
Tumbler, babies cleaning, bl mk, 3½" 375.00

Tapestries

Basket, Rose Tapestry, bl mk, 5" H 450.00

Bell, peacock, bl mk 245.00
Creamer & sugar bowl, Rose Tapestry, bl mk 450.00
Dresser box, Rose Tapestry, 3-color, bl mk, 2¼x3¼" 275.00
Hair receiver, courting scene, bl mk 335.00
Hair receiver, Rose Tapestry, 3-color, bl mk, 4¼" 350.00
Hatpin holder, Rose Tapestry, pk, bl mk 450.00
Nappy, cottage & waterfall w/gold trim, clover shape, bl mk 235.00
Nappy, girl w/geese, bl mk, 3" 315.00
Nappy, Rose Tapestry, leaf shape, bl mk 315.00
Pitcher, girl w/muff, pinched spout, bl mk, cream sz 325.00
Pitcher, polar bears, bl mk, water sz 2,000.00
Pitcher, Rose Tapestry, 3-color, bl mk, cream sz, 3" 265.00
Planter, Rose Tapestry, 3-color, bl mk, 3" 250.00
Plate, peacock, bl mk, gold trim, 9" 950.00
Plate, Rose Tapestry, bl mk, 6" 200.00
Powder box, castle scene, bl mk 315.00
Powder box, courting scene, bl mk 350.00
Powder box, Rose Tapestry, bl mk, 4" dia 350.00
Sugar bowl, courting scene, bl mk 350.00
Sugar shaker, Rose Tapestry, orange, cork closure, bl mk 550.00
Tray, dresser; Canterbury flower, bl mk 465.00
Trinket box, Rose Tapestry, pk & wht, oval, bl mk, 4½" 225.00
Vase, cows, bl mk, 4" 350.00
Vase, goat scene, bulbous, bl mk, 7" 475.00
Vase, Rose Tapestry, bl mk, 4" 360.00
Vase, Rose Tapestry, bl mk, 5" 380.00
Vase, Rose Tapestry, hdls, bl mk, 3½" 335.00

Royal Bonn

Royal Bonn is a fine-paste porcelain, ornately decorated with scenes, portraits, or florals. The factory was established in the mid-1800s in Bonn, Germany; however, most pieces found today are from the latter part of the century.

Ewer, floral, pk & bl on cream w/much gold, 13" 485.00
Umbrella stand, irises, prof pnt touch-up, 18x11" 395.00
Vase, Dutch women, sgn, Gleaners series, 6¼" 595.00
Vase, floral, gold & mc, sm neck hdls, pre-1890, 20x5" 365.00
Vase, floral, gold & orange on brn & yel, 8x5" 95.00
Vase, floral, gold on pk to bl, 8x3⅞" 65.00
Vase, lady, sgn Muller, upright hdls, 4-scallop top, 11" 495.00
Vase, men watch artist/bk: scene, sgn, gold dragon hdls, 27" 1,800.00
Vase, rooster/hen/chicks, sgn, 8" 500.00
Vase, roses, appl knotted 'cord' at neck, sgn Liefs, ftd, 50" 3,000.00
Vase, roses, mc on yel w/gold, ca 1900, crown mk, 11¼" 295.00
Vase, sand tapestry mc florals in panels, cylindrical, 8½" 125.00
Vase, spider mums, Nouveau hdls, 8½" 95.00
Vase, 2 ladies pick wheat, sgn, hdls, 6¼" 675.00

Royal Copenhagen

The Royal Copenhagen Manufactory was established in Denmark in about 1775 by Frantz Henrich Muller. When bankruptcy threatened in 1779, the Crown took charge. The fine dinnerware and objects of art produced after that time carry the familiar logo, the crown over three wavy lines. See also Limited Edition Plates.

Bowl, floral, #2357, 11" 300.00
Cup & saucer, chocolate; Flora Danica, set of 4 ....1,350.00
Cup & saucer, demitasse; floral on wht, sgn, 1930s 55.00
Decanter, Rosenburg Castle, bl & wht, 9¾" 48.00

Figurine, boy w/dog, #782, 7½"	275.00
Figurine, boy w/pig, #848	395.00
Figurine, boy w/2 calves, #1858, 7½x9"	475.00
Figurine, boy w/2 geese, #2139	275.00
Figurine, children playing, #1568, 4½"	200.00
Figurine, children reading, #1567, 3⅞"	150.00
Figurine, duck, #1993, 2¼x4¼"	135.00
Figurine, girl & boy hugging dog, ca 1975, #707, 5¾x6¾"	400.00
Figurine, girl braiding hair, #1323, 8"	275.00
Figurine, girl knitting, #1314, 6"	340.00
Figurine, girl w/doll, #1938, 5"	250.00
Figurine, girl w/goose, #528, 7½"	200.00
Figurine, girl w/teddy bear, #1879, 5⅛"	475.00
Figurine, girl w/2 goats, #694, 9x7½"	475.00
Figurine, lady on bench sewing, #1317, 9"	275.00
Figurine, Leda & Swan, blanc de chine, 8"	275.00

Figurine, seated man wearing tam o' shanter, 8", $275.00; Fishmonger with catch, 9", $250.00.

Figurine, nude on rock, #4027	195.00
Figurine, Pan w/goat, #1012-498, 5"	250.00
Figurine, pigs, 2 recumbent, ca 1966, #683	135.00
Figurine, rooster, ca 1961, #1127, 3¼x5½"	70.00
Figurine, 2 geese, #609, 7"	200.00
Lamp base, stoneware, 3 stylized frogs, Alex Salto, 21"	1,800.00
Plaque, angel & 2 sleeping babes relief, wht parian, 6"	27.50
Plate, Flora Danica, 10", set of 6	2,300.00
Plate, salad; Flora Danica, 7½", set of 6	1,600.00
Soup plate, Flora Danica, 8¾", set of 6	1,800.00
Teapot, dogwood & butterfly, ca 1963, #9103	110.00
Vase, rose branches up corners, roses around shoulders, 10"	375.00
Wine cooler, Flora Danica, 6½"	1,700.00

Royal Copley

Royal Copley is a decorative type of pottery made by the Spaulding China Company in Sebring, Ohio, from 1942 to 1957. They also produced two other major lines — Royal Windsor and Spaulding. Royal Copley was primarily marketed through five-and-ten cent stores; Royal Windsor and Spaulding were sold through department stores, gift shops, and jobbers. Items trimmed in gold are worth 25% to 50% more than the same item with no gold trim.

For more information we recommend *Royal Copley* and *More About Royal Copley* by Leslie and Marjorie Wolfe, edited by our advisor for this category, Joe Devine; he is listed in the Directory under Iowa. These books have been brought back by popular demand and include updated values.

Ashtray, affectionate birds, heart shaped, emb mk, 5½"	16.00
Ashtray, bow & ribbon, emb mk	20.00
Ashtray, leaf, gr stamp, 5"	6.00

Ashtray, leaf & bird, gr stamp, 5½"	9.00
Ashtray, lily pad w/bird, gr stamp, 5"	9.00
Ashtray, mallard, paper label, 2"	10.00
Ashtray, straw hat w/bow tie, emb mk, 5"	12.00
Bank, pig, paper label or gr stamp, lg, 7½"	45.00
Bank, pig w/bow tie, paper label, 6¼"	30.00
Bank, teddy bear, paper label, 7½"	65.00
Bowl, bird perched on side, gr stamp, 4"	10.00
Coaster, pheasants flying, paper label, 4⅝"	17.00
Figurine, Airedale, paper label, 6½"	20.00
Figurine, Blackamoor, paper label, 8½"	20.00
Figurine, canary, paper label, 5½"	35.00
Figurine, cockatoo, paper label, 7¼"	34.00
Figurine, kingfisher, paper label, 5"	22.00
Figurine, Oriental boy holding jar, paper label, 7½"	15.00
Figurine, rooster, feet hidden, wht only, paper label, 8"	50.00
Figurine, skylark on stump, full body, paper label, 5"	12.00
Figurine, sparrow w/open beak, 5"	15.00
Figurine, swallow w/extended wings, full body, paper label, 7"	40.00
Figurine, titmouse on stump, full body, paper label, 8"	25.00
Figurine, vireo, paper label, 4½"	15.00
Figurine, wren, paper label, sm, 3½"	18.00
Lamp, clown, retooled planter, paper label, 7½"	65.00
Lamp, cocker spaniel, 10"	54.00
Lamp, dancing lady, orig shade	65.00
Lamp, Oriental figurine	35.00
Pitcher, Pome Fruit, gr stamp, 8"	26.00
Planter, barefoot boy, paper label, 7½"	20.00
Planter, big apple & finch, paper label, 6½"	15.00
Planter, birdhouse w/bird, paper label, 8"	50.00
Planter, blk & wht dog at mailbox, paper label, 8½"	55.00
Planter, cockatiel on kidney-shaped planter, w/label, 8½"	40.00
Planter, duck & mailbox, US Mail on box, paper label, 6¾"	45.00
Planter, duck & wheelbarrow, paper label, 3¾"	14.00
Planter, hummingbird on flower, paper label, 5¼"	25.00
Planter, Indian boy w/drum, paper label, 6½"	15.00
Planter, jumping salmon, gray only, paper label, 6½x11½"	45.00
Planter, jumping salmon, mc, paper label, 6½x11½"	54.00
Planter, mature wood duck, paper label, 7¼"	18.00
Planter, Oriental boy w/basket on bk, paper label, 8"	28.00
Planter, Oriental boy w/basket on ground, emb mk, 7¾"	14.00
Planter, resting poodle, paper label, 6½"	36.00
Planter, rooster, paper label, 8"	25.00
Planter, wide-brim hat girl, hangs or rests on table, mk, 7½"	28.00
Planter, woodpecker on floral stump, gr stamp mk, 6¼"	15.00
Planter, wren on tree stump, paper label, 6¼"	18.00
Plaque planter, fruit, emb mk, 6¾"	18.00
Plaque planter, The Mill, Amsterdam Holland, emb mk, 8"	40.00
Vase, bud; parrot on branch, raised letters, gr stamp mk, 5"	12.00
Vase, Floral Elegance, gr stamp, 8"	18.00
Vase, goldfinch on stump, paper label, 6½"	18.00
Vase, Oriental-style dragons, ftd, paper label, 5¼"	10.00
Vase, star & angel, depression for candle, paper label, 6¾"	28.00
Vase, 2 fish swimming, gold trim, cylindrical, emb mk, 8"	18.00
Vase/planter, bird in flight, paper label, 7¼"	20.00
Wall pocket, bamboo, paper label, 7"	35.00

Royal Crown Derby

The Royal Crown Derby company can trace its origin back to 1848. It first operated under the name of Locker & Co. but by 1859 had become Stevenson, Sharp & Co. Several changes in ownership occured until 1866 when it became known as the Sampson Hancock Co. The

Derby Crown Porcelain Co. Ltd. was formed in 1876, and these companies soon merged. In 1890 they were appointed as a manufacturer for the Queen and began using the name Royal Crown Derby.

In the early years considerable 'Japan ware' decorated in Imari pattern using red, blue and gold in oriental patterns was popular. They excelled in their ability to use gold in the decoration, and some of the best flower painters of all time were employed. Nice vases or plaques signed by any of these artists will bring thousands of dollars: Gregory, Mosley, Rouse, Gresley and D'esir'e Leroy. We have observed porcelain plaques decorated with flowers signed by Gregory selling at auction for as much as $12,000.00. If you find signed pieces and are not sure of your values, it would be best if possible to have it appraised by someone very knowledgeable regarding current market values.

As is usual among most other English factories, nearly all of the vases produced by Royal Crown Derby came with covers. If they are missing, deduct 40% to 45%. There are several well-illustrated books available from antique book sellers to help you learn to identify this ware. The back stamps used after 1891 will date every piece except dinnerware. The company is still in business producing outstanding dinnerware and Imari-decorated figures and serving pieces. They also produce custom (one only) sets of table service for the wealthy of the world. The advisors for this category are Henry and Geneva Tyler, who are listed in the Directory under Florida.

Bowl, fruit; Mikado **48.00**
Bowl, mc florals w/gold, w/lid, 3x5" **67.50**
Bowl, vegetable; Imari-style pattern, w/lid, 11½" L **275.00**
Creamer, Oriental figures, bl on wht w/gold, bone china, 3⅛" **22.50**
Creamer, Vine **105.00**
Cup, floral sprays w/gold, fluted & scalloped **7.50**
Cup & saucer, demitasse; Geishas & gardener, bl & wht w/gold ..**67.50**
Cup & saucer, Derby Posies **55.00**
Cup & saucer, Imari **98.00**
Cup & saucer, Mandarin **55.00**
Cup & saucer, Vine **78.00**
Figurine, sphinx on base, facing pr, 1820s, 6", EX **675.00**
Plate, dinner; Derby Posies **55.00**
Plate, dinner; Mikado **68.00**
Plate, Imari, 7" **78.00**
Plate, Imari-style pattern, 10", set of 12 ....**3,000.00**

Potpourri jar, florals on ivory, with lid, #544/2658, ca 1885, 8¾x6", $850.00.

Sugar bowl, Imari, w/lid **185.00**
Teacup, Mikado **65.00**
Teapot, floral/birds on gr to wht, 5x5" **125.00**
Tureen, sauce; Imari-style pattern, 8½" L, +undertray **650.00**
Tureen, soup; Imari-style pattern, 16½" L, +undertray **1,200.00**
Vase, florals/gold on cream, gold hdls, cobalt lid/ft, 12" **1,100.00**

Royal Doulton, Doulton

The range of wares produced by the Doulton Company since its inception in 1815 has been vast and varied. The earliest wares produced in the tiny pottery in Lambeth, England, were salt-glazed pitchers, plain and fancy figural bottles — all utility-type stoneware geared to the practical needs of everyday living. The original partners, John Doulton and John Watts, saw the potential for success in the manufacture of drain and sewage pipes and during the 1840s concentrated on these highly lucrative types of commercial wares. Watts retired from the company in 1854, and Doulton began experimenting with a more decorative style of product. As time went by, many glazes and decorative effects were developed, among them Faience, Impasto, Silicon, Carrara, Marqueterie, Chine, and Rouge Flambe. Tiles and architectural terra cotta were an important part of their manufacture. Late in the nineteenth century at the original Lambeth location, fine artware was decorated by such notable artists as Hannah and Arthur Barlow, George Tinworth, and J.H. McLennan. Stoneware vases with incised animal drawings, gracefully shaped urns with painted scenes, and cleverly modeled figurines rivaled the best of any competitor.

In 1882 a second factory was built in Burslem which continues even yet to produce the famous figurines, character jugs, series ware, and table services so popular with collectors today. Their Kingsware line, made from 1899 to 1946, featured flasks and flagons with drinking scenes, usually on a brown-glazed ground. Some were limited editions, while others were commemorative and advertising items. The Gibson Girl series, twenty-four plates in all, was introduced in 1901. It was drawn by Charles Dana Gibson and is recognized by its blue and white borders and central illustrations, each scene depicting a humorous or poignant episode in the life of 'The Widow and Her Friends.' Dickensware, produced from 1911 through the early 1940s, featured illustrations by Charles Dickens, with many of his famous characters. The Robin Hood series was introduced in 1914; the Shakespeare series #1, portraying scenes from the Bard's plays, was made from 1914 until World War II. The Shakespeare series #2 ran from 1906 until 1974 and was decorated with featured characters. Nursery Rhymes was a series that was first produced in earthenware in 1930 and later in bone china. In 1933 a line of decorated children's ware, the Bunnykin series, was introduced; it continues to be made to the present day. About 150 'bunny' scenes have been devised, the earliest and most desirable being those signed by the artist Barbara Vernon. Most pieces range in value from $60.00 to $120.00.

Factors contributing to the value of a figurine are age, color, and detail. Those with a limited production run and those signed by the artist or marked 'Potted' (indicating a pre-1939 origin) are also more valuable. After 1920 wares were marked with a lion — with or without a crown — over a circular 'Royal Doulton.' Our advisor for this category is Nicki Budin; she is listed in the Directory under Ohio.

Animals and Birds

Dog, Airedale, HN1024, sm **265.00**
Dog, Alsation, NH1116, med **165.00**
Dog, Boxer, CH Warlord of Mazelain, HN2643 ....**145.00**
Dog, Bulldog, brindle, HN1044, sm **225.00**
Dog, Bulldog, K-1 ....**125.00**
Dog, Cairn, begging, HN2589 ....**75.00**
Dog, Cairn, HN1034, med **275.00**
Dog, Cairn, HN1035, sm **110.00**
Dog, Cavin Terrier, HN1035 ....**125.00**
Dog, Chow, K-15 ....**75.00**
Dog, Cocker Spaniel, HN1002, lg **350.00**
Dog, Cocker Spaniel, HN1021, sm **115.00**
Dog, Cocker Spaniel, K-9 ....**65.00**

Dog, Cocker Spaniel w/pheasant, HN1028, med 175.00
Dog, Collie, HN1058, med 185.00
Dog, Collie, HN1059, sm 275.00
Dog, Dachshund, HN1129, sm 175.00
Dog, Dachshund, K-17 ....75.00
Dog, Doberman Pinscher, #2645, sm 185.00
Dog, English Foxhound, #1026, med 425.00
Dog, English Setter, #1050, med 155.00
Dog, Fox Terrier, #1014, sm 115.00
Dog, Greyhound, #1065, lg 1,400.00
Dog, Irish Setter, #1054, lg 625.00
Dog, Irish Setter, #1056, sm 155.00
Dog, Labrador, HN2667, med 165.00
Dog, Pekinese, HN1012, sm 95.00
Dog, Pekinese, HN1040, 3⅛x3¾" 195.00
Dog, Scottish Terrier, K-18 ....70.00
Dog, Springer Spaniel, #2516, med 275.00
Dog, Terrier, HN1099 ....150.00
Dog, Terrier in basket, HN2587 ....75.00
Drake, HN806 ....150.00
Elephant, HN2644, 5½" 150.00
Fox, recumbent, #147 ....225.00
Hare, K-37, recumbent 125.00
Kitten, HN2582 ....85.00
Lamb, HN2505 ....215.00
Mallard on rock, HN853 ....275.00
Owl, HN173, red cloak, rare 2,000.00
Penguin, K-22 ....245.00
Persian cat, HN2539, wht 165.00
Persian cat, HN999, blk & wht 150.00
Piglet, HN2653 ....225.00

Character Jugs

Three Musketeers: Athos, D6439; Porthos, D6440; Aramis, D6641, 1956, each 7½", $375.00 for the set.

Anne Boleyn, D6644, lg 125.00
Annie Oakley, D6732, med 85.00
Apothecary, D6574, sm 70.00
Arriet, D6208, lg 200.00
Arriet, D6256, tiny 185.00
Arry, D6249, mini 85.00
Auld Mac, D5823, lg 110.00
Buz Fuz, D5858, sm 95.00
Cap'n Cuttle, D5842, sm 95.00
Captain Hook, D6601, sm 360.00
Captain Hook, D6605, mini 350.00
Catherine of Aragon, D6643, lg 145.00
Clown, wht, D6322, lg 950.00
Dick Turpin, D6535, sm 70.00
Falstaff, D6287, lg 230.00
Fat Boy, D5840, odd sz 225.00
Fat Boy, D5840, sm 95.00

Fortune Teller, D6503, sm 295.00
Friar Tuck, D6321, lg 395.00
Geronimo, D6733, med 125.00
Gondolier, D6589, lg 575.00
Gondolier, D6592, sm 365.00
Granny, D5521, lg 110.00
Grant & Lee, D6698, lg 285.00
Gulliver, D6560, lg 635.00
Gunsmith of Williamsburg, D6587, mini 55.00
Henry VIII, D6642, lg 110.00
Jarge, D6295, sm 180.00
John Barleycorn, D6041, mini 65.00
John Peel, D5731, sm 68.00
John Peel, D6259, tiny 235.00
Mad Hatter, D6602, sm 78.00
Mikado, D6507, sm 275.00
Mr Micawber, D6138, A, mini 55.00
Mr Pickwick, D6260, tiny 210.00
North American Indian, D6614, 1966, sm 50.00
Old Charley, D5527, A, sm 45.00
Old King Cole, D6037, A, sm 115.00
Paddy, D5753, lg 135.00
Parson Brown, D5529, sm 55.00
Porthos, D6440, lg 110.00
Punch & Judy, D6593, sm 360.00
Regency Beau, D6562, sm 480.00
Sam Johnson, D6296, sm 175.00
Sam Weller, D6064, A, lg 150.00
Sam Weller, D6140, mini 60.00
Scaramouche, D6558, lg 650.00
Scaramouche, D6564, mini 350.00
Shakespeare, D6689, lg 110.00
Simple Simon, D6374, lg 470.00
Tam O'Shanter, D6632, lg 130.00
Toby Philpots, D6043, mini 45.00
Town Crier, D6530, lg 180.00
Town Crier, D6537, sm 85.00
Ugly Duchess, D6607, mini 250.00
Ugly Duchess, sm 235.00
Veteran Motorist, D6633, lg 115.00
Vicar of Bray, D5615, lg 195.00
Viking, D6496, lg 185.00
Viking, D6502, sm 110.00
Viking, D6526, mini 120.00
Walrus & Carpenter, D6608, mini 50.00

Figurines

A Courting, HN2004, 7¼" 485.00
Adrienne, HN2304, bl 175.00
Affection, HN2236 ....125.00
Afternoon Tea, HN1747, 5¼" 400.00
Alexandra, HN2398 ....180.00
Angelina, HN2013 ....845.00
Anna, HN2802, Kate Greenaway 150.00
Annette, HN1550, gr skirt 500.00
Antoinette, HN1850 ....1,150.00
Autumn Breezes, HN2147 ....295.00
Autumn Glory, HN2766 ....135.00
Baby Bunting, HN2108 ....265.00
Bachelor, HN2319 ....225.00
Beachcomber, HN2487, matt 185.00
Bess, HN2002 ....225.00
Biddy, HN1513, red 175.00

Blacksmith, HN2782	170.00
Blue Beard, HN2105, bl robe, 2nd version	415.00
Boatman, HN2417, Men of the Sea	150.00
Bride, HN2166, pk, 2nd version	225.00
Bridesmaid, HN2874, 4th version	110.00
Bridget, HN2070	325.00
Bunny, HN2214	175.00
Camille, HN1586	700.00
Captain, HN2260	250.00
Carolyn, HN2112	300.00
Carpet Seller, HN1464, 9¼"	275.00
Cavalier, HN2716, 2nd version	250.00
Choir Boy, HN2141	130.00
Christmas Morn, HN1992	235.00
Christmas Parcels, HN2851	245.00
Circe, HN1249	2,500.00
Clockmaker, HN2279	225.00
Clothilde, HN1598	665.00
Collinette, HN1998, bl cloak	615.00
Cookie, HN2218	175.00
Coralee, HN2307, yel	150.00
Cup of Tea, HN2322	175.00
Daisy, HN1575	485.00
Darling, HN1985, 2nd version	95.00
Delight, HN1772, 1st version	195.00
Dorothy, HN3098	235.00
Drummer Boy, HN2679	350.00
Embroidering, HN2855	175.00
Favourite, HN2249	175.00
Fiona, HN2694	145.00
First Waltz, HN2862	200.00
Fortune Teller, HN2159	450.00
Gay Morning, HN2135	275.00
Genevieve, HN1962	250.00
Genie, HN2989	165.00
Golden Days, HN2274	175.00
Good King Wenceslas, HN2118	375.00
Helmsman, HN2499	225.00
Her Ladyship, HN1977	300.00
Huntsman, HN2492, 3rd version	195.00
Indian Temple Dancer, HN2830, limited edition	1,500.00
Innocence, HN2842	160.00
Jack, HN2060	165.00
Jane, HN2806, yel gown	150.00
Janice, HN2165	350.00
Jean, HN2032	250.00
Jersey Milkmaid, HN2057	200.00
Karen, HN1994	450.00
Kitten, HN2583	75.00
Lady Anne Neville, HN2006	685.00
Lady April, HN1958, red & purple	315.00
Lady Charmian, HN1949, 1st version	250.00
Laurianne, HN2719	150.00
Lavinia, HN1955	120.00
Leisure Hour, HN2055, 6¾"	395.00
Lesley, HN2410	195.00
Lily, HN1798	150.00
Little Boy Blue, HN2062	125.00
Lobster Man, HN2317	185.00
Lori, Kate Greenaway, HN2801	125.00
Love Letter, HN2149	325.00
Lydia, HN1908, red gown	130.00
Margaret, HN1989	350.00
Marigold, HN1447	475.00

Master Sweep, HN2205, 8⅝"	450.00
Memories, HN1856, bl gown	365.00
Nana, HN1766	475.00
New Companions, HN2770	175.00
Olga, HN2463	165.00
Once Upon a Time, HN2047	450.00
Orange Lady, HN1953, 8¾"	265.00
Paisley Shawl, HN1988, 2nd version	175.00
Penelope, HN1901	295.00
Pensive Moments, HN2704	150.00
Phyllis, HN1420	675.00
Polka, HN2156	235.00
Polly Peachum, HN694, dk pk dress	465.00
Potter, HN1493	450.00
Premiere, HN2343	165.00
Priscilla, HN1337	450.00
Professor, HN2281	185.00
Rag Doll, HN2142	95.00
Rose, HN1368	75.00
Schoolmarm, HN2223	265.00
Shore Leave, HN2254	195.00

Silks and Ribbons, HN2017, $165.00.

Solitude, HN2810	195.00
Spinning, HN2390, limited edition	1,300.00
Stitch in Time, HN2352	200.00
Suitor, HN2132	365.00
Sweet & Twenty, HN1298	275.00
Sweeting, HN1935	125.00
Taking Things Easy, HN2680	195.00
Tootles, HN1680	125.00
Toymaker, HN2250	350.00
Tulips, HN1334	2,000.00
Vera, HN1730, gr dress	925.00
Veronica, HN1517	365.00
Viking, HN2375	250.00
Virginia, HN1693	500.00
Wardrobe Mistress, HN2145	450.00
Wistful, HN2396	285.00
Young Widow, HN1399	3,150.00

Flambe

Alligator, rare	1,500.00
Cat, #2259	225.00
Cat, seated, #9	130.00
Confucious, #3314	195.00

Dragon, #2085 ....450.00
Drake, #137 ....65.00
Drake, standing, #806 ....275.00
Duck, #112 ....60.00
Fox, #29 ....295.00
Fox, #42, lg, 13" L 465.00
Fox, recumbent, 5" 365.00
Frog, #1162 ....495.00
Guinea, #69 ....495.00
Hippo, 3¼x6¾" 1,250.00
Monkeys, pr embracing 350.00
Owl, #2249 ....300.00
Rabbit, ears tucked, #43 ....465.00
Salmon, 12¼" 995.00
Tiger, stalking, 6x13" 525.00
Tortoise, #101, 1x3" 545.00
Vase, landscape, 14" 575.00
Vase, Sung, gourd shape w/sides lobed in bl, blk, gr or red, 7" 495.00
Wizard, #3121 ....195.00

Series Ware

Ashtray, Dickensware, Mr Squeers, E series, 4" 80.00
Ashtray, Ships, trading ketch, mc, 5¼" sq 78.00
Bowl, Bobby Burns, 7½" 150.00
Bowl, Nursery Rhymes, There Was a Little Man..., 6" 70.00
Bowl, salad; Bayeux Tapestry, Battle of Hastings, 6" 98.00
Candlestick, King Arthur's Knights, 2 knights, mc, 1924, 6½" ...110.00
Candlestick, Ships, trading ketch, mc, 1924, 6½" 110.00
Candlesticks, Woodlands, 7", pr 85.00
Coffeepot, Moorish Gate, merchants, 7" 155.00
Creamer, Nursery Rhumes, Little Man, 1905, 3¼" 98.00
Creamer & sugar bowl, Gnomes, w/lid 235.00
Cup & saucer, Australia Gum Trees, w/house, mc 70.00
Fern pot, Dutch People, 5" 100.00
Jardiniere, Shakespeare, Ophelia/Hamlet, mk, 8¾x10" ...325.00
Loving cup, King Arthur's Knights, 2 knights, mc, hdls, 6" ...385.00
Mug, King Arthur's Knights, 2 knights, dtd 1921, 5½" ...265.00
Nut dish, Dickensware, Sam Weller 50.00
Pitcher, Coaching Days, 6½" 195.00
Pitcher, Dickensware, Bill Sykes, 5" 185.00
Pitcher, Eglington Tournament, D2792, 13½" 525.00
Pitcher, Gondoliers, D3039, 7¼" 225.00
Pitcher, Jackdaw of Rheims, D2532, 4" 200.00
Pitcher, Jacobean, D1011, 7¾" 350.00
Pitcher, Medieval Minstrels, mk, 7½x4½" 135.00
Pitcher, Shakespeare, Romeo, 4½" 90.00
Plaque, Gleaners, women & boys w/grain, mk, 15½" 245.00
Plate, Am Buildings, Mt Vernon, dk bl, commemorative, 10" 95.00
Plate, Am Buildings, US Capitol, WA DC, commemorative, 10" ..95.00
Plate, Australian Views, Aborigines w/Weapons, 10½" 50.00
Plate, Australian Views, Koala Bears, 10½" 50.00
Plate, Canada, Rose & Thistle, 10½" 85.00
Plate, Canadian Views, Lake Louise & Victoria, 10½" 55.00
Plate, Canadian Views, Vermillion Lake & Mt Rundle, 10½" 60.00
Plate, Canterbury Pilgrims, Scene of Becket's Martydom, 10⅜" .165.00
Plate, Castles & Churches, Rochester Castle, bl & wht, 10¼" 85.00
Plate, Castles & Churches, Rochester Castle, mc, 10⅜" 85.00
Plate, Coaching Days, coach on hill, 5⅝" 55.00
Plate, Dickensware, Artful Dodger, Noke, scalloped, 10" 125.00
Plate, Dickensware, Sam Weller & Pickwick, 10" 95.00
Plate, Falconry, 3 ladies, man & falcon, mc, 10¼" 85.00
Plate, Flowers, prunus, pk on dk gr, dtd 1917, 8½" 75.00
Plate, Flowers, prunus on wht, cobalt border, 8⅝" 110.00

Plate, Flowers, yel nasturtiums on wht, 1915, 8½" 85.00
Plate, Gaffers, ¾-view, mc, dtd 1928, 8½" 78.00
Plate, Golf, Caddy Blowing Ball, 10" 400.00
Plate, Gondoliers, lady w/fan & man in gondola, 1909, 10½" 160.00
Plate, Haystacks, church in bkground, 1907, 10⅝" 95.00
Plate, Historic US, Commodore MacDonnough Victory, 9⅝" ...200.00
Plate, Home Waters, sailboats & townscape, Grace, 13" 150.00
Plate, Jackdaw of Rheims, Many a Knight..., 1906, 8" 60.00
Plate, Jackdaw of Rheims, 10" 80.00
Plate, Nautical History, Sir Francis Drake, 1907, 8" 170.00
Plate, Old English Inns, Bear's Head, 10½" 60.00
Plate, Old Rustic Inns, Cobham, 10" 60.00
Plate, Professionals, Doctor, 10⅜" 75.00
Plate, Professionals, Parson, 1934, 10⅜" 75.00
Plate, Proverbs, vintage border, 10" 65.00
Plate, sandwich; Australia Gum Trees, w/house, mc, 1935, 5¾" ...60.00
Plate, Shakespeare, Portia, mc, 7⅜" 80.00
Teapot stand, Old Moreton Hall, entrance, 6½" 95.00
Tile, Canterbury Pilgrims 125.00
Toothpick holder, Woodland, cottages & church, mc, 1938, 2½" ..90.00
Tray, Shakespeare, Katharine, 15½" 155.00
Vase, Babes in Woods, flow bl w/gold, 6½" 265.00
Vase, Dickensware, Cap'n Cuttle, early mk, 4⅝" 90.00
Vase, Welsh Ladies, 2 ladies by fence, mk, 3⅜" 120.00

Stoneware

Biscuit jar, cow frieze, SP rim/lid, H Barlow, 7¾" 950.00
Crock, utility; mustard yel & beige panels, 1858-90, 6x5" 130.00
Jug, mc floral, Lambeth, 8¼" 130.00
Loving cup, mc floral, silver lip mk Sheffield, Lambeth, 6" 220.00
Loving cup, tavern scenes, Lambeth, 6¼" 120.00
Loving cup, tavern scenes, 3 hound hdls, Lambeth, 5½" 160.00
Mug, hunters relief, wht/brn/tan, 3-hdld, dtd 1899, 1⅜" 425.00
Pitcher, Christopher Columbus commemorative, Lambeth, 9" ...225.00
Pitcher, Coronation of King Edward VII 1902, Lambeth, 8" 250.00
Pitcher, Egyptian frieze, tan/brn, pewter lid, 1884, 8" 495.00
Pitcher, hunters relief, wht/tan/brn, 1869-72, 7½" 475.00
Pitcher, utility; mustard yel & beige panels, 1858-90, 2¼" 98.00
Pitcher, Victoria, mc, Lambeth, 6" 300.00
Pitcher, Victoria, silver lip w/London hallmk, Lambeth, 5¼" 240.00
Vase, horses & sheep, fleur-de-lis band, H Barlow, 16" 1,555.00
Vase, mc floral w/gold, sgn, Lambeth, 10⅛" 335.00
Vase, pk roses, Carrara Ware, pre-1891, 8⅞" 235.00

Toby Jugs

Charrington, One Toby Leads to Another 350.00
Falstaff, D6020 ....140.00
Jolly Toby, D6109 ....90.00
Mr Pickwick, D6261 ....195.00
Old Charley, D6069 ....325.00
Old Charley, 5" 275.00
Sam Weller, D6265 ....150.00
Sherlock Holmes, D6661 ....120.00
Sir Frances Drake, D6660, A, lg 110.00
Sir Winston Churchill, lg 140.00
Sir Winston Churchill, D6172, sm 155.00
Squire, D6319 ....275.00
Town Crier, Doultonville, 5" 185.00

Miscellaneous

Ashtray, Winston Churchill commemorative, 1941, 4⅝" 45.00

Beaker, hunt scene, brass rim 65.00
Beaker, Wedding, Princess of Wales, 1981 ....40.00
Bust, Mr Pickwick, D6049 ....70.00
Pitcher, fish pattern slip decor, 1902, 13½" 375.00
Plate, turkeys/holly/mistletoe on wht, gr rim, Burslem, 10" 85.00
Ring dish, owl figural, brn & tan, 4x3¼" 165.00
Teapot, Charley 1,800.00
Teapot, Sairey Gamp 1,800.00
Teapot, Tony Weller 2,200.00
Vase, Arts & Crafts-style floral medallion on blended mc, 12½" ..200.00
Vase, cherry blossoms, spherical w/bottle neck, Burslem, 10" 125.00
Vase, Doune Castle, bl transfer, ovoid, 1911, 7½" 500.00
Vase, gold body w/sm spirals, flower band, 3 hdls/ft, 8x9" 800.00
Vase, HP florals w/gold, Doulton & Slater, 1886, 10⅞" 275.00
Vase, lilies/leaves, wht/gold/pk/wine on bk mottle, 1875, 14" .1,200.00
Vase, stylized floral/leaf, squeezebag decor, Slater's, 16½" 180.00
Wall mask, Sweet Anne, HN1590 ....450.00

Royal Dux

The Duxer Porzellan Manufactur was established by E. Eichler in 1860. Located in what is now Duchcov, Czechoslovakia, the area was known as Dux, Bohemia, until WWI. The war brought about changes in both the style of the ware as well as the mark. Prewar pieces were modeled in the Art Nouveau or Greek Classical manner and marked with 'Bohemia' and a pink triangle containing the letter 'E.' They were usually matt glazed in green, brown, and gold. Better pieces were made of porcelain, while the larger items were of pottery. After the war the ware was marked with the small pink triangle but without the Bohemia designation; 'Made in Czechoslovakia' was added. The style became Art Deco, with cobalt blue a dominant color.

Vase, lily with two nymphs at rim, cream with gray and gilt details, triangular mark, 21½", $1,650.00.

Centerpc, maid w/bird at elbow centers floriform, 1900, 13" 880.00
Centerpc, organic bowl, 1 maid below, 2nd on rim, 15" 770.00
Centerpc, standing maid, lg leaves form vase & 2 bowls, 21" 700.00
Centerpc, swans/sailboat, boy & girl ea end, 13½" L 250.00
Centerpc, 3-D maid stands by trunk stem, 2nd on rim, 18" 635.00
Figurine, boy at pond, gold trim, #1866, 13" L 300.00
Figurine, camel w/driver, man sits basket atop bundle, 20" 690.00
Figurine, crane, pk triangle mk, 7" 70.00
Figurine, dancer in mauve midrif, gold skirt, no shoes, 22" 350.00
Figurine, doe, head down, on leafy base, #0177, 8x10½" 175.00
Figurine, fox, recumbent, dk brn w/wht, Deco style 45.00
Figurine, he w/arm around her shoulders, she w/lamb, 15" 650.00
Figurine, man w/scroll & seated lady, pk triangle mk, 12½" 1,135.00
Figurine, mother w/child near basket, pk triangle mk, 8½" 425.00
Figurine, nude seated on rocky ledge dries ft w/cloth, 22" 800.00
Vase, grapes & plums w/gold, pk triangle mk, 17", pr 375.00

Vase, standing lady w/vase by waterway on gr, 12", pr 550.00

Royal Flemish

Royal Flemish was introduced in the late 1880s and was patented in 1894 by the Mt. Washington Glass Company. Transparent glass was enameled with one or several colors and the surface divided by a network of raised lines suggesting leaded glasswork. Some pieces were further decorated with enameled florals, birds, or Roman coins. Our advisors for this category are Betty and Clarence Maier; they are listed in the Directory under Pennsylvania.

Cologne, butterflies/floral, gold/bl on frost, bulbous, 5¾" 5,000.00
Ewer, shield w/griffin, 1546 on banner, gold rope hdl, 10" 3,850.00
Goblet, gold flowers/lines on autumn tones, cone stem, 5" 2,200.00
Pitcher, fish/seaweed, mc/gold, helmet spout, mk/#d, 7x8" 6,800.00
Vase, gold lines/mc floral, cup neck w/disk, ovoid body, 9" 3,900.00
Vase, roses/berries/floral w/rnd medallions, label, 13x8" 3,700.00
Vase, spear panels/griffin heads/florals, lobed neck, 15" 3,600.00

Royal Haeger, Haeger

In 1871 David Henry Haeger, a young son of German immigrants, purchased a brick factory at Dundee, Illinois, and began an association with the ceramic industry that his descendants have pursued to the present time. David's bricks had rebuilt Chicago after their great fire in 1871. By 1914 they had ventured into the field of commerical artware. Vases, figurines, lamp bases, and gift items in a pastel matt glaze carried the logo of the company name written over the bar of an 'H.' From 1929 to 1933, they produced a line of dinnerware which they marketed through Marshall Fields. Ware produced before the mid-thirties sometimes is found with a paper label; these are of special interest. 'Royal Haeger,' their premium line designed in 1938 by Royal Hickman, is highly desirable with collectors today. The mark 'Royal Haeger' (in raised lettering) was used during the thirties and forties; later a paper label in the shape of a crown was used.

Fast becoming popular with today's collectors is the Earth Graphic Wraps line, first introduced in the mid-'70s. These one-of-a-kind pieces consist of rough, raised formations on backgrounds of marigold, white, fern and brown, in both matt and glossy finishes.

The Macomb plant, built in 1939, primarily made ware for the florist trade. A second plant, built there in 1969, produces lamp bases. For those interested in learning more about the subject, we recommend *Collecting Royal Haeger* by our advisors, Lee Garmon and Doris Frizzell; both are listed in the Directory under Illinois.

Ashtray, R-1272, free-form, 11" L 8.00
Ashtray, R-1359, pear shape, 7" L 9.00
Ashtray, R-1471, abstract fish, 13" L 10.00
Bookend/planter, R-641, stallion, 8½" 12.00
Bookends, R-1144, water lily, 5", pr 45.00
Bowl, console; R-611, fish, 12" L 10.00
Bowl, R-373, appl fruit on side, 20" L 45.00
Bowl, R-510, dolphin, 15" W 12.00
Bowl, R-562, Pei Tung, 9½" 25.00
Bowl, R-819, acanthus leaf, 14" L 10.00
Box, R-689, shallow, 10½" W 8.00
Candle holder, R-1174, Rococo, 6½" 10.00
Candle holder, R-203, fish, dbl, 5", ea 20.00
Candle holder, R-511, dolphin, 10¾" 15.00
Candle holder, R-622, Chinese figure, yel, 5" 12.00
Candy box, R-590, Hawaiian, w/lid, 8" dia 35.00

Candy box, R-664, polar bear, w/lid, 7½" W 35.00
Cigarette box, R-684, turtle figural, w/lid, 9½" L 30.00
Figurine, #3427, musical Madonna, 11½" 45.00
Figurine, #3670, peasant girl w/geese, 17½" 150.00
Figurine, #505, mermaid, reclining, 21" 75.00
Figurine, R-101, rooster, head down, 12" 30.00
Figurine, R-102, rooster, head up, 12" 30.00
Figurine, R-1131, leopard, head bk, tail up, sitting, 8" 55.00
Figurine, R-1224, gypsy girl, 16½" 75.00
Figurine, R-162, dbl race horses w/jockey, 9" 50.00
Figurine, R-167, greyhound, head up, 9" 50.00
Figurine, R-168, nude torso, 14" 50.00
Figurine, R-305, giraffe, head & neck, 19" 150.00
Figurine, R-350, pheasants on ped, 14" L 25.00
Figurine, R-375A, polar bear cub, sitting, 3" 20.00
Figurine, R-479, prospector w/burros, 11½" L 55.00
Figurine, R-493, Egyptian cat, head down, 6½" 30.00
Figurine, R-539, elephant, 9" 30.00
Figurine, R-596, Barn Yard Riders, horse w/3 riders, 14" L 150.00
Figurine, R-618, Thought 150.00
Figurine, R-648, leopard, sitting, 6" 20.00
Figurine, R-649, leopard, recumbent, 7" L 20.00
Figurine, R-695, lion 50.00
Figurine, R-734, Collie 50.00
Figurine, R-740, giraffe & young, head & neck, 15" 125.00
Figurine, R-759, Temple Goddess 35.00
Figurine, R-896, cat sleeping, 7" L 30.00
Figurine, R-991, stag, standing, 7" 30.00
Flower block, R-359, 2 birds, 11" W 35.00
Planter, R-639, circus leopard, 12½" L 75.00
Planter, R-754, donkey cart, 11¼" L 15.00
Planter, R-834, turtle, 11" L 25.00
Planter, R-869, gazelle, 14" 45.00
Planter, R-984, log form, 11" L 12.00
TV planter, R-1239, bronco, 12" L 50.00
Vase, #3417, musical birthday, 8" 45.00
Vase, console; R-248, Plume Feather, 10" 20.00
Vase, R-1401, lg swan, 12½" 25.00
Vase, R-1492, 3-legged, 10" 15.00
Vase, R-222, frog sitting on rnd spiral, 12" 25.00
Vase, R-298, cornucopia shell, 11" L 20.00
Vase, R-467, flying goose, 16¼" L 50.00
Vase, R-501, beehive w/flowers, 7" 15.00
Vase, R-616, tulip form, 8" 12.00
Vase, R-660, birds & sprigs, 14" 25.00
Vase, R-888, Goose Quills, 17½" 55.00
Wall pocket, R-724, rocking horse 15.00
Wall pocket, R-745, grapevine 12.00
Window box, R-851, oblong, 10" L 12.00

Royal Rudolstadt

The hard-paste porcelain that has come to be known as Royal Rudolstadt was produced in Thuringia, Germany, in the early 18th century. Various names and marks have been associated with this pottery. One of the earliest was a hay fork symbol associated with Johann Frederichvon Schwarzburg-Rudolstadt, one of the first founders. Variations, some that included an 'R,' were also used. In 1854 Earnst Bohne produced wares that were marked with an anchor and the letters 'EB.' Examples commonly found today were made during the late 1800s and early 20th century. These are usually marked with an 'RW' within a shield under a crown and the words 'Crown Rudolstadt.' Items marked 'Germany' were made after 1890.

Cake plate, floral, HP/transfer, 12-sided, hdls, 11x12" 50.00
Chocolate set, Nouveau poppies w/gold, sgn F Kahn, pot+5 c/s .425.00
Leaf fish, mc MOP w/much gold, 6" 15.00
Nappy, roses, mc on pastel w/gold, 5⅜" 12.00
Tea set, Golliwogs, child sz, 23-pc 225.00
Vase, floral, purple on cream, rtcl w/gold, 1887, 9½" 195.00
Vase, mc morning glories w/gold, relief scrolls, 12½x5¾" 135.00

Royal Vienna

In 1719 Claude Innocentius de Paquier established a hard-paste porcelain factory in Vienna where he made highly ornamental wares similar to the type produced at Meissen. Early wares were usually unmarked; but after 1744, when the factory was purchased by the Empress, the Austrian shield (often called 'beehive') was stamped on under the glaze. In the following listings, values are for hand-painted items unless noted otherwise. Decal-decorated items would be considerably lower.

Note: An influx of Japanese reproductions on the market have influenced values to decline on genuine old Royal Vienna. Buyer beware! On new items the beehive mark is over the glaze, the weight of the porcelain is heavier, and the decoration is obviously decaled. Our advisor for this category is Madeleine France; she is listed in the Directory under Florida.

Coffee service, allegorical reserves with cobalt and gilt, 7" pot, creamer and sugar bowl with lid, eight cups and saucers (total twenty pieces), $2,200.00.

Candlesticks, mythical scenes, maroon & gold, 5½", pr 525.00
Chocolate pot, ladies & cherub w/flowers & gold, 9" 225.00
Cup & saucer, demitasse; portrait of maid on blk, w/gilt 650.00
Ewer, lady/angel, sgn Pojche, gold hdls/etc, 5½" 650.00
Jug, Schonteer: monk w/empty stein on red w/gilt, wear, 7" 350.00
Lamp, lady on wine w/gilt, sgn Wrigel, hdls/ftd, 12½" 800.00
Lamp, temple sacrifice & scene on sq ft, cobalt, Seller, 15" 1,700.00
Plate, mermaids luring man from boat, sgn Perges, 9¾" 1,000.00
Plate, peasants in field, beehive mk, 10" 150.00
Plate, seminude w/cherub, wine/gold border, sgn, 7" 115.00
Plate, Titians Tochter, girl w/fruit, gr/gilt rim, sgn, 8" 225.00
Plate, Traumerei, Egyptian lady/cockatoos, sgn Wagner, 9½" 650.00
Stein, pheasant/men w/stein/floral, porc inlay lid, 4" 1,550.00
Urn, courting couple on rose w/gold, w/lid, 5½" 400.00
Urn, ladies in garden panels, florals & gold, hdls, 10¾" 350.00
Urn, lady on red lustre/gold, pk scene panels, sq base, 26" 1,100.00
Urn, portait on cobalt, sgn Walter, gold hdls, sq ft, 7" 350.00
Vase, Bachantan, lady/putti on dk gr w/gilt, ftd, 38" 18,700.00
Vase, Colonial couple, cobalt & gold, beehive mk, 6¼x2¾" 195.00
Vase, Cupid in garden w/Venus, bk: Cupid, titled, 22x6" 2,800.00

Vase, lady's portrait, floral on bl, sgn Berg, gold/hdls, 6" **400.00**
Vase, lady's portrait, sgn Donali, maroon & gold lustre, 9¾" ...**1,050.00**
Vase, maids/pool reserve on cobalt w/gold, beehive mk, 11x7" ..**800.00**
Vase, Solitude, nude on gr/red lustre w/gilt, hdls, 9" **1,500.00**
Vase, 4 children as seasons, mk, 3" **225.00**

Roycroft

Near the turn of the century, Elbert Hubbard established the Roycroft Printing Shop in East Aurora, New York. Named in honor of two 17th-century printer-bookbinders, the print shop was just the beginning of a community called Roycroft, which came to be known worldwide. Hubbard became a popular personality of the early 1900s, known for his talents in a variety of areas from writing and lecturing to manufacturing. The Roycroft community became a meeting place for people of various capabilities and included shops for the production of furniture, copper, leather items, and a multitude of other wares which were marked with the Roycroft symbol, an 'R' within a circle below a stylized cross. Hubbard lost his life on the Lusitania in 1915; production in the community continued until the Depression.

Interest is strong in the field of Arts and Crafts in general and in Roycroft items in particular. Copper items are evaluated to a large extent by the condition of the original patina that remains. In the listings that follow, values reflect the worth of items retaining their original patina unless condition is otherwise described. Our advisor for this category is Bruce Austin; he is listed in the Directory under New York.

Andirons, S-shaped wrought iron w/spiral & twist detail, EX .**1,600.00**
Ash stand, tray removes, 9" dia, 26" **425.00**
Bench, #46, Ali Baba, flat surface, bark underneath, 42" **5,000.00**
Book, Book of Songs, leather bound, EX **50.00**
Book, Little Journeys: Great Business Men, MIB **150.00**
Book, Motto Book..., red poppies on brn paper, EX **100.00**
Book rack, oak w/orig finish, mk, 5x15½x6" **325.00**
Book stand, Little Journeys; tenon/key built, rfn top, mk **525.00**
Bookcase, #086, 33-degree, 16-pane door, orig, 55x40" **4,750.00**
Bookcase, 33-degree, ldgl door, appl columns, mk, rpr, 55" **7,500.00**
Bookends, #304, repousse sq Viennese Secessionist floral **200.00**
Bookends, #329, abstract tooled floral, EX patina **275.00**
Bookends, appl leaf, crimped top, 5x4" **275.00**
Bookends, brass washed w/rnd pull on riveted strap, 5x4" **250.00**
Bookends, canted corners, owl design, 4x6", EX **300.00**
Bookends, copper w/brass wash, cvd ship, 5½", pr **200.00**
Bookends, ring attached to lg sq w/tooled strap, 5", pr **275.00**
Bowl, brass finish, crimped, worn patina, 2x7" **175.00**
Bowl, centerpc; rolled rim, 4x10" **800.00**
Bowl, incurvate, 3-ftd, mk, 4x10" **900.00**
Bowl vase, brass wash, lg upright leaves design, 3", EX **300.00**
Box, hammered/tooled brass hdls & top pc, EX patina, 3x10x5" ...**1,600.00**
Bracelet, Roycroft, sterling w/emb floral medallion, ⅜" **375.00**
Buffet, quarter-sawn, ldgl doors, copper hdw, mk, 46x42" **6,250.00**
Cabinet, china; ldgl doors, copper hdw/quarter-sawn oak, 57" ..**8,500.00**
Calling card holder, leather, w/card inside **250.00**
Candlesticks, rnd bobeches, 4 strap sides & ft, 12", EX, pr **1,200.00**
Chair, office; swivel base, no arms, 1 broad bk slat, EX **2,500.00**
Chair, office; 1 vertical bk-slat, short arms, 41", M **1,100.00**
Chair, side; #030, waisted bk-splat, MacMurdo ft, mk, 43" **600.00**
Chair, side; ash, 3 horizontal slats, new leather, mk, 37" **325.00**
Chair, side; 1 broad/1 thin bk-slat, rpl seat/finish, 6 for **2,000.00**
Chandelier, inverted 2-band 17" dome on 3 heavy chains, mk ..**7,000.00**
Chandelier, 3 torch-shaped lights, electrified, VG **4,750.00**
Desk, #901, drop-front, strap hinges, MacMurdo ft, mk, rfn ..**3,400.00**
Footstool, 14x12x17", VG **600.00**

Frame, horizontal w/arching top, 5x6" **300.00**
Humidor, brass finish, appl top/base twist, lid finial, 8" **300.00**

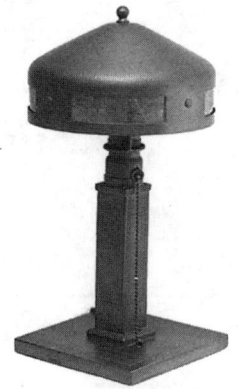

Lamp, 7" domical shade with rectangular mica panels on hammered copper square standard and base, #903, ca 1905, 13½", $1,400.00.

Luggage rack, walnut, 6-plank top, tenon/key built, mk, EX **600.00**
Necklace, 1½" sterling 3-side pendant w/orb................................**250.00**
Nut set, bowl w/tube in center holding cracker+picks, 5x8" **300.00**
Nut set, 9" bowl+4 ind, w/ladle, mk, EX **650.00**
Pedestal, #080, mahog w/keyed tenons top/bottom, rstr, 50" ...**4,000.00**
Pin tray, early, 4¾" dia, EX **225.00**
Poker chip holder, 6-compartment, ftd, w/lid, 7", EX **550.00**
Stand, sq top, splay legs, orig finish, 19x12" **1,200.00**
Table, dining; 48" dia top, 5-leg, massive, +4 leaves **3,750.00**
Table, may be from inn, enhanced orig finish, mk, 30x74x74" ..**3,200.00**
Tray, gr tooled design at rim, cleaned, 6" dia, VG **95.00**
Tray, heavy gauge, hdls, lt cleaning, 15" dia **500.00**
Tray, repousse border, slim oval w/hdls, mid-period, rfn, 22" **500.00**
Vase, #239, bulbous base, flaring mouth, 4x6", EX **600.00**
Vase, Am Beauty, long flaring cylinder neck, rfn, 21x8" **1,600.00**
Vase, appl silver device, rolled-in rim, EX patina, 6" **1,900.00**
Vase, Arts & Crafts design, gr wash, cylindrical, 10" **2,000.00**
Vase, flat flaring rim, heavy gauge, 8¾x4" **650.00**
Vase, floral w/gr wash on copper cylinder, 7", EX **600.00**
Vase, geometric silver o/l, cylindrical, 6x3" **1,000.00**
Vase, scalloped wavy rim, 8¾x3" **700.00**
Vase, shouldered, orb mk, 4½" **250.00**
Vase, 3 full-length angle hdls over smooth panels, 6¾" **1,600.00**

Rozenburg

Some of the most innovative and original Art Nouveau ceramics were created by the Rozenberg factory at The Hague in The Netherlands between 1885 and 1916. Some pieces are similar to Gouda. Rozenburg also made highly prized eggshell ware, so called because of its very thin walls; this is eagerly sought after by collectors. T.A.C. Colenbrander was their artistic leader, with Samuel Schellink and J. Kok designing many of the eggshell pieces.

Cup & saucer, nasturtiums, sgn Schellink, octagonal, 1905 ....**1,600.00**
Jug, chrysanthemums, sgn Schellink, 1910s, w/lid, rpr, 6¼" **1,550.00**
Pitcher, exotic birds, brn/ochre on terra cotta, 7" **325.00**
Plaque, mc floral, earthenware, ca 1910, 8⅞" **400.00**
Plate, 2 birds/vines/flower, vivid colors, 11" **485.00**
Vase, abstracts, gr/brn/bl, flared neck, ftd bulbous body, 12" ..**1,650.00**
Vase, floral, baluster shape, earthenware, 1893, pnt mk, 15" **250.00**
Vase, floral on cream, sgn Sterken, 1903, 8⅞" **7,000.00**
Vase, irises, sqd bottle form, sgn Schellink, 1901, 10" **1,800.00**
Vase, pelican, 3 pk orchids, cobalt/mc Deco motif, 4" **575.00**

Rubena

Rubena glass was made by several firms in the late 1800s. It is a blown art glass that shades from clear to red. See also Art Glass Baskets; Cruets; Sugar Shakers; Salts; specific manufacturers.

Bowl, centerpc; swirl w/ruffled rim, NP base, 8x10" 225.00
Bowl, wavy reverse swirl, trifold rim w/pinched points, 6" 250.00
Creamer, 4-lobed top, cut star bottom, clear hdl 95.00
Pitcher, gold trim, bulbous, clear hdl, 2x2¾" 85.00
Syrup, opal Coin Spot, crystal hdl, metal top, 6½" 275.00
Tumbler, Hobnail, 4" 67.50
Tumbler, HP florals, 3½x2¾" 55.00

Rubena Verde

Rubena Verde glass was introduced in the late 1800s by Hobbs, Brockunier, and Company of Wheeling, West Virginia. Its transparent colors shade from red to green. Our advisor for this category is Mike Roscoe; he is listed in the Directory under Michigan. See also Art Glass Baskets; Cruets; Sugar Shakers; Salts.

Basket, Dmn Quilt, clear thorn hdl 275.00
Cup, wht floral, ribbed, 2¾" 120.00
Pickle castor, Invt T'print, bulbous; SP fr & tongs 350.00
Pitcher, floral enamel, 7½" 550.00
Pitcher, Invt T'print, quatrelobe top, 6½" 285.00
Shakers, HP floral, pewter lid, 4½", pr 200.00
Syrup, Hobnail, clear hdl, pewter top 650.00
Vase, HP floral, bl ribbon, ribbed, cylindrical, ruffled, 11" 195.00
Vase, lily form w/folded & scalloped rim, 5" 250.00

Ruby Glass

Produced for over one hundred years by every glasshouse of note in this country, ruby glass has been used to create decorative items such as one might find in gift shops, utilitarian bottles and kitchenware, figurines, and dinnerware lines such as were popular in the Depression era. For further information and study, we recommend *Ruby Glass of the 20th Century* by our advisor, Naomi Over; she is listed in the Directory under Colorado.

Pitcher, Anchor Hocking, $35.00;
Matching juice tumblers, $6.00 each.

Basket, Daisy & Button, oval, Fenton 15.00
Bonbon, crimped, 7¼" 25.00

Bowl, ruffled rim, Blenko shape #3744, 3¼" H 15.00
Bowl, scalloped, 4-toed, Cambridge, 6" 60.00
Bubble, Blenko, mid-1930s, 5" 20.00
Candlesticks, metal stem, 8½", pr 95.00
Cigarette jar, ship's lantern form, w/lid 35.00
Creamer & sugar bowl, Hostmaster line, New Martinsville 55.00
Cup, measuring; 16-oz 28.00
Figurine, bird, Swedish Glass, 4" 18.00
Finger bowl, 4¾", +saucer 25.00
Goblet, wine; chrome stem 8.00
Lamp, oil; Viking, 9" 22.50
Marmalade, Eyewinker, LG Wright, 8¾" 40.00
Nappy, Oyster & Pearl, Anchor Hocking, 6½" 15.00
Pickle dish, Anchor Hocking, 1940s, 6" 15.00
Pitcher, High Point, Anchor Hocking, 80-oz 40.00
Pitcher, hostess; Roly Poly, Macbeth-Evans, 32-oz 65.00
Pitcher, reeded, Imperial, 80-oz 100.00
Plate, luncheon; Anchor Hocking, 7¾" 6.00
Tumbler, iced tea; Bubble, Anchor Hocking, 16-oz 15.00
Vase, Heirloom, pitcher form, 9" 50.00
Vase, Hoover, Anchor Hocking, 9" 18.00

Ruby-Stained Souvenirs

Ruby-flashed or ruby-stained glass was made through the application of a thin layer of color over clear. It was used in the manufacture of some early pressed tableware and from the Victorian era well into the 20th century for souvenir items which were often engraved on the spot with the date, location, and buyer's name.

Canoe, Cranberry Lake NJ, worn lettering 25.00
Creamer, Button Arches, Gettysburg 1863, 2¾" 25.00
Creamer, Triple Triangle 40.00
Goblet, T'print, allover pattern, Reading PA, 5¾" 28.00
Toothpick holder, Button Arches, Lancaster PA, 2⅝x2⅝" 30.00
Toothpick holder, Corona 35.00
Tumbler, Button Arches, Sarasota Springs, 3⅞x3" 30.00
Tumbler, Inverted Heart, 3¾x3⅛" 32.00
Wine, King's Crown, allover pattern, Renovo PA, 3¾" 22.00
Wine, Sunk Honeycomb 20.00

Rugs

Hooked rugs are treasured today for their folk-art appeal. It was a craft that was introduced to this country in about 1830 and flourished its best in the New England states. The prime consideration is not age but artistic appeal. Scenes with animals, buildings, and people; patriotic designs; or whimsical themes are preferred. Those with finely conceived designs, great imagination, interesting color use, etc., demand higher prices. Condition is, of course, also a factor. Marked examples bearing the stamps of 'Frost and Co.,' 'Abenakee,' 'C.R.,' and 'Ouia' are highly prized. Note: the rugs listed here are rag unless noted otherwise. See also Orientalia, Rugs.

Basket of flowers on bl w/blk border, PA, 1943, 24x39" 220.00
Bear, navy-blk on gray w/pk border, 22x33" 580.00
Boy w/pony cart, mc, crocheted edge, 1900s, 17x33" 330.00
Cat & dog in field of hearts, mc, 22x41", EX 1,500.00
Cat on platform, 4-color, minor rpr, 20x38" 275.00
Cats, blk on gray w/mc floral border, worn, 24x30" 330.00
Cows, horse & flowering tree, mc, 38x38", EX 1,750.00
Floral, ca 1900, rebacked, 25x38" 250.00

Geometric border (wide), mc, minor wear & fading, 64x35" 380.00
Geometrics, shades of gray-bl, lt wear, 107x37" 415.00
House in landscape, 1900s, 31x52", EX 330.00
Medallions & roses on variegated beige, rprs, 46x88" 360.00
PA, bl-gray w/wht & bl warp, 180x36" 88.00
PA, mc stripes w/bl & wht warp, lt wear, 186x36" 110.00
Rooster, hen & chicks, mc w/blk border, 31x45" 155.00
Rooster crowing at sunrise, mc, 18½x32" 50.00
Roses, mc on blk w/leafy scroll border, damage, 27x46" 85.00
Sailboat, semicircular, 5-color, fading/wear, 17½x33" 140.00
Squirrel amid scrolls, 4-color, scalloped felt border, 37x21" 150.00
Swan on pond, 3-color, mtd on stretcher, 26x36" 385.00
Trotting horse, blk on brn tones, lt wear/soil, 29x39" 225.00
2 Scottish terriers, 1900s, 26x46", EX 400.00

RumRill

George Rumrill designed and marketed his pottery designs from 1933 until his death in 1942. During this period of time, four different companies produced his works. Today the most popular designs are those made by the Red Wing Stoneware Company from 1933 until 1936 and Red Wing Potteries from 1936 until early 1938. Some of these lines include Trumpet Flower, Classic, Manhattan, and Athena, the Nudes.

For a period of months in 1938, Shawnee took over the production of RumRill pottery. This relationship ended abruptly, and the Florence Pottery took over and produced his wares until the plant burned down. The final producer was Gonder. Pieces from each individual pottery are easily recognized by their designs, glazes, and/or signatures. It is interesting to note that the same designs were produced by all three companies. They may be marked RumRill or with the name of the specific company that made them. Our advisors for this category are Wendy and Leo Frese; they are listed in the Directory under Texas.

Basket, #285, Riviera, Classic Group, 8" 35.00
Basket, #438, Pompeian, Sylvan Group, 8½" 50.00
Bookends, #396, blk matt, Novelties Group, 7", pr 300.00
Candle holder, #539, Marigold, Manhattan Group, 14½", ea 90.00
Candle holder, #563, wht, Athena Group, 10", ea 300.00
Console bowl, #271, Dutch Blue, Classic Group, 14½" 75.00
Console bowl, #303, lilac, Grecian Group, 11½" 60.00
Console bowl, #419, aqua, Continental Group, 19" 125.00
Dealer's sign, wht scroll 350.00
Ewer, #220, Pompeian, Continental Group, 10" 60.00
Ewer, #448, Pompeian, Sylvan Group, 9½" 50.00
Vase, #T-1, wht, floor type, 18" 200.00
Vase, #215, Goldenrod, Miscellaneous Group, 6" 75.00
Vase, #259, wht, Swan Group, 6" 45.00
Vase, #308, wht, Florentine Group, 10" 50.00
Vase, #401, gr, Grecian Group, 12" 95.00
Vase, #486, Dutch Blue, Trumpet Flower Group, 7" 75.00
Vase, #570, gr, Athena Group, 10" 400.00
Vase, #599, Pompeian, Miscellaneous Group, 9" 50.00
Vase, #613, gr, Vintage Group, 12" 75.00

Ruskin

This English pottery operated near Birmingham from 1989 until 1935. Its founder was W. Howson Taylor, and it was named in honor of the reknown author and critic, John Ruskin. The earliest marks were 'Taylor' in block letters and the initials 'WHT,' the smaller W and H superimposed over the upright leg of a larger T. Later marks included the Ruskin name.

Bowl, mc crystalline, 5" 200.00
Vase, cobalt lustre, flat shoulder, 6x3" 75.00
Vase, gr drip on gun-metal mottle, flat shoulder, 8x4" 200.00
Vase, mc crystalline, 8" 325.00
Vase, orange lustre mottle w/gr shamrock band, 7½" 225.00
Vase, red to plum mottle, bulbous bottom, mk/1910, 8" 800.00
Vase, yel lustre w/platinum highlights, trumpet neck, 7½" 150.00

Russel Wright Dinnerware

Russel Wright, one of America's foremost industrial designers, also designed several lines of ceramic dinnerware, glassware, and aluminum ware that are now highly sought-after collectibles. His most popular dinnerware then and with today's collectors, American Modern, was manufactured by the Steubenville Pottery Company from 1939 until 1959. It was produced in a variety of solid colors in assortments chosen to stay attune with the times. Casual (his first line sturdy enough to be guaranteed against breakage for ten years from date of purchase) is relatively easy to find today — simply because it has held up so well. During the years of its production, the Casual line was constantly being restyled, some items as many as five times. Early examples were heavily mottled, while later pieces were smoothly glazed and sometimes patterned. The ware was marked with Wright's signature and 'China by Iroquois.' It was marketed in fine department stores throughout the country. After 1950 the line was marked 'Iroquois China by Russel Wright.'

To calculate values for items in American Modern, add 100% to the suggested prices in the following listings for examples in these colors: White, Bean Brown, Cantaloupe, and Glacier Blue. In Casual, Brick Red and Aqua items go for around 200% more than any other color, while those in Avocado Yellow are priced lower than suggested values. Values are given for glassware in coral and seafoam; other colors are 10% to 15% less. For those wanting to learn more about the subject, we recommend *The Collector's Encyclopedia of Russel Wright Designs* (with updated values) by our advisor, Ann Kerr. She is listed in the Directory under Ohio.

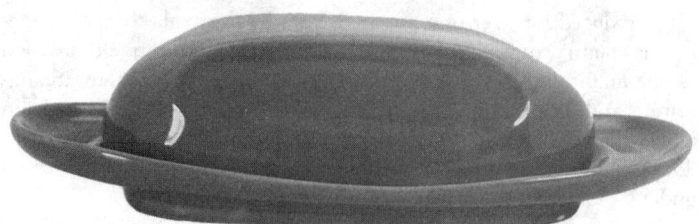

Restyled butter dish, aqua, very rare item in rare color, no determined value.

American Modern

Bowl, child's 75.00
Bowl, salad 75.00
Bowl, vegetable 22.00
Butter dish 185.00
Coffeepot, AD 75.00
Coffeepot, 8x8½" 150.00
Creamer 10.00
Cup & saucer 15.00
Hostess set, plate & cup 85.00
Pickle dish 16.00
Pitcher, water 100.00
Plate, chop 30.00
Plate, dinner; 10" 10.00

Plate, salad; 8" 12.00
Ramekin, ind, w/lid 150.00
Relish rosette 150.00
Salad fork & spoon 90.00
Shakers, pr 14.00
Stack server 165.00
Sugar bowl, w/lid 14.00
Teapot, 6x10" 75.00

Casual

Asbestos pad 30.00
Bowl, cereal; 5" 8.00
Bowl, fruit; restyled, 5¾" 8.00
Bowl, open vegetable; 10" 40.00
Bowl, soup; 11½-oz 18.00
Butter dish, regular colors, restyled, ¼-lb 150.00
Casserole, deep, 4-qt, 8" 65.00
Casserole, open, 10" 40.00
Coffeepot, AD; 4½" 75.00
Cookware, 6-qt 175.00
Creamer, lg family sz 30.00
Creamer, restyled 15.00
Cup & saucer, coffee 12.00
Cup & saucer, restyled 10.00
Dutch oven 125.00
Gravy bowl, 12-oz, 5¼" 12.00
Gravy stand, 7½" 15.00
Lid for open divided vegetable bowl 20.00
Lid for water pitcher 30.00
Lid for 4-qt casserole 20.00
Mug, 13-oz 65.00
Percolator 175.00
Pitcher, water; restyled, 2-qt 126.00
Plate, chop; 13⅞" 28.00
Plate, dinner; 10" 10.00
Plate, party; w/cup 75.00
Platter, oval, 10¼" 40.00
Shakers, stacking, pr 12.00
Sugar bowl, restyled 20.00
Sugar bowl, stacking, 4" 12.00

Glass

American Modern, chilling bowl, 12-oz, 3x5½" 100.00
American Modern, cocktail, 3-oz, 2½" 25.00
American Modern, cordial, 2" 38.00
American Modern, dbl old-fashioned 45.00
American Modern, dessert dish, 2" 40.00
American Modern, goblet, 4" 40.00
American Modern, pilsner, rare, 7" 100.00
American Modern, sherbet, 2½" 25.00
American Modern, tumbler, iced tea; 13-oz 30.00
American Modern, tumbler, juice; 4" 30.00
American Modern, tumbler, water; 4½" 30.00
American Modern, wine, 3" 25.00
Eclipse, old-fashioned 15.00
Eclipse, shot glass 10.00
Flair, tumbler, iced tea; 14-oz 65.00
Flair, tumbler, juice; 6-oz 50.00
Flair, tumbler, water; 11-oz 50.00
Pinch, tumbler, iced tea; 14-oz 35.00
Pinch, tumbler, juice; 6-oz 35.00
Pinch, tumbler, red, any sz 125.00

Pinch, tumbler, water; 11-oz 35.00
Snow glass, bowl, salad/vegetable; rnd 165.00
Snow glass, bowl, vegetable; oval, w/lid/tray/platter 175.00
Snow glass, candle holders, pr 200.00
Snow glass, plate, salad 65.00
Snow glass, shakers, pr 110.00
Snow glass, sugar bowl, w/lid & tray 85.00
Snow glass, tumbler, iced tea; 14-oz 150.00
Snow glass, tumbler, juice; 5-oz 150.00

Highlight

Bowl, divided vegetable; Citron or Nutmeg 35.00
Bowl, oval vegetable; Citron or Nutmeg 55.00
Bowl, soup or cereal; Citron or Nutmeg, either sz 30.00
Bowl, vegetable; rnd, White, Pepper, or Blueberry 60.00
Butter dish, White, Pepper, or Blueberry 125.00
Casserole (Bain Marie), Citron or Nutmeg 100.00
Cup & saucer, AD; Citron or Nutmeg 50.00
Lid for soup, White, Pepper or Blueberry 50.00
Mug, Citron or Nutmeg 55.00
Pitcher, White, Pepper or Blueberry, w/lid 100.00
Plate, bread & butter; Citron or Nutmeg 10.00
Plate, dinner; White, Pepper or Blueberry 30.00
Platter, rnd, Citron or Nutmeg, sm 55.00
Sugar bowl, White, Pepper or Blueberry 40.00

Spun Aluminum

Russel Wright's aluminum ware may not have been especially well accepted in its day — it tended to damage easily and seems to have had only limited market appeal — but today's collectors feel quite differently about it, as is apparent in the suggested values noted in the following listings.

Beverage set 400.00
Bowl 75.00

Bun warmer, wood knob and handle, 10", $65.00.

Casserole 85.00
Flower ring 125.00
Ice bucket 75.00
Relish rosette, lg 125.00
Serving accessory, sm 115.00
Smoking stand 650.00
Spaghetti set, 3-pc 400.00
Vase, 12" 110.00
Waste basket 110.00

Sterling

Bowl, bouillon; 7-oz 12.00

Bowl, onion soup; 10-oz 20.00
Bowl, soup; 6½" 15.00
Coffee bottle 95.00
Creamer, ind, 3-oz 12.00
Cup, demitasse; 3½-oz 55.00
Pitcher, water; 2-qt 65.00
Plate, bread & butter; 6¼" 5.00
Plate, dinner; 10¼" 12.00
Platter, oval, 10½" 17.00
Teapot, 10-oz 65.00

Miscellaneous

Bauer, ash dish, #10A, 5½" sq 300.00
Bauer, pillow base, #1A 850.00
Bauer, vase, tall, #5A, 22" 1,000.00
Bauer, vase/planter, #16A, 7½" 600.00
Book, Guide to Easier Living, R Wright, EX 75.00
Display sign, Iroquois Casual Cookware, lg 300.00
Flair, creamer 10.00
Flair, lug soup 12.00
Flair, tumbler 15.00
Harker White Clover, casserole, clover decor, w/lid, 2-qt 50.00
Harker White Clover, creamer, clover decor 14.00
Harker White Clover, pitcher, clover decor, w/lid, 2-qt 65.00
Harker White Clover, plate, jumbo; clover decor, 10" 16.00
Home Decorator, bowl, oval vegetable; shallow 12.00
Home Decorator, cup & saucer 9.00
Home Decorator, sugar bowl, w/lid 13.00
Ideal Adult Kitchen Ware, butter dish 45.00
Ideal Adult Kitchen Ware, decanter, juice 30.00
Ideal Adult Kitchen Ware, tumbler, either sz 25.00
Ideal Children's Toy Dishes, boxed set 150.00
Ideal Children's Toy Dishes, serving items, ea 20.00
Knowles, creamer & sugar bowl, w/lid 35.00
Knowles, cup & saucer 14.00
Knowles, plate, dinner; 10¾" 15.00
Knowles, platter, oval, 13" 18.00
Knowles, sauce boat 30.00
Linen runner, scarf, or mat, ea, minimum value 25.00
Mary Wright, Country Gardens, plate 75.00
Mary Wright, cup & saucer 100.00
Meladur, cup, 7-oz 8.00
Meladur, plate, compartmented, 9½" 10.00
Meladur, plate, service; 10" 10.00
Price list of American Modern 35.00
Residential, bowl, divided vegetable 18.00
Residential, bowl, fruit 13.00
Residential, plate, dinner 5.00
Theme Formal, mug 100.00
Theme Formal, tumbler 250.00

Russian Art

Before the Revolution in 1917, many jewelers and craftsmen created exquisite marvels of their arts, distinctive in the extravagant detail of their enamel work, jeweled inlays, and use of precious metals. These treasures aptly symbolized the glitter and the romance of the glorious days under the reign of the Tsars of Imperial Russia. The most famous of these master jewelers was Carl Faberge (1852-1920), goldsmith to the Romanovs. Following the tradition of his father, he took over the Faberge workshop in 1870. Eventually Faberge employed more than 500 assistants and set up workshops in Moscow, Kiev, and London as well as in St. Petersburg. His specialties were enamel work, clockwork automated figures, carved animal and human figures of precious or semiprecious stones, cigarette cases, small boxes, scent flasks, and his best-known creations, the Imperial Easter Eggs — each of an entirely different design. By the turn of the century, his influence had spread to other countries, and his work was revered by royalty and the very wealthy. The onset of the war marked the end of the era. Very little of his work remains on the market, and items that are available are very expensive. But several of his contemporaries were goldsmiths whose work can be equally enchanting. Among them are Klingert, Ovchinnikov, Smirnov, Ruckert, Loriye, Cheryatov, Kuzmichev, Nevalainen, Adler, Sbitnev, Third Artel, Wakewa, Holmstrom, Britzin, Wigstrom, Orlov, Nichols, and Plincke. Most of them produced excellent pieces similar to those made by Faberge between 1880 and 1910.

Perhaps the most important bronze Russian artist was Eugenie Alexandrovich Lanceray (1847-87). From 1875 until 1887, he modeled many equestrian groups of falconers and soldiers ranging in height from about 20" to 30". Some of them bear the Chopin foundry mark; they are presently worth from $4,000.00 up. Other excellent artists were Schmidt Felling (19th Century), who specialized in mounted figures of cossacks wearing military uniforms, and Nicholas Leiberich (late 19th century), who also specialized in equestrian groups. Most of the pieces made by the above artists were signed and had the foundry mark (Chopin, Woerfell, etc.)

Russian porcelain is another field where Imperial connections have undoubtedly added to the interest of collectors and museums worldwide. The most important factories were: Imperial Russian Porcelain, St. Petersburg (or Petrograd or Leningrad, 1744-1917); Gardner, Moscow (1765-1872); Kuznetsoff, St. Petersburg and Moscow (1800-1900); Korniloff, St. Petersburg (1800-1900); and Babunin, St. Petersburg (1800-1900).

Beaker, repousse/chased silver, gilt int, ball ft, 1761, 2½" 700.00
Cigarette box, silver w/enamel portraits, malachite clasp 1,375.00
Cigarette case, silver, Ivanov, 1873 ....260.00
Cigarette case, wht metal, CCCP/plane/factory emb, 4½" 1,400.00

Silver easter egg, Pavel Ovchinnikov, chased and engraved to appear as basketwork, gilt interior, on silver gilt stand, ca 1896-1908, 4½", $1,300.00.

Egg, porc w/HP floral on lt gr, Imperial Porc Factory, 1890 ....700.00
Egg, wht w/gold crowned monogram for Alexandra, 1900, 2½" .385.00
Figurine, peasant mother & child, porc, Gardner, 1885, 6⅝" 750.00
Hot water kettle, silver, Faberge, Moscow, 1900, 12"+stand ...3,300.00
Icon, silver, riza cased, Madonna & Child, Moscow, 1863, 11" .1,200.00
Icon, silver-gilt, Christ Pantocreator, Moscow, 1884, 8¾" 2,500.00
Icon, silver-gilt/pearls/jewels, mother of Kazan, 1775, 13" 1,200.00
Inkwell & tray, silver w/HP birds/flowers, Bradley, 1890s, 8" ..1,650.00
Match holder, lacquered papier-mache, peasant lady, 1800s 450.00
Salt cellar, scroll & star champleve, red/gr/wht, mk NK, 2½" 425.00
Salt cellar, silver w/mc HP florals, mk, 2" dia 225.00
Spoon, champleve enamel, blk/red/bl, stylized decor, 5", pr 550.00
Spoon, enameled, mk CK, Gustav Klingert, 1896, 4½" 115.00
Spoon, silver-gilt & enamel, floral, twist hdl, ca 1900, 7" 250.00

Stirrup cup, silver, ram's head form, ruby eyes, 1860s, 3" **2,800.00**
Tankard, silver, 4 eng bands, floral finial, lyre hdl, 1850 ....**495.00**
Tea set, silver-gilt & enamel, floral finial/decor, 3-pc **4,700.00**
Teapot, enamel w/fighting cocks, onyx set in hdl, #84, 6" **900.00**
Teapot, silver w/eng band, ivory hdl/finial, Dubrovin, 1800 ....**650.00**
Tray, silver, appl dragonfly/leaf/spider, Ovchinnikov, 13" **2,000.00**
Waste bowl, silver w/enamel floral, 1880s, 4" **700.00**

Sabino

Sabino art glass was produced by Marius-Ernest Sabino in France during the 1920s and '30s. It was made in opalescent, frosted, and colored glass and was designed to reflect the Art Deco style of that era. In 1960 using molds he modeled by hand, Sabino once again began to produce art glass using a special formula he himself developed that was characterized by a golden opalescence. Although the family continued to produce glassware for export after his death in 1971, they were never able to duplicate Sabino's formula.

Charger, 3 swimming nudes, spirals, 11¾" **545.00**
Figurine, butterfly, sgn, 5¾", NM **350.00**
Figurine, butterfly, 2¾" **30.00**
Figurine, cherub, sm **28.00**
Figurine, L'i Lole, nude seated in lotus position, 8½" **2,000.00**
Figurine, nude w/doves, 6½" **350.00**
Figurine, nude w/long flowing hair, opal, 7" **500.00**

Lamp base, Lex Oiseaux, six frosted panels with birds and flowering branches, gilt bronze mounts, #4449, 32", $3,850.00.

Vase, birds of paradise, bulbous, 9½" **1,100.00**
Vase, Enlacements, blown, 5" **325.00**
Vase, flock of swallows/2 setting suns, 7" **125.00**
Vase, Gaiete, 8 dancers, ca 1920s, 14" **1,800.00**
Vase, overlapping concentric arcs, flared/ftd U-form, 6" **345.00**
Vase, Vallon, 10¾" **950.00**

Salesman's Samples and Patent Models

Salesman's samples and patent models are often mistaken for toys or homemade folk art pieces. They are instead actual working models made by very skilled craftsmen who worked as model-makers. Patent models were made until the early 1900s. After that, the patent office no longer required a model to grant a patent. The name of the inventor or the model-maker and the date it was built is sometimes noted on the patent model. Salesman's samples were occasionally made by model-makers, but often they were assembled by an employee of the company.

These usually carried advertising messages to boost the sale of the product. Though they are still in use today, the most desirable examples date from the 1800s to about 1945.

Many small stoves are incorrectly termed a 'salesman's sample'; remember that no matter how detailed one may be, it must be considered a toy unless accompanied by a carrying case, the indisputable mark of a salesman's sample.

Bowl, livestock watering; CI w/wooden base, 11x14x9", EX **15.00**
Buckboard, AH Spiller Builder, pnt wood, 1800s, 29" **1,955.00**
Buggy, dr's, leather seats, brass running gear, 21" L, EX **1,500.00**
Clothes wringer, wood & CI, M **200.00**
Decoy, Canada goose, Wildfowler Factory, NM pnt, sm dents ...**400.00**
Decoy, Mallard drake, Hays Factory, EX orig pnt, hairline **500.00**
Dumbwaiter, Storm Mfg, Pat Apr 19, 1883, 17¼x5½x5½" **700.00**
Gate latch, wood & iron, Pat Dec 1, 1874, 11x10" **100.00**
Lock, combination safe; Sargent & Greenleaf NY, 1875, 5¼" **250.00**
Pan, Royal Super Ware, aluminum, 3" (w/hdl), 1¼" dia **135.00**
Pump, bronze & CI, Lewis Kirk on brass plate, 28½" **175.00**
Scrubbing machine, dvtl cherry w/cast brass mts, 11½" **100.00**
Ski binder, metal & wood, Caroll Pressed Metal Co, 24x2½" **45.00**
Skis, Oxford, West Paris, Maine, 24", pr **100.00**
Steam injector, Sellers, Pat Apr 24, 1860, 22½", EX **1,000.00**
Steam slide valve mechanism, brass/steel/mahog, 25" L **400.00**

Salt Shakers

The screw-top salt shaker was invented by John Mason in 1858. In 1871 when salt became more refined, some ceramic shakers were molded with pierced tops. 'Christmas' shakers, so called because of their December 25, 1877, patent date, were fitted with a rotary agitator designed to break up any lumps in the salt. There are four types: Christmas Barrel (rare in cranberry and amethyst); Christmas Panel (rare in colors); Christmas Pearl (opaque, pearly white with painted decor); and Octagon Waffle (clear, thick glass made in three sizes with a rotary agitator, sometimes having undated tops). The dated tops and patented agitators were produced by Dana K. Alden of Boston, who contracted with various glasshouses to make the glass bodies. The Christmas Barrel and Christmas Panel patterns were produced by Boston and Sandwich (though the Christmas Barrel was made elsewhere as well). Alden contracted with Mt. Washington to make the Christmas Pearl pattern, and Waffle Octagon was made by several glass factories, McKee and Federal among them. Both of the latter patterns were made as late as 1900. Identical shakers which have no agitator or dated top are the companion peppers; these fetch about 30% less than the salts on today's markets.

Today's Victorian salt shaker collectors' interest primarily encompasses art glass, decorated cranberry and ruby, and custard and colored opalescent examples. (See also specified categories.) If you would like to learn more abut Victorian glass salt shakers, we recommend *The World of Salt Shakers, Second Edition*, by Mildred and Ralph Lechner; their address may be found in the Directory under Virginia. (Mildred and Ralph deal only in Victorian shakers; please do not contact them with questions pertaining to novelty types.) In the following listings, prices are for single shakers unless noted 'pair.' Values are for old, original shakers. Some of these may have been reproduced, and this will be noted in the description.

Beaded Oval Mirror, bl opaque, Challinor/Taylor, 1866-91, 3¼" ..**60.00**
Beaded Twist, wht opaque, vertical ribs, Gillinder, 1890s, 3¾" **35.00**
Beads & Bulges, cranberry, Consolidated, 1894-1900, 3⅜" **85.00**
Block & Star, bl opaque, Fenton, 1955-56, 2¾" **30.00**
Bulging Loops, yel cased **105.00**
Bulging Petal, bl opaque **48.00**

Button Arches, ruby stained, Oriental Glass Co, ca 1906 ....40.00
Cambridge #1035, crystal, cut florals, 1935-45, 3⅛" 20.00
Christmas Barrel, amber, w/lid (dtd) & agitator, Alden 100.00
Christmas Barrel, apple gr, w/lid, & agitator 110.00
Christmas Barrel, cobalt, w/lid & agitator, +pepper, pr 200.00
Christmas Barrel, cranberry, w/lid & agitator 325.00
Christmas Barrel, cranberry, w/lid & agitator, +pepper & fr, pr ..600.00
Christmas Barrel, dk amethyst, w/lid & agitator 100.00
Christmas Barrel, gr, w/lid & agitator, 2½" 70.00
Christmas Barrel, peacock bl, w/lid & agitator, +pepper, pr 250.00
Christmas Panel, amethyst, w/lid & agitator 250.00
Christmas Panel, cranberry, w/lid & agitator 300.00
Christmas Panel, sapphire bl, w/lid & agitator 225.00
Clematis & Scroll, bl opaque, on orig glass stand, pr 115.00
Cord & Tassle, Dbl; pk opaque, Consolidated, 1894-1900, 2" 60.00
Corn, custard opaque, tapered ear, Dithridge, 1894-1901, 3⅛" 65.00
Cosmos, wht opaque w/yel floral, Consolidated, ca 1900, 3⅜" 47.00
Cotton Bale, bl opaque, Consolidated, 1894-1900, 2⅝" 35.00
Dbl Deck, wht opaque, corn over scrolls, Dithridge, 2¾" 35.00
Ear, gr opaque, Dithridge, 1894-1900, 3" 45.00
Fenton Swirl, lt pk opaque, ca 1954, 3⅛" 35.00
Findlay, Spattered; frosted crystal mc dots, Dalzell, 1888-90, 3" .125.00
Flared Rib, bl opaque, 1894-1900, 3" 35.00
Floral Neck, wht opaque opal w/red & gilt goofus pnt, 3⅛" 25.00
Flower Band, pigeon blood, Lancaster Glass, ca 1901 ....85.00
Forget-Me-Not, bl 30.00
Forget-Me-Not, pk opaque, Challinor 45.00
Gaudy Scroll, wht opal, 1900-08, 2½" 15.00
Grape, gilted opalware opaque, Eagle, 1900-10, 3⅞" 18.00
Hobnail, bl opal, Fenton, 1950-54, 2¾" 23.00
Horseshoe & Aster, vaseline, Challinor/Taylor, 1890s, 3½" 90.00
Iowa, clear w/EX gold, US Glass, 2¾" 40.00
Jefferson Optic, amethyst 45.00
Jefferson Optic, sapphire bl w/HP wht Shasta daisies, pr 155.00
Josephine's Fan, Robinson, 2⅝" 20.00
Leaf, 4-Sided; gr opaque w/decor, Gillinder, 1890-96, 2⅜" 31.00
Leaf & Flower, rose stain & HP decor, Hobbs, 1890-92, 3¼" 100.00
Little Acorn, bl opaque, US Glass, 6¼" 30.00
Long Petal Daisy, gr opaque, Consolidated, 1904, 3½" 75.00
Loop & Daisy, Mt WA 85.00
Minnesota, bulbous, US Glass, 2¾" 37.00
Moon & Stars Jeweled, amber-stained crystal, Co-op Flint, 1896 ..36.00
Octagon Waffle, w/agitator & dtd 1877 lid, 3" 50.00
Palm Leaf, pk 30.00
Panelled Sprig, cranberry 85.00
Petticoat, vaseline w/EX gold, 3" 65.00
Pineapple & Fans, ruby-stained crystal, Heisey, 1896-97, 2⅞" 60.00
Poppy, pk irid carnival, flowers & wedges, Imperial, 1975-82, 3" .15.00
Quilted Pineapple 40.00
Rabbit, HP gilted opalware opaque, Eagle, 1900-10, 2⅝" 35.00
Radiant, worn gold, Pat 1887 top, ca 1887, 3" 90.00
Rib, Pointed; bl opaque, Dithridge, 1896-1902, 2⅞" 40.00
Rib & Scroll, lime gr opaque, Consolidated, 1904-05, 3" 46.00
Ribbed Melon, wht opaque opalware, 1890-97, 2⅝" 38.00
Ring Neck, pk & wht opaque, Hobbs, 1889-90, 3" 135.00
Roman Rosette, clear w/ruby stain, US Glass, 3" 80.00
Scroll, Bottom; bl opaque, Consolidated, 1896-1902, 2⅝" 45.00
Seashell, chocolate & off-wht slag, Challinor/Taylor, 1890s, 3⅜" .87.00
Six-Beaded Panel, bl opaque, 1897, 1901, 3⅝" 40.00
Spider Web, pk opaque, emb web overall, Dithridge, 1894-97 .....40.00
Square S, bl opaque, S on side, Challinor/Taylor, 1890s, 3¼" 35.00
Swirl & Leaf, pk opaque, swirls in middle, Dithridge, 1894-1900 ..65.00
Tall Pansy, bl opaque, 1894-1900, 3⅝" 35.00
Tapered Scroll, pk opaque 55.00

Tapered Scroll, pk slag 185.00
Texas, US Glass, 2¾" 30.00
Thistle & Fern, frosted w/Goofus decor, McKee, 1901-06, 2⅜" 70.00
Thousand Eye, vaseline, hobnails w/diamonds, Adams, 1880........50.00
Three Face, clear frosted, 2⅝" (+) 125.00
Thrush, wht opaque, bird on branch, Dalzell, 1890s, 2¾" 135.00
Valencia Waffle, bl, blocks & stars, Adams, 1883-87, 3" 30.00
Vertical Opal Ribbon, clear w/wht opal stripes, 2½" 36.00
Vine 25.00
Winsome, 6 concave vertical panels, Riverside, 3⅛" 20.00

Novelty

Those interested in novelty shakers will enjoy *Salt and Pepper Shakers, Volumes I, II, III,* and *IV* by Helene Guarnaccia, and *The Collector's Encyclopedia of Salt and Pepper Shakers, Figural and Novelty, Volumes I* and *II,* by Melva Davern. Both are available at your local library or from Collector Books. Note: 'Mini' shakers are no taller than 2". Instead of having a cork, the user was directed to 'use tape to cover hole.' Our advisor for Novelty Salt Shakers is Judy Posner; she is listed in the Directory under Pennsylvania. See also Regal; Occupied Japan; other specific manufacturers.

Advertising, Bud Man, 1970s, pr 275.00
Advertising, Coors, beer bottle, pottery, pr 55.00
Advertising, Dairy Queen Girls, pr 275.00
Advertising, Elsie's children (Beulah & Beauregard), pr 85.00
Advertising, Farmwell Feeds, farmer figural, pr 185.00
Advertising, Harvey Railroad Girls, pr 225.00
Advertising, Homepride Flour, Fred, hard plastic, English, pr......85.00
Advertising, Magic Chef, milk glass, pr 75.00
Advertising, Magic Chef, plastic, pr 65.00
Advertising, Magic Chef, pottery, pr 110.00
Animal, cocker spaniel, realistic, pr 28.00
Animal, giraffe, realistic, pr 16.00
Animal, hippo chefs 'Cook' & 'Cookie,' Lefton, pr 24.00
Animal, monkey, sitting, realistic, pr 16.00
Animal, monkey & palm tree, pr 22.00
Animal, monkey mother w/hanging baby, pr 22.00
Animal, 3 Wise Monkeys, 1-pc set 45.00
Anthromorphic, banana head fellow, pr 26.00
Anthromorphic, cactus people, happy & sad, pr 50.00
Anthromorphic, coffeepot-head boy & teapot-head girl, pr 38.00
Anthromorphic, fork & spoon couple, brn skin tone, pr 55.00
Anthromorphic, keg cowgirl & mug cowboy, PY, EX, pr 85.00

Banana people, paper Japan sticker, 3½", $25.00 for the pair.

Character, barber chair & hair clippers, pr 45.00
Character, circus clown elephant, ruffled collar, pr 28.00
Character, drunk & lamppost, pr 22.00
Character, frog musican playing instrument, pr 45.00

Character, Ike, head stacks on shoulders, pr 95.00
Character, Indian chief & brave, detailed, pr 35.00
Character, martini & aspirin, old version, pr 36.00
Comic, Bonzo pup, bl scarf & cane, pr 22.00
Comic, Kayo & Moon Mullins, chalkware, early, pr 65.00
Comic, Popeye & Olive Oyl, old, pr 250.00
Comic, Snoopy & Woodstock, pr 75.00
Comic, Vallona Star, man in doghouse/woman w/rolling pin, pr ..95.00
Comic, Wimpy w/hamburger, brn skin tone, pr 225.00
Disney, Donald Duck condiment set, tongue is spoon 325.00
Disney, Mickey & Minnie Mouse, Leeds, pr 45.00
Disney, Mickey Mouse, Dan Brechner Imports, pr 225.00
Disney, Pinocchio, early, pr 195.00
Disney, Pinocchio & Stromboli's girl marionette, pr 150.00
Disney, Snow White napkin holder w/dwarf shakers, Enesco 550.00
Disney, Winnie the Pooh & Rabbit, Enesco, pr on tray 295.00
Mini, change purse & pocket watch, pr 28.00
Mini, cowboy boot, pr 30.00
Mini, cowboy hat & gun & holster, pr 35.00
Mini, gold thread & needle, pr 30.00
Mini, jam jar & pan of rolls, pr 35.00
Mini, Old King Cole & fiddlers, bone china, pr 125.00
Mini, straw holder & ice cream soda, pr 30.00
Mini, thermos & lunch pail, pr 32.00
Nude or naughty, nude to waist couple, brn skin tones, pr 58.00
Nude or naughty, outhouse couple, Hurry I Can Hardly Wait, pr ..42.00
Nursery rhyme/fairy tale, Arab on magic carpet, pr 45.00
Nursery rhyme/fairy tale, cat & fiddle, blk & wht, pr 30.00
Nursery rhyme/fairy tale, Gingham Dog & Calico Cat, pr 35.00
Nursery rhyme/fairy tale, Mary & lamb, pr 25.00
Nursery rhyme/fairy tale, Robin Hood, pr 45.00
Nursery rhyme/fairy tale, Snow White, not mk Disney, '30s, pr .275.00
Vegetable people, beet & carrot head ladies, pr 35.00
Vegetable people, carrot fellow, winking, pr 22.00
Vegetable people, corn & turnip head ladies, pr 28.00
Vegetable people, cucumber fellow, pr 24.00
Vegetable people, pea & beet fellows, pr 35.00

Salts, Open

Before salt became refined, processed, and free-flowing as we know it today, it was necessary to serve it in a salt cellar. An innovation of the early 1800s, the master salt was placed by the host and passed from person to person. Smaller individual salts were a part of each place setting. A small silver spoon was used to sprinkle it onto the food.

If you would like to learn more about the subject of salts, we recommend *5,000 Open Salts*, written by William Heacock and Patricia Johnson, with many full-color illustrations and current values. Our advisor for this category is Chris Christensen; he is listed in the Directory under California. In the listings below, the numbers refer to *Open Salts* by Johnson and Heacock and *Pressed Glass Salt Dishes* by L.W. and D.B. Neal. Lines with 'repro' within the description reflect values for reproduced salts.

Key:
EPNS — electroplated nickel silver   HM — hallmarked

Cameo, Art Glass, and Miscellaneous

Daum Nancy, windmill scene, HJ-10 ....850.00
Daum Nancy, winter scene 950.00
Doulton, Lambeth, sterling HM rim, HJ-1851, ca 1900 ....85.00
Intaglio, animals or butterfly HP, sgn, HJ-159 ....45.00

Intaglio, bl, gr, etc, unsgn, HJ-215 ....15.00
Lutz, red/wht/gold striping, blown, ftd master, 1½x⅞" 60.00
Millefiori: European, HJ-609, ca 1900, 2" dia 450.00
Monot & Stumpf, HJ-19, ca 1900, ind 95.00
Moorcroft, sterling HM rim, London, HJ-1762, ca 1920 ....65.00
Mt Washington, HJ-35 to HJ-44, unsgn 95.00
Opal w/vaseline ruffles, HJ-72 ....110.00
Plique-a-jour, Viking boat, Norway, 930S, HJ-83, 2½" 750.00
Royal Doulton, sterling HM rim, HJ-1870, ca 1873 ....115.00
Sowerby, bl slag, HJ-385 ....110.00
Sowerby, cream opaque, HJ-385 ....75.00
Sowerby, HJ-385 & HJ-2090, sgn & #d, ea 75.00
Sowerby, purple slag, HJ-385, ca 1880 ....95.00
Steuben, Calcite, ped ft, HJ-34 ....225.00
Tiffany, bl, ruffled top, sgn, HJ-30 ....375.00
Tiffany, pulled ears, sgn, HJ-3 ....275.00
Tiffany, witch's pot, sgn, HJ-1 ....275.00
Webb, Burmese, HJ-75, ca 1890, 1¾" dia 650.00
Webb, 2-color, sgn, HJ-84 ....900.00
Wedgwood, sterling rim, sgn, HJ-1850, ca 1897 ....160.00

China and Porcelain

Austria, HP, mk, HJ-1272, rnd, ind 12.00
Belleek, HP, ruffled top, mk, HJ-1310, rnd, ind 35.00
Celery salt, HP, HJ-1720, ind 15.00
Dresden, attached flowers, HJ-1689, ind 45.00
Elfinware, heavy decor, sgn Germany, HJ-1270, ind 30.00
Elfinware, Japan, HJ-1222, ind 10.00
Elfinware, tub, sgn Germany, HJ-1250, ind 25.00
Elfinware, wheelbarrow, sgn Germany, HJ-1244, ind 65.00
Haviland, HJ-1400, ind 35.00
HP, artist sgn, scalloped ft, HJ-1390, ind 20.00
Limoges, HP, mk, HJ-1275, rnd, ind 12.00
Meissen, HJ-1595, sq, ind 60.00
Nippon, celery salt, HJ-1714, ind 10.00
Nippon, HP, HJ-1365, ind 10.00
Nippon, HP, ped ft, HJ-1495, ind 20.00
Nippon, HP floral tub, HJ-1454, ind 20.00
Pickard, HJ-1569, sq, ind 45.00
Royal Bayreuth, animal decor, ped ft, HJ-1666, ind 135.00
Royal Bayreuth, figural claw, HJ-1667, ind 75.00
Royal Copenhagen, HJ-1332, ind 25.00
Royal Worcester, HJ-1861, ca 1862, ind 120.00
Satsuma, HJ-1931, ca 1940-60, ind 25.00

Cut Glass

Clark, ped ft, sgn, HJ-3009 ....25.00
Cranberry, ped ft, etched, HJ-123, ca 1890 ....110.00
Dmn Point, HJ-3101 ....15.00
English Strawberry & Dmn Cut, oval tub, HJ-2857 ....35.00
Faceted, HJ-2919 ....10.00
Hawkes, sgn, HJ-3064 ....55.00
Heart, spade, dmn, club, HJ-3034 to HJ-3035, 4 for 160.00
J Hoare, sgn, HJ-3166 ....45.00
Waterford, ped ft, sgn, HJ-3698, ca 1970 ....45.00
Waterford type, gr, ped ft, HJ-601, ca 1860 ....150.00
Waterford type, ped ft, HJ-3699, ca 1860 ....75.00
Zippered, HJ-3088 ....10.00

Doubles

Austria Hungary, HM sterling, w/mustard, HJ-751, 1850s, M 350.00

Automobile, pressed glass, mk Pontieux, HJ-3764 ....55.00
European, 800 sterling, figural, cobalt inserts, HJ-2062 ....125.00
French, cobalt pressed glass, HJ-2087 ....55.00
French, pressed glass figural, HJ-3777 ....35.00
French, sterling HM, cobalt insert, HJ-761, ca 1845 ....150.00
German, HP porc, HJ-1150 ....45.00
KPM, figural, porc, HJ-1155 to HJ-1156, ca 1860, ea 295.00
KPM, porc, wht w/gold border, HJ-1142 ....35.00
Meissen, porc, w/hdl, HJ-1169 ....125.00
Quimper, porc, sgn, HJ-1134 ....110.00
Quimper, porc, sgn, old, HJ-1135 ....65.00

Lacy Glass

American, non-flint, ca 1920-40, repro, VG 45.00
Avon, #3506, repro 5.00
French, amber, non-flint, #1771, ca 1920-40, repro, VG 65.00
Metro Museum of Art, vaseline, bl, etc, MMA, repro, VG 15.00
Neal BF-1, basket of flowers, #3462, VG 75.00
Neal BF-1B, opal, basket of flowers, chip on leg 175.00
Neal BS-2, opal, Beaded Scroll, Sandwich, NM 175.00
Neal BS-3, chalk wht, Beaded Scroll, Sandwich, EX 400.00
Neal BS-3, dk opaque violet, Beaded Scroll 750.00
Neal BT-2, cobalt, boat, Stourbridge, NM 850.00
Neal BT-8, cobalt, boat, Sandwich, VG 950.00
Neal BT-9, opal, boat, NM 400.00
Neal BT-9, violet, boat, NM 500.00
Neal CD-3, w/lid, NM 700.00
Neal CN-1A, crown, Sandwich, NM 125.00
Neal CT-1A, chariot, Sandwich, VG 175.00
Neal DI-18, divided, French, NM 175.00
Neal DI-4, sapphire, divided, NM 900.00
Neal DI-8, dbl, #3460, roughage on bottom 140.00
Neal DS-11, opal, Strawberry Dmn, Sandwich, NM 420.00
Neal EE-3B, eagles on 4 corners, VG 175.00
Neal EE-3B, opal, eagle, NM 350.00
Neal GA-2, cobalt, Cathedral Windows, leg chipped 195.00
Neal GA-2A, med bl, Gothic Arch, minor chips 400.00
Neal HN-18A, opal, ftd, #4460, VG 250.00
Neal MV-1, dk aqua, sq/ftd, Mt Vernon Glass Co, EX 240.00
Neal NE-1A, wht opaque, NE Glass Co, EX 175.00
Neal NE-1A, wht opaque, NE Glass Co, minor roughage, NM ..225.00
Neal NE-5, lt gr, NE Glass Co, NM 300.00
Neal OG-2, heart, NE Glass Co, EX 125.00
Neal OG-4, violet bl, oval, Pittsburgh, EX 700.00
Neal OL-17, minor chips, 3½" L 45.00
Neal OL-9, oblong, Pittsburgh, EX 275.00
Neal OO-1, dk amethyst, octagonal oblong, Sandwich, EX 425.00
Neal OO-1A, NM 60.00
Neal OP-1, ftd, Sandwich, EX 200.00
Neal OP-17, oblong, Sandwich, NM 200.00
Neal OP-2, clambroth, ftd oval, Sandwich, NM 300.00
Neal PE-1, beaded base, Providence Flint Glass, NM 100.00
Neal PO-4, cobalt, Peacock Eye, NM 750.00
Neal PR-1C, violet-bl, Peacock Eye, rnd, Sandwich, NM 700.00
Neal RP-17, rnd w/ped base, Sandwich, EX 210.00
Neal SC-16, cobalt, French, EX 1,200.00
Neal SC-6, cobalt, scroll, EX 425.00
Neal SD-2A, Strawberry Dmn, paw ft, Sandwich, NM 50.00
Neal SD-4, Strawberry Dmn, Sandwich, EX 100.00
Neal SD-7, cobalt, Strawberry Dmn, Sandwich, NM 400.00
Neal SL-14, opal, shell, Sandwich, EX 225.00
Neal SN-1B, clambroth, stag's horn, EX 225.00
Neal WN-1, wagon, Sandwich, EX 450.00

Pressed Pattern Glass, Clear

Beaded Acorn Leaf Band, HJ-3609, flint, master 65.00
Bearded Head, HJ-3636, master 40.00
Bird & Berry, sgn Degenhart, HJ-998, ind 35.00
Bird & Berry, unsgn Degenhart, HJ-998, ind 25.00
Bow Tie, HJ-2548, ind 25.00
Brazilian, HJ-2572, ind 15.00
Butterfly, HJ-3539, master 45.00
Chicken, covered, sgn Vallerysthal, HJ-958 to HJ-960, ind 55.00
Daisy & Button, LG Wright, HJ-875 & HJ-876, repro, ind, ea 5.00
English Hobnail, HJ-2680, ind 8.00
Euchre, HJ-3018 to HJ-3021, ind, ea 12.00
Faceted, HJ-2910, ind 6.00
Heisey, Fancy Loop, HJ-2674, ind 25.00
Heisey, Fandango, HJ-2673, ind 30.00
Heisey, tub, sgn, HJ-2850 ....25.00
Horseshoe, HJ-3741, ind 27.00
Liberty Bell 1776-1876, HJ-2689, ind 55.00
Moon & Star, HJ-3044, 1940s, ind 15.00
Moon & Star, ped ft, HJ-3044, old, ind 45.00
Open Plaid, HJ-3567, master 15.00
Panelled Grape Band, HJ-3516, master 35.00
Roman Key, HJ-3582, flint, master 55.00
Sawtooth Circle, HJ-3540, master 25.00
Snail, HJ-2656, ind 28.00
Stippled Bowl, HJ-3589, flint, master 65.00
Tree of Life, 'SALT,' HJ-3581, master 75.00
Tulip w/Sawtooth, HJ-3621, master 35.00
Turtle, HJ-3758, ind 35.00
Washington Centennial, HJ-3510, master 55.00

Pressed Pattern Glass, Colored

Bird & Berry, McKee, vaseline, amber or bl, HJ-997, ind, ea 55.00
Daisy & Button Triangle, bl, old, HJ-442, ind 25.00
Jersey Swirl, bl, HJ-426, ind 25.00
Moon & Star, all colors, repros, HJ-870, ind, ea 5.00
Tub, unmk Heisey, pk or gr, HJ-2850, ind, ea 25.00
Two-Panel, bl, gr or amber, HJ-429, ind, ea 20.00
Two-Panel, bl, gr or vaseline, HJ-564, master, ea 25.00
Wildflower w/turtle base, amber, HJ-506, master 150.00

Silverplate

American, cobalt liner, mk W&S, HJ-653 ....15.00
American, ruby liner, mk Derby, HJ-319 ....75.00
American, Victorian, crackle glass liner, Meriden, HJ-4215 ....85.00
English, ornate, w/babies, gold wash, ca 1880 ....125.00
English, ruby liner, paw ft, ca 1900 ....75.00
English, set of 4 w/spoons, ca 1880, MIB 100.00
English, vaseline ruffled Webb insert, HJ-95, ca 1880 ....225.00
European, vaseline ruffled liner, HJ-91, ca 1880 ....125.00

Sterling and Continental Silver

American, ped ft, HJ-4034, ca 1930 ....35.00
Dutch, cobalt liner, HM, HJ-713, ca 1880, 4-pc set 300.00
English, gr liner, HJ-379, ind 75.00
French, cobalt liner, HJ, HJ-720, ca 1845, master 175.00
French, liner & spoon, HJ-3937, ind 135.00
German, HJ-4286, ca 1800, master, pr 500.00
German 800, HJ-3983 ....45.00
Gorham, medallion, ped ft, HJ-3976, ca 1860 ....175.00

Gorham, plain, HJ-3992, ca 1920 ....**30.00**
Gorham, ruby liner, HJ-323, ca 1890 ....**150.00**
Russian, chair, HM, HJ-4735, ca 1890 ....**450.00**
Swan, cut glass w/835 sterling wings, old, HJ-4287 ....**55.00**

Swedish, M. Troller, stylized lizards, #925/#830, approximately 15 troy ounces, 8⅛", $935.00 for the pair.

Viking, Norway boat, plique-a-jour **1,750.00**
Viking, 900, Norway boat, enameled, HJ-2002 ....**125.00**
Viking, 900, Norway boat, HJ-4260, w/stopper **75.00**

Samplers

American samplers were made as early as the the colonial days; even earlier examples from 17th-century England still exist today. Changes in style and decorative motif are evident down through the years. Verses were not added until the late 17th century. By the 18th century, samplers were used not only for sewing experience but also as an educational tool. Young ladies, who often signed and dated their work, embroidered numbers and letters of the alphabet and practiced fancy stitches as well. Fruits and flowers were added for borders; birds, animals, and Adam and Eve were popular subjects. Later houses and other buildings were included. By the 19th century, the American Eagle and the little red schoolhouse had made their appearances.

Many factors bear on value: design and workmanship, strength of color, the presence of a signature and/or a date (both being preferred over only one or the other, and earlier is better), and, of course, condition.

ABCs, numbers, verse, with roses and landscape work, multicolor threads on linen, signed, ca 1820, 18x17½", EX, $5,500.00.

ABCs, 4-color silk on homespun linen, sgn/1810, 17x10" **660.00**
ABCs (bold), 2-color on homespun, sgn, stains, fr, 14x11" **470.00**
ABCs & house, homespun, sgn/1809, fr, 18x11⅜" **600.00**
ABCs/Adam & Eve/buildings/etc, homespun, 174_, 43x10" ...**1,100.00**
ABCs/flower/birds/people/etc, initials/1836, fr, 11x14" **275.00**
ABCs/flowers/animals, homespun, sgn/1831, fading, fr, 25x18" .**550.00**

ABCs/flowers/chain, mc on homespun, sgn/1811, fr, 17x11" **275.00**
ABCs/flowers/German inscription, homespun, 1834, fr, 18x15" ..**495.00**
ABCs/geometrics/crowns/etc, homespun, sgn/1775, fr, 24x15" ...**550.00**
ABCs/hearse/gate keeper/etc, homespun, 1806, fr, 17x26" **1,485.00**
ABCs/house/dog/flag/etc, homespun, sgn, fr, 19x19" **1,700.00**
ABCs/house/trees/fence, homespun linen, sgn/1829, 18x14" ...**4,500.00**
ABCs/house/verse, 8-color, homespun, sgn/1824, 19x19", EX ..**3,650.00**
ABCs/house/willows/etc, homespun, sgn, fr, 21x17" **1,800.00**
ABCs/trees/tomb, sgn/1838, holes/stains, fr, 15x14" **660.00**
ABCs/verse, linen, sgn/1820, 16½x16½", EX **975.00**
ABCs/verse/buildings/etc, homespun, sgn/1780s, 17x15", VG ...**770.00**
ABCs/verse/flowers, homespun, sgn/1820, wear, fr, 17x9" **745.00**
ABCs/verse/flowers/etc, homespun, sgn, 17x12", VG **250.00**
ABCs/verse/flowers/etc, homespun, sgn/1814, fading, 23x22" **660.00**
ABCs/verse/wreath/etc, homespun, sgn/1832, fr, 25x23" **1,850.00**
ABCs/verses/inscription, sgn/1831, lt stain, 17x13" **690.00**
ABCs/10 Commandments in verse, homespun, 1899, 22x24" **600.00**
Adam & Eve/flowers/angels, homespun, sgn/1826, fr, 20x16" **990.00**
Alphanumerics/borders, homespun, sgn/1769, sm holes, 17x9" ..**850.00**
Alphanumerics/flowers, homespun, 1748, holes, fr, 17x25" **385.00**
Family record/flowers, homespun, sgn/1798, fr, 21x18" **500.00**
Family record/flowers/etc, homespun, 1788, wear, fr, 15x19" **275.00**
Geometric designs, some cut work, homespun, fr, 18½x10" **660.00**
House/flowers/trees/etc, homespun, sgn/1774, 19x16", VG **770.00**
Verse/Adam & Eve/tree/serpent/etc, sgn/1787, 17x18" **2,300.00**
Verse/church/house/etc, homespun, sgn/1828, fr, 18x18", VG ...**415.00**
Verse/flowers/angels/etc, homespun, 176_, wear, 29x24" **300.00**
Verse/flowers/birds/etc, homespun, sgn, damage, fr, 18x18" **525.00**
Verse/flowers/tree, homespun, sgn/1812, stains, 18x13" **300.00**
Verse/house/peacocks, homespun, boy's signature, 19x15" **2,000.00**
4-line verse/lg stag/flowers, sgn/dtd 1837, 19x14", VG **430.00**
6-line verse/lg house (detailed, 1801 over door), sgn, 22x21" **670.00**

Sandwich Glass

The Boston and Sandwich Glass Company was founded in 1820 by Deming Jarves in Sandwich, Massachusetts. Their first products were simple cruets, salts, half-pint jugs, and lamps. They were attributed as being one of the first to perfect a method for pressing glass, a step toward the manufacture of the 'lacy' glass which they made until about 1840. Many other types of glass were made there — cut, colored, snakeskin, hobnail, and opalescent among them. After the Civil War, profits began to dwindle due to the keen competition of the Western factories which were situated in areas rich in natural gas and easily accessible sand and coal deposits. The end came with an unreconcilable wage dispute between the workers and the company, and the factory closed in 1888. See also Cup Plates; Lacy Glass; Salts, Open; other specific types of glass.

Bottle, scent; Icicle, cranberry, orig overshot stopper, 9½" **475.00**
Bottle, scent; Loop, emerald gr, orig stopper, 8", EX **825.00**
Bottle, scent; teal gr, smooth base, orig Cologne label, 6½" **300.00**
Bottle, scent; turq opal, missing stopper, 1860s, 5⅛" **130.00**
Candlesticks, Petal & Loop, canary, 7, NM, pr **320.00**
Decanter, b3m, GV-8, flared mouth, period stopper, 1-pt **200.00**
Lamp, acanthus leaves on bl opaque base/wht opaque font, 12" ..**965.00**
Lamp, cut dbl o/l, pressed Baroque base, 1870s, 12½", EX **7,150.00**
Lamp, cut dbl o/l & gold w/gilt brass & marble base, 9½" **980.00**
Lamp, cut dbl o/l quatrefoil, marble base, 1850s, 12" **865.00**
Lamp, pressed cup plate base w/blown font, knop stem, 5¼" **880.00**
Lamp, Sweetheart, canary, dbl drop oil burner, late, 10" **285.00**
Lamp, 3-step base w/short stem, conical font, w/burner, 5⅛" ..**1,200.00**
Tumbler, b3m, GII-18, pale bl, tooled rim, pontil scar, 3⅛" **280.00**

Vase, Loop, canary, gauffered rim, knop base, 10" 375.00
Vase, pk satin w/camphor hdls, rib swirl, tooled rim, 10" 425.00
Vase, T'print, canary, tall knop std, 11½", (1 M/1 EX), pr 700.00
Wine, Sandwich Star, rare 215.00

Sarreguemines

Sarreguemines, France, is the location of Utzschneider and Company, founded in 1770, producers of majolica, transfer-printed dinnerware, figurines, and novelties which are usually marked 'Sarreguemines.'

Pitchers, head forms, 3½", $75.00 each.

Basket, quilted gr w/leopard skin crystals, Etna, 9" 225.00
Cup & saucer, strawberries, majolica, oversz 35.00
Figurine, Madonna standing & praying, creamware, 15" 70.00
Pitcher, brn crystalline, Etna, squat, 6x7" 195.00
Pitcher, man's face, night watchman, 7½" 230.00
Plate, Notre Dame 30.00
Plate, oyster; 6 shell wells, dk gr, 9¾" 100.00
Plate, soldiers transfer, 8½" 65.00
Vase, gr crackled, bulbous w/cylinder neck, 10" 200.00
Vase, Mid-Eastern decor, 8½" 398.00

Satin Glass

Satin glass is simply glassware with a velvety matt finish achieved through the application of an acid bath. This procedure has been used by many companies since the 20th century, both here and abroad, on many types of colored and art glass. See also Mother-of-Pearl.

Bowl, centerpc; bl shaded w/floral, SP ft, 8x10½" 225.00
Bowl, gr, emb X border, bent-up sides, ruffled/scalloped, 12" 150.00
Bowl, purple, 14" 300.00
Cookie jar, Fleurette, pk o/l, 6¼x5½" 195.00
Creamer, bl shaded w/floral, 6x4¾" 235.00
Ewer, peach shaded w/flowers & birds, thorn hdl, 13" 245.00
Jam dish, pk w/blk incised birds & berries, SP fr, 6½x4" 165.00
Pitcher, amber o/l, emb swirls, frosted reed hdl, 6½" 65.00
Pitcher, pk Hobnail, sqd mouth, camphor hdl, 7" 250.00
Rose bowl, cream w/mc/gold maidenhair fern, 8-crimp, 2¾" 75.00
Rose bowl, pk, florals & scrolls, 4x4⅜" 145.00
Rose bowl, pk o/l w/clear mat-su-noke & thorny base, 4x3" 395.00
Rose bowl, yel, emb shell around base, crimped, 3¾x4½" 65.00
Sweetmeat, pk o/l w/cream flowers/tan leaves, 3½x4½" 195.00
Vase, bl o/l, birds & appl jewels, ewer form, 10¾" 145.00
Vase, emb swirl on bl, ruffled top, 8½x4⅝", pr 198.00
Vase, ivory w/gold leaves & spirals, English, 5" 60.00
Vase, pk, ribbed, bulbous, 6¾", pr 150.00
Vase, pk o/l w/birds & floral, ruffled, 9½x4", pr 185.00

Vase, pk/wht/yel swirled stripes, ribbed, ruffled, 5" 100.00
Vase, rose w/appl mat-su-noke, frosted hdls, bulbous, 6" 350.00

Satsuma

Satsuma is a type of fine cream crackle-glaze pottery or earthenware made in Japan as early as the 17th century. The earliest wares, made at the original kiln in the Satsuma province, were enameled with only simple florals. By the late 18th century, a floral brocade (or nishikide design) was favored, and similar wares were being made at other kilns under the direction of the Lord of Satsuma. In the early part of the 19th century, a diaper pattern was added to the florals. Gold and silver enamels were used for accents by the latter years of the century. During the 1850s, as the quality of goods made for export to the western world increased and the style of decoration began to evolve toward becoming more appealing to the Westerners, human forms such as Arhats, Kannon, geisha girls, and samurai warriors were added. Today the most valuable pieces are those marked 'Kinkozan,' 'Shuzan,' 'Ryuzan,' and 'Kozan.' The genuine Satsuma 'mon' or mark is a cross within a circle — usually in gold on the body or lid, or in red on the base of the ware. Character marks may be included.

Caution: Much of what is termed 'Satsuma' comes from the Showa Period (1926 to the present); it is not true Satsuma but a simulated type, a cheaper pottery with heavy enamel. Our advisor for this category is Norma Angelo; she is listed in the Directory under New York.

Basket, floral/butterflies, Edo period, 3x3½" 185.00
Bowl, 3 figures on ornate ground w/florals, oval, 9¼" 130.00
Creamer, florals/beading, Edo period, 3½" 85.00
Jar, florals w/gold, jeweled rtcl neck, dome lid, 9¾" 225.00
Jar, immortals/attendants frieze, drum hdls, w/lid, sgn, 11" 750.00
Jar, seated Orientals, bk: children, allover mc/gilt, 16" 900.00
Kogo, bijin/children by well, mc on gilt, Hozan, 3½" 300.00
Plate, cranes, floral on scalloped edge, Edo period, 7" 90.00
Plate, floral/butterflies, rtcl edge, Edo period, 7½" 135.00
Teapot, birds on lt gr, bamboo spout/hdl, ca 1885, +2 c/s 110.00
Vase, bijin/landscape reserves, keyfret band, 1800s, 12", pr 1,650.00
Vase, birds/flowering trees/bldgs, dragon hdls, 5" 150.00
Vase, figural/floral panel, figural finial, 1900s, 7" 250.00
Vase, florals/fans w/genre panels & still life, slim, 9" 400.00
Vase, genre scene cartouch on brocade, 3 scroll ft, 3½x3½" 500.00
Vase, lg mc flowers, fine crackle, Awata, 1905, 12" 115.00
Vase, panels w/beauties, flowers & scene, bulbous, 4½" 150.00
Vase, samurai/beauties/parade/mums, w/gilt, long neck, 10" 600.00
Vase, 3 scenic panels on cobalt w/gold, hexagonal, sgn, 7" 275.00

Scales

In today's world of pre-measured and pre-packaged goods, it is difficult to imagine the days when such products as sugar, flour, soap, and candy first had to be weighed by the grocer. The variety of scales used at the turn of the century was highly diverse; at the Philadelphia Exposition in 1876, one company alone displayed over three hundred different weighing devices. Among those found today, brass, cast-iron, and plastic models are the most common. Fancy postal scales in decorative wood, silver, marble, bronze, and mosaic are also to be found.

A word of caution on the values listed: these values range from a low for those items in fair to good condition to the upper values for items in excellent condition. Naturally, items in mint condition could command even higher prices, and they often do. Also, these are **retail** prices that suggest what a collector will pay for the object. When you sell to a dealer, expect to get much less. These estimated values have been prepared by a committee of the International Society of Antique Scale Collectors under the direction of Robert Stein and George Mallis. The values noted are averages taken from various auction and other catalogues in the possession of the Society members. Among these, but not limited to, are the following: Joel L. Malter & Co., Inc., Encino, CA; *Collectors Journal of Ancient Art*, Joel L. Malter & Co., Inc.; Nobody's Bizness But Our Own, Storrs, CT; Craig A. Whitford Numismatic Auctions; *Auktion Alt Technic*, Auction Team, Koln, Germany; *Waaqgen Auktion Essen*, Auktion Karla W. Schenk-Behrens, Essen, Germany.

Those seeking additional information concerning antique scales are encouraged to contact the International Society of Antique Scale Collectors, whose address can be found in the Directory under Clubs, Newsletters, and Catalogs.

Key:
ap — arrow pointer
bal — balance
bm — base metal
br — brass
Brit — British
Can — Canadian
Col — Colonial
CW — Civil War
cwt — counterweight
Engl — English
eq — equal arm
Euro — European
FIS — Fairbanks Infallible
   Scale Co.

h — hanging
hcp — hanging counterpoise
hh — hand held
l+ — label with foreign coin values
lb w/i — labeled box with
   instructions
lph — letter plate or holder
pend — pendulum
PP — Patent Pending
st — sterling
tt — torsion type
ua — unequal arm
wt — weight

The Computing Scale Company, Dayton, Ohio, store type, $120.00.

Analytical (Scientific)

Am, eq, mahog w/br & ivory, late 1800s, 14x16x8", $200 to **400.00**

Apothecary (Druggist)

Am, tt bal, 2 marble pans/oak base, 1880s, 8x15x8", $150 to **250.00**

Assay

Am, eq, mahog box w/br & ivory, plaque/drw, 1890s, $250 to ...**350.00**

Coin: Equal Arm Balance, American

Am, blk japanned metal, eagle on lid, late 19th C, $125 to **225.00**
Col, oak 6-part box, Col moneys, Boston, 1720-75, $600 to ...**1,200.00**
Post Col to CW, oak 6-part box, label+, 1843, $400 to **1,000.00**

Coin: Equal Arm Balance, English

Charles I, wooden box w/11 Briot weights, 1640s, $900 to **1,500.00**
1-pc wood box, rnd wts, label, Freeman, 1760s, $250 to **450.00**
6-pc oak box, coin wts label, Thos Harrison, 1750s, $200 to **450.00**

Coin: Equal Arm Balance, French

Solid wood box w/recesses, 5 sq wts, A Gardes, 1800s, $250 to ..**800.00**
Solid wood box, 12 sq wts, J Reyne, Bourdeau, 1694, $400 to .**1,000.00**
1-pc oval box, nested/fractional wts, label, 1700s, $250 to **400.00**
1-pc oval box, no wts, label of Fr/Euro coins, 1700s, $150 to **250.00**
1-pc walnut box, nested wts, Charpentier label, 1810, $275 to ..**675.00**

Coin: Equal Arm Balance, Miscellaneous

Amsterdam, 1-pc box w/32 sq wts, label, late 1600s, $1000 to .**2,800.00**
Cologne, full set of wts & full label, late 1600s, $1200 to **2,800.00**

Counterfeit Coin Detectors, American

Allender Pat, lb w/i, cwt, Nov 22, 1855, 8½", $350 to **750.00**
Allender PP, rocker, labeled box, cwt, 1850s, 8½", $450 to **750.00**
Allender PP, space for $3 gold pc, lb w/i, cwt, 1855, $350 to **750.00**
Allender PP, space for $3 gold pc, no box/cwt, 1855, $275 to **375.00**
Allender Warranted, rocker, no box or cwt, 1850s, $250 to **475.00**
McNally-Harrison Pat 1882, rocker, cwt, JT McNally..., $275 to .**500.00**
McNally-Harrison Pat 1882, rocker, cwt/box, FIS, $400 to **750.00**
McNally-Harrison...1882, rocker, CI base, no cwt/box, $250 to .**400.00**
Thompson, Z-formed rocker, Berrian Mfg, 1877 Pat, $175 to **350.00**

Counterfeit Coin Detectors, English

Folding, Guinea, self rising, labeled box, 1850s, $125 to **175.00**
Folding, Guinea, self rising, wooden box, pre-1800, $175 to **275.00**
Rocker, simple, no maker's name or cb, end cap box, $85 to **125.00**
Rocker, w/maker's name & cb, end cap box, $120 to **150.00**

Diamond

Am, eq w/carat wts, 5" box, Kohlbusch, ca 1900, $175 to **225.00**

Postal

In the listings below an asterisk (*) was used to indicate that any one of several manufacturers' or brand names might be found on particular set of scales. Some of the American-made pieces could be marked Pelouze, Lorraine, Hanson, Kinsbury, IDL, Newman, Accurate, Ideal, B-T, Marvel, Reliance, Victor, Liberty, Gem, Superior, Landers-Frary-Clark, Chatillon, Triner, American Bank Service, or Weiss. European/U.S.-made scales marked with an asterisk (*) could be marked Salter, Peerless, Pelouze, Sturgis, L.F.&C., Alderman, G. Little, or S&D. English-made scales with the asterisk (*) could be marked Josh. & Edmd. Ratcliff, R.W. Winfield, S. Mordan, STS (Samuel S. Turner), W.&T. Avery, Parnall & Sons, S&P, or H.B. Wright. There may be other manufacturers as well.

Brit/Can Bal, eq, br or CI on base, *, 4"-15", $100 to **750.00**
Engl Bal, eq/Roberval, gilt or st, on stand, *, 3"-8", $500 to **2,500.00**
Engl Bal, eq/Roberval, plain to ornate, *, 3"-8", $100 to **2,500.00**
Engl Spring, candlestick, br or st, *, 3½"-15", $100 to **500.00**
Engl Spring, CI, br or NP fr, Salter, ozs/lbs, 7"-10", $25 to **200.00**
Engl Steelyard, ua, 1- or 2-beam, h lph, *, 4"-15", $100 to **1,500.00**
Euro pend, gravity, br, CI or NP fr on base, oz/grams, $75 to **350.00**

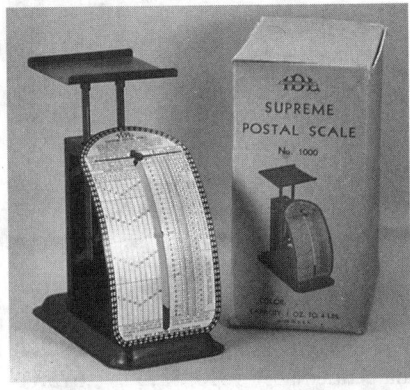

Supreme Postal Scale No 1000, 1 oz. up to 4 lbs., MIB, $40.00.

Euro pend, gravity, 2-arm, bm, br or NP, *, 6"-9", $50 to 300.00
Euro/US Spring, br or NP, pence/etc, h or hh, *, 4"-17", $10 to .. 100.00
US pend, gravity, metal, pnt face, ap, hcp, sm, $20 to 100.00
US Spring, pnt base metal, *, 2½"- 8", $10 to 80.00
US Spring, pnt bm, *, mtd on inkstand, 2½"-8", $75 to 250.00
US Spring, pnt bm, rnd glass-covered face, *, 8"-10", $25 to 100.00
US Spring, SP, oblong base, *, 2½"-8", $100 to 200.00
US Spring, st, oblong base, *, 2½"-8", $200 to 500.00
US Steelyard, ua, CI, *, 5"-13" beam, 4½"-12" base, $25 to 100.00

Schafer and Vater

Established in 1890 by Gustav Schafer and Gunther Vater in the Thuringia, a region of southwest Germany; by 1913 this firm employed two hundred workers. The original factory burned in 1918, but production and export continued until WWII. It is unlikely that they exported after the Wall was built.

Schafer & Vater's range was wide, and not all pieces are marked with the nine-point star (with 'R' inside) under a crown, but the collector soon learns to recognize their styles, color washes and wonderful sense of whimsy. The pieces without the marks are often impressed with a four-digit mold number and a two-digit artist mark. Although often marked 'Made in Germany' with blue or black ink, it is rare to find a piece with a crown and star mark in ink. Pieces that are ink-marked in this manner also have a splotch of glaze over the mark to protect it. None of the impressed-marked pieces are glazed underneath.

Another hallmark of this pottery is the fine texture of the clay used in production. Mined locally, it was rich with kaolin and resulted in a finished product with velvety texture and very fine grain. The glazed bisque pieces may be multicolored, decorated in brown and blue washes, and occasionally left entirely white. The glazes may be clear, iridescent or Tiffany type. Jasper items come in may colors, often layered for effect. Blue, green, pink, and lavenders are common, but brown, gray, ivory and other colors were used as well. Some items are decorated in more than one of these colors and may have white insets reminiscent of the traditional cameo (or one with an intricate floral or whimsical animals), Grecian scenes, comic characters and more. The light slip wash over some of the jasper items hugs the details and highlights intricate features of their fine modeling. Any jasper container is invariably glazed on the inside, and many of the dresser pieces and vases are 'jeweled' with spots of richly colored glaze applied as accents.

Many Schafer and Vater items find a place with cross-over collectibles such hatpin holders, dresser sets, match strikers, shaving mugs, razor banks, toothpick holders, tea sets, cups and saucers, and animal figures. The company was an authorized manufacturer of Rose O'Neill Kewpies. They made naughties and nudes well as 'nippers' or 'giveaways,' small glazed bottles used at the turn of the century to hold gifts of liquor for hotel and restaurant patrons. The giveaway bottles and the figural pitchers are very collectible. Many were made in a multitude of

sizes, ranging from 3" to 11". The liquor bottles were often sold with trays and shot glasses that would complement the figure.

The market for Schafer and Vater is highly volatile at this writing. As new collectors continue to enter the market, supply and demand definitely drive the price structure. Our advisor for this category is Dawn Ricker; she is listed in the Directory under Michigan. Anyone interested in the formation of a collector's society is welcome to contact her.

Ash keeper, baseball player, pnt loss 110.00
Bottle, A Ticklish Time 210.00
Bottle, boy holding bottle, gray jasper 175.00
Candle holder, rose, gr & wht 60.00
Figurine, lady looking down front of gown 225.00
Figurine, lady putting on stocking, rpr 125.00
Figurine, Mr Adam 250.00
Figurine, The Golfer 225.00
Figurine, The Masseuse 300.00
Hair receiver, angel & Cupid, mc on sq shape 75.00
Hair receiver, Art Nouveau decor w/jewels, kidney shape 90.00
Hair receiver, rose, wht & gr 40.00
Hatpin holder, cameo, cartouches, bl & pk 210.00
Hatpin holder, Egyptian head, brown jasper w/pk, jeweled 260.00
Hatpin holder, Egyptian head, lav & gr 225.00
Hatpin holder, geisha girl, lav 150.00
Hatpin holder, roses on tower, gr & wht 90.00
Hatpin holder/wall pocket, cameo 250.00
Humidor, Art Nouveau lady smoking, mold flaw 300.00
Humidor, Art Nouveau lady smoking, pk & gr 525.00
Match striker, Art Nouveau lady's head, smoking, chip 200.00
Pipe, woman's head 225.00
Pitcher, bl jasper w/ram-head spout 75.00
Pitcher, Dutch girl w/purse, holding wine jug, 3½" 125.00
Pot, Egyptian head, brn & pk 100.00
Tea set, cameo, 3-pc set, missing 1 lid 425.00
Vase, boy w/lg shoe & lobster, flake 120.00
Vase, dbl; roses, mc 60.00

Scheier

The Scheiers began their ceramics careers in the late 1930s and soon thereafter began to teach their craft at the University of New Hampshire. After WWII they cooperated with the Puerto Rican government in establishing a native ceramic industry, an involvement which would continue to influence their designs. In the fifties they retired and moved to Mexico; they currently reside in Arizona.

Bowl, bl mottle w/central brn swirl, brn ext, 2x15" 300.00
Bowl, gun-metal matt w/irid highlights, ftd, 4½x6" 350.00
Pastel, handmade paper, woman w/3 eyes+2 chicks, 1974, 17x12" .400.00
Plate, cvd fish & heads, blk on brn, 9" 300.00
Plate, 3 stylized faces (1 in fish), bl/purple matt, 9" 425.00
Sand/wood/nail painting, fertility scene, mc, rpr, 33x15" 700.00
Vase, aqua w/brn bkground exposed, thin walls, 3½x5½" 200.00
Vase, cvd co-joined human figures/faces, bl tones, 15x6" 800.00
Vase, dk bl over yel, U-form, 3¾x5" 200.00
Vase, dk gray/bl to chocolate, cvd lines, narrow neck, 7x5" 300.00
Vase, figures cvd inside fish forms, bulb w/stick neck, 5" 450.00
Vase, stylized lady in ovals, brn/speckled wht, 10½" 1,100.00

Schlegelmilch Porcelain

Authority Mary Frank Gaston, who is our advisor, has completed four volumes of *The Collector's Encyclopedia of R.S. Prussia* with full-color illustrations and current values. Mold numbers appearing in some of the listings refer to these books. You will find Mrs. Gaston's address in the Directory under Texas.

Key:
BM — blue mark   SM — steeple mark
GM — green mark   RM — red mark

E.S. Germany

Fine chinaware marked 'E.S. Germany' or 'E.S. Prov. Saxe' was produced by the E.S. Schlegelmilch factory in Suhl in the Thuringia region of Prussia from sometime after 1861 until about 1925.

Bowl, flowers & ferns, shell mold, mk, 4¾x8¼" 145.00
Cake plate, roses reserve on MOP w/gold, open hdls, 11" 200.00
Candy dish, 4 portrait medallions, Recamier, 7" 175.00
Celery vase, apples w/mc trim, mk, 12" 95.00
Chamberstick, bl flowers, cobalt inner border, mk, 2x6" 120.00
Cup & saucer, Queen Louise portrait, floral reserves, mk 185.00
Egg dish, pastel flowers, gold ruffled rim, center hdl, mk 450.00
Plate, lady's portrait, scalloped gold rim, hdls, mk, 9½" 175.00
Plate, spotted horse, mk, 7" 85.00
Urn, Cupids & flowers on pk, unmk, w/lid, 12½" 195.00
Vase, lady w/doves, gargoyles in relief at hdls, mk, 12" 1,350.00
Vase, lady w/peacock, lady w/doves on verso, mk, 10" 850.00
Vase, mythological, pearl lustre, mk, 6" 130.00

R.S. Germany

In 1869 Reinhold Schlegelmilch began to manufacture porcelain in Suhl in the German province of Thuringia. In 1894 he established another factory in Tillowitz in upper Silesia. Both areas were rich in resources necessary for the production of hard-paste porcelain. Wares marked with the name 'Tillowitz' and the accompanying 'R.S. Germany' phrase are attributed to Reinhold. The most common mark is a wreath and star in a solid color under the glaze. Items marked 'R.S. Germany' are usually more simply decorated than R.S. Prussia. Some reflect the Art Deco trend of the 1920s. Certain hand-painted floral decorations and themes such as 'Sheepherder,' 'Man with Horses,' and 'Cottage' are especially valued by collectors — those with a high-gloss finish or on Art Deco shapes in particular. Not all hand-painted items were painted at the factory. Those with an artist's signature but no 'Hand Painted' mark indicate that the blank was decorated outside the factory.

R.S. Germany bowl, iris with pearl lustre finish, lettuce mold, 9", $300.00.

Bowl, lady w/cows near cottage, hdls, mk, 10" 235.00
Bowl, roses, 3-corner, 3-hdld, mk 95.00
Bowl, vegetable; orange poppy 45.00
Cake plate, magnolias, gold rim, mk, 10" 75.00

Cake plate, poppies on gray, pierced hdls, 10" **75.00**
Cake plate, roses, sm roses/daisies ribbed border, hdls, 10" **70.00**
Celery dish, roses, open hdl, mk, 12⅝" **95.00**
Chocolate pot, peach & wht flowers, 10½" **175.00**
Mug, scuttle; pk poppies, mk, 3½" **110.00**
Pitcher, milk; roses & clover, 4" **95.00**
Vase, boy, house, windmill & stream, gr mk, 4" **125.00**
Vase, church scene, salesman's sample, 4" **95.00**
Vase, lilies, wht on lt gr, hdls, 5½" **95.00**

R.S. Poland

'R.S. Poland' is a mark attributed to Reinhold Schlegelmilch's factory in Tillowitz, Silesia. It was in use for a few years after 1945.

Bowl, Rembrandt's Nightwatch on gray-gr, mk, 1½x5⅜" **145.00**
Dresser set, roses w/gold trim, 4-pc on 12½x9" tray **565.00**
Ewer, golden pheasants, left handed, 6¼" **460.00**
Flower holder pheasants, attached metal frog, mk, 7" **750.00**
Server, lav & pk roses w/gold trim, center hdl, 8x11" dia **525.00**
Tray, bird on branch, floral/geometric border, mk, 14" **115.00**
Vase, cavaliers, mk, 4" **315.00**
Vase, cottage & lady w/sheep, ornate gold hdls, mk, 10" **650.00**
Vase, crowned cranes, salesman's sample, 3½x1½" **815.00**
Vase, turkey, salesman's sample, unmk, 3½" **500.00**

R.S. Prussia

Art porcelain bearing the mark 'R.S. Prussia' was manufactured by Reinhold Schlegelmilch from the late 1870s to the early 1900s in a Germanic area known until the end of WWI as Prussia. The vast array of mold shapes in combination with a wide variety of decorations is the basis for R.S. Prussia's appeal. Themes can be categorized as figural (usually based on a famous artist's work), birds, florals, portraits, scenics, and animals.

Berry set, florals, leaf mold, unmk, 7-pc **495.00**
Berry set, roses, mc on turq, carnation mold, 7-pc **500.00**
Berry set, surreal dogwood, red mk, 7-pc **265.00**
Bowl, autumn leaves & purple berries, 10" **150.00**
Bowl, centerpiece; carnations w/in & w/out, mk **1,750.00**
Bowl, Dice Players, ribbon & jewel mold, rstr, 10½" **1,450.00**
Bowl, Easter lilies, feather mold, 9" **250.00**
Bowl, floral, carnation mold, RM, 10½" **350.00**
Bowl, floral, emb medallions & scrolls, mk, 3½x10½" **385.00**
Bowl, floral center, scenic medallions, Tiffany border, 9" **500.00**
Bowl, geometric & cattail medallions w/gold, emb decor, 3x10" .**250.00**
Bowl, grapes & peaches w/gold, RM, 10¾" **385.00**
Bowl, lilies, wht & gr on purple & orange lustre, RM, 3x11" **400.00**
Bowl, mixed fruit, icicle mold, RM, 8½" **275.00**
Bowl, poppies on wht, floral & cobalt sides, unmk, 10¼ **965.00**
Bowl, roses, pk on pearly wht w/lav, bl & gold trim, RM, 10¼" .**325.00**
Bowl, roses & daisies, deep, mk, 10½" **250.00**
Bowl, roses & hydrangeas, unmk, 9" **115.00**
Bowl, roses & much gold, scalloped, RM, 10" **265.00**
Bowl, roses & red berries, ftd, scalloped, RM, 7" **110.00**
Bowl, swan & gazebo, RM, 10¾" **625.00**
Bowl, swan medallions & swallows, gold border, RM, 11" **650.00**
Bowl, 4 portrait medallions, gr Tiffany border, mk, 9" **450.00**
Cake plate, chickens, duck & swallows, glossy, 9¾" **1,000.00**
Cake plate, floral center, cherubs & ladies, Tiffany finish **475.00**
Cake plate, floral on cobalt, open hdls, 11" **425.00**
Cake plate, hidden image, RM **425.00**
Cake plate, mums on cobalt, open hdls, 9½" **235.00**

Cake plate, pk roses w/teal leaves on wht, 10¾" 215.00
Cake plate, roses in basket on gold/br/brn/wht, 12" 275.00
Celery dish, reflecting poppies & daisies, portraits, RM 650.00
Celery vase, mill scene, sawtooth mold, RM, 12½" 475.00
Celery vase, roses on lav, RM, 9" 200.00
Cracker jar, lilies, lily mold, RM 425.00
Cracker jar, pk roses, melon shape, steeple-type lid, RM 525.00
Cracker jar, red roses, mold #509A, mk 200.00
Cracker jar, roses & snowballs, RM 400.00
Creamer & sugar bowl, cherubs & roses, egg mold, w/lid 425.00
Creamer & sugar bowl, fruit decor, RM 250.00
Creamer & sugar bowl, mc roses w/gold, ped base, scalloped 385.00
Creamer & sugar bowl, pk & wht florals, ornate mold 225.00
Creamer & sugar bowl, summer season on satin, RM 1,200.00
Creamer & sugar bowl, swan on satin, RM 425.00
Cup & saucer, dogwood, much detail & gold, RM 45.00
Cup & saucer, pheasant & swallow, worn gold, mk 200.00
Cup & saucer, purple & wht violets, unmk 115.00
Cup & saucer, roses on bl satin, ftd, RM 100.00
Hair receiver, pk roses on dmn shape, mk 115.00
Ink blotter, floral on cobalt 395.00
Jam jar, dogwood & carnations, Tiffany finish, RM, w/tray 265.00
Letter holder, Countess Litta, ornate, unmk 295.00
Mustache cup, floral, RM 235.00
Mustache cup, gold leaves on bl to lav 235.00
Nut set, peach roses, RM, 8-pc 560.00
Pitcher, milk; pk carnations, morning-glory mold, 5" 165.00
Pitcher, roses, red/pk on gr, gold hdl, scalloped base, 5" 125.00
Pitcher, tankard; floral, carnation mold, RM, 11½" 800.00
Pitcher, tankard; pk & red roses, carnation mold, mk, 11½" 695.00
Pitcher, tankard; poppies, pk on gr, scrolled rim, mk, 12" 500.00
Pitcher, tankard; red & wht roses on satin, unmk, 11½" 495.00
Plaque, duck among evergreens, pierced eyelets, RM, 6" 355.00
Plate, fruit decor, iris mold, RM, 9" 235.00
Plate, hidden image lady, blown-out iris mold, 11" 450.00
Plate, lilies, pk & red on gr w/gold, RM, 8½" 175.00
Plate, Madame Lebrun, steeple mk, 8½" 525.00
Plate, roses & daisies on gr w/lav, leaf variation mold, 12" 225.00
Plate, swan, icicle mold, RM, 8¾" 225.00
Plate, swan scenic, lav & bl, unmk, 8½" 195.00
Plate, turkey & evergreens, RM, 8½" 525.00
Plate, yel & wht flowers w/gold bands, unmk, 7½" 115.00
Relish tray, Melon Boys, point & clover mold, RM, 9½" 695.00
Sugar shaker, pk roses w/gold, 4¾" 250.00
Tea set, classical scene w/cobalt, mk, serves 6 ....350.00
Tea set, floral w/much gold, RM, 3-pc 265.00
Tea set, pk & wht roses, mk, child sz, 9-pc 650.00
Tea set, roses w/gold, unmk, child sz, 12-pc 600.00

R.S. Prussia teapot, Queen Louise, unmarked, 8½", $800.00.

Teapot, floral, much jewelling, scalloped base 395.00
Teapot, roses, iris mold, RM 300.00
Teapot, roses on pastel gr, sq ped ft, unmk, 5¾x7½" 135.00
Teapot, wht floral on shaded pastels, ped ft, unmk, 6¼x7" 135.00
Toothpick holder, floral, 3-hdld, RM 295.00
Toothpick holder, pk roses, stipple mold 155.00
Toothpick holder, swans swimming, unmk 110.00
Tray, bread; carnations, lily-of-valley mold, leaf form, 12½" 145.00
Tray, dresser; hanging basket, icicle mold 360.00
Tray, pk roses w/bl & gr, unmk, 11½x7" 225.00
Tray, snowball & roses, ribbon & jewel mold, RM, 12x7½" 300.00
Tray, swans, icicle mold, RM, 11x7" 495.00
Urn, cottage & mill scene, unmk, w/lid, 12½", pr 3,475.00
Vase, Colonial couple & pk roses, ftd, 7½" 550.00
Vase, Colonial man's portrait, sm rose ft, 7½" 650.00
Vase, mill scene, jewels, ped base, 10" 775.00
Vase, parrot on lav w/much gold, mk, 5⅜" 295.00
Vase, woman in swing, RM, 4½" 550.00

R.S. Suhl, E.S. Suhl

Porcelains marked with this designation are attributed to Reinhold Schlegelmilch's Suhl factory.

Cake plate, floral w/floral border, hdls, 10" 140.00
Coffee set, Angelica Kauffmann scene, 9" pot+cr/sug+6 c/s 1,675.00
Cup & saucer, Nightwatch, brn tones 55.00
Vase, Melon Boys, flared sides, mk, 9½" 1,150.00
Vase, sunflowers, hdls, 6¾" 110.00
Wall plaque, daisies, 10½" 130.00

R.S. Tillowitz

R.S. Tillowitz-marked porcelains are attributed to Reinhold Schlegelmilch's factory in Tillowitz, Silesia.

Bowl, lilacs w/bl & gold tracing, oval, 10" 65.00
Bowl, pheasants, scalloped, oval, open hdls, mk, 10" L 265.00
Creamer & sugar bowl, lilies, wht on shaded gr 185.00
Cup & saucer, demitasse; wht flowers, mk 65.00
Nut dish, peonies & snowballs on cream, openwork, mk, 6" 95.00
Plate, poinsettias, pk on ivory to gr, hdls, 9¾" 60.00
Plate, stylized butterfly border w/gold, gold hdls, mk, 7" 38.00
Tray, floral, bl on gr w/much gold, pierced hdls, 4x8" 45.00
Tray, relish; azaleas/foliage on yel & brn, hdls, 10½" 40.00
Tray, sm floral, bl on gr, heavy gold, pierced hdls, 4x8" 30.00
Vase, golden pheasant, plain mold, 6" 260.00

Schneider

The Schneider Glass Company was founded in 1914 at Epinay-sur-seine, France. They made many types of art glass, some of which sandwiched designs between layers. Other decorative devices were applique and carved work. These were marked 'Charder' or 'Schneider.' During the twenties commercial artware was produced with Deco motifs cut by acid through two or three layers and signed 'LeVerre Francais' in script or with a section of inlaid filigrane. Our advisor for this category is Don Williams; he is listed in the Directory under Missouri. See also Le Verre Francais.

Bowl, etch band of sqs on lid, clear to lt gr, bubbly, 6½" 745.00
Bowl, finger; orange mottle, wrought leaf fr, 3" 125.00
Compote, clear bubbly shallow bowl, pk mottled ped, 4x12" 345.00
Compote, lime gr opal on amethyst base, knop stem, sgn 595.00

Compote, orange mottle to bl in swirl pattern, CI base, 16" **1,200.00**
Ewer, orange w/dk bl mottle, 3 appl spikes, 13x7", EX **700.00**
Pitcher, purple to red cased, amethyst hdl, bulbous body, 7" **485.00**
Vase, bl mottle, gourd shape, mk, 13" **375.00**
Vase, bubbly orange, brn streaks/prunts, stick neck, 24" **1,300.00**
Vase, cameo geometrics/chevrons, purple on clear, ftd, 8" **865.00**
Vase, clear to yel, part cased in clear coils, lav ft, 7" **1,000.00**
Vase, cobalt mottle over yel, tapered/shouldered, 14" **275.00**
Vase, mc mottle, flared rim, bulbous body, 10" **495.00**
Vase, orange crystal ribbed cylinder, blk disk base, 11½" **200.00**
Vase, orange mottle cylinder w/cup rim, blk disk base, 14½" **225.00**
Vase, pk mottle, clear/yel int, 3 prunts, stick neck, 20" **575.00**
Vase, purple mottle w/orange & yel inclusions, wine ft, 16" **1,200.00**
Vase, yel cased w/brn & bl splotches between layers, 12x7" **400.00**
Vase, yel/orange mottle, trumpet form w/cushion ft, 19" **575.00**

Schoolhouse Collectibles

Schoolhouse collectibles bring to mind memories of a bygone era when the teacher rang her bell to call the youngsters to class in a one-room schoolhouse where often both the 'hickory stick' and an apple occupied a prominent position on her desk. Our advisor for this category is Kenn Norris; he is listed in the Directory under Texas.

Bell, hand; brass ferrule, wood hdl, sq shoulder, 6x11" **70.00**
Bell, teacher's desk; cast brass, Pat 4-8-1856 ....**20.00**
Blackboard eraser, Andrews' Dustless..., wool & felt, 6" L **6.00**

Book, Friends and Neighbors, Dick and Jane second grade reader, Scott Foresman, 1941, EX, $35.00.

Book, Dick & Jane, girl on swing cover, Elson, 1936, EX **80.00**
Book, Fun w/Dick & Jane, 1946-47, EX **22.00**
Book, Learning To Live Together (Dick & Jane), 1947, EX **20.00**
Book, McGuffey's Eclectic Primer, ca 1900, 60-pg, VG **125.00**
Book, We Work & Play (Dick & Jane), 1946-47, EX **40.00**
Book cards, Sally, Dick & Jane, 19x20", 18 pgs **195.00**
Chalk holder, wooden, 3⅛" **10.00**
Desk, beech w/pine base, dvtl case, 5-drw, rfn, 41x31x22" **440.00**
Desk, master's, pine w/yel grpt over earlier red, 34x28x25" **200.00**
Desk, master's, rfn walnut, dvtl drw & gallery, 42x32" **715.00**
Desk, poplar Country Hepplewht, worn bl rpt, 32x36x23" **880.00**
Globe, Goldthwaites Folding..., Chicago, Pat 1898, EX **600.00**
Globe, Kittinger, 12", on trn wood stand, 36" overall **335.00**
Globe, terrestrial; Ginn & Heath, mid-1800s, 9½", EX **1,200.00**
Ink jar, Sanford's, ceramic, wire lock, wire/wood bail, 9" **125.00**
Lunch box, pail type, metal, bail hdl, 4x4¼" **15.00**
Lunch box, pressboard, riveted corners, leather hdl, 7⅜x4⅛" **42.00**
Number fr, home use, wooden, 100 beads, 8¼x9" **45.00**
Pencil sharpener, saxaphone, CI, Germany, 1⅝" **35.00**

Pencil sharpener, Scottie dog, red celluloid, 1½" **35.00**
Slate, bentwood oak fr, bottom tacked together, 7⅝x11" **75.00**
Stickers, yel & orange pumpkins, mk L&B, Germany, 1900s **65.00**
Water colors, tin container, Milton Bradley, 2⅞x5¼" **18.00**

Pencil Boxes

Among the most common of school-related collectibles are the many classes of pencil boxes. Generally from the period of the 1870s to the 1940s, these boxes were made in many hundred different styles. Materials included tin, wood (thin frame and solid hardwood) and leather; later fabric and plastics were used. Most pencil boxes were in a basic, rectangular configuration, though rare examples were made to resemble other objects. These included rolling pins, ball bats, and nightsticks. Pencil boxes are still to be found at reasonable prices, though collectors have lately noticed this field. All boxes listed below are in very-good to near-mint condition. Our advisors for pencil boxes are Sue and Lar Hothem, authors of *School Collectibles of the Past*; they are listed in the Directory under Ohio.

Cb tube w/wooden ends, metal twist caps, advertising, 1x9⅞" **28.00**
Fabric, flip lid, #926, Eagle Pencil Co, gr, 2x9⅝" **10.00**
Plastic, 3-color, #555 Sterling Multiplier, w/sharpener, 7⅞" **12.00**
Suede leather, profile of Indians, eraser pocket, 2⅝x8¼" **8.00**
Tin, hinged lift lid, mc camping scene, Wallace, 3⅝x8" **40.00**
Tin, sliding lid, 1-compartment, dk bl w/sm pnt flowers, 7⅝" **18.00**
Wooden, Art Nouveau cvd lid, metal hinges, 1930s, 8¾" **25.00**
Wooden, lift lid, litho European scenes, Germany, 8½" **18.00**
Wooden, lift lid, Oriental motif, blk pnt, w/lock, 8½" **20.00**
Wooden, red pnt top, varnished, grooves cut lengthwise, 7⅞" **30.00**
Wooden, slide-top, advertising, 9" ruler, str-edge, 9¼" **32.00**
Wooden, swing-top, advertising, floral decal, 8¾" **27.00**
Wooden, 1-level slide-top, single or dbl compartments, 9¼" **24.00**
Wooden, 4-level, 1 compartment per level, floral decal, 9¼" **70.00**

Schoop, Hedi

Swiss-born Hedi Schoop started her ceramics business in North Hollywood in 1940. With a talented crew of about twenty decorators, she produced figurines, figure-vases, console sets, TV lamps, and other decorative housewares — much of which was accented with gold or platinum trim. Schoop's pottery closed after a fire destroyed the building in 1958. Marks are impressed or printed. For further information we recommend *The Collector's Encyclopedia of California Pottery* by our advisor, Jack Chipman; he is listed in the Directory under California.

Cookie jar, Queen, rare **1,100.00**
Figurine, dancer w/arms over head, turq/wht/gold **85.00**
Figurine, Dutch girl on gr base, 10" **85.00**
Figurine, French man & lady, 13", pr **200.00**
Figurine, lady in peach w/gr, basket on side, 13" **95.00**
Figurine, Mexican lady, scarf over hat, baskets on side, 12" **75.00**
Planter, lady reading book before opening, 9" **65.00**
Planter, lady w/basket on head, bl, pk & wht, 13" **85.00**
Vase, cock crowing, sponged decor **65.00**
Vase, Maria, lady figural, 12½" **85.00**
Vase/planter, lady in long gown w/basket, appl flowers, 12½" **90.00**

Scouting Collectibles

Boy Scouts

Scouting was founded in England in 1907 by a retired Major General, Lord Robert Baden-Powell. Its purpose is the same today as it was then — to help develop physically strong, mentally alert boys and to teach them basic fundamentals of survival and leadership. The movement soon spread to the United States, and in 1910 a Chicago publisher, William Boyce, set out to establish Scouting in America. The first World Scout Jamboree was held in 1911 in England. Baden-Powell was honored as the Chief Scout of the World. In 1926 he was awarded the Silver Buffalo Award in the United States. He was knighted in 1929 for distinguished military service and for his Scouting efforts. Baden-Powell died in 1941. For more information you may contact our advisor, R.J. Sayers, author of *Guide to Scouting Collectibles*, whose address (and ordering information regarding his book) may be found in the Directory under North Carolina.

Auto radiator cap, BSA, #1529, full 1st Class, 1924-29	**75.00**
Auto windshield transfer, BSA, #3475, 1924-29, 4½x2½"	**10.00**
Belt buckle, National Jamboree, Max Sibler, bronze, 1969	**35.00**
Bookends, Sea Scout, #1726, brass, 1937-45, pr	**20.00**
Coin, National Jamboree, brass, 1950	**5.00**
Combination tool kit, BSA, #1186, interlocking, 1925-32	**10.00**
Compass, BSA, #1088, 1912-17	**22.00**
Drinking cup, BSA, collapsible, full logo, brass/NP, 1912-17	**20.00**
Field glasses, BSA, #1077, 1912-17	**50.00**
Fire-making kit, BSA, #1532, bow & leather thong, 1925-32	**15.00**
First Aid kit, BSA, Bauer & Black	**20.00**
Flag, National Jamboree, w/logo, 1957, 36x60"	**50.00**
Flag, patrol; BSA, silk screened, 40 issued, 1912-17, ea	**15.00**
Flashlight, BSA, #1278, 90-degree style, gr over brass, 1925-32	**10.00**
Flint & steel kit, BSA, #1505, 1925-32	**7.50**
Guard rope, BSA, #1276, snap fastener & ring, 15-ft, 1925-32	**5.00**
Harmonica, BSA, #1256, mk Marine Band, 1924-29	**25.00**
Hatchet, BSA, #1507, Collins, w/sheath #1507, 1924-29	**29.00**
Lantern, BSA, Dietz Kerosene, Pat 1910	**40.00**
Lantern, BSA, Just-Rite, 1912-17	**22.00**
Mess kit, Official Scout; #1001, breaks down, 1912-17	**22.00**
Microscope, BSA, #1085, brass, 1912-17	**100.00**
Neckerchief, National Jamboree, Chorus Staff, limited #, 1953	**50.00**
Neckerchief, National Jamboree, cotton, 1950	**22.00**
Patch, BSA, Eagle, tan, type 1	**150.00**
Patch, Canoe Staff, crossed paddles, 1940	**15.00**
Patch, National Jamboree, canvas, 1950, 3"	**27.00**
Patch, National Jamboree, Chaplin's Staff, 1989	**10.00**
Patch, National Jamboree, Special Conservation Staff, 1960	**55.00**
Patch, National Jamboree, Transportation Staff, 1989	**9.00**
Patch, National Order of Arrow, 1958	**22.00**
Pennant, National Jamboree, bl felt, 1953	**12.00**
Pennant, World Jamboree, wool, 1929	**75.00**
Pin, hat; Commissioner's, screw bk, bl/silver, #268, 1924-29	**90.00**
Pin, Scoutmaster's, 1st Class, gr enamel, 1912-17, 1½"	**125.00**
Pocketknife, BSA, Remington, RH54, w/sheath, 1-blade, 7"	**50.00**
Pocketknife, BSA, Ulster, #1503, 1924-29	**22.00**
Pocketknife, BSA, Ulster, brass & steel, 4-blade, 4", MIB	**65.00**
Record, BSA, BS Bugle Calls, #3703, 78 rpm, 1924-29	**10.00**
Sewing kit, BSA, standard, #1061, 1912-17	**22.00**
Shakers, National Jamboree, w/logo, 1973, pr	**4.00**
Song book, BSA, #3023, 1912-17	**10.00**
Trumpet, BSA, Rexcraft, #1064, w/logo, 1912-17	**60.00**
Watch fob, Patrol Leaders, blk silk ribbon, gold clasp, 1912-17	**125.00**
Wristwatch, BSA, #1380, 'Day-nite' type, 1924-29	**30.00**
Wristwatch, BSA, #1547, 6-jewel, w/leather strap, 1925-32	**25.00**

Girl Scouts

Collecting Girl Scout memorabilia is a hobby that is growing nationwide. When Sir Baden-Powell founded the Boy Scout Movement in England, it proved to be too attractive and too well adaped to youth to limit its great opportunities to boys alone. The sister organization, known in England as the Girl Guides, quickly followed and was equally successful. Mrs. Juliette Low, an American visitor to England and a personal friend of the father of Scouting, realized the tremendous future of the movement for her own country, and with the active and friendly cooperation of the Baden-Powells, she founded the Girl Guides in America, enrolling the first patrols in Savannah, Georgia, in March 1912. In 1915 National Headquarters were established in Washington, D.C., and the name was changed to Girl Scouts. The first National Convention was held in 1914, and each succeeding year has shown growth and increased enthusiasm in this steadily growing army of girls and young women who are learning in the happiest ways to combine patriotism, outdoor activities of every kind, skill in every branch of domestic science, and high standards of community service. Today there are over 400,000 girl Scouts and more than 22,000 leaders. Mr. Sayers is also our Girl Scout advisor. (See previous column.)

Armband, GSA, Senior Service	**20.00**
Book, Nature; GSA, for leaders	**5.00**
Calendar, GSA, 1920	**70.00**
Camera, Univex, GSA, 1937	**35.00**
Cap, Den Mother's, Garrison type, bl, w/pin, 1960s	**5.00**
Compact, unofficial, bronze, w/mirror, 1½" sq	**20.00**
Cookie box, autograph by Babe Ruth, 1940s	**200.00**
Diary, GSA, gr cover, 1930	**10.00**
Doll, uniform; GSA, Madam Hendren, rare, 1920-22	**200.00**
Doll, uniform; GSA, Terri Lee, hard plastic, 1949-53, 16"	**20.00**
Drinking cup, GSA, collapsible, aluminum, 1950	**5.00**
Flag, GSA, Brownie, sm, 1930s	**25.00**
Flag, signal; GSA, wooden hdls, 1920	**15.00**
Flag, troop; GSA, wool, 1930s	**30.00**
Handbook, GSA, tan cover, 1920	**25.00**
Locket, unofficial, brass, opens to hold picture, sm	**20.00**
Manual, Sectional; National Jamboree, 1964	**3.00**
Medal, Silver; GSA, Life Saving, Maltese cross, gr ribbon, 1916	**300.00**
Paper dolls, GSA, uniforms, pins, etc, 6x9" sheets, 51, complete	**20.00**
Patch, GSA, Treasurer's, gr twill, 1937	**10.00**
Postcard, GSA, scout w/flag, WWI, 1915	**7.00**
Poster, GSA, Cookie Drive, color litho, 1923	**100.00**
Poster, GSA, 1st issue, girl in uniform, 1917	**75.00**
Ring, GSA, gold w/gr stone	**10.00**
Scarf, National Jamboree, silk, w/logo, 1960	**7.00**
Whistle, cylinder, GSA, 1920s	**20.00**

Scrimshaw

The most desirable examples of the art of scrimshaw can be traced back to the first half of the 19th century to the heyday of the whaling industry. Some voyages lasted for several years, and conditions on board were often dismal. Sailors filled the long hours by using the tools of their trade to engrave whale teeth and make boxes, pie crimpers (jagging wheels), etc., from the bone and teeth of captured whales. Eskimos also made scrimshaw, sometimes borrowing designs from the sailors who traded with them.

Beware of fraudulent pieces; fakery is prevelant in this field. If you're in doubt, it's best to deal with reputable people who guarantee the items they sell. There are also many carved teeth that are actually made of plastic. A listing of these plastic items has been published by the Kendall Whaling Museum in Sharon, Massachusetts. Our advisor for this category is John Rinaldi; he is listed in the Directory under Maine. See also Powder Horns.

Bodkin, tortoise-shell spacer, monkey-fist top, 1840s, 5¼" **695.00**
Bodkin, trn, cvd & scribed, 19th C, 4⅜" **215.00**
Busk, heart top, drapes/flower/star/tree/flag, 19th C, 12" **700.00**
Busk, whale bone, sperm whale/ship/eagle/flag/boat, 1800s, 12" ..**800.00**
Busk, whalebone, verse amid 2 Am eagles, 19th C, 13½" **2,800.00**
Cane, fancy rope-twist cvd shaft, wood spacers, 1840s, 33" **1,985.00**
Cane, narwhal tusk, simple form, cvd rings, 1840s, 34¾" **2,250.00**
Clock tower, 2 eng 4½" teeth on baleen base, 1840s, 5x8¾" ...**2,275.00**
Clothespins, whalebone, chamfered edges, 1860s, 4½", 6 for **495.00**
Cribbage board, walrus tusk, EX cvg, Eskimo sgn/ 1903, 23" ...**2,150.00**
Crimper, cvd 1-pc curved hdl, serrated ivory wheel, 1850s, 2¼" ..**795.00**
Crimper, whale ivory, swan neck & head, 19th C, 4⅝" **2,000.00**
Swift, whale ivory, fist-form clamp, 1840-50, 22" L **4,580.00**
Tooth, EX cvg by Naval Engagement Engraver, 19th C, 5½" .**3,300.00**
Tooth, lady & sailor/lady & flowers, mc, 1840s, 5x2⅝", pr **1,785.00**
Tooth, lady's portrait ea side, ca 1850, 7x3¼", EX **1,820.00**
Tooth, ornate cvgs by Thistle Engraver, 6½x2¼", pr **3,375.00**
Tooth, sperm whale, chipmunk/bird/nest, 19th C, 5¼" **975.00**
Vase, hollowed tooth, baleen spacers, trn stem, 19th C, 6¾" ..**1,250.00**
Whistle, lady's leg form, wood disk at knee, 19th C, 4⅛" **925.00**

Sebastians

Sebastian miniatures were first produced in 1938 by Prescott W. Baston in Marblehead, Massachusetts. Since then more than six hundred have been modeled. These figurines have been sold through gift shops all over the country, primarily in the New England states. In 1976 Baston withdrew his Sebastians from production. Under an agreement with the Lance Corporation of Hudson, Massachusetts, one hundred designs were selected to be produced by that company under Baston's supervision. Those remaining were discontinued. In the time since then, the older figurines have become very collectible. Price is determined by three factors: 1) in production/out of production; 2) labels — color of oval label, i.e. red, blue, green, etc.; Marblehead label, a green and silver palette-shaped label used until 1977; or no label; 3) condition. If there is no label and the varnish coat is quite yellowed, then it is considered to be of the Marblehead era. Dates are merely copyright dates and have no particular significance in regard to value. (Signed) 'P.W. Baston' should only have impact on price when the signature is an actual autograph. Most pieces are manufactured with an imprinted 'P.W. Baston' on the base. Baston died in 1984; the miniatures are now being done by P.W. Baston, Jr.

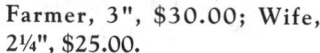

Farmer, 3", $30.00; Wife, 2¼", $25.00.

Christmas Morning **30.00**
Darned Well He Can **250.00**
David Copperfield & Wife, Marblehead era **40.00**
Diedrich Knickerbocker, Marblehead era **50.00**

Gathering Tulips **100.00**
Gay Nineties Gibson Girl at Home, 3½" **30.00**
Grocery Store, Marblehead label **62.50**
House of 7 Gables, Marblehead era...**60.00**
James Madison, pewter **65.00**
Lobster Man, Marblehead era..**55.00**
Mark Antony, Marblehead era..**65.00**
Micawber, Marblehead label **50.00**
Oliver Twist & Beetle, Marblehead label **50.00**
Paul Revere **45.00**
Penny Shop, Marblehead label **50.00**
Pilgrims, Marblehead label **50.00**
Pioneer Village, Marblehead era **65.00**
Robert E Lee & Traveler, Marblehead era...............................**90.00**
Sampling the Stew, Marblehead era...**55.00**
Scrooge **25.00**
Scuba Diver **375.00**
Son of the Desert **200.00**
Spirit of '76, Marblehead label **68.00**
Stagecoach, Marblehead era..**65.00**
Weaver & Loom, Marblehead label **60.00**

Sevres

Fine-quality porcelains have been made in Sevres, France, since the early 1700s. Rich ground colors were often hand painted with portraits, scenics, and florals. Some pieces were decorated with transfer prints and decalcomania; many were embellished with heavy gold. These wares are the most respected of all French porcelains. Their style and designs have been widely copied, and some of the items listed below are Sevres-type wares.

Box, dk bl, couple in garden on lid, oval, 8½" L **250.00**
Box, ivory inset w/army scene, serpentine, metal mts, 6" **635.00**
Centerpc, bsk/gilt, 3 standing maids support rtcl bowl, 15" **1,200.00**
Figurine, Agnes Morel, lav gown, 9" **150.00**
Plate, Elisa Boneparte, sgn O Brun, 9½" **115.00**
Plate, exotic bird in garden, 3 rim reserves, gilt, 10", pr **200.00**
Plate, Mme de Cencin portrait, sgn G Perier, 8¾" **105.00**
Plate, Mme Elisabeth, sgn Morin, floral rim, 9⅞" **185.00**
Plate, 3 ladies & Cupid, floral border w/gold, 10¾"+fr **225.00**
Tray, couple in swing, hdls, w/in bronze flower-cast fr, 16" **750.00**
Tray, 18th-C couple on cobalt w/gold, sgn Collier, 11¼" **600.00**
Tureen, soup; pk/floral bands, bird crest, gold hdls/ft, 15" **745.00**

Urn, 18th-century couple in garden, lady beyond, foliate ring handles, gilt-bronze mounts, with lid, 28", $2,600.00.

Urn, Colonial figures on cobalt, 3-hdld, bronze mts, 35" **1,250.00**
Urn, couple in garden/gold on bl, sgn, ormolu hdls/mts, 5½" **275.00**
Urn, lady's portrait, sgn, cobalt trim, ormolu mts, 11" **395.00**
Urn, pr in garden, sgn, dome lid, bronze mts/hdls, 27" **2,300.00**
Vase, gilt leaves & band on bl/brn mottle, 1914, 17" **1,375.00**

Sewer Tile

Whimsies, advertising novelties, and other ornamental items were sometimes made in potteries where the primary product was simply tile.

Bird on stump, signed EJE, 9½", $425.00; Lion on plinth, signed EJE, 6½x9", $95.00; Staffordshire-style spaniel, signed EJE, 10½", $120.00.

Ashtray, stump form, 2½x4" 28.00
Birdhouse w/attached perch & roof w/gr glaze, 8" 330.00
Bookend, Indian w/headdress, 5½" 45.00
Boundary markers, mk NUW 33, chips, 45", pr 550.00
Bulldog, minor chips, 9" 250.00
Cat, jeweled eyes, rpr, 9" 65.00
Cat, seated, pnt eyes, minor chips, 5" 65.00
Cat, yel pnt traces, chip, 7¼" 140.00
Collie on rectangular base, tooled details, 11¼" 550.00
Dog, seated, olive-gr, crudely molded, 7" 50.00
Duck, initialed, 6¾" 330.00
Eagle on log paperweight w/FOE, 1944, 8" 40.00
Fish, open mouth, scale details, early 1900s, 8" 125.00
Frog, advertising label on base, 4¼" L 105.00
Frog, sm chip on base, 7¼" 160.00
Lady's shoe, sm chip, 6" 60.00
Lamp, tree form, orig electric fittings, 11¾" 65.00
Lion on rectangular base, tooled details, 9¼" 385.00
Lion on stepped base, tooled details, chips, 9¼" 275.00
Owl on stump, base flakes, 5⅜" 85.00
Planter, elf, pointed cap, cut-out mouth & eyes, 13", EX 150.00
Planter, log shape w/tooled bark, chips, 15½" 35.00
Planter, stump form, splayed 'roots,' 6¾x9" 50.00
Plaque, crane, old mc pnt, 6¼x11" 88.00
Squirrel, EX tooling & detail, chips, 8⅜" 66.00

Sewing Items

Sewing collectibles continue to intrigue collectors, and fine 19th-century and earlier pieces are commanding higher prices due to increased demand and scarcity. Complete needlework boxes and chatelaines in original condition are rare. But even though they may be incomplete, as long as boxes contain fittings of the period and the chains of the chatelaine are intact and contemporary with the style and the individual holders original and matching the brooch, they should be considered prime additions to any collection. As 19th-century items become harder to find, new trends in collecting develop. Among them are needlebooks, many of which were decorated with horses, children, beautiful ladies, etc. Some were giveaways printed with advertisements of products and businesses. Even early pins are collectible; the earliest were made in two parts with the round head attached separately. Pin disks, pin cubes, and other pin holders make interesting additions to a sewing collection as well.

Tape measures are now popular. Victorian figurals command premium prices. Early wooden examples of transferware and Tunbridge ware have gained in popularity as have figurals of vegetable ivory, celluloid, and other early plastics. From the 20th century, tatting shuttles made of plastics as well as bone, brass, sterling, and wood decorated with Art Nouveau, Deco, and more modern designs are in demand; so are darning eggs, stillettos, and thimbles. Because of the decline in the popularity of needlework after the 1920s (due to increased production of machine-made items), many novelty-type items were made in an attempt to regain consumer interest, and many collectors today find them appealing.

Watch for reproductions. Sterling thimbles are being made in Holland and in the U.S. and are available in many designs from the Victorian era. But the originals are usually plainly marked, either in the inside apex or outside on the band. Avoid testing gold and silver thimbles for content; this often destroys the inside marks. Instead, research the manufacturer's mark; this will often denote the material as well. Even though the reproductions are well finished, they do not have the manufacturers' marks. Many thimbles are being made specifically for the collectible market; reproductions of porcelain thimbles are also found. Prices should reflect the age and availability of these thimbles. Our advisor for this category is Marjorie Geddes; she is listed in the Directory under Oregon.

Bobbin holder, cast brass & iron w/emb floral & shield, 5" **95.00**
Box, base metal, Clark's ONT advertising on bl, 3x5x2" **35.00**
Box, folk art tree/bird cvg sgn AWS, ped base, 34x12" **360.00**
Box, gold & blk chinoiserie lacquer, fitted int, 14" **650.00**
Box, poplar w/red & blk foliate stencil, cylindrical, 7x9" **600.00**
Box, satinwood w/faceted-head steel tacks, 8" **245.00**
Box, wood reed & woven braided straw, 7½" L **90.00**
Buttonhole cutter, brass w/sliding retractable knife, Pat 72 ....**16.50**
Buttonhole cutter, hand-wrought hatchet form, line decor, 4½" .**190.00**
Case, leather, 4-section, w/orig tools **50.00**

Lady's chatelaine, sterling, with five matched and engraved tools on chains, Whiting and Davis, dated 1898, $1,500.00.

Clip, chatelaine; SP, ornate, 2" 95.00
Darner, blown, amber glass, foot shape, EX 50.00
Darner, blown, blk glass w/sterling repousse hdl, 4½", VG 55.00
Darner, blown, clear w/red/wht/bl swirls, pontil scar, 4½" 120.00
Darner, blown, dk gr glass, ball-shape working end, 5¼", EX 70.00
Darner, blown, milk glass, ridged hdl, 6" 70.00

Darner, blown, milk glass w/red & bl splotches, 4¼" 100.00
Darner, maple, 1" ball-shaped working end, 5¾" 17.50
Darner, sterling, end opens, beads on hdl, for gloves 175.00
Darner, sterling, glove w/twist hdl, loop for chatelaine 145.00
Darner, sterling, repousse hdl w/loop, 4" 98.00
Darner, sterling, rope-patterned hdl, opens to hold needles 150.00
Darner, sterling, Webster floral, for glove 165.00
Darner, wood, wht pnt, for gloves 65.00
Darning egg, celluloid, hand decor, w/hdl 15.00
Emery, gr taffeta heart shape, 2", VG 37.50
Emery, satin cat figural, stamped Japan 60.00
Emery, silk strawberry form, silk flowers at top w/tassel, EX 45.00
Emery, sterling, closed filigree case from chatelaine 195.00
Emery, sterling acorn figural w/suede fabric, 1", EX 145.00
Emery, tomato figural, sterling top, silk cushion 195.00
Etui, gilt metal, mythological scenes, birds; complete 750.00
Gauge, hem; sterling openwork heart w/repousse roses, 4½" 145.00
Gauge, knitting needle; celluloid, Good Shepard Yarns, 6½" 12.50
Knitting guards, blk celluloid, 1¾", pr 55.00
Knitting guards, celluloid, tube shape w/blk elastic, pr 35.00
Knitting guards, eng 800 silver w/chain, pr 125.00
Knitting guards, sterling, lady's shoes, Victorian, pr 225.00
Knitting sheath, trn wood, brass liner, 1800s, 7¾" 175.00
Knitting sheath, wood, goose wing 185.00
Measure, brass, teapot form, 1½" dia, EX 195.00
Measure, brass, turtle figural, 1890s, EX 145.00
Measure, celluloid, basket of flowers form, Germany 85.00
Measure, celluloid, bear figural, Japan 110.00
Measure, celluloid, cottage form 145.00
Measure, celluloid, deer figural, mc details, Germany, 2" 165.00
Measure, celluloid, dog figural w/wavy fur, on gr pillow 145.00
Measure, celluloid, fruit basket form, 1" dia, EX 60.00
Measure, celluloid, Indian boy figural 145.00
Measure, celluloid, kangaroo & baby figural 115.00
Measure, celluloid, lady bug figural, Germany 65.00
Measure, celluloid, Mammy figural, NM 285.00
Measure, celluloid, parrot figural, gr 185.00
Measure, celluloid, pig figural w/red hat tape, M 55.00
Measure, celluloid, sailing ship form 85.00
Measure, celluloid, sandpiper figural on ped, glass eyes, EX 45.00
Measure, celluloid, scallop shell form, 1½" 67.50
Measure, celluloid, Scottie & pup figural 145.00
Measure, celluloid, Sears Roebuck Plows advertising, mc, EX 60.00
Measure, celluloid, terrier by log figural, mc details, 2¼" 145.00
Measure, celluloid, 2-story house form, mc details, 2" 145.00
Measure, Lydia Pinkham, disk type, 1½" 60.00
Measure, Mauchline Ware, butter churn form, self-winding, 2" .155.00
Measure, metal, drum form, mirror 1 side, farm scene other, 2" 55.00
Measure, metal, pecking chick figural, Germany, 1890s, EX 265.00
Measure, MOP/brass, cage form 50.00
Measure, plastic, apple form, M 30.00
Measure, plastic, Calvert Whiskey bottle form, 3¼" 45.00
Measure, plush, bear figural, Japan 30.00
Measure, Tunbridge, bbl form w/inlay top & bottom (no tape) 60.00
Measure, vegetable ivory, bbl form, Stanhope in hdl, 1" 165.00
Nanny pin, brass, attached horseshoe medallion w/hair filling ...275.00
Nanny pin, brass w/amethyst stone 245.00
Nanny pin, brass w/gold stone center, end unscrews, 2" 185.00
Needle book, printed fabric, bonnet form 12.00
Needle book, sterling, repousse, 2¼" sq 165.00
Needle book, Tartan Ware, Wm Hall Needles, 3x5", EX 165.00
Needle book, Tunbridge, mosaic, flannel pages, 2¼x1½" 85.00
Needle case, beading on bone, ca 1850s, 3½", VG 195.00
Needle case, Beatrice, accordion fold, emb floral 375.00

Needle case, bone, flat style, pull-off cap, 1830s, 2" 145.00
Needle case, brass, Avery, w/easel, Victorian 495.00
Needle case, brass, butterfly, mk au Louvre, Victorian 575.00
Needle case, brass, shield w/rose, Victorian 350.00
Needle case, celluloid, umbrella form, 3¾" 125.00
Needle case, gold wash on silver, floral repousse, Fr, 3½" 185.00
Needle case, Palais Royal, MOP, pansy medallion, 1825, 3x½" ..850.00
Needle case, sterling, appl fleur-de-lis ea side, 3" 95.00
Needle case, sterling, eng decor, flat, narrow, 2¼", EX 75.00
Pin holder, Mauchline Ware, disk form, NH souvenir, 2" dia 135.00
Pincushion, lady's slipper form, leather w/glass beading, 4" L 95.00
Pincushion, pig figural, sterling, hallmk, 1" 165.00
Pincushion, shoe form, sterling, 1980s 95.00
Pincushion, turtle nodder, base metal, glass eyes, Japan 25.00
Pincushion clamp, pnt wood, mirror on reverse, 7½", EX 125.00
Ribbon threader, Salem witch, sterling, in case, mk D Low 450.00
Ribbon threader, sterling, dbl-ended, narrow 26.50
Scissors, base metal, stork figural, 4" 20.00
Scissors, cut steel, eng shanks, 4" 50.00
Scissors, embroidery, base metal, cross design, Japan 20.00
Scissors, embroidery, figural swan hdls 250.00
Scissors, embroidery, gilt-over-sterling hdls, cross design 85.00
Scissors, embroidery, MOP urn figural hdls 395.00
Scissors, gilt joining band, cvd MOP hdls, 4½" 265.00
Scissors, gilt over metal, Fr style, 4", M 160.00
Scissors, nickel silver, lady's legs form, MOP hdls, 1¾" 235.00
Scissors, souvenir, Louis & Clark Expo, 6" 165.00
Scissors, souvenir, Washington DC medallion in hdl, 6" 135.00
Scissors, sterling, beading & feather design, unmk, 3¾" 125.00
Scissors, sterling, floral daisy at base of shanks, EX 90.00
Scissors charm, sterling, stork figural, 1½" 60.00
Sewing kit, wood, bullet shape, int spools, 3½" 35.00
Spool, MOP top w/cvd design, metal shaft, bone base, 1½" 45.00
Spool holder, brass, holds 24 spools, 2-tiered, 16x8" 235.00
Spool holder, SP, 2 floral bands 65.00
Stencil, quilting; base metal, 6-petal flower, 3¾" 15.00
Tatting shuttle, brass, heavy, 3¼x¾" 60.00
Tatting shuttle, celluloid, Lydia Pinkham, NM 85.00
Tatting shuttle, MOP, 2½x¾" 115.00
Tatting shuttle, sterling, Foster & Bailey, cartouche/floral 145.00
Tatting shuttle, sterling, Webster, eng dmn in center 195.00
Tatting shuttle, Tartan Ware, slim style, lt wear 185.00
Tatting shuttle, tortoise, slim, 2¼x½ " 150.00
Thimble, chased gold band of roses & leaves on sterling 130.00
Thimble, Crown mk, sterling, floral band, appl rolled rim 65.00
Thimble, Joseph Swan & Son..., sterling, carnelian stone 70.00
Thimble, Simons, chased gold band 65.00
Thimble, Simons, sterling, cherubs, Pat Nov 21, '05, EX 250.00
Thimble, Simons, sterling, snail border, reeded rim 55.00
Thimble, Simons, Vermicelli style 78.00
Thimble, sterling, cherubs Simons' design, repro 40.00
Thimble, sterling, orchid-pattern band, VG 95.00
Thimble holder/case, brass egg form, Queen Victoria portrait 185.00
Thimble holder/case, brass egg form, 1¾", w/2" chain 87.50
Thimble holder/case, from chatelaine, ornate, hallmarked 165.00
Thimble holder/case, mahog, acorn form, pull-off cap, 2¾" 68.00
Thimble holder/case, MOP egg shape, 1¾", +brass chain loops 75.00
Thimble holder/case, Tartan Ware, egg shape, Stuart 245.00
Thimble holder/case, treen, bottle w/Mauchline scene 185.00
Thimble holder/case, vegetable ivory, acorn form, 1½", EX 115.00
Thimble holder/case, vegetable ivory, cvd, 2½", +thimble 180.00
Thimble holder/case, wooden egg shape on pedestal, blk/wht 85.00
Thimble stand, base metal, cat on 2½" dia base 78.00
Thimble stand, base metal, dog figural, emb floral base, 3" dia 65.00

Thimble stand, base metal, lady figural on rnd base, 2½" 45.00
Thimble stand, base metal, turtle figural, 1¼x2¾" 48.00
Thread winder, bl glass, tubular, 1½x2½" 125.00
Thread winder, ivory, rectangular, flat, 2" 45.00
Thread winder, MOP, rnded corners, flat, 1½" 60.00
Winding clamp, ivory, from fitted needlework box, 4", pr 485.00
Winding clamp, treen, grain pnt, English, 1860s 250.00

Sewing Machines

The fact that Thomas Saint, an English cabinetmaker, invented the first sewing machine in 1790 was unknown until 1874 when Newton Wilson, an English sewing machine manufacturer and patentee, chanced on the drawings included in a patent specification describing methods of making boots and shoes. By the middle of the 19th century, several patents were granted to American inventors, among them Isaac M. Singer, whose machine used a treadle. These machines were ruggedly built, usually of cast iron. By the 1860s and '70s, the sewing machine had become a popular commodity, and the ironwork became more detailed and ornate.

Though rare machines are costly, many of the old oak treadle machines (especially these brands: Davis, Home, Household, National, New Home, Singer, Weed, Wheeler & Wilson, and Willcox & Gibbs) have only nominal value. Our advisor for this category is Peter Frei; he is listed in the Directory under Massachusetts. Refer to *Toy and Miniature Sewing Machines* by Glenda Thomas for more information.

Child's, Am Girl, Delta Specialty, 1930s-40s, 6x4x8¾", EX 110.00
Child's, Casige, ornate pnt florals, pre-WWII, 5x2x5", EX 125.00
Child's, Eldredgette, MIB 135.00

Child's functional treadle machine, metal and wood, 30" tall, EX, $250.00.

Child's, Junior Miss, blk enamel, Artcraft, 1940s, 6½", EX 85.00
Child's, KAYanEE Sew Master, metal body, 6", EX 25.00
Child's, Little Mary Mix Up, gr enamel, ca 1930s, 7", EX 65.00
Child's, Little Missy, Lindstrom, Pat 1889 ....210.00
Child's, Little Mother, Artcraft Metal Products, 1940s, 8", EX 75.00
Child's, Muller #6, NP CI, wooden base, pre-WWII, 6", EX 130.00
Child's, Sew Mistress, M in orig case 60.00
Child's, Singer, cast metal, blk enamel w/NP, 1926, EX 125.00
Child's, Singer Featherweight #221, blk, complete, w/case 335.00
Child's, Singer Sewhandy #20, beige pnt, 1950s, EX 110.00
Child's, Smith & Egge Automatic, 1901, 6¾x6", EX 250.00
Eldredge Automatic, 1880s, complete, EX 145.00

Florence, CI, belt driven, Pat Nov 12, 1850, 16" L, EX 250.00
Wilcox & Gibbs, complete, ca 1883 ....75.00

Shaker Items

The Shaker community was founded in America in 1776 at Niskeyuna, New York, by a small group of English 'Shaking Quakers.' The name referred to a group dance which was part of their religious rites. Their leader was Mother Ann Lee. By 1815 their membership had grown to more than one thousand in eighteen communities as far west as Indiana and Kentucky. But in less than a decade, their numbers began to decline until today only a handful remain. Their furniture is prized for its originality, simplicity, workmanship, and practicality. Few pieces were signed. Some were carefully finished to enhance the natural wood; a few were painted.

Although other methods were used earlier, most Shaker boxes were of oval construction with overlapping 'fingers' at the seams to prevent buckling as the wood aged. A box in original paint will often fetch triple the price of an unpainted box; number of fingers and size should also be considered.

Although the Shakers were responsible for weaving a great number of baskets, their methods are not easily distinguished from those of their outside neighbors, and it is nearly impossible without first-hand knowledge to positively attribute a specific example to their manufacture. They were involved in various commercial efforts other than woodworking — among them sheep and dairy farming, sawmilling, and pipe and brick making. They were the first to raise crops specifically for seed and to market their product commercially. They perfected a method to recycle paper and were able to produce wrinkle-free fabrics. Our advisor for this category is Nancy Winston; she is listed in the Directory under New Hampshire. Standard two-letter state abbreviations have been used throughout the following listings.

Key:
bj — bootjack   NL — New Lebanon
CB — Canterbury   PH — Pleasant Hill
EF — Enfield   SDL — Sabbathday Lake
ML — Mt. Lebanon   WV — Watervliet

Basket, reed & raffia, hinged lid, minor damage, 7½" L 25.00
Basket, woven splint, bentwood hdl, SDL, 7¾x16" dia 198.00
Basket, woven splint, bentwood hdl, some age, 7¾x13" 125.00
Basket, woven splint, faded blk & red, Union Village, 24x17" ...125.00
Bench, kneeling; rfn poplar w/red stain, SLD, 6½x41x6" 275.00
Bin, wood; poplar w/trn pegs, old worn pnt, 38x35x19" 385.00
Box, bentwood beech & pine, copper tacks, 6¾" 125.00
Box, bentwood pine, copper tacks, old varnish, 8¾" 125.00
Box, blanket; pine, 1-drw, red stain, CB, 1800s, 25x33x17" 8,250.00
Box, ochre pnt, oval, paper label: bee's wax, 14½" 5,500.00
Box, sewing; mixed woods w/red stain, drw, compartment, 6⅝" .550.00
Box, sewing; walnut & maple, 1-drw, tambour door, 8¾" 295.00
Box, sewing; 3-finger, copper tacks, SDL, 8" 235.00
Box, storage; bentwood, 3-finger, old bl-gr pnt, 10½" 500.00
Box, 2-finger, yel varnish, inscr/1882, 4⅝" 4,000.00
Box, 3-finger, bl pnt, New England, 1850s, 8x11¼x4¼" 3,750.00
Box, 3-finger, hardwood & pine, copper tacks, 6⅛" L 395.00
Box, 3-finger, oval, CT, 3½x9x6" 865.00
Box, 4-finger, old bl pnt, pine & hardwood, 11¾" L 2,200.00
Box, 4-finger, oval, New England, 1880s, 3¼x8¾" 250.00
Candlestand, rfn walnut, tripod base, 1-brd rpl top, 27x19" 600.00
Chair, ladderbk side; cherry/tiger maple, 3-slat, 1840s, 42" 880.00
Chair, weaver's, ladderbk, 2-slat, tape seat, 34" 200.00
Chairs, 3-slat bk, tape seat, pnt traces, KY, 35½", 4 for 880.00
Chest, blanket; pine, dvtl drw, bracket ft, rfn, ML, 18x38" 1,300.00

Churn, staved w/wooden bands, worn red stain, ML, 14½" 350.00
Cloak hanger, long wood hdl, brass wire hook, 60¾" 77.00
Cupboard, butternut, 2 doors & 10 drw, EF, 1850s, 104x62" ...2,300.00
Cupboard, poplar & cherry, paneled doors, rprs, 36x28" 560.00

Cupboard, stepback style, natural pine, three paneled doors, Watervliet, NY, ca 1830, 84x43x16", $1,800.00.

Desk, sewing; poplar, 3 dvtl drw, step-bk top, MA, 36x19" 660.00
Drying rack, cherry, 3 bars on trestle ft, rfn, 37x30" 300.00
Footstool, slanted top w/trn ft, ML label, 7x11½x11½" 525.00
Foot warmer, dvtl walnut, tin int, velvet cover, ML, 7x8" 275.00
Grater, punched tin w/wooden bkbrd, ML, 29" 50.00
Mold, bee's wax; wooden, ML, 2" dia, pr 120.00
Niddy noddy, old finish, ML, 18½" 95.00
Pail, ochre pnt, 6", EX 1,500.00
Rocker, #0, w/arms, NL, 1870s, rfn, 23½" 1,045.00
Rocker, #3, w/arms, ladderbk, rfn stain, rpl seat, ML, 33" 325.00
Rocker, #6, w/arms, tape seat, orig dk finish, ML, 41½" 880.00
Rocker, #6, w/arms & bar, tape seat, NL, 1880-1900, 43" 750.00
Rocker, armless, maple, Harvard MA, mid-1800s, 41½" 2,000.00
Rocker, armless; maple, CB, rfn, 33½" 330.00
Rocker, maple, slat bk, red stain, EF, 1800s, 39½" 3,575.00
Rocker, w/arms, worn orig finish, rpl tape seat, ML, 38" 825.00
Rocker w/arms, 4-slat ladderbk, old rfn, 43" 550.00
Rug, shag; mc knitted woolens on cotton ground, 1890s, 24x40" .150.00
Shovel, grain; wooden, SDL, rfn, 36" 250.00
Stand, sewing; 3-tier, hardwood w/cherry stain, 8" 195.00
String holder, laminated walnut & maple, EF, rpr, 3⅜x4⅜" 250.00
Swift, w/table clamp, orig yel varnish, 20" 275.00
Table, birch, 1-drw, CB, 24½x28x17" 9,350.00
Table, poplar/pine, dvtl drw, tapered legs, WV, 28x37x22" 880.00
Table, work; Hepplewht, breadbrd top, stain traces, 56x40" 600.00
Table, work; poplar/pine, 1 drop-leaf, worn, SDL, 44x28" 175.00
Teakettle, tin, old rprs, ML, 7"+swivel hdl 165.00
Tub, rnd staves w/wooden bands, worn patina, 6¾x18" 275.00

Shaving Mugs

Between 1865 and 1920, the personalized shaving mug became very popular, with the occupational shaving mugs enjoying their greatest popularity. Most men having occupational mugs would frequent the barber shop several times a week where their mugs were clearly visible for all to see in the barber's rack. As a matter of fact, this display was in many ways the index of the individual town or neighborhood.

During the first twenty years, blank mugs were almost entirely imported from France, Germany and Austria and were hand painted in this country. Later on, some china was produced by local companies. It is noteworthy that American vitreous china is inferior to the imported Limoges and is subject to extreme crazing.

Artists employed by the American barber supply companies were, for the most part extremely talented and were capable of executing any design the owner required, depicting his occupation, fraternal affiliation or sport. When the mug was completed, the name was always added (as was the gold trim) in varying degrees, depending on the price paid by the customer. This price was determined by the barber who added his markup to that of the barber supply company. As mentioned above, the popularity of the occupational shaving mug diminished with the advent of World War I and the introduction by Gillette of the safety razor, later followed by the blue laws forcing barber shops to close on Sundays, thereby eliminating the political and social discussions for which the barber shops were so well noted.

Occupational shaving mugs are the most sought after of the group which would include those with sport affiliations. Fraternal mugs, although desirable, do not command the same price as the occupationals. Occasionally, you will find the owner's occupation together with his fraternal affiliation. This combination could add anywhere between 25% to 50% to the price. Price is dependent on the execution of the painting, rarity of the subject and detail. Some subjects can be done very simply; others can be done in extreme detail, commanding substantially higher prices. It is fair to say, however, that the rarity of the occupation will dictate the price. Mugs which have lost the gold through wear lose between 20% and 30% of their value immediately. This would not apply to the gold trim around the rim, but to the loss of the name itself. Our advisor for this category is Burton Handelsman; he is listed in the Directory under New York.

Character, Egyptian lady, bsk, purple & gr, M 595.00
Fraternal, Shriner symbol & gold scrolls 235.00
Fruit vignettes, T&V Limoges 170.00
Millersville Shooting Club, Eisemann 325.00
Occupational, baker, pretzel, name, gold trim 225.00
Occupational, blacksmith, man at forge, T&V Limoges 425.00
Occupational, bricklayer, 5 men working 250.00
Occupational, Dr driving 1-horse buggy, name in gold 475.00
Occupational, farmer plowing, wear on gold 300.00
Occupational, furniture dealer, furniture, T&V Limoges 600.00
Occupational, hunter, dog, rabbit & horn, Koken, Limoges 175.00
Occupational, ice wagon driver, EX gold, T&V Limoges 850.00
Occupational, livestock dealer, steer's & horse's heads, T&V 300.00
Occupational, painter, man on scaffold, Kern 600.00
Occupational, postman delivering mail 2,900.00
Occupational, roofer/tinsmith, man on roof, worn gold 750.00
Occupational, storekeeper, store int, line in hdl 600.00
Occupational, tailor, man at work, Made in USA 475.00
Occupational, trainman, locomotive & tender, EX 225.00
Occupational, undertaker, horse-drawn hearse 1,550.00
Patriotic, eagle/flags/shield/etc, T&V Limoges 110.00
Photographic, town scene, name of town at bottom, EX 100.00
SP, floral decor, w/insert, Superior Co 75.00
18th-century tavern int, dancers lithophane 75.00

Shawnee

The Shawnee Pottery Company operated in Zanesville, Ohio, from 1937 to 1961. They produced inexpensive novelty ware (vases, flowerpots, and figurines) as well as a very successful line of figural cookie jars, creamers, and salt and pepper shakers.

They also produced three dinnerware lines, the first of which, Valencia, was designed by Louise Bauer in 1937 for Sears & Roebuck. A starter set was given away with the purchase of one of their refrigerators. Second and most popular was the King Corn line. It was produced from 1946 to 1954, when the colors were changed to a lighter yellow for the kernels and darker green for the shucks. This variation was called Queen Corn. (Our values are for yellow corn prices unless white is noted in the description.) Their third dinnerware line, produced after 1954, was called Lobsterware. It was made in either black, brown, or gray; lobsters were usually applied to serving pieces and accessory items.

For further study we recommend these books: *The Collector's Guide to Shawnee Pottery* by our advisors, Janice and Duane Vanderbilt, who are listed in the Directory under Indiana; and *Shawnee Pottery, An Identification and Value Guide*, by Jim and Bev Mangus, who are listed in Ohio.

Cookie Jars

Basketweave, hexagon form, mk USA, minimum value 50.00
Beanpot, Snowflake, w/decal, mk USA, minimum value 50.00
Drum Major, mk USA 10, minimum value 200.00
Dutch Boy, cold pnt, mk USA, minimum value 65.00
Dutch Boy, striped pants, mk USA, minimum value 125.00
Dutch Girl, gold & decal, mk USA, minimum value 250.00
Dutch Girl, pnt under glaze, mk USA, minimum value 75.00
Elephant, Sitting; cold pnt, mk USA, minimum value 75.00
Elephant, Sitting; gold trim & decals, mk USA 350.00
Fruit Basket, mk Shawnee 84, minimum value 125.00
Jo Jo the Clown, mk Shawnee 12, minimum value 300.00
Jug, pnt flowers, mk USA, minimum value 75.00
Little Chef, gr, mk USA, minimum value 75.00
Muggsy, gold trim & decals, Pat Muggsy USA, minimum value .550.00
Owl, mk USA, minimum value 125.00
Puss'n Boots, mk Pat Puss'n Boots, minimum value 150.00

Puss 'n Boots, gold with decals, marked Pat Puss 'n Boots, $375.00 minimum value.

Sailor Boy, gold & decals, mk USA, minimum value 550.00
Smiley the Pig, apples, mk USA, minimum value 350.00
Smiley the Pig, gold & decals, mk USA, minimum value ...:......275.00
Smiley the Pig, plums, mk USA, minimum value 325.00
Smiley the Pig, toupee, gold & decals, minimum value 375.00
Winnie the Pig, bl collar, gold trim, mk USA, minimum value .350.00
Winnie the Pig, chocolate base, Winnie 61, minimum value 300.00
Winnie the Pig, clover bud, Pat Winnie USA, minimum value .300.00

Corn Line

Bowl, cereal; mk #94 ....45.00
Bowl, mixing; mk #6, 6" 30.00
Bowl, vegetable; mk #95 ....35.00
Butter dish, mk #72 ....50.00

Creamer, gold trim, mk USA 60.00
Creamer, mk #70 ....25.00
Cup, #90 ....30.00
Mug, #69 ....45.00
Pitcher, mk #71 ....65.00
Pitcher, wht corn, gold trim, mk USA 100.00
Pitcher, wht corn, mk USA 70.00
Plate, mk #68, 10" 30.00
Plate, mk #93, 8" 25.00
Platter, mk #96, 12" 45.00
Relish dish, mk #79 ....17.00
Saucer, mk #91 ....12.00
Shakers, Indian corn, pr 65.00
Shakers, lg, pr 25.00
Sugar bowl, w/lid, mk #78 ....30.00
Sugar shaker, wht corn 75.00
Teapot, mk #65, 10-oz 175.00
Teapot, wht corn, gold trim, mk USA, 30-oz 120.00

Kitchen Ware

Casserole, fruit in basketweave bowl form, mk Shawnee 83 ....70.00
Coffeepot, Sunflower, mk USA 175.00
Creamer, Elephant, gold trim, mk Pat USA 150.00
Creamer, Puss 'n Boots, mk Pat Puss'n Boots 45.00
Creamer, quill decor, ball form, mk USA 12 ....125.00
Creamer, Smiley the Pig, bl & yel, mk Shawnee 86 ....50.00
Lobster, shakers, lobster hdls, brn, pr 45.00
Lobster, spoon holder 175.00
Lobster, sugar bowl, Kenwood, #907 ....22.50
Pitcher, Bo Peep, gold w/decals, mk Pat Bo Peep 200.00
Pitcher, Charlie Chicken, gold trim, mk Chanticleer 250.00
Pitcher, Charlie Chicken, mk Pat Chanticleer 70.00
Pitcher, Flower & Fern, jug form 50.00
Pitcher, Pennsylvania Dutch, mk USA 64 ....95.00
Pitcher, Smiley the Pig, apple, mk Pat Smiley USA 175.00
Pitcher, Smiley the Pig, peach flower, mk Pat Smiley 125.00
Shakers, Charlie Chicken, gold trim, lg, pr 125.00
Shakers, cottage, mk USA 9, sm, pr 175.00
Shakers, ducks, sm, pr 35.00
Shakers, Farmer Pig, gold trim, sm, pr 100.00
Shakers, Muggsy, lg, pr 100.00
Shakers, Smiley, gr bib w/gold & decals, lg, pr 200.00
Shakers, Swiss boy & girl, gold trim, lg, pr 75.00
Shakers, Winnie & Smiley, gold trim, sm, pr 100.00
Shakers, Winnie & Smiley, heart decor, lg, pr 100.00
Shakers, Winnie & Smiley, sm, pr 55.00
Sugar bowl, Bucket, mk Great Northern USA 1042 ....55.00
Sugar bowl, Pennsylvania Dutch, jug form, mk USA 100.00
Teapot, Clover Bud, mk USA 125.00
Teapot, elephant, gold trim, mk USA 175.00
Teapot, Granny Ann, gr apron, mk Pat Granny Ann 80.00
Teapot, Snowflake, mk USA 40.00
Teapot, Tom Tom, mk Tom the Piper's Son Pat USA 70.00
Teapot, Tulip, mk USA 50.00
Valencia, chop plate, 13" 55.00
Valencia, creamer & sugar bowl, bl & yel, mk 12.00
Valencia, nappy, 9½" 17.00
Valencia, pitcher, water; mk 45.00
Valencia, plate, tangerine, 10" 15.00

Miscellaneous

Bank, bulldog 130.00

Bank, Howdy Doody, mk USA Bob Smith 375.00
Cigarette box, emb trademk, mk USA 225.00
Figurine, Oriental playing mandolin, lg, pr 40.00
Figurine, tumbling bear, gold & decals 110.00
Flowerpot, emb leaves, attached saucer, mk Shawnee USA 465 ..12.00
Lamp, girl w/mandolin, low base, unmk 35.00
Lamp base, Champ the Dog 20.00
Miniature, cornucopia, mk USA 15.00
Miniature, pitcher, mk USA 15.00
Planter, canopy bed, mk Shawnee 734 ....60.00
Planter, clown w/pot, mk USA 619 ....15.00
Planter, Colonial lady, gold trim, mk USA 616 ....35.00
Planter, fawn by stump, gold trim, mk USA 535 ....18.00
Planter, Irish Setter, mk USA 10.00
Planter, pig & wheelbarrow, mk USA 14.00
Planter, pony, curly mane & tail, mk Shawnee 506 ....40.00
Planter, poodle on bicycle, mk USA 712 ....32.00
Planter, rabbit & cabbage, wht, mk USA 10.00
Vase, bulbous, mk Kenwood USA 2014, 10" 22.00
Vase, hdls, gold trim, mk USA 878, 8" 22.00
Vase, iris emb on wht fan form, mk USA, 6" 18.00
Wall pocket, bow, gold trim, mk USA 434 ....35.00

Shearwater

Since 1928 generations of the Peter, Walter, and James McConnell Anderson families have been producing figurines and artwares in their studio at Ocean Springs, Mississippi. Their work is difficult to date. Figures from the twenties and thirties won critical acclaim and have continued to be made to the present time. Early marks include a die-stamped 'Shearwater' in a dime-sized circle, a similar ink stamp, and a half-circle mark. Any older item may still be ordered in the same glazes as it was originally produced, so many pieces on the market today may be relatively new. However, the older marks are not currently in use. Currently produced Blacks and pirates figurines are marked with a hand-incised 'Shearwater' and/or a cypher formed with an 'S' whose bottom curve doubles as the top loop of a 'P' formed by the addition of an upright placed below and to the left of the S. Many are dated, '93, for example. These figures are generally valued at $35.00 to $50.00 and are available at the pottery or by mail order. New decorated and carved pieces are very expensive, starting at $400.00 to $500.00 for a 6" pot.

Bowl, rtcl floral shoulder, lt gr semi-matt, sgn MA, 4x6½" 400.00
Figurine, pirate, 6½" 45.00
Lamp, Blk Minstrel player, wht 75.00
Tile, advertising; textured turq irid, 6x11" 200.00
Vase, bl over rose, hdls, mk, 5" 135.00
Vase, Blk figures & animals, bl/gr/gold flambe w/gold, 11½" 450.00
Vase, red copper lustre, gourd shape, 6" 210.00
Vase, stylized curtain motif, gr metallic, Anderson, '46, 9½" 700.00

Sheet Music

Sheet music is often collected more for its colorful lithographed covers, rather than for the music itself. Transportation songs (which have pictures or illustrations of trains, ships, and planes), Ragtime and Blues, Comic characters (especially Disney), Sports, Political, and Expositions are eagerly sought after. Much of the sheet music on the market today is valued at under $5.00; some of the better examples are listed here. Values are given for examples in excellent to near-mint condition unless otherwise noted.

Our advisor for this category is Jeannie Peters; she is listed in the Directory under Ohio.

Red Wing, by Kerry Mills and Thurland Chattaway, color Indian cover, 1907, NM, $40.00.

Abraham, Irving Berlin, 1942 ....10.00
Afraid, Rex Allen photo cover, 1949 ....5.00
After Taps, WWII, 1918 ....15.00
After the First of July, cover by Pfeiffer, 1919 ....15.00
All or Nothing, Rogers & Hammerstein II, from Oklahoma, 1943 .5.00
Amapola, Jimmy Dorsey photo cover, 1924 ....5.00
America Lindbergh Is Your Boy, c 1927, EX 10.00
American Guard March, by Arthur Bergh, March, 1924 ....15.00
American Patrol, Meacham, 1885 ....10.00
Anytime, Eddy Arnold & Eddie Fisher photo cover, 1921 ....5.00
At Long Last Love, Movie: You Never Know 5.00
At Peace w/the World, Irving Berlin, 1926 ....10.00
Baby Mine, Movie: Dumbo (Disney), 1941 ....15.00
Beale St Blues, WC Handy, Blues, 1916 ....10.00
Beautiful Star of Heaven, Drumheiler, 1905 ....10.00
Bianica, Musical: Kiss Me Kate, 1948 ....5.00
Boys From Yankee Land, WWI, 1916 ....15.00
Breeze From Alabama, A; Scott Joplin, 1902 ....50.00
Bring Back My Loving Man, Irving Berlin, 1911 ......15.00
Down in the Depths, Cole Porter, Movie: Red, Hot & Blue, 1936 .5.00
Dream Dancing, Cole Porter, Movie: You'll Never Get Rich, 1941 .5.00
Easy Street, Toby Claude photo cover, 1905 ....10.00
Easy Winners, Scott Joplin, 1901 ....50.00
Go Away Little Girl, Donny Osmond photo cover, 1962 ....5.00
Good-Bye Flo, George M Cohan 15.00
He's a Rag Picker, Moss & Potter photo cover, 1914 ....15.00
He's a Right Guy, Movie: Something for the Boys, 1942 ....5.00
How Do You Do?, Movie: Song of the South, 1946 ....10.00
I Beg of You, Elvis Presley, 1957 ....20.00
I've Got My Washing To Do, Janette Davis photo cover 5.00
Java Jive, King Sisters photo cover, Jazz 5.00
Jesse James, Eileen Barton, 1954 ....5.00
Jim Crow Polka, Performers in Blk face, 1847 ....50.00
Just a Girl That Men Forget, Ulis & Lee photo cover, 1923 ....10.00
Just an Echo in the Valley, Bing Crosby photo cover, 1932 ....30.00
King Cotton March, John Philip Sousa, 1898 ....30.00
Kiss Me Goodnight, Guy Lombardo photo cover, 1935 ....5.00
Laugh & Call It Love, Bing Crosby photo cover, 1938 ....10.00
Let's Go, Movie: Toot Toot, 1918 ....8.00
Let's Go Home, Ila Grannon photo cover, 1908 ....10.00
Let's Sing a Gay Little Spring Song, Movie: Bambi (Disney), 1942 .10.00
Lies, Rudy Vallee photo cover, 1931 ....10.00
Light's Out, Rudy Vallee photo cover, 1935 ....8.00
Lincoln Centennial Grand March, President Lincoln 50.00
Little Toot, Movie: Melody Time (Disney), 1948 ....10.00
Little White Lies, Kate Smith Deco cover, 1930, EX ...20.00
Look Out for Jimmy Valentine, Gus Edwards photo cover, 1910 ..10.00

Lord! Have Mercy on a Married Man; Dochstader cover, 1911 ....20.00
Love Lives Forever, John Philip Sousa, 1918 ....20.00
Love Me Tender, Elvis Presley photo cover, 1956 ....25.00
Love of My Life, Movie: The Pirate, 1948 ....5.00
Lullaby of Broadway, Movie: Al Jolson Story, 1932 ....15.00
Magic Is the Moonlight, Movie: Bathing Beauty, 1944 ....5.00
My Baby's Arms, Musical: Ziegfeld Follies, 1919 ....15.00
My Best Girl's a Corker, Washburn Sisters, 1895 ....15.00
My Mammy, Movie: Al Jolson Story, 1929 ....20.00
My Own, Edith Mason photo cover, 1905 ....10.00
Rose of Washington Square, Fanny Brice photo cover, 1920 ....20.00
Route 66, Nat King Cole photo cover, 1946 ....3.00
Ship Named USA, President Wilson photo cover, 1915 ....50.00
Short'nin' Bread, Eddy Nelson photo cover, 1928 ....100.00
Underneath the Stars, Dolly Sisters photo cover, 1915 ....5.00
When Uncle Joe Steps Into France, Eddie Cantor cover, 1918 ....25.00

Shelley

In 1872 Joseph Shelley became partners with James Wileman, owner of Foley China Works, thus creating Wileman & Co. in Stoke-on-Trent. Twelve years later James Wileman withdrew from the company, though the firm continued to use his name until 1925 when it became known as Shelley Potteries, Ltd. Like many successful 19th-century English potteries, this firm continued to produce useful household wares as well as dinnerware of considerable note. In 1896 the beautiful Dainty White shape was introduced, and it is regarded by many as synonymous with the name Shelley. In addition to the original Dainty 6-Flute design, other lovely shapes were produced: 12-Flute, 14-Flute, Oleander, Queen Anne, and the more modern shapes of Vogue, Regent, and Eve.

Though often overlooked, striking earthenware was produced under the direction of Frederick Rhead and later Walter Slater and his son Eric. Many notable artists contributed their talents in designing unusual, attractive wares: Rowland Morris, Mabel Lucie Attwell, and Hilda Cowham, to name but a few.

In 1966 Allied English Potteries acquired control of the Shelley Company, and by 1967 the last of the exquisite Shelley China had been produced to honor remaining overseas orders. In 1971 Allied English Potteries merged with the Doulton group. Our advisors for this category are Lila and Fred Shrader; they are listed in the Directory under California.

Key: MLA — Mabel Lucie Attwell

Ashtray, Dainty Blue, 6½" dia 42.00
Ashtray, Dainty White w/pk dots, 3½" dia 24.00
Ashtray, Drifting Leaves, 3½" sq 15.00
Ashtray, Whitehorse Whiskey, blk & wht, 6" sq 55.00
Bowl, cereal; Lilac Time, 6-flute, 6¼" 45.00
Bowl, cereal; Rose-Pansy-Forget Me Not, 6-flute, 6½" 40.00
Bowl, cereal; Serenity, 6½" 25.00
Bowl, cream soup; Dainty White, w/underplate 35.00
Bowl, cream soup; Rosebud, 6-flute, w/underplate 79.00
Bowl, flat soup; Rosebud, 6-flute, 7½" 65.00
Bowl, flat soup; Woodland (scenic), 7½" 75.00
Bowl, fruit; Cloisonne, bl, 5½" 25.00
Bowl, fruit; Glorious Devon, 6-flute, 5½" 35.00
Bowl, rimmed soup; Blue Iris, Queen Anne shape, 8¼" 65.00
Bowl, rimmed soup; Dainty Blue, 8" 75.00
Bowl, rimmed soup; Syringa, 6-flute, 8" 65.00
Bowl, vegetable; Dainty Blue, 6-flute, hdls, w/lid, 9½" 245.00
Bowl, vegetable; Hedgerow, oval, 9" 125.00
Bowl, vegetable; Regency, 6-flute, hdls, w/lid, 9½" 195.00

Bowl, vegetable; Rosebud, 6-flute, hdls, w/lid, 9½" 200.00
Bowl, vegetagle; Rosebud, 6-flute, 9½" 145.00
Box, Coronation George V (1911), w/lid, 2" dia 85.00
Box, Heraldic, Butter of Pitlochry, w/lid, 2" dia 75.00
Box, Violets, 6-flute, w/lid, 3½x3½" 135.00
Butter dish, DuBarry, 7½" dia 75.00
Butter dish, Heather (scenic), 7½" dia 125.00
Butter dish, Maytime (Chintz), 7½" dia 175.00
Butter dish, Regency, oblong shape, 6-flute 110.00
Butter dish, Rosebud, 6-flute, 7½" dia 145.00
Butter pat, Bridal Spray, 6-flute 55.00
Butter pat, Daffodil 42.00
Butter pat, Dainty Pink 60.00
Butter pat, Gordy's & seaside scene on lt bl 55.00
Butter pat, Harebell, Oleander shape 75.00
Butter pat, Lowestaft 45.00
Butter pat, Rosebud, 6-flute 55.00
Cake plate, Campanula, 6-flute, ped ft, 8" 175.00
Cake plate, Dainty White w/bl polka dots, 6-flute, ped ft 195.00
Cake plate, Old Sevres, 6-flute, ped ft, 8" 145.00
Cake plate, Primrose, 6-flute, tab hdls, 9" sq 95.00
Cake plate, Wildflowers, 14-flute, tab hdls, 8½" dia 100.00
Cake plate, Windflower, 6-flute, tab hdls, 9" sq 125.00
Candle holder, Cloisonne, 9" 195.00
Candle holder, pnt flowers on blk matt, 7" 95.00
Candle holder, sm flower & leaves (enamel-like), 9" 225.00
Candy dish, Bridal Rose, 5" dia 32.00
Candy dish, Dainty Blue, 5" dia 42.00
Candy dish, Iris, 14-flute, 5½" sq 40.00
Candy dish, Primrose, 6-flute, 5" dia 40.00
Chamber set, pnt flowers on blk matt, pitcher+bowl+5 pcs 375.00
Chamberstick, Maytime, w/finger ring, 5" dia 95.00
Cheese dish, Bridal Rose (aka Rose Spray), w/domed lid 325.00
Children's ware, bowl (Baby's Plate), cute decor, 8" 110.00
Children's ware, cup & saucer, MLA animals 110.00
Children's ware, plate, Hilda Cowham scene, 8" 60.00
Children's ware, plate, MLA animals, 8" 95.00
Children's ware, teapot, mushroom house, 4½" 450.00
Chocolate pot, Heavenly Blue, 6-flute, 5½" 165.00
Chocolate pot, Indian Peony, 6½" 125.00
Cigarette holder, Bramble, 6-flute 35.00
Cigarette holder, Melody (Chintz) 39.00
Coffeepot, Blue Poppy, 6-flute, 8-cup 245.00
Coffeepot, Flashes & Flowers (Deco), Queen Anne, 8-cup 350.00
Coffeepot, Regency, 6-cup 145.00
Coffeepot, Summer Glory (Chintz) 185.00
Condiment set, Rosebud, shakers+mustard w/lid+tray 225.00
Creamer & sugar bowl, Bridal Rose, 6-flute, w/lid, med sz 100.00
Creamer & sugar bowl, Daffodil Time, med sz 55.00
Creamer & sugar bowl, Dainty Blue, 6-flute, w/lid, med sz 125.00
Creamer & sugar bowl, gold & blk panels, Queen Anne, w/lid ..145.00
Creamer & sugar bowl, Lily of the Valley, 6-flute, +tray 150.00
Creamer & sugar bowl, pastoral scene, Queen Anne, med sz 125.00
Cup & saucer, banded Bridal Rose, Henley shape 55.00

Cup and saucer, Blue Rock, six-flute, $55.00

Cup & saucer, Blue Poppy, 6-flute 57.00
Cup & saucer, Countryside (Chintz) 60.00
Cup & saucer, Dainty Blue, 6-flute 58.00
Cup & saucer, demi; Bramble, 6-flute 50.00
Cup & saucer, demi; Dainty shape w/floral hdl 65.00
Cup & saucer, demi; Iris, Regent shape 50.00
Cup & saucer, demi; Maytime (Chintz), Henley shape 58.00
Cup & saucer, demi; Sheraton, Gainsborough shape 35.00
Cup & saucer, fruit decor in cup, Oleander shape 60.00
Cup & saucer, Harebell, Oleander shape 54.00
Cup & saucer, Indian Peony, Gainsborough shape 50.00
Cup & saucer, Medallion, Queen Anne shape 50.00
Cup & saucer, Old Bow, enameling, Gainsborough shape ...57.00
Cup & saucer, Pansy, 6-flute, lg 58.00
Cup & saucer, scenics, Henley shape 55.00
Cup & saucer, Shamrock, 14-flute 55.00
Egg cup, Dainty White w/polka dots, 6-flute, sm 55.00
Egg cup, Regency, 6-flute, lg 55.00
Egg cup, Wild Anenome, 6-flute, sm 55.00
Ginger jar, Harmony Drip Ware, w/lid, 9½" 195.00
Gravy boat, Duchess, Gainsborough shape, w/underplate 90.00
Gravy boat, Hedgerow, Oleander shape, w/underplate 140.00
Gravy boat, Lily of the Valley, 6-flute, w/underplate 175.00
Horseradish container, Begonia, 6-flute, w/lid & underplate 150.00
Jam container, Bramble, 6-flute, w/lid 75.00
Jam container, Old Sevres, w/lid & underplate 110.00
Kitchen reminder, MLA vegetable people, 6x8" 120.00
Lamp base, Harmony Drip Ware, cone shape w/wide ft, 10" 225.00
Muffin, Lilac Time, 6-flute, w/lid, 9" 165.00
Muffin, Old Sevres, w/lid, 9" 135.00
Muffin, scattered flowers, mk Ideal, w/lid 65.00
Mug, Dainty Blue, 6-flute, 4¾" 95.00
Mug, Rosebud, 6-flute, 4¾" 75.00
Mustard container, Begonia, 6-flute, w/lid & underplate 125.00
Mustard container, Blue Daisy, w/lid 75.00
Napkin ring, Lily of the Valley 65.00
Pitcher, Honeysuckle, 6-flute, 7½" 125.00
Pitcher, Pansies (sm, scattered), Queen Anne shape, 6½" 95.00
Pitcher, utilitarian ware w/bl stripe at base, 6½" 55.00
Plate, Begonia, 6-flute, 10½" 60.00
Plate, Begonia, 6-flute, 8" 38.00
Plate, Bridal Rose, 6-flute, 10½" 70.00
Plate, Bridal Rose, 6-flute, 8" 38.00
Plate, Garland of Flowers, Queen Anne shape, 10¼" 85.00
Plate, Harebell, Oleander shape, 6" 22.00
Plate, Harebell, Oleander shape, 8" 32.00
Plate, Heather (scenic), 10½" 65.00
Plate, Heather (scenic), 8" 38.00
Plate, Maytime (Chintz), 8" 45.00
Plate, Old Sevres, 10½", in ¾" sterling fr 165.00
Plate, Old Sevres, 8" 38.00
Plate, Sheraton, 10½" 42.00
Plate, Sheraton, 7½" 28.00
Platter, Bridal Rose, Oleander shape, 14x11" 225.00
Platter, Bridal Rose, 6-flute, 16x13½" 285.00
Platter, Dainty Blue, 6-flute, 12x10" 200.00
Platter, Indian Peony, 14x12" 95.00
Platter, Wild Anenome, 6-flute, 14x12" 210.00
Pudding mold, Crayfish, utilitarian ware, 6x8" 95.00
Relish dish, Old Bow, Gainsborough shape, 5x8½" 45.00
Relish dish, Rose & Red Daisy, 6-flute, 5x9" 100.00
Shakers, Blue Rock, 6-flute, cylindrical, 3½", pr 100.00
Shakers, Dainty White, 6-flute, pear shape, 4", pr 55.00
Snack set, Stocks, cup+intented 8" sq plate 75.00

Tankard, Festival of Empire series, 7" 200.00
Tankard, Indian Peony, 7" 55.00
Tea & toast set, Blue Rock, 6-flute, cup+6x9" plate 85.00
Tea & toast set, Rosebud, 6-flute, cup+5x8" plate 75.00
Teapot, Daffodil Time, 6-cup 145.00
Teapot, Dainty White w/polka dots, 6-flute, 6-cup 245.00
Teapot, DuBarry, 8-cup 145.00
Teapot, Hedgerow, Oleander shape, 6-cup 195.00
Teapot, Phlox, Regent shape, 6-cup 165.00
Toast rack, Dainty White, 5-bar 45.00
Toast rack, Harebell, 3-bar 75.00
Toast rack, Primrose (Chintz) 95.00
Tray, sandwich; Begonia, 6-flute, 4½x11½" 145.00
Tray, sandwich; Serenity, 4½x11½" 65.00
Tray, tea; Bridal Rose, 6-flute, oval, 16" 450.00
Tray, triple; Dainty Pink, 6-flute, w/hdl, lg 225.00
Vase, Moorcroft style, bulbous, 8" 440.00
Vase, Moresque, pnt decor, cone shape, 7½" 275.00

Shenandoah

The Shenandoah Valley, extending from Virginia to Pennsylvania, is well known for the fine pottery made there from the early 1800s until the turn of the century. It is characterized by bright, clear glazes in a variety of colors or in compination. Many small potteries were involved. Items marked 'Bell' indicate one of the large companies.

Jug, clear w/brn & gr sponging, sm flakes, 2¾" 50.00
Jug, clear w/gr circles & brn daubs, strap hdl, hairline, 5" 40.00
Pitcher, yel/gr/brn mottle, incised shoulder line, 7", EX 800.00
Spittoon, gr/orange/yel mottle w/manganese splotches, 7", NM .490.00

Silhouettes

Silhouette portraits were made by positioning the subject between a bright light and a sheet of white drawing paper. The resulting shadow was then traced and cut out, the paper mounted over a contrasting color and framed. The hollow-cut process was simplified by an invention called the Physiognotrace, a device that allowed tracing and cutting to be done in one operation. Experienced silhouette artists could do full-length figures, scenics, ships, or trains freehand. Some of the most famous of these artists were Charles Peale Polk, Charles Wilson Peale, William Bache, Doyle, Edouart, Chamberlain, Brown, and William King. Though not often seen, some silhouettes were completely painted or executed in wax. Examples listed here are hollow-cut unless noted.

Key:
bk — backing   p — profile
c/p — cut and pasted   wc — watercolor
fl — full length

Boy w/bow & arrow, fl, c/p, gilt fr, 12⅜x8½" 1,100.00
Family, men/lady/girl, fl, c/p, identified, 1838, fr, 12x16" 330.00
Family set of 10, p, birth dates from 1777 to 1820, fr, 12x8" 825.00
Lady, p, blk cloth bk, mahog veneer fr, 7¾x6" 95.00
Lady, p, blk w/red & gilt detail, 1826, fr, 5x4¼" 415.00
Lady, p, ink, worn rvpt glass, brass fr, 5⅞x5⅛" 200.00
Lady, p, ink detail, identified, 1829, gilt fr, 3¾" 195.00
Lady, p, ink detail, rvpt glass, blk fr, 6x5" 60.00
Lady, p, pencil detail, pin-prick floral mat, fr, 14x14" 635.00
Lady in long dress holds book, hair up, c/p, fr, 13x8½" 210.00

Man, p, blk ink & gilt detail, identified, fr, 5½x4⅞" 360.00
Man, p, charcoal gouache, ink & gilt, fr, 8x6¾" 360.00
Man, p, ink & gold wash, blk lacquer fr w/gilt, 5¼x4½" 465.00
Man, p, ink/pencil/ink wash, convex glass fr, 5¼" dia 75.00
Man, p, minor stain, maple veneer fr, 7¾x6¼" 165.00
Man, p, minor stains, modern fr, 6x5" 55.00
Man, p, pencil/ink details, identified, 1829, 5½x4½" 330.00
Man & lady, p, blk cloth bk, ink details, fr, 5¾x8½" 75.00
Man & lady, p, ink details, sgn Doyle, pr in gilt fr, 7x10" 415.00
Man & lady, p, ink/wc, emb brass fr, 5⅛x4½", pr 715.00
Man on chair w/book & glasses, wc scenic bk, gilt fr, 13x12" 310.00
Man w/horse, ink/gouache on paper, sgn/1840, fr, 15x17" 690.00
Man w/queue, p, blk silk bk, old fr, 5x4" 250.00
Man w/sword, fl, identified, 1838, fr, 14x10" 300.00
Man w/top hat & cane, fl c/p, sepia ink, Edouart/1843, 14x11" ..465.00
Mother/2 children, fl, c/p, ink-wash bk, Edouart/1843, 14x11" ..5,500.00
Officer, p, charcoal gouache/ink/gilt, fr, 5⅜x4½" 220.00
Youth, p, blk cut w/wht & red detail, stain, 5⅝x4" 140.00
Youth, p, emb label: Museum, 7x5½" 250.00
Youth, p, red & bl ink detail, NP fr w/convex glass, 4½" 95.00

Silver

Coin Silver

The mark 'Coin Silver' was used after the 1830s to indicate items
made with 900 parts of silver to every 1000 parts of content.

Key:
gw — gold washed   t-oz — troy ounce

A Tyler, New Orleans; cup, chased/emb floral sprig, 1850, 4" 350.00
AG Storm, tongs 55.00
Benedict, spoon, 8¼" 65.00
Daniel Jackson, tablespoon, coffin 75.00
DM Spurgin, ladle, rattail hdl, 7½" 415.00
E Lownes, Phila; teapot, floral band at shoulder, 1820s, 10" 950.00
E Pro Filet, Natches, MS; mustard ladle, 1800s 350.00
E&D Kinsey, tablespoon, rattail hdl, 8¾" 20.00
E&D Kinsey, teaspoon, rattial hdl, 5¾", 3 for 25.00
Gorham, cup, leaves/pods/stippling/name/1860, ftd, 4" 225.00
GR Dunning, NY; spoon, 8¾" 32.50
Harding, olive fork 40.00
Harrington & Hunnewell, serving spoon, 7½" 20.00
HP Buckley, New Orleans; emb/eng floral sprig, 1855, 4" 275.00
Hyde-Goodrich, baby cup, plain w/beaded hdl, 1800s 85.00
Hyde-Goodrich, beaker, heart band at base, monogram, 1850s ..425.00
Hyde-Goodrich, tablespoon, fiddle hdl, eng initials, pr 150.00
J Draper, tablespoon 55.00
JA Clark, spoon, 9" 45.00
Jaccard, St Louis; tablespoon, Threaded Fiddle 50.00
JB Jones, Boston; porringer, ca 1835, 9-t-oz, 5½" 865.00
JG Libby, Boston; teaspoon, 6⅛", 3 for 25.00
JH Morse, teaspoon 20.00
Joel Sayre, NY; teapot, mid-band, leaf final, ball ft, 5" 495.00
N Roth, Utica, sugar shovel, Fiddle 50.00
P Chitry, NY/Phila; tea service, gadroon bands, 76-t-oz, 4-pc .3,500.00
Pear & Bacall, spoon, 9" 55.00
S Hildeburn, spoon, 9" 75.00
S&R, tablespoon, oval, ca 1800 ....65.00
Smith & Sharp, London; goblet, early 1800s, 4" 100.00
T Richards, tablespoon, 3-masted ship crest on bk, ca 1805 ....650.00
Thomas Baker, spoon, 9" 75.00

Tift & Whiting, goblet, 5½" 95.00
Unmk Am, saucepan, dome lid, wood hdl, 1800, 6" 465.00
WP Bingham, spoon, 8¼" 60.00
Zahn & Jackson, spoon, 9" 50.00

Flatware

Silver flatware is being collected today either to replace missing
pieces of heirloom sets or in lieu of buying new patterns, by those who
admire and appreciate the style and quality of the older ware. Prices vary
from dealer to dealer; some pieces are harder to find and are therefore
more expensive. Items such as olive spoons, cream ladles, lemon forks,
etc., once thought a necessary part of a silver service, may today be slow to
sell; as a result, dealers may price them low and make up the difference on
items that sell more readily. Many factors enter into evaluation. Popular
patterns may be high due to demand though easily found, while scarce
patterns may be passed over by collectors who find them difficult to
reassemble. See also Tiffany, Silver. Our advisors for this category are Rick
Spencer and JoAnn Kilmer; they are listed in the Directory under Utah.

Acorn, partial flatware service, Georg Jensen, thirty-two pieces, $2,090.00.

Antique Lily Engraved, oyster ladle, Whiting, 1902, 11½" 225.00
Avalon, berry spoon, Internat'l, 1900 ....150.00
Avalon, chocolate spoon, Internat'l, 1900 ....25.00
Avalon, fish slice, Internat'l, 1900, 11¾" 200.00
Avalon, jelly spoon, Internat'l, 1900 ....90.00
Avalon, pickle fork, Internat'l, 1900 ....57.50
Avalon, pie server, FH, Internat'l, 1900 ....295.00
Avalon, stuffing spoon, Internat'l, 1900, 12½" 425.00
Ben Franklin, bouillon spoon, Towle, 1904 ....22.00
Ben Franklin, cheese cleaver, Towle, 1904 ....25.00
Ben Franklin, iced teaspoon, Towle, 1904 ....22.00
Ben Franklin, knife, Towle, 1904, 8⅞" 30.00
Brocade, cheese server, Internat'l, 1950 ....20.00
Brocade, cocktail fork, Internat'l, 1950 ....17.00
Brocade, cold meat fork, Internat'l, 1950 ....55.00
Brocade, cream soup, Internat'l, 1950 ....25.00
Brocade, gravy ladle, Internat'l, 1950 ....55.00
Brocade, sugar spoon, Internat'l, 1950 ....25.00
Brocade, tablespoon, Internat'l, 1950 ....42.00
Brocade, tomato server, Internat'l, 1950 ....70.00
Buttercup, knife, Gorham, 1899, 8½" 25.00
Buttercup, pie trowel, Gorham, 1899, 9" 200.00
Buttercup, teaspoon, Gorham, 1899 ....16.00
Buttercup, 4-pc place setting, Gorham, 1899 ....105.00
Canterbury, berry spoon, Towle, 1893 ....75.00
Canterbury, jelly server, Towle, 1893 ....35.00
Canterbury, tomato server, Towle, 1893 ....95.00
Chantilly, bouillon spoon, Gorham, 1895 ....25.00
Chantilly, cocktail fork, Gorham, 1895 ....17.00
Chantilly, cream soup spoon, Gorham, 1895 ....25.00

Chantilly, fork, Gorham, 1895, 6⅞"	25.00
Chantilly, luncheon fork, Gorham, 1895	25.00
Chantilly, teaspoon, Gorham, 1895, 5¾"	17.00
Chrysanthemum, bouillon spoon, Durgin, 1893	50.00
Cleota, salt spoon, Internat'l, 1905	30.00
Clovelly, butter spreader, Reed & Barton, 1912	15.00
Clovelly, gumbo, Reed & Barton, 1912	19.00
Clovelly, knife, Reed & Barton, 1912, 9½"	22.00
Clovelly, sugar spoon, Reed & Barton, 1912	19.00
Cottage, dinner fork, Gorham, 1861	40.00
Courtship, cold meat fork, Internat'l, 1936	50.00
Courtship, fork, Internat'l, 1936, 7⅛"	19.00
Courtship, gumbo, Internat'l, 1936	21.00
Courtship, jelly server, Internat'l, 1936	17.00
Courtship, tablespoon, Internat'l, 1936	36.00
Courtship, teaspoon, Internat'l, 1936	12.00
Etruscan, coffee spoon, Gorham, 1913	22.00
Etruscan, jelly server, Gorham, 1913	28.00
Fairfax, iced teaspoon, Gorham, 1910	20.00
Fairfax, salad fork, Gorham, 1910	22.00
Fairfax, teaspoon, Gorham, 1910	13.00
Fairfax, 4-pc place setting, Gorham, 1910	105.00
Fontainebleau, sugar shell, Gorham, 1880	55.00
Fontana, fork, Towle, 1957, 7⅛"	20.00
Fontana, gravy ladle, Towle, 1957	50.00
Fontana, salad fork, Towle, 1957	21.00
Fontana, sugar spoon, Towle, 1957	18.00
Fontana, tablespoon, Towle, 1957	38.00
Fontana, teaspoon, Towle, 1957	16.00
Francis I, 4-pc place setting	135.00
French Provincial, baby fork, Towle, 1949	16.00
French Provincial, butter spreader, Towle, 1949	15.00
French Provincial, gravy ladle, Towle, 1949	48.00
French Provincial, luncheon fork, Towle, 1949	20.00
French Provincial, nut spoon, Towle, 1949	23.00
French Provincial, sugar spoon, Towle, 1949	17.00
French Provincial, tablespoon, Towle, 1949	42.00
Georgian, bouillon spoon, Towle, 1898	35.00
Georgian, butter spreader, Towle, 1898	35.00
Georgian, lemon fork, Towle, 1898	25.00
Georgian, luncheon fork, Towle, 1898	35.00
Georgian, salad fork, Towle, 1898	40.00
Georgian, salt spoon, Towle, 1898	15.00
Georgian, teaspoon, Towle, 1898	30.00
Georgian, tomato server, Towle, 1898	85.00
Grande Baroque, cream spoon, Wallace, 1941	33.00
Grande Baroque, fork, Wallace, 1941, 7⅜"	30.00
Grande Baroque, teaspoon, Wallace, 1941	16.00
Grande Baroque, 4-pc place setting, Wallace, 1941	125.00
Imperial Chrysanthemum, berry scoop, Gorham, 1894	225.00
Imperial Chrysanthemum, cream ladle, Gorham, 1894	90.00
Imperial Chrysanthemum, dessert spoon, Gorham, 1894	40.00
Imperial Chrysanthemum, dinner fork, Gorham, 1894	50.00
Imperial Chrysanthemum, teaspoon, Gorham, 1894	35.00
King George, butter spreader, Gorham, 1894	30.00
King George, dessert spoon, Gorham, 1894	40.00
King George, dinner knife, Gorham, 1894	35.00
King George, teaspoon, Gorham, 1894	25.00
King Richard, cheese server, Towle, 1932	26.00
King Richard, dinner knife, Towle, 1932	35.00
King Richard, fork, Towle, 1932, 7¼"	30.00
King Richard, master butter spreader, Towle, 1932	35.00
King Richard, oval soup, Towle, 1932	45.00
King Richard, place spoon, Towle, 1932, 6"	20.00

King Richard, sugar spoon, Towle, 1932	33.00
King Richard, 4-pc place setting, Towle, 1932	125.00
Lancaster, luncheon fork, Gorham, 1897	35.00
Lancaster, rnd soup, Gorham, 1897	30.00
Lancaster, salad fork, Gorham, 1897	45.00
Lark, nut spoon, Reed & Barton, 1960	20.00
Lark, pie server, Reed & Barton, 1960	25.00
Lark, sauce ladle, Reed & Barton, 1960	25.00
Lark, sugar spoon, Reed & Barton, 1960	18.00
Lily, butter spreader, Whiting, 1902	40.00
Lily, dinner fork, Whiting, 1902	65.00
Lily, luncheon fork, Whiting, 1902	35.00
Lily, rnd soup, Whiting, 1902	50.00
Louis XV, cream soup, Whiting, 1891	40.00
Louis XV, fish slice, 1891, 11¾"	300.00
Louis XV, luncheon fork, Whiting, 1891	30.00
Lyric, cold meat fork, Gorham, 1940	50.00
Lyric, fork, Gorham, 1940, 7¼"	20.00
Lyric, gravy ladle, Gorham, 1940	45.00
Lyric, lemon fork, Gorham, 1940	10.00
Lyric, salad fork, Gorham, 1940	20.00
Lyric, sugar spoon, Gorham, 1940	20.00
Lyric, tablespoon, Gorham, 1940	37.00
Lyric, 4-pc place setting, Gorham, 1940	85.00
Madeira, fork, Towle, 1948, 7⅜"	20.00
Madeira, jelly server, Towle, 1948	21.00
Madeira, master butter spreader, Towle, 1948	16.00
Madeira, salad fork, Towle, 1948	19.00
Mt Vernon, teaspoon, Lunt, 1905, 5¾"	12.00
Mythologique, bouillon spoon, Gorham, 1894	40.00
Mythologique, cocktail fork, Gorham, 1894	35.00
Mythologique, cold meat fork, Gorham, 1894	150.00
Mythologique, ice cream fork, Gorham, 1894	65.00
Mythologique, tablespoon, Gorham, 1894	85.00
Old Baronial, beef fork, Gorham, 1898	50.00
Old Baronial, bouillon spoon, Gorham, 1898	20.00
Old Baronial, cold meat fork, Gorham, 1898	70.00
Old Baronial, fork, Gorham, 1898, 6⅞"	20.00
Old Baronial, fork, Gorham, 1898, 7⅝"	27.00
Old Baronial, fruit Spoon, Gorham, 1898	20.00
Repousse, sugar tongs, Kirk	35.00
Rose Solitaire, baby fork, Towle, 1954	19.00
Rose Solitaire, butter spreader, Towle, 1954	15.00
Rose Solitaire, cold meat fork, Towle, 1954	55.00
Rose Solitaire, soup spoon, Towle, 1954	23.00
Rose Solitaire, sugar spoon, Towle, 1954	21.00
Royal Danish, fish serving fork, Internat'l, 1939, 9⅛"	125.00
Sea Rose, dessert spoon, Gorham, 1958	25.00
Sea Rose, gravy ladle, Gorham, 1958	47.00
Sea Rose, master butter spreader, Gorham, 1958	21.00
Sea Rose, pie server, Gorham, 1958	25.00
Sea Rose, sugar spoon, Gorham, 1958	17.00
Sea Rose, teaspoon, Gorham, 1958	11.00
Sir Christopher, cream ladle, Wallace, 1936	50.00
Sir Christopher, demitasse spoon, Wallace, 1936	22.00
Sir Christopher, dinner knife, Wallace, 1936	35.00
Sir Christopher, salad fork, Wallace, 1936	30.00
Sir Christopher, serving spoon, Wallace, 1936	70.00
Sir Christopher, 4-pc place setting, Wallace, 1936	125.00
Strasbourg, luncheon fork	20.00
Strasbourg, teaspoon	15.00
Stratford, luncheon fork, Internat'l, 1902	20.00
Versailles, bouillon spoon, Gorham, 1888	35.00
Versailles, coffee spoon, Gorham, 1888	30.00

Versailles, knife, Gorham, 1888, 7½"	42.00
Versailles, pie server, Gorham, 1888	225.00
Versailles, salad-serving fork, Gorham, 1888	200.00
Violet, berry spoon, Wallace, 1904	185.00

Hollow Ware

Until the middle of the 19th century, the silverware produced in America was custom made on order of the buyer directly from the silversmith. With the rise of industrialization, factories sprung up that manufactured silverware for retailers who often added their trademark to the ware. Silver ore was mined in abundance, and demand spurred production. Changes in style occurred at the whim of fashion. Repousse decoration (relief work) became popular about 1885, reflecting the ostentatious preference of the Victorian era. Later in the century, Greek, Etruscan, and several classic styles found favor. Today the Art Deco styles of this century are very popular with collectors.

In the listings that follow, manufacturer's name or trademark is noted first; in lieu of that information, listings are by country. Weight is given in troy ounces. See also Tiffany, Silver.

Key: t-oz — troy ounce

Samuel Kirk, coffeepot, scroll and rocaille cartouch surrounds coat-of-arms and initialed crest, scroll spout and handle, engraved flowers, thistle finial, 1830-1846, gross weight 43 oz. 10 dwt., 11¼", $1,430.00.

A Stone, bud vase, cylinder w/flaring base, 1918, 8", pr	1,500.00
A Stone, candlesticks, fluted baluster stems, 1918, 11", pr	2,200.00
A Stone, coffeepot, ivory stick hdl, 3-ftd, monogram, 7"	990.00
Aage Weimar, coffee set, floral finials, ebony hdl, 3-pc	880.00
Blk-Starr-Frost, coffee service, octagonal, 7-pc, 100-t-oz	1,000.00
Blk-Starr-Frost, pitcher, floral repousse, lyre hdl, 12"	1,650.00
Chinese, punch bowl, repousse dragon, mk, 1800s, 38-t-oz	1,800.00
Continental, fruit basket, rtcl ribbons/ropes, glass int, 12"	990.00
Danish, waste bowl, lion/ring hdls, 1900, 10-t-oz	250.00
Elmore, pitcher, vasiform w/eng scrolls, scroll hdl, 10"	975.00
English, salver, Georgian, shell/gadroon border, 1896, 11"	440.00
French, hot water pot, swirl lid, 3-leg pear shape, 1800s	500.00
Gale-Willis, wine flagon, beaded trim, C-hdl, 1868, 12½"	465.00
Geo Jensen, bowl, Bernadotte, scalloped/lobed, ftd, 8½"	1,495.00
Geo Jensen, compote, Grape, spiral stem, #263B, 7½x7"	1,750.00
Geo Jensen, goblet, Rohde, openwork flute/bead stem, 4", pr	1,725.00
Geo Jensen, pitcher, ebony hdl w/leaf & berry terminal, 6¾"	2,000.00
Geo Jensen, salts, modeled as owls w/hardstone eyes, 2½", pr	440.00
Geo Jensen, sauce boat, Grape, grapes on ft/hdl, #296, 7x9"	3,500.00
Gorham, bonbon, shaped pie-crust rim, monogram, 6"	50.00
Gorham, cup, figural repousse, C-scroll hdl, 1800s	230.00
Gorham, demi cup/saucer, Florenz, Lenox liners, 12 in case	1,650.00
Gorham, nut stands, rtcl, beaded edge, set of 12	230.00
Gorham, pitcher, classical urn shape, 1917, 11"	700.00
Gorham, pitcher, eng decor/crest, vasiform, 9"	600.00
Gorham, powder box, floral repousse, gilt int, rnd, 1800s	330.00

Gorham, sweets comport, rtcl fan/rosette/garland border	50.00
Gorham, tea/coffee set, Maintenon, 7-pc	7,500.00
Gorham, tea/coffee tray, cut-out hdls, eng sides, 27" tray	1,980.00
Gorham, tea/coffee tray, shell/feather emb border w/hdls	1,485.00
Gorham, vegetable dish, Maintenon, scroll hdl, lid, 13"	990.00
Gorham, vegetable dish, serpentine, eng lid/border, 14"	550.00
Henry Chawner, att; teapot stand, Geo III, monogram, 7"	350.00
Henry Nutting, att; vegetable dish, shell-eng lid, 1800, 10"	600.00
James Hewitt, brandy warmer, hammered pear shape, 1786	1,485.00
James Lloyd, att; castor, Geo III, urn finial, 1809, 7½"	465.00
JE Caldwell, fruit bowl, vermeil int, floral repousse, 8½"	495.00
JE Caldwell, soup tureen, gadrooned, pineapple finial	1,265.00
John Eames, creamer & sugar, bright-cut border/base, wreath	600.00
John Eames, hot water urn, lion-head/ring hdls, reeding, 18"	5,500.00
John Roberts, candlesticks, Geo III, reeded, 12¾", pr	2,000.00
Josh Healy, castor, Geo I, cylindrical, 1723	565.00
Kalo, vase, hammered, bulbous base, flared lip, mk, 7"	1,100.00
Kirk & Sons, fruit bowl, ftd, 20-t-oz, 9"	185.00
Kirk & Sons, salver, repousse border, claw/ball ft, 9"	550.00
Kirk & Sons, vegetable dish, griffin finial, allover repousse	3,500.00
Loring-Andrews, pitcher, allover repousse floral, 1850, 9"	440.00
Marshall Field, male & female pheasants, 17", pr	2,600.00
Persian, tray, floral eng/monogram, serpentine, 12½"	230.00
R Garrard, bowl, beading on ft, 1830s, 7x10"	750.00
Reed & Barton, tea tray, eng cartouch, serpentine, 25"	1,800.00
RM EH, monteith bowl, mask/ring hdls, inscribed, 10½"	3,500.00
Robert Salmon, vegetable dish, Geo III, threaded border, 11"	700.00
Rogers, water pitcher, plain oval w/C-hdl, 32-t-oz, 10"	550.00
S Alexander, creamer, ribbed edge, melon form, 1808	300.00
Shreve & Co, tea/coffee set, strapwork edging, 1900, 5-pc	1,750.00
Thome, charger, gadrooned scalloped edge, monogram, 22"	990.00
Unmk Am, fruit compote, sq plinth, replica, 8"	495.00
Wallace, demitasse set, Nouveau swirling florals, 27-t-oz	1,100.00
Wm Kidney, coffeepot, emb scrolls, eng crest, 1728, 10"	1,000.00

Silver Lustre Ware

Much of the ware known as silver lustre was produced in the 1800s in Staffordshire, England. This type of earthenware was entirely covered with the metallic silver glaze. It was most popular prior to 1840 when the technique of electroplating was developed and silverplated wares came into vogue. Later in the century, artisans used silver lustre to develop designs on vases and other decorative ware.

Creamer, emb strawberry band, rectanglar, scroll hdl, 4"	45.00
Loving cup, red flower on bl marbleized, wear, 5"	385.00
Master salt, allover silver, ftd, 2x3" dia	50.00
Pitcher, floral w/dalmation & bird, wear, 5⅝"	110.00
Pitcher, reserves: Little Bony & Jack Frost, 6", VG	170.00

Silver Overlay

The silver overlay glass made during the 1800s was decorated with a cut-out pattern of sterling silver applied to the surface of the ware.

Cruet, gr w/heavy floral/scroll o/l sgn Alvin, 7"	750.00
Decanter, cranberry cut to clear w/roses o/l sgn Alvin, 12"	1,850.00
Decanter, cranberry to rubena w/grapes o/l, 12"	350.00
Inkwell, bright gr w/wild rose/lattice o/l, monogram, 4x3"	650.00
Rose bowl, emerald w/allover rose o/l sgn Alvin, 4½x5"	725.00
Tumbler, grapes & leaves on crystal, 3½x2¼"	40.00
Vase, blk w/bubble ball stem, allover Deco o/l, 13"	545.00

Vase, clear w/Deco roses o/l, o/l rim & ft, 12x7" 575.00
Vase, cranberry w/daisy o/l, flared, ftd, 10" 1,350.00
Vase, cranberry w/mums o/l, shouldered, disk ft, 12x5" 300.00
Vase, cranberry w/roses o/l & monogram crest, dtd 1899, 5x3" ..150.00
Vase, emerald w/carnations o/l sgn Pat, 3½x5½" 725.00
Vase, emerald w/floral o/l, squat, 2½x3" 275.00
Vase, emerald w/Nouveau florals, 14" 1,850.00
Vase, emerald w/scrolls/floral/shield o/l sgn Alvin, 7" 500.00
Vase, gr, spider webb o/l, trumpet form, 12" 375.00
Vase, turq w/floral/scroll o/l sgn Fine #d Silver, 2¾x2½" 500.00

Silverplate

Silverplated hollow ware is fast becoming the focus of attention for many of today's collectors. Pricing is based on pieces in excellent condition. Serving pieces and knives are priced to reflect the values of examples that retain their original blades. Our advisors for this category are Rick Spencer and JoAnn Kilmer; they are listed in the Directory under Utah. See also Railroadiana, Silverplate.

Key:
gw — gold wash   hh — hollow handle

Flatware

Adam, 1917, Oneida, pierced nut spoon 24.00
Alhambra, 1907, Wm Rogers, cold meat fork 35.00
Alhambra, 1907, Wm Rogers, youth fork 12.00
Ambassador, 1919, Rogers Bros, cocktail fork 8.00
Ancestral, 1924, Rogers Bros, fruit knife 12.00
Ancestral, 1924, Rogers Bros, salad fork 8.00
Arbutus, 1908, Rogers Bros, sugar spoon 16.00
Arbutus, 1908, Rogers Bros, teaspoon 12.00
Berkshire, 1897, Rogers Bros, cream ladle 32.00
Berkshire, 1897, Rogers Bros, soup ladle 85.00
Bird of Paradise, 1923, Oneida Community, dinner fork 12.00
Bride's Bouquet, 1908, Alvin, cream ladle 35.00
Bride's Bouquet, 1908, Alvin, teaspoon 15.00
Century, 1923, Holmes & Edwards, berry spoon 75.00
Century, 1923, Holmes & Edwards, ice cream fork 20.00
Charter Oak, 1906, Rogers Bros, gravy ladle 40.00
Charter Oak, 1906, Rogers Bros, oval soup 20.00
Charter Oak, 1906, Rogers Bros, twisted butter spreader 24.00
Chester, 1900, Rogers Bros, ice cream fork 20.00
Chester, 1900, Rogers Bros, teaspoon 10.00
Classic Filigree, 1937, Wallace, dessert server 20.00
Daffodil, 1950, Internat'l, baby spoon 15.00
Diana (aka Berwick), 1904, Rogers Bros, soup ladle 95.00
Eternally Yours, 1941, Internat'l, baby spoon 15.00
Eternally Yours, 1941, Internat'l, viande fork 15.00
Eternally Yours, 1941, Internat'l, viande knife 15.00
Evening Star, 1950, Oneida, teaspoon 9.00
First Love, 1937, Rogers Bros, baby fork 9.00
First Love, 1937, Rogers Bros, iced teaspoon 15.00
Flair, 1956, Internat'l, baby spoon 10.00
Flair, 1956, Internat'l, iced teaspoon 10.00
Floral, 1902, Wallace, cake server 55.00
Floral, 1902, Wallace, dinner fork 18.00
Floral, 1902, Wallace, ice cream spoon 45.00
Floral, 1902, Wallace, soup ladle 125.00
Floral, 1902, Wallace, strawberry fork 50.00
Flower de Luce, 1904, Oneida, dinner fork, hh 18.00
Flower de Luce, 1904, Oneida, dinner knife, hh 23.00
Flower de Luce, 1904, Oneida, salad fork 15.00

Grosvenor, 1921, Oneida, dinner fork 18.00
Grosvenor, 1921, Oneida, ind butter spreader 9.00
Hanover, 1901, Wm Rogers, bouillon spoon 15.00
Holly, 1904, Smith, cold meat fork 110.00
Holly, 1904, Smith, dinner knife, hh 50.00
Holly, 1904, Smith, gumbo soup 38.00
Holly, 1904, Smith, tablespoon 32.00
Isabella, 1913, Wm Rogers, gravy ladle 30.00
Isabella, 1913, Wm Rogers, tablespoon 18.00
Jubilee, 1953, Internat'l, sugar spoon 8.00
La Concorde, 1910, Wm A Rogers, salad fork 30.00
La Concorde, 1910, Wm A Rogers, cold meat fork 30.00
La Vigne, 1908, Oneida, bouillon spoon 18.00
La Vigne, 1908, Oneida, butter spreader 20.00
La Vigne, 1908, Oneida, dinner knife, hh 70.00
La Vigne, 1908, Oneida, pastry fork 30.00
La Vigne, 1908, Oneida, tea strainer 115.00
La Vigne, 1908, Oneida, teaspoon 10.00
Laurel, 1878, Rogers Bros, cake knife 75.00
Lilyta, 1909, Stratford, bouillon spoon 10.00
Lilyta, 1909, Stratford, dinner fork 15.00
Lilyta, 1909, Stratford, sugar spoon 16.00
Morning Star, 1948, Oneida, iced teaspoon 8.00
Moselle, 1906, World, cake serving fork 175.00
Moselle, 1906, World, cold meat fork 75.00
Moselle, 1906, World, dinner knife 35.00
Moselle, 1906, World, pickle fork, long hdl 95.00
Moselle, 1906, World, teaspoon 15.00
Moss Rose, 1949, Nat'l, demitasse spoon 12.00
Moss Rose, 1949, Nat'l, teaspoon 10.00
Mystic, 1903, Meriden Britannia, demitasse spoon 15.00
Nenuphar, 1904, American Silver, tablespoon 18.00
Old Colony, 1911, Rogers Bros, berry spoon 48.00
Old Colony, 1911, Rogers Bros, pickle fork 22.00
Olive, 1800s, nut pick 15.00
Olive, 1800s, pastry fork 12.00
Orange Blossom, 1910, Rogers Bros, citrus spoon 18.00
Orange Blossom, 1910, Rogers Bros, dinner knife, hh 50.00
Orient (aka Venice), 1904, Rockford, dinner fork 18.00
Orient (aka Venice), 1904, Rockford, 5 o'clock spoon 12.00
Queen Anne, 1910, Rogers Bros, cold meat fork 18.00
Raphael, 1896, Rogers & Hamilton, sugar spoon 22.00
Rose & Leaf, 1937, Nat'l, gravy ladle 24.00
Silver Renaissance, 1971, Internat'l, dinner knife, hh 30.00
Silver Renaissance, 1971, Internat'l, gravy ladle 40.00
Thistle, 1906, Simmons Hardware, dinner fork 18.00
Thistle, 1906, Simmons Hardware, master butter spreader 18.00
Thistle, 1906, Simmons Hardware, tablespoon 15.00
Vintage, 1904, Rogers Bros, berry spoon 75.00
Vintage, 1904, Rogers Bros, cold meat fork 35.00
Vintage, 1904, Rogers Bros, cream ladle 42.00
Vintage, 1904, Rogers Bros, fork, hh 25.00
Vintage, 1904, Rogers Bros, grapefruit spoon 23.00
Vintage, 1904, Rogers Bros, iced teaspoon 65.00
Vintage, 1904, Rogers Bros, mustard spoon, long hdl 90.00
Vintage, 1904, Rogers Bros, olive spoon 85.00
Vintage, 1904, Rogers Bros, salad fork 38.00
Vintage, 1904, Rogers Bros, soup ladle 110.00
White Orchid, 1953, Oneida, baby spoon 12.00

Hollow Ware

Baby cup, First Love 35.00
Bowl, vegetable; Queen Anne, octagonal, w/lid, Robert Ensko ..185.00

Silverplate

Butter bowl, cow & ring hdl, bl glass liner 275.00
Butter dish, cow finial, w/insert & butter knife, Barbour 150.00
Butter dish, lift-up adjustable top, #1649 ....110.00
Candlelabra, 3-light, ornate Nouveau style, English, 22", pr 600.00
Candlesticks, emb/eng floral, grotesque masks, 1800s, 12", pr 220.00
Coffeepot, Egyptian Revival, sphinx heads, Taunton 250.00
Coffeepot, emb/eng floral, acorn finial, Victorian, 9" 75.00
Cracker barrel, loop finial, bail hdl, Empire Mfg 100.00
Ladle, punch; Holly, hh, Smith 450.00
Ladle, soup; Flower de Luce, Oneida 65.00
Ladle, soup; Hanover, Wm A Rogers 85.00
Lemonade server, eng fans etc, Aesthetic style, rtcl stand, 20" ...825.00
Pitcher, water; Ancestral 135.00
Pitcher, water; Assyrian head, tilts, on stand, ceramic liner 900.00
Pitcher, water; Coronation, Community 325.00
Pitcher, water; Eternally Yours 135.00
Plate, scalloped pie-crust rim, eng crest, 3 scroll ft, 10" 65.00
Poultry set, Bird of Paradise 48.00
Roast cover, gadrooned sides, ornate hdl, oval, 16" 465.00
Shakers, Grosvenor, Oneida Community, pr 45.00
Tea service, eng garlands, 1920s, 12½" coffeepot+3 pcs 330.00
Tea set, Grosvenor, 3-pc 250.00
Tea urn, Neoclassic style, reeded spigot, ftd sq vase, 23" 825.00
Tea/coffee, geometric bands, Aesthetic, Meriden, 5-pc 935.00
Tea/coffee service, heritage, International, 7-pc 1,100.00
Toothpick holder, Dutch girl holds scrolled holder, Tufts 130.00
Toothpick holder, griffin hdls 50.00
Tray, bread; Grosvenor, Oneida Community 45.00
Tray, chased/eng w/plain center, bun ft, wood hdls, 27" 200.00
Tray, eng foliage/scrollwork, C-scroll rim, oval, 25" 300.00
Tray, fruit center medallion, claw ft, Tufts 60.00
Tray, Georgian style, raised edge w/appl scrollwork, hdls, 23" 465.00
Tray, rtcl gallery w/hdls, chased/eng w/plain center, 24" 200.00
Tureen, soup; stag finial, Rococo emb sides, hdls/ftd, 15" 500.00

Sheffield

Coffeepot, pear shape w/ebony hdl 220.00
Dish, eng crest, shell/foliate scrolls on rim, 1820s, 16" L 300.00
Hot water urn, sq base, ball ft, ivory hdls, urn finial, 23" 750.00
Sauce boat, urn finial, lion-head/ring hdls, pr 350.00
Sweets urn, classical form w/scroll hdls, glass liner, 10" 200.00
Tea urn, Geo IV, 15½" 450.00
Tea/coffee set, bright cut, Walker & Hall, 4-pc 350.00
Teapot, eng monogram, gadrooned borders, ball ft, 6" 125.00

Sinclaire

In 1904 H.P. Sinclaire and Company was founded in Corning, New York. For the first sixteen years of production, Sinclaire used blanks from other glassworks for his cut and engraved designs. In 1920 he established his own glass-blowing factory in Bath, New York. His most popular designs utilize fruits, flowers, and other forms from nature. Most of Sinclaire's glass is unmarked; items that are carry his logo: an 'S' within a wreath with two shields.

Bowl, amethyst, ftd spittoon shape, 10" 75.00
Bowl, canoe w/eng flowers, 11x7½" 175.00
Bowl, cut, Assyrian variation (no hobstar), low, 10" 475.00
Candlesticks, golden amber, cut prisms, 9", pr 95.00
Candlesticks, inverted lip cut w/stars, low, 4" dia, pr 100.00
Compote, amber, stemmed, #11916, 6½" 50.00
Compote, cut & eng florals, 5½" 90.00

Compote, gr ribbed & opaque wht, 10" 195.00
Teapot, cut, florals & thistles, appl hdl & spout 400.00
Tray, eng leaves, 5-section, 10x14" 160.00
Vase, bl irid, 5" 175.00
Vase, Colonial Bl, #13001, 7¾" 100.00
Vase, cut, geometrics & hobstars, rayed base, wide rim, 10" 195.00
Vase, eng bulbous bowl on pencil stem, 12" 465.00
Vase, olive gr, #13012, 12" 75.00

Sitzendorf

The Sitzendorf factory began operations in East Germany in the mid-1800s, adopting the name of the city as the name of their company. They produced fine porcelain groups, figurines, etc., in much the same style and quality as Meissen and the Dresden factories. Much of their ware was marked with a crown over the letter 'S' and a horizontal line with two slash marks.

Compote, appl florals, rtcl, 2-part, ca 1887, 4½" 150.00
Figurine, Colonial lady w/basket, sgn, 5½" 60.00
Figurine, Mary of Burgundy, 8" 165.00
Lamp, perfume; owls (2) w/glass eyes, porc, mk, 6" 200.00
Vase, appl flowers & cupid w/bow, ca 1887, 12½" 300.00
Vase, 3 winged cherubs support egg w/appl flowers & vines, 7" ..250.00

Slag Glass

Slag glass is a marbleized opaque glassware made by several companies from about 1870 until the turn of the century. It is usually found in purple or caramel (see Chocolate Glass), though other colors were also made. Pink is rare and very expensive.

Blue, basket, cherries/leaves in relief, crimped/ruffled, 9" 75.00
Blue, humidor, drum shape, cap-shaped finial, 6½x5¼" 250.00
Pink, Invt Fan & Feather, butter dish, ftd, 6x8" 1,200.00
Pink, Invt Fan & Feather, creamer & sugar bowl, 4½", 6½" 1,200.00
Pink, Invt Fan & Feather, cruet 1,400.00
Pink, Invt Fan & Feather, jelly compote, scalloped rim, 4½x5" ..550.00
Pink, Invt Fan & Feather, pitcher, water 1,500.00
Pink, Invt Fan & Feather, punch cup 300.00
Pink, Invt Fan & Feather, sauce dish, 4" 265.00
Pink, Invt Fan & Feather, shakers, rare, pr 1,200.00
Pink, Invt Fan & Feather, spooner 425.00
Pink, Invt Fan & feather, toothpick holder 650.00
Pink, Invt Fan & Feather, tumbler 400.00
Purple, Beads & Bark, vase, novelty 50.00

Purple candy dish, Indiana Glass, $55.00.

Purple, Jenny Lind, compote, 7¾x8½" 165.00
Purple, oil lamp, emb spears, clear font, 13" 145.00
Purple, Oval Medallion, spooner 85.00
Purple, Panel & Waffle mold, compote, w/lid, 8x8" 80.00
Purple, Panel & Waffle mold, vase, ftd, scalloped, 8" 48.00
Purple, plate, lattice edge, 13" 85.00
Purple, Scroll w/Acanthus, creamer & sugar bowl 100.00
Purple, Scroll w/Acanthus, spooner 75.00
Purple, vase, paneled sides, 8" 90.00
Red, vase, mc/gold decor at top, 7" 60.00

SMF (Schramberg/Wheelock Black Forest)

Since 1918 the Schramberger Majolica Factory in Schramberg, Wurttemberg, Germany, has produced majolica, stoneware, and porcelain. Various marks were used (Schramberg, and Wheelock 'Black Forest' Hand Painted Pottery), but the common link is the SMF insignia. They produced a number of hand-painted pieces, but those of most interest to collectors are painted in gaudy colors in bizarre designs on equally bizarre shapes. As a result it is often referred to as the 'poor man's Clarice Cliff.' Collectors will note that most pieces bear an incised mold number, a painter's number, and the SMF mark. Of special note are the pieces marked Gobelin, followed by a number (or simply G and the number). Gobelin wares have a gray background with as many as ten colors used in the design. The number denotes particular color combinations. For example, Gobelin 3 pieces will be painted in green and orange leaves and yellow eyes, along with other colors specific to that design. Expect to find Gobelin-numbered pottery in various unusual shapes. It is not uncommon to find pieces that are chipped, and a perfect piece should be valued by its owner. Our advisor for this category is Ralph Winslow; he is listed in the Directory under Kansas.

Basket, G5, SMF, 4" 45.00
Candle holder, floral, 4-color, 4", ea 50.00
Creamer, G2, Wheelock 20.00
Planter, G3, SMF, 3¾" 60.00
Planter, G6, SMF, 4½" 60.00
Syrup, floral, SMF, 4½" 25.00
Tray, floral, #54, SMF 30.00
Trivet, floral, 4-color 35.00
Vase, floral, blk & orange, SMF, 6½" 30.00
Vase, floral, Wheelock, 4¼" 25.00
Vase, G1, 8-color, 7" 70.00
Vase, G4, 7-color, #57, 4½" 45.00
Vase, G4, 7-color, hdls, 9" 75.00

Smith Bros.

Alfred and Harry Smith founded their glassmaking firm in New Bedford, Massachusetts. They had been formerly associated with the Mt. Washington Glass Works, working there from 1871 to 1875 to aid in establishing a decorating department. Smith glass is valued for its excellent enameled decoration on satin or opalescent glass. Pieces were often marked with a lion in a red shield. Our advisors for this category are Betty and Clarence Maier; they are listed in the Directory under Pennsylvania.

Biscuit jar, florals, lav/bl on cream, melon ribs, 5" dia 325.00
Biscuit jar, gold floral, melon ribbed, 6-lobe SP lid, 5½" 375.00
Bowl, asters on cream, beaded rim, spherical, 3½x5½" 125.00
Creamer, floral, raised gold on biscuit, metal trim, 3" 150.00
Decanter, gold irises/spirals on wht, 8-sided, paneled, lg 800.00

Humidor, pansies, bl on tan, ribbed base/lid, 6x4" 250.00
Pitcher, gold floral branch on glossy wht, 8" 198.00
Syrup, ribbed conical shape w/florals 395.00
Vase, carnations on yel to cream, pinched sides, 4½" 300.00
Vase, daisies on baluster shape w/emb rope, lion mk, 6¼" 150.00

Snow Babies

During the last quarter of the 19th century, snow babies — little figurals in white snowsuits — originated in Germany. They were made of sugar candy and were often used as decorations for Christmas cakes. Later on they were made of marzipan, a confection of crushed almonds, sugar, and egg whites. Eventually porcelain manufacturers began making them in bisque. They were popular until WWII. These tiny bisque figures range in size from 1" up to 7" tall. Quality German pieces bring very respectable prices on the market today. Beware of reproductions. Our advisor for this category is Linda Vines; she is listed in the Directory under New Jersey.

Adult skier, mica coat & hat, blk pants, Germany, 2½" 45.00
Babies, no snow, 2 atop snowball, American flag, Germany, 3" .150.00

Two babies dancing, Germany, 2", $165.00. (Photo courtesy of Linda L. Vines.)

Babies, 2 holding baby bottle, Germany, 2" 200.00
Babies, 3 on sled, Germany, 3" L 225.00
Baby, jtd at shoulders & hips, Germany, 5" 250.00
Baby, no snow, pulling sled, red suit, Germany, 2" 75.00
Baby pulling sled, Germany, 2" 150.00
Baby riding on silver plane, Germany, 1½" 165.00
Baby riding on snow bear, Germany, 2½" 150.00
Baby standing on wooden skis, Germany, 3" 175.00
Baby standing or sitting, Germany, 1" 40.00
Baby w/seal & red ball, Germany, 2½" 165.00
Baby w/seal & ball in snow globe, Japan baby/USA globe, 5" 110.00
Baby w/tennis racket, Germany, 2" 150.00
Children (2), no snow, sitting on sled, Germany, 2½" 75.00
Doll, bsk shoulderhead & limbs, cloth body, Germany, 7" 450.00
Elf, no snow, on tummy or sitting, red suit, Germany, 1½" 30.00
Santa atop snow bear, Germany, 2½" 200.00
Santa climbing over log fence, Germany, 2" 110.00
Santa in yel train, toys on bk, Germany, 3" 200.00
Santa in yel train, toys on bk, Japan, 3" 65.00
Santa riding in sled pulled by reindeer, Germany, 2½" 150.00
Santa riding motorcycle, pixie on bk, Germany, 2" 150.00
Snow bear sitting or walking, Germany, 2" 75.00

Snuff Boxes

As early as the 17th century, the Chinese began using snuff. By the early 19th century, the practice had spread to Europe and America. It was used by both the gentlemen and the ladies alike, and expensive snuff boxes and bottles were the earmark of the genteel. Some were of silver or gold set with precious stones or pearls, while others contained music boxes. In the following listings, the dimension noted is length. See also Orientalia, Snuff Bottles.

Continental 18k gold, rectangular with angled corners, hunting paraphernalia flanked by flowers, engraved anchor and scrolls on back, B&C hallmark, 3½" long, $1,800.00.

Agate top, enameled sides, oval, chased ormolu mts, 3"	150.00
Birch bark, eng decor w/German inscriptions, hinged, 4"	95.00
Brass w/eng MOP sides, tortoise-shell top & bottom, 2⅝"	360.00
Burl w/scratch-cvd initials, 3⅞", EX	85.00
Cvd whalebone, flowerpot decor, 1800s, 3½x¾x3½"	260.00
Gilt & lacquer, Zachary Taylor portrait, Old Rough..., 3½"	1,150.00
Mull, made from animal hoof, polished, sm	65.00
Papier-mache, revelers in gentlemen's club, English, 4¼" dia	650.00
Pewter, eng florals, JP Jennson, lt wear, 3½"	150.00
Pewter w/eng decor, hinged lid w/monogram, 1½x2x3"	95.00
Silver, repousse w/frolicking cherubs & lovers, Continental	150.00
Walnut, brass mt, cvd top, dtd 1679, Chas II, 3½" dia	500.00

Soap Hollow Furniture

In the Mennonite community of Soap Hollow, Pennsylvania, the women made and sold soap; the men made handcrafted furniture. Rare today, these pieces were stenciled, grain painted, and beautifully decorated with inlaid escutcheons. These pieces are becoming very sought after. When well kept, they are very distinctive and beautiful. The items described in these listings were recently sold through Merle S. Mishlers Auctions, RD 2, Hollsopple, Pennsylvania. All are in excellent condition unless othewise noted. Our advisors for this category represent DLK Nostalgia and Collectibles; they are listed in the Directory under Pennsylvania.

Chest, blanket; grpt maroon & blk, no stencil, sm, G-	350.00
Chest, blanket; grpt w/blk lid, fruit/florals w/gold, 1882	2,900.00
Chest, blanket; maroon w/gold stencil, rnd escutcheon, 1856	2,000.00
Chest, lt w/dk lid, stenciled flower, sgn ST, 1890, VG	650.00
Chest, 4 lg/2 sm drws w/decor, enamel pulls, sgn, 1851, EX+	4,600.00
Chest, 4 lg/3 sm drws, stencil, enamel pulls, sgn, 1883, EX+	5,400.00
Chest of drws, bk brd, hidden lock, stencil, sgn HS, 1879, EX	5,500.00
Chest of drws, redwood, 1841, EX	750.00
Cupboard, corner; maroon w/blk, stencil, 1856, EX	11,500.00

Soapstone

Soapstone is a soft talc in rock form with a smooth, greasy feel from whence comes its name. In colonial times it was extracted from out-croppings in large sections with hand saws, carted by oxen to mills, and fashioned into useful domestic articles such as foot warmers, cooking utensils, inkwells, etc. During the early 1800s, it was used to make heating stoves and kitchen sinks. Most familiar today are the carved vases, bookends, and boxes made in China during the Victorian era.

Cigarette/match holder, phoenix birds/eng, red, 3½x4"	65.00
Figurine, Buddha, gr, 2½"	32.00
Figurine, seated deity, 9"	85.00
Toothpick holder, tan/wht, cylindrical, 2"	28.00
Vase, monkey 1 end, bird at other, lt gray w/rust, 9" L	85.00

Soda Fountain Collectibles

The first soda water sales in the United States occurred in the very late 1790s in New York and New Haven, Connecticut. By the 1830s soda water was being sold in drug stores as a medicinal item, especially the effervescent mineral waters from various springs around the country. By this time the first flavored soda water appeared at an apothecary shop in Philadelphia.

The 1830s also saw the first manufacture of devices to make soda water. The first marble soda fountain made its appearance in 1857 as a combination ice shaver and flavor-dispensing apparatus. By the 1870s the soda fountain was an established feature of the neighborhood drug store.

The fountains of this period were large, elaborate marble devices with druggists competing with each other for business by having fountains decorated with choice marbles, statues, mirrors and gas lamps.

In 1903 the fountain completed its last major evolution with the introduction of the 'front' counter service we know today. (The soda clerk faced the customer when drawing soda.)

By this time ice cream was a standard feature being served as sundaes, ice cream sodas, and milk shakes. Syrup dispensers were just being introduced as 'point-of-sale' devices to sell various flavorings from many different companies. Straws were commonplace, especially those made from paper. Fancy and unusual ice cream dippers were in daily use, and they continued to evolve, reaching their pinnacle with the introduction of the heart-shaped dipper in 1927.

This American business has provided collectors today with an almost endless supply of interesting and different articles of commerce. One can collect dippers, syrup dispensers, glassware, milk shakers, advertising, and catalogs.

Collectors need to be made aware of decorating pieces that are fantasy items: copper ice cream cones, a large copper ice cream dipper, and a copper ice cream soda glass. These items have no resale value. Our advisors for this category are Joyce and Harold Screen; they are listed in the Directory under Maryland. See also Advertising.

Displays: Pola Maid Ice Cream Cone, composition with cast iron, brown with ivory top, red and black lettering, 48", $600.00; Carrara's Ice Cream Cone, papier-mache, electric, man comes out of cone, red lettering, 40½", $1,900.00.

Banana split dish, Heisey Greek Key	25.00
Banana split dish, Tea Room, pk	40.00
Banana split dish, wht milk glass	20.00
Container, Borden's Malted Milk, aluminum, w/top	40.00

Container, Borden's Malted Milk, label under glass, w/lid, EX ...400.00
Container, Horlick's Malted Milk, label under glass, w/lid 300.00
Cup, Cudahy's Rexoma 35.00
Cup, Fry's Hot Chocolate 15.00
Cup, Howell's Orange Julep, wht china 35.00
Cup, Mavis Chocolate wht china 50.00
Dipper, Clewell's, tin, tubular hdl 25.00
Dipper, Cold Dog, cylinder 600.00
Dipper, Delmonico, N&E Co, key top release 125.00
Dipper, Dover slicer, single trigger 400.00
Dipper, Gilchrist, banana split 425.00
Dipper, Gilchrist, rnd bowl, #31, sz 16 ....25.00
Dipper, Gilchrist, rnd bowl, #31, sz 40 ....125.00
Dipper, Hamilton Beach, sz 12, MIB 25.00
Dipper, heart shape, EX 3,000.00
Dipper, Kingery, dbl scraper, metal hdl 425.00
Dipper, McLaren Icy-Pi sandwich 125.00
Dipper, MD Baking Co, rnd bowl, sz 8 ....200.00
Dipper, Pie-Alamoder 1,200.00
Dipper, United Products, sandwich, EX 200.00
Dispenser, Buckeye, dancing satyrs on base, orig pump 1,500.00
Dispenser, Cherry Bon, figural cherry 2,250.00
Dispenser, Dr Swett's Root Beer, tree stump, orig pump 2,000.00
Dispenser, Fowler's Cherry Smash, 5¢, orig pump 1,300.00
Dispenser, Fowler's Root Beer, w/orig pump 750.00
Dispenser, Ginger Mint Julep 600.00
Dispenser, Hires 'Muni-Maker,' complete 2,000.00
Dispenser, ice cream cone; Mosteller, glass tube, EX 350.00
Dispenser, Johnson's Cold Fudge, bl china, w/lid 175.00
Dispenser, Liggett's Grape Juice, china, no bottle 600.00
Ice cream measure, turn key release on bottom, 1-qt 75.00
Menu holder, Fairmont Ice Cream, celluloid 45.00
Mixer, A&W, Chicago, mechanical, floor model 850.00
Mixer, Arnold, sq motor housing, electric 125.00
Mixer, Liquid Carbonic, electric 125.00
Mug, A&W Root Beer, glass, lg or sm, ea....................................15.00
Mug, Bardwell's Root Beer, bl salt glaze 125.00
Mug, Hall & Lyons Root Beer, china 150.00
Mug, Hunter's Root Beer, stoneware 75.00
Mug, Jim Dandy Root Beer, stoneware 100.00
Mug, Kravemor Root Beer, stoneware 75.00
Mug, Rochester Root Beer, glass 35.00
Mug, Schuster's Root Beer, stoneware 70.00
Soda glass, Allen's Red Tame Cherry 100.00
Soda glass, Cherry Smash, etched, w/syrup line 100.00
Soda glass, Dr Brown's Celery Tonic 45.00
Soda glass, Fox's Cherry, w/syrup line 75.00
Soda glass, Green River, optic, w/syrup line 50.00
Soda glass, Moxie, orange band, glass hdl 125.00
Soda glass, Vin Fizz 60.00
Straw dispenser, Grape Smash 800.00
Straw dispenser, Sani-Straw, mechanical, horizontal 300.00
Syrup bottle, Cherry Smash, label under glass, w/cap 200.00
Syrup bottle, Moonshine, brn glass, w/cap 175.00
Syrup bottle, Orange, etched, w/cap 30.00
Syrup bottle, Rustles, label under glass, w/cap 150.00
Syrup bottle, vanilla, wht pnt label 20.00
Wafer holder, Ergos 60.00
Wafer holder, wht porc 60.00

South Jersey Glass

As early as 1739, Caspar Wistar established a factory in Salem

County, taking advantage of the large beds of sand suitable for glass blowing and the abundant forests available for fueling his furnaces. Scores of glassworks followed, many of which were short-lived. It is generally conceded that aside from the early works of Wistar and the Harmony Glass Works, which emerged from the Glassboro factory originally founded by the Strangers, the finest quality glassware was blown after 1800. In the 1850s coal was substituted for the wood as fuel. Though a more efficient source of heat, the added cost of transporting the coal inland proved to be the downfall of many of the smaller factories, and soon many had failed.

Glassware can be attributed to this area through the study of colors, shapes, and decorative devices that were favored there; but because techniques were passed down through generations of South Jersey Glass blowers, without documentation it is usually impossible to identify the specific factory that produced it. Our advisor for this category is Mark Vuono; he is listed in the Directory under Connecticut.

Bowl, clear w/wht loopings, ftd, 5¾" H 185.00
Creamer, aqua, flaring lip w/pouring spout, crude hdl, 3¾" 265.00
Jug, grotesque face, J Reinhart...NC..93, gr w/bl, 13½" 195.00
Pitcher, amber, swirled, folded rim, pinched spout, 6" 100.00
Pitcher, aqua, lily pads, curled-end hdl, appl base, 8x6" 2,250.00
Pitcher, lt gr, 4 lily-pad pulls, threaded lip, 6" 825.00

Spangle Glass

Spangle glass, also known as Vasa Murrhina, is cased art glass characterized by the metallic flakes embedded in its top layer. It was made both abroad and in the United States during the latter years of the 19th century, and it was reproduced in the 1960s by the Fenton Art Glass Company.

Vasa Murrhina was a New England distributor who sold glassware of this type manufactured by a Dr. Flower of Sandwich, Massachusetts. Flower had purchased the defunct Cape Cod Glassworks in 1885 and used the facilities to operate his own company. Since none of the ware was marked, it is very difficult to attribute specific examples to his manufacture. See also Art Glass Baskets; Fenton.

Bottle, scent; gold w/mica, HP butterflies w/gold, 5x3¾" 395.00
Bowl, gold shaded w/mica, wht int, clear ruffle, 2¾x8" 95.00
Bowl, pk w/bl w/appl clear drippings/ft, 3-lobe rim, 5x6" 325.00
Condiment set, cranberry w/mica, 3-pc in SP fr, 6" 225.00
Creamer, cobalt w/gold flecks, appl amber hdl w/gold, 5" 200.00
Creamer, cobalt w/silver mica, clear hdl 110.00

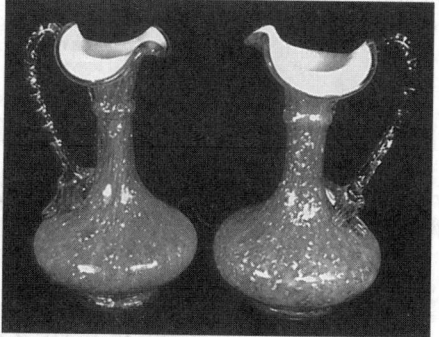

Ewers, cased pink with mica, clear handles, 9½", $750.00 for the pair.

Ewer, dk wine, wht int, clear rim/thorn hdl, dbl-bulb, 8" 375.00
Rose bowl, mc spatter w/mica swirls, 3¼x4" 110.00

Spangle Glass (continued)

Sweetmeat, pk w/silver flecks, HP leaves & flowers, 6" dia 110.00
Tumbler, gr w/much mica, 3⅞x2⅝" 45.00
Tumbler, mc spatter w/silver mica, emb swirl, 3¾x2¾" 70.00
Tumbler, peach & wht spatter w/mica, 3½x2½" 45.00
Vase, jack-in-pulpit; mc spatter w/silver mica, fluted, 7" 85.00
Vase, pk w/silver mica, wht int, ruffled, 9x3½" 100.00
Vase, red w/gold mica, 5½" 80.00
Vase, yel w/silver mica, crystal edge, wht int, bulbous, 4" 95.00

Spatter Glass

Spatter glass, characterized by its multicolor 'spatters,' has been made from the late 19th century to the present by American glass houses as well as those abroad. Although it was once thought to have been made entirely by workers at the 'end of the day' from bits and pieces of leftover scrap, it is now known that it was a standard line of production. See also Art Glass Baskets.

Basket, 4-color, wht int, clear thorn hdl, 8x5" 175.00
Bowl, cased mc, sqd clear rim, polished pontil, 7" 90.00
Box, patch; yel/wht/clear 150.00
Candlesticks, 5-color, 8¾x3⅞", pr 135.00
Jar, 4-color w/crystal shell trim, clear finial, 6x3⅝" 68.00
Pitcher, Invt T'print, maroon & wht, bulbous, clear hdl, 8" 110.00
Rose bowl, mc, plain rim, 5½x5½" 80.00
Tumbler, mc w/wht int, emb swirls, 4" 55.00

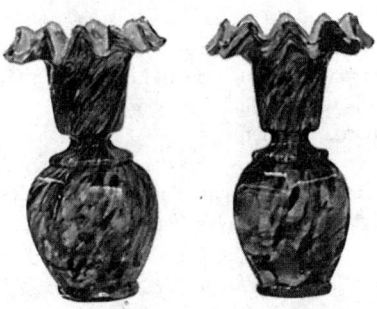

Vase, cased multicolor spatter, fluted rim, 7½", $195.00 for the pair.

Vase, bl w/lt bl spatter, clear ruffle, 11x6½", pr 395.00
Vase, rainbow pastel o/l, clear thorn hdls, 9" 95.00
Vase, yel & wht, appl clear leaf & hdl, 6¾x4¼" 95.00
Watch holder, bl & wht dish in ormolu fr, 7x3¾x4¼" 165.00

Spatterware

Spatterware is a general term referring to a type of decoration used by English potters beginning in the late 1700s. Using a brush or a stick, brightly colored paint was dabbed onto the soft-paste earthenware items, achieving a spattered effect which was often used as a border. Because much of this type of ware was made for export to the United States, some of the subjects in the central design — the schoolhouse and the eagle patterns, for instance — reflect American tastes. Yellow, green, and black spatterware is scarce and highly valued by collectors.

In the descriptions that follow, the color listed after the item indicates the color of the spatter. The central design is identified next, and the color description that follows that refers to the design.

Our advisor for this category is Diane Patalano; she is listed in the Directory under New Jersey.

Coffeepot, rainbow, 3-color, w/Adam's Rose, 8-sided, 8", VG ..2,550.00
Creamer, bl, star, red, chip, 4½" 85.00
Creamer, cow form, blk & brn stripes w/gr base, 5" 470.00
Creamer, yel, profile tulip, red/gr/blk, shell spout, 4½" 2,350.00
Cup & saucer, gr, peafowl, yel/bl/red, miniature 130.00
Cup & saucer, rainbow, bl/red, NM 225.00
Cup & saucer, red, parrot, gr/bl/red, mismatch saucer, NM 400.00
Cup & saucer, red/yel, carnation, rare, EX 1,350.00
Pitcher, red, molded leaf design at spout, 9¾" 250.00
Plate, bl, Adam's Rose, 7" 140.00
Plate, bl, eagle & shield, bl, stain, 8¼" 150.00
Plate, bl, peafowl, yel/red/gr, 8" 360.00
Plate, bl, peafowl, 4-color, stain, 7⅝" 135.00
Plate, bl, rose, red/gr/blk, Walker, 8½" 275.00
Plate, bl, schoolhouse, 3-color, stain, 8⅜" 330.00
Plate, rainbow, bull's eye, red & gr, stains, 7½" 275.00
Plate, red, peafowl, 4-color, wear, 8¼" 250.00
Plate, red, peafowl, 4-color, 8⅜" 470.00
Plate, red/bl/yel, tulip, red/yel/gr, wear, 9½" 140.00
Platter, bl, cowboys & wild horses, red, 12⅜", EX 195.00
Sauce dish, bl/purple, red bud w/gr leaves, Davenport, 5" 220.00
Saucer, bl, rooster, bl/yel/red, 6" 210.00
Saucer, gr, peafowl, 4-color, stains, 5¾" 110.00
Saucer, red, dove, yel/bl/red, 5½", NM 210.00
Saucer, red, peafowl, 4-color, rpr, 4⅛" 60.00
Saucer, red, peafowl, 4-color, underneath chip, 5⅜" 160.00
Sugar bowl, bl, fort, 3-color, rpr, 4⅛" 55.00
Sugar bowl, bl & purple, rose, 3-color, minor rpr, 4¼" 330.00
Sugar bowl, red, rose, red/gr/blk, 7½" 275.00
Tea bowl, brn & gr, peafowl, 4-color, mini 66.00
Tea bowl & saucer, bl, house, 4-color, mini, EX 160.00
Tea bowl & saucer, bl, peafowl, 4-color, mini 95.00
Tea bowl & saucer, bl, rooster, 4-color, wear 440.00
Tea bowl & saucer, gr, peafowl, 4-color, rpr 165.00
Tea bowl & saucer, gr, peafowl, 4-color, NM 470.00
Tea bowl & saucer, purple, rose, red, gr & blk 260.00
Tea bowl & saucer, red, deer, blk 360.00
Tea bowl & saucer, red, peafowl, 4-color, minor rpr 550.00
Tea bowl & saucer, red, peafowl, 4-color, VG 165.00
Tea bowl & saucer, red & bl, flower, red & gr 110.00
Tea bowl & saucer, yel, tulip, 3-color, stain/flake 850.00
Teapot, gr, peafowl, 3-color, oval w/C hdl, 4x7", VG 300.00
Teapot, red & gr rainbow, rpr, 7" 220.00
Toddy, bl red & purple segments, peafowl, 3-color, chip, 5¼" 470.00
Waste bowl, bl, eagle & shield, bl, hairline, 6½" 120.00

Cut-Sponge

Cup & saucer, bl, snowflake, mk SB, NM 75.00
Plate, bl, snowflake, mk SB, 7¾", NM 70.00
Plate, bl star rim w/dk gr Os, dk gr rim stripe, 6" 30.00
Plate, gr/bl spatter rim, blk band around mc floral, 7½" 230.00
Soup plate, bl, bull's eye w/floral rim, gr stars, 8½", VG 45.00

Spectacles

Collectors of Americana are beginning to appreciate the charm of antique optical items, and those involved in the related trade find them particularly fascinating. Anyone, however, cannot help but notice the evolution of technology apparent when viewing a collection of old eye ware and at the same time admire the primitive ingenuity involved in its construction.

Eyeglasses case, sterling, eng Nouveau floral, mk Blackington 60.00
Spectacles, brass fr, rnd lenses, wide extending temporals, EX 120.00
Spectacles, coin silver, mk Kippen, M in papier-mache case 150.00
Spectacles, coin silver, narrow temporals, mk Wilcox, EX 135.00
Spectacles, octagonal w/gr glass, fold-in side lenses, 1800s 95.00
Spectacles, Pinz-nez style, brass fr, Birmingham, Pat 1892 ....36.00
Spectacles, preacher type w/bun-shaped lenses, EX 45.00
Spectacles, steel fr, Benjamin Martin type, 1750s, EX 400.00
Spectacles, steel fr, lg gr rnd lenses, turn-pin temporals 115.00
Spectacles, steel fr, oval lenses, wide dbl temporals, folding 88.00
Spectacles, steel fr, rnd lenses, wide short temporals 140.00
Spectacles, tortoise-shell fr, oval lenses, str temporals 75.00
Spectacles, wht metal, oval lenses, mk Pebbles, EX in case 75.00

Spelter

Spelter figurines are cast from commercial zinc and coated with a metallic patina. The result is a product very similar to bronze in appearance, yet much less expensive.

Figurine, Can't You Talk?, child and dog, 5x7½", $85.00.

Bookends, Scotty heads, silvered, 20th C, 4½x5", pr 70.00
Clock, mantel; modeled as horse w/attendant, GE, 17" 125.00
Figure, Coup de Soleil, Coupe de Vent, bronzed, 20", pr 350.00
Lamp, Nouveau maid under leafy arch w/sm lights, 32" 450.00
Lamp, peasant girl w/flower basket on head, oil burner, 13" 65.00
Lamp, Psyche figural, 4 leafy stem lights, frog/snail, 36" 1,250.00
Urn, patinated floral, marble base, ormolu ft, 15", pr 250.00

Spode-Copeland

The Spode Works was established in 1770 in England by Josiah Spode I and continued to operate under that title until 1843. Their earliest products were typical underglaze blue-printed patterns. After 1790 a translucent porcelain body was the basis for a line of fine enamel-decorated dinnerware. Stone china was introduced in 1805, often in patterns reflecting an Oriental influence. In 1833 William Taylor Copeland purchased the company, having been Spode's business partner. Copeland continued the buiness in much the same traditon as the Spode-Copeland partnership. Spode was the Royal Potter for years, providing many exquisite items for Royal Families. They employed paintresses to decorate the merchandise by hand. Most of the Spode-Copeland wares were marked with one of

several variations that incorporate the firm's name, making identification possible. The Spode Company merged with Worcester Royal Porcelain Company in 1976 and became Royal Worcester Spode Limited. This company was then purchased by Derby International in 1988. The two firms separated in 1989. The holding company is the Porcelain and Fine China Companies Limited, a division of Derby International. Spode china is still being manufactured today at exactly the same location where Josiah Spode I began in 1770. Robert Copeland, a descendent of William Taylor Copeland, resides in England. He writes books and lectures on Spode. Our advisor for this category is Don Haase; he is listed in the Directory under Washington.

Bowl, cereal; Billingsley Rose 35.00
Bowl, cereal; Byron 28.00
Bowl, cereal; Mayflower 28.00
Bowl, cream soup; Gainsborough, w/underplate 38.00
Bowl, cream soup; Tower, pk 38.00
Bowl, fruit; Billingsley Rose 25.00
Bowl, fruit; Chelsea Garden 48.00
Bowl, fruit; Tower, bl or pk, ea 25.00
Bowl, rim soup; Aster, 7" 35.00
Bowl, rim soup; Billingsley Rose, 7" 35.00
Bowl, salad; Cowslip, 7½" 28.00
Bowl, vegetable; Billingsley Rose, oval, 9" 85.00
Bowl, vegetable; Bridal Rose, bone china, 8" sq 245.00
Bowl, vegetable; Camilla; oval, bone china, 9" 85.00
Bowl, vegetable; Chelsea Garden, oval, bone china, 9" 175.00
Bowl, vegetable; Cowslip, 9" 85.00
Bowl, vegetable; Irene, oval, bone china 175.00
Butter pat, Chelsea Garden 42.00
Butter pat, Heath & Rose 25.00
Butter pat, Mayflower 25.00
Butter pat, Tower, pk 25.00
Chop plate, Irene, bone china, 13" 225.00
Chop plate, Tower, bl, 15" 185.00
Coffeepot, Billingsley Rose, 8-cup 165.00
Coffeepot, Gloucester, bl, 8-cup 165.00
Coffeepot, Tower, 8-cup 165.00
Creamer, Billingsley Rose 45.00
Creamer, Chelsea Garden 95.00
Creamer, Florence 45.00
Creamer, Tower, pk 45.00
Cup & saucer, Aster 39.00
Cup & saucer, Buttercup 39.00
Cup & saucer, Chelsea Garden, bone china 69.00
Cup & saucer, Cowslip 39.00
Cup & saucer, Mayflower 39.00
Cup & saucer, Rosebriar 39.00
Cup & saucer, Shanghai, bone china 69.00
Cup & saucer, Tower, bl 39.00
Egg cup, Gainsborough 32.00
Gravy boat, Camilla, earthenware 110.00
Gravy boat, Chelsea Garden 195.00
Gravy boat, Patricia 110.00
Jug, Tower, bbl shape, 6" 67.50
Pitcher, Jasper, classical figures on lt bl, Copeland, 4" 75.00
Pitcher, milk; Greek Brown 85.00
Plate, bread & butter; Tower, pk 25.00
Plate, Camilla, bl, pk, or gr, 5¼", ea 22.00
Plate, Christmas Tree, center brass hdl, 10½" 45.00
Plate, dinner; Rosebriar 35.00
Plate, dinner; Billingsley Rose 35.00
Plate, dinner; Cowslip 35.00

Plate, dinner; Dresden Rose Savoy	69.00
Plate, dinner; Greek Brown	25.00
Plate, dinner; Irene, bone china	69.00
Plate, dinner; Primrose, red	69.00
Plate, dinner; Rosebriar	35.00
Plate, dinner; Ruins	75.00
Plate, dinner; Shanghai, bone china	69.00
Plate, dinner; Tower, pk or bl, ea	35.00
Plate, luncheon; Aster	32.00
Plate, luncheon; Buttercup	32.00
Plate, luncheon; Chelsea Wicker	32.00
Plate, luncheon; Fairy Dell	32.00
Plate, salad; Billingsley Rose	28.00
Plate, salad; Camilla, bl, pk, or gr, ea	28.00
Plate, salad; Chelsea Garden	49.00
Plate, salad; Moss Rose	28.00
Plate, salad; Wild Flower	28.00
Platter, Billingsley Rose, 17"	175.00
Platter, Chelsea Garden, 13"	170.00
Platter, chop; Irene, 13"	215.00
Platter, Cowslip, 15"	145.00
Platter, Gainsborough, 17"	175.00
Platter, Greek Brown, 13"	125.00
Platter, Tower, bl, 15"	155.00
Sugar bowl, Billingsley Rose	45.00
Sugar bowl, Chelsea Garden	125.00
Sugar bowl, Claudia, bone china	125.00
Sugar bowl, Dresden Rose Savoy, bone china	125.00
Sugar bowl, Florence	45.00
Sugar bowl, Tower	45.00
Teakettle, Tower, pk, red mk	400.00
Teapot, Tower, bl, 6-cup	145.00
Teapot, Tower, bl, 8-cup	165.00

Spongeware

Spongeware is a type of factory-made earthenware that was popular during the last quarter of the 19th century. It was decorated by dabbing color onto the drying ware with a sponge, leaving a splotched design at random or in simple patterns. Sometimes a solid band of color was added. The vessel was then covered with a clear glaze and fired at a high temperature. Blue on white is the most preferred combination, but green on ivory, orange on white, or those colors in combination may also occasionally be found.

Bean pot, mc chicken wire sponging, ca 1890s, 5¾"	175.00
Bowl, bl/wht, scalloped, rectangular, 8½", EX	200.00
Bowl, bl/wht, wht band, 6x13"	275.00
Bowl, brn/wht, emb scrolls, 1870s, 5½x10½"	125.00
Bowl, soup; brn/cream, sponging at rim, 2¼x9½", NM	40.00
Jug, bl/wht, Grandmother's Maple Syrup..., wire bail, 5½"	660.00
Mush cup, flowing bl sponging, 5x8", +8" saucer	215.00
Pitcher, bl/wht, 6¾"	165.00
Pitcher, tankard, bl/wht, 2-pc mold, 1850s, 9"	235.00
Plate, bl/wht, relief-molded rim, 1880s, 8½"	100.00
Plate, bl/wht, rim hdls, 10"	150.00
Platter, bl/wht, oval, 1840s, 13x9"	165.00
Platter, bl/wht, scalloped, rectangular, 12½"	200.00
Platter, bl/wht, Trenton NJ, 12x8"	350.00
Platter, bl/wht, 11¼"	145.00
Sauce boat, bl/wht, lion & unicorn mk, 7" L	325.00
Toothbrush holder, flowing bl, scalloped, emb scrolls, 6"	260.00
Wash pitcher, wide bl base band, 12"	235.00

Spoons

Souvenir spoons have been popular remembrances since the 1890s. The early hand-wrought examples of the silversmith's art are especially sought and appreciated for their fine craftsmanship. Commemorative, personality-related, advertising, and those with Indian busts or floral designs are only a few of the many types of collectible spoons. In the following listings, spoons are entered by city, character, or occasion. Our advisor for this category is Margaret Alves; she is listed in the Directory under Connecticut.

Key:
B — bowl
BR — bowl reverse
emb — embossed
eng — engraved

FF — full figure
GW — gold wash
H — handle
HR — handle reverse

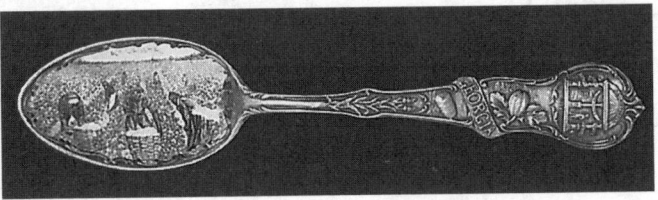

Georgia on stem, Blacks picking cotton enameled in bowl, State Capitol on the back, ca 1900-1930, 5¾", $125.00.

Alaska & totem pole w/cutouts on H; Anchorage etched in B	36.00
Annapolis Naval Academy B; military H	65.00
Atlantic City etched in B; twist H	12.50
Baby in scales emb on H; plain B; Watson	35.00
Black Hills SD in B; miner FF H; Indian FF HR	120.00
Brooklyn Bridge view eng in GW B; twist H; Whiting	24.00
Canada on H; seal on finial; plain B; Watson	27.50
Catalina eng in B; Indian head FF H	30.00
Catalina Island eng in B; lg fish finial H	30.00
Catholic Church Extension Society B; symbols on H	50.00
Chicago & emb Indian head H; plain B	17.50
Chief Seattle eng B; totem pole FF H	40.00
Christian Endeavor 1881, demitasse	30.00
City Hall Detroit MI eng B; Indian FF H	35.00
Confederate Monument Alexandria LA in B; Louisiana on H	120.00
DePauw in B; girl graduate FF H; Watson	32.00
Dillingham Alaska on H; fish finial; plain B	27.50
Empire State & Capitol buildings on H; Brooklyn Bridge in B	27.50
Everett WA courthouse in B; chinook salmon FF H	22.50
Girl Graduate hdl, 1906, 3¼"	35.00
Grover Cleveland emb on H; White House view in B	22.50
Hamilton OH emb in B; sheaves of wheat on H; leaves on HR	13.50
Harry Truman finial H; Berlin Airlift in B	45.00
IL Central Bridge scene in B; Cairo IL on H	40.00
Independence Hall & Liberty Bell on H; plain B	24.00
Kansas, sunflower on H; Capitol building in B	32.50
Lake Placid NY eng in heart-shaped B; cherub finial H; Watson	34.00
Liberty Bell emb in B; emb eagle on H; mk 90 Holland	8.50
Milwaukee & soldiers' monument in B; beaver cutout in H	17.50
Minne-ha-ha Falls emb/HP B; State H; GW	85.00
Mission San Gabriel eng B; City of Angels on H	35.00
Mt Hood view eng in B; salmon FF H	34.00
Mt Ranier eng in B; chinook salmon FF H	26.50
Nashville & Jackson's birthplace in B; state seal on H	12.00

Niagara Falls emb in B; Indian FF H; Ellis, 5¾" 155.00
Old KY Home eng B; KY on H 35.00
Pan American 1901 Expo eng B 45.00
Pike's Peak eng B; plain H; demitasse 15.00
Rocky Mtns & miners emb on H; miners emb in B 40.00
San Antonio emb on H; Alamo view emb in B 27.50
Santa Cruz in B; scroll H 10.00
Seattle & totem pole on H; plain B 12.50
Shamrocks/harps/thistle on H; Liberty & Law emb in B 48.00
St Louis Union Station eng B; FF woman H 35.00
Steamer Robert Fulton in B; salmon on H 32.50
Stevens House Lake Placid NY in B; scroll H; GW, demitasse 14.00
Stork FF H; birth data in B; Reed & Barton, 6" 24.00
Summit of Pike's Peak & scene in B; acorn & leaf H 27.50
Taconic Trail pnt B; cut-out Indian H 35.00
Tappin ND in B; blown-out face in rose on H; Manchester 55.00
Union Station Dayton OH in B; plain H 18.50
Vatican emb view in B; Pope Leo portrait on H 22.50
Wapakoneta OH courthouse in B; Justice FF H 58.00
Washington Monument eng B; monument FF H 25.00
Westerly RI & man's head finial H; plain B; Howard, demitasse ..20.00
World's Columbian Expo & Columbus H; ship in B; Alvin 60.00
Yellowstone Park, elk/bear on H; Old Faithful Inn in B 40.00
Yellowstone Park pnt B; cut-out H 30.00
Zanesville eng in B; floral H; Simpson-Hall-Miller 35.00

Sporting Goods

When sports cards became so widely collectible several years ago, other types of related memorabilia started to interest sports fans. Now they search for baseball uniforms, autographed baseballs, game-used bats and gloves, and all sorts of ephemera. Although baseball is America's all-time favorite, other sports have their own groups of interested collectors. Our advice for this category comes from Paul Longo Americana, Box 490, Chatham Rd., South Orleans, Cape Cod, Massachusetts 02662. See also Target Balls.

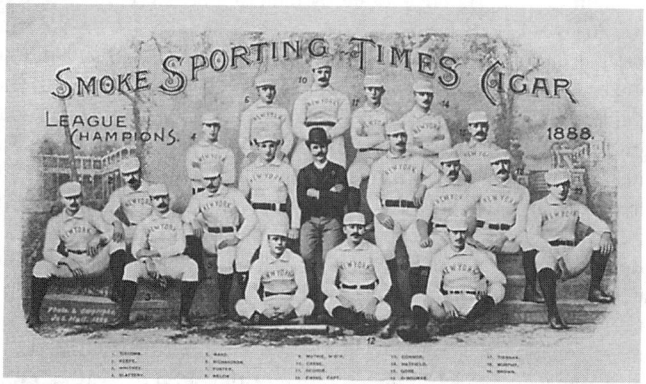

Trade card, Smoke Sporting Times Cigar, sepia drawing after photo by J. Hall Studios of the New York Giants, 1888 World Champions, EX, $1,400.00.

Baseball, Official Am Assoc, sgn by Cy Young w/2 photos 1,500.00
Baseball, sgn, Carl Yastrzemski, M in case 35.00
Baseball, sgn, Jim Palmer, M in case 25.00
Baseball, sgn Pete Rose, M in case 35.00
Bat, Little League Triple Crown, sgn Mickey Mantle 50.00
Bat, Our Leader, prof model, 1950s, EX 30.00
Book, Babe Ruth Story, 1st edition, 1948, EX 45.00

Book, Baseball Rules, 1958, M 12.00
Book, Gold w/Great Masters...First Tee, Turner, 1922, EX 20.00
Book, How To Play Tennis, Spalding Primer Series, 1914, EX 40.00
Book, It's Good To Be Alive, Roy Campanella, 1974, EX 12.00
Book, My Turn at Bat, Ted Williams, photos, 1969, NM 15.00
Book, Spalding's Official Baseball Guide, 1886, 160-pg, EX 140.00
Booklet, Big League Secrets, 1959 ....10.00
Button, Ali/Frazier Fight, 'I'm the Greatest,' 1971, 3½" 12.00
Candy bar, Reggie Jackson, waxed paper wrapper, Curtiss 12.00
Cereal box, Jim Palmer on Wheaties, unopened, M 20.00
Diecut, Michael Jordan, cb, 15" 5.00
Glove, baseball; sgn Bob Allison, EX 15.00
Glove, baseball; Triple Crown, Mickey Mantle, NM 50.00
Glove, softball; Rawlings Official AW-15, 1930s, EX 20.00
Gloves, boxing; sgn Muhammad Ali, w/case 300.00
Helmet, football; Franklin, red & beige compo, EX 75.00
Helmet, football; red compo, hutch type, MIB 75.00
Jersey & pants, Babe Ruth, Wilson, 1930s, child sz 200.00
Magazine, Baseball, Brooks Robinson cover, 1971, NM 8.00
Mask, softball catcher's; Rigidbilt, foam face pads, early 50.00
Membership kit, Hank Aaron, 715 Club 35.00
Mitt, catcher's; darkly oiled, 1930s 40.00
Mitt, catcher's; Roy Campenella, EX 65.00
Pennant, New Jersey Nets, NBA, 3 autographs 30.00
Pennant, Stanford, felt, w/beanie hat 30.00
Photo, Jack Dempsey portrait, 1930s 30.00
Photo, Montreal Canadians hockey team, 1937, 5x9" 65.00
Pin, lapel; NY Mets World Series souvenir, 1969 ....15.00
Program, Baseball 1920 World Series, Dodgers & Indians, EX .1,000.00
Program, Chicago Black Hawks Stanley Cup, 1970-71 ....20.00
Program, Olympic souvenir; Berlin, 1936, EX 65.00
Program, 1932 Olympics, M 50.00
Program/score card, Cincinnati Reds, Crosley Field, 1960 ....15.00
Program/score card, Yankees/Cleveland, 1950 ....25.00
Program/score card, Yankees/Washington, 1947, EX 25.00
Record book, Official Major League Baseball, 1972, M 12.00
Ring, Cleveland Indians, enameled, 1940s, EX 125.00
Shoulder pads, football; Bill Ingram Rawlings 'Plebe,' EX 50.00
Spring score book, Detroit Tigers, Marchant Stadium FL, 1972 ...10.00
Stamps, Major League Baseball, 9 sheets (81 stamps), 1988 ....20.00
Ticket, Stanford-California football game, 1932, unused, M 45.00
Tie clip, Remington Arms, gold-tone shotgun form 15.00
Trophy, Arlington Country Club Golf, Wilcox SP, 1911, 11" ...130.00
Trophy, yachting, lady figural top, SP & metal, 1930s, 13" 75.00
Wristwatch, Harlem Globetrotters 40.00

St. Clair

The St. Clair Glass Company began as a small family-oriented operation in Elwood, Indiana, in 1941. Most famous for their lamps, the family made numerous small items of carnival, pink and caramel slag, and custard glass as well. Later, paperweights became popular production pieces; many command considerably high prices on today's market. Weights are stamped and usually dated, while small production pieces are often unmarked. For further information we recommend *St. Clair Glass Collector's Book* by Bonnie Pruitt, available from our advisor, Ted Pruitt, who is listed in the Directory under Indiana.

Bookends, wht ribbon style, 4", pr 325.00
Bottle, scent; carnival glass 100.00
Buffalo, red, Joe St Clair 200.00
Candle holder, floral paperweight base 85.00
Candle holders, chocolate, w/finger hold, sgn Joe St Clair, pr 120.00

Covered dish, dolphin, cobalt 100.00
Creamer, aqua floral base, sgn Joe St Clair 55.00
Doorstop, Little Bo Peep 525.00
Figurine, bird, bl sulfide, lg 95.00
Figurine, turtle, sulfide 175.00
Lamp, yel lilies, gr base, 21" 210.00
Lamp base, pk slag, kerosene burner 250.00
Miniature, pear, carnival glass 100.00
Miniature, strawberry 100.00
Miniature, tomato 100.00
Paperweight, bl heart sulfide w/names, sgn Bob & Maud 58.00
Paperweight, butterfly, controlled bubbles, etched 325.00
Paperweight, cameo, windowed 300.00
Paperweight, dove sulfide 165.00
Paperweight, flower, windowed, sgn Paul St Clair 200.00
Paperweight, mc ribbon, sgn Joe St Clair 75.00
Paperweight, wht floral base, sgn Joe St Clair 30.00
Plate, Kewpie, cobalt 225.00
Toothpick holder, dog's head, gr opaque 75.00
Toothpick holder, Fan & Feather, gr carnival 30.00
Toothpick holder, flower sulfide 75.00
Toothpick holder, Santa, sgn Joe St Clair 200.00
Toothpick holder, Shriner's hat (fez), red 200.00
Toothpick holder, swan hdl, Peach Glow 45.00
Tumbler, Invt Fan & Feather, pk slag 35.00
Wine, Panel Grape, ice bl carnival 65.00

Staffordshire

Scores of potteries sprang up in England's Staffordshire district in the early 18th century; several remain to the present time. (See also specific companies.) Figurines and groups were made in great numbers; dogs were favorite subjects. Often they were made in pairs, each a mirror image of the other. They varied in heights from 3" or 4" to the largest, measuring 16" to 18". From 1840 until about 1900, portrait figures were produced to represent specific characters, both real and fictional. As a rule these were never marked.

The Historical Ware listed here was made throughout the district; some collectors refer to it as Staffordshire Blue Ware. It was produced as early as 1820, and because much was exported to America, it was very often decorated with transfers depicting scenic views of well-known American landmarks. Early examples were printed in a deep cobalt. By 1830 a softer blue was favored, and within the next decade black, pink, red, and green prints were used. Although sometimes careless about adding their trademark, many companies used their own border designs that were as individual as their names.

This ware should not be confused with the vast amounts of modern china (mostly plates) made from early in the century to the present. These souvenir or commemorative items are usually marketed through gift stores and the like. (See Rowland and Marsellus.) See also specific manufacturers. Our advisor for Historical Staffordshire is William Kurau; he is listed in the Directory under Pennsylvania.

Key:
blk — black   l/b — light blue
gr — green   m/b — medium blue
d/b — dark blue   m-d/b — medium dark blue

Historical

Basket & undertray, Dorney Court, d/b, Wood, 11" 1,350.00
Bowl, Bird Cage, d/b, Adams, 6¼", EX 110.00

Bowl, Bywell Castle, d/b, bluebell border, Adams, 12" 795.00
Bowl, lovers in woods, grape border, d/b, 6½", NM 160.00
Coffeepot, Lafayette at Franklin's Tomb, d/b, dome top, 11" ..1,200.00
Coffeepot, Lafayette at Franklin's Tomb, d/b, rpr, 11½" 770.00
Coffeepot, Wadsworth Tower, d/b, high dome, Wood, 10½" ..2,350.00
Creamer, Bird Cage, Adams, NM 295.00
Creamer, Castle Toward, d/b, entwined hdls, Hall 375.00
Creamer, Christmas Eve, Wilkie's Designs, Clews, d/b, 5½" 250.00
Creamer, Lafayette at Franklin's Tomb, d/b, 5¾" 500.00
Creamer, Richard Jordan, purple, hairline, 5" 375.00
Cup & saucer, handleless; Basket of Flowers, d/b, Adams, NM ..110.00
Cup & saucer, handleless; Christmas Eve, d/b, Wilkie, Clews 225.00
Cup & saucer, handleless; dogs, d/b, Clews 195.00
Cup & saucer, handleless; Farm Horses, d/b 235.00
Cup & saucer, handleless; Fruit, d/b, fluted rim 155.00
Cup & saucer, handleless; horse-drawn sleigh, Wood 330.00
Cup & saucer, handleless; India dome building, d/b, Adams 150.00
Cup & saucer, handleless; Lovers in Tropical Forest, d/b 165.00
Cup & saucer, handleless; Sleigh Ride, d/b, Wood 325.00
Cup & saucer, handleless; Washington, red 140.00
Cup plate, Batalha Portugal, m/b, 3⅞" 145.00
Cup plate, Battersea Park NY, d/b, 3⅝" 360.00
Cup plate, bridge scene, d/b, Wood, 3¾" 160.00
Cup plate, Columbus, gr, Adams, 4" 85.00
Cup plate, English country scene, d/b, pk lustre, 3⅞" 78.00
Cup plate, Fakeer's Rock, d/b, Hall, 4¼" 165.00
Cup plate, hyena, m/b, Quadrupeds series, 4" 150.00
Cup plate, Italian Scenery, Santa Croce, m/b, 4⅝" 66.00
Cup plate, Landing of Lafayette, d/b, Clews, 3", EX 280.00
Cup plate, Shirley House, m/b, Wood, 3¾" 185.00
Cup plate, soldier & girl, m/b, 3⅞" 88.00
Cup plate, Vale of Wyoming, l/b, Wilkes-Barre, 4" 155.00
Cup plate, Worcester Cathedral, d/b, Hall, 3⅞" 175.00
Cup plate, 3 children, d/b, 3¾" 85.00
Mug, John Gilpin & horse, blk, chip, 2½" 105.00
Pitcher, floral, d/b, poor rpr, 7½" 275.00
Pitcher, Lafayette at Franklin's Tomb, d/b, rpr, 7¼" 600.00
Pitcher, Lafayette at Franklin's Tomb, d/b, Wood, 7" 750.00
Plate, Am & Independence, States border, d/b, Clews, 10½" 330.00
Plate, Arms of Rhode Island, d/b, Mayer, 8½" 475.00
Plate, Baltimore & OH RR (level), d/b, Wood, 10¼" 600.00
Plate, beehive, d/b, Stevenson & Williams, 8½" 185.00
Plate, Boston State House, m/b, 9½" 195.00
Plate, Cadmus, d/b, Enoch Wood & Sons, 10¼", EX 605.00
Plate, Cascade de Grecy, d/b, Wood, 7⅝" 155.00
Plate, Castle of Furstenfel, d/b, 8⅝" 120.00
Plate, Castle Ruins, l/b, Clews, wear, 6⅛" 30.00
Plate, Castskill Mtn house, red, 10¼" 195.00
Plate, City Hall NY, m/b, Ridgway, 9⅞" 275.00
Plate, City Hotel NY, d/b, Stevenson, 8⅝" 325.00
Plate, City Hotel NY, m/b, Stevenson, 8¾" 300.00
Plate, Commodore MacDonnough's Victory, d/b, Wood, rpr, 10" ..330.00
Plate, Commodore MacDonnough's Victory, d/b, Wood, 6½" ...330.00
Plate, Commodore MacDonnough's Victory, d/b, Wood, 7⅝" ..425.00
Plate, Commodore MacDonnough's Victory, d/b, Wood, 9", NM .325.00
Plate, Dam & Water Works Philadelphia, d/b, 10" 440.00
Plate, Dartmouth, d/b, 8¼" 330.00
Plate, dog, d/b, Quadrupeds series, 6⅜" 165.00
Plate, Dunraven Gladmorgan, d/b, Wood, 6½" 60.00
Plate, English Country scene w/hunters, d/b, 10⅜" 160.00
Plate, Fairmount Near Phila, d/b, Stubbs, wear, 10⅜" 300.00
Plate, fruit, floral & acanthus border, d/b, 5½" 70.00
Plate, fruit & flowers, d/b, Stubbs & Kent, 10", EX 95.00
Plate, Gen WH Harrison...Thames 1813, gr, stain, 9½" 1,980.00

Plate, Ghaut of Cutwa, d/b, floral/scroll rim, Adams, 9", VG **95.00**
Plate, Greenwich, d/b, Clews, 8⅞" **165.00**
Plate, Harvard College, brn, Wood, 10½" **165.00**
Plate, Hawthornden Edinburghshire, m/b, Adams, 8¾", EX **120.00**
Plate, Insane Hospital Boston, m/b, Ridgway, 7¼" **250.00**
Plate, Italian Scenery Bridge of Lucano, d/b, Wood, 10", EX **120.00**
Plate, LaGrange Residence of Lafayette, d/b, Wood, 10" **265.00**
Plate, Lakes of Killarny, d/b, 6½" **55.00**
Plate, Landing of Fathers at Plymouth, m/b, 7⅝" **150.00**
Plate, Landing of Gen Lafayette, d/b, Clews, rpr, 6¾" **165.00**
Plate, Landing of Gen Lafayette, d/b, Clews, 10⅛" **325.00**
Plate, Library Philadelphia, m/b, flakes, 8⅛" **170.00**
Plate, Llanarth Court Mornmouthshire, d/b, Hall, 10" **195.00**
Plate, Millenium, brn, Stubbs, 10½" **175.00**
Plate, Montreal, brn, Davenport, 7" **195.00**
Plate, Nahant Hotel Near Boston, d/b, 8⅝" **325.00**
Plate, otter, d/b, Quadrupeds series, 8⅝" **275.00**
Plate, Park Theatre NY, m/b, minor glaze flake, 10" **275.00**
Plate, Peace & Plenty, d/b, Clews, 10¼" **395.00**
Plate, Rural Homes, d/b, Wood, 9⅛" **115.00**
Plate, Sailboat, men digging in foreground, d/b, 9" **395.00**
Plate, Southampton Hampshire, d/b, Wood, 7⅝", EX **220.00**
Plate, St Phillip's Chapel, d/b, Wood, 10¼" **195.00**
Plate, States, d/b, Clews, 10⅝" **475.00**
Plate, States w/American & Independence, d/b, Clews, 8¾" **360.00**
Plate, Steamboat, men pulling boat ashore, d/b, 8" **395.00**
Plate, toddy; Moral Maxims, 5⅞" **75.00**
Plate, toddy; ship, d/b, shell border, Wood, 5⅝" **220.00**
Plate, Upper Ferry Bridge Over...Schuylkill, d/b, 8½", EX **185.00**
Plate, Upper Ferry Bridge Over...Schuylkill, m/b, 8¾" **110.00**
Plate, Valentine, Wilkie's Designs, d/b, Clews, 8⅞" **99.00**
Plate, View Near Florence, d/b, Wood, 8½" **165.00**
Plate, Villa in Regents Park London, d/b, Adams, 10", EX **150.00**
Plate, Wardour Castle, d/b, Wood, grapevine border, 10" **175.00**
Plate, Wells Cathedral, d/b, Clews, 10" **160.00**
Plate, Winter View of Pittsfield MA, d/b, Clews, 7¾" **360.00**
Platter, Am & Independence, d/b, gap in pattern, 16⅝" **1,045.00**
Platter, Clarence Terrace, d/b, Adams, 10¾" **875.00**
Platter, Columbus (OH), d/b, wear/stains, 14½" **880.00**
Platter, Falls of Niagara, red, Adams, 20" **1,125.00**
Platter, Grecian Scenery, m/b, wear/flakes, 13" **75.00**
Platter, Harper's Ferry, red, Adams, 16½" **495.00**
Platter, Hermitage en Dauphine, d/b, Wood, 14¾" **695.00**
Platter, Houghton Conquest House, d/b, 21½" **1,050.00**

Platter, Landing of General Lafayette at Castle Garden..., dark blue, octagonal, Clews, 1819-1836, 17", NM, $935.00.

Platter, London Views Clarence Terrace..., d/b, Wood, 11", EX ..**190.00**
Platter, Lucerne, l/b, wear/glaze chips, 20" **190.00**

Platter, Military School West Point, red, Adams, 17½" **695.00**
Platter, moose, d/b, Hall's Quadruped, 15¼" **1,400.00**
Platter, Oriental scene, d/b, 12¾" **450.00**
Platter, Peace, Plenty, d/b, Clews, 19" **880.00**
Platter, Post Office Dublin, d/b, Tams Anderson, 17", NM **825.00**
Platter, Residence of the Late Richard Jordan, purple, 19½" **965.00**
Platter, View From Fort Putnam, l/b, Ridgway, 15¼" **360.00**
Platter, well & tree; Antique Scenery, NE View Lancaster, 21" .**370.00**
Platter, Winter View of Pittsfield Mass, d/b, Clews, rpr, 15" **715.00**
Soup, hunter fires at ducks over dogs, d/b, Wood, 8¼" **185.00**
Soup, Marmora, 10⅜", 6 for **265.00**
Soup, shepherds w/cottage & windmill, l/b, 10" **65.00**
Soup, Warwick Castle, d/b, Wood, 9⅜" **175.00**
Soup, Winter View of Pittsfield MA, d/b, Clews, 10⅜" **415.00**
Sugar bowl, English scene, d/b, Adams, mismatched lid, 6" **165.00**
Sugar bowl, Lafayette at Franklin's Tomb, d/b, Wood, 6⅝" **635.00**
Sugar bowl, Mounted Zebra, d/b, lion hdls, Rogers, prof rpr **375.00**
Sugar bowl, Oriental scene, d/b, 7" **250.00**
Sugar bowl, WA at Tomb w/Scroll in Hand, d/b, rpr rim, 4½" .**1,025.00**
Sugar bowl, zebra & horse, d/b, rstr, 5¾" **165.00**
Teapot, Lafayette at Franklin's Tomb, d/b, rpr, 8¼" **1,045.00**
Tray, Landing of Lafayette, d/b, Clews, 6", EX **1,250.00**
Tureen, sauce; dead game, d/b, rpr **425.00**
Tureen, scenic, grape border, d/b, rose finial, 8", +tray, VG **510.00**
Wash pitcher & bowl, Lafayette at Tomb of Franklin, d/b, lg .**2,350.00**

Miscellaneous

Bank, cottage, mc, 4½" **150.00**
Clock, man w/pipe, lady w/lamp at sides, 12" **225.00**
Clock watch holder, surmounted by 2 lovebirds & 3 ladies, 10" .**250.00**
Figurine, bear, porc, gray & gr, chips, 3⅝" **100.00**
Figurine, boy & dog, mc, minor wear, 6⅞" **325.00**
Figurine, clown, mc, 4" **200.00**
Figurine, cottage, mc, 4½" **150.00**
Figurine, couple by fence pour water from well, 9½" **180.00**
Figurine, couple w/fruit, seated & barefoot, 8¾" **125.00**
Figurine, courting couple w/flower baskets, 17" **275.00**
Figurine, elderly milkmaid pouring from pitcher to glass, 6" **70.00**
Figurine, Fortune Teller, gypsy w/baby & lady, 12", EX **225.00**
Figurine, Garibaldi, man w/scroll, gold trim, 19" **300.00**
Figurine, general on horsebk, plumed hat, 12" **225.00**
Figurine, girl holding basket, yel & brn mottle, 1800s, 4½" **115.00**
Figurine, Highlander w/bagpipes, 4½" **60.00**
Figurine, Highlander w/deer & dog, mc w/gold, flaking, 10" **140.00**
Figurine, Highlander w/wild boar & dog, 17½" **350.00**
Figurine, hunter w/quail in hand & at ft, 15½" **200.00**
Figurine, Jobson, cobbler w/spaniel at side, 6" **120.00**
Figurine, lady w/bouquet in lap kisses bird on hand, 7¼" **200.00**
Figurine, lady w/wood bundle, man w/jug, on base, 13" **300.00**
Figurine, lion, tan & gilt w/glass eyes, 12½", pr **330.00**
Figurine, Lord & Lady Stanhope drawing water, 9" **325.00**
Figurine, man in tricorner hat on horse, 7" **300.00**
Figurine, man w/mandolin, lady w/tambourine, 8½", EX **125.00**
Figurine, Mother's Rescue, lady & child/eagle & eaglets, 16" **550.00**
Figurine, Napoleon in classic stance w/eagle at side, 12" **300.00**
Figurine, Napoleon w/rolled document, wear, 7½" **125.00**
Figurine, Pomona, lady w/overflowing cornucopia, 7¼" **675.00**
Figurine, Prince of Wales astride, wht w/flesh tones, 12" **350.00**
Figurine, Red Riding Hood & brn wolf, 5½" **325.00**
Figurine, Red Riding Hood & wolf, rprs, 14" **225.00**
Figurine, Roman in toga beside pillar & spaniel, 16" **200.00**
Figurine, Shakespeare, ermine cape & manuscript, 11½", EX **300.00**
Figurine, Shakespeare w/books & papers on pillar, 17½" **275.00**

Figurine, soldier on horsebk w/tricolor flag, 11" 300.00
Figurine, spaniel, copper lustre spots, dk stain, 6¾" 135.00
Figurine, spaniel, gr lustre, 10½", pr 220.00
Figurine, spaniel, red accents, 12", pr 410.00
Figurine, spaniel, rust color, 9½", pr 400.00
Figurine, spaniel, rust mottle, 12", pr 160.00
Figurine, spaniel, wht w/copper lustre spots, 9½x5" 225.00
Figurine, St John w/goose, wht w/enamel & gilt, 11¼" 215.00
Figurine, Tenderness, couple w/lamb, sgn Walton, 6¼" 325.00
Figurine, Tom holds Little Eva, quote on base, 7½" 650.00
Figurine, Wallace as Highland warrior, 16" 400.00
Figurine, William Tell w/quiver, gold trim, 20" 315.00
Figurine, youth w/violin & book reclining on cushion, 8¼" 175.00
Mug, cat & 3 kittens, brn transfer w/mc pnt, 2⅝" 120.00
Mug, child in dog cart blk transfer, mc enamel, 2⅝" 140.00
Mug, emb pub scenes & frog, mc, oversz, 4¾" 150.00
Mug, horse blk transfer w/gr enameling, 2½" 100.00
Pitcher, red Adam's Rose type w/gr & bl, Wood, 10", VG 260.00
Pitcher, toby, mc, wear, 9⅜" 110.00
Teapot, Garden Sports, pk transfer, dolphin hdl, 7x12", VG 160.00
Vase, cow & milkmaid, mc, wear, 8½" 580.00
Vase, leaping stag pursued by hounds form, 11¾", pr 350.00
Vase, spaniel (wht) before gr tree trunk, 14" 250.00
Vase, spill; Highland hunter w/bow beside tree trunk, 17" 400.00
Vase, spill; Highland lad & lass by tree w/2 lambs, 8¾" 150.00
Vase, spill; Highland lad & lassie & fawn by tree, 7" 250.00
Vase, spill; Highland lass w/birdhouse & dog by tree, 7", EX 125.00
Vase, spill; lady w/lamb at ft beside tree w/appl florals, 9" 300.00
Vase, spill; lovers by tree & trellis w/dog, 13", EX 275.00

Stained Glass

There are many factors to consider in evaluating a window or panel of stained glass art. Besides the obvious factor of condition, intricacy, jeweling, beveling, and the amount of selenium (red, orange, and yellow) present should all be taken into account. Remember, repair work is itself an art and can be very expensive. Our advisor for this category is Carl Heck; he is listed in the Directory under Colorado.

Lamps

Duffner-Kimberly, flowers/leaves/vines, shallow, 28" 4,500.00
Duffner-Kimberly, 22" Louis XV-shaped shade; sgn gilt std ..11,000.00
Gorham, 17" allover tulip shade; bronze std, 24" 2,500.00
Unmk, 18" conical shade w/flowers; stick-form std, 26" 1,750.00
Unmk, 18 bell-shaped shade w/flowers; Nouveau std; 24" 2,200.00
Unmk, 20" dome shade w/tulip band; bronze std, 26", EX 850.00
Unmk, 20" wisteria cone shade w/irreg edge, bronze std, 25" ..2,200.00
Unmk, 22" apple blossom shade; 24" 2,000.00
Unmk, 22" floral-border shade w/irreg edge; bronze std, EX 700.00

Miscellaneous

Foliate frame forms arch for center panel with vegetable still life, 23½x35⅜" with frame, $950.00.

Chandelier, 24½" pond lily dome shade, irreg rim 1,950.00
Fire screen, 3-panel, sqs/bull's eye, brass frwork, 25x30" 2,250.00
Hanging shade, floral/fruit, cone w/bent-down sides, 26" 1,000.00
Shade, Dutch girls & windmills, 24½" dia 900.00
Window, Arts & Crafts, florals & geometrics, 1902, 35x70" 475.00
Window, Prairie School, rectangles/sqs, 3-color, 41x54" 600.00

Stanford

The Stanford Pottery Co. was founded in 1945 in Sebring, Ohio. One of the founders was George Stanford, a former manager at Spaulding China (Royal Copley). They continued in operations until the factory was destroyed by a fire about 1961. They produced a Corn Line, similar to that of the Shawnee Company, that is today becoming very collectible. Most examples are marked (either Stanford Sebring Ohio or with a paper label), so there should be no difficulty in distinguishing one from the other.

In addition to their Corn line, they produced planters and figurines, many of which were black trimmed with gold, made to be sold as pairs or sets. Wall pockets and vases were made as well. In 1949 they introduced a line called Tomatoe Ware, consisting of a cookie jar, grease jar, salt and pepper shakers, creamer and sugar bowl, mustard jar, marmalade jar, etc. These were shaped as bright red tomatoes with green leaves and stems (often used as lid finials), and were marketed under the name 'The Pantry Parade.' Our advisor for this category is Joe Devine; he is listed in the Directory under Iowa.

Corn Line, butter dish 45.00
Corn Line, cookie jar 85.00
Corn Line, creamer & sugar bowl 45.00
Corn Line, pitcher, 7½" 55.00
Corn Line, relish tray 35.00
Corn Line, shakers, pr 25.00
Corn Line, spoon rest 25.00
Corn Line, teapot 60.00
Planter, drum major or majorette, ea 15.00
Planter, Dutch boy or girl by tulip, blk w/gold trim, ea 15.00
Tomatoe Ware, cookie jar 50.00
Tomatoe Ware, creamer 25.00
Tomatoe Ware, grease jar 25.00
Tomatoe Ware, marmalade jar 25.00
Tomatoe Ware, mustard jar 25.00
Tomatoe Ware, sugar bowl 25.00
Wall pocket, bird, bl & cobalt w/gold trim 28.00

Stangl

Stangl Pottery was one of the longest-existing potteries in the United States, having as its beginning in 1814 the Sam Hill Pottery, becoming the Fulper Pottery which gained eminence in the field of art pottery (ca. 1860), and then coming under the aegis of Johann Martin Stangl. The German-born Stangl joined Fulper in 1910 as chemical engineer, left for a brief stint at Haeger in Dundee, Illinois, and rejoined Fulper as general manager in 1920. He became president of the firm in 1928. Although Stangl's name was on much of the ware from the late twenties onward, the company's name was not changed officially until 1955. J.M. Stangl died in 1972; the pottery continued under the ownership of Wheaton Industries until 1978, then closed. Stangl is best known for its extensive Birds of America line, styled after Audubon; its brightly colored, hand-carved, hand-painted dinnerware; and its great variety of giftware, including its dry-brushed gold lines. For more information we recommend *Stangl Pottery* by Harvey Duke; for ordering information refer to the listing for Nancy and Robert Perzel, Popkorn Antiques (our advisors for this category), in our Directory under New Jersey.

Birds

#3250E, Drinking Duck	75.00
#3274, Penguin	500.00
#3276, Bluebird	88.00
#3276D, Bluebirds, 8½"	150.00
#3400, Lovebird, revised version, 5½"	50.00
#3401D, Wrens, brn, revised version	90.00
#3401D, Wrens, tan, old version	250.00
#3402, Oriole, 3¼"	60.00
#3405, Cockatoo, 6"	55.00
#3406, Kingfisher	75.00
#3408, Bird of Paradise	100.00
#3443, Flying Duck, bl, 9"	300.00
#3443, Flying Duck, teal gr	350.00
#3444, Cardinal, pk glossy, 6"	85.00
#3444, Cardinal, red matt	125.00
#3445, Rooster, gray	200.00
#3445, Rooster, yel, 9"	165.00
#3446, Hen, gray	175.00
#3446, Hen, yel, 7"	165.00
#3447, Prothonatary Warbler	75.00
#3448, Bl-Headed Vireo	65.00
#3449, Parrot (Paraquet)	145.00
#3452, Painted Bunting	90.00
#3454, Key West Quail Dove, both wings up, 9"	750.00
#3454, Key West Quail Dove, 1 wing up, 9"	275.00
#3455, Shoveler Duck	1,200.00
#3456, Cerulean Warbler, 4½"	65.00
#3457, Pheasant, walking, 7¼x15"	1,500.00
#3460, Lovebird, old	90.00
#3490D, Red Starts, pr	210.00
#3581, Chickadees	225.00
#3582D, Parakeets, bl	225.00
#3583, Parula Warbler	65.00
#3584, Cockatoo, 11⅜"	245.00

#3589, Indigo Bunting, $65.00.

#3590, Carolina Wren	165.00
#3591, Brewer's Blackbird	105.00
#3592, Titmouse	55.00
#3593, Nuthatch	55.00
#3596, Grey's Cardinal	80.00
#3597, Wilson Warbler, yel, 3½"	50.00
#3599D, Hummingbirds	250.00

#3627, Rivoli Hummingbird	125.00
#3629, Broadbill Hummingbird	125.00
#3634, Allen Hummingbird	85.00
#3716, Blue Jay w/leaf	550.00
#3757, Scissor-Tailed Flycatcher, 11"	600.00
#3758, Magpie, 11x7"	800.00
#3813, Evening Grosbeak	120.00
#3815, Western Bluebird	400.00
#3848, Golden Crown Kinglet	85.00
#3849, Goldfinch	95.00
#3922, European Finch	800.00
#3924, Yel-Throated Warbler	400.00

Miscellaneous

Amber Glo, bowl, fruit; 5⅝"	8.00
Amber Glo, saucer	4.00
Animal, buffalo, #3246	350.00
Animal, cat, sitting, orange, 8½", NM	200.00
Animal, dog, sitting, #3280	400.00
Animal, draft horse, #3244	200.00
Animal, elephant, #3249, 3"	225.00
Animal, giraffe, #3248	400.00
Antique Gold Peacock, chop plate	150.00
Apple Delight, mug	20.00
Apple Delight, pitcher, 2-qt	35.00
Apple Delight, plate, luncheon	10.00
Ashtray, Canada goose, oval, #3926	30.00
Ashtray, mallard duck, #3915	40.00
Bittersweet, mug	20.00
Bittersweet, pitcher, 1-qt	17.50
Bittersweet, plate, dessert	5.00
Blossom Time, ashtray/coaster, #3886	12.00
Blossom Time, cigarette box, #3386	38.00
Blue Daisy, celery tray	20.00
Blue Daisy, plate, 10"	10.00
Blueberry, butter dish	30.00
Blueberry, cup & saucer	12.00
Blueberry, gravy boat	15.00
Blueberry, plate, 6"	6.00
Blueberry, plate, 8"	10.00
Book matches, Stangl Pottery	8.00
Carnival, condiment tray, #415	15.00
Carnival, plate, sandwich; metal hdl	10.00
Carnival, shakers, pr	8.00
Chicory, bowl, fruit	9.00
Chicory, cup	10.00
Colonial, bowl, salad; hdls, 8"	20.00
Colonial, carafe, w/stopper	50.00
Colonial, custard cup	7.50
Colonial, platter, 12" dia	26.00
Colonial, sugar bowl	12.00
Cosmos, ashtray, 5½"	25.00
Country Garden, bowl, cereal; 5½"	18.00
Country Garden, butter dish, ¼-lb	35.00
Country Garden, creamer	12.00
Country Garden, mug	25.00
Country Garden, pitcher, 1-pt	20.00
Country Garden, plate, 10"	18.00
Country Garden, plate, 12½"	40.00
Country Garden, shakers, pr	20.00
Country Garden, sugar bowl, w/lid	12.00
Country Garden, teapot	65.00
Country Life, bowl, fruit; w/pony	75.00

Country Life, bowl, fruit; w/rooster 45.00
Country Life, cup & saucer 40.00
Country Life, plate, farmer's wife, 10" 165.00
Country Life, plate, 6" 25.00
Dealer's sign, Antique Gold 75.00
Dealer's sign, tulips in 1 corner, 4x7" 150.00
Festival, bowl, Terra Rose, deep, 11½" 75.00
Festival, bowl, Terra Rose, 9" 35.00
Festival, cup & saucer, Terra Rose 15.00
Festival, nappy, Terra Rose, loop hdl, 7" 20.00
Festival, plate, Terra Rose, 10" 15.00
Festival, plate, Terra Rose, 8¼" 10.00
Festival, plate, Terra Rose, 9¼" 12.00
First Love, plate, 10" 15.00
Fruit, creamer & sugar bowl 27.50
Fruit, plate, dinner 17.50
Fruits & Flowers, creamer 6.00
Fruits & Flowers, cup & saucer 12.00
Garland, coffee warmer 20.00
Garland, plate, 10" 16.00
Golden Blossom, bowl, soup; 7¼" 10.00
Golden Blossom, cup & saucer 11.00
Golden Blossom, egg cup 12.00
Golden Blossom, mug 20.00
Golden Blossom, platter, 12" dia 26.50
Grape, cup & saucer 12.50
Kiddieware, bowl, Little Bo Peep 75.00
Kiddieware, cup, Little Bo Peep or Little Boy Blue, ea 60.00
Kiddieware, cup, Peter Rabbit 100.00
Kiddieware, divided dish, 3-part, ABCs, wht clay ...100.00
Kiddieware, divided dish, 3-part, Kitten Capers 100.00
Kiddieware, plate, Gingerbread Boy 175.00
Kiddieware, plate, Humpty Dumpty, gr border 150.00
Kiddieware, plate, Peter Rabbit, Lunning (artist) 175.00
Match holder, rabbit on scroll base, #3533, 4x4" 350.00
Orchard Song, cup & saucer 12.50
Orchard Song, plate, 8" 10.00
Orchard Song, server, center hdl 6.00
Pig bank, Antique Gold, paper label, 5½x3½" 100.00
Pig cactus pot, unpnt, #1076C 100.00
Plate, w/silkscreened Stangle 04764 Since 1805, 9" ...100.00
Postcard, Stangl wig stands ad 7.00
Powder box, Deco lady, Fulper porc, Martin Stangl cipher, 6" ...130.00
Prelude, creamer & sugar bowl 22.00
Prelude, plate, 10" 15.00
Provincial, bowl, divided vegetable 25.00
Provincial, bowl, lug soup; 5½" 10.00
Provincial, bowl, salad; 11" 35.00
Provincial, butter dish 35.00
Provincial, casserole, w/lid 40.00
Provincial, chop plate, 14½" 35.00
Provincial, cup & saucer 12.50
Provincial, pickle tray 15.00
Provincial, plate, luncheon; 8" 10.00
Provincial, plate, salad; 6" 5.00
Provincial, sugar bowl, w/lid 12.00
Sculptured Fruit, bowl, 8" 30.00
Sculptured Fruit, saucer 5.00
Thistle, bowl, lug soup 15.00
Thistle, creamer & sugar bowl, w/lid 26.50
Thistle, cup & saucer 11.00
Thistle, plate, 6" 5.00
Thistle, teapot 55.00
Thistle, tray, condiment 28.00

Tulip, cookie jar, Bean Pot 60.00
Tulip, gravy tray 15.00
Water Lily, plate, 10" 15.00
Wig stand, blond, wood base 225.00
Wig stand, brunette, wood base 200.00

Stanley Tools

The Stanley company was founded in Connecticut in 1854, and over the years has absorbed more than a score of tool companies already in existence. By the second decade of the 20th century, having long since solidified their position as the source for tools of the highest grade, the company enjoyed worldwide prestige. Through both World Wars, they were recognized as one of the nation's premier producers of wartime goods. Industrial arts classes introduced baby boomers to Stanley tools and provided yet another impetus to expansion and recognition. Overall, the company's growth and development has kept an easy pace along with the economy of the nation, and it continues today as a leader in the field of tool production.

Two factors to consider when evaluating a tool are these: age and condition. One of their earliest trademarks (1854-1857) is 'A. Stanley,' found only on rules. In the early twenties, their now-familiar 'sweetheart' trademark, the letters SW and a heart shape within the confines of a modified rectangle, was adopted. They continued to use this trademark until it was discontinued in 1933. Many other variations were used as well, some of which contain a patent date. A study of these marks will help you determine the vintage of your tools. Condition is extremely important, and though a light cleaning is acceptable, you should never attempt to 'restore' a tool by sanding, repainting or replacing parts that may be damaged or missing. Tools listed below are for those in average as-found condition, ranging from very good to excellent.

For more information, we recommend *Antique and Collectible Stanley Tools*, written by our advisor, John Walter, who is listed in the Directory under Ohio.

Angle divider, #30 ....50.00
Bench bracket, #203 ....30.00
Bevel, ship carpenter's; #42½ 200.00
Drill, breast; #722 ....20.00
Drill, hand; #626 ....10.00
Gauge, cutting; #70½ 75.00
Gauge, marking; #61 ....10.00
Gauge, mortise; #67 ....40.00
Hammer, saddler's; #5 ....30.00
Hammer, shoemaker's; #6 ....100.00
Knife, razor blade; #199 ....5.00
Level, Brook's Pat Universal; #26 ....1,000.00
Level, carpenter's; w/plumb, #1½ 50.00

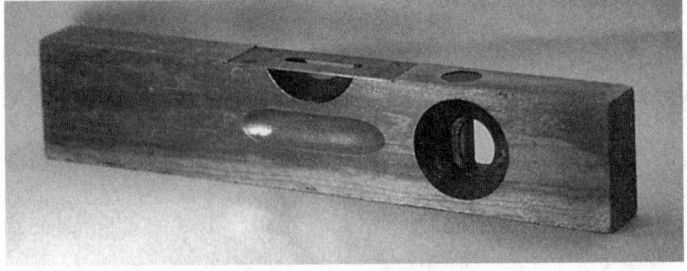

Carpenter's plumb and level, hardwood and brass, #104, 12", EX, $10.00.

Level, mason's; w/plumb, #20 ....40.00
Mallet, tinner's; #4 ....15.00
Plane, block; #15, type 2 (1871-85) 100.00
Plane, circular; #13, type 1, 1867-71 ....1,200.00
Plane, tongue & groove; #48 ....60.00
Scraper, veneer; #12½ 85.00

Statue of Liberty

Long before she began greeting immigrants in 1886, the Statue of Liberty was being honored by craftsmen both here and abroad. Her likeness was etched on blades of the finest straight razors from England, captured in finely detailed busts sold as souvenirs to Paris fairgoers in 1878, and presented on colorfully lithographed trade cards, usually satirical, to American shoppers. Perhaps no other object has been represented in more forms or with such frequency as the universal symbol of America. Liberty's keepsakes are also universally accessible. Delightful souvenir models created in 1885 to raise funds for Liberty's pedestal are frequently found at flea markets, while earlier French bronze and terra cotta Liberties have been auctioned for over $100,000.00. Some collectors hunt for the countless forms of 19th-century Liberty memorabilia, while many collections were begun in anticipation of the 1986 Centennial with concentration on modern depictions. Our advisor for this category is Mike Brooks; he is listed in the Directory under California.

Bookmark, fabric, Bartholdi Souvenir, 1886 ....25.00
Charm bracelet, 1939 World's Fair 45.00
Coffeepot, enameled scene on metal, 11" 200.00
Cup, pewter, ca 1905 ....35.00
Invitation to inauguration, by President Cleveland 150.00
Knife, scrimshaw hdl 110.00
Lamp base, wht metal, clock at base, ca 1885, 20", EX 300.00
Medal, American Liberty Day, 1916 ....30.00
Medal, Emma Lazarus, Magnes Museum 40.00
Model, CI w/NP & silver flame, Committee model, 36", EX ..11,000.00
Model, Democratic Nat'l Convention, NY, 1924 ....35.00
Photograph, Liberty nearing completion, 1886 ....85.00
Smoking stand, figural, copper-plated cast metal, EX 150.00
Spoon, Liberty figural hdl, SP, 5¾", EX 77.00
Statue, pot metal w/silver finish, 9" 25.00
Watercolor, harbor scene, JW Goppard, 21x15", EX 220.00

Steamship Collectibles

For centuries, ocean-going vessels with their venturesome officers and crews were the catalyst that changed the unknown aspects of our world to the known. Changing economic conditions, unfortunately, have now placed the North American shipping industry in the same jeopardy as the American passenger train. They are becoming a memory. The surge of interest in railroad collectibles and the railroad-related steamship lines has lead collectors to examine the whole spectrum of steamship collectibles. Our advisors for this category are Lila and Fred Shrader; they are listed in the Directory under California.

Key:
BS – back stamped   TM – top mark
NBS – no back stamp   SL – side logo
TL – top logo

Dinnerware

Ashtray, Cunard (Foley), tan w/blk & dk tan stripe 42.00

Ashtray, Holland-America, ship's logo, NBS, 5½" dia 15.00
Bowl, cereal; Alaska SS, TL, NBS, 6½" 45.00
Bowl, rimmed soup; IMM, Katherine, TM, NBS, 9¼" 35.00
Butter pat, American Mail, red & bl logo & stripes, TM 75.00
Butter pat, CN, Maritime, NBS 25.00
Butter pat, Mobil, TL, NBS 48.00
Butter pat, Munson SS, TL, NBS 65.00
Cup & saucer, Alaska SS, TL, NBS 55.00
Cup & saucer, Anchor Line, bl anchor logo, NBS 75.00
Cup & saucer, Georgian Bay Line flag logo, NBS 85.00
Cup & saucer, Union Castle, flag & banner logo, NBS 40.00
Egg cup, Union Castle Line, belt logo, sm 40.00
Plate, Bank Line, house flag w/Bank Line banner, 8" 25.00
Plate, CP, British Columbia Coast SS, Tremblant, TM, 9½" 75.00
Plate, Cunard, Snowflake, BS, 9½" 35.00
Plate, Dollar Line, house flag w/$ sign+life ring 50.00
Plate, Eastern SS, 'E' house flag enclosed in ring, 8½" 45.00
Plate, GNPSS, Pacific Coast, TM house flag, NBS, 9½" 85.00
Plate, Royal Cruise Line, TM crown over waves, 10" 12.00
Teapot, Guion Line, SL w/Xd British & Am flags+name, 4-cup ..85.00
Toothpick holder, CP, BCCSS, SL, NBS, 2" 95.00

Miscellaneous

Annual pass, Mallory Steamship Co, bright bl, 1915 ....38.00
Annual pass, Wilson Steamboat Co, pictorial, 1914, EX 45.00
Ashtray, French Line, bl glass 12.50
Ashtray, Matson Lines, SS Lurline silkscreen logo on glass 6.50
Ashtray, SS France, gold 'France' on cobalt glass, 4" dia 12.50
Ashtray, US Lines, Bakelite stars border, eagle center 12.00
Baggage sticker, US Lines, Tourist Class, 1955, 3¼" dia 3.50
Baggage tag, US Lines 6.00
Book, Along the North Coast, Davies, 1925 ....40.00
Booklet, Canada SS Lines, R&O, Niagara to the Sea, 1916 ....24.00
Booklet, Ericsson Line, Philadelphia to Jamestown Expo, 1907 ..35.00
Booklet, Seeing Seattle by Water, 1930 ....8.00
Brochure, Cunard Line Mediterranean Cruise, Feb 1952, EX 6.00
Brochure, Matson, Hawaii on SS Lurline & SS Matsonia, 1961 .....6.00
Brochure, NAL, Sunlit Norway Calls, 1936 ....15.00
Brochure, Sweden-American Lines, 1939 Midsummer Excursions ..11.00
Brochure, Wilmington Trans Co, Catalina Isthmus, 1932 ....20.00
Brooch, Donaldson Line, crossed flags, TSS Letitia, EX 25.00
Button, uniform; Dollar Line, brass w/logo, ¾" 5.00
Chair, deck; SS Queen Elizabeth, teak w/brass fittings, G 250.00
Coffeepot, Matson, SP, BS, ind sz 45.00
Cuff links, NAL, NAL house flag on brass, pr 18.00
Decanter, cut, St Louis & New Orleans Anchor Line, 1880s 100.00
Envelope, Louisville & Cincinnati Mailboat postmk, 1874 ....45.00
Fan, Delta Line in script on pennant, folds 15.00
Fork, place; Cunard Lines, Romney, 3-tine, 7¾" 17.50
Iced teaspoon, Dollar Line TM, SP 22.00
Map, Alaska SS, N Pacific Coast to Alaska, 1925, 24x36" 110.00
Menu, Alaska SS, Crumrine illus, 1941 ....25.00
Menu, CPSS, Empress to Canada, scenic, 1959 ....5.00
Menu, Cunard, Mauretania, scenic sketch, 1931 ....19.00
Napkin, Canada SS Co, R&O woven in wht on wht, 22" sq 25.00
Napkin, Hamburg America Line, woven wht on wht, 22" sq 25.00
Passenger list, Drottningholm, 1936 ....15.00
Passenger list, SS Berlin, 1895, 5x7" 17.50
Passenger list, SS United States, dk bl, 2-pc, 1955 ....12.00
Pen, Pittsburgh Steamship & house flag by Waterman 45.00
Place mat, Munson Steamship embr in corner, wht on wht 28.00
Playing cards, Am Mail Line logo, in case, 52+2 Jokers 35.00
Postcard, Amerika Lines, interior, mc, ca 1900, M in envelope ..65.00

Postcard, D&C Line, Steamer City of Cleveland, mailed 1909 ......**7.50**
Postcard, Ferry-Astoria, Oregon, blk & wht real photo **12.00**
Postcard, Mallory Liner entering Galveston Harbor **5.00**
Towel, P&O, bl stripe, 14x21" **12.50**
Tray, Alaska SS, SP, TL, 7x9" **65.00**

Steins

Steins have been made from pottery, pewter, glass, stoneware, and porcelain, from very small up to the four-liter size. They are decorated by etching, in-mold relief, decals, and occasionally they may be hand painted. Some porcelain steins have lithophane bases. Collectors often specialize in a particular type — faience, regimental, or figural — while others limit themselves to the products of only one manufacturer. Our advisor for this category is Ron Fox; he is listed in the Directory under New York. See also Mettlach.

Key:
L — liter
lith — lithophane
POG — print over glaze
PUG — print under glaze
tl — thumb lift

Character steins, all pottery, left to right: #1227, Barbell, Steinzeugwerke, ½-L, $330.00; #1140, Bowling pin, Steinzeugwerke, ½-L, $265.00; Munich Child, Reinemann, 1-L, $360.00.

Character, artillery shell, porc, lith, wear on lid, ½-L **300.00**
Character, artillery shell, stoneware, pnt wear, ½-L **188.00**
Character, barmaid finial on keg form, porc, 5½" **130.00**
Character, bowling pins, pottery, scratches, ½-L **120.00**
Character, bowling pins, pottery, 1-L **220.00**
Character, cucumber & fish, pottery, no lid, ½-L **175.00**
Character, drunken monkey, porc, Schierholz, hairline, ½-L **275.00**
Character, football, porc, platinum on hdl, wear, ½-L **250.00**
Character, Frauenkirche Tower, porc, M Pauson, rpr, ½-L **1,075.00**
Character, Frauenkirche Tower, porc, M Pauson, 1-L, NM **1,130.00**
Character, Gentleman Dog, porc, Schierholz, 1980s, ½-L **465.00**
Character, Gentleman Fox, porc, Schierholz, poor rpr, ½-L **745.00**
Character, Gentleman Rabbit, porc, Schierholz, rpr, ½-L, EX ...**935.00**
Character, Happy Radish, porc, tan, Schierholz, rpr, ½-L **275.00**
Character, Happy Radish, pottery, rpr/chip, ½-L **200.00**
Character, Indian, porc, E Bohne Sohne, .3-L **495.00**
Character, lady, pottery, rpr strap, ½-L, EX **190.00**
Character, monk, porc, hunter lith, ½-L **220.00**
Character, monk, porc, lith w/faint line, ½-L **275.00**
Character, monk, pottery, ½-L **275.00**
Character, monk, stoneware, Merkelbach & Wick, rpr, ½-L **165.00**
Character, monkey, pottery, Diesinger, chips/lid dent, ½-L **285.00**

Character, monkey, pottery, Steinzeugwerke, rpr, ½-L **200.00**
Character, Munich Child, porc, lith, Schierholz, ½-L, NM **580.00**
Character, Munich Child, porc, rpr pewter shank, ½-L **188.00**
Character, Munich Child, pottery, Reinemann, ½-L **330.00**
Character, nun, porc, lith, slight wear, ½-L **360.00**
Character, nun, pottery, Merkelbach & Wick, rpr, ¼-L **190.00**
Character, old lady, porc, 1-L **240.00**
Character, pig, pottery, JW Remy, ½-L **415.00**
Character, rooster, porc, Schierholz, 1980s, ½-L **525.00**
Character, Sad Radish, porc, Schierholz, chip, ½-L **240.00**
Character, skull & devil, porc, E Bohne Sohne, ¼-L **798.00**
Character, Von Moltke, porc, Schierholz, 1980s, ½-L **360.00**
Glass, blown, amber, HP scene, pewter lid, ½-L **440.00**
Glass, blown, bl flashed, etched building, clear lid, .1-L **175.00**
Glass, blown, clear to cranberry shaded, pewter lid, ½-L **220.00**
Glass, blown, cut, gold beading, pewter strap rpr, ½-L **210.00**
Glass, blown, eng priest, pewter lid, early 1800s, ½-L **1,300.00**
Glass, blown, eng stag, pewter lid w/dachshund, ½-L **600.00**
Glass, blown, faceted, SP lid w/Wilhelm I finial, ½-L **165.00**
Glass, blown, gr, cut decor, SP lid, ½-L, NM **275.00**
Glass, blown, HP: building on gr, red glass lid, .2-L **130.00**
Glass, blown, red flashed, Zum Andeken..., gr glass lid, .2-L **120.00**
Glass, blown, transfer/HP: fireman, pewter lid, ½-L **188.00**
Glass, blown: mc florals, very worn, .3-L **75.00**
Military, pottery, Bavarian, soldier & lady on lid, rpr, ½-L **120.00**
Military, pottery, Unteroffz-Korps Reiter..., .35-L **330.00**
Military, stoneware, Iron Cross/1914, pewter lid, ½-L **170.00**
Porc, HP: Angelica, porc inlaid lid, mk w/beehive, ½-L **2,640.00**
Porc, transfer: hunters, couple lith, pewter lid, ½-L, NM **230.00**
Pottery, etch: dwarfs, inlaid lid, flake, .3-L **155.00**
Pottery, etch: Faust & Gretchen, Remy, inlaid lid, ½-L **230.00**
Pottery, etch: lovers, Gambrinus finial, pewter lid, 1-L **155.00**
Pottery, relief & transfer: hunters, mc, pewter lid, 1-L **125.00**
Pottery, relief: barmaid, pewter lid, ½-L **60.00**
Pottery, relief: bowling, mc, pewter lid, 2-L **160.00**
Pottery, relief: couple, Diesinger, mc, pewter lid, ½-L **75.00**
Pottery, relief: dwarfs, tan/brn/blk, pewter lid, ½-L **100.00**
Pottery, relief: Gambrinus, pewter lid, 2-L **245.00**
Pottery, relief: man on bicycle, pewter lid, ½-L **330.00**
Pottery, relief: monk, mc, music box base, ½-L **85.00**
Pottery, relief: musicians, DRGM, pewter lid, ½-L, EX **188.00**
Pottery, relief: Solomon, pewter lid, hairlines, 3-L **245.00**
Pottery, relief: 3 panels of knights, pewter lid, 2½-L **340.00**
Pottery, transfer: bowling, Merkelbach & Wick, ½-L **110.00**
Pottery, transfer: bowling, pewter lid, scratch, ½-L **120.00**
Pottery, transfer: fireman, pewter lid w/dent, chip, ½-L **70.00**
Pottery, transfer: Nach des tages..., pewter lid, ½-L **175.00**
Regimental, porc, Bayr 3 Artl Regt...1896-98, lith, ½-L **360.00**
Regimental, porc, Feld Artl...Strassburg, 1896-98, lith, ½-L **325.00**
Regimental, porc, Inft Regt Nr 123...1903-05, ½-L, NM **265.00**
Regimental, porc, Leib Regt...Munchen 1908-10, lion tl, ½-L .**350.00**
Regimental, porc, Pionier...Riesa 1911-13, Saxon tl, ½-L **1,155.00**
Regimental, porc, 10 Feld Art...1902-04, lion tl, ½-L, NM **900.00**
Regimental, porc, 16 Reiter Rgt...1921-33, eagle tl, ½-L **495.00**
Regimental, porc, 2 Comp Inft Regt 145, 1908-11, ½-L, NM **415.00**
Regimental, porc, 2 Comp Jager Bat...1906-08, eagle tl, ½-L .**1,200.00**
Regimental, pottery, Reiterschwadron...1941, rpl lid, ½-L **155.00**
Regimental, pottery, SMS Blucher...1913, eagle tl, rpr, 1-L **900.00**
Regimental, SMS Torpedoboot V.181...1910-13, eagle tl, 1-L .**1,450.00**
Stoneware, incised: floral, cobalt/salt glaze, 1880s, 2½-L **275.00**
Stoneware, relief/etch: cards, pewter lid, ½-L, NM **100.00**
Stoneware, relief: Art Nouveau, Gerz, pewter lid, .3-L **165.00**
Stoneware, relief: cavalier, Whites Utica, ½-L, NM **265.00**
Stoneware, relief: couples, porc lid, Regensburg, ½-L **100.00**

Stoneware, relief: drinking scene, bl/brn, Whites Utica, ½-L **385.00**
Stoneware, relief: figures moving log, mc, Whites Utica, .4-L **745.00**
Stoneware, relief: harvest scenes, porc inlaid lid, 1-L, NM **110.00**
Stoneware, relief: hunters, pewter lid, Regensburg, rpr, 1-L **100.00**
Stoneware, relief: Iron Cross/Wilhelm II/F Josef, ½-L, NM **465.00**
Stoneware, relief: Regensburg, porc lid w/jester, 1-L **135.00**
Stoneware, relief: soldiers/Iron Cross, 1914, ½-L **200.00**
Stoneware, relief: tavern scene, Whites Utica, 2-L, NM **300.00**
Stoneware, relief: trombone player, Whites Utica, ½-L **350.00**
Stoneware, transfer/HP: Aenanen Stiftungsfest, 1851-1911, ½-L ...**200.00**
Stoneware, transfer/HP: Spaten-Brau, Munchen, pewter lid, .4-L ...**230.00**
Stoneware, transfer: hat-maker scene, pewter lid, ½-L **210.00**
Third Reich, pottery, swastika w/labor corp symbol, ½-L, NM ...**385.00**
Third Reich, pottery, Unteroffizier-Korps..., pewter lid, ½-L **385.00**
Third Reich, stoneware, Aufkl...Wurzburg, helmet finial, ½-L ...**855.00**
Third Reich, stoneware, Erinnerung...1940-42, metal lid, ½-L ...**855.00**

Steuben

Carder Steuben glass was made by the Stueben Glass Works in Corning, New York, while under the direction of Frederick Carder from 1903 to 1932. Perhaps the most popular types of Carder Steuben glass are Gold Aurene which was introduced in 1904 and Blue Aurene, introduced in 1905. Gold and Blue Aurene objects shimmer with the lustrous beauty of their metallic iridescence. Carder also produced other types of 'Aurenes' including Red, Green, Yellow, Brown, and Decorated, all of which are very rare. Aurene also was cased upon Calcite glass. Some pieces had paper labels.

Other types of Carder Steuben include Cluthra, Cintra, Florentia, Rosaline, Ivory, Ivorene, Jades, Verre de Soie; there are many more.

Frederick Carder's leadership of Steuben ended in 1932, and the production of colored glassware soon ceased. Since 1932 the tradition of fine Steuben art glass has been continued in crystal.

Our advisor for this category is Thomas P. Dimitroff; he is in the Directory under New York. In the following listings, examples are signed unless noted otherwise.

Key: ACB — acid cut back

Bonbon, Bl Aurene & Calcite **225.00**
Bottle, Rosaline, ball stopper, Alabaster insert, 6¾" **375.00**
Bottle, scent; amber, 8 ribs, blown stopper, #2183, 4½" **235.00**
Bottle, scent; Gold Aurene, #1414, 7½" **485.00**
Bottle, scent; Verre de Soie, eng florals, sterling top, 5" **350.00**
Bottle, scent; Verre de Soie, ribs, amber stopper, 7" **300.00**
Bottle, scent; Verre de Soie, Rosaline/Calcite stopper, #1455 ....**375.00**
Bowl, ACB, Chinese decor, Gold Aurene/Calcite, #6283, 4x7" .**2,500.00**
Bowl, ACB, Chinese decor, Rosaline on Alabaster, w/lid, 3" ..**1,400.00**
Bowl, Bl Aurene, #2851, 10" **750.00**
Bowl, Bl Aurene, ribbed, scalloped, #564, 3" **450.00**
Bowl, Bl Aurene, 3 appl ft, #7986, 2¾x10" **900.00**
Bowl, centerpc; Blk Jade, ribbed, oval, #6890, 12½" **350.00**
Bowl, centerpc; Gold Aurene & Calcite, 3x12" **500.00**
Bowl, centerpc; Ivorene, #7563, 6x14" **950.00**
Bowl, clear bubbles w/bl threading, ruffled, 8½" **200.00**
Bowl, Gold Aurene, #2887, 4x6" **220.00**
Bowl, Gold Aurene, petal rim, 3x6½", +underplate **450.00**
Bowl, Gold Aurene, ruffled/stretched border, #171, 1¾x6½" **300.00**
Bowl, Gold Aurene & Calcite, stretch irid, #3200, 10" **450.00**
Bowl, Grotesque, bl, #7537, 13" **800.00**
Bowl, Grotesque, gr to clear, 4½" **325.00**
Bowl, Ivorene w/Bl Aurene rim wrap, 4x10" **770.00**
Bowl, Pomona Gr, #3176, 10" **200.00**

Bowl, Pomona Gr, fold-down rim, ribbed, #3579, 14½" **225.00**
Bowl, topaz, #3200, 10" **85.00**
Bowl, Verre de Soie Dmn Quilt w/gr threading, 10", +sticks **440.00**
Bowl vase, Dk Bl Jade, like #6962, 6½x9½" **2,000.00**

Bust of Ross Coffin Purdy, F. Carder Cire Perdue, #42, 6¼", $4,850.00.

Candlesticks, Grotesque, fishhook std on dome ft, 11", pr **300.00**
Candlesticks, Pomona Gr, ribbed/shaped, stepped base, 10", pr .**450.00**
Candlesticks, Rosa twist stem, gr ribs (top & base), 12", pr **675.00**
Candlesticks, topaz, dbl-twist stem, 10", pr **550.00**
Charger, Bl Aurene w/silver highlights, 14" **850.00**
Compote, clear w/controlled bubbles & topaz threading, 5x6¾" .**175.00**
Compote, Flemish Bl, 4x6" **200.00**
Compote, Gold Aurene, trumpet-form base, #6241, 4" **650.00**
Compote, Rosaline w/Alabaster ft, 8" **350.00**
Cordial, Gold Aurene **250.00**
Creamer & sugar bowl, ruby threads on crystal, 2½", 2" **175.00**
Cup & saucer, demitasse; Gold Aurene, +sterling liner & saucer ...**250.00**
Figurine, elephant, trunk up, on half sphere, glossy ivory, 6" **800.00**
Figurine, Oriental lady, Wht Jade, #7133, +floral block, 9" **700.00**
Finger bowl, Gold Aurene & Calcite, +6" underplate **375.00**
Finger bowl, Gold Aurene w/bl irid, #818, 3¾", +plate **200.00**
Goblet, ivory, ftd, #7040, 4¾" **150.00**
Goblet, Oriental Poppy, 8¼" **450.00**
Goblet, wheel-cut bowls, Pomona Gr trn stems, 6½", set of 12 ..**1,200.00**
Goblet/vase, Rosalene w/Alabaster ft, 6" **220.00**
Lamp, Gr Jade, ACB Bristol design, #7426 ....**800.00**
Paperweight, controlled bubbles, cranberry int, 4½x5" **450.00**
Perfume, Gold Aurene, melon ribs, flame stopper, #1455, 4½" ..**800.00**
Perfume, Gr Jade, teardrop stopper, #6237, 10" **850.00**
Perfume set, blk threading on clear, sgn, 3-pc **550.00**
Pitcher, Gold Aurene, #1523, 8" **900.00**
Plate, Celeste Bl, 10", 10 for **200.00**
Plate, Cluthra, pk, lg bubbles, 6½" **250.00**
Plate, Gold Aurene, crackled irid, 7½", set of 6 ....**1,200.00**
Plate, Gold Aurene, 8" **250.00**
Powder box, Gr Jade w/Alabaster ball ft & finial, 5½" **350.00**
Salt cellar, Gold Aurene, #2660 ....**250.00**
Salt cellar, Gold Aurene, ftd, #3067 ....**250.00**
Sculpture, Tree of Life, Jacob Landau, #3295, 14" **16,500.00**
Shade, Calcite w/Gold Aurene int, #2984, 4¾" H, pr **200.00**
Shade, Gold Aurene & Calcite, ribbed, #2524, 2½" **175.00**
Shade, leaves, plum w/gold tips on opal, #2476, 5¾" **400.00**
Sherbet, Bl Aurene & Calcite, w/underplate **375.00**
Sherbet, Gold Aurene & Calcite, 3¾", +underplate **160.00**
Tumbler, iced tea; amethyst, #5192 ....**125.00**
Tumbler, Verre de Soie, monogrammed, 4", set of 6 ....**450.00**

Vase, ACB, Chang variant, Gr Jade & textured Alabaster, 8" ...900.00
Vase, ACB, exotic birds/branches, Gr Jade to Alabaster, 9" 850.00
Vase, ACB, geese/trees, Plum Jade/Amethyst Cintra, hdls, 13" .2,100.00
Vase, ACB, 3 pussy willow trees, dk bl on wht frost, 6" 3,100.00
Vase, Agnus Dei, eng winged bull, Sidney Waugh, #8207, 7" 465.00
Vase, Bl Aurene, classic form, #2683, 6" 700.00
Vase, Bl Aurene, classic form, paper label, 4" 300.00
Vase, Bl Aurene, pulled feathers, #735, 4½" 1,200.00
Vase, Bl Aurene, 3-prong stump, #2744, 6" 1,100.00
Vase, Bl Aurene on Calcite, trumpet form, #743, 6" 650.00
Vase, Bl Aurene w/opal & gold vines & leaves, fan form, 9" ..2,900.00
Vase, bubbly crystal w/gr reeding, #2163, 6" 110.00
Vase, Celeste Bl, ribbed, #2105 ....125.00
Vase, Celeste Bl, ribbed, folded rim, ped ft, #2907, 8¼" 225.00
Vase, Celeste Bl, 12" 225.00
Vase, Celeste Bl w/appl threading, 5½" 125.00
Vase, clear w/bl threading on flared rim, 5¾x8" 175.00
Vase, Cluthra, bl, classic form, fleur-de-lis mk, 6" 900.00
Vase, Cluthra, blk to wht w/clear tooled base, 3-sided, 12" 750.00
Vase, Cluthra, dk bl, classic form, silver label, 8" 1,300.00
Vase, Cluthra, gr to wht, conical, 5½" 450.00
Vase, crystal bubbly glass w/gr reeding, #2163, 6" 175.00
Vase, Gold Aurene, #2080, classic form, 10" 600.00
Vase, Gold Aurene, #455, 12½" 1,200.00
Vase, Gold Aurene, bl highlights, 2½x2" 300.00
Vase, Gold Aurene, flared 4-lobe rim, dented sides, #131B, 5" ...600.00
Vase, Gold Aurene, trumpet shape, #2909, 5½" 550.00
Vase, Gold Aurene, upright scroll hdls, classic form, 11½" 1,300.00
Vase, Gold Aurene & Calcite, ruffled, #1644, 6" 250.00
Vase, Gr Jade, int swirls, #6215, 8" 225.00
Vase, Gr Jade, ribbed, 12" 325.00
Vase, Grotesque, amethyst, #7090, ca 1920, 11" 495.00
Vase, Iridized Oriental Poppy, #6500, 6x5" 2,200.00
Vase, Ivorene, #6512, 5" 225.00
Vase, Ivorene, ribbed, flared, #357, 4¾" 250.00
Vase, lily; Gold Aurene & Calcite, #743, 8" 500.00
Vase, Lt Bl Jade, ped base, classic shape, 7" 950.00
Vase, Pomona Gr, faintly ribbed, rectangular, sgn, 3x9½x6" 150.00
Vase, Rosa, faint ribs, appl glass prunts at shoulder, 7" 125.00
Vase, Rosaline w/Alabaster ped ft, 9" 300.00
Vase, Selenium Ruby, #6030, 7" 425.00
Vase, Spanish Gr, random bubbles, fan form, #6287, 8" 175.00
Vase, Verre de Soie, bulbous, flared ruffled rim, ftd, 5¾" 225.00
Vase, Verre de Soie, ftd, 10" 350.00
Vase, Verre de Soie, 19" 700.00
Vase, yel irid w/appl electric bl leaves, drilled, 11x4" 900.00
Wine, Gold Aurene & Calcite, 6¾" 250.00

Stevengraphs

A Stevengraph is a small picture made of woven silk resembling an elaborate ribbon, created by Thomas Stevens in England in the latter half of the 1800s. They were matted and framed by Stevens, usually with his name appearing on the mat or, more commonly, the trade announcement on the back of the mat. He also produced silk postcards and bookmarks, all of which have 'Stevens' woven in silk on one of the mitered corners. Anyone wishing to learn more about Stevengraphs is encouraged to contact the Stevengraph Collectors' Association, whose address can be found in the Directory under Clubs, Newsletters, and Catalogs.

Are You Ready? 150.00
Crystal Palace (inside), orig mat, G 285.00
Dick Turpin's Last Ride on His Blk Bess, Hogarth, VG 150.00

The First Innings, 2x6", EX, $550.00.

First Innings, G 300.00
God Speed the Plough, G 150.00
Grace Darling, EX 165.00
Mrs Cleveland, VG 135.00
Present Time (60 Miles an Hour), EX 175.00
Present Time (60 Miles an Hour), M 285.00
Start, NM 175.00
Struggle, EX 155.00
Victoria Queen of Empire on Which Sun Never Sets, VG 150.00
Wellington & Blugher, G 165.00

Miscellaneous

Bookmark, Behold the Man, blk fr, G 50.00
Bookmark, Garibaldi, United Italy 135.00
Bookmark, Home Sweet Home, VG 65.00
Bookmark, Present From Crystal Palace, G 50.00
Bookmark, Remember Me 65.00
Bookmark, Robert Burns, VG 70.00
Bookmark, To My Son, G 40.00
Postcard, Ann Hathaway's Cottage 40.00
Postcard, RMS Lusitania 75.00

Stevens and Williams

Stevens and Williams glass was produced at the Brierly Hill Glassworks in Stourbridge, England, for nearly a century, beginning in the 1830s. They were credited with being among the first to develop a method of manufacturing a more affordable type of cameo glass. Other lines were also made — silver deposit, alexandrite, and engraved rock crystal, to name but a few. Our advisor for this category is Don Williams; he is listed in the Directory under Missouri.

Basket, amber o/l, appl strawberries on gr branches, 7x7½" 1,250.00
Basket, butterflies & flowers, pk on wht, 8¾" 965.00
Basket, pk opal o/l w/appl strawberry, 6x6½x4½" 1,600.00
Bottle, amber w/crystal shell applique, peacock finial, 11" 495.00
Bowl, MOP rubena verde satin swirl, shell form, 3½", +plate 800.00
Bowl, sapphire bl w/lg appl pk flower, clear X hdls, 10" 650.00
Bowl, wht w/pk int, amber trim & berry prunts, 4x11" 450.00
Lamp, gr w/4 appl amber ft, appl branches, cut-bk shade, 14" 900.00
Pitcher, allover wine/yel pulled design, rose int, 8½" 600.00
Pitcher, vertical yel/wht/clear stripes, str sides, 9" 400.00
Pitcher, wht w/pk int, appl bl/gr flower, amber hdl, 2¾" 235.00
Rose bowl, aqua o/l satin, box-pleated top, 4⅜x5⅜" 195.00
Rose bowl, bl opal stripe satin, box-pleated top, 4¼x4¼" 145.00
Rose bowl, mat-su-noke florals on thorny vine, w/base, 3½x3" ..585.00
Rose bowl, rose shaded w/emb basketweave, pleated top, 6x4½" .450.00
Rose bowl, turq swirl, box-pleated top, 3¾x4" 195.00
Sweetmeat, bl, wht & clear frosted stripes, SP fr, 6x4¼" 100.00
Tankard, chartreuse gr/wht/clear stripes, SP rim, 9", +tumbler ...500.00
Vase, bl o/l, appl red cherries w/clear leaves, 4½x3¼" 155.00

Vase, Blurina, thorn ft, rolled rim, att, 4" 350.00
Vase, bud; cranberry w/clear mat-su-noke, 5" 350.00
Vase, cameo floral, wht on bl, 5" 1,500.00
Vase, coral o/l w/clear opal ruffle, appl leaves, 12x4" 395.00
Vase, lime gr satin swirl, cone ft, flared lip, 10½" 300.00
Vase, lt bl, dk bl int, appl pk floral/amber leaves, 4½" 135.00
Vase, MOP pk to rose w/gold florals, bottle shape, 7" 800.00
Vase, MOP reverse rubena verde swirl, 10" 470.00
Vase, MOP rubena swirl, 6¾" 485.00
Vase, pk o/l, appl flowers, ruffled top, 5" 120.00
Vase, pk o/l, floral intaglio, opal scroll ft, 4x1½" 165.00
Vase, pk o/l w/gr ruffle, appl leafy branch, 5¾x5¼" 165.00
Vase, wht o/l, pk int, amber rigaree, appl amber leaves/ft, 9" 265.00
Vase, wht o/l, rose int, appl leaves & ruffle, 7½" 225.00
Vase, wht o/l w/appl amber plums, red/amber leaves, ftd, 10" 200.00
Vase, wht o/l w/pk int & amber ruffle, appl leaves, 4" 115.00

Stickley

Among the leading proponents of the Arts and Crafts Movement, the Stickley brothers — Gustav, Leopold, Charles, Albert, and John George — were at various times and locations separately involved in designing and producing furniture as well as decorative items for the home. (See Arts and Crafts for further information.) The oldest of the five Stickley brothers was Gustav; his work is the most highly regarded of all. He developed the style of furniture referred to as Mission. It was strongly influenced by the type of furnishings found in the Spanish missions of California — utilitarian, squarely built, and simple. It was made most often of oak, and decoration was very limited or non-existent. The work of his brothers display adaptations of many of Gustav's ideas and designs. His factory, the Craftsman Workshop, operated in Eastwood, New York, from the late 1890s until 1915, when he was forced out of business by larger companies who copied his work and sold it at much lower prices. Among his shopmarks are the early red decal containing a joiner's compass and the words 'Als Ik Kan,' the branded mark with very similar components, and paper labels.

The firm known as Stickley Brothers was located first in Binghamton, New York, and then Grand Rapids, Michigan. Albert and John George made the move to Michigan, leaving Charles in Binghamton (where he and an uncle continued the operation under a different name). After several years John George left the company to rejoin Leopold in New York. (These two later formed their own firm called L. & J.G. Stickley.) The Stickley Brothers Company under Albert's sole direction produced furniture that featured fine inlay work, decorative cutouts, and leaned strongly toward a style of Arts and Crafts with an English influence. It was tagged with a paper label 'Made by Stickley Brothers, Grand Rapids', or with a brass plate or decal with the words 'Quaint Furniture,' an English term he chose to refer to his product. In addition to his furniture, he made metal furnishings as well.

The workshops of the L. & J.G. Stickley Company first operated under the name 'Onondaga Shops.' Located in Fayetteville, New York, their designs were often all but copies of Gustav's work. Their products were well made and marketed, and their business was very successful. Their decal labels contained all or a combination of the words 'Handcraft' or 'Onondaga Shops,' along with the brothers' initials and last name. The firm continues in business today. Our advisor for this category is Bruce Austin; he is listed in the Directory under New York. Note: When only one dimension is given for tables, it is length.

Charles Stickley

Cabinet, china; 6-pane door ea side 1 lg glass door, no mk 3,750.00
Chair, side; 9-spindle bk, drop-in cushion, brand, EX 450.00

Rocker, arm; like Gustav #2615, att, orig, 35", VG 250.00
Rocker, no arm; #2617, 3-slat bk, worn orig, 34", VG 140.00
Table, like Gustav #609, rnd top/lower shelf, 36", VG 850.00

Gustav Stickley

Gustav Stickley copper and amber glass lantern on riveted iron support with oak base, 19x12", EX, $4,500.00.

Armchair, #2604, scoop crest over 3-slat bk, decal, EX 950.00
Armchair, #324, fixed-bk, 5-slat sides, decal, NM 1,900.00
Armchair, #326, 5-slat bk, orig leather seats, brand, 8 for 4,500.00
Armchair, #349½ A, ladderbk, corbels under arm, EX 1,100.00
Bench, child's; #215, 2 horizontal bk slats, cut-bk side, VG 950.00
Bookcase, #715, 12-pane door, orig hdw/finish, mk, 56x36" ...4,000.00
Bookcase, #715, 16-pane door, orig hdw, no mk, rfn, 56", VG ..3,750.00
Bookcase, #716, 2 16-pane doors, label/brand, 56x43", EX 4,250.00
Bookcase, #717, 2 8-pane doors, rstr finish, mk, 56x42" 4,500.00
Bride's chest, long corbels, strap hdw, all orig, decal, 41" 8,000.00
Cabinet, china; #815, 16-pane doors, orig finish, decal, 64" 2,750.00
Cabinet, music; #70, 10 amber panes, label, cleaned, 46" 2,750.00
Cabinet, smoker's; #89, 1 drw/door, arched toebrd, mk, EX 1,500.00
Chair, Morris; #336, rope foundation, faceted pegs, rfn, VG ...5,000.00
Chair, Morris; #369, 5-slat drop arm, orig finish, brand 6,250.00
Chair, side; #1299, Thornden, 2 broad slats in bk, decal, EX 550.00
Chair, side; #1304, 2 broad slats in bk, no seat, decal, EX 350.00
Chair, side; #306, ladderbk, new seat, orig finish, decal 425.00
Chair, side; #308, 'H' bk slat, no mk, rfn, rough, 4 for 1,100.00
Chair, side; #338, 3-slat bk, arched seat rail, no mk, VG, pr 375.00
Chair, side; #354½ , V-bk, 5-slat, poor rfn, set of 4, G 2,100.00
Chair, side; #370, ladderbk, rpl leather, brand, set of 6 ....2,500.00
Chair, side; wicker, X-pattern in bk, orig, no mk, 33", VG 225.00
Chest of drw, #626, 2 drw over 3, no mk, rfn, 43x36", VG 2,400.00
Chest of drw, #911, 2 short/2 long drws, mirror, brand, rfn 2,500.00
Costumer, dbl post w/6 hooks, recoated, mk, 72", VG 1,900.00
Desk, #731, drop-front, 2 short over 1 long drw, brand, NM ...1,600.00
Footstool, #300, sq stretcher, rpl leather, rfn, no mk 200.00
Footstool, #302, short flared ft, orig leather, decal, M 600.00
Highchair, #388, 3 bk slats, rush seat, no tray, decal, M 850.00
Lantern, #830, 4 glass panes, copper fr w/6 open sqs, 10" 1,700.00
Lantern, 4 hammered glass panels, rpl cap/rfn, 25" w/chain 650.00
Plant stand, #660, overhanging top, 4 splay legs, rpr, VG 1,200.00
Rocker, arm; #2603, U-bk w/3 slats, decal, worn orig finish 850.00
Rocker, arm; #311½, V-bk w/5 slats, rpl rush, decal, EX 500.00
Rocker, arm; #319, notched bk w/4 slats, open arms, no mk, VG .950.00
Rocker, arm; #321½ , V-bk, 5-slat, rpl seat, decal, 35" 500.00
Rocker, arm; #397, 3-slat bk, brand, rpl leather, 43", EX 1,600.00
Rocker, arm; child's, #344, open arm ladderbk, new seat 750.00
Rocker, arm; child's, 3 bk slats, rpr arm, decal, rpl leather 250.00
Rocker, sewing; 4-slat bk, rope seat foundation, decal, M 450.00
Rug, Craftsman, drugget style, Greek Key border, 48x74" 400.00

Screen, #81, 3 embr linen panels (rpl), decal, 59x57" 1,600.00
Server, #802, 2-drw, lower shelf, brand, 42" L, EX 3,000.00
Settee, #161, concave crest over 3 vertical slats, decal, M 3,250.00
Settle, #226, even-arm, 5 slats on side, 1 in bk, mk, 60", EX 7,000.00
Settle, #616, 4 horizontal bk slats, open arms, 50", VG 1,800.00
Sideboard, #814, plate rail, 2 doors/3 drws over 1, mk, EX 4,000.00
Table, #609, leather top & lower shelf, label, 36" dia, VG 4,250.00
Table, #626, X-stretcher base, label/decal, rfn top, 40" dia 1,500.00
Table, #638, clip-corner drop-leaf, gate legs, rfn, 30x40" 1,400.00
Table, child's; #658, rnd top, 4 legs, decal, orig, VG 850.00
Table, dining; #656, 54" dia top, sq ped w/curved ft, mk, EX .3,750.00
Table, director's; #631½ , branded, 72" L 13,500.00
Table, dressing; #907, swivel mirror, 5 drws, decal, EX 2,500.00
Table, library; #651, flat top/shelf, no mk, rstr finish 1,100.00
Table, library; #653, 1-drw, lower shelf, decal, 48", VG 1,500.00
Table, side; #654, arched X-stretchers, decal, 24" dia, VG 650.00
Table, tea; #604, 4 str legs, rfn, 26x20" dia 700.00
Telephone stand, #605, sq top/shelf, decal, 30x14", M 1,100.00
Tray, #355, hammered copper w/hdls, no mk, cleaned, 23" L ...325.00
Tray, hammered copper w/emb pods in wide rim, 20" dia, VG .7,500.00
Umbrella stand, #382, emb leaf, 2 leaf hdls, no pan, wear, 26" ...750.00
Wardrobe, mirror w/in, X-hatched front, EX grain, mk, 64x41" ..4,500.00
Window seat, #178, slat bk/sides, str crest rail, decal, EX 1,300.00

L. & J.G. Stickley

Armchair, #426, curved arm, 4-slat sides, mk, EX 2,000.00
Armchair, #816, 6-slat bk, decal, rfn, rough, VG 300.00
Ashtray, hammered copper, cleaned, 6½" dia, VG 300.00
Bookcase, 2 12-panel doors, tenon/key built, no mk, rfn, 57" ..4,000.00
Cabinet, china; #746, 2 doors w/6-pane top, mk, 62x44", EX .5,500.00
Chair, Morris; #830, corbels under open arms, mk, 39", VG ...1,100.00
Chair, side; #328, 4-slat bk, decal, orig seat/finish, VG 260.00
Chair, side; #808, 5-slat peaked-crest bk, mk, EX, 8 for 7,000.00
Chair, side; 5-slat peaked-crest bk, new leather, no mk, rfn 450.00
Daybed, #292, 4-slat ends, decal, color added, 80", VG 2,800.00
Desk, #601, letter rack in bkbrd, lower shelf, 34", VG 700.00
Frame, arched top, flaring sides, pegged, orig finish, 12x14½" 650.00
Magazine stand, #46, 3-slat side, 4-shelf, no mk, rfn, 42" 1,200.00
Rocker, arm; #421, corbels under open arms, orig, 39", EX 1,600.00
Rocker, arm; #485, 6-slat sides, recovered orig cushions, VG ..1,700.00
Rocker, arm; #499, slant arm w/5 slats, decal, rstr, G 1,500.00
Rocker, no arm; #809, 5-slat peaked-crest bk, no mk 220.00
Server, blind drw over open shelf, sm bk splash, mk, 32x32" 600.00
Settle, #232, even-arm, 5-slat bk, new leather/rfn, 72" 3,250.00
Sideboard, #709, 3 sm drw ea side 2 doors over 2 drw, 54" L ...2,250.00
Sideboard, #745, plate rack, door ea side 4 sm drw, label 2,900.00
Sideboard, like #734, plate rail, 2 doors+4 drw over 1, rfn 2,700.00
Smoking set, hammered copper, 17" tray+4 pcs, EX 350.00
Stand, #601, 14" dia top, X-stretcher, label, M 950.00
Stand, #603, 20" dia 3-brd top, X-stretchers, decal, rfn top 650.00
Table, book; #516, 7 slats/shelf on all 4 sides, EX 6,500.00
Table, breakfast; 4-leg, 48x35", +4 3-slat chairs, mk, rfn 3,600.00
Table, dining; #713, ped base, no mk, orig, 40" dia 2,900.00
Table, dining; #722, 4-leg w/X-stretchers, decal, 48" 2,250.00
Table, lamp; 36" dia top, sm rnd lower shelf, rfn, decal 1,300.00
Table, library; #520, 2-drw, lower shelf, decal, wear, 42" 700.00
Table, side; #576, cut corners, sq lower shelf, no mk, VG 650.00
Table, tea; #513, 30" dia top & shelf, orig blk finish, M 1,300.00
Telephone stand, sq top & stretcher, decal, rstr finish 750.00

Stickley Bros.

Armchair, #728½ , 6-slat bk, corbeled arms, rfn, 41", VG 750.00

Ashtray, #17, hammered copper w/raised spade design, 7", VG ..175.00
Chair, Morris; open arm, tapered legs, new leather, mk 700.00
Cup, hammered copper, 3-hdl, no mk, minor wear, 4¾" 275.00
Hall stand, splay bk w/X-bar at top, attached umbrella stand 600.00
Magazine stand, #4743, 5-shelf, wide slat ea splay side, VG 750.00
Music stand, #670, 4-shelf, label, orig finish, 39", EX 3,200.00
Plant stand, sq top, tapered column, sq ftd base, 34x13" 650.00
Plant stand, X-base, splay legs, arched apron, mk, G 650.00
Rocker, arm; #728, 6 slats in bk/sides, spring seat, rfn, 38" 850.00
Server, 1-drw w/orig hdw, lower shelf, mk, 34" W, VG 950.00
Settle, #3563, even-arm, 2-slat sides, 6 in bk, mk, 75", VG 1,300.00
Settle, 2-section, ea w/4 slats, new leather, metal tag, EX 1,000.00
Stand, #111, hex top, 3 splayed legs ea w/cut-out floral 500.00
Table, dining; 48" dia, sq base w/corbeled ft, tag, VG 2,200.00
Umbrella stand, #180, copper hexagon w/raised dome ea panel .650.00
Vase, hammered copper, 3 C hdls extend above rim, #63, 12" ...175.00
Wastebasket, canted 4-slat sides, cut-out top brd, no mk, VG 800.00

Stiegel

Baron Henry Stiegel produced glassware in Pennsylvania as early as 1760, very similar to glass being made concurrently in Germany and England. Without substantiating evidence, it is impossible to positively attribute a specific article to his manufacture. Although he made other types of glass, today the term Stiegel generally refers to any very early ware made in shapes and colors similar to those he is known to have produced — especially that with etched or enameled decoration. It is generally conceded, however, that most glass of this type is of European origin. Our advisor for this category is Mark Vuono; he is listed in the Directory under Connecticut.

Bottle, half-post, mc enameling, pewter cap, 6⅜" 260.00
Bottle, mc bird/floral, 6-color, threaded pewter top, 5¾" 500.00
Bowl, cobalt, 16-dmn bowl, appl ft, pot stones, 5x4¼" 275.00
Mug, eagle/floral, 5-color, appl strap hdl, 4½" 1,000.00
Mug, mc floral & deer, 5¼" 415.00
Salt, master; cobalt, Dmn Quilt, ftd, 3x2" 575.00
Salt, master; cobalt, paneled/flared w/folded rim, knop stem 700.00
Tumbler, mc florals w/birds, 4" 250.00

Stocks and Bonds

Scripophily (scrip-awfully), the collecting of 'worthless' old stocks and bonds, gained recognition as an area of serious interest around the mid-1970s. Today there are an estimated 5,000 collectors in the United States and 15,000 worldwide. Collectors who come from numerous business fields mainly enjoy its hobby aspect, though there are those who consider scripophily an investment. Some collectors like the historical significance that certain certificates have. Others prefer the beauty of older stocks and bonds that were printed in various colors with fancy artwork and ornate engravings. Even autograph collectors are found in this field, on the lookout for signed certificates.

Many factors help determine the collector value: autograph value, age of the certificate, the industry represented, whether it is issued or not, its attractiveness, condition, and collector demand. Certificates from the mining, energy, and railroad industries are the most popular with collectors. Other industries or special collecting fields include banking, automobiles, aircraft, and territorials. Serious collectors usually prefer only issued certificates that date from before 1910. Unissued certificates are usually worth one-fourth to one-tenth the value of one that has been issued. Inexpensive issued common stocks and bonds dated between the 1930s and 1980s usually retail between $1.00 to $10.00.

Those dating between 1890 and 1930 usually sell for $10.00 to $50.00. Those over one hundred years old retail between $25.00 and $100.00 or more, depending on the quantity found and the industry represented. Some stocks are one of a kind while others are found by the hundreds or even thousands, especially railroad certificates. Autographed stocks normally sell anywhere from $100.00 to $1,000.00. A formal collecting organization for scripophilists is known as The Bond and Share Society with an American chapter located in New York City.

Our advisor for this category is Warren Anderson; he is listed in the Directory under Utah. In many of the following listings, two-letter state abbreviations immediately follow company name. All are in fine condition unless noted otherwise.

Key:
cp — coupon   U — unissued
I/C — issued/cancelled   vgn — vignette
I/U — issued/uncancelled

Allen Sarsaparilla, ME/1893, State Arms, dog & deer vgns, I/C ...**80.00**
Am Settlement, KS Territory/1856, eagle on bl, I/C **120.00**
Argonaut Gold Mining, CO/1896, lady vgn, gr seal, I/U **35.00**
Bank of NC, NC/1864, reapers & portraits vgns, ABNCo, I/C ..**135.00**
Bay State Mining, MI/1865, red seal, rubber stamped, I/C **130.00**
Big Revenue Gold Bullion Mining, AZ Territory/1906, vgn, I/U .**35.00**
Bullion Hill Mining, NV/1906, blk on bl w/gold seal, I/U **25.00**
Cashier Mining & Milling, WA/1903, 3 vgns, I/U **25.00**
Chemical Hand Fire Extinguisher, Portland ME/1880s, U, M **30.00**
City of Indianapolis, IN/1875, building vgns, IC **55.00**
Coleman Farm Mill, NY/1859, farming vgns, Hatch Litho, I/C **55.00**
Confederate Loan, 1864, registered 4%, battle scene **35.00**
Confederate States of Am, $1,000 w/cancelled coupon, EX **95.00**
Consolidated Silver Mining, NY/1866, mining scene, I/C, NM ...**90.00**
Crown Head Gold Mining, ME/1889, seal vgn, blk/wht, I/U **30.00**
Dearborn Truck, DE/1920, eagle vgn on bl, I/C **50.00**
Doman Helicopters, DE/1956, eagle on cliff vgn, I/C **50.00**
Dr Pepper, CO/1927, fancy border on bl, I/C **110.00**
Fame Mutual Insurance, PA/1860, lady w/trumpet vgn, I/C **30.00**
Four Metals Mining Co, AZ Territory/1905, 4 vgns, I/U **20.00**
Golden Treasure Mining & Tunnel Co, CO/1900, bl seal, I/U **40.00**
Grand Pacific Gold Mining, CA/1903, 3 vgns, I/U **20.00**
Grand River Valley RR, MI/1903, station vgn, ABNCo, I/C **35.00**
Imperial Gold Mining, MT/1896, ornate artwork, gold seal, I/U ..**25.00**
IN Advertising Auto Speedway, IN/1921, Mercury vgn on gr, I/C .**35.00**
Internat'l Life Assurance...of London, NY/1857, gray/blk, I/U **50.00**
Kinney Steamship, OH/1925, lady w/shield vgn, I/C **45.00**
Kora Temple, ME/1908, Magi on camel, 3-color border, NM **70.00**
Liggett/Myers Tobacco, NJ/1912-25, steamship vgn, sgn, IC **22.00**
Marmon Motor Car, IN/1930, allegorical figures vgn, ABNCo ..**150.00**
Merchants Union Express, NY/1868, handshake vgn, Hatch, I/C ..**95.00**
Morley Sewing Machines, ME/1890s, State arms, ships vgn, I/C ..**30.00**
Mountain Top Mining, CO/1918, eagle vgn, gold seal, I/U **20.00**
Nashville & Decatur RR, TN/1886, 2 train vgns, I/C **30.00**
New Mexico Mining, NM/1867, prospectors vgn, I/C **75.00**
NY Central Sleeping Car, 1886, train/steamer vgn, sgn WS Webb ..**65.00**
Oil Fields Corp, AR/1925, gusher vgn, brn seal, I/U **15.00**
Ophir Development Co, NM/1916, mining vgn, gold seal, I/U **25.00**
Oxford Linen Mills, ME/1910, machine vgn, I/U **20.00**
People's Ice, San Francisco/1876, train/river vgn, IC **35.00**
Peoria & Bureau Valley RR, IL/1875, Indian vgn, ABNCo, I/C ...**55.00**
Philadelphia Rapid Transit, PA/1926, trolley/subway/bus vgns **18.00**
Pierce-Arrow Car, NY/1935, man & emblem vgns, ABNCo, I/C .**135.00**
Potomac Oil Co, AZ Territory/1902, vgn, gold seal, I/U **25.00**
Roston & Chelsea RR, 186_, red print, no illus, U **5.00**
Salmon River & Porcupine Mining, WA/1899, mining vgn, I/U .**30.00**

St Lucie Rod & Gun Club, FL/1928, State arms, seal, I/C **50.00**
Staten Island Rapid Transit RR, NY/1883, typeset, I/C **60.00**
Tintic Co, ME/1904, eagle vgn, ABNCo, I/C **25.00**
Union Oil Co of CO, CO/1924, gusher vgn, orange print, I/U **15.00**
United Southern Oil Co #2, TX/1919, gusher vgn, gr border, I/U ..**15.00**
Upper Potomac Steamboat Co, VA/1875, PH Troth, 11x13", EX ..**22.50**
US Worsted, MA/1923, sheep herds vgn, ABNCo, I/C **40.00**
Vesuvius Mines, OR/1909, 3 vgns, gold border, I/U **25.00**
Walt Disney, DE/19__, allegorical woman vgn, CBNCo, U **110.00**
Wiling Gold Mining Co, AZ Territory/1906, 3 vgns, I/U **20.00**
WY-NV Mining Co, WY/1905, 3 vgns, gr seal & border, I/U **25.00**
1st Nat'l Bank of Ouray, CO/1889, miners vgn, blk/wht, I/C **35.00**

Stoneware

There are three broad periods of time that collectors of American pottery can look to in evaluating and dating the stoneware and earthenware in their collections. Among the first permanent settlers in America were English and German potters who found a great demand for their individually turned wares. The early pottery was produced from red and yellow clays scraped from the ground at surface levels. The earthenware made in these potteries was fragile and coated with lead glazes that periodically created health problems for the people who ate or drank from it. There was little stoneware available for sale until the early 1800s, because the clays used in its production were not readily available in many areas, and transportation was prohibitively expensive. The opening of the Erie Canal and improved roads brought about a dramatic increase in the accessibility of stoneware clay, and many new potteries began to open in New York and New England.

Collectors have difficulty today locating earthenware and stoneware jugs produced prior to 1840, because few have survived intact. These ovoid or pear-shaped jugs were designed to be used on a daily basis. When cracked or severely chipped, they were quickly discarded. The value of handcrafted pottery is often determined by the cobalt decoration it carries. Pieces with elaborate scenes (a chicken pecking corn, a bluebird on a branch, a stag standing near a pine tree, a sailing ship, or people) may easily bring $1,000.00 to $12,000.00 at auction.

After the Civil War there was a need and a national demand for stoneware jugs, crocks, canning jars, churns, spittoons, and a wide variety of other pottery items. The competition among the many potteries reached the point where only the largest could survive. To cut costs, most potteries did away with all but the simplest kinds of decoration on their wares. Time-consuming brush-painted birds or flowers quickly gave way to more simply executed swirls or numbers and stenciled designs. The coming of home refrigeration and Prohibition in 1919 effectively destroyed the American stoneware industry. See also Bennington, Stoneware.

Key: c/s — cobalt on salt glaze

Churn, bird on floral branch, White and Wood, Binghamton, New York, 1883-87, 17½", $4,600.00.

Bottle, emb eagle w/shield, c/s, AP Donaghho...PA, 9¾" 965.00
Bowl, emb scroll, c/s, Bristol glaze, Whites Utica, 7", EX 140.00
Bowl, milk; brushed c/s, appl hdls & spout, H Smith, 11" 1,100.00
Butter pail, orchid, c/s, att Whites Utica, chips, 6-qt 400.00
Churn, #4/bird w/worm, c/s, John Burger..., 1855, rpr, 18½" ...2,200.00
Churn, #4/flower (thick), c/s, OL & AK Ballard...VT, 17", EX ..650.00
Churn, #5/bird & flowers, c/s, Whites Utica, 1865, 5-gal, EX .3,700.00
Churn, #5/flower, c/s, hairline, 19" 275.00
Cooler, #6/bird & lg plume, c/s, Cage City...1886, 6-gal, EX ...875.00
Cooler, #6/bird on plume, c/s, Satterlee & Morey, 2-hdl, rstr 400.00
Cooler, bl molded bands, c/s, bbl shape, pewter spigot, 11" 90.00
Cooler, flower basket, cobalt on Bristol, Improved..., 11", EX .2,500.00
Crock, #1/bird (dotted), c/s, W Roberts...NY, ovoid, 7½", EX ...350.00
Crock, #2 in wreath, c/s, Burger & Co..., 1878, 2-gal, EX 130.00
Crock, #2/daffodil, c/s, Burger & Co..., 1878, 2-gal, 9", EX 170.00
Crock, #2/flower, c/s, Bross Bros Sterling PA, 9½" 150.00
Crock, #2/flower, c/s, NA White & Son Utica NY, 9" 140.00
Crock, #2/plume, c/s, C Boynton & Co Troy, ca 1829, 2-gal 250.00
Crock, #2/plume (simple), c/s, N Clark & Co, 1830s, 11", EX ...140.00
Crock, #3/bird, c/s, D Weston...NY, 1860s, 10", EX 455.00
Crock, #3/daisy & buds, c/s, J Burger Jr..., 1885, 3-gal, EX 250.00
Crock, #3/dragonfly, c/s, hairlines, 10½" 75.00
Crock, #3/flower (dbl), c/s, Harrington & Burger, 3-gal, EX ...1,550.00
Crock, #3/grapes, c/s, AK Ballard...VT, 1870s, prof rpr, 10" 300.00
Crock, #4/bird on floral plume, c/s, Whites Utica, 4-gal, EX 500.00
Crock, #4/flower (dbl), c/s, John Burger..., 1855, 4-gal, NM ...1,000.00
Crock, #4/flower (ornate), c/s, John Burger..., rpr, 4-gal 1,300.00
Crock, #4/flower (stylized), c/s, Haxtun & Co, 4-gal, EX 160.00
Crock, #4/flowers (ornate), c/s, N Clark...Lyons, 13½", EX 825.00
Crock, #4/house & palms, c/s, Whittemore, 1865, 11", EX 3,500.00
Crock, #4/1876 in wreath, c/s, Ottman Bros...NY, 11½", EX 375.00
Crock, #5/bird, c/s, J Burger Jr..., 1880s, rpr, 5-gal 1,000.00
Crock, #5/birds (3), c/s, West Troy NY..., 1880s, 12", EX 1,100.00
Crock, #5/flower, c/s, J Mantell Penn Yan, rpr, 5-gal, 13½" 825.00
Crock, #5/flower (dbl/3-D), c/s, John Burger..., 1855, 5-gal 1,250.00
Crock, #5/orchid (4-petal), c/s, NA White & Son, 5-gal, EX 650.00
Crock, #6/birds (2), Ottman Bros...NY, c/s, 1870s, 13", EX 1,050.00
Crock, bird/notes, c/s, unsgn, ca 1860, chip, 1-gal 240.00
Crock, bird/quillwork, c/s, N Clark, Lyons NY, 10½" 1,155.00
Crock, flower, c/s, F___ & Son, Taunton, Mass, 7x8" 250.00
Crock, 1832, c/s, Clark & Fox Athens, chips, 2-gal, 11" 425.00
Crock, 1853/LH, c/s, unsgn, ovoid, ca 1853, 4-gal, 15" 280.00
Crock lid, zigzag border w/cobalt infill, 14¾" dia 600.00
Cuspidor, gray salt glaze w/brn highlights, 8½", EX 55.00
Jar, #2/bird on branch, c/s, Whites Utica, chips, 2-gal 550.00
Jar, #2/flourish, c/s, 12¾" 75.00
Jar, #2/flower, c/s, S Blair Cortland, 1830s, 2-gal, EX 240.00
Jar, #2/flower (triple), c/s, J Shepard Jr, 1857, 2-gal 700.00
Jar, #3, c/s, freehand & stencil, Hamilton & Jones..., 14" 95.00
Jar, #3/flower bouquet, c/s, Whites Utica NY, 1865, 3-gal 800.00
Jar, #3/tulip (brushed), c/s, T Reed, chip, 13¼" 550.00
Jar, #4, c/s, Jas Hamilton & Co, Greensboro PA, 15", EX 185.00
Jar, #5/flower (stylized), c/s, Troy NY Pottery, 5-gal, EX 350.00
Jar, flower (brushed), c/s, N Clark, ovoid, hdls, 13", NM............290.00
Jar, flower (brushed), c/s, 8¾", EX 100.00
Jar, flowers (2), c/s, Cortland, 1860s, 1-gal, 9", EX 210.00
Jar, molasses; Albany slip, Lyons NY, 1870s, 1-gal, 9", EX 35.00
Jar, narrow mouth, unsgn, 1840s, 6" 30.00
Jar, preserve; #2/flower (triple), c/s, Cortland, 2-gal, EX 375.00
Jar, preserve; AP Donaghho, Parkersburg WV c/s, 8½" 95.00
Jar, preserve; elf, c/s, w/lid, unsgn, 1860s, chip, 1-gal 525.00
Jar, preserve; flower, c/s, JB Caire..., 1850s, 1-gal 220.00
Jar, preserve; flower, c/s, 10" 75.00
Jug, #1/flower (simple), c/s, I Seymour Troy, 1825, 11½" 250.00

Jug, eagle with ribbon dated 1776 and 1876, cobalt on salt glaze, New York Stoneware Co., dated 1876, flakes, 19½", $2,800.00.

Jug, #1/upsidedown stamp, c/s, DW Graves..., 1-gal, EX 110.00
Jug, #2/bird on branch, c/s, Whites Utica, 13½" 425.00
Jug, #2/bird on branch, W Roberts...NY, 1870s, 14", EX 975.00
Jug, #2/flower, c/s, Burger & Lang, Rochester NY, ovoid, 15" 290.00
Jug, #2/flower, c/s, WH Farrar & Co..., 1840s, 2-gal, EX 260.00
Jug, #2/flower (triple), c/s, Evan R Jones...PA, 1880s, 2-gal 200.00
Jug, #2/flowers (2), c/s, P Mugler...NY, 1850s, rpr, 14" 600.00
Jug, #2/man's profile (folky), c/s, unsgn, 1840, 2-gal, EX 1,450.00
Jug, #2/paddle-tail bird, c/s, NA White..., 1885, 2-gal, EX 625.00
Jug, #3/bird & plume, c/s, A Wheeler..., 1870s, chip, 3-gal 700.00
Jug, #3/bird on branch, c/s, hairlines, 15⅝" 440.00
Jug, #3/flower, c/s, ovoid, hairline, 16" 165.00
Jug, #3/flower (stylized), c/s, OL & AK Ballard...VT, 16", EX 200.00
Jug, #3/2 birds w/flourish, c/s, S Hart, Fulton, 14" 825.00
Jug, #4/bird w/stylized wings, c/s, dbl ear hdls, 14½" 150.00
Jug, #4/flower, c/s, F Stetzenmeyer..., 1855, rstr, 4-gal 700.00
Jug, #5/flower, c/s, IM Mead, Mogadore, OH, rstr, 18½" 385.00
Jug, Albany slip, Kauffman Latimer...Ohio, 13½" 88.00
Jug, batter; flower, c/s, Cowden & Wilcox, complete, 9" 1,700.00
Jug, bird on branch, c/s, West Troy Pottery, hdl rpr, 12" 275.00
Jug, C Scrack's Varnish Mfg...Phila, ovoid, 16", EX 120.00
Jug, feather foliage, c/s, rope spiral hdl, J Holloway, 10⅜" 1,325.00
Jug, flower (dbl), c/s, J Shepard Jr..., 1860s, 3-gal, EX 375.00
Jug, flower (dbl/brushed), c/s, Riedinger..., 1870s, 13½", EX 210.00
Jug, foliage w/flourish, c/s, Ottman Bros Fort Edward NY, 12" 185.00
Jug, stencil: c/s, CB Somerville & Co Staunton VA, 11" 275.00
Pitcher, #1 in circle/flower, c/s, 10½" 100.00
Pitcher, Albany slip, sm flakes, 9¾" 50.00
Pitcher, Albany slip w/emb label: Auburn NY, ovoid, 11", EX 85.00
Pitcher, bl & wht sponging, Albany slip int, 11¼" 195.00
Pitcher, brn-gray salt glaze, strap hdl, pinched spout, 10¾" 165.00
Pitcher, emb hunting scenes, Bristol glaze, ca 1900, 6¾" 160.00
Pot, cream; #5/flower (dbl), c/s, T Harrington..., 14", EX 350.00
Pot, plume, c/s, AK Ballard...VT, 1870s, 2-gal, 10½", EX 200.00
Vase, flower & butterfly, c/s, att Whites Utica, 9", EX 280.00

Store

Perhaps more more than any other yesteryear establishment, the country store evokes the most nostalgic feelings for folks old enough to remember its charms — barrels for coffee, crackers, and big green pickles; candy in a jar for the grocer to weigh on shiny brass scales; beheaded chickens in the meat case outwardly devoid of nothing but feathers. Today mementos from this segment of Americana are being collected by those who 'lived it' as well as those less fortunate! Our advisor for this category is Charles Reynolds; he is listed in the Directory under Virginia. See also Advertising; Scales.

Bag holder, wood fan shape w/stencil, Pat 1810, holds 8 szs 325.00

Bill clip, bronze finish, heavily emb, Pat 1871 & 1874 ....27.50
Bill holder, National Cash Register 15.00
Bill holder, steel, Congress, wall hanging 20.00
Bill hook, emb iron, Pat 1872 ....25.00
Broom display holder, wavy wire, 24 hoops, 18x17", EX 80.00
Display case, counter; slanted, oak & glass, 34x21x10", EX 210.00
Jar, pressed glass, paneled sides, w/lid, 17¾" 165.00
Mannequin, compo lady, dress & pnt shoes, w/stand, '40s, 24" ..230.00
Package sealer, National, NP CI, dispenses & moistens tape 95.00
Peanut warmer, aluminum, peanut finial, 1930s, EX 160.00
Price marker, Monarch, Deco style 85.00
Scoop, brass, ring base, 22" 75.00
Scoop, brass on copper, ring base, oval, 12" 45.00
Scoop, brass w/wood hdl, 8" 30.00
Scoop, candy; brass, sgn Diamond C, 4x4x9" 40.00
Shot dispenser, CI & oak, Pat 1879 ....475.00
Sign, cash register; Get a Receipt, brass, 2-sided, 6x14", EX 150.00

Stoves

Antique stoves' desirability is based on two criteria: their utility and
their decorative value. It's the latter that adds an 'antique' premium to the
basic functional value that could be served just as well by a modern stove.
Sheer age is usually irrelevant. Decorative features that enhance desirability
include fancy, embossed ornamentation, nickel-plated trim, mica windows,
ceramic tiles, and (in cooking stoves) water reservoirs and high warming
closets rather than mere high shelves. The less sheet metal and the more
cast iron, the better. Look for crisp, sharp designs in preference to those
made from worn or damaged and repaired foundry patterns. Stoves with a
pastel porcelain finish can be very attractive; blue is a favorite, white is least
desirable. Chrome trim dates a stove to circa 1933 or later and is a good
indicator of a post-antique stove. Though purists prefer the earlier models
trimmed in nickel rather than chrome, there is now considerable amount of
public interest in these post-antique stoves as well, and some people are
willing to pay a good price for these appliance-era 'classics.'

Among stove types, base burners (with self-feeding coal magazines)
are the most desirable. Then come the upright, cylindrical 'oak' stoves,
kitchen ranges, and wood parlors. Cannon stoves approach the margin
of undesirability; laundries and gasoline stoves plunge through it.

There's a thin but continuing stream of desirable antique stoves
going to the high-priced Pacific Coast market. Interest in antique stoves
is least in the Deep South. Demand for wood/coal stoves is strongest in
areas where firewood is affordable and storage of it is practical. Demand
for antique gas ranges has become strong, especially in metropolitan
markets, and interest in antique electric ranges is starting to surface.
The market for antique stoves is so limited and the variety so bewilder-
ing that a consensus on a going price can hardly emerge. They are only
worth something to the right individual, and prices realized depend very
greatly on who happens to be in the auction crowd. Even an expert's
appraisal will usually miss the realized price by a substantial percent.

The term 'parlor stove' as we use it here is very general and encompasses at least eight distinct types recognized by the stove industry: cottage parlor, double-cased airtight, circulator, cylinder, oak, base burner,
Franklin, and the fireplace heater.

In judging condition look out for deep rust pits, warped or burnt-
out parts, unsound firebricks, poorly fitting parts, poor repairs, and
empty mounting holes indicating missing trim. Search meticulously for
cracks in the cast iron. Our listings reflect auction prices of completely
restored, safe, and functional stoves, unless indicated otherwise.

Base Burners

Art Amherst #15, NP trim, tiles, 11" urn, 50x25x28" 1,875.00

Detroit Emerald Jewel #14, NPCI, 54"+15" brass urn 1,550.00
Favorite #30, Piqua OH, fancy CI, mica windows, 52"+14" urn ..2,000.00
Ransom Art Denmark #15, Albany..., tiles/NP/mica, 1887, VG .4,500.00
Thos Caffney Waverly #12, Boston MA, 40x20x22" 1,875.00

Box Stoves

J.H. Shear Albany, N.Y. #4, cast-iron
column stove, 56", EX, $2,000.00.

A Belanger Barge #34, scrollwork, CI, 1905, sm 190.00
BF&M Co #1, front load, early legs, 1800s, 17x13x14" 125.00
E Eaton #24, Amherst NH, schoolhouse type, 24x38x16" 435.00
Unknown, parlor type, reeded column sides, 1830s, 25x37x17" .500.00
Walker & Pratt Laconia, ornate CI, NP foot rail, 1860s, 35" 125.00

Franklin Stoves

AC Barstow Parlor Franklin #5, ornate CI, 1852, 35x24x38" 375.00
Atlanta Franklin #8M, CI, 2-burner, coal/wood, EX 125.00
Corner-type fireplace, #214, CI, 1915, 31x24" 1,560.00
Iron Foundry...NH, ornate CI, grate missing, 1820s, 37x26x32" ..200.00
Noyes & Nutter Kineo #16, fireplace, 1870s, 32x23x20" 185.00

Parlor Stoves

Albany #2, CI, 2-column, ornate, urn atop, 40x32" 250.00
Anthony, Davy & Co Lady Washington, CI, 1848, 26"+7" urn .280.00
B&H Radiant Handwarmer Cool Morning, Pat 1893-94, 33" 435.00
C Williams Forest #91, CI, 1870, 27" 375.00
Cooperative Cycle #23, rnd coal burner, mica door, ornate 125.00
De Soto #1, CI, Pat 1854, 42x26x21" 685.00
JC Fletcher's Pat 1853, Fuller Warren & Morrison, 45", EX 850.00
JS&M Peckham Rosedale #23, 1870s, 33"+10" swivel-top dome .250.00
Newberry-Filley Oven Parlor #7, Pat 1855, 34x22x27" 250.00
Palace Pat 1873 A Bradley & Co, Pittsburgh PA, 46", VG 325.00
Portland Radiant #22, CI, top loading, mica window 215.00
SH Ransom, ornate CI, rnd air intake, Pat 1846, 26x14" urn 275.00
Somersworth Oak #18, rnd oak/coal burner, NP trim, 1894 ....250.00
Standard Lighting Globe Incandescent, kerosene heater, 29" 315.00
Vose & Co #5 Temple, CI, Pat 1854, 44", EX 800.00
Weir Glenwood #25, oven in top, NP trim, mica 875.00
Wood/Bishop Eva, CI, Pat 1865, 8" urn, 29x27" 215.00

Ranges (Gas)

Cribben-Sexton Univ, 4-burner, gr/cream, high oven, '27, VG .375.00

Detroit Jewel, 4-burner, blk/NP, glass oven door, 1918, VG **500.00**
Magic Chef, 6-burner/2-oven, warming closet, 1932, EX **2,500.00**
Magic Chef, 6-burner/2-oven, warming closet, 1937, rstr **6,000.00**
Weir Insulated Glenwood, 6-burner/2-oven, wht, 1932, rstr ..**4,125.00**

Ranges (Wood and Coal)

Cribben-Sexton Universal, bl porc, high closet/no reservoir ...**2,750.00**
Home Comfort, gray graniteware, reservoir, warming ovens, NM .**1,000.00**
Kalamazoo, tan enamel, 1937, EX **315.00**
Quick Meal, bl porc, EX **3,125.00**
Weir Glenwood E, ornate CI, ca 1890, oven: 11x20x22" **815.00**
Wood/Bishop Home Clarion, CI, 1907, oven: 12x19x19" **750.00**
Wood/Bishop New Clarion #8, low closet, 1882, 32x28x46" ..**1,875.00**

Stove Manufacturers' Toy Stoves

Buck's Jr Range, St Louis MO, new body/pnt/recast parts, 26" ...**850.00**

Buck's Junior 2, cast iron with nickel trim, ca 1900, 23x22", EX original, $1,760.00.

Charter Oak #503, GF Filley, St Louis MO, 14x12x25", EX ...**2,050.00**
Dainty, Reading Stove Works, PA, 7x13x8", VG **150.00**
Great Majestic Jr, Majestic Mfg, 31x16x23", M **5,650.00**
Karr, Qualified, bl porc w/NP, Belleville IL, 1925, EX **2,500.00**
Karr Range, Belleville IL, bl porc, old model, 21½x13x9" **3,100.00**
Karr repro, Qualified, bl porc w/NP, 1950s, EX **2,500.00**
Little Eva T Southard, NYC, 8½x14x11", G **350.00**
Little Fanny, CI, minor rust, EX **300.00**
Little Willie, CI, EX **75.00**
Royal American, Bridgeford, Louisville KY, 14x12x10", G **950.00**

Toy Manufacturers' Toy Stoves

Arcade Hotpoint range, pnt CI, tan & gr, VG **130.00**
Arcade Roper, pnt CI & sheet metal w/silver trim, 6", EX **100.00**
Arcade Roper, range, pnt CI, gas type, door opens, 4½", EX **70.00**
Bing, cook stove, bl steel, brass trim, 16½", VG **600.00**
Crescent, cook stove, plated CI & steel, 4-burner, 11½", EX **230.00**
Eagle, cook stove, CI & steel, 6-burner, 11", EX **110.00**
Eagle, Hubley, Lancaster PA, NP, recast parts **450.00**
Eclipse, CI, EX **175.00**
Kenton Royal, CI & steel, 4-burner, ornate, 10", VG **100.00**
Kenton Royal, pnt CI & steel, 4-burner, no pipe, rpt, 10", VG **45.00**
Little Giant, unmk/unidentified, 7½x8½x11", EX orig **675.00**
Novelty, Kenton Hdwe, bl pnt/NP trim, rfn, 13x6½x8½" **600.00**
Pet, The; Young Bros, Albany NY, 10½x6x8½" **165.00**
Rival, J&E Stevens, Cromwell CT, 14x9x16", M, +2 kettles ..**1,350.00**
Rival, J&E Stevens, Cromwell CT, 1895, 13x7½x18½", G **240.00**

Royal, plated CI, stovepipe, shield shape, 16", G **85.00**
Triumph, Kenton Hdwe, OH, 14x8½x19", G **195.00**

Strawberry Soft Paste and Lustre Ware

Strawberry lustre is a general term for pearlware and semiporcelain decorated with hand-painted strawberries, veins, tendrils, and pink lustre trim. Strawberry soft paste is decorated creamware without the pink lustre trim. Both types were made by many manufacturers in England in the 19th century, most of whom never marked their ware.

Coffeepot, dome lid, soft paste, 12", NM **1,800.00**
Cup & saucer, pearl ware, pk/red int bands, EX **325.00**
Plate, soft paste, Davenport, ca 1810, 6½" **185.00**
Sauce boat, lustre, 6" **175.00**
Teapot, squat, 1820s, 6", VG **525.00**
Teapot, vine border, ftd, 11", EX **600.00**

Stretch Glass

Stretch glass, produced from 1916 until after 1930, was made in an effort to emulate the fine art glass of Tiffany and Carder. The glassware was sprayed with a special finish while still hot, and a reheating process caused the coating to contract, leaving a striated, crepe-like iridescence. Northwood, Imperial, Fenton, Diamond, Lancaster, and the United States Glass Company were the largest manufacturers of this type of glass. See also specific companies.

Bobeches, vaseline, scalloped rim, pr **30.00**
Bowl, amber, flared rim, 12" **35.00**
Bowl, baked apple; vaseline, 6½" **24.00**
Bowl, bl, 4-sided, ped ft, Northwood, 8½" **45.00**
Bowl, bl opaque, ribbed, flared, Northwood, 3x9½" **42.00**
Bowl, centerpc; gr, flared, 11" **38.00**
Bowl, custard opaque, Northwood #617 ....**75.00**
Bowl, Dbl Scroll, amberina, fluted, Imperial **100.00**
Candlesticks, Dmn, gr, hollow, 9¾", pr **60.00**
Candlesticks, vaseline, twist, blk edge decor, US Glass, pr **125.00**
Compote, Russett, Northwood #637 ....**70.00**
Compote, wht, bl band, orange flowers, Lancaster, 8¾x5¼" **40.00**
Compote, wht, HP florals, Lancaster, 3¾x10" **45.00**
Pitcher, lemonade; Celeste Bl, cobalt hdl, Fenton **130.00**
Plate, amberina, 14-panel, 8" **55.00**
Plate, salad; vaseline **15.00**
Plate, wht, 8" **12.00**
Puff box, Wisteria, Fenton, #743, w/lid **45.00**
Sherbet, amberina, ribbed, ftd, 3⅜x4" **40.00**
Tumbler, lemonade; wht, cobalt hdl **28.00**
Vase, pk, dolphin hdls, fan form, 6" **55.00**
Vase, red, flared, 7¾" **95.00**
Vase, Ribbed Optic, HP florals, Lancaster, 6" **48.00**

String Holders

Today, if you want to wrap and secure a package, you have a variety of products to choose from: cellophane tape, staples, etc. But in the 1800s, string was about the only available binder; thus the string holder, either the hanging or counter type, was a common and practical item found in most homes and businesses. Chalkware and ceramic figurals from the 1930s and 1940s contrast with the cast- and wrought-iron examples from the 1800s to make for an interesting collection. Our advisor for this category is Charles Reynolds; he is listed in the Directory under Virginia.

Ceramic, Blk porter, Fredericksburg Art Pottery, 6½", M 150.00
Ceramic, String Swallow, bird & house 20.00
Chalkware, Dutch boy w/pipe, EX pnt 45.00
Chalkware, old lady in rocker 32.00
Chalkware, sailor w/pipe, eyes to side 35.00
Chalkware, strawberry w/face, EX 40.00
China, cat's face, Holt Howard China, 1958 ....30.00
CI, ball type, hinged, ca 1910, EX 110.00
CI, compote shape w/emb leaves, tall finial on lid, 10" 125.00
CI, mechanical, ball runs on track 365.00
CI, spherical w/trn wooden base, 7" dia 66.00
CI, SSS for the Blood, rtcl insert, EX pnt, 4⅞" 195.00
CI, Tabby, mc pnt, 1880s, 5⅝" 900.00
Treen, EX trn/detail, lid w/hole & finial, metal cutter, 3" 185.00

Sugar Shakers

Sugar shakers (or muffineers, as they were also called) were used during the Victorian era to sprinkle sugar and spice onto breakfast muffins, toast, etc. They were made of art glass, in pressed patterns, and in china. See also specific types and manufacturers. Our advisor for this category is Jeff Bradfield; he is listed in the Directory under Virginia.

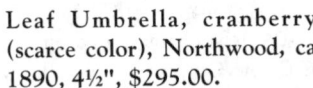
Leaf Umbrella, cranberry (scarce color), Northwood, ca 1890, 4½", $295.00.

Acorn, bl opaque 200.00
Acorn, wht opaque 115.00
Acorn, wht opaque w/decor 175.00
Apple Blossom, milk glass w/decor 165.00
Argus Swirl, wht opaque w/decor 95.00
Banded Portland 80.00
Beatty Rib, bl opal 250.00
Chrysanthemum Base Swirl, cranberry 350.00
Coin Spot, bl opal, ring neck 170.00
Coin Spot, dk bl, wide waist 185.00
Cone, bl cased 150.00
Cone, gr opaque 165.00
Cone, pk cased 200.00
Cranberry, bulbous optic base 250.00
Cranberry, Optic Panel, orig beaded lid 150.00
Daisy & Fern, cranberry opal 325.00
Daisy & Fern, wht opal 160.00
Florette, pk cased satin 250.00
Forget-Me-Not, bl, Challinor 140.00
Hobnail, amber 120.00
Invt T'print, cranberry, tapered 185.00

Many Lobes, wht satin w/EX decor 110.00
Melon, bl floral, Gillinder 195.00
Paneled Daisy 125.00
Paneled Sprig, milk glass w/HP decor 75.00
Parian Swirl, bl satin 195.00
Parian Swirl, bl satin w/HP decor 225.00
Parian Swirl, cranberry 235.00
Parian Swirl, wht opaque w/decor 135.00
Plain Band, Heisey 40.00
Portland 55.00
Quilted Phlox, amethyst 185.00
Quilted Phlox, bl opaque 200.00
Quilted Phlox, milk glass w/HP floral 165.00
Quilted Phlox, pk cased 225.00
Reverse Swirl, vaseline opal 250.00
Ribbed Opal Lattice, bl 185.00
Ribbed Opal Lattice, cranberry 300.00
Ribbed Pillar, pk & wht spatter 175.00
Ring & Ribs, milk glass w/HP decor 125.00
Ring Neck, cranberry satin spatter 175.00
Snail 85.00
Spanish Lace, cranberry opal 295.00
Spanish Lace, vaseline opal 245.00
Venetian Diamond, cranberry 225.00
Windemere Fan, peach bloom w/HP floral 275.00
Windows, bl opal 295.00

Sunderland Lustre

Sunderland lustre was made by various potters in the Sunderland district of England during the 18th and 19th centuries. It is characterized by a splashed-on application of the pink lustre, which results in an effect sometimes referred to as the 'cloud' pattern. Some pieces are transfer printed with scenes, ships, florals, or portraits.

Bowl, hunt scenes, blk transfer w/mc pnt & pk lustre, 8½" 200.00
Jar, Sailor's Farewell, blk transfer w/mc enamel, 5½", EX 150.00
Pitcher, Crimea w/verse, blk transfer, mc trim, 7½" 330.00
Pitcher, Ship Caroline/Shipright Arms, blk transfer, 11½" 140.00
Plaque, Best of All God Is w/Us, blk transfer, 5¾x6¾" 285.00
Plaque, He That Believeth..., blk transfer, 5¾x6¾" 300.00
Plaque, In Memory of...1853, brn enamel inscription, 7⅝x8½" ..550.00
Plaque, Prepare To Meet..., blk transfer, mc Gabriel, 8x8¾" 415.00
Plate, fluted rim, Staffordshire, 6¾" 68.00

Surveying Instruments

The practice of surveying offers a wide variety of precision instruments primarily for field use, most of which are associated with the recording of distance and angular measurements. These instruments were primarily made from brass; the larger examples were fitted with tripods and protective cases. These cases also held accessories for the instruments, and these can sometimes play a key part in their evaluation. Instruments in complete condition and showing little use will have much greater values than those that appear to have had moderate or heavy use. Instruments were never polished during use, and those that have been polished as decorator pieces are of little interest to most avid collectors. Our advisor for this category is Dale Beeks; he is listed in the Directory under Idaho.

Alidade, coast survey-style high post; Buff & Buff, 1930s, M 325.00
Alidade, explorer's, W&LE Gurley, 1945, 8¾" scope, 4" dia 150.00

Chain, gunter's, Am, 4-pole, swivel hdl, 100 links, 1900s **200.00**
Chain, link; J Chesterman England, brass, ca 1900, NM **225.00**
Clinometer, W&LE Gurley, mahog/brass, 2¼" level vial, '20s **300.00**

Vernier compass, W. & L.E. Gurley, Troy, New York, brass, in labeled wooden case, $600.00.

Compass, Charles Heffricht Phila, dry card, 1840s, EX in box ...**350.00**
Compass, dip; W&LE Gurley Troy NY, brass, mid-1800s, 4¾" ..**285.00**
Compass, JR Cameron...Liverpool, dry card, wooden bowl, 6½" ..**250.00**
Compass, LJ Harri Amsterdam, flat top, 9½", EX in box **325.00**
Compass, vernier, Keuffel & Esser NY & Chicago, ca 1894, 4½" ..**550.00**
Compass, W&LE Gurley NY, brass, ca 1910, 3½" needle **325.00**
Compass, Wm J Young, 1870s, 15½" mahog case **865.00**
Dial/clinometer, miner's, unmk European, 1800s, brass, 9½" **225.00**
Level, dumpy, CL Berger & Sons, 1930s, 14" scope, 7" vial **200.00**
Level, dumpy, Dietzgen Chicago, 1950s, 18" scope, 7" vial **150.00**
Level, dumpy, Kolesch & Co NY, 1 post, 1920s, 11½" scope **175.00**
Level, precision; CL Berger & Sons, ca 1945, 17¾" scope **300.00**
Level, Stadia hand; Keuffel & Esser, 1920, 10½" scope **250.00**
Level, wye, Blunt & Co NY, 1880s, 18" external scope, 9" vial ..**400.00**
Level, wye, engineer's, F Eckle, 1880s, 17" scope, 9" vial **350.00**
Level, wye, engineer's, R Witcomb Cinci, 1855, 15" scope **475.00**
Level, wye, Kolesch & Co NY, 1900s, 18" scope, 8" vial **225.00**
Level/transit, AS Aloe MO, 1930s, 11¾" scope, 3½" **375.00**
Theodolite, balloon; Keuffel & Esser NY, 1930s, 10" scope **225.00**
Theodolite, FE Brandis...NY, CI & brass, 11" oval, EX in box .**1,200.00**
Transit, AS Aloe MO, 1900s, 8½" scope, 5" compass, 6½" **250.00**
Transit, Buff & Buff, 1930, 11½" scope, 6¼", EX **375.00**
Transit, CL Berger & Sons, 1942, 9¾" scope, 5½" **300.00**
Transit, engineer's, Keuffel & Esser, A fr, 1911, 6¼" **550.00**
Transit, engineer's, W&LE Gurley, 1890s, 11" scope, 4½" dia ...**500.00**
Transit, FE Brandis Sons, 1900s, 10" scope, 5" vial, 6¼" **750.00**
Transit, Hellgate; W&LE Gurley, truss fr, 1926, 8½" scope **275.00**
Transit, JW Queen Phila, 1870s, 10½" scope, 6¾" **500.00**
Transit, Keuffel & Esser NY, ca 1890, 10" scope, 6", EX **550.00**
Transit, Keuffel & Esser NY, ca 1924, 11¼" scope, 6¼" **400.00**
Transit, W&LE Gurley NY, ca 1929, 9¾" scope, 5" vial, +box ..**225.00**
Transit, W&LE Gurley NY, 1920s w/1916 truss fr, 6¼" vial **300.00**
Transit, WF Holzke NY, ca 1875, 9½" scope, 4¼" vials **700.00**
Transit, Young & Sons Phila, ca 1899, 10" scope, 6" **400.00**

Swarovski Crystal

The Swarovski family has been perfecting the glassmaker's art in Wattens, Austria, since 1895. Collectible figurines and desk items were introduced in 1977, and the Swarovski Collectors Society (SCS) was created in 1987. Featuring lead content of 30%+, these 'Silver Crystal' limited edition decorative accessories have attracted a following of over 200,000 dedicated collectors worldwide. Some designs were distributed regionally, making persuit of retired items an interesting challenge that spans the globe. Most items have an etched mark on the underside. The first mark was a block-style SC. In 1989 the mark was changed to a Swan. Marks on larger items also include the name Swarovski. SCS figurines are further identified with the year and designer's initials. The periodical *Swan Seekers News*, published by Maret Webb, our advisor for this category, is available if you want more information about retired Swarovski items. Her address is listed in the Directory under Arizona. Prices listed below reflect the presence of complete original packing and enclosures, without which prices are compromised 10% to 35%.

Bear, Giant; #7637nr112, 4½" **1,300.00**
Bear, King Size; #7637nr92, 3¾" **1,100.00**
Bear, Mini; #7670nr32, 1⅛" **100.00**
Cat, Med; metal tail, #7634nr52, 2" **300.00**
Gold Hummingbird, #7552nr100 ....**900.00**
Hedgehog w/silver whiskers, #7630nr30, 1¼" **360.00**
Hedgehog w/silver whiskers, #7630nr60, 2⅜" **360.00**
Pig, Lg; #7638nr65, 1¾" L **200.00**
Rhodium Hummingbird, #7552nr200 ....**2,000.00**
Swan, Mini; #7658nr27, 1" **100.00**
1981 Christmas ornament **325.00**
1987 'Togetherness' the Lovebirds, #do1x861 ....**3,500.00**
1988 'Partnership' the Woodpeckers, #do1x881 (w/mirror) **1,200.00**
1988 Cactus SCS renewal gift **150.00**
1989 'Armour' the Turtledoves, #do1x891 ....**700.00**
1990 'Lead Me' the Dolphins, #do1x901 ....**1,000.00**
1990 Orlando 'Dumbo,' blk eyes, clear hat, #7640nr100 ....**950.00**
1991 'Care for Me' the Seals, #do1x911 ....**360.00**
1992 'Save Me' the Whales, #do1x921 ....**330.00**
1993 'Inspiration Africa' the Elephant, #do1x931 ....**480.00**

Swastika Keramos

Swastika Keramos was a line of artware made by the Owens China Co., of Minerva, Ohio, around 1902-04. It is characterized either by a coralene type of decoration (similar to the Opalesce line made by the J.B. Owens Pottery Company of Zanesville) or by the application of metallic lustres, usually in simple designs. Shapes are often plain and handles squarish and rather thick, suggestive of the Arts and Crafts style.

Pitcher, gold tone, 10½" **375.00**
Vase, curdled wht on gold irid w/gr, hdls, #706E, 8" **150.00**
Vase, floral, red & gr w/blk on copper irid, 8" **300.00**
Vase, gold veins on glossy wht w/gr, appl coralene, hdls, 8" **160.00**

Syracuse

Syracuse was a line of fine dinnerware and casual ware which was made for nearly a century by the Onondaga Pottery Company of Syracuse, New York. Early patterns were marked O.P. Company. Collectors of American dinnerware are focusing their attention on reassembling some of their many lovely patterns. In 1966 the firm became officially known as the Syracuse China Company in order to better identify with the name of their popular chinaware. Many of the patterns were marked with the shape and color names (Old Ivory, Federal, etc.), not the pattern names. By 1971 dinnerware geared for use in the home was discontinued, and the company turned to the manufacture of hotel, restaurant, and other types of commercial tableware. Our advisor for this category is Mary Delucchi; she is listed in the Directory under California.

Arcadia, bowl, vegetable; w/lid **88.00**
Arcadia, cake plate, hdls **48.00**
Arcadia, cream soup w/underplate **32.00**

Arcadia, cup & saucer, demitasse 30.00
Arcadia, plate, dessert; 7⅛" 18.00
Arcadia, plate, dinner; 9¾" 26.00
Arcadia, plate, salad; 8" 16.00
Arcadia, platter, 12" 45.00
Arcadia, platter, 14" 57.50
Arcadia, rim soup 26.00
Avalon, cream soup & underplate, gold trim 32.00
Avalon, cup & saucer, gold trim 32.00
Avalon, plate, bread & butter; gold trim 16.00
Avalon, plate, dinner; gold trim, 10¼" 25.00
Bombay, bowl, fruit; gold trim 20.00
Bombay, bowl, vegetable; gold trim, w/lid 98.00
Bombay, chop plate, gold trim 87.50
Bombay, cup & saucer, gold trim 30.00
Bombay, gravy boat, gold trim 67.50
Bombay, plate, bread & butter; gold trim 16.00
Bombay, plate, dinner; gold trim 26.00
Bombay, platter, gold trim, 14" 42.50
Bombay, platter, gold trim, 16" 65.00
Bombay, teapot, gold trim 98.00
Bracelet, gravy boat, w/underplate 98.00
Bracelet, plate, dinner; 9¾" 40.00
Bracelet, plate, salad 26.00
Bracelet, platter, 14" 75.00
Briarcliff, bowl, cereal 32.00
Briarcliff, bowl, fruit 20.00
Briarcliff, creamer 32.00
Briarcliff, cup & saucer 30.00
Briarcliff, plate, dessert; 7⅛" 17.50
Briarcliff, plate, dinner; 10" 27.50
Briarcliff, sugar bowl 37.50
Carvel, bowl, vegetable; oval 42.00
Carvel, platter, 14" 67.50
Carvel, sugar bowl, w/lid 37.50
Diane, bowl, vegetable; rnd 130.00
Diane, plate, dinner 67.50
Gardenia, bowl, cereal 27.50
Gardenia, plate, dinner 27.50
Gardenia, plate, luncheon 22.00
Governor Clinton, bowl, cereal 20.00
Governor Clinton, cream soup & underplate 22.50
Jefferson, bowl, vegetable; w/lid 98.00
Jefferson, chop plate 88.00
Jefferson, cup & saucer 32.00
Jefferson, plate, dinner; 10¼" 30.00
Jefferson, plate, salad; 8" 20.00
Jefferson, platter, 12" 67.50
Jefferson, rim soup 26.00
Jefferson, teapot 98.00
Lady Mary, bowl, fruit 20.00
Lady Mary, creamer 32.00
Lady Mary, plate, salad; 8" 20.00
Lady Mary, platter, 12" 57.50
Lady Mary, platter, 14" 67.50
Lady Mary, platter, 8" 32.00
Lady Mary, sugar bowl 36.00
Lyric, bowl, fruit 22.00
Lyric, cup & saucer 32.00
Lyric, plate, dinner 26.50
Lyric, plate, salad 22.00
Lyric, rim soup 27.50
Meadow Breeze, bowl, vegetable; rnd 88.00
Meadow Breeze, cup & saucer 40.00

Meadow Breeze, plate, dinner 37.50
Meadow Breeze, plate, salad 26.00
Meadow Breeze, platter, 14" 127.50
Meadow Breeze, sugar bowl, w/lid 57.50
Minuet, cup & saucer 32.50
Minuet, plate, dinner 36.00
Queen Anne, cup & saucer 67.50
Queen Anne, plate, salad; sq 37.50
Sharon, bowl, fruit 20.00
Sharon, bowl, vegetable; oval, 10" 47.50
Sharon, creamer 32.00
Sharon, cup & saucer 30.00
Sharon, plate, salad 17.50
Sharon, platter, 14" 47.50
Sharon, sugar bowl 37.50
Sherwood, bowl, vegetable; oval 47.50
Sherwood, cup & saucer 30.00
Sherwood, gravy boat 67.50
Sherwood, plate, dinner 32.00
Sherwood, platter, 12" 45.00
Sherwood, platter, 14" 65.00
Sherwood, platter, 16" 77.50
Stansbury, bowl, fruit 20.00
Stansbury, bowl, vegetable; oval, 10½" 55.00
Stansbury, bowl, vegetable; oval, 9¼" 47.50
Stansbury, creamer 32.50
Stansbury, cup & saucer 37.50
Stansbury, plate, dinner 25.00
Stansbury, platter, 14" 65.00
Stansbury, sugar bowl 37.50
Suzanne, bowl, vegetable; oval 67.50
Suzanne, cup & saucer 37.50
Suzanne, plate, bread & butter 17.50
Suzanne, plate, dinner 32.50
Suzanne, plate, salad 20.00
Whitby, cake plate, 1 hdl 65.00
Whitby, cup & saucer 30.00

Syrups

Values are for old, original syrups. Beware of reproductions! See also various manufacturers and specific types of glass. Our advisor is Jeff Bradfield; he is listed in the Directory under Virginia.

Alba, milk glass, HP lav florals 80.00
Baby Invt T'print, gr 125.00
Banded Portland, pk stain 375.00
Brittanic, amber stained 325.00
Broken Column 125.00
Button Arches, ruby stained 225.00
Chrysanthem Base Swirl, bl opal 285.00
Coin Spot, bl opal, bulbous (+) 145.00
Coin Spot, bl opal, 9 Panel 240.00
Coin Spot & Swirl, bl 150.00
Coin Spot & Swirl, clear opal 90.00
Cone, pk cased 250.00
Cord Drapery, amber 350.00
Currier & Ives, amber 185.00
Daisy & Button, bl, pewter top 175.00
Daisy & Fern, bl opal, bulbous (+) 225.00
Feather, gr 350.00
Flat Flower, bl 325.00
Florette, pk cased satin 225.00

Flower Mold, bl 495.00
Grape & Leaf, gr opaque 250.00
Guttate, pk cased (+) 290.00
Heart w/T'print, pewter top 100.00
Herringbone, gr 495.00
Hobbs Optic, rubena 235.00
Invt T'print, amber, pinched base 175.00
Invt T'print, bl, Hobbs 140.00
Invt T'print, rubena 285.00
Michigan, pewter top 125.00
Reverse Swirl, bl opal 295.00
Thousand Eye, amber 80.00
Torpedo, ruby stained 220.00
Wildflower, bl 315.00

Tamac Pottery

At the close of World War II, finding jobs almost nonexistent for homecoming military men, Leonard Tate and Allen Macauley decided to take advantage of an offer made by the state of Oklahoma who was trying to encourage industry by offering free factory sites for new businesses. Their wives had both worked as designers for same company, so the foursome decided to combine efforts and past experiences and thus formed 'Tamac' pottery, a conglomeration of the two last names.

The company was organized in September 1946, in Henry and Zoma Tate's garage, (Leonard Tate's parents) in Perry, Oklahoma; production was very limited. They expanded in 1948 and were able to produce over three hundred pieces of earthenware daily.

The Tates and Macauleys were directly responsible for all phases of Tamac production: designing and making the molds, mixing the Oklahoma and Kansas clays, final processing, and shipping. They had customers in every state as well as foreign countries, and they operated an outlet store as well.

About seventy various pieces of Tamac pottery were produced, mainly buffet/dinnerware. Other 'specialty' pieces included candle holders, ashtrays, vases, and table centerpieces. One of their most popular sellers was the barbeque line, designed for casual entertaining and backyard dining. It consisted of tray-like plates with unique coffee mugs having non-traditional handles.

Six colors were produced, each with a 'frosted' rim of a different color. The six colors were: Frosty Pine, Avocado, Frosty Fudge, Honey, Raspberry, and Butterscotch. The Frosty Pine and Avocado (both with dark green bases) are the most readily available. Few items, mainly 'specialty' pieces, were manufactured in Raspberry.

In 1950 the Macauleys sold their shares to the Tates. The business expanded and by 1952 required bank financing which proved impossible to obtain. As a result, the plant was sold in September of that year to Earl, Raymond and Bettye Bechtold. (Earl was a brother to Zoma Tate.) With only eight employees, the pottery produced about 250,000 pieces a year, shipping their product to ten states and four foreign countries, those being Canada, Australia, Germany, and Belgium. Most of their sales, however, were made at the plant itself. The motto of the pottery was 'See it Made'.

Raymond Bechtold was the active manager of the business and added more than thirty-five pieces to the line, among them the juice pitcher and juice glasses, breakfast plate and mug, covered casserole, decanter and goblet set, teapot, demitasse line, chocolate pitcher, and bud vase. These items are now among the most sought after. Bechtold also experimented with new colors in the accessory and floral lines such as Raspberry, Sky Blue, and Bronze. Only Raspberry was popular, and the others were quickly phased out.

Raymond Bechtold assumed full control of the pottery in 1960 and operated it until February, 1965, when he sold it to Mrs. Lenita Moore.

Mrs. Moore's mother had been a long-time employee of the plant and was the active manager. The pottery operated until 1970 when it closed and the final auction was held. The building still stands and is used for storage.

Tamac pottery can easily be identified by its unique design and the stamp on the bottom of each piece: 'TAMAC Perry, Okla USA.' Some earlier pieces carry the etched 'TAMAC' mark.

Our advisors for this category are Bob and Dondee Klein. They are listed in the Directory under Oklahoma.

Ashtray, bridge 8.00
Ashtray, Oklahoma 15.00
Ashtray, rnd 15.00
Ashtray, 3-corner 8.00
Bird, 3-dimensional, any color, ea 30.00
Bowl, centerpc; dish garden 20.00
Bowl, centerpc; S-shape 17.50
Bowl, serving; 2-qt 18.00
Bowl, serving; 4-qt 30.00
Butter dish, no lid 9.00
Candle holder, dbl 25.00
Candle holder, single 18.00
Casserole, w/lid, 2-qt 30.00
Chocolate pot, tall & thin 55.00
Coffee cup, hdls 5.00
Coffee mug, w/finger insert 9.00
Creamer, demitasse 10.00
Creamer, 8-oz 8.00
Cup, demitasse 12.00
Decanter, wine; w/stopper 60.00
Goblet, wine; 6-oz 13.00
Pitcher, juice; 24-oz 15.00
Pitcher, 2-qt 25.00
Pitcher, 4-qt 35.00
Planter vase, no tray, 5x6" dia 20.00
Planter vase, w/tray & drain hole 15.00
Plate, barbeque; 15" 12.00
Plate, dinner; 10" 8.00
Platter, turkey; 18" 35.00
Saucer 3.00
Saucer, demitasse 7.00
Shakers, pr 10.00
Spoon holder 15.00
Sugar bowl, demitasse 10.00
Sugar bowl, w/lid 10.00
Teapot, short & squat 50.00
Toothpick holder 7.00
Tumbler, juice; 4-oz 10.00
Tumbler, 16-oz 8.00
Vase, free-form, 5½" 25.00
Violet planter, w/tray & drain hole 17.00
Wall vase/pocket, 5" 12.50

Target Balls

Prior to 1880 when the clay pigeon was invented, blown glass target balls were used extensively for shotgun competitions. Approximately 2¾" in diameter, these balls were hand blown into a three-piece mold. All have a ragged hole where the blowpipe was twisted free. Target balls date from approximately 1840 (English) to World War I, although they were most widely used in the 1870-1880 period. Common examples are unmarked except for the blower's code — dots, crude numerals, etc. Some balls are embossed in a dot or diamond pattern so they were more likely to shatter when struck by shot, and some have names and/or patent dates. When evaluating condition, bubbles and other minor manufacturing imperfections are acceptable; cracks are not. The prices below are for mint condition examples.

Amber w/emb ribs, horizontal or vertical	150.00
Bogardus' Glass Ball Pat'd April 10 1877, amber, Am	350.00
Bogardus' Glass Ball Pat'd April 10 1877, other than amber, Am	800.00
CTB Co, blk pitch, Pat dates on bottom, Am	250.00
Dmn Quilt w/plain center band, ground top, Am	150.00
Dmn Quilt w/shooter emb in 2 panels, clear, English	300.00
Dmn Quilt w/shooter emb in 2 panels, gr or purple, English, ea	300.00
For Hockey's Pat Trap, gr, English	500.00
Great Western Gun Works, Pittsburgh, amber, Am	900.00
Gurd & Son, London, Ontario, amber, Canadian	500.00
Ilmenau (Thur) Sophiehutte, amber, Dmn Quilt, Germany	425.00
Ira Paine's Filled Ball Pat Oct 23 1877, amber, Am	250.00
Ira Paine's Filled Ball Pat Oct 23 1877, other than amber, Am	800.00
NB Glass Works Perth, other than pale gr, English	200.00
NB Glass Works Perth, pale gr, English	100.00
Plain, amber w/mold mks	65.00
Plain, clear w/mold mks	1,000.00
Plain, cobalt w/mold mks	150.00
T Jones, Gunmaker, Blackburn, pale bl, English	150.00
WW Greener, St Mary's Works, various colors, English, ea	250.00

Related Memorabilia

Trap, DUVROCK, with black pitch birds, $150.00.

Ball thrower, dbl; old red pnt, ME Card, Pat...78, 79, VG	900.00
Clay birds, Winchester, Pat May 29 1917, 1 flight in box	100.00
Pitch bird, blk DUVROCK	1.00
Shell, dummy, w/single window, any brand	35.00
Shell, dummy shotgun, Winchester, window w/powder, 6"	125.00
Shell set, dummy, Gamble Stores, 2 window shells, 3 cut out	125.00
Shell set, dummy, Winchester, 5 window shells	175.00
Shell set, dummy shotgun, Peters, 6 window shells+full box	175.00
Shotshell loader, rosewood/brass, Parker Bros, Pat 1884	50.00
Target, Am sheet metal, rod ends mk Pat Feb 8 '21, set	25.00
Target, blk japanned sheet metal, Bussy Patentee, London	50.00
Target, BUST-O, blk or wht breakable wafer	20.00
Trap, MO-SKEET-O, w/birds	150.00

Tea Caddies

Because tea was once regarded as a precious commodity, special boxes called caddies were used to store the tea leaves. They were made from various materials: porcelain, carved and inlaid woods, and metals ranging from painted tin or tole to engraved silver. Our advisor for this category is Tina Carter; she is listed in the Directory under California.

Amboyna wood, Sheraton, canted corners, 7½"	350.00
Burl veneer w/inlay & ivory escutcheon, brass ball ft, 17½"	210.00
Burl w/ivory bands, Regency, swollen sides, dome lid	990.00
Burl walnut Regency, sarcophagus shape, banded inlay, 6x8"	595.00
Burl walnut w/kingwood banding, flat lid/sides, Victorian, 9"	175.00
China, genre scenes HP on wht, 6x4x3"	125.00
Chinoiserie lacquer w/gilt, lead insert, 8½", EX	300.00
Figured mahog veneer Hplwht, ivory inlay escutcheon, 14"	315.00
Figured wood w/2 inner compartments & mixing bowl, 13¾"	575.00
Fruitwood, England, 1800s, rpl knop, 4¾"	350.00
Mahog case, fitted tole int, 5½x10x5¾", EX	200.00
Mahog sarcophagus shape w/ivory escutcheon & beads, Regency	250.00
Mahog veneer w/inlay, brass escutcheon, rpl ft, 10¾"	195.00
Mahog w/satinwood inlay & ivory escutcheon, 7¼"	200.00
Pearlware, comic English figures, 4-color, no lid, 5¼"	95.00
Rosewood veneer, dbl int lids, 10" L, EX	215.00
Silver, bright cut, octagonal w/rampant lion finial, 1870	2,000.00
SP, Oriental decor, ball ft, Acme SP Co, EX	150.00
Tortoise, fluted sq-center sunburst on front, dome lid, 7"	1,100.00
Tortoise, MOP inlay, serpentine front, 8"	1,400.00
Tortoise, rnded corners, ivory bun ft, 1850s, 5x6¾"	2,300.00

Tea Leaf Ironstone

Tea Leaf Ironstone became popular in the 1880s when middle-class American housewives became bored with the plain white stone china that English potters had been exporting to this country for nearly a century. The original design has been credited to Anthony Shaw of Longport, who decorated the plain ironstone with a hand-painted copper lustre design of bands and leaves. Originally known as Lustre Band and Sprig, the pattern has since come to be known as Tea Leaf Lustre. It was produced with minor variations by many different firms both in England and the United States. By the early 1900s, it had become so commonplace that it had lost much of its appeal.

Items marked Red Cliff are reproductions made from 1950 until 1980 for this distributing and decorating company of Chicago, Illinois. Hall China provided many of the blanks.

Bone dish, scalloped, Meakin	65.00
Bowl, crimped edge, Wilkinson, 3⅜x9½" sq	67.50
Bowl, sauce; Adams Micratex, 5½"	7.50
Bowl, sauce; scalloped, sq, gold lustre, Powell Bishop, 4½"	12.00
Bowl, sauce; simple, sq, Meakin, 4¼"	14.00
Bowl, vegetable; Cable style, w/lid, Burgess	175.00
Bowl, vegetable; Fish Hook, ftd, w/lid, Meakin, 11x7"	175.00
Bowl, vegetable; Fish Hook, w/lid, Meakin 10½" dia	175.00
Bowl, vegetable; medallion finial & hdl, Mellor-Taylor	165.00
Bowl, vegetable; Pagoda hdl, ridged, sq, w/lid, Wedgwood	195.00
Bowl, vegetable; Ribbed Pagoda, 8-sided, w/lid, 7x11"	225.00
Bowl, vegetable; Sunburst shape, ftd, w/lid, Shaw, 5½x11½"	225.00
Butter dish, Fish Hook, no drain, Meakin	125.00
Butter dish, Fish Hook, w/drain, Meakin	150.00
Butter dish, simple, no drain, Wedgwood, 5½" sq	150.00
Butter dish, simple, w/drain, Wedgwood, 5½" sq	165.00
Butter dish, vertical ribs w/leaf finial, sq, Mellor-Taylor	140.00
Butter pat, Meakin, 2¾" sq	15.00
Butter pat, unmk, 2¾"	12.50
Cake plate, 8-sided, Adams Micratex, 11⅛x8¾"	50.00
Coffeepot, Bamboo, Meakin, 9"	195.00
Creamer, Adams Micratex, 3"	55.00
Creamer, Bamboo, Meakin, 6½"	150.00
Creamer, Morning Glory, Elsmore & Forster	275.00
Creamer, plain, rnd, Meakin, 5¾"	155.00

Cup & saucer, Adams Micratex 25.00
Cup & saucer, Chelsea type, Johnson Bros, 2⅝", 3½" 75.00
Cup & saucer, Fish Hook, Meakin, 2¼", 3½" 75.00
Cup & saucer, handleless; Meakin, 3", 3½" 95.00
Cup & saucer, Meakin, 3", 3½" 75.00
Cup & saucer, Morning Glory, Var Portland, Elsmore & Forster ..140.00
Cup & saucer, Shaw, 3⅛", 3½" 75.00
Cup & saucer, Square Ridged, Wedgwood 75.00
Cup plate, unmk, 3½" 55.00
Gravy boat, Fish Hook, Meakin, w/underplate, 2¾x8" ...75.00
Gravy boat, simple, sq, unmk 45.00
Pitcher, milk; Bamboo, Meakin, 7½" 295.00
Plate, Adams Micratex, 6⅛" 7.00
Plate, Chinese Pattern, Shaw, 7⅜" 17.50
Plate, Chinese Pattern, Shaw, 9½" 30.00
Plate, Cloverleaf Variant, gold lustre, unmk Bridgewood, 4⅝" 15.00
Plate, gold lustre variant, Bufords Porc, 7½" 12.00
Plate, Meakin, 10" 35.00
Plate, Meakin, 6¾" 10.00
Plate, Meakin, 8" 12.00
Plate, Mellor-Taylor, 9" 20.00
Plate, Morning Glory, Portland shape, Elsmore & Forster, 7" 37.50
Plate, soup; flanged, Meakin, 8¾" 30.00
Plate, Wedgwood, 9" 20.00
Plate, Wheat, w/lustre, Elsmore & Forster, 7¾" 24.00
Plate, Wilkinson, 8" 22.00
Platter, oval, Wilkinson, 11" 45.00
Platter, rectangular, Meakin, 12¾x9⅛" 55.00
Platter, rectangular, Meakin, 14x10" 55.00
Platter, ribbed, rectangular, Wedgwood, 12" 60.00
Platter, Wedgwood, 13x9½" 60.00
Sauce boat, medallion finial, bracket ft, Mellor-Taylor, lid & tray .245.00
Shaving mug, Meakin, 3¼x3½" 175.00
Shaving mug, 12-sided, Shaw 195.00
Sugar bowl, Bamboo, w/lid, Grindley 85.00
Sugar bowl, Fish Hook, w/lid, Meakin, 7" 85.00
Sugar bowl, gold lustre, w/lid, unmk 48.00
Sugar bowl, Lily of the Valley, Shaw, 5½x6½" 145.00
Sugar bowl, Morning Glory, Elsmore & Forster 225.00
Sugar bowl, w/lid, Adams Microtex, 5" 60.00
Teapot, Chinese shape, Shaw, 10" 345.00
Teapot, Morning Glory, Elsmore & Forster 375.00
Toothbrush holder, Meakin, 5" 185.00
Toothbrush holder, Mellor-Taylor 165.00
Tray, service; Anthony Shaw, pierced hdls 125.00
Tureen, sauce; Bamboo, Meakin, +lid/ladle/underplate ..375.00
Wash set, Lily of the Valley, Shaw, pitcher & bowl+5 pcs 1,200.00

Teapots

The custom of drinking tea has resulted in the production of many tea-related collectibles; the most popular is the teapot. The first teapots were manufactured in the Chinese village of Yixing during the late 16th century and were no bigger than the tiny cups previously used for tea drinking. Amazingly these same tiny teapots are still being used today.

A wide range of teapots can be found by the avid searcher; those most readily available today were produced from about 1870 to the present. Almost every pottery and porcelain manufacturer in Europe as well as in America have produced teapots. Some are purely functional, others decorative and whimsical. Refer to various manufacturers' names for further listings. Our advisor for this category is Tina M. Carter, listed in the Directory under California. Her book, *Teapots*, is available at bookstores or direct from the author.

Franciscan, U.S.A., Tiempo shape, ear-shaped handle, 1947, $50.00.

Automobile, gr glaze, no mk, 8" L 300.00
Barge, brn, emb mk, S Derbyshire, England, lg 75.00
Barge, raised floral design on brn, 'A Present...,' 1800s, 10" 1,000.00
Bone china, bl/wht/gold, SYP, Wedgwood, England, ca 1905-06 .125.00
Brn earthenware, Sadler, England, floral & gold decor 45.00
Buff sharkskin, tan, slip decor, unmk Japan, ca 1920 ....32.00
Bunny, mk England, ca 1960, 6-cup 45.00
Cat figural, paw spout, blk/gray/cream, US Zone Germany, 9" 45.00
Charles & Diana, brn pottery, Wales CM, 2½" 78.00
China, bees/leaves on cream, bee finial, Occupied Japan, 6x5" 38.00
China, dk brn w/gold floral & beadwork, Tunstall England, 6x9" ..32.00
Copper, ball ft, Art Deco style, China 38.00
Dbl spout, earthenware, slip decor, ca 1890 ....85.00
Dmn shape, brn w/HP flowers in formal rows, England, #405097 .35.00
Dog figural, sitting on haunches, upraised legs form spout 45.00
Elf figural, HP, label E&R, Western Germany 45.00
Ellgreave, Wood & Sons, England, ironstone w/floral 35.00
Fitz & Floyd, Christopher Columbus, ltd ed, recent 90.00
Flow bl, man seated, legs outstretched, conical hat, 8x9" 50.00
Gr lustre, HP, Royal Hanover, Germany, 6½" 75.00
Horizontal lines, bulbous, Susie Cooper, England 65.00
HP decor, mk Wade, +matching cr/sug 55.00
HP floral, Bonn, Germany, 4-cup 45.00
Iced Tea dispenser, brn, USA, 2-pc 175.00
Jasperware, bl/wht, Wedgwood, dtd 20th C, 6-cup 190.00
John Bull figural, wht porc 90.00
Lipton's, oval & ribbed, Fraunfelter, ca 1930 ....35.00
Ming Tea Co, Made in Japan, w/label, 1½-cup 18.00
Pyrex mk, blown glass, etched flowers, 6-cup 48.00
Rococo style, HP gold, appl flowers, mk Italy, 10" 38.00
Rudolph the Red Nosed Reindeer, Japan, +cr/sug 65.00
Snow White w/Dwarfs, musical, Walt Disney Productions 50.00
Souvenir, cobalt, Washington DC, Germany, mini 28.00
SP, Sheffield, England, electro-plated nickel silver, wood hdl 40.00
Spode's Tower, bl/wht transfer, London shape, England, VG 45.00
Tank, gr w/silver details, Made in England, 8½" L 200.00
Tea for Two, man in tux hdl, girl in gown forms pot, Japan 45.00
Torquay, scene & motto, Watcombe, England, 1½-cup 45.00
Weller, majolica, wooded scene, mk USA, ca 1930, VG 48.00
WWII, Esc to US by Royal Navy or Allied Fleets, brn, England ..38.00

Teco

Teco artware was made by the American Terra Cotta and Ceramic Company, located near Chicago, Illinois. The firm was established in 1886 and until 1901 produced only brick, sewer tile, and other redware. Their early glaze was inspired by the matt green made popular by Grueby. 'Teco Green' was made for nearly ten years. It was similar to Grueby's yet with a subtle silver-gray cast. The company was one of the first in the United States to perfect a true crystalline glaze. The only decoration used was through the modeling and glazing techniques; no hand painting was attempted. Favored motifs were naturalistic leaves and flowers. The company broadened their lines to include garden pottery and faience tiles and panels. New matt glazes (browns, yellows, blue, and rose) were added to the green in 1910. By 1922 the artware lines were discontinued; the company was sold in 1930.

Values are dictated by size and shape, with architectural and organic forms being more desirable. Teco is usually marked with a vertical impressed device comprised of a large 'T' to the left of the remaining three letters.

Ashtray, gr, crimped rim, Gates design, 4½" dia 250.00
Bookends, Rebecca at the Well, brn/ivory on gr, 7", NM 475.00
Bowl, gr, shallow w/recessed incurvate rim, 1¾x8½" 325.00
Bowl, gr, shallow w/4 broad ft, Mundie design, 10" 750.00
Bowl, gr w/gun metal, strong twisting leaves mold, 2½x9" 850.00
Bowl vase, gray, 3-ftd, Albert design, 3x7" 300.00
Charger, gr, emb monogram, Gates design, #501, 10½" 500.00
Figurine, pelican on base, sgn 295.00
Inkwell, gr, dome w/sm opening, #128, 2¼x3" 225.00
Jardiniere, gr, bowl form w/3 lg buttress ft, Mundie, 8x10" 3,250.00
Pitcher, gr, concave sides, vine hdl emerges from rim, 9" 800.00
Pitcher, gr, lg integral hdl, 4x5" 300.00
Vase, caramel & red crystalline, stick neck, #2919/93, 5½" 375.00
Vase, gr, bulbous bottom, Gates design, 4" 400.00
Vase, gr, buttress hdls on classic form, tiny rpr, 7" 850.00
Vase, gr, classic shape, #660, 26x12" 3,750.00
Vase, gr, classic shape w/ribbing, #356, 4x4" 375.00
Vase, gr, cylindrical w/2 full-length buttresses, 7" 750.00
Vase, gr, flaring form w/full-length vertical hdls, rpr, 11" 1,100.00
Vase, gr, hdls at rim issuing from ea of 4 sqd panels, 9" 3,000.00
Vase, gr, long rim-to-shoulder hdls, #283, 9½x5" 750.00
Vase, gr, ovoid w/flared rim & closed angle hdls, 6½" 900.00
Vase, gr, ovoid w/short neck, #166C, 5½x3¼" 475.00
Vase, gr, short flared lip, closed sqd hdls, Gates design, 6" 1,000.00
Vase, gr, tapered top, bulb bottom, #205, rpr lip, 10x9" 700.00
Vase, gr, 2 integral rim-to-width hdls, F Albert #283, 9½" 750.00
Vase, gr, 4 curving rim-to-low width buttresses, rstr, 12x5" 750.00
Vase, gr, 4 full-length buttresses, Gates #436, 7x2½" 1,100.00
Vase, gr, 4 integral rim-to-width hdls, #297A, 6x9" 2,600.00
Vase, gr, 4 open buttresses, #403, base chip, 8x6" 1,200.00
Vase, gr crystalline, bulbous base, concave cylinder, 13" 900.00
Vase, gr crystalline, ribbed bulb bottom, 7-point rim, 10x8" ...1,800.00
Vase, gr w/charcoal, tapered w/4 buttresses, 10x4", EX 1,600.00
Vase, gr/blk mottle, triangular w/flat shoulder, 7¾" 1,300.00
Vase, gray, cylindrical w/ring neck, Gates design, 6" 260.00
Vase, leathery gr, 3 3-leaf rtcl in bulb bottom, ftd, 9" 1,000.00
Vase, leathery gray, dbl-gourd w/4 buttress hdls, 6½" 1,250.00
Vase, lt gr, buttressed floriform, Moreau design, 11½" 1,200.00
Vase, lt pk, ovoid w/sqd buttress ea side, Gates #427, 5½" 600.00
Vase, rose, tulip in 4 upright buttresses, #423, rpr, 12" 800.00
Vase, taupe speckled, ruffled neck, bulbous bottom, 5x4" 375.00

Teddy Bear Collectibles

The story of Teddy Roosevelt's encounter with the bear cub has been oft recounted with varying degrees of accuracy, so it will suffice to say that it was as a result of this incident in 1902 that the teddy bear got his name. These appealing little creatures are enjoying renewed popularity with collectors today. To one who has not yet succumbed to their obvious charms, one bear seems to look very much like another. How to tell the older ones? Look for long snouts, jointed limbs, large feet and felt paws, long curving arms, and glass or shoe-button eyes. Most old bears have a humped back and are made of mohair stuffed with straw or excelsior. Cute expressions, original clothes, a nice personality, and, of course, good condition add to their value. Steiff bears in mint condition may go for a minimum of $100.00 per inch (for a small bear) up to $200.00 per inch (for one 20" high or larger). These are easily recognized by the trademark button within the ear. For further information we recommend *Teddy Bears, Annalee's & Steiff Animals*, by Margaret Fox Mandel, available from Collector Books. See also Toys, Steiff.

Key: jtd — jointed

Bears

Light golden mohair, shoe-button eyes, hump, felt pads, ca 1906, 16", EX, $1,000.00; Blond mohair, shoe-button eyes, hump, worn fur, replaced pads, ca 1906, 13", $250.00; Golden mohair, shoe-button eyes, hump, felt pads, slightly worn fur, ca 1906, 15", $950.00; Cinnamon plush, shoe-button eyes, hump, worn fur, replaced pads, ca 1910, 14", $550.00.

Alpha Farnell, long mohair, glass eyes, 1920s, 14", NM 1,850.00
Am, beige mohair, long snout, glass eyes, early, 11", EX 345.00
Am, Hecla, wht mohair, ca 1907, 14", EX 1,250.00
Berg, gold acrylic plush, heart medallion, tag, 3½" 65.00
Chad Valley, gold mohair, rexine pads, 14½", M 375.00
Clemmons, yel mohair, felt pads, glass eyes, growler, 15", VG 350.00
English, Pooh bear, gold, flat feet, glass eyes, 18½", NM 1,400.00
German, brn mohair, glass eyes, pnt details, 1927, 15", EX 350.00
German, gold mohair w/lg ears & eyes, orig pads, 17", EX 1,400.00
German, gold plush, glass eyes, 20", NM 265.00
German, gray mohair w/cotton print body, glass eyes, 10" 250.00
German, growler, bl mohair, felt pads, 19" 300.00
German, growler, short mohair, cloth pads, glass eyes, 19" 200.00
German, wht mohair, plastic brads on outside, 5", EX 65.00
Hermann, frosted mohair, open mouth, 1940s, 21", NM 265.00
Hermann, growler, beige mohair, glass eyes, 1940-50, 14", EX ...200.00
Hermann, growler, brn short mohair, glass eyes, 1940s, 20", EX .400.00
Hermann, growler, frosted mohair, shaved snout, 1930s, 16", EX .415.00
Hermann, orange mohair, long snout, straw filled, 14", NM 200.00
Hermann, sleepy, on tummy, red collar, glass eyes, 9", M 195.00
Hermann, wht cotton plush, inset snout, ca 1940s, 15", EX 265.00
Ideal, gold mohair, twill nose, button eyes, 1910, 20", M 400.00
Ideal, gold mohair, twill nose, glass eyes, 1920s, 18", EX 375.00
Knickerbocker, blond/gold long mohair, glass eyes, 12", EX 250.00
Knickerbocker, brn mohair, glass eyes, 1940s, 14", NM 250.00
Knickerbocker, brn mohair, inset snout, on all 4s, 9x13", M 350.00
Knickerbocker, cinnamon fur, tin eyes w/decals, 15", M 415.00
Schuco, Bellhop, yes/no, button eyes, orig suit, '20s, 14", NM ..3,750.00
Schuco, blond mohair, glass eyes, flat cb ft, 14", EX 665.00

Schuco, fully jtd, brn mohair, metal eyes, orig ribbon, 4", M **385.00**
Schuco, fully jtd, gold mohair, 3" **275.00**
Schuco, fully jtd, gold mohair over metal, 2½", M **250.00**
Schuco, fully jtd, gold mohair over metal, 5", NM **350.00**
Schuco, fully jtd, wht, metal eyes, 1950s, 2½", M **265.00**
Schuco, fully jtd, wht mohair, cb ft, 1940s, 25", EX **1,375.00**
Schuco, gray mohair w/sheared cream snout, glass eyes, 14", M .**850.00**
Schuco, music yes/no, curly hair, 1940s, 24", EX **3,000.00**
Schuco, Tricky, yes/no, w/tag & ribbon, 21", NM **2,350.00**
Schuco, yes/no, lt tan mohair, US Zone, 12", M **975.00**
Steiff, bl collar w/bell, w/button & tag, 6", M **275.00**
Steiff, caramel mohair, red tag/orig ribbon, 5½", M **260.00**
Steiff, cinnamon mohair, button eyes, w/button, '05, 20", EX .**2,500.00**
Steiff, curly cinnamon mohair, 1905, 20", EX **2,500.00**
Steiff, fully jtd, beige mohair, no ID, 3½", NM **185.00**
Steiff, gold mohair, button eyes, 1908, 20", M **2,500.00**
Steiff, gold mohair, glass eyes, w/button/tag, '10s, 24", EX **3,000.00**
Steiff, gold mohair, orig red ribbon, 1940s, w/button, 11", M **495.00**
Steiff, gold mohair, w/button, 1950s, 13", M **665.00**
Steiff, vanilla mohair w/long snout, button eyes, 1904, 17", NM .**2,750.00**
Steiff, wht fluffy mohair, w/button, 1950s, 21", M **2,250.00**
Steiff, wht long mohair, w/button, ca 1907, 14", EX **1,700.00**
Steiff, wht mohair, w/tag, 1950s, 13", M **875.00**

Telephones

Since Alexander Graham Bell's first successful telephone communication, the phone itself has undergone a complete evolution in style as well as function. Early models, especially those wall types with ornately carved oak boxes, are of special interest to collectors. Also of value are the candlestick phones from the early part of the century and any telephone-related memorabilia.

American Electric, candlestick, dial type, rstr, working **225.00**
American Telecom, 1972, EX **40.00**
Automatic Electric, beige, 3-slot pay phone, 1950s, EX orig **150.00**
Bell System, candlestick, operator's issue **90.00**
Cradle style, off-wht plastic, 1930s, 6x8x5" **100.00**
Kellogg, oak, wall type, EX **235.00**
Leich, wall phone, crank type, complete, EX orig **225.00**
North Electric, Cleveland, oak, wall type **265.00**
Stromberg-Carlson Mfg, candlestick **100.00**
Table model, golden oak w/glass panel, 40", EX orig **2,600.00**
Utica Fire Alarm, candlestick, NP brass **200.00**
Western Electric, brass, candlestick style, 1904 ....**175.00**
Western Electric, brass, candlestick w/dial **240.00**
Western Electric, Model AA1, w/dial, subset, EX **500.00**
Western Electric, wall type, space saver, non-dial, 1920s **35.00**
Western Electric, walnut, wall type, 2-box, 1890s, EX **600.00**

Blue Bell Paperweights

First issued in the early 1900s, these bell-shaped glass weights were used as giveaways and by telephone company executives to prevent stacks of papers from blowing off their desks in the days of overhead fans. Over the years they have all but vanished — some taken by retiring employees, others accidently broken. The weights came to be widely used as advertising by individual telephone companies; and as the smaller companies merged to form larger companies, more and more new weights were created. They were widely distributed with the opening of the first transcontinental telephone line in 1915. The weight embossed 'Opening of Trans-Pacific Service, Dec. 23, 1931,' in peacock blue glass is very rare, and the price is negotiable. In 1972 the first Pio-

neer bell paperweights were made to sell to raise funds for the charities the Pioneers support. This has continued to the present day. These bell paperweights have also become 'collectibles.' For further study we recommend *Blue Bell Paperweights, 1992 Revised Edition*, by Jacqueline Linscott; she is listed in the Directory under Florida.

Bell System C&P Telephone Co & Associated..., ice bl **225.00**
Bell System New York Telephone Co, peacock **125.00**
Bell System the Central District & Printing..., peacock **400.00**
Missouri & Kansas Telephone Co, peacock **100.00**
Pacific Bell, crystal w/old cobalt bl bell glass in center **50.00**
Pays 7% Mountain States Telephone, peacock **175.00**
Southwestern Telegraph & Telephone, peacock **300.00**
Telephone Pioneers of America-1994, red **40.00**
The Southwestern Telegraph & Telephone Company, cobalt ...**375.00**

Related Memorabilia

Sign, Alberta Government Telephones, blue and white double-sided porcelain, wooden frame, 21x21", $300.00.

Directory, New England, 1907 ....**30.00**
Sign, Bell Telephone, porc, 5x20", M **175.00**
Sign, Public Telephone, 11x11" **85.00**
Sign, Public Telephone System, flanged, 18x18" **100.00**
Sign, Southwestern Bell Business Office, porc, flanged, M **350.00**
Sign, Telephone Office, porc, EX **135.00**
Switchboard, Western Electric, 1-operator, ca 1930, 57x27x35" ..**100.00**

Telescopes

Antique telescopes were sold in large quantities to sailors, astronomers, voyeurs, and the military, but survive in relatively few numbers because their glass lenses and brass tubes were easily damaged. Even scarcer are antique reflecting telescopes, which use a polished metal mirror to magnify the world. Telescopes used for astronomy give an inverted image, but most old telescopes were used for marine purposes and have more complicated optics that show the world right-side up. Spyglasses are smaller, hand-held telescopes that collapse into their tube and focus by drawing out the tube to the correct length. A more compact instrument with three or four sections is also more delicate, so sailors usually preferred a single-draw spyglass. They are almost always made of brass, though nickel silver or silverplate was used on occasion. They're usually covered with leather, or (less often) rosewood veneer. Solid wood barrel spyglasses (with a brass draw tube) tend to be early and rare. Before the middle of the 1800s, makers put their names in elaborate script on the smallest drawtube, but as 1900 approached, most switched to plain block printing. British instruments from WWI are commonly found by a variety of makers but sharing a format of a 2" objective, 30" length with three draws extended, a tapered main tube, and sometimes low- and high-powered oculars and a beautiful leather case. U.S. Navy WWII spyglasses are quite common but nevertheless have outstanding optics. They focus by twisting the eyepiece, a feature which makes them weatherproof. The Quartermaster (Q.M.) 16x spyglass is 31" long, with a tapered barrel, and a 2½" objective. The Officer of the Deck (O.D.D.) has a 23" cylinder with a 1½" objective. Very massive, short, brass telescopes are usually gunsights or ship equipment and have little interest to most collectors. World War II marked the first widespread use of coated optics, which can be recognized by a colored film on the objective lens. Collectible post-WWII telescopes include early refractors by Unitron or Fecker and reflectors by Cave or Questar. Modern spotting scopes often use a prism to erect the image and are of great interest if made by the best makers, two of which are Nikon and Zeiss. Several modern makers still use lacquered brass, and many replica instruments have been reproduced.

A telescope with no maker's name is much less interesting than a signed instrument, and 'Made in France' is the most common mark on old spyglasses. Dollond of London made instruments for 200 years, making theirs possibly the most common name on antiques. Because of their important technical innovations and very high quality, Dollond telescopes are always valuable. Bardou, Paris, is another relatively common name; they were a prolific maker for many years, making telescopes of very high quality that were sold through Sears. Alvin Clark and Sons were the most prolific early American makers, from the 1850s to the 1920s, and their astronomical telescopes are of great historical import.

Spyglasses are delicate instruments that were subject to severe use under all weather conditions. Cracked or deeply scratched optics are impossible to repair and lower the value considerably. Most lenses are doublets, two lenses glued together, and deteriorated cement is common. This looks like crazed glaze and is fairly difficult to repair. Dents in the tube and damaged or missing leather covering can usually be fixed. The best test of a telescope is to use it; the image should be sharp and clear. Accessories, eyepieces, erecting prisms, or quality cases can add significantly to value. The following prices assume that the telescope is in very good to fine condition. We give the objective lens (obj.) diameter, which is the most important measurement of a telescope.

Our advisor for this category is Peter Abrahams, who studies and collects telescopes and other optics. Please contact him, especially to exchange reference material. Mr. Abrahams is listed in the Directory under Oregon.

Key:
obj — objective lens   ODD — Officer of the Deck

Bardou & Son, Paris, 4-draw, 50 mm obj, leather cover, 36" 220.00
Bausch & Lomb, 1-draw, 45 mm obj, wrinkle pnt, 17" 90.00
Brashear, 3½" obj, brass, tripod, w/eyepieces 3,800.00
Cary, London (script), 2" obj, tripod, w/3 eyepieces 2,200.00
Clark, Alvan, 4" obj, iron mt on wood legs, 48" 4,000.00
Dallmeyer, London (script), 2½" obj, SP, 5-draw, 49" 450.00
Dolland, London (script), 2-draw, 2" obj, leather cover 160.00
Dollond, London (block), 2-draw, 2" obj, leather cover 220.00
Dollond, London (script), 2-draw, 2" obj, leather cover 300.00
Dollond, London (script), 3" obj, brass, 40", on tripod 2,500.00
France or Made in France, 30 mm obj, 3-draw, lens cap 80.00
McAlister (script), 3½" obj, brass, 45", tripod 3,000.00
Mogey, 3" obj, brass, 40", on tripod, w/4 eyepieces 2,000.00
Queen & Co (script), 70 mm obj, 6-draw, wood veneer, 50" 650.00
Questar, 3½" dia reflecting, on astro mt, 1950s 1,200.00
Short, James; 3" dia reflecting, brass cabriole tripod 2,500.00
Tel Sct Regt Mk 2 S, many maker's names, UK WWI 120.00
Unitron, 4" obj, wht, 60", on tripod, many accessories 1,800.00
US Navy, Bu Ships, Mk II, 10-Power, 1943, ODD 80.00
US Navy, Quarter Master Spyglass, 16X, Mk II, in box 220.00
USN Quarter Master Mk II, 16 power, 31", EX in box 275.00
Vion, Paris, 40 Power, 3-draw, 40 mm obj, leather cover, 21" 95.00
Wollensak Mirroscope, 1950s, 2" dia, 12" L, leather case 150.00
Wood bbl, rnd taper, 1½" obj, signed, 1800s 300.00
Wood bbl, 8-sided, 1½" obj, 1700s, 30" 1,500.00

Zeiss Asiola, 60 mm obj prism spotting scope, pre-WWII 450.00

Televisions

Many early TVs have escalated in value in the last few years. Pre-1943 sets (usually with only one to five channels) are often worth $500.00 to $5,000.00. Unusually styled small-screen wooden 1940s TVs are 'hot'; but most metal, Bakelite, and large-screen sets are still shunned by collectors. 1950s color TVs with 16" or smaller tubes are valuable; larger color sets are not. Our advisor for this category is Harry Poster; author of *Poster's Radio & Television Price Guide 1920-1990, 2nd Edition*; he is listed in the Directory under New Jersey.

Admiral, #17T11, Bakelite 7" tabletop, 1948 ....100.00
Air King, A-1001, 10" wide console, 1949 ....100.00
Andrea, C-VK12, continuous tuner to right, 12" console 100.00
Arvin, #2160, simple console version of #2161, 1950 ....25.00
Automatic, TV-1649, sq lines, 1950, 16" 50.00
Bendix, #2001, rnded corners, 1950, 10" tabletop 100.00
CBS-Columbia, #23C59, console w/dbl doors 25.00
Crosley, #9-403, continuous tuner to left, 10" tabletop 60.00
DuMont, RA-102, Club, pnt tabletop w/12" screen behind doors ..200.00
Emerson, #644, porthole-look screen, 12" tabletop 75.00
Fada, S-1030, wooden tabletop, 1950 ....35.00
General Electric, #801, 10" console w/AM radio, 1947 ....125.00
General Electric, HM-226, 5-channel tuner, prewar, 12" 4,000.00
Hallicrafters, #860, 15" combination w/dbl doors, 1950, lg 50.00
Motorola, #21C2, wooden 21" with 4 spindle legs 25.00
Motorola, #7-TV2, 7" Bakelite tabletop, 1948 ....65.00
National, TV-1601, 16" simple-style tabletop, 1949 ....50.00
Olympic, TV-928, 10" mirror-in-lid type w/phonograph/radio ...100.00
Philco, #49-1280, wooden 12" w/dbl doors, 1949, lg 50.00

Raytheon/Belmont, #7DX22-P, 1948, 7", $150.00.

Raytheon/Belmont, M-1101, 12" porthole-look tabletop, 1949 .100.00
RCA, TRK-12, 12" mirror-in-lid console, w/radio, 1939 ....3,000.00
Silvertone, #133, 12" wooden console w/pull-out phonograph 50.00
Sparton, #4941, 10" mahog tabletop, 1949 ....100.00
Stromberg-Carlson, TC-125-HM, wooden 12" tabletop 125.00
Tele-Tone, TV-300, blk Bakelite 10" tabletop, 1950 ....100.00
Videodyne, #10TV, wooden 10" tabletop, 13-channel tuner 275.00
Westinghouse, H-610, 10" tabletop, 4 knobs, 1948 ....65.00
Zenith, #28T96, 16" porthole-look screen 75.00
Zenith, G-2322, brn Bakelite tabletop, 12" screen, 1950 ....65.00

Teplitz

Teplitz, in Bohemia, was an active art pottery center at the turn of the century. The Amphora Pottery Works was only one of the firms that operated there. (See Amphora.) Art Nouveau and Art Deco styles were favored, and much of the ware was hand decorated with the primary emphasis on vases and figurines. Items listed here are marked 'Teplitz' or 'Turn,' a nearby city. Our advisor for this category is Jack Gunsaulus; he is listed in the Directory under Michigan.

Bowl, irises/whiplash hdls, rtcl, wht/gold/blk/gr, ftd, 13" **1,300.00**
Vase, abstract, bl/rose/gr irid, ovoid, 6" **200.00**
Vase, appl nude boy & girl on lustre w/vintage, Wahliss, 10" ..**1,050.00**
Vase, Arab w/sword, HP, Stellmacher, 7¾" **230.00**
Vase, bees/purple flowers on gilt rtcl hdls, slim neck, 11" **450.00**
Vase, emb Nouveau lady's head, branch hdls, Crownoakware, 13" ..**375.00**

Vase, girl stringing flowers on white, RS&K Teplitz, 7", $750.00.

Vase, gold spider web on cobalt, rtcl top & hdl, 20" **750.00**
Vase, lady's portrait on gr-gold w/cobalt, red mk, 6¾" **300.00**
Vase, leaf swags, geometric hdls, rtcl neck, mc, #d, 5x6" **270.00**
Vase, mother & child portrait on gr w/gold, 7x4" **325.00**
Vase, night scene, gr on bl, HP gold bees, gourd form, 6" **300.00**
Vase, Nouveau lady's profile on gr w/gold, prof rpr, 18" **950.00**
Vase, Nouveau lady/landscape, much gold, swirl mold, 7x6" ...**1,400.00**
Vase, profile of girl, bk: scene, gilt, tulip neck, 6" **550.00**
Vase, stylized tree form, emb lav leaves on gold, 10x6" **200.00**
Vase, trees w/emb red mushrooms, rtcl top w/gold, ovoid, 6" **550.00**
Vase, 2-sided scenic in triangular panels, #635, 5½x5½" **400.00**

Terra Cotta

Terra cotta is a type of earthenware or clay used for statuary, architectural facings, or domestic articles. It is unglazed, baked to durable hardness, and characterized by the color of the body which may range from brick red to buff.

Bust, boy & girl on single base, sgn/#d, Fr, 1925, 11¾x10" **195.00**
Figure, calvaryman on horsebk, sgn T Howard, blk pnt, 23" **400.00**
Figure, hunter in loincloth, mk India, 9¼" **95.00**
Umbrella stand, emb dragons w/gilt, 24" **72.50**

Thermometers

Few objects man has invented have been so eloquently expressed both functionally and artistically as the ubiquitous thermometer. Developed initially by Galileo as a scientific device, thermometers slowly evolved into decorative objets d'art, functional household utensils, and eye-catching advertising specialties. Most American thermometers manufactured early in the 20th century were produced by Taylor (Tycos), and today their thermometers remain the most plentiful on the market. Decorative thermometers manufactured before 1800 are now ensconced in the permanent collections of approximately a dozen European museums. Because of their fragility, few devices of this era have survived in private collections. Nowadays most antique thermometers find their way to market through estate sales.

Insofar as sheer beauty, uniqueness, and scientific accuracy, decorative thermometers are far superior to the ordinary and inexpensive versions which carry advertising. Decorative thermometers run the gamut from plain tin household varieties to the highly ornate creations of Tiffany and Bradley and Hubbard. They have been manufactured from nearly every conceivable material — oak, sterling, brass, and glass being the favorites — and have tested the artistry and technical skills of some of America's finest craftsmen. Ornamental models can be found in free-hanging, wall-mounted, or desk/mantel versions. The largest collection of decorative thermometers — some 600 specimens — is housed at the Thermometer Collectors Club of America headquarters in Sacramento, California.

Thermometer prices are based on age, ornateness, and whether mercury or alcohol is used as the filler in the tube. A broken or missing tube will cut at least 40% off the value. (Only one company in the world makes replacement tubes.) A magnificent Tiffany custom-made thermometer mounted on a 30" elephant tusk set on a silver pedestal recently sold at a Christies' auction for $18,400.00. Virtually all American-made thermometers available today as collectors' items were made between 1875 and 1940. The Golden Age of decoratives ended in the early 1940s as modern manufacturing processes and materials robbed them of their natural distinctiveness.

Key:
br — brass	pmc — permacolor
F&C — Fahrenheit & Celsius	R&C — Reamer & Celcius
F&R — Fahrenheit & Reamer	sc — scales
hyg — hygrometer	stl — stainless
mrc — mercury	

Alexandre, desk, scimitar figural, brass sc/mrc, 9" **430.00**
Anonymous, cvd wood squirrel, glass R sc, mrc, 1905, 10" **625.00**
Anonymous, desk, alabaster w/eagle, br R&C sc, mrc, 1895 ....**875.00**
Anonymous, desk, brass conquistador figural, brass sc/mrc **430.00**
Anonymous, desk, love scene, silver metal, br R&C sc, mrc, 8" .**830.00**
Anonymous, pendant, sterling case, ivory F sc, mrc, 1880, 5" .**1,250.00**
Anonymous, wall, giltwood fr, ivory, F sc, mrc, 1790, 10x3½" ...**3,100.00**
Blk/Starr/Frost, desk, barometer, stl, F&C, mrc, '10, 11" **2,200.00**
Carpenter & Westley, desk, ivory w/glass dome mrc, 1880, 6" ...**950.00**
Casella London, wall, maxi/minimum, 2 units, wood, plastic sc .**400.00**
Cheshire Silversmiths, desk, br candelabra, mrc, 1875, 10" **4,500.00**
Chevallier, L'ingre, wall, ivory/mahog, R&C sc, 1880, 11x3" .**2,350.00**
Clark, desk, ivory ped, crown, mrc, 1904, 7" **400.00**
Cloister, inkwell, stl bk & base w/angels at side, 1901 ....**1,050.00**
CW Wilder...NH, bear & billboard br figural, mrc, 6½" **525.00**
Desk, cvd walrus tusk, 2-tier disk base, inlay sc, 1860, 9" **430.00**
Dixey of London, wall, wood, F sc, mrc, 1900, 9" **350.00**
Dixie, W (London); desk, gilt/br, Gothic, SP sc, mrc, 8" **790.00**
Dollard London, hanging, mahog fr, sterling sc/mrc, 1810, 18" ...**4,600.00**
Dollard of London, wall, mahog, F sc, mrc, 1860, 12" **4,500.00**
Dring & Fage, desk, marble, ivory sc, mrc, 1880, 6" **1,500.00**
Dring & Fage, wall mahog, porc F sc, mrc, 1860, 28x5" **2,500.00**
Farley, travel, walnut base mt, ivory F&C sc, mrc, 5" **900.00**
Gilbert & Co, travel, silver eng sc, mrc, 1850, 8" **630.00**
Gloucester Scientific, sterling case, glass front, pmc, 42" **1,600.00**
Heath & Wing, figural calendar, br w/porc sc, mrc, 1870 ....**1,000.00**
Moreau, desk, mahog, R&C sc, spiral tube, mrc, 1860, 6½x5½" .**1,725.00**
Pairpoint, desk, sterling picture fr, mrc, 1907, 5" **600.00**
Rowley & Sons, travel, ivory sc, mrc, 1894, 4", +case **350.00**

Somalvico, Jos; desk, figural, flared base, br sc, mrc, 10" **650.00**
Taylor, ped, br, 3-sided, F sc, alcohol, 1900, rare, 6" **3,200.00**
Taylor Castle St, wall mahog, sterling F sc, mrc, 1860, 12" **4,100.00**
Tiffany, amber glass w/grapes, gold mt, brass/mrc, '06, 8x12" ..**2,400.00**
Tiffany, desk, elephant tusk, sterling F sc, mrc, 1890, 33" **18,400.00**
Tiffany, gr glass w/pine needles, brass sc/mrc, '02, 8x12" **2,800.00**
Tiffany & Co, desk, sterling, br sc/mrc, 1900, rare, 3x5" **1,600.00**
Wall, Fr gilt, wood fr, silver eng, F&R sc, mrc, 1776, 10x14" ..**3,600.00**
West, desk, Gothic design, br, 1900, 12" **1,360.00**
Whitehead & Hoag, Lambrecht's Polymeter, wall, mrc, 9" **890.00**
Wise, desk, Tunbridge, twin columns, mrc, 1870, 5" **1,750.00**

1000 Faces China

So named because of its many hand-painted faces, much of this chinaware was made during the '30s through the '50s (some even earlier). Though many pieces are unmarked, others are marked 'Made in Japan.' There are two primary patterns, 'Black Face' and the 'Gold' pattern, and variations exist. Both designs employ many colors. Dinner plates usually are decorated with an outer-most 'ring of color' (two or three hues) containing a simple design which is often flowers. The inner ring is usually comprised of many colors radiating from the center circle which may be done in a primary color (red, for instance) with a design such as a dragon or clouds painted in gold. 'Black Face' is distinguishable by its range of colors — primarily red, white, and yellow with some green and blue — and the black hand-painted faces. The 'Gold' pattern is also multicolored but is dominated by the gold throught the design, and the faces themselves are gold as well. Other variations include '1000 Men in Robes' and '1000 Faces' with black or blue rims on the saucers and cups. These pieces seem to be very scarce. In the listings that follow, all items are marked 'Made in Japan' (MIJ) unless noted otherwise. Our advisor for this category is Suzi Hibbard; she is listed in the Directory under California.

Cup & saucer, blk faces **40.00**
Cup & saucer, demitasse; gold **25.00**
Cup & saucer, gold **35.00**
Plate, blk, 10" **45.00**
Plate, 6" **10.00**
Shakers, pr **18.00**
Snack set, 8½" L **45.00**
Soup set, blk faces, 3-pc **75.00**
Sweetmeat set, gold, 15-pc, serves 6 ....**150.00**
Sweetmeat set, w/lacquer box, 6", 5-pc **75.00**
Tea set, blk faces, 15-pc, serves 6 ....**150.00**
Tea set, gold, 15-pc, serves 6 ....**125.00**
Teapot, gold, dragon spout, 7" **50.00**

Tiffany

Louis Comfort Tiffany was born in 1848 to Charles Lewis and Harriet Young Tiffany of New York. By the time he was eighteen, his father's small dry goods and stationery store had grown and developed into the world-renowned Tiffany and Company. Preferring the study of art to joining his father in the family business, Louis spent the next six years under the tutelage of noted artists. He returned to America in 1870 and until 1875 painted canvases that focused on European and North African scenes. Deciding the more lucrative approach was in the application of industrial arts and crafts, he opened a decorating studio called Louis C. Tiffany and Co., Associated Artists. He began seriously experimenting with glass, and eschewing traditionally painted-on details, he instead learned to produce glass with qualities that could sug-

gest natural textures and effects. His experiments broadened, and he soon concentrated his efforts on vases, bowls, etc., that came to be considered the highest achievements of the art. Peacock feathers, leaves and vines, flowers and abstracts were developed within the plane of the glass as it was blown. Opalescent and metallic lustres were combined with transparent color to produce stunning effects. Tiffany called his glass Favrile, meaning handmade.

In 1900 he established Tiffany Studios and turned his attention full time to producing art glass, leaded-glass lamp shades and windows, and household wares with metal components. He also designed a complete line of jewelry which was sold through his father's store. He became proficiently accomplished in silverwork and produced such articles as hand mirrors embellished with peacock feather designs set with gems and candlesticks with Favrile glass inserts.

Tiffany's work exemplified the Art Nouveau style of design and decoration, and through his own flamboyant personality and business acumen he perpetrated his tastes onto the American market to the extent that his name became a household word. Tiffany Studios continued to prosper until the second decade of this century when due to changing tastes his influence began to diminish. By the early 1930s the company had closed.

Serial numbers were assigned to much of Tiffany's work, and letter prefixes indicated the year of manufacture: A-N for 1896-1900, P-Z for 1901-1905. After that, the letter followed the numbers with A-N in use from 1906-1912; P-Z from 1913-1920. O-marked pieces were made especially for friends of relatives; X indicated pieces not made for sale.

Our listings are primarily from the auction houses in the East where Tiffany sells at a premium. All pieces are signed unless noted otherwise.

Glass

Basket, Yel Pastel w/vertical leaves, in hdld fr #516, 7" **770.00**
Bowl, butterscotch opal w/raised Dmn Quilt, pastel ft, 6" **575.00**
Bowl, cobalt irid, low ped ft, 3x11½" **1,045.00**
Bowl, feathers, gold on dk bl irid, early, no mk, 4x6" **600.00**
Bowl, gold, emb ribs, 2x6½" **250.00**
Bowl, gold, ribbed, ruffled, 2x4" **250.00**
Bowl, gold, scalloped leaf form, 3½x10" **750.00**
Bowl, gold, vertical ribs, 4x10¾" **1,000.00**
Bowl, gold w/red highlights, ruffled, 5", +underplate **475.00**
Bowl, Gr Pastel, feathered ribs in wht, 4x12" **650.00**
Bowl, nut; gold, scalloped, 2¾" **175.00**
Candlesticks, gold cup/shaft in 3-strap bronze ft, 10", pr **5,500.00**
Compote, cobalt irid, stretched edge, shallow bowl, 6½x5" **880.00**
Compote, gold, flared rim & ft, 3¾x8" **770.00**
Compote, gold irid w/stretch at rim, 3x5¼" **425.00**
Compote, Yel Pastel, feathered ribs in wht, 8½x9" **1,100.00**
Cordial, amber irid, 4¾", set of 6 ....**800.00**
Cordial, gold, pinched sides, 1¾" **250.00**
Creamer, Gr Pastel, crystal hdl, base flake, 5" **150.00**
Decanter, amber w/2 gold irid borders, 11", EX **550.00**
Finger bowl, gold w/platinum highlights, 2x4", +underplate **260.00**
Finger bowl, Pk Pastel, 5" **375.00**
Finger bowl, purple & gr irid, plain, +underplate **325.00**
Plaque, bl/purple irid, stretch edge, no mk, 10½" dia **225.00**
Plate, gold, pulled design underneath, 5½" **110.00**
Plate, Gr Pastel, 8½" **190.00**
Plate, Optic Rib, deep bl w/wht center, sgn, 7" **375.00**
Plate, pk w/opal star center, 10¾", pr **425.00**
Salt cellar, bl-gold, tooled design, spherical, 2" **275.00**
Shade, feathers, gr/gold on opal, 5½x3¾" **800.00**
Shade, feathers, gr/gold on yel opal, 4½x7½", EX **1,050.00**
Sherbet, gold, Prince style, flared/shallow bowl, 3½", 6 for **935.00**

Toothpick holder, bl irid base, gold cup, 1⅞" 285.00
Toothpick holder, gold irid, dimpled sides, 1¾" 225.00
Tumbler, mirror lustre, dimpled sides, sgn, 2¼", pr 275.00
Vase, abstract floral, gr/gold/copper w/red irid on turq, 6" 6,500.00
Vase, amber agate w/bl irid, appl twigs & berries, 2½" 2,640.00
Vase, amber w/gold irid, int spiral stripes, angle sides, 3¾" 660.00
Vase, Bl Pastel, ped ft, 2¾" 200.00
Vase, bl w/purple & gr irid, ribbed/elongated on ped ft, 9" 2,300.00
Vase, bl w/purple & gr irid, ribbed/pinched, irreg top, 4½" 1,400.00
Vase, brn/cream striped irid w/pk highlights, #7039H, 9½" 2,000.00
Vase, bubble stripes on purple-gr, tapered neck, #3611P, 4½" .5,000.00
Vase, bud; dk gr & gold irid, bronze base, 12" 550.00
Vase, cobalt irid, wide dimpled waist, 2½" 700.00
Vase, cvd leaves/vines, gr on gold w/pk & bl irid, 8½" 3,750.00
Vase, Cypriote, pitted/textured gold, long bottle form, 13" 4,400.00
Vase, drapes/swirls, wht/gr/gold irid EX highlights, 4x5" 2,100.00
Vase, emb florals on gold, bronze ft, sgn, 13" 1,175.00
Vase, feathers, bl/gr/irid on gr, wht cased, shouldered, 2" 900.00
Vase, feathers, gr on gold, wide flared & crimped top, 3⅕" 550.00
Vase, feathers, gr on pk & opal, ruffled goblet form, 14" 3,250.00
Vase, feathers, wht/gr on gold lily, bronze base #1043, 12" 850.00
Vase, feathers on gr/gold base, wht ruffle w/gold int, 5½x7" 1,200.00
Vase, floriform; feathers, gr/ivory, shaped cone body, 6" 2,200.00
Vase, floriform; feathers, shouldered cone, dome ft 17" 4,750.00
Vase, floriform; hearts/vines, #1515 9307M, 6" 1,500.00
Vase, floriform; leaves/stems in gr w/red cup, 12" 1,100.00
Vase, free-form; bl-gr, LCT V970, 4¾" 600.00
Vase, gold, flared rim, 3x4½" 375.00
Vase, gold, ftd trumpet form, sgn, 10" 990.00
Vase, gold, pulled hdls, 3½" 525.00
Vase, gold, wide classic form, 17", EX 2,970.00
Vase, gold translucent w/wht shoulder & lip, ftd/hdls, 2" 600.00
Vase, gold w/EX highlights, waisted/ribbed ftd trumpet, 8" 950.00
Vase, gold w/EX irid, classic form, #7082/1538, 13" 2,900.00
Vase, gold w/mc enameled base, trumpet form, mk, 16¼" 1,500.00
Vase, gold 10-ribbed blossom in artichoke bronze ft, 16" 1,100.00
Vase, ivory/lt gold w/bl & pk irid highlights, hdls, 3" 375.00
Vase, ivy, gr on gold, sgn, 5x5" 1,250.00
Vase, leaves/vines, gold on ivory, shouldered, 4x6" 1,700.00
Vase, leaves/vines in gr, wht/red millefiori, #R1210, 6½" 3,750.00
Vase, lg swirled shoulder band, silver on med bl irid, 5x4" 2,100.00
Vase, peacock bl irid, trumpet form, bronze base, 12" 600.00
Vase, peacock feathers on bl-gr, bulbed shoulder, 12½" 15,400.00
Vase, pulled 'Vs'/waves, purple/gr irid on gold, 6½" 2,800.00
Vase, Purple Pastel, clear base, trumpet form, 12" 1,500.00
Vase, swirls, wht/gr on gold/gr, bulb w/ringed neck, 4" 3,250.00
Vase, Tel El Amarna, can neck w/zigzag band, bulbous, 6x5" ..3,500.00
Vase, waves at top & base, gold/gr/opal, ribbed, 6x4½" 1,300.00
Vase, wavy band, gold on gold, U-form, 2½" 400.00
Vase, wavy shoulder band, gold on blk to bl lava, 3x4" 2,700.00
Vase, wht opal irid, pulled hdls, 2½" 625.00
Vase, yel/ivory, pulled hdls at width, ball form, 1½" 400.00
Vase, yel/orange mottle w/int crackled webbing, 5¾" 1,100.00
Vase, zippered ribs, lt bl gold on med bl, wht cased, 6" 5,000.00
Vase, 2 Egyptian-influence bands, bl/gr on blk irid, 8x6" 1,950.00

Lamps

Lamp prices seem to be getting stronger, especially for leaded lamps with lighter colors (red, blue, purples). Bases that are unusual or rare have brought good prices and added to the value of the more common shades that sold on them. Bases with enamel or glass inserts are very much in demand. Our advisor for Tiffany lamps is Carl Heck; he is listed in the Directory under Colorado.

Key: c-b — counter-balance

Desk lamp, green and white leaded glass shell-form shade; stylized, lobed base with twisted vine arms, stamped mark/monogram/#25890, 14¼", $8,800.00.

Base, floor, c-b, 5 tall slim ft, #468, 55", EX 1,600.00
Base, foliate molding/coiled wires, 3-socket, #S1550, 26" 4,950.00
Base, stick form on wide base, gr/brn patina, #581, 24", EX 1,750.00
Bridge, damascene 10" gold domical shade; harp base, 59" 4,000.00
Candle, bl-gr irid shade, gold column, swirl rib std, 14" 850.00
Candle, gold, feathered column, swirl rib std, sgn 2X, 12" 1,300.00
Candle, gold, honeycomb pattern, metal fitter, 13½" 1,450.00
Candle, gold, irid column, swirl rib std, 14½" 1,600.00
Candle, gold w/EX highlights shade & twisted base, 13" 1,200.00
Desk, bronze ½-cylinder Zodiac shade adjusts, 14", EX 1,600.00
Desk, damascene 8" gr/platinum shade; c-b 1-arm std #S207 ..2,800.00
Desk, damascene 9" shade w/cvd insects; #369 std, M 4,250.00
Desk, gooseneck w/feathered shade in gr/pearl, sgn 2X, 12x13" ..2,000.00
Desk, irid amber cased 7" dome shade; harp std, #419 base 2,250.00
Desk, linenfold amber 7½" shade; c-b #415 std, 15", EX 4,500.00
Desk, linenfold 12 panel gr shade; bronze std; #5-39524, 16" ..2,700.00
Desk, red-brn pulled feather bell shade; harp base #416, 12" ...2,000.00
Desk, rtcl-band 7" bronze shade; harp std, base #419, 13", EX .1,850.00
Desk, swirled 7" dome shade w/in harp std #418, 13½" 3,000.00
Floor, damascene 10" ribbed irid dome shade; 4-ftd harp std ...5,500.00
Floor, damascene 12" shade; 5-leg harp std, #423 base, 58" 6,500.00
Lily, 10-light, EX irid/sgn shades; lily-pad base #381, 22" 19,000.00
Lily, 12-light, all shades sgn; lily-pad base #382, M 16,100.00
Lily, 12-light, gold sgn shades; lily-pad base #382, 21", EX ...11,000.00
Lily, 18-light, ea sgn; on lily-pad base #383 ....32,000.00
Shade, candle lamp; feathers, gr on wht w/gold, 5" 900.00
Shade, feathers, dk gr on irid opal, 6x5¾" 700.00
Shade, feathers, gr on gold, 4¼x6¼" 900.00
Shade, feathers, gr on gold, 5¼" 500.00
Shade, feathers, red on glossy opal, LCT #0671, 4¼" 1,800.00
Shade, King Tut, silvery bl irid on gold, 4½" 750.00
Shade, ldgl, swirling leaves, 18" dia 5,500.00
Shade, yel & gold bronze pulled decor on yel, LCT #4103, 2¾" .250.00
Table, ldgl 14" daffodil shade; 3-leg fuel canister #26536 ....20,700.00
Table, ldgl 14" dogwood shade; 3-leg adjustable std #482 ....19,000.00
Table, ldgl 15" daffodil shade; gold dore std, 22", EX 8,000.00
Table, ldgl 16" acorn-band shade; 3-arm std #9916 ....5,500.00
Table, ldgl 16" acorn-band shade; 4-ftd leaf-emb #6847 std 6,000.00
Table, ldgl 16" crocus shade (EX); bronze Greek urn std 7,500.00
Table, ldgl 16" pansy shade; 3-arm std #580 w/favrile stems ..29,900.00
Table, ldgl 16" peacock shade; std #10976 w/favrile jewels ...66,300.00
Table, ldgl 16" tulip-cluster shade; std #6845 ....13,200.00
Table, ldgl 18" peony dome shade; std #357 ....37,500.00
Table, ldgl 20" Greek Key band cone shade; std #528 ....12,650.00
Table, ldgl 22" Greek Key band shade; ornate 6-ftd #550 std .17,600.00
Table, ldgl 22" tulip shade; Empire base #550 w/gr patina 65,200.00

Metal Work

Items are bronze unless noted otherwise.

Candlesticks, bronze with alligator finish, slender standard with acanthus leaves supporting candle cup with removable bobeche, marked, 10½", $1,380.00 for the pair.

Ash receiver, Artichoke, gold dore, #1651, 25" 800.00
Ash stand, glass liner in strapwork bowl, #1649, 28", EX 350.00
Ash stand, Nouveau design, match holder, insert, #2066, 29", G .500.00
Blotter ends, owl pattern, #1181, 19", pr 175.00
Bowl, gold dore w/etched fruit & flower band, MOP inset, 9" 150.00
Bowl, twisted wire trim, 5 enamel disks, 14", +undertray, EX 400.00
Box, flower forms/raised nodules w/in circle, #10031, 9x6" 650.00
Box, geometric, pk/red enamel on gold dore, #350, 2½x6½" 700.00
Box, stamp; 19th Century, gr/bl jewels, gold patina, #1624 ....900.00
Bud holder, 10 clear glass tubes in bronze base #721, 9", VG 450.00
Candlestick, cup in 3-stem cradle on 4 long curved legs, G 500.00
Candlestick, 2 jeweled cups on leaf base #6075, 3¾x7x8" 3,800.00
Candlesticks, fluted cup w/6-leaf support, #1210, 11", pr ...1,300.00
Candlesticks, jeweled cup, 3 4-toed ft, #1200, 12½", pr 3,750.00
Candlesticks, 4 curved legs, paw ft, sq base, #1201, 12", pr 1,035.00
Card receiver, gold dore, gr enamel, 8" 250.00
Clock, Grapevine, #2375, 10x6½x5¾" 2,700.00
Clock, Zodiac, hexagonal base, rnd face, #1075, 3x4½" 750.00
Compote, gold dore/mc enamel, rtcl flower hdls, #522, 12" 350.00
Desk set, Zodiac, letter rack/fr/2 boxes/calendar+2 pcs 1,150.00
Desk set, Zodiac, orig patina, inkwell/pen tray/blotter ends 425.00
Frame, dbl; Pine Needle, rnded corners, #954, 10x16" 2,875.00
Frame, Grapevine, #919, 14" 4,600.00
Frame, long amber glass segments in bronze, #54, 13" 4,300.00
Frame, Venetian, #5454, 12x9" 1,000.00
Frame, Zodiac, #912, 7x8", VG 500.00
Frame, Zodiac, #920, 14x12", EX 1,100.00
Frame, Zodiac, #942, 8" 865.00
Frame, 18k gold, line border, 11" 16,000.00
Humidor, cylindrical, #308, 3½", EX 150.00
Inkwell, allover butterflies, orange irid glass well, 3x5" 4,800.00
Inkwell, cvd/hammered Arts & Crafts motif, EX patina, #1112 .550.00
Inkwell, rtcl well blown w/gr glass, hinged, #27035, 4" 1,000.00
Paperweight, Boston Bulldog, gold dore 450.00
Paperweight, lion, gold dore, 5" L 700.00
Paperweight, setter, Shando 825.00
Plate, Moorish design, brn/red on gold dore, #1612A, 10" 200.00

Pottery

Bowl, dogwood blossoms on wht bsk, in-making rim chip, 2x5" .225.00
Vase, allover trumpet vines/leaves on gr gloss, rstr, 12" 1,100.00
Vase, antique gr/bl matt, 3 hdls above center width, 9", EX 550.00
Vase, bud; emb maple seed pods on mustard satin matt, 5¼" ..1,400.00
Vase, emb leaves on ivory, bulb w/can neck, hairline, 4¾" 1,000.00
Vase, leaves/vines relief, natural colors, squat base, 6" 500.00

Vase, lilies emb on gr mottle, waisted/incurvate, 15" 3,450.00

Silver

Asparagus dish, floral-cast ends, claw ft, w/liner, 13½" 2,300.00
Bowl, floral repousse, 3¼x8" 550.00
Bowl, rtcl twig-form base, Truex design, 26-oz 1,100.00
Box, cigarette; plain w/eng crest, 7½" 150.00
Cake basket, etched Regency decor, swing hdl, 10½" 750.00
Candle followers, w/linenfold shade, 5½", pr 625.00
Plate, 4 wreath reserves: couples/crests, 11", set of 6 ....3,700.00
Platter, Chrysanthemum, scratches/lt dent, 22" 5,200.00
Punch bowl, presentation, plain w/flaring ft, 10" 1,900.00
Roast platter, molded edge, 58-oz, 18" 1,300.00
Rose bowl, Regency style, SP liner/frog, monogram, 12" dia 935.00
Smoker's set, 8 rnd ashtrays & 8 match urns 150.00
Sweets tazza, ribbon/latticinio border, pr, 28-oz 1,485.00
Tazza, repousse floral, shell/scroll border, monogram, 3½" H 385.00
Tray, Chrysanthemum, monogram, scratches/dents, 13" 2,860.00
Tray, molded border, 28-oz, 13" dia 200.00
Tray, molded border, 74-oz, 18" 1,100.00
Vase, fluted rim, 1900, 9" 495.00
Vase, slim w/scroll hdls extending above rim, 18" 3,100.00
Wine, flaring w/slender knobbed stems, set of 12 ....985.00

Tiffin Glass

The Tiffin Glass Company was founded in 1887 in Tiffin, Ohio, one of the many factories composing the U.S. Glass Company. Its early wares consisted of tablewares and decorative items such as lamps and globes. Among the most popular of all Tiffin products was the black satin glass produced there during the 1920s. In 1959 U.S. Glass was sold, and in 1962 the factories closed. The plant was re-opened in 1963 as the Tiffin Art Glass Company. Products from this period were tableware, hand-blown stemware, and other decorative items.

Those interested in learning more about Tiffin glass are encouraged to contact the Tiffin Glass Collectors' Club, whose address can be found in the Directory under Clubs, Newsletters, and Catalogs. See also Black Glass; Glass Animals.

Bowl, Cherokee Rose, crimped rim, 12½" 75.00
Bowl, cream soup; Cadena 20.00
Bowl, cream soup; Fuchsia, #5831 ....30.00
Bowl, Fuchsia, #5902, 7¼" 30.00
Bowl, Twilight, ftd wishbone shape, 6½" 75.00
Candle holder, Juno, gr 32.50
Candlestick, Cadena, pk or yel, ea 32.50
Celery tray, June Night, 10½" 30.00
Champagne, Adam, pk 30.00
Champagne, Cherokee Rose, saucer type, 5½" 18.00
Champagne, Classic 22.50
Champagne, Flanders, saucer type 15.00
Champagne, June Night, #17403, 5½-oz 19.00
Champagne, Persian Pheasant, 5½-oz 21.00
Champagne, Shawl Dancer 42.50
Comport, Flanders, #5831, tall, 6¾" W 95.00
Cordial, #14199 Line 20.00
Cordial, #14199 Line, gr 30.00
Cordial, June Night, #17403, 1-oz 40.00
Creamer & sugar bowl, June Night 38.00
Cup, Cadena 25.00
Cup & saucer, Flanders, ftd 47.50
Cup & saucer, Fontaine, Twilight, blown 125.00

Cup & saucer, La Fleure, yel **45.00**
Goblet, cocktail; Cadena, pk or yel, 5¼", ea **25.00**
Goblet, water; Brookmar **24.00**
Goblet, water; Cadena, pk or yel, 7½" **35.00**
Goblet, water; Cerice, #3075 ....**24.00**
Goblet, water; Fairfax, platinum trim **18.00**
Goblet, water; Flanders **25.00**
Goblet, water; Flanders, pk **40.00**
Goblet, water; Fuchsia, 7½" **25.00**
Goblet, water; June Night **24.00**
Goblet, water; Kingsley **18.00**
Goblet, water; Mystic **15.00**
Goblet, water; Persian Pheasant, 8½" **28.00**
Goblet, water; Rose **25.00**
Pilsner, Classic **47.50**
Pitcher, Arcadian, gr hdl & ft **375.00**
Plate, Cadena, pk or yel, 6", ea **8.00**
Plate, Fairfax, platinum trim, 8" **12.00**
Plate, Flanders, 8" **12.00**
Plate, June Night, 8¼" **14.00**
Plate, La Fleure, 7¼" **12.00**
Plate, Twilight, 8" **22.50**
Relish, Fuchsia, #5902, 3-part **35.00**
Saucer, Cadena **10.00**
Server, Juno, pk, center hdl **75.00**
Shakers, June Night, ruffled, pr **80.00**
Sherbet, Brookmar, tall **16.00**
Sherbet, Byzantine, tall **18.00**
Sherbet, Cherokee Rose, #17399 ....**16.00**
Sherbet, Cherokee Rose, #17403 ....**20.00**
Sherbet, Fairfax, platinum trim **15.00**
Sherbet, Flanders, pk, tall **28.00**
Sherbet, June Night, tall **18.00**
Sherbet, Mystic, tall **12.00**
Sherbet, Persian Pheasant, 7" **20.00**
Sherbet, Wisteria, tall, #17501 ....**22.00**
Sherry, June Night, #17403, 2-oz **45.00**
Sherry, Shawl Dancer **52.50**
Sugar bowl, Cerice **25.00**
Tumbler, iced tea; Brookmar, ftd **28.00**
Tumbler, iced tea; Fairfax, platinum trim, ftd **18.00**
Tumbler, iced tea; Flanders, ftd, 12-oz **20.00**
Tumbler, iced tea; Fuchsia, ftd, 10-oz **30.00**
Tumbler, iced tea; Persian Pheasant, ftd **24.00**
Tumbler, iced tea; Wisteria, ftd **25.00**
Tumbler, juice; Cadena, pk or yel, ftd, 4¼" **27.50**
Tumbler, juice; June Night, ftd **20.00**
Tumbler, juice; Persian Pheasant, ftd **24.00**
Tumbler, juice; Wisteria, #17394 ....**25.00**
Vase, bud; Cherokee Rose, 8" **45.00**
Vase, Twilight & Smoke, #6551, 10" **250.00**
Wine, Cadena, 6" **25.00**

Tiles

Though originally strictly functional, tiles were being produced in various colors and used as architectural highlights as early as the Ancient Roman Empire. By the 18th century, Dutch tiles were decorated with polychrome landscapes and figures. During the 19th century, there were over a hundred companies in England involved in the manufacture of tile. By the Victorian era, the use of decorative tiles had reached its peak. Special souvenir editions, campaign and portrait tiles, and Art Nouveau motifs with lovely ladies and stylized examples from

nature were popular. Today all of these are very collectible. See also specific manufacturers.

Franklin, Dutch girl & old man w/pipe on pier, self fr, 6" **190.00**
Germany, A Present From Wales **15.00**
Hamilton, pine branch w/pine cones & needles, mk, 6" sq, EX ..**125.00**
Italian, landscape w/figures, 1800s, fr, 12x8" **550.00**
LA Pressed Brick Co, mtns/trees, mc, in mahog fr, 6" sq **2,600.00**
Low, JG&JF; Shylock, I'll Have My Bond, 8¼x4¾" **295.00**
Low, JG&JF; Woodsman & Axe, dk brn majolica, rstr, 8x4½" ..**275.00**
Minton, cows, brn & bl, fr, 8x8" **60.00**
Moravian, Indian Making Fire, mosaic style, mc, 5½" sq **180.00**
Moravian, skier, mc matt & glossy, unmk, 4½" sq **150.00**
Pardee, heron by water, mc, mk, 4¼" sq, NM **150.00**
Pardee, 4 Delft animal tiles w/in lg tile base, no mk, 10" **175.00**
Trent, lady's profile, burgundy majolica, 6" sq, NM **350.00**
Trent, Renaissance boy in high relief, amber, nicks, 6" sq **135.00**
US Encaustic Tile, Walt Whitman (?) portrait, olive gr, 6" sq ...**295.00**
Walrich, brn tree in field, yel sun, 5½" sq **575.00**
Walrich, trees & mtn landscape, 3-color, unmk, 5½" sq **560.00**

Tinware

In the American household of the 17th and 18th centuries, tinware items could be found in abundance, from food containers to foot warmers and mirror frames. Although the first settlers brought much of their tinware with them from Europe, by 1798 sheets of tin plate were being imported from England for use by the growing number of American tinsmiths. Tinwares were often decorated either by piercing or painted designs which were both freehand and stenciled. (See Toleware.) By the early 1900s, many homes had replaced their old tinware with the more attractive aluminum and graniteware.

In the 19th century, tenth wedding anniversaries were traditionally celebrated by gifts of tin. Couples gave big parties, dressed in their wedding clothes, and reaffirmed their vows before their friends and family who arrived bearing (and often wearing) tin gifts, most of which were quite humorous. Anniversary tin items may include hats, cradles, slippers and shoes, rolling pins, etc. See also Primitives and Kitchen Collectibles.

Wall sconces, oval reflection disks, Deer Isle, Maine, 19th century, 15", EX, $1,760.00 for the pair.

Biscuit cutter, heavy wire hdl **47.00**
Box, salt; drum shape w/hinged lid, hangs **125.00**
Butter press, long tube, open star design, wooden pusher **70.00**
Cabinet; spice, 8 oval drws **295.00**
Can, milk; bail hdl, w/lid, 1-gal **32.00**
Cheese-drainer mold, brass hanging loop, 2¾x6⅝" dia **125.00**
Cheese-drainer mold, pierced, heart shape, tubular ft, 3x6x6" **350.00**
Churn, syllabub; narrow, domed lid, wire hdl on dasher, tall **75.00**
Coffee grinder, dk tin, handmade, iron hopper & hdl **200.00**
Coffee maker, 2-pc w/drip top, cast leaf & ring hdl, 14" **85.00**
Coffeepot, gooseneck, punched band on hinged lid, 11" **130.00**
Coffeepot, minor rpr, 16"+swivel hdl **175.00**

Coffeepot, stick spout, strap hdl, emb Mason's, 8½", EX 75.00
Coffeepot, 4-pc, early, 1-cup 78.00
Colander, strap hdls, brass screen, attached rim base, sm 24.00
Cookie press, tube shape, wooden pusher w/heart design 125.00
Cracker pricker/cutter, oblong w/scalloped edge 70.00
Cutter, doughnut; hand soldered, flat top w/hold, 2¾x2⅞" 15.00
Dust pan, old, sm 18.00
Egg coddler, holds 2 tiers of 4 eggs, ftd, side hdls 275.00
Funnel, sm holes for straining, 6½x6¼" 20.00
Ice cream dipper, cone shape, CI hdl, Pat 1878, 8" 30.00
Ladle, cup shape w/pour spout, long hook hdl, early 28.00
Lunch box, Moore's Pat, folding, red & blk pnt, 1911, EX 50.00
Match holder, dbl pockets, w/striker, orig japanning, EX 30.00
Matchbox holder, punched floral, 4¾x2¾x1⅝" 35.00
Measure, Dover, flared rim, 1-pt 34.00
Measure, raised rings, 1-gal 42.00
Measure, raised rings, 1-pt 30.00
Measure, raised rings, 1-qt 32.00
Measure, 1-cup, VG 10.00
Measure, ½-cup, VG 15.00
Mold, ring form, heavy, w/hanging loop 25.00
Oil can w/spout, sloped shoulders, wood grip on bail, 14x11" 45.00
Pan, muffin; Self Rising Up & Up Cake Flour, 6-hole 28.00
Pastry sheet, curved bottom, w/tin rolling pin 650.00
Pie pan, sunburst design in bottom & initials HM 11.50
Pitcher, strap hdl, hand soldered, 7⅝x5½" 60.00
Pitcher & bowl, early 250.00
Rack, potato baking, 6 rnded points, dtd 1909, 2¼x13½" 40.00
Roaster, chestnut; 2-pc skillet shape, iron hdl, 1870s, 8¾" 90.00
Sconce, pcd mirrors, strap arms, crimped saucer, 10", pr 600.00
Sconce, ribbed bk w/rnded crimped top, ½-rnd base, 13" 140.00
Scoop, triangular bottom, stick hdl, Pat Oct 19, 1897, 7"+hdl 45.00
Skimmer, molasses; wood & dk tin, 10x5¾"+4" hdl 50.00
Spittoon, handmade, slanted removable lid, 3¼x6" dia 40.00
Sugar shaker, star-pierced dome lid, appl base ring, 5½" 55.00
Teapot, pewter finial, 8" 105.00
Toddy warmer, folding hdl, hinged lid 275.00

Tobacciana

Tobacciana is the generally accepted term used to cover a field of collecting that includes smoking pipes, cigar molds, cigarette lighters, humidors — in short, any article having to do with the practice of using tobacco in any form. Perhaps the most valuable variety of pipes is the meerschaum, hand carved from hydrous magnesium, an opaque white-gray or cream-colored mineral of the soapstone family. (Much of this is now mined in Turkey which has the largest meerschaum deposit in the world, though there are other deposits of lesser significance around the globe.) These figural bowls often portray an elaborately carved mythological character, an animal, or a historical scene. Amber is sometimes used for the stem. Other collectible pipes are corn cob (Missouri Meerschaum) and Indian peace pipes of clay or catlinite. (See American Indian Art.)

Chosen because it was the Indians who first introduced the white man to smoking, the cigar store Indian was a symbol used to identify tobacco stores in the 19th century. The majority of them were hand carved between 1830 and 1900 and are today recognized as some of the finest examples of early wood sculptures. When found they command very high prices.

For further information on lighters, refer to *Collector's Guide to Cigarette Lighters* by James Flanagan. Our advisor for this category is Chuck Thompson; he is listed in the Directory under Texas. Chris Rossiter assisted with pipe listings; you will find him listed in the Directory under Wisconsin. See also Advertising; Snuff Boxes.

Bag, cigar; canvas pouch type, advertising, ca 1890-1910, EX 4.50
Box, cigarette; colored wood, nacre & inlay, fitted int, 7" 105.00
Box, cigaros; The Overland, unopened 32.00
Case, cigar; cb giveaway, gold stamped lettering, NM 7.50
Case, cigar; emb leather w/rigid sides, holds 4, EX 7.50
Case, cigar; silver repousse, emb Nouveau decor, 4" 22.50
Case, cigar; sterling, emb florals, 5x2¼" 30.00
Case, cigarette; blk enamel w/rhinestones, clip, Volupte 120.00
Case, hard leather, Hamburg fire of 1842, map on bk 300.00
Case, silver, Nouveau aces, 1880s, 2½x3½", EX 400.00
Cheroot holder, meerschaum, Venus & Cupid, 6", EX, +case 135.00
Cheroot holder, meerschaum, 2 racing horses, amber stem, case ..360.00

Cigar lighter, Midland Jump Spark, push lever to ignite wick, wood base, restored, ca 1900, 16x7", $275.00.

Cigarette card, A Kodak at the Zoo, England, 1924, complete 30.00
Cigarette card, Lucky Charms, 1923, complete set of 50 ....30.00
Cigarette pack, Egyptian Prettiest, 1934, full, NM 15.00
Cigarette pack, Formal, blk & gold, 1944, full, NM 15.00
Cigarette pack, Murad, CA tax stamp in place, full, NM 6.00
Cigarette pack, Phantom, 1953, full, NM 10.00
Cigarette pack, Royal Bengals, full 27.50
Cigarette pack, Sheffield #5, 1940, full, NM 10.00
Cigarette papers, Bull Dog 5¢, NM 60.00
Cigarette papers, Duke's Mixture, bl bkground, M 7.00
Cigarette papers, Kite, M 10.00
Cigarette papers, Pride of Reidsville, gr bkground, M 36.00
Cigarette papers, Yum Yum, NM 50.00
Cutter, cigar; Harvard, key wind, EX 325.00
Cutter, cigar; mechanical, key wind, figure on top, 10½", G 225.00
Cutter, cigar; spring-operated blade, 4x7½" 48.00
Cutter, plug; Brown's Mule, RJ Reynolds, CI, counter-top, '30s ...95.00
Cutter, plug; Champion Knife Improved..., pnt CI, 19", EX 65.00
Cutter, plug; Griswold Erie #1, CI, 21" 155.00
Cutter, plug; Reading Hardware Standard, pnt CI, 17", EX 65.00
Lighter, Chase, ball shape, table style 150.00
Lighter, Chase Featherweight, tortoise 100.00
Lighter, Dunhill, pistol form, trigger opens top, 6x4½", EX 350.00
Lighter, Dunhill, pocket type 75.00
Lighter, Dunhill, Silent Flame, Sally Rand 100.00
Lighter, Dunhill, w/tape measure, rare 450.00
Lighter, gilt brass & dk bronze w/cupid base, 8⅝" 85.00
Lighter, Nestles/Nescafe, musical 75.00
Lighter, Occupied Japan, airplane, chrome 200.00
Lighter, Occupied Japan, baseball 75.00
Lighter, Occupied Japan, piano 100.00
Lighter, Occupied Japan, rocket 100.00
Lighter, Occupied Japan, ship, chrome, M 200.00
Lighter, Oldtime, copper, counter-top style, lg 22.50

Lighter, pipe; Nimrod 10.00
Lighter, Ronson, Leona, brass w/enameling, 4" 75.00
Lighter, Ronson, Queen Anne, SP, lg 60.00
Lighter, Ronson, Varaflame Comet, MIB 22.00
Lighter, Supreme, musical, Smoke Gets In Your Eyes, pocket sz ...35.00
Lighter, Thorens, automatic 100.00
Lighter, Zippo, American School of Aviation, MIB 75.00
Lighter, Zippo, Clark Candy Bar 55.00
Lighter, Zippo, Laurel Mtn Express 35.00
Lighter, Zippo, military logo, 1940s, MIB 100.00
Lighter, Zippo, Philip Morris 45.00
Lighter, Zippo type, Heineken logo on leather-like grain, 1" 25.00
Package, Trump Long Cut, sealed paper, playing cards, 1900s, EX ..55.00
Smoke set, metal w/brass floral medallions, Gold Crest, 2-pc 45.00
Tongs, pipe; wrought steel, EX detail, polished, 11½" 440.00

Pipes

Meerschaum: Pipe, Bacchanalian scene, amber stem, 8⅝", with fitted case, $650.00; Cheroot holder, two galloping horses, amber stem (damaged), 7⅛", with fitted case, $360.00; Pipe, deer (buck, doe and fawn) beside bellflower bowl, amber and meerschaum stem, amber mouthpiece (damaged), 11⅝", with fitted case, $470.00.

Amber bowl & stem w/18k gold band on skull-shaped bowl, 8½" .850.00
Amber cigarillo, lady's leg shape w/garter & high-top shoe 175.00
Blown glass, clear bowl & stem, HP floral decor 50.00
Blown glass, cranberry, MIE 125.00
Burled wood bowl, Bakelite mouthpc, 6½" 35.00
Burled wood bowl, birch stem, NP trim, horn mouthpc, Czech 45.00
Clay, early golf-club shape, short (nose warmer), 1700s 20.00
Clay, lady's bust form, red mouthpc insert, Fr, 1840s 50.00
Clay, plain bowl, church-warden type, 17" 17.00
Clay, Punch-&-Judy-shaped bowl, Dutch made, 1920s, 7½" 30.00
Clay, skull-shaped bowl, MIE, 6" 20.00
Meerschaum, amber mouthpc, 4½" 35.00
Meerschaum, eagle holding egg, amber mouthpc, 6½" 175.00
Meerschaum, horn stem, Bakelite mouthpc, 8½" 75.00
Meerschaum, king's head-form bowl, silver crown lid, amber stem ..375.00
Meerschaum, man's head, plumed helmet, color stain, 6", +case .325.00
Meerschaum, Popeye's head-form bowl, Bakelite stem, 1940s 115.00
Meerschaum, stag running by stump, amber mouthpc 275.00
Porcelain, HP Maltese cross, dtd 1917 ....100.00
Porcelain, hunting scene, deer-horn stem, red mouthpc 65.00
Porcelain, lady's portrait, birch stem, red mouthpc 17.00
Porcelain, monkey's head bowl w/pnt, birch stem, red mouthpc ..375.00
Porcelain, occupational type, farmer plowing 75.00
Porcelain, regimental, birch stem, helmet lid 550.00
Shell w/meerschaum insert, cherry-wood stem, amber mouthpc ...75.00
Wood, cvd bust of Civil War soldier, Kepi lid, Bakelite stem 65.00
Wood, Grenadier guard cvd bowl (lg), Bakelite stem 375.00

Wood, hunting scene relief cvg, silver lid, Germany, ca 1900 ......45.00

Toby Jugs

The delightful jug known as the Toby dates back to the 18th century, when factories in England produced them for export to the American colonies. Named for the character Toby Philpots in the song *The Little Brown Jug*, the Toby was fashioned in the form of a jolly fellow, usually holding a jug of beer and a glass. The earlier examples were made with strict attention to details such as fingernails and teeth. Originally representing only a non-entity, a trend developed to portray well-known individuals such as George II, Napoleon, and Ben Franklin. Among the most-valued Tobies are those produced by Ralph Wood I in the late 1700s. By the mid-1830s Tobies were being made in America. See also Doulton, Lenox, and Occupied Japan.

Falstaff, Staffordshire, 1800s, 9" 190.00
Man in bl coat, yel vest, Staffordshire, 800s, 9¾" 180.00
Man in red coat, Hearty Good Fellow, Staffordshire, 11½" 240.00
Man standing, Bennington type, 1800s, 9½" 100.00
Man w/jug, pearlware, mc sponging, w/lid, 10", NM 1,100.00
Napoleon, mc w/gold, A Evans, Phila PA, 9¾" 250.00
Pratt, seated, jug on knee, pipe between ft, rstr/chips, 10" 885.00
Salt-glazed stoneware, man w/jug, w/lid, ca 1840, 10", VG 210.00
Seated w/pitcher on knee, translucent mc, 1780s, chips, 9" 275.00
Shepherd w/staff, soft paste, mk/#d, German, 5" 65.00
Walton, seated, pitcher on knee, ribbon mk, lines/rprs, 10" 1,100.00

Toleware

The term 'toleware' originally came from a French term meaning 'sheet iron.' Today it is used to refer to paint-decorated tin items, most popular from 1800 to 1850s. The craft was very popular in Pennsylvania, Connecticut, Maine, and New York state. Early toleware has a very distinctive look. The surface is dull and unvarnished; background colors range from black to cream. Geometrics are quite common, but florals and fruits were also popular motifs. Items made after 1850 were often stenciled, and gold trim was sometimes added.

American toleware is usually found in practical, everyday forms — trays, boxes, and coffeepots are most common — while French examples might include candlesticks, wine coolers, jardinieres, etc. Be sure to note color and design when determining date and value, but condition of the paint is the most important worth-assessing factor. Our advisors for this category are Barbara and Frank Pollack; they are listed in the Directory under Illinois. In the listings that follow, the dimension given for boxes and trays indicates length. Unless noted otherwise, values are for examples with average wear.

Bowl, punch; scenes w/gilt, rim to hold glasses, hdls, VG 260.00
Box, dee; dome top, plums, 4-color, japanned, 6½", VG 200.00
Box, deed; floral, gold on blk, molded lid, 9½" 110.00
Box, deed; orig gr pnt w/red & gold stripes, 6½", EX 65.00
Box, deed; swags on orig dk japanning, soldered rpr, 4⅜" 85.00
Box, spice; floral, 3-color on blk, hinged lid, 3" sq 75.00
Box, spice; worn orig mustard pnt w/blk stencil, 14" 95.00
Can, milk; floral, 4-color on blk, 10¼" 95.00
Candle lantern, gold on brn japanning, mica panels, 1865, 5" ...195.00
Canister, floral, 3-color on blk, resoldered cap, 8¼" 120.00
Coffeepot, floral, 4-color on blk, EX orig pnt, 8½" 220.00
Coffeepot, floral in leaf reserve, blk w/mc, str sides, 9" 475.00
Coffeepot, floral reserve on blk, 3-color bands, stick spout, 8" 425.00

Coffeepot, floral/fruit, 5-color, japanned, gooseneck, 11" 900.00
Creamer, floral, mc on blk, rpt, hinged lid, 4¼" 135.00
Creamer, floral, 2-color on dk brn japanning, hinged lid, 4" 200.00
Creamer, floral, 4-color on dk brn japanning, wear, 4" 415.00
Cuspidor, smoked wht w/red stripes & gold stencil, 8¼" 15.00
Foot warmer, floral, 3-color on orig brn, complete, 8½" 275.00
Lamp, lard-burning, old blk & gold rpt, 6¾", EX 165.00
Lantern, half-circle w/glass front, worn red pnt, 9½" 175.00
Mug, leaf band, yel/blk on red, strap hdl, 1¾x2" 325.00
Mug, mc fruit & flowers on blk, unpnt rim, 4¾" 40.00
Sugar bowl, floral, 2-color on blk japanning, worn, 3½" 140.00
Syrup, floral, 3-color, japanned, hinged lid, 4", EX 575.00
Syrup, floral/fruit, 3-color, japanned, hinged lid, worn, 4" 275.00
Tea caddy, floral, 2-color on brn japanning, 6¼" 75.00
Tea caddy, floral, 3-color, japanned, oval, 5½", EX 145.00
Tea caddy, floral, 3-color on blk, commas on lid, 4½" 165.00
Tea caddy, floral, 3-color on brn japanning, 5⅜" 85.00
Tea caddy, floral, 4-color on brn japanning, 6¾" 165.00
Tea caddy, floral, 4-color on dk brn japanning, wear, 5¼" 415.00
Tray, apple; japanned w/band of cherries/plums/flowers, 12" 210.00
Tray, floral band, 5-color on blk, 9x12" 300.00

Tools

Before the Civil War, tools for the most part were handmade. Some were primitive to the point of crudeness, while others reflected the skill of those who took pride in their trade. Increasing demand for quality tools and the dawning of the age of industrialization resulted in tools that were mass-produced. Factors important in evaluating antique tools are scarcity, usefulness, and portability. Those with a manufacturer's mark are worth more than unmarked items. When no condition is indicated, the items listed here are assumed to be in excellent condition. Our advisor for this category is Jim Calison; he is listed in the Directory under New York. See also Keen Kutter; Stanley; Winchester.

Saddle horn fencing tool, cast iron, Atomic Glaskin Mfg., $40.00.

Bit & brace, cooper's; brass on wood, minimum value 200.00
Broadaxe, goosewing; Northern PA Germanic type, minimum value .450.00
Cabin hinges, smith/farrier, bent horseshoes, pr 35.00
Calipers, iron w/brass jointer 31.50
Chalk-line reel, mortised, hickory, 18th century 110.00
Corner brace, metal w/wood fixtures 75.00
Dividers, pearwood, brass fittings & wing tips, lg sz 45.00
Hole punch, B Smith, iron w/incised sprig, brass plate, 5½" 75.00
Hoof scraper, wooden hdl, steel files 20.00
Horseshoes calk remover, factory stamped, wooden, eye to hang ..20.00
Jack, carriage; oak, iron teeth, lifted axle, minimum value 100.00
Jack, coach; hickory, iron joiner, minimum value 110.00
Jointer, cooper's, barrel maker, long, about 72" 175.00

Jointer, cooper's, maple, about 36" 85.00
Maul, burl; wht oak hdl, 18th century, minimum value 55.00
Measure, log; brass & wood 115.00
Oilstone, smith's, walnut box 70.00
Plane, rabbet; maple, wide eye 65.00
Plane, special purpose; all metal, cuts inside curve 35.00
Rasp, hoof; dbl end, steel 17.00
Saw, burl; cherry hdl, fine tooth, signed 85.00
Scraper, cooper's, pull type, maple hdl, brass ferrule 40.00
Scribe, timber; T Dixon & Sons, wrought iron w/incising, 6" 80.00
Spokeshave, wheelwright's, adj tang blade, cherry & brass, sm 40.00
Square, set try, cherry, polished iron, brass-bound blade 47.50
Sugar nippers, iron, 8", EX 90.00
Wagon wheel hubs, hickory, iron axle throats & bands 45.00
Witchet, hardwoods, brass-lined throat, 2-blade, 1840s 225.00

Toothbrush Holders

Most of the collectible toothbrush holders were made in prewar Japan and were modeled after popular comic-strip and Disney characters. Since many were made of bisque and decorated with unfired enamel, it's not uncommon to find them in less-than-perfect paint, a factor you must consider when attempting to assess their values. Our advisor for this category is Marilyn Cooper, author of *Pictorial Guide to Toothbrush Holders*; she is listed in the Directory under Texas.

Blk crow, tan & wht lustre, Japan, 5¾" 130.00
Boy by postbox holder, mc matt, Japan, 4¼" 55.00
Boy in top hat, tube tray, tan & wht lustre, Japan, 5½" 70.00
Boy w/violin & dog, Japan (Goldcastle), 5½" 75.00
Butcher, Japan (Goldcastle), 5¼" 80.00
Circus dog, tray, Japan, 4½" 80.00
Clown juggling, tray, Japan, 5" 85.00
Clown w/mask, tray, Japan (Goldcastle), 5½" 115.00
Dutch couple kissing, tube tray, Japan, 6" 55.00
Dutch girl, Japan, 4¾" 70.00
Giraffe, beige, tube tray, Japan, 6" 115.00
Little Orphan Annie & Sandy on couch, bsk, Famous Artists Syn .125.00
Lone Ranger, chalkware, 1940s, NM 75.00
Mickey Mouse, jtd arm, Japan, Disney, 5", EX 400.00
Old King Cole, china, Japan, 5¼" 90.00
Sailors on anchor, tray, Japan, 5½" 65.00
Skippy, jtd arm, bsk, mc, Japan, 5¾" 95.00
Soldier, tube tray, red & blk, Japan, 6" 75.00
Three Little Pigs, porc, Goldcastle, 4" 95.00

Toothpick Holders

Once common on every table, the toothpick holder was relegated to the china cabinet near the turn of the century. Fortunately, this contributed to their survival. As a result, many are available to collectors today. Because they are small and easily displayed, they are a very popular collectible. They come in a wide range of prices to fit every budget. The rare ones have been reproduced and, unfortunately, are being offered for sale right along with the originals. These 'repros' should be priced in the $10.00 to $30.00 range. Unless you're sure of what you're buying, choose a reputable dealer. In addition to pattern glass, you'll find examples in china, bisque, art glass, and various metals. Toothpick holders in the listings that follow are glass unless noted otherwise. Some toothpick holders have been reproduced. Beware of reproductions. Values here are for originals. Our advisor for this category is Judy A. Knauer; she is listed in the Directory under Pennsylvania.

Acorn, pk to wht 75.00
Amberina, Dmn Quilt, EX color, sq rim, 2¼" 200.00
Atlanta, frosted 60.00
Banded Portland, Maiden Blush 60.00
Banded Portland, pk 60.00
Beaded Swirl & Disk, amber 60.00
Beatty Honeycomb, wht opal 50.00
Bees in Basket 45.00
Blazing Cornucopia, purple eyes 35.00
Box-in-Box, red stained w/wht florals 60.00
Boy w/Pack, amber 45.00
Burmese, shiny, sq top, Mt WA, 2½" 350.00
Capitol 34.00
Cat on pillow, bl 60.00
Cat on pillow, clear 45.00
Cat on pillow, vaseline 60.00
Champion, gr 55.00
Colorado, gr 35.00
Columbia, vaseline w/gold 75.00
Crisscross, wht opal 165.00
Cut glass, ped base 75.00
Daisy & Button, clear w/red collar, kettle shape 60.00
Delaware, gr w/gold 75.00
Diamond Spearhead, vaseline opal 65.00
Diamond w/Peg, ruby stained, souvenir 45.00
Double Dahlia w/Lens 60.00
Empress 55.00
Eureka, National's, ruby stained 75.00
Fiber Bundle, milk glass 30.00
Finecut, bl, hat form 22.50
Florette, gr 60.00
Harvard, gr 50.00
Illinois 35.00
Inverted T'print, amberina, bulbous 195.00
Inverted T'print w/ring base, cranberry 75.00
Iris w/Meander, bl opal 90.00
Iris w/Meander, gr opal 70.00
Jefferson Optic, bl 65.00
Jefferson Optic, gold scrolls & wht leaves 85.00
Jefferson Optic, gr, souvenir 65.00
Jefferson's Colonial, gr 68.00
Man w/hat, clear, rare 110.00
Manhattan 32.00
Manhattan, gr stain 36.00
Massachusetts 50.00
Minnesota, gr 125.00
Palm Leaf, pk & wht 65.00
Peerless 30.00
Pineapple, shiny, lt gr 110.00
Pleating, ruby stained 60.00
Prize 42.50
Punty Band, ruby, souvenir, Heisey 60.00
Radiant, etched 40.00
Reverse Swirl, cranberry opal 235.00
Ribbed Pillar, frosted 75.00
Ribbed Pillar, glossy 60.00
Ribbed Spiral, vaseline opal 115.00
Ruby T'print, etched 48.00
Scalloped Swirl, ruby stained 60.00
Scroll w/Acanthus, apple gr w/decor 145.00
Scrolled Shell 30.00
Shell & Seaweed, maroon seaweed on milk glass 50.00
Shell & Seaweed, pk 65.00
Spearpoint Band (Gothic) 30.00

Tacoma 20.00
Tapered Bulge, wht opal w/HP cabin in snow, rare 165.00
Texas 35.00
Trophy, gr 22.00
Truncated Cube, ruby stained 40.00
Valise, amber 50.00
Winged Scroll, gr w/gold 450.00

Torquay Pottery

Torquay is a unique type of pottery made in the South Devon area of England as early as 1867. At the height of productivity, at least a dozen companies flourished there, producing simple folk pottery from the area's natural red clay. The ware was both wheel turned and molded and decorated under the glaze with heavy slip resulting in low-relief nature subjects or simple scrollwork. Three of the best-known of these potteries were: Watcombe (1867-1962); Aller Vale (in operation from the mid-1800s, producing domestic ware and architectural products); and Longpark (1890 until 1957). Watcombe and Aller Vale merged in 1901 and operated until 1962 under the name of Royal Aller Vale and Watcombe Art Pottery.

A decline in the popularity of the early classical terra-cotta styles (urns, busts, figures, etc.) lead to the introduction of painted and glazed, terra-cotta wares. During the late 1880s white clay wares, both turned and molded, were decorated with colored glazes (Stapleton ware, grotesque molded figures, ornamental vases, large jardiniers, etc.). By the turn of the century, the market for art pottery was diminishing, so the potteries turned to wares decorated in colored slips (Barbotine, Persian, Scrolls, etc.).

Motto wares were introduced in the late 19th century by Aller Vale and taken up in the present century by the other Torquay potteries. This eventually became the 'bread and butter' product of the local industry. This was perhaps the most famous type of ware potted in this area because of the verses, proverbs, and quotations that decorated it. This was achieved by the sgraffito technique — scratching the letters through the slip to expose the red clay underneath. The most popular patterns were Cottage, Black Cockerel, Multi-Cockerel, and a scrollwork design called Scandy. Other popular decorations were Kerswell Daisy, ships, kingfishers, applied bird decorations, Art Deco styles, Egyptian ware and many others. Aller Vale ware may sometimes be found marked 'H.H. and Company,' a firm who assumed ownership from 1897 to 1901. 'Watcombe Torquay' was an impressed marked used from 1884 to 1927.

Our advisors for this category are Jerry and Gerry Kline; they are listed in the Directory under Ohio. If you're interested in joining a Torquay club, the address of The North American Torquay Society is given under Clubs, Newsletters, and Catalogs.

Left to right: Vase, Daffodil on green, 3-handled, Longpark, 8", $225.00; Pitcher, Scrolls on white, impressed Aller Vale, 5¾", $300.00; Pitcher, Sandringham, blue Scrolls on white, Aller Vale, 8½", $200.00; Bottle vase, colored Scrolls on cream, 'B-1,' Aller Vale, 6", $250.00; Vase, Scrolls on blue, 'B-3,' Aller Vale, 8", $175.00.

Art Pottery

Ashtray, rabbit figure, 'Who Burnt the Tablecloth,' 5x4¾" 95.00
Candlestick, Tintern Abbey, Longpark, 8⅛" 250.00
Chamberstick, Scrolls, wht clay, A-1, Aller Vale, 2½" 300.00
Figure, cat, gr, Watcombe, 8½" 750.00
Loving cup, commemorative, Tommy Adkins, 'God Bless,' 4½" 275.00
Pitcher, Cottage, Dorset, mk Collard-Dorset-Poole, 4½" 200.00
Pitcher, Scrolls, pinched spout, A-1, Aller Vale, 4¾" 175.00
Pitcher, Scrolls, Sandringham, pierced rim, Aller Vale, 8¼" 235.00
Pitcher, Scrolls, 3-pinch top, B-2, Aller Vale, 8¼" 250.00
Teapot, Faience, Old Mill Lyme Regis, Watcombe, chip, 5" 275.00
Vase, Flowers, glazed terra cotta, bbl shape, Watcombe 175.00
Vase, Ladybird on gr, 2-hdl, Aller Vale, 8" 350.00
Vase, Scrolls, 5-finger funnel, Aller Vale, sm chip, 8" 200.00
Vase, Scrolls on gr, 5-spout, B-2, Longpark 225.00
Vase, Windmill, 2-hdl, Watcombe, 6" 200.00

Devon Motto Ware

Basket, Cockerel, oval, 'Homemade Preserves,' 5" 125.00
Basket, Cottage, 'Gather Roses While You May,' 4x5¼x4" 65.00
Bean pot, Scandy, 'Beccles Gude Folks...,' 3¼x3¼" 55.00
Biscuit barrel, Cottage, Watcombe, 'Help Yourself,' 6" 300.00
Bottle, scent; Devonshire violets, crown stopper, 4" 45.00
Bottle, scent; Violets, sealed, cork top 40.00
Bowl, Scandy, Exeter, 'Keep Your Breath...,' 5¼" 75.00
Candlestick, Cottage, Longpark, 'Llanfairfechan...,' 4½" 90.00
Carafe, Cottage, Sea gull, Babbacombe, w/stopper, 4½" 90.00
Chamberstick, Cottage, 'Pleasant Dreams,' 3½" 65.00
Chamberstick, Sailing Ships, 'Many Are Called...,' 3¾" 45.00

**Cheese keeper, 'Help Yourself to the Cheese,'
Cottage and Pre-Scandy, 6⅝x7¾" plate, impressed
Watcombe, 'Cheese' on 4½x5⅝" lid, $400.00.**

Condiment holder, w/shakers, egg cup & mustard, 3½" 195.00
Creamer, Cockerel, 'Help Yerzel Ter Cream,' 2¼" 40.00
Creamer, Scandy, tadpoles, Longpark, motto, 3¼" 30.00
Cup, Blk Cockerel, Longpark, 'Jack & Jill Went...,' 2¾" 80.00
Cup & saucer, Cottage, 'Caernavron/Bore Da' 45.00
Cup & saucer, Cottage, Watcombe, motto, 3¾", 8¼" 35.00
Cup & saucer, Scandy, Aller Vale, w/motto 55.00
Egg cup, Cockerel, ped ft, 'Fresh Laid,' 2¾" 40.00
Egg cup, Kingfisher, ped ft, deep saucer, sgn England 35.00
Hatpin holder, Daffodil, Watcombe, brn ground, 4½" 250.00
Hatpin holder, Scandy, Longpark, 'Keep Me on...Table,' lg 100.00
Inkwell, Scandy, 'Us Be Always...,' Longpark, 1¾" 95.00
Jam dish, Cottage, 'Help Yourself...,' 2½x5¼" 48.00
Jam dish, Scandy, 'Elp Yerzel Tu Jam,' skillet form, 5" dia 75.00
Jam jar, Cottage, Watcombe, 'Guid Volks Be...,' 4x3⅛" 55.00
Jardiniere, Parrot, ruffled edge, 7⅜" 175.00
Jug, puzzle; Kerswell Daisy, Aller Vale, 'Here Gentlemen' 250.00

Jug, Ship, hdl through pierced rim, Hastings, 'Make Hay,' 6" 275.00
Match striker, Cockerel, 'A Match for Any Man,' lg 125.00
Mug, Cottage, 'Drink & Be Merry,' 4⅜x3⅜" 80.00
Mug, Cottage, 'Up to the Lips & Over...,' 3¾x3¼" 80.00
Mug, Cottage, Dartmouth, 'Kind Words Are Music,' 3¾" 100.00
Mug, shaving; Multi-Cockerel, Longpark, motto, 4" 300.00
Mustard pot, Cottage, 'Saltburn by the Sea...,' 1¾x2½" 50.00
Pitcher, Cockerel, Longpark, 'Better Do One Thing,' 4¼" 65.00
Pitcher, Colored Cockerel, Longpark, 'There Would Be...,' 6" ..185.00
Pitcher, Cottage, 'A Thing of Beauty...,' bbl shape, 3½x3" 50.00
Pitcher, Cottage, 'Gretna Green,' 2¼x1¾" 45.00
Pitcher, Cottage, 'Little Tommy Tucker,' child sz, 2" 45.00
Pitcher, Rosy Sunset, 'Don't Take 2 Bites of a Cherry,' 6" 95.00
Pitcher, Scandy, Aller Vale, 'Do Not Hurry...,' 4½" 55.00
Plate, Cottage, 'To Thine Own Sel Be True,' 8¼" 95.00
Plate, Cottage, Dartmouth, 8" 42.50
Plate, Cottage, DMW, 'There's No Wealth But Life,' 5" 35.00
Pot, chamber; Kingfisher, gold & bl, Hele Cross, 5" dia 200.00
Salt cellar, Scandy, Longpark, 'Be Aisy w/Tha...,' 1¾x2½" 50.00
Shakers, Cottage, Watcombe, 'No Road Is Long...,' pr 50.00
Sugar basin, Cottage, ped ft, 'Doo Good in Time...,' 2⅞" 55.00
Sugar bowl, Scandy, Aller Vale, 'Take a Little Sugar' 35.00
Sugar bowl, Scandy, Watcombe, 'Sweeten to Your Liking' 37.00
Teapot, Blk Cockerel, Longpark, 'Du'ee 'Ave...,' 5" 175.00
Teapot, Cockerel, 'Du'll Make Yourzels at 'Ome,' 3¼" 150.00
Teapot, Cottage, 'Daunt'ee Worry But 'Ave...,' 4¾x5" 125.00
Teapot stand, Scandy, Longpark, motto 85.00
Tile, Widecombe Moor, heavily potted, 5¾x4⅝" 150.00
Toast rack, Cottage, Watcombe, 'Take a...,' 5 rails 175.00
Tray, dresser; Blk Cockerel, Longpark, 10¾x7¾" 350.00
Tray, pen; Multi-Cockerel, 2⅞x9¼" 150.00
Tumbler, Scandy, 'Every Blade of Grass...,' 3¾" 60.00
Vase, Kerswell Daisy, Aller Vale, 'Life Has Many Shadows', 5¾" .225.00
Vase, Scandy, 'Empty Bbls...,' no mk, mini, 2¼" 85.00
Vase, udder; Scandy, Aller Vale, 'Many Are Called...,' 3½" 125.00

Tortoise Shell

The outer shell of several species of land turtles, called tortoises, was once commonly used to make brooches, combs, small boxes, and novelty items. It was often used for inlay as well. The material is easily recognized by its mottled brown and yellow coloring. Because some of these turtles are now on the endangered list, such use is prohibited.

Box, glove; ivory edge, brass escutcheon, bun ft, lg 900.00
Box, Oriental cvg on lid, oval, 4" 110.00
Box, pill; dome lid 90.00
Card case, raised panel on lid, 4½" 175.00
Card case, rnded rectangle w/oval ends 60.00
Card case, serpentine, 4½" 275.00
Clock, traveling; octagonal, rnd brass bezel, sm 120.00
Compact, rectangular w/appl silver medallion 260.00
Miniature, guitar, MOP inlay, 5" 70.00
Miniature, mandolin, MOP inlay, 5½" 100.00
Miniature, mandolin, MOP inlay, 8" 150.00
Purse, gilt metal w/oval shell in lid, serpentine, sm 100.00

Tortoise Shell Glass

By combining several shades of glass — brown, clear, and yellow — glass manufacturers of the 19th century were able to produce an art glass that closely resembled the shell of the tortoise. Some of this type of glassware was manufactured in Germany. In America it was made by several firms, the most prominent of which was the Boston and Sandwich Glass Works.

Bottle, scent; amber stopper, silver collar, 4½" 250.00
Bowl, 3½x8½" 90.00
Pitcher, appl amber hdl, 8½" 125.00
Platter, 16" dia 95.00
Tumbler, 3½x2½" 125.00

Toys

The prices shown in this edition reviews auction reports, known sales, and sales lists. We have shown prices of toys in various conditions and noted which toys sold with boxes. To get the most out of this guide, when you see the same toys with different prices, you must consider these important factors. On occasion, a toy will bring a much higher than normal price at auction. This is 'auction fever.' Sometimes a collector simply wants to add a toy to his collection, and to him price is not as important as availability.

Toys can be classified into at least two categories: early collectible toys with an established history and the newer toys. The antique toys are easier to evaluate. A great deal of research has been done on them, and much data is available. The newer toys are just beginning to be studied; relative information is only now being published, and the lack of production records makes it difficult to know how many may be available. Often warehouse finds of these newer toys can change the market. This has happened with battery-operated toys and to some extent with robots. Review past issues of this guide. You will see the changing trends for the newer toys. All toys become more important as collectibles when a fixed period of manufacture is known. When we know the numbers produced and documentation of the makers is established, the prices become more predictable.

The best way to learn about toys is to attend toy shows and auctions. This will give you the opportunity to compare prices and condition. The more collectors and dealers you meet, the more you will learn. There is no substitute for holding a toy in your hand and seeing for yourself what they are. If you are going to be a serious collector, buy all the books you can find. Read every article you see. Knowledge is vital to building a good collections. Study all books that are available. These are some of the most helpful: *American Toy Cars and Trucks* by Lillian Gottschalk; *Toy Autos 1890-1939*, the Peter Ottenheimer Collection; *Collecting the Tin Toy Car, 1950-1970*, by Dale Kelley; *Arcade Toys* by Al Aune; *The Art of the Tin Toy* by David Pressland; *Lehmann Toys* by Cieslik; *The History of Martin Mechanical Toys* by Marchand; *Mechanical Toys* by Spilhaus; *American Antique Toys* by Barenholtz, McClintock, and Holland; *American Clockwork Toys* by Whitton; *The George Brown Sketchbook* by Edith Barenholtz; *Toy Dreams* by Kitahara; *Collecting Toys*, *Collecting Toy Soldiers*, and *Collecting Toy Trains*, *An Identification & Value Guide #3*, by Richard O'Brien; *Occupied Japan Toys With Prices* by David Gould and Donna Crevar-Donaldson; *Evolution of the Pedal Car and Other Riding Toys, 1844-1970s*, by Neil Wood; *Toys of the Sixties, A Pictorial Guide* by Bill Bruegman; and *Fisher-Price, A Historical, Rarity & Value Guide, 1931-1963*, by John Murray and Bruce Fox. Other informative books (published by Collector Books) are *Schroeder's Collectible Toys, Antique to Modern*, by Sharon and Bob Huxford; *Motorcycle Toys, Antique & Contemporary*, by Sally Gibson-Downs and Christine Gentry; *Mego Toys* by Wallace M. Chrouch, *Collector's Encyclopedia of Disneyana,* by David Longest and Michael Stern; *Stern's Guide to Disney Collectibles* by Michael Stern; *Modern Toys, American Toys, 1830-1980*, by Linda Baker; *Character Toys and Collectibles, Antique and Collectible Toys* and *Toys, Antiques &*

Collectibles, both by David Longest; *Collector's Guide to Tootsietoys* by David Richter; *Collectible Male Action Figures* by Paris and Susan Manos; and *Matchbox Toys, 1948-1993*, by Dana Johnson. *The Dictionary of Toys Sold in America, Vol. I & II*, by Earnest and Ida Long are good for identification and dating.

Our advisor for all toys except Farm Toys, Guns, Steiff, Toy Soldiers and Trains is Jon Thurmond; he is listed in the Directory under Missouri. In the listings that follow, toys are listed by manufacturer's name if possible, otherwise by type. Condition is given when known. Measurements are given when appropriate and available; if only one dimension is noted, it is the greater one — height if the toy is vertical, length if it is horizontal. See also Children's Things; Personalities. For toy stoves, see Stoves.

Key:
b/o — battery operated   NP — nickel plated
cl — celluloid   w/up — wind-up
jtd — jointed

Company or Country of Manufacturer

AC Williams, Coupe, pnt CI, NP wheels, chips, 4¼", VG 75.00
AC Williams, Mack Stake Truck, pnt CI, rubber tires, 4¾", VG .75.00
Acme, Dick Tracy Movie Viewer, cb & plastic, 1955, M on card .125.00
Alps, Airport Service Helicopter, tin litho, b/o, 13", VG 75.00
Alps, Batmobile, tin & plastic, b/o, 1966, 11½", EX 400.00
Alps, BMW Turbo Race Car, plastic, b/o, 11", MIB 85.00
Alps, Coney Island Rocket Ride, tin, b/o, '50s, 6x14", NMIB 650.00
Alps, Hiller Hornet Helicopter, tin litho, remote, 12", VG 125.00
Alps, Real Sound Highway Patrol, tin litho, b/o, 11½", MIB 85.00
Arcade, Bell Telephone Truck w/Pole Trailer, CI, 9", 8", EX 450.00
Arcade, Buick Coupe, CI, NP driver, 8½", NM 5,450.00

Arcade, Buick Sedan, painted cast iron, 8½", VG+, $2,750.00.

Arcade, Bus, CI, NP driver, G pnt/partial rpt, 13", VG 1,750.00
Arcade, Car Carrier, CI w/steel trailer, carries 4, 24½", EX 650.00
Arcade, Car Carrier, CI w/steel trailer, 19½", EX 350.00
Arcade, Car Carrier w/Tractor & Trailer, CI, 14", EX 350.00
Arcade, Century of Progress Greyhound Lines Bus, CI, 7¼", EX ..250.00
Arcade, Chester Gump Cart, pnt CI, much wear, 7½", G 350.00
Arcade, Chevrolet Coupe, pnt CI, disk wheels, 8¼", VG 650.00
Arcade, Chevy Sedan, CI, NP wheels, 8½", EX 850.00
Arcade, Contractor's Dump Wagon, pnt CI, orig decal, 13", VG .165.00
Arcade, Dbl Decker Bus, CI, 3 passengers on roof, 1930s, 8", EX ..500.00
Arcade, Dbl Decker Bus, CI, 6 figures, ca 1927, 8", EX 700.00
Arcade, Dump Truck, CI, old rpt, 7¼", VG 165.00
Arcade, Fageol Bus, CI, NP w/gold trim, rpt, 8", VG 55.00
Arcade, Fageol Bus, CI, NP wheels, rpt/rpl, 12¼", VG 195.00
Arcade, Fire Trailer Truck, CI, 3 figures, 2-pc, 16½", EX 450.00
Arcade, Flat Top Cab, CI, nickel driver, balloon tires, 8", EX 700.00
Arcade, Ford Rumble-Seat Roadster, CI, NP grill, 6½", EX 600.00
Arcade, Ford Sedan, CI, NP grill, 6½", EX 1,200.00

Arcade, Greyhound Bus, CI, 1940s style, 8¾", G- 225.00
Arcade, Ice Delivery Truck, pnt CI, NP trim, 7", VG 310.00
Arcade, Internat'l Dump Truck, CI, rubber wheels, 11⅛", EX 350.00
Arcade, Internat'l Harvester Dump Truck, CI, NP driver, 10½", EX ...550.00
Arcade, Internat'l Harvester Dump Truck, CI, NP driver, 10½", VG ..375.00
Arcade, Internat'l Stake Truck, CI, NP grill, 11½", EX 950.00
Arcade, Ladder Truck, CI, NP driver, EX pnt, 18" 500.00
Arcade, Mack Dump Truck, CI, rpl driver, rpt, 12", VG 165.00
Arcade, Model T Coupe, CI, NP wheels, 2-door, 7", EX 425.00
Arcade, Model T Coupe, CI, 4-door, 6½", G 275.00
Arcade, Model T Pickup Truck, CI, NP driver/wheels, 8½", EX .500.00
Arcade, Model T Sedan, CI, center door, 6¼", EX 200.00
Arcade, Model T Sedan, CI, NP wheels, 2-door, 6½", EX 350.00
Arcade, Paddle Wheel Boat, CI, worn NP, 7½", VG 80.00
Arcade, Panama Digger, CI, molded-in figures, 13", EX 1,350.00
Arcade, Pontiac Sedan, CI, NP grill, rubber tires, 6½", EX 1,200.00
Arcade, Scraper, CI, NP wheels, 5", EX 125.00
Arcade, Snub Nose Ice Truck, CI, w/driver, 1930s, 7", EX 200.00
Arcade, Touring Car, CI, NP driver, 6¼", EX 400.00
Arcade, Touring Car, CI, NP wheels, no driver, 6¼", EX 250.00
Arcade, World's Fair Tour Bus, CI, worn graphics, VG 125.00
Arcade, Wrecker Truck, CI, rubber wheels, 5½", VG 95.00
Arcade, Yel Cab, CI, cowl lights, no driver, 8", VG 525.00
Arcade, Yel Cab, CI, NP wheels, w/driver, 5", NM 725.00
Arcade, Yel Cab, CI, w/driver, spare missing, 7¼", G 175.00
Arcade, Yel Cab Coupe, CI, rpl figure, rstr, 9" 900.00
Arcade, 4-Car Tractor Trailer Car Carrier, CI, 10", EX 250.00
Arcade, 4-Car Transport, CI w/steel trailer, 11", EX 150.00
Arcade, 4-Car Transport, CI w/steel trailer, 15¼", NM 675.00
Arnold, Monkey on Trike, tin litho w/up, working, 3½", VG 160.00
Bandai, #7 Hot Rod, pnt & litho tin, friction, 7¾", EX 70.00
Bandai, Dump Truck, tin litho, lever top, 1950s, 9", VG 50.00
Bandai, Ferrari Racer, pnt tin, b/o, working, 9", VG in box 55.00
Bandai, Highway Patrol Car, tin litho, b/o, 11", MIB 75.00
Bandai, Old Fashioned Fire Engine, tin litho, friction, 6½", VG ..25.00
Bandai, Old Timer Touring Car, pnt & litho tin, friction, 5", G ..25.00
Bandai, Vacation Set, pnt & litho tin, b/o, nonworking, 17", EX .140.00
Bing, Battleship, tin litho, 2-stack, clockwork, 16", G 700.00
Bing, Model T Coupe, tin litho w/up, man driver, 6½", EX 440.00
Bing, Model T Phaeton, tin litho w/up, lady driver, 6½", EX 470.00
Bing, Model T Roadster, tin litho w/up, couple, 6¼", EX 500.00
Bing, Model T Sedan, tin litho w/up, lady driver, 6½", EX 470.00
Bing, Race Car, tin litho w/up, w/driver, 5½", EX 635.00
Bing, Steam Locomotive & Cars, pnt CI w/up, 24", VG 110.00
Bing, Touring Car, tin litho, working, 9½", EX 550.00
Bing, Town Car, tin litho, clockwork, 7", EX 800.00
Bing, Van, tin litho, clockwork, 8", NM 1,200.00
Bliss, Fire House, litho on wood, 12½x10x3½", EX 775.00
Bliss, Noah's Ark, mk The Wonder, no animals, 10x22x6", EX .400.00
British Zone Germany, Jaguar XK120 Sport coupe, w/up, 6", M ..200.00
Buddy L, Aerial Ladder Truck, hydraulic, pnt steel, 26", G 210.00
Buddy L, Aerial Ladder Truck, pnt steel, rstr, 38", NM 425.00
Buddy L, Auto Wrecker, pnt steel, 27", EX 1,500.00
Buddy L, Chain Lift Dump Truck, pnt steel, 23½", VG 200.00
Buddy L, Dump Truck, pnt steel, no tailgate, 17", VG 50.00
Buddy L, Dump Truck, pnt steel, partial decal, 25", VG 240.00
Buddy L, Dump Truck, pnt steel, rstr, 23½" 300.00
Buddy L, Express Body Truck, pnt steel, partial decal, 25", VG ..300.00
Buddy L, Express Line Moving Van, pnt steel, 25", VG 375.00
Buddy L, Fire Truck w/Ladders, pnt steel, decals, 26", VG 350.00
Buddy L, Flivver Pickup, pnt steel, partial decal, 11", G 500.00
Buddy L, Flivver Roadster, pnt steel, orig decal, 11", G 525.00
Buddy L, Greyhound Bus, pnt steel w/bell, 16¼", G 55.00
Buddy L, Ice Delivery Truck, pnt steel, repro cover, 26", EX 600.00

Buddy L, Outdoor RR Box Car, pnt steel, 8-wheel, 21", G 250.00
Buddy L, Outdoor RR Caboose, pnt steel, 8-wheel, 19", G 650.00
Buddy L, Outdoor RR Locomotive & Tender, pnt steel, 33½", G ..450.00
Buddy L, Outdoor RR Tank Car, pnt steel, 8-wheel, 19", G 95.00
Buddy L, Outdoor RR Track, 3 str sections, 48", EX 40.00
Buddy L, Station Wagon, pnt wood/paper/plywood, 18½", G- 90.00
Buddy L, Station Wagon, pressed steel/plastic/wood, 15", G 30.00
Buddy L, Tank Line Truck, pnt steel, rstr, 25½" 600.00
Buddy L, Town & Country Convertible, pnt wood, 18½", G 75.00
Buddy L, Wrecking Truck, pnt steel, b/o lights, 18", VG 125.00
Buffalo Toy Works, Jackpot Slot Machine, metal, 6", EX 50.00
Carette, Limousine, pnt & litho tin, clockwork, 9", EX 1,980.00
Carette, Limousine, pnt tin, clockwork, w/head lamp, 9", G ...1,485.00
Carette, Phaeton, tin litho, rpl driver, 6", EX 220.00
Carette, Racecar #5, tin litho, rubber wheels, 9", EX 7,375.00
Carette, River Boat w/Sailors, pnt tin, clockwork, 7½", VG 770.00
Carette, Roadster, tin litho, clockwork, 10½", EX 4,625.00
Carette, Speedboat, pnt tin, clockwork, 10½", G 635.00
Carette, Town Car, tin litho, clockwork, 12", EX 3,850.00
Carpenter, Doctor's Cart, pnt CI, rpl figure/bench, 10", G 75.00
Champion, Ladder Truck, CI, NP wheels, 2 firemen, 7½", G 100.00
Chein, Hercules Ferris Wheel, tin litho w/up, working, 17", VG+ .250.00
Chein, Popeye in Barrel, tin litho w/up, nonworking, 7", G 200.00
Chein, Popeye in Barrel, tin litho w/up, 7", EX in box 900.00

Chein, Roller Coaster, tin lithographed wind-up, 10x20", MIB, $550.00.

Chein, Royal Blue Bus, pnt & litho tin, 18", G 250.00
Chein, Santa, tin litho w/up walker, 5½", EX 600.00
China, Motorcycle w/Sidecar, tin litho w/up, 7¼", EX 10.00
China, Sparking Police Patrol, tin litho, friction, 8", MIB 25.00
China, 1950 Cadillac Sedan, tin litho, friction, 10½", MIB 45.00
Converse, City Delivery Wagon, pnt tin, 11¼", VG 95.00
Courtland, Checker Cab, tin litho w/up, 6", VG 90.00
Cragston, Automatic Train & Station, tin, b/o, 9x4", MIB 188.00
Cragston, Greyhound Bus, tin, friction, 9¼", MIB 180.00
Criterion, Hula Hoop Monkey, tin & plastic w/up, 10", NMIB ..110.00
De Camp, tiger, hide covered, glass eyes, clockwork, 14", EX 300.00
Dent, Open Touring Car, CI, metal wheels, 2 figures, 9½", G 300.00
Distler, Fire Truck, tin litho, clockwork, 6 men, 15½", EX 525.00
Distler, Limousine, tin litho, inertia drive, 5¾", G 155.00
Distler, Open Touring Car, tin litho w/up, nonworking, 6", VG .155.00
Europe, Santa, papier-mache/wire/lead/cb w/up, 9¼", EX 1,300.00
Fischer, Limousine, tin litho, clockwork, 13", EX 2,200.00
Fischer, Ornithopter, tin litho & cl, clockwork, 9", EX 2,000.00
Fischer, Town Coupe, tin litho, clockwork, 9½", EX 3,850.00
Fisher-Price, Boom Boom Popeye, #491, 1937, EX 300.00
Fisher-Price, Bucky Burro, #166, 1955, NM 250.00
Fisher-Price, Butch the Pup, #333, 1952, M 75.00
Fisher-Price, Dog Cart Donald, #149, 1936, EX 700.00
Fisher-Price, Duckie Family, #799, 1940, NM 195.00

Fisher-Price, Jumbo Jitterbug, #422, 1940, EX 225.00
Fisher-Price, Merry Mousewife, #662, 1962, M 50.00
Fisher-Price, Merry Mutt, #473, 1949, EX 50.00
Fisher-Price, Nosey Pup, #445, 1956, VG 40.00
Fisher-Price, Peter Bunny Engine, #715, 1941, EX 225.00
Fisher-Price, Quacko Duck, #300, 1939, EX 100.00
Fisher-Price, Mini-Snowmobile, #705, 1979, EX 50.00
Fisher-Price, Snoopy Sniffer, #181, 1961, M 40.00
Fisher-Price, Teddy Xylophone, #752, old litho version, 1946, EX ...350.00
Fisher-Price, Walt Disney's Donald Duck, #208, 1936, G 200.00
Fisher-Price, Wheel Horse, #200, 1934, EX 285.00
Fleischman, Cruise Liner, pnt tin, clockwork, 20", EX 685.00
Fleischman, Flying Boat, tin, clockwork, rpt, 18", EX 5,170.00
Fontaine Fox, Toonerville Trolley, tin w/up, 1922, 7½", EX 850.00
Germany, #501 Dump Truck, metal w/up, 16", EX in box 175.00
Germany, Graf Zeppelin DLZ 127, tin litho, clockwork, 15", EX .635.00
Germany, Gyrocopter, tin litho, clockwork, 3¼", EX 275.00
Germany, Indian Motorcycle, tin litho, no mechanism, 4½", EX .600.00
Germany, Indian Motorcycle, tin litho w/up, 4½", EX 1,100.00
Germany, Motorcycle & Rider, tin litho w/up, 5", G 55.00
Germany, Toonerville Trolley, pnt & litho tin w/up, 5", G 600.00
Germany, Zeppelin, tin litho, clockwork, paper props, 7", G 525.00
Germany, Zeppelin, tin litho, clockwork, 10", EX 685.00
Girard, Air Express, tin litho, ratchet noisemaker, 9", EX 245.00
Girard, Fire Chief Siren Coupe, pnt steel, b/o, 14", G 140.00
Gunthermann, Airplane, w/2 propellers, tin litho w/up, 9", VG ..2,200.00
Gunthermann, Bicycle, tin litho, clockwork, 8", EX 1,650.00
Gunthermann, Dbl Phaeton Car, tin litho, clockwork, 7", EX .1,980.00
Gunthermann, Musical Clown, pnt tin, clockwork, 8", G 385.00
Gunthermann, Open Touring Car, pnt & litho tin, rare, 9", VG .3,850.00
Gunthermann, Open Town Car, tin litho, rubber tires, 9", EX 3,525.00
Gunthermann, Paris-Berlin Car, tin litho, clockwork, 6", EX .1,375.00
Gunthermann, Rear Entry Tonneau, tin litho, clockwork, 8", G .1,375.00
Gunthermann, Town Car, tin litho, clockwork, 10½", G 6,050.00
Gunthermann, Vis-a-Vis Car, tin litho, clockwork, 9", EX 4,400.00
Gunthermann, Wright Bros Type Airplane, tin w/up, 7", EX .1,000.00
Hans Erbel, Town Car, tin litho, rpl roof, 11½", EX 4,950.00
Hartland, Cochise on horse, MIB 265.00
Hartland, General Robert E Lee on horse, MIB 245.00
Hartland, Lone Ranger, 9½", MIB 275.00
Hartland, Tonto on horse, NM 200.00
Hartland, Willy Mays figure, NM 240.00
Hess, Avanti Race Car, tin litho, inertia drive, 5", EX 1,325.00

Hubley, Huber Road Roller, painted cast iron, 8", EX, $750.00.

Hubley, Bell Telephone Truck, pnt CI, 9", w/accessories, VG ...375.00
Hubley, Bremen Airplane, CI, minor pnt wear, 7½", VG 415.00
Hubley, Chrysler Airflow, CI, NP chassis, rpt, 6", VG 170.00
Hubley, Chrysler Airflow, pnt CI, NP trim, 8", G 600.00

Hubley, Coupe, CI, 2-door, 7", EX 200.00
Hubley, Fire Truck, pnt CI, red & yel wheels, 5½", VG 50.00
Hubley, Grasshopper, pnt CI, NP legs, 4½", EX 200.00
Hubley, Hose Reel Ladder Truck, CI, NP wheels, 5½", G 35.00
Hubley, Ladder Fire Truck, CI, rpl tires, 8", G 35.00
Hubley, Ladder Fire Truck, CI, transitional style, 23", EX 800.00
Hubley, Ladder Wagon, CI, bl w/yel wheels, 7½", G 70.00
Hubley, Lincoln Zephyr Sedan & House Trailer, CI w/NP, 14", VG .475.00
Hubley, Lindy Airplane, CI, gear-driven, rpl wing, 10", VG 500.00
Hubley, Lindy Monoplane, pnt CI, NP trim, recast wing, 9", VG ..350.00
Hubley, Lindy Monoplane, pnt CI, NP trim, rpl cowl, 9¼", EX .725.00
Hubley, Log Wagon, pnt CI, 2 oxen, Blk driver, 15¼", VG 525.00
Hubley, Patrol Wagon, CI, molded-in figures, 6½", EX 110.00
Hubley, Police Cycle & Sidecar, pnt CI, rpl figure, 8½", VG 450.00
Hubley, Road Roller, CI, w/driver, partial rpt, 14", EX 550.00
Hubley, Royal Circus Calliope Wagon, CI, some rpt, 16", EX ..2,500.00
Hubley, Royal Circus Horse-Drawn Giraffe Wagon, CI, 15½", G .1,400.00
Hubley, Surrey, pnt CI & sheet steel, rpl figure, 14", VG 250.00
Ives, Dumping Coal Wagon, pnt CI, Blk driver, brn mule, 13", VG .725.00
Ives, Gun Boat, tin litho, 2-stack, clockwork, 12½", VG 125.00
Ives, Horse-Drawn Fire Patrol Wagon, CI, 18", G 400.00
Ives, Horse-Drawn Fire Pumper, CI, clockwork, 18", G- 350.00
Ives, Negro Preacher, compo, clockwork, working, 10½", EX .5,200.00
Ives, Ocean Liner, tin litho, 1-stack, 2-mast, 10½", G 200.00
Ives, Ocean Liner New York, tin litho, clockwork, 13½", G 275.00
Japan, Allied Van Lines Truck, tin, friction, 9", MIB 170.00
Japan, Army Helicopter, tin litho & plastic w/up, 8", VG 30.00
Japan, Attacking Martian, tin, b/o, earliest version, 11", NMIB .250.00
Japan, Bell Ringing Santa Claus, tin/rubber/plush, b/o, 8", NM ...95.00
Japan, Bull & Boy, tin litho w/up, 9", EX 95.00
Japan, Clown Bump Car, tin litho, friction, 7", VG 85.00
Japan, Cowboy w/Lariat, tin litho w/up, cl head, 8¼", EX 35.00
Japan, Driving Pet #1, tin litho, friction, 1950s, 7", MIB 150.00
Japan, Fantasy Car, tin litho & plastic, friction, 9¾", G 50.00
Japan, Ferrari 365 GT BB, tin litho, b/o, working, NMIB 50.00
Japan, Flying Space Car, tin, friction, 1950s, 7x7", EX 465.00
Japan, Ford Mustang, barking dog inside, b/o, 13½", EX 650.00
Japan, Greyhound Bus, tin litho, b/o, nonworking, 7¼", G 40.00
Japan, Greyhound Bus, tin litho, friction, 11", VG 40.00
Japan, Happy Pup Car, tin litho, friction, 8", VG 40.00
Japan, Highway Patrol Car, tin litho, friction, 9", NMIB 95.00
Japan, Horse Transport Van, tin litho, friction, 9", MIB 150.00
Japan, John's Farm Truck, tin litho w/NP, b/o, 9", G 25.00
Japan, Loop Plane, tin litho, b/o, 9x9x5", NM 120.00
Japan, Loop Plane, tin litho, b/o, 9x9x5", NMIB 225.00
Japan, Mars Patrol Spacemobile, tin friction, 1950s, 6", EX 185.00
Japan, Mighty Robot, tin litho w/up, sparks, 5", MIB 150.00
Japan, Motorcycle Racer, tin litho, friction, 3½", NM 90.00
Japan, Mr Robot, tin litho, b/o, nonworking, 11", VG in box 300.00
Japan, Old Time Ford, tin litho, friction, 8", EX 30.00
Japan, Overland Express Train, tin litho, b/o, 16½", MIB 150.00
Japan, Police Auto Motorcycle, tin litho, friction, 8", EX 35.00
Japan, Robo Tank, tin & plastic, b/o, 5½x4", NM 300.00
Japan, Rocket Race, tin litho w/up, 1950s, 7", NM 300.00
Japan, Santa Claus Cycle, tin & cl w/up, 1950s, 4", MIB 135.00
Japan, Shasta Trailer, pnt tin, 9¾", VG 70.00
Japan, Space Super Jet Gun, tin & plastic, friction, 9", MIB 95.00
Japan, Sparkling Tank, tin w/up, pre-1940s, 5", NMIB 140.00
Japan, Studebaker Pickup, pnt tin, 1950s, 10", G 40.00
Japan, Thunderbolt Cap Firing Tank, tin, friction, 8", MIB 120.00
Japan, US Passenger Ship, tin litho, friction, 6½", NMIB 40.00
Japan, Walking Drummer, tin litho & cl w/up, 8¾", VG 95.00
Japan, Walking Robot, tin w/up, 7", EX 130.00
Japan, 1970 Camaro Z-28, tin w/NP, b/o, nonworking, 10", VG ..45.00

JML, Three-Wheeler Motorcycle, tin litho, clockwork, 14", VG ..770.00
Jones & Bixler, Army Motor Truck, CI, rpl driver, rpt, 15", VG ..325.00
KBN, Town Car, tin litho, clockwork, w/driver, 10½", VG ..11,750.00
Kenton, #21 Toy-Lands Treasure Chest Box, cb, 14x11", VG 20.00
Kenton, Air Mail Plane, pnt CI, 7", VG 475.00
Kenton, Buckeye Ditch Digger, CI, lt rust, 12½", VG 325.00
Kenton, Buckeye Ditch Digger, CI, NP gears/etc, 9", EX 300.00
Kenton, Car & House Trailer, pnt CI w/NP, rubber tires, 10", VG .450.00
Kenton, Cement Mixer Truck, CI, NP chute & drum, 8", EX 700.00
Kenton, Covered Wagon, 15", MIB 525.00
Kenton, Delivery Wagon, pnt CI, 2 horses, 14¾", VG 110.00
Kenton, Fire Engine, CI, 3 horses, molded-in figure, 10", MIB ...185.00
Kenton, Fire Truck, CI, no pnt or driver, 5¾", G 35.00
Kenton, Hansom Cab, pnt CI, 15¾", MIB 385.00
Kenton, Jaeger Cement Mixer Truck, CI, NP drum, 9", NM ..1,000.00
Kenton, Jaeger Cement Mixer Truck, CI, NP drum, 9¼", EX 725.00
Kenton, Ladder Truck, CI, rpr/rpl, 17½", G 200.00
Kenton, Mixer Truck, CI, NP drum, rubber tires, 7¼", VG 250.00
Kenton, Motorized Pumper, CI, molded-in driver, 7½", G 95.00
Kenton, Nash Sedan, CI, EX pnt, 4-door, 8", EX 5,200.00
Kenton, Open Touring Car, CI, 3 figures, 9", EX 400.00
Kenton, Overland Circus, pnt CI, 14", MIB 500.00
Kenton, Patrol Wagon, CI, bl pnt, missing figures, 6½", G 35.00
Kenton, Police Patrol Car, pnt CI, 4 repro figures, 9", VG 190.00
Kenton, Pumper, CI, molded-in driver, NP wheels, 5½", G 35.00
Kenton, Pumper, CI, molded-in driver, rubber tires, 7", EX 80.00
Kenton, Racer, pnt CI, rpl driver, 7", G 70.00
Kenton, Road Scraper, CI, NMIB 200.00
Keystone, Coal Car, pnt steel, rstr, 19" 50.00
Keystone, Dump Truck, pnt steel, Packard type, 26", VG 180.00
Keystone, Ladder Truck, pnt steel, 2 ladders, 28", G 300.00
Keystone, Sand Loader, pnt steel, chain op, 17½", G 50.00
Keystone, US Army Troop Carrier, pnt steel, canvas top, 26", EX .200.00
Keystone, Water Tower Truck, pnt steel, rstr, 32" 450.00
Ki Co, Motorcycle, tin litho, clockwork, 8½", EX 7,150.00
Kilgore, Rumble Seat Roadster, CI, no driver, 8", EX 250.00
Kilgore, Sea Gull Flying Boat, pnt CI, steel wheels, 8¼", VG 525.00
Kingsbury, Airflow Sedan, pressed steel w/up, rpt, 15", G 160.00
Kingsbury, Car & Trailer, pnt steel, 1930s style, 24", EX 150.00
Kingsbury, Fire Pumper, tin w/up, poor pnt, 9½" 195.00
Knickerbocker, monkey, stuffed, orig clothes, 13½", VG 25.00
KO, Bump 'N Go Car, pnt & litho tin, friction, 6¾", VG 35.00
KO, Hustling Bulldozer, tin, friction, 6", MIB 120.00
KO, Space Dog, tin litho, friction, sparks, 6", MIB 360.00
Lehmann, Alabama Coon Jigger, pnt & tin litho, 7", EX in box ..650.00
Lehmann, Balky Mule, pnt & litho tin w/up, 7¼", G 155.00
Lehmann, Dare Devil, tin litho w/up, working, 7", G 350.00
Lehmann, New Century Cycle, pnt & litho tin, 5", G 450.00
Lehmann, Tap-Tap, pnt & litho tin w/up, working, 7", VG 225.00
Lehmann, Zig-Zag, pnt & litho tin w/up, working, 5", G 825.00
Lesney, Jumbo the Elephant, tin w/up, 1950, 4", NM 775.00
Lesney, Muffin the Mule, tin, jtd, 1951, 5½", EX 250.00
Lindstrom, Santa, tin litho w/up, 8", VG 120.00
Linemar, Olive Oyl on Tricycle, tin w/up, rprs, 4", EX 250.00
Lionel, Peter Rabbit Chick-Mobile, compo & steel w/up, 9½", EX .625.00
Marklin, Sand Dumper Cart, CI/tin/wood, ca 1895, 15½", EX ..450.00
Marklin, Train Station, tin, bright pnt, 7½x11x5", EX 1,000.00
Marx, Amos 'N Andy Taxi, tin litho w/up, working, 8", VG 650.00
Marx, Army Bomber, tin litho w/up, 14" wingspan, EX 275.00
Marx, Batman Shooting Range, tin/plastic/metal, '55, EX in box .215.00
Marx, BO Plenty, tin litho w/up, 8¼", VG 190.00
Marx, Busy Bridge, tin litho w/up, 1930s style, 24", G 350.00
Marx, Campus Car, tin litho w/up, working, 5½", EX 250.00
Marx, Charleston Trio, tin litho w/up, working, 7¾", G 500.00

Marx, Charlie McCarthy Benzine Buggy, tin litho w/up, 8", VG ..400.00
Marx, City Coal Truck, tin litho w/up, working, 13", G 95.00
Marx, Climbing Fireman, tin litho w/up, 21", VG 300.00
Marx, Coupe, pnt & litho steel, b/o, nonworking, 15", G+ 100.00
Marx, Dump Truck, pnt steel, b/o lights, 10½", VG 60.00
Marx, Eagle Air Scout Airplane, tin litho, 1920s, 25½", EX 575.00
Marx, Honeymoon Express, tin litho w/up, 1950s, 9" dia, NM ...175.00
Marx, Hoppo the Monkey, tin litho w/up, 8", VG 130.00
Marx, Joe Penner, tin litho w/up, 8", EX 650.00
Marx, Johnny Tremain figure, w/horse & accessories, MIB 225.00
Marx, Lone Ranger Range Rider, tin w/up, 1938, 11", NMIB ..650.00
Marx, Lonesome Pine Trailer, tin litho, 8", VG 140.00
Marx, Main Street, tin litho w/up, 1920s style, 24", VG 375.00
Marx, Merchant's Transfer Truck, tin litho w/up, 11", G 100.00
Marx, Pinocchio the Acrobat, tin w/up, 17", G+ in EX box 350.00
Marx, Pioneer Air Express Airplane, tin litho, 1920s, 24", EX ...635.00
Marx, Police Motorcycle, tin litho w/up, 4½", G 130.00
Marx, Popeye & Olive Oyl Jigger, tin litho, clockwork, 9", VG ..750.00
Marx, Popeye Express, tin litho w/up, stationary parrot, 8", EX ..600.00
Marx, Popeye Pilot Airplane, tin litho, clockwork, 9", G 375.00
Marx, Popeye w/Parrot Cages, tin litho w/up, 8¼", G 350.00
Marx, Reversing Sedan, tin litho w/up, nonworking, 15", G 170.00
Marx, Roadside Rest Service Station w/Car, clockwork, 13½", VG ..675.00
Marx, Seawolf Submarine, tin litho, friction, 8", VG 150.00
Marx, Speed King Racer, tin litho w/up, nonworking, 16", G 125.00
Marx, Streamline Coupe, pnt & litho tin, clockwork, 14", G 95.00
Marx, Subway Express, tin litho w/up, 9¼", EX 250.00
Marx, Toyland Milk Wagon, tin litho w/up, 9", G 175.00
Mattel, Dancing Dude Music Box, metal/paper litho/cloth, NMIB .130.00
Meccano, Biplane, pressed steel, from kit, 12½", EX 385.00
Meccano, Passenger Biplane, pressed steel, from kit, 14", EX 415.00
MetalCraft, Heinz Truck, pressed steel, b/o lights, rstr, 12", EX .275.00
Moko, Limousine, tin litho, clockwork, rpl doors, 9", G 360.00
Mueller Kadeder, Zeppelin Go Round, pnt tin w/up, 10½", VG .770.00
Nat'l Products, Batman & Robin Walkie Talkies, b/o, '73, MIB ...100.00
Nat'l Products, Superman Movie Viewer, cb/plastic, M on card ...45.00
Nosco, Hot Rod Car, pnt plastic, friction, nonworking, 9", VG ...45.00
Nylint, Tri-Wheel Motorcycle Delivery, tin w/up, 7", NM 240.00
Occupied Japan, Banjo Playing Monkey, tin & plush w/up, 5", MIB .115.00
Pratt & Letchworth, Hanson Cab, pnt CI, rpl roller, 12", VG ...500.00
Pratt & Letchworth, Horse-Drawn Fire Pumper, CI, 17", G- 375.00
Pride Lines, Donald Duck Hand Car, pnt steel, 9½", NMIB 650.00
Pride Lines, Mickey Hand Car, pnt steel, 9½", EX in box 750.00
Pride Lines, Santa Hand Car, pnt steel, 9½", EX in box 300.00
Rich Toys, Borden's Milk Wagon, tin litho/wood, rprs, 18", VG .250.00
S&E Japan, Trigger Action Plane, tin, friction, 8", MIB 105.00
Schuco, Airplane Radiant 5600, b/o, 18½", EX 100.00
Schuco, Angel, tin w/up, cloth dressed, 5", EX 1,485.00
Schuco, Boy w/Girl, tin & cl w/up, cloth dressed, 5", VG 145.00
Schuco, Charlie Chaplin, tin w/up, cloth dressed, 6½", VG+ .1,700.00
Schuco, Clown Drummer, tin w/up, cloth dressed, 4½", EX 160.00
Schuco, Clown Violinist, tin w/up, cloth dressed, 4½", EX 175.00
Schuco, Clown w/Boy, tin w/up, cloth dressed, 5", VG 660.00
Schuco, Drinking Monk, tin w/up, cloth dressed, 5", EX 125.00
Schuco, Drinking Mouse, tin w/up, cloth dressed, 4", EX 175.00
Schuco, Monkey Drummer, tin w/up, cloth dressed, 4½", NM ...200.00
Schuco, Rabbit, tin w/up, cloth dressed, 6¼", EX 1,100.00
Schylling, Whirly-Bird Helicopter, tin litho, friction, 10", EX 15.00
Slik, Sand & Gravel Truck, pnt metal, rubber tires, 13", G 10.00
Strauss, Ham & Sam, tin litho w/up, working, 6", NM 1,200.00
Strauss, Ham & Sam, tin litho w/up, 6", G 250.00
Strauss, Tombo Coon Jigger, tin litho w/up, 10¼", G 600.00
Structo, Dump Truck, pnt tin, red w/orange wheels, 18", G 160.00
Structo, Ladder Truck, pnt tin, rstr, 18" 275.00

Structo, Tank Truck, pnt pressed steel, rstr, 26" 275.00
Structo, Tractor Trailer, pnt aluminum, 22", G 35.00
Tipp, Hindenburg Zeppelin, tin litho, clockwork, 11", EX 825.00
Tipp, Race Car #32, tin litho, clockwork, 16", EX 2,975.00
TN, Circus Jet, tin litho, b/o, 12", EX in box 120.00
TN, Drumming Indian, cloth/vinyl/tin, b/o, 12", VG 25.00
TN, Gunboat, tin litho w/up, nonworking, 6¾", VG 30.00
TN, Helicopter, tin litho, friction, 10½", VG 30.00
TN, Hot Rod, pnt & litho tin, friction, 7", EX 85.00
TN, Hy-Que Monkey, tin litho/cloth, b/o, 17", VG 45.00
TN, Mechanical Circus Seal, tin & plush w/up, 6", MIB 70.00
TN, Old Time Auto, tin litho, friction, 7½", VG 30.00
Tootsietoy, Andy Gump Car, pnt cast metal, 2¾", G 350.00
Tootsietoy, Boat Tail Roadster, #233, EX 18.00
Tootsietoy, Buick Roadster, #6001, NM 60.00
Tootsietoy, Chevrolet Deluxe Panel Truck, EX 25.00
Tootsietoy, Civilian Jeep, M 27.50
Tootsietoy, Ford Ranch Wagon, 3", NM 22.50
Tootsietoy, Hook & Ladder truck, #1040, EX 24.50
Tootsietoy, International Tractor, NM 17.50
Tootsietoy, Oldsmobile Brougham, #6303, EX 45.00
Tootsietoy, Submarine, #128, EX 7.50
Tootsietoy, 1907 Stanley Steamer, NM 22.00
TPS, Happy Hippo, tin litho w/up, 6x6", NM 435.00
TPS, Happy the Violinist, tin & plush w/up, 9", NMIB 250.00
TPS, Playful Puppy, tin litho w/up, M in wrapper 85.00
Union Mfg, Steam Launch, polished brass, Little Pet, 13", EX ..1,450.00
Unique Art, GI Joe & K-9 Pups, tin litho w/up, 9", EX 225.00
Unique Art, GI Joe Jeep, tin litho w/up, 6¾", EX 275.00
Unique Art, Kiddy Cyclist, tin litho w/up, working, 8¼", EX 200.00
Unique Art, Li'l Abner Dogpatch Band, tin litho, working, 9", VG .350.00
Unique Art, Lincoln Tunnel, tin litho w/up, 24", VG 220.00
USA, Robot Lamp, metal & plastic, electric, 1950s, 12", NM ...330.00
W Germany, Apollo Saucer, tin friction, 1950s, 4" dia, MIB 150.00
White, Four-Seat Touring Car, pnt tin, 10", EX 2,500.00
Wilkins, Blk Man in Cart, pnt CI, mule drawn, 10½", VG 250.00
Wilkins, Horse-Drawn Hanson Cab, CI, no driver, 11", VG 225.00
Wolverine, Car & Trailer, tin litho, 1940s style, 28", EX 190.00
Wolverine, Merry Go Round, tin litho, lever op, 11", VG 160.00
Wolverine, Mystery Car, pnt & litho tin, clockwork, 13", VG ...120.00
Wolverine, Sunny Andy Kiddie Kampers, tin w/up, w/scout, EX ..350.00
Wolverine, Zilotone, tin litho, clockwork, 6 disks, 7½", EX 2,000.00
Wolverine, Zilotone, tin litho w/up, 3 disks, working, VG 1,500.00
Wyandotte, Airplane, pnt steel, NP propellers, 9½", VG 70.00
Wyandotte, Ambulance, pnt steel, NP grille, 11", VG 120.00
Wyandotte, Boat-Tail Racer, pnt steel, b/o lights, 8½", VG 100.00
Wyandotte, Humphrey Mobile, tin litho w/up, 8½", VG 500.00
Wyandotte, Monoplane, pnt steel, 7", G 40.00
Wyandotte, Pan Am Clipper, pnt steel/brass/NP, 9", EX 275.00
Wyandotte, Sedan, pnt pressed steel, 6½", VG 55.00
Wyandotte, Stake Truck, pnt steel, wood milk cans, 12", G 110.00

Farm Toys

Combine, Case, wht metal, G 175.00
Hay loader, Vindex, M 525.00
Hay wagon, pnt wood, iron wheels, cloth-covered horse, 26", EX ..350.00
Mowing machine, Wilkins, rpt CI, 10½", G 2,250.00
Plow, Internat'l Harvester, 3-bottom, red pnt, 8", G 16.50
Threshing machine, Arcade, McCormick-Deering, pnt CI, 9½", VG .350.00
Threshing machine, Arcade, red/wht/bl pnt CI, rprs, 10½", VG ..100.00
Tractor, Arcade, Allis Chalmers, w/dump wagon, 12½", EX 275.00
Tractor, Arcade, Fordson, pnt CI, orig decal, 5¾", VG 375.00
Tractor, Arcade, McCormick-Deering, pnt CI, 10", G 215.00

Tractor, Ertl, Case, #2590 ....62.50
Tractor, Hubley, steam boiler in front, early 1920s, 4¾" 65.00
Tractor, Japan, Allis Chalmers type, friction, 5", EX 27.50
Tractor, McCormick-Deering, CI, rpl figure, rpt, 7½", VG 100.00
Tractor, Minneapolis Moline, cast driver, ca 1956, EX 24.00
Truck, pickup; Internat'l Harvester, plastic & metal, EX 125.00
Wagon, Internat'l Harvester, red pnt, rubber wheels, 4½" 9.00
Wagon, Wilkins, pnt CI & sheet metal, horse & driver, 14", G .195.00

Guns: Cast-Iron Cap Guns

Though toy guns were patented as early as the 1850s, the cap pistol was not invented until 1870, when paper caps that were primarily developed to detonate muzzleloaders became available. Some of the earlier models were very ornate and were occasionally decorated with figural heads. Most are marked with the name of their manufacturer; Ace, Daisy, Bulldog, Victor, and Excelsior are the most common. Caution! Reproductions exist.

Our advisor for toy guns is James Schleyer, nationally recognized author, collector, and appraiser of toy guns. He is listed in the Directory under Virginia. Please include a SASE when requesting information. See also Toy Gun Purveyors listed in the Directory under Clubs, Newsletters and Catalogs.

Kilgore cast-iron cap guns from the 1940s, Long Tom (top), light grips, 10⅜", rare, M, $500.00; Roy Rogers, polished, gray grips, EX, $650.00.

American, Kilgore, revolving cylinder, 1940, 9⅜", VG 250.00
Army 45 Auto, Hubley, 1945, 6½", M 135.00
Atta Boy, single shot, Hubley, 1935, 4", G- 30.00
Bango, eng, jewels, Stevens, 1940, 7½", VG 70.00
Big Bill, single shot, Kilgore, 1935, 4⅞", M 65.00
Big Horn, revolving cylinder, Kilgore, 1940, 8⅝", M 400.00
Big Scout, single shot, Stevens, 1930, 9⅜", VG 110.00
Billy the Kid, single shot, Stevens, 1940s, 6¾", G- 100.00
Border Patrol, automatic, Kilgore, 1935, 4½", VG 65.00
Buc-A-Roo, single shot, Kilgore, 1940, 7¾", M 100.00
Buffalo Bill, single shot, Kenton, 1930, rare, 13½", VG 45.00
Buffalo Bill, single shot, Stevens, 1890, rare, 11¾", G- 235.00
Bulldog, single shot, Hubley, 1935, 6", G 35.00
Bunker Hill, single shot, National, 1925, 5¼", M 95.00
Captain, automatic, Kilgore, 1940, 4¼", VG 65.00
Champ, automatic, Star Medallion, Hubley, 1940, 5", EX 100.00
Chief, single shot, Dent, 1935, 7½", VG 110.00
Colt, single shot, Stevens, 1900, 5½", EX 75.00
Cowboy, Hubley, 1940, 8", VG 65.00
Cowboy King, Stevens, 1940, 9", M 250.00
Dick, automatic, Hubley, 1930, 4⅛", VG 45.00
Doughboy, automatic, Kilgore, 1920, 4⅞", VG 100.00
Eagle, single shot, Hubley, 1935, 8½", VG 125.00

G-Man, automatic, Kilgore, 1935, 5¼", G- 45.00
Gene Autry, dummy, Kenton, 1940, rare, 8⅜", M 325.00
Gene Autry, eng, Kenton, 1940, rare, 6½", VG 300.00
Gene Autry, repeater, NP, Kenton, 1940, 8⅜", VG 220.00
Invincible, Kilgore, 1935, 5¼", G- 45.00
Lasso 'Em Bill, revolving cylinder, Kilgore, 1930, 9", EX 275.00
Lawmaker, blk, Kenton, 1940, 8⅜", M 210.00
Lone Eagle, revolving cylinder, Kilgore, 1930, 5¼", EX 150.00
Lone Ranger, NP, Kilgore, 1940, rare, 8¼", M 345.00
Long Boy, single shot, Kilgore, 1920, 11⅛", VG 135.00
Long Tom, revolving cylinder, Kilgore, 1940, rare, 10⅜", M 500.00
Mohican, single shot, Dent, 1930, 6¼", EX 65.00
National Auto, National, 1915, 3¾", G- 25.00
Officer's Pistol, automatic, Kilgore, 1940, rare, 6", M 250.00
Pawnee Bill, Stevens, 1940, 7⅝", VG 135.00
Peacemaker, gold, Stevens, 1940, 8½", M 175.00
Pirate, dbl bbl, Hubley, 1940, 9⅜", M 145.00
Presto, automatic, Kilgore, 1940, 5⅛", VG 65.00
Rodeo, single shot, Hubley, 1940, 7", EX 50.00
Roy Rogers, polished, Kilgore, 1940, rare, 10¼", EX 650.00
Scout, single shot, Stevens, 1890, 7", VG 75.00
Six Shooter, revolving cylinder, Kilgore, 1940, 6½", VG 85.00
Spitfire, automatic, Kilgore, 1940, 4⅝", EX 90.00
Texan, revolving cylinder, NP, Hubley, 1940, 9¼", M 185.00
Texan Jr, Hubley, 1940, 8⅛", VG 70.00
Trooper Safety, repeater, Kilgore, 1925, 10¼", M 145.00
Two Time, rubber band, Kenton, 1929, 9¼", VG 135.00
Warrior, repeater, NP, Kilgore, 9", EX 145.00
Wild West, single shot, Kenton, 1920s, rare, 11½", M 285.00
101 Ranch, single shot, Hubley, 1930, 11½", VG 225.00
2-in-1, rubber band, Stevens, 1930, 9¼", VG 110.00
49-er, Stevens, 1940, 9", M 250.00

Guns: Early-Style Figural Guns and Cap Bombs

Admiral Dewey Bomb, CI, Grey Iron, 1900, 1¾", EX 185.00
Butting Match, CI, Ives, 1885, 5", EX 375.00
Cannon, CI, Kenton, 1900, 4⅞", VG 450.00
Chinese Must Go, CI, Ives, 1880, 4¾", G- 275.00
Clown on Powder Keg, CI, Ives, 1890s, 3¾", VG 350.00
Devil's Head Bomb, CI, .22 blank, Ives, 1880, 2¼", VG 250.00
Dog's head Bomb, CI, Ives, 1880, 2⅛", EX 130.00
Double-Face Man, CI, Ives, 1890, 1⅝", G- 85.00
George Washington Bomb, CI, 1900, 1¼", EX 225.00
Hobo Bomb, CI, Ideal, 1890s, 2", G- 90.00
Liberty Bell Bomb, CI, 1876, 2⅜", EX 125.00
Lightening Express, CI, Kenton, 1900, 5", EX 475.00
Punch & Judy, CI, Ives, 1880s, 5¼", VG 500.00
Sea Serpent, CI, Stevens, 1890, 3½", EX 600.00
Yellow Kid Bomb, CI, Grey Iron, 1900, 1½", VG 135.00

Pedal Cars and Ride-On Toys

AG Spalding & Bros Target Kite Mark 1, cloth & wood, 60", EX ...120.00
BMC Tractor, pnt steel, chain drive, 37", VG 50.00
C Higgins Boy's Bicycle, red & wht w/yel, 60", M rstr 330.00
Garton Kidillac Cadillac, pressed steel, rstr pnt, 43", EX 225.00
John Deere Tractor, pressed steel/cast aluminum, 20", +trailer ..235.00
Keystone Locomotive, pnt steel, NP trim, rstr, 26" 150.00
Keystone Pullman Train Car, pressed steel, rstr, 25" 145.00
Keystone Steam Shovel, pnt steel, metal wheels, 21", VG 65.00
Keystone Wrecker, pnt steel, rstr, 19" 100.00
Marx Fire Truck, pnt steel, missing steering wheel, 31", G- 110.00
Olson Blk Hawk Airplane, pnt sheet metal, recent, 51", M 1,100.00

Wards, Hawthorne Girl's Bicycle, gr & cream, 70", M 250.00

Penny Toys

Airplane, tin litho, open cockpit w/pilot, 5", EX 250.00
Airplane w/Hanger, tin litho, Germany, 3", EX 465.00
Auto Coach w/Driver, tin litho, Meier, 3¼", VG 110.00
Beetle, tin litho, legs move as wheels turn, 1900s, 1⅞", NM 185.00
Carousel, pnt/litho tin, Meier, 2¾", EX 875.00
Horseless Carriage, tin litho, Meier, rare, 3¾", EX 950.00
Man w/Wheelbarrow, tin litho, 3", EX 120.00
Open Touring Car, tin litho, Distler, 3½", EX 120.00
Pool Player, tin litho, animated, Kellerman, 4", EX 120.00
Reindeer on Platform, tin litho, Germany, 4", EX 220.00
Sedan Delivery, tin litho, Germany, 4", EX 200.00
Squirrel Cage Whistle, tin litho, Germany, 4½", EX 165.00
Vis-a-Vis Car, tin litho, inertia mechanism, Meier, 3", EX 365.00

Pipsqueaks

Pipsqueak toys were popular among the Pennsylvania Germans. The earliest had bellows made from sheepskin. Later cloth replaced the sheepskin, and finally paper bellows were used.

Cat, cloth over wood/compo, glass eyes, ribbon, label, 4" 115.00
Dog, seated, papier-mache, orig blk/mc pnt, rpl/damage, 4½" 50.00
Parrot, papier-mache, mc pnt, faint squeak, 6⅝", VG 50.00
Peacock, papier-mache, 4-color pnt, silent, lt wear, 5¾" 265.00
Rooster, papier-mache, mc pnt, spring legs, 7", VG 155.00
Rooster, papier-mache, orig pnt/gilt, spring legs, 8", EX 265.00
Rooster in cage, wood, printed paper & feathers, 6¾", G 40.00
Rooster in house, paper on wood, Germany, 6½", VG 200.00

Pull Toys

Camel on platform, painted tin, offset wheels, American, early, 9", VG, $2,700.00.

Clown disk revolves, bellringer, tin, 9½" 110.00
Duck, papier-mache on wooden base w/cb wheels, mc pnt, 4" ...120.00
Felix the Cat w/2 mice, tin litho, 1930s, 7½", EX 950.00
Horse, wood & papier-mache, fiber tail, 7¼x6½" 165.00
Horse & wagon, tin & steel, w/bell, 13½", VG 95.00
Kicking mule, bellringer, pnt CI, ca 1900, 7¾", EX+ 1,200.00
Kitten on wheels, cloth-covered compo, tin wheels, 8", VG 130.00
Sheep, wood/wool/papier-mache, tin wheels, lt wear, 7¼" 360.00

Schoenhut

Bear, glass eyes, open mouth, worn brn pnt, 4" 350.00
Bulldog, pnt eyes, regular, NM 685.00
Camel, Arabian; glass eyes, regular, EX 1,200.00

Camel, Bactrian, pnt eyes, reduced, EX 300.00
Clown, bsk head, regular, EX 200.00
Donkey, pnt eyes, regular, NM 85.00
Elephant, glass eyes, worn tusks, EX pnt, regular 100.00
Golfer Man, regular, EX 450.00
Happy Hooligan, EX 1,500.00
Hippopotamus, pnt eyes, regular, EX 365.00
Hobo, pressed wood head, reduced, NM 425.00
Horse, wht, pnt eyes, reduced, VG 120.00
Ladder, EX 15.00
Lady Acrobat, wooden pressed head, regular, NM 450.00
Leopard, pnt eyes, reduced, NM 380.00
Milk wagon, Fairmount Farms, 24", EX 950.00
Naturalist, EX 1,750.00
Negro Dude, wooden pressed head, regular, VG 345.00
Ostrich, pnt eyes, reduced, EX 385.00
Polar Bear, pnt eyes, regular, NM 895.00
Rhino, glass eyes, regular, NM 950.00
Rhino, pnt eyes, rpl horn, slight wear, regular 340.00
Table, EX 32.00
Teddy Roosevelt, NM 2,000.00
Tent, 24x36", EX 1,850.00
Tiger, pnt eyes, regular, EX 375.00
Zebra, glass eyes, some fading, 7" 375.00
Zebra, pnt eyes, regular, NM 550.00

Steiff

Margaret Steiff began making her felt stuffed toys in Germany in the late 1800s. The animals she made were tagged with an elephant in a circle. Her first teddy bear, made in 1903, became such a popular seller that she changed her tag to a bear. Felt stuffing was replaced with excelsior and wool; when it became available, foam was used. In addition to the tag, look for the 'Steiff' ribbon and the button inside the ear. For further information we recommend *Teddy Bears and Steiff Animals,* a full-color identification and value guide by Margaret Fox Mandel, available Collector Books or your public library. See also Teddy Bears.

Baboon, Coco, sitting, worn ruff, w/tags & button, 10½", NM ... 400.00
Boar, plastic tusks, no ID, 6x8", VG 85.00
Bulldog, mohair w/velvet muzzle, unmk, 4", VG 55.00
Coral Fish, Puff, bl & gr wool, w/button & tag, 2", M 30.00
Cow, Bessy, w/udders, orig collar & bell, tag only, 6x9", M 265.00
Dog, Cockie, googly eyes, w/button & tag, 8", EX 115.00
Dog, Floppy (poodle), unmk baby toy, 9", EX 55.00
Dog, Raudi, orig collar & tag, 9x9", VG 145.00
Dog, Snobby Poodle, gray, jtd, orig collar, full ID, 8x7½", M 150.00
Duck, mc, w/button & tag, 4x5", M 85.00
Fawn, Bambi, velvet, w/button, 5x4", EX 85.00
Goose, w/button & tag, 4½", M 145.00
Hamster, Goldy, Dralon, w/button & tag, 7", VG 35.00
Hamster, Goldy, w/buttons & tags, 3½", M 120.00
Lion, standing, w/button, 3½x4", EX 65.00
Owl, Wittie, w/button & tag, 8½", EX 95.00
Owl, Wittie puppet, w/button & tags, M 85.00
Parrot, hand puppet, w/button & tag, M 250.00
Penguin, Peggy, w/button & tags, 3", NM 95.00
Pig, pk, w/button & tag, 2", VG 135.00
Puppy, Mopsey, swivel head, brass button, 5", M 55.00
Rabbit, Manni, w/button & tags, 4½", M 95.00
Rabbit, Ossi, orig ribbon, w/button & tags, 8x5", M 95.00
Raccoon, Molly Raggy, w/full ID, 8", NM 75.00
Tiger, fully jtd, w/button, M 350.00
Tiger, recumbent, chest tag, 9", M 110.00

Zebra, w/button & tag, 6x5", M 75.00

Toy Soldiers

Unique to this country are what are called 'Dimestore' soldiers; they were made by various companies from the 1930s until sometime in the 1950s. The most common are Barclay, Manoil, and Jones (hollow cast lead); Grey Iron (cast iron); and Auburn (rubber). They're about 4 to 4½" high. They were sold in Woolworth and Kresge's 5 & 10 Stores (most for just five cents), hence the name 'Dimestore.' Marx made tin soldiers for use in target gun games; these sell for about $4.00. Condition is most important as these toys were made to play with. They're most often found with much of the paint worn off. In the listings that follow, prices are for examples in excellent condition which means they show very little wear. Please remember that these pieces are only representative. There were over 600 made, plus a number of others by minor makers such as Tommy Toy and All-Nu, all of which are higher priced. Serious collectors should to refer to *Collecting Toys* (1993) or *Toy Soldiers,* (1992) both by Richard O'Brien, Books Americana, Inc. Reference numbers are those used in O'Brien's books and are considered the standard for the hobby. Another very popular toy soldier has been made by Britains of England since 1893. They are smaller and more detailed than 'Dimestores,' and variants number in the thousands. O'Brien's 'Toy Soldier' book has over 200 pages devoted to Britains and other foreign makers. Our advisor for this category is Tim O'Callaghan; he is listed in the Directory under Michigan.

Auburn, A002, infantry private 12.00
Auburn, A006, Foreign Legion private 18.00
Auburn, A009, officer marching 12.00
Auburn, A014, Red Cross doctor 32.00
Auburn, A015, nurse, wht 32.00
Auburn, A019, signalman 58.00
Auburn, A020, sniper, crawling, rifle on bk 70.00
Auburn, A021, standing, throwing hand grenade 22.00
Auburn, A030, sound detector 38.00
Auburn, A034, running w/ammo box 37.50
Auburn, A036, motor scout 40.00
Barclay, B007, flagbearer, cast helmet 20.00
Barclay, B013, sniper firing, long stride, tin helmet 22.00
Barclay, B023, officer w/sword, short stride 27.00
Barclay, B030, bugler, long stride, tin helmet 18.00
Barclay, B035, West Point officer, short stride 18.00
Barclay, B041, Italian officer 200.00
Barclay, B054, Naval officer, short stride, tin helmet 95.00
Barclay, B058, marine in dress uniform 28.00
Barclay, B067, telephone operator 18.00
Barclay, B071, sentry 17.00
Barclay, B086, sharpshooter, short stride 20.00
Barclay, B092, soldier w/gas mask charging, cast helmet 28.00
Barclay, B101, machine gunner long stride, kneeling 20.00
Barclay, B104, wounded, tin helmet 17.00
Barclay, B107a, bayonetting, cast helmet 285.00
Barclay, B111, cook peeling potatoes 24.00
Barclay, B132, w/field phone, cast helmet 65.00
Barclay, B146, surgeon & soldier 120.00
Barclay, B201, flagbearer, WWII helmet 22.00
Barclay, B211, marching 24.00
Barclay, B233, kneeling & firing, WWII, khaki 12.00
Barclay, B236, bugler 12.00
Barclay, B256, wounded head & arm 30.00
Grey Iron, G003, Colonial color bearer, rare 365.00
Grey Iron, G005, cadet, early version 18.00
Grey Iron, G021, carrying ammo boxes 95.00

Grey Iron, G023, doughboy w/bayonet 22.00
Grey Iron, G024, cavalryman, early 35.00
Grey Iron, G029, doughboy charging 15.00
Grey Iron, G034, cavalryman, sm 32.00
Grey Iron, G043, Royal Canadian mounted policeman 45.00
Grey Iron, G061, machine gunner 15.00
Grey Iron, G066, sailor, wht uniform 16.00
Grey Iron, G098, wounded, on crutches 42.00
Grey Iron, G105, soldier helping wounded man 260.00
Grey Iron, G111, Foreign Legion bomber 38.00
Jones, J007, litter bearer 110.00
Jones, J012, seated, w/rifle 75.00
Jones, J014, prone, firing rifle 120.00
Jones, J018, ammunition carrier, scarce 385.00
Jones, J019, motorcycle rider 110.00
Jones, J028, doctor w/medical bag 78.00
Jones, J029, standing & firing rifle 110.00
Jones, J032, marching, carrying rifle 115.00
Manoil, M001, flag bearer, hollow base 78.00
Manoil, M003, flag bearer 30.00
Manoil, M010, officer, 2nd version 78.00
Manoil, M015, drummer 36.00
Manoil, M023, sailor, hollow base 45.00
Manoil, M025, marine, hollow base 70.00
Manoil, M035, doctor, khaki 32.00
Manoil, M039, machine gunner, seated 25.00
Manoil, M048, sniper 20.00
Manoil, M058a, stretcher carrier w/medical kit, # on bk 95.00
Manoil, M062, soldier charging w/bayonet 38.00
Manoil, M066, kneeling w/bayonet 65.00
Manoil, M080, motorized machine gunner 45.00
Manoil, M084, sitting, eating 48.00
Manoil, M088, parachute jumper 22.00
Manoil, M101, lineman & telephone pole w/oval base 90.00
Manoil, M187, flag bearer, WWII, smaller sz 32.00

Trains

Electric trains were produced as early as the late 19th century. Names to look for are Lionel, Ives, and American Flyer.

The following listings were prepared by our advisor, Bruce C. Greenberg (see the Directory under Maryland), and are taken from his comprehensive publications on Lionel, American Flyer, and Ives trains. The prices presented are the most common versions of each item. In many cases, there are several other variations often having a substantially higher value. Identification numbers given in the listings below actually appear on the item.

Key: Std Gauge — Standard Gauge

American Flyer 21210, S Gauge diesel engine, VG 90.00
American Flyer 21801, S Gauge diesel engine, EX 100.00
American Flyer 282, S Gauge engine w/tender, EX 60.00
American Flyer 287, S Gauge engine w/tender, EX 100.00
American Flyer 295, S Gauge engine w/tender, EX 225.00
American Flyer 300AC, S Gauge engine w/tender, EX 50.00
American Flyer 499, S Gauge electric engine, EX 550.00
Ives 10, O Gauge steam engine w/tender, 1930, G 75.00
Ives 1100, O Gauge steam engine w/tender, 1917-22, EX 175.00
Ives 1117, O Gauge steam engine w/tender, 1915-16, EX 250.00
Ives 17, O Gauge steam engine w/tender, 1917-25, EX 250.00
Ives 1764, Wide Gauge electric engine, repro, EX 425.00
Ives 1764, Wide Gauge electric engine, 1930, EX 3,000.00
Ives 3218, O Gauge electric engine, 1914-16, VG 275.00

Ives 3235, Wide Gauge electric engine, 1924-25, EX 200.00
Ives 3236, Wide Gauge electric engine, 1926-27, G 125.00
Ives 3237, Wide Gauge electric engine, 1930, G 700.00
Ives 3242, Wide Gauge electric engine, 1924-26, EX 300.00
Ives 3251, O Gauge electric engine, 1919-27, VG 100.00
Ives 3255, O Gauge electric engine, 1925, EX 275.00
Lionel 10, Std Gauge electric engine, 1925-29, G 100.00
Lionel 152, O Gauge electric engine, 1917-26, EX 140.00
Lionel 1664, 027 Gauge steam engine w/tender, 1938-42, EX 85.00
Lionel 1666, 027 Gauge steam engine w/tender, 1938-42, EX 160.00
Lionel 1668, 027 Gauge steam engine w/tender, 1937-41, EX 140.00
Lionel 1689, 027 Gauge steam engine w/tender, 1936-37, G 65.00
Lionel 1835, Std Gauge steam engine, 1934-39, VG 625.00
Lionel 2035, 027 Gauge steam engine w/tender, 1950-51, VG 90.00
Lionel 225, O Gauge steam engine w/tender, 1938-42, EX 400.00
Lionel 229, 027 Gauge diesel engine A unit only, 1961, EX 120.00
Lionel 231, 027 Gauge diesel engine, 1961-63, EX 120.00
Lionel 2359, O Gauge diesel engine, 1961, EX 295.00
Lionel 2360, O Gauge electric engine, 1956-58, 61-63, G 425.00
Lionel 237, 027 Gauge steam engine w/tender, 1963-66, EX 60.00
Lionel 238, O Gauge steam engine w/tender, 1936-38, EX 210.00
Lionel 249, 027 Gauge steam engine w/tender, 1958, EX 50.00
Lionel 252, O Gauge electric engine, 1926-32, EX 140.00
Lionel 253, O Gauge electric engine, 1924-32, G 95.00
Lionel 318, Std Gauge electric engine, 1924-32, G 125.00
Lionel 38, Std Gauge electric engine, 1913-24, VG 125.00
Lionel 392E, Std Gauge steam engine, 1932-39, EX 1,150.00
Lionel 600, 027 Gauge diesel engine, 1955, G 95.00
Lionel 614, 027 Gauge diesel engine, 1959-60, EX 210.00
Lionel 637, O Gauge steam engine w/tender, 1958-63, G 80.00

Trade Signs

Trade signs were popular during the 1800s. They were usually made in an easily recognizable shape that one could mentally associate with the particular type of business it was to represent, especially appropriate in the days when many customers could not read!

Pocketknife, carved and painted wood, movable blades, inscribed New York Cutlery Co., ca 1900, 30", EX, $3,000.00.

Boot, rubber w/pin striping, Ales Goodyear Shoe Co, 36", EX ...935.00
Butcher's tools, CI, bull finial, 17x15", EX 350.00
Cod fish, pnt sheet metal, 1800s, 30½" 750.00
Dbl-bbl shotgun w/ramrod, cvd/pnt wood, 1800s, 100" 1,100.00
Key shape, Keys Made, enamel on metal, locksmith's, EX 150.00
Mortar & pestle, trn wood, sheet zinc lid, rpt, mortar: 11" 285.00
Powder horn form w/rpt horses & riders, 43" L 330.00
Watch, CI & tin, worn pnt, 22x16", EX 625.00

Watch, wood, iron stem, gold-pnt numerals, 15" dia 885.00
Watch, wood w/cast ring, Bulova, mc pnt, 28" dia 195.00
Watch, zinc w/old worn blk & gold rpt, 19¼" 195.00

Tramp Art

'Tramp' is considered a type of Folk Art. In America it was primarily made from the end of the Civil War through the 1930s. It comes from carving and decorating methods which are much older, originating mostly from Germany and Scandinavia. 'Trampen' probably refers to the itinerant stages of Middle Ages craft apprenticeship. The carving techniques were also used for practice. Tramp Art was perpetuated by soldiers in the Civil War and primarily practiced where there was a plentiful and free supply of materials such as cigar boxes and fruit crates. The belief that this work was done by tramps and hobos as payment for room or meals is generally incorrect. The larger pieces especially, would have required a lengthy stay in one place.

There is a great variety of tramp art, from boxes and frames, which are most common, to large furniture and intricate objects. The most common method of decoration is chip carving with several layers built one on top of another. There are several variations of that form and others such as 'Crown of Thorns,' an interlocking method, which are completely different. The most common finishes were lacquer or stain, although paints were also used. The value of Tramp Art varies according to size, detail, surface, and complexity. The new collector should be aware that Tramp Art is being made today. While some sell it as new, others are offering it as old. In addition, many people mistakenly use the term as a catchall phrase to refer to other forms of construction — expecially things they are uncertain about. Our advisor is Matt Lippa; he is listed in the Directory under Alabama.

Dresser, one large and three small drawers, carved roses and leaves, 13" to top of mirror, EX, $450.00.

Box, built-up lid & sides, leather strap on front, 8x10x9" 115.00
Box, built-up notched layers, red pnt w/gilt, 3x7x5" 100.00
Box, built-up notched-cvd rectangular sides, lid removes, 10" 250.00
Box, built-up rectangle panels allover, 8x8x10", EX 150.00
Box, comb; simple V-bk, appl strips, stamped eagle, 8x9x4" 35.00
Box, dbl ped, built-up panels, 2 on lid/front/bk, 10" L 120.00
Box, dbl ped, built-up pyramids & strips, lid removes, 8x10x7" ..475.00
Box, hinged lid w/mirror, built-up triangles, 8x9x11" 650.00
Box, jewelry; tiered octagonal-shaped layers, 5x5x4¼" 90.00
Box, jewelry; tin-fr sq mirror w/in, 2-tier, appl hearts, 6" 200.00
Box, layered, 2 lg leaves on lid, dmn designs, sm ft, 12" W 190.00
Box, layered & notch-cvd, brass stars/lock/bail hdl, 8½" L 220.00
Box, layered geometrics, extended ft, 5x8x10" 320.00
Box, layered notched-cvd sides & ped base, 6x7x12" 170.00
Box, mirror, 4 step-down tiers of drw, appl strips, 18" 170.00

Box, mirror panels, built-up geometrics/rosettes, 6x10x10" 350.00
Box, overall notch cvg, layered, 3½x9x6" 110.00
Box, sewing; fabric panels, pincushion on lid, stars/anchors 310.00
Box, sewing; ftd, front drw, pincushion, 5x5x7" 70.00
Box, shaving; cvd lines/razors/snake/mug, mirror, 9x17x9" 320.00
Box, slide lid, base drw, layered, appl dmns, 7x10x6", VG 190.00
Box, wall; shield-shape bk, box at top/base, rosettes, 12x7" 50.00
Clock stand, 3-step base (1 w/drw), rosette at peak, 21" 325.00
Comb case, chip-cvd hearts/dmns/moon/etc, 2-tier, 10x6x3" 225.00
Dresser, ornate chip cvg, 4-drw, late 1800s, 21½x15x10" 425.00
Frame, chip-cvd, old varnish, silver/gold/bronze pnt, 36x28" 715.00
Frame, chip-cvd w/porc button trim, eagle crest, 18x14" 250.00
Frame, dbl; X corners, overall notch-cvd layers, 4x6" openings 120.00
Frame, notched-cvd built-up layers, 7x9½" 110.00
Frame, sm sqs in built-up layers, 12x9" 100.00
Frame, 3-tiered dmn shapes ea corner, chip-cvd, 10x8x3¾" 65.00
Magazine rack, 3-layer applique on bkbrd, notched, 19x17x6" ...140.00
Mirror, built-up geometrics, sq in corners, gilt, 19x16" 85.00
Mirror, scalloped/shaped/notch-cvd, built-up band, 17x16" 300.00
Sewing stand, box over lower shelf, notch-cvd legs, 29x12x9" ...180.00
Table lamp, shaft w/balls/dmns/sqs, stepped base, overall: 29" 275.00
Table lamp, sq, 2 lg layered sqs ea side, overall: 19" 140.00
Wall pocket/comb box, dbl-arch bkbrd w/notched edges, 6x7x2" ..90.00

Traps

Though of interest to collectors for many years, trap collecting has gained in popularity over the past ten years in particular, causing prices to appreciate rapidly. Traps are usually marked on the pan as to manufacturer, and the condition of these trademarks are important when determining their value. Grading is as follows:

Good: one-half of pan legible.
Very Good: legible in entirety, but light.
Fine: legible in entirety, with strong lettering.
Mint: in like-new, shiny condition.

Our advisor for this category is Boyd Nedry; he is listed in the Directory under Michigan. Prices listed here are for traps in fine condition.

Abbey McLeod, #4, rnd base, Pat 1897 ....400.00
Acme, wood snap, mousetrap 20.00
Adirondak Instant Death, pan model 325.00
Alligator Game Trap, #2, w/teeth 165.00
Ampco, self-setting gopher trap 15.00
Armstrong's Cockroach & Waterbug trap 25.00
Arrow, #1, single underspring 50.00
Automatic, The World's Finest Mouse Trap, blk metal 20.00
Basic, wood snap, mousetrap 4.00
Black Hole, gopher trap 10.00
Blake & Lamb, #0, single underspring, Pat 1859 ....100.00
Blake & Lamb, #44, dbl underspring, w/teeth 35.00
Briddell Escape Proof, 7-hole pan 12.00
Cabella's, #2, dbl coil spring 10.00
Chasse, wood, 3-hole choker, mousetrap 30.00
Clayton, killer 100.00
Clincher, #1, long spring 65.00
Clipper, killer 75.00
Cooks Quick Catch, wood snap, rat trap 15.00
Cosey, w/trip bar 30.00
Crescent, #1½, w/cast pan, single long spring 150.00
Cush-In-Grip, #1, w/rubber jaw 30.00
Dauffer, killer 30.00
Death Clamp, 4" 30.00
Delusion, tin & wood, mousetrap 45.00

Destro, metal, mousetrap 18.00
Diamond, #22, dbl long spring, dbl jaw 18.00
Diamond, #51 Walloper, coil spring 45.00
Dover, metal, rat trap 18.00
Dwight, #1, single long spring 350.00
Eclipse, #2, underspring 35.00
Economy, #2, dbl long spring 40.00
Epp Chain Trap 125.00
Eureka Rat Trap, Buhl Bros, Detroit MI, wood snap 14.00
Evans, brass, fish & mousetrap 225.00
Feemster, metal, mousetrap 30.00
Fox, blk metal snap, rat trap 4.00
Funsten Float trap 350.00
Gabriel Fish & Game Trap 250.00
Gibbs, #2, dbl coil spring 18.00
Gibbs Live Muskrat 350.00
Good, wood snap, mousetrap 8.00
Handforged bear trap, 31" L 375.00
Handforged beaver trap 150.00
Hawley & Norton, #4, dbl long spring 30.00
Hector, #0, single long spring 35.00
Hellcat, Eagle Lock Co, metal, mousetrap 18.00
Herters, #0, single long spring 65.00
IOA, Browncamp Hwd Co, wood snap, rat trap 15.00
Iron Cat, metal snap, mousetrap 30.00
Jack Frost, brass trigger, killer 15.00
Jillson, rat trap, 2" sz 135.00
Joker, #3, wood snap, rat trap 15.00
Juby English, killer 40.00
Kangaroo, 'Triumph' #1 underspring 8.00
Ketchem, fits on fruit jar, mousetrap 22.00
King Bee, 'Triumph' #0 underspring 15.00
Kleeflock Killer 20.00
Knapp, #1½, dbl coil spring 6.00
Kriket, #1, jump trap 7.00
Little Champ, plastic 1-hole choker, mousetrap 15.00
Lohman, #4 dbl coil spring, unmk 20.00
Luths Hwd Co, wood snap, mousetrap 5.00
Marsh Special, 'Victor' #1, single long spring 10.00
Mascot, #1, single long spring 8.00
McGill, all steel, mousetrap 6.00
Montgomery, #1½, dbl coil spring 6.00
Morrison Selfset, metal, mousetrap 12.00
Newhouse, #0, single long spring 45.00
Newhouse, #15, bear trap 325.00
Newhouse, #31½, single long spring 175.00
Northwoods, #1½, dbl coil spring 5.00
Northwoods, #3, dbl coil spring 17.00
Northwoods, blk metal snap, mousetrap 2.00
Oberto, #400, dbl underspring 30.00
Official Mouse Trap, Animal Trap Co, wood snap 10.00
Oneida, tin, 5-hole choker, mousetrap 18.00
Oneida Community, #2, dbl underspring 10.00
Otto Kampfe Mfg Co, glass, live mousetrap 85.00
Pioneer, #3, dbl long spring 8.00
Prott, #1¼, Racine Wisc 35.00
PS Mfg Co, #2, dbl long spring 40.00
PS&W Co, #0, single long spring 25.00
Quigley, wood snap, mousetrap 8.00
Reddick, Niles Mich, spear-type mole trap 14.00
Rice, Improved, killer 20.00
Runway, red tin, mousetrap 16.00
Sabo Den Trap 95.00
Sargent, #22, dbl long spring 95.00

Schene, #4, dbl coil spring 95.00
Schulyer, folding rat trap 25.00
Short Stop, wood snap, rat trap 6.00
Stoptheif, #3, killer 22.00
Sure Catch, mousetrap 4.00
Taylor FC Sure Kill, mole trap 20.00
Trailzend, #2, long spring 45.00
Triple J, Erskine Minn, 4-jaw killer 20.00
Triumph, #2xt, dbl long spring 22.00
Triumph, #34x, dbl coil spring 100.00
True Value, #1, single long spring 7.00
Union Hardware, #2, dbl long spring 70.00
Unique Coon Trap, plastic PVC pipe 70.00
Victor, #4, dbl long spring 18.00
Victor, #40, 2 traps in 1 ....50.00
Victor Black Cat, 4-hole choker, mousetrap 8.00
Warren Safety, gopher trap 6.00
Webley, #4, dbl long spring 40.00
Zip, metal snap, mousetrap 14.00

Trenton

Trenton, New Jersey, was an area that supported several pottery companies from the mid-1800s until the late 1960s. A consolidation of several smaller companies that occurred in the 1890s was called Trenton Potteries Company. Each company produced their own type of wares independent of the others.

Bowl, ivory, vertical ribs, ftd, attached flower frog, 11" 10.00
Bowl, turq semigloss, 10" 48.00
Vase, cornucopia form, 6" 17.50
Vase, cream, hdls, 7⅝x6" 24.00
Vase, pk, star ink stamp, 8" 35.00
Vase, turq, Deco shape, flat pillow form 22.50

Trivets

Although strictly a decorative item today, the original purpose of the trivet was much more practical. They were used to protect table tops from hot serving dishes, and irons heated on the kitchen range were placed on trivets during use to protect work surfaces. The first patent date was 1869; many of the earliest trivets bore portraits of famous people or patriotic designs. Florals, birds, animals, and fruit were other favored motifs. Watch for remakes of early original designs. Some of these are marked Wilton, Emig, Wright, Iron Art, and V.M. for Virginia Metalcrafters. However, many of these reproductions are becoming collectible in the '90s. Expect to pay considerably less for these than for the originals, since they are abundant.

Brass

Cut-out pattern, 4-legged, 5x10x6½" 75.00
Heart w/greyhound cutout, 3 cutouts in hdl, 9" 98.00
Hearts & dmns cutouts, 9" 35.00
Horseshoe, 1888 in center, w/hdl, EX 85.00
Rtcl heart shape, trn wood hdl, 1849, 11¼" 125.00
Star (lg) contained in heavy ring, 6" 95.00
Tilt-top tea table form, 6 heart cutouts in center, 12" 365.00

Cast Iron

Butterfly, 9½" 80.00

Cleveland w/horseshoe, blk pnt, 5" 100.00
Eagle & God Bless Our Home, 10" 65.00
Floral scrolls, blk rpt, 10" 95.00
Floral w/star hdl, 9" 72.50
Garfield w/horseshoe, 5" 85.00
George Washington, 9½" 65.00
Girl's face, rare, 8" 155.00

Good Luck on horseshoe, marked British Made, 6", $35.00.

Good Luck, Pat'd 1888 ....45.00
Grapes & scrolls, 8" 45.00
Hearts, rare, 9½" 130.00
Hearts & quatrefoils, 8½" 65.00
Horseshoe w/moose, flags & eagle, old mc rpt, 8¼" 60.00
Leaf w/in circle, blk rpt, 6" 115.00
Lyre, 7¼" 40.00
Rectangular w/columns, hairline, 10" 75.00
Scrolls & hearts in circle, blk rpt, 8" 95.00
SR Fox & Co St Louis MO, blk rpt, 9" 30.00
Star & braid, buffed, 8" 75.00
Star & fans, blk rpt, 9½" 60.00
Tulip, mk SB Miller, 8" 50.00
2 birds, hdl rpr, blk rpt, 11" 40.00

Wrought Iron

Heart shape, pitted, 9¾" 300.00
Iron shape w/shoe ft, 13¾" 12.50
Rectangular, 4 legs w/penny ft, wood hdl, 14x11" 65.00
Rnd, 3-legged, 7x9" 100.00
Scroll details, trn wood hdl, 13¼" 75.00
Triangular, high legs w/paw-like ft, 9" 40.00
3 crimped flared rods w/in shield shape, wood hdl, 10", EX 100.00

Trolls

The first trolls to come to the United States were molded after a 1952 design by Marti and Helena Kuuskoski of Tampere, Finland. The first trolls to be mass-produced in America were molded from wood carvings made by Thomas Dam of Denmark. As the demand for these trolls increased, several U.S. manufacturers were licensed to produce them. The most noteworthy of these were Uneeda Doll Company's Wishnik line and Inga Kykins Scandia House True Trolls. Thomas Dam continued to import his Dam Things line. Today trolls are enjoying a renaissance as baby boomers try to recapture their childhood. As a result values are rising.

The troll craze from the '60s spawned many items other than troll dolls such as wall plaques, salt and pepper shakers, pins, squirt guns, rings, clay trolls, lamps, Halloween costumes, animals, lawn ornaments, coat racks, notebooks, folders, and even a car.

In the '70s, '80 and '90s new trolls were produced. While these are attractive to some collectors, the avid troll collector still prefers those produced in the '60s. Remember trolls must be in mint condition to receive top dollar. For further study we recommend *Collector's Guide to Trolls* by Pat Peterson. Our advisor for this category is Roger Inouye; he is listed in the Directory under California.

Blk, vinyl, jtd neck, inserted eyes/lashes, Dam Things, 18" 165.00
Bride, blk mohair, gray plastic eyes, orig clothes, 5½" 30.00
Brother Bear, vinyl, jtd neck only, 7" 90.00
Clown, insert eyes, mk Dam on bk, 4" 25.00
Common, 10" 50.00
Common, 12" 60.00
Common, 15" minumum 80.00
Common, 2½-3", minimum 15.00
Common, 4", from $20 to 25.00
Common, 7", from $30 to 40.00
Cow 65.00
Giraffe 70.00
Groovies, rhinestone eyes, mohair, 1-pc clothes, 3" 20.00
Horse, lav mohair, gr & yel saddle, mk, 2½" 40.00
Monkey, vinyl, jtd neck only, all orig, mk USA, 8" 90.00
Moon monster, peach mohair, gold eyes, vinyl, mk L Khem, 3" ...20.00
Mouse, brn hair, brn glass eyes, blk nose, pnt whiskers, 5" 70.00
Sailor, blond mohair, amber glass eyes, Dam, 12" 150.00
Turtle 55.00
Vampire, jtd neck, wht hair, brn plastic eyes, unmk, 3" 10.00
Viking, vinyl, molded tooth/helmet, rabbit fur beard, all orig, 7" 70.00
Werewolf, blk hair, pnt face, plastic, Hong Kong, 1980s, 3¾" 15.00
Willy Fox, vinyl, jtd neck, fur on stomach, 7" 90.00
2-headed, pk hair/bl eyes on right, wht/gold on bk, 3" 40.00

Trunks

The first use of the term 'trunk' can be traced back to Egyptian times, when hollowed out tree sections were used to transport goods of commerce. In the the days of steamboat voyages, stagecoach journeys, and railroad travel, trunks were used to transport clothing and personal belongings.

The most desirable trunks are flat tops, 24" to 38" long, from the late 1800s, preferably in restored condition. Embossed dome tops (rounded on top to better accommodate milady's finery) from the 1880s, 24" to 38" long, in complete original condition are very desirable as well. On the other hand, ca 1870s flush tin trunks, even in mint condition, inspire very little collector interest.

Unless the trunk is complete (retaining all original trays and compartments), its value is considerably lessened. If parts are absent or broken, the trunk is judged incomplete. All interiors differ; some had upper lid compartments, others did not. Our advisor is Doris Harroff; she is listed in the Directory under Indiana.

Dome top, emb decor, 1880s, 24" to 38", complete, $75 to 175.00
Flat top, orig, 1880-1900, 24" to 38", complete, $75 to 125.00
Flat top, orig, 1880-1900, 24" to 38", complete, rstr, $300 to 425.00
Leather trim w/brass tacks on pine, 19x10x9" 110.00
Stagecoach, flat or dome, pre-1860s, 24" to 38", rstr, up to 475.00

Tuthill

The Tuthill Glass Company operated in Middletown, New York, from 1902 to 1923. Collectors look for signed pieces and those in an identifiable pattern. Condition is of utmost importance, and examples with brilliant cutting and intaglio (natural flowers and fruits) combined fetch the highest prices.

Bonbon, notching, eng flowers/leaves, star center, 8-sided 90.00
Bowl, eng rose w/in dmn & star-cut miters, 9" 350.00
Celery dish, stars/X-hatching/fans, 12" 150.00
Compote, floral intaglio, 6" dia 215.00
Mayonaise set, phlox, 3", 2-pc 300.00
Nappy, phlox & geometric cuttings, hobstar in middle, hdls 195.00
Nappy, vintage cutting, blown blank, hdls, 5" 225.00
Tazza, Evening Primrose, allover intaglio, 5x7" 325.00
Tazza, vintage cutting, 4x6" 225.00
Tray, Wild Rose, allover cutting, 8x5" 250.00
Vase, bud; intaglio floral/dmn-point cutting, 16" 175.00
Vase, Intaglio, 3 fruits/geometrics, waisted/3-ftd, 12½" 600.00

Typewriters

The first commercially successful typewriter was the Sholes and Glidden, introduced in 1874. By 1882 other models appeared, and by the 1890s dozens were on the market. At the time of the First World War, the ranks of typewriter-makers thinned, and by the 1920s only a few survived.

Collectors informally divide typewriter history into the pioneering period, up to about 1890; the classic period, from 1890 to 1920; and the modern period, since 1920. There are two broad classifications of early typewriters: (1) Keyboard machines, in which depression of a key prints a character and via a shift key prints up to three different characters per key. (2) Index machines, in which a chart of all the characters appears on the typewriter; the character is selected by a pointer or dial and is printed by operation of a lever or other device. Even though index typewriters were simpler and more primitive than keyboard machines, they were none-the-less a later development, designed to provide a cheaper alternative to the standard keyboard models that were selling for upwards of $100.00. Eventually second-hand keyboard typewriters supplied the low-price customer, and index typewriters vanished except as toys. Both classes of typewriters appeared in a great many designs.

It is difficult, if not impossible, to assign standard market prices to early typewriters. Unlike collectors of postage stamps, carnival glass, etc., few people collect typewriters, so there is no active marketplace from which to draw stable prices. Also, condition is a very important factor, and typewriters can vary infinitely in condition. A third factor to consider is that an early typewriter achieves its value mainly through the skill, effort, and patience of the collector who restores it to its original condition, in which case its purchase price is insignificant. Some unusual-looking early typewriters are not at all rare or valuable, while some very ordinary-looking ones are scarce and could be quite valuable. No general rules apply. When no condition is indicated, the items listed below are assumed to be in excellent, unrestored condition. Our advisor for this category is Mike Brooks; he is listed in the Directory under California.

Oliver Standard Visible #9, VG, $60.00.

Berwin, tin, 1950s, MIB 20.00
Blickensderfer #5, dtd 1892, VG 65.00
Blickensderfer Electric, NM 2,000.00
Boston, index 2,000.00
Brooks, EX 500.00
Corona, folding, EX 25.00
Crandall 600.00
Crown, index, EX 600.00
Hall, index, EX 700.00
Keystone 1,200.00
O'Dell #2, EX 265.00
Oliver Standard Visible Writer, old upright keys, NM 85.00
Peoples, index 300.00
Royal #10, 1922, EX 50.00
Sholes & Glidden, 1874 ....11,500.00
Smith-Corona #4, portable, 1920s, EX in case 42.00
Underwood Standard, dtd 1912, EX 28.00
Victor, index, rare, EX 500.00
World, index, EX 125.00

Uhl Pottery

Founded in Evansville, Indiana, in 1849 by German immigrants, the Uhl Pottery was moved to Huntingburg, Indiana, in 1908 because of the more suitable clay available there. They produced stoneware — Acorn Ware jugs, crocks, and bowls — which were marked with the acorn logo and 'Uhl Pottery.' They also made mugs, pitchers, and vases in simple shapes and solid glazes marked with a circular ink stamp containing the name of the pottery and 'Huntingburg, Indiana.' The pottery closed in the mid-1940s. Those seeking additional information about Uhl pottery are encouraged to contact the Uhl Collectors' Society, whose address is listed in the Directory under Clubs, Newsletters, and Catalogs.

Ashtray, acorn, brn 250.00
Ashtray, brn, #140 ....50.00
Ashtray, pig, wht 175.00
Bowl, batter; bl, mk, 10" 90.00
Bowl, mixing; basketweave, bl, 6" 95.00
Bowl, mixing; reverse pyramid, bl, 9" 75.00
Bowl, Tulip, pk, #119, 5½" 45.00
Candle holder, bl, w/shield, hand trn 300.00
Candlestick, bl, w/hdl, hand trn, 5½" 300.00
Cookie jar, globe, brn 60.00
Cookie jar, yel, #522 ....70.00
Feeder, Acorn, buttermilk, wht, ½-gal 100.00
Feeder, dog, bl, #144 ....120.00
Feeder, Scottie dog, pk, #128 ....90.00
Jar, Acorn Ware, 10-gal 90.00
Jar, Acorn Ware, 4-gal 50.00
Jar, butter; bl, mk, 2-lb 45.00
Jar, grease; pk 75.00
Jar, ice water; Acorn Ware, 5-gal 275.00
Jar, preserve; Acorn Ware, brn on wht, 1-gal 85.00
Jar, steam table; Acorn Ware, wht, 6½" 50.00
Jug, Acorn Ware, brn on wht, 3-gal 55.00
Jug, Acorn Ware, wht, 5-gal 70.00
Jug, Baseball, wht, mini 60.00
Jug, bellied form, bl, #175, 1-pt 45.00
Jug, canteen, brn, ½-pt 30.00
Jug, Egyptian, bl, #125, 25-oz 75.00
Jug, Grecian, bl, #162, 25-oz 75.00
Jug, harvest; Acorn Ware, w/air vent, wire bail, 1-gal 135.00

Jug, Merry Christmas, brn on wht, 1939, mini 225.00
Jug, shoulder; Great Smoky Mtns advertising, mini 175.00
Jug, sorghum; Acorn Ware, brn on wht, dbl hdls, 8-gal 120.00
Mug, coffee; bl, 8-oz 60.00
Pitcher, acid; brn, mk, 1-gal 75.00
Pitcher, bl, ice restrainer, 5-pt 100.00
Pitcher, bl & wht sponging, bellied, 1-gal 400.00
Pitcher, Lincoln, bl, incised mk, 2-qt 500.00
Pitcher, Lincoln, bl, incised mk, 3-qt 650.00
Pitcher, Lincoln, bl, 1-pt 275.00
Pitcher, Lincoln, bl, 1-qt 375.00
Pitcher, Lincoln, bl, ½-pt 225.00
Pitcher, rustic, brn, bbl form, 100-oz 60.00
Plate, bl, mk, 6" 50.00
Plate, pk, mk, 10" 70.00
Porch pedestal, brn, mk C-15, 16" 65.00
Porch pot, brn, mk C-14, 14" dia 50.00
Shoe, baby, tied shoestring, wht, mk 55.00
Shoe, Dutch, bl, #2 ....55.00
Shoes, lady's slippers, wht, mk, mini, pr 90.00
Stein, bbl, bl, 16-oz 100.00
Stein, flagon, tan, 12-oz 20.00
Stein, grape, bl, 16-oz 115.00
Teapot, bl, #131, 2-cup 250.00
Teapot, brn, #143, 8-cup 80.00
Teapot, pk, #132, 4-cup 200.00
Vase, bl, #157, 5" 70.00
Vase, bud; #22, wht, 3" 35.00
Vase, bud; #24, wht, mk, 3½" 125.00
Vase, bud; #30, yel, 4½" 65.00
Vase, cemetery; bl, 5" dia 55.00
Vase, cut flower, bl, mk, #116, 5" 60.00
Vase, cut flower, blk, #114, 10" 35.00
Vase, orange blossom, yel, #118, 4" 45.00
Wren house, terra cotta, #525 ....285.00

Ungemach Pottery Company

Fred Ungemach began his career as a boy, jiggering for the Nelson McCoy Pottery of Roseville, Ohio. Later he worked for Thomas Watt in Hawthorne, Pennsylvania, then he returned to Roseville to work for the Ransbottom Pottery. In 1938 with the help of his daughter Mary who was an employee of the Brush Pottery, he opened his own company in Roseville. The business was first known as the South Fork Pottery, but after several years and a number of expansions, the name was changed to the Ungemach Pottery Company (UPCO).

In June 1950 a flood demolished the plant, but it reopened in three weeks and continued to expand. In April 1966 the plant was struck by lightening and was destroyed again, but by September of the same year they were back in production. Then in 1984 the pottery was sold to the Friendship Pottery of Roseville, Ohio.

Ungemach produced a full line of wares including kitchen items, planters, vases, and novelty pieces and during the 1940s and '50s obtained an exclusive contract with Walt Disney Productions, Burbank, California, to produce Disney character planters. These pieces were marked with Disney copyrights only. Their other production pieces are marked in a variety of ways — 'Ungemach, UPCO, Roseville.' A few are not marked at all. Our advisors for this category are Brenda and Jerry Siegel; they are listed in the Directory under Missouri.

Bowl, fluted, rnd, brn, #762 ....7.00
Bowl, fruit; yel, #779, 7" 8.00
Bread server, brn, mk Roseville, #630, 10" 8.00

Bread server, rust & brn, oval, #797 ....9.00
Candy server, bl, 10" 11.00
Lamp, snowman's head, blk, red & gr pnt, no mk, 8½" 24.00
Planter, bonsai, wht, #289, 9x6x3½" 10.00
Planter, cactus, yel, 8" 8.00
Planter, chalice, brn, mk Flora Plant UPCO, rare, 8" 16.00
Planter, fluted star, tan, 5" 6.00
Planter, hand thrown, gr, #489, 8" 9.00
Planter, octagonal, tan, #755 ....6.00
Planter, rnd, tan, 6½" 4.00
Planter, rnd, wht, #610, 4½" 4.00
Strawberry pot, gr, 4" 6.00

Unger Brothers

The Art Nouveau silver produced by Unger Brothers, who operated in Newark, New Jersey, from the early 1880s until 1909, is fast becoming very popular with today's collectors. In addition to tableware, they also made brushes, mirrors, powder boxes, and the like for milady's dressing table as well as jewelry and small personal accessories such as match safes and flasks. They often marked their products with a circle seal containing an intertwined 'UB' and '925 fine sterling.' In addition to sterling, a very limited amount of gold was also used. Note: This company made no pewter items; Unger designs may occasionally be found in pewter, but these are copies. Items dated in the mark or signed 'Birmingham' are English (not Unger).

Ashtray, man-in-moon, Nouveau lady formed by pipe smoke 525.00
Bodkins, ornate, graduated 3-pc set 250.00
Buckle, belt; lady's, Nouveau cherubs, low V-form, sterling 165.00

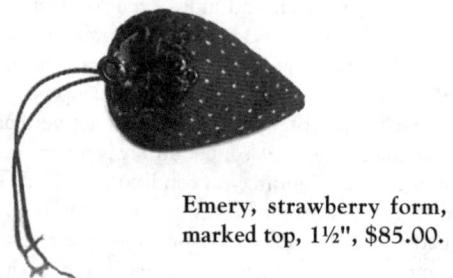

Emery, strawberry form, marked top, 1½", $85.00.

Jelly cake server, Passaic, pierced 295.00
Mirror, hand; Love's Dream 275.00
Sifter, Douvaine, sm 120.00
Tea strainer, Art Nouveau, needs hdl rpl 95.00
Teether, figural boy w/overalls & cap, MOP hdl, 4", EX 195.00
Thimble case, walnut figural, chatelaine loop, unlined, 1" 265.00

Universal

Universal Potteries Incorporated operated in Cambridge, Ohio, from 1934 to 1956. Many lines of dinnerware and kitchen items were produced in both earthenware and semiporcelain. In 1956 the emphasis was shifted to the manufacture of floor and wall tiles, and the name was changed to the Oxford Tile Company, Division of Universal Potteries. The plant closed in 1976. Our advisor for this category is Ted Haun; he is listed in the Directory under Indiana.

Ballerina, bowl, cereal 5.00
Ballerina, bowl, soup 6.00

Ballerina, chop plate 15.00
Ballerina, creamer & sugar bowl 20.00
Ballerina, cup & saucer, demitasse 20.00
Ballerina, egg cup 12.00
Ballerina, gravy boat 10.00
Ballerina, shakers, pr 12.00
Calico Fruit, bowl, mixing; 9" 15.00
Calico Fruit, creamer 11.00
Calico Fruit, cup 8.00
Calico Fruit, platter 12.00
Calico Fruit, refrigerator jug, w/lid 35.00
Calico Fruit, sugar bowl, w/lid 14.00
Calico Fruit, utility shaker 12.00
Cattail, batter set (batter pitcher & syrup w/lids on tray) 250.00
Cattail, bowl, berry; 5¼" 4.00
Cattail, bowl, mixing; 6" 15.00
Cattail, bowl, soup; 7¾" 7.00
Cattail, bowl, str sides, 5" 8.00
Cattail, bowl, 6¼" 7.00
Cattail, bowl, 7" 10.00
Cattail, cake lifter 12.00
Cattail, cake safe, tin 17.00

Cattail, casserole, with lid, made for Sears, 8½" diameter, $22.50.

Cattail, cookie jar 75.00
Cattail, cup & saucer 10.00
Cattail, pie baker, 10" 17.00
Cattail, pie server 25.00
Cattail, plate, 9" 12.00
Cattail, scales, metal 35.00
Cattail, teapot 20.00
Red Poppy, pie plate 8.00
Zinnias, casserole 13.00

University City

Located in University City, Missouri, this pottery operated for only five years (1910-1915), but because of the outstanding potters associated with it, produced notable artware. The company's founder was Edward Gardner Lewis, and among the well-known artists he employed were Adelaide Robineau, Frederick Rhead, Taxile Doat, and Julian Zsolnay.

Vase, bl/wht crystalline, mk UC 1913 TD, 7", EX 1,750.00
Vase, dk bl/buff/umber speckled, amber shoulder, 7½" 1,100.00
Vase, honey/bl/wht crystalline, mk UC 1912, 6¾" 2,200.00
Vase, ivory crystalline, str sides, oval rim & body, 3⅝" 650.00
Vase, pk to gray gloss, bl UC mk, 1910, 3" 450.00
Vase, yel/orange crystalline sunbursts on wht, 5¾" 425.00

Val St. Lambert

Since its inception in Belgium at the turn of the 19th century, the Val St. Lambert Cristalleries has been involved in the production of

high quality glass, producing some cameo. The factory is still in production. Our advisor for this category is Don Williams; he is listed in the Directory under Missouri.

Bottle, scent; cut-bk cranberry floral, faceted stopper, 5½" 250.00
Punch bowl, ruby cut to clear w/circles & chevrons, 7x12" 400.00
Vase, cameo arrowhead leaves/vines in violet, stick neck, 10" ...350.00
Vase, cameo roses, cobalt on gold geometrics, cylindrical, 10" ...450.00
Vase, ruby cut to clear w/ovals etc, dmn band, cut stem, 10" 400.00

Valentines

Handmade Valentines date back to the mid-1700s in the United States; as time went on, increased interest resulted in other types of Valentine cards being made. Today Valentine collectors are not the only ones who buy; Valentines are often considered a desirable addition to other collections as well — Black memorabilia, advertising, transportation memorabilia, Walt Disney, cartoon and movie characters, etc. Besides examples representing these areas, 3-dimensionals and mechanical Valentines (1860s to the present) are becoming highly prized by many collectors. There are six qualifying specifications to consider when evaluating a Valentine card: age, size, category, manufacturer, artist signature, and condition. Our advisor for this category is Katherine Kreider; she is listed in the Directory under California.

Key: HCPP — honeycomb paper puff

Mechanical, flower opens to reveal girl's face, 1910-15, 6x4½", NM, $30.00.

Airplane, 2-D, chromolitho, MIG, 1920s, 4⅜x3½x3" 30.00
Ambassador, 3-D, train, 1960, 7x10", EX 35.00
Ballerina, chromolitho, HCPP tutu, MIG, 1927, 5¼x4½", EX 30.00
Big-eyed child rides mechanical duck, 5½x7", VG 35.00
Big-eyed girl in bonnet, mechanical, litho, MIG, '23, 8x5", EX 45.00
Black child under sprinkling can, USA, 1940s, 5½x3½", NM 35.00
Brownie & Cub Scout, USA, 1950s, 6x3¼", EX 15.00
Cagney, James; USA, 1935, 5⅞x3½", EX 45.00
Cherub w/butterfly net, 2-D, litho, MIG, 4x2½x1½", NM 55.00
Cinderella-type coach, 3-D w/HCPP, 1900s, 11¼x13x6", VG 95.00
Cobweb, HP orig, 1850, 8x9", EX 250.00
Dopey, mechanical, Walt Disney Enterprises, 4¼x3", NM 75.00
Dutch boy w/orig pc of Wrigley's gum, 6½x3½", NM 75.00
Geppetto on raft, mechanical, Walt Disney Productions, '39, EX ..65.00
Goat & cart, girl delivers milk, tab stand, USA, 10x7", VG 35.00
Halls Bros, dog w/felt ears, 1940s, 8½x6¾", VG 15.00
Harp, litho stands w/tab accented w/Victorian scraps, 7", EX 75.00
HCPP basket & hearts, litho cherubs, ca 1925, 8½", EX 85.00
Hot air balloon, litho w/orig ribbon, MIG, 9½x4", NM 150.00
Kautz, artist paints portrait, mechanical, '25, 6x4½", EX 35.00
Kautz, cat, mechanical, tab stand, USA, 1925, 4½x3½", NM 35.00
Loverville Telephone Card, cast-metal phone, 4x3¼", EX 75.00

Mechanical, airplane, 1940s-50s, 3¼x4½", EX 8.00
Mechanical, bear on stump, Stecher Litho, tab stand, 5", EX 25.00
Mechanical, cow, head & neck move, USA, '40s, 7¼x4¾", NM ...20.00
Mechanical, gypsy, USA, 6½x2¼", NM 15.00
Mechanical, miner panning for gold, Canada, 5½x3", EX 15.00
Mechanical, Russian bear & child, tab stand, MIG, 8½", EX 55.00
Nister, boy & girl, litho, Bavaria, 1900s, 4¾x3", EX 35.00
Olive Oyle & Popeye, USA, 1940s, 5¾x5", EX 45.00
St Bernard dog, w/orig chain to doghouse, MIG, 10", VG 75.00
Tuck, Artistic Series, carriage/Blk Child/3-D flowers, 7", VG 95.00
Tuck, horse-drawn carriage, 3-D, 6½x10⅜x4½", EX 175.00
3-D Victorian scene in open heart, To My..., MIG, 3½", NM 75.00

Van Briggle

The Van Briggle Pottery of Colorado Springs, Colorado, was established in 1901 by Artus Van Briggle, whose early career had been
shaped by such notables as Karl Langenbeck and Maria Nichols Storer.
His quest for several years had been to perfect a completely flat matt
glaze, and upon accomplishing his goal, he opened his pottery. His wife,
Anne, worked with him, and they, along with George Young, were
responsible for the modeling of the wares. Their work typified the flow
and form of the Art Nouveau movement, and the shapes they designed
played as important a part in their success as their glazes. Some of their
most famous pieces were Despondency, Lorelei, and Toast Cup. Increasing demand for their work soon made it necessary to add to their quarters as well as their staff. Although much of the ware was eventually
made from molds, each piece was carefully trimmed and refined before
the glaze was sprayed on. Their most popular colors were Persian Rose,
Ming Blue, and Mustard Yellow.

Van Briggle died in 1904, but the work was continued by his wife.
New facilities were built; and by 1908, in addition to their artware,
tiles, gardenware, and commercial lines were added. By the twenties the
emphasis had shifted from art pottery to novelties and commercial
wares. As late as 1970, reproductions of some of the early designs continued to be made. Until about 1920 most pieces were marked with the
date and shape number; after that the AA mark was used.

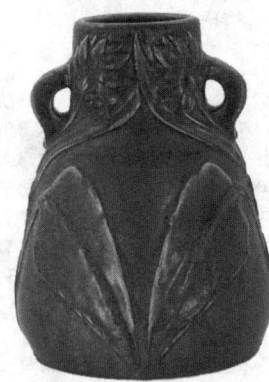

Vase, sunflowers on green
(rare color), dated 1903,
#49, 10x7", $2,250.00.

Bowl, dragonflies, maroon/bl, 1919, 2½x8", +frog 475.00
Bowl, floral, bl w/exposed cream, #297, '05, 2½x6", +frog 425.00
Bowl, lotus flower form, 8-sided, Persian Rose, 1920, 10" 300.00
Bowl, maroon matt w/bl highlights, imp mk, 1911, 2x9" 250.00
Candlesticks, gr to maroon, flared ft, 1920s, 9", pr 275.00
Lamp, leaves, bl on red matt, bulbous, imp mk, 5" 150.00
Lamp, Persian Rose, floral base, w/orig shade, 1920, 7½" 200.00
Lamp base, 3 lizards at wide base, bl/gr crystalline, '13, 12" 650.00
Pitcher, gr textured, bulbous, bulbous lip, 1905, 4¼x6" 550.00
Vase, Arts & Crafts floral on thick stems, bl/gr, '20s, 11" 500.00

Vase, daffodils/swirling stems, wine/med gr, #367, 1906, 9" 1,500.00
Vase, Despondency, nude man at rim, bl/maroon, '20s, 13" 2,000.00
Vase, dk bl & gr, spherical w/pinched-in waist, 1904, 6" 500.00
Vase, Dos Cabezas, 2 women in flowing gowns, bl, 1914, 8" ...5,000.00
Vase, Dos Cabezas, 2 women in flowing gowns, plum, 8", EX .6,000.00
Vase, dragonflies, maroon/bl, #9, 1920s, 6½" 450.00
Vase, dragonflies at shoulder, bl w/tan highlights, 1920, 7" 375.00
Vase, floral, brn, 1908-11, 2" 300.00
Vase, floral (stylized), lt/med bl on tan, 1918, 11x10" 1,000.00
Vase, floral on bulbous shoulder, gr, 1904-06, 4" 500.00
Vase, floral on low width, lt bl/cream clay, #105, 1904, 4½" 550.00
Vase, floral on shoulder & 4-panel sides, brn, 1907, 6x4" 500.00
Vase, floral/leaves, maroon w/gr-brn, hdls, #39, 1904, 10" 1,725.00
Vase, flower buds on tall stems, mustard mottle, 1906, 9½x4" ..1,100.00
Vase, flower buds/leaves, lt bl, #789, 1916, 6¼" 250.00
Vase, gr/maroon, wide shoulder, #320, 1906, 10x8" 800.00
Vase, gr/rose broken glaze, bulbous, #378, 1905, 14½" 2,600.00
Vase, Indian heads (3) around top, Persian Rose, 1930s, 12" 550.00
Vase, Indian heads (3) around top, turq, 1950s, 11½", EX 190.00
Vase, irises, purple/gr on cream w/exposed clay, 1906, 14" 2,500.00
Vase, irises (lg), brn/gr, hdls at low width, #137, 1903, 14" 3,500.00
Vase, leaves, dk gr w/red clay exposed, #651, '07-12, 6", NM 475.00
Vase, leaves, feathered lav/gray, ear hdls, #506, '07-12, 5" 300.00
Vase, leaves, feathery bl, #389, 1907-12, 4½x4½" 425.00
Vase, leaves (full-length, stylized), mauve, 1905, 9x4" 700.00
Vase, leaves (upright), feathered wine/gr, #453, '07-12, 6" 400.00
Vase, leaves (4), bl, #857, 1915, 5" 500.00
Vase, leaves at shoulder, alligatored dk gr/bl, '07-12, 4x5" 850.00
Vase, leaves at top, Mountain Craig Brn/gr, ca '30s, 3½x5" 150.00
Vase, long-stem floral, 3-color, #131, 1903, 8x3" 6,900.00
Vase, mistletoe at swollen shoulder, bl/gr, 1907-12, 4½" 350.00
Vase, moths, Persian Rose, #684, 1926-32, 3x3" 150.00
Vase, Nouveau floral, maroon, hdls, wide bottom, '03, 8x8" ...2,500.00
Vase, peacock feathers, lav on apple gr, #62, 1903, 12", NM ..2,000.00
Vase, poppies, med/lt bl, ca 1930s, 8x4" 290.00
Vase, poppies on whiplash stems, 2-tone bl, 4x3" 230.00
Vase, poppies/pods, maroon/gr, #794, 1916, 8x4", NM 1,000.00
Vase, robin's egg bl, shouldered, 1905, 4¼x2" 300.00
Vase, roses, pk/gr on pk, #400, 1906, crazing/flakes, 14x8" 1,600.00
Vase, spider reserve, red/gr on brn, EX mold, 1902, 4½" 1,300.00
Vase, stylized daisies, gr/purple w/exposed clay, '07-12, 7" 425.00
Vase, swirling leaves/stems cvd on burgundy, '20s, 7½x5" 550.00
Vase, tulips, Persian Rose, ca 1930s, 8" 190.00
Vase, tulips (long stems), bl crystalline, 1912, 6x6" 950.00
Vase, woman w/flowing hair, arms around rim, bl/gr, '20s, 9½" ..850.00
Vase, 3 egrets encircle body, bl, ca 1930s, 15½" 475.00

Vance Avon

Although pottery had been made in Tiltonville, Ohio, since about
1880, the ware manufacturered there was of little significance until after
the turn of the century when the Vance Faience company was organized for the purpose of producing quality artware. By 1902 the name
had been changed to the Avon Faience company, and late in the same
year it and three other West Virginia potteries incorporated to form the
Wheeling Potteries Company. The Avon branch operated in
Tiltonville until 1905 when production was moved to Wheeling. Art
pottery was discontinued.

From the beginning, only skilled craftsmen and trained engineers
were hired. Wm. P. Jervis and Frederick Hurten Rhead were among the
notable artists responsible for designing some of the early artware. Some
of the ware was slip decorated under glaze, while other pieces were
molded with high-relief designs. Examples with squeeze-bag decoration

by Rhead are obviously forerunners of the Jap Birdimal line he later developed for Weller. Ware was marked 'Vance F. Co.'; 'Avon F. Co., Tiltonville'; or 'Avon W. Pts. Co.'

Vase, floral, squeeze-bag decor, WP&S Co, 5½x5½", NM 1,200.00
Vase, stylized scenic, mc, squat w/long neck, 6", EX 220.00
Vase, stylized trees, squeeze bag, bulbous w/can neck, 6" 550.00

Vaseline

Vaseline, a greenish-yellow colored glass produced by adding uranium oxide to the batch, was produced during the Victorian era. It was made in smaller quantities than other colors and lost much of its popularity with the advent of the electric light. It was used for pressed tablewares, vases, whimseys, souvenir items, oil lamps, perfume bottles, drawer pulls and doorknobs. Pieces have been reproduced, and some factories still make it today in small batches. Vaseline glass will flouresce under an ultraviolet light. Our advisor for this category is Terry Fedosky; she is listed in the Directory under Kentucky.

Bottle, scent; emb ovals, faceted vaseline stopper, 4¾x2" 110.00
Bottle, scent; Ribbed Pillar mold, blown stopper, 6¼x4½" 750.00
Candlestick, flint, NE Glass, 1890s, 10¼x5" dia 200.00
Candlesticks, Swirl, short, 1938, pr 55.00
Creamer, Wildflower 50.00
Goblet, Wildflower, 5" 30.00
Pitcher, Daisy & Button w/Crossbars 120.00
Spoon holder, notched, metal base, 1890 ....95.00
Sugar bowl, Gothic Arch, flint, 3½" 150.00
Sugar bowl, Maple Leaf, Gillinder & Sons, 1880, w/lid 125.00
Sugar bowl, Starburst & Pinwheel, w/lid 45.00
Vase, allover pressed pattern, scalloped ft, 6x3", pr 95.00

Verlys

Verlys art glass, produced in France after 1931 by the Holophane Company of Verlys, was made in crystal with acid-finished relief work in the Art Deco style. Colored and opalescent glass was also used. In 1935 an American branch was opened in Newark, Ohio, where very similar wares were produced until the factory ceased production in 1951. French Verlys was signed with one of three mold-impressed script signatures, all containing the company name and country of origin. The American-made glassware was signed 'Verlys' only, either scratched with a diamond-tipped pen or impressed in the mold. There is very little if any difference in value between items produced in France and America. Though some seem to feel that the French should be higher priced (assuming it to be scarce), many prefer the American-made product.

In June of 1955, about sixteen Verlys molds were leased to the A.H. Heisey Company. Heisey's versions were not signed with the Verlys name, so if an item is unsigned it is almost certainly a Heisey piece. The molds were returned to Verlys of America in July 1957. Our advisor for this category is Don Frost; he is listed in the Directory under Oregon.

Ashtray, Swallow, crystal etched, 4¾" 85.00
Bowl, Birds & Bees, clear on frost, shallow, 2¼x11⅝" 250.00
Bowl, Birds & Bees, Directoire bl, 2¼x11⅝" 450.00
Bowl, Chrysanthemum, 6¼x10⅛" 385.00
Bowl, Poissons (fish), crystal etched, 11¾x7⅞x19¼" 800.00
Bowl, Poissons (fish), Directoire bl opal, 11¾x7⅞x19¼" 1,500.00
Bowl, Poppies, clear/frosted, 13½" 325.00
Bowl, 3 molded orchids, frosted, shallow, 14" 375.00
Box, Chrysanthemums, topaz, 5¼" 375.00

Vase, Alpine Thistle, opal, shouldered, 9" 625.00
Vase, Butterflies, opal, 5x5" 185.00
Vase, Lovebirds, flat-sided U-form, clear/frost, 5" 145.00
Vase, Mandarin, crystal etched, 9½" 400.00
Vase, Seasons, wheat Autumn/dancer Spring, Schmitz, 8x5" ..1,000.00
Vase, Thistle, topaz, 9¾" 750.00

Vernon Kilns

Vernon Potteries Ltd. was established by Faye G. Bennison in Vernon, California, in 1931. The name was later changed to Vernon Kilns; until it closed in 1958, dinnerware, specialty plates and figurines were their primary products. Among its wares most sought after by collectors today are items designed by such famous artists as Rockwell Kent, Walt Disney, Don Blanding, Jane Bennison, and May and Vieve Hamilton. Authority Maxine Nelson has compiled a lovely book, *Collectible Vernon Kilns*, with full-color photos, current prices and an index; you will find her listed in the Directory under California.

Bennison, bowl, pierced base 135.00
Brown-Eyed Susan, bowl, fruit; 5½" 8.00
Brown-Eyed Susan, bowl, tab hdls, 6⅛" 12.00
Brown-Eyed Susan, bowl, 9" 20.00
Brown-Eyed Susan, carafe, w/lid, 8" 35.00
Brown-Eyed Susan, chop plate, 12⅜" 20.00
Brown-Eyed Susan, creamer & sugar bowl, w/lid 35.00
Brown-Eyed Susan, cup & saucer 10.00
Brown-Eyed Susan, gravy boat 18.00
Brown-Eyed Susan, plate, 10" 12.00
Brown-Eyed Susan, plate, 6" 5.00
Brown-Eyed Susan, shakers, pr 15.00
Bubbles, mug, child's 75.00
Casual California, mug 15.00
Coastline, cup & saucer 25.00
Coastline, plate, 9½" 35.00
Dis 'n Dot, casserole, w/lid, 8" 45.00
Dis 'n Dot, coffeepot 55.00
Dis 'n Dot, teapot 55.00
Early California, bowl, fruit; 5½" 5.00
Fantasia, bowl, Sprite, solid color, 3x10½" 250.00
Fantasia, bowl, winged nymph, HP, 2½x12" 375.00
Fantasia, figurine, elephant standing, #24, Disney 350.00
Fantasia, figurine, hippo, #32 ....595.00
Fantasia, figurine, hippo in tutu, #34, Disney, 1940 ....350.00
Fantasia, figurine, satyr, 4½" 200.00
Fantasia, plate, Nutcracker, 9½" 165.00
Fantasia, shakers, Hop & Lo mushrooms, pr 150.00
Fantasia, vase, Diana, wht glossy, ca 1940, 10" 500.00
Figurine, Baby Weems 235.00
Figurine, Dumbo, recumbent, 1941 ....175.00

Figurine, Evelyn Venable (movie star), lady in long green and gray coat, sculpted by Janice Pettee, 11½", $1,500.00.

Frontier Days, bowl, salad; ind, 5½"	20.00
Gingham, plate, salad; 7¼"	7.00
Gingham, shakers, pr	12.00
Gingham, teapot	35.00
Hamilton, plate, rippled, 9½"	25.00
Hamilton, vase, spheres, No 4	125.00
Hawaiian Flowers, chop plate, 12¼"	85.00
Hawaiian Flowers, coffeepot	195.00
Hawaiian Flowers, creamer & sugar bowl	75.00
Hawaiian Flowers, cup & saucer	25.00
Hawaiian Flowers, plate, 8½"	20.00
Hawaiian Flowers, plate, 9½"	30.00
Hawaiian Flowers, shakers, pr	35.00
Hawaiian Flowers, tureen	325.00
Homespun, bowl, divided vegetable; 11½"	20.00
Homespun, bowl, fruit; 5½"	5.00
Homespun, bowl, mixing; 5", 8", 9", set of 3	75.00
Homespun, bowl, salad; 10½"	85.00
Homespun, bowl, vegetable; 9"	15.00
Homespun, bowl, 1-pt	12.00
Homespun, butter dish	35.00
Homespun, casserole, ind, w/lid	20.00
Homespun, chop plate, 14"	40.00
Homespun, coaster	25.00
Homespun, coffee server	35.00
Homespun, creamer, regular	10.00
Homespun, creamer & sugar bowl, w/lid	25.00
Homespun, cup & saucer	12.00
Homespun, cup & saucer, demitasse	25.00
Homespun, egg cup	18.00
Homespun, mug, 9-oz	25.00
Homespun, pitcher, streamlined, 1-pt	20.00
Homespun, plate, 6½"	4.00
Homespun, plate, 9½"	10.00
Homespun, platter, 12½"	17.00
Homespun, platter, 14"	30.00
Homespun, shakers, pr	15.00
Homespun, sugar bowl, w/lid	12.00
Homespun, syrup, drip-cut top	45.00
Lei Lani, plate, 10½"	40.00
Lei Lani, plate, 9½"	35.00
Moby Dick, chop plate, 12½"	175.00
Moby Dick, plate, brn, 9"	60.00
Monterey, shakers, pr	15.00
Organdie, bowl, fruit; 5½"	4.00
Organdie, bowl, mixing; 5"	18.00
Organdie, bowl, serving; oval, 10"	20.00
Organdie, carafe	35.00
Organdie, casserole, w/lid	30.00
Organdie, creamer	8.00
Organdie, creamer & sugar bowl, w/lid	20.00
Organdie, plate, 7½"	6.00
Organdie, plate, 9½"	8.00
Organdie, platter, 12½"	15.00
Organdie, server, 2-tier	15.00
Organdie, shakers, pr	8.50
Plate, Camino Real, 14"	40.00
Plate, Chicago IL, 10½"	16.00
Plate, Chinatown, San Francisco CA, 10½"	17.50
Plate, Cocktail Hour Bicardi, 8½"	45.00
Plate, Florida, 10½"	12.00
Plate, Liszt, 8½"	25.00
Plate, McAlister OK, 50th Anniversary, 10½"	12.00
Plate, St Louis commemorative, Van Gelder, 1945, 10½"	12.50

Plate, Texas Foley's Store, mc, 10½"	27.50
Plate, Williamsburg VA, mc, 10½"	15.00
Raffia, cup & saucer	6.00
Raffia, plate, 10"	8.00
Raffia, plate, 6"	3.00
Raffia, platter, 13"	15.00
Salamina, cup & saucer	50.00
Salamina, plate, chop; 14"	400.00
Salamina, plate, chop; 17"	575.00
Salamina, plate, dinner; 9½"	125.00
Salamina, sugar bowl, w/lid, regular	100.00
Salamina, tumbler	110.00
Tam O'Shanter, bowl, divided vegetable	30.00
Tam O'Shanter, bowl, fruit; 5½"	15.00
Tam O'Shanter, creamer	8.00
Tam O'Shanter, cup & saucer	7.00
Tam O'Shanter, plate, salad; 7½"	5.00
Tam O'Shanter, plate, 6¼"	3.00
Tam O'Shanter, plate, 9½"	9.00
Tam O'Shanter, shakers, pr	16.00
Tickled Pink, cup & saucer	10.00
Tickled Pink, plate, 10"	8.00
Tickled Pink, plate, 7½"	7.50
Tickled Pink, shakers, pr	10.00

Vistosa

Vistosa was produced from about 1938 through the early forties. It was Taylor, Smith, and Taylor's answer to the very successful Fiesta line of their nearby competitor, Homer Laughlin. Vistosa was made in four solid colors: mango red, cobalt blue, light green, and deep yellow. 'Pie crust' edges and a dainty five-petal flower molded into handles and lid finials made for a very attractive yet nevertheless commercially unsuccessful product. Our advisor for this category is Ted Haun; he is listed in the Directory under Indiana.

Bowl, salad; ftd	125.00
Bowl, 5¾"	8.00
Bowl, 8½"	24.00
Chop plate, 13"	18.00
Chop plate, 15"	35.00
Creamer	10.00
Cup & saucer	15.00
Egg cup	22.50
Gravy boat	90.00
Pitcher, cobalt	75.00
Pitcher, red	75.00
Plate, salad; 7"	8.00
Plate, 7"	7.00
Plate, 9"	10.00
Plate, 9"	18.00
Shakers, pr	15.00
Sugar bowl, w/lid	95.00
Teapot	95.00

Volkmar

Charles Volkmar established a workshop in Tremont, New York, in 1882. He produced artware decorated under the glaze in the manner of the early barbotine work done at the Haviland factory in Limoges, France. He relocated in 1888 in Menlo Park, New Jersey, and together with J.T. Smith established the Menlo Park Ceramic Company for the production of art tile. The partnership was dissolved in 1893. From

1895 until 1902, Volkmar located in Corona, New York, first under the name Volkmar Ceramic Company, later as Volkmar and Cory, and for the final six years as Crown Point. During the latter period he made art tile, blue under-glaze Delft-type wares, colorful polychrome vases, etc. The Volkmar Kilns were established in 1903 in Metuchen, New Jersey, by Volkmar and his son. Wares were marked with various devices consisting of the Volkmar name, initials, or 'Crown Point Ware.'

Vases: American Indian portraits in Limoges style, artist signed, ca 1885, 11¼", VG, $2,500.00 for the pair.

Bowl, gr matt, irreg leaves form upright sides, 3½x9½" 275.00
Lamp base, mums, yel on brn gloss, bulbous, CPW, 11x6" 425.00
Pitcher, cider; gr matt, ovoid, 8½", +4 mugs 460.00
Plaque, pastoral scene w/house, natural colors, sgn, 9x16" 4,675.00
Plaque, Stadt Uys, 1st Public Bldg in NY 1642, 1895, 11" 320.00
Tile, duck silhouette outlined in squeeze-bag, gr matt, 8¼" 585.00
Tile, trees landscape, bl & gr matt, 6" sq, EX 800.00

Volkstedt

There were several porcelain factories in and around Volkstedt, Province of Thuringia, the original and earliest one established in 1762 by George Heinrich Macheleid. Others soon followed, producing many fine porcelain figures and groups in the Scheib-Alsbach, Potschappel, and Sitzendorf style. The 'crossed hayforks' mark was used from 1787 to 1800 by Christian Nonne; it was later modified with the addition of a crown by R. Ekhart (1906-08). An 'M' crossed by a 'V' with a crown was used from 1907-47 by Muller, who used an oval-shaped diamond with an 'M,' 'V' and a crown from 1910-1960. The Greiner Bros. mark was a double crossed 'G' and a crown, in use from 1850-1920.

Bowl, 3-D maid, lilies at rim, gilt, 10" H, NM 460.00
Figurine, boy playing flute, dog at side, mk, 5" 125.00
Figurine, lady in lacy skirt w/bonnet & flowers, 1930, 9½" 250.00
Figurine, Tea Time, ladies at table, 7x8" 295.00

Wade

The Wade Group of Potteries originated in 1810 with a small, single-oven pottery near Chesterton, just west of Burslem, England. This pottery, first owned by a Henry Hallen, was eventually taken over by George Wade who had opened his own pottery in the latter part of the 19th century, on Hall Street, Burslem. In the early 19th century, George Wade combined the two businesses into one pottery — the George Wade Pottery, located on High Street, Burslem. This pottery was named the Manchester Pottery; it still stands and is in business today.

Both the original Hallen Pottery and the newer George Albert Wade, Pottery specialized in pottery items for the textile industry, then booming in nothern England. In 1906 Wade's son, George Albert Wade, joined the company, and in 1919 the pottery name was changed to George Wade and Son Ltd.

George Wade's brothers, Albert and William, had interests in two

other potteries, Wade Heath & Co. Ltd., founded in 1867 as Wade, Colclough and Lingard (changed to Wade & Co. in 1887, and to Wade Heath & Co. Ltd. in 1927), and J.&W. Wade & Co. founded in the late 19th century with a name change, also in 1927, to A.J. Wade & Co. Together the potteries manufactured decorative tiles, teapots, and other related dinnerware. In 1938 Wade Heath took over the Royal Victoria Pottery, also in Burslem, and began producing a wide range of figurines and other decorative items. The A.J. Wade & Co. pottery ceased production in 1970 but the main building was not sold and reopened recently as The Pottery Store. The Royal Victoria Pottery is still in production but is now referred to as Hill Top.

In 1947 a new pottery was opened in Portadown, Northern Ireland, to produce both industrial ceramics and Irish porcelain giftware. In 1958 all the Wade potteries were amalgamated, becoming the Wade Group of Potteries. The most recent addition to the group is Wade (PDM) Limited, a marketing arm for the advertising ware made by Wade Heath at the Royal Victoria Pottery. Wade (PDM) Limited was incorporated in 1969. In 1989 the Wade Group of Potteries was bought out by Beauford engineering. With this takeover, Wade Heath and George Wade & Son Ltd. were combined to form Wade Ceramics. Wade (Ireland) Ltd. and Wade (PDM) Ltd. became subsidiaries of Wade Ceramics. In 1990 Wade (Ireland) Ltd. changed its name to Seagoe Ceramics Limited. In April, 1993, Seagoe Ceramics Limited ceased the production of table and gift ware to concentrate on industrial ceramics. The pottery, although still owned by Beauford, is no longer part of the Wade Group.

For those interested in learning more about Wade pottery, we recommend *The World of Wade* and *The World of Wade, Book 2*, by Ian Warner and Mike Posgay; Mr. Warner is listed in the Directory under Canada.

Bristo-Kid shakers, girl (salt) & boy (pepper), ea 98.00
Disney Figurine, Madam Mim 200.00
Disney Figurine, Merlin as a Turtle 215.00
Nursery Favourite, Goosey Gander, orig 150.00
Nursery Favourite, Goosey Gander, 1991 reissue 35.00
Nursery Favourite, Jack or Jill, ea 45.00
Nursery Favourite, King Cole or Queen of Hearts, ea 55.00
Nursery Favourite, Mary Mary, orig 55.00
Nursery Favourite, Mary Mary, 1990 reissue.............................35.00
Nursery Favourite, Old Woman in Shoe, orig.............................130.00
Nursery Favourite, Old Woman in Shoe, 1991 reissue....................32.00
Nursery Favourite, Polly Kettle, orig 55.00
Nursery Favourite, Polly Kettle, 1990 reissue..............................35.00
Nursery Favourite, Tom Piper, orig..55.00
Nursery Favourite, Tom Piper, 1990 reissue...............................35.00
Sophisticated Lady, Roxanne, Emily, or Felicity, ea....................100.00
Sophisticated Lady, Susannah..110.00
TV Pet, Bengo, Chee-Chee, Mitzi, or Simon, ea 60.00
TV Pet, Droopy Jr, Percy or Bruno, ea 100.00
TV Pet, Fifi 45.00
TV Pet, Pepi 55.00
Wade (Ireland) Ltd, Raindrops coffeepot 80.00
Wade (Ireland) Ltd, Raindrops creamer & sugar bowl, ea..............28.00
Wade (Ireland) Ltd, Raindrops teapot.......................................75.00
Wade (PDM) Ltd, bottle pourers (bird or animal figures), ea 65.00
Wade (PDM) Ltd, Charrington's Beer toby mug..........................175.00
Wade (PDM) Ltd, VAT 69 water jug, 4½" 36.00
Wade (PDM) Ltd, Waiter tray, tin, 12½" sq................................18.00
Whimsy, cockatoo, 1950s...45.00
Whimsy, crocodile, 1950s...55.00
Whimsy, Dog Dish, terrier, 1950s 45.00
Whimsy, piglet, 1950s..65.00
Whimsy, Salada Tea Village store canister, 1950s.........................95.00
Whimsy, Shire horse, orig, 1950s (watch for crude repro) 200.00
Whimsy, Slow-Fe, tortoise, 1950s 55.00

Whimsy, swan, orig, 1950s (watch for crude repro)......................180.00
Whimsy, Village Store Canisters, 1950s, set of 4..........................280.00

Wallace China

Dinnerware with a Western theme produced by the Wallace China Company, who operated in California from 1931 until 1964, has become very popular. Artist Till Goodan designed three lines, Rodeo, Pioneer Trails, and Boots and Saddle, which they marketed under the package name Westward Ho. When dinnerware with a western theme became so popular just a few years ago, Rodeo was reproduced, but the new trademark includes neither 'California' or 'Wallace China.'

Our advisor for this category is Marv Fogleman; he is listed in the Directory under California. If you'd like to learn more about this company, we recommend *The Collector's Encyclopedia of California Pottery* by Jack Chipman.

Boots & Saddle, ashtray, 5½" 55.00
Boots & Saddle, pitcher, disk 375.00
Boots & Saddle, plate, 7" 40.00
Chuckwagon, plate, 9" 50.00
El Rancho, bowl, vegetable; oval, 12" 160.00
El Rancho, plate, grill 65.00
Little Buckaroo set, 3-pc 600.00
Longhorn, platter, oval, 15¼" 180.00
Pioneer Trails, plate, bl on wht, 10½" 80.00
Pioneer Trails, platter, Till Goodan, 15¼" 200.00
Rodeo, bowl, flat soup; 9" 300.00
Rodeo, bowl, vegetable; oval 195.00
Rodeo, creamer, mini 95.00
Rodeo, mug & saucer 90.00
Rodeo, pitcher, water; disk style 450.00
Rodeo, plate, 7" 60.00
Westward Ho (brands only), bowl, chili; 5¾" 55.00
Westward Ho (brands only), bowl, fruit; 5" 40.00
Westward Ho (brands only), cup & saucer, demi 125.00
Westward Ho (brands only), cup & saucer, 3" 45.00
Westward Ho (brands only), custard, 4" dia 40.00
Westward Ho (brands only), shaker, sm 45.00

Walley

The Walley Pottery operated in West Sterling, Massachusetts, from 1898 to 1919. Never more than a one-man operation, Walley himself handcrafted all his wares from local clay. The majority of his pottery was simple and unadorned. Though it was usually glazed in matt green, on occasion you may find high- and semi-gloss green as well as matt glazes in blue, cream, brown, and red. The most rare and desirable examples of his work are those with applied or relief-carved decorations. Some pieces are marked 'WJW.'

Vase, brn over bl/gr drip, shouldered, mk WJW, 3⅜" 220.00
Vase, brn/khaki flambe, ½-hdls, no mk, 8x6" 165.00
Vase, gr mottled semi-matt, bottle form, WJW, 6¾x4" 800.00
Vase, leathery gr matt, incised initials, 3x3½" 185.00

Walrath

Frederick Walrath was a studio potter who worked from around the turn of the century until his death in 1920. He was located in Rochester, New York, until 1918 when he became associated with the Newcomb Pottery in New Orleans, Louisiana.

Bowl, gray matt, incised mk, 8" 100.00
Figurine, mountain lion on rock, gr/brn matt, 5x7" 800.00
Figurine, reclining nude, brn on gr matt, mk, EX mold, 3x5½" ..450.00
Flower holder, nude kneels w/arm extended, wht, 5x5" 375.00
Paperweight, scarab form, brn-gr, 3½" 200.00
Vase, floral/leaves, yel on cafe-au-lait, 3¾x4½" 1,200.00
Vase, repeating floral stalk, 3-color, spherical, 3½x4" 800.00

Walter, A.

Almaric Walter was employed from 1904 through 1914 at Verreries Artistiques des Freres Daum in Nancy, France. After 1919 he opened his own business where he continued to make the same type of quality objets d'art in pate-de-verre glass as he had earlier. His pieces are signed A. Walter, Nancy H. Berge Sc.

Box, florals at rim, gr pod on lid w/pk bud finial, 5" dia 1,700.00
Jar, lg scarabs w/curling antennae on yel/gr/orange, 7" dia 6,600.00
Pendant, orchids, amber/wine on mottle, gold bezel, 1¾" dia 550.00
Tile, seashells/lg crab emb in hexagon, 7" 900.00
Tray, frog/lily pads at side, mk AH, 2½x6½" 1,725.00
Tray, hermit crab/snail on rim of shell shape, 4x9" 2,500.00
Tray, lg cockatoo perched on rim, 6½x6½" 2,700.00

Walters, Carl

Trained as a painter, Walters began designing ceramics about 1921. He is best known for his sculpted and painted animal forms.

Sculpture, tropical fish swimming on coral reef on molded plinth, mauve, rust and turquoise, earthenware, signed, 1927, 12¾", $2,640.00.

Bowl, geometrics, blk on turq, 3½x6" 150.00
Charger, stylized Persian motif, blk/turq/gr gloss, 15" 825.00
Vase, chicken form, maroon/blk on wht, 11" 330.00

Wannopee

The Wannopee Pottery, established in 1892, developed from the reorganization of the financially insecure New Milford Pottery Company of New Milford, Connecticut. They produced a line of mottledglazed pottery called 'Duchess' and a similar line in porcelain. Both were marked with the impressed sunburst 'W' with 'porcelain' added to indicate that particular body type.

In 1895 semiporcelain pitchers in three sizes were decorated with relief medallion cameos of Beethoven, Mozart, and Napoleon. Lettuce Leaf ware was first produced in 1901 and used actual leaves in the modeling. Scarabronze, made in 1895, was their finest artware. It featured simple Egyptian shapes with a coppery glaze. It was marked with a scarab, either impressed or applied. Production ceased in 1903.

Bowl, Lettuce Leaf, #212, lg, NM 125.00
Candlestick, dk bl irid, twist stem, 12", NM 150.00
Ewer, shaded brn & gr, compressed body, 4¾" 50.00
Lamp, gr/bl/blk irid, can insert, 2-light, wicker shade, 18" 700.00
Vase, Scarabronze, appl scarab/emb Egyptian, rstr, 12x6" 200.00

Warwick

The Warwick China Company operated in Wheeling, West Virginia, from 1887 until 1951. They produced both hand-painted and decaled plates, vases, teapots, coffeepots, pitchers, bowls, and jardinieres featuring lovely florals or portraits of beautiful ladies done in luscious colors. Backgrounds were usually blendings of brown and beige, but ivory was also used (and on rare occasion, pink). Various marks were employed, all of which incorporate the Warwick name. For a more thorough study of the subject, we recommend *Warwick, A to W*, a supplement to *Why Not Warwick* by our advisor, Donald C. Hoffmann; his address can be found in the Directory under Illinois. In an effort to inform the collector/dealer, Mr. Hoffman now has a video available that identifies the company's decals and their variations by number. These numbers are contained within the following listings (VT #1, VT #2, etc.)

Mug, brn, Dickens, rnd hdl, VT #3, 4" 65.00
Mug, brn, Dickens, sq hdl, VT #1 & #2, 4" 75.00
Mug, brn, dogs, rnd hdl, VT #10, 4" 90.00
Mug, brn, fraternal order, rnd hdl, VT #3, 4" 65.00
Mug, brn, fraternal order, rnd hdl, VT #4, 4" 80.00
Mug, brn, fraternal order, sq hdl, VT #2, 4" 70.00
Mug, brn, friar, finger-hole hdl, VT #10, 3" 65.00
Mug, brn, friar, finger-hole hdl, VT #4 & #5, 3" 50.00
Mug, brn, friar, finger-hole hdl, VT #6, 3" 60.00
Mug, brn, friar, finger-hole hdl, VT #7 & #9, 3" 55.00
Mug, brn, friar, sq hdl, VT #1 & #2, 4" 70.00
Mug, brn, friar, sq hdl, VT #3, 4" 60.00
Mug, brn, Indians, rnd hdl, VT #6, 4" 100.00
Mug, brn, Indians, rnd hdl, VT #8, 4" 85.00
Mug, brn, monk, rnd hdl, VT #3, 4" 60.00
Mug, charcoal, friar, rnd hdl, VT #10, 4" 90.00
Mug, charcoal, monk, rnd hdl, VT #2, 4" 95.00
Mug, matt brn, fraternal order, rnd hdl, VT #4, 4" 80.00
Mug, matt brn, monk, rnd hdl, VT #1/#2/#3, 4" 75.00
Mug, matt tan-brn, fisherman, sq hdl, VT #2, 4" 80.00
Mug, matt tan-brn, monks, sq hdl, VT #1 & #2, 4" 75.00
Mug, pk-gr, monks, sq hdl, VT #1 & #2, 4" 95.00
Mug, red, fisherman, rnd hdl, VT #2, 4" 80.00
Mug, red, fisherman, sq hdl, VT #1 & #2, 4" 75.00
Plate, brn, left side, friar, VT #9, 10" 100.00
Plate, brn to cream, friar, VT #12 & #16, 10" 95.00
Plate, brn to yel, dog, VG #7, 10" 115.00
Plate, gr to cream, friar, VT #14, 10" 100.00
Spirit jug, brn, Dickens, VT #1 & #2 ....220.00
Spirit jug, brn, fisherman, VT #2 ....235.00
Spirit jug, brn, floral, VT #9 ....290.00
Spirit jug, brn, Indian, VT #9 ....250.00
Spirit jug, brn, portrait, VT #3 ....285.00
Spirit jug, matt tan-brn, VT #12 ....280.00
Stein, brn, Dickens, ring hdl, VT #1, 5" 75.00
Stein, brn, friar, ring hdl, VT #4, 5" 85.00
Stein, brn, friar, ring hdl, VT #7, 5" 90.00
Stein, brn, friar, ring hdl, VT #9, 5" 80.00
Stein, brn, Indian, ring hdl, VT #6, 5" 115.00
Stein, brn, monk, ring hdl, VT #1, 5" 70.00

Stein, brn, monk, ring hdl, VT #3, 5" 85.00
Stein, charcoal, friar, ring hdl, VT #15, 5" 95.00
Stein, red, monk, ring hdl, VT #2, 5" 80.00
Tankard, brn, Dickens, ring hdl, VG #1, 15" 260.00
Tankard, brn, Dickens, ring hdl, VG #1, 15", +6 5" steins 750.00
Tankard, brn, Dickens, rnd hdl, VT #2, 10" 220.00
Tankard, brn, dog, rnd hdl, VT #7, 10" 250.00
Tankard, brn, FOE old style, ring hdl, VT #2, 15", +6 steins 880.00
Tankard, brn, fraternal order, ring hdl, VT #3, 15" 230.00
Tankard, brn, friar, ring hdl, VT #10, 13" 230.00
Tankard, brn, friar, ring hdl, VT #11, 13" 240.00
Tankard, brn, friar, ring hdl, VT #11, 15", +6 5" steins 775.00
Tankard, brn, friar, rnd hdl, VT #1, 10" 240.00
Tankard, brn, friar, rnd hdl, VT #15, 10" 200.00
Tankard, brn, friar, sq hdl w/bar, VT #1, 10" 230.00
Tankard, brn, fruit, ring hdl, VT #8, 13" 265.00
Tankard, brn, Indian, ring hdl, VT #4, 15" 295.00
Tankard, brn, Indian, ring hdl, VT #4, 15", +6 5" steins 800.00
Tankard, brn, monk, sq hdl w/bar, #VT #2, 10" 245.00
Tankard, brn, opera decor, ring hdl, VT #3, +6 5" steins 1,000.00
Tankard, brn, portrait, ring hdl, VT #23, 15" 300.00
Tankard, brn, portrait, ring hdl, VT #4, 13" 245.00
Tankard, brn, portrait, ring hdl, VT #54, 15" 325.00
Tankard, matt bl, fraternal order, sq hdl, VT #1, 10" 300.00
Tankard, matt brn, fisherman, sq hdl w/bar, VT #1, 10" 300.00
Tankard, red, fisherman, sq hdl w/bar, VT #2, 10" 260.00
Vase, Geran, brn, floral, VT #9, 11" 245.00
Vase, Geran, charcoal, floral, VT #13, 11" 260.00
Vase, Grecian, brn, floral, VT #14, 8" 240.00
Vase, Grecian, red, floral, VT #2, 8" 250.00
Vase, Grecian, red, portrait, VT #35, 8" 235.00
Vase, Helene, brn, floral, VT #22, 12" 245.00
Vase, Helene, brn, floral, VT #9, 12" 230.00
Vase, Helene, wht, birds, VT #4, 12" 260.00
Vase, Henrietta, brn, floral, VT #9, 10" 235.00
Vase, Hibiscus, brn, dogs, VT #5, 11½" 300.00
Vase, Hibiscus, charcoal, VT #30, 11 2/2" 320.00
Vase, Hyacinth, brn, floral, VT #10, 11" 240.00
Vase, Hyacinth, red, portrait, VT #36, 11" 235.00
Vase, Iris, brn, floral, VT #14, 9¾" 145.00
Vase, Iris, brn, floral, VT #9, 9¾" 140.00
Vase, Iris, brn, nut decor, VT #14, 9¾" 150.00
Vase, Lemonade, brn, floral, VT #5, 6½" 150.00
Vase, Lemonade, pk, portrait, VT #6, 6½" 230.00
Vase, Leomonade, wht, birds, VT #3, 6½" 190.00
Vase, Lily, brn, floral, VT #9, 9½" 200.00
Vase, Lily, charcoal, floral, VT #13, 9½" 235.00
Vase, Lily, charcoal, nude, VT #30, 9½" 250.00
Vase, Louise, brn, floral, VT #23, 9½" 265.00
Vase, Louise, pk, portrait, VT #9, 9½" 290.00
Vase, Magnolia, floral, VT #9, 10½" 250.00
Vase, Maria, brn, floral, VT #15, 10½" 245.00
Vase, Maria, charcoal, portrait, VT #29, 10½" 260.00
Vase, Maria, pk, portrait, VT #6, 10½" 285.00
Vase, Nasturtium, brn, floral, VT #10, 12¼" 250.00

Wash Sets

Before the days of running water, bedrooms were standardly equipped with a wash bowl and pitcher as a matter of necessity. A 'toilet set' was comprised of the pitcher and bowl, toothbrush holder, covered commode, soap dish, shaving dish, and mug. Some sets were even more elaborate. Through everyday usage, the smaller items were often broken, and today it is unusual to find a complete set.

Porcelain sets decorated with florals, fruits, or scenics were produced abroad by Limoges in France; some were imported from Germany and England. During the last quarter of the 1800s and until after the turn of the century, American-made toilet sets were manufactured in abundance. Tin and graniteware sets were also made.

Chesapeake Pottery, Algerian #654 decor, 5-pc set 400.00
Chrysanthemum, Buffalo, pitcher+bowl 255.00
English, bl-gr florals, pitcher+bowl+toothbrush holder+pot 375.00
Gaudy Staffordshire, mc florals, 11", 13" dia, 2 pcs 495.00
Homer Laughlin, gold floral/sprigs, pitcher+bowl+5 pcs 575.00
Leonard-Vienna, HP forest/gold trim, 8-pcs, rpr, chips 500.00
Minton, child's, gr ivy on cream, 7" pitcher+9½" bowl 295.00
Old Paris, floral & scrollwork panels on wht, pitcher+bowl 625.00
Royal Coronaware, floral, blk w/mc trim, 15¾" dia, 2 pcs 260.00
Staffordshire, dk bl seashell & flower border, 12" dia, 2 pcs 85.00

Watch Fobs

Watch fobs have been popular since the last quarter of the 19th century. They were often made by retail companies to feature their products. Souvenir, commemorative, and political fobs were also produced. Of special interest today are those with advertising, heavy equipment in particular. Some of the more pricey fobs are listed here, but most of those currently available were produced in such quantities that they are relatively common and should fall into a price range of $3.00 to $10.00. Our advisor for this category is Tony George; he is listed in the Directory under California.

Abraham Fur Co, St Mouis MO 150.00
Alaska Yukon Pacific Exposition, Nouveau ladies 75.00
Allis Chalmers HD 21 Cat 65.00
Atkins, bl porc 70.00
Aultman Taylor, rooster 65.00
Avery, tractor 65.00
Bronco Brand Overalls, diecut 125.00
Bucyrus Erie 40.00
Buick, auto, enamel 50.00
Burrough's Adding Machines 100.00
Case Cross, motor 85.00
Case Tractor 50.00
Clarke's Pure Rye 50.00
Confederate Reunion, Biloxi, 1930 ....150.00
Cyrus McCormick, medallion 25.00
Dr Pepper Billiken 85.00
Fidelity Flour, porc 75.00
Fordson Tractor 40.00
Germer Stoves, stove diecut 50.00
Gold Dust Twins 225.00
Gold Medal Flour 65.00
Hampshire Swine, porc 50.00
Happy Cow Feed, celluloid 50.00
Heinz, girl in wht cap 50.00
International Harvester, red, wht & bl 50.00
International Livestock Expo, 1920 ....125.00
Jefferson, Friend of Personal Liberty, VA Whiskey, 1½x2" 40.00
JI Case, steam engine, EX color 25.00
John Deere, MOP 75.00
Kellogg's Corn Flakes 50.00
Kiwanis Arrowhead, South Bend, 1923 ....35.00
Le Tourneau, enameled 85.00
Masonic, Atlanta 1914, enamel w/compass 45.00

McCormick-Deering Farm Machines, enamel 45.00
Moonshine Corn Whiskey, silver, 1½", EX 60.00
National Fidelity & Casualty, emb eagle 65.00
Order of Cootie, WWI military 18.00
Oshkosh Beer, porc 150.00
Peters Weatherbird Shoes 60.00
Round Oak Stoves 225.00
Rumely, tractor 65.00
Russell, steam engine 85.00
Sam Rosenthal & Bros, boy holds trousers, 1890s 32.00
San Antonio, Alamo, 1931 ....65.00
Savage Arms Co, gun diecut 125.00
Tenison Saddle Co, saddle shape, Dallas TX 275.00
Texas Portland Cement 50.00
Tomlinson, chair diecut 60.00
Twinkies Shoe Co, inset compass, brass, early 295.00
WWI, 57th Infantry, sterling 75.00

Watch Stands

Watch stands were decorative articles designed with a hook from which to hang a watch. Some displayed the watch as the face of a grandfather clock or as part of an interior scene with figures in period costumes and contemporary furnishings. They were popular products of Staffordshire potters and silver companies as well.

Bone prisoner-of-war work watch holder in the form of gazebo, early 1800s, 10x7x5", EX, $950.00.

Architectural, wooden, mc pnt, Austrian, 1800s, 13" 265.00
Bronze, cornucopias, griffins on stepped base, Chas X, 9" 825.00
Bronze cherub w/padded shield for watch, marble base, 7" 200.00
Chalk, domed base holds wood/papier-mache doll, 14", VG 425.00
Cvd walnut, Am, mid-1800s, 11½", EX 450.00
Eagle on sphere, plated base metal, 6½" 250.00
Gilt bronze, Saracen Warrior, malachite base, 1820, 7" 220.00
Grandfather clock, wood, Japan, early 1900s, 8" 200.00
Neoclassical giltwood, Chronos figure, Austrian, 1800s, 10" 365.00
Oak w/allover cvd/punched design, circle fr in top, rpr, 7" 195.00
2 facing cherubs, red pad for watch, 6" 200.00

Watches

First made in the 1500s in Germany, early watches were actually small clocks, suspended from the neck or belt. By 1700 they had become the approximate shape and size we know today. The first watches produced in America were made in 1810. The well-known Waltham Watch Company was established in 1850. Later, Waterbury produced inexpensive watches which they sold by the thousands.

Open-face and hunting-case watches of the 1890s were often solid gold or gold-filled and were often elaborately decorated in several colors of gold. Gold watches became a status symbol in this decade and were worn by both men and women on chains with fobs or jeweled slides. Ladies sometimes fastened them to their clothing with pins often set with jewels. The chatelaine watch was worn at the waist, only one of several items such as scissors, coin purses, or needle cases, each attached by small chains.

Most turn-of-the-century watch cases were gold-filled; these are plentiful today. Sterling cases, though interest in them is on the increase, are not in great demand. Our advise for this category comes from Maundy International Watches, Antiquarian Horologists, price consultants and researchers for many watch reference guides and books on Horology. Their firm is a leading purveyor of antique watches of all kinds. They are listed in the Directory under Kansas. For character-related watches, see Personalities.

Key:

adj — adjusted	k/s — key set
brg — bridge plate design	k/w — key wind
d/s — double sunk dial	l/s — lever set
fbd — finger bridge design	mvt — movement
g/f — gold-filled	o/f — open face
g/j/s — gold jewel setting	p/s — pendant set
h/c — hunter case	r/g/p — rolled gold plate
HCI#P — heat, cold,	s — size
isochronism & position	s/s — single sunk dial
adjusted	s/w — stem wind
j — jewel	w/g/f — white gold-filled
k — karat	y/g/f — yellow gold-filled

Gold pocketwatch with ornate tricolored gold flowers and green leaves, gold hands on white face, marked .0585 with crown in circle and a bell surrounded by five stars, inside marked Union/No. 37763, late 1800s, M in original leather case (not shown), $1,500.00 to $3,500.00.

Am Watch Co, 0s, 7j, #1891, 14k, h/c, Am Watch Co 575.00
Am Watch Co, 12s, 17j, #1894, 14k, o/f, Royal 275.00
Am Watch Co, 12s, 21j, #1894, 14k, h/c 575.00
Am Watch Co, 16s, 11j, #1872, p/s, silver h/c, Park Road 425.00
Am Watch Co, 16s, 15j, #1899, y/g/f, h/c 190.00
Am Watch Co, 16s, 16j, #1884, 5-min, coin silver, Repeater .4,500.00
Am Watch Co, 16s, 17j, #1888, Railroader 625.00
Am Watch Co, 16s, 19j, #1872, 14k, h/c, Am Watch Co 3,250.00
Am Watch Co, 16s, 21j, #1888, o/f, 14k, Riverside Maximus .1,475.00
Am Watch Co, 16s, 21j, #1899, y/g/f, l/s, o/f, Crescent St 325.00
Am Watch Co, 16s, 21j, #1908, y/g/f, o/f, Grade #645 ....250.00
Am Watch Co, 16s, 23j, #1908, o/f, 18k, Premier Maximus, MIB .9,000.00
Am Watch Co, 16s, 23j, #1908, y/g/f, o/f, adj, RR, Vanguard ...325.00
Am Watch Co, 16s, 23j, #1908, y/g/f, o/f, Vanguard Up/Down ..685.00
Am Watch Co, 18s, #1857, silver h/c, k/w Samuel Curtiss 3,450.00

Am Watch Co, 18s, 11j, #1857, k/w, 1st run, PS Barlett 450.00
Am Watch Co, 18s, 11j, #1857, silver h/c, k/w, DH&D 1,425.00
Am Watch Co, 18s, 11j, #1857, silver h/c, k/w, s/s, Ellery, EX ...350.00
Am Watch Co, 18s, 15j, #1877, k/w, RE Robbins 395.00
Am Watch Co, 18s, 15j, #1883, y/g/f, 2-tone, Railroad King 650.00
Am Watch Co, 18s, 17j, #1883, y/g/f, o/f, Crescent Street 175.00
Am Watch Co, 18s, 17j, #1892, HC, Canadian Pacific Railway .1,400.00
Am Watch Co, 18s, 17j, #1892, y/g/f, o/f, Sidereal, rare 1,950.00
Am Watch Co, 18s, 17j, 25-yr, y/g/f, o/f, s/s, PS Bartlett 165.00
Am Watch Co, 18s, 21j, #1892, y/g/f, o/f, d/s, Crescent St 325.00
Am Watch Co, 18s, 21j, #1892, y/g/f, o/f, Grade #845 ....250.00
Am Watch Co, 18s, 21j, #1892, y/g/f, o/f, Pennsylvania Special .1,650.00
Am Watch Co, 18s, 7j, #1857, k/w, CT Parker, scarce 2,650.00
Am Watch Co, 6s, 7j, #1873, y/g/f, h/c, Am Watch Co 195.00
Auburndale Watch Co, 18s, 7j, k/w, l/s, Lincoln 1,250.00
Aurora Watch Co, 18s, 11j, o/f, k/w, h/c 550.00
Aurora Watch Co, 18s, 15 ruby j, k/w, h/c 1,400.00
Ball (Elgin), 18s, 17j, o/f, silver, Official RR Standard 525.00
Ball (Hamilton), 16s, 21j, #999, g/f, o/f, l/s 365.00
Ball (Hamilton), 16s, 23j, #998, y/g/f, o/f, Elinvar 900.00
Ball (Hamilton), 18s, 19j, #999, g/f, o/f, l/s 450.00
Ball (Hampden), 18s, 17j, o/f, adj, RR, Superior Grade 1,375.00
Ball (Illinois), 12s, 19j, w/g/f, o/f 250.00
Ball (Waltham), 16s, 17j, y/g/f, o/f, Commercial Std 225.00
Ball (Waltham), 16s, 21j, o/f, Official Standard 365.00
Columbus, 18s, 11-15j, k/w, k/s 550.00
Columbus, 18s, 15j, o/f, l/s 240.00
Columbus, 18s, 15j, y/g/f, o/f, Jay Gould 925.00
Columbus, 18s, 21j, y/g/f, h/c, train on dial, Railway King 625.00
Columbus, 18s, 23j, 14k h/c, Columbus King 2,250.00
Columbus, 6s, 11j, 14k h/c 495.00
Cornell, 18s, 15j, s/w, JC Adams 725.00
Cornell, 18s, 15j, silver h/c, k/w, John Evans 540.00
Dudley, 12s, #1, 14k, o/f, flip-bk case, Masonic 3,450.00
Elgin, 10s, 18k, h/c, k/w, k/s, s/s, Gail Borden 775.00
Elgin, 12s, 15j, 14k, h/c 450.00
Elgin, 12s, 17j, 14k, h/c, GM Wheeler 495.00
Elgin, 16s, 15j, doctor's, 4th model, 14k, 2nd sweep hand 1,650.00
Elgin, 16s, 15j, 14k, h/c 575.00
Elgin, 16s, 21j, g/f, 3 fbd, grade #72-91, scarce 1,975.00
Elgin, 16s, 21j, y/g/f, g/j/s, o/f, BW Raymond 325.00
Elgin, 16s, 21j, y/g/f, g/j/s, 3 fbd 395.00
Elgin, 16s, 21j, y/g/f, o/f, l/s, RR, Father Time 295.00
Elgin, 16s, 23j, up/down indicator, BW Raymond 850.00
Elgin, 17s, 7j, k/w, orig silver case, Leader 250.00
Elgin, 18s, 11j, silver, h/c, k/w, gilded, MG Odgen 285.00
Elgin, 18s, 15j, o/f, d/s, k/w, silveroid, RR, BW Raymond 285.00
Elgin, 18s, 15j, silver h/c, Penn RR dial, BW Raymond k/w mvt .2,250.00
Elgin, 18s, 15j, 14k, k/w, k/s, h/c, HL Culver 1,245.00
Elgin, 18s, 17j, silveroid, BW Raymond 285.00
Elgin, 18s, 21j, y/g/f, o/f, Father Time 325.00
Elgin, 18s, 23j, y/g/f, o/f, 5-position, RR, Veritas 485.00
Elgin, 6s, 11j, 14k, h/c 400.00
Elgin, 6s, 15j, 20-yr, y/g/f, h/c, s/s 150.00
Fredonia, 18s, 11j, y/g/f, h/c, k/w 425.00
Hamilton, #4992B, 16s, 22j, o/f, steel case 280.00
Hamilton, #910, 12s, 17j, 20-yr, y/g/f, o/f, s/s 125.00
Hamilton, #912, 12s, 17j, y/g/f, o/f, adj 125.00
Hamilton, #920, 12s, 23j, 14k, o/f 495.00
Hamilton, #922MP, 12s, 18k case, Masterpiece (sgn) 1,400.00
Hamilton, #925, 18s, 17j, y/g/f, h/c, s/s, l/s 240.00
Hamilton, #928, 18s, 15j, y/g/f, o/f, s/s 160.00
Hamilton, #933, 18s, 16j, h/c, nickel plate, low serial # 1,400.00
Hamilton, #938, 18s, 17j, 10k, y/g/f, adj 625.00

Hamilton, #940, 18s, 21j, NP, coin silver, o/f 285.00
Hamilton, #946, 18s, 23j, y/g/f, o/f, g/j/s, EX 625.00
Hamilton, #947, 18s, 23j, 14k, h/c, orig/sgn, EX 6,450.00
Hamilton, #950, 16s, 23j, y/g/f, o/f, l/s, sgn d/s 575.00
Hamilton, #965, 16s, 17j, 14k, p/s, h/c, brg, scarce 1,100.00
Hamilton, #972, 16s, 17j, y/g/f, g/j/s, o/f, d/s, l/s, adj 175.00
Hamilton, #974, 16s, 17j, 20-yr, y/g/f, o/f, s/s 150.00
Hamilton, #992, 16s, 21j, y/g/f, o/f, adj, d/s, dbl roller 265.00
Hamilton, #992B, 16s, 21j, y/g/f, o/f, l/s, Bar/Crown 350.00
Hampden, 12s, 17j, w/g/f, o/f, thin model, Aviator 150.00
Hampden, 16s, 17j, o/f, adj 100.00
Hampden, 16s, 17j, y/g/f, h/c, s/w 225.00
Hampden, 16s, 21j, g/j/s, y/g/f, NP, h/c, Dueber, ¾-mvt 240.00
Hampden, 16s, 21j, o/f, adj, dbl roller, Special Railway 325.00
Hampden, 16s, 7j, gilded, NP, ¾-mvt 100.00
Hampden, 18s, 15j, k/w, mk on mvt, Railway 1,150.00
Hampden, 18s, 15j, s/w, gilded, JC Perry 250.00
Hampden, 18s, 15j, silver, k/w, h/c, Hayward 240.00
Hampden, 18s, 15j, y/g/f, damascened, h/c, Dueber 200.00
Hampden, 18s, 21j, y/g/f, g/j/s, h/c, New Railway 280.00
Hampden, 18s, 21j, y/g/f, o/f, d/s, l/s, N Am Railway 325.00
Hampden, 18s, 23j, y/g/f, d/s, adj, New Railway 365.00
Hampden, 18s, 23j, 14k, h/c, Special Railway 950.00
Hampden, 18s, 7-11j, k/w, gilded, Springfield Mass 240.00
Howard, E; 16s, 15j, s/w, 14k h/c, Series V, L sz 1,400.00
Howard, E; 18s, 15j, h/c, silver case, k/w, Series I, N sz 1,950.00
Howard, E; 18s, 15j, h/c, 14k case, k/w, Series II, N sz 1,950.00
Howard, E; 18s, 15j, 18k h/c, k/w, Series II, N sz 3,400.00
Howard, E; 18s, 17j, 25-yr, y/g/f, o/f, orig case 495.00
Howard, E; 6s, 15j, s/w, 18k h/c, Series VI, G sz 1,650.00
Howard (Keystone), 12s, 23j, 14k, h/c, brg, Series 8 ....940.00
Howard (Keystone), 16s, 17j, y/g/f, o/f, Series 9 ....295.00
Howard (Keystone), 16s, 21j, y/g/f, o/f, RR Chronometer II 450.00
Howard (Keystone), 16s, 23j, y/g/f, o/f, Series 0, jeweled bbl 695.00
Illinois, 0s, 7j, 14k, l/s, h/c 325.00
Illinois, 12s, 17j, y/g/f, o/f, d/s dial 95.00
Illinois, 16s, 17j, silver h/c, RR King 750.00
Illinois, 16s, 17j, y/g/f, o/f, d/s, Bunn, EX 385.00
Illinois, 16s, 19j, y/g/f, o/f, d/s, 60-hr, Sangamo Special 1,095.00
Illinois, 16s, 21j, g/j/s, h/c, Burlington 295.00
Illinois, 16s, 21j, o/f, d/s, Santa Fe Special 395.00
Illinois, 16s, 21j, y/g/f, o/f, s/s, Bunn Special 325.00
Illinois, 16s, 23j, y/g/f, o/f, d/s, RR, Bunn Special 700.00
Illinois, 16s, 23j, y/g/f, stiff bow, o/f, Sangamo Special 795.00
Illinois, 18s, 11j, #1, silver, k/w, Alleghany 340.00
Illinois, 18s, 11j, #3, o/f, s/w, l/s, Comet 250.00
Illinois, 18s, 11j, Forest City 225.00
Illinois, 18s, 15j, #1, adj, k/w, k/s, Stuart 1,550.00
Illinois, 18s, 15j, #1, y/g/f, k/w, h/c, gilt, Bunn 1,600.00
Illinois, 18s, 15j, k/w, k/s, gilt, Railway Regulator 675.00
Illinois, 18s, 15j, s/w, silveroid 95.00
Illinois, 18s, 17j, g/j/s, adj, B&O RR Special (Hunter), h/c 1,495.00
Illinois, 18s, 17j, h/c, s/w, NP, coin silver, Bunn 425.00
Illinois, 18s, 17j, o/f, d/s, adj, silveroid case, Lakeshore 325.00
Illinois, 18s, 17j, o/f, s/w, 5th pinion, Miller 325.00
Illinois, 18s, 21j, g/j/s, g/f, o/f, A Lincoln 340.00
Illinois, 18s, 21j, g/j/s, o/f, adj, B&O RR Special 2,250.00
Illinois, 18s, 21j, g/j/s, o/f, adj, B&O RR Special 1,575.00
Illinois, 18s, 21j, 14k, g/j/s, h/c, Bunn Special 1,575.00
Illinois, 18s, 23j, g/j/s, Bunn Special 625.00
Illinois, 18s, 24j, g/j/s, adj, o/f, Chesapeake & Ohio 3,450.00
Illinois, 18s, 24j, g/j/s, Bunn Special 825.00
Illinois, 18s, 26j, g/j/s, o/f, Ben Franklin USA 6,500.00
Illinois, 18s, 26j, 14k, Penn Special 6,500.00
Illinois, 18s, 7j, #3, Interior 240.00

Illinois, 18s, 7j, #3, silveroid, America 225.00
Illinois, 18s, 9-11j, o/f, k/w, s/s, silveroid case, Hoyt 275.00
Illinois, 8s, 13j, ¾-mvt, Rose LeLand, scarce 450.00
Ingersoll, 16s, 7j, wht base metal, Reliance 45.00
Lancaster, 18s, 7j, o/f, k/w, k/s, eng case 350.00
Marion US, 18s, h/c, k/w, k/s, ¾-plate, Asa Fuller 495.00
Marion US, 18s, 15j, nickel plate, h/c, s/w, Henry Randel 675.00
Melrose Watch Co, 18s, 7j, k/w, k/s 495.00
New York Watch Co, 18s, 7j, silver, h/c, k/w, Geo Sam Rice 375.00
New York Watch Co, 19j, low sz #, wolf's teeth wind 2,500.00
Patek Philippe, 12s, 18j, 18k, o/f 2,400.00
Patek Philippe, 16s, 20j, 18k, h/c 3,400.00
Rockford, 16s, 17j, y/g/f, h/c, brg, dbl roller 225.00
Rockford, 16s, 21j, #515, y/g/f 275.00
Rockford, 16s, 21j, g/j/s, o/f, grade #537, rare 1,425.00
Rockford, 16s, 23j, 14k, o/f, mk Doll on dial/mvt 2,250.00
Rockford, 18s, 15j, o/f, k/w, silver case 175.00
Rockford, 18s, 17j, silveroid w/mc dial, fancy mvt/hands 275.00
Rockford, 18s, 17j, y/g/f, o/f, Winnebago 275.00
Rockford, 18s, 21j, o/f, King Edward 425.00
Seth Thomas, 18s, 17j, #2, g/j/s, adj, Henry Molineux 950.00
Seth Thomas, 18s, 17j, Edgemere 150.00
Seth Thomas, 18s, 25j, g/j/s, g/f, Maiden Lane 3,250.00
Seth Thomas, 18s, 7j, ¾-mvt, bk: eagle/Liberty model 275.00
South Bend, 12s, 21j, dbl roller, Grade #431 ....225.00
South Bend, 12s, 21j, orig o/f, d/s, Studebaker 325.00
South Bend, 18s, 21j, g/j/s, h/c, Studebaker 925.00
South Bend, 18s, 21j, 14k, h/c 995.00
Swiss, 18s, 18k, h/c, 1-min, Repeater, High Grade 4,250.00

Waterford

The Waterford Glass Company operated in Ireland from the late 1700s until 1851 when the factory closed. One hundred years later (in 1951) another Waterford glassworks was instituted that produced glass similar to the 18th century wares — crystal glass, usually with cut decoration. Today Waterford is a generic term referring to the type of glass first produced there.

Bowl, centerpiece; Masterpiece Collection, ftd, 10" 950.00
Brandy, Lismore 65.00
Carafe, water; Lismore 139.00
Carafe, wine; Lismore 189.00
Claret, Colleen 75.00
Cocktail, Kylemore 79.00
Cordial, Kylemore 60.00
Flute, Cashel, 6" 102.00
Goblet, Sheila, 8-oz 79.00
Goblet, water; Colleen 75.00
Knife, hors d'oeuvre 95.00
Lamp, Masterpiece Collection, 31" 1,975.00

Mustard jar, square, with ladle, 3¼", $135.00.

Old-fashioned, dbl; Comeragh	88.00
Rose bowl, Carina	98.00
Saucer champagne, Colleen, 4⅜"	75.00
Saucer champagne, Kylemore	83.00
Shakers, Lismore, ftd, pr	150.00
Sherry, Sheila	65.00
Sherry, Traymere	70.00
Tumbler, Colleen, 10-oz	58.00
Tumbler, Colleen, 12-oz	65.00
Tumbler, water; Lismore, lg	75.00
Wine, Eileen	75.00
Wine, Kylemore	83.00

Watt Pottery

The Watt Pottery Company was established in Crooksville, Ohio, on July 5, 1922. From approximately 1922 until 1935, they manufactured hand-turned stone containers — jars, jugs, milk pans, preserve jars, and various sizes of mixing bowls, usually marked with a cobalt blue acorn stamp. In 1936 production of these items was discontinued, and the company began to produce kitchen utility ware and ovenware such as mixing bowls, spaghetti bowls and plates, canister sets, covered casseroles, salt and pepper shakers, cookie jars, ice buckets, pitchers, bean pots, and salad and dinnerware sets. Most Watt ware is individually hand-painted with bold brush strokes of red, green, or blue contrasting with the natural buff color of the glazed body. Several patterns were produced: Apple, Autumn Foliage, Cherry, Dutch Tulip, Morning Glory, Rio Rose, Rooster, Tear Drop, Starflower, and Tulip, to name a few. Much of the ware was made for advertising premiums and is often found stamped with the name of the retail company.

Tragedy struck the Watt Pottery Company on October 4, 1965, when fire completely destroyed the factory and warehouse. Production never resumed, but the ware they made has withstood many years of service in American kitchens and is today highly regarded and prized by collectors. The vivid colors and folk art-like execution of each cheerful pattern create a homespun ambiance that will make Watt pottery a treasure for years to come.

For further study we recommend *Watt Pottery, An Identification and Price Guide,* by our advisors for this category, Sue and Dave Morris, who are listed in the Directory under Iowa. For the address of the *Watt's News* newsletter, see the section on Clubs, Newsletters, and Catalogs.

Apple, bean pot, w/lid, #76	190.00
Apple, bowl, cereal; #94	45.00
Apple, bowl, mixing; #64	50.00
Apple, creamer, #62	110.00
Apple, ice bucket, w/lid	225.00
Apple, pie plate, #33	150.00
Apple, pitcher w/ice lip, #17	300.00
Apple, shakers, hourglass shape, pr	275.00
Apple, sugar bowl (open), #98	225.00
Autumn Foliage, bowl, mixing; #7	35.00
Autumn Foliage, pie plate, #33	100.00
Autumn Foliage, pitcher, #15	85.00
Autumn Foliage, shakers, hourglass shape, pr	200.00
Banded, casserole, bl/wht bands, w/lid, 8" dia	55.00
Cherry, bowl, cereal; #52	55.00
Cherry, pitcher, #15	125.00
Cherry, salt shaker, bbl shape	65.00
Dutch Tulip, bowl, mixing; #65	150.00
Dutch Tulip, bowl, spaghetti; #39	250.00
Dutch Tulip, cheese crock, w/lid, #80	850.00
Eagle, canister, #72	225.00

Kitch-N-Queen, bowl, mixing; ribbed, #8	45.00
Kla-Ham'rd, casserole, w/lid, #43-19	45.00
Morning Glory, bowl, mixing; #8	135.00
Morning Glory, sugar bowl (open), #98	225.00
Rio Rose, bowl, spaghetti; 13" dia	75.00
Rio Rose, casserole, w/lid, 8" dia	90.00
Rio Rose, plate, dinner	85.00
Rooster, baking dish, rectangular	1,000.00
Rooster, bowl, #73	150.00
Rooster, creamer, #62	250.00
Rooster, pitcher, #16	135.00
Rooster, shakers, bbl shape, pr	400.00
Silhouette (gr or brn starflower), cookie jar, w/lid, #21	165.00
Starflower, bowl, #73	75.00
Starflower, casserole, Fr hdl, w/lid, #18, ind	150.00
Starflower, grease jar, w/lid, #47	250.00
Starflower, mug, #501	100.00
Starflower, pitcher, #15	65.00
Tear Drop, bean server, #75, ind	30.00
Tear Drop, bowl, mixing; #7	35.00
Tear Drop, pitcher, #15	65.00
Tulip, bowl, mixing; #64	100.00
Tulip, casserole, ribbed, w/lid, #600	250.00
Tulip, creamer, #62	185.00
Tulip, pitcher, #16	200.00
White Daisy, bowl, mixing; #8	85.00

Wave Crest

Wave Crest is a line of decorated opal ware (milk glass) patented in 1892 by the C.F. Monroe Co. of Meriden, Connecticut. They made a full line of items for every room of the house, but they are probably best known for their boxes and vases. Most items were hand painted in various levels of decoration, but more transfers were used in the later years prior to the company's demise in 1916. Floral themes are common; items with the scenics and portraits are rarer and more highly prized. Many pieces have ornately scrolled ormolu and brass handles, feet and rims attached. Early pieces were often signed with a black mark; later a red banner mark was used, and occasionally a paper label may be found. However, the glass is quite distinctive and has not been reproduced, so even unmarked items are easy to recognize. Our advisors for this category are Dolli and Wilfred Cohen; they are listed in the Directory under California. Note: There is no premium for signatures on Wave Crest. Values are given for hand-decorated pieces that are *not* worn.

Box, Swirl, with hand-painted morning glories, 3¼x5½", $550.00.

Atomizer, floral, ball form, all orig	350.00
Biscuit jar, wht w/floral transfer, no embossing, 8"	225.00
Bonbon, floral on wht, metal rim & hdl, 1½x5¼"	300.00
Bonbon, Swirl, floral, rare brass lid	400.00
Bowl/tray, Swirl, florals, gold-washed ormolu w/hdls, 6¾"	245.00
Box, Baroque Shell, floral, orig lining, 7" dia	750.00

Box, Collars & Cuffs, Puffy, HP florals, 6" 950.00
Box, HP floral on bl w/blown-out swirls, hinged lid, 3½" 350.00
Box, Puffy, forget-me-nots on lt pk, 5" dia 450.00
Box, Swirl, floral, ftd, orig lined, 7" 750.00
Box, Swirl, floral, 3x4½" dia 265.00
Box, Swirl, floral w/gray traceries, ormolu ft, 6x7" dia 675.00
Box, Swirl, pk floral on scrolled gilded blk band, 6" dia 550.00
Box, Swirl, shoreline/sailing vessel/scrolls/flowers, 5½" dia 550.00
Card holder, roses, 2½x4" 295.00
Cologne, ribbon & floral, swirl-emb neck, str sides, stopper 350.00
Ewer, rose on gr/beige, glass body, ormolu top/ft, 16" 235.00
Humidor, Egg Crate, floral/Tobacco, ormolu corner mts, 4x5" 600.00
Humidor, Swirl, roses/turq scroll panels, cylindrical, 7" 650.00
Humidor, 3 bulldogs/Guardsmen, brass lid w/sponge holder 525.00
Jardiniere, floral, beaded rim w/gold, 7" 550.00
Lamp, 10" molded floral decor shade & font, ormolu base, 22" 750.00
Photo receiver, Puffy, wild roses, ormolu rim, 4x5½" 375.00
Photo receiver, scrolled panels w/bl daisies ea side, 4" L 450.00
Plaque, river scene, ormolu fr, cartouch form, 13x8" 1,500.00
Shakers, Erie Twist, peach & lt bl HP florals, pr 250.00
Shakers, Tulip, HP floral, pr 125.00
Sweetmeat, Swirl, wild roses/pk swirled panels, 3½" 325.00
Vase, mums, mc on lt pk, wht beaded rim, 10" 575.00

Weapons

Among the varied areas of specialization within the broad category of weapons, guns are by far the most popular. Muskets are among the earliest firearms; they were large-bore shoulder arms, usually firing black powder with separate loading of powder and shot. Some ignited the charge by flintlock or caplock, while later types used a firing pin with a metallic cartridge. Side arms, referred to as such because they were worn at the side, include pistols and revolvers. Pistols range from early single-shot and multiple barrels to modern types with cartridges held in the handle. Revolvers were supplied with a cylinder that turned to feed a fresh round in front of the barrel breech. Other firearms include shotguns, which fired round or conical bullets and had a smooth inner barrel surface, and rifles, so named because the interior of the barrel contained spiral grooves (rifling) which increased accuracy. For further study we recommend *Modern Guns, Tenth Edition*, by Russell Quertermous and Steve Quertermous, available at your local bookstore. All weapons but swords are under the advisement of Steve Howard, see the Directory under California. See also Militaria.

Key:
bbl — barrel	mag — magazine
cal — caliber	mgn — magnum
conv — conversion	mod — modified
cyl — cylinder	oct — octagon
f/l — flintlock	o/u — over/under
f/s — full stock	p/b — patch box
ga — gauge	perc — percussion
hdw — hardware	/s — stock
h/s — half stock	

Carbines

Austrian, 70 cal perc, CI hdw, 14½" bbl, G 250.00
Ball & Williams US Civil War, 44 cal, 22" oct bbl, G 1,700.00
Barnett, perc, .577 cal, walnut/s, 23" rifled bbl, EX 625.00
Comblain, f/s w/swivels, dtd 1889, 25½" 11mm bbl, EX 1,000.00
Dreyse Artillery, 16mm rifled, f/s, dtd 1870 & 71, 23" bbl, EX ..1,300.00
Inland US M1, 30 cal, flash-hider bbl, folding/s, EX 575.00
Martini Henry, 45 cal, mk Enfield 1885 on fr, 21¼" bbl, EX 300.00

Maynard 1st Model, mk p/b, saddle ring, 22" bbl, VG 2,300.00
Sharps & Hankins Navy, orig leather cover on 24" bbl, EX 750.00
Sharps New Model 1863, iron furniture, no p/b, VG 1,050.00
Snider, 54 cal, breech loading, dtd 1876, 21½" bbl, G 400.00
Spencer US Civil War, 52 cal, 22" rnd bbl, G 1,800.00
Spencer 1865, 20" bbl w/o Stabler cut-off, EX 2,000.00
Springfield Armory Krag 1895, orig cleaning rod, VG 325.00
Springfield 1807 f/l, perc conv, dtd 1809, EX 3,300.00
Tower, f/l, 65 cal, f/s, 28" bbl, 7" saddle ring, EX 3,100.00
Underwood US M1, 30 cal, military sights, w/pouch & sling, G ...400.00
Winchester US M1, 30 cal, military sights, 18" bbl, EX 325.00
Winchester US M1 Paratrooper, 30 cal, Xd cannons on grip, EX ..650.00
Winchester 1886, 50 cal, full mag, 22" bbl, G 2,250.00
Winchester 1892, 44/40 cal, w/saddle ring, 20" bbl, EX 1,700.00

Muskets

Brescia, perc, 72 cal, 1863 on lock, 40½" smooth bbl, VG 450.00
Daniel Gilbert US 1795, f/l, 69 cal, 44¼" bbl, VG 1,500.00
Enfield Musketoon, .577 cal, lock dtd 1861, 24" bbl, EX 1,450.00
French 1842, stamped lock, dtd 1849 on 41" bbl, EX, +bayonet ...625.00
German Military, .60 cal, 41½" rifled bbl oct at breech, EX ..1,500.00
H Flagg & US M 1842 perc, 69 cal, f/s, 42" bbl, G, +bayonet 600.00
L Pomeroy M 1816, eagle on lock, 1829 on bbl, EX, +bayonet ..1,550.00
Lindsay 2-Shot Rifle, w/US bayonet & scabbard, M/unissued .4,100.00
Norfolk 1861, eagle on lock, rifled bbl dtd 1863, EX 2,200.00
P Girard Fusil 1717, f/l, 70 cal, 47" bbl, EX 1,400.00
R&C Leonard 1808, f/l, 69 cal, f/s, 42⅝" bbl, G 550.00
Revolutionary War M 1763 St Etienne f/l, 75 cal, 45" bbl, G .4,000.00
Savage US M 1861, 58 cal, f/s, dtd 1863, 40" rifled bbl, VG 650.00
Snider, 39" bbl w/London proofs, f/s, EX rstr, +bayonet 350.00
Springfield Type 1-Type 2 transitional, 1863, EX, +bayonet ..3,500.00
Springfield 1795 Type III f/l, dtd 1812, EX 1,300.00
Springfield 1842, eagle on lock, mk bbl, VG, +bayonet 775.00
Tower, perc conv, f/s w/brass mts, 39" bbl, EX 500.00
US Model 1861-63, 58 cal, Roberts conv to cartridge, 37" bbl ...700.00
US Springfield 1808, f/l, 69 cal, 44¾" bbl, G 2,000.00
US 1884 Trap Door, mk breech block, 32⅝" bbl, EX 500.00
Wickham, perc conv, 1861 pattern hammer, rpl nipple, EX 550.00
Winchester Hotkiss 1st Model, w/US Socket bayonet, EX 550.00
Winchester Winder, 22 short cal, 28" take-down bbl, EX 650.00

Pistols

Beretta 1934 Pocket, 380 ACP cal, rubber grips, 3⅜" bbl, G 250.00
Browning Renaissance Hi-Power, 9mm, eng, 5" bbl, M 1,300.00
Colt Nat'l Automatic Match, 45 ACP cal, 5" bbl, EX 450.00
Colt Woodsman, 22 LR cal, target sights, 4½" bbl, VG 350.00
Colt 1902 Military Automatic, 38 rimless cal, 6" bbl, VG 650.00
Colt 1903 Hammer Pocket Automatic, 38 rimless cal, 4½" bbl, G ..300.00
Colt 1905, 45 ACP cal, checkered wood grips, 5" bbl, G 400.00
Colt 1908, 25 ACP cal, wood grips, 2" bbl, G 175.00
Harrington & Richardson Self Loading, 25 ACP cal, 2" bbl, M .250.00
Mauser Broom Handle, 30 Mauser cal, wood grips, 5½" bbl, G .375.00
Mauser Pocket, 25 ACP cal, wood grips, 3" bl, EX 150.00
Smith & Wesson 1913, 35 ACP cal, gold on grips, 3½" bbl, EX ...275.00
US Springfield Armory 1911 Army, 45 ACP cal, 5" bbl, G 450.00
Walther #4, 32 ACP cal, rubber grips, 3⅜" bbl, G 90.00
Walther PPK Pre-War Pocket w/Nazi Proof, 32 cal, 3¼" bbl, EX ...775.00
Wm W Marstrom Derringer, 32 cal rimfire, 3" bbl, G 400.00

Revolvers

Apache Nuckle-Duster, 32 cal, 1⅝" cyl, 6-shot, w/dagger, G ..1,600.00

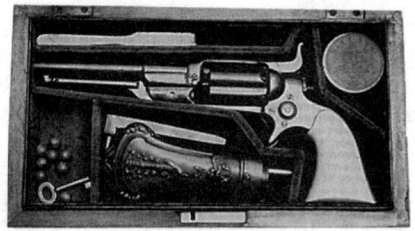

Colt Root Model 1855 sidehammer revolver, Type (rare) 5A, 4½" round barrel, 31 caliber, marked with patent date of September 10, 1860, ivory pistol grips, EX in case, $2,900.00.

Butterfield Army, 41 cal, 5-shot, dtd 1855, 7" bbl, VG 2,200.00
Colt Combat Python, 357 mag cal, rubber grips, 3" bbl, M 600.00
Colt New Service, 455 Eley cal, rubber grips, 5" bbl, VG 350.00
Colt Police Positive, 38 Special cal, wood grips, 4" bbl, M 300.00
Colt 1851 Navy, 36 cal, 7½" bbl, G 650.00
Colt 1860 Army, 44 cal, 8" bbl, EX 900.00
Colt 1877 Lightening, 41 long cal, 4½" bbl w/ejector rod, VG ...550.00
Manhattan 36 Series II, 5-shot cyl, 6½" bbl, VG 500.00
Martial Colt Single Action, US on fr, dtd 1890, rstr 4,500.00
Rogers & Spencer, 44 cal, 7½", EX 1,250.00
Smith & Wesson M&P, 38 Special cal, wood grips, 2" bbl, M ...160.00
Smith & Wesson Regulation Police, 32 long cal, 3¼" bbl, M 400.00
Webley Mark IV, 38 S&W cal, blk rubber grips, 5" bbl, EX 100.00

Rifles

Colt AR-15 SP1, 223 cal, military sights, 22" bbl, EX 675.00
Frank Wesson Single Shot Bicycle, 32 cal, 12" oct bbl, G 450.00
German Model 98 Military, Nazi proof, 8mm cal, 24" bbl, M 350.00
Greene Single Shot, 53 cal, breech loading, f/s, 35" bbl, G 700.00
Japanese Bolt Action Single Shot, 1 mm cal, 32" bbl, VG 775.00
Mannlicher 1888, 8mm cal, 28" bbl, VG 250.00
Mannlicher 1908, 8mm cal, f/s, scope, 20" bbl, G 625.00
Marlin Model 1890, 38-40 cal, EX 310.00
Marlin Model 1894, 25-20 cal, EX 470.00
Marlin 39A Lever Action, 22 LR cal, 24" rnd bbl, VG 175.00
Peabody Side Hammer, 50 cal, military mks, 33" bbl, EX 800.00
Remington US 03A3 (Sniper), 30/06 cal, 24" bbl, VG 750.00
Remington 121, 22 LR cal, aluminum buttplate, 24" bbl, G 175.00
Remington 721 Sporting, 300 mag cal, Tasco scope, 26" bbl, VG ..325.00
Savage 99, 300 cal, pistol grips, 24" bbl, G 225.00
Springfield US 1903 Military, 30/06 cal, 24" bbl, EX 650.00
Sringfield US 1903 w/1906 alterations, 30/06 cal, 24" bbl, VG ..800.00
Stevens Reliable Pocket #42, 22 LR cal, 9" bbl, VG 500.00
Unmk Kentucky, 38 cal, dbl triggers, 44" oct bbl, EX 600.00
US Springfield 1903 Mark I Military, 30/06 cal, 24" bbl, VG 375.00
US 1884 Trap Door Cadet, 45/70 cal, 29½" bbl, G 500.00
Wilson & Co Trial Bolt Action, f/s, 32" bbl, EX, +bayonet 500.00
Winchester US 1917, 30/06, NM, +bayonet & scabbard 550.00
Winchester 1885 Lo-Wall Single Shot, 22 WRF cal, 24" bbl, G ..625.00
Winchester 64 Deluxe, 30/30 cal, half mag, 24" rnd bbl, EX 900.00
Winchester 73, 38-40 cal, EX 550.00
Winchester 94, 32-40 cal, EX 300.00

Shotguns

AH Ansley Fox A Grade, 30" full & mod bbls, eng, VG 900.00
Belgium, 12 ga, 27½" full- & mod-choke bbls, VG 450.00
Beretta, 12 ga, 29½" full-choke o/u bbls, M 550.00
Browning A-5 Classic Semiautomatic, 12 ga, 28" mod bbl, NM ...700.00

Browning BPS Ducks Unlimited, 12 ga, pump action, 28" bbl, EX ..350.00
Dakin, 20 ga, detachable side locks, 26" bbls, EX 1,000.00
Ithaca Grade 2, 16 ga, dbl triggers, 30" bbls, EX 300.00
LC Smith, hammer action, 30" mod bbls, VG 200.00
Parker DH Grade, 12 ga, 32" reblued bbls, EX 700.00
Parker GH Grade, 12 ga, 30" full-choke Damascus bbls, EX ...1,200.00
Parker VH, 20 ga, 28" full- & mod-choke bbls, G 1,150.00
Ranger, 12-ga, 28" bbls, EX 200.00
Remington, 12 ga, hammer action, 27" Damascus bbls, VG 175.00
Remington, 23 ga, pump action, 30" mod-choke bbls, EX 200.00
Winchester 24, 12 ga, dbl triggers & extractors, 30" bbls, EX 375.00
Winchester 42, 410 ga, pump action, 28" full-choke bbl, EX 800.00
WW Greener 10 ga, hammer action, 29¾" bbls, EX 275.00

Swords

All swords listed below are priced 'with scabbard.'

Ames 1860 US Naval Cutlass, logo on grip, 32¼", EX 550.00
Bavarian Infantry officer's, brass hdl, WWI era, 40", EX 250.00
Cavalry Model 1913, 'Patten' model, mk 35" blade, 44", EX 225.00
English Infantry officer's, urn-shaped pommel, 1840s, 38", EX ...450.00
Foot officer's, eng grip w/eagle, ca 1850, 38½", EX 500.00
German Nazi Police officer's, Clemens & Jung Solingen, 39", EX .200.00
German WWII Army officer's saber, Horster, Solingen, 38", EX ..500.00
Infantry officer's, eagle-head pommel, 1820-50, 33", G 200.00
Infantry officer's saber, 5-ball guard & bowl, 1820s, 33", G 175.00
Mounted Artillery officer's saber, bl & gold decor, 1840s, 35" 800.00
N Star, stirrup iron hilt, leather-covered grip, 34" blade 350.00
Naval cutlass, 'corn-cob' hdl, figure-8 guard, 1800-18, 34", G ...450.00
NCO's Artillery saber, brass guard, wood grip, 1830s, 33½" 150.00
Revolutionary War Fr Grenadier saber Model 1767, 29", G 250.00
Seaman's cutlass, brass deguard & grip, ca 1814, 22¾", G 275.00
Standard US Eagle Head, gold decor on 30" blade, 36", EX 350.00
Tiffany & Co Calvary saber, iron bow, 1860s, 41", G 275.00
US Model 1860 Staff, eagle/clam-shell guard, 36", G 110.00

Weather Vanes

The earliest weather vanes were of handmade wrought iron and were generally simple angular silhouettes with a small hole suggesting an eye. Later copper, zinc, and polychromed wood with features in relief were fashioned into more realistic forms. Ships, horses, fish, Indians, roosters, and angels were popular motifs. In the 19th century, silhouettes were often made from sheet metal. Wooden figures became highly carved and were painted in vivid colors. E.G. Washburne and Company in New York was one of the most prominent manufacturers of weather vanes during the last half of the century. Two-dimensional sheet metal weather vanes are increasing in value due to the already heady prices of the full-bodied variety. Originality, strength of line, and patination help to determine value. When no condition is indicated, the items listed below are assumed to be in excellent condition.

Key:
fb — full-bodied   f/fb — flattened full-bodied

Circus horse, 2-part pressed tin, 14x12" on 28" arrow 270.00
Cow, copper & zinc, att Cushing & White, verdigris, 27" 2,100.00
Cow, pnt sheet metal, 17x22", EX 460.00
Cow, tin, worn silver-gray pnt, 15x9", on CI & copper arrow 225.00
Cow, zinc w/copper spire & steel fr, CI arrow, 55" H 165.00
Eagle, copper, old gold rpt, battered, 28" wingspan 115.00
Eagle, copper, wooden ball & metal ft rpl, rprs, 18x18" 75.00

Fish, wood body w/lead & copper fittings, 31" **200.00**
Fox, CI f/fb, on rod w/scrolls & directionals, 1850, 32" **1,500.00**
Halley's Comet banner, 60", EX **1,750.00**
Handsaw, pnt wood on copper base, 23½" **490.00**
Horse, hollow sheet copper w/CI head, rstr, 27x24" **580.00**
Horse, prancing, tin, old pnt, 1900s, 9½x8" on 21" arrow **185.00**
Horse, running, copper, cast head, early, 16" **325.00**
Horse, running, copper, gold rpt, Am, 1800s, 29½" **1,265.00**
Horse, running, zinc & copper, gold pnt traces, 1880s, 26" **2,300.00**
Horse, running silhouette, sheet iron, rpt, 28" **715.00**
Horse, sheet tin & iron, gold pnt, 11x10½" on 22" arrow **235.00**
Horse, zinc w/old silver rpt, 14½" **105.00**
Morgan horse, sheet metal, Am, early 1900s, 28½x33" **600.00**
Pig, sheet metal, pnt decor, 42", EX **2,070.00**
Rooster, cast & molded copper, zinc legs, worn pnt, 24x19x2" ..**1,800.00**
Rooster, CI w/rpl sheet metal tail, 22½" **800.00**
Rooster, copper, gilt verdigris, 1800s, 23", EX **1,850.00**
Rooster, copper, hollow body, old gold pnt, 12½"+base **825.00**
Rooster, cvd & pnt wood, 12x15", EX **1,050.00**
Rooster, galvanized tin, unpnt, 17½x15"+support rod **350.00**
Rooster, sheet iron, riveted, old blk pnt, 20½" **880.00**
Steam locomotive, sheet metal, Am, late 1800s, worn pnt, 64" ..**2,300.00**

Weaving

Early Americans used a variety of tools and a great amount of time to produce the material from which their clothing was made. Soaked and dried flax was broken on a flax brake to remove waste material. It was then tapped and stroked with a scutching knife. Hackles further removed waste and separated the short fibers from the longer ones. Unspun fibers were placed on the distaff on the spinning wheel for processing into yarn. The yarn was then wound around a reel for measuring. Three tools used for this purpose were the niddy-noddy, the reel yarn winder, and the click reel. After it was washed and dyed, the yarn was transferred to a barrel-cage or squirrel-cage swift and fed onto a bobbin winder.

Today flax wheels are more plentiful than the large wool wheels, since they were small and could be more easily stored and preserved. The distaff, an often-discarded or misplaced part of the wheel, is very scarce. French spinners from the Quebec area painted their wheels. Many have been stripped and refinished by those unaware of this fact. Wheels may be very simple or have a great amount of detail, depending upon the owner's ethnic background and the maker's skill.

Flax clock winder, 6 trn arms, trn finial, pnt w/striping, 43" **400.00**
Hatchel, hardwood, w/red & blk pnt, rnd bed of nails, 30½" **160.00**
Hatchel, hardwood, worn wht pnt w/mc floral decor, 25" **80.00**
Hatchel, star-punched tin on brd under spikes dtd 1773, 14" **170.00**
Niddy noddy, chestnut, old soft patina, 18½" **65.00**
Niddy noddy, chip cvd, old varnish, 18" **200.00**
Reel, EX detail & chip cvg, orange & blk striping, 1847, 36" **195.00**
Spinning wheel, corner type, tripod base, trn legs etc, rfn **425.00**
Spinning wheel, hardwood, old pnt, trn details, 42", EX **300.00**
Spinning wheel, oak, chip cvd & trn detail, rprs, 35½" **250.00**
Spinning wheel, Saxony type, orange/blk striping, sgn Fox **525.00**
Spinning wheel, Saxony type, punch decor, trn legs/etc **350.00**
Spinning wheel, Saxony type, sgn/dtd 1820, trn legs, rfn, EX **325.00**
Yarn winder, metal, adjustable, clamps on, Pats 1860 & 1867 ......**95.00**

Webb

Thomas Webb and Sons have been glassmakers in Stourbridge, England, since 1837. Besides their fine cameo glass, they have also made enameled ware and pieces heavily decorated with applied glass ornaments. The butterfly is a motif that has been so often featured that it tends to suggest Webb as the manufacturer. Our advisor for this category is Don Williams; he is listed in the Directory under Missouri. See also specific types of glass such as Alexandrite, Burmese, Mother-of-Pearl, and Peachblow.

Bottle, scent; brn satin w/gold floral, silver cap, 4" **425.00**
Bowl, brn to tan satin, gold butterfly/prunus, 2½x3" **295.00**
Bowl, clear rigaree & berry prunts on amber o/l, 5x4¾" **210.00**
Bowl, fish & aquatic plants on yel satin w/gold, 4¼" **250.00**
Bowl, gold flowers on bl triple o/l, fluted rim, 3¾x7" **245.00**
Bowl, 3 clear leaves & berry on pk o/l, 3½x3¼" **275.00**
Rose bowl, brn shaded satin w/gold flowers & butterfly, 3" **275.00**
Rose bowl, brn shaded w/gold prunus, 2½x2½" **295.00**
Rose bowl, ivory w/heavy gold flowers, clear ped ft, 3¾" **95.00**
Rose bowl, rose satin w/bl morning glories, petal ft **220.00**
Vase, bl satin, gold floral/dragonfly, 5¾", pr **200.00**
Vase, brn to tan w/gold floral/bug, fluted stick neck, 9" **325.00**
Vase, ivory opaque w/gold floral & butterfly, mk, 3¼x2½" **195.00**
Vase, pk cased w/florals & butterfly on front, 10" **165.00**
Vase, rose to gr satin, bottle form, 9½x4½" **495.00**
Vase, shiny mahog w/silver floral/gold vines, tapered, 5" **175.00**

Cameo

Vase, Oriental-style florals and scrolls on elongated bottle form, crystal cased to red and layered with yellow over white, Gem mark, 7⅛", $8,250.00.

Bottle, scent; floral, wht on red, tapered, silver top, 5" **750.00**
Bottle, scent; floral on cranberry, lay down, SP lid, 10" **3,850.00**
Bottle, scent; fuchsia, wht/cranberry/citron, SP cap, 6" **3,500.00**
Bowl, morning glories, wht on lime gr, 5¼" **500.00**
Lamp, floral/butterfly, wht on bl, 9" **3,300.00**
Perfume flask, floral, wht on turq, silver hinged lid, 5" **920.00**
Perfume flask, violets/insects, wht on yel, lay down, 2½" **575.00**
Rose bowl, dragonfly etc, wht on red, miniature, 1" **750.00**
Rose bowl, ferns, bl/wht on citron, 2¾" **2,000.00**
Rose bowl, passion flower, bk: firefly, wht on rose, 1½" dia **1,000.00**
Rose bowl, scrolls/floral on ivory, 2¾" **500.00**
Vase, allover floral, ivory, hdls, stem ft, 4" **3,500.00**
Vase, butterfly/acorns/mums, wht on peachblow, 9" **2,500.00**
Vase, cyclamen/butterfly/neck bands, wht on citron, 5" **1,550.00**
Vase, floral, pk/wht on gold irid, 6" **2,300.00**
Vase, floral, red/wht on yel, bulbous bottom, 8" **2,860.00**
Vase, floral/creatures, ivory, elephant hdls/stick neck, 9" **4,700.00**
Vase, floral/2 insects, wht/red on lime, stick neck, 14" **3,250.00**
Vase, fuchsia, wht on cranberry, dimpled sides, 7" **1,600.00**
Vase, fuchsia vines, bk: ferns & leaves, wht on pk, 4½" **900.00**
Vase, leaves, wht on red, stick neck, cupped rim, 8½" **2,100.00**
Vase, leaves/butterflies, red/wht on yel, bottle form, 6" **2,400.00**

Vase, morning glories, 3-color on bl, gold scrolls, 6x5" **2,700.00**
Vase, nasturtiums/butterfly, wht on rose, 2" **500.00**
Vase, roses, red/wht on yel, bottle form, 14" **2,700.00**
Vase, roses, wht/red on citron, ovoid w/rnd ft, 4" **600.00**
Vase, wild rose/buds, pk/wht on citron, stick neck, 3½" **1,100.00**

Wedgwood

Josiah Wedgwood established his pottery in Burslem, England, in 1759. He produced only molded utilitarian earthenwares until 1770 when new facilities were opened at Etruria for the production of ornamental wares. It was there he introduced his famous Basalt and Jasperware. Jasperware, an unglazed fine stoneware decorated with classic figures in white relief, was usually produced in blues; but it was also made in ground colors of green, lilac, yellow, black, or white. Occasionally three or more colors were used in combination. It has been in continuous production to the present day and is the most easily recognized of all the Wedgwood lines. Jasper-dip is a ware with a solid-color body or a white body that has been dipped in an overlay color. It was introduced in the late 1700s and is the type most often encountered on today's market.

Though Wedgwood's Jasperware was highly acclaimed, on a more practical basis his improved creamware was his greatest success. Due to the ease with which it could be potted and because its lighter weight significantly reduced transportation expenses, Wedgwood was able to offer 'chinaware' at affordable prices. Queen Charlotte was so pleased with the ware that she allowed it to be called 'Queen's Ware.' Most creamware was marked simply 'Wedgwood.' ('Wedgwood & Co.' and 'Wedgewood' are marks of other potters.) From 1769 to 1780, Wedgwood was in partnership with Thomas Bentley; artwares of the highest quality may bear the 'Wedgwood & Bentley' mark indicating this partnership. Moonlight Lustre, an allover splashed-on effect of pink intermingling with gray, brown, or yellow, was made from 1805 to 1815. Porcelain was made, though not to any great extent, from 1812 to 1822. Bone china was produced before 1822 and after 1872. These types of wares were marked 'WEDGWOOD' (with a printed 'Portland Vase' mark after 1872). Stone china and Pearlware were made from about 1820 to 1875. Examples of either may be found with a printed or impressed mark to indicate their body type. During the late 1800s, Wedgwood produced some fine parian and majolica. Creamware, hand painted by Emile Lessore, was sold from about 1860 to 1875. From the 20th century, several lines of lustre wares — Butterfly, Dragon, and Fairyland (designed by Daisy Makeig-Jones) — have attracted the collector and, as their prices suggest, are highly sought after and admired.

Nearly all of Wedgwood's wares are clearly marked. 'WEDGWOOD' was used before 1891, after which time 'ENGLAND' was added. Most examples marked 'MADE IN ENGLAND' were made after 1905. A detailed study of all marks is recommended for accurate dating. See also Majolica.

Key:
WW — Wedgwood
WWE — Wedgwood England
WWMIE — Wedgwood Made in England

Ashtray, Jasper, bl, WWE, ca 1981, 4" **22.50**
Basket, Creamware, rust line decor, raffia hdl, WW, ca 1840 .....**235.00**
Basket, Creamware, WWE, ca 1925 ....**120.00**
Biscuit barrel, Jasper, cobalt, baluster, WWE **265.00**
Biscuit barrel, Jasper, cobalt, SP trim, WW **325.00**
Biscuit barrel, Jasper, lt gr, rstr SP trim, WW **325.00**
Biscuit jar, bone china, Imari colors, SP trim, WW, 5" **350.00**
Bowl, Basalt, incurvate rim, WW, 9¾" **325.00**
Bowl, Dragon Lustre, gr, lt gr int, 9" **500.00**

Bowl, Dragon Lustre, orange, bl/gr int w/tigers, 9" **495.00**
Bowl, Fairyland Lustre, elves on bell branch, #Z5360, 9¼" **4,000.00**
Bowl, Fairyland Lustre, fairy in lg hat, WW, #Z4968, 3x7" **3,500.00**
Bowl, Glazed Drabware, thin gold band, oval, WW, ca 1820 .....**120.00**
Bowl, Hummingbird Lustre, bl w/orange int, WW, 4½" **325.00**
Bowl, Hummingbird Lustre, geese borders, WW, 4½x10" **535.00**
Bowl, Jasper, lt bl, WWE, 2x4¾" **75.00**
Box, Basalt, Cupid sharpening arrow on lid, oval, WWE **65.00**
Box, Basalt, Rosso Egyptian decor, WWE, ca 1977, 3¾" sq ...**145.00**
Box, bone china, Wild Strawberry, hexagonal, WWE, ca 1981 ....**45.00**
Box, Jasper, bl, WWE, ca 1981 ....**120.00**
Box, Jasper, lilac, pentagonal, WWE, ca 1960 ....**120.00**
Box, Jasper, lilac, WWE, 1¾" dia **100.00**
Box, Jasper, lilac, WWE, 4" sq **125.00**
Box, Jasper, Portland bl, octagonal, WWE, 1½x3" **220.00**
Box, Jasper, Portland bl, WWE, 1½x4" dia **220.00**
Box, Jasper, Primrose on lt bl, octagonal, WWE **120.00**
Box, Jasper, taupe, scallops, shell finial, WWE, 3¾" dia **98.00**
Box, Jasper, terra cotta, WWE, 4" sq **230.00**
Brooch, Jasper, lt bl, sterling fr, WW, 1½" dia **235.00**
Brooch, Jasper, olive gr, set in 10k gold, WW, ⅞x1" **255.00**
Brooch, Jasper, 3-color, sterling fr, WW, 1¼x1½" **425.00**
Bust, Dwight Eisenhower, Basalt, WWE, 8½" **175.00**
Butter pat, Creamware, Eastern Flowers, WW **55.00**
Butter scoop, Creamware, WW, ca 1825 ....**245.00**
Cake plate, Jasper, lt bl, WWE, 9½" **75.00**
Calendar plate, Creamware, WWE, 1900 ....**145.00**
Cameo, Jasper, cobalt dipped, WW, 1x1½" **130.00**
Candlesticks, Basalt, Muses, WWE, ca 1900, 6¾", pr **665.00**
Candlesticks, Creamware, red/bl, Etruria, 9", pr **210.00**
Candlesticks, Jasper, lt bl, WW, 6¼", pr **350.00**
Chess pc, Basalt, Arnold Machine design, WWE, 1964 ....**125.00**
Cigarette jar, Jasper, sage gr, WWE, ca 1960, 4" **145.00**
Cigarette lighter, Jasper, lt bl, boat shape, WWE, 3½" **58.00**
Clock, Jasper, cobalt, WWE, EX **525.00**
Coffee can & saucer, AD; bone china, yel w/silver, WWE **40.00**
Coffee cup & saucer, AD; Jasper, terra cotta, WW **195.00**
Compact, Jasper, lt bl, Stratton, M in orig fabric case **110.00**
Comport, Gr Glaze, Victorian yel-gr, WW, 4½" **230.00**
Comport, Jasper, terra cotta, WWE, 3¾x6" **245.00**
Creamer, Basalt, checkerboard pattern, helmet shape, WW, 3⅛" ..**300.00**
Creamer, Drabware, lt brn, WW, ca 1840, 2½x5" **170.00**
Creamer, Drabware, wht florals, WW, ca 1830 ....**200.00**
Creamer, Jasper, blk, St Louis shape, WWE **145.00**
Creamer, Jasper, lt bl, St Louis shape, WWE, 2¼x3½" **100.00**
Creamer, Jasper, lt bl, WWE, 1975, MIB **75.00**
Creamer, stoneware, cobalt vintage, WW, ca 1810 ....**225.00**
Cup, Stella, yel & copper lustre, gr scrolls, hdls, ftd **110.00**
Cup & saucer, Creamware, gr floral, WW, ca 1882 ....**26.00**
Cup & saucer, demitasse; Basalt, WW, ca 1850 ....**120.00**
Cup & saucer, handleless; Basalt, no decor, WE, 2½x3" **75.00**
Cup & saucer, Jasper, cobalt, pear shape, WWE, ca 1937 .....**200.00**
Cup & saucer, Jasper, lt bl, WWE, ca 1975, MIB **60.00**
Custard set, Jasper, sage gr, WWE, tray+4 cups w/lids **800.00**
Dish, Creamware, dk bl Ferrara decor, leaf shape, WW, 8x10" ...**230.00**
Dish, Moonlight Lustre, shell form, 1810, 11" **325.00**
Easter egg, Jasper, bl, WWE, 1977 ....**70.00**
Egg box, Jasper, lt bl, WWE, lg **60.00**
Figure, Basalt, nude male, WW **1,125.00**
Figure, Jasper, Terpsichore, wht on bl base, WWE, 10" **525.00**
Game dish, Caneware, glazed int, rabbit finial, WW, 12x8" **565.00**
Humidor, Jasper, lt gr, acorn finial, MIE, 8x5½" **435.00**
Humidor, Jasper, lt gr, acorn finial, WWE, 1900, 8x5½" **425.00**
Inkstand, Drabware, glazed, WW, ca 1845 ....**525.00**

Jam jar, Jasper, lt bl, WW, SP lid 230.00
Jardiniere, Jasper, cobalt, England, 6x7" 400.00
Jardiniere, Jasper, cobalt, MIE, 4½x5" 245.00
Jardiniere, Jasper, cobalt, WWE, 4½x5" 295.00
Jardiniere, Jasper, lt bl, WWE, ca 1900, 8¼x7⅛" 500.00
Jardiniere, Jasper, lt bl, WWE, 4¼x4¾" 145.00
Jardiniere, Jasper, olive gr, WWE, 6¼x7¼" 335.00
Match striker, Jasper, cobalt, Classical figures, WWE, 3¾" 225.00
Matchbox, Basalt, gilt Egyptian decor, oblong, WWE, ca 1978 ..120.00
Matchbox, Jasper, lilac, oblong, WWE, ca 1960 ....135.00
Matchbox holder, Jasper, lt bl, WW, 3¾x6" dia 120.00
Medallion, Jasper, lt bl, Elizabeth II & Phillip, WWE, pr 295.00
Medallion, Jasper, lt bl, Trinity Church, WWE 100.00
Mug, Christmas; Jasper, Houses of Parliament, WWE, 1974 ....65.00
Mug, Creamware, ivory matt, Keith Murray, WWE 95.00
Mug, Creamware, Royal Wedding, WWE, 1981 ....50.00
Mug, toothbrush; bl transfer, WW 130.00
Napkin rings, bone china, Clementine, WWE, 4 for 100.00
Pendant, Jasper, lt bl, sterling fr, WWE, ca 1960 ....95.00
Pin tray, Jasper, pk, oblong, WWE, 6" 98.00
Pitcher, Basalt, Victoria BC, WWE, 3½" 130.00
Pitcher, bone china, purple lustre, Ferrara, WWE 120.00
Pitcher, Cambridge Ale, Redware, WW, 5¼" 120.00
Pitcher, cream; Basalt, Clover, Rose, Thistle, Harp, WW, 3¼" ..200.00
Pitcher, Creamware, dk bl-gr, WW, 7" 230.00
Pitcher, Gr Glaze, vintage, WWE, 7½" 200.00
Pitcher, Jasper, bleeding gr, Franklin & WA, WWE, 3¾" 325.00
Pitcher, Jasper, bronze lustre, Fallow deer, WWE, ca 1900 ....145.00
Pitcher, Jasper, lilac, Etruscan shape, MIE, ca 1960 ....230.00
Pitcher, lemonade; Creamware, silver lustre, WWE, +6 tumblers .365.00
Pitcher, Majolica, Washington/Lincoln, WW, ca 1876, 5½", EX .350.00
Pitcher, tankard; Jasper, lt gr, WWE, 4⅝" 125.00
Plaque, Fairyland Lustre, Elves in Pine Tree, 7½x11" 5,950.00
Plate, Christmas; Jasper, Trafalgar Sq, 2nd Ed, WWE, 1970 ....75.00
Plate, Christmas; Jasper, Windsor Castle, 1st Ed, WWE, 1969 .....95.00
Plate, Creamware, Albion College, WWE, ca 1952 ....35.00
Plate, Creamware, Bl Willow, Etruria, WWE, ca 1905 ....100.00
Plate, Creamware, Ivanhoe, mc, WWE 145.00
Plate, Creamware, Japonica, shell shape, WW, ca 1870 ....45.00
Plate, Glazed Drabware, Capri, WW, ca 1840, 8" 120.00
Plate, Glazed Drabware, gold trim, WW, ca 1830, 7" 75.00
Plate, Glazed Drabware, gold trim, WW, 1830s, 9¾" 130.00
Plate, Gr Glaze, Sunflower, WW, 8" 100.00
Plate, Jasper, lt bl, Cupid, WWE, 8" 80.00
Plate, Jasper, terra cotta, WWE, 9½" 165.00
Plate, Moonlight Lustre, shell shape, WW, ca 1810 ....265.00
Plate/barometer, Jasper, lilac, WWE, 8" 350.00
Platter, Creamware, blk litho, Santa Barbara Mission, WWE 95.00
Posy pot, Jasper, blk, WWE, 3¼" 75.00
Posy pot, Jasper, lilac, Seasons, WWE, ca 1960, 3½", pr 145.00
Potpourri, Caneware, cobalt vintage, WW, rpr, mini 245.00
Potpourri, Jasper, wht, WW, ca 1910, mini 445.00
Ring tree, Jasper, lt bl, WWE, ca 1910 ....215.00
Shell, Moonlight Lustre, WW, 1½x8¼" 370.00
Spill vase, Basalt, Muses, WW, ca 1850, 6½" 230.00
Sugar bowl, Jasper, cobalt, WWE, 5½" dia 150.00
Sugar bowl, Jasper, lt bl, WWE 80.00
Sugar bowl & creamer, Jasper, lilac, w/lid, WWE, ca 1980 ....300.00
Tankard, bone china, Wild Strawberry, WWE, mini 38.00
Tankard, Jasper, cobalt dipped, WWE, ca 1905, 4" 100.00
Tea set, bone china, Liberty, WWE, 1919, 11-pc 2,275.00
Tea set, bone china, yel on wht w/gold, WW, ca 1878, 3-pc 685.00
Tea set, stoneware, platinum over copper, WWE, 3-pc 735.00
Teapot, Basalt, Canada decor, WW, 5" 125.00

Teapot, Basalt, Capri, WW, ca 1840, lg 650.00
Teapot, Basalt, Victoria BC, WWE, lg 135.00
Teapot, Caneware, Rosso decor, WW, ca 1805, rpr, lg 420.00
Teapot, Glazed Drabware, parapet shape, WW 255.00
Teapot, Jasper, lt bl, WWE, ca 1975 ....120.00
Thimble, Jasper, lt bl, Snowflake, WWE, ca 1981 ....25.00
Tile, calendar; Creamware, WWE, 1907 ....100.00
Tile, stoneware, Ganymede & Eagle, blk/rust, WW, 6x6"+fr 400.00
Toothpick holder, Jasper, cobalt, castle & figures, WWE, 1¾" ...125.00
Tray, bone china, Nautilus, WWE 45.00
Tray, Jasper, blk, club shape, WWE 48.00
Tray, Jasper, blk, spade shape, WW, ca 1890 ....75.00
Tray, Jasper, dk bl, Tower of London, WWE 37.50
Tray, Jasper, lilac, WWE, ca 1960, 9¾x7½" 175.00
Tray, Jasper, lt bl, Josiah Wedgood, WW Collector's Society 50.00
Tray, Jasper, lt bl, Taurus, WWE 22.50
Tray, Jasper, pk, heart shape, WWE 55.00
Tray, Jasper, Rosso Antico/blk, City of London, WWE, 4½" dia ..75.00
Tray, Jasper, solid lt bl, Heart, WWE, ca 1976 ....35.00
Vase, bone china, Imari colors, hexagonal, WW, ca 1880, 7" 230.00
Vase, bud; Jasper, terra cotta, WWE, 5" 145.00
Vase, Creamware, chartreuse, hdls, WWE, ca 1935, 9" 345.00
Vase, Creamware, Imari colors, Etruria, WWE, 9¼" 265.00
Vase, Fairyland Lustre, Candlemas, w/lid, 8½" 4,500.00
Vase, Fairyland Lustre, Imps on Bridge, Z5360, rpr, 12" 5,000.00
Vase, Jasper, cobalt, classical figures, WWE, 6¼x3" 225.00
Vase, Jasper, lt bl, Cupid finial, ovoid, WW, ca 1825, 9½" 1,550.00

Weil Ware

Max Weil came to the United States in the 1940s, settling in California. There he began manufacturing dinnerware, figurines, cookie jars, and wall pockets. American clays were used, and the dinnerware was all hand decorated. Weil died in 1954; the company closed two years later. The last backstamp to be used was the outline of a burro with the words 'Weil Ware — Made in California.' Many unmarked pieces found today originally carried a silver foil label; but you'll often find a four-digit handwritten number series, especially on figurines. For further study we recommend *The Collector's Encyclopedia of California Pottery* by our advisor, Jack Chipman. He is listed in the Directory under California.

Butter dish, Blossom, ¼-lb 27.50
Cigarette box & ashtray, Ming Tree 36.00
Cup & sucer, Rose 12.00
Dish, Dogwood, divided, sq, 10½" 15.00

Figure of a girl in blue gown with pink shawl, 10½", $35.00.

Figurine, boy w/wheelbarrow, #4005 ....**25.00**
Figurine, Buddy, boy, 7" **22.00**
Plate, Bamboo, dinner sz **10.00**
Platter, Blossom, 13" **22.00**
Shelf sitter, Oriental girl, lime gr & purple, mk, 9" **35.00**
Vase, bud; Ming Tree, w/coralene, #946, 6" **20.00**
Vase, girl in gr dress sits between 2 bud vases **35.00**
Vase, girl in loose dress, hands to hair, vase behind, 11" **35.00**

Weller

The Weller Pottery Company was established in Zanesville, Ohio, in 1882, the outgrowth of a small one-kiln log cabin works Sam Weller had operated in Fultonham. Through an association with Wm. Long, he entered the art pottery field in 1895, producing the Lonhuda Ware Long had perfected in Steubenville six years earlier. His famous Louwelsa line was merely a continuation of Lonhuda and was made in at least five hundred different shapes until 1924. Many fine lines of artware followed under the direction of Charles Babcock Upjohn, Art Director from 1895 to 1904: Dickens Ware (1st Line), under-glaze slip decorations on dark backgrounds; Turada, featuring applied ivory bands of delicate openwork on solid dark brown backgrounds; and Aurelian, similar to Louwelsa, but with a brushed-on rather than blended ground. One of their most famous lines was 2nd Line Dickens, introduced in 1900. Backgrounds, characteristically caramel shading to turquoise matt, were decorated by sgraffito with animals, golfers, monks, Indians, and scenes from Dickens novels. The work is often artist signed. Sicardo, 1903, was a metallic lustre line in tones of rose, blue, green, or purple with flowing Art Nouveau patterns developed within the glaze.

Frederick Hurten Rhead, who worked for Weller in 1903 to 1904, created the prestigious Jap Birdimal line decorated with geisha girls, landscapes, storks, etc., accomplished through application of heavy slip forced through the tiny nozzle of a squeeze bag. Other lines to his credit are L'Art Nouveau, produced both in high-gloss brown and matt pastels, and 3rd Line Dickens, often decorated with Cruikshank's illustrations in relief. Other early artware lines were Eocean, Floretta, Hunter, Perfecto, Dresden, Etched Matt, and Etna.

In 1920 John Lessel was hired as Art Director, and under his supervision several new lines were created. LaSa, LaMar, Marengo, and Besline attest to his expertise with metallic lustres. The last of the artware lines and one of the most sought-after by collectors today is Hudson, first made during the early 1920s. Hudson, a semimatt glazed ware, was beautifully artist decorated on shaded backgrounds with florals, animals, birds, and scenics. Notable artists often signed their work, among them Hester Pillsbury, Dorothy England Laughead, Ruth Axline, Claude Leffler, Sarah Reid McLaughlin, E.L. Pickens, and Mae Timberlake.

During the thirties Weller produced a line of gardenware and naturalistic life-sized figures of dogs, cats, swans, geese, and playful gnomes. The Depression brought a slow, steady decline in sales, and by 1948 the pottery was closed. For a more thorough study we recommend *The Collector's Encyclopedia of Weller Pottery* by Sharon and Bob Huxford, available at your local library or from Collector Books.

Arcadia, vase, emb leaves allover, #A-11, 8½" **45.00**
Arcadia, vase, leaves form fan shape, 8x15" **55.00**
Ardsley, vase, cattails form fan-shaped body, mk, 8" **100.00**
Ardsley, vase, irises & leaves form body, mk, 7" **125.00**
Athens, vase, classical figures in medallions, unmk, 10" **450.00**
Athens, vase, swags & medallions, unmk, 10" **450.00**
Atlas, dish, star form, #C-2, 2" **22.50**
Atlas, vase, star form, bl w/ivory int, mk, 10½" **60.00**
Aurelian, ewer, cavalier, sgn Fouts, cylindrical, 16½" **1,300.00**
Aurelian, lamp, banquet; irises, sgn Schnieder, 27" **1,550.00**

Aurelian, mug, cherries, sgn, 6" **140.00**
Aurelian, vase, dog w/game in mouth, pillow form, 7½x8" **1,375.00**
Aurelian, vase, floral, C Terry, 18" **1,650.00**
Aurelian, vase, floral, sgn EA, bulbous, 7" **215.00**
Aurelian, vase, floral, sgn TJW, cylindrical, 16" **1,000.00**
Aurelian, vase, floral w/silver o/l at top, sgn HM, 11½" **1,350.00**
Baldin, Blue; vase, apples, unmk, 11" **325.00**
Baldin, vase, apples on brn, mk, 7" **165.00**
Barcelona, candle holder, floral, bl on brn, unmk, 2x5" **90.00**
Barcelona, vase, floral on brn, hdls, mk, 6½" **150.00**
Bedford, umbrella stand, long-stemmed florals, gr matt, 20" **350.00**
Bedford, vase, florals form rim, long stems, glossy, 8" **115.00**
Besline, vase, floral w/lustre, classic form, unmk, 12" **535.00**
Blo' Red, vase, paper label, 9½" **125.00**
Blo' Red, vase, 14" **200.00**
Blue Decorated, vase, rose & wht roses, 9" **175.00**
Blue Drapery, candlestick, floral, unmk, 9½" **85.00**
Blue Drapery, vase, floral, slim form, unmk, 8" **40.00**
Blue Drapery, vase, floral, unmk, 4" **30.00**
Blue Ware, comport, fruit swags on bl, mk, 5½" **185.00**
Blue Ware, jardiniere, 2 angels on bl, unmk, 8½" **190.00**
Blue Ware, vase, classic figure on bl, cylindrical, mk, 8½" **185.00**
Bonito, candle holders, floral on cream, 1½", pr **60.00**
Bonito, vase, floral on cream, hdls, ftd, 5" **85.00**
Bonito, vase, floral on cream, sm hdls, gr int, 10" **215.00**
Bouquet, bowl vase, floral on gr, incurvate rim, #B-8, 4" **27.50**
Bouquet, vase, floral, scalloped rim, ftd, #B-5, 5½" **30.00**
Breton, bowl, emb florals at top, gr, incurvate rim, unmk, 4" **85.00**
Brighton, bluebird, #3 inside, 6" **275.00**
Brighton, cardinal on stump, sgn MH, unmk, 5½" **400.00**
Brighton, parrot, mk, 13½" **950.00**
Brighton, parrot w/spread wings, hanging, unmk, 15" **1,350.00**
Brighton, penguins on base, unmk, 5" **700.00**
Brighton, pheasant, 7x11½" **600.00**
Brighton, wall vase, bird on perch, 9½" **165.00**
Brighton, wall vase, dbl bud; bird on perch, unmk, 12" **300.00**
Burntwood, plate, Odd Fellows, Wildey Picnic on tan, 7" **200.00**
Burntwood, urn, floral on tan, brn rim & base, unmk, 6½" **135.00**
Burntwood, vase, floral on tan, brn rim, slim form, unmk, 7" **115.00**
Burntwood, vase, floral on tan, brn rim & base, unmk, 7" **135.00**
Burntwood, vase, floral on tan, 6-sided, mk, 5" **85.00**
Cactus, figurine, boy w/bag, brn, mk, 5" **82.50**
Cactus, figurine, camel, brn, mk, 4" **70.00**
Cactus, figurine, duck, gr, mk, 4½" **82.50**
Camelot, vase, wht on lt tan, very wide bulbous bottom, 7½" **400.00**
Cameo, basket, floral, wht on gr, shaped hdl, 7½" **40.00**
Cameo, vase, floral, ivory on brn, hdls, ftd, mk, 13" **75.00**
Cameo, vase, floral, wht on bl, ornate hdls, unmk, 5" **30.00**
Cameo Jewell, umbrella stand, 22" **550.00**
Candis, basket, hanging; gr w/gr wash on wht, unmk, 5½" **85.00**
Candis, vase, gr w/gr wash on wht, mk, 9" **80.00**
Chase, vase, hunt scene, ivory on brn, unusual color, 10½" **375.00**
Chase, vase, hunt scene, wht on bl, bulbous, mk, 6½" **255.00**
Chase, vase, hunt scene in silver o/l, ftd, 12" **475.00**
Chengtu, ginger jar, Chinese Red, 12" **215.00**
Chengtu, urn, Chinese Red, mk, 5½" **75.00**
Chengtu, vase, Chinese Red, 4-sided slim form, w/label, 8" **85.00**
Classic, bowl, wht, rtcl rim, mk, 8" **35.00**
Classic, window box, gr, rtcl rim, paper label & mk, 4" **65.00**
Claywood, bowl, floral, tan & brn, unmk, 2" **55.00**
Claywood, bowl, mouse band, tan on brn, unmk, 2" **85.00**
Claywood, candle holder, floral, tan & brn, unmk, 5" **55.00**
Claywood, vase, floral, tan & brn, unmk, 3" **55.00**
Coppertone, ashtray, frog at side, mk, 6½" **165.00**

Coppertone, figurine, frog w/banjo, mk, 7½" 1,000.00
Coppertone, vase, flared cylinder w/sm ft, unmk, 6½" 125.00
Coppertone, vase, slim form, hdls, 15½" 550.00
Copra, basket, floral, 4-ftd, mk, 11" 215.00
Copra, vase, floral on brn, ring hdls, ftd, 10" 215.00
Cornish, jardiniere, berries on branch on brn, 7" 75.00
Creamware, mug, floral, unmk, 5" 115.00
Creamware, planter w/liner, Coat-of-Arms pattern, 3½" 50.00
Creamware, vase, floral, classic form, mk, 11½" 325.00
Cretone, vase, deer & florals, brn on ivory, bulbous, 8" ...265.00
Darsie, flowerpot, emb tassels on ivory, 5½" 25.00
Darsie, vase, emb tassels on gr, mk, 5½" 22.50
Delsa, ewer, floral on bl, squat, shaped rim, #10, 7" 27.50
Dickens I, loving cup, floral, 3-hdld, 5½" 325.00
Dickens I, mug, floral on brn, sgn, 7" 200.00
Dickens I, vase, Chief Hollowhorn Bear, sgn, 13" 2,000.00
Dickens I, vase, floral, classic form, 11" 365.00
Dickens I, vase, lady's portrait, pillow form, 7" 2,000.00
Dickens II, humidor, Irishman, sgn RD, unmk, 6½" 975.00
Dickens II, mug, Black Bird portrait, sgn UJ, 6" 700.00
Dickens II, mug, shield & figures, glossy, 5½" 800.00
Dickens II, tankard, draped nude, Pickens, 12" 2,600.00
Dickens II, vase, fish, bulbous, ring hdls, 9½" 1,700.00
Dickens II, vase, floral, tan on brn, 9½" 350.00
Dickens II, vase, girl on lily pad, Dusenbery, 12" 1,500.00
Dickens II, vase, golfer in landscape, sgn, 8¾x4" 1,600.00
Dickens II, vase, swordsmen, sgn LJB, hdls, 5½" 650.00
Dickens III, flask vase, Dombey & Son, #d, 7½" 475.00
Dickens III, mug, man w/pipe portrait, unmk, 4" 465.00
Dickens III, teapot, Captain Cuttle, sgn, #5055, 7" 775.00
Dickens III, vase, W Micawber/D Copperfield, 10½" 700.00
Dresden, vase, windmill on bl, cylindrical w/indents, 10½" 600.00
Dunton, umbrella stand, exotic birds & floral branches, 23" ...1,350.00
Dupont, bowl, flower baskets on cream, unmk, 3" 45.00
Dupont, jardiniere, flower baskets on cream, unmk, 7½" 115.00
Dupont, vase, flower baskets, cylindrical, 10" 115.00
Dynasty, vase, gr runs on bl, ring hdls, 6" 45.00
Elberta, bowl, console; boat shape w/integral hdls, 11½" L 35.00
Eocean, basket, cherries on brn, wht ft, unmk, 6½" 250.00
Eocean, flask vase, dog, sgn L Blake, 7½" 1,000.00
Eocean, Late Line; vase, bud; floral, umk, 6½" 85.00
Eocean, vase, floral, Levi Burgess, 6½x4½" 425.00
Eocean, vase, floral, sgn EP, 4 sm hdls at rim, #9613, 10½" 450.00
Eocean, vase, floral, tub hdls, unmk, 9" 200.00
Eocean, vase, fruit on brn shaded, sm hdls, cylindrical, 16" 500.00
Eocean, vase, owl on limb, sgn EB, 10½" 1,400.00
Eocean, vase, wild roses, sgn ML, rim hairline, 12" 300.00
Eocean Rose, vase, dogwood branches, 6x5" 300.00
Eocean Rose, vase, leaves on pk to dk gr, multi-hdld, 13" 800.00
Etched Matt, vase, tulips on caramel, sgn Ferrell, 10" ...375.00
Ethel, vase, fan form, mk, 6" 50.00
Ethel, vase, mk, 11½" 225.00
Etna, mug, vintage, angle hdl, cylindrical, #9005, 5" 115.00
Etna, vase, floral, pk on brn to tan, waisted, 5½" 110.00
Etna, vase, frog & snake, gourd form, mk, 6½" 550.00
Etna, vase, lg pk rose, classic form, unmk, 10½" 225.00
Etna, vase, lizard, gourd form, brn to pk shaded, 4½" 450.00
Etna, vase, pansies, gourd form, 6½" 115.00
Evergreen, bowl, console; scalloped rim, mk, 5" 60.00
Evergreen, candlesticks, flat rnd shape, 1½", pr 60.00
Fairfield, vase, cherubs band, cylindrical, unmk, 9½" 110.00
Flask, All's Well, unmk, 4" 165.00
Flask, Never Dry, unmk, 6" 165.00
Flask, Old Kentucky, lady's form, unmk, 5" 165.00

Flask, Suffer-E-Get, unmk, 6" 165.00
Flemish, Blue; vase, floral, flared cylinder, mk, 6½" 120.00
Flemish, inkwell, birds & flowers, unmk, 7x4½" 400.00
Flemish, jardiniere, floral, 3-ftd, unmk, 8" 115.00
Flemish, jardiniere, lg florals, mk, 8" 225.00
Flemish, jardiniere, ornate floral panels, unmk, 7½" 135.00
Flemish, tub, floral, tub hdls, 3½" 75.00
Flemish, umbrella stand, ornate floral panels, 21½" 365.00
Fleron, vase, gr, folded rim, mk, 9" 115.00
Florala, bowl, console; floral band at rim, unmk, 11" 45.00
Florala, candle holders, mc florals, flared ft, 5", pr 55.00
Florenzo, basket, floral on ivory, gr at rim & hdl, 5½" ...75.00
Florenzo, planter, roses on ivory, gr at rim, mk, 3½" 40.00
Floretta, ewer, floral on brn, mk, 4½" 70.00
Floretta, ewer, fruit emb on brn, cylindrical, mk, 10½" ...125.00
Floretta, Matt; tankard, fruit on branch, sgn CD, 13½" ...400.00
Floretta, vase, floral, pk on brn shades, slim, 5½" 165.00
Floretta, vase, fruit on gr, squat, flared rim, unmk, 12" ..325.00
Floretta, vase, vintage, shouldered cylinder, 15" 325.00
Forest, jardiniere, trees landscape, earth tones, unmk, 8½" 400.00
Forest, pitcher, woodland scene, hi-gloss, mk, 5" 175.00
Forest, planter, woodland scene, tub hdls, mk, 6" 115.00
Forest, vase, woodland scene, flared cylinder, unmk, 8" ..115.00
Forest, window box, woodland scene, rectangular, 14½" L 325.00
Fruitone, vase, bud; long stick neck, 11½" 75.00
Fruitone, vase, 6-sided, mk, 8" 125.00
Garden ornament, Fisher Boy, mk, 21" 1,950.00
Garden ornament, Pan w/Fife, mk, 16½" 1,300.00
Geode, stars & comets, bl on ivory, globular, 5½" 175.00
Glendale, vase, bird, butterfly & flowers, classic form, 12" 450.00
Glendale, vase, dbl bud; bird between 2 stumps, unmk, 7" 225.00
Gloria, bowl, floral on gr, #G-15, 3½" 30.00
Gloria, vase, iris on gr, #G-13, 5" 35.00
Graystone Garden Ware, rabbit, sgn CW, mk, 7½x13" 1,100.00
Graystone Garden Ware, Regal birdbath, unmk, 21½" 275.00
Graystone Garden Ware, Sunray birdbath w/fountain, 33½" 600.00
Greenbriar, vase, marbleized colors, unmk, 6" 55.00
Greora, strawberry pot, 4-pocket, mk, 8½" 165.00
Greora, vase, triangular w/3 ft, unmk, 4½" 45.00
Hobart, bowl, gr, flower form, unmk, 8x9½" 90.00
Hobart, figurine, girl w/flowers, gr, unmk, 8½" 200.00
Hobart, figurine, girl w/skirt held wide, mk, 11" 200.00
Hobart, figurine, nude girl kneeling, gr, unmk, 4½" 215.00
Hobart, vase, dbl bud; nude between trunk forms, pk, 10" 265.00
Hudson, bowl, floral on wht, unmk, 4" 135.00

Hudson, vase, lily pads
and water lilies, signed,
10¾", $700.00.

Hudson, vase, bud; floral on bl, unmk, 10" 135.00
Hudson, vase, cottage & lg poplar, M Timberlake, 8¾" 2,000.00
Hudson, vase, floral, maroon & gr on wht, 6¾" 325.00

Hudson, vase, floral band on bl, cylindrical, 8½" 175.00
Hudson, vase, floral on bl to pk, sgn, hdls, mk, 8" 825.00
Hudson, vase, floral on lav band, block mk, 11" 160.00
Hudson, vase, floral on wht, 6-sided, mk, 9½" 185.00
Hudson, vase, harvest landscape, Pillsbury, mk, 8" 1,650.00
Hudson, vase, iris, sgn Axline, cylindrical, 8½" 350.00
Hudson, vase, irises, Pillsbury, classic form, unmk, 15" 1,350.00
Hudson, vase, lady on bl, cylindrical, mk, 13½" 1,500.00
Hudson, vase, lg floral, bulbous, hdls, 13½" 1,100.00
Hudson, vase, lotus blossom on lt gr to yel, 9½" 190.00
Hudson, vase, orchids, sgn MT, classic form, 15½" 1,350.00
Hudson, vase, parrot on floral branch, Timberlake, hdls, 14" ..2,000.00
Hudson, vase, purple & wht lilacs, classic form, 12" 1,100.00
Hudson, vase, rider in western landscape, Timberlake, 9" 1,650.00
Hudson, vase, river & mtn scenic, Pillsbury, 8" 1,200.00
Hudson, vase, roses, ivory on lt gr, heavy crazing, 10" 275.00
Hudson, vase, sampan scenic on bl, sgn, classic form, 27½" ..10,000.00
Hudson, vase, sm floral, England, 8x3½" 325.00
Hudson, vase, styled flowers, D England, 5½" 325.00
Hudson Light, vase, floral, bulbous, 4½" 150.00
Hudson Light, vase, floral, mauve on bl-gray to cream, 10" 325.00
Hudson Light, vase, floral on cream, mk, 9" 300.00
Hudson Perfecto, vase, chrysanthemums, Leffler, bulbous, 9½" ..850.00
Hudson Perfecto, vase, irises, cylindrical, 9" 215.00
Hudson Perfecto, vase, irises, Leffler, classic form, 13½" 1,300.00
Hunter, vase, duck swimming, squat ewer form, 7" 500.00
Hunter, vase, elk on brn, hdls, #343, 6½" 700.00
Ivoris, basket, emb florals, mk, 5" 55.00
Ivoris, vase, emb floral, 3 buttress ft, mk, 6" 35.00
Ivory, jardiniere, geometric decor, mk, 7 /12" 125.00
Ivory, jardiniere, squirrels in tree, unmk, 5" 55.00
Ivory, vase, satyrs, flared cylinder, unmk, 15" 200.00
Ivory, window box, classical figures, mk, 8x20½" 375.00
Ivory, window planter, floral, 6x15½" 155.00
Jap Birdimal, pitcher, oil; sailing ships, sgn HMR, 10½" 900.00
Jap Birdimal, vase, bird in flight, wht on gray, unmk, 7" 400.00
Jap Birdimal, vase, landscape, bl on pk, flared cylinder, 14" 700.00
Jap Birdimal, vase, Oriental lady, unmk, 4" 575.00
Jewell, vase, cylindrical, flared ft & sm rim, 9" 350.00
Kenova, vase, emb floral vine, bulbous, mk, 5½" 250.00
Kenova, vase, emb frog on side, dk brn matt, 6¾", NM 475.00
Klyro, planter, floral, sq, mk, 4" 55.00
Klyro, wall pocket, floral, paper label, 7½" 100.00
Knifewood, humidor, hunting dog, unmk, 7" 425.00
Knifewood, vase, daisies on brn, mk, 7" 115.00
Knifewood, vase, floral, glossy, bulbous, 4½" 90.00
L'Art Nouveau, bank, ear of corn form, unmk, 8" 285.00
L'Art Nouveau, bank, sunflower form, mk, 2x4" 135.00
L'Art Nouveau, mug, floral, 5" 225.00
L'Art Nouveau, vase, classic figure & flowers, unmk, 17½" 600.00
L'Art Nouveau, vase, lady in reserve, glossy, shouldered, 12" 375.00
La Sa, vase, cross & flowers, sgn, bulbous, 3½" 135.00
La Sa, vase, palms scenic, sgn, classic form, 13½" 475.00
Lamar, lamp, scenic, unmk, 16" 425.00
Lamar, vase, scenic, flared cylinder, 7½" 175.00
Lebanon, vase, figure on camel, unmk, 9" 425.00
Lonhuda, vase, floral, sgn AH, integral hdls, #820, 4½" 185.00
Lorbeek, bowl, sq shape w/rtcl rim, 2½x10½" 52.50
Lorbeek, candle holders, stepped base, 2½", pr 85.00
Louella, hair receiver, floral on shirred ground, 3" 55.00
Louella, vase, floral on shirred ground, ruffled, 8" 120.00
Louwelsa, Blue; vase, floral, bulbous w/1 integral hdl, 3" 350.00
Louwelsa, Blue; vase, floral, cylindrical, 10½" 800.00
Louwelsa, Blue; vase, floral, sgn LM, slim form, flared rim, 10" ..675.00
Louwelsa, candle holder, floral, sgn HL, slim, 9" 150.00
Louwelsa, clock, floral, 10½" 850.00
Louwelsa, ewer, floral, long slim neck, ruffled rim, 6½" 160.00
Louwelsa, ewer, floral, sgn KK, 12" 450.00
Louwelsa, jardiniere, mums on brn, ruffled rim, 9½" 275.00
Louwelsa, mug, portrait, sgn Ferrell, #432, 6½" 850.00
Louwelsa, star w/lid, floral on brn, mk, 2½" 275.00
Louwelsa, tankard, leaves/berries, MB, 6" 160.00
Louwelsa, vase, floral, sgn MM, cylindrical, angle hdls, 11" 285.00
Louwelsa, vase, Indian portrait, Levi Burgess, str sides, 11" 950.00
Louwelsa, vase, lady's portrait, sgn RGT, bulbous, 11" 1,400.00
Louwelsa, vase, pansies w/silver o/l, classic form, 6½" 2,250.00
Louwelsa, vase, vintage, sgn E Roberts, classic form, 25" 2,000.00
Lustre, candlestick, orange, flared base, mk, 8" 45.00
Lustre, vase, Cloudburst, bulbous, sm str rim, unmk, 10½" 225.00
Lustre, vase, dk orange, squat w/integral hdls, unmk, 4½" 75.00
Lustre, vase, orange, on Glendale shape, experimental, 8½" 275.00
Lustre, vase, pk, cylindrical, unmk, 8½" 60.00
Malverne, bowl, console; floral, twig hdl, unmk, 2x14½" 115.00
Malverne, circle vase, floral branch forms hdl, mk, 8" 65.00
Malverne, wall pocket, leaves, unmk, 11" 135.00
Mammy Line, sugar bowl, 2 children at sides, w/lid, 3½" 300.00
Mammy Line, syrup pitcher, Mammy figural, mk, 6" 400.00
Mammy Line, teapot, Mammy figural, mk, 8" 650.00
Manhattan, pitcher, floral, gr on gr, ring hdl, 10" 95.00
Manhattan, vase, emb leaves, gr on gr, hdls, mk, 8" 65.00
Marbleized, bowl, incurvate rim, 1½x7" 45.00
Marbleized, comport, tall std, flared ft, 8" 85.00
Marbleized, jardiniere, incurvate rim, mk, 10" 265.00
Marbleized, vase, slim w/flared rim & ft, mk, 9½" 115.00
Marvo, frog, emb foliage, gray, unmk, 2" 27.50
Marvo, pitcher, emb foliage on brn, 8" 115.00
Marvo, vase, emb foliage, gr, cylindrical, 8½" 55.00
Matt, vase, cvd iris, ivory/yel on gr, 10" 700.00
Melrose, basket, grapes & flowers on pk, twig hdl, mk, 10" 175.00
Melrose, bowl, console; roses, ruffled rim, hdls, 5x8½" 110.00
Minerva, vase, cranes, cylindrical, mk, 8½" 425.00
Mirror Black, bowl, slightly shaped rim, 11" 55.00
Mirror Black, vase, classic form, mk, 9" 60.00
Modeled Etched Matt, vase, roses on stem, bulbous, 6½" 225.00
Monochrome, bowl, bl, unmk, 3½x10" 42.50
Monochrome, comport, gr, flared std, incurvate rim, 10" 65.00
Montego, vase, gr runs on brn, angle hdls, mk, 8" 100.00
Muskota, bowl, turtle form, mk, 4½x9½" 300.00
Muskota, fence, mk, 5" 165.00
Muskota, figurine, boy fishing, unmk, 6½" 300.00
Muskota, figurine, elephant, mk, 7½x12½" 1,100.00
Muskota, figurine, girl w/flowers & hat, unmk, 9" 400.00
Muskota, figurine, girl w/watering can, unmk, 7" 255.00
Muskota, figurine, nude on rock, mk, 8" 275.00
Muskota, flower frog, swan form, unmk, 2½x6" 115.00
Noval, bowl, fruit on ivory w/blk trim, unmk, 3½x9½" 70.00
Noval, vase, floral, pk on cream w/blk trim & hdls, 6" 60.00
Novelty, ashtray, 3 pigs at side, unmk, 4" 75.00
Novelty, butterfly, red, unmk, 3" 150.00
Novelty, dragonfly, unmk, 3½" 150.00
Novelty, kangaroo & pouch, unmk, 5½" 80.00
Novelty, pin tray, rose at side of ruffled rim, sgn DE, 2½" 90.00
Novelty, plate, Dickens Pottery, SA Weller, 12½" 1,900.00
Novelty, vase, Indian's portrait, St Louis World's Fair, 6½" 550.00
Novelty, vase, St Louis 1904, unmk, 3" 175.00
Oak Leaf, basket, #G-1, 7½" 55.00
Oak Leaf, planter, bl, mk, 6" 30.00
Panella, bowl, floral, 3-ftd, 3½" 22.50

Panella, vase, floral, gourd shape, low hdls, mk, 6½" 18.00
Paragon, vase, emb florals, bulbous, 7½" 85.00
Parian, wall pocket, flower in dmn shape, unmk, 10" 175.00
Pastel, circle vase, emb decor, turq, mk, 6" 40.00
Patra, basket, floral on brn, mk, 5½" 85.00
Patra, vase, floral on brn, sm gr hdls, shape #6, 4½" 35.00
Patricia, planter, pelican figural, ivory, mk, 5" 85.00
Patricia, vase, ivory, goose-head hdls, mk, 7" 60.00
Pearl, basket, pearls & florals in cream, unmk, 6½" 135.00
Pearl, candle holders, pearls & florals on cream, 8½", pr 135.00
Pearl, wall vase, pearls & florals on cream, mk, 8" 175.00
Perfecto, ewer, ear of corn, sgn A Haubrich, #580/4, 12" 700.00
Perfecto, ewer, florals w/long stems, #580/2, unmk, 12" 475.00
Pumila, vase, long-stem flowers form rim, mk, 9½" 55.00
Ragenda, urn, draped decor emb on pk, mk, 6½" 45.00
Ragenda, vase, draped decor emb on bl ball form, mk, 9" 65.00
Raydance, vase, ivory, emb leaves, sm hdls, flared rim, 7½" 30.00
Roba, ewer, floral on swirled body, branch hdl, 6" 40.00
Roba, vase, cornucopia; floral on brn, mk, 5½" 22.50
Roma, candlestick, triple; floral, unmk, 9" 135.00
Roma, comport, floral on ivory, 2 low hdls on base, unmk, 5" 85.00
Roma, comport, floral swags, tall ped, 9½" 115.00
Roma, console w/liner, vintage on ivory, twig hdls, 18" L 165.00
Roma, vase, dbl bud; floral on ivory, mk, 8½" 85.00
Roma, vase, floral wreath on ivory, cylindrical, unmk, 6½" 75.00
Roma, wall pocket, roses & bow on ivory, mk, 7" 225.00
Rosella, vase, dbl; floral on pk, mk, 5" 65.00
Rosemont, jardiniere, fruit branch on gridwork, mk, 5" 100.00
Rosemont, vase, bird on branch on blk, classic form, mk, 10" 350.00
Rudlor, vase, emb floral on gr, hdls, mk, 9" 40.00
Rudlor, vase, emb landscape on gr, sm hdls, #S-16, 10" 65.00
Sabrinian, vase, bud; shell form, mk, 7" 110.00
Sabrinian, vase, shell forms body, sea-horse hdls, 12" 275.00
Sabrinian, window box, shells form sides, 3½x9" 175.00
Sicardo, figurine, striding panther, rstr ear, mk, 16" L 2,500.00
Sicardo, figurine, Tambourine Boy, purple lustre, unmk, 9½" .3,500.00
Sicardo, vase, cloverleaves, cylindrical, no mk, 4" 345.00
Sicardo, vase, emb poppies, 11" 3,500.00

Sicardo vases: gold-green flowers on dark purple to gold, two-handled tapering pot shape, 6", $1,000.00; Gold-green flowers and dots on dark purple, pink and green, unusual waisted form, 9", $1,200.00.

Sicardo, vase, floral, gold on purple, hdls, teardrop form, 7" 950.00
Sicardo, vase, floral, gr irid, slim form, unmk, 6" 450.00
Sicardo, vase, floral, purple lustre, trumpet neck, 15½" 1,750.00
Sicardo, vase, floral on purple lustre, gourd form, 3½" 350.00
Sicardo, vase, shamrocks, gr irid, bulging base, 6" 900.00
Sicardo, vase, stars, silver/bl on burgundy, waisted, 6" 550.00
Sicardo, vase, swirling mistletoe, gold/lav, ovoid, 7x3¾" 550.00
Silvertone, basket, floral, twig hdl, mk, 13" 250.00
Silvertone, vase, floral, long angle hdls, mk, 10" 225.00
Silvertone, vase, floral, ruffled rim, hdls, 8½" 300.00

Softone, vase, bl, bulbous, mk, 10" 45.00
Softone, vase, dbl bud; pk, mk, 9" 25.00
Stellar, vase, stars on blk, globular, mk, 5" 175.00
Stellar, vase, wht stars on med bl, 7x7" 550.00
Sydonia, vase, cornucopia; gr speckled, mk, 8" 45.00
Sydonia, vase, dbl; 2 trumpet-like forms, gr, mk, 7½" 55.00
Teapot, gold decor on pk, mk, 6" 67.50
Teapot, gold-gr, mk, 4" 45.00
Tivoli, vase, classic form w/ftd floral base, unmk, 9½" 115.00
Trellis, wall shelf, turq, unmk, 10½" 115.00
Turada, humidor, appl filigree, 5½" 300.00
Turada, lamp base, appl filigree, 8" 850.00
Turada, mug, appl filigree, #562/7 on base 300.00
Turkis, vase, angle hdls, mk, 5½" 85.00
Turkis, vase, integral hdls, mk, 4" 30.00
Tutone, bowl, console; floral, w/frog, 3½", 1½" 110.00
Tutone, vase, floral, bulbous, 4" 40.00
Tutone, vase, floral on gr, mk, 11" 110.00
Velva, vase, floral, sm uptrn hdls, ftd, mk, 9" 65.00
Velvetone, batter jug, blended pastels, 10" 150.00
Velvetone, pitcher, blended pastels, 10" 135.00
Voile, vase, fruit-filled trees, fan form, unmk, 8" 70.00
Warwick, jardiniere, floral on brn wood grain, mk, 7" 135.00
Warwick, planter, floral, twig hdl, mk, 3½" 70.00
Wild Rose, vase, floral, pk on gr, low hdls, 8½" 28.00
Wild Rose, vase, floral, pk on gr, 4-ftd, hdls, 7½" 28.00
Woodcraft, bowl, plums on brn, unmk, 3½" 70.00
Woodcraft, bowl, vining twigs form body w/openwork, ftd, 3½" ...70.00
Woodcraft, candle holder, tree trunk form, 8½" 60.00
Woodcraft, jardiniere, bird at side of stump form, 5½" 300.00
Woodcraft, lamp, owl perched by knothole on trunk form, 16" ..850.00
Woodcraft, vase, fruit on branch, flared cylinder, unmk, 13" 150.00
Woodrose, bowl, roses on brn, tub form w/hdls, 2½x8½" 52.50
Woodrose, vase, roses on brn, tub form w/hdls, 4" 37.50
Xenia, vase, poppies, wine/gr on gray-bl, waisted, 11" 800.00
Zona, jardiniere, bl ribs on ivory, floral band w/blk, 7" 135.00
Zona, pickle dish, ivory w/brn twig hdl, 11" L 55.00
Zona, pitcher, bird, cylindrical, unmk, 7" 115.00
Zona, pitcher, fruit on branch, twig hdl, mk, 6" 45.00
Zona, pitcher, lg pk floral, bl trim at rim & hdl, unmk, 7½" 135.00
Zona, plate, baby's, squirrels, ABC rim, unmk, 7½" 90.00
Zona, plate, fruit branch along rim, unmk, 10" 22.50

West Coast Pottery

Founded in Burbank, California, West Coast Pottery has become known for finely decorated artware and novelties.

Basket vase, #207, 9" 50.00
Bowl, oval, #453, 12½" 50.00
Candle holder, #576C, w/label 25.00
Pitcher, mk, 6½" 75.00
Vase, dk gr & brn, scalloped, #117, 8" 32.00
Vase, leaf design, w/label, 6½" 55.00
Vase, pk & bl, w/label, 5¼" 55.00
Vase, shell design, #904, 7" 45.00
Vase, swan form, 7" 15.00
Wall pocket, vintage, gr & red, #437, 10" 32.00

Western Americana

The collecting of Western Americana encompasses a broad spectrum of memorabilia and collectibles. Examples of various areas within the main stream would include the following fields: weapons, bottles, photographs, mining/railroad artifacts, cowboy paraphernalia, farm and ranch implements, maps, barbed wire, tokens, Indian relics, saloon/gambling items, and branding irons. Some of these areas have their own separate listings in this book. Western Americana is not only a collecting field but is also a collecting *era* with specific boundries. Depending upon which field the collector decides to specialize in, prices can start at a few dollars and run into the thousands.

Our advisor for this category is Bill Mackin, author of *Cowboy and Gunfighter Collectibles* (order from the author); he is listed in the Directory under Colorado.

Bit, Canon City, silver inlay	550.00
Bit, Ed Klapmeir, Miles City MT, silver mtd w/stones, EX	850.00
Bit, Eddie Hulbert, silver mtd	1,350.00
Bit, GS Garcia, lg kissing bird concho	950.00
Bit, spade type, silver inlay, 1800s, all orig	600.00
Branding iron, wrought iron, opening at top for stick, 18"	38.00
Bridle, Navajo, silver & turq	1,900.00
Bridle, Yuma Territory, hitched horsehair, EX	1,950.00
Bridle, Yuma Territory Prison, mc horsehair, rosettes	4,700.00
Buckle set, Ranger, sterling, mk Bohlin Hollywood	375.00
Buckskin outfit, Bohlin on sterling buttons, NM	350.00
Chap, JT Reishacher, step-in style, fringed, EX	800.00
Chaps, Bohlin, batwing, Silver Dollar conchos, cvd belt	1,900.00
Chaps, Johnson Trading Co, Dillon MT, w/decor, EX	415.00
Chaps, Vanco, mk Cowboy Batwing Chaps, studded, 1920s, NM	7,500.00
Chaps, Wyeth, batwing, spotted shield pattern, EX	1,000.00
Cuffs, Al Furstnow, tooled leather, M, pr	600.00
Cuffs, Bohlin, tooled leather, pr	1,000.00
Cuffs, FA Meanea, tooled leather, NM	850.00
Gun belt & holster, Bohlin, cvd leather w/silver buckles	700.00
Hat band, Bohlin, beaded, M	100.00
Lap robe, buffalo hide, EX	115.00
Letterhead & letter, Sells-Floto, from Buffalo Bill, EX	1,300.00
Poster, Buffalo Bill & Famous Generals, Hoen, 24x34", EX	2,400.00
Program, Buffalo Bill, 1893, NM	550.00
Reata, rawhide, long, early, EX	375.00
Rope, mc hitched horsehair, EX	1,250.00
Saddle, Bohlin, leather, plain, M	1,400.00
Saddle, parade; Bohlin, hand-tooled leather, silver mts	8,750.00
Saddle, US Packer, EX	500.00
Saddle bags, blk angora, old & orig, EX	950.00
Saddle bags, Connely Bros, hand cvd, EX	500.00
Saddle bags, spotted woolly type, minor rstr	425.00
Spur straps, Jos Sullivan Ft Benton MT, bib style, EX	725.00
Spurs, Buermann, Cowpuncher's Favorites, dbl button, pr	125.00
Spurs, Buermann, drop shank, jingle bobs, pr	275.00
Spurs, Buermann, drop shank, silver mtd, pr	650.00
Spurs, Buermann Hercules, bronze drop, shank, pr	325.00
Spurs, Buermann star AB, silver inlay, pre-1920, pr	850.00
Spurs, Buremann CA style, drop shank, chains	285.00
Spurs, Cates, silver-mtd eagle, pr	450.00
Spurs, cavalry, brass, 1888, pr	135.00
Spurs, CP Shipley, dbl mtd, fancy, pr	2,500.00
Spurs, Crockett, CI w/silver o/l, 1920s	495.00
Spurs, Crockett, silver-mtd eagle, split heel band, EX, pr	500.00
Spurs, Crockett, silver-mtd fish, pr	475.00
Spurs, Eddie Hulbert, dbl mtd, gold on silver, M, pr	4,250.00
Spurs, GS Garcia, Dandy #75, 1914, NM, pr	6,500.00
Spurs, McChesney, lady's leg, silver mtd, EX, pr	720.00
Spurs, McChesney pattern #1, silver mtd, EX, pr	950.00
Spurs, Mexican, Charro, 1800s, lg, pr	650.00
Spurs, OA Vogal, iron, rare, scarce, pr	475.00

Spurs, Oscar Crockett, mk Gal Leg, rare pattern, pr	2,900.00
Spurs, Schnitger, dbl mtd, EX, pr	1,800.00

Western Pottery Manufacturing Company

This pottery was originally founded as the Denver China and Pottery Company; William Long was the owner. The company's assets were sold to a group who in 1905 formed the Western Pottery Manufacturing Company, located at 16th Street and Alcott in Denver, Colorado. By 1926, 186 different items were being produced, including crocks, flowerpots, kitchen items, and other stoneware. The company dissolved in 1936.

Seven various marks were used during the years, and values may be higher for items that carry a rare mark. Numbers within the descriptions refer to specific marks, see the line drawings. Prices may vary depending on demand and locale. Our advisors for this category are Cathy Segelke and Pat James; they are listed in the Directory under Colorado.

Churn, #2, hdl, 4-gal, M	75.00
Churn, #2, hdl, 5-gal, M	65.00
Churn, #2, no lid, 5-gal, G	80.00
Crock, #4, bail lip, 4-gal, G	55.00
Crock, #4, hdl, no lid, 8-gal, M	90.00
Crock, #4, ice water; bl/wht sponge pnt, 3-gal, NM	30.00
Crock, #4, 2-gal, M	32.00
Crock, #4, 6-gal, EX	72.00
Crock, #4b, 20-gal, M	200.00
Crock, #4b, 22x17½", 15-gal, NM	150.00
Crock, #5, bail lip, 1½-gal, M	45.00
Crock, #5, no lid, 6-gal, M	70.00
Crock, #6, wire hdl, 10-gal, NM	100.00
Crock, #6, 2-gal, NM	30.00
Crock, #6, 3-gal, M	40.00
Crock, #6, 4-gal, M	50.00
Crock, #6, 5-gal, NM	60.00
Foot warmer, #6, M	50.00
Jug, #6, brn/wht, 1-gal, EX	25.00
Jug, #6, brn/wht, 5-gal, M	75.00
Rabbit feeder, #1, EX	25.00
Rabbit waterer, #1, M	25.00

Westmoreland

Originally titled the Specialty Glass Company, Westmoreland began operations in East Liverpool, Ohio, producing utility items as well as tableware in milk glass and crystal. When the company moved to Grapeville, Pennsylvania, in 1890, lamps, vases, covered animal dishes, and decorative plates were introduced. Prior to 1920 Westmoreland was a major manufacturer of carnival glass and soon thereafter added a line of lovely reproduction art glass items. High-quality milk glass became their speciality, accounting for about 90% of their production. Black glass was introduced in the 1940s, and later in the decade ruby-stained pieces and items decorated in the Mary Gregory style became fashionable. By the 1960s colored glassware was being produced, examples of which are very popular with collectors today. Early pieces were marked with a paper label; by the 1960s the ware was embossed with a superimposed 'WG.' The last mark was a circle containing 'Westmoreland' around the perimeter and a large 'W' in the center. The company closed in 1985. See also Animal Dishes with Covers; Carnival Glass. Note: Though you may find pieces very similar to Westmoreland's, their Della Robbia has no bananas among the fruits relief.

Urn, Roses and Bows on milk glass, 12½", $125.00.

Appetizer, Panelled Grape, milk glass, 3-part	60.00
Ashtray, Beaded Grape, milk glass, sq, 6½"	15.00
Banana boat, Doric, milk glass, high ped	25.00
Banana boat, Ring & Petal, milk glass, tall	45.00
Basket, Panelled Grape, milk glass, split hdl, oval, 6½"	22.50
Basket, Swirl & Ball, amber, 5"	18.50
Bowl, Beaded Grape, milk glass, ftd, w/lid, 9"	45.00
Bowl, Doric, milk glass, oval, crimped, 12"	35.00
Bowl, Doric, milk glass, 9"	25.00
Bowl, English Hobnail, lilac opal, hdls	45.00
Bowl, Old Quilt, milk glass, 8"	50.00
Bowl, Panelled Grape, milk glass, ftd, crimped, 6"	40.00
Bowl, Panelled Grape, milk glass, lipped, 9"	50.00
Bowl, Panelled Grape, milk glass, oval, lipped, ftd, 11"	60.00
Bowl, Sawtooth, amber, flared, ftd, 12"	50.00
Bowl, wedding; Roses & Bows, milk glass, HP decor, w/lid, 8"	100.00
Butter dish, Old Quilt, milk glass, ¼-lb	37.00
Butter dish, Panelled Grape, milk glass	35.00
Cake salver, Beaded Grape, milk glass, low std	60.00
Cake salver, Panelled Grape, milk glass, 10½"	90.00
Candelabra, English Hobnail, milk glass, 2-light, pr	80.00
Candle holders, American Hobnail, milk glass, pr	20.00
Candle holders, Doric, milk glass, 4½", pr	20.00
Candle holders, Doric, Yel Mist, pr	20.00
Candle holders, Old Quilt, milk glass, pr	28.00
Candle holders, Panelled Grape, milk glass, 4", pr	25.00
Candle holders, Panelled Grape, MOP, pr	30.00
Candle holders, Spiral, milk glass, tall, pr	25.00
Candle holders, Thousand Eye, crystal, 5", pr	37.50

Candle holders, Thousand Eye, milk glass, 3-ball, pr	30.00
Candy dish, Argonaut Shell, Antique bl, ftd, w/lid	65.00
Candy dish, English Hobnail, milk glass, ftd, w/lid	25.00
Candy dish, Old Quilt, milk glass, low, sq, ftd	25.00
Candy dish, Panelled Grape, milk glass, ruffled, 3-ftd	25.00
Candy dish, Panelled Grape, milk glass, w/lid, 7"	35.00
Candy dish, Swirl & Ball, amber, w/lid	25.00
Celery tray, Old Quilt, milk glass, flat, 10"	30.00
Celery vase, Old Quilt, milk glass, ftd, 6"	28.00
Cheese dish, Old Quilt, milk glass	55.00
Compote, American Hobnail, crystal, 8x7"	30.00
Compote, Dolphin Shell, milk glass, 8"	35.00
Compote, Old Quilt, milk glass, 8-sided ft, 7"	15.00
Compote, Panelled Grape, milk glass, crimped, 9"	75.00
Compote, Panelled Grape, milk glass, w/lid, 7"	30.00
Cordial, Thousand Eye, crystal	9.00
Creamer, Old Quilt, milk glass, lg	15.00
Creamer & sugar bowl, American Hobnail, milk glass	12.00
Creamer & sugar bowl, Maple Leaf, milk glass	20.00
Creamer & sugar bowl, Old Quilt, milk glass, ind	22.00
Creamer & sugar bowl, Panelled Grape, milk glass, ind	35.00
Creamer & sugar bowl, Panelled Grape, milk glass, w/lid, lg	50.00
Cruet, American Hobnail, milk glass	15.00
Cup, Beaded Edge, milk glass	6.00
Cup, punch; Old Quilt, milk glass	15.00
Cup, punch; Panelled Grape, milk glass	12.00
Cup, punch; Three Fruits, milk glass	10.00
Cup & saucer, American Hobnail, milk glass	12.00
Cup & saucer, English Hobnail, milk glass	12.00
Cup & saucer, Panelled Grape, milk glass	18.00
Epergne, Panelled Grape, milk glass, 2-pc, 11½" bowl	150.00
Flower holder, English Hobnail, milk glass, ftd	15.00
Goblet, American Hobnail, milk glass	12.50
Goblet, Colonial, Bermuda Bl	8.00
Goblet, Panelled Grape, milk glass	15.00
Goblet, water; Della Robbia, milk glass	15.00
Goblet, water; Della Robbia, red stain	25.00
Goblet, water; Old Quilt, milk glass	15.00
Honey dish, Beaded Grape, milk glass, w/lid, 4"	15.00
Ivy ball, Panelled Grape, milk glass	40.00
Mayonnaise, American Hobnail, milk glass	7.50
Mayonnaise, Panelled Grape, milk glass, ftd	25.00
Nut bowl, Panelled Grape, milk glass, 6½"	18.00
Pansy basket, Panelled Grape, milk glass, split hdl, 5"	20.00
Pitcher, Colonial, Bermuda Bl	45.00
Pitcher, Old Quilt, milk glass, 1-pt	35.00
Pitcher, Old Quilt, milk glass, 1-qt	35.00
Pitcher, Panelled Grape, lilac opal, 1-qt	55.00
Pitcher, Panelled Grape, milk glass, ftd, 1-qt	30.00
Pitcher, Panelled Grape, milk glass, 1-pt	30.00
Plate, Beaded Edge, flower center, milk glass, 7"	13.00
Plate, Beaded Edge, peach center, milk glass, 7"	12.00
Plate, dinner; Beaded Edge, milk glass	14.00
Plate, Old Quilt, milk glass, 8½"	20.00
Plate, Panelled Grape, milk glass, 10½"	38.00
Plate, Panelled Grape, milk glass, 6¼"	15.00
Plate, torte; Della Robbia, red stain, 14"	90.00
Punch set, Fruit, milk glass, 15-pc	250.00
Relish, Old Quilt, milk glass, 3-part, 9"	40.00
Rose bowl, American Hobnail, lilac opal, 4½"	15.00
Rose bowl, American Hobnail, milk glass	12.50
Rose bowl, Panelled Grape, milk glass	25.00
Shakers, Beaded Grape, milk glass, pr	25.00
Shakers, Della Robbia, red stain, ftd, pr	60.00

Shakers, Old Quilt, milk glass, pr **14.00**
Shakers, Panelled Grape, milk glass, allover pattern, flat, pr **18.00**
Shakers, Panelled Grape, milk glass, allover pattern, ftd, pr **18.00**
Sherbet, Beaded Edge, strawberries, milk glass **16.00**
Sherbet, Panelled Grape, milk glass **16.00**
Sherbet, Thousand Eye, milk glass, low **9.00**
Sugar bowl, Lacy Edge, milk glass, w/lid **32.00**
Syrup, Old Quilt, milk glass **30.00**
Tumbler, Beaded Edge, milk glass, ftd **15.00**
Tumbler, iced tea; Old Quilt, milk glass **12.00**
Vase, bud; Roses & Bows, milk glass, hexagonal, 10" **28.00**
Vase, Panelled Grape, milk glass, ftd, 6" **22.00**
Window box, Panelled Grape, milk glass, 5x9" **30.00**

Wheatley, T. J.

In 1880 after a brief association with the Coultry Works, Thomas J. Wheatley opened his own studio in Cincinnati, Ohio, claiming to have been the first to discover the secret of under-glaze slip decoration on an unbaked clay vessel. He applied for and was granted a patent for his process. Demand for his ware increased to the point that several artists were hired to decorate the ware. The company incorporated in 1880 as the Cincinnati Art Pottery, but until 1882 it continued to operate under Wheatley's name. Ware from this period is marked 'T.J. Wheatley' or 'T.J.W. and Co.,' and it may be dated.

Sand jar, blk drip over lt bl, #610, 30", NM, pr **1,300.00**
Tile, lion in relief, brick red w/gr, unmk, 8" **135.00**
Vase, cvd band on feathered gr matt, 5½x9" **450.00**
Vase, Grueby-style leaves, gr curdled matt, 13", NM **2,000.00**
Vase, leathery gr matt, bulbous/waisted, flared rim, 6" **375.00**
Vase, upright leaves/stems/berries, gr matt, 6x5", NM **650.00**
Vase, 4 long buttress hdls on flaring body, gr matt, 18x9" **5,500.00**

Whieldon

Thomas Whieldon was regarded as the finest of the Staffordshire potters of the mid-1700s. He produced marbled and black Egyptian wares as well as tortoise shell, a mottled brown-glazed earthenware accented with touches of blue and yellow. In 1754 he became a partner of Josiah Wedgwood. Other potters produced similar wares, and today the term Whieldon is used generically.

Plates, multicolor splashes on brown mottle with patterned rims, ca 1765, 9½", $285.00 each; Teapot, pineapple shape with green leaves on body, dolphin handle, repair, ca 1760, 4½", $1,760.00.

Basket, yel/brn stripes, ribbed, oval w/arched hdl, 3", EX **230.00**
Cat on plinth, yel & gray splashes, ca 1800, 2½" **425.00**
Coffeepot, gr/yel/brn streaky glaze, rpr, 9" **835.00**
Creamer, cauliflower mold, cream/gr, w/lid, 1765, 6", EX **825.00**
Mustard pot, gr/ochre/b/l/brn mottle, twisted C-hdl, 3", VG **700.00**
Plate, emb floral sprigs, brn tortoise shell w/bl & gr, 5" **150.00**
Platter, tortoise shell w/bl & gr, emb rim, rpr, 10⅜" **300.00**
Teapot, cauliflower, cream/gr, 1765, rstr, 3¾" **300.00**
Teapot, cauliflower, deep gr, ca 1760, lg, NM **1,200.00**
Teapot, clouded ware, brn/yel/gr tortoise shell, 1750s, 5¼" **385.00**
Wall vase, brn mottle, cornucopia w/bust of lady, rstr, 11" **825.00**

Wicker

Wicker is the basket-like material used in many types of furniture and accessories. It may be made from bamboo cane, rattan, reed, or artificial fibers. It is airy, lightweight, and very popular in hot regions. Imported from the Orient in the 18th century, it was first manufactured in the United States in about 1850. The elaborate, closely-woven Victorian designs belong to the mid- to late 1800s, and the simple styles with coarse reedings usually indicate a post-1900 production. Art Deco styles followed in the twenties and thirties. The most important consideration in buying wicker is condition — it can be restored, but only by a professional. Age is an important factor, but be aware that 'Victorian-style' furniture is being manufactured today.

Key:
HB — Heywood Brothers   H/W — Heywood-Wakefield
WR — Wakefield Rattan Co.

Armchair, H/W, bent rod fr w/U-seat, narrow bk/apron, 1900 ...**400.00**
Armchair, scrolls & beadwork, serpentine bk & arms, 1890s **350.00**
Basket, pnt geometric design, leather finged hdls, 21x14" **180.00**
Chair, corner; fancy scrollwork, cane seat, HB, 1890s, EX **745.00**
Chair, platform rocker; ornate lyre bk, arched legs **450.00**
Chaise lounge, animal design, metal loop springs, Home Comfort .**1,350.00**
Cradle, tight weave, wht pnt, hanging, EX **900.00**
Desk, wooden shelved superstructure, 1-drw, HW, 43x75" **825.00**
Easel, elaborate top/apron, beaded, 1895, 75" **3,000.00**
Highchair, fine-woven bk, wooden tray & footrest, 1900s **375.00**
Plant stand, machine-woven fiber w/shelf, trn legs, 1920s **155.00**
Planter, 26" dia bowl w/4-leg scroll-support base, 44" **350.00**
Record player, Wakefield, crank type, natural, 45" H, EX **400.00**
Sewing basket, 2-door, wht pnt, EX **200.00**
Stroller, bentwood hdl, wire/tin wheels, doll sz, VG **155.00**
Table, dining; fine-woven skirting under wood top, ped ft, 42" ..**525.00**
Tea caddy, simple style, wht pnt, EX **325.00**
Tea cart, tight weave, child sz, EX **300.00**
Vanity, tight weave, wht pnt, child sz, EX **200.00**

Willets

The Willets Manufacturing Company of Trenton, New Jersey, produced a type of belleek porcelain during the late 1880s and 1890s. Examples were often marked with a coiled snake that formed a 'W' with 'Willets' below and 'Belleek' above. Not all Willet's is factory decorated. Items painted by amateurs outside the factory are worth considerably less. In the listings below, all items are belleek unless noted otherwise. Our advisor for this category is Mary Frank Gaston. You will find her address in the Directory under Texas.

Bowl, gold leaves fr red flower, dragon hdls, 4½x11" **500.00**

Bowl, lav thistles w/leafy stems, gold hdls, 7¼" 350.00
Bowl, platinum decor, 3½x7½" 80.00
Compote, bk roses, bl rim band, gold hdls, sq, ftd, 4½x6" 325.00
Creamer & sugar bowl, florals w/gold scrolls & hdls, 3", 2½" 175.00
Cup & saucer, chocolate; purple w/gold dragon hdl & monogram .60.00
Hair receiver, gold berries & branches, scalloped, 2" 125.00
Pitcher, roses along rim, trailing stems, cylindrical, 7¾" 225.00
Pitcher, tankard, grapes, sgn Skillman, gold scroll hdl, 14" 350.00
Pitcher, tankard, grapes on leafy branches, 14½" 400.00
Plate, butterflies, bl & yel on cream, NLH, 1917, 10½" 175.00
Stein, grapes & vines, gold dragon hdl, inscr base, 5½" 275.00
Vase, Am Beauty roses on mc, artist sgn, oviform, 15" 400.00
Vase, birds in brn/tan/wht, cylindrical, gr mk, 17½" 495.00
Vase, flowing flowers on gr matt, bulbous base, 14" 400.00
Vase, mc roses, tapered, 12" 350.00
Vase, nude in veils blowing bubbles, 15¾" 1,150.00
Vase, peacock feather panels alternate w/gr, Saie, 12" 225.00
Vase, roses, pk & red on bl to gr, gold ruffled rim, 10" 300.00
Vase, roses w/trailing brn stems, Snyder, cylindrical, 8" 200.00

Willow Ware

Willow Ware, inspired no doubt by the numerous patterns of the blue and white Nanking imports, has been popular since the late 18th century and has been made in as many variations as there were manufacturers. English transfer wares by such notable firms as Allerton and Ridgway are the most sought after and the most expensive. Japanese potters have been producing Willow-patterned dinnerware since the late 1800s, and American manufacturers have followed suit. Although blue is the color most commonly used, mauve, black, and even multicolor Willow Ware may be found. Complementary glassware, tinware, and linens have also been made. In addition to 'Allerton' and 'Ridgway,' both companies used the possessive forms of their names in marking their wares (i.e. Allerton's, Ridgway's). For further study we recommend the book *Blue Willow*, with full-color photos and current prices, by Mary Frank Gaston. You will find her address in the Directory under Texas. In the following listings, if no manufacturer is noted, the ware is unmarked. See also Buffalo.

Cream soup, 5¾", with matching underplate, 7", $25.00 for the set.

Bowl, berry; Adams 8.00
Bowl, berry; Bourne & Leigh, sm 6.00
Bowl, cereal; Japan, 6¼" 10.00
Bowl, cereal; Royal, 6¼" 6.00
Bowl, coupe soup; Ridgway, 7½" 22.00
Bowl, cream soup; Japan 12.00
Bowl, fruit; England, 5" 6.00
Bowl, fruit; gr, Royal USA, gr, 5½" 4.50
Bowl, pk, Royal, 6¼" 7.00
Bowl, soup; flat, 7½" 9.50

Bowl, soup; Ridgway, 8¾" 24.00
Bowl, soup; Royal USA, gr, flat, 8⅜" 9.50
Bowl, vegetable; Allerton 60.00
Bowl, vegetable; Homer Laughlin, oval 25.00
Bowl, vegetable; Japan, oval, 10" 30.00
Bowl, vegetable; L Straus, Burslem England, deep, 8x6½" 55.00
Butter dish, Allerton 190.00
Butter pat, Allerton, 3⅛" 25.00
Coffeepot & warmer, Japan, pre-1960 ....150.00
Compote, Adams, ca 1850 ....250.00
Cookie canister, rnd 150.00
Creamer, Japan, 3½" 16.00
Creamer, Shenango, ind 20.00
Creamer & sugar bowl, Allerton 100.00
Creamer & sugar bowl, Japan, oval 30.00
Creamer & sugar bowl, Ridgway 100.00
Cup & saucer, chili; Japan 35.00
Cup & saucer, Japan, inside decal 14.00
Cup & saucer, USA, stacking 4.00
Egg cup, dbl; Japan 22.00
Egg cup, unmk Am 12.00
Gravy boat, Ridgway 50.00
Gravy boat, Woods 65.00
Pitcher, juice; Japan, 10" 70.00
Pitcher, L Straus, Burslem England, ½-gal, 9" 150.00
Plate, Adams, luncheon sz 15.00
Plate, Adams, salad sz 12.00
Plate, Allerton, luncheon sz 22.00
Plate, Booth's, gold trim, dinner sz 25.00
Plate, Booth's, gold trim, salad sz 20.00
Plate, Buff, heavy, 5½" 10.00
Plate, England, 10" 7.00
Plate, England, 6¼" 4.00
Plate, grill; Japan 12.00
Plate, grill; Japan, 10¾" 15.00
Plate, grill; Moriyama, 11" 18.00
Plate, Japan, 6¼" 5.00
Plate, Maastricht, 6" 10.00
Plate, Ridgway, dinner sz 22.00
Plate, Ridgway, luncheon sz 20.00
Plate, Royal, pk, 10" 9.00
Plate, Royal USA, gr, 10" 9.50
Plate, Royal USA, gr, 6¼" 3.50
Plate, unmk Am, 9" 7.00
Platter, Allerton, 11¼x9⅛" 100.00
Platter, Homer Laughlin, 12" 25.00
Platter, Japan, 13" 22.00
Platter, Ridgway, med 100.00
Platter, Royal, pk, 13x10" 30.00
Platter, Staffordshire type, 16" 100.00
Platter, Woods, oval, 14½" 55.00
Saucer, England, 5½" 8.00
Shakers, England, pr 55.00
Snack plate & cup set 20.00
Toaster, rare 1,795.00
Toby mug, Japan 300.00
Toothpick holder, unmk 85.00

Winchester

The Winchester Repeating Arms Company lost their important government contract after WWI and of necessity turned to the manufacture of sporting goods, hardware items, tools, etc., to augment their gun production. Between 1920 and 1931, over 7,500 different items, each marked 'Winchester Trademark U.S.A.,' were offered for sale by thousands of Winchester Hardware stores throughout the country. After 1931 the firm became Winchester-Western. Unless noted otherwise, values are for examples in EX condition. Our advisor for this category is James Anderson; he is listed in the Directory under Minnesota. See also Knives.

Axe, VG	95.00
Battery, radio; 7x8x3", G	85.00
Bit, auger; WZ4-16, 13 szs, ¼-1", ea	20.00
Brace, bit; W18, 8"	85.00
Calendar, 1912, VG	700.00
Can, gun oil, Winchester Repeating Arms, 5x2½", NM	40.00
Can opener, EX	75.00
Case, pocketknife display, counter-top style w/drw, EX	295.00
Catalog, guns, 1925	100.00
Chisel, #4512, ¼"	50.00
Cutlery set, ivory hdls, EX	175.00
Display, gun solvent, w/6 full bottles, ca 1950s	125.00
Drill bit	20.00
Fan, paper, ornate, EX	125.00
Fishing fly, M on card	85.00
Fishing plug, 3-hook, EX	450.00
Fishing plug, 5-hook, EX	600.00
Golf club, G	125.00
Hammer, machinist; WM2, 24-oz	85.00
Hatchet, VG	90.00
Hockey puck, VG	140.00
Ice pick, wood hdl, #9501, 8½"	85.00
Iron, electric, VG	150.00
Knife, steel, wooden hdl, #1761, 17"	65.00
Lawn mower, VG	275.00
Lawn sprinkler, rare, G	195.00
Level, iron, W36/24, 24"	125.00
Meat grinder, #12, clean	45.00
Meat grinder, W31	75.00
Mold, 44/40 caliber, VG+	60.00
Padlock, 2 keys	145.00
Percussion caps, dtd 1912, orig unopened pack	15.00
Plane, block; W103, 5½"	75.00
Plane, block; W60, 6"	75.00
Plane, dbl-end block; W130, 7¾"	95.00
Plane, fillister; W78, 8½"	125.00
Plane, jack; W/5, 14"	95.00
Plane, jointer; W7, 22"	125.00
Plane, metal, #3089, 7"	135.00
Plane, metal, W013, 5½", EX	125.00
Plane, scraper; W12, 6", VG	125.00
Pliers, #2495	50.00
Pliers, mk Oct Special, EX	50.00
Pliers, side cutting; W206	50.00
Pliers, slip joint; W150	40.00
Pocketknife, red, gold & blk hdl, #1051, EX	250.00
Pocketknife, 2-blade, EX	200.00
Print, Norman Rockwell, 'Stagecoach,' EX	90.00
Punch, center; unused, ⅜"	45.00
Razor, straight; W44, EX	100.00
Razor strop, #8385, VG	125.00
Reamer, sq; unused, orig hanging tag	75.00
Reel, #2242	125.00
Rod, baitcasting; in orig case	150.00
Rod, fly; bamboo, 9-ft, EX	295.00
Rod, fly; 8-ft, NM	325.00

Rule, folding; W32, w/caliper, 12"	95.00
Rule, folding; W61, 24"	75.00
Saw, crosscut; W3003	125.00
Saw, meat; #28, 24", VG	125.00
Saw, wood; W85	85.00
Scissors, clean, 10"	45.00
Screwdriver, VG	35.00
Shells, 9mm shot, M in sealed box	150.00
Sign, counter; stands up, EX	175.00
Space heater, w/cord, VG	175.00
Spatula	75.00
Spoke shave, W91, 10"	75.00
Square, steel; W14, 24"	60.00
Tennis racquet, EX	175.00
Thermometer, very clean	135.00
Tube, cb, for fishing shot	45.00
Wire cutters, #2166, 6"	65.00
Wrench, brake adjusting; VG	55.00
Wrench, monkey; WB15, 15"	75.00
Wrench, open end; W623, 4 szs, ea	30.00
Wrench, pipe; WWP6, 6", VG+	95.00
Wrench, W23, 4½"	30.00

Windmill Weights

Windmill weights were used to protect the windmill's plunger rod from damage during high winds by adding weight that slowed down the speed of the blades.

Bull, Fairbury, CI, no pnt, 18¼x24½x1¼"	750.00
Bull, unmk Fairbury, CI, old pnt, 1940s, 38-lb, 24x18"	770.00
Horse, bob-tailed, CI, free-standing, #58, 17x18"	365.00
Horse, long-tailed, Demster, old blk pnt, 37-lb, 21½"	1,000.00

Hummer rooster, marked E 184, poor paint, $350.00.

Moon crescent, Fairbanks Morse, 1900, 22-lb, 11x6⅝"	185.00
Rooster, Elgin, rainbow tail, EX pnt, 60-lb, 18x16x3"	875.00
Rooster, Hummer, old pnt, ca 1900, 8⅞x9⅞x1¾", EX	500.00
Rooster, Mogul; Elgin, hollow body, old blk pnt, 21"	2,300.00
Spear, Challenge, CI, no pnt, 35-lb, 24"	800.00
Star, US Wind Engine, no pnt, ca 1890s, 14½x14½x3"	425.00

Winfield

The Winfield Pottery was founded in 1929 in Pasadena, California. The artware and giftware items they made were marked Winfield, Pasadena, sometimes with the date added. In 1946 the line of more than 400 shapes was licensed to the American Ceramic Products Company of Santa Monica who began using the Winfield trade name on their semi-porcelain dinnerware. The Winfield Pottery from then on marked their output 'Gabriel.' Both companies closed during the early 1960s.

Blue Pacific, cheese dish 30.00
Desert Dawn, chop plate, 14" sq 30.00
Desert Dawn, plate, bread & butter 5.00
Desert Dawn, saucer 2.50
Dragon Flower, gravy boat 15.00
Dragon Flower, plate, 10" 8.00
Tiger Iris, bowl, vegetable; 9⅛" 10.00
Tiger Iris, cup & saucer 4.00
Tiger Iris, shakers, pr 8.00

Wire Ware

Two thousand years B.C. wire was made by cutting sheet metal into strips which were shaped with mallet and file. By the late 13th century, craftsmen in Europe had developed a method of pulling these strips through progressively smaller holes until the desired gauge was obtained. During the Industrial Revolution of the late 1800s, machinery was developed that could produce wire cheaply and easily; and it became a popular commercial commodity. It was used to produce large items such as garden benches and fencing as well as innumerable small pieces for use in the kitchen or on the farm. Beware of reproductions. Our advisor for this category is Rosella Tinsley; she is listed in the Directory under Kansas.

Basket, fruit; rnd openwork designs, ca 1900, 5x14" 85.00
Basket, gathering; stationary hdl, 8½"+hdlx7" 55.00
Basket, onion; wire in circles, bulged-out sides 85.00
Basket, vegetable; fine wire, folds flat including hdls 24.00
Biscuit pricker, heavy wire spikes, loop hdl, 2¼" dia 55.00
Bottle holder, circular, top hdl, ftd 32.50
Bucket, heavy wire in dmn design, flared top, bail hdl, 12x12" 55.00
Calling card basket, fancy twisted wire w/wire ft, 7½" dia 70.00
Carpet beater, braided design, oval shape w/wood hdl 22.00
Carrier, bottle; heavy twisted wire, holds 6, 4x13½x9"+hdl 45.00
Comb holder, twisted, fancy top, hangs 95.00
Compote, fancy, sm rnd scalloped base, lg bowl top 125.00
Compote, triangular basket w/trn-down rim, ped ft, 7x9" 65.00
Dish drainer, twisted wire w/4 wire ft, early 1900s, 15" dia 75.00
Egg tongs, heavy oval circular wire, squeeze hdl, 11" L 45.00
Fly cover, screen wire, dk tin band, wooden knob, 8½" 50.00
Ladle, pea skimmer; twisted, wooden hdl, 1890s, 9¼" 30.00
Lifter, fruit jar; collapsible, jar fits inside 12.00
Lifter, plate, adjustable slide, ca 1890s, rare, 18" 75.00
Napkin holder, twisted, easel bk, stands 75.00
Pot scrubber, wire rings, old 28.00
Rolling pin holder, fine twisted wire, 4 hearts, old, EX 65.00
Rolling pin holder, heavy wire, hangs vertically 50.00
Settee, twisted wire & scrolls, arms, 36", EX 395.00
Sieve, on oblong wires that slide into bowl, ca 1890 ....22.00
Soap dish, twisted, ornate, hanging 70.00
Sponge holder, heavy, hooks on side of tub, EX 32.00
Sponge holder, twisted, loop hanger 95.00
Tea ball, screen wire, tin banding, lock fastener, 2¼" oval 28.00
Tray, egg; looped wires in wooden fr, holds 6 dozen, 24x12" 45.00
Tray, tea; twisted wire, 6½" dia 37.50
Trivet, fine wire in circles, ftd, 14" dia 75.00
Trivet, twisted, ftd, some rust, 1¼x9" dia 55.00
Vegetable washer, ball shaped, top hdls, 2-pc 55.00
Whisk, tined loop w/twisted hdl, Germany, 8", EX 18.00

Witch Balls

Witch balls were a Victorian fad touted to be meritorious toward

ridding the house of evil spirits, thus warding off sickness and bad luck. Folklore would have it that by wiping the dust and soot from the ball, the spirits were exorcised. It is much more probable, however, considering the fact that such beautiful art glass was used in their making, that the ostensive Victorians perpetrated the myth rather tongue-in-cheek while enjoying them as lovely decorations for their homes.

Amber, blown, 5" dia 85.00
Blk amethyst, sm sheared opening on 1 end, 1870-90, 4¼" 85.00
Cobalt, open pontil 1 end, many bubbles, 1860-90, 8" 150.00
Cobalt, pontil scars on ball & stand, Am, 1835-50, 9¾" 400.00
Dk gr-aqua, 5", in matching vase w/6" dia lip, att S Jersey 925.00
Nailsea, aqua w/wht loopings, New England, 1850s, 6¾", pr 485.00
Nailsea, clear w/cranberry, bl & wht loopings, 4¾" 440.00
Nailsea, clear w/wht looping, 5½" 110.00
Wht w/pk & red loopings, crudely made, att Sandwich, 4¼" 185.00

Wood Carvings

Wood sculptures represent an important section of American folk art. Wood carvings were made not only by skilled woodworkers such as cabinetmakers, carpenters, etc., but by amateur 'whittlers' as well. They take the form of circus-wagon figures, carousel animals, decoys, busts, figurines, and cigar-store Indians. Oriental artists show themselves to have been as proficient with the medium of wood as they were with ivory or hardstone. See also Carousel Animals; Decoys; Tobacciana.

Birdhouse, plywood w/cut-out bamboo segments, 1900s, 5½x7" .120.00
Boar, appl cvd ears, incised cvd on bk, 3½x5" 80.00
Bowler w/ball, mc pnt, ca 1940, 7½x3x3" 40.00
Bust of Lincoln on ped, mc pnt, ca 1900, 6" 110.00
Bust of Washington, mc pnt, ca 1900, 4" 140.00
Chain, cvd from 1 pc, hook 1 end, 63" 85.00
Chain, cvd from 1 pc, 17 links, 30" 80.00
Dog's head, old brn pnt w/some wht, ca 1900, 4" 15.00
Dr w/medical bag, mc pnt, early 1900s, 5" on 2½" dia base 85.00
Duck in flight, yel button eyes, mc pnt, 1930s, 11x7x4¾" 125.00
Eagle, EX pnt, early 1800s, 32", on later columnar stand 3,165.00
Eagle, old mc pnt, EX detail, minor damage to wing, 8½" 330.00
Eagle, pine, old finish, ca 1900, 9x18" wingspan 440.00
Eagle, primitive style, old varnish, 16" wingspan 50.00
Eagle, Schimmel style, wings spread, 3-color pnt, 12x7" 270.00
Elderly lady, pnt details, cloth dress w/lace, 1900s, 6½" 85.00
Head of bald man, pine, pnt details, early 1900s, 6½" 85.00
Horse, front leg raised, blk pnt, 1920s, 10x8x2½" 110.00

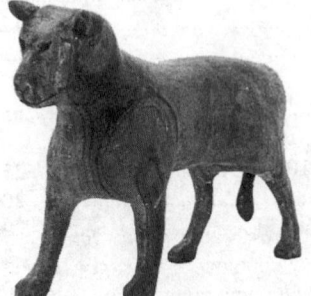

Lion, natural finish, 6x8", $250.00.

Man, mc pnt, felt hat, jtd arms, ca 1900, 8½" 30.00
Man on base, articulated, mc pnt, 1880s, 9¼" 110.00
Parrot, EX detail, orig mc pnt, wire nails, 19½" 195.00
Parrot, glass eyes, orig pnt, OH, 11½" 330.00

Roadrunner, glass eyes, orig pnt, OH, 30" **550.00**
Rooster, pine, EX detail, varnish, sgn, 1950s, 12¾" **170.00**
Rooster, pine w/gesso & pnt, ind feathers, rpr/pnt loss, 12" **1,275.00**
Squirrel, EX detail, orig varnish, 6½" **35.00**
Tiger, realistic pnt, 1800s, 25x32" **5,000.00**

Woodenware

Woodenware (or treenware, as it is sometimes called) generally refers to those wooden items such as spoons, bowls, food molds, etc., that were used in the preparation of food. Common during the 18th and 19th centuries, these wares were designed from a strictly functional viewpoint and were used on a day-to-day basis. With the advent of the Industrial Revolution which brought it new materials and products, much of the old woodenware was simply discarded. Today original hand-crafted American woodenware is extremely difficult to find.

Burl bowls: deep with flat rim, New England, 1800s, 4x10½", $750.00; Oval with shaped ends, carved handles, Plains Indians, 1800s, 14¼" long, $2,600.00; Deep circular form, New England, 1800s, 5x12¼", $850.00.

Apple butter stirrer, dk patina, 74" **40.00**
Bowl, ash burl, EX figure, stained finish, 4½x12" **825.00**
Bowl, ash burl, EX figure & color, rim crack, 5½x16" **600.00**
Bowl, ash burl, old dk patina, 7½x21½" **825.00**
Bowl, ash burl w/ G figure, old rfn, 4x12½" **600.00**
Bowl, ash burl w/G figure, 2⅛x6¼" **330.00**
Bowl, burl, EX figure, soft patina, G wear, 4½x14" **935.00**
Bowl, burl, trn, Am, 1800s, 9", EX **375.00**
Bowl, curly maple, red traces, wear/crack, 5¼x17" **360.00**
Bowl, curly maple, rfn, 6¾x19¾x18¾" **440.00**
Bowl, harvest; poplar, old rpr, 42½" L **300.00**
Bowl, maple, EX patina, 4x13" **60.00**
Bowl, old red rpt, 5½x18½" **195.00**
Bowl, Pease, flared rim, ftd, old varnish, 3⅝x7" **330.00**
Bowl, Pease, ftd, old varnish, 4⅜x4½" **120.00**
Bowl, poplar, worn blk & red stripes on ext, 4x20" **125.00**
Bowl, poplar, worn patina w/red traces, 11x29" **385.00**
Box, salt; pine, hinged lid, curved-up bk w/hanging hole **70.00**
Bucket, grease; cvd from 1-pc pine, strap holds lid, 10½" **130.00**
Bucket, sap; dk tin bands, orig mustard pnt, 9½x12", EX **95.00**
Bucket, staved, bail hdl, old bl-gray pnt, 6¼x8¾" **45.00**
Bucket, staved, dk tin bands, wire bail hdl, 5¾x6¾" **42.00**
Butter paddle, ash burl w/G figure, 8½" **300.00**
Butter paddle, birch, curved flat bowl, hook-end hdl, 9¾" **95.00**
Butter paddle, cherry wood, hand cvd, oblong, 4" hdl **50.00**
Butter paddle, curly maple, dished curved blade, 9¾" **250.00**

Butter paddle, curly maple, hook-end hdl, rfn, 8¾" **165.00**
Butter paddle, maple w/some curl, bird's-head hdl, 10" **225.00**
Butter paddle, pine, cvd, wide rnd shoulder, hook hdl **35.00**
Butter paddle, primitive, 10½" **25.00**
Butter roller, trn wood, vining decor, soft patina, 14" **226.00**
Cake/cookie press, 2 sqs: washer lady/dogs jump hoops, 6½" **175.00**
Cheese drainer, cradle shape, pegged sides, 1840s **245.00**
Cookie board, hardwood, 12 designs, minor damage, 3⅜x13½" .**195.00**
Cookie board, hardwood w/tin border, 3 coiled snakes, 7x10" **120.00**
Cookie board, walnut, 15 designs including Masonic, 6x10" **85.00**
Cookie mold, cherry, 4 ovals w/rabbit/bird/etc, 3⅝x4¾" **165.00**
Cookie mold, cherry, 6 rectangles w/crown/rabbit/etc, 3x6" **165.00**
Cookie mold, maple, 4 rectangles w/sheaf/berry/etc, 4½x5¼" **165.00**
Cookie mold, poplar, flower urns & dog w/tree, 3⅝x5" **195.00**
Cookie mold, poplar, 4 rectangles w/fish/basket/etc, 3⅜x4" **150.00**
Cookie mold, poplar, 8 rectangles w/snake/flower/etc, 3x7⅝" **110.00**
Cookie mold, 6 circles w/lady/animals/etc, cherry, 4¼x6⅝" **275.00**
Cookie roller/meat pounder, maple, 2½" dia, 14" L **45.00**
Cutting board, pig shape, worn red pnt, 9¼x7¼" **35.00**
Dipper, maple w/some curl, 9¼" **105.00**
Firkin, bentwood swing hdl, 10¾x11⅜" **175.00**
Firkin, copper tacks in bands, swing hdl, 9½x9¾" **150.00**
Firkin, staved, old red pnt, w/lid, 14½x15" **195.00**
Firkin, staves w/split sapling bands, old red pnt, 5¾x6¾" **150.00**
Jar, bulbous, old varnish, 3¾" **170.00**
Jar, Pease, bulbous, ftd, old varnish, 4⅞" **240.00**
Jar, Pease, bulbous, varnish, wire bail w/wood hdl, 3⅜" **440.00**
Jar, Pease, from 2¼" to 3", graduated set of 4 ....**726.00**
Jar, Pease, ftd, old varnish, sm crack in lid, 2½" **65.00**
Jar, Pease, ftd, old varnish, 5¼" **138.00**
Jar, Pease, old varnish w/red pnt on bottom, bail hdl, 9½" **990.00**
Jar, poplar w/orig red sponged flame graining, 7½" **535.00**
Measure, bentwood, tin bands, 7" dia **40.00**
Measure, dbl staved, dk tin bands, peck & half peck, G **110.00**
Noggin, age crack, rfn, 5" **35.00**
Noggin, rfn, 10¾" **75.00**
Paddle, burl, worn natural patina, 13½" **60.00**
Peal, pine, 13" oval shape w/8" thick hdl **110.00**
Rolling pin, cookie; narrow grooves, stationary hdls, 12" **50.00**
Rolling pin, hdl up sides & across top, sm 8¼" roller **290.00**
Rolling pin, maple, rnd knob hdl 1 end, 1880s, 1-pc, 18½" **40.00**
Rolling pin, springerle, 12 designs, 5¾" roller, 3¾" hdls **150.00**
Rolling pin, walnut, cvd floral & foliage, trn hdls, 12" **160.00**
Scoop, bird's-eye maple, old rfn, 8½" **45.00**
Scoop, cranberry; flat bottom, 15x10½x5"+12" hdl **220.00**
Scoop, hooded, early nails, old bl-gray pnt, 1850s **140.00**
Scoop, maple, 3-pc, cylinder shaped, old varnish, 12¾" L **80.00**
Sieve, bentwood, laced, no bottom band, fine screen, 13" **36.00**
Slaw board, walnut, head-shape hdl, eye is hanging hole, 20" **500.00**
Thread caddy, Pease, 2 compartments, old varnish, #593 ....**275.00**
Thread caddy, Pease, 2 compartments, old varnish, 6" **200.00**
Trencher, early, much wear, 10½" **105.00**
Trencher, oblong, EX patina, 18x10⅝x3¾" **160.00**
Trencher, some wear, 3x9x17" **140.00**

Woodworking Machinery

Vintage cast-iron woodworking machines are monuments to the highly skilled engineers, foundrymen, and machinists who devised them, thus making possible the mass production of items ranging from clothespins, boxes, and barrels to decorative moldings and furniture. Though attractive from a nostalgic viewpoint, many of these machines are bought by the hobbyist and professional alike, to be put into actual use — at far less cost than new equipment. Many worth-assessing factors must be considered; but as a general rule, a machine in good condition is worth about 65¢ a pound (excluding motors). A machine needing a lot of restoration is not worth more than 35¢ a pound, while one professionally rebuilt and with a warranty can be calculated at $1.10 a pound. Modern, new machinery averages over $3.00 a pound. Two of the best sources of information on purchasing or selling such machines are *Vintage Machines — Searching for the Cast Iron Classics*, by Tom Howell, and *Used Machines and Abused Buyers* by Chuck Seidel from *Fine Woodworking*, November/December 1984. Prices quoted are for machines in good condition, less motors and accessories. Our advisor for this category is Mr. Dana Martin Batory; he is listed in the Directory under Ohio. No phone calls, please.

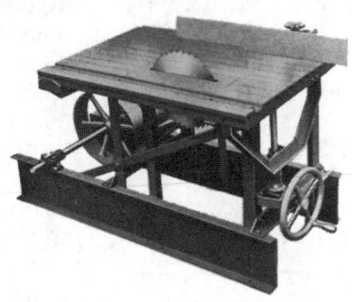

Parks 'Champion' 24" rip and cut-off saw, ca 1925, $350.00.

American Saw Mill Machinery Company, 1931

Band saw, Monarch Line, #X25, 30" built-in ball-bearing motor .770.00
Jointer, Monarch Line, #XII, ball bearing, 12" 1,040.00
Jointer, Monarch Line, ball-bearing bench, 8" 475.00
Mortiser, Monarch Line, #XI, hollow chisel, motorized 345.00
Planer, Monarch Line, single surface, 30" 2,600.00
Sander, Monarch Line, #X8, ball-bearing drum & disk 560.00
Table saw, Monarch Line, Universal, ball bearing, 14" 1,140.00

Blue Star Products, 1939

Band saw, #1200, 12" floor model 85.00
Drill press, #500, 12" bench model 30.00
Lathe, #1001, 72" bed, 12" swing 60.00
Table saw, #800, 8" 95.00

Boice-Crane Power Tools, 1937

Band saw, #800, 14" 100.00
Jointer, #950, 4" 50.00
Lathe, #1100, gap bed 50.00
Table saw, #1500, tilting arbor, 10" 100.00

Crescent Machine Company, 1921

Band saw, 36" 975.00
Mortiser, hollow chisel 525.00
Table saw, cut-off; 16" 550.00
Universal Wood-Worker #59, 5 machines in 1 ....2,050.00

Defiance Machine Works, 1910

Band saw, 28" 520.00
Planer, 4-roll, single surface, 24" 1,300.00
Table saw, #2, hand feed, 20" 650.00

Table saw, #2, power feed, 20" 1,100.00

Gallmeyer & Livingston Company, 1927

Band saw, Union, 20" 390.00
Combination, Union #86, Universal 8" saw/6" jointer 340.00
Jointer, Union, motor on arbor, 8" 370.00
Shaper, Union, dbl spindle 780.00
Table saw, Union #7, 7" 210.00

G.N. Goodspeed Company, 1876

Boring machine, upright 225.00
Planer, New & Improved, Pony, 24" 900.00
Sawing & boring machine 200.00
Table saw, 12" 200.00

Greenlee Bros. & Company, 1925

Borer, #355, single spindle, vertical 520.00
Mortiser, #225, hollow chisel 750.00
Swing saw, #445, belt driven, heavy, 40" 975.00
Table saw, #478, dbl arbor, 18" 1,625.00
Tenoner, #530, sash, door & cabinet, ball bearing 1,530.00

Hoyt & Brother Company, 1888

Band scroll & resawing machine, #1194, 20" 1,700.00
Boring machine, Universal, vertical, single spindle 360.00
Dovetailing machine, 13" 490.00
Jointer, Perfection, 8" 450.00
Planer, matcher & surfacer, New Combined, #2, 24" 5,200.00
Planer & polishing machine, 42" 2,600.00
Planing & matching machine, #7, 13" 3,250.00
Saw, cut-off; swing, 14" 260.00
Scroll saw, #1 ....300.00
Shingle machine, Grand Mogul, 2-block, automatic feed 2,210.00
Table saw, #2, 14" 800.00
Tenoning machine, #2 ....650.00
Universal Wood-Worker, 5 machines in 1 ....1,500.00
Wood shaper, dbl spindle 850.00

J. D. Wallace & Company, 1940

Band saw, 16" 210.00
Grinder & sander, disk; Wonder, 12" 100.00
Grinder & sander, disk; Wonder, 16" 165.00
Grinder & sander, spindle; Wonder 150.00
Jointer, 4" 15.00
Jointer, 6" 65.00
Lathe, 6x24" 115.00
Saw, circular (table saw); Universal, 7" 75.00
Saw, circular; plain, 7" 65.00

L. Power & Company, 1888

Mortiser & borer, #2 ....780.00
Planer & matcher (combined), #5, 24" 5,525.00
Shaper, single spindle, reversible 585.00
Table saw, self feed, 14" 715.00

Ober Manufacturing Company, 1889

Rip saw, self feed, 14" 725.00

Saw, swing cut-off, 18" 275.00
Shaper, saw & jointer combination 400.00

Oliver Machinery Company, 1922

Band saw, #17, 30" 925.00
Sander, vertical & disk, #34, 24" 1,475.00
Shaper, #483, high speed, dbl spindle 1,300.00
Table saw, #32, Variety, 12" 500.00

Parks Ball Bearing Machine Company, 1925

Band saw, H-62, Jewel, 22" 250.00
Planer, H-117, Endurance, 20" 950.00
Sander, H-139, Peerless, flexible belt 650.00
Saw, H-97, swing cut-off, Alert, 12" 225.00

P.B. Yates Machine Company, 1917

Jointer, #199, 12" 1,235.00
Planer, #160, dbl surface, 20" 5,000.00
Rip saw, #255, self feed, circular, 20" 1,235.00
Saw, #232, swing cut-off, 16" 260.00

S.A. Woods Machine Company, 1876

Circular resawing machine, Joslin's Improved, 50" 2,275.00
Molding machine, #1, 2-roll, 12" 2,275.00
Planer, panel; Improved, 20" 520.00
Planer, Pat Improved, shop surface, 30" 1,430.00

Sprunger Power Tools, 1950s

Band saw, 14" 60.00
Jigsaw, 20" 40.00
Lathe, gap bed, 10" 50.00
Table saw, tilt arbor, 10¼" 75.00

Worcester Porcelain Company

The Worcester Porcelain Company was deeded in 1751. During the first or Dr. Wall period (so called for one of its proprietors), porcelain with an Oriental influence was decorated in underglaze blue. Useful tablewares represented the largest portion of production, but figurines and decorative items were also made. Very little of the earliest wares were marked and can only be identified by a study of forms, glazes, and the porcelain body, which tends to transmit a greenish cast when held to light. Late in the fifties, a crescent mark was in general use, and rare examples bare a facsimile of the Meissen crossed swords. The first period ended in 1783, and the company went through several changes in ownership during the next eighty years. The years from 1783-1792 are referred to as the Flight period. Marks were a small crescent, a crown with 'Royal,' or an impressed 'Flight.' From 1792-1807 the company was known as Flight and Barr and used the trademark 'F&B' or 'B,' with or without a small cross. From 1807-1813 the company was under the Barr, Flight, and Barr management; this era is recognized as having produced porcelain with the highest quality of artistic decoration. Their mark was 'B.F.B.' From 1813-1840 many marks were used, but the most usual was 'F.B.B.' under a crown to indicate Flight, Barr, and Barr. In 1840 the firm merged with Chamberlain, and in 1852 they were succeeded by Kerr and Binns. The firm became known as Royal Worcester in 1862. The production was then marked with a circle with '51' within and a crown on top. The date of manufacture was incised into the bottom or

stamped with a letter of the alphabet, just under the circle. In 1891 Royal Worcester England was added to the circle and crown. From that point on each piece is dated with a code of dots or other symbols. After 1891 most wares had a blush color ground. Prior to that date it was ivory. Most shapes were marked with a unique number.

During the early years they produced considerable ornamental wares with a Persian influence. This gave way to a Japanesque influence. James Hadley is most responsible for the Victorian look. He is considered the 'best ever' designer and modeller. He was joined by the finest porcelain painters. Together they produced pieces with very fine detail and exquisite painting and decoration. Figures, vases and tableware were produced in great volume and are highly collectible. During the 1890s they allowed the artists to sign some of their work. Pieces signed on the face by the Stintons, Baldwyn, Davis, Raby, Austin, Powell, Sedgley and Rushton (not a complete list) are in great demand. The company is still in production. There is an outstanding museum on the company grounds in Worcester, England.

The advisors on this category are Henry and Geneva Tyler in Florida. Note: most pieces had lids or tops (if there is a flat area on the top lip, chances are it had one), if missing deduct 30 to 40%.

Bottle, scent; pansies in yel/purple w/gold, rnd, 4" 250.00
Bough pot, reserve w/Venus & Cupid, w/gold, Chamberlain, 7x9" ..825.00
Bowl, florals w/in & w/out, shell form w/hdl, 6½" 200.00
Candlesticks, bamboo shoot w/stalk hdl, floral/gilt, 6", pr 275.00
Cornucopia, flower form, leaf base, gold satin, #891C, 4x3¾" 115.00
Creamer, floral sprays, gold, 4" 120.00
Cup & saucer, demi; loose bl netting, gold stork/butterfly 750.00
Cup & saucer, frogs/snake 2-tone relief w/gilt, 1882, 6½" 275.00
Ewer, allover florals/gold, lizard hdl, 1883, 11½x6" 750.00
Ewer, floral sprays, rtcl rim/hdl, gold collar, 11" 700.00
Ewer, floral/gilt, rtcl bulbous neck, ornate hdl, 10" 750.00
Figurine, Parula Warblers on Sweet Bay Flowers, #3536/#3537 ..800.00
Figurine, Yellow-Headed Blackbirds on Spider Wart, pr 1,300.00
Figurines, Evening Dew/Morning Dew, ca 1892, 16½", pr 2,900.00
Flower holder, toad on branch entwined w/snake, bl/wht, 7" 685.00
Ice jug, tusk hdls, ca 1895, 10" 450.00
Jug, owl on branch, moonlit sky, serpent hdl, ca 1885, 11¼" 935.00
Lamp, mc floral w/gold, scroll hdls, 17" to top of harp 175.00
Mortuary urn, gilt swans, #1256, ca 1889 ....3,400.00
Pitcher, cobalt w/floral, lg gargoyle as hdl, 13" 280.00
Plate, hunt scene, gr/red/gold leaf border, 1800, 9¾" 145.00
Plate, Tewkesbury village scene, Nickolls, 1953, 10¾" 225.00
Tray, flora/gilt, 3-section, scalloped, central hdl, 11" 235.00
Vase, allover rtcl leaf work, 4x2¾" 400.00
Vase, bird in flight on beige w/blk enameling, Hadley, 4" 375.00
Vase, daisies/wisteria/gilt, sqd ornate hdls, long neck, 12" 500.00
Vase, dolphin top, raised gilt on decor, shape #13, 1890s, 15" 975.00
Vase, florals w/gold, appl rope & bow, 1886 mk, 6x5½" 350.00
Vase, florals/thistles/gilt, trumpet neck/base, hdls, 11" 750.00
Vase, flying swans on bl, Baldwyn, #1572, ca 1904, 10½" 4,000.00
Vase, gilt flowers, angle hdls, #1071, ca 1888 ....2,500.00
Vase, lg owl, spherical w/sm hdls at stick neck, 7", pr 700.00
Vase, lilacs w/gold, rtcl, hdls, #1200, 13½x7" 1,075.00
Vase, parrots, gold on mc ground, rtcl hdls, 16½x7" 2,900.00
Vase, pierced cherubs masks, hawk support, w/lid, #G/11, 9" 495.00
Vase, Sabrina, fish, lt bl on shaded cobalt, cylinder, 5" 165.00
Vase, shell on gilt seaweed support, rnd base, 8½" 325.00
Vase, thistles & flowers on yel, scroll hdls, ftd, 16" 1,400.00

World's Fairs and Expos

Since 1851 and the Crystal Palace Exhibition in London, World's

Fairs and Expositions have taken place at a steady pace. Many of them commemorate historical events. The 1904 Louisiana Purchase Exposition, commonly known as the St. Louis World's Fair, celebrated the 100th anniversary of the Louisiana Purchase agreement between Thomas Jefferson and Napoleon in 1803. The 1893 Columbian Exposition, known as The Chicago World's Fair, commemorated the 400th anniversary of the discovery of America by Columbus in 1492. (Both of these fairs were held one year later than originally scheduled.) The multitude of souvenirs from these and similar events have become a growing area of interest to collectors in recent years. Many items have a 'crossover' interest into other fields: i.e., collectors of postcards and souvenir spoons eagerly search for those from various fairs and expositions. For additional information collectors may contact World's Fairs Collectors Society (WFCS), whose address is in the Directory under Clubs, Newsletters, and Catalogs, or our advisor, D.D. Woollard, Jr. His address is listed in the Directory under Missouri.

Key:
T&P — Trylon & Perisphere   WF — World's Fair

1876 Centennial, Philadelphia

Bandanna, Centennial; linen, mc buildings, 26x26" 150.00
Bird's-eye view, buildings identified, 17½x28" 50.00
Cake plate, glass, Declaration of Independence 1776-1876, 10" ...50.00
Half dollar, wht metal, Liberty Bell/Independence, M 20.00
Medal, wht metal, 1st in War, 1st in Peace..., EX in box 16.00
Ribbon, silk, Father of Our country..., mc, 10", EX 48.00
Slipper, frosted glass, Expo mk, Gillinder, 6" 70.00
Ticket, admission; overprinted 50¢ 10.00
View book, Centennial Pocket Album, red/blk/gold cover, EX 25.00

1893 Columbian, Chicago

Charm, gold-plated brass, bust of Cleveland & Expo mks, rnd 35.00
Cup, china, Government Building, England, 2½" 60.00
Guide, Official; illus, 192-pg 20.00
Handkerchief, mc embr on blk silk, 13x14", EX 50.00
Medal, aluminum, Landing of Columbus/Discovery of Am, EX 15.00
Napkin ring, wht metal, World's Fair '93 Chicago, EX 20.00
Paperweight, glass, Machinery Hall, rectangular 25.00
Plate, china, To Castille & Leon...1492, mc, 9", EX 50.00
Plate, Machinery Building, Wedgwood china, 8½" 55.00
Playing cards, Columbian Souvenir, complete deck 100.00
Postcard, Official Souvenir, Goldsmith 15.00
Razor, Columbian Expo Chicago 1893, blk hdl, MIG, EX 75.00
Ribbon, woven silk, Machinery Hall, orig bk, 2¼x7½" 150.00
Scarf, silk, Viking Ship Souvenir 1893 embr, 17", VG 25.00
Spoon, SP, Administration Building in bowl, Leonard 10.00
Stickpin, gold-tone metal, I Will, EX 25.00
Table scarf, red & wht linen, 23x39", EX 50.00
Ticket, Chicago Day, w/stub 17.50
Tray, lead, Landing of Columbus, 8x5½", EX 25.00
Tumbler, clear glass w/frosted Administration Building, 3½" 40.00
Watch case opener, nickel, Keystone Watch Case Co, NM 20.00

1898 Trans-Mississippi

Pin-bk button, Iowa Day, celluloid, 1¼" 30.00
Pin-bk button, PA Day, celluloid, 1¾" 40.00
Spoon, SP, Administration Building, 5½" 35.00

1901 Pan American

Miniature frying pan, brass, Meet Me At..., lid pops open, EX 28.00

Paperweight, glass, Temple of Music, faded 25.00
Pin-bk, mc celluloid, MO Pan-Am Expo Buffalo 1901..., EX 20.00
Playing cards, Official Pan-Am..., bridge deck, EX in box 50.00
Pocket mirror, celluloid, Electric Tower, 2¼" 60.00
Ribbon, woven silk, Electric Tower, 3½x5" 55.00
Token, aluminum, World's Great Wonder Niagara Falls, EX 7.50
Tumbler, juice; crystal, Pan-Am Expo & buffalo etch, gold rim ...18.00

1904 St. Louis

Booklet, Singer Story of Louisiana Purchase, mc cover, 20-pg 10.00
Case, cigar; leather cover w/burned-in design, 3¼x5¼", EX 25.00
Measure, celluloid, Cascade WF...1904, sepia toned, EX 35.00

Mug, General Grant's log cabin transfer, $75.00.

Paperweight, clear glass, mc scene, Pat'd Oct 2, 1866, EX 60.00
Paperweight, seashells in glass 20.00
Pocketknife, aluminum fr, 2-blade, Liberal Arts Building, EX 50.00
Postcard, woven silk, Cascade Gardens, fr, M 250.00
Razor, hard rubber hdl w/Horticulture Building engr, rpr, EX 40.00
Ribbon, silk, Festival Hall..., blk & wht transfer, 10¾x5¼" 35.00
Stein, stoneware, Balance of Electricity, ½-liter, M 300.00
Tip tray, aluminum, Souvenir of..., mc litho, MIG, 3x5" 26.00
Token, brass, Palace of Liberal Arts, NM 20.00
Toothpick holder, ceramic, cream & orange, 2¼", EX 36.00

1905 Lewis and Clark

Handkerchief, cotton, Foreign Exhibits Building embr, 14½" 10.00
Medal, brass, Louis & Clark Centennial... in wreath, EX 75.00
Pin-back button, celluloid, Sighting the Pacific, 1½" 35.00
Poster stamps, sheet of 12 ....17.50
Token, Louis & Clark, map of Louisiana, EX 24.00

1907 Jamestown

Guide, Jamestown, Williamsburg & Yorktown, 1607-1907, 48-pg, EX ..12.50
Mandolin harp, Special Jamestown Model..., Schmidt, EX 150.00
Plate, tin, John Smith & Pocahontas, mc pnt, 10", EX 110.00
Program, Kiralfy's Pocahontas, 16-pg, EX 10.00
Watch fob, NP, oval, strap type 35.00

1909 Alaska Yukon Pacific

Pin tray, base metal, Fine Arts Building, scalloped, 5½x4" 15.00
Pin tray, copper-plated base metal, scalloped, 4¼" dia 10.00
Postcard, mc, Carnation Milk, Gr Grass Year 'Round..., EX 20.00
Scarf, magenta silk, various buildings, 19" sq, EX 40.00

1915 Panama Pacific

Badge, celluloid, Admit One, Opening Day..., w/ribbon 25.00
Cent, elongated, Administration Building, 1¼", VG 10.00
Photo folder, Official Souvenir #12, 22 mc views, unused 12.50
Postcard, ship scene, opens to sz of 4, NM 8.00
Tin, Ridgway's Tea, mc fair views, 4x4x6", EX 50.00
View book, Official, mini 12.50

1926 Sesquicentennial

Badge, bar; brass, Welcome Great Council of Penna, w/ribbon 10.00
Badge, employee; brass w/blk enamel, EX 55.00
Bank, CI, Proclaim Liberty...1776-1926, 3½", EX 40.00
Compact, brass w/red & gr glass stones, fair mks, oval, EX 88.00
Ribbon, silk, 150 Yrs of Am Independence, 6x4", EX 88.00
Tapestry, mc woven cloth, patriotic images, 1926, 24x48", EX 80.00

1933 Chicago

Ashtray, glass & rubber tire form, Firestone, 5½" 37.00
Bank, tin litho, Am Can Co 25.00
Book, Official Guide, illus, 1933, 176-pg 15.00
Book, Our Trip Through Fields, blk & wht, 47-pg, EX 10.00
Bookmark, brass w/bl enamel, Federal & States...Sky Ride, 4½" 5.00
Cane, wood w/brass tag, Century of Progress..., 36" 15.00
Litho, bird's-eye view, mc, 10x51" 60.00
Map, Chicago & Century of Progress, Std Oil, mc, EX 10.00
Parasol, paper & wood, red/wht/bl, 1933 Chicago, 24", EX 22.50
Pencil, Eagle Automatic, bl & silver, 10½", MIB 20.00
Plate, ceramic, Ft Dearborn, bl on wht, Pickard, 7¾" sq 30.00
Playing cards, comet logo, complete deck 30.00
Poster, Go! Century of Progress..., red/gr/blk/wht, 13x19", EX 40.00
Ring, sterling silver, Century of Progress, adjustable band 30.00
Tapestry, mc woven cloth, Ft Dearborn, Chicago WF 1933, 19" sq .55.00
Tie clip, comet logo 15.00
Wallet, leather, gold stamped, w/ID card & 1934 calendar, NM ..12.50

1939 New York

Bank, mc pnt on wht metal, Underwood Typewriter Co, 2½", EX ..36.00
Book, Official Guide, illus, 256-pg 20.00
Cake server, SP, NY WF 1939 & Washington on hdl, 10", EX 32.50
Fish knife, 5" mc Lucite hdl w/4" stainless blades, WF mk, EX 45.00
Hat, lady's uniform; bl & orange cloth, patch on front, EX 25.00
Jacket, police; blk gabardine, WF Expo buttons, EX 120.00
Lamp base, ceramic, T&P shape, Made in England 100.00
Pin-bk, celluloid, Employee's Friend, bl/wht/orange, EX 10.00
Playing cards, complete deck, M, sealed 40.00
Sheet music, Yours for a Song, T&P pictured 30.00
Swizzle stick, cobalt glass, Brass Rail (restaurant), 6" 6.00

1939 San Francisco

Bookmark, butterfly form, yel on acetate w/paper, M in pkg 25.00
Comb, amber plastic in gold-tone case w/brass medallion, EX 30.00
Compact, brushed brass, Golden Gate Internat'l Expo eng, MIB .30.00
Pillow sham, mc fair views, 17", sq, EX 18.00
Token, aluminum, Road of Streamliners & Challengers, EX 8.00
Wallet, leather w/WF mk & sailing ship, VG 20.00

1962 Seattle

Bottle opener, steel w/mc enamel, Space Needle, MIB 15.00

Scarf, silk, fair images & Space Needle, mc, 30" sq, VG 5.00
Tray, mc pnt on tin, fair scenes & Space Needle, 11" dia 3.50

1964 New York

Booklet, Look's Guide to NY WF, color map, 34-pg, EX 5.00
Magazine, Nat'l Geographics, World's Fair in NY Reopens, EX 5.00
Paperweight, base metal, Unisphere, US Steel, 2½x5½" 5.00
Postcard mailer, Unisphere on cover, 14 mc views, M 3.00
Record, Triumph of Man, orig record jacket, EX 15.00
Tray, copper plated, 9 fair buildings & scenes, 6x4½" 10.00
Tray, metal, Unisphere, mc pnt, 11¾", EX 10.00

Wright, Frank Lloyd

Born in Richland Center, Wisconsin, in 1869, Wright became a pioneer in architectural expression, developing a style referred to as 'prairie.' From early in the century until he died in 1959, he designed houses with whose rooms were open, rather than divided by walls in the traditional manner. They exhibited low, horizontal lines and strongly projecting eaves, and he filled them with furnishings whose radical aesthetics complemented the structures to perfection. Several of his homes have been preserved to the present day, and collectors who admire his ideas and the unique, striking look he achieved treasure the stained glass windows, furniture, chinaware, lamps, and other decorative accessories made by Wright.

Chairs, barrel style, refinished, ca 1906, 29x21x18", VG, $3,500.00 each.

Cabinet, #2008, Taliesan trim, 28x20x22", VG 900.00
Chest, #2000, 6 drw+2 doors, Taliesan trim, 52x37", EX 1,500.00
Coffee table, slate top on cruciform base, no mk, 36" dia 1,200.00
Dresser, #2001, w/open shelving unit #2006, rfn, 76x62", VG .5,000.00
Dresser, #2001, 65", w/mirror #2003, EX 1,500.00
Headboard, #2001, Taliesan trim, king-sz, EX 1,100.00
Lounge chairs, #2001, uphl seat/octagonal bk, 28", EX, pr 500.00
Print, Wasmuth #XVII, house, ext & floor plan, sgn, 25x16" 750.00
Sofa, Taliesan design to base, 101", VG 950.00
Table, #452-C, sq top/base, Taliesan edge, rfn, 12x26x26", EX .2,000.00
Table, side; #2000, top shelf rests on center divider, EX 700.00
Table, slate top, cruciform base w/Taliesan trim, 22" dia 1,300.00
Window, geometrics in wht/red/clear, 33x16", EX 2,900.00

Wrought Iron

Until the middle of the 19th century, almost all the metal hand forged in America was made from a material called wrought iron. When wrought iron rusts it appears grainy, while the mild steel that was used later shows no grain but pits to an orange-peel surface. This is an important aid in determining the age of an ironwork piece.

Candle stand, tripod base, OH, 62½" 300.00
Chain, hook ea end, ca 1800s, 62" 70.00
Dipper, tooled date of 1845 on hdl, polished, 10½" 75.00
Dipper & fork, 19", pr 45.00
Fork, brass & copper inlay w/tooling, 16½" 200.00
Fork, 2-tine, wraparound loop w/teardrop opening, 1870s, 21" 55.00
Fork, 3-tine, GD Miller stamp on hdl, 25" 77.50
Fork, 3-tine claw, flattened ribbon hdl w/eye, 17¾" 100.00
Hinges, ram's horn scroll, 16", pr 140.00
Latch hdl, leaf ends, missing thumb pc, 12" 28.00
Meat hook, crown hanger w/5 hooks, twist detail, 22" H 275.00
Pan, fireplace; arched hdl w/iron loop at arch top, 14" dia 70.00
Peel, ram's horn hdl, 46½" 105.00
Peel, ram's horn hdl, 48" L 160.00
Poker, open-work heart at end, ca 1900, 14¾" 85.00
Rack, scrolls & 5 hooks, hangs, 18x18" 185.00
Skillet, primitive, pitted, 9½" dia, 11" hdl 15.00
Spatula & fork, hdls w/eng florals & initials, ea: 10½" 450.00
Spider, hook hdl terminal, 3-legged, 8½x12", L: 36" 85.00
Tasting ladle, brass floral inlay, hook hdl, 10" 160.00
Thumb latch, ornate top plate, leaf-shape bottom plate, PA, 12" .125.00
Trammel, sawtooth, some pitting, 48" 220.00
Wafer iron, detailed crucifix, August Kopf...1795, 30" 55.00

Yellow Ware

Ranging in color from buff to deep mustard, yellow ware which almost always has a clear glaze can be slip banded, plain, Rockingham decorated, flint enamel glazed, or mocha decorated. Mocha-decorated pieces are usually the most expensive and desirable. The majority of pieces are plain and do not bear a manufacturer's mark. Yellow ware which was primarily produced in the United States, England, and Canada was popular from the mid-19th century to the early 20th century. A utilitarian ware, it was first domestically produced in New York, New Jersey, Pennsylvania, and Vermont. With more than thirty active potteries, East Liverpool, Ohio, became the center for yellow ware production. After experiencing several years of dramatic price increases, the market has begun to stabilize. Note: Because this was a utilitarian type of everyday pottery, yellow ware is often found with signs of heavy use and damage; this would of course decrease its value. For further information we recommend *Collecting Yellow Ware, An Identification and Value Guide*, written by our advisor, John Michel, and Lisa S. McAllister. Mr. Michel's address is in the Directory under New York.

Jar, seaweed and blue rings, 4¾", $375.00; Mug, green seaweed and rings, 3½", $210.00.

Bowl, batter; emb decor, wht int, JE Jeffords Phila 165.00
Bowl, mixing; seaweed on wht, 4x8" 265.00
Bowl, tea; 2 wide wht bands, US, 1850-90, 6" dia 125.00

Chamber pot, wht band, 1850s 95.00
Colander, multi-banded in bl, 13" 700.00
Cup, measure; Spearpoint & Flower, Ohio, 1890-1920, 6" 250.00
Custard cup, 3 bl bands, early 1900s, 3¼x3⅛" 27.50
Fish flask, English, 10½" L 1,500.00
Foot warmer, wedge shape, 1800s 275.00
Inkwell, dbl, dog-head lids 235.00
Jar, canning; w/lid, 5", NM 155.00
Ladle, rare, 10", minimum value 750.00
Mold, dmn shape, mini 175.00
Mold, ear of corn, octagonal, 6" L 110.00
Mold, heart shape, mini 245.00
Mold, melon shape, mini 200.00
Mold, parrot on branch, 4-lobed sides, late 1800s, 10x8" 525.00
Mold, pinwheel 100.00
Mug, narrow brn & wht bands 225.00
Mug, seaweed band in bl, brn band border, 3x4" 325.00
Mug, wht band, ribbed strap hdl, 3⅞" 125.00
Mug, wht bands, unmk, 1850s 95.00
Mustard pot, 2 bl incised bands, 4½" 345.00
Pepper pot, bl mocha decor 650.00
Pepper pot, wht & bl bands 550.00
Pie plate, 13" 125.00
Pie plate, 8" 75.00
Pie plate colander, 13" 500.00
Pitcher, brn sponging, minor wear, 5½" 75.00
Pitcher, lovebirds emb medallion, Midwestern, ca 1900 ....525.00
Pitcher, Morning Glory & Basketweave, Midwestern, ca 1900 ..200.00
Pitcher, peacock relief, Midwestern, ca 1900, scarce 525.00
Pitcher, slip decor, lift lug, 1860-90, 10" 465.00
Pitcher, slip dots form flowers, slip bands, Midwestern, 1900s 150.00
Plate, bread; Westward Expansion, 6¼" 150.00
Plate, dinner; Western Expansion, 11" 225.00
Plate, salad; Westward Expansion, 8¾" 175.00
Spice jar, emb wheat, 3¾" 195.00
Teapot, tapered hexagon, 6" 215.00

Zanesville Art Pottery

In 1900 the Zanesville Roofing Tile Company changed its name to the Zanesville Art Pottery Company and began the manufacture of standard-glaze art pottery as well as cobalt blue jardinieres. David Schmidt (1847-1922) was president of the concern during its twenty years of operation, and Albert Radford was general manager for a short time around 1901. The plant burned in 1901, possibly due to arson, and again in 1910 but was rebuilt both times. In 1920 the plant was sold to S.A. Weller and became Weller Plant No. 3. All identified pieces of the company's art pottery are impressed 'La Moro' with a shape number. Our advisor for this category is James L. Murphy; he is listed in the Directory under Ohio.

Vase, poppies, standard glaze, sgn M Gray, cylindrical, 15" 330.00
Vase, roses, emb leaves, standard glaze, #844, 7½" 175.00

Zanesville Glass

Glassware was produced in Zanesville, Ohio, from as early as 1815 until 1851. Two companies produced clear and colored hollowware pieces in five characteristic patterns: 1) diamond faceted, 2) broken swirls, 3) vertical swirls, 4) perpendicular fluting, 5) plain, with scalloped or fluted rims and strap handles. The most readily identified product is perhaps the whiskey bottles made in the vertical swirl pattern, often called globular swirls because of their full, round bodies. Their necks vary in width; some have a ringed rim and some are collared. They were made in several colors; amber, light green, and light aquamarine are the most common. Our advisor for this category is Mark Vuono; he is listed in the Directory under Connecticut.

Chestnut-shaped Grandfather's flask, golden amber, twenty-four broken-rib pattern swirled to the right, open pontil, sheared lip, 8⅛", NM, $950.00.

Bottle, amber, blown, 24 swirled ribs, globular, stain, 7½" **415.00**
Bottle, aqua, 24-rib broken swirl, club shape, 8¼" **110.00**
Bottle, aqua w/HP florals, 24 swirled ribs, 7½" **85.00**
Bottle, golden amber, 24-rib left swirl, globular, 7⅝" **500.00**
Bottle, med amber, 24-rib right swirl, globular, 8½" **425.00**
Flask, chestnut; amber, 24 vertical ribs, 4⅝" **330.00**

Zell

The Georg Schmider United Zell Ceramic Factories has a long and colorful history. Affectionately called 'Zell' by those who are attracted to this charming German-Dutch type tin-glazed earthenware, this ware came into production in the latter part of the last century.

Typical scenes are set against lush green backgrounds with windmills on the distant horizon. Into the scenes appear typically garbed girls (long dresses with long white aprons and lowland bonnet-headgear) being teased or admired by little boys attired in pantaloon-type trousers and short rust-colored jackets. There are variations on this theme and occasionally a collector may even find an animal motif or even a Kate Greenaway-like decoration.

While Zell produced a wide range of wares and even quite recently (1970s) introduced an entirely hand-painted hen/rooster ware; it is this early charming German-Dutch theme ware that is coveted and collected by increasing numbers of devoted collectors. Our advisors for this category are Fred and Lila Shrader; they are listed in the Directory under California.

Bowl, boy & girl strolling, 4"+tab hdls **45.00**
Bowl, vegetable; 2 boys near road, harbor beyond, 9½" **85.00**
Cup, boy skulking down road, 4" H, 12-oz **50.00**
Cup & saucer, 2 sm girls, doll sz **55.00**
Tumbler, boy w/smoking pipe strolling down path, 6-oz **40.00**

Zsolnay

Only until the past decade has the production of the Zsolnay factory become more correctly understood. In the beginning they produced only cement; industrial and kitchen ware manufacture began in the 1850s, and in the early 1870s a line of decorative architectural and art pottery was initiated which has continued to the present time.

The city of Pecs (pronounced Paach) is the major provincial city of southwest Hungary close to the Yugoslav border. The old German name for the city was Funfkirchen, meaning 'Five Churches.' (The 'five-steeple' mark became the factory's logo in 1878.)

Although most Americans only think of Zsolnay in terms of the bizarre, reticulated examples of the 1880s and '90s and the small 'Eosine' green figures of animals and children that have been produced since the 1920s, the factory went through all the art trends of major international art potteries and produced various types of forms and decorations. The 'golden period,' circa 1895-1920, is when its Art Nouveau (Sezession in Austro-Hungarian terms) examples were unequalled. Vilmos Zsolnay was a Renaissance man devoted to innovation, and his children carried on the tradition after his death in 1900. Important sculptors and artists of the day were employed (usually anonymously) and married into the family, creating a dynasty.

Nearly all Zsolnay is marked, either impressed 'Zsolnay Pecs' or with the 'five steeple' stamp. Variations and form numbers can date a piece fairly accurately. For the most part, the earlier ethnic historical-revival pieces do not bring the prices that the later Sezession and second Sezession (Deco) examples do. Our advisor for this category is John Gacher; he is listed in the Directory under Rhode Island.

Bowl, exotic bird on floral branch w/in, mc irid, 9" **400.00**
Figurine, 2 wrestling bears, gr/bl irid, sgn/1911, 13" **1,265.00**
Jug, thistles/butterflies, purple on gold/brn, mc hdl, 12" **450.00**
Mirror, leaf ea corner, berries around mirror, irid, 21x16" **350.00**
Plaque, cvd scene: man/horse/cart/windmill, irid fr, 10x16" **865.00**

Vase, blue iridescent with draped green spirals, deeply ruffled irregular rim, #4626, ca 1985-86, 12", $550.00.

Vase, bl irid decor on cream, gr/gilt neck, baluster, 3" **500.00**
Vase, gold/bl irid swirl, 1903, 6" **300.00**
Vase, hawk/fruit trees, mc irid, baluster, #36-48-5385, 10" **2,300.00**
Vase, irid, 3-D maid on shoulder, lobed rim, long neck, 9" **175.00**
Vase, irid streaks, sq flared/twisted neck, bulb base, 12" **175.00**
Vase, leaves at base, red irid on bl/gr irid, ribs, rpr, 6½" **375.00**
Vase, maid w/flowing hair/gown hugs cylinder, irid, 17" **2,640.00**
Vase, rtcl outer panels w/pods & frogs, gr irid, 4½" **1,600.00**
Vase, seated satyr & standing maid on shoulder, purple, 18" ...**4,000.00**
Vase, turq/gold w/appl rtcl teardrops, wing hdls, 7½x6½" **80.00**

Advisory Board

The editors and staff take this opportunity to express our sincere gratitude and appreciation to each person who has in any way contributed to the preparation of this guide. We believe the credibility of our book is greatly enhanced through their efforts. See each advisor's Directory listing for information concerning their specific areas of expertise.

You will notice that at the conclusion of some of the narratives the advisor's name is given. This is optional and up to the discretion of each individual. Simply because no name is mentioned does not indicate that we have no advisor for that subject. Our board grows with each issue and now numbers nearly 450; if you care to correspond with any of them or anyone listed in our Directory, you must send a SASE with your letter. If you are seeking an appraisal, first ask about their fee, since many of these people are professionals who must naturally charge for their services. Because of our huge circulation, every person who allows us to publish their name runs the risk of their privacy being invaded by too many phone calls and letters. We are indebted to every advisor and very much regret losing any one of them. By far, the majority of those we lose give that reason. Please help us retain them on our board by observing the simple rules of common courtesy. Take the differences in time zones into consideration; some of our advisors tell us they often get phone calls in the middle of the night. For suggestions that may help you evaluate your holdings, see the Introduction.

AAA Antique Shop
Nappanee, Indiana

Peter Abrahams
Lake Oswego, Oregon

Charles and Barbara Adams
Middleboro, Massachusetts

Jay Adams
Clifton, New Jersey

Geneva D. Addy
Winterset, Iowa

Charles Alexander
Indianapolis, Indiana

Margaret Alves
Shelton, Connecticut

James Anderson
New Brighton, Minnesota

Suzy McLennan Anderson
Holmdel, New Jersey

Tim Anderson
Provo, Utah

Warren R. Anderson
Cedar City, Utah

Norma Angelo
Jamestown, New York

Dorothy Malone Anthony
Fort Scott, Kansas

John Apple
Racine, Wisconsin

Dick and Ellie Archer
St. Augustine, Florida

Una Arnbal
Ames, Iowa

Bruce Austin
Pittsford, New York

Rod Baer
Vienna, Virginia

Wayne and Gale Bailey
Dacula, Georgia

Mrs. Lillian Baker, Fellow IBA,
Cambridge, England
Gardena, California

Roger Baker
Woodside, California

Robert Banks
Brookeville, Maryland

Jim Barker
Bethlehem, Pennsylvania

Kit Barry
Brattleboro, Vermont

Henry Bartsch
Rockaway, Oregon

Mark Bassett
Lakewood, Ohio

Daniel J. Batchelor
Oswego, New York

Dana Martin Batory
Crestline, Ohio

Joyce Bee
Sandy, Oregon

D.R. Beeks
Coeur d'Alene, Idaho

Scott Benjamin
Elyria, Ohio

Phyllis and Tom Bess
Tulsa, Oklahoma

Robert Bettinger
Mt. Dora, Florida

John E. Bilane
Union, New Jersey

Dale Blann
Vincennes, Indiana

Clarence H. Bodine, Jr.
New Hope, Pennsylvania

Sandra V. Bondhus
Unionville, Connecticut

Clifford Boram
Monticello, Indiana

Dick and Waunita Bosworth
Kansas City, Missouri

Jeff Bradfield
Dayton, Virginia

Tom Bradshaw
Ventura, California

Larry Brenner
Manchester, New Hampshire

William J. Brinkley
McLeansboro, Illinois

Mike Brooks
Oakland, California

Jim Broom
Effingham, Illinois

David L. Brown
Victoria, British Columbia, Canada

Rick Brown
Newspaper Collector's Society of
America
Lansing, Michigan

Mike Bruner
Ortonville, Michigan

Nicki Budin
Worthington, Ohio

Robert C. Butz
Newbury Park, California

Jim Calison
Wallkill, New York

Carol and Jim Carlton
Englewood, Colorado

Fran Carter
Coos Bay, Oregon

Tina M. Carter
El Cajon, California

Cerebro
East Prospect, Pennsylvania

Jackie Chamberlain
Wickenburg, Arizona

Mick and Lorna Chase
Cookeville, Tennessee

Pat and Chris Christensen
Costa Mesa, California

Jack Chipman
Venice, California

Debbie and Randy Coe
Hillsboro, Oregon

Wilfred and Dolli Cohen
Santa Ana, California

Richard Cohn
St. Paul, Minnesota

Lillian M. Cole
Flemington, New Jersey

Marilyn Cooper
Houston, Texas

J.W. Courter
Kevil, Kentucky

Susan Cox
El Cajon, California

Rosalind Cranor
Blacksburg, Virginia

Ron Damaska
New Brighton, Pennsylvania

John Danis
Rockford, Illinois

Patricia M. Davis
Wilmington, Delaware

Gael deCourtivron
Sarasota, Florida

Norm Vigue
Stoughton, Massachusetts

Linda L. Vines
Upper Montclair, New Jersey

Stephen Visakay
West Caldwell, New Jersey

Mark Vuono
Stamford, Connecticut

John W. Waddell
Mineral Wells, Texas

Jim Waite
Farmer City, Illinois

John Walter
Marietta, Ohio

Ian Warner
Brampton, Ontario, Canada

Cara Washburn
Osseo, Wisconsin

Maret Webb
Phoenix, Arizona

Marty Webster
Ann Arbor, Michigan

Pastor Frederick S. Weiser
New Oxford, Pennsylvania

BA Wellman
Westminster, Massachusetts

Rosie J. Wells
Canton, Illinois

Kaye and Jim Whitaker
Lynnwood, Washington

John 'Grandpa' White
Denver, Colorado

Douglass White
Orlando, Florida

Margaret and Kenn Whitmyer
Gahanna, Ohio

Steven Whysel
Bentonville, Arkansas

Doug Wiesehan
St. Charles, Missouri

James R. Wilkins
Duncanville, Texas

Juanita Wilkins
Lima, Ohio

Don Williams
Kirksville, Missouri

Neil Williams
Springfield, Massachusetts

Ron L. Willis
Moore, Oklahoma

Roy M. Willis
Lebanon Junction, Kentucky

Jack D. Wilson
Chicago, Illinois

Ralph Winslow
Overland Park, Kansas

Nancy Winston
Northwood, New Hampshire

Jo Ellen Winther
Arvada, Colorado

Raphael C. Wise
West Palm Beach, Florida

D.D. Woollard, Jr.
Bridgeton, Missouri

Bill Wright
New Albany, Indiana

Libby Yalom
Adelphi, Maryland

Darlene Yohe
Stuttgart, Arkansas

Catherine Yronwode
Forestville, California

Charles S. Zayic
Ellsworth, Maine

Audrey Zeder
Long Beach, California

Auction Houses

We wish to thank the following auction houses whose catalogs have been used as sources for pricing information. Many have granted us permission to reproduce their photographs as well.

A-1 Auction Service
P.O. Box 540672, Orlando, FL 32854; 407-839-0004. Specializing in American antique sales

America West Archives
Anderson, Warren
P.O. Box 100, Cedar City, UT 84721; 801-586-9497; Publishes 26-page illustrated catalog 6 times a year that includes auction section of scarce and historical early western documents, letters, autographs, stock certificates, and other important ephemera. Subscription: $15 per year

Andre Ammelounx
The Stein Company
P.O. Box 136, Palatine, IL 60078; 708-991-5927 or (Fax) 708-991-5947. Specializing in steins, catalogs available

Anthony J. Nard & Co.
US Rt. 220, Milan, PA 18831; 717-888-9404 or (Fax) 717-888-7723

Arman Absentee Auctions
16 Sixth St, Stamford, CT 06905; 203-928-5838. Specializing in American glass, Historical Staffordshire, English soft paste, paperweights

Barry, Kit
109 Main St., Brattleboro, VT 05301; 802-254-3634. Specializing in ephemera and related auctions

Bertoia & Brady Auctions
2413 Madison Ave., Vineland, NJ 08360; 609-692-4092

Bider's
241 S. Union St., Lawrence, MA 01843; 508-688-4347 or 508-683-3944. Antiques appraised, purchased, and sold on consignment

Brian Riba Auctions Inc.
P.O. Box 53, Main St., S. Glastonbury, CT 06073; 203-633-3076

Butterfield & Butterfield
220 San Bruno Ave., San Francisco, CA 91043; 415-861-7500 or (Fax) 415-861-8951.
Also located at: 7601 Sunset Blvd., Los Angeles, CA 90046; 213-850-7500 or (Fax) 213-850-5843. Fine Art Auctioneers and Appraisers since 1865

C.E. Guarino
Box 49, Denmark, ME 04022

Cerebro
P.O. Box 327, E. Prospect, 17317; 717-252-2400 or 800-69-LABEL. Specializing in antique advertising labels, especially cigar box labels, cigar bands, food labels, firecracker labels. Holds semiannual auction on tobacco ephemera. Consignments accepted.

Charles E. Kirtley
P.O. Box 2273, Elizabeth City, NC 27096; 919-335-1262. Specializing in World's Fair, Civil War, political, advertising and other American collectibles

Cherry Land Auctions
Ronald D. Millard
P.O. Box 4086, Tequesta, FL 33469; 407-743-0010. Specializing in postcard mail auctions

Cincinnati Art Gallery
635 Main St., Cincinnati, OH 45202; 513-381-2128. Specializing in American art pottery, American and European fine paintings, watercolors

Col. Doug Allard
P.O. Box 460, St. Ignatius, MT 59865-0460; 406-745-2951 or (Fax) 406-745-2961

Collectors Auction Services
326 Seneca St., Oil City, PA 16301; 814-677-6070. Specializing in advertising, oil and gas, toys, rare museum and investment-quality antiques

David Rago
P.O. Box 3592, Station E, Trenton, NJ 08629; 609-397-9374 Gallery: 17 S. Main St., Lambertville, NJ 08530. Specializing in American art pottery and Arts & Crafts

Doyle Auctioneers & Appraisers
109 Osborne Hill Rd., Fishkill, NY 12524; 914-896-9492. Thousands of collectibles offered: call for free calendar of upcoming events

Dunbar's Gallery
Leila and Howard Dunbar
76 Haven St., Milford, MA 01757; 508-634-8697 or (Fax) 508-634-8698.

Dynamite Auctions
Franklin Antique Mall & Auction Gallery
1280 Franklin Ave., Franklin, PA 16323; 814-432-8577 or 814-786-9211

Du Mouchelles
409 Jefferson Ave., Detroit, MI 48226

Early Auction Co.
123 Main St., Milford, OH 45150

Garth's Auctions Inc.
2690 Stratford Rd., Box 369, Delaware, OH 43015; 614-362-4771

The Glass Menagerie, bimonthly newsletter
Susan Candelaria, Editor
5440 El Arbol, Carlsbad, CA 92008

Glass-Works Auctions
James Hagenbuch
102 Jefferson, East Greenville, PA 18041; 215-679-5849. America's leading auction company in early American bottles and glass

Greenberg Auctions
7566 Main St., Sykesville, MD 21784. Specializing in trains: Lionel, American Flyer, Ives, Marx, HO

Guernsey's
136 E. 73rd St., New York, NY 10021; 212-794-2280. Specializing in carousel figures

Hake's Americana & Collectibles
Specializing in character and personality collectibles along with all artifacts of popular culture for over 20 years. To receive a catalog for their next 3,000-item mail/phone bid auction, send $5 to Hake's Americana, P.O. Box 1444M, York, PA 17405

Hanna-Whysel Auctioneers & Appraisers
Steven Whysel
109 N. Main, Bentonville, AR, 72712; 501-273-7770. Antiques and art auctions

Horst Auctioneers
Horst Auction Center
50 Durlach Rd. (corner of Rt. 322 & Durlach Rd., West of Ephrata), Ephrata, Lancaster County, PA 17522; 717-859-1331 or 717-738-3080. Voices of Experience

Jack Sellner
Sellner Marketing of California
P.O. Box 308, Fremont, CA 94536; 415-745-9463

James D. Julia
P.O. Box 210, Showhegan Rd., Fairfield, ME 04937

James R. Bakker Antiques, Inc.
James R. Bakker
370 Broadway, Cambridge, MA 02139; 617-864-7067. Specializing in American paintings, prints and decorative arts

John Toomey Gallery
818 North Blvd., Oak Park, IL 60301; 708-383-5234 or (Fax) 708-383-4828. Specializing in furniture and decorative arts of the Arts & Crafts, Art Deco and Modern Design movements; Modern Design Expert: Richard Wright

Joy Luke Fine Arts Brokers and Auctioneers
The Gallery
300 East Grove St., Bloomington, IL 61701; 309-828-5533

Ken Farmer Realty & Auction Company
1122 Norwood St., Radford, VA 24141; 703-639-0939 or (Fax) 703-639-1759

L.R. 'Les' Docks
Box 691035, San Antonio, TX 78269-1035. Providing occasional mail-order record auctions, rarely consigned; the only consignments considered are exceptionally scarce and unusual records

Litchfield, Auction Gallery
425 Bantam Rd., P.O. Box 1337, Litchfield, CT 06759; 203-567-3126 or (Fax) 203-567-3266

Lloyd Ralston Toys
447 Stratford Rd., Fairfield, CT 06432

Manion's International Auction House, Inc.
P.O. Box 12214, Kansas City, KS 66112

Maritime Auctions
R.R. 2, Box 45A, York, ME 03909; 207-363-4247

McMasters Doll Auctions
P.O. Box 1755, 5855 Glenn Highway Rd., Cambridge, OH 43725; 614-432-4320 or (Fax) 614-432-3191

Mid-Hudson Auction Galleries
One Idlewild Ave., Cornwall-on-Hudson, NY 12520; 914-534-7828 or (Fax) 914-534-4802

Monsen & Baer,
Annual Perfume Bottle Auction
Monsen, Randall; and Baer, Rod
Box 529, Vienna, 22183; 743-242-1357. Cataloged auctions of perfume bottles. We purchase, sell, and accept consignments. Specializing in commercial, Czechoslovakian, Lalique, Baccarat, Victorian, crown top, factices, miniatures

Noel Barrett Antiques & Auctions
P.O. Box 1001, Carversville, PA 18913; 215-297-5109 or (Fax) 215-297-0457

Nostalgia Co.
21 S. Lake Dr., Hackensack, NJ 07601; 201-488-4536

Phillips
406 E. 79th St., New York, NY 10021

The Political Gallery
1325 W. 86th St., Indianapolis, IN 46260; 317-257-0863. Publishes quarterly catalogs

Postcards International
P.O. Box 2930, New Haven, CT 06515-0030; 203-865-0814 or (Fax) 203-495-8005

Refinders
737 Barberry Rd., Highland Park, IL 60035; 708-831-1102 or 708-831-1160. Refinders will find your wants from 1860-1960

Rex Stark Auctions
49 Wethersfield Rd., Bellingham, MA 02019

Richard A. Bourne Co. Inc.
Estate Auctioneers & Appraisers
Box 141, Hyannis Port, MA 02647; 617-775-0797

Richard Opfer Auctioneering, Inc.
1919 Greenspring Dr., Timonium, MD 21093; 301-252-5035

Roan, Inc.
Box 118, R.D. 3, Cogan Station, PA 17728

Ron Fox Auctions
Ron Fox
83 Morris St., Brentwood, NY 11717; 516-231-0633 or (Fax) 516-952-7719. Specializing in steins; auctions with illustrated catalogs and video tapes

Skinner, Inc.
Auctioneers & Appraisers of Antiques and Fine Arts
The Heritage on the Garden, 63 Park Plaza, Boston, MA 02116; 617-350-5400 or (Fax) 617-350-5429. Second address: 357 Main Street, Boston, MA 01740; 508-779-6241 or (Fax) 508-779-5144

Soldiers Trunk
60 Craigs Rd., Windsor, CT 06095; 203-688-0580. Specializing in American and foreign military items; 4 catalog issues for $20

Sotheby Parke Bernet, Inc.
980 Madison Ave., New York, NY 10021

Tradewinds Auctions
Henry and Nancy Taron
24 Magnolia, Ave., Manchester-By-The-Sea, MA 01944

Treadway Gallery, Inc.
2029 Madison Rd., Cincinnati, OH 45208; 513-321-6742 or (Fax) 513-871-7722. Specializing in American Art Pottery; American and European art glass; European ceramics; Italian glass; fine American and European paintings and graphics; and furniture and decorative arts of the Arts & Crafts, Art Nouveau, Art Deco and Modern Design Movements. Modern Design expert: Thierry Lorthioir. Members: National Antique Dealers Association, American Art Pottery Association, International Society of Appraisers, American Ceramic Arts Society, Ohio Decorative Arts Society, Art Gallery Association of Cincinnati.

Weschler's
Adam A. Weschler & Son
905 E. St. N.W., Washington, DC 20004

Willis Henry Auctions
22 Main St., Marshfield, MA 02050

Directory of Contributors

When contacting any of the buyers/sellers listed in this part of the Directory by mail, you must include an SASE (stamped, self-addressed envelope) if you expect a reply. As hectic as our lifestyles are, the time it saves them is probably worth more to them than the price of a stamp. Not only that, but trying to decipher someone's handwritten name and address can be very frustrating. Sometimes even zip codes are unreadable, and even more time is required to double check zip code numbers. And in the end, if 'Rosen' becomes 'Rirer' and 'Ave. 5' becomes 'Ave. S,' even if the person you contacted was gracious enough to answer you, you probably won't ever know he did. Many of these people are professional appraisers and there will be a fee for their time and service. Find out up front. Include a clear photo if you want an item identified. Most items cannot be described clearly enough to make an identification without a photo.

If you call and get their answering machine, when you leave your number so that they can return your call, tell them to call back collect. And please take the differences in time zones into consideration. 7:00 AM in the midwest is only 4:00 AM in California! And if you're in California, remember that even 7:00 PM is too late to call the east coast. Most people work and are gone during the daytime. Even some of our antique dealers say they prefer after-work phone calls. Don't assume that a person who deals in a particular field will be able to help you with related items. They may seem related to you when they are not.

Please, we need your help. This book sells in such great numbers that allowing their names to be published can create a potential nightmare for each advisor and contributor. Please do your part to help us minimize this, so that we can retain them on our board and in turn pass their experience and knowledge on to you through our book. Many of our people tell us that even with the occasional problem, they feel that the good outweighs the bad and makes all their hard work worthwhile.

Alabama

Dole, Pat
9825 Red Mill Rd.
Birmingham, 35215; 205-833-9853. Specializing in Purinton pottery

Lippa, Matt; and Schaaf, Elizabeth
Artisans
R.R. 1, Box 20-C, Mentone, 35984; 205-634-4037. Specializing in folk art, quilts, painted and folky furniture, tramp art, whirligigs, windmill weights

Luckey, Carl
Carl F. Luckey Communications
R.R. 4, Box 301, Lingerlost Trail, Killen, 35645. Freelance writer specializing in art, antiques, and collectibles. No telephone calls will be accepted; SASE required for correspondence.

Arizona

Chamberlain, Jackie
Jackie Chamberlain Antiques
P.O. Box 20842, Wickenburg, 85358. Specializing in holiday collectibles, antique reference books, pewter ice-cream molds, rare out-of-print books. Holiday slide program available for rent

Chase Collectors Society
c/o Barry L. Van Hook
2149 Jibsail Loop, Mesa, 85202-5524; 602-838-6971. Publishes (6 issues per year) newsletter, *Art Deco Reflections* (sample copy $1); Membership: $5

Ellwood, J.M.
7077 E. Main #4, Scottsdale, 85251; 602-947-9679. Specializing in cast-iron banks, toys, irons, trivets, doorstops and miscellaneous cast iron

Schaut, Jim and Nancy
Aquarius Antiques
P.O. Box 10781, Glendale, 85318; 602-878-4293. Specializing in automobilia, racing memorabilia, auto toys; Authors of *American Automobilia*, 1994

Webb, Maret
Swan Seekers Network
4118 E. Vernon Ave., Phoenix, 85008-2333; Phone & Fax: 602-957-6294; Business hours: 8:30 a.m. - 5:00 p.m., M.S.T., Mon. — Fri. Publishes *Swan Seekers News* and *Swan Seekers Marketplace* periodicals ($28 in US per year, $38 foreign). Specializing in Swarovski crystal

Arkansas

Gifford, David Edwin
Arkansas Pottery Research
P.O. Box 7617, Little Rock, 72217; 501-664-0902. Historian/author/collector of Arkansas art pottery from 1905 to 1932. Seeking all information and company literature on the Ouachita Pottery, Niloak Pottery, and Camark Pottery companies as well as quality pieces marked Ouachita Hot Springs, Niloak Patent Pend'G, LeCamark or Hywood Art Pottery, will answer queries — LSASE please

Hall, Doris and Burdell
B&B Antiques
P.O. Box 1501, Fairfield Bay, 72088-0501 or 210 W. Sassafras Dr., Morton, IL 61550-1245. Authors of *Morton's Potteries: 99 Years* (Vols. I and II). Specializing in Morton pottery, American dinnerware, early American pattern glass, historical items

Whysel, Steven
Antique & Art Galleries Ltd., Inc.
109 N. Main, Bentonville, 72712; 501-273-7770. Specializing in Art Nouveau, full line, books and art

Yohe, Darlene
Timberview Antiques
P.O. Box 343, Stuttgart, 72160; 501-673-3437. Specializing in American pattern glass, historical glass, Victorian pattern glass, carnival glass, and custard glass

California

Baker, Mrs. Lillian
15237 Chanera Ave., Gardena, 90249. Author Collector Books on antique, collectible, and high-fashion costume jewelry, hatpins and hatpin holders, miniatures

Baker, Roger
Baker's Lady Luck Emporium
Box 620417, Woodside, 94062. Specializing in Saloon Americana — advertising, gambling, bar bottles, cigar lighters, match safes, bowie knives, dirks, daggers, cowboy hats, spurs, chaps, saddles, barber items: bottles, shaving mugs, razors

Bradshaw, Tom
325 Carol Dr., Ventura, 93003; 805-641-1470. Specializing in antique Bohemian glass

Brooks, Mike
7335 Skyline, Oakland, 94611; 510-339-1751. Specializing in typewriters, transistor radios, early televisions, Statue of Liberty

Butz, Robert C.
Collector's Wedgwood
P.O. Box 462, Newbury Park, 91319. Specializing in Wedgwood

Carter, Tina M.
882 S. Mollison, El Cajon, 92020; 619-440-5043. Specializing in teapots, tea-related items, tea tins, children's and toy tea sets, coffeepots, etc.; Book on teapots available. Send $15.50 (includes postage) or $16.41 for CA residents, Canada: add $2, to above address

Chipman, Jack
California Spectrum
P.O. Box 1079, Venice, 90291. Specializing in California ceramics; author of *Collector's Encyclopedia of California Pottery*, autographed copies available from author for $24.95+$3.50 postage and handling+(CA) tax of $2.35

Christensen, Pat and Chris
1067 Salvador St., Costa Mesa, 92626. Specializing in open salts

Cohen, Wilfred and Dolli
Antiques & Art Glass
P.O. Box 27151, Santa Ana, 92799; 714-545-5673 (best to phone after 6:00 p.m. Pacific time). Specializing in Wave Crest (C.F. Monroe); Victorian era art and pattern glass (salt shakers, toothpick holders, syrups, cruets, sugar shakers, tumblers, biscuit jars, table and pitcher sets); art and cameo glass open salts; custard and ruby stain glass; burmese, peachblow and amberina glass; pottery by Moorcroft (pre-1935 only); Buffalo (Deldare and Emerald ware); and Polia Pillin. Please include SASE for reply.

Cox, Susan N.
237 E. Main St., El Cajon, 92020; 619-447-0800. Specializing in California pottery and Frankoma

Delucchi, Mary
P.O. Box 4265, Stockton 95204; 209-956-4645

Ehrhard, J. David
Psycho-Ceramic Restorations
c/o Showcase Antiques, 60 N. Lake Ave., Pasadena. 91101; Specializing in restoration of ceramics, collects Susie Cooper and British pottery, Mabel Lucie Attwell

Enge, Delleen
Franciscan Dinnerware Matching Service
323 E. Matilija, Ste. 112, Ojai, 93023

Escoe, Adrienne S., Member
Glass Knife Collectors Club
4448 Ironwood Ave., Seal Beach, 90740; 310-430-6479; Specializing in glass knives; E-mail: adrienne_escoe@wwire.net.

Fogleman, Marv
Marv's Memories
1914 W. Carriage Dr., Santa Ana, 92704. Specializing in Western dinnerware, Metlox, Mikasa, and Franciscan

George, Tony
22431-B160 Antonio Pkwy., #252, Rancho Santa Margarita, 92688; 714-589-6075. Specializing in watch fobs

Giacomini, Mary Jane
P.O. Box 404, Ferndale, CA 95536-0404; 707-786-9464. Author of *American Bisque, a Collector's Guide with Prices*; Specializing in American Bisque pottery, cookie jars

Gibson, Pat
38280 Guava Dr., Newark, 94560; 510-792-0586. Specializing in R.A. Fox

Harrison, Gwynne
P.O. Box 1, Mira Loma, 91752-0001; 909-685-5434. Specializing in Autumn Leaf (Jewel Tea)

Hibbard, Suzi
WanderWares
2570 Walnut Blvd. #20, Walnut Creek, 94596; 510-947-1076. Specializing in Dragonware, 1000 Faces china, Oriental china. Inquiries should be accompanied by SASE

Howard, Steve
101 1st St., Suite 404, Los Altos, 94022; 510-484-4488. Specializing in antique American firearms, bowie knives, Western Americana, old advertising, and vintage gambling items

Inouye, Roger
765 E. Franklin Ave., Pomona, 91766; 909-623-1368. Specializing in Trolls

Kreider, Katherine
Kingsbury Productions
4555 N. Pershing Ave., Suite 33-138, Stockton, 95207; 209-467-8438. Specializing in Valentines

Main Street Antique Mall
237 E Main Street
El Cajon, 92020; 619-447-0800

Maurer, Oveda L.
Oveda Maurer Antiques
34 Greenfield Ave., San Anselmo, 94960; 415-454-6439. Specializing in 18th-century and early 19th-century American furniture, lighting, pewter, and hearthware

Nelson, Maxine
873 Marigold Ct., Carlsbad, 92009. Specializing in Vernon Kilns; author of *Collectible Vernon Kilns*; autographed copies available from the author for $24.95+$2.50 postage & handling (CA sale tax: $1.93); SASE appreciated for inquiries

Paper Pile Quarterly
Ada Fitsimmons, Editor
P.O. Box 337, San Anselmo, 94979; 619-322-3525. Sales and features magazine serving paper collectors and dealers since 1980, quarterly cataloged sales, large advertising section; Subscription: $17 per year (shipped 1st class)

Pardini, Dick
3107 N. El Dorado St., Dept. SAPG, Stockton, 95204-3412; 209-466-5550 (recorder may answer). Specializing in California Perfume Company items dating from 1886 to 1928: buyer and information center. Not interested in items that have Avon, Perfection, or Anniversary Keepsake markings. California Perfume Company offerings must be accompanied by a photo, Xerox copy, or sketching along with a condition report and, most important, price wanted. Inquiries require large SASE; not necessary if offering items for sale

Roller, Gayle
829 Valley Crest Dr., Vista, 92084. Specializing in Hagen-Renaker

Sanford, Steve and Martha
230 Harrison Ave., Campbell, 95088; 408-978-8408. Specializing in Brush-McCoy

Shrader, Fred and Lila
Shrader Antiques
2025 Hwy. 199, Crescent City, 95531; 707-458-3525. Specializing in railroad, steamship and other transportation memorabilia; Shelley china, Buffalo china, Niloak, and Zell

Stella's Collectibles
Memory Lanes Antique Mall
20740 S. Figueroa St., Carson, (Space 214) 90745; 310-316-7198; PCH Antique Mall Long Beach (Space 129); Santa Monica Antique Market (Space 113); Westchester Faire Mall (Space 320-326); The Enchanted Castle, 169 N. Main, Lake Elsinore (Space 25). Specializing in quality glass, china, figurines and plates

Thornton, Don
Off Beat Books
1345 Poplar Ave., Sunnyvale, 94087. Specializing in eggbeaters; author of *Beat This: The Eggbeater Chronicles* ($28.95 including postage and handling).

Webb, Frances Finch
1589 Gretel Lane, Mountain View, 94040. Specializing in Kay Finch ceramics

Yronwode, Catherine
6632 Covey Rd., Forestville, 95436; 707-887-2424. Specializing in pre-1950 collectible plastic

Zeder, Audrey
6755 Coralite St. S., Long Beach, 90808 (appointment only). Specializing in British Royal Commemorative Souvenirs (mail-order catalog available). Author (Wallace-Homestead) of *British Royal Commemoratives*

Canada

Brown, David L.
Stevengraph Collectors Assn.
2103-2829 Arbutus Rd., Victoria, British Columbia, V8N 5X5; 604-477-9896. Specializing in Stevengraphs

Melis, Mirko
Marcelle Antiques
P.O. Box 53039, 5100 Erin Mills Pkwy., Mississauga, Ontario, L5M 4Z5; 905-689-1648. Specializing in American and European art glass, Russian works of art (enamels, porcelains, silver, etc.), English and Continental glass and china, member of Antique Appraisal Association of America, Inc., and AADA (Associated Antique Dealers of America, Inc.)

Old China Patterns Limited
1560 Brimley Rd., Unit 1, Scarborough, Ontario, MIP369; 416-299-8880 or (Fax) 416-299-4721. Specializing in discontinued china dinnerware, matching service (since 1966), charter member I.A.D.M.

Warner, Ian
P.O. Box 93022, 499 Main St. S., Brampton, Ontario, L6Y 4V8; 905-453-9074 or (Fax) 905-453-2931. Specializing in Wade porcelain and Swankyswigs, author of *The World of Wade*, Co-author: Mike Posgay

Colorado

Carlton, Carol and Jim
8115 S. Syracuse St., Englewood, 80112; 303-773-8616. Specializing in Broadmoor, Coors and other Colorado pottery

Heck, Carl
Carl Heck Decorative Arts
Box 8416, Aspen, 81612; 970-925-8011. Specializing in original Tiffany lamps, art glass, windows and chandeliers. Also reverse-painted and leaded-glass table lamps, stained and beveled glass windows, bronzes, paintings, etc.; Buy and sell. Please include SASE for reply

Mackin, Bill
Author of *Cowboy and Gunfighter Collectibles*; available from author: 1137 Washington St., Craig, 81625; 303-824-6717, Paperback: $22; 1993-94 updated Price Guide: $9. Specializing in old and fine spurs, guns, gun leather, cowboy gear, Western Americana (Collection in the Museum of Northwest Colorado, Craig)

Over, Naomi L.
8909 Sharon Lane, Arvada, 80002; 303-424-5922. Specializing in ruby glassware, author of *Ruby Glass of the 20th Century*, available from author for $24 (includes shipping and handling)

Segelke, Cathy; and James, Pat
Brush, 303-847-3758 (Cathy) or 308-847-3759 (Pat). Specializing in crocks, Western Pottery Mfg. Co. (Denver, CO)

Toohey, Marlena
703 S. Pratt Pky., Longmont, 80501; 303-678-9726. Specializing in black glass; book available from author for $20 (includes shipping and handling)

White, John 'Grandpa'
Grandpa's Depot
Denver Union Station, 1616 17th St., Denver, 80202; 303-892-1177 or (Fax) 303-573-5505. Specializing in railroad-related items, catalogs available

Winther, Jo Ellen
8449 W. 75th Way, Arvada, 80005; 800-872-2345 or 303-421-2371. Specializing in Coors

Connecticut

Alves, Margaret
84 Oak Ave., Shelton, 06484; 203-924-4768. Specializing in spoons: plated, sterling, silver, pre-1920s

Bondhus, Sandra V.
Box 100, Unionville, 06085; 203-678-1808. Author of *Quimper Pottery: A French Folk Art Faience*; specializing in Quimper pottery

Harned, Denise
P.O. Box 330373, Elmwood, 06133-0373. Author of *Griswold Cast Collectibles*. Specializing in Griswold cast iron and aluminum

Kilbride, Mrs. Richard J.
81 Willard Terrace, Stamford, 06903; 203-322-0568. Has available for sale: *Art Deco Chrome, The Chase Era*, and *Art Deco Chrome, Book 2, A Collector's Guide, Industrial Design in the Chase Era*

MacSorley, Earl
823 Indian Hill Rd., Orange, 06477; 203-387-1793 (after 7:00 p.m.). Specializing in nutcrackers, Bessie Pease Gutmann prints, figural lift-top spittoons

Postcards International
Shapiro, Marty
P.O. Box 2930, New Haven, 06515-0030; 203-865-0814 or (Fax) 203-495-8005. Specializing in vintage picture postcards

Rivera, Ted
Box 163, Torrington, 06790; 203-489-4325. Specializing in inkwells and inkstands; Co-author of *Inkstands and Inkwells: A Collector's Guide*

Roenigk, Martin
Mechantiques
26 Barton Hill, E. Hampton, 06424; 203-267-8682. Specializing in mechanical musical instruments, music boxes, band organs, musical clocks and watches, coin pianos, orchestrions, monkey organs, automata, mechanical birds and dolls, etc.

Thalberg, Bruce
Mountain View Dr., Weston, 06883; 203-227-8175. Specializing in canes and walking sticks: novelty, carved, and Black

Van Deusen, Hobart D.
28 The Green, Watertown, 06795; 203-945-3456. Specializing in Canton, SASE required when requesting information

Vuono, Mark
306 Mill Rd., Stamford, 06903; 203-357-0892 (10 a.m. to 5:30 p.m. E.S.T.). Specializing in historical flasks, blown 3-mold glass, blown American glass

Delaware

Davis, Patricia M.
700 Greenhill Ave., Wilmington, 19805; 302-658-2992

District of Columbia

Durham, Ken and Jackie (By appointment)
909 26 St. N.W., Washington, D.C. 20037. Specializing in counter-top arcade machines, trade stimulators, and vending machines; 16-page illustrated list: $2; Send SASE for free list of books on coin-operated machines

England

Pedel, Alan
Hidden Treasures
Marwood Lee, Barnstaple, Devon, EX31 4EB; 011-44-271-75166 (anytime). Specializing in pie birds and most other collectibles

Florida

Archer, Dick and Ellie
Artiques
419 Sevilla Dr., St. Augustine, 32086; 904-797-4678. Specializing in Victorian silverplate: figurals, fancy hollow ware, and collectibles

Bettinger, Robert
P.O. Box 333, Mt. Dora, 32757; 904-735-3575. Specializing in American art pottery

Cohen, Joel
Cohen Books & Collectibles
P.O. Box 810310, Boca Raton, 33481; 407-487-7888. Specializing in Disneyana

deCourtivron, Gael
Cocaholics
4811 Remington Dr., Sarasota, 34234; 813-355-2652 or 813-359-2652. Specializing in Coca-Cola memorabilia.

Dodds, Rebecca
Silver Flute
Box 39644, Ft. Lauderdale, 33339. Specializing in jewelry

Donnelly, Ron
Saturday Heroes
Box 7047, Panama City Beach, 32413. Specializing in Big Little Books, movie posters, premiums, western heroes, character collectibles, early Disney. For inquiries include SASE

France, Madeleine
P.O. Box 15555, Ft. Lauderdale, 33318; 305-584-0009. Specializing in top-quality perfume bottles: Rene Lalique, Steuben, Czechoslovakian, DeVilbiss, Baccarat, Commercials

Hudson, Hardy
Our Antiques Market
5453 Lake Howell Rd., Winter Park, 32792; 407-657-2100 from 11:00 a.m. to 6:00 p.m. Specializing in majolica, American art pottery; Buying one piece or entire collections; Also buying Weller animals, rare Roseville, Kay Finch

Lawrence, Judy and Cliff
1169 Overcash Dr., Dunedin, 34698; 813-734-4742. Specializing in fountain pens, dip pens, and mechanical pencils

Linscott, Jacqueline C.
3557 Nicklaus Dr., Titusville, 32780. Specializing in Blue Bell paperweights; author of *1992 Revised Edition, Blue Bell Paperweights*, complete with history, illustrations, and price guide; Available from author for $12 (includes postage and handling)

Linscott, Len
Line Jewels-Insulators
3557 Nicklaus Dr., Titusville, 32780. Specializing in glass and porcelain insulators. Also glass insulator books by CD number (LSASE required)

McNerny, Kathryn
118 Creek Hollow Lane, Middleburg, 32068. Author (Collector Books) on blue and white stoneware, primitives, tools

Millard, Ronald D.
Cherry Land Auctions
P.O. Box 4086, Tequesta, 33469; 407-743-0010. Specializing in postcard mail auctions

New World Maps, Inc.
Charles R. Neuschafer
1123 S. Broadway, Lantana, 33462-4522; 407-586-8723. Buys and sells antique and collectible maps, specializing in 20th-century road maps; Columnist for *Paper Collectors Marketplace* and member of International Map Dealers Association

Parker, Alton B.
6127 Dartmouth Dr., Bradenton, 34207-4730; 813-756-0386. Specializing in Azalea china, Depression Glass, Roseville pottery

Supnick, Mark
2771 Oakbrook Manor, Ft. Lauderdale, 33332. Author of *Collecting Hull Pottery's Little Red Riding Hood* ($12.95 postage paid). Specializing in American pottery

Tyler, Henry
13 Bellevue Dr., Treasure Island, 33706

White, Douglass
Classic Interiors & Antiques
2042 N. Rio Grande, Suite E, Orlando, 32804; 407-839-0004. Specializing in Fulper, Arts & Crafts furniture

Wise, Raphael C.
The Collector's Stop
12018 Suellen Circle, West Palm Beach, 33414; 407-793-0986. Specializing in Wedgwood Jasper Ware, Rosenthal, Moorcroft, Buffalo Deldare and Emerald Ware, Heisey, contemporary paperweights, English porcelains

Georgia

Bailey, Wayne and Gale
P.O. Box 173, Dacula, 30211; 404-963-5736. Specializing in Goebels (Friar Tuck)

Glenn, Walter
Geode Ltd.
3393 Peachtree Rd., Atlanta, 30326; 404-261-9346. Specializing in Frankart

Hartley, Glenn, Sr.
Fire Mark Circle of the Americas
2859 Marlin Dr., Chamblee, 30341-5119; 404-451-2651. Specializing in fire marks, Methodist, Masonic, Foremost Dairies, Goodyear

Joiner, John R.
52 Jefferson Pkwy., Apt. D, Newnan, 30263; 404-502-9565. Specializing in commercial aviation collectibles

Idaho

Beeks, D.R.
P.O. Box 2515, Coeur d'Alene, 83814; 208-667-0830. Specializing in instruments of early science, technology, and medicine. Also surveying instruments, microscopes

Illinois

Ammelounx, Andre
The Stein Auction Company
P.O. Box 136, Palatine, 60078; 708-991-5927 or (Fax) 708-991-5947. Specializing in steins, catalogs available

The Barrel Antique Mall
5850 S St Road, I-55 Exit 90, Springfield, 62707; 217-585-1438

Brinkley, Wm. J.
Brinkley Galleries
401 S. Washington Ave., McLeansboro, 62859. Specializing in Meissen, Dresden, European porcelains, American porcelains (Cybis)

Broom, Jim
Box 65, Effingham, 62401. Specializing in opalescent pattern glassware

Danis, John
11028 Raleigh Ct., Rockford, 61115; 815-963-0757 or (Fax) 815-877-6042. Specializing in R. Lalique

Feldman, Arthur M.
Arthur M. Feldman Gallery
1815 St. Johns Ave., Highland Park, 60035; 708-432-8858. Specializing in Judaica and antiques

Frizzell, Doris
Doris' Dishes
5687 Oakdale Dr., Springfield, 62707; 217-529-3873. Specializing in Royal Haeger, and Depression Glass; Co-author (Collector Books) of Royal Haeger book

Gandolfo, Dan
The Goofus Connection
3 S. 577 Elizabeth Ave., Warrenville, 60555; 708-393-9115. Specializing in Goofus glass

Garmon, Lee
1529 Whittier St., Springfield, 62704; 217-789-9574. Specializing in Royal Haeger, Royal Hickman, glass animals; Co-author (Collector Books) of *Glass Animals and Figural Flower Frogs of the Depression Era* and *Collecting Royal Haeger*

Griffith, Woody
Chicago, 312-975-1957. Specializing in DeVilbiss, perfumes, Jewel Tea, Noritake, Hall

Hall, Doris and Burdell
B&B Antiques
210 W. Sassafras Dr., Morton, 61550-1245 or P.O. Box 1501, Fairfield Bay, AR 72088-1501. Authors of *Morton's Potteries: 99 Years* (Vols. I and II). Specializing in Morton pottery, American dinnerware, early American pattern glass, historical items

Haussmann, Richard A., Past President, Aurora Historical Society
Aurora, 60507

Hilst, Randy
1221 Florence #4, Pekin, 61554; 309-346-2710. Specializing in general line including fishing and hunting collectibles

Hoffmann, Pat and Don, Sr.
1291 N. Elmwood Dr., Aurora, 60506; 708-859-3435. Authors of *Warwick, A to W*, a supplement to *Why Not Warwick? China Collector's Guide*; video regarding Warwick decals currently available. Specializing in Warwick china

The Home Place Antiques
Durham, William; Galaway, William
615 S. State St., Belvidere, 61008; 815-544-0577. Specializing in Tea Leaf ironstone and white ironstone

Hooks, Dee
Dee's China Shop
P.O. Box 142, Lawrenceville, 62439-0142; 618-943-2741. Specializing in R.S. Prussia, Royal Bayreuth, Haviland, other fine china

Hopp, Dennis Carl
Midcentury
642½ W. Addison, Chicago, 60613; 312-549-5405. Specializing in 20th-century glass, pottery, enamels, metal

Hurney, George and Mary
Glass Connection (Mail-order only)
312 Babcock Dr., Palatine, 50067; 708-359-3839. Specializing in Depression Glass and Paden City glass (not advising on pottery)

The Illinois Antique Center
320 S.W. Commercial St.
Peoria, IL 61602

International Society of Antique Scale Collectors
Bob Stein, President
176 W. Adams, Suite 1706, Chicago, 60603; 312-263-7500. Publishes *Equilibrium* Magazine; President's newsletter; Annual membership directory; Out-of-print catalogs; Annual convention.

John Toomey Gallery
818 N. Blvd, Oak Park, IL 60301

Lake Forest Antiquarians
c/o John Batzel, Ph. D.
P.O. Box 841, Lake Forest, 60045; 708-234-1990. Specializing in antique English and Continental silver

Long, Dee
112 S. Center, Lacon, 61540. Specializing in reamers

Lotton, Charles
Lotton Art Glass
1938 177th St., Lansing, 60438; 708-474-4022. Specializing in art glass

Lubliner, Larry
Refinders mail/telephone auction
737 Barberry Rd., Highland Park, IL 60035; 708-831-1102 or 708-831-1160. Refinders will find your wants from 1860-1960

Martin, Jim
R.R. 1, 1091 215th Ave., Monmouth, 61462; 309-734-2703. Specializing in Old Sleepy Eye, Monmouth Pottery, Western Stoneware

Meyer, Larry
4001 Elmwood, Stickney, 60402; 708-749-1564. Specializing in fire grenades

Miller, Larry; Strickfaden, Dick
218 Devron Circle, E. Peoria, 61611-1605. Specializing in German and Czechoslovakian Erphila

Ochsner, Grace
Grace Ochsner Doll House
1636 E. County Rd. 2700, Niota, 62358; 217-755-4362. Specializing in piano babies, bisque German dolls

Owen, Larry and Sally
Specializing in Morten Studio dogs, etc.

Pollack, Frank and Barbara
(Appointment only)
1214 Green Bay Rd., Highland Park, 60035; 708-433-2213. Specializing in American country antiques and art

Pustelniak, Dick and Mary
Mary's Antiques
R.R. 2, Box 10, Paris, 61944; 217-465-5185.

Randy's Ol' Time Collectibles
Illinois Antique Center
100 Walnut St., Peoria, 61602; 309-346-2710. Specializing in general line, including hunting and fishing collectibles

Rastello, Lisa
Milkweed Antiques
5N531 Ancient Oak Lane, St. Charles, 60175; 708-377-4612. Specializing in Depression-era collectibles

Rhoden, Joan and Charles
Memories/Rhoden's Antiques
605 N. Main, Georgetown, 61846; 217-662-8046. Specializing in Heisey and other elegant glassware, general line antiques. Co-authors of *Those Wonderful Yard-Long Prints and More*, and *More Wonderful Yard-Long Prints*, illustrated value guides

Rodrick, Tammy
Stacey's Treasures
R.R. 2, Box 163, Sumner, 62466. Specializing in antiques and collectibles

Spencer, Dick
Glass and More (Shows only)
1203 N. Yale, O'Fallon, 62269; 618-632-9067. Specializing in Cambridge, Fenton, Fostoria, Heisey, etc.

Spiess, Greg
230 E. Washington, Joliet, 60433; 815-722-5639. Specializing in Odd Fellows lodge items

Stifter, Donna & Craig
P.O. Box 6514, Naperville, 60540; 708-717-7949. Specializing in Pepsi-Cola, Coca-Cola and other soda-pop brand collectibles

Stretch Glass Society
Attention: Joanne Rodgers
P.O. Box 573, Hampshire, 60140. Membership: $12 per year; quarterly newsletter, annual convention

Waite, Jim
112 N. Main St., Farmer City, 61842; 800-842-2593. Specializing in Sebastians

Weldi-Skinner, Mary
1656 W. Farragut Ave., Chicago, 60640. Specializing in American and European art pottery, designer collectibles

Wells, Rosalie J. 'Rosie'
R.R. 1S, E. Wells Dr., Canton, 61520; 1-800-445-8745. Publishes *The Ornament Collector*,™ *Precious Collectibles*®, and *Collectors' Bulletin*™. She also publishes the *Weekly Collectors' Gazette* and annual price guides for Precious Moments® Collectibles, Hallmark Ornament Collectibles, and Hallmark's Merry Miniatures. Rosie has hosted eight International Conventions for Precious Moments Collectors and also hosts the semiannual Midwest Collectibles Fest, held in St. Charles, IL, each March and October. For Hot Tips call 1-900-420-3713 ext. 307 for Precious Moments® and ext. 306 for Hallmark ornament news. In Canada: 1-900-451-5323 ext. 101 for Hot Tips on Precious Moments® news, Hallmark ornaments and other popular limited edition collectibles and ornaments. Rosie also offers a touch-tone 900 line (1-900-740-7575) for callers to record Voice Ads to reach American collectors. Call 'Rosie' at 309-668-2211 for information on limited edition collectibles.

Westover, Elaine;
Treasurer/Membership information
Abingdon Pottery Collectors Club
210 Knox Hwy. 5, Abingdon, 61410. 309-462-3267. Specializing in collecting and preservation of Abingdon pottery

Wilson, Jack D.
P.O. Box 81974, Chicago, 60681-0974; 312-282-9553. Specializing in Phoenix and Consolidated glass; Buying Ruba Rombic; Author of *Phoenix & Consolidated Art Glass: 1926-1980*; Secretary of Phoenix and Consolidated Glass Collectors' Club; Editor of *Phoenix & Consolidated Glass Collectors' News & Views* Newsletter (bimonthly); Membership: $25 (single), $35 (couple) per year

Yester-Daze Glass
c/o Illinois Antique Center
Peoria, 309-347-1679. Specializing in Depression Glass, pottery and Florence ceramics

Indiana

AAA Antique Shop
US 6 West, Nappanee, 46550; 219-773-4912. Specializing in trunks

Alexander, Charles
221 E. 34th St., Indianapolis, 46205; Specializing in American dinnerware

Black Creek Antiques
18405 St. Rd. 37, Harlan, 46743. Specializing in primitives, general antiques and collectibles

Blann, Dale
President of Uhl Collectors' Society
4 Appaloosa Dr., Vincennes, 47591; 812-886-5895. Contact for membership and newsletter information

Boram, Clifford
Antique Stove Information Clearinghouse
Monticello; Free consultation by phone only: 219-583-6465

Cochron, Ruby
4255 S. Lynhurst Dr., Indianapolis, 46221; 317-856-6089. Specializing in Jewel Tea and Hall

Crossroads Antique Mall
311 Holiday Square, Seymour, 47274; 812-522-5675. Open 7 days a week

Doll Adoption Agency, Etc.
Faulkner, Joan
1149 Buchanan St., Plainfield, 46168; 317-839-6092. Specializing in dolls, jewelry, and miscellaneous smalls

Edwards, Bill
620 W. 2nd, Madison, 47250. Author (Collector Books) on Carnival Glass

Fisher, Todd
Crossroads Antique Mall
311 Holiday Square, Seymour, 47274; 812-522-5675. Open 7 days a week

Fred, James A.
Antique Radio Labs
R.R. 1, Box 41, Cutler, 46920; 317-268-2214. Specializing in radios made from 1922 to 1950

Garrett, Jerry and Sandi
Jerry's Antiques (Shows only)
1807 W. Madison St., Kokomo, 46901; 317-457-5256. Specializing in Greentown glass, old postcards

Gilley, Betty
Gilley's Antiques
1209 W. Main St., Plainfield, 46168; 317-839-8779. Specializing in pottery, china, furniture

Gilley's Antique Mall and Collectibles
1209 W. Main (US 40), Plainfield, 46168; 317-839-8779. Open daily from 10 a.m. to 5 p.m., features booths with over 250 dealers; outdoor summer weekend flea market

Haisley, Gary
Old Tyme Toy Mall
542 Circle Dr., Fairmount, 46928; 317-948-5479. Specializing in farm toys of the '40s through '70s, cast-iron farm toys, Vindex and Arcade

Haun, Ted
2426 N. 700 East, Kokomo, 46901; 317-628-3640. Specializing in American pottery and china, '50s items, Russel Wright designs

Heiss, Virginia
7777 N. Alton Ave., Indianapolis, 46268; 317-875-6797. Specializing in Muncie, AMACO, Brandt Steele, Marblehead, Kenton Hills

Keagy, William and June
P.O. Box 106, Bloomfield, 47424; 812-384-3471. Co-authors of *Those Wonderful Yard-Long Prints and More*, and *More Wonderful Yard-Long Prints*, illustrated value guides

Old Storefront Antiques
P.O. Box 357, Dublin, 47335; 317-478-4809. Specializing in country store items, tins, primitives, pharmaceuticals, advertising, etc. Active in mail order with catalogs available. Information requires LSASE

Pruitt, Ted
3382 W. 700 N., Anderson, 46011. *St. Clair Glass Collector's Book*, available ($15 each) from Ted at above address

Scowden, Virgil
Williamsport, 47993; 317-762-3408 or 317-762-3178. Antiques museum, general line, tours

Slater, Thomas D.
The Political Gallery
1325 W. 86th St., Indianapolis, 46260; 317-257-0863. Specializing in political and sports memorabilia

Stofft, Marvin and Jeanette
Marnette Antiques
Tell City, 47586; 812-547-5707. Specializing in Ohio art pottery, buy and sell

Swayzee Antique Mall
115 N. Washington St., Swayzee, 46986; 317-922-7903

Vanderbilt, Duane and Janice
4040 W. Over Dr., Indianapolis, 46268; 317-875-8932. Authors (Collector Books) of *Collector's Guide to Shawnee Pottery*

Webb's Antique Mall
over 400 Quality Dealers
200 W. Union St., Centerville, 47330

Wright, Bill
325 Shady Dr., New Albany, 47150. Specializing in knives: Bowie, hunting, military, and jackknives

Iowa

Addy, Geneva D.
Winterset, 50273; 515-462-3027

Arnbal, Una
Woodland Antiques
242 Trail Ridge Rd., Ames, 50014; 515-292-1005. Specializing in china, glass, Lomonosov figurines, Danish collector plates

DeGood, Hal and Meredith
The Baggage Car
3100 Justin Dr., Suite B, Des Moines, 50322; 515-270-9080. Specializing in Hallmark collectibles; publishers of Hallmark newsletter

DeLozier, Loretta
1101 Polk St., Bedford, 50833; 712-523-2289. Author (Collector Books) of *Collector's Encyclopedia of Lefton China, Identification & Values*. Specializing in Lefton china

Devine, Dennis; Norman; and Joe
D & D Antique Mall
1411 3rd St., Council Bluffs, 51503; 712-323-5233 or 712-328-7305. Specializing in furniture, phonographs, collectibles, general line. Joe Devine: Royal Copley collector

Jaarsma, Ralph
De Pelikaan Antieks
812 Washington St., c/o Red Ribbon Antique Mall, Pella, 50219. Specializing in Dutch antiques

Morris, Susan
P.O. Box 656, Panora, 50216. Specializing in Watt pottery and Purinton pottery; Author of *Watt Pottery — An Identification and Value Guide* and *Purinton Pottery — An Identification and Value Guide*

Nichols, Harold J.
632 Agg, Ames, 50010; 515-292-9167. Author of *McCoy Cookie Jars from the First to the Last*. Specializing in Roseville, Weller, McCoy

Picek, Louis
Main Street Antiques
110 W. Main St., Box 340, West Branch, 52358. Specializing in folk art, country Americana, the unusual

Westmoreland Glass Society
Jim Fisher, President
513 5th Ave., Coralville, 52241; 319-354-5011. Membership: $15 (single) or $25 (household)

Kansas

Anthony, Dorothy Malone
World of Bells Publications
802 S. Eddy, Fort Scott, 66701; 316-223-3404. Specializing in publishing and selling books on all types of small bells

Maundy International
P.O. Box 13208-G, Shawnee Mission, 66282; 1-800-235-2866. Specializing in watches — antique pocket and vintage wristwatches

McCormick, John and Marilyn
P.O. Box 3174, Shawnee, 66226; 913-441-0793. Specializing in Gonder pottery

Rash, Jim
135 Alder Ave., Pleasantville, 08232; 609-646-4125. Specializing in advertising, cereal, and cartoon figures

Smies, David
Pops Collectibles
Box 522, 315 So. 4th, Manhattan, 66502; 913-776-1433. Specializing in coins, stamps, cards, tokens, Masonic collectibles

Snyder, Charlie and Rose
Charlie's Collectables
R.R. 4, Box 79, Independence, 67301; 316-331-6259. Specializing in cookie jars and accessories, salt and pepper shakers, pottery

Street, Patti
Currier & Ives Newsletter
P.O. Box 504, Riverton, 66770; 316-848-3529

Tinsley, Rosella
105 15th St., Osawatomie, 66064; 913-755-3237. Specializing in primitives, kitchen, farm, woodenware, and miscellaneous (phone calls only)

Winslow, Ralph
4008 W. 100 Terrace, Overland Park, 66207. Specializing in Dryden and Shramberg pottery

Kentucky

Courter, J.W.
3935 Kelley Rd., Kevil, 42053; 502-488-2116. Specializing in Aladdin lamps; Author of *Aladdin — The Magic Name in Lamps*, softbound, 180 pages; and *Aladdin Electric Lamps*, hardbound, 229 pages

Fedosky, Terry
R.R. 1, Box 118, Symsonia, 42082. Specializing in vaseline glass

Florence, Gene
Box 7186H, Lexington, 40522. Author (Collector Books) on Depression Glass, Occupied Japan

Johnson, Wes, Sr.
RFD, Glenview, 40025. Specializing in Cracker Jack: toys, point of sale, packages, etc.; Checkers Confection, Schoenhut toys, Victor Toy Oats, Universal Theatre (Chicago), old toys; Please include SASE

Willis, Roy M.
Heartland of Kentucky Decanters and Steins
P.O. Box 428, Lebanon Jct., 40150; Huge selection of limited edition decanters and beer steins — open showroom. Include large self-addressed envelope (two stamps) with correspondence. Fee for appraisals. Decanter price guide (listings only, no pictures): $5.00 PPD.

Maine

Hathaway, John
Hathaway's Antiques
3 Mills Rd., Bryant Pond, 04219; 207-665-2124. Specializing in fruit jars; mail order a specialty

Rinaldi, John
Nautical Antiques Related Items
Box 765, Dock Square, Kennebunkport, 04046; 207-967-3218. Specializing in nautical antiques, 19th- & 20th-century American paintings; Annual Fall catalog: $3

Zayic, Charles S.
Americana Advertising Art P.O. Box 57, Ellsworth, 04605; 207-667-7342. Specializing in early magazines, early advertising art, illustrators

Maryland

Banks, Robert
18901 Gold Mine Court, Brookeville, 20833. Specializing in American flags of historical significance and exceptional design

Ezell, Elaine; Newhouse, George
Cruets Cruets Cruets
P.O. Box 1609, Pasadena, 21122-1609; 410-255-6777. Specializing in cruets, glass, porcelain and pottery

Greenberg, Bruce C., Ph. D.
7566 Main St., Sykesville, 21784. Specializing in toy trains; author of comprehensive publications on Lionel, American Flyer, and Ives trains

Humphrey, George C.
4932 Prince George Ave., Beltsville, 20705; 301-937-7899. Specializing in John Rogers groups

Meadows, John, Jean and Michael
Meadows House Antiques
919 Stiles St., Baltimore, 21202; 410-837-5427. Specializing in antique wicker; rustic, twig, and old hickory furniture; quilts; tramp art

Michels, John
Jamm Enterprises
1658 Hardwick Rd., Baltimore, 21286; 410-825-3636. Specializing in watch holders and small clocks

Rudisill's Alt Print Haus
Rudisill, John and Barbara
P.O. Box 199, Worton, 21678; 410-778-9290. Specializing in Currier & Ives

Screen, Harold and Joyce
2804 Munster Rd., Baltimore, 21234; 410-661-6765 (after 6:00 p.m. E.S.T.). Specializing in soda fountain 'tools of the trade' and paper: catalogs, *Soda Fountain Magazine*, etc.

Yalom, Libby
The Shoe Lady
P.O. Box 7146, Adelphi, 20783; 301-422-2026. Specializing in glass and china shoes

Massachusetts

Adams, Charles and Barbara
Middleboro, 02346; 508-947-7277. Specializing in Bennington (brown only)

Dunbar's Gallery
Leila and Howard Dunbar
76 Haven St., Milford, 01757; 508-634-8697 or (Fax) 508-634-8698. Specializing in advertising and toys

Frei, Peter
P.O. Box 500, Brimfield, 01010; 1-800-942-8968. Specializing in sewing machines, adding machines, typewriters, and hand-powered vacuum cleaners; SASE required with correspondence

Hess, John A.
Fine Photographic Americana
P.O. Box 3062, Andover, 01810; 508-470-0327. Specializing in 19th-century photography

Longo, Paul J.
Paul Longo Americana
Box 490, Chatham Rd., South Orleans, Cape Cod, 02662; 508-255-5482. Specializing in political pins, ribbons, banners, autographs, old stocks and bonds, baseball and sports memorabilia of all types

MacLean, Dale
Dale's
593 High St., Dedham, 02026; 617-326-3010. Specializing in Dedham pottery

Mallis, A. George
788 Stony Hill Rd., Wilbraham, MA 01095-02202. Specializing in antique scales

Morin, Albert
668 Robbins Ave. #23, Dracut, 01826; 508-454-7907. Specializing in miscellaneous Akro Agate and Westite

Owings, K.C., Jr.
Antiques Americana
Box 19, N. Abington, 02351; 617-857-1655. Specializing in Civil War, Revolutionary War, autographs, documents, books, antiques

Vigue, Norm
62 Bailey St., Stoughton, 02072; 617-344-5441. Buying and selling TV, western, cartoon-show collectibles, animation art and 1-sheets, radio cereal premiums, and board games

Wellman, BA
88 State Rd W. Homestead Farms #2, Westminster, 01473-1435. Specializing in all areas of American ceramics with video book, identification and price guides available on Ceramic Arts Studio

Williams, Neil
73 Jamestown Dr., Springfield, 01108; 413-739-7797. Specializing in Planters Peanuts

Michigan

Brown, Rick
Newspaper Collectors' Society of America
Box 19134-S, Lansing, 48901; 517-887-1255 or (Fax) 517-887-2194. Specializing in newspapers

Bruner, Mike
2615 Echo Lane, Ortonville, 48462; 810-627-6351. Specializing in lightning rod balls

Gunsaulus, Jack
Gray's Gallery/Jack's Corner Bookstore
583 W. Ann Arbor Trail, Plymouth, 48170. Specializing in porcelain, books, jewelry, glass

Haas, Norman
264 Clizbe Rd., Quincy 49802; 517-639-8537. Specializing in American art pottery

Hoppe, Gordon
10120 32 Ave. N., Plymouth, 55441-3110; 612-546-7461. Specializing in Roseville

Marsh, Linda K.
1229 Gould Rd., Lansing, 48917. Specializing in Degenhart glass

Nedry, Boyd W.
728 Buth Dr., Comstock Park, 49321; 616-784-1513. Specializing in traps (including mice, rat, and fly traps) and trap-related items

Newbound, Betty
4567 Chadsworth, Commerce, 48382. Author (Collector Books) on Blue Ridge dinnerware. Specializing in collectible china and glass

Nickel, Mike
A Nickel's Worth
P.O. Box 456, Portland, 48875; 517-647-7646. Specializing in Roseville, Weller, Rookwood and other important American art pottery, Venetian/Murano glass, Art Deco

O'Callaghan, Tim
46878 Betty Hill, Plymouth, 48170; 313-459-4636. Specializing in dime-store soldiers, also Ford Motor Co., and 'Old Ironsides' (USS Constitution) memorabilia

Oates, Joan
685 S. Washington, Constantine, 49042; 616-435-8353. Specializing in Phoenix Bird chinaware

Ricker, Dawn V.
39145 Marne, Sterling Heights, 48313; 801-566-0891. Schafer & Vater collector

Webster, Marty
2756 Kimberly Rd., Ann Arbor, 48104; 313-665-2030. Specializing in California porcelain and pottery

Minnesota

Anderson, James
Box 12704, New Brighton, 55112; 612-484-3198. Specializing in old fishing lures and reels, also tackle catalogs, posters, calendars, Winchester items

Gallagher, Jerry
420 1st Ave. N.W., Plainview, 55964; 507-534-3511. Specializing in Morgantown research; matching service for Morgantown, Heisey, Fostoria, Cambridge, Duncan, and Tiffin. Publisher of *A Handbook of Old Morgantown Glass* ($35+$4 shipping & handling), Morgantown 1931 catalog reprint (sold out), *Morgantown Colors* placard ($4 postpaid), and *The Morgantown Newscaster*, triannual journal of the Morgantown Collectors of America, Inc. (subscription: $15 per year)

Harrigan, John
1900 Hennepin, Minneapolis, 55403; 612-872-0226. Specializing in Battersea (English enamel) boxes

Ketcham, Steve
Steve Ketcham Antiques (Shows and mail order only)
Box 24114, Edina, 55424; 612-920-4205. Specializing in early American bottles; early Red Wing stoneware (no art pottery or dinnerware); advertising signs, trays, trade cards, pocket mirrors, etched beer and shot glasses. Please include SASE for reply

Nelson, C.L.
Box 222, Spring Park, 55384; 612-473-5625. Specializing in 18th-, 19th- and 20th-century pottery and porcelain, among others: Gaudy Welsh, ABC plates, relief-molded jugs

Podpeskar, Doug
624 Jones St., Eveleth, 55734-1631; 218-744-4854. Specializing in Red Wing dinnerware. Prefers letters with clear photos of items to be identified along with SASE for return

Schoneck, Steve
P.O. Box 56, Newport, 55055; 612-459-2980. Specializing in American art pottery, 20th-century decorative arts, Handicraft Guild of Minneapolis

Missouri

Bine, John and Judy
32 San Carlos Dr., St. Charles, 63303; 314-940-0878. Specializing in glassware

Bosworth, Dick and Waunita
Kansas City Trade Winds
7307 N.W. 75th St., Kansas City, 64152. Specializing in American art pottery, Parrish prints, art glass, Arts & Crafts furniture, lighting

Farris, Sandra
Red Bow Antiques
Bertrand, 314-683-6867. Specializing in pottery, art glass, collectibles

International Rose O'Neill Club
Contact Karen Stewart
P.O. Box 668, Branson, 65616. Dues: $7 (single) or $10 (family) includes newsletter *Kewpiesta Kourier*, published quarterly

Old World Antiques
1715 Summit, Kansas City, 64108
Branch Location: 4436 State Line
Rd., Kansas City, 66103. Specializing in 18th- and 19th-century
furniture, paintings, accessories,
clocks, medical and scientific
instruments, chandeliers, sconces,
Sabino and much more

Our McCoy Matters
Lynch, Kathy
McCoy Publications, P.O. Box
14255, Parkville, 64152. Subscription: $24 per year (6 issues)

Roberts, Brenda
Country Side Antiques
R.R. 2, Marshall, 65340. Specializing in Hull pottery and
general line. Author of *Collectors
Encyclopedia of Hull Pottery*,
*Roberts' Ultimate Encyclopedia of
Hull Pottery* and *The Companion
Guide to Robert's Ultimate Encyclopedia of Hull Pottery*, all with
accompanying price guides;
SASE required

Siegel, Brenda and Jerry
Tower Grove Antiques
3308 Meramec, St. Louis, 63118;
314-352-9020. Specializing in
Ungemach pottery

Scott, John and Peggy
Scotty's Antiques
4650 S. Leroy, Springfield, 65810;
417-887-2191. Specializing in
Depression-era glassware and pottery

Smith, Pat
Independence
Author (Collector Books) of doll
book series

Stout, Elizabeth M.
152 Highway F., Defiance, 63341;
314-987-2223. Specializing in
calendar plates

Thurmond, Jon and Carolyn
Collectorholics
15006 Fuller, Grandview, 64030;
816-322-0906. Specializing in
1950s-1980s character, space, and
unusual toys

Wiesehan, Doug
D & R Farm Antiques
4535 Hwy. H, St. Charles, 63301.
Specializing in salesman's samples
and patent models, antique toys,
farm toys, metal farm signs

Williams, Don
P.O. Box 147, Kirksville 63501; 816-
627-8009 (between 8 a.m. and 6
p.m.). Specializing in art glass; SASE
required with all correspondence

Woollard, D.D., Jr.
11614 Old St. Charles Rd.,
Bridgeton, 63044; 314-739-4662.
Specializing in World's Fair &
Exposition memorabilia

Nebraska

Larsen, Robert V.
3214 19th St., Columbus, 68601
Specializing in old hatpins and
hatpin holders

New Hampshire

Brenner, Larry
Brenner Antiques
1005 Chestnut St., Manchester,
03104; 603-625-8203. Specializing in Royal Bayreuth

Winston, Nancy
Willow Hollow Antiques
RFD 1, Box 550, Northwood,
03261; 603-942-5739. Specializing
in Shaker baskets, primitives, country smalls, paper Americana, toys

New Jersey

Adams, Jay (Mail order only)
245 Lakeview Ave., Suite 208,
Clifton, NJ 07011; 201-365-5907.
Specializing in Depression-era
china and glass

Anderson, Suzy McLennan
Heritage Antiques & Appraisal
Services
65 E. Main St., Holmdel, 07733;
908-946-8801 or (Fax) 908-946-
1036. Specializing in American furniture and decorative accessories

Bilane, John E. (Mail order only)
2065 Morris Ave., Apt. 109,
Union, 07083. Specializing in
antique glass cup plates

Cole, Lillian M., Editor of *Piebirds
Unlimited* Newsletter
14 Harmony School Rd., Flemington, 08822; 908-782-3198. Specializing in pie birds, pie funnels, pie vents

Dezso, Doug
864 Paterson Ave., Maywood,
07607-2119; 201-488-1311. Specializing in nodders (German),
candy containers, Tonka

Doorstop Collectors of America
Doorstopper newsletter
Jeanie Bertoia
2413 Madison Ave., Vineland,
08630; 609-692-4092. Membership: $20 per year, includes 2
newsletters and convention. Send
2-stamp SASE for sample

Litts, Elyce
P.O. Box 394, Morris Plains,
07950; 201-361-4087. Author
(Collector Books) of *Collector's
Encyclopedia of Geisha Girl Porcelain*

Lockwood, Howard J.
Box 191, Fort Lee, 07024; 201-
692-9780. Specializing in Italian
glass of the 20th century

Meschi, Edward J.
129 Pinyard Rd., Monroeville,
08343; 609-358-7293 or (Fax)
609-358-7293. Specializing in
Durand art glass, Icart etching,
Maxfield Parrish prints, Rookwood pottery, and other fine arts

Patalano, Diane
34 Holly Dr., Upper Saddle River
07458. Specializing in banks,
spatterware, various antiques and
collectibles

Perzel, Robert and Nancy
Popkorn
4 Mine St. (near Main St.), P.O.
Box 1057, Flemington, 08822;
908-782-9631. Specializing in
Stangl dinnerware, birds, and artware; Depression Glass

Poster, Harry
Vintage TVs
Box 1883, S. Hackensack, 07606;
Days: 201-794-9606; 24-Hour Fax:
201-794-9553; Phone: 201-410-
7525. Writes *Poster's Radio and
Television Price Guide*. Specializes
in vintage televisions, transistor
radios, 3-D stereo cameras

Rago, David
9 S. Main St., Lambertville,
08530; 609-397-9374. Specializing in Arts & Crafts, art pottery

Rash, Jim
135 Alder Ave., Pleasantville,
08232; 609-646-4125. Specializing in advertising dolls

Rosen, Barbara
6 Shoshone Trail, Wayne, 07470.
Specializing in figural bottle
openers and antique dollhouses

Steinfeld, Milt
633 Westfield Ave., Box 457,
Westfield, 07091. Specializing in
collectible glass and china, Victorian silverplate, and other small
collectibles

Vines, Linda L.
Yesterday Once More
P.O. Box 721, Upper Montclair,
07043; 201-783-4990. Specializing in Snow Babies, all holidays
(Christmas, Easter, Halloween),
dolls, toys, and Steiff

Visakay, Stephen
Vintage Cocktail Shakers (By
appointment)
P.O. Box 1517, W. Caldwell,
07007-1517. Specializing in vintage cocktail shakers

New Mexico

Hardisty, Don
Artistic Restorations: Specializing
in Bossons and Hummels
3020 E. Majestic Ridge, Las
Cruces, 88011; 505-522-3721 or
800-BOSSONS (267-7667); Fax
available: 505-522-7909

Manns, William
P.O. Box 6459, Santa Fe, 87502;
800-266-5767. Co-author of
Painted Ponies, hard-bound edition (226 pages), available from
author for $39.95+$4 shipping.
Specializing in carousel art and
western antiques

New York

Angelo, Norma
205 Huxley Ave., Jamestown,
14701; 716-483-3752. Specializing in Oriental porcelain

Austin, Bruce A.
1 Hardwood Hill Rd., Pittsford,
14534; 716-387-9820 (evenings);
716-475-2879 (week days). Specializing in clocks and Arts &
Crafts furnishings and accessories

Batchelor, Daniel J.
R.R. 10, Box 1010, Oswego,
13126. Specializing in Pairpoint,
Handel, Bradley and Hubbard
lamps; Photo and SASE required
with all correspondence

Calison, Jim
Tools of Distinction
Wallkill, 12589; 914-895-8035.
Specializing in antique and collectible tools, buying and selling

Dimitroff, Thomas P.
Dimitroff's Antiques (Appointment only)
140 E. First St., Corning, 14830; 607-962-6745. Specializing in Steuben and cut glass

Doyle, Robert A.
Doyle Auctioneers & Appraisers
109 Osborne Hill Rd., Fishkill, 12524. Thousands of collectibles offered, call for free calendar of upcoming auctions

Fer-Duc Inc.
Ferrara, Joseph
Box 1303, Newburgh, 12550; 914-565-5990. Specializing in American art pottery (Ohr, Rookwood, Zanesville), 19th- and 20th-century American paintings

Fox, Ron
Ron Fox Auctions
83 Morris St., Brentwood, 11717; 516-231-0633 or Fax: 516-952-7719. Specializing in steins; auctions with illustrated catalogs and video tapes

Gerson, Roselyn
P.O. Box 40, Lynbrook, 11563; 516-593-8746. Author/collector specializing in unusual, gadgetry, figural compacts and vanity bags/purses

Greguire, Helen
Helen's Antiques
103 Trimmer Rd., Hilton, 14468; 716-392-2704. Specializing in graniteware (any color), Carnival Glass lamps and shades, Carnival Glass lighting of all kinds; Author (Collector Books) of *The Collector's Encyclopedia of Graniteware, Colors, Shapes & Values*, (updated values, $27.95 postage paid); Second book on graniteware now available (same price); Also available is *Carnival in Lights*, featuring Carnival glass, lamps, shades, etc. ($13.45 (postage paid); All available at above address. Also interested in unusual and rare toasters

Handelsman, Burton
18 Hotel Dr., White Plains, 10605; 914-428-4480 (home) and 914-761-8880 (office). Specializing in occupational shaving mugs, accessories

Herley, Patrick J.
P.O. Box 606, E. Setauket, 11733; 516-928-6052. Specializing in Goss china

Jordan, Ruth E.
Meridale, 13806; 607-746-2082. Specializing in cut glass, American Brilliant period

Laun, H. Thomas and Patricia
Little Century
215 Paul Ave., Syracuse, 13206; 315-437-4156. Summer residence: 35109 Country Rte. 7, Cape Vincent, 13618; 315-654-3244. Specializing in firefighting collectibles

Malloy, Alex G.
Alex G. Malloy, Inc.
P.O. Box 38, South Salem, 10590; 203-438-0396. Specializing in ancient and medieval coins; antiquities, numismatic literature

Malitz, Lucille
Lucid Antiques
Box KH, Scarsdale, 10583; 914-636-7825. Specializing in lithophanes, medical antiques, stanhopes, antique kaleidoscopes

Meisel, Louis K. and Susan P.
Meisel Decorative Arts Gallery
133 Prince St., New York City, 10012. Specializing in Clarice Cliff and 20th-century designs in jewelry, watches, toys, unusual vintage bicycles, and model sailboats

Michel, John and Barbara
Americana Blue
200 E. 78th St., 18E, New York City, 10021; 212-861-6094. Specializing in yellow ware, cast iron, and tramp art

Owens, Lowell
Owens' Collectibles
12 Bonnie Ave., New Hartford, 13413. Specializing in beer advertising

Pisello, Faye
577 Lake St., Wilson, 14172. Specializing in Brownies by Palmer Cox

Rifken, Blume J.
Author of *Silhouettes in America — 1790-1840 — a Collector's Guide*. Specializing in American antique silhouettes from 1790 to 1840

Safir, Charlotte F.
1349 Lexington Ave., 9-B, New York City, 10128; 212-534-7933. Specializing in cookbooks, children's books (out-of-print only)

Schleifman, Roselle
Ed's Collectibles/The Rage
16 Vincent Rd., Spring Valley, 10977; 914-356-2121. Specializing in Duncan & Miller, elegant glass

Smyth, Carole and Richard
Carole Smyth Antiques
P.O. Box 2068, Huntington, 11743; 516-673-8666. Authors of *The Burning Passion — Antique and Collectible Pyrography*, available from authors at above address for $19.95+$3 postage (New York State residents add 8.5% sales tax)

Steinbock, Nancy
Nancy Steinbock Posters & Prints
518-438-1577. Specializing in posters: travel, war, literary, advertising

Tuggle, Robert
105 W. St., New York City, 10023; 212-595-0514. Specializing in John Bennett, Anglo-Japanese china

Van Kuren, Jean and Dale
Ruth's Antiques, Inc.
9060 Main St., Clarence, 14031; 716-632-1630. Specializing in Buffalo pottery, general line

Van Patten, Joan F.
Box 102, Rexford, 12148. Author (Collector Books) of books on Nippon and Noritake

North Carolina

Degenhardt, Richard K.
Sugar Hollow Farm
124 Cypress Point, Hendersonville, 28739; 704-696-9750. Author of *Belleek, The Complete Collectors' Guide and Illustrated Reference*. Specializing in Belleek (The only Belleek is the Irish. Established by legal action in 1929)

Hughes, Kathy (Mrs. Paul)
Tudor House Galleries
1401 E. Blvd., Charlotte, 28203; 704-377-4748. Specializing in relief-molded Jugs, 18th- and 19th-century English pottery and 19th-century oil paintings

Kirtley, Charles E.
P.O. Box 2273, Elizabeth City, 27096; 919-335-1262. Specializing in monthly auctions and bid sales dealing with World's Fair, Civil War, political, advertising, and other American collectibles

Sayers, R.J.
Southeastern Antiques & Appraisals
14 Longbranch Rd., Pisgah Forest, 28768. Specializing in Boy Scout collectibles, Pisgah Forest pottery, primitive American furniture; Author of *Guide to Scouting Collectibles*, available from author for $24.95+$4 postage

North Dakota

Farnsworth, Bryce
1334 14½ St. South, Fargo, 58103; 701-237-3597. Specializing in Rosemeade pottery; If writing for information, please send a picture if possible, also phone number and best time to call

Ohio

Bassett, Mark
P.O. Box 771233, Lakewood, 44017. Specializing in Cowan, American and European art pottery, Art Deco.

Batory, Mr. Dana Martin
402 E. Bucyrus St., Crestline, 44827. Specializing in antique woodworking machinery, old and new woodworking machinery catalogs. In order to prepare a definitive history on American manufacturers of woodworking machinery, Dana is interested in acquiring by loan, gift, or photocopy, any and all documents, catalogs, manuals, photos, personal reminiscences, etc., pertaining to woodworking machinery and/or their manufacturers. **No phone calls please.**

Benjamin, Scott
P.O. Box 611, Elyria, 44036; 216-365-9534. Specializing in gas globes; Co-author of *Gas Pump Globes*, listing nearly 4,000 gas globes with over 400 photos, prices, rarity guide, histories, and reproduction information. Currently available from author

Blair, Betty
Golden Apple Antiques
216 Bridge St., Jackson, 45640; 614-286-4817. Specializing in art pottery, Watt, cookie jars, chocolate molds, general line

Briggs, Karen
Toledo, 419-478-7453. Specializing in glass, china, pottery, knives

Budin, Nicki
Curio Cabinet
679 High St., Worthington, 43085; 614-885-1986. Specializing in Royal Doulton

China Specialties, Inc.
19238 Dorchester Circle, Strongsville, 44136; 216-238-2528. Specializing in Autumn Leaf

Cincinnati Auction Gallery
635 Main St., Cincinnati, 45202; 513-381-2128. Specializing in American art pottery (especially Rookwood), American and European fine paintings, watercolors

Collectors of Findlay Glass
P.O. Box 256, Findlay, 45840. An organization dedicated to the study and recognition of Findlay glass; *The Melting Pot* Newsletter published quarterly; Convention held annually; Membership: $10 per year

Collings, Sam and Becky
Hardtimes Glassware
202 Brook Dr., Brookfield, 44403; 216-448-8986. Specializing in Depression Glass and Fenton

DeGenaro, Steve
P.O. Box 5662, Youngstown, 44504. Specializing in post-mortem photos, mourning collectibles

Distel, Ginny
Distel's Antiques
4041 S.C.R. 22, Tiffin, 44883; 419-447-5832. Specializing in Tiffin glass

Ebner, Rita and John
Cracker Barrel Antiques
4540 Helen Rd., Columbus, 43232. Specializing in door knockers, cast-iron bottle openers, Griswold

Ferguson, Maxine
1380 Bussemer, Zanesville, 43701.

Forsythe, Ruth A.
Box 327, Galena, 43021. Author of *Made in Czechoslovakia*, Books I and II

Graff, Shirley
4515 Grafton Rd., Brunswick, 44212. Specializing in Pennsbury pottery

Guenin, Tom
Box 454, Chardon, 44024. Specializing in antique telephones and antique telephone restoration

Hamlin, Jack & Treva
R.R. 4, Box 150, Kaiser St., Proctorville, 45669; 614-886-7644. Specializing in Currier and Ives by Royal China Co.

Harnish, Jerry and Ellen
Old Tyme Toy Mall/Booth #3
110 Main St., Bellville, 44813; 419-886-4782. Specializing in G.I. Joe

Hothem, Lar
Hothem House
Box 458, Lancaster, 43130. Specializing in books about Indians and artifacts

Kao, Fern Larking
Lustre Pitcher Antiques
P.O. Box 312, Bowling Green, 43402; 419-352-5928. Specializing in jewelry, sewing implements, ladies' accessories

Kerr, Ann
P.O. 437, Sidney, 45365; 513-492-6369. Author (Collector Books) of *Collector's Encyclopedia of Russel Wright Designs* and *Fostoria, an Identification and Value Guide*. Specializing in work of Wright, interested in 20th-century decorative arts

Kitchen, Lorrie
Toledo, 419-478-3815. Specializing in Depression-era glass, Hall china, Fiesta, Blue Ridge, Shawnee

Klender, James and Grace
Town & Country Antiques & Collectibles
P.O. Box 447, Pioneer, 43554; 419-737-2880. Specializing in Depression Glass and general line

Kline, Mr. and Mrs. Jerry and Gerry
Members of North American Torquay Society and Torquay Pottery Collectors' Society
604 Orchard View Dr., Maumee, 43537; 419-893-1226. Specializing in collecting Torquay pottery

Mathes, Richard
P.O. Box 1408, Springfield, 45501-1408; 513-324-6917. Specializing in buttonhooks

Mondloch, Dee and Tony
Precious & Few
709 N. Union St., Fostoria, 44830; 419-435-2987. Specializing in Tiffin glass

Moore, Carolyn
445 N. Prospect, Bowling Green, 43402. Specializing in primitives, yellow ware, graniteware

Murphy, James L.
1023 Neil Ave., Columbus, 43201; 614-297-0746. Specializing in Radford and Vance Avon

National Imperial Glass Collectors' Society, Inc.
P.O. Box 534, Bellaire 43906. Dues: $12 per year (plus $1 for each additional member in the same household), quarterly newsletter, convention every June

Nelson, Norman
2267 E. Erie, Lorain, 44052; 216-288-4977. Specializing in jukeboxes

Osborne, Ruth
5954 State Rte. 505, Georgetown, 45121. Specializing in vintage clothing, lamps, jewelry. Please, no phone calls.

Peters, Jeannie L.
Mt. Washington Antiques
3742 Kellogg, Cincinnati, 45226; 513-231-6584. Specializing in sheet music

Pierce, David
27544 Black Rd., P.O. Box 248, Danville, 43014; 614-599-6394. Specializing in Glidden pottery

Radel, Erle and Janice
Rapids Renovations & Antiques
Grand Rapids. Specializing in furniture and fine jewelry, (collectors only) Labino art glass

Rees, Debbie
Zanesville.
Specializing in Watt, Roseville juvenile and other Roseville pottery, Zanesville area pottery, cookie jars, and Steiff

Riebel, James; Krause, Terry
Pottery Peregrinators
Zanesville, 614-452-7687. Specializing in American art pottery, Nicodemus, and Carnival Glass

Roscoe, Mike
3351 Lagrange, Toledo, 43608; 419-244-6935. Specializing in toys, advertising, coin-operated machines, furniture, and miscellaneous

Rothrock, Ken and Joan
Silver Spoon Antiques
Millikin Hotel, 101 S. Main, Bowling Green, 43402; 419-354-6606. Specializing in silver, linen, smalls

Rouppas, William
Frogtown
Box 822, Toledo, 43601; 419-475-1235. Specializing in unique collectibles

Trainer, Veronica
Bayhouse
Box 40443, Cleveland, 44140; 216-871-8584. Specializing in beaded and enamelled mesh purses

Tucker, Dan
Toledo, 419-478-3815. Specializing in Depression-era glass, Hall china, Fiesta, Blue Ridge, Shawnee

Vroman, Bill & Judy
739 Eastern Ave., Fostoria, 44830; 419-435-5443. Collectors of Jewel Tea or Autumn Leaf, buying and selling all types of fine antiques

Walker, Bunny
Box 502, Bucyrus, 44820; 419-562-8355. Specializing in Steiff teddy bears, penny toys, pottery

Walter, John
The Old Tool Shop
208 Front St., Marietta, 45750; 614-373-9973. Specializing in all types of antique tools

Whitmyer, Margaret and Kenn
Box 30806, Gahanna, 43230. Author (Collector Books) on children's dishes. Specializing in Depression-era collectibles

Wilkins, Juanita
The Bird of Paradise
Lima. Specializing in R.S. china, Old Ivory china, colored pattern glass, lamps, and jewelry

Young, Mary
1040 Greenridge Dr., Kettering, 45429. Author (Collector Books) of *Collector's Guide to Paper Dolls*

Oklahoma

Bess, Phyllis and Tom
14535 E. 13th St., Tulsa, 74108; 918-437-7776. Authors of *Frankoma Treasures*, and *Frankoma and Other Oklahoma Potteries*. Specializing in Frankoma and Oklahoma pottery

Klein, Bob and Dondee
1002 Walnut Court, Guthrie, 73044; 405-282-6545. Specializing in Tamac pottery

Moore, Art and Shirley
2145 S. Norfolk Ave., Tulsa, 74114; 918-747-4164. Specializing in Lu Ray Pastels, Depression Glass

Scott, Roger R.
4250 S. Oswego, Tulsa, 74135; 918-742-8710 or (Fax) 918-583-1226. Specializing in Victor and RCA Victor trademark items along with Nipper

Willis, Ron L.
2110 Fox Ave., Moore, 73160. Specializing in militaria

Oregon

Abrahams, Peter
1948 Mapleleaf Rd., Lake Oswego, 97034; 503-636-2988. Specializing in telescopes, binoculars, microscopes. Peter studies and collects optics: telescopes, binoculars, hand magnifiers, and microscopes. He especially seeks reference material on these subjects, including books, catalogs, repair manuals, and histories

Bartsch, Henry
Antique Registers
2050 N. Hwy. 101, Rockaway Beach, 97136; 503-355-2932. Specializing in antique cash registers; Co-author of *Antique Cash Registers 1880-1920*. Written insurance appraisals are provided by Mr. Bartsch for a $25 fee; Please include register's model, serial number, condition and 3 keeper photographs.

Bird, Leah and Walt
Bird's Nest
P.O. Box 4502, Medford, 97501; 503-779-3028. Specializing in vintage clothing (pre-1940s), beaded and mesh purses, buttons

Brady, Glen
P.O. Box 3933, Central Point, 97502; 503-772-0350. Specializing in Ertl and Tonka, construction and logging toys, pressed steel, diecast toy trucks, Smokey the Bear items

Brown, Marcia
Sparkles
6959 Pinehurst, Central Point, 97502; 503-826-3039. Specializing in rhinestone jewelry

Buzan, James
Antique Workshop
17935 Monticello Dr., Gladstone, 97027-1338; 503-655-7686 (evenings). Specializing in fine art tile and decorative arts

Carter, Fran (Appointment only)
Box 3220, Coos Bay, 97420; 503-888-5780. Specializing in estate sales

Coe, Debbie and Randy
Coes Mercantile
1240 S.E. 40th, Hillsboro, 97123; 503-640-9122. Specializing in elegant Depression-era glass, art pottery

Couts, Rick and Melissa
Intellasearch
1361 N. 4th St., Lakeview, 97630; 1-800-947-5390. Specializing in America's antiques and collectibles data base service

Cox, Billy & Thelma, Owners
Medford Antique Mall
1 West 6th St., Medford 97501; 503-773-4983

Frost, Donald M.
Country Estate Antiques (Appointment only)
17875 N.W. Tillamook Dr., Portland, 97229; 503-531-3563. Specializing in fine glass and porcelain

Geddes, Marjorie
P.O. Box 5875, Aloha, 97007; 503-649-1041. Specializing in sewing items, open salts, Florence ceramics, California figurines, miscellaneous small and elegant collectibles

Hamilton, Hope and Harvey
300 Luman Rd. #195, Phoenix, 97535; 503-535-2410. Specializing in Royal Hickman

Hertager, Vanita J.
P.O. Box 833, Phoenix, 97535; 503-535-7419. Specializing in buttons (sew-ons), plastic, pins, jewelry

Hirshman, Susan and Larry
Everyday Antiques
542 Siskiyou Blvd., Ashland, 97520; 503-482-9411. Specializing in china, glassware, kitchenware

Main Antique Mall
30 N. Riverside, Medford, 97501; 503-779-9490. Quality products and services for the serious collector, dealer, or those just browsing

Matthews, Kathy and Skip
Second Childhood Antiques and Collectibles
1154 Grande Ave., Astoria, 97103; 503-325-6543. Specializing in Disneyana, toys, and character collectibles

Miller, Don and Robby
P.O. Box 508, Talent, 97540; 503-535-1231 Specializing in milk bottles, TV Siamese cat lamps, seltzer bottles, red cocktail shakers

Morris, Thomas G.
Prize Publishers
P.O. Box 8307, Medford, 97504; 503-779-3164. Author of *The Carnival Chalk Prize*, Books I and II, pictorial price guides on carnival chalkware figures with brief histories and values for each

Rich, Shirley
424 Highland Dr., Medford, 97504; 503-772-8395. Specializing in milk bottles

Ringering, David
Belle Ringer Antiques
1480 Tumalo Dr. S.E., Salem, 97301; 503-585-8253. Specializing in Rowland & Marsellus and other souvenir/historical china with scenes of buildings, parks, and other tourist attractions of the 1890s-1930s. Feel free to contact David if you have any questions about Rowland & Marsellus or other souvenir china. He will be happy to answer questions about souvenir china.

Roberts, Fred
Bah Humbug Collectibles, 503-776-3826

Wright, Patricia
P.O. Box 83, Phoenix, 97535; 503-535-2095. Specializing in half dolls, Christmas and Halloween decorations

Pennsylvania

Barker, Jim
Toastermaster Antique Appliances
P.O. Box 41, Bethlehem, 18016; 610-439-0751. Specializing in early electric toasters and fans; Porcelier and Royal Rochester items wanted

Barrett, Noel
Rosebud Antiques
P.O. Box 1001, Carversville, 18913; 215-297-5109. Specializing in toys

Bodine, Clarence H., Jr., Proprietor
East/West Gallery
41B Ferry St., New Hope, 18938; 908-782-3430 (evenings). Specializing in antique Japanese woodblock prints, netsuke, inro, tsuba

Cerebro
P.O. Box 327, East Prospect, 17317; 717-252-2400 or 800-69-LABEL. Fax: 717-252-3685. Specializing in antique advertising labels, especially cigar box labels, cigar bands, food labels, firecracker labels

Damaska, Ron
738 9th Ave., New Brighton, 15066; 412-843-1393. Specializing in Fry cut glass, match holders, oil lamps, silver; SASE required when requesting information

DLK Nostalgia & Collectibles
P.O. Box 5112, Johnstown, 15904. Specializing in corkscrews and openers, Art Deco, clocks, toys, breweriana, football cards, radios, militaria, antique guns, robots, battery-operated toys, miscellaneous

Garvin, Joann
P.O. Box 182, Beaver Falls, 15010; 412-843-3999. Specializing in Fiesta

Gottuso, Bob
Bojo
P.O. Box 1403, Cranberry Township, 16066; Phone/Fax: 412-776-0621. Specializing in Beatles, Elvis, Kiss, Monkees, licensed Rock 'N Roll memorabilia

Hagenbuch, James
Glass-Works Auction
102 Jefferson, East Greenville, 18041; 215-679-5849. America's leading auction company in early American bottles and glass

Hain, Henry F., III
Antiques & Collectibles
2623 N. Second St., Harrisburg, 17110; 717-238-0534. Lists available of items for sale

Hinton, Michael C.
246 W. Ashland St., Doylestown, 18901; 215-345-0892. Owns/ operates Bucks County Art & Antiques Company and Chem-Clean Furniture Restoration Company. Specializing in quality restorations of a wide range of art and antiques from colonial to contemporary. Catalog of paintings and frames available

Holland, William
William Holland Fine Arts
1708 E. Lancaster Ave., Paoli, 19301; 610-648-0369 or (Fax) 610-647-4448. Specializing in Louis Icart etchings and oils, Art Nouveau and Art Deco items; Author of *Louis Icart: The Complete Etchings* and *The Collectible Maxfield Parrish*

Irons, Dave
Dave Irons Antiques
223 Covered Bridge Road, Northampton, 18067; 610-262-9335. Author of *Irons By Irons* (soft-cover); Available from author, (over 1,600 irons pictured, contains current information and price ranges, collecting hints, news of trends, and information for proper care of irons). Specializing in pressing irons, country furniture, primitives, quilts, accessories

Kamm, George
George Kamm Paperweights
24-SP Townsend Ct., Lancaster, 17603; 717-872-7858. Specializing in antique and contemporary paperweights – color brochure published bimonthly. $5 annual fee (refundable). Sample on request (#10 SASE required)

Knauer, Judy A.
National Toothpick Holder Collectors' Society
1224 Spring Valley Lane, West Chester, 19380; 610-431-3477. Specializing in toothpick holders and Victorian glass

The Krauses
Krause, Gail
97 W. Wheeling St., Washington, 15301; 412-228-5034. Author of book on Duncan glass

Kurau, William
Box 457, Lampeter, 17537; 717-464-0731. Specializing in historical Staffordshire. Please include SASE when requesting information

Lindsay, Ralph
P.O. Box 21, New Holland, 17557. Specializing in target balls. SASE required with correspondence

Maier, Clarence and Betty
Mail order: The Burmese Cruet
Box 432, Montgomeryville, 18936; 215-855-5388. Specializing in Victorian art glass

Marks, Mariann Katz
1416 Main, Honesdale, 18431. Author (Collector Books) of *Majolica Pottery, Second Series*. Specializing in collecting, buying, and selling American and English majolica of the Victorian period; LSASE required for mail-order list. Enclose photo and price wanted with offers to sell

Merchants Square Mall
Jim & Annetta Vitez, Managers
1901 S. 12th St., Allentown, 18103; 610-797-7743

Oster, Frederick
Frederick W. Oster Fine Violins
1529 Pine St., Philadelphia, 19102; 215-545-1100 or (Fax) 215-735-3634. Specializing in rare and antique instruments of the violin family, as well as antique stringed and wind instruments

Posner, Judy
R.D. 1, Box 273, Effort, 18330; 717-629-6583. Specializing in figural pottery, cookie jars, salt and peppers, Black memorabilia, Disneyana, character and advertising collectibles; buy, sell & trade

Rosso, Philip J. and Philip Jr.
Wholesale Glass Dealers
1815 Trimble Ave., Port Vue, 15133; 412-678-7352. Specializing in Westmoreland glass

Weiser, Pastor Frederick S.
55 Kohler School Rd., New Oxford, 17350; 717-624-4106. Specializing in frakturs and other Pennsylvania German documents

Rhode Island

Dumont, Louise
579 Old Main St., Coventry, 02816; 401-828-2799. Winter address: 319 Hawthorne Blvd, Leesburg, FL 34748; 904-787-6060. Specializing in cookie jars, Abingdon

Gacher, John
The Zsolnay Store
152 Spring St., Newport, 02840; 401-841-5060. Specializing in Zsolnay, Fischer, Amphora, and Austro-Hungarian art pottery

The Occupied Japan Club
c/o Florence Archambault
29 Freeborn St., Newport, 02840-1821. Publishes bimonthly newsletter, *The Upside Down World of an O.J. Collector*. SASE required when requesting information

South Carolina

Roerig, Fred and Joyce
R.R. 2, Box 504, Walterboro, 29488; 803-538-2487. Specializing in cookie jars; Authors of *Collector's Encyclopedia of Cookie Jars, an Illustrated Value Guide*, publishers of *Cookie Jarrin' With Joyce: The Cookie Jar Newsletter*

Tennessee

Chase, Mick and Lorna
Fiesta Plus
380 Hawkins Crawford Rd., Cookeville, 38501; 615-372-8333. Specializing in Fiesta, Franciscan, Metlox, other American dinnerware

Grist, Everett
6503 Slater Rd., Suite H, Chattanooga, 37412-3955; 615-855-4032. Specializing in covered animal dishes and marbles

Hudson, Murray
Murray Hudson Antiquarian Books & Maps
109 S. Church St., Box 163, Halls, 38040; Fax & phone: 900-836-9057 or phone 800-748-9946. Specializing in antique maps, globes and books with maps, atlases, explorations, travel guides, geographies, surveys, etc.

Texas

Cooper, Marilyn
8408 Lofland Dr., Houston, 77055; 713-465-7773. Specializing in figural toothbrush holders, Pez

Dockery, Rod
4600 Kemble St., Ft. Worth, 76103; 817-536-2168. Specializing in milk glass; SASE required with correspondence

Docks, L.R. 'Les'
Shellac Shack; Discollector
Box 691035, San Antonio, 78269-1035. Author of *American Premium Record Guide*. Specializing in vintage records

Frese, Leo and Wendy
Three Rivers Collectibles
Box 551542, Dallas, 75355; 214-341-5165. Specializing in Rum-Rill, Red Wing pottery and stoneware, Hull

Gaston, Mary Frank
Box 342, Bryan, 77806. Author (Collector Books) on china and metals

Gibbs, Carl, Jr.
P.O. Box 131584, Houston, 77219-1584; 713-521-9661. Author of *Collector's Encyclopedia of Metlox Potteries*, autographed copies available from author for $24.95 plus $3 shipping and handling

Malowanczyk, Abby and Wlodek
Collage-20th Century Classics
3017-B Routh St., Dallas, 75201; 214-880-0020 or (Fax) 214-351-6208. Specializing in architect-designed furniture and decorative arts from the modern movement

Norris, Kenn
Schoolmaster Auctions
P.O. Box 4830, 208 Kerr St., Sanderson, 79848; 915-345-2640. Specializing in school-related items and barbed wire

Pringle, Joyce M.
Chip & Dale Collectables
3500 S. Cooper St., Arlington, 76015. Specializing in Boyd, Summit, and Mosser glass

Silvermintz, Karen
5254 Vanderbilt, Dallas, 75206; 214-826-1107. Specializing in dinnerware, Russel Wright, mid-century glass and pottery

Smith, Allan
1806 Shields Dr., Sherman, 75090. Specializing in children's lunch boxes, Coca-Cola, Dr. Pepper, Pepsi Cola, RC Cola, and western stars' items

Thompson, Chuck
Chuck Thompson & Associates
P.O. Box 11652, Houston, 77293. Send LSASE for free list of Chuck's tobacciana publications; Thompson specializes in smokers' ashtrays with and without advertising imprints. His research includes ashtrays designed for homes, automobiles, ocean liners, hotels, trains, and any place where 'ash receivers' were provided to accommodate smokers.

Tucker, Richard and Valerie
Argyle Antiques
P.O. Box 262, Argyle, 76226; 817-464-3752 or (Fax) 817-464-7293. Specializing in windmill weights, shooting gallery targets, figural lawn sprinklers and cast-iron advertising paperweights

Waddell, John
2903 Stan Terrace, Mineral Wells, 76067. Specializing in buggy steps

Wilkins, James R.
Olden Year Musical Museum
Box 381951, Duncanville, 75138-1951; 214-298-5587. Specializing in music boxes, phonographs, grind organs, nickelodeons

Utah

Anderson, Tim
Box 461, Provo, 84603. Specializing in autographs; Buys single items or collections — historical, movie stars, US Presidents, sports figures, and pre-1860 correspondence. Autograph questions? Please include photocopies of your autographs with possible and enclose a SASE for guaranteed reply.

Anderson, Warren R.
America West Archives
P.O. Box 100, Cedar City, 84721; 801-586-9497. Specializing in old stock certificates and bonds, western documents and books, financial ephemera, autographs, maps, photos. Author of *Owning Western History*, with 75+ photos of old documents and recommended reference guide. Available ($18 soft cover or $28 hardback, postpaid) from author

Killmer, Jo
Antiques, Etc.
260 N. University Ave., Provo, 84604; 801-375-1211. Specializing in silverplate patterns, also sterling, china, general line of antiques, Roseville

Spencer, Rick
3953 S. Renault Circle, West Valley, 84119; 801-973-0805. Specializing in silverware, Old McDonald by Regal, Shawnee, Van Telligen, salt and pepper shakers

Vermont

Barry, Kit
109 Main St., Brattleboro, 05301; 802-254-3634. Author of *Reflections 1* and *Reflections 2*. Specializing in advertising trade cards and ephemera in general

Virginia

Bradfield, Jeff
Jeff's Antiques
90 Main St., Dayton, 22821; 540-879-9961. Also located in Pat's Antique Mall (I-81), Exit 227, Verona. Specializing in candy containers, toys, postcards, sugar shakers, lamps, furniture, pottery, and advertising items

Cranor, Rosalind
P.O. Box 859, Blacksburg, 24063. Specializing in Elvis collectibles; Author of *Elvis Collectibles* and *Best of Elvis Collectibles* (each at $19.95+$1.75 postage), available from author

Flanigan, Vicki
Flanigan's Antiques
P.O. Box 1662, Winchester, 22601. Specializing in antique dolls and hand fans

Friend, Terry
839 Glendale Rd., Galax, 24333; 703-236-9027 after 9:30 p.m. E.S.T. Specializing in coffee mills; SASE required

Haigh, Richard
10607 Baypines Lane, Richmond, 23233; 804-741-5770. Specializing in Locke Art, Steuben

Harold, James P.
2200 Columbia Pike, Arlington, 22204-4422. Specializing in pink lustre ware

Lechner, Mildred and Ralph
Box 554, Mechanicsville, 23111; 804-737-3347. Author (Collector Books) on glass salt shakers. Specializing in art and pattern glass salt shakers circa 1870-1940. Directors of Antique and Art Glass Salt Shakers Society Club, 1991-92. **Please note:** Mildred and Ralph have absolutely **NO** involvement or dealings concerning novelty salt shakers or their values

Monsen, Randall; and Baer, Rod
Monsen & Baer
Box 529, Vienna, 22183; 703-242-1357. Specializing in perfume bottles, Roseville pottery, Art Deco

Reynolds, Charles
Reynolds Toys
2836 Monroe St., Falls Church, 22042; 703-533-1322. Specializing in limited-edition mechanical and still banks, figural bottle openers

Schleyer, Jim
Toy Gun Purveyors
Box 243-S, Burke, 22015. Specializing in toy guns

Tutton, John
R.R. 4, Box 929, Front Royal, 22630; 703-635-7058. Specializing in milk bottles

Washington

Haase, Don (Mr. Spode)
D&D Antiques
P.O. Box 818, Mukilteo, 98275; 206-348-7443. Specializing in Spode china

Jackson, Denis C., Editor
The Illustrator Collector's News
P.O. Box 1958, Sequim, 98382; 206-683-2559. Copy of recent sample: $3. Specializing in old magazines and illustrations such as: Rose O'Neill, Maxfield Parrish, pinups, Marilyn Monroe, Norman Rockwell, etc.

Payne, Sharon A.
Antiquities & Art
9104 163rd Ave. NE, Granite Falls, 98252; 206-691-4847. Specializing in Cordey

Rothe, Linda
P.O. Box 17438, Seattle, 98107. Specializing in Black Americana

Wheeler-Tanner Escapes
Tanner, Joseph and Pamela
3024 E. 35th Ave., Spokane, 99223; 509-448-8457. Specializing in handcuffs, leg shackles, balls and chains, restraints and padlocks of all kinds (including railroad) locking and non-locking devices; Also Houdini memorabilia: autographs, photos, posters, books, letters, etc.

Whitaker, Jim and Kaye
Eclectic Antiques
P.O. Box 475S, Lynnwood, 98046; 206-774-6910. Specializing in Josef Originals and motion lamps. Please include SASE

West Virginia

Fostoria Glass Society of America, Inc.
Box 826, Moundsville, 26041. Specializing in Fostoria glass

Wisconsin

Apple, John
John Apple Antiques
1720 College Ave., Racine, 53403; 414-633-3086. Specializing in brass cash registers and parts

Fortney, Daniel
Suite 713, Chalet at the River, 823 N. 2nd St., Milwaukee, 53203. Specializing in china and glass

Knapper, Mary
Phoneco, Inc.
207 E. Mill Rd., P.O. Box 70, Galesville, 54630; 608-582-4124. Specializing in telephones, antique to modern

Matzke, Gene
Gene's Badges & Emblems
2345 S. 28th St., Milwaukee, 53215; 414-383-8995. Specializing in police badges, leg irons, old police photos, fire badges (old), patches, old handcuffs, and memorabilia

Rice, Ferill J.
302 Pheasant Run, Kaukauna, 54130. Specializing in Fenton art glass

Rossiter, Chris
Box 264, Cleveland, 53015; 414-693-8086. Specializing in pipes (especially porcelains) also collecting toys and English military

Washburn, Cara
Washburn Antiques
751 E. Thomas St., Osseo, 54758; 715-597-2666 (M-F). Specializing in glass (over 6,000 pieces), tools, toys, furniture, general merchandise

Clubs, Newsletters and Catalogs

Abingdon Pottery Collectors Club
Elaine Westover, Membership and Treasurer
210 Knox Hwy. 5, Abingdon, IL 61410; 309-462-3267. Specializing in collecting and preservation of Abingdon pottery

Akro Agate Collectors Club
Clarksburg Crow quarterly newsletter
Roger Hardy
10 Bailey St., Clarksburg, WV 26301-2524; 304-624-4523 (evenings) or West End Antiques, 97 Milford St., Clarksburg, WV 26301; 304-624-7600 (week days). Annual membership fee: $20

America West Archives
Anderson, Warren
P.O. Box 100, Cedar City, UT 84721; 801-586-9497; 26-page illustrated catalogs issued 6 times a year. Has both fixed-price and auction sections offering early western documents, letters, stock certificates, autographs, and other important ephemera. Subscription: $15 per year

American Antique Deck Collectors
52 Plus Joker Club
Clear the Decks, quarterly publication
Ray Hartz, President
P.O. Box 1002, Westerville, OH 43081; 614-891-6296. Specializing in antique playing cards

American Bell Association, Int., Inc.
c/o The Bell Tower
P.O. Box 19443, Indianapolis, IN 46219. Dorothy Malone Anthony, Past President

Antique & Art Glass Salt Shaker Collectors' Society (AAGSSCS)
2832 Rapidan Trail, Maitland, FL 32751

Antique & Collectors Reproduction News
Antiques Coast to Coast
c/o Lorna Bambrook
Box 71174, Des Moines, IA 50325; 515-270-8994 or (subscriptions only) 800-227-5531. Monthly newsletter, subscription: $32 per year in US; $41 in Canada

Antique Purses Catalog: $4
Bayhouse
P.O. Box 40443, Bay Village, OH 44140; 216-871-8584. Includes colored photos of beaded and enameled mesh purses.

Antique Radio Club of America
81 Steeplechase Rd., Devon, PA 19333

Antique Souvenir Collectors' News
Gary Leveille, Editor
P.O. Box 562, Great Barrington, MA 01230

Antique Stove Association
Clifford Boram, Secretary
417 N. Main St., Monticello, IN 47960. Inquiries should be accompanied by SASE and marked 'Urgent' in red

Antique Trader Weekly
Kyle D. Husfloen, Editor
P.O. Box 1050, Dubuque, IA 52004. Featuring news about antiques and collectibles, auctions and events; listing over 165,000 buyers and sellers in every edition. Subscription: $32 (52 issues) per year

Antique Wireless Association
Ormiston Rd., Breesport, NY 14816

Appraisers National Association
120 S. Bradford Ave., Placentia, CA 92670; 714-579-1082. Founded in 1982 by Dr. David Long, Ph.D, President of the College for Appraisers, to provide for a standardization of educational requirements for certification of its appraiser members and assure the public that A.N.A. appraisers not only have a broad range of knowledge in personal property valuation, but are held to the highest ethical and professional standards in the industry.

Arkansas Pottery Collectors' Society
P.O. Box 7617, Little Rock, AR 72217
Arts & Crafts Quarterly
9 S. Main St., Lambertville, NJ 08530; 609-397-9374

Ashtray Journal, a Newsletter for Ashtray Collectors
Chuck Thompson
Box 11652, Houston, EX 77293; For collectors of smoker's ashtrays, from inexpensive advertising ashtrays to valuable works of art; Subscribers receive free ads bimonthly newsletter; Subscription: $14.95 per year; Sample: $3.95

Association of Coffee Mill Enthusiasts
c/o John E. White, Treasurer
5941 Wilkerson Road, Rex, GA 30273; Annual dues: $30, covers cost of quarterly newsletter and copy of membership roster

Autographs of America
Tim Anderson
P.O. Box 461, Provo, UT 84603. Free sample catalog of hundreds of autographs for sale

Avon Times (National Newsletter Club)
c/o Dwight or Vera Young
P.O. Box 9868, Dept P., Kansas City, MO 64134. Inquiries should be accompanied by large SASE

The Beer Stein Journal
Gary Kirsner, Publisher
P.O. Box 8807, Coral Springs, FL 33075; 305-344-9856 or Fax: 305-344-4421. Published quarterly; Subscriptions $20 per year in USA

Black Memorabilia Catalog
Judy Posner
R.D. 1, Box 273 SC, Effort, PA 18330; 717-629-6583. Send $2 and LSASE. Buy-Sell-Trade

Boyd's Art Glass Collectors Guild
P.O. Box 52, Hatboro, PA 19040-0052

British Royal Commemorative Souvenirs Mail Order Catalog
Audrey Zeder
6755 Coralite St. S, Long Beach, CA 90808

The Buttonhook Society
Box 287, White Marsh, MD 21162. Publishes bimonthly newsletter *The Boutonneur*, which promotes collecting of buttonhooks and shares research and information contributed by members

California Perfume Company
For information contact Dick Pardini
3107 North El Dorado St., Dept. SAPG, Stockton, CA 95204-3412. Information requires large SASE; not necessary when offering items for sale

Candy Container Collectors of America
P.O. Box 352, Chelmsord, MA 01824-0352
Or contact: Jeff Bradfield
90 Main St., Dayton, VA 22821

The Cane Collector's Chronicle
Linda Beeman
15 2nd St. N.E., Washington, D.C. 20002; $30 for 4 issues

The Carousel News & Trader
87 Parke Ave. W., Suite 206, Mansfield, OH 44902. A monthly magazine for the carousel enthusiast. Subscription: $22 per year, sample: $3

The Carousel Shopper Resource Catalog
Box 47, Dept PC, Millwood, NY 10546; Only $2 (+50¢ postage); A full-color catalog featuring dealers of antique carousel art offering single figures or complete carousels, museums, restoration services, organizations, full-size reproductions, books, cards, posters, auction services and other hard-to-find items for carousel enthusiasts

Central Florida Insulator Collectors
557 Nicklaus Dr., Titusville, FL 32780

Ceramic Arts Studio Catalog Reprints
BA Wellman
88 State Road W., Homested Farms #2, Westminster, MA, 01473-1435. Also available: Video Book identification and price guides for Ceramic Arts Studio

Ceramic Arts Studio Collector's Association
P.O. Box 46, Madison, WI 53701; 608-241-9138. Publishes newsletter, *CAS Collector*, a 22-page bimonthly; Annual membership: $15; Sample copy: $3. Inventory record and price guide also available

Character Collectibles Catalog
Judy Posner
R.D. 1, Box 273 SC, Effort, PA 18330; 717-629-6583. Send $2 and LSASE. Buy-Sell-Trade

Chase Collectors Society
c/o Barry L. Van Hook
2149 W. Jibsail Loop, Mesa, AZ
85202-5524; 602-838-6971. Publishes newsletter *Art Deco Reflections*, Membership: $10, Sample copy of newsletter: $1

Chicagoland Antique Amusements Slot Machine & Jukebox Gazette
Ken Durham, Editor
P.O. Box 2426, Dept. S, Rockville, MD 20852. 20-page newspaper published twice a year. Subscription: 4 issues for $10, Sample: $5

Coin-Op Newsletter
Ken Durham, Publisher
909 26th St. N.W., Washington, D.C. 20037. Subscription (10 issues): $24 per year, Sample: $5

The Cola Clan
Alice Fisher, Treasurer
2084 Continental Drive N.E., Atlanta, GA 30345

Collectors of Findlay Glass
P.O. Box 256, Findlay, OH 45840. An organization dedicated to the study and recognition of Findlay glass, newsletter *The Melting Pot*, published quarterly; Convention held annually; Membership: $10 per year

The Compact Collectors
Roselyn Gerson
P.O. Box S, Lynbrook, NY 11563. Publishes *Powder Puff* Newsletter, which contains articles covering all aspects of compact collecting, restoration, vintage ads, patents, history, and articles by members and prominent guest writers. Seeker and sellers column offered free to members

Cookie Jar Catalog
Judy Posner
R.D. 1, Box 273 SC, Effort, PA 18330; 717-629-6583. Send $2 and LSASE. Buy-Sell-Trade

Cookie Jarrin' with Joyce:
The Cookie Jar Newsletter
R.R. 2, Box 504, Walterboro, SC 29488

The Copley Courier
1639 N. Catalina St., Burbank, CA 91505.

Currier & Ives Catalog
Rudisill's Alt Print Haus
P.O. Box 199, Worton, MD 21678. Please include LSASE

Currier & Ives Quarterly Newsletter
c/o Patti Street
P.O. Box 504, Riverton, KS 66770; 316-848-3529. Subscription: $12 per year (includes 2 free ads)

The Cutting Edge, quarterly publication of the Glass Knife Collectors Club
Wilbur Peterson
711 Kelly Dr., Lebanon, TN 37087; 615-444-4303. Subscription: $5 per year, Sample: $1.25

The Dedham Pottery Collectors Society Newsletter, published quarterly
Jim Kaufman, Publisher
248 Highland St., Dedham, MA 02026; 800-283-8070. Subscription: $18

Depression Glass Daze
Teri Steel, Editor/Publisher
Box 57, Otisville, MI 48463; 313-631-4593. The nation's marketplace for glass, china, and pottery

Disneyana Catalog
Judy Posner
R.D. 1, Box 273 SC, Effort, PA 18330; 717-629-6583. Send $2 and LSASE. Buy-Sell-Trade

Docks, L.R. 'Les'
Shellac Shack
Box 691035, San Antonio, TX 78269-1035. Send $2 for a 72-page catalog of 78s that Docks wants to buy, the prices he will pay, and shipping instructions

Doorstop Collectors of America
Doorstopper Newsletter
Jeanie Bertoia
2413 Madison Ave., Vineland, NJ 08630; 609-692-4092; Membership: $20 per year, includes 2 newsletters and convention. Send 2-stamp SASE for sample

Doyle Auctioneers & Appraisers
Doyle, Robert A.
109 Osborne Hill Rd., Fishkill, NY 12524; 800-551-5161. Newsletter: *Auction Opportunities, Inc.*, for $25 per year

Dragonware Club
c/o Suzi Hibbard
2570 Walnut Blvd. #20, Walnut Creek, CA 94596; 510-947-1076. Inquiries should be accompanied by SASE. All contributions are welcome

Drawing Room of Newport
Gacher, John
152 Spring St., Newport, RI 02840; 401-841-5060. Book on Zsolnay available

Eggcup Collector's Corner
67 Stevens Ave., Old Bridge, NJ 08857. Issued quarterly; subscriptions $18 per year (checks made out to Joan George). Sample copies $5

The Elegance of Old Ivory Newsletter
Box 1004, Wilsonville, OR 97070

Fenton Art Glass Collectors of America, Inc.
Williamstown, WV 26187

Fiesta Collector's Quarterly Newsletter
19238 Dorchester Circle, Strongsville, OH 44136. Subscription: $12 per year

Figural Bottle Opener Collectors
c/o Donna Kitzmiller
117 Basin Hill Rd., Duncannon, PA 17020. Please include SASE

Fire Mark Circle of Americas
Glen Hartley, Sr.
2859 Marlin Dr., Chamblee, GA 30341-5119; 404-451-2651. Specializing in fire marks

Fostoria Glass Society of America, Inc.
P.O. Box 826, Moundsville, WV 26041

Frankoma Family Collectors Association
c/o Nancy Littrell
P.O. Box 32571, Oklahoma City, OK 73123-0771. Membership dues: $20; Includes quarterly newsletter, annual convention

Friar Tuck Collectors Club
P.O. Box 173, Dacula, GA 30211; 404-963-5736. Quarterly newsletter, annual convention, write or call for membership application and information

H.C. Fry Society
P.O. Box 41, Beaver, PA 15009. Founded in 1983 for the sole purpose of learning about Fry glass; Publishes *Shards*, quarterly newsletter

GAR Post 20 Mem. Assn.
Richard A. Haussmann, Chaplain
P.O. Box 1865, Aurora, 60507

George Kamm Paperweights
24-SP Townsend Court, Lancaster, PA 17603; 717-872-7858. Specializing in antique and contemporary paperweights; Color brochure published bimonthly, $5 annual fee (refundable); Sample on request (requires #10 SASE)

Glass Knife Collector's Club
Wilbur Peterson
711 Kelly Dr., Lebanon, TN 37087

Gonder Pottery Collectors' Newsletter
c/o John and Marilyn McCormick
P.O. Box 3174, Shawnee, KS 66226

Grandpa's Depot & Caboose
John 'Grandpa' White
Denver Union Station, 1616 17th St. Denver, CO 80202; 303-892-1177 or (Fax) 303-573-5505. Publishes catalogs on railroad-related collectibles

Hake's Americana & Collectibles
Specializing in character and personality collectibles along with artifacts of popular culture for over 20 years. To receive a catalog for their next 3,000-item mail/phone bid auction, send $3 to:
Hake's Americana
P.O. Box 1444M, York, PA 17405

Ice Screamer
c/o Duvall Sollers
P.O. Box 132, Monkton, MD 21111. Published bimonthly, dues: $15 per year; annual convention late June

The Illustrator Collector's News (TICN)
Denis C. Jackson, Editor
P.O. Box 1958, Sequim, WA 98382; Fax 206-683-2559. Subscription: $17 per year; $3 for sample copy of bimonthly publication. Publishes price and identification guides on various illustrators and magazines, write for further information

Indiana Historical Radio Society
245 N. Oakland Ave., Indianapolis, IN 46201

International Association of Calculator Collectors, *International Calculator Collector* Newsletter
Guy Ball, Co-Editor
14561 Livingston St., Tustin, CA 92680-2618. Subscription: $8 per year ($12 foreign), published quarterly

International Club for Collectors of Hatpins & Hatpin Holders (ICC of H&HH)
Lillian Baker, Founder
15237 Chanera Ave., Gardena, CA 90249; 213-329-2619. Monthly *Points* newsletter and *Pictorial Journal*

International Nippon Collectors Club (INCC)
c/o Phil Fernkes
112 Oak Ave N., Owatonna, MN 55060. Publishes newsletter 6 times a year, holds annual convention

International Perfume and Scent Bottle Collectors Association
Randall B. Monsen, Membership Secretary P.O. Box 529, Vienna, VA 22193 or Fax: 703-242-1357. Membership: $35 (USA) or $48 (Foreign). Newsletter published quarterly

International Rose O'Neill Club
Contact Karen Stewart
P.O. Box 668, Branson, MO 65616. Publishes quarterly newsletter *Kewpiesta Kourier*. Dues: (includes newsletter) $7 (single) or $10 (family)

International Society of Antique Scale Collectors
Bob Stein, President
176 West Adams, Suite 1706, Chicago, IL 60603; 312-263-7500. Publishes *Equilibrium* Magazine; Quarterly President's Newsletter; Annual membership directory and out-of-print scale catalogs, holds annual convention

Kitchen Antiques & Collectibles News Newsletter
Kollectors of Old Kitchen Stuff
Dana & Darlene DeMore, Editors
4645 Laurel Ridge Dr., Harrisburg, PA 17110; 717-545-7320. Subscription: $24 per year for 6 issues of *Kitchen Antiques & Collectibles News*

The Lady's Gallery, color-glossy magazine of fashion, decorative arts, and collectibles
Subscription: $23.95 (US, 6 issues) per year; Call 800-622-5676 for further information

The Laughlin Eagle
Joan Jasper, Publisher
Richard Racheter, Editor
1270 63rd Terrace S., St. Petersburg, FL 33705; Subscription: $14 (4 issues) per year, Sample issue: $4

Line Jewels-Insulators
3557 Nicklaus Dr., Titusville, FL 32780. Books/price guides (not sold separately) available: *Most About Glass Insulators* and *Insulators Vol. 1* and *Vol. II*. For information, send long SASE.

Mabel Lucie Attwell Catalogs
c/o Showcase Antiques
60 N. Lake Ave., Pasadena, CA 91101; 818-577-9660

Majolica Mail Order Catalog
Items from the collection of Mariann Katz Marks
P.O. Box 750, Honesdale, PA 18431. Please send LSASE for majolica listing

Marble Collectors' Society of America
P.O. Box 222, Trumbull, CT 06611
Claire Block, Secretary
Publishes *Marble Mania*, gathers and disseminates information to further the hobby of marbles and marble collecting. $12 adds your name to the contributor mailing list ($21 covers 2 years)

Mike's General Store
52 St. Anne's Rd., Winnepeg, Manitoba, Canada R2M 2Y3; 204-255-3464. Catalog subscription: $6 per issue or next 4 issues for $20

Morgantown Collectors of America
Jerry Gallagher
420 1st Ave. N.W., Plainview, MN 55964; 507-534-3511. *The Morgantown Newscaster*, triannual journal for research of Morgantown Glass only; affiliated with no club. Subscription: $15 per year. Morgantown 1931 Catalog Reprint (presently out of print). *Morgantown Colors* placard: $4 postpaid. A *Collector's Handbook of Morgantown Glass, Volume I*, 256 pages, includes 8 color plates and 1,800+ illustrations, $35+$4 insured shipping and handling; Order from the author at above address. SASE required for answers to queries

Mt. Washington Art Glass Society
P.O. Box 24094, Fort Worth, TX 76124-1094. Publishes *MWAGS Review*, to educate, inform and provide helpful information to anyone interested in art glass; holds annual convention. Subscription/membership: $20 per individual or $25 for 2 persons in 1 household

Mystic Lights of the Aladdin Knights, bimonthly newsletter
c/o J.W. Courter
3935 Kelley Rd., Kevil, KY 40253; 502-488-2116. Information requires LSASE

National Association of Avon Collectors
c/o Connie Clark
6100 Walnut, Dept. P, Kansas City, MO 64113. Information requires large SASE

National Association of Miniature Enthusiasts (N.A.M.E.)
Box 2621, Anaheim, CA 92804-0621; 714-871-NAME

National Autumn Leaf Collectors' Club
c/o Gwynne Harrison
P.O. Box 1, Mira Loma, CA 91752-0001; 909-685-5434

National Blue Ridge Newsletter
Norma Lilly
144 Highland Dr., Blountville, TN 37617. Subscription: $15 per year (6 issues)

National Cambridge Collectors, Inc.
P.O. Box 416, Cambridge, OH 43725

National Graniteware Society
P.O. Box 10013, Cedar Rapids, IA 52410

National Greentown Glass Assoc.
1807 W. Madison, Kokomo, IN 46901

National Imperial Glass Collectors' Society, Inc.
P.O. Box 534, Bellaire, OH 43906. Dues: $12 per year (+$1 for each additional member of household), quarterly newsletter, convention every June

National Insulator Association
1315 Old Mill Path, Broadview Heights, OH 44147

National Milk Glass Collectors' Society and *Opaque News*, quarterly newsletter
c/o Helen D. Storey
46 Almond Dr., Cocoa Townes, Hershey, PA 17033. Please include SASE

National Reamer Association
c/o Larry Branstad
R.R. 3, Box 67, Frederic, WI 54837

National Toothpick Holder Collectors' Society
Joyce Ender, Treasurer
Box 246, Sawyer, MI 49125. Dues: $15 (single) or $20 (couple) per year (includes monthly *Toothpick Bulletin*.) Annual convention held in August

National Valentine Collectors Association
Evalene Pulati
P.O. Box 1404, Santa Ana, CA 92702; 714-547-1355. Specializing in Valentines and love tokens

New England Society of Open Salt Collectors
c/o Mimi Waible P.O. Box 177, Sudberry, MA 01776; 508-443-3613. Dues: $5 per year

New York Decorative Ceramic Society
9 S. Main St., Lambertville, NJ 08530. Meetings held 4-6 times a year in New York and New Jersey, at museums, galleries, and collectors' homes

Newspaper Collector's Society of America
Rick Brown
Box 19134-S, Lansing, MI 48901; 517-887-1255 or (Fax) 517-887-2194

North American Torquay Society
Jerry and Gerry Kline, Archivists
604 Orchard View Dr., Maumee, OH 43537. Quarterly newsletter sent to members; Information and membership form requires #10 SASE

North American Trap Collectors' Association
c/o Tom Parr
P.O. Box 94, Galloway, OH 43119-0094. Dues: $15 per year; Publishes bimonthly newsletter

The Occupied Japan Club
c/o Florence Archambault
29 Freeborn St., Newport, RI 02840-1821. Publishes *The Upside Down World of an O.J. Collector*, a bimonthly newsletter. Information requires SASE

Old Storefront Antiques
P.O. Box 357, Dublin, IN 47335; 317-478-4809. Publishes catalogs on store items, primitives, advertising, profession-related, etc. Each is available for $1.50 or all 17 for $17 postpaid. Include LSASE

Old Stuff
Donna and Ron Miller, Publishers
336 N. Davis, P.O. Box 1084,
McMinnville, OR 97128; 503-434-
5386. Published 6 times annually;
Copies by mail: $3 each; Annual
subscription: $12 ($20 in Canada)

On the LIGHTER Side, bimonthly newsletter
International Lighter Collectors
Judith Sanders, Editor
136 Circle Dr., Quitman, TX
75783; 903-763-2795 or (Fax) 903-
763-4953. Annual convention held
in different cities in the US; Subscription fees: Overseas rate, US
and Canada rate, and a Junior &
Senior Citizen rate. Please include
SASE when requesting information

Open Salt Collectors of the
Atlantic Regions (O.S.C.A.R.)
Lee Anne Gommer, Secretary
56 Northview Dr., Lancaster, PA
17601. Dues: $5 per year

Open Salt Seekers of the West,
Northern California Chapter
Sarah Kawakami, Secretary
2005 Pitnam St., Antioch, CA
95409; 510-757-9603. Dues: $5
per year

Open Salt Seekers of the West,
Southern California Chapter
Pat and Chris Christensen,
Newsletters
1067 Salvador, Costa Mesa, CA 92626;
714-540-1225. Dues: $5 per year

Our McCoy Matters
Kathy Lynch, Editor
McCoy Publications, P.O. Box
14255, Parkville, MO 64152.
Subscription: $24 for 6 issues

Paper Pile Quarterly Magazine
Ada Fitzsimmons, Editor
P.O. Box 337, San Anselmo, CA
94979; 619-322-3525. Sales and
features magazine serving paper
collectors and dealers since 1980,
quarterly cataloged sales, large
advertising section. Subscription:
$17 per year (shipped 1st class)

Paperweight Collectors' Association, Inc
P.O. Box 1059, Easthampton, MA
01027; 413-527-2598. Membership:
$15 per person or $25 per couple.
Publishes 5 newsletters a year; Bian-
nual conventions to promote and
study paperweights. Annual bulletin not included with dues

Pen Collectors of America
P.O. Box 821449, Houston, TX
77282-1449; Phone/Fax: 713-496-
2290. Published quarterly newsletter,
Pennant; annual membership fee:
$25. (Includes publication and
access to extensive reference library)

Pen Fancier's Club
1169 Overcash Dr., Dunedin, FL
34698. Publishes bimonthly catalog
of pens and mechanical pencils. Subscription: $18 per year, Sample: $3

Phoenix and Consolidated Glass
Collectors' Club
Jack D. Wilson, Secretary/Editor
(club newsletter) P.O. Box
81974, Chicago, IL 60681-0974;
312-282-9553.
Membership: $25 (single) or $35
(couple) per year

Phoenix Bird Discoveries Newsletter
Joan Oates
685 S. Washington, Constantine,
MI 49042; 616-435-8353. Subscription: $8 per year (2 issues)

Pie Birds Unlimited Newsletter
Lillian M. Cole
14 Harmony School Rd., Flemington, NJ 08822; 908-782-3198.
Specializing in pie birds, pie funnels, pie vents

The Political Gallery
Thomas D. Slater
1325 W. 86th St., Indianapolis, IN
46260; 317-257-0863. Specializing
in political and sports memorabilia

Powder Puff Compact Collectors'
Chronicle
P.O. Box 40, Lynbrook, NY
11563; 516-593-8746

Purinton Pastimes
P.O. Box 9394, Arlington, VA
22219. Newsletter for Purinton
pottery enthusiasts; Subscription:
$10 per year

R. Lalique
John Danis
11028 Raleigh Ct., Rockford, IL
61115; 815-963-0757 or (Fax)
815-877-6042

Red Wing Collectors Society
c/o Doug Podpeskar, membership
information 624 Jones St.,
Eveleth, MN 55734-1631; 218-
744-4854. Please include SASE
when requesting information

Rosevilles of the Past Newsletter
Jack Bomm, Editor
P.O. Box 656, Clarcona, FL
32710-0656. $19.95 per year for 6
to 12 newsletters

Rosie Wells Enterprises, Inc.
R.R. 1S, E. Wells Dr., Canton, IL
61520. Write for free literature;
Publishes secondary market price
guides for Precious Moments® collectibles, Hallmark ornaments and
Hallmark's Merry Miniatures. Rosie
has hosted International Conventions for Precious Moments Collectors and hosts the semiannual
Midwest Collectibles Fest, both
held in St. Charles, IL. For Hot
Tips on collectibles call 1-900-420-
3713 ext. 307 for Precious
Moments®, Hallmark ornaments
and other popular limited edition
collectibles and ornaments. Also
available: a touch-tone 900 line for
callers to record Voice Ads to reach
collectors across the U.S.A., 1-900-
740-7575. For additional information call 1-800-445-8745. Ask
about the informational kit available to clubs for writing constitu-
tions, planning meetings, etc.
Collectibles information line: call
309-668-2211.

Salt & Pepper Shakers Catalog
Judy Posner
R.D. 1, Box 273 SC, Effort, PA
18330; 717-629-6583. Send $2
and LSASE. Buy-Sell-Trade

Salt & Pepper Novelty Shakers Club
Irene Thornburg
581 Joy Road, Battle Creek, MI
49017; 616-963-7953. Publishes
quarterly newsletter; Holds annual convention; Dues: $20 per year
in US, Canada and Mexico ($5
extra for couple)

Shawnee Pottery Collectors' Club
P.O. Box 713, New Smyrna
Beach, FL 32170-0713. Monthly
nation-wide newsletter. SASE (c/o
Pamela Curran) required when
requesting information. Optional:
$3 for sample of current newsletter

Shelley National China Club
c/o LaDonna Douglass
P.O. Box 5802, Chokoloskee, FL
33925. Membership $25 per year, 4
quarterly newsletters, plus many
other benefits. 4 years old and
growing, 1995 National convention in Chicago, build large Shelley
database and links to British club

Southern Oregon Antiques &
Collectibles Club
P.O. Box 508, Talent, OR 97540;
503-535-1231 Meets 1st Wednes-
day of the month, promotes 2
shows a year in Medford, OR

Spoonville Scoop
Alves, Margaret
84 Oak Ave., Shelton, 06484;
203-924-4768. Specializing in
spoons: plated, sterling, silver,
pre-1920s. Subscription: $8 per
year (published bimonthly)

Stanley Tool Collector News
c/o The Old Tool Shop
208 Front St., Marietta, OH
45750. Features articles of interest, auction results, price trends,
classified ads, etc. Subscription:
$20 per year; Sample: $6.95

Stevengraph Collectors Assoc.
David L. Brown
2103-2829 Arbutus Rd., Victoria,
British Columbia, Canada, V8N
5X5; 604-477-9896

Stretch Glass Society
P.O. Box 573, Hampshire, IL
60140. Membership: $12; quarter-
ly newsletter, annual convention

Surveyors Historical Society
Identification Committee
D.R. Beeks
P.O. Box 2515, Coeur d'Alene,
ID 83814; 208-667-0830

Susie Cooper Catalogs
J. David Ehrhard
c/o Showcase Antiques
60 N. Lake Ave., Pasadena, CA
91101; 818-577-9660

Swan Seekers Network
Maret Webb
4118 E. Vernon Ave., Phoenix, AZ
85008-2333; Telephone and Fax:
602-957-6294, 8:30 a.m. - 5:00
p.m. M.S.T., Mon. — Fri. Publishes *Swan Seekers News* and *Swan
Seekers Marketplace* periodicals ($28
per year U.S., $38 foreign). Spe-
cializing in Swarovski crystal

Table Toppers
1340 West Irving Park Rd., P.O.
Box 161, Chicago, IL 60613; 312-
769-3184. Membership: $18 (single)
per year, which includes *Table Topics,* a bimonthly newsletter for those
interested in table-top collectibles

The Tanner Restraints Collection 3024 E. 35th, Spokane, WA 99223; 509-448-8457. 40-page catalog of magician/escape artist equipment from trick and regulation padlocks, handcuffs, leg shackles and straight jackets to picks and pick sets. Books on all of the above and much more. Catalog: $3

Tea Leaf Club International 222 Powderhorn Dr., Houghton Lake, MI 48629. Publishes *Tea Leaf Readings* Newsletter. Membership: $20 (single) or $25 (couple) per year

Tea Talk
Tina M. Carter, Teapot Columnist Diana Rosen/Lucy Roman, Editors P.O. Box 860, Sausalito, CA 94966; 415-331-1557. Subscription: $17.95 per year; Sample: $2

Thermometer Collectors' Club of America
Richard Porter, Vice President 6130 Rampart Dr., Carmichael, CA 95608

Thimble Collectors International 6411 Montego Rd., Louisville, KY 40228

Three Rivers Depression Era Glass Society
Meetings held 1st Monday of each month at DeMartino's Restaurant, Carnegie, PA
For more information call: Edith A. Putanko at John's Antiques & Edie's Glassware, Rte 88 & Broughton Rd, Bethel Park, PA 15102; 412-831-2702

Tiffin Glass Collectors P.O. Box 554, Tiffin, OH 44883. Meetings at Seneca Cty. Museum on 2nd Tuesday of each month

Tobacco Antiques and Collectibles Market
Chuck Thompson, Publisher P.O. Box 11652, Houston, TX 77293. Subscription: $9.95 (12 issues); $19.95 in Canada and Mexico; All other foreign countries: $30 for 6 issues

Tops & Bottoms Club (Rene Lalique perfumes only) c/o Madeleine France P.O. Box 15555, Ft. Lauderdale, FL 33318

Toy Gun Collectors of America Newsletter
Jim Buskirk, Editor & Publisher 175 Cornell St., Windsor, CA 95492; 707-837-9949. Published quarterly, covers both toy and BB guns. Dues: $15 per year

Toy Gun Purveyors c/o Jim Schleyer Box 243-S, Burke, VA 22015. An international club that fosters the collecting of valuable and rare toy guns. SASE required when requesting information

The Trade Card Journal
Kit Barry 109 Main St., Brattleboro, VT 05301; 802-254-3634. A quarterly publication on the social and historical use of trade cards

Uhl Collectors' Society Dale Blann, President 4 Appaloosa Dr., Vincennes, IN 47591; 812-886-5895.
Tom Eubelhor, Secretary/Treasurer 233 E. Timberlin Lane, Huntingburg, IN 47542; 812-482-9575.
Tim Hodges, Newsletter 1378 W. Andrew Lane, Jasper, IN 47546; 812-482-3016. For membership and newsletter information contact any of the above.

Vaseline Glass Newsletter
Jerry Chambers 2163 Pomona Place, Fairfield, CA 94533; 707-425-6166 after 4:30 p.m. P.S.T.

Vernon Views, newsletter for Vernon Kilns collectors P.O. Box 945, Scottsdale, AZ 85252. Published quarterly beginning with the spring issue, $10 per year

Vintage Fashion & Costume Jewelry Newsletter/Club P.O. Box 265, Glen Oaks, NY 11004; 718-969-2320 or 718-939-3095. Year's subscription (4 issues): $15 in US; $20 in Canada; $25 International. Back issues available at $5 each

Walking Stick Notes
Cecil Curtis, Editor 4051 E. Olive Rd., Pensacola, FL 32514. Quarterly publication with limited distribution

Watt's News Newsletter, for Watt pottery enthusiasts c/o Watt Collectors Association P.O. Box 184, Galesburg, IL 61402-0184. Subscription: $10 per year; quarterly newsletter, annual convention

Westmoreland Glass Society Jim Fisher, President 513 5th Ave., Coralville, IA 52241; 319-354-5011. Membership: $15 (single) or $25 (household)

The Whimsey Club c/o Christopher Davis 522 Woodhill, Newark, NY 14513. *Whimsical Notions*, quarterly newsletter; Dues: $5 per year. Annual meeting in Rochester, NY, in April during Genessee Valley Bottle Collectors' Show

The White Ironstone China Association, Inc. R.D. #1, Box 23, Howes Cave, NY 12092. Publishes newsletter; $25 individual; $30 for 2 persons at same address

The Willow Word
Mary Lina Berndt, Publisher P.O. Box 13382, Arlington, TX 76094. Each bimonthly issue contains 20 pages of articles, photographs and full-color 'centerfold.' Subscription: $20 in US, $22 in Canada, $25 overseas (US funds only)

World's Fair Collectors' Society, Inc. *Fair News*, monthly newsletter Michael R. Pender, Editor P.O. Box 20806, Sarasota, FL 34238; 813-923-2590. Dues: $17 per year in USA, $18 in Canada, and $27 overseas

The Zsolnay Store 152 Spring St., Newport, RI 02840; 401-841-5060. Zsolnay book available

Index

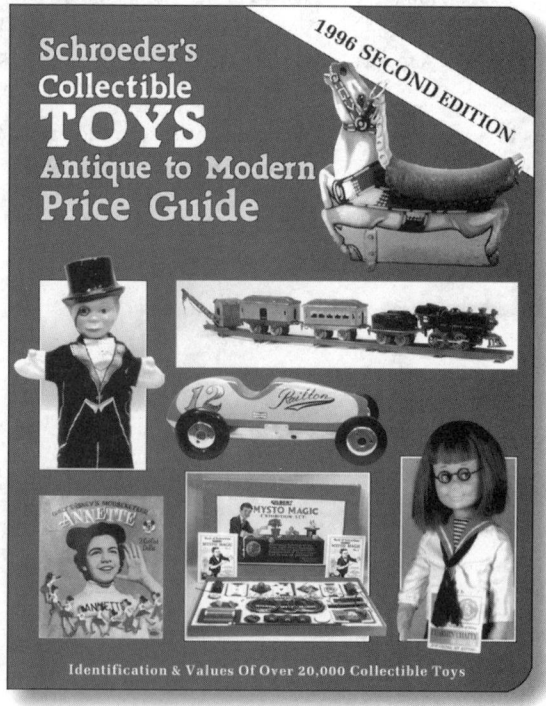